CRIMINAL PROCEDURES

CRIMINAL PROCEDURES

Cases, Statutes, and Executive Materials

Second Edition

MARC L. MILLER
Professor of Law
Emory University School of Law

RONALD F. WRIGHT
Professor of Law
Wake Forest University School of Law

1185 Avenue of the Americas, New York, NY 10036
www.Aspenpublishers.com

Permissions
Aspen Publishers
1185 Avenue of the Americas
New York, NY 10036

Printed in the United States of America.

1 2 3 4 5 6 7 8 9 0

ISBN 0-7355-2483-1

Library of Congress Cataloging-in-Publication Data

Miller, Marc (Marc Louis)
Criminal procedures : cases, statutes, and executive materials / Marc L. Miller, Ronald F. Wright.—2nd ed.
p. cm.
Includes index.
ISBN 0-7355-2483-1
1. Criminal procedure—United States—Cases. I. Wright, Ronald F., 1959- . II. Title.
KF9618.M52 2003
345.73′05—dc21

2003040445

About Aspen Publishers

Aspen Publishers, headquartered in New York City, is a leading information provider for attorneys, business professionals, and law students. Written by preeminent authorities, our products consist of analytical and practical information covering both U.S. and international topics. We publish in the full range of formats, including updated manuals, books, periodicals, CDs, and online products.

Our proprietary content is complemented by 2,500 legal databases, containing over 11 million documents, available through our Loislaw division. Aspen Publishers also offers a wide range of topical legal and business databases linked to Loislaw's primary material. Our mission is to provide accurate, timely, and authoritative content in easily accessible formats, supported by unmatched customer care.

To order any Aspen Publishers title, go to *www.aspenpublishers.com* or call 1-800-638-8437.

To reinstate your manual update service, call 1-800-638-8437.

For more information on Loislaw products, go to *www.loislaw.com* or call 1-800-364-2512.

For Customer Care issues, e-mail CustomerCare@aspenpublishers.com; call 1-800-234-1660; or fax 1-800-901-9075.

Aspen Publishers
A Wolters Kluwer Company

For our fathers, Howard Miller and Ronald Wright

Summary of Contents

Contents		*xi*
Preface		*xxxiii*
Acknowledgments		*xxxix*
PART ONE ■ GATHERING INFORMATION		**1**
I.	The Border of Criminal Procedure: Daily Interactions Between Citizens and Police	3
II.	Brief Searches and Stops	33
III.	Full Searches of People and Places: Basic Concepts	129
IV.	Searches in Recurring Contexts	213
V.	Arrests	285
VI.	Remedies for Unreasonable Searches and Seizures	335
VII.	Technology and Privacy	395
VIII.	Interrogations	463
IX.	Identifications	577
X.	Complex Investigations	621
PART TWO ■ EVALUATING CHARGES		**673**
XI.	Defense Counsel	675
XII.	Pretrial Release and Detention	759
XIII.	Charging	797
XIV.	Jeopardy and Joinder	877
PART THREE ■ RESOLVING GUILT AND INNOCENCE		**931**
XV.	Discovery and Speedy Trial	933
XVI.	Pleas and Bargains	993

XVII. Decisionmakers at Trial 1085
XVIII. Witnesses and Proof 1169

PART FOUR ■ MEASURING PUNISHMENT AND REASSESSING GUILT 1245

XIX. Sentencing 1247
XX. Appeals 1345
XXI. Habeas Corpus 1393

Table of Cases 1455
Index 1469

Contents

Preface *xxxiii*
Acknowledgments *xxxix*

PART ONE
GATHERING INFORMATION **1**

I. *The Border of Criminal Procedure: Daily Interactions Between Citizens and Police* ***3***

A. Police as Community Caretakers 4
Oregon Revised Statutes §133.033 4
Indianapolis Police Department Job Description: Patrol Officer 4
State v. Michael Dube *6*
State v. Robert Stowe *7*
Notes 9

B. Police Enforcement of Civility 10
State v. Stanley Janisczak *10*
Notes 13

C. Control of Gangs and Kids 15
City of Chicago v. Jesus Morales *16*
Notes 21
Problem 1-1. Juvenile Curfews 22
Notes 23

D. Traditional and Community Policing 24
Brown, Community Policing: A Practical Guide for Police Officials 26
Packer, The Limits of the Criminal Sanction 29
Notes 31

II. *Brief Searches and Stops* ***33***

A. Brief Investigative Stops of Suspects 36
Delaware Code tit. 11, §1902 36
Alaska Statutes §28.35.182(a) 37
Notes 37
1. Consensual Encounters and "Stops" 38
United States v. Sylvia Mendenhall *38*
Wesley Wilson v. State *41*
Notes 45
Problem 2-1. Tickets, Please 47
Notes 48
2. Grounds for Stops: Articulable, Individualized Reasonable Suspicion 49
State v. Theodore Nelson *50*
State v. David Dean *51*
Notes 53
Illinois v. William aka "Sam" Wardlow *56*
Notes 58
3. Pretextual Stops 60
People v. Frank Robinson *60*
Notes 65
4. Criminal Profiles and Race 68
Samir Quarles v. State *69*
Notes 72
Problem 2-2. Race and Witness Descriptions 74
Notes 75
Verniero, Interim Report of the State Police Review Team Regarding Allegations of Racial Profiling 76
Problem 2-3. Racial Profiling After September 11 83
Notes 83
B. Brief Administrative Stops 84
City of Indianapolis v. James Edmond *84*
Iowa Code §321K.1 89
Notes 89
Problem 2-4. Airport Checkpoints After September 11 93
C. Gathering Information Without Searching 93
1. Plain View 94
State v. Mihai Bobic *94*
Steven Dewayne Bond v. United States *96*
Notes 98
Problem 2-5. Plain View from a Ladder 100

Problem 2-6. The Friendly Skies 100
Problem 2-7. Super Bowl Coverage 101
Notes 101
2. Abandoned Property 103
Dominick Moran v. State *103*
Notes 105
D. Brief Searches of Individuals 106
1. Frisks for Weapons 106
John Terry v. Ohio *107*
Notes 114
2. The Scope of a *Terry* Search 115
Commonwealth v. Arthur Crowder *116*
Arkansas Code §16-81-206 118
Montana Code §46-5-402 118
Notes 119
Larry Hiibel v. District Court *121*
Problem 2-8. Frisking Car and Driver 126
Notes 126

III. *Full Searches of People and Places: Basic Concepts* ***129***

A. Origins of the Fourth Amendment and Its Analogs 129
1. General Search Warrants 130
John Entick v. Nathan Carrington *130*
The Writs of Assistance 132
Notes 133
2. American Limits on General Warrants and Other Searches 135
3. The Language of the Fourth Amendment and Its Analogs 136
B. Probable Cause 138
1. Defining Probable Cause 138
Problem 3-1. Applying Different Probable Cause Standards 140
Virgil Brinegar v. United States *141*
Notes 144
2. Sources of Information to Support Probable Cause 146
a. Confidential Informants 146
State v. Timothy Barton *146*
State v. Randall Utterback *152*
Notes 155
b. Anonymous Sources 157
Danny Bradley v. State *158*
Notes 161
3. Can a Statute or Rule Clarify the Assessment of Probable Cause? 162
Arkansas Rule of Criminal Procedure 13.1 162
Iowa Code §808.3 162
Iowa Rule of Criminal Procedure 2.36, Form 2 163
Iowa Rule of Criminal Procedure 2.36, Form 3 164
Notes 164

C. Warrants 165
1. The Warrant Requirement and Exigent Circumstances 166
Marvin Hawkins v. State *166*
Notes 168
2. Requirements for Obtaining Warrants 170
a. Neutral and Detached Magistrate 170
State ex rel. Eustace Brown v. Jerry Dietrick *170*
Notes 173
b. Particularity in Warrants 174
Bell v. Clapp *174*
Grummon v. Raymond *175*
Notes 176
Problem 3-2. Errors in a Facially Valid Warrant 179
Notes 180
3. Execution of Warrants 180
Steiney Richards v. Wisconsin *180*
Notes 183
4. So You Like Warrants? 185
a. Anticipatory Warrants 186
State v. Craig Parent *186*
Notes 188
b. Administrative Warrants 189
Roland Camara v. Municipal Court of San Francisco *189*
Notes 193
D. Consensual Searches 194
1. Components of a Voluntary Choice 194
Merle Schneckloth v. Robert Bustamonte *195*
Pittsfield, Maine, Police Department Consent-to-Search Form 199
Philadelphia Police Department Directive 7, Appendix A 199
Problem 3-3. Consent After a Traffic Stop 200
Notes 200
Problem 3-4. Scope of Consent 202
Notes 203
2. Third-Party Consent 204
Problem 3-5. Lessor Consenting for Lessee 204
Problem 3-6. Co-tenant Consenting for Co-tenant 204
Problem 3-7. Parent Consenting for Child 204
Problem 3-8. Child Consenting for Parent 205
Arkansas Rule of Criminal Procedure 11.2 205
Notes 205
State v. Reinaldo Maristany *206*
Notes 209
Problem 3-9. Consent Through Lease Provisions 210
Notes 210

IV. *Searches in Recurring Contexts* ***213***

A. "Persons" 214
1. Searches Incident to Arrest 214
Arkansas Rule of Criminal Procedure 12.2 214
Annotated Laws of Massachusetts ch. 276, §1 214
State v. Marc Hufnagel *214*
Notes 218
Problem 4-1. Search Incident to (But After) Arrest 220
Notes 220
2. Intrusive Body Searches 221
Arkansas Rule of Criminal Procedure 12.3 221
Tennessee Code §40-7-121 222
Revised Code of Washington §§10.79.080, 10.79.130, 10.79.140 222
Notes 224
People v. Eric More *225*
Notes 227
B. "Houses" and Other Places 229
1. The Outer Boundaries of Houses 229
Constitution of Michigan art. 1, §11 230
State v. Theresa Dixson *230*
Notes 233
Problem 4-2. Apartment Curtilage 235
Problem 4-3. Houses Without Walls? 235
2. Workplaces 236
State v. Edwin Bonnell *236*
Notes 239
3. Schools and Prisons 240
In the Matter of Gregory M. *241*
Oklahoma Statutes tit. 70., §24-102 245
Notes 245
Problem 4-4. Gun Lockers 247
Board of Education of Independent School District No. 92 of Pottawatomie County v. Lindsay Earls *248*
Notes 253
Problem 4-5. Jail Cell Search 254
Notes 254
C. "Papers" 256
Edward Boyd v. United States *256*
Notes 259
D. "Effects" 262
1. Inventory Searches 262
State v. Jackie Hundley *262*
Notes 265
Problem 4-6. Creating Inventory Searches 267
2. Cars and Containers 267
State v. Eileen Pierce *268*
Notes 272

California v. Charles Acevedo 274
Notes 281
Problem 4-7. Mobile . . . Homes 284

V. *Arrests* ***285***

A. Stop or Arrest? 285
Nevada Revised Statutes §171.123 286
Arkansas Rule of Criminal Procedure 3.1 286
In re M.E.B. *286*
Notes 289

B. Arrest Warrants 291
Blackstone, Commentaries on the Laws of England 291
State v. Jason Kiper *291*
Notes 296

C. Police Discretion in the Arrest Decision 297
Blackstone, Commentaries on the Laws of England 297
Oklahoma Statutes tit. 22, §40.3 298
Connecticut General Statutes §46b-38b 298
Iowa Code §236.12 298
Sherman & Berk, The Minneapolis Domestic Violence Experiment 299
Notes 303
Problem 5-1. Arrests and Curfews 306
Problem 5-2. Racial Patterns in Arrests 306
Notes 307

D. Paper Arrests: Citations 309
New York Criminal Procedure Law §§150.10, 150.20, 150.60 309
Revised Statutes of Nebraska §§29-435, 29-427 310
Patrick Knowles v. Iowa *311*
Gail Atwater v. City of Lago Vista *312*
Notes 318

E. Use of Force in Making Arrests 320
Blackstone, Commentaries on the Laws of England 320
Tennessee v. Edward Garner *320*
Notes 327
Frisby, Florida's Police Continuum of Force 329
Notes 332
Problem 5-3. Ruby Ridge 333

VI. *Remedies for Unreasonable Searches and Seizures* ***335***

A. Origins of the Exclusionary Rule 335
Fremont Weeks v. United States *336*
Notes 337
People v. Charles Cahan *338*

Dollree Mapp v. Ohio *343*
Notes 347
B. Limitations on the Exclusionary Rule 350
1. Evidence Obtained in "Good Faith" 350
Commonwealth v. Louis Edmunds *351*
Notes 357
Problem 6-1. Objective Good Faith 359
Texas Code of Criminal Procedure art. 38.23 359
Colorado Revised Statutes §16-3-308 360
Problem 6-2. Unwarranted Good Faith 360
Notes 361
2. Causation Limits: Inevitable Discovery and Independent Source 362
Crispus Nix v. Robert Anthony Williams *362*
Notes 367
3. Standing to Challenge Illegal Searches and Seizures 370
Louisiana Constitution art. 1, §5 370
State v. Gary Wood *370*
Problem 6-3. Place of Business 373
Notes 374
C. Additions and Alternatives to the Exclusionary Rule 375
1. Administrative Remedies 376
Chemerinsky with Hoffman, Levenson, Paz, Rice, & Sobel, An Independent Analysis of the Los Angeles Police Department's Board of Inquiry Report on the Rampart Scandal 377
St. Paul, Minnesota, Ordinances §§102.01-102.04 381
Notes 382
2. Tort Actions and Criminal Prosecutions 383
Office of the Attorney General of Tennessee, Opinion 81-212 384
Consent Decree, *United States v. City of Los Angeles* *385*
Problem 6-4. Clear as a Post 388
Notes 390
Problem 6-5. Legislative Remedies 394

VII. *Technology and Privacy* ***395***

A. Enhancement of the Senses 395
Charles Katz v. United States *396*
Danny Lee Kyllo v. United States *398*
Notes 403
Commonwealth v. William Martin *404*
Notes 407
Problem 7-1. Beepers 409
Problem 7-2. Eye in the Sky 410
Notes 410

B. Wiretapping 412
1. Judicial Limits on Wiretaps 412
Roy Olmstead v. United States *412*
Notes 414
2. Statutory Wiretapping Procedures 414
18 U.S.C. §2511 417
New Jersey Statutes §2A:156A-4 418
State v. John Worthy *418*
Notes 422
Problem 7-3. Minimization 425
Notes 427
3. Bugs on Agents 431
State v. Charles Reeves *431*
Notes 437
4. Wiretaps to Fight Terrorism and Crime 437
Problem 7-4. Crack in the Wall? 438
C. Records in the Hands of Third Parties 440
18 U.S.C. §3121 440
18 U.S.C. §3123 441
Damon Richardson v. State *441*
Notes 445
Problem 7-5. Total Information Awareness 446
Notes 447
D. Nongovernmental Infringement of Privacy ("Private Privacy") 450
State v. Adam Nemser *451*
Notes 453
Rita Plaxico v. Glenn Michael *455*
Notes 458
Georgia Code §16-11-62 459
Notes 459

VIII. *Interrogations* ***463***

A. Voluntariness of Confessions 464
1. Physical Abuse and Deprivations 464
Ed Brown v. Mississippi *465*
Notes 467
2. Promises and Threats 470
State v. Charles Strain *470*
Problem 8-1. Parental Promises 472
Notes 473
3. Police Lies 475
State v. John Kelekolio *476*
Notes 480
B. *Miranda* Warnings 482
1. The *Miranda* Revolution 483
Ernesto Miranda v. Arizona *483*
Louisiana Constitution art. 1, §13 495
Massachusetts General Laws, ch. 276, §33A 495
Notes 496

2. Triggering *Miranda* Warnings 499
 a. "Custody" 499
  State v. Burt Smith *499*
  Problem 8-2. (Non)Custody: Police Assistance 504
  Problem 8-3. (Non)Custody: Phoning Home 505
  Notes 505
 b. "Interrogation" 506
  Rhode Island v. Thomas Innis *506*
  Problem 8-4. Blurting 511
  Problem 8-5. Public Safety Motivation 512
  Notes 512
3. Form of Warnings 514
  State v. John Reed *515*
  Notes 522
C. Invocation and Waiver of *Miranda* Rights 524
  Vermont Statutes tit. 13, §§5234, 5237 524
  State v. Jason Williams *525*
  Problem 8-6. Ambiguous Assertion 529
  Problem 8-7. Ambiguous Waiver 530
  Notes 530
  Problem 8-8. Capacity to Waive 533
  Notes 534
D. Effect of Asserting *Miranda* Rights 535
  Robert Minnick v. Mississippi *536*
  State v. Kevin Stanley *540*
  Notes 543
E. Sixth Amendment Right to Counsel During Investigations 544
  R.H. Kuhlmann v. Joseph Wilson *545*
  Problem 8-9. Christian Burial Speech 549
  Notes 551
F. *Miranda:* Cures, Impacts, and Alternatives 552
1. Cures and Remedies for *Miranda* Violations 552
  State v. Hosie Van Smith *553*
  Notes 557
  Problem 8-10. Inevitable Discovery 559
  Note 559
2. Systemwide Impacts 560
  Cassell & Hayman, Police Interrogation in the 1990s: An Empirical Study of the Effects of *Miranda* 560
  Notes 563
3. Alternatives to *Miranda* 566
  Texas Code of Criminal Procedure art. 38.22 567
  Donald Stephan v. State *568*
  Notes 573
  United Kingdom, Criminal Justice and Public Order Act of 1994, §34 576
  Notes 576

IX. *Identifications* **577**

A. Risks of Mistaken Identification 577
Haber & Haber, Experiencing, Remembering and Reporting Events 578
Notes 584
B. Exclusion of Identification Evidence 585
1. Exclusion on Right to Counsel Grounds 586
United States v. Billy Joe Wade *586*
People v. Freddie Hawkins *590*
New York City Police Department, Legal Bureau, Eyewitness Identification Procedures: Lineups 594
Notes 595
2. Exclusion on Due Process Grounds 598
State v. Livio Alphonso Ramirez *598*
Problem 9-1. Prompting in a Lineup 603
Problem 9-2. Wigs and Mustaches 603
New York City Police Department, Legal Bureau, Eyewitness Identification Procedures: Showups 604
Notes 605
Farmer, Attorney General Guidelines for Preparing and Conducting Photo and Live Lineup Identification Procedures 607
Problem 9-3. Photo Lineups 609
Problem 9-4. Videotaped Lineups 610
Notes 611
C. Other Remedies for Improper Identification Procedures 612
State v. McKinley Cromedy *613*
Notes 618

X. *Complex Investigations* **621**

A. Selection and Pursuit of Targets 621
1. Selective Investigations 621
U.S. Environmental Protection Agency Memorandum 622
Ah Sin v. George Wittman *624*
Dennis Baluyut v. Superior Court *625*
Problem 10-1. Selection of Participants 627
Notes 628
2. Entrapment Defenses 630
State v. Anna Lee *630*
American Law Institute, Model Penal Code §2.13 635
Missouri Revised Statutes §562.066 635
Notes 636
Problem 10-2. Outrageous Government Conduct 638
Cincinnati Police Division, Procedure Manual §12.131, Confidential Informant Management and Control 639
Notes 640

Problem 10-3. The Mayor 642
Problem 10-4. Rolling Drunks 644
B. The Investigative Grand Jury 644
1. Grand Jury Secrecy 645
Federal Rule of Criminal Procedure 6 646
Colorado Revised Statutes §16-5-204(d) 646
Problem 10-5. Selecting Witnesses 646
Notes 647
2. Immunity for Witnesses 650
Commonwealth v. Patricia Swinehart *650*
Notes 655
3. Document Subpoenas 658
United States v. R. Enterprises, Inc. *659*
Ohio Revised Code §2939.12 662
Arkansas Statutes §16-43-212 662
Notes 662
Problem 10-6. Subpoena Versus Search Warrant 664
Notes 664
United States v. Webster Hubbell *666*
Notes 671

PART TWO
■
EVALUATING CHARGES 673

XI. *Defense Counsel* *675*
A. When Will Counsel Be Provided? 675
1. Types of Charges 676
Clarence Earl Gideon v. Louie Wainwright *677*
In re Advisory Opinion to the Governor (Appointed Counsel) *680*
Alabama v. LeReed Shelton *683*
Florida Rule of Criminal Procedure 3.111 688
Vermont Statutes tit. 13, §§5231, 5201 688
Notes 689
Problem 11-1. Lawyers and Experts 692
Note 692
2. Point in the Proceedings 693
Alabama Rule of Criminal Procedure 6.1(a) 694
Missouri Supreme Court Rules 31.01, 31.02 694
Joy Friedman v. Commissioner of Public Safety *694*
Problem 11-2. Psychiatric Examinations 699
Notes 699
B. Selection and Rejection of Counsel 702
State v. Joseph Spencer *702*
Notes 707

C. Adequacy of Counsel 709
Charles Strickland v. David Washington 710
Michael Bruno v. State 716
Problem 11-3. *Cronic* Errors 722
Notes 723
American Bar Association, Defense Function Standards 727
Rule 33, Court of Common Pleas, Cuyahoga County, Ohio 727
Problem 11-4. More Objective Competence Standards 728
Notes 729
D. Systems for Providing Counsel 729
Smith & DeFrances, Indigent Defense 730
State v. Leonard Peart 732
State v. Delbert Lynch 737
American Bar Association, Model Rule of Professional Conduct 1.5(d) 742
Problem 11-5. Flat Fees for Service 742
Problem 11-6. The Neighborhood Defender 743
Notes 744
E. The Ethics of Defending Criminals 749
Speeches of Lord Erskine 749
Dos Passos, The American Lawyer 749
American Bar Association and Association of American Law Schools, Professional Responsibility: Report of the Joint Conference 750
Kaplan, Defending Guilty People 752
Cutler, Is a Lawyer Bound to Support an Unjust Cause? A Problem of Ethics 753
Letter from William Townsend 755
Notes 755

XII. *Pretrial Release and Detention* ***759***

A. Pretrial Release 760
1. Method of Release 760
Vera Institute of Justice, Fair Treatment for the Indigent: The Manhattan Bail Project 760
Alabama Rules of Criminal Procedure 7.2, 7.3 765
Reaves & Perez, Pretrial Release of Felony Defendants, 1992 766
Notes 768
2. Who Sets Bail? 772
Donald Westerman v. Christine Cary 773
Notes 776
B. Pretrial Detention 778
U.S. Constitution Amendment VIII 778
Tennessee Constitution art. 1, §§15, 16 779

18 U.S.C. §3142(e), (f) 779
United States v. Anthony Salerno *780*
New Mexico Constitution art. II, §13 786
Virginia Code §19.2-120 787
Notes 788
Feroz Abbasi v. Secretary of State *791*

XIII. *Charging* ***797***

A. Police Screening 798
Philadelphia Police Department Directive 50 799
Houston Police Department General Order 500-7 800
Notes 801
B. Prosecutorial Screening 802
1. Declination and Diversion 802
a. Declination Policies 803
U.S. Department of Justice, United States Attorneys' Written Guidelines for the Declination of Alleged Violations of Federal Criminal Laws 803
Statement of Assistant Attorney General Philip Heymann 805
Revised Code of Washington §9.94A.411(1) 807
Notes 808
b. Diversion of Defendants 811
Montana Code §46-16-130 812
State v. Wallace Baynes *813*
Office of the District Attorney Orleans Parish, Louisiana, Diversionary Program 817
Notes 818
2. Encouraging or Mandating Criminal Charges 820
Florida Statutes §741.2901 821
Wisconsin Statutes §968.075 822
Prosecution Guidelines for Duluth, Minnesota 822
Italian Constitution art. 112 823
German Code of Criminal Procedure 152(2) 823
West Virginia Code §7-4-1 823
Notes 824
3. Private Prosecution 827
Wisconsin Statutes §968.02 827
State v. Donald Culbreath *827*
Problem 13-1. Private Money, Public Prosecutions 832
Notes 833
4. Selection of Charges and System 836
a. Selection Among Charges 836
U.S. Department of Justice, Principles of Federal Prosecution 836
Minnesota Statutes §388.051 836
State v. Tanya Caskey *837*

Florida Prosecuting Attorneys' Association, Statement Concerning Implementing of Habitual Offender Laws 838
Problem 13-2. Available Charges 840
Notes 840
b. Selection of System 842
Snyder, Sickmund, & Poe-Yamagata, Juvenile Transfers to Criminal Court in the 1990's: Lessons Learned from Four Studies 842
Kristy Maddox v. State *848*
Notes 851
Problem 13-3. Federal Day 854
Note 854
5. Selective Prosecution 855
United States v. Christopher Armstrong *855*
Notes 860
C. Grand Jury and Judicial Screening 863
New York Constitution art. 1, §6 864
Illinois Annotated Statutes ch. 725, para. 5/111-2 864
State v. Eric Edmonson *864*
Notes 868
State v. Gabriel Kahlbaun *871*
Notes 875

XIV. *Jeopardy and Joinder* ***877***

A. Double Jeopardy 877
1. Multiple Sovereigns 878
Alfonse Bartkus v. Illinois *878*
U.S. Attorneys' Manual §9-2.031, Dual Prosecution and Successive Prosecution Policy (*Petite* Policy) 883
New Jersey Statutes §2C:1-11 886
Ohio Revised Code §2925.50 886
Problem 14-1. Rodney King's Attackers 886
Notes 888
2. "Same Offence" 890
Robert Taylor v. Commonwealth *891*
State v. James Lessary *894*
New York Criminal Procedure Law §40.20 898
Notes 898
Problem 14-2. Multiplicity 901
Notes 902
3. Collateral Estoppel 903
Avery Ferrell v. State *903*
Notes 909
B. Joinder 910
1. Discretionary Joinder and Severance of Offenses 911
Federal Rule of Criminal Procedure 8(a) 911

Federal Rule of Criminal Procedure 13 911
Federal Rule of Criminal Procedure 14 912
Vermont Rule of Criminal Procedure 8(a) 912
Vermont Rule of Criminal Procedure 14 912
Damian Long v. United States *913*
Problem 14-3. Compulsory Joinder 919
Problem 14-4. Protective Order 919
Notes 921
2. Joint Trials of Defendants 923
Federal Rule of Criminal Procedure 8(b) 924
Vermont Rule of Criminal Procedure 8(b) 924
Vermont Rule of Criminal Procedure 14(b)(2) 924
Problem 14-5. Antagonistic Brothers 926
Notes 928

PART THREE
■
RESOLVING GUILT AND INNOCENCE 931

XV. *Discovery and Speedy Trial* ***933***

A. Discovery 933
1. Prosecution Disclosures 934
Problem 15-1. Exchanging Words 934
North Carolina General Statutes §15A-903 936
New Jersey Court Rule 3:13-3 937
Notes 938
Problem 15-2. Discovery from Victims 941
Rauland Grube v. State *942*
Hawaii Penal Procedure Rule 16 949
Utah Criminal Procedure Rule 16 950
Notes 950
Problem 15-3. Preserving Evidence 954
2. Defense Disclosures 955
Pennsylvania Rule of Criminal Procedure 573(c) 956
State v. John Lucious *957*
Notes 961
3. Discovery Ethics 963
Michael Hitch v. Pima County Superior Court *963*
Notes 969
B. Speedy Trial Preparation 970
1. Pre-accusation Delay 971
New York Criminal Procedure Law §30.10 971
State v. Shane Trompeter *972*
Problem 15-4. Child Victims 974
Notes 975
2. Speedy Trial After Accusation 977
State v. David Magnusen *977*

Notes 984
18 U.S.C. §3161 987
18 U.S.C. §3162 988
California Penal Code §1382 988
California Penal Code §1387 989
Problem 15-5. Whose Delay? 989
Notes 991

XVI. *Pleas and Bargains* ***993***

A. Bargain About What? 994
Federal Rule of Criminal Procedure 11(a), (c) 994
People v. Gregory Lumzy *995*
Problem 16-1. Waiving Right to Appeal a Sentence 998
Problem 16-2. Dealing Away Double Jeopardy 999
Notes 999

B. Categorical Restrictions on Bargaining 1003
1. Legislative Limits 1003
California Penal Code §1192.7 1004
New York Criminal Procedure Law §220.10 1005
Revised Code of Washington §§9.94A.450, 9.94A.460 1005
Notes 1006
2. Judicial Rules 1007
Raymond Espinoza v. Hon. Gregory Martin *1008*
Problem 16-3. Bargaining Ban in a Lower Court 1012
Notes 1013
3. Prosecutorial Guidelines 1014
U.S. Department of Justice, Principles of Federal Prosecution (1980) 1015
28 U.S.C. §994(a)(2)(E) 1018
U.S. Sentencing Guidelines §§6B1.2, 6B1.4 (Policy Statements) 1018
Prosecutors' Handbook on Sentencing Guidelines ("The Redbook") 1019
Plea Policy for Federal Prosecutors ("Thornburgh Bluesheet") 1022
Department of Justice Policies ("Terwilliger Bluesheet") 1023
Charging and Plea Decisions ("Reno Bluesheet") 1024
Notes 1025
State v. Reynaldo Lagares *1027*
Problem 16-4. Statewide Bargaining Guidelines 1030
Notes 1030
4. Victim Consultation 1032
Maine Revised Statutes tit. 15, §812; tit. 17-A, §§1172, 1173 1032
State v. Michael McDonnell *1033*
Notes 1036

C. Validity of Individual Plea Bargains 1037
1. Lack of Knowledge 1037
Federal Rule of Criminal Procedure 11(b) 1038
State v. Donald Ross *1038*
United States v. Angela Ruiz *1040*
Notes 1043
2. Involuntary Pleas 1045
a. *Alford* Pleas 1046
Federal Rule of Criminal Procedure 11(b) 1046
North Carolina v. Henry Alford *1046*
Notes 1049
Problem 16-5. An Offer You Can't Refuse 1050
Notes 1051
b. Judicial Overinvolvement 1051
State v. Landour Bouie *1052*
Notes 1057
D. Making and Breaking Bargains 1059
State v. Librado Sanchez *1060*
Problem 16-6. Breaking Bargains 1064
Notes 1066
Problem 16-7. Remedies for Broken Bargains 1068
Notes 1069
E. The Future of Bargaining 1070
1. Legitimacy of Bargaining 1070
Alschuler, Implementing the Criminal Defendant's Right to Trial: Alternatives to the Plea Bargaining System 1070
Easterbrook, Plea Bargaining as Compromise 1072
Notes 1074
2. Efforts to Ban Bargaining 1075
Commonwealth v. John Battis *1075*
George Edwards v. People *1076*
Wright & Miller, The Screening/Bargaining Tradeoff 1078
Notes 1083

XVII. *Decisionmakers at Trial* ***1085***

A. Judge or Jury? 1086
1. Availability of Jury Trial 1086
State v. Kent Bowers *1087*
Maryland Courts and Judicial Proceedings Code §12-401 1090
Notes 1091
2. Waiver of Jury Trial 1093
State v. Robert Dunne *1093*
Notes 1098
B. Selection of Jurors 1100
1. Voir Dire 1101
Andrew Hill v. State *1101*

Commonwealth v. Brian Glaspy *1104*
Problem 17-1. Defendant Bias and Voir Dire 1107
Notes 1107
2. Dismissal for Cause 1109
Texas Code of Criminal Procedure art. 35.16 1109
State v. Bobby Ray Hightower *1111*
Notes 1113
3. Peremptory Challenges 1114
James Batson v. Kentucky *1116*
Rodney Lingo v. State *1122*
Notes 1129
Problem 17-2. Extending *Batson* 1133
Notes 1133
C. Jury Deliberations and Verdicts 1136
1. Instructions to Deadlocked Juries 1136
New York Criminal Procedure Law §310.30 1136
Daniel Bailey v. State *1136*
Notes 1139
Georgia Constitution art. 1, §1, para. XI 1142
Montana Code §46-16-110 1142
Problem 17-3. Non-unanimous Verdicts 1142
Notes 1143
2. Jury Nullification 1147
Fully-Informed Jury Association, Jurors' Handbook: A Citizen's Guide to Jury Duty 1148
Problem 17-4. Juries and Social Justice 1149
Notes 1150
D. The Public as Decisionmaker 1153
1. Public Access to Trials 1153
State v. Barry Garcia *1154*
Notes 1160
2. Community Courts 1161
Feinblatt & Berman, Responding to the Community: Principles for Planning and Creating a Community Court 1163
Notes 1166

XVIII. *Witnesses and Proof* ***1169***

A. Burden of Proof 1170
1. Reasonable Doubt 1170
Steve Winegeart v. State *1170*
Steele & Thornburg, Jury Instructions: A Persistent Failure to Communicate 1176
Problem 18-1. A Doubt with a Reason 1179
Notes 1180
Problem 18-2. Words and Numbers 1181
Problem 18-3. Presumed Innocent or Not Guilty? 1182
Notes 1182

2. Presumptions 1184
State v. John Deal *1185*
Notes 1189
B. Confrontation of Witnesses 1191
1. The Value of Confrontation 1191
Michael Brady v. State *1191*
Notes 1197
Désiré Doorson v. Netherlands *1200*
Notes 1205
2. Unavailable Prosecution Witnesses 1205
Kevin Gray v. Maryland *1206*
Notes 1211
3. Unavailable Topics 1213
Johnny Carroll v. State *1213*
Problem 18-4. Evidence Off Limits 1218
Notes 1219
C. Self-Incrimination Privilege at Trial 1221
Eddie Dean Griffin v. California *1222*
Kevin Sean Murray v. United Kingdom *1225*
Problem 18-5. Telling the Jury 1231
Problem 18-6. Pre-arrest Silence 1231
Notes 1232
D. Ethics and Lies at Trial 1235
State v. Troy Jones *1236*
People v. Victor Reichman *1240*
Notes 1243

PART FOUR

■

MEASURING PUNISHMENT AND REASSESSING GUILT 1245

XIX. *Sentencing* ***1247***

A. Who Sentences? 1247
1. Indeterminate Sentencing 1248
Samuel Williams v. New York *1248*
United States v. Oliver North, Government's Sentencing Memorandum *1251*
Sentencing Memorandum on Behalf of Oliver North 1253
United States v. Oliver North, Transcript *1257*
Notes 1258
2. Legislative Sentencing 1260
Code of Hammurabi 1261
U.S. Sentencing Commission, Mandatory Minimum Penalties in the Federal Criminal Justice System 1261
Notes 1262

Problem 19-1. Sentence of Constitutional Proportions 1266
3. Sentencing Commissions 1266
ABA Standards for Criminal Justice Sentencing Standard 18-1.3(a) 1267
Parent, Structuring Criminal Sentencing 1267
Tonry, Sentencing Guidelines and Their Effects 1271
Notes 1272
B. Revisiting Investigations and Charges 1275
1. Revisiting Investigations 1275
State v. Anthony Soto *1276*
Problem 19-2. Learning a Lesson 1278
Problem 19-3. Reversing the Exclusion 1278
Notes 1279
2. Revisiting Charging Decisions: Relevant Conduct 1281
U.S. Sentencing Guidelines §1B1.3(a) 1282
Florida Rule of Criminal Procedure 3.701(d)(11) 1282
State v. Douglas McAlpin *1282*
Notes 1285
Problem 19-4. Double Counting and Double Jeopardy 1287
Notes 1288
C. Revisiting Pleas and Trials 1290
1. Revisiting Proof at Trial 1290
Charles Apprendi v. New Jersey *1291*
Notes 1298
2. Revisiting Jury Verdicts and Guilty Pleas 1299
United States v. Vernon Watts *1299*
Notes 1304
United States Sentencing Guidelines §3E1.1 1304
Problem 19-5. Trial Penalty or Reward for Plea? 1305
Notes 1305
D. New Information About the Offender and the Victim 1307
1. Offender Information 1307
a. Criminal History 1307
Melvin Tunstill v. State *1308*
Washington State Sentencing Guidelines, Implementation Manual 1310
California Penal Code §667 ("Three Strikes") 1311
Problem 19-6. Striking Out 1311
Problem 19-7. Personal History and Prospects 1312
Notes 1313
b. Cooperation in Other Investigations 1315
Robert Matos v. State *1315*
U.S. Sentencing Guidelines §5K1.1 1317
Notes 1317
2. New Information About the Victim and the Community 1318
Terry Nichols v. Commonwealth *1319*

Michigan Constitution §24 1321
Problem 19-8. Vulnerable Victim 1321
Notes 1321
Problem 19-9. Community as Victim 1323
Problem 19-10. Local Conditions 1324
Notes 1325

E. Race and Sentencing 1326
1. Race and the Victims of Crime 1327
Warren McCleskey v. Ralph Kemp *1329*
Notes 1334
2. Race and Discretionary Decisions Affecting Punishment 1335
Freddie Stephens v. State *1335*
Notes 1340
Problem 19-11. The Crack-Powder Differential 1341
Notes 1342

XX. *Appeals* ***1345***

A. Who Appeals? 1345
1. Right to Appeal 1345
Arkansas Statutes §16-91-101 1346
Arkansas Rule of Criminal Procedure 24.3(b) 1346
California Penal Code §1237.5 1346
California Rule of Court 31(d) 1346
Notes 1346
2. Appeals by Indigent Defendants 1348
George Smith v. Lee Robbins *1348*
Notes 1353
3. Interlocutory Appeals 1354
Delaware Code tit. 10, §§9902, 9903 1354
State v. Matthew Medrano *1355*
Notes 1359

B. Appellate Review of Factual Findings 1361
Elbert Clewis v. State *1363*
Problem 20-1. Wrong Place, Wrong Time? 1369
Notes 1370

C. Retroactivity 1371
State v. Curtis Knight *1372*
Notes 1376
Problem 20-2. Ex Post Facto 1378

D. Harmless Error 1379
Federal Rule of Criminal Procedure 52 1381
Tennessee Criminal Procedure Rule 52 1381
People v. Walter Budzyn *1381*
Notes 1390

XXI. *Habeas Corpus* ***1393***

A. History and Theory of Habeas Corpus 1394

U.S. House of Representatives, Suspension of the Habeas Corpus 1396
Yaser Esam Hamdi v. Donald Rumsfeld *1400*
Notes 1404

B. The Availability of Post-Conviction Review 1406
1. Cognizable Subject Matter 1406
42 Pennsylvania Consolidated Statutes §9543(a) 1406
Oklahoma Statutes, tit. 22, §1089(c) 1408
People v. Kurtis Washington *1408*
Notes 1413
2. Procedural Bars 1414
Idaho Code §19-4901 1415
Dennis Jackson v. Commissioner *1416*
Notes 1419
Problem 21-1. Successive Petitions 1423
Notes 1425
3. Collateral Review of Ineffective Assistance Claims 1425
Flango, Habeas Corpus in State and Federal Courts 1426
42 Pennsylvania Consolidated Statutes §9543 1429
Donald Duncan v. Dareld Kerby *1429*
Notes 1432

C. Federal Habeas Corpus Review of State Convictions 1434
1. Expansion 1435
Edward Fay v. Charles Noia *1436*
Notes 1442
2. Contraction 1444
Frank Dean Teague v. Michael Lane *1444*
Notes 1450
Problem 21-2. New Law 1453
Notes 1454

Table of Cases ***1455***
Index ***1469***

Preface

The American criminal justice system is huge, complex, and varied. Federal, state and local governments together spend around $150 billion each year on policing, prosecution, trial, and punishment. They employ over 2 million persons in criminal justice activities. In an average year, they make more than 15 million arrests and obtain about 1 million felony convictions. More than 1.4 million people serve time each year in U.S. prisons, another 600,000 are held in jail on any given day, and another 4.6 million are on probation or parole.

Criminal cases are prosecuted by more than 2,400 prosecutors' offices, which employ about 29,000 attorneys and about 50,000 additional staff. Thousands of attorneys work as public defenders or as defense counsel in private practice. Thousands of judges hear cases in trial and appellate courts. Lawyers often find their first jobs in the criminal justice system. Some stay for life.

Criminal procedure is the body of law governing this collection of systems. The law of criminal procedure directs — or at least attempts to direct — the actions of police officers, prosecutors, defense attorneys, judges, and other government officials. Criminal procedure limits the way the government may interact with citizens, suspects, defendants, convicted offenders, and victims.

The federal government, every state government, and many local governments operate criminal justice systems. All spend time, effort, and money each year running and reshaping their systems. There is no one criminal procedure: Each system follows its own set of rules, controlled to different degrees by outside authorities. Procedural rules come from many sources, including constitutions, legislatures, courts, and executive branch agencies. Because the issues of criminal procedure are common and accessible — unlike, say, antitrust law — a wealth of less formal constraints, including community views and the media, also shape procedure. We have titled this casebook "Criminal Procedures" to reflect these multiple layers and sources of law.

The Approach in This Casebook

A criminal procedure casebook must impose some order on the morass of cases, rules, and practices that describe criminal justice systems. One accepted way to make this material accessible for newcomers is to focus on the role of one important institution, the United States Supreme Court, and on one important source of law, the United States Constitution.

Since the days of the Warren Court, starting in 1953, the Supreme Court has influenced criminal justice systems in profound ways. It made the Bill of Rights in the federal Constitution a shaping force for every criminal justice system. The Warren Court made the story of criminal procedure, told from the point of view of the Supreme Court, compelling. The main topics of controversy were police practices: stops, searches, and interrogations. Other decisions of the Court created a basic framework for providing defendants with counsel and for conducting criminal trials. For years, the focus on the Supreme Court's constitutional rulings guided students through the questions that most concerned judges and lawyers.

But the story of this one institution has shown less explanatory power as time passes. The traditional issues on the Court's constitutional criminal procedure docket now occupy less of the attention of judges, attorneys, defendants, victims, and others concerned about criminal justice. Most criminal defendants do not go to trial. Many have no complaints about illegal searches or coerced confessions. These defendants and their lawyers care about pretrial detention, the charges filed, the plea agreements they can reach with the prosecutor, and their sentences.

The central questions have shifted in light of changes in the workload, politics, funding, and structure of criminal justice institutions. For example, the question of *whether* indigent defendants will get counsel has become a question of *what* counsel they will get. New crime-fighting strategies — such as community policing and curfews — and changes in technology raise new questions and place old questions in a new light. For judges, sentencing questions in particular have attained a higher priority: Determining the proper sentence in some systems now requires more time for court personnel than resolution of guilt or innocence.

The U.S. Supreme Court leaves important dimensions of most procedural issues unresolved and thus leaves other institutions free to innovate. They have done so. The issues of current importance in criminal procedure are being shaped in multiple institutions, including state courts, legislatures, and executive branch agencies.

This book adopts a panoramic view of criminal procedure, emphasizing the interaction among, and variety within, criminal justice systems. In our opinion, students in an upper-level course such as criminal procedure can and should move beyond the skills of case synthesis and beyond an ability to appreciate the role of only one institution. Our materials emphasize the following themes and objectives.

- *Procedural variety.* In each area we present competing rules from the federal and state systems. We also occasionally examine procedures from earlier times or from non-U.S. systems. Review of different possible procedural rules encourages critical analysis and helps identify the assumptions held and judgments made in designing each criminal system.
- *Materials from multiple institutions.* In addition to leading U.S. Supreme Court cases, we make extensive use of state high court cases, statutes, rules of procedure, and police and prosecutorial policies, and encourage readers to consider the interactions among multiple institutions. Examining the efforts of

different institutions to achieve similar goals highlights the reality of procedural innovation and reform.

- *Real-world perspective.* We focus on procedures and issues of current importance to defendants, lawyers, courts, legislators, and the public. We devote the most attention to the issues arising in the largest number of cases.
- *Street-level federalism.* Federal law, typically in the form of constitutional decisions by the U.S. Supreme Court, still plays an important role guiding the investigation and prosecution of high-volume street crimes. The interactions of police with citizens and suspects are the workaday setting for issues of criminal justice. The impact of abstract constitutional doctrine on these daily interactions raises important theoretical questions about federal-state relations and interactions among jurisdictions and governmental institutions.
- *Political context.* Materials trace the political environment surrounding different institutions and issues. We explore the impact that public concerns, such as drug trafficking, domestic abuse, and treatment of crime victims, have on procedural rules.
- *Impact of procedures.* We consider the impact that different procedures have on law enforcers, lawyers, courts, communities, defendants, and victims. We emphasize primary materials but include social science studies as well, especially when they have been the basis for procedural reform. This perspective keeps in mind the managerial needs of criminal justice: Any legal rule must apply to multitudes of defendants in overcrowded systems.

By studying the various ways in which state and local systems have answered crucial procedural questions, students become aware of a fuller range of policy alternatives. They form a more complete picture of the complex and interactive workings of the criminal justice system. Our goal in emphasizing the variety within criminal procedure is to train lawyers who know both the current law and how to shape better law down the road.

Conceptual Anchors

Our emphasis on variation does not lead us to survey all 50 states on each issue; this casebook is not a treatise. Rather, the materials highlight the majority and minority views on each topic, as well as the federal view. The major positions on each topic are usually summarized in the first note following the principal materials. Truly distinctive answers to problems are mentioned occasionally as a point of comparison to the leading approach, but the uniqueness of the position is always highlighted.

The book addresses a wide range of U.S. Supreme Court precedents, including the recognized core of essential cases and many of the most recent important Supreme Court decisions. Some U.S. Supreme Court cases are discussed in other sources. State supreme court decisions summarizing and critiquing a U.S. Supreme Court decision, or a line of cases, prove effective teaching tools since the state cases tend to highlight the competing doctrinal positions. State supreme court opinions by and large show less interest in the positions of individual justices than do U.S. Supreme Court decisions and pay less attention to questions about consistency with past decisions. State supreme court opinions often provide provocative factual settings that show how principles operate in practice. They tend to present succinctly the textual and institutional arguments favoring a procedural requirement, the values furthered by the rules, and their likely effects on police, suspects, and communities. State courts vary by jurisdiction and issue in the extent to which they respect, reject, or sidestep federal constitutional doctrine.

Studying a variety of possible answers to important procedural questions has an unexpected effect: Through criticism and contrast it provides students with a firmer grasp of the federal approach, including current federal constitutional criminal procedure, than does presentation of federal law alone. Students become better equipped to understand what is truly important about the current norms. Short "problems" throughout the book also enable readers to apply and integrate basic concepts.

The state cases appearing in this book take every conceivable position with respect to Supreme Court precedent, ranging from total agreement, to complete rejection, to subtle variations in interpretation and emphasis. For a large number of state cases that focus on state constitutional or statutory questions, the position of the U.S. Supreme Court is simply irrelevant. The case selection does not lean toward decisions merely because they reject the U.S. Supreme Court view — the "new federalism" approach. These materials are not a battle cry for state court independence; they simply reflect the vibrancy of state supreme courts and state law.

The Second Edition

The second edition of this book responds to changes in the field, incorporating emerging themes and major issues. Such themes and issues — the turning points in the law — emerge at least as often from dramatic events outside the courtroom as from blockbuster judicial decisions. Such dramatic and unexpected "drivers" of change in criminal procedure over the five years since the first edition of this book appeared include increasing attention to issues of race, especially the so-called DWB ("driving while black") stops on American highways, the Rampart scandal in Los Angeles, and the "innocence" projects that have revealed strings of wrongful convictions. This edition records the first legal echoes within domestic criminal procedure of the attacks on September 11, 2001, and the emerging war on terrorism.

We have made changes in every chapter. Some of those changes reflect actual changes in doctrine, while others reflect the advice of teachers and students about cases and materials that worked well in the classroom, and other cases and materials that might be improved. Recent significant U.S. Supreme Court cases appearing in this edition include Chicago v. Morales, Illinois v. Wardlow, Indianapolis v. Edmond, Bond v. United States, Atwater v. City of Lago Vista, Kyllo v. United States, Alabama v. Shelton, United States v. Ruiz, Apprendi v. New Jersey, and Smith v. Robbins. Some of these cases, such as *Morales,* wrestle with significant new questions. Others, such as *Shelton,* emphasize the interplay among key actors in the criminal justice system. A few older Supreme Court cases were added, such as Brinegar v. United States, because those cases take on new importance in light of post–September 11 events.

The new edition also includes some changes in topics covered. The chapter on forfeiture was removed from the print volume; few teachers said they had time in their "adjudication" or "survey" courses to teach these materials. An updated version of that chapter is available for teachers who want to use it. The chapters on sentencing and race in sentencing have both been shortened and combined into a single chapter, with the emphatic focus on race still in place. The habeas corpus chapter has been added to this print volume.

The overall goal of these changes is a book that remains fresh and engaging. We note that the product of these changes is a significantly shorter book.

Criminal Procedure Courses

This book covers the full spectrum of procedure, from casual police-citizen interactions to appeals. Part One examines police activities, including stops, investigations, searches, arrests, interrogations, and identifications. This is the heart of the basic criminal procedure course, often labeled the police practices course. It is typically taught in either three or four classroom hours.

Most law schools now offer a second procedure course — often called the bail-to-jail course — which focuses on the regulation of prosecutors, defense counsel, and courts before and during trial. Part Two examines procedural issues before trial, including the provision of defense counsel, and Part Three explores adjudication of guilt through both the most common method (plea bargains) and the most prominent (trials). Sometimes survey or advanced courses include an introduction to the new law of sentencing and the procedures governing appeals and collateral review of convictions. Part Four provides a relatively quick introduction to sentencing and post-conviction review.

The materials throughout this volume address interrelated themes; criminal procedure is a relatively coherent field. It is not necessary, however, to study the materials on police practices before those on adjudication. Within each course, teachers can approach these topics both from a variety of perspectives and from a number of different doctrinal starting points. Students should not be surprised if their professor presents chapters in an order different from what we have used or adds chapters, cases, or other materials to the course.

Procedure, Politics, and Reform

This book reminds readers regularly about the political environment shaping the work of every institutional actor in criminal justice. The materials consider the changing political priorities that make enforcement especially urgent for certain criminal laws — those punishing drug trafficking, environmental crimes, and sexual assault, to name a few. Such high-priority enforcement efforts influence criminal procedure more generally. Terrorism is the newest and saddest law enforcement priority, and we consider the potential impact of new priorities and doctrines aimed at terrorists on domestic criminal procedure and for more typical crimes.

Students who appreciate the handful of basic political struggles that time and again shape procedural debates will be better able to direct changes in the system and to influence decisions in close cases. The struggles center on questions such as these: Do we trust the police? How important is it to treat suspects similarly? Should we explicitly consider the costs of procedures?

The priorities built into this textbook suggest a return to the treatment of criminal procedure as a genuine procedure course, not a course in constitutional adjudication. The constitutional component remains an indispensable part of the course but is not the sum total of criminal procedure.

The return to a fuller conception of criminal procedure offers enormous opportunities to those who study the system and to those who will soon participate in its operation and evolution. When many institutions can shape a legal system, there are many opportunities for change. We hope each student will complete this course with a sense of the drama and the special challenges of each case and of the entire process. We hope each student will leave school ready to create procedures more sound than those that exist today.

Marc Miller
Ron Wright

Mammoth Lakes, California
Winston-Salem, North Carolina
February 2003

Acknowledgments

Creating the second edition of this book powerfully reminded us of how communities make work more fun and make final products better. Our debts extend to our friends and colleagues, our institutions, our students, our teachers, and our families.

Advice from colleagues around the country came at many stages. Special appreciation goes to Doug Berman, Steve Easton, Sandra Guerra Thompson, Alan Michaels, and David Yellen, who offered periodic suggestions as they taught from the book. We have also learned from two extensive published reviews of this book. See Robert Weisberg, A New Legal Realism for Criminal Procedure, 49 Buff. L. Rev. 909 (2001), and Stephanos Bibas, The Real-World Shift in Criminal Procedure, J. Crim. L. & Criminology (Winter 2003).

Some of the teachers who have used this book contacted us on occasion to suggest improvements that should be evident in this volume. They include Frank Bowman, Darryl Brown, Nancy Gertner, Lenese Herbert, Jim Jacobs, Sam Kamin, Tracey Meares, Kenneth Nunn, David Orentlicher, Leonard Orland, Anne Poulin, Sadiz Reza, Natsu Saito, Jonathan Simon, Rick Singer, and Kate Stith. Steve Turner, the director of the Wilsonville, Oregon, public library, helped us find greater clarity throughout the book.

Scholars who provided wise counsel on the first edition still very evident in the revised volume include Albert Alschuler, Akhil Amar, Barbara Babcock, Adolph Dean, Nora Demleitner, George Fisher, Dan Freed, Mark Hall, Mark Harris, Andrew Kull, Gerard Lynch, William Mayton, Alan Palmiter, Aaron Rappaport, Stephen Schulhofer, Charles Shanor, Michael Smith, Charles Weisselberg, Bert Westbrook, and Deborah Young.

We have both been graced with great teachers, all of whom became friends. We can trace in these pages the influence of Norval Morris, Frank Zimring, Edward Levi,

Richard Epstein, Philip Kurland, David Currie, James Boyd White, Owen Fiss, Robert Burt, Peter Schuck, Steven Duke, and Judges Frank Johnson and John Godbold.

Over the years we have worked on this project with many fine students whose energy renewed our own. They include Wes Camden, Tyronia Morrison, and Alice Shanlever. Exceptional commitment on the first edition came from Nathan Adams, Sean Monaghan, Daniel Terner, and Roger Abramson.

We have made heavy demands on our libraries and technology experts, and owe special thanks on the second edition to Marcia Baker, Terry Gordon, and Will Haines. Bibliographic help with the initial edition came from Deborah Keene, Holliday Osborne, John Perkins, Lori Levy, William Morse, Stuart Myerberg, and Erika Wayne. Radine Robinson and Beverly Marshall have provided steady administrative support: It is a miracle they have not asked to work with faculty other than us.

We also have debts to many of the hard-working and visionary lawyers in the criminal justice system. A few who provided special assistance are Harry Connick and Tim McElroy of the District Attorney's office in New Orleans; Numa Bertel of the Orleans Indigent Defender Program; Judge Camille Buras of the District Court in New Orleans; Lawson Lamar and William Vose of the State Attorney's office in Orange County, Florida; and Patricia Jessamy of the State's Attorney's office in Baltimore, Maryland. We appreciate the willingness of police departments and prosecutorial and defender offices to give us copies of their policies and manuals.

Family debts for so consuming a project are hard to recognize in print, and even harder to repay in life. Joanna Wright (age 13), ever the curious one, showed an interest in everything from exclusionary rules to font sizes. Andrew Wright (age 15) asked questions to remind us that justice for real people must be the bottom line for any legal procedure. Owen Miller, who made his appearance on November 22, 2002, as this second edition went to press, has yet to ask many questions, but he already makes it clear that he will. Conversations with our brothers Travis Wright, who is a police officer, and Craig Miller, who for years worked on justice reform projects and now teaches inner-city high school students history and government, helped us remember that criminal procedure rules guide the behavior of people in very different settings. Other family members (especially Alex Miller, Renata Miller, Katy Miller, Denis Wright, Kyung Ah Wright, and the Ohlingers and Mannings) read parts of the manuscript and forgave us the piles of papers and disks at every family gathering.

Our parents have been our teachers, our friends, and our models. Ron's father, Ronald F. Wright, Sr., died when Ron was a law student, but his energy and optimism pervade this book. Marc's father, Howard, for many years a law professor, provided steady advice from beginning to end. Our mothers, Marian and Shirley, showed a confidence that kept our destination in mind when work seemed nothing but roads.

This book sits between covers only because of the daily encouragement and advice of Amy Wright and Christina Cutshaw. Putting up with writing projects is not part of the wedding vows; perhaps it should be.

---

pany. Reprinted by permission of The Yale Law Journal Company and Fred B. Rothman & Company.

Paul G. Cassell & Bret S. Hayman, Police Interrogation in the 1990s: An Empirical Study of the Effects of *Miranda,* 43 UCLA L. Rev. 839 (1996). Copyright © 1996 by The Regents of the University of California. All Rights Reserved. Reprinted by permission of the authors and the UCLA Law Review.

Erwin Chemerinsky, An Independent Analysis of the Los Angeles Police Department's Board of Inquiry Report on the Rampart Scandal. Copyright © 2000 by the author. Reprinted with permission.

Frank Easterbrook, Plea Bargaining as Compromise, 101 Yale L.J. 1969 (1992). Copyright © 1992 by The Yale Law Journal Company. Reprinted by permission of The Yale Law Journal Company and Fred B. Rothman & Company.

Victor E. Flango, Habeas Corpus in State and Federal Courts (1994). Copyright © 1994 by the National Center for State Courts. Reprinted with permission.

David Frisby, Florida's Police Continuum of Force, Trial Advocate Quarterly (July 1993). Copyright © 1993 by the Florida Defense Lawyers Association. Reprinted with permission.

Fully Informed Jury Association, Jurors Handbook: A Citizen's Guide to Jury Duty (last modified Feb. 2, 1997) http://www.fija.org/juror-handbook.htm. Reprinted by permission of the Fully Informed Jury Association.

John Griffiths, Ideology in Criminal Procedure, or a Third "Model" of the Criminal Process, 79 Yale L.J. 359 (1970). Copyright © 1970 by The Yale Law Journal Company. Reprinted by permission of The Yale Law Journal Company and Fred B. Rothman & Company.

Ralph Norman Haber & Lyn Haber, Experiencing, Remembering and Reporting Events, 6 Psych. Pub. Pol. & L. 1057-1091 (2000). Copyright © 2000 by the American Psychological Association. Reprinted with permission.

John Kaplan, Defending Guilty People, 7 Univ. Bridgeport L. Rev. 223 (1986). Copyright © 1986 by the University of Bridgeport Law Review Association. Reprinted by permission of the Quinnipiac Law Review.

Herbert Packer, The Limits of the Criminal Sanction (1968). Reprinted with the permission of Stanford University Press, www.sup.org. Copyright © 1968 by Herbert L. Packer.

Dale Parent, Structuring Criminal Sentences: The Evolution of Minnesota's Sentencing Guidelines (1988). Copyright © 1988 by Butterworth Legal Publishers. Reprinted with permission from LEXIS Law Publishing, Charlottesville, VA (800) 446-3410. All Rights Reserved.

Reena Raggi, Local Concerns, Local Insights, 5 Fed. Sentencing Rep. 306 (1993). Copyright © 1993, Vera Institute of Justice. Reprinted with permission of the author.

Lawrence W. Sherman and Richard A. Berk, The Minneapolis Domestic Violence Experiment. Washington, D.C., Police Foundation, 1984. Reprinted with permission of the Police Foundation.

Walter Steele & Elizabeth Thornburgh, Jury Instructions: A Persistent Failure to Communicate, 67 N.C. Law Rev. 77 (1988). Copyright © 1988, North Carolina Law Review Association. Reprinted with permission.

William J. Stuntz, The Substantive Origins of Criminal Procedure, 105 Yale L.J. 393 (1995). Copyright © 1995 by The Yale Law Journal Company. Reprinted by permission of The Yale Law Journal Company and Fred B. Rothman & Company.

Michael Tonry, The Sentencing Commission and Its Guidelines, from The Sentencing Commission and Its Guidelines by Andrew von Hirsch, Kay A. Knapp, and Michael Tonry. Copyright © 1987 by Andrew von Hirsch, Kay Knapp, and Michael Tonry. Reprinted with the permission of Northeastern University Press.

Barbara Underwood, Ending Race Discrimination in Jury Selection: Whose Right Is It, Anyway? 92 Colum. L. Rev. 725 (1992). Reprinted by permission of the author and the Columbia Law Review.

Vera Institute of Justice, Fair Treatment for the Indigent: The Manhattan Bail Project, in Ten-Year Report, 1961-1971. Reprinted by permission of Vera Institute of Justice, Inc.

Ronald Wright & Marc Miller, The Screening/Bargaining Tradeoff, 55 Stan. L. Rev. 29 (2002). Copyright © 2002 by the Board of Trustees of the Leland Stanford Junior University. Reprinted with permission.

CRIMINAL PROCEDURES

PART ONE

GATHERING INFORMATION

I

The Border of Criminal Procedure: Daily Interactions Between Citizens and Police

Criminal procedure shapes the behavior of police, prosecutors, defense attorneys, and courts as they investigate crimes, prosecute, defend, and adjudge defendants, and sentence criminals. Many institutions create procedural rules to regulate the criminal justice process.

Looking at police work, for example, there are rules regarding when and how police can stop, search, and arrest suspects. But not all aspects of police activity are subject to rules. For example, no state has legal procedures telling police officers how they should talk with people on their rounds. But why not? When a legal system allows some kinds of police activities to fall outside the bounds of formal legal rules, what conception of the police and their function does that legal system endorse?

A society's vision of ordinary or desirable police behavior determines the "border" of criminal procedure — that is, the point where the law, in the form of rules from whatever source, comes to guide and limit police activity. This chapter explores that border. It suggests that assumptions about the *ordinary* behavior of the police shape the procedures that govern the *exceptional* confrontations between citizens and officers.

Modern criminal procedure assumes that the police initiate contact with citizens while "engaged in the often competitive enterprise of ferreting out crime." Johnson v. United States, 333 U.S. 10 (1948). But the police do many things in addition to ferreting out crime. The cases in Section A involve police-initiated actions that are expressly aimed at a purpose other than enforcing the criminal law — actions often referred to as the "community caretaker" function of police. Should police and citizens have different powers and responsibilities when the police are acting outside their law enforcement mode? In the cases in Section B, citizens have initiated the relationship by commenting on police behavior, usually in colorful (though rarely original) terms. In Section C, we consider the power of police to control the movement of kids, gang members, and other people. The chapter concludes with an examination of different philosophies of policing, asking whether a change in overall philosophy should produce changes in the relevant procedural rules governing the police.

A. POLICE AS COMMUNITY CARETAKERS

Any description of police work (and, therefore, any set of procedural rules to control the police) must reckon with the wide variety of functions that the police perform. Police officers interact with most citizens, most of the time, without giving a thought to making an arrest or gathering evidence of a crime. It is estimated that police officers devote roughly 70 percent of their time to matters other than criminal enforcement. The following materials — drawn from statutes, police department manuals, and cases — offer concrete images of police attempting to accomplish something other than enforcing the criminal law. The police might view their task as defusing domestic disputes, or moving people out of dangerous or unhealthy situations, or offering guidance to young people, or something else. How should procedural rules that apply to the police account for these different functions? Should there be different rules for the police when they pursue "community caretaker" objectives rather than "law enforcement" objectives?

■ OREGON REVISED STATUTES §133.033

(1) [A]ny peace officer of this state . . . is authorized to perform community caretaking functions.

(2) As used in this section, "community caretaking functions" means any lawful acts that are inherent in the duty of the peace officer to serve and protect the public. "Community caretaking functions" includes, but is not limited to:

(a) The right to enter or remain upon the premises of another if it reasonably appears to be necessary to:

(A) Prevent serious harm to any person or property;

(B) Render aid to injured or ill persons; or

(C) Locate missing persons.

(b) The right to stop or redirect traffic or aid motorists or other persons when such action reasonably appears to be necessary to:

(A) Prevent serious harm to any person or property;

(B) Render aid to injured or ill persons; or

(C) Locate missing persons. . . .

■ INDIANAPOLIS POLICE DEPARTMENT JOB DESCRIPTION: PATROL OFFICER

% TIME	*CRITICAL TASKS*
15%	1. Patrols assigned area in vehicle and on foot; maintains high patrol visibility to assist in crime prevention; actively performs routine beat patrol, concentrating on high incident areas, to detect possible

% TIME	*CRITICAL TASKS*
	criminal activities or needs for service; regularly checks businesses and residential areas; monitors radio broadcasts by Communications and other officers to ensure awareness of activities in area and to provide assistance, if needed; identifies, reports, and responds to suspicious activities or needs for service.
14%	2. Performs variety of police-community relations functions; meets and talks with citizens, providing information and advising of safety measures; visits local businesses to determine needs for service; assists motorists, providing directions; talks with juveniles in district to establish rapport; makes presentations to neighborhood organizations and block clubs. . . .
12%	3. Performs duties relating to service and assistance (lost child, injured persons, walk-aways, prowlers, abandoned vehicles, dog bites, civil law disputes, vehicle inspections, etc.). . . .
10%	4. Receives emergency and non-emergency radio runs and information from Communications; . . . responds to run, using siren and/or red lights in emergencies. . . .
10%	5. Prepares reports (incident reports, capias information sheets, probable cause affidavits, accident reports, arrest slips, [uniform traffic tickets], property slips, inter-departments, etc.) relating to activities in accordance with General Orders/Department Directives; observes and records events. . . .
8%	6. Performs duties relating to criminal investigation and apprehension; responds to scenes of possible criminal activity through radio runs, notification, or observation; assesses scene to determine situation needs (assistance from other officers, ambulance, detective, K-9, etc.); provides assistance to victim(s); searches and secures crime scene; interviews victims and witnesses to determine and verify nature of offense and identify suspect(s); notifies Communications of descriptions for broadcast; assists in pursuit (foot and vehicular) and/or apprehension of suspects; interrogates suspects, advising of Constitutional rights; makes arrests using only that force necessary; conducts search of arrested suspects; ensures suspects are transported to appropriate detention area and evidence is secured; advises victims of procedures to follow in prosecution.
6%	7. Performs duties relating to disturbances and domestic violence; . . . evaluates situation to determine needs (assistance from other officers, ambulance, etc.); administers first aid, if needed; assists in resolution of conflicts; subdues violent subject using only that physical force necessary; makes arrests as needed to preserve peace . . . ; advises victim of possible courses of action.
5%	8. Performs duties relating to traffic enforcement; observes traffic violations; stops vehicles; checks registration and licenses for status; advises driver of violation committed and need to maintain safe driving practices; conducts or requests breathalyzer tests, if indicated; issues citations and makes arrests to enforce law, advising violator of rights. . . .
5%	9. Performs duties relating to accident investigation and assistance; . . . assists in extraction of victims and provision of first aid; secures scene

% TIME	*CRITICAL TASKS*
	to prevent further incidents; conducts investigation, gathering evidence, taking statements, and preparing diagrams; conducts or requests breathalyzer tests, if indicated; issues citations and makes arrests to enforce law, advising violator of rights. . . .
5%	10. Testifies in court; prepares for testimony, reviewing reports and notes; meets with victims, witnesses, detectives, defense attorneys, and representatives from Prosecutor's Office to review case; . . . presents testimony in accordance with Department policy. . . .

The following two cases explore the extent to which the community caretaker function gives the police additional authority, beyond their traditional law enforcement powers, to involve themselves with the lives of citizens. When must police officers rely on criminal enforcement powers? Do citizens have a "right to be let alone"?

■ STATE v. MICHAEL DUBE

655 A.2d 338 (Me. 1995)

Wathen, C.J.

Michael Dube appeals from his conviction of endangering the welfare of a child, entered in the District Court following Dube's conditional guilty plea. The defendant challenges the District Court's denial of his motion to suppress [evidence that he claims was] obtained as a result of an illegal search. We vacate the Judgment of conviction.

On July 4, 1993, two officers of the Sanford Police Department responded to a call from the custodian of the apartment building in which defendant lived with his family. Defendant was not at home and the custodian needed to enter the apartment to stop sewage or water from leaking into the apartments below. The custodian had his own key but asked the police officers to accompany him to verify that he was only dealing with the emergency. When they entered the kitchen, the officers were struck with an "incredible smell of urine and feces." There was a puddle of urine on the kitchen floor, and an open diaper containing human feces that appeared to have been walked through by a baby. The feces had been tracked throughout the apartment. The officers watched the custodian [work on toilets on the first and second floors]. From where they stood on the landing, the officers could see into the three bedrooms. In the baby's bedroom and the children's bedroom, they saw clothes strewn on the floor covered with animal and human feces. There were at least 75-100 individual feces "right beside the baby's crib," and a similar number around the bunk beds and more in the hallway.

Officer Beaulieu called the Sanford Police Department to request that the Department of Human Services (DHS) send a caseworker to the apartment. He also radioed for another police unit to bring a camera. The officers asked the custodian to "stand by," and when he finished with the repairs the custodian waited on the sidewalk. About five minutes later, two officers arrived with a camera and Officer Beaulieu took pictures of parts of the apartment, and then went outside to wait with the custodian. When two DHS workers arrived, they were shown around the apartment by Officer Beaulieu. Thereafter, defendant and his family returned home, and he was charged with endangering the welfare of a child. . . .

Defendant argues that the initial entry into the apartment by the police officers was unlawful and a violation of the fourth amendment proscription against unreasonable searches. [We have noted] that a police officer has a legitimate role as a public servant to assist those in distress and to maintain and foster public safety. Local police officers frequently engage in community caretaking functions, totally divorced from the detection, investigation, or acquisition of evidence relating to the violation of a criminal statute.

In this case, the custodian had a statutory right to enter the apartment in response to an emergency, and the court found that it was reasonable for the police to accompany him. During the time that the officers were on the premises performing a lawful police function, their observations, made with their natural senses, without acting to enhance their view, [were proper].

Defendant next argues that even if the officers' initial entry was lawful, their continued presence at some point became unlawful. We agree. Although the officers were lawfully on the premises during the time the custodian was dealing with the plumbing emergency, their continued presence after the repairs were completed was unlawful. [The law required them at that point to leave the apartment and obtain a warrant before proceeding with any further searches. Although the photographs only recorded what was in plain sight,] the photographs were taken after the custodian had finished his repairs. [O]nce the repairs were complete, the justification for the presence of the police in the apartment ceased. . . . We are required to vacate the judgment. . . .

■ STATE v. ROBERT STOWE

635 So. 2d 168 (La. 1994)

Marcus, J.

Defendant was charged by bill of information with the offense of second degree battery. After trial by jury, defendant was found guilty as charged, and was sentenced to serve 60 months at hard labor. . . .

On the afternoon of September 4, 1991, Officer Gary Taylor of the Olla Police Department responded to a report of an injured person walking along Highway 125. Upon arriving at the scene, Officer Taylor observed two men, Reverend Allen Scott McDowell, who was responsible for placing the call, and defendant. Defendant, who was in an intoxicated state, had earlier had a fight with his wife and apparently punched through a window, resulting in a deep cut on his right arm which was dripping blood. Officer Taylor wrapped a towel around defendant's arm in an attempt to stop the blood flow. Defendant responded in a belligerent manner, cursing very loudly. Officer Taylor attempted to reason with him and tried to take him to get medical attention for his arm. Defendant refused and became increasingly hostile and threatening. Traffic began to back up, since defendant and the officer were standing in the middle of the highway. Realizing that he was unable to reason with defendant, Officer Taylor advised him that he was under arrest for disturbing the peace. At this point, defendant suddenly hit Officer Taylor in the head, knocking him backwards across the road and into a roadside ditch. [Eventually, with] the assistance of Reverend McDowell and a bystander,

Ken Evans, the officer put his handcuffs on defendant and placed him in his patrol car. . . .

Defendant contends that the state failed to prove he committed second degree battery. . . . Having reviewed the evidence in the light most favorable to the prosecution, we find that a rational trier of fact could have found beyond a reasonable doubt that the state proved that defendant intentionally inflicted extreme physical pain on Officer Taylor without his consent. . . .

Defendant argues the officer's decision to "force his will" upon him after he refused the officer's assistance meant the officer "impliedly consented" to this physical confrontation.* In essence, defendant argues he was simply exercising his right to resist an unlawful arrest. We find no merit to this argument. Clearly, on the basis of defendant's offensive and derisive language in the middle of a public highway, plus his visibly intoxicated condition, Officer Taylor was justified in believing that defendant was acting "in a manner which would foreseeably disturb or alarm the public." Therefore, Officer Taylor had probable cause to arrest him for . . . disturbing the peace. Since Officer Taylor was engaged in making a lawful arrest, he did not consent to the battery.

ORTIQUE, J., dissenting.

I respectfully dissent. I do not perceive that the defendant acted as monstrously as depicted by the majority. Au contraire, I discern a deeply disturbed individual who was consumed with emotional hurt and, therefore, oblivious to the physical hurt portended by his bleeding forearm. I perceive an individual who, while walking down the road, was seeking solace within himself, minding his own business, disturbing no one.

After a man of the cloth became concerned about defendant due to his injured forearm, he offered defendant assistance. Defendant declined his assistance, as well as that offered by the law enforcement officer who had been called to the scene by the clergyman. Defendant made it apparent to all of his "rescuers" that he did not require their assistance and resented their interference in his internal misery. Nonetheless, his rescuers persisted in their attempts to force medical attention on him until traffic backed-up. After these rescuers created a spectacle, causing traffic to back-up, the determined officer thought to win the now public battle of wills by placing defendant under arrest. Defendant, however, did not yield to this unlawful exercise of governmental power. He resisted. . . . In my opinion, at all times, defendant acted like a man who desired to be left alone but was compelled to fend off well-intentioned, but clearly unwanted interference to achieve his objective.

The officer's refusal to leave defendant alone was an unconstitutional seizure of his person in violation of the 4th Amendment of the United States Constitution and Article 1, §5 of the Louisiana Constitution of 1974. These provisions guarantee a citizen's right to be free of unwarranted seizures of their person. Implicit within their protection is the restraint on officers from detaining law abiding citizens against their will and from forcing on them unwanted attention or assistance. Herein, the officer offered defendant a towel to stem the bleeding. Defendant apparently agreed to accept this assistance. Then the officer insisted on doing more: to aid defendant, to impress the clergyman or to satiate his own ego? The officer detained defendant, in an unwarranted determination to impose his will on the defendant.

* This paragraph appeared in footnote 3 in the original opinion.—EDS.

Defendant had not violated any law. He merely had walked down the road injured. Any drunkenness on his part had not disturbed the peace, i.e., his actions had not "foreseeably disturbed or alarm[ed] the public" within the meaning of [the disturbing-the-peace statute]. Rather, defendant's "crime" was bleeding in public and not accepting the additionally offered aid. It was only in retaliation of the officer's continuous and persistent breach of his constitutional right to be left alone and free of unwanted governmental interference, that defendant used any offensive or derisive words. Thus, while I do not condone the manner in which defendant expressed it, I respect his defense of his constitutional rights. . . .

Louisiana has long held to the rule of law that a citizen has the right to resist an unlawful arrest. In this state, the right to resist an unlawful arrest is even considered statutory as it has been codified. . . . To the extent that Officer Taylor wished to be helpful, his deeds are to be applauded. But to take unwarranted advantage of another, under color of being helpful or under color of law is importunately disputatious. . . .

Under the facts, as I perceive them, the contest of wills should have ended in a draw. No lawful arrest was made. Society's demand for vengeance under these circumstances is egregious. . . .

Notes

1. *Community caretakers: majority view.* Most states have recognized the community caretaking function of police in case law. This concept often arises when courts relax the usual restrictions on searches and seizures that apply during a criminal investigation. For instance, in People v. Ray, 981 P.2d 928 (Cal. 1999), the court validated the decision by police officers to enter an apartment without a warrant. On Christmas day, neighbors reported that the door to the apartment had been open all day. The front room appeared to have been ransacked. The officers entered and found crack cocaine inside. The court declared that warrants are not required in these situations, because community caretaking functions are "totally unrelated to the criminal investigation duties of the police." In this setting, officers who enter an apartment "view the occupant as a potential victim, not as a potential suspect." These functions, the court said, are necessary in an impersonal society: "Many of us do not know the names of our next-door neighbors. Because of this, tasks that neighbors, friends or relatives may have performed in the past now fall to the police." Justice Mosk, in a dissenting opinion, saw less benign effects from viewing the police this way: "I strongly disagree with the assumption that the warrantless search of a residence, under nonexigent circumstances, can be justified on the paternalistic premise that 'We're from the government and we're here to help you.'"

The U.S. Supreme Court has also recognized the community caretaking function. Colorado v. Bertine, 479 U.S. 367 (1987) ("Inventory searches are not subject to the warrant requirement because they are conducted by the government as part of a 'community caretaking' function, 'totally divorced from the detection, investigation, or acquisition of evidence relating to the violation of a criminal statute.'") (quoting Cady v. Dombrowski, 413 U.S. 433 (1973)).

2. *Distinguishing community caretaker functions from criminal enforcement.* As suggested by the Oregon statute, the Indianapolis job description, and the *Dube* and *Stowe* cases, the community caretaker function of the police can cover a wide variety of activities, including examination of abandoned vehicles and assisting drunks.

Should community caretaker authority be defined and limited by statute or ordinance? Would the Oregon statute provide a different outcome in *Dube* or *Stowe*? As explained in *Dube*, a community caretaker function can change to a crime control function. What factors might identify such a shift in function? If a police department receives a 911 call reporting unusual noises behind the neighbor's house, should that be treated as a "crime control" or a community caretaker episode? What if a patrol officer responds to a burglar alarm? What if 95 percent of burglar alarm calls are false calls? Review the job description of a patrol officer in Indianapolis, and attempt to sort the various duties into the community caretaker or the crime control category.

3. *Adjusted procedural controls for different police roles.* The *Dube* court suggests that it is appropriate to have higher procedural requirements for police officers who are investigating a crime, and to apply more lax requirements to officers acting in a community caretaker function. What features of community caretaker functions might justify this different treatment? Are caretaker functions less intrusive for citizens? Do those activities produce less severe consequences than a criminal investigation? Do police encounter a greater variety of situations during community caretaking, making it less amenable to general rules than the conduct of a criminal investigation? Could a legal system subject all police activity—whether or not directed toward criminal law enforcement—to the same procedural requirements? See Debra Livingston, Police, Community Caretaking and the Fourth Amendment, 1998 U. Chi. Legal Forum 261.

4. *Resisting unlawful arrest and other unlawful demands.* The Louisiana court in *Stowe* indicated that citizens may resist an unlawful arrest. This is not true in every state: Some require citizens to submit to unlawful arrests by police officers. State v. Locken, 322 N.E.2d 51 (Ill. 1974) (resisting even an unlawful arrest by a known officer is a violation of state law); State v. Moyorga, 901 S.W.2d 943 (Tex. Crim. App. 1995). Would you extend this rule to require citizens to comply with a police demand (proper or improper) that a person leave a dangerous place, such as a roadside?

B. POLICE ENFORCEMENT OF CIVILITY

Police and citizens have very many exchanges that do not enter the casebooks and that are not governed by statutes or other rules. Because of the informal and personal nature of many of these exchanges, they will often be resolved in the streets, or in police precincts and prosecutors' offices, without ever becoming a source of formal (or traceable) conflict. But the lack of formality in day-to-day exchanges between police and citizens does not mean the exchanges are unimportant. These low-level interactions—at the border of criminal procedure—may be the place where trust and distrust, abuse and respect, are firmly established in the public mind.

■ STATE v. STANLEY JANISCZAK

579 A.2d 736 (Me. 1990)

COLLINS, J.

Stanley W. Janisczak appeals from a judgment of conviction entered after a jury trial [for obstructing government administration]. Janisczak argues that the evidence of his actions presented at trial was insufficient to sustain this conviction because his actions deserve constitutional protection under both the First Amendment to the Federal Constitution and article I, §4 of the Maine Constitution. We agree with the defendant, and we vacate the judgment of conviction.

The case . . . arises from the disruptive conduct in which Janisczak engaged in the town of Richmond on December 26, 1988, while protesting the arrest of Nicholas Kovtuschenko by several police officers. Early that evening, Officer George Mele of the Richmond Police pulled over a van with a blown-out tail light on Main Street in Richmond. The van was driven by Nicholas Kovtuschenko. While running a license check, Officer Mele discovered that Kovtuschenko's driver's license was then under suspension. When Officer Mele informed Kovtuschenko that he was under arrest for operating with a suspended license and asked him to step out of the motor vehicle, Kovtuschenko refused, and quickly rolled up the windows and locked the doors of the van.

In response to Officer Mele's request for assistance, four other officers, including Corporal Bill Robbins of the Richmond Police, soon arrived at the scene. Kovtuschenko remained locked in his van for an hour to an hour-and-a-half, intermittently yelling and blowing the horn. Despite repeated attempts, the officers were not able to persuade Kovtuschenko to surrender himself. . . . As time wore on, a crowd of 35 to 40 spectators gathered directly across the street from the van, [and] about 15 spectators also assembled on the side of the street where the van was stopped. Many members of the crowd began shouting at the police officers, telling them to leave Kovtuschenko alone. At some point the defendant Janisczak joined the crowd; he was notable because he was "one of those hollering" early on.

[At one point, Corporal Robbins reached through the van's open window to unlock the door, but Kovtuschenko twisted his arm and rolled the window up. Eventually, Corporal Robbins broke the van's window with a flashlight.] With the help of two other officers, Corporal Robbins opened the van's door and pulled Kovtuschenko from the van. Kovtuschenko, who is a large man according to Officer Mele's testimony, resisted being placed in handcuffs and refused to put his arms behind his back. All five of the officers present were needed to wrestle Kovtuschenko to the ground, and it took between a minute and a minute-and-a-half to place handcuffs on him.

While the police were struggling to control Kovtuschenko, Janisczak "bolted" from the crowd of spectators up to the officers, shouting. The crowd, now 30-40 strong, was "hollering" and "all screaming" at the police officers. Janisczak stood one or two feet behind Corporal Robbins yelling at the officers. According to Corporal Robbins he appeared to be "very hostile" as he shouted "you don't have the right to do that," and "you are violating his rights," and "don't beat on him." Robbins testified that Janisczak called the officers abusive names, including "something [like] you fucking assholes or you jerks . . . very vulgar language and just offensive language." Janisczak voiced his protests throughout the period in which the officers struggled to place handcuffs on Kovtuschenko. One officer testified that Janisczak's yelling and name calling broke his concentration. When Robbins believed that the other officers had Kovtuschenko in control, he turned to Janisczak and ordered him, by name, to "get the hell out of here." Janisczak stepped within inches of Robbins, and within two or three feet of Kovtuschenko, and said "fuck you." Corporal Robbins immediately placed Janisczak under arrest. At no point did Janisczak make physical contact with the officers before he was placed under arrest.

Janisczak argues that there was insufficient evidence presented at trial to sustain his conviction for obstructing government administration. . . . The portion of the obstructing government administration statute relevant to this appeal states that a person "is guilty of obstructing government administration if he uses . . . intimidation . . . or engages in any criminal act with the intent to interfere with a public servant performing or purporting to perform an official function." [W]e confine our review to whether there was adequate evidence that Janisczak, with the intent to interfere with the arrest, either intimidated the officers present or engaged in a criminal act.

Our review of the record indicates that there was insufficient evidence of intimidation presented to sustain Janisczak's conviction for obstructing government administration on that basis. [A]lthough all five of the officers who were present at the scene testified at trial, none stated that he was put in fear by the defendant. Nor did any officer present testimony from which a jury reasonably could infer that one or more of the officers was afraid of Janisczak or his actions.

We now direct our attention to whether there was sufficient evidence to substantiate a finding that Janisczak engaged in a criminal act with the intent to obstruct the arrest. The Superior Court instructed the jury that the only criminal act it needed to consider was disorderly conduct . . . , which prohibits intentionally or recklessly causing annoyance to others in a public place by intentionally making "loud and unreasonable noises."

Janisczak argues that the conduct for which he could be found criminally liable under the disorderly conduct statute — intentionally making loud and unreasonable noises — falls, in these circumstances, within the scope of constitutionally protected speech, and, therefore, evidence of his conduct may not be used to convict him. We agree.

As a preliminary point, we observe that Janisczak's right to freedom of speech is placed directly at issue in the circumstances of this case by the definition of disorderly conduct. . . . This section does not prohibit any actions other than the making of "loud and unreasonable noises," except to the extent that other actions may contribute to the "unreasonable" character of the noises made. The record reflects that Janisczak moved up to within several feet of an ongoing and physical arrest, and shouted his protests in crude and vulgar language. Although Janisczak's close proximity to the officers as they wrestled with Kovtuschenko may have made Janisczak's shouts more "unreasonable" . . . than his shouts would have been had he remained at a greater distance from the area of the arrest, this section of the disorderly conduct statute was not intended, as we read it, to make criminal the act of standing close to an arrest. Given that the only noises Janisczak made were his vulgar and abusive protests, the only criminal act that he could have committed under this section was his enunciation of these verbal protests. The act of verbally protesting a police arrest falls within the scope of our constitutional protections over speech, see State v. John W., 418 A.2d 1097 (Me. 1980), unless, as discussed below, the State has a compelling interest in prohibiting the particular speech used.

In *John W.,* a case in which we vacated a [disorderly conduct conviction] of a juvenile who verbally harassed police officers after they arrested his sister, we examined the scope of our constitutional protections of speech:

> Our fundamental interest in free speech demands the existence of a compelling governmental interest to justify legislative restrictions upon it. Such a compelling governmental interest has been found to exist in the prohibition of . . . fighting words.

"[Words] which by their very utterance inflict injury or tend to incite an immediate breach of the peace do not enjoy constitutional protection." Chaplinsky v. New Hampshire, 315 U.S. 568 (1942).

[I]f Janisczak's words were merely vulgar they must be accorded constitutional protection, even if they reasonably could be found to have "annoyed" the police officers within the meaning of the disorderly conduct statute. On the other hand, the State may properly prohibit "fighting words" and "speech that produces or is likely to produce a clear and present danger of substantive evils" that Maine may constitutionally seek to prevent. . . .

As we apply this test, we place special emphasis on the fact that the vulgar and abusive language used by the defendant here was addressed not at an ordinary civilian, but at a group of police officers. In *John W.*, we acknowledged that police officers are "trained to exercise a higher degree of restraint than the average citizen." We articulated a presumption that unlike a civilian:

> a police officer would not so readily respond violently to conduct of the sort engaged in by John W. To constitute a violation of the [disorderly conduct] statute in these circumstances the conduct must be egregiously offensive, so offensive as to have a direct tendency to cause a violent response even from a police officer. [E]pithets directed at police officers are not fighting words merely because they might be so if directed at some other person. The nature of the experience, training, and responsibilities of police officers must be considered in determining whether a given defendant's language constituted fighting words.

The evidence in the present case indicates that the brunt of Janisczak's vulgar language was directed at Corporal Robbins, who by his own testimony had been a full-time police officer in Richmond for four years at the time of Janisczak's arrest, and had been a part-time officer in Richmond for four years before that. We determine that Janisczak's words, directed at an officer of such rank and experience, were not so egregiously offensive to him that they may be deemed "fighting words." Put simply, the defendant's words and actions were not likely to incite Corporal Robbins, or, indeed, the other officers present, to an immediate breach of the peace. Nor are we persuaded that in the circumstances of this case Janisczak's words and conduct created a clear and present danger of other substantive evils that the State may permissibly prohibit. . . . Therefore, we conclude that our societal interest in free and unfettered expression outweighs any danger that could have resulted from Janisczak's vulgar words, and that Janisczak's words were constitutionally protected. On this basis, we determine that there was insufficient evidence presented at trial to find that Janisczak engaged in disorderly conduct. . . .

Notes

1. *Police enforcement of civility: majority view.* Appellate cases involving arrests for incivility toward police officers are rare. One reason might be that citizens are rarely uncivil toward police, though this seems unlikely. Sometimes police arrest citizens for direct interference with their duties and charge them with obstruction or interfering with an arrest or assault, but in the absence of physical contact police more often respond with the indirect charge of disorderly conduct. Prosecutors refuse to charge some of these arrests, and trial courts dismiss others.

Most state appellate decisions reverse disorderly conduct convictions based solely on profane insults directed toward police officers. See Jones v. State, 798 So. 2d 1241 (Miss. 2001). But a few sustain such convictions. In City of St. Paul v. Morris, 104 N.W.2d 902 (Minn. 1960), two officers entered a restaurant at 1:30 A.M. and arrested three people (including the half brother of the defendant, Robert Morris), for consuming liquor in a restaurant not licensed for such consumption. As the officers left the restaurant, Morris walked behind them asking the officers why they were arresting his brother. The defendant then said to the officers two or three times, "You white mother f___kers, what are you picking on us for, why don't you pick on the white people?" The officers then arrested Morris. Other patrons of the restaurant were close enough to hear what Morris said, but he used a normal tone of voice and there was no noise, fighting, violence, or threats among the other patrons. The ordinance in question made it a misdemeanor for a person to make "any noise, riot, disturbance or improper diversion." The appellate court upheld Morris' conviction because the ordinance "embraces acts which corrupt the public morals or outrage the sense of public decency." The officers had no special duty to tolerate such verbal abuse: "there is no sound reason why officers must be subjected to indignities such as present here, indignities that go far beyond what any other citizen might reasonably be expected to endure." Although the dissenting opinion stressed the racial tension evident in the conflict, the majority believed that the case raised no racial issue: "under the particular facts involved, we have no doubt that the expression would be equally provocative and offensive to any citizen, regardless of race." For a more recent example of a court sustaining a conviction based on abusive language directed at a police officer, see Commonwealth v. Jones, 880 S.W.2d 544 (Ky. 1994) (upholding a disorderly conduct conviction when a woman protesting the presence of military vehicles at a parade called an officer a "Nazi pig motherfucker"); Bailey v. State, 972 S.W.2d 239 (Ark. 1998) (rejecting First Amendment challenge to disorderly conduct statute by defendant who shouted racial epithets at arresting officer).

What differences might explain the different outcomes in *Janisczak* and *Morris*? Could you imagine a court today not seeing a racial issue involved based on facts like those in *Morris?* What has changed?

2. *Nonjudicial procedural rules for enforcing civility.* Were the officers in these cases really concerned with "disorderly conduct," or were they concerned with something else? If you were responsible for training police, would you recommend that officers enforce civility, both among citizens and toward officers? Would you draft a policy that offers guidance on this question?

3. *The capacity of the police to tolerate abuse.* How does the Maine court in *Janisczak* view the need for police officers to tolerate abusive outbursts by citizens? Does the court hold police officers to higher standards of tolerance than might be expected of ordinary citizens? Should the tolerance expected of an officer depend on rank and experience?

4. *The capacity of the police to impose punishment.* How upset do you think Corporal Robbins was after the appellate court reversed Janisczak's conviction for resisting arrest? Appellate courts often dismiss charges of disorderly conduct or resisting arrest after a citizen directs profanity toward an officer. Why might such decisions not deter officers from making such arrests? Perhaps the answer comes from the observation made by some police officers that "If you can't give 'em a rap, you can still give 'em a ride."

5. *Officer Manners: police civility guidelines.* Should police officers themselves speak and act politely if they insist on civil treatment from citizens? Can police departments do anything to compel their officers to act politely? In 1999, New York City's mayor and police chief promulgated civility guidelines for police officers. The guidelines appear on a card given to all NYPD officers. One side of the card listed "NYPD Department Values," including pledges to "value human life, respect the dignity of each individual and render our services with courtesy and civility," and to "maintain a higher standard of integrity than is generally expected of others because so much is expected of us." The reverse side of the card reminded officers, when addressing the public, to "introduce yourself to members of the public during the course of your duties," to "respect each individual, his or her cultural identity, customs and beliefs," and to "explain to the public in a courteous, professional demeanor the reason for your interaction with them and apologize for any inconvenience." The reaction to the new policy among police officers was mixed. The president of the Patrolmen's Benevolent Association called the plan "patronizing" to police officers. One officer said "They're going to want us to be robots soon." Henri Cauvin and John Marzulli, Nice NYPD on Way—Giuliani Orders Police to Show Good Manners, N.Y. Daily News, Apr. 7, 1999 at 4. Should polite cops be granted greater discretion and power than impolite cops?

C. CONTROL OF GANGS AND KIDS

Not everyone will respond civilly to police requests, and the police often desire more formal control than the combination of words and either fear or respect allow. Laws such as gang and loitering ordinances and curfews provide a more formal and enforceable basis for control of citizens by police. These laws exist not only at the border of criminal procedure, but at the borders of government powers and individual rights more generally. These cases raise the most basic questions of our government: What powers *must* government have? What powers *may* government have? What powers must government *not* have?

In 1992, the city of Chicago passed an ordinance, §8-4-015 of the Municipal Code, giving police authority to disrupt loitering by gang members.

> (a) Whenever a police officer observes a person whom he reasonably believes to be a criminal street gang member loitering in any public place with one or more other persons, he shall order all such persons to disperse and remove themselves from the area. Any person who does not promptly obey such an order is in violation of this section. . . .
>
> (c) As used in this section:
>
> (1) "Loiter" means to remain in any one place with no apparent purpose.
>
> (2) "Criminal street gang" means any ongoing organization, association in fact or group of three or more persons, whether formal or informal, having as one of its substantial activities the commission of one or more [enumerated] criminal acts . . . , and whose members individually or collectively engage in or have engaged in a pattern of criminal gang activity. . . .
>
> (e) Any person who violates this Section is subject to a fine of not less than $100 and not more than $500 for each offense, or imprisonment for not more than six

> months, or both. In addition to or instead of the above penalties, any person who violates this section may be required to perform up to 120 hours of community service. . . .

In 1997 the Illinois Supreme Court held that the ordinance violated the U.S. Constitution. City of Chicago v. Jesus Morales, 687 N.E.2d 53 (Ill. 1997). The city petitioned the U.S. Supreme Court for certiorari. The Supreme Court's decision follows.

■ CITY OF CHICAGO v. JESUS MORALES

527 U.S. 41 (1999)

STEVENS, J.

In 1992, the Chicago City Council enacted the Gang Congregation Ordinance, which prohibits "criminal street gang members" from "loitering" with one another or with other persons in any public place. The question presented is whether the Supreme Court of Illinois correctly held that the ordinance violates the Due Process Clause of the Fourteenth Amendment to the Federal Constitution.

Before the ordinance was adopted, the city council's Committee on Police and Fire conducted hearings to explore the problems created by the city's street gangs, and more particularly, the consequences of public loitering by gang members. Witnesses included residents of the neighborhoods where gang members are most active, as well as some of the aldermen who represent those areas. . . . The council found that a continuing increase in criminal street gang activity was largely responsible for the city's rising murder rate, as well as an escalation of violent and drug-related crimes. It noted that in many neighborhoods throughout the city, "the burgeoning presence of street gang members in public places has intimidated many law abiding citizens." Furthermore, the council stated that gang members "establish control over identifiable areas . . . by loitering in those areas and intimidating others from entering those areas; and [m]embers of criminal street gangs avoid arrest by committing no offense punishable under existing laws when they know the police are present. . . ."

Two months after the ordinance was adopted, the Chicago Police Department promulgated General Order 92-4 to provide guidelines to govern its enforcement. That order purported to establish limitations on the enforcement discretion of police officers "to ensure that the anti-gang loitering ordinance is not enforced in an arbitrary or discriminatory way." The limitations confine the authority to arrest gang members who violate the ordinance to sworn "members of the Gang Crime Section" and certain other designated officers, and establish detailed criteria for defining street gangs and membership in such gangs. In addition, the order directs district commanders to "designate areas in which the presence of gang members has a demonstrable effect on the activities of law abiding persons in the surrounding community," and provides that the ordinance "will be enforced only within the designated areas." The city, however, does not release the locations of these "designated areas" to the public. During the three years of its enforcement, the police issued over 89,000 dispersal orders and arrested over 42,000 people for violating the ordinance.[7] . . .

7. City of Chicago, R. Daley & T. Hillard, Gang and Narcotic Related Violent Crime: 1993-1997, p.7 (June 1998). The city believes that the ordinance resulted in a significant decline in gang-related homicides. It notes that in 1995, the last year the ordinance was enforced, the gang-related homicide rate fell by 26%. In 1996, after the ordinance had been held invalid, the gang-related homicide rate rose 11%. However, gang-related homicides fell by 19% in 1997, over a year after the suspension of the ordinance. . . .

The basic factual predicate for the city's ordinance is not in dispute. As the city argues in its brief, "the very presence of a large collection of obviously brazen, insistent, and lawless gang members and hangers-on on the public ways intimidates residents, who become afraid even to leave their homes and go about their business. That, in turn, imperils community residents' sense of safety and security, detracts from property values, and can ultimately destabilize entire neighborhoods." The findings in the ordinance explain that it was motivated by these concerns. We have no doubt that a law that directly prohibited such intimidating conduct would be constitutional,[17] but this ordinance broadly covers a significant amount of additional activity. Uncertainty about the scope of that additional coverage provides the basis for respondents' claim that the ordinance is too vague. . . .

Vagueness may invalidate a criminal law for either of two independent reasons. First, it may fail to provide the kind of notice that will enable ordinary people to understand what conduct it prohibits; second, it may authorize and even encourage arbitrary and discriminatory enforcement.

[T]he term "loiter" may have a common and accepted meaning, but the definition of that term in this ordinance — "to remain in any one place with no apparent purpose" — does not. It is difficult to imagine how any citizen of the city of Chicago standing in a public place with a group of people would know if he or she had an "apparent purpose." If she were talking to another person, would she have an apparent purpose? If she were frequently checking her watch and looking expectantly down the street, would she have an apparent purpose? . . .

The city's principal response to this concern about adequate notice is that loiterers are not subject to sanction until after they have failed to comply with an officer's order to disperse. "[W]hatever problem is created by a law that criminalizes conduct people normally believe to be innocent is solved when persons receive actual notice from a police order of what they are expected to do." We find this response unpersuasive for at least two reasons.

First, the purpose of the fair notice requirement is to enable the ordinary citizen to conform his or her conduct to the law. No one may be required at peril of life, liberty or property to speculate as to the meaning of penal statutes. Although it is true that a loiterer is not subject to criminal sanctions unless he or she disobeys a dispersal order, the loitering is the conduct that the ordinance is designed to prohibit. If the loitering is in fact harmless and innocent, the dispersal order itself is an unjustified impairment of liberty. . . . Because an officer may issue an order only after prohibited conduct has already occurred, it cannot provide the kind of advance notice that will protect the putative loiterer from being ordered to disperse. Such an order cannot retroactively give adequate warning of the boundary between the permissible and the impermissible applications of the law.

Second, the terms of the dispersal order compound the inadequacy of the notice afforded by the ordinance. It provides that the officer "shall order all such persons to disperse and remove themselves from the area." This vague phrasing raises a host of questions. After such an order issues, how long must the loiterers remain apart? How far must they move? If each loiterer walks around the block and they

17. In fact the city already has several laws that serve this purpose. See, e.g., Ill. Comp. Stat. ch. 720 §§5/12-6 (1998) (Intimidation); 570/405.2 (Streetgang criminal drug conspiracy); 147/1 et seq. (Illinois Streetgang Terrorism Omnibus Prevention Act); 5/25-1 (Mob action). . . .

meet again at the same location, are they subject to arrest or merely to being ordered to disperse again? . . .

The Constitution does not permit a legislature to set a net large enough to catch all possible offenders, and leave it to the courts to step inside and say who could be rightfully detained, and who should be set at large. This ordinance is therefore vague not in the sense that it requires a person to conform his conduct to an imprecise but comprehensible normative standard, but rather in the sense that no standard of conduct is specified at all.

The broad sweep of the ordinance also violates the requirement that a legislature establish minimal guidelines to govern law enforcement. . . .

It is true, as the city argues, that the requirement that the officer reasonably believe that a group of loiterers contains a gang member does place a limit on the authority to order dispersal. That limitation would no doubt be sufficient if the ordinance only applied to loitering that had an apparently harmful purpose or effect, or possibly if it only applied to loitering by persons reasonably believed to be criminal gang members. But this ordinance, for reasons that are not explained in the findings of the city council, requires no harmful purpose and applies to nongang members as well as suspected gang members. . . .

We recognize the serious and difficult problems testified to by the citizens of Chicago that led to the enactment of this ordinance. We are mindful that the preservation of liberty depends in part on the maintenance of social order. However, in this instance the city has enacted an ordinance that affords too much discretion to the police and too little notice to citizens who wish to use the public streets. . . .

O'Connor, J., concurring in part.

[The ordinance] fails to provide police with any standard by which they can judge whether an individual has an "apparent purpose." Indeed, because any person standing on the street has a general "purpose"— even if it is simply to stand— the ordinance permits police officers to choose which purposes are permissible. Under this construction the police do not have to decide that an individual is "threaten[ing] the public peace" to issue a dispersal order. [T]he ordinance applies to hundreds of thousands of persons who are not gang members, standing on any sidewalk or in any park, coffee shop, bar, or other location open to the public. . . .

Nevertheless, there remain open to Chicago reasonable alternatives to combat the very real threat posed by gang intimidation and violence. For example, the Court properly and expressly distinguishes the ordinance from laws that require loiterers to have a "harmful purpose," from laws that target only gang members, and from laws that incorporate limits on the area and manner in which the laws may be enforced. In addition, the ordinance here is unlike a law that "directly prohibit[s]" the "presence of a large collection of obviously brazen, insistent, and lawless gang members and hangers-on on the public ways," that intimidates residents. Indeed, as the plurality notes, the city of Chicago has several laws that do exactly this. . . .

Breyer, J., concurring in part.

[The ordinance does not] limit in any way the range of conduct that police may prohibit. . . . Since one always has some apparent purpose, the so-called limitation invites, in fact requires, the policeman to interpret the words "no apparent purpose" as meaning "no apparent purpose except for. . . ." And it is in the ordinance's delegation to the policeman of open-ended discretion to fill in that blank that the problem lies. To grant to a policeman virtually standardless discretion to close off major portions of the city to an innocent person is, in my view, to create a major, not a "minor," limitation upon the free state of nature. . . .

The ordinance is unconstitutional, not because a policeman applied this discretion wisely or poorly in a particular case, but rather because the policeman enjoys too much discretion in every case. [T]he city of Chicago may no more apply this law to the defendants, no matter how they behaved, than could it apply an (imaginary) statute that said, "It is a crime to do wrong," even to the worst of murderers. . . .

SCALIA, J., dissenting

The citizens of Chicago were once free to drive about the city at whatever speed they wished. At some point Chicagoans (or perhaps Illinoisans) decided this would not do, and imposed prophylactic speed limits designed to assure safe operation by the average (or perhaps even subaverage) driver with the average (or perhaps even subaverage) vehicle. This infringed upon the "freedom" of all citizens, but was not unconstitutional.

Similarly, the citizens of Chicago were once free to stand around and gawk at the scene of an accident. At some point Chicagoans discovered that this obstructed traffic and caused more accidents. They did not make the practice unlawful, but they did authorize police officers to order the crowd to disperse, and imposed penalties for refusal to obey such an order. Again, this prophylactic measure infringed upon the "freedom" of all citizens, but was not unconstitutional.

Until the ordinance that is before us today was adopted, the citizens of Chicago were free to stand about in public places with no apparent purpose — to engage, that is, in conduct that appeared to be loitering. In recent years, however, the city has been afflicted with criminal street gangs. . . . Once again, Chicagoans decided that to eliminate the problem it was worth restricting some of the freedom that they once enjoyed. The means they took was similar to the second, and more mild, example given above rather than the first: Loitering was not made unlawful, but when a group of people occupied a public place without an apparent purpose and in the company of a known gang member, police officers were authorized to order them to disperse, and the failure to obey such an order was made unlawful. The minor limitation upon the free state of nature that this prophylactic arrangement imposed upon all Chicagoans seemed to them (and it seems to me) a small price to pay for liberation of their streets. The majority today invalidates this perfectly reasonable measure . . . by elevating loitering to a constitutionally guaranteed right, and by discerning vagueness where . . . none exists.

[The ordinance is not vague.] The criteria for issuance of a dispersal order under the Chicago Ordinance could hardly be clearer. . . .

The Court [argues] that the "apparent purpose" test is too elastic because it presumably allows police officers to treat de minimis "violations" as not warranting enforcement. But such discretion . . . is no different with regard to the enforcement of this clear ordinance than it is with regard to the enforcement of all laws in our criminal-justice system. Police officers (and prosecutors) have broad discretion over what laws to enforce and when. . . .

The fact is that the present ordinance is entirely clear in its application, cannot be violated except with full knowledge and intent, and vests no more discretion in the police than innumerable other measures authorizing police orders to preserve the public peace and safety. [T]he majority's real quarrel with the Chicago

Ordinance is simply that it permits (or indeed requires) too much harmless conduct by innocent citizens to be proscribed. . . .

But in our democratic system, how much harmless conduct to proscribe is not a judgment to be made by the courts. So long as constitutionally guaranteed rights are not affected, and so long as the proscription has a rational basis, all sorts of perfectly harmless activity by millions of perfectly innocent people can be forbidden — riding a motorcycle without a safety helmet, for example, starting a campfire in a national forest, or selling a safe and effective drug not yet approved by the FDA. All of these acts are entirely innocent and harmless in themselves, but because of the risk of harm that they entail, the freedom to engage in them has been abridged. The citizens of Chicago have decided that depriving themselves of the freedom to "hang out" with a gang member is necessary to eliminate pervasive gang crime and intimidation — and that the elimination of the one is worth the deprivation of the other. This Court has no business second-guessing either the degree of necessity or the fairness of the trade. . . .

THOMAS, J., dissenting.

. . . Gangs fill the daily lives of many of our poorest and most vulnerable citizens with a terror that the Court does not give sufficient consideration, often relegating them to the status of prisoners in their own homes. The city of Chicago has suffered the devastation wrought by this national tragedy. Last year, in an effort to curb plummeting attendance, the Chicago Public Schools hired dozens of adults to escort children to school. The youngsters had become too terrified of gang violence to leave their homes alone. The children's fears were not unfounded. In 1996, the Chicago Police Department estimated that there were 132 criminal street gangs in the city. Between 1987 and 1994, these gangs were involved in 63,141 criminal incidents, including 21,689 nonlethal violent crimes and 894 homicides. Many of these criminal incidents and homicides result from gang "turf battles," which take place on the public streets and place innocent residents in grave danger. . . .

As part of its ongoing effort to curb the deleterious effects of criminal street gangs, the citizens of Chicago sensibly decided to return to basics. The ordinance does nothing more than confirm the well-established principle that the police have the duty and the power to maintain the public peace, and, when necessary, to disperse groups of individuals who threaten it.

[I]t is important to note that the ordinance does not criminalize loitering per se. Rather, it penalizes loiterers' failure to obey a police officer's order to move along. A majority of the Court believes that this scheme vests too much discretion in police officers. Nothing could be further from the truth. Far from according officers too much discretion, the ordinance merely enables police officers to fulfill one of their traditional functions. Police officers are not, and have never been, simply enforcers of the criminal law. They wear other hats — importantly, they have long been vested with the responsibility for preserving the public peace.

In order to perform their peace-keeping responsibilities satisfactorily, the police inevitably must exercise discretion. Indeed, by empowering them to act as peace officers, the law assumes that the police will exercise that discretion responsibly and with sound judgment. That is not to say that the law should not provide objective guidelines for the police, but simply that it cannot rigidly constrain their every action. By directing a police officer not to issue a dispersal order unless he "observes a person whom he reasonably believes to be a criminal street gang member loitering in any public place," Chicago's ordinance strikes an appropriate balance between those two extremes. Just as we trust officers to rely on their experience and expertise in order to make spur-of-the-moment determinations about amorphous legal standards such as "probable cause" and "reasonable suspicion," so we must trust them to determine whether a group of loiterers contains individuals (in this case members of criminal street gangs) whom the city has determined threaten the public peace. . . .

Today, the Court focuses extensively on the "rights" of gang members and their companions. It can safely do so — the people who will have to live with the consequences of today's opinion do not live in our neighborhoods. Rather, the people who will suffer from our lofty pronouncements are people . . . who have seen their neighborhoods literally destroyed by gangs and violence and drugs. They are good, decent people who must struggle to overcome their desperate situation, against all odds, in order to raise their families, earn a living, and remain good citizens. As one resident described, "There is only about maybe one or two percent of the people in the city causing these problems maybe, but it's keeping 98 percent of us in our houses and off the streets and afraid to shop." By focusing exclusively on the imagined "rights" of the two percent, the Court today has denied our most vulnerable citizens the very thing that Justice Stevens elevates above all else — the "freedom of movement." And that is a shame. I respectfully dissent.

Notes

1. *Order maintenance.* Is order maintenance (or as Justice Thomas labels it, "peace-keeping") a crime control function or a community caretaker function? Should police have the general authority to ask citizens to "move on"? If you were a member of the Chicago City Council, could you draft a constitutional gang ordinance that would serve similar purposes to the ordinance struck down in *Morales?* State and federal cases on gang and order maintenance provisions are uncommon. Why?

In February 2000, the city of Chicago amended its anti-loitering ordinance to address the Court's concerns as expressed in *Morales.* The new ordinance prohibits loitering "under circumstances that would warrant a reasonable person to believe the purpose *or effect* of that behavior is to enable a criminal street gang to establish control over identifiable areas" (emphasis added). The ordinance itself now requires the police superintendent to designate "hot zones" of gang or narcotics activity, where the police may enforce the ordinance. The superintendent must consult community groups (along with various law enforcement officials) when designating the hot zones. Would the amended ordinance survive a constitutional challenge? Does it reinforce community crime control efforts?

2. *Community control of police.* The opinions of the Justices in *Morales* reveal different visions of "ordinary" policing and the ordinary methods of controlling police. For the plurality and concurring Justices, pre-announced rules of law are necessary to hold police discretion to an acceptable minimum; legislators and judges control the police through formal sources of law. For the dissenting Justices, police discretion is perfectly ordinary, even desirable. Control of the police comes from political pressure on elected officials at the local level rather than from pre-announced rules. Are these visions realistic about the power of legal rules or political pressure to influence police operations? Professors Dan Kahan and Tracey Meares argue that doctrines granting broad discretion to police officers (including loitering laws) are

more defensible today than in the 1960s because of the rising political power of African Americans in the nation's inner cities. Techniques formerly used to harass and exclude African Americans from public life could now become the tools of minority communities to free themselves from rampant criminality. Kahan and Meares, The Coming Crisis of Criminal Procedure, 86 Geo. L.J. 1153 (1998); see also Debra Livingston, Police Discretion and the Quality of Life in Public Places: Courts, Communities, and the New Policing, 97 Colum. L. Rev. 551 (1997). Is their vision of democratic accountability realistic?

3. *Community crime control.* Scholars have argued lately that crime control must come first from the community rather than the police. Hearkening back to work by sociologists in the 1930s and 1940s, these scholars argue that crime policies, including police authority, must be understood in the context of "place" or "social meaning." Pursuing this theme of localized and contextual understandings of crime and police power, Professor Tracey Meares has argued in favor of police strategies that reinforce the relationship between the police department and neighborhood organizations such as churches. See Meares, Place and Crime, 73 Chicago-Kent L. Rev. 669 (1998). So long as the notion of community is kept local and democratic, should community representatives (the police) have greater powers, such as the power to direct people to "move on"?

4. *Community crime control antecedents.* There are historic antecedents for today's forms of community crime control. Professor Jonathan Simon describes the thousand-year-old tradition of "frankpledge" in England, where each frankpledge group (originally 100 households) was held collectively responsible for crime control. From the tenth through the fifteenth centuries, free adult males had a legal obligation to "report offenses committed by other members of the group and to be financially obligated for any failure to produce the offender at presentment." During the "view of the frankpledge," the male population gathered before representatives of the crown and local elites. The officials collected taxes and fines, registered newcomers, and took reports on crime. In this way, the frankpledge system "integrated crime control into the everyday lives of the common people and local government." Simon, Poor Discipline: Parole and the Social Control of the Underclass 18-20 (1993). The frankpledge system created strong incentive for private social control of criminal behavior. Does it resemble crime control in small towns in the United States today? Is the frankpledge compatible with a mobile society? How does the relationship between citizen and police officer in a community policing model resemble the frankpledge?

Problem 1-1. Juvenile Curfews

At 10:35 P.M., 15-year-old David Simmons and a friend were skateboarding in a Panora, Iowa, shopping center. A police officer issued citations to them for violating a Panora juvenile curfew ordinance, which provided as follows:

1. It is unlawful for any minor [under 18] to be or remain upon any of the alleys, streets or public places or places of business and amusement in the city between the hours of 10 P.M. and 5 A.M. of the following day.
2. The curfew shall not apply to any minor who is accompanied by a guardian, parent or other person charged with the care and custody of such minor, or

other responsible person over 18 years of age, nor shall the restriction apply to any minor who is traveling between his home or place of residence and the place where any approved place of employment, church, municipal or school function is being held.

3. It is unlawful for any parent, guardian or other person charged with the care and custody of any minor to allow or permit such minor to be in or upon any of the streets, alleys, places of business, or amusement or other public places within the curfew hours except as provided in subsection 2.
4. It is unlawful for any person, firm or corporation operating a place of business or amusement to allow or permit any minor to be in or upon any place of business or amusement operated by them within the curfew hours except as provided in subsection 2.
5. Any peace officer of this city while on duty is hereby empowered to arrest any minor who violates the curfew. Upon arrest, the minor shall be returned to the custody of the parent, guardian or other person charged with the care and custody of the minor.

Simmons was found guilty of violating the curfew ordinance. The penalty imposed was a $1 fine plus surcharge and costs. Simmons appealed the conviction, with strong support from his parents. The Simmons family also asked the city council to repeal or amend the curfew ordinance.

As an appellate court judge, how would you rule on his appeal? Is the ordinance constitutional? As a member of the city council, would you vote to repeal or amend the ordinance? Compare City of Panora v. Simmons, 445 N.W.2d 363 (Iowa 1989).

Notes

1. *Juvenile curfews: majority position.* Many state and local governments have passed laws empowering the police to enforce a "curfew" on persons less than 18 years old. The practice is becoming commonplace: In 1996, about 80 percent of cities with populations over 30,000 had a nighttime youth curfew, up from 70 percent in 1995. See William Ruefle and K. M. Reynolds, Keep Them at Home: Juvenile Curfew Ordinances in 200 American Cities (U.S. Dept. of Justice 1996). Constitutional challenges to these laws fail more often than they succeed. The challengers argue that the curfews are unconstitutionally vague and interfere with fundamental rights such as the "right to travel" or the right of parents to make basic parenting decisions without governmental interference. Among the small number of high state courts ruling on the question, most have upheld the statutes or ordinances, noting that they do not simply ban juveniles from being "present" in public after dark. Instead, they allow juveniles to be outdoors for certain legitimate reasons or in the company of a parent. See In re J. M., 768 P.2d 219 (Colo. 1989). Most (but not all) federal courts of appeals have also rejected these constitutional challenges. See Hutchins v. District of Columbia, 188 F.3d 531 (D.C. Cir. 1999); Schleifer v. City of Charlottesville, 159 F.3d 843 (4th Cir. 1998).

2. *Adult curfews.* There is a long and largely disreputable history of adult curfews in the United States. Before the Civil War, curfew laws in the South designated times when slaves could be on the streets. During the late 1800s, curfew ordinances flourished in places where there were large numbers of immigrants, because of fears that

immigrants would not properly supervise their children. In 1941, emergency curfews were imposed on American citizens of Japanese ancestry. A variety of adult curfew, loitering, and vagrancy laws were invalidated in the late 1960s through the early 1980s as violations of the basic right of adult citizens to go where they want, whenever they want. See Papachristou v. City of Jacksonville, 405 U.S. 156 (1972) (striking down a vagrancy ordinance); Kolender v. Lawson, 461 U.S. 352 (1983) (rejecting a California statute requiring citizens who loiter to account for their presence and show "reasonable and reliable" identification when required by a police officer; Lawson detained about 15 times during two-year period for walking in isolated areas at late hours). The Supreme Court reaffirmed this line of cases by striking down the gang loitering ordinance in Chicago v. Morales, 527 U.S. 41 (1999). In a society terrified of crime, should courts reconsider the validity of adult curfew laws? Is the right to prowl at 3 A.M. essential to a free country?

3. *Police as enforcers: curfews as control measures.* For the first half of the twentieth century police departments (and sometimes the police chief acting alone) were given the power to set curfews. The remnants of this allocation of authority can be seen in statutes such as Rhode Island §11-9-11, which empowers the police commissioners or police chief to designate "curfew streets." In other states, courts have struck down such arrangements as excessive delegations of state legislative power. See, e.g., Thistlewood v. Trial Magistrate for Ocean City, 204 A.2d 688 (Md. Ct. App. 1964) (invalidating a curfew imposed by a committee of the police chief, mayor, and solicitor because of improper delegation); State v. Grant, 216 A.2d 790 (N.H. 1966) (reviewing history of police authority to set curfew hours and upholding delegation of authority to department).

4. *Police as parents: curfews as social welfare.* As a parent, how would you feel about a local curfew law? Would your decision depend on the sanctions attached to the law? Would it depend on your view of the police purpose when enforcing a curfew? Are police exercising a crime control function or a community caretaker function (or something else entirely) when they enforce a curfew?

D. TRADITIONAL AND COMMUNITY POLICING

The idea of what police do, and how they do it, is far from a static concept. From the introduction of police into municipalities in the mid-nineteenth century until the 1940s, local political leaders controlled police departments through job patronage and through investigating complaints from citizens. Police officers in this period responded to a wide variety of social needs including, but not limited to, crime control. The "reform era" followed, lasting from the 1940s until the 1980s. During this period, according to scholars George Kelling and Mark Moore,

> [r]eformers rejected politics as the basis of police legitimacy. . . . Civil service eliminated patronage and ward influences in hiring and firing police officers. In some cities . . . even the position of chief of police became a civil service position to be attained through examination. . . . Concern for separation of police from politics did not focus only on chiefs, however. In some cities, such as Philadelphia, it became illegal for patrol officers to live in the cities they patrolled.
>
> [P]olice in the reform era moved to narrow their functioning to crime control and criminal apprehension. Police agencies became *law enforcement* agencies. Their goal was

to control crime. Their principal means was the use of criminal law to apprehend and deter offenders. Activities that drew the police into solving other kinds of community problems . . . were identified as "social work," and became the object of derision. . . .

During the era of reform policing, the new model demanded an impartial law enforcer who related to citizens in professionally neutral and distant terms. No better characterization of this model can be found than television's Sergeant Friday whose response, "Just the facts, ma'am," typified the idea: impersonal and oriented toward crime solving rather than responsive to the emotional crisis of a victim.

[Reformers rejected foot patrol] as an outmoded, expensive frill. . . . Receipt of demand for police services was centralized. No longer were citizens encouraged to go to "their" neighborhood police officers or districts; all calls went to a central communications facility. When 911 systems were installed, police aggressively sold 911 and rapid response to calls for service as effective police service. . . .

O. W. Wilson developed the theory of preventive patrol by automobile as an anti-crime tactic. He theorized that if police drove conspicuously marked cars randomly through city streets and gave special attention to certain "hazards" (bars and schools, for example), a feeling of police omnipresence would be developed. In turn, that sense of omnipresence would both deter criminals and reassure good citizens.

Kelling and Moore, From Political to Reform to Community: The Evolving Strategy of Police, in Community Policing: Rhetoric or Reality (Jack Greene and Stephen Mastrofski eds. 1988).

When random patrol fell out of favor, departments created variations on the basic themes of the "reform" or "professional model" of policing. Departments used "directed" or "saturation" patrols to concentrate officers in problem areas, rather than spreading them randomly across an entire city. But these crackdowns on particular areas failed to produce long-lasting reductions in crime and undermined the relationship between police departments and the communities they served. David A. Kessler and Diane Borella, Taking Back Druid Hills: An Evaluation of a Community Policing Effort in Birmingham, Alabama, 19 Law & Policy 95 (1997).

In the past 20 years a new conception of the police function has emerged: "community policing." In its broadest outlines, community policing shifts control over police resources from central police management to the community level. Community policing broadens the goals of policing to include community order beyond crime control, and recognizes that fear of crime is a serious matter in its own right. The philosophy encourages officers to discuss with citizens in the community the most likely places where crime might occur, and to make those targets less appealing, rather than waiting to respond after a crime occurs. In these sweeping terms, it is difficult to find many police officers, or many departments, that have not embraced this change.

As these changes in police function become pervasive, the trend toward community policing may shift individual and public perceptions of what the police do. In turn, this change may require us to rethink much of modern criminal procedure, which is firmly anchored to the reform-era conception of policing. The following material describes in more detail the origin of the community-policing movement and some of its characteristics.

As you read the description below of this changing philosophy of policing, keep in mind its possible effect on procedural rules. If you were a city council member, would you pass an ordinance to give the police greater powers to "problem solve"? For instance, recall the curfew and "civility" cases from the previous sections. It is possible that departments adopting the community-policing philosophy should get greater leeway in enforcing civility or juvenile curfews. With the shift to community policing, are procedural controls on the police *less* important or feasible, or are they *more* important than ever — to prevent the officers from making arbitrary and discriminatory use of their more frequent interactions with the public?

■ COMMUNITY POLICING: A PRACTICAL GUIDE FOR POLICE OFFICIALS
LEE BROWN
(1989)

[In] response to problems such as crime, drugs, fear, and urban decay, the police have begun experimenting with new approaches to their tasks. Among the most prominent new approaches is the concept of community policing. Viewed from one perspective, it is not a new concept; the principles can be traced back to some of policing's oldest traditions. . . .

The evolution to community policy is not complete. What is commonly called traditional policing remains this country's dominant policing style. From its introduction in the 1930s through the 1970s, when it reached its peak of popularity, traditional policing has developed a number of identifying characteristics, such as the following:

- The police are *reactive* to incidents. The organization is driven by calls for police service.
- *Information* from and about the community is limited. Planning efforts focus on internally generated police data.
- *Planning* is narrow in its focus and centers on internal operations such as policies, procedures, rules, and regulations.
- *Recruitment* focuses on the spirit of adventure rather than the spirit of service.
- *Patrol officers* are restrained in their role. They are not encouraged or expected to be creative in addressing problems and are not rewarded for undertaking innovative approaches.
- *Training* is geared toward the law enforcement role of the police even though officers spend only 15 to 20 percent of their time on such activities.
- *Management* uses an authoritative style and adheres to the military model of command and control.
- *Supervision* is control-oriented as it reflects and reinforces the organization's management style.
- *Rewards* are associated with participating in daring events rather than conducting service activities.
- *Performance evaluations* are based not on outcomes but on activities. The number of arrests made and the number of citations issued are of paramount importance.
- *Agency effectiveness* is on the basis of data — particularly crime and clearance rates — from the FBI's Uniform Crime Reports.
- *Police departments* operate as entities unto themselves, with few collaborative links to the community.

For 40 years, traditional policing ostensibly served the public well, primarily because it was seen as a marked improvement over the policing style it had replaced — one that was characterized by negative political control and widespread corruption. Traditional policing gave citizens a false sense of security about police officers' ability to ensure the safety of the community. That the policing style might not be as effective as it seemed came into sharp focus by the middle of the 1960s and early 1970s when riots and protests exploded with rampant regularity across America. . . .

Although it is an operating style, community policing is also a *philosophy* of policing that contains several interrelated components. All are essential to the community policing concept and help distinguish it from traditional policing.

> **Results v. process.** The first component of the community policing philosophy is an orientation toward problem solving. . . .
>
> **Values.** Community policing also relies heavily on the articulation of policing values that incorporate citizen involvement in matters that directly affect the safety and quality of neighborhood life. . . .
>
> **Accountability.** Because different neighborhoods have different concerns, desires, and priorities, it is necessary to have an adequate understanding of what is important to a particular neighborhood. To acquire such an understanding, officers must interact with residents on a routine basis and keep them informed of police efforts to fight and prevent neighborhood crime. As the communication continues, a cooperative and mutually beneficial relationship develops between the police and the community. Inherent in this relationship is the requirement that officers keep residents abreast of their activities. . . .
>
> **Decentralization.** The decentralization of authority and structure is another component of community policing. . . .
>
> **Empowerment of beat officers.** Rather than simply patrolling the streets, beat officers are encouraged to initiate creative responses to neighborhood problems. . . .
>
> **Supervision and management.** Under community policing, the role of persons at all levels within the organization changes. For example, the patrol officer becomes the "manager" of his beat, while the first-line supervisor assumes responsibility for facilitating the problem-solving process by training, coaching, coordinating, and evaluating the officers under him. Management's role is to support the process by mobilizing the resources needed to address citizen concerns and problems. . . .
>
> **Training.** Also changed under community policing are all aspects of officer training. At the recruit level, cadets are provided information about the complexities and dynamics of the community and how the police fit into the larger picture. Cadet training also enables the future officer to develop community-organizing skills, leadership abilities, and a problem-solving perspective on the basis of the understanding that such efforts will be more effective if departmental and community resources are used in concert. . . .
>
> **Performance evaluation.** With the changed roles for all personnel comes the need for a revised system for evaluating officer performance. Rather than simply

counting numbers (e.g., number of citations issued, number of arrests made, number of calls handled), performance quality is on the basis of the officer's ability to solve problems and involve the community in the department's crime-fighting efforts. The criterion then becomes the *absence* of incidents such as criminal offenses, traffic accidents, and repeat calls-for-service.

Managing calls-for-service. Inherent in the community policing philosophy is the understanding that all police resources will be managed, organized, and directed in a manner that facilitates problem solving. For example, rather than directing a patrol car to each request for police service, alternative response methods are used whenever possible and appropriate. Such alternative techniques include the taking of incident reports over the telephone, by mail, or in person at police facilities; holding lower-priority calls; and having officers make appointments with an individual or a group. The result is more time available for officers to engage in problem-solving and community-organizing activities that lead to improvements in the quality of neighborhood life. Equally important, officers will be able to remain in their beats and handle those calls that require an on-scene response. . . .

By definition, then, community policing is *an interactive process between the police and the community to mutually identify and resolve community problems.* . . .

Questions Asked and Answered . . .

- *Is community policing social work?* Community policing calls for an expansion of the role of the police in that it focuses on problems from the citizen's point of view. Experience has shown that the concerns of citizens are often different from what the police would say they are. For example, before listening to citizens' concerns became routine, officers assumed that the public worried most about major crimes such as rape, robbery, and burglary. After talking with the people who live and work in their beat, officers found that the community's main concerns were quality-of-life issues such as abandoned cars and houses, loud noises, and rowdy youngsters. . . .
- *Will community policing result in less safe neighborhoods?* By any standard, the police working alone have been unable to control crime effectively. Experience has shown that increased citizen involvement results in more efficient crime control efforts. . . . Because community policing includes the public as a full partner in the provision of crime-prevention and crime-fighting services, it stands to reason that public safety will *increase* rather than decrease.
- *Will officers be reluctant to enforce the law under community policing?* . . . In most neighborhoods, only a small percentage of the population commits illegal acts. The goal of community policing is to become a part of the law-abiding majority and thereby develop a partnership to effectively deal with the law-violating minority. Experience has shown that if police work closely with the "good" citizens, the "bad" ones are either displaced or driven out of the area. It, therefore, is incorrect to suggest that as the police develop close relationships with the citizens in their beat, law violators will not be arrested. . . .
- *Will access to community policing be distributed fairly?* This question would be appropriate only if community policing were no more than a program; however

it is an overall operating *style* and philosophy of policing. Nowhere among the tenets of community policing is there anything that would, in and of itself, result in the unequal distribution of services between the poor and the affluent. By its very nature, community policing calls for the appropriate delivery of services to [meet the unique needs of] all neighborhoods. . . .

■ THE LIMITS OF THE CRIMINAL SANCTION HERBERT PACKER

(1968)

The kind of criminal process we have depends importantly on certain value choices that are reflected, explicitly or implicitly, in its habitual functioning. The kind of model we need is one that permits us to recognize explicitly the value choices that underlie the details of the criminal process. . . . It will take more than one model, but it will not take more than two. [I call my] two models the Due Process Model and the Crime Control Model. . . .

Crime Control Values

The value system that underlies the Crime Control Model is on the basis of the proposition that the repression of criminal conduct is by far the most important function to be performed by the criminal process. The failure of law enforcement to bring criminal conduct under tight control is viewed as leading to the breakdown of public order and thence to the disappearance of an important condition of human freedom. [T]he Crime Control Model requires that primary attention be paid to the efficiency with which the criminal process operates to screen suspects, determine guilt, and secure appropriate dispositions of persons convicted of crime. Efficiency of operation is not, of course, a criterion that can be applied in a vacuum. By "efficiency" we mean the system's capacity to apprehend, try, convict, and dispose of a high proportion of criminal offenders whose offenses become known. . . .

The model, in order to operate successfully, must produce a high rate of apprehension and conviction, and must do so in a context where the magnitudes being dealt with are very large and the resources for dealing with them are very limited. There must then be a premium on speed and finality. Speed, in turn, depends on informality and on uniformity; finality depends on minimizing the occasions for challenge. The process must not be cluttered up with ceremonious rituals that do not advance the progress of a case. Facts can be established more quickly through interrogation in a police station than through the formal process of examination and cross-examination in a court. It follows that extra-judicial processes should be preferred to judicial processes, informal operations to formal ones. But informality is not enough; there must also be uniformity. Routine, stereotyped procedures are essential if large numbers are being handled. The model that will operate successfully on these presuppositions must be an administrative, almost a managerial, model. The image that comes to mind is an assembly-line conveyor belt down which moves an endless stream of cases, never stopping, carrying the cases to workers who stand at fixed stations and who perform on each case as it comes by the same small but essential operation that brings it one step closer to being a finished product, or, to exchange the metaphor for the reality, a closed file. . . .

What is a successful conclusion? One that throws off at an early stage those cases in which it appears unlikely that the person apprehended is an offender and then secures, as expeditiously as possible, the conviction of the rest, with a minimum of occasions for challenge, let alone post-audit. By the application of administrative expertness, primarily that of the police and prosecutors, an early determination of probable innocence or guilt emerges. Those who are probably innocent are screened out. Those who are probably guilty are passed quickly through the remaining stages of the process.

[T]here have to be devices for dealing with the suspect after the preliminary screening process has resulted in a determination of probable guilt. The focal device, as we shall see, is the plea of guilty; through its use, adjudicative fact-finding is reduced to a minimum. . . .

Due Process Values

If the Crime Control Model resembles an assembly line, the Due Process Model looks very much like an obstacle course. Each of its successive stages is designed to present formidable impediments to carrying the accused any further along in the process. . . .

The Due Process Model encounters its rival on the Crime Control Model's own ground in respect to the reliability of fact-finding processes. The Crime Control Model . . . places heavy reliance on the ability of investigative and prosecutorial officers, acting in an informal setting in which their distinctive skills are given full sway, to elicit and reconstruct a tolerably accurate account of what actually took place in an alleged criminal event. The Due Process Model rejects this premise and substitutes for it a view of informal, nonadjudicative fact-finding that stresses the possibility of error. People are notoriously poor observers of disturbing events. . . . Considerations of this kind all lead to a rejection of informal fact-finding processes as definitive of factual guilt and to an insistence on formal, adjudicative, adversary fact-finding processes in which the factual case against the accused is publicly heard by an impartial tribunal and is evaluated only after the accused has had a full opportunity to discredit the case against him.

[M]ore is at stake than simply an evaluation of what kinds of fact-finding processes, alone or in combination, are likely to produce the most nearly reliable results. The stumbling block is this: how much reliability is compatible with efficiency? Granted that informal fact-finding will make some mistakes that can be remedied if backed up by adjudicative fact-finding, the desirability of providing this backup is not affirmed or negated by factual demonstrations or predictions that the increase in reliability will be *x* percent or *x* plus *n* percent. It still remains to ask how much weight is to be given to the competing demands of reliability (a high degree of probability in each case that factual guilt has been accurately determined) and efficiency (expeditious handling of the large numbers of cases that the process ingests). . . .

All of this is only the beginning of the ideological difference between the two models. [The values of the Due Process Model could] be expressed in, although not adequately described by, the concept of the primacy of the individual and the complementary concept of limitation on official power. The combination of stigma and loss of liberty that is embodied in the end result of the criminal process is viewed as being the heaviest deprivation that government can inflict on the individual. Furthermore, the processes that culminate in these highly afflictive sanctions are seen as in themselves coercive, restricting, and demeaning. Power is always subject to abuse — sometimes subtle, other times, as in the criminal process, open and ugly. Precisely because of its potency in subjecting the individual to the coercive power of the state, the criminal process must, in this model, be subjected to controls that prevent it from operating with maximal efficiency. According to this ideology, maximal efficiency means maximal tyranny. . . .

Notes

1. *Are your police community police?* Do you recognize the police approach described by former Houston police chief (and later federal drug czar) Lee Brown in the activities and attitudes of your local police? Are there any dangers in the community policing approach?

Periodic surveys of local police departments show that the rhetoric and practices of community policing are spreading quickly in the United States. As of 1999, 64 percent of all local police departments employed at least some "community police" officers; 21 percent of all full-time sworn police officers in the nation were devoted to community policing. On an operational level, police departments in 1999 reported greater use of foot and bicycle patrol, assignment of officers to fixed geographic beats, outreach to neighborhood associations and other community organizations, surveys of citizens about their satisfaction with police services, and use of computers for crime mapping. Bureau of Justice Statistics, Community Policing in Local Police Departments, 1997 and 1999 (February 2001, NCJ 184794). How might each of these activities carry out the "community policing" philosophy?

2. *Allocation of police services.* Brown says that community policing calls for the "appropriate delivery of services" to all neighborhoods. If poor neighborhoods and rich neighborhoods both want more police services, what principles should be used to allocate resources? Suppose the burglary rate in an affluent area is so low, and the presence of private security services so high, that the police department decides to eliminate police presence entirely for that neighborhood. Is this a rational choice? A fair one?

3. *Whom do the police serve?* What do you think about Brown's suggestion that society is divided into a majority of law-abiding "us" and a minority of law-breaking "them"? Will this view of society produce different procedural rules than a view in which the distinction, over time, is not so clear between who is law abiding and who is a law breaker? Are "us" or "them" more likely to engage in minor violations of the law (such as speeding)? Income tax evasion? Stock fraud? See Arnold Loewy, Protecting Citizens from Cops and Crooks, 62 N.C. L. Rev. 329 (1984).

4. *Potential impact on criminal procedure.* Community policing tends to give more authority to the officer on the beat and to give supervisors less control over daily activities and choices of patrol officers. Does this development make it difficult to enforce procedural requirements? Is the decentralizing of authority inconsistent with the very idea of uniform rules of procedure influencing all police officers? As you read cases on searches and seizures in Chapters 2-7, ask yourself how many of the police in these cases were acting in a community policing mode. Would your view of the cases, or the proper rules, change if the police adopted a different philosophy?

5. *Herbert Packer's models of criminal procedure and the community policing philosophy.* Professor Herbert Packer created a way of thinking about criminal procedure that has remained highly influential to this day. His "Crime Control" and "Due Process" models offer a way to identify some of the values and assumptions of different approaches to procedural controversies. You might find it useful to refer to these models as organizing principles from time to time as you think about difficult procedural questions later in this course. How do Packer's two models differ in their description of police work? Do the two models share any assumptions about policing? Would a shift to "community" policing be more appealing to a Crime Control advocate or to a Due Process advocate? Or does community policing promote forms of policing that Packer's account does not address at all? Consider an alternative method of thinking about the criminal process, proposed by John Griffiths:

> . . . Packer's [model] rests not upon two but upon a single, albeit unarticulated, basic conception of the nature of the criminal process — that it is a battleground of fundamentally hostile forces, where the only relevant variable is the "balance of advantage." [Packer] assumes disharmony, fundamentally irreconcilable interests, a state of war. We can start from an assumption of reconcilable — even mutually supportive — interests, a state of love. [There is] a "real-world" institution which occasionally inflicts punishments on offenders for their offenses but which is nonetheless built upon a fundamental assumption of harmony of interest and love. [I therefore offer] a "Family Model" of the criminal process. [People operating within the Family Model would accept] the idea that criminals are just people who are deemed to have offended — that we are all . . . both actual and potential criminals. . . .
>
> What other implications would follow from a Family Model? For one thing, that ideology would necessarily be accompanied by a basic faith in public officials; everyone would assume, as a general matter, that if a public official has a particular role or duty, he can be expected to carry it out in good faith and using his best judgment. . . . Basic faith in public officials would revolutionize American criminal procedure. We are all used to the proposition that legal procedures — indeed, the organization of government in general — must be designed with the bad man, or the man who will unwittingly misuse his powers, primarily in mind. . . . Our assumption that the state and the individual are in battle compels us to believe that any "discretion" — any active responsibility going beyond the umpiring role of a judge — will necessarily be exercised either on behalf of the individual's interest or on behalf of the state's. We see only Packer's two poles as the possible outcomes of discretion.

Griffiths, Ideology in Criminal Procedure, or a Third "Model" of the Criminal Process, 79 Yale L.J. 359 (1970).

II

Brief Searches and Stops

Police officers sometimes restrict the movement of individuals ("seize" them) or intrude into their privacy to obtain information ("search" them). But in most of these encounters, the stop or search does not last very long or intrude very deeply. Courts and legislatures have established rules to control these encounters between government agents and the public. Yet the restrictions on this police behavior are not as demanding as the rules that apply when government agents attempt to carry out a full-blown search or seizure. This chapter deals with efforts to regulate these lesser searches and seizures.

One of the most important legal constraints on these brief searches and seizures comes from the Fourth Amendment to the U.S. Constitution, which provides as follows:

> The right of the people to be secure in their persons, houses, papers, and effects, against unreasonable searches and seizures, shall not be violated, and no Warrants shall issue, but upon probable cause, supported by Oath or affirmation, and particularly describing the place to be searched, and the persons or things to be seized.

The Fourth Amendment and its analogs in state constitutions have spawned a huge and complex case law. They have also shaped many state and federal statutes, as well as prosecutorial office guidelines and police department directives and training manuals. To understand the complex law of search and seizure, it is helpful (and probably necessary) to approach the material with some general conceptual framework. Two different frameworks for organizing the extensive modern law of search and seizure suggest themselves in the cases and other legal materials.

The traditional framework for searches and seizures begins with the oft-repeated remark that the Fourth Amendment incorporates a strong preference for search warrants (that is, a judicial determination that a proposed search is justified), that warrantless searches are generally considered unreasonable, and that exceptions to the "warrant requirement" are "jealously and carefully drawn." State and federal courts invoke this theme. This preference for warrants grows out of the apparent emphasis on limited warrants in the constitutional text. Some statutes also implicitly make warrants the standard and unwarranted searches truly exceptions. For example, Mont. Code Ann. §46-5-101 provides that

> [a] search of a person, object, or place may be made and evidence, contraband, and persons may be seized . . . when a search is made: (1) by the authority of a search warrant; or (2) in accordance with judicially recognized exceptions to the warrant requirement.

Before the late 1960s, the number of recognized exceptions to the warrant requirement were indeed fairly few. Most prominent were two umbrella categories, exigent circumstances and consent. Warrants were generally required unless the police could show exigent circumstances or consent to search or seize. Within the category of exigent circumstances, courts developed exceptions to the warrant requirement such as risk of flight, destruction of evidence, or an officer's personal observation of a crime.

In the traditional framework, the justification necessary to proceed with a valid search or seizure, whether carried out with or without a warrant, was probable cause. Once a court was convinced that the government's activity amounted to a "search" or "seizure," the court insisted that the government show probable cause to justify its action. A sensible approach for the study of search and seizure in such a legal system is to start with the foundational elements — the process for warrants and the standard of probable cause — and then to identify and study the exceptions.

Organizing a field according to its foundational rules and exceptions works well if the rules are ordinarily followed and the exceptions are modest. But in the modern law of search and seizure the exceptions have swallowed the traditional rules. In doing so, they have changed the entire framework and the best way to study searches and seizures.

Modern search and seizure law is astoundingly complex and contradictory. A survey of current "exceptions" to the warrant requirement — some of which appear in this chapter, and others in Chapters 3 and 4 — suggests how unwieldy the traditional framework has become. A partial list would include exigent circumstances (such as flight or destruction of evidence), the direct observation of crime, plain view, open fields, community caretaker functions, brief investigative stops, brief frisks for weapons, inventory searches, protective sweeps, automobile searches, border searches, school searches, prison searches, arrests in public places, searches incident to arrest, fire investigations, and administrative searches. See Craig Bradley, Two Models of the Fourth Amendment, 83 Mich. L. Rev. 1468 (1985).

What has caused such complexity in this area of the law? Three changes, marked by three U.S. Supreme Court cases decided in 1967 and 1968, rearranged the doctrinal foundations of search and seizure law. Because these cases appear at different points in the book, a preview here is useful.

The first key case was Katz v. United States, 389 U.S. 347 (1967). In *Katz,* the U.S. Supreme Court changed the method of deciding whether a person had an interest that the Fourth Amendment would protect. In other words, it redefined the basic *conceptual framework* for deciding whether the government had engaged in a "search" that is subject to constitutional limitations. In doing so, the Court moved away from concepts of protected physical spaces (property) and toward concepts of individual privacy.

Katz was convicted of transmitting gambling information by telephone across state lines; crucial evidence in the case came from a wiretap of a public phone booth. The intermediate appeals court found no Fourth Amendment violation and upheld Katz's conviction because the listening device had been placed on the outside of the telephone booth, and thus there was "no physical entrance into the area occupied" by Katz. This was a straightforward application of the "trespass" theory of unreasonable searches, with historical origins in the tort suits that the targets of unreasonable searches filed against the officers who had improperly invaded their property interests. But the Supreme Court reversed Katz's conviction, finding that the Fourth Amendment protected Katz against having his conversation in a telephone booth recorded by the government. The Court described the key doctrinal shift as follows:

> [T]he parties have attached great significance to the characterization of the telephone booth from which the petitioner placed his calls. The petitioner has strenuously argued that the booth was a "constitutionally protected area." The Government has maintained with equal vigor that it was not. But this effort to decide whether or not a given "area," viewed in the abstract, is "constitutionally protected" deflects attention from the problem presented by this case. For the Fourth Amendment protects people, not places. What a person knowingly exposes to the public, even in his own home or office, is not a subject of Fourth Amendment protection. But what he seeks to preserve as private, even in an area accessible to the public, may be constitutionally protected.

What are the implications of deciding that the Fourth Amendment "protects people, not places"? The shift to a privacy analysis has drawn a larger number and variety of governmental actions into Fourth Amendment territory. It is far easier to make a claim about "expectations of privacy" in a host of situations than it would be to make a claim based on property interests. As the courts have applied the Fourth Amendment to new settings, they have generated new law and departed more frequently from the concepts of probable cause and warrants.

The second key case to transform search and seizure doctrine is Terry v. Ohio, 392 U.S. 1 (1968), which we will study in section D of this chapter. *Terry* moved beyond the relative simplicity of having a single *standard*— probable cause — to assess the validity of searches and seizures. *Terry* recognized a major category of limited stops and searches that law enforcement officers could conduct on the basis of reasonable suspicion — a standard less than probable cause. By recognizing that standards other than probable cause would be appropriate for justifying various kinds of searches and seizures, the Court invited more deviations from the traditional doctrinal core of the Fourth Amendment.

The third key case is Camara v. Municipal Court, 387 U.S. 523 (1967), which created a new *method* for determining what justification the government would need for a search and what process it would follow to establish that justification. In *Camara,* the Supreme Court approved the granting of warrants for municipal building code enforcement inspections. These inspections took place on the basis of general administrative needs for inspecting an area, without requiring any individualized suspicion that a property owner was violating the law. The Court in *Camara* declared that the Fourth Amendment applied to both civil and criminal law enforcement efforts. With such a diversity of governmental purposes and activities at issue, the complexity of search and seizure doctrine was bound to increase. Furthermore, the opinion in *Camara* announced that it would "balance" competing interests to determine the level of justification and the type of warrant process the government would need to follow before conducting a search: "[T]here can be no ready test for determining reasonableness other than by balancing the need to search against the invasion which the search entails."

These cases have fractured search and seizure doctrine and increased the overall complexity of the law. Whether these changes are good or bad, they have made search and seizure law more difficult to learn and apply.

Perhaps some new principle or calculus offers a more satisfying synthesis of these changes in the law than the traditional framework of warrants and probable cause can offer. As you study the materials in the next few chapters, try to construct a coherent explanation for the cases and laws that govern searches and seizures.

In particular, consider the explanatory value of a calculus that weighs three recurring factors in determining the "reasonableness" of a search or seizure: (1) the privacy interest of the person subject to a search; (2) the government's interest in conducting the search; and (3) the degree of intrusion from the search. The balancing of these three factors may solve such crucial puzzles as the level of justification necessary to support the search (such as probable cause, reasonable suspicion, or no individualized suspicion) and the time when the government must give its justification (before the search to obtain a warrant, or after the fact when the target challenges the search).

You will have the opportunity to test this conceptual framework, along with the more traditional framework that emphasizes probable cause and warrants, and to analyze a wide array of government efforts to collect information. The following materials begin with the briefest and most common government searches and seizures.

A. BRIEF INVESTIGATIVE STOPS OF SUSPECTS

Countless times each day, a police officer or some other government agent stops to talk with a member of the general public. Some citizens take part in these conversations willingly; others are more reluctant but feel obliged to stay and continue the conversation. A few do not cooperate at all. What authority does the officer have to insist that a citizen stop for a few moments during an investigation?

■ DELAWARE CODE TIT. 11, §1902

(a) A peace officer may stop any person abroad, or in a public place, who the officer has reasonable ground to suspect is committing, has committed or is about to commit a crime, and may demand the person's name, address, business abroad and destination.

(b) Any person so questioned who fails to give identification or explain the person's actions to the satisfaction of the officer may be detained and further questioned and investigated.

■ ALASKA STATUTES §28.35.182(a)

A person commits the offense of failure to stop at the direction of a peace officer . . . if the person, while driving or operating a vehicle or motor vehicle . . . knowingly fails to stop as soon as practical and in a reasonably safe manner under the circumstance when requested or signaled to do so by a peace officer.

Notes

1. *Three types of encounters: conversations, stops, and arrests.* These statutes set out a typical set of requirements for police officers who stop a person in a vehicle or on foot in public. While more than 30 states codify these requirements in statutes or rules of criminal procedure, others announce the requirements in judicial opinions. Most are not recent innovations; for instance, the Delaware statute above was adopted in 1951 and is based on the Uniform Arrest Act of 1940. The Supreme Court ratified the constitutionality of this framework in Terry v. Ohio, 392 U.S. 1 (1968), a case we discuss later in this chapter. If you were a police officer, would you prefer explicit statutory authority to stop suspects, or would you rather see the power established and developed in case law? See George Dix, Nonarrest Investigatory Detentions in Search and Seizure Law, 1985 Duke L.J. 849.

These statutes assume the existence of three different levels of controls on the officer. On the first level, where the police officer does not "stop" a person at all but merely engages in a conversation, the officer does not need to justify the decision to focus attention on one person. On the second level, where the officer "stops" a person for a brief time but not long enough to qualify as an arrest, the officer must have "reasonable suspicion" before making the stop. Reasonable suspicion has also been described as "individualized" or "articulable" suspicion. On the third level, where the officer detains a person for a longer time or in a more coercive way, there is an "arrest." Constitutions, statutes, and rules of procedure all require that the officer show "probable cause" that the individual has committed a crime.

Thus, for the brief encounters we are now exploring, there are three questions to resolve: Was the encounter a "stop" subject to constitutional or statutory limits at all? If the incident was a stop, did the government agent have adequate grounds to justify the stop? Did the stop amount to an arrest?

2. *The prevalence of stops and consensual encounters.* Consensual conversations and stops (particularly traffic stops) are the two most common forms of interaction between the police and the public. According to a 1999 national survey, about 21 percent of all persons age 16 or older had at least one contact with a police officer during the year. About half of those contacts occurred during a motor vehicle stop; another 20 percent of the contacts happened when people reported a crime to the police. Only about three percent of the contacts occurred because the officer suspected the person of a crime. Bureau of Justice Statistics, Contacts Between Police and the Public: Findings from the 1999 National Survey (February 2001, NCJ 184957).

3. *Ambiguous statutory language.* Will defense counsel and prosecutors in Delaware agree on what constitutes a "reasonable ground" for a stop under the statute? Will they agree on how long the "further" questioning can last under the statute? How should the trial court resolve their disagreements? What sources will be

relevant? Is the court's task here the same as when parties dispute the meaning of some phrase that has developed through the common law? As you read further in this chapter, take special note of the methods courts use to resolve conflicts about the meaning of ambiguous statutory language.

1. Consensual Encounters and "Stops"

Conversations change direction. Sometimes a conversation between a police officer and a member of the public will begin as a "consensual encounter" but will transform into a "stop" without the officer's announcement of this fact in so many words. What marks the difference between consensual encounters and coercive stops?

■ UNITED STATES v. SYLVIA MENDENHALL

446 U.S. 544 (1980)

STEWART, J.

[Sylvia Mendenhall] arrived at the Detroit Metropolitan Airport on a commercial airline flight from Los Angeles early in the morning on February 10, 1976. As she disembarked from the airplane, she was observed by two agents of the Drug Enforcement Administration (DEA), who were present at the airport for the purpose of detecting unlawful traffic in narcotics. After observing the respondent's conduct, which appeared to the agents to be characteristic of persons unlawfully carrying narcotics,[1] the agents approached her as she was walking through the concourse, identified themselves as federal agents, and asked to see her identification and airline ticket. The respondent produced her driver's license, which was in the name of Sylvia Mendenhall, and, in answer to a question of one of the agents, stated that she resided at the address appearing on the license. The airline ticket was issued in the name of "Annette Ford." When asked why the ticket bore a name different from her own, the respondent stated that she "just felt like using that name." In response to a further question, the respondent indicated that she had been in California only two days. Agent Anderson then specifically identified himself as a federal narcotics agent and, according to his testimony, the respondent "became quite shaken, extremely nervous. She had a hard time speaking."

After returning the airline ticket and driver's license to her, Agent Anderson asked the respondent if she would accompany him to the airport DEA office for further questions. She did so, although the record does not indicate a verbal response to the request. The office, which was located up one flight of stairs about 50 feet from where the respondent had first been approached, consisted of a reception area

1. The agent testified that the respondent's behavior fit the so-called "drug courier profile"—an informally compiled abstract of characteristics thought typical of persons carrying illicit drugs. In this case the agents thought it relevant that (1) the respondent was arriving on a flight from Los Angeles, a city believed by the agents to be the place of origin for much of the heroin brought to Detroit; (2) the respondent was the last person to leave the plane, "appeared to be very nervous," and "completely scanned the whole area where [the agents] were standing"; (3) after leaving the plane the respondent proceeded past the baggage area without claiming any luggage; and (4) the respondent changed airlines for her flight out of Detroit.

adjoined by three other rooms. At the office the agent asked the respondent if she would allow a search of her person and handbag and told her that she had the right to decline the search if she desired. She responded: "Go ahead." She then handed Agent Anderson her purse, which contained a receipt for an airline ticket that had been issued to "F. Bush" three days earlier for a flight from Pittsburgh through Chicago to Los Angeles. The agent asked whether this was the ticket that she had used for her flight to California, and the respondent stated that it was.

A female police officer then arrived to conduct the search of the respondent's person. . . . The policewoman explained that the search would require that the respondent remove her clothing. . . . As the respondent removed her clothing, she took from her undergarments two small packages, one of which appeared to contain heroin, and handed both to the policewoman. The agents then arrested the respondent for possessing heroin. It was on the basis of this evidence that the District Court denied the respondent's motion to suppress. . . .

The Fourth Amendment provides that "the right of the people to be secure in their persons, houses, papers, and effects, against unreasonable searches and seizures, shall not be violated. . . ." The Fourth Amendment's requirement that searches and seizures be founded upon an objective justification, governs all seizures of the person, including seizures that involve only a brief detention short of traditional arrest. Terry v. Ohio, 392 U.S. 1 (1968). Accordingly, if the respondent was "seized" when the DEA agents approached her on the concourse and asked questions of her, the agents' conduct in doing so was constitutional only if they reasonably suspected the respondent of wrongdoing. But "obviously, not all personal intercourse between policemen and citizens involves 'seizures' of persons. Only when the officer, by means of physical force or show of authority, has in some way restrained the liberty of a citizen may we conclude that a 'seizure' has occurred." *Terry,* 392 U.S., at 19, n.16.

The distinction between an intrusion amounting to a "seizure" of the person and an encounter that intrudes upon no constitutionally protected interest is illustrated by the facts of Terry v. Ohio, which the Court recounted as follows: "Officer McFadden approached the three men, identified himself as a police officer and asked for their names. . . . When the men 'mumbled something' in response to his inquiries, Officer McFadden grabbed petitioner Terry, spun him around so that they were facing the other two, with Terry between McFadden and the others, and patted down the outside of his clothing." Obviously the officer "seized" Terry and subjected him to a "search" when he took hold of him, spun him around, and patted down the outer surfaces of his clothing. What was not determined in that case, however, was that a seizure had taken place before the officer physically restrained Terry for purposes of searching his person for weapons. The Court "assume[d] that up to that point no intrusion upon constitutionally protected rights had occurred." The Court's assumption appears entirely correct in view of the fact [that police officers enjoy the liberty possessed by every citizen] to address questions to other persons. . . .

We adhere to the view that a person is "seized" only when, by means of physical force or a show of authority, his freedom of movement is restrained. Only when such restraint is imposed is there any foundation whatever for invoking constitutional safeguards. The purpose of the Fourth Amendment is not to eliminate all contact between the police and the citizenry, but to prevent arbitrary and oppressive interference by enforcement officials with the privacy and personal security of individuals. As long as the person to whom questions are put remains free to disregard the questions and walk away, there has been no intrusion upon that person's liberty or privacy as would under the Constitution require some particularized and objective justification.

Moreover, characterizing every street encounter between a citizen and the police as a "seizure," while not enhancing any interest secured by the Fourth Amendment, would impose wholly unrealistic restrictions upon a wide variety of legitimate law enforcement practices. The Court has on other occasions referred to the acknowledged need for police questioning as a tool in the effective enforcement of the criminal laws. Without such investigation, those who were innocent might be falsely accused, those who were guilty might wholly escape prosecution, and many crimes would go unsolved. In short, the security of all would be diminished.

We conclude that a person has been "seized" within the meaning of the Fourth Amendment only if, in view of all of the circumstances surrounding the incident, a reasonable person would have believed that he was not free to leave.[6] Examples of circumstances that might indicate a seizure, even where the person did not attempt to leave, would be the threatening presence of several officers, the display of a weapon by an officer, some physical touching of the person of the citizen, or the use of language or tone of voice indicating that compliance with the officer's request might be compelled. In the absence of some such evidence, otherwise inoffensive contact between a member of the public and the police cannot, as a matter of law, amount to a seizure of that person.

On the facts of this case, no "seizure" of the respondent occurred. The events took place in the public concourse. The agents wore no uniforms and displayed no weapons. They did not summon the respondent to their presence, but instead approached her and identified themselves as federal agents. They requested, but did not demand to see the respondent's identification and ticket. Such conduct without more, did not amount to an intrusion upon any constitutionally protected interest. The respondent was not seized simply by reason of the fact that the agents approached her, asked her if she would show them her ticket and identification, and posed to her a few questions. Nor was it enough to establish a seizure that the person asking the questions was a law enforcement official. In short, nothing in the record suggests that the respondent had any objective reason to believe that she was not free to end the conversation in the concourse and proceed on her way, and for that reason we conclude that the agents' initial approach to her was not a seizure.

Our conclusion that no seizure occurred is not affected by the fact that the respondent was not expressly told by the agents that she was free to decline to cooperate with their inquiry, for the voluntariness of her responses does not depend upon her having been so informed. We also reject the argument that the only inference to be drawn from the fact that the respondent acted in a manner so contrary to her self-interest is that she was compelled to answer the agents' questions. It may happen that a person makes statements to law enforcement officials that he later regrets, but the issue in such cases is not whether the statement was self-protective, but rather whether it was made voluntarily. [The court also held that Mendenhall had "voluntarily" proceeded to the DEA office, and consented to the search of her person.]

6. We agree with the District Court that the subjective intention of the DEA agent in this case to detain the respondent, had she attempted to leave, is irrelevant except insofar as that may have been conveyed to the respondent.

■ WESLEY WILSON v. STATE

874 P.2d 215 (Wyo. 1994)

TAYLOR, J.

[L]imping severely, Wesley Wilson . . . walked rapidly eastbound on 12th Street in Casper, Wyoming on the morning of June 21, 1991. At 12:31 A.M., Officer Kamron Ritter . . . of the Casper Police Department watched Wilson's "lunging" steps and pulled his patrol car over to the sidewalk. Officer Ritter, believing that a fight may have taken place, asked if Wilson was okay and what happened to his leg. Wilson responded that he had twisted his ankle at a party. Smelling alcohol on Wilson's breath, Officer Ritter requested identification which Wilson provided. Officer Ritter radioed for a routine warrants check with the National Crime Information Center (NCIC) and local files. This initial encounter with Wilson lasted about a minute and a half.

The conversation with Wilson was interrupted when Officer Ritter detected smoke coming from 12th Street, west of where he was standing. At the same time, two motorcyclists stopped and reported to Officer Ritter that a fire was burning in a building [one block] up the street. Before leaving to check on the fire, Officer Ritter told Wilson to "stay in the area."

Officer Ritter reported the fire to the police dispatcher. . . . After about eight minutes at the scene of the fire, Officer Ritter returned to check on Wilson. He had limped about 40 feet farther east and was attempting to cross 12th Street. As additional fire trucks approached, Officer Ritter helped Wilson cross the street. Officer Ritter then told Wilson to go to a nearby corner and "wait" while the officer returned to the fire scene.

As Officer Ritter provided traffic control, the police dispatcher radioed, at 12:41 A.M., that Wilson had two outstanding arrest warrants. Officer Ritter and Officer Terry Van Oordt then walked down the block to where Wilson was sitting on a lawn at the corner watching the fire. When the officers approached Wilson, they informed him of the outstanding warrants and asked him to stand. Wilson told the officers it was difficult to stand with his injured ankle. The officers noticed an oily patch on the right shoulder of the shirt Wilson was wearing. Both officers touched the stained area and found an oily substance. Wilson volunteered, "What are you doing? I don't smell like smoke." The officers proceeded to arrest Wilson on the outstanding warrants. The following morning, in custody, Wilson made a voluntary statement implicating himself in starting the fire.

At a suppression hearing, Officer Ritter testified about his concerns for Wilson's safety during their initial encounter and that he had no suspicions of Wilson's involvement in the fire or of arresting him for public intoxication. Officer Ritter stated he followed routine Casper Police Department procedure to get the names of subjects police come in "contact" with "at that time of night" and "always" run a warrants check. Officer Ritter said he wanted Wilson to wait until the results of the warrants check were received. During their second encounter, when Officer Ritter helped Wilson cross the street, the officer testified he still had no suspicion of Wilson's potential involvement in the fire but wanted Wilson to wait for the completion of the warrants check. . . .

Wilson, who did not testify at the hearing, argued that the stop was illegal and the evidence gathered from the stop [including his statements about smoke and his confession] should be suppressed.* [The district court denied the suppression motion, and the jury convicted Wilson of felony property destruction.]

Wilson's statement of the issues presumes his appeal is one based on provisions of both the United States Constitution and the Wyoming Constitution. The language of Wyo. Const. art. 1, §4 differs somewhat from its federal counterpart in providing:

> The right of the people to be secure in their persons, houses, papers and effects against unreasonable searches and seizures shall not be violated, and no warrant shall issue but upon probable cause, supported by affidavit, particularly describing the place to be searched or the person or thing to be seized.

[However,] we are unable to consider the impact of those differences in this situation because Wilson . . . failed to offer any argument supporting an independent state constitutional claim. . . . The Fourth Amendment to the United States Constitution grants

> the right of the people to be secure in their persons, houses, papers, and effects, against unreasonable searches and seizures, shall not be violated, and no Warrants shall issue, but upon probable cause, supported by Oath or affirmation, and particularly describing the place to be searched, and the persons or things to be seized.

[The] decision of the United States Supreme Court in Terry v. Ohio, 392 U.S. 1 (1968) marked the initial recognition by the United States Supreme Court of some lesser standard than probable cause for intrusion upon constitutionally guaranteed rights. In *Terry,* a police officer, observing specific conduct which his training and experience taught him was indicative of criminal behavior, conducted a limited seizure to investigate his reasonable suspicions. In the course of such a seizure, the United States Supreme Court approved a limited search for weapons for the protection of the police officer. . . .

From this genesis, a general recognition of the rich diversity of police-citizen encounters has emerged. [T]hree categories or tiers of interaction between police and citizens may be characterized. The most intrusive encounter, an arrest, requires justification by probable cause to believe that a person has committed or is committing a crime. The investigatory stop represents a seizure which invokes Fourth Amendment safeguards, but, by its less intrusive character, requires only the presence of specific and articulable facts and rational inferences which give rise to a reasonable suspicion that a person has committed or may be committing a crime. The least intrusive police-citizen contact, a consensual encounter, involves no restraint of liberty and elicits the citizen's voluntary cooperation with non-coercive questioning.

The proper test for determining when a police-citizen encounter implicates Fourth Amendment rights as a seizure was initially outlined in United States v. Mendenhall, 446 U.S. 544 (1980). [The Court] found no seizure had occurred where federal drug agents approached a woman walking through an airport and requested her identification. [The *Mendenhall* standard] creates an objective test, which makes the subjective intent of the police officer irrelevant unless it is

* The ordinary remedy for the violation of the defendant's constitutional rights is the exclusion of the evidence obtained as a result of the improper seizure during the prosecution's case at trial. Exclusion is not the only possible remedy. See discussion in Chapter 6.—Eds.

conveyed to the person being detained, and like all search and seizure cases, the inquiry is very fact oriented. The reasonable person standard also means the subjective perceptions of the suspect are irrelevant to the court's inquiry.

[A]n analytical difficulty imposed by [this] standard lies in the determination of whether a reasonable person "would have believed that he was not free to leave" when being questioned by a police officer. We find useful instruction in the Model Code of Pre-Arraignment Procedure, §110.1 commentary at 259-60 (A.L.I. 1975):

> The motives that lead one to cooperate with the police are various. To put an extreme case, the police may in purely precatory language request a person to give information. Even if he is guilty, such a person might accede to the request because he has been trained to submit to the wishes of persons in authority, or because he fears that a refusal will focus suspicion, or because he believes that concealment is no longer possible and a cooperative posture tactically or psychologically preferable. Regardless of the particular motive, the cooperation is clearly a response to the authority of the police.
>
> By specifically authorizing law enforcement officers . . . to seek cooperation, the Code rejects the notion that a damaging response to an inquiry from a policeman can never be "voluntary." . . . The extra pressures to cooperate with what is known to be an official request require no further justification than that the request was made in the performance of law enforcement functions. That there exist such pressures seems to us, far from being regrettable, to be a necessary condition of the police's capacity to operate reasonably effectively within their limited grant of powers.

The critical distinction between the position advanced by Wilson and that argued by the State is which type of encounter occurred in this case. Wilson basically contends that he was seized without reasonable suspicion during the period when his identification was being checked for possible warrants. The State asserts that Wilson was never seized in a manner that would implicate Fourth Amendment rights, until he was validly arrested on the outstanding warrants. . . .

The initial encounter between Officer Ritter and Wilson was prompted by the officer's concerns for the safety of a citizen. The officer conducted himself in a reasonable manner by simply pulling his patrol car to the curb to talk with Wilson. No flashing lights or siren sounds were used to signal Wilson to stop. The community caretaker function . . . permits police to act in a manner that enhances public safety. The police officer's observation of specific and articulable facts, Wilson's lunging walk with a severe limp, reasonably justified a brief inquiry into his condition and the possible cause, such as whether Wilson was a victim of criminal conduct. This portion of the initial encounter between Officer Ritter and Wilson occurred in a consensual atmosphere which implicates no Fourth Amendment interest.

When Officer Ritter requested Wilson's name and identification and Wilson complied, the encounter remained consensual. A request for identification is not, by itself, a seizure. Indeed, a reasonable person in physical distress should feel less intimidated by a police officer's offer to help and a request for identification than someone stopped at random. . . .

After obtaining Wilson's identification, Officer Ritter radioed for the NCIC and local warrants check. Despite the request for the computerized warrants check, the encounter remained consensual. Officer Ritter had not imposed any restriction on Wilson's freedom to leave as the warrants check was instituted. . . .

The initial encounter ended when Officer Ritter detected smoke and the two motorcyclists stopped to report a fire. At that point, Officer Ritter told Wilson to "stay in the area." [No seizure occurred at this point] because, when left unattended, [Wilson] limped away from the immediate area where the questioning had occurred. . . .

When Officer Ritter left the fire scene and returned to check on Wilson for the second time, [he] assisted Wilson across the street by grabbing him at the elbow and supporting his weight. [The] physical touching in this instance did not effect a seizure. A reasonable person would not believe that an officer's assistance in crossing a street would represent a restriction on the person's freedom to leave. The aid Officer Ritter provided ensured Wilson's safety by removing him from the path of emergency vehicles.

After Officer Ritter and Wilson crossed the street, the officer instructed Wilson to go to a specific street corner and wait. We hold a seizure occurred at the point when Wilson complied with the instruction to wait given by Officer Ritter in their second encounter. As Officer Ritter directed traffic, he could see Wilson sitting in front of a retail store at the specific corner the officer had directed. The persistence of Officer Ritter in returning to check on Wilson only supplements the determination that a seizure occurred. The show of authority by Officer Ritter restrained Wilson's liberty. A reasonable person would have believed he or she was not free to leave. With his seizure, Wilson's Fourth Amendment right to be free of unreasonable intrusions was implicated.

The narrow issue remaining is whether a brief detention for the purpose of completing a computerized warrants check is an unreasonable seizure. [It] is Casper Police Department policy to conduct NCIC and local warrants checks of everyone police "contact" late at night. The meaning of a "contact" was never defined. However, a seizure to conduct a computerized identification check without reasonable suspicion is not permitted. We acknowledge that where police have been unable to locate a person suspected of involvement in a past crime, the ability to briefly stop that person, ask questions, or check identification in the absence of probable cause promotes the strong government interest in solving crimes and bringing offenders to justice. However, we do not find in the circumstances of Officer Ritter's encounter with Wilson justification for a seizure . . . for the purpose of investigating past crime. . . . Officer Ritter questioned Wilson and requested his identification solely on the basis of the officer's concern for a citizen's safety. The officer lacked any reasonable suspicion of past criminal conduct. . . . When no observed violation of law is present, the intrusion required to run an NCIC or warrants check requires reasonable suspicion of criminal conduct. . . .

Officer Ritter admitted in his testimony that at no time during the first or second encounters did he possess any articulable facts sufficient to create a reasonable suspicion of past or present criminal conduct. Acting in a community caretaker function, Officer Ritter stopped Wilson to inquire about his condition and ensure his safety. A seizure for the purpose of completing an NCIC and local warrants check was impermissible as a matter of law. . . .

In a society burdened by crime, the protection of individual liberties requires difficult choices. All of us want to be able to freely walk the streets of our cities and towns. While we cannot and should not tolerate crime and lawlessness, we equally cannot tolerate the abrogation of basic liberties. Permitting a seizure, without reasonable suspicion of criminal behavior, to complete a computerized identification check of a police "contact" represents an unreasonable intrusion on basic liberties. . . .

The decision of the district court to deny suppression is reversed and this case is remanded for retrial without the tainted evidence.

THOMAS, J., dissenting.

I must dissent from the majority opinion in this case. . . . The contact between the officer and Wilson never went beyond the elicitation of Wilson's voluntary cooperation so as to become a seizure. [Wilson never asked to leave.] The officer testified he would not have pursued Wilson if he had chosen to leave because he had no reason to detain him if Wilson did not consent. . . . Laying aside the question whether there was any constraint upon Wilson's freedom to leave, an elapsed period of ten minutes, during which the officer's attention was devoted to the fire and traffic direction, is not unreasonable. The record reveals, of the ten minutes, Wilson was in the presence of the officer less than three minutes. . . .

The American bench needs to understand that its invocation of the premise of protecting Constitutional rights in reversing criminal convictions has contributed to the development of a society in which violence stalks our streets and fear permeates our neighborhoods. Every decision that tightens the cuffs with which we shackle our law enforcement officers contributes to such evolution. We must remember this rule applies to serial killers and multiple rapists as well as to inept firebugs who are simply a nuisance to property, until someone dies in the fire. . . .

In my judgment, the real question to be addressed in this case is: What was going on that was wrong? The obvious answer is it was wrong for Wilson to set fire to another citizen's garage-workshop. . . . The conclusion Wilson's conviction should not be upheld because of an academic fascination with the supposed wrongful conduct of the police officer does not serve the interests of the citizens of Wyoming and their property rights, which are not constitutionally subordinated to the rights of their persons. . . . I most vigorously dissent.

Notes

1. *Definition of a "stop": majority position.* Most American jurisdictions have chosen to define a "stop" along the lines set out in United States v. Mendenhall, 446 U.S. 544 (1980). An encounter between a police officer and a citizen becomes a "stop" when a reasonable person in that situation would not "feel free to leave" or to refuse to cooperate. Jurisdictions have generally adopted this definition in judicial decisions construing the state constitution rather than settling the question through statutes or rules of procedure. Is this the same "reasonable person" you met in Torts?

2. *Does reality matter?* In theory, empirical inquiries could help us answer the question of whether a reasonable person would "feel free to leave" in a given situation. How would you gather such information for a court to use? Did the Wyoming court in *Wilson* show any curiosity about the best method for finding a psychologically realistic answer to the question? See Daniel J. Steinbock, The Wrong Line Between Freedom and Restraint: The Unreality, Obscurity, and Incivility of the Fourth Amendment Consensual Encounter Doctrine, 38 San Diego L. Rev. 507 (2001).

3. *The relevant pool.* The concept of the "reasonable person" is familiar in tort law and substantive criminal law. Courts applying the reasonable person concept are sometimes willing to consider particular features of the victim (age or gender, for instance) in their definition of a reasonable person. In effect, courts will

sometimes narrow the relevant "pool" of persons from which the reasonable person is drawn.

Should the reasonable person standard for purposes of defining a "stop" consider the experiences and perceptions of different racial groups in their dealings with the police? Different genders? There is ample sociological and survey evidence that black males perceive the police to be more discriminatory and abusive than do white males. If a court is convinced that black males are more likely than other groups to submit passively to police encounters, should it account for this in the totality of the circumstances that go into the definition of a "stop"? See Devon W. Carbado, (E)Racing the Fourth Amendment, 100 Mich. L. Rev. 946, 974-1003 (2002).

4. *Routine check for warrants.* The court ultimately found that Ritter did not seize Wilson when he first requested a warrant check. Do you agree? Did Ritter "seize" Wilson without reasonable suspicion when he followed police department policy and requested an NCIC and warrant check on the person he "contacted" at night? The court concludes that Ritter later detained Wilson for the purpose of "completing" the warrant check. Did Ritter ever tell Wilson that he intended to complete the warrant check before releasing him? Does the status of a warrant check as a "stop" depend on how often police officers allow the individual to walk away before the check is complete? Or is it more important to know how this particular citizen (or a "reasonable" citizen) *believes* the officer would react? Can we measure an actual reasonable person's belief or response? See State v. Daniel, 12 S.W.3d 420 (Tenn. 2000) (officers approach young men in parking lot of convenience store; request for their identification did not "seize" them until the officers held onto the ID cards to run computer check for warrants).

5. *Limiting stops to investigations of serious crimes.* Should stops be available to police officers investigating misdemeanors? Most states have granted this power to the police, although there are exceptions. See N.Y. Crim. Proc. Law §140.50 (grants power to stop only when officer suspects commission of felony or the most serious misdemeanors); State v. Duvernoy, 195 S.E.2d 631 (W. Va. 1973) (limiting power to stop to investigate nonviolent offenses). Does your position on this issue depend on how effective a policy of investigative stops can be in preventing specific crimes? See Gordon Whitaker, Charles Phillips, Peter Haas, and Robert Worden, Aggressive Policing and the Deterrence of Crime, 7 Law & Poly. 395 (1985) (investigative stops have strong negative effects on rate of robberies, auto theft, vandalism; smaller effects on rates of burglaries and thefts of property from autos). Does it depend on the racial makeup of the police force?

6. *Stopping those suspected of past crimes.* The American Law Institute's Model Code of Pre-Arraignment Procedure (1975), in §110.2(c), empowers an officer to stop any person she reasonably suspects of committing, in the past, "a felony involving danger of forcible injury to persons or of appropriation of or damage to property." Why does the Model Code not allow stops to investigate less serious crimes committed in the past? Courts typically allow these stops to investigate past crimes, even less serious crimes. But see United States v. Hensley, 469 U.S. 221 (1985) ("[I]f police have a reasonable suspicion, grounded in specific and articulable facts, that a person they encounter was involved in or is wanted in connection with a completed felony, then a . . . stop may be made to investigate that suspicion"). Which is more susceptible to abuse; stops to investigate completed crimes or stops to investigate potential crimes?

7. *Stopping witnesses on reasonable suspicion.* If a police officer has reasonable suspicion to believe that a person is a witness to a crime, can the officer insist that the

potential witness give a name and address? Several states have statutes authorizing the police to detain potential witnesses for a short time to obtain their names and addresses. For instance, Rule 3.5 of the Arkansas Rules of Criminal Procedure authorizes short detentions of potential witnesses, but only if the crime involved is a felony. See also Mont. Code Ann. §46-5-403 (stop and search when occupant of vehicle is witness to crime). The ALI's Model Code, §110.2(b), allows officers to stop witnesses near the scene of misdemeanors and felonies involving "forcible injury to persons or of appropriation or danger to property." Other statutes, however, do not confine this power to felony cases. Given that the police officer intends only to question a witness and not to develop and file criminal charges against that person, should these stops be subject to different limits from stops of suspects?

8. *Duration of stop and subject matter of questions.* When an officer stops a car based on reasonable suspicion that a traffic violation has occurred, it creates an opportunity to investigate other crimes. But the opportunity is limited. It is clear that the stop can only last as long as it would ordinarily take to complete a routine traffic citation. See State v. Ballard, 617 N.W.2d 837 (S.D. 2000) (officer informs motorist that traffic stop is over, but detains at location long enough to call drug-sniffing dogs; improper stop extending beyond duration of traffic stop). It is less clear whether there are any limits on the subjects that an officer can discuss during the limited time available during a traffic stop. State and federal courts are currently split on this question. How would you frame an argument for limiting the subject matter of any questions?

Problem 2-1. Tickets, Please

At 3:30 A.M. on January 23, Battaglia, an investigator from the Sheriff's Department boarded a bus just as it arrived in Albany from New York City. Battaglia wore civilian clothing with his police badge prominently displayed on his coat. Two uniformed officers accompanied him. Battaglia announced to the fifteen passengers on board that he was conducting a drug interdiction. He said that he would ask everyone to produce bus tickets and identification. Battaglia then walked to the rear of the bus and saw Rawle McIntosh and a female companion sitting in the last row of seats. Battaglia noticed that McIntosh pushed a black jacket between himself and his companion. He asked McIntosh for his identification and bus ticket. Battaglia inspected the driver's license and ticket he provided, and asked him about his travel plans. Battaglia then returned the identification and the ticket to McIntosh, and asked the two passengers to stand. As they stood, the jacket remained on the seat. Noticing a bulge in the pocket of the jacket, Battaglia reached into the pocket and found cocaine.

Did Battaglia "stop" McIntosh? If so, exactly when did the stop happen? Would there be a stop if Battaglia questioned McIntosh about his identity and his travel plans without requesting or holding the ticket and identification document? See People v. McIntosh, 755 N.E.2d 329 (N.Y. 2001).

Now suppose that McIntosh refused to provide the proof of his identity when Officer Battaglia requested it, and he is prosecuted under a statute punishing any person for refusing to provide proof of identity when a police officer makes such a request. The state legislature passed this statute in the aftermath of the terrorist attacks in New York City on September 11, 2001. Is the statute constitutional?

Notes

1. *Asking for name and identification.* Does a stop occur whenever a police officer asks for a person to produce proof of identity? Does it matter how the officer asks for the identification card or how quickly she returns the card? How could anyone feel free to leave when an officer is holding his driver's license? More than 20 state legislatures have passed statutes empowering police officers to ask for identification. In other states, the judiciary has permitted the police to make this request without specific statutory authority. If a statute authorizes a request for identification only upon reasonable suspicion (as statutes typically do), does that suggest that any police request for a citizen's identification is a stop? Apart from asking for name and identification, are there certain questions a police officer might ask that should automatically convert a conversation into a stop?

Could a statute explicitly oblige citizens to comply with the request for identification and allow officers to restrain citizens who refuse to do so? Is that what the Delaware statute allows? There is little litigation so far over the question of whether such a statute is constitutional. The questions become more immediate in light of the September 11 terrorist attacks. Some states have now increased the amount of information included on drivers' licenses: some now require a picture where none appeared before, and some include a fingerprint. If drivers' licenses started including DNA information about the card holder, would a legislature become less willing to give the police power to see the card on demand? The law in other countries, such as Germany and France, explicitly empowers police officers to insist that people identify themselves. What would you want to know about these laws to determine whether they offer useful guidance for legislatures in the United States?

2. *Seizures in close quarters.* In Florida v. Bostick, 501 U.S. 429 (1991), the Court considered an encounter between police officers and a suspected drug courier who consented to a search of his luggage during questioning on a bus. Terrance Bostick was reclining on the back seat of the Greyhound bus bound from Miami to Atlanta when two officers wearing badges and sheriff's department jackets boarded the bus during a rest stop. The officers proceeded to the rear of the bus, stood in the aisle in front of Bostick, and questioned him about his destination. They requested that he produce his ticket and identification. After returning the documents, the officers stated that they were narcotics agents in search of illegal drugs. Then they asked for Bostick's consent to search his bag, telling him that he did not have to consent. He did consent, and they discovered cocaine in the bag. The Supreme Court decided that the agents did not "stop" Bostick when they questioned him on the bus. Although Bostick was not literally "free to leave" during the questioning because the officers were blocking the aisle of the bus, the Court concluded that a reasonable person in Bostick's position could have felt "free to decline the officers' requests or otherwise terminate the encounter." Compare United States v. Drayton, 122 S. Ct. 2105 (2002) (no "stop" when two officers question passengers on bus while standing behind passenger's seat, one officer remains at front of bus watching passengers).

3. *The reasonable person standard and the guilty suspect.* When trying to determine whether police seized a person during a conversation, courts have often stated that the exchange amounts to a seizure only if a "reasonable person" would conclude that he is not free to go. In Florida v. Bostick, the defendant argued that any person carrying contraband in a piece of luggage would not freely consent to a search of the

luggage in his presence. Hence, he argued, his agreement to allow the search of his bag demonstrated that he did not feel free to leave. The court replied that the reasonable person standard "presupposes an innocent person." Does this standard lead to the conclusion that *any* refusal to engage in a conversation with a police officer amounts to reasonable suspicion for a stop? What if a jurisdiction adopts a more subjective standard from the citizen's perspective (e.g., did the person actually believe she was free to leave)?

2. *Grounds for Stops: Articulable, Individualized Reasonable Suspicion*

To justify a "stop," the government agent must be able to articulate a reasonable suspicion that the person has committed or will commit a crime. Exactly how can an officer establish reasonable suspicion? This concept is among the most commonly invoked in criminal procedure. Judges and lawyers applying the concept speak with apparent assurance about its meaning. Yet it is surprisingly difficult to find a precise definition of reasonable suspicion. And even a precise standard will leave enormous difficulties when applied to varied circumstances.

Judicial decisions, statutes, and rules of procedure use somewhat different verbal formulations to describe the justification needed for a low-level stop. Some formulations, especially those of the U.S. Supreme Court, emphasize the difference between reasonable suspicion and probable cause (the level of proof necessary to justify an arrest or a full-blown search):

> The Fourth Amendment requires some minimal level of objective justification for making the stop [that] is considerably less than proof of wrongdoing by a preponderance of the evidence. We have held that probable cause means a fair probability that contraband or evidence of a crime will be found, and the level of suspicion required for [reasonable suspicion] is obviously less demanding than that for probable cause. The concept of reasonable suspicion, like probable cause, is not readily, or even usefully, reduced to a neat set of legal rules. . . . In evaluating the validity of a stop such as this, we must consider the totality of the circumstances — the whole picture. [United States v. Sokolow, 490 U.S. 1 (1989).]

Some formulations emphasize that reasonable suspicion must be *more* than a guess and that it must be based on objective and articulable facts about an individual:

> [I]n justifying the particular intrusion the police officer must be able to point to specific and articulable facts which, taken together with rational inferences from those facts, reasonably warrant that intrusion. . . . And in determining whether the officer acted reasonably in such circumstances, due weight must be given, not to his inchoate and unparticularized suspicion or "hunch," but to the specific reasonable inferences which he is entitled to draw from the facts in light of his experience. [Terry v. Ohio, 392 U.S. 1 (1968).]

Still other formulations insist that the reasonable suspicion standard is fact-sensitive, and the facts necessary to meet the standard will change from one context to another.

> The following are among the factors to be considered in determining if the officer has grounds to "reasonably suspect": (1) The demeanor of the suspect; (2) The gait and

manner of the suspect; (3) Any knowledge the officer may have of the suspect's background or character; (4) Whether the suspect is carrying anything, and what he is carrying; (5) The manner in which the suspect is dressed, including bulges in clothing, when considered in light of all of the other factors; (6) The time of the day or night the suspect is observed; (7) Any overheard conversation of the suspect; (8) The particular streets and areas involved; (9) Any information received from third persons, whether they are known or unknown; (10) Whether the suspect is consorting with others whose conduct is "reasonably suspect"; (11) The suspect's proximity to known criminal conduct; (12) Incidence of crime in the immediate neighborhood; (13) The suspect's apparent effort to conceal an article; (14) Apparent effort of the suspect to avoid identification or confrontation by the police. [Ark. Stat. §16-81-203.]

As used in [the following sections], unless the context requires otherwise: . . . "Reasonably suspects" means that a peace officer holds a belief that is reasonable under the totality of the circumstances existing at the time and place the peace officer acts. [Oregon Rev. Stat. §131.605.]

■ STATE v. THEODORE NELSON

638 A.2d 720 (Me. 1994)

GLASSMAN, J.

Theodore Nelson appeals from the judgment entered . . . on a jury verdict finding him guilty of operating a motor vehicle while under the influence of intoxicating liquor. . . . We agree with Nelson that because the stop of his motor vehicle was unlawful, the District Court erred in not granting Nelson's motion to suppress the evidence secured as a result of the stop and we vacate the judgment. . . .

At the hearing before the District Court on Nelson's motion to suppress, the sole witness presented was Officer Michael Holmes, who testified as follows: On December 24, 1991, at approximately 1:30 A.M., while on patrol . . . , he observed an unoccupied automobile he knew belonged to Bruce Moore, a former neighbor of his, in a well-lit parking lot at a housing complex for the elderly located on North Main Street. Because the police department within the prior two weeks had received several complaints of theft during the nighttime, Officer Holmes took up an observation post in a small parking lot adjacent to the driveway to the complex and approximately 50 to 100 yards from the Moore automobile. He observed a white pickup truck occupied by a driver, later identified as Nelson, and one passenger enter the driveway to the complex. The pickup was backed into a parking space beside the Moore vehicle, the motor was shut off, and the headlights extinguished leaving the parking lights illuminated. With the use of binoculars, Officer Holmes recognized the passenger as Moore. He observed each of the occupants of the pickup starting to drink from a 16-ounce Budweiser can. There was no evidence that Officer Holmes observed anything unusual about the appearance of either occupant. After approximately forty-five to fifty minutes, Moore left the pickup truck and entered his own vehicle. The headlights of the pickup truck were turned on and it was again driven past Officer Holmes onto North Main Street. As the pickup passed his observation site, Officer Holmes immediately "pulled out behind it, and turned on [his] blue lights, [and] made an enforcement stop." Nelson promptly brought the pickup to a stop. At no time did Officer Holmes observe anything unusual about the operation of the pickup. There was no evidence of mechanical defects to the pickup or of excessive speed. He stopped the pickup because he "observed the operator . . .

drinkin' a can of beer [and suspected that] the person may be under the influence of intoxicating liquor." The District Court held "Officer Holmes had reasonable articulable suspicion to stop the Defendant's vehicle," and denied Nelson's motion to suppress evidence secured as a result of the claimed illegal stop. . . .

Every person is protected from unreasonable intrusions by police officers and other governmental agents by the Fourth Amendment to the United States Constitution and article I, section 5 of the Maine Constitution. An investigatory stop is justified if at the time of the stop the officer has an articulable suspicion that criminal conduct has taken place, is occurring, or imminently will occur, and the officer's assessment of the existence of specific and articulable facts sufficient to warrant the stop is objectively reasonable in the totality of the circumstances. . . . It is well established that the suspicion for the stop must be based on information available to the officer at the time of the stop and cannot be bolstered by evidence secured by the stop. . . .

In the instant case, we find a clear deficiency in the evidence supporting the reasonableness of the suspicion. The record reveals that the officer observed nothing to support his suspicion that Nelson was operating under the influence of alcohol other than Nelson's consumption of a single can of beer over the course of nearly one hour. An adult's consumption of liquor in a motor vehicle is neither a crime nor a civil violation. The reasonable suspicion standard requires more than mere speculation. There was no evidence that the officer observed indicia of physical impairment or anything unusual in Nelson's appearance. Officer Holmes testified that the pickup truck was not being operated in an erratic manner. The officer offered no reason for his stop of the motor vehicle other than his suspicion that Nelson was under the influence of alcohol.

Based on the whole picture presented by this case, it cannot be said that it was objectively reasonable to believe that criminal activity was afoot. Accordingly, the court should have granted Nelson's motion to suppress the evidence secured as a result of the illegal stop. Judgment vacated.

Collins, J., dissenting.

. . . The stop in this instance was not based on mere speculation that Nelson was driving while under the influence. Rather, the officer had observed Nelson drinking a 16-ounce beer, at 1:30 in the morning on Christmas Eve, while parked in the parking lot of a housing complex for the elderly from which several complaints of theft had been registered. These observed facts, in combination with the recognition of the common practice in American society of having a second beer, gave the officer an articulable suspicion that Nelson was operating his truck while under the influence of alcohol. The officer's suspicion was objectively reasonable given the totality of the circumstances. As such, I believe the stop was justified and I would affirm the trial court.

■ STATE v. DAVID DEAN

645 A.2d 634 (Me. 1994)

Rudman, J.

[David Dean entered a conditional plea of guilty to charges of operating a vehicle under the influence of alcohol. He now appeals on the ground that the stop was not justified by reasonable suspicion.] The underlying facts are undisputed. At approximately 11:00 P.M. on Tuesday, April 13, 1993, Officer Dennis Sampson of the South Paris Police Department spotted Dean's car while Sampson was patrolling a new residential development on Cobble Hill Road. The road is a dead end, and the development was uninhabited during weekdays. Sampson was patrolling the area at the request of the development's property owners after a number of complaints of vandalism. No complaint had been made that night, and Dean's driving was unremarkable. Sampson stopped him solely because of his presence at that particular time and place. Sampson "wanted to see what they was up to, see if they were landowners or property owners, get some names in case we did have problems up in that area." The District Court, in a well-reasoned opinion, ruled that Sampson had the necessary "reasonable suspicion" to justify the stop. . . .

Dean's contention is that Officer Sampson did not entertain any suspicion that Dean was engaged in criminal activity. Dean raises the specter of random stops in any high-crime area, justified solely by the fact that the person detained happens to be in that area. The District Court, however, understood Dean's contentions and explicitly made the required findings:

> Now, I'll point out that the facts in this case suggest that this particular defendant was driving along a dead-end road at nighttime. The — the structures in the area were uninhabited, and it had been an area which had been the scene of a variety of criminal behavior which, in fact, brought . . . if not residents then the property owners to the police. They asked for increased surveillance. Ordinarily, the officer could not have stopped this particular vehicle. But under the circumstances, given the fact that this occurred well after dark, that the place was virtually uninhabited, that it was a dead-end street and [an area] in which a substantial amount of crime had been perpetrated in the recent past — I find that the officer acted properly because he reasonably suspected, based on prior reports of criminal activity in the area, that this particular Defendant could be engaged in such behavior. . . .

The only real issue is whether the two articulable facts relied on by the court can yield a reasonable suspicion. Those two facts are: (1) Dean's presence in an area of recent crime reports; and (2) the apparent absence of any reason to be in an uninhabited area at night. It is well-settled that a person's mere presence in a high crime area does not justify an investigatory stop. However, the combination of the recent criminal activity with other articulable facts — in this case, the time of day and the fact that the area was uninhabited — creates a reasonable suspicion. Many cases uphold a finding of a reasonable suspicion on similar facts.

In a recent decision, also involving police surveillance of an area due to several complaints, we held that the District Court erred by failing to grant the defendant's motion to suppress. State v. Nelson (Me. 1994). . . . In the *Nelson* case, however, the defendant was sitting in a truck in the parking lot of an occupied housing complex. Dean, in contrast, was driving through an uninhabited development site on a dead end street at 11:00 at night. His situation is distinguishable from that of the defendant in *Nelson*.

Dean's situation is more analogous to that of the defendant in State v. Fitzgerald, 620 A.2d 874 (Me. 1993). After dark, a police officer spotted Fitzgerald's car entering a private turn-around, known to be the site of frequent illegal trash dumping, and posted with "no trespassing" signs by the owner. When the officer's vehicle drove into the turn-around, the defendant was standing next to his car. The defendant then got into his car and drove away. The officer stopped the defendant's vehicle, saw that the defendant displayed evidence of being under the influence of alcohol, and arrested him for operating under the influence. Although the officer never witnessed any illegality or impropriety (Fitzgerald never violated the no trespassing signs), we affirmed the finding that the officer had a reasonable and articulable suspicion, "based on the previous littering and trespassing," the fact that Fitzgerald was outside his car in the dark when the officer approached, and the fact that Fitzgerald tried to leave when he saw the cruiser. Similarly, Officer Sampson's suspicion of Dean was engendered by prior complaints combined with other facts — the time of night and the absence of any apparent reason to be in an uninhabited housing development.

But for Dean's intoxication, this would have been a brief investigatory stop. An investigatory stop of a motor vehicle is normally a minimal intrusion by the state into a person's affairs. Balancing the facts on which Officer Sampson relied to make the stop against Dean's right to be free from any arbitrary intrusions by the State, we find the District Court's findings that the officer's suspicion was reasonable and the stop was justified are not clearly erroneous.

Glassman, J., dissenting.

I respectfully dissent. We have recently reemphasized that the reasonable articulable suspicion standard requires "more than mere speculation" on the part of the police officer to sustain an investigatory stop. State v. Nelson (Me. 1994). Dean's behavior in driving out of a dead-end street at 11:00 P.M. on a Tuesday was in no sense illegal or even inherently suspicious, and the officer's desire to "see what [Dean] was up to" stems, at best, from a hunch.[1] A mere hunch will not justify a stop, and the officer's reasons for stopping the vehicle must not be a mere pretext or ruse. . . .

As the court notes, it is well settled that a person's mere presence in a high-crime area does not justify an investigatory stop. What the court regards as "other articulable facts" justifying the stop, in reality, are mere speculations entertained by the officer because of Dean's presence on a public way in an area where there had been complaints of vandalism or other damage to property. Each of the cases cited by the court to support its position involves additional facts beyond the defendant's mere presence in a crime area, e.g., police observed unusual behavior by the defendant, intrusion onto private property, the unusual operation of a vehicle, or the vehicle's unusual location. The constitutional right to be free from an illegal stop should not be abridged solely on the basis of the day of the week or time of day a car is being operated on a public way. . . .

Notes

1. *Components of reasonable suspicion: majority position.* Courts typically do not specify the general categories of facts that could support a finding of reasonable

1. The court seeks to distinguish *Nelson* by noting that Nelson was sitting in a pickup truck parked in the parking lot of an occupied housing complex whereas Dean was observed driving a motor vehicle on a public way leading out of a largely uninhabited residential development site. This is inapposite because the surroundings in which the police observed Nelson were not at issue in that case, which turned on whether merely drinking a can of beer in a parked car provided a reasonably articulable suspicion that a crime had taken place. This case turns on the site of the stop.

suspicion. In virtually all cases, however, the conduct of the suspect said to be the basis for reasonable suspicion does not violate the criminal law. The observer must infer from the observed facts that there is some correlation between the legal conduct observed and the suspected criminal acts. The officer may observe something resembling criminal conduct (such as the legal acts necessary to prepare for a crime); she might also observe the suspect taking an action that could be designed to hide a crime or to avoid contact with the police (such as avoiding eye contact with the officer or running away from the scene). See Sibron v. New York, 392 U.S. 40 (1968). The surroundings of the suspect are another common component of reasonable suspicion: For instance, presence near a crime scene at the time of a crime would be significant, especially if the suspect has no other apparent reason to be in that location. See State v. Maya, 493 A.2d 1139 (N.H. 1985) (defendant near scene of recent burglary at 1 A.M., street virtually deserted). How strong should the correlation be between this innocent conduct and the suspected criminal conduct to establish reasonable suspicion? Why do courts and other legal institutions scrupulously avoid answering this question in terms of numeric probabilities?

A study of stops in New York City gives us one indication of the level of certainty police officers believe in practice to be enough for reasonable suspicion. During a two-year period, a specialized Street Crimes Unit made 45,000 stops, with about 20 percent of those stops resulting in an arrest or criminal charges. See Jeffrey Goldberg, The Color of Suspicion, N.Y. Times Magazine, June 20, 1999, p.85. Do these figures indicate that police officers have 20 percent confidence that a crime has been or is about to be committed when they make a stop? If so, is that enough certainty?

2. *Do standards matter?* Are *Nelson* and *Dean* consistent; that is, do they reflect a single standard of reasonable suspicion? If you were representing Nelson and Dean, where would you rather argue the case: under the statutory definition of reasonable suspicion in Oregon or Arkansas or the judicial definition in Maine? Do different formulations of the reasonable suspicion standard make any difference in the outcomes?

3. *Objective basis.* The basis for reasonable suspicion turns on the facts available to the officer; it does not matter whether the officer holds an actual suspicion. In fact, the officer might wrongly believe that reasonable suspicion exists for one crime, when in fact reasonable suspicion exists for another crime. Should the "reasonable suspicion" promote more careful evaluation of facts by police officers? Can an objective standard accomplish this?

4. *Seriousness of crime.* Would the reasonable suspicion determination in *Dean* have turned out differently if the suspected crime had been murder instead of vandalism of property? Was the police officer in *Nelson* concerned about a different crime from the one he ultimately charged? Should the seriousness of the crime committed or soon to be committed affect the determination of reasonable suspicion? See State v. Pully, 863 S.W.2d 29 (Tenn. 1993) (upholding stop to investigate tip of man armed with shotgun); Commonwealth v. Hawkins, 692 A.2d 1068 (Pa. 1997) (rejects concept of fluctuating reasonable suspicion standard based on seriousness of crime suspected; no "gun exception" to reasonable suspicion requirement).

5. *Codified definitions of reasonable suspicion.* This section began with examples of statutes defining reasonable suspicion. Similar definitions appear in some states' rules of criminal procedure. The statutory examples draw on language familiar in

judicial opinions defining the same concept; that is, they codify the common law. Would the presence of such a statute or rule affect a court's willingness to elaborate on the meaning of reasonable suspicion or to adjust it over time?

6. *Role of appellate courts in defining reasonable suspicion.* Under the "totality of the circumstances" test, the factfinder at the trial level takes a central role in deciding whether reasonable suspicion exists. What contributions might an appellate court make? Could an appeals court bring more predictability to the process by describing the sorts of factors that should receive more or less weight? For instance, should an appellate court declare that conduct "as consistent with innocent activity as with criminal activity" should receive little or no weight? See Irwin v. Superior Court of Los Angeles County, 462 P.2d 12, 14 (Cal. 1969) (adopting innocent conduct limit); State v. O'Meara, 9 P.3d 325 (Ariz. 2000) ("totality of circumstances" test for reasonable suspicion allows court to consider conduct susceptible of an innocent explanation; here, unusual meeting in parking lot with drivers switching among four vehicles established reasonable suspicion for stop).

In Ornelas v. United States, 517 U.S. 690 (1996), the U.S. Supreme Court held that appellate courts would determine for themselves, under a de novo standard, the presence or absence of reasonable suspicion. This standard, the Court said, would prevent the affirmance of opposite decisions on identical facts from different judicial districts, and would allow appellate courts to unify precedent and clarify the legal principles at stake, providing law enforcement officers with the tools to reach correct determinations beforehand. At the same time, the Court declared that a reviewing court must give "due weight" to factual inferences drawn by resident judges. In United States v. Arvizu, 534 U.S. 266 (2002), the Court applied this standard of review to affirm a trial judge's finding of reasonable suspicion. A Border Patrol agent stopped Arvizu while driving on an unpaved road in a remote area of southeastern Arizona, and discovered over 100 pounds of marijuana in the minivan. The officer became suspicious when the driver of the minivan slowed dramatically after the patrol car appeared, and the children in the back seat waved to the officer in an "abnormal" and "mechanical" fashion, off and on for about five minutes. While each of these facts was "susceptible to innocent explanations" when viewed in isolation, the trial judge nevertheless could consider them as part of the "totality of the circumstances" to establish reasonable suspicion. An appellate court should not "casually" reject factors such as these "in light of the District Court's superior access to the evidence and the well-recognized inability of reviewing courts to reconstruct what happened in the courtroom." Is this a de novo standard of review at work?

7. *Anonymous tips as the basis for reasonable suspicion.* Ordinarily, the police obtain reasonable suspicion based on their own observations and investigations. But on occasion, the police receive information from an anonymous informant that might contribute later to a finding of "reasonable suspicion." The U.S. Supreme Court has stated that anonymous tips can contribute to a reasonable suspicion finding only if the police can find independent corroboration of "significant details" of the informant's information. Alabama v. White, 496 U.S. 325 (1990). Those significant details must amount to more than innocent conduct that any person could observe. The anonymous tip, standing alone without corroboration, cannot justify a brief seizure of the suspect. See Florida v. J.L., 529 U.S. 266 (2000) (anonymous tip says that young black male standing at a particular bus stop and wearing a plaid shirt was carrying a gun; not enough for reasonable suspicion).

■ ILLINOIS v. WILLIAM aka "SAM" WARDLOW

528 U.S. 119 (2000)

Rehnquist, C.J.

Respondent Wardlow fled upon seeing police officers patrolling an area known for heavy narcotics trafficking. Two of the officers caught up with him, stopped him and conducted a protective pat-down search for weapons. Discovering a .38-caliber handgun, the officers arrested Wardlow. We hold that the officers' stop did not violate the Fourth Amendment to the United States Constitution.

On September 9, 1995, Officers Nolan and Harvey were working as uniformed officers in the special operations section of the Chicago Police Department. The officers were driving the last car of a four car caravan converging on an area known for heavy narcotics trafficking in order to investigate drug transactions. The officers were traveling together because they expected to find a crowd of people in the area, including lookouts and customers.

As the caravan passed 4035 West Van Buren, Officer Nolan observed respondent Wardlow standing next to the building holding an opaque bag. Respondent looked in the direction of the officers and fled. Nolan and Harvey turned their car southbound, watched him as he ran through the gangway and an alley, and eventually cornered him on the street. Nolan then exited his car and stopped respondent. He immediately conducted a protective pat-down search for weapons because in his experience it was common for there to be weapons in the near vicinity of narcotics transactions. During the frisk, Officer Nolan squeezed the bag respondent was carrying and felt a heavy, hard object similar to the shape of a gun. The officer then opened the bag and discovered a .38-caliber handgun with five live rounds of ammunition. The officers arrested Wardlow. The Illinois trial court denied respondent's motion to suppress, finding the gun was recovered during a lawful stop and frisk. Following a stipulated bench trial, Wardlow was convicted of unlawful use of a weapon by a felon. The [Illinois Supreme Court] reversed Wardlow's conviction, concluding that the gun should have been suppressed because Officer Nolan did not have reasonable suspicion. . . .

This case, involving a brief encounter between a citizen and a police officer on a public street, is governed by the analysis we first applied in Terry v. Ohio, 392 U.S. 1 (1968). In *Terry*, we held that an officer may, consistent with the Fourth Amendment, conduct a brief, investigatory stop when the officer has a reasonable, articulable suspicion that criminal activity is afoot. While "reasonable suspicion" is a less demanding standard than probable cause and requires a showing considerably less than preponderance of the evidence, the Fourth Amendment requires at least a minimal level of objective justification for making the stop. The officer must be able to articulate more than an inchoate and unparticularized suspicion or hunch of criminal activity.

Nolan and Harvey were among eight officers in a four car caravan that was converging on an area known for heavy narcotics trafficking, and the officers anticipated encountering a large number of people in the area, including drug customers and individuals serving as lookouts. It was in this context that Officer Nolan decided to investigate Wardlow after observing him flee. An individual's presence in an area of expected criminal activity, standing alone, is not enough to support a reasonable, particularized suspicion that the person is committing a crime. Brown v. Texas, 443 U.S. 47 (1979). But officers are not required to ignore the relevant characteristics of a location in determining whether the circumstances are sufficiently suspicious to warrant further investigation. Accordingly, we have previously noted the fact that the stop occurred in a "high crime area" among the relevant contextual considerations in a *Terry* analysis.

In this case, moreover, it was not merely respondent's presence in an area of heavy narcotics trafficking that aroused the officers' suspicion but his unprovoked flight upon noticing the police. Our cases have also recognized that nervous, evasive behavior is a pertinent factor in determining reasonable suspicion. Headlong flight — wherever it occurs — is the consummate act of evasion: it is not necessarily indicative of wrongdoing, but it is certainly suggestive of such. In reviewing the propriety of an officer's conduct, courts do not have available empirical studies dealing with inferences drawn from suspicious behavior, and we cannot reasonably demand scientific certainty from judges or law enforcement officers where none exists. Thus, the determination of reasonable suspicion must be based on commonsense judgments and inferences about human behavior. We conclude Officer Nolan was justified in suspecting that Wardlow was involved in criminal activity, and, therefore, in investigating further.

Such a holding is entirely consistent with our decision in Florida v. Royer, 460 U.S. 491 (1983), where we held that when an officer, without reasonable suspicion or probable cause, approaches an individual, the individual has a right to ignore the police and go about his business. And any refusal to cooperate, without more, does not furnish the minimal level of objective justification needed for a detention or seizure. But unprovoked flight is simply not a mere refusal to cooperate. Flight, by its very nature, is not "going about one's business"; in fact, it is just the opposite. Allowing officers confronted with such flight to stop the fugitive and investigate further is quite consistent with the individual's right to go about his business or to stay put and remain silent in the face of police questioning. . . .

STEVENS, J., concurring in part and dissenting in part.

The State of Illinois asks this Court to announce a "bright-line rule" authorizing the temporary detention of anyone who flees at the mere sight of a police officer. Respondent counters by asking us to adopt the opposite per se rule — that the fact that a person flees upon seeing the police can never, by itself, be sufficient to justify a temporary investigative stop of the kind authorized by *Terry*. The Court today wisely endorses neither per se rule. . . .

Although I agree with the Court's rejection of the per se rules proffered by the parties, unlike the Court, I am persuaded that in this case the brief testimony of the officer who seized respondent does not justify the conclusion that he had reasonable suspicion to make the stop.

. . . The question in this case concerns "the degree of suspicion that attaches to" a person's flight — or, more precisely, what "commonsense conclusions" can be drawn respecting the motives behind that flight. A pedestrian may break into a run for a variety of reasons — to catch up with a friend a block or two away, to seek shelter from an impending storm, to arrive at a bus stop before the bus leaves, to get home in time for dinner, to resume jogging after a pause for rest, to avoid contact with a bore or a bully, or simply to answer the call of nature — any of which might coincide with the arrival of an officer in the vicinity. A pedestrian might also run because he or she has just sighted one or more police officers. [T]here are unquestionably circumstances in which a person's flight is suspicious, and undeniably instances in which a person runs for entirely innocent reasons.[3]

Given the diversity and frequency of possible motivations for flight, it would be profoundly unwise to endorse either per se rule. The inference we can reasonably draw about the motivation for a person's flight, rather, will depend on a number of different circumstances. Factors such as the time of day, the number of people in the area, the character of the neighborhood, whether the officer was in uniform, the way the runner was dressed, the direction and speed of the flight, and whether the person's behavior was otherwise unusual might be relevant in specific cases. . . .

[A] reasonable person may conclude that an officer's sudden appearance indicates nearby criminal activity. And where there is criminal activity there is also a substantial element of danger — either from the criminal or from a confrontation between the criminal and the police. These considerations can lead to an innocent and understandable desire to quit the vicinity with all speed. Among some citizens, particularly minorities and those residing in high crime areas, there is also the possibility that the fleeing person is entirely innocent, but, with or without justification, believes that contact with the police can itself be dangerous, apart from any criminal activity associated with the officer's sudden presence.[7]

[In this case, the] entire justification for the stop is articulated in the brief testimony of Officer Nolan, [who stated,] "He looked in our direction and began fleeing." No other factors sufficiently support a finding of reasonable suspicion. Though respondent was carrying a white, opaque bag under his arm, there is nothing at all suspicious about that. Certainly the time of day — shortly after noon — does not support Illinois' argument. Nor were the officers responding to any call or report of suspicious activity in the area. . . .

The State, along with the majority of the Court, relies as well on the assumption that this flight occurred in a high crime area. Even if that assumption is accurate, it is insufficient because even in a high crime neighborhood unprovoked flight does not invariably lead to reasonable suspicion. On the contrary, because many factors providing innocent motivations for unprovoked flight are concentrated in high crime areas, the character of the neighborhood arguably makes an inference of guilt less appropriate, rather than more so. . . .

Notes

1. *"Bad neighborhoods" and reasonable suspicion: majority position.* An officer trying to establish reasonable suspicion will at times rely on the amount of crime occurring

3. Compare, e.g., Proverbs 28:1 ("The wicked flee when no man pursueth: but the righteous are as bold as a lion") with Proverbs 22:3 ("A shrewd man sees trouble coming and lies low; the simple walk into it and pay the penalty"). I have rejected reliance on the former proverb in the past, because its "ivory-towered analysis of the real world" fails to account for the experiences of many citizens of this country, particularly those who are minorities. See California v. Hodari D., 499 U.S. 621, 630, n.4 (1991) (Stevens, J., dissenting). That this pithy expression fails to capture the total reality of our world, however, does not mean it is inaccurate in all instances.

7. See Johnson, Americans' Views on Crime and Law Enforcement: Survey Findings, National Institute of Justice Journal 13 (Sept.1997) (reporting study by the Joint Center for Political and Economic Studies in April 1996, which found that 43% of African-Americans consider "police brutality and harassment of African-Americans a serious problem" in their own community); Casimir, Minority Men: We Are Frisk Targets, N.Y. Daily News, Mar. 26, 1999, p.34 (informal survey of 100 young black and Hispanic men living in New York City; 81 reported having been stopped and frisked by police at least once; none of the 81 stops resulted in arrests).

recently in the neighborhood. The government typically does not support the assertion with any statistical analysis of reported crimes, but bases the claim on the impressions of the officer and reports of community opinion about neighborhoods. See Ex parte Tucker, 667 So. 2d 1339 (Ala. 1995); Commonwealth v. Cheek, 597 N.E.2d 1029 (Mass. 1992). If you were a judge evaluating the claim of reasonable suspicion, would the reputation of the neighborhood for crime play any part in your decision? If you were a police officer, how might you strengthen such claims? See Margaret Raymond, Down on the Corner, Out in the Street: Considering the Character of the Neighborhood in Evaluating Reasonable Suspicion, 60 Ohio St. L.J. 99 (1999); cf. Brown v. Texas, 443 U.S. 47 (1979) ("The fact that appellant was in a neighborhood frequented by drug users, standing alone, is not a basis for concluding that appellant himself was engaged in criminal conduct").

2. *Neighborhood as proxy for race?* The neighborhoods described in court as "high crime" areas are often the homes for poor and minority residents. Do the demographics of some neighborhoods make crimes committed or reported there easier to notice or remember? Do more crimes occur in poorer neighborhoods because of subtle signals that disorder is tolerated there — the so-called "broken windows" theory of policing? If this is true, then it would make sense to direct more stop and frisk activity in places where police find the greatest physical and social disorder. A study of New York City policing by Jeffrey Fagan and Garth Davies, however, found that neighborhood characteristics such as racial composition and poverty levels are better predictors of stop and frisk activity than the presence of physical disorder in the neighborhood. They conclude that policing in New York City "is not about disorderly places . . . but about policing poor people in poor places." Fagan and Davies, Street Stops and Broken Windows: *Terry,* Race and Disorder in New York City, 28 Fordham Urban L.J. 457 (2000). If you were a police chief and a reporter called a similar study about your department to your attention, how would you respond?

3. *Avoiding or fleeing the police as basis for reasonable suspicion.* The officers in *Wardlow* noted that the suspect tried to flee the scene and considered the flight to be one factor contributing to reasonable suspicion. Would a suspect's flight from the police be enough, standing alone, to establish reasonable suspicion of criminal activity? Compare In re D.M., 781 A.2d 1161 (Pa. 2001) (reasonable suspicion based on anonymous tip regarding man with gun, plus flight from police) with State v. Hicks, 488 N.W.2d 359 (Neb. 1992) (flight upon approach of police vehicle not sufficient to justify investigative stop).

4. *Seizure by pursuit.* In California v. Hodari D., 499 U.S. 621 (1991), the Court assumed that a suspect's flight, standing alone, did not create reasonable suspicion. Nevertheless, the Court ruled that the officer needed no individualized suspicion to pursue Hodari because the pursuit did not amount to a "seizure" under the federal constitution. Two officers wearing police department jackets rounded a corner in their patrol car and saw four or five young men gathered around a small car parked at the curb. When the group saw the officers' car approaching, they began to run away. The officers were suspicious and gave chase. One officer left the patrol car and took a route that placed him in front of one of the fleeing suspects. The suspect, looking behind as he ran, did not turn and see the officer until the two were quite close. At that point, he tossed away what appeared to be a small rock and ran in the opposite direction. A moment later, the officer tackled the suspect, handcuffed him, and radioed for assistance. The rock the suspect had discarded was crack cocaine.

The Court held that there was no "stop" until the officer tackled Hodari; the pursuit by the officer was not enough.

Courts in about 30 states, reviewing similar cases under their state constitutions, have reached the same conclusion. See State v. Smith, 39 S.W.3d 739 (Ark. 2001). However, most of the remaining states insist that pursuit might sometimes qualify as a seizure. Seizures occur when the "totality of the circumstances" reasonably indicate that the person is not free to leave. See Jones v. State, 745 A.2d 856 (Del. 1999). How might a court reach the conclusion that a person can feel "free to leave," despite the fact that a police officer is chasing her and shouting "stop"? Is it because the suspect is in fact trying to leave? Would it matter if the suspect paused momentarily before or during flight? See State v. Rogers, 924 P.2d 1027 (Ariz. 1996).

5. *Discretion to stop and the definition of crimes.* There is a powerful relationship between reasonable suspicion and the substantive criminal law. If a legislature creates a crime such as "drug loitering," it empowers the police to stop people based on innocent behavior (such as standing on a corner or making signals) that is often a precursor to more harmful criminal activity, such as drug trafficking. See Mich. Comp. L. §750.167(1)(j) (disorderly conduct where a person knowingly loiters in or about a place where an illegal occupation or business is being conducted); Andrew D. Leipold, Targeted Loitering Laws, 3 U. Pa. J. Const. L. 474 (2001). If you were counsel to a police department, would you ask the city council to pass such an ordinance, or would you rather formulate a profile within the department itself?

3. *Pretextual Stops*

An officer needs reasonable suspicion that a crime has been or will be committed before stopping a person for an investigation. But when the officer has multiple reasons to stop a person, including reasonable suspicion of one crime and a hunch that the person has committed another crime, must the suspicion and the purpose match? In other words, does the police officer invalidate a stop when the crime that she reasonably suspects is only a "pretext" to justify a stop that she intends to use while investigating some other crime? State courts were split on this subject until the U.S. Supreme Court addressed it in Whren v. United States, 517 U.S. 806 (1996). The case created a new shorthand term in criminal procedure: "*Whren* stops" refer to traffic stops based on reasonable suspicion of a traffic violation, but intended to further the investigation of some other crime. Now virtually all state courts addressing this question respond much like the New York court in the following case.

■ PEOPLE v. FRANK ROBINSON

767 N.E.2d 638 (N.Y. 2001)

SMITH, J.

The issue [in these consolidated cases] is whether a police officer who has probable cause to believe a driver has committed a traffic infraction violates article I, §12 of the New York State Constitution when the officer, whose primary motivation is to conduct another investigation, stops the vehicle. We conclude that there is no violation, and we adopt Whren v. United States, 517 U.S. 806 (1996), as a matter of state law.

People v. Robinson. On November 22, 1993, New York City police officers in the Street Crime Unit, Mobile Taxi Homicide Task Force were on night patrol in a marked police car in the Bronx. Their main assignment was to follow taxicabs to make sure that no robberies occurred. After observing a car speed through a red light, the police activated their high intensity lights and pulled over what they suspected was a livery cab. After stopping the cab, one officer observed a passenger, the defendant, look back several times. The officers testified that they had no intention of giving the driver a summons but wanted to talk to him about safety tips. The officers approached the vehicle with their flashlights turned on and their guns holstered. One of the officers shined his flashlight into the back of the vehicle, where defendant was seated, and noticed that defendant was wearing a bullet proof vest. After the officer ordered defendant out of the taxicab, he observed a gun on the floor where defendant had been seated. Defendant was arrested and charged with criminal possession of a weapon and unlawfully wearing a bullet proof vest. Defendant moved to suppress the vest and gun, arguing that the officers used a traffic infraction as a pretext to search the occupant of the taxicab. The Court denied the motion, and defendant was convicted of both charges. . . .

People v. Reynolds. On March 6, 1999, shortly after midnight, a police officer, on routine motor patrol in the City of Rochester, saw a man he knew to be a prostitute enter defendant's truck. The officer followed the truck and ran a computer check on the license plate. Upon learning that the vehicle's registration had expired two months earlier, the officer stopped the vehicle. The resulting investigation did not lead to any charges involving prostitution. Nevertheless, because the driver's eyes were bloodshot, his speech slurred and there was a strong odor of alcohol, police performed various field sobriety tests, with defendant failing most. . . . Defendant was charged with driving while intoxicated, an unclassified misdemeanor, and operating an unregistered motor vehicle, a traffic infraction. Defendant's motion to suppress was granted by the Rochester City Court which dismissed all charges.

People v. Glenn. On November 7, 1997, plainclothes police officers were on street crime patrol in an unmarked car in Manhattan. They observed a livery cab make a right hand turn without signaling. An officer noticed one of three passengers in the back seat lean forward. The police stopped the vehicle to investigate whether or not a robbery was in progress. A police officer subsequently found cocaine on the rear seat and, after he arrested defendant, found additional drugs on his person. Defendant was charged with criminal possession of a controlled substance in the third degree and criminally using drug paraphernalia in the second degree. He contended that the drugs should be suppressed, asserting that the traffic infraction was a pretext to investigate a robbery. After his motion to suppress was denied, he pleaded guilty to one count of criminal possession of a controlled substance. . . .

Discussion. The Supreme Court, in Whren v. United States, 517 U.S. 806 (1996), unanimously held that where a police officer has probable cause to detain a person temporarily for a traffic violation, that seizure does not violate the Fourth Amendment to the United States Constitution even though the underlying reason for the stop might have been to investigate some other matter. In *Whren,* officers patrolling a known drug area of the District of Columbia became suspicious when several young persons seated in a truck with temporary license plates remained at a stop sign for an unusual period of time, and the driver was looking down into the lap of the passenger seated on his right. After the car made a right turn without signaling, the police stopped it, assertedly to warn the driver of traffic violations, and saw two plastic bags of what appeared to be crack cocaine in Whren's hands.

After arresting the occupants, the police found several quantities of drugs in the car. The petitioners were charged with violating federal drug laws. The petitioners moved to suppress the drugs, arguing that the stop was not based upon probable cause or even reasonable suspicion that they were engaged in illegal drug activity and that the police officer's assertion that he approached the car in order to give a warning was pretextual. The District Court denied suppression. . . .

The Supreme Court held that the Fourth Amendment had not been violated because "as a general matter, the decision to stop an automobile is reasonable where the police have probable cause to believe that a traffic violation has occurred." The stop of the truck was based upon probable cause that the petitioners had violated provisions of the District of Columbia traffic code. The Court rejected any effort to tie the legality of the officers' conduct to their primary motivation or purpose in making the stop, deeming irrelevant whether a reasonable traffic police officer would have made the stop. According to the Court, "Subjective intentions play no role in ordinary, probable-cause Fourth Amendment analysis." Thus, the "Fourth Amendment's concern with 'reasonableness' allows certain actions to be taken in certain circumstances, whatever the subjective intent." More than forty states and the District of Columbia have adopted the objective standard approved by *Whren* or cited it with approval.

In each of the cases before us, defendant argues that the stop was pretextual and in violation of New York State Constitution, article I, §12. . . . We hold that where a police officer has probable cause to believe that the driver of an automobile has committed a traffic violation, a stop does not violate article I, §12 of the New York State Constitution. In making that determination of probable cause, neither the primary motivation of the officer nor a determination of what a reasonable traffic officer would have done under the circumstances is relevant. . . .

The real concern of those opposing pretextual stops is that police officers will use their authority to stop persons on a selective and arbitrary basis. *Whren* recognized that the answer to such action is the Equal Protection Clause of the Constitution. We are not unmindful of studies . . . which show that certain racial and ethnic groups are disproportionately stopped by police officers, and that those stops do not end in the discovery of a higher proportion of contraband than in the cars of other groups. The fact that such disparities exist is cause for both vigilance and concern about the protections given by the New York State Constitution. Discriminatory law enforcement has no place in our law. . . .

The alternatives to upholding a stop based solely upon reasonable cause to believe a traffic infraction has been committed put unacceptable restraints on law enforcement. This is so whether those restrictions are based upon the primary motivation of an officer or upon what a reasonable traffic police officer would have done under the circumstances. Rather than restrain the police in these instances, the police should be permitted to do what they are sworn to do — uphold the law. . . .

To be sure, the story does not end when the police stop a vehicle for a traffic infraction. Our holding in this case addresses only the initial police action upon which the vehicular stop was predicated. The scope, duration and intensity of the seizure, as well as any search made by the police subsequent to that stop, remain subject to the strictures of article I, §12, and judicial review. . . .

The dissenters concede that . . . an individualized determination of probable cause will generally provide an objective evidentiary floor circumscribing police conduct and thereby prevent the arbitrary exercise of search and seizure power. However, [the] dissenters assert that because motor vehicle travel is so much a part of our lives and is minutely regulated, total compliance with the law is impossible. We see no basis for this differentiation. While New Yorkers may ubiquitously disobey parts of the Vehicle and Traffic Law, that does not render its commands unenforceable. As noted by the unanimous United States Supreme Court, "we are aware of no principle that would allow us to decide at what point a code of law becomes so expansive and so commonly violated that infraction itself can no longer be the ordinary measure of the lawfulness of enforcement." *Whren,* 517 U.S. at 818.

Because the Vehicle and Traffic Law provides an objective grid upon which to measure probable cause, a stop based on that standard is not arbitrary in the context of constitutional search and seizure jurisprudence. Contrary to the dissent's view, probable cause stops are not based on the discretion of police officers. They are based on violations of law. An officer may choose to stop someone for a "minor" violation after considering a number of factors, including traffic and weather conditions, but the officer's authority to stop a vehicle is circumscribed by the requirement of a violation of a duly enacted law. In other words, it is the violation of a statute that both triggers the officer's authority to make the stop and limits the officer's discretion. . . .

The dissent also raises the spectre of "repeatedly documented" racial profiling in the search and seizure context. There is no claim in any of the three cases before us that the police officers engaged in racial profiling. But, if racial profiling is the analytical pivot of our colleagues' dissent, their remedy misses the mark. The dissenters' "reasonable police officer" standard does little to combat or reduce the likelihood of racially-motivated traffic stops, since, in their view, an officer's primary motivation is irrelevant.

We conclude, for a number of reasons, that the "reasonable police officer" test should not be followed. The dissenters maintain that under the "reasonable police officer" test, prosecution of a traffic violation would be appropriate even if the stop were pretextual and the other evidence suppressed. . . . We do not see how, in the context before us, a court may separate the fruits of a stop (often a gun or drugs) from the supposed illegality of the stop itself. It would seem that if the stop is arbitrary and, therefore, unlawful, it must be so for all purposes. In the name of protecting the rights of New Yorkers, the dissenters' result would be all too ironic: A police officer could "arbitrarily" stop someone for speeding and the stop would be valid, but a gun seen in plain view in the car during the stop would be suppressed as unlawfully seized.

The invention of the automobile has changed the fabric of American life. While the vast majority of New Yorkers own or drive vehicles, the frequency of their time on the road cannot recast the functional parameters of the Fourth Amendment or article 1, §12. We agree with *Whren* that the reasonable officer standard would result in inappropriate selective enforcement of traffic laws. How is a court to know which laws to enforce? . . . We are simply not free to pick and choose which laws deserve our adherence. If a statute improperly impairs our constitutional liberties, whatever the source, there is a remedy.

We are not confounded by the proposition that police officers must exercise their discretion on a daily basis. Nor are we surprised at the assertion that many New

Yorkers often violate some provision of the Vehicle and Traffic Law. But we cannot equate the combination of police officer discretion and numerous traffic violations as arbitrary police conduct. . . . In the cases before us, [we have] a standard that constrains police conduct — probable cause under the Vehicle and Traffic Law and its related regulations that govern the safe use of our highways. . . .

LEVINE, J., dissenting.

[I]n the context of pretextual traffic stops — traffic infraction stops that would not have been made but for the aim of the police to accomplish an otherwise unlawful investigative seizure or search — the existence of probable cause that the infraction was committed is manifestly insufficient to protect against arbitrary police conduct. That is so for two reasons. First, motor vehicle travel is one of the most ubiquitous activities in which Americans engage outside the home. Second, it is, by an overwhelming margin, the most pervasively regulated activity engaged in by Americans. . . .

The confluence of the foregoing factors — the dependency of the vast majority of Americans upon private automobile transportation and the virtual impossibility of sustained total compliance with the traffic laws — gives the police wide discretion to engage in investigative seizures, only superficially checked by the probable cause requirement for the traffic infraction that is the ostensible predicate for the stop. . . . Sadly, the pretext stop decisions in lower State and Federal courts confirm that the traffic infraction probable cause standard has left the police with the ability to stop vehicles at will for illegitimate investigative purposes. Typically, the stops are conducted as part of a drug interdiction program by a law enforcement agency. The vehicle and occupants appear to fit within a "drug courier" profile and the driver or occupants may have engaged in some other innocuous behavior which arouses a surmise of criminal conduct. The officer then follows the vehicle until some traffic code violation is observed. At that point, or even later, the vehicle is pulled over and the officer proceeds with the investigation. All occupants may be directed to exit the vehicle; the driver also may be interrogated and asked to consent to a search of the vehicle. . . .

Moreover, as has been repeatedly documented, . . . drug courier interdiction through traffic infraction stops has a dramatically disproportionate impact on young African-American males. Yet both the majority and the *Whren* Court dismiss the relevance of such disparate treatment in the constitutional search and seizure context. They instead suggest that the remedy lies in invoking the Federal Constitution's Equal Protection Clause. The same studies that recognize the existence of a disparate racial impact, however, also demonstrate the inadequacy of the Equal Protection Clause as a remedy for those abuses. A racial profiling claim under the Equal Protection Clause is difficult, if not impossible, to prove. The Equal Protection Clause prohibits race-based selective enforcement of the law only when such enforcement "had a discriminatory effect and . . . was motivated by a discriminatory purpose." United States v Armstrong, 517 U.S. 456 (1996). . . . Moreover, the problems of proof in establishing an equal protection claim may be all but insurmountable. Putting aside the unquestionably expensive and time-consuming process of assembling statistical evidence, it is debatable whether the requisite data would even be available. Supreme Court precedent also suggests that minority motorists alleging that a pretextual traffic stop constituted a denial of equal protection must show that similarly situated white motorists could have been stopped, but were not.

[The petitioners in *Whren*] urged the adoption of an objective standard by which to judge police exploitation of arbitrary traffic code enforcement to conduct investigative stops: whether a reasonable police officer, under the circumstances, would have made the stop for the reasons given. Despite the objective nature of that test, the Supreme Court's primary reason for rejecting it was that it was "driven by subjective considerations"— that is, the improper motivation of the seizing officer to conduct an otherwise unjustified investigative stop. . . . This criticism, in our view, misses the mark. The petitioners in *Whren* claimed that the officers' seizure was unreasonable because it was arbitrary, not because it was either unjustified or improperly motivated. . . .

The *Whren* Court offered only two other reasons for rejecting the test suggested by the petitioners. The first was that "police enforcement practices, even if they could be practicably assessed by a judge, vary from place to place and from time to time. We cannot accept that the search and seizure protections of the Fourth Amendment are so variable . . . and can be made to turn upon such trivialities." Under well-established Federal and State search and seizure doctrine, however, the . . . the basic determination of reasonable suspicion or even probable cause to support a search or seizure will almost always vary from place to place and time to time, depending on the particular circumstances confronting an officer.

[The opinion in *Whren*] also claimed in substance that accepting petitioners' position would place Judges in the role of deciding what traffic code provisions are to be enforced at all. . . . Adoption of the [reasonable officer standard] would do nothing of the sort. It does nothing more than set an objective standard, the violation of which would deprive law enforcement officers only of the use of evidence of crimes unrelated to the traffic infraction obtained in investigative stops effected through arbitrary enforcement of the traffic laws. As to the infraction itself, . . . prosecution of the underlying traffic infraction is not based upon evidence obtained through exploitation of the initial stop, but upon observations made before the stop. . . .

Next to be addressed on these appeals is the standard we would adopt to determine whether the stops in these cases were pretextual. . . . Defendants urge that we adopt a subjective test, whether the "primary motivation" for the stop was to investigate criminal activity rather than to prosecute the traffic offense ostensibly justifying the seizure. We would reject that test [because] courts and commentators have noted the difficulty, if not futility, of basing the constitutional validity of searches or seizures on judicial determinations of the subjective motivation of police officers. . . . Thus, we prefer an objective [standard:] would a reasonable officer assigned to Vehicle and Traffic Law enforcement in the seizing officer's department have made the stop under the circumstances presented, absent a purpose to investigate serious criminal activity of the vehicle's occupants. Whether the stop was carried out in accordance with standard procedures of the officer's department would be a highly relevant inquiry in that regard. . . .

Notes

1. *Pretextual stops: majority position.* Under the federal constitution, courts refuse to question the legitimacy of allegedly pretextual stops, so long as the officer "could have" properly stopped the vehicle based on evidence of a traffic offense. According

to the Supreme Court in Whren v. United States, 517 U.S. 806 (1996), any effort to determine whether a reasonable officer "would have" stopped a vehicle for traffic violations alone would be too uncertain: "While police manuals and standard procedures may sometimes provide objective assistance, ordinarily one would be reduced to speculating about the hypothetical reaction of a hypothetical constable — an exercise that might be called virtual subjectivity." The *Whren* decision convinced most states that at one time employed the "would have" doctrine to change approaches for purposes of the state constitution. At this point, over 40 states follow the *Whren* decision. See Gama v. State, 920 P.2d 1010 (Nev. 1996); State v. Vineyard, 958 S.W.2d 730 (Tenn. 1997).

One of the few remaining exceptions is the state of Washington. In State v. Ladson, 979 P.2d 833 (Wash. 1999), officers on proactive gang patrol noticed a driver who was rumored to be involved in gang and drug activity. They followed the car and stopped the driver after noticing that the license plate tabs had expired. Their primary reason for the stop was to investigate drug activity, and they found drugs in the passenger's possession. The Washington Supreme Court called pretextual stops "a triumph of form over substance" and worried that approving such searches would mean that "nearly every citizen would be subject to a *Terry* stop simply because he or she is in his or her car." As for how to determine whether a given stop is pretextual, the court adopted a "totality of the circumstances" approach. Trial courts may inquire both about the subjective intent of the officer as well as the objective reasonableness of the officer's behavior to determine whether a stop was pretextual or not. If you wanted to learn whether judicial controls of pretextual stops are workable in practice, what aspect of the Washington system would you study most closely?

2. *State constitutions and the federal constitution.* In *Robinson,* the New York court pointed out that both the state and federal constitutions contain provisions to limit police searches and seizures and to protect privacy. State courts must interpret both constitutional provisions when a litigant presents the issue. The state courts must adhere to the decisions of the U.S. Supreme Court as to the meaning of the federal constitution. State law enforcement officers must comply with certain provisions of the federal constitution — those applicable to the states because the due process clause of the Fourteenth Amendment "incorporates" them. Today, most of the specific Bill of Rights protections for criminal defendants and for citizens generally have been "incorporated" to apply against the states and their agents. See Akhil Reed Amar, The Bill of Rights: Creation and Reconstruction (1998) and Michael Kent Curtis, No State Shall Abridge: The Fourteenth Amendment and the Bill of Rights (1986).

However, a state's supreme court has the ultimate judicial authority over the meaning of its own state constitution. It might interpret the state constitution (or some other provision of state law, such as a statute) to place restrictions on law enforcement officers different from what the federal constitution might require. The federal courts, including the U.S. Supreme Court, must allow a state supreme court's decision in a criminal case to stand so long as the decision does not flatly conflict with binding federal law and rests on "independent and adequate" state law grounds. Periodically, we will consider cases about procedural issues in which state law gives different answers from federal law or asks different procedural questions altogether. This variety in criminal procedure in different jurisdictions makes it possible for lawyers to argue for procedural innovations that might not be apparent from studying federal law alone.

3. *Reading minds.* Do judicial controls on pretextual stops require the judge to read the officer's mind? Is it truly possible to declare that a stop was pretextual based on "objective" evidence (such as the prevalence of traffic stops in that situation, or the officer's compliance with a police department's internal rules about traffic stops)? Or is some finding about subjective intent implicit in any pretext case? Perhaps a court's position on pretext claims reflect an underlying assumption about the trustworthiness of police officers. If a court is unwilling to attempt to control pretextual stops, is it implicitly deciding that the police ordinarily make good faith decisions that ought to be encouraged rather than discouraged? Is it making any implicit claims about the truthfulness of police testimony in the ordinary case? See Angela Davis, Race, Cops, and Traffic Stops, 51 U. Miami L. Rev. 425 (1997). Consider how defense attorneys and prosecutors might explain the relevance of a particular officer's habits in making traffic stops. See State Highway Patrol Trooper Barry Washington Is on the Prowl for Drugs, San Antonio Express-News July 25, 1996 (trooper seizes more than 1,000 pounds of marijuana and 20,000 grams of cocaine each year; stops up to 40 drivers daily, spending about four minutes with each; sends average of two drug suspects per week into court system).

4. *Highways as a special arena.* The pretext issue takes on special urgency on the highways. Over half of all contacts between adults and police officers take place during traffic stops. In a given year, the police stop about ten percent of all drivers. See Bureau of Justice Statistics, Characteristics of Drivers Stopped by Police, 1999 (2001, NCJ 191548). The vehicle's equipment and the driver's conduct are also regulated in minute detail, allowing a wide variety of stops. The potential grounds for stops cover everything from bumper height, to tire tread, to burned-out license tag light, or the ever-popular "changing lanes without signaling."

Does a healthy legal system depend on lax enforcement of certain laws? In this imperfect world, how many cars and drivers can go for long without some minor violation, such as tag lights or lane violations? If police officers can develop reasonable suspicion against any driver if they persist in the effort, does the *Whren* decision effectively repeal the reasonable suspicion limit for police power on the highways? How does the majority opinion in the New York case answer this question?

5. *Arbitrary enforcement.* Is the pretext doctrine necessary to prevent arbitrary enforcement decisions by the police (including possible harassment of racial minorities), or are other legal doctrines available to prevent arbitrary policing? See David Harris, "Driving While Black" and All Other Traffic Offenses: The Supreme Court and Pretextual Traffic Stops, 87 J. Crim. L. & Criminology 544 (1997) (describing disproportionate stops of African Americans and Hispanics in Colorado, Florida, Illinois, and Maryland; large-scale study in Florida showed almost 70 percent of drivers stopped were African American or Hispanic, although they constitute about 5 percent of drivers on that highway; Maryland state police records show 75 percent of drivers stopped were African Americans). Would a challenge based on the equal protection clause of the Constitution be available (or sufficient) to respond to any police use of race as a basis for selecting drivers to stop? See Tracy Maclin, Race and the Fourth Amendment, 51 Vand. L. Rev. 333 (1998).

6. *Police responses to pretext claims.* If you were legal counsel to a police department in a jurisdiction adopting the reasonable officer "would" test for pretext (such

as Washington state), what advice would you give the department? For instance, what charges should the arresting officer file — the original offense justifying the stop or the more serious offense or both? What sorts of reasons should an officer give to justify an initial stop? Will the officer fare better if he identifies some grounds for stopping a car other than a traffic violation? See Scott v. State, 877 P.2d 503 (Nev. 1994) (officer stopped car because vehicle might have been stolen). Can the officer overcome the claim of pretext by arguing that he routinely stops several vehicles per month based on similar traffic violations? State v. Wilson, 867 P.2d 1175 (N.M. 1994) (officer testifies that he stops six to eight cars every month for failure to use seat belts, stop upheld).

7. *Department-level pretexts.* Some individual police officers use traffic stops as a means to enforce drug laws. Are pretext claims by defendants stronger or weaker when the use of pretext (such as traffic stops to look for drugs) is a department policy instead of just an individual officer's decision? Other departments (for example, the Kansas City Police Department) use reasonable suspicion stops of cars and persons as a general policy with the goal of finding weapons and enforcing firearms laws. A study of the Kansas City program, which began in 1991, concluded that gun seizures in the 80-by-10-block target area increased by 65 percent, while seizures in a comparable beat went down slightly. Gun crimes in the target beat decreased by 49 percent and increased slightly in the comparison beat. See Lawrence Sherman, James Shaw, and Dennis Rogan, The Kansas City Gun Experiment, National Institute of Justice, Research in Brief, NCJ 150855 (Jan. 1995). Would a challenge to this Kansas City practice be more difficult than the challenges to the various individual stops in *Robinson*?

8. *Traffic stop statutes.* A number of state legislatures have passed statutes authorizing certain types of traffic stops and disapproving others. Oregon Rev. Stat. §810.410(3)(b) provides as follows: "A police officer [may] stop and detain a person for a traffic violation for the purposes of investigation reasonably related to the traffic violation, identification and issuance of citation." Would this statute change the outcome in a case like *Robinson*? Is a statute prohibiting the police from acting with certain purposes likely to work?

4. *Criminal Profiles and Race*

The police officer in the field is not left entirely to her own devices when deciding whether apparently innocent facts are actually indicators of criminal activity. Both police departments and legislative bodies offer guidance on the types of conduct that might create grounds for a stop. Police departments periodically create "criminal profiles," which are lists of personal characteristics and behaviors said to be associated with particular types of crime (most commonly drug trafficking). Sometimes these profiles are quite specific, while at other times they are relatively short and general. An officer hoping to explain after the fact why she stopped a person might describe the features of the profile that the suspect matched.

The criminal profiles developed in police departments often remain informal and unwritten. Do these "profiles"— collective judgments about suspicious activity — add any weight to the individual police officer's judgment in the field as the officer tries to establish reasonable suspicion? Do they have anything in common with claims of expertise by an individual police officer?

■ SAMIR QUARLES v. STATE

696 A.2d 1334 (Del. 1997)

WALSH, J.

In this appeal from the Superior Court, the appellant, Samir Quarles seeks a reversal of a ruling that denied his motion to suppress evidence of illegal drugs seized from his person during a street encounter with police. . . . We conclude that under a totality of circumstances test the conduct of the appellant, measured from the perspective of experienced police officers, provided a specific and articulable basis for a limited investigative stop. . . .

At approximately 10:00 P.M. on the date in question, Officers Looney and Solge went to the terminal to meet a bus arriving from New York City. Based on their past experience, the officers were aware that the bus in question was often used by persons acting as drug couriers. It was their intention to conduct surveillance of persons departing the bus with the hope of intercepting the flow of drugs into the city. As they watched, fifteen to twenty passengers disembarked from the bus with two individuals, later identified as Quarles and Thomas, exiting last.

Although Quarles and Thomas were conversing as they left the bus, their conversation "came to an abrupt halt" as soon as they observed two uniformed officers standing nearby. The conversation was not reinitiated once the pair passed the officers. The pair then stood motionless on the sidewalk for a few moments before turning to walk north toward Second Street in the opposite direction of the police. The police observed as Quarles began walking at a faster pace ahead of Thomas, who eventually caught up with Quarles after some distance. As Quarles and Thomas proceeded quickly toward Second Street, Quarles looked back on three different occasions to determine the location of the police officers. When Quarles and Thomas reached the intersection of Second and French Streets they turned west on Second Street. After they turned the corner, Quarles observed a third officer, Officer Cunningham, sitting in his patrol car in a parking lot a short distance ahead on Second Street. Upon observing Cunningham's vehicle, Quarles backtracked to the corner and looked around to determine where the two officers on foot were located. According to the officers, Quarles and Thomas seemed "kind of surprised" and in a quandary as to what direction to proceed. At that point Officers Looney and Solge approached the pair and Officer Solge asked if he could speak to them. Quarles and Thomas agreed to speak with the officers.

In the meantime, Officer Cunningham, who had been in radio contact with the other two officers, proceeded the wrong way on Second Street, against traffic, and parked his vehicle partially on the sidewalk prior to joining the group gathered at the corner. The defendants gave inconsistent statements as to their destination and appeared nervous in answering questions about their origin and destination. They were advised that the police were checking for drugs and/or weapons couriers and were asked if they had any drugs or contraband on their persons. The police requested permission to conduct a search of their persons as well as of a bag carried by Quarles. . . . The police proceeded to search both Quarles' bag and his person, uncovering a large quantity of cocaine in Quarles' boot. . . .

Under the Fourth Amendment, a police seizure can be justified only when, based upon specific and articulable facts which, taken together with rational inferences from those facts, reasonably warrant the belief that a crime is being or has been committed. Under this standard, the courts must look for a minimal level of

objective "justification" for making the stop. United States v. Sokolow, 490 U.S. 1 (1989). This burden of proof is "considerably less" than proof by a preponderance of the evidence and less demanding than probable cause. When conducting its analysis, the court must consider the totality of the circumstances, the "whole picture," as viewed through the eyes of a police officer who is experienced in discerning the ostensibly innocuous behavior that is indicative of narcotics trafficking.

The United States Supreme Court has stated that the circumstances must be evaluated under an objective/subjective standard as opposed to a purely objective standard. This reflects the reality that:

> [m]uch of the drug traffic is highly organized and conducted by sophisticated criminal syndicates. The profits are enormous. And many drugs . . . may be easily concealed. As a result, the obstacles to detection of illegal conduct may be unmatched in any other area of law enforcement.

It logically follows that a pattern of behavior interpreted by an untrained observer as innocent could justify an investigatory stop when viewed by experienced law enforcement agents who are cognizant of current drug trafficking operations. United States v. Cortez, 449 U.S. 411 (1981). In *Cortez,* the United States Supreme Court cautioned that terms like "articulable reasons" and "founded suspicion" are not self-defining. But the Court noted that any assessment of police conduct must be two-pronged, based upon: (1) "all the circumstances," including objective observations and "consideration of the modes or patterns of operation of certain kinds of law-breakers"; and (2) the inferences and deductions that a trained officer could make which "might well elude an untrained person." We believe that standard is an appropriate one for use by courts reviewing the conduct of detaining officers, and we adopt it here.

In our case, the officers relied upon specific factors together with a "drug courier profile" to justify their articulable suspicion. Although the use of "profiling" is vigorously debated in academic circles, it has been accepted by the United States Supreme Court. The Court has stated that a "profile," alone, will not justify a seizure, but when considered in conjunction with police observations, a seizure could be warranted even though the "non-profile" observations by themselves would not justify an investigatory stop. Moreover, the fact that the articulated factors "may be set forth in a 'profile' does not somehow detract from their evidentiary significance as seen by a trained agent." *Sokolow,* 490 U.S. at 9-10.

Here the "profile" characteristics were: (1) the defendants came into Wilmington via bus from New York (a known drug source city); (2) they carried no luggage; (3) they came in at night, typically when law enforcement activity is at a minimum; and (4) they traveled as a pair. This profile was compiled relying upon police experience, based on past arrests of individuals bringing drugs into the City of Wilmington. The "non-profile" factors relied upon by police were: (1) the defendants' startled reaction to uniformed police officers upon exiting the bus (ceasing their conversation); (2) quickly leaving the bus terminal in a direction away from the officers; (3) the defendants' repeated glances over their shoulders to see if the officers were following them both before and after turning the corner; (4) rapid stride; and (5) abrupt about face upon seeing a marked police car.

When assessing the relevance of these factors the focus is not on whether the particular conduct is "innocent" or "guilty" but the degree of suspicion that attaches to particular types of conduct. Courts have recognized that wholly lawful and innocent conduct descriptive of a large segment of the population can justify the suspicion that criminal activity is afoot.

When Quarles exited the New York bus in Wilmington, he and his companion satisfied a number of well known "drug courier profile" characteristics. While this fact alone would not justify a seizure, when combined with the other specific instances of suspicious and odd behavior, police were justified in effectuating a seizure. This Court notes that the conclusions reached by the officers as to Quarles' behavior were based in large part upon their personal experiences in conducting drug courier surveillance at the bus station. Combined, the officers conducted surveillance at the bus station over 90 times, approximately two to three times a month, with, over the past year, Officer Looney personally arresting 12 people for carrying drugs through the station.

The two arresting officers, drawing on their experience of observing hundreds of people move through the bus station, were able to conclude that Quarles' behavior was abnormal and suspicious when compared to other passengers.[5] Quarles' suspicious behavior and the "drug profile," when taken as a whole from the perspective of one who is trained in narcotics detection, produces a reasonable articulable suspicion that a crime was afoot. We therefore conclude that the police officers had a sufficient basis upon which to support an initial stop to question Quarles.

The safeguarding of a citizen's rights against unreasonable stops and seizures by police officers is a cherished protection under the Fourth Amendment and this Court's obligation to advance those rights is clear. But this Court should not turn a blind eye to the realities of society's war against drugs and the experience of the police in combating that problem. We are entitled to test the actions of the police by the exacting standards of the Fourth Amendment jurisprudence, but we should be reluctant to substitute an academic analysis for the on the spot judgment of trained law enforcement officers. . . .

Veasey, C.J., dissenting.

. . . I submit, respectfully, that the majority opinion rests on a novel rationale — unprecedented deference to subjective police observations based solely upon law enforcement experience. The majority correctly states that . . . "any curtailment of a person's liberty by the police must be supported at least by a reasonable and articulable suspicion that the person seized is engaged in criminal activity." The key words here are "reasonable" and "articulable." These are objective tests. . . . Hunches and subjective impressions of experienced police officers will not suffice. . . .

In this case police did not rely on intelligence reports that drugs were being carried on the bus or that defendant, or anyone fitting his description, was transporting drugs to Wilmington. . . . There were no suspicious hand signals or papers passed secretly. [T]he data available to Officers Cunningham, Looney, and Solge at the time they seized Quarles completely lacked specificity and could not have raised a justifiable suspicion that Quarles was engaged in wrongdoing. . . .

Moreover, I question whether the four benign facts cited by the majority establish a profile. . . . These four facts taken as a whole might well describe a number of

5. With over 90 surveillance operations at the bus station, if each night only one bus carrying twenty passengers came into the station, the two arresting officers would have witnessed the behavior of over 1800 passengers. This vast experience gave the officers an adequate frame of reference for detecting abnormal or suspicious behavior.

innocent people. New York City is only 120 miles from Wilmington. Nighttime travel with a companion and without luggage is hardly remarkable. As for New York City being a "known drug source city," what city is not infested with drugs and drug suppliers? Even the trial judge here concluded, "The mere fact that they exited a bus coming from New York City would not give rise to a reasonable suspicion." . . .

At bottom, the majority opinion attaches a novel, and outcome-determinative, deference to experienced police eyes without any expert or empirical evidence. . . . If the precedent embodied in the majority opinion is taken to its logical extreme, police experience alone, and without articulable expert analysis or meticulous police work . . . , will almost always support the seizure. . . .

This case is about constitutional protections that the judicial branch of government is obliged to enforce for the protection of innocent citizens, as well as reprehensible drug traffickers who poison our citizens. With the utmost deference, I must state my concern that the rationale and the unprecedented reach of the majority opinion is dangerous and could lead to a pernicious erosion of our liberty.

Notes

1. *Criminal profiles in the courts: majority position.* The strong majority of courts presented with stops based on facts listed in a criminal profile will not allow the match with the profile, standing alone, to constitute reasonable suspicion. However, most courts also say that the appearance of an observed fact in a profile gives that fact added weight in the reasonable suspicion calculus. See State v. Staten, 469 N.W.2d 112 (Neb. 1991) (airline passengers fitting drug courier profile may be detained up to one hour). A significant minority of states have rejected or criticized any reliance on the use of profiles to add any weight to facts observed in the field. Commonwealth v. Lewis, 636 A.2d 619 (Pa. 1994). The federal law on profiles seems agnostic, placing no independent weight — positive or negative — on the existence of a profile. See United States v. Sokolow, 490 U.S. 1 (1989); Florida v. Royer, 460 U.S. 491 (1983) (reasonable suspicion established). Some state courts reject particular components of a profile without rejecting the reliance on profiles generally. See Derricott v. State, 611 A.2d 592 (Md. 1992) (criticizing profile that apparently included race of suspect); Crockett v. State, 803 S.W.2d 308 (Tex. Crim. App. 1991) (no evidence that drug dealers purchase train tickets with cash more frequently than other people).

2. *Dueling profiles and discretion.* Courts seem especially skeptical about profiles phrased broadly enough to "describe a very large category of presumably innocent travelers, who would be subject to virtually random seizures" if a mere match to such a profile were enough to justify a search or seizure. Reid v. Georgia, 448 U.S. 438 (1980). Drug courier profiles sometimes are written broadly enough to attach suspicion both to a particular characteristic (such as exiting a plane first or making eye contact with another passenger) and to its opposite (exiting a plane last or avoiding eye contact with another passenger). What exactly is the problem with a declaration that a particular behavior and its opposite are both suspicious? Judicial opinions dealing with challenges to the use of a criminal profile almost never list the complete provisions of the profile. What does this mean to the attorney hoping to challenge the reliability of the profile as a method of establishing reasonable suspicion?

3. *Officer expertise and subjective standards.* Should the particular expertise of the investigating officer have any bearing on a finding of reasonable suspicion? Or

should the court accept only those inferences that any "reasonable person" (that is, a citizen) would draw from the observed facts? If you are willing to account for the special experience of a particular police officer in establishing reasonable suspicion, is this consistent with your views on the "reasonable person" standard we encountered earlier, dealing with the definition of a "stop"? See United States v. Cortez, 449 U.S. 411 (1981) ("when used by trained law enforcement officers, objective facts, meaningless to the untrained, can be combined with permissible deductions from such facts to form a legitimate basis for suspicion of a particular person").

4. *Collective judgments and expertise.* Stops based on criminal profiles differ from other reasonable suspicion stops because they attempt to give the officer on the street the benefit of the collective experience of other officers or the collective judgments of political authorities. The officer makes the stop not only based on his own expertise in law enforcement but also because the "profile" places significance on certain facts. Which is a stronger basis for believing that certain apparently innocent facts are actually indications of criminal activity: the individual training and experience of the officer making the stop or the statistical and collective experience of police in the department? As the attorney for a person stopped, which of the two bases would you prefer to test on cross-examination? See Wayne LaFave, Controlling Discretion by Administrative Regulations: The Use, Misuse, and Nonuse of Police Rules and Policies in Fourth Amendment Adjudication, 89 Mich. L. Rev. 442 (1990).

5. *Package profiles.* Recall that courts distinguish between "consensual" encounters that do not involve a seizure at all (and therefore require no justification) and stops that do require reasonable suspicion. If the seizure amounts to a full arrest, the government must show probable cause. The same framework applies to property. When the government takes possession (temporary or permanent) of property and the owner later challenges that control as an unconstitutional seizure, courts ask whether the governmental control amounted to a "stop" of the property that required reasonable suspicion.

The U.S. Supreme Court has held that postal authorities must have reasonable suspicion to detain a mail package for a short time and probable cause to seize it outright. United States v. Van Leeuwen, 397 U.S. 249 (1970). The postal service has developed profiles for identifying packages carrying illegal narcotics: packages meeting the profile are delayed for further inspection (often by drug-sniffing dogs) and for controlled delivery to the addressee. One such profile lists the following characteristics: (1) size and shape of the package; (2) package taped to close or seal all openings; (3) handwritten or printed labels; (4) unusual return name and address; (5) unusual odors coming from the package; (6) fictitious return address; and (7) destination of the package. See State v. Cooper, 652 A.2d 995 (Vt. 1994); 39 U.S.C. §3623(d) (Postal Service "shall maintain one or more classes of mail for the transmission of letters sealed against inspection. . . . No letter of such a class of domestic origin shall be opened except under authority of a search warrant authorized by law").

Often the challenges to detentions of property involve delays in delivering luggage to airline passengers waiting in baggage claims areas. A brief detention of the luggage also effectively detains the person. Should this make a difference in a court's evaluation of the government's handling of the property?

6. *Efficiency in proof?* Is the problem with criminal profiles that the government has not written specific profiles and has not shown rigorously how the profile

features are common to a great number of criminal defendants? Consider a profile constructed as follows. A group of more than 40 representatives from law enforcement agencies in the Phoenix area developed a profile for stopping suspected automobile thieves transporting stolen vehicles to Mexico. The profile was based on an analysis of 10,000 auto thefts in the area over a 17-month period. The profile indicated which vehicles were targeted most often by the thieves: sedans and pickup trucks manufactured by Ford and Chevrolet within the last three years. In addition, the records indicated that the driver of a stolen car would probably be a male between 17 and 27 years of age; he would usually be alone; he would have no apparent luggage; if there was a passenger, there would be no children; and the car's license plate would show a registration to either Pima or Maricopa County. This profile fit only a small percentage of those people driving between Tucson and Nogales. See State v. Ochoa, 544 P.2d 1097 (Ariz. 1976). Could profiles, when carefully constructed and meticulously proven in early cases, prevent duplicative presentation of evidence in later cases?

Problem 2-2. Race and Witness Descriptions

On February 21, at approximately 4:15 A.M., Nancy Henderson approached an automatic teller machine on Main Street. While she was operating the teller machine, but before completing her transaction, someone grabbed her from behind and said, "this is a stick-up" and "I want your money." During a brief struggle, the man pressed a hard, blunt object into her back. He forced Henderson from the front of the bank to a parking lot in back of the building. She gave her money to the man. The man then declared that he planned to rape Henderson. He forced her to walk to the front of the bank and ordered her to get into the driver's seat of her car, threatening to "blow her brains out" if she did not comply. The man positioned himself next to Henderson in the front passenger seat, and directed her where to drive the car.

As Henderson drove, she noticed a pizza shop that appeared to be open. She accelerated the car in that direction and jumped the curb. Then she got out of the car and ran screaming for help. Several people emerged from the shop. During the confusion, the assailant walked away. The police were called, and arrived at the pizza shop within minutes. Henderson described her assailant as "a black male, 5′11″ to 6′2″, wearing a ski cap, had a mustache, was wearing a light-colored coat, dark pants, white tennis shoes and had medium to dark skin." The police dispatcher sent this description to all officers on patrol.

At 5:25 A.M., another officer on patrol stopped Daniel Coleman in the parking lot of a restaurant located approximately one-half of a mile from the pizza shop. Coleman fit the general description of the assailant, except that he had a goatee as well as a mustache and was not wearing a coat or a cap. The officer questioned Coleman briefly about his identity and destination. Coleman stated that he was coming from his girlfriend's home and that he was on his way to work. During this discussion, another officer drove by with Henderson in the car. She was unable to identify Coleman as her assailant. The officer detained Coleman for a total of about 10 minutes, then released him.

Later that morning, the police viewed a videotape taken by a camera installed near the automatic teller machine. Both of the police officers who had seen

Coleman earlier that morning during his brief detention viewed the videotape and identified the assailant on the videotape as Coleman. Coleman was arrested at his place of employment and charged with robbery and attempted rape. When the officers first stopped Coleman, did they have reasonable suspicion? If they ignored information about the race of the suspect, would they have reasonable suspicion? See Coleman v. State, 562 A.2d 1171 (Del. 1989).

Notes

1. *Race and witness descriptions: majority position.* Most courts allow the police to rely on race as one among many components of reasonable suspicion, particularly if the police use the racial element of a description received from a victim or witness of the crime. Note, Developments in the Law—Race and the Criminal Process, 101 Harv. L. Rev. 1473 (1988). Can you imagine a jurisdiction that would bar any use of race in establishing reasonable suspicion, thus requiring the police to point to other factors? For witness identifications, could the police rely on descriptions of clothing or facial hair, while being barred from using information about skin color?

On the other hand, police officers will at times rely on a suspect's race in cases where no witness has described the perpetrator, or even where there is no report of a crime at all. This most often occurs when a person appears to be "out of place": for instance, a black person in a predominantly white neighborhood. Courts have divided on whether such a fact can be the primary component of reasonable suspicion. See, e.g., State v. Dean, 543 P.2d 425 (Ariz. 1975) (Mexican male in dented car in predominantly white neighborhood, reasonable suspicion); State v. Mallory, 337 N.W.2d 391 (Minn. 1983) (black male stopped in white neighborhood where burglary by a black male had occurred recently, reasonable suspicion); State v. Barber, 823 P.2d 1068 (Wash. 1992) (presence of black person in white neighborhood can never amount to reasonable suspicion standing alone).

Officers also sometimes rely on the race of the suspect when it is difficult to articulate other specific grounds for suspicion; courts now tend to invalidate stops in such cases. See United States v. Bellamy, 619 A.2d 515 (D.C. 1993) (no reasonable suspicion where officer stops four black youths in car who teased him about violence against police); Commonwealth v. Phillips, 595 N.E.2d 310 (Mass. 1992) (no reasonable suspicion where Boston police implement policy to "search on sight" young black males suspected of membership in gangs). If most American jurisdictions allow race as one "factor" that contributes to a finding of reasonable suspicion, won't there necessarily be cases where race provides the extra marginal evidence to obtain reasonable suspicion? Would this be objectionable discrimination, or a plausible reaction to probabilities familiar to the police? See Sheri Lynn Johnson, Race and the Decision to Detain a Suspect, 93 Yale L.J. 214 (1983).

2. *Patterns of discrimination in stops.* When the Supreme Court first considered the validity of stops based on reasonable suspicion, in Terry v. Ohio, 392 U.S. 1 (1968), advocates and commentators objected to the police practice, pointing to evidence that police used stops in a discriminatory manner to harass African Americans. More recent observers of police practices argue that officers still choose to stop a disproportionate number of black males. Michael Brown, Working the Street: Police Discretion and the Dilemmas of Reform 166 (1981) ("Race, the field

observations [of police] reveal, is one of the most salient criteria to patrolmen in deciding whether or not to stop someone"). How might the attorney for an individual who is stopped go about establishing this sort of claim?

Defendants have only rarely convinced courts to outlaw the use of pretextual stops or criminal profiles, but a related claim has achieved more success outside the courts. The related claim is that police stop motorists based at least partly on their race. Such claims are often described in public debates as the creation of a crime called "driving while black" or "DWB."

Claims of DWB are difficult for a criminal defendant to litigate, but state and federal governments now regularly investigate patterns of traffic and drug stops on highways. The New Jersey Attorney General conducted one such investigation. Law enforcement officials prepared the report excerpted below in the aftermath of a tragic shooting incident in 1998 on the New Jersey Turnpike. Troopers were accused of firing 11 shots into a van containing four young men on their way to a basketball tryout. The shots wounded two black men and a Hispanic man. The officers said that they initially stopped the van because it was speeding, and opened fire when the van backed up to hit them. The shooting triggered protests and an internal investigation of claims that officers used racial profiling during stops and investigations on the highway.

■ INTERIM REPORT OF THE STATE POLICE REVIEW TEAM REGARDING ALLEGATIONS OF RACIAL PROFILING PETER VERNIERO, ATTORNEY GENERAL

(April 20, 1999)

. . . This Interim Report specifically focuses on the activities of state troopers assigned to patrol the New Jersey Turnpike. [T]he Turnpike is widely believed to be a major drug corridor, thereby providing the State Police with both the impetus and the opportunity to engage in drug interdiction tactics that appear to be inextricably linked to the "racial profiling" controversy. [B]ased upon the information that we reviewed, minority motorists have been treated differently than nonminority motorists during the course of traffic stops on the New Jersey Turnpike. For the reasons set out fully in this Report, we conclude that the problem of disparate treatment is real — not imagined. This problem . . . is more complex and subtle than has generally been reported.

[We] define "racial profiling" broadly to encompass any action taken by a state trooper during a traffic stop that is based upon racial or ethnic stereotypes and that has the effect of treating minority motorists differently than nonminority motorists. We have thus elected not to limit our review to a trooper's initial decision to order a vehicle to pull over. Rather, we also consider a host of other actions that may be taken by State Police members throughout the course of a traffic stop, such as ordering the driver or passengers to step out, subjecting the occupants to questions that are not directly related to the motor vehicle violation that gave rise to the stop, summoning a drug-detection canine to the scene, or requesting permission to conduct a consent search of the vehicle and its contents. . . .

Our review has revealed two interrelated problems that may be influenced by the goal of interdicting illicit drugs: (1) willful misconduct by a small number of State Police members, and (2) more common instances of possible de facto discrimination by officers who may be influenced by stereotypes and may thus tend to treat minority motorists differently during the course of routine traffic stops, subjecting them more routinely to investigative tactics and techniques that are designed to ferret out illicit drugs and weapons. . . .

The obvious and necessary remedy to deal with those officers who intentionally violate the civil rights of minority motorists is to ensure swift discipline and criminal prosecutions, taking full advantage of New Jersey's official misconduct laws. . . . As to the problem occasioned by the disparate treatment of minorities based on subtle or even subconscious stereotypes, the solution lies not only in clearly and precisely explaining once and for all what conduct is prohibited, but also, as importantly, in clearly explaining in *positive* terms how stops are to be conducted. . . .

Our review has shown that over the years, conflicting messages have been sent regarding the official policy to prohibit any form of race-based profiling. This situation should be rectified by developing a clear and consistent message. We propose that as a matter of policy for the New Jersey State Police, race, ethnicity, and national origin should not be used at all by troopers in selecting vehicles to be stopped or in exercising discretion during the course of a stop (other than in determining whether a person matches the general description of one or more known suspects). In making this recommendation, we propose going beyond the minimum requirements of federal precedent because, simply, it is the right thing to do and because the Executive Branch, no less than its judicial counterpart, has an independent duty to ensure that our laws are enforced in a constitutional, efficient, and even-handed fashion. . . .

Stops. We have received and compiled information regarding stops by troopers assigned to the Moorestown and Cranbury stations from the monthly stop data. . . . Four of every ten stops (40.6 percent) made during the period for which data are available involved black, Hispanic, Asian or other nonwhite people. . . .

Searches. It is obvious from the data provided that very few stops result in the search of a motor vehicle. For example, in those instances for which we have data permitting comparisons between stops and searches, only 627 (0.7 percent) of 87,489 stops involved a search. [T]he available data indicate that the overwhelming majority of searches (77.2 percent) involved black or Hispanic persons. Specifically, of the 1,193 searches for which data are available, 21.4 percent involved a white person, more than half (53.1 percent) involved a black person, and almost one of every four (24.1 percent) involved a Hispanic person.

. . . Not surprisingly, most consent searches do not result in a "positive" finding. . . . Specifically, 19.2 percent of the searches we considered resulted in an arrest or seizure of contraband. Accounting for race and ethnicity, 10.5 percent of the searches that involved white motorists resulted in an arrest or seizure of contraband, 13.5 percent of the searches that involved black motorists resulted in an arrest or seizure, and 38.1 percent of the searches of Hispanic motorists resulted in an arrest or seizure.

Arrests. [During the years 1996 through 1998], there were a total of 2,871 arrests [for crimes other than drunk driving]. Of these, 932 (32.5 percent) involved white persons, 1,772 (61.7 percent) involved black persons, and 167 (5.8 percent) involved persons of other races.

Interpretations of the Data and Areas of Special Concern

. . . Information and analysis compiled by the Public Defender's Office . . . suggests that troopers who enjoyed a wider ambit of discretion, by virtue of the nature of their duty assignment, stopped and ticketed minority motorists more often. Specifically, the Public Defender's statistical expert compared the tickets issued on 35 randomly selected days by three different State Police units: (1) the Radar Unit, which uses radar-equipped vans and chase cars and exercises comparatively little discretion; (2) the Tactical Patrol Unit, which focuses on motor vehicle enforcement in particular areas and exercises somewhat greater discretion; and, (3) the Patrol Unit, which is responsible for general law enforcement and exercises the most discretion. [T]he Radar Unit was found to have issued 18% of its tickets to African-Americans, the Tactical Patrol Unit issued 23.8% of its tickets to African-Americans, and the Patrol Unit issued 34.2% of its tickets to African-Americans. . . . We are concerned by what may be a pattern that when state troopers are permitted more discretion by virtue of their duty assignment, they tended during the time periods examined to ticket African-Americans more often. . . .

One need not be a racist to violate the Equal Protection Clause. . . . Many if not most of the problems and concerns we address in this Report will require that the State Police take a new look at the issue of racial profiling precisely because honest, nonbigoted officers throughout the ranks of the State Police could scarcely believe that they were engaged in or tolerated any form of discrimination.

The potential for the disparate treatment of minorities during routine traffic stops may be the product of an accumulation of circumstances that can contribute to the use of race or ethnicity-based criteria by creating the unintended message that the best way to catch drug traffickers is to focus on minorities. To some extent, the State Police as an organization may have been caught up in the martial rhetoric of the "war on drugs," responding to the call to arms urged by the public, the Legislature, and the Attorney General's Statewide Narcotics Action Plans of 1987 and 1993.

[T]he officially stated policy has always been to condemn reliance upon constitutionally impermissible factors. The message in these official policies, however, was not always clear and may have been undermined by other messages in both official and unofficial policies. . . . The State Police official policy prohibiting racial profiling was announced in a 1990 Standard Operating Procedure. Ironically, the problem of the reliance upon stereotypes may have unwittingly been exacerbated by the issuance of this [1990 Procedure. It] included a discussion of the "sufficiency of objective facts to establish reasonable suspicion or probable cause," explaining that . . . personal characteristics such as race, age, sex, length of hair, style of dress, type of vehicle, and number of occupants of a vehicle "may not be utilized as facts relevant to establish reasonable suspicion or probable cause *unless the [State Police] member can identify and describe the manner in which a characteristic is directly and specifically related to particular criminal activity*." (Emphasis added.) [This] portion of the Standard Operating Procedure, read literally, suggests that a person's race *may* be relied upon by a State Police member if he or she is able to identify and describe the manner in which race is directly and specifically related to a particular criminal activity. This exception has the very real capacity to swallow the rule, and opens the door (or at least fails to shut the door) to the use of stereotypes, especially those that have been "validated" by tautological and self-serving intelligence reports and profiles. . . .

With respect to training programs, no one can seriously question the right, indeed the obligation, of the State Police to alert troopers to the existence and activities of criminal organizations that they might encounter. . . . The problem, however, is that in providing this kind of training, inadequate attention may have been paid to the possibility that subtle messages in these lectures and videos would reinforce preexisting stereotypes by, for example, focusing mostly on criminal groups that happen to be comprised of minority citizens or foreign nationals. These kinds of messages may have been further reinforced by statistics compiled by State Police and disseminated to troopers in seminars and bulletins. The very fact that information concerning the racial characteristics of drug traffickers was provided to troopers assigned to patrol duties could have suggested that such characteristics are a legitimate, relevant factor to be taken into account or "kept in mind" in exercising police discretion during a traffic stop.

The State Police reward system, meanwhile, gave practical impetus to the use of these inappropriate stereotypes about drug dealers. [E]vidence has surfaced that minority troopers may also have been caught up in a system that rewards officers based on the quantity of drugs that they have discovered during routine traffic stops. (An internal audit of State Police motor vehicle stops recorded on the Moorestown Station radio logs between May 1, 1996 and July 31, 1996 shows that 34.3% of the 3,524 stops that were conducted by nonminority troopers involved minority motorists. An essentially identical proportion (33.3%) of the 1,751 total stops that were conducted by minority troopers involved minority motorists.) . . . The typical trooper is an intelligent, rational, ambitious, and career-oriented professional who responds to the prospect of rewards and promotions as much as to the threat of discipline and punishment. The system of organizational rewards, by definition and design, exerts a powerful influence on officer performance and enforcement priorities. . . .

The Critical Distinction Between Legitimate Crime Trend Analysis and Impermissible Racial Profiling

Today we propose to make clear, as a matter of policy if not settled law, that race, ethnicity, and national origin are inappropriate factors that State Police members should not rely upon at all in selecting vehicles to be stopped or in exercising discretion during the course of a stop (other than in determining whether a person matches the general description of one or more known suspects).

[We] start with a discussion of the legitimate use of law enforcement's "collective knowledge and experience." Sophisticated crime analysis is sorely needed if police agencies are to remain responsive to emerging new threats and enforcement opportunities. The law is thus well-settled that in appropriate factual circumstances, police may piece together a series of acts, which by themselves seem innocent, but to a trained officer would reasonably indicate that criminal activity is afoot. State v. Patterson, 270 N.J. Super. 550, 557 (Law Div. 1993). As the court in *Patterson* correctly noted, "it is appropriate and legitimate police work to develop a so-called 'profile' based upon observations made in investigating the distribution or transportation of illicit drugs." Using these and other means, the police can develop a pattern of criminal wrongdoing that justifies their suspicions when they observe features that are in accord with the principal aspects of that pattern. . . . This regularized police experience reflects the collection of historical and intelligence information, careful crime trend analysis, and an examination of the methods of operations, the so-called "modus operandi," of drug traffickers and others engaged in various types of criminal activity. . . .

While police agencies are permitted, indeed are expected, to conduct crime trend analysis and to train officers as to those facts and circumstances that, while innocent on their face, provide a reasonable basis for suspecting criminal activity, the law also provides that certain factors may not be considered by law enforcement. In State v. Kuhn, 213 N.J. Super. 275 (App. Div. 1986), the court held that police are not permitted to draw any inferences of criminal activity from a suspect's race. The court in State v. Patterson expounded on this point, noting that, "[c]ertainly the police cannot conclude that all young, male African-Americans are suspected of involvement in the illicit drug trade." . . .

One need not be a constitutional scholar to understand that race, ethnicity, or national origin cannot be the sole basis for initiating a motor vehicle stop. On this point, everyone seems to agree. The law is far less clear, and opinions within and outside the criminal justice system become far more diverse, with respect to the question whether there are any circumstances when police may legitimately consider these kinds of personal traits and characteristics in drawing rational inferences about criminal activity. No one disputes, of course, that police can take a person's race into account in deciding whether the person is the individual who is described in a "wanted" bulletin; in this instance, race or ethnicity is used only as an "identifier." The issue, rather, and one that has not yet been definitely or at least uniformly resolved by the courts, is whether race, ethnicity, or national origin may be considered as one among an array of factors to infer that a particular individual is more likely than others to be engaged in criminal activity.

We believe that when finally confronted with this issue, the New Jersey Supreme Court would likely . . . hold, based upon independent state constitutional grounds if necessary, that race may play no part in an officer's determination of whether a particular person is reasonably likely to be engaged in criminal activity. In any event, . . . we need not wait for the courts to reach this conclusion before we propose a clear rule to be followed by state troopers assigned to patrol duties. . . .

The Importance of Perceptions

Our findings and our proposed remedial steps are based in part on statistics . . . that document actual practices and procedures. We think it important to add, however, that law enforcement policy cannot be divorced from public opinion and public perceptions. The New Jersey State Police, no less than any other law enforcement agency, [must] remain responsive to public needs and expectations if it is to achieve its ultimate mission to protect and to serve. [P]erceptions concerning the magnitude and impact of the problem vary widely. . . .

To help to explain the nature of these issues we now confront and to put the problem and the proposed remedial steps in perspective, we find it useful to cite to a *Star Ledger/Eagleton* poll that was conducted in early May 1998. The poll showed that while the overall job performance rating of the State Police is quite positive in New Jersey, there is a major racial divide among Garden State residents. Black and white New Jerseyans have markedly different views of troopers' fairness in the enforcement of the laws, even-handed treatment of all drivers, judgment in deciding whom to pull over, and courteousness in dealing with stopped motorists. The poll revealed that the vast majority of African-Americans in New Jersey feel that State Police members treat minorities worse than others, and that troopers target cars to pull over based on the race and age of the people in the cars. In stark contrast, the majority of white New Jerseyans feel that troopers treat all motorists the same and seem highly satisfied with all aspects of their job performance. . . .

The Circular Illogic of Race-Based Profiles

. . . We turn now to the specific assumption that is at the heart of the racial profiling controversy: the notion that a disproportionate percentage of drug traffickers and couriers are black or Hispanic, so that race, ethnicity, or national origin can serve as a reliable, accurate predictor of criminal activity. The proponents of this view point to empirical evidence, usually in the form of arrest and conviction statistics, that would appear at first blush to demonstrate quite conclusively that minorities are disproportionately represented among the universe of drug dealers.

The evidence for this conclusion is, in reality, tautological and reflects as much as anything the initial stereotypes of those who rely upon these statistics. To a large extent, these statistics have been used to grease the wheels of a vicious cycle — a self-fulfilling prophecy where law enforcement agencies rely on arrest data that they themselves generated as a result of the discretionary allocation of resources and targeted drug enforcement efforts. . . .

The most obvious problem in relying on arrest statistics, of course, is that these numbers refer only to persons who were found to be involved in criminal activity. . . . Arrest statistics, by definition, do not show the number of persons who were detained or investigated who, as it turned out, were not found to be trafficking drugs or carrying weapons. Consistent with our human nature, we in law enforcement proudly display seized drug shipments or "hits" as a kind of trophy, but pay scant attention to our far more frequent "misses," that is, those instances where stops and searches failed to discover contraband. . . .

Remedial Steps

[T]he State Police has already undertaken a series of initiatives to address these issues, beginning in 1990 with a comprehensive Standard Operating Procedure governing the conduct of motor vehicle stops. That SOP included a number of important and innovative safeguards, including a requirement that state troopers have a reasonable, articulable suspicion to believe that evidence of a crime would be found before asking for permission to conduct a consent search, and a requirement that all consents to search be reduced to writing.

The State Police have also issued policies and procedures that require troopers to advise the dispatcher as to the racial characteristics of motorists who are stopped, that require troopers to record this information on patrol logs, and that prohibit the practice of "spotlighting" vehicles to ascertain the racial characteristics of the occupants of vehicles that have not yet been ordered to pull over. . . . Most recently, pursuant to the Governor's and Attorney General's initiative, State Police vehicles were equipped with video cameras that can be used to provide conclusive evidence of the conduct of motor vehicle stops. . . .

[A] trooper who is bent on finding drugs will . . . engage in comparatively protracted patrol stops, since his or her objective would not be simply to issue a summons or warning, but rather to undertake a full-blown criminal investigation. For this reason, we propose the establishment of a system that would allow supervisors and the State Police hierarchy to monitor the duration of road stops. If, for example, the median length of patrol stops by a given officer is shown to be correlated to the race, ethnicity, or national origin of motorists, that circumstance would trigger the "early warning system" and require appropriate follow-up investigation and explanation. . . .

The Department of Law and Public Safety should prepare and make public on a quarterly basis aggregate statistics compiled pursuant to the databases created in accordance with the recommendations of this Interim Report, detailing by State Police station the proportion of minority and nonminority citizens who were subject to various actions taken by State Police members during the course of traffic stops.

The Superintendent should within 120 days of this Report issue a comprehensive Standard Operating Procedure creating and establishing a protocol for the use of an "early warning system" to detect and deter the disparate treatment of minority citizens by State Police members assigned to patrol duties. . . . The protocol for use of the "early warning system" should provide for the routine supervisory review of videotapes, patrol officer logs, Traffic Stop Report forms, Search Incident forms, and any other patrol work product. The protocol should also provide for regularly conducted audits of enforcement patterns including traffic stops, the issuance of motor vehicle summons, and search and arrest activity. . . .

The Superintendent should within 90 days of this Report issue a single, comprehensive Standard Operating Procedure [regarding traffic stops]. In preparing the Standard Operating Procedure, the following should be considered:

1. Before exiting his or her police vehicle, a State Police member will inform the dispatcher of the exact reason for the stop (e.g., speeding, 70 mph), a description of the vehicle and, when possible, a description of its occupants (i.e., the number of occupants and the apparent race and gender).
2. A system should be established to monitor the exact duration of all stops.
3. When the patrol vehicle is equipped with a video camera, the State Police person will ensure that the camera is activated before exiting the patrol vehicle and will not turn the camera off until the detained vehicle has been released and departs the scene.
4. In the case of routine stops, the State Police member will at the outset of the stop introduce him or herself by name and inform the driver as to the reason for the stop. The member should not wait for the driver to inquire as to the reason for the stop, which may not be readily apparent to the driver. . . .
6. At the conclusion of the vehicle stop, the State Police person will inform the dispatcher as to the stop outcome (e.g., warning, summons, etc.). . . .
7. All State Police members conducting a motor vehicle traffic stop must utilize a Traffic Stop Report form, which shall record all officer action information necessary for immediate supervisory review or to supplement information recorded by the Computer Aided Dispatch System. . . .
8. All Traffic Stop Report forms are to be reviewed by supervisory personnel at the conclusion of all duty shifts. The information contained in the reports should be entered into the "early warning system" database. . . .

Although the racial profiling issue has gained state and national attention recently, the underlying conditions that foster disparate treatment of minorities have existed for decades in New Jersey and throughout the nation, and will not be changed overnight. Even so, we firmly believe that this Interim Report represents a major step, indeed a watershed event, signaling significant change. We thus hope that this Report, once fully implemented through the issuance of new and comprehensive Standard Operating Procedures, a monitoring system, training, and other reforms, will ensure that New Jersey is a national leader in addressing the issue of racial profiling.

Problem 2-3. Racial Profiling After September 11

On October 25, 2001, the Wall Street Journal ran an editorial by Senior Editor Jason Riley. He began by noting that all 19 of the hijackers on September 11 were Arabic, practitioners of Islam, and from "known state incubators of terrorism" in the Middle East.

> Before [September 11], those Americans who favored [racial] profiling were few in number, and those willing to say so aloud were fewer still. President Bush and [Attorney General] Ashcroft had gone on record condemning racially motivated police stops, which surprised no one. To the American public and the media, racial profiling was a major no-no; it evoked images of state troopers targeting black highway motorists for traffic violations in order to search for drugs.
>
> Not much effort has gone into distinguishing between America's pre-September understanding of this controversial police procedure and the current effort to preempt future terror strikes on the basis of all we know about the perpetrators. Instead we get polls purporting to show a shift in public attitudes about profiling. . . .
>
> Two respected pollsters have reported that blacks, the frequent targets of profiling in the U.S., are now more likely than other racial groups to favor it. Seventy-one percent of black respondents to a Gallup poll, and 54% in a Zogby poll, said they want Arab-looking travelers singled out for extra scrutiny at airports. . . .
>
> In part, what the polls speak to is the uselessness of the term "racial profiling." . . . Regardless of what the polls say, black Americans haven't suddenly decided that "driving while black" is no longer a problem that needs addressing. . . . More plausibly, [black Americans], to their credit, are making a distinction that the media are ignoring. Whatever you want to call it, they're saying, what's happening now is a logical and legitimate response given our knowledge of the adversary, and quite different from previous debates we had over whether random black drivers were stopped along the highway.

Has the acceptability of racial profiling changed after September 11? Is some profiling acceptable, and some unacceptable? Does that depend on the consequences of being "profiled"? Has the term profiling come to mean so many things that it may not mean any specific thing?

Notes

1. *DWB claims.* Claims that police officers stop drivers because of their race and not their behavior are not new, but have become much more prominent over the past several years after a series of prominent law review articles, and some litigation in New Jersey and Maryland. These civil lawsuits, along with defenses raised in criminal proceedings, have produced only modest success. Based on cases such as Whren v. United States, 517 U.S. 806 (1996), described above, most courts have found no constitutional violation. See Tracey Maclin, The Fourth Amendment on the Freeway, 3 Rutgers Race and the Law Rev. 117, 117-128 (2001); American Civil

Liberties Union, Driving While Black: Racial Profiling on Our Nation's Highways (June 1999).

If racial bias in stops, searches, and arrests is so high, why have so few defendants challenged police action on these grounds, at least as far as indicated by published case reports? Note the concern of the New Jersey Attorney General's Office that its report might encourage such litigation: "We cannot prevent defendants from raising these issues in future motions to suppress evidence, but we wish to make clear that as to any such future challenges, we will be prepared to fully and fairly litigate the question whether any particular defendant was, in fact, a victim of unconstitutional conduct by the State Police warranting the suppression of reliable evidence of guilt."

2. *DWB legislation.* With DWB making little or no headway as a constitutional claim, state legislatures have taken the lead in efforts to monitor, limit, and sanction racially biased traffic stops. See David A. Harris, Addressing Racial Profiling in the States: A Case Study of the "New Federalism" in Constitutional Criminal Procedure, 3 Pa. J. Const. L. 367 (2001). The statutes pursue different strategies. An Oklahoma statute, 22 Okla. Stat. §34.3, directly forbids the use of race as the "sole" basis for stopping or detaining a person, and makes racial profiling a misdemeanor. The statute also calls for law enforcement agencies to adopt and publicize "a detailed written policy that clearly defines the elements constituting racial profiling." A California statute, Penal Code §13519.4, requires training of officers in topics related to cultural diversity. A Missouri statute, Mo. Stat. §590.650, provides for mandatory collection of data about the race of motorists whom the police stop and search. Which of these strategies is most likely to reduce the amount of racial profiling?

Apart from legislation on the subject, many police departments have now adopted internal guidelines calling on officers to record the age, gender, and race or ethnicity of every person they stop in traffic. See Bureau of Justice Statistics, "Traffic Stop Data Collection Policies for State Police, 1999" (2000) (NCJ 180776). What (or who) might convince a police department to adopt such a policy?

B. BRIEF ADMINISTRATIVE STOPS

Among the brief stops and searches that government agents carry out, some are subject to less restrictive rules because of their routine administrative nature. These brief stops are carried out on large numbers of people and further government interests apart from criminal law enforcement. The U.S. Supreme Court determined, in Camara v. Municipal Court, 387 U.S. 523 (1967), that the Fourth Amendment could place limits on government activities even when they are not directed at enforcement of the criminal laws. These "administrative" stops and searches sometimes take place even when the government agents have no reasonable suspicion to believe that a law has been violated. We begin with non-individualized stops of drivers.

■ CITY OF INDIANAPOLIS v. JAMES EDMOND

531 U.S. 32 (2000)

O'Connor, J.

. . . In August 1998, the city of Indianapolis began to operate vehicle checkpoints on Indianapolis roads in an effort to interdict unlawful drugs. The city conducted six such roadblocks between August and November that year, stopping 1,161 vehicles and arresting 104 motorists. Fifty-five arrests were for drug-related crimes, while 49 were for offenses unrelated to drugs. The overall "hit rate" of the program was thus approximately nine percent.

The parties stipulated to the facts concerning the operation of the checkpoints by the Indianapolis Police Department (IPD) for purposes of the preliminary injunction proceedings instituted below. At each checkpoint location, the police stop a predetermined number of vehicles. Approximately 30 officers are stationed at the checkpoint. Pursuant to written directives issued by the chief of police, at least one officer approaches the vehicle, advises the driver that he or she is being stopped briefly at a drug checkpoint, and asks the driver to produce a license and registration. The officer also looks for signs of impairment and conducts an open-view examination of the vehicle from the outside. A narcotics-detection dog walks around the outside of each stopped vehicle.

The directives instruct the officers that they may conduct a search only by consent or based on the appropriate quantum of particularized suspicion. The officers must conduct each stop in the same manner until particularized suspicion develops, and the officers have no discretion to stop any vehicle out of sequence. . . . According to Sergeant [Marshall] DePew, checkpoint locations are selected weeks in advance based on such considerations as area crime statistics and traffic flow. The checkpoints are generally operated during daylight hours and are identified with lighted signs reading, "NARCOTICS CHECKPOINT ___ MILE AHEAD, NARCOTICS K-9 IN USE, BE PREPARED TO STOP." Once a group of cars has been stopped, other traffic proceeds without interruption until all the stopped cars have been processed or diverted for further processing. Sergeant DePew also stated that the average stop for a vehicle not subject to further processing lasts two to three minutes or less.

Respondents James Edmond and Joell Palmer were each stopped at a narcotics checkpoint in late September 1998. Respondents then filed a lawsuit on behalf of themselves and the class of all motorists who had been stopped or were subject to being stopped in the future at the Indianapolis drug checkpoints. Respondents claimed that the roadblocks violated the Fourth Amendment of the United States Constitution and the search and seizure provision of the Indiana Constitution. Respondents requested declaratory and injunctive relief for the class, as well as damages and attorney's fees for themselves. . . .

The Fourth Amendment requires that searches and seizures be reasonable. A search or seizure is ordinarily unreasonable in the absence of individualized suspicion of wrongdoing. While such suspicion is not an irreducible component of reasonableness, we have recognized only limited circumstances in which the usual rule does not apply. For example, we have upheld certain regimes of suspicionless searches where the program was designed to serve "special needs, beyond the normal need for law enforcement." See, e.g., Vernonia School Dist. 47J v. Acton, 515 U.S. 646 (1995) (random drug testing of student-athletes); Treasury Employees v. Von Raab, 489 U.S. 656 (1989) (drug tests for United States Customs Service employees seeking transfer or promotion to certain positions). We have also allowed searches for certain administrative purposes without particularized suspicion of misconduct, provided that those searches are appropriately limited. See, e.g., New York v. Burger, 482 U.S. 691 (1987) (warrantless administrative inspection of premises of "closely regulated" business).

We have also upheld brief, suspicionless seizures of motorists at a fixed Border Patrol checkpoint designed to intercept illegal aliens, United States v. Martinez-Fuerte, 428 U.S. 543 (1976), and at a sobriety checkpoint aimed at removing drunk drivers from the road, Michigan Dept. of State Police v. Sitz, 496 U.S. 444 (1990). In addition, in Delaware v. Prouse, 440 U.S. 648 (1979), we suggested that a similar type of roadblock with the purpose of verifying drivers' licenses and vehicle registrations would be permissible. In none of these cases, however, did we indicate approval of a checkpoint program whose primary purpose was to detect evidence of ordinary criminal wrongdoing. . . .

In *Sitz,* we evaluated the constitutionality of a Michigan highway sobriety checkpoint program. The *Sitz* checkpoint involved brief suspicionless stops of motorists so that police officers could detect signs of intoxication and remove impaired drivers from the road. Motorists who exhibited signs of intoxication were diverted for a license and registration check and, if warranted, further sobriety tests. This checkpoint program was clearly aimed at reducing the immediate hazard posed by the presence of drunk drivers on the highways, and there was an obvious connection between the imperative of highway safety and the law enforcement practice at issue. The gravity of the drunk driving problem and the magnitude of the State's interest in getting drunk drivers off the road weighed heavily in our determination that the program was constitutional.

In *Prouse,* we invalidated a discretionary, suspicionless stop for a spot check of a motorist's driver's license and vehicle registration. The officer's conduct in that case was unconstitutional primarily on account of his exercise of "standardless and unconstrained discretion." We nonetheless acknowledged the States' "vital interest in ensuring that only those qualified to do so are permitted to operate motor vehicles, that these vehicles are fit for safe operation, and hence that licensing, registration, and vehicle inspection requirements are being observed." Accordingly, we suggested that "questioning of all oncoming traffic at roadblock-type stops" would be a lawful means of serving this interest in highway safety.

We further indicated in *Prouse* that we considered the purposes of such a hypothetical roadblock to be distinct from a general purpose of investigating crime. [We considered the State's primary interest in this setting to be roadway safety.] Not only does the common thread of highway safety thus run through *Sitz* and *Prouse,* but *Prouse* itself reveals a difference in the Fourth Amendment significance of highway safety interests and the general interest in crime control.

It is well established that a vehicle stop at a highway checkpoint effectuates a seizure within the meaning of the Fourth Amendment. The fact that officers walk a narcotics-detection dog around the exterior of each car at the Indianapolis checkpoints does not transform the seizure into a search. See United States v. Place, 462 U.S. 696 (1983). Just as in *Place,* an exterior sniff of an automobile does not require entry into the car and is not designed to disclose any information other than the presence or absence of narcotics. . . . Rather, what principally distinguishes these checkpoints from those we have previously approved is their primary purpose.

As petitioners concede, the Indianapolis checkpoint program unquestionably has the primary purpose of interdicting illegal narcotics. In their stipulation of facts, the parties repeatedly refer to the checkpoints as "drug checkpoints" and describe them as "being operated by the City of Indianapolis in an effort to interdict unlawful drugs in Indianapolis." In addition, the [operating] directives instruct officers to "advise the citizen that they are being stopped briefly at a drug checkpoint." . . .

Because the primary purpose of the Indianapolis narcotics checkpoint program is to uncover evidence of ordinary criminal wrongdoing, the program contravenes the Fourth Amendment.

Petitioners propose several ways in which the narcotics-detection purpose of the instant checkpoint program may instead resemble the primary purposes of the checkpoints in *Sitz* and *Martinez-Fuerte*. Petitioners state that the checkpoints in those cases had the same ultimate purpose of arresting those suspected of committing crimes. Securing the border and apprehending drunk drivers are, of course, law enforcement activities, and law enforcement officers employ arrests and criminal prosecutions in pursuit of these goals. If we were to rest the case at this high level of generality, there would be little check on the ability of the authorities to construct roadblocks for almost any conceivable law enforcement purpose. Without drawing the line at roadblocks designed primarily to serve the general interest in crime control, the Fourth Amendment would do little to prevent such intrusions from becoming a routine part of American life. . . .

Nor can the narcotics-interdiction purpose of the checkpoints be rationalized in terms of a highway safety concern similar to that present in *Sitz*. The detection and punishment of almost any criminal offense serves broadly the safety of the community, and our streets would no doubt be safer but for the scourge of illegal drugs. Only with respect to a smaller class of offenses, however, is society confronted with the type of immediate, vehicle-bound threat to life and limb that the sobriety checkpoint in *Sitz* was designed to eliminate. . . .

Of course, there are circumstances that may justify a law enforcement checkpoint where the primary purpose would otherwise, but for some emergency, relate to ordinary crime control. For example, . . . the Fourth Amendment would almost certainly permit an appropriately tailored roadblock set up to thwart an imminent terrorist attack or to catch a dangerous criminal who is likely to flee by way of a particular route. The exigencies created by these scenarios are far removed from the circumstances under which authorities might simply stop cars as a matter of course to see if there just happens to be a felon leaving the jurisdiction. . . .

Petitioners argue that our prior cases preclude an inquiry into the purposes of the checkpoint program. For example, they cite Whren v. United States, 517 U.S. 806 (1996) . . . to support the proposition that "where the government articulates and pursues a legitimate interest for a suspicionless stop, courts should not look behind that interest to determine whether the government's 'primary purpose' is valid." These cases, however, do not control the instant situation.

In *Whren,* we held that an individual officer's subjective intentions are irrelevant to the Fourth Amendment validity of a traffic stop that is justified objectively by probable cause to believe that a traffic violation has occurred. . . . In so holding, we expressly distinguished cases where we had addressed the validity of searches conducted in the absence of probable cause. [W]hile subjective intentions play no role in ordinary, probable-cause Fourth Amendment analysis, programmatic purposes may be relevant to the validity of Fourth Amendment intrusions undertaken pursuant to a general scheme without individualized suspicion. . . .

Petitioners argue that the Indianapolis checkpoint program is justified by its lawful secondary purposes of keeping impaired motorists off the road and verifying licenses and registrations. If this were the case, however, law enforcement authorities would be able to establish checkpoints for virtually any purpose so long as they also included a license or sobriety check. For this reason, we examine the available evidence to determine the primary purpose of the checkpoint program. While we recognize the challenges inherent in a purpose inquiry, courts routinely engage in this enterprise in many areas of constitutional jurisprudence as a means of sifting abusive governmental conduct from that which is lawful. . . .

Because the primary purpose of the Indianapolis checkpoint program is ultimately indistinguishable from the general interest in crime control, the checkpoints violate the Fourth Amendment. . . .

REHNQUIST, C.J., dissenting.

The State's use of a drug-sniffing dog, according to the Court's holding, annuls what is otherwise plainly constitutional under our Fourth Amendment jurisprudence: brief, standardized, discretionless, roadblock seizures of automobiles, seizures which effectively serve a weighty state interest with only minimal intrusion on the privacy of their occupants. Because these seizures serve the State's accepted and significant interests of preventing drunken driving and checking for driver's licenses and vehicle registrations, and because there is nothing in the record to indicate that the addition of the dog sniff lengthens these otherwise legitimate seizures, I dissent. . . .

Petitioners acknowledge that the "primary purpose" of these roadblocks is to interdict illegal drugs, but this fact should not be controlling. [T]he question whether a law enforcement purpose could support a roadblock seizure is not presented in this case. The District Court found that another "purpose of the checkpoints is to check driver's licenses and vehicle registrations," and the written directives state that the police officers are to "look for signs of impairment." . . . That the roadblocks serve these legitimate state interests cannot be seriously disputed, as the 49 people arrested for offenses unrelated to drugs can attest. . . .

Because of the valid reasons for conducting these roadblock seizures, it is constitutionally irrelevant that petitioners also hoped to interdict drugs. In Whren v. United States, we held that an officer's subjective intent would not invalidate an otherwise objectively justifiable stop of an automobile. The reasonableness of an officer's discretionary decision to stop an automobile, at issue in *Whren,* turns on whether there is probable cause to believe that a traffic violation has occurred. The reasonableness of highway checkpoints, at issue here, turns on whether they effectively serve a significant state interest with minimal intrusion on motorists. . . . Once the constitutional requirements for a particular seizure are satisfied, the subjective expectations of those responsible for it, be it police officers or members of a city council, are irrelevant. It is the objective effect of the State's actions on the privacy of the individual that animates the Fourth Amendment. Because the objective intrusion of a valid seizure does not turn upon anyone's subjective thoughts, neither should our constitutional analysis. . . .

[T]he checkpoints' success rate — 49 arrests for offenses unrelated to drugs [or 4.2 percent of the motorists stopped] — only confirms the State's legitimate interests in preventing drunken driving and ensuring the proper licensing of drivers and registration of their vehicles. These stops effectively serve the State's legitimate interests; they are executed in a regularized and neutral manner; and they only minimally intrude upon the privacy of the motorists. They should therefore be constitutional.

[Expectations] of privacy in an automobile and of freedom in its operation are significantly different from the traditional expectation of privacy and freedom in one's residence. This is because automobiles, unlike homes, are subjected to pervasive and continuing governmental regulation and controls. The lowered expectation of privacy in one's automobile is coupled with the limited nature of the intrusion: a brief, standardized, nonintrusive seizure. . . .

Because of these extrinsic limitations upon roadblock seizures, the Court's newfound non-law-enforcement primary purpose test is both unnecessary to secure Fourth Amendment rights and bound to produce wide-ranging litigation over the "purpose" of any given seizure. Police designing highway roadblocks can never be sure of their validity, since a jury might later determine that a forbidden purpose exists. . . .

■ IOWA CODE §321K.1

1. The law enforcement agencies of this state may conduct emergency vehicle roadblocks in response to immediate threats to the health, safety, and welfare of the public; and otherwise may conduct routine vehicle roadblocks only as provided in this section. Routine vehicle roadblocks may be conducted to enforce compliance with the law regarding any of the following:

a. The licensing of operators of motor vehicles.

b. The registration of motor vehicles.

c. The safety equipment required on motor vehicles.

d. The provisions of chapters 481A and 483A [dealing with fish and game conservation].

2. Any routine vehicle roadblock conducted under this section shall meet the following requirements:

a. The location of the roadblock, the time during which the roadblock will be conducted, and the procedure to be used while conducting the roadblock, shall be determined by policymaking administrative officers of the law enforcement agency.

b. The roadblock location shall be selected for its safety and visibility to oncoming motorists, and adequate advance warning signs, illuminated at night or under conditions of poor visibility, shall be erected to provide timely information to approaching motorists of the roadblock and its nature.

c. There shall be uniformed officers and marked official vehicles of the law enforcement agency or agencies involved, in sufficient quantity and visibility to demonstrate the official nature of the roadblock.

d. The selection of motor vehicles to be stopped shall not be arbitrary.

e. The roadblock shall be conducted to assure the safety of and to minimize the inconvenience of the motorists involved.

Notes

1. *Automobile checkpoints: majority position.* As the opinion in *Edmond* makes clear, the federal constitution imposes different requirements on sobriety checkpoints and drug enforcement checkpoints. In Michigan Department of Police v. Sitz, 496 U.S. 444 (1990), the Court upheld a sobriety checkpoint where officers stopped vehicles without reasonable suspicion. The opinion emphasized the importance of

neutral guidelines for carrying out the roadblock, formulated by supervisors or others besides the officers in the field. Those guidelines reduced both the "objective" intrusion (the duration of the stop and the intensity of the questioning) and the "subjective" intrusion of the stop (the anxiety of law-abiding drivers when unaware of the purpose of the stop). On the other hand, after the ruling in *Edmond*, governments may not conduct suspicionless stops at drug enforcement checkpoints.

State courts are split on whether suspicionless sobriety checkpoints violate their state constitutions, with a strong majority (nearly 40 states) mirroring the federal position. See State v. Mikolinski, 775 A.2d 274 (Conn. 2001). A minority (about 10) require individualized suspicion before a vehicle stop may occur at a sobriety checkpoint. This group includes Michigan, the state whose appeals court decision was reversed in *Sitz*, which in turn rejected the U.S. Supreme Court's *Sitz* opinion on state constitutional grounds. Sitz v. Department of Police, 506 N.W.2d 209 (Mich. 1993). See also Pimental v. Dept. of Transportation, 561 A.2d 1348 (R.I. 1989).

2. *Driver's license and other safety reasons for checkpoints.* Police in many jurisdictions stop vehicles without individualized suspicion at a checkpoint to verify the validity of the operators' licenses, and they follow much the same procedures for license checkpoints as they do for sobriety checkpoints. The Iowa statute above approves of roadblocks for purposes of enforcing safety equipment laws but not for purposes of enforcing drunk driving laws. Does this distinction make sense?

The U.S. Supreme Court has approved of license checkpoints so long as they are carried out in a way that does not leave officers in the field with discretion to select the vehicles to stop. Delaware v. Prouse, 440 U.S. 648 (1979). Some states have rejected license checkpoints under their state constitutions. State v. Sanchez, 856 S.W.2d 166 (Tex. Crim. App. 1993) (license and insurance checkpoint set up by four officers); State v. Hicks, 55 S.W.3d 515 (Tenn. 2001) (license checkpoint).

Government agents enforcing health and safety laws other than traffic laws also find it useful to stop and question motorists and persons outside their cars. See People v. McHugh, 630 So. 2d 1259 (La. 1994) (upholding statute authorizing suspicionless stops of hunters who are leaving state wilderness area to inspect hunting license and to request permission to inspect game); but see State v. Medley, 898 P.2d 1093 (Idaho 1995) (disallowing, in an opinion by Justice Trout, a game management checkpoint because of officer discretion in stopping vehicles and presence of criminal law enforcement officials). What set of safety and health concerns convinced the Iowa legislature to pass Section 321K.1?

3. *Which programmatic purpose?* Justice O'Connor, in her majority opinion in *Edmond*, says that "programmatic purposes may be relevant" even though an officer's subjective intentions normally do not matter in evaluating the reasonableness of a seizure. We encountered this issue earlier, in discussing "pretextual" stops. Is it any easier for courts to determine the purpose of a program than to determine the intentions of a particular officer? What sources of evidence are available to the court making this factual finding? See Crowell v. State, 994 P.2d 788 (Okla. Crim. App. 2000) (use of narcotics detection dog to sniff cars not enough to show that safety roadblock was a pretext for drug enforcement); State v. DeBooy, 996 P.2d 546 (Utah 2000) (checkpoint set up for purpose of detecting drunk driving and controlled substance violations, vehicle equipment violations, compliance with seat belt and child restraint laws, and compliance with insurance and registration laws violated state and federal constitutions; multiple purposes made checkpoint overbroad).

4. *Warrant clause and reasonableness clause.* A court ruling on the constitutionality of a suspicionless checkpoint stop confronts a question of legal text that we will encounter time and again in search and seizure issues. Recall that the text of the Fourth Amendment provides as follows: "The right of the people to be secure . . . against unreasonable searches and seizures, shall not be violated, and no Warrants shall issue, but upon probable cause. . . ." The first phrase (up to the word "violated") is known as the "reasonableness clause"; the second, the "warrant clause." What is the proper relationship between these clauses? Is the warrant clause a modifier to the reasonableness clause, defining the quintessential "reasonable" search and seizure, or do the clauses have independent meaning? If we are free to define reasonableness apart from the presence of a warrant and probable cause, then courts will need to determine in many different settings the proper measure of reasonableness. But if reasonableness is defined only in light of the warrant and probable cause requirements, then reasonableness in most settings becomes only a matter of determining how feasible it is to require police to show probable cause and obtain warrants.

Sobriety checkpoints take place in the absence of any probable cause or reasonable suspicion to believe that a driver being stopped is violating the law. The Supreme Court in *Sitz* and the other courts that have upheld sobriety checkpoints have used a "balancing" methodology to determine that individualized suspicion is not necessary. These courts balance the needs of law enforcement against the intrusiveness of the search and the individual's interest in privacy. Did the majority opinion in *Edmond* also balance interests? Should courts engage in balancing at all when it comes to constitutionally protected privacy interests? Or should they conclude that the Fourth Amendment and its equivalents have already struck a balance for all cases, requiring individualized suspicion for any "seizure" or "search"?

5. *Effectiveness of sobriety checkpoints.* Is it relevant in weighing the government's interest to determine the effectiveness of a particular set of roadblock guidelines in catching drunk drivers? Would a roadblock that produces one arrest for every 100 cars stopped be more constitutionally suspect than a roadblock that produces one arrest for every 20 cars stopped? How might police supervisors change guidelines to increase the number of arrests? Perhaps courts, police, and legislatures could consider some measure of effectiveness besides the number of arrests. Would courts be more likely to validate sobriety checkpoints if the government shows decreases in alcohol-related fatal crashes? See Ralph Hingson, Prevention of Drinking and Driving, 20 Alcohol Health & Research World 223-224 (1996) (reporting such decreases in Australia and Tennessee after widespread use of sobriety checkpoints).

6. *Advance notice and neutral plans.* The guidelines for conducting roadblocks often provide for two types of notice. First, there are markers at the scene of the roadblock, announcing to oncoming drivers the purpose of the stop. Second, some guidelines require advance notice in the local media that roadblocks will be taking place in the area on particular days, without announcing the exact locations of the roadblocks. This advance notice is designed to increase the deterrent effect of the roadblocks by influencing the choices of all potential drivers who hear about the stops and to decrease the anxiety of drivers who encounter a roadblock. Such notice was part of the Michigan guidelines considered by the Supreme Court in *Sitz.*

If you were writing roadblock guidelines for a police department, would you include provisions for advance notice? Will such advance notice achieve its purposes? Some courts have concluded that advance notice is not constitutionally required. See People v. Banks, 863 P.2d 769 (Cal. 1993). A few states modify the typical procedures by allowing random stops and giving officers more discretion. See State v. Davis, 464 S.E.2d 598 (W. Va. 1995) (allowing random stops). Who is in a position to know if the police adequately follow the plan for stopping and questioning drivers? Should the plan be written? If the state's legislature has passed a statute similar to the Iowa statute above, is any further written plan necessary?

7. *Roadblocks to find particular criminal suspects.* Police will occasionally receive information about the location of a suspect for a serious crime and will search all vehicles leaving the area. At least ten states give police explicit statutory authority to set up roadblocks to find criminal suspects. See Idaho Code §19-621. Courts evaluating these roadblocks tend to approve them more readily if the crime is serious and the officers administer the roadblock in an evenhanded way that minimizes the delay and other intrusions. What if a car approaching a roadblock makes a U-turn or exits the highway in an apparent attempt to avoid the roadblock? Does that give the police reasonable suspicion to pursue and stop the vehicle? See Commonwealth v. Scavello, 734 A.2d 386 (Pa.1999) (properly executed turn to avoid passing through roadblock not a basis for stop).

8. *Fixed and roving stops for immigration enforcement.* Customs and immigration officials routinely stop vehicles crossing the border into the country, and vehicles passing fixed checkpoints near the border. There are criminal sanctions for certain violations of the immigration laws; indeed, immigration crimes have become one of the most frequent charges in the federal courts (along with drug and fraud cases). While the Supreme Court has disapproved of "roving" suspicionless stops of vehicles, it has upheld suspicionless stops of cars for brief questioning at fixed checkpoints at or near the border. See United States v. Martinez-Fuerte, 428 U.S. 543 (1976) (approves fixed checkpoint stops for brief questioning); United States v. Brignoni-Ponce, 422 U.S. 873 (1975) (disapproves roving stops in interior for questioning about immigration status); United States v. Ortiz, 422 U.S. 891 (1975) (disapproves roving immigration stops away from border to search interior of car); cf. United States v. Villamonte-Marquez, 462 U.S. 579 (1983) (approves suspicionless boarding of vessels at sea to inspect documentation). The Court has required reasonable suspicion for unusually long detentions of persons at the border. See United States v. Montoya de Hernandez, 473 U.S. 531 (1985).

9. *Legislative intent in statutory construction.* Does the Iowa statute reprinted above require each of the listed conditions for a roadblock to be valid? Courts faced with questions about the meaning of a statute will often look beyond the actual language of the statute and will read the language in light of the "legislative intent." Sometimes this legislative intent will be expressed in the "legislative history," a set of documents such as committee reports that discuss the statute before its passage or statements of legislators during floor debates on the bill. Such materials occupy a prominent place in federal statutory construction, although Justice Scalia and several other federal judges have argued for less reliance on legislative history. See INS v. Cardoza-Fonseca, 480 U.S. 421, 452 (1987) (Scalia, J., concurring); William Mayton, Law Among the Pleonasms: The Futility and Aconstitutionality of Legislative History in Statutory Interpretation, 41 Emory L.J. 113 (1992).

Legislative history is generally less influential in most states. Many state courts do not consider legislative history at all because the state does not even maintain or publish such materials. Other state courts have legislative history available but discount it because it is difficult to know when statements of a single committee or a single legislator reflect the collective views of all those voting for a bill. Nevertheless, even those state courts that ignore or discount legislative history will inquire into the "purpose" of the statute. They might surmise this purpose from the language and structure of the statute (perhaps contained in the title of the statute or in a preamble explicitly stating the statute's purpose) or from a familiarity with the general history of the perceived problem and the statutory solution.

This effort to identify a statutory "purpose" gives courts the opportunity to read different statutes, perhaps passed and amended at different times, as a coherent and rational whole, furthering social purposes of the current day. In an influential text from 1958, Henry Hart and Albert Sacks expressed the interpreting judge's obligation this way: A judge interpreting a statute with ambiguous language "must resolve the uncertainty . . . in a way which is consistent with other established applications of [the statute.] And he must do so in the way which best serves the principles and policies it expresses. If the policy of the [statute] is open to doubt, the official should interpret it in the way which best harmonizes with more basic principles and policies of law." The Legal Process: Basic Problems in the Making and Application of Law 147 (William Eskridge and Phillip Frickey eds. 1994) (1958).

What was the intent of the Iowa legislature in passing its roadblock statute? What would a court need to know to answer this question? If a court determines the general "purpose" of the statute and applies the statute in a way that furthers that purpose, whose "intent" is it furthering?

Problem 2-4. Airport Checkpoints After September 11

You are an associate in a firm representing Los Angeles International Airport (LAX). Airport authorities have decided to install the Secure 2000 scanner. The Secure 2000 is a back-scatter X-ray system for detecting weapons and contraband hidden under a person's clothing. The Secure 2000 covertly scans persons for hidden weapons and explosives as they walk down a hallway. Almost immediately, an image of the person and any concealed objects appears on the monitor. Metal guns and knifes can be detected, as well as nonmetallic objects such as drugs and explosives. The image allows a view under clothes and, indeed, under the skin's surface.

Airport officials ask whether they can implement the Secure 2000 in all of the hallways leading to the terminals. If so, do they need to post a notice, and what does any notice need to say? They ask what authorities should do if the scanner reveals drugs, but not weapons.

C. GATHERING INFORMATION WITHOUT SEARCHING

Thus far, we have focused on various stops (that is, brief seizures) of persons and their property. We now turn to brief searches, the least intrusive efforts by government agents to collect private information from individuals.

Just as there are some encounters with police that do not count as a "seizure," there are some government efforts to gather information from individuals that do not amount to a "search" at all. Where there is no search, there is no constitutional requirement for the government to justify its efforts to gather information. Under the Fourth Amendment and most of its state equivalents, there is no search within

the meaning of the Constitution when the government intrudes into some place or interest where the person has no "reasonable expectation of privacy." The definition contains both a subjective and an objective component. The target of the search must actually expect privacy, and that expectation must be one that society is prepared to recognize as reasonable.

This definition of a "search," now prominent in the case law of every state, derives from Katz v. United States, 389 U.S. 347 (1967). Before *Katz*, searches were defined in terms of property rights. A government agent performed a "search" within the meaning of the constitution when he or she "trespassed" on a protected area. Now under the *Katz* "reasonable expectation of privacy" test, a search might occur even if there is no trespass into a protected place. In the materials that follow, ask yourself what factors might make an expectation of privacy "reasonable."

1. *Plain View*

One of the least intrusive forms of information-gathering occurs when the police simply notice what is in open view of others. Under the Fourth Amendment and its equivalents, there is no reasonable expectation of privacy in matters left within open view. Hence, no "search" has occurred to be evaluated under federal or state law. But when is an item in "open" or "plain" view?

■ STATE v. MIHAI BOBIC

996 P.2d 610 (Wash. 2000)

TALMADGE, J.

We are asked in this case to determine whether an officer's warrantless search of a commercial storage unit was constitutional when the search was made through a small, preexisting hole in an adjoining storage unit. . . . Under the circumstances of this case, we agree the evidence the officers obtained from the storage unit was in open view. . . .

Mihai Bobic and Igor Stepchuk were charged with numerous crimes arising from a sophisticated auto theft conspiracy. Bobic, Stepchuk, or their confederates stole vehicles and stripped them of their contents and key parts. They stored the stolen car parts and other stolen goods in various commercial storage facilities. Insurance carriers subsequently sold the hulks of the cars left by the thieves at auto auctions. Bobic, Stepchuk, or their confederates then purchased the hulks at those auto auctions, giving them clear title to the vehicles. They then reassembled the vehicles with the stolen car parts and sold them.

Detective Kelly Quirin became suspicious about certain auto thefts and his investigation uncovered a possible connection between auto thefts and storage facilities. On March 1, 1994, Quirin obtained and executed a search warrant to examine certain units at a Shurgard Storage facility. After searching the units in accordance with the warrant, the facility's manager told Quirin that one of the units at his facility, unit E-71, might be connected with stolen vehicles. . . . On March 8, Quirin went to the storage facility with another officer and asked to look at unit E-71, which was locked. The manager let the officers into an unrented, unlocked storage unit next door to unit E-71. Upon entering the unit, the officers saw a preexisting hole, "maybe big enough to stick your pinky finger in or a little bigger," about four feet off the ground. (The walls of the units go up to the ceiling.) Quirin looked through the hole, and without aid of a flashlight was able to see items in unit E-71. Based on this information, Quirin obtained a search warrant for unit E-71 and recovered stolen goods.

[Stepchuk and Bobic were charged with theft, trafficking in stolen property, and conspiracy.] Prior to trial, Bobic moved to suppress the evidence recovered during the search of unit E-71. During his pretrial suppression hearing, Bobic testified [that a friend rented unit E-71, but he and the friend shared the unit. Bobic placed a lock on the door of the unit. The rental agreement] permitted the manager to open a unit at any time to uncover illegal activities.[1] . . . After a lengthy trial in King County Superior Court, Bobic and Stepchuk were convicted [and Bobic] appealed the lower court's denial of both his motion to suppress evidence seized from unit E-71. . . .

Washington's constitution provides that "[n]o person shall be disturbed in his private affairs, . . . without authority of law." Const. Art I., §7. A violation of this right turns on whether the State has unreasonably intruded into a person's private affairs. In contrast, a search occurs under the Fourth Amendment if the government intrudes upon a reasonable expectation of privacy. Thus, Washington's "private affairs inquiry" is broader than the Fourth Amendment's "reasonable expectation of privacy inquiry."

Detective Quirin's observations do not constitute a search because the objects under observation were in "open view." Under the open view doctrine, when a law enforcement officer is able to detect something by utilization of one or more of his senses while lawfully present at the vantage point where those senses are used, that detection does not constitute a search. Here, the detective was lawfully inside the adjoining unit because the manager had given him permission to enter. Furthermore, it appears from the record that the detective's observations were made without extraordinary or invasive means and could be seen by anyone renting the unit. [Detective Quirin was able to "look in[to the hole] with one eye"; not utilizing a flashlight because "[t]he hole wasn't big enough to be able to look at to have the flashlight and your eye next to it to see in."].

Bobic contends the search here must nonetheless fail because it invaded a protected privacy interest and was more intrusive than the search in *State v. Rose,* 909 P.2d 280 (1996). In *Rose,* the officer's search was likely *more* intrusive because he looked with the aid of a flashlight through a window into the defendant's residence during the evening. Here, the detective did not peer through a curtained window; he did not wait until something incriminating came into sight or hearing; and he did not attempt to create a better vantage point.

Moreover, a commercial storage unit is not the kind of location entitled to special privacy protection. For example, a person's home is entitled to heightened constitutional protection relative to other locations. We decline to determine that a commercial storage unit has any special protected status. . . .

1. The rental agreement states, in pertinent part: ". . . The Storage Unit may not be used for any unlawful purpose . . . nor will Tenant keep in the Storage Unit any . . . substances whose storage or use is regulated or prohibited by local, state or federal law or regulation. . . . Tenant shall give the Landlord permission to enter the Storage Unit at any time for the purpose of removing and disposing of any property in the Storage Unit in violation of this provision. . . . Tenant represents to Landlord that all personal property to be stored by Tenant in the Storage Unit will belong to Tenant only, and not to any third parties. . . ."

In this case, notwithstanding the troubling image of a police officer peering through a peephole in a storage unit, the trial court did not err in denying Bobic's motion to suppress because there was no "search"; the contents of the unit were in open view as that doctrine is understood in our law where the officer was legally at the vantage point, the vantage point was not artificially improved, and the officer perceived what he did with his unaided vision. . . .

■ STEVEN DEWAYNE BOND v. UNITED STATES

529 U.S. 334 (2000)

REHNQUIST, C.J.

This case presents the question whether a law enforcement officer's physical manipulation of a bus passenger's carry-on luggage violated the Fourth Amendment's proscription against unreasonable searches. We hold that it did.

Petitioner Steven Dewayne Bond was a passenger on a Greyhound bus that left California bound for Little Rock, Arkansas. The bus stopped, as it was required to do, at the permanent Border Patrol checkpoint in Sierra Blanca, Texas. Border Patrol Agent Cesar Cantu boarded the bus to check the immigration status of its passengers. After reaching the back of the bus, having satisfied himself that the passengers were lawfully in the United States, Agent Cantu began walking toward the front. Along the way, he squeezed the soft luggage which passengers had placed in the overhead storage space above the seats.

Petitioner was seated four or five rows from the back of the bus. As Agent Cantu inspected the luggage in the compartment above petitioner's seat, he squeezed a green canvas bag and noticed that it contained a "brick-like" object. Petitioner admitted that the bag was his and agreed to allow Agent Cantu to open it. Upon opening the bag, Agent Cantu discovered a "brick" of methamphetamine. The brick had been wrapped in duct tape until it was oval-shaped and then rolled in a pair of pants.

Petitioner was indicted for conspiracy to possess, and possession with intent to distribute, methamphetamine. . . . He moved to suppress the drugs, arguing that Agent Cantu conducted an illegal search of his bag. Petitioner's motion was denied, and the District Court found him guilty on both counts and sentenced him to 57 months in prison.

[It] is undisputed here that petitioner possessed a privacy interest in his bag. But the Government asserts that by exposing his bag to the public, petitioner lost a reasonable expectation that his bag would not be physically manipulated. The Government relies on our decisions in California v. Ciraolo, 476 U.S. 207 (1986), and Florida v. Riley, 488 U.S. 445 (1989), for the proposition that matters open to public observation are not protected by the Fourth Amendment. In *Ciraolo,* we held that police observation of a backyard from a plane flying at an altitude of 1,000 feet did not violate a reasonable expectation of privacy. Similarly, in *Riley,* we relied on *Ciraolo* to hold that police observation of a greenhouse in a home's curtilage from a helicopter passing at an altitude of 400 feet did not violate the Fourth Amendment. We reasoned that the property was "not necessarily protected from inspection that involves no physical invasion," and determined that because any member of the public could have lawfully observed the defendants' property by flying overhead, the defendants' expectation of privacy was "not reasonable and not one that society is prepared to honor."

But *Ciraolo* and *Riley* are different from this case because they involved only visual, as opposed to tactile, observation. Physically invasive inspection is simply more intrusive than purely visual inspection. For example, in Terry v. Ohio, 392 U.S. 1 (1968), we stated that a "careful [tactile] exploration of the outer surfaces of a person's clothing all over his or her body" is a "serious intrusion upon the sanctity of the person, which may inflict great indignity and arouse strong resentment, and is not to be undertaken lightly." Although Agent Cantu did not "frisk" petitioner's person, he did conduct a probing tactile examination of petitioner's carry-on luggage. Obviously, petitioner's bag was not part of his person. But travelers are particularly concerned about their carry-on luggage; they generally use it to transport personal items that, for whatever reason, they prefer to keep close at hand.

Here, petitioner concedes that, by placing his bag in the overhead compartment, he could expect that it would be exposed to certain kinds of touching and handling. But petitioner argues that Agent Cantu's physical manipulation of his luggage "far exceeded the casual contact [petitioner] could have expected from other passengers." The Government counters that it did not.

Our Fourth Amendment analysis embraces two questions. First, we ask whether the individual, by his conduct, has exhibited an actual expectation of privacy; that is, whether he has shown that he sought to preserve something as private. Here, petitioner sought to preserve privacy by using an opaque bag and placing that bag directly above his seat. Second, we inquire whether the individual's expectation of privacy is "one that society is prepared to recognize as reasonable."[2] When a bus passenger places a bag in an overhead bin, he expects that other passengers or bus employees may move it for one reason or another. Thus, a bus passenger clearly expects that his bag may be handled. He does not expect that other passengers or bus employees will, as a matter of course, feel the bag in an exploratory manner. But this is exactly what the agent did here. We therefore hold that the agent's physical manipulation of petitioner's bag violated the Fourth Amendment.

BREYER, J., dissenting.

Does a traveler who places a soft-sided bag in the shared overhead storage compartment of a bus have a "reasonable expectation" that strangers will not push, pull, prod, squeeze, or otherwise manipulate his luggage? Unlike the majority, I believe that he does not.

Petitioner argues . . . that even if bags in overhead bins are subject to general "touching" and "handling," this case is special because Agent Cantu's physical manipulation of petitioner's luggage far exceeded the casual contact he could have expected from other passengers. But the record shows the contrary. . . . On the occasion at issue here, Agent Cantu "felt a green bag" which had "a brick-like object in it." He explained that he felt "the edges of the brick in the bag," and that . . . "when squeezed, you could feel an outline of something of a different mass inside of it." Although the agent acknowledged that his practice was to "squeeze [bags] very hard," he testified that his touch ordinarily was not "[h]ard enough to break something

2. The parties properly agree that the subjective intent of the law enforcement officer is irrelevant in determining whether that officer's actions violate the Fourth Amendment. See Whren v. United States, 517 U.S. 806 (1996) (stating that "we have been unwilling to entertain Fourth Amendment challenges based on the actual motivations of individual officers"). This principle applies to the agent's acts in this case as well; the issue is not his state of mind, but the objective effect of his actions.

inside that might be fragile." Petitioner also testified that Agent Cantu "reached for my bag, and he shook it a little, and squeezed it."

How does the "squeezing" just described differ from the treatment that overhead luggage is likely to receive from strangers in a world of travel that is somewhat less gentle than it used to be? I think not at all. Eagan, Familiar Anger Takes Flight with Airline Tussles, Boston Herald, Aug. 15, 1999, p.8 ("It's dog-eat-dog trying to cram half your home into overhead compartments"). The trial court . . . viewed the agent's activity as "minimally intrusive touching." . . .

Privacy itself implies the exclusion of uninvited strangers, not just strangers who work for the Government. Hence, an individual cannot reasonably expect privacy in respect to objects or activities that he knowingly exposes to the public. . . . Of course, the agent's purpose here — searching for drugs — differs dramatically from the intention of a driver or fellow passenger who squeezes a bag in the process of making more room for another parcel. But in determining whether an expectation of privacy is reasonable, it is the effect, not the purpose, that matters. Few individuals with something to hide wish to expose that something to the police, however careless or indifferent they may be in respect to discovery by other members of the public. Hence, a Fourth Amendment rule that turns on purpose could prevent police alone from intruding where other strangers freely tread. . . .

Nor can I accept the majority's effort to distinguish "tactile" from "visual" interventions, even assuming that distinction matters here. Whether tactile manipulation (say, of the exterior of luggage) is more intrusive or less intrusive than visual observation (say, through a lighted window) necessarily depends on the particular circumstances.

If we are to depart from established legal principles, we should not begin here. At best, this decision will lead to a constitutional jurisprudence of "squeezes," thereby complicating further already complex Fourth Amendment law, increasing the difficulty of deciding ordinary criminal matters, and hindering the administrative guidance (with its potential for control of unreasonable police practices) that a less complicated jurisprudence might provide. At worst, this case will deter law enforcement officers searching for drugs near borders from using even the most nonintrusive touch to help investigate publicly exposed bags. At the same time, the ubiquity of nongovernmental pushes, prods, and squeezes (delivered by driver, attendant, passenger, or some other stranger) means that this decision cannot do much to protect true privacy. Rather, the traveler who wants to place a bag in a shared overhead bin and yet safeguard its contents from public touch should plan to pack those contents in a suitcase with hard sides, irrespective of the Court's decision today. For these reasons, I dissent.

Notes

1. *Items in plain view: majority position.* If an officer sees an item in plain view, no search has occurred under state or federal law. To qualify for plain view treatment, the police officer must view the item from a place where she has a right to be. The officer might have legal access to the place because it is open to the general public — some state courts, such as those in Florida and Hawaii, call this situation "open view" rather than "plain view." An officer might also have reason to view some item from a vantage point not open to the general public. For instance, the officer might

be executing an arrest warrant or might be present in a "community caretaker" capacity. If the officer has a proper reason to be in that non-public location, the discovery of new information from that vantage point is not considered a search. In either setting, plain view or open view, the courts conclude that the target of the investigation has no reasonable expectation of privacy in the item within view of the officer.

What matters other than the location of the officer making the observation? As the Washington court indicates in *Bobic,* the amount of police effort involved in reaching the location might matter. The use of technological enhancements such as flashlights might matter. The nature of the location (a home versus a commercial storage facility) could matter. The U.S. Supreme Court has indicated in several cases that any physical movement of an item makes it much more difficult to claim that the item observed was in plain view. See Arizona v. Hicks, 480 U.S. 321 (1987) (stereo receiver moved inches to observe serial number was not in plain view). Does the opinion in Bond v. United States offer any guidance on the relevance of the *purpose* of the person observing or touching an item? Do you think that Bobic or Bond makes the stronger case that the government conducted a search?

2. *Location of the item; seizing versus viewing.* After an officer has seen some contraband or evidence of a crime in plain view, he may want to seize the item. Even when there has been no "search" of an item in plain view, there are some additional requirements the officer must meet before seizing the item. His ability to complete the seizure will depend primarily on where the item is located. If it is located in an unprotected area (such as the open bed of a pickup truck or an apartment where the officer already has obtained legal access) the officer may seize the item so long as there is probable cause to believe that it is contraband or evidence of a crime or otherwise subject to seizure. If the item is located in a protected area (such as the interior of a building that the officer observes from a point outside), most courts require the officer to obtain a search warrant or to explain why an exception to the warrant requirement is necessary. See Coolidge v. New Hampshire, 403 U.S. 443 (1971) (warrantless seizure of item in plain view is acceptable if officer observes item from lawful location, the discovery is inadvertent, its incriminating nature is immediately apparent, and officer has lawful right of access to the object).

3. *Incriminating nature of the item in plain view.* State and federal courts also require that the incriminating nature of the item in plain view be "immediately apparent" before the officer can *seize* an item in plain view. When the item in plain view is an illicit drug or other contraband, the incriminating nature of the item is easy to see. In other cases, the incriminating nature of the item might not be apparent to the average observer, but the police officer conducting the search will often know enough about the ongoing investigation to link the items she sees to the crime she is investigating. See State v. Chrisman, 514 N.W.2d 57 (Iowa 1994) (tennis shoes incriminating in light of footprints at crime scene). The incriminating nature of the item is "immediately apparent" if there is probable cause to believe that it is evidence of a crime.

4. *Police "inadvertence" in obtaining the plain view.* Under federal law and the law of most states, the police may observe and seize an item in plain view, even if the officer intended to find it. See Horton v. California, 496 U.S. 128 (1990):

> Evenhanded law enforcement is best achieved by the application of objective standards of conduct, rather than standards that depend upon the subjective state of mind of the

officer. The fact that an officer is interested in an item of evidence and fully expects to find it in the course of a search should not invalidate its seizure if the search is confined in area and duration by the terms of a warrant or a valid exception to the warrant requirement.

A minority of states take up a suggestion in older U.S. Supreme Court cases and insist that the police officer "inadvertently" discover the item in plain view before the officer can seize it. If the officer had reason to expect the discovery, he cannot seize the item. See Commonwealth v. Balicki, 762 N.E.2d 290 (Mass. 2002). Why don't most courts care about the motives of the police officer in obtaining the plain view? What police purpose might be objectionable? Is this debate over "inadvertence" the same as the disagreement reviewed above over "pretextual" stops, or are different interests at stake here?

5. *Plain smell and plain hearing.* If it is possible for an officer to notice an object in "plain view" without conducting a search, is it possible for the officer to notice a "plain smell" without conducting a search? There are cases in which the officer, standing in a proper location, smells something that creates some suspicion or evidence of a crime. Mazen v. Seidel, 940 P.2d 923 (Ariz. 1997) (smell of burnt marijuana). The same can be said of an investigation based on something an officer hears when standing in a legally sanctioned location (plain hearing): There is no "search" here in the constitutional sense. We will consider the "plain feel" doctrine in section D of this chapter.

Problem 2-5. Plain View from a Ladder

Special Agent Forsythe became aware that football gambling forms were circulating in the town of Farrell. After receiving a tip about the source of the gambling forms, Forsythe began to keep watch at a local print shop. During one October evening, Forsythe noticed that the presses inside the shop were operating, but due to the location and size of the windows, he was unable to observe what was being printed from his position off the premises. The sills of the windows were seven feet off the ground, so they prevented any view into the shop by someone standing on the ground outside the building. To remedy this problem, Forsythe mounted a four-foot ladder that he placed on the railroad tracks abutting the print shop property. From a distance of 15 to 20 feet, he observed through a side window some "Las Vegas" football parlay sheets being run off the press. Did Agent Forsythe conduct a "search" within the meaning of state or federal constitutions? Compare Commonwealth v. Hernley, 263 A.2d 904 (Pa. Super. Ct. 1970).

Problem 2-6. The Friendly Skies

Officer Greg Bohlen, an undercover narcotics investigator, received an anonymous telephone call informing him that Bernard Henderson was cultivating and selling marijuana from his home. Bohlen watched the residence carefully for several days but did not observe any illegal activity. Several months later, another officer received a second anonymous call implicating Henderson in marijuana trafficking. Bohlen was unable to obtain a law enforcement helicopter to fly over the property, so he arranged for the use of a helicopter operated by a television station, KUSA. KUSA agreed to provide a helicopter to Officer Bohlen in exchange for the right to report on the drug investigation. On the morning of the scheduled flyover, Bohlen received another anonymous telephone call about Henderson, indicating that Henderson was growing five-foot-tall marijuana plants in a shed behind his house.

Officer Bohlen, the helicopter pilot, and a photographer for KUSA made four or five passes over Henderson's residence during a period of approximately five minutes. Officer Bohlen observed a shed, located about 100 yards away from the house. The shed had a plastic roof with "green plant material" (as Bohlen later described it in a warrant application) growing underneath the plastic. Bohlen stated that the helicopter stayed between 500 and 700 feet in altitude. He based his altitude estimate on his experience flying in helicopters. Although he could not describe the plants in detail, based on his special education in drug identification and on his law enforcement experience, Officer Bohlen concluded that the plants were marijuana. A later warranted search of the property and the house produced marijuana plants, along with guns, scales, and other drug paraphernalia. The defendant has filed a motion to suppress the evidence. Will the judge grant it? Compare Henderson v. People, 879 P.2d 383 (Colo. 1994).

Problem 2-7. Super Bowl Coverage

About 100,000 people attended the Super Bowl in Tampa, Florida in January, 2001. As they passed through turnstiles to enter the stadium, hidden cameras scanned and recorded each of their faces. In a command post at the stadium, computers compared the digitized images of fans and workers to the photos of suspected terrorists and known criminals contained in the files of local police, the FBI and state agencies. The computers operated at the rate of a million images a minute. The cameras identified 19 people with criminal histories, none of them very serious. The Tampa Police Department gave no public notice of their plans to use this technology at the Super Bowl. A spokesperson said the Department wanted to screen for pickpockets and other potential scam artists drawn to the huge event and for potential terrorists who wanted to use its worldwide television audience to make a political statement. The owners of the technology allowed the Tampa police to try the equipment without charge, hoping to convince other police agencies to purchase the program for regular use. Did the Tampa Police Department conduct searches when it used this technology? If you were a member of a city council, would you authorize the purchase of this technology for a reasonable price? See Louis Sahagun and Josh Meyer, "Secret Cameras Scanned Crowd at Super Bowl for Criminals," Los Angeles Times, February 1, 2001.

Notes

1. *Flyovers and reasonable expectations of privacy: majority position.* Recall that under the Fourth Amendment and its state equivalents, the government has not engaged in a search if it has invaded no "reasonable expectation of privacy." One difficult question about the definition of a search arises when government agents place themselves in unusual—but not necessarily illegal—positions for observing

wrongdoing. A situation of this sort that appears frequently in appellate cases is the "flyover" of property by police officers searching for evidence of a crime.

In Florida v. Riley, 488 U.S. 445 (1988), the Supreme Court determined that police observing the defendant's backyard from a helicopter flying in legal air space did not conduct a search for Fourth Amendment purposes. The defendant lived in a mobile home located on five acres of property. A greenhouse near the residence was obscured from view by a fence, trees, and shrubs. As the result of an anonymous tip, a police helicopter made two passes over the property at an altitude of 400 feet. The observing officer viewed what he thought was marijuana growing in the greenhouse, because two roof panels were missing. One of the primary factors in determining whether the defendant's expectation of privacy was unreasonable was that the helicopter was flying in navigable airspace within the Federal Aviation Administration guidelines. Thus, the Court relied on the fact that the observation itself was legal. The Court also considered the minimal intrusiveness of the observations: the helicopter never "interfered with respondent's normal use of the greenhouse or other parts of the curtilage." Furthermore, "no intimate details connected with the use of the home or curtilage were observed, and there was no undue noise, and no wind, dust, or threat of injury." See also California v. Ciraolo, 476 U.S. 207 (1986) (no search when police officer observes property from fixed-wing aircraft 1,000 feet above property in legal airspace). Do you believe the Supreme Court should have ruled in *Ciraolo* and *Riley* that the government conducted a search? Should the answer depend on whether the police have routine access to helicopters and planes?

Virtually all state courts have agreed with the U.S. Supreme Court's view that a flyover is not a "search" so long as the police aircraft stays within airspace where private aircraft could travel and does not create too much noise, dust, or threat of injury. See Commonwealth v. One 1985 Ford Thunderbird Automobile, 624 N.E.2d 547 (Mass. 1993); but see Commonwealth v. Oglialoro, 579 A.2d 1288 (Pa. 1990) ("search" occurred when helicopter hovered 50 feet above pole barn in "navigable" airspace but created hazard). How might a defendant dispute the government's factual claim about the flight pattern of the aircraft?

2. *Subjective expectations of privacy.* Many courts asking whether government agents have engaged in a search employ a two-part analysis taken from the concurring opinion of Justice Harlan in Katz v. United States, 389 U.S. 347 (1967). A litigant hoping to establish a "search" under the Fourth Amendment must meet "a twofold requirement, first that a person ha[s] exhibited an actual (subjective) expectation of privacy and, second, that the expectation be one that society is prepared to recognize as 'reasonable.'" Later opinions of the U.S. Supreme Court and of state courts repeat this formulation, but they also suggest that the objective component alone might be enough: a subjective expectation of privacy will not always be a precondition to a conclusion that a search has occurred. See United States v. White, 401 U.S. 745 (1971). Could you imagine courts holding otherwise, that is, insisting on a subjective expectation of privacy before finding that a search took place?

3. *Legal entitlement versus likelihood of observation.* Suppose a litigant could show that flyovers at 500 feet above the property in question are very rare. In what way would this be relevant to the definition of a search? Would such a defendant need to argue that there is a legitimate expectation of lax enforcement of the narcotics laws? Could there be some moral (but extralegal) objection to the police conduct that makes more reasonable an expectation of avoiding such scrutiny?

4. *Police observation versus public observation.* Let us assume that reasonable and law-abiding people leave some things visible to a few members of the public that they would rather not expose to the sustained scrutiny of the police. Can police officers make observations from any place open to the public, or should they be expected to remain outside some areas open to some members of the public? Does the defendant's argument on the "search" issue get stronger when police officers flying over a property must apply their expertise to interpret what they see below (such as an assertion that a building is "typical" of those used to grow marijuana)?

5. *Other sense enhancements.* So long as the government agent remains in a position properly available to her, many state courts allow the agent to use various devices to get a clearer or closer look at the items in plain view. The clearest cases involve commonly used devices such as flashlights. See State v. Brooks, 446 S.E.2d 579 (N.C. 1994) (officer walking up to car and shining light inside is not a search). A few state and federal courts have been willing to go farther, allowing government agents to use vision-enhancing devices not readily available to most viewers. See Dow Chemical Co. v. United States, 476 U.S. 227 (1986) (no search when agents in airplane over chemical plant use precision aerial-mapping camera). See Chapter 7.

2. *Abandoned Property*

As we have seen, reasonable expectations of privacy do not attach to property or activities in "plain view" or "open view." Thus, efforts to see such property are not searches in the constitutional sense. The same can be said for property that a person has abandoned, even though it does not lie within plain view of the public or government agents. The following case explores whether a government agent rummaging through a person's trash is conducting a "search."

■ DOMINICK MORAN v. STATE

644 N.E.2d 536 (Ind. 1994)

DEBRULER, J.

[The Indiana State Police (ISP) operated a business supplying hydroponic equipment as a way to identify individuals who might be cultivating marijuana. Two frequent purchasers of hydroponic equipment were Moran and Holland. At 5:00 A.M. one winter morning,] two ISP officers drove to Holland's house in a pickup truck. The house sat back fifty feet from the street. Several plastic garbage cans were sitting about a foot from the street in front of the house, near the mail box. They had lids. They had been set out for the trash pickup scheduled for that day. The contents of the cans included both loose material and material in several common opaque plastic garbage bags. The cans were emptied into the back of the pickup truck and taken to the ISP office, where the garbage bags were opened and sifted through for contraband and evidence. ISP officers found a green leafy material later determined to be marijuana plant clippings. [The clippings formed part of the basis for a search warrant which produced additional evidence of marijuana production. After being charged, the defendants unsuccessfully moved to suppress the evidence.]

Turning for the moment to the subject of appellants' federal claim, we conclude that the trial court and the court of appeals were correct in rejecting appellants' federal constitutional claim based upon the Fourth Amendment. Clearly, it afforded no protection against the acts of these police in taking and inspecting the trash set out by appellants at the curb for pickup. California v. Greenwood, 486 U.S. 35 (1988). That case governs the federal claim, but not the state constitutional claim.

Returning to the state claim at hand, we note . . . that other states have considered this issue under their own search and seizure provisions with divergent results. In State v. Hempele, 567 A.2d 792 (N.J. 1990), the Supreme Court of New Jersey . . . found that there was an expectation of privacy in garbage as against police intrusion. In State v. DeFusco, 620 A.2d 746 (Conn. 1993), the Supreme Court of Connecticut followed the *Greenwood* path in applying its own search and seizure provision. The court found no expectation of privacy in trash. The legal analysis in each case tracks the two-prong test from Katz v. United States, 389 U.S. 347 (1967), namely 1) did the person exhibit an actual expectation of privacy; and 2) does society recognize that expectation as reasonable? . . .

We do not lightly entertain intrusions on those things that we regard as private, i.e. concealed and hidden. However, at the same time the inhabitants of this state have always valued neighborliness, hospitality, and concern for others, even those who may be strangers. Here, an open front walk leading to the front porch of a house is accurately judged by the passerby to be an open invitation to seek temporary shelter in the event of a sudden downpour. Stepping on that part of a yard next to the street or sidewalk to seek shade from a tree or to pick edible yet valueless plants growing in the lawn has been regarded proper conduct. It is permissible for children at play on the street or in the alley to examine the contents of garbage cans to find interesting items, so long as they do not make a mess. It is not infrequent that valuable items are placed in the trash in hopes that someone passing by will see them there and will take them and make good use of them. It has often been said that if you do not want others to know what you drink, don't put empties in the trash. . . .

One who places trash bags for collection intends for them to be taken up, and is pleased when that occurs. Here, the police did not trespass upon the premises to get the bags. They came by early in the morning when their actions were unlikely to be seen in the neighborhood and commented about. There was no disturbance. Appellants claim that local ordinances regulating the manner in which trash is to be set out and handled supports their claim for suppression. The police here conducted themselves in the same manner as would be appropriate for those whose duty it was to pick up. Given these attendant circumstances, and while realizing that Hoosiers are not entirely comfortable with the idea of police officers casually rummaging through trash left at curbside, we cannot say that the police activity here was unreasonable under Article 1, Section 11 of the Indiana Constitution and that the police must refrain from such conduct. . . .

SHEPARD, C.J., not participating.

I fully expected to sit in this appeal, until a spate of press reports appeared just before the decision was to be issued. Recent publicity about my own experience as the target of a trash search,* suggests to me that recusal is the best course. For the moment at least, I do not feel dispassionate on the subject of trash searches.

* During election season, a judge on Indiana's intermediate appeals court hired a private investigator to search the garbage of Chief Justice Shepard's home to uncover evidence of abuse of alcohol or use of marijuana.—EDS.

DICKSON, J., concurring and dissenting.

[I] remain convinced that Indiana citizens should be able to dispose of their trash without relinquishing their privacy. The waste products from homes can reveal intimate details of private religious beliefs, finance, political interests, medical and legal matters, personal relationships, and numerous other confidential matters. In today's predominantly urban and suburban society, it is no longer reasonable (and in many situations unlawful) privately to burn or bury unwanted waste. People must necessarily rely upon governmental or commercial trash collection systems to achieve anonymous disposal. The contents of sealed trash containers intended for such disposal ought to be deemed as included among the "papers and effects" protected against unreasonable search and seizure by Section 11 of Indiana's Bill of Rights.

When there is reasonable cause to believe that the contents of a particular home's curbside trash may provide evidence of specific criminal activity, the police may seek a warrant authorizing its search and seizure. This assures a proper balance between effective law enforcement and the preservation of personal privacy free from unfettered government intrusion. I therefore conclude that it is unreasonable under Article 1, Section 11 of the Indiana Constitution to permit warrantless searches and seizures by police of private trash left for curbside pick-up and disposal.

Notes

1. *Garbage searches: majority rule.* As the Indiana court indicated, states have gone in different directions on searches of garbage. The U.S. Supreme Court in California v. Greenwood, 486 U.S. 35 (1988), held that there is no reasonable expectation of privacy in trash put out for collection; thus, there is no constitutionally relevant search if government agents inspect the trash. Over half the states have adopted this same view. See State v. Hillman, 834 P.2d 1271 (Colo. 1992). A smaller group (fewer than a dozen) have held in various contexts that there is a reasonable expectation of privacy in garbage, while a good number of high state courts still have not confronted the issue. See State v. Boland, 800 P.2d 1112 (Wash. 1990). How did the majority in *Moran* know what Hoosiers collectively would consider reasonable? Wasn't Chief Justice Shepard in a special position to understand this issue?

Some have pointed out that the government, under the reasoning of *Greenwood*, can defeat a widely-shared expectation of privacy simply by announcing that it plans to conduct a particular form of investigation, thus defeating any expectation of privacy. See Anthony G. Amsterdam, Perspectives on the Fourth Amendment, 58 Minn. L. Rev. 349, 384 (1974). If most Americans today still have an expectation of privacy in their curbside garbage bags, isn't there a reasonable expectation of privacy regardless of what the Supreme Court held in *Greenwood*? See Christopher Slobogin & Joseph Schumacher, Reasonable Expectations of Privacy and Autonomy in Fourth Amendment Cases: An Empirical Look at "Understandings Recognized and Permitted by Society," 42 Duke L.J. 727 (1993) (public survey measuring perceived intrusiveness of various investigative techniques). Should the courts announce decisions about reasonable expectations of privacy on a tentative basis, and overrule themselves if most people don't take the decision to heart?

2. *Local values and consent.* Do you agree with the court that diverse local conditions within this country are a major factor in determining whether an expectation of privacy is reasonable? Is the court saying that Moran implicitly consented to this gathering of information by living in Indiana?

3. *Trash in the curtilage or open fields?* Courts give the highest protection to claims of privacy for activities in the home. The privacy interests in a home or building also extend to the area under the eaves and immediately surrounding the building, an area known as the "curtilage." Thus, it could matter where the trash is placed. If the police inspect garbage kept in containers beside a home prior to the day appointed for collection, have they conducted a "search"? The fact that the police inspected trash behind a home rather than on the street has been significant to a few courts. See State v. Hempele, 576 A.2d 793 (N.J. 1990) (finding a "search"). Would it be significant whether sanitation workers ordinarily collect trash from the curb or from cans behind the house? The protection of privacy in a home or building does not extend beyond the curtilage to cover items found at a greater distance. The U.S. Supreme Court has created a special set of rules, known as the "open fields" doctrine, to judge whether a search has occurred on real property far outside the bounds of a home. The doctrine creates a blanket rule stating that searches do not occur in open fields. See Chapter 4, Section B.

4. *Computer "trash" cans.* Most electronic message systems allow the computer user to delete messages, but the deleted messages are recoverable until further events take place (e.g., the user turns off the system, or some manager of the computer system empties the electronic "trash can"). Similarly, it is possible under some circumstances to recover copies of electronic documents or files that a user has attempted to delete. If the government discovers evidence of a crime in these deleted but recoverable messages or files, was there a search at all? If there was a search, was it justified by implied consent?

D. BRIEF SEARCHES OF INDIVIDUALS

The police conduct a great variety of searches, ranging from brief and less intrusive searches of persons or property, up to extensive and very invasive searches. The number of legal standards — constitutional and otherwise — available to limit these searches is not nearly so large. As you read in this section about brief searches of individuals, consider whether the fit between police practices and available legal standards is sufficiently tight and whether different legal standards are likely to change actual behavior.

1. *Frisks for Weapons*

Police encounter people every day who carry hidden handguns. One time-honored police response to this threat is the "frisk," a brief search of a suspect's body. The frisk was a reality long before American courts resolved the question of whether or how the law would regulate the practice. The following case lays out the constitutional controls over frisks, controls at work in every U.S. jurisdiction.

■ JOHN TERRY v. OHIO

392 U.S. 1 (1968)

WARREN, C.J.

This case presents serious questions concerning the role of the Fourth Amendment in the confrontation on the street between the citizen and the policeman investigating suspicious circumstances.

Petitioner Terry was convicted of carrying a concealed weapon. [The] prosecution introduced in evidence two revolvers and a number of bullets seized from Terry and a codefendant, Richard Chilton, by Cleveland Police Detective Martin McFadden. At the hearing on the motion to suppress this evidence, Officer McFadden testified that while he was patrolling in plain clothes in downtown Cleveland at approximately 2:30 in the afternoon, [he noticed two men, Chilton and Terry, who "didn't look right."] His interest aroused, Officer McFadden took up a post of observation in the entrance to a store 300 to 400 feet away from the two men. "I get more purpose to watch them when I seen their movements," he testified. [One of the men walked away from the corner and past some stores, paused for a moment and looked in a store window, then walked on a short distance, turned around and walked back toward the corner, pausing once again to look in the same store window. Then the second man went through the same series of motions. Each of the two men repeated this ritual five or six times. A third man, Katz, approached them and engaged them briefly in conversation, then walked away. Chilton and Terry resumed their earlier routine. After this had gone on for 10 to 12 minutes, the two men walked off together, following the route taken earlier by Katz.]

By this time Officer McFadden had become thoroughly suspicious. He testified that . . . he suspected the two men of "casing a job, a stick-up," and that he considered it his duty as a police officer to investigate further. He added that he feared "they may have a gun." Thus, Officer McFadden followed Chilton and Terry and saw them stop in front of Zucker's store to talk to [Katz]. Deciding that the situation was ripe for direct action, Officer McFadden approached the three men, identified himself as a police officer and asked for their names. . . . When the men "mumbled something" in response to his inquiries, Officer McFadden grabbed petitioner Terry, spun him around so that they were facing the other two, with Terry between McFadden and the others, and patted down the outside of his clothing. In the left breast pocket of Terry's overcoat Officer McFadden felt a pistol. He reached inside the overcoat pocket, but was unable to remove the gun. At this point, keeping Terry between himself and the others, the officer ordered all three men to enter Zucker's store. As they went in, he removed Terry's overcoat completely, removed a .38-caliber revolver from the pocket and ordered all three men to face the wall with their hands raised. Officer McFadden proceeded to pat down the outer clothing of Chilton and [Katz]. He discovered another revolver in the outer pocket of Chilton's overcoat, but no weapons were found on Katz. The officer testified that he only patted the men down to see whether they had weapons, and that he did not put his hands beneath the outer garments of either Terry or Chilton until he felt their guns. . . . Chilton and Terry were formally charged with carrying concealed weapons.

[The trial court concluded that McFadden did not have probable cause to search or arrest the men, but nonetheless upheld the validity of the search.] The court distinguished between an investigatory "stop" and an arrest, and between a "frisk" of the outer clothing for weapons and a full-blown search for evidence of crime. The frisk, it held, was essential to the proper performance of the officer's investigatory duties, for without it "the answer to the police officer may be a bullet, and a loaded pistol discovered during the frisk is admissible." [The court found Terry and Chilton guilty in a bench trial.]

I

The Fourth Amendment provides that "the right of the people to be secure in their persons, houses, papers, and effects, against unreasonable searches and seizures, shall not be violated. . . ." This inestimable right of personal security belongs as much to the citizen on the streets of our cities as to the homeowner closeted in his study to dispose of his secret affairs. [However,] what the Constitution forbids is not all searches and seizures, but unreasonable searches and seizures. Unquestionably petitioner was entitled to the protection of the Fourth Amendment as he walked down the street in Cleveland. The question is whether in all the circumstances of this on-the-street encounter, his right to personal security was violated by an unreasonable search and seizure.

[I]t is frequently argued that in dealing with the rapidly unfolding and often dangerous situations on city streets the police are in need of an escalating set of flexible responses, graduated in relation to the amount of information they possess. For this purpose it is urged that distinctions should be made between a "stop" and an "arrest" (or a "seizure" of a person), and between a "frisk" and a "search." Thus, it is argued, the police should be allowed to "stop" a person and detain him briefly for questioning upon suspicion that he may be connected with criminal activity. Upon suspicion that the person may be armed, the police should have the power to "frisk" him for weapons. If the "stop" and the "frisk" give rise to probable cause to believe that the suspect has committed a crime, then the police should be empowered to make a formal "arrest," and a full incident "search" of the person. This scheme is justified in part upon the notion that a "stop" and a "frisk" amount to a mere minor inconvenience and petty indignity, which can properly be imposed upon the citizen in the interest of effective law enforcement on the basis of a police officer's suspicion.

On the other side the argument is made that the authority of the police must be strictly circumscribed by the law of arrest and search as it has developed to date in the traditional jurisprudence of the Fourth Amendment. It is contended with some force that there is not — and cannot be — a variety of police activity which does not depend solely upon the voluntary cooperation of the citizen and yet which stops short of an arrest based upon probable cause to make such an arrest. The heart of the Fourth Amendment, the argument runs, is a severe requirement of specific justification for any intrusion upon protected personal security, coupled with a highly developed system of judicial controls to enforce upon the agents of the State the commands of the Constitution. Acquiescence by the courts in the compulsion inherent in the field interrogation practices at issue here, it is urged, would constitute an abdication of judicial control over, and indeed an encouragement of, substantial interference with liberty and personal security by police officers whose judgment is necessarily colored by their primary involvement in the often competitive enterprise of ferreting out crime. This, it is argued, can only serve to exacerbate police-community tensions in the crowded centers of our Nation's cities.

In this context we approach the issues in this case mindful of the limitations of the judicial function in controlling the myriad daily situations in which policemen and citizens confront each other on the street. . . . Street encounters between citizens and police officers are incredibly rich in diversity. They range from wholly friendly exchanges of pleasantries or mutually useful information to hostile confrontations of armed men involving arrests, or injuries, or loss of life. Moreover, hostile confrontations are not all of a piece. Some of them begin in a friendly enough manner, only to take a different turn upon the injection of some unexpected element into the conversation. Encounters are initiated by the police for a wide variety of purposes, some of which are wholly unrelated to a desire to prosecute for crime. . . .

II

Our first task is to establish at what point in this encounter the Fourth Amendment becomes relevant. That is, we must decide whether and when Officer McFadden "seized" Terry and whether and when he conducted a "search." There is some suggestion in the use of such terms as "stop" and "frisk" that such police conduct is outside the purview of the Fourth Amendment because neither action rises to the level of a "search" or "seizure" within the meaning of the Constitution. We emphatically reject this notion. It is . . . nothing less than sheer torture of the English language to suggest that a careful exploration of the outer surfaces of a person's clothing all over his or her body in an attempt to find weapons is not a "search." . . . It is a serious intrusion upon the sanctity of the person, which may inflict great indignity and arouse strong resentment, and it is not to be undertaken lightly.

The danger in the logic which proceeds upon distinctions between a . . . "frisk" and a "search" is twofold. It seeks to isolate from constitutional scrutiny the initial stages of the contact between the policeman and the citizen. And by suggesting a rigid all-or-nothing model of justification and regulation under the Amendment, it obscures the utility of limitations upon the scope, as well as the initiation, of police action as a means of constitutional regulation. [A] search which is reasonable at its inception may violate the Fourth Amendment by virtue of its intolerable intensity and scope. The scope of the search must be strictly tied to and justified by the circumstances which rendered its initiation permissible. . . .

In this case there can be no question, then, that Officer McFadden "seized" petitioner and subjected him to a "search" when he took hold of him and patted down the outer surfaces of his clothing. We must decide whether at that point it was reasonable for Officer McFadden to have interfered with petitioner's personal security as he did. And in determining whether the seizure and search were "unreasonable" our inquiry is a dual one — whether the officer's action was justified at its inception, and whether it was reasonably related in scope to the circumstances which justified the interference in the first place.

III

If this case involved police conduct subject to the Warrant Clause of the Fourth Amendment, we would have to ascertain whether "probable cause" existed to justify the search and seizure which took place. However, that is not the case. We do not retreat from our holdings that the police must, whenever practicable, obtain advance judicial approval of searches and seizures through the warrant procedure, or that in most instances failure to comply with the warrant requirement can only be excused by exigent circumstances. But we deal here with an entire rubric of police conduct—necessarily swift action predicated upon the on-the-spot observations of the officer on the beat—which historically has not been, and as a practical matter could not be, subjected to the warrant procedure. Instead, the conduct involved in this case must be tested by the Fourth Amendment's general proscription against unreasonable searches and seizures.

Nonetheless, the notions which underlie both the warrant procedure and the requirement of probable cause remain fully relevant in this context. In order to assess the reasonableness of Officer McFadden's conduct as a general proposition, it is necessary first to focus upon the governmental interest which allegedly justifies official intrusion upon the constitutionally protected interests of the private citizen, for there is no ready test for determining reasonableness other than by balancing the need to search [or seize] against the invasion which the search or seizure entails. And in justifying the particular intrusion the police officer must be able to point to specific and articulable facts which, taken together with rational inferences from those facts, reasonably warrant that intrusion. [When a judge assesses the reasonableness of a search or seizure,] it is imperative that the facts be judged against an objective standard: would the facts available to the officer at the moment of the seizure or the search warrant a man of reasonable caution in the belief that the action taken was appropriate? Anything less would invite intrusions upon constitutionally guaranteed rights based on nothing more substantial than inarticulate hunches, a result this Court has consistently refused to sanction. And simple good faith on the part of the arresting officer is not enough. If subjective good faith alone were the test, the protections of the Fourth Amendment would evaporate, and the people would be secure in their persons, houses, papers, and effects, only in the discretion of the police.

Applying these principles to this case, we consider first the nature and extent of the governmental interests involved. One general interest is of course that of effective crime prevention and detection; it is this interest which underlies the recognition that a police officer may in appropriate circumstances and in an appropriate manner approach a person for purposes of investigating possibly criminal behavior even though there is no probable cause to make an arrest. [In this case, it] would have been poor police work indeed for an officer of 30 years' experience in the detection of thievery from stores in this same neighborhood to have failed to investigate this behavior further.

The crux of this case, however, is not the propriety of Officer McFadden's taking steps to investigate petitioner's suspicious behavior, but rather, whether there was justification for McFadden's invasion of Terry's personal security by searching him for weapons in the course of that investigation. We are now concerned with more than the governmental interest in investigating crime; in addition, there is the more immediate interest of the police officer in taking steps to assure himself that the person with whom he is dealing is not armed with a weapon that could unexpectedly and fatally be used against him. Certainly it would be unreasonable to require that police officers take unnecessary risks in the performance of their duties. American criminals have a long tradition of armed violence, and every year in this country many law enforcement officers are killed in the line of duty, and thousands more are wounded. Virtually all of these deaths and a substantial portion of the injuries are inflicted with guns and knives.

In view of these facts, we cannot blind ourselves to the need for law enforcement officers to protect themselves and other prospective victims of violence in situations where they may lack probable cause for an arrest. When an officer is justified in believing that the individual whose suspicious behavior he is investigating at close range is armed and presently dangerous to the officer or to others, it would appear to be clearly unreasonable to deny the officer the power to take necessary measures to determine whether the person is in fact carrying a weapon and to neutralize the threat of physical harm.

We must still consider, however, the nature and quality of the intrusion on individual rights which must be accepted if police officers are to be conceded the right to search for weapons in situations where probable cause to arrest for crime is lacking. Even a limited search of the outer clothing for weapons constitutes a severe, though brief, intrusion upon cherished personal security, and it must surely be an annoying, frightening, and perhaps humiliating experience. . . .

Petitioner does not argue that a police officer should refrain from making any investigation of suspicious circumstances until such time as he has probable cause to make an arrest; nor does he deny that police officers in properly discharging their investigative function may find themselves confronting persons who might well be armed and dangerous. Moreover, he does not say that an officer is always unjustified in searching a suspect to discover weapons. Rather, he says it is unreasonable for the policeman to take that step until such time as the situation evolves to a point where there is probable cause to make an arrest. When that point has been reached, petitioner would concede the officer's right to conduct a search of the suspect for weapons, fruits or instrumentalities of the crime, or "mere" evidence, incident to the arrest.

[The problem with this line of reasoning, however, is that] it fails to take account of traditional limitations upon the scope of searches, and thus recognizes no distinction in purpose, character, and extent between a search incident to an arrest and a limited search for weapons. The former, although justified in part by the acknowledged necessity to protect the arresting officer from assault with a concealed weapon, is also justified on other grounds, and can therefore involve a relatively extensive exploration of the person. A search for weapons in the absence of probable cause to arrest, however, must, like any other search, be strictly circumscribed by the exigencies which justify its initiation. Thus it must be limited to that which is necessary for the discovery of weapons which might be used to harm the officer or others nearby, and may realistically be characterized as something less than a "full" search, even though it remains a serious intrusion. . . .

Our evaluation of the proper balance that has to be struck in this type of case leads us to conclude that there must be a narrowly drawn authority to permit a reasonable search for weapons for the protection of the police officer, where he has reason to believe that he is dealing with an armed and dangerous individual, regardless of whether he has probable cause to arrest the individual for a crime. The officer need not be absolutely certain that the individual is armed; the issue is whether a reasonably prudent man in the circumstances would be warranted in the belief that his safety or that of others was in danger. And in determining whether the officer acted reasonably in such circumstances, due weight must be given, not to his inchoate and unparticularized suspicion or "hunch," but to the specific reasonable inferences which he is entitled to draw from the facts in light of his experience.

IV

We must now examine the conduct of Officer McFadden in this case to determine whether his search and seizure of petitioner were reasonable, both at their inception and as conducted. He had observed Terry, together with Chilton and another man, acting in a manner he took to be preface to a "stick-up." We think on the facts and circumstances Officer McFadden detailed before the trial judge a reasonably prudent man would have been warranted in believing petitioner was armed and thus presented a threat to the officer's safety while he was investigating his suspicious behavior. The actions of Terry and Chilton were consistent with McFadden's hypothesis that these men were contemplating a daylight robbery—which, it is reasonable to assume, would be likely to involve the use of weapons. . . . We cannot say his decision at that point to seize Terry and pat his clothing for weapons was the product of a volatile or inventive imagination, or was undertaken simply as an act of harassment; the record evidences the tempered act of a policeman who in the course of an investigation had to make a quick decision as to how to protect himself and others from possible danger, and took limited steps to do so.

The manner in which the seizure and search were conducted is, of course, as vital a part of the inquiry as whether they were warranted at all. The Fourth Amendment proceeds as much by limitations upon the scope of governmental action as by imposing preconditions upon its initiation. . . . We need not develop at length in this case, however, the limitations which the Fourth Amendment places upon a protective seizure and search for weapons. These limitations will have to be developed in the concrete factual circumstances of individual cases. Suffice it to note that such a search, unlike a search without a warrant incident to a lawful arrest, is not justified by any need to prevent the disappearance or destruction of evidence of crime. The sole justification of the search in the present situation is the protection of the police officer and others nearby, and it must therefore be confined in scope to an intrusion reasonably designed to discover guns, knives, clubs, or other hidden instruments for the assault of the police officer.

The scope of the search in this case presents no serious problem in light of these standards. Officer McFadden patted down the outer clothing of petitioner and his two companions. He did not place his hands in their pockets or under the outer surface of their garments until he had felt weapons, and then he merely reached for and removed the guns. He never did invade Katz' person beyond the outer surfaces of his clothes, since he discovered nothing in his pat-down which might have been a weapon. Officer McFadden confined his search strictly to what was minimally necessary to learn whether the men were armed and to disarm them once he discovered the weapons. He did not conduct a general exploratory search for whatever evidence of criminal activity he might find.

V

We conclude that the revolver seized from Terry was properly admitted in evidence against him. . . . Each case of this sort will, of course, have to be decided on its own facts. We merely hold today that where a police officer observes unusual conduct which leads him reasonably to conclude in light of his experience that criminal activity may be afoot and that the persons with whom he is dealing may be armed and presently dangerous, where in the course of investigating this behavior he

identifies himself as a policeman and makes reasonable inquiries, and where nothing in the initial stages of the encounter serves to dispel his reasonable fear for his own or others' safety, he is entitled for the protection of himself and others in the area to conduct a carefully limited search of the outer clothing of such persons in an attempt to discover weapons which might be used to assault him. Such a search is a reasonable search under the Fourth Amendment, and any weapons seized may properly be introduced in evidence against the person from whom they were taken. Affirmed.

HARLAN, J., concurring.

[I]f the frisk is justified in order to protect the officer during an encounter with a citizen, the officer must first have constitutional grounds to insist on an encounter, to make a forcible stop. . . . Where such a stop is reasonable, however, the right to frisk must be immediate and automatic if the reason for the stop is, as here, an articulable suspicion of a crime of violence. Just as a full search incident to a lawful arrest requires no additional justification, a limited frisk incident to a lawful stop must often be rapid and routine. There is no reason why an officer, rightfully but forcibly confronting a person suspected of a serious crime, should have to ask one question and take the risk that the answer might be a bullet. . . . Upon the foregoing premises, I join the opinion of the Court.

DOUGLAS, J., dissenting.

[F]risking petitioner and his companions for guns was a "search." But it is a mystery how that "search" . . . can be constitutional by Fourth Amendment standards, unless there was "probable cause" to believe that (1) a crime had been committed or (2) a crime was in the process of being committed or (3) a crime was about to be committed.

The opinion of the Court disclaims the existence of "probable cause." If loitering were in issue and that was the offense charged, there would be "probable cause" shown. But the crime here is carrying concealed weapons; and there is no basis for concluding that the officer had "probable cause" for believing that that crime was being committed. Had a warrant been sought, a magistrate would, therefore, have been unauthorized to issue one, for he can act only if there is a showing of "probable cause." We hold today that the police have greater authority to make a "seizure" and conduct a "search" than a judge has to authorize such action. We have said precisely the opposite over and over again.

In other words, police officers up to today have been permitted to effect arrests or searches without warrants only when the facts within their personal knowledge would satisfy the constitutional standard of probable cause. At the time of their "seizure" without a warrant they must possess facts concerning the person arrested that would have satisfied a magistrate that "probable cause" was indeed present. The term "probable cause" rings a bell of certainty that is not sounded by phrases such as "reasonable suspicion." Moreover, the meaning of "probable cause" is deeply imbedded in our constitutional history. . . .

The infringement on personal liberty of any "seizure" of a person can only be "reasonable" under the Fourth Amendment if we require the police to possess "probable cause" before they seize him. Only that line draws a meaningful distinction between an officer's mere inkling and the presence of facts within the officer's personal knowledge which would convince a reasonable man that the person seized has committed, is committing, or is about to commit a particular crime. . . .

To give the police greater power than a magistrate is to take a long step down the totalitarian path. Perhaps such a step is desirable to cope with modern forms of lawlessness. But if it is taken, it should be the deliberate choice of the people through a constitutional amendment. Until the Fourth Amendment . . . is rewritten, the person and the effects of the individual are beyond the reach of all government agencies until there are reasonable grounds to believe (probable cause) that a criminal venture has been launched or is about to be launched.

There have been powerful hydraulic pressures throughout our history that bear heavily on the Court to water down constitutional guarantees and give the police the upper hand. That hydraulic pressure has probably never been greater than it is today. Yet if the individual is no longer to be sovereign, if the police can pick him up whenever they do not like the cut of his jib, if they can "seize" and "search" him in their discretion, we enter a new regime. The decision to enter it should be made only after a full debate by the people of this country.

Notes

1. *Frisks for weapons: majority position.* The *Terry* opinion addressed both stops and frisks, and approved a framework already in place in some states at that point. It allowed the police to seize a person for a short time based on reasonable suspicion. We explored this question in section A of this chapter. But the Court considered the brief search — the frisk — to be the "crux" of this case. On the question of frisks, *Terry* has been very influential in the state systems; all the states now approve of frisks for weapons based on some justification less than probable cause. The majority take this position by statute, while others authorize such frisks through judicial rulings.

2. *Grounds for a* Terry *search.* Exactly what justification must an officer have before she performs a pat-down search? Why do both Chief Justice Warren and Justice Harlan distinguish between the justification needed for the initial stop and the justification needed for the brief search? Was Justice Douglas right to be concerned that government agents could manipulate too easily any standard less than probable cause?

Some state courts have declared that the police automatically have reasonable suspicion to frisk a person suspected of involvement in drug crimes and burglary. See State v. Evans, 618 N.E.2d 162, 169 (Ohio 1993); State v. Scott, 405 N.W.2d 829, 832 (Iowa 1987). Does the *Terry* opinion leave room for courts to make categorical judgments about reasonable suspicion to frisk, or does it require individualized findings in each case?

3. *Prevalence of frisks.* How often do frisks happen? According to a nationwide survey in 1999, police officers search 4.3 percent of the drivers they stop. Bureau of Justice Statistics, Contacts between Police and the Public (2001). In New York City, a study of stops and frisks over a 15-month period in 1998 and 1999 showed over 175,000 stops and frisks. This worked out to about 24 frisks for every 1000 residents. The New York City Police Department's "Stop & Frisk" Practices: A Report to the People of the State of New York, From the Office of the Attorney General Eliot Spitzer at 97-100 (1999) (see *http://www.oag.state.ny.us/press/reports/stop_frisk/stop_frisk.html*). How would you go about determining how often your local police department conducts frisks?

4. Terry *searches before* Terry. Do you believe that police officers frisked suspects based on something less than probable cause before Detective McFadden decided to do so in Cleveland in 1963? Police officers in some states had statutes or department rules explicitly authorizing them to search for weapons without probable cause to arrest. The Uniform Arrest Act of 1942 provided that "A peace officer may search for a dangerous weapon any person whom he has stopped or detained to question . . . whenever he has reasonable ground to believe that he is in danger if the person possesses a dangerous weapon." Rule 470 of the Chicago Police Department in 1933 also recognized a brief search for weapons without having probable cause: "[When] stopping and questioning a suspicious character [the police officer] shall be on guard against the use of any concealed or deadly weapon by such person. He shall be justified at such times in passing his hands over the clothing for the purpose of finding any deadly weapons." Many other police departments allowed frisks based on grounds less than probable cause but never openly acknowledged the practice.

Only a handful of state courts before 1968 ever explicitly addressed whether police could perform these brief searches without probable cause, with a slight majority of courts approving of the practice. Why did the issue not arise in the Supreme Court until 1968? See Wayne LaFave, "Street Encounters" and the Constitution: *Terry, Sibron, Peters,* and Beyond, 67 Mich. L. Rev. 40 (1968).

5. *The law and self-preservation.* Did the Supreme Court have any choice other than to approve of brief searches for weapons? If police officers felt that their lives were in jeopardy, would they not carry out the search regardless of the legal consequences? If Justice Douglas had written the opinion for the Court, what would have been the impact of the decision on police behavior and on the law of criminal procedure?

6. *Frisks in foreign systems.* In Great Britain, the Police and Criminal Evidence Act of 1984 provides that a constable can stop and search a person in a "public place" based on "reasonable grounds for suspecting" a search will reveal stolen or contraband articles. This level of justification is the same for a full-blown arrest, but it seems to correspond more closely to the American "reasonable suspicion" standard than to the "probable cause" standard. According to the government-issued Code of Practice for the Exercise by Police Officers of the Statutory Powers of Stop and Search, §3.5, a "search" occurring in a "public place" must be limited to a search of the outer garments, while a more thorough search can occur at the police station. In what ways do these legal provisions differ from the law of frisks in the United States? Do you believe that police practices in Great Britain reflect these differences in law? The law in France authorizes the police to conduct an identity check procedure that resembles the American stop and frisk, but the French procedure does not require individualized suspicion and may last up to four hours. See Richard S. Frase, Comparative Criminal Justice as a Guide to American Law Reform: How Do the French Do It, How Can We Find Out, and Why Should We Care? 78 Calif. L. Rev. 542, 576 (1990).

2. *The Scope of a* Terry *Search*

The frisk for weapons in *Terry* proceeds on a reduced level of justification (reasonable suspicion) because of the especially urgent nature of government's objective in that setting (the safety of the officer and others in the area) and the limited nature of the search. Could a search based on reasonable suspicion also serve other non-safety purposes, such as collecting evidence of a crime? What if the search is a bit more intrusive than a weapons frisk? In short, how far do *Terry* searches extend?

■ COMMONWEALTH v. ARTHUR CROWDER

884 S.W.2d 649 (Ky. 1994)

ROSENBERG, J.

The issue in this case is whether the seizure of a "bindle"[1] of drugs incident to a *Terry* patdown search violated the prohibition on "unreasonable searches and seizures" in the Fourth Amendment of the Constitution of the United States and §10 of the Kentucky Constitution.

[Twelve days prior to the incident involved in this proceeding, Arthur Crowder was arrested on a charge of trafficking in marijuana by Louisville police officer Brian Nunn. The sale had occurred on the corner of 22nd and Garland Streets.] On May 16, Officer Nunn was in the area once more, this time patrolling in a vehicle with Officer David Sanford. Nunn again saw Crowder at the corner of 22nd and Garland. When Crowder saw the police officers, he turned his back on them and started to walk off. Nunn stopped the car and told Sanford to detain Crowder and pat him down. Nunn stopped to talk to two women on the corner, but he did not charge them with any offense.

Officer Sanford testified that he did as Nunn ordered. He said in patting Crowder down, he was looking for weapons as a safety precaution. He did not feel any weapons, but felt some keys in Crowder's pocket. Additionally, he felt something in Crowder's left front pocket. Sanford testified "it felt like it may have been a bindle of drugs," and he reached into the pocket to get it out. He said it felt "like a small gumball." In fact, the substance was wrapped in a corner of a cut-off plastic bag, and turned out to be .016 of an ounce of cocaine. [Crowder was indicted for illegal possession of cocaine. He moved to suppress the evidence on the ground that the search for drugs exceeded the permissible scope of a *Terry* search; the trial court denied the motion.

In the recent Supreme Court case of Minnesota v. Dickerson, 508 U.S. 366 (1993)], two Minneapolis police officers on patrol observed respondent leaving a building they considered to be a crack house. . . . When the suspect made eye contact with one of the police officers, he halted and walked in the opposite direction into an alleyway. Based on the suspect having left the building known as a "crack house" and his decision to walk away from them, the police officers followed respondent into the alley and ordered him to submit to a *Terry* search. The search revealed no weapons, but the officer conducting the patdown search noticed a small lump in the front pocket of the suspect's nylon jacket. He then reached into the suspect's pocket and retrieved a small plastic bag containing one-fifth of one gram of crack cocaine.

1. "Bindle: slang: a small package, envelope, or paper containing a narcotic (as morphine, heroin, or cocaine; also: a small quantity of a narcotic: a narcotic dose." Meriam-Webster Third New International Dictionary (1986).

The United States Supreme Court held, as did the Supreme Court of Minnesota, that the further exploration of the suspect's pockets after determining that it contained no weapon "over-stepped the bounds of the strictly circumscribed search for weapons allowed under *Terry*" and the Fourth Amendment's protection against unreasonable searches and seizures. The Supreme Court reiterated the narrow limits on the permissibility of a *Terry* patdown search as an exception to the warrant requirement:

> [A] protective search — permitted without a warrant and on the basis of reasonable suspicion less than probable cause — must be strictly limited to that which is necessary for the discovery of weapons which might be used to harm the officer or others nearby. If the protective search goes beyond what is necessary to determine if the suspect is armed, it is no longer valid under *Terry* and its fruits will be suppressed.

The Supreme Court then went on to examine whether a "plain feel" rule might be applicable if the police discovers contraband through the sense of touch during an otherwise lawful search. The Court concluded that a narrowly drawn exception to the warrant requirement is appropriate when: (1) the requirements of *Terry* are otherwise complied with; and (2) the non-threatening contraband is immediately apparent from the sense of touch. The Supreme Court based its decision by analogy to the plain view cases, noting that in either case, the Fourth Amendment's requirement that an officer have probable cause to believe that the item is contraband before seizing it ensures against excessively speculative seizures. [T]here has been no invasion of the suspect's privacy beyond that already authorized by the officer's search for weapons. [I]f the nonthreatening contraband is immediately apparent from the sense of touch, during an otherwise lawful patdown, an officer should not be required to ignore it.

In applying these principles to the facts in *Dickerson,* the Supreme Court held, however, that the seizure of the cocaine was unconstitutional because the officer had exceeded the bounds of *Terry* in conducting the patdown search. . . . Once having concluded that the suspect's pocket contained no weapon, the officer had no basis for a continued exploration of the pocket. . . .

By applying the Supreme Court's analysis to this case, the same result follows. Even acknowledging the propriety of the *Terry* search in light of defense counsel's concession [that officer Nunn had sufficient basis for a frisk], it is clear from the record that Officer Sanford did not immediately recognize what he felt in Crowder's pocket as drugs. Sanford testified it "felt like it may have been a bindle of drugs"; and that "it felt like a small gumball." He then reached into the pocket to get it out. Since the nature of the non-threatening contraband was not immediately apparent to Officer Sanford when conducting the patdown, his further exploration of Crowder's pocket was not authorized by *Terry*. . . . Therefore the search was constitutionally invalid, as was the resulting seizure of the cocaine.

Finally, Crowder urges that this Court should reject the limited plain touch exception adopted in *Dickerson* as being violative of §10 of the Kentucky Constitution. To be sure, this Court has held that the Kentucky Constitution may, in certain circumstances, provide greater protection from the infringement of individual liberties than the federal constitution. [However, an] examination of Section 10 of the Constitution of Kentucky and the Fourth Amendment to the Constitution of the United States reveals little textual difference. The language used is virtually the same and only the arrangement of the words is different. [Accordingly,] the limited application of a plain feel exception to the warrant requirement in connection with a valid *Terry* search . . . does not violate §10 of the Kentucky Constitution. The decision of the Court of Appeals is affirmed.

LAMBERT, J., concurring.

Despite the views expressed hereinafter, but being unable to meaningfully distinguish between the case at bar and the decision of the United States Supreme Court in Minnesota v. Dickerson, . . . I am compelled by [the supremacy clause of the U.S. Constitution] to concur in the result reached by the majority. Nevertheless, I write separately to express my disagreement with the *Dickerson* case.

Simply stated, the issue is whether a police officer, rightfully engaged in a *Terry* patdown search, may seize an item encountered which is known or reasonably believed to be contraband. [O]ne sworn to enforce the law should not be required to turn a blind eye to the commission of a crime in his presence simply because the initial search was for something other than the contraband discovered. [T]here is nothing unreasonable about the seizure of items of contraband when the search which brought about the discovery was lawful.

The decision of the Supreme Court in Minnesota v. Dickerson amounts to hair-splitting in the extreme. The opinion acknowledges the right of police officers to conduct a *Terry* patdown search in a proper case, but prohibits seizure of contraband discovered in the course of the search unless the contraband is immediately apparent as such. Thus, . . . the police officer must, on discovery of an item or object on the person of a suspect, simultaneously conclude that the object is not a weapon and that it is contraband other than a weapon. Such decisions must be made instantaneously and as a part of the same thought process. No further inquiry as to the nature of the object is permitted.

It is unrealistic to require such superhuman conduct. A far more rational rule would be to permit seizure of any item of contraband discovered in the course of a *Terry* search. Of course, no search would be permitted after it was determined that the suspect was unarmed, but any item suspected of being contraband and discovered in the course of the search for weapons should be subject to seizure and the convoluted process required by *Dickerson* entirely avoided.

■ ARKANSAS CODE §16-81-206

(a) A law enforcement officer who has detained a person . . . may, if he reasonably suspects that the person is armed and presently dangerous to the officer or others, search the outer clothing of the person and the immediate surroundings for, and seize, any weapon or other dangerous thing which may be used against the officer or others.

(b) In no event shall that search be more detailed than is reasonably necessary to ensure the safety of the officer or others.

■ MONTANA CODE §46-5-402

A peace officer who has lawfully stopped a person . . . (1) may frisk the person and take other reasonably necessary steps for protection if the officer has reasonable cause to suspect that the person is armed and presently dangerous to the officer or another person present; (2) may take possession of any object that is discovered during the course of the frisk if the officer has probable cause to believe the object is a deadly weapon. . . .

Notes

1. *"Plain feel": majority position.* Under the "plain feel" or "plain touch" doctrine, if an officer conducts a properly circumscribed *Terry* search for weapons and feels an object that is not a weapon, the officer can seize the item if it is "immediately apparent" that the item is contraband or evidence of a crime. Minnesota v. Dickerson, 508 U.S. 366 (1993). Most state courts to consider the question also have adopted a "plain feel" doctrine under their state constitutions. See People v. Champion, 549 N.W.2d 849 (Mich. 1996). While accepting the basic contours of the doctrine, many courts apply it strictly. Courts have declared that commonplace items touched during a frisk cannot be seized, because it cannot be "immediately apparent" that the item is contraband or evidence. Ex parte Warren, 783 So. 2d 86 (Ala. 2000) (plain feel doctrine does not permit seizure of Tic Tac box felt during frisk, despite officer's prior experience that such boxes contain drugs); State v. James, 795 So. 2d 1146 (La. 2000) (film canister).

The high court in New York rejected the "plain touch" doctrine entirely under its state constitution. The court in People v. Diaz, 612 N.E.2d 298 (N.Y. 1993) explained its position as follows:

> The identity and criminal nature of a concealed object are not likely to be discernible upon a mere touch or pat within the scope of the intrusion authorized by *Terry*. While in most instances seeing an object will instantly reveal its identity and nature, touching is inherently less reliable and cannot conclusively establish an object's identity or criminal nature. Moreover, knowledge concerning an object merely from feeling it through an exterior covering is necessarily based on the police officer's expert opinion. . . .
>
> Finally, an opinion of a police officer that the object touched is evidence of criminality will predictably, at least in some circumstances, require a degree of pinching, squeezing or probing beyond the limited intrusion allowed under *Terry*. The proposed "plain touch" exception could thus invite a blurring of the limits to *Terry* searches and the sanctioning of warrantless searches on information obtained from an initial intrusion which, itself, amounts to an unauthorized warrantless search.

What kind of training—formal and informal—would you expect to occur within police departments in jurisdictions that adopt a "plain feel" rule? Should courts evaluate plain feel cases based on what a reasonable officer would know or on what the officer in question knew?

2. *Superhuman conduct.* Is Justice Lambert correct in arguing that the police must perform superhuman feats before the plain touch doctrine will validate their seizures arising out of weapons frisks? If so, is that a reason to relax the requirements of the doctrine or to abandon its use altogether? What might Officer Sanford have done or said differently to have changed the outcome?

3. *Reasonable suspicion for nonweapons frisks?* The Supreme Court has insisted that a frisk of a person designed to obtain evidence of a crime cannot be based on

reasonable suspicion; the officer must have probable cause that the evidence will be on the person, even if the brief search is no more intrusive than a weapons frisk. See Ybarra v. Illinois, 444 U.S. 85 (1979) (frisk of customer in bar where search warrant was being executed). How exactly will the courts make the distinction between permissible weapons frisks and impermissible evidence frisks?

4. *Frisk statutes.* Would the court in *Crowder* have decided the case any differently if a statute identical to the Arkansas statute had been in effect in Kentucky? What outcome under the Montana statute? Are the police in a better position, generally speaking, in states with a frisk statute or in those where the authority to frisk is based entirely on judicial opinions?

5. *Are courts the agents of legislators or independent interpreters?* Suppose an Arkansas court is convinced that the statute regarding the scope of frisks is badly flawed because it does not authorize a frisk beyond the "outer clothing." Should the court feel free to "fix" the problem created by the legislature? Are there canons of construction that would allow a court to read this statute to allow more intrusive (and effective) frisks?

As we have seen earlier, courts look to several different sources of guidance in interpreting the meaning of ambiguous statutory language. They sometimes resort to canons of construction to determine the "plain meaning" of the statutory text. They also often consult the legislative history to determine the legislature's intent in passing the statute. Alternatively, they may refer to the statute's title or language to ascertain the legislative purpose. These different sources may point in different directions in a particular case. What weight will a court give to the various sources of guidance?

The answer to such a question depends on the court's objective: Does the court view itself as an agent of the legislature, or is the court to exercise its own best judgment about how to give meaning to the language? Courts have not agreed on this question. On the one hand, most probably adhere to the view that they interpret statutes as agents of the legislature, to put into effect what the legislators intended in a specific setting (or what they *would have* intended for the setting if they had thought of it). As Justice Oliver Wendell Holmes once stated, "If my fellow citizens want to go to Hell I will help them. It's my job." 1 Holmes-Laski Letters 249 (Mark DeWolfe Howe ed. 1953).

On the other hand, many courts *act* as if they have an independent responsibility to make sense of statutory language. Professor Ernst Freund captured this independent view of courts as interpreters of statutes with the following advice in 1917: "In cases of genuine ambiguity courts should use the power of interpretation consciously and deliberately to promote sound law and sound principles of legislation." Ernst Freund, Interpretation of Statutes, 65 U. Pa. L. Rev. 207 (1917). What objective of statutory interpretation would a court be endorsing if it were to interpret the Arkansas frisk statute to allow frisks of the person beyond the outer clothing?

6. *Purses, briefcases, and bags.* Police also commonly extend protective *Terry* searches to purses, briefcases, and other items a suspect might be holding at the time of a stop. Although the officer might reduce the danger of any weapons in a purse or bag by placing it well out of reach of the suspect, neither courts nor police department rules have required the police to do so. They must, however, start with a "frisk" of the exterior of a cloth bag, and may not open the bag to search its contents if the initial frisk confirms that there is no weapon inside.

■ LARRY HIIBEL v. DISTRICT COURT

59 P.3d 1201 (Nev. 2002)

YOUNG, C.J.

The pertinent issue before us is whether NRS 171.123(3), which requires a person stopped under reasonable suspicion by a police officer to identify himself or herself, violates the Fourth Amendment of the United States Constitution. We conclude NRS 171.123(3) does not violate the Fourth Amendment because it strikes a balance between constitutional protections of privacy and the need to protect police officers and the public.

In pertinent part, NRS 171.123 provides:

> 1. Any peace officer may detain any person whom the officer encounters under circumstances which reasonably indicate that the person has committed, is committing or is about to commit a crime. . . .
>
> 3. The officer may detain the person pursuant to this section only to ascertain his identity and the suspicious circumstances surrounding his presence abroad. Any person so detained shall identify himself, but may not be compelled to answer any other inquiry of any peace officer.
>
> 4. A person may not be detained longer than is reasonably necessary to effect the purposes of this section, and in no event longer than 60 minutes.

In response to a call from police dispatch, Humboldt County Sheriff's Deputy Lee Dove drove to the scene where a concerned citizen had observed someone striking a female passenger inside a truck. There, Dove spoke to the concerned citizen and was directed to a parked truck. When Dove approached the truck, he noticed skid marks in the gravel, suggesting the truck had been parked in a sudden and aggressive manner. Dove saw Larry D. Hiibel standing outside the truck and thought he was intoxicated based on his eyes, mannerisms, speech, and odor. Hiibel's minor daughter was in the passenger side of the truck. When Dove asked Hiibel to identify himself, Hiibel refused. Instead, Hiibel placed his hands behind his back and challenged the officer to take him to jail.

Hiibel said he would cooperate but was unwilling to provide identification, because he did not believe he had done anything wrong. After eleven requests for identification, to no avail, Dove arrested Hiibel. Dove described the situation as follows:

> During my conversation with Mr. Hiibel, there was a point where he became somewhat aggressive. I felt based on me not being able to find out who he was, to identify him, I didn't know if he was wanted or what his situation was, I wasn't able to determine what was going on crimewise in the vehicle, based on that I felt he was intoxicated, and how he was becoming aggressive and moody, I went ahead and put him in handcuffs so I could secure him for my safety, and put him in my patrol vehicle.

Hiibel was charged and found guilty of resisting a public officer. . . . The justice of the peace in Humboldt County determined that "[Hiibel] was asked only for identification and failure to provide identification obstructed and delayed Dove as a public officer in attempting to discharge his duty." . . . Evidence "over and above simply failing to identify himself" was found to support Hiibel's arrest and conviction, which included Dove's suspicion that Hiibel engaged in driving under the influence. . . .

Fundamental to a democratic society is the ability to wander freely and anonymously, if we so choose, without being compelled to divulge information to the government about who we are or what we are doing. See Papachristou v. City of Jacksonville, 405 U.S. 156 (1972). This "right to be let alone"—to simply live in privacy—is a right protected by the Fourth Amendment and undoubtedly sacred to us all.

Yet, this right to privacy is not absolute. Like all freedoms we enjoy, it includes both limitations and responsibilities. One such limitation to the right of privacy is reasonableness. The Fourth Amendment only protects against "unreasonable" invasions of privacy, or searches and seizures, by the government. The United States Supreme Court has twice expressly refused to address whether a person reasonably suspected of engaging in criminal behavior may be required to identify himself or herself. Brown v. Texas, 443 U.S. 47, 53 n.3 ("We need not decide whether an individual may be punished for refusing to identify himself in the context of a lawful investigatory stop which satisfies Fourth Amendment requirements."); Kolender v. Lawson, 461 U.S. 352, 361-62 n.10 (1983) (holding that a California statute requiring an individual who loitered or wandered the streets to produce "credible and reliable" identification to an officer upon request of a police officer was unconstitutional on vagueness grounds, but refusing to consider whether the statute violated the Fourth Amendment). Therefore, the issue is unresolved.

Traditionally, in resolving issues implicating the Fourth Amendment right to privacy, the following touchstone question has been asked: Is the invasion of privacy reasonable? Reasonableness is determined by balancing the public interest and the individual's right to personal security free from arbitrary interference by law officers. Considerations involve the weighing of the gravity of the public concerns served by the seizure, the degree to which the seizure advances the public interest, and the severity of the interference with individual liberty. A primary concern is to assure that an individual's reasonable expectation of privacy is not subject to arbitrary invasions solely at the unfettered discretion of officers in the field.

Balancing these interests, we conclude that any intrusion on privacy caused by NRS 171.123(3) is outweighed by the benefits to officers and community safety. The public interest in requiring individuals to identify themselves to officers when a reasonable suspicion exists is overwhelming. The United States Supreme Court has recognized that "American criminals have a long tradition of armed violence, and every year in this country many law enforcement officers are killed in the line of duty, and thousands more are wounded." [*Terry,* 392 U.S. at 23]. The most dangerous time for an officer may be during an investigative stop—when a suspect is approached and questioned.

Judicial notice is taken that in the year 2000, fifty-one officers were murdered in the line of duty. These homicides occurred as follows: thirteen during traffic stops/pursuits, twelve during arrest situations, ten during ambushes, eight during responses to disturbance calls, six during investigations of suspicious persons, and two during prisoner transport.[20] Of the suspects who committed these killings, twenty had been previously arrested for crimes of violence, nine had previously assaulted a

20. Federal Bureau of Investigation, U.S. Dep't of Justice, Law Enforcement Officers Killed and Assaulted, 2000, at 28 (2001), at *http://www.fbi.gov/ucr/killed/00leoka.pdf* (last visited Nov. 12, 2002).

police officer, and twelve were on probation or parole. Moreover, 15,915 officers were assaulted that year. If the officers referenced in these statistics had known the identity and history of their attackers prior to being assaulted or killed, perhaps some of these incidents could have been prevented.

Knowing the identity of a suspect allows officers to more accurately evaluate and predict potential dangers that may arise during an investigative stop. It follows that an officer making a reasonable investigatory stop should not be denied the opportunity to protect himself from attack by a hostile suspect. For example, the suspect may be a former felon or wanted for an outstanding arrest warrant. Such persons pose a heightened risk of danger to officers and the public during investigatory encounters.

Additionally, if suspects are not legally required to identify themselves, what could an officer do if a suspicious person were loitering outside a daycare center or school? Perhaps that person is a sex offender. How are officers to enforce restraining orders? Or, how are officers to enforce curfew laws for minors without a requirement to produce identification? In these situations, it is the observable conduct that creates a reasonable suspicion, but it is the requirement to produce identification that enables an officer to determine whether the suspect is breaking the law.

Most importantly, we are at war against enemies who operate with concealed identities and the dangers we face as a nation are unparalleled. Terrorism is "changing the way we live and the way we act and the way we think."[24] During the recent past, this country suffered the tragic deaths of more than 3,000 unsuspecting men, women, and children at the hands of terrorists; seventeen innocent people in six different states were randomly gunned down by snipers; and our citizens have suffered illness and death from exposure to mail contaminated with Anthrax. We have also seen high school students transport guns to school and randomly gun down their fellow classmates and teachers. It cannot be stressed enough: "This is a different kind of war that requires a different type of approach and a different type of mentality."[25] To deny officers the ability to request identification from suspicious persons creates a situation where an officer could approach a wanted terrorist or sniper but be unable to identify him or her if the person's behavior does not rise to the level of probable cause necessary for an arrest. . . .

The requirements of NRS 171.123(3) are also reasonable and involve a minimal invasion of personal privacy. Reasonable people do not expect their identities — their names — to be withheld from officers. Rather, we reveal our names in a variety of situations every day without much consideration. For instance, it is merely polite manners to introduce ourselves when meeting a new acquaintance. A person's name is given out on business cards, credit cards, checks, and driver's licenses, to name a few more instances. In addition, everyone is required to reveal government issued identification to airport officials and are subject to random searches before proceeding to flight gates. Asking a suspect to state his or her name when an officer has an articulable suspicion is nominal in comparison.

To hold that a name, which is neutral and non-incriminating information, is somehow an invasion of privacy is untenable. Such an invasion is minimal at best. The suspect is not required to provide private details about his background, but

24. Interview by Tony Snow with Senator Tom Daeschle, United States Senate, Washington, D.C. (Oct. 21, 2002), *http://www.foxnews.com/story/0,2933,66236,00.html.*

25. President George W. Bush, Address During a News Conference (Oct. 11, 2001), *http://www.cnn.com/2001/US/10/11/gen.bush.transcript/index.html.*

merely to state his name to an officer when reasonable suspicion exists. The Supreme Court held it reasonable for officers to pat down and frisk a person during an investigative stop. As the Court recognized in Terry v. Ohio, 392 U.S. 1 (1968), "it would be unreasonable to require that police officers take unnecessary risks in the performance of their duties." Requiring identification is far less intrusive than conducting a pat down search of one's physical person.

Here, Hiibel was suspected of domestic violence against his minor daughter and driving under the influence of alcohol. Based on skid marks in the gravel, it appeared that Hiibel parked his truck in a quick and aggressive manner. Hiibel refused eleven requests by officers to identify himself. Instead, Hiibel placed his hands behind his back and challenged the deputy to take him to jail. An ordinary person would conclude it was Hiibel who was unreasonable, not the law. . . .

Maupin, J., concurring.

I join in the result reached by the majority, stressing again that NRS 171.123 is narrowly written, and that its requirement that persons reasonably suspected of criminal misconduct be required to identify themselves to police during brief investigatory stops is a commonsense requirement for the protection of the public and law enforcement officers. I write separately to note that the majority has not somehow overreacted to the dangers presented by the war against domestic and international terrorism. Our decision today is truly related to the ability of police to properly and safely deal with persons reasonably suspected of criminal misconduct, here, domestic violence and driving under the influence of alcohol. . . .

Agosti, J., dissenting.

[The] right to wander freely and anonymously, if we so choose, is a fundamental right of privacy in a democratic society. [Detaining] a person and requiring him to identify himself constitutes a seizure of his person subject to the requirements of the Fourth Amendment, Brown v. Texas, 443 U.S. 47 (1979). In light of these constitutional requirements, the United States Supreme Court has stated that although the officers may question the person, the detainee need not answer any questions. Furthermore, unless the detainee volunteers answers and those answers supply the officer with probable cause to arrest, the detainee must be released. . . .

Anonymity is encompassed within the expectation of privacy, a civil liberty that is protected during a *Terry* stop. . . . The majority concludes that the governmental interest in police safety outweighs an individual's interest in his right to keep private his identity. The majority relies upon FBI statistics about police fatalities and assaults to support its argument. However, it does not provide any evidence that an officer, by knowing a person's identity, is better protected from potential violence. In *Terry*, the United States Supreme Court addressed the issue of officer safety by carving out an exception to the Fourth Amendment to allow a police officer to make certain that the person being detained "is not armed with a weapon that could unexpectedly and fatally be used against him" when the officer reasonably believes "he is dealing with an armed and dangerous individual." The purpose of such a search is to ensure the detainee is not armed with a weapon that could be immediately used against a police officer, not to ensure against a detainee's propensity for violence based upon a prior record of criminal behavior.

It is well known that within the context of a *Terry* stop an officer's authority to search is limited to a pat-down to detect weapons. The officer may investigate a hard object because it might be a gun. An officer may not investigate a soft object he detects, even though it might be drugs. Similarly, an officer may not detect a wallet and remove it for search. With today's majority decision, the officer can now, figuratively, reach in, grab the wallet and pull out the detainee's identification. So much for our right to be left alone or as the majority says — to wander freely and anonymously if we choose.

The majority avoids the fact that knowing a suspect's identity does not alleviate any threat of immediate danger by arguing that a reasonable person cannot expect to withhold his identity from police officers, as we reveal our names to different people everyday. What the majority fails to recognize, however, is that when we give our names to new acquaintances, business associates and shop owners, we do so voluntarily, out of friendship or to complete a transaction. With the heightened security at airports, for example, passengers are required to provide picture identification. But non-passengers are free to wander that portion of the airport that is unsecured without showing an ID. Purchasing an airline ticket is a business transaction, and the airlines may condition the sale on knowing who is the purchaser. In contrast, being forced to identify oneself to a police officer or else face arrest is government coercion — precisely the type of governmental intrusion that the Fourth Amendment was designed to prevent. Furthermore, it is not necessary to have one's name on a credit card or checkbook in order to effect a purchase. A dedicated libertarian, for example, might deliberately eschew financial institutions, credit cards and checkbooks, engaging solely in cash transactions, in order to jealously protect his individual rights, especially his right to be anonymous, to be left alone, to wander freely.

Finally, the majority also makes an emotional appeal based upon fear and speculation by arguing that the police would be powerless to protect innocent children from sex offenders, to enforce restraining orders, and to enforce curfews for minors. What the majority fails to recognize is that it is the observable conduct, not the identity, of a person, upon which an officer must legally rely when investigating crimes and enforcing the law.

The majority further appeals to the public's fear during this time of war "against an enemy who operates with a concealed identity." Now is precisely the time when our duty to vigilantly guard the rights enumerated in the Constitution becomes most important. To ease our guard now, in the wake of fear of unknown perpetrators who may still seek to harm the United States and its people, would sound the call of retreat and begin the erosion of civil liberties. The court must not be blinded by fear. I am reminded of a statement by Justice Felix Frankfurter . . . in another search and seizure case involving individual liberties protected by the Fourth Amendment:

> [W]e are in danger of forgetting that the Bill of Rights reflects experience with police excesses. It is not only under Nazi rule that police excesses are inimical to freedom. It is easy to make light of insistence on scrupulous regard for the safeguards of civil liberties when invoked on behalf of the unworthy. It is too easy. History bears testimony that by such disregard are the rights of liberty extinguished, heedlessly at first, then stealthily, and brazenly in the end. [Davis v. United States, 328 U.S. 582 (1946).]

The terrorist threat has shaken our complacency. Our way of life is threatened as never before. At this time, this extraordinary time, the true test of our national courage is not our necessary and steadfast resolve to defend ourselves against terrorist activity. The true test is our necessary and steadfast resolve to protect and safeguard the rights and principles upon which our nation was founded, our constitution and our personal liberties. I dissent from the majority's retreat from this challenge.

Problem 2-8. Frisking Car and Driver

Around 12:30 A.M., police officers Josephine Copland and Jess Segundo were patrolling West Oliwood, investigating narcotics sales in that area. As they waited at an intersection for a traffic signal to change, they saw a red Lexus drive through the intersection with a tail light burned out. Officers Copland and Segundo immediately stopped the Lexus, although they typically would not stop a car based only on a problem with the tail light.

When the driver, Steven Worth, pulled over and stopped, he started to move about the inside the vehicle, back and forth in the front seat, and ducked down below the seat. When Officers Copland and Segundo exited their cruiser and approached on foot, they ordered Worth to step out of his vehicle.

Officer Copland ordered Worth to move away from his vehicle, and began examining the interior of the Lexus. She looked around and under the seats and found nothing suspicious. Officer Copland then opened the glove compartment and found what looked to her like a hand-rolled cigarette. Upon picking up and examining the cigarette, she discovered it was filled with tobacco. Officer Copland reached over and lifted the lever next to the driver's seat to disengage the trunk latch. Moving outside to the back of the car, she looked inside the trunk and found an expensive-looking sets of golf clubs inside a golf bag. Officer Copland noticed a number of bulges within the golf bag, and she began to unzip the bag's various pockets. In the largest pocket, which ran the length of the bag, Copland discovered a sawed-off shotgun.

Meanwhile, Officer Segundo was examining Worth. She performed a pat down search of Worth's outer clothing. As part of this frisk, Officer Segundo patted down the knit stocking cap Worth wore, which was rolled over on the edges. Officer Segundo felt a hard object on the right side of Worth's hat. Officer Segundo was not sure what this hard object was, and she reached inside the hat. Grabbing the hard object with her fingers, she felt what she believed (based upon her previous experience) to be crack cocaine. Officer Segundo then removed two pieces of suspected crack cocaine from the hat and arrested Worth for possession of that illegal substance.

Steven Worth was charged with possession of crack cocaine and with possession of an illegal firearm. He filed a motion prior to trial asking the court to suppress the gun recovered from the golf bag and the drugs recovered from his stocking cap. How would you argue in support of the motion?

Notes

1. Terry *searches of stopped cars.* Although a pat-down search of a person should expose any guns or other large weapons hidden in the clothing, a person stopped while riding in a car might hide a weapon somewhere in the vehicle. How can an officer protect herself from a suspect who keeps a weapon somewhere nearby, but not on his person? The U.S. Supreme Court, in Michigan v. Long, 463 U.S. 1032

(1983), stated that police officers who stop a vehicle and frisk the driver standing outside the car may conduct a further "protective" search of the passenger compartment and any containers inside it that might contain a large weapon such as a gun. Under the federal constitution, the police must have a reasonable suspicion that there may be weapons in the vehicle before the protective search takes place.

Most state courts (all but about a half dozen) allow police to conduct protective searches of stopped cars, on terms identical to federal law. They allow the officers to conduct a protective search of the interior and any containers inside (but only those large enough to contain a weapon) if the officers reasonably suspect that there are dangerous weapons in the vehicle. These courts reason that the search of a vehicle is just as important to the officer's safety as a frisk of the person under *Terry*. See State v. Wilkins, 692 A.2d 1233 (Conn. 1997). However, the high court in New York decided in People v. Torres, 543 N.E.2d 61 (N.Y. 1989), that police officers could not search the interior of a stopped vehicle for weapons based only on reasonable suspicion. The *Torres* court suggested that the officer stopping the vehicle can reduce any risk by separating the suspect from the vehicle. How might the majority of courts respond to this argument? Would you draw a distinction between a pat-down search of the driver and placing the driver into the patrol car during the stop? See Wilson v. State, 745 N.E.2d 789 (Ind. 2001) (pat-down search of motorist prior to placing him in police car during routine traffic stop violated Fourth Amendment; pat-down search was not supported by particularized reasonable suspicion that motorist was armed).

2. *Orders to exit a vehicle.* When an officer stops a vehicle, he will sometimes but not always ask the driver to get out of the vehicle, out of concern for his own safety. The U.S. Supreme Court has concluded that this intrusion on the driver is minimal and that the officer needs no justification (other than the reasonable suspicion necessary to stop the car) for ordering the driver to get out of the car. Pennsylvania v. Mimms, 434 U.S. 106 (1977); cf. Commonwealth v. Gonsalves, 711 N.E.2d 108 (Mass. 1999) (state constitution requires reasonable suspicion of danger before officer may order driver or passenger out of stopped car; court expresses concern that automatic power could be "invitation to discriminatory enforcement"). In Maryland v. Wilson, 519 U.S. 408 (1997), the court extended *Mimms* to hold that officers may order a *passenger* in the car to get out, without any grounds to believe that the passenger is dangerous. Some states previously had rejected that position. See State v. Smith, 637 A.2d 158 (N.J. 1994) (order to passenger to get out of car stopped for minor traffic infraction must be based on articulable suspicion that passenger poses danger). The great majority of state courts now follow *Wilson*. Cf. People v. Jackson, 45 P.3d 1237 (Colo. 2002) (police may request identification of passenger in stopped vehicle without individualized suspicion); but see State v. Mendez, 970 P.2d 722 (Wash. 1999). Should the police treat the driver and the passenger differently? Is one any more or less dangerous than the other? Is the intrusion on drivers and passengers the same?

3. Terry *stops and requests for identification.* The Nevada court in the *Hiibel* case decided an issue that has received surprisingly little attention: Does the police officer's power to stop a pedestrian include the power to insist that the person provide some identification? Is the argument in favor of this power the same as the argument favoring an automatic order to exit a vehicle during a traffic stop?

III

Full Searches of People and Places: Basic Concepts

We now move from brief searches and stops to more extended and complete searches. This chapter describes the origins of the Fourth Amendment and the language of analogous provisions in state constitutions. Then it introduces the three concepts that dominate the case law governing full searches: probable cause, warrants, and consent. Probable cause is the usual justification required to validate a full search. The judicial warrant is the procedure meant to ensure careful and early assessment of probable cause. To obtain a warrant, a government agent must demonstrate to a judge or magistrate, before the search happens, that the plan is justified. The last of the basic concepts, consent, may be the most important of all because police obtain consent from private parties for a large proportion of the searches they conduct. Following this chapter's survey of the most important tools for analyzing full searches, Chapter 4 applies these concepts in several contexts that recur time and again in judicial decisions and in the field.

A. ORIGINS OF THE FOURTH AMENDMENT AND ITS ANALOGS

The police force is a nineteenth-century invention; the repressive government officers that most infuriated the colonists were tax and customs inspectors. These officials often carried out their work by using general warrants, which were broad grants of authority from the king of England or his representatives to search homes and businesses. One goal of this section is to identify the characteristics of government searches that constitutional drafters found most objectionable. Many historians and judges have stated that Americans were especially concerned with "general warrants." Why were general warrants troubling to colonial lawyers? Did any other characteristics of government searches, apart from their reliance on general warrants, also draw colonial criticism?

1. *General Search Warrants*

In the 1760s, a series of English cases addressed the validity of general search warrants. The cases were civil tort actions against the individuals who issued and executed the warrants. The plaintiff in the following case, John Entick, published a series of pamphlets critical of the government. A minister of the government, Lord Halifax, considered the pamphlets libelous. He issued to his subordinates a "warrant" authorizing them to search for Entick (without specifying a place where they could look) and to seize him and his papers (without specifying which ones). Halifax's subordinates (or "messengers") executed the warrant and seized a great many of Entick's papers. Entick later brought a tort suit against Carrington, one of the messengers who had executed the warrant. The issue on appeal was whether the warrant was authorized by law (giving the searcher a legal defense) or was beyond the scope of the law, perhaps exposing those who created and executed the warrant to liability for the improper search.

■ JOHN ENTICK v. NATHAN CARRINGTON

95 Eng. Rep. 807 (K.B. 1765)

In trespass; the plaintiff declares that the defendants . . . broke and entered the dwelling-house of the plaintiff . . . and continued there four hours without his consent and against his will, and all that time disturbed him in the peaceable possession thereof, and . . . searched and examined all the rooms, &c. in his dwelling-house, and all the boxes &c. so broke open, and read over, pryed into, and examined all the private papers, books, &c. of the plaintiff there found, whereby the secret affairs, &c. of the plaintiff became wrongfully discovered and made public; and took and carried away . . . printed pamphlets, &c. &c. of the plaintiff there found. [The defendants say] the plaintiff ought not to have his action against them, because they say, that before the supposed trespass . . . the Earl of Halifax was, and yet is, one of the Lords of the King's Privy Council, and one of his principal Secretaries of State, and that the earl . . . made his warrant under his hand and seal directed to the defendants, by which the earl did in the King's name authorize and require the defendants, taking a constable to their assistance, to make strict and diligent search for the plaintiff, mentioned in the said warrant to be the author . . . of several weekly very seditious papers . . . containing gross and scandalous reflections and invectives upon His Majesty's Government, and upon both Houses of Parliament, and him the plaintiff having found, to seize and apprehend and bring together with his books and papers in safe custody, before the Earl of Halifax to be examined. [The defendants argued that such warrants have frequently been granted by Secretaries of State since the Glorious Revolution of 1688 and have never been controverted. The jury found that the agents of Lord Halifax had committed the acts described by the plaintiff and was willing to award damages of 3,000 pounds if the court concluded that these facts constituted a trespass.]

[We] shall now consider the special justification, whether [the defense to a tort claim for trespass] can be supported in law, and this depends upon the jurisdiction of the Secretary of State; for if he has no jurisdiction to grant a warrant to break open doors, locks, boxes, and to seize a man and all his books, &c. in the first instance upon an information of his being guilty of publishing a libel, the warrant will not justify the defendants: it was resolved . . . in the case of Shergold v. Holloway, that a justice's warrant expressly to arrest the party will not justify the officer, there being no jurisdiction. The warrant in our case was an execution in the first instance, without any previous summons, examination, hearing the plaintiff, or proof that he was the author of the supposed libels; a power claimed by no other magistrate whatever . . . ; it was left to the discretion of these defendants to execute the warrant in the absence or presence of the plaintiff, when he might have no witness present to see what they did; for they were to seize all papers, bank bills, or any other valuable papers they might take away if they were so disposed; there might be nobody to detect them.

[In the case of Wilkes v. Wood (1763), involving a member of the House of Commons who had published an attack on the King and his ministers], all his books and papers were seized and taken away; we were told by one of these messengers that he was obliged by his oath to sweep away all papers whatsoever; if this is law it would be found in our books, but no such law ever existed in this country; our law holds the property of every man so sacred, that no man can set his foot upon his neighbour's close without his leave; if he does he is a trespasser, though he does no damage at all; if he will tread upon his neighbour's ground, he must justify it by law. [W]e can safely say there is no law in this country to justify the defendants in what they have done; if there was, it would destroy all the comforts of society; for papers are often the dearest property a man can have. This case was compared to that of stolen goods; . . . but in that case the justice and the informer must proceed with great caution; there must be an oath that the party has had his goods stolen, and his strong reason to believe they are concealed in such a place; but if the goods are not found there, he is a trespasser; the officer in that case is a witness; there are none in this case, no inventory taken; if it had been legal many guards of property would have attended it. We shall now consider the usage of these warrants since the [Glorious] Revolution [of 1688]; if it began then, it is too modern to be law; the common law did not begin with the Revolution; the ancient constitution which had been almost overthrown and destroyed, was then repaired and revived; the Revolution added a new buttress to the ancient venerable edifice. [T]his is the first instance of an attempt to prove a modern practice of a private office to make and execute warrants to enter a man's house, search for and take away all his books and papers in the first instance, to be law, which is not to be found in our books. It must have been the guilt or poverty of those upon whom such warrants have been executed, that deterred or hindered them from contending against the power of a Secretary of State and the Solicitor of the Treasury, or such warrants could never have passed for lawful till this time. We are . . . all of opinion that it cannot be justified by law. [I]f a man is punishable for having a libel in his private custody, as many cases say he is, half the kingdom would be guilty in the case of a favourable libel, if libels may be searched for and seized by whomsoever and wheresoever the Secretary of State thinks fit. . . . Our law is wise and merciful, and supposes every man accused to be innocent before he is tried by his peers: upon the whole, we are all of opinion that this warrant is wholly illegal and void. One word more for ourselves; we are no advocates for libels, all Governments must set their faces against them, and whenever they come before us and a jury we shall set our faces against them; and if juries do not prevent them they may prove fatal to liberty, destroy Government and introduce anarchy; but tyranny is better than anarchy, and the worst Government better than none at all. Judgment for the plaintiff.

The English controversy in the 1760s over general warrants was familiar to American colonists. A similar practice was creating a popular uproar in the colonies at about this time. Customs agents of the English government, who enforced the highly unpopular and widely flouted tax laws for imports and exports, had all the powers of their English counterparts as they searched for taxable goods. Their power to search for goods sometimes took the form of "writs of assistance." Like a general warrant, the writ of assistance authorized the agent to search private premises, without specifying the place to search or the things to seize. These writs contained no real time limitation, for they expired only upon the death of the king. The writs also obligated all government officials and all subjects of the Crown to assist the customs agent in the search. A reporter of proceedings in the court in the Massachusetts Bay colony offers the following example of a 1755 application for a writ of assistance.

■ THE WRITS OF ASSISTANCE

Quincy's Rep. (Mass.) App., 1:402-404, 453

To the Honourable his Majestys Justices of his Superiour Court for said Province to be held at York in and for the County of York on the third Tuesday of June 1755.

HUMBLY SHEWS Charles Paxton Esqr: That he is lawfully authorized to Execute the Office of Surveyor of all Rates Duties and Impositions arising and growing due to his Majesty at Boston in this Province & cannot fully Exercise said Office in such Manner as his Majestys Service and the Laws in such Cases Require Unless Your Honours who are vested with the Power of a Court of Exchequer for this Province will please to Grant him a Writ of Assistants, he therefore prays he & his Deputys may be Aided in the Execution of said office within his District by a Writ of Assistants under the Seal of this Superiour Court in Legal form & according to Usage in his Majestys Court of Exchequer & in Great Britain, & your Petitioner &Ca:

CHAS PAXTON

[The court issued the writ in the following form:]

GEORGE the Second by the Grace of God of Great Britain, France and Ireland King, Defender of the Faith &c — To all and singular Justices of the Peace, Sheriffs and Constables, and to all other our officers and Subjects within said Prov. & to each of you Greeting —

WHEREAS the Commissioners of our Customs have by their Deputation dated the 8th day of Jany 1752, assignd Charles Paxton Esqr Surveyor of all Rates, Duties, and Impositions arising and growing due within the Port of Boston in said Province as by said Deputation at large appears, WE THEREFORE command you and each of you that you permit ye said C.P. and his Deputies and Servants from Time to time at his or their Will as well in the day as in the Night to enter and go on board any Ship, Boat or other Vessell riding lying or being within or coming to the said Port or any Places or Creeks appertaining to said Port, such Ship, Boat or Vessell then & there found to View & Search & strictly to examine in the same, touching the Customs and

Subsidies to us due, And also in the day Time together with a Constable or other public officer inhabiting near unto the Place to enter and go into any Vaults, Cellars, Warehouses, Shops or other Places to search and see whether any Goods, Wares or Merchandises, in ye same Ships, Boats or Vessells, Vaults, Cellars, Warehouses, Shops or other Places are or shall be there hid or concealed, having been imported, ship't or laden in order to be exported from or out of the said Port or any Creeks or Places appertain'g to the same Port; and to open any Trunks, Chests, Boxes, fardells [packages] or Packs made up or in Bulk, whatever in which any Goods, Wares, or Merchandises are suspected to be packed or concealed and further to do all Things which of Rt and according to Law and the Statutes in such Cases provided, is in this Part to be done: And We strictly command you and every of you that you, from Time to Time be aiding and assisting to the said C.P. his Deputies and Servants and every of them in the Execution of the Premises in all Things as becometh: Fail not at your Peril.

Notes

1. *The battle over general warrants and writs of assistance.* The English legal system was rejecting general warrants at the same time colonial officials in America were relying on such warrants more heavily. Lord Camden's decision in Entick v. Carrington is one of several decisions to declare that there was no statutory or other legal authority for general warrants in England. An equally famous decision, Wilkes v. Wood, 19 Howell's State Trials 1153 (C.P. 1763), involved a member of Parliament (John Wilkes) who wrote a series of pamphlets critical of the government and, like John Entick, became the target of government agents executing a general warrant. Did the *Entick* court simply want to encourage Parliament to enact clearer legislation authorizing such warrants? Does the opinion reveal any deeper concerns about their use?

Writs of assistance issued in the American colonies in the 1760s provoked arguments and protests similar to those found in the *Entick* decision. In a now famous (but at the time losing) argument against the validity of writs of assistance, James Otis criticized the writs in these terms:

> Now one of the most essential branches of English liberty, is the freedom of one's house. A man's house is his castle; and while he is quiet, he is as well guarded as a prince in his castle. This writ, if it should be declared legal, would totally annihilate this privilege. Custom house officers may enter our houses when they please—we are commanded to permit their entry—their menial servants may enter—may break locks, bars and every thing in their way—and whether they break through malice or revenge, no man, no court can inquire—bare suspicion without oath is sufficient.

2 Legal Papers of John Adams 113, 142 (L. Wroth and H. Zobel eds., 1965); see generally M. H. Smith, The Writs of Assistance Case (1978).

2. *Fourth Amendment history in the Supreme Court.* The concerns of the Constitution's framers figure into current interpretations of the Fourth Amendment. While the role of history rises and falls in different eras of the Supreme Court's search and seizure jurisprudence, history appears to be on the upswing lately. Consider this assertion by Justice Scalia in Wyoming v. Houghton, 526 U.S. 295, 299-300 (1999): "In

determining whether a particular governmental action violates [the Fourth Amendment], provision, we inquire first whether the action was regarded as an unlawful search or seizure under the common law when the Amendment was framed. Where that inquiry yields no answer, we must evaluate the search or seizure under traditional standards of reasonableness. . . ." See David A. Sklansky, The Fourth Amendment and Common Law, 100 Colum. L. Rev. 1739, 1745-70 (2000) (Justices in earlier periods focused on general warrants and writs of assistance and generalized from those controversies to the underlying evils; current Justices read constitution in light of eighteenth century common law practices).

3. *What were the offensive characteristics of searches?* Can we isolate the offensive characteristics of general warrants? Did the *Entick* court express concern about the lack of an explanation for a proposed search before it began? Was it concerned with the fact that a government official issued the warrant to his own subordinates? Why does it matter that the general warrants and writs of assistance name no particular target or place for a search? Notice also that the *Entick* court seemed troubled by the fact that the searches under these warrants took place with no witnesses present. What evils would witnesses help prevent? How did the *Entick* court describe a search for "stolen goods"? Was that sort of search more palatable than a search under a general warrant? Try to identify, from these materials, a definition of general warrants that will enable you to spot their possible reemergence in modern doctrine and practice.

4. *Warranted searches and reasonable searches.* The incidents discussed most during constitutional debates involved *warranted* searches rather than warrantless searches. See Thomas Y. Davies, Recovering the Original Fourth Amendment, 98 Mich. L. Rev. 547, 551 (1999) ("the Framers understood 'unreasonable searches and seizures' simply as a pejorative label for the inherent illegality of any searches or seizures that might be made under general warrants"). Warrants issued from an authority with proper jurisdiction became a legal defense for the government officer in any tort suit against him for trespass during the search or seizure. As William Blackstone put it in his influential treatise on the common law of the period, "a lawful warrant will at all events indemnify the officer, who executes the same ministerially." 4 William Blackstone, Commentaries on the Laws of England *286. A messenger executing a warrant could defend against a tort suit by proving that the search was successful. Thus, warrants diminished the power of the jury in a tort suit to control government officers. See Akhil Amar, Fourth Amendment First Principles, 107 Harv. L. Rev. 757 (1994); compare Ronald J. Allen & Ross M. Rosenberg, The Fourth Amendment and the Limits of Theory: Local Versus General Theoretical Knowledge, 72 St. John's L. Rev. 1149, 1169 (1998) (arguing that juries were not granted general power to determine reasonableness of searches).

5. *The civil origins of criminal procedure.* The great English cases that helped to define the central concepts for limiting government searches were not criminal but civil cases. What impact has this had on the criminal procedure doctrines that have emerged? Professor William Stuntz offers the following thesis:

> The most famous and important search and seizure cases of the eighteenth, nineteenth, and twentieth centuries involve government officials rummaging through private papers, subpoenaing private documents, or eavesdropping on telephone conversations. . . . The results of this history can be seen today both in what the law regulates and in what it leaves alone. If the law of search and seizure now seems obsessed with

> evaluating the privacy interest in jacket pockets or paper bags, that is a consequence of the strong tradition of using Fourth and Fifth Amendment law as a shield against government information-gathering — a tradition that has more to do with protecting free speech than with regulating the police. [I]f the law all but ignores police violence outside of interrogation rooms, if it pays more attention to what police officers can see than to what they can do, that too is a consequence of the Fourth and Fifth Amendments' odd history. [That history deals] with the substantive law of crimes, with what activities the government should and should not be able to punish.

Stuntz, The Substantive Origins of Criminal Procedure, 105 Yale L.J. 393 (1995).

6. *Recent appearance of police departments.* The creators of the Fourth Amendment and the earliest analogs in state constitutions did not anticipate possible abuses by professional police officers, because police departments did not exist at the time. Most law enforcement was carried out by amateurs: citizens who volunteered (or who grudgingly took their turn) as constable or night watchman. There were local sheriffs, but they had no professional staff. Police departments as we think of them did not appear, even in the largest American cities, until late in the nineteenth century. See Lawrence M. Friedman, Crime and Punishment in American History 27-30 (1993); Carol Steiker, Second Thoughts About First Principles, 107 Harv. L. Rev. 820, 830-838 (1994). Does this major change in circumstance make history less relevant for interpreting the Fourth Amendment than it is for other constitutional language? See Anthony Amsterdam, Perspectives on the Fourth Amendment, 58 Minn. L. Rev. 349 (1974) (treating history as unhelpful).

2. *American Limits on General Warrants and Other Searches*

In June 1776, just before the American colonies declared their independence, Virginia adopted a Declaration of Rights that included this provision:

> That general warrants, whereby any officer or messenger may be commanded to search suspected places without evidence of a fact committed, or to seize any person or persons not named, or whose offense is not particularly described and supported by evidence, are grievous and oppressive, and ought not to be granted.

The Maryland constitution expanded the concern from general warrants to "all warrants." The Pennsylvania Declaration of Rights in the Constitution of 1776 explained the connection between the limits on searches and warrants, and the basic rights of the people:

> That the people have a right to hold themselves, their houses, papers, and possessions free from search and seizure, and therefore warrants without oaths or affirmations first made, affording a sufficient foundation for them, and whereby any officer or messenger may be commanded or required to search suspected places, or to seize any person [or his] property, not particularly described, are contrary to that right, and ought not to be granted.

When the debate shifted from state constitutions to the new proposed federal constitution, many of the ratifying conventions in the states stipulated that they were approving the proposed federal constitution under the assumption that individual rights were implicit within the document and that an express Bill of Rights would soon be added. The First Congress elected under the new constitution immediately took up the task of drafting constitutional amendments dealing with basic liberties. James Madison presented to the House of Representatives a package of amendments, including one that addressed the problem of improper warrants:

> The rights of the people to be secured in their persons, their houses, their papers, and their other property, from all unreasonable searches and seizures, shall not be violated by warrants issued without probable cause, supported by oath or affirmation, or not particularly describing the places to be searched, or the persons or things to be seized.

After a House committee made some slight changes in language, the amendment came to the full House for a vote. At this point, some remarkable things happened. Rep. Egbert Benson of New York suggested that the provision was "good as far as it went" but was not sufficient. He proposed inserting the phrase "and no warrant shall issue" after the word "violated," so as to create two clauses, one addressing unreasonable searches and seizures generally and the other focused on warrants. Voting records of the convention showed that the House voted down Benson's proposed change "by a considerable majority." After the vote, the House appointed a committee to collect and summarize the various amendments it had approved over several days of debate. This so-called Committee of Three (which included Benson) placed on its list the search and seizure provision—as Benson had proposed amending it! The Senate and House both approved the language in this form, and the state conventions also ratified the text as follows:

> The right of the people to be secure in their persons, houses, papers, and effects, against unreasonable searches and seizures, shall not be violated, and no Warrants shall issue, but upon probable cause, supported by oath or affirmation, and particularly describing the place to be searched, and the persons or things to be seized.

See Nelson Lasson, The History and Development of the Fourth Amendment to the United States Constitution 100-103 (1937); Edward Dumbauld, The Bill of Rights and What It Means Today 35-42 (1957).

3. *The Language of the Fourth Amendment and Its Analogs*

Courts did not treat the Fourth Amendment as a limit on the power of *state* governments (where most crimes are tried) until Wolf v. Colorado, 338 U.S. 25 (1949). Although the federal Bill of Rights originally applied only to the federal government, the Fourteenth Amendment (passed after the Civil War) declared that "no state shall deprive any person of . . . liberty without due process of law." During the 1940s and 1950s, the Supreme Court decided a series of cases, declaring that many of the rights guaranteed in the federal Bill of Rights were such a fundamental part of "due process" that they should apply to the states. The due process clause selectively "incorporated" these rights against state governments. See George C. Thomas, III, When Constitutional Worlds Collide: Resurrecting the Framers' Bill of Rights and Criminal Procedure, 100 Mich. L. Rev. 145 (2001). Before and after *Wolf*, however, states had their own constitutional limitations on state government action, parallel to the Fourth Amendment.

Today all states have a constitutional provision limiting the power of the government to conduct searches and seizures. About half of the states have a provision that tracks the language of the Fourth Amendment, some with only minor modifications. Other states have variations on the Fourth Amendment language that include additional procedural requirements. A typical requirement appears in article II, section 7 of the Colorado constitution, which says that affidavits must be in writing and that the person or thing to be seized must be described "as near as may be." A few states take aim at the specific problem of general warrants. For example, article I, section 7 of the Tennessee constitution states that "general warrants, whereby an officer may be commanded to search suspected places, without evidence of the fact committed, or to seize any person or persons not named, whose offenses are not particularly described and supported by evidence, are dangerous to liberty and ought not to be granted."

Other states emphasize the range of protected privacy rights of individuals. Article I, section 5 of the Louisiana constitution guarantees that the "person, property, communications, houses, papers, and effects" of every person shall be secure against "invasions of privacy." Arizona and Washington State frame the protection even more generally: "No person shall be disturbed in his private affairs, or his home invaded, without authority of law." The constitutions of about ten states contain express protections for individual "privacy" rights. A number of these state constitutional provisions grew out of recent constitutional conventions, some as recent as the 1990s. See Robert Williams, Are State Constitutional Conventions a Thing of The Past? The Increasing Role of the Constitutional Commission in State Constitutional Change, 1 Hofstra L. & Pol'y Symp. 1 (1996).

The varying language of these Fourth Amendment analogs creates room for differing interpretations of the scope of the rights they protect. But variation in language is not determinative: Some states with provisions identical to the Fourth Amendment have interpreted their language differently from one another and differently from federal law; other states with substantially different language in their constitutions have interpreted it in the same way that the U.S. Supreme Court interprets the Fourth Amendment.

In light of the Fourth Amendment and these state provisions, consider three basic issues that underlie many difficult questions regarding the law of search and seizure:

- *The interaction between probable cause and reasonableness.* Do the Fourth Amendment and its state constitutional analogs provide one standard to determine the validity of government searches and seizures? Is that standard probable cause or reasonableness? Are searches without probable cause presumptively (or conclusively) unreasonable? If reasonableness is not defined by reference to probable cause, how should it be defined?
- *The preference for warrants.* Do you think the Fourth Amendment or its state analogs were meant to require that all (or most) searches and seizures take place only after the issuance of a warrant? Or are warrants merely a mechanism for obtaining prior review of the "reasonableness" of searches and seizures, but otherwise not preferred? In other words, how strong is the presumption for warrants?
- *The nature of warrants.* For searches based on warrants, what limits should be placed on the issuance, content, or effect of warrants? Can warrants be issued

for more than one person or place? Do warrants need to specify the crime suspected or the nature of the evidence to be sought? Should time limits be placed on the execution of warrants?

What information, principles, or logic should interpreters use to answer these questions? Should the intent of the framers of each provision matter? Can definitions change over time or in different contexts? The remainder of this chapter explores these questions.

B. PROBABLE CAUSE

The two most important standards in modern criminal procedure for justifying stops, searches, and seizures are reasonable suspicion (examined in Chapter 2) and probable cause. Probable cause is the central standard of traditional search and seizure law, and it continues to govern a large portion of full-fledged searches and seizures, including those based on warrants.

1. *Defining Probable Cause*

Probable cause is constantly applied but only rarely defined. Perhaps this is because the assessment of probable cause is an inherently fact-laden, case-specific sort of judgment. While some situations arise frequently enough for standards to develop (for example, how information from an unnamed informant should be assessed to determine probable cause), general principles are difficult to deduce.

A close analysis of case law and a handful of statutes suggest that general definitions of probable cause do exist and that there is some interesting variation among those definitions. The most common definition emerges from language used by the Supreme Court in Brinegar v. United States, 338 U.S. 160, 175-176 (1949), reprinted below. Four elements, not all of which are present in every definition, tend to capture the variation in definitions of probable cause.

Reasonable to whom. Most jurisdictions focus on the assessment that a "reasonably prudent" or "cautious" person would make in deciding whether probable cause exists. Some jurisdictions, however, focus on the information that a *police officer* knows. Would officers make the same connections and assessment as a citizen without law enforcement experience or training? Kentucky requires the assessment of probable cause to be reasonable to the magistrate. Would experienced magistrates make the same assessments as police?

Strength of inference. Several formulations define the required strength of the link between the facts offered and the conclusion that criminal activity has occurred. One common formulation says the magistrate must determine whether the facts suggest a "probability of criminal activity." Another says the magistrate must determine whether the facts are sufficient "to believe an offense has been committed." Yet another standard requires that the investigator "believe or consciously entertain a strong suspicion that the person is guilty." A few jurisdictions require merely that there be a "substantial basis for concluding that the articles mentioned are probably present" at the place to be searched.

Can these formulations be translated into probabilities of criminal activity? For example, do some of them mean less than 50 percent, while others mean a 50-50 chance, and still others mean more likely than not? Alone among the states, Oregon answers this question by statute. Oregon Rev. Stat. §131.005(11) states that probable cause "means that there is a substantial objective basis for believing that more likely than not an offense has been committed and a person to be arrested has committed it."

Comparison to other standards. Some jurisdictions not only define the probable cause standard but also suggest its limits through comparison with other procedural standards. For example, several states say that probable cause is "more than mere suspicion or possibility but less than certainty." Some states note that the determination of probable cause requires less confidence that a crime has occurred than is required for guilt (that is, judgment beyond a reasonable doubt). As we saw in Chapter 2, the "reasonable suspicion" demands less of a showing by police than probable cause.

Quality of information. Some jurisdictions enhance their general definition of probable cause by requiring that the assessment be based on evidence that is reliable, trustworthy, or credible. The following chart excerpts typical language from the case law, constitutional provisions, and statutes in selected states.

State	*Information to Be Considered*	*Quality of Information*	*Perspective*	*Nature of Belief*	*Degree of Certainty*
Arizona	Facts and circumstances,	based on trustworthy information [such that a]	person of reasonable caution [would believe that]	items are related to criminal activity and likely to be found at the place described.	The showing is one of criminal activity, not the rigorous standard required for admissibility of evidence at trial.
California	A particularized suspicion or facts [sufficient]	to entertain a strong suspicion [such that a]	person of ordinary caution [would find that the]	object of the search is in the particular place to be searched.	The government need not demonstrate certainty.
Colorado	Sufficient facts [that a]		person of reasonable caution [would conclude that]	contraband or evidence of criminal activity is located at the place to be searched.	This judgment is one of reasonableness, not pure mathematical probability.
Connecticut	All information set forth in affidavit [such that the]	totality of the circumstances [could lead a]	magistrate [to conclude that]	contraband or evidence will be found in a particular place [with a]	fair probability.
South Dakota	The existence of facts and circumstances within the knowledge of the magistrate [such that a]		reasonable prudent man [would conclude that]	an offense has been or is being committed and the property exists at the place designated [to a]	probability.

Problem 3-1. Applying Different Probable Cause Standards

Consider the following two searches in light of the California and Connecticut standards.

Case 1: One afternoon, Captain Lee and Sergeant Hurter were on patrol in what they described as a "high crime area." Lee, Hurter, and four other officers in two other patrol cars stopped at 1225 6th Alley East, where five or six persons were gathered in front of a shot house (a private residence where illegal whiskey is sold by the shot). Officers had executed a search warrant at this residence two to three weeks earlier. As a result of that search, the owner of the residence had been arrested and charged with the illegal sale of alcohol. Officers during that earlier search found a small quantity of illegal drugs on the front porch, presumably left by people sitting there who dispersed when the police arrived at the house.

The house was located in a mostly African American neighborhood, and the people gathered in front of the house were African American men. Between the porch of the house and the roadway there was a small yard, and there was no sidewalk. Some of the men, including Eddie Tucker, were standing in the yard abutting the roadway, and some were in the roadway leaning on a parked car. There had been no calls or complaints to the police that day concerning any illegal activity at the house or pertaining to any of the people gathered in front of the house. Neither Lee nor Hurter knew Tucker at that point.

The officers testified that they were not aware of anything illegal occurring among the men, but as Lee exited the car, he noticed that Tucker (who was about three feet away from him) had a large bulge in one of his front pants pockets. For safety reasons, Lee asked Tucker what was in his pocket and told him to take whatever it was out so that it could be seen. Tucker took from his pocket a black 35mm film canister with its lid closed. Both officers knew at this point that the object was a film canister and was not a weapon.

Lee then directed his attention to another of the persons present, and Hurter asked Tucker what was in the canister. In response, Tucker put the canister behind his back. Sergeant Hurter then asked to see the canister. Tucker handed the canister to Hurter, who opened it and found five $10 bags of marijuana packaged in cellophane. Did Officer Hurter have probable cause to search the canister? Compare Ex parte Tucker, 667 So. 2d 1339 (Ala. 1995).

Case 2: At 3:20 A.M. on June 10, the Dothan Police Department received a call saying that shots had been fired at the Johnson Homes apartment complex. Officer Jerry Watkins responded to the call. As Watkins arrived, he saw four people standing outside behind the apartments, arguing. The people yelled for Officer Watkins to stop, but when he did, one of the people standing in the group started running. A second man in the group told Watkins that the person who ran away was Kenneth Moffitt, and that Moffitt "had a gun." Watkins followed Moffitt because he believed that he "would probably be pretty dangerous if he was out there shooting." Moffitt ran into the back door of an apartment, and Watkins followed a few seconds later. Watkins searched the kitchen and the living room, and noticed some cocaine on a television, but Moffitt was not in either of those rooms. Officer Watkins then went into the bedroom across the hall, where a small child was sitting on a bed pointing under the bed. Watkins found Moffitt on the floor under the bed. Did Officer

Watkins have probable cause to enter the apartment? Compare Ex parte Moffitt, ___ So. 2d ___, 2002 WL 254129 (Ala., Feb. 22, 2002).

■ VIRGIL BRINEGAR v. UNITED STATES

338 U.S. 160 (1949)

RUTLEDGE, J.

. . . At about six o'clock on the evening of March 3, 1947, Malsed, an investigator of the Alcohol Tax Unit, and Creehan, a special investigator, were parked in a car beside a highway near the Quapaw Bridge in northeastern Oklahoma. The point was about five miles west of the Missouri-Oklahoma line. Brinegar drove past headed west in his Ford coupe. Malsed had arrested him about five months earlier for illegally transporting liquor; had seen him loading liquor into a car or truck in Joplin, Missouri, on at least two occasions during the preceding six months; and knew him to have a reputation for hauling liquor. As Brinegar passed, Malsed recognized both him and the Ford. He told Creehan, who was driving the officers' car, that Brinegar was the driver of the passing car. Both agents later testified that the car, but not especially its rear end, appeared to be "heavily loaded" and "weighted down with something." Brinegar increased his speed as he passed the officers. They gave chase. After pursuing him for about a mile at top speed, they gained on him as his car skidded on a curve, sounded their siren, overtook him, and crowded his car to the side of the road by pulling across in front of it. The highway was one leading from Joplin, Missouri, toward Vinita, Oklahoma, Brinegar's home. [The officers searched the car and found 13 cases of liquor. Brinegar was charged with importing intoxicating liquor into Oklahoma from Missouri in violation of the federal statute that forbids such importation contrary to the laws of any state. The trial judge denied the motion to suppress. Even though the facts described above did not constitute probable cause, the judge believed that certain statements Brinegar made after he was stopped gave the officers probable cause to search].

The crucial question is whether there was probable cause for Brinegar's arrest, in the light of prior adjudications on this problem, more particularly Carroll v. United States, 267 U.S. 132 (1925), which on its face most closely approximates the situation presented here. The *Carroll* [court ruled] that the facts presented amounted to probable cause for the search of the automobile there involved.

In the *Carroll* case three federal prohibition agents and a state officer stopped and searched the defendants' car on a highway leading from Detroit to Grand Rapids, Michigan, and seized a quantity of liquor discovered in the search. About three months before the search, the two defendants and another man called on two of the agents at an apartment in Grand Rapids and, unaware that they were dealing with federal agents, agreed to sell one of the agents three cases of liquor. Both agents noticed the Oldsmobile roadster in which the three men came to the apartment and its license number. Presumably because the official capacity of the proposed purchaser was suspected by the defendants, the liquor was never delivered.

About a week later the same two agents, while patrolling the road between Grand Rapids and Detroit on the lookout for violations of the National Prohibition Act, were passed by the defendants, who were proceeding in a direction from Grand Rapids toward Detroit in the same Oldsmobile roadster. The agents followed the defendants for some distance but lost trace of them. Still later, on the occasion of the search, while the officers were patrolling the same highway, they met and passed the defendants, who were in the same roadster, going in a direction from Detroit toward Grand Rapids. Recognizing the defendants, the agents turned around, pursued them, stopped them about sixteen miles outside Grand Rapids, searched their car and seized the liquor it carried.

This Court ruled that the information held by the agents, together with the judicially noticed fact that Detroit was "one of the most active centers for introducing illegally into this country spirituous liquors for distribution into the interior," constituted probable cause for the search.

Obviously the basic facts held to constitute probable cause in the *Carroll* case were very similar to the basic facts here. . . . In each instance the officers were patrolling the highway in the discharge of their duty. And in each before stopping the car or starting to pursue it they recognized both the driver and the car, from recent personal contact and observation, as having been lately engaged in illicit liquor dealings. Finally, each driver was proceeding in his identified car in a direction from a known source of liquor supply toward a probable illegal market, under circumstances indicating no other probable purpose than to carry on his illegal adventure.

[There were also variations in details of the proof in the two cases.] In *Carroll* the agent's knowledge of the primary and ultimate fact that the accused were engaged in liquor running was derived from the defendants' offer to sell liquor to the agents some three months prior to the search, while here that knowledge was derived largely from Malsed's personal observation, reinforced by hearsay; the officers when they bargained for the liquor in *Carroll* saw the number of the defendants' car, whereas no such fact is shown in this record; and in *Carroll* the Court took judicial notice that Detroit was on the international boundary and an active center for illegal importation of spirituous liquors for distribution into the interior, while in this case the facts that Joplin, Missouri, was a ready source of supply for liquor and Oklahoma a place of likely illegal market were known to the agent Malsed from his personal observation and experience as well as from facts of common knowledge.

Treating first the two latter and less important matters, in view of the positive and undisputed evidence concerning Malsed's identification of Brinegar's Ford, we think no significance whatever attaches, for purposes of distinguishing the cases, to the fact that in the *Carroll* case the officers saw and recalled the license number of the offending car while this record discloses no like recollection. Likewise it is impossible to distinguish the *Carroll* case with reference to the proof relating to the source of supply, the place of probable destination and illegal market, and consequently the probability that the known liquor operators were using the connecting highway for the purposes of their unlawful business.

There were of course some legal as well as some factual differences in the two situations. Under the statute in review in *Carroll* the whole nation was legally dry. Not only the manufacture, but the importation, transportation and sale of intoxicating liquors were prohibited throughout the country. Under the statute now in question only the importation of such liquors contrary to the law of the state into which they are brought and in which they were seized is forbidden. . . .

In this case, the record shows that Brinegar had used Joplin, Missouri, to Malsed's personal knowledge derived from direct observation, not merely from hearsay as seems to be suggested, as a source of supply on other occasions within the preceding six months. It also discloses that Brinegar's home was in Vinita, Oklahoma, and that

Brinegar when apprehended was traveling in a direction leading from Joplin to Vinita, at a point about four or five miles west of the Missouri-Oklahoma line. Joplin, like Detroit in the *Carroll* case, was a ready source of supply. But unlike Detroit it was not an illegal source. So far as appears, Brinegar's purchases there were entirely legal. And so, we may assume for present purposes, was his transportation of the liquor in Missouri, until he reached and crossed the state line into Oklahoma.

This difference, however, is insubstantial. For the important thing here is not whether Joplin was an illegal source of a supply; it is rather that Joplin was a ready, convenient and probable one for persons disposed to violate the Oklahoma and federal statutes. That fact was demonstrated fully, not only by the geographic facts, but by Malsed's direct and undisputed testimony of his personal observation of Brinegar's use of liquor dispensing establishments in Joplin for procuring his whiskey. Such direct evidence was lacking in *Carroll* as to Detroit, and for that reason the Court resorted to judicial notice of the commonly known facts to supply that deficiency. Malsed's direct testimony, based on his personal observation, dispensed with that necessity in this case.

The situation relating to the probable place of market, as bearing on the probability of unlawful importation, is somewhat different. Broadly on the facts this may well have been taken to be the State of Oklahoma as a whole or its populous northeastern region. From the facts of record we know, as the agents knew, that Oklahoma was a "dry" state. At the time of the search, its law forbade the importation of intoxicating liquors from other states. . . . This fact, taken in connection with the known "wet" status of Missouri and the location of Joplin close to the Oklahoma line, affords a very natural situation for persons inclined to violate the Oklahoma and federal statutes to ply their trade. The proof therefore concerning the source of supply, the place of probable destination and illegal market, and hence the probability that Brinegar was using the highway for the forbidden transportation, was certainly no less strong than the showing in these respects in the *Carroll* case.

Finally, as for the most important potential distinction, namely, that concerning the primary and ultimate fact that the petitioner was engaging in liquor running, Malsed's personal observation of Brinegar's recent activities established that he was so engaged quite as effectively as did the agent's prior bargaining with the defendants in the *Carroll* case. He saw Brinegar loading liquor, in larger quantities than would be normal for personal consumption, into a car or a truck in Joplin on other occasions during the six months prior to the search. He saw the car Brinegar was using in this case in use by him at least once in Joplin within that period and followed it. And several months prior to the search he had arrested Brinegar for unlawful transportation of liquor and this arrest had resulted in an indictment which was pending at the time of this trial. . . .

Guilt in a criminal case must be proved beyond a reasonable doubt and by evidence confined to that which long experience in the common-law tradition, to some extent embodied in the Constitution, has crystallized into rules of evidence consistent with that standard. These rules are historically grounded rights of our system, developed to safeguard men from dubious and unjust convictions, with resulting forfeitures of life, liberty and property. . . .

In dealing with probable cause, however, as the very name implies, we deal with probabilities. These are not technical; they are the factual and practical considerations of everyday life on which reasonable and prudent men, not legal technicians, act. The standard of proof is accordingly correlative to what must be proved.

The substance of all the definitions of probable cause is a reasonable ground for belief of guilt. And this means less than evidence which would justify condemnation or conviction. [It] has come to mean more than bare suspicion: Probable cause exists where the facts and circumstances within [the officers'] knowledge and of which they had reasonably trustworthy information [are] sufficient in themselves to warrant a man of reasonable caution in the belief that an offense has been or is being committed.

These long-prevailing standards seek to safeguard citizens from rash and unreasonable interferences with privacy and from unfounded charges of crime. They also seek to give fair leeway for enforcing the law in the community's protection. Because many situations which confront officers in the course of executing their duties are more or less ambiguous, room must be allowed for some mistakes on their part. But the mistakes must be those of reasonable men, acting on facts leading sensibly to their conclusions of probability. The rule of probable cause is a practical, nontechnical conception affording the best compromise that has been found for accommodating these often opposing interests. Requiring more would unduly hamper law enforcement. To allow less would be to leave law-abiding citizens at the mercy of the officers' whim or caprice.

The troublesome line posed by the facts in the *Carroll* case and this case is one between mere suspicion and probable cause. That line necessarily must be drawn by an act of judgment formed in the light of the particular situation and with account taken of all the circumstances. No problem of searching the home or any other place of privacy was presented either in *Carroll* or here. Both cases involve freedom to use public highways in swiftly moving vehicles for dealing in contraband, and to be unmolested by investigation and search in those movements. In such a case the citizen who has given no good cause for believing he is engaged in that sort of activity is entitled to proceed on his way without interference. But one who recently and repeatedly has given substantial ground for believing that he is engaging in the forbidden transportation in the area of his usual operations has no such immunity, if the officer who intercepts him in that region knows that fact at the time he makes the interception and the circumstances under which it is made are not such as to indicate the suspect going about legitimate affairs.

This does not mean, as seems to be assumed, that every traveler along the public highways may be stopped and searched at the officers' whim, caprice or mere suspicion. The question presented in the *Carroll* case lay on the border between suspicion and probable cause. But the Court carefully considered that problem and resolved it by concluding that the facts within the officers' knowledge when they intercepted the *Carroll* defendants amounted to more than mere suspicion and constituted probable cause for their action. We cannot say this conclusion was wrong, or was so lacking in reason and consistency with the Fourth Amendment's purposes that it should now be overridden. Nor, as we have said, can we find in the present facts any substantial basis for distinguishing this case from the *Carroll* case. Accordingly the judgment is affirmed.

Notes

1. *Applying different standards?* Which of the cases described in Problem 3-1 offers a stronger basis — in other words, a stronger argument for probable cause — for

a search? Does the relative strength of the cases depend on the standard applied to them, or are all the standards stronger for one of the cases? Consider the Connecticut standard. Can you add (or subtract) a fact that would make a weaker case for probable cause? Would you change different facts to make the case for finding probable cause stronger or weaker under the California standard?

2. *Probable cause and probabilities.* Does probable cause translate into a level of certainty the same as the preponderance of the evidence standard at trial? Courts in all jurisdictions have long insisted that probable cause is something less than "beyond a reasonable doubt" and something more than "mere suspicion," but they have shied away from equating it with the preponderance standard. See Ronald Bacigal, The Fourth Amendment in Flux: The Rise and Fall of Probable Cause, 1979 U. Ill. L.F. 763; Illinois v. Gates, 462 U.S. 213 (1983) (probable cause requires "only the probability, and not a prima facie showing of criminal activity"). In a survey of more than 150 federal judges, about one-third believed that "probable cause" required 50 percent certainty, with the next largest groups of judges calling for 40 percent and 30 percent certainty. See C. M. A. McCauliff, Burdens of Proof: Degrees of Belief, Quanta of Evidence, or Constitutional Guarantees? 35 Vand. L. Rev. 1293 (1982). Does this mean that the judges would not sustain the validity of a search of a house when the police know that one of three possible locations contains evidence of a serious crime? See Joseph Grano, Probable Cause and Common Sense: A Reply to the Critics of *Illinois v. Gates,* 17 U. Mich. J.L. Ref. 465 (1984).

3. *Police expertise in assessing probable cause.* Courts often recognize that officers will rely on their training and experience in assessing probable cause. See Ornelas v. United States, 517 U.S. 690 (1996) ("a reviewing court should take care both to review findings of historical fact only for clear error and to give due weight to inferences drawn from those facts by resident judges and local law enforcement officers. [A] police officer may draw inferences based on his own experience in deciding whether probable cause exists. To a layman the sort of loose panel below the back seat arm rest in the automobile involved in this case may suggest only wear and tear, but to Officer Luedke, who had searched roughly 2,000 cars for narcotics, it suggested that drugs may be secreted inside the panel"). As a trial judge in a suppression hearing, would you attribute the same level of expertise to all officers or to those within a particular unit of the police department (such as the narcotics squad)? Or would you insist on some particularized showing of experience from each police officer trying to establish probable cause?

What many jurisdictions refer to as the "fellow officer" rule allows officers in one department to rely on determinations made by other police departments that suspects should be detained, arrested, or searched. The validity of the search is tested by determining whether the initial police department in fact had grounds for the search or arrest.

4. *Actual knowledge of officer.* Does one assess probable cause based on what the officer(s) on the scene actually relied on to justify the search or on facts that were available to the officer, whether or not she relied on them? Courts have not entirely agreed on this question, but the existence of probable cause usually depends on the facts available to the officer in the field, not just on facts the officer actually relied on to justify a search or seizure. But see Wilson v. State, 874 P.2d 215 (Wyo. 1994) (considering only facts relied on by officer). Recall the discussion in Chapter 2 of "pretextual" stops, and the choice discussed there between objective and subjective standards in criminal procedure. If courts approve of any search

that *could* have been justified, are they creating too great a temptation for police perjury?

Some jurisdictions test probable cause based on the collective information the police have, even if no individual officer holds all of that information. See Woodward v. State, 668 S.W.2d 337 (Tex. Crim. App. 1984); In re M. E. B., 638 A.2d 1123 (D.C. 1993). Does this doctrine give the police too much opportunity for *post hoc* rationalization of the individual officer's decision to conduct a search? What, if anything, is wrong with justifying a search after the fact, based on events that truly did occur?

2. *Sources of Information to Support Probable Cause*

The information needed to show probable cause comes from sources as varied as victims, other witnesses, anonymous sources, confidential informants, and police officers themselves. In the abstract, which of these sources would you expect to be most reliable? Can we judge reliability in the abstract? Jurisdictions have reached different conclusions, and have used different standards, in answering these questions. This section considers how courts assess information from different sources, with particular attention to confidential informants and anonymous sources.

a. Confidential Informants

Much as the law of evidence shows a mistrust of hearsay, so the law of probable cause shows a mistrust of informants, who provide information to the police but are often not available to be questioned further when the time comes to assess probable cause. The U.S. Supreme Court has developed a specialized set of rules for judging the reliability of information from informants. The following two cases trace the impact of a major change in the Supreme Court's approach to such questions.

■ STATE v. TIMOTHY BARTON

594 A.2d 917 (Conn. 1991)

PETERS, J.

The sole issue in this appeal is whether . . . article first, §7, of the Connecticut constitution permits a court to determine the existence of probable cause on the basis of the "totality of the circumstances" when it reviews a search warrant application based on information provided to the police by a confidential informant. The state charged the defendant, Timothy Barton, with possession of over a kilogram of marihuana with intent to sell and with possession of marihuana . . . after police, acting under the authority of a warrant, had searched his home and had seized more than fifty pounds of marihuana there. The defendant moved to suppress the seized evidence, and the trial court granted the defendant's motion on the ground that the affidavit accompanying the search warrant application failed to state the informant's "basis of knowledge." The charges were subsequently dismissed with prejudice. [W]e reverse.

[O]fficers of the Winsted police department, acting on the authority of a search and seizure warrant obtained that day on the basis of information provided by a confidential informant, searched the defendant's apartment. . . . In the course of their search, the police found some fifty-two pounds of marihuana wrapped in clear plastic bags and kept in larger garbage bags in a bedroom. When the defendant returned home after midnight, the police arrested him.

[At the hearing on the defendant's motion to suppress this evidence, the trial court] applied the two-pronged analysis mandated by this court's decision in State v. Kimbro, 496 A.2d 498 (Conn. 1985), which requires a magistrate, in determining whether probable cause exists for a search or seizure, to evaluate both the "basis of knowledge" and the "veracity" or "reliability" of an informant upon whose information the police have relied. Spinelli v. United States, 393 U.S. 410 (1969); Aguilar v. Texas, 378 U.S. 108 (1964). In the circumstances of this case, [the trial court] concluded that the affidavit in support of the search warrant did not adequately set forth the unnamed informant's basis of knowledge and therefore failed to establish probable cause. . . .

In the present appeal, the state urges us to overrule our holding in State v. Kimbro, and to adopt the "totality of the circumstances" standard for determining probable cause used in the federal courts pursuant to the decision of the United States Supreme Court in Illinois v. Gates, 462 U.S. 213 (1983). . . . We agree with the state that application of the standards mandated by *Kimbro* has resulted at times in unduly technical readings of warrant affidavits, and we reject such an inappropriate methodology. . . .

In Illinois v. Gates, the United States Supreme Court rejected the "complex superstructure of evidentiary and analytical rules" that had evolved from its earlier decisions in Aguilar v. Texas and Spinelli v. United States. [T]he "two-pronged" *Aguilar-Spinelli* test provides a method for evaluating the existence of probable cause consistent with the requirements of the fourth amendment when a search warrant affidavit is based upon information supplied to the police by a confidential informant. The issuing judge must be informed of (1) some of the underlying circumstances relied on by the informant in concluding that the facts are as he claims they are, and (2) some of the underlying circumstances from which the officer seeking the warrant concluded (a) that the informant, whose identity need not be disclosed, was credible, or (b) that the information was reliable. When the information supplied by the informant fails to satisfy the *Aguilar-Spinelli* test, probable cause may still be found if the warrant application affidavit sets forth other circumstances — typically independent police corroboration of certain details provided by the informant — that bolster the deficiencies.

The *Gates* court identified two principal flaws in the *Aguilar-Spinelli* test. First, because courts and commentators had generally regarded the two prongs of the test to be entirely independent of each other, courts had struggled to formulate rules regarding what types of information and what types of corroboration might satisfy each of the prongs. Specifically, some courts had concluded that independent police investigation might corroborate the "reliability" of the information, but could never satisfy the "basis of knowledge" prong of the test, while ample "self-verifying details" might establish that the informant had personal knowledge of the alleged activity and thus could satisfy the "basis of knowledge" prong, but could never compensate for a deficiency in the "veracity" or "reliability" prong. The "elaborate set of legal rules" that had resulted from this emphasis on the independent character of the two prongs had led courts, in many cases, to dissect warrant applications in an excessively technical manner, "with undue attention being focused on isolated issues that [could not] sensibly be divorced from the other facts presented to the magistrate." Such a result was inconsistent with the nature of a probable cause determination, which, as the *Gates* court noted, involves a "practical, nontechnical conception."

The second principal flaw in the application of the *Aguilar-Spinelli* test, according to the *Gates* court, was that the test had caused reviewing courts, both at suppression hearings and at appellate levels, to test the sufficiency of warrant affidavits by de novo review. Such de novo review, in the view of the *Gates* majority, was inconsistent with the constitution's "strong preference for searches conducted pursuant to a warrant." A reviewing court should rather determine whether the magistrate issuing the warrant had a "substantial basis" for concluding that a search would uncover evidence of criminal activity.

In rejecting the complex structure of rules that had evolved from *Aguilar* and *Spinelli,* however, the *Gates* court did not reject out of hand the underlying concerns that had originally been expressed in *Aguilar.* In that case, the United States Supreme Court invalidated a search warrant supported by an affidavit that stated only that the "[a]ffiants have received reliable information from a credible person," without stating any of the underlying circumstances that would support a finding of probable cause. The *Aguilar* court ruled that such a conclusory affidavit failed to state a factual basis on which a neutral and detached magistrate could determine the existence of probable cause. In *Gates,* the court reaffirmed that the "veracity" or "reliability" and the "basis of knowledge" inquiries formulated in *Aguilar* remain "highly relevant" in the determination of probable cause and should be regarded as "closely intertwined issues that may usefully illuminate the commonsense, practical question" of the existence of probable cause to believe that contraband or evidence is located in a particular place. The *Gates* court abandoned only a "rigid compartmentalization" of the inquiries and denied that the court had ever intended them to be understood as "entirely separate and independent requirements to be rigidly exacted in every case."

In the place of the "compartmentalized" *Aguilar-Spinelli* test, the *Gates* court directed lower courts to apply a "totality of the circumstances" analysis more consistent with traditional assessments of probable cause. While still employing the analytical frame of reference established in *Aguilar,* a "totality of the circumstances" analysis permits a judge issuing a warrant greater freedom to assess "the relative weights of all the various indicia of reliability (and unreliability) attending an informant's tip." . . . The task of a subsequent court reviewing the magistrate's decision to issue a warrant is to determine whether the magistrate had a "substantial basis" for concluding that probable cause existed. The court's decision in *Gates* emphasized the necessity of a case-by-case analysis of probable cause based on all of the facts presented to the judge issuing the warrant, not merely on those capable of categorization as indicating the "veracity" or "basis of knowledge" of a particular informant.

[We turn now to a reconsideration of our 1985 decision in State v. Kimbro.] *Kimbro* did not rely upon historical analysis to determine the standard by which probable cause should be measured. We relied, rather, upon our determination that the *Aguilar-Spinelli* test, "with its two prongs of 'veracity' or 'reliability' and 'basis of knowledge,' offers a practical and independent test under our constitution that predictably guides the conduct of all concerned, including magistrates and law enforcement officials, in the determination of probable cause." We regarded the *Gates* "totality of the circumstances" analysis as an "amorphous standard" that inadequately safeguarded the rights of individuals to be free from unjustified intrusions. Upon careful review of that determination, we agree with the conclusion of the United States Supreme Court in *Gates* that the two prongs of the *Aguilar-Spinelli* test are highly relevant evidentiary questions that a magistrate issuing the warrant must consider in deciding whether probable cause for a search or seizure exists, but that they are not wholly independent and dispositive constitutional tests for which de novo review exists at a suppression hearing.

In reaching our present conclusion we return to first principles. Article first, §7, of our constitution . . . safeguards the privacy, the personal security, and the property of the individual against unjustified intrusions by agents of the government. One of the principal means by which the warrant requirement protects the privacy and property of the individual is by the interposition of a neutral and detached magistrate who must judge independently the sufficiency of an affidavit supporting an application for a search warrant. Whether applying the fourth amendment or article first, §7, of our own constitution, we have frequently recognized that a magistrate issuing a warrant cannot form an independent opinion as to the existence of probable cause unless the affidavit supporting the warrant application sets forth some of the facts upon which the police have relied in concluding that a search is justified. . . .

When a police officer seeking a search warrant relies on hearsay information supplied by confidential informants rather than on personal knowledge and observations, certain additional facts are necessary to ensure that the magistrate's decision to issue the warrant is informed and independent. [The *Aguilar* decision began with the commonsensical premise] that confidential informants are themselves often "criminals, drug addicts, or even pathological liars" whose motives for providing information to the police may range from offers of immunity or sentence reduction, promises of money payments, or "such perverse motives as revenge or the hope of eliminating criminal competition." Because such an informant's reliance on rumors circulating on the street is not unlikely and the veracity of such an informant is questionable, a magistrate reviewing a search warrant application based on such an informant's word can best assess the probable reliability of the information if she or he is informed of some of the predicate facts that indicate how the informant gained his information and why the police officer believes that the information is reliable in order to decide, independently, whether the police officer's inferences from the informant's statements are reasonable.

In *Kimbro,* we expressed concern that the "fluid" totality of the circumstances analysis approved in the fourth amendment context of Illinois v. Gates would inadequately inform magistrates and law enforcement officials of their obligation to scrutinize the information gathered from confidential police informants with appropriate caution. In construing article first, §7, of our constitution to require continued application of the *Aguilar-Spinelli* test, we sought to make clear certain benchmarks to guide the discretion of our judges in reviewing ex parte applications for search and seizure warrants based on confidential informants' tips.

Nonetheless, over time, the case law applying the *Aguilar-Spinelli* test has come to be encrusted with an overlay of analytical rigidity that is inconsistent with the underlying proposition that it is the constitutional function of the magistrate issuing the warrant to exercise discretion in the determination of probable cause. That discretion must be controlled by constitutional principles and guided by the evidentiary standards developed in our prior cases, but it should not be so shackled by rigid analytical standards that it deprives the magistrate of the ability to draw reasonable inferences from the facts presented. To the extent that *Kimbro* stands for the proposition that the exercise of discretion by a magistrate is reviewable only according to fixed analytical standards, it is overruled.

Our adoption of a "totality of the circumstances" analysis does not mean, however, that a magistrate considering a search warrant application should automatically defer to the conclusion of the police that probable cause exists. Such deference would be an abdication of the magistrate's constitutional responsibility to exercise an independent and detached judgment to protect the rights of privacy and personal security of the people of Connecticut.

In essence, our adoption of a "totality of the circumstances" analysis of the probable cause requirement of article first, §7, of our constitution means simply this: When a search warrant affidavit is based on information provided to the police by confidential informants, the magistrate should examine the affidavit to determine whether it adequately describes both the factual basis of the informant's knowledge and the basis on which the police have determined that the information is reliable. If the warrant affidavit fails to state in specific terms how the informant gained his knowledge or why the police believe the information to be trustworthy, however, the magistrate can also consider all the circumstances set forth in the affidavit to determine whether, despite these deficiencies, other objective indicia of reliability reasonably establish that probable cause to search exists. In making this determination, the magistrate is entitled to draw reasonable inferences from the facts presented. When a magistrate has determined that the warrant affidavit presents sufficient objective indicia of reliability to justify a search and has issued a warrant, a court reviewing that warrant at a subsequent suppression hearing should defer to the reasonable inferences drawn by the magistrate. . . .

In adopting the *Gates* "totality of the circumstances" analysis, as we have here construed it, as the standard of analysis applicable to article first, §7, of our constitution, we do not intend to dilute the constitutional safeguards of the warrant requirement. This court has both the constitutional duty to construe article first, §7, in a way that adequately protects the rights of individuals in Connecticut and also the supervisory responsibility, as the overseer of the judiciary in Connecticut, to ensure that the standards adopted here require law enforcement officers to provide magistrates with adequate information on which to base their decisions in an ex parte context. . . .

We now consider the affidavit presented in this case in light of the proper constitutional standards. [The critical paragraph of the affidavit] provides: "That the affiants state on Sunday, August 7, 1988 Sgt. Gerald O. Peters received information from a confidential informant at police headquarters pertaining to Tim Barton who resides at 232 Perch Rock Trail, Winsted, Connecticut, first floor that Barton has in his apartment a large quantity of marijuana in plastic garbage bags, which are kept in a closet. That the informant also provided Sergeant Peters of [*sic*] a sample of the marijuana that is in the bags. A field test of the marijuana substance that was provided to Sgt. Peters was field tested and the test results was [*sic*] positive for cannibas [*sic*] substance. The informant further stated that Tim Barton operates a Texas registered vehicle and after being away for approximately one week Barton returned home on Saturday, August 6, 1988 and unloaded several large plastic bags in the evening hours. The informant further stated that shortly after that four to five people arrived at the Barton apartment and stayed a short while and then left with plastic garbage bags." . . .

Reviewing the allegations set forth in the third paragraph of the affidavit in this case, the Appellate Court concluded that the affidavit failed to establish probable cause because it was defective under the "basis of knowledge" prong of the *Aguilar-Spinelli* test mandated by *Kimbro.* The Appellate Court cited the following deficiencies: (1) the affidavit did not expressly indicate that the informant had ever been inside the defendant's apartment; (2) the details regarding the truck and the carrying in and out of garbage bags were "innocuous"; (3) the affidavit did not indicate that the informant had said that he had purchased the marihuana from the defendant, or that he had observed the defendant "constantly in possession" of marihuana in the apartment; and (4) the informant did not give a detailed description of the apartment but merely alleged that the garbage bags were in a closet. We agree that the affidavit does not expressly state that the informant had personal knowledge of the facts described. Legitimate law enforcement efforts, however, should not be unduly frustrated because a police officer, in the haste of a criminal investigation, fails to recite his information in particular formulaic phrases. Probable cause does not depend upon the incantation of certain magic words. Having reviewed the circumstances described by the informant, we conclude that the affidavit provided a substantial basis for the magistrate's inference that the informant was reporting events that he had personally observed.

[Details from the affidavit] support an inference that the informant was sufficiently acquainted with the defendant to have known of a week-long absence and to have been present to observe the defendant's activities upon his return. When considered together with the detail that the garbage bags were kept in a closet and with the fact that the informant provided the police with a marihuana sample purportedly from the same bags, these details support a reasonable, commonsense inference that the informant had personally observed the events he reported and had secured the marihuana sample directly from the defendant at his apartment. . . . Although the magistrate could have properly exercised his discretion to reject the warrant application or to require the affiants to supplement it or corroborate some of its details we conclude that the inference drawn by the magistrate that the informant had firsthand knowledge of the defendant's activities was not unreasonable.

[We also conclude] that the affidavit provided a substantial basis for the magistrate's inference that the informant's information was reliable. The first circumstance supporting an inference of "veracity" or "reliability" is the fact that the informant was not anonymous. . . . Because his identity was known to the police, the informant could expect adverse consequences if the information that he provided was erroneous. Those consequences might range from a loss of confidence or indulgence by the police to prosecution for the class A misdemeanor of falsely reporting an incident . . . had the information supplied proved to be a fabrication.

More significantly, however, the informant supplied the police with a sample of a substance that the police tested and confirmed to be marihuana. By entering the police station with the marihuana in his possession and by exhibiting the marihuana to the police, the informant rendered himself liable to arrest, conviction, and imprisonment. . . . Although the warrant application would have unquestionably been stronger if the affiants had bolstered the reliability of the informant by independently corroborating some of the details he reported we conclude that the affidavit sufficiently set forth some of the underlying circumstances from which the police could have concluded that the informant was credible or that his information was reliable.

As our discussion of this affidavit demonstrates, the determination of an informant's "veracity" or "reliability" and "basis of knowledge" remains highly relevant under the constitutional standard announced in this decision. . . . This is a marginal case; the magistrate could reasonably have demanded more information. We will not invalidate a warrant, however, merely because we might, in the first instance, have reasonably declined to draw the inferences that were necessary here. Having reviewed all the circumstances presented to the magistrate in this affidavit, we conclude that the affidavit provided a substantial basis for concluding that probable cause existed. We accordingly reverse the judgment of the Appellate Court [and] remand the case to the trial court for further proceedings.

GLASS, J., concurring in part, dissenting in part.

I concur in the result reached by the majority in this case because, unlike the majority, I conclude that the disputed warrant meets the established requirements of the time honored *Aguilar-Spinelli* test. Because I disagree with the majority's decision to scrap the *Aguilar-Spinelli* test by overruling State v. Kimbro . . . I write separately in dissent. . . .

Dressed today in Connecticut constitutional finery, the *Gates* approach relegates the principles pertinent to the "veracity" and "basis of knowledge" prongs of the *Aguilar-Spinelli* test to the status of "relevant considerations" among the amorphous "totality of the circumstances." The purported relevance of these "considerations," however, is belied by the majority's suggestion that despite "deficiencies" under both prongs of the *Aguilar-Spinelli* test, a warrant may yet derive sufficient sustenance from the "totality of the circumstances" to satisfy the mandates of our constitution. The majority thus appears to have strayed even further beyond the strictures of *Aguilar-Spinelli* than the *Gates* majority, which proposed that "a deficiency in one [of the prongs of the *Aguilar-Spinelli* test] may be compensated for . . . by a strong showing as to the other, or by some other indicia of reliability." Under the majority's evident reading of *Gates,* a warrant deficient under both prongs of the *Aguilar-Spinelli* test, nevertheless, complies with Connecticut constitutional requirements where the "totality of the circumstances" permit. [Magistrates and police officers,] unfettered by meaningful standards by which to discharge their respective functions in the warrant process, are now granted the unbridled play to accord weight to their subjective preferences in determining the "circumstances" whose "totality" permissibly adds up to probable cause. . . .

The *Aguilar-Spinelli* test, in my opinion, allows ample room for the application of common sense and the evaluation of the unique facts presented by particular cases. I do not, therefore, share the majority's desire to strip probable cause determinations of the "fixed, analytical standards" of *Aguilar-Spinelli* that have served to protect the free men and women of Connecticut from unreasonable government intrusion in a way that the standardless *Gates* approach, I submit, will never do. . . . In my view, the Connecticut constitution is not a document so fragile that a swift stroke of the federal pen suffices, as is allowed today, to erode the substantive protections found not six years ago to be afforded thereunder to the citizens of this state.

■ STATE v. RANDALL UTTERBACK

485 N.W.2d 760 (Neb. 1992)

PER CURIAM

[A] search warrant, to be valid, must be supported by an affidavit establishing probable cause [founded on articulable facts.] When a search warrant is obtained on the strength of an informant's information, the affidavit in support of the issuance of the search warrant must (1) set forth facts demonstrating the basis of the informant's knowledge of criminal activity and (2) establish the informant's credibility, or the informant's credibility must be established in the affidavit through a police officer's independent investigation. The affidavit must affirmatively set forth the circumstances from which the status of the informant can reasonably be inferred.

To determine the sufficiency of an affidavit used to obtain a search warrant, this jurisdiction has adopted the "totality of the circumstances" test set forth by the U.S. Supreme Court in Illinois v. Gates, 462 U.S. 213 (1983). The issuing magistrate must make a practical, commonsense decision whether, given the totality of the circumstances set forth in the affidavit before him, including the veracity and basis of knowledge of the persons supplying hearsay information, there is a fair probability that contraband or evidence of a crime will be found in a particular place. . . .

At approximately 7 A.M. on March 1, 1990, a Fremont police detective and six or seven fellow law enforcement officers executed a no-knock search warrant at Utterback's home. Utterback shared his home with his wife and infant child. In various containers discovered at various locales in the Utterback house, police found 25 separate plastic bags which contained a total of 570 grams of marijuana. . . .

The warrant which the officers executed authorized a search for automatic weapons, drug paraphernalia, and various controlled substances. The police detective obtained the warrant on the previous day from a Dodge County judge. The sworn affidavit executed by the police detective to obtain the search warrant states in pertinent part:

> On February 28, 1990, your affiant was advised by an *individual who is neither a paid nor habitual informant* that a second individual named "Randy" was engaged in the distribution and sale of controlled substances at the residence [at 321 North K Street]. The informant advised that "Randy" lived at the above described residence with his wife. The informant gave a physical description of "Randy" which matches the physical description of Randy Utterback contained in Fremont Police Dept. files. *The informant advised your affiant that in the past six months (the informant) had purchased marijuana from "Randy" at the residence described above,* and had observed other sales of illegal drugs at said residence. The informant further advised your affiant that (the informant) had been inside said residence within the last five days, and had seen a large quantity of marijuana, and lesser quantities of hashish, cocaine, LSD, and PCP. The informant indicated to your affiant that (the informant) was very familiar with illegal drugs, and the information furnished to your affiant indicated such knowledge.
>
> The informant further indicated to your affiant that (the informant) had observed what (the informant) believed to be an AK 47 assault rifle and an Uzi submachine gun in said residence, together with other weapons. The informant advised your affiant that (the informant) had personally inspected these weapons, and that they were loaded with ammunition. The informant gave a description of these weapons to your affiant, and that description is consistent with an AK 47 assault rifle and an Uzi submachine gun.
>
> Your affiant personally drove by the above described residence and observed an older model blue station wagon parked in the driveway of said residence bearing Nebraska license plate No. 5-B8618. According to records of the Dodge County Treasurer said vehicle is registered to Randy and/or Marla Utterback. Your affiant personally checked the records of the Fremont Department of Utilities and determined that the utilities were registered to Marla Utterback. . . .

Utterback argues that the search warrant was invalid in that the affidavit failed to establish the veracity of the confidential informant. To credit a confidential source's information in making a probable cause determination, the affidavit should support an inference that the source was trustworthy and that the source's accusation of criminal activity was made on the basis of information obtained in a reliable way.

Among the ways in which the reliability of an informant may be established are by showing in the affidavit to obtain a search warrant that (1) the informant has given reliable information to police officers in the past, see State v. Hoxworth, 358 N.W.2d 208 (Neb. 1984); (2) the informant is a citizen informant, see State v. Duff, 412 N.W.2d 843 (Neb. 1987); (3) the informant has made a statement that is against his or her penal interest, see State v. Sneed, 436 N.W.2d 211 (Neb. 1989); and (4) a police officer's independent investigation establishes the informant's reliability or the reliability of the information the informant has given, see United States v. Stanert, 762 F.2d 775 (9th Cir. 1985).

Nowhere in the detective's affidavit to obtain the search warrant in this case is there an averment that the detective's informant had given reliable information in the past, nor is there an averment that the informant was a "citizen informant." [Our prior cases have defined a citizen informant as]

> a citizen who purports to be the victim of or to have been the witness of a crime who is motivated by good citizenship and acts openly in aid of law enforcement. [E]xperienced stool pigeons or persons criminally involved or disposed are not regarded as "citizen-informants" because they are generally motivated by something other than good citizenship. . . .

The status of a citizen informant cannot attach unless the affidavit used to obtain a search warrant affirmatively sets forth the circumstances from which the existence of the status can reasonably be inferred. Here, there is nothing in the detective's affidavit used to obtain a search warrant even hinting that the informant was "motivated by good citizenship."

The State argues that the assertion in the detective's affidavit that "[t]he informant advised your affiant that in the past six months (the informant) had purchased marijuana from 'Randy' at the residence described above" was a statement against the penal interest of the informant. An admission by an informant that he or she participated in the crime about which the informant is informing carries its own indicia of reliability, since people do not lightly admit a crime and place critical evidence of that crime in the hands of police.

The act of purchasing marijuana is not a statutorily proscribed act in Nebraska. [Statutes] prohibit the possession of marijuana and . . . being under its influence, but nowhere in the statutes of the State of Nebraska is the purchase of marijuana expressly prohibited. There is nothing in the affidavit used to obtain the search warrant in this case that would establish, unequivocally, that the informant could be prosecuted for the crimes of possession or being under the influence of marijuana. [W]hen the informant in this case admitted to purchasing marijuana he did not make a statement against his penal interest.

The fourth method of determining the veracity of a confidential informant is through corroboration. Here, the affidavit reveals only that the police corroborated that Utterback lived at the described address, that the car in the driveway was registered to him, that the utilities at the house were registered to Utterback's wife, and that Utterback's physical description matched that given by the informant. If the police had chosen to corroborate the information regarding any criminal activities of Utterback's rather than merely corroborating these innocent details of his life, or had the affidavit contained other corroborative sources of information about the same alleged criminal activity of Utterback's, the veracity of the informant might have been established in the affidavit. However, no such corroboration is reflected in the detective's affidavit used to obtain the search warrant in this case.

We conclude that the affidavit in support of obtaining the search warrant herein fails to establish the veracity and reliability of the confidential informant and that the county judge was clearly wrong in determining that it supported a finding of probable cause to issue a search warrant. . . .

Notes

1. Gates *versus* Aguilar-Spinelli: *majority position.* In Illinois v. Gates, 462 U.S. 213 (1983), the Supreme Court upheld a trial court's finding of probable cause on the following facts. The police received an anonymous letter on May 3 alleging that a husband and wife were engaged in selling drugs; that the wife would drive their car to Florida on May 3 to be loaded with drugs, and the husband would fly down in a few days to drive the car back; that the car's trunk would be loaded with drugs; and that the suspects were storing over $100,000 worth of drugs in their basement. A police officer determined the address of the couple and learned that the husband made a reservation on a May 5 flight to Florida. A federal drug enforcement agent confirmed that the husband took the flight, stayed overnight in a motel room registered in the wife's name, and left the following morning with a woman in a car bearing an Illinois license plate issued to the husband, heading north on an interstate highway. These facts were sufficient under the "totality of the circumstances" test. Could they also support probable cause under the *Aguilar-Spinelli* test?

More than 30 states have adopted the *Gates* "totality of the circumstances" standard, though a handful of states such as Massachusetts, New Mexico, and Tennessee (fewer than 10) have retained the *Aguilar-Spinelli* analysis, relying on state constitutions or statutes. See, e.g., State v. Cordova, 784 P.2d 30 (N.M. 1989). Why have these states rejected the *Gates* standard? A number of jurisdictions have adopted a "totality of the circumstances" test but have emphasized the continuing relevance of the *Aguilar-Spinelli* analysis. Is this a preferable compromise position?

The *Barton* court in Connecticut switched from its earlier choice of *Aguilar-Spinelli* to the *Gates* standard, saying the *Aguilar-Spinelli* analysis had become "encrusted with an overlay of analytical rigidity." What evidence did the court offer to support this conclusion? What evidence could the court have offered? If the claim about "encrustation" is hyperbole, what other reasons might have moved the court to the *Gates* standard?

2. *Fact-based probable cause analysis.* Both *Barton* and *Utterback* adopt the "totality of the circumstances" standard of *Gates.* Which set of facts provided stronger support for a finding of probable cause? Which confidential informant provided greater detail? Which description could a police officer verify more easily? Do you

agree with the court in *Utterback* that an admitted purchase of marijuana is not an admission against penal interest because purchasing is not a crime?

The "totality" standard, as the court said in *Barton,* is designed to place more responsibility for the probable cause finding in the hands of the factfinder on the scene: the magistrate reviewing the application for a warrant. Should other institutions allow magistrates to make probable cause determinations by their own lights or should they attempt to standardize the probable cause determination? See Ornelas v. United States, 517 U.S. 690 (1996) (underlying facts reviewed for clear error, ultimate determination of probable cause reviewed de novo). Do you imagine that magistrates see similar fact patterns repeatedly, ones amenable to legal rules? Or do the warrant applications present such different fact patterns that they cannot usefully be compared?

3. *Legal standards and legal cultures.* How different are the alternative legal standards at issue in these cases? If you were concerned about limiting police powers at a time of rising fear about crime, would you rather be in a state with the *Aguilar-Spinelli* standard or in a state with a legal culture suspicious of government abuses where the courts use the *Gates* standard? Attorneys and others who train police officers very often emphasize the facts central to the *Aguilar-Spinelli* standard, even in jurisdictions that have adopted the *Gates* standard under the state constitution. See Corey Fleming Hirokawa, Making the "Law of the Land" the Law on the Street: How Police Academies Teach Evolving Fourth Amendment Law, 49 Emory L.J. 295 (2000). Why do they make such a choice?

4. *Prevalence of confidential informants.* While officers rely heavily on their own observations in unwarranted searches, cases involving search warrants more often turn on evidence obtained from confidential informants. A survey of warrants issued in drug cases in San Diego in 1998 found that 64 percent of the warrant applications included information from confidential informants, and a quarter of the applications offered information from anonymous tips. Most of the applications gave little information about the informant's reliability or track record; the little information offered appeared in standard boilerplate language. However, in almost all cases depending on information from confidential informants (95 percent of them), the police corroborated the tip by conducting a "controlled buy" of narcotics. See Laurence A. Benner and Charles T. Samarkos, Searching for Narcotics in San Diego: Preliminary Findings from the San Diego Search Warrant Project, 36 Cal. W. L. Rev. 221, 238-243 (2000).

5. *The presumption in favor of "citizen informants."* As suggested in dicta in *Utterback,* most courts presume information provided by victims and witnesses to be sufficiently reliable to serve as a basis for finding probable cause without additional proof that the source is credible or the information reliable. See Frette v. Springdale, 959 S.W.2d 734 (Ark. 1998); People v. Donnelly, 691 P.2d 747 (Colo. 1984). Why? Does a person lose the status of "citizen informant" if she receives a reward for the information? What if the police pay the citizen small amounts of cash for meals or transportation? See People v. Cantre, 95 A.D.2d 522 (N.Y. App. Div. 1983). Can victims or witnesses be liable to suspects for the torts of malicious prosecution or false arrest if they file a complaint with an intent other than the investigation or prosecution of the suspect?

6. *Informer's privilege.* Should suspects be able to challenge information provided by a confidential informant, even at the stage of establishing probable cause? Courts and legislatures have long recognized an "informer's privilege" that allows

the government to withhold the name of a confidential informant. Drawing on well-established common law roots in the law of evidence, the Supreme Court in McCray v. Illinois, 386 U.S. 300 (1967), explained the privilege in these terms: "Whether an informer is motivated by good citizenship, promise of leniency or prospect of pecuniary award, he will usually condition his cooperation on an assurance of anonymity — to protect himself and his family from harm, to preclude adverse social reactions. . . . Revelation of the dual role played by such persons ends their usefulness to the government and discourages others from entering into a like relationship."

Typically, the law allows a magistrate or judge (but not the suspect) to learn the informer's identity and to examine the informer in camera if there is some reason to disbelieve the informer's statements. Disclosure is also allowed in exceptional cases, as when the defense must call the informer as an important witness at trial or when the prosecution calls the informer as a witness without revealing his or her role in the application for a search warrant. In practice, officers submitting warrant applications often do not provide any case-specific reasons for keeping the informant's name confidential, and provide little basis for judging the informant's past performance. See Laurence A. Benner and Charles T. Samarkos, Searching for Narcotics in San Diego: Preliminary Findings from the San Diego Search Warrant Project, 36 Cal. W. L. Rev. 221 (2000).

Should the informer's privilege apply when *all* the information supporting a search warrant is withheld from the defendant as confidential? Justice Mosk of the California Supreme Court, in a dissenting opinion in People v. Hobbs, 873 P.2d 1246 (Cal. 1994) characterized this problem as follows:

> A search warrant containing no information other than the address of a home to be searched. Not a word as to what the government seeks to discover and seize. A government informer, his — or, indeed, her — identity kept secret from the suspect, the suspect's counsel, and the public. Both the suspect and counsel barred from a closed proceeding before a magistrate. No record of the proceeding given to the suspect or counsel. Based entirely on the foregoing, a court order approving an unrestricted search of the suspect's home. Did this scenario occur in a communist dictatorship? Under a military junta? Or perhaps in a Kafka novel? No, this is grim reality in California in the final decade of the 20th century.

What if another court — say, the Idaho Supreme Court — reads Justice Mosk's observation, then re-reads Kafka and decides to eliminate the informer's privilege? Could a legal system function if it took the position that no deprivation of liberty, including a search or seizure, could take place without full disclosure to the suspect after the search or arrest?

b. Anonymous Sources

Should courts treat anonymous sources like citizen informants, with presumptions of reliability, or like confidential informants, with a requirement that police show the informant is trustworthy or the information is accurate? Consider the following modern-day "wanted" poster, soliciting anonymous and confidential informants, along with the case below.

WANTED: Information

Do you want to help keep Anaconda-Deer Lodge County
DRUG FREE in the 1990s?
HERE'S YOUR CHANCE!
If you know or suspect that someone is dealing in drugs . . .
TURN THEM IN
Fill out the information below, clip it out, and mail to:

Jim Connors, Police Chief
Anaconda, MT
or phone 555-5242
All information will be kept strictly confidential

- -

Who? (name) ____________________ Age ____
Where? (address) ____________________
City, State ____________________
What? Coke ________ Crank ________ Grass ________
Any other info ____________________

■ DANNY BRADLEY v. STATE

609 N.E.2d 420 (Ind. 1993)

DEBRULER, J.

. . . At approximately 2:00 A.M. on November 4, 1989, appellant knocked on the motel room door of Janet McLaughlin and Mary Lou Leonard, who were staying at a Knights Inn in Indianapolis. Appellant told them that they had left their key in the door. Leonard thanked appellant and told him she would retrieve the key later. She watched him walk away and waited a few minutes to be sure he had left. When Leonard opened the door, appellant pushed his way inside the room with a gun in his hand, knocking Leonard to the ground. Appellant ordered the women to the corner of the room and threatened to kill them if they looked at him. He placed a coat over their heads and proceeded to ransack the room. Appellant took the women's purses, jewelry, and luggage, then told the women to stick their hands out so he could take their wedding bands. Leonard begged to be allowed to use soap to take off her rings, which had not been removed in years. Appellant refused and in the process of removing her rings he broke her finger. After the assailant left, the women notified the police and gave a description of their attacker. They were interviewed by Detective Sergeant Steven Gibbs and then taken to a hospital for treatment of Leonard's finger, as well as a laceration on her head and bruises.

The following Monday Detective Gibbs received an anonymous phone call advising him that appellant had committed the robbery. He obtained a search warrant, and on November 7th he and another officer executed the warrant at 2021 N. Bellefontaine, Bradley's address, finding several pieces of stolen property. Kerry Thomas, the mother of Bradley's children, was in the house and was wearing some of the jewelry taken from Leonard and McLaughlin. The search warrant was based on the following affidavit . . . :

> Det/Sgt Steven T Gibbs of the Marion CSD swears or affirms that he believes and has good cause to believe . . . that certain property hereinafter described is concealed in the following described residence, to wit: a two story yellow frame house with white trim and an enclosed brick porch with the numbers 2021 in the window and located at 2021 N Bellefontaine, Indpls, Marion County, Indiana.
>
> The property is described as follows: A light colored small automatic pistol; a grey sweatshirt with wide red stripes down the sleeves; two diamond rings, a diamond cross necklace, two maroon suitcases, a ladies Gucci watch, a black ladies purse; a maroon John Romaine purse and credit cards and identification in the names of Mary Lou Leonard and Janet M McLaughlin; which constitutes unlawfully obtained property and evidence of an offense.
>
> In support of your affiant's assertion of probable cause, your affiant would show the court that he has received the following facts from a reliable informant which facts the informant stated to be within the informant's personal knowledge, to wit: On 11-6-89 the informant made a phone call to Det/Sgt Steve Gibbs. The informant stated that he knew an armed robbery had occurred at a motel room near Shadeland Ave the previous Friday or Saturday. The informant said that two older white women had a black male force his way into their motel room and display a weapon. The informant stated that luggage, jewelry, cash and credit cards were taken and that one lady had been injured. The informant stated that this robbery had been done by a Denny Bradley who resides at 2021 Bellefontaine, and that Bradley has a prior history of robbery arrests.
>
> Your affiant believes and has probable cause to believe that the informant's information is reliable, based upon the following facts within your affiant's personal knowledge, to wit: On 11-4-89 (the previous Saturday) at about 2:41 A.M. Det/Sgt Gibbs was sent to 7101 E 21st St, the Knights Inn Motel, room 309 (a block east of Shadeland) to investigate an armed robbery. There I found Mary Lou Leonard wf55 and Janet McLaughlin wf56. They stated that a black male forced his way into their motel room and robbed them at gunpoint. They described all the property mentioned above by the informant as being taken with the exception of the credit cards. Mrs. Leonard had her left finger broken by the robber as he took her wedding band. On 11-6-89 Det/Sgt Gibbs phoned both Leonard and McLaughlin and they stated that their credit cards had also been taken. To your affiant's knowledge, there has been no publicity of this incident prior to receiving the informant's phone call. Checking criminal histories Det/Sgt Gibbs found a Danny Bradley living at 2021 N Bellefontaine with prior robbery arrests. Therefore, your affiant respectfully requests the court to issue a search warrant directing the search for and seizure of the above-described property.

I.C. 35-33-5-2(b) requires that an affidavit in support of probable cause which is based on hearsay either "contain reliable information establishing the credibility of the source and of each of the declarants of the hearsay and establishing that there is a factual basis for the information furnished" or "contain information that establishes that the totality of the circumstances corroborates the hearsay." Neither of these requirements have been met.

The affidavit does not establish the credibility of the source. The affiant twice states that the informant was reliable, when, in actuality, the informant was anonymous. Gibbs testified at the hearing on the motion to suppress that the caller was anonymous, that he did not recognize the voice, and, to Gibbs' knowledge, that he had never before provided information to the police. . . .

Additionally, there is no information establishing a factual basis for the tip from which a court could test the informant's conclusion that appellant was the perpetrator of the crime or Gibbs' conclusion that evidence of the crime would be found at the address to be searched. Gibbs swore that the informant stated the information was within his personal knowledge but sets forth in the affidavit no information which would allow a court to draw that conclusion. For example, there is no declaration that the informant witnessed or participated in the crime or that appellant told the informant the details of the crime, nor is there a statement that the informant personally observed the fruits of that crime in the possession of appellant or at his residence. Nor does the tip contain an "explicit and detailed description of alleged wrongdoing, along with a statement that the event was observed firsthand," which would entitle the tip to greater weight than might otherwise be the case "if we entertain some doubt as to an informant's motives." Illinois v. Gates, 462 U.S. 213 (1983). The tip simply does not contain that level of intimate detail which would lead a court to infer that the informant obtained the information from the perpetrator himself. There is merely a recitation of some facts of the crime and an allegation that appellant was the criminal.

There is also insufficient information to establish that the totality of the circumstances corroborates the hearsay. The fact that a Danny Bradley with prior robbery arrests was found in the computer to reside at the address given in the tip, and that a crime fitting the description of the one related by the informant had actually occurred does not constitute probable cause to believe that the anonymous caller was telling the truth, or that a search at that address would yield fruits of the crime. The corroboration did not involve the verification of accurate predictions of future actions of a third party, an important factor in *Gates*, which would give a court a substantial basis to believe that the informant had access to reliable information concerning illegal activities, but merely confirmed "easily obtained facts and conditions existing at the time of the tip." Although Gibbs testified at the suppression hearing that he did not relate the details of the crime to the motel staff or to the media, he could not state that the victims or other personnel present at the crime scene did not discuss the crime. Indeed, as appellant points out, the hospital record of Leonard's treatment discloses that she was robbed at gunpoint. Gibbs' corroboration of the informant's tip simply establishes that the informant knew of the crime and knew of appellant. It does not provide a connection between the crime and appellant or between the stolen property and the place searched. We therefore find that this affidavit does not meet the requirements of I.C. 35-33-5-2 and that the warrant to search 2021 N. Bellefontaine did not issue upon probable cause. . . . Accordingly, we reverse appellant's convictions and remand this cause to the trial court for a new trial.

GIVAN, J., dissenting.

. . . When reading the affidavit in its entirety, it becomes quite clear that the affiant was representing to the trial court that the information received from an informant was thought by the affiant to be reliable because the caller described the crime in detail including the fact that credit cards had been taken. The officer felt the information was reliable based upon what he knew at that time concerning the crime. However, he did not know that credit cards had been taken and he called the victims to verify that such had occurred. This strengthened his conclusion that the information was reliable. . . . The trial court did not err in refusing to suppress the evidence obtained in the search.

Notes

1. *Anonymous tips and probable cause: majority position.* Courts do not adopt a special framework for assessing probable cause based on information from an anonymous tip. They apply the same basic framework—whether it be *Gates* or *Aguilar-Spinelli*—used to assess the reliability of named and confidential informants. A number of the classic cases on the sources of probable cause, including Illinois v. Gates, 462 U.S. 213 (1983), involved tips from anonymous sources. Of course, the police in such cases face the major difficulty of establishing the reliability of the source without knowing the identity of the source. While a track record for the source might not be available, and an "admission against penal interest" cannot bolster the credibility of an anonymous source, it is still possible that the police will be able to corroborate some details of the tip. See State v. Griggs, 34 P.3d 101 (Mont. 2001) (corroborated facts in anonymous tip must be suspicious and associated with criminal activity to establish probable cause).

In a jurisdiction following the *Aguilar-Spinelli* approach to probable cause, how often will information from an anonymous informant satisfy both prongs? In a *Gates* jurisdiction, would you expect the showing for "basis of knowledge" to be much higher than usual in an anonymous informant case? In assessing the reliability of an anonymous source, does it matter to you whether the anonymous tipster uses a telephone call (as in *Bradley*) or submits a written tip (as requested in the "wanted" poster)? Governments, corporations and "watchdog" organizations often maintain "whistle blower" sites on the internet, to encourage employees and others who know about wrongdoing to share the information. Should those sites allow for anonymous submissions? See Lisa Guernsey, Whistle-Blower Sites Mine Clues Amid Mountains of Suspicion, New York Times, Feb. 21, 2002.

2. *Anonymous tips and reasonable suspicion to stop vehicles.* In Chapter 2, we considered the "reasonable suspicion" necessary to justify a police stop of a person or vehicle. Sometimes anonymous tips give the police a reason to stop a person. Typically, courts require the officer to confirm some of the details that the anonymous tipster related before reasonable suspicion is present. In one common fact pattern, an anonymous tip identifies a driver who might be driving while intoxicated. If the officer stops the vehicle on the basis of the anonymous tip without first developing some independent basis for reasonable suspicion, courts will frequently overturn the stop.

The U.S. Supreme Court has addressed the use of anonymous tips to establish reasonable suspicion to stop a driver suspected of drug activity. In Alabama v. White, 496 U.S. 325, 332 (1990), an anonymous caller gave police specific information about the future travel plans of an alleged drug dealer. The Court agreed that the tip, together with police efforts to corroborate the tip by following the vehicle for a time, amounted to reasonable suspicion, despite the anonymity of the source: "[I]f a tip has a relatively low degree of reliability, more information will be required to establish the requisite quantum of suspicion than would be required if the tip were more reliable." The fact that the tip predicted future behavior, which the police were able to verify, gave it extra weight:

> What was important was the caller's ability to predict respondent's future behavior, because it demonstrated inside information — a special familiarity with respondent's affairs. . . . Because only a small number of people are generally privy to an individual's

> itinerary, it is reasonable for police to believe that a person with access to such information is likely to also have access to reliable information about that individual's illegal activities. When significant aspects of the caller's predictions were verified, there was reason to believe not only that the caller was honest but also that he was well informed, at least well enough to justify the stop.

Compare Florida v. J.L., 529 U.S. 266 (2000) (anonymous caller reported that a young black male standing at a particular bus stop and wearing a plaid shirt was carrying a gun; officers saw three black males, one of whom was wearing a plaid shirt; officers observed no gun and no unusual movements; not sufficient basis for reasonable suspicion to stop and frisk). Police departments typically record their 911 calls, and many employ caller ID technology. Should courts adapt their anonymous tip jurisprudence to this change in technology?

3. Can a Statute or Rule Clarify the Assessment of Probable Cause?

If a jurisdiction were committed to obtaining consistent determinations of probable cause, would it help if a statute or criminal procedure rule specified the factors for assessing probable cause? Do the following statutes adopt the *Aguilar-Spinelli* or the *Gates* standard? Apply the following statutes to the facts in *Barton* and *Utterback.* Would you reach a different outcome in either of those cases?

■ ARKANSAS RULE OF CRIMINAL PROCEDURE 13.1

(b) [If] an affidavit or testimony is based in whole or in part on hearsay, the affiant or witness shall set forth particular facts bearing on the informant's reliability and shall disclose, as far as practicable, the means by which the information was obtained. An affidavit or testimony is sufficient if it describes circumstances establishing reasonable cause to believe that things subject to seizure will be found in a particular place. Failure of the affidavit or testimony to establish the veracity and bases of knowledge of persons providing information to the affiant shall not require that the application be denied, if the affidavit or testimony viewed as a whole, provides a substantial basis for a finding of reasonable cause to believe that things subject to seizure will be found in a particular place.

■ IOWA CODE §808.3

[T]he magistrate shall endorse on the application the name and address of all persons upon whose sworn testimony the magistrate relied to issue the warrant together with the abstract of each witness' testimony, or the witness' affidavit. However, if the grounds for issuance are supplied by an informant, the magistrate shall identify only the peace officer to whom the information was given. The application or sworn testimony supplied in support of the application must establish the credibility of the informant or the credibility of the information given by the informant. The magistrate may in the magistrate's discretion require that a witness upon whom the applicant relies for information appear personally and be examined concerning the information.

■ IOWA RULE OF CRIMINAL PROCEDURE 2.36, FORM 2

An application for a search warrant shall be in substantially the following form: . . .

Being duly sworn, I, the undersigned, say that at the place (and on the person(s) and in the vehicle(s)) described as follows:

in _________ County, there is now certain property, namely:
which is:
___ Property that has been obtained in violation of law.
___ Property, the possession of which is illegal.
___ Property used or possessed with the intent to be used as the means of committing a public offense or concealed to prevent an offense from being discovered.
___ Property relevant and material as evidence in a criminal prosecution.

The facts establishing the foregoing ground(s) for issuance of a search warrant are as set forth in the attachment(s) made part of this application.

ATTACHMENT
Applicant's name: ____
Occupation: ______________________________ No. of years: _________
Assignment: ______________________________ No. of years: _________
Your applicant conducted an investigation and received information from other officers and other sources as follows:
(_________ See attached investigative and police reports.) . . .

INFORMANT'S ATTACHMENT (Note: Prepare separate attachment for each informant.)
Peace officer _________ received information from an informant whose name is: _________
___ Confidential because disclosure of informant's identity would:
___ Endanger informant's safety;
___ Impair informant's future usefulness to law enforcement.

The informant is reliable for the following reason(s):
___ The informant is a concerned citizen who has been known by the above peace officer for years and who:
___ Is a mature individual.
___ Is regularly employed.
___ Is a student in good standing.
___ Is a well-respected family or business person.
___ Is a person of truthful reputation.
___ Has no motivation to falsify the information.
___ Has no known association with known criminals.
___ Has no known criminal record.
___ Has otherwise demonstrated truthfulness. (State in the narrative the facts that led to this conclusion.)
___ Other:
___ The informant has supplied information in the past _____ times.

___ The informant's past information has helped supply the basis for ______ search warrants.
___ The informant's past information has led to the making of ______ arrests.
___ Past information from the informant has led to the filing of the following charges: ______________________________
___ Past information from the informant has led to the discovery and seizure of stolen property, drugs, or other contraband.
___ The informant has not given false information in the past.
___ The information supplied by the informant in this investigation has been corroborated by law enforcement personnel. (Indicate in the narrative the corroborated information and how it was corroborated.)
___ Other: ______________________________
The informant has provided the following information: ______________________________

■ IOWA RULE OF CRIMINAL PROCEDURE 2.36, FORM 3

An endorsement on a search warrant shall be in substantially the following form: . . .

1. In issuing the search warrant, the undersigned relied upon the sworn testimony of the following person(s) together with the statements and information contained in the application and any attachments thereto. The court relied upon the following witnesses:

Name	Address
______________	______________
______________	______________
______________	______________

2. Abstract of Testimony. (As set forth in the application and the attachments thereto, plus the following information.)

3. The undersigned has relied, at least in part, on information supplied by a confidential informant (who need not be named) to the peace officer(s) shown on Attachment(s) __________.

4. The information appears credible because (select):

___ A. Sworn testimony indicates this informant has given reliable information on previous occasions; or,

___ B. Sworn testimony indicates that either the informant appears credible or the information appears credible for the following reasons (if credibility is based on this ground, the magistrate MUST set out reasons here):

____

____

5. The information (is/is not) found to justify probable cause.

6. I therefore (do/do not) issue the warrant.

Notes

1. *Statutes and probable cause determinations: majority position.* Only one state (Oregon) offers a general statutory definition of probable cause. However, most states do have statutes or rules of procedure instructing magistrates how to determine whether probable cause exists before issuing a warrant. The statutes often

specify the types of sources a magistrate may consider and the inquiries a magistrate must make when assessing "hearsay" information or other questionable sources.

Iowa courts have concluded that the state legislature, in passing section 808.3, was repudiating the decision of the Supreme Court in Illinois v. Gates, 462 U.S. 213 (1983). See State v. Swaim, 412 N.W.2d 568 (Iowa 1987) (interpreting language in statute, "shall include a determination that the information appears credible," as a rejection of *Gates*). What purposes might the other two provisions reprinted above serve?

2. *Rules as requirements and rules as nonbinding guidance.* What should be the effect of a failure to check any boxes on the Iowa form to show why an informant was reliable, in a case where a reviewing court believes that the information provided to the magistrate was enough for probable cause? See State v. District Court of Black Hawk County, 472 N.W.2d 621 (Iowa 1991) (invalidating search warrant based on form application with no checks indicating informant's basis of knowledge). Such checklists are also developed as part of police and prosecutorial manuals. The lists often take the form of computer software, used to prompt an officer to answer specific questions while constructing an application for a search warrant. Should failure to follow a written executive branch guideline have the same effect on review of probable cause as failure to follow an identical rule of criminal procedure? Should the question simply be whether probable cause exists, with the forms or checklists, whatever their origins, merely serving as evidence for the court assessing or reviewing the probable cause determination?

C. WARRANTS

The U.S. Supreme Court and state supreme courts say it often: Searches and seizures ordinarily must be carried out under warrants obtained from neutral magistrates. See, e.g., Trupiano v. United States, 334 U.S. 699, 705 (1948) ("It is a cardinal rule that, in seizing goods and articles, law enforcement agents must secure and use search warrants wherever reasonably practicable"). Look back at the language of the Fourth Amendment and its equivalents. How would you respond to an argument that searches can be conducted only pursuant to warrants?

Even if an absolute warrant requirement is not plausible, the constitutional language and the oft-stated judicial "preference" for warrants might lead to the expectation that *most* searches are conducted pursuant to a warrant, with exceptions to the warrant requirement being just that — exceptions, and therefore uncommon. Does a judicial preference for warrants mean that warrants are common in practice? It is difficult to determine what proportion of searches are carried out based on warrants, but the current appellate case law suggests a great majority of searches in most contexts are conducted without first obtaining a warrant.

What advantage might warranted searches offer over searches supported by probable cause but no warrant? After all, in both cases, exclusion of evidence will typically be available to remedy any improper searches.

The special contributions of the warrant involve the timing of the decision and the identity of the decision maker. For warranted searches, the determination of probable cause must occur before the search begins. By settling the issue early, a warrant prevents the use of hindsight. If the probable cause issue waits until after the search produces evidence, judges may feel pressure to accept a search that was based on nothing more than a lucky guess. Some police officers might also feel tempted to lie about the original basis for their search. And for warranted searches, a judicial officer decides whether probable cause is present, rather than the law enforcement officers who are in the thick of the chase. See William Stuntz, Warrants and Fourth Amendment Remedies, 77 Va. L. Rev. 881 (1991).

1. The Warrant Requirement and Exigent Circumstances

Perhaps the largest "exception" to the preference for warrants is the presence of exigent circumstances. When exigent circumstances appear, there is no need for police to obtain a warrant before conducting a search. Exigent circumstances include situations in which an immediate search or seizure is needed to protect the safety of an officer or the public, or when the suspect might escape or destroy evidence. In what proportion of all searches and seizures would you imagine that there is some risk that one of these events might occur? How much risk must the government accept before the circumstances become "exigent"? Can the government take any actions to decrease (or increase) these risks?

■ MARVIN HAWKINS v. STATE

626 N.E.2d 436 (Ind. 1993)

DeBruler, J.

[After receiving information that Marvin Hawkins was selling crack cocaine in his house, the police used an informant to execute a "controlled buy" at the residence.] Prior to the buy, officers searched the informant for drugs and gave her fifty dollars in cash which the police had previously photocopied. . . . Officer Gillum drove the informant to appellant Hawkins' residence while additional officers maintained visual surveillance of the house. The informant entered the house and returned within two or three minutes with a rock-like substance. Officer Gillum met her in his police car, took the informant a safe distance from appellant Hawkins' residence, and field tested the substance. The field test indicated the presence of cocaine. Thereafter, Officer Gillum advised the other officers via police radio that the substance tested positive for cocaine and then he returned to appellant Hawkins' residence.

Officers Neal, Gillum, and Vollmar approached the front door of appellant Hawkins' house. Additional officers waited at the rear door. At approximately 10:57 p.m., Officer Neal knocked on the door. Neal identified himself, and demanded that the door be opened. The officers testified that someone approached the door and asked what they wanted, then withdrew from the doorway. Officer Neal re-identified himself and again demanded that the door be opened. After this subsequent demand, Officer Neal kicked in the door and entered the residence followed by the other officers. Appellant was knocked to the floor by the door as it flew open. Neal testified that he did not remember hearing anyone running inside before forcing open the door. Vollmar testified that he heard no running before the door was forced open. Gillum heard no running but believed the door was forced open because one of the other officers had heard running. Once the officers forcibly entered the premises, they definitely heard the sound of people toward the back of the house. [The officers arrested the occupants of the house and noticed cocaine, razor blades and shot gun shells placed on a table.]

After securing the premises, Officer Gillum met Dave Eiler, an investigator from the prosecutor's office, at the courthouse where they prepared a request for a search warrant. Around midnight, Officer Gillum and Eiler went to Judge Barnet's home, gave testimony, and received a warrant to search appellant Hawkins' residence. The testimony included a description of the cocaine seen after entry was made. [The officers executed the search warrant and seized several firearms, $885 in cash, including $45 of the buy money used by the informant, and a jar of coins. The government admitted this evidence at trial over the defendant's objections.]

When a search is conducted without a warrant, the State bears the burden of justifying the search by proving that one of the exceptions to the warrant requirement applied. In this case, the State argues that the search was legal because it was necessary to prevent the loss of evidence and the escape of the perpetrators. Appellant Hawkins contends that the State had the opportunity to obtain a valid search warrant prior to forcibly entering his house.

Generally, warrantless entry into the home for purposes of arrest or search are prohibited by the Fourth Amendment of the United States Constitution. Article I, §11 of the Indiana Constitution mirrors the federal protection. Under these constitutional guarantees, a search and seizure must be supported by a judicially issued warrant unless exigent circumstances exist that place the search and seizure within certain narrowly defined exceptions. The burden is on the prosecution to demonstrate exigent circumstances to overcome the presumption of unreasonableness that accompanies all warrantless home entries.

One such exception permits the State to enter a home when government agents believe evidence may be destroyed or removed before a search warrant is obtained. The police must have an objective and reasonable fear that the evidence is about to be destroyed. Moreover, exigent circumstances cannot be created by police officers to justify warrantless searches.

Officer Gillum testified that crack houses typically have a high volume of customers. Therefore, the police believed that they might lose the "buy money" via subsequent sales transactions. Notwithstanding Officer Gillum's testimony, the record does not support his claim that appellant Hawkins' house was as busy as a "drive-in restaurant." The record shows that only fifteen transactions were executed within the house during the preceding two-week period. During the evening of [the arrest], a Wednesday, the police did not observe any additional traffic at the home after the informant left appellant Hawkins' house. . . .

The officers testified that they heard nothing after Neal knocked on the front door and identified himself, nor did they believe the occupants had any idea that the police were initiating a raid. As officers waited at the door they did not hear people running. It was only after an officer kicked the front door open that people began to run within the house.

Courts should not be reticent in enforcing the constitutional rule restricting the search of a person's home without a warrant or consent, and therefore, demand a genuine showing of an emergency before they will excuse the police's failure to obtain a warrant. In this case, we believe that the State has made no such showing. Prior to the warrantless entry, the police properly executed a controlled buy. Officers, stationed in front and behind appellant Hawkins' house, maintained visual surveillance of the premises following the drug purchase. It took a little more than an hour for Officer Gillum to meet with a member of the prosecutor's staff and prepare a probable cause affidavit, travel to Judge Barnet's home, obtain a judicially authorized search warrant, and return to appellant Hawkins' house.

In our view, the State failed to show that they were faced with circumstances making it impractical to wait for a search warrant before entering the premises. Consequently, the evidence seized by the officers after the warrantless entry was illegally obtained and it was error to allow its introduction at trial. . . .

GIVAN, J., dissenting.

[The record shows that immediately] after a purchase of cocaine had been made at the house in question, the officer went to the door, knocked, identified himself, and asked that the door be opened. He could see a person on the other side of the door with a lit cigarette who asked what was wanted. When the officer re-identified himself and repeated his demand, the cigarette glow disappeared and the officer heard running. It was then that the door was forced open.

At trial, the officers testified that they knew from the informant that crack cocaine was in the house and that the informant had used marked bills in paying for the cocaine purchased. The officer testified that there was going and coming from the house, and he was fearful that the drugs and the marked money would disappear before a warrant could be obtained. This was ample evidence of exigent circumstances from which the trial court could determine that the warrantless search was justified. However, the majority opinion reweighs this evidence and comes to the opposite conclusion. This is an improper invasion of the prerogative of the trial court in the weighing of evidence. This Court has repeatedly stated that it is improper for this Court to reweigh evidence on appeal. I cannot justify reversal of this case. . . .

Notes

1. *Exigent circumstances: majority position.* The two grounds for exigent circumstances argued by the state in this case — the destruction of possible evidence or escape of suspects — are two of the most common grounds for arguing that the police need not obtain a judicial warrant. See People v. Blasius, 459 N.W.2d 906 (Mich. 1990) (exigent circumstances must be based on "more than a mere possibility" of immediate destruction or removal of evidence). Are there exigent circumstances in all cases dealing with evidence (such as narcotics) that is easy to destroy or remove? In all cases where private parties will have access to the area while the police seek a warrant? Exigent circumstances might also be based on possible danger to the investigating officers or to citizens in the area where the search is to take place. The danger might involve the use of a weapon on the premises, an item creating a risk of fire or explosion, or the possible presence of persons needing medical care, among other things. See People v. Higbee, 802 P.2d 1085 (Colo. 1990) (search for bomb); Minnesota v. Olson, 495 U.S. 91, 100 (1990) (exigent circumstances might be based on hot pursuit of a fleeing felon, imminent destruction of evidence, the need to prevent a suspect's escape, or "the risk of danger to the police or to other persons"). Exigent circumstances can vary with the seriousness of the crime; the showing becomes more difficult as the crime under investigation becomes less serious. See Welsh v. Wisconsin, 466 U.S. 740 (1984) ("application of the exigent-circumstances ex-

ception in the context of a home entry should rarely be sanctioned when there is probable cause to believe that only a minor offense [such as driving while intoxicated] has been committed").

When do inconvenient circumstances become "exigent"? That is, how much extra risk must the police accept before they may conclude that obtaining a warrant would be too difficult? There was conflicting testimony in *Hawkins* about the amount of traffic at the house on the evening of the controlled purchase and arrest. Was it feasible for the police to wait to enter the house only after another potential purchaser entered and then started to leave the house? Could they detain any person leaving the premises until officers returned with a warrant?

Exigent circumstances are not the only cases in which courts will allow a warrantless search. As we saw in Chapter 2, many less intrusive searches may be conducted without a warrant. And as we will discover in Chapter 4, searches "incident to arrest" and searches of vehicles may take place without warrants. For each case involving warrantless searches, ask yourself what kind of argument the state makes and whether you have seen it before. It is useful to make a list of the variety of justifications for warrantless searches.

2. *Creating exigencies.* The majority and the dissent disagree over whether the officers in this case heard running inside the house after they knocked. Does it matter whether they heard running? What does the court mean when it says that "exigent circumstances cannot be created by police officers to justify warrantless searches"? Will it suffice for the police to argue that they had some legitimate and independent justification for taking the course of action that created the exigent circumstances? Compare State v. Alayon, 459 N.W.2d 325 (Minn. 1990) (approving exigent circumstances arising after questioning of drug dealer at suspected location of evidence, because questioning was necessary to establish which of two locations he was using) with Dunnuck v. State, 786 A.2d 695 (Md. 2001) (no exigent circumstances when police observed indoor marijuana plant through window and created exigent circumstances by knocking on door and announcing their connection to drug task force; state offered no evidence as to time it would take to get a warrant).

3. *Maintaining the status quo while seeking a warrant.* May the police enter or remain on the premises long enough to prevent the destruction of evidence or other harms that could occur while they seek a warrant? See Illinois v. McArthur, 531 U.S. 326 (2001) (police obtain probable cause of presence of illegal narcotics in home; occupant required to remain outside home two hours with police officer present while other officers seek search warrant); Segura v. United States, 468 U.S. 796 (1984) (search valid where police officers remained in apartment 19 hours until warrant was obtained); Commonwealth v. Martino, 588 N.E.2d 651 (Mass. 1992) (search valid when officer is posted outside apartment to prevent removal of items from inside until warrant is obtained and seizes item from attorney attempting to carry it away from premises). If it requires too many police officers for too long a period to maintain the status quo, do the police then have exigent circumstances?

4. *The special status of homes.* Courts strike down warrantless searches most often in the context of searches of homes. Many of the exceptions to the warrant requirement applicable outside the home do not apply in the same way within a home, and courts tend to demand greater justifications for warrantless searches of a house. If police get an anonymous report of a burglary in progress, and find a window broken, do they have justification for a warrantless search? Some courts extend the special protection provided homes to other areas. Indiana, for example, has found

a similar preference for warrants when the police search parked and impounded cars. Brown v. State, 653 N.E.2d 77 (Ind. 1995):

> With respect to automobiles generally, it may safely be said that Hoosiers regard their automobiles as private and cannot easily abide their uninvited intrusion. . . . Americans in general love their cars. It is, however, particularly important, in the state which hosts the Indy 500 automobile race, to recognize that cars are sources of pride, status, and identity that transcend their objective attributes. We are extremely hesitant to countenance their casual violation, even by law enforcement officers who are attempting to solve serious crimes.

2. *Requirements for Obtaining Warrants*

Procedures for obtaining warrants typically appear in state statutes, local code provisions, and local rules of court. These rules specify such things as who can issue warrants, the form and content of warrant applications, and the allowable scope of warrants. Several procedural requirements appear on the face of the Fourth Amendment and its analogs. Warrants must be issued by a "neutral and detached magistrate." Most constitutions require the applicant to specify the targeted place and the items or person sought. Some also require that the warrant application be in writing or under oath.

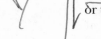

a. Neutral and Detached Magistrate

While there are occasional cases litigating the constitutional requirement of a "neutral and detached magistrate," issues of judicial neutrality are more often litigated under judicial ethics rules. Indeed, ethics rules have become a standard avenue for the regulation of lawyers and judges throughout the criminal process, as influential today in practical terms as constitutional provisions.

■ STATE EX REL. EUSTACE BROWN v. JERRY DIETRICK

444 S.E.2d 47 (W. Va. 1994)

MILLER, J.

[W]e consider whether the Circuit Court of Jefferson County was correct in holding that a search warrant issued by a magistrate was void because the magistrate was married to the chief of police and one of his officers had procured the warrant. The lower court determined that because the magistrate was married to the chief of police there was a violation of Canon 3C(1) and 3C(1)(d) of the Judicial Code of Ethics. The former provision requires the recusal of a judge if his impartiality might reasonably be questioned; the latter requires disqualification where the judge's spouse has an interest in the proceeding.[3] We have not had occasion to consider this particular question.

3. The applicable provisions in 1992 of the Judicial Code of Ethics . . . were in Canon 3C(1) and 3C(1)(d):

> A judge should disqualify himself in a proceeding in which his impartiality might reasonably be questioned, including but not limited to instances where: . . .

Initially, we note that independent of the Judicial Code of Ethics, the United States Supreme Court has interpreted the Fourth Amendment to the United States Constitution to require that a search warrant be issued by a "neutral and detached magistrate." In Shadwick v. City of Tampa, 407 U.S. 345 (1972), the Supreme Court held that the office of magistrate, in order to satisfy the neutral and detached standard "requires severance and disengagement from activities of law enforcement." By way of illustration, the Supreme Court in *Shadwick* pointed to its earlier case of Coolidge v. New Hampshire, 403 U.S. 443 (1971), where it voided a search warrant issued by the state's attorney general because he "was actively in charge of the investigation and later was to be chief prosecutor at trial." Similarly, in Lo-Ji Sales, Inc. v. New York, 442 U.S. 319 (1979), the magistrate was found not to be neutral and detached when he "allowed himself to become a member, if not the leader, of the search party which was essentially a police operation." In Connally v. Georgia, 429 U.S. 245 (1977), the Supreme Court determined that a magistrate who was compensated based on a fee for the warrants issued could not be considered neutral and detached. It relied on its earlier case of Tumey v. Ohio, 273 U.S. 510 (1927), which invalidated on due process principles the payment of the village mayor, when he acted as a judge, from costs collected in criminal cases brought before him in which there was a conviction.

We afforded the same protection for a neutral and detached magistrate under our search and seizure constitutional provision in . . . State v. Dudick, 213 S.E.2d 458 (W. Va. 1975):

> The constitutional guarantee under W. Va. Const., Article III, §6 that no search warrant will issue except on probable cause goes to substance and not to form; therefore, where it is conclusively proved that a magistrate acted as a mere agent of the prosecutorial process and failed to make an independent evaluation of the circumstances surrounding a request for a warrant, the warrant will be held invalid and the search will be held illegal.

As the foregoing law indicates, where there is a lack of neutrality and detachment in the issuance of the search warrant, it is void. Aside from the constitutional requirements for a neutral and detached magistrate as to warrants, similar standards are imposed by Canon 3C of the Judicial Code of Ethics relating to the disqualification of a judge. The Code defines those situations when a judge may be precluded from presiding over a case. The underlying rationale for requiring disqualification is based on principles of due process. . . .

Canon 3C(1) contains an initial general admonition that "[a] judge should disqualify himself in a proceeding in which his impartiality might reasonably be questioned[.]" This admonition is followed by a number of specific instances when disqualification is required. . . . In this case, in addition to the general disqualification standard, it is claimed that the more specific disqualification test contained in Canon 3C(1)(d)(iii) applies. This provision requires disqualification if the judge's spouse has "an interest that could be substantially affected by the outcome of the proceeding[.]" This disqualification is claimed to apply if Chief Boober appeared

---

(d) he or his spouse, or a person within the third degree of relationship to either of them, or the spouse of such a person:

(i) is a party to the proceeding, or an officer, director, or trustee of a party; . . .

(iii) is known by the judge to have an interest that could be substantially affected by the outcome of the proceeding;

(iv) is to the judge's knowledge likely to be a material witness in the proceeding. . . .

before his wife to seek a warrant. . . . We have no case law on this point, but we agree with cases from other jurisdictions that support the disqualification.

For example, the Louisiana court in State v. LaCour, 493 So. 2d 756 (La. Ct. App. 1986), set aside a criminal conviction because it found that the judge should have disqualified himself because his son was prosecuting the defendant on another criminal charge in a different county. . . . In Smith v. Beckman, 683 P.2d 1214 (Colo. Ct. App. 1984), the judge's wife was an assistant prosecutor. The record showed that the prosecutor's office had screened her from cases that were before her husband. The court concluded that his disqualification in all criminal cases was warranted because of the appearance of impropriety. . . . The critical point in the court's view was the perception of the closeness created by the marital relationship:

> A husband and wife generally conduct their personal and financial affairs as a partnership. In addition to living together, a husband and wife are also perceived to share confidences regarding their personal lives and employment situations. Generally, the public views married people as "a couple," as "a partnership," and as participants in a relationship more intimate than any other kind of relationship between individuals. In our view the existence of a marriage relationship between a judge and a deputy district attorney in the same county is sufficient to establish grounds for disqualification, even though no other facts call into question the judge's impartiality. . . .

We believe that the foregoing cases and the language in Canon 3C(1) and 3C(1)(d)(i) of the Judicial Code of Ethics relating to the disqualification of a judicial official when his or her impartiality might reasonably be questioned if the official's spouse is a party to the proceeding would foreclose a magistrate from issuing a warrant sought by his or her spouse who is a police officer. However, this situation did not occur here.

The search warrant was issued at the request of Sergeant R. R. Roberts of the Ranson police force. At the hearing below, Magistrate Boober testified that she was the on-call magistrate for emergency matters that might occur after 4:00 P.M. and before 8:00 A.M. the next morning when the magistrate office would be open for normal business.

Magistrate Boober also stated that she was not related to Sergeant Roberts and had no contact with him except through the magistrate system. She also stated that she made an independent review of the affidavit for the search warrant. Her husband's name did not appear on the affidavit nor was there any discussion about her husband with Sergeant Roberts.

There was no evidence to show any actual bias or partiality on the part of Magistrate Boober. The entire argument centered on an implied partiality because of the magistrate's relationship to Chief Boober. We indicated earlier that any criminal matters which the magistrate's husband is involved with cannot be brought before her because of their spousal relationship. We decline to extend such a per se rule with regard to the other members of the Ranson police force. The fact that a magistrate's spouse is the chief of police of a small police force does not automatically disqualify the magistrate, who is otherwise neutral and detached, from issuing a warrant sought by another member of such police force. However, a small police force[14] coupled with the chief's active role in a given case may create an appearance

14. The 1993 West Virginia Blue Book gives the population of the City of Ranson at 2,890. According to the [briefs], there are six other police officers in addition to the Chief of Police.

of impropriety that would warrant a right to challenge the validity of a search warrant. Certainly, prudence dictates that Magistrate Boober's involvement with warrants from the Ranson police force should be severely curtailed. . . .

Finally, we are asked to extend the rule of necessity to allow Magistrate Boober to handle warrants when she is the on-call magistrate. The rule of necessity is an exception to the disqualification of a judge. It allows a judge who is otherwise disqualified to handle the case to preside if there is no provision that allows another judge to hear the matter. . . .

The rule of necessity is an exception to the general rule precluding a disqualified judge from hearing a matter. Therefore, it is strictly construed and applied only when there is no other person having jurisdiction to handle the matter that can be brought in to hear it. . . . We would not sanction the use of the rule were it to be offered if Chief Boober appeared seeking the search warrant. In the case of the other police officers from Ranson, we decline to utilize the rule simply because we do not find that Magistrate Boober is automatically barred from issuing warrants at their request. There may be circumstances that can be shown that would cast a shadow over the magistrate's impartiality. In that event, a motion to suppress the evidence obtained under the warrant may be made, and the issue will be resolved at a hearing. . . . The matter is remanded for a further hearing with regard to the warrant if the relators below desire to challenge it on the basis that there are additional facts, other than her marriage to Chief Boober, that demonstrate Magistrate Boober was not neutral and detached. . . .

Notes

1. *Who issues warrants? Majority view.* Most states (more than 30) allow only judges and magistrates to issue warrants. Some state statutes require that magistrates be lawyers, while others list no special statutory qualifications. Magistrates are generally appointed by a judge. They are thus subject to removal by judges or city officials and lack some of the usual privileges accorded to judicial officers. A smaller group of states allow functionaries — who go by titles such as "clerk magistrates," "ministerial recorders," clerks of court, or court commissioners — to issue search warrants. In West Virginia, mayors have the power to issue search warrants pursuant to violations of city ordinances. W. Va. Code §8-10-1. New Mexico allows the state secretary of finance and administration to authorize state agencies to issue search warrants. N.M. Stat. Ann. §6-5-9.

As noted in *Dietrick,* the Supreme Court, in Connally v. Georgia, 429 U.S. 245 (1977), found unconstitutional a system that compensated magistrates for each warrant they issued. What if, to encourage protection of individual rights, magistrates were paid for warrants they refused to issue?

2. *Neutrality in outcomes.* What if a defendant can show that a particular magistrate has never refused a warrant or approves warrants 98 percent of the time? A major empirical study of the search warrant process in seven jurisdictions made the following observations about the number of warrant applications denied by magistrates:

> It is unfortunate, though not surprising, that documents are not routinely collected that reveal the number of applications that are denied by magistrates. Normally a

> rejected application is destroyed or revised by the applicant. According to our observations and interviews, the rate of outright rejection is extremely low. Most of the police officers interviewed could not remember having a search warrant application turned down. The estimates by the judges interviewed varied on the number of rejections from almost never to about half. Of the 84 warrant proceedings observed, 7 resulted in denial of the application (8 percent).

Richard van Duizend, Paul Sutton, and Charlotte Carter, The Search Warrant Process: Preconceptions, Perceptions, Practices 26-27 (1985). A more recent study of warrant practices in one jurisdiction noted that some judges handled far more than their share of warrant applications. Of the 24 judges available for duty, six judges issued almost three-fourths of the search warrants. Laurence A. Benner and Charles T. Samarkos, Searching for Narcotics in San Diego: Preliminary Findings from the San Diego Search Warrant Project, 36 Cal. W. L. Rev. 221, 226 (2000). Could a defendant strengthen her challenge to the neutrality of a magistrate by demonstrating that the police apply to the particular magistrate in question for search warrants far more often than to other available magistrates?

b. Particularity in Warrants

Remember that the Fourth Amendment, in language echoed in many state provisions, says that "no Warrants shall issue, but upon probable cause, supported by Oath or affirmation, and particularly describing the place to be searched, and the persons or things to be seized." The following classic state cases explore the requirement that warrants be supported by "Oath or affirmation" and that they "particularly" describe the place to be searched and the persons or things to be seized. This "particularity" requirement captures an essential part of the distinction between valid warrants and invalid general warrants.

■ BELL v. CLAPP

10 Johns. 263 (N.Y. 1813)

PER CURIAM

The matter set forth in the plea is a justification of the trespass. The search warrant was founded on oath, and the information stated that one hundred barrels of flour had been stolen from the wharf, in the first ward, by Richard and Isaac Jaques, and that the same, or a part thereof, was concealed in a cellar of Gideon Jaques. The plea then states that the warrant, being under the hand and seal of the magistrate . . . , and being directed to the constables and marshals, authorized and required them to enter the said cellar, in the day-time, and search for the flour, and to bring it, together with the said Gideon, or the person in whose custody it might be found, before the justice; that in pursuance of the warrant, the defendants, the one being a constable and the other a marshal, did go to the cellar, which was part and parcel of the dwelling-house of the plaintiff, and, after being refused entrance, did open the door by force, and seize the flour in as peaceable a manner as possible. This, then, was a valid warrant duly executed by these officers. The warrant had all the essential qualities of a legal warrant. It was founded on oath, and was specific as to place and object, and the stolen goods were taken, and taken in as peaceable a manner as the nature of the case admitted.

In Entick v. Carrington . . . Lord Camden admitted a search warrant, so well guarded, to be a lawful authority. The warrant did not state in whom the property of the flour resided, nor was this essential to its validity: a person may even be indicted and convicted of stealing the goods of a person unknown. Nor did it affect the legality of the warrant that it directed the officer to bring Jaques, to whom the cellar belonged, or the person in whose custody the flour might be found. It was impossible for any warrant to be more explicit and particular; and it would, probably, have been the duty of the officer to have arrested any person in possession of the stolen goods at the place designated, without any directions in the warrant, and to have carried him before the justice for examination.

Sir Mathew Hale, in one part of his treatise, denies to the officer the right of breaking open the door, on a warrant to search for stolen goods. But he, afterwards, admits this power in the officer, if the door be shut, and if upon demand it is refused to be opened. This past opinion is founded on the better reason, for search warrants are often indispensable to the detection of crimes; and they would be of little or no efficacy without this power attached to them. All the checks which the English law, and which even the constitution of the United States, have imposed upon the operation of these search warrants, and with the manifestation of a strong jealousy of the abuses incident to them, would scarcely have been thought of, or have been deemed necessary, if the warrant did not communicate the power of opening the outer door of a house. . . .

The defendants are, accordingly, entitled to judgment upon the demurrers. Judgment for the defendants.

■ GRUMMON v. RAYMOND

1 Conn. 40 (1814)

REEVE, C.J.

That this warrant was such as no justice ought to have issued will be admitted; for it is not only a warrant to search for stolen goods supposed to be concealed in a particular place, but it is a warrant to search all suspected places, stores, shops and barns in Wilton. Where those suspected places were in Wilton is not pointed out, or by whom suspected: so that all the dwelling-houses and out-houses within the town of Wilton were by this warrant made liable to search. The officer also was directed to search suspected persons, and arrest them. By whom they were suspected, whether by the justice, the officer, or complainant, is not mentioned; so that every citizen of the United States within the jurisdiction of the justice to try for theft, was liable to be arrested and carried before the justice for trial. The warrant was this: Search every house, store or barn within the town of Wilton, that is suspected of having certain bags concealed in it, said to be stolen, and all persons who are suspected of having stolen them. This is a general search-warrant, which has always been determined to be illegal, not only in cases of searching for stolen goods, but in all other cases. . . .

Should it be asked, if a justice issues a warrant which has some defect in it, so that the person arrested cannot be held by it, is the justice liable? I answer, he is not, if he aims at issuing a process which the law recognizes, and fails through some oversight or mistake. . . . From the case of Entick v. Carrington, we have the opinion of the Chief Justice, that if a warrant which is against law be granted, such as no justice of the peace or other magistrate, high or low, has power to issue, the justice who issues and the officer who executes it are liable in an action of trespass. And no man can hesitate to say, that the law knows of no such warrant as one to arrest suspected persons without naming them, without any complaint, against any person, leaving it to the officer to suspect whom he pleases, or to arrest every person that any other person suspects. . . .

This purports to be a search-warrant for stolen goods; and the law requires, that before any justice can have power to issue a warrant in such case, certain requisites be complied with. . . . There must be an oath by the applicant that he has had his goods stolen, and strongly suspects that they are concealed in such a place; and the warrant cannot give a direction to search any other place than the particular place pointed out. By the complaint on record in writing, it does not appear that any oath was made that the bags were stolen; nor that any place was pointed out where they were concealed; both of which were necessary, and without them no warrant could issue.

But it is said, that from the warrant under the hand of the justice it appears, that there was an oath that the bags were stolen; and that they were concealed at Aaron Hyatt's, or some other place. It is true, the justice so says; but it will be remarked, that he says, "as will appear by the complaint"; and upon examination of that, there is no oath ever made that there was any felony, or any place pointed out where the stolen bags were supposed to be; so that the justice had no jurisdiction over the case so as to issue a search-warrant.

But admitting that the warrant under the hand of the justice presents to us correctly the facts, it will not help the defendants; for there is no place pointed out, only at Aaron Hyatt's or somewhere else, which is equivalent to saying, that they were somewhere concealed. This would not be sufficient to warrant the issuing of a search-warrant.

If it should be contended, that it would authorize the issuing of a warrant to search Aaron Hyatt's, yet it laid no foundation to search any other place, for no other place is mentioned; and notwithstanding this, the warrant directs all suspected places in Wilton to be searched, whether houses, barns or stores; and under a warrant so issued the plaintiff was arrested. . . .

The justice, therefore, was liable to this action, and the officer also who executed it; for although an officer is not always liable when he executes an improper warrant; yet this is in a case where it does not appear on the face of the warrant that it is illegal. It may, for any thing that the officer can discover, be legal; and in such case, it is his duty to obey, and to presume that it is lawful. But an officer is bound to know the law; and when the warrant, on the face of it, appears to be illegal, and he executes it, he is liable to the person arrested. Such was the present case.

Notes

1. *Particular description of place to be searched: majority position.* The nineteenth-century opinions in *Bell* and *Grummon* reflect some very modern concerns. Both state and federal constitutions require that the warrant name with "particularity" the place to be searched and the things to be seized. When a warrant lists property in an urban setting, the street address (including the apartment number, where

relevant) is usually particular enough to allow the searching officer "with reasonable effort [to] ascertain and identify the place intended." Steele v. United States, 267 U.S. 498 (1925). Property in a rural setting might be described without an address.

What was the difference between the alternative phrasing in the warrants in *Bell* and *Grummon*? Would a warrant listing more than one place to search ever be valid? Does it matter if different people own or occupy the properties? Compare State v. Mehner, 480 N.W.2d 872 (Iowa 1992) (validating warrant listing two house trailers with different occupants) with Brewer v. State, 244 P.2d 1154 (Okla. Crim. App. 1952) (invalidating warrant listing two apartments and barn occupied by different families).

Warrants tend to be more specific about the place to be searched than about any persons to be searched. Why is that? If you were a magistrate, what sort of evidence would convince you to issue a warrant authorizing the search of a specific bar and "all persons" found on those premises? See State v. Thomas, 540 N.W.2d 658 (Iowa 1995) (invalidating warrant; application noted numerous prior arrests and controlled purchases of crack cocaine, and observations by undercover officers that most persons present in bar possessed narcotics or weapons).

2. *Particular description of things to be seized: majority position.* Warrants authorize searches for particular objects. The types of objects that may be seized vary somewhat from state to state, although the general categories are fruits, instrumentalities, and evidence of crime. See Ill. Stat. ch. 725, §5/108-3(a) ("any judge may issue a search warrant for the seizure of [any] instruments, articles or things designed or intended for use or which are or have been used in the commission of, or which may constitute evidence of, the offense in connection with which the warrant is issued; or contraband, the fruits of crime, or things otherwise criminally possessed"). The Fourth Amendment requirement of particularity "makes general searches . . . impossible and prevents the seizure of one thing under a warrant describing another. As to what is taken, nothing is left to the discretion of the officer executing the warrant." Marron v. United States, 275 U.S. 192 (1927). What sort of description in the warrant would leave "nothing" to the discretion of the officer? See People v. Brown, 749 N.E.2d 170 (N.Y. 2001) (warrant naming four particular items plus authorizing search for "any other property the possession of which would be considered contraband" was overbroad).

Like the federal constitution, most state constitutions and statutes also require a description of the items (or persons) being sought and an explanation for why the applicant believes that the items (or persons) are at the location sought. See Ohio Rev. Code §2933.24(A) (search warrant shall "particularly name or describe the property to be searched for and seized, the place to be searched, and the person to be searched").

3. *"[S]upported by Oath or affirmation."* According to Richard van Duizend, Paul Sutton, and Charlotte Carter, The Search Warrant Process (1985), every state requires some form of sworn statement to accompany an application for a search warrant. See State v. Tye, 636 N.W.2d 473 (Wis. 2001) (lack of sworn statement supporting warrant requires suppression). Most states allow the statement to be oral; only Missouri and Pennsylvania expressly forbid oral statements to support a search warrant.

4. *Warrants "in writing" and telephonic warrants.* A majority of states have statutes requiring that warrants be in writing. A number of state constitutions also expressly

provide for written warrants. See Neb. Rev. Stat. §29-830; R.I. Const. Art. 1, §6. Requiring warrants to be in writing does not preclude their electronic transmission. See Mich. Comp. Laws §780.651.

Despite the prevalence of constitutional provisions and statutes calling for warrants obtained by testimony made under oath and "in writing," a growing number of states have statutes authorizing the police to obtain warrants over the telephone. Consider, for example, Kan. Stat. Ann. §22-2502(a):

> A search warrant shall be issued only upon the oral or written statement, including those conveyed or received by telefacsimile communication, of any person under oath or affirmation which states facts sufficient to show probable cause that a crime has been or is being committed and which particularly describes a person, place or means of conveyance to be searched and things to be seized. Any statement which is made orally shall be either taken down by a certified shorthand reporter, sworn to under oath and made part of the application for a search warrant, or recorded before the magistrate from whom the search warrant is requested and sworn to under oath. Any statement orally made shall be reduced to writing as soon thereafter as possible. If the magistrate is satisfied that grounds for the application exist or that there is probable cause to believe that they exist, the magistrate may issue a search warrant.

Why does Kansas insist that the person seeking the warrant swear to the statement under oath? Why does the state go to the trouble and expense of reducing the statements to writing? Does the availability of telephonic warrants mean that police can claim exigent circumstances in far fewer cases? One survey of warrant practices discovered that officers rarely used the available procedures for telephonic and electronic search warrants. Laurence A. Benner and Charles T. Samarkos, Searching for Narcotics in San Diego: Preliminary Findings from the San Diego Search Warrant Project, 36 Cal. W. L. Rev. 221, 223 (2000). Why might police officers decline to use such procedures when they are available?

5. *Plain view seizures.* You may recall, from Chapter 2, the "plain view" doctrine, which declares that the police may seize evidence, contraband, or the fruits or instrumentalities of crime that come within the "plain view" of police officers during proper execution of a valid warrant. See Horton v. California, 496 U.S. 128 (1990) (item in plain view is seizable if its incriminating character is immediately apparent to police). Does this authorization to seize items not named in the warrant effectively eliminate any requirement that the warrant "particularly name" the property to be seized?

6. *The advantage for police of warrants listing small items.* The nature of the items sought will determine the permissible scope of the search. If police are looking for an elephant, the search will be limited to places an elephant might hide. If police are looking for a field mouse, the scope of the search would be much broader. See, e.g., State v. Apelt, 861 P.2d 634 (Ariz. 1993) (because warrant included receipts, police could conduct a very detailed search and had a higher possibility of additional "plain view" discovery of evidence than in a more narrowly circumscribed search). Would it be ethical to advise police to include small items such as receipts in all warrant applications?

7. *The "four corners" rule.* If a defendant challenges the sufficiency of a warrant during a suppression hearing, statutes and court rules in most jurisdictions (and constitutional rulings in a few others) prevent the government from supplementing the warrant application itself with information that the officers knew at the time but

failed to present to the magistrate. Some also prevent the government from relying on any information supplementing the application, even if it was actually presented to the magistrate. People v. Sloan, 538 N.W.2d 380 (Mich. 1995). The government's defense of the warrant, in other words, must come from within the "four corners" of the application. Why have the states embraced this view?

8. *Challenges to facially sufficient warrants.* Defendants sometimes will concede that the facts set forth in the warrant amount to probable cause but contend that the factual basis for the warrant is untrue. The Supreme Court has held (and state courts have largely agreed) that if a defendant makes a preliminary showing of false statements in the warrant application, the trial court must grant a hearing on the question. Under Franks v. Delaware, 438 U.S. 154 (1978), the defendant's preliminary showing must demonstrate that the government "knowingly and intentionally, or with reckless disregard for the truth," included a false statement in the warrant affidavit. The attack must be "more than conclusory," and must point out "specifically with supporting reasons" the portion of the warrant affidavit that is claimed to be false. It also must be accompanied by affidavits or reliable statements of witnesses, or a satisfactory explanation of their absence. If the unreliable evidence was necessary to the government's showing of probable cause, the defendant gets a hearing and must establish his or her claims by a preponderance of the evidence before the fruits of the search or seizure are excluded from evidence.

Problem 3-2. Errors in a Facially Valid Warrant

Officer Holden observed a confidential informant make two illegal purchases of weapons at 916 Varney Street. Both times, the informant entered the building, returned with the weapons, and told Holden that he made the purchases in the "last apartment, of two, on the left" in a hallway down a flight of stairs. With this information, Holden applied for and obtained a warrant to search the apartment. The affidavit accompanying the application described the premises as follows:

> First-floor corner apartment, 916 Varney Street, described as a four-story red-brick structure with a green-colored solid door, with the number 916 affixed to the outside of the main entryway. The corner apartment is described as down one flight of stairs where three apartment doors are situated with two on the left side and one on the right side, the door is tan in color and is the second door on the left side in the main hallway at the end of the hall.

Prior to executing the warrant, Holden sent the informant into the building for a third time. After returning outside, he told Holden that the apartment subject to the warrant had a rug in front of the door. When Holden entered the hallway of the building, he realized that the informant was mistaken: There were two doors on the right side of the hallway and only one on the left. Holden decided to search the sole apartment on the left because there was a rug outside the door. He discovered evidence of weapons violations.

In a suppression hearing, will the court treat the evidence as the product of a valid warranted search? Compare Buckner v. United States, 615 A.2d 1154 (D.C. 1992).

Notes

1. *Awareness of the error.* In this problem, the officer was aware of the inaccuracy in the warrant before executing it. Does it make a difference if the officer remains unaware of the inaccuracy until she has begun the search? See Maryland v. Garrison, 480 U.S. 79 (1987) (warrant listing third floor as single apartment, when it was actually divided into separate apartments, could be executed because officers were reasonable in not discovering the inadvertent error in the warrant).

2. *The wrong jurisdiction.* Is an otherwise valid warrant still valid if it is executed by police accidentally acting outside of their jurisdiction? See People v. Martinez, 898 P.2d 28 (Colo. 1995) (error in jurisdiction, despite violating statute, not fatal).

3. Execution of Warrants

Once the police have obtained a valid warrant, they must "execute" it. That is, the police carry out a search within the limits described in the warrant, and "return" it to the magistrate who issued the warrant. The return serves as a report about the search. Recall that the court in Entick v. Carrington expressed some concern about the lack of any return for a general warrant, and thus the enforcement officer who conducted the search would not be accountable for completing the job properly. Does a return prevent abuses by searchers?

Specific procedure rules and statutes address the details of executing warrants. For instance, rules determine the total time that can elapse between issuance and execution of a search warrant. All but three states prescribe a deadline for serving a warrant, at which time the warrant expires. This period ranges from two days (North Carolina and Pennsylvania) to 60 days (Arkansas). The typical time span is 10 days (the period employed in more than 30 states plus the federal system). Maryland and Virginia allow 15 days. Ohio and Texas allow three days, Illinois and Kansas allow four days, and Delaware allows three days for night searches and 10 days for daytime searches. Apparently, it is common for police to delay the execution of a warrant after the judge issues it. As one might expect, searches are far more likely to produce the expected evidence if they are executed promptly. See Laurence A. Benner and Charles T. Samarkos, Searching for Narcotics in San Diego: Preliminary Findings from the San Diego Search Warrant Project, 36 Cal. W. L. Rev. 221, 223 (2000).

■ STEINEY RICHARDS v. WISCONSIN

520 U.S. 385 (1997)

STEVENS, J.

. . . On December 31, 1991, police officers in Madison, Wisconsin obtained a warrant to search Steiney Richards' hotel room for drugs and related paraphernalia. The search warrant was the culmination of an investigation that had uncovered substantial evidence that Richards was one of several individuals dealing drugs out of hotel rooms in Madison. The police requested a warrant that would have given advance authorization for a "no-knock" entry into the hotel room, but the magistrate explicitly deleted those portions of the warrant.

The officers arrived at the hotel room at 3:40 A.M. Officer Pharo, dressed as a maintenance man, led the team. With him were several plainclothes officers and at least one man in uniform. Officer Pharo knocked on Richards' door and, responding to the query from inside the room, stated that he was a maintenance man. With the chain still on the door, Richards cracked it open. [When Richards] opened the door he saw the man in uniform standing behind Officer Pharo. He quickly slammed the door closed and, after waiting two or three seconds, the officers began kicking and ramming the door to gain entry to the locked room. [The] officers testified that they identified themselves as police while they were kicking the door in. When they finally did break into the room, the officers caught Richards trying to escape through the window. They also found cash and cocaine hidden in plastic bags above the bathroom ceiling tiles.

Richards sought to have the evidence from his hotel room suppressed on the ground that the officers had failed to knock and announce their presence prior to forcing entry into the room. The trial court denied the motion, concluding that the officers could gather from Richards' strange behavior when they first sought entry that he knew they were police officers and that he might try to destroy evidence or to escape. The judge emphasized that the easily disposable nature of the drugs the police were searching for further justified their decision to identify themselves as they crossed the threshold instead of announcing their presence before seeking entry.

[The Wisconsin Supreme Court] found it reasonable — after considering criminal conduct surveys, newspaper articles, and other judicial opinions — to assume that all felony drug crimes will involve "an extremely high risk of serious if not deadly injury to the police as well as the potential for the disposal of drugs by the occupants prior to entry by the police." [The] court concluded that exigent circumstances justifying a no-knock entry are always present in felony drug cases.

[In Wilson v. Arkansas, 514 U.S. 927 (1995), we held that the Fourth Amendment incorporates the common law requirement that police officers entering a dwelling must knock on the door and announce their identity and purpose before attempting forcible entry. At the same time, we recognized that the "flexible requirement of reasonableness should not be read to mandate a rigid rule of announcement that ignores countervailing law enforcement interests." In particular, we stated] that the knock-and-announce requirement could give way under circumstances presenting a threat of physical violence, or where police officers have reason to believe that evidence would likely be destroyed if advance notice were given. It is indisputable that felony drug investigations may frequently involve both of these circumstances. The question we must resolve is whether this fact justifies dispensing with case-by-case evaluation of the manner in which a search was executed.

The Wisconsin court explained its blanket exception as necessitated by the special circumstances of today's drug culture, and the State asserted at oral argument that the blanket exception was reasonable in felony drug cases because of the convergence in a violent and dangerous form of commerce of weapons and the destruction of drugs. But creating exceptions to the knock-and-announce rule based on the "culture" surrounding a general category of criminal behavior presents at least two serious concerns.

First, the exception contains considerable overgeneralization. For example, while drug investigation frequently does pose special risks to officer safety and the preservation of evidence, not every drug investigation will pose these risks to a substantial degree. For example, a search could be conducted at a time when the only individuals present in a residence have no connection with the drug activity and thus will be unlikely to threaten officers or destroy evidence. Or the police could know that the drugs being searched for were of a type or in a location that made them impossible to destroy quickly. In those situations, the asserted governmental interests in preserving evidence and maintaining safety may not outweigh the individual privacy interests intruded upon by a no-knock entry.[5] Wisconsin's blanket rule impermissibly insulates these cases from judicial review.

A second difficulty with permitting a criminal-category exception to the knock-and-announce requirement is that the reasons for creating an exception in one category can, relatively easily, be applied to others. Armed bank robbers, for example, are, by definition, likely to have weapons, and the fruits of their crime may be destroyed without too much difficulty. If a per se exception were allowed for each category of criminal investigation that included a considerable — albeit hypothetical — risk of danger to officers or destruction of evidence, the knock-and-announce element of the Fourth Amendment's reasonableness requirement would be meaningless.

Thus, the fact that felony drug investigations may frequently present circumstances warranting a no-knock entry cannot remove from the neutral scrutiny of a reviewing court the reasonableness of the police decision not to knock and announce in a particular case. Instead, in each case, it is the duty of a court confronted with the question to determine whether the facts and circumstances of the particular entry justified dispensing with the knock-and-announce requirement.

In order to justify a "no-knock" entry, the police must have a reasonable suspicion that knocking and announcing their presence, under the particular circumstances, would be dangerous or futile, or that it would inhibit the effective investigation of the crime by, for example, allowing the destruction of evidence. This standard — as opposed to a probable cause requirement — strikes the appropriate balance between the legitimate law enforcement concerns at issue in the execution of search warrants and the individual privacy interests affected by no-knock entries. This showing is not high, but the police should be required to make it whenever the reasonableness of a no-knock entry is challenged.

Although we reject the Wisconsin court's blanket exception to the knock-and-announce requirement, we conclude that the officers' no-knock entry into Richards' hotel room did not violate the Fourth Amendment. We agree with the trial court . . . that the circumstances in this case show that the officers had a reasonable suspicion that Richards might destroy evidence if given further opportunity to do so.

The judge who heard testimony at Richards' suppression hearing concluded that it was reasonable for the officers executing the warrant to believe that Richards

5. The State asserts that the intrusion on individual interests effectuated by a no-knock entry is minimal because the execution of the warrant itself constitutes the primary intrusion on individual privacy and that the individual privacy interest cannot outweigh the generalized governmental interest in effective and safe law enforcement. While it is true that a no-knock entry is less intrusive than, for example, a warrantless search, the individual interests implicated by an unannounced, forcible entry should not be unduly minimized. As we observed in *Wilson,* the common law recognized that individuals should have an opportunity to themselves comply with the law and to avoid the destruction of property occasioned by a forcible entry. These interests are not inconsequential. Additionally, when police enter a residence without announcing their presence, the residents are not given any opportunity to prepare themselves for such an entry. . . . The brief interlude between announcement and entry with a warrant may be the opportunity that an individual has to pull on clothes or get out of bed.

knew, after opening the door to his hotel room the first time, that the men seeking entry to his room were the police. Once the officers reasonably believed that Richards knew who they were, the court concluded, it was reasonable for them to force entry immediately given the disposable nature of the drugs.

In arguing that the officers' entry was unreasonable, Richards places great emphasis on the fact that the magistrate who signed the search warrant for his hotel room deleted the portions of the proposed warrant that would have given the officers permission to execute a no-knock entry. But this fact does not alter the reasonableness of the officers' decision, which must be evaluated as of the time they entered the hotel room. [A number of States give magistrate judges the authority to issue "no-knock" warrants if the officers demonstrate ahead of time a reasonable suspicion that entry without prior announcement will be appropriate in a particular context. The practice of allowing magistrates to issue no-knock warrants seems entirely reasonable when sufficient cause to do so can be demonstrated ahead of time. But, as the facts of this case demonstrate, a magistrate's decision not to authorize a no-knock entry should not be interpreted to remove the officers' authority to exercise independent judgment concerning the wisdom of a no-knock entry at the time the warrant is being executed.]

Accordingly, although we reject the blanket exception to the knock-and-announce requirement for felony drug investigations, the judgment of the Wisconsin Supreme Court is affirmed.

Notes

1. *Use of force in executing warrants and "knock and announce."* Most states have statutes requiring a police officer executing a search warrant to "knock and announce"—that is, to knock on the door before entering, to identify himself as a police officer, and to explain the purpose for seeking entry. See 18 U.S.C. §3109. Those with no statute on point have recognized the doctrine through judicial opinions. Only after entrance has been refused may the officer use force to enter. The knock-and-announce requirement derives from the common law. See Semayne's Case, 77 Eng. Rep. 194 (K.B. 1603). It also has constitutional dimensions: A failure to knock and announce can have some bearing on the constitutional "reasonableness" of a search or seizure. See Wilson v. Arkansas, 514 U.S. 927 (1995).

2. *No-knock entry.* There are important exceptions to the knock-and-announce requirement. Typically, the police may enter without notice if they have enough reason to believe that notice would endanger themselves or some other party, or would allow for the destruction of evidence or the escape of a suspect. In most states with a statute codifying the no-knock principle, the statute also explicitly lists some exceptions to this requirement. In other states, the courts have interpreted the statutory or common law knock-and-announce requirement to allow for no-knock entry under such exigent circumstances. See Commonwealth v. Means, 614 A.2d 220 (Pa. 1992). What common household sounds might justify a forcible no-knock entry to execute a search? See also United States v. Ramirez, 523 U.S. 65 (1998) ("no knock" searches that cause property damage subject to same reasonableness standard as those causing no damage). A number of courts allow police officers to enter without announcing their true intentions if they can gain entry through a ruse such as pretending to be the "pizza man." Adcock v. Commonwealth, 967 S.W.2d 6 (Ky. 1998);

State v. Eleneki, 993 P.2d 1191 (Haw. 2000). Is entry through a ruse consistent with the rationale of the knock-and-announce principle?

As we saw in Richards v. Wisconsin, the exceptions to the knock-and-announce requirement cannot be phrased too broadly. However, on the specific facts of that case, the officers' decision to enter the location unannounced might be constitutionally reasonable. See People v. Krueger, 675 N.E.2d 604 (Ill. 1996) (striking down portion of knock-and-announce statute because it allows prior possession of firearm by occupant of building to be an exigent circumstance excusing failure to knock and announce).

3. *Limits on nighttime searches.* Another common subject for statutes and codes of criminal procedure is the time of day or night an officer may execute a search warrant. More than a dozen states have rules or statutes explicitly authorizing the execution of a search warrant at night, without any special showing or procedures. See Ind. Code §35-33-5-7(c); Ga. Code §17-5-26. However, roughly 30 states have statutes or procedural rules imposing some legal limit on the execution of search warrants at night beyond the usual requirements for daytime warrants. The most common limitation is specific authorization by the magistrate, without requiring the government to make any particular special showing. See Hope v. State, 570 A.2d 1185 (Del. 1990) (nighttime execution of warrant properly authorized by magistrate as required by statute, even though magistrate gave no reasons supporting need for nighttime search). States might also require the government agents to make some special showing before conducting a search at night. See Mo. Rev. Stat. §542.291 ("The search may be made at night if making it during the daytime is not practicable"); Minn. Stat. §626.14 (search warrant may be served only between 7 A.M. and 8 P.M. unless court "determines on the basis of facts stated in the affidavits that a nighttime search outside those hours is necessary to prevent the loss, destruction, or removal of the objects of the search or to protect the searchers or the public"). These restrictions on searches at night are often very detailed. Where detailed statutes or procedure rules loom larger than any constitutional requirements, does that necessarily make procedure clearer? Does it prevent investigators, attorneys, and judges from creating their own special requirements for special settings? See Coleman v. State, 826 S.W.2d 273 (Ark. 1992) (approving night search based on warrant application containing boilerplate language taken from procedure rules requiring government to show facts establishing special need for night search).

4. *Witnesses and returns.* The law in Germany and France requires searches of a home to be witnessed by a resident or someone else not working for the police. See Richard S. Frase and Thomas Weigend, German Criminal Justice as a Guide to American Law Reform: Similar Problems, Better Solutions?, 18 B.C. Int'l & Comp. L. Rev. 317 (1995). In the United States, officers executing a search warrant must fill out the "return," describing to the issuing judge the results of the search. Do these two requirements provide comparable protections to the owner of property that is searched?

5. *Burden of proof.* Most jurisdictions encourage greater police use of search warrants by shifting the burden of proof at a suppression hearing. While the government bears the burden of proof for warrantless searches that are challenged at a suppression hearing, the defendant must carry the burden of proof for warranted searches. State v. Staten, 469 N.W.2d 112 (Neb. 1991); City of Xenia v. Wallace, 524 N.E.2d 889 (Ohio 1988). There is, however, a sizable group of states placing the burden of coming forward and the burden of persuasion on the prosecution for all motions to

suppress. See Kan. Stat. Ann. §22-3216 ("the burden of proving that the search and seizure were lawful shall be on the prosecution"); Mo. Rev. Stat. §542.296.

6. *Ride-alongs and reasonableness.* Some police departments allow members of the public or the media to ride along in their patrol cars and to observe the police at work. From time to time, the ride-along guest might observe the officers as they execute a search or arrest warrant in a home. Does the presence of media or other ride-along observers make a warranted search any less reasonable? What if the observers are taking pictures or filming the events for television viewers? See Wilson v. Layne, 526 U.S. 603 (1999) (team of officers entered the home at 6:45 A.M., accompanied by reporter and photographer from newspaper; court held that bringing media into home during arrest was unreasonable because presence of the reporters inside the home was not "related to the objectives of the authorized intrusion" and did not "assist the police in their task"). As a public relations officer with the local police department, what policy might you draft for the participation of interested citizens or members of the media during searches or seizures?

4. *So You Like Warrants?*

There is surprisingly little empirical literature on how often warrants are actually used across different jurisdictions and for different kinds of searches (for example, for different suspected crimes). The general perception, supported by the limited and outdated evidence now available, is that the police conduct most searches, across most crime categories, in most jurisdictions, without obtaining warrants. Consider the following introduction from the van Duizend et al. study of the warrant process:

> [W]arrants do not serve as a primary safeguard of privacy because they are sought in relatively few cases. . . . The most detailed study of warrants prior to this one—the American Bar Foundation's survey of the Administration of Criminal Justice conducted in the late 1950s—found 29 search warrants issued in Detroit, 30 in Milwaukee, and 17 in Wichita during 1956. Following the application of the "exclusionary rule" to state court decisions, there was a substantial increase in the use of search warrants, although the number remains a small proportion of all criminal cases. In Boston, for example, the number of search warrants issued annually averaged 693 between 1961 and 1976. Moreover, the types of cases in which warrants were used appear to be quite limited, according to the literature. . . . Krantz, Gilman, Benda and Hallstrom (1979), in their study of Boston police practices found that 83 percent of the warrants issued during 1976 in the city's three busiest district courts "were to investigate suspected violations of the narcotic drug laws or vice laws." Such offenses accounted for less than 12 percent of all arrests nationally for that year.
>
> [A] serious question has been raised about the intensity and objectivity of the review, since search warrant applications appear to be rejected quite infrequently by reviewing magistrates. Federal data on state court wiretapping and eavesdropping warrants under the 1968 Omnibus Crime Control and Safe Streets Act show that of 5,563 applications made from 1969 through 1976, only 15 were denied. . . . A more recent survey of Virginia magistrates revealed [that 11.4 percent of the magistrates believed that the police have the best knowledge of the facts of the case, and that the magistrate should generally issue the warrant]. The impact of such a philosophy may be heightened by judge-shopping practices and by the fact that many magistrates authorized to issue search warrants are neither lawyers nor required to have any legal training. . . .

What could courts or legislatures or police departments do to encourage police officers to use warrants more often and to make warrants a more significant form of protection against improper searches and seizures? One possibility is to make the warrant requirement a true requirement, subject only to an exception for necessity. In other words, if a warrant can be obtained, it must be obtained or the search will be held invalid. Another approach would be to judge warrantless searches under a different, tougher standard than searches conducted pursuant to a warrant. A third possibility would be to encourage the use of telephonic warrants. For example, a jurisdiction might allow oral statements to support warrant requests, put cellular phones in police cars, and arrange to have a magistrate available "on call." Consider as well the two approaches we explore in this section, both of which might encourage the use of search warrants.

a. Anticipatory Warrants

The prototypical application for a search warrant describes events that have already occurred and infers from those facts the probable cause to believe that a crime has been committed and that the items sought will be found at the named location. But this creates a timing problem. The officer completes the application after gathering the relevant facts establishing probable cause and before the search takes place. The minutes or hours necessary to obtain a warrant may not be available after the confirmation of probable cause but before the search must happen. To relieve this problem, can the application anticipate future events?

■ STATE v. CRAIG PARENT

867 P.2d 1143 (Nev. 1994)

Per Curiam

. . . On July 1, 1992, an anonymous informant telephoned Detective Wygnanski of the Washoe County Consolidated Narcotics Unit. The informant told Wygnanski that respondent Parent would arrive, via Continental Airlines, at the Reno Cannon Airport, from New Orleans, on July 3, 1992. The informant stated that Parent would be with two women and he would have cocaine concealed inside a baby powder bottle in his baggage. The informant also provided Wygnanski with a physical description of Parent, his social security number, his FBI number, and his date of birth. Wygnanski confirmed the fact that Parent was scheduled to fly on Continental Airlines to Reno on July 3, 1992. On July 2, 1992, Wygnanski obtained a search warrant from a justice of the peace. Execution of the warrant was conditioned upon the arrival of Continental Airlines flight number 781 from New Orleans on July 3, 1992.

On July 3, 1992, Parent and two women arrived at the Reno Cannon Airport. Police officers observed the threesome once the threesome exited the airplane. Parent played a slot machine and entered the airport bar before retrieving his luggage from the luggage carousel. The police officers arrested Parent shortly after he retrieved his luggage. A police officer found 3.7 grams of cocaine in a baby powder bottle which was located inside one of appellant's bags.

[The state charged Parent with narcotics crimes, and Parent moved to suppress the evidence, which the trial court granted.] In his motion to suppress, Parent argued that the justice of the peace improperly issued the search warrant because NRS 179.035 requires that the offense for which the search was obtained be committed before the search warrant issues. . . .

NRS 179.035 provides (emphasis added):

> A warrant may be issued . . . to search for and seize any property:
>
> 1. Stolen or embezzled in violation of the laws of the State of Nevada, or of any other state or of the United States;
>
> 2. *Designed or intended for use or which is or has been used as the means of committing a criminal offense;* or
>
> 3. When the property or things to be seized consist of any item or constitute any evidence which tends to show that *a criminal offense has been committed,* or tends to show that a particular person has committed a criminal offense. . . .

At the time that the justice of the peace issued the search warrant, Parent had not yet entered the State of Nevada and had not yet committed a crime within the State of Nevada. The district court and the parties relied exclusively on NRS 179.035(3) in their analysis of this issue. Although NRS 179.035(3), at least arguably, contains language that might require that a crime actually have been committed at the time a warrant is issued,[2] NRS 179.035(2), which clearly applies to the facts of this case, has no such language. . . . The "intended for use" language of [NRS 179.035(2)] indicates that it is not necessary that the crime be committed before the magistrate issues the search warrant.

Although the district court is correct in noting that this court has not expressly approved of anticipatory search warrants, the clear weight of authority holds that anticipatory search warrants are not unconstitutional per se. . . . Anticipatory search warrants are not unreasonable and are therefore permissible under the Fourth Amendment to the United States Constitution. In United States v. Garcia, 882 F.2d 699 (2d Cir. 1989), the Second Circuit Court of Appeals provided a model for analysis of whether the issuance of an anticipatory search warrant is proper. We find the analysis persuasive. In that case, the court stated the following:

> We recognize that any warrant conditioned on what may occur in the future presents some potential for abuse. Magistrates and judges should therefore take care to require independent evidence giving rise to probable cause that the contraband will be located at the premises at the time of the search. . . . Moreover, when an anticipatory warrant is used, the magistrate should protect against its premature execution by listing in the warrant conditions governing the execution which are explicit, clear, and narrowly drawn so as to avoid misunderstanding or manipulation by government agents.
>
> Finally, as with other search warrants, anticipatory warrants require that a magistrate give careful heed to the fourth amendment's requirement that the warrant "particularly describe the place to be searched, and the persons or things to be seized." Of course, the scope of the search under an anticipatory warrant should be no narrower than the scope of the search which would be allowed under the "exigent circumstances" exception.

In this case, Officer Wygnanski's oral affidavit in support of the application for an anticipatory search warrant revealed that Wygnanski received a telephone call

2. One might argue, however, that NRS 179.035(3) requires only that a crime have been committed at the time property is seized; the statute is silent with respect to the timing of the issuance of the warrant. . . .

from an anonymous informant. The informant told Wygnanski that Parent, who resides in New Orleans, is a driver for an organized crime figure named Frank Kerazy. The informant told Wygnanski that Parent is six foot one, a white male with green eyes, brown wavy hair, and a moustache. Further, the informant told Wygnanski that Parent's FBI number is 259273JA1, that Parent has a long criminal history, that Parent would arrive in Reno on July 3rd at approximately 1:26 P.M., on flight number 781 Continental Airlines from New Orleans to Denver, and that Parent would be flying with two women by the names of Jodie and Stephanie. The informant told Wygnanski that Parent would bring approximately four ounces of cocaine which would be packaged in a baby powder bottle and would be disguised within the baby powder.

Wygnanski verified with the State of Louisiana that Parent had prior convictions for aggravated burglary, resisting arrest, causing substantial bodily harm to a police officer, resisting a police officer, first degree murder, armed robbery, aggravated burglary and attempted armed robbery. Parent's FBI record was expunged on September 28, 1989. Wygnanski also verified the fact that Parent would be flying into Reno on July 3rd on Continental Airlines.

The magistrate provided protection against premature execution of the warrant by requiring that the warrant be served only after the arrival of Continental Airlines flight number 781 from New Orleans on July 3, 1992. Finally, the warrant particularly described the place to be searched and persons or things to be seized. The warrant provided that the evidence to be seized consisted of cocaine, packaging materials, U.S. currency, and writings with names, addresses or phone numbers. The warrant provided that the police were permitted to search all luggage, purses, personal clothing, and the persons of the three suspects at the Reno Cannon Airport.

The issuance of the anticipatory search warrant and subsequent search in this case were authorized by state statute and did not violate the Fourth Amendment to the United States Constitution. The district court erred in suppressing the evidence obtained as a result of the search. . . .

Notes

1. *Anticipatory warrants: majority position.* The courts in over half of the states have upheld the use of anticipatory search warrants, while courts in about 10 states have held that such warrants violate constitutional or (more typically) statutory requirements. Even in some states where the law allows a magistrate to issue anticipatory warrants in some circumstances, practice might vary from county to county and from judge to judge. See Commonwealth v. Glass, 754 A.2d 655 (Pa. 2000). Many cases upholding anticipatory warrants in general nonetheless reject the warrant in a particular instance as being based on insufficient information to support a finding of probable cause — even probable cause contingent on future events. See, e.g., State v. Canelo, 653 A.2d 1097 (N.H. 1995). Why might anticipatory warrants be subject to a higher level of reversals than traditional warrants?

2. *Predicting the future.* Are anticipatory warrants likely to involve magistrates in reviewing a larger number of searches? Do they remove the magistrate from effective review, or do they involve the magistrate even more closely than usual in examining warrant applications? What would the officers in *Parent* have done if Jodie and Stephanie had not appeared on the flight with Craig? What if Craig appeared with shortly trimmed hair rather than "wavy" hair?

Suppose that investigators plan to send a paid informant into two specific locations to purchase illegal drugs. They are confident that the informant will be able to purchase the drugs at one of the two locations, but they are uncertain which location is correct. Could they obtain an anticipatory search warrant for the two locations, conditioned on a positive field test showing that the substance purchased was indeed cocaine? See State v. Gillespie, 530 N.W.2d 446 (Iowa 1995). Would the names of the targets contribute to the showing of probable cause? the dates or the addresses? Does this application amount to a request for the magistrate to preapprove a standard police operating procedure?

3. *Defining warrant-use policies.* Suppose you serve as counsel to the judicial conference of a state. What guidelines might you set for magistrates to avoid abuse of anticipatory warrants? Would you allow the police to lay out alternative sequences of events or alternative locations or descriptions? Would you insist that the magistrate include as a condition in the warrant every detail that the police relate in the application? Over what time span might an anticipatory warrant be valid? What kinds of information might you require to form the basis of both present information and expectation of future events?

4. *Virtues of anticipatory warrants.* If anticipatory warrants are both allowed and encouraged in a particular state, what might that do to the state's doctrines regarding exigent circumstances when the police have reasonable expectations that a situation requiring a search will occur? Should courts require police to obtain anticipatory search warrants instead of waiting for exigent circumstances when the police have sufficient information to expect that exigent circumstances will arise? See Commonwealth v. Killackey, 572 N.E.2d 560 (Mass. 1991) (rejecting requirement that police obtain anticipatory warrant if they can). Will anticipatory warrants reinvigorate the warrant requirement?

b. Administrative Warrants

Anticipatory warrants, considered in the preceding section, encourage the use of warrants. Another way to encourage the use of warrants is to allow a standard lower than probable cause (or a different kind of probable cause) for searches when the investigators obtain prior review and approval by magistrates, leaving the ordinary probable cause standard for warrantless searches.

The following case is pivotal in Fourth Amendment jurisprudence. Not only did it open up the possibility of a reduced standard of probable cause in certain settings, but it also established the importance of "balancing" the competing interests in different categories of Fourth Amendment cases. The balancing methodology enables a court to decide what level of justification the government must present to support a valid search in different contexts.

■ ROLAND CAMARA v. MUNICIPAL COURT OF SAN FRANCISCO

387 U.S. 523 (1967)

WHITE, J.

. . . On November 6, 1963, an inspector of the Division of Housing Inspection of the San Francisco Department of Public Health entered an apartment building to make a routine annual inspection for possible violations of the city's Housing Code. The building's manager informed the inspector that appellant, lessee of the ground floor, was using the rear of his leasehold as a personal residence. Claiming that the building's occupancy permit did not allow residential use of the ground floor, the inspector confronted appellant and demanded that he permit an inspection of the premises. Appellant refused to allow the inspection because the inspector lacked a search warrant.

[The inspector returned on several later occasions without a search warrant. When Camara refused to allow him to enter, he was charged with refusing to permit a lawful inspection, a misdemeanor. Camara argued that the charges against him were unconstitutional, because they derived from illegitimate power of government agents to search without probable cause or a warrant.]

[In this Court's cases interpreting the Fourth Amendment,] one governing principle, justified by history and by current experience, has consistently been followed: except in certain carefully defined classes of cases, a search of private property without proper consent is "unreasonable" unless it has been authorized by a valid search warrant. . . .

In Frank v. Maryland, 359 U.S. 360 (1959), this Court upheld the conviction of one who refused to permit a warrantless inspection of private premises for the purposes of locating and abating a suspected public nuisance. . . . We proceed to a re-examination of the factors which persuaded the *Frank* majority to adopt this construction of the Fourth Amendment's prohibition against unreasonable searches.

To the *Frank* majority, municipal fire, health, and housing inspection programs "touch at most upon the periphery of the important interests safeguarded by the Fourteenth Amendment's protection against official intrusion," because the inspections are merely to determine whether physical conditions exist which do not comply with minimum [regulatory standards]. We may agree that a routine inspection of the physical condition of private property is a less hostile intrusion than the typical policeman's search for the fruits and instrumentalities of crime. . . . But we cannot agree that the Fourth Amendment interests at stake in these inspection cases are merely "peripheral." It is surely anomalous to say that the individual and his private property are fully protected by the Fourth Amendment only when the individual is suspected of criminal behavior. For instance, even the most law-abiding citizen has a very tangible interest in limiting the circumstances under which the sanctity of his home may be broken by official authority, for the possibility of criminal entry under the guise of official sanction is a serious threat to personal and family security. . . . Like most regulatory laws, fire, health, and housing codes are enforced by criminal processes. . . .

The *Frank* majority suggested, and appellee reasserts, two other justifications for permitting administrative health and safety inspections without a warrant. First, it is argued that these inspections are "designed to make the least possible demand on the individual occupant." The ordinances authorizing inspections are hedged with safeguards, and at any rate the inspector's particular decision to enter must comply with the constitutional standard of reasonableness even if he may enter without a warrant. [For instance, the San Francisco Code requires that the inspector display proper credentials, that he inspect "at reasonable times," and that he not obtain entry by force except in emergencies.] In addition, the argument proceeds, the warrant process could not function effectively in this field. The decision to inspect an entire municipal area is based upon legislative or administrative assessment of broad factors such as the area's age and condition. Unless the magistrate is to review such policy matters, he must issue a "rubber stamp" warrant which provides no protection at all to the property owner.

In our opinion, these arguments unduly discount the purposes behind the warrant machinery contemplated by the Fourth Amendment. Under the present system, when the inspector demands entry, the occupant has no way of knowing whether enforcement of the municipal code involved requires inspection of his premises, no way of knowing the lawful limits of the inspector's power to search, and no way of knowing whether the inspector himself is acting under proper authorization. These are questions which may be reviewed by a neutral magistrate without any reassessment of the basic agency decision to canvass an area. . . . The practical effect of [the current] system is to leave the occupant subject to the discretion of the official in the field. This is precisely the discretion to invade private property which we have consistently circumscribed by a requirement that a disinterested party warrant the need to search. We simply cannot say that the protections provided by the warrant procedure are not needed in this context; broad statutory safeguards are no substitute for individualized review, particularly when those safeguards may only be invoked at the risk of a criminal penalty. . . .

In summary, we hold that administrative searches of the kind at issue here are significant intrusions upon the interests protected by the Fourth Amendment, [and] that such searches when authorized and conducted without a warrant procedure lack the traditional safeguards which the Fourth Amendment guarantees to the individual. . . . Because of the nature of the municipal programs under consideration, however, these conclusions must be the beginning, not the end, of our inquiry. . . .

The Fourth Amendment provides that, "no Warrants shall issue, but upon probable cause." Borrowing from more typical Fourth Amendment cases, appellant argues not only that code enforcement inspection programs must be circumscribed by a warrant procedure, but also that warrants should issue only when the inspector possesses probable cause to believe that a particular dwelling contains violations of the minimum standards prescribed by the code being enforced. We disagree.

In cases in which the Fourth Amendment requires that a warrant to search be obtained, "probable cause" is the standard by which a particular decision to search is tested against the constitutional mandate of reasonableness. To apply this standard, it is obviously necessary first to focus upon the governmental interest which allegedly justifies official intrusion upon the constitutionally protected interests of the private citizen. . . .

Unlike the search pursuant to a criminal investigation, the inspection programs at issue here are aimed at securing city-wide compliance with minimum physical standards for private property. The primary governmental interest at stake is to prevent even the unintentional development of conditions which are hazardous to public health and safety. Because fires and epidemics may ravage large urban areas, because unsightly conditions adversely affect the economic values of neighboring structures, numerous courts have upheld the police power of municipalities to impose and enforce such minimum standards even upon existing structures. . . . There is unanimous agreement among those most familiar with this field that the only effective way to seek universal compliance with the minimum standards required by municipal codes is through routine periodic inspections of all structures.

[Camara contends, first], that his probable cause standard would not jeopardize area inspection programs because only a minute portion of the population will refuse to consent to such inspections, and second, that individual privacy in any event should be given preference to the public interest in conducting such inspections. The first argument, even if true, is irrelevant to the question whether the area inspection is reasonable within the meaning of the Fourth Amendment. The second argument is in effect an assertion that the area inspection is an unreasonable search. Unfortunately, there can be no ready test for determining reasonableness other than by balancing the need to search against the invasion which the search entails. But we think that a number of persuasive factors combine to support the reasonableness of area code-enforcement inspections. First, such programs have a long history of judicial and public acceptance. Second, the public interest demands that all dangerous conditions be prevented or abated, yet it is doubtful that any other canvassing technique would achieve acceptable results. Many such conditions — faulty wiring is an obvious example — are not observable from outside the building and indeed may not be apparent to the inexpert occupant himself. Finally, because the inspections are neither personal in nature nor aimed at the discovery of evidence of crime, they involve a relatively limited invasion of the urban citizen's privacy. . . .

Having concluded that the area inspection is a "reasonable" search of private property within the meaning of the Fourth Amendment, it is obvious that "probable cause" to issue a warrant to inspect must exist if reasonable legislative or administrative standards for conducting an area inspection are satisfied with respect to a particular dwelling. Such standards, which will vary with the municipal program being enforced, may be based upon the passage of time, the nature of the building (e.g., a multi-family apartment house), or the condition of the entire area, but they will not necessarily depend upon specific knowledge of the condition of the particular dwelling. It has been suggested that so to vary the probable cause test from the standard applied in criminal cases would be to authorize a "synthetic search warrant" and thereby to lessen the overall protections of the Fourth Amendment. But we do not agree. The warrant procedure is designed to guarantee that a decision to search private property is justified by a reasonable governmental interest. But reasonableness is still the ultimate standard. If a valid public interest justifies the intrusion contemplated, then there is probable cause to issue a suitably restricted search warrant. Such an approach [recognizes] the competing public and private interests here at stake and, in so doing, best fulfills the historic purpose behind the constitutional right to be free from unreasonable government invasions of privacy.

[M]ost citizens allow inspections of their property without a warrant. Thus, as a practical matter and in light of the Fourth Amendment's requirement that a warrant specify the property to be searched, it seems likely that warrants should normally be sought only after entry is refused unless there has been a citizen complaint or there is other satisfactory reason for securing immediate entry. . . .

In this case, [there was no emergency demanding immediate access, yet] no warrant was obtained and thus appellant was unable to verify either the need for or the appropriate limits of the inspection. [We] conclude that appellant had a constitutional right to insist that the inspectors obtain a warrant to search and that appellant may not constitutionally be convicted for refusing to consent to the inspection. . . .

Clark, J., dissenting.

Today the Court renders . . . municipal experience, which dates back to Colonial days, for naught by . . . striking down hundreds of city ordinances throughout the country and jeopardizing thereby the health, welfare, and safety of literally millions of people. But this is not all. It prostitutes the command of the Fourth Amendment that "no Warrants shall issue, but upon probable cause" and sets up in the health and safety codes area inspection a newfangled "warrant" system that is entirely foreign to Fourth Amendment standards. . . .

There is nothing here that suggests that the inspection was unauthorized, unreasonable, for any improper purpose, or designed as a basis for a criminal prosecution; nor is there any indication of any discriminatory, arbitrary, or capricious action affecting the appellant. . . . The majority say, however, that under the present system the occupant has no way of knowing the necessity for the inspection, the limits of the inspector's power, or whether the inspector is himself authorized to perform the search. [A]ll of these doubts raised by the Court could be resolved very quickly. Indeed, the inspectors all have identification cards which they show the occupant and the latter could easily resolve the remaining questions by a call to the inspector's superior or, upon demand, receive a written answer thereto. . . .

The Court then addresses itself to the propriety of warrantless area inspections. [T]hese boxcar warrants will be identical as to every dwelling in the area, save the street number itself. I daresay they will be printed up in pads of a thousand or more — with space for the street number to be inserted — and issued by magistrates in broadcast fashion as a matter of course. I ask: Why go through such an exercise, such a pretense? As the same essentials are being followed under the present procedures, I ask: Why the ceremony, the delay, the expense, the abuse of the search warrant? In my view this will not only destroy its integrity but will degrade the magistrate issuing them and soon bring disrepute not only upon the practice but upon the judicial process. It will be very costly to the city in paperwork incident to the issuance of the paper warrants, in loss of time of inspectors and waste of the time of magistrates and will result in more annoyance to the public. . . .

Notes

1. *Do administrative warrants honor the Fourth Amendment or undermine it?* Does the majority or dissent in *Camara* do greater honor to the Fourth Amendment? Would the Court have been truer to the Fourth Amendment if it had allowed administrative searches on the basis of their reasonableness, modest intrusion, and general applicability, subject to careful guidelines, rather than craft a new kind of warrant? Would the Court have been truer still to the Fourth Amendment if it had barred administrative searches absent consent or individualized suspicion of a civil or criminal violation?

Have you seen administrative warrants before, in another context? Review now the eighteenth-century writ of assistance reprinted in section A of this chapter. Are there significant differences between that writ and the administrative warrants described in the *Camara* decision?

2. *Statutory guidance.* The authority for such warrants is often in statutes. Does a legislative imprimatur help to validate the idea of administrative warrants? Does the legislative approval of the practice answer concerns about the discretion or priorities of police supervisors or field officers? Consider the following language from Mich. Stat. §333.7504(2):

> A magistrate . . . upon proper oath or affirmation showing probable cause, may issue a warrant for the purpose of conducting an administrative inspection authorized by this

article or the rules promulgated under this article and seizures of property appropriate to the inspection. Probable cause exists upon showing a valid public interest in the effective enforcement of this article or the rules promulgated under this article sufficient to justify administrative inspection of the area, premises, building, or conveyance in the circumstances specified in the application for the warrant. . . .

3. *Sliding scales.* One of the justifications for allowing administrative search warrants appears to be the modestly invasive nature of the searches they justify. The Supreme Court has declared that the balancing method of determining the reasonableness of a search is available whenever there is a "special need" beyond the normal need for law enforcement. New York v. Burger, 482 U.S. 691 (1987).

Should this "lesser invasion/lesser justification" idea be limited to the context of administrative searches, or should the principle be taken more broadly to require a rough correlation between the intrusiveness of any search (warranted or warrantless) and the justification the government must offer? Is a sliding scale of searches a workable concept? Can it be reconciled with the traditional limits of a warrant requirement and probable cause?

4. *Administrative warrants in highly regulated industries.* There is an important exception to the requirement that the government obtain an administrative warrant. If the target of the search is engaged in a "highly regulated industry," the Supreme Court and an overwhelming number of state courts have concluded that an administrative warrant is not necessary. Instead, the government must show that the warrantless search is necessary, that there is an adequate substitute for the warrant to limit the discretion of the field agent, and that the inspection is limited in time, place, and scope. Donovan v. Dewey, 452 U.S. 594 (1981) (statute authorizing warrantless safety inspections of coal mines). The regulation in question must apply to a focused group of people or enterprises; regulations covering all or most employers, however intrusive, do not eliminate the need for an administrative warrant. Marshall v. Barlow's, Inc., 436 U.S. 307 (1978) (inspection to enforce OSHA workplace safety rules invalid). Is this exception available because of the consent of the targets? That is, does a liquor or firearms retailer understand when going into the business that warrantless searches will occur?

D. CONSENSUAL SEARCHES

The police can conduct a full search *without a warrant* and *without probable cause* if the target of the search consents. In most jurisdictions, the police conduct far more consensual searches than those justified by probable cause or a search warrant. Indeed, one might ask whether a consensual search is a "search" (within the meaning of the constitution) at all. As you read these materials, compare consensual searches with intrusions, covered in Chapter 2, that are not considered "searches" at all.

1. Components of a Voluntary Choice

Any valid consent to search must be "voluntary," yet this choice rarely takes place in a setting ideally suited to rational deliberation of all available options. What are the minimum elements of voluntariness necessary to make a consensual search legally acceptable?

■ MERLE SCHNECKLOTH v. ROBERT BUSTAMONTE

412 U.S. 218 (1973)

STEWART, J.

[While on routine patrol in Sunnyvale, California, at approximately 2:40 A.M., Police Officer James Rand stopped an automobile when he observed that one headlight and its license plate light were burned out. Six men were in the vehicle. When the driver, Joe Gonzalez, could not produce a driver's license, Rand asked the others for identification. Only Joe Alcala produced a license,] and he explained that the car was his brother's. After the six occupants had stepped out of the car at the officer's request and after two additional policemen had arrived, Officer Rand asked Alcala if he could search the car. Alcala replied, "Sure, go ahead." Prior to the search no one was threatened with arrest and, according to Officer Rand's uncontradicted testimony, it "was all very congenial at this time." [The police officer asked Alcala, "Does the trunk open?" Alcala said, "Yes," and opened up the trunk.] Wadded up under the left rear seat, the police officers found three checks that had previously been stolen from a car wash.

[Bustamonte was brought to trial in a California court on a charge of possessing a check with intent to defraud. The trial judge denied the motion to suppress the checks, and on the basis of the checks and other evidence he was convicted. After his failure to obtain relief on appellate review in state court, Bustamonte challenged his conviction in federal habeas corpus proceedings.]

[T]he State concedes that when a prosecutor seeks to rely upon consent to justify the lawfulness of a search, he has the burden of proving that the consent was, in fact, freely and voluntarily given. The precise question in this case, then, is what must the prosecution prove to demonstrate that a consent was "voluntarily" given. . . .

The most extensive judicial exposition of the meaning of "voluntariness" has been developed in those cases in which the Court has had to determine the "voluntariness" of a defendant's confession for purposes of the Fourteenth Amendment. . . . In determining whether a defendant's will was over-borne in a particular case, the Court has assessed the totality of all the surrounding circumstances — both the characteristics of the accused and the details of the interrogation. Some of the factors taken into account have included the youth of the accused; his lack of education, or his low intelligence; the lack of any advice to the accused of his constitutional rights; the length of detention; the repeated and prolonged nature of the questioning; and the use of physical punishment such as the deprivation of food or sleep. . . .

The significant fact about all of these decisions is that none of them turned on the presence or absence of a single controlling criterion; each reflected a careful scrutiny of all the surrounding circumstances. In none of them did the Court rule that the Due Process Clause required the prosecution to prove as part of its initial burden that the defendant knew he had a right to refuse to answer the questions that were put. While the state of the accused's mind, and the failure of the police to advise the accused of his rights, were certainly factors to be evaluated in assessing the "voluntariness" of an accused's responses, they were not in and of themselves determinative.

Similar considerations lead us to [conclude] that the question whether a consent to a search was in fact "voluntary" or was the product of duress or coercion, express or implied, is a question of fact to be determined from the totality of all the circumstances. While knowledge of the right to refuse consent is one factor to be taken into account, the government need not establish such knowledge as the sine qua non of an effective consent. As with police questioning, two competing concerns must be accommodated in determining the meaning of a "voluntary" consent — the legitimate need for such searches and the equally important requirement of assuring the absence of coercion.

In situations where the police have some evidence of illicit activity, but lack probable cause to arrest or search, a search authorized by a valid consent may be the only means of obtaining important and reliable evidence. . . . And in those cases where there is probable cause to arrest or search, but where the police lack a warrant, a consent search may still be valuable. If the search is conducted and proves fruitless, that in itself may convince the police that an arrest with its possible stigma and embarrassment is unnecessary, or that a far more extensive search pursuant to a warrant is not justified. In short, a search pursuant to consent may result in considerably less inconvenience for the subject of the search, and, properly conducted, is a constitutionally permissible and wholly legitimate aspect of effective police activity.

But the Fourth and Fourteenth Amendments require that a consent not be coerced, by explicit or implicit means, by implied threat or covert force. For, no matter how subtly the coercion was applied, the resulting "consent" would be no more than a pretext for the unjustified police intrusion against which the Fourth Amendment is directed. . . .

The problem of reconciling the recognized legitimacy of consent searches with the requirement that they be free from any aspect of official coercion cannot be resolved by any infallible touchstone. To approve such searches without the most careful scrutiny would sanction the possibility of official coercion; to place artificial restrictions upon such searches would jeopardize their basic validity. . . . In examining all the surrounding circumstances to determine if in fact the consent to search was coerced, account must be taken of subtly coercive police questions, as well as the possibly vulnerable subjective state of the person who consents. Those searches that are the product of police coercion can thus be filtered out without undermining the continuing validity of consent searches. In sum, there is no reason for us to depart in the area of consent searches, from the traditional definition of "voluntariness."

The approach of [those courts ruling] that the State must affirmatively prove that the subject of the search knew that he had a right to refuse consent, would, in practice, create serious doubt whether consent searches could continue to be conducted. There might be rare cases where it could be proved from the record that a person in fact affirmatively knew of his right to refuse — such as a case where he announced to the police that if he didn't sign the consent form, "[you] are going to get a search warrant;" or a case where by prior experience and training a person had clearly and convincingly demonstrated such knowledge. But more commonly where there was no evidence of any coercion, explicit or implicit, the prosecution would nevertheless be unable to demonstrate that the subject of the search in fact had known of his right to refuse consent. . . .

One alternative that would go far toward proving that the subject of a search did know he had a right to refuse consent would be to advise him of that right before eliciting his consent. That, however, is a suggestion that has been almost universally repudiated by both federal and state courts, and, we think, rightly so. For it would be thoroughly impractical to impose on the normal consent search the detailed requirements of an effective warning. Consent searches are part of the standard investigatory techniques of law enforcement agencies. They normally occur on the highway, or in a person's home or office, and under informal and unstructured conditions. The circumstances that prompt the initial request to search may develop quickly or be a logical extension of investigative police questioning. . . . These situations are a far cry from the structured atmosphere of a trial where, assisted by counsel if he chooses, a defendant is informed of his trial rights. And, while surely a closer question, these situations are still immeasurably far removed from "custodial interrogation" where, in Miranda v. Arizona, 384 U.S. 436 (1966), we found that the Constitution required certain now familiar warnings as a prerequisite to police interrogation. . . .

It is said, however, that a "consent" is a "waiver" of a person's rights under the Fourth and Fourteenth Amendments. The argument is that by allowing the police to conduct a search, a person "waives" whatever right he had to prevent the police from searching. It is argued that under the doctrine of Johnson v. Zerbst, 304 U.S. 458 (1938) to establish such a "waiver" the State must demonstrate "an intentional relinquishment or abandonment of a known right or privilege." But these standards were enunciated in *Johnson* in the context of the safeguards of a fair criminal trial [such as waiver of counsel at trial or] the right to confrontation, to a jury trial, and to a speedy trial, and the right to be free from twice being placed in jeopardy. . . .

The protections of the Fourth Amendment are of a wholly different order, and have nothing whatever to do with promoting the fair ascertainment of truth at a criminal trial. [T]he Fourth Amendment protects the security of one's privacy against arbitrary intrusion by the police. . . . It is no part of the policy underlying the Fourth and Fourteenth Amendments to discourage citizens from aiding to the utmost of their ability in the apprehension of criminals. Rather, the community has a real interest in encouraging consent, for the resulting search may yield necessary evidence for the solution and prosecution of crime, evidence that may insure that a wholly innocent person is not wrongly charged with a criminal offense. [It] would be unrealistic to expect that in the informal, unstructured context of a consent search, a policeman, upon pain of tainting the evidence obtained, could make the detailed type of examination demanded by *Johnson*. . . .

It is . . . argued that the failure to require the Government to establish knowledge as a prerequisite to a valid consent, will relegate the Fourth Amendment to the special province of "the sophisticated, the knowledgeable and the privileged." We cannot agree. The traditional definition of voluntariness we accept today has always taken into account evidence of minimal schooling, low intelligence, and the lack of any effective warnings to a person of his rights; and the voluntariness of any statement taken under those conditions has been carefully scrutinized to determine whether it was in fact voluntarily given.

Our decision today is a narrow one. We hold only that when the subject of a search is not in custody and the State attempts to justify a search on the basis of his consent, the Fourth and Fourteenth Amendments require that it demonstrate that the consent was in fact voluntarily given, and not the result of duress or coercion, express or implied. Voluntariness is a question of fact to be determined from all the circumstances, and while the subject's knowledge of a right to refuse is a factor to be taken into account, the prosecution is not required to demonstrate such knowledge as a prerequisite to establishing a voluntary consent. . . .

MARSHALL, J., dissenting.

[I would] have thought that the capacity to choose necessarily depends upon knowledge that there is a choice to be made. But today the Court reaches the curious result that one can choose to relinquish a constitutional right — the right to be free of unreasonable searches — without knowing that he has the alternative of refusing to accede to a police request to search. I cannot agree, and therefore dissent.

[The Court] imports into the law of search and seizure standards developed to decide entirely different questions about coerced confessions. . . . The inquiry in a case where a confession is challenged as having been elicited in an unconstitutional manner is . . . whether the behavior of the police amounted to compulsion of the defendant. [N]o sane person would knowingly relinquish a right to be free of compulsion. Thus, the questions of compulsion and of violation of the right itself are inextricably intertwined. The cases involving coerced confessions, therefore, pass over the question of knowledge of that right as irrelevant, and turn directly to the question of compulsion.

[W]hen a search is justified solely by consent . . . , the needs of law enforcement are significantly more attenuated, for probable cause to search may be lacking but a search permitted if the subject's consent has been obtained. Thus, consent searches are permitted, not because such an exception to the requirements of probable cause and warrant is essential to proper law enforcement, but because we permit our citizens to choose whether or not they wish to exercise their constitutional rights. . . .

If consent to search means that a person has chosen to forgo his right to exclude the police from the place they seek to search, it follows that his consent cannot be considered a meaningful choice unless he knew that he could in fact exclude the police. . . . I can think of no other situation in which we would say that a person agreed to some course of action if he convinced us that he did not know that there was some other course he might have pursued. . . .

If one accepts this view, the question then is a simple one: must the Government show that the subject knew of his rights, or must the subject show that he lacked such knowledge? I think that any fair allocation of the burden would require that it be placed on the prosecution. . . . If the burden is placed on the defendant, all the subject can do is to testify that he did not know of his rights. And I doubt that many trial judges will find for the defendant simply on the basis of that testimony. [The government, however, might demonstrate the subject's knowledge of his rights by showing his responses at the time of the search.] Denials of knowledge may be disproved by establishing that the subject had, in the recent past, demonstrated his knowledge of his rights, for example, by refusing entry when it was requested by the police. The prior experience or training of the subject might in some cases support an inference that he knew of his right to exclude the police.

The burden on the prosecutor would disappear, of course, if the police, at the time they requested consent to search, also told the subject that he had a right to refuse consent and that his decision to refuse would be respected. . . . The Court contends that if an officer paused to inform the subject of his rights, the informality of the exchange would be destroyed. I doubt that a simple statement by an officer of an individual's right to refuse consent would do much to alter the informality of the exchange, except to alert the subject to a fact that he surely is entitled to know. It is not without significance that for many years the agents of the Federal Bureau of Investigation have routinely informed subjects of their right to refuse consent, when they request consent to search. . . .

I must conclude, with some reluctance, that when the Court speaks of practicality, what it really is talking of is the continued ability of the police to capitalize on the ignorance of citizens so as to accomplish by subterfuge what they could not achieve by relying only on the knowing relinquishment of constitutional rights. Of course it would be "practical" for the police to ignore the commands of the Fourth Amendment, if by practicality we mean that more criminals will be apprehended, even though the constitutional rights of innocent people also go by the board. But such a practical advantage is achieved only at the cost of permitting the police to disregard the limitations that the Constitution places on their behavior, a cost that a constitutional democracy cannot long absorb. . . .

■ PITTSFIELD, MAINE, POLICE DEPARTMENT CONSENT-TO-SEARCH FORM

I, ___, have been informed by ___ and ___ who made proper identification as (an) authorized law enforcement officers of the Pittsfield PD . . . of my CONSTITUTIONAL RIGHT not to have a search made of the premises and property owned by me and/or under my care, custody and control, without a search warrant. Knowing of my lawful right to refuse to consent to such a search, I willingly give my permission to the above named officers to conduct a complete search of the premises and property, including all buildings and vehicles, both inside and outside of the property located at ___.

The above said officers further have my permission to take from my premises and property, any letters, papers, materials or any other property or things which they desire as evidence for criminal prosecution in the case or cases under investigation. This written permission to search without a search warrant is given by me to the above officers voluntarily and without any threats or promises of any kind, at ___ A.M./P.M. on this ___ day of ___, at ___ (place).

■ PHILADELPHIA POLICE DEPARTMENT DIRECTIVE 7, APPENDIX A

[O]fficers will ensure they provide the consenting party with the following warnings:

1. that the consenting party has the right to require the police to obtain a search warrant, and
2. that he/she has the right to refuse to consent to a search. . . .

If the person is in police custody, three additional warnings must be provided:

1. that any items found can and will be confiscated and may be used against them in court;

2. they have the right to consult with an attorney before making a decision to consent; and
3. that they have the right to withdraw their consent at any time.

Problem 3-3. Consent After a Traffic Stop

Robert Robinette was driving his car at 69 miles per hour in a 45-mile-per-hour construction zone on the Interstate. Deputy Roger Newsome, who was on drug interdiction patrol at the time, stopped Robinette for a speeding violation. Before Newsome approached Robinette's vehicle, he decided to issue Robinette only a verbal warning, which was his routine practice regarding speeders in that construction zone. Newsome approached Robinette's vehicle and requested his driver's license. Robinette handed over his license, and Newsome returned to his vehicle to check it. Finding no violations, Newsome returned to Robinette's vehicle. Newsome then asked Robinette to get out of his car and step to the rear of the vehicle. Robinette complied with Newsome's request and stood between his car and the deputy's cruiser. Newsome returned to his vehicle to activate the cruiser's video camera so that he could videotape his interaction with Robinette. Newsome then issued a verbal warning regarding Robinette's speed and returned Robinette's driver's license.

After returning the license, Newsome said to Robinette, "One question before you go: Are you carrying any illegal contraband in your car? Any weapons of any kind, drugs, anything like that?" When Robinette said that he did not have any contraband in the car, Newsome asked if he could search the vehicle. Robinette hesitated briefly, then answered "yes." Upon his search of Robinette's vehicle, Newsome found a small amount of marijuana. Newsome then put Robinette and his passenger in the back seat of the cruiser and continued the search. As a result of this extended search, Newsome found a pill inside a film container; the pill was later determined to be an illegal narcotic. Newsome always asked permission to search the cars he stopped for speeding violations. He had followed this procedure more than 800 times during the previous 12 months. Was Robinette's consent valid? Compare State v. Robinette, 653 N.E.2d 695 (Ohio 1995); Ohio v. Robinette, 519 U.S. 33 (1996).

Notes

1. *Voluntariness of consent: majority position.* Almost all state courts agree with *Bustamonte* that a "totality of the circumstances" determines whether a person consented to a search, and that it is not necessary to inform the person of the right to refuse consent. See Commonwealth v. Cleckley, 738 A.2d 427 (Pa. 1999); but see State v. Johnson, 346 A.2d 66 (N.J. 1975) (party consenting to search must understand right to refuse consent). Whose perceptions of the totality of the circumstances will determine whether the choice was voluntary? Should a court adopt the viewpoint of the person being searched, the officer, or an objective "reasonable person"? Courts have tended to adopt the objective point of view. People v. Henderson, 210 N.E.2d 483 (Ill. 1965). Why would a "reasonable" person who knows that evidence of a crime is present on the premises ever consent to a search? There is considerable evidence in psychological studies that people unreflectively defer to the wishes of authority figures, including police officers. Is this a sufficient explanation?

2. *Proof of knowledge.* As a prosecutor, how would you try to prove that a person who consented to a search knew that she had the power to refuse? As police counsel, would you recommend that your officers use a consent form in all cases when they wish to search on the basis of consent? Would it increase the chance that the courts would validate consent searches? Would this practice result in a loss of too many searches? Should the form contain explicit notice that the person can refuse to consent? Note that Directive 7 from the Philadelphia Police Manual provides for some warnings not required as a matter of federal constitutional law. The manual also calls for consent searches only when there is no probable cause and no chance to get a warrant. Why would a police manual contain such provisions?

3. *Consent based on inevitability of a search.* Is consent voluntary when the police claim to have the authority to search immediately, or as soon as they obtain a warrant? In Bumper v. North Carolina, 391 U.S. 543 (1968), the police officer said to a homeowner, "I have a warrant," but the prosecution later justified the search as a consensual search rather than relying on a warrant. The court held that the homeowner's consent to the search was not voluntary because it was induced by a "show of authority" by the police. Was the consent involuntary because of some knowledge the homeowner did not have, such as the invalidity of the warrant? Or was it because the police affirmatively misrepresented the range of options open to her?

Suppose the officer had said, "I can get a warrant if you don't consent." Would your answer change if she had said, "I will seek a warrant"? See State v. Brown, 783 P.2d 1278 (Kan. 1989). Would consent be voluntary if the police ask to search a home while saying that if the owner insists that they obtain a warrant, they plan to return with their "blue lights and sirens blazing" for the benefit of the neighbors?

4. *"Knock and talk" practices.* Police departments encourage their officers to obtain consent to search in many settings. The practice provokes some serious challenges in the setting of searches in a home. When police officers approach a home with no probable cause to search, and plan to request consent to search, this "knock and talk" practice raises difficult factual issues about whether the resident's consent is truly voluntary. Given the special sensitivity of searches in a home, a few jurisdictions declare that officers who approach a home for the sole purpose of obtaining consent to search the home must inform the resident that he or she does not have to consent. State v. Bustamante-Davila, 983 P.2d 590 (Wash. 1999). Most jurisdictions, however, leave the voluntariness of such consensual searches to the factfinding of the trial judge in the individual case. State v. Smith, 488 S.E.2d 210 (N.C. 1997) ("knock and talk" policy of police department does not violate constitution per se).

5. *Consent while in custody.* Does the driver of a vehicle stopped for a traffic violation voluntarily consent to a search of the car if told that the alternative is to be arrested and taken to jail (and the officer has lawful authority to do just that for traffic violators)? Can a suspect already in custody consent to a search? In United States v. Watson, 423 U.S. 411 (1976), the court approved of a consensual search of a car owned by a person who had been taken into custody in a restaurant and was being held on a public street. As in *Bustamonte,* the Court held that the lack of notice about the right to refuse consent did not make the choice involuntary in this setting. See Reynolds v. State, 592 So. 2d 1082 (Fla. 1992) (use of handcuffs to restrain suspect does not necessarily foreclose granting of consent to search; one factor among totality of circumstances); People v. Anthony, 761 N.E.2d 1188 (Ill. 2001) (suspect

wordlessly assuming frisk position after officer's request to search his person is too ambiguous to establish consent; actions might indicate acquiescence to authority).

6. *Consent after a traffic stop.* The Supreme Court held, in Ohio v. Robinette, 519 U.S. 33 (1996), that a police officer asking for consent to search the car at the conclusion of a valid traffic stop need not inform the motorist that he is free to leave and may refuse to consent to the search. However, the Ohio Supreme Court on remand held that the officer's failure to inform the motorist that the stop was over still amounted to one important factor showing lack of consent in the case. State v. Robinette, 685 N.E.2d 762 (Ohio 1997). Courts in other jurisdictions state that consent obtained after a traffic stop deserves heightened review to ensure the voluntariness of the consent. State v. George, 557 N.W.2d 575 (Minn. 1997); Ferris v. State, 735 A.2d 491 (Md. 1999). In fact, a small group of states (fewer than a half dozen) insist that police may not request consent to search a car stopped for traffic violations unless they have reasonable suspicion of some criminal activity other than the traffic matter. See State v. Carty, 790 A.2d 903 (N.J. 2002). Are these decisions consistent with Schneckloth v. Bustamonte? Is knowledge about the power to refuse consent more important for stopped automobile drivers than for others who are asked to consent to a search?

7. *Capacity to consent.* Should consent be harder for officers to obtain when the person whose consent is in question is intoxicated, mentally disabled, young, unsophisticated, or does not speak English well? The majority in *Bustamonte* wrote as follows: "The traditional definition of voluntariness we accept today has always taken into account evidence of minimal schooling [and] low intelligence." Doesn't this position require a subjective viewpoint? Courts take intoxication, mental capacity, and maturity into account in evaluating consent but often find such individuals able to consent nonetheless. See, e.g., State v. McDowell, 407 S.E.2d 200 (N.C. 1991) (defendant's girlfriend able to consent even though she was "mentally retarded"). Should a person with more education and worldliness have more difficulty arguing their consent to a search was involuntary? Indeed, after taking this course would you be able to claim your consent to a search was involuntary on any grounds short of torture?

Problem 3-4. Scope of Consent

Trooper Galbreath of the state police stopped Ellis for speeding. By chance, Detective Aviola of a drug crimes unit in the state police drove by the stopped car at this time and recognized Ellis. Two weeks earlier, Aviola had received an anonymous tip concerning Ellis's involvement in drug trafficking. The caller had told Aviola that Ellis carried narcotics in some type of box with a magnet attached to it, either under the hood or above the wheel well in the trunk.

Aviola pulled over and asked Ellis for consent to "search the vehicle" for weapons and narcotics. When Ellis agreed, Aviola checked the trunk, the wheel wells, and the interior of the vehicle and found nothing. Then he opened the hood and found a black box attached to the frame of the vehicle by a round magnet bolted to its back. Aviola opened the box and found inside a clear plastic bag containing approximately 14 grams of cocaine. During the search, Ellis was seated on the curb by the passenger side of the vehicle. Did Ellis consent to Aviola's search under the hood? Compare State v. Ellis, 604 A.2d 419 (Del. 1991) (unpublished).

Notes

1. *Scope of consent: majority position.* A consent search is valid only if the government agent conducting the search remains within the bounds of the consent granted. The Supreme Court has held that "[t]he standard for measuring the scope of a suspect's consent under the Fourth Amendment is that of 'objective' reasonableness—what would the typical reasonable person have understood by the exchange between the officer and the suspect?" Florida v. Jimeno, 500 U.S. 248 (1991). Virtually all state courts deciding this question have reached the same conclusion. A court will determine the exact coverage of the agreement by reviewing the language that the officer and the target of the search used, much as a court would examine the language used by contractual parties to determine the meaning of their agreement. Would the use of written consent forms tend to help or hurt police departments in this inquiry? If a person consents generally to a search of his "person" or his "vehicle," does that general statement include consent to search all areas within those bounds? A court will typically find it significant if the government agent tells the search target what he is looking for. If the officer is seeking illegal narcotics, the search might be more thorough and intrusive while still remaining within the bounds of the consent. But a number of courts have insisted that an officer obtain specific consent before searching the crotch area. See Davis v. State, 594 So. 2d 264 (Fla. 1992).

2. *Withdrawal of consent.* A person who has consented to a search can withdraw that consent (or restrict its scope) at any time before the completion of the search. However, the person must make an unequivocal withdrawal, through words or actions or both. An action withdrawing consent must be clearly inconsistent with the prior consent, such as a refusal to open a door or a container.

3. *Duration of consent.* While it is clear that a person must withdraw consent through clear language or action, does that mean that a consent to search remains effective indefinitely, allowing a search several days after the grant of consent? Most courts conclude that an open-ended consent to search contains an implied time limitation: The search must be conducted as soon as it is reasonably possible to do so. State v. Brochu, 237 A.2d 418 (Me. 1967). But do some circumstances suggest a consent with longer duration? In Caldwell v. State, 393 S.E.2d 436 (Ga. 1990), the defendant called the police at 3:00 P.M. to report the stabbing of her children, invited the police into her apartment, and asked them to search for evidence that would lead to the arrest of the murderer. She then left the premises to spend the night with relatives. The search continued until 10:00 P.M. the day of the murder, and for several hours the next day. The court concluded that the consent remained valid for the entire period of the search.

4. *Retroactive consent.* There have been times when the police have begun a search, without legal authority, before they obtain consent. Most courts conclude that it is possible for the target of the search to consent retroactively to any portions of the search that occurred before the consent was given. Should it matter whether the target of the search is *aware* of what the police have found during the preconsent phase of the search? If the consent is framed generally without any reference to portions of the search already complete, should the reviewing court assume that the consent extends to all portions of the search or only to the portions taking place after the grant of consent? See State v. Weaver, 874 P.2d 1322 (Or. 1994) (retroactive consent is possible, but not present here where the written consent form did not explicitly mention the preconsent portion of search).

2. *Third-Party Consent*

The police can obtain the consent to search property either from the target of the search herself or from some third party. Of course, the third party's consent must be voluntary, just as with the target of the search. In addition, the third party must have the authority (or at least the apparent authority) to consent to the search. The third party's authority to consent to a search of property "does not rest upon the law of property, with its attendant historical and legal refinements, but rests rather on mutual use of the property by persons generally having joint access or control for most purposes." In such a setting, the target of the search has "assumed the risk" that another person with access to the property will consent to a search. United States v. Matlock, 415 U.S. 164 (1974). How might this standard apply in the following problems? Would any recurring fact make a difference to a reviewing court?

Problem 3-5. Lessor Consenting for Lessee

Police officers investigating a robbery wanted to search the hotel room of a suspect. They approached the night clerk and asked him if Joey Stoner was living at the hotel. The clerk replied that Stoner lived in room 404 but was out at the time. The officers then asked for permission to enter the room, explaining that Stoner may have committed a robbery and might be hiding the gun in his room. The clerk replied, "In this case, I will be more than happy to give you permission and I will take you directly to the room." The officers found a pistol and other evidence in the room. Was this a valid consensual search? Compare Stoner v. California, 376 U.S. 483 (1964).

Problem 3-6. Co-tenant Consenting for Co-tenant

Gina owned a house, which she rented to her son Dale and another man, Thomas. At about 2:00 A.M. on August 30, several acquaintances of Dale and Thomas were at the house. Two of the guests left for about 30 minutes and returned with more than a half-pound of marijuana. Thomas was upset that there was marijuana in the house and complained to Dale, but Dale seemed unconcerned.

Thomas went to the police, where he signed a consent to search the house for the marijuana. Several officers went to the house, drew their weapons and entered the house without knocking or announcing their purpose or authority. They found marijuana in baggies in a black leather jacket in the kitchen and arrested the guest who owned the jacket. In plain view in the living room was a "sawed off" or "short barreled" shotgun belonging to Dale. Was this a valid consensual search? Compare In re Welfare of D. A. G., 474 N.W.2d 419 (Minn. 1991).

Problem 3-7. Parent Consenting for Child

During a murder investigation, police officers went to a suspect's house and asked his mother for consent to search his room. The suspect, who was 23 years old, slept and stored his clothes and other property in a bedroom upstairs in the house and sporadically paid his mother rent for the room. His mother had regular access to the room for purposes of collecting his laundry. She also stored her sewing machine in the room. Although the room was usually unlocked, on this day it was locked. The suspect's mother opened the door with a key and allowed the police to search his room. They found in the closet a jacket with blood stains matching the blood of the murder victim. Was this a valid consensual search?

Problem 3-8. Child Consenting for Parent

Joe Harmon and Dorothy Rader had been living together in her home, but she had been trying to convince him to move out. Ms. Rader's children, including her 15-year-old daughter, Marie, also lived in the home. Joe killed another man and made little effort to conceal the crime from Dorothy or Marie. He told them which rifle he had used and showed them two rings he had removed from the victim. Marie and her mother did not report the crime at first because they were afraid of Joe. When Joe left town to appear in court on a speeding charge, however, Marie went to the police and reported the murder. She signed a form consenting to the search of her mother's house. She told the police that she knew about consent searches, having seen her father (who was a police officer in another state) execute one. When she accompanied the officers to the house, her mother was not at home. She described the rifle used in the murder and told the officers that they would find the rifle in the gun cabinet. The officers found the weapon. She also took from her finger one of the two rings that Joe had taken from the victim. Was this a valid consensual search? Compare Harmon v. State, 641 S.W.2d 21 (Ark. 1982).

■ ARKANSAS RULE OF CRIMINAL PROCEDURE 11.2

The consent justifying a search and seizure can only be given, in the case of: (a) search of an individual's person, by the individual in question or, if the person is under 14 years of age, by both the individual and his parent, guardian, or a person in loco parentis; (b) search of a vehicle, by the person registered as its owner or in apparent control of its operation or contents at the time consent is given; and (c) search of premises, by a person who, by ownership or otherwise, is apparently entitled to give or withhold consent.

Notes

1. *Presence or absence of target and consenting party.* In Problem 3-6, the target of the search was present during the search and did not consent. Would the analysis change if the target of a search leaves explicit instructions to others with joint control over the property that she does not wish for them to authorize any searches? Or if the consenting party is not at the scene of the search? The court in United States v. Matlock, 415 U.S. 164 (1974), addressed these questions obliquely when it spoke of valid third-party consent against an "absent, nonconsenting" person with an interest in the property. State and federal courts have almost always upheld third-party consents when they contradicted the explicit instructions of the absent search

target. There is more disagreement about whether third-party consent is effective when the target of the search is present and objecting to the search or when the consenting party is not present. Compare State v. Leach, 782 P.2d 1035 (Wash. 1989) (no valid consent when target is present and objecting) with People v. Sanders, 904 P.2d 1311 (Colo. 1995) (approving of search of trailer, consent obtained from occupant not present, target of search present and not consenting to search).

2. *Unequal interests in property.* What happens if the consenting party has a clearly lesser interest in the property than the target of the search? Suppose the target of the search pays rent on an apartment, while the consenting third party is a frequent long-term guest. Should the third party in that setting be able to override the objections of the party with the stronger claim on the property? A few courts require a third party to have at least an equal interest with other owners before allowing that person to consent to a search of the property, at least when the superior interest holder is present and objecting to the search. See Silva v. State, 344 So. 2d 559 (Fla. 1977). Is the principle here that the third party's interests derive from the first party's and therefore cannot override the first party's privacy? The situation often arises when the police obtain consent from one occupant of an automobile to search the vehicle or some property inside. See Johnson v. State, 905 P.2d 818 (Okla. Crim. App. 1995) (driver's consent cannot override lack of consent from actual owner of vehicle or property in vehicle, present at scene). Would a special rule for automobiles be appropriate or useful?

3. *Antagonism.* Many third-party consent cases involve spouses or others in a similar relationship. Sometimes one spouse will consent to a search in an effort to injure a partner during a time of conflict. Is it reasonable for the police to rely on consent if it is clear that one party intends only to harm the target of the search? A few older cases held that an "angry wife" could not consent to a search of household property because she was not acting in the interest of the husband and could not be considered an agent for purposes of consenting to the search. See Kelley v. State, 197 S.W.2d 545 (Tenn. 1946) (during police visit to home after domestic violence, wife cannot consent to search for moonshine liquor). Courts no longer take this approach, arguing that a third party's consent to search no longer depends on an agency relationship with the target of the search; it depends instead on her own interest in the common property. See State v. Bartram, 925 S.W.2d 227 (Tenn. 1996). Is there any way to argue, consistent with the "assumption of the risk" analysis of *Matlock,* that third-party consent is not valid when granted primarily to injure the target of the search?

4. *Consent forms and policies.* Would you advise a police department to adopt a special version of its consent-to-search forms for third-party consent searches? Would you advise the police to adopt any rules regarding the proper procedure for obtaining third-party consent?

■ STATE v. REINALDO MARISTANY

627 A.2d 1066 (N.J. 1993)

STEIN, J.

[State] Troopers Frank Trifari and Thomas Colella were patrolling the southbound lane of Interstate 95 when they observed a 1988 Oldsmobile with out-of-state license plates proceeding in the left-hand lane for approximately one-half mile. The troopers stopped the car for failing to keep right. . . . The troopers approached the car and asked the driver, Gerald Green, for his license and registration. Both Green and the passenger, defendant Reinaldo Maristany, appeared nervous as they searched for the papers. When Green failed to produce credentials, Trifari asked him to step out of the car and walk to the rear of the vehicle. Defendant remained in the passenger seat.

Trifari questioned Green and defendant separately. Green explained that he was returning from a visit with his sick aunt in New York. However, defendant claimed that he and Green had been visiting defendant's children in New York. Because of the inconsistent responses and apparent nervousness, Trifari requested Green's consent to search the car and trunk. When asked if the trunk contained any luggage, Green indicated that a blue canvas bag and brown suitcase were inside. . . .

Trifari and Green were standing at the rear of the car; [Maristany] was sitting on the front hood. After Trifari advised Green of his right to refuse consent, Green acquiesced in the search and signed a consent-to-search form that authorized Trifari to "conduct a complete search of trunk portion of vehicle including blue canvas bag, brown suitcase, also includes interior portion of vehicle."

[Trifari found no contraband in the car's interior. Green removed the keys from the ignition and opened the trunk for the trooper's inspection.] In the blue canvas gym bag, Trifari found three kilograms of cocaine. The bag did not have any identification tags and was empty except for the cocaine. A search of the brown suitcase revealed no contraband. . . . A further search of the car uncovered a rental agreement, indicating that the car had been rented to a Bernadette Harvey. [After his arrest, Green claimed that the blue bag belonged to Maristany and that he had no knowledge of its contents.]

At the suppression hearing, relying on Green's statement at headquarters, defense counsel argued that Green did not own the blue gym bag, and therefore his consent to search was invalid. . . . The State urged the court to consider the trooper's state of mind at the time of the search. According to the State, nothing had indicated that defendant owned the gym bag, and the trooper had been presented with a driver who showed apparent ownership and control of the car and who consented to its search. The State argued that under those circumstances the search had been valid. . . .

To justify a search on the basis of consent, the State must prove that the consent was voluntary and that the consenting party understood his or her right to refuse consent. See State v. Johnson, 346 A.2d 66 (N.J. 1975). Consent may be obtained from the person whose property is to be searched, from a third party who possesses common authority over the property, or from a third party whom the police reasonably believe has authority to consent. . . . The validity of the search depends largely on whether Trooper Trifari, at the time of the search, had a reasonable basis for believing that Green had the authority to consent to a search of the blue gym bag. After reviewing the facts and circumstances known to Trooper Trifari, we are satisfied that the officer reasonably relied on Green's consent to search the car and its contents.

Absent evidence that the driver's control over the car is limited, a driver has the authority to consent to a complete search of the vehicle, including the trunk, glove compartment, and other areas. In that connection, some federal courts have expressed the view that a driver's apparent authority to consent to a search of the vehicle includes the authority to permit a search of luggage belonging to other passengers. Other courts, however, have determined that a driver's authority to consent to a general search of a car does not necessarily include the authority to consent to a search of every container found within the vehicle. For example, a driver's consent to search a car does not extend to containers in which the driver has disclaimed ownership because the officer is under no misapprehension as to the limit of [the driver's] authority to consent. In addition, a driver may not consent to a search of another's private property contained within the car.

As the driver, Green had immediate possession of and control over the vehicle. By possessing the keys to the car and trunk, Green displayed sufficient control over all areas of the vehicle to enable him to consent to its search. Green exercised that control when he consented to a search of the car and voluntarily opened the trunk for the trooper's inspection. In addition, Green's knowledge of the contents of the trunk, prior to the search, further supported the belief that Green had apparent authority to consent.

Once the trunk had been opened, there was nothing to alert Trooper Trifari that both, none, or only one of the bags belonged to Green. Neither bag contained identification. Further, the type of luggage, a canvas gym bag and a suitcase, did not compel the conclusion that one bag belonged to each of the occupants. If, at the time of the search, Green had denied ownership of the gym bag, or defendant had claimed ownership of the bag, we might conclude that the officer's reliance on Green's consent was unreasonable. However, under these circumstances, for Trooper Trifari to believe that Green had apparent authority to consent to the search of both the gym bag and the brown suitcase was objectively reasonable.

[The] better law-enforcement practice would be for police officers specifically to inquire and attempt to ascertain ownership of luggage in a vehicle with several occupants, rather than rely on the driver's consent to search. However, validity of the search does not depend on whether the trooper used the best procedure, but rather on whether the officer's conduct was objectively reasonable under the circumstances. . . .

POLLOCK, J., concurring in part and dissenting in part.

[The majority opinion] puts a premium on ignorance. [As] long as police officers do not know whose property they are searching, they can search at will. Consequently, I respectfully dissent. . . .

The majority states correctly that the validity of the search depends on whether Trooper Trifari had a reasonable basis for believing that Green had the authority to consent to the search of the blue gym bag. Specifically, the fact-sensitive determination accompanying an application of the apparent authority rule shall "be judged against an objective standard: would the facts available to the officer at the moment warrant a [person] of reasonable caution in the belief that the consenting party had authority to consent to a search of luggage in the trunk of a car?" Illinois v. Rodriguez, 497 U.S. 177, 188 (1990). The facts known to Trooper Trifari would have left a reasonable person in doubt about Green's authority to consent to search both bags. . . .

Shortly after the stop, Trooper Trifari ordered Green to walk to the rear of the car. He asked Green where he and Maristany had started their trip. Trooper Trifari left Green at the rear of the car with Trooper Colella and approached Maristany, who was still sitting in the passenger seat. Trifari ordered Maristany to sit on the hood of the car, facing forward, under Colella's observation. Returning to the rear of the car, Trifari asked Green to consent to a search of the car. Significantly, Maristany was too far away to hear this exchange. . . .

Trooper Trifari did not have to hurry because of fear for his safety. Prudently, he had called for back-up assistance. He had ample opportunity to engage in further questioning without endangering himself and Trooper Colella or their investigation. He should have followed his question to Green about the contents of the trunk with the next logical question: Who owns the bags? [He] would have had to ask one more question, but that is a small price to pay for honoring the Constitution.

The majority's approach will likely encourage police officers to avoid inquiring into the facts of similar future situations. The State's burden of proof cannot be met if police officers, faced with an ambiguous situation, nevertheless proceed without making further inquiry. . . . As a practical matter, the requirement to make further inquiries in an ambiguous situation can be easily met. As a matter of law, the inquiry is constitutionally compelled.

Notes

1. *Apparent authority: majority position.* In a number of third-party consent cases, as in *Maristany,* the third party does not actually have authority to consent to the search. Several state courts concluded that these searches are still constitutional so long as the officer has a reasonable belief that the third-party had authority to consent. The Supreme Court endorsed this "apparent authority" rule in Illinois v. Rodriguez, 497 U.S. 177 (1990). In that case, the police searched an apartment based on the consent of a former lover of the tenant, who did not have actual authority to consent to a search of the apartment. Justice Scalia's opinion gave these reasons for adopting the rule:

> It is apparent that in order to satisfy the "reasonableness" requirement of the Fourth Amendment, what is generally demanded of the many factual determinations that must regularly be made by agents of the government — whether the magistrate issuing a warrant, the police officer executing a warrant, or the police officer conducting a search or seizure under one of the exceptions to the warrant requirement — is not that they always be correct, but that they always be reasonable. . . . Because many situations which confront officers in the course of executing their duties are more or less ambiguous, room must be allowed for some mistakes on their part. But the mistakes must be those of reasonable men, acting on facts leading sensibly to their conclusions of probability.
>
> [W]hat we hold today does not suggest that law enforcement officers may always accept a person's invitation to enter premises. Even when the invitation is accompanied by an explicit assertion that the person lives there, the surrounding circumstances could conceivably be such that a reasonable person would doubt its truth and not act upon it without further inquiry. As with other factual determinations bearing upon search and seizure, determination of consent to enter must be judged against an objective standard: would the facts available to the officer at the moment warrant a man of reasonable caution in the belief that the consenting party had authority over the premises?

The majority of states addressing this question both before and after *Rodriguez* have reached the same conclusion, approving of searches based on apparent rather than actual authority to consent. See State v. McCaughey, 904 P.2d 939 (Idaho 1995). A few states, however, have disagreed. See State v. McLees, 994 P.2d 683 (Mont. 2000).

2. *Are consent searches reasonable?* One might view consent as a method of making any search a reasonable one. Alternatively, one might say that consent makes reasonableness irrelevant because the party consenting to the search decides not to insist on the probable cause or valid warrant or other circumstances that would make a search reasonable. The latter view might lead a court to reject the apparent authority doctrine: If the search is unreasonable, then actual consent is necessary to salvage it. If, on the other hand, police act reasonably when they conduct a consensual search, then consent that is invalid for reasons not apparent to the police does not make their actions any less reasonable. Is there a principled basis for deciding between these two views?

3. *Voluntariness revisited.* While following *Bustamonte,* courts have stated that consent must still be voluntary, even if the consenting party lacks full knowledge of the nature of his rights. By allowing police to proceed on the apparent authority rather than the actual authority of third parties, have the majority of courts effectively eliminated the voluntariness requirement for a sizable group of cases? Are police training policies and practices likely to increase the number of consent searches based on the apparent authority of third parties?

Problem 3-9. Consent Through Lease Provisions

In response to long-standing problems with drug trafficking and handgun violence in public housing developments in the city, organized groups of tenants urge the housing authority to require all public housing residents to sign leases consenting to police searches of their apartments for drugs or weapons at any time during the lease period. The housing authority tentatively agrees to the plan. In any public housing development where a majority of tenants vote to adopt the plan, the housing authority will include in every lease a provision consenting to searches of the apartment during the lease period.

As legal counsel for the housing authority, what advice would you offer about this plan? Would you amend it?

Notes

1. *Prospective consent and conditioning of government benefits.* Courts limit the extent to which a landlord may waive a tenant's privacy rights and consent to police searches. They enforce lease terms allowing the landlord access only for inspections or emergencies. But suppose the lease includes an explicit clause giving prospective consent for weapons or drug searches. Would you allow tenants prospectively to give consent to searches? If so, should the consent be limited to searches of an individual's home or might it extend to searches of the person?

In Wyman v. James, 400 U.S. 309 (1971), the Supreme Court held that governments could condition the provision of social services (in this instance, Aid to Families with Dependent Children) on agreements to allow home access by aid workers on the grounds that home visits were not searches. To the extent the visits had the appearance of searches, they were reasonable. Finally, relying on *Camara,* the Court noted that the penalty for refusing caseworkers access was termination of benefits, not criminal sanctions.

What arguments would you make for and against applying Wyman v. James to a public housing lease condition allowing prospective searches? The general issue raised here — known as the doctrine of "unconstitutional conditions"— is whether the conditions that the government places on receipt of government support are unconstitutional. The question arises in a variety of contexts, including, for example, the ability of a state university to condition participation on an athletic team on a student's willingness to agree to random or periodic drug tests. See Lynn Baker, The Prices of Rights: Toward a Positive Theory of Unconstitutional Conditions, 75 Cornell L. Rev. 1185 (1990).

2. *Group consent.* Can a majority of a defined group consent for all members of the group? In the public housing situation, if a majority of residents sign leases allowing random searches, do the police have to check a list of who has agreed to the searches or can they treat the situation as one of "group consent"? Could a majority of residents agree to install a metal detector at the entrance to the complex? What percentage of residents would be needed to consent to searches in the common areas of the building?

If collective consent is not allowed as a basis to waive the rights of an entire group, could collective behavior, such as a series of gunshots in a project or a group fight, serve as an exigency that justifies multiple apartment searches? See Pratt v. Chicago Housing Authority, 848 F. Supp. 792 (N.D. Ill. 1994) (rejecting broad-scale searches and sweeps of multiple apartment units, including searches of "closets, drawers, refrigerators, cabinets and personal effects," days after multiple, random gunfire was heard throughout a complex, and despite consent from many tenants).

IV

Searches in Recurring Contexts

Chapters 2 and 3 introduced the basic elements of search and seizure analysis. This chapter explores the recurring situations in which courts, legislatures, and executive branch agencies have applied those elements. Most of these situations actually happen quite often; others appear often in court opinions and statutes but happen less frequently in actual practice.

Review of these commonly encountered problems will offer some worthwhile practice in using concepts introduced in the previous two chapters. Will the government practice be considered a "search" within the meaning of the federal or state constitution? What showing does the government need to make to justify the search: reasonable suspicion, probable cause, or something else? Is a warrant necessary? Is the search acceptable because the target (or someone else with authority) consented to the search, either explicitly or implicitly?

This chapter is divided into categories identified in the text of the Fourth Amendment and many of its analogs. Remember that the Fourth Amendment secures the right of the people to be secure "in their persons, houses, papers, and effects, against unreasonable searches and seizures." Section A considers searches of "persons," along with searches of places or objects based on their proximity to persons. Section B considers issues raised during searches of "houses" and then expands the inquiry to cover other searches where the location of the search matters in creating the relevant legal rules. Section C considers an historic debate (with modern statutory echoes) about the proper treatment of private "papers," a debate that goes to the heart of the types of limits our legal system now places (and refuses to place) on government searches. Section D considers searches of personal property (or "effects"), including searches of cars and containers, which are among the most common recurring situations in law enforcement.

A. "PERSONS"

Searches of the human body intrude into privacy more clearly than most other searches. Do the legal rules about searches of the person reflect the special intrusiveness of these searches? Consider what distinctions in principle or policy explain the various search rules adopted.

1. Searches Incident to Arrest

When government agents arrest a person, it has long been clear that they may search the person "incident" to the arrest, without any probable cause or reasonable suspicion to believe that the search will produce any weapon or anything else connected to the crime. This automatic "search incident to arrest" was established in English common law and became part of the law of the American colonies from the very earliest times.

The "search incident to arrest" also extends beyond the body of the arrestee to include areas nearby. But just how near? As a matter of both common law and constitutional law, the answer to this question has fluctuated over time. As Judge Learned Hand once wrote, with typical understatement, "When a man is arrested, the extent to which the premises under his direct control may be searched has proved a troublesome question." United States v. Poller, 43 F.2d 911 (2d Cir. 1930).

■ ARKANSAS RULE OF CRIMINAL PROCEDURE 12.2

An officer making an arrest and the authorized officials at the police station or other place of detention to which the accused is brought may conduct a search of the accused's garments and personal effects ready to hand, the surface of his body, and the area within his immediate control.

■ ANNOTATED LAWS OF MASSACHUSETTS CH. 276, §1

A search conducted incident to an arrest may be made only for the purposes of seizing fruits, instrumentalities, contraband and other evidence of the crime for which the arrest has been made, in order to prevent its destruction or concealment; and removing any weapons that the arrestee might use to resist arrest or effect his escape. Property seized as a result of a search in violation of the provisions of this paragraph shall not be admissible in evidence in criminal proceedings.

■ STATE V. MARC HUFNAGEL

745 P.2d 242 (Colo. 1987)

Mullarkey, J.

. . . On October 21, 1986, Hufnagel was indicted by the grand jury on charges of selling cocaine and a warrant for his arrest was issued. In the afternoon of the same day, Sheriff Masters, Undersheriff Walters, and Sergeant Berg went to Hufnagel's condominium for the purpose of executing the arrest warrant. The officers did not have a search warrant. When the officers arrived at the defendant's condominium, the door to his unit was open and Undersheriff Walters called out the defendant's name. The defendant, who had been asleep on a sofa in the living area downstairs, responded by calling out "Hello" or "Yo." The officers entered the unit at the top of the stairs leading down to the living area. They saw an eighteen-inch billy club in the entry way and a hatchet downstairs near a fireplace. The officers went downstairs, asked Hufnagel to stand up, and told him that he was under arrest for selling cocaine. He did not overtly resist the arrest, but he was slow to follow their instructions. The officers were in plain clothes and, although armed, did not display their weapons.

Within approximately five minutes after the officers first made verbal contact with the defendant, he was arrested, handcuffed, and led out of the condominium unit. The exact sequence of events within the five minutes is not entirely clear from the record or from the trial court's findings. It is apparent that Hufnagel was patted down for weapons shortly after he stood up and, at that time, he was standing near the sofa and an adjacent, octagonal end table about eighteen inches high. One or two of the officers turned Hufnagel around and handcuffed him with his hands behind his back while Sheriff Masters felt around the edge of the sofa for weapons. As the defendant was being handcuffed, Sheriff Masters saw him look at the end table. Concerned by the defendant's glance, the sheriff flipped open a door in the end table and, inside, he saw a white box. Since the box had no lid, he saw that it contained several baggies, each of which held a white substance which he believed was cocaine. He picked up the box and examined its contents without removing them. He then put the box back into the end table and closed the door.

At approximately the same time that Sheriff Masters searched the sofa and end table, Sergeant Berg made a cursory search of the rest of the condominium to make sure no one else was present. Two of the officers then took the defendant to the sheriff's office; the third remained behind to guard the premises. Later on the same day, Sheriff Masters executed an affidavit for a search warrant, based in part on his observation of the cocaine in the defendant's end table. The warrant was executed, and additional evidence was found and seized.

The defendant moved to suppress the evidence found during the warrantless search incident to his arrest. He conceded that the arrest had been valid, but argued that because he could not have reached into the end table, the search had not been limited to the area within his immediate control. After a hearing, the trial court found as matters of fact that the defendant had been handcuffed before Sheriff Masters searched the sofa and end table and that the door to the end table had been completely closed prior to the search. Based on his finding that the defendant was handcuffed with his hands behind his back, the judge reasoned that the defendant would not have been able to reach into the end table to remove a weapon or to destroy evidence. Therefore, he concluded that the search violated the fourth amendment's prohibition on unreasonable searches and granted the defendant's first motion to suppress. [Because the search warrant was issued on the basis of information obtained in the search incident to the arrest, the trial court concluded that all evidence obtained in the warranted search should also be suppressed.]

As the defendant notes, a warrantless search is generally presumed to be unreasonable and in violation of the fourth amendment. The prosecution has the burden of showing that such a search falls within an exception to the warrant requirement. In this case, the People rely on the well-settled rule that, when making a lawful arrest, law enforcement officers may search the arrestee's person and the area within the arrestee's immediate control. See Chimel v. California, 395 U.S. 752 (1969). In *Chimel*, the Supreme Court explained that:

> It is entirely reasonable for the arresting officer to search for and seize any evidence on the arrestee's person in order to prevent its concealment or destruction. And the area into which an arrestee might reach in order to grab a weapon or evidentiary items must, of course, be governed by a like rule. A gun on a table or in a drawer in front of one who is arrested can be as dangerous to the arresting officer as one concealed in the clothing of the person arrested. There is ample justification, therefore, for a search of the arrestee's person and the area "within his immediate control"— construing that phrase to mean the area from within which he might gain possession of a weapon or destructible evidence.

The trial court found that the end table door was within "lunging" distance of the defendant and its finding is supported by the record. The end table was directly adjacent to the sofa on which the defendant had been sleeping. When he sat up, he was approximately one to two feet from the end table. He stood up when the officers came downstairs, but did not leave "a very narrow confinement of [the] vicinity" of the end table, according to Sheriff Masters' testimony, and moved only "a few feet," according to his own testimony. This evidence indicates that, prior to being handcuffed, the defendant could have reached the end table and grabbed a weapon or destructible evidence from inside it.

In spite of this, the trial court found that the search was unreasonable because the defendant was handcuffed. We disagree. The search was reasonable in scope and time and was confined to items within the defendant's immediate control. First, it is clear that the police did not engage in a general search of the defendant's home. The search was limited to two items, the sofa and the adjacent end table, which were brought to the officers' attention by the defendant's conduct. As discussed above, Hufnagel had been sleeping on the sofa when the police arrived and he stared at the end table while he was being arrested. Second, the events occurred within a very short time span; the officers spent a total of only about five minutes in the condominium unit. The defendant was not secured when he looked at the end table but he was secured by the time Sheriff Masters flipped open the door. As these findings demonstrate, whether the handcuffs clicked shut before or after the end table search is a matter of split-second timing. We think it would be unwise and highly artificial to make the validity of a search incident to an arrest turn on such a fine point of timing.[2]

Third, the sofa and end table were within the defendant's immediate control. It is well established that, when a search of the arrestee and the area immediately around him or her is incident to a valid, custodial arrest, no additional justification is required for the search. The United States Supreme Court has stated that "the potential dangers lurking in all custodial arrests make warrantless searches of items within the 'immediate control' area reasonable without requiring the arresting

2. This position has been persuasively explained by Professor LaFave: . . . "A highly sophisticated set of rules, qualified by all sorts of ifs, ands, and buts and requiring the drawing of subtle nuances and hairline distinctions, may be the sort of heady stuff upon which the facile minds of lawyers and judges eagerly feed, but [such rules] may be 'literally impossible of application by the officer in the field.'" LaFave, "Case-by-Case Adjudication" Versus "Standardized Procedures": The *Robinson* Dilemma,1974 Sup. Ct. Rev. 127.

officer to calculate the probability that weapons or destructible evidence may be involved." United States v. Chadwick, 433 U.S. 1 (1977); see also United States v. Robinson, 414 U.S. 218 (1973). This court also has stated that such a search requires no independent justification. Therefore, we have declined to make a separate determination in each case as to whether the arresting officers had reason to believe that the arrestee would grab a weapon or evidence from the surrounding area. As explained below, the danger inherent in any custodial arrest also leads us to hold that a search incident to arrest is constitutional even if the arrestee is handcuffed prior to the search.

Chimel did not decide the exact boundaries of the search incident to arrest exception to the warrant requirement. Therefore, courts have interpreted the exception in a variety of ways. Many courts have considered the fact that the arrestee was handcuffed as one factor in determining the reasonableness of the search. To determine the legal effect of handcuffing an arrestee, courts using this approach have considered the practical effects handcuffs have on the arrestee's "lunging" distance. For example, handcuffs do not completely eliminate an arrestee's ability to reach and grab items. Further, since handcuffs can fail, it is reasonable for the arresting officer to search the area the arrestee could reach after breaking free from them.

Other courts have adopted a rule that a search of the area immediately around the arrestee, made contemporaneously with or immediately following the arrest, is constitutional even if the arrestee is physically unable to reach the area searched at the time of the search.

We believe the second approach, permitting officers to make a reasonable search incident to arrest regardless of whether the arrestee is handcuffed, is the most realistic approach and serves the purposes behind *Chimel.* Arrests are necessarily tense, risky events when many things are happening at once. The difficulty of imposing an orderly chronology after the fact is apparent in this case. Police officers, who must act quickly, cannot reasonably be expected to pay attention to the exact time at which the arrestee is handcuffed and then to make an accurate guess as to how much a reviewing court will think the handcuffs restrict that particular arrestee's "lunging" distance under all the circumstances. . . .

A case-by-case analysis considering all the circumstances of such a search would be impracticable. Further, a case-by-case analysis is not required by *Chimel.* In *Chimel,* the United States Supreme Court rejected the prosecution's argument that an unlimited, warrantless search of an arrestee's house was justified whenever an individual was arrested at home, explaining that "under such an unconfined analysis, Fourth Amendment protection in this area would approach the evaporation point." Instead, the Court concluded that, while legitimate needs of arresting officers to protect themselves and to preserve evidence made warrantless searches "of the person arrested and the area within his reach" reasonable, those needs did not justify "more extensive searches." The Court's goal was to develop a rule that would allow police officers to protect themselves and to preserve evidence without eviscerating arrestees' fourth amendment rights. This goal can be met by limiting searches incident to arrests to the area immediately around the arrestee and the time contemporaneous with or immediately following the arrest.

Therefore, we hold that the People need not show that the arrestee was physically able to reach the exact place searched at the exact second it was searched in order to justify a search incident to arrest. Instead, the prosecution can meet its burden of showing that a warrantless search was reasonable by showing, as it did here, that it was contemporaneous with or immediately following the defendant's arrest and was limited to the area immediately around him. Because we conclude that Sheriff Masters' observation of the contents of the end table was made during a valid search incident to a lawful arrest, we reverse the trial court's order suppressing the evidence found in both searches. . . .

Notes

1. *Search incident to arrest: majority position.* Under the long-standing doctrine of "search incident to arrest," the police may search the person of an arrestee, along with some area near the arrestee, without any independent probable cause or warrant to support the search. As for the amount of area the police may search "incident" to the arrest, the federal standard appears in Chimel v. California, 395 U.S. 752 (1969). The search may extend to the area within the "immediate control" of the arrestee, that is, the area in which the arrestee could reach a weapon or destroy evidence. State courts have by and large adopted this same standard under their state constitutions and statutes. However, as the *Hufnagel* case from Colorado makes clear, there are real disagreements over how to apply this standard. *Hufnagel* represents a strong minority position on the question of handcuffs: A larger group of state courts will consider the fact that an arrestee was handcuffed at the time of a search when determining the area within the "immediate control" of an arrestee.

Whether a suspect is handcuffed at the time of a search incident to arrest is only one of a host of facts that courts have used to assess the validity of searches in particular cases. Other factors include: (a) whether there are multiple defendants; (b) whether there are confederates of the suspect nearby who might destroy evidence; (c) whether the officers are between the suspect and the area or object to be searched; (d) whether the officers have control over the area or object to be searched; and (e) any postarrest movement by the arrestee (for example, to get dressed). Which of these factors is subject to the control of the officer? Doesn't assessment of these factors depend on the justification underlying searches incident to arrest?

In the *Hufnagel* case from Colorado, what were the critical factors justifying the search of the end table as a search incident to arrest? How far away from Hufnagel was the end table when the officers entered the apartment? When Hufnagel gave the fatal glance?

2. Chimel *and its predecessors.* The law defining the permissible scope of searches incident to arrest has gone through many changes over the past 70 years. Flexible as *Chimel* may seem, it narrowed the prior rule of Harris v. United States, 331 U.S. 145 (1947), and United States v. Rabinowitz, 339 U.S. 56 (1950), which allowed searches of multiple-room dwellings as searches incident to arrest. An earlier strand of Supreme Court cases — notably Go-Bart Importing Co. v. United States, 282 U.S. 344 (1931), and Trupiano v. United States, 334 U.S. 699 (1948) (rejected by *Rabinowitz*) — suggested that where a search warrant could be obtained before the arrest, it should be.

The court in *Hufnagel,* echoing the U.S. Supreme Court in *Chimel,* justified searches incident to arrest based on the need to find relevant evidence before it is destroyed and the need to protect officers from harm by discovering possible weapons. Which of the two basic justifications supports a more expansive view of searches incident to arrest? What additional theories might justify expansion or contraction of searches incident to arrest? Do the justifications for searches incident to arrest apply most strongly before, during, or after arrest?

3. *Automatic authorization to search.* The distinctive feature of the search incident to arrest is its automatic quality: The police need no justification for the search beyond the justification for the arrest. See United States v. Robinson, 414 U.S. 218 (1973). There is no need to suspect that the person himself is holding a weapon or evidence of a crime; there is no need to suspect that the area within the arrestee's immediate control holds weapons, contraband, or evidence. Is this another example of the courts adopting a "bright line" rule to make the police officer's job more manageable? See Ronald Dworkin, Fact Style Adjudication and the Fourth Amendment, 48 Ind. L.J. 329 (1973).

Statutes in England allow different searches incident to arrest than does American law. Under section 18 of the Police and Criminal Evidence Act of 1984, the constable may search the *premises* of any arrested person (regardless of where the arrest takes place) if there are "reasonable grounds" to believe that the premises contain evidence of the offense that is the basis of the arrest or some similar offense. Section 32 of the Act allows the constable to search a *person,* if the person to be searched has been arrested at a place other than a police station, and if "the constable has reasonable grounds for believing that the arrested person may present a danger to himself or others." The constable may also search the arrested person for evidence of a crime, or for anything he or she might use to escape custody, but only if the constable has "reasonable grounds for believing" that such items will be found in the search. Finally, section 32 also allows the constable "to enter and search any premises in which [the arrested person] was when arrested . . . for evidence relating to the offence for which he has been arrested," but once again, only if the constable has "reasonable grounds for believing that there is evidence . . . on the premises." If an American jurisdiction were to adopt this statute, would it change the practices of the police during arrests in a significant way? Would the police be in greater danger?

4. *Comparison to* Terry *searches.* Courts allow searches of the person incident to arrest to be more intensive than *Terry* searches. See United States v. Robinson, 414 U.S. at 224-229. Why? How long can a search incident to arrest take? Is there any kind of search, either of the person or of a place, that would not be allowed within the justification of a search incident to arrest?

5. *A "life cycle" for procedure issues?* For some time after *Chimel,* state supreme courts actively explored the scope of the area of "immediate control" of the arrestee, considering issues such as the impact of handcuffing the suspect. In recent years the number of cases involving searches incident to arrest in the U.S. and state supreme courts has decreased, and the validity of such searches has been left to trial courts to decide on the facts of each case, with only occasional appeals to lower appellate courts. What characteristics of a criminal procedure issue will make it appear on the docket of a state supreme court? Is there a "life cycle" for criminal procedure issues, in which they become prominent in different institutions in predictable patterns?

6. *Protective sweeps.* Although *Chimel* rejected searches of entire rooms or multiple rooms as part of a search incident to arrest, such searches may still be allowed at the time of arrest on other grounds. One justification for a full-house search is to discover persons who may pose a threat to officers conducting the arrest. In Maryland v. Buie, 494 U.S. 325 (1990), the Supreme Court upheld two sorts of "protective sweeps" outside the area within the "immediate control" of the arrestee.

First, the arresting officers may look in closets and other places immediately adjoining the place of the arrest from which another person might launch an attack on the officers. This search needs no justification beyond the simple fact of the arrest. Second, the officers may search other areas in the house for any persons who might pose a danger to them, but only if they have a reasonable suspicion that the "sweep" will reveal the presence of such a person. In either case, the search is limited to places where a person may be found.

Almost all state courts addressing this subject also allow police to make "protective sweeps" of the premises where an arrest takes place, under the same two-stage analysis that the *Buie* court used. See Reasor v. State, 12 S.W.3d 813, 817 (Tex. Crim. App. 2000). Should multiple-room searches for potential accomplices be allowed even when there are no reasonable grounds to believe such accomplices pose a danger to officers but when there is a reasonable suspicion that parties to a multiparty offense are likely to be present or that persons in the house may destroy evidence?

Problem 4-1. Search Incident to (But After) Arrest

An officer looking through binoculars saw a man with a plaid shirt and a blue backpack leaving a field of marijuana plants in a remote, unpopulated canyon. The officer and his partner followed the man in the plaid shirt, whose name turned out to be Howard Boff, and arrested him on a deserted dirt road after he sat down and placed the backpack on the ground about five feet from his body.

The officers drove Boff and his backpack to the sheriff's office, about 45 minutes away in Dove Creek. Three hours after placing Boff in custody, the police officers opened the backpack without a search warrant and found marijuana. Was the search valid as a search incident to arrest? Compare People v. Boff, 766 P.2d 646 (Colo. 1988).

Notes

1. *Subsequent searches: how much time?* Until 1974 the Supreme Court required that searches incident to arrest be "substantially contemporaneous with the arrest." See, e.g., Vale v. Louisiana, 399 U.S. 30 (1970). In 1974 the Court decided United States v. Edwards, 415 U.S. 800, in which it upheld a search of defendant's clothing for paint chips 10 hours after he was arrested. State courts have generally allowed searches at the police station, well after the time of arrest, of objects "immediately associated with the person" that could have been searched at the time of arrest, including clothing, wallets, and purses. See Commonwealth v. Stallworth, 781 A.2d 110 (Pa. 2001). Professor Myron Moskovitz, based on telephone interviews with police officers and written training materials from various police departments, concluded that police officers typically handcuff a suspect before searching the vicinity, but they usually obtain a warrant to search an area if they have already removed the arrestee from the scene. Moskovitz, A Rule in Search of a Reason: An Empirical Reexamination of *Chimel* and *Belton*, 2002 Wis. L. Rev. 657, 666-67. This practice, he concludes, is based on police views about the reasonableness of searches rather than their reading of what the courts might allow.

2. *Searches prior to arrest.* The rationale for a search incident to arrest may be strongest immediately prior to arrest, when officers are searching for the person to

be arrested or have reasonable grounds to believe that weapons may be present or that evidence might be destroyed. Courts typically allow pre-arrest searches, on the basis of "exigent circumstances," to find a suspect when police are otherwise lawfully within the premises. Courts may also allow pre-arrest searches of areas too small to conceal the offender but large enough to conceal weapons, at least during a "hot pursuit" of the defendant. See Warden v. Hayden, 387 U.S. 294 (1967) (during search for suspect, officer looks in washing machine and discovers evidence). Should such searches generally be allowed as part of arrests within homes? Should officers be able to conduct a "search incident to arrest" beyond the scope of a *Terry* search if they find a person they believe to be the suspect but are not certain?

2. *Intrusive Body Searches*

Strip searches and body cavity examinations are among the most intrusive searches that government agents perform. The police sometimes conduct these searches in the field, either before an arrest or incident to arrest. Sometimes they conduct these searches with the suspect's consent. At other times, officers carry out strip searches at the police station or in a jail or other detention facility, either as part of standard booking procedures or in response to police concerns about an individual.

In recent years, legislatures rather than courts have created the legal limits for these searches. Most states now have statutes placing some limits on the use of strip searches and body cavity searches, and courts have in turn largely ceased their efforts to regulate such searches. Reprinted below are a few examples of these statutes. They highlight how legislatures develop legal rules different from those that courts develop.

Consider the differences between the legislative and judicial rules governing pre-arrest and postarrest searches. Should the extremely intrusive nature of the search technique require some showing beyond probable cause and a judicial warrant in any setting? Or should the regulation of strip searches be more substantial in the field (because of possible abuse), or in the station house (because of the more controlled setting)? Strip search statutes generally require that any allowable strip or body cavity search take place in clean, private surroundings and that the police officers conducting the search must be of the same sex as the person being examined.

As you examine the following three statutes, consider (1) the different levels of justification required for such searches, (2) any special procedures or additional actors who must approve the search, and (3) the use of alternatives to body cavity and strip searches. Then, based on these elements, rank the following statutes in terms of their potential to minimize the number of strip and body cavity searches. What information would you collect to test your assumptions about the impact of different procedures in actual practice?

■ ARKANSAS RULE OF CRIMINAL PROCEDURE 12.3

(a) Search of an accused's blood stream, body cavities, and subcutaneous tissues conducted incidental to an arrest may be made only:

(i) if there is a strong probability that it will disclose things subject to seizure and related to the offense for which the individual was arrested; and

(ii) if it reasonably appears that the delay consequent upon procurement of a search warrant would probably result in the disappearance or destruction of the objects of the search; and

(iii) if it reasonably appears that the search is otherwise reasonable under the circumstances of the case, including the seriousness of the offense and the nature of the invasion of the individual's person.

■ TENNESSEE CODE §40-7-121

(b) No person shall be subjected to a body cavity search by a law enforcement officer or by another person acting under the direction, supervision or authority of a law enforcement officer unless such search is conducted pursuant to a search warrant. . . .

(c) The issue of whether a person subjected to a body cavity search consented to such search is irrelevant and shall not be considered in determining whether the search was a valid one under the provisions of this section, unless the consent is in writing on a preprinted form and contains the following language:

> **Waiver of Warrant Requirement and Consent to Search Body Cavities**
> I knowingly and voluntarily consent to have my body cavities searched immediately by law enforcement personnel in the manner provided by the laws of Tennessee. By signing this consent form, I knowingly and voluntarily waive my right to require that a warrant be obtained from an appropriate judge or magistrate before my body cavities are searched. I understand that a body cavity search may involve both visual and physical probing into my genitals and anus. I understand that I would not be prejudiced or penalized by declining to give my consent to be searched in this manner.

■ REVISED CODE OF WASHINGTON §§10.79.080, 10.79.130, 10.79.140

§10.79.080

(1) No person may be subjected to a body cavity search by or at the direction of a law enforcement agency unless a search warrant is issued. . . .

(2) No law enforcement officer may seek a warrant for a body cavity search without first obtaining specific authorization for the body cavity search from the ranking shift supervisor of the law enforcement authority. Authorization for the body cavity search may be obtained electronically: PROVIDED, That such electronic authorization shall be reduced to writing by the law enforcement officer seeking the authorization and signed by the ranking supervisor as soon as possible thereafter.

(3) Before any body cavity search is authorized or conducted, a thorough pat-down search, a thorough electronic metal-detector search, and a thorough clothing search, where appropriate, must be used to search for and seize any evidence of a crime, contraband, fruits of crime, things otherwise criminally possessed, weapons, or other things by means of which a crime has been committed or reasonably appears about to be committed. No body cavity search shall be authorized or conducted unless these other methods do not satisfy the safety, security, or evidentiary concerns of the law enforcement agency.

(4) A law enforcement officer requesting a body cavity search shall prepare and sign a report regarding the body cavity search. . . .

§10.79.130

(1) No person [in custody at a holding, detention, or local correctional facility, regardless of whether an arrest warrant or other court order was issued before the person was arrested, may] be strip searched without a warrant unless:

(a) There is a reasonable suspicion to believe that a strip search is necessary to discover weapons, criminal evidence, contraband, or other thing concealed on the body of the person to be searched, that constitutes a threat to the security of a holding, detention, or local correctional facility;

(b) There is probable cause to believe that a strip search is necessary to discover other criminal evidence concealed on the body of the person to be searched, but not constituting a threat to facility security; or

(c) There is a reasonable suspicion to believe that a strip search is necessary to discover a health condition requiring immediate medical attention.

(2) For the purposes of subsection (1) of this section, a reasonable suspicion is deemed to be present when the person to be searched has been arrested for:

(a) A violent offense . . . ;

(b) An offense involving escape, burglary, or the use of a deadly weapon; or

(c) An offense involving possession of a drug or controlled substance . . .

§10.79.140

(1) A person [in custody at a holding, detention, or local correctional facility, regardless of whether an arrest warrant or other court order was issued before the person was arrested or otherwise taken into custody] who has not been arrested for an offense within one of the categories specified in RCW 10.79.130(2) may nevertheless be strip searched, but only upon an individualized determination of reasonable suspicion or probable cause as provided in this section.

(2) With the exception of those situations in which reasonable suspicion is deemed to be present under RCW 10.79.130(2), no strip search may be conducted without the specific prior written approval of the jail unit supervisor on duty. Before any strip search is conducted, reasonable efforts must be made to use other less-intrusive means, such as pat-down, electronic metal detector, or clothing searches, to determine whether a weapon, criminal evidence, contraband, or other thing is concealed on the body, or whether a health condition requiring immediate medical attention is present. The determination of whether reasonable suspicion or probable cause exists to conduct a strip search shall be made only after such less-intrusive means have been used and shall be based on a consideration of all information and circumstances known to the officer authorizing the strip search, including but not limited to the following factors:

(a) The nature of the offense for which the person to be searched was arrested;

(b) The prior criminal record of the person to be searched; and

(c) Physically violent behavior of the person to be searched, during or after the arrest.

Notes

1. *Strip search statutes: majority position.* In most places, state statutes and police department policies place special limits on strip searches and body cavity searches. More states have statutes or rules addressing this sort of search than virtually any other specific search technique (with the exception of electronic eavesdropping, which we consider in Chapter 7). Is it possible to bar all strip searches? Why does the Washington legislature provide so much more guidance for searches conducted once a person is in custody? Apart from responding to abuses in specific cases, what else might explain the willingness of so many legislatures to address this topic? If legislatures were to leave this question to courts, what standards would courts apply?

2. *Strip searches for misdemeanors and infractions.* Public attention is often drawn to strip searches conducted on people suspected only of minor offenses. See Edwards v. State, 759 N.E.2d 626 (Ind. 2001) (warrantless and suspicionless strip search of misdemeanor arrestees violates federal and state constitutions). Legislatures often claim to sharply limit strip searches for minor offenses. Consider the following illustration from California Penal Code §4030(f):

> No person arrested and held in custody on a misdemeanor or infraction offense, except those involving weapons, controlled substances or violence . . . shall be subjected to a strip search or visual body cavity search prior to placement in the general jail population, unless a peace officer has determined there is reasonable suspicion based on specific and articulable facts to believe such person is concealing a weapon or contraband, and a strip search will result in the discovery of the weapon or contraband. No strip search or visual body cavity search or both may be conducted without the prior written authorization of the supervising officer on duty. The authorization shall include the specific and articulable facts and circumstances upon which the reasonable suspicion determination was made by the supervisor. . . .

How much protection for citizens suspected of minor offenses does this statute provide? Why do some legislatures create different presumptions for drug and violent offenders? In these states, how important for the ultimate impact of these rules is the definition of a drug or violent offender?

Other state legislatures have passed such statutes in response to notorious and newsworthy cases involving strip searches. See Mary Beth G. v. City of Chicago, 723 F.2d 1263 (7th Cir. 1983) (civil suit brought by women arrested for outstanding parking tickets, challenging city policy requiring a strip search and body cavity search of all women arrested and detained in city lockups, regardless of charges; Illinois legislature amended arrest statute to prohibit strip searches of persons arrested for traffic, regulatory, or misdemeanor offenses absent a reasonable belief that the arrestee is concealing weapons or controlled substances on her person). Often the motivation for these statutes is not the facts of a particular case but the judgment in a lawsuit. Hundreds of lawsuits based on strip suits have been filed in recent years, including one civil lawsuit in New York City that resulted in a settlement for $50,000,000 based on strip searches conducted as part of a "quality of life" policing strategy promoted by former Mayor Rudy Giuliani. See Terry Golway, "Here's the Naked Truth About Strip Searches," New York Observer, Mon. Feb. 12, 2001 (class action lawsuit on behalf of 65,000 citizens who were strip searched after arrest for minor offenses).

3. *The relative virtues of process and substantive standards.* Among the statutes addressing strip searches and body cavity searches, there are two distinct limiting techniques at work. Some of the statutory provisions contain substantive "standards," describing a subclass of cases not eligible for this type of search (such as those accused of particular offenses or cases where the police do not have adequate reason to believe that the search will succeed). Others focus on the process of authorizing such a search (by requiring a judicial warrant or supervisor approval or a written record of any decision to conduct such a search). Which regulatory technique offers greater protection to citizens: more intricate process requirements or higher substantive standards?

4. *The mouth exception.* Most of the body cavity statutes do not cover searches of the mouth. Would you expect statutes to have separate mouth search statutes? Why or why not? See State v. Peterson, 515 N.W.2d 23 (Iowa 1994) (upholding forced search of mouth as search incident to arrest).

5. *Consent to strip searches.* Some statutes bar consent to strip searches, others allow consent, still others require special procedures for obtaining consent, and several say nothing about consent. In a jurisdiction whose statute says nothing about consent, what arguments would you make to a court that it should enforce special consent rules for strip and body cavity searches?

Probable cause, a term captured in the text of the Fourth Amendment and many of its analogs, is the core standard for determining when the government may search a place or person. But it is not the only standard. The investigatory searches and stops described in Chapter 2 are governed by the "reasonable suspicion" standard, considered to be less demanding than probable cause. A few other searches — often bodily searches of a highly intrusive nature — are allowed only when the government makes a showing that is even more demanding than probable cause.

The strip search statutes suggest that legislatures will sometimes step in to define sharper limits or higher standards for intrusive body searches. Consider, for example, how the Arkansas, Tennessee and Washington strip search statutes would apply to the following case. Where legislatures have not acted to limit highly intrusive searches, courts have stepped in to fill that gap.

■ PEOPLE v. ERIC MORE

764 N.E.2d 967 (N.Y. 2002)

LEVINE, J.

Defendant was convicted of criminal possession of a controlled substance in the third degree, criminal possession of a controlled substance in the fifth degree, resisting arrest and false personation. The drug possession counts related to 2.37 grams of crack cocaine which the police extracted from defendant's rectum during a strip search incident to his arrest. . . .

Prior to trial, defendant moved to suppress the drugs seized from his person. At the suppression hearing, a detective in the Troy Police Department Special Operations Unit testified that he and several other officers entered an apartment after obtaining the tenant's permission to do so. The tenant told the police that individuals in the apartment were "cutting up cocaine" for sale and that one of the subjects was wanted on an arrest warrant for assaulting a police officer. Upon entering the apartment, the detective saw defendant sitting on a couch with a woman on his lap. He also saw a "crack pipe and small piece of white rocklike substance" on a nearby table. Based upon his training and experience, the detective believed the substance was crack cocaine. The police arrested defendant and the woman, ordered them onto the floor, handcuffed them and conducted a "quick pat-down" search for weapons. No weapons were found.

The police then separated defendant and the female in order to strip search them. Defendant initially cooperated by taking off most of his clothes, but at some point he protested and scuffled with the officers. During the search, which took place in a bedroom, the police removed a plastic bag, an outer portion of which they saw protruding from defendant's rectum. The bag contained several individually wrapped pieces of a white rock-like substance, which later tested positive for cocaine. Drugs were also recovered from defendant's female companion.

In his motion to suppress the drugs seized from his person, defendant focused his challenge on the legality of his arrest and the strip search incident thereto. He claimed that the arrest was effected without probable cause, presumably as a pretext to justify the search of his person. In addition, he specifically averred that the body cavity search was "illegal and effected in the absence of probable cause, in the absence of a warrant and in the absence of any exigency." County Court denied the motion to suppress in all respects. . . .

The Supreme Court of the United States addressed the constitutionality of a seizure involving an intrusion into the human body in Schmerber v. California, 384 U.S. 757 (1966). Recognizing that it was "writ[ing] on a clean slate," the Court held that the police were justified in requiring a person arrested for driving while under the influence of alcohol to submit to a blood test to determine blood alcohol level. The Court framed the relevant issues as "whether the police were justified in requiring petitioner to submit to the blood test, and whether the means and procedures employed in taking his blood respected relevant Fourth Amendment standards of reasonableness."

After concluding that the police had probable cause to arrest the petitioner for driving while under the influence of alcohol, the Supreme Court determined that seizures involving intrusions beyond the body's surface cannot be justified simply because they are made incident to a lawful arrest. The Court reasoned that although a "full search" of a person is allowed incident to a lawful arrest in order to disarm the suspect or preserve evidence, the considerations permitting such a search "have little applicability with respect to searches involving intrusions beyond the body's surface." The Fourth Amendment "forbids any such intrusions on the mere chance that desired evidence might be obtained." Rather, there must exist a "clear indication" that desired evidence will be found. In the absence of such an indication, the Fourth Amendment mandates that the police "suffer the risk that such evidence may disappear unless there is an immediate search."

Moreover, even where there is a "clear indication" that incriminating evidence will be retrieved if the bodily intrusion is permitted, "[s]earch warrants are ordinarily required for searches of dwellings, and *absent an emergency,* no less could be required where intrusions into the human body are concerned." Indeed, as the Court stressed, the "importance of informed, detached and deliberate determinations of the issue whether or not to invade another's body in search of evidence of guilt is indisputable and great." The police were not required to obtain a search warrant in *Schmerber* only because of the existence of exigent circumstances—the officer there "might reasonably have believed that he was confronted with an emergency, in which the delay necessary to obtain a warrant, under the circumstances, threatened 'the destruction of evidence.'"

Finally, the *Schmerber* Court concluded that the procedure used to extract the blood from the petitioner was itself reasonable and conducted in a reasonable manner. In upholding the seizure, the Court noted that its decision to allow the intrusion into the petitioner's body "under stringently limited conditions" did not indicate that the Fourth Amendment "permits more substantial intrusions, or intrusions under other conditions."

Undoubtedly, body cavity searches incident to an arrest are at least as intrusive as blood test procedures. This Court has referred to them as "invasive" and "degrading," People v. Luna, 535 N.E.2d 1305 (N.Y. 1989), and other courts have similarly described them. [The court cited federal cases from the First and Seventh Circuits.]

On the suppression record before us, we conclude that the body cavity search of defendant incident to his arrest was unreasonable and invalid. Even assuming that the extraction of the drugs satisfied all of *Schmerber*'s other requirements, the People failed to offer any evidence of exigent circumstances to justify dispensing with the warrant requirement—that a neutral, detached magistrate determine that the search is justified and will be conducted in a reasonable manner. This record is devoid of any evidence from which an officer "might reasonably have believed that he was confronted with an emergency, in which the delay necessary to obtain a warrant" posed a threat to the officer's personal safety or of the destruction of the evidence. Notably, no police officer testified that, despite the available means of incapacitating defendant and keeping him under full surveillance, an immediate body cavity search was necessary to prevent his access to a weapon or prevent his disposing of the drugs. Nor was there any evidence the police were concerned that the drugs—which were wrapped in plastic—could have been absorbed into defendant's body. The absence of exigent circumstances dictates the conclusion that the body cavity search here was unreasonable. . . .

Notes

1. *Probable cause "plus": majority position.* Some courts require the government to justify the use of an especially intrusive bodily search with something more than probable cause. Does the New York court in *More* require some "plus," in addition to probable cause? When the government uses invasive medical techniques to carry out a bodily search, the relevant standard under the federal constitution appears in Schmerber v. California, 384 U.S. 757 (1966). There the Court approved the use of evidence derived from a blood sample that a physician had taken from a suspect. The Court found the search reasonable because (1) there was a "clear indication" that the blood sample would produce evidence of a crime; (2) the test was "commonplace" and involved almost no risk or trauma; and (3) the test was conducted in a "reasonable manner," carried out by a physician in a hospital environment. See also Rochin v. California, 342 U.S. 165 (1952) (forced administration of emetic solution to induce vomiting in suspect who had swallowed capsules; barred by due process). Some state courts interpret *Schmerber* to require only probable cause, but most

take this language to mean that the government must show exigent circumstances or evidence stronger than probable cause to justify the taking of blood.

When an especially intrusive search technique takes place in the field rather than in a health care facility, some courts absolutely forbid the practice (regardless of the government's level of certainty that the search will be successful) under the due process clause of the federal or state constitution. See State v. Hodson, 907 P.2d 1155 (Utah 1995) (condemning use of throat hold and the pointing of a gun at suspect's head to convince him to spit out drugs in his mouth). It is more common, however, for courts to approve of searches involving force during an arrest. See State v. Thompson, 505 N.W.2d 673 (Neb. 1993) (approving use of choke hold to prevent suspect from swallowing narcotics).

What role will police expertise play in jurisdictions where officers are left with some discretion to conduct highly intrusive searches in the field? For example, in *More,* how could the police determine before the search whether or not any secreted drugs were in a form which might be destroyed or disappear with further delay? Did More's consent make the search valid in this case? Even if More withdrew his consent, would a judge issue a warrant on the facts of More? Would the baggie and its contents "inevitably" be discovered when a strip search was conducted at the station as part of standard processing before placing the suspect in a jail cell?

2. *Orders for saliva, urine, and bite casts.* When a police officer or prosecutor requests a saliva sample, or a plaster cast of a suspect's "bite," should the request be treated as an administrative processing request, or as a search? If the request is treated as a search, are these searches intrusive body searches? Some jurisdictions require police or prosecutors to obtain a court order when a suspect refuses to consent to providing saliva or a bite cast. The majority of states require only reasonable suspicion or "reasonable grounds to suspect" that the person has been involved in a crime and that the information will be relevant to that offense. See, e.g., In re Nontestimonial Identification Order Directed to R.H., 762 A.2d 1239 (Vt. 2000).

3. *Orders for nonintrusive identification evidence.* Should nonintrusive nontestimonial requests, for example for handwriting, voice, and hair samples and other evidence involving the physical state of the suspect be governed by a reasonable suspicion standard, since such information does not require intrusive body searches? See Iowa Code §§810.1-.6 (governing collection of nontestimonial identification evidence including "fingerprints, palm prints, footprints, measurements, hair strands, handwriting samples, voice samples, photographs, blood and saliva samples, ultraviolet or black-light examinations, paraffin tests, and lineups"). Under Iowa Code §810.6, nontestimonial identification orders require the government to establish each of the following:

1. That there is probable cause to believe that a felony described in the application has been committed.
2. That there are reasonable grounds to suspect that the person named or described in the application committed the felony and it is reasonable in view of the seriousness of the offense to subject that person to the requested nontestimonial identification procedures.
3. That the results of the requested nontestimonial identification procedures will be of material aid in determining whether the person named or described in the application committed the felony.
4. That such evidence cannot practicably be obtained from other sources.

In Keith Bousman v. District Court, 630 N.W. 2d 789 (Iowa 2001), the Iowa Supreme Court held that this statute and the federal and Iowa constitutions required only reasonable suspicion in support of an order to obtain saliva for a DNA test. The court also held that reasonable suspicion was all that is required to support a brief investigatory detention to gather this information. Is the compelled presence of a suspect at the police station for a physical sample an arrest? If so, why don't the federal and state constitutions require probable cause for the suspect's detention or forced presence, even if they do not require probable cause to compel the nontestimonial evidence?

4. *Noninvasive medical search techniques.* The pumping of a stomach is one medical technique that typically requires the probable cause "plus" showing. Would you require the probable cause "plus" only for physically invasive techniques? How about the use of an X-ray, followed by administration of a laxative? See People v. Thompson, 820 P.2d 1160 (Colo. Ct. App. 1991) (higher justification required for laxative but not for X-ray). Would most people rather be subject to an unwanted X-ray or an unwanted laxative? Which of these procedures can go forward without the assistance of a doctor? A number of cases have approved the taking of a blood sample based only on a showing of probable cause. Would a justification higher than probable cause be necessary if the police officer uses a "stun gun" (a weapon that produces 0.00006 of an amp of electricity to cause muscle contractions and a resulting loss of balance) to disable a resisting suspect long enough to draw the blood sample? See McCann v. State, 588 A.2d 1100 (Del. 1991).

B. "HOUSES" AND OTHER PLACES

We move now to searches of "houses" and other common searches in which the location of the search plays a major part in the legal analysis. Recall from Chapter 2 that the Fourth Amendment and most analogous state provisions protect only a "reasonable expectation of privacy." In Katz v. United States, 389 U.S. 347 (1967), the Supreme Court declared that the Fourth Amendment "protects people, not places." Nevertheless, the location of a search still matters a great deal. We consider in this section searches and seizures that take place in several important recurring locations: in or near homes, workplaces, and institutions such as schools and prisons.

1. *The Outer Boundaries of Houses*

Searches of homes have always presented some of the easiest cases for limiting the power of the government to search. Recall that the most infamous searches of the late eighteenth century—which most influenced the framers of the Fourth Amendment—were searches of homes. But it is not always so easy to tell where a home leaves off and where the rest of the world begins. The area immediately surrounding the home, known as the "curtilage," receives the same protection as the home itself. Areas beyond the curtilage, known as "open fields," traditionally received no Fourth Amendment protection at all. The Supreme Court in United

States v. Dunn, 480 U.S. 294, 300-301 (1987), defined the boundary between the curtilage and the open field as follows:

> the extent of the curtilage is determined by factors that bear upon whether an individual reasonably may expect that the area in question should be treated as the home itself. [The] central component of this inquiry [is] whether the area harbors the intimate activity associated with the sanctity of a man's home and the privacies of life. [We] believe that curtilage questions should be resolved with particular reference to four factors: the proximity of the area claimed to be curtilage to the home, whether the area is included within an enclosure surrounding the home, the nature of the uses to which the area is put, and the steps taken by the resident to protect the area from observation by people passing by.

What functions or features of the home explain the strong protections the law affords to privacy there?

■ CONSTITUTION OF MICHIGAN ART. I, §11

The person, houses, papers and possessions of every person shall be secure from unreasonable searches and seizures. No warrant to search any place or to seize any person or things shall issue without describing them, nor without probable cause, supported by oath or affirmation. The provisions of this section shall not be construed to bar from evidence in any criminal proceeding any narcotic drug, firearm, bomb, explosive or any other dangerous weapon, seized by a peace officer outside the curtilage of any dwelling house in this state.

■ STATE v. THERESA DIXSON

766 P.2d 1015 (Or. 1988)

GILLETTE, J.

The issue in these criminal cases, combined for purposes of appeal, is whether the search and seizure provision in the Oregon Constitution protects land outside the "curtilage" of a residence. . . .

Sheriff's deputies received an informant's tip that marijuana was growing on heavily forested land owned by the Rogge Lumber Company. . . . The officers requested and received the company's permission to search the property for marijuana. [They] drove onto the property by way of a public road until they reached a dirt logging road the informant had described as leading to the marijuana. Unknown to the officers, this road extended onto property [where Lorin and Theresa Dixson lived]. The dirt road had fallen into disuse and no longer was passable by car. The trunk of a large tree lay across the road and, a little further on, a wire cable with a "No Hunting" sign on it stretched across the road. The officers left their car and walked past the fallen tree and wire cable. Just past the cable was another dirt road running along a fence line. This road also had a wire cable and "No Hunting" sign stretched across it. The officers continued walking down this second road. At a bend in the road, they encountered another "No Hunting" sign. The area was rural and covered with thick brush. The officers were able to see marijuana plants only after pushing aside the brush. The plants, which were on the Dixsons' property, were not visible at ground level except from that property. [The officers returned the next day and arrested the defendants near the plants. After charges were filed, the defendants filed a motion to suppress the evidence, based on both the state and federal constitutions.]

The state argues that this court should adopt an "open fields" exception to Article I, section 9, for the reasons expressed in the majority opinion in Oliver v. United States, 466 U.S. 170 (1984). In *Oliver,* the police, without first obtaining a warrant, went to Oliver's farm to investigate reports that he was raising marijuana there. They drove past Oliver's house to a locked gate with a "No Trespassing" sign on it. On foot, they followed a path around the gate and along the road for several hundred yards. As they passed a barn and a parked camper, they heard someone standing by the camper shout, "No hunting is allowed, come back up here." The officers identified themselves and approached the camper, but found no one. They continued walking until they found a field of marijuana over a mile from Oliver's house. . . .

The *Oliver* majority relied on the following rationale for holding that the Fourth Amendment does not protect land outside the curtilage of a dwelling. First, the language of the amendment expressly protects from unreasonable search and seizure only "persons, houses, papers, and effects." The majority concluded that the framers of the Fourth Amendment "would have understood the term 'effects' to be limited to personal, rather than real, property." Second, at common law, a distinction was drawn between the curtilage of a home and other land surrounding the home. In the majority's view, this distinction bolstered its conclusion that the framers of the Fourth Amendment did not intend to extend its protection to land outside the curtilage; it also demonstrated that society historically has had a reduced expectation of privacy in such land.

Third, land outside the curtilage of a dwelling "do[es] not provide the setting for those intimate activities that the Amendment is intended to shelter from government interference or surveillance"; thus, those who perform the activities typically conducted in such areas do not require or expect a great deal of privacy. Finally, the desirability of a uniform rule and the problems inherent in fashioning and enforcing a case-by-case approach outweigh any privacy interests that may exist in land outside the curtilage of a dwelling.

The state [argues] that the above reasons wholly justify an interpretation of Article I, section 9, that parallels the federal rule. Although in interpreting Article I, section 9, we are not bound either by the Supreme Court's holding in *Oliver* or by its method of tackling the problem, we will examine its underlying rationale, to the extent that they are pertinent to an Article I, section 9, inquiry.

At the outset, [a caveat is] in order. [The term "open fields"] encompasses lands that are neither fields nor, in any fair sense of the word, open; the open fields doctrine denies Fourth Amendment protection to all undeveloped and unoccupied land outside the curtilage of a residence. We therefore frame the question presented by this case in what we believe to be more realistic terms — not whether the requirements of Article I, section 9, are subject to an exception for "open fields," but whether that provision prohibits unreasonable searches and seizures conducted on land that falls outside the curtilage of a dwelling.

The Textual Argument

The state argues that, because Article I, section 9, like the Fourth Amendment, expressly protects "persons, houses, papers and effects," the state provision should be interpreted the same way that the United States Supreme Court has interpreted the Fourth Amendment. That argument has some obvious validity, because the language of a constitutional provision must have some meaning if it is to be interpreted in any principled manner. On the other hand, Article I, section 9, has acquired a meaning over the years that is hard to reconcile with the literal interpretation advocated by the state.

Our prior decisions establish that Article I, section 9, does not protect property alone; in a broader sense, it also protects an individual's "privacy interest," which we have defined as an interest in freedom from certain forms of governmental scrutiny. [A] literal interpretation of Article I, section 9, would afford no protection from such things as the police interception of a private telephone conversation from a public telephone booth. . . .

There is a second problem with the literal interpretation proposed by the state. If we were to rely on the language of Article I, section 9, to limit its protection to "persons, papers, houses, and effects [i.e., personal property]," that interpretation necessarily would exclude all kinds of real property except houses. There would be no principled way to distinguish, based on the language itself, office buildings, churches, schools, commercial establishments, and the like, from other kinds of real property. The drafters of Article I, section 9, are unlikely to have intended to exclude from its protections all real property except houses, i.e., structures where people customarily reside. The scope of the section is broader than a literal reading of its terms.

We conclude that we cannot rely on a literal reading of Article I, section 9. To hold that the provision applies only to those items specifically enumerated therein would undermine the rationale that we have identified as the touchstone of Article I, section 9 — the right to be free from intrusive forms of government scrutiny — and would open up prior decisions of this court . . . to serious question. We decline to take that step. Article I, section 9, protects the privacy of the individual from certain kinds of governmental scrutiny. If the individual has a privacy interest in land outside the curtilage of his dwelling, that privacy interest will not go unprotected simply because of its location. . . .

The Argument Based on the Uses to Which Land Outside the Curtilage of a Dwelling Is Put

[Under Article I, section 9,] the question is whether governmental intrusions into privately owned land would significantly impair an individual's interest in freedom from scrutiny, i.e., his privacy. The answer is: That depends.

Areas such as "the vast expanse of some western ranches or . . . the undeveloped woods of the Northwest" described by the *Oliver* majority may involve little or no privacy interest. Some areas of this state contain large unmarked tracts of land in which it is difficult to tell where one piece of property ends and another begins. The public may be in the habit of using these areas to hike, fish, hunt or camp. However lonely a person usually may be in such places, he or she has no true privacy in them.

On the other hand, owners of even large tracts may, at some expense, take steps to keep out intruders. In this society, signs, such as "No Trespassing" signs, the erection of high, sturdy fences and other, similar measures are all indications that the possessor wishes to have his privacy respected. Allowing the police to intrude into private land, regardless of the steps taken by its occupant to keep it private, would be a significant limitation on the occupant's freedom from governmental scrutiny. Article I, section 9, does not permit such freewheeling official conduct. The remaining question is whether it is possible to fashion a workable test to enable the police to determine whether a particular intrusion constitutes a search under the state constitution. It is.

CASE-BY-CASE ANALYSIS

The rule we announce today is simple and objective. An individual's privacy interest in land he or she has left unimproved and unbounded is not sufficient to trigger the protections of Article I, section 9. Thus, it is not sufficient that the property in question is privately owned, or that it is shielded from view by vegetation or topographical barriers, because those features do not necessarily indicate the owner's intention that the property be kept private. A person who wishes to preserve a constitutionally protected privacy interest in land outside the curtilage must manifest an intention to exclude the public by erecting barriers to entry, such as fences, or by posting signs. This rule will not unduly hamper law enforcement officers in their attempts to curtail the manufacture of and trafficking in illegal drugs, because it does not require investigating officers to draw any deduction other than that required of the general public: if land is fenced, posted or otherwise closed off, one does not enter it without permission or, in the officers' situation, permission or a warrant.

In the present case, the defendants (or someone) had blocked access to their property with cables and posted "No Hunting" signs. However, on this record there was no objective reason for the officers to believe that, in addition to the restriction on hunting, other uses such as hiking were forbidden. In this state, with its expanses of rough and open country, hiking, camping and the like commonly occur on land that is owned by large companies and individuals. See generally, ORS §105.655-.680, dealing with public recreational use of private lands. Unless they intended to hunt, neither the officers nor anyone else would have understood the posted signs to be intended to exclude them from the property entirely. The state carried its burden of showing that there was no violation of the Oregon Constitution in the officer's actions. . . .

Notes

1. *Open fields: majority position.* Under the federal constitution, there is no "search" when officers discover something in "open fields," land beyond the boundaries of a home and its curtilage. The decision in Oliver v. United States, 466 U.S. 170 (1984), affirming the traditional "open fields" doctrine, came as a surprise. After the Supreme Court declared in Katz v. United States, 389 U.S. 347 (1967), that the Fourth Amendment protected expectations of privacy rather than property interests, most lower courts assumed that the old per se rule allowing warrantless and suspicionless searches of open fields was no longer tenable. The *Oliver* decision, however, reaffirmed the traditional "open fields" doctrine (based on Hester v. United States, 265 U.S. 57 (1924)). See Stephen Saltzburg, Another Victim of Illegal Narcotics: The Fourth Amendment (as Illustrated by the Open Fields Doctrine), 48 U. Pitt. L. Rev. 1 (1986).

State courts considering the "open fields" question since 1984 are divided. A sizable group has followed the Supreme Court in *Oliver:* for items discovered on property outside the curtilage, no search takes place and no case-by-case consideration of "expectations of privacy" is necessary. This group includes more than 15 states with rulings on the subject from their high courts and a slightly larger group of states with rulings from intermediate appellate courts. Roughly 10 states have parted company with the federal rule, like the Oregon court in *Dixson.* These courts have ruled that, under state statutes or constitutions, police must have a warrant to enter private property if the owner has taken enough measures to prevent entry onto the land by the public. The adequacy of the property owner's efforts to maintain privacy on the land might be measured case by case or with a relatively clear rule (as in Oregon).

2. *Curtilage.* Many cases, both state and federal, have declared that the constitutional protection of privacy is at its highest in the home and the area immediately surrounding it, known as the "curtilage." Does the Michigan constitution make this distinction between the home and all other places explicit?

Even in jurisdictions that allow warrantless and suspicionless searches of open fields, a search of the "curtilage" still has to be supported by a warrant and probable cause. Thus, the definition of "curtilage" can be important. As indicated above, United States v. Dunn, 480 U.S. 294 (1987), announced several factors that are now widely used to determine whether property is curtilage: (1) the proximity of the area to the home; (2) whether the area is included within an enclosure surrounding the home; (3) the nature of the uses to which the area is put; and (4) the steps taken by the resident to protect the area from observation. In *Dunn,* federal agents suspected that the defendant was operating a drug laboratory in a barn on a ranch. The barn sat 60 yards from a house; a waist-high wooden fence with locked gates enclosed the front of the barn. A fence surrounded the perimeter of the property, and several barbed-wire fences crossed the interior of the property (including a fence surrounding the ranch house and running between the barn and the house). The agents crossed the perimeter fence, several of the barbed-wire fences, and the wooden fence in front of the barn. The court held that the barn was not within the curtilage of the ranch house.

The *Dunn* case and many others deal with searches of alleged "curtilage" areas in a rural or wooded setting. Are these definitions based on assumptions about land use and habits that do not apply in urban and suburban areas? For instance, would you conclude that a "search" of an item in the curtilage had occurred if police officers walked onto the front porch of a home, rang the doorbell, and then picked up a pair of boots, covered with plaster dust, sitting on a box on the porch (attempting to match the tread of the boots to white footprints found on the carpet at a burglary scene)? See State v. Portrey, 896 P.2d 7 (Or. Ct. App. 1995). Does the rule in *Dunn* encourage development of property and discourage landowners from maintaining private wildlife areas? Is a home best characterized as a place of activity and industry?

3. *Categories covered by constitutional texts.* The Oregon court was willing to conclude that real property was included within the "persons, houses, papers and effects" that are protected from unreasonable searches and seizures. Does it matter what the constitutional framers considered to be the meaning of "effects" or "houses"? Where would a lawyer discover the framers' views on this question? Would it matter if the final category were called "possessions" instead of "effects"? See Brent v. Commonwealth, 240 S.W. 45 (Ky. 1922) (term "possessions" means "the intimate things about one's person"); Falkner v. State, 98 So. 691 (Miss. 1924) (term "possessions" embraces "all of the property of the citizen"); State v. Pinder, 514 A.2d 1241 (N.H. 1986) (term "possessions" does not include real property beyond curtilage).

4. *Crime scene searches.* Police often search crime scenes. Do they need to obtain warrants at any point? Officers can secure a crime scene without a warrant. Officers can also conduct an initial search in response to emergency situations such as assisting a victim, searching for other victims, or searching for an offender. Police may also seize evidence in plain view during their emergency search and while securing the crime scene. However, in Mincey v. Arizona, 437 U.S. 385 (1978), the U.S Supreme Court rejected a "crime scene exception" to the Fourth Amendment, and said that police should have obtained a warrant before they conducted a detailed four-day search of an apartment following the murder of an undercover officer. Following *Mincey,* some state courts allowed warrantless crime scene searches when they were more immediate than the extended search in *Mincey.* See e.g., State v. Hatten, 315 S.E.2d 893 (Ga. 1984) (allowing six-hour crime scene search in homicide case where police found bloodstained sheet on the bed, a bullet in the bathroom ceiling, empty cartridge casings on the bedroom floor, and the weapon and ammunition in the yard, on grounds that "to require that police officers cease their search and to obtain a warrant defies logic and common sense.") However, in Flippo v. West Virginia, 528 U.S. 11 (1999), the U.S. Supreme Court reaffirmed *Mincey* and rejected the warrantless search of a briefcase found (closed) during a murder scene investigation of a vacation cabin in a state park. The briefcase belonged to the husband of the victim, who had called the police to investigate; it contained pictures that established his motive for the murder. How often do defendants raise crime scene warrant issues? How do defendants and their lawyers know what police do at crime scenes, and when they do it? Are courts likely to issue search warrants for crime scenes that are more sweeping than for other kinds of investigations? See 22 Okl. St. Ann. §1230 (creating exception for daytime search warrant presumption for search of crime scenes).

Problem 4-2. Apartment Curtilage

Police officers obtained a search warrant for a residence at 251-B Marietta Road that was part of a duplex approximately 60 yards from the road and hidden from view. They searched apartment B of the duplex, which was specified in the warrant, and then searched the grounds and found a plastic bag containing five pounds of marijuana in bushes near the private driveway. Apartment A was closer to the left half of the driveway, which was shaped like a stethoscope; apartment B was closer to the right half. The plastic bag was found among bushes seven to eight feet to the left of the driveway leading to apartment A, outside the stethoscope, approximately 30 yards from the house. No fence enclosed the yard. Was this a valid search? Compare Espinoza v. State, 454 S.E.2d 765 (Ga. 1995).

Problem 4-3. Houses Without Walls?

Mooney beat and strangled Branford and stole from him some coins, a videocassette recorder, and his car. Several days later, the police arrested Mooney in connection with the murder and robbery. Shortly after midnight on the night when police took Mooney into custody, Detective Morro met Mooney's girlfriend, Spencer. She took Morro to the place where Mooney had been living at the time of the murder: a bridge abutment underneath the highway overpass by the State Street entrance ramp to the interstate highway. The abutment was separated from the entrance ramp roadway by a steep embankment that was covered by crushed stone and heavy underbrush. The state department of transportation owns the property involved.

Morro climbed up the embankment and, using a flashlight to illuminate the area, saw several items, including a blanket used as a mattress, a rolled-up sleeping bag, a closed cardboard box, a suitcase, a small closed duffel bag, and paper trash. Mooney, using the metal and cement beams of the highway support structure as shelves, had placed all of his belongings on the beams, with the exception of the duffel bag, the blanket, and the trash, which were left on the ground. Morro opened the duffel bag and found in it a paper bag containing a large number of quarters. He did not open the other items at that time. Morro then called the police department evidence officers to the scene. They photographed and tagged all of the items and brought them to the police department, where they were opened and inventoried. The cardboard box contained a pair of white pants stained with what was later determined to be blood.

Mooney had been living under the bridge abutment for about one month; he had no other home. He was the only person occupying that space. Although he would leave the area every day, he would secure his belongings so that they could not be seen from the bottom of the embankment because he was worried about theft. At night, he slept there behind a bush. Mooney knew that the area was state property and that there was no reason why someone else could not enter or live in the area where he was living. Mooney once encountered an employee of the department of transportation who happened upon his resting place during a maintenance inspection of the bridge.

Mooney moved to suppress the quarters and the white pants from evidence. Will the motion succeed? Would it succeed if Morro had seized the property, carried it to the police station, and obtained a warrant before opening the box and duffel bag? Compare State v. Mooney, 588 A.2d 145 (Conn. 1991).

2. *Workplaces*

Although the Fourth Amendment and its state analogs extend to "homes," all courts have extended the protection against unreasonable searches and seizures to other locations. The nature of the place can profoundly influence the reasonableness of the search. Given the amount of time many people spend in the workplace, it should come as no surprise that police searches of the workplace generate plenty of disputes. In addition to the location of the search, these cases also sometimes raise questions about the relationship between the government and a private employer who participates to some degree in a search.

■ STATE v. EDWIN BONNELL

856 P.2d 1265 (Haw. 1993)

LEVINSON, J.

The [State] appeals from orders of the District Court [granting] motions to suppress evidence obtained as a result of warrantless covert video surveillance — spanning a year in duration and conducted by the Maui Police Department (MPD) — of the defendants' "break room" located in their place of employment, the Lahaina Post Office. We affirm.

The defendants are postal workers employed at the United States Post Office located in downtown Lahaina, on the Island of Maui. All were charged . . . with one or more counts of gambling (a misdemeanor). [U.S. Postal Inspector Keith Silva received two anonymous letters alleging that gambling, involving two postal service employees, was taking place in the downtown Lahaina post office. Silva's superiors sent copies of the letters to the Maui Police Department. At the request of the MPD, Silva met with several police officers to plan an investigation, and they decided to use hidden video cameras. Technicians from the postal inspector's office installed the video system at the post office. During those four days,] post office employees were falsely advised that the technicians were installing smoke detectors and a burglar alarm. The surveillance system's hidden cameras were strictly visual; there was no audio component. A total of four cameras were installed. Two were placed in a position to record events at the public counter area. A third was placed in the ceiling of the supervisor's office. The final camera was placed inside a smoke detector in the break room and focused on the area of the break room table. Once installed, the cameras ran twenty-four hours a day for the duration of the investigation. [Officer Benjamin Nu was] one of the two MPD police officers assigned to investigate the alleged gambling. Nu and the other officer monitored the video data . . . five days a week (Mondays through Fridays) during regular work hours, from 7:00 or 7:30 A.M. until 4:30 or 5:00 P.M.

[Each defendant testified that] he or she had an actual subjective expectation of privacy in the break room for the following reasons: (1) the break room was not a public place; rather, access was limited to post office employees and authorized visitors; (2) the break room was not visible to the public service area of the post office or from outside the building; (3) "activities" in the break room could not be "overheard" by persons not present; [and (4)] there was no provision in the employee manual or collective bargaining agreement addressing or authorizing the use of video surveillance. . . .

The dispositive question presented in this appeal is whether the covert video surveillance of the employee break room of the post office constituted an illegal search within the meaning of the fourth amendment to the United States Constitution and/or article I, section 7 of the Constitution of the State of Hawaii.[2] . . .

It is well settled that an area in which an individual has a reasonable expectation of privacy is protected by article I, section 7 of the Hawaii Constitution and cannot be searched without a warrant. That being the case, any warrantless search of a constitutionally protected area is presumptively unreasonable unless there is both probable cause and a legally recognized exception to the warrant requirement. . . .

Given the deliberation with which the videotape surveillance was undertaken and its yearlong duration, there were obviously no special or exigent circumstances that would have justified a warrantless search in this case; it can hardly be said that the MPD was faced with any sort of "emergency." It therefore follows that if the

2. Article I, section 7 of the Constitution of the State of Hawaii provides: "The right of the people to be secure in their persons, houses, papers and effects against unreasonable searches, seizures, and invasions of privacy shall not be violated; and no warrants shall issue but upon probable cause, supported by oath or affirmation, and particularly describing the place to be searched and the persons or things to be seized or the communications sought to be intercepted.". . .

warrantless and covert video surveillance of the employee break room was a search in the constitutional sense, then the videotapes and any other evidence obtained as a result thereof are tainted by the surveillance and must be suppressed as "fruits of the poisonous tree."[5]

This Court has adopted the following two-part test, borrowed from the concurring opinion of Justice Harlan in Katz v. United States, 389 U.S. 347, 361 (1967), to determine when a person's expectation of privacy may be deemed reasonable: "First, one must exhibit an actual, subjective expectation of privacy. Second, that expectation must be one that society would recognize as objectively reasonable." [The testimony at the suppression hearing clearly established the subjective expectations of the employees.] Accordingly, we must ascertain whether the record before us supports the district court's findings and conclusion that the [defendants' expectations were objectively reasonable.]

The State contends that there can be no reasonable expectation of privacy in a place, activity or object which a defendant exposes to open view. The State further urges . . . that "the openness and non-exclusivity of the breakroom area and the openness with which the gambling activities were conducted precluded any reasonable expectation of privacy from surveillance, personal or remote, open or covert." We disagree. . . .

In assessing the reasonableness of an expectation of privacy, we consider, inter alia, the nature of the area involved, the precautions taken to insure privacy, and the type and character of the governmental invasion employed. A person may have a subjective expectation of privacy that is objectively reasonable in some area of his or her workplace. Such an expectation is not defeated merely because the area is accessible to others. This is precisely because what a person seeks to preserve as private, even in an area accessible to the public, may be constitutionally protected. Privacy does not require solitude. Even "private" business offices are often subject to the legitimate visits of coworkers, supervisors, and the public, without defeating the expectation of privacy unless the office is so open to fellow employees or the public that no expectation of privacy is reasonable.

In the present case, the employee break room was neither a public place nor subject to public view or hearing. Only postal employees and invited guests were allowed in it. Accordingly, the defendants were in a position to regulate their conduct as a function of present company. Moreover, when seated in the break room, the defendants could see anyone approaching and could avoid being surprised by an untrusted intruder.

[T]he State's reliance on the "open view" doctrine is misplaced. In the open view situation, the observation takes place from a non-intrusive vantage point. The governmental agent is either on the outside looking outside or on the outside looking inside at that which is knowingly exposed to the public. By contrast, the video surveillance at issue in this appeal involved the yearlong observations, from the "inside looking inside," of a smoke detector-obscured "seeing eye" video camera occupying a grossly intrusive vantage point and targeting activity that by no stretch of the imagination can be regarded as having been knowingly exposed to the public.

5. Although we are not required in this appeal to delineate the requirements for video surveillance [under] article I, section 7 of the Hawaii Constitution in order to support the issuance of a search warrant, we nevertheless emphasize that the showing of necessity needed to justify the use of video surveillance is higher than the showing needed to justify other search and seizure methods, including bugging. The use of a video camera is an extraordinarily intrusive method of searching. . . .

We now address the type and character of the governmental invasion—video surveillance—leveled against the defendants in the present case. . . . Television surveillance in criminal investigations is indeed reminiscent of the telescreens by which Big Brother in George Orwell's *1984* maintained visual surveillance of the entire population of "Oceania," the miserable country depicted in that anti-utopian novel. . . . Accordingly, based on the "totality of the circumstances" present in the record before us, we hold that the defendants had an objectively reasonable privacy expectation that they would not be videotaped by government agents in the employee break room. . . .

The State's final argument on appeal is that the covert video surveillance operation "was a joint operation of the police and postal inspectors, the former concerned with state gambling violations and the latter with employer investigation of work-related employee misconduct." From this premise the State makes the leap of logic that the district court therefore erred in suppressing the fruits of the operation. We cannot accept the State's strained position.

However the record in this appeal is massaged, the fact remains that the MPD approached Inspector Silva to solicit his "cooperation" in investigating suspected criminal violations of state law. On a daily and yearlong basis, two MPD officers monitored and recorded the data transmitted by the hidden video cameras. The actions of the MPD resulted in criminal prosecutions by the Maui Prosecutor's Office. We are not dealing here with a federal administrative appeal. . . . We hold that the district court was not clearly erroneous in finding that the MPD conducted a criminal investigation.

Because (1) the defendants had actual, subjective expectations of privacy that society would recognize as objectively reasonable that they would not be the objects of covert video surveillance in the employee break room, [and (2) the] recorded observations were the product of a criminal investigation, we affirm the district court's findings of fact, conclusions of law, and suppression orders.

Notes

1. *Privacy interests in the workplace: majority position.* American courts have overwhelmingly decided that workers can hold some reasonable expectation of privacy in items kept at their workplace and in their activities at the workplace. The crucial question, as identified in the *Bonnell* opinion from Hawaii, is whether the workers have some control over access to the area. Yet the Fourth Amendment and its state analogs speak only about government searches of "persons, houses, papers and effects." Is a workplace a "house"? What is the justification for treating the workplace as a protected area? What would a society be like that did not limit searches in workplaces?

The government has plenty of reasons to collect information in the workplace. What begins as routine regulatory enforcement might end in a criminal prosecution. For instance, immigration agents may question employees in their workplace about their immigration status. Because of the limited intrusion involved, the questioning does not amount to a "seizure," even if workplace rules require the employees to remain on the site when the government agents arrive. INS v. Delgado, 466 U.S. 210 (1984). Does the access of regulators to the workplace strengthen or weaken the privacy interest of workers in their place of employment?

2. *Private searches.* The federal and state constitutions reach only searches conducted by government agents. A private employer can conduct any sort of search she chooses without engaging in an "unreasonable" search or seizure within the meaning of the federal constitution. See Burdeau v. McDowell, 256 U.S. 465 (1921). Statutes and common law rules (or contracts) may limit the private employer's searching power. However, if a private employer acts at the government's behest, a search can become "state action." Assuming that the U.S. Postal Service (now a nongovernmental corporation) could be considered a private employer, was the search in *Bonnell* a "private" search?

Does the power of private employers to gather information about their employees affect the reasonable expectations of privacy that an employee might have in the workplace? Employers may monitor telephone conversations or read computer files at the workplace. Private parties routinely collect and use information about their customers. Credit card companies can track where and what a consumer buys and can sell that information to merchants. As the editors of The Economist magazine put it, as we lose control over our privacy, "[t]he chief culprit is not so much Big Brother as lots of little brothers, all gossiping with each other over computer networks." The Economist, February 10, 1996, at 27. Are statutory protections for privacy in the workplace likely to be enacted? Would they be effective?

The private security industry employs more personnel than federal, state and local governments combined. As Professor David Sklansky points out, the growing number of private security forces might entail a shift in some of the most basic tenets of criminal procedure. He suggests that this trend will create a body of criminal procedure law that is deconstitutionalized, defederalized, tort-based, and heavily reliant both on legislatures and on juries. See Sklansky, The Private Police, 46 UCLA L. Rev. 1165 (1999).

3. *Government as employer.* If a government agent wishes to search a workplace in the private sector, she usually needs probable cause and a warrant, or consent. But if the government agent represents a government employer conducting a search of a *government* workplace, different constitutional rules apply. Neither a warrant nor probable cause is necessary when the government employer is conducting (1) a noninvestigatory work-related search (such as retrieving a file) or (2) an investigation of work-related misconduct. The Supreme Court in O'Connor v. Ortega, 480 U.S. 709 (1987), concluded that the reasonable suspicion standard was the best method of accommodating the employee's privacy interests with the public employer's interests apart from law enforcement. Workplace searches that are based on some neutral criteria, but not on individualized suspicion, may also be acceptable. See State v. Ziegler, 637 So. 2d 109 (La. 1994).

3. Schools and Prisons

When searches take place in institutions such as schools and prisons, courts tend to evaluate them much more generously than searches of homes or workplaces. These searches fall into a category sometimes known as "administrative" searches, where the government has purposes for its search other than enforcement of the criminal law. In such settings, warrants are often unnecessary, and the level of justification required does not rise to the level of probable cause. As you read the following materials, try to identify the elements of these searches that lead courts to place fewer controls on them than they do for searches in other settings. Could the arguments used to explain the looser supervision of searches in these contexts apply more broadly to others?

■ IN THE MATTER OF GREGORY M.

627 N.E.2d 500 (N.Y. 1993)

LEVINE, J.

. . . On November 29, 1990 appellant, then 15 years old, arrived at the high school he attended in The Bronx without a proper student identification card. He was directed by a school security officer to report to the office of the Dean to obtain a new card. In accordance with school policy, he was required to leave his cloth book bag with the security officer until he had obtained the proper identification. When appellant tossed the book bag on a metal shelf before proceeding beyond the school lobby to the Dean's office, the security officer heard a metallic "thud" which he characterized as "unusual." He ran his fingers over the outer surface of the bottom of the bag and felt the outline of a gun. The security officer then summoned the Dean who also discerned the shape of a gun upon feeling the outside of appellant's book bag. The bag was brought to the Dean's office and opened by the head of school security, revealing a small hand gun later identified as a .38 Titan Tiger Special. A juvenile delinquency petition was filed in Family Court accusing appellant of [weapons violations]. Family Court denied appellant's motion to suppress the gun. . . .

We affirm [the denial of the appellant's motion to suppress]. Although minimally intrusive, the purposeful investigative touching of the outside of appellant's book bag by the school security officer (i.e., to acquire knowledge about the bag's contents) falls marginally within a search for constitutional purposes. Also, appellant is quite correct in contending that the metallic thud heard by the security officer when appellant put the book bag down was by itself insufficient to furnish a reasonable suspicion that the bag contained a weapon. We conclude, however, that a less rigorous premonition concerning the contents of the bag was sufficient to justify the investigative touching of the outside of the bag. When that touching disclosed the presence of a gun-like object in the bag, there was reasonable suspicion to justify the search of the inside of the bag.

In People v. Scott D., 315 N.E.2d 466 (1974), this Court held that students attending public schools are protected by the constitutional ban against unreasonable searches and seizures. *Scott D.* involved a school search of a student for illegal drugs. We further held in *Scott D.* that inherent in determining whether a school search was reasonable is a "balancing of basic personal rights against urgent social necessities" and that, "[g]iven the special responsibility of school teachers in the control of the school precincts and the grave threat, even lethal threat, of drug abuse among school children, the basis for finding sufficient cause for a school search will be less than that required outside the school precincts."

Employing an analysis similar to that of People v. Scott D., the United States Supreme Court in New Jersey v. T.L.O., 469 U.S. 325 (1985), also concluded that the Fourth Amendment of the United States Constitution applies to searches of students by school authorities, but held that less cause is required to justify such a search than is required of law enforcement authorities searching persons or their effects outside school premises. Thus, the Supreme Court held that a determination of the appropriate standard of reasonableness to govern a certain class of searches requires a balancing: "On one side of the balance are arrayed the individual's legitimate expectations of privacy and personal security; on the other, the government's need for effective methods to deal with breaches of public order." The Court in New Jersey v. T.L.O. held that, ordinarily, searches by school authorities of the persons or belongings of students may be made upon "reasonable grounds for suspecting that the search will turn up evidence that the student has violated or is violating either the law or the rules of the school." The Court applied the reasonable suspicion standard in validating a teacher's full search of the inside of a student's purse for cigarettes, during which evidence of her involvement in drug dealing was revealed.

We agree that for searches by school authorities of the persons and belongings of students, such as that conducted in New Jersey v. T.L.O., the reasonable suspicion standard adopted in that case for Fourth Amendment purposes is also appropriate under our State Constitution (N.Y. Const., art. I, §12). In the instant case, however, the investigative touching of the outer surface of appellant's book bag falls within a class of searches far less intrusive than those which, under New Jersey v. T.L.O., require application of the reasonable suspicion standard. Applying the balancing process required under People v. Scott D. and New Jersey v. T.L.O., it is undeniable that appellant had only a minimal expectation of privacy regarding the outer touching of his school bag by school security personnel, even for purposes of learning something regarding its contents, when he left the bag with the security officer pursuant to the school policy requiring this until he obtained a valid identification card. On the other hand, it seems equally undeniable that, in the balancing process, prevention of the introduction of hand guns and other lethal weapons into New York City schools such as this high school is a governmental interest of the highest urgency. The extreme exigency of barring the introduction of weapons into the schools by students is no longer a matter of debate.

Thus, the balancing process ordained by People v. Scott D. and New Jersey v. T.L.O. leads to the conclusion that a less strict justification applies to the limited search here than the reasonable suspicion standard applicable for more intrusive school searches. In this regard, we find it noteworthy that the Supreme Court in New Jersey v. T.L.O. specifically disclaimed that its decision made some quantum of individualized suspicion an essential element of every school search.* The Supreme Court has elsewhere made it clear that, at least outside the context of criminal investigations by law enforcement officers, individualized suspicion is not a constitutional floor below which any search must be deemed unreasonable. There may be circumstances in which, because the privacy interests involved in the case are minimal and are overborne by the governmental interests in jeopardy if a higher standard were enforced, a search may be reasonable despite the absence of such suspicion. See Skinner v. Railway Labor Executives' Assn., 489 U.S. 602 (1989) [approving of drug testing of railway employees involved in train accidents or safety incidents]; United States v. Martinez-Fuerte, 428 U.S. 543 (1976) [brief suspicionless stops of vehicles for questioning at immigration checkpoint at fixed location].

* Footnote 8 of the *T.L.O.* opinion reads as follows: "We do not decide whether individualized suspicion is an essential element of the reasonableness standard we adopt for searches by school authorities. In other contexts, however, we have held that although some quantum of individualized suspicion is usually a prerequisite to a constitutional search or seizure, . . . the Fourth Amendment imposes no irreducible requirement of such suspicion."—Eds.

We need not apply these precedents, however, to sustain the actions of the school authorities in the instant case.

Because appellant's diminished expectation of privacy was so clearly outweighed by the governmental interest in interdicting the infusion of weapons in the schools, we think the "unusual" metallic thud heard when the book bag was flung down — quite evidently suggesting to the school security officer the possibility that it might contain a weapon — was sufficient justification for the investigative touching of the outside of the bag, thus rendering that limited intrusion reasonable (and not based on mere whim or caprice) for constitutional purposes. Our application in the instant case of a graduated standard of reasonableness is, of course, sanctioned by and premised on the minimal nature of the search, and that it was conducted by school officials for the special needs of school security and not for a criminal investigative purpose. Once the touching of the outer surface of the bag revealed the presence of a gun-like object inside, school authorities had a reasonable suspicion of a violation of law justifying the search of the contents of the bag.

[D]espite vague professions to the contrary, the dissent is contending that reasonable suspicion is a constitutional floor for purposes of all types of searches, however limited, in a school setting or elsewhere, and irrespective of who conducts the search. [The dissent] supports this position by reliance on Terry v. Ohio, 392 U.S. 1 (1968), and [related New York cases]. The Supreme Court in *Terry* described the intrusion in that case as "a careful exploration of the outer surfaces of a person's clothing all over his or her body in an attempt to find weapons" and characterized it as "a serious intrusion upon the sanctity of the person, which may inflict great indignity." [The Court called the frisk a "limited search" only because] it must be limited to that which is necessary for the discovery of weapons which might be used to harm the officer or others nearby.

People v. Diaz, 612 N.E.2d 298 (N.Y. 1993), declined to extend the *Terry* warrantless search exception to a frisk disclosing other forms of contraband. "Once an officer has concluded that no weapon is present, the search is over and there is no authority for further intrusion." *Diaz* and *Terry* simply do not apply to a less intrusive touching of the outside of a book bag by school personnel, after possession of the bag had been lawfully relinquished. . . . Thus, Family Court's denial of appellant's motion to suppress should be upheld. . . .

TITONE, J., dissenting.

Acknowledging that there was not even a "reasonable suspicion" of criminality, the Court nevertheless holds that the school security guard was entitled to conduct a search of appellant's book bag. In so ruling, the Court has reduced the privacy protections of the Fourth Amendment and of article I, §12 of the State Constitution below all previously recognized minimum thresholds. While I too am horrified by the recent escalation of deadly weapons in the public schools, I cannot agree that the problem should be remedied by a contraction of even the minimal privacy rights that the Supreme Court has accorded to school children, particularly when there exist other, less intrusive remedies. . . .

The teaching of New Jersey v. T.L.O., on which the majority places heavy reliance, is that search warrants are not constitutionally required for school searches and that such searches may be justified by a lesser showing of reasonable suspicion. Nothing in *T.L.O.*, however, suggests that the serious intrusion of a search may be upheld on even less than reasonable suspicion, much less on the gossamer thread of what the Court has labeled an "unusual" metallic thud. . . .

The majority begins its analysis with the premise that the "investigative touching" of the outside of appellant's book bag was somehow "far less intrusive" than other types of searches. [But] an investigative touching of a closed container requires a degree of pinching, squeezing or probing beyond the limited intrusion allowed under Terry v. Ohio. . . .

The majority also attempts to justify its decision on the theory that appellant had only a "minimal" expectation of privacy "regarding the outer touching of his school bag" when he left it with a security officer pursuant to a school policy. This sweeping conclusion, however, remains unexplained. Significantly, the Supreme Court [in *T.L.O.*] has specifically rejected the contention that a child has a drastically diminished expectation of privacy in articles of personal property that are carried into school. . . .

A further reason offered by the majority for reducing the quantum of information necessary to conduct a school search such as this one is the unquestionably compelling need to prevent the introduction of hand guns and other lethal weapons into the schools. I find this aspect of the majority's rationale unconvincing for several reasons. First, the reduction of students' privacy rights that the majority sanctions is not narrowly tailored to address weapon-related criminal activities. While the search in this case happened to disclose a weapon, the sequence of events that led to that disclosure here could just as easily lead in another case to the discovery of some other illegality or rule infraction such as the possession of drugs or cigarettes. Second, there exist other, more effective means of interdicting weapons in public schools, namely, the installation of metal detectors at the front door. . . .

Third, and most importantly, the constitutional privacy guarantees in our Federal and State Constitutions exist precisely to protect citizens from governmental overreaching in the name of the exigencies of law enforcement. [The majority's rationale is] dangerous, since the same rationale may be trotted out to justify virtually any governmental excess that is aimed at a currently troublesome or rampant form of crime. [T]he need for judicial intervention to bolster the privacy protections would concomitantly increase, rather than diminish, with an increase in the public pressure on law enforcement authorities to take all necessary steps to obliterate a new crime threat. . . .

Finally, even if it is assumed that some lesser showing than the reasonable suspicion approved by the Supreme Court is permissible in these circumstances, the majority has not given any indication of the nature of that showing or of what the lower limits of that showing might be. . . . If, as the majority admits, the "thud" was not sufficient to furnish reasonable suspicion that the bag contained a gun, it is difficult to see how that "thud" could have "evidently suggest[ed] to the school security officer the possibility that [the bag] might contain a weapon." The distinction between a "reasonable suspicion" and an "evident suggestion" is not at all clear to me and will probably be even less meaningful to the school authorities who have to implement this new standard. The significance of the majority's reference to a "premonition" that is "less rigorous" than reasonable suspicion is even more opaque.

The closest the majority has come to actually objectifying the standard it has used is its characterization of the "thud" the guard heard as "unusual." However, what made this sound so "unusual" is far from clear. Students' book bags routinely contain such unexceptional items as make-up cases, portable cassette players and other consumer electronic devices, all of which would likely produce a metallic "thud" when dropped on a hard surface such as a counter. Even more importantly, the "unusual" nature of an event or circumstance does not provide a sound basis for a search of an individual's personal effects. Without more, such an amorphous touchstone would permit intrusions on the most arbitrary of predicates, including a student's "unusual" manner of dress, gait or speech.

. . . While we all have a vital interest in preventing weapons from entering our public school classrooms, that interest could have been served in this case without seriously undermining the student's constitutional rights by either asking the student about the contents of his bag upon his return or by insisting that he empty it or leave it with the guard before re-entering the building. In any event, while I do not advocate anything as sweeping as an over-all constitutional floor of "reasonable suspicion" that would be applicable in all situations, I cannot concur in the majority's decision to sustain this search on a showing that falls well below the minimum requirements approved by the Supreme Court for searches conducted on school premises. Accordingly, I dissent. . . .

■ OKLAHOMA STATUTES TIT. 70, §24-102

The superintendent, principal, teacher, or security personnel of any public school in the State of Oklahoma, upon reasonable suspicion, shall have the authority to detain and search or authorize the search, of any pupil or property in the possession of the pupil when said pupil is on any school premises, or while in transit under the authority of the school, or while attending any function sponsored or authorized by the school, for dangerous weapons, controlled dangerous substances, . . . intoxicating beverages, . . . or for missing or stolen property if said property be reasonably suspected to have been taken from a pupil, a school employee or the school during school activities. The search shall be conducted by a person of the same sex as the person being searched and shall be witnessed by at least one other authorized person, said person to be of the same sex if practicable.

The extent of any search conducted pursuant to this section shall be reasonably related to the objective of the search and not excessively intrusive in light of the age and sex of the student and the nature of the infraction. In no event shall a strip search of a student be allowed. No student's clothing, except cold weather outerwear, shall be removed prior to or during the conduct of any warrantless search. . . .

Pupils shall not have any reasonable expectation of privacy towards school administrators or teachers in the contents of a school locker, desk, or other school property. School personnel shall have access to school lockers, desks, and other school property in order to properly supervise the welfare of pupils. School lockers, desks, and other areas of school facilities may be opened and examined by school officials at any time and no reason shall be necessary for such search. Schools shall inform pupils in the student discipline code that they have no reasonable expectation of privacy rights towards school officials in school lockers, desks, or other school property.

Notes

1. *Lesser protections in school: majority position.* The decision of the U.S. Supreme Court in New Jersey v. T.L.O., 469 U.S. 325 (1985), reached the same conclusion

as had many of the state courts considering earlier challenges to searches by school officials. Because of the special environment of the school, these courts concluded that neither a warrant nor probable cause was necessary to justify a search by school officials, even if the evidence found during the search ultimately led to a criminal or juvenile conviction. Instead, reasonable suspicion was all that was typically necessary to support a valid search. State courts and legislatures visiting this question have continued to take the position that warrants and probable cause are unnecessary in this environment; the statutes printed above are typical in this respect. Compare In re Randy G., 28 P.3d 239 (Cal. 2001) (reasonable suspicion not required to justify school security officer's temporary detention of student).

2. *Individualized suspicion, less than reasonable.* The New York court in *Gregory M.* allowed a search to go forward on the basis of information about an individual student (a backpack making a "thud") that did not amount to reasonable suspicion. Do you agree with the court that the "thud" was not enough for reasonable suspicion? Instead of expanding its own definition of reasonable suspicion, the court decided to recognize a lower level of suspicion in the school context, "evident suggestion." What does the court accomplish (if anything) by creating a new category rather than expanding an old one? Should the new standard apply to exterior touching of purses and backpacks outside the school setting?

3. *Searches of school-owned areas.* School authorities grant students access to lockers and other areas for storage of personal property; sometimes school administrators inform students (either by posting signs or by providing individual notice) that they might search the lockers from time to time. See New Jersey v. T.L.O., 469 U.S. at 338 n.5 (reserving question of proper standard for searches of lockers and desks); Md. Educ. Code §7-308 (authorizes searches of school-owned areas); S.C. Stat. §59-63-1120 (search of school property or student's personal belongings). Under such circumstances, is it reasonable for a student to expect any privacy at all in the locker area? What if the school assumes but does not announce its power to search lockers and exercises that power periodically? Would the same analysis apply to searches of dormitory rooms by school officials in state-supported universities?

4. *School officials as criminal law enforcers.* Part of the justification that courts often give for the relaxed requirements for valid searches in schools is the noncriminal purpose of the searches. School administrators can conduct searches based on reasonable suspicion of a violation of "either the law or the rules of the school." *T.L.O.*, 469 U.S. at 341. But what happens if law enforcement officials approach school officials and ask them to conduct the search? What if the law enforcement agent who initiates the search is stationed full time at the school? Most courts have used the probable cause standard for searches carried out by school officials at the request of the police. Courts use the reasonable suspicion standard for searches initiated by a police officer assigned full time or part time as a liaison to the school. See People v. Dilworth, 661 N.E.2d 310 (Ill. 1996). Should it matter whether the searching police officer has a regular relationship with the school?

Would your analysis change if school officials have a general duty to cooperate with criminal law enforcement rather than an intent to do so in a particular case? For instance, Tenn. Code Ann. §49-6-4209 imposes on school officials the legal duty to help enforce the criminal law: "It is the duty of a school principal who has reasonable suspicion to believe, either as a result of a search or otherwise, that any student is committing or has committed any violation of [criminal laws against possession of weapons or drugs], upon the school ground . . . to report [the] suspicion to the appropriate law enforcement officer." Searches in the school context have attracted the attention of about 20 state legislatures. A few statutes place limits on who can conduct searches, or the crimes to be investigated. Others require schools to notify parents about any searches, or to develop a standard search "plan."

5. *Scope of search.* The *T.L.O.* court stated that a search by school officials justified by reasonable suspicion still must be "reasonably related to the objectives of the search and not excessively intrusive in light of the age and sex of the student and the nature of the infraction." State statutes usually provide more specific guidance on the type of searches available to school officials. Oklahoma's law, reprinted above, is typical in its prohibition on strip searches. Suppose that a school official has reasonable suspicion of truancy but also guesses that the student is carrying cigarettes or drugs. Is any sort of search possible once an official has reasonable suspicion of any criminal offense or rule infraction? See Coronado v. State, 835 S.W.2d 636 (Tex. Crim. App. 1992) (search of clothing, locker, and auto based on reasonable suspicion of truancy held unreasonable).

Problem 4-4. Gun Lockers

One Friday night in November, students at Madison High School reported hearing gunshots as they left the school following a basketball game. School security guards found spent casings on school grounds the next day. By the following Monday morning, the school staff and security personnel were receiving more reports of guns present in the school building and on school buses, and rumors that a shootout would occur at the school that day. Some staff members and students asked to leave the school out of fear for their safety.

The school principal, Jude, ordered school security personnel to begin a random search of student lockers as a preventive measure while he interviewed selected students. The public school handbook indicates that "lockers are the property of the school system and subject to inspection as determined necessary or appropriate." Students are prohibited from putting private locks on their lockers.

Siena, a Madison High School security aide, searched the school lockers. Using a pass key, he opened the lockers and visually inspected the lockers' contents, moving some articles to see more clearly, and patted down coats in the lockers. Siena did not search every student locker. He chose lockers initially on the lower level of the building, where the largest crowds gathered. He also took care to search the lockers of any known "problem" students and any locker where he saw groups of students congregating.

Altogether, Siena conducted between 75 and 100 locker searches before he opened Baker's locker. At the time, Siena did not know who was assigned to the locker. Baker did not have a history of prior weapon violations, nor did the school officials suspect his involvement in the recent gun incidents. Siena removed a coat from the locker and immediately believed it to be unusually heavy. He found a gun in the coat.

Was the search legal? How would you resolve the case under the constitutional standards described in the *Gregory M.* case? Under the Oklahoma statute reprinted above? Compare Isiah B. v. State, 500 N.W.2d 637 (Wis. 1993).

■ BOARD OF EDUCATION OF INDEPENDENT SCHOOL DISTRICT NO. 92 OF POTTAWATOMIE COUNTY v. LINDSAY EARLS

122 S. Ct. 2559 (2002)

THOMAS, J.

The Student Activities Drug Testing Policy implemented by the Board of Education of Independent School District No. 92 of Pottawatomie County requires all students who participate in competitive extracurricular activities to submit to drug testing. Because this Policy reasonably serves the School District's important interest in detecting and preventing drug use among its students, we hold that it is constitutional.

The city of Tecumseh, Oklahoma, is a rural community located approximately 40 miles southeast of Oklahoma City. . . . In the fall of 1998, the School District adopted the Student Activities Drug Testing Policy (Policy), which requires all middle and high school students to consent to drug testing in order to participate in any extracurricular activity. In practice, the Policy has been applied only to competitive extracurricular activities sanctioned by the Oklahoma Secondary Schools Activities Association, such as the Academic Team, Future Farmers of America, Future Homemakers of America, band, choir, pom pom, cheerleading, and athletics. Under the Policy, students are required to take a drug test before participating in an extracurricular activity, must submit to random drug testing while participating in that activity, and must agree to be tested at any time upon reasonable suspicion. The urinalysis tests are designed to detect only the use of illegal drugs, including amphetamines, marijuana, cocaine, opiates, and barbituates, not medical conditions or the presence of authorized prescription medications. . . .

Respondent Lindsay Earls was a member of the show choir, the marching band, the Academic Team, and the National Honor Society. Respondent Daniel James sought to participate in the Academic Team. Together with their parents, Earls and James brought a 42 U.S.C. §1983 action against the School District, challenging the Policy both on its face and as applied to their participation in extracurricular activities. They alleged that the Policy violates the Fourth Amendment as incorporated by the Fourteenth Amendment and requested injunctive and declarative relief. [The District Court granted summary judgment to the School District, but the Tenth Circuit reversed.]

Searches by public school officials, such as the collection of urine samples, implicate Fourth Amendment interests. We must therefore review the School District's Policy for "reasonableness," which is the touchstone of the constitutionality of a governmental search. In the criminal context, reasonableness usually requires a showing of probable cause. The probable-cause standard, however, is peculiarly related to criminal investigations and may be unsuited to determining the reasonableness of administrative searches where the Government seeks to *prevent* the development of hazardous conditions. The Court has also held that a warrant and finding of probable cause are unnecessary in the public school context because such requirements "would unduly interfere with the maintenance of the swift and informal disciplinary procedures [that are] needed." New Jersey v. T.L.O., 469 U.S. 325, 340-341 (1985).

Given that the School District's Policy is not in any way related to the conduct of criminal investigations, respondents do not contend that the School District requires probable cause before testing students for drug use. Respondents instead argue that drug testing must be based at least on some level of individualized suspicion. It is true that we generally determine the reasonableness of a search by balancing the nature of the intrusion on the individual's privacy against the promotion of legitimate governmental interests. But we have long held that the Fourth Amendment imposes no irreducible requirement of individualized suspicion. In certain limited circumstances, the Government's need to discover such latent or hidden conditions, or to prevent their development, is sufficiently compelling to justify the intrusion on privacy entailed by conducting such searches without any measure of individualized suspicion. Treasury Employees v. Von Raab, 489 U.S. 656 (1989) [allowing drug testing of customs employees in drug enforcement positions]; Skinner v. Railway Labor Executives' Assn., 489 U.S. 602 (1989) [allowing drug testing of railway employees after train accidents]. Therefore, in the context of safety and administrative regulations, a search unsupported by probable cause may be reasonable when "special needs, beyond the normal need for law enforcement, make the warrant and probable-cause requirement impracticable." *T.L.O.* at 351.

Significantly, this Court has previously held that "special needs" inhere in the public school context. While schoolchildren do not shed their constitutional rights when they enter the schoolhouse, "Fourth Amendment rights . . . are different in public schools than elsewhere; the 'reasonableness' inquiry cannot disregard the schools' custodial and tutelary responsibility for children." Vernonia School Dist. 47J v. Acton, 515 U.S. 646, 656 (1995). In particular, a finding of individualized suspicion may not be necessary when a school conducts drug testing.

In *Vernonia,* this Court held that the suspicionless drug testing of athletes was constitutional. The Court, however, did not simply authorize all school drug testing, but rather conducted a fact-specific balancing of the intrusion on the children's Fourth Amendment rights against the promotion of legitimate governmental interests. Applying the principles of *Vernonia* to the somewhat different facts of this case, we conclude that Tecumseh's Policy is also constitutional.

We first consider the nature of the privacy interest allegedly compromised by the drug testing. As in *Vernonia,* the context of the public school environment serves as the backdrop for the analysis of the privacy interest at stake and the reasonableness of the drug testing policy in general. A student's privacy interest is limited in a public school environment where the State is responsible for maintaining discipline, health, and safety. Schoolchildren are routinely required to submit to physical examinations and vaccinations against disease. Securing order in the school environment sometimes requires that students be subjected to greater controls than those appropriate for adults.

Respondents argue that because children participating in nonathletic extracurricular activities are not subject to regular physicals and communal undress, they have a stronger expectation of privacy than the athletes tested in *Vernonia.* [However], students who participate in competitive extracurricular activities voluntarily subject themselves to many of the same intrusions on their privacy as do athletes. Some of these clubs and activities require occasional off-campus travel and communal undress. All of them have their own rules and requirements for participating students that do not apply to the student body as a whole. For example, each of the competitive extracurricular activities governed by the Policy must abide by the rules of the Oklahoma Secondary Schools Activities Association, and a faculty sponsor monitors the students for compliance with the various rules dictated by the clubs and activities. . . . We therefore conclude that the students affected by this Policy have a limited expectation of privacy.

Next, we consider the character of the intrusion imposed by the Policy. Urination is an excretory function traditionally shielded by great privacy. But the degree of intrusion on one's privacy caused by collecting a urine sample depends upon the manner in which production of the urine sample is monitored. Under the Policy, a faculty monitor waits outside the closed restroom stall for the student to produce a sample and must "listen for the normal sounds of urination in order to guard against tampered specimens and to insure an accurate chain of custody." . . . This procedure is virtually identical to that reviewed in *Vernonia*. . . .

In addition, the Policy clearly requires that the test results be kept in confidential files separate from a student's other educational records and released to school personnel only on a "need to know" basis. Respondents nonetheless contend that the intrusion on students' privacy is significant because the Policy fails to protect effectively against the disclosure of confidential information and, specifically, that the school "has been careless in protecting that information: for example, the Choir teacher looked at students' prescription drug lists and left them where other students could see them." But the choir teacher is someone with a "need to know," because during off-campus trips she needs to know what medications are taken by her students. . . . This one example of alleged carelessness hardly increases the character of the intrusion.

Moreover, the test results are not turned over to any law enforcement authority. Nor do the test results here lead to the imposition of discipline or have any academic consequences. Rather, the only consequence of a failed drug test is to limit the student's privilege of participating in extracurricular activities. Indeed, a student may test positive for drugs twice and still be allowed to participate in extracurricular activities. . . . Given the minimally intrusive nature of the sample collection and the limited uses to which the test results are put, we conclude that the invasion of students' privacy is not significant.

Finally, this Court must consider the nature and immediacy of the government's concerns and the efficacy of the Policy in meeting them. This Court has already articulated in detail the importance of the governmental concern in preventing drug use by schoolchildren. The drug abuse problem among our Nation's youth has hardly abated since *Vernonia* was decided in 1995. In fact, evidence suggests that it has only grown worse. As in *Vernonia,* "the necessity for the State to act is magnified by the fact that this evil is being visited not just upon individuals at large, but upon children for whom it has undertaken a special responsibility of care and direction." The health and safety risks identified in *Vernonia* apply with equal force to Tecumseh's children. Indeed, the nationwide drug epidemic makes the war against drugs a pressing concern in every school.

Additionally, the School District in this case has presented specific evidence of drug use at Tecumseh schools. Teachers testified that they had seen students who appeared to be under the influence of drugs and that they had heard students speaking openly about using drugs. A drug dog found marijuana cigarettes near the school parking lot. Police officers once found drugs or drug paraphernalia in a car driven by a Future Farmers of America member. And the school board president reported that people in the community were calling the board to discuss the "drug situation." We decline to second-guess the finding of the District Court that "viewing the evidence as a whole, it cannot be reasonably disputed that the School District was faced with a 'drug problem' when it adopted the Policy." . . .

We also reject respondents' argument that drug testing must presumptively be based upon an individualized reasonable suspicion of wrongdoing because such a testing regime would be less intrusive. [We] question whether testing based on individualized suspicion in fact would be less intrusive. Such a regime would place an additional burden on public school teachers who are already tasked with the difficult job of maintaining order and discipline. A program of individualized suspicion might unfairly target members of unpopular groups. The fear of lawsuits resulting from such targeted searches may chill enforcement of the program, rendering it ineffective in combating drug use. In any case, this Court has repeatedly stated that reasonableness under the Fourth Amendment does not require employing the least intrusive means, because the logic of such elaborate less-restrictive-alternative arguments could raise insuperable barriers to the exercise of virtually all search-and-seizure powers. . . .

Within the limits of the Fourth Amendment, local school boards must assess the desirability of drug testing schoolchildren. In upholding the constitutionality of the Policy, we express no opinion as to its wisdom. Rather, we hold only that Tecumseh's Policy is a reasonable means of furthering the School District's important interest in preventing and deterring drug use among its schoolchildren. . . .

BREYER, J., concurring.

. . . When trying to resolve this kind of close question involving the interpretation of constitutional values, I believe it important that the school board provided an opportunity for the airing of these differences at public meetings designed to give the entire community the opportunity to be able to participate in developing the drug policy. The board used this democratic, participatory process to uncover and to resolve differences, giving weight to the fact that the process, in this instance, revealed little, if any, objection to the proposed testing program.

[A] contrary reading of the Constitution, as requiring "individualized suspicion" in this public school context, could well lead schools to push the boundaries of "individualized suspicion" to its outer limits, using subjective criteria that may "unfairly target members of unpopular groups," or leave those whose behavior is slightly abnormal stigmatized in the minds of others. . . .

GINSBURG, J., dissenting.

Seven years ago, in Vernonia School Dist. 47J v. Acton, 515 U.S. 646 (1995), this Court determined that a school district's policy of randomly testing the urine of its student athletes for illicit drugs did not violate the Fourth Amendment. In so ruling, the Court emphasized that drug use "increased the risk of sports-related injury" and that Vernonia's athletes were the "leaders" of an aggressive local "drug culture" that had reached "epidemic proportions." Today, the Court relies upon *Vernonia* to permit a school district with a drug problem its superintendent repeatedly described as "not major" to test the urine of an academic team member solely by reason of her participation in a nonathletic, competitive extracurricular activity—participation associated with neither special dangers from, nor particular predilections for, drug use. . . . The particular testing program upheld today is not reasonable, it is capricious, even perverse: Petitioners' policy targets for testing a student population least likely to be at risk from illicit drugs and their damaging effects. I therefore dissent.

[The Court points to] the voluntary character of both interscholastic athletics and other competitive extracurricular activities. . . . The comparison is enlightening. While extracurricular activities are "voluntary" in the sense that they are not required for graduation, they are part of the school's educational program; for that reason, the petitioner . . . is justified in expending public resources to make them available. Participation in such activities is a key component of school life, essential in reality for students applying to college, and, for all participants, a significant contributor to the breadth and quality of the educational experience. Students "volunteer" for extracurricular pursuits in the same way they might volunteer for honors classes: They subject themselves to additional requirements, but they do so in order to take full advantage of the education offered them.

Voluntary participation in athletics has a distinctly different dimension: Schools regulate student athletes discretely because competitive school sports by their nature require communal undress and, more important, expose students to physical risks that schools have a duty to mitigate. . . . Competitive extracurricular activities other than athletics, however, serve students of all manner: the modest and shy along with the bold and uninhibited. Activities of the kind plaintiff-respondent Lindsay Earls pursued — choir, show choir, marching band, and academic team — afford opportunities to gain self-assurance. . . .

Finally, the nature and immediacy of the governmental concern faced by the Vernonia School District dwarfed that confronting Tecumseh administrators. Vernonia initiated its drug testing policy in response to an alarming situation: "[A] large segment of the student body, particularly those involved in interscholastic athletics, was in a state of rebellion . . . fueled by alcohol and drug abuse as well as the students' misperceptions about the drug culture." Tecumseh, by contrast, repeatedly reported to the Federal Government during the period leading up to the adoption of the policy that "types of drugs [other than alcohol and tobacco] including controlled dangerous substances, are present [in the schools] but have not identified themselves as major problems at this time." 1998-1999 Tecumseh School's Application for Funds under the Safe and Drug-Free Schools and Communities Program. . . .

Nationwide, students who participate in extracurricular activities are significantly less likely to develop substance abuse problems than are their less-involved peers. See, *e.g.*, N. Zill, C. Nord, & L. Loomis, Adolescent Time Use, Risky Behavior, and Outcomes 52 (1995) (tenth graders "who reported spending no time in school-sponsored activities were . . . 49 percent more likely to have used drugs" than those who spent 1-4 hours per week in such activities). Even if students might be deterred from drug use in order to preserve their extracurricular eligibility, it is at least as likely that other students might forgo their extracurricular involvement in order to avoid detection of their drug use. Tecumseh's policy thus falls short doubly if deterrence is its aim: It invades the privacy of students who need deterrence least, and risks steering students at greatest risk for substance abuse away from extracurricular involvement that potentially may palliate drug problems.

[Schools'] tutelary obligations to their students require them to "teach by example" by avoiding symbolic measures that diminish constitutional protections. "That [schools] are educating the young for citizenship is reason for scrupulous protection of Constitutional freedoms of the individual, if we are not to strangle the free mind at its source and teach youth to discount important principles of our government as mere platitudes." West Virginia Bd. of Ed. v. Barnette, 319 U.S. 624, 637 (1943). . . .

Notes

1. *Drug testing in schools: majority position.* When the Supreme Court first addressed drug testing in schools in Vernonia School District 47J v. Acton, 515 U.S. 646 (1995), the issue had received little attention in courts or legislatures. The existing statutes and cases validated drug testing of students based on reasonable suspicion of illegal drug use without addressing mandatory random testing. See Tenn. Code Ann. §49-6-4213 (reasonable suspicion testing). In the years between *Vernonia* and *Earls,* very few school districts adopted a policy of random drug testing. See Ronald F. Wright, The Abruptness of *Acton,* 36 Crim. L. Bull. 401 (2000). Do you expect the number of districts adopting this policy to increase more quickly after the *Earls* decision? If you were sitting on a state supreme court addressing a challenge to a random testing program, would your ruling turn on the types of students subject to the program (for example, all athletes, or all students at particular grade levels)? Would it depend on the uses the school makes of the test results (such as counseling, school sanctions, or criminal prosecution)?

2. *Drug testing in other contexts: majority position.* Drug testing occurs more frequently in workplaces than in schools. Some employers require a drug test of all job applicants and probationary employees; among current employees, reasonable suspicion testing is more common. If the employer is a private party, the Fourth Amendment and its state analogs do not apply. Only statutes and common law theories are available to limit the employer's choices, and those statutes tend to regulate but not bar use of random drug testing. See Ariz. Rev. Stat. §23-493.04 (allowing testing "for any job-related purposes"); Minn. Stat. §181.951 (allowing reasonable suspicion testing for all employees and random testing for "safety sensitive" employees); see also Twigg v. Hercules Corp., 406 S.E.2d 52 (W. Va. 1990) (drug testing by private employer will not violate public policy grounded in potential intrusion of person's right to privacy when it is conducted by employer based on reasonable, good faith, objective suspicion of employee's drug usage or while employee's job responsibility involves public safety or safety of others).

As for public employers, courts have upheld testing programs against most challenges. It is clear that when a public employer has reasonable suspicion of drug use by an employee, drug testing is acceptable. Specific incidents (such as an accident involving a train) might give the employer reasonable suspicion, or at least some individualized suspicion, to test for drug use among the employees involved in the incident. See Skinner v. Railway Labor Executives' Assn., 489 U.S. 602 (1989). Courts have even approved random or routine drug testing, at least for job categories in which drug use presents a special concern for the employer. In National Treasury Employees Union v. Von Raab, 489 U.S. 656 (1989), the Court upheld a program requiring a urinalysis from any Customs Service employee seeking a transfer to a position involving drug interdiction or the carrying of a firearm. Does this opinion suggest that a police department could insist on random drug testing for all of its officers? See McCloskey v. Honolulu Police Department, 799 P.2d 953 (Haw. 1990) (upholding such a program); Guiney v. Police Commissioner of Boston, 582 N.E.2d 523 (Mass. 1991) (striking down such a program). For all members of the Narcotics

Bureau within the department? See Delaraba v. Police Dept., 632 N.E.2d 1251 (N.Y. 1994) (upholding such a program). Collective labor agreements will sometimes limit the power of an employer to implement drug testing. See Fraternal Order of Police, Miami Lodge 20 v. City of Miami, 609 So. 2d 31 (Fla. 1992).

Would you argue that some public employees (within the police department or otherwise) should be subject to drug testing only after officials obtain a warrant based on probable cause? See Chandler v. Miller, 520 U.S. 305 (1997) (Georgia's requirement that candidates for state office pass drug test did not fit within "closely guarded category" of constitutionally permissible suspicionless searches, and were not sufficiently related to requirements of public office).

Problem 4-5. Jail Cell Search

McCoy's first two trials on charges of armed robbery and attempted murder of a police officer ended in mistrials. After his third trial, the jury convicted McCoy, but an appellate court reversed the conviction. On the eve of the scheduled date for the fourth trial, the assistant state attorney assigned to the case, Ketchum, and a police officer, Hagerman, went to McCoy's cell at the local pretrial detention facility.

Hagerman, following instructions from Ketchum, first removed McCoy and his cellmate and then searched the cell for anything McCoy may have written that might contain incriminating statements. As Hagerman searched, Ketchum stood in the doorway of the cell. Hagerman found on a table in the cell a number of depositions, transcripts, offense reports, and personal notes. He seized McCoy's copies of depositions of four state witnesses, which consisted of some 70 pages and included McCoy's copious handwritten notes in the margins. Several of the handwritten notes were incriminating.

McCoy presented no particular security problems at the detention facility, and there was no concrete information suggesting that the papers in his cell would contain incriminating information. How will the trial court rule on his motion to suppress the handwritten notes found on the depositions? Compare McCoy v. State, 639 So. 2d 163 (Fla. Dist. Ct. App. 1994).

Notes

1. *Searches of prison cells: majority position.* State and federal appellate courts have traditionally given a lot of latitude to the decisions of the administrators of prisons, jails, and other detention facilities. They point out the exceptional need for order in such a setting. The Supreme Court in Hudson v. Palmer, 468 U.S. 517 (1984), made a particularly strong statement of this view when it held that the Fourth Amendment does not place any limits on a prison guard's search of the prison cell of a convicted offender. The prisoner in that case claimed that a prison guard had searched his cell and destroyed his property solely to harass the prisoner. The Court replied:

> A right of privacy in traditional Fourth Amendment terms is fundamentally incompatible with the close and continual surveillance of inmates and their cells required to ensure institutional security and internal order. We are satisfied that society would insist

> that the prisoner's expectation of privacy always yield to what must be considered the paramount interest in institutional security.

468 U.S. at 527-528. A concern for the security and order of prisons led the Court to hold that "the Fourth Amendment has no applicability to a prison cell." Virtually all state courts to consider this question have followed the *Hudson* case and concluded that their analogous state constitutional provisions also have no application to searches of prison cells. Should the exemption from the Fourth Amendment apply only when searches are motivated by the need for order and security in the jail or prison? If so, how should a court determine what motivated the search?

2. *Pretrial detainees versus convicted offenders.* Some persons confined in a cell have been convicted of a crime, while others have only been accused of a crime. Should a pretrial detainee have a "reasonable expectation of privacy" in a cell when a convicted offender would not? The Supreme Court spoke indirectly to this issue in Bell v. Wolfish, 441 U.S. 520 (1979), when it held that the Fourth Amendment protects neither sentenced nor pretrial detainees from a prison policy requiring inmates to undergo strip and body cavity searches after all contact visits with non-inmates. The Court stated that the security concerns at issue for convicted offenders also exist for pretrial detainees. State courts have split on the question whether constitutional privacy protections apply differently to pretrial detainees and convicted offenders. See DeLancie v. Superior Court, 647 P.2d 142 (Cal. 1982) (invalidating sheriff's routine practice of monitoring conversations between pretrial detainees and visitors); State v. Martin, 367 S.E.2d 618 (N.C. 1988) (search of pretrial detainee's cell by jailer not subject to Fourth Amendment reasonableness test). Does the lack of a reasonable expectation of privacy, as announced in Hudson v. Palmer, derive from the nature of the person's status (convicted of a crime) or from the nature of the place (a prison)?

3. *Places categorically out of reach of the constitution?* Do *Hudson* and the cases following its lead establish "Fourth-Amendment-free zones"? If prison officials are free to act without legal limits, how will this affect the present or future conduct of the prisoners being punished for violating the criminal law? Are there any alternatives? Consider State v. Berard, 576 A.2d 118 (Vt. 1990) (search and seizure provision in state constitution applies to prison searches, but "special needs" of prison environment allow warrantless random searches of cells). Is *Berard* an improvement over *Hudson* from a prisoner's point of view? From society's point of view? Cf. United States v. Knights, 534 U.S. 112 (2001) (constitution allows police with reasonable suspicion of criminal behavior to conduct a warrantless search of home of a probationer who is subject to a probation condition authorizing warrantless searches).

In Ferguson v. City of Charleston, 532 U.S. 67 (2001), the Supreme Court returned to the question of drug testing in special institutional settings. A state hospital instructed its staff to identify pregnant patients at risk for drug abuse, to test those patients for drug abuse, and to report positive tests to the police. Patients who tested positive for cocaine use were arrested and prosecuted for child abuse. The Court held that this testing was an unreasonable search. Given the amount of cooperation between the hospital and criminal prosecutors in this program, the tests served no "special needs" apart from the State's "general law enforcement interest." The central purpose of the program was the use of criminal law enforcement to coerce patients into substance abuse treatment. Drug testing in these circumstances was a search that was not accomplished through consent and not supported by probable cause.

C. "PAPERS"

There are several methods available to the government to inspect "papers" during criminal law enforcement. One method, which we will explore in Chapter 10, is to issue a subpoena from a grand jury or an administrative agency. The government might also rely on statutory requirements for certain types of businesses to maintain records and to allow the government access to those records. On the other hand, if the government attempts to search and seize papers without using a subpoena or a record-keeping requirement, it must comply with traditional Fourth Amendment requirements: showing probable cause to believe that the papers will provide evidence of a crime, and perhaps obtaining a warrant.

Are there some papers, however, that are so intimately personal that the government cannot obtain them, even if it demonstrates probable cause and obtains a warrant? We start with one of the most important early Supreme Court cases on the Fourth Amendment. The answer that the Court gave in 1886 to the question of "private papers" searches is not the same answer that legal institutions, by and large, give today. This classic opinion, however, does offer us a chance to consider an alternative form of privacy protection, in which rules would absolutely bar the government from searching some areas, regardless of the justifications it might have to conduct the search.

■ EDWARD BOYD v. UNITED STATES

116 U.S. 616 (1886)

BRADLEY, J.

[The government brought this forfeiture action to obtain 35 cases of glass that Boyd and others allegedly imported from England without paying the proper customs duties. At trial, it became important to show the quantity and value of the glass contained in 29 cases previously imported. The trial court ordered Boyd to produce the invoices for the cases. He did so, but objected to the constitutionality of the 1874 statute giving the judge the power to make such an order. Other provisions of the same statute, which were passed in 1863 and 1867, empowered the judge to issue a warrant to a marshal or customs collector to enter private premises and obtain any papers, books, or invoices that might tend to prove the government's allegations in a civil forfeiture suit under the customs laws. The jury in this case heard the evidence relating to the invoices and rendered a verdict for the United States.]

The clauses of the Constitution, to which it is contended that these laws are repugnant, are the fourth and fifth amendments. . . . The fifth article, amongst other things, declares that no person "shall be compelled in any criminal case to be a witness against himself." . . .

Is a search and seizure, or, what is equivalent thereto, a compulsory production of a man's private papers, to be used in evidence against him in a proceeding to forfeit his property for alleged fraud against the revenue laws — is such a proceeding for such a purpose an "unreasonable search and seizure" within the meaning of the fourth amendment of the Constitution? or, is it a legitimate proceeding? It is contended by the counsel for the government, that it is a legitimate proceeding, sanctioned by long usage, and the authority of judicial decision. No doubt long usage, acquiesced in by the courts, goes a long way to prove that there is some plausible ground or reason for it in the law. . . .

But we do not find any long usage, or any contemporary construction of the Constitution, which would justify any of the acts of Congress now under consideration. [T]he act of 1863 was the first act in this country, and, we might say, either in this country or in England, so far as we have been able to ascertain, which authorized the search and seizure of a man's private papers, or the compulsory production of them, for the purpose of using them in evidence against him in a criminal case, or in a proceeding to enforce the forfeiture of his property. Even the act under which the obnoxious writs of assistance were issued did not go as far as this, but only authorized the examination of ships and vessels, and persons found therein, for the purpose of finding goods prohibited to be imported or exported, or on which the duties were not paid, and to enter into and search any suspected vaults, cellars, or warehouses for such goods.

The search for and seizure of stolen or forfeited goods, or goods liable to duties and concealed to avoid the payment thereof, are totally different things from a search for and seizure of a man's private books and papers for the purpose of obtaining information therein contained, or of using them as evidence against him. . . . In the one case, the government is entitled to the possession of the property; in the other it is not. The seizure of stolen goods is authorized by the common law; and the seizure of goods forfeited for a breach of the revenue laws, or concealed to avoid the duties payable on them, has been authorized by English statutes for at least two centuries past; and the like seizures have been authorized by our own revenue acts from the commencement of the government. . . .

But, when examined with care, it is manifest that there is a total unlikeness of these official acts and proceedings to that which is now under consideration. In the case of stolen goods, the owner from whom they were stolen is entitled to their possession; and in the case of excisable or dutiable articles, the government has an interest in them for the payment of the duties thereon, and until such duties are paid has a right to keep them under observation, or to pursue and drag them from concealment; and in the case of goods seized on attachment or execution, the creditor is entitled to their seizure in satisfaction of his debt. . . . Whereas, by the proceeding now under consideration, the court attempts to extort from the party his private books and papers to make him liable for a penalty or to forfeit his property.

In order to ascertain the nature of the proceedings intended by the fourth amendment to the Constitution under the terms "unreasonable searches and seizures," it is only necessary to recall the contemporary or then recent history of the controversies on the subject, both in this country and in England. The practice had obtained in the colonies of issuing writs of assistance to the revenue officers, empowering them, in their discretion, to search suspected places for smuggled goods, which James Otis [in 1761] pronounced "the worst instrument of arbitrary power, the most destructive of English liberty, and the fundamental principles of law, that ever was found in an English law book;" since they placed "the liberty of every man in the hands of every petty officer." . . .

These things, and the events which took place in England immediately following the argument about writs of assistance in Boston, were fresh in the memories of those who achieved our independence and established our form of government. [The opinion of Lord Camden in the 1765 case of Entick v. Carrington] is regarded as one of the permanent monuments of the British Constitution, and is quoted as such by the English authorities on that subject down to the present time. As every American statesmen, during our revolutionary and formative period as a nation, was undoubtedly familiar with this monument of English freedom, and considered it as the true and ultimate expression of constitutional law, it may be confidently asserted that its propositions were in the minds of those who framed the fourth amendment to the Constitution, and were considered as sufficiently explanatory of what was meant by unreasonable searches and seizures. . . .

The principles laid down in [Entick v. Carrington] affect the very essence of constitutional liberty and security. They reach farther than the concrete form of the case then before the court, with its adventitious circumstances; they apply to all invasions on the part of the government and its employes of the sanctity of a man's home and the privacies of life. It is not the breaking of his doors, and the rummaging of his drawers, that constitutes the essence of the offence; but it is the invasion of his indefeasible right of personal security, personal liberty and private property [that violates the constitutional principle]. Breaking into a house and opening boxes and drawers are circumstances of aggravation; but any forcible and compulsory extortion of a man's own testimony or of his private papers to be used as evidence to convict him of crime or to forfeit his goods, is within the condemnation of that judgment. In this regard the fourth and fifth amendments run almost into each other.

Can we doubt that when the fourth and fifth amendments to the Constitution of the United States were penned and adopted, the language of Lord Camden was relied on as expressing the true doctrine on the subject of searches and seizures, and as furnishing the true criteria of the reasonable and "unreasonable" character of such seizures? [Could the men who proposed those amendments have approved of statutes such as those at issue here?] It seems to us that the question cannot admit of a doubt. They never would have approved of them. The struggles against arbitrary power in which they had been engaged for more than 20 years, would have been too deeply engraved in their memories to have allowed them to approve of such insidious disguises of the old grievance which they had so deeply abhorred. . . .

We have already noticed the intimate relation between the two amendments. They throw great light on each other. For the "unreasonable searches and seizures" condemned in the fourth amendment are almost always made for the purpose of compelling a man to give evidence against himself, which in criminal cases is condemned in the fifth amendment; and compelling a man "in a criminal case to be a witness against himself," which is condemned in the fifth amendment, throws light on the question as to what is an "unreasonable search and seizure" within the meaning of the fourth amendment. And we have been unable to perceive that the seizure of a man's private books and papers to be used in evidence against him is substantially different from compelling him to be a witness against himself. We think it is within the clear intent and meaning of those terms. . . .

Though the proceeding in question is divested of many of the aggravating incidents of actual search and seizure, yet, as before said, it contains their substance and essence, and effects their substantial purpose. . . . We think that the notice to produce the invoice in this case, the order by virtue of which it was issued, and the law which authorized the order, were unconstitutional and void, and that the inspection by the district attorney of said invoice, when produced in obedience to said notice, and its admission in evidence by the court, were erroneous and unconstitutional proceedings. . . .

MILLER, J., concurring.

. . . While the framers of the Constitution had their attention drawn, no doubt, to the abuses of this power of searching private houses and seizing private papers, as practiced in England, it is obvious that they only intended to restrain the abuse, while they did not abolish the power. Hence it is only unreasonable searches and seizures that are forbidden, and the means of securing this protection was by abolishing searches under warrants, which were called general warrants, because they authorized searches in any place, for the thing. This was forbidden, while searches founded on affidavits, and made under warrants which described the thing to be searched for, the person and place to be searched, are still permitted. . . .

Notes

1. *The erosion of* Boyd: *property and privacy.* The *Boyd* court notes that the government could seize contraband or proceeds of a crime but not papers containing evidence of a crime, because only in the former cases does the government have a proprietary interest in the item stronger than that of the private party. The constitution, under this reading, reinforces the protections of property law.

The linkage between property law and unreasonable searches has changed. For one thing, as we have seen, the definition of a "search" now depends on the "reasonable expectations of privacy" of the target of the search, and not on whether the government has trespassed on any property interest of the target. Katz v. United States, 389 U.S. 347 (1967). For another thing, most courts have now abandoned a traditional limitation on the search power known as the "mere evidence" rule. Under that rule, the government could search for and seize contraband, instrumentalities, or fruits of crime but not mere evidence of crime. Again, the reasoning was grounded in property law: The government had a superior claim to contraband and the like (which the private party had no right to own), but the private party had a superior claim to innocent property that provided evidence of a crime. The U.S. Supreme Court abandoned the mere evidence rule in Warden v. Hayden, 387 U.S. 294 (1967). Every state now interprets its own constitution to allow such searches.

Why might searches of papers become more common after the rejection of the mere evidence rule? Does the mere evidence rule offer more protection to some classes of search targets than to others? See Eric Schnapper, Unreasonable Searches and Seizures of Papers, 71 Va. L. Rev. 869 (1985).

2. *The erosion of* Boyd: *self-incrimination and unreasonable searches.* The *Boyd* court also suggested that the Fourth and Fifth Amendments throw light on each other, or provide mutually reinforcing protections. A search of a person's papers is equivalent to a demand that the person make incriminating testimony. This aspect of the *Boyd* case has also fallen by the wayside. In several cases, such as Andresen v. Maryland, 427 U.S. 463 (1976), the Supreme Court has declared that a search of a person's documents does not amount to compelled "testimony" because the person created the documents voluntarily and does not have to participate in the government's later search or seizure of the documents. Again, state courts have followed suit.

3. *The erosion of* Boyd: *private papers.* Federal and state courts have left more room to wonder if there is still an absolute bar to the search or seizure of private papers such as diaries. The Supreme Court has allowed searches and seizures of business records, see Andresen v. Maryland, but has not squarely addressed private papers.

By and large, state courts have taken the next step to conclude that there is no absolute bar to the search of private papers. See State v. Andrei, 574 A.2d 295 (Me. 1990). Every so often, a court says or intimates that some private papers (so long as the papers themselves were not used to commit a crime) might be beyond the reach of a government search, even if supported by probable cause and a warrant. See State v. Bisaccia, 213 A.2d 185 (N.J. 1965). Georgia has passed an unusual statute protecting "private papers" from searches:

> [A judicial officer] may issue a search warrant for the seizure of the following: (1) Any instruments, articles, or things, including the private papers of any person, which are designed, intended for use, or which have been used in the commission of the offense in connection with which the warrant is issued; . . . or (5) Any item, substance, object, thing, or matter, other than the private papers of any person, which is tangible evidence of the commission of the crime for which probable cause is shown.

Ga. Code Ann. §17-5-21(a). Does this statutory protection from searches re-create the now-abandoned requirements of *Boyd?* Would it prevent a search for an illegal lottery ticket? For a list of telephone numbers of purchasers of illegal narcotics? If you were restricting the scope of this statute, how might you define "private" papers? See Sears v. State, 426 S.E.2d 553 (Ga. 1993) (interpreting section to bar search for documents only when covered by privilege, such as attorney-client or doctor-patient).

The Model Code of Pre-Arraignment Procedure, §SS210.3(2), exempts a limited group of papers from search or seizure: "things subject to seizure . . . shall not include personal diaries, letters, or other writings or recordings, made solely for private use or communication to an individual occupying a family, personal or other confidential relation, other than a relation in criminal enterprise, unless such things have served or are serving a substantial purpose in furtherance of a criminal enterprise." This Model Code provision has not earned a following in the states. It is more common to find a statute such as Del. Code Ann. tit. 11, §2305(5), which allows searches for any "[p]apers, articles or things which are of an evidentiary nature pertaining to the commission of a crime. . . ."

4. *Extra particularity in search warrants for private papers.* While it is not often that a legal system will absolutely bar all searches for private papers, it is more common to see judges insist on extra particularity in a warrant authorizing a search for books or papers. See Lo-Ji Sales, Inc. v. New York, 442 U.S. 319 (1979); Tattered Cover, Inc. v. City of Thornton, 44 P.3d 1044 (Colo. 2002). Will a more specific warrant address the special intrusiveness of a search for papers? Consider this argument by Telford Taylor, from his renowned essay on the Fourth Amendment:

> [W]here personal papers are concerned, specificity of category is no real safeguard against the most grievous intrusions on privacy, as was pointed out over two hundred years ago during the House of Commons debates on general warrants: "Even a particular warrant to seize seditious papers alone, without mentioning the titles of them, may prove highly detrimental, since in that case, all a man's papers must be indiscriminately examined. . . ." Of course, a search for a tiny object, such as a stolen or smuggled diamond, which can be concealed among papers or in some other small recess, may

involve much the same kind of ransacking search. But at least in such a case it is unnecessary to read papers. [Two Studies in Constitutional Interpretation 67-68 (1969).]

5. *Private records held by third parties: banking records.* Many types of sensitive personal documents, such as banking records or medical records, are held by institutions on behalf of their customers. When government agents investigating a crime try to obtain these records, does the legal system allow the institution to deny the request? Under the Fourth Amendment, the Supreme Court in United States v. Miller, 425 U.S. 435 (1976), decided that a bank's customer has no reasonable expectation of privacy in records relating to the customer's account:

> All of the documents obtained, including financial statements and deposit slips, contain only information voluntarily conveyed to the banks and exposed to their employees in the ordinary course of business. . . . The depositor takes the risk, in revealing his affairs to another, that the information will be conveyed by that person to the Government.

Two years earlier, the California Supreme Court in Burrows v. Superior Court, 529 P.2d 590 (Cal. 1974), set out an argument in favor of giving bank customers standing to challenge unreasonable searches of bank records relating to their accounts:

> A bank customer's reasonable expectation is that, absent compulsion by legal process, the matters he reveals to the bank will be utilized by the bank only for internal banking purposes. . . . For all practical purposes, the disclosure by individuals or business firms of their financial affairs to a bank is not entirely volitional, since it is impossible to participate in the economic life of contemporary society without maintaining a bank account. In the course of such dealings, a depositor reveals many aspects of his personal affairs, opinions, habits and associations. . . .

State courts have divided on the constitutional question, with a strong majority following *Burrows*. See People v. Jackson, 452 N.E.2d 85 (Ill. 1983) (following *Burrows*); State v. Thompson, 810 P.2d 415 (Utah 1991) (same); State v. Schultz, 850 P.2d 818 (Kansas 1993) (following *Miller*).

Several legislatures have also declared that banking customers may challenge the reasonableness of government efforts to search their banking records. Congress adopted the Right to Financial Privacy Act, 12 U.S.C. §§3401 et seq., as a repudiation of the *Miller* decision: "The Court did not acknowledge the sensitive nature of these records." 1978 U.S.C.C.A.N. 9305. The act requires that the bank customer have notice and an opportunity to object before the financial institution complies with a subpoena seeking the records. About one-third of the states have enacted an equivalent of the Right to Financial Privacy Act. See, e.g., Mo. Rev. Stat. §§408.683 et seq. We will explore the subpoena power and the gathering of documents in complex investigations in Chapter 10.

Do these statutes and cases provide enough protection by allowing the customer to insist that any search of records be reasonable? Should they provide instead for a much higher level of justification by the government to support a search of banking records (similar to bank secrecy provisions in some other nations)? Would a reinvigorated *Boyd* present an absolute bar to a search of banking records? Would you take the same position on a proposed statute protecting the records relating to rentals of videotaped movies?

D. "EFFECTS"

We now turn to the final interest mentioned in the text of the Fourth Amendment, "effects." Given the variety of property that falls within the meaning of this phrase, and the variety of places where a search of effects could take place, it is difficult to find a unifying theme for all these searches. There are a few settings, however, in which courts and others have created special search rules about personal property. We begin with the "inventory" practices of police departments, the routine methods they use to process the property of those who are taken into custody. We then survey the complex rules surrounding that most American form of personal property, the automobile.

1. Inventory Searches

When police officers take a person into custody, some of his personal property comes with him. When the government holds a person's property, it must use ordinary care to maintain the property; the department therefore may need to keep records of the property. This process of examining and storing personal property can often produce evidence of a crime.

■ STATE v. JACKIE HUNDLEY

619 N.E.2d 744 (Ill. 1993)

HEIPLE, J.

[A]t approximately 10 P.M., State Trooper Anthony Grace was on routine patrol when he came across what appeared to have been a one-car accident. . . . Trooper Grace observed a 1986 blue Mercury automobile in a ditch. A utility pole had been broken off and a part of it was stuck under the car. Downed power lines were lying across the highway. Hundley, the owner and operator of the car, was not present. From an examination of the scene, the trooper was able to conclude that the car had left the traveled portion of U.S. 136, crossed an embankment, crashed through a fence and come to rest in the ditch after colliding with and breaking off a utility pole. Closer inspection of the car revealed that the doors were locked.

Trooper Grace called for a tow truck to remove the vehicle. He then used a mechanical device called a "slim jim" to open the car's locked door. He testified that this was done so that he could shift the transmission into neutral to avoid towing damage.

Since defendant was not present, Trooper Grace conducted an inventory search of the car prior to its removal by the tow truck to an unguarded storage facility. In the course of his search, he found a closed, snap-top cigarette case which he opened. Inside the cigarette case, he found a snorting tube containing cocaine. The trooper testified that he opened the cigarette case because in his experience he had found women often put their drivers' licenses and money in these containers. No purse or other valuables were found in the vehicle. Trooper Grace testified that he prepared an inventory list pursuant to State police policy and gave copies of it to his commanding sergeant and the tow truck operator. No inventory form was introduced into evidence at the suppression hearing. At the conclusion of the hearing, the court received into evidence the State police general order which contains the policy and procedure to be followed during a warrantless inventory search of an impounded vehicle. Identified as section 13-4(a)(2) of the General Order of the Illinois State Police, it provides:

> An examination and inventory of the contents of all vehicles/boats towed or held by authority of Division personnel shall be made by the officer who completes the Tow-In Recovery Report. This examination and inventory shall be restricted to those areas where an owner or operator would ordinarily place or store property or equipment in the vehicle/boat; and would normally include front and rear seat areas, glove compartment, map case, sun visors, and trunk and engine compartments.

Trooper Grace's authority for ordering the car towed and impounded is grounded in statute.

An inventory search is a judicially created exception to the warrant requirement of the fourth amendment. Three requirements must be satisfied for a valid warrantless inventory search of a vehicle: (1) the original impoundment of the vehicle must be lawful, South Dakota v. Opperman, 428 U.S. 364 (1976); (2) the purpose of the inventory search must be to protect the owner's property and to protect the police from claims of lost, stolen, or vandalized property and to guard the police from danger; and (3) the inventory search must be conducted in good faith pursuant to reasonable standardized police procedures and not as a pretext for an investigatory search, Colorado v. Bertine, 479 U.S. 367 (1987).

In Florida v. Wells, 495 U.S. 1 (1990), the Supreme Court again affirmed the validity of warrantless inventory searches which follow a standardized police procedure requiring the opening of closed containers in impounded vehicles. Differing on its facts from the instant case, however, in *Wells* the defendant had been stopped for driving under the influence of alcohol and the trooper forced open a locked suitcase in the trunk of the car. Defendant Wells had given permission to inventory the trunk of the car but had not given permission to the officer to force open the locked suitcase. The Court held that since the Florida Highway Patrol had no policy whatsoever with respect to the opening of closed containers, the marijuana which was found in the locked suitcase was properly suppressed. The Court stated, however, that police should be allowed sufficient latitude to determine whether a particular container should or should not be opened in light of the nature of the search and characteristics of the container itself.

Considering the applicable law as applied to the facts of the instant case, we believe that the general order of the Illinois State Police is adequate to the situation. More particularly, based on the unique circumstances of the towing of an unattended vehicle following a wreck, we believe that the officer's decision to open the cigarette case, because in his experience he had found women often put their drivers' licenses and money in these containers, was a reasonable exercise of judgment on the officer's part. Accordingly, the judgments of the appellate court and circuit court are reversed. The cause is remanded to the circuit court for further proceedings. . . .

FREEMAN, J., dissenting.

I conclude that the warrantless inventory search of defendant's automobile was not sufficiently regulated to satisfy the fourth amendment to the United States Constitution. Accordingly, I respectfully dissent.

. . . The record contains the following additional facts. Defendant's friend, Tom Main, whom the trooper also knew, was present at the accident scene. The trooper did not relinquish possession of defendant's automobile to Main because defendant and not Main was the car's registered owner. The next morning, defendant and Main went to the storage facility and attempted to retrieve her car. . . .

Routine inventory searches of automobiles are generally constitutional because an individual's diminished expectation of privacy in an automobile is outweighed by three governmental interests: protection of the police from danger; protection of the police against claims and disputes over lost or stolen property; and protection of the owner's property while it remains in police custody. However, a warrantless inventory search of an automobile must not be unrestrained. The search must be conducted in accordance with established police department rules or policy. . . . Indeed, this is the rationale for the "inventory exception" to the fourth amendment's warrant requirement. Justice Powell explained in *Opperman* as follows:

> Inventory searches, however, are not conducted in order to discover evidence of crime. The officer does not make a discretionary determination to search based on a judgment that certain conditions are present. Inventory searches are conducted in accordance with established police department rules or policy and occur whenever an automobile is seized.

Thus, based on *Opperman*, "what is needed in the vehicle inventory context . . . is not probable cause but rather a regularized set of procedures which adequately guard against arbitrariness."

These principles apply to the opening of a closed container during a vehicle inventory search. In Colorado v. Bertine, 479 U.S. 367 (1987), the United States Supreme Court held that a police officer may open a closed container while conducting a routine inventory search of an impounded vehicle. The Court emphasized that police department procedures in that case mandated the opening of closed containers.

Standardized criteria or an established routine governing inventory searches must limit an officer's discretion in two ways. First, it must limit the officer's discretion regarding whether to search a seized vehicle. Second, the pre-existing criteria or routine must limit an officer's discretion regarding the scope of an inventory search, particularly with respect to the treatment of closed containers.

However, the majority opinion in *Wells* included the following dictum: "A police officer may be allowed sufficient latitude to determine whether a particular container should or should not be opened in light of the nature of the search and characteristics of the container itself." Four justices concurred in the judgment. They objected to the above-quoted dictum. Indeed, Justices Brennan and Blackmun each feared that "this dictum will be relied on by lower courts in reviewing the constitutionality of particular inventory searches." This exact fear has been fulfilled by the majority in the present case. . . .

Illinois State Police General Order §13-4(a)(2) does not save this search. This provision is very similar to the Florida Highway Patrol policy at issue in *Wells*. As with the general order, the Florida Highway Patrol policy did not specifically refer to closed containers, but rather required a general inventory of articles in the vehicle. As with the Florida Highway Patrol policy, the general order does not limit an officer's discretion regarding the scope of an inventory search, particularly with respect to the treatment of closed containers. . . .

The majority upholds the warrantless inventory search in the present case also because the trooper's opening of defendant's closed cigarette case constituted "a reasonable exercise of judgment on the officer's part." However, the very essence of an inventory search is that a police officer does not exercise any discretion. The officer does not decide to search based on his or her judgment that certain conditions are present. A police officer cannot be given complete, if any, discretion in choosing whether to search or not to search closed containers found during an inventory search.

The inventory search in the present case did not meet fourth amendment requirements. The trooper did not open defendant's closed cigarette case based on any standard police policy, including the general order. Rather, he testified that he acted based on "his experience." The trooper's personal experience does not constitute a standard police procedure. . . .

HARRISON, J., dissenting.

The majority's disposition runs directly counter to the holding of Florida v. Wells. . . . Closed containers are not mentioned anywhere in the general order promulgated by our State police for inventory searches.

The majority attempts to distinguish this case from *Wells* on the grounds that the search here involved an unattended car towed after a wreck, whereas the search in *Wells* came after the defendant's car was impounded following his arrest for drunk driving and the arresting officer directed employees of the impoundment facility to unlock a locked suitcase found in the trunk. I agree that these factual differences exist, but am at a loss to understand their legal significance. Nothing in *Wells'* analysis turns on the circumstances giving rise to the inventory search. In determining whether police have the right to open closed containers found in the course of an inventory search, the threshold inquiry is whether a policy exists which specifically authorizes the procedure. Absent such a policy, opening closed containers during an inventory search violates the fourth amendment, regardless of why the inventory search was originally undertaken. . . .

Notes

1. *Inventory searches: majority position.* Inventory searches serve "administrative caretaking functions" of protecting against property damage claims and protecting police from dangerous items rather than enforcing criminal law. As a result, the Supreme Court has held that the federal constitution allows a routine (and warrantless) inventory search of impounded automobiles or other personal property without probable cause or individualized suspicion. South Dakota v. Opperman, 428 U.S. 364 (1976). The Supreme Court, in cases such as Colorado v. Bertine, 479 U.S. 367 (1987), has insisted that the inventory search occur under the guidance of "standardized" regulations. According to Florida v. Wells, 495 U.S. 1 (1990), the rules must address the proper treatment of containers found in a car, although those rules may leave some discretion to the officer conducting the inventory to open some containers and to leave others unopened. Most state courts also allow the police to conduct inventory searches without any special justification, so long as the inventory proceeds according to standard rules. The recurring issues in litigation deal with the specificity of the inventory rules and the amount of discretion those

rules leave to the police officer in deciding whether to impound a vehicle and whether to open containers. See, e.g., State v. Hathman, 604 N.E.2d 743 (Ohio 1992) (rejecting field inventory search of plastic bag in trunk under spare tire where officer testified that procedure was to "inventory everything accessible to him"). Do police departments need inventory rules at all? Would consensual inventory searches (and routine requests for that consent) address the problems of safeguarding property in vehicles?

2. *The impoundment decision.* Some jurisdictions address the inventory process at the first possible point and impose various limits on the initial decision whether to impound a vehicle or to leave it at the scene. See Fair v. State, 627 N.E.2d 427 (Ind. 1993) (prosecution must demonstrate (1) that the belief that the vehicle posed some threat or harm to the community or was itself imperiled was consistent with objective standards of sound policing, and (2) that the decision to combat that threat by impoundment was in keeping with established departmental routine or regulation); State v. Huisman, 544 N.W.2d 433 (Iowa 1996) (impoundment decision must be made "according to standardized criteria," and "an administrative or caretaking reason to impound" must exist). Others, such as the Colorado rules reviewed in *Bertine,* leave some discretion to the individual officer to act within guidelines in deciding whether to impound a car in the first place.

3. *Least intrusive means and investigatory intent.* Defendants often argue that their vehicle was impounded, or the contents inventoried, despite less intrusive means to achieve the stated goals of inventory searches, such as leaving the car where it sits, leaving it with another person, or getting the defendant to sign liability waivers (thus removing the interest in protecting officers against a lawsuit for harm to the personal property). Only a handful of jurisdictions (fewer than a half dozen) recognize such claims when it comes to closed containers; however, a larger group (about 15) require police to give an arrestee a reasonable chance to provide for alternative custody of a vehicle before it is impounded. See, e.g., State v. Perham, 814 P.2d 914 (Haw. 1991) (closed containers). Most courts focus only on whether the administrative rules were followed and whether those rules provide adequate guidance. Isn't a "least intrusive means" test one way to guarantee that officers do not use inventory searches to investigate crimes? Are less intrusive methods easier to see in hindsight than at the moment of decision? The Supreme Court has rejected the argument that the "least intrusive means" is a requirement of the federal constitution. Illinois v. Lafayette, 462 U.S. 640 (1983).

In Colorado v. Bertine, the Supreme Court said that inventory searches could be challenged if they were conducted "in bad faith or for the sole purpose of investigation." Is examination of "bad faith" consistent with the general rejection of "pretext" claims? See Chapter 2. Most state courts discussing inventory searches require that the officer conducting the inventory show "good faith" and prohibit use of the inventory as a "pretext" for a search for incriminating evidence. See State v. West, 862 P.2d 192 (Ariz. 1993). How will this "bad faith" come to light? What if an officer admits to "dual" purposes for an inventory search? See State v. Hauseman, 900 P.2d 74 (Colo. 1995).

4. *Inventory searches of personal belongings at the station.* Inventory searches apply to personal items carried by a person who is arrested and placed in detention. What arguments can you make that the justification for inventory searches is stronger for inventory of personal belongings than for cars? What arguments can you make that the privacy interest of the individual is stronger for personal belongings, especially those held in pockets, outside of public view (such as the content of wallets or

purses)? Most states impose fewer restrictions on inventory searches of personal belongings than on inventory searches of cars. See Oles v. State 993 S.W.2d 103 (Tex. Crim. App. 1999) (police did not need probable cause or warrant to take a second look at clothing that had been seized from a defendant a week earlier as part of inventory of his belongings after his arrest). Should similar rules apply to the personal property of civil detainees, such as those who are extremely intoxicated or who suffer from mental illness? See State v. Carper, 876 P.2d 582 (Colo. 1994); Morris v. State, 908 P.2d 931 (Wyo. 1995).

5. *Procedures whose validity turns on the adequacy of executive rules.* There are several types of searches, like inventory searches, in which courts have approved of procedures only when there is a regularized process for police to follow. Consider, for example, the legitimacy of sobriety checkpoints, where the U.S. Supreme Court and state courts have approved only of checkpoints governed by detailed rules. See Chapter 2; Wayne LaFave, Controlling Discretion by Administrative Regulations: The Use, Misuse, and Nonuse of Police Rules and Policies in Fourth Amendment Adjudication, 89 Mich. L. Rev. 442 (1990). Who should issue inventory rules? Should they be determined by statute? If you were the general counsel to a police department, would you have a responsibility to maximize police power to conduct inventory searches? If police officers are concerned about the length and complexity of the inventory forms and process, how might you address that concern?

Problem 4-6. Creating Inventory Searches

Pursuant to a search warrant, officers entered a house where they found four individuals, including Nancy Filkin, who did not reside there. Filkin and the other three individuals were arrested and removed from the premises. The officer who placed her under arrest did not notice whether Filkin was carrying a purse. However, Deputy Richard McKinny, who transported Filkin to the county jail, testified that she had it with her when he transported her to the jail.

Upon arrival at the county jail, McKinny took Filkin to the female booking area, removed her handcuffs, and remained present during the booking process. The standard operating procedure during the booking process at the county jail was to inventory personal items, to assure that the detainee carries no contraband objects into the jail, and to produce an accurate record so that the prisoner gets everything back when she is released. The search is also designed to protect the safety of the officers. The standard operating procedure for a purse is to remove all items to ensure that it contains no money or valuables.

A female corrections officer inventoried Filkin's closed purse under the watchful eye of McKinny. In the process, the officers discovered and opened a black film canister. The canister contained, among other things, a small self-seal bag holding .05 grams of methamphetamine.

Filkin has filed a motion to suppress the drugs found in the black film canister. How would you rule? Compare State v. Filkin, 494 N.W.2d 544 (Neb. 1993).

2. *Cars and Containers*

Of all the forms of personal property protected from unreasonable searches and seizures, cars and the containers inside them have generated the most litigation.

There are distinctive constitutional and statutory rules involving car searches. When reading the following cases, be sure to distinguish the various rationales available to the police to search a car and its contents, and note the ways that the analysis changes because the search involves a car.

■ STATE v. EILEEN PIERCE

642 A.2d 947 (N.J. 1994)

STEIN, J.

This appeal concerns the scope of a police officer's authority to conduct a search of articles contained in the passenger compartment of an automobile following the arrest of the driver for operating the vehicle while his license is suspended. The State supports the validity of the search by relying on New York v. Belton, 453 U.S. 454 (1981), which held that "when a policeman has made a lawful custodial arrest of the occupant of an automobile, he may, as a contemporaneous incident of that arrest, search the passenger compartment of that automobile." Defendant contends that both the custodial arrest of the driver and the incidental search of the vehicle constituted violations of rights protected by the Fourth Amendment of the United States Constitution and article I, paragraph 7 of the New Jersey Constitution. . . .

The facts are essentially undisputed. On August 19, 1989, Officer Rette of the Manalapan Township Police Department stopped a 1986 Ford van owned and operated by co-defendant Nicholas Grass for speeding, the officer having clocked the vehicle's speed at fifty-one miles per hour in a forty-mile-per-hour zone. The other occupants of the vehicle were defendant, Pierce, and co-defendant Eugene Bernardo. The officer requested and received Grass's Pennsylvania driver's license and vehicle registration. Officer Rette communicated by radio with his headquarters, and learned that Grass's driver's license had been suspended. The officer then ordered Grass to step out of the van and informed Grass that he was arresting him for driving an automobile while his license was suspended. Officer Rette conduced a pat-down search of Grass, handcuffed him, and placed him in the rear of his patrol car, which he had parked directly behind the van.

Officer Rette returned to the van and ordered Pierce and Bernardo to get out of the vehicle and to produce identification. Pierce stated that she had no identification; Bernardo produced a New Jersey driver's license. The officer conducted a pat-down search of both passengers to determine if they were armed, and found no weapons. By this time, a state trooper and a police officer from another municipality had arrived on the scene to provide back-up.

Officer Rette then entered the van to search its interior while the back-up officers secured Pierce and Bernardo behind the van. He first observed a "large hunting-type knife" on the front console. The officer also saw behind the driver's seat a metal camera case with two latches, one fastened and the other unfastened. He opened the case and found a revolver with "four loaded rounds of .357 magnum ammunition and also two spent rounds." The officer also found in the van [two] motorcycle gang jackets." . . . Officer Rette testified that the jacket he identified as "the female's jacket . . . had a patch on the back stating 'Nick's property.'" The officer stated that he found in a pocket of that jacket a cellophane packet containing a trace amount of white powder that laboratory tests later showed to be cocaine. The officer testified that he had searched the van within two or three minutes after he had handcuffed Grass and secured him in the patrol car. Bernardo and Pierce were arrested and, together with Grass, were indicted [on weapons and narcotics violations.]

[O]ver the course of several decades the Supreme Court successively expanded and contracted the scope of police authority to conduct warrantless searches incident to arrests. . . . In 1969 the Supreme Court decided Chimel v. California, 395 U.S. 752 (1969), . . . restricting the constitutionally-permissible scope of a search incident to an arrest. [In *Belton*], the Court applied *Chimel*'s holding to an automobile search incident to the arrest of the occupants. A New York State trooper stopped a vehicle for speeding, and while examining the driver's license and registration smelled the odor of burned marijuana. The trooper also observed an envelope marked "Supergold" on the floor of the car and suspected that it contained marijuana. The trooper ordered the four occupants to step out of the car, and placed them under arrest for possession of marijuana. He patted down each of them, and directed them to stand in separate areas. Finding marijuana in the envelope, the trooper then searched each of the occupants and also searched the passenger compartment of the vehicle. A black leather jacket on the back seat belonged to Belton. When the trooper unzipped one of the pockets, he found cocaine.

[T]he Supreme Court endorsed the view that Fourth Amendment protections "can only be realized if the police are acting under a set of rules which, in most instances, makes it possible to reach a correct determination beforehand as to whether an invasion of privacy is justified in the interest of law enforcement." The Court, stressing its adherence to "the fundamental principles established in the *Chimel* case," adopted "the generalization that articles inside the relatively narrow compass of the passenger compartment of an automobile are in fact generally, even if not inevitably, within the area into which an arrestee might reach in order to grab a weapon or evidentiary item." Accordingly, the Court upheld the validity of the *Belton* search, holding

> that when a policeman has made a lawful custodial arrest of the occupant of an automobile, he may, as a contemporaneous incident of that arrest, search the passenger compartment of that automobile [and] may also examine the contents of any containers found within the passenger compartment, for if the passenger compartment is within reach of the arrestee, so also will containers in it be within his reach.

. . . The Court's holding encompassed only the interior of an automobile's passenger compartment, not the trunk. In applying the *Belton* rule, federal courts have generally sustained vehicular searches even if the arrestee has been removed from the vehicle and handcuffed.

The Court's holding in *Belton* has been widely criticized. Professor LaFave, whose endorsement of bright-line rules to guide police officers in resolving Fourth Amendment issues the *Belton* majority quoted approvingly, concludes that *Belton* "does a disservice to the development of sound Fourth Amendment doctrine." He observes that because the automobile search authorized by *Belton* is not based on probable cause, the decision creates the risk that "police will make custodial arrests which they otherwise would not make as a cover for a search which the Fourth Amendment otherwise prohibits." . . .

Most of the state courts that have addressed the issue apply the *Belton* rule, although several state courts have declined to follow *Belton*. . . . No case has heretofore required us to consider the *Belton* holding in the context of our State Constitution because most warrantless automobile searches conducted by police officers are sustainable on other grounds. Our courts have relied primarily on the automobile exception first established in Carroll v. United States, 267 U.S. 132 (1925), which "holds a search warrant unnecessary when the police stop an automobile on the highway and have probable cause to believe that it contains contraband or evidence of a crime." An obvious explanation for reliance by law-enforcement officials on the "automobile exception" is that the very same facts that constitute probable cause to arrest a vehicle's occupant often will afford police officers probable cause to believe that the vehicle contains evidence of crime or contraband. . . .

In addition, we have applied the holding of Michigan v. Long, 463 U.S. 1032 (1983), in which the Supreme Court sustained the validity of a weapons search in the passenger compartment of an automobile when the police officers had a reasonable belief that the driver posed a threat to their safety. The Court observed that a weapons search was "permissible if the police officer possesses a reasonable belief based on specific and articulable facts which, taken together with the rational inferences from those facts, reasonably warrant the officer in believing that the suspect is dangerous and the suspect may gain immediate control of weapons." . . .

Hence, irrespective of the *Belton* rule, warrantless vehicle searches in New Jersey are sustainable either under the so-called "automobile exception" on the basis of probable cause, or in connection with a search for weapons based on an objectively-reasonable belief that an occupant of the vehicle is dangerous and may gain access to weapons. We must now determine whether our State Constitution will permit application of the *Belton* rule to sustain a warrantless vehicular search solely on the basis of an arrest for a motor-vehicle offense.

We first sustain the validity of the custodial arrest of co-defendant Grass for operating a motor vehicle during the period in which his driver's license had been suspended. [O]peration of a motor vehicle by a person whose license is suspended is one of the more serious Title 39 offenses, and one that poses grave danger to the public. We note that the Motor Vehicle Code authorizes suspension of a driver's license only for serious offenses, or an accumulation of offenses, that directly implicate the public safety. [H]owever, the broad statutory authorization to arrest those who commit any violation of the Motor Vehicle Code embraces [minor offenses], and the arbitrary and unreasonable exercise of the statutory arrest power in respect of minor traffic offenses could infringe on constitutionally-protected rights. [We hold] that under article I, paragraph 7 of the New Jersey Constitution the rule of *Belton* shall not apply to warrantless arrests for motor-vehicle offenses. . . .

We rest that conclusion on several grounds. Initially, we note that the rationale for the Supreme Court's decision in *Chimel,* the analytical source for the Court's holding in *Belton,* is less persuasive when offered to justify the need for a vehicular search following an arrest for a traffic offense. The Court in *Chimel* observed that an arresting officer might reasonably search the arrestee and the adjacent area to remove weapons that the arrestee might use to effect escape or resist arrest, and to locate evidence pertinent to the arrest to prevent its concealment or destruction. That justification for a warrantless vehicular search diminishes significantly when the basis for the arrest is a routine violation of one of the motor vehicle statutes.

We are mindful that police officers are at risk whenever they make a vehicular stop, and that a significant percentage of assaults on police officers occur in the course of traffic stops. Nevertheless, out of the substantial number of ordinary citizens who might on occasion commit commonplace traffic offenses, the vast majority are unarmed. Moreover, when the predicate offense is a motor-vehicle violation, the vehicle stopped by police would not ordinarily contain evidence at risk of destruction that pertains to the underlying offense, except in the case of . . . driving while intoxicated [and] operating a vehicle while possessing controlled dangerous substances. . . . In addition, motorists arrested for traffic offenses almost invariably are removed from the vehicle and secured. When an arrestee, as was the case with Grass, has been handcuffed and placed in the patrol car, and the passengers are removed from the vehicle and frisked, the officer's justification for searching the vehicle and the passengers' clothing and containers is minimal. Thus, in the context of arrests for motor-vehicle violations, the bright-line *Belton* holding extends the *Chimel* rule beyond the logical limits of its principle. [We] perceive that the *Belton* rule, as applied to arrests for traffic offenses, creates an unwarranted incentive for police officers to "make custodial arrests which they otherwise would not make as a cover for a search which the Fourth Amendment otherwise prohibits." . . .

Our holding . . . poses no obstacle to law enforcement or to the ability of police officers to take precautions necessary for their safety. Thus, our holding does not affect the right of a police officer, following a valid custodial arrest for a motor-vehicle violation or for a criminal offense, to conduct a search of the person of the arrestee solely on the basis of the lawful arrest. In addition, . . . police officers are authorized under the "automobile exception" to make warrantless searches of vehicles that they have stopped on the highway whenever they have probable cause to believe that a vehicle contains contraband or evidence of a crime. [V]ehicle searches sustainable under the "automobile exception" and based on probable cause stand on firmer ground than those that depend for their validity on a judicially-created exception to the warrant requirement, such as the *Belton* rule, which requires no proof of probable cause.

Moreover, under circumstances in which police officers possess a reasonable belief that a vehicle's driver or occupants pose a threat to their safety, a weapons search of the vehicle is permissible in accordance with *Long*. . . . Finally, in the event of an arrest for a traffic offense in which the arrestee remained in or adjacent to the vehicle, with the result that the vehicle was within the area of the arrestee's "immediate control," a contemporaneous search of the vehicle could be sustainable under *Chimel*, but not based on *Belton*'s automatic application of *Chimel*.

On this record, however, the search of Grass's vehicle following his arrest depends entirely on whether *Belton* applies. [No one suggests] that the search was based on probable cause to believe that the vehicle contained contraband or evidence of crime or on the officer's reasonable belief that Grass or the occupants posed a threat to his safety. Accordingly, because we hold that the *Belton* rule cannot sustain the search, the evidence of cocaine found in Pierce's jacket must be suppressed. . . .

HANDLER, J., concurring.

. . . Under *Chimel* the area that the police can search incident to an arrest is that which is within the "immediate control" of the arrestee. In the context of an arrest involving occupants of a motor vehicle, *Belton* defines that physical area to include the passenger compartment. . . . In the context of an arrest associated with the use of a motor vehicle, when an arrestee remains near the vehicle, the entire passenger compartment is likely to be within the control of the arrestee. However, when an arrestee has been physically restrained, removed from proximity to the vehicle, and placed in the patrol car, typically the vehicle is no longer within the control of the arrestee. Further, under those circumstances, there is considerably less likelihood that the ensuing search will any longer be "a contemporaneous incident of the arrest." That is because "control" is the defining dimension of the reasonableness of the search, and its application necessarily turns on particular facts.

The element of "control" as the factor determining the reasonableness of a search incident to an arrest is to be understood in the sense of the physical and temporal capacity of the arrestee in light of surrounding circumstances. That understanding is exemplified by *Belton.* There, a sole officer searched the stopped automobile. Even though the officer had advised the four suspects that they were "under arrest," the suspects stood near the car while the officer searched it.

In contrast, the evidence in this case suggests that the search occurred after the arrest of the driver had been completed by his physical restraint and actual removal to the patrol car and, therefore, was not contemporaneous with the arrest of the driver, and that the area searched, the van, was no longer within the physical control of the arrestee. . . .

Although I agree that *Belton* established a "bright line" by defining the passenger compartment of a vehicle to be within the "grabbable" area of a recent occupant of the vehicle, I am persuaded by the *Belton* Court's stated intention not to alter *Chimel* that the concept of control must still have real meaning and be applied in light of surrounding circumstances. I believe that *Belton*'s requirement that the search be a "contemporaneous incident of the arrest" provides that meaning and must be interpreted consistent with the analytical construct established in *Chimel*. . . .

The search here was invalid, under both *Belton* and *Chimel,* for the straightforward and narrow reason that it was not a "contemporaneous" incident of the arrest and the passenger compartment was no longer within the "immediate control" of Grass once he had been physically restrained and removed and placed in the patrol car. Accordingly, I concur in the judgment of the Court.

Notes

1. *Search of an automobile incident to arrest: majority position.* As noted by the court in *Pierce,* the largest group of states (about 30) have followed the Supreme Court's decision in New York v. Belton, 453 U.S. 454 (1981), applying the law of searches incident to arrest to drivers and occupants of cars. See State v. Murrell, 764 N.E.2d 986 (Ohio 2002). About half as many states (roughly 15) have rejected the bright-line rule of *Belton* and have required a case-by-case analysis of the scope of searches of cars incident to arrest. In some of these states, the officers must have reason to fear for their safety (or reason to believe evidence will be destroyed) before they search any area in the vehicle beyond what is within the immediate control of the arrestee. See, e.g., State v. Brown, 588 N.E.2d 113 (Ohio 1993); Vasquez v. State, 990 P.2d 476 (Wyo. 1999). Doesn't every jurisdiction need to draw some line to settle the question of when searches of cars incident to arrest (the *Belton* rule) will no longer apply? Where should courts (or legislatures) draw this line? Cf. Glasco v. Commonwealth, 513 S.E.2d 137 (Va. 1999) (defendant who had voluntarily left his vehicle when initially contacted by arresting officer was a recent occupant of vehicle, permitting search of interior of vehicle incident to arrest).

2. *Passengers and searches of cars incident to arrest.* There was some doubt over the years whether a search of a car incident to the arrest of the driver could also reach property that clearly belonged to a passenger who is not arrested. The Supreme Court resolved this question in Wyoming v. Houghton, 526 U.S. 295 (1999). In that case, an officer stopped a vehicle for speeding and noticed a hypodermic syringe in the driver's shirt pocket. When the driver admitted that he used the syringe to take drugs, the officer arrested him and ordered two female passengers out of the car. He searched the passenger compartment of the car for contraband and discovered drugs in a purse on the back seat belonging to one of the passengers. The Court upheld the search, emphasizing once again the need for bright-line rules that are easy for officers to apply in the field. Do you predict that state courts will follow this application of Belton as they interpret their own constitutions? See State v. Ray, 620 N.W.2d 83 (Neb. 2000) (officer may inspect passenger's knapsack found in passenger compartment, although passenger not arrested at the time).

3. *Scope of car searches incident to arrest: trunks and hatchbacks.* The court in *Belton* did not define the scope of "passenger compartment." Almost all courts have held that hatchbacks that can be reached from the passenger compartment, however awkwardly, may be subject to a search incident to arrest. See, e.g., Stout v. State, 898 S.W.2d 457 (Ark. 1995) (spare tire area in hatchback station wagon); United States v. Olguin-Rivera, 168 F.3d 1203 (10th Cir. 1999) (rear cargo area of sport utility vehicle, covered by retractable vinyl covering).

The search incident to arrest approved in *Belton* applies only to "the interior of the passenger compartment of an automobile and does not encompass the trunk." Thus, state courts have not allowed police officers to rely on the "search incident to arrest" rationale when they search a trunk. See State v. Neely, 462 N.W.2d 105 (Neb. 1990). Trunk searches will usually be justified instead by probable cause (under the automobile exception) or as inventory searches.

4. *Searches incident to arrest for minor offenses.* In *Pierce* the New Jersey court limited the powers of the police to conduct searches of cars incident to the arrest of the driver or an occupant automatically when the arrest is for a traffic offense. States are fairly evenly divided on this question. The larger group of courts rejects any rule limiting the power to conduct searches of cars incident to arrest on the basis of the severity of the offense. See State v. Cook, 530 N.W.2d 728 (Iowa 1995) (search incident to citation for seat belt violation). Among the courts limiting the availability of searches incident to arrest for minor offenses, some base their decisions on readings of the state constitutions, while others base the outcome on a restricted reading of the statute granting arrest authority to the officer for minor traffic offenses. See State v. Brown, 588 N.E.2d 113 (Ohio 1992).

Should courts (or legislatures or police departments) limit the kind of offenses that may serve as the basis for car searches? What about using a broken license-plate light bulb, or the absence of a front (but not a rear) license plate, as a basis for an arrest and corresponding search?

5. *The "new judicial federalism."* On many constitutional questions arising in the criminal process, the New Jersey Supreme Court and many others have taken positions different from the federal view under their own state constitutions. One of the recurring questions — on which state courts have reached a wide range of positions — is how much deference state courts should give to U.S. Supreme Court decisions when the state courts are interpreting state law that is analogous to federal provisions. The degree of deference has shifted in response to highly publicized

calls, led by Supreme Court Justice William Brennan, for independent state constitutional decision-making. See William Brennan, Jr., State Constitutions and the Protection of Individual Rights, 90 Harv. L. Rev. 489 (1977); James Gardner, The Failed Discourse of State Constitutionalism, 90 Mich. L. Rev. 761 (1992); Barry Latzer, The New Judicial Federalism and Criminal Justice: Two Problems and a Response, 22 Rutgers L.J. 863 (1991).

6. *Independent and adequate state grounds.* The U.S. Supreme Court reviews questions of federal law, but cannot question a state court's interpretation of state law. When a state court discusses both state and federal law in its decision (and you have now seen how commonly that occurs), how does the U.S. Supreme Court decide whether it can review the decision? Under Michigan v. Long, 463 U.S. 1032 (1983), the Court requires a "plain statement" sufficient to show that "the federal cases are being used only for the purpose of guidance, and do not themselves compel the result that the court has reached." An assertion by the state court that it has relied independently on state law will not suffice. If the discussion of state law is "interwoven with the federal law, and . . . the adequacy and independence of any possible state law ground is not clear from the face of the opinion," the Supreme Court will treat the decision as one resting on federal law. Is this an appropriate test for judging the intentions of a state court? Does a state court risk reversal if it cites any U.S. Supreme Court cases at all? See Pennsylvania v. Labron, 518 U.S. 938 (1996) (taking jurisdiction and reversing in case where state court cited two federal decisions along with multiple state decisions); Commonwealth v. Labron, 690 A.2d 228 (Pa. 1997) (on remand, reinstating earlier decision and "explicitly not[ing] that it was, in fact, decided upon independent state grounds").

7. *Lower courts?* Should the U.S. Supreme Court continue to refer to both state supreme courts and federal district and circuit courts as "lower" courts? Certainly the U.S. Supreme Court has power in our federal system to review decisions in state courts based on federal law. But since state supreme courts are the final authority on state questions, would it not be more appropriate for the U.S. Supreme Court to refer to the state high courts by a more respectful name? Should state supreme courts refer to the U.S. Supreme Court as "the High Court"?

■ CALIFORNIA v. CHARLES ACEVEDO

500 U.S. 565 (1991)

BLACKMUN, J.

This case requires us once again to consider the so-called "automobile exception" to the warrant requirement of the Fourth Amendment and its application to the search of a closed container in the trunk of a car. On October 28, 1987, Officer Coleman of the Santa Ana Police Department received a telephone call from a federal drug enforcement agent in Hawaii. The agent informed Coleman that he had seized a package containing marijuana which was to have been delivered to the Federal Express Office in Santa Ana and which was addressed to J.R. Daza at 805 West Stevens Avenue in that city. The agent arranged to send the package to Coleman instead. Coleman then was to take the package to the Federal Express office and arrest the person who arrived to claim it.

Coleman received the package on October 29, verified its contents, and took it to the Senior Operations Manager at the Federal Express office. At about 10:30 A.M.

on October 30, a man, who identified himself as Jamie Daza, arrived to claim the package. He accepted it and drove to his apartment on West Stevens. He carried the package into the apartment.

At 11:45 A.M., officers observed Daza leave the apartment and drop the box and paper that had contained the marijuana into a trash bin. Coleman at that point left the scene to get a search warrant. About 12:05 P.M., the officers saw Richard St. George leave the apartment carrying a blue knapsack which appeared to be half full. The officers stopped him as he was driving off, searched the knapsack, and found 1 1/2 pounds of marijuana.

At 12:30 P.M., respondent Charles Steven Acevedo arrived. He entered Daza's apartment, stayed for about 10 minutes, and reappeared carrying a brown paper bag that looked full. The officers noticed that the bag was the size of one of the wrapped marijuana packages sent from Hawaii. Acevedo walked to a silver Honda in the parking lot. He placed the bag in the trunk of the car and started to drive away. Fearing the loss of evidence, officers in a marked police car stopped him. They opened the trunk and the bag, and found marijuana.

Respondent was charged in state court with possession of marijuana for sale. . . . He moved to suppress the marijuana found in the car. The motion was denied. He then pleaded guilty but appealed the denial of the suppression motion. We granted certiorari to reexamine the law applicable to a closed container in an automobile, a subject that has troubled courts and law enforcement officers since it was first considered in United States v. Chadwick, 433 U.S. 1 (1977). . . .

In Carroll v. United States, 267 U.S. 132 (1925), this Court established an exception to the warrant requirement for moving vehicles, for it recognized "a necessary difference between a search of a store, dwelling house or other structure in respect of which a proper official warrant readily may be obtained, and a search of a ship, motor boat, wagon or automobile, for contraband goods, where it is not practicable to secure a warrant because the vehicle can be quickly moved out of the locality or jurisdiction in which the warrant must be sought." It therefore held that a warrantless search of an automobile, based upon probable cause to believe that the vehicle contained evidence of crime in the light of an exigency arising out of the likely disappearance of the vehicle, did not contravene the Warrant Clause of the Fourth Amendment. . . .

In United States v. Ross, 456 U.S. 798 (1982), we held that a warrantless search of an automobile under the *Carroll* doctrine could include a search of a container or package found inside the car when such a search was supported by probable cause. The warrantless search of Ross' car occurred after an informant told the police that he had seen Ross complete a drug transaction using drugs stored in the trunk of his car. The police stopped the car, searched it, and discovered in the trunk a brown paper bag containing drugs. We decided that the search of Ross' car was not unreasonable under the Fourth Amendment. [If] probable cause justifies the search of a lawfully stopped vehicle, it justifies the search of every part of the vehicle and its contents that may conceal the object of the search. . . .

Ross distinguished the *Carroll* doctrine from the separate rule that governed the search of closed containers. The Court had announced this separate rule, unique to luggage and other closed packages, bags, and containers, in United States v. Chadwick, 433 U.S. 1 (1977). In *Chadwick,* federal narcotics agents had probable cause to believe that a 200-pound double-locked footlocker contained marijuana. The agents tracked the locker as the defendants removed it from a train and carried it through the station to a waiting car. As soon as the defendants lifted the locker into the trunk of the car, the agents arrested them, seized the locker, and searched it. In this Court, the United States did not contend that the locker's brief contact with the automobile's trunk sufficed to make the *Carroll* doctrine applicable. Rather, the United States urged that the search of movable luggage could be considered analogous to the search of an automobile. The Court rejected this argument because, it reasoned, a person expects more privacy in his luggage and personal effects than he does in his automobile. Moreover, it concluded that as "may often not be the case when automobiles are seized," secure storage facilities are usually available when the police seize luggage.

In Arkansas v. Sanders, 442 U.S. 753 (1979), the Court extended *Chadwick*'s rule to apply to a suitcase actually being transported in the trunk of a car. In *Sanders*, the police had probable cause to believe a suitcase contained marijuana. They watched as the defendant placed the suitcase in the trunk of a taxi and was driven away. The police pursued the taxi for several blocks, stopped it, found the suitcase in the trunk, and searched it. Although the Court had applied the *Carroll* doctrine to searches of integral parts of the automobile itself (indeed, in *Carroll*, contraband whiskey was in the upholstery of the seats), it did not extend the doctrine to the warrantless search of personal luggage "merely because it was located in an automobile lawfully stopped by the police." Again, the *Sanders* majority stressed the heightened privacy expectation in personal luggage and concluded that the presence of luggage in an automobile did not diminish the owner's expectation of privacy in his personal items.

In *Ross*, the Court endeavored to distinguish between *Carroll*, which governed the *Ross* automobile search, and *Chadwick*, which governed the *Sanders* automobile search. It held that the *Carroll* doctrine covered searches of automobiles when the police had probable cause to search an entire vehicle, but that the *Chadwick* doctrine governed searches of luggage when the officers had probable cause to search only a container within the vehicle. Thus, in a *Ross* situation, the police could conduct a reasonable search under the Fourth Amendment without obtaining a warrant, whereas in a *Sanders* situation, the police had to obtain a warrant before they searched. . . .

The facts in this case closely resemble the facts in *Ross*. In *Ross*, the police had probable cause to believe that drugs were stored in the trunk of a particular car. Here, the [California courts] concluded that the police had probable cause to believe that respondent was carrying marijuana in a bag in his car's trunk. Furthermore, for what it is worth, in *Ross*, as here, the drugs in the trunk were contained in a brown paper bag.

This Court in *Ross* rejected *Chadwick*'s distinction between containers and cars. It concluded that the expectation of privacy in one's vehicle is equal to one's expectation of privacy in the container, and noted that "the privacy interests in a car's trunk or glove compartment may be no less than those in a movable container." [T]he time and expense of the warrant process would be misdirected if the police could search every cubic inch of an automobile until they discovered a paper sack, at which point the Fourth Amendment required them to take the sack to a magistrate for permission to look inside. We now must decide the question deferred in *Ross:* whether the Fourth Amendment requires the police to obtain a warrant to open the sack in a movable vehicle simply because they lack probable cause to search the entire car. We conclude that it does not.

[A] container found after a general search of the automobile and a container found in a car after a limited search for the container are equally easy for the police to store and for the suspect to hide or destroy. In fact, we see no principled distinction in terms of either the privacy expectation or the exigent circumstances between the paper bag found by the police in *Ross* and the paper bag found by the police here. Furthermore, by attempting to distinguish between a container for which the police are specifically searching and a container which they come across in a car, we have provided only minimal protection for privacy and have impeded effective law enforcement.

The line between probable cause to search a vehicle and probable cause to search a package in that vehicle is not always clear, and separate rules that govern the two objects to be searched may enable the police to broaden their power to make warrantless searches and disserve privacy interests. . . . At the moment when officers stop an automobile, it may be less than clear whether they suspect with a high degree of certainty that the vehicle contains drugs in a bag or simply contains drugs. If the police know that they may open a bag only if they are actually searching the entire car, they may search more extensively than they otherwise would in order to establish the general probable cause required by *Ross*. . . . We cannot see the benefit of a rule that requires law enforcement officers to conduct a more intrusive search in order to justify a less intrusive one.

To the extent that the *Chadwick-Sanders* rule protects privacy, its protection is minimal. Law enforcement officers may seize a container and hold it until they obtain a search warrant. . . . And the police often will be able to search containers without a warrant, despite the *Chadwick-Sanders* rule, as a search incident to a lawful arrest. . . .

Finally, the search of a paper bag intrudes far less on individual privacy than does the incursion sanctioned long ago in *Carroll*. In that case, prohibition agents slashed the upholstery of the automobile. This Court nonetheless found their search to be reasonable under the Fourth Amendment. If destroying the interior of an automobile is not unreasonable, we cannot conclude that looking inside a closed container is. In light of the minimal protection to privacy afforded by the *Chadwick-Sanders* rule, and our serious doubt whether that rule substantially serves privacy interests, we now hold that the Fourth Amendment does not compel separate treatment for an automobile search that extends only to a container within the vehicle.

The *Chadwick-Sanders* rule not only has failed to protect privacy but also has confused courts and police officers and impeded effective law enforcement. The conflict between the *Carroll* doctrine cases and the *Chadwick-Sanders* line has been criticized in academic commentary. One leading authority on the Fourth Amendment, after comparing *Chadwick* and *Sanders* with *Carroll* and its progeny, observed: "These two lines of authority cannot be completely reconciled, and thus how one comes out in the container-in-the-car situation depends upon which line of authority is used as a point of departure." 3 W. LaFave, Search and Seizure 53 (2d ed. 1987).

The discrepancy between the two rules has led to confusion for law enforcement officers. For example, when an officer, who has developed probable cause to believe that a vehicle contains drugs, begins to search the vehicle and immediately discovers a closed container, which rule applies? The defendant will argue that the fact that the officer first chose to search the container indicates that his probable cause extended only to the container and that *Chadwick* and *Sanders* therefore require a warrant. On the other hand, the fact that the officer first chose to search in the most obvious location should not restrict the propriety of the search. The *Chadwick* rule, as applied in *Sanders,* has devolved into an anomaly such that the more likely the police are to discover drugs in a container, the less authority they have to search it. We have noted the virtue of providing clear and unequivocal guidelines to the law enforcement profession. The *Chadwick-Sanders* rule is the antithesis of a "clear and unequivocal" guideline.

[Justice Stevens argues in dissent] that law enforcement has not been impeded because the Court has decided 29 Fourth Amendment cases since *Ross* in favor of the government. . . . In each of these cases, the government appeared as the petitioner. The dissent fails to explain how the loss of 29 cases below, not to mention the many others which this Court did not hear, did not interfere with law enforcement. The fact that the state courts and the Federal Courts of Appeals have been reversed in their Fourth Amendment holdings 29 times since 1982 further demonstrates the extent to which our Fourth Amendment jurisprudence has confused the courts. . . .

The interpretation of the *Carroll* doctrine set forth in *Ross* now applies to all searches of containers found in an automobile. In other words, the police may search without a warrant if their search is supported by probable cause. [However, probable] cause to believe that a container placed in the trunk of a [vehicle] contains contraband or evidence does not justify a search of the entire [vehicle]. In the case before us, the police had probable cause to believe that the paper bag in the automobile's trunk contained marijuana. That probable cause now allows a warrantless search of the paper bag. The facts in the record reveal that the police did not have probable cause to believe that contraband was hidden in any other part of the automobile and a search of the entire vehicle would have been without probable cause and unreasonable under the Fourth Amendment. . . .

Until today, this Court has drawn a curious line between the search of an automobile that coincidentally turns up a container and the search of a container that coincidentally turns up in an automobile. The protections of the Fourth Amendment must not turn on such coincidences. We therefore interpret *Carroll* as providing one rule to govern all automobile searches. . . .

SCALIA, J., concurring in the judgment.

I agree with the dissent that it is anomalous for a briefcase to be protected by the "general requirement" of a prior warrant when it is being carried along the street, but for that same briefcase to become unprotected as soon as it is carried into an automobile. On the other hand, I agree with the Court that it would be anomalous for a locked compartment in an automobile to be unprotected by the "general requirement" of a prior warrant, but for an unlocked briefcase within the automobile to be protected. I join in the judgment of the Court because I think its holding is more faithful to the text and tradition of the Fourth Amendment, and if these anomalies in our jurisprudence are ever to be eliminated that is the direction in which we should travel.

The Fourth Amendment does not by its terms require a prior warrant for searches and seizures; it merely prohibits searches and seizures that are "unreasonable." What it explicitly states regarding warrants is by way of limitation upon their issuance rather than requirement of their use. For the warrant was a means of insulating officials from personal liability assessed by colonial juries. An officer who searched or seized without a warrant did so at his own risk; he would be liable for trespass, including exemplary damages, unless the jury found that his action was "reasonable." If, however, the officer acted pursuant to a proper warrant, he would be absolutely immune. See Bell v. Clapp, 10 Johns. 263 (N.Y. 1813). By restricting the issuance of warrants, the Framers endeavored to preserve the jury's role in regulating searches and seizures. . . .

Even before today's decision, the "warrant requirement" had become so riddled with exceptions that it was basically unrecognizable. . . . Our intricate body of law regarding "reasonable expectation of privacy" has been developed largely as a means of creating these exceptions, enabling a search to be denominated not a Fourth Amendment "search" and therefore not subject to the general warrant requirement.

Unlike the dissent, therefore, I do not regard today's holding as some momentous departure, but rather as merely the continuation of an inconsistent jurisprudence that has been with us for years. . . . In my view, the path out of this confusion should be sought by returning to the first principle that the "reasonableness" requirement of the Fourth Amendment affords the protection that the common law afforded. I have no difficulty with the proposition that that includes the requirement of a warrant, where the common law required a warrant; and it may even be that changes in the surrounding legal rules (for example, elimination of the common-law rule that reasonable, good-faith belief was no defense to absolute liability for trespass) may make a warrant indispensable to reasonableness where it once was not. But the supposed "general rule" that a warrant is always required does not appear to have any basis in the common law, and confuses rather than facilitates any attempt to develop rules of reasonableness in light of changed legal circumstances. . . .

STEVENS, J., dissenting.

. . . The Fourth Amendment is a restraint on Executive power. The Amendment constitutes the Framers' direct constitutional response to the unreasonable law enforcement practices employed by agents of the British Crown. Over the years — particularly in the period immediately after World War II and particularly in opinions authored by Justice Jackson after his service as a special prosecutor at the Nuremburg trials — the Court has recognized the importance of this restraint as a bulwark against police practices that prevail in totalitarian regimes. This history is, however, only part of the explanation for the warrant requirement. The requirement also reflects the sound policy judgment that, absent exceptional circumstances, the decision to invade the privacy of an individual's personal effects should be made by a neutral magistrate rather than an agent of the Executive.

[In United States v. Chadwick, we] concluded that neither of the justifications for the automobile exception could support a similar exception for luggage. We first held that the privacy interest in luggage is substantially greater than in an automobile. Unlike automobiles and their contents, we reasoned, luggage contents are not open to public view, except as a condition to a border entry or common carrier travel; nor is luggage subject to regular inspections and official scrutiny on a continuing basis. Indeed, luggage is specifically intended to safeguard the privacy of personal effects, unlike an automobile, whose primary function is transportation. We then held that the mobility of luggage did not justify creating an additional exception to the Warrant Clause. Unlike an automobile, luggage can easily be seized and detained pending judicial approval of a search. . . .

In its opinion today, the Court recognizes that the police did not have probable cause to search respondent's vehicle and that a search of anything but the paper bag that respondent had carried from Daza's apartment and placed in the trunk of his car would have been unconstitutional. Moreover, as I read the opinion, the Court assumes that the police could not have made a warrantless inspection of the bag before it was placed in the car. Finally, the Court also does not question the fact that, under our prior cases, it would have been lawful for the police to seize the container and detain it (and respondent) until they obtained a search warrant. Thus, all of the relevant facts that governed our decisions in *Chadwick* and *Sanders* are present here whereas the relevant fact that justified the vehicle search in *Ross* is not present.

The Court does not attempt to identify any exigent circumstances that would justify its refusal to apply the general rule against warrantless searches. Instead, it advances these three arguments: First, the rules identified in the foregoing cases are confusing and anomalous. Second, the rules do not protect any significant interest in privacy. And, third, the rules impede effective law enforcement. None of these arguments withstands scrutiny.

The "Confusion"

. . . In the case the Court decides today, the California Court of Appeal . . . had no difficulty applying the critical distinction. Relying on *Chadwick*, it explained that "the officers had probable cause to believe marijuana would be found only in a brown lunch bag and nowhere else in the car. We are compelled to hold they should have obtained a search warrant before opening it." The decided cases . . . provide no support for the Court's concern about "confusion." The Court instead relies primarily on predictions that were made by Justice Blackmun in his dissenting opinions in *Chadwick* and *Sanders*. The Court, however, cites no evidence that these predictions have in fact materialized. . . .

To the extent there was any "anomaly" in our prior jurisprudence, the Court has "cured" it at the expense of creating a more serious paradox. For surely it is anomalous to prohibit a search of a briefcase while the owner is carrying it exposed on a public street yet to permit a search once the owner has placed the briefcase in the locked trunk of his car. One's privacy interest in one's luggage can certainly not be diminished by one's removing it from a public thoroughfare and placing it — out of sight — in a privately owned vehicle. Nor is the danger that evidence will escape increased if the luggage is in a car rather than on the street. In either location, if the police have probable cause, they are authorized to seize the luggage and to detain it until they obtain judicial approval for a search. Any line demarking an exception to the warrant requirement will appear blurred at the edges, but the Court has certainly erred if it believes that, by erasing one line and drawing another, it has drawn a clearer boundary.

The Privacy Argument

. . . To support its argument that today's holding works only a minimal intrusion on privacy, the Court suggests that "[i]f the police know that they may open a bag only if they are actually searching the entire car, they may search more extensively than they otherwise would in order to establish the general probable cause required by Ross." [T]his fear is unexplained and inexplicable. Neither evidence uncovered in the course of a search nor the scope of the search conducted can be used to provide post hoc justification for a search unsupported by probable cause at its inception.

The Court also justifies its claim that its holding inflicts only minor damage by suggesting that, under New York v. Belton, 453 U.S. 454 (1981), the police could have arrested respondent and searched his bag if respondent had placed the bag in the passenger compartment of the automobile instead of in the trunk. In *Belton,* however, the justification for stopping the car and arresting the driver had nothing to do with the subsequent search, which was based on the potential danger to the arresting officer. The holding in *Belton* was supportable under a straightforward application of the automobile exception. I would not extend *Belton*'s holding to this case, in which the container — which was protected from a warrantless search before it was placed in the car — provided the only justification for the arrest. Even accepting *Belton*'s application to a case like this one, however, the Court's logic extends its holding to a container placed in the trunk of a vehicle, rather than in the passenger compartment. And the Court makes this extension without any justification whatsoever other than convenience to law enforcement.

THE BURDEN ON LAW ENFORCEMENT

The Court's suggestion that *Chadwick* and *Sanders* have created a significant burden on effective law enforcement is unsupported, inaccurate, and, in any event, an insufficient reason for creating a new exception to the warrant requirement. Despite repeated claims that *Chadwick* and *Sanders* have "impeded effective law enforcement," the Court cites no authority for its contentions. Moreover, all evidence that does exist points to the contrary conclusion. In the years since *Ross* was decided, the Court has heard argument in 30 Fourth Amendment cases involving narcotics. In all but one, the government was the petitioner. All save two involved a search or seizure without a warrant or with a defective warrant. And, in all except three, the Court upheld the constitutionality of the search or seizure.

In the meantime, the flow of narcotics cases through the courts has steadily and dramatically increased. No impartial observer could criticize this Court for hindering the progress of the war on drugs. On the contrary, decisions like the one the Court makes today will support the conclusion that this Court has become a loyal foot soldier in the Executive's fight against crime.

Even if the warrant requirement does inconvenience the police to some extent, that fact does not distinguish this constitutional requirement from any other procedural protection secured by the Bill of Rights. It is merely a part of the price that our society must pay in order to preserve its freedom. . . . I respectfully dissent.

Notes

1. *Searches of containers in cars: majority position.* In California v. Acevedo, the Court resolved the tension between two lines of its earlier cases. It allowed warrantless searches of containers within automobiles so long as the police have probable cause to believe that either the car as a whole or the container itself holds contraband or evidence. Very few state courts have rejected the Court's holding in Acevedo as they have interpreted their state constitutions. But see State v. Savva, 616 A.2d 774 (Vt. 1991). Even in the handful of courts that do require exigent circumstances for containers in cars, the rule applies only to containers in the trunk or other areas not covered by a search incident to arrest. This widespread endorsement of *Acevedo*

differs from the more skeptical reception that the Court's decision in New York v. Belton received (as discussed in the previous section). Why did *Acevedo* develop such a strong following, while *Belton* did not?

The Court made it clear in Wyoming v. Houghton, 526 U.S. 295 (1999), that the *Acevedo* rule also applied to any containers owned by passengers rather than the driver. Police officers with probable cause to search a car may inspect a passengers' belongings inside the car if they are capable of concealing the object of the search. Passengers, just like drivers, possess a reduced expectation of privacy when it comes to property inside cars. Would requiring a warrant in this setting encourage drivers to hide contraband in containers belonging to passengers?

2. *Containers (effects) not in cars.* The decision in the federal courts to apply the automobile exception to containers in cars creates an inconsistency between the status of the containers inside and outside a car. For containers outside of cars, police apparently must find one of the many familiar exigencies to justify a warrantless examination of its contents. In jurisdictions that follow the federal rule, a container becomes subject to warrantless search, so long as the officer has probable cause, as soon as it is placed in a car. Will this wrinkle in the law change a police officer's strategy for the timing of an arrest of a suspect holding a container?

3. *The variety of grounds for searching cars.* As in many areas of search and seizure law, the government may use a number of justifications for a search of an automobile and its contents. A lawyer must assess all the possible theories.

a. The automobile exception to the warrant requirement. In Carroll v. United States, 267 U.S. 132 (1925), the Supreme Court upheld a warrantless search by two federal prohibition agents looking for liquor hidden in the upholstery of an automobile. The Court allowed warrantless searches, based on probable cause, of automobiles and other vehicles because "the vehicle can be quickly moved out of the locality or jurisdiction." A second theory justifying reduced Fourth Amendment protection for cars, developed in a series of later cases, is that cars are subject to public view and to pervasive state regulation. Car owners have lower reasonable expectations of privacy than, for example, homeowners.

The power of the police to search cars and other conveyances without a warrant has become known as the "automobile exception." This is an exception to the warrant requirement but not to the probable cause requirement: To exercise this power, police must have probable cause to believe that the car contains evidence or contraband. If police have probable cause, under the automobile exception they may stop the car and conduct a search. A search may be rejected if it exceeds the scope justified by objects which police, based on their finding of probable cause, expect to discover.

The largest group of state courts (about half) have fully embraced the federal view and require no warrant for any search of an automobile. In effect, these courts conclusively presume that exigent circumstances are present for any search of a car, even if the particular car in question was unlikely to move while the officers sought a warrant. A minority of state courts (roughly 15) still explicitly or implicitly require the government to show exigent circumstances to support a warrantless search of a car. The mobility of a car makes this showing quite easy in the ordinary case, but defendants can rebut a presumption of exigency by showing that the car was parked and locked or was otherwise not mobile. See State v. Kock, 725 P.2d 1285 (Or. 1986) (rejecting warrantless search of employee's parked car after viewing employee put box of diapers in back and return to building).

b. The application of Terry *to cars.* A separate justification for car searches stems from the application of *Terry* searches to cars. As we saw in Chapter 2, the Supreme Court approved such searches in Michigan v. Long. Such searches must satisfy the requirements of *Terry.* In other words, the officer must have a proper basis for stopping the car. Then the officer may automatically order the driver and any passengers out of the car. At that point, if the officer has reasonable suspicion to believe there are weapons in the car, she can search in the passenger compartment, in any areas that could contain an accessible weapon, such as under the seats and inside containers large enough for a weapon.

c. Inventory searches and searches incident to arrest. As we saw earlier in this chapter, other justifications for a search include the need for an inventory of the contents of a vehicle when the vehicle is impounded, or a search of the vehicle when an officer is arresting one of its occupants.

4. *Warrant preferences before or after seizure.* Are the police required to obtain a warrant before searching a vehicle if they can obtain one? The Supreme Court in *Carroll* suggested that the automobile exception would apply only "where it is not practicable to secure a warrant." Modern federal decisions generally allow car searches in most situations even when it is clear that a warrant could have been obtained. See, e.g., Chambers v. Maroney, 399 U.S. 42 (1970). What about a warrant preference for searches of vehicles after they are seized? Can a car search that could have been conducted in the field — under any of the car-search justifications — be conducted later, in the police station? Here, too, courts typically have allowed post-seizure warrantless searches. See, e.g., United States v. Johns, 469 U.S. 478 (1985); Michigan v. Thomas, 458 U.S. 259 (1982).

Where the police could obtain a warrant, as in a station-house search, some state courts declare that a warrant is "preferred" but not constitutionally required. See State v. Ray, 265 N.W.2d 663 (Minn. 1978). Does such a declaration in a judicial opinion mean anything? Does it change behavior?

5. *Viewing the exterior of cars.* The rules for searching the interior of cars do not apply to examination of the exterior of cars. Following the familiar expectation of privacy analysis of *Katz,* courts have held that no Fourth Amendment issue is raised when police examine the outside of a car or take a picture of it. Courts have also typically refused to apply the Fourth Amendment to examinations of the tread, tire wear, and even the removal of dirt or small samples of paint. See, e.g., Cardwell v. Lewis, 417 U.S. 583 (1974); State v. Skeleton, 795 P.2d 349 (Kan. 1990). Examination of the contents of a car from the outside, including the use of sight, smell, or even a flashlight to enhance the view, usually falls outside the limits of the Fourth Amendment so long as the car is parked in a place that is otherwise accessible to the police.

What about the viewing of the VIN (vehicle identification number)? In cases involving police efforts to obtain the VIN, courts agree that if the VIN is visible through the front windshield (as it is on all modern cars), and the officer simply reads it, there is no search. If the officer must reach into the car, open the door, lift the hood, or look under the vehicle to read the VIN or inspect some other feature of the car, some courts (a minority) still hold that no search has occurred. See, e.g., New York v. Class, 475 U.S. 106 (1986); Wood v. State, 632 S.W.2d 734 (Tex. Crim. App. 1982). About twice as many states, however, conclude that probable cause is required to move items inside a car, open a door, or lift a hood before viewing a VIN. State v. Larocco, 794 P.2d 460 (Utah 1990).

6. *Warrants reconsidered: what is the exception and what is the rule?* After studying the automobile exception, searches of cars incident to arrest, and inventory searches, look again at the following oft-repeated statement, quoted here from United States v. Ross, 456 U.S. 798 (1982), in a manner that emphasizes the statement's pedigree:

> We reaffirm the basic rule of Fourth Amendment jurisprudence stated by Justice Stewart for a unanimous Court in Mincey v. Arizona, 437 U.S. 385, 390: "The Fourth Amendment proscribes all unreasonable searches and seizures, and it is a cardinal principle that 'searches conducted outside the judicial process, without prior approval by judge or magistrate, are per se unreasonable under the Fourth Amendment — subject only to a few specifically established and well-delineated exceptions.' Katz v. United States, 389 U.S. 347, 357."

Consider Justice Scalia's observation in California v. Acevedo, that the warrant requirement has become "so riddled with exceptions" that it is "basically unrecognizable." Is this a problem courts and legislatures should care about, or have they developed an acceptable replacement for a strong warrant requirement? See Joseph Grano, Rethinking the Fourth Amendment Warrant Requirement, 19 Am. Crim. L. Rev. 603 (1982); Phyllis Bookspan, Reworking the Warrant Requirement: Resuscitating the Fourth Amendment, 44 Vand. L. Rev. 473 (1991); Tracey Maclin, The Central Meaning of the Fourth Amendment, 35 Wm. & Mary L. Rev. 197 (1993).

Problem 4-7. Mobile . . . Homes

Robert Williams, an agent of the Drug Enforcement Administration, watched Charles Carney approach a youth in downtown San Diego. The youth accompanied Carney to a Dodge Mini Motor Home parked in a nearby lot, a few blocks from the courthouse. Carney and the youth closed the window shades in the motor home. Williams had previously received uncorroborated information that another person who used the same motor home was exchanging marijuana for sex. Williams, with assistance from other agents, watched the motor home for the entire one and one-quarter hours that Carney and the youth remained inside. When the youth left the motor home, the agents followed and stopped him. The youth told the agents that he had received marijuana in return for allowing Carney sexual contacts.

At the agents' request, the youth returned to the motor home and knocked on its door; Carney stepped out. The agents identified themselves as law enforcement officers. Without a warrant or consent, one agent entered the motor home and observed marijuana, plastic bags, and a scale of the kind used in weighing drugs on a table.

Assess the validity of the warrantless search. Compare California v. Carney, 471 U.S. 386 (1985).

V Arrests

Every year, police in the United States make about 15 million arrests. Arrests are a serious intrusion on liberty, and our legal systems place several types of controls on them. The constraints come from constitutions, statutes, police department rules, the common law of torts, and elsewhere. Despite these multiple limits, police officers in the field still make the most important decisions about arrests.

This chapter surveys the legal rules and institutions that limit the arrest power and studies the operation of that power within (and sometimes outside) those legal boundaries. Section A considers the distinction between arrests and the lesser restraints on liberty known as "stops." Section B identifies the limited situations in which a warrant is necessary to complete a valid arrest. Section C focuses on legal rules dealing with the police officer's decision *not* to make an arrest in certain settings. Section D continues with the theme of police discretion in the arrest decision, looking to the use of the citation power as an alternative to arrests. And finally, Section E introduces the limits on the officer's use of force in carrying out an arrest.

A. STOP OR ARREST?

Police often find it necessary to restrain an individual from moving away from a particular place. They might do so to protect themselves or others from harm. They might do so to investigate a completed crime or to prevent an ongoing or future one. As we saw in Chapter 2, not all of these restraints are equally intrusive, and the different levels of restraint are subject to different legal controls. Some are consensual encounters, some are stops, and some are arrests. How do legal systems distinguish the different types of police efforts to control the movement of citizens? Answers to this question appear in statutes, in cases, and in the interaction between the two.

■ NEVADA REVISED STATUTES §171.123

1. Any peace officer may detain any person whom the officer encounters under circumstances which reasonably indicate that the person has committed, is committing or is about to commit a crime. . . .

4. A person must not be detained longer than is reasonably necessary to effect the purposes of this section, and in no event longer than 60 minutes. The detention must not extend beyond the place or the immediate vicinity of the place where the detention was first effected, unless the person is arrested.

■ ARKANSAS RULE OF CRIMINAL PROCEDURE 3.1

A law enforcement officer lawfully present in any place may, in the performance of his duties, stop and detain any person who he reasonably suspects is committing, has committed, or is about to commit (1) a felony, or (2) a misdemeanor involving danger of forcible injury to persons or of appropriation of or damage to property, if such action is reasonably necessary either to obtain or verify the identification of the person or to determine the lawfulness of his conduct. An officer acting under this rule may require the person to remain in or near such place in the officer's presence for a period of not more than 15 minutes or for such time as is reasonable under the circumstances. At the end of such period the person detained shall be released without further restraint, or arrested and charged with an offense.

■ In re M.E.B.

638 A.2d 1123 (D.C. 1993)

King, J.

Appellant, who was 16 years of age at the time of the offense, was found guilty of second-degree murder based largely upon his confession. On appeal he claims that the confession should have been suppressed because it was tainted by the illegal arrest that preceded it. We conclude that the confession was properly admitted by the trial judge. Accordingly, we affirm.

On May 31, 1990, Lloyd Copeland was shot twice at the doorway of a laundromat . . . at approximately 2:35 P.M. He was pronounced dead shortly afterward. [Within 15 minutes, police on the scene broadcast a lookout for a black male, 17 to 18 years old, wearing a black Guess jean outfit with shorts and a white T-shirt. The suspect was 5′8″, with a slim build, dark complexion, and a "Philly" style haircut. At 3:07, a citizen named Tracy Harris called the police to say that she had seen the suspect on Joliet Street, wearing Guess jeans and a Bart Simpson T-shirt. She also said that the suspect was standing with another male, wearing a black and white T-shirt. Homicide Detective Pamela Reed interviewed Harris, who said that she had been inside the store next door to the laundromat when she heard shots. Harris saw A., then a 14-year-old juvenile, whom she knew, standing next to the decedent's body. She also said that the person she had seen with A. on Joliet Street (later identified as M.E.B.) had also been with A. just before the shooting occurred.] Detective Reed informed the dispatcher of the information she had received from Harris and the dispatcher rebroadcast that information. . . .

After interviewing Harris and calling the dispatcher, Detective Reed went to the scene of the shooting, where she interviewed other witnesses. It was then she learned that immediately before the shooting the decedent and two other young males had been engaged in an argument inside the laundromat. One witness informed Detective Reed that the gunman was one of the two males who had argued with decedent. . . .

At 3:50 P.M., [before Detective Reed had relayed her new information to the dispatcher,] Officer Pierce and Officer Strong took A. and appellant (who was wearing a black and white shirt) into custody. . . . The two were told that they were not under arrest. They were both handcuffed and then transported to the crime scene 10-15 blocks away. They remained at the crime scene for 5-10 minutes, and then were directed to go to a location on Galveston Street, a trip which took another 2-3 minutes, where Harris identified both A. and appellant as the two she had seen earlier. Before the identification procedures were conducted, however, A. informed Detective Reed that appellant was the shooter. Thereafter, appellant was placed under arrest and transported to the homicide division office where he confessed that he had shot the decedent.

[Before trial, M.E.B. moved to suppress the confession, claiming that it was the product of an illegal arrest. The trial judge denied the motion, and appellant was convicted. He now contends that] (1) the restraints to which he was subjected, between the time he was stopped on the street through the time of the identification, constituted an arrest, which can be supported only by a showing of probable cause (which was concededly lacking); [and] (2) that none of the information received by Detective Reed after the broadcast initiated by her may be used in determining whether the information available rose to the level of reasonable suspicion. . . .

The question presented here . . . is whether the police conduct, in handcuffing appellant, placing him in the rear of the police vehicle, and driving him from the point where he was stopped on the street to other locations for identification purposes, converted the *Terry* stop into an arrest requiring probable cause. As noted, the government concedes, and we agree, that there was insufficient evidence, at the time appellant was stopped, to establish probable cause. Thus, if the seizure of M.E.B. went beyond an investigative stop and amounted to an arrest, then the police conduct was unlawful. We conclude that it did not.

Before we address this point, we find it helpful to consider the differences between the purpose for an arrest on one hand, and a *Terry* stop on the other. Generally, an arrest is effected when the police have made a determination to charge the suspect with a criminal offense and custody is maintained to permit the arrestee to be formally charged and brought before the court. A *Terry* seizure, on the other hand, involves a more temporary detention, designed to last only until a preliminary investigation either generates probable cause or results in the release of the suspect. There is no evidence that the officers meant to formally charge A. and appellant when they put them into the police vehicle. In fact, although this is not controlling, A. and appellant were specifically told they were not under arrest.[2] Here the two detainees were only wanted "for questioning," a phrase incompatible with an intent to arrest.

2. The police may not, however, in the absence of probable cause, take someone into custody for purposes of interrogation in the hopes that something incriminating will be elicited. See Dunaway v. New York, 442 U.S. 200 (1979) (detention to conduct a custodial interrogation — regardless of the label applied to the detention — is an arrest which must be supported by probable cause).

We have held that *Terry* permits the police to transport a suspect, especially one thought to be involved in a serious felony, from the place of apprehension to another location for identification purposes. The trial court found that between 12 and 17 minutes elapsed between the initial stop and the identification. [T]he trial court concluded that since it was necessary to transport appellant approximately 14-19 blocks to two separate locations, the passage of time did not convert the detention to an arrest.

The measure of the scope of permissible police action in any investigative stop depends on whether the police conduct was reasonable under the circumstances. Here, the police first transported appellant to the scene of the shooting, a trip that took four to five minutes. Had the identification procedures occurred then, it would be clear that . . . no arrest would be considered to have occurred. Upon arriving at that location, however, it took the officers between five and ten minutes to learn that the prospective identification witnesses were somewhere else. It then took two to three minutes to reach the second location, where the identification procedures promptly took place. The trial judge found that, under the circumstances, the delays were reasonable [and] concluded that the police conduct, in so transporting appellant, did not convert the custody status of appellant from a "detention for investigation" to a "formal arrest." We find no basis for concluding otherwise.

Nor do we believe that the handcuffing of appellant during the period he was in the scout car, under these circumstances, changed the character of his custody. Although we have never addressed the question of whether handcuffing a detainee converts a *Terry* detention to an arrest, we have observed that the "protection of the officer making the stop . . . is of paramount importance. It has been called the rationale of *Terry*." Here . . . the police had reasonable grounds to suspect that appellant and his companion were involved in a murder that had occurred just over an hour earlier. It appears to be undisputed that the police followed their usual practice and frisked both appellant and A. before they were handcuffed. Officer Pierce testified that he told both A. and appellant that they were not under arrest. They were then placed in the car to be transported.

The cases uniformly hold that the officers' safety is a significant factor to be weighed in determining whether the restraint chosen by the officers converts the stop to an arrest. Here the two detainees were suspected of possible involvement in a murder, and they were to be transported, in the back of a patrol car, for a dozen or more blocks. We cannot say that the additional restraint caused by the handcuffing was such an intrusion that the handcuffing transformed the character of the restraint to an arrest. We have assumed that the two were frisked, but even a frisk does not ensure that weapons will be discovered. See Nelson v. United States, 601 A.2d 582 (D.C. 1991) (pat down by arresting officer discovered no weapon; full search by transporting officer discovered a knife in arrestee's pocket). We are satisfied, therefore, that there was a significant basis in this record for the trial court to conclude the handcuffing was a reasonable precaution under the circumstances.

We note also that other courts have generally upheld the use of handcuffs in the context of a *Terry* stop where it was reasonably necessary to protect the officers' safety or to thwart a suspect's attempt to flee. In short, handcuffing the detainee, like length of detention, place of detention, and other considerations, is simply one factor, among many, that the trial judge must consider in weighing whether a detention for investigation crossed the line into the realm of arrest. We are satisfied that [the trial judge] properly weighed those factors in ruling that the line had not been crossed, and that no arrest had taken place until after the identification procedures were completed, and A. had implicated appellant.

[We also must] determine whether the information obtained by Detective Reed, after she initiated her first broadcast, may be considered in assessing the adequacy of the basis for a *Terry* stop and detention. Appellant contends that it may not be considered, because a later broadcast, taking into account the new information, was not communicated to the officers who stopped A. and appellant on the street. Specifically, appellant argues that the information learned by Detective Reed after her broadcast, namely that two people, one of whom might reasonably have been appellant, were arguing with decedent inside the laundromat just before the decedent was shot by A. at the door of the laundromat, may not be considered when determining whether there were adequate grounds for the stop. The government conceded in its brief that, until Detective Reed received that final piece of information, sufficient grounds for a *Terry* stop were lacking. . . . Thus, if the after-acquired information, relating to M.E.B.'s presence during the argument in the laundromat, cannot be considered in the calculus, then the so-called *Terry* stop was unlawful.

The "collective knowledge" doctrine is firmly established in this jurisdiction in a line of cases going back at least 30 years. . . . The correct test is whether a warrant if sought could have been obtained by law enforcement agency application which disclosed its corporate information, not whether any one particular officer could have obtained it on what information he individually possessed.

Applying that test to the facts of this case, the question becomes, what was the "corporate information" available at the time Officers Pierce and Strong effected the stop? The answer is that the "corporate information" available consisted of information provided by the officers who first arrived on the murder scene; information provided to Detective Reed, both before and after the broadcast (but before the *Terry* stop); and observations made by Officers Pierce and Strong when they found A. and appellant still together, approximately 40 minutes after they were last seen by Harris on Joliet Street. [T]hat information was sufficient to establish the required reasonable suspicion to support a *Terry* stop and detention. [W]hen faced with a fast moving sequence of events involving a number of police officers, a citizen's rights are protected if, at the time of the intrusion, the information collectively known to the police is constitutionally sufficient to justify that intrusion. . . . For the reasons stated, the judgment of the trial court is affirmed.

Notes

1. *Arrest versus stop: majority position.* The difference between an arrest (requiring probable cause) and an investigative detention (requiring reasonable suspicion) turns on several different factors. Courts look to the amount of time the detention lasts, the techniques (such as handcuffs) used to restrain the suspect, the location of the suspect (including the distance covered during any transportation of the suspect), and what the police officers say and intend about the purposes of the detention. The judicial opinions often say, using a circular definition, that an arrest takes place when a reasonable person would believe that he or she is under arrest. Medford v. State, 13 S.W.3d 769 (Tex. 2000) (arrest is complete "when a person's liberty of movement is successfully restricted or restrained, whether this is achieved by an officer's physical force or the suspect's submission to the officer's authority [and]

only if a reasonable person in the suspect's position would have understood the situation to constitute a restraint on freedom of movement of the degree which the law associates with formal arrest.").

2. *Time of detention.* The amount of time that the police detain a person is among the most important facts in determining whether a seizure amounted to an arrest or merely a stop. In Florida v. Royer, 460 U.S. 491 (1983), the Supreme Court stated that an investigative detention "must be temporary and last no longer than is necessary to effectuate the purpose of the stop." Most states allow for a flexible determination of the time necessary to convert a stop into an arrest. Why do the Nevada statute and the Arkansas rule choose such different time limits (15 minutes and 60 minutes)? Did the legislators in the two states have different concerns in mind? Courts deciding cases in the absence of a statute also pay close attention to the amount of time elapsed. While the absolute number of minutes in a detention is important, courts also judge the length of the detention in light of the purposes of the stop and the time reasonably needed to effectuate those purposes, including the diligence of officers in pursuing the investigation. See United States v. Sharpe, 470 U.S. 675 (1985) (approves of 20-minute automobile stop for purpose of investigating potential narcotics violations); People v. Garcia, 11 P.3d 449 (Colo. 2000) (length of valid investigatory stop measured as time required for officers to diligently complete investigation given complexity of situation and protection of personal safety).

Is the amount of time allowed for an investigative stop the kind of factor amenable to bright-line rules? Is it the kind of factor that can be undermined by the use of general standards such as "reasonableness"? If you were to draft a bright-line rule, would you include an "escape" valve for exceptional situations? If you prefer a rule in this situation, would you want that rule to be determined by the legislature or the courts? Do rules or standards as a class tend to favor prosecution or defense?

3. *Conditions of detention.* What can be more typical of arrest than being handcuffed and placed in the back of a police cruiser? If this is true, how can the District of Columbia and the majority of state courts find that being handcuffed and placed in the back of a cruiser does not, alone, convert an investigative stop into an arrest? See State v. Blackmore, 925 P.2d 1347 (Ariz. 1996) (burglary suspect stopped at gunpoint, handcuffed, placed in back seat of police cruiser; no arrest). Which is more indicative of arrest, the handcuffs or the seat in the police car? Would you support a bright-line rule stating that handcuffs = arrest?

4. *Location of detention.* Why do both the Arkansas rule and the Nevada statute require that the detained person remain in the vicinity of the initial stop? Most of the cases on this question allow officers to transport a suspect to some other location nearby to complete an investigation, but longer trips can convert the stop into an arrest. Taking a suspect to the police station is also a key factor in the cases. Can a person be taken to the police station and still not be under arrest? See Dunaway v. New York, 442 U.S. 200 (1979) (recognizing possibility of nonarrest detention based on reasonable suspicion for questioning at police station; however, arrest without probable cause occurred here where defendant was taken to police station for questioning without being told he was under arrest); Collins-Draine v. Knief, 617 N.E.2d 679 (Ill. 2000) (bounds of stop exceeded if officer unnecessarily holds suspect or transports suspect to police station; holding at jail for five hours).

5. *The "collective" or "corporate" knowledge doctrine.* The court in *M.E.B.* discussed briefly the "collective knowledge" doctrine. Like the District of Columbia court, most courts will assess probable cause or reasonable suspicion based on the collective

information the police have, even if no individual officer or department holds all of that information at the moment of a stop or arrest. See State v. Richards, 588 N.W.2d 594 (S.D. 1998). Does this doctrine give the police too much opportunity for post hoc rationalization of the individual officer's decision to conduct a search? What, if anything, is wrong with justifying a search after the fact, based on events that truly did occur?

B. ARREST WARRANTS

In Chapter 3, we explored the various ways that the law supposedly encourages the use of a judicial warrant to authorize an officer to conduct a full search. Yet, despite the often-stated "preference" for warrants, most searches take place without a warrant. The same is true for arrests. There are legal rules encouraging or requiring warrants before a police officer can arrest a person in some settings (in particular, arrests made in a home). But in reality, most arrests take place without a warrant. As you read the following materials on the coverage of the warrant requirement for arrests, keep in mind the types of arrests that these rules do not cover.

■ COMMENTARIES ON THE LAWS OF ENGLAND WILLIAM BLACKSTONE

Vol. 3, p.288 (1768)

An arrest must be by corporal seising or touching the defendant's body; after which the bailiff may justify breaking open the house in which he is, to take him: otherwise he has no such power; but must watch his opportunity to arrest him. For every man's house is looked upon by the law to be his castle of defence and asylum, wherein he should suffer no violence. Which principle is carried so far in the civil law, that for the most part not so much as a common citation or summons, much less an arrest, can be executed upon a man within his own walls.

■ STATE v. JASON KIPER

532 N.W.2d 698 (Wis. 1995)

GESKE, J.

[Jason Kiper] was arrested and convicted for possession with intent to deliver a controlled substance. However, Kiper argues that his arrest and conviction were based upon evidence illegally seized at his home when a police officer sought to execute an arrest warrant for a third party, David J. Wanie. According to Kiper, the evidence seized should have been suppressed because . . . prior to his entry, the police officer lacked probable cause to believe that Wanie resided in the apartment[, and] no exigent circumstances existed at the time the police officer entered the apartment, establishing an exception to the warrant requirement. . . .

The issue before this court is whether police entry into Kiper's home is controlled by Steagald v. United States, 451 U.S. 204 (1981), or Payton v. New York, 445 U.S. 573 (1980). [In *Payton,* the Supreme Court held that an arrest warrant carries with it the implicit authority to search the home of the arrestee if there is reason to believe the suspect is inside. In *Steagald,* the Court held that a search warrant is ordinarily required to enter the home of a third party to execute an arrest warrant for a person believed to be present there.]

For the reasons set forth below, we . . . hold that *Steagald* is controlling in this case. Accordingly, the police officer was required to obtain a search warrant prior to entering Kiper's apartment to execute an arrest warrant for Wanie. Absent the search warrant, the police entry was illegal, and any and all statements Kiper made to the police, as well as any evidence seized from Kiper's apartment, ought to have been suppressed. Further, neither consent nor exigent circumstances existed at the time of the police officer's entry which would have established an exception to the requirement for the search warrant.

[Wanie was convicted of permitting an unauthorized minor to drive, and fined $55. When Wanie failed to pay the fine, a warrant issued for his arrest. On December 31, about a month after issuance of the warrant, Green Bay police officer Todd Thomas sought to execute the arrest warrant. The face of the warrant indicated two addresses, but Thomas knew that Wanie no longer lived at either address. Instead, Thomas went to Kiper's home, believing he might find Wanie there since he had seen him at the same location six weeks earlier while on another call. Thomas knocked on the front door, and a young man named Jason Mianecki opened the door.]

Thomas asked if "David Wane was there," mispronouncing Wanie's last name. Shortly after Mianecki responded "no," Thomas saw the person he believed to be Wanie inside the apartment, near the doorway. Thomas then said that a warrant had been issued for "Mr. Wane." Wanie responded that "Wane" wasn't there and walked away from the doorway area toward the kitchen. [However, Thomas recognized Wanie (and his distinctive haircut) from a photograph he had consulted in his squad car, and from an encounter six weeks earlier, so] he entered the apartment and followed Wanie down the hallway toward the bedrooms. At that point, Thomas asked Wanie to identify himself, which he did.

While in the hallway, Wanie attempted to close one of the bedroom doors. Thomas told him to stop and, through the partially closed doorway, saw drug paraphernalia and smelled the odor of marijuana. Thomas entered the bedroom, told Wanie to sit on the couch, and saw Kiper standing next to a number of items located on the floor, including a metal lock box, scales, a bong, and drugs.

[A second officer arrived on the scene, and they took Wanie and Kiper into custody. The trial court denied Kiper's motion to suppress the evidence Thomas had discovered inside the apartment.] The resolution of this case requires a three-part analysis: (1) did the police have probable cause to believe Wanie was a resident of and present in Kiper's apartment prior to the time of entry; (2) are the facts of this case controlled by *Steagald,* such that a search warrant was required to enter Kiper's apartment; and (3) did exigent circumstances exist at the time Thomas entered the apartment, establishing an exception to the warrant requirement?

. . . Courts generally have assumed that the quantum of evidence required to show probable cause is the same whether one is concerned with an arrest warrant or a search warrant. It is true that both types of warrants serve to subject the probable-cause determination of police officers to judicial review and assessment. However, an arrest warrant and a search warrant each protect distinct interests under the fourth amendment. For example, requiring a warrant to arrest protects an individual from unreasonable seizure because a magistrate or judge may issue the document only upon a showing that probable cause exists to believe the subject sought has committed a criminal offense. . . .

By contrast, the prerequisite of a warrant to search "serves to protect the privacy interest of the individual in his home and possessions from the unjustified intrusion of the police by requiring a showing of probable cause to believe that the legitimate object of a search is situated in a particular place." [The] duty of the judge issuing the warrant is to make a practical, common-sense decision whether . . . there is a fair probability that contraband or evidence of a crime will be found in a particular place.

[T]he evidence supports a finding that Thomas lacked probable cause to believe Wanie was a resident of Kiper's apartment on December 31, 1992. According to his own testimony, Thomas knew only that Wanie had moved from the two addresses noted on the face of the arrest warrant, had no known present address, and that Wanie was present at Kiper's apartment six weeks earlier. Without more substantial evidence, any belief held by Thomas that Wanie may have resided at the apartment constituted no more than mere suspicion. Additionally, the fact that Wanie approached the doorway area from inside the apartment after Mianecki answered the door does not, without more, prove that Wanie exercised control or dominion over the premises. Instead, Wanie's movement toward the doorway merely confirms his presence in the apartment. Because there is insufficient evidence to conclude that Wanie resided in Kiper's apartment, we must now apply a *Steagald* analysis. . . .

In 1980, the Supreme Court decided *Payton,* a [challenge to] New York statutes authorizing police officers to enter a private residence without a warrant to make a routine felony arrest. [Payton] was sought by police as a suspect in the murder of a gas station manager. When the police went to Payton's apartment to arrest him, they did not have either an arrest warrant or a search warrant. Hearing music playing inside the apartment, they called for emergency assistance and subsequently used crowbars to break open the door and enter the apartment. Upon entry, the police discovered that no one was present; however, they did seize a .30-caliber shell casing which was later admitted into evidence during Payton's murder trial.

[T]he Supreme Court held that, absent consent or exigent circumstances, the fourth amendment prohibits the police from effecting a warrantless entry into a suspect's home in order to make a routine felony arrest without an arrest warrant. In particular, the Court reasoned:

> The Fourth Amendment protects the individual's privacy in a variety of settings. In none is the zone of privacy more clearly defined than when bounded by the unambiguous physical dimensions of an individual's home — a zone that finds its roots in clear and specific constitutional terms: "The right of the people to be secure in their . . . houses . . . shall not be violated." That language unequivocally establishes the proposition that at the very core [of the Fourth Amendment] stands the right of a man to retreat into his own home and there be free from unreasonable governmental intrusion. . . . In terms that apply equally to seizures of property and to seizures of persons, the Fourth Amendment has drawn a firm line at the entrance to the house. Absent exigent circumstances, that threshold may not reasonably be crossed without a warrant.

In 1981, the Supreme Court [in *Steagald*] extended the discussion of the right of privacy in the home to include the concerns of third parties by considering the issue of "whether an arrest warrant — as opposed to a search warrant — is adequate to protect the Fourth Amendment interests of persons not named in the warrant, when their homes are searched without their consent and in the absence of exigent circumstances." [F]ederal agents learned from an informant that the subject of an arrest warrant, Ricky Lyons, could be found at Steagald's home during a certain 24-hour period. The agents entered the home without consent, searching for Lyons. Lyons was not found. However, the agents discovered cocaine, which discovery led to Steagald's prosecution on federal drug charges. [The Supreme Court held] that, absent consent or exigent circumstances, the agents were required to secure a search warrant to enter Steagald's home to look for Lyons.

[T]he agents used the arrest warrant for Lyons as legal authority to enter Steagald's home, based on a belief that Lyons might be a guest there. Regardless of how reasonable this belief might have been, it was never subjected to the detached scrutiny of a judicial officer. As a consequence,

> while the warrant in this case may have protected Lyons from an unreasonable seizure, it did absolutely nothing to protect petitioner's privacy interest in being free from an unreasonable invasion and search of his home. Instead, petitioner's only protection from an illegal entry and search was the agent's personal determination of probable cause. In the absence of exigent circumstances, we have consistently held that such judicially untested determinations are not reliable enough to justify an entry into a person's home to arrest him without a warrant, or a search of a home for objects in the absence of a search warrant.

[I]f only an arrest warrant were required in this type of situation, police would be free to search the homes of all the suspect's friends and acquaintances. Finally, the Court stated that an underlying purpose of the fourth amendment was to protect against abuses by law enforcement officers similar to that experienced in the Colonies with writs of assistance: police were given the unfettered discretion to choose which homes to search. . . .

Having already held that prior to his entry Thomas did not have probable cause to believe Wanie was a resident of Kiper's apartment, we now conclude that Thomas needed a search warrant to enter the apartment to look for and execute the arrest warrant for Wanie. Thomas could not use the arrest warrant as legal authority to enter Kiper's home based on the simple belief that Wanie might be there, because that belief was never subjected to the neutral and detached scrutiny of a judicial officer.

The state argues that regardless of the scope of the arrest warrant's authorization, Thomas was able to make a lawful and warrantless entry into Kiper's apartment on the grounds of exigent circumstances. We agree that if exigent circumstances developed during an attempt to identify and arrest Wanie, Thomas could have lawfully entered the apartment without a search warrant. However, the facts of this case do not indicate that any exigency existed at any time during Thomas's encounter with Wanie at Kiper's apartment.

The basic test to determine whether exigent circumstances exist is an objective one: Whether a police officer under the circumstances known to the officer at the time reasonably believes that delay in procuring a warrant would gravely endanger life or risk destruction of evidence or greatly enhance the likelihood of the suspect's escape. As a result, this court has identified four factors which constitute the exigent circumstances required for a warrantless entry: (1) an arrest made in "hot pursuit,"

(2) a threat to safety of a suspect or others, (3) a risk that evidence will be destroyed, and (4) a likelihood that the suspect will flee.

The state claims that exigent circumstances were created . . . when Thomas encountered Wanie, because the officer feared Wanie might try to evade custody by fleeing through a rear apartment exit. However, we conclude that the facts of this case did not combine to create "extreme emergency conditions"[18] or the equivalent of "hot pursuit," justifying a warrantless police entry. Green Bay police were in receipt of an arrest warrant for Wanie nearly a month before he was seen at Kiper's apartment on December 31, 1992. Further, there is nothing in Thomas's testimony during the suppression hearing to indicate that police regarded Wanie's apprehension as a primary objective.

We acknowledge that a fundamental concern for police "is that persons, as opposed to objects, are inherently mobile, and thus officers seeking to effect an arrest may be forced to return to the magistrate several times as the subject of the arrest warrant moves from place to place." *Steagald.* However, Wanie's mobility did not create an exigency or an impediment to law enforcement as much as it created an inconvenience for police, who, once aware of his presence at Kiper's apartment, were required to secure a search warrant to gain entry. Additionally, Thomas testified that the presence of Wanie in Kiper's apartment posed no threat to the safety of anyone present. . . .

In Welsh v. Wisconsin, 466 U.S. 740 (1984), the United States Supreme Court considered the issue of whether "the Fourth Amendment prohibits the police from making a warrantless night entry of a person's home in order to arrest him for a nonjailable traffic offense." The facts revealed that Welsh was observed erratically driving his car, causing it to swerve off the road into a field. Even though a witness suggested that he remain with the car and wait for assistance, Welsh walked away from the scene. Police checked the car's registration and, without obtaining a warrant, proceeded to Welsh's home, wherein he was arrested for driving a motor vehicle while under the influence of an intoxicant. . . . Though probable cause existed to arrest Welsh, the Supreme Court concluded that the warrantless entry into Welsh's home violated the fourth amendment because the police did not establish the existence of exigent circumstances. The Court reasoned:

> Our hesitation in finding exigent circumstances, especially when warrantless arrests in the home are at issue, is particularly appropriate when the underlying offense for which there is probable cause to arrest is relatively minor. . . .

Applying the *Welsh* standard to the instant case, we conclude that Thomas was not faced with exigent circumstances during his encounter with Wanie at Kiper's apartment. The arrest warrant for Wanie resulted from his failure to pay a $55 fine for violating a municipal ordinance. . . .

Accordingly, we reverse the decision of the court of appeals. Under *Steagald,* Thomas was required to obtain a search warrant prior to entering Kiper's apartment to execute an arrest warrant for Wanie. Absent the warrant, consent or exigent circumstances, police entry into the apartment was illegal, and all statements Kiper

18. In United States v. Santana, 427 U.S. 38 (1976), the Supreme Court stated that "hot pursuit" may justify a warrantless entry into one's home to execute an arrest because the police must act quickly to apprehend a fleeing criminal suspect or to prevent the imminent destruction of evidence.

made to the police, as well as any evidence seized from his apartment, should have been suppressed. . . .

STEINMETZ, J., dissenting.

[Under] the totality of the circumstances, Officer Thomas had probable cause to believe that Wanie was residing in Kiper's home. Officer Thomas had confronted Wanie in the same apartment approximately six weeks earlier. From this confrontation, he thought that Wanie might be residing there. This suspicion alone would fall short of probable cause to believe that Wanie was residing at the apartment. However, Officer Thomas's suspicion rose to the level of probable cause when Wanie, who had no known present address, emerged from inside the apartment, approached Officer Thomas at the apartment door, and told him that "Wane" was not there. Wanie's presence in the apartment and his response to Officer Thomas, after Mianecki had already acknowledged Officer Thomas's presence, is consistent with a reasonable inference that Wanie had dominion or control over the premises. . . .

Even if I were to conclude, which I do not, that Officer Thomas was required to secure a search warrant, I would nonetheless disagree with the majority's conclusion that exigent circumstances did not exist justifying Officer Thomas's entry into the apartment. I would conclude that Officer Thomas's observation of Wanie in the doorway coupled with his reasonable fear that Wanie might flee out a back door to the apartment provides a sufficient basis for a finding of exigent circumstances. A police officer who has an arrest warrant for a suspect should not be forced to stand outside the open front door of the suspect's residence and watch as the suspect walks out the back door. Regardless of the severity of the offense underlying the arrest warrant, if the officer is in possession of an arrest warrant, the officer may enter the home and arrest the suspect. Under these circumstances, the severity of the underlying offense is simply irrelevant. The arrest warrant gives the officer legal authority to enter the premises and arrest the suspect. For these reasons, I dissent. . . .

Notes

1. *Warrants for arrests in a home: majority position.* The federal constitution allows a police officer to make an arrest in a public place without a warrant. When the arrest takes place in a home, however, warrants become more important. As the *Kiper* decision from Wisconsin explained, the federal constitution requires only an arrest warrant to justify entry into a suspect's home to carry out the arrest, along with some "reason to believe" the suspect is within. Payton v. New York, 445 U.S. 573 (1980); Kirk v. Louisiana, 122 S.Ct. 2458 (2002) (reaffirms *Payton*). This is often the first place a police officer will look when trying to execute an arrest warrant. When an officer enters a third party's home to arrest a suspect, he must have a search warrant, based on probable cause to believe that the suspect (the object of the search) is present in that location. Virtually all state courts have used this same framework under their state constitutions. See Vasquez v. State, 739 S.W.2d 37 (Tex. Crim. App. 1987).

In what ways are arrest warrants different from search warrants? Do you view *Kiper* (and the Supreme Court decisions it relies upon — *Steagald, Payton,* and *Welsh*) as highly protective of suspects' rights? Nonsuspects' rights? Which is the most important case in terms of limiting police search powers while pursuing an arrest?

2. *Warrantless arrests in public places.* The U.S. Constitution does not require warrants for arrests made in a public place, even if the arresting officer could easily have obtained a warrant. In United States v. Watson, 423 U.S. 411 (1976), the Court upheld statutes and regulations granting Postal Service officers the power to make warrantless arrests for felonies. The Court deferred to Congress's judgment about the meaning of the Fourth Amendment and also relied on "the ancient common-law rule that a peace officer was permitted to arrest without a warrant for a misdemeanor or felony committed in his presence as well as for a felony not committed in his presence if there was reasonable ground for making the arrest," noting that the common law rule had prevailed under state and federal law. See N.D. Cent. Code §29-06-15 (allowing warrantless arrests for misdemeanors only when they are committed in the presence of the arresting officer; exceptions for traffic offenses and domestic violence assaults).

3. *Is crime seriousness a basis for exigency?* Why should exigent circumstances for entering homes vary based on the seriousness of the alleged crime committed? Is the *Welsh* rule biased in favor of those socioeconomic classes more likely to commit "minor" offenses, such as driving while intoxicated?

C. POLICE DISCRETION IN THE ARREST DECISION

Police officers remain the critical decisionmakers for arrests. This section considers recent legal reforms that could have contradictory effects on police discretion in arrests. First, statutes have expanded the power of the police to arrest a person without adhering to traditional common law and statutory requirements that the police obtain an arrest warrant in some contexts. In most states, these reforms have eliminated the need for an arrest warrant in most settings. Second, while police officers generally have discretion to decide whether to arrest, statutes and police department rules in special areas now guide the officers in their arrest decisions once there is probable cause to believe that the person has committed a crime. Prominent examples of both of these trends — one expanding the officer's discretion to arrest and the other restricting it — appear in cases involving domestic violence. We begin with the traditional common law rule, which requires a warrant to arrest a person for lesser crimes committed outside the officer's presence.

■ COMMENTARIES ON THE LAWS OF ENGLAND
WILLIAM BLACKSTONE
Vol. 4, p.287 (1769)

A warrant may be granted . . . ordinarily by justices of the peace. This they may do in any cases where they have a jurisdiction over the offence [and] this extends undoubtedly to all treasons, felonies, and breaches of the peace; and also to all such offences as they have power to punish by statute. [The constable] may, without warrant, arrest any one for a breach of the peace, committed in his view, and carry him before a justice of the peace. And, in case of felony actually committed, or a dangerous wounding whereby felony is likely to ensue, he may upon probable suspicion arrest the felon.

■ OKLAHOMA STATUTES TIT. 22, §40.3

A. A peace officer shall not discourage a victim of rape, forcible sodomy or domestic abuse from pressing charges against the assailant of the victim.

B. A peace officer may arrest without a warrant a person anywhere, including his place of residence, if the peace officer has probable cause to believe the person within the preceding seventy-two hours has committed an act of domestic abuse . . . although the assault did not take place in the presence of the peace officer. A peace officer may not arrest a person pursuant to this section without first observing a recent physical injury to, or an impairment of the physical condition of, the alleged victim. . . .

■ CONNECTICUT GENERAL STATUTES §46b-38b

(a) Whenever a peace officer determines upon speedy information that a family violence crime . . . has been committed within his jurisdiction, he shall arrest the person or persons suspected of its commission and charge such person or persons with the appropriate crime. The decision to arrest and charge shall not (1) be dependent on the specific consent of the victim, (2) consider the relationship of the parties or (3) be based solely on a request by the victim.

(b) No peace officer investigating an incident of family violence shall threaten, suggest or otherwise indicate the arrest of all parties for the purpose of discouraging requests for law enforcement intervention by any party. Where complaints are received from two or more opposing parties, the officer shall evaluate each complaint separately to determine whether he should seek a warrant for an arrest.

■ IOWA CODE §236.12

1. If a peace officer has reason to believe that domestic abuse has occurred, the officer shall use all reasonable means to prevent further abuse including but not limited to the following:

a. If requested, remaining on the scene as long as there is a danger to an abused person's physical safety without the presence of a peace officer, [or] assisting the person in leaving the residence.

b. Assisting an abused person in obtaining medical treatment necessitated by an assault. . . .

c. Providing an abused person with immediate and adequate notice of the person's rights. The notice shall consist of handing the person a copy of the following statement written in English and Spanish, asking the person to read the card and whether the person understands the rights:

> You have the right to ask the court for the following help on a temporary basis:
>
> (1) Keeping your attacker away from you, your home and your place of work.
>
> (2) The right to stay at your home without interference from your attacker.
>
> (3) Getting custody of children and obtaining support for yourself and your minor children if your attacker is legally required to provide such support.
>
> (4) Professional counseling for you, the children who are members of the household, and the defendant.

You have the right to seek help from the court to seek a protective order with or without the assistance of legal representation. . . .

You have the right to file criminal charges for threats, assaults, or other related crimes. You have the right to seek restitution against your attacker for harm to yourself or your property.

If you are in need of medical treatment, you have the right to request that the officer present assist you in obtaining transportation to the nearest hospital or otherwise assist you.

If you believe that police protection is needed for your physical safety, you have the right to request that the officer present remain at the scene until you and other affected parties can leave or until safety is otherwise ensured.

The notice shall also contain the telephone numbers of safe shelters, support groups, or crisis lines operating in the area.

2. a. A peace officer may, with or without a warrant, arrest a person . . . if, upon investigation, . . . the officer has probable cause to believe that a domestic abuse assault has been committed which did not result in any injury to the alleged victim.

b. Except as otherwise provided in subsection 3, a peace officer shall, with or without a warrant, arrest a person [if] the officer has probable cause to believe that a domestic abuse assault has been committed which resulted in the alleged victim's suffering a bodily injury.

c. Except as otherwise provided in subsection 3, a peace officer shall, with or without a warrant, arrest a person [if] the officer has probable cause to believe that a domestic abuse assault has been committed with the intent to inflict a serious injury.

d. Except as otherwise provided in subsection 3, a peace officer shall, with or without a warrant, arrest a person [if] the officer has probable cause to believe that a domestic abuse assault has been committed and that the alleged abuser used or displayed a dangerous weapon in connection with the assault.

3. As described in subsection 2, paragraph "b," "c," or "d," the peace officer shall arrest the person whom the peace officer believes to be the primary physical aggressor. . . . Persons acting with justification . . . are not subject to mandatory arrest. In identifying the primary physical aggressor, a peace officer shall consider the need to protect victims of domestic abuse, the relative degree of injury or fear inflicted on the persons involved, and any history of domestic abuse between the persons involved. A peace officer's identification of the primary physical aggressor shall not be based on the consent of the victim to any subsequent prosecution or on the relationship of the persons involved in the incident, and shall not be based solely upon the absence of visible indications of injury or impairment.

■ THE MINNEAPOLIS DOMESTIC VIOLENCE EXPERIMENT
LAWRENCE SHERMAN AND RICHARD BERK

(1984)

[T]he Minneapolis domestic violence experiment was the first scientifically controlled test of the effects of arrest for any crime. It found that arrest was the most effective of three standard methods police use to reduce domestic violence. The other police methods — attempting to counsel both parties or sending assailants away from home for several hours — were found to be considerably less effective in deterring future violence in the cases examined. [The] preponderance of evidence in the Minneapolis study strongly suggests that the police should use arrest in most domestic violence cases. . . .

Policing Domestic Assaults

Police have typically been reluctant to make arrests for domestic violence, as well as for a wide range of other kinds of offenses, unless a victim demands an arrest, a suspect insults an officer, or other factors are present. [Two surveys] of battered women who tried to have their domestic assailants arrested report that arrest occurred in only ten percent [and] three percent of the cases. Surveys of police agencies in Illinois and New York found explicit policies against arrest in the majority of the agencies surveyed. Despite the fact that violence is reported to be present in one-third to two-thirds of all domestic disturbances police respond to, police department data show arrests in only five percent of those disturbances in Oakland, . . . and six percent in Los Angeles County. . . .

The apparent preference of many police for separating the parties rather than arresting the offender has been attacked from two directions over the past 15 years. The original critique came from clinical psychologists who agreed that police should rarely make arrests in domestic assault cases and argued that police should mediate the disputes responsible for the violence. A highly publicized demonstration project teaching police special counseling skills for family crisis intervention failed to show a reduction in violence, but was interpreted as a success nonetheless. By 1977, a national survey of police agencies with 100 or more officers found that over 70 percent reported a family crisis intervention training program in operation. Although it is not clear whether these programs reduced separation and increased mediation, a decline in arrests was noted for some. Indeed, many sought explicitly to *reduce* the number of arrests.

By the mid 1970's, police practices were criticized from the opposite direction by feminist groups. Just as psychologists succeeded in having many police agencies respond to domestic violence as "half social work and half police work," feminists began to argue that police put "too much emphasis on the social work aspect and not enough on the criminal." Widely publicized lawsuits in New York and Oakland sought to compel police to make arrests in every case of domestic assault, and state legislatures were lobbied successfully to reduce the evidentiary requirements needed for police to make arrests for misdemeanor domestic assaults. Some legislatures are now considering statutes requiring police to make arrests in these cases.

The feminist critique was bolstered by a study showing that for 85 percent of a sample of spouse killings, police had intervened at least once in the preceding two years. For 54 percent of those homicides, police had intervened five or more times. But it was impossible to determine from the data whether making more or fewer arrests would have reduced the homicide rate.

How the Experiment Was Designed

[To] find which police approach was most effective in deterring future domestic violence, . . . the Minneapolis Police Department agreed to conduct a classic experiment. A classic experiment is a research design that allows scientists to discover the effects of one thing on another by holding constant all other possible causes of those effects. The design of the experiment called for a lottery selection, which ensured that there would be no difference among the three groups of suspects receiving the different police responses. The lottery determined which of the three responses police officers would use on each suspect in a domestic assault case. According to the lottery, a suspect would be arrested, or sent from the scene of the assault for eight hours, or given some form of advice, which could include mediation at an offender's discretion. In the language of the experiment, these responses were called the arrest, send, and advice treatments. The design called for a six-month follow-up period to measure the frequency and seriousness of any future domestic violence in all cases in which the police intervened.

The design applied only to simple (misdemeanor) domestic assaults, where both the suspect and the victim were present when the police arrived. Thus, the experiment included only those cases in which police were empowered, but not required, to make arrests under a recently liberalized Minnesota state law. The police officer must have probable cause to believe that a cohabitant or spouse had assaulted the victim within the past four hours. Police need not have witnessed the assault. Cases of life-threatening or severe injury, usually labeled as a felony (aggravated assault), were excluded from the design.

The design called for each officer to carry a pad of report forms, color coded for the three different police responses. Each time the officers encountered a situation that fit the experiment's criteria, they were to take whatever action was indicated by the report form on the top of the pad. The forms were numbered and arranged for each officer in an order determined by the lottery. . . .

Anticipating something of the background of the victims in the experiment, a predominantly minority, female research staff was employed to contact the victims for a detailed, face-to-face interview, to be followed by telephone follow-up interviews every two weeks for 24 weeks. The interviews were designed primarily to measure the frequency and seriousness of victimizations caused by a suspect after police interventions. The research staff also collected criminal justice reports that mentioned suspects' names during the six-month follow-up period.

Conduct of the Experiment

As is common in field experiments, the actual process in Minneapolis suffered some slippage from the original plan. [The experiment ran from March 17, 1981] until August 1, 1982, and produced 314 case reports. . . . Ninety-nine percent of the suspects targeted for arrest actually were arrested; 78 percent of those scheduled to receive advice did; and 73 percent of those to be sent out of the residence for eight hours actually were sent. One explanation for this pattern . . . is that mediating and sending were more difficult ways for police to control a situation. There was a greater likelihood that an officer might have to resort to arrest as a fallback position. . . .

Results

[Two] measures of repeat violence were used in the experiment. One was a police record of an offender repeating domestic violence during the six-month follow-up period. . . . A second kind of measure came from the interviews in which victims were asked if there had been a repeat incident with the same suspect, broadly defined to include an assault, threatened assault, or property damage. . . .

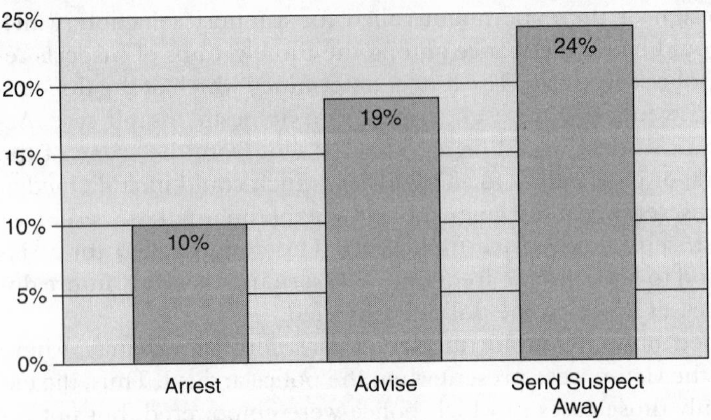

Figure 1. Percentage of Repeat Violence Over Six Months for Each Police Action (Office Records N = 314)

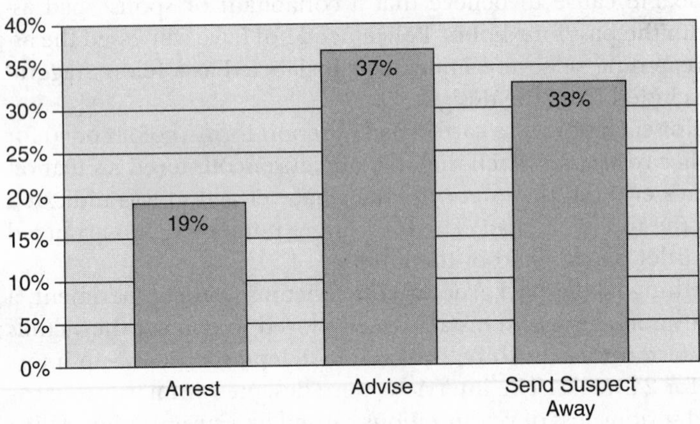

Figure 2. Percentage of Repeat Violence Over Six Months for Each Police Action (Victim Interviews N = 161)

Figure 1 shows the results taken from the police records on subsequent violence. The arrest treatment is clearly an improvement over sending the suspect away, which produced two and a half times as many repeat incidents as arrest. The advice treatment was statistically not distinguishable from the other two police actions.

Figure 2 shows a somewhat different picture. According to the victims' reports of repeat violence, arrest is still the most effective police action. But the advise category, not sending the suspect away, produced the worst results, with almost twice as much violence as arrest. Sending the suspect away produced results that were not statistically distinguishable from the results of the other two actions. It is not clear why the order of the three levels of repeat violence is different for these two ways of measuring the violence. But it is clear that arrest works best by either measure.

Additional statistical analysis showed that these findings were basically the same for all categories of suspects. Regardless of the race, employment status, educational level, criminal history of the suspect, or how long the suspect was in jail when arrested, arrest still had the strongest violence reduction effect. There was one factor, however, that seemed to govern the effectiveness of arrest: whether the police showed interest in the victim's side of the story.

Figure 3 shows what happens to the effect of arrest on repeat violence incidents when the police do or do not take the time to listen to the victim, at least as the victim

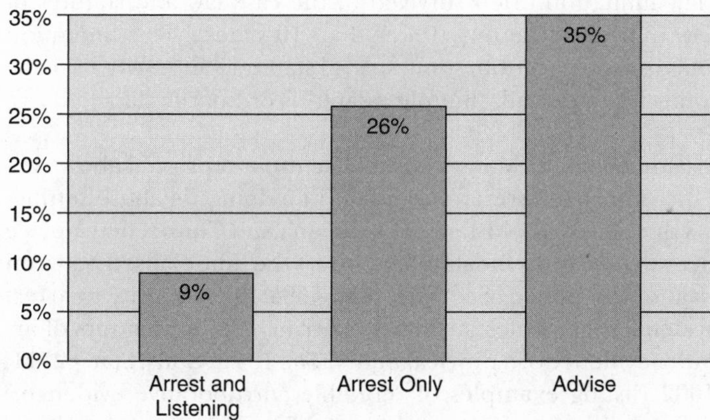

Figure 3. Percentage of Repeat Violence Over Six Months for Each Police Action and Listening to Victim (Victim Interviews N = 194)

perceives it. If police do listen, that reduces the occurrence of repeat violence even more. But if the victims think the police did not take the time to listen, then the level of victim-reported violence is much higher. One interpretation of this finding is that by listening to the victim, the police "empower" her with their strength, letting the suspect know that she can influence their behavior. If police ignore the victim, the suspect may think he was arrested for arbitrary reasons unrelated to the victim and be less deterred from future violence.

Conclusions and Policy Implications

It may be premature to conclude that arrest is always the best way for police to handle domestic violence, or that all suspects in such situations should be arrested. A number of factors suggest a cautious interpretation of the findings, [such as the small sample size, the fact that most arrested suspects in Minneapolis spent the night in jail, and biases in the interview and follow-up process].

But police officers cannot wait for further research to decide how to handle the domestic violence they face each day. They must use the best information available. This experiment provides the only scientifically controlled comparison of different methods of reducing repeat violence. And on the basis of this study alone, police should probably employ arrest in most cases of minor domestic violence. . . .

As a result of the experiment's findings, the Minneapolis Police Department changed its policy on domestic assault in early March of 1984. The policy did not make arrest 100 percent mandatory. But it did require officers to file a written report explaining why they failed to make an arrest when it was legally possible to do so. . . . If the findings are truly generalizeable, the experiment will help ultimately to reduce one of the most common forms of violent crime.

Notes

1. *Common law arrest powers and domestic abuse.* As the passage from Blackstone indicates, officers at common law did not have authority to make a warrantless arrest of a person who committed a misdemeanor out of the presence of the officer, even if the officer had probable cause to believe that the person had committed the

crime. This common law limitation often survived in the case law and statutes of states and is still the law in a few locations (fewer than 10 states). This limitation makes it difficult for police officers, without some special statutory authority, to make arrests in the typical domestic abuse call. "Simple assault" is ordinarily classified as a misdemeanor.

2. *The variety of legislative solutions.* Many statutes, like those reprinted above, expand the authority of the officer to arrest an assailant in a domestic abuse setting. Note the different limits that states (for instance, Oklahoma and Connecticut) place on this expanded arrest power. Why do the statutes address the time elapsed between the injury and the arrival of the police? See N.H. Stat. §594:10 (authority to arrest without warrant for misdemeanor domestic abuse occurring within six hours of arrest). Why do some require evidence of a physical injury? See 18 Pa. Cons. Stat. §2711; W. Va. Code §48-27-1002 (listing examples of "credible corroborative evidence," such as contusions, missing hair, torn clothing, damaged furnishings on premises).

In addition to expanding police authority to arrest in the domestic abuse setting, some of the statutes encourage or require officers to respond in ways other than arresting the assailant. For instance, about a dozen states require the officer on the scene to provide the victim with information about health care and legal protection from further abuse. Why do some statutes call for an automatic warning, such as the one set forth in the Iowa statute? It is also common for statutes to require the officer responding to the call to report the incident to the prosecutor's office, regardless of the arrest decision.

Finally, more than a dozen states have passed statutes encouraging or mandating arrest as the proper police response to evidence of domestic violence. Is the Iowa statute an example of a mandatory statute? While a few statutes only require probable cause that a domestic violence offense has occurred, other statutes impose a number of different preconditions on the mandatory arrest duty of the police. See Utah Code Ann. §77-36-2.2 ("shall arrest" if there is evidence of recent serious injury, or use of dangerous weapon, or probable cause to believe there is potential of continued violence toward victim); Mo. Rev. Stat. §455.085 ("shall" arrest for second incident within 12 hours). Why does Iowa direct a police officer to arrest the person the officer believes to be the "primary physical aggressor," and how does the statute define that term?

The statutes reprinted here do not exhaust the legislative responses to this problem. Other relevant approaches include a Florida statute directing state agencies to collect detailed annual statistics about the enforcement of that state's domestic violence arrest policy and subsequent incidents of violence. See Fla. Stat. §943.1702. Some statutes emphasize training of officers that stresses the criminal nature of domestic abuse rather than the "social work" approach to the problem. Idaho Code §6316.

As the Sherman and Berk study demonstrates, local ordinances or police department policies might adopt a mandatory arrest policy, or a strong preference for arrests, even when state statutes do not. Indeed, about 90 percent of all police departments have policies dealing with domestic violence; about three quarters of the departments have policies to encourage arrest in at least some domestic violence situations. See Bureau of Justice Statistics, Local Police Departments 1999 (May 2001, NCJ 186478); Dallas Police Department General Order 307.01 (officer to submit report explaining reason for making no arrest when there is reason to believe family violence offense has occurred).

3. *Arrest statutes for other crimes.* For some other controversial offenses, statutes in many states provide for arrest powers that are broader than common law arrest doctrine would support. One common example is a statute that approves warrantless arrests whenever a driver violates the traffic code or commits related offenses such as driving under the influence. See N.D. Cent. Code §29-06-15(1)(f). These driving violation arrest statutes find additional authority in the quasicontractual nature of the agreement between the citizen and the state represented by the driver's license: The citizen, it is argued, grants the state additional arrest powers if she exercises the option to drive.

4. *Arrest quotas.* Police department policies *other* than those calling for automatic or presumed arrests in some situations can have a powerful effect on individual officers' arrest decisions. How will officers respond to a departmental policy that evaluates and rewards officers based on the number of arrests they make? See Howie Carr, Arresting Memo Puts State Cops in a Pinch, Boston Herald, Oct. 21, 1998, at 1 (quoting internal memorandum of Massachusetts State Police, reviewing arrest journal and calling for "corrective action" to "increase the level of activity" because arrests are a "valid indicator" but not the only indicator of good performance). Is there a plausible legal basis for challenging a system of "arrest quotas" in court? Disputes over these policies more often arise during labor negotiations between police officer unions and department administrators. See Thomas Ott, Police Sergeants, Lieutenants Say Mentor Unfair, Cleveland Plain Dealer, Feb. 25, 1999, at 4B (describing a labor dispute centering on a system of arrest and ticket quotas).

5. *History and changes in legal rules.* Lawyers typically face questions about the application or validity of a *current* rule. Because they are not trained as historians and have limited time and resources, it can be difficult for lawyers to trace the evolution of policies and rules even over fairly brief periods of time. One of the notable aspects of the Sherman and Berk policy paper is its effective use of recent history (the past 20 years) to build an argument for a particular policy position.

The story told by Sherman and Berk offers a telling reminder: Prior policies were passionately supported by smart and principled people, and those policies, too, were bolstered by varying amounts of research. This realization should serve as a warning against assuming that current policies are necessarily an improvement over earlier ones and that the current policy is the best possible policy — the end of the line. About the only thing that can be said with confidence about any policy in effect 10 to 20 years from now is that its proponents will view current policy — the current generation's views — as misguided and ineffective.

6. *The virtues of social science methods.* How persuasive is the bottom line in the analysis of the Minneapolis experiment? If you were the police chief in another city or a legislator in another state, would you change policy on the basis of this publication? If so, what would your new policy be?

This policy brief, and the movement it captured, is a notable example of the possible influence of social science on criminal procedure. Many states and police departments adopted some version of an "automatic" arrest policy (although most are not truly mandatory arrest policies but strongly encourage such arrests). Despite the warnings about the need for further research, the Minneapolis study was central in promoting these policy changes. A more complete description of the research for the original experiment can be found in Lawrence Sherman and Richard Berk, The Specific Deterrent Effects of Arrest for Domestic Assault, 49 Am. Soc. Rev. 261 (1984).

7. *"More research is needed": an important caveat.* A series of replication experiments in six cities only partially confirmed the dramatic findings in Minneapolis. In three cities, the use of arrest actually *increased* later domestic violence. The use of arrest had more of a deterrent effect on suspects who were employed than on those who were unemployed. Arrest also had a positive effect in *neighborhoods* with high rates of employment, and negative effects in neighborhoods with low employment rates. See, e.g., Lawrence W. Sherman, The Police, in James Q. Wilson & Joan Petersilia, Eds., Crime 327, 336–338 (1995) (describing replication studies in Omaha, Charlotte, Milwaukee, Colorado Springs, Dade County); Joel Garner, Jeffrey Fagan, and Christopher Maxwell, Published Findings from the Spouse Assault Replication Program: A Critical Review, 11 J. Quantitative Criminology 3 (1995) (noting methodological inconsistencies in replication studies and urging policymakers to use caution in interpreting the results).

Despite the lack of successful replication, policies favoring arrest in domestic assault situations generally have remained in force, and new policies encouraging arrest are still being adopted. Why hasn't the more recent research on domestic assaults and arrest policies produced more targeted policies (for instance, a policy calling for arrest only if the suspect is employed)? Is it easier to apply the gas than the brakes? See Donna Coker, Crime Control and Feminist Law Reform in Domestic Violence Law: A Critical Review, 4 Buff. Crim. L. Rev. 801, 831–33 (2001) (mandatory arrest policies increase "dual arrests" of both partners and increase removal of children from home). If you were police chief, or mayor, and were convinced that the original Minneapolis experiment was not replicable, what would you do?

Problem 5-1. Arrests and Curfews

The local police department is considering a rule that would require officers to take into custody every juvenile found outdoors after an established curfew hour. The department hopes the new rule will reduce the crime rate by and against juveniles. A recent study found that 40 percent of crimes after curfew are committed against juveniles and that an unknown but significant percentage of all crimes — especially property crimes — are also committed by juveniles.

How would you design a study to test whether the proposed arrest policy would reduce either crimes generally or the percentage of crimes against juveniles? How would you convince the local police department to participate in the study? Would you tell the media about the study?

Problem 5-2. Racial Patterns in Arrests

In the early 1980s, police officers in Georgia arrested more white suspects than black suspects for drug offenses. In a typical year, officers arrested about 10,000 white suspects and 5,000 to 7,000 black suspects. Beginning in the mid-1980s, law enforcement officials decided to increase their emphasis on enforcement of the narcotics laws. As a result, the number of white suspects arrested each year on drug charges increased slightly, while a much steeper increase occurred in arrests of black suspects. Between 1990 and 1995, black suspects accounted for about 119,000 drug arrests; white suspects accounted for about 58,000 arrests, less than a third of the total. The disparity was stronger for cocaine cases than for marijuana cases. About 85 percent of all cocaine arrestees were black, while just over 40 percent of the marijuana arrestees were black.

When these figures are adjusted for the number of blacks and whites in the general population of the state, the arrest rate for African Americans was more than 10,200 arrests (over the five-year period) for every 100,000 black residents of the state. The comparable rate for whites was about 1,600 arrests for every 100,000 white residents. Even for marijuana arrests, where the racial disparities were least pronounced, the adjusted rate of arrest for blacks was about 2,600 per 100,000, while the rate for whites was around 1,200 per 100,000. National surveys at the time suggested that a slightly larger proportion of blacks than whites used illicit drugs. These surveys showed that blacks used drugs at a rate about 20 percent higher than whites.

As a concerned high-ranking police official, how might you react to these developments? Officers in the department tell you that more blacks are arrested for drug trafficking because they tend to make more sales on street corners and other places visible to the public, while white users and sellers tend more often to conduct their operations indoors. Would it address the disparity problem to issue a departmental policy making arrest mandatory whenever a police officer develops probable cause that a narcotics offense has taken place, no matter how small? See Jamie Fellner, Stark Racial Disparities Found in Georgia Drug Law Enforcement, 7 Overcrowded Times (October 1996).

Notes

1. *The competing (or complementary) explanations.* For most crimes that generate large numbers of arrests in this country, African Americans are arrested in numbers disproportionate to their percentage of the general population. The disproportion is usually much less dramatic than the numbers described above for drug arrests in Georgia. But the differences are present, nonetheless, for many crimes in many different places (but not for all crimes or places). How might one explain this persistent and discomfiting fact?

Some have postulated racial bias, whether conscious or unconscious, on the part of arresting police officers. See Coramae Richey Mann, Unequal Justice (1993). Consistent with this view, one study of the processing of arrests by prosecutors suggested that blacks were arrested on less stringent legal criteria than whites. John Hepburn, Race and the Decision to Arrest: An Analysis of Warrants Issued, 15 J. Research Crime & Delinq. 54 (1978). Others conclude that blacks are arrested more often because they more often violate the criminal law. Alfred Blumstein, On the Racial Disproportionality of the United States' Prison Populations, 73 J. Crim. L. & Criminology 1259 (1982). Those who rely on this explanation point to surveys of victims regarding the race of the offenders in their cases (regardless of whether the police were ever involved or whether an arrest was ever made): The information from victims about the race of criminal perpetrators roughly corresponds to the racial makeup of arrestees.

Another line of explanation suggests, based on observations from field studies, that police officers are more likely to arrest suspects who are antagonistic toward them and that black suspects are more likely to meet this description. See Donald

Black, The Social Organization of Arrest, 23 Stan. L. Rev. 1087 (1971). Still another group of researchers has argued that police arrest black suspects more frequently because black complainants (who are most often the victims of crimes by black perpetrators) request arrest more often than white complainants. See Richard Lundman, Richard Sykes, and John Clark, Police Control of Juveniles: A Replication, 15 J. Research Crime & Delinq. 74 (1978). Others suggest that blacks are more likely to encounter police officers in poorer neighborhoods and that police officers are more likely to use their discretion to arrest in such neighborhoods. Douglas Smith, Christy Visher, and Laura Davidson, Equity and Discretionary Justice: The Influence of Race on Police Arrest Decisions, 75 J. Crim. L. & Criminology 234 (1984). Do these various explanations for racial disparity in arrest rates conflict with one another or are they reconcilable?

2. *Field influences on arrest discretion.* Certain recurring facts about the situations that police officers encounter will often influence their decision whether to arrest. Criminologists studied police practices in two cities in 1996 and 1997, tracking situations where citizens requested that an officer control another person, either through advice, warning, an order to leave another person alone, an order to leave the scene, or arrest. According to the study, officers granted the citizen's most restrictive request in about 70 percent of the cases. The strength of evidence against the person was the single strongest factor in determining whether the officer arrested. However, officers were less likely to grant the requests of citizens having a close relationship with the suspect. Male officers, officers with less experience, and officers with stronger proclivity for community policing were all more likely to grant citizen request. See Stephen D. Mastrofski, Jeffrey B. Snipes, Roger B. Parks, & Christopher D. Maxwell, The Helping Hand of the Law: Police Control of Citizens on Request, 38 Criminology 307 (May 2000). See also Richard Lundman, Demeanor or Crime? The Midwest City Police-Citizen Encounters Study, 32 Criminology 631, 648-49 (1994) (hostile or impolite verbal responses from suspect affect arrest decision). What other factors would you expect to influence this decision?

3. *The ethics of police experiments.* Does it trouble you that the Minneapolis police treated similar domestic assault cases differently in the same time period? Do the police have an obligation to apply one, consistent policy at any one time? The recommendation that police officers pursue an arrest policy, in Minneapolis and elsewhere, was not based on a prediction that more arrests would lead to more domestic assault prosecutions. Is there an ethical issue with police using arrest when they know there will not be a prosecution? Does arrest become a form of punishment without trial?

4. *Expungement of arrest records.* Arrests have consequences beyond the initial detention. An arrest record might influence police decisions months or years later about who to investigate, or prosecutorial decisions about whether to charge a person with a new crime. But what if the original arrest was unfounded? Many states provide for "expungement" of arrest records if they do not result in conviction. The state laws vary greatly as to the crimes where they apply (for instance, some make arrests for sex crimes ineligible for expungement). They use different events to judge which arrests were unsubstantiated and therefore subject to expungement: Some use acquittal only, while others include any dismissal without adjudication. Some of them are self-executing, while others depend on a formal request from the arrestee. Should expungement be available automatically (and immediately) whenever a case is dismissed without a prosecution? See Mich. Comp. Laws 28.243(5); 20 ILCS 2630/5.

D. PAPER ARRESTS: CITATIONS

An arrest is not the only method available to initiate a criminal prosecution or to secure a defendant's presence at judicial proceedings. There are some circumstances when a police officer will issue a "citation" or "appearance ticket" to a person, requiring the person to appear in court regarding a crime the officer believes the person has committed. As in other areas of police officer discretion not to arrest, legal reforms in this field are moving in different directions. On the one hand, the range of offenses where the officer can use citation rather than arrest is expanding. On the other hand, in some limited circumstances the law restricts the officer to using a citation instead of an arrest.

■ NEW YORK CRIMINAL PROCEDURE LAW §§150.10, 150.20, 150.60

§150.10

An appearance ticket is a written notice issued and subscribed by a police officer or other public servant . . ., directing a designated person to appear in a designated local criminal court at a designated future time in connection with his alleged commission of a designated offense. . . .

§150.20

1. Whenever a police officer is authorized . . . to arrest a person without a warrant for an offense other than a class A, B, C or D felony, [the officer may] instead issue to and serve upon such person an appearance ticket.

2. (a) Whenever a police officer has arrested a person without a warrant for an offense other than a class A, B, C or D felony . . . such police officer may, instead of bringing such person before a local criminal court and promptly filing or causing the arresting peace officer or arresting person to file a local criminal court accusatory instrument therewith, issue to and serve upon such person an appearance ticket. The issuance and service of an appearance ticket under such circumstances may be conditioned upon a deposit of pre-arraignment bail. . . .

§150.60

If after the service of an appearance ticket and the filing of a local criminal court accusatory instrument charging the offense designated therein, the defendant does not appear in the designated local criminal court at the time such appearance ticket is returnable, the court may issue a summons or a warrant of arrest based upon the local criminal court accusatory instrument filed.

Commission Staff Notes on Desk Appearance Ticket Provisions (1970 Comment)*

[An appearance ticket] is issued and served by a police officer or other public servant who has observed the commission of a minor offense, and it requires the

* This is considered the legislative history for these provisions. The following excerpts mix paragraphs from the report for different statutory sections.—Eds.

offender to appear in a designated court upon a designated return date to answer a charge which the issuer of the ticket will formally file in the court some time after the issuance. In terms of basic function, an appearance ticket is used in some minor cases as a compassionate substitute for an arrest without a warrant, which is also employed to require or compel the court appearance of an offender against whom no formal charges have as yet been lodged.

On a state-wide basis, the use of appearance tickets is at present largely confined to traffic infraction cases. In New York City, however, numerous non-police public officials and employees, such as those of the Sanitation, Fire, Building and Markets Departments, are authorized to issue and serve such tickets in cases involving offenses peculiarly within their ambits. . . .

The theory of the proposed section is that under present law the virtues and advantages of the appearance ticket have not been sufficiently exploited. . . . The results to be expected from the new appearance ticket scheme are (1) an immense saving of police time, (2) elimination of much expense and embarrassment to defendants charged with minor offenses who are excellent risks to appear in court when required, and (3) above all, a significant reduction of that portion of our jail population consisting of unconvicted defendants awaiting trial or other disposition of their cases.

The advantages to the police may be partly appreciated by picturing the predicament of a police officer who observes the commission of a misdemeanor or petty offense by a person whom he either knows to be a resident of the community or whom he finds to have solid roots therein. Absent the appearance ticket device, two very awkward and unsatisfactory courses of action are available to the officer. Normal procedure requires him to arrest the defendant and, dropping his regular duties, take him to the station house to book him, and then to take him to a local criminal court where a formal information must be filed, the defendant arraigned, bail set, and so on. The even less appealing and equally time consuming alternative entails the officer first going to the court himself, filing an information against the defendant, obtaining a summons or a warrant of arrest and then returning to find the defendant and serve or execute such process; and all this in a case in which the simple issuance of an appearance ticket would almost certainly accomplish the same end result.

■ REVISED STATUTES OF NEBRASKA §§29-435, 29-427

§29-435

Except as provided in section 29-427, for any offense classified as an infraction, a citation shall be issued in lieu of arrest or continued custody. . . .

§29-427

Any peace officer having grounds for making an arrest may take the accused into custody or, already having done so, detain him further when the accused fails to identify himself satisfactorily, or refuses to sign the citation, or when the officer has reasonable grounds to believe that (1) the accused will refuse to respond to the citation, (2) such custody is necessary to protect the accused or others when his continued liberty would constitute a risk of immediate harm, (3) such action is necessary in order to carry out legitimate investigative functions, (4) the accused has no ties to the jurisdiction reasonably sufficient to assure his appearance, or (5) the accused has previously failed to appear in response to a citation.

■ PATRICK KNOWLES v. IOWA

525 U.S. 113 (1998)

REHNQUIST, C.J.

An Iowa police officer stopped petitioner Knowles for speeding, but issued him a citation rather than arresting him. The question presented is whether such a procedure authorizes the officer, consistently with the Fourth Amendment, to conduct a full search of the car. We answer this question "no."

Knowles was stopped in Newton, Iowa, after having been clocked driving 43 miles per hour on a road where the speed limit was 25 miles per hour. The police officer issued a citation to Knowles, although under Iowa law he might have arrested him. The officer then conducted a full search of the car, and under the driver's seat he found a bag of marijuana and a "pot pipe." Knowles was then arrested and charged with violation of state laws dealing with controlled substances.

Before trial, Knowles moved to suppress the evidence so obtained. He argued that the search could not be sustained under the "search incident to arrest" exception recognized in United States v. Robinson, 414 U.S. 218 (1973), because he had not been placed under arrest. At the hearing on the motion to suppress, the police officer conceded that he had neither Knowles' consent nor probable cause to conduct the search. He relied on Iowa law dealing with such searches.

Iowa Code Ann. §321.485(1)(a) provides that Iowa peace officers having cause to believe that a person has violated any traffic or motor vehicle equipment law may arrest the person and immediately take the person before a magistrate. Iowa law also authorizes the far more usual practice of issuing a citation in lieu of arrest or in lieu of continued custody after an initial arrest.[1] Section 805.1(4) provides that the issuance of a citation in lieu of an arrest "does not affect the officer's authority to conduct an otherwise lawful search." The Iowa Supreme Court has interpreted this provision as providing authority to officers to conduct a full-blown search of an automobile and driver in those cases where police elect not to make a custodial arrest and instead issue a citation — that is, a search incident to citation. See State v. Meyer, 543 N.W.2d 876, 879 (Iowa 1996). Based on this authority, the trial court denied the motion to suppress and found Knowles guilty. . . .

In *Robinson,* we noted the two historical rationales for the "search incident to arrest" exception: (1) the need to disarm the suspect in order to take him into custody, and (2) the need to preserve evidence for later use at trial. But neither of these underlying rationales for the search incident to arrest exception is sufficient to justify the search in the present case.

We have recognized that the first rationale — officer safety — is both legitimate and weighty. The threat to officer safety from issuing a traffic citation, however, is a

1. Iowa law permits the issuance of a citation in lieu of arrest for most offenses for which an accused person would be "eligible for bail." See Iowa Code Ann. §805.1(1). In addition to traffic and motor vehicle equipment violations, this would permit the issuance of a citation in lieu of arrest for such serious felonies as second-degree burglary and first-degree theft, both bailable offenses under Iowa law. The practice in Iowa of permitting citation in lieu of arrest is consistent with law reform efforts. See 3 W. LaFave, Search and Seizure §5.2(h), p.99, and n.151 (3d ed. 1996).

good deal less than in the case of a custodial arrest. In *Robinson,* we stated that a custodial arrest involves "danger to an officer" because of "the extended exposure which follows the taking of a suspect into custody and transporting him to the police station." . . . A routine traffic stop, on the other hand, is a relatively brief encounter and is more analogous to a so-called *Terry* stop than to a formal arrest.

This is not to say that the concern for officer safety is absent in the case of a routine traffic stop. It plainly is not. But while the concern for officer safety in this context may justify the "minimal" additional intrusion of ordering a driver and passengers out of the car, it does not by itself justify the often considerably greater intrusion attending a full field-type search. Even without the search authority Iowa urges, officers have other, independent bases to search for weapons and protect themselves from danger. For example, they may order out of a vehicle both the driver, Pennsylvania v. Mimms, 434 U.S. 106, 111 (1977) (per curiam), and any passengers, Maryland v. Wilson, 519 U.S. 408, 414 (1997); perform a "patdown" of a driver and any passengers upon reasonable suspicion that they may be armed and dangerous, Terry v. Ohio, 392 U.S. 1 (1968); conduct a "*Terry* patdown" of the passenger compartment of a vehicle upon reasonable suspicion that an occupant is dangerous and may gain immediate control of a weapon, Michigan v. Long, 463 U.S. 1032 (1983); and even conduct a full search of the passenger compartment, including any containers therein, pursuant to a custodial arrest, New York v. Belton, 453 U.S. 454, 460 (1981).

Nor has Iowa shown the second justification for the authority to search incident to arrest — the need to discover and preserve evidence. Once Knowles was stopped for speeding and issued a citation, all the evidence necessary to prosecute that offense had been obtained. No further evidence of excessive speed was going to be found either on the person of the offender or in the passenger compartment of the car.

Iowa nevertheless argues that a "search incident to citation" is justified because a suspect who is subject to a routine traffic stop may attempt to hide or destroy evidence related to his identity (e.g., a driver's license or vehicle registration), or destroy evidence of another, as yet undetected crime. As for the destruction of evidence relating to identity, if a police officer is not satisfied with the identification furnished by the driver, this may be a basis for arresting him rather than merely issuing a citation. As for destroying evidence of other crimes, the possibility that an officer would stumble onto evidence wholly unrelated to the speeding offense seems remote.

In *Robinson,* we held that the authority to conduct a full field search as incident to an arrest was a "bright-line rule," which was based on the concern for officer safety and destruction or loss of evidence, but which did not depend in every case upon the existence of either concern. Here we are asked to extend that "bright-line rule" to a situation where the concern for officer safety is not present to the same extent and the concern for destruction or loss of evidence is not present at all. We decline to do so. . . .

■ GAIL ATWATER v. CITY OF LAGO VISTA

532 U.S. 318 (2001)

SOUTER, J.

The question is whether the Fourth Amendment forbids a warrantless arrest for a minor criminal offense, such as a misdemeanor seatbelt violation punishable only by a fine. We hold that it does not.

In Texas, if a car is equipped with safety belts, a front-seat passenger must wear one, and the driver must secure any small child riding in front. Violation of either provision is a misdemeanor punishable by a fine not less than $25 or more than $50. Texas law expressly authorizes "any peace officer [to] arrest without warrant a person found committing a violation" of these seatbelt laws, Transp. Code §543.001, although it permits police to issue citations in lieu of arrest.

In March 1997, Petitioner Gail Atwater was driving her pickup truck in Lago Vista, Texas, with her 3-year-old son and 5-year-old daughter in the front seat. None of them was wearing a seatbelt. Respondent Bart Turek, a Lago Vista police officer at the time, observed the seatbelt violations and pulled Atwater over. According to Atwater's complaint (the allegations of which we assume to be true for present purposes), Turek approached the truck and "yelled" something to the effect of "we've met before" and "you're going to jail."[1] He then called for backup and asked to see Atwater's driver's license and insurance documentation, which state law required her to carry. When Atwater told Turek that she did not have the papers because her purse had been stolen the day before, Turek said that he had "heard that story two hundred times."

Atwater asked to take her frightened, upset, and crying children to a friend's house nearby, but Turek told her, "you're not going anywhere." As it turned out, Atwater's friend learned what was going on and soon arrived to take charge of the children. Turek then handcuffed Atwater, placed her in his squad car, and drove her to the local police station, where booking officers had her remove her shoes, jewelry, and eyeglasses, and empty her pockets. Officers took Atwater's "mug shot" and placed her, alone, in a jail cell for about one hour, after which she was taken before a magistrate and released on $310 bond.

Atwater was charged with driving without her seatbelt fastened, failing to secure her children in seatbelts, driving without a license, and failing to provide proof of insurance. She ultimately pleaded no contest to the misdemeanor seatbelt offenses and paid a $50 fine; the other charges were dismissed. Atwater and her husband, petitioner Michael Haas, filed suit in a Texas state court under 42 U.S.C. §1983, [alleging that the City] had violated Atwater's Fourth Amendment "right to be free from unreasonable seizure," and sought compensatory and punitive damages.

[A]n examination of the common-law understanding of an officer's authority to arrest sheds light on the obviously relevant, if not entirely dispositive, consideration of what the Framers of the Amendment might have thought to be reasonable. . . . Atwater's specific contention is that "founding-era common-law rules" forbade peace officers to make warrantless misdemeanor arrests except in cases of "breach of the peace," a category she claims was then understood narrowly as covering only those nonfelony offenses "involving or tending toward violence." Although her historical argument is by no means insubstantial, it ultimately fails. We [find that] the common-law commentators (as well as the sparsely reported cases) reached divergent conclusions with respect to officers' warrantless misdemeanor arrest power. . . .

On one side of the divide there are certainly eminent authorities supporting Atwater's position. . . . James Fitzjames Stephen and Glanville Williams both seemed

1. Turek had previously stopped Atwater for what he had thought was a seatbelt violation, but had realized that Atwater's son, although seated on the vehicle's armrest, was in fact belted in. Atwater acknowledged that her son's seating position was unsafe, and Turek issued a verbal warning.

to indicate that the common law confined warrantless misdemeanor arrests to actual breaches of the peace. See 1 J. Stephen, A History of the Criminal Law of England 193 (1883) ("The common law did not authorise the arrest of persons guilty or suspected of misdemeanours, except in cases of an actual breach of the peace either by an affray or by violence to an individual"); G. Williams, Arrest for Breach of the Peace, 1954 Crim. L. Rev. 578, 578 ("Apart from arrest for felony . . ., the only power of arrest at common law is in respect of breach of the peace"). . . .

The great commentators were not unanimous, however, and there is also considerable evidence of a broader conception of common-law misdemeanor arrest authority unlimited by any breach-of-the-peace condition. Sir Matthew Hale, Chief Justice of King's Bench from 1671 to 1676, wrote in his History of the Pleas of the Crown that, by his "original and inherent power," a constable could arrest without a warrant "for breach of the peace and some misdemeanors, less than felony." 2 M. Hale, The History of the Pleas of the Crown 88 (1736). . . .

A second, and equally serious, problem for Atwater's historical argument is posed by the "divers Statutes," M. Dalton, Country Justice ch. 170, §4, p.582 (1727), enacted by Parliament well before this Republic's founding that authorized warrantless misdemeanor arrests without reference to violence or turmoil. [T]he legal background of any conception of reasonableness the Fourth Amendment's Framers might have entertained would have included English statutes, some centuries old, authorizing peace officers (and even private persons) to make warrantless arrests for all sorts of relatively minor offenses unaccompanied by violence. The so-called "nightwalker" statutes are perhaps the most notable examples. From the enactment of the Statute of Winchester in 1285, through its various readoptions and until its repeal in 1827, night watchmen were authorized and charged "as . . . in Times past" to "watch the Town continually all Night, from the Sun-setting unto the Sun-rising" and were directed that "if any Stranger do pass by them, he shall be arrested until Morning. . . ."

An examination of specifically American evidence is to the same effect. Neither the history of the framing era nor subsequent legal development indicates that the Fourth Amendment was originally understood, or has traditionally been read, to embrace Atwater's position. . . . During the period leading up to and surrounding the framing of the Bill of Rights, colonial and state legislatures, like Parliament before them, regularly authorized local peace officers to make warrantless misdemeanor arrests without conditioning statutory authority on breach of the peace. See, e.g., First Laws of the State of Connecticut 214–215 (authorizing warrantless arrests of "all Persons unnecessarily travelling on the Sabbath or Lord's Day"). . . .

Nor does Atwater's argument from tradition pick up any steam from the historical record as it has unfolded since the framing, there being no indication that her claimed rule has ever become woven into the fabric of American law. The story, on the contrary, is of two centuries of uninterrupted (and largely unchallenged) state and federal practice permitting warrantless arrests for misdemeanors not amounting to or involving breach of the peace.

[There are] numerous early- and mid-19th-century decisions expressly sustaining (often against constitutional challenge) state and local laws authorizing peace officers to make warrantless arrests for misdemeanors not involving any breach of the peace. See, e.g., Mayo v. Wilson, 1 N.H. 53 (1817) (upholding statute authorizing warrantless arrests of those unnecessarily traveling on Sunday against challenge based on state due process and search-and-seizure provisions). . . . Small wonder, then, that today statutes in all 50 States and the District of Columbia permit warrantless misdemeanor arrests by at least some (if not all) peace officers without requiring any breach of the peace, as do a host of congressional enactments.

[But] Atwater does not wager all on history. Instead, she asks us to mint a new rule of constitutional law on the understanding that when historical practice fails to speak conclusively to a claim grounded on the Fourth Amendment, courts are left to strike a current balance between individual and societal interests by subjecting particular contemporary circumstances to traditional standards of reasonableness. . . .

If we were to derive a rule exclusively to address the uncontested facts of this case, Atwater might well prevail. She was a known and established resident of Lago Vista with no place to hide and no incentive to flee, and common sense says she would almost certainly have buckled up as a condition of driving off with a citation. In her case, the physical incidents of arrest were merely gratuitous humiliations imposed by a police officer who was (at best) exercising extremely poor judgment. Atwater's claim to live free of pointless indignity and confinement clearly outweighs anything the City can raise against it specific to her case.

But we have traditionally recognized that a responsible Fourth Amendment balance is not well served by standards requiring sensitive, case-by-case determinations of government need, lest every discretionary judgment in the field be converted into an occasion for constitutional review. Often enough, the Fourth Amendment has to be applied on the spur (and in the heat) of the moment, and the object in implementing its command of reasonableness is to draw standards sufficiently clear and simple to be applied with a fair prospect of surviving judicial second-guessing months and years after an arrest or search is made. . . .

At first glance, Atwater's argument may seem to respect the values of clarity and simplicity, so far as she claims that the Fourth Amendment generally forbids warrantless arrests for minor crimes not accompanied by violence or some demonstrable threat of it (whether "minor crime" be defined as a fine-only traffic offense, a fine-only offense more generally, or a misdemeanor). But the claim is not ultimately so simple, nor could it be, for complications arise the moment we begin to think about the possible applications of the several criteria Atwater proposes for drawing a line between minor crimes with limited arrest authority and others not so restricted.

One line, she suggests, might be between "jailable" and "fine-only" offenses, between those for which conviction could result in commitment and those for which it could not. The trouble with this distinction, of course, is that an officer on the street might not be able to tell. It is not merely that we cannot expect every police officer to know the details of frequently complex penalty schemes, but that penalties for ostensibly identical conduct can vary on account of facts difficult (if not impossible) to know at the scene of an arrest. Is this the first offense or is the suspect a repeat offender? Is the weight of the marijuana a gram above or a gram below the fine-only line? Where conduct could implicate more than one criminal prohibition, which one will the district attorney ultimately decide to charge? And so on.

But Atwater's refinements would not end there. She represents that if the line were drawn at nonjailable traffic offenses, her proposed limitation should be qualified by a proviso authorizing warrantless arrests where "necessary for enforcement of the traffic laws or when [an] offense would otherwise continue and pose a danger to others on the road." . . . The proviso only compounds the difficulties.

Would, for instance, either exception apply to speeding? [Is] it not fair to expect that the chronic speeder will speed again despite a citation in his pocket, and should that not qualify as showing that the "offense would . . . continue" under Atwater's rule? . . . Atwater's rule therefore would not only place police in an almost impossible spot but would guarantee increased litigation over many of the arrests that would occur. . . .

An officer not quite sure that the drugs weighed enough to warrant jail time or not quite certain about a suspect's risk of flight would not arrest, even though it could perfectly well turn out that, in fact, the offense called for incarceration and the defendant was long gone on the day of trial. Multiplied many times over, the costs to society of such underenforcement could easily outweigh the costs to defendants of being needlessly arrested and booked. . . .

Just how easily the costs could outweigh the benefits may be shown by asking, as one Member of this Court did at oral argument, "how bad the problem is out there." The very fact that the law has never jelled the way Atwater would have it leads one to wonder whether warrantless misdemeanor arrests need constitutional attention, and there is cause to think the answer is no. [A]nyone arrested for a crime without formal process, whether for felony or misdemeanor, is entitled to a magistrate's review of probable cause within 48 hours. . . . Many jurisdictions, moreover, have chosen to impose more restrictive safeguards through statutes limiting warrantless arrests for minor offenses. [The Court cited statutes from eight states.] It is of course easier to devise a minor-offense limitation by statute than to derive one through the Constitution, simply because the statute can let the arrest power turn on any sort of practical consideration without having to subsume it under a broader principle. It is, in fact, only natural that States should resort to this sort of legislative regulation, for, as Atwater's own *amici* emphasize, it is in the interest of the police to limit petty-offense arrests, which carry costs that are simply too great to incur without good reason.

. . . The upshot of all these influences, combined with the good sense (and, failing that, the political accountability) of most local lawmakers and law-enforcement officials, is a dearth of horribles demanding redress. [T]he country is not confronting anything like an epidemic of unnecessary minor-offense arrests. . . . Accordingly, we confirm today [that if] an officer has probable cause to believe that an individual has committed even a very minor criminal offense in his presence, he may, without violating the Fourth Amendment, arrest the offender.

O'CONNOR, J., dissenting.

[H]istory is just one of the tools we use in conducting the reasonableness inquiry. And when history is inconclusive, as the majority amply demonstrates it is in this case, we will evaluate the search or seizure under traditional standards of reasonableness by assessing, on the one hand, the degree to which it intrudes upon an individual's privacy and, on the other, the degree to which it is needed for the promotion of legitimate governmental interests. In other words, in determining reasonableness, each case is to be decided on its own facts and circumstances. . . .

A custodial arrest exacts an obvious toll on an individual's liberty and privacy, even when the period of custody is relatively brief. The arrestee is subject to a full search of her person and confiscation of her possessions. If the arrestee is the occupant of a car, the entire passenger compartment of the car, including packages therein, is subject to search as well. The arrestee may be detained for up to 48 hours without having a magistrate determine whether there in fact was probable cause for the arrest. Because people arrested for all types of violent and nonviolent offenses may be housed together awaiting such review, this detention period is potentially dangerous. And once the period of custody is over, the fact of the arrest is a permanent part of the public record. . . .

Because a full custodial arrest is such a severe intrusion on an individual's liberty, its reasonableness hinges on the degree to which it is needed for the promotion of legitimate governmental interests. In light of the availability of citations to promote a State's interests when a fine-only offense has been committed, I cannot concur in a rule which deems a full custodial arrest to be reasonable in every circumstance. . . . Instead, I would require that when there is probable cause to believe that a fine-only offense has been committed, the police officer should issue a citation unless the officer is able to point to specific and articulable facts which, taken together with rational inferences from those facts, reasonably warrant the additional intrusion of a full custodial arrest. . . .

At bottom, the majority offers two related reasons why a bright-line rule is necessary: the fear that officers who arrest for fine-only offenses will be subject to personal 42 U.S.C. §1983 liability for the misapplication of a constitutional standard, and the resulting systematic disincentive to arrest where arresting would serve an important societal interest. These concerns are certainly valid, but they are more than adequately resolved by the doctrine of qualified immunity.

If, for example, an officer reasonably thinks that a suspect poses a flight risk or might be a danger to the community if released, he may arrest without fear of the legal consequences. Similarly, if an officer reasonably concludes that a suspect may possess more than four ounces of marijuana and thus might be guilty of a felony, the officer will be insulated from liability for arresting the suspect even if the initial assessment turns out to be factually incorrect. . . .

The record in this case makes it abundantly clear that Ms. Atwater's arrest was constitutionally unreasonable. . . . The Court's error, however, does not merely affect the disposition of this case. The *per se* rule that the Court creates has potentially serious consequences for the everyday lives of Americans. A broad range of conduct falls into the category of fine-only misdemeanors. In Texas alone, for example, disobeying any sort of traffic warning sign is a misdemeanor punishable only by fine, as is failing to pay a highway toll, and driving with expired license plates. Nor are fine-only crimes limited to the traffic context. In several States, for example, littering is a criminal offense punishable only by fine.

[Unbounded] discretion carries with it grave potential for abuse. The majority takes comfort in the lack of evidence of "an epidemic of unnecessary minor-offense arrests." But the relatively small number of published cases dealing with such arrests proves little and should provide little solace. Indeed, as the recent debate over racial profiling demonstrates all too clearly, a relatively minor traffic infraction may often serve as an excuse for stopping and harassing an individual. After today, the arsenal available to any officer extends to a full arrest and the searches permissible concomitant to that arrest. An officer's subjective motivations for making a traffic stop are not relevant considerations in determining the reasonableness of the stop. But it is precisely because these motivations are beyond our purview that we must vigilantly ensure that officers' poststop actions—which are properly within our reach—comport with the Fourth Amendment's guarantee of reasonableness. . . .

Notes

1. *Citations as supplement to arrest: majority position.* Every state gives its law enforcement officers the authority to issue citations (or "appearance tickets") for the violation of some criminal laws. Citations are ordinarily available to address traffic violations, but they are increasingly available for minor nontraffic violations of the criminal law — sometimes all "infractions" or specified misdemeanors. See Cincinnati Police Department Procedure Manual §12.555 (adults charged with misdemeanor offenses are eligible for Notice to Appear, except for specified misdemeanors such as weapons offense, second DUI offense, and three pending summons). The limited evidence on the use of the citation power suggests that officers do not commonly replace arrests with citations outside the traffic enforcement area.

Some foreign jurisdictions make extensive use of devices such as citations to give police officers an alternative to custodial arrest. For instance, in Queensland, Australia, police can issue a "notice to appear" (NTA) for any criminal offense. The NTA can be issued in the field or after taking the person into custody. It is used most frequently for traffic violations, prostitution, drugs, and weapons charges. If police officers in the United States had similarly broad powers to use citations, do you believe they would use it in similar categories of cases? Would citation in the field or at the station prove more popular?

2. *Citations as replacement for arrest.* Almost half of the states now have statutes that attempt to control the choice between citations and arrests for certain traffic offenses. Some simply state that the officer "shall" use the citation, while others (such as the Nebraska statute reprinted above) require the citation unless the officer can demonstrate one of the designated exceptions. Will a law such as the Nebraska statute effectively limit the use of arrest? On the constitutional level, the *Atwater* decision held that the federal constitution does not limit a police officer's power to arrest for a minor crime. Before *Atwater,* state courts were reluctant to declare that state constitutions required use of a citation rather than an arrest. See Barbara Salken, The General Warrant Requirement of the Twentieth Century? A Fourth Amendment Solution to Unchecked Discretion to Arrest for Traffic Offenses, 62 Temple L. Rev. 221 (1989). Is there any reason to think the trend in the state courts will change after the *Atwater* decision? See State v. Bauer, 36 P.3d 892 (Mont. 2001) (state constitution prevents arrests for non-jailable offense of possession of alcohol by minor).

What concerns, if any, might there be with the extensive use of citations? It might help in answering this question to consider it from a number of different perspectives — police, courts, civil rights groups, minority groups, and various kinds of possible defendants. Another way to think about the policy and justice implications of such a reform is to summarize its effect this way: Citations make arrests easier for the police.

3. *Search incident to citation: majority position.* Prior to the Supreme Court's 1998 ruling in *Knowles,* very few courts addressed the question of whether police could conduct a search incident to citation. Why did state courts develop so little case law on this subject? Was the practice of "search incident to citation" simply too rare to generate much litigation? Or was the practice common but unchallenged because prosecutors used other techniques to avoid appellate rulings on the subject? Here, as with many issues surrounding arrest and detention, police department policies often supplement statutes and judicial doctrine. See Phoenix Police Manual Order

No. B-5(5)(D) (prohibiting search incident to issuance of a citation). Does *Knowles* apply outside the traffic stop context? See Lovelace v. Commonwealth, 522 S.E.2d 856 (Va. 1999) (applies to brief detention of pedestrian to issue summons).

New York City adopted a policy linking desk appearance tickets with fingerprint checks. When officers detain a person to issue the DAT, the person must now remain in police custody until a computerized fingerprint check is complete. The department issues about 80,000 DATs each year. The change in policy was designed to prevent the erroneous release of parole violators and fugitives from justice who present false identification to an officer making a stop. In some cases, it takes up to eight hours to complete a check of a person's fingerprints and criminal record. See David Kocieniewski and Michael Cooper, Police to Tighten the Scrutiny of All Suspects Under Arrest, New York Times, May 28, 1998, at A1. Imagine that you are a legal advisor to the chief of police in another jurisdiction who is contemplating a similar change in policy. What are the legal and policy consequences of this change? How will the officers in the department react to it? How will prosecutors react? Should the chief expect any particular public reaction?

4. *Pretextual arrests and limiting factors.* Recall the discussion from Chapter 2 about pretextual stops. Are the arguments any stronger or weaker to place controls on pretextual arrests — arrests motivated by some factor other than a desire to enforce some law that the officer has probable cause to believe the suspect has violated? Courts have given comparable treatment to claims about pretextual stops and arrests. See Arkansas v. Sullivan, 532 U.S. 769 (2001) (arrest based on probable cause does not violate Fourth Amendment even if arrest was motivated by desire to conduct search incident to arrest); State v. Hofmann, 537 N.W.2d 767 (Iowa 1995); but see State v. Sullivan, 74 S.W.3d 215 (Ark. 2002) (state constitution bars pretextual arrests for misdemeanor punishable by 90 days in jail).

The court in *Atwater* mentioned several practical limits on the willingness of police officers to arrest for minor crimes, including the amount of time and effort it takes to process an arrest. Does the arrest actually have to happen before the search incident? Could the officer announce an arrest, conduct the search, and then convert the arrest to a citation? See Wayne A. Logan, An Exception Swallows a Rule: Police Authority to Search Incident to Arrest, 19 Yale L. & Pol'y Rev. 381, 406-14 (2001) (distinguishes custodial and non-custodial arrests; argues that search incident should only happen if the officer actually does carry out a custodial arrest).

The *Atwater* court also mentioned the prospect that legislatures would pass statutes to limit any abuses of the arrest power. Under what political circumstances would a state legislature take action to limit the arrest authority of the police? See People v. McKay, 41 P.3d 59 (Cal. 2002) (state statute allows arrest for improper bicycle riding; even if it did not, arrest in violation of statute would not amount to Fourth Amendment violation).

5. *Arrests for minor crimes and race.* Does the officer's discretion to choose between arrest and citation for minor crimes create more risk of racial discrimination in enforcement? If you were advising a police department about a proposed campaign to stop and ticket more drivers who fail to use seatbelts, and you knew that Latino and African American drivers use seat belts less frequently than other drivers, what advice would you give about carrying out this program? See Ana Beatriz-Cholo, Seat-Belt Drive Targets Latinos, L.A. Times, May 22, 2001, at B3. In the context of drug crimes, could you exercise arrest discretion in a way that equalizes the impact of enforcement on suburban and urban neighborhoods? See Tracey L. Meares &

Dan M. Kahan, Law and (Norms of) Order in the Inner City, 32 Law & Soc'y Rev. 805, 816-19 (1998).

E. USE OF FORCE IN MAKING ARRESTS

The prior sections of this chapter have focused on *whether* an officer should make an arrest. In addition, the legal system pays attention to *how* a police officer makes an arrest. Legal controls are most vigorous when a suspect resists the officer's effort to make the arrest and the officer must use force — either deadly or non-deadly — to complete the arrest.

■ COMMENTARIES ON THE LAWS OF ENGLAND WILLIAM BLACKSTONE

Vol. 4, p.289 (1769)

[I]n case of felony actually committed, or a dangerous wounding whereby felony is likely to ensue, [the constable] may upon probable suspicion arrest the felon; and for that purpose is authorized (as upon a justice's warrant) to break open doors, and even to kill the felon if he cannot otherwise be taken.

■ TENNESSEE v. EDWARD GARNER

471 U.S. 1 (1985)

White, J.

This case requires us to determine the constitutionality of the use of deadly force to prevent the escape of an apparently unarmed suspected felon. We conclude that such force may not be used unless it is necessary to prevent the escape and the officer has probable cause to believe that the suspect poses a significant threat of death or serious physical injury to the officer or others.

At about 10:45 P.M. on October 3, 1974, Memphis Police Officers Elton Hymon and Leslie Wright were dispatched to answer a "prowler inside call." Upon arriving at the scene they saw a woman standing on her porch and gesturing toward the adjacent house. She told them she had heard glass breaking and that "they" or "someone" was breaking in next door. While Wright radioed the dispatcher to say that they were on the scene, Hymon went behind the house. He heard a door slam and saw someone run across the backyard. The fleeing suspect, who was [Edward Garner], stopped at a 6-feet-high chain link fence at the edge of the yard. With the aid of a flashlight, Hymon was able to see Garner's face and hands. He saw no sign of a weapon, and, though not certain, was "reasonably sure" and "figured" that Garner was unarmed. He thought Garner was 17 or 18 years old and about 5′5″ or 5′7″ tall.[2] While Garner was crouched at the base of the fence, Hymon called out "police, halt" and took a few steps toward him. Garner then began to climb over the fence.

2. In fact, Garner, an eighth-grader, was 15. He was 5′4″ tall and weighed somewhere around 100 or 110 pounds.

Convinced that if Garner made it over the fence he would elude capture,[3] Hymon shot him. The bullet hit Garner in the back of the head. Garner was taken by ambulance to a hospital, where he died on the operating table. Ten dollars and a purse taken from the house were found on his body.

In using deadly force to prevent the escape, Hymon was acting under the authority of a Tennessee statute and pursuant to Police Department policy. The statute provides that "[if], after notice of the intention to arrest the defendant, he either flee or forcibly resist, the officer may use all the necessary means to effect the arrest." Tenn. Code §40-7-108. The Department policy was slightly more restrictive than the statute, but still allowed the use of deadly force in cases of burglary. The incident was reviewed by the Memphis Police Firearm's Review Board and presented to a grand jury. Neither took any action.

Garner's father then brought this action, [seeking damages for asserted violations of Garner's constitutional rights.] After a 3-day bench trial, the District Court entered judgment for all defendants. [The trial court concluded that] Hymon had employed the only reasonable and practicable means of preventing Garner's escape. Garner had "recklessly and heedlessly attempted to vault over the fence to escape, thereby assuming the risk of being fired upon." . . .

Whenever an officer restrains the freedom of a person to walk away, he has seized that person. While it is not always clear just when minimal police interference becomes a seizure there can be no question that apprehension by the use of deadly force is a seizure subject to the reasonableness requirement of the Fourth Amendment.

A police officer may arrest a person if he has probable cause to believe that person committed a crime. [The state argues] that if this requirement is satisfied the Fourth Amendment has nothing to say about how that seizure is made. This submission ignores the many cases in which this Court, by balancing the extent of the intrusion against the need for it, has examined the reasonableness of the manner in which a search or seizure is conducted. To determine the constitutionality of a seizure "[we] must balance the nature and quality of the intrusion on the individual's Fourth Amendment interests against the importance of the governmental interests alleged to justify the intrusion." We have described "the balancing of competing interests" as "the key principle of the Fourth Amendment." Because one of the factors is the extent of the intrusion, it is plain that reasonableness depends on not only when a seizure is made, but also how it is carried out.

[The balancing process] demonstrates that, notwithstanding probable cause to seize a suspect, an officer may not always do so by killing him. The intrusiveness of a seizure by means of deadly force is unmatched. The suspect's fundamental interest in his own life need not be elaborated upon. The use of deadly force also frustrates the interest of the individual, and of society, in judicial determination of guilt and punishment. Against these interests are ranged governmental interests in effective law enforcement. It is argued that overall violence will be reduced by encouraging the peaceful submission of suspects who know that they may be shot if they flee. Effectiveness in making arrests requires the resort to deadly force, or at least the meaningful threat thereof. "Being able to arrest such individuals is a condition precedent to the state's entire system of law enforcement."

3. When asked at trial why he fired, Hymon stated . . . that the area beyond the fence was dark, that he could not have gotten over the fence easily because he was carrying a lot of equipment and wearing heavy boots, and that Garner, being younger and more energetic, could have outrun him.

Without in any way disparaging the importance of these goals, we are not convinced that the use of deadly force is a sufficiently productive means of accomplishing them to justify the killing of nonviolent suspects. The use of deadly force is a self-defeating way of apprehending a suspect and so setting the criminal justice mechanism in motion. If successful, it guarantees that that mechanism will not be set in motion. And while the meaningful threat of deadly force might be thought to lead to the arrest of more live suspects by discouraging escape attempts, the presently available evidence does not support this thesis. The fact is that a majority of police departments in this country have forbidden the use of deadly force against nonviolent suspects. If those charged with the enforcement of the criminal law have abjured the use of deadly force in arresting nondangerous felons, there is a substantial basis for doubting that the use of such force is an essential attribute of the arrest power in all felony cases. Petitioners and appellant have not persuaded us that shooting nondangerous fleeing suspects is so vital as to outweigh the suspect's interest in his own life.

The use of deadly force to prevent the escape of all felony suspects, whatever the circumstances, is constitutionally unreasonable. It is not better that all felony suspects die than that they escape. Where the suspect poses no immediate threat to the officer and no threat to others, the harm resulting from failing to apprehend him does not justify the use of deadly force to do so. It is no doubt unfortunate when a suspect who is in sight escapes, but the fact that the police arrive a little late or are a little slower afoot does not always justify killing the suspect. A police officer may not seize an unarmed, nondangerous suspect by shooting him dead. The Tennessee statute is unconstitutional insofar as it authorizes the use of deadly force against such fleeing suspects.

It is not, however, unconstitutional on its face. Where the officer has probable cause to believe that the suspect poses a threat of serious physical harm, either to the officer or to others, it is not constitutionally unreasonable to prevent escape by using deadly force. Thus, if the suspect threatens the officer with a weapon or there is probable cause to believe that he has committed a crime involving the infliction or threatened infliction of serious physical harm, deadly force may be used if necessary to prevent escape, and if, where feasible, some warning has been given. As applied in such circumstances, the Tennessee statute would pass constitutional muster.

It is insisted that the Fourth Amendment must be construed in light of the common-law rule, which allowed the use of whatever force was necessary to effect the arrest of a fleeing felon, though not a misdemeanant. As stated in Hale's posthumously published Pleas of the Crown:

> [If] persons that are pursued by these officers for felony or the just suspicion thereof . . . shall not yield themselves to these officers, but shall either resist or fly before they are apprehended or being apprehended shall rescue themselves and resist or fly, so that they cannot be otherwise apprehended, and are upon necessity slain therein, because they cannot be otherwise taken, it is no felony.

2 M. Hale, Historia Placitorum Coronae 85 (1736). See also 4 W. Blackstone, Commentaries *289. Most American jurisdictions also imposed a flat prohibition against the use of deadly force to stop a fleeing misdemeanant, coupled with a general privilege to use such force to stop a fleeing felon.

The State and city argue that because this was the prevailing rule at the time of the adoption of the Fourth Amendment and for some time thereafter, and is still in force in some States, use of deadly force against a fleeing felon must be "reasonable." It is true that this Court has often looked to the common law in evaluating the reasonableness, for Fourth Amendment purposes, of police activity. On the other hand, it "has not simply frozen into constitutional law those law enforcement practices that existed at the time of the Fourth Amendment's passage." Because of sweeping change in the legal and technological context, reliance on the common-law rule in this case would be a mistaken literalism that ignores the purposes of a historical inquiry.

It has been pointed out many times that the common-law rule is best understood in light of the fact that it arose at a time when virtually all felonies were punishable by death. Though effected without the protections and formalities of an orderly trial and conviction, the killing of a resisting or fleeing felon resulted in no greater consequences than those authorized for punishment of the felony of which the individual was charged or suspected. Courts have also justified the common-law rule by emphasizing the relative dangerousness of felons.

Neither of these justifications makes sense today. Almost all crimes formerly punishable by death no longer are or can be. And while in earlier times the gulf between the felonies and the minor offences was broad and deep, today the distinction is minor and often arbitrary. Many crimes classified as misdemeanors, or nonexistent, at common law are now felonies. These changes have undermined the concept, which was questionable to begin with, that use of deadly force against a fleeing felon is merely a speedier execution of someone who has already forfeited his life. They have also made the assumption that a "felon" is more dangerous than a misdemeanant untenable. Indeed, numerous misdemeanors involve conduct more dangerous than many felonies.

There is an additional reason why the common-law rule cannot be directly translated to the present day. The common-law rule developed at a time when weapons were rudimentary. Deadly force could be inflicted almost solely in a hand-to-hand struggle during which, necessarily, the safety of the arresting officer was at risk. Handguns were not carried by police officers until the latter half of the last century. Only then did it become possible to use deadly force from a distance as a means of apprehension. As a practical matter, the use of deadly force under the standard articulation of the common-law rule has an altogether different meaning—and harsher consequences—now than in past centuries. . . .

In evaluating the reasonableness of police procedures under the Fourth Amendment, we have also looked to prevailing rules in individual jurisdictions. The rules in the States are varied. Some 19 States have codified the common-law rule, though in two of these the courts have significantly limited the statute. Four States, though without a relevant statute, apparently retain the common-law rule. Two States have adopted the Model Penal Code's provision verbatim.* Eighteen others allow, in slightly varying language, the use of deadly force only if the suspect has

* Section 3.07(2)(b) of the Model Penal Code provides:

The use of deadly force is not justifiable . . . unless (i) the arrest is for a felony; and (ii) the person effecting the arrest is authorized to act as a peace officer or is assisting a person whom he believes to be authorized to act as a peace officer; and (iii) the actor believes that the force employed creates no substantial risk of injury to innocent persons; and (iv) the actor believes that (1) the crime for which the arrest is made involved conduct including the use or threatened use of deadly force; or (2) there is a substantial risk that the person to be arrested will cause death or serious bodily harm if his apprehension is delayed.

—Eds.

committed a felony involving the use or threat of physical or deadly force, or is escaping with a deadly weapon, or is likely to endanger life or inflict serious physical injury if not arrested. . . .

It cannot be said that there is a constant or overwhelming trend away from the common-law rule. In recent years, some States have reviewed their laws and expressly rejected abandonment of the common-law rule. Nonetheless, the long-term movement has been away from the rule that deadly force may be used against any fleeing felon, and that remains the rule in less than half the States.

This trend is more evident and impressive when viewed in light of the policies adopted by the police departments themselves. Overwhelmingly, these are more restrictive than the common-law rule. The Federal Bureau of Investigation and the New York City Police Department, for example, both forbid the use of firearms except when necessary to prevent death or grievous bodily harm. For accreditation by the Commission on Accreditation for Law Enforcement Agencies, a department must restrict the use of deadly force to situations where "the officer reasonably believes that the action is in defense of human life . . . or in defense of any person in immediate danger of serious physical injury." A 1974 study reported that the police department regulations in a majority of the large cities of the United States allowed the firing of a weapon only when a felon presented a threat of death or serious bodily harm. Overall, only 7.5 percent of departmental and municipal policies explicitly permit the use of deadly force against any felon; 86.8 percent explicitly do not. In light of the rules adopted by those who must actually administer them, the older and fading common-law view is a dubious indicium of the constitutionality of the Tennessee statute now before us.

Actual departmental policies are important for an additional reason. We would hesitate to declare a police practice of long standing "unreasonable" if doing so would severely hamper effective law enforcement. But the indications are to the contrary. There has been no suggestion that crime has worsened in any way in jurisdictions that have adopted, by legislation or departmental policy, rules similar to that announced today. . . .

Nor do we agree with [the state] that the rule we have adopted requires the police to make impossible, split-second evaluations of unknowable facts. We do not deny the practical difficulties of attempting to assess the suspect's dangerousness. However, similarly difficult judgments must be made by the police in equally uncertain circumstances. See, e.g., Terry v. Ohio, 392 U.S. 1 (1968). Nor is there any indication that in States that allow the use of deadly force only against dangerous suspects, the standard has been difficult to apply or has led to a rash of litigation involving inappropriate second-guessing of police officers' split-second decisions. Moreover, the highly technical felony/misdemeanor distinction is equally, if not more, difficult to apply in the field. An officer is in no position to know, for example, the precise value of property stolen, or whether the crime was a first or second offense. . . .

The [district court did not determine whether Garner presented a danger of physical harm to Officer Hymon or others.] The court did find, however, that Garner appeared to be unarmed, though Hymon could not be certain that was the case. Restated in Fourth Amendment terms, this means Hymon had no articulable basis to think Garner was armed.

[These facts do not justify the use of deadly force.] Officer Hymon could not reasonably have believed that Garner—young, slight, and unarmed—posed any threat. Indeed, Hymon never attempted to justify his actions on any basis other than the need to prevent an escape. [T]he fact that Garner was a suspected burglar could not, without regard to the other circumstances, automatically justify the use of deadly force. Hymon did not have probable cause to believe that Garner, whom he correctly believed to be unarmed, posed any physical danger to himself or others.

The dissent argues that the shooting was justified by the fact that Officer Hymon had probable cause to believe that Garner had committed a nighttime burglary. While we agree that burglary is a serious crime, we cannot agree that it is so dangerous as automatically to justify the use of deadly force. The FBI classifies burglary as a "property" rather than a "violent" crime. Although the armed burglar would present a different situation, the fact that an unarmed suspect has broken into a dwelling at night does not automatically mean he is physically dangerous. This case demonstrates as much. In fact, the available statistics demonstrate that burglaries only rarely involve physical violence. During the 10-year period from 1973-1982, only 3.8 percent of all burglaries involved violent crime.[23]

[We] hold that the statute is invalid insofar as it purported to give Hymon the authority to act as he did. [The] case is remanded for further proceedings consistent with this opinion. So ordered.

O'CONNOR, J., dissenting.

[Although] the circumstances of this case are unquestionably tragic and unfortunate, our constitutional holdings must be sensitive both to the history of the Fourth Amendment and to the general implications of the Court's reasoning. By disregarding the serious and dangerous nature of residential burglaries and the longstanding practice of many States, the Court effectively creates a Fourth Amendment right allowing a burglary suspect to flee unimpeded from a police officer who has probable cause to arrest, who has ordered the suspect to halt, and who has no means short of firing his weapon to prevent escape. I do not believe that the Fourth Amendment supports such a right, and I accordingly dissent.

The facts below warrant brief review because they highlight the difficult, split-second decisions police officers must make in these circumstances. . . . As Officer Hymon walked behind the house, he heard a door slam. He saw Edward Eugene Garner run away from the house through the dark and cluttered backyard. Garner crouched next to a 6-foot-high fence. Officer Hymon thought Garner was an adult and was unsure whether Garner was armed because Hymon "had no idea what was in the hand [that he could not see] or what he might have had on his person." In fact, Garner was 15 years old and unarmed. Hymon also did not know whether accomplices remained inside the house. . . .

The precise issue before the Court deserves emphasis. . . . The issue is not the constitutional validity of the Tennessee statute on its face or as applied to some hypothetical set of facts. Instead, the issue is whether the use of deadly force by Officer

23. The dissent points out that three-fifths of all rapes in the home, three-fifths of all home robberies, and about a third of home assaults are committed by burglars. These figures mean only that if one knows that a suspect committed a rape in the home, there is a good chance that the suspect is also a burglar. That has nothing to do with the question here, which is whether the fact that someone has committed a burglary indicates that he has committed, or might commit, a violent crime. The dissent also points out that this 3.8% adds up to 2.8 million violent crimes over a 10-year period, as if to imply that today's holding will let loose 2.8 million violent burglars. The relevant universe is, of course, far smaller. At issue is only that tiny fraction of cases where violence has taken place and an officer who has no other means of apprehending the suspect is unaware of its occurrence.

Hymon under the circumstances of this case violated Garner's constitutional rights. Thus, the majority's assertion that a police officer who has probable cause to seize a suspect "may not always do so by killing him," is unexceptionable but also of little relevance to the question presented here. . . . The question we must address is whether the Constitution allows the use of such force to apprehend a suspect who resists arrest by attempting to flee the scene of a nighttime burglary of a residence.

[We must balance] the important public interest in crime prevention and detection and the nature and quality of the intrusion upon legitimate interests of the individual. In striking this balance here, it is crucial to acknowledge that police use of deadly force to apprehend a fleeing criminal suspect falls within the "rubric of police conduct . . . necessarily [involving] swift action predicated upon the on-the-spot observations of the officer on the beat." Terry v. Ohio, 392 U.S. 1 (1968). The clarity of hindsight cannot provide the standard for judging the reasonableness of police decisions made in uncertain and often dangerous circumstances. . . .

The public interest involved in the use of deadly force as a last resort to apprehend a fleeing burglary suspect relates primarily to the serious nature of the crime. Household burglaries not only represent the illegal entry into a person's home, but also "[pose] real risk of serious harm to others." According to recent Department of Justice statistics, "[three-fifths] of all rapes in the home, three-fifths of all home robberies, and about a third of home aggravated and simple assaults are committed by burglars." During the period 1973-1982, 2.8 million such violent crimes were committed in the course of burglaries. Victims of a forcible intrusion into their home by a nighttime prowler will find little consolation in the majority's confident assertion that "burglaries only rarely involve physical violence." Moreover, even if a particular burglary, when viewed in retrospect, does not involve physical harm to others, the "harsh potentialities for violence" inherent in the forced entry into a home preclude characterization of the crime as [innocuous or nonviolent.]

Because burglary is a serious and dangerous felony, the public interest in the prevention and detection of the crime is of compelling importance. Where a police officer has probable cause to arrest a suspected burglar, the use of deadly force as a last resort might well be the only means of apprehending the suspect. With respect to a particular burglary, subsequent investigation simply cannot represent a substitute for immediate apprehension of the criminal suspect at the scene. Indeed, the Captain of the Memphis Police Department testified that in his city, if apprehension is not immediate, it is likely that the suspect will not be caught. Although some law enforcement agencies may choose to assume the risk that a criminal will remain at large, the Tennessee statute reflects a legislative determination that the [provision will] assist the police in apprehending suspected perpetrators of serious crimes and provide notice that a lawful police order to stop and submit to arrest may not be ignored with impunity. . . .

Against the strong public interests justifying the conduct at issue here must be weighed the individual interests implicated in the use of deadly force by police officers. The majority declares that "[the] suspect's fundamental interest in his own life need not be elaborated upon." This blithe assertion hardly provides an adequate substitute for the majority's failure to acknowledge the distinctive manner in which the suspect's interest in his life is even exposed to risk. [The] officer's use of force resulted because the suspected burglar refused to heed [his command to halt] and the officer reasonably believed that there was no means short of firing his weapon to apprehend the suspect. Without questioning the importance of a person's interest in his life, I do not think this interest encompasses a right to flee unimpeded from the scene of a burglary. The legitimate interests of the suspect in these circumstances are adequately accommodated by the Tennessee statute: to avoid the use of deadly force and the consequent risk to his life, the suspect need merely obey the valid order to halt.

A proper balancing of the interests involved suggests that use of deadly force as a last resort to apprehend a criminal suspect fleeing from the scene of a nighttime burglary is not unreasonable within the meaning of the Fourth Amendment. Admittedly, the events giving rise to this case are in retrospect deeply regrettable. No one can view the death of an unarmed and apparently nonviolent 15-year-old without sorrow, much less disapproval. Nonetheless, the reasonableness of Officer Hymon's conduct for purposes of the Fourth Amendment cannot be evaluated by what later appears to have been a preferable course of police action. [I]nstead, the question is whether it is constitutionally impermissible for police officers, as a last resort, to shoot a burglary suspect fleeing the scene of the crime. . . .

I cannot accept the majority's creation of a constitutional right to flight for burglary suspects seeking to avoid capture at the scene of the crime. Whatever the constitutional limits on police use of deadly force in order to apprehend a fleeing felon, I do not believe they are exceeded in a case in which a police officer has probable cause to arrest a suspect at the scene of a residential burglary, orders the suspect to halt, and then fires his weapon as a last resort to prevent the suspect's escape into the night. I respectfully dissent.

Notes

1. *Deadly force: majority position.* In the wake of *Garner,* most states now have statutes either meeting or surpassing the constitutional minimum described in that decision. More than 30 states follow the Model Penal Code provisions on the use of force; more than a dozen of these states adopted (or reaffirmed) this position after the decision in *Garner.* Other states enforce the constitutional requirements through judicial decisions. Police departments now routinely adopt written policies regarding the use of deadly force, even departments that ordinarily do not maintain written operational guidelines. In fact, over 98 percent of the police deparments serving jurisdictions with populations greater than 2500 have adopted written deadly force policies. About 90 percent of all police departments have written policies on nondeadly force. Bureau of Justice Statistics, Local Policy Departments 1999 (May 2001, NCJ 186478).

Is the limit on the use of force in *Garner* workable in the real world? Are the situations in which police can use deadly force after *Garner* sufficiently clear to allow police to anticipate and train for those situations? Does *Garner* create an incentive for perjury by officers being sued for their use of force?

2. *Civil remedies for excessive force during arrest.* The *Garner* decision may strike a familiar chord — not from the study of criminal procedure but from the study of torts. The standard avenue for claims of use of excessive force during arrest — including both deadly and nondeadly force — is a civil suit by the arrestee, usually against the officer or officers and the department. Claims are made under state tort law, federal civil rights laws, or both. Defendants often do not seek to exclude evidence because arrest alone does not always produce any evidence to exclude. Other

remedies and responses to improper searches and seizures, including excessive use of force, are considered in Chapter 6.

3. *Excessive nondeadly force.* The police need not use deadly force to provoke a claim that they used force improperly to carry out an arrest. Many civil damage claims are founded on incidents involving nondeadly force used during arrests. See, e.g., Samaniego v. City of Kodiak, 2 P.3d 78 (Alaska 2000). The use of nondeadly force raises potential claims under the Fourth Amendment that an unreasonable seizure occurred. See Graham v. Connor, 490 U.S. 386 (1989). But in much of the litigation over nondeadly force, traditional doctrines of tort law govern. The question in such cases is often whether the officer reasonably believed such force to be necessary to accomplish a legitimate police purpose. Are civil juries less capable of evaluating claims of negligence or gross negligence by the police than they are in other types of tort cases? See Geoffrey Alpert and William Smith, How Reasonable Is the Reasonable Man? Police and Excessive Force, 85 J. Crim. L. & Criminology 481 (1994).

4. *Changing times.* What societal changes since 1985 might be the basis for arguing that the Supreme Court should reverse *Garner?* What about the emergence of crack cocaine or the presence of Uzis and Mac 10s? The increase in the number of homicides among youth? What if researchers found an increase in the number of killings committed by burglars?

Since the early 1970s, in a trend that *Garner* has reinforced, killings of citizens by police have decreased substantially, as have killings of police by citizens. See Samuel Walker, Taming the System 25-33 (1993). These changes occurred despite a largely stable, high homicide rate nationwide and dramatically increasing levels of homicide among youth in urban centers. See Alfred Blumstein, Youth Violence, Guns, and the Illicit-Drug Industry, 86 J. Crim. L. & Criminology 10 (1995). To the extent the reduction in police killings (and killings of police) can be attributed to *Garner,* does this positive social change justify the original decision? Should courts intentionally conduct experiments, or is experimentation the sole province of legislatures, executive branch agencies, nonprofit foundations, and academics?

5. *Racial patterns in the use of excessive force.* Criminologists have extensively studied police use of deadly force; one researcher summarized the thrust of the studies as follows: "The literature on police use of deadly force has produced two major findings. First, researchers report extreme variation in rates of police shooting among American jurisdictions. Second, regardless of its geographic scope, the research invariably reports that the percentage of police shootings involving black victims far exceeds the percentage of blacks in the population." James Fyfe, Blind Justice: Police Shootings in Memphis, 73 J. Crim. L. & Criminology 707 (1982); see also Jerome Skolnick and James Fyfe, Above the Law: Police and the Excessive Use of Force (1993). In some places, this pattern might be explained by the disproportionate number of black suspects involved in the most serious violent crimes. In other places, such as Memphis (the location of the shooting in *Garner*) between 1969 and 1976, African Americans were more likely to be injured or killed, even after controlling for seriousness of the suspected crime. Should the *Garner* court have mentioned this sort of evidence as support for its decision?

Police departments have devoted much attention to their policies for the use of force, both deadly and nondeadly. Their efforts go far beyond the constitutional requirements set out in *Garner* or in state constitutional decisions. The following materials suggest, both directly and more obliquely, the forces that compel police departments to develop these rules.

■ FLORIDA'S POLICE CONTINUUM OF FORCE
DAVID FRISBY
12 Trial Advocate Quarterly 37 (1993)

[The] Florida Department of Law Enforcement Bureau of Criminal Justice Standards and Training (FDLE/CJST) in the early 1980's recognized a civil vulnerability of Florida police agencies. [FDLE/CJST created the Use of Force Subcommittee to develop state standards and curricula on use of force]. This committee met formally for the first time in 1986. It completed its initial charge in 1990.

Its product consisted of a use of force matrix and a list of approved police arrest techniques. The arrest techniques had been medically reviewed by a committee of medical doctors and legally reviewed by a committee of attorneys. Both pronounced the techniques appropriate in the context of the use of force matrix. . . . The standard of care established by the police use of force matrix became Florida's official standard of care. . . .

Continuum of Force/Levels of Resistance Matrix

The matrix defines the relationship between the proper use of force by a police officer and the resistance offered by the offender. The levels of resistance to lawful police authority are broken down into six categories.

Resistance Levels

Presence is the first level of resistance. This level of resistance occurs when a person breaks the law by the nature of his very presence in a place, as in a trespass.

The second level of resistance is verbal resistance. A person can violate the law and subject himself to arrest by his speech. Disorderly conduct and variations of "Fire" shouted in a movie theater are typical examples. Verbal resistance, however, is usually a response to a police officer's direction or command.

The third level of resistance is passive physical resistance. Passive physical resistance involves more than mere presence or speech. It occurs when a law breaker, by action or inaction, physically resists the action or direction of a lawful authority. A shoplifter who sits and must be carried away from the store is exhibiting passive resistance.

The fourth level of resistance is active physical resistance. This level includes such behavior as pulling away or fleeing arrest.

The fifth level is aggressive physical resistance. When a person turns his active resistance against the police officer or against another person he achieves this level. Aggressive physical resistance need not necessarily be effective, just threatening.

The sixth level is aggravated physical resistance. An officer is faced with aggravated physical resistance when a resistor makes overt, hostile, attacking movements, with or without a weapon, with the apparent intent and ability to cause death or great bodily harm.

Florida Use of Force / Levels of Resistance Matrix

Resistance Levels	Arrival	Interview Stance	Touch (consoling)	Verbal Direction	Dialogue	Restraint Devices	Transporters	Take Downs	Pain Compliance	Counter Moves	Intermediate Weapons	Incapacitation	Deadly Force
6 Aggravated Physical	†	†	†	†	†	†	†	†	†	†	†	†	†
5 Aggressive Physical	†	†	†	†	†	†	†	†	†	†	†	†	
4 Active Physical	†	†	†	†	†	†	†	†	†	†	†		
3 Passive Physical	†	†	†	†	†	†	†	†	†				
2 Verbal	†	†	†	†	†	†							
1 Presence	†	†	†	†									
Response Levels	Official Presence 1		Verbal Control 2			Physical Control 3					Intermediate Weapons 4	Incapacitating Conduct 5	Deadly Force 6

Areas with crosses represent suggested, acceptable, beginning response levels. Any response in an area without a cross requires explanation.

Response Levels

As the name suggests, the police continuum of force theory defines a spectrum of police response starting at a low level of police response and moving to a high level. It gives rules for escalating and de-escalating the use of force. The police continuum of force sets a standard and makes it clear when a particular example of force is within guidelines or outside acceptable practice. As with the law-breaker's resistance, the police continuum of force defines six levels of police response or police force.

The first and lowest level of police force is presence. Before an officer can even give a lawful command he must establish presence by establishing his identity and authority. He can do this by presenting himself in uniform or by presenting a badge, credentials, and announcing his authority. Presence is often enough force to convince a lawbreaker to stop his unlawful activity.

The second level of force is verbal direction. A police officer uses this force when he requests or commands, verbally or with body language. The third level of force is physical control. Physical control is the most complex level and will be discussed in greater detail later. The fourth level is alternate weapons. This level of force includes the use of police batons, chemical irritants, and stun guns. It is the level automatically in effect whenever the various police specialty weapons are used to obtain compliance. The fifth level of force is incapacitating force. As the name suggests, this level of force is intended to incapacitate a lawbreaker temporarily. Incapacitation techniques include some strikes and blows.

Level six is deadly force. This level of force is reached whenever firearms are used. It is force which is likely to cause serious bodily harm or even death. The deadly force category also includes baton strikes to the head, the use of police vehicles against other occupied vehicles and any other techniques defined as deadly by the local police administration.

The police continuum of force matrix relates these levels of police response to the levels of resistance. It gives a police officer guidance about where to enter the continuum matrix based on the particular bad behavior from the lawbreaker. . . .

Police response in level three is divided into subcategories. Transporters are techniques which are designed to move an arrested person from one place to another. Pain compliance techniques are designed to cause pain but not injury. Such a technique might be appropriate to separate a determined trespasser from a fence when he insists on holding tight. The techniques called takedowns, designed to place an arrestee on the ground for handcuffing, compose another subcategory. The very use of handcuffs, leg irons and other restraint devices is also a level three subcategory. Finally blocks, strikes and reactive techniques designed to control but not incapacitate are classified as level three countermoves. Striking a lawbreaker's hand which is bringing up a weapon is an example of a countermove.

General Rules

There are some general rules for the use of the continuum of force. Usually an officer will escalate up the continuum step by step until the law enforcement goal is achieved. He must then de-escalate as much as possible, consistent with maintaining control. An officer may by-pass steps in the continuum if he can explain why the lesser force would not be effective. An officer who exceeds the recommended level of force must document acceptable justification. For example, an officer might easily justify bypassing intermediate steps and initiating a level four or five response to recapture a desperate escaped murderer. . . .

Local police administrators routinely exercise their legitimate power to set force guidelines different from those of the state. Some department administrators move particular techniques to different places in the continuum because of sensitivity to community feelings. Sometimes they forbid certain types of force. For example, a few police departments in Florida have banned the use of the police baton. This type of practice might lead to increased civil liability if an officer found it necessary to use greater police force because his baton (a level four tool) was not available. Sensitive administrators weigh the benefits of varying from state standards carefully. . . .

Notes

1. *Detailed guidance.* Almost all major metropolitan police departments have adopted policies dealing with the use of force, and most of them describe a "continuum" of force similar to the one used in Florida. Most, however, do not have the same level of detail as the Florida policy. See Phoenix Police Department General Order A-8, Addendum A (listing seven levels of force without matching levels to particular conduct). How do you suppose the law enforcement community received the Florida guidelines on the use of force? If you were one of the attorneys asked to review the guidelines during the drafting process, would you have suggested more or fewer categories? Would you change any of the boxes to add or eliminate a particular response level to a particular resistance level? If you were chief of police in Jacksonville, would you issue cards with this chart for every member of the force? Would you publish this chart in the local newspaper?

2. *Extent of the use of force.* The prescribed responses in the lower and middle range of the grid prove just as important as the higher levels of force and resistance because police officers use the lower levels of force much more frequently. One national survey of police use of force during 1991 calculated the following average rates of use, per 1,000 officers, for various techniques of applying force during arrests: 490 uses of handcuffs or leg restraints, 130 incidents of unholstering a weapon, 36 uses of batons, 22 uses of flashlights, 3 civilians shot at but not hit, 0.9 persons shot and killed, and 0.2 persons shot and wounded. Antony Pate and Lorie Fridell, Police Use of Force: Official Reports, Citizen Complaints, and Legal Consequences 74 (1993).

The Department of Justice collects statistics regarding use of "excessive force by law enforcement officers," as required by §210402 of the Violent Crime Control and Law Enforcement Act of 1994. In 1996, an estimated 44.6 million persons had a face-to-face contact with a police officer. Of those 44.6 million, an estimated 500,000 persons were hit, pushed, choked, threatened with a flashlight, restrained by a police dog, threatened or actually sprayed with chemical or pepper spray, threatened with a gun, or experienced some other form of force. See Lawrence Greenfeld, Patrick Langan, and Steven Smith, Police Use of Force: Collection of National Data (January 1998, NCJ-165040). Police officers use, display, or threaten to use weapons in about 5 percent of all arrests. They use only weaponless techniques (such as grabbing, pushing, or holding) in roughly 15 percent of arrests. National Institute of Justice, Use of Force by Police: Overview of National and Local Data (October 1999, NCJ-176330).

3. *High-speed chases.* Sometimes police officers must pursue suspects in automobiles, and those pursuits at high speed sometimes result in injuries to the police

officers, the suspect, and third parties. More than 90 percent of law enforcement agencies have policies restricting the use of high-speed chases. Most of those policies appeared in the 1970s; about half of the policies have been updated since then to place tighter controls on the occasions for engaging in a high-speed chase. These policies allow high-speed chases more readily to chase suspects involved in more dangerous crimes. Geoffrey Alpert, Police Pursuit: Policies and Training, NCJ 164831 (1997); Cal. Pen. Code §13519.8 (mandating creation of department policies). States must waive their sovereign immunity before they can be held liable in tort for injuries resulting from high-speed chases. In what types of cases would you imagine that states have waived their immunity?

Federal law is not hospitable to constitutional tort claims based on high-speed chases. In Sacramento County, California v. Lewis, 523 U.S. 833 (1998), the court affirmed the lower court's dismissal of a suit brought by the estate of a passenger on a motorcycle who was killed after the police and the driver of the motorcycle engaged in a high-speed chase. The court held that the high-speed police chase there did not amount to a Fourth Amendment "seizure" because the chase did not terminate the passenger's "freedom of movement through means intentionally applied." A plaintiff must show that the officers have an "intent to harm suspects physically."

4. *Public scrutiny of use of force.* Public scrutiny of police departments often centers on the use of force. Newspapers routinely publish articles about high visibility cases, especially those resulting in the payment of tort damages by the city; they might also review the department's use of force policies more generally. For instance, a 1998 series of articles in the Washington Post reviewed the use of force by officers in the District of Columbia. Over a five-year period, "D.C. officers shot and killed 57 people — three more than police reported in Chicago, which has three times the police force and five times the population." Jeff Leen, Jo Craven, David Jackson, and Sari Horwitz, D.C. Police Lead Nation in Shootings; Lack of Training, Supervision Implicated as Key Factors, Washington Post, Nov. 15, 1998, at A1. What political incentives do city council members or police officials face when newspapers publish such summaries about the use of force?

Problem 5-3. Ruby Ridge

When Randy Weaver failed to appear in court on federal weapons charges, federal marshals decided to arrest him at his home in Ruby Ridge, Idaho. While several agents were walking around the property before approaching the house, a gun battle erupted between the marshals and Weaver's 14-year-old son, who was out walking and carrying a rifle when he encountered the agents. Weaver's son and one of the marshals died in the firefight.

The federal government was aware that other adults and children were on the Weaver property and that Weaver and his family owned and used a large number of firearms. As a result, the FBI sent several SWAT teams and a hostage rescue team to support the marshals in their effort to apprehend Weaver.

The FBI has general policies regarding the use of deadly force by its agents. The standard FBI rules at that time stated that an agent could use deadly force if the agent or some third party is threatened with "grievous" bodily injury. However, when FBI tactical teams are deployed, specialized "rules of engagement" can supplement the general policy. Rules of engagement are instructions that clearly indicate what action agents should take when confronted, threatened, or fired upon by someone. The on-scene commander formulates the rules of engagement. The special rules of engagement in effect at Ruby Ridge stated:

> If any adult in the compound is observed with a weapon after the surrender announcement is made, deadly force can and should be employed to neutralize this individual. If any adult male is observed with a weapon prior to the announcement, deadly force can and should be employed, if the shot can be taken without endangering any children.

The on-scene commander discussed these rules of engagement with supervisors within the FBI but not with legal counsel for the agency.

There were many interpretations of the rules of engagement among the FBI SWAT teams deployed to the Ruby Ridge site. One SWAT team leader recalled the rules as "if you see Weaver or Harris outside with a weapon, you've got the green light." Another member of a SWAT team remembered the rules as, "if you see 'em, shoot 'em."

During the ensuing siege, a member of the FBI's hostage rescue team shot and killed Weaver's wife while she was standing behind a door, holding her 10-month-old baby. Kevin Harris, a member of the Weaver household, was also shot. After the siege ended, Weaver was acquitted of criminal charges. He brought a civil suit against the government and settled the case for $3.1 million. Kevin Harris also filed a civil action against the government and its agents. See Harris v. Roderick, 126 F.3d 1189 (9th Cir. 1997). During Senate hearings on the matter, the FBI announced a new policy on deadly force. The new policy read as follows:

> *Use of Deadly Force Policy*
>
> a. Deadly Force. Officers may use deadly force only when necessary, that is, when the officer has a reasonable belief that the subject of such force poses an imminent danger of death or serious physical injury to the officer or to another person.
>
> b. Fleeing Felons. Deadly force may be used to prevent the escape of a fleeing subject if there is probable cause to believe:
>
> (1) the subject has committed a felony involving the infliction or threatened infliction of serious physical injury or death; and
>
> (2) the escape of the subject would pose an imminent danger of death or serious physical injury to the officer or to another person.
>
> *Use of Nondeadly Force*
>
> If force other than deadly force reasonably appears to be sufficient to accomplish an arrest or otherwise accomplish the law enforcement purpose, deadly force is not necessary.
>
> *Verbal Warnings*
>
> If feasible and if to do so would not increase the danger to the officer or others, a verbal warning to submit to the authority of the officer shall be given prior to the use of deadly force.

See 60 Fed. Reg. 54,569 (October 24, 1995). The policy applies to all federal law enforcement agents. Is each component of the new federal deadly force policy required by *Garner*? Were the Ruby Ridge rules of engagement consistent with *Garner*? Would you recommend the same deadly force policy for the police officers in Memphis responding to calls about crimes in progress?

VI

Remedies for Unreasonable Searches and Seizures

We have seen how the Fourth Amendment and its analogs, along with many statutes, rules, and internal police policies, condemn certain searches and seizures as unreasonable. We now consider the various methods available to remedy the government's violations of law.

A. ORIGINS OF THE EXCLUSIONARY RULE

The texts of the Fourth Amendment and its state constitutional analogs do not usually specify the remedy for the victim of an illegal search or seizure. Up until the twentieth century, courts remedied these violations of the law by allowing the victims to sue the offending government agents in tort (typically for trespass). But when criminal defendants also asked the courts during criminal proceedings to exclude the wrongfully obtained evidence, state and federal courts rejected the suggestion unanimously. As Justice Joseph Story once put it:

> If it is competent or pertinent evidence, and not in its own nature objectionable, as having been created by constraint, or oppression, such as confessions extorted by threats or fraud, the evidence is admissible on charges for the highest crimes, even though it may have been obtained by a trespass upon the person, or by any other forcible and illegal means. The law deliberates not on the mode, by which it has come to the possession of the party, but on its value in establishing itself as satisfactory proof.

United States v. La Jeune, 26 F. Cas. 832 (C.C.D. Mass. 1822); see also Commonwealth v. Dana, 43 Mass. (2 Met.) 329 (1841). The Supreme Court suggested for the first time in Boyd v. United States, 116 U.S. 616 (1886), that exclusion of evidence might be the proper remedy for evidence obtained through a violation of both the

Fourth and Fifth Amendments. A later case, Adams v. New York, 192 U.S. 585 (1904), curtly dismissed the exclusion remedy for a Fourth Amendment violation alone. The following case was the Court's next word on the subject of remedies for illegal searches and seizures.

■ FREMONT WEEKS v. UNITED STATES

232 U.S. 383 (1914)

DAY, J.

[The defendant was convicted of using the mails for the purpose of transporting lottery tickets, in violation of §213 of the Criminal Code. At the time of his arrest at the Union Station in Kansas City, Missouri, police officers went to the defendant's house to search it. A neighbor told them where to find the key, and they entered the house and took various papers from his room. Later in the same day police officers returned with the United States Marshal, who thought he might find additional evidence,] and, being admitted by someone in the house, probably a boarder, in response to a rap, the Marshal searched the defendant's room and carried away certain letters and envelopes found in the drawer of a chiffonier. Neither the marshal nor the police officers had a search warrant.

The defendant filed in the cause before the time for trial a "Petition to Return Private Papers, Books and Other Property" [claiming that officers of the government had seized his books and papers] "in violation of Sections 11 and 23 of the Constitution of Missouri and of the 4th and 5th Amendments to the Constitution of the United States." [He further argued that the District Attorney's plans to use the papers and property as evidence in the case against him would violate his constitutional rights. The trial court denied the petition.] Among the papers retained and put in evidence were a number of lottery tickets and statements with reference to the lottery, taken at the first visit of the police to the defendant's room, and a number of letters written to the defendant in respect to the lottery, taken by the Marshal upon his search of defendant's room. . . .

The effect of the Fourth Amendment is to put the courts of the United States and Federal officials, in the exercise of their power and authority, under limitations and restraints as to the exercise of such power and authority, and to forever secure the people, their persons, houses, papers and effects against all unreasonable searches and seizures under the guise of law. This protection reaches all alike, whether accused of crime or not, and the duty of giving to it force and effect is obligatory upon all entrusted under our Federal system with the enforcement of the laws. The tendency of those who execute the criminal laws of the country to obtain conviction by means of unlawful seizures and enforced confessions, the latter often obtained after subjecting accused persons to unwarranted practices destructive of rights secured by the Federal Constitution, should find no sanction in the judgments of the courts which are charged at all times with the support of the Constitution and to which people of all conditions have a right to appeal for the maintenance of such fundamental rights.

[This case] involves the right of the court in a criminal prosecution to retain for the purposes of evidence the letters and correspondence of the accused, seized in his house in his absence and without his authority, by a United States Marshal holding no warrant for his arrest and none for the search of his premises. . . . If letters and private documents can thus be seized and held and used in evidence against a citizen accused of an offense, the protection of the Fourth Amendment declaring his right to be secure against such searches and seizures is of no value, and, so far as those thus placed are concerned, might as well be stricken from the Constitution. The efforts of the courts and their officials to bring the guilty to punishment, praiseworthy as they are, are not to be aided by the sacrifice of those great principles established by years of endeavor and suffering which have resulted in their embodiment in the fundamental law of the land. The United States Marshal . . . acted without sanction of law, doubtless prompted by the desire to bring further proof to the aid of the Government, and under color of his office undertook to make a seizure of private papers in direct violation of the constitutional prohibition against such action. . . . To sanction such proceedings would be to affirm by judicial decision a manifest neglect if not an open defiance of the prohibitions of the Constitution, intended for the protection of the people against such unauthorized action.

The [Government contends that the correct rule of law is] that the letters having come into the control of the court, it would not inquire into the manner in which they were obtained, but if competent would keep them and permit their use in evidence. Such proposition, the Government asserts, is conclusively established by certain decisions of this court. [This doctrine,] that a court will not in trying a criminal cause permit a collateral issue to be raised as to the source of competent testimony, has the sanction of so many state cases that it would be impracticable to cite or refer to them in detail. [The editor of one legal publication has explained the rule as follows:] "Such an investigation is not involved necessarily in the litigation in chief, and to pursue it would be to halt in the orderly progress of a cause, and consider incidentally a question which has happened to cross the path of such litigation, and which is wholly independent thereof."

It is therefore evident that [our prior cases] afford no authority for the action of the court in this case, when applied to in due season for the return of papers seized in violation of the Constitutional Amendment. [Prior cases were distinguishable, however, because they involved] application of the doctrine that a collateral issue will not be raised to ascertain the source from which testimony, competent in a criminal case, comes. . . . The right of the court to deal with papers and documents in the possession of the District Attorney and other officers of the court and subject to its authority [is clearly established.] That papers wrongfully seized should be turned over to the accused has been frequently recognized in the early as well as later decisions of the courts.

We therefore reach the conclusion that the letters in question were taken from the house of the accused by an official of the United States acting under color of his office in direct violation of the constitutional rights of the defendant; that having made a seasonable application for their return, which was heard and passed upon by the court, there was involved in the order refusing the application a denial of the constitutional rights of the accused, and that the court should have restored these letters to the accused. In holding them and permitting their use upon the trial, we think prejudicial error was committed. . . .

Notes

1. *Evidentiary fruits of illegal searches.* Would the exclusionary rule described in the *Weeks* case apply to contraband seized illegally? Would it prevent the government

from introducing evidence *derived* from illegally obtained papers rather than the papers themselves? In Silverthorne Lumber Co. v. United States, 251 U.S. 385 (1920), the government had illegally seized corporate papers, returned them before trial, and then issued a subpoena duces tecum to obtain the documents through proper means. The Court declared that the exclusionary rule prevented such a method of curing the effects of an illegal seizure: Exclusion means "that not merely evidence [illegally] acquired shall not be used before the Court but that it shall not be used at all." In Agnello v. United States, 269 U.S. 20 (1925), the Court excluded from evidence some cocaine that was seized illegally.

2. *The states and the exclusionary rule after 1949.* Because the *Weeks* opinion was based on the federal Bill of Rights, which did not at that time apply to the states, state courts and legislatures were free to adopt or reject the exclusionary remedy. Only a handful of states adopted an exclusionary rule prior to the *Weeks* opinion. See State v. Sheridan, 96 N.W. 730 (Iowa 1903); State v. Slamon, 50 A. 1097 (Vt. 1901). The *Weeks* opinion did not change this trend in the state courts. Most took the view of Judge Benjamin Cardozo in People v. Defore, 150 N.E. 585 (N.Y. 1926), in which he tartly summarized the exclusionary rule as follows: "There is no blinking the consequences. The criminal is to go free because the constable has blundered. . . . The pettiest peace officer would have it in his power through overzeal or indiscretion to confer immunity upon an offender for crimes the most flagitious."

Thus, for the first half of this century the exclusionary remedy applied only in the federal system and a handful of states. As of 1926, fewer than 15 states had adopted the exclusionary rule and more than 30 had rejected it. Even after the Supreme Court decided to apply the Fourth Amendment to state law enforcement officers in Wolf v. Colorado, 338 U.S. 25 (1949), it did not insist that state courts exclude improperly seized evidence. They were still free to adopt remedies other than the exclusionary rule. About half of the states continued to rely on civil remedies for victims of illegal searches and on criminal charges against police officers who violated the law. But by the 1950s, judges and commentators started having doubts about the success of alternatives to the exclusionary rule — at that time, not just alternatives but the only remedies available in many states.

■ PEOPLE v. CHARLES CAHAN

282 P.2d 905 (Cal. 1955)

TRAYNOR, J.

Defendant and 15 other persons were charged with conspiring to engage in horse-race bookmaking and related offenses. [After a trial without a jury, the court found one defendant not guilty, and all the other defendants, including Cahan, guilty.]

Most of the incriminatory evidence introduced at the trial was obtained by officers of the Los Angeles Police Department in flagrant violation of the United States Constitution (4th and 14th Amendments), the California Constitution (art. I, §19), and state and federal statutes. Gerald Wooters, an officer attached to the intelligence unit of that department testified that after securing the permission of the chief of police to make microphone installations* at two places occupied by

* Section 653h of the Penal Code provided: "Any person who, without consent of the owner, lessee, or occupant, installs or attempts to install or use a dictograph in any house . . . is guilty of a misdemeanor;

defendants, he, Sergeant Keeler, and Officer Phillips one night at about 8:45 entered one "house through the side window of the first floor," and that he "directed the officers to place a listening device under a chest of drawers." Another officer made recordings and transcriptions of the conversations that came over wires from the listening device to receiving equipment installed in a nearby garage. . . . Section 653h of the Penal Code does not and could not authorize violations of the Constitution. . . .

The evidence obtained from the microphones was not the only unconstitutionally obtained evidence introduced at the trial over defendants' objection. In addition there was a mass of evidence obtained by numerous forcible entries and seizures without search warrants. [The officers testified that they obtained evidence by kicking open a door in one location, and by breaking a window at another.]

Thus, without fear of criminal punishment or other discipline, law enforcement officers, sworn to support the Constitution of the United States and the Constitution of California, frankly admit their deliberate, flagrant acts in violation of both Constitutions and the laws enacted thereunder. It is clearly apparent from their testimony that they casually regard such acts as nothing more than the performance of their ordinary duties for which the city employs and pays them.

[Both] the United States Constitution and the California Constitution make it emphatically clear that important as efficient law enforcement may be, it is more important that the right of privacy guaranteed by these constitutional provisions be respected. [The] contention that unreasonable searches and seizures are justified by the necessity of bringing criminals to justice cannot be accepted. It was rejected when the constitutional provisions were adopted and the choice was made that all the people, guilty and innocent alike, should be secure from unreasonable police intrusions, even though some criminals should escape. Moreover, the constitutional provisions make no distinction between the guilty and the innocent, and it would be manifestly impossible to protect the rights of the innocent if the police were permitted to justify unreasonable searches and seizures on the ground that they assumed their victims were criminals. Thus, when consideration is directed to the question of the admissibility of evidence obtained in violation of the constitutional provisions, it bears emphasis that the court is not concerned solely with the rights of the defendant before it, however guilty he may appear, but with the constitutional right of all of the people to be secure in their homes, persons, and effects.

The constitutional provisions themselves do not expressly answer the question whether evidence obtained in violation thereof is admissible in criminal actions. Neither Congress nor the Legislature has given an answer, and the courts of the country are divided on the question. The federal courts and those of some of the states exclude such evidence. In accord with the traditional common-law rule, the courts of a majority of the states admit it, and heretofore the courts of this state have admitted it.

The decision of the United States Supreme Court in Wolf v. Colorado, 338 U.S. 25 (1949), that the guarantee of the Fourth Amendment applies to the states through the Fourteenth [Amendment,] does not require states like California that have heretofore admitted illegally seized evidence to exclude it now. The

---

provided, that nothing herein shall prevent the use and installation of dictographs by a regular salaried police officer expressly authorized thereto by the head of his office . . . when such use and installation are necessary in the performance of their duties in detecting crime and in the apprehension of criminals."—Eds.

exclusionary rule is not "an essential ingredient" of the right of privacy guaranteed by the Fourth Amendment, but simply a means of enforcing that right, which the states can accept or reject. . . .

The rule admitting the evidence has been strongly supported by both scholars and judges. Their arguments may be briefly summarized as follows:

The rules of evidence are designed to enable courts to reach the truth and, in criminal cases, to secure a fair trial to those accused of crime. Evidence obtained by an illegal search and seizure is ordinarily just as true and reliable as evidence lawfully obtained. The court needs all reliable evidence material to the issue before it, the guilt or innocence of the accused, and how such evidence is obtained is immaterial to that issue. It should not be excluded unless strong considerations of public policy demand it. . . .

Exclusion of the evidence cannot be justified as affording protection or recompense to the defendant or punishment to the officers for the illegal search and seizure. It does not protect the defendant from the search and seizure, since that illegal act has already occurred. If he is innocent or if there is ample evidence to convict him without the illegally obtained evidence, exclusion of the evidence gives him no remedy at all. Thus the only defendants who benefit by the exclusionary rule are those criminals who could not be convicted without the illegally obtained evidence. Allowing such criminals to escape punishment is not appropriate recompense for the invasion of their constitutional rights; it does not punish the officers who violated the constitutional provisions; and it fails to protect society from known criminals who should not be left at large. For his crime the defendant should be punished. For his violation of the constitutional provisions the offending officer should be punished. As the exclusionary rule operates, however, the defendant's crime and the officer's flouting of constitutional guarantees both go unpunished. . . .

Opponents of the exclusionary rule also point out that it is inconsistent with the rule allowing private litigants to use illegally obtained evidence, and that as applied in the federal courts, it is capricious in its operation, either going too far or not far enough. So many exceptions to the exclusionary rule have been granted the judicial blessing as largely to destroy any value it might otherwise have had. . . .

Finally it has been pointed out that there is no convincing evidence that the exclusionary rule actually tends to prevent unreasonable searches and seizures and that the disciplinary or educational effect of the court's releasing the defendant for police misbehavior is so indirect as to be no more than a mild deterrent at best.

Despite the persuasive force of the foregoing arguments, we have concluded that evidence obtained in violation of the constitutional guarantees is inadmissible. We have been compelled to reach that conclusion because other remedies have completely failed to secure compliance with the constitutional provisions on the part of police officers with the attendant result that the courts under the old rule have been constantly required to participate in, and in effect condone, the lawless activities of law enforcement officers.

When, as in the present case, the very purpose of an illegal search and seizure is to get evidence to introduce at a trial, the success of the lawless venture depends entirely on the court's lending its aid by allowing the evidence to be introduced. . . . Out of regard for its own dignity as an agency of justice and custodian of liberty the court should not have a hand in such dirty business.

Courts refuse their aid in civil cases to prevent the consummation of illegal schemes of private litigants; a fortiori, they should not extend that aid and thereby permit the consummation of illegal schemes of the state itself. It is morally incongruous for the state to flout constitutional rights and at the same time demand that its citizens observe the law. The end that the state seeks may be a laudable one, but it no more justifies unlawful acts than a laudable end justifies unlawful action by any member of the public. Moreover, any process of law that sanctions the imposition of penalties upon an individual through the use of the fruits of official lawlessness tends to the destruction of the whole system of restraints on the exercise of the public force that are inherent in the concept of ordered liberty. . . . "Our Government is the potent, the omnipresent teacher. For good or for ill, it teaches the whole people by its example. Crime is contagious. If the Government becomes a lawbreaker, it breeds contempt for law, it invites everyman to become a law unto himself; it invites anarchy." Olmstead v. United States, 277 U.S. 438 (1928) (Brandeis, J., dissenting).

[If the constitutional guarantees against unreasonable searches and seizures] were being effectively enforced by other means than excluding evidence obtained by their violation, a different problem would be presented. If such were the case there would be more force to the argument that a particular criminal should not be redressed for a past violation of his rights by excluding the evidence against him. Experience has demonstrated, however, that neither administrative, criminal nor civil remedies are effective in suppressing lawless searches and seizures. The innocent suffer with the guilty, and we cannot close our eyes to the effect the rule we adopt will have on the rights of those not before the court. "The difficulty with [other remedies] is in part due to the failure of interested parties to inform of the offense. No matter what an illegal raid turns up, police are unlikely to inform on themselves or each other. If it turns up nothing incriminating, the innocent victim usually does not care to take steps which will air the fact that he has been under suspicion." Irvine v. California, 347 U.S. 128 (1954). Moreover, even when it becomes generally known that the police conduct illegal searches and seizures, public opinion is not aroused as it is in the case of other violations of constitutional rights. Illegal searches and seizures lack the obvious brutality of coerced confessions and the third degree and do not so clearly strike at the very basis of our civil liberties as do unfair trials or the lynching of even an admitted murderer. . . . There is thus all the more necessity for courts to be vigilant in protecting these constitutional rights if they are to be protected at all. People v. Mayen, 205 P. 435 (Cal. 1922) [rejecting the exclusionary rule in California] was decided over 30 years ago. Since then case after case has appeared in our appellate reports describing unlawful searches and seizures against the defendant on trial, and those cases undoubtedly reflect only a small fraction of the violations of the constitutional provisions that have actually occurred. On the other hand, reported cases involving civil actions against police officers are rare, and those involving successful criminal prosecutions against officers are nonexistent. In short, the constitutional provisions are not being enforced.

Granted that the adoption of the exclusionary rule will not prevent all illegal searches and seizures, it will discourage them. Police officers and prosecuting officials are primarily interested in convicting criminals. Given the exclusionary rule and a choice between securing evidence by legal rather than illegal means, officers will be impelled to obey the law themselves since not to do so will jeopardize their objectives. [If] courts respect the constitutional provisions by refusing to sanction their violation, they will not only command the respect of law-abiding citizens for themselves adhering to the law, they will also arouse public opinion as a deterrent to lawless enforcement of the law by bringing just criticism to bear on law enforcement officers who allow criminals to escape by pursuing them in lawless ways.

It is contended, however, that the police do not always have a choice of securing evidence by legal means and that in many cases the criminal will escape if illegally obtained evidence cannot be used against him. This contention is not properly directed at the exclusionary rule, but at the constitutional provisions themselves. It was rejected when those provisions were adopted. In such cases had the Constitution been obeyed, the criminal could in no event be convicted. He does not go free because the constable blundered, but because the Constitutions prohibit securing the evidence against him. . . .

In developing a rule of evidence applicable in the state courts, this court is not bound by the decisions that have applied the federal rule, and if it appears that those decisions have developed needless refinements and distinctions, this court need not follow them. . . . Under these circumstances the adoption of the exclusionary rule need not introduce confusion into the law of criminal procedure. Instead it opens the door to the development of workable rules governing searches and seizures and the issuance of warrants that will protect both the rights guaranteed by the constitutional provisions and the interest of society in the suppression of crime. . . .

SPENCE, J., dissenting.

I dissent. The guilt of the appellant is clearly demonstrated by the record before us. . . . In adopting and adhering to the nonexclusionary rule, the law of the State of California has thereby been kept in harmony with the law of the great majority of the other states and of all the British commonwealths; as well as in line with the considered views of the majority of the most eminent legal scholars. Only the federal courts and the courts of a relatively few states have adopted the judicially created exclusionary rule. . . .

The experience of the federal courts in attempting to apply the exclusionary rule does not appear to commend its adoption elsewhere. The spectacle of an obviously guilty defendant obtaining a favorable ruling by a court upon a motion to suppress evidence or upon an objection to evidence, and thereby, in effect, obtaining immunity from any successful prosecution of the charge against him, is a picture which has been too often seen in the federal practice. . . . Furthermore, under the present federal practice, the trial of the accused is interrupted to try the question of whether the evidence was in fact illegally obtained. This question is often a delicate one, and the main trial is at least delayed while the question of whether some other person has committed a wrong in obtaining the evidence has been judicially determined. . . .

[I cannot] ascertain from the majority opinion in the present case the nature of the rule which is being adopted to supplant the well established nonexclusionary rule in California. Is it the exclusionary rule as interpreted in the federal courts with all its technical distinctions, exceptions, and qualifications . . . ? [Neither] the federal courts nor the courts of any of the few states which adopted the exclusionary rule have apparently found a satisfactory solution to [the] problem of developing "workable rules," and it seems impossible to contemplate the possibility that this court can develop a satisfactory solution. At best, this court would have to work out such rules in piecemeal fashion as each case might come before it. In the meantime, what rules are to guide our trial courts in the handling of their problems? If the nonexclusionary rule can be said to have one unquestioned advantage, it is the advantage of certainty. . . .

If, however, reasons may be said to exist for a change in the established policy of this state, I believe that the Legislature, rather than the courts, should make such change. This is particularly true in a situation such as the present one, when the change of policy should be accompanied by "workable rules" to implement such change. . . . In this connection, it is worthy of note that bills have frequently been introduced in the Legislature to accomplish precisely that which is accomplished by the majority opinion, to wit: the supplanting of the nonexclusionary rule by the so-called exclusionary rule, without prescribing any "workable rules" for the latter's application. In the recent legislative sessions of 1951 and of 1953, such bills have been introduced but none has ever been brought to a vote in either house. Under the circumstances, it would be far better for this court to allow the Legislature to deal with this question of policy. . . .

Returning to the precise situation presented by the record before us, it may be conceded that the illegality in obtaining the evidence was both clear and flagrant. It may be further conceded that the crimes which defendants conspired to commit were not in the class of the more serious public offenses. The fact remains, however, that the exclusionary rule, as adopted by the majority, is a rule for all cases and that it deprives society of its remedy against the most desperate gangster charged with the most heinous crime merely because of some degree of illegality in obtaining the evidence against him. . . .

In my opinion, the cost of the adoption of the exclusionary rule is manifestly too great. It would be far better for this state to adhere to the nonexclusionary rule, and to reexamine its laws concerning the sanctions to be placed upon illegal searches and seizures. If the present laws are deemed inadequate to discourage illegal practices by enforcement officers, the Legislature might well consider the imposition of civil liability for such conduct upon the governmental unit employing the offending officer, in addition to the liability now imposed upon the officer himself. It might also consider fixing a minimum amount to be recovered as damages in the same manner that a minimum has been fixed for the invasion of other civil rights. These methods would be far more effective in discouraging illegal activities on the part of enforcement officers and such methods would not be subject to the objection, inherent in the adoption of the exclusionary rule, that "It deprives society of its remedy against one lawbreaker because he has been pursued by another." Irvine v. California, 347 U.S. 128 (1954). . . .

■ DOLLREE MAPP v. OHIO

367 U.S. 643 (1961)

CLARK, J.

On May 23, 1957, three Cleveland police officers arrived at appellant's residence in that city pursuant to information that "a person [was] hiding out in the home, who was wanted for questioning in connection with a recent bombing, and that there was a large amount of policy paraphernalia being hidden in the home." Miss Mapp and her daughter by a former marriage lived on the top floor of the two-family dwelling. Upon their arrival at that house, the officers knocked on the door and demanded entrance but appellant, after telephoning her attorney, refused to admit them without a search warrant. They advised their headquarters of the situation and undertook a surveillance of the house.

The officers again sought entrance some three hours later when four or more additional officers arrived on the scene. When Miss Mapp did not come to the door immediately, at least one of the several doors to the house was forcibly opened[2] and the policemen gained admittance. Meanwhile Miss Mapp's attorney arrived, but the officers, having secured their own entry, and continuing in their defiance of the law, would permit him neither to see Miss Mapp nor to enter the house. It appears that Miss Mapp was halfway down the stairs from the upper floor to the front door when the officers, in this highhanded manner, broke into the hall. She demanded to see the search warrant. A paper, claimed to be a warrant, was held up by one of the officers. She grabbed the "warrant" and placed it in her bosom. A struggle ensued in which the officers recovered the piece of paper and as a result of which they handcuffed appellant because she had been "belligerent" in resisting their official rescue of the "warrant" from her person. Running roughshod over appellant, a policeman "grabbed" her, "twisted [her] hand," and she "yelled [and] pleaded with him" because "it was hurting." Appellant, in handcuffs, was then forcibly taken upstairs to her bedroom where the officers searched a dresser, a chest of drawers, a closet and some suitcases. They also looked into a photo album and through personal papers belonging to the appellant. The search spread to the rest of the second floor including the child's bedroom, the living room, the kitchen and a dinette. The basement of the building and a trunk found therein were also searched. The obscene [books and pictures] for possession of which she was ultimately convicted were discovered in the course of that widespread search.

At the trial no search warrant was produced by the prosecution, nor was the failure to produce one explained or accounted for. [The Ohio Supreme Court affirmed the conviction because] the evidence had not been taken "from defendant's person by the use of brutal or offensive physical force against defendant." The State says that even if the search were made without authority, or otherwise unreasonably, it is not prevented from using the unconstitutionally seized evidence at trial.

[I]n the year 1914, in the *Weeks* case, this Court for the first time held that in a federal prosecution the Fourth Amendment barred the use of evidence secured through an illegal search and seizure. This Court has ever since required of federal law officers a strict adherence to that command which this Court has held to be a clear, specific, and constitutionally required — even if judicially implied — deterrent safeguard without insistence upon which the Fourth Amendment would have been reduced to a form of words.

[Thirty-five years later, in Wolf v. Colorado, 338 U.S. 25 (1949)], the Court decided that the *Weeks* exclusionary rule would not then be imposed upon the States as "an essential ingredient of the right." The Court's reasons for not considering essential to the right to privacy, as a curb imposed upon the States by the Due Process Clause, that which decades before had been posited as part and parcel of the Fourth Amendment's limitation upon federal encroachment of individual privacy, were bottomed on factual considerations.

While they are not basically relevant to a decision that the exclusionary rule is an essential ingredient of the Fourth Amendment as the right it embodies is

2. A police officer testified that "we did pry the screen door to gain entrance"; the attorney on the scene testified that a policeman "tried . . . to kick in the door" and then "broke the glass in the door and somebody reached in and opened the door and let them in. . . ."

vouchsafed against the States by the Due Process Clause, we will consider the current validity of the factual grounds upon which *Wolf* was based.

The Court in *Wolf* first stated that "the contrariety of views of the States" on the adoption of the exclusionary rule of *Weeks* was "particularly impressive"; and, in this connection, that it could not "brush aside the experience of States which deem the incidence of such conduct by the police too slight to call for a deterrent remedy by overriding the States' relevant rules of evidence." While in 1949, prior to the *Wolf* case, almost two-thirds of the States were opposed to the use of the exclusionary rule, now, despite the *Wolf* case, more than half of those since passing upon it, [including California], by their own legislative or judicial decision, have wholly or partly adopted or adhered to the *Weeks* rule.

[T]he second basis elaborated in *Wolf* in support of its failure to enforce the exclusionary doctrine against the States was that "other means of protection" have been afforded the right to privacy.[7] The experience of California [described in People v. Cahan] that such other remedies have been worthless and futile is buttressed by the experience of other States. . . . It, therefore, plainly appears that the factual considerations supporting the failure of the *Wolf* Court to include the *Weeks* exclusionary rule when it recognized the enforceability of the right to privacy against the States in 1949, while not basically relevant to the constitutional consideration, could not, in any analysis, now be deemed controlling. . . .

Today we once again examine *Wolf*'s constitutional documentation of the right to privacy free from unreasonable state intrusion, and, after its dozen years on our books, are led by it to close the only courtroom door remaining open to evidence secured by official lawlessness in flagrant abuse of that basic right, reserved to all persons as a specific guarantee against that very same unlawful conduct. We hold that all evidence obtained by searches and seizures in violation of the Constitution is, by that same authority, inadmissible in a state court.

Since the Fourth Amendment's right of privacy has been declared enforceable against the States through the Due Process Clause of the Fourteenth, it is enforceable against them by the same sanction of exclusion as is used against the Federal Government. Were it otherwise, then just as without the *Weeks* rule the assurance against unreasonable federal searches and seizures would be "a form of words," valueless and undeserving of mention in a perpetual charter of inestimable human liberties, so too, without that rule the freedom from state invasions of privacy would be so ephemeral and so neatly severed from its conceptual nexus with the freedom from all brutish means of coercing evidence as not to merit this Court's high regard as a freedom "implicit in the concept of ordered liberty." . . . Therefore, in extending the substantive protections of due process to all constitutionally unreasonable searches — state or federal — it was logically and constitutionally necessary that the exclusion doctrine — an essential part of the right to privacy — be also insisted upon as an essential ingredient of the right newly recognized by the *Wolf* case. . . . To hold otherwise is to grant the right but in reality to withhold its privilege and enjoyment. . . .

This Court has not hesitated to enforce as strictly against the States as it does against the Federal Government the rights of free speech and of a free press, the rights to notice and to a fair, public trial, including, as it does, the right not to be convicted by use of a coerced confession, however logically relevant it be, and without

7. Less than half [23] of the States have any criminal provisions relating directly to unreasonable searches and seizures. . . .

regard to its reliability. And nothing could be more certain than that when a coerced confession is involved, "the relevant rules of evidence" are overridden. . . . Why should not the same rule apply to what is tantamount to coerced testimony by way of unconstitutional seizure of goods, papers, effects, documents, etc.? . . .

Moreover, our holding that the exclusionary rule is an essential part of both the Fourth and Fourteenth Amendments is not only the logical dictate of prior cases, but it also makes very good sense. There is no war between the Constitution and common sense. Presently, a federal prosecutor may make no use of evidence illegally seized, but a State's attorney across the street may, although he supposedly is operating under the enforceable prohibitions of the same Amendment. Thus the State, by admitting evidence unlawfully seized, serves to encourage disobedience to the Federal Constitution which it is bound to uphold. Moreover, . . . the very essence of a healthy federalism depends upon the avoidance of needless conflict between state and federal courts. . . . Federal-state cooperation in the solution of crime under constitutional standards will be promoted, if only by recognition of their now mutual obligation to respect the same fundamental criteria in their approaches. . . .

There are those who say, as did Justice (then Judge) Cardozo, that under our constitutional exclusionary doctrine "the criminal is to go free because the constable has blundered." In some cases this will undoubtedly be the result. But . . . there is another consideration — the imperative of judicial integrity. The criminal goes free, if he must, but it is the law that sets him free. Nothing can destroy a government more quickly than its failure to observe its own laws, or worse, its disregard of the charter of its own existence. . . .

The ignoble shortcut to conviction left open to the State tends to destroy the entire system of constitutional restraints on which the liberties of the people rest. Having once recognized that the right to privacy embodied in the Fourth Amendment is enforceable against the States, and that the right to be secure against rude invasions of privacy by state officers is, therefore, constitutional in origin, we can no longer permit that right to remain an empty promise. Because it is enforceable in the same manner and to like effect as other basic rights secured by the Due Process Clause, we can no longer permit it to be revocable at the whim of any police officer who, in the name of law enforcement itself, chooses to suspend its enjoyment. Our decision, founded on reason and truth, gives to the individual no more than that which the Constitution guarantees him, to the police officer no less than that to which honest law enforcement is entitled, and, to the courts, that judicial integrity so necessary in the true administration of justice. . . .

HARLAN, J., dissenting.

[It] cannot be too much emphasized that what was recognized in *Wolf* was not that the Fourth Amendment as such is enforceable against the States as a facet of due process, . . . but the principle of privacy "which is at the core of the Fourth Amendment." It would not be proper to expect or impose any precise equivalence, either as regards the scope of the right or the means of its implementation, between the requirements of the Fourth and Fourteenth Amendments. [Unlike the Fourteenth, which states a general principle only, the Fourth] is a particular command, having its setting in a pre-existing legal context on which both interpreting decisions and enabling statutes must at least build. . . .

I would not impose upon the States this federal exclusionary remedy. . . . Our concern here, as it was in *Wolf*, is not with the desirability of that rule but only with the question whether the States are Constitutionally free to follow it or not as they may themselves determine, and the relevance of the disparity of views among the States on this point lies simply in the fact that the judgment involved is a debatable one. . . .

The preservation of a proper balance between state and federal responsibility in the administration of criminal justice demands patience on the part of those who might like to see things move faster among the States in this respect. Problems of criminal law enforcement vary widely from State to State. One State, in considering the totality of its legal picture, may conclude that the need for embracing the *Weeks* rule is pressing because other remedies are unavailable or inadequate to secure compliance with the substantive Constitutional principle involved. Another, though equally solicitous of Constitutional rights, may choose to pursue one purpose at a time, allowing all evidence relevant to guilt to be brought into a criminal trial, and dealing with Constitutional infractions by other means. Still another may consider the exclusionary rule too rough-and-ready a remedy, in that it reaches only unconstitutional intrusions which eventuate in criminal prosecution of the victims. Further, a State after experimenting with the *Weeks* rule for a time may, because of unsatisfactory experience with it, decide to revert to a non-exclusionary rule. And so on. . . . For us the question remains, as it has always been, one of state power, not one of passing judgment on the wisdom of one state course or another. . . .

I regret that I find so unwise in principle and so inexpedient in policy a decision motivated by the high purpose of increasing respect for Constitutional rights. But in the last analysis I think this Court can increase respect for the Constitution only if it rigidly respects the limitations which the Constitution places upon it, and respects as well the principles inherent in its own processes. In the present case I think we exceed both, and that our voice becomes only a voice of power, not of reason.

Notes

1. *Power and reason.* Was *Mapp* an appropriate interpretation of the due process clause? Do you believe that conditions had changed significantly between 1949 (the date of the *Wolf* decision) and 1961 (the date of *Mapp*)? Mapp's attorney did not ask the court to overturn the *Wolf* decision, but the American Civil Liberties Union, appearing as *amicus curiae,* raised the issue.

2. *Empirical evidence on the benefits of the exclusionary rule.* The *Cahan* court stated that "there is no convincing evidence that the exclusionary rule actually tends to prevent unreasonable searches and seizures" and that it was "a mild deterrent at best." It is quite difficult to estimate the real impact of the exclusionary rule on police and magistrate practices because the effect of the rule (if any) would be to produce a nonevent. That is, the exclusionary rule would, in theory, prevent improper searches and seizures from occurring. Some have attempted to measure the effects of the exclusionary rule by tracking either the number of search and arrest warrants sought or the number of arrests completed in the same location before and after the exclusionary rule took effect. In some locations, the number of warrants sought went up and the number of arrests went down after *Mapp,* but in other locations there was little or no change.

Others have estimated the deterrent effect of the exclusionary rule by asking police officers themselves how the prospect of losing evidence in a case would affect their decisions in the field. The authors of one survey of 547 police officers in four northeastern cities concluded that roughly half of the officers would comply with a known constitutional requirement, while 15 percent expressed a willingness to violate a known legal requirement in several specific situations calling for a search or seizure. The remaining officers were not aware of their legal obligations in the situations described. William Heffernan and Richard Lovely, Evaluating the Fourth Amendment Exclusionary Rule: The Problem of Police Compliance with the Law, 24 U. Mich. J.L. Ref. 311 (1991). A 1987 study of the narcotics division of the Chicago Police Department concluded that the exclusionary rule has a substantial deterrent impact. Myron Orfield, The Exclusionary Rule and Deterrence: An Empirical Study of Chicago Narcotics Officers, 54 U. Chi. L. Rev. 1016 (1987).

A 1997 survey of law enforcement officers in Ventura County, California, offered more equivocal evidence about the deterrent effects of the exclusionary rule. About 20 percent of the officers responding to the survey said that the risk of exclusion of evidence was their primary concern in deciding whether to conduct a search or seizure, while nearly 60 percent considered suppression to be an "important" concern. Officers who had "lost" evidence because of improper searches or seizures in past cases were no more likely than other officers to give correct answers to hypothetical search and seizure questions. See Timothy Perrin, H. Mitchell Caldwell, Carol Chase and Ronald Fagan, If It's Broken, Fix It: Moving Beyond the Exclusionary Rule — A New and Extensive Empirical Study of the Exclusionary Rule and a Call for a Civil Administrative Remedy to Partially Replace the Rule, 83 Iowa L. Rev. 669 (1998).

3. *Empirical evidence on the costs of the exclusionary rule.* More effort has gone into measuring the "costs" of the exclusionary rule. A number of studies have estimated the number of convictions that the government loses because of concerns about exclusion of evidence obtained from an improper search or seizure. The estimates of arrests lost range from 0.6 percent to 2.35 percent of all felony arrests, with a higher proportion (in the range of 3 to 5 percent) of arrests on drug and weapons charges. Thomas Davies, A Hard Look at What We Know (and Still Need to Learn) about the "Costs" of the Exclusionary Rule: The NIJ Study and Other Studies of "Lost" Arrests, 1983 Am. B. Found. Res. J. 611.

Assuming we knew with some confidence how many cases are lost because of improper searches or seizures, how many would be too many? Perhaps the answer depends on whether the exclusionary rule should function as a "sanction" to signal that conduct is wrong and completely intolerable, or as a "price" that tolerates some of the behavior so long as it produces more good than harm overall. See Sharon Davies, The Penalty of Exclusion — A Price or Sanction? 73 S. Cal. L. Rev. 1275 (2000).

4. *The imperative of judicial integrity.* The courts in *Mapp* and *Cahan* each mentioned that the exclusionary rule would serve multiple purposes. In addition to deterring violations of the Constitution, it would also protect judicial integrity. Today, however, the Supreme Court describes the purpose of the exclusionary rule solely in terms of deterrence. See United States v. Janis, 428 U.S. 433, 458 (1976) ("considerations of judicial integrity do not require exclusion of the evidence"). Is the exclusionary rule necessary to protect the integrity of courts? Do courts undermine their integrity when they accept evidence in *civil* cases that was obtained contrary to law? Is the "truth seeking" function of the criminal process the best guarantee of judicial integrity, and does the exclusionary rule harm the truth-seeking function?

5. *Exclusion for violation of state constitutions, statutes, and procedure rules.* When a state court concludes that a search or seizure violated the state constitution rather than the federal constitution, exclusion is almost always the remedy the court adopts. Although exclusion is not required by federal law in such a case (regardless of whether the evidence is offered in state or federal criminal proceedings), state courts will typically choose exclusion as the proper remedy under state law.

When a search or seizure violates the provisions of a statute (state or federal) rather than a constitution, courts try to determine which remedy the legislature intended. Sometimes an explicit provision in a statute makes this relatively easy. See Ill. Stat. Ann. ch. 720, §5/14-5 (exclusion of any evidence obtained in violation of eavesdropping statute); Or. Stat. §136.432 ("A court may not exclude relevant and otherwise admissible evidence in a criminal action on the grounds that it was obtained in violation of any statutory provision unless exclusion of the evidence is required by . . . (1) The United States Constitution or the Oregon Constitution; (2) The rules of evidence governing privileges and the admission of hearsay; or (3) The rights of the press").

In other cases, the statutory language does not address remedies, and the legislative history is unhelpful. In such cases, courts tend to use the exclusion remedy for statutory violations when the search or seizure infringed in a "significant" way on "substantial" rights of the defendant. Compare People v. McKinstry, 843 P.2d 18 (Colo. 1993) (no exclusion for failure to include affiant's name in warrant application, as required by statute) with People v. Taylor, 541 N.E.2d 386 (N.Y. 1989) (exclusion required for violation of statutory requirement of contemporaneous recording of evidence supporting warrant application). What remedy would you expect state courts to select when police officers violate departmental policies as they gather evidence?

6. *Silver platters.* It is clear that a federal court cannot receive evidence that state officers obtain in violation of federal law. That is, the state officers may not present the evidence to their federal counterparts on a "silver platter." See Elkins v. United States, 364 U.S. 206 (1960). The same rule prevents federal officers from presenting evidence to a state court if they obtained it in violation of the federal constitution. But the "silver platter doctrine" does not operate in all possible combinations. Officers from some other jurisdiction (federal or state) may obtain evidence in violation of state law (constitutional or statutory) and present that evidence in the federal courts or in the courts of another state. Local rules about search and seizure do not export to the courts of other jurisdictions. As the reach of federal criminal law grows and the overlap between state and federal criminal justice increases, does the argument get stronger for applying local search and seizure rules in the courts of other jurisdictions? How would traditional conflicts of laws doctrine resolve this issue?

7. *International adoption of exclusionary rule.* Although judges in the United States sometimes claim that no other country in the world uses an exclusionary rule, the claim is not true. For instance, in Germany, judges must consider whether admission of evidence obtained illegally would violate the constitutionally protected privacy interests of the defendant. German judges balance in each case the defendant's interests in privacy against the importance of the evidence and the seriousness of the offense charged. In practice, however, German judges rarely exclude evidence obtained through improper searches. England uses an attenuated case-by-case form of the exclusionary rule as a remedy for improper searches or seizures. The common

law rule allowed courts to admit evidence in a criminal trial no matter how it was obtained. This rule is now codified in §78 of the Police and Criminal Evidence Act of 1984. Exclusion is available to English judges as a remedy today, but they are reluctant to withhold strong evidence of guilt from the jury. In Canada, exclusion happens more frequently. The constitutionally based Charter of Rights and Freedoms gives the accused a basis for excluding evidence that was obtained improperly. Evidence is excluded only if a breach of a Charter right or freedom is demonstrated and if the admission of the evidence in the trial would tend to bring the administration of justice "into disrepute." More serious violations are more likely to result in exclusion. Craig Bradley, *Mapp* Goes Abroad, 52 Case Western Res. L. Rev. 375 (2001). In general, judges in other countries distinguish between "real" evidence and interrogation evidence, and are more likely to exclude interrogation evidence. Why would courts make this distinction?

The basis for the exclusionary rule in these and other countries focuses more on judicial integrity than deterrence of police misconduct. If courts in the United States were to emphasize once again the "imperative of judicial integrity," would that open the way to an exclusionary rule that is applied less consistently than it is today?

B. LIMITATIONS ON THE EXCLUSIONARY RULE

We have traced the history of the adoption of the exclusionary rule as a remedy for illegal searches and seizures. The exclusionary rule was a highly controversial choice of remedies at the time of *Weeks, Cahan,* and *Mapp,* and it remains so today. Reservations about the exclusionary rule have not yet led any U.S. legal system to abandon the remedy, but they have led to some serious limitations on its applicability and effects.

1. Evidence Obtained in "Good Faith"

■ COMMONWEALTH v. LOUIS EDMUNDS

586 A.2d 887 (Penn. 1991)

Cappy, J.

The issue presented to this court is whether Pennsylvania should adopt the "good faith" exception to the exclusionary rule as articulated by the United States Supreme Court in the case of United States v. Leon, 468 U.S. 897 (1984). We conclude that a "good faith" exception to the exclusionary rule would frustrate the guarantees embodied in Article I, Section 8, of the Pennsylvania Constitution. Accordingly, the decision of the Superior Court is reversed. . . .

The pertinent facts can be briefly summarized as follows. On August 5, 1985 State Police Trooper Michael Deise obtained a warrant from a district magistrate to search a white corrugated building and curtilage on the property of the defendant. [The information in the warrant affidavit came from confidential informants and from a later helicopter flyover of the property. When Trooper Deise and three other troopers went to Edmunds's property to execute the warrant, they discovered 17 growing marijuana plants inside the building, rather than outside the building as the informants had alleged. Prior to trial on drug charges, Edmunds moved to suppress the marijuana seized from the building] on the ground that the warrant was constitutionally defective, and probable cause was lacking, because the warrant failed to set forth a time frame in which the informants had observed the marijuana.

Recognizing that the affidavit of probable cause was deficient on its face, the trial court granted the request of the district attorney to convene a supplemental suppression hearing. . . . The express purpose of this hearing was to allow the district attorney to provide oral supplementation of the facts set forth in the written affidavit and warrant, in order to establish a "good faith" exception to the exclusionary rule under the auspices of *Leon.* [District Justice Tlumac] testified that Trooper Deise appeared in her office . . . and related his conversation with the two anonymous informants. She stated that Trooper Deise thereafter dictated the affidavit, which she typed verbatim. She then prepared and issued the search warrant. [She was under the impression that the informants had seen the marijuana the day before Trooper Deise had sought the warrant.]

Upon the close of the supplemental suppression hearing, the trial court found that . . . this warrant would be incapable of establishing probable cause to justify the search of defendant's property. The warrant failed to set forth a time frame from which a neutral and detached magistrate could reasonably infer that the criminal conduct observed was recent and would most likely still be in progress at the time the warrant was requested. [The trial court nevertheless admitted the evidence, because the trooper acted in "good faith" in executing the defective warrant.]

Our starting point must be the decision of the United States Supreme Court in *Leon.* In *Leon,* the Supreme Court in 1984 departed from a long history of exclusionary rule jurisprudence dating back to Weeks v. United States (1914) and Mapp v. Ohio (1961). The Court in *Leon* concluded that the Fourth Amendment does not mandate suppression of illegally seized evidence obtained pursuant to a constitutionally defective warrant, so long as the police officer acted in good faith reliance upon the warrant issued by a neutral and detached magistrate.

In *Leon,* police officers in Burbank, California, had initiated a drug investigation after receiving a tip from a confidential informant that large quantities of cocaine and methaqualone were being sold from a residence. The informant had indicated that he witnessed a sale of methaqualone approximately five months earlier. The Burbank police set up a surveillance of three residences, [and used their observations there to seek a search warrant. A magistrate mistakenly issued the warrant even though the officers had not established probable cause. The search uncovered large quantities of cocaine and methaqualone.]

Justice White, writing for the majority in *Leon,* first indicated that the exclusionary rule was not a "necessary corollary of the Fourth Amendment." Although . . . Mapp v. Ohio had suggested that the exclusion of illegally seized evidence was part-and-parcel of the Fourth Amendment's guaranty, the *Leon* Court took the position that the exclusionary rule operates as "a judicially created remedy designed to safeguard Fourth Amendment rights generally through its deterrent effect, rather than a personal constitutional right of the party aggrieved."

Justice White went on to conclude that the issue of whether the exclusionary rule should be imposed in a particular case "must be resolved by weighing the costs and benefits" of precluding such evidence from the prosecution's case. On the costs side of the analysis, Justice White declared that the exclusionary rule incurs "substantial social costs" in terms of "impeding unacceptably the truthfinding functions of judge and jury." As a result, Justice White noted that "some guilty defendants may go free or receive reduced sentences as a result of favorable plea bargains."

On the benefits side of the analysis, Justice White indicated that the sole purpose of the exclusionary rule under the Fourth Amendment was to "deter police misconduct rather than to punish the errors of judges and magistrates." Given this goal, Justice White concluded that there was no reason to presume that judges or magistrates would be more inclined to "ignore or subvert" the Fourth Amendment if evidence seized pursuant to a defective warrant were admissible. The majority wrote: "Although there are assertions that some magistrates become rubber stamps for the police and others may be unable effectively to screen police conduct . . . we are not convinced that this is a problem of major proportions."

The Court in *Leon* found that the argument that the exclusionary rule "deters future inadequate presentations" by police officers or prevents "magistrate shopping" was "speculative." . . . The *Leon* majority therefore concluded that, where a police officer is acting in objective good faith, based upon a search warrant duly issued by a neutral magistrate or judge, the Fourth Amendment does not require exclusion of such evidence, even where it is later determined that probable cause was lacking for the warrant. Unless the police officer acted "knowingly" or "recklessly" in providing false information to the magistrate, or the affidavit of probable cause is "so lacking in indicia of probable cause as to render official belief in its existence unreasonable," the evidence is admissible. . . .

This Court has long emphasized that, in interpreting a provision of the Pennsylvania Constitution, we are not bound by the decisions of the United States Supreme Court which interpret similar (yet distinct) federal constitutional provisions. [Independent analysis of state constitutions] is a positive expression of the jurisprudence which has existed in the United States since the founding of the nation.

[In Pennsylvania, a court considering differences between state and federal constitutional provisions will analyze] at least the following four factors: 1) text of the Pennsylvania constitutional provision; 2) history of the provision, including Pennsylvania case-law; 3) related case-law from other states; 4) policy considerations, including unique issues of state and local concern, and applicability within modern Pennsylvania jurisprudence. . . . Depending upon the particular issue presented, an examination of related federal precedent may be useful as part of the state constitutional analysis, not as binding authority, but as one form of guidance. . . .

The text of Article I, Section 8 of the Pennsylvania Constitution [provides:] "The people shall be secure in their persons, houses, papers and possessions from unreasonable searches and seizures, and no warrant to search any place or to seize any person or things shall issue without describing them as nearly as may be, nor without probable cause, supported by oath or affirmation subscribed to by the affiant." Although the wording of the Pennsylvania Constitution is similar in language to the Fourth Amendment of the United States Constitution, we are not bound to interpret the two provisions as if they were mirror images, even where the text is similar or identical.

[Pennsylvania's] Constitution was adopted on September 28, 1776, a full ten years prior to the ratification of the U.S. Constitution. [It] was drafted in the midst of the American Revolution, as the first overt expression of independence from the

British Crown. The Pennsylvania Constitution was therefore meant to reduce to writing a deep history of unwritten legal and moral codes which had guided the colonists from the beginning of William Penn's charter in 1681. . . . Thus, contrary to the popular misconception that state constitutions are somehow patterned after the United States Constitution, the reverse is true. The federal Bill of Rights borrowed heavily from the Declarations of Rights contained in the constitutions of Pennsylvania and other colonies. . . .

With respect to Article I, Section 8 of the present Pennsylvania Constitution, which relates to freedom from unreasonable searches and seizures, that provision had its origin prior to the Fourth Amendment, in [the original Commonwealth] Constitution of 1776, drafted by the first convention of delegates chaired by Benjamin Franklin. The primary purpose of the warrant requirement was to abolish "general warrants," which had been used by the British to conduct sweeping searches of residences and businesses, based upon generalized suspicions. Therefore, . . . the issue of searches and seizures unsupported by probable cause was of utmost concern to the constitutional draftsmen. Moreover, as this Court has stated repeatedly in interpreting Article I, Section 8, that provision is meant to embody a strong notion of privacy, carefully safeguarded in this Commonwealth for the past two centuries.

The history of Article I, Section 8, thus indicates that the purpose underlying the exclusionary rule in this Commonwealth is quite distinct from the purpose underlying the exclusionary rule under the Fourth Amendment, as articulated by the majority in *Leon*. The United States Supreme Court in *Leon* made clear that, in its view, the sole purpose for the exclusionary rule under the Fourth Amendment was to deter police misconduct. . . . This reinterpretation differs from the way the exclusionary rule has evolved in Pennsylvania. . . .

Like many of its sister states, Pennsylvania did not adopt an exclusionary rule until the United States Supreme Court's decision in *Mapp* required it to do so. However, at the time the exclusionary rule was embraced in Pennsylvania, we clearly viewed it as a constitutional mandate. . . . During the first decade after *Mapp*, our decisions in Pennsylvania tended to parallel the cases interpreting the Fourth Amendment. However, beginning in 1973, our case-law began to reflect a clear divergence from federal precedent. The United States Supreme Court at this time began moving towards a metamorphosed view, suggesting that the purpose of the exclusionary rule is not to redress the injury to the privacy of the search victim but, rather, to deter future unlawful police conduct. At the same time this Court began to forge its own path under Article I, Section 8 of the Pennsylvania Constitution, declaring with increasing frequency that Article I, Section 8 of the Pennsylvania Constitution embodied a strong notion of privacy, notwithstanding federal cases to the contrary. . . . Thus, the exclusionary rule in Pennsylvania has consistently served to bolster the twin aims of Article I, Section 8; to-wit, the safeguarding of privacy and the fundamental requirement that warrants shall only be issued upon probable cause. . . .

Citizens in this Commonwealth possess such rights, even where a police officer in "good faith" carrying out his or her duties inadvertently invades the privacy or circumvents the strictures of probable cause. To adopt a "good faith" exception to the exclusionary rule, we believe, would virtually emasculate those clear safeguards which have been carefully developed under the Pennsylvania Constitution over the past 200 years.

A number of states other than Pennsylvania have confronted the issue of whether to apply a "good faith" exception to the exclusionary rule, under their own constitutions, in the wake of *Leon.* [The court reviewed the decisions of eight states approving of *Leon* and 11 rejecting *Leon* on constitutional or statutory grounds.]

We similarly conclude that [allowing] the judicial branch to participate, directly or indirectly, in the use of the fruits of illegal searches would only serve to undermine the integrity of the judiciary in this Commonwealth. From the perspective of the citizen whose rights are at stake, an invasion of privacy, in good faith or bad, is equally as intrusive. This is true whether it occurs through the actions of the legislative, executive or the judicial branch of government.

We recognize that, in analyzing any state constitutional provision, it is necessary to go beyond the bare text and history of that provision as it was drafted 200 years ago, and consider its application within the modern scheme of Pennsylvania jurisprudence. An assessment of various policy considerations, however, only supports our conclusion that the good faith exception to the exclusionary rule would be inconsistent with the jurisprudence surrounding Article I, Section 8.

First, such a rule would effectively negate the judicially created mandate reflected in the Pennsylvania Rules of Criminal Procedure, in [Rule 2003, which] relates to the requirements for the issuance of a warrant, and provides in relevant part:

> (a) No search warrant shall issue but upon probable cause supported by one or more affidavits sworn to before the issuing authority. The issuing authority, in determining whether probable cause has been established, may not consider any evidence outside the affidavits.
>
> (b) At any hearing on a motion for the return or suppression of evidence, or for suppression of the fruits of evidence, obtained pursuant to a search warrant, no evidence shall be admissible to establish probable cause other than the affidavits provided for in paragraph (a).

Rule 2003 thus adopts a "four corners" requirement, and provides that only evidence contained within the four corners of the affidavit may be considered to establish probable cause. . . . Although Rule 2003 is not constitutionally mandated by Article I, Section 8, . . . it reflects yet another expression of this Court's unwavering insistence that probable cause exist before a warrant is issued, and only those facts memorialized in the written affidavit may be considered in establishing probable cause, in order to eliminate any chance of incomplete or reconstructed hindsight. [W]e have chosen to adopt that Rule as an administrative matter, and that Rule has now stood in Pennsylvania for 17 years.

In the instant case, probable cause — as defined under Pennsylvania law — is lacking. Two lower courts have so held; we concur. Applying the federal *Leon* test would not only frustrate the procedural safeguards embodied in Rule 2003, but would permit the admission of illegally seized evidence in a variety of contexts where probable cause is lacking, so long as the police officer acted in "good faith." In *Leon* itself probable cause was absent entirely, yet illegally seized evidence was admitted into evidence. We cannot countenance such a wide departure from the text and history of Article I, Section 8, nor can we permit the use of a "good faith" exception to effectively nullify Pa. R. Crim. P. 2003. . . .

A second policy consideration which bolsters our conclusion is that the underlying premise of *Leon* is still open to serious debate. Although it is clear that the exclusionary rule presents some cost to society, in allowing some guilty defendants to go free, the extent of the costs are far from clear. A number of recent studies have indicated that the exclusion of illegally seized evidence has had a marginal effect in allowing guilty criminals to avoid successful prosecution.[15] . . . Equally as important, the alternative to the exclusionary rule most commonly advanced — i.e., allowing victims of improper searches to sue police officers directly — has raised serious concern among police officers.[17]

A third policy consideration which compels our decisions is that, given the recent decision of the United States Supreme Court in Illinois v. Gates, 462 U.S. 213 (1983), adopting a "totality of the circumstances test" in assessing probable cause, there is far less reason to adopt a "good faith" exception to the exclusionary rule. We have adopted Gates as a matter of Pennsylvania law. . . . As a number of jurists have pointed out, the flexible *Gates* standard now eliminates much of the prior concern which existed with respect to an overly rigid application of the exclusionary rule.

Finally, the dangers of allowing magistrates to serve as "rubber stamps" and of fostering "magistrate-shopping," are evident under *Leon*. As the instant case illustrates, police officers and magistrates have historically worked closely together in this Commonwealth. Trooper Deise and District Justice Tlumac prepared the warrant and affidavit with Trooper Deise dictating the affidavit while the magistrate typed it verbatim.

There is no suggestion here that Trooper Deise and District Justice Tlumac acted other than in utmost "good faith" when preparing the warrant. Nevertheless, we are mindful of the fact that both state and federal interpretations of the Fourth Amendment require a warrant to be issued by a "neutral and detached magistrate," because . . . there is a requirement of an independent determination of probable cause. . . .

It must be remembered that a District Justice is not a member of the executive branch — the police — but a member of the judiciary. By falling within the judicial branch of government, the District Justice is thus charged with the responsibility of being the disinterested arbiter of disputes and is charged further with acting as the bulwark between the police and the rights of citizens. Unless and until a magistrate independently determines there is probable cause, no warrant shall issue.

This is not to say that we distrust our police or district justices; far from it. We, in fact, have no doubt that police officer's and district justices in Pennsylvania are intelligent, committed and independent enough to carry out their duties under the scheme which has evolved over the past 30 years, in order to safeguard the rights of our citizens. However, requiring "neutral and detached magistrates" furthers the twin aims of safeguarding privacy and assuring that no warrant shall issue but upon probable cause. As such, we see no reason to eliminate this requirement, for if we did, we would eviscerate the purpose of requiring warrants prior to searches. "If it ain't broke, don't fix it."

15. See Nardulli, The Societal Costs of the Exclusionary Rule: An Empirical Assessment, 1983 A. B. Found. Research J. 585. In this study of nine mid-sized counties in Illinois, Michigan and Pennsylvania, the author found that motions to suppress physical evidence were filed in fewer than five percent of the 7,500 cases studied, and such motions were successful in only seven-tenths of a percent of all cases. A 1979 study prepared by the General Accounting Office at the request of Congress reported that only four-tenths of a percent of all cases declined for prosecution by federal prosecutors were declined primarily because of illegal search problems. Restated in terms of all arrests, the study shows that only two-tenths of a percent of all felony arrests are declined for prosecution because of potential exclusionary rule problems. . . .

17. See Note, The Exclusionary Rule and Deterrence: An Empirical Study of Chicago Narcotics Officers, 54 U. Chi. L. Rev. 1016, 1053 (1987). In a survey of 26 Chicago narcotics officers, all 26 believed that the exclusionary rule was preferable to a system where police officers were sued directly.

Thirty years ago, when the exclusionary rule was first introduced, police officers were perhaps plagued with ill-defined, unarticulated rules governing their conduct. However, the past 30 years have seen a gradual sharpening of the process, with police officers adapting well to the exclusionary rule. . . . Although the exclusionary rule may place a duty of thoroughness and care upon police officers and district justices in this Commonwealth, in order to safeguard the rights of citizens under Article I, Section 8, that is a small price to pay, we believe, for a democracy.

Papadakos, J., concurring.

I am compelled to concur in the result because Rule 2003(a) of the Pennsylvania Rules of Criminal Procedure is absolute in requiring that the affidavit of probable cause supporting the issuance of a search warrant must be complete on its face in every essential detail, and that no testimony is permitted after its execution to fill in the blanks. . . .

In view of the clear, unequivocal command of Rule 2003(a), I see no reason for the majority to reinvent the wheel and re-express the rationale underpinning the judicially created rule of procedure. It's all been said before. . . . Since the majority apparently does not wish to change the rule to avoid the absurdity of excluding the evidence obtained by the police through no misconduct on their part, I see no need for the in-depth re-analysis given by the majority. Were the rule not so absolute on its face, I would gladly join [Justice McDermott] in dissent, for my sympathies and reason lie in his expression of outrage in the result of cases such as this.

McDermott, J., dissenting.

Today we have abandoned the 27 year history of this Court's restrictive use of the exclusionary rule to only those instances where its application would deter misconduct by law enforcement authorities. Now that we have ignored that history and have decided to employ it even in cases where police officers have fulfilled their every obligation to protect the individual constitutional rights of citizens, I dissent.

Until this day we have dutifully followed the canons of the Fourth Amendment prescribed by the Supreme Court of the United States through hundreds of cases. We . . . were obliged to ignore a mountain of illegal contraband that otherwise was palpable indicia of guilt. There is no doubt that the social cost has been more than criminals freed to try again. It has generated a disbelief and a growing disrespect in the efficacy of law that stands mute in the presence of incontrovertible evidence of fire and lets the house burn down because the fireman arrived before he was properly called.[2] United States v. Leon, 468 U.S. 897 (1984), does not open the gates to unauthorized search, it does not dissolve the need for probable cause. It simply and properly shifts the responsibility for determining probable cause to a neutral magistrate and frees the police of his or her mistakes. . . .

The instant case is a classic illustration. The defect in the affidavit of probable cause was that the time of the offense was not specified. What was told the magistrate was that the contraband was "growing," a clear indication of present tense. The informants told the police that they saw it growing and the magistrate was told that it

2. One rationale, other than deterrence, that has been offered for the use of the exclusionary rule is "the imperative of judicial integrity." However, this rationale has been criticized because [the] layman finds the judicial integrity rationale difficult to grasp, [and] many lawyers think the highest integrity of the adjudicative aspect of the criminal process lies in the separation of the guilty from the innocent on the basis of all the relevant evidence available.

was growing and he issued a search warrant on that premise. When the police arrived it was still growing. All concerned acted in good faith. To suppress the evidence because a date was not specified with exactitude under those circumstances dwindles into practiced absurdity.

The United States Supreme Court has made it abundantly clear that suppression of evidence seized without probable cause is not a constitutional right. This Court has made that clear as well. See Commonwealth v. Miller, 518 A.2d 1187 (Pa. 1986) ("[T]he exclusionary rule is a judicially created device designed to deter improper governmental action in the course of criminal investigations and prosecutions. It is not a personal right of the accused"). The United States Supreme Court has made it equally clear that suppression of evidence seized without probable cause is mandated to contain police action. Likewise, we have approved the suppression of evidence only where it will have the benefit of deterring similar police misconduct in the future.

In interpreting our Constitution we are, as are our sister states, always free to give more than that allowed under Federal Constitutional interpretation. I would choose to accept the rationale of the Supreme Court and recognize the "good faith exception" of *Leon* to the exclusionary rule as have 18 of our sister states. . . . Like the United States Supreme Court, I find no evidence that the judiciary has run beyond its responsibilities, or that if they do we cannot correct them. The Supreme Court of the United States is a world landmark for the protection of constitutional rights. What they require we enforce; what they allow we ought not deter except upon clear evidence of positive need. The United States Supreme Court has recognized a positive need to allow, under the canons of *Leon,* a good faith exception. To do otherwise is to provide a sanctuary for the lawless elements seeking profit, particularly in the growing human misery of addiction. . .

Notes

1. *Good faith exception: majority position.* About 15 states have decided, like Pennsylvania, not to adopt a good faith exception to exclusionary rules under their state constitutions. Another group of roughly 25 states has explicitly adopted *Leon* under state constitutions. See State v. Eason, 629 N.W.2d 613 (Wis. 2001). A few states have codified the good faith exception. See, e.g., Tex. Code Crim. Proc. art. 38.23, reprinted later in this chapter. Do you agree with the Pennsylvania court that a state rejecting the good faith exception will maintain stronger privacy protections and stronger control over the quality of warranted searches? If you were directing a police training program in a state that had adopted *Leon,* would that decision affect your training priorities or your recommendations to police officers?

2. *Objective good faith and perjury.* As the *Edmunds* court mentions, the officer's good faith reliance on the warrant under *Leon* must be "objectively reasonable." There is no objective good faith when (1) the officer gives to the magistrate information that the officer knew or should have known was false; (2) the magistrate "wholly abandon[s]" the judicial role; (3) the affidavit is "so lacking in indicia of probable cause" that it would be "entirely unreasonable" for a well-trained officer to believe probable cause existed; or (4) the warrant is so facially deficient that the officer could not reasonably believe it is valid. *Leon,* 468 U.S. at 923. How would a criminal defendant prove that an officer gave false information to the magistrate?

In one limited survey, Chicago prosecutors and judges estimated that police officers lie in 20 to 50 percent of all the affidavits they submit to obtain warrants. Myron Orfield, Deterrence, Perjury, and the Heater Factor: An Exclusionary Rule in the Chicago Criminal Courts, 63 U. Colo. L. Rev. 75 (1992).

The "four corners" rule, mentioned in the *Edmunds* case from Pennsylvania, is one traditional technique to prevent perjury or other inaccurate police testimony. Is it possible to adopt the good faith exception while continuing to insist that any facts related to the reasonableness of the search appear within the warrant application and supporting affidavits? See State v. Davidson, 618 N.W.2d 418 (Neb. 2000) (inquiry into officers' good faith is not limited to four corners of warrant affidavit).

3. *What counts as a cost?* Are criminal convictions lost because the exclusionary rule is the chosen remedy or are the lost convictions simply the cost of having the Fourth Amendment and its analogs? Since the exclusionary rule arguably returns the parties to their relative positions before the constitutional violation took place, one might consider it a backward-looking "tort" remedy. On the other hand, if one is convinced that the value of the remedy to the defendant (avoiding a criminal conviction) far exceeds the value of any lost privacy, then the difference in value between the loss to the defendant and the loss to the government might be considered a "cost" of the exclusionary rule rather than a cost of the constitutional provision. One might prefer a remedy that more closely matches the defendant's actual loss. Which is the most appropriate measure?

4. *Good faith exceptions to rules or statutes.* The *Edmunds* court partly based its decision on the perceived conflict between a rule of procedure and the proposed good faith exception to the exclusionary remedy. As we saw in Chapters 2 and 3, many states have rules and statutes that supplement or clarify the requirements of the Fourth Amendment and its analogs. Consider Iowa Code §808.3, reprinted in Chapter 3. Would that statute prevent an Iowa court from adopting a good faith exception to the state exclusionary rule? See State v. Beckett, 532 N.W.2d 751 (Iowa 1995). Does the Pennsylvania rule or the Iowa statute say anything about remedies for violations? If a statute or rule regarding searches or seizures is silent about remedies, should a court presume that exclusion is the proper remedy? Should it make this presumption more readily for statutes than for the constitution?

5. *Good faith reliance on rules or statutes.* Rules or statutes can also work in favor of a good faith exception. In Illinois v. Krull, 480 U.S. 340 (1987), the court extended the good faith exception of *Leon* to include searches by officers who relied in good faith during a search or seizure on a statute later declared to be unconstitutional. Does the exclusionary rule help to "deter" the legislature from passing unconstitutional legislation regarding searches and seizures?

6. *Good faith reliance on others.* The *Leon* decision allows police officers to rely on determinations by a magistrate. In Arizona v. Evans, 514 U.S. 1 (1995), the Court allowed a good faith exception to the exclusionary rule when an officer relied on an inaccurate record showing an outstanding arrest warrant for a person he had stopped. The record was inaccurate because an employee of the clerk of the court had failed to update a computer database. Would the outcome be any different if the police department, rather than the court, had employed the clerk? See State v. White, 660 So. 2d 664 (Fla. 1995) (applying "fellow officer rule" and excluding evidence).

Problem 6-1. Objective Good Faith

The Drug Squad of the Boulder Police Department received an anonymous letter, postmarked from Kansas City, which read as follows:

> This letter is to inform you that the person described below is an active drug dealer and warrants investigation. This is based on firsthand knowledge and eyewitness accounts by me and others. Below are some facts that may help you.
>
> Name: Jeff; Age: 35-40; Height: 5′9″; Weight: 170 lbs.; Race: white; Features: Bald on the top of his head. Crooked front teeth. Address: Lives in Boulder, Colorado, and is a student at the university.
>
> Vehicle: Two-door van with a large window on the driver's side. The passenger side has a sliding door. Color is steel blue. License plate number is MXS 518 or MSX 518, Colorado.
>
> Drugs are collected at a music store located in Kansas City just north of the intersection of 39th and Main on the east side of the street. The collection times may coincide with the vacation times of the university in Colorado. The drugs are then taken to Boulder for resale.
>
> We hope that this information will help you and are sorry that we must remain anonymous as other innocent people may get involved.
>
> Your friends in Kansas City.

Detective Kurt Weiler began an investigation, and confirmed that the vehicle described was registered to Jeffrey Leftwich, that Leftwich was 37 years old, and that his appearance matched the description in the letter. A call to the Kansas City Police Department confirmed that the music store described in the letter was in a "high drug" area.

During spring break at the university, officers noted that no vehicles were parked outside Leftwich's trailer residence. The day after spring break ended, an officer observed a car parked in the driveway of the residence. The parked car belonged to a person who had been convicted two years earlier of possessing cocaine. The next day, officers noted that Leftwich's Ford van was parked in the driveway. Further inquiries confirmed that Leftwich had traveled to Kansas City during spring break.

Detective Weiler then prepared an affidavit for a search warrant for Leftwich's home. The chief deputy district attorney reviewed the affidavit and advised Detective Weiler that the affidavit presented a close case and that a judge might not sign it. Weiler nonetheless filed the application and a district court judge issued a warrant. During the search of Leftwich's home, Weiler found a triple-beam balance and some marijuana.

Assuming that a reviewing court would conclude that the warrant was not supported by probable cause, would the good faith exception apply? Recall that the officer's good faith must be "objectively" reasonable. If this officer did not qualify for the good faith exception, how often will the exception apply in those states adopting it? Compare People v. Leftwich, 869 P.2d 1260 (Colo. 1994).

■ TEXAS CODE OF CRIMINAL PROCEDURE ART. 38.23

(a) No evidence obtained by an officer or other person in violation of any provisions of the Constitution or laws of the State of Texas, or of the Constitution or laws of the United States of America, shall be admitted in evidence against the accused on the trial of any criminal case. . . .

(b) It is an exception to the provisions of subsection (a) of this Article that the evidence was obtained by a law enforcement officer acting in objective good faith reliance upon a warrant issued by a neutral magistrate based on probable cause.

■ COLORADO REVISED STATUTES §16-3-308

(1) Evidence which is otherwise admissible in a criminal proceeding shall not be suppressed by the trial court if the court determines that the evidence was seized by a peace officer . . . as a result of a good faith mistake or of a technical violation.

(2) As used in subsection (1) of this section:

(a) "Good faith mistake" means a reasonable judgmental error concerning the existence of facts or law which if true would be sufficient to constitute probable cause.

(b) "Technical violation" means a reasonable good faith reliance upon a statute which is later ruled unconstitutional, a warrant which is later invalidated due to a good faith mistake, or a court precedent which is later overruled. . . .

(4) (a) It is hereby declared to be the public policy of the state of Colorado that, when evidence is sought to be excluded from the trier of fact in a criminal proceeding because of the conduct of a peace officer leading to its discovery, it will be open to the proponent of the evidence to urge that the conduct in question was taken in a reasonable, good faith belief that it was proper, and in such instances the evidence so discovered should not be kept from the trier of fact if otherwise admissible. . . .

(b) It shall be prima facie evidence that the conduct of the peace officer was performed in the reasonable good faith belief that it was proper if there is a showing that the evidence was obtained pursuant to and within the scope of a warrant, unless the warrant was obtained through intentional and material misrepresentation.

Problem 6-2. Unwarranted Good Faith

Three undercover police officers went to the Brook Hollow Inn to set up a surveillance of possible illegal activities in one of the rooms. The manager checked the officers into a room that she believed to be vacant. However, when the officers entered the room they noticed that clothing and luggage had been left in the room. One officer called the registration desk to confirm that they were in the right room. Another officer opened the doors of the television cabinet and found cocaine there. After the officers had left the room, Charles Farmer arrived at the room and let himself in with his key. He called the manager from the phone in the room and told her that he had paid for another day and still occupied the room. The manager told Farmer that a terrible mistake had been made.

Would a court in Colorado exclude from evidence the cocaine found in the room? What about a court in Texas? Would this evidence be admissible under *Leon*? Compare Farmer v. State, 759 P.2d 1031 (Okla. Crim. App. 1988).

Notes

1. *Statutory exclusion.* A number of states have passed statutes calling in general terms for the exclusion of evidence obtained through illegal searches or seizures. Would this sort of statute make it more difficult for a court to justify the creation of good faith exceptions or other limitations on the state's exclusionary rule? On the other hand, several jurisdictions have passed statutes allowing admission of evidence obtained illegally, so long as the officer acted in good faith. Some of these statutes (including Colorado's) were enacted before the Supreme Court decided *Leon* in 1984. Would the passage of such a statute affect your analysis in Problem 6-2?

2. *Evidence excluded in which proceedings?* The statutes printed above all address admission of evidence in criminal proceedings. Federal and state constitutions require the exclusion of evidence from the government's case-in-chief at a criminal trial. However, the exclusionary rule usually does not operate in other proceedings. For instance, the government can use such evidence in grand jury proceedings and in most administrative proceedings. See INS v. Lopez-Mendoza, 468 U.S. 1032 (1984) (exclusion does not apply in civil deportation proceedings). Courts deciding whether to follow the exclusionary rule in various types of proceedings have often relied on the reasoning of the Supreme Court in United States v. Calandra, 414 U.S. 338 (1974). The Court there decided that the exclusionary rule would not apply to grand jury proceedings because the rule would have little additional deterrent value on police, given that the evidence was already excludable from any criminal trial. Would this reasoning apply to investigators for the Immigration and Naturalization Service, or others like them, whose principal task is to enforce civil laws? State courts often engage in a balancing test to determine the benefits and costs of excluding evidence from different kinds of proceedings. The exclusionary rule is generally applied to "quasi-criminal" proceedings before judges or administrative agencies such as proceedings to forfeit property (because of its connection with criminal activity). See, e.g., Commonwealth v. One 1985 Ford Thunderbird Automobile, 624 N.E.2d 547 (Mass. 1993). But see Pennsylvania Board of Probation and Parole v. Scott, 524 U.S. 357 (1998) (parole boards are not required by federal law to exclude evidence obtained in violation of Fourth Amendment). Is the deterrent value of the exclusionary rule in quasi-criminal proceedings any greater than in other civil proceedings? A number of state statutes and court rules clarify whether illegally obtained evidence may be admitted in various types of proceedings. See, e.g., La. Code Evid. art. 1101.

3. *Impeachment.* The government can also use improperly obtained evidence as the basis for impeaching a defendant if she testifies at a criminal trial. The Court in United States v. Havens, 446 U.S. 620 (1980), reasoned that exclusion in such cases would not deter police because the usefulness of evidence for impeachment purposes is so difficult to predict. At the same time, allowing the evidence to form the basis of impeachment questions would discourage defendants from committing perjury. See also James v. Illinois, 493 U.S. 307 (1990) (illegally obtained evidence may *not* be used to impeach defense witnesses other than defendant; such impeachment not necessary to discourage perjury of witnesses other than defendant). A few state courts have either rejected or limited the use of illegally obtained evidence for impeachment. See Commonwealth v. Fini, 531 N.E.2d 570 (Mass. 1988) (no impeachment allowed); State v. Brunelle, 534 A.2d 198 (Vt. 1987) (impeachment allowed only if defendant's testimony directly contradicts evidence obtained illegally; not available generally to call defendant's credibility into question).

2. *Causation Limits: Inevitable Discovery and Independent Source*

Long before *Wolf* and *Mapp,* it was clear that the exclusionary rule applied not only to evidence obtained during an improper search or seizure but also to any "fruits," that is, evidence the government later developed on the basis of leads obtained during an improper search or seizure. The exclusionary rule, it is said, applies to the "fruit of the poisonous tree."

But a government error early in an investigation cannot bar all subsequent investigation. Courts have wrestled over how far to extend the impact of government errors — what harms can be said to be "caused" by, or fairly attributed to, the initial violation? Federal and state courts have placed several causal limitations on the fruit-of-the-poisonous-tree doctrine. Two widely acknowledged limitations are known as the "independent source" and "inevitable discovery" rules. Though these are often described as "exceptions" to the exclusionary rule, each amounts to a conclusion that the government would have obtained the evidence in question even without the illegal enforcement activity; thus, the violation did not "cause" the government to hold the evidence.

■ CRISPUS NIX v. ROBERT ANTHONY WILLIAMS

467 U.S. 431 (1984)

BURGER, C.J.

We granted certiorari to consider whether, at respondent Williams' second murder trial in state court, evidence pertaining to the discovery and condition of the victim's body was properly admitted on the ground that it would ultimately or inevitably have been discovered even if no violation of any constitutional or statutory provision had taken place.

On December 24, 1968, 10-year-old Pamela Powers disappeared from a YMCA building in Des Moines, Iowa, where she had accompanied her parents to watch an athletic contest. Shortly after she disappeared, Williams was seen leaving the YMCA carrying a large bundle wrapped in a blanket; a 14-year-old boy who had helped Williams open his car door reported that he had seen "two legs in it and they were skinny and white."

Williams' car was found the next day 160 miles east of Des Moines in Davenport, Iowa. Later several items of clothing belonging to the child, some of Williams' clothing, and an army blanket like the one used to wrap the bundle that Williams carried out of the YMCA were found at a rest stop on Interstate 80 near Grinnell, between Des Moines and Davenport. A warrant was issued for Williams' arrest.

Police surmised that Williams had left Pamela Powers or her body somewhere between Des Moines and the Grinnell rest stop where some of the young girl's clothing had been found. On December 26, the Iowa Bureau of Criminal Investigation initiated a large-scale search. Two hundred volunteers divided into teams began the search 21 miles east of Grinnell, covering an area several miles to the north and south of Interstate 80. They moved westward from Poweshiek County, in which Grinnell was located, into Jasper County. Searchers were instructed to check all roads, abandoned farm buildings, ditches, culverts, and any other place in which the body of a small child could be hidden.

Meanwhile, Williams surrendered to local police in Davenport, where he was promptly arraigned. Williams contacted a Des Moines attorney who arranged for an attorney in Davenport to meet Williams at the Davenport police station. Des Moines police informed counsel they would pick Williams up in Davenport and return him to Des Moines without questioning him. Two Des Moines detectives then drove to Davenport, took Williams into custody, and proceeded to drive him back to Des Moines. During the return trip, one of the policemen, Detective Leaming, began a conversation with Williams, saying:

> I want to give you something to think about while we're traveling down the road. . . . They are predicting several inches of snow for tonight, and I feel that you yourself are the only person that knows where this little girl's body is . . . and if you get a snow on top of it you yourself may be unable to find it. And since we will be going right past the area [where the body is] on the way into Des Moines, I feel that we could stop and locate the body, that the parents of this little girl should be entitled to a Christian burial for the little girl who was snatched away from them on Christmas [E]ve and murdered. [A]fter a snow storm [we may not be] able to find it at all.

Leaming told Williams he knew the body was in the area of Mitchellville — a town they would be passing on the way to Des Moines. He concluded the conversation by saying "I do not want you to answer me. . . . Just think about it."

Later, as the police car approached Grinnell, Williams asked Leaming whether the police had found the young girl's shoes. After Leaming replied that he was unsure, Williams directed the police to a point near a service station where he said he had left the shoes; they were not found. As they continued to drive to Des Moines, Williams asked whether the blanket had been found and then directed the officers to a rest area in Grinnell where he said he had disposed of the blanket; they did not find the blanket. At this point Leaming and his party were joined by the officers in charge of the search. As they approached Mitchellville, Williams, without any further conversation, agreed to direct the officers to the child's body.

The officers directing the search had called off the search at 3 P.M., when they left the Grinnell Police Department to join Leaming at the rest area. At that time, one search team near the Jasper County-Polk County line was only two and one-half miles from where Williams soon guided Leaming and his party to the body. The child's body was found next to a culvert in a ditch beside a gravel road in Polk County, about two miles south of Interstate 80, and essentially within the area to be searched.

In February 1969 Williams was indicted for first-degree murder. [He was convicted at trial, but this Court overturned the conviction because] Detective Leaming had obtained incriminating statements from Williams by what was viewed as interrogation in violation of his right to counsel. Brewer v. Williams, 430 U.S. 387 (1977). This Court's opinion noted, however, that although Williams' incriminating statements could not be introduced into evidence at a second trial, evidence of the body's location and condition "might well be admissible on the theory that the body would have been discovered in any event, even had incriminating statements not been elicited from Williams."

At Williams' second trial in 1977 in the Iowa court, the prosecution did not offer Williams' statements into evidence, nor did it seek to show that Williams had directed the police to the child's body. However, evidence of the condition of her body as it was found, articles and photographs of her clothing, and the results of post mortem medical and chemical tests on the body were admitted. The trial court concluded that the State had proved by a preponderance of the evidence that, if the search had not been suspended and Williams had not led the police to the victim, her body would have been discovered "within a short time" in essentially the same condition as it was actually found. The trial court also ruled that if the police had not located the body, "the search would clearly have been taken up again where it left off, given the extreme circumstances of this case and the body would have been found in short order."

In finding that the body would have been discovered in essentially the same condition as it was actually found, the court noted that freezing temperatures had prevailed and tissue deterioration would have been suspended. The challenged evidence was admitted and the jury again found Williams guilty of first-degree murder; he was sentenced to life in prison. . . .

The . . . vast majority of all courts, both state and federal, recognize an inevitable discovery exception to the exclusionary rule. We are now urged to adopt and apply the so-called ultimate or inevitable discovery exception to the exclusionary rule. Williams contends that evidence of the body's location and condition is "fruit of the poisonous tree," i.e., the "fruit" or product of Detective Leaming's plea to help the child's parents give her "a Christian burial," which this Court had already held equated to interrogation. He contends that admitting the challenged evidence violated the Sixth Amendment whether it would have been inevitably discovered or not. Williams also contends that, if the inevitable discovery doctrine is constitutionally permissible, it must include a threshold showing of police good faith.

The doctrine requiring courts to suppress evidence as the tainted "fruit" of unlawful governmental conduct had its genesis in Silverthorne Lumber Co. v. United States, 251 U.S. 385 (1920); there, the Court held that the exclusionary rule applies not only to the illegally obtained evidence itself, but also to other incriminating evidence derived from the primary evidence. The holding of *Silverthorne* was carefully limited, however, for the Court emphasized that such information does not automatically become "sacred and inaccessible. . . . If knowledge of [such facts] is gained from an independent source, they may be proved like any others. . . ."

Wong Sun v. United States, 371 U.S. 471 (1963), extended the exclusionary rule to evidence that was the indirect product or "fruit" of unlawful police conduct, but there again the Court emphasized that evidence that has been illegally obtained need not always be suppressed, stating:

> We need not hold that all evidence is "fruit of the poisonous tree" simply because it would not have come to light but for the illegal actions of the police. Rather, the more apt question in such a case is whether, granting establishment of the primary illegality, the evidence to which instant objection is made has been come at by exploitation of that illegality or instead by means sufficiently distinguishable to be purged of the primary taint.

The Court thus pointedly negated the kind of good-faith requirement advanced by [Williams]. Although *Silverthorne* and *Wong Sun* involved violations of the Fourth Amendment, the "fruit of the poisonous tree" doctrine has not been limited to cases in which there has been a Fourth Amendment violation. . . .

The core rationale consistently advanced by this Court for extending the exclusionary rule to evidence that is the fruit of unlawful police conduct has been that this admittedly drastic and socially costly course is needed to deter police from violations of constitutional and statutory protections. This Court has accepted the argument that the way to ensure such protections is to exclude evidence seized as a result of such violations notwithstanding the high social cost of letting persons obviously guilty go unpunished for their crimes. On this rationale, the prosecution is not to be put in a better position than it would have been in if no illegality had transpired.

By contrast, the derivative evidence analysis ensures that the prosecution is not put in a worse position simply because of some earlier police error or misconduct. The independent source doctrine allows admission of evidence that has been discovered by means wholly independent of any constitutional violation. That doctrine, although closely related to the inevitable discovery doctrine, does not apply here; Williams' statements to Leaming indeed led police to the child's body, but that is not the whole story. The independent source doctrine teaches us that the interest of society in deterring unlawful police conduct and the public interest in having juries receive all probative evidence of a crime are properly balanced by putting the police in the same, not a worse, position that they would have been in if no police error or misconduct had occurred. When the challenged evidence has an independent source, exclusion of such evidence would put the police in a worse position than they would have been in absent any error or violation. There is a functional similarity between these two doctrines in that exclusion of evidence that would inevitably have been discovered would also put the government in a worse position, because the police would have obtained that evidence if no misconduct had taken place. Thus, while the independent source exception would not justify admission of evidence in this case, its rationale is wholly consistent with and justifies our adoption of the ultimate or inevitable discovery exception to the exclusionary rule. . . .

If the prosecution can establish by a preponderance of the evidence that the information ultimately or inevitably would have been discovered by lawful means — here the volunteers' search — then the deterrence rationale has so little basis that the evidence should be received.[5] Anything less would reject logic, experience, and common sense.

The requirement that the prosecution must prove the absence of bad faith . . . would place courts in the position of withholding from juries relevant and undoubted truth that would have been available to police absent any unlawful police activity. Of course, that view would put the police in a worse position than they would have been in if no unlawful conduct had transpired. And, of equal importance, it wholly fails to take into account the enormous societal cost of excluding truth in the search for truth in the administration of justice. Nothing in this Court's prior holdings supports any such formalistic, pointless, and punitive approach. . . .

A police officer who is faced with the opportunity to obtain evidence illegally will rarely, if ever, be in a position to calculate whether the evidence sought would inevitably be discovered. . . . On the other hand, when an officer is aware that the

5. As to the quantum of proof, we have already established some relevant guidelines. . . . In Lego v. Twomey, 404 U.S. 477, 488 (1972), we observed "from our experience [that] no substantial evidence has accumulated that federal rights have suffered from determining admissibility by a preponderance of the evidence" and held that the prosecution must prove by a preponderance of the evidence that a confession sought to be used at trial was voluntary. We are unwilling to impose added burdens on the already difficult task of proving guilt in criminal cases by enlarging the barrier to placing evidence of unquestioned truth before juries. Williams argues that the preponderance-of-the-evidence standard used by the Iowa courts is inconsistent with United States v. Wade, 388 U.S. 218 (1967). [Inevitable] discovery involves no speculative elements but focuses on demonstrated historical facts capable of ready verification or impeachment and does not require a departure from the usual burden of proof at suppression hearings.

evidence will inevitably be discovered, he will try to avoid engaging in any questionable practice. In that situation, there will be little to gain from taking any dubious "shortcuts" to obtain the evidence. Significant disincentives to obtaining evidence illegally — including the possibility of departmental discipline and civil liability — also lessen the likelihood that the ultimate or inevitable discovery exception will promote police misconduct. See Bivens v. Six Unknown Federal Narcotics Agents, 403 U.S. 388 (1971). In these circumstances, the societal costs of the exclusionary rule far outweigh any possible benefits to deterrence that a good-faith requirement might produce.

[Three lower courts] independently reviewing the evidence have found that the body of the child inevitably would have been found by the searchers. Williams challenges these findings, asserting that the record contains only the "post hoc rationalization" that the search efforts would have proceeded two and one-half miles into Polk County where Williams had led police to the body. When that challenge was made at the suppression hearing preceding Williams' second trial, the prosecution offered the testimony of Agent Ruxlow of the Iowa Bureau of Criminal Investigation. Ruxlow had organized and directed some 200 volunteers who were searching for the child's body. The searchers were instructed "to check all the roads, the ditches, any culverts. . . . If they came upon any abandoned farm buildings, they were instructed to go onto the property and search those abandoned farm buildings or any other places where a small child could be secreted." Ruxlow testified that he marked off highway maps of Poweshiek and Jasper Counties in grid fashion, divided the volunteers into teams of four to six persons, and assigned each team to search specific grid areas. . . . Although he had previously marked off into grids only the highway maps of Poweshiek and Jasper Counties, Ruxlow had obtained a map of Polk County, which he said he would have marked off in the same manner had it been necessary for the search to continue.

The search had commenced at approximately 10 A.M. and moved westward through Poweshiek County into Jasper County. At approximately 3 P.M., after Williams had volunteered to cooperate with the police, Detective Leaming, who was in the police car with Williams, sent word to Ruxlow and the other Special Agent directing the search to meet him at the Grinnell truck stop and the search was suspended at that time. Ruxlow also stated that he was "under the impression that there was a possibility" that Williams would lead them to the child's body at that time. The search was not resumed once it was learned that Williams had led the police to the body, which was found two and one-half miles from where the search had stopped in what would have been the easternmost grid to be searched in Polk County. There was testimony that it would have taken an additional three to five hours to discover the body if the search had continued; the body was found near a culvert, one of the kinds of places the teams had been specifically directed to search.

On this record it is clear that the search parties were approaching the actual location of the body, and we are satisfied, along with three courts earlier, that the volunteer search teams would have resumed the search had Williams not earlier led the police to the body and the body inevitably would have been found. [The] case is remanded for further proceedings consistent with this opinion. It is so ordered.

BRENNAN, J., dissenting.

To the extent that today's decision adopts this "inevitable discovery" exception to the exclusionary rule, it simply acknowledges a doctrine that is akin to the "independent source" exception first recognized by the Court in Silverthorne Lumber Co. v. United States, 251 U.S. 385 (1920). In particular, the Court concludes that unconstitutionally obtained evidence may be admitted at trial if it inevitably would have been discovered in the same condition by an independent line of investigation that was already being pursued when the constitutional violation occurred. . . . I agree that in these circumstances the "inevitable discovery" exception to the exclusionary rule is consistent with the requirements of the Constitution.

In its zealous efforts to emasculate the exclusionary rule, however, the Court loses sight of the crucial difference between the "inevitable discovery" doctrine and the "independent source" exception from which it is derived. When properly applied, the "independent source" exception allows the prosecution to use evidence only if it was, in fact, obtained by fully lawful means. It therefore does no violence to the constitutional protections that the exclusionary rule is meant to enforce. The "inevitable discovery" exception is likewise compatible with the Constitution, though it differs in one key respect from its next of kin: specifically, the evidence sought to be introduced at trial has not actually been obtained from an independent source, but rather would have been discovered as a matter of course if independent investigations were allowed to proceed.

In my view, this distinction should require that the government satisfy a heightened burden of proof before it is allowed to use such evidence. The inevitable discovery exception necessarily implicates a hypothetical finding that differs in kind from the factual finding that precedes application of the independent source rule. To ensure that this hypothetical finding is narrowly confined to circumstances that are functionally equivalent to an independent source, and to protect fully the fundamental rights served by the exclusionary rule, I would require clear and convincing evidence before concluding that the government had met its burden of proof on this issue. Increasing the burden of proof serves to impress the factfinder with the importance of the decision and thereby reduces the risk that illegally obtained evidence will be admitted. Because the lower courts did not impose such a requirement, I would remand this case for application of this heightened burden of proof by the lower courts in the first instance. I am therefore unable to join either the Court's opinion or its judgment.

Notes

1. *Inevitable discovery: majority position.* Along with the federal system, every state except Texas and Washington recognizes an "inevitable discovery" exception to exclusion. Under this doctrine, a court may use evidence obtained as the fruit of an illegal search or seizure if the government *would have* learned about evidence through proper techniques or channels without the illegal search or seizure ever taking place. Consider State v. Daugherty, 931 S.W.2d 268 (Tex. Crim. App. 1996) (statutory exclusion rule does not include inevitable discovery exception). The inevitable discovery exception is a potentially large limit on exclusion, particularly if one is willing to presume that the police (or interested citizens) are often capable of solving important crimes and would more often than not find the evidence. The level of certainty required in predicting the "inevitability" of the discovery is the key issue. Under federal law, the government must prove by a preponderance of the evidence the underlying facts necessary to conclude that the discovery was inevitable. Note

the distinction between the standard of proof necessary to establish the underlying facts and the level of certainty necessary to reach the conclusion that discovery was "inevitable." Compare State v. Sugar, 527 A.2d 1377 (N.J. 1987) (body buried in shallow ground would have inevitably been discovered because defendant was attempting to sell the property and prospective buyers would have smelled decomposing body; meets clear and convincing evidence requirement of state law) with Commonwealth v. O'Connor, 546 N.E.2d 336, 340 (Mass. 1989) (question is whether specific facts demonstrate that discovery by lawful means was "certain as a practical matter").

2. *Potential limits on inevitable discovery doctrine.* A number of state courts endorsing the inevitable discovery exception to the exclusionary rule take great pains to say that they do not consider it a "blanket" exception and that it might be used in some circumstances but not in others. See, e.g., State v. Ault, 724 P.2d 545 (Ariz. 1986) (inevitable discovery doctrine does not apply to illegal search or seizure of items in a home); People v. Stith, 506 N.E.2d 911 (N.Y. 1987) (inevitable discovery exception does not apply to "primary evidence" obtained at time of illegal search; applies only to indirect fruits of illegal search). Should special limits on the coverage of inevitable discovery be based on the strength of the privacy or possessory interests at stake, on the likelihood that discovery was indeed inevitable, or on some other factor? Sometimes the willingness of a court to apply this exception depends on how serious the judges believe the violation to be. Compare Lee v. State, 774 A.2d 1183 (Md. App. 2001) (inevitable discovery doctrine cannot save evidence seized in violation of the knock-and-announce rule), with People v. Stevens, 597 N.W.2d 53 (Mich. 1999) (inevitable discovery allows admission of evidence seized in violation of knock-and-announce rule).

What if the police deliberately conduct an illegal search, knowing that discovery of any evidence is inevitable (say, during a later inventory search)? Should courts apply the inevitable discovery exception only when the police act in "good faith"? Only when the lawful investigative process is under way before the violation takes place? See Commonwealth v. Benoit, 415 N.E.2d 818 (Mass. 1981) (refusing to apply inevitable discovery exception to unwarranted search, even though warrant could have been obtained).

The opinions in Nix v. Williams discussed the relevant standard of proof. Most state courts have embraced the federal position and use a preponderance standard. Fewer than a half dozen require the government to show that discovery was inevitable by "clear and convincing" evidence. See Smith v. State, 948 P.2d 473 (Alaska 1997). In the typical pretrial motion to suppress, the standard of proof is a preponderance of the evidence. The defendant carries the burden of proof for warranted searches; the government carries the burden for warrantless searches. Do the factual and legal questions surrounding inevitable discovery justify any changes from the ordinary rules about standard of proof and burden of proof?

3. *Inevitable discovery and statutory remedies.* Does the Oregon statute above enact the inevitable discovery exception in the form most often endorsed in the majority of cases? Despite the importance of the issue, and the variety of positions a state might take on this exception to the exclusionary rule, very few states have a statute addressing "inevitable discovery." Why have the legislatures remained silent? If the legislature has adopted a statutory form of the exclusionary rule without providing for an inevitable discovery exception, should a court nevertheless be willing to create the exception?

4. *Independent source: majority position.* All but a few states have declared that the exclusionary rule does not apply to evidence obtained after an improper search or seizure if the government also learned of the evidence through an "independent source." The independent source is distinct from the inevitable discovery exception because it is based on an untainted source that *actually did* lead the police to the evidence in question. For instance, if officers improperly enter a building without a warrant and discover evidence of a crime but later obtain a warrant based on information in their possession before they entered the building, the evidence is not excluded. The basis for the proper warranted search was "independent" of anything the police learned during the improper search. See Murray v. United States, 487 U.S. 533 (1988); Segura v. United States, 468 U.S. 796 (1984); compare People v. Weiss, 978 P.2d 1257 (Cal. 1999) (prosecution does not have to show that particular magistrate would have issued warrant if affidavit had not contained illegally obtained information; independent source applies if police would have sought warrant even without tainted information, and redacted affidavit was sufficient for probable cause). In light of this doctrine, do the police have anything to lose by routinely conducting a "preliminary" search before seeking a search warrant? See William Stuntz, Warrants and Fourth Amendment Remedies, 77 Va. L. Rev. 881 (1991).

5. *Harmless error for improper arrests.* If an arrest is improper, the defendant might argue that his very presence in the courtroom is the result of illegal government action, and a conviction would be barred. Both state and federal courts have uniformly rejected this argument because the use of properly obtained evidence to obtain a conviction in criminal proceedings cures any error in the arrest. United States v. Crews, 445 U.S. 463 (1980) (illegal arrest does not taint otherwise valid eyewitness identification of arrestee); Frisbie v. Collins, 342 U.S. 519 (1952) (illegal arrest is no bar to prosecution); State v. Fleming, 502 A.2d 886 (Conn. 1986). Like the inevitable discovery and independent source rules, the *Frisbie* rule is based on the idea that the illegal government action was not a legally sufficient "cause" of any harm to the defendant.

6. *Attenuation.* Even when there is a causal linkage between an improper search or seizure and some evidence obtained later, the evidence can still be admitted if the link is sufficiently "attenuated." An analogy from the law of torts might be the concept of "proximate cause." For instance, in United States v. Ceccolini, 435 U.S. 268 (1978), a police officer during a conversation with a friend at her workplace wrongfully peered into an envelope in the room and discovered gambling paraphernalia, which belonged to the friend's boss. The friend agreed months later to testify against her boss in criminal proceedings. Even though the improper search of the package was a "but for" cause of the government's access to this testimony, it was not excluded because the witness's willingness to testify was more important than the improper search. In this type of case, courts will not exclude the evidence because, they say, police are unlikely to anticipate the chain of events linking their illegal search to some later source of evidence and therefore will not be deterred by the threat of exclusion. Could the officer in *Ceccolini* have anticipated that an unlawful search of the envelope might create an opportunity for his friend to provide evidence in a criminal trial? See also Stuart v. State, 36 P.3d 1278 (Idaho 2001) (police illegally recorded conversations between attorney and defendant; testimony of witnesses named in those conversations sufficiently attenuated to be admitted).

3. Standing to Challenge Illegal Searches and Seizures

One other major limitation on the exclusionary rule restricts the number of people who can challenge an allegedly illegal search or seizure. In some jurisdictions, this is known as the "standing" doctrine. This limitation applies when the government improperly intrudes on a reasonable privacy expectation of one person and finds evidence implicating a second person in a crime. Can the second person challenge the unreasonable intrusion?

■ LOUISIANA CONSTITUTION ART. I, §5

Any person adversely affected by a search or seizure conducted in violation of this Section shall have standing to raise its illegality in the appropriate court.

■ STATE v. GARY WOOD

536 A.2d 902 (Vt. 1987)

ALLEN, C.J.

The defendant appeals his conviction of aiding in the concealment of stolen property. . . . He claims error in the trial court's denial of his pretrial motion to suppress the product of a warrantless search by state police officers. The trial court denied the motion, concluding that the defendant lacked standing to challenge the search under the Fourth Amendment of the United States Constitution, and Chapter I, Article 11 of the Vermont Constitution. We hold that the defendant has standing to challenge the search under the Vermont Constitution, and reverse the court's ruling. . . .

The challenged evidence in this case is testimony, documents and other evidence identifying a car and two motorcycles as well as the vehicles themselves. These vehicles were seized by a state police officer from the yard of a summer camp where the defendant was staying. The officer conducted the search that yielded the vehicles, without a warrant, as part of an investigation into the theft of stolen motorcycles from members of the "Blue Knights" motorcycle club.

The defendant, his wife and child occupied a trailer situated on the summer camp property. . . . The defendant and his family had stayed in the trailer for two weeks before the search. The defendant's wife had been given permission to stay in the trailer by its owner, who was the caretaker of the premises and the brother of the owner of the land upon which the camp and trailer were located. The camp caretaker was an acquaintance of the defendant and knew that he was on the property. The caretaker observed the defendant on the property on two occasions, and although he never expressly told the defendant he could stay, he never told him to leave. The camp caretaker often allowed people to stay at the camp on a casual basis in this manner, and the camp and trailer were generally left unlocked. Cars and other motor vehicles were left from time to time on the property with the caretaker's permission.

The search and seizure were conducted while the defendant was away from the camp. After determining that the vehicles were stolen, the officer impounded them, and the defendant was charged with aiding in the concealment of stolen property. . . .

The trial court's determination under Rakas v. Illinois, 439 U.S. 128 (1978), that the defendant lacked standing to challenge the search in this case highlights the change that has occurred in Fourth Amendment standing analysis. The *Rakas* standard is markedly different from and more stringent than that announced in its predecessor, Jones v. United States, 362 U.S. 257 (1960), for it both altered the focus of Fourth Amendment analysis, and increased the burden imposed upon a defendant seeking to invoke the protection of the Fourth Amendment.

Rakas transformed the review of an accused's Fourth Amendment claim. . . . Before that decision, . . . the inquiry into a defendant's capacity to raise a Fourth Amendment challenge was viewed as a collateral question of standing. Standing analysis explored whether the claim was being presented by one "whose rights were violated by the search itself," rather than "aggrieved solely by the introduction of damaging evidence" obtained by a search that violated the Fourth Amendment rights of another. Alderman v. United States, 394 U.S. 165 (1969). An accused seeking to challenge a search that invaded the rights of someone other than the accused was viewed as a third party to the search, and denied standing to raise the challenge, because Fourth Amendment rights are personal rights which, like some other constitutional rights, may not be vicariously asserted.

In those cases where the State contested the defendant's allegation that "he himself was a victim of an invasion of privacy," the preliminary standing analysis ensured that the defendant was invoking his personal Fourth Amendment rights. Thus, in *Alderman,* it was held that only a defendant whose conversations were improperly overheard could rely on the protection of the Fourth Amendment, while co-conspirators or co-defendants could not vicariously invoke that defendant's interest, and in United States v. Jeffers, 342 U.S. 48 (1951), it was determined that the accused was advancing his rights rather than those of his two aunts, in whose hotel room he was staying. . . .

Rakas worked a major change in the federal approach to standing analysis. In adopting the "legitimate expectation of privacy" test, the Court declared that its assessment of a defendant's capacity to challenge a search focuses on the substantive merits of the defendant's Fourth Amendment claim rather than on "any theoretically separate, but invariably intertwined concept of standing." The collateral inquiry into whether the defendant was asserting personal rights was transformed into an evaluation of whether the defendant had asserted an interest in privacy sufficient to deserve Fourth Amendment protection. This substantive inquiry is now to be conducted in addition to the defendant's challenge to the reasonableness of the search whenever a defendant makes a Fourth Amendment claim. . . . The collateral question of standing has thus evolved into a substantive inquiry of equal, if not greater, importance than the resolution of the defendant's challenge to the government's evidence-gathering technique.

Rakas also established that a defendant seeking to present a Fourth Amendment challenge under its "legitimate expectation of privacy" test bears a greater burden than had been required under the previous standing analysis. Until *Rakas,* "anyone legitimately on the premises [searched]" could raise a Fourth Amendment challenge. Jones v. United States, 362 U.S. 257 (1960). This formula was set aside in *Rakas*. . . .[5]

5. . . . . If dissatisfaction with the exclusionary rule is in fact the rationale behind *Rakas,* it is incompatible with Article Four of the Vermont Constitution, which provides each individual a "guaranteed right to a remedy at law" for a harm that is suffered. Restricting the availability of the exclusionary rule as the remedy for a violation of Article 11 merely because of dissatisfaction with that remedy would be inconsistent with this guarantee.

In replacing the *Jones* standard with the "legitimate expectation of privacy" test, *Rakas* further decided that the privacy interest must be demonstrated through

> a source outside of the Fourth Amendment, either by reference to concepts of real or personal property law or to understandings that are recognized and permitted by society. One of the main rights attaching to property is the right to exclude others, and one who owns or lawfully possesses or controls property will in all likelihood have a legitimate expectation of privacy by virtue of this right to exclude.

While the ability to raise a Fourth Amendment challenge does not necessarily depend on an actual property interest after *Rakas,* according to this pronouncement, a defendant challenging a search must exhibit an interest in the area searched demonstrably greater than that which would have been sufficient under the previous test of whether the defendant was "legitimately on the premises." . . .

Neither the focus of the federal test away from judicial review of a challenged search nor its curtailment of the scope of the protected right to be free from unlawful governmental conduct is compatible with Article 11. In drafting Article 11, the framers of the Declaration of Rights vested responsibility and authority in the judiciary to review and restrain overreaching searches and seizures by the government. The federal test limits this judicial function, and it cannot be relied upon to promote the central purpose of Article 11.

Vermont's constitutional Declaration of Rights, of which Article 11 is an integral part, sets forth the "natural, inherent, and unalienable" rights of the citizenry. Vt. Const. Ch. I, Art. 1. . . . In fashioning the Declaration of Rights, the authors of our constitution entrusted the judiciary with the primary responsibility in the preservation of this constitutional order. . . . Under Article 11, the reviewing court determines whether the search was lawful, or whether the exclusionary rule must be applied to remedy an unlawful search.

The legal check operates in this manner each time a court scrutinizes the post-search challenge of an accused upon a motion to suppress. The current federal test curtails this function of the judiciary by focusing on the defendant's ability to present a challenge rather than on the challenge itself, and by unduly limiting the class of defendants who may invoke the right to be free from unlawful searches and seizures. The federal test thus frustrates the design of Article 11, and we decline to adopt it.[7]

Article 11 itself establishes the scope of the protected right, and defines who may invoke its protection. The right of the people "to hold themselves, their houses, papers, and possessions, free from search or seizure," defines a right dependent on a possessory interest, with equal recognition accorded to the item seized and the area intruded upon. By delineating the right as a possessory interest, Article 11 premises the protected right upon an objectively defined relationship between a person and the item seized or place searched, as opposed to a subjective evaluation

7. The failure of the "legitimate expectation of privacy" test to promote restraint of officer discretion in the field through the use of search warrants is illustrated by United States v. Payner, 447 U.S. 727 (1980). In *Payner* the district court found that "the Government affirmatively counsels its agents that the Fourth Amendment standing limitation permits them to purposefully conduct an unconstitutional search and seizure of one individual in order to obtain evidence against third parties." Although this finding was acknowledged by the Court in *Payner,* challenged evidence was held admissible based upon the conclusion that the defendant had not demonstrated a legitimate expectation of privacy in the challenged evidence.

of the legitimacy of the person's expectation of privacy in the area searched. Accordingly, a defendant need only assert a possessory, proprietary or participatory interest in the item seized or the area searched to establish standing to assert an Article 11 challenge.

This test gives the proper scope to Article 11, ensuring that a defendant with a protected Article 11 interest may challenge a search which intrudes upon this interest. The preliminary inquiry into the defendant's standing looks no further than to determine whether the protected interest exists. If that interest is established, the reviewing court shifts its focus to the primary assessment of the substantive Article 11 challenge.

This standard simplifies the analysis that must be made by courts and those who follow our decision in deciding whether a warrant was required as a prerequisite to a search. The federal test has been inconsistently applied. . . . By contrast, the possessory interest test is more easily applied because it is based on an objective inquiry into the relationship between the suspect and the item to be seized or the place searched, rather than a subjective analysis of the suspect's expectation of privacy.

In this case, defendant has not asserted a possessory, proprietary or participatory interest in the car and two motorcycles which were seized, and therefore must demonstrate such an interest in the grounds of the trailer, or the area searched, to establish his standing to present his Article 11 claim. The court's findings, with support in the record, demonstrate defendant's possessory interest in the trailer. The camp caretaker gave express permission to his wife to use the trailer, and at least tacit approval to the defendant. Moreover, the defendant and his family resided in the trailer for two weeks before his arrest. This possessory interest in the trailer sustains his standing under the curtilage doctrine to challenge a search of the open space situated within a common enclosure belonging to a dwelling house. The trial court erred in determining that the defendant lacked standing to challenge the legality of the search of the camp yard. The matter must be remanded for a hearing on the merits of the suppression motion. . . .

Problem 6-3. Place of Business

A citizen in Eagen, Minnesota was walking by a ground-floor apartment and saw through the window several people putting white powder into bags. He called the police, and Officer James Thielen went to Apartment 103 to investigate. Thielen looked in the same window through a gap in the closed blind and observed Wayne Carter, Melvin Johns, and Kimberly Thompson putting the powder into bags for several minutes. While other officers began to prepare affidavits for a search warrant, Thielen remained at the apartment building to keep watch. He then saw Carter and Johns leave the building and drive away. Police stopped the car, and noticed in the passenger compartment some drug paraphernalia and a handgun. They arrested Carter and Johns, and an inventory search of the vehicle uncovered 47 grams of cocaine in plastic sandwich bags.

After seizing the car, the police returned to Apartment 103 and arrested Thompson. A warranted search of the apartment revealed cocaine residue on the kitchen table and plastic baggies similar to those found in the car. Thompson was the lessee of the apartment. Carter and Johns lived in Chicago and had come to the apartment for the sole purpose of packaging the cocaine. They had never been to the apartment before and were in the apartment for less than three hours. In return for the use of the apartment, Carter and Johns had given Thompson one-eighth of an ounce of the cocaine.

Carter and Johns were charged with narcotics crimes, and they moved to suppress all evidence obtained from the apartment and the car. Do they have a sufficient privacy interest in the apartment to challenge any illegal search that may have happened there? Compare Minnesota v. Carter, 525 U.S. 83 (1998).

Notes

1. *Standing: majority position.* A slight majority of states follow the federal "legitimate expectation of privacy" approach when they determine who may invoke the exclusionary rule to remedy an illegal search or seizure. Others, like the Vermont court in *Wood,* use some form of the older "legitimately on the premises" test for standing. Often, these courts say that a defendant challenging an illegal search or seizure must demonstrate a "proprietary, possessory, or participatory interest" in the premises searched or the property seized. Try to imagine situations in which the federal test and the "legitimately on the premises" test produce different results.

The Supreme Court attempted, in Rakas v. Illinois, 439 U.S. 128 (1978), to eliminate any distinction between a person's "standing" to challenge an illegal search and the "extent of a particular defendant's rights" under the Fourth Amendment. Rights against unreasonable searches and seizures, said the Court, are personal rights and third parties may not assert them. See Roger Kirst, Constitutional Rights of Bystanders in the War on Crime, 28 N.M. L. Rev. 59 (1998). What would be the consequences of allowing a criminal defendant to challenge an allegedly improper search of a third party's property? Why require standing *at all* for a litigant who hopes to challenge governmental misconduct, particularly if deterrence of government wrongdoing is the central purpose of the exclusionary rule?

2. *Standing for searches of residences, business premises, and cars.* Even though a defendant, under the federal (and majority) rule, must show a "legitimate" expectation of privacy in the premises searched or the property seized, this does not preclude challenges by those who do not own or lease property. The easier cases to decide involve the search of a residence, where the defendant lives full time even though another person owns or leases the residence. Courts in that setting have no trouble in concluding that the person living in the house may challenge a search of any common area in the house or any area within the special control of the defendant. How might these residential cases apply to business premises?

More difficult cases involve guests and others who are present in a residence for shorter periods. In Minnesota v. Olson, 495 U.S. 91 (1990), the Court recognized standing for an overnight guest at an apartment: "[s]taying overnight in another's home is a longstanding social custom that serves functions recognized as valuable by society." On the other hand, the Court in Minnesota v. Carter, 525 U.S. 83 (1998), concluded that defendants present in an apartment only for a few hours did not have a "legitimate expectation of privacy" in the premises. What could be said in favor of allowing dinner guests to challenge the admission of evidence obtained when the police make a warrantless entry of a home to arrest the guest or search her possessions? What if the police illegally search the purse of one person and find inside some contraband belonging to another person? See Rawlings v. Kentucky, 448 U.S. 98 (1980) (denying standing in such a setting).

Should it matter whether a challenged search takes place after a traffic stop rather than in a residence? See State v. Bowers, 976 S.W.2d 379 (Ark. 1998) (passenger has standing to challenge search of car after illegal stop, even though passenger has no possessory interest in the car).

3. *"Automatic" standing for possessory crimes.* Special rules sometimes apply to defendants charged with possessory offenses, such as possession of stolen property or narcotics. The defendant in such a case faces a dilemma. For purposes of standing, she often must establish some ownership interest in the premises that were illegally searched, but for purposes of defending against the charges, she would prefer to deny any connection with the contraband or the premises searched. At one time, most American courts responded to this difficulty by granting "automatic" standing to any defendant who chose to challenge a search or seizure in a possessory crime case. See Jones v. United States, 362 U.S. 257 (1960). Later, the Supreme Court took a different approach to the problem. It held, in Simmons v. United States, 390 U.S. 377 (1968), that the government could not use at trial the defendant's testimony at a suppression hearing, if it was given for the purpose of establishing standing. Because of this "immunity" for the defendant's testimony, the Court decided that "automatic" standing was no longer necessary to protect a defendant. In addition, a defendant might establish a "legitimate" expectation of privacy in some premises searched without necessarily admitting ownership of contraband. See United States v. Salvucci, 448 U.S. 83 (1980). A sizable minority of states have retained the "automatic" standing rule for possessory offenses. Some have explained that the "immunity" for the defendant's testimony at a suppression hearing is not adequate because the testimony still might be used to impeach the defendant's trial testimony. See State v. Alston, 440 A.2d 1311 (N.J. 1981). Can you think of any other reasons to retain the "automatic" standing rule?

4. *"Target" standing.* Should a court give any special treatment to a claim that the police *intentionally* conducted an illegal search against one party for the purpose of obtaining evidence against another party? In United States v. Payner, 447 U.S. 727 (1980), the Supreme Court applied its usual rules of standing in such a case. A few other courts, however, have responded to purposefully illegal searches of this sort by granting standing to the "target" of the search, even if the target had no legitimate expectation of privacy (or any other interest) in the premises that were searched. See Waring v. State, 670 P.2d 357 (Alaska 1983). What difficulties might a court encounter in applying the "target" standing rule? How often will the doctrine be relevant?

C. ADDITIONS AND ALTERNATIVES TO THE EXCLUSIONARY RULE

As we have seen, the exclusionary rule is not available in many cases to enforce the rights against unreasonable searches and seizures. Are there any credible alternatives to the exclusionary rule? Would you embrace any (or all) of these remedies as replacements to the exclusionary rule, or would you adopt them as *additional* remedies and wait for proof of their viability?

1. *Administrative Remedies*

Police officers are sworn to uphold the law, and supervisors within a police department must ensure that the rank-and-file officers obey the law during criminal investigations. Many police departments hire legal counsel to train and advise investigating officers. What other steps might a police department or a local government adopt to discourage illegal searches and seizures?

Events in Los Angeles in the late 1990s offer a fascinating window into a police department's efforts to punish and prevent misbehavior by individual officers. In 1998, eight pounds of cocaine were found missing from a police evidence locker in the Los Angeles Police Department's Rampart division. Investigations led to officer Raphael Perez, a member of Rampart's elite anti-gang unit known as CRASH, for Community Resources Against Street Hoodlums. Like criminals everywhere, Officer Perez told prosecutors that he had information about other officers that he would trade for a reduced sentence of five years. The information from Officer Perez (much of it later confirmed from independent sources) revealed one of the largest patterns of police misconduct in U.S. history.

Perez told investigators a wild tale of police conspiring to frame innocent suspects, beating suspects, and covering up unjustified shootings. For example, he said that two officers in particular — Brian Hewitt and Daniel Lujan — were well known for administering street justice:

> Actually, [Hewitt's] biggest forte was thumping people. He just had this thing about beating people up while they were handcuffed. . . . I saw Officer Hewitt hit this guy so hard in the neck that the guy flipped backward and onto the floor. . . . Let's say [Hewitt] catches you dirty, he would rather beat you up, beat you to a pulp, and then say, "OK, we're even now, right?"

Hundreds of felony cases were tainted by alleged police misconduct. Dozens of officers were fired, relieved of duty, suspended, or quit. The city faced possible civil damages of hundreds of millions of dollars.

Almost every governmental institution that might respond to police abuse did so, including the police department, the Los Angeles District Attorney, the mayor, the city council, and federal civil rights enforcers. The Los Angeles Police assembled a Board of Inquiry to study the corruption scandal. A 362-page Board of Inquiry report blamed the calamity on poor hiring, the isolation of the special CRASH unit, and "rogue cops." L.A. Police Chief Bernard C. Parks explained:

> [T]he Board of Inquiry report . . . points out in graphic detail [that] people with troubling backgrounds have been hired as police officers. We need to tighten up that hiring process. Individuals with criminal records or with histories of violent behavior or narcotics involvement have no place in this department. We need to make sure that field officers are supervised closely and that supervisors have the courage to take corrective action when necessary. I recognize there is a fine line between smothering officers under a stifling bureaucratic blanket and beefing up supervision. The Board of Inquiry report tells us how to walk that fine line and how to do it effectively. . . .
>
> As the members of the Board of Inquiry have emphasized, we do not need to reinvent the wheel, introduce a flock of new programs or institute revolutionary approaches to police work. What we do need to do is emphasize a scrupulous adherence to existing policies and standards. We must enhance our ability to detect any individual

or collective pattern of performance that falters. We must have the courage to deal with those who are responsible for failures. If we do not do all those things, another Rampart will surely occur.

Chief Parks issued an 18-page order detailing his response to the Rampart scandal, including abolition of the CRASH name in favor of generic "gang details," a limited three-year tour of duty with the new special anti-gang units, and new requirements for members and supervisors of the units.

Chief Parks fired Hewitt (one of the officers that Perez had specifically accused) for the alleged beating of Ismael Jimenez, a gang member. In doing so, Parks followed the recommendation of the Board of Rights, a panel of officers who hear disciplinary cases. Evidence compiled by LAPD detectives against Hewitt included samples of blood splattered on the walls of the Rampart Station, which were matched to the victim's DNA; testimony from an emergency room doctor detailing the victim's injuries; testimony from several citizens and law enforcement personnel; and a piece of carpet from the Rampart Station that was soaked with the victim's bloody vomit.

But county prosecutors, citing a lack of evidence, twice declined to file charges against Hewitt. The prosecutors concluded that there was insufficient evidence to prove in court that Hewitt assaulted Jimenez. The office argued there were no witnesses, except possibly another gang member, and no photographs of his injuries.

Eventually, the federal government entered the scene, with an extensive civil rights investigation of the LAPD. Federal officials wanted to know whether Los Angeles ever implemented the recommendations of the 1991 Christopher Commission report, issued following the Rodney King beating and the trials of the officers who beat him. Los Angeles received federal funds to implement those prior recommendations.

■ AN INDEPENDENT ANALYSIS OF THE LOS ANGELES POLICE DEPARTMENT'S BOARD OF INQUIRY REPORT ON THE RAMPART SCANDAL

ERWIN CHEMERINSKY, WITH PAUL HOFFMAN, LAURIE LEVENSON, R. SAMUEL PAZ, CONNIE RICE & CAROL SOBEL

September 11, 2000

On March 1, 2000, The Police Department's Board of Inquiry released its report on the "Rampart Area Corruption Incident." This report, [prepared at the request of the Police Protective League], analyzes the Board of Inquiry report and its recommendations. My overall conclusion is that the Board of Inquiry report unjustifiably minimized the magnitude of the scandal and failed to recommend the major changes necessary to reform the Los Angeles Police Department. The Board of Inquiry report is the management account of the Rampart scandal. The Board of Inquiry was created by the management of the Los Angeles Police Department to study the Rampart scandal and it reflects the views of the Department's leadership, greatly understating the problem and sparing management from criticism. . . .

1. The Board of Inquiry Report Fails to Identify the Extent of the Problem and, Indeed, Minimizes Its Scope and Nature.

Crucial, basic questions must be answered in appraising the extent of the Rampart scandal and the magnitude of the problems confronting the Los Angeles Police Department. How many officers in the Rampart Division CRASH unit participated in illegal activities? How many officers in this unit and in the Rampart Division knew of illegal activity and were complicit by their silence? How high within the Department was there some knowledge of illegal activities by Rampart officers? Was there similar illegal activity in other CRASH units, in other specialized units, and in other divisions?

The Board of Inquiry report provides no answer to these questions. Nonetheless, the Board of Inquiry minimizes the problem, calling it the "Rampart Incident," saying that the problem was a result of a "few" officers, and declaring that corruption is not a problem throughout the Department. These conclusions are at odds with everything that we learned in preparing this report and with the Justice Department's investigation which concluded that abuses occur "on a regular basis."

To ensure that there is a complete and adequate investigation to determine the full extent of the problem, I recommend [that the City of Los Angeles create an independent commission] with the mandate of thoroughly investigating the Los Angeles Police Department, including assessing the extent and nature of police corruption and lawlessness. . . . The Commission should be external to the Police Department and report to the Mayor, the City Council, the City Attorney, the Police Commission, and the people of Los Angeles. Officers with knowledge of wrong-doing in connection with the Rampart scandal should be encouraged to reveal what they know by granting them immunity from discipline for their failure to reveal wrong-doing previously. . . .

2. The Board of Inquiry Report Fails to Recognize That the Central Problem Is the Culture of the Los Angeles Police Department, Which Gave Rise to and Tolerated What Occurred in the Rampart Division and Elsewhere.

The culture within the Los Angeles Police Department gave rise to the Rampart scandal and allowed it to remain undetected for so long. Every police department has a culture — the unwritten rules, mores, customs, codes, values, and outlooks — that creates the policing environment and style. . . . The culture of the Los Angeles Police Department emphasizes control and the exclusion of scrutiny by outsiders, including the Police Commission and its Inspector General, as well as courts and prosecutors. The culture of the Los Angeles Police Department exercises control over the rank and file officers through a highly stratified, elaborate discipline system that enforces voluminous rules and regulations, some of them very petty. The result is a startling degree of alienation and hostility to the management of the Department. The culture of the Los Angeles Police Department, as documented by the Christopher Commission, emphasizes overly aggressive policing, resulting in the use of excessive force.

Most importantly, a code of silence is deeply embedded in the Los Angeles Police Department. . . . The code of silence is reinforced in many ways, as the Department punishes whistleblowers and those who expose the wrong-doing of others.

Changing the culture of the Police Department and reforming its practices will require many dramatic changes, including a shift from overly aggressive police tactics and a mentality that excludes outside oversight, to one that emphasizes community policing and seeks to end the code of silence. This change will not happen voluntarily. [There] must be judicial enforcement of reforms, either through a consent decree or a court order as part of a judgment.

3. The Board of Inquiry Report Fails to Consider the Need for Structural Reforms in the Department, Including Reforming the Police Commission, Strengthening the Independence and Powers of the Inspector General, and Creating Permanent Oversight Mechanisms for the Department.

The Board of Inquiry report identifies no problems with the structure of the Police Department and apparently does not see this as in any way responsible for the Rampart scandal. . . . One essential change is to create a full-time, paid Police Commission and to change the manner of selecting and removing Commissioners to ensure greater independence. Under the Los Angeles City Charter, the Police Commission is the manager for all aspects of the Department, except for police discipline which is the responsibility of the Chief of Police. The Police Commission does not exist only for oversight or policy-making; it is the Department's manager. This task cannot be effectively done by a part-time, unpaid Commission.

Under the Charter, all Commissioners are appointed by, and are removable by, the Mayor. The problem is that Commissioners then are much more likely to reflect one philosophy and, at times, refrain from expressing a difference of opinion because of the risk of being removed by the Mayor or not reappointed. If the Mayor is strongly aligned with the Police Chief, and the Commissioners are seen as aligned with the Mayor, then there is an inherent erosion of public confidence in the Police Commission. That, of course, is exactly the situation today. Mayor Richard Riordan has been outspoken in his support of Police Chief Bernard Parks and Parks' policies. . . . The appointment authority should be dispersed (such as by having the Mayor appoint two police commissioners and having one each by the President of the City Council, the City Attorney, and the City Controller). Removal of a commissioner should require approval of the City Council. . . .

There must be a substantial strengthening of the independence of the Inspector General. . . . The first Inspector General saw her role and powers gutted as she was instructed that she could not report to the Police Commission and could not have access to case files. . . . The Inspector General needs more protection from removal and clearer authority to investigate any matter, unimpeded by the Police Commission.

Finally, there must be an external oversight mechanism for the worst abuses by LAPD officers. A permanent special prosecutor should be created, ideally in the Attorney General's office, to conduct criminal investigations and prosecutions of illegal activity by officers.

4. The Board of Inquiry Report Unduly Minimizes the Problems in the Police Department's Disciplinary System.

. . . Serious problems remain at every step of the disciplinary system. Many have expressed the view that it is too difficult to file complaints against police officers.

Many in the public believe that the system does not adequately discipline wrongdoers. Many officers have expressed a complete loss of faith in the fairness of the system. Many see the Chief of Police as exercising undue control over the process and using it arbitrarily to protect some (especially command staff) from discipline and to persecute others. We cannot emphasize enough the deep distrust we heard voiced by many officers in the police disciplinary system. . . .

The Board of Inquiry recommends strengthening the disciplinary system, especially by increasing the powers of the Internal Affairs division and the authority of the Chief of Police. These recommendations fail to deal with the serious distrust in the system among officers or with any of the underlying problems in the disciplinary system. . . .

Assignments to Internal Affairs are for limited time periods, usually no more than two or three years for most individuals, some for far shorter time periods. This turnover in personnel in Internal Affairs often results in significant turnover in handling a single case. More insidiously, it means that officers from Internal Affairs soon will be returning to work with the same officers that they were disciplining. . . .

The Charter provides that disciplinary charges against police officers are adjudicated by a Board of Rights comprised of two command officers and one civilian. . . . The Board of Inquiry report flatly rejects any change in the disciplinary system. In light of the crisis of confidence in the existing system this is an untenable position. There must be reform and there are many options to be explored. One possibility . . . would be to reconstitute the Board of Rights to include one command officer, one officer of the rank of Sergeant II or higher, and one civilian. Another would be binding arbitration. Another, likely the most promising, would be a citizen review board. . . .

. . . There are serious problems with how officer involved shootings are investigated by the LAPD. As described in the Board of Inquiry report, the practice is that officers are not separated, but are allowed to remain together, return to the station, wait together, meet with the same attorney together, then go back to the scene of the shooting (with the same lawyer consulting multiple officers) and walk through, discuss the evidence and compare stories and develop a scripted smoothly choreographed version of the facts. . . .

In preparing the OIS report, the officer's version of the facts is included in the summary of the shooting, but the tape recorded statements of the witnesses are only summarized. Thus, when the report is approved by the OIS supervisors, any contradictory statements are not included. When the report is widely disseminated to the Use of Force Board, the Police Commission, the Inspector General, the Chief of Police and others, the one-sided version of the facts almost invariably lead to the conclusion that the use of force was within policy. Overall, the present OIS procedure is designed to protect the City and LAPD officers from liability. . . .

Conclusion

. . . Reform is not an event, but a process that will take many years to complete. The hope is that this crisis provides a unique opportunity for reform. This opportunity must not be squandered. . . .

■ ST. PAUL, MINNESOTA, ORDINANCES §§102.01-102.03

SECTION 102.01 . . .

(b) The [police-civilian internal affairs review commission] shall review all complaint investigations concerning members of the police department . . . completed by the internal affairs unit of the police department and subsequent investigations thereof related to alleged acts of excessive force, inappropriate use of firearms, discrimination, . . . poor public relations and such other complaints as may be referred to it by the mayor and/or the chief of police. The commission shall also collect and review summary data on complaints received and report to the mayor and council any patterns which may merit further examination.

SECTION 102.02

(a) There is hereby created a police-civilian internal affairs review commission consisting of seven voting members to be appointed by the mayor and approved by the council. . . . Five members shall be citizen members and two shall be members of the Saint Paul Police Federation as shall be recommended by the police chief to the mayor for appointment. Members shall, to the extent possible, be representative of the city's diversity of neighborhoods, races and cultures, abilities, incomes and sexual orientations. . . .

SECTION 102.03 . . .

(b) Each member of the commission shall, prior to assuming official duties, participate in a training program which shall include topics related to police work, investigation, relevant law, cultural diversity, gender, sexual orientation, disability and the emotional impact of abuse. They shall also participate in ride-alongs with an officer on actual patrol duties. . . .

(d) The investigatory materials prepared by the internal affairs unit of the police department or independent investigators under contract to the city are considered data collected in furtherance of an active investigation and will be reviewed by the commission. The meetings of the commission on such matters will be closed . . . excepting to members of the commission and such other participants as approved by the chair of the commission and the police chief and that will facilitate the review process of the commission.

(e) The commission may request [that] individuals appear before it to state facts to supplement files. The commission may also request internal affairs staff to gather such additional information as may be needed for a determination by the commission. The commission may . . . hire a private investigator as approved by the mayor or chief of police. The commission shall have the power to subpoena witnesses to compel their appearance before it. . . .

(g) The commission, after review and deliberation of an investigation, shall, by majority vote, make its recommendation on the case. Such recommendation by the commission shall be upon a finding that the complaint be sustained; or the complaint not be sustained; or that the officer be exonerated; or the complaint is unfounded; or that the matter does not involve guilt or a lack thereof, but rather a failure of a departmental policy to address the situation. The commission shall also, by majority vote, make a recommendation as to any action to be taken concerning an involved officer. . . .

(j) In the event the chief of police disagrees with the action recommended by the commission, the chief shall notify the commission, in writing, of the action he or she intends to impose. The commission chair and chief of police shall have five working days to discuss any concerns they may have before any action is finalized. This provision does not prohibit the chief of police from taking immediate action in any case. . . .

Notes

1. *Police review boards.* Most police departments of any size have a section (often called "Internal Affairs" or "IAD") that reviews police officer conduct. Sometimes cities establish review boards to help internal affairs divisions or to reconsider the IAD findings. See, e.g., Code of Winston-Salem, North Carolina §§2-242 to 2-253. Sometimes special boards are set up to investigate particular allegations of police abuse. More controversial and less common are review boards entirely outside the police department. Sometimes private groups establish their own independent or citizen review boards, but these nongovernmental boards lack the power to compel the police department to share information or to compel testimony. What are the advantages of an official review board? Who should be its members? What powers should the board have? Review boards often focus on serious misconduct by officers. How should review boards handle low-level but repeated complaints? If review boards do not handle such complaints, who will? See Sean Hecker, Race and Pretextual Traffic Stops: An Expanded Role for Civilian Review Board, 28 Colum. Hum. Rts. L. Rev. 551 (1997).

2. *Internal versus external review.* Are internal and external review bodies likely to reach the same results? Two separate reports assessing allegations of "testilying" and other illegal practices by Philadelphia police in the early 1990s reached widely differing conclusions: The internal report identified rogue officers; the external review found fundamental problems with the training and policies of the department. What are the advantages and disadvantages of an "independent" review board? How can internal review efforts be tied to salary raises and promotion decisions? For a comparison of "internal," "external," and "hybrid" forms of police review based on survey research of police attitudes and citizen complaints, see Douglas Perez, Common Sense About Police Review (1996). The very *existence* of police review panels, particularly those with citizen members, can reduce the number of citizen complaints against police. See Liqun Cao and Bu Huang, Determinants of Citizen Complaints Against Police Abuse of Power, 28 Journal of Criminal Justice 203-213 (May/June 2000) (NCJ 183359). Why might this be true?

3. *Review by the media.* Sometimes newspapers or local TV stations will examine allegations of police misconduct. As with unofficial citizen review boards, the formal power of reporters to obtain information is limited, but of course reporters can disclose to the public any refusals to share information. An additional limit on the use of the media to shape officer and department behavior is the risk of libel suits brought by officers against reporters and newspapers. See, e.g., Costello v. Ocean County Observer, 643 A.2d 1012 (N.J. 1994).

4. *Early warning systems.* Police chiefs have a slogan: Ten percent of the officers cause ninety percent of the problems. How can police managers identify the officers who need special training or removal from the field? Some departments (just over a fourth of all departments nationwide) use "early warning" systems to select officers who might benefit from training or other intervention. See Samuel Walker, Geoffrey P. Alpert, and Dennis J. Kenney, Early Warning Systems: Responding to the Problem Police Officer (July 2001, NCJ 188565). Data collection systems flag officers for special attention if they are involved in some requisite number of citizen complaints, firearm discharges, use-of-force reports, civil litigation, high speed pursuits, or vehicular damage. The supervisors of officers so identified review the incidents and counsel the officer; sometimes the department sends the officer to special training classes. Assuming that plaintiffs in civil lawsuits could subpoena this data about individual officers, does it help or hurt the department during the litigation? Do early warning systems encourage inactive policing?

5. *Renegade cops or renegade police culture?* No one defends the brutality of the individual Rampart officers. But is the problem, as the Los Angeles Police Department and its defenders suggest, with bad cops and weak supervision, or is there a wider problem with the culture of policing? What different responses are called for by the two kinds of problems?

2. *Tort Actions and Criminal Prosecutions*

The most common private remedy for illegal searches prior to the use of the exclusionary rule was a tort action against the officer who violated the law during the search. Any victim of a wrongful search (not just those who later face criminal charges) can, in theory, bring a lawsuit against the officer conducting the search, or against the police department or other governmental units, requesting damages or other relief. The search victim might sue in state court based on state common law torts such as false imprisonment or trespass; she might also look to a state statute granting a civil cause of action for wrongful searches or seizures. Some victims also rely on a federal statute, 42 U.S.C. §1983, which creates a cause of action in federal court against any "person" who acts "under color of" state law to deprive another person of federal constitutional or statutory rights.

These lawsuits have not become a common method of dealing with improper searches or seizures. The plaintiffs in such cases face several substantial legal obstacles: The most important are the doctrines of "sovereign immunity" protecting the state or local government from suit, and "qualified immunity," which protects individual police officers who act with "good faith."

But private enforcement is not the only possibility. In 1994, Congress passed legislation (now codified at 42 U.S.C. §14141) that prohibits state and local governments from engaging in "a pattern or practice of conduct by law enforcement officials" that deprives persons of "rights, privileges, or immunities secured or protected by the Constitution or laws of the United States." The statute authorizes the U.S. Department of Justice to sue in federal court for injunctive and declaratory relief to eliminate the pattern or practice. The Civil Rights Division of the Justice Department filed such a suit against the Los Angeles Police Department in the wake of the Rampart scandal described above; the consent decree resolving that suit is excerpted below. What are the relative merits of public and private civil enforcement?

■ OFFICE OF THE ATTORNEY GENERAL OF TENNESSEE, OPINION 81-212

April 29, 1981

[The District Attorneys General Conference has] requested an opinion on the following questions regarding the responsibility and liability of state criminal investigators. . . . 1) Does a state criminal investigator enjoy immunity from civil liability for acts or omissions within the performance of his official duties? 2) If a state criminal investigator is named as a defendant in a civil action for such acts or omissions is he entitled to legal representation by the state? 3) If a judgment for money damages is rendered against a state criminal investigator for such acts or omissions will the state indemnify him for the judgment? . . .

1) [The criminal investigator would] be entitled to claim a defense of qualified immunity in defense of complaints regarding the manner in which the investigator effected an arrest, conducted a search, or performed other investigatory duties. In defense of a cause of action alleging the deprivation of federal constitutional rights a criminal investigator is entitled to a qualified executive immunity. The doctrine of qualified immunity operates to bar the award of damages against a government official who acts in good faith in accordance with state law and administrative procedures.

The criminal investigator, like any other government official, will not be liable for damages in an action alleging a violation of constitutional rights unless: (1) the official violated a known and unquestioned settled constitutional right of the plaintiff; or (2) the official acted with the intention to maliciously single out the plaintiff to violate the plaintiff's constitutional rights. This doctrine does not require criminal investigators, or any other government official, to predict the future development of constitutional law. . . .

Under the prevailing view in this country a peace officer who arrests someone with probable cause is not liable for false arrest simply because the innocence of the suspect is later proved. A policeman's lot is not so unhappy that he must choose between being charged with dereliction of duty if he does not arrest when he has probable cause, and being mulcted in damages if he does. Though the matter is not entirely free from doubt, the same consideration would seem to require excusing him from liability for acting under a statute that he [believed] to be valid but that was later held unconstitutional on its face or as applied.

[As several courts have stated, the] standard governing police conduct is composed of two elements, the first is subjective and the second is objective. Thus the officer must allege and prove not only that he believed, in good faith, that his conduct was lawful, but also that his belief was reasonable. Thus, investigating officers, like school officials, mental hospital officials and prison officials, must prove that they did not know and should not have known that they were violating the constitutional rights of the plaintiff as well as that they did not act with the intent to cause harm to the plaintiff.

2) State employees may be represented by the Attorney General in civil actions which allege acts or omissions within the employee's scope of employment. Tenn. Code Ann. §§8-6-109 to 8-6-110. However, a state employee may retain private counsel to represent him in such a civil action for damages whose fees may be paid by the Defense Counsel Commission. Tenn. Code Ann. §8-42-101 et seq. The Defense Counsel Commission is only authorized to pay attorneys fees to those state

employees who acted within the scope of their employment or under apparent lawful authority or orders in furtherance of their duties.

3) There is no state statutory authority for the indemnification of a state employee against whom a judgment for compensatory or punitive damages is awarded in either state or federal court.

■ CONSENT DECREE, UNITED STATES v. CITY OF LOS ANGELES

Civil No. 00-11769 GAF, June 15, 2001

1. The United States and the City of Los Angeles, a chartered municipal corporation in the State of California, share a mutual interest in promoting effective and respectful policing. They join together in entering this settlement in order to promote police integrity and prevent conduct that deprives persons of rights, privileges, or immunities secured or protected by the Constitution or laws of the United States.

2. In its Complaint, plaintiff United States alleges that the City of Los Angeles, the Los Angeles Board of Police Commissioners, and the Los Angeles Police Department (collectively, "the City defendants") are violating 42 U.S.C. §14141 by engaging in a pattern or practice of unconstitutional or otherwise unlawful conduct that has been made possible by the failure of the City defendants to adopt and implement proper management practices and procedures. In making these allegations, the United States recognizes that the majority of Los Angeles police officers perform their difficult jobs in a lawful manner. . . .

13. The term "Categorical Uses of Force" means (i) all incidents involving the use of deadly force by an LAPD officer; (ii) all uses of an upper body control hold by an LAPD officer and can include the use of a modified carotid, full carotid or locked carotid; (iii) all uses of force by an LAPD officer resulting in an injury requiring hospitalization, commonly referred to as a law enforcement related injury . . . incident; (iv) all head strikes with an impact weapon; (v) all other uses of force by an LAPD officer resulting in a death, commonly known as a law enforcement activity related death . . . incident; and (vi) all deaths while the arrestee or detainee is in the custodial care of the LAPD, commonly referred to as an in-custody death. . . .

Management and Supervisory Measures to Promote Civil Rights Integrity

39. The City has taken steps to develop, and shall establish a database containing relevant information about its officers, supervisors, and managers to promote professionalism and best policing practices and to identify and modify at-risk behavior (also known as an early warning system). This system shall be a successor to, and not simply a modification of, the existing computerized information processing system known as the Training Evaluation and Management System ("TEAMS"). The new system shall be known as "TEAMS II". . . .

41. TEAMS II shall contain information on the following matters:

a. all non-lethal uses of force that are required to be reported in LAPD "use of force" reports or otherwise are the subject of an administrative investigation by the Department; . . .

c. all officer-involved shootings and firearms discharges, both on-duty and off-duty . . .

d. all other lethal uses of force;

e. all other injuries and deaths that are reviewed by the LAPD Use of Force Review Board . . .

f. all vehicle pursuits and traffic collisions; . . .

h. with respect to the foregoing clauses (a) through [f], the results of adjudication of all investigations (whether criminal or administrative) and discipline imposed or non-disciplinary action taken;

i. all written compliments received by the LAPD about officer performance;

j. all commendations and awards;

k. all criminal arrests and investigations known to LAPD of, and all charges against, LAPD employees;

l. all civil or administrative claims filed with and all lawsuits served upon the City or its officers . . . resulting from LAPD operations and known by the City, the Department, or the City Attorney's Office; . . .

n. all arrest reports, crime reports, and citations made by officers, and all motor vehicle stops and pedestrian stops that are required to be documented in the manner specified in paragraphs 104 and 105;

o. assignment and rank history, and information from performance evaluations for each officer;

p. training history and any failure of an officer to meet weapons qualification requirements; and

q. all management and supervisory actions taken pursuant to a review of TEAMS II information, including non-disciplinary actions. . . .

47. The protocol for using TEAMS II shall include the following provisions and elements:

a. The protocol shall require that, on a regular basis, supervisors review and analyze all relevant information in TEAMS II about officers under their supervision to detect any pattern or series of incidents that indicate that an officer, group of officers, or an LAPD unit under his or her supervision may be engaging in at-risk behavior. . . .

c. The protocol shall require that LAPD managers on a regular basis review and analyze relevant information in TEAMS II about subordinate managers and supervisors in their command regarding the subordinate's ability to manage adherence to policy and to address at-risk behavior.

d. The protocol shall state guidelines for numbers and types of incidents requiring a TEAMS II review by supervisors and managers (in addition to the regular reviews required by the preceding subparagraphs), and the frequency of these reviews. . . .

g. The protocol shall require that all relevant and appropriate information in TEAMS II be taken into account when [deciding matters of] pay grade advancement, promotion, assignment as . . . a Field Training Officer, or when preparing annual personnel performance evaluations. . . .

k. The protocol shall require regular review by appropriate managers of all relevant TEAMS II information to evaluate officer performance citywide, and to evaluate and make appropriate comparisons regarding the performance of all LAPD units in order to identify any patterns or series of incidents that may indicate at-risk behavior. . . .

Incidents, Procedures, Documentation, Investigation, and Review

58. The LAPD shall continue its policy of notifying the County of Los Angeles District Attorney's Office whenever an LAPD officer, on or off-duty, shoots and injures any person during the scope and course of employment. In addition, the LAPD shall notify the District Attorney's Office whenever an individual dies while in the custody or control of an LAPD officer or the LAPD, and a use of force by a peace officer may be a proximate cause of the death. . . .

69. The Department shall continue to have the Use of Force Review Board review all Categorical Uses of Force. The LAPD shall continue to have Non-Categorical Uses of Force reviewed by chain-of-command managers at the Division and Bureau level. . . .

73. All detainees and arrestees brought to an LAPD facility shall be brought before a watch commander for inspection. The watch commander shall visually inspect each such detainee or arrestee for injuries as required by LAPD procedures and, at a minimum, ask the detainee or arrestee the questions required by current LAPD procedures, which are: 1) "Do you understand why you were detained/arrested?"; 2) "Are you sick, ill, or injured?"; 3) "Do you have any questions or concerns?". . . .

78. The Department shall continue to require officers to report to the LAPD without delay: any conduct by other officers that reasonably appears to constitute (a) an excessive use of force or improper threat of force; (b) a false arrest or filing of false charges; (c) an unlawful search or seizure; (d) invidious discrimination; (e) an intentional failure to complete forms required by LAPD policies and in accordance with procedures; (f) an act of retaliation for complying with any LAPD policy or procedure; or (g) an intentional provision of false information in an administrative investigation or in any official report, log, or electronic transmittal of information. . . . Failure to voluntarily report as described in this paragraph shall be an offense subject to discipline if sustained. . . .

97. [T]he City shall develop and initiate a plan for organizing and executing regular, targeted, and random integrity audit checks, or "sting" operations . . . to identify and investigate officers engaging in at-risk behavior, including: unlawful stops, searches, seizures (including false arrests), [or] uses of excessive force. . . . These operations shall also seek to identify officers who discourage the filing of a complaint or fail to report misconduct or complaints. . . . The Department shall use the relevant TEAMS II data, and other relevant information, in selecting targets for these sting audits. . . .

103. LAPD officers may not use race, color, ethnicity, or national origin (to any extent or degree) in conducting stops or detentions, or activities following stops or detentions, except when . . . officers are seeking one or more specific persons who have been identified or described in part by their race, color, ethnicity, or national origin. . . .

104. [T]he Department shall require LAPD officers to complete a written or electronic report each time an officer conducts a motor vehicle stop. . . . The report shall include the following: (i) the officer's serial number; (ii) date and approximate time of the stop; (iii) reporting district where the stop occurred; (iv) driver's apparent race, ethnicity, or national origin; (v) driver's gender and apparent age; (vi) reason for the stop . . . ; (vii) whether the driver was required to exit the vehicle; (viii) whether a pat-down/frisk was conducted; (ix) action taken, to include check boxes

for warning, citation, arrest, completion of a field interview card, with appropriate identification number for the citation or arrest report; and (x) whether the driver was asked to submit to a consensual search of person, vehicle, or belongings, and whether permission was granted or denied. . . .

105. [T]he Department shall require LAPD officers to complete a written or electronic report each time an officer conducts a pedestrian stop. . . .

Community Outreach and Public Information

155. For the term of this Agreement, the Department shall conduct a Community Outreach and Public Information program for each LAPD geographic area. The program shall require . . . at least one open meeting per quarter in each of the 18 geographic Areas for the first year of the Agreement, and one meeting in each Area annually thereafter, to inform the public about the provisions of this Agreement, and the various methods of filing a complaint against an officer. . . .

156. The LAPD shall prepare and publish on its website semiannual public reports. . . . Such reports shall include aggregate statistics broken down by each LAPD geographic area and for the Operations Headquarters Bureau, and broken down by the race/ethnicity/ national origin of the citizens involved, for arrests, information required to be maintained pursuant to paragraphs 104 and 105, and uses of force. Such reports shall include a brief description of [audits completed] and any significant actions taken as a result of such audits or reports, (ii) a summary of all discipline imposed during the period reported by type of misconduct, broken down by type of discipline, bureau and rank, and (iii) any new policies or changes in policies made by the Department to address the requirements of this Agreement. . . .

Problem 6-4. Clear as a Post

Prison guards twice handcuffed inmate Larry Hope to a "hitching post," once for two hours, and the other time for seven hours. On the second occasion, Hope was given water only once or twice and was given no bathroom breaks. A guard taunted Hope about his thirst. He first gave water to some dogs, then brought the water cooler closer to Hope, removed its lid, and kicked the cooler over, spilling the water onto the ground. Hope filed a civil claim under 42 U.S.C. §1983 against three guards who had either ordered or actually hitched him to the post. The district court entered judgment for the guards, finding they were entitled to qualified immunity.

The doctrine of qualified immunity protects state actors from suit despite their participation in constitutionally impermissible conduct, if their actions did not violate "clearly established statutory or constitutional rights of which a reasonable person would have known." Harlow v. Fitzgerald, 457 U.S. 800, 818 (1982). In Hope's case, the U.S. Supreme Court held that a situation could be factually novel, and yet violate "clearly established" rights:

> As we have explained, qualified immunity operates to ensure that before they are subjected to suit, officers are on notice their conduct is unlawful. For a constitutional right to be clearly established, its contours must be sufficiently clear that a reasonable official would understand that what he is doing violates that right. This is not to say that an official action is protected by qualified immunity unless the very action in question has

> previously been held unlawful, but it is to say that in the light of pre-existing law the unlawfulness must be apparent.

Hope v. Pelzer, 122 S. Ct. 2508 (2002). The high court found that several sources of law — including Eleventh Circuit precedent, Alabama Department of Corrections regulations from 1993, and a 1994 U.S. Department of Justice report — put the prison guards on notice that their actions were unconstitutional. Also relevant, perhaps, was that in 1995 Alabama was the only State that handcuffed prisoners to hitching posts if they either refused to work or disrupted other work squads. Perhaps notice of the unconstitutionality of the act also came from the cruelty of the act itself: "Hope was treated in a way antithetical to human dignity — he was hitched to a post for an extended period of time in a position that was painful, and under circumstances that were both degrading and dangerous."

The Supreme Court remanded another case for reconsideration in light of *Hope*. In Vaughan v. Cox, 264 F.3d 1027 (11th Cir. 2001), Jerry Vaughan filed suit under §1983, claiming that Deputy Fred Cox and Sheriff Mike Yeager of Coweta County, Georgia, used excessive force during a police chase. In the early morning of January 5, 1998, the Sheriff's Department received a report that a red pickup truck with a silver tool box in its bed had been stolen from a service station along the interstate highway near Atlanta. The report included the information that the suspect, a white male wearing a white T-shirt, was believed to be heading north on the interstate.

Deputy Cox joined the pursuit. In an attempt to determine whether the vehicle was indeed the stolen truck, Deputy Cox sped up and passed the truck, which was traveling near the speed limit. He observed two men in the cab. The man in the passenger's seat, Vaughan, matched the description of the suspect. Cox's suspicions confirmed, he and a fellow deputy in another car decided to use a "rolling roadblock" to stop the vehicle. In a rolling roadblock, officers surround a suspect's vehicle with their police cars and reduce speed, in the hope that the suspect will slow down as well. Deputy Cox moved in front of the truck and applied his brakes. The truck rammed into the back of Cox's cruiser.

The driver of the truck, Freddy Rayson, did not pull over following the collision, but instead accelerated while staying in the same lane of traffic. Deputy Cox decided to reposition his vehicle behind the truck. He unholstered his sidearm and rolled down the passenger side window, in case Rayson made aggressive moves in his direction. Cox then shifted his cruiser one lane to the left and slowed to allow the truck to pass by him. As soon as his cruiser was even with the pickup, Deputy Cox turned on his rooftop lights. Rayson accelerated to 85 miles per hour. Cox then fired three rounds into the truck. Cox later testified that he fired because the pickup swerved as if to smash into his cruiser. Vaughan disagreed, maintaining that the truck made no motion in the direction of Cox's vehicle. The third bullet fired from Cox's weapon punctured Vaughan's spine, paralyzing him below the chest.

The Eleventh Circuit held that Deputy Cox should be shielded from suit based on qualified immunity since "a reasonable officer in Deputy Cox's position could have believed that he had sufficient probable cause to apply deadly force." A reasonable officer in Cox's position could have concluded that the suspects, who were fleeing down a major highway at 85 miles per hour in a pickup and apparently were not about to stop, posed a serious threat of harm to other motorists.

The Eleventh Circuit also found "that the law was not sufficiently established on the day of the shooting that Deputy Cox knew that he needed to warn the occupants of the truck before firing his weapon." The Eleventh Circuit noted that the U.S. Supreme Court had found in Tennessee v. Garner, 471 U.S. 1 (1985), that a police officer must warn a suspect of the potential application of deadly force "where feasible," but the *Garner* Court made no effort to define under what factual situations such a warning would be necessary. What will be the result on remand as the court applies the *Hope* decision to the facts of *Vaughan*? What else would you need to know to predict the outcome?

Notes

1. *The availability of tort remedies for police misconduct.* All states and the federal system offer some kind of tort (or tort-like) remedies for some kinds of police misconduct. In the federal system, private claims can arise under 42 U.S.C. §1983 (civil rights), the Federal Tort Claims Act, or directly under the Constitution in suits known as *Bivens* actions, after Bivens v. Six Unknown Named Agents of Federal Bureau of Narcotics, 403 U.S. 388 (1971). Remedies in federal court may include money damages, injunctive relief, or consent decrees entered between parties in lieu of further litigation. In many states recovery is allowed under statutes providing generally for tort claims against the government and its agents, subject to limitations for sovereign immunity (for governments) and official immunity (for individual officers). Claims may also be made under specialized tort statutes. Surprisingly, very few states have promulgated statutes specifically addressing actions by citizens against the police.

2. *The invisibility of tort claims.* Despite the long history of tort actions to remedy unconstitutional and excessive police action, it is extremely difficult to find any reported cases involving successful claims. Indeed, there are more law review articles discussing tort actions than reported decisions. See, e.g., John C. Jeffries, Jr., Disaggregating Constitutional Torts, 110 Yale L.J. 259 (2000); Susan Bandes, Patterns of Injustice: Police Brutality in the Courts, 47 Buff. L. Rev. 1275-1341 (1999).

The almost complete absence of reported decisions might suggest that tort remedies are entirely illusory, and that the legal barriers to recovery are too high (at least too high to make tort suits a plausible remedy, either for the purposes of the claimant or as a behavior-shaping device). But some plaintiffs who sue the government for improper police conduct do recover damages, despite immunities and other obstacles. Newspapers regularly carry stories of settlements or jury verdicts in civil suits dealing with officer misconduct. The most frequent basis for these claims is excessive use of force.

Cities tend to settle most of these suits for relatively small amounts, with a few high-visibility cases receiving larger settlements or jury verdicts after trial. The unadorned numbers show some large total payments in some cities and much smaller total payments elsewhere. From 1994 to 1996, for example, New York City paid about $70 million as settlements or judgments in claims alleging improper police actions. By contrast, San Jose, California, paid only $27,500 in settlements and judgments involving police misconduct cases in 1993 and $71,500 in 1992. In 1993, Detroit spent more than 8 percent of its operating budget, or $27.5 million, on police misconduct damages. San Francisco paid less than $2 million between 1990 and 1994 to alleged victims of police brutality. Of 31 cases contested in court, city attorneys won all but two, and the city paid $234,600 to the two successful plaintiffs. The city settled 25 cases out of court for $1.54 million, usually in amounts of $10,000 to $20,000. See Dennis Opatrny, Little Danger of Sudden Wealth in Suing the SFPD, City Fights Claims for Misconduct Hard, Rarely Pays Much, San Francisco Examiner, June 11, 1995. Would you devote a major portion of your private practice to representing such clients? What would you need to know before concluding that such a practice would be financially viable?

The news accounts of settlements raise the classic tort question whether civil suits have any impact on police practices. In Pittsburgh, annual civil judgments and settlements exceeding $1 million between 1990 and 1996 convinced the city council to create a citizen police-review board. Many of the settlements, however, include a provision keeping the settlement terms secret. The settlements are often paid from the city's general budget rather than the police department budget, and the officer whose conduct led to the lawsuit is not routinely disciplined as a result of the city's financial loss. Despite these limits, does the amount of money that cities pay to tort plaintiffs each year suggest that civil liability is working reasonably well?

Scholarly debate often centers on section 1983 litigation in the federal courts rather than state tort claims. Professor Theodore Eisenberg studied section 1983 litigation conducted in the Central District of California (which includes Los Angeles) during 1975 and 1976. Of the 212 cases he examined, only two plaintiffs received substantial damages. Theodore Eisenberg, Section 1983: Doctrinal Foundations and an Empirical Study, 67 Cornell L. Rev. 482 (1982). A random nationwide sampling of section 1983 litigation during 1991 concluded that cases alleging assault by an arresting officer constituted 6 percent of all 1983 suits filed. That percentage would amount to about 1,500 of the roughly 25,000 section 1983 filings. Cases alleging assault by an arresting officer take longer to process than any other type of section 1983 claim (an average of 721 days). The study concluded that plaintiff success on these claims is relatively rare but is difficult to pinpoint. Roger Hanson and Henry Daley, Challenging the Conditions of Prisons and Jails: A Report on Section 1983 Litigation (1995, NCJ 151652).

3. *Qualified good faith immunity for individuals.* The legal barriers to tort claims are very high. State and federal courts have created protections known as a "qualified good faith immunity" or "official immunity" for police officers sued in tort for the illegal acts they commit during the course of their employment. The immunity is "qualified" because an officer loses it when she subjectively knows that she is violating the rights of the victim or when she objectively should know that she is violating those rights. Does the doctrine of qualified immunity mean that damages will be unavailable in all cases where *Leon* would create a good faith exception to the exclusionary rule? Does it leave plaintiffs without a remedy? See Malley v. Briggs, 475 U.S. 335 (1986) (officer's good faith immunity from tort liability for improper warranted search is same scope as *Leon* good faith exception to exclusionary rule). The high standards required for plaintiffs to cross the qualified immunity threshold were clarified, and may have been lowered a tad, in Hope v. Pelzer, 122 S. Ct. 2508 (2002), where the court held that new factual situations could nonetheless violate "clearly established" rights.

4. *Sovereign immunity and waiver.* Often the victim of an improper search or seizure will prefer to sue the state or local government rather than the judgment-proof individual officer who violated the law. Under traditional common law principles, such a suit is not possible under state law because of the doctrine of "sovereign immunity," which insulates the government from any monetary claims. Most states

have passed statutes that partially waive their sovereign immunity, so they will pay for some wrongdoing committed by state employees (on a respondeat superior basis). Under these tort claims acts, the lawsuit against the state or local government usually becomes the only cause of action for the wrongdoing; the plaintiff can no longer sue the individual employee. However, almost all of these statutes contain exceptions. For instance, most provide that the state or local government will not be liable for "discretionary" actions of officials. Some also exempt any action by officials engaged in the "enforcement" of any law or judicial order. See S.C. Code §15-78-60.

Section 1983 does not create respondeat superior liability for state or local government. A plaintiff can sue a local government based on the actions of its police officers only if the officer was acting pursuant to a "policy" or "practice" endorsed by the government.

5. *Costs and indemnity for judgments.* As the Attorney General's Opinion indicates, Tennessee statutes allow the state to pay for the police officer's legal representation so long as the officer was acting within the scope of authority, but they do not allow the state to indemnify the officer for the amount of any judgment paid to the plaintiff. Many states do have statutes authorizing indemnification. See, e.g., Ky. Code §16.185. Do such statutes compromise the power of tort suits to deter officers from making improper searches and seizures? Some states also have statutes authorizing the trial court to order a losing plaintiff to pay the attorney's fees and costs of the defendants if the suit was not substantially justified. See, e.g., Md. State Govt. Code §12-309. Do these statutes affect the viability of tort suits as an alternative to the exclusionary rule? See Richard Emery and Ilann Maazel, Why Civil Rights Lawsuits Do Not Deter Police Misconduct: The Conundrum of Indemnification and a Proposed Solution, 28 Fordham Urb. L.J. 587 (2000).

6. *Limitations on equitable relief.* Sometimes plaintiffs want injunctive relief rather than, or in addition to, money damages. Historically, courts were not willing to issue injunctions against individuals or agencies in law enforcement for illegal searches or seizures, no matter how egregious. See Harmon v. Commissioner of Police, 174 N.E. 198 (Mass. 1931) (injunction denied after multiple warrantless searches of premises for liquor, destruction of property during searches); Monte Vulture Social Club v. Wallander, 68 N.Y.S.2d 657 (Sup. Ct. 1947) (injunction denied against police setting curfew hours for social and political clubs in East Harlem).

Although injunctions are now considered a legitimate response to some search and seizure violations, they are still not as widely used as exclusion or damages. When relief is sought in federal court for actions of state actors, federal courts may be reluctant to order or affirm injunctive relief on federalism grounds. Another limitation on the availability of injunctions is the standing doctrine. Who has standing to challenge a police policy or practice? When a plaintiff seeks injunctive relief rather than damages, the Supreme Court has held that the plaintiff must show a likelihood of future harm. In City of Los Angeles v. Lyons, 461 U.S. 95 (1983), a plaintiff who was challenging the use of "chokeholds" by the police department had no standing to obtain injunctive or declaratory relief (as opposed to damages). Although the police had used the chokehold on Adolph Lyons in a situation where the officers faced no threat of injury, Lyons could not demonstrate a "substantial likelihood" that he personally would be choked again in the future. Is this standing limitation applicable mostly to use of force policies? Is it possible to identify the likely future victim of any type of illegal police policies (say, the use of sobriety checkpoints near bars)?

State courts may not be constrained by similarly strict standing doctrines, and the federalism concerns will not be present. Is an injunction inherently more intrusive than damage awards or exclusion of evidence in criminal proceedings? Should it be reserved for certain types of violations by law enforcement officials? Keep in mind that an injunction gives a court continuing jurisdiction over the controversy; the court can impose contempt sanctions on any defendant violating the terms of an injunction.

7. *Who benefits from a damages remedy?* Unlike the exclusion remedy, a tort suit can benefit victims of illegal searches and seizures who commit no crime or who are not charged with a crime. This feature of tort suits could make them a better remedy for those injured in the past; does it affect the relative ability of these remedies to prevent future violations? Think about the connection between remedies and rights. If tort suits were the primary method for enforcing the Fourth Amendment, would courts see different types of parties raising these claims? Would the scope of privacy rights change if the remedy were to change? See Christopher Slobogin, Why Liberals Should Chuck the Exclusionary Rule, 1999 U. Ill. L. Rev. 363 (1999) (arguing that exclusionary rule is structurally unable to deter either individual police officers or to shape department behavior, and recommending an administrative damages regime for Fourth Amendment violations). In light of the number of components necessary to create a new remedial scheme and the history of ineffective remedies earlier in this century, how much confidence would you have in an "improved" tort remedy? Would you encourage legislators to adopt such a remedy as a supplement to exclusion for some trial period? Is such a trial period constitutionally required to ensure that people have some effective remedy for violations of the Fourth Amendment and its equivalents?

8. *Federal involvement in police review.* Over the past several years, the U.S. Department of Justice has entered into a series of consent decrees with local and state police departments around the country, focusing on issues such as racial bias in stops, use of deadly force, and mistreatment of citizens. Under 42 U.S.C. §14141, known as the "Police Misconduct Provision," the Department can sue in federal court to prohibit state and local governments from engaging in "a pattern or practice of conduct by law enforcement officials" that deprives persons of "rights, privileges, or immunities secured or protected by the Constitution or laws of the United States." Since 1994, DOJ has investigated dozens of matters under the authority of 14141, and entered several settlements, including the consent decree in Los Angeles. Other consent decrees or "memoranda of understanding" resolved federal lawsuits against Pittsburgh, Cincinnati, Steubenville (Ohio), Highland Park (Illinois), the state of New Jersey, Montgomery County (Maryland), and the District of Columbia (see *http://www.usdoj.gov/crt/split/*). Does the Los Angeles consent decree suggest the promise of this new avenue for structural reform? What are the most important aspects of the decree? The Los Angeles Consent Decree requires a lot of data, recordkeeping, and monitoring. Can you access this important information? Why did Los Angeles agree to this burdensome decree? See James Turner, Police Accountability in the Federal System, 30 McGeorge L. Rev. 991 (1999).

9. *Criminal charges.* It is possible for a prosecutor to file criminal charges against an officer who conducts an illegal search or seizure, either under general criminal statutes (such as false imprisonment or trespass) or under statutes expressly covering police violations of civil rights. See 18 U.S.C. §§241, 242. U.S. Attorneys have to get central DOJ clearance to bring criminal charges against a police officer. Does the

potential for criminal charges help prevent illegal searches and seizures? Would these criminal statutes become more effective if they were amended to compel prosecutors to file charges whenever there is probable cause?

Local prosecutors are charged with the duty of prosecuting crimes, whether they are committed by citizens or officers. But do prosecutors aggressively prosecute police officers, with whom they work on a daily basis? Evidence from Los Angeles suggests a hesitation to prosecute officers spanning many decades. For example, according to news reports, from 1977-87, LAPD officers were involved in 571 shootings; many victims were unarmed civilians. But only one officer was indicted. Special units have been created in the district attorney's office, only to be underfunded, and eventually disbanded. In a bizarre twist to the Rampart scandal, at one point Chief Parks ordered his detectives to deny county prosecutors access to information regarding the ongoing Rampart corruption investigation on the grounds that District Attorney Gil Garcetti had mishandled the six-month probe, and had given the LAPD bad legal advice and could no longer be trusted. Garcetti's response: "This chief is accountable to the justice system. If [Parks] wants to test this in court, we are going to win."

Should state legislatures create crimes specific to violations by police officers? See State v. Groom, 947 P.2d 240 (Wash. 1997) (first reported appellate case involving prosecution under 1921 statutes, and which makes it a gross misdemeanor "for any policeman or other peace officer to enter and search any private dwelling house or place of residence without the authority of a search warrant issued upon a complaint as by law provided").

Problem 6-5. Legislative Remedies

You work as an adviser to a state senator who wants to limit or abolish the exclusionary rule and to replace it with a genuinely effective, alternative set of tort remedies. Draft a statute creating, to the extent possible, effective remedies for illegal searches and seizures. The remedies can include tort damages, injunctions, and  police department training requirements and promotion rules, among other options. The senator has always valued your candid opinion. When you submit this proposal to her, will you recommend that the array of new remedies replace the exclusionary rule?

VII

Technology and Privacy

There was of course no way of knowing whether you were being watched at any given moment. . . . It was even conceivable that they watched everybody all the time. . . . You had to live—did live, from habit that became instinct—in the assumption that every sound you made was overheard, and . . . every moment scrutinized.

George Orwell, *1984*

The cases, statutes, and executive branch policies we have examined thus far have revealed social forces at work, shaping the basic rules constraining searches and seizures. At times and in places where protection of privacy or individual liberty are paramount or where the police are perceived skeptically, the rules of criminal procedure tend to be more restrictive. Where crime control takes the upper hand or where the police are perceived as largely benign, police are given greater power and discretion.

The collective attitudes that influence criminal procedures are constantly shifting. One force that can change attitudes is technology, which alters the ability both to conceal and to detect information. In this chapter, we consider how typical rules governing searches and seizures change when the government uses various technologies to enhance its powers to collect information that no human sense could otherwise detect.

A. ENHANCEMENT OF THE SENSES

New technologies allow searches of vast databases or observation of daily activities such as how people drive and what they say on the phone or in e-mail. These technologies raise new questions about the limits on state power and the right to privacy. You should consider not only whether the limits on today's devices (such as wiretaps,

X-rays, and pen registers) have been resolved wisely but whether there is a solid foundation of principle and practice that can resolve questions about the flood of new observation and search technologies on the horizon.

Under the widely adopted test in Katz v. United States, 389 U.S. 347 (1967), a "search" subject to constitutional limitations takes place when the government intrudes into a person's "reasonable expectation of privacy." Applying this test, when a government agent sees something in plain view, there is no "search" that is subject to constitutional limits. See Chapter 2, section C. But can the same be said of an item that an officer sees (or smells or hears) with the aid of some device that offers a clearer or closer view or a louder sound or a stronger smell? Since the *Katz* standard first appeared in 1967, federal and state courts have wrestled with a variety of investigative technologies, often on a technology-by-technology basis. Consider whether either of the following two cases provides a useful framework for assessing high technology searches in other contexts.

■ CHARLES KATZ v. UNITED STATES

389 U.S. 347 (1967)

STEWART, J.

The petitioner was convicted [of] transmitting wagering information by telephone from Los Angeles to Miami and Boston, in violation of a federal statute. At trial the Government was permitted, over the petitioner's objection, to introduce evidence of the petitioner's end of telephone conversations, overheard by FBI agents who had attached an electronic listening and recording device to the outside of the public telephone booth from which he had placed his calls. In affirming his conviction, the Court of Appeals rejected the contention that the recordings had been obtained in violation of the Fourth Amendment, because "there was no physical entrance into the area occupied by [the petitioner]."

[T]he parties have attached great significance to the characterization of the telephone booth from which the petitioner placed his calls. The petitioner has strenuously argued that the booth was a "constitutionally protected area." The Government has maintained with equal vigor that it was not. But this effort to decide whether or not a given "area," viewed in the abstract, is "constitutionally protected" deflects attention from the problem presented by this case. For the Fourth Amendment protects people, not places. What a person knowingly exposes to the public, even in his own home or office, is not a subject of Fourth Amendment protection. But what he seeks to preserve as private, even in an area accessible to the public, may be constitutionally protected. . . .

No less than an individual in a business office, in a friend's apartment, or in a taxicab, a person in a telephone booth may rely upon the protection of the Fourth Amendment. One who occupies it, shuts the door behind him, and pays the toll that permits him to place a call is surely entitled to assume that the words he utters into the mouthpiece will not be broadcast to the world. To read the Constitution more narrowly is to ignore the vital role that the public telephone has come to play in private communication.

The Government contends, however, that the activities of its agents in this case should not be tested by Fourth Amendment requirements, for the surveillance technique they employed involved no physical penetration of the telephone booth from which the petitioner placed his calls. It is true that the absence of such penetration was at one time thought to foreclose further Fourth Amendment inquiry, Olmstead v. United States, 277 U.S. 438 (1928), for that Amendment was thought to limit only searches and seizures of tangible property. But the premise that property interests control the right of the Government to search and seize has been discredited. Thus, although a closely divided Court supposed in *Olmstead* that surveillance without any trespass and without the seizure of any material object fell outside the ambit of the Constitution, we have since departed from the narrow view on which that decision rested. Indeed, we have expressly held that the Fourth Amendment governs not only the seizure of tangible items, but extends as well to the recording of oral statements, overheard without any technical trespass under local property law. Silverman v. United States, 365 U.S. 505 (1961). Once this much is acknowledged, and once it is recognized that the Fourth Amendment protects people — and not simply "areas" — against unreasonable searches and seizures, it becomes clear that the reach of that Amendment cannot turn upon the presence or absence of a physical intrusion into any given enclosure.

[T]he Government's position is that its agents acted in an entirely defensible manner: They did not begin their electronic surveillance until investigation of the petitioner's activities had established a strong probability that he was using the telephone in question to transmit gambling information to persons in other States, in violation of federal law. Moreover, the surveillance was limited, both in scope and in duration, to the specific purpose of establishing the contents of the petitioner's unlawful telephonic communications. The agents confined their surveillance to the brief periods during which he used the telephone booth,[14] and they took great care to overhear only the conversations of the petitioner himself. . . .

The Government urges that, because its agents . . . did no more here than they might properly have done with prior judicial sanction, we should retroactively validate their conduct. That we cannot do. It is apparent that the agents in this case acted with restraint. Yet the inescapable fact is that this restraint was imposed by the agents themselves, not by a judicial officer. . . . Over and again this Court has emphasized that the mandate of the Fourth Amendment requires adherence to judicial processes, and that searches conducted outside the judicial process, without prior approval by judge or magistrate, are per se unreasonable under the Fourth Amendment — subject only to a few specifically established and well-delineated exceptions. . . . These considerations do not vanish when the search in question is transferred from the setting of a home, an office, or a hotel room to that of a telephone booth. Wherever a man may be, he is entitled to know that he will remain free from unreasonable searches and seizures. . . . It is so ordered.

HARLAN, J., concurring.

[As] the Court's opinion states, "the Fourth Amendment protects people, not places." The question, however, is what protection it affords to those people. Generally, as here, the answer to that question requires reference to a "place." My understanding of the rule that has emerged from prior decisions is that there is a twofold requirement, first that a person have exhibited an actual (subjective) expectation of privacy and, second, that the expectation be one that society is prepared to

14. Based upon their previous visual observations of the petitioner, the agents correctly predicted that he would use the telephone booth for several minutes at approximately the same time each morning. The petitioner was subjected to electronic surveillance only during this predetermined period. Six recordings, averaging some three minutes each, were obtained and admitted in evidence. They preserved the petitioner's end of conversations concerning the placing of bets and the receipt of wagering information.

recognize as "reasonable." Thus a man's home is, for most purposes, a place where he expects privacy, but objects, activities, or statements that he exposes to the "plain view" of outsiders are not "protected" because no intention to keep them to himself has been exhibited. On the other hand, conversations in the open would not be protected against being overheard, for the expectation of privacy under the circumstances would be unreasonable. . . .

BLACK, J., dissenting.

[The Fourth Amendment's] first clause protects "persons, houses, papers, and effects, against unreasonable searches and seizures. . . ." These words connote the idea of tangible things with size, form, and weight, things capable of being searched, seized, or both. The second clause of the Amendment still further establishes its Framers' purpose to limit its protection to tangible things by providing that no warrants shall issue but those "particularly describing the place to be searched, and the persons or things to be seized." A conversation overheard by eavesdropping, whether by plain snooping or wiretapping, is not tangible and, under the normally accepted meanings of the words, can neither be searched nor seized. . . . Yet the Court's interpretation would have the Amendment apply to overhearing future conversations which by their very nature are nonexistent until they take place. . . .

Tapping telephone wires, of course, was an unknown possibility at the time the Fourth Amendment was adopted. But eavesdropping (and wiretapping is nothing more than eavesdropping by telephone) was . . . an ancient practice which at common law was condemned as a nuisance. In those days the eavesdropper listened by naked ear under the eaves of houses or their windows, or beyond their walls seeking out private discourse. There can be no doubt that the Framers were aware of this practice, and if they had desired to outlaw or restrict the use of evidence obtained by eavesdropping, I believe that they would have used the appropriate language to do so in the Fourth Amendment. They certainly would not have left such a task to the ingenuity of language-stretching judges. . . .

Since I see no way in which the words of the Fourth Amendment can be construed to apply to eavesdropping, that closes the matter for me. In interpreting the Bill of Rights, I willingly go as far as a liberal construction of the language takes me, but I simply cannot in good conscience give a meaning to words which they have never before been thought to have and which they certainly do not have in common ordinary usage. I will not distort the words of the Amendment in order to "keep the Constitution up to date" or "to bring it into harmony with the times." . . .

With this decision the Court has completed, I hope, its rewriting of the Fourth Amendment, which started only recently when the Court began referring incessantly to the Fourth Amendment not so much as a law against unreasonable searches and seizures as one to protect an individual's privacy. . . . Few things happen to an individual that do not affect his privacy in one way or another. . . .

■ DANNY LEE KYLLO v. UNITED STATES

533 U.S. 27 (2001)

SCALIA, J.

This case presents the question whether the use of a thermal-imaging device aimed at a private home from a public street to detect relative amounts of heat within the home constitutes a "search" within the meaning of the Fourth Amendment.

In 1991 Agent William Elliott of the United States Department of the Interior came to suspect that marijuana was being grown in the home belonging to petitioner Danny Kyllo, part of a triplex on Rhododendron Drive in Florence, Oregon. Indoor marijuana growth typically requires high-intensity lamps. In order to determine whether an amount of heat was emanating from petitioner's home consistent with the use of such lamps, at 3:20 A.M. on January 16, 1992, Agent Elliott and Dan Haas used an Agema Thermovision 210 thermal imager to scan the triplex. Thermal imagers detect infrared radiation, which virtually all objects emit but which is not visible to the naked eye. The imager converts radiation into images based on relative warmth — black is cool, white is hot, shades of gray connote relative differences; in that respect, it operates somewhat like a video camera showing heat images. The scan of Kyllo's home took only a few minutes and was performed from the passenger seat of Agent Elliott's vehicle across the street from the front of the house and also from the street in back of the house. The scan showed that the roof over the garage and a side wall of petitioner's home were relatively hot compared to the rest of the home and substantially warmer than neighboring homes in the triplex. Agent Elliott concluded that petitioner was using halide lights to grow marijuana in his house, which indeed he was. Based on tips from informants, utility bills, and the thermal imaging, a Federal Magistrate Judge issued a warrant authorizing a search of petitioner's home, and the agents found an indoor growing operation involving more than 100 plants. Petitioner was indicted on one count of manufacturing marijuana. . . . He unsuccessfully moved to suppress the evidence seized from his home and then entered a conditional guilty plea.

[T]he District Court found that the Agema 210 "is a non-intrusive device which emits no rays or beams and shows a crude visual image of the heat being radiated from the outside of the house"; it "did not show any people or activity within the walls of the structure"; "[t]he device used cannot penetrate walls or windows to reveal conversations or human activities"; and "[n]o intimate details of the home were observed." Based on these findings, the District Court upheld the validity of the warrant that relied in part upon the thermal imaging. . . .

At the very core of the Fourth Amendment stands the right of a man to retreat into his own home and there be free from unreasonable governmental intrusion. With few exceptions, the question whether a warrantless search of a home is reasonable and hence constitutional must be answered no.

On the other hand, the antecedent question of whether or not a Fourth Amendment "search" has occurred is not so simple under our precedent. The permissibility of ordinary visual surveillance of a home used to be clear because, well into the 20th century, our Fourth Amendment jurisprudence was tied to common-law trespass. See, e.g., Olmstead v. United States, 277 U.S. 438 (1928). Visual surveillance was unquestionably lawful because "the eye cannot by the laws of England be guilty of a trespass." Boyd v. United States, 116 U.S. 616 (1886) (quoting Entick v. Carrington, (K.B.1765)). We have since decoupled violation of a person's Fourth Amendment rights from trespassory violation of his property, but the lawfulness of warrantless visual surveillance of a home has still been preserved. As we observed in California v. Ciraolo, 476 U.S. 207 (1986), "[t]he Fourth Amendment protection of the home has never been extended to require law enforcement officers to shield their eyes when passing by a home on public thoroughfares."

One might think that the . . . validating rationale would be that examining the portion of a house that is in plain public view, while it is a "search" despite the absence of trespass, is not an "unreasonable" one under the Fourth Amendment. But in fact we have held that visual observation is no "search" at all — perhaps in order to preserve somewhat more intact our doctrine that warrantless searches are presumptively unconstitutional. In assessing when a search is not a search, we have applied somewhat in reverse the principle first enunciated in Katz v. United States, 389 U.S. 347 (1967). [Under *Katz,*] a Fourth Amendment search occurs when the government violates a subjective expectation of privacy that society recognizes as reasonable. We have subsequently applied this principle to hold that a Fourth Amendment search does *not* occur — even when the explicitly protected location of a *house* is concerned — unless the individual manifested a subjective expectation of privacy in the object of the challenged search, and society is willing to recognize that expectation as reasonable. . . .

The present case involves officers on a public street engaged in more than naked-eye surveillance of a home. We have previously reserved judgment as to how much technological enhancement of ordinary perception from such a vantage point, if any, is too much. While we upheld enhanced aerial photography of an industrial complex in Dow Chemical v. United States, 476 U.S. 227 (1986), we noted that we found "it important that this is *not* an area immediately adjacent to a private home, where privacy expectations are most heightened."

It would be foolish to contend that the degree of privacy secured to citizens by the Fourth Amendment has been entirely unaffected by the advance of technology. For example . . . the technology enabling human flight has exposed to public view (and hence, we have said, to official observation) uncovered portions of the house and its curtilage that once were private. The question we confront today is what limits there are upon this power of technology to shrink the realm of guaranteed privacy.

The *Katz* test — whether the individual has an expectation of privacy that society is prepared to recognize as reasonable — has often been criticized as circular, and hence subjective and unpredictable. See Posner, The Uncertain Protection of Privacy by the Supreme Court, 1979 S. Ct. Rev. 173. While it may be difficult to refine *Katz* when the search of areas such as telephone booths, automobiles, or even the curtilage and uncovered portions of residences are at issue, in the case of the search of the interior of homes — the prototypical and hence most commonly litigated area of protected privacy — there is a ready criterion, with roots deep in the common law, of the minimal expectation of privacy that *exists,* and that is acknowledged to be *reasonable.* To withdraw protection of this minimum expectation would be to permit police technology to erode the privacy guaranteed by the Fourth Amendment. We think that obtaining by sense-enhancing technology any information regarding the interior of the home that could not otherwise have been obtained without physical intrusion into a constitutionally protected area, constitutes a search — at least where (as here) the technology in question is not in general public use. This assures preservation of that degree of privacy against government that existed when the Fourth Amendment was adopted. On the basis of this criterion, the information obtained by the thermal imager in this case was the product of a search.

The Government maintains, however, that the thermal imaging must be upheld because it detected "only heat radiating from the external surface of the house." The dissent makes this its leading point, contending that there is a fundamental difference between what it calls "off-the-wall" observations and "through-the-wall surveillance." But just as a thermal imager captures only heat emanating from a house, so also a powerful directional microphone picks up only sound emanating from a house — and a satellite capable of scanning from many miles away would pick up only visible light emanating from a house. We rejected such a mechanical interpretation of the Fourth Amendment in *Katz,* where the eavesdropping device picked up only sound waves that reached the exterior of the phone booth. Reversing that approach would leave the homeowner at the mercy of advancing technology — including imaging technology that could discern all human activity in the home. While the technology used in the present case was relatively crude, the rule we adopt must take account of more sophisticated systems that are already in use or in development.[3] . . .

The Government also contends that the thermal imaging was constitutional because it did not "detect private activities occurring in private areas." . . . In the home, [however], *all* details are intimate details, because the entire area is held safe from prying government eyes. . . . Limiting the prohibition of thermal imaging to "intimate details" would not only be wrong in principle; it would be impractical in application, failing to provide a workable accommodation between the needs of law enforcement and the interests protected by the Fourth Amendment. To begin with, there is no necessary connection between the sophistication of the surveillance equipment and the "intimacy" of the details that it observes — which means that one cannot say (and the police cannot be assured) that use of the relatively crude equipment at issue here will always be lawful. The Agema Thermovision 210 might disclose, for example, at what hour each night the lady of the house takes her daily sauna and bath — a detail that many would consider "intimate"; and a much more sophisticated system might detect nothing more intimate than the fact that someone left a closet light on. We . . . would have to develop a jurisprudence specifying which home activities are "intimate" and which are not. And even when (if ever) that jurisprudence were fully developed, no police officer would be able to know *in advance* whether his through-the-wall surveillance picks up "intimate" details — and thus would be unable to know in advance whether it is constitutional. . . .

We have said that the Fourth Amendment draws "a firm line at the entrance to the house." That line, we think, must be not only firm but also bright — which requires clear specification of those methods of surveillance that require a warrant. While it is certainly possible to conclude from the videotape of the thermal imaging that occurred in this case that no "significant" compromise of the homeowner's privacy has occurred, we must take the long view, from the original meaning of the Fourth Amendment forward. . . . Where, as here, the Government uses a device that is not in general public use, to explore details of the home that would previously have been unknowable without physical intrusion, the surveillance is a "search" and is presumptively unreasonable without a warrant. Since we hold the Thermovision

3. The ability to "see" through walls and other opaque barriers is a clear, and scientifically feasible, goal of law enforcement research and development. The National Law Enforcement and Corrections Technology Center, a program within the United States Department of Justice, features on its Internet Website projects that include a "Radar-Based Through-the-Wall Surveillance System," "Handheld Ultrasound Through the Wall Surveillance," and a "Radar Flashlight" that "will enable law officers to detect individuals through interior building walls." *www.nlectc.org/techproj/* (visited May 3, 2001). Some devices may emit low levels of radiation that travel "through-the-wall," but others, such as more sophisticated thermal imaging devices, are entirely passive, or "off-the-wall" as the dissent puts it.

imaging to have been an unlawful search, it will remain for the District Court to determine whether, without the evidence it provided, the search warrant issued in this case was supported by probable cause — and if not, whether there is any other basis for supporting admission of the evidence that the search pursuant to the warrant produced. . . .

STEVENS, J., dissenting.

There is, in my judgment, a distinction of constitutional magnitude between "through-the-wall surveillance" that gives the observer or listener direct access to information in a private area, on the one hand, and the thought processes used to draw inferences from information in the public domain, on the other hand. The Court has crafted a rule that purports to deal with direct observations of the inside of the home, but the case before us merely involves indirect deductions from "off-the-wall" surveillance, that is, observations of the exterior of the home. Those observations were made with a fairly primitive thermal imager that gathered data exposed on the outside of petitioner's home but did not invade any constitutionally protected interest in privacy. . . . What a person knowingly exposes to the public, even in his own home or office, is not a subject of Fourth Amendment protection. That is the principle implicated here.

[The] ordinary use of the senses might enable a neighbor or passerby to notice the heat emanating from a building, particularly if it is vented, as was the case here. Additionally, any member of the public might notice that one part of a house is warmer than another part or a nearby building if, for example, rainwater evaporates or snow melts at different rates across its surfaces. Such use of the senses would not convert into an unreasonable search if, instead, an adjoining neighbor allowed an officer onto her property to verify her perceptions with a sensitive thermometer. Nor, in my view, does such observation become an unreasonable search if made from a distance with the aid of a device that merely discloses that the exterior of one house, or one area of the house, is much warmer than another. Nothing more occurred in this case.

Thus, the notion that heat emissions from the outside of a dwelling is a private matter [covered under] the Fourth Amendment (the text of which guarantees the right of people "to be secure *in* their . . . houses" against unreasonable searches and seizures) is not only unprecedented but also quite difficult to take seriously. Heat waves, like aromas that are generated in a kitchen, or in a laboratory or opium den, enter the public domain if and when they leave a building. A subjective expectation that they would remain private is not only implausible but also surely not one that society is prepared to recognize as reasonable. [Based] on what the thermal imager showed regarding the outside of petitioner's home, the officers concluded that petitioner was engaging in illegal activity inside the home. It would be quite absurd to characterize their thought processes as "searches." . . . For the first time in its history, the Court assumes that an inference can amount to a Fourth Amendment violation.

[Public] officials should not have to avert their senses or their equipment from detecting emissions in the public domain such as excessive heat, traces of smoke, suspicious odors, odorless gases, airborne particulates, or radioactive emissions, any of which could identify hazards to the community. In my judgment, monitoring such emissions with sense-enhancing technology, and drawing useful conclusions from such monitoring, is an entirely reasonable public service. On the other hand, the countervailing privacy interest is at best trivial. [Society will not] suffer from a rule requiring the rare homeowner who both intends to engage in uncommon activities that produce extraordinary amounts of heat, and wishes to conceal that production from outsiders, to make sure that the surrounding area is well insulated.

[The contours of the] new rule are uncertain because its protection apparently dissipates as soon as the relevant technology is "in general public use." Yet how much use is general public use is not even hinted at by the Court's opinion, which makes the somewhat doubtful assumption that the thermal imager used in this case does not satisfy that criterion.[5] In any event, putting aside its lack of clarity, this criterion is somewhat perverse because it seems likely that the threat to privacy will grow, rather than recede, as the use of intrusive equipment becomes more readily available. . . .

Although the Court is properly and commendably concerned about the threats to privacy that may flow from advances in the technology available to the law enforcement profession, it has unfortunately failed to heed the tried and true counsel of judicial restraint. Instead of concentrating on the rather mundane issue that is actually presented by the case before it, the Court has endeavored to craft an all-encompassing rule for the future. It would be far wiser to give legislators an unimpeded opportunity to grapple with these emerging issues rather than to shackle them with prematurely devised constitutional constraints.

Notes

1. *Thermal imaging: majority position.* State and federal law enforcement authorities started using thermal imaging—also commonly referred to as forward-looking infra-red radar or "FLIR"—in the late 1980s. In 1991, the U.S. District Court for the District of Hawaii upheld the constitutionality of thermal imaging without a warrant, analogizing the examination of the heat emitted from the house to examination of garbage left at the curb, and to the molecules sniffed by a dog during the warrantless external examination of a bag, approved by the Supreme Court in United States v. Place, 462 U.S. 696 (1983). See United States v. Penny-Feeney, 773 F. Supp. 220 (D. Haw. 1991). Federal circuit courts of appeal before *Kyllo* largely followed this analysis. In contrast, three of the four state supreme courts that addressed the constitutionality of thermal imaging deemed it unconstitutional, with Washington State and Montana resting their decisions on state grounds. See Commonwealth v. Gindlesperger, 743 A.2d 898 (Pa. 1999); State v. Young, 867 P.2d 593 (Wash. 1994); State v. Siegal, 934 P.2d 176 (Mont. 1997); but see LaFollette v. Commonwealth, 915 S.W.2d 747 (Ky. 1996) (not a search under Fourth Amendment). In *Kyllo,* decided 10 years after the first of the thermal imaging cases appeared in federal courts, the Supreme Court held that thermal imaging of a home is a search under the Fourth Amendment. The decision surprised many observers, who saw many doctrinal avenues in the court's existing doctrine for the court to find that thermal imaging was a not a search at all.

2. *New doctrine for new technology?* Both the majority and dissent in *Kyllo* recognize that the *Katz* test, based on individual and societal expectations of privacy, created

5. The record describes a device that numbers close to a thousand manufactured units; that has a predecessor numbering in the neighborhood of 4,000 to 5,000 units; that competes with a similar product numbering from 5,000 to 6,000 units; and that is "readily available to the public" for commercial, personal, or law enforcement purposes. . . .

an inherent tension with new technologies for observation and investigation. First, as a technology becomes widespread it might become unreasonable for an individual to hold a subjective expectation of privacy. If humans develop Superman's X-ray vision, we will all subjectively need to recognize that our walls (and perhaps our clothes) no longer create an barrier to observation. Second, as technology becomes more widespread, members of society might be less and less willing to recognize individual subjective preferences as reasonable. Is either element of the *Katz* test modified by *Kyllo,* or does the court simply apply *Katz* to find that thermal imaging is a search? Will *Kyllo* lead federal or state courts to reconsider the use of helicopters, planes, and high magnification cameras to gather information? Does *Kyllo* provide a doctrinal framework that will help courts, legislatures, and executive agencies to resolve questions about the use of other search technologies in the future?

3. *Home sweet home.* The majority in *Kyllo* finds thermal imaging inappropriate for the home, which it calls the "prototypical" area of protected privacy. Will the holding be read to apply only to technological searches of the home? The majority also qualifies its holding by observing that the image here provided information "that would previously have been unknowable without physical intrusion." Could an observer know about heat emanating from a home without physical intrusion? Will *Kyllo* be limited only to devices that provide information that would have required "physical intrusion"?

4. *Cheap technology and cheap doctrine.* The majority in *Kyllo* limited its holding to devices that are "not in general public use." But it does not define "general public use." Is this language part of the holding, or merely dicta? Will this limitation pose the same kind of continual erosion as the original "expectation" doctrine of *Katz,* since technology often becomes cheaper and more widespread over time?

For many years, law enforcement officers have relied on dogs and their powerful sense of smell to track fleeing suspects. More recently, that sense of smell has become a useful way for the government to detect the presence of illegal drugs and other contraband. Do constitutional limits on searches apply to police officers who enhance their own olfactory skills with a canine's keener senses? In the following decision the Pennsylvania court describes how most jurisdictions react to such constitutional claims and carves out its own position.

■ COMMONWEALTH v. WILLIAM MARTIN

626 A.2d 556 (Pa. 1993)

FLAHERTY, J.

The questions raised by this case are whether police acted lawfully in utilizing a trained dog to sniff appellant Martin's satchel for the presence of illegal drugs; and whether police were required, after the dog had alerted to the presence of drugs, to secure a search warrant before they could open the satchel and examine its contents.

On June 27, 1989 five members of the Montgomery County narcotics enforcement team were having lunch in a restaurant in King of Prussia, Pennsylvania. At approximately 1:55 P.M., two men entered the restaurant and were seated. One of them carried a black satchel with an antenna protruding. The men sat at the table briefly, then moved two or three feet to another table, where, without prior greeting or conversation, they joined two other men who were already seated at the second table. One of the men already seated was appellant Martin. . . .

At approximately 2:10 P.M., drinks were served and the man with the black satchel placed it on the table and pushed it across to Martin while looking around in what police characterized as a suspicious manner. Martin, who also was looking around "furtively," took the satchel and placed it on his lap. [Martin placed his hands in the satchel,] then placed the satchel on the table and pushed it back to the first man. The men then raised their glasses as if making a toast. The detectives believed at this point that a drug deal was in progress and that the toast was the consummation of the deal. The detectives communicated their suspicions to the Upper Marion Police and requested that additional officers [and a trained drug detection dog] be positioned outside the restaurant and out of sight. . . .

At approximately 2:30 P.M., two of the suspected drug dealers, not Martin, exited the restaurant and approached a black Ford that was parked in the lot. One of the men opened the trunk and the other retrieved a small brown gym bag from the trunk. The two shook hands and the one who had retrieved the bag entered a taxi and left. The man who had opened the trunk returned to the restaurant, where he rejoined Martin and the other man. Other police units stopped the taxi within several miles of the restaurant. [The occupant] consented to a search of his person and belongings. The search revealed a small amount of marijuana. The police radioed this information to the detectives at the restaurant. . . .

At approximately 2:55 P.M., the three men remaining in the restaurant left their table, exited the restaurant, and approached the same Ford automobile parked in the lot. Each man carried a satchel. As the men prepared to enter the vehicle, detectives approached, guns drawn but at their sides, and indicated that they wanted to know what had occurred in the restaurant. Martin was directed to place his brown satchel on the ground. One of the detectives then directed the trained dog to perform a sniff search of Martin's brown satchel. The dog indicated to its handler that the satchel contained drugs. Thereupon, one of the detectives opened the satchel and found a small quantity of marijuana, an address book, and $70,500 in consecutively numbered $100 bills. Martin was then arrested. The dog then sniffed the car and alerted to the trunk area. Subsequent search of the trunk revealed 38 pounds of marijuana in bricks. The remaining two men were then placed under arrest. [In denying the motion to suppress evidence obtained from Martin's satchel, the trial court found that the cumulative observations of the detectives in the restaurant, combined with the canine alert, established probable cause to believe that drugs would be found in the satchel.]

In Commonwealth v. Johnston, 530 A.2d 74 (1987), we held that use of a trained dog to sniff for the presence of drugs was, under Article I, Section 8 of the Pennsylvania Constitution, a search. The search in *Johnston* concerned a storage locker, a place. . . . Although the federal courts do not consider a canine sniff search a "search" for Fourth Amendment purposes, see United States v. Place, 462 U.S. 696 (1983), we held in *Johnston* that a canine sniff is a search under Article I, Section 8 of the Pennsylvania Constitution, but because it involves a minimal intrusion and is directed to a compelling state interest in eradicating illegal trafficking in drugs, the sniff search may be carried out on the basis of an articulated "reasonable suspicion," not probable cause. We saw this as a constitutional middle ground between requiring probable cause to believe that a crime has been or is being committed or that contraband or evidence of a crime will be discovered, and requiring nothing at all before police would be permitted to conduct a sniff search.

This middle ground approach was acceptable in *Johnston* because police intrusion was minimal, because the intrusion was directed solely at contraband drugs, and because much of the law enforcement utility of drug detection dogs would be lost if full-blown warrant procedures were required. In this case, however, the search is that of a person, not a place, and accordingly, we believe that different interests are implicated. [T]he principal object of [Article I, Section 8 and the Fourth] Amendment is the protection of privacy rather than property. Further, although privacy may relate both to property and to one's person, an invasion of one's person is, in the usual case, more severe intrusion on one's privacy interest than an invasion of one's property.

Because the search in this case involved Martin's person, we believe that in addition to being lawfully in place at the time of the search, the police must have probable cause to believe that a canine search of a person will produce contraband or evidence of a crime. Reasonable suspicion of criminal activity will not suffice. Moreover, because the intrusion concerns the person, we also hold that once the police have probable cause and a sniff search has been conducted pursuant to that probable cause, before any search, beyond that permitted by Terry v. Ohio, 392 U.S. 1 (1968), may be conducted (patting down outer garments to check for weapons upon reasonable suspicion that the suspect may be armed), the police must secure a search warrant and they may detain the suspect for a reasonable time while the warrant is sought.

We are aware of the view that allowing the search without a warrant would be less intrusive than seizing the person of the suspect while a magistrate decides whether the search should be conducted at all. It is our view, however, that in the event the suspect wishes to resist the search by refusing to consent, the propriety of a search is best determined by a magistrate. . . .

Applying these requirements to this case, the search fails constitutional muster. First, although it may be that there was reasonable suspicion of criminal activity on the facts of this case, there was no probable cause. But even assuming probable cause, which would validate the sniff search, police did not secure a warrant to conduct the actual search of the satchel. It was error, therefore, to admit into evidence that which was seized as a result of the illegal search. Reversed and remanded for a new trial.

MONTEMURO, J., dissenting.

Today the majority has placed a choke collar on law enforcement and pulled it tight. I dissent.

[Although I do not believe] that a seizure of a satchel is a search of a person, focusing on nomenclature misses the point. The reasonableness of a search is not determined by the name we affix to a particular intrusion. Rather, the proper focus of our inquiry should be on the scope and degree of the intrusion. A search of a personal effect may, under certain circumstances, be more intrusive than a search of a place. However, this fact does not automatically trigger the traditional probable cause analysis. For example, under appropriate circumstances limited searches and seizures of one's person with less than probable cause are permitted. Terry v. Ohio, 392 U.S. 1 (1968). . . . The proper analysis focuses on whether the sniff search of a satchel is a more severe intrusion than the sniff search of a commercial storage facility permitted in *Johnston*. . . .

Here, the police, while conducting a brief investigatory stop, directed a drug detection dog to sniff a satchel that was placed on the ground. The present search, like the one in *Johnston,* implicated privacy interests protected by our constitution in an inherently less intrusive manner than a traditional search. The sniff search only provided police with the limited information of whether contraband was present, and therefore was unlikely to intrude, except marginally, upon an innocent person's rights. The additional inconvenience of a brief sniff search conducted during a valid investigatory stop was minimal. Further, the subject of the investigation was reasonably protected from police harassment, annoyance and humiliation since both the investigatory stop and the canine sniff were supported by reasonable suspicion. Thus, the limited intrusion in the present case was not qualitatively different from the sniff search permitted in *Johnston.* . . .

The effect of this unwarranted restraint on law enforcement will . . . be the elimination of the use of dogs trained in narcotics detection. Under the majority's standard, the police must have probable cause to believe the satchel contains contraband before conducting a sniff search. If the dog sniff indicates the presence of drugs, then nothing has been gained because the police already had probable cause to believe that the satchel contained contraband. However, if the dog sniff does not indicate the presence of drugs, then the police are in a quandary. [D]epending on the facts of the case, the probable cause determination may be undermined. At the very least, the evidence of probable cause would be equivocal. It stands to reason that the police will not use a technique, which they are not required to use, that could only work to undermine their law enforcement efforts. [In effect,] the police are told to discard an unintrusive tool that was utilized to meet a compelling need. . . .

Notes

1. *Are dog sniffs searches? Majority position.* As the court in *Martin* notes, in United States v. Place, 462 U.S. 696 (1983), the Supreme Court held that dog sniffs are not searches and therefore are not subject to the constraints of the Fourth Amendment. *Place* involved a sniff of a suspect's luggage at the airport. The Court held as follows:

> A "canine sniff" by a well-trained narcotics detection dog, however, does not require opening the luggage. It does not expose noncontraband items that otherwise would remain hidden from public view, as does, for example, an officer's rummaging through the contents of the luggage. Thus, the manner in which information is obtained through this investigative technique is much less intrusive than a typical search. Moreover, the sniff discloses only the presence or absence of narcotics, a contraband item. Thus, despite the fact that the sniff tells the authorities something about the contents of the luggage, the information obtained is limited. This limited disclosure also ensures that the owner of the property is not subjected to the embarrassment and inconvenience entailed in less discriminate and more intrusive investigative methods.
>
> In these respects, the canine sniff is sui generis. We are aware of no other investigative procedure that is so limited both in the manner in which the information is obtained and in the content of the information revealed by the procedure. Therefore, we conclude that . . . exposure of respondent's luggage, which was located in a public place, to a trained canine . . . did not constitute a "search" within the meaning of the Fourth Amendment.

The largest group of state courts have read their state constitutions and statutes in a similar fashion to conclude that use of canines to sniff items in public places does not qualify as a "search." See, e.g., State v. Morrow, 625 P.2d 898 (Ariz. 1981). A strong minority, however, treat a canine sniff as a "search" under the state constitution. These holdings tend to appear in cases in which the dog is brought into a private area or to the edge of such an area (for instance, up to the front door of a home). These courts typically require the police to demonstrate reasonable suspicion — not probable cause — to carry out the canine sniff search. See People v. Unruh, 713 P.2d 370 (Colo. 1986); People v. Dunn, 564 N.E.2d 1054 (N.Y. 1990).

2. *Plain view and sense enhancements: majority position.* Remember that it is no search for an officer to view objects within "plain" view when the officer is justified in being in a particular place — whether in a home during execution of a warrant or in an area based on consent or some exception to the warrant requirement. See Chapter 2, section C. Most courts draw an analogy between "plain view" and the use of familiar tools that enhance human senses of sight or hearing to provide light, change or magnify a view, or magnify a voice. They often ask whether the officer (or a group of officers) could have made the observation by using normal senses from a permissible location. If the answer to this question is "yes," courts often conclude that the evidence collection is not a search at all; if not, they are more inclined to consider it a search and then evaluate whether the search was reasonable.

More often than not, a court reviewing a police officer's use of sense-enhancing devices will conclude that the officer did not conduct a "search." See United States v. Lee, 274 U.S. 559 (1927) (use of searchlight on boat not a search because it is "comparable to use of a marine glass or a field glass"); Dow Chemical Co. v. United States, 476 U.S. 227 (1986) (no search when government uses $22,000 aerial mapping camera during overflight of plant suspected of environmental crimes); State v. Wacker, 856 P.2d 1029 (Or. 1993) (applying *Katz* analysis and finding no search where police used light-enhancing "starscope" to watch occupants in car parked outside tavern at night). As with other aspects of search and seizure doctrine, the shift in *Katz* from a property-based conception to a privacy-based conception of the Fourth Amendment makes it more difficult for courts to reach categorical conclusions about the use of any particular technological sense-enhancement. The amount of effort a government agent expends in obtaining a "plain" view, the nature of the location observed, the place from which the observation is made, and the public familiarity with a device may all be relevant. Courts are more ready, for example, to find observations into the home (but not cars) to be "searches." State v. Knight, 621 P.2d 370 (Haw. 1980) (use of high-powered binoculars to look into greenhouse was a search). Even the use of a simple flashlight can be a search if the officer illuminates a space that could not be perceived without awkward viewing and added light, such as peering under the covering on the bed of a pickup truck through a narrow opening. State v. Tarantino, 368 S.E.2d 588 (N.C. 1988) (search when officer shines flashlight through cracks in rear wall of storage shed). Remember that even when use of a sense-enhancing device constitutes a search, a court must address further questions: It must determine what level of justification the government must have to support the search, and then it must evaluate whether the search was reasonable given those particular facts.

3. *An area ripe for statutory precision?* Do questions about the use of technological enhancement of the senses require answers too precise for judges to give? Can

statutes, with their greater possible detail, better limit the misuse of technology? Should police be limited, for example, to use of binoculars of a certain magnification? Statutes have become the most common method of regulating some technological search devices. These include wiretapping, tracking devices, and pen registers, which are all topics later in this chapter, as well as the "beeper" device described in the following problem.

Problem 7-1. Beepers

In August, Agent Rottinger of the Drug Enforcement Administration (DEA) learned that James Karo ordered 50 gallons of ether from a government informant, Carl Muehlenweg of Graphic Photo Design. Muehlenweg told Rottinger that Karo planned to use the ether to extract cocaine from clothing he had imported into the United States. The agents obtained a court order authorizing the installation and monitoring of a beeper in one of the cans of ether. With Muehlenweg's consent, agents substituted their own can containing a beeper for one of the cans in the shipment and then painted all 10 cans to give them a uniform appearance.

On September 20, agents saw Karo pick up the ether from Muehlenweg. They followed Karo to his house, using visual and beeper surveillance. At one point later that day, agents determined by using the beeper that the ether was still inside the house, but they later determined that it had been moved undetected to the house of a person named Richard Horton, where they located it using the beeper. The next day, the beeper was no longer transmitting from Horton's house, and agents traced the beeper to a self-storage facility.

Agents detected the smell of ether coming from locker 15 and learned from the manager that Horton had rented that locker using an alias. The agents obtained consent from the manager of the facility to install a closed-circuit video camera in a locker that had a view of locker 15. On February 6, agents monitoring the video camera saw a man and a woman removing the cans from the locker and loading them onto the rear bed of Horton's pickup truck.

At about 6 P.M. on February 6, the pickup left the driveway and traveled along public highways to Taos. During the trip, the agents kept the two vehicles under both physical and electronic surveillance. When the vehicles arrived at a house in Taos rented by Horton, the agents did not maintain tight surveillance for fear of detection. When the vehicles left the Taos residence, agents determined, using the beeper monitor, that the beeper can was still inside the house. Again on February 7, the beeper revealed that the ether can was still on the premises. At one point, agents noticed that the windows of the house were wide open on a cold windy day, leading them to suspect that the ether was being used. On February 8, the agents obtained a warrant to search the Taos residence based in part on information derived through use of the beeper. DEA agents executed the warrant on February 10, and seized cocaine and laboratory equipment.

Karo was indicted for conspiracy to possess cocaine with intent to distribute it. The trial court granted Karo's pretrial motion to suppress the evidence seized from the Taos residence on the grounds that the initial warrant to install the beeper in the ether container was invalid as an unauthorized "seizure" and that the continued tracking of the beeper as it moved among and inside various homes and the storage locker constituted an unauthorized "search." How would you rule on appeal?

Problem 7-2. Eye in the Sky

Advances in technology are making it easier for police to use video cameras for surveillance of pedestrian areas and busy street intersections. Earlier technologies used analog videotape and were wired to monitoring locations through fiber-optic cable. New cameras use digital images that can be stored and manipulated more easily. The new cameras can be operated by radio commands and can transmit images wirelessly, saving the cost of installing cable.

Police in many jurisdictions are experimenting with video cameras posted in public places. Over two million cameras have been deployed in Great Britain, at busy intersections and in public gathering areas. Many cities in the United States have installed a cameras at intersections to record the license plates of cars that disobey traffic signals; private firms operate the cameras in exchange for a large portion of the revenue from traffic tickets issued.

In Washington, D.C., the police department now has more than a dozen cameras mounted in downtown areas, monitoring such sites as the White House, the National Mall, and Union Station, as well as others attached to police helicopters. Eventually, the system could include more than 200 cameras in stations of the Washington Metro system, another 200 cameras in public schools, and 100 more planned for installation by the city traffic department at busy intersections. The first neighborhood to add camera surveillance will probably be Georgetown, a shopping district popular with tourists and college students.

The signals from the cameras all feed into a control room in police headquarters, called the Joint Operations Command Center. The center has 40 video stations angled around a wall of floor-to-ceiling screens. The cameras are programmed to scan public areas automatically, and officers can take over manual control if they see something they want to examine more closely. Eventually, the system could include "biometric" software that will permit an automated match between a face in the crowd and a computerized photo of a suspect.

If you were asked to testify before a state legislature about the legal implications of camera surveillance, what would you say? If it is implemented and a driver receives an automatic ticket in the mail for failing to stop completely at a stop sign or for driving through an intersection while the traffic light is red, what claims might she make? Compare Jess Bravin, D.C. Cops Build Surveillance Network; New System Will Link Hundreds of Public Cameras, Wall St. Journal, Feb. 13, 2002.

Notes

1. *Beepers: federal position.* In United States v. Knotts, 460 U.S. 276 (1983), the Court held that no search took place when police attached a beeper to a drum of chloroform (a chemical used for making drugs) and then followed the movements of the car using the beeper when they lost visual contact. The Court held that "[a] person travelling in an automobile on public thoroughfares has no reasonable expectation of privacy in his movements from one place to another." In United States v. Karo, 468 U.S. 705 (1984), the Court held that no seizure took place when the DEA planted a beeper in a drum of ether (another precursor chemical), finding that there was no "meaningful interference with an individual's possessory interests in that property." The *Karo* Court also held that there was no "search" when the

drum was transferred to the defendant. However, the Court found that a search occurred when agents used the beeper to track movements within a house.

> In this case, had a DEA agent thought it useful to enter the Taos residence to verify that the ether was actually in the house and had he done so surreptitiously and without a warrant, there is little doubt that he would have engaged in an unreasonable search within the meaning of the Fourth Amendment. For purposes of the Amendment, the result is the same where, without a warrant, the Government surreptitiously employs an electronic device to obtain information that it could not have obtained by observation from outside the curtilage of the house. . . . The monitoring of an electronic device such as a beeper is, of course, less intrusive than a full-scale search, but it does reveal a critical fact about the interior of the premises that the Government is extremely interested in knowing and that it could not have otherwise obtained without a warrant. . . .

There have been relatively few decisions about beepers by state supreme courts since *Knotts* and *Karo,* suggesting that the use of beepers is limited. Most of the state supreme court decisions have held — contrary to the decisions in *Karo* and *Knotts*— that placing beepers in a car or commercial object is a search. See People v. Oates, 698 P.2d 811 (Colo. 1985); State v. Campbell, 759 P.2d 1040 (Or. 1988).

2. *Beeper statutes.* Mobile tracking devices receive more attention in statutes than in constitutional decisions. The statutes generally treat the use of beepers as a search that must be supported by reasonable suspicion, and some statutes require judicial authorization. For example, a Pennsylvania statute, 18 Pa. Cons. Stat. §5761, authorizes the use of "mobile tracking devices" only after applying for a judicial order and demonstrating reasonable suspicion. The judicial order authorizes the use of the device only for 90 days. The statute also prevents use of a mobile tracking device to track movement within "an area protected by a reasonable expectation of privacy" unless "exigent circumstances" are present or the government has obtained a judicial order "supported by probable cause."

What explains the prevalence of statutes rather than case law on this question? Does legislation such as the Pennsylvania statute handle all the significant problems? More generally, are statutes of this sort a basis for concluding that legislative procedure tends to create higher barriers than judicial decisions to police action? Has legislation regarding beepers created such onerous conditions that authorities now rarely use the device?

3. *Distinguishing beepers from dogs.* Beepers reveal some information that, at least in theory, would be available to an officer observing a suspect from a legal vantage point. In this sense, beepers differ from dog sniffs because the dog accomplishes what even the most diligent or discerning officer could not. But as the Supreme Court recognized in *Karo,* a beeper can also reveal information (such as the presence or movement of objects within a building) that would not be available to an observing officer at the scene. Do you agree that these different sorts of information deserve different treatment in the law?

4. *Tracing traffic.* In the "beeper" cases, courts often point out that a beeper simply reveals the target's location on public highways, something the police could monitor without the special device (and without violating the Fourth Amendment) if they had enough time and resources to follow in another vehicle. Could the same argument apply to other devices now in use, such as police surveillance cameras mounted at stop signs? Does the analysis change if the observation technologies become pervasive? See Robert Weisberg, IVHS, Legal Privacy, and the Legacy of

Dr. Faustus, 11 Santa Clara Computer & High Tech. L.J. 75 (1995). Does the fact that the camera "never sleeps" convert this gathering of publicly available information into a constitutionally regulated "search"? If current doctrines do not answer this question, what principles should apply to the development or use of pervasive information-gathering technologies?

B. WIRETAPPING

Wiretapping is just one of many technologies that provide the capacity to observe or hear more than would be possible with human senses. This section considers the evolution of the procedures governing wiretapping, from judicial doctrine to statute. The first subsection looks at Olmstead v. United States, one of the earliest wiretapping cases. This case, along with Katz v. United States, set the stage for Congress and state legislatures to occupy the wiretapping field, largely unrestricted by precedent and other limits on judicial authority. The remainder of this section highlights the recurring features of these wiretapping statutes, and reviews some difficult choices about how to extend this regulation to some specialized settings.

1. *Judicial Limits on Wiretaps*

■ ROY OLMSTEAD v. UNITED STATES

277 U.S. 438 (1928)

TAFT, C.J.

The petitioners were convicted . . . of a conspiracy to violate the National Prohibition Act by unlawfully possessing, transporting and importing intoxicating liquors and maintaining nuisances, and by selling intoxicating liquors. Seventy-two others in addition to the petitioners were indicted. Some were not apprehended, some were acquitted and others pleaded guilty.

The evidence in the records discloses a conspiracy of amazing magnitude to import, possess and sell liquor unlawfully. . . . Olmstead was the leading conspirator and the general manager of the business. . . . Of the several offices in Seattle the chief one was in a large office building. In this there were three telephones on three different lines. There were telephones in an office of the manager in his own home, at the homes of his associates, and at other places in the city. . . .

The information which led to the discovery of the conspiracy and its nature and extent was largely obtained by intercepting messages on the telephones of the conspirators by four federal prohibition officers. Small wires were inserted along the ordinary telephone wires from the residences of four of the petitioners and those leading from the chief office. The insertions were made without trespass upon any property of the defendants. They were made in the basement of the large office building. The taps from house lines were made in the streets near the houses. The gathering of evidence continued for many months. . .

The [Fourth] Amendment itself shows that the search is to be of material things — the person, the house, his papers or his effects. The description of the warrant necessary to make the proceeding lawful, is that it must specify the place to be searched and the person or things to be seized. . . . It is plainly within the words of the

Amendment to say that the unlawful rifling by a government agent of a sealed letter is a search and seizure of the sender's papers or effects. The letter is a paper, an effect, and in the custody of a Government that forbids carriage except under its protection. The United States takes no such care of telegraph or telephone messages as of mailed sealed letters. The Amendment does not forbid what was done here. There was no searching. There was no seizure. The evidence was secured by the use of the sense of hearing and that only. There was no entry of the houses or offices of the defendants.

By the invention of the telephone, 50 years ago, and its application for the purpose of extending communications, one can talk with another at a far distant place. The language of the Amendment can not be extended and expanded to include telephone wires reaching to the whole world from the defendant's house or office. The intervening wires are not part of his house or office any more than are the highways along which they are stretched. . . .

Congress may of course protect the secrecy of telephone messages by making them, when intercepted, inadmissible in evidence in federal criminal trials, by direct legislation, and thus depart from the common law of evidence. But the courts may not adopt such a policy by attributing an enlarged and unusual meaning to the Fourth Amendment. . . .

BRANDEIS, J., dissenting.

[At least six] prohibition agents listened over the tapped wires and reported the messages taken. Their operations extended over a period of nearly five months. The typewritten record of the notes of conversations overheard occupies 775 typewritten pages. [The Government concedes] that if wire-tapping can be deemed a search and seizure within the Fourth Amendment, such wire-tapping as was practiced in the case at bar was an unreasonable search and seizure, and that the evidence thus obtained was inadmissible. . . .

When the Fourth and Fifth Amendments were adopted, [f]orce and violence were then the only means known to man by which a Government could directly effect self-incrimination. It could compel the individual to testify — a compulsion effected, if need be, by torture. It could secure possession of his papers and other articles incident to his private life — a seizure effected, if need be, by breaking and entry. Protection against such invasion of the sanctities of a man's home and the privacies of life was provided in the Fourth and Fifth Amendments by specific language. . . . Subtler and more far-reaching means of invading privacy have become available to the Government. Discovery and invention have made it possible for the Government, by means far more effective than stretching upon the rack, to obtain disclosure in court of what is whispered in the closet.

Moreover, in the application of a constitution, our contemplation cannot be only of what has been but of what may be. The progress of science in furnishing the Government with means of espionage is not likely to stop with wire-tapping. Ways may some day be developed by which the Government, without removing papers from secret drawers, can reproduce them in court, and by which it will be enabled to expose to a jury the most intimate occurrences of the home. Advances in the psychic and related sciences may bring means of exploring unexpressed beliefs, thoughts and emotions. . . . Can it be that the Constitution affords no protection against such invasions of individual security?

[The] tapping of one man's telephone line involves the tapping of the telephone of every other person whom he may call, or who may call him. As a means of espionage, writs of assistance and general warrants are but puny instruments of tyranny and oppression when compared with wire-tapping.

The makers of our Constitution undertook to secure conditions favorable to the pursuit of happiness. They recognized the significance of man's spiritual nature, of his feelings and of his intellect. . . . They conferred, as against the Government, the right to be let alone — the most comprehensive of rights and the right most valued by civilized men. To protect that right, every unjustifiable intrusion by the Government upon the privacy of the individual, whatever the means employed, must be deemed a violation of the Fourth Amendment. . . .

Notes

1. *Constitutional interpretation.* Recall that the Supreme Court overruled *Olmstead* in Katz v. United States, 389 U.S. 347 (1967). Despite their great difference in doctrine and bottom line, *Olmstead* and *Katz* are both splendid examples of constitutional decision making. They each raise some of the foundational issues in any difficult constitutional context: What do the words of the various provisions mean? Should interpretation be limited to the words? If not, what principles limit the power of the court from acting as a superlegislature by interpreting words? On the question of the role a court plays when interpreting the meaning of constitutional terms such as "persons," "houses," or "effects"— much less concepts such as "privacy" and "reasonableness"— consider the following exchange:

> "There's glory for you!"
>
> "I don't know what you mean by 'glory,'" Alice said.
>
> Humpty Dumpty smiled contemptuously. "Of course you don't — till I tell you. I meant there's a nice knock-down argument for you."
>
> "But 'glory' doesn't mean 'a nice knock-down argument,'" Alice objected.
>
> "When I use a word," Humpty Dumpty said in rather a scornful tone, "it means just what I choose it to mean — neither more nor less."
>
> "The question is," said Alice, "whether you can make words mean so many different things."
>
> "The question is," said Humpty Dumpty, "which is to be the master — that's all."

Lewis Carroll, Through the Looking-Glass and What Alice Found There 269 (Martin Gardner ed., 1960).

2. *Wiretap cases between* Olmstead *and* Katz. Even before *Katz,* the Supreme Court had begun to place limits on electronic eavesdropping. In Silverman v. United States, 365 U.S. 505 (1961), the Court found that the government violated the Fourth Amendment when it inserted a "spike mike" into a heating duct. Although the Court concluded that the government had committed a trespass, it emphasized that its decision did "not turn upon the technicality of a trespass upon a party wall as a matter of local law. It is based upon the reality of an actual intrusion into a constitutionally protected area."

2. *Statutory Wiretapping Procedures*

Congress took up the Supreme Court's invitation in the *Olmstead* opinion to regulate wiretapping by statute. Indeed, Congress followed the specific recommendation in Chief Justice William Howard Taft's opinion that wiretap evidence be made inadmissible in federal court. Section 605 of the Federal Communications Act of 1934 stated that no person "shall intercept any communication *and* divulge or publish" the communication to any other person, unless the sender authorizes the interception. This relatively broad ban on wiretapping (at least when coupled with "divulging") barred the use in federal court of most intercepted conversations obtained through tapping the telephones of criminal defendants. Because Congress focused on the admissibility of the evidence and not on its collection, federal agents continued to use wiretaps in investigations. Where the evidence could be used in state prosecutions, federal agents would provide it to the state under what was known as the "silver platter" doctrine (because the federal agents could offer the tainted evidence to the state prosecutors "on a silver platter").

The 1934 statutory limits on federal law enforcement changed when the United States Congress enacted Title III of the Omnibus Crime Control and Safe Streets Act of 1968, which established procedures for authorized wiretapping. The provisions in Title III reflected not only the new constitutional emphasis on privacy in *Katz*, but the specific concerns that led the United States Supreme Court in 1967— the same year as *Katz*— to reject New York's wiretap statute in Berger v. New York, 388 U.S. 41 (1967). The key provision in the New York statute, authorizing ex parte wiretapping orders, provided as follows:

> An ex parte order for eavesdropping . . . may be issued by any justice of the supreme court or judge of a county court . . . upon oath or affirmation of a district attorney, or of the attorney-general or of an officer above the rank of sergeant of any police department . . . , that there is reasonable ground to believe that evidence of crime may be thus obtained, and particularly describing the person or persons whose communications . . . are to be overheard or recorded and the purpose thereof, and, in the case of a telegraphic or telephonic communication, identifying the particular telephone number or telegraph line involved. . . . Any such order shall be effective for the time specified therein but not for a period of more than two months unless extended or renewed by the justice or judge who signed and issued the original order upon satisfying himself that such extension or renewal is in the public interest. . . .

The Court concluded that the statute violated the Fourth Amendment (applicable to New York through the Fourteenth Amendment), 388 U.S. at 58-60:

> We believe the statute here is [unconstitutional]. First, . . . eavesdropping is authorized without requiring belief that any particular offense has been or is being committed; nor that the "property" sought, the conversations, be particularly described. The purpose of the probable-cause requirement of the Fourth Amendment . . . is thereby wholly aborted. Likewise the statute's failure to describe with particularity the conversations sought gives the officer a roving commission to "seize" any and all conversations. It is true that the statute requires the naming of "the person or persons whose communications, conversations or discussions are to be overheard or recorded. . . ." But this does no more than identify the person whose constitutionally protected area is to be invaded rather than "particularly describing" the communications, conversations, or discussions to be seized. As with general warrants this leaves too much to the discretion of the officer executing the order.
>
> Secondly, authorization of eavesdropping for a two-month period is the equivalent of a series of intrusions, searches, and seizures pursuant to a single showing of probable cause. Prompt execution is also avoided. During such a long and continuous (24 hours

a day) period the conversations of any and all persons coming into the area covered by the device will be seized indiscriminately and without regard to their connection with the crime under investigation. Moreover, the statute permits, and there were authorized here, extensions of the original two-month period — presumably for two months each — on a mere showing that such extension is "in the public interest." . . . This we believe insufficient without a showing of present probable cause for the continuance of the eavesdrop. . . .

Finally, the statute's procedure, necessarily because its success depends on secrecy, has no requirement for notice as do conventional warrants, nor does it overcome this defect by requiring some showing of special facts. On the contrary, it permits unconsented entry without any showing of exigent circumstances. Such a showing of exigency, in order to avoid notice, would appear more important in eavesdropping, with its inherent dangers, than that required when conventional procedures of search and seizure are utilized. Nor does the statute provide for a return on the warrant thereby leaving full discretion in the officer as to the use of seized conversations of innocent as well as guilty parties. In short, the statute's blanket grant of permission to eavesdrop is without adequate judicial supervision or protective procedures.

Before the enactment of Title III in 1968, many states (like the federal government, under the Federal Communications Act of 1934) prohibited wiretapping. After Title III, most states amended their own wiretap laws, authorizing the government to conduct wiretaps under judicial supervision. Wiretapping throughout the United States and in most other countries is now controlled by procedures specified in statutes. The Supreme Court has never considered the constitutionality of Title III, but lower federal courts have affirmed its constitutionality, and state courts have upheld similar state statutes.

Portions of Title III and selected provisions from several state statutes follow. Title III served as the model for most states and for many non-U.S. jurisdictions. The provisions in state statutes selected for this section highlight different policy choices than the federal act. Because of the special difficulties in reading and parsing statutory materials, the provisions address only two sets of questions: (1) the basic coverage of the protections for electronic communications and (2) judicial administration of wiretap requests. The statutory schemes governing wiretaps are quite complex and raise many additional issues, a few of which are covered in notes. See generally Clifford Fishman and Anne McKenna, Wiretapping and Eavesdropping (2d ed. 1995).

Wiretap statutes treat government searches through electronic surveillance differently from other searches. First, the wiretap statutes decide for all cases the question debated as a matter of Fourth Amendment interpretation in *Olmstead* and *Katz:* They declare that wiretaps are searches. Second, Congress and the state legislatures have left little room for the many varieties of exigent circumstances that government agents rely on every day to conduct warrantless searches. If agents want to use wiretaps, they must seek a warrant.

While the federal and state statutes do not invite claims of exigency, this highly proceduralized structure does not cover every "intercepted communication." First, most statutes exclude from the wiretap warrant process conversations that are recorded with the consent of one of the parties.

Second, the statutes do not apply to all kinds of communications, though the coverage of wiretap statutes has expanded well beyond traditional taps such as those seen in *Olmstead* and *Katz.* The federal wiretap statute originally applied to communications transmitted over a wire, but now it protects wire, oral, and electronic communications, as do most of the state statutes. A wire communication includes any transfer of the human voice by means of a wire, cable, or other connection between the sender and the recipient. See 18 U.S.C. §§2510(4), (18). Electronic communications include those not carried by sound waves, such as electronic mail, video teleconferences, and other data transfers. 18 U.S.C. §2510 (12). Under the federal statute, an "interception" of one of these types of communications occurs when a person uses "any electronic, mechanical, or other device" to make an "aural acquisition" of the "contents" of the communication. How well do these statutory definitions account for future technological changes in communications?

Third, the statutes may not apply to recording of conversations out of the governing jurisdiction or in another country. This question often arises when prosecutors wish to introduce conversations between a party in a different jurisdiction and a second party in the prosecutors' jurisdiction. Should a New Jersey statute control law enforcement efforts to intercept calls placed to or from another state? Between two other states? In a federal system, with many different governments intercepting communications (and regulating those interceptions), how will courts resolve conflicts among the different statutory schemes? Will law enforcement agencies convince states to engage in a "race to the bottom" in the regulation of wiretapping? The following two statutes illustrate common features of wiretap statutes.

■ 18 U.S.C. §2511

(1) Except as otherwise specifically provided in this chapter any person who—

(a) intentionally intercepts, endeavors to intercept, or procures any other person to intercept or endeavor to intercept, any wire, oral, or electronic communication; . . .

(c) intentionally discloses, or endeavors to disclose, to any other person the contents of any wire, oral, or electronic communication, knowing or having reason to know that the information was obtained through the interception of a wire, oral, or electronic communication in violation of this subsection;

(d) intentionally uses, or endeavors to use, the contents of any wire, oral, or electronic communication, knowing or having reason to know that the information was obtained through the interception of a wire, oral, or electronic communication in violation of this subsection; . . . shall be punished as provided [elsewhere in this statute] or shall be subject to suit. . . .

(2)(c) It shall not be unlawful under this chapter for a person acting under color of law to intercept a wire, oral, or electronic communication, where such person is a party to the communication or one of the parties to the communication has given prior consent to such interception.

(d) It shall not be unlawful under this chapter for a person not acting under color of law to intercept a wire, oral, or electronic communication where such person is a party to the communication or where one of the parties to the communication has given prior consent to such interception unless such communication is intercepted for the purpose of committing any criminal or tortious act in violation of the Constitution or laws of the United States or of any State.

■ NEW JERSEY STATUTES §2A:156A-4

It shall not be unlawful under this act for: . . .

b. Any investigative or law enforcement officer to intercept a wire, electronic or oral communication, where such officer is a party to the communication or where another officer who is a party to the communication requests or requires him to make such interception;

c. Any person acting at the direction of an investigative or law enforcement officer to intercept a wire, electronic or oral communication, where such person is a party to the communication or one of the parties to the communication has given prior consent to such interception; provided, however, that no such interception shall be made without the prior approval of the Attorney General or his designee or a county prosecutor or his designee. . . .

■ STATE v. JOHN WORTHY

661 A.2d 1244 (N.J. 1995)

HANDLER, J.

This case involves the application of the New Jersey Wiretap and Electronic Surveillance Control Act to tape-recorded telephone conversations between a consenting out-of-state caller and the unsuspecting defendant in New Jersey. . . .

Investigator Michael DiGiorgio is a member of the Narcotics Strike Force of the Gloucester County Prosecutor's Office. On April 1, 1991, Gordon Todd Skinner, a cooperating informant residing in Oklahoma, contacted DiGiorgio. Skinner, who had been indicted in New Jersey on charges of distribution of controlled dangerous substances, provided DiGiorgio with information regarding a telephone conversation he had had with defendant John Worthy, a resident of Paulsboro, New Jersey. DiGiorgio was familiar with both Skinner and Worthy from prior drug-related investigations. Skinner informed DiGiorgio that Worthy had, during the course of the conversation, described his existing cocaine-distribution network in Paulsboro and Philadelphia, Pennsylvania. Worthy indicated to Skinner that he wanted to expand his network to include the sale of marijuana, and allegedly proposed to purchase marijuana from Skinner. That alleged conversation between Worthy and Skinner was not recorded or transcribed. . . .

Based on the information provided by Skinner, DiGiorgio decided to initiate an investigation of Worthy and to "conduct a 'reverse' purchase of marijuana where Skinner would sell the drugs to defendant in New Jersey." DiGiorgio directed Skinner to record any future conversations with Worthy. The State concedes that "at that point Mr. Skinner was working . . . under the color of law." DiGiorgio did not seek prior approval from the Attorney General or her designee or a county prosecutor to determine "that there existed a reasonable suspicion that evidence of criminal conduct would be derived from such interception." N.J.S.A. 2A:156A-4c. DiGiorgio stated that he did not seek prior authorization because "basically I didn't believe I needed [it]."

On April 5, 1991, Skinner placed a call from Oklahoma to John Worthy. Skinner recorded the conversation, and later mailed the original tape to DiGiorgio. [During the taped conversation, Skinner and Worthy discussed possible payment terms for a sale of marijuana. Skinner placed and recorded another call from Oklahoma to

Worthy on May 28. The two men discussed the quantity and quality of marijuana for sale. During a third recorded call on May 31 from Skinner to Worthy, they settled on the time and place to complete the sale in New Jersey.]

On June 10, 1991, DiGiorgio applied, for the first time, for authorization for a consensual interception from the Gloucester County Prosecutor. In seeking the authorization, DiGiorgio [informed the prosecutor about the telephone calls and other aspects of the investigation up until that time, and described the location in Gloucester County where the transaction was scheduled to take place]. The prosecutor approved the request on June 10, 1991. Fearful that Worthy would not purchase the marijuana in Gloucester County due to a prior arrest there, DiGiorgio changed the location of the "reverse" purchase to a hotel in Cumberland County [and obtained authorization from the Cumberland County prosecutor].

A few hours after receiving authorization, DiGiorgio instructed Skinner, now in New Jersey, to make a series of telephone calls to Worthy, who was then at a residence in Pennsylvania. Each call was recorded and retained as evidence by DiGiorgio on audio cassettes. [In these calls, Worthy and Skinner made final arrangements for their rendezvous. When Worthy arrived at the designated hotel room and completed the sale, he was arrested.] Defendants moved to suppress the three taped telephone conversations originating from Oklahoma, and all evidence seized by police on June 12, 1991, and to dismiss the indictment. The trial court ordered the suppression of the three recorded conversations initiated from Oklahoma and of the intercepts of June 12, 1991. . . .

In general, the New Jersey Wiretap and Electronic Surveillance Control Act (Wiretap Control Act or Act) prohibits the interception of conversations. In certain exceptional circumstances, however, a conversation may be intercepted. Thus, "it shall not be unlawful," under the Act, for

> any person acting at the direction of an investigative or law enforcement officer to intercept a wire, electronic or oral communication, where such person is a party to the communication or one of the parties to the communication has given prior consent to such interception; provided, however, that no such interception shall be made unless the Attorney General or his designee or a county prosecutor within his authority determines that there exists a reasonable suspicion that evidence of criminal conduct will be derived from such interception. [N.J.S.A. 2A:156A-4c.]

Defendants contend that the State is not entitled to rely on this exception because Skinner, although consenting to the interception of his phone conversation with defendant, did so at the direction of DiGiorgio, "an investigative or law enforcement officer," who had not obtained the requisite prior authorization from "the Attorney General, [her] designee, or a county prosecutor within his authority."

The first major issue is whether the initial preauthorization interceptions of the telephonic communications violated the terms of the Wiretap Control Act. That issue, in turn, poses the antecedent question of whether the New Jersey statute applies to the interception of telephone conversations originating from an out-of-state telephone. State v. Minter, 561 A.2d 570 (N.J. 1989), identifies the circumstances under which the Wiretap Control Act may be applied to the interception of such communications.

In *Minter,* federal law enforcement agents arranged for an informant to place telephone calls from Morrisville, Pennsylvania to the defendant's office in Trenton. The purpose of the calls was to attempt to make a controlled purchase of drugs from the defendant. The calls were recorded. Because the federal wiretap act does not require law enforcement officials to obtain supervisory authorization prior to recording a conversation where one of the parties has given consent to the wiretap, see 18 U.S.C.A. §2511(2)(c), the agents sought no such authorization. [T]he federal agents eventually closed their investigation. The evidence, including the recorded conversations, was later turned over to New Jersey law enforcement officers. The defendant was thereafter indicted for conspiracy to distribute cocaine. Prior to trial, he moved to suppress the wiretap evidence, claiming that the failure of the federal agents to obtain prior authorization required the suppression of the recorded conversations in a state prosecution. The motion was denied.

Reasoning that state wiretap law cannot bind federal officers, the *Minter* majority perceived the critical question to involve the existence . . . of an agency relationship between the federal and state investigators. Accordingly, the Court remanded the matter for a determination of the actual nature of the relationship between the federal and state investigators. . . . The Court ruled that "if a purpose of the investigation is for a State prosecution, the federal agents can, in effect, be deemed agents of the State prosecutors, thus subject to the provisions of N.J.S.A. 2A:156A-4(c)." [T]he fact that the targeted defendant was in New Jersey was sufficient to call into operation the New Jersey statute. . . .

We are satisfied that the application of the Wiretap Control Act in these circumstances does not constitute an impermissible or extra-territorial extension of the statute because the telephone calls, though originating from an out-of-state telephone, involved conversations with a person in New Jersey. As implicitly recognized in *Minter,* there can be no doubt that the legislative concern for privacy embraces the privacy interest that a resident in New Jersey has in telephone conversations that originate from an out-of-state telephone.

The powerful privacy concerns generated by the spectre of government-directed wiretapping exist even with respect to the consensual interception of such communications, at least when the non-consenting party is in New Jersey. In imposing a requirement of prior prosecutorial approval before the police may direct a "consensual" wiretap, the Legislature sought to safeguard personal privacy. . . . Thus, in accordance with the principles enunciated in *Minter,* the New Jersey Wiretap Control Act applies to the interception of out-of-state telephone calls when a person located in New Jersey is a party, when the interception is undertaken for the purpose of investigating criminal activity in this State, and when New Jersey law enforcement officers direct, or cooperate in, the interception.

We next consider whether the initial interceptions violated the Wiretap Control Act and must be suppressed. The Act, N.J.S.A. 2A:156A-21a, provides that an "aggrieved person . . . may move to suppress the contents of any intercepted wire, electronic or oral communication, or evidence derived therefrom, on the grounds that . . . the communication was unlawfully intercepted." If the motion is granted, "the entire contents of all intercepted wire, electronic or oral communications obtained during or after any interception which is determined to be in violation of this act . . . , or evidence derived therefrom, shall not be received in the trial, hearing or proceeding."

We are aware that some courts have determined that not every failure to comply with the Wiretap Control Act mandates suppression of the interception. Courts have rather applied the remedy of suppression only to those statutory requirements considered "critical."

The trial court determined that the requirement of prosecutorial approval was "substantive," in that it protected citizens from overly zealous and completely discretionary law-enforcement practices. Indeed, it is the sole protection applicable in cases of consensual interceptions. . . . Although the statutory condition for the interception of a consensual wiretap is less onerous than, and hence not as protective of privacy as, the conditions that surround the nonconsensual interception of conversations, it cannot be doubted that the Legislature viewed the requirement of supervisory approval as an indispensable protection for the privacy interests implicated even in consensual telephone wiretaps. The history of the statutory provision strongly evidences that intent. The 1968 New Jersey Wiretap Control Act did not prohibit or regulate consensual interceptions. But after observing six years of operation, the Legislature revised the Wiretap Control Act to provide for prosecutorial oversight and prior approval of consensual interceptions [in 1975].

The State . . . contends that no deterrent effect would be served by suppression of the evidence, given the benign nature of the officer's conduct. That argument is misplaced. The statute contains no good-faith exception. . . . Application of the exclusionary rule encourages respect for protected rights and care in following prescribed procedures among law enforcement officials and departments.

The Legislature, by amending the New Jersey Wiretap Control Act, intended to protect privacy interests to a greater extent than does the federal wiretap statute. That was accomplished by interposing prosecutorial review between law-enforcement officers and the citizenry. This review is clearly critical to achieving the desired protection of privacy that the Legislature envisioned, especially in light of its singular nature. In not seeking prosecutorial review, Officer DiGiorgio failed to comply with an essential requirement of the statute; therefore, the conversations were unlawfully intercepted and must be suppressed according to the statute's own terms.

The State asserts that even if the recorded calls initiated from Oklahoma are suppressed, the "New Jersey communications, intercepted after the consent of two local prosecutors had been obtained, are not tainted and therefore admissible." As originally enacted, the Wiretap Control Act provided that "if the motion is granted, the contents of the intercepted wire or oral communication, or evidence derived therefrom, shall not be received in evidence in the trial, hearing or proceeding." In State v. Dye, 291 A.2d 825 (N.J. 1972), the Court refused to suppress two and one-half hours of incriminating conversations gleaned from 105 hours of indiscriminate recording by law-enforcement officials pursuant to a warrant. The Court held that "those illegally taken may be suppressed, or excluded at the trial, but those within the warrant do not become so tainted as to bar their receipt in evidence." . . .

Dissatisfaction with the *Dye* decision was evident throughout the 1975 legislative hearings, which considered the conditions to be imposed on consensual wiretaps as well as the clarification and extension of the suppression remedy. The Legislature, as a result, clarified and strengthened the suppression remedy of section 21 as follows: "If the motion is granted, the entire contents of all intercepted wire or oral communications obtained during or after any interception which is determined to be in violation of this act . . . , or evidence derived therefrom, shall not be received in evidence in the trial, hearing or proceeding." A plain and strict reading of the amended statute supports the proposition that all evidence derived from the illegal interception — the conversations recorded by that interception, conversations recorded after the unlawful interception, and other evidence "derived" from the illegal interception — shall be excluded.

It is clear, in this case, that the later-seized evidence was derived from the unlawful interceptions. Both the trial court and the Appellate Division found that the subsequent interceptions were impermissibly tainted by the prior unlawful interception. . . . Examining the totality of the circumstances, the [trial] court determined that "the disputed evidence in this case . . . is inextricably tied to the illegal intercepts that have been previously suppressed." The Appellate Division adopted the trial court's determination that "the prosecutors' consents cannot be considered intervening circumstances since they were based entirely on the information obtained through the unlawful interception of the Oklahoma communications." We concur in the determinations reached by the lower courts that the evidence is impermissibly tainted. Both applications for authorization relied entirely on the illegally intercepted communications. . . .

The State next argues that, even if tainted, the evidence would have inevitably been discovered wholly independently of the recording of Skinner's and Worthy's conversations. More precisely, the State argues that Worthy would have been apprehended for the drug offenses he actually committed through investigative efforts that would have occurred inevitably and independently of the investigation involving the unlawful wiretap interception. Defendant answers that the plain language of N.J.S.A. 2A:156A-21 does not allow for an exception based on "inevitable discovery." In light of the Legislature's obvious concern for privacy and its express and consistent recognition of the need for an effective exclusionary rule to assure the protection of privacy, it is not reasonable to impute a legislative intent to undermine that exclusionary rule with such an exception.

In State v. Sugar, 495 A.2d 90 (1985), this Court adopted an "inevitable discovery" exception to the judicially-created exclusionary rule applicable to an unreasonable search and seizure. The exception applied when:

> (1) proper, normal and specific investigatory procedures would have been pursued in order to complete the investigation of the case; (2) under all of the surrounding relevant circumstances the pursuit of those procedures would have inevitably resulted in the discovery of the evidence; and (3) the discovery of the evidence through the use of such procedures would have occurred wholly independently of the discovery of such evidence by unlawful means.

[Even if the inevitable discovery exception were to apply, the] State has failed to show by clear and convincing evidence the likelihood of a separate investigation that would have led to the detection of defendant's participation in the crimes charged in the indictment. . . .

Notes

1. *Consensual intercepts: majority view.* Most state wiretap statutes follow the federal lead and do not protect interceptions of communications if at least one of the parties to the communication consents to the interception. About a dozen states require the consent of both parties before a conversation may be recorded (absent judicial authorization). See, e.g., 18 Pa. Cons. Stat. §5704(4) ("It shall not be unlawful under this chapter for [a] person to intercept a wire, electronic or oral communication, where all parties to the communication have given prior consent to such

interception"). New Jersey takes the unusual position of allowing consensual interceptions while creating some protection for such interceptions when a government agent who is involved in the conversation provides the consent. How would a legislator justify the decision to treat these communications differently from those receiving the full protection of the wiretap statute? Why did the New Jersey legislature require only executive branch review of these interceptions? Will the state attorney general or county prosecutor ever rebuff a police request to seek third-party consent to record a conversation?

2. *Statutes and federalism.* The language of the federal wiretap statute in Title III applies both to federal and state law enforcement officers. The supremacy clause in Article VI of the U.S. Constitution declares that federal legislation is "the supreme Law of the Land." Thus, federal legislation can create binding legal obligations on state law enforcement officials. But is the converse true? Can state statutes (for instance, those regulating wiretaps more stringently than federal law) create binding obligations on federal law enforcement officers operating within the state? Does it matter whether the evidence that the federal agents collect is presented in a state or federal prosecution? See 18 U.S.C. §2516(2).

3. *Statutes and extraterritorial behavior.* The most far-reaching issue in the *Worthy* case was the extraterritorial effect of the wiretap statute. How important would a state wiretap statute be if it applied only to monitoring of calls between two people located within the state where the crime was committed? Are you satisfied that the New Jersey court interpreted this statute properly on this issue? Is there any legal limitation on the authority of a state legislature to prohibit monitoring activity occurring outside state boundaries? Would you answer questions about extraterritoriality differently if law enforcement agents of another *country* monitored a telephone call between one person in the state and another person in the foreign country and presented the evidence of a criminal violation to state officials? In State v. Capolongo, 647 N.E.2d 1286 (N.Y. 1995), the court faced just this question, in a case involving the interception in Toronto of a telephone conversation between the Canadian suspect and the defendant, located in New York. The interception of the phone call did not comply with New York statutory requirements, but the court held that this interception did not violate New York's privacy act because the government agents took action in Toronto rather than in New York. The Court also distinguished efforts to control wiretapping by investigators from efforts to control the use of wiretap evidence by prosecutors within the state:

> While New York law governing acquisition of wiretap evidence in New York State is, by its terms, inapplicable to the methods by which foreign law enforcement officials procure wiretap evidence, New York law does at a minimum control the conduct of New York prosecutors seeking to introduce wiretap evidence into our courts. The statutory procedure applicable to admissibility of electronic eavesdropping evidence—independent of any questions concerning the authorization and acquisition of such evidence—obligated the People to provide defendant, within 15 days of arraignment, with copies of the Canadian wiretap warrant and affidavits to permit him to investigate grounds for suppression.
>
> States differ on whether to allow prosecutors to employ wiretap evidence seized in another jurisdiction pursuant to conduct that would clearly render that evidence inadmissible under the State's own standards. Some adhere to the Federal view that the overriding purpose of the exclusionary rule is to deter unlawful governmental conduct, and that one State's laws have no deterrent effect on conduct of governmental agents

> of another jurisdiction. Support also exists for approaching the question as a choice-of-law problem, and choosing the law either of the forum State or the State where the seizure occurred. In another case, therefore, we will be called to decide whether to apply our State law to suppress foreign electronic eavesdropping evidence that offends our State standards.

Would the outcome change if both callers were located in the foreign country during the telephone call and discussed a crime that had occurred in the state?

4. *The exclusion remedy.* If a government wiretap violates a constitutional provision, then the constitutional remedy (exclusion of the evidence) will take hold. But what if the government violates statutory limits on wiretapping that are not mandated by the constitution? The state and federal wiretap statutes almost uniformly contain their own exclusionary remedy for at least some statutory violations. See 18 U.S.C. §2515 (designating exclusion as the remedy for unlawful interceptions of wire and oral communications but not electronic communications). In United States v. Giordano, 416 U.S. 505 (1974), the Supreme Court interpreted the federal remedial statute to apply only to violations of provisions that play "a central role in the statutory scheme." The New Jersey court in *Worthy* applied a similar test to its state statutory remedy. How does a court determine which statutory provisions are "central" and which are peripheral if the statute itself does not say so? Does it depend on the number of cases in which the government is likely to violate the provision? Is the intent of the investigating officer(s) relevant? Note that the federal statute reprinted above and most state statutes also provide for civil and criminal sanctions against individuals who intentionally violate those statutes.

5. *Applying remedial doctrines in a statutory environment.* The New Jersey court in *Worthy* was not receptive to the government's argument for "good faith" and "inevitable discovery" exceptions that would have forgiven or ignored the police officer's unintentional statutory violation. Courts may feel reluctant to apply doctrines first developed in areas left largely to judicial development (such as a "good faith" exception to the exclusionary remedy) to areas controlled largely by statute. Is the possibility of legislatures acting more broadly across the field of criminal procedure a reason for courts generally to hesitate developing new doctrines of their own?

6. *Statutory procedure.* Wiretap statutes raise a set of institutional questions for students of criminal procedure. Congress and state legislatures over the past two or three generations have taken a much more active hand in criminal procedure questions. Hardly a legislative session goes by without the passage of some new statute affecting the investigation and prosecution of crime. Wiretap statutes were one of the earliest and most prominent examples of "statutory procedure": an area in which legislatures take the leading role in setting the legal limits on practices in the field.

Legislatures have considerably greater flexibility than courts to fashion procedural rules. Legislatures can, for example, create new institutions or allocate funds to support new procedures. But if legislatures have such flexibility, and are free to adopt or ignore any nonconstitutional precedents on the topic, what principles should legislatures rely on in crafting wise rules? Are there any general drafting principles, apart from the content of a statute, that can tell readers whether a law is well-drafted?

What is the role left to courts when an entire area has been occupied by statutory procedure? Does the judicial role become more administrative and fact-oriented? In the *Worthy* case, the New Jersey court recognized that suppression would be an appropriate remedy only for statutory violations that were "substantive" or "critical." This was not a distinction drawn in the New Jersey statute, but a rule the New Jersey court (like other courts) had developed in applying complex statutory procedure.

7. *Statutory interpretation in a constitutional area.* Are the principles of statutory interpretation the same for statutes with constitutional dimensions? The statutory text itself is the starting point, of course, and certain interpretive conventions, called "canons of construction," may enable the interpreter to place the language in context or resolve ambiguous language. In American courts, judges also try to apply statutory language in a manner most consistent with the perceived "purpose" of the legislation. In some jurisdictions (especially under federal law), the judge will settle on a statutory purpose by looking to the intent of the legislators who passed the statute, as embodied in specific sources such as committee reports and floor debates. Do any of these interpretive techniques change when a statute deals with a subject that has been the subject of constitutional litigation, such as the law of searches and seizures? Will courts interpreting a wiretap statute tend to be guided more by their own (or a "judicial") view of prudent legal controls on government investigations, and consider themselves less obliged to carry out the expressed views of legislators who voted for the bill? In other words, does a constitutional aura around a statute increase the judiciary's interpretive powers?

8. *The changing response to developing phone-like technologies.* Starting in the 1970s state and federal courts battled over whether wiretap statutes covered conversations made on cordless or cellular phones. The majority of jurisdictions refused to extend the existing statutes governing "wire" communications to wireless exchanges. Federal law now directly addresses these communications. In the Electronic Communications Privacy Act of 1986, 18 U.S.C. §2510(1), Congress protected conversations over cellular phones, and in the Communications Assistance for Law Enforcement Act, 47 U.S.C. §1001, enacted in 1994, Congress extended this protection to conversations on cordless phones. If the problem of unprotected wireless communications first appeared regularly in appellate decisions in the 1970s, and did not lead to specific statutory coverage until 1994 (and even then, not in every state), what does this say about the adaptability of the legal system? Do you conclude from this story that statutes are not capable of responding to changing conditions, because they are too rigid and too difficult to amend? Should legislatures address new technologies quickly, or should courts extend laws to cover them unless and until legislatures say otherwise? For example, what privacy should be recognized in voice or data communications conveyed through satellites? Does it matter whether the user knows that the communication bounces off a satellite?

Problem 7-3. Minimization

Beginning in 1989, the Harford County Narcotics Task Force and Baltimore County authorities jointly investigated Carl Briscoe for suspected cocaine distribution. Along the way, the investigators began to suspect that Roland Mazzone, who lived in Baltimore County, was involved in the distribution ring. On June 19, 1991, the State's Attorney for Baltimore County filed ex parte applications with the Circuit Court to intercept and record conversations on two telephones (one at Mazzone's home, the other at his business, the Valley View Inn) from June 20 to July 20, 1991. A circuit court judge approved the applications and, on June 19, signed orders authorizing the interceptions. The orders authorized the wiretaps, and placed certain conditions on the operation of the wiretap, including a statement in the orders that the interceptions be conducted "in such a way as to minimize the interception of communications not otherwise subject to interception under Title III or the Maryland wiretap provisions."

At the time the orders were signed, the court also approved written "minimization guidelines," formulated by the State's Attorney. The guidelines included a section on privileged communications:

> Under Maryland Law, we will be concerned with privileged communications involving lawyer-client, husband-wife, priest-penitent, accountant-client and psychologist-patient relationship. Contact the above listed Assistant State's Attorneys for Baltimore County for instructions if you anticipate that you are about to monitor such a conversation and cannot affirmatively decide to minimize it completely. If it appears that the communication does discuss the commission of a designated crime itself, the privilege is breached and the whole conversation is to be monitored. If it appears that the communication might discuss the commission of a designated crime then spot monitoring shall be employed. If the communication does not involve the commission of a crime then the privilege applies absolutely and must be completely minimized as soon as the speakers identify themselves. All husband and wife communications are privileged; but discussions which involve the commission of the designated crime may be intercepted. All other communications must be minimized and spot monitoring must be employed carefully.

On July 12, 1991, after the State's Attorney filed further ex parte applications, the court issued new orders to continue the interceptions for an additional 30 days. The court approved a new set of written minimization guidelines, prepared by the State's Attorney, which stated that the minimization guidelines approved on June 19 "will also apply to the operational procedures" authorized on July 12, except for the following changes:

> Information gathered from the wiretaps conducted over Roland Mazzone's residence telephone as well as the business telephone of the Valley View Inn has identified Mazzone's wife, Elizabeth Ann, as being involved in this illegal controlled dangerous substance operation. Thus the privilege that is afforded to them under Maryland Law as husband and wife is breached during the interception of conversations that pertain to Mazzone's illegal drug activity.

During the investigation, the investigating officers learned that David Vita was Mazzone's supplier. Specifically, the officers collected evidence that on June 30, 1991, Mazzone paid Vita $14,000 and received from Vita a kilo of cocaine. Agents recorded dozens of phone calls between Roland and Elizabeth. Two provided incriminating evidence. In the first conversation, Roland called Elizabeth and she told him that he should not "come home empty-handed," meaning that he should bring some cocaine home with him. In the second conversation, Elizabeth called Roland at his business to inform him that Vita had arrived at their house.

Before trial, Mazzone moved to suppress all communications intercepted pursuant to the wiretap orders. He argued that the wiretap orders were illegal because the minimization guidelines misstated Maryland law on the marital communication privilege and therefore illegally authorized interception of privileged communications. The marital communications privilege is codified at §9-105. It provides that "one spouse is not competent to disclose any confidential communication between the spouses occurring during their marriage." As Mazzone suggests, Maryland courts have indeed interpreted the marital communications privilege to apply even when the communication furthers a crime.

As the trial judge in this case, you must rule on Mazzone's motion to suppress. Section 10-408(i) of the state wiretap law permits suppression of "any intercepted wire, oral, or electronic communication, or evidence derived therefrom" when "the interception was not made in conformity with the order of authorization."

When evaluating the validity of a wiretap order, Maryland courts distinguish between "preconditions" and "post conditions." Preconditions include the actions that investigators must take before a judge may issue an ex parte wiretap order and the inclusion of certain provisions required to be in the wiretap order. One such precondition is the requirement in §10-408(e)(3) that "every order and extension thereof shall contain a provision that the authorization to intercept . . . shall be conducted in such a way as to minimize the interception of communications not otherwise subject to interception under this subtitle." Maryland courts say that failure of a precondition requires suppression of all the evidence obtained under the wiretap.

Post conditions are the actions that must be taken after the judge issues a valid wiretap order, including compliance with the minimization mandate in the order. Imperfect compliance with a post condition does not require suppression of the evidence obtained under the wiretap order, so long as the level of compliance is "reasonable under the circumstances." Maryland case law designates the following ten factors to be considered in determining the reasonableness of minimization:

> (1) the nature and scope of the crime being investigated; (2) the sophistication of those under suspicion and their efforts to avoid surveillance through such devices as coded conversations; (3) the location and the operation of the subject telephone; (4) government expectation of the contents of the call; (5) the extent of judicial supervision; (6) the duration of the wiretap; (7) the purpose of the wiretap; (8) the length of the calls monitored; (9) the existence of a pattern of pertinent calls, which the monitoring agents could discern so as to eliminate the interception of non-pertinent calls; (10) the absence of monitoring of privileged conversations.

As the trial judge, how would you rule? Would you suppress all the wiretap evidence? Only the recorded calls between husband and wife? None of the statements? Compare State v. Mazzone, 648 A.2d 978 (Md. 1994).

Notes

1. *Minimization: majority view.* Wiretap statutes require the government to "minimize" the number of conversations "intercepted." This limitation prevents the government from listening to all conversations at a given telephone. Instead, agents must stop listening to a call if it does not fall within the coverage of the wiretap order. However, the minimization requirement is not enforced rigorously in some jurisdictions. In Scott v. United States, 436 U.S. 128 (1978), the Supreme Court held that the monitoring and recording of the entirety of virtually all calls received on a tapped phone over a 30-day period was reasonable under the Fourth Amendment

and was not a violation of the statute. The Court noted that the extent of the criminal activity under investigation, the extent to which the phone was used for illegal purposes, and the frequent use of ambiguous language in the conversations justified the full monitoring of every call. Admittedly, the officers knew about the "minimization" requirement contained in the statute and in the judge's order and took no steps to reduce the number of conversations they intercepted. Nevertheless, the Supreme Court decided that the relevant question was not the good faith of the officers (or the lack thereof) but the "objective" reasonableness of the scope of the interceptions. On the basis of the *Scott* opinion, would you advise an officer executing a wiretap order that there is no longer an effective minimization requirement under federal law? Should agents make different minimization efforts at the end of a wiretap period than they do at the beginning of the period? A minority of states have rejected the *Scott* decision in reading their own state wiretap statutes and insist that the good faith of the officers is relevant in determining whether they complied with the minimization requirement. See State v. Thompson, 464 A.2d 799 (Conn. 1983); State v. Catania, 427 A.2d 537 (N.J. 1981). If a target suspects the government is listening to her communications, how could she take advantage of a minimization requirement in jurisdictions where it is enforced?

2. *Wiretap reports.* State and federal wiretap statutes require various types of reports from the prosecutors executing the order. First, they routinely empower the judge issuing the order to require periodic reports from the officers about the progress of the investigation. Some also require the administrative office of the judiciary or the chief prosecutor to assemble periodic statistics on the overall number of wiretaps and to describe the characteristics of those investigations. The report goes to the legislature. See 18 U.S.C. §2519; Conn. Gen. Stat. §54-41o. As a legislator, which features of these investigations would you want to hear about? At the termination of the interception order, the officers must seal the tapes and records and "return" or file them immediately with the court to prevent tampering. Under certain circumstances, particularly if the target of a wiretap later faces criminal charges based on the wiretap evidence, the target must receive notice that the wiretap took place and must be told about its methods and results. As defense counsel, what would you want to know about the wiretap?

3. *Special showing of probable cause.* The court issuing a wiretap order under the typical statute must be convinced that probable cause exists as to several facts: (a) an individual has committed, is committing, or is about to commit a crime designated in the statute; (b) communications about that offense will be obtained through an interception; and (c) the particular facility to be monitored will be used in connection with the offense. See 18 U.S.C. §2518(3); Or. Rev. Stat. §133.724(3). How does this compare to the probable cause finding to support an ordinary search warrant?

Wiretap orders are available only to investigate crimes designated in the statute. While the federal statute includes an extensive list of federal and state crimes, some state statutes are far more selective. Most state statutes extend to violent crimes and narcotics offenses. Compare Utah Code §77-23a-8 (extensive list of crimes punishable by more than one year in prison) with Okla. Stat. tit. 13, §176.7 (murder and drug investigations). The applicant has an incentive to list as many crimes as possible to increase the scope of the permissible interceptions that may take place.

4. *Specifying the target.* Wiretap statutes typically require that applications specify the identity of the person whose communications are to be intercepted, "if known." See, e.g., 18 U.S.C. §2518(1)(b)(iv). Do statutory provisions such as these mean that

a person specified in the application must take part in every intercepted conversation, or can the government intercept conversations at the specified facility between two people who were not specified in the application? See United States v. Kahn, 415 U.S. 143 (1974) (approving of interception of conversation between two persons not named in application, where application mentioned "others unknown"); cf. Commonwealth v. Westerman, 611 N.E.2d 215 (Mass. 1993) (no state statutory provision for intercepting conversations of "others unknown"; target named in application must participate in all intercepted communications).

Wiretap statutes also require the application to describe the "nature and location" of the facility from which the communication is to be intercepted. In 1986, Congress amended the federal wiretap statute to allow applications for "roving wiretaps" and "roving oral intercepts." See 18 U.S.C. §2518(11). The USA PATRIOT Act, passed soon after the terrorist attacks of September 11, 2001, expanded the authority for roving wiretaps. More than a dozen states followed suit. See, e.g., Fla. Stat. Ann. §§934.09(10), (11). Under these provisions, the government may intercept any communication of a designated individual about a suspected crime, wherever the communication takes place. The application for a roving wiretap must specify, to a greater extent than an ordinary wiretap application, the targeted individuals. It must also set out facts demonstrating that a wiretap at a specific facility would be ineffective because the target has a purpose to thwart interception by changing facilities. Is the "roving wiretap" the equivalent of a search warrant that fails to "particularly describe" the place to be searched?

5. *Other investigative procedures.* Some items included in the wiretap application are analogous to (but more specific than) the kinds of information government agents present in typical applications for search warrants. But some of the information required for wiretaps is entirely new. One important example is the requirement in 18 U.S.C. §2518(c) that government agents describe any "other investigative procedures" that have been tried and an explanation of why those procedures failed or why they "reasonably appear" unlikely to succeed or are "likely" to be too dangerous. The provisions are designed to encourage the government to try measures other than wiretapping as the initial steps in an investigation. As the Court stated in United States v. Kahn, 415 U.S. 143 (1974), interceptions should not be permitted if "traditional investigative techniques would suffice to expose the crime." Courts often note that the "other procedures" provisions do not require the government to show that no other means would work, or that all other means have been tried and failed, but only that some reasonable effort has been made. See Commonwealth v. Fenderson, 571 N.E.2d 11 (Mass. 1991).

6. *Authority to apply for wiretaps.* Although any police officer can typically apply for an ordinary search warrant, a more limited group of law enforcement officials may apply for an interception order. The federal wiretap statute requires a senior Justice Department official or a United States Attorney (or a designee) to approve any application. See 18 U.S.C. §2516. The Oregon statute is typical in requiring the elected district attorney to apply for the interception order. Or. Rev. Stat. §133.724(1). Other statutes allow state-level officials (such as the attorney general) to apply for an order or to comment on the applications of others. See Neb. Rev. Stat. §86-703. Do these provisions successfully promote political accountability for law enforcement decisions? Does a statute create more or less protection for liberty and privacy by centralizing enforcement choices in the hands of politically accountable officials? Should the governor have authority to request a wiretap?

7. *Duration of wiretaps.* All wiretap statutes limit the total length of surveillance allowed. For example, 18 U.S.C. §2518(5) provides that wiretap orders should not authorize interceptions "for any period longer than is necessary to achieve the objective of the authorization, nor in any event longer than thirty days." The judge can grant extensions of a wiretap order if the government renews the application, again for no longer than 30 days. Some state statutes authorize shorter periods of time for surveillance. For example, New Jersey is more restrictive than Title III on the length of initial approvals and the length and number of possible extensions except for racketeering and some narcotics offenses, where the periods are longer. N.J. Stat. §2A:156A-12(f), (g).

8. *The dilemma of placing details in the application.* The application will, in most cases, find its way to the target of the wiretap after the interceptions are complete. 18 U.S.C. §2518(8)(d). Thus, details about the investigation and its goals that are included in the application will likely be available to defense counsel at trial. Does this suggest that the applicant should include as few details as possible? On the other hand, wouldn't a wide range of specified individuals, crimes, and conversations lead to a wiretap order with a broader scope?

9. *The frequency of wiretaps.* The Administrative Office of the U.S. Courts reports the annual number of wiretap orders issued at the request of both federal and state law enforcement officials. A single court order can involve many telephones. The annual number of wiretap orders remained fairly constant during the 1980s, but increased during the last decade:

1985: 784	1991: 856	1996: 1,149	1999: 1,350
1987: 673	1993: 976	1997: 1,186	2000: 1,190
1989: 763	1995: 1,058	1998: 1,329	2001: 1,491

Of the 1,491 orders issued in 2001, the three leading states were New York (425), California (130), and Illinois (128). The number of wiretap orders issued each year appears to be remarkably low, at least by comparison to the number of searches (both warranted and warrantless) that take place each year. Do the multiple statutory requirements for obtaining a court order, one piled on the other, make the overall process so burdensome that government agents rarely find wiretaps worth the effort?

Looking at the number of wiretaps makes wiretapping seem like a fairly modest practical concern. Another perspective, however, is to consider the number of conversations reached by court-ordered wiretaps. According to the Department of Justice, each wiretap request approved in 2001 reached an average of 86 persons and 1,565 conversations (over two million total conversations). The orders remained in effect for a combined 53,574 days. See Administrative Office of the U.S. Courts, 2001 Wiretap Report.

Connecticut requires a special showing from any applicant after the courts issue the first 35 interception orders in a given year. The applicant must show the court why any subsequent requests are based on an emergency situation that "may result in imminent peril to the public health, safety and welfare." See Conn. Gen. Stat. §54-41c(12). How do you suppose the legislature settled on the number 35? Would it be possible for judges, in the absence of a statute, to scrutinize government wiretap requests differently if the number of requests gets too large?

3. *Bugs on Agents*

Katz firmly established that a search occurs when a government agent plants an electronic bug in a flower vase and leaves the vase in a person's home. But what if a government agent attaches the bug to a flower, places the flower in his lapel, and then converses with a suspect? Which should be the determinative fact — that a conversation is taking place between two people (one of whom could be an agent or could choose to recount that conversation to authorities) or that electronic devices are recording the conversation?

■ STATE v. CHARLES REEVES

427 So. 2d 403 (La. 1983)

BLANCHE, J.

On our initial review of this case, we held that the warrantless monitoring of a conversation through the use of an electronic transmitter concealed on the person of one of the parties to the communication violates Article 1, §5 of our 1974 Louisiana Constitution. After careful consideration on rehearing, we must reverse our original finding, and in so doing, we affirm the conviction and sentence imposed upon the defendant by the trial court. The use of electronic surveillance equipment, which is hidden from view on the person of a consenting party to a conversation, does not "invade the privacy" of the other party or parties in the conversation within the meaning of our Constitution, and, therefore, the warrant requirement does not attach.

[Alvin Pilley, an employee of the Department of Elections, informed the State Attorney General's office] that he was being pressured by his supervisors to contribute money to the campaign of Commissioner Jerry Fowler. In addition, Pilley exposed a procedure approved by certain employees of the Department of Elections whereby he could receive reimbursement for any contributions he made to the campaign fund by filing false state travel expense vouchers. . . .

With Pilley's consent, the investigators concealed an electronic transmitter on his person in order to overhear and record his conversations with other employees of the Department of Elections concerning the falsification of the travel vouchers as a means to reimburse Pilley for [a] $100 contribution. . . . Pilley wore the electronic transmitter into the voting machine warehouse in Lake Charles. Investigators were posted outside in two cars. One of these cars was equipped with machines to receive and tape record the transmissions. . . .

Once inside the warehouse, Pilley engaged in conversations with several Department of Elections employees. Among them was the defendant, Charles Reeves, who was . . . also Pilley's supervisor. During his recorded colloquy with Pilley, the defendant made several statements concerning the false travel vouchers. [The government later brought charges against Reeves for committing perjury during grand jury testimony. After the trial court denied a motion to suppress the tape recordings, the government used them to prove the falsehood of some of his testimony.

In our original opinion in this case, we] interpreted the language of our 1974 Constitution Article 1, §5, which protects a person's "communications" against unreasonable "invasions of privacy," to proscribe the admission of evidence secured through electronic surveillance of any type when such surveillance was conducted without compliance with the warrant requirement. However, we failed to analyze properly this constitutional protection. Although the defendant's conversations were surely "communications" within the meaning of Article 1, §5, the manner in which the conversations were monitored, by consensual electronic surveillance, did not "invade the privacy" of Charles Reeves. . . .

Unlike the U.S. Constitution, [Article 1, §5 of our constitution] explicitly protects every person's "communications" from "unreasonable invasions of privacy."[1] The present case necessitates the interpretation of "communications" and "invasions of privacy," those terms in Article 1, §5 of the 1974 Louisiana Constitution which are not found in the Fourth Amendment. . . . Prior Louisiana jurisprudence provides us with little guidance in this formidable task. Therefore, an analysis of the transcripts of the Louisiana Constitutional convention and an examination of other sources of reference are essential to our understanding of Article 1, §5.

Without question, the members of the Committee on Bill of Rights and Elections, who drafted Article 1, §5 of the 1974 Louisiana Constitution, were aware of the potential threat to privacy posed by governmental electronic surveillance. The original proposal for Article 1, §5, which was tentatively adopted by the Committee on April 17, 1973, would have prohibited all forms of electronic surveillance, with or without a warrant. Delegate Jenkins, the author of this draft, argued that such a ban was necessary to protect the communications of innocent persons from governmental electronic intrusion.

On May 19, 1973, however, the initial draft was revised. [The Committee] eliminated the ban on electronic surveillance. However, the word "communications" was inserted in the list of persons, property, houses, papers, and effects in Article 1, §5. In this way, the members of the Committee insured and made it explicit that each person's communications would be free from unreasonable searches, seizures, or invasions of privacy. . . . Clearly, the Framers intended the defendant's intercepted conversations to be "communications" and protected by Article 1, §5 from invasions of privacy. Unfortunately, the transcripts do not reveal the intention of the delegates as to the second and more difficult question—whether consensual electronic surveillance is an "invasion of privacy." . . .

Our jurisprudence sheds little light upon the meaning of privacy and its relationship to electronic surveillance. . . . The United States Supreme Court, on the other hand, has examined intensively the effect of electronic surveillance upon one's privacy in construing the Fourth Amendment. In Katz v. United States, 389 U.S. 347 (1967), the Court was confronted with the problem of the Government's employment of nonconsensual electronic surveillance without a warrant. Federal agents had attached an electronic listening device to the outside of a public telephone booth to overhear and record the defendant's telephone conversations inside the booth. [The Court held that] the Government's activities in electronically listening to and recording the defendant's words violated the privacy upon which he justifiably relied while using the telephone booth.

The United States Supreme Court arrived at a different conclusion when consensual as opposed to nonconsensual electronic surveillance was employed by

1. Every person shall be secure in his person, property, communications, houses, papers, and effects against unreasonable searches, seizures, or invasions of privacy. No warrant shall issue without probable cause supported by oath or affirmation. . . .

the Government to secure evidence. In United States v. White, 401 U.S. 745 (1971), the Court held that consensual electronic surveillance was not subject to the warrant requirement, for it did not invade the constitutionally "justifiable" expectations of privacy of the defendant.

The facts in *White* are very similar to our present case. A government informer concealed a radio transmitter on his person and engaged in conversations with the defendant. By monitoring the frequency of the transmitter carried by the informant, government agents were able to overhear certain incriminating statements by the defendant. No warrant had been obtained. . . . Justice White, in speaking for the Court, observed that each person who enters into a conversation assumes certain risks which are not protected by the Fourth Amendment. One such risk . . . is that his listener may be a police agent who may report their conversation to the authorities immediately following their encounter. In those circumstances, the Fourth Amendment is not violated, for the person's constitutionally "justifiable" expectations of privacy are not invaded. . . . Justice White found that no different result was required where a police officer or agent, who conceals his identity and is a party to the conversation, wears an electronic device:

> Concededly a police agent who conceals his police connections may write down for official use his conversations with a defendant and testify concerning them, without a warrant authorizing his encounters with the defendant and without otherwise violating the latter's Fourth Amendment rights. For constitutional purposes, no different result is required if the agent instead of immediately reporting and transcribing his conversations with defendant, either (1) simultaneously records them with electronic equipment which he is carrying on his person, (2) or carries radio equipment which simultaneously transmits the conversations either to recording equipment located elsewhere or to other agents monitoring the transmitting frequency. If the conduct and revelations of an agent operating without electronic equipment do not invade the defendant's constitutionally justifiable expectations of privacy, neither does a simultaneous recording of the same conversations made by the agent or by others from transmissions received from the agent to whom the defendant is talking and whose trustworthiness the defendant necessarily risks.[13]

We agree with United States v. White that consensual electronic surveillance involves different privacy considerations than non-consensual electronic surveillance. Moreover, we believe that the "invasion of privacy" provision in Article 1, §5 of the 1975 Louisiana Constitution does not prohibit warrantless consensual surveillance. However, we choose not to adopt the analysis of the Supreme Court in *White*. Rather, we prefer to follow our previous decisions and examine the effect of the constitutional guarantee against "invasions of privacy" on consensual electronic surveillance in light of the test articulated by Justice Harlan in *Katz*, [which requires "first, that a person have exhibited an actual (subjective) expectation of privacy and, second, that the expectation be one that society is prepared to recognize as 'reasonable.'"]

13. The majority of the states have recognized a distinction between consensual and nonconsensual surveillance. [The court cited cases from Arizona, Arkansas, Colorado, Connecticut, Georgia, Illinois, Indiana, Kansas, Kentucky, Maryland, Massachusetts, Minnesota, Mississippi, New Jersey, North Carolina, Ohio, Oklahoma, Pennsylvania, Texas, Virginia, and West Virginia.]

We find that the defendant Reeves, a victim of consensual electronic surveillance, did not exhibit a subjective expectation of privacy. No other conclusion is possible when we examine the defendant's privacy interests in the statements made to Pilley in the three following hypothetical situations: (1) Pilley does not contact the police before the conversation takes place (i.e., he is not a police agent), but he voluntarily reports the defendant to the authorities immediately after the termination of the communication. At this time, Pilley repeats the conversation to the police. (2) Pilley is a police agent, but he wears no electronic devices. (3) Pilley is a police agent, and he conceals an electronic transmitting device on his person.

Clearly, in the first situation, the defendant has no subjective expectation of privacy. Reeves, by entering into the conversation, should realize that Pilley, or any other party to the communication, may violate his confidence and disclose to others, including the police, the incriminating remarks made therein. Though the violation of a confidence is rarely contemplated by the declarant, his knowledge of the risk (disclosure) is ever present and destroys his subjective expectation that the communication will forever remain a secret (private). Accordingly, unless there is honor among thieves, disclosure to another by one who possesses knowledge of the other's misdeeds is a fact of life that precludes the subjective expectation of privacy. Similarly, Reeves possesses no subjective expectation of privacy in the second situation. What difference would it make that he did not know to whom he was speaking and that his "friend" to whom he was making these disclosures of illegal activity was in fact a police officer or police informer? The fact remains that the risk that his confidence will be violated and that his disclosures may be repeated to others is the same regardless whether made to a false friend or police informer. . . .

The third situation is our present case. As in the second hypothetical, Reeves expects and accepts the risk that Pilley is a possible police agent. Pilley's presence as an informant, therefore, does not invade the subjective expectations of privacy of the defendant. One aspect of Reeves' encounter with Pilley has been altered by this third situation, however. Hidden from view on Pilley's person is an electronic transmitter. In our original opinion, we found that the presence of the transmitter dramatically changes the effect on the privacy interests of the defendant who engages in the conversation:

> A party speaking in private conversation does not knowingly expose his conversation to the public simply because an unknown party is surreptitiously hearing and recording every word that is being spoken. A confidence repeated by a false friend is received by others with attendant circumstances of the friend's credibility and memory. . . . While there is no indication that the delegates sought to protect a person against betrayal by his confidant, clearly they sought to eliminate the danger that an official record is being made of what we say to unknown government agents at their unfettered discretion.

Thus, our first review of this case hinged the invasion of the defendant's privacy on the fact that the electronic equipment recorded his conversation word-for-word. We failed to realize, however, that the risk of disclosure includes the manner of disclosure. As illustrated by our previous hypotheticals, the defendant enters into the conversation knowing that his confidences may be disclosed to anyone by the listener. He also must realize that this disclosure could take any form. To decide otherwise would force this court to speculate as to which form of disclosure a person risks and which one he does not anticipate when entering into a conversation. Such theoretical line drawing is result oriented. For example, how can we conclude that a declarant foresees and risks that his listener is a police agent who will testify in court against him, and then rationally decide that the same speaker cannot anticipate and risk that the listener will tape his conversation and play it in court as in this present case? We cannot. The risk that his confidence will be violated and his disclosures may be repeated to others is the same. He assumes this risk upon entering the conversation. Therefore, we find that the defendant exhibited no actual expectation of privacy.

If we assume, arguendo, that the defendant did exhibit a subjective expectation of privacy, is this the type of expectation which society at large would recognize as reasonable? We think not. Society seeks to foster truth, not to suppress it. The presence of the electronic transmitter has but one effect. Instead of the informant committing the conversation to memory, a machine tapes each and every sentence of the communication. . . . Surely, society would not consider reasonable an expectation of privacy which would result in a more inaccurate version of the events in question. [W]e hold that the manner in which these communications were intercepted, through warrantless consensual electronic surveillance, did not invade his privacy within the meaning of La. Const. art. 1, §5. . . .

LEMMON, J., concurring.

[The specter of the "Orwellian Big Brother"] is and should be of grave concern to the courts, as well as to legislative bodies. However, the Legislature (despite the general awareness of the advances in technology available for "electronic surveillance") enacted in 1980 an "Electronic Surveillance" statute, which (like its federal predecessor and counterpart) explicitly exempted from its scope police electronic interception of a conversation when one of the parties consents. See R.S. 15:1303 B(3); 18 U.S.C. §2511(2)(c). The fact that the members of the legislative branch approved such procedures only six years after the adoption of the [Louisiana] Constitution certainly indicates that those elected representatives of the people did not believe such action to be an unreasonable invasion of the privacy of a person's communications. . . . If the fears expressed by the dissenters later materialize, the Legislature may be persuaded to adopt the added protections of probable cause or judicial supervision to govern the present situation and to provide the law-abiding citizens with greater protection from "electronic surveillance" than is required by the state and federal constitutions. The legislators (more so than this court) reflect the views of the people whom they represent. . . .

DIXON, C.J., dissenting.

With all due respect, I dissent. The Louisiana Constitutional Convention, by literally including protection for communications and against the invasion of privacy, certainly intended to strengthen those rights so valuable to free people. . . . The only serious relevant argument in the Committee on Bill of Rights and Elections about protecting private communications was whether to prohibit absolutely all invasions of private communications, or to permit such invasions upon warrant supported by probable cause.[1] . . . If the majority really thinks there is an important freedom

1. Mr. Guarisco: "Let me make this comment, that before we adopted 'communications' you could do it without a warrant. Now we are at least requiring a warrant to do it. So we have improved upon it." Documents of the Louisiana Constitutional Convention of 1973.

interest in preventing wholesale police intrusion into private communications, it should simply apply the same rule that this state and the federal government do before permitting a policeman (the "consenting" party) to search a home—he must obtain a warrant from a magistrate, based on probable cause. . . .

DENNIS, J., dissenting.

With all due respect for my brethren in the majority, I am shocked by the methodology and the results of their opinion. . . . Placed in proper perspective, the majority's reasoning that it has the power to dispense with the warrant safeguard for certain communications because no delegate said anything to the contrary in committee is a flimsy excuse for avoiding the obvious fact that the delegates and the people intended to defend all communications, just as they intended to defend all houses, by making a search or seizure outside the judicial process, without prior approval by a magistrate or a judge, per se unreasonable under article 1 §5. [T]he people of this state adopted the constitution by popular vote; the delegates were merely authorized to draft the instrument and submit it to the electorate. Therefore, the function of this court in interpreting the constitution is not so much to determine how it was understood by its framers as how it was understood by the people adopting it. . . . The majority opinion breaches all of our time-honored, common sense precepts of constitutional construction by using a committee's silence which actually supports the meaning of a plain and unambiguous provision to judicially overrule it. . . .

The majority's "reasonable expectation" approach is circular and meaningless, leading it to adopt an untenable policy that a person has no reasonable expectation of security in his communications. . . . Since it is the task of the law to form and project, as well as mirror and reflect, we should not, as judges, merely recite the expectations and risks without examining the desirability of saddling them upon society. . . . For those more extensive intrusions that significantly jeopardize the sense of security which is the paramount concern of Fourth Amendment liberties, I am of the view that more than self-restraint by law enforcement officials is required and at the least warrants should be necessary. . . .

The majority's argument that we should imitate a number of states which have recognized a distinction between consensual and nonconsensual surveillance, is unconvincing. Of the states listed, only three have express constitutional provisions relative to the right of privacy. And, only one of the cases from these states construes its constitutional right to privacy to allow warrantless consensual electronic monitoring. However, among states with affirmative constitutional guarantees of the right to privacy or specific protections of communications against unreasonable invasion, the majority rule would appear to be to the contrary. [The dissent cited decisions from Florida, Alaska, Montana, and Michigan.]

Like a blindfolded Houdini, the majority opinion writer eludes uncontradicted convention history, wiggles free of plain words in the constitution and discovers a gap in the document no other scholar knew existed, to find, after all, that, whenever this court wishes, private communications can be seized or intercepted without a warrant and without probable cause supported by oath or affirmation. . . . Under the majority's interpretation, words do not mean what they seem. Although the constitution expressly guarantees the security of "communications," it provides no more, and perhaps less, protection than if the word had been left out. . . .

Notes

1. *Bugs on government agents: majority position.* As the opinions in the *Reeves* case from Louisiana indicate, a substantial majority of the states take the federal position as stated in United States v. White, 401 U.S. 745 (1971). Under this reasoning, a conversation between a government agent and a suspect does not become a "search," subject to constitutional limitations, when the agent uses a device to transmit or record the conversation. State courts that have rejected *White* have often relied on distinctive language in a state constitution or a distinctive state constitutional history. See Commonwealth v. Blood, 507 N.E.2d 1029 (Mass. 1987). Did *Reeves* reach the best interpretation of the distinctive language and history of the Louisiana constitutional provision?

A number of state courts that originally rejected *White* have reconsidered their decision (sometimes many years later) and have embraced the federal position. See People v. Collins, 475 N.W.2d 684 (Mich. 1991) (overruling 1975 decision that had rejected *White*); Melanie Black Dubis, The Consensual Electronic Surveillance Experiment: State Courts React to *United States v. White,* 47 Vand. L. Rev. 857 (1994). If a state court has rejected the federal view on a constitutional question, does that decision remain a questionable authority for its entire life span? Is there something special about the issue of consensual electronic surveillance that made these courts willing to reconsider their earlier independent stances?

2. *Confusing bugs and people.* Is the tape recording or transmission of a conversation with a government agent a consensual search, or is it no search at all? Is there any difference between "consent" and "assumption of the risk"? When a recording device is on an agent, doesn't the microphone simply serve as a more accurate way to capture and re-create statements? Should the rules be different when the technological enhancement changes the listener's capacity for recollection, but not the capacity to hear the evidence in the first place?

4. *Wiretaps to Fight Terrorism and Crime*

Just as wiretaps are useful for criminal investigations, they can also be useful for espionage. During the Cold War, the FBI and the CIA investigated possible agents of foreign governments operating within the United States. Congressional hearings during the 1970s, however, brought to light some abuses of domestic intelligence, including wiretaps and other surveillance of leaders of the civil rights movement and critics of the Vietnam War. In 1978, Congress passed the Foreign Intelligence Surveillance Act (FISA), creating new legal limits on domestic surveillance of suspected foreign agents.

The provisions of FISA require agents of the government to obtain judicial approval for their wiretaps. The order comes from a specialized federal court, known as the FISA court. While FISA does require probable cause to believe that the target is acting as an agent of a foreign power, the application for a surveillance order under FISA does not require the same detailed showing that is necessary for an ordinary criminal wiretap order under Title III. To prevent criminal investigators from using FISA wiretaps to avoid the more burdensome aspects of Title III, federal courts interpreted the statutes to require a clear separation between criminal and foreign intelligence investigations.

After the terrorist attacks of September 11, 2001, Congress passed the USA PATRIOT Act. One set of provisions in the Act made it easier for different groups of investigators to share information obtained from a FISA wiretap order. As you read the following problem, consider whether the new regime for wiretap orders under FISA will become more commonplace in a wide range of criminal investigations.

Problem 7-4. Crack in the Wall?

You are a judge on the Foreign Intelligence Surveillance Court of Review — a special federal appellate court created by Congress in FISA in 1978 to handle appeals from the FISA court. The Foreign Intelligence Surveillance Court of Review did not hear a single case in its first 25 years of statutory existence. After September 11 and the passage of the USA PATRIOT Act, the first appeal arrives, and the government has filed it. The high-stakes questions for the court are these:

(1) Is the order of the FISA court setting limits on the government in this case valid?
(2) Is the new rule of the FISA court (calling for the government to disclose connections between any FISA application and any ongoing criminal investigations) required by or allowed by the statute?
(3) Is the amendment of FISA by the USA PATRIOT Act constitutional?

As part of its investigation into suspected terrorist groups after the September 11 attacks, the government applied to the FISA court for an order authorizing electronic surveillance. The government's application included some detailed information to support its contention that the target, a United States citizen, was conspiring with others in international terrorism. The FISA court granted the order, but it also placed some limits on the government. The order said that

> law enforcement officials shall not make recommendations to intelligence officials concerning the initiation, operation, continuation or expansion of FISA searches or surveillances. Additionally, the FBI and the Criminal Division of the Department of Justice shall ensure that law enforcement officials do not direct or control the use of the FISA procedures to enhance criminal prosecution, and that advice intended to preserve the option of a criminal prosecution does not inadvertently result in the Criminal Division's directing or controlling the investigation using FISA searches and surveillances toward law enforcement objectives.

To ensure the Justice Department followed these strictures, the court also fashioned a "chaperone requirement." A unit of the Justice Department, the Office of Intelligence Policy and Review (OIPR), composed of 31 lawyers and 25 support staff, must be invited to all meetings between the FBI and the Criminal Division to coordinate their efforts "to investigate or protect against foreign attack, international terrorism, or clandestine intelligence activities by foreign powers." If representatives of OIPR are unable to attend such meetings, "OIPR shall be apprized of the substance of the meetings in writing so that the Court may be notified at the earliest opportunity." Finally, the FISA court issued a new procedural rule, Rule 11, stating that "all FISA applications shall include informative descriptions of any ongoing criminal investigations of FISA targets, as well as the substance of any consultations between the FBI and criminal prosecutors at the Department of Justice."

The FISA court's restrictions were designed to build a "wall" between intelligence officials and law enforcement officers in the Executive branch. Drawing on many other judicial interpretations of FISA, the court meant to approve applications only when the "government's objective is not primarily directed toward criminal prosecution of the foreign agents for their foreign intelligence activity."

Under FISA, the court can approve of electronic surveillance to "obtain foreign intelligence information" if the government shows probable cause to believe that the target is "an agent of a foreign power" and that the communication facility to be monitored "is being used, or is about to be used" by the agent. 50 U.S.C. §1805(a)(3). The statute defines "foreign intelligence information" as

> information that relates to, and if concerning a United States person is necessary to, the ability of the United States to protect against—A) actual or potential attack or other grave hostile acts of a foreign power or an agent of a foreign power; B) sabotage or international terrorism by a foreign power or an agent of a foreign power; or C) clandestine intelligence activities by an intelligence service or network of a foreign power or by an agent of a foreign power.

50 U.S.C. §1801(e)(1). It defines an agent of a foreign power to include any person who "knowingly engages in clandestine intelligence gathering activities . . . which activities involve or may involve a violation of the criminal statutes of the United States" or those involving international terrorist acts, defined as "violent acts or acts dangerous to human life that are a violation of the criminal laws of the United States or of any State."

Section 1804 of FISA requires a national security official to certify in the application that "the purpose" of the surveillance was to obtain foreign intelligence information. That same certification must include a statement of "the basis of the certification that (i) the information sought is the type of foreign intelligence information designated." FISA includes "minimization procedures" designed to prevent the acquisition or sharing within the government of material gathered in an electronic surveillance that is unnecessary to the government's need for foreign intelligence information. 50 U.S.C. §1801(h).

Before 2001, the Department of Justice followed some internal procedures that limited contacts between the FBI and the Criminal Division in cases where FISA surveillance or searches were being conducted by the FBI for foreign intelligence purposes. The 1995 version of those internal procedures states that "the FBI and Criminal Division should ensure that advice intended to preserve the option of a criminal prosecution does not inadvertently result in either the fact or the appearance of the Criminal Division's directing or controlling the foreign intelligence investigation toward law enforcement purposes." Under these procedures, OIPR became a "wall" to prevent the FBI intelligence officials from communicating directly with the Criminal Division about their investigations.

The USA PATRIOT Act made some important changes to this statutory structure. It changed the certification requirement of Section 1804 to declare that "a significant purpose" of the surveillance was to obtain foreign intelligence information (as opposed to "the purpose" under FISA). The statute also explicitly authorized federal officers who conduct foreign intelligence surveillance to "consult with

Federal law enforcement officers to coordinate efforts to investigate or protect against" attack, sabotage, international terrorism, or clandestine intelligence activities by foreign agents. 50 U.S.C. §1806(k)(1).

In 2002, the Attorney General modified the 1995 internal procedures. The new procedures eliminated the "directing or controlling" language and allowed the exchange of advice among the FBI, OIPR, and the Criminal Division regarding "the initiation, operation, continuation, or expansion of FISA searches or surveillance."

The government has appealed the order of the FISA court in this case, and also challenges the validity of the court's new Rule 11. Is the FISA court's order in this case consistent with the statute, as amended? Is the order compelled by the constitution? Compare In re Sealed Case, 310 F.3d 717 (Foreign Intelligence Surveillance Court of Review 2002).

C. RECORDS IN THE HANDS OF THIRD PARTIES

Just as technology enables government investigators to monitor a suspect's conversations, it can also enable the government to make the most of available information by assembling small bits of scattered information into larger patterns. When electronic documents are in private hands, courts must confront the question whether an individual maintains any expectation of privacy in those documents. Government access to such records may allow collection of a huge range of information because of the sheer quantity of data that business databases contain, together with the ability to computerize a search of that information.

As we have seen, wiretap statutes tightly regulate the government's electronic eavesdropping on telephone conversations, face-to-face conversations, or electronic communications. Wiretaps can occur only after the government invests extraordinary effort in a detailed application to a judge, and the judge approves the application. Both federal and state law place lesser protections on records of communications held in third party storage, including telephone records, e-mail, and voice mail. The statutes in this area, such as 18 U.S.C. §§2701-2709, give law enforcement officers access, ordinarily pursuant to a warrant or court order or under a subpoena in some cases. The warrant or subpoena used in this setting does not include the exceptionally detailed information necessary for a wiretap order.

A less demanding set of restrictions apply to a third form of communications evidence: the government's use of trap and trace devices and "pen registers," which identify the source and destination of calls made to and from a particular telephone. Devices such as pen registers inspired the passage of many statutes that both obligate the telephone company to cooperate in the use of pen registers and limit the cases in which government may seek a pen register.

■ 18 U.S.C. §3121

(a) [N]o person may install or use a pen register or a trap and trace device without first obtaining a court order. . . .

(c) A government agency authorized to install and use a pen register or trap and trace device under this chapter or under State law shall use technology reasonably available to it that restricts the recording or decoding of electronic or other impulses to the dialing, routing, addressing, and signaling information utilized in the processing and transmitting of wire or electronic communications so as not to include the contents of any wire or electronic communications.

■ 18 U.S.C. §3123

(a) . . . Upon an application made under [this statute], the court shall enter an ex parte order authorizing the installation and use of a pen register or trap and trace device . . . if the court finds that the attorney for the Government [or the State law enforcement or investigative officer] has certified to the court that the information likely to be obtained by such installation and use is relevant to an ongoing criminal investigation. [The law enforcement] agency shall ensure that a record will be maintained which will identify—

(i) any officer or officers who installed the device and any officer or officers who accessed the device to obtain information from the network;

(ii) the date and time the device was installed, the date and time the device was uninstalled, and the date, time, and duration of each time the device is accessed to obtain information;

(iii) the configuration of the device at the time of its installation and any subsequent modification thereof; and

(iv) any information which has been collected by the device.

(b) An order issued under this section —

(1) shall specify —

(A) the identity, if known, of the person to whom is leased or in whose name is listed the telephone line to which the pen register or trap and trace device is to be attached;

(B) the identity, if known, of the person who is the subject of the criminal investigation;

(C) the attributes of the communications to which the order applies, including the number or other identifier and, if known, the location of the telephone line or other facility to which the pen register or trap and trace device is to be attached or applied, and, in the case of an order authorizing installation and use of a trap and trace device [requested by state law enforcement officials], the geographic limits of the order; and

(D) a statement of the offense to which the information likely to be obtained by the pen register or trap and trace device relates. . . .

(c) An order issued under this section shall authorize the installation and use of a pen register or a trap and trace device for a period not to exceed sixty days. . . . Extensions of such an order may be granted, but only upon an application for an order under [this statute] and upon the judicial finding required by subsection (a) of this section. The period of extension shall be for a period not to exceed sixty days.

■ DAMON RICHARDSON v. STATE

865 S.W.2d 944 (Tex. Crim. App. 1993) (en banc)

CLINTON, J.

Appellant was convicted of the offense of engaging in organized criminal activity . . . and the jury assessed punishment at life confinement in the penitentiary and a $10,000 fine. On appeal he contended . . . that the trial court erred in overruling his motion to suppress evidence obtained by use of a pen register because the use of the pen register was a search in contemplation of Article I, §9 of the Texas Constitution; therefore, Article 18.21 [of the Texas Code of Criminal Procedure] is unconstitutional insofar as it authorizes a search without requiring a showing of probable cause.[1] . . .

In March of 1988, officers of the Texas Department of Public Safety were involved in an extensive investigation of a suspected drug ring operating in Lubbock County. The investigation centered around appellant, who was in the Lubbock County Jail awaiting trial for capital murder, and several other individuals residing at the Seven Acres Lodge, a motel in Lubbock. Despite appellant's incarceration, officers believed that he was controlling a cocaine and crack distribution organization using the telephones located in the county jail, by placing calls to a private telephone located at the Seven Acres Lodge. Due to the difficulty in investigating this case through customary investigative techniques, the officers sought court orders authorizing electronic surveillance to assist in their identification of co-conspirators and the modus operandi of the alleged trafficking organization.

On March 30, 1988, in accordance with the provisions of Article 18.21, the officers applied for and received a court order authorizing the installation of a pen register to catalogue the telephone numbers dialed from (806) 555-4729, a telephone at the Seven Acres Lodge. The officers then combined this information with other information outlined in a 56-page affidavit signed by Officer J.A. Randall, and on April 13, 1988, applied for and received a court order authorizing the wiretapping and recording of communications on the same telephone line. The wiretap intercepted numerous incriminating telephone conversations involving appellant and other targeted suspects. [A second pen register was ordered on April 14, and was installed to record numbers dialed from a limited use telephone in the Lubbock County Jail. Prior to trial, Richardson moved to suppress the evidentiary fruit of the pen registers, arguing that the use of a pen register was a search under Article I, §9 of the Texas Constitution.]

Ultimately, in the context of both the Fourth Amendment and Article I, §9, whether the government's installation and use of a pen register constitutes a search necessarily depends upon whether appellant has a "legitimate expectation of privacy" in the numbers he dialed on the telephone. . . . For purposes of the Fourth Amendment, a 5-3 majority of the Supreme Court has held that the installation and use of a pen register is not a search. This is so, the Court observed, because an individual "in all probability" entertains no actual expectation of privacy in the phone numbers he dials, and, even if he did, such an expectation is not "legitimate." Smith v. Maryland, 442 U.S. 735 (1979). The majority reasoned that telephone users "typically know that they must convey numerical information to the phone company; that the phone company has facilities for recording this information; and that the

1. Article 18.21 authorizes Texas law enforcement's use of pen registers as a means of electronic surveillance. A pen register is a mechanical or electronic device that attaches to a telephone line and is capable of recording outgoing numbers dialed from that line but is not capable of recording the origin of an incoming communication to that line or the content of a communication carried between that line and another line. Although Article 18.21 does establish a number of prerequisites to the issuance of a court order authorizing the use of a pen register, the statute does not require an applicant show probable cause. The statute merely requires that the application state the installation and utilization of the pen register will be material to the investigation of a criminal offense. . . .

phone company does in fact record this information for a variety of legitimate business purposes." Telephone users, therefore, cannot have an actual expectation that the numbers they dial will remain private.

The *Smith* majority further reasoned that even if an individual did have an actual expectation that the numbers he dials would remain secret, such an expectation is not one that society would recognize as reasonable. To the majority, the disclosure of the telephone numbers was similar to other cases in which the Court held that a person has no legitimate expectation of privacy in information he voluntarily turns over to third parties. In particular, the Court noted United States v. Miller, 425 U.S. 435 (1976), which held that the government could access a bank depositor's financial records, including the depositor's monthly statement, checks and deposit slips, without probable cause. The *Miller* Court noted "that the Fourth Amendment does not prohibit the obtaining of information revealed to a third party and conveyed by him to government authorities, even if the information is revealed on the assumption that it will be used only for a limited purpose and the confidence placed in the third party will not be betrayed." Thus, the bank depositor who has voluntarily disclosed certain financial information to the bank and, necessarily, its employees, takes the risk that the information will be conveyed by the bank or its employees to the government. Having assumed this risk, the bank depositor has no legitimate expectation of privacy.

Similarly, the caller who has voluntarily disclosed the telephone number to the telephone company has assumed the risk that the telephone company would reveal these numbers to the police. For this reason the telephone caller has no legitimate expectation of privacy in the telephone numbers dialed. The installation and use of a pen register to record these numbers is therefore not a search under the Fourth Amendment, and no warrant is required.

The Supreme Court's holding in *Smith* has not gone without criticism. Quite the contrary, a number of legal commentators have rejected the Court's holding as making "a mockery of the Fourth Amendment." 1 W. LaFave, Search and Seizure: A Treatise on the Fourth Amendment §2.7(b), at 507 (2d ed. 1987). . . . LaFave agreed with Justice Marshall's dissent that the mere fact that a telephone user may know the telephone company can monitor his calls for internal reasons does not necessarily mean that he expects "this information to be made available to the public in general or the government in particular." [It] makes no sense to say that the telephone subscriber . . . is fair game for unrestrained police scrutiny merely because he has surrendered some degree of his privacy for a limited purpose to those with whom he is doing business. . . .

In addition to the commentators, numerous state courts have criticized the Supreme Court's holding in *Smith.* At least seven States have rejected the reasoning of *Smith,* holding that their state constitutions provide an individual with a protected privacy interest in the telephone numbers dialed from a telephone. [The court cited cases from New Jersey, California, Pennsylvania, Colorado, Washington, Idaho, and Hawaii.] All but one of these cases involve construction of a state constitutional provision that is substantially similar to our Article I, §9. . . .

We agree [with these decisions]. The mere fact that a telephone caller has disclosed the number called to the telephone company for the limited purpose of obtaining the services does not invariably lead to the conclusion that the caller has relinquished his expectation of privacy such that the telephone company is free to turn the information over to anyone, especially the police, absent legal process.

Certainly it is true that a general or indiscriminate disclosure of what otherwise may seem private information by its very nature evinces the lack even of a subjective expectation of privacy. Thus, the drug vendor . . . hawking his wares on the street, does not even demonstrate a subjective belief that his activities will remain private. Even if he did, the open nature of the disclosure obviates any possibility that the public would share his belief, and thus he cannot claim an objectively reasonable expectation of privacy. . . .

But whether an individual "assumes the risk" that a more limited disclosure will open the door to public disclosure depends, we think, upon the reasonableness of his subjective belief (if any) that the disclosure will in fact go no further. A selective disclosure may evidence a subjective expectation of privacy; the circumstances in which information is related to a third party may show a unilateral or even a mutual understanding that the information will remain confidential. This is not an understanding that society is invariably willing to recognize as legitimate, however, for society may have no particular stake in the matter. Thus, a subjective expectation of privacy despite a limited disclosure is not always a "reasonable" one.

There are some subjective expectations of privacy, however, that society does sanction as legitimate in spite of limited, confidential disclosure. We would not want to say, for example, that society does not recognize the confidentiality of information imparted to a physician behind the closed doors of an examination room. That certain facts may be revealed in the necessarily candid process of diagnosis and treatment does not mean we no longer have a collective interest in insulating them from public scrutiny. On the contrary, society accepts — indeed, positively insists — that such information, although of necessity partly exposed, should nevertheless retain its essentially private character. In view of this societal imperative, it is hardly fair to reason that the patient "assumed the risk" of public disclosure because of the forthrightness with which he spoke to his doctor.

Although the argument is not quite as compelling, we believe it would be likewise unfair to hold that the customer "assumes the risk" of public disclosure of a number he dials on the telephone. Other than for billing purposes, the telephone company itself has no interest in memorializing that information. Moreover, the telephone company is fiercely protective of what it considers the privacy interest of its customers even in the information it does record in the ordinary course of business — as any private citizen will discover if he attempts to obtain the telephone bill of another customer without that other's express permission.[8] It goes without saying that telecommunications are pervasive in our society. The telephone company's vigilance in protecting from public disclosure the uses to which its customers put their telephones reflects a value that is equally pervasive. As with information imparted to a doctor, we share a common understanding that the numbers we call remain our own affair, and will go no further. Thus, society recognizes as objectively reasonable the expectation of the telephone customer that the numbers he dials as a necessary incident of his use of the telephone will not be published to the rest of the world.

8. On page 37 of the prefatory pages of the 1992-1993 Greater Austin Telephone Directory printed by Southwestern Bell we find the heading, "Your Rights As a Customer." Under the subheading, "Telecommunications Privacy," we find the following assurance: "We fully safeguard every individual's right to privacy as an essential aspect of our service. We carefully strive to protect communications services from unlawful wiretapping or other illegal interception. Customer service records, credit information and related confidential personal account information are fully protected."

It follows that the use of a pen register may well constitute a "search" under Article I, §9 of the Texas Constitution. The question remaining is whether such a search would be "unreasonable" in the absence of probable cause. If so, then to the extent it authorizes a court ordered pen register without a showing of probable cause, Article 18.21 violates Article I, §9. Because the court of appeals did not decide the question of reasonableness . . . we remand the cause for further disposition.

CAMPBELL, J., dissenting.

The majority perceives the question presented to be the abstract one of whether the State's use of a pen register may constitute a "search" under Article I, §9, of the Texas Constitution. Clearly, however, that is not the question presented. The true question presented is whether appellant has shown that he, as a pretrial detainee in a county jail, had a reasonable expectation of privacy in the telephone numbers he dialed on the jail telephone. [The dissent argued that the appellant had no reasonable expectation of privacy in calls made from jail, and that in any case society would be unwilling to accept such an expectation of privacy.]

Notes

1. *Pen registers as "searches": majority position.* Most state supreme courts ruling on the constitutional question have concluded (unlike the Supreme Court in Smith v. Maryland, 442 U.S. 735 (1979)), that use of a pen register is a "search" within the meaning of the constitution. The cases also conclude that it is a search for the government to compel a telephone company to provide access to *existing* records, as opposed to the creation of new records, which takes place with a pen register. But see Saldana v. State, 846 P.2d 604 (Wyo. 1993) (no violation of state constitution to subpoena toll records for unlisted number).

The federal statute reprinted above has analogs in almost 40 states. The statutes often authorize the use of a pen register after obtaining a court order, based on a showing that the pen register is "likely" to produce information that is "material" or "relevant" to a criminal investigation. See Fla. Stat. §934.33. Are statutes such as these consistent with the conclusion of many state courts that using a pen register is a constitutionally regulated "search"? These statutes also compel the telephone company to cooperate with the government in placing an authorized pen-register device on a telephone. Would telephone companies oppose the passage of a pen-register statute? For discussion of bank secrecy statutes, see Chapter 4, section C.

2. *Electronic Communications Privacy Act.* The Electronic Communications Privacy Act of 1986, 18 U.S.C. §2703, prohibits any "provider of electronic communications" services to the public from disclosing the contents of electronic communications it stores during the transmission process. The statute does not apply to the internal computer networks of computers operated by many employers; it covers instead any provider of electronic communications or computing services to the public, if the transmission occurs on a system that affects interstate or foreign commerce. Despite the statute's general protection from disclosure of electronic message contents, it creates an exception for disclosure to the government. The statute requires the government to obtain a warrant (based on probable cause) before it can obtain an electronic communication that has been in "electronic storage"

for less than 180 days. For communications stored for more than 180 days, the government can obtain them without probable cause if it notifies the owner of the communication and obtains a subpoena or a court order based on "specific and articulable facts showing that there are reasonable grounds to believe that the contents of a wire or electronic communication . . . are relevant and material to an ongoing criminal investigation." Why the different treatment for messages stored longer than 180 days?

Are Internet service providers (ISPs) required to provide the government with records of usage by its users? If the records being requested by the government involve e-mail and communications, they might be covered by the Electronic Communications Privacy Act. But what if the materials sought by the government are not communications, but stored files and documents? Is the delivery of such information by the service provider a matter covered solely by the contractual relationship between the user and the provider?

Problem 7-5. Total Information Awareness

In the months following the terrorist attacks on the World Trade Towers and the Pentagon in September 2001, the Department of Defense began planning for a data system to identify and stop terrorists. The system would allow the government to collect in one database all the publicly available information about an individual's purchases and other electronic transactions. Sophisticated computer programs could then "mine" this data to uncover patterns of behavior by people who make purchases or transactions that raise suspicions of terrorism. For instance, investigators might use the database to identify people who take commercial flying or scuba diving lessons, or people who purchase large amounts of fertilizer. A government Web site, sponsored by the Department's "Information Awareness Office," describes the program's objective like this:

> Currently, terrorists are able to move freely throughout the world, to hide when necessary, to find unpunished sponsorship and support, to operate in small, independent cells, and to strike infrequently. . . . This low-intensity/low-density form of warfare has an information signature, albeit not one that our intelligence infrastructure and other government agencies are optimized to detect. In all cases, terrorists have left detectable clues that are generally found after an attack. Even if we could find these clues faster and more easily, our counter-terrorism defenses are spread throughout many different agencies and organizations at the national, state, and local level. To fight terrorism, we need to create a new intelligence infrastructure to allow these agencies to share information and collaborate effectively, and new information technology aimed at exposing terrorists and their activities and support systems. . . . The key to fighting terrorism is information.

The Web site also describes the sorts of "transactional data" for individuals that would be deposited in the Total Information Awareness database: "financial, educational, travel, medical, veterinary, country entry, place/event entry, transportation, housing, critical resources, government, communications." The individual identifiers would be removed from these transactions until the "data mining" process identified persons who called for further investigation. See *http://www.darpa.mil/iao/TIASystems.htm.* The logo for the government office is a pyramid with the all-seeing eye, gazing upon a globe (the same graphic that appears on the dollar bill), and the agency's motto is "Knowledge is power."

The columnist William Safire expressed the concerns of civil libertarians and advocates of limited government about this program:

> Every purchase you make with a credit card, every magazine subscription you buy and medical prescription you fill, every Web site you visit and e-mail you send or receive, every academic grade you receive, every bank deposit you make, every trip you book and every event you attend — all these transactions and communications will go into what the Defense Department describes as "a virtual, centralized grand database." To this computerized dossier on your private life from commercial sources, add every piece of information that government has about you — passport application, driver's license and bridge toll records, judicial and divorce records, complaints from nosy neighbors to the F.B.I., your lifetime paper trail plus the latest hidden camera surveillance — and you have the supersnoop's dream: a "Total Information Awareness" about every U.S. citizen.

Safire, You Are a Suspect, N.Y. Times, p.35, Nov. 14, 2002. He argued that "the government's infinite knowledge about you is its power over you."

Michael Scardaville of the Heritage Foundation, however, supported the program: "Only those already identified as terrorists have anything to fear." He described as follows the safeguards on privacy the system would use:

> Even if they wanted to, TIA employees simply won't have time to monitor who plays football pools, who has asthma, who surfs what websites, or even who deals cocaine or steals cars. They'll begin with intelligence reports about people already suspected of terrorism. . . . Those already identified as terrorists or potential terrorists by the intelligence community then could be monitored through existing public and private databases to build an in-depth portfolio, including contacts and frequent activities. . . These portfolios should enable authorities to determine whom to watch and where to find them when they suspect a terror strike is imminent. Access to this information should be limited to those with appropriate clearances as well as by need to know, and programmers are hard at work on filters for these purposes.

Scardaville proposed limiting database access to the FBI, the CIA, and the Department of Homeland Security. The TIA program could develop "limited spinoffs" for use by state and local law enforcement and for those working for aviation security or monitoring for epidemics and biological warfare. Scardaville, Targeting Terrorists, National Review, Nov. 25, 2002. As a member of Congress, would you vote to fund the development of this program? Do adequate safeguards exist to prevent administrators of this system (administrators who will come from different political perspectives and personal backgrounds over the years) from misusing the data in the Total Information Awareness system?

Notes

1. *Access to transaction records and encryption.* The government can obtain access to transactional information in the hands of third parties (such as retailers) by warrant or subpoena. More frequently, however, the third party consents to provide the information. When it comes to stored communications, however, none of these

techniques will give the government access to information that has been "encrypted" to make it unreadable to anyone other than the intended recipient, who holds the encryption "key." During the 1990s, the federal government proposed a series of schemes to require the creators of encryption software to give the government a "key" to unlock the encryption, a key that the government would only be able to use after demonstrating probable cause to search. During 1996 congressional hearings on this question, FBI Director Louis Freeh made the case for government access to encrypted messages:

> [C]onventional encryption not only can prevent electronic surveillance efforts, which in terms of numbers are conducted sparingly, but it also can prevent police officers on a daily basis from conducting basic searches and seizures of computers and files. Without an ability to promptly decrypt encrypted criminal or terrorist communications and computer files, we in the law enforcement community will not be able to effectively investigate or prosecute society's most dangerous felons or, importantly, save lives in kidnappings and in numerous other life and death cases. . . .
>
> In a very fundamental way, conventional encryption has the effect of upsetting the delicate legal balance of the Fourth Amendment, since when a judge issues a search warrant it will be of no practical value when this type of encryption is encountered. Constitutionally-effective search and seizure law assumes, and the American public fully expects, that with warrant in hand law enforcement officers will be able to quickly act upon seized materials to solve and prevent crimes, and that prosecutors will be able to put understandable evidence before a jury. Conventional encryption virtually destroys this centuries old legal principle.

What did Director Freeh fear if unbreakable communications are allowed? What "delicate legal balance" did he find in the Fourth Amendment? In the end, the federal government abandoned its plans to require software developers to provide a key for its products to the government.

2. *Combinations of government-held information.* Once the government gains access to information, is any search or seizure issue involved in how the government uses the information? U.S. Treasury Department regulations describe an ongoing government program, known as "FinCEN," designed to make the most of the information scattered in various government files. The records that FinCEN reviews are based on reports that banks and other institutions and individuals must submit to comply with federal statutes and regulations. By using computers to combine and analyze the information held legitimately in various government files, law enforcers can obtain a more complete picture of an individual's activities or can note trends among certain groups of people that could justify closer scrutiny. This particular program focuses on financial crimes, such as tax evasion or money laundering. Does this technique hold promise for other sorts of investigations? How might one construct an argument that the assembling of many existing bits of data about an individual, contained in different records, creates new information that should be deemed a "search" regulated by the constitution?

Most search and seizure law relates to the government's initial access to information. The FinCEN program offers an example of government *use* of information to which it has undeniable access. Is the use of information relevant to the constitutional requirement of "reasonableness"? Consider Federal Rule of Criminal Procedure 41(e): "A person aggrieved by an unlawful search and seizure or by the deprivation of property may move . . . for the return of the property." See Harold Krent,

Of Diaries and Data Banks: Use Restrictions Under the Fourth Amendment, 74 Tex. L. Rev. 49 (1995). If a legislature, or some executive policymaker, decided to place some limit on the government's use of legitimately obtained information, what sort of limit would be feasible? Should the statute or policy impose a time limit on the use of the information? Should it force the government to use the information only in the enforcement of specified laws?

3. *DNA databases.* The kinds of data held by the government extend beyond financial records. One especially powerful class of information is genetic information, revealed through chemical patterns in an individual's DNA. Most states have now firmly established the validity, as an evidentiary matter, of some types of DNA evidence. Beyond the evidentiary and technical aspects of DNA evidence, its use can be quite dramatic. DNA evidence has proven the innocence of some people wrongly convicted.

But individual use of DNA to establish whether a known individual was (or was not) the likely offender is very different from having a broad database that allows the government to match any genetic material to a particular person. A database containing genetic information about many individuals, and perhaps an entire population, might allow investigators who find hairs, blood, semen, or mucus to identify quickly the most likely suspects.

What only a few years ago sounded like science fiction increasingly sounds like science fact. Every state in the country has passed legislation authorizing a DNA database made up of samples from various categories of citizens, most often groups of criminal offenders or suspects. The military obtains genetic information from every member of the armed services. Some states collect identifying information, such as fingerprints, as part of providing basic services, such as a driver's license. It may not be long until the basic elements of citizenship and commerce obligate individuals to provide a sample of their DNA.

The development of genetic databases raises a huge range of issues. Those issues focus on how the information is obtained, how it may be used, and who will have access to it. Take Massachusetts as an example. The legislature passed in 1997 a statute authorizing collection and analysis of DNA samples from defendants convicted of any of the 33 enumerated felonies. The law applied retroactively to those currently incarcerated, on probation, or on parole as a result of such a conviction. If a conviction is later dismissed, relevant DNA records may be expunged by court order. Law enforcement officers and correction personnel are authorized to use "reasonable force" to collect the DNA samples. Once samples are collected, the state crime laboratory performs "DNA typing tests" to generate numerical identification information. This numerical identifier becomes part of the state DNA database, and is also forwarded to the Federal Bureau of Investigation for storage and maintenance in a national index system.

The Massachusetts Act limits access to the information obtained from DNA samples. The crime lab forwards a DNA record to local police departments, to the Department of Correction, to a sheriff's department, to the parole board, or to prosecuting officers on written or electronic request. The crime lab also must disclose DNA records to "local, state and federal criminal justice and law enforcement agencies, including forensic laboratories serving such agencies, for identification purposes in order to further official criminal investigations or prosecutions." Defendants who are charged with crimes as a result of a DNA database search are provided with a copy of their own DNA record. The director of the crime lab also has discretion to release DNA records for identifying victims of mass disasters or for "advancing other humanitarian purposes."

If you, as an attorney in Massachusetts, hoped to challenge the constitutionality of this law, who would be your ideal client? What constitutional texts and doctrines would you invoke? As Director of the state crime laboratory, what regulations would you issue to address any potential constitutional or political difficulties? The Massachusetts statute has survived an initial constitutional challenge. Landry v. Attorney General, 709 N.E. 2d 1085 (Mass. 1999); see also State v. Olivas, 856 P.2d 1076 (Wash. 1993) (en banc).

4. *Compensating the innocent imprisoned.* DNA evidence has led to an impressive number of overturned convictions over the last decade or more. Though little careful analytic work has yet been published examining these cases, two important lessons emerge from these cases. First, the most common source of wrongful convictions is erroneous identification evidence, especially in cases where the identifications formed a central part of the case. Second, wrongful convictions seem far more likely to be uncovered when some advocate is investigating the case: These cases do not uncover themselves. When a person is freed after years of imprisonment for a crime they did not commit, should the government compensate them?

D. NONGOVERNMENTAL INFRINGEMENT OF PRIVACY ("PRIVATE PRIVACY")

Criminal procedure and its constitutional superstructure speak to the relationship between citizens' privacy and their government's power to invade that privacy. On the other hand, infringement of privacy rights by nongovernmental actors has historically been left to private law. Tort claims for trespass, conversion, assault, battery, libel, slander, and invasion of privacy allow private parties to recover damages, and a handful of criminal charges reinforce those privacy interests.

There are various private actors who might collect information about criminal suspects, including family members, friends, employers, teachers, or roommates. Private security firms employ a growing number of people to prevent and ferret out crime. Although the legal questions of how to regulate the behavior of private security personnel are looming larger all the time, these questions have not yet received much attention from lawyers, legislators, courts, or scholars. Professor David Sklansky has argued that

> [t]he neglect is increasingly indefensible. The private security industry already employs significantly more guards, patrol personnel, and detectives than the federal, state, and local governments combined, and the disparity is growing. Increasingly, private security firms patrol not only industrial facilities and commercial establishments but also office buildings, shopping districts, and residential neighborhoods. . . .

Sklansky, The Private Police, 46 UCLA L. Rev. 1165 (1999). If traditional principles of policing do not limit the actions of private security forces, what law and principles will?

Since traditional constitutional limits on searches and seizures do not apply to "private" searches, police and prosecutors might simply encourage private actors to conduct searches and interrogations, and then turn over their evidence to the authorities. However, courts hold private searchers to public standards when the private action is conducted "at the behest of" or "in partnership with" government authorities. What factors should courts use to determine whether private searches are really public searches in disguise? Should the increasing number of private security personnel lead to the regulation of more private searches? Should private police officers who act like public police officers, but for the color of the uniform, be held to public search standards?

■ STATE v. ADAM NEMSER

807 A.2d 1289 (N.H. 2002)

NADEAU, J.

. . . The defendant, a Dartmouth College undergraduate, was charged with possession of marijuana. He moved to suppress, alleging that the entry and search of his room by Dartmouth Safety and Security (DSS) officers violated the Fourth and Fourteenth Amendments to the Federal Constitution, and Part I, Article 19 of the State Constitution. The defendant argued that the DSS officers are agents of the State, to whom the requirements of the Fourth and Fourteenth Amendments and Part I, Article 19 apply.

The trial court found:

> [T]he DSS officers (1) do not jointly train with the Hanover Police Department or other law enforcement officers or agencies, (2) do not take specific direction from public law enforcement officials, (3) were not, in the Nemser case, acting at the specific direction or behest of Hanover Police Officers, (4) were not trained or directed by the Hanover Police Department or any other public law enforcement agency in formulating their policy and protocols and, (5) that they were not supplied with any equipment or other accessories or information by the Hanover Police Department to either assist them in or lead them to the discovery of the items seized in the present case.

Nevertheless, the court found a sufficient relationship between DSS and the Hanover Police Department to apply constitutional restrictions to the search at issue, and granted the motion to suppress. The State appealed. The defendant relies upon both the State and Federal Constitutions. We address his State Constitutional claim first, using federal cases merely to aid our analysis under the State Constitution. . . .

The protections against unreasonable searches and seizures apply only to State action. Thus, evidence obtained by a private party may be admissible even if secured through the most outrageous behavior by the private party. Constitutional restrictions do apply, however, to a seizure of evidence by a private party acting as an agent of law enforcement. This "agency rule" prevents the police from having a private individual conduct a search or seizure that would be unlawful if performed by the police themselves.

The State argues that the trial court erred in finding that the DSS officers acted as agents of the State in seizing contraband from the defendant. Because the determination whether an agency relationship exists is fact-driven, we [will] uphold a trial court's finding of an agency relationship unless it is unsupported by the record or clearly erroneous.

A conclusion that an agency relationship existed requires proof of some affirmative action by a governmental official prior to the search that can reasonably be seen to have induced the search by the private party. [T]wo kinds of governmental action will meet this standard. The first is the government's prior agreement with a third party that the latter should act to obtain evidence from a defendant. Whether the agreement is formal or informal, there will be some responsive communication between the parties, and the exchange will evince an understanding that the third party will be acting on the government's behalf or for the government's benefit. Second, a prior governmental request for help may have the same effect, even though the third party who acts upon it may make no reply back to the government but responds simply by taking the action that a government official has requested.

The trial court found "no express agreement between the State and College," but rather an "implicit understanding." Specifically, the court found:

> The College's agents conduct private area searches of drugs, not necessarily in plain view or with consent, and seize contraband, hold it for however long DSS determines, and the State won't prosecute any such agents and won't object to securing a search warrant [to retrieve contraband in DSS's possession] to "legalize" the process by cloaking the search with judicial approval. . . .

Robert McEwen, college proctor and director of DSS, testified that it is against college policy for students to possess drugs. As of June 1995, the college's policy with regard to controlled substances encountered by DSS officers was to destroy drug paraphernalia and small quantities of contraband and to report to the Hanover Police Department the rare instances in which large quantities of drugs were discovered or DSS suspected drug trafficking. The question was occasionally raised, however, whether DSS officers, being private citizens, risked arrest if they took possession of contraband in the course of their duties.

Mr. McEwen expressed this concern to Nicholas Giaccone, Hanover Chief of Police, in a letter dated June 12, 1995. Chief Giaccone replied that he did not believe that DSS officers met any of the recognized exemptions to the law prohibiting possession of a controlled substance, but that, as a practical matter, he would not be inclined to charge a DSS officer coming into possession of such substances in the course of his or her duties.

Chief Giaccone testified that a meeting between college and governmental officials was held "to discuss the issue of controlled substances," but that no agreement or consensus on college policy was reached. Subsequently, the college sent Chief Giaccone a letter, dated April 8, 1996, detailing the policy it had instituted. Senior Associate Dean Daniel Nelson, on the other hand, testified that the policy the college wanted to implement was discussed at the meeting and that the "Hanover police said that that was agreeable to them, and [the letter confirmed the] sense of the meeting." Nevertheless, Dean Nelson stated that the policy was "our policy; it's not a policy dictated by Hanover police or by the county attorney, but it's a policy that we developed."

The policy, as found by the trial court, is that DSS officers initially decide, in their own discretion, whether any illegal substance they discover is a small or "personal use" quantity, which they will confiscate, or a large quantity, which they will not confiscate. When large quantities of drugs or evidence of drug trafficking is observed,

DSS reports the matter to the Hanover Police Department. When a small quantity of contraband is seized,

> [it] is retained at the DSS Office for an indeterminate, variable length of time, solely in the discretion of college officials. Thereafter, at some point the Hanover Police Department is notified by DSS and the Hanover Police then seek the issuance of a Search Warrant because the college position mandates that a search warrant be presented by the police before the contraband is relinquished by the college security force.

Chief Giaccone testified that the policy outlined in the April 8 letter was not "particularly something that [he] was thrilled at," but that, as he told the county attorney, "this is what they came up with and this is what we're gonna have to live with." He also testified that he was not aware of any instance in which one of his officers directed a DSS officer to search for drugs or had prior knowledge that a DSS officer would find drugs.

We conclude that these facts do not support the existence of an agency relationship. We do not discern in them an inducement by the State to search on its behalf, but rather a grudging acceptance by the Hanover Police Department of the unilateral decisions of a private party over which it believed it had no control. Mere knowledge of another's independent action does not produce vicarious responsibility absent some manifestation of consent and the ability to control. In addition, the facts do not evince an understanding that the third party will be acting on the government's behalf or for the government's benefit. Instead, the college acted for its own purposes in enforcing its own policy against drug possession by students. . . .

This case differs factually from State v. Heirtzler, 789 A.2d 634 (N.H. 2001), in which "there was an agreement that [a police officer] would inform school officials of suspicious behavior when he did not have probable cause to investigate." Here, DSS officers acted unilaterally and unaided by police in furtherance of the college's own interests. Accordingly, we conclude that the trial court's finding of an agency relationship is clearly erroneous.

Notes

1. *Private searches: majority view.* Courts uniformly asses whether there is a sufficiently close link between a private search and government agents in deciding whether evidence found or obtained from a private search should be admitted. Courts look to a variety of factors, including prior agreements between private actors and government agents that a private agent will conduct a search. The application of this loose standard, however, leads to varying outcomes, both across and within jurisdictions. For example, the year before *Nemser,* the New Hampshire Supreme Court decided a case involving a high school student, and held that two assistant principals were acting in concert with a police officer stationed at the school when the principals conducted a search of a student with consent but without probable cause.

> The fundamental concern of the agency rule is to curb unconstitutional activity by government; it is meant to prevent the government from circumventing the rights of a defendant by securing private parties to do what it cannot. [Officer Bennette] conceded that a "silent understanding" existed between him and school officials that passing

> information to the school when he could not act was a technique used to gather evidence otherwise inaccessible to him due to constitutional restraints. The school, by "a mere wink or nod" or something more concrete, agreed to investigate certain potential criminal matters on the State's behalf or for its benefit.

See State v. Heirtzler, 789 A.2d 634 (N.H. 2001). Is *Heirtzler* still good law after *Nemser?* Does deference to the trial court's fact-intensive inquiry explain the different outcome in the two cases? Does the full-time presence of a police officer on the high school campus explain the difference?

While all U.S. jurisdictions declare that the constitutional limits on searches and seizures do not apply to truly private searches, that has not always been the case. Between 1979 and 1985, Montana applied the constitutional guarantees against unreasonable searches and seizures to private searches, noting that government agents might use private actors to sidestep constitutional limits. See State v. Helfrich, 600 P.2d 816 (Mont. 1979), reversed by State v. Long, 700 P.2d 153 (Mont. 1985). Although the reasons given by Montana courts have only become stronger since 1985, with the increase in the number of private security agents, no other state has followed Montana's brief experiment.

One important class of searches are conducted by agents who constantly work with the government, such as bail bond agents. See, e.g., State v. Collins, 790 A.2d 660 (Md. 2001) (bail bond agents were acting as state actors for purposes of the Fourth Amendment due to the extent of the participation by the police officer who accompanied them as part of "service to stand by" procedure). More generally, bail bond agents raise the question whether government regulation of private actors or industries should be a factor in determining whether searches they conduct should be constrained by the rules for the police.

2. *Searches by private security.* The number of private security agents is striking. David Sklansky found that:

> as of 1990, there were 393,000 "proprietary," or in-house, security guards throughout the United States (i.e., guards employed directly by the owner of the property they protect), and 520,000 employees of "contract" guard companies (i.e., companies that hire out guards). [Guards] constitute all but 2-5% of those employed by contract guard companies. The more conservative figure of 5% yields 484,000 contract guards and 877,000 guards overall. There were roughly 600,000 sworn law enforcement officers throughout the country in 1990.

Private Police, 46 UCLA L. Rev. 1165 at n.27 (1999). If the government abolished its police force and a jurisdiction relied entirely on private security, would constitutional limits on search and seizure apply? Should private security agents stay within the same restrictions as other private actors?

3. *Searches by family members.* A mother searching through her teenage son's room may make her child feel like he lives in a police state, but any contraband she might find and report to the police is still admissible as evidence. Sometimes, however, family members interests will be even more at odds than the run-of-the-mill battles between teenagers and their parents. Consider Virdin v. State, 780 A.2d 1024 (Del. 2001), where the parents of a missing girl asked police to accompany them to the apartment she shared with her husband, who was a suspect.

> [T]wo critical factors in the instrument or agent analysis are whether the government knew of and acquiesced in the intrusive conduct and whether the private party's

purpose in conducting the search was to assist law enforcement agents or to further [its] own ends. Other useful criteria are whether the private actor acted at the request of the government and whether the government offered the private actor a reward.

The analysis is a highly factual one that must take into account the totality of the circumstances. The defendant bears the burden of proving that the private party was acting as an instrument or agent of the government. . . . We conclude that the trial court's determination that the Yuns were not acting as state agents finds substantial support in the record. . . . In the two days leading up the discovery of the body, she engaged in frantic efforts to locate her daughter, including driving to area hospitals, calling various people who might have seen Stefanie, and visiting the apartment by herself early on Monday morning. Her decision to go back to the apartment with Sergeant Timmons, and later with Corporal Graham (together with her husband, Mike Yun), was motivated by an urgent concern for her daughter's safety, and was not related to assisting with a police investigation. The record reflects that the Yuns requested that the police accompany them because of concern about a confrontation with the defendant.

To what extent was Ms. Yun's subjective motivation for inviting the police to accompany here critical to this decision? Should the test for whether a search is private or public turn on the subjective motivations of any of the actors? See also Commonwealth v. Harris, 2002 WL 31618533 (Pa. Nov. 20, 2002) (no constitutional rights implicated where state received photocopies of letters from murder defendant to his accomplice, originals of which were intercepted and copied by accomplice's brother, absent any indication that accomplice's brother was acting as state agent); State v. Brockman, 528 S.E.2d 661 (S.C. 2000) (private search where mother called police to settle domestic dispute with son, then searched son's moped in front of officers).

In many instances, alleged invasions of privacy may occur entirely as a result of the actions of private individuals. What protections do individuals have if other individuals or businesses (but not state agents) invade their privacy? Do traditional protections against invasion of privacy by individuals and private businesses provide enough protection in the information-driven, highly technological modern state?

■ RITA PLAXICO v. GLENN MICHAEL

735 So.2d 1036 (Miss. 1999)

SMITH, J.

This is an appeal from a judgment of the Circuit Court of Tippah County, Mississippi, dismissing with prejudice, Rita Plaxico's invasion of privacy claim which is based upon the sub-tort of intentional intrusion upon seclusion or solitude. . . .

Glenn Michael and his wife were divorced. They had one female child who was about six years old at the time of trial. The Chancellor gave custody of the child to Michael's wife in the Divorce Decree. Michael's former wife and child lived in a cabin that had been rented by Michael as the family home prior to their divorce. Plaxico moved into the cabin with Michael's former wife and his child sometime after the divorce. Michael was later informed that his ex-wife was having a relationship with the Plaintiff, Rita Plaxico. Michael wanted to modify the child custody based on the fact that his former wife and Plaxico were romantically involved with each other.

One night in June, 1993, Michael slipped up to a window in the cabin through which he witnessed Plaxico and his former wife having sexual relations. He left to retrieve a camera from his vehicle. After doing so, he returned and took three photographs of Plaxico, who was sitting in bed naked. However, the bed covers covered her from the waist down. Michael had the photographs developed and delivered the pictures to his attorney. He then, on November 16, 1993, filed for modification of child custody. Michael testified that he did not show the photographs to anyone other than his lawyer. His lawyer produced the photographs to Michael's former wife's attorney in response to discovery requests in the child custody matter pending between Michael and his former wife in which the Chancellor granted Michael the custody of his child. Plaxico became aware of the photographs through Michael's former wife's attorney. . . .

Plaxico subsequently filed suit for invasion of privacy. She claimed that Michael intentionally intruded upon her seclusion and solitude, and she suffered damages as a result of this tort. She further testified and acknowledged that she and Michael's former wife were lovers and had engaged in sexual relations. [The trial court heard all the evidence, then ruled that Michael had a qualified privilege to protect his child when he obtained the evidence of the relationship between Plaxico and his former wife. The trial court then dismissed the complaint with prejudice and ordered Plaxico to pay the costs of the proceeding.]

In order for Plaxico to prevail in this action, she must prove all elements of the sub-tort to invasion of privacy, intentional intrusion upon seclusion or solitude. In Candebat v. Flanagan, 487 So. 2d 207 (Miss. 1986), we stated that actions for the invasion of privacy as a tort have received universal recognition in the United States. In fact, every state except Rhode Island provides either statutory or common law relief for it. . . . The tort of invasion of privacy is comprised of four distinct and separate sub-torts which are as follows:

1. The intentional intrusion upon the solitude or seclusion of another;
2. The appropriation of another's identity for an unpermitted use;
3. The public disclosure of private facts; and
4. Holding another to the public eye in a false light.

Candebat, 487 So. 2d at 209. In the case at bar, it is the first of the sub-torts which is at issue, the intentional intrusion upon the solitude or seclusion of another. [T]o recover for an invasion of privacy, a plaintiff must meet a heavy burden of showing a substantial interference with his seclusion of a kind that "would be highly offensive to the ordinary, reasonable man, as the result of conduct to which the reasonable man would strongly object." Restatement Second of Torts, §652B, comt. d (1977). Further, the plaintiff must show some bad faith or utterly reckless prying to recover on an invasion of privacy cause of action. However, the general rule is that there is no requirement of publication or communication to a third party in cases of intrusion upon a plaintiff's seclusion or solitude.

In the present case, Plaxico did not prove each element of intentional intrusion upon solitude or seclusion of another. Plaxico was in a state of solitude or seclusion in the privacy of her bedroom where she had an expectation of privacy. However, we conclude that a reasonable person would not feel Michael's interference with Plaxico's seclusion was a substantial one that would rise to the level of gross offensiveness as required to prove the sub-tort of intentional intrusion upon seclusion or solitude.

No one would dispute that parents have a predominant and primary interest in the nurture and care of their children. In child custody matters the best interest of the child is the polestar consideration. Here, Michael became concerned about the welfare of his daughter, who was in the custody of his former wife. Michael's former wife subleased a cabin from him, and invited Plaxico to be her roommate. His concern was based on numerous rumors of an illicit lesbian sexual relationship between Plaxico and his former wife. Michael decided that it was not in the best interests of his daughter to allow her to remain in the custody of her mother, and he wanted to obtain custody of the child. It is of no consequence that the mother was having an affair with another woman. She could have been carrying on an illicit affair with a man in the home where the child was, and any father would feel that this too was inappropriate behavior to be carried on in the presence of the child. A modification would still be desired by the parent.

In the present case, Michael did want to file for modification of child custody. However, he had no proof that there actually was lesbian sexual relationship which could be adversely affecting his minor child. In order to obtain such proof, he went to the cabin, peered through the window and took pictures of the two women engaged in sexual conduct. Three pictures were actually developed which were of Plaxico in a naked state from her waist up in her bed. Michael believed that he took these pictures for the sole purpose to protect his minor child. Although these actions were done without Plaxico's consent, this conduct is not highly offensive to the ordinary person which would cause the reasonable person to object. In fact, most reasonable people would feel Michael's actions were justified in order to protect the welfare of his minor child. Therefore, the elements necessary to establish the tort of intentional intrusion upon solitude or seclusion are not present. . . .

BANKS, J., dissenting.

. . . In my view, peeping into the bedroom window of another is a gross invasion of privacy which may subject one to liability for intentional intrusion upon the solitude or seclusion of that other. See Restatement (Second) of Torts 652B cmt. b, illus. 2 (1977) (invasion of privacy would occur if private investigator, seeking evidence for use in a lawsuit, looks into plaintiff's bedroom window with telescope for two weeks and takes intimate photographs).

The trial court found refuge in what it found to be a qualified privilege to see to the best interest of a child. Neither rumors concerning an ex-wife's lifestyle nor a parent's justifiable concern over the best of interests of his child, however, gave Michael license to spy on a person's bedroom, take photographs of her in a seminude state and have those photographs developed by third parties and delivered to his attorney thereby exposing them to others. While it is not my view that the publication to others is necessary for tort liability here, I make reference to it to demonstrate the highly offensive nature of the behavior here involved.

[W]e have observed that "the end does not justify the means. . . . Our society is one of law, not expediency. . . ." I regret that today's majority here does not follow these worthy ideals.

McRae, J., dissenting.

. . . Ms. Plaxico, the paramour of Michael's ex-wife, however, was not a party to the custody proceedings. As the majority points out, it matters not whether Michael's former wife was involved in a lesbian or a heterosexual relationship. Michaels [sic] was not at liberty to peek in the women's bedroom window, an act that can only be characterized as voyeuristic. Nor was he at liberty to take photographs of Plaxico and share them with his attorney. At best, only pictures of his former wife could possibly be characterized as helpful to Michael's case. As to Plaxico, any privilege allowed Michael is misplaced. . . .

Notes

1. *Privacy torts: majority position.* As the court in *Plaxico* notes, every state but Rhode Island provides a cause of action for "intentional intrusion upon the solitude or seclusion of another." Some states allow the action as part of common law tort doctrine; in others a cause of action for invasion of privacy appears in state statutes. For instance, a Nebraska Statutes §20-203 provides that "Any person, firm, or corporation that trespasses or intrudes upon any natural person in his or her place of solitude or seclusion, if the intrusion would be highly offensive to a reasonable person, shall be liable for invasion of privacy."

Whether based in common law or statutory causes of actions, the law of intentional intrusion on seclusion is relatively unformed, and a general Westlaw or Lexis search of all federal and state cases produces fewer than 100 reported cases, with many of those cases focused on "false light" claims. See, e.g., Mauri v. Smith, 929 P.2d 307 (Or. 1996) (reversing summary judgment against police officers who entered apartment without authority or consent); Sabrina W. v. Willman, 540 N.W.2d 364 (Neb. App. 1995). Is this an area of social interaction generally in need of greater legal regulation? If not, are there avenues other than civil tort claims to bolster a sense (and perhaps the reality) of individual privacy, and to limit invasions of privacy by private actors? Are there some actors in particular, such as firms that gather and sell information about individuals, that call for particular regulation?

2. *Reasonableness is not a rose.* In Shakespeare's "Romeo and Juliet," Juliet says "What's in a name? That which we call a rose, by any other word would smell as sweet." Although "reasonableness" goes by the same name in both public constitutional criminal and private tort law, it plays widely varying roles in these different contexts. For starters, judges typically apply the constitutional rules of search and seizure; juries usually assess tort claims. Nominally the government must bear the burden of showing that its searches and seizures are reasonable; in a tort suit, the plaintiff must show that the defendant's behavior was unreasonable. What are the virtues and vices of reasonableness as a method for assessing government or private behavior? What are the alternatives? Which institutions should develop more precise reasonableness rules of the road?

3. *The media and privacy.* More familiar than claims for physical invasion of privacy are claims that someone, often a media outlet, has published information that invades the claimant's privacy. It is important to distinguish such claims from claims that another person has reported false information or portrayed the claimant in a false light, which includes causes of action for defamation, libel, and slander. See James A. Albert, The Liability of the Press for Trespass and Invasion of Privacy in

Gathering the News — A Call for the Recognition of a Newsgathering Tort Privilege, 45 N.Y.L. Sch. L. Rev. 331 (2002).

■ GEORGIA CODE §16-11-62

It shall be unlawful for:

(1) Any person in a clandestine manner intentionally to overhear, transmit, or record . . . the private conversation of another which shall originate in any private place;

(2) Any person, through the use of any device, without the consent of all persons observed, to observe, photograph, or record the activities of another which occur in any private place and out of public view; provided, however, that it shall not be unlawful:

> (B) For an owner or occupier of real property to use for security purposes, crime prevention, or crime detection any device to observe, photograph, or record the activities of persons who are on the property or an approach thereto in areas where there is no reasonable expectation of privacy; or
>
> (C) To use for security purposes, crime prevention, or crime detection any device to observe, photograph, or record the activities of persons who are within the curtilage of the residence of the person using such device . . . ;

(3) Any person to go on or about the premises of another or any private place, except as otherwise provided by law, for the purpose of invading the privacy of others by eavesdropping upon their conversations or secretly observing their activities;

(4) Any person intentionally and secretly to intercept by the use of any device, instrument, or apparatus the contents of a message sent by telephone, telegraph, letter, or by any other means of private communication; . . .

(5) Any person to divulge to any unauthorized person or authority the content or substance of any private message intercepted lawfully . . . ; or

(6) Any person to sell, give, or distribute, without legal authority, to any person or entity any photograph, videotape, or record, or copies thereof, of the activities of another which occur in any private place and out of public view without the consent of all persons observed; or

(7) Any person to commit any other acts of a nature similar to those set out in paragraphs (1) through (6) of this code section which invade the privacy of another.

Notes

1. *Private wiretaps: majority position.* Many state wiretap and privacy acts provide some limitation on the private recording of conversations. Often these acts are broadly phrased to apply to conversations transmitted through a variety of means, and courts have applied them to new communications technologies such as e-mail. For example, wiretap statutes often bar or limit nonconsensual private recording of conversations, and they create private claims when individuals violate these restrictions. They include recovery of presumed damages. See 18 U.S.C. §2520; Wash. Rev. Code §9.73.030. Some of the wiretap statutes also create criminal sanctions for wrongful interceptions of "communications." See Conn. Gen. Stat. §53a-189. About a dozen states require mutual consent for recording of conversations, while others

require only the consent of one person, leaving the risk on anyone who converses that the other person may record. Which of these positions better reflects the social contract to which you would like to be a party?

The federal wiretap statute and some state statutes provide for statutory damages within sharp limits when actual damages are not great or cannot be proven. Why not allow more substantial statutory damages? Some state statutes authorize attorney's fees in statutory damage cases for interception of private communications. What effect do you think attorney's fees provisions have generally? In the enforcement of privacy rights?

There is less established state law regulating relationships between employers and employees. What rights would you recognize in a "workplace privacy act"? Is the better presumption — as a matter of technology or social policy — that communications intended to be private should be protected by law, or that communications that can be read by employers or other third parties should be presumed nonprivate, absent contractual agreements to the contrary? Would you choose instead to leave concerns about privacy to negotiations in the free market?

2. *Data privacy and e-mail.* Can you imagine settings where the collection, collation, analysis, or distribution of otherwise public information should be prohibited? See Juliana Spaeth, Mark J. Plotkin, and Sandra C. Sheets, Privacy, Eh! 4 Vand. J. Ent. L. & Prac. 29 (2002); Pamela Samuelson, A New King of Privacy? Regulating Uses of Personal Data in the Global Information Economy, 87 Cal. L. Rev. 751 (1999) (reviewing Paul M. Schwartz and Joel R. Reidenberg, Data Privacy Law (1996)).

Should individuals have enforceable privacy interests against nongovernmental parties with respect to e-mail that resides on third-party or corporate computers? Does the answer depend on the nature of the contract between the person and the third party or the person's employer? Reasonable expectations of privacy? See Larry Gantt, An Affront to Human Dignity: Electronic Mail Monitoring in the Private Sector Workplace, 8 Harv. J.L. & Tech. 345 (1995); David Neil King, Privacy Issues in the Private-Sector Workplace: Protection from Electronic Surveillance and the Emerging "Privacy Gap," 67 S. Cal. L. Rev. 441 (1994).

3. *Voluntary privacy limits in commerce.* News stories in 1998 described efforts by the National Retail Federation, which represents a wide range of companies including various department stores and discount warehouses, to voluntarily set policies regarding the use of information gathered about customers. Will businesses develop privacy policies as strong or stronger than those that a legislature or agency might develop? Will consumers be able to negotiate for higher levels of privacy?

4. *A growth area.* In general, legal controls over private searches have remained anemic compared to the controls on government agents, while the conflict between private searches and individual privacy has gotten sharper. Citizens are likely to demand that this discrepancy be addressed. The development of a richer conception of privacy and associated laws is likely to be the focus of major developments over the next decade and beyond.

Technology gives private searchers more capacity than ever to learn about their targets. The possibilities are stunning. Private investigative firms, through access to computer databases, can assemble a person's long-distance telephone toll records, bank account balances, credit card activity, and medical treatment history. Firms will sell unlisted telephone numbers and bank account numbers, information about a person's salary, or lists of someone's stocks, bonds, and mutual funds. The information sometimes comes from databases built on information that the government sells out of its own records. See Nina Bernstein, Electronic Eyes: What the Computer Knows, N.Y. Times, September 15, 1997, at A1.

If private collection of information becomes common enough and intrusive enough, it would make almost meaningless any limitations on searches by public agents. In an atmosphere in which the law does not limit private collection of private information, there is less and less room for a "reasonable expectation of privacy" against government. Should legislatures begin to demarcate areas of privacy within employment, neighborhood, and perhaps even family relationships? Should courts take another look at fundamental property rights in light of the erosion of privacy in all walks of life? Should individuals be allowed to use whatever technologies they like to listen, watch, or smell other people so long as there is no technical invasion or trespass?

VIII

Interrogations

Some crimes go unsolved unless the perpetrator confesses. Confessions are especially important in some violent crimes, such as murder and robbery; they are less important in possession crimes or transactional crimes (such as drug offenses or fraud), where a greater range of testimonial and physical evidence is often available. Beyond these general observations, however, it is hard to determine the exact number and types of cases in which police interrogation is necessary to solve the crime.

Many police officers are convinced that interrogations and confessions are indispensible in a broad range of cases. Field studies have certainly confirmed that the police interrogate the great majority of all suspects in custody. In a 1994 survey of police interrogation practices in Salt Lake City, the police questioned 79 percent of all suspects, whether or not in custody. Paul Cassell and Bret Hayman, Police Interrogation in the 1990s: An Empirical Study of the Effects of *Miranda,* 43 UCLA L. Rev. 839 (1996). Earlier studies also showed high rates of interrogation, something more than 90 percent of all suspects in custody. Project, Interrogations in New Haven: The Impact of *Miranda,* 76 Yale L.J. 1519 (1967); James Witt, Non-Coercive Interrogation and the Administration of Criminal Justice: The Impact of *Miranda* on Police Effectuality, 64 J. Crim. L. & Criminology 320 (1973).

If a suspect does provide the police with incriminating information, this has a considerable effect on the later processing of her case. People who confess to the police are more likely to be charged with a crime, less likely to have the charges against them dismissed, more likely to plead guilty, more likely to be convicted, and more likely to receive a more serious punishment. See Richard Leo, Inside the Interrogation Room, 86 J. Crim. L. & Criminology 266 (1996). Jurors consider evidence of a confession by the defendant to be among the most important types of information that a prosecutor can present. See Saul Kassin and Katherine Neumann, On the Power of Confession Evidence: An Experimental Test of the Fundamental Difference Hypothesis, 21 Law & Hum. Behav. 469 (1997).

In short, the confession of a criminal suspect can be a pivotal moment in the investigation and processing of a criminal case. What are the legal obligations of the police and other government agents who interrogate suspects in the hope of obtaining an outright confession or some admission leading to incriminating evidence?

A. VOLUNTARINESS OF CONFESSIONS

Courts have a long-standing concern about the voluntariness of confessions. An involuntary confession, the courts have long declared, cannot be a valid source of prosecution evidence. However, the precise reasons why involuntary confessions are considered objectionable, and the factors that can demonstrate the involuntariness of the confession, have shifted over the years. The following materials consider the impact of physical abuse, promises, threats, and lies on those courts considering whether a confession is voluntary.

1. *Physical Abuse and Deprivations*

Not so long ago, police in the United States used physical violence widely when they interrogated suspects. In 1931, the National Commission on Law Observance and Enforcement (known as the Wickersham Commission) collected evidence from current and former police officers and from many observers of police interrogation practices. The Commission concluded as follows:

> The third degree — the inflicting of pain, physical or mental, to extract confessions or statements — is widespread throughout the country. Physical brutality is extensively practiced. The methods are various. They range from beating to harsher forms of torture. The commoner forms are beating with the fists or with some implement, especially the rubber hose, that inflicts pain but is not likely to leave permanent visible scars.
>
> The method most commonly employed is protracted questioning. By this we mean questioning — at times by relays of questioners — so protracted that the prisoner's energies are spent and his powers of resistance overcome. . . . Methods of intimidation adjusted to the age or mentality of the victim are frequently used alone or in combination with other practices. The threats are usually of bodily injury. They have gone to the extreme of procuring a confession at the point of a pistol or through fear of a mob. . . .
>
> In considerably over half of the States, instances of the third degree practice have occurred in the last 10 years. . . . Fifteen representative cities were visited during the last 12 months by our field investigators. In 10 of them there was no doubt as to the existence of third-degree practices at that time. The practice is by no means confined to cities. Over one-third of the cases judicially reported since 1920 arose in places of less than 10,000 inhabitants.

Some police officers argued that third-degree tactics were justified, for a number of reasons (again, as summarized by the Wickersham Commission):

- [T]he third degree is used only against the guilty.
- [O]bstacles in the way of the police make it almost impossible to obtain convictions except by third-degree methods. [T]hrough intimidation, bribery, and

all kinds of political connections criminals are often set free. . . . Consequently they hope to build up such a solid case on the basis of a confession that the prisoner will, in spite of all obstacles, be convicted.

- [P]olice brutality is an inevitable and therefore an excusable reaction to the brutality of criminals.
- [R]estrictions on the third degree may impair the morale of the police.
- [T]he existence of organized gangs in large cities renders traditional legal limitations outworn.

How might you reply to each of these arguments? Could these same arguments be relevant in discussing other interrogation techniques that do not involve physical violence or intimidation?

Five years after the Wickersham Commission report appeared, the Supreme Court issued a major ruling on the question of coerced confessions. As early as 1897, the Court had considered the validity of confessions obtained by federal law enforcement officers, concluding in Bram v. United States, 168 U.S. 532 (1897), that the Fifth Amendment's self-incrimination clause limited coercive police interrogations. However, the Fifth Amendment did not apply to the states at that point, and it was unclear whether federal law placed any limits on the use of an involuntary confession in state court.

■ ED BROWN v. MISSISSIPPI

297 U.S. 278 (1936)

HUGHES, C.J.

The question in this case is whether convictions, which rest solely upon confessions shown to have been extorted by officers of the State by brutality and violence, are consistent with the due process of law required by the Fourteenth Amendment of the Constitution of the United States.

[Ed Brown, Henry Shields, and Yank Ellington] were indicted for the murder of one Raymond Stewart, whose death occurred on March 30, 1934. They were indicted on April 4, 1934, and were then arraigned and pleaded not guilty. Counsel were appointed by the court to defend them. Trial was begun the next morning and was concluded on the following day, when they were found guilty and sentenced to death.

Aside from the confessions, there was no evidence sufficient to warrant the submission of the case to the jury. [Defendants testified] that the confessions were false and had been procured by physical torture. The case went to the jury with instructions, upon the request of defendants' counsel, that if the jury had reasonable doubt as to the confessions having resulted from coercion, and that they were not true, they were not to be considered as evidence.

[The state supreme court refused to overturn the convictions on appeal.] The grounds of the decision were (1) that immunity from self-incrimination is not essential to due process of law, and (2) that the failure of the trial court to exclude the confessions after the introduction of evidence showing their incompetency, in the absence of a request for such exclusion, did not deprive the defendants of life or liberty without due process of law. . . .

That the evidence established that [the confessions] were procured by coercion was not questioned. . . . There is no dispute as to the facts upon this point and as they are clearly and adequately stated in the dissenting opinion of Judge Griffith . . . — showing both the extreme brutality of the measures to extort the confessions and the participation of the state authorities — we quote this part of his opinion in full, as follows:

> The crime with which these defendants, all ignorant negroes, are charged, was discovered about one o'clock P.M. on Friday, March 30, 1934. On that night one Dial, a deputy sheriff, accompanied by others, came to the home of Ellington, one of the defendants, and requested him to accompany them to the house of the deceased, and there a number of white men were gathered, who began to accuse the defendant of the crime. Upon his denial they seized him, and with the participation of the deputy they hanged him by a rope to the limb of a tree, and having let him down, they hung him again, and when he was let down the second time, and he still protested his innocence, he was tied to a tree and whipped, and still declining to accede to the demands that he confess, he was finally released and he returned with some difficulty to his home, suffering intense pain and agony. The record of the testimony shows that the signs of the rope on his neck were plainly visible during the so-called trial. A day or two thereafter the said deputy, accompanied by another, returned to the home of the said defendant and arrested him, and departed with the prisoner towards the jail in an adjoining county, but went by a route which led into the State of Alabama; and while on the way, in that State, the deputy stopped and again severely whipped the defendant, declaring that he would continue the whipping until he confessed, and the defendant then agreed to confess to such a statement as the deputy would dictate, and he did so, after which he was delivered to jail.
>
> The other two defendants, Ed Brown and Henry Shields, were also arrested and taken to the same jail. On Sunday night, April 1, 1934, the same deputy, accompanied by a number of white men, one of whom was also an officer, and by the jailer, came to the jail, and the two last named defendants were made to strip and they were laid over chairs and their backs were cut to pieces with a leather strap with buckles on it, and they were likewise made by the said deputy definitely to understand that the whipping would be continued unless and until they confessed, and not only confessed, but confessed in every matter of detail as demanded by those present; and in this manner the defendants confessed the crime, and as the whippings progressed and were repeated, they changed or adjusted their confession in all particulars of detail so as to conform to the demands of their torturers. When the confessions had been obtained in the exact form and contents as desired by the mob, they left with the parting admonition and warning that, if the defendants changed their story at any time in any respect from that last stated, the perpetrators of the outrage would administer the same or equally effective treatment. . . .
>
> The evidence upon which the conviction was obtained was the so-called confessions. Without this evidence a peremptory instruction to find for the defendants would have been inescapable. The defendants were put on the stand, and by their testimony the facts and the details thereof as to the manner by which the confessions were extorted from them were fully developed, and it is further disclosed by the record that the same deputy, Dial, under whose guiding hand and active participation the tortures to coerce the confessions were administered, was actively in the performance of the supposed duties of a court deputy in the courthouse and in the presence of the prisoners during what is denominated, in complimentary terms, the trial of these defendants. This deputy was put on the stand by the state in rebuttal, and admitted the whippings. It is interesting to note that in his testimony with reference to the whipping of the defendant Ellington, and in response to the inquiry as to how severely he was whipped, the deputy stated, "Not too much for a negro; not as much as I would have done if it were left to me." Two others who had participated in these whippings were introduced and admitted it — not a single witness was introduced who denied it. . . .

The State stresses the statement in Twining v. New Jersey, 211 U.S. 78 (1908), that "exemption from compulsory self-incrimination in the courts of the States is not secured by any part of the Federal Constitution." . . . But the question of the right of the State to withdraw the privilege against self-incrimination is not here involved. The compulsion to which the quoted statements refer is that of the processes of justice by which the accused may be called as a witness and required to testify. Compulsion by torture to extort a confession is a different matter.

The State is free to regulate the procedure of its courts in accordance with its own conceptions of policy, unless in so doing it "offends some principle of justice so rooted in the traditions and conscience of our people as to be ranked as fundamental." The State may abolish trial by jury. It may dispense with indictment by a grand jury and substitute complaint or information. But the freedom of the State in establishing its policy is the freedom of constitutional government and is limited by the requirement of due process of law. Because a State may dispense with a jury trial, it does not follow that it may substitute trial by ordeal. The rack and torture chamber may not be substituted for the witness stand. The State may not permit an accused to be hurried to conviction under mob domination — where the whole proceeding is but a mask — without supplying corrective process. The State may not deny to the accused the aid of counsel. Nor may a State, through the action of its officers, contrive a conviction through the pretense of a trial which in truth is "but used as a means of depriving a defendant of liberty through a deliberate deception of court and jury by the presentation of testimony known to be perjured." Mooney v. Holohan, 294 U.S. 103 (1935). And the trial equally is a mere pretense where the state authorities have contrived a conviction resting solely upon confessions obtained by violence. . . . It would be difficult to conceive of methods more revolting to the sense of justice than those taken to procure the confessions of these petitioners, and the use of the confessions thus obtained as the basis for conviction and sentence was a clear denial of due process. . . .

In the instant case, the trial court was fully advised by the undisputed evidence of the way in which the confessions had been procured. The trial court knew that there was no other evidence upon which conviction and sentence could be based. Yet it proceeded to permit conviction and to pronounce sentence. The conviction and sentence were void for want of the essential elements of due process. . . .

Notes

1. *Disappearance of the third degree.* Thirty-six years after the appearance of the Wickersham Commission report, another national commission reported the virtual disappearance of physical coercion as an interrogation technique: "today the third degree is almost non-existent." President's Commission on Criminal Justice and the Administration of Justice, The Challenge of Crime in a Free Society (1967). Physical brutality and intimidation disappeared in part because of political pressure from the public, outraged by the findings of the Wickersham Commission and countless similar news accounts. Would these practices have disappeared, even without the Supreme Court's ruling in *Brown?* During the 30 years following *Brown,* due process claims of involuntary confessions became a staple of the Supreme Court docket. The Court ultimately decided more than 30 such cases. Over time, the nature of the police conduct in question shifted away from physical violence or threats

of violence to more subtle physical deprivations and psychological coercion. However, the move away from physical deprivation happened slower in some places than others. In particular, physical abuse of black defendants in Southern states continued through the 1940s. See Michael Klarman, Is the Supreme Court Sometimes Irrelevant?: Race and the Southern Criminal Justice System in the World War II Era, 89 Journal of American History 119 (2002).

2. *Physical deprivations: modern limits.* Although physical abuse such as striking a suspect has largely disappeared from interrogations in this country, one can still find examples of physical deprivations, such as depriving a suspect of food or sleep for some period of time. Courts say that some deprivations are tolerable while others are not. Up to a point, interrogators can limit the sleep or food available to the suspect. See Payne v. Arkansas, 356 U.S. 560 (1958) (confession coerced when defendant given two sandwiches during 40-hour detention and interrogations). What if the interrogator fails to provide the suspect with a cigarette?

After the physical coercion in police interrogations withered away, the legal system still faced questions about psychological manipulation during interrogations. If the *Brown* court prohibited the use of "coerced" or "involuntary" confessions, what types of psychological pressures might qualify under that standard? One recurring source of psychological pressure that has been influential with courts has been the extended isolation of the defendant from family, friends, legal counsel, and other support. See Fikes v. Alabama, 352 U.S. 191 (1957) (isolation for more than a week, confession involuntary).

3. *Length of interrogation.* Interrogators find greater success with suspects after lengthier interrogation sessions. A prominent training manual lists the time available for interrogation as one of the most basic conditions for obtaining a confession: "Criminal offenders . . . ordinarily will not admit their guilt unless questioned under conditions of privacy, and for a period of perhaps several hours." Fred Inbau, John Reid, and Joseph Buckley, Criminal Interrogations and Confessions (3d ed. 1986). Criminologist Richard Leo, who observed about 180 police interrogations, conducted a statistical study concluding that the length of an interrogation is one of the strongest determinants of its success. Richard Leo, Inside the Interrogation Room, 86 J. Crim. L. & Criminology 266 (1996). At the same time, lengthy interrogations create a risk that a court will later find any confession to be involuntary. Ashcraft v. Tennessee, 322 U.S. 143 (1944) (continuous 36-hour interrogation, confession involuntary); State v. Mayes, 825 P.2d 1196 (Mont. 1992) (suspect awake for more than 30 hours, questioned continually, separated from children, confession involuntary). There is no clear time limit that will create an involuntary confession under the "totality of the circumstances," but many interrogators believe that the risk goes up once the session extends past three or four hours.

4. *Delay in presenting a suspect to a judicial officer.* The rules of criminal procedure in most jurisdictions require the police to arrange for the suspect's prompt appearance before a judicial officer. The rules in some states specify a time period. See Ariz. R. Crim. Proc. 4.1 ("A person arrested shall be taken before a magistrate without unnecessary delay. If the person is not brought before a magistrate within 24 hours after arrest, he or she shall immediately be released"); Cal. Penal Code §825 (defendant shall "be taken before the magistrate without unnecessary delay, and, in any event, within 48 hours after his or her arrest, excluding Sundays and holidays"). The Supreme Court has declared that any violation of the time rules contained in the Federal Rules of Criminal Procedure will require suppression of confessions

obtained as a result of that delay. This requirement (declared under the Court's so-called supervisory power over federal law enforcement) is known as the *McNabb-Mallory* rule, after McNabb v. United States, 318 U.S. 332 (1943), and Mallory v. United States, 354 U.S. 449 (1957). Although most states have a time-limit provision in their rules of procedure, most state courts have rejected the *McNabb-Mallory* rule and have declared instead that a violation of the timeliness requirement will not lead to automatic suppression but will be one part of the "totality of the circumstances" that could indicate an involuntary confession. Fewer than 10 states follow the per se federal rule. Some states have special rules (embodied in statutes, court rules, or constitutional due process rulings) requiring prompt presentation of *juveniles* to a judicial officer. See W. Va. Code, §49-5-8(d); In re Steven William T., 499 S.E.2d 876 (W. Va. 1997) (when a juvenile is taken into custody, he must immediately be taken before a referee, circuit judge, or magistrate; confession obtained as a result of the delay will be invalid where it appears that the primary purpose of the delay was to obtain a confession from the juvenile).

5. *Vulnerability of suspect.* The Court in *Brown* mentioned the "ignorance" of the suspects. Many other cases assessing the voluntariness of a confession for due process purposes have also considered the vulnerability of the suspect. A suspect who is especially young or who is suffering from illness or injury will be more likely to succeed in claiming that a confession was involuntary. See Beecher v. Alabama, 408 U.S. 234 (1972) (suspect confesses while under influence of morphine and in pain from gunshot wound, confession involuntary); Haley v. Ohio, 332 U.S. 596 (1948) (15-year-old interrogated with no advice from family or friends, confession involuntary). Conversely, a suspect who is mature and well educated will find it more difficult to sustain a claim of involuntariness.

6. *Torture, truth, and need.* Exactly what is objectionable about relying on confessions obtained through torture? If the problem is unreliable information, could that be cured by an evidentiary rule requiring independent corroboration of anything learned through physical abuse of a suspect? If the objection is abuse of police powers, could that risk be addressed through procedures specifying when physical coercion would be allowed, and the types of physical techniques the police could use? Are there situations in which torture may still be justified? What if the life of a hostage is at stake, or there is a possibility of great loss of life from an act of terror? See John Langbein, Torture and the Law of Proof (1977).

These questions are not merely academic. In the aftermath of the terrorist attacks in New York City and Washington on September 11, 2001, lawyers and government officials started to anticipate settings where torture might be appropriate. See Jonathan Alter, "Time to Think About Torture," Newsweek Nov. 5, 2001, p. 45 ("In this autumn of anger, even a liberal can find his thoughts turning to . . . torture. OK, not cattle prods or rubber hoses, at least not here in the United States, but something to jump-start the stalled investigation of the greatest crime in American history").

The legitimacy of the limited use of physical torture is still a live issue in many places in the world. In 1999, the Israeli Supreme Court banned the use of physical force by General Security Service interrogators. For decades, their methods included violently shaking the suspects' upper torsos, forcing them to crouch, handcuffing them in painful positions, placing filthy sacks over their heads, and depriving them of sleep. Critics of the Supreme Court's decision argued that force is necessary in a "ticking bomb situation," when the General Security Service suspects that a terror attack is about to take place, but does not know where, and has to find out to prevent loss of life. The Supreme Court's decision noted that in such a case, a court might accept the argument that physical force was necessary. Deborah Sontag, Israel Court Bans Most Use of Force in Interrogations, N.Y. Times, Sept. 7, 1999 at A1.

2. *Promises and Threats*

Only rarely does a suspect volunteer a confession without any effort by the police to convince the suspect that a confession would be worthwhile. When an interrogator tries to convince a suspect of the value of a confession, is it proper to make promises or threats of any type? Are these techniques objectionable for the same reasons that one might object to physical torture during interrogations?

■ STATE v. CHARLES STRAIN

779 P.2d 221 (Utah 1989)

HOWE, Assoc. C.J.

Defendant Charles Nicholas Strain appeals his jury conviction of second degree murder. [Strain] was arrested on February 20, 1986, in Scottsdale, Arizona, on a fugitive warrant issued in the state of Idaho. [Four hours after his arrest,] Detective Peter Bell of the Utah County, Utah, Sheriff's office questioned him about the shooting death of defendant's sixteen-year-old stepdaughter, Deanna, whose decomposed body had been found some five years earlier in Spanish Fork Canyon, Utah. Throughout this initial three-hour interview, defendant maintained his innocence with respect to that death. The following morning, Detective Bell resumed his questioning. This session was followed by another interrogation that evening by Detective Bell and also by Utah County Deputy Sheriff Scott Carter. The interrogation culminated in defendant's signing a statement, admitting the killing. He was subsequently charged with second degree murder.

Prior to trial, defendant filed a motion to suppress his confession [because of] threats and promises made to him by Detective Bell which allegedly rendered his confession involuntary. [The trial court denied the motion and admitted the confession into evidence. Defendant was found guilty of second degree murder. Strain] contends that the trial court erred by failing to suppress his confession because it was obtained through coercion by Detective Bell. Such a claim, if valid, would render the confession involuntary as being violative of defendant's fifth and fourteenth amendment rights against self-incrimination. Specifically, defendant contends that Detective Bell threatened a first degree murder charge against him and possible execution, if convicted of that charge, if he did not admit his involvement in the homicide of his stepdaughter. Set alongside this threat was an alleged promise by Bell which offered defendant the lesser charge of second degree murder if he admitted involvement in the murder. Detective Bell denied making such a promise to defendant.

Over the years, both federal and state courts have struggled with the concept of voluntariness and have employed several formulations in their attempts to apply it. Several courts have stated that a confession of the accused must be the product or result of a "free and unconstrained choice." Other courts have defined the concept of voluntariness by insisting that the confession be "freely self-determined," or the product of "rational intellect and free will." Another perspective frames the issue as "whether the defendant's will was overborne at the time he confessed." [The] determination of voluntariness of confessions requires the court to consider "the totality of all the surrounding circumstances — both the characteristics of the accused and the details of the interrogation." Schneckloth v. Bustamonte, 412 U.S. 218 (1973); State v. Hegelman, 717 P.2d 1348 (Utah 1986). The mere representation to a defendant by officers that they will make known to the prosecutor and to the court that he cooperated with them, or appeals to the defendant that full cooperation would be his best course of action, have been recognized as not coercive. However, as the State freely admits in the instant case, most courts have found a confession involuntary where a threat to pursue a higher charge if the accused did not confess, or a promise to pursue a lesser charge if he did confess, was exhortative.

The record indicates that during the course of the February 27, 1986 morning interrogation, Detective Bell made the following statement to defendant:

> Now, what I'm trying to tell you right now Charlie is, all you have to do . . . the only thing that is keeping you from going back to the State of Utah and looking at a possible execution on a first degree murder charge or a second degree murder charge, which is some jail time. The only thing that keeps between them two, is "yes, I did or no I didn't." Yes, second degree murder, no, I didn't, I will prove that you did and you are looking at a possible execution date in the State of Utah. That's all I want to hear from you Charlie, all I want to hear is yes or no. All I want to hear is, is there going to be first degree murder or second degree murder. . . .

Later, Detective Bell repeated this line of interrogation.

> [J]ust tell me right now, let's just (not understandable), yes for jail time or no, we are going to go to trial and for possible execution. That's all I want to hear from you is just yes or no.

Defendant immediately asked, "Just that simple?" Upon this response, Detective Bell then framed his dichotomous proposal into what easily would have been taken as an offer or a promise of leniency:

> Just that simple. And I can guarantee it Charlie, I can guarantee it's that simple. My God, this thing has been drug on for five years. The little girl's body up in the canyon, the soul was crying for justice.

Not only did Detective Bell threaten a first degree murder charge and possible execution if convicted, we believe that he also crossed the line when he offered defendant a promise as evidenced by his personal guarantee. The detective's offer was framed strictly in terms which offered defendant a second degree murder charge and jail time for his "yes, I did." . . .

Upon Bell's extension of this promise of leniency, defendant attempted to relate his philosophy of life but was interrupted by Detective Bell: "I don't want to hear it Charlie. All I want to hear is yes or no." [Soon afterward,] Detective Bell offered defendant a moment to think. Then after one final push by Bell, defendant began to admit his involvement in the murder which eventually resulted in a signed statement that evening admitting culpability for the killing.

It is clear that the statements made by Detective Bell to defendant were impermissibly coercive because they carried a threat of greater punishment or a promise for lesser punishment depending on whether he confessed. The State, however, urges us to affirm the admission of the confession because looking at the "totality of all the surrounding circumstances," the improper statements of Detective Bell did not induce defendant to confess. The State points out that defendant was an adult in his forties and familiar with the criminal justice system. Certain statements made by defendant in the course of the interrogation indicated that he little cared whether he lived or died. He stated that he had "no life left"; that he did not care if he were executed; and that he cared only about the persons he would leave behind.

While in Bram v. United States, 168 U.S. 532 (1897), the statement was made that any threat or promise, however slight, renders a confession involuntary and inadmissible, later cases do not repeat that rigid rule but follow the totality of all the circumstances test. [For example, in] People v. Conte, 365 N.W.2d 648 (Mich. 1984) . . . the Supreme Court of Michigan rejected the strict per se test sometimes attributed to Bram v. United States, and adopted "the simple rule that a confession caused by a promise of leniency is involuntary and inadmissible."

In the instant case, the trial court did not address the defendant's contention that [his] confession was the result of coercive threats and promises made by the interrogating officers. We therefore do not have before us an adequate record upon which we can determine the question of voluntariness. There is no testimony of defendant as to what considerations prompted his confession. As earlier stated, while coercive threats and promises were made to him, he also made statements which indicate that the improper statements of the officers did not induce him to confess.

We therefore remand this case to the trial court for an evidentiary hearing to determine the voluntariness of defendant's confession under a "totality of all the surrounding circumstances." If the confession is found to have been voluntarily given, the conviction is affirmed. However, if the confession is found to have been involuntarily made, a new trial should follow.

Problem 8-1. Parental Promises

The strangled and stabbed body of Sharon Johnson, then in an advanced stage of pregnancy, was found at a construction site. Police Sergeant Roland Lamy was assigned to the case and learned from Tony Pfaff that the victim's husband, Ken Johnson, had solicited Pfaff to move the victim's car shortly after the time of the murder. Investigation into Pfaff's background revealed that 19-year-old Jason Carroll worked with Pfaff and that Carroll had not reported for work on the night of the murder. Lamy first interviewed Carroll at the National Guard Armory. He admitted having been at the murder scene with Pfaff and Johnson but admitted no other involvement in the murder. After completing a written statement to this effect, Carroll indicated he was tired and, agreeing to continue the interview three days later, went home with his parents.

The next morning, however, Carroll told his parents that he wanted to recant his previous statements to the police. Karen Moore, the defendant's mother and a local police officer, arranged for an interview with her colleague, Captain Leo Morency. Carroll drove himself and his mother to the police station, where, at about 1:30 P.M., he met Lamy and Morency in Morency's office, which measured about 10 feet by 10 feet and had two outside windows. State Police Sergeant Neal Scott soon joined the interview. Carroll denied any knowledge of the murder. In a sometimes raised voice, Lamy repeatedly said he did not believe Carroll. At about 2:45 P.M., Carroll asked to have his mother present. While Lamy went to get Moore, Carroll told the officers in the room that his statement of the day before was true, and that he was afraid of Johnson and Pfaff. When Moore entered the interview room, Lamy told her that she was entering as the suspect's mother, not as a police officer, and that, although she was not to assist the police in their interrogation, she was free to do anything she wanted as the defendant's mother.

The interview resumed, and at about 3:20 P.M., Morency activated an audio tape recorder. During the recorded portion of the interview, Moore began to question her son aggressively. Both she and Lamy used raised voices at times, and several times Carroll began to cry. Throughout the interrogation, Carroll repeatedly expressed his desire to confess, saying, "I have to let it go," "I want so much to get this over and out of my life," "I just want to get this over with," and "It's not gonna be easy like this, just to spit it out, I can't, I want to so much." At one point, the following exchange took place about the benefits of telling the truth:

Moore: The longer you put off telling the truth, the harder it is gonna be, and the worse it is gonna be on yourself because you still have a chance to save your ass, my dear. I don't want to see you go to prison. . . .

Carroll: I don't want to go to prison either Ma.

Lamy: Then tell us the truth.

Carroll stated several times that he was afraid of how Pfaff and Johnson would react if he told of their involvement in the incident. Lamy responded:

> And if you're afraid, and you tell us what you're afraid of, including Mr. Johnson, we can take care of protecting you. We can't take care of protecting something we don't understand. Protection for your safety is commensurate on you convincing us that you want to be truthful. You haven't done that to me. Look, I understand that you are afraid. We already told you, if you get to the bottom dollar here and tell us the truth, we will then discuss your safety.

Lamy also assured Carroll that, as far as he knew, Johnson was living in Rhode Island, had no money, and was being monitored.

Carroll finally admitted that he had agreed with Pfaff to participate in the murder for $2,000, that he had helped Pfaff trick the victim into driving from a mall to the construction site, that he had been the first to stab the victim, that he had helped move the victim's car after the murder, and that his own pocket knife was the murder weapon. At this point, Carroll broke down and, in tears, said, "I just want to go home. I want to go home. I want to go home." The defendant was charged with capital murder. Was the confession voluntary? Compare State v. Carroll, 645 A.2d 82 (N.H. 1994).

Notes

1. *Police promises: majority position.* Most jurisdictions have not taken literally the Supreme Court's prohibition on the use of confessions obtained through "any sort of threats or . . . any direct or implied promises, however slight." Bram v. United States, 168 U.S. 532 (1897). Some promises or threats, standing alone, are indeed enough to render a confession "involuntary." These would include promises to re-

duce (or decline to file) charges, threats to file more serious charges, or promises to seek more or less serious punishment for the crime. See Lynumn v. Illinois, 372 U.S. 528 (1963) (suspect told that cooperation could lead to lesser charges; failure to co-operate would mean loss of custody of children, confession involuntary); Beavers v. State, 998 P.2d 1040 (Alaska 2000) (threat that suspect would be "hammered" if he did not talk made confession presumptively involuntary, but state could rebut presumption). They could also include threats to refuse to protect the suspect from mob violence or from a dangerous co-conspirator. Interrogators can, however, make many other promises or threats without invalidating a confession. They can promise to inform the prosecutor about the defendant's cooperation in making a statement, to have the prosecutor discuss lesser charges, or to arrange for treatment programs or similar activities. What distinguishes the acceptable from the unacceptable promises? See McLeod v. State, 718 So. 2d 727 (Ala. 1998) (confession voluntary despite officer's promise to make cooperation known to prosecutor and trial court). When the police make promises or threats to a juvenile suspect, the government has a somewhat more difficult burden to meet in showing that the confession was voluntary. See State v. Presha, 748 A.2d 1108 (N.J. 2000) (courts should consider parent's absence during interview as a highly significant factor in judging voluntariness of juvenile's statement); In re G.O., 727 N.E.2d 1003 (Ill. 2000) (juvenile's confession should not be suppressed simply because he was denied the opportunity to confer with a parent during interrogation, but that factor may be relevant in determining voluntariness).

The government carries the burden of proving that a confession was voluntary, and the standard of proof is preponderance of the evidence. State v. Agnello 593 N.W.2d 427 (Wis.1999) (voluntariness of confession need be shown only by a preponderance, not beyond reasonable doubt). As the Utah court in *Strain* indicated, even after a defendant demonstrates that the police made an improper promise or threat, he must also prove that the promise or threat "induced" the confession. How would Strain prove this fact during the hearing before retrial?

2. *Do innocent people confess?* Do innocent people really confess to crimes they did not commit? Some legal systems treat all confessions as questionable evidence by requiring "corroboration" of any confession in order to sustain a criminal conviction. See, e.g., Ark. Code §16-89-111(d). A number of psychologists have investigated the circumstances that lead people to make false confessions. A Royal Commission in Great Britain summarized the findings as follows:

> There is no way of establishing the frequency of false confessions: a retracted confession may nevertheless be true, and defendants who have made false confessions may have reasons of their own for adhering to them. However, there is now a substantial body of research which shows that there are four distinct categories of false confession:
>
> (i) people may make confessions entirely voluntarily as a result of a morbid desire for publicity or notoriety; or to relieve feelings of guilt about a real or imagined previous transgression; or because they cannot distinguish between reality and fantasy;
>
> (ii) a suspect may confess from a desire to protect someone else from interrogation and prosecution;
>
> (iii) people may see a prospect of immediate advantage from confessing (e.g., an end to questioning or release from the police station), even though the long-term consequences are far worse (the resulting confessions are termed "coerced-compliant" confessions); and

(iv) people may be persuaded temporarily by the interrogators that they really have done the act in question (the resulting confessions are termed "coerced-internalized" confessions).

Report of the Royal Commission on Criminal Justice 57 (1993) (Runciman Commission). See generally Richard Ofshe and Richard Leo, The Social Psychology of Police Interrogation: The Theory and Classification of True and False Confessions, 16 Studies L. Pol. & Socy. 189 (1997); Welsh White, False Confessions and the Constitution: Safeguards Against Untrustworthy Confessions, 32 Harv. C.R.-C.L. L. Rev. 105 (1997).

The availability of videotapes and other recordings of many interrogations in recent years has created a rich field for psychological and sociological research. Richard Ofshe and Richard Leo have used these materials to develop a model of true and false confessions that emphasizes the misuse of standard interrogation techniques as a major cause of false confessions. They pay particular attention to the "post-admission" portion of an interrogation, when a suspect provides the details that can corroborate or repudiate the suspect's admission of guilt. See Ofshe and Leo, The Decision to Confess Falsely: Rational Choice and Irrational Action, 74 Denv. U. L. Rev. 979 (1997).

Leo and Ofshe also surveyed a collection of 60 cases in which the government arrested and prosecuted a suspect based entirely on a confession that was probably false. They conclude that such confessions have a powerful influence on the later decisions of investigators, prosecutors, and triers of fact. See Richard Leo and Richard Ofshe, The Consequences of False Confessions: Deprivations of Liberty and Miscarriages of Justice in the Age of Psychological Interrogation, 88 J. Crim. L. & Criminology 429 (1998); but see Paul Cassell, The Guilty and the "Innocent": An Examination of Alleged Cases of Wrongful Conviction from False Confessions, 22 Harv. J.L. & Pub. Poly. 523 (1999) (analyzing cases of alleged false confessions and concluding that virtually all defendants were indeed guilty of the crime charged); Leo & Ofshe, The Truth About False Confessions and Advocacy Scholarship, 37 Crim. L. Bull. (July/Aug. 2001).

3. *Frequency of false confessions.* How often do suspects confess to crimes they did not commit, and how often do such false confessions lead to an erroneous conviction? Paul Cassell has estimated the number of wrongful convictions based on false confessions. He concludes that rate of wrongful convictions is "somewhere between 1 in 2,400 convictions and 1 in 90,000 convictions, depending on what assumptions one makes." Most of the wrongful convictions he identifies involve suspects with some mental impairment. Cassell, Protecting the Innocent from False Confessions and Lost Confessions—And from *Miranda,* 88 J. Crim. L. & Criminology 497, 502 (1998). For a discussion of the uncertainties involved in this sort of estimate, see Richard Leo and Richard Ofshe, Using the Innocent to Scapegoat *Miranda:* Another Reply to Paul Cassell, 88 J. Crim. L. & Criminology 557 (1998).

3. Police Lies

Police often know facts that suspects do not know and can use those facts to expose a suspect's false story or to encourage a silent suspect to talk. Sometimes police only pretend to know something: They make assertions that are untrue or unsupported, such as stating that a co-defendant has confessed or that a victim has died (or is alive). Other times police create props, in the form of physical evidence, to increase the chance of obtaining a confession. Are all police lies in the interrogation room a fair and legal part of the "often competitive enterprise of ferreting out crime"? If not, where should courts or police agencies draw the line?

■ STATE v. JOHN KELEKOLIO

849 P.2d 58 (Haw. 1993)

LEVINSON, J.

On January 6, 1991, Kelekolio, a "Handi-van" driver, allegedly kidnapped his lone passenger (hereinafter referred to as "the complainant"), drove the van he was operating into a parking lot, and sexually assaulted her. The complainant, who suffers from Down's Syndrome, is a mentally retarded woman and functions at the cognitive level of a four- to seven-year-old child. At the time, Kelekolio was transporting the complainant to her place of employment, . . . where she was receiving vocational training in food service. [Kelekolio was charged with sexual assault and kidnapping.]

The Honolulu Police Department (HPD) arrested Kelekolio on January 7, 1991, at 1:30 P.M. Because Kelekolio was transferred from the Pearl City station to the Honolulu station after dinner hours, he did not receive a meal that evening. Commencing at 8:45 A.M. on January 8, 1991, HPD Detective Dennis Kim conducted a forty-five minute interview of Kelekolio. . . .

While testifying at the voluntariness hearing and at trial, Detective Kim acknowledged that he made two false statements during Kelekolio's interview, namely that: (1) the police possessed physical evidence of sexual activity that incriminated Kelekolio; and (2) bruises on the complainant's arms and legs indicated that force had been used. Detective Kim further testified that the false statements were deliberate lies, prompted by his dissatisfaction with Kelekolio's inconsistent versions of the incident and designed to elicit a truthful statement from Kelekolio. Detective Kim explained that, at a seminar on interrogation techniques, he had been instructed to mislead suspects during interviews in order to extract truthful confessions.

In Kelekolio's fourth and final version of the incident, he admitted to Detective Kim that: (1) he had stopped the Handi-van at the parking lot; (2) the complainant had taken off her clothes; (3) he had inserted his penis into the complainant's vagina; and (4) immediately thereafter, he had withdrawn and ejaculated into the complainant's hand. Following these disclosures, Kelekolio vehemently denied any use of force despite the fact that Detective Kim had maintained that there were bruises on the complainant's body.

During the interview, Kelekolio claimed that the complainant had referred to sexual activities that she had purportedly engaged in with her "boyfriend Tony." Detective Kim disputed both that the complainant had a boyfriend and that Tony existed at all. In these respects, Detective Kim was engaging in bald assertion, inasmuch as he had no knowledge as to whether the complainant had a boyfriend or whether there was a "Tony."

[The trial court determined that Kelekolio made the statement voluntarily and admitted it into evidence at trial.] Kelekolio testified that his admissions to Detective Kim during the interview, proffered in his fourth version of the incident, were lies; rather, he testified that he had admitted to having intercourse with the complainant only to satisfy Detective Kim so that he would be allowed to go home and see his family. . . .

On appeal, Kelekolio contends that his audiotaped statement to Detective Kim was not freely and voluntarily given, but rather was "coerced." Instead of accepting his initial denial of any wrongdoing at face value, Kelekolio complains that Kim repeatedly exhorted him to tell the "whole story" and wheedled a confession out of him through trickery and lies — i.e., Kim's misrepresentations regarding (1) evidence of sexual activity implicating Kelekolio, and (2) the presence of bruises on the complainant's arms and legs, implying the use of force. Kim's tactics, Kelekolio argues, amounted to "mental or psychological" coercion, thereby rendering his consequent statement involuntary and inadmissible. We disagree.

Under the fifth amendment to the United States Constitution and article 1, section 10 of the Hawaii Constitution, "[n]o person shall . . . be compelled in any criminal case to be a witness against" himself or herself. When a confession or inculpatory statement is obtained in violation of either of these provisions, the prosecution will not be permitted to use it to secure a defendant's criminal conviction.

. . . The basic considerations that require exclusion of confessions obtained through coercion are the inherent untrustworthiness of involuntary confessions, a desire that criminal proceedings be accusatorial rather than inquisitorial and a desire that the police not become law breakers in the process of achieving society's valid law enforcement objectives. The burden is on the prosecution to show that the statement was voluntarily given and not the product of coercion. The burden is particularly heavy in cases where the defendant is under arrest. . . .

Kelekolio complains that, instead of accepting his initial denial of sexual contact of any kind with the complainant, Detective Kim repeatedly challenged the completeness of his account and enjoined him to tell "the whole story" until he finally admitted to sexual penetration. In effect, Kelekolio seeks to fault Kim for urging him to tell the truth, although he does not suggest that Kim's exhortations were accompanied by any sort of threat or promise.

Kelekolio's argument is unavailing, however, because [we have held in past cases that] mere advice from the police that it would be better for the accused to tell the truth when unaccompanied by either a threat or promise does not render a subsequent confession involuntary. This is precisely because such exhortations to tell the truth, are calculated to enhance, rather than diminish, the trustworthiness of an accused's inculpatory statement or confession. Accordingly, the proposition that a police interrogator's unwillingness to accept a suspect's initial version of events at face value amounts to "coercion" per se is not only naive and disingenuous, but falls of its own weight; were we to accept it, the legitimate right of law enforcement agencies to seek voluntary confessions would be rendered nugatory.

We next consider Kelekolio's claim that Detective Kim's use of deliberate misrepresentations regarding the existence of incriminating evidence of sexual activity and bruises on the complainant's arms and legs constituted "coercion" that was mental and psychological in nature, thereby rendering his confession involuntary.

At the outset, we note that

> [i]t is by now well established that certain interrogation techniques, either in isolation, or as applied to the unique characteristics of a particular suspect, are so offensive to a civilized system of justice that they must be condemned under the Due Process Clause of the Fourteenth Amendment. . . . To assure that the fruits of such techniques are never used to secure a conviction, due process also requires that a jury not hear a confession unless and until the trial judge or some other independent decisionmaker has determined that it was freely and voluntarily given.

Crane v. Kentucky, 476 U.S. 683 (1986). We therefore address the question whether, considering the totality of the circumstances surrounding Kelekolio's interview, Detective Kim's deliberate misrepresentations were of a character likely to produce an untrustworthy confession or of such a nature as to transform the investigative process into an "inquisition." For the reasons set forth below, we answer the question in the negative.

The current view of the United States Supreme Court on the subject appears to be reflected in Frazier v. Cupp, 394 U.S. 731 (1969). In *Frazier,* the police, in the course of questioning the petitioner (Frazier), misrepresented to him that his co-defendant (Rawls) had already confessed to the offense with which they were charged and thereafter obtained a confession from Frazier. The entire interrogation lasted slightly more than an hour. . . . On habeas corpus review of Frazier's murder conviction, the Court, through Justice Marshall, ruled as follows:

> [Frazier presses the argument] that his confession was involuntary and that it should have been excluded for that reason. The trial judge, after an evidentiary hearing during which the tape recording [of Frazier's confession] was played, could not agree with this contention, and our reading of the record does not lead us to a contrary conclusion. . . . The questioning was of short duration, and [Frazier] was a mature individual of normal intelligence. The fact that the police misrepresented the statements that Rawls had made is, while relevant, insufficient in our view to make this otherwise voluntary confession inadmissible. These cases must be decided by viewing the "totality of the circumstances," . . . and on the facts of this case we can find no error in the admission of [Frazier's] confession.

[The Court then quoted from secondary sources a general rule regarding the relation between police deception and the voluntariness of a resulting confession: Most cases reject challenges to the voluntariness of a confession when the use of subterfuge alone has no tendency to produce an untrue confession. To support such a claim, the subterfuge employed must involve a "collateral inducement which has a tendency to stimulate a confession irrespective of guilt." Annotation, Admissibility of Confession as Affected by Its Inducement through Artifice, Deception, Trickery, or Fraud, 99 A.L.R.2d 772 (1965 & Supp. 1992).]

Consistent with the foregoing annotation, compare People v. Thompson, 785 P.2d 857 (Cal. 1990) (interrogating officers falsely represented to defendant that (1) his car had been connected with scene of victim's death by tire tracks and soil samples, (2) physical evidence linked to victim found in his car, and (3) rope fibers found in his bedroom; confession held voluntary and admissible), . . . with State v. Nelson, 748 P.2d 365 (Haw. 1987) (confession extracted from defendant through "prayer and exorcism" and reference by police to biblical suggestion that "confession can save one from the wrath of God" made it "difficult to determine where the police officer ended and the savior began"; confession held involuntary and inadmissible).

In our view, the relevant case law and scholarly authority, including that cited above, is amenable to the formulation of a rule by which to measure the legitimacy of the use of "deception" by the police in eliciting confessions or inculpatory statements from suspects and arrestees. That rule, which we now adopt, is that employment by the police of deliberate falsehoods intrinsic to the facts of the alleged offense in question will be treated as one of the totality of circumstances surrounding the confession or statement to be considered in assessing its voluntariness; on the other hand, deliberate falsehoods extrinsic to the facts of the alleged offense, which are of a type reasonably likely to procure an untrue statement or to influence an accused to make a confession regardless of guilt, will be regarded as coercive per se, thus obviating the need for a "totality of circumstances" analysis of voluntariness.

Although the foregoing rule will, of course, have to be applied on a case-by-case basis, some examples of intrinsic falsehoods [that other courts have considered] would include such misrepresentations regarding the existence of incriminating evidence as (1) placement of the defendant's vehicle at the crime scene, (2) physical evidence linked to the victim found in the defendant's car, (3) discovery of the murder weapon, (4) a claim that the murder victim is still alive, (5) presence of the defendant's fingerprints on the getaway car or at the crime scene, (6) positive identification of the defendant by reliable witnesses, and (7) discovery of a nonexistent witness. Some examples [from other cases] of extrinsic falsehoods — of a type reasonably likely to procure an untrue statement or to influence an accused to make a confession regardless of guilt — would include (1) assurances of divine salvation upon confession, (2) promises of mental health treatment in exchange for a confession, (3) assurances of treatment in a "nice hospital" (in which the defendant could have his personal belongings and be visited by his girlfriend) in lieu of incarceration, in exchange for a confession, (4) promises of more favorable treatment in the event of a confession, (5) misrepresentations of legal principles, such as (a) suggesting that the defendant would have the burden of convincing a judge and jury at trial that he was "perfectly innocent" and had nothing to do with the offense, (b) misrepresenting the consequences of a "habitual offender" conviction, and (c) holding out that the defendant's confession cannot be used against him at trial, and (6) misrepresentations by an interrogating police officer, who is a close friend of the defendant, that the defendant's failure to confess will get the officer into trouble with his superiors and jeopardize the well-being of the officer's pregnant wife and children, see Spano v. New York, 360 U.S. 315 (1959).

Because Detective Kim's deliberate misrepresentations to Kelekolio were intrinsic to the facts of the present offenses and because we determine from the totality of the circumstances surrounding Kelekolio's audiotaped statement, based on our review of the entire record, that the misrepresentations were not of a type that would reasonably induce a false confession, we hold that Detective Kim's use of deception did not render Kelekolio's inculpatory statements involuntary.

Notwithstanding our holding, we emphasize that we are not purporting to enunciate a bright line per se rule that the use of intrinsic factual deception cannot, given the totality of circumstances surrounding any given statement, result in an involuntary confession. Rather, the rule that we formulate today merely declines to foreclose the admissibility of confessions, as a per se matter, procured in part through the use of this kind of deception. Such confessions remain subject to "totality of circumstances" analysis, and may still be the product of interrogation techniques that are so offensive to a civilized system of justice that they must be condemned under principles of due process.[17] . . .

Notes

1. *Police lies: majority position.* Most jurisdictions take the same view as the Hawaii court in *Kelekolio:* Only some police lies will produce a per se "coerced" confession, while others will ordinarily not be enough standing alone to make the confession inadmissible under the "totality of the circumstances." See Frazier v. Cupp, 394 U.S. 731 (1969). What would be the impact of a legal rule barring the use of any confession obtained because of police lies? See Margaret Paris, Faults, Fallacies, and the Future of Our Criminal Justice System: Trust, Lies and Interrogations, 3 Va. J. Soc. Poly. & L. 3 (1995); Deborah Young, Unnecessary Evil: Police Lying in Interrogations, 28 Conn. L. Rev. 425 (1996). Not every court categorizes police lies in the same manner as the *Kelekolio* court: "intrinsic" lies that do not produce coerced confessions standing alone, and "extrinsic" lies that do produce coerced confessions. Consider the lists in the *Kelekolio* opinion of "intrinsic" and "extrinsic" falsehoods. Do you agree that the extrinsic falsehoods are more likely to produce a false confession than the intrinsic falsehoods on the list? See State v. McConkie, 755 A.2d 1075 (Maine 2000) (involuntary statement when officer said during police station interview that suspect's statement would "stay confidential"; officers may not affirmatively mislead suspects about the uses to which their statements may be put). Will two or three lies about "intrinsic" matters combine to produce a coerced confession when a single lie about an extrinsic fact might not? See State v. Grey, 907 P.2d 951 (Mont. 1995).

2. *False physical evidence and false friends.* Is there any relevant difference between verbal lies about evidence against a defendant and the creation of false physical evidence against a suspect (for instance, forging a report from the forensics laboratory)? See Sheriff, Washoe County v. Bessey, 914 P.2d 618 (Nev. 1996) (no due process violation when interrogators use falsified report); Jerome Skolnick and Richard Leo, The Ethics of Deceptive Interrogation, 11 Crim. Just. Ethics 3 (Winter/Spring 1992). Another type of lie that especially troubles courts is the use of "false friends," when the questioner asks the suspect to confess out of friendship or sympathy. In Spano v. New York, 360 U.S. 315 (1959), cited by the *Kelekolio* court, the questioner was a friend of the suspect and stated (falsely) that if he did not obtain a statement, he would lose his job and his source of support for his family. The resulting confession was held to be involuntary.

3. *Bad confessions or bad police?* Over time the Supreme Court has shifted its views on what constitutes an "involuntary" confession for purposes of the federal constitution. In Bram v. United States, 168 U.S. 532 (1897), the Court concluded that a

17. As an example of the latter, see State v. Cayward, 552 So. 2d 971 (Fla. App. 1989) (confession extracted from sex-assault defendant through use of police-fabricated "scientific" reports purporting to establish that semen stains on victim's underwear came from defendant; court ruled that use of such "falsely contrived scientific documents" brought to mind "the horrors of less advanced centuries in our civilization when magistrates at times schemed with sovereigns to frame political rivals," being "precisely one of the parade of horribles civics teachers have long taught their pupils that our modern judicial system was designed to correct" and thereby offending "traditional notions of due process of law").

coerced confession was a violation of the Fifth Amendment's self-incrimination clause. Hence, the emphasis was on the state of mind of the suspect — the question was whether the statement was "compelled." By 1936, in Brown v. Mississippi, the Court shifted its emphasis to the due process clause as the relevant limitation on the use of coerced confessions. But the Court still seemed most concerned with interrogation practices, such as physical torture in *Brown,* that made the confession, as a matter of fact, "involuntary" and therefore quite possibly false. Later decisions indicated that the state of mind of the defendant, and the consequent risk of false confessions, was not the only concern of courts evaluating the "voluntariness" of a confession. In cases such as Rogers v. Richmond, 365 U.S. 534 (1961), the Court barred use of confessions that were obtained through trickery (a false order to arrest the suspect's ill wife). Even if police conduct does not create a risk of false confession from the defendant, some morally objectionable interrogation tactics might still lead a court to conclude that the confession was "involuntary" based on the totality of the circumstances. The Supreme Court has suggested that wrongful police coercion is "a necessary predicate to the finding that a confession is not 'voluntary'" under federal law. Colorado v. Connelly, 479 U.S. 157 (1986). If the interrogators have not acted wrongfully (for instance, in failing to appreciate a suspect's unusually limited mental capacity), then the fact that the suspect was coerced is not sufficient.

4. *How common is police lying?* One criminologist who observed more than 180 police interrogations in 1992 and 1993 noted that police officers lied to the suspect in about 30 percent of all the interrogations he observed. This technique, he concluded, was among the most effective methods of obtaining a confession or admission but it was less effective than appeals to the suspect's conscience, identifying contradictions in the story the suspect was telling, or offering excuses for the suspect's alleged conduct. Richard Leo, Inside the Interrogation Room, 86 J. Crim. L. & Criminology 266, 278 (1996). What obstacles might prevent one from learning how often police lie during interrogations? See Laurie Magid, Deceptive Police Interrogation Practices: How Far Is Too Far?, 99 Mich. L. Rev. 1168 (2001) (arguing that deception should be permitted unless it creates an unreasonable risk that an innocent person would falsely confess; until statistically sound research on random sample of confession cases demonstrates the size of this problem, no drastic limit on deceptive techniques is justified).

5. *Training police to lie.* A widely used training manual for police interrogators advises readers to accuse the suspect of committing the crime and if necessary to lie about the evidence available to the police or about other matters: "[T]he vast majority of criminal offenders are reluctant to confess and must be psychologically persuaded to do so, and, unavoidably, by interrogation procedures involving elements of trickery or deceit. The legality of such procedures is well established." Fred Inbau, John Reid, Joseph Buckley, Criminal Interrogation and Confessions 216 (3d ed. 1986). Is there a difference between this line of argument and the arguments used to justify the "third degree"? What ethical boundaries should limit police lies or unenforceable (but legally valid) promises? Christopher Slobogin has applied the work of moral philosopher Sissela Bok to the ethics of police lies during interrogations, and concludes that many lies told to "publicly-targeted suspects" are ethically justifiable, especially in cases where police begin the interrogation with strong independent grounds to suspect the target's guilt. Slobogin, Deceit, Pretext, and Trickery: Investigative Lies by the Police, 76 Or. L. Rev. 775 (1997); but see Margaret Paris, Lying to Ourselves, 76 Or. L. Rev. 817 (1997) (applying Bok's framework to conclude

that almost all police lies during interrogations are ethically unjustified because investigators have alternatives to lying). Consider the ethics implicit in the observation of Justice Hugo Black dissenting in a case involving the enforcement of treaties with Native Americans: "Great nations, like great men, should keep their word," FPC v. Tuscarora Indian Nation, 362 U.S. 99 (1960) (Black, J., dissenting).

B. *MIRANDA* WARNINGS

It can be very difficult for a court to determine after the fact whether a confession was "voluntary." In a series of cases between 1936 and 1964, the Supreme Court attempted to highlight the various facts that might, in the "totality of the circumstances," deprive the suspect of the "power of resistance." Fikes v. Alabama, 352 U.S. 191 (1957). As the cases proliferated, it became clear that a great many facts could be relevant to the question of voluntariness. The Supreme Court, perhaps out of frustration with the repeated and difficult application of the "voluntariness" test it had created under the due process clause, began a search in the late 1950s for a more effective and easily administered method of stopping interrogation abuses.

The Court turned first to the possibility of requiring defense lawyers to be present during at least some interrogations. In a series of opinions, several members of the Court indicated that due process required that any suspect in custody should be able to obtain an attorney from the moment of arrest. See Spano v. New York, 360 U.S. 315 (1959). These tentative suggestions soon led to a holding, under the Sixth Amendment right to counsel (rather than the due process clause), that defendants in at least some interrogations had the right to have an attorney present. In Massiah v. United States, 377 U.S. 201 (1964), the defendant had already been indicted for violating narcotics laws and had retained defense counsel when the government recruited his friend to collect more evidence against him. The government placed a radio transmitter in his friend's car. Then the friend struck up a conversation with Massiah in the car about the crimes.

The Court invalidated the use of the confession that Massiah made in the car. The use of the confession at trial, the Court said, violated Massiah's Sixth Amendment right to counsel in all "criminal proceedings." Although these circumstances did not amount to physical or psychological coercion under the customary due process analysis, the Court said that an effective right to counsel "must apply to indirect and surreptitious interrogations as well as those conducted in the jailhouse." The *Massiah* decision created a method for courts to invalidate confessions on the basis of a clear rule, one that could apply regardless of the conditions during the interrogation. But if the rule were applied only to suspects who have already been indicted or to those who are tricked into a confession outside the police station, its impact would be small.

The right to counsel during custodial interrogations occurring *before* indictment received its clearest declaration in Escobedo v. Illinois, 378 U.S. 478 (1964), decided just weeks after *Massiah*. The investigators in that murder case obtained a confession from Escobedo by preventing him from consulting with his retained attorney (who was present at the police station) during the interrogation. The investigators kept Escobedo handcuffed and standing during the interrogation, and they arranged a confrontation with a second suspect, who accused Escobedo of the killing.

Some of the language in the opinion referred broadly to the importance of the presence of counsel at interrogation, which the Court now called a "critical stage" in the criminal process and which was thus covered by the Sixth Amendment right to counsel during a "prosecution." The opinion suggested that all interrogations of persons in custody would have to take place in the presence of counsel:

> The right to counsel would indeed be hollow if it began at a period when few confessions were obtained. There is necessarily a direct relationship between the importance of a stage to the police in their quest for a confession and the criticalness of that stage to the accused in his need for legal advice. [N]o system worth preserving should have to fear that if an accused is permitted to consult with a lawyer, he will become aware of, and exercise, these rights. [378 U.S. at 488.]

However, the opinion also lent itself to a narrower reading by emphasizing some of the distinctive facts of the case in its holding:

> We hold, therefore, that where, as here, the investigation is no longer a general inquiry into an unsolved crime but has begun to focus on a particular suspect, the suspect has been taken into police custody, the police carry out a process of interrogations that lends itself to eliciting incriminating statements, the suspect has requested and been denied an opportunity to consult with his lawyer, and the police have not effectively warned him of his absolute constitutional right to remain silent, the accused has been denied "the Assistance of Counsel" in violation of the Sixth Amendment to the Constitution . . . and that no statement elicited by the police during the interrogation may be used against him at a criminal trial. [378 U.S. at 490-491.]

Escobedo suggested the possibility that the Sixth Amendment might require the government to provide suspects with counsel before any interrogation, and the decision sparked a national debate among state courts. Most states restricted the holding to situations in which a defendant had requested counsel, but some states tried to forecast the direction of the Supreme Court and required the government to provide counsel when an interrogation reached the "accusatory" or "critical" stage. See People v. Dorado, 394 P.2d 952 (Cal. 1964) ("The defendant who does not realize his rights under the law and who therefore does not request counsel is the very defendant who most needs counsel"); Neuenfeldt v. State, 138 N.W.2d 252 (Wis. 1965). A few states went in a different direction, requiring police to advise suspects about their right to assistance of counsel and their right to remain silent. See State v. Mendes, 210 A.2d 50 (R.I. 1965). In 1966, two years after *Escobedo,* the Supreme Court decided Miranda v. Arizona.

1. The Miranda *Revolution*

■ ERNESTO MIRANDA v. ARIZONA

384 U.S. 436 (1966)

WARREN, C.J.

The cases before us raise questions which go to the roots of our concepts of American criminal jurisprudence: the restraints society must observe consistent with the Federal Constitution in prosecuting individuals for crime. More specifically, we deal with the admissibility of statements obtained from an individual who is subjected to custodial police interrogation and the necessity for procedures which assure that the individual is accorded his privilege under the Fifth Amendment to the Constitution not to be compelled to incriminate himself.

We dealt with certain phases of this problem recently in Escobedo v. Illinois, 378 U.S. 478 (1964). We granted certiorari in these cases [to explore some facets of the problems] of applying the privilege against self-incrimination to in-custody interrogation, and to give concrete constitutional guidelines for law enforcement agencies and courts to follow. . . .

We start here, as we did in *Escobedo,* with the premise that our holding is not an innovation in our jurisprudence, but is an application of principles long recognized and applied in other settings. . . . Our holding will be spelled out with some specificity in the pages which follow but briefly stated it is this: the prosecution may not use statements, whether exculpatory or inculpatory, stemming from custodial interrogation of the defendant unless it demonstrates the use of procedural safeguards effective to secure the privilege against self-incrimination. By custodial interrogation, we mean questioning initiated by law enforcement officers after a person has been taken into custody or otherwise deprived of his freedom of action in any significant way.[4] As for the procedural safeguards to be employed, unless other fully effective means are devised to inform accused persons of their right of silence and to assure a continuous opportunity to exercise it, the following measures are required. Prior to any questioning, the person must be warned that he has a right to remain silent, that any statement he does make may be used as evidence against him, and that he has a right to the presence of an attorney, either retained or appointed. The defendant may waive effectuation of these rights, provided the waiver is made voluntarily, knowingly and intelligently. If, however, he indicates in any manner and at any stage of the process that he wishes to consult with an attorney before speaking there can be no questioning. Likewise, if the individual is alone and indicates in any manner that he does not wish to be interrogated, the police may not question him. The mere fact that he may have answered some questions or volunteered some statements on his own does not deprive him of the right to refrain from answering any further inquiries until he has consulted with an attorney and thereafter consents to be questioned.

I.

The constitutional issue we decide in each of these cases is the admissibility of statements obtained from a defendant questioned while in custody or otherwise deprived of his freedom of action in any significant way. In each, the defendant was questioned by police officers, detectives, or a prosecuting attorney in a room in which he was cut off from the outside world. In none of these cases was the defendant given a full and effective warning of his rights at the outset of the interrogation process. In all the cases, the questioning elicited oral admissions, and in three of them, signed statements as well which were admitted at their trials. They all thus share salient features — incommunicado interrogation of individuals in a

4. This is what we meant in *Escobedo* when we spoke of an investigation which had focused on an accused.

police-dominated atmosphere, resulting in self-incriminating statements without full warnings of constitutional rights.

An understanding of the nature and setting of this in-custody interrogation is essential to our decisions today. . . . From extensive factual studies undertaken in the early 1930's . . . it is clear that police violence and the "third degree" flourished at that time. [These practices] are undoubtedly the exception now, but they are sufficiently widespread to be the object of concern. Unless a proper limitation upon custodial interrogation is achieved — such as these decisions will advance — there can be no assurance that practices of this nature will be eradicated in the foreseeable future. [Furthermore, this] Court has recognized that coercion can be mental as well as physical, and that the blood of the accused is not the only hallmark of an unconstitutional inquisition.

Interrogation still takes place in privacy. Privacy results in secrecy and this in turn results in a gap in our knowledge as to what in fact goes on in the interrogation rooms. A valuable source of information about present police practices, however, may be found in various police manuals and texts which document procedures employed with success in the past, and which recommend various other effective tactics. These texts are used by law enforcement agencies themselves as guides.[9] . . .

The officers are told by the manuals that the "principal psychological factor contributing to a successful interrogation is privacy — being alone with the person under interrogation." The efficacy of this tactic has been explained as follows:

> [The subject] is more keenly aware of his rights and more reluctant to tell of his indiscretions or criminal behavior within the walls of his home. Moreover his family and other friends are nearby, their presence lending moral support. In his own office, the investigator possesses all the advantages. The atmosphere suggests the invincibility of the forces of the law.

To highlight the isolation and unfamiliar surroundings, the manuals instruct the police to display an air of confidence in the suspect's guilt and from outward appearance to maintain only an interest in confirming certain details. The guilt of the subject is to be posited as a fact. The interrogator should direct his comments toward the reasons why the subject committed the act, rather than court failure by asking the subject whether he did it. Like other men, perhaps the subject has had a bad family life, had an unhappy childhood, had too much to drink, had an unrequited desire for women. The officers are instructed to minimize the moral seriousness of the offense, to cast blame on the victim or on society. These tactics are designed to put the subject in a psychological state where his story is but an elaboration of what the police purport to know already — that he is guilty. Explanations to the contrary are dismissed and discouraged. . . .

9. The methods described in Inbau & Reid, Criminal Interrogation and Confessions (1962), are a revision and enlargement of material presented in three prior editions of a predecessor text, Lie Detection and Criminal Interrogation (3d ed. 1953). The authors and their associates are officers of the Chicago Police Scientific Crime Detection Laboratory and [they] say that the techniques portrayed in their manuals reflect their experiences. [This manual, together with O'Hara, Fundamentals of Criminal Investigation (1956),] have had rather extensive use among law enforcement agencies and among students of police science, with total sales and circulation of over 44,000.

When the techniques described above prove unavailing, the texts recommend they be alternated with a show of some hostility. One ploy often used has been termed the "friendly-unfriendly" or the "Mutt and Jeff" act:

> In this technique, two agents are employed. Mutt, the relentless investigator, who knows the subject is guilty and is not going to waste any time. . . . Jeff, on the other hand, is obviously a kindhearted man. He has a family himself. He has a brother who was involved in a little scrape like this. He disapproves of Mutt and his tactics and will arrange to get him off the case if the subject will cooperate. He can't hold Mutt off for very long. The subject would be wise to make a quick decision. . . .

The manuals also contain instructions for police on how to handle the individual who refuses to discuss the matter entirely, or who asks for an attorney or relatives. The examiner is to concede him the right to remain silent. "This usually has a very undermining effect. [A] concession of this right to remain silent impresses the subject with the apparent fairness of his interrogator." After this psychological conditioning, however, the officer is told to point out the incriminating significance of the suspect's refusal to talk:

> Joe, you have a right to remain silent. That's your privilege and I'm the last person in the world who'll try to take it away from you. . . . But let me ask you this. Suppose you were in my shoes and I were in yours and you called me in to ask me about this and I told you, "I don't want to answer any of your questions." You'd think I had something to hide, and you'd probably be right in thinking that. That's exactly what I'll have to think about you, and so will everybody else. So let's sit here and talk this whole thing over. . . .

In the event that the subject wishes to speak to a relative or an attorney, the following advice is tendered:

> The interrogator should respond by suggesting that the subject first tell the truth to the interrogator himself rather than get anyone else involved in the matter. If the request is for an attorney, the interrogator may suggest that the subject save himself or his family the expense of any such professional service, particularly if he is innocent of the offense under investigation. The interrogator may also add, "Joe, I'm only looking for the truth, and if you're telling the truth, that's it. You can handle this by yourself."

From these representative samples of interrogation techniques, the setting prescribed by the manuals and observed in practice becomes clear. . . . Even without employing brutality, the "third degree" or the specific stratagems described above, the very fact of custodial interrogation exacts a heavy toll on individual liberty and trades on the weakness of individuals. . . .

In these cases, we might not find the defendants' statements to have been involuntary in traditional terms. Our concern for adequate safeguards to protect precious Fifth Amendment rights is, of course, not lessened in the slightest. In each of the cases, the defendant was thrust into an unfamiliar atmosphere and run through menacing police interrogation procedures. The potentiality for compulsion is forcefully apparent, for example, in State v. Miranda, 401 P.2d 721 (Ariz. 1965), where the indigent Mexican defendant was a seriously disturbed individual with pronounced sexual fantasies, and in People v. Stewart, 400 P.2d 97 (Cal. 1965), in which the defendant was an indigent Los Angeles Negro who had dropped out of school in the sixth grade. [I]n none of these cases did the officers undertake to afford appropriate safeguards at the outset of the interrogation to insure that the statements were truly the product of free choice. . . .

The current practice of incommunicado interrogation is at odds with one of our Nation's most cherished principles — that the individual may not be compelled to incriminate himself. Unless adequate protective devices are employed to dispel the compulsion inherent in custodial surroundings, no statement obtained from the defendant can truly be the product of his free choice. From the foregoing, we can readily perceive an intimate connection between the privilege against self-incrimination and police custodial questioning. . . .

II.

[T]he constitutional foundation underlying the privilege is the respect a government — state or federal — must accord to the dignity and integrity of its citizens. To maintain a fair state-individual balance, to require the government to shoulder the entire load, to respect the inviolability of the human personality, our accusatory system of criminal justice demands that the government seeking to punish an individual produce the evidence against him by its own independent labors, rather than by the cruel, simple expedient of compelling it from his own mouth. In sum, the privilege is fulfilled only when the person is guaranteed the right to remain silent unless he chooses to speak in the unfettered exercise of his own will.

The question in these cases is whether the privilege is fully applicable during a period of custodial interrogation. . . . An individual swept from familiar surroundings into police custody, surrounded by antagonistic forces, and subjected to the techniques of persuasion described above cannot be otherwise than under compulsion to speak. As a practical matter, the compulsion to speak in the isolated setting of the police station may well be greater than in courts or other official investigations, where there are often impartial observers to guard against intimidation or trickery. . . .

Our holding [in *Escobedo*] stressed the fact that the police had not advised the defendant of his constitutional privilege to remain silent at the outset of the interrogation. . . . A different phase of the *Escobedo* decision was significant in its attention to the absence of counsel during the questioning. [And] *Escobedo* explicated another facet of the pre-trial privilege, noted in many of the Court's prior decisions: the protection of rights at trial. That counsel is present when statements are taken from an individual during interrogation obviously enhances the integrity of the fact-finding processes in court. . . . Without the protections flowing from adequate warnings and the rights of counsel, all the careful safeguards erected around the giving of testimony, whether by an accused or any other witness, would become empty formalities in a procedure where the most compelling possible evidence of guilt, a confession, would have already been obtained at the unsupervised pleasure of the police. . . .

III.

It is impossible for us to foresee the potential alternatives for protecting the privilege which might be devised by Congress or the States in the exercise of their creative rule-making capacities. Therefore we cannot say that the Constitution necessarily requires adherence to any particular solution for the inherent compulsions of the interrogation process as it is presently conducted. Our decision in no way creates a constitutional straitjacket which will handicap sound efforts at reform, nor is it intended to have this effect. . . . However, unless we are shown other procedures which are at least as effective in apprising accused persons of their right of silence and in assuring a continuous opportunity to exercise it, the following safeguards must be observed.

At the outset, if a person in custody is to be subjected to interrogation, he must first be informed in clear and unequivocal terms that he has the right to remain silent. For those unaware of the privilege, the warning is needed simply to make them aware of it — the threshold requirement for an intelligent decision as to its exercise. More important, such a warning is an absolute prerequisite in overcoming the inherent pressures of the interrogation atmosphere. It is not just the subnormal or woefully ignorant who succumb to an interrogator's imprecations, whether implied or expressly stated, that the interrogation will continue until a confession is obtained or that silence in the face of accusation is itself damning and will bode ill when presented to a jury.[37] . . . The Fifth Amendment privilege is so fundamental to our system of constitutional rule and the expedient of giving an adequate warning as to the availability of the privilege so simple, we will not pause to inquire in individual cases whether the defendant was aware of his rights without a warning being given. . . .

The warning of the right to remain silent must be accompanied by the explanation that anything said can and will be used against the individual in court. This warning is needed in order to make him aware not only of the privilege, but also of the consequences of forgoing it. It is only through an awareness of these consequences that there can be any assurance of real understanding and intelligent exercise of the privilege. Moreover, this warning may serve to make the individual more acutely aware that . . . he is not in the presence of persons acting solely in his interest.

The circumstances surrounding in-custody interrogation can operate very quickly to overbear the will of one merely made aware of his privilege by his interrogators. Therefore, the right to have counsel present at the interrogation is indispensable to the protection of the Fifth Amendment privilege under the system we delineate today. Our aim is to assure that the individual's right to choose between silence and speech remains unfettered throughout the interrogation process. A once-stated warning, delivered by those who will conduct the interrogation, cannot itself suffice to that end among those who most require knowledge of their rights. . . . Even preliminary advice given to the accused by his own attorney can be swiftly overcome by the secret interrogation process. Thus, the need for counsel to protect the Fifth Amendment privilege comprehends not merely a right to consult with counsel prior to questioning, but also to have counsel present during any questioning if the defendant so desires.

The presence of counsel at the interrogation may serve several significant subsidiary functions as well. If the accused decides to talk to his interrogators, the assistance of counsel can mitigate the dangers of untrustworthiness. With a lawyer present the likelihood that the police will practice coercion is reduced, and if

37. [In] accord with our decision today, it is impermissible to penalize an individual for exercising his Fifth Amendment privilege when he is under police custodial interrogation. The prosecution may not, therefore, use at trial the fact that he stood mute or claimed his privilege in the face of accusation.

coercion is nevertheless exercised the lawyer can testify to it in court. The presence of a lawyer can also help to guarantee that the accused gives a fully accurate statement to the police and that the statement is rightly reported by the prosecution at trial.

[An individual's] failure to ask for a lawyer does not constitute a waiver. No effective waiver of the right to counsel during interrogation can be recognized unless specifically made after the warnings we here delineate have been given. The accused who does not know his rights and therefore does not make a request may be the person who most needs counsel. . . .

Accordingly we hold that an individual held for interrogation must be clearly informed that he has the right to consult with a lawyer and to have the lawyer with him during interrogation under the system for protecting the privilege we delineate today. As with the warnings of the right to remain silent and that anything stated can be used in evidence against him, this warning is an absolute prerequisite to interrogation. . . .

If an individual indicates that he wishes the assistance of counsel before any interrogation occurs, the authorities cannot rationally ignore or deny his request on the basis that the individual does not have or cannot afford a retained attorney. The financial ability of the individual has no relationship to the scope of the rights involved here. The privilege against self-incrimination secured by the Constitution applies to all individuals. . . . In fact, were we to limit these constitutional rights to those who can retain an attorney, our decisions today would be of little significance. The cases before us as well as the vast majority of confession cases with which we have dealt in the past involve those unable to retain counsel. . . .

In order fully to apprise a person interrogated of the extent of his rights under this system then, it is necessary to warn him not only that he has the right to consult with an attorney, but also that if he is indigent a lawyer will be appointed to represent him. Without this additional warning, the admonition of the right to consult with counsel would often be understood as meaning only that he can consult with a lawyer if he has one or has the funds to obtain one. . . .

Once warnings have been given, the subsequent procedure is clear. If the individual indicates in any manner, at any time prior to or during questioning, that he wishes to remain silent, the interrogation must cease. At this point he has shown that he intends to exercise his Fifth Amendment privilege; any statement taken after the person invokes his privilege cannot be other than the product of compulsion, subtle or otherwise. Without the right to cut off questioning, the setting of in-custody interrogation operates on the individual to overcome free choice in producing a statement after the privilege has been once invoked. If the individual states that he wants an attorney, the interrogation must cease until an attorney is present. At that time, the individual must have an opportunity to confer with the attorney and to have him present during any subsequent questioning. If the individual cannot obtain an attorney and he indicates that he wants one before speaking to police, they must respect his decision to remain silent.

This does not mean, as some have suggested, that each police station must have a "station house lawyer" present at all times to advise prisoners. It does mean, however, that if police propose to interrogate a person they must make known to him that he is entitled to a lawyer and that if he cannot afford one, a lawyer will be provided for him prior to any interrogation. . . . If the interrogation continues without the presence of an attorney and a statement is taken, a heavy burden rests on the government to demonstrate that the defendant knowingly and intelligently waived his privilege against self-incrimination and his right to retained or appointed counsel. . . .

An express statement that the individual is willing to make a statement and does not want an attorney followed closely by a statement could constitute a waiver. But a valid waiver will not be presumed simply from the silence of the accused after warnings are given or simply from the fact that a confession was in fact eventually obtained. . . . Moreover, where in-custody interrogation is involved, there is no room for the contention that the privilege is waived if the individual answers some questions or gives some information on his own prior to invoking his right to remain silent when interrogated.

Whatever the testimony of the authorities as to waiver of rights by an accused, the fact of lengthy interrogation or incommunicado incarceration before a statement is made is strong evidence that the accused did not validly waive his rights. . . . Moreover, any evidence that the accused was threatened, tricked, or cajoled into a waiver will, of course, show that the defendant did not voluntarily waive his privilege. The requirement of warnings and waiver of rights is a fundamental with respect to the Fifth Amendment privilege and not simply a preliminary ritual to existing methods of interrogation. . . .

The principles announced today deal with the protection which must be given to the privilege against self-incrimination when the individual is first subjected to police interrogation while in custody at the station or otherwise deprived of his freedom of action in any significant way. It is at this point that our adversary system of criminal proceedings commences, distinguishing itself at the outset from the inquisitorial system recognized in some countries. . . .

Our decision is not intended to hamper the traditional function of police officers in investigating crime. When an individual is in custody on probable cause, the police may, of course, seek out evidence in the field to be used at trial against him. Such investigation may include inquiry of persons not under restraint. General on-the-scene questioning as to facts surrounding a crime or other general questioning of citizens in the fact-finding process is not affected by our holding. . . .

In dealing with statements obtained through interrogation, we do not purport to find all confessions inadmissible. Confessions remain a proper element in law enforcement. Any statement given freely and voluntarily without any compelling influences is, of course, admissible in evidence. . . .

IV.

In announcing these principles, we are not unmindful of the burdens which law enforcement officials must bear, often under trying circumstances. [O]ur decision does not in any way preclude police from carrying out their traditional investigatory functions. Although confessions may play an important role in some convictions, the cases before us present graphic examples of the overstatement of the "need" for confessions. In each case authorities conducted interrogations ranging up to five days in duration despite the presence, through standard investigating practices, of considerable evidence against each defendant. . . .

Over the years the Federal Bureau of Investigation has compiled an exemplary record of effective law enforcement while advising any suspect or arrested person, at the outset of an interview, that he is not required to make a statement, that any statement may be used against him in court, that the individual may obtain the services of an attorney of his own choice and, more recently, that he has a right to free counsel if he is unable to pay. . . .

The experience in some other countries also suggests that the danger to law enforcement in curbs on interrogation is overplayed. The English procedure since 1912 under the Judges' Rules is significant. As recently strengthened, the Rules require that a cautionary warning be given an accused by a police officer as soon as he has evidence that affords reasonable grounds for suspicion; they also require that any statement made be given by the accused without questioning by police. The right of the individual to consult with an attorney during this period is expressly recognized. . . .

It is also urged upon us that we withhold decision on this issue until state legislative bodies and advisory groups have had an opportunity to deal with these problems by rule making. We have already pointed out that the Constitution does not require any specific code of procedures for protecting the privilege against self-incrimination during custodial interrogation. Congress and the States are free to develop their own safeguards for the privilege, so long as they are fully as effective as those described above in informing accused persons of their right of silence and in affording a continuous opportunity to exercise it. In any event, however, the issues presented are of constitutional dimensions and must be determined by the courts. . . .

V.

Because of the nature of the problem and because of its recurrent significance in numerous cases, we have to this point discussed the relationship of the Fifth Amendment privilege to police interrogation without specific concentration on the facts of the cases before us. We turn now to these facts to consider the application to these cases of the constitutional principles discussed above. . . .

On March 13, 1963, petitioner, Ernesto Miranda, was arrested at his home and taken in custody to a Phoenix police station. He was there identified by the complaining witness. The police then took him to Interrogation Room No. 2 of the detective bureau. There he was questioned by two police officers. The officers admitted at trial that Miranda was not advised that he had a right to have an attorney present. Two hours later, the officers emerged from the interrogation room with a written confession signed by Miranda. At the top of the statement was a typed paragraph stating that the confession was made voluntarily, without threats or promises of immunity and "with full knowledge of my legal rights, understanding any statement I make may be used against me."[67]

At his trial before a jury, the written confession was admitted into evidence over the objection of defense counsel, and the officers testified to the prior oral confession made by Miranda during the interrogation. Miranda was found guilty of kidnapping and rape. He was sentenced to 20 to 30 years' imprisonment on each count, the sentences to run concurrently. On appeal, the Supreme Court of Arizona held that Miranda's constitutional rights were not violated in obtaining the confession

67. One of the officers testified that he read this paragraph to Miranda. Apparently, however, he did not do so until after Miranda had confessed orally.

and affirmed the conviction. In reaching its decision, the court emphasized heavily the fact that Miranda did not specifically request counsel.

We reverse. From the testimony of the officers and by the admission of respondent, it is clear that Miranda was not in any way apprised of his right to consult with an attorney and to have one present during the interrogation, nor was his right not to be compelled to incriminate himself effectively protected in any other manner. Without these warnings the statements were inadmissible. The mere fact that he signed a statement which contained a typed-in clause stating that he had "full knowledge" of his "legal rights" does not approach the knowing and intelligent waiver required to relinquish constitutional rights. . . .

HARLAN, J., dissenting.

[T]he new rules are not designed to guard against police brutality or other unmistakably banned forms of coercion. Those who use third-degree tactics and deny them in court are equally able and destined to lie as skillfully about warnings and waivers. Rather, the thrust of the new rules is to negate all pressures, to reinforce the nervous or ignorant suspect, and ultimately to discourage any confession at all. The aim in short is toward "voluntariness" in a utopian sense, or to view it from a different angle, voluntariness with a vengeance. To incorporate this notion into the Constitution requires a strained reading of history and precedent and a disregard of the very pragmatic concerns that alone may on occasion justify such strains. . . .

It is most fitting to begin an inquiry into the constitutional precedents by surveying the limits on confessions the Court has evolved under the Due Process Clause of the Fourteenth Amendment. This is so because these cases show that there exists a workable and effective means of dealing with confessions in a judicial manner. . . .

The earliest confession cases in this Court emerged from federal prosecutions and were settled on a nonconstitutional basis, the Court adopting the common-law rule that the absence of inducements, promises, and threats made a confession voluntary and admissible. [A] new line of decisions, testing admissibility by the Due Process Clause, began in 1936 with Brown v. Mississippi, and must now embrace somewhat more than 30 full opinions of the Court. While the voluntariness rubric was repeated in many instances, the Court never pinned it down to a single meaning but on the contrary infused it with a number of different values. To travel quickly over the main themes, there was an initial emphasis on reliability, supplemented by concern over the legality and fairness of the police practices, in an "accusatorial" system of law enforcement, and eventually by close attention to the individual's state of mind and capacity for effective choice. The outcome was a continuing re-evaluation on the facts of each case of how much pressure on the suspect was permissible.

Among the criteria often taken into account were threats or imminent danger, physical deprivations such as lack of sleep or food, repeated or extended interrogation, limits on access to counsel or friends, length and illegality of detention under state law, and individual weakness or incapacities. Apart from direct physical coercion, however, no single default or fixed combination of defaults guaranteed exclusion, and synopses of the cases would serve little use because the overall gauge has been steadily changing, usually in the direction of restricting admissibility. . . .

There are several relevant lessons to be drawn from this constitutional history. The first is that with over 25 years of precedent the Court has developed an elaborate, sophisticated, and sensitive approach to admissibility of confessions. It is "judicial" in its treatment of one case at a time, flexible in its ability to respond to the endless mutations of fact presented, and ever more familiar to the lower courts. Of course, strict certainty is not obtained in this developing process, but this is often so with constitutional principles, and disagreement is usually confined to that borderland of close cases where it matters least.

The second point is that in practice and from time to time in principle, the Court has given ample recognition to society's interest in suspect questioning as an instrument of law enforcement. Cases countenancing quite significant pressures can be cited without difficulty, and the lower courts may often have been yet more tolerant. . . .

I turn now to the Court's asserted reliance on the Fifth Amendment, an approach which I frankly regard as a *trompe l'oeil.* The Court's opinion in my view reveals no adequate basis for extending the Fifth Amendment's privilege against self-incrimination to the police station. Far more important, it fails to show that the Court's new rules are well supported, let alone compelled, by Fifth Amendment precedents. . . .

Examined as an expression of public policy, the Court's new regime proves so dubious that there can be no due compensation for its weakness in constitutional law. [The] Court has not and cannot make the powerful showing that its new rules are plainly desirable in the context of our society, something which is surely demanded before those rules are engrafted onto the Constitution and imposed on every State and county in the land.

Without at all subscribing to the generally black picture of police conduct painted by the Court, I think it must be frankly recognized at the outset that police questioning allowable under due process precedents may inherently entail some pressure on the suspect and may seek advantage in his ignorance or weaknesses. The atmosphere and questioning techniques, proper and fair though they be, can in themselves exert a tug on the suspect to confess, and in this light to speak of any confessions of crime made after arrest as being "voluntary" or "uncoerced" is somewhat inaccurate, although traditional. . . . The Court's new rules aim to offset these minor pressures and disadvantages intrinsic to any kind of police interrogation. . . .

What the Court largely ignores is that its rules impair, if they will not eventually serve wholly to frustrate, an instrument of law enforcement that has long and quite reasonably been thought worth the price paid for it. There can be little doubt that the Court's new code would markedly decrease the number of confessions. To warn the suspect that he may remain silent and remind him that his confession may be used in court are minor obstructions. To require also an express waiver by the suspect and an end to questioning whenever he demurs must heavily handicap questioning. And to suggest or provide counsel for the suspect simply invites the end of the interrogation. . . .

While passing over the costs and risks of its experiment, the Court portrays the evils of normal police questioning in terms which I think are exaggerated. Albeit stringently confined by the due process standards interrogation is no doubt often inconvenient and unpleasant for the suspect. However, it is no less so for a man to be arrested and jailed, to have his house searched, or to stand trial in court, yet all this may properly happen to the most innocent given probable cause, a warrant, or an indictment. Society has always paid a stiff price for law and order, and peaceful interrogation is not one of the dark moments of the law. . . .

It is also instructive to compare the attitude in this case of those responsible for law enforcement with the official views that existed when the Court undertook . . .

major revisions of prosecutorial practice prior to this case. . . In Mapp v. Ohio, 367 U.S. 643 (1961), which imposed the exclusionary rule on the States for Fourth Amendment violations, more than half of the States had themselves already adopted some such rule. In Gideon v. Wainwright, 372 U.S. 335 (1963), . . . an amicus brief was filed by 22 States and Commonwealths urging that [the Court extend the right to counsel to indigents in state court]; only two States besides that of the respondent came forward to protest. By contrast, in this case new restrictions on police questioning have been opposed by the United States and in an amicus brief signed by 27 States and Commonwealths, not including the three other States which are parties. No State in the country has urged this Court to impose the newly announced rules, nor has any State chosen to go nearly so far on its own. [T]he FBI falls sensibly short of the Court's formalistic rules. For example, there is no indication that FBI agents must obtain an affirmative "waiver" before they pursue their questioning. . . .

In closing this [discussion] of policy considerations attending the new confession rules, some reference must be made to their ironic untimeliness. There is now in progress in this country a massive re-examination of criminal law enforcement procedures on a scale never before witnessed. [L]egislative reform is rarely speedy or unanimous, though this Court has been more patient in the past. But the legislative reforms when they come would have the vast advantage of empirical data and comprehensive study, they would allow experimentation and use of solutions not open to the courts, and they would restore the initiative in criminal law reform to those forums where it truly belongs. . . .

WHITE, J., dissenting.

Decisions like these cannot rest alone on syllogism, metaphysics or some ill-defined notions of natural justice, although each will perhaps play its part. . . . First, we may inquire what are the textual and factual bases of this new fundamental rule. To reach the result announced on the grounds it does, the Court must stay within the confines of the Fifth Amendment, which forbids self-incrimination only if compelled. [T]he Court concedes that it cannot truly know what occurs during custodial questioning, because of the innate secrecy of such proceedings. It extrapolates a picture of what it conceives to be the norm from police investigatorial manuals. . . . Judged by any of the standards for empirical investigation utilized in the social sciences the factual basis for the Court's premise is patently inadequate. . . .

Even if one were to postulate that the Court's concern is not that all confessions induced by police interrogation are coerced but rather that some such confessions are coerced and present judicial procedures are believed to be inadequate to identify the confessions that are coerced and those that are not, it would still not be essential to impose the rule that the Court has now fashioned. Transcripts or observers could be required, specific time limits, tailored to fit the cause, could be imposed, or other devices could be utilized to reduce the chances that otherwise indiscernible coercion will produce an inadmissible confession.

On the other hand, even if one assumed that there was an adequate factual basis for the conclusion that all confessions obtained during in-custody interrogation are the product of compulsion, the rule propounded by the Court would still be irrational, for, apparently, it is only if the accused is also warned of his right to counsel and waives both that right and the right against self-incrimination that the inherent compulsiveness of interrogation disappears. But if the defendant may not answer without a warning a question such as "Where were you last night?" without having his answer be a compelled one, how can the Court ever accept his negative answer to the question of whether he wants to consult his retained counsel or counsel whom the court will appoint? . . .

The obvious underpinning of the Court's decision is a deep-seated distrust of all confessions. As the Court declares that the accused may not be interrogated without counsel present, absent a waiver of the right to counsel, and as the Court all but admonishes the lawyer to advise the accused to remain silent, the result adds up to a judicial judgment that evidence from the accused should not be used against him in any way, whether compelled or not. . . . I see nothing wrong or immoral, and certainly nothing unconstitutional, in the police's asking a suspect whom they have reasonable cause to arrest whether or not he killed his wife or in confronting him with the evidence on which the arrest was based, at least where he has been plainly advised that he may remain completely silent. . . . Particularly when corroborated, as where the police have confirmed the accused's disclosure of the hiding place of implements or fruits of the crime, such confessions have the highest reliability and significantly contribute to the certitude with which we may believe the accused is guilty. Moreover, it is by no means certain that the process of confessing is injurious to the accused. To the contrary it may provide psychological relief and enhance the prospects for rehabilitation. . . .

Much of the trouble with the Court's new rule is that it will operate indiscriminately in all criminal cases, regardless of the severity of the crime or the circumstances involved. It applies to every defendant, whether the professional criminal or one committing a crime of momentary passion. [It cannot] be claimed that judicial time and effort, assuming that is a relevant consideration, will be conserved because of the ease of application of the new rule. Today's decision leaves open such questions as whether the accused was in custody, whether his statements were spontaneous or the product of interrogation, whether the accused has effectively waived his rights, and whether nontestimonial evidence introduced at trial is the fruit of statements made during a prohibited interrogation. [I]f further restrictions on police interrogation are desirable at this time, a more flexible approach makes much more sense than the Court's constitutional straitjacket which forecloses more discriminating treatment by legislative or rule-making pronouncements. . . .

■ LOUISIANA CONSTITUTION ART. 1, §13

When any person has been arrested or detained in connection with the investigation or commission of any offense, he shall be advised fully of the reasons for his arrest or detention, his right to remain silent, his right against self incrimination, his right to the assistance of counsel and, if indigent, his right to court appointed counsel.

■ MASSACHUSETTS GENERAL LAWS, CH. 276, §33A

The police official in charge of the station or other place of detention having a telephone wherein a person is held in custody, shall permit the use of the telephone, at the expense of the arrested person, for the purpose of allowing the arrested person to communicate with his family or friends, or to arrange for release on bail, or to engage the services of an attorney. Any such person shall be informed forthwith upon his arrival at such station or place of detention, of his right to so use the telephone, and such use shall be permitted within one hour thereafter.

Notes

1. *The constitutional basis for* Miranda. What is the legal basis of the *Miranda* decision? The Court indicated that the warnings and the right to counsel it was announcing were requirements of the Fifth Amendment's self-incrimination clause. Later, the Court refined this position and stated that the *Miranda* rights were "prophylactic" rules that were not, strictly speaking, required by the Fifth Amendment but were necessary to prevent violations of the self-incrimination privilege. See Michigan v. Tucker, 417 U.S. 433 (1974). Why do you suppose the Court based its ruling on the Fifth Amendment rather than the Sixth Amendment's right to counsel? If the *Miranda* warnings are a prophylactic rule rather than a constitutional requirement, did the Court have the authority to impose this requirement on state as well as federal law enforcement officers? See Joseph Grano, Confessions, Truth, and the Law (1993). The opinion in *Miranda* creates a relatively detailed set of obligations. Some states and law enforcement agencies, prior to 1966, used warnings to increase the likelihood that a confession would be found voluntary. Would the Court have been wiser to announce more general principles and hope for legislation or police rules to appear before providing any needed specification?

2. *State adoption and modification of* Miranda. The *Miranda* requirements apply to law enforcement officials in all the states. What would occur if the Supreme Court were to modify the *Miranda* decision? A few states, such as Louisiana and Massachusetts, have independently adopted under their state constitutions or statutes a set of required warnings similar to those in *Miranda.* See Traylor v. State, 596 So. 2d 957 (Fla. 1992). Others declare that *Miranda* has no basis in the state constitution. See State v. Bleyl, 435 A.2d 1349 (Me. 1981). Does the Louisiana provision reprinted above impose any requirements different from what the Court required in *Miranda?*

3. *The coercive environment and the "infinite regress" problem.* The *Miranda* opinion is premised on the view that interrogation of a suspect in a police station is inherently coercive. Do you agree with this premise? If so, what makes the interrogation coercive? Is there any legal or practical consequence if a suspect refuses to speak? Consider again the words of the Fifth Amendment: Are you convinced that interrogation in a police station "compels" a person to be a "witness" against himself? As you answer these questions, keep in mind the physical environment of a typical custodial interrogation. The interrogation rooms are designed to isolate suspects, for instance, by locating the rooms in the rear of the building, often with no windows for viewing persons outside the room. The room will contain only a table and a few chairs. Consider also the subject matter of the conversation, and the assertions a questioner will often make. If interrogation is inherently coercive, isn't the decision to waive the right to counsel also made in the same setting? Could the Court respond to this problem by requiring a more specific warning about waiver? A warning about the warning?

4. *The value of confessions.* Was the *Miranda* court casting doubt on the value of confessions generally, as compared to other forms of evidence? Dean Wigmore offered the following classic defense of interrogating suspects:

> An innocent person is always helped by an early opportunity to tell his whole story; hundreds of suspected persons every day are set free because their story thus told bears the marks of truth. Moreover, and more important, every guilty person is almost always ready and desirous to confess as soon as he is detected and arrested. . . . The nervous pressure of guilt is enormous; the load of the deed done is heavy; the fear of detection fills the consciousness; and when detection comes the pressure is relieved and the deep sense of relief makes confession a satisfaction. At that moment he will tell all, and tell it truly. . . . And this expedient, if sanctioned, saves the State a delay and expense in convicting him after he has reacted from his first sensations, has yielded to his friends' solicitations, and comes under the sway of the natural human instinct to struggle to save himself by the aid of all technicalities.
>
> In the case of professional criminals, who usually work in groups, there is often no hope of getting at the group until one of them has "peached," and given the clues to the police. . . . A thorough questioning of the first suspected person who is caught makes possible the pursuit of the right trail for the others.

2 John Henry Wigmore, A Treatise on the Anglo-American System of Evidence §851 (2d ed. 1923). Do you agree with Wigmore that interrogation and confession is a positive good, or would you argue instead that it is a necessary evil? An unnecessary evil?

5. *Liberal or conservative?* Was *Miranda* a liberal or conservative ruling? Did it legitimize police interrogation through the use of a routine and inconsequential warning? Did it foreclose more intrusive and less predictable judicial supervision of interrogation techniques? Early opinions among police officers about the wisdom of *Miranda* were mixed. Some officers believed that it was a damaging and unnecessary impediment to effective interrogations; others believed that the required warnings were appropriate and would further the professionalism of police work. See Otis Stephens, Robert Flanders, and Lewis Cannon, Law Enforcement and the Supreme Court: Police Perceptions of the *Miranda* Requirements, 39 Tenn. L. Rev. 407 (1972). Over the years, police opinion about the decision has become markedly more positive.

6. *Constitutional foundations of* Miranda, *revisited.* Soon after the *Miranda* decision, Congress enacted 18 U.S.C. §3501, stating that the admissibility of statements made by federal defendants while in police custody should turn only on whether or not they were voluntarily made. While the statute instructed the judge to consider any warnings given to the suspect about the right to silence or to consult an attorney, the "presence or absence" of any such warnings "need not be conclusive on the issue of voluntariness of the confession." For the statute to be tested in court, federal investigators and prosecutors had to try to enforce it, and that happened rarely. For many years and through many administrations, federal prosecutors appear to have made only modest use of §3501. See Paul Cassell, The Statute That Time Forgot: 18 U.S.C. §3501 and the Overhauling of *Miranda,* 85 Iowa L. Rev. 175, 197-225 (1999). The most likely explanation is that §3501 was such a stark rejection of the Supreme Court's decision that most federal prosecutors felt they should not, and perhaps could not, rely upon it, since they are sworn to uphold the constitution.

The Supreme Court finally spoke to the issue in Dickerson v. United States, 530 U.S. 428 (2000). The defendant in the case gave incriminating evidence against himself in an interview that proceeded without proper *Miranda* warnings (although the interrogation was not otherwise coercive). The key question was whether *Miranda* announced a constitutional rule or was merely a regulation of evidence used in federal court. Congress retains the ultimate authority to modify or set aside any judicially created rules of evidence and procedure, but Congress may not legislatively supersede Court decisions interpreting and applying the Constitution.

The Court held that *Miranda,* "being a constitutional decision of this Court, may not be in effect overruled by an Act of Congress, and we decline to overrule *Miranda* ourselves." Over the years, the Court made conflicting statements about the constitutional basis for *Miranda.* Many later decisions referred to *Miranda* as a "prophylactic" rule rather than a constitutional requirement in its own right. See New York v. Quarles, 467 U.S. 649 (1984) (warnings not required when questions were necessitated by an immediate threat to public safety); Harris v. New York, 401 U.S. 222 (1971) (prosecution can use confession obtained in violation of *Miranda* for impeachment purposes if confession was not coerced). But in the end, the fact that *Miranda* applied to proceedings in state court demonstrated that the rule was constitutionally required. The court also pointed out that principles of stare decisis weighed against overruling *Miranda:*

> *Miranda* has become embedded in routine police practice to the point where the warnings have become part of our national culture. [Our] subsequent cases have reduced the impact of the *Miranda* rule on legitimate law enforcement while reaffirming the decision's core ruling that unwarned statements may not be used as evidence in the prosecution's case in chief.
>
> The disadvantage of the *Miranda* rule is that statements which may be by no means involuntary, made by a defendant who is aware of his "rights," may nonetheless be excluded and a guilty defendant go free as a result. But experience suggests that the totality-of-the-circumstances test which §3501 seeks to revive is more difficult than *Miranda* for law enforcement officers to conform to, and for courts to apply in a consistent manner.

Justice Scalia, in dissent, argued that the Court was claiming for itself "the power, not merely to apply the Constitution but to expand it, imposing what it regards as useful 'prophylactic' restrictions upon Congress and the States. That is an immense and frightening antidemocratic power, and it does not exist." *Miranda,* he argued, was not an acceptable interpretation of the Fifth Amendment, because of "its palpable hostility toward the act of confession per se, rather than toward what the Constitution abhors, compelled confession."

7. *Real* Miranda *reforms.* Again and again courts and commentators have noted that the *Miranda* court left open "potential alternatives for protecting the privilege which might be devised by Congress or the States," and allowed legislative solutions different from *Miranda* warnings, so long as the alternatives were "at least as effective in apprising accused persons of their right of silence and in assuring a continuous opportunity to exercise it." If *Miranda* warnings are problematic for law enforcement, why hasn't Congress or a state legislature enacted alternatives more substantial than §3501? What form might this legislation take?

2. *Triggering* Miranda *Warnings*

Like any rule or legislative provision, *Miranda* generates some problems of application. Which conversations between police and suspects make the warnings necessary?

a. "Custody"

Miranda warnings do not need to be given before *every* conversation between police and citizens. There are two conditions that trigger a need for warnings: First, the suspect must be in custody, and second, the officers must be conducting an interrogation. Even though judges, police, and commentators often join the concepts in the phrase "custodial interrogation," it is important to evaluate custody and interrogation separately.

Interviews and interrogations often occur outside custodial settings. There have been few studies of noncustodial interrogations. One study of police work in Salt Lake City during a six-week period found that 30 percent of all interviews occurred in noncustodial settings, including examinations at the crime scene, during field investigations, and during arranged interviews. See Paul Cassell and Bret Hayman, Police Interrogation in the 1990s: An Empirical Study of the Effects of *Miranda,* 43 UCLA L. Rev. 839 (1996). The 30-percent figure relates to full-blown interrogations: It substantially understates the total amount of questions, inquiries, comments, and exchanges that police conduct outside of custodial settings. In noncustodial interrogations, the police are not required to give *Miranda* warnings, and when interrogations are challenged, prosecutors will often argue first that an interrogation was noncustodial, and second (if the interrogation is held to be custodial) that the suspect was properly warned.

■ STATE v. BURT SMITH

546 N.W.2d 916 (Iowa 1996)

SNELL, J.

[The leading suspects in the murder of a woman in Iowa were four juveniles in Missouri: twins Burt and Derek Smith, Blake Privitt, and Jayson Speaks.] Three of the four juveniles were then under the supervision of the Missouri juvenile court. . . . Iowa Sheriff Tad Kamatchus and Iowa department of criminal investigation agent David Fees met with Mike Waddle, the director of juvenile court services, [who] informed the Iowa officers they were in his jurisdiction and he required Missouri juvenile procedures be followed or he would not facilitate the interviews. The Iowa officers agreed to proceed under the Missouri rules.

The officers then proceeded to the juvenile center in Kirksville, Missouri. Each of the juveniles was present with his mother and was interviewed twice. Each was interviewed individually, accompanied by his mother. The initial interview was preceded by a discussion between the officers and the mother. At that time each mother was told that her son was to be interviewed regarding any information he might have relating to the killing of a woman in Iowa. Each mother orally consented to the interview of her son. Before the interviews, director Waddle read to each juvenile from a written form explaining the juvenile's rights. . . . The first interviews lasted from twenty to forty minutes. None of the boys incriminated himself. . . . After consent by his mother and himself each boy was then fingerprinted. After the first interview, each boy was asked to remain at the center and was placed in a separate room. Food and drink were provided, and the juveniles were allowed supervised restroom breaks. At the conclusion of all four interviews, officers noted inconsistencies leading them to believe the boys had not been completely honest. The boys were again interviewed — this time in reverse order: Blake Privitt, who had been interviewed last during the first series, was interviewed first and had a twenty-minute wait between interviews. Jayson Speaks waited approximately two hours. The Smith boys waited several hours before they were interviewed the second time. During this wait, they were not allowed to speak with their mother although she had asked to speak with them. At the beginning of the second interview each boy was briefly reminded of his rights. One by one the boys made incriminating statements regarding [the] killing.

The four juveniles were subsequently charged in Iowa with first-degree murder and first-degree robbery. All four moved to suppress their statements as having been obtained in violation of U.S. Constitutional and Iowa statutory rights, specifically Iowa Code chapter 232. [The district court concluded that the second set of interviews violated the statutory safeguards for juveniles, and the statements were therefore involuntary under section 232.45.]

The initial question with which we are faced in examining defendants' challenge to the interview procedure is whether the defendants were in fact in the custody of law enforcement officials at the time of the second interviews. If the defendants were in fact in custody at this time, then they are entitled to the full compliment of constitutional rights accorded by Miranda v. Arizona, 384 U.S. 436 (1966). In addition, provided they were in fact in custody at the time of the second interviews, because the defendants are juveniles they would be accorded additional procedural safeguards under Iowa Code chapter 232, Missouri Code chapter 211, and Missouri Supreme Court Rules 122.01 and 122.05,* the portions of the code governing juvenile justice proceedings. . . .

* The court was referring to the following code provisions. Iowa Code 232.45(9) provides:

> [S]tatements made by the child after being taken into custody . . . are admissible as evidence in chief provided that the court finds the statements were voluntary. In making its determination, the court may consider any factors it finds relevant and shall consider the following factors:
> a. Opportunity for the child to consult with a parent, guardian, custodian, lawyer or other adult.
> b. The age of the child.
> c. The child's level of education.
> d. The child's level of intelligence.
> e. Whether the child was advised of the child's consititutional rights.
> f. Length of time the child was held in shelter care or detention before making the statement in question.
> g. The nature of the questioning which elicited the statement.
> h. Whether physical punishment such as deprivation of food or sleep was used upon the child during the shelter care, detention, or questioning.

Rev. Stat. Mo. §211.059(1) provides as follows:

> When a child is taken into custody by a juvenile officer or law enforcement official . . ., the child shall be advised prior to questioning:
> (1) That he has the right to remain silent; and
> (2) That any statement he does make to anyone can be and may be used against him; and
> (3) That he has a right to have a parent, guardian or custodian present during questioning; and

In Miranda v. Arizona, the Supreme Court . . . held the privilege against self-incrimination applied to informal coercion by law enforcement officers as well as it did to formal coercion and required a defendant be advised of his rights prior to any custodial interrogation: "By custodial interrogation, we mean questioning initiated by law enforcement officers after a person has been taken into custody or otherwise deprived of his freedom of action in any significant way. . . ."

The *Miranda* decision left in its wake much confusion on the question of the determination of custody. The Supreme Court and most state courts faced with the question seemed to basically reiterate the *Miranda* definition of custody and then proceed to find or not find custody based upon the facts of the particular situation. See Oregon v. Mathiason, 429 U.S. 492 (1977) (per curiam) (holding a parolee held at a police station for questioning was not in custody because he was free to leave at any time); Beckwith v. United States, 425 U.S. 341 (1976) (holding a suspect in a tax case not in custody when questioned at a private home); Orozco v. Texas, 394 U.S. 324 (1969) (holding a defendant placed under arrest in his own bedroom was in custody as he was not free to leave); Mathis v. United States, 391 U.S. 1 (1968) (holding a suspect questioned while incarcerated for other charges was not free to leave, and therefore was in custody).

Most cases decided in this time period analyzed custody under one of two approaches: a subjective test examining whether the particular defendant and/or the officer thought the defendant was in custody; or an objective or reasonable person test—whether a reasonable person in that situation would have thought he was in custody. Most courts looking at this issue applied the objective, reasonable person test.

In 1984 the Supreme Court revisited the question of custody for *Miranda* purposes and unequivocally adopted the objective reasonable person test as the standard in making the determination. In Berkemer v. McCarty, 468 U.S. 420 (1984), the Court was faced with the question whether a motorist detained for a routine traffic stop was in custody so as to be entitled to the safeguards provided under *Miranda*. The Court first acknowledged that even a routine traffic stop such as the one at issue was a significant curtailment of the freedom of action of the driver as it is a crime to refuse to stop or drive away from a policeman. . . . In holding that such a stop did not result in custody, the Court explained "the only relevant inquiry is how a reasonable man in the suspect's position would have understood his situation." The Court stated it was inappropriate to take into consideration a "policeman's unarticulated plan" as to the future arrest of a suspect as this had no bearing on the objective belief of a reasonable person in the situation.

[The question is whether in the absence of actual arrest the authorities say or do something that indicates to the defendant that he would not be allowed to depart. Applying this standard] requires examination of the totality of the circumstances with no one particular fact or factor being determinative of the issue. For instance, courts have held custody is not implicated merely because questioning takes place at the police station or the defendant is the sole subject of a police investigation. . . .

---

(4) That he has a right to consult with an attorney and that one will be appointed and paid for him if he cannot afford one

—Eds.

Our court has also utilized this approach, most recently in State v. Scott, 518 N.W.2d 347 (Iowa 1994), and State v. Deases, 518 N.W.2d 784 (Iowa 1994). In *Scott,* we examined the question whether a brief detention and pat down search of a motorist and his passenger constituted a custodial situation. In concluding such was not the case, we explained [that] the ultimate inquiry is simply whether there was a formal arrest or restraint on freedom of movement of the degree associated with formal arrest.

At nearly the same time, we considered State v. Deases, in which we examined the question whether a correctional officer's interrogation of a prisoner was custodial. [We] adopted a four factor test from the Ninth Circuit as guidance in making such a determination:

> Relevant factors in making this determination include the language used to summon the individual, the purpose, place and manner of the interrogation, the extent to which the defendant is confronted with evidence of his guilt, and whether the defendant is free to leave the place of questioning.

One additional factor is apparent in the present case which we deem worthy of note. In none of our cases dealing with the reasonable person standard have we been faced with the situation we have presently, that is, juvenile defendants. This brings us to the question whether the reasonable person standard should take into consideration the age of the defendants. In Haley v. Ohio, 332 U.S. 596 (1948), the Supreme Court examined the validity of a confession of a fifteen-year-old defendant who had been held fifteen hours and questioned by police in relay teams. He was also denied access to his attorney and his mother for two days. [W]e believe the reasoning applied is relevant to our case:

> What transpired would make us pause for careful inquiry if a mature man were involved. And when, as here, a mere child — an easy victim of the law — is before us, special care in scrutinizing the record must be used. . . . He cannot be judged by the more exacting standards of maturity. That which would leave a man cold and unimpressed can overawe and overwhelm a lad in his early teens. This is the period of instability which the crisis of adolescence produces. [We] cannot believe that a lad of tender years is a match for police in such a contest.

Because we too see the danger of overwhelming a minor defendant, as has our Legislature by passing the many protections afforded juveniles in the Iowa Code, we hold it is appropriate to consider the age of the defendants as an additional factor in making a determination as to custody status.

The district court . . . determined the defendants were in custody for the purposes of constitutional analysis and the attendant rights under chapter 232 [during the second series of interviews]. The first fact to be analyzed under the reasonable person test is the way in which the defendants were summoned to the place of the questioning. In this case, all four defendants were voluntarily brought to the juvenile center by their mothers at the request of juvenile authorities.[2] Prior to coming they were told they would be questioned regarding a murder investigation. Although coming to the center voluntarily is not alone enough to negate a finding of

2. Defendants urge the fact they were on probation supports a finding of custody as they felt compelled to appear at the juvenile facility so as not to violate the terms of their probation. This is not an appropriate consideration, however, as the standard to be applied in determining the overall custodial character of the situation is that of the reasonable person in the defendant's situation, not taking into account any prior record or possible guilt of the defendant.

custody, it is indicative of the state of mind of a reasonable person in the situation. Furthermore, where a defendant's presence is involuntary, a finding of custody is much more likely.

In addition, we must examine the purpose, place, and manner of the interrogation. In the instant case, the purpose of the second interviews was clearly to attempt to get the defendants to tell the truth about their involvement in the murder. It was prompted by the inconsistencies in the stories they related during the first series of interviews. In looking at this fact, however, we must keep in mind the warning of *Berkemer,* that an officer's unarticulated plan has no bearing on the question whether a suspect is in custody at a particular time. . . .

The nature of the juvenile center, the place in which the interviews took place, clearly weighs against a finding of custody. The record shows that the interview site was not intimidating. It was described by more than one witness as being very "family-centered" and warm — not at all like a typical police station or jail. In addition, it was a completely separate facility, attached neither to any police station nor any jail. The center had recently undergone remodeling and consisted of a waiting area complete with a fish tank, a conference room, several offices to house juvenile officers, and typical restroom and break areas. The center was also recently recarpeted and refurnished following the remodeling. Additionally, the officers and other employees present on the day of the interviews were dressed casually in civilian clothes. The record also indicates that uniformed officers were not summoned until the second round of interviews was completed. These facts favor a finding that a reasonable person in the situation of the defendants would not believe himself to be in custody.

Another step in determining whether a reasonable person in the position of the defendants would feel as if he were in custody is to examine the manner in which the defendants were interviewed. We must examine whether a confrontational and aggressive style is utilized in questioning, or whether the circumstances seem more relaxed and investigatory in nature. Again, an examination of the totality of the circumstances surrounding the manner of the second series of interviews reveals they were not conducted in a coercive manner. One fact of particular significance is the number of law enforcement officers taking part in the interview process. . . . In the case at bar, only two Iowa officers were present, and one of them, Agent Fees, was absent from the room during much of the questioning because he was helping fingerprint the other defendants. The style of questioning during the second series of interviews was clearly not coercive or threatening. The interviews themselves were rather brief in duration, lasting only from twenty to forty minutes. Testimony showed the interviews each began with a detailed reminder of the defendant's *Miranda* rights, along with a verbal explanation of their significance. The interviewer then explained to the defendant that his initial interview had some discrepancies from what the other defendants had stated, and the defendant was then urged to share the rest of the information he knew relating to the murder. During the course of these interviews, the questioners did not raise their voices, make any threats, or promise any favors or leniency. They conducted the entire interview in a calm and respectful manner. Mrs. Smith herself, the mother of two of the defendants, even admitted in her testimony that neither officer used an accusatory tone toward either of her sons. Furthermore, when Mrs. Smith and Mrs. Speaks each became emotionally distraught upon learning of their sons' involvement in the slaying, the officers ended the interviews so the women could have some time to collect their thoughts.

Defendants further urge the extent of time they were forced to wait between interviews ranging from twenty minutes for Blake Privitt to six and one-half hours for

Burt Smith, transforms the situation into a custodial one. Although defendants are certainly correct in their assertion this is a relevant inquiry, such a time lapse, by itself, is not sufficient to establish a custodial situation. Testimony presented at the hearing tended to establish the juveniles were detained for only the time period necessary to complete the interviews. It goes without saying that when the same officers are separately questioning four different individuals, there will necessarily be a gap in time during which the later questioned defendants will be forced to wait. A waiting period of this nature does not create a custodial situation.

The facts surrounding the wait tend to show it was merely a necessary procedure in order to separately interview the four defendants. The defendants were kept in separate rooms in order to prevent them from collaborating and establishing a consistent but untrue story. Additionally, the supervisory control over the defendants was minimal — they were under no type of physical restraint and were taken to wait in pleasantly furnished offices at the center. At no time were they placed in anything resembling a cell of any kind nor did any of the defendants ask or attempt to leave the building. . . .

Another factor which we examine is the extent to which the defendant is confronted with evidence of his guilt. Here, the facts again point us to a finding the defendants were not in custody. The officers questioning the defendants made it clear to them that their stories did not match and used this fact as a tool with which to urge the defendants to provide more information; however, no particular evidence was discussed or disclosed to the defendants. The officers merely did what they could to persuade the defendants to tell the truth.

Our final consideration in making a custody determination is the degree to which a reasonable person in the situation of the defendant would believe he was free to leave. One obvious factor we must examine is the degree of physical restraint imposed on the defendants during the interview process. The defendants in the instant case were subjected to no physical restraint of any kind. They were allowed soda, food, and restroom breaks throughout the process; the Smith brothers were even allowed to smoke. Defendants take issue with the fact their restroom breaks were supervised; however, in this situation such monitoring was clearly warranted in order to prevent the defendants from collaborating and developing matching stories which would contaminate further interviews. Because of this danger, an officer accompanied the defendants on their restroom breaks, and the defendants were not allowed to contact one another during the course of or between the interviews. This was a minimal restriction on their actions merited by the dangers inherent in the circumstances. This was not a case where the defendants were held incommunicado or placed in a holding cell; rather, they were interviewed in an unimposing newly remodeled juvenile center. . . .

In our de novo review, we have determined none of the defendants was in custody during the first or second interviews by the law enforcement officials of the State of Iowa. For this reason, we hold all statements given by them and the rifle subsequently discovered may be introduced in evidence of the crime at trial of the defendants. . . .

Problem 8-2. (Non)Custody: Police Assistance

Shortly after midnight, Police Officer Gene Sheldon was dispatched to the residence of Marvin and Linda Dyer on an emergency call. Ms. Dyer was reportedly suffering from a pleurisy attack. Officer Sheldon arrived at the same time as an ambulance. He followed the ambulance crew into the house and found Ms. Dyer seated on the floor of the bathroom. Emergency medical technicians convinced her to leave the house to seek medical attention. After the rescue unit had left to take Ms. Dyer to the clinic, Officer Sheldon asked Mr. Dyer what had happened, and Mr. Dyer admitted that he had hit his wife. While Sheldon spoke with Mr. Dyer in one room, a volunteer firefighter stayed with the six children in the next room. After a few moments of conversation, Mr. Dyer said that he wanted to go to bed and "if anybody comes back to the bedroom all they are going to hear is a loud bang." Sheldon stopped Mr. Dyer from leaving the room by standing in the hallway. He convinced Mr. Dyer to sit down. About two hours after Officer Sheldon had arrived at the house, Ms. Dyer returned in the ambulance. Mr. Dyer went outside and Officer Sheldon placed him under arrest. Did Mr. Dyer make his statements while in custody? See State v. Dyer, 513 N.W.2d 316 (Neb. 1994).

Problem 8-3. (Non)Custody: Phoning Home

A bicycle was reported as stolen to the police department. As part of his investigation of the theft, Detective Fred Patterson contacted by telephone several juveniles he suspected may have been involved, including J.C. With each juvenile, Patterson made the telephone contact without the presence of a parent, guardian, or other responsible adult. A state statute requires police officers to allow parents of juveniles to be present during any custodial interrogation. J.C. made several incriminating statements over the phone, so Detective Patterson later contacted him at home. In the presence of his mother and older brother, J.C. refused to speak further with the officer. J.C. was then taken into custody and charged with theft in a juvenile proceeding. Did Detective Patterson obtain the evidence against J.C. in violation of statute? See In the Interest of J.C., 844 P.2d 1185 (Colo. 1993).

Notes

1. *Subjective versus objective test for custody: majority position.* Federal and state courts determine whether a suspect is in "custody" for purposes of *Miranda* by using an objective test: Would a reasonable person in the suspect's position believe that she has been constrained in a manner akin to an arrest? See Berkemer v. McCarty, 468 U.S. 420 (1984). The particular officer's intentions about the suspect's freedom to leave, and the suspect's actual views about whether she was free to leave, are not controlling under this approach. See Stansbury v. California, 511 U.S. 318 (1994) (officer's subjective and undisclosed view concerning whether the person being interrogated is a suspect is irrelevant to the assessment of whether the person is in custody). Many circumstances — the location of the interrogation, the suspect's reason for coming there, the number of officers present, the defendant's conduct after the interrogation — can have a bearing on this objective test. An interrogation does not have to occur in a police station to be custodial. See Orozco v. Texas, 394 U.S. 324 (1969) (custodial interrogation when four police officers wake suspect in bedroom at 4 A.M. and question him). By the same token, an interrogation does not become custodial whenever it occurs within a police station. See California v. Beheler, 463 U.S. 1121

(1983) (suspect arrives at station voluntarily, is told he is not under arrest, and leaves after brief interrogation); Dye v. State, 717 N.E.2d 5 (Ind. 1999) (suspect not in custody when interrogated at police station after being driven there handcuffed in back of police vehicle; suspect was told he was not under arrest, and was handcuffed only because department policy required it). When a suspect is "asked" to come to the station, is it a voluntary appearance? If a police officer asks a suspect "to have a seat" in the patrol car, is the suspect in custody? See State v. Gesinger, 559 N.W.2d 549 (S.D. 1997) (no custody); People v. Taylor, 41 P.3d 681 (Colo. 2002) (roadside stop of driver became custodial for *Miranda* purposes after passenger was arrested on outstanding warrant, officers searched car without consent, and one officer kept driver standing in one place outside car). Is "custody" a wise line, or does it invite police to interrogate suspects in noncustodial settings? What other lines might be drawn? Warnings for all interrogations? A more subjective standard of custody?

2. *"Stop" versus "custody."* Recall that, for purposes of the Fourth Amendment, a "stop" occurs when a reasonable person would not "feel free to leave" (see Chapter 2). If an officer questions a person during such an investigative stop, has a custodial interrogation occurred for purposes of *Miranda*? In Berkemer v. McCarty, 468 U.S. 420 (1984), the Supreme Court decided that a traffic stop does not amount to "custody" under *Miranda*. State courts both before and after *Berkemer* reached the same conclusion. How is an investigative stop different from interrogation in the police station? How are they similar?

3. *Compelled appearances in legal proceedings.* Is a person in "custody" when a court orders her to appear in legal proceedings to answer questions? Under the U.S. Constitution, the courts have concluded that compulsory process is not "custody" for purposes of *Miranda*. See United States v. Mandujano, 425 U.S. 564 (1976) (no *Miranda* warnings required for witnesses compelled to appear before grand jury); State v. Monteiro, 632 A.2d 340 (R.I. 1993) (same); Minnesota v. Murphy, 465 U.S. 420 (1984) (no warnings necessary during required interview with probation officer); but see Estelle v. Smith, 451 U.S. 454 (1981) (suspect is in custody when compelled to attend interview with state-paid psychologist who will testify at sentencing). Given that a refusal to comply with an order to appear can lead to a jail term for contempt, how is this situation different from custodial interrogation in a police station?

b. "Interrogation"

A suspect's conversations while in custody might not rise to the level of interrogations and therefore might not require *Miranda* warnings. Of the many conversations taking place between police officers and suspects, which qualify as "interrogations" that trigger *Miranda* warnings in custodial settings? Again, have the courts drawn the line wisely?

■ RHODE ISLAND v. THOMAS INNIS

446 U.S. 291 (1980)

STEWART, J.

In Miranda v. Arizona, 384 U.S. 436 (1966), the Court held that, once a defendant in custody asks to speak with a lawyer, all interrogation must cease until a lawyer is present. The issue in this case is whether the respondent was "interrogated" in violation of the standards promulgated in the *Miranda* opinion.

[S]hortly after midnight, the Providence police received a telephone call from Gerald Aubin, . . . a taxicab driver, who reported that he had just been robbed by a man wielding a sawed-off shotgun [near Mount Pleasant]. While at the Providence police station waiting to give a statement, Aubin noticed a picture of his assailant on a bulletin board [on a poster relating to the murder of a taxicab driver five days earlier. That picture was of Innis].

At approximately 4:30 A.M. on the same date, Patrolman Lovell, while cruising the streets of Mount Pleasant in a patrol car, spotted [Innis, arrested him, and advised him of his *Miranda* rights. Within minutes, Sergeant Sears and Captain Leyden arrived at the scene, and each of them also gave Innis *Miranda* warnings.] The respondent stated that he understood those rights and wanted to speak with a lawyer. Captain Leyden then directed that the respondent be placed in a "caged wagon," a four-door police car with a wire screen mesh between the front and rear seats, and be driven to the central police station. Three officers, Patrolmen Gleckman, Williams, and McKenna, were assigned to accompany the respondent to the central station. They placed the respondent in the vehicle and shut the doors. Captain Leyden then instructed the officers not to question the respondent or intimidate or coerce him in any way. The three officers then entered the vehicle, and it departed.

While en route to the central station, Patrolman Gleckman initiated a conversation with Patrolman McKenna concerning the missing shotgun. As Patrolman Gleckman later testified:

> At this point, I was talking back and forth with Patrolman McKenna stating that I frequent this area while on patrol and [that because a school for handicapped children is located nearby,] there's a lot of handicapped children running around in this area, and God forbid one of them might find a weapon with shells and they might hurt themselves.

Patrolman McKenna apparently shared his fellow officer's concern: "I more or less concurred with him [Gleckman] that it was a safety factor and that we should, you know, continue to search for the weapon and try to find it." While Patrolman Williams said nothing, he overheard the conversation between the two officers: "He [Gleckman] said it would be too bad if the little — I believe he said a girl — would pick up the gun, maybe kill herself." The respondent then interrupted the conversation, stating that the officers should turn the car around so he could show them where the gun was located. . . . At the time the respondent indicated that the officers should turn back, they had traveled no more than a mile, a trip encompassing only a few minutes. The police vehicle then returned to the scene of the arrest where a search for the shotgun was in progress. There, Captain Leyden again advised the respondent of his *Miranda* rights. The respondent replied that he understood those rights but that he "wanted to get the gun out of the way because of the kids in the area in the school." The respondent then led the police to a nearby field, where he pointed out the shotgun under some rocks by the side of the road.

[The trial court denied Innis's motion to suppress the evidence regarding the gun, concluding that Innis had waived his *Miranda* rights. The jury returned a verdict of guilty on all counts.] We granted certiorari to address for the first time the meaning of "interrogation" under Miranda v. Arizona. . . .

The starting point for defining "interrogation" in this context is, of course, the Court's *Miranda* opinion. There the Court observed that "[by] custodial interrogation, we mean questioning initiated by law enforcement officers after a person has been taken into custody or otherwise deprived of his freedom of action in any significant way." This passage and other references throughout the opinion to "questioning" might suggest that the *Miranda* rules were to apply only to those police interrogation practices that involve express questioning of a defendant while in custody.

We do not, however, construe the *Miranda* opinion so narrowly. The concern of the Court in *Miranda* was that the "interrogation environment" created by the interplay of interrogation and custody would "subjugate the individual to the will of his examiner" and thereby undermine the privilege against compulsory self-incrimination. The police practices that evoked this concern included several that did not involve express questioning. For example, [the Court mentioned] the use of psychological ploys, such as to posit "the guilt of the subject," to "minimize the moral seriousness of the offense," and "to cast blame on the victim or on society." It is clear that these techniques of persuasion, no less than express questioning, were thought, in a custodial setting, to amount to interrogation.

This is not to say, however, that all statements obtained by the police after a person has been taken into custody are to be considered the product of interrogation. [It is clear] that the special procedural safeguards outlined in *Miranda* are required not where a suspect is simply taken into custody, but rather where a suspect in custody is subjected to interrogation. "Interrogation," as conceptualized in the *Miranda* opinion, must reflect a measure of compulsion above and beyond that inherent in custody itself.

We conclude that the *Miranda* safeguards come into play whenever a person in custody is subjected to either express questioning or its functional equivalent. That is to say, the term "interrogation" under *Miranda* refers not only to express questioning, but also to any words or actions on the part of the police (other than those normally attendant to arrest and custody) that the police should know are reasonably likely to elicit an incriminating response from the suspect. The latter portion of this definition focuses primarily upon the perceptions of the suspect, rather than the intent of the police. This focus reflects the fact that the *Miranda* safeguards were designed to vest a suspect in custody with an added measure of protection against coercive police practices, without regard to objective proof of the underlying intent of the police. A practice that the police should know is reasonably likely to evoke an incriminating response from a suspect thus amounts to interrogation.[7] But, since the police surely cannot be held accountable for the unforeseeable results of their words or actions, the definition of interrogation can extend only to words or actions on the part of police officers that they should have known were reasonably likely to elicit an incriminating response.[8]

7. This is not to say that the intent of the police is irrelevant, for it may well have a bearing on whether the police should have known that their words or actions were reasonably likely to evoke an incriminating response. In particular, where a police practice is designed to elicit an incriminating response from the accused, it is unlikely that the practice will not also be one which the police should have known was reasonably likely to have that effect.

8. Any knowledge the police may have had concerning the unusual susceptibility of a defendant to a particular form of persuasion might be an important factor in determining whether the police should have known that their words or actions were reasonably likely to elicit an incriminating response from the suspect.

Turning to the facts of the present case, we conclude that the respondent was not "interrogated" within the meaning of *Miranda.* It is undisputed that the first prong of the definition of "interrogation" was not satisfied, for the conversation between Patrolmen Gleckman and McKenna included no express questioning of the respondent. Rather, that conversation was, at least in form, nothing more than a dialogue between the two officers to which no response from the respondent was invited.

Moreover, it cannot be fairly concluded that the respondent was subjected to the "functional equivalent" of questioning. It cannot be said, in short, that Patrolmen Gleckman and McKenna should have known that their conversation was reasonably likely to elicit an incriminating response from the respondent. There is nothing in the record to suggest that the officers were aware that the respondent was peculiarly susceptible to an appeal to his conscience concerning the safety of handicapped children. Nor is there anything in the record to suggest that the police knew that the respondent was unusually disoriented or upset at the time of his arrest.

The case thus boils down to whether, in the context of a brief conversation, the officers should have known that the respondent would suddenly be moved to make a self-incriminating response. Given the fact that the entire conversation appears to have consisted of no more than a few offhand remarks, we cannot say that the officers should have known that it was reasonably likely that Innis would so respond. This is not a case where the police carried on a lengthy harangue in the presence of the suspect. Nor does the record support the respondent's contention that, under the circumstances, the officers' comments were particularly "evocative." It is our view, therefore, that the respondent was not subjected by the police to words or actions that the police should have known were reasonably likely to elicit an incriminating response from him. . . .

MARSHALL, J., dissenting.

I am substantially in agreement with the Court's definition of "interrogation" within the meaning of Miranda v. Arizona, 384 U.S. 436 (1966). In my view, the *Miranda* safeguards apply whenever police conduct is intended or likely to produce a response from a suspect in custody. [T]he Court requires an objective inquiry into the likely effect of police conduct on a typical individual, taking into account any special susceptibility of the suspect to certain kinds of pressure of which the police know or have reason to know.

I am utterly at a loss, however, to understand how this objective standard as applied to the facts before us can rationally lead to the conclusion that there was no interrogation. . . . Since the car traveled no more than a mile before Innis agreed to point out the location of the murder weapon, Officer Gleckman must have begun almost immediately to talk about the search for the shotgun. . . . One can scarcely imagine a stronger appeal to the conscience of a suspect — any suspect — than the assertion that if the weapon is not found an innocent person will be hurt or killed. And not just any innocent person, but an innocent child — a little girl — a helpless, handicapped little girl on her way to school. The notion that such an appeal could not be expected to have any effect unless the suspect were known to have some special interest in handicapped children verges on the ludicrous. . . . I firmly believe that this case is simply an aberration, and that in future cases the Court will apply the standard adopted today in accordance with its plain meaning.

STEVENS, J., dissenting.

[In] my view any statement that would normally be understood by the average listener as calling for a response is the functional equivalent of a direct question, whether or not it is punctuated by a question mark. The Court, however, takes a much narrower view. It holds that police conduct is not the "functional equivalent" of direct questioning unless the police should have known that what they were saying or doing was likely to elicit an incriminating response from the suspect. This holding represents a plain departure from the principles set forth in *Miranda.*

[Once a suspect cuts off questioning,] the police are prohibited from making deliberate attempts to elicit statements from the suspect. Yet the Court is unwilling to characterize all such attempts as "interrogation," noting only that "where a police practice is designed to elicit an incriminating response from the accused, it is unlikely that the practice will not also be one which the police should have known was reasonably likely to have that effect."[8]

[In] order to give full protection to a suspect's right to be free from any interrogation at all, the definition of "interrogation" must include any police statement or conduct that has the same purpose or effect as a direct question. Statements that appear to call for a response from the suspect, as well as those that are designed to do so, should be considered interrogation. By prohibiting only those relatively few statements or actions that a police officer should know are likely to elicit an incriminating response, the Court today accords a suspect considerably less protection. Indeed, since I suppose most suspects are unlikely to incriminate themselves even when questioned directly, this new definition will almost certainly exclude every statement that is not punctuated with a question mark from the concept of "interrogation."

The difference between the approach required by a faithful adherence to *Miranda* and the stinted test applied by the Court today can be illustrated by comparing three different ways in which Officer Gleckman could have communicated his fears about the possible dangers posed by the shotgun to handicapped children. He could have:

(1) directly asked Innis: "Will you please tell me where the shotgun is so we can protect handicapped schoolchildren from danger?"
(2) announced to the other officers in the wagon: "If the man sitting in the back seat with me should decide to tell us where the gun is, we can protect handicapped children from danger," or
(3) stated to the other officers: "It would be too bad if a little handicapped girl would pick up the gun that this man left in the area and maybe kill herself."

In my opinion, all three of these statements should be considered interrogation because all three appear to be designed to elicit a response from anyone who in fact knew where the gun was located. Under the Court's test, on the other hand, the form of the statements would be critical. The third statement would not be interrogation because in the Court's view there was no reason for Officer Gleckman to believe that Innis was susceptible to this type of an implied appeal; therefore, the

8. This factual assumption is extremely dubious. I would assume that police often interrogate suspects without any reason to believe that their efforts are likely to be successful in the hope that a statement will nevertheless be forthcoming.

statement would not be reasonably likely to elicit an incriminating response. Assuming that this is true, then it seems to me that the first two statements, which would be just as unlikely to elicit such a response, should also not be considered interrogation. But, because the first statement is clearly an express question, it would be considered interrogation under the Court's test. The second statement, although just as clearly a deliberate appeal to Innis to reveal the location of the gun, would presumably not be interrogation because (a) it was not in form a direct question and (b) it does not fit within the "reasonably likely to elicit an incriminating response" category that applies to indirect interrogation.

As this example illustrates, the Court's test creates an incentive for police to ignore a suspect's invocation of his rights in order to make continued attempts to extract information from him. If a suspect does not appear to be susceptible to a particular type of psychological pressure, the police are apparently free to exert that pressure on him despite his request for counsel, so long as they are careful not to punctuate their statements with question marks. And if, contrary to all reasonable expectations, the suspect makes an incriminating statement, that statement can be used against him at trial. The Court thus turns *Miranda*'s unequivocal rule against any interrogation at all into a trap in which unwary suspects may be caught by police deception. . . .

In any event, I think the Court is clearly wrong in holding, as a matter of law, that Officer Gleckman should not have realized that his statement was likely to elicit an incriminating response. The Court implicitly assumes that, at least in the absence of a lengthy harangue, a criminal suspect will not be likely to respond to indirect appeals to his humanitarian impulses. [This assumption] is directly contrary to the teachings of police interrogation manuals, which recommend appealing to a suspect's sense of morality as a standard and often successful interrogation technique. . . .

Moreover, there is evidence in the record to support the view that Officer Gleckman's statement was intended to elicit a response from Innis. Officer Gleckman, who was not regularly assigned to the caged wagon, was directed by a police captain to ride with respondent to the police station. . . . The record does not explain why, notwithstanding the fact that respondent was handcuffed, unarmed, and had offered no resistance when arrested by an officer acting alone, the captain ordered Officer Gleckman to ride with respondent. It is not inconceivable that two professionally trained police officers concluded that a few well-chosen remarks might induce respondent to disclose the whereabouts of the shotgun. This conclusion becomes even more plausible in light of the emotionally charged words chosen by Officer Gleckman. . . .

Problem 8-4. Blurting

A suspect in a shooting was taken into custody. The suspect asked to talk with the detectives investigating the case, but they told him that he could do so only after his fingerprints were taken and after he had executed a written waiver of his *Miranda* rights. While a different detective was taking the prints, the suspect blurted out, "This is really going to fuck me up." The detective immediately asked why, and the suspect said that he had handled the gun in question on the previous day but that it had jammed. The detective stopped the defendant from saying anything further. Later tests of the gun yielded no identifiable fingerprints. Was the suspect "interrogated"? Compare Commonwealth v. Diaz, 661 N.E.2d 1326 (Mass. 1996).

Problem 8-5. Public Safety Motivation

At approximately 12:30 A.M., a young woman approached Police Officers Frank Kraft and Sal Scarring and told them that she had just been raped by a black male, approximately six feet tall, who was wearing a black jacket with the name "Big Ben" printed in yellow letters on the back. She told the officers that the man, who was carrying a gun, had just entered a nearby supermarket.

The officers drove the woman to the supermarket, and Officer Kraft entered the store while Officer Scarring radioed for assistance. Officer Kraft quickly spotted Benjamin Quarles, who matched the description given by the woman, approaching a checkout counter. When Quarles saw Kraft, he turned and ran toward the rear of the store, and Kraft pursued him with a drawn gun. Kraft lost sight of him for several seconds but spotted him again and ordered him to stop and put his hands over his head.

Although more than three other officers had arrived on the scene by that time, Officer Kraft was the first to reach Quarles. He frisked him and discovered an empty shoulder holster. After handcuffing him, Officer Kraft asked him where the gun was. Quarles nodded in the direction of some empty cartons and responded, "the gun is over there." Officer Kraft then retrieved a loaded .38-caliber revolver from one of the cartons, formally placed Quarles under arrest, and read him his *Miranda* rights from a printed card. Quarles indicated that he would be willing to answer questions without an attorney present. Officer Kraft then asked him if he owned the gun and where he had purchased it. Quarles answered that he did own it and that he had purchased it in Miami.

If you were a judge convinced that all of Quarles's statements should be admitted into evidence, how might you draft an opinion to explain this position? Compare New York v. Quarles, 467 U.S. 649 (1984).

Notes

1. *Interrogation by known government agents: majority position.* Virtually all jurisdictions follow the *Innis* definition of "interrogation": words or actions that the police "should know are reasonably likely to elicit an incriminating response from the suspect." See Drury v. State, 793 A.2d 567 (Md. 2002) (functional equivalent of interrogation when officer places tire iron and stolen goods in front of suspect and says they will be dusted for fingerprints). Did the Court apply this test appropriately on the facts of *Innis?* If not, what definition of "interrogation" could better account for the outcome of the case? This definition applies not only in those cases when the police initiate a conversation; it also reaches some cases in which the suspect asks a question or makes a statement, and the officer responds in a way that leads the suspect to make an incriminating reply.

2. *Booking questions.* The definition of an "interrogation" sometimes becomes an issue when a police officer who processes the routine paperwork and fingerprints as part of the suspect's detention makes some comment that elicits an incriminating

response from the suspect. In Pennsylvania v. Muniz, 496 U.S. 582 (1990), the Supreme Court determined that some, but not all, of the questions asked of a defendant during a routine booking on DWI charges were "interrogations" that required *Miranda* warnings. Routine questions asking for the suspect's name, address, height, weight, eye color, date of birth, and current age were not considered interrogations. When, however, the booking officer asked the suspect the date of his sixth birthday and the suspect was unable to calculate it, the officer's question qualified as an interrogation. What is it about most of the booking questions that takes them outside the coverage of *Miranda*? Is it the routine nature of booking questions? Consider again the facts of Problem 8-4. See also State v. Goseland, 887 P.2d 1109 (Kan. 1994) (during booking paperwork, officer remarks to suspect in narcotics case, "You need to find something else to do with your life" and suspect replies "No, I'll not stop selling dope, because then you all would not have anything to do"; no interrogation, because officer always makes this remark to suspects being booked); Franks v. State, 486 S.E.2d 594 (Ga. 1997) (interrogation occurs when during booking, officer asks suspect about bandage on arm).

3. *Interrogation by unknown government agents: majority position.* In all the interrogations we have considered so far, the suspect was aware that the person asking questions was a police officer. But is there an "interrogation" when a suspect in custody is talking with a person that he does not believe to be an agent of the police? The Supreme Court and state high courts say no. In Illinois v. Perkins, 496 U.S. 292 (1990), the Supreme Court held that no *Miranda* warnings were necessary when police placed an undercover agent in same cellblock with a murder suspect detained on other charges, and during discussion of possible escape, the agent asked if the suspect had ever "done" anybody. The Court held that "[c]onversations between suspects and undercover agents do not implicate the concerns underlying *Miranda*." But weren't the undercover agent's words "reasonably likely to elicit an incriminating response"? If so, what explains the inapplicability of *Miranda* when undercover agents ask the questions?

4. *"Public safety" exception to* Miranda: *majority position.* In New York v. Quarles, the Court concluded that even though the officer had conducted a custodial interrogation without giving *Miranda* warnings, the suspect's confession was not obtained contrary to the Constitution. The officer's questions about the gun were necessary not only to solve a completed crime but to prevent future crimes or accidents involving the missing gun. The need for "answers to questions in a situation posing a threat to the public safety outweighs the need for the prophylactic rule protecting the Fifth Amendment's privilege against self-incrimination." 467 U.S. at 657. Even if the officer did not ask the questions with the actual purpose of preventing a future mishap with the weapon, a court could later infer a public safety purpose for the questions from the surrounding circumstances. About half the states allow a "public safety" or related "rescue" exception to *Miranda;* the other half have not confronted the question. See People v. Attebury, 624 N.W.2d 912 (Mich. 2001) (applying public safety exception).

Although *Quarles* was partly justified by the idea that warnings about the right to silence are a "prophylactic" rule rather than an actual requirement, the Court has now rejected that reasoning in Dickerson v. United States, 530 U.S. 428 (2000). Will the Supreme Court now reconsider *Quarles*? See Susan Klein, *Miranda*'s exceptions in a Post-*Dickerson* World, 91 J. Crim. L. & Criminology 567 (2001); George C. Thomas III, Separated at Birth But Siblings Nonetheless: *Miranda* and the Due Process Notice Cases, 99 Mich. L. Rev. 1081 (2001).

5. *Purpose of custody.* While the public safety exception recognizes the potential importance of the purpose of *questioning,* the purpose of a suspect's *custody* does not alter *Miranda* requirements. When a defendant is being detained on the basis of one violation and is questioned about a different potential violation, the interrogators still must give *Miranda* warnings. See Mathis v. United States, 391 U.S. 1 (1968) (*Miranda* warnings necessary when IRS agent poses questions about tax returns to person serving state criminal sentence).

3. Form of Warnings

The *Miranda* decision designated four topics that warnings would need to cover before a custodial interrogation could take place. However, the Court did not specify the precise language that the police must use to convey these warnings. How much variation in the language of the warnings is tolerable? When is variation necessary?

In California v. Prysock, 453 U.S. 355 (1981), the Supreme Court confirmed that a "verbatim recital" of the words in the *Miranda* opinion is not necessary to give an adequate warning to a suspect before an interrogation. The warning in that case told the suspect of his right to have an attorney present prior to and during questioning, and of his "right to have a lawyer appointed at no cost if he could not afford one." This was sufficient, even though it might have left the suspect with the impression that an appointed lawyer would become available only after questioning. In Duckworth v. Eagan, 492 U.S. 195 (1989), the Supreme Court considered the constitutionality of an Indiana *Miranda* warning that said, among other things, "we have no way of giving you a lawyer, but one will be appointed for you, if you wish, if and when you go to court." The Court held the warning complied with *Miranda,* noting that "*Miranda* does not require that attorneys be producible on call, but only that the suspect be informed, as here, that he has the right to an attorney before and during questioning, and that an attorney would be appointed for him if he could not afford one. . . . *Miranda* requires only that the police not question a suspect unless he waives his right to counsel."

State courts have also determined that their constitutions allow for some variety (and some ambiguity) in the way the warnings are phrased. A few state statutes provide for additional warnings to some suspects (especially juveniles) before interrogation, but state courts have hesitated to conclude that statutes dealing with warnings for suspects require a particular verbal formula. See, e.g., State v. Bittick, 806 S.W.2d 652 (Mo. 1991) (interpreting warnings listed in Mo. Rev. Stat. §600.048.1). Why haven't more state courts insisted on a uniform and unambiguous method of conveying the *Miranda* warnings? Wouldn't an "inflexible" rule be both realistic and easy to administer because police officers could simply read the warnings from a pocket-sized card?

Some situations might call for additional warnings. A suspect may waive the right to counsel because the prospect of waiting in custody may be unappealing, or because no specific attorney has been identified, or because the suspect doubts that the attorney ultimately assigned to the case will be capable. But what if counsel retained for a specific suspect is available at the police station? Do the interrogating officers have any obligation to allow the attorney to consult with the client before questioning continues? Must they tell the suspect of the presence of a particular attorney when the additional warning could affect the waiver decision?

■ STATE v. JOHN REED

627 A.2d 630 (N.J. 1993)

HANDLER, J.

In this case, the jury convicted defendant, John Reed, of knowing murder and aggravated criminal sexual contact. Defendant had confessed to those crimes and that confession constituted critically important evidence. The admissibility of defendant's confession presents the sole issue on this appeal. The police refused, before and during defendant's interrogation, to inform defendant that an attorney, who had been brought to police headquarters by a friend of defendant, was present and sought to confer with him. The issue is whether that refusal by the police violated defendant's constitutional rights, including the privilege against self-incrimination, and therefore rendered defendant's confession inadmissible.

[Fran Varga called the police Monday at 8:00 A.M. to inform them that her roommate and boyfriend, John Reed, had found the dead body of Susan Green, one of Reed's coworkers. He found Green's body on the floor of her own apartment, with fifty-three stab wounds. When detectives Shedden and Importico arrived at the scene, they asked Reed some questions, but had difficulty understanding his answers because Reed suffered from a speech impediment and tended to stutter severely when nervous. He told them that the victim had called him the previous Friday night, afraid because a stranger had been trying to enter her apartment. The stranger had disappeared by the time Reed had arrived to help. He found the body, he said, when he stopped by her apartment on his way to work on Monday morning.

The detectives asked Reed to go to the prosecutor's office to give a statement and provide "elimination" fingerprints. Varga drove him to the prosecutor's office, where they arrived just before 11:00 A.M. The detectives isolated Reed in an interrogation room, and asked Varga to remain in the waiting room. Varga called an attorney, and told him that she and Reed were at the prosecutor's office, that the police were about to question Reed, and that she and Reed needed an attorney. The attorney, William Aitken, agreed to come to the station immediately. Varga informed a police officer that Aitken was on the way.

Meanwhile, Chief Richard Thornburg instructed detectives Shedden and Importico to move Reed to the Major Crimes Building, located a few blocks away. Instead of taking Reed past the area where Varga was waiting and down the elevator, the officers led him down four flights of stairs near the interrogation room and out the back door of the building. Reed signed a *Miranda* waiver form, then gave a different account of the events than he had given earlier.

At approximately 11:25 A.M., Aitken arrived at the prosecutor's office and consulted with Varga. He approached the prosecutor who would eventually present the case against Reed and told him that he was there to represent both Varga and Reed. The prosecutor informed Aitken that Reed was a witness and not a suspect, and stated that, in any event, Aitken had "no right to walk into an investigation." Aitken gave the prosecutor a business card, and the prosecutor assured Aitken that the police would call him if and when Reed requested an attorney. No one informed Reed that a lawyer retained by Varga was waiting to see him.

After a second waiver of *Miranda* rights around noon, Reed spoke with another interrogator, Lt. Mazzei, and told a story markedly different from the second account he had provided Thornburg, Importico, and Shedden. According to Mazzei, in the third version of the defendant's story, defendant had actually witnessed Green being murdered when, looking through Green's front window, defendant had seen a "black man" repeatedly stabbing her. After detectives confronted him with the inconsistency, and after further questioning, Reed admitted that he had killed Green. After waiving his *Miranda* rights for a third time, Reed confessed on tape. He explained that he had killed Green in self-defense during a heated argument. The confession was taped at 3:52 P.M.]

Prior to trial, defense counsel moved to suppress defendant's confession on the ground that defendant had not knowingly, voluntarily, and intelligently waived his *Miranda* rights. [The trial court denied the motion because] the police had no duty to inform defendant of the attorney's presence.

[In] Moran v. Burbine, 475 U.S. 412 (1986), [the U.S. Supreme Court] held, as a matter of federal constitutional law, that the police had no obligation to advise a defendant that a third party had summoned an attorney to advise him and that, in the absence of a request by the defendant himself, an attorney's presence at the police station does not affect the right of the police to interrogate him.

In *Moran,* the defendant was in police custody for a burglary. While the defendant was in custody, the police received information connecting the defendant with a murder. The police proceeded to interrogate the defendant about the murder, even though they were aware that a public defender, retained by the defendant's sister in connection with the burglary charge, had called to say that she would act as the defendant's attorney if the police placed him in a lineup or interrogated him. Although the police assured the public defender that they had no plans to question the defendant that evening, nevertheless, shortly after the phone call, the police began interrogating the defendant about the murder. Before each interrogation session, the police informed the defendant of his *Miranda* rights and had him sign waiver forms, but they never informed him that his sister had retained a public defender to assist him or that the public defender was trying to reach him.

Writing for the majority, Justice O'Connor held that the actions of the police did not violate the defendant's fifth, sixth, or fourteenth amendment rights. After noting that the voluntariness of the waiver was not at issue, the Court found that there was no question concerning the defendant's understanding of the *Miranda* warnings and of the consequences of waiving them. In the Court's view, the failure of the police to inform the defendant that an attorney was available to assist him was irrelevant to the question whether he had knowingly waived his rights. . . .

The majority decision in *Moran* signaled a marked departure from the fifth amendment jurisprudence that state and federal courts had established prior to *Moran.* At the time *Moran* was decided, many courts had held that when the police fail to inform a suspect that an attorney is actually available and seeking to render assistance, any subsequent waiver of the suspect's *Miranda* rights was invalid. [The court cited cases from Colorado, Delaware, Florida, Illinois, Louisiana, Massachusetts, North Carolina, Ohio, Oklahoma, Oregon, Pennsylvania, and West Virginia.] [S]ince 1986, several state courts have had occasion to consider or reconsider the issue presented in *Moran.* Some of those courts . . . have expressly rejected *Moran* on the grounds that its holding offends state-constitutional provisions protecting the privilege against self-incrimination and due process rights. [The court cited cases from California, Connecticut, Delaware, Florida, Oregon, and Texas. The California case was subsequently overruled by a constitutional amendment.]

Defendant's case now compels this Court to look to its own State law to determine the standards that should govern the conduct of law-enforcement officers in undertaking the custodial interrogation of a suspect and, specifically, to determine whether law-enforcement officers in conducting such interrogation must inform the suspect that an attorney retained on his or her behalf is present and seeks to provide assistance.

In New Jersey, the right against self-incrimination is founded on a common-law and statutory — rather than a constitutional — basis. . . . The common-law right against self-incrimination was first codified in New Jersey in 1855. Subsequently, the Legislature incorporated the right against self-incrimination in its enactment of the Rules of Evidence. Thus, although lacking a constitutional provision expressly establishing the right, the privilege against self-incrimination has been an integral thread in the fabric of New Jersey common law. . . .

In effectuating the privilege against self-incrimination, this Court has recognized that ancillary rights, regardless of their legal characterization and derivation, are essential to preserving the privilege against self-incrimination. This Court has found those ancillary rights may be given even greater protection under our State law than that accorded the federal right. We have done so, for example, with respect to the right to remain silent, the use of pre-arrest silence, the use of post-arrest silence, the information that must be given with respect to the consequences of incriminating statements, the right to terminate interrogation, and the right to counsel. . . .

The right to counsel has been the object of special judicial solicitude. . . . The significance of the right to counsel as an adjunct of the privilege against self-incrimination is evidenced by the special requirements that are affixed to that right. It is not sufficient to advise a suspect subjected to custodial interrogation only that he or she has a generalized right to an attorney. It is essential to inform the suspect that, if the suspect cannot afford one, an attorney will be provided at State expense. It is also essential that the suspect be clearly informed that he or she may ask for counsel at any time during custodial interrogation, and, additionally, that interrogation will be stopped any time the defendant desires counsel. Further, a suspect need not be articulate, clear, or explicit in requesting counsel; any indication of a desire for counsel, however ambiguous, will trigger entitlement to counsel. State v. Bey, 548 A.2d 887 (N.J. 1988).

Our decisional law on the state right against self-incrimination is based on the understanding that the privilege is defined by the ancillary rights, like the right to counsel during custodial interrogation. Moreover, the protections afforded by those ancillary rights provide a metric by which to measure the strength of the privilege. The history of our case law reflects a strong commitment to enhance those ancillary rights to forestall the possible use of coerced confessions. Our own jurisprudence and legal traditions, in light of the distinctive origin and development of the privilege against self-incrimination in New Jersey, impel us to maximize the protections of the ancillary rights, including especially the right to counsel, to vindicate fully the privilege against self-incrimination.

Many state courts, as already noted, have interpreted their respective state constitutions to require that a suspect exposed to custodial interrogation be apprised of the presence of an attorney seeking to render assistance. Courts have offered different rationales for imposing that duty. Some have based the duty on the fundamental constraints that govern the waiver of the right against self-incrimination. Those constraints are invariably expressed in terms of whether the waiver is "knowing, intelligent, and voluntary."[2] . . . Other courts have derived the duty from notions of due process that insist on reasonable police conduct. . . .

However, we need not engage in an extended debate over the different approaches to dealing with the standards governing the validity of a waiver in this context. For while courts may differ on the rationale for imposing the duty to inform a suspect that an attorney is waiting to confer, they agree on one supervening principle: the atmosphere of custodial interrogation is inherently coercive and protecting the right against self-incrimination entails counteracting that coercion. . . .

The lesson to be drawn from this debate is that a waiver of the right against self-incrimination which, by all subjective indicia, appears knowing, intelligent, and voluntary, may still be deemed invalid when elicited in an atmosphere of coercion. That is because the determination of the subjective mental state that leads to a waiver is often so problematic. As *Miranda* itself observed, "Assessments of the knowledge the defendant possessed, based on information as to his age, education, intelligence, prior contact with authorities, can never be more than speculation; a warning is a clearcut fact." That observation also applies to voluntariness and coercion. . . . Accordingly, the most practical means to overcome coercion will be through normative rules that apply reasonable, specific, and objective standards. . . .

In rejecting the exclusive focus . . . on the subjective knowledge of defendant, we are simply acknowledging that the ancillary rights, after all, are not designed merely to impart subjective knowledge. The central idea that inheres in the concept of a voluntary waiver is "freedom from coercion." That realization . . . is at the very heart of the jurisprudence of *Miranda*. . . . The ancillary rights of *Miranda* establish objective standards and although the strict application of those standards will sometimes prove overinclusive, they constitute an indispensable counterweight to the inherently coercive nature of custodial interrogation.

[O]ur decision today should be governed by a two-fold purpose: to enhance the reliability of confessions by reducing the inherent coercion of custodial interrogation and diminish the likelihood of unreasonable police conduct in those situations where police, knowing that an attorney has been retained for the suspect and is asking for contact with his or her client, are desperate to acquire a confession before the suspect speaks with the attorney.

The State nevertheless contends that the police had no duty to inform defendant about Aitken's presence because Aitken could not be considered defendant's attorney. The State stresses that defendant never requested an attorney and that Aitken had no legal authority to invoke defendant's rights, and could not exercise, for defendant, the right to counsel. The State thus claims that because no attorney-client relationship existed between defendant and Aitken, law-enforcement authorities could not possibly have interfered in that relationship and defendant's right to counsel.

2. At least one commentator has argued that in order for a suspect's confession to be valid, the suspect should be provided with "as complete an understanding of his tactical position as possible." See George Dix, Mistake, Ignorance, Expectation of Benefit and the Modern Law of Confessions, 1975 Wash. U. L.Q. 275, 330-331. On this view, deprivation of "crucial information" can convert what otherwise would be a noncoercive situation into a coercive situation. . . . The difficulty with this position is that it is unacceptably overinclusive: it would encompass information such as the death of a critical witness, the successful escape of an accomplice, and the destruction of crucial evidence. Certainly, each of these bits of information would play an important part in the suspect's understanding of his or her "tactical position" and, accordingly, in the suspect's decision to confess.

In most cases in which courts have held that the police had a duty, in the absence of a request by the suspect, to inform the suspect of the presence or availability of an attorney during police interrogation, that attorney had been contacted by a member of the suspect's family or a close friend, or had represented the suspect on previous charges and had voluntarily appeared at the police station, or the attorney had the apparent authority to represent the suspect. However, other courts have held that the police have no duty to inform the suspect of an attorney's presence if the attorney was unknown to the suspect or was truly a volunteer who had not been retained by anyone on behalf of the suspect. . . .

We are satisfied that an attorney-client relationship should be deemed to exist under such circumstances between the suspect and an attorney when the suspect's family or friends have retained the attorney or where the attorney has represented or is representing the suspect on another matter. When, to the knowledge of the police, such an attorney is present or available, and the attorney has communicated a desire to confer with the suspect, the police must make that information known to the suspect before custodial interrogation can proceed or continue. Further, we hold that the failure of the police to give the suspect that information renders the suspect's subsequent waiver of the privilege against self-incrimination invalid per se.

Our holding is essential to give effect to the right to counsel that, in turn, effectuates the privilege against self-incrimination. Moreover, our holding is supported in large measure by the special and essential role lawyers play in realizing the purpose of the right against self-incrimination. . . . Our holding is also consistent with the Rules of Professional Conduct of the American legal profession. The American Bar Association's Standards for Criminal Justice are unequivocally clear about the need for the earliest possible provision of counsel for an accused in custody. Standards 5-5.1; 5-7.1. . . .

We do not, however, ground our decision on the right to counsel contained in the Sixth Amendment to the federal constitution. In *Moran,* the United States Supreme Court, noting that the Sixth Amendment right to counsel did not attach before the initiation of adversary judicial proceedings, found that because the defendant had not been formally charged, the actions of the police had not violated his right to counsel.

Nor do we base our holding on the state constitutional right to counsel. N.J. Const., art. 1, §10. In this regard we note that under New York law, a suspect's right to counsel attaches once the police know or have been apprised of the fact that the defendant is represented by counsel or that an attorney has communicated with the police for the purpose of representing the defendant and this right is not dependent upon the existence of a formal retainer. . . . Under the law of our State, although the right to counsel is implicated in the exercise of the privilege against self-incrimination in the pre-indictment stage of a criminal prosecution, it is not the right to counsel that is constitutionally guaranteed once a defendant has been indicted.

Although we have, today, undoubtedly made explicit an additional responsibility of the State in its conduct toward criminal defendants, we do not believe that burden to be a heavy one. The duty to inform, that we place upon the State, is narrow and specific. It arises only where counsel has made known that he or she has been retained to represent the person held in custody, is present or readily available, and makes a request to consult with the suspect in a reasonably diligent, timely and pertinent fashion.

We do not make incumbent upon the attorney the duty to communicate directly with the interrogating officers. That communication will not, most times, be possible. Rather, whenever the attorney has communicated his presence and desire to confer with the suspect to an agent of the State in a position to contact the interrogating officers, we will impute to those officers knowledge of the attorney's presence and desire to confer with the suspect. Thus, the police need do no more than receive and convey what has already been communicated: that an identified attorney retained for a person in custody is available to assist that person if he or she requests such assistance. . . .

We are satisfied that our holding will fully serve considerations of public policy and not undermine the proper and effective administration of criminal justice. . . . Prior to *Moran,* a majority of states followed a rule similar to the one we enunciate today, without any apparent diminishment in the effectiveness of their law-enforcement agencies. In the states, since 1986, that have rejected *Moran,* no evidence exists that the police have been seriously hindered in their efforts to uphold the law.

[We reject] the dissent's contention that the rule we enunciate today is unfairly biased against the "indigent defendant with no previous experience with law enforcement who is arrested while alone." It is probably true that such a person will be less likely to have a lawyer contacted to see him or her. In an ideal world, every defendant would have the family, friends, financial means, time, energy, and personal resources to mount the best defense. But we do not live in an ideal world.

Regrettably, reality compels us to tolerate significant differences in the empirical operation of the constitutional rules we enunciate. Would anyone dispute, after all, that the Sixth Amendment right to counsel is experienced differently by a well educated defendant with access to any trial lawyer in the country and unlimited financial resources to present a defense, than by an illiterate and indigent defendant, without family or friends, who must rely on a highly competent and committed, but overworked, public defender? Yet we have never taken a disparity in the actual ability of differently-situated defendants to make use of a right as an argument against affording that right. Accordingly, the fact that not every suspect will benefit from the rule we announce today is no reason to deny the benefits of that rule to those suspects who may be advantaged by it.

[T]he police conduct in this case illustrates the close correlation between police conduct that can increase the inherently coercive atmosphere of custodial interrogation and conduct that is excessive, shocking, and fundamentally unfair and therefore violative of due process. We are presented with a prosecutor misstating to an attorney retained to represent a client that the client was a witness not a suspect, and refusing to allow that attorney access to the client, thus violating the rules of his profession.[4] In turn, the police hurried defendant down a back stairway to prevent defendant from seeing his girlfriend or the attorney retained to represent him. This, in turn, prompted the police to aver that taking four flights of stairs to exit a building was "more convenient" than using the elevator next to which defendant's girlfriend was coincidentally sitting. We think that in this case the law-enforcement officers were under great pressure to secure a confession. To prevent defendant from speaking with his attorney, the police engaged in conduct that, if not egregious,

4. Our own Rules of Professional Conduct state as a "special responsibility of a prosecutor" the duty to "make reasonable efforts to assure that the accused has been advised of the right to, and the procedure for obtaining, counsel and has been given reasonable opportunity to obtain counsel." RPC 3.8(b).

exemplifies the ways in which the inherently coercive atmosphere of custodial interrogation can be materially increased in the efforts to obtain a confession.

[P]olice and prosecutorial behavior, in denying defendant access to counsel, did not well serve the investigative function. Such conduct does not promote public esteem for the law, and it substantially increases the possibility that a suspect's confession will be involuntary. At a minimum, such conduct must not be encouraged by the courts. . . .

STEIN, J., concurring.

[I]nforming a suspect of the right to the presence of an attorney is qualitatively different from informing a suspect of both the right to the presence of an attorney and that the attorney is already in the stationhouse. In the first instance, the suspect may reject the offer out of fear that the police will interpret the request for an attorney as an acknowledgment of guilt, or the suspect may view with skepticism the offer by police to provide an unknown attorney. But if the attorney is already present, the same suspect may conclude that consultation with the attorney outweighs any risk of antagonizing the police, particularly if the suspect has had a prior relationship with the attorney or if friends or family have retained the attorney. Thus, the presence and availability of a retained attorney is critical information that qualitatively affects the exercise by a suspect of the right to consult with counsel. When that information is withheld, the suspect's waiver of the right to counsel and to remain silent is more abstract than real, becoming, in effect, a waiver of a theoretical right that is uninformed by the material knowledge that retained counsel, present and available to assist the suspect in the full exercise of his or her rights, is just outside the door. That the suspect may ultimately reject the offer and waive his or her right is irrelevant to whether the uninformed waiver is knowing and intelligent. . . .

CLIFFORD, J., dissenting.

The importance of the right to counsel in protecting suspects against compelled self-incrimination can hardly be overstated. This Court has traditionally been most solicitous of that right. We have determined that any indication of a suspect's desire for counsel — even if not articulate, clear, or explicit — triggers the right. But today the Court extends that treasured right even farther, concluding that the right to counsel can attach even if a suspect expressly and voluntarily waives that right. That goes too far. . . .

Reed, a quality-control inspector whose work required the reading of complex manuals and engineering drawings, understood that he had the right to an attorney. He understood that an attorney would be provided if he could not afford one. He understood that he could ask for counsel at any time during the investigation and that the interrogation would cease at that point. Fully understanding all of the foregoing, defendant waived those rights — three times. Therefore, the failure to inform defendant of attorney Aitken's desire to communicate cannot be viewed as a violation of defendant's *Miranda* rights. And it should not be viewed as contrary to New Jersey's equivalent common-law protections. . . .

Philosophical as well as practical concerns lead me to disagree with my colleagues' conclusion. First, [a] mentally-competent person's constitutional rights may be asserted only by that person. Therefore, I part company with the Court in its conclusion that a third party — in this case, the attorney in waiting — can assert a suspect's right against self-incrimination.

Moreover, the Court's rule creates an illogical or unfair advantage for some suspects. Those suspects who are taken into custody in the presence of others, or who have previously obtained a private attorney, or who have previously required the services of a public defender — and therefore are more likely to be the beneficiaries of someone's call to an attorney on their behalf — will be found to have been coerced if not alerted should an attorney arrive at the station house. On the other hand, the indigent defendant with no previous experience with law enforcement who is arrested while alone — and hence "out of the loop" as far as legal assistance is concerned — although subjected to identical interrogation techniques will have knowingly and voluntarily waived the right to counsel. The rule therefore results in two classes of suspects and favors those who are more likely to have access to counsel. Such intolerable incongruities result when the emphasis shifts to events entirely unrelated to the suspect's knowledge rather than focusing on the sole person who matters in evaluating the validity of a suspect's waiver — the suspect.

Furthermore, the rule the Court fashions today risks increasing the likelihood of police coercion. Police officers of flexible rectitude who know that the right to question a suspect may terminate once an attorney makes known his or her availability to assist a suspect may be tempted to "turn up the heat" to secure a confession in what the officers may perceive as a limited window of opportunity. The right the Court creates intensifies rather than diminishes the pressure on law-enforcement officers to cut corners in the effort to extract an incriminating statement.

Likewise, the duty of police to inform a suspect that an attorney seeks to communicate with the suspect raises a number of other issues that the Court will surely need to address before long. For example, how quickly must the police relay the information that an attorney is available? If an attorney calls the police station, is the officer receiving the call obliged immediately to put aside all other matters and race to inform the investigating officers? Does the right attach at the time of communication or at some reasonable time thereafter? . . .

I need hardly add that my resolution of this case in no way constitutes an endorsement of the deplorable bumbling of the law-enforcement personnel who lied to Ms. Varga and Aitken and who scurried through the basement to hide defendant from the attorney who sought to confer with him. I join the majority in its denouncement of such foolishness. However, [the purpose of the majority's decision — to enhance the reliability of confessions by reducing the inherent coercion of custodial interrogation — is] adequately served by careful administering of the *Miranda* warnings, fully complied with in this case, and punctilious observance of the procedures laid out in our case law. . . .

Notes

1. *Informing a suspect about an available retained attorney: majority position.* The Supreme Court decided in Moran v. Burbine, 475 U.S. 412 (1986), that the police had no obligation to tell a suspect about an available attorney if the suspect has already waived the *Miranda* rights. Supreme courts in more than half the states have now faced this issue; a clear majority have disagreed with the Supreme Court and taken the same position as the *Reed* court. Compare Commonwealth v. Mavredakis, 725 N.E.2d 169 (Mass. 2000) (rejecting *Moran*) with Ajabu v. State, 693 N.E.2d 921 (Ind. 1998) (following *Moran* and collecting cases). If an elected prosecutor lived in a

jurisdiction following the approach of the Supreme Court in *Moran,* how might she explain this position to a civic organization — say, the Elks Club or the high school's Honor Society? If a prosecutor approves of this practice, does that cast any light on what she understands her primary responsibility to be? How might an elected prosecutor explain a decision such as the one in *Reed* from New Jersey? Do these questions help to explain why so many states have rejected *Moran?*

2. *Weighting decisions.* If most state courts reject a position taken by the U.S. Supreme Court, what weight should a later state court place on the Supreme Court opinion when interpreting its own state constitution? Should it carry less weight than recent opinions from the highest courts of sister states? Equivalent weight? On what theory of inter-court relations might such a Supreme Court opinion carry greater weight than later decisions from other state courts?

3. *"For or against" warning.* Some police officers tell suspects that anything they say during an interrogation can be used "for or against" the suspect. Why do you suppose they phrase the warning this way? Is it an acceptable variation on the *Miranda* warnings? See State v. Stanley, 613 A.2d 788 (Conn. 1992) (approving of "for or against" statement on printed waiver form when it is accompanied by other "against" statements); State v. Melvin, 319 A.2d 450 (N.J. 1974) (criticizing a "for or against" warning but finding no constitutional error); Dunn v. State, 721 S.W.2d 325 (Tex. Crim. App. 1986) (error to give "for or against" warning).

4. *The "fifth right."* The *Miranda* opinion, after describing the four warnings now known as the *Miranda* warnings, added the following: If the suspect "indicates in any manner that he does not wish to be interrogated, the police may not question him." 384 U.S. at 445. The opinion also refers to "the right to refrain from answering any further inquiries." Should the police be expected to warn suspects about this "fifth right" to cut off questioning? Courts considering this question have almost uniformly said no. See, e.g., State v. Mitchell, 482 N.W.2d 364 (Wis. 1992). If the suspect does indeed have the right to cut off questioning, why should the police be obliged to tell suspects about some of their rights but not this one? Would warnings about this right have any greater effect than the four existing warnings? Cf. United States v. Lombera-Camorlinga, 206 F.3d 882 (9th Cir. 2000) (failure to inform arrested non-citizen of Vienna Convention right to contact consul does not require suppression of statement).

5. *Changing the subject.* There is no constitutional requirement that the police warn a suspect about the subject matter of an interrogation. Thus, if the interrogator begins talking about one crime but then inquires about another, there is no need to highlight this fact for the suspect. See Colorado v. Spring, 479 U.S. 564 (1987); State v. Randolph, 370 S.E.2d 741 (W. Va. 1988).

6. *Translation of* Miranda *warnings.* A suspect who has difficulty understanding English must receive the warnings in her own language. For this reason, some police departments maintain a standardized translation of the *Miranda* warnings in languages commonly spoken in the area. See State v. Santiago, 556 N.W.2d 687 (Wis. 1996).

7. Miranda *on the stand.* Defense attorneys at suppression hearings will sometimes ask a testifying police officer the exact manner in which she administered the *Miranda* warnings. In cases in which the officer administered the warnings without reading them from a card, the attorney might ask for a rendition of the warnings on the stand. If the officer, in the stress of the moment, is unable to state the warnings accurately (or translates them improperly, in cases in which the officer administered warnings in another language), how would you rule on the suppression motion?

C. INVOCATION AND WAIVER OF *MIRANDA* RIGHTS

After the police give a *Miranda* warning, a suspect may invoke the right to counsel or to silence, or waive these rights and submit to the interrogation. Most suspects waive the right to counsel and the right to silence after receiving *Miranda* warnings. Waiver occurs in at least three-quarters of all custodial interrogations (and probably more). Thus, the legal rules dealing with waiver and invocation of interrogation rights affect more cases than any other aspect of the vast legal doctrine surrounding *Miranda.* In this section, we review how courts determine whether a suspect has invoked or waived *Miranda* rights.

Suspects typically use language that leaves some doubt about their invocation or waiver of the right to counsel or silence. The rules for handling ambiguous words or actions suggesting invocation or waiver can have a huge practical impact: If only crystal clear invocation is valid, there will be more waivers, while if courts insist that government agents treat a range of ambiguous statements or actions as assertions of *Miranda* rights, assertion will be more common. When the suspect makes an ambiguous statement or takes action that might be a waiver of *Miranda* rights, when must the police clarify the waiver before proceeding with the interrogation?

■ VERMONT STATUTES TIT. 13, §§5234, 5237

§5234

(a) If a person who is being detained by a law enforcement officer . . . is not represented by an attorney under conditions in which a person having his own counsel would be entitled to be so represented, the law enforcement officer, magistrate, or court concerned shall:

(1) Clearly inform him of the right of a person to be represented by an attorney and of a needy person to be represented at public expense; and

(2) If the person detained or charged does not have an attorney and does not knowingly, voluntarily and intelligently waive his right to have an attorney when detained or charged, notify the appropriate public defender that he is not so represented. . . .

(d) Information . . . given to a person by a law enforcement officer under this section gives rise to a rebuttable presumption that the information was effectively communicated if:

(1) It is in writing or otherwise recorded;

(2) The recipient records his acknowledgment of receipt and time of receipt of the information; and

(3) The material so recorded under paragraphs (1) and (2) of this subsection is filed with the court next concerned.

§5237

A person who has been appropriately informed under section 5234 of this title may waive in writing, or by other record, any right provided by this chapter, if the court, at the time of or after waiver, finds of record that he has acted with full awareness of his rights and of the consequences of a waiver and if the waiver is otherwise according to law. The court shall consider such factors as the person's age, education, and familiarity with the English language, and the complexity of the crime involved.

■ STATE v. JASON WILLIAMS

535 N.W.2d 277 (Minn. 1995)

ANDERSON, J.

[Jason Ryan Williams, a 16-year-old black male, was referred for prosecution as an adult on charges arising from his involvement in a double homicide and an attempted homicide. The crimes took place in the home of Julie Hage and her two children, Nicole and Mathew, ages three and four. The killer had used a knife and a shotgun, and had stolen several items of personal property from the victims' home, including an automobile. At approximately 10:15 P.M. that evening, an officer noticed the missing car on the road, and ordered the driver to stop. Other squad cars arrived, and the officers arrested the car's five occupants (including Williams) and took them to the Brooklyn Park police department for questioning. Interviews later that night with the other occupants of the car revealed that Williams had told the others that he had stolen the car and that he had cut his hand while shooting a shotgun.]

At approximately 5:20 A.M., Williams was taken from his detention cell to an interview room located across the hall. The interview room measured 10 feet, 8 inches long by 7 feet, 5 inches wide. The room had no exterior windows. Two banks of lights, each containing three 48-inch tube fluorescent bulbs, illuminated the room's only furniture: one table, measuring 48 inches long by 30 inches wide, and three chairs. Detectives Bozovsky and Christensen were waiting in the interview room when Williams arrived. They introduced themselves and sat at opposite ends of the table, while Williams sat between them with his back to the door. . . . Williams was not wearing handcuffs.

After Williams sat down, Detective Bozovsky orally recited a full *Miranda* warning and asked Williams if he understood the rights of which he had just been advised. Williams responded affirmatively. Bozovsky then asked Williams if he was willing to talk with them. Williams responded that he was willing to talk.

Williams had not yet been informed about the homicide investigation. Instead, he was questioned about being in a stolen car. Williams initially maintained that he had stolen the car from a black man who had left the keys in its ignition while parked outside of a south Minneapolis liquor store. . . . Approximately 45 minutes into the interview, Detective Bozovsky informed Williams that the car he had been riding in had been stolen from the home of people who had been murdered. Bozovsky stated that he suspected Williams had injured his hand during the murders. Bozovsky next said that he wanted Williams's side of the story because if he didn't explain "how it happened people would believe the worst about what had happened." Williams denied any involvement in the homicides. When Detective Christensen explained that the homicide scene would be processed for fingerprints and blood analysis, Williams responded that neither his fingerprints nor his blood would be found at the homicide scene.

Detective Christensen continued to hypothesize about the homicides and explained to Williams that if the adult female victim had been sexually assaulted, physical evidence, such as semen, could be traced back to the assailant. Williams emphatically denied that anything like that had happened, and Christensen accused him of lying. Williams then lost his composure, stood up from his chair, turned towards Christensen and said, "I don't have to take any more of your bullshit." Then Williams walked out of the interrogation room, into the hall, and back to his detention cell, where he was placed by the detention officer. This episode occurred approximately one hour into the interview. Williams never said that he wanted to stop answering questions. Christensen testified that he was shocked by Williams's behavior because, in over 17 years of police experience, a suspect had never stood up and simply walked out of the interview room. Christensen interpreted Williams's behavior to be a "temper tantrum."

To allow Williams some time to "cool off," Detectives Christensen and Bozovsky left the detention center area of the police department. After a few minutes, another officer informed them that Mathew Hage was being treated at the hospital and was expected to survive. [The two detectives decided to inform Williams about the new development in the case.] Approximately five minutes after leaving the detention center area, Detective Bozovsky entered Williams's detention cell. Bozovsky, who "never got the impression [Williams] didn't want to talk to me," sat down next to Williams, who was calmly lying on his bed. Detective Christensen did not enter the cell, because Williams's earlier behavior indicated that he was angry at Christensen for calling him a liar. Instead, Christensen stood on the door threshold, attempting to avoid creating hostility towards Williams.

Detective Bozovsky informed Williams that Mathew was expected to survive. Bozovsky then told Williams that Mathew would be able to identify him, an assertion that Bozovsky admitted was "pure speculation." Bozovsky then asked Williams if he would like to tell his side of the story. At that point, Williams nodded affirmatively, and while tears welled up in his eyes, he admitted that he had been in the house. Detective Christensen then entered Williams's cell and, in an attempt to comfort Williams, addressed Williams in a calm, soft tone, "You understand that I was just doing my job." Williams nodded that he understood and shook hands with Christensen. Bozovsky then asked Williams whether he wanted to talk with them further in the detention cell or whether he wanted to return to the interview room. Williams chose to return to the interview room.

Williams and the two detectives returned to the same interview room they had previously been in and resumed their prior seating arrangements. Williams had regained his composure, and Bozovsky fully advised him of his *Miranda* rights for the second time. Williams again said he understood his rights, and when the detectives asked whether he was willing to talk with them, Williams responded affirmatively. During the first half hour of the ultimately hour-long interview, Williams told the detectives his version of what occurred at the Hage residence. . . . Although no one told Williams that he had the [statutory] right to have a parent or guardian present, at no time during the two-hour questioning period did Williams request to speak with a lawyer, parent, or guardian. . . . The interview ended at approximately 7:28 A.M. . . .

When an accused suspect invokes the right to remain silent, custodial interrogation must cease. Miranda v. Arizona, 384 U.S. 436 (1966). In response to Detective Christensen's accusation that he was lying about his involvement in the homicides, Williams stood up from his chair, turned towards Christensen, said "I don't have to take any more of your bullshit," and walked out of the interview room. By this behavior, Williams claims that he invoked his right to remain silent while being questioned at the police department. Williams further claims that the interrogating officers failed to scrupulously honor his invocation because they returned to question him only five minutes after his invocation. . . . Before analyzing whether the detectives scrupulously honored Williams's invocation of his right to remain silent, we must first determine whether he effectively invoked his right to remain silent.

In the right to counsel context, we note that generally the police and the court must examine the language used by a defendant in determining whether a defendant has attempted to invoke the right to counsel. It is difficult to imagine what behavior a defendant could use to clearly convey the desire to speak with counsel. In contrast, a suspect can attempt to convey a desire to remain silent in various ways that do not necessarily require that words be used at all. . . .

A suspect's hostile behavior during custodial interrogation might be in response to a number of stimuli. It can express everything from physical discomfort to reluctance to talk. Without oral explanation, it is often ambiguous as to what message a suspect's behavior is intended to convey. Therefore, before it can be said that a suspect has unequivocally and unambiguously invoked the right to remain silent, we hesitate to go beyond the language used by the suspect to examine the behavior of the suspect. . . .

Thus, to unambiguously invoke the right to remain silent, we conclude that a suspect's hostile behavior, standing alone, is ordinarily insufficient, and we conclude that the language used by the suspect must sufficiently articulate the desire to remain silent. To hold otherwise would encourage judicial second-guessing of police officers as to the meaning of a suspect's actions. . . .

Williams never said that he wanted to stop answering questions. In addition, Williams never exhibited a general refusal to answer any of the questions the detectives wanted to ask. Instead, he expressed insult when Detective Christensen accused him of lying. Although we recognize that a suspect who answers some questions does not thereby deprive himself of the right to refrain from answering other questions, we conclude, as did the trial court, that Williams's hostile response to Christensen's specific accusation, occurring after approximately one hour of questioning, does not constitute an unequivocal and unambiguous invocation of his right to remain silent.

Indeed, the detectives testified that Williams was apparently angry at only Detective Christensen because Christensen had called him a liar; but Detective Bozovsky "never got the impression he didn't want to talk to me." Christensen explained that he and Bozovsky could not know whether Williams wanted to talk with them unless they went back into Williams's detention cell and informed him of the new development in the case. . . .

This court has not addressed whether an ambiguous or equivocal request to remain silent is sufficient to implicate *Miranda*'s protections. In the context of an ambiguous or equivocal invocation of *Miranda*'s right to counsel protection, when an accused utters a statement that is arguably subject to a construction that the accused is invoking his right to counsel, this court has held that all further questioning must stop, except narrow questioning designed to clarify the accused's true desires respecting counsel may continue. State v. Robinson, 427 N.W.2d 217 (Minn. 1988).

Recently, however, in Davis v. United States, 512 U.S. 452 (1994), the Supreme Court declined to adopt a rule requiring officers to ask clarifying questions when an accused ambiguously or equivocally requests counsel. Instead, the Court held that if the accused's statement is not an unambiguous or unequivocal request for counsel, the officers have no obligation to stop questioning him. The Court adopted this position partially in an attempt to minimize the chance of a confession being suppressed due to subsequent judicial second-guessing of police officers as to the meaning of the accused's statement regarding counsel.

In deciding whether to adopt the clarifying approach in the right to remain silent context, we recognize that *Miranda*'s prophylactic procedural safeguards are designed to protect two distinct rights: the right to counsel contained in the Sixth Amendment and the privilege against compelled self-incrimination contained in the Fifth Amendment. When an accused attempts to invoke his right to counsel, he indicates that he feels comfortable dealing with the authorities only with the assistance of counsel. See Edwards v. Arizona, 451 U.S. 477 (1981) (holding that questioning must cease and police may not re-approach the accused when the accused requests counsel, an additional protection beyond those provided in the right to remain silent context). That is not the case in the right to remain silent context, and therefore, fewer procedural safeguards are appropriate when the accused invokes the right to remain silent. Because the Supreme Court has held that the Constitution does not require police officers to confine their questioning to clarifying questions when an accused ambiguously or equivocally attempts to invoke his right to counsel, Davis v. United States, it follows by even greater logic that the Constitution does not require such a clarifying approach when an accused ambiguously or equivocally attempts to invoke his right to remain silent. See Michigan v. Mosley, 423 U.S. 96 (1975) (distinguishing between the procedural safeguards triggered by a request to remain silent and the greater procedural safeguards triggered by a request for an attorney).

[We] conclude that nothing short of an unambiguous or unequivocal invocation of the right to remain silent will be sufficient to implicate *Miranda*'s protections. Recognizing that *Miranda* protects two distinct rights, with more protection afforded the right to counsel, we decline to adopt the clarifying approach in the right to remain silent context.

Because Williams's desire with respect to his right to remain silent was ambiguous or equivocal at best, and because questioning may continue when the defendant has not clearly indicated a desire to stop answering questions, Detectives Bozovsky and Christensen were allowed to return to Williams's cell to question him. The detectives appropriately allowed Williams some time to calm down before returning to question him. Five minutes apparently provided Williams with sufficient time to compose himself. When Detective Bozovsky entered Williams's detention cell, Williams was calmly lying on his bed and Williams had regained his composure by the time he returned to the interview room. In addition, by informing Williams of Mathew's condition, Bozovsky merely informed Williams of the possible charges or evidence against him, which is not improper.

As a result of Detective Bozovsky's subsequent questions, Williams revealed that he did not desire to remain silent, and indicated instead that he wanted to return to the interrogation room to talk with them further. We conclude that Williams failed to effectively invoke his right to remain silent. . . .

For a statement obtained from an accused during custodial interrogation to be admissible, the state must prove by a preponderance of the evidence both that the accused knowingly, intelligently, and voluntarily waived his right against self-incrimination, and that the accused freely and voluntarily gave the statement. . . . In the present case, Williams was fully advised of his *Miranda* rights three different times within a two-hour period. Each time, Williams responded that he understood his rights and that he was willing to talk. That Williams was not again advised of his *Miranda* rights before being informed that Mathew was expected to survive does not necessarily taint his confession. Detective Bozovsky had advised Williams of his rights just one hour earlier, and this warning easily covered the second interview. [The] state has met its burden of proving that Williams knowingly and intelligently waived his rights. [The court went on to conclude, in light of Williams's many previous experiences with the juvenile justice system, that the conditions of his detention and interrogation did not render his confession involuntary.]

PAGE, J., dissenting in part.

I respectfully dissent . . . from that part of the court's decision which holds that Williams was equivocal in invoking his right to remain silent when he broke off the interrogation with Detectives Christensen and Bozovsky.

The United States Supreme Court, in Miranda v. Arizona, 384 U.S. 436 (1966), recognized the need to protect a defendant's right to both consult with an attorney and remain silent. Specifically referring to the invocation of the right to remain silent, the Court stated "if the individual indicates in any manner, at any time prior to or during questioning, that he wishes to remain silent, the interrogation must cease." The invocation of the right to remain silent requires that all questioning cease in order to prevent "police from persisting in repeated efforts to wear down the accused's resistance and make him change his mind."

Here, the manner utilized by Williams to indicate that he did not wish to be interrogated further was to remove himself from the interrogation room. The court's argument appears to be that in standing up, turning toward Detective Christensen, and saying "I don't have to take any more of your bullshit," then walking out of the room, Williams left some doubt as to whether he wanted the interrogation to continue. I believe, however, that there was nothing equivocal, uncertain, or doubtful in the manner he chose to invoke his right to remain silent. By leaving the interrogation room, Williams made a clearer and stronger statement of his desire to remain silent than any verbal statement he could have made. The message to be taken from Williams' walking out of the interrogation room in the manner he did was that he did not want to talk to the officers any longer and that he did not want the officers to talk to him any longer. [T]he fact that Williams may have been angry when he invoked his right to remain silent does not make an unequivocal invocation of the right any less effective. Having unequivocally invoked his right to remain silent, Williams was entitled to have the right "scrupulously" honored. Michigan v. Mosley, 423 U.S. 96 (1975). . . .

Problem 8-6. Ambiguous Assertion

A sheriff's deputy, Sergeant Brosig, arrested Bonnie Walkowiak on charges of bringing drugs into a prison. Upon Walkowiak's arrival at the sheriff's department, Brosig gave her a copy of a standardized rights form which lists the *Miranda* rights. Brosig read this form to Walkowiak, and she signed it to indicate that she understood these rights. Sometime after Walkowiak signed the *Miranda* form she told Brosig that she had an attorney from another case and asked Brosig whether he thought she needed an attorney. Brosig replied that he could not answer that question and that she would have to decide it for herself. Brosig then told Walkowiak that he could not talk to her about the incident at the prison until she signed the waiver portion of the rights form. Walkowiak signed the form, then made inculpatory statements to Brosig. Did Walkowiak invoke her right to counsel? Did Brosig respond legally? Appropriately? See State v. Walkowiak, 515 N.W.2d 863 (Wis. 1994).

Problem 8-7. Ambiguous Waiver

Willie Thomas Butler and Elmer Lee robbed a gas station in Goldsboro, North Carolina, and shot the station attendant. The attendant was paralyzed but survived. FBI agents arrested Butler in the Bronx and advised him of his *Miranda* rights, then took him to the FBI office in nearby New Rochelle. There, after the agents determined that Butler had an eleventh grade education, he was given the Bureau's "Advice of Rights" form to read. When asked if he understood his rights, he replied that he did. Butler refused to sign the waiver at the bottom of the form. He was told that he did not have to speak or sign the form but that the agents would like for him to talk to them. He replied, "I will talk to you but I am not signing any form." Butler then admitted to the agents that on the day of the robbery he and Lee had been drinking heavily and had decided to rob a gas station. He claimed, however, that Lee had actually carried out the robbery alone. At no time did Butler request counsel or attempt to terminate the agents' questioning. Why was Butler more willing to talk than he was to sign a waiver? Did Butler waive his *Miranda* rights? Is more factfinding necessary to answer this question? Compare North Carolina v. Butler, 441 U.S. 369 (1979).

Notes

1. *Ambiguous assertion of* Miranda *rights: majority position.* The judicial opinions on ambiguous assertions of *Miranda* rights divide into three groups. A small group has stated that any statements that might be interpreted as an assertion of rights puts an end to the interrogation. A second group holds that when a suspect makes an ambiguous statement that could be an assertion of rights, the interrogator must stop the questioning about the crime and obtain a clarification about the meaning of the statement. The last group, represented by Davis v. United States, 512 U.S. 452 (1994), declares that a suspect must make a clear and unequivocal statement to invoke *Miranda* rights. As the *Williams* court from Minnesota discusses, it is possible for a court to take different approaches to ambiguous assertions of the two distinct *Miranda* rights, silence and counsel. Some courts also require officers to ask clarifying questions before the *initial* waiver, and require suspects to make an unambiguous statement to *reinvoke* their *Miranda* rights after an initial waiver. See State v. Leyva, 951 P.2d 738 (Utah 1997).

Even if the suspect uses unambiguous words, she must use them at the right time. Courts have not allowed suspects to make "anticipatory assertions" of rights, before interrogation begins. See, e.g., Sapp v. State, 690 So. 2d 581 (Fla. 1997); People v. Villalobos, 737 N.E.2d 639 (Ill. 2000). Although a questioner may continue questioning after an ambiguous statement from a suspect, courts sometimes require them to respond to clear questions from the suspect that do not invoke *Miranda* rights. See Almeida v. State, 737 So. 2d 520 (Fla. 1999) (suspect asks "Well, what good is a lawyer going to do?"; questioner must reply that decision belongs to suspect).

2. *Interaction among supreme courts.* In Davis v. United States, 512 U.S. 452 (1994), the Supreme Court addressed an issue that many state courts had already answered, and it adopted a position taken by a minority of state courts until that time. Should the positions of state courts on a question of federal constitutional law have any significance when the U.S. Supreme Court considers the question? If so, is their significance any different from that of lower federal courts? What if the state opinions are explicitly grounded on state constitutional provisions with language similar or identical to the federal provision in question? Since *Davis* there has been strong movement in state courts toward the "unambiguous assertion" position. See State v. Eastlack, 883 P.2d 999 (Ariz. 1994) (follows *Davis,* although officer asked clarifying questions); People v. Arroya, 988 P.2d 1124 (Colo. 1999) (mother suspected of killing her child cries during interrogation; detective asks if she wants a break; she replies "I don't wanna talk no more"; this was unambiguous invocation, not request for a break). A few courts have reaffirmed their earlier allegiance to some other approach. See State v. Hoey, 881 P.2d 504 (Haw. 1994). How would you explain the apparent, but incomplete, influence of the U.S. Supreme Court on state supreme courts deciding this question, one that arises often in every jurisdiction?

3. *Ambiguous waiver: majority position.* There are many instances in which a defendant says or does something that might be interpreted to constitute a waiver (rather than an assertion) of *Miranda* rights. This could be something as simple as refusing to answer any questions about waiver but discussing the crime with the interrogating officer. In North Carolina v. Butler, 441 U.S. 369 (1979), the basis for Problem 8-7, the Court said that "an explicit statement of waiver is not invariably necessary to support a finding that the defendant waived the right to remain silent or the right to counsel guaranteed by the *Miranda* case." Virtually all state courts have agreed that a suspect can implicitly waive *Miranda* rights through conduct or ambiguous statements. But see Commonwealth v. Bussey, 404 A.2d 1309 (Pa. 1979) (requires explicit waiver). Does the Vermont statute reprinted above prevent the use of a confession obtained after a suspect orally waives his rights but refuses to sign any waiver form? See State v. Caron, 586 A.2d 1127 (Vt. 1990). What would be the likely effect of a legal rule requiring explicit *and* written waiver of *Miranda* rights? What legal institution or private group would most likely be responsible for creating such a rule? The Vermont statute is taken in large part from the Model Public Defender Act, adopted in 1970 by the National Conference of Commissioners on Uniform State Laws. In Connecticut v. Barrett, 479 U.S. 523 (1987), the suspect said he was willing to talk about the offense but was unwilling to make a written statement without an attorney present. The Court treated this as a valid partial waiver of the right to counsel. Should the police be required in this setting to explain to a defendant the rules of evidence making it possible to use oral statements at trial?

4. *Musing about counsel.* For a sample of the statements about legal counsel that have failed to qualify as an "unambiguous" assertion of the right to counsel, consider the following discussion from Midkiff v. Commonwealth, 462 S.E.2d 112 (Va. 1995):

> Midkiff relies on the statement, "I'll be honest with you, I'm scared to say anything without talking to a lawyer," to support the contention that his confession should be suppressed because he invoked his right to counsel. . . . In prior decisions, we have been

> faced with the task of evaluating statements similar to the one that Midkiff asserts is a clear invocation of his right to counsel. We have held that defendants' questions, "Do you think I need an attorney here?," "You did say I could have an attorney if I wanted one?," and "Didn't you say I have the right to an attorney?," fell short of being clear assertions of the right to counsel. Further, the United States Supreme Court recently held that the statement, "Maybe I should talk to a lawyer," was not an invocation of the right to counsel. . . .

Cf. Lucas v. State, 538 S.E.2d 44 (Ga. 2000) (suspect invoked right to counsel by saying "my lawyer told me, the one I talked to, not to say nothing").

5. *Silence as waiver.* Given that an implicit waiver is possible, can the police establish a waiver by showing that they gave proper *Miranda* warnings to the suspect and she later confessed to the crime without ever mentioning the waiver of rights? See Tague v. Louisiana, 444 U.S. 469 (1980) (confession excluded where officer read *Miranda* rights to suspect and could not recall whether he asked petitioner whether he understood the rights). Is there a waiver if the suspect indicates an understanding of the rights but does not discuss waiver at all before confessing to the crime? Does your answer depend on how close together the confession and the expression of understanding about the rights are? Does it depend on who initiates the conversation about the crime after the suspect says that she understands the rights?

6. *Standard of proof for waiver.* In Lego v. Twomey, 404 U.S. 477 (1972), the Court ruled that the constitution requires the government to show that a confession was voluntary by a preponderance of the evidence. The same standard of proof applies when the government must prove the knowing and intelligent waiver of *Miranda* rights. Colorado v. Connelly, 479 U.S. 157 (1986). In both cases, the Court emphasized the distinction between proving the essential elements of a crime (which bears directly on the reliability of the jury's verdict) and establishing the voluntariness of a confession (which bears on the admissibility of evidence). Most state courts have also adopted the preponderance standard. See, e.g., People v. Clark, 857 P.2d 1099 (Cal. 1993); but see State v. Gerald, 549 A.2d 792 (N.J. 1988) (beyond reasonable doubt); State v. Griffith, 612 A.2d 21 (R.I. 1992) (clear and convincing evidence). Do doubts about the validity of a waiver of *Miranda* rights translate into doubts about the accuracy of the prosecution's evidence?

7. *Why do suspects waive their rights?* Can a suspect gain anything by talking to the police? Perhaps suspects believe they can convince the officers to look elsewhere for the culprit or to drop the investigation. Observers of interrogations say that it is standard practice for police interrogators at the beginning of an interrogation to encourage the suspect to speak with the officer as a way of telling "his side" of the story and to learn more about the evidence the police have collected. The officer will be careful to engage in small talk, to cover routine booking questions, and to talk about the advantages of waiver before allowing the suspect to answer any questions about *Miranda* rights. At that point, the questioner will often speak of the *Miranda* waiver as a formality that is surely very familiar to the suspect. If the suspect announces a decision about waiver too early, the officer has no opportunity to persuade the suspect to waive, and the relevant legal rules make it difficult to follow up after an invocation of rights. David Simon, Homicide: A Year on the Killing Streets (1991); Richard A. Leo and Welsh S. White, Adapting to *Miranda:* Modern Interrogators' Strategies for Dealing with the Obstacles Posed by *Miranda,* 84 Minn. L. Rev. 397 (1999). Suspects with a prior felony record are far less likely than other suspects to

waive their *Miranda* rights. Richard Leo, Inside the Interrogation Room, 86 J. Crim. L. & Criminology 266 (1996) (prior felons four times more likely than those with no prior record to invoke *Miranda* rights). In hindsight, if the Warren Court was concerned about the coercive nature of the interrogation environment in the police station, was it a mistake to allow a suspect to waive the right to silence without an attorney present?

Problem 8-8. Capacity to Waive

Donald Cleary forced his way into a home, struggled with the occupant, held her at gunpoint, and fled. About an hour later, an investigator from the state's attorney's office and a sergeant from the sheriff's department stopped defendant as he was driving his truck because he fit the general description of the assailant. The sergeant read Cleary his *Miranda* rights twice, and Cleary signed a statement purporting to waive those rights. He then confessed, admitting that he had entered the victim's house and accosted her, and that he had intended to rape her.

At the hearing on the defense motion to suppress this statement, Cleary relied on expert testimony from a psychiatrist, Dr. Robert Linder. Linder had evaluated Cleary in connection with several prior criminal charges. He estimated that Cleary had an IQ of 65, which translated into a mental age between ten and twelve, and only a limited ability to read and write. Cleary was 26 years old at the time of the hearing. Dr. Linder testified that Cleary had difficulty thinking abstractly and anticipating future events, which would limit his ability to comprehend the language of the *Miranda* warnings. He conceded, however, that Cleary could understand that he did not have to talk to the police, that he could speak with an attorney if he wished, and that he could stop answering questions whenever he chose. However, he believed that Cleary might have difficulty understanding the future legal impact of waiving his rights. Dr. Linder believed that Cleary would not be able to look beyond his immediate concerns to a future court proceeding in which comments he had made earlier would be used against him. Instead, Cleary would speak to police to take the shortest route to his immediate needs — to please the officers, to make himself feel better, and to go home.

Under cross-examination, Dr. Linder conceded that defendant had undergone a learning process through his prior contacts with the police and court system. Cleary had been questioned in previous arson and sexual assault investigations, and now understood that the prosecutor sought to put him in jail. Those previous charges had all been dismissed. He was declared incompetent to stand trial for one of the charges.

Cleary's former mental health services counselor also testified, and estimated his mental capacity to be that of a seven- or eight-year-old child and his emotional level to be that of a four- or five-year-old child. Cleary himself testified at the hearing that he spoke to the officers because he thought they would help him and because he could not leave until he spoke to them.

According to the U.S. Supreme Court in Fare v. Michael C., 442 U.S. 707, 725 (1979), an analysis of a defendant's capacity to waive *Miranda* rights requires a "totality-of-the-circumstances approach," that mandates an evaluation of the defendant's "age, experience, education, background, and intelligence," and an inquiry into "whether he has the capacity to understand the warnings given him, the nature of his Fifth Amendment rights, and the consequences of waiving those rights." Courts typically say that a suspect's mental impairment is a highly significant circumstance to be considered among all the others in deciding the voluntariness question.

The trial judge found that Cleary had attended special education classes in school through the eleventh grade and had limited ability to read, write, and do mathematics. He read at a second-grade level. He had also participated in programs for mentally retarded adults and continued to work actively with two counselors. She stated that Cleary, "in spite of his intellectual limitations, has the ability to learn and puts his learning to practical use." For example, Cleary operated his own logging business for seven years. He purchased and maintained equipment for the business and negotiated bank loans, timber contracts, and truck transportation for his timber. Cleary had a driver's license, maintained a vehicle, was knowledgeable about how it worked, and purchased parts for it.

Assume that the trial court rules that Cleary voluntarily waived his *Miranda* rights. Recall that the government carries the burden of proof on questions of the voluntariness of a waiver. As an appellate judge, would you conclude that this ruling was an abuse of discretion? Cf. State v. Cleary, 641 A.2d 102 (Vt. 1994).

Notes

1. *Capacity to waive under* Miranda: *majority position.* Analysis of the capacity of suspects to waive their *Miranda* rights is highly case-specific. Courts often assess a variety of factors in response to claims of incapacity, such as whether a defendant had prior experience with the criminal justice system, the defendant's intelligence and education, mental illness, vocabulary and literacy, state of intoxication, and emotional state. Courts also look at the conduct of the police in eliciting a confession. For example, the U.S. Supreme Court in Colorado v. Connelly, 479 U.S. 157 (1986), considered a case involving the confession of a suspect who suffered from a psychosis. Because the police could not reasonably have known about the condition and did not engage in any "overreaching" conduct during the interrogation, the Court held that the waiver of *Miranda* rights was knowing and voluntary. See also State v. Chapman, 605 A.2d 1055 (N.H. 1992). How are the police interrogators to determine whether and to what degree a suspect is mentally disabled?

Appellate courts defer to trial court judgments of capacity; the appellate case law is full of decisions affirming a trial court's finding of waiver, even on fairly dramatic facts. Is a per se rule or rebuttable presumption of incapacity appropriate for some defendants? See Morgan Cloud, George B. Shepherd, Alison Nodvin Barkoff, and Justin V. Shur, Words Without Meaning: The Constitution, Confessions, and Mentally Retarded Suspects, 69 U. Chi. L. Rev. 495 (2002) (authors tested sample of mentally impaired individuals to determine if they could understand *Miranda* warnings; in contrast to control group of nondisabled persons, mentally impaired suspects do not understand context in which interrogation occurs, legal consequences of confessing, meaning of sentences comprising warnings, or warnings' individual words).

2. *Intoxication and capacity to waive.* Suspects under the influence of alcohol or drugs very rarely convince a court that they did not have the capacity to waive their *Miranda* rights. In State v. Keith, 628 A.2d 1247 (Vt. 1993), for example, the court

affirmed a finding of valid waiver where defendant had a blood-alcohol level of .203 at the time he was interrogated and gave several inconsistent stories of his whereabouts at the time of a suspicious fire. James Keith had refused to sign the waiver form, saying, "every time I sign something I get in trouble," but he was willing to talk to Sergeant Bombardier of the arson squad, who later expressed his belief that the defendant was just "playing head games." Courts in these cases often point out that the defendant voluntarily got himself into the intoxicated condition. Does the blameworthiness of the defendant have any bearing on her capacity to waive rights? Is a claim that intoxication negates the capacity to waive *Miranda* rights different from the claim that the influence of alcohol or drugs eliminates criminal responsibility for purposes of substantive criminal law?

3. *Juveniles.* The youth of a suspect in custody can be an important factor for courts determining whether the suspect has the capacity to make a knowing and voluntary waiver. Most states follow the totality-of-the-circumstances rule of Fare v. Michael C., 442 U.S. 707 (1979). See Commonwealth v. Williams, 475 A.2d 1283 (Pa. 1984). A few states, however, require that a juvenile consult with an "interested adult" before she can waive *Miranda* rights. See In re K.W.B., 500 S.W.2d 275 (Mo. 1973); Conn. Gen. Stat. Ann. §46b-137(a). Is a per se consultation rule appropriate for juveniles as a group? Perhaps your answer to this question will depend on how many juveniles you believe will misunderstand the rights explained to them. One empirical study, which sought to determine the capacity of juveniles to comprehend the meaning and significance of their *Miranda* rights, concluded that juveniles younger than 15 years old typically did not adequately comprehend their *Miranda* rights and that one-third to one-half of 15-year-olds showed an inadequate understanding of the *Miranda* warnings. The study further found that 55.3 percent of the children demonstrated an inadequate understanding of at least one of the four warnings, and that 63.3 percent of the juveniles misunderstood at least one of the crucial words used in the standard *Miranda* warnings. Adequate understanding of the warnings was achieved by only 20.9 percent of the juveniles. See Thomas Grisso, Juveniles' Capacities to Waive *Miranda* Rights: An Empirical Analysis, 68 Calif. L. Rev. 1134 (1980).

4. *Language barriers.* Courts have also treated language barriers as one circumstance that might contribute to a finding of incapacity. See People v. Jiminez, 863 P.2d 981 (Colo. 1993) (suspect spoke no English and little Spanish, mostly Kickapoo; no valid waiver when warnings were delivered in Spanish); State v. Leuthavone, 640 A.2d 515 (R.I. 1994) (Laotian with limited English language skills had warnings and written statement translated by companion and co-defendant; court allows use of confession because suspect appeared to understand the translation, even if not the full strategic implications of waiver; to hold otherwise would encourage people to remain "willfully ignorant" of English). How might you argue for resolving language-barrier cases with a more clear-cut rule than the approach taken for alcohol, mental disability, or youthfulness claims?

D. EFFECT OF ASSERTING *MIRANDA* RIGHTS

The *Miranda* opinion appeared to bar police efforts to change a suspect's decision after he or she invoked *Miranda* rights during an interrogation: "If the individual indicates in any manner, at any time prior to or during questioning, that he wishes to remain silent, the interrogation must cease. At this point, he has shown that he intends to exercise his Fifth Amendment privilege; any statement taken after the person invokes his privilege cannot be other than the product of compulsion, subtle or otherwise." It later became clear, however, that a suspect could waive *Miranda* rights even after initially invoking them. Indeed, the police in some circumstances can take actions to encourage this later waiver.

The U.S. Supreme Court distinguished between the effects of invoking the *right to silence* and the *right to counsel.* In Michigan v. Mosley, 423 U.S. 96 (1975), the Court upheld the use of a confession despite the fact that the suspect earlier invoked his right to silence. Under the circumstances of that case, the Court concluded that the police "scrupulously honored" Mosley's initial invocation of the privilege, even though they had initiated a later conversation about the criminal investigation that led to his waiver and confession. In Edwards v. Arizona, 451 U.S. 477 (1981), however, the Court insisted on a different rule for those who invoke the right to counsel: Such a person "is not subject to further interrogation by the authorities until counsel has been made available to him, unless the accused himself initiates further communication, exchanges or conversations with the police." 451 U.S. at 484. Consider the following judicial efforts to apply these rules regarding waiver after an initial invocation.

■ ROBERT MINNICK v. MISSISSIPPI

498 U.S. 146 (1990)

KENNEDY, J.

To protect the privilege against self-incrimination guaranteed by the Fifth Amendment, we have held that the police must terminate interrogation of an accused in custody if the accused requests the assistance of counsel. Miranda v. Arizona, 384 U.S. 436 (1966). We reinforced the protections of *Miranda* in Edwards v. Arizona, 451 U.S. 477, 484-485 (1981), which held that once the accused requests counsel, officials may not reinitiate questioning "until counsel has been made available" to him. The issue in the case before us is whether *Edwards'* protection ceases once the suspect has consulted with an attorney.

Petitioner Robert Minnick and fellow prisoner James Dyess escaped from a county jail in Mississippi and, a day later, broke into a mobile home in search of weapons. In the course of the burglary they were interrupted by the arrival of the trailer's owner, Ellis Thomas, accompanied by Lamar Lafferty and Lafferty's infant son. Dyess and Minnick used the stolen weapons to kill Thomas and the senior Lafferty. Minnick's story is that Dyess murdered one victim and forced Minnick to shoot the other. Before the escapees could get away, two young women arrived at the mobile home. They were held at gunpoint, then bound hand and foot. Dyess and Minnick fled in Thomas' truck, abandoning the vehicle in New Orleans. The fugitives continued to Mexico, where they fought, and Minnick then proceeded alone to California. Minnick was arrested in Lemon Grove, California, on a Mississippi warrant, some four months after the murders.

The confession at issue here resulted from the last interrogation of Minnick while he was held in the San Diego jail. . . . Minnick was arrested on Friday, August 22, 1986. Petitioner testified that he was mistreated by local police during and after the arrest. The day following the arrest, Saturday, two FBI agents came to the jail to interview him. Petitioner testified that he refused to go to the interview, but was told he would "have to go down or else." The FBI report indicates that the agents read petitioner his *Miranda* warnings, and that he acknowledged he understood his rights. He refused to sign a rights waiver form, however, and said he would not answer "very many" questions. Minnick told the agents about the jailbreak and the flight, and described how Dyess threatened and beat him. Early in the interview, he sobbed "it was my life or theirs," but otherwise he hesitated to tell what happened at the trailer. The agents reminded him he did not have to answer questions without a lawyer present. According to the report, "Minnick stated 'Come back Monday when I have a lawyer,' and stated that he would make a more complete statement then with his lawyer present." The FBI interview ended.

After the FBI interview, an appointed attorney met with petitioner. Petitioner spoke with the lawyer on two or three occasions, though it is not clear from the record whether all of these conferences were in person. On Monday, August 25, Deputy Sheriff J.C. Denham of Clarke County, Mississippi, came to the San Diego jail to question Minnick. Minnick testified that his jailers again told him he would "have to talk" to Denham and that he "could not refuse." Denham advised petitioner of his rights, and petitioner again declined to sign a rights waiver form. Petitioner told Denham about the escape and then proceeded to describe the events at the mobile home. According to petitioner, Dyess jumped out of the mobile home and shot the first of the two victims, once in the back with a shotgun and once in the head with a pistol. Dyess then handed the pistol to petitioner and ordered him to shoot the other victim, holding the shotgun on petitioner until he did so. Petitioner also said that when the two girls arrived, he talked Dyess out of raping or otherwise hurting them.

Minnick was tried for murder in Mississippi. He moved to suppress all statements given to the FBI or other police officers, including Denham. The trial court denied the motion with respect to petitioner's statements to Denham, but suppressed his other statements. Petitioner was convicted on two counts of capital murder and sentenced to death. On appeal, petitioner argued that the confession to Denham was taken in violation of his rights to counsel under the [Fifth Amendment].

In *Miranda,* we indicated that once an individual in custody invokes his right to counsel, interrogation "must cease until an attorney is present"; at that point, "the individual must have an opportunity to confer with the attorney and to have him present during any subsequent questioning." *Edwards* gave force to these admonitions. [An] accused who requests an attorney, "having expressed his desire to deal with the police only through counsel, is not subject to further interrogation by the authorities until counsel has been made available to him, unless the accused himself initiates further communication, exchanges, or conversations with the police."

Edwards is designed to prevent police from badgering a defendant into waiving his previously asserted *Miranda* rights. The rule ensures that any statement made in subsequent interrogation is not the result of coercive pressures. *Edwards* conserves judicial resources which would otherwise be expended in making difficult determinations of voluntariness, and implements the protections of *Miranda* in practical and straight-forward terms.

The merit of the *Edwards* decision lies in the clarity of its command and the certainty of its application. [This] specificity, which benefits the accused and the State alike, has been thought to outweigh the burdens that the decision in *Miranda* imposes on law enforcement agencies and the courts by requiring the suppression of trustworthy and highly probative evidence even though the confession might be voluntary under traditional Fifth Amendment analysis. . . .

In context, the requirement that counsel be "made available" to the accused refers to more than an opportunity to consult with an attorney outside the interrogation room. . . . A single consultation with an attorney does not remove the suspect from persistent attempts by officials to persuade him to waive his rights, or from the coercive pressures that accompany custody and that may increase as custody is prolonged. The case before us well illustrates the pressures, and abuses, that may be concomitants of custody. Petitioner testified that though he resisted, he was required to submit to both the FBI and the Denham interviews. In the latter instance, the compulsion to submit to interrogation followed petitioner's unequivocal request during the FBI interview that questioning cease until counsel was present. The case illustrates also that consultation is not always effective in instructing the suspect of his rights. One plausible interpretation of the record is that petitioner thought he could keep his admissions out of evidence by refusing to sign a formal waiver of rights. If the authorities had complied with Minnick's request to have counsel present during interrogation, the attorney could have corrected Minnick's misunderstanding, or indeed counseled him that he need not make a statement at all. We decline to remove protection from police-initiated questioning based on isolated consultations with counsel who is absent when the interrogation resumes.

The exception proposed [here] would undermine the advantages flowing from *Edwards*' "clear and unequivocal" character. Respondent concedes that even after consultation with counsel, a second request for counsel should reinstate the *Edwards* protection. We are invited by this formulation to adopt a regime in which *Edwards*' protection could pass in and out of existence multiple times prior to arraignment, at which point the same protection might reattach by virtue of our Sixth Amendment jurisprudence. . . .

In addition, adopting the rule proposed would leave far from certain the sort of consultation required to displace *Edwards*. Consultation is not a precise concept, for it may encompass variations from a telephone call to say that the attorney is en route, to a hurried interchange between the attorney and client in a detention facility corridor, to a lengthy in-person conference in which the attorney gives full and adequate advice respecting all matters that might be covered in further interrogations. And even with the necessary scope of consultation settled, the officials in charge of the case would have to confirm the occurrence and, possibly, the extent of consultation to determine whether further interrogation is permissible. The necessary inquiries could interfere with the attorney-client privilege.

Added to these difficulties in definition and application of the proposed rule is our concern over its consequence that the suspect whose counsel is prompt would lose the protection of *Edwards,* while the one whose counsel is dilatory would not. There is more than irony to this result. There is a strong possibility that it would distort the proper conception of the attorney's duty to the client and set us on a course at odds with what ought to be effective representation.

Both waiver of rights and admission of guilt are consistent with the affirmation of individual responsibility that is a principle of the criminal justice system. It does not detract from this principle, however, to insist that neither admissions nor waivers are effective unless there are both particular and systemic assurances that the coercive pressures of custody were not the inducing cause. . . .

Edwards does not foreclose finding a waiver of Fifth Amendment protections after counsel has been requested, provided the accused has initiated the conversation or discussions with the authorities; but that is not the case before us. There can be no doubt that the interrogation in question was initiated by the police; it was a formal interview which petitioner was compelled to attend. Since petitioner made a specific request for counsel before the interview, the police-initiated interrogation was impermissible. Petitioner's statement to Denham was not admissible at trial. . . .

SCALIA, J., dissenting.

. . . Minnick was [provided] an attorney, with whom he consulted several times. . . . As Minnick testified at a subsequent suppression hearing:

> I talked to [my attorney] two different times and — it might have been three different times. . . . He told me that first day that he was my lawyer and that he was appointed to me and to not to talk to nobody and not tell nobody nothing and to not sign no waivers and not sign no extradition papers or sign anything and that he was going to get a court order . . . to restrict anybody talking to me outside of the San Diego Police Department.

[Today the Court] holds that, because Minnick had asked for counsel during the interview with the FBI agents, he could not — as a matter of law — validly waive the right to have counsel present during the conversation initiated by Denham. That Minnick's original request to see an attorney had been honored, that Minnick had consulted with his attorney on several occasions, and that the attorney had specifically warned Minnick not to speak to the authorities, are irrelevant. That Minnick was familiar with the criminal justice system in general or *Miranda* warnings in particular (he had previously been convicted of robbery in Mississippi and assault with a deadly weapon in California) is also beside the point. The confession must be suppressed, not because it was "compelled," nor even because it was obtained from an individual who could realistically be assumed to be unaware of his rights, but simply because this Court sees fit to prescribe as a "systemic assurance" that a person in custody who has once asked for counsel cannot thereafter be approached by the police unless counsel is present. Of course the Constitution's proscription of compelled testimony does not remotely authorize this incursion upon state practices.

[*Miranda*] recognized that a State could establish that the suspect "knowingly and intelligently waived . . . his right to retained or appointed counsel." For this purpose, the Court expressly adopted the "high standard of proof for the waiver of constitutional rights" set forth in Johnson v. Zerbst, 304 U.S. 458 (1938). The *Zerbst* waiver standard, and the means of applying it, are familiar: Waiver is "an intentional relinquishment or abandonment of a known right or privilege," and whether such a relinquishment or abandonment has occurred depends "in each case, upon the particular facts and circumstances surrounding that case, including the background, experience, and conduct of the accused." . . .

Edwards, however, broke with this approach, holding that a defendant's waiver of his *Miranda* right to counsel, made in the course of a police-initiated encounter after he had requested counsel but before counsel had been provided, was per se involuntary. The case stands as a solitary exception to our waiver jurisprudence. It does, to be sure, have the desirable consequences described in today's opinion. . . . But so would a rule that simply excludes all confessions by all persons in police custody. The value of any prophylactic rule (assuming the authority to adopt a prophylactic rule) must be assessed not only on the basis of what is gained, but also on the basis of what is lost. . . .

In this case, of course, we have not been called upon to reconsider *Edwards,* but simply to determine whether its irrebuttable presumption should continue after a suspect has actually consulted with his attorney. Whatever justifications might support *Edwards* are even less convincing in this context.

[T]he *Edwards* rule rests upon an assumption similar to that of *Miranda* itself: that when a suspect in police custody is first questioned he is likely to be ignorant of his rights and to feel isolated in a hostile environment. This likelihood is thought to justify special protection against unknowing or coerced waiver of rights. After a suspect has seen his request for an attorney honored, however, and has actually spoken with that attorney, the probabilities change. The suspect then knows that he has an advocate on his side, and that the police will permit him to consult that advocate. He almost certainly also has a heightened awareness (above what the *Miranda* warning itself will provide) of his right to remain silent. . . .

Under these circumstances, an irrebuttable presumption that any police-prompted confession is the result of ignorance of rights, or of coercion, has no genuine basis in fact. After the first consultation, therefore, the *Edwards* exclusionary rule should cease to apply. . . . If and when postconsultation police inquiry becomes so protracted or threatening as to constitute coercion, the *Zerbst* standard will afford the needed protection. . . .

Today's extension of the *Edwards* prohibition is the latest stage of prophylaxis built upon prophylaxis. [We] have gone far beyond any genuine concern about suspects who do not know their right to remain silent, or who have been coerced to abandon it. [We should] rejoice at an honest confession, rather than pity the "poor fool" who has made it; and we should regret the attempted retraction of that good act, rather than seek to facilitate and encourage it. To design our laws on premises contrary to these is to abandon belief in either personal responsibility or the moral claim of just government to obedience. . . .

■ STATE v. KEVIN STANLEY

613 A.2d 788 (Conn. 1992)

BORDEN, J.

[During an argument over a rock thrown at a car window, the defendant allegedly shot Javin Green three or four times; he died later at a hospital.] On December 3, 1989, the defendant was arrested for a shooting unrelated to this case. He was taken to the New Haven police department at approximately 3 A.M. At that time, the defendant was also a suspect in the Green murder. At police headquarters, Detective Joseph Pettola gave the defendant a *Miranda* rights waiver form, which was read to him, and advised him of his *Miranda* rights. The defendant indicated that he understood his rights. . . . The defendant refused to sign the waiver form. When Pettola asked the defendant whether he wanted to discuss the other shooting, the defendant said that he had had a gun, that he had fired it in the air and that he did not want to talk further about the incident. When asked about the shooting in this case, the defendant refused to speak about the incident, at which point the police questioning, which had lasted approximately five minutes, was terminated. The defendant never requested an attorney. Pettola then escorted the defendant to a detention area.

At 8 A.M., Detective Gilbert Burton arrived at the New Haven police department and picked up the defendant at a lineup. Before picking up the defendant, Burton had asked another police officer to ask the defendant if he was willing to talk with him, and the defendant had indicated that he was willing to do so. Burton then took the defendant to an interview room, where he informed the defendant that he was going to question him about the Green murder. Burton then read a *Miranda* rights waiver form to the defendant. The defendant read the form, initialed each line identifying a protected right and signed the bottom of the form, at which point a taped interview ensued. During the interview, Burton periodically turned off the tape recorder "to explain questions or to make [the defendant] more aware of what was going on" or to "think of a question to ask." The interview began at 8:45 A.M. and ended at 9:25 A.M. The tape recording lasted for approximately fifteen minutes. . . . Although the defendant denied shooting Green, he admitted that he had been at the scene of the shooting and that Green had been threatening his younger brother.

[The defendant filed a motion to suppress the statement.] The trial court concluded, relying on Michigan v. Mosley, 423 U.S. 96 (1975), that the police could reinterrogate a defendant who had waived his right to remain silent if the defendant waived those rights at the subsequent interrogation. The court further stated that Connecticut case law permits reinterrogation of an accused after an initial election to remain silent when, as in this case, the two interviews are separate, when the first interrogation ceased immediately upon the defendant's invocation of his right to remain silent, when new *Miranda* warnings are given before reinterrogation, and when no attorney was requested. [The trial court went on to conclude that the defendant's waiver was knowing, intelligent, and voluntary. On appeal, Stanley claims that] the statement should not have been admitted pursuant to Michigan v. Mosley, because the defendant's right to terminate police interrogation after he had invoked his right to remain silent was not scrupulously honored. We disagree.

In Michigan v. Mosley, the defendant was arrested for robbery. After effecting the arrest, a police officer advised the defendant of his *Miranda* rights and had him read and sign the constitutional rights notification certificate. When the officer began to interrogate him about the robbery, the defendant refused to talk and the officer then ceased the interrogation. The questioning lasted approximately twenty minutes. At no time during the questioning did the defendant request to speak with a lawyer. Approximately two hours later, another police officer brought the defendant to an interview room in order to interrogate him about a separate incident, a murder. That officer advised the defendant of his *Miranda* rights and had him sign the constitutional rights form. During the interrogation, the defendant made a statement implicating himself in the murder. That interrogation lasted approximately fifteen minutes and at no point during its course did the defendant request to speak with a lawyer. The defendant moved to suppress the statement.

The United States Supreme Court held that "the admissibility of statements obtained after the person in custody has decided to remain silent depends under *Miranda* on whether his right to cut off questioning was scrupulously honored." The court then concluded that the defendant's right to cut off questioning was fully respected because: (1) the first interrogating police officer had immediately ceased his interrogation when the defendant invoked his right to remain silent; (2) the second interrogating police officer had waited a significant period of time, more than two hours, before reinterrogating the defendant; (3) the reinterrogation concerned a crime unrelated to the first interrogation; and (4) before the second interrogation began, the defendant had been advised of his *Miranda* rights and had waived those rights.

The only arguable difference between this case and *Mosley* is that in the present case the second interrogating officer, Burton, questioned the defendant about the same crime, the Green murder, about which the first interrogating officer, Pettola, had questioned the defendant. The sole basis of the defendant's argument is that because the subsequent interrogation by the police concerned the same crime about which the defendant had previously refused to talk, the police, per se, failed scrupulously to honor the defendant's fifth amendment right to remain silent. . . .

We do not interpret *Mosley* to stand for the proposition that the police can never reinterrogate a suspect, who has invoked his right to remain silent, regarding the same crime about which he had refused to talk. [The court cited decisions from the Second, Fifth, Eighth, and Ninth Circuits, and from Arkansas, Colorado, and Illinois; it noted contrary authority from the District of Columbia and Pennsylvania.] In *Mosley,* the fact that the second officer's interrogation involved a separate crime from the first interrogation was only one factor that the court considered when concluding that the defendant's right to remain silent had been scrupulously honored. The court also considered the fact that the first interrogating police officer immediately ceased his interrogation when the defendant invoked his right to remain silent, that the second interrogating police officer waited a significant period of time, more than two hours, before reinterrogating the defendant, and that before the second interrogation began the defendant was fully advised of his *Miranda* rights and waived those rights.

Indeed, a broader interpretation of *Mosley* would result in a per se proscription of any further questioning by the police once the defendant invokes his right to remain silent. In essence, the defendant's interpretation of *Mosley* would limit the opportunity of the police to reinterrogate a defendant to those situations where the defendant is under suspicion for more than one crime. This result is contrary to the reasoning in *Mosley,* which refused to "create a per se proscription of indefinite duration upon any further questioning by any police on any subject, once the person in custody has indicated a desire to remain silent." The court further noted that such a per se prohibition "would transform the *Miranda* safeguards into wholly irrational obstacles to legitimate police investigative activity, and deprive suspects of an opportunity to make informed and intelligent assessments of their interests." Under the defendant's interpretation, only those defendants under suspicion for more than one crime would have the "opportunity to make informed and intelligent assessments of their interests."

The purpose of the "scrupulously honor" test is to avoid situations where the police fail "to honor a decision of a person in custody to cut off questioning, either by refusing to discontinue the interrogation upon request or by persisting in repeated efforts to wear down his resistance and make him change his mind." Considering the facts in the present case, we conclude that the police did not persist "in repeated efforts to wear down [the defendant's] resistance and make him change his mind."

In this case, after the defendant was arrested, Pettola fully advised him of his *Miranda* rights. The defendant said he understood them. Pettola interrogated the defendant about an unrelated assault and also about the murder in this case. When the defendant refused to talk about the murder, Pettola immediately ceased the interrogation. This interrogation, during which the defendant did not request a lawyer, lasted only five minutes. Approximately five hours later, longer than the two hour period in *Mosley,* Burton brought the defendant to an interview room to interrogate him about the murder. He had first asked another police officer to speak to the defendant to determine if the defendant would speak with him, which the defendant agreed to do. Burton read the defendant his *Miranda* rights. The defendant again stated that he understood his rights and initialed each protected right. During the course of the interview the defendant made incriminating statements. That interrogation lasted approximately forty-five minutes and the defendant again did not request a lawyer. Based on the foregoing, we conclude that the defendant's right to remain silent was scrupulously honored. . . .

Notes

1. *Effect of invoking right to counsel: majority position.* The Supreme Court now applies the two-part test elaborated in Oregon v. Bradshaw, 462 U.S. 1039 (1983), to determine whether a suspect's statement is admissible when made after an earlier invocation of the right to counsel. First, the court asks who "initiated" any post-invocation conversation about the crime. If the police initiate the conversation (by word or deed), then they violate Edwards v. Arizona, 451 U.S. 477 (1981), and the confession must be suppressed. If the suspect initiates "a generalized discussion about the investigation," a court will proceed to the second step and ask whether the defendant waived the right to counsel knowingly and intelligently, despite the earlier invocation of the right. In *Bradshaw,* the defendant "initiated" the conversation by asking, "Well, what is going to happen to me now?" This basic approach has also met with approval in most state courts. See, e.g., State v. Olivera, 647 N.E.2d 926 (Ill. 1995). However, it is not always easy to determine who "initiates" a "generalized" conversation about the investigation. For instance, what should a police officer do if a suspect who has invoked the right to counsel asks, after a lineup procedure, "What happened?"

As the decision in *Minnick* shows, the Supreme Court has been unwilling to recognize many alternative methods of reopening an interrogation of the suspect who has asked for an attorney. See also Arizona v. Roberson, 486 U.S. 675 (1988) (*Edwards* rule applies even when the second interrogation deals with unrelated crime). Does the *Edwards* rule sufficiently protect the suspect's privilege against self-incrimination? New York provides that a suspect who has invoked the right to counsel should never be allowed to initiate a conversation with the police about the crime unless counsel is present. See People v. Cunningham, 400 N.E.2d 360 (N.Y. 1980) (barring any interrogation after invocation of right to counsel unless waiver made with attorney present). This position has attracted virtually no following among the other states. State v. Piorkowski, 700 A.2d 1146 (Conn. 1997) (rejects New York rule on waiver, defendant may make post-arraignment waiver of counsel in counsel's absence). Why do you suppose so many jurisdictions decline to take this approach?

2. *Effect of invoking right to silence: majority position.* As the *Stanley* case from Connecticut indicates, it is easier for the police to initiate a new interrogation after a suspect has invoked the right to silence, as opposed to the right to counsel. Most state courts have read their state constitutions to reach results consistent with the holding in Michigan v. Mosley, 423 U.S. 96 (1975). See State v. Crump, 834 S.W.2d 265 (Tenn. 1992). As the *Stanley* case suggests, it is still not entirely clear which of the various facts in *Mosley* were essential to the holding there. See Wilson v. State, 562

S.E.2d 164 (Ga. 2002) (reinterrogation under *Mosley* not available for same crime after 17 hour interval; later interrogation must address different crime). Is it appropriate to place different obligations on the police, depending on which right the defendant invokes? What practical differences are there, if any, between the invocation of the right to counsel and the right to silence? Consider People v. Pettingill, 578 P.2d 108 (Cal. 1978) (rejecting the *Mosley* rule and disallowing any government initiation of interrogation after invocation of right to silence).

3. *Effect of invoking rights: foreign practice.* Under the government-issued Code of Practice in Great Britain, authorities may continue to question a suspect even after he has asserted a right to silence, so long as the continued questioning is not oppressive. They may question suspects who request a solicitor only under "exigent circumstances" and a few other exceptional cases. Code of Practice for the Detention, Treatment, and Questioning of Persons by the Police, para. 6.6. See also Craig Bradley, The Emerging International Consensus as to Criminal Procedure Rules, 14 Mich. J. Intl. L. 171 (1993).

E. SIXTH AMENDMENT RIGHT TO COUNSEL DURING INVESTIGATIONS

The Fifth Amendment to the U.S. Constitution, as interpreted in *Miranda,* is not the only source of a right to counsel during the investigate stage of the criminal process. Indeed, the Sixth Amendment provides an explicit right to counsel: "In all criminal prosecutions, the accused shall enjoy the right to . . . have the Assistance of Counsel for his defence." Recall that shortly before it decided *Miranda,* the U.S. Supreme Court suggested, in Escobedo v. Illinois, 378 U.S. 478 (1964), that the Sixth Amendment right to counsel might apply before the start of any formal criminal process. But it eventually became clear that the Sixth Amendment right to counsel attaches only after the initiation of formal proceedings, which typically means some form of charging (initial arraignment, indictment or information). State courts have given the same meaning to state constitutions.

The Sixth Amendment thus provides an alternative — and indeed a clear, textually-based alternative — right to counsel after charging. This separate source of a right to counsel for some defendants raises the fundamental question whether the scope and impact of the Fifth and Sixth Amendment rights to counsel are the same. For example, must defendants be informed of the Sixth Amendment right to counsel, or is the notice regarding the Fifth Amendment right to counsel — through *Miranda* — sufficient? Must a defendant assert the Sixth Amendment right, or does it automatically attach after charging? Will the detailed rules that govern notice, assertion and waiver of the right to counsel under *Miranda* also apply after indictment?

Part D examined the effect of assertion of the Fifth Amendment right to counsel under *Miranda.* The following case and problem examine the effect of asserting a Sixth Amendment right to counsel after charges are filed. Notice any differences between the standards applied under the two constitutional clauses. The specific legal question is whether a government agent can ask subsequent questions to the defendant after the Sixth Amendment counsel right attaches; the factual question within this legal framework is whether various assertions or settings "deliberately elicit" a confession from the defendant.

■ R.H. KUHLMANN v. JOSEPH WILSON

477 U.S. 436 (1986)

POWELL, J.

In the early morning of July 4, 1970, respondent and two confederates robbed the Star Taxicab Garage in the Bronx, New York, and fatally shot the night dispatcher. Shortly before, employees of the garage had observed respondent, a former employee there, on the premises conversing with two other men. They also witnessed respondent fleeing after the robbery, carrying loose money in his arms. After eluding the police for four days, respondent turned himself in. Respondent admitted that he had been present when the crimes took place, claimed that he had witnessed the robbery, gave the police a description of the robbers, but denied knowing them. Respondent also denied any involvement in the robbery or murder, claiming that he had fled because he was afraid of being blamed for the crimes.

After his arraignment, respondent was confined in the Bronx House of Detention, where he was placed in a cell with a prisoner named Benny Lee. Unknown to respondent, Lee had . . . entered into an arrangement with Detective Cullen, according to which Lee agreed to listen to respondent's conversations and report his remarks to Cullen. . . . Cullen instructed Lee not to ask respondent any questions, but simply to "keep his ears open" for the names of the other perpetrators.

Respondent first spoke to Lee about the crimes after he looked out the cellblock window at the Star Taxicab Garage, where the crimes had occurred. Respondent said, "someone's messing with me," and began talking to Lee about the robbery, narrating the same story that he had given the police at the time of his arrest. Lee advised respondent that this explanation "didn't sound too good,"[1] but respondent did not alter his story.

Over the next few days, however, respondent changed details of his original account. Respondent then received a visit from his brother, who mentioned that members of his family were upset because they believed that respondent had murdered the dispatcher. After the visit, respondent again described the crimes to Lee. Respondent now admitted that he and two other men, whom he never identified, had planned and carried out the robbery, and had murdered the dispatcher. Lee informed Cullen of respondent's statements and furnished Cullen with notes that he had written surreptitiously while sharing the cell with respondent.

[After the trial court denied the motion to suppress Lee's evidence, the] jury convicted respondent of common-law murder and felonious possession of a weapon. On May 18, 1972, the trial court sentenced him to a term of 20 years to life on the murder count and to a concurrent term of up to 7 years on the weapons count. [Wilson] filed a petition for federal habeas corpus relief. Respondent argued, among other things, that his statements to Lee were obtained pursuant to police investigative methods that violated his constitutional rights. After considering Massiah v. United States, 377 U.S. 201 (1964), the District Court for the Southern District of New York denied the writ on January 7, 1977. The record demonstrated

1. At the suppression hearing, Lee testified that, after hearing respondent's initial version of his participation in the crimes, "I think I remember telling him that the story wasn't—it didn't sound too good. Things didn't look too good for him." At trial, Lee testified to a somewhat different version of his remark: "Well, I said, look, you better come up with a better story than that because that one doesn't sound too cool to me, that's what I said."

"no interrogation whatsoever" by Lee and "only spontaneous statements" from respondent.

[Our earlier cases in this area] left open the question whether the Sixth Amendment forbids admission in evidence of an accused's statements to a jailhouse informant who was "placed in close proximity but [made] no effort to stimulate conversations about the crime charged." Our review of the line of cases beginning with Massiah v. United States, 377 U.S. 201 (1964), shows that this question must . . . be answered negatively.

The decision in *Massiah* had its roots in . . . Spano v. New York, 360 U.S. 315 (1959). Following his indictment for first-degree murder, the defendant in Spano retained a lawyer and surrendered to the authorities. Before leaving the defendant in police custody, counsel cautioned him not to respond to interrogation. The prosecutor and police questioned the defendant, persisting in the face of his repeated refusal to answer and his repeated request to speak with his lawyer. The lengthy interrogation involved improper police tactics, and the defendant ultimately confessed. Following a trial at which his confession was admitted in evidence, the defendant was convicted and sentenced to death. Agreeing with the Court that the confession was involuntary and thus improperly admitted in evidence under the Fourteenth Amendment, [two] concurring Justices also took the position that the defendant's right to counsel was violated by the secret interrogation. As Justice Stewart observed, an indicted person has the right to assistance of counsel throughout the proceedings against him. The defendant was denied that right when he was subjected to an "all-night inquisition," during which police ignored his repeated requests for his lawyer.

The Court in *Massiah* . . . held that, once a defendant's Sixth Amendment right to counsel has attached, he is denied that right when federal agents "deliberately elicit" incriminating statements from him in the absence of his lawyer. The Court adopted this test, rather than one that turned simply on whether the statements were obtained in an "interrogation," to protect accused persons from "indirect and surreptitious interrogations as well as those conducted in the jailhouse. In this case, Massiah was more seriously imposed upon . . . because he did not even know that he was under interrogation by a government agent." Thus, the Court made clear that it was concerned with interrogation or investigative techniques that were equivalent to interrogation, and that it so viewed the technique in issue in *Massiah*.[20]

In United States v. Henry, 447 U.S. 264 (1980), the Court applied the *Massiah* test to incriminating statements made to a jailhouse informant. [The] informant had engaged the defendant in conversations and "had developed a relationship of trust and confidence with [the defendant] such that [the defendant] revealed incriminating information." This Court [found a *Massiah* violation because] the Government informant "deliberately used his position to secure incriminating information from [the defendant] when counsel was not present." Although the informant had not questioned the defendant, the informant had "stimulated" conversations with the defendant in order to "elicit" incriminating information. The Court emphasized that those facts, like the facts of *Massiah*, amounted to "indirect and surreptitious interrogation" of the defendant.

20. The defendant in *Massiah* made the incriminating statements in a conversation with one of his confederates, who had secretly agreed to permit Government agents to listen to the conversation over a radio transmitter. The agents instructed the confederate to "engage Massiah in conversation relating to the alleged crimes."

Earlier this Term, we applied the *Massiah* standard in a case involving incriminating statements made under circumstances substantially similar to the facts of *Massiah* itself. In Maine v. Moulton, 474 U.S. 159 (1985), the defendant made incriminating statements in a meeting with his accomplice, who had agreed to cooperate with the police. During that meeting, the accomplice, who wore a wire transmitter to record the conversation, discussed with the defendant the charges pending against him, repeatedly asked the defendant to remind him of the details of the crime, and encouraged the defendant to describe his plan for killing witnesses. The Court concluded that these investigatory techniques denied the defendant his right to counsel on the pending charges.[21] Significantly, the Court emphasized that, because of the relationship between the defendant and the informant, the informant's engaging the defendant "in active conversation about their upcoming trial was certain to elicit" incriminating statements from the defendant. Thus, the informant's participation "in this conversation was the functional equivalent of interrogation."

As our recent examination of this Sixth Amendment issue in *Moulton* makes clear, the primary concern of the *Massiah* line of decisions is secret interrogation by investigatory techniques that are the equivalent of direct police interrogation. Since "the Sixth Amendment is not violated whenever — by luck or happenstance — the State obtains incriminating statements from the accused after the right to counsel has attached," a defendant does not make out a violation of that right simply by showing that an informant, either through prior arrangement or voluntarily, reported his incriminating statements to the police. Rather, the defendant must demonstrate that the police and their informant took some action, beyond merely listening, that was designed deliberately to elicit incriminating remarks.

It is thus apparent that the Court of Appeals erred in concluding that respondent's right to counsel was violated under the circumstances of this case. . . . The state court found that Officer Cullen had instructed Lee only to listen to respondent for the purpose of determining the identities of the other participants in the robbery and murder. The police already had solid evidence of respondent's participation. The court further found that Lee followed those instructions, that he "at no time asked any questions" of respondent concerning the pending charges, and that he "only listened" to respondent's "spontaneous" and "unsolicited" statements. The only remark made by Lee that has any support in this record was his comment that respondent's initial version of his participation in the crimes "didn't sound too good." [T]he Court of Appeals focused on that one remark and gave a description of Lee's interaction with respondent that is completely at odds with the facts found by the trial court. In the Court of Appeals' view, "[s]ubtly and slowly, but surely, Lee's ongoing verbal intercourse with [respondent] served to exacerbate [respondent's] already troubled state of mind."[24] After thus revising some of the trial court's findings, and ignoring other more relevant findings, the Court of Appeals concluded that the police "deliberately elicited" respondent's incriminating statements. This

21. The Court observed, however, that where the defendant makes "[i]ncriminating statements pertaining to other crimes, as to which the Sixth Amendment right has not yet attached," those statements "are, of course, admissible at a trial of those offenses."

24. Curiously, the Court of Appeals expressed concern that respondent was placed in a cell that overlooked the scene of his crimes. For all the record shows, however, that fact was sheer coincidence. Nor do we perceive any reason to require police to isolate one charged with crime so that he cannot view the scene, whatever it may be, from his cell window.

conclusion conflicts with the decision of every other state and federal judge who reviewed this record. . . . The judgment of the Court of Appeals is reversed, and the case is remanded for further proceedings consistent with this opinion. . . .

BURGER, C.J., concurring.

. . . This case is clearly distinguishable from United States v. Henry, 447 U.S. 264 (1980). There is a vast difference between placing an "ear" in the suspect's cell and placing a voice in the cell to encourage conversation for the "ear" to record. . . .

BRENNAN, J., dissenting.

The Sixth Amendment guarantees an accused, at least after the initiation of formal charges, the right to rely on counsel as the "medium" between himself and the State. Accordingly, the Sixth Amendment imposes on the State an affirmative obligation to respect and preserve the accused's choice to seek the assistance of counsel, and therefore the determination whether particular action by state agents violates the accused's right to counsel must be made in light of this obligation. . . . As we explained in *Henry*, where the accused has not waived his right to counsel, the government knowingly circumvents the defendant's right to counsel where it "deliberately elicits" inculpatory admissions, that is, "intentionally creates a situation likely to induce [the accused] to make incriminating statements without the assistance of counsel."

In *Henry*, we found that the Federal Government had "deliberately elicited" incriminating statements from Henry based on the following circumstances. The jailhouse informant, Nichols, had apparently followed instructions to obtain information without directly questioning Henry and without initiating conversations concerning the charges pending against Henry. . . . Nichols, we noted, "was not a passive listener; . . . he had some conversations with Mr. Henry while he was in jail and Henry's incriminatory statements were the product of this conversation."

In deciding that Nichols' role in these conversations amounted to deliberate elicitation, we also found three other factors important. First, Nichols was to be paid for any information he produced and thus had an incentive to extract inculpatory admissions from Henry. Second, Henry was not aware that Nichols was acting as an informant. "Conversation stimulated in such circumstances," we observed, "may elicit information that an accused would not intentionally reveal to persons known to be Government agents." Third, Henry was in custody at the time he spoke with Nichols. This last fact is significant, we stated, because "custody imposes pressures on the accused [and] confinement may bring into play subtle influences that will make him particularly susceptible to the ploys of undercover Government agents." We concluded that by "intentionally creating a situation likely to induce Henry to make incriminating statements without the assistance of counsel, the Government violated Henry's Sixth Amendment right to counsel."

In the instant case, as in *Henry*, the accused was incarcerated and therefore was "susceptible to the ploys of undercover Government agents." Like Nichols, Lee was a secret informant, usually received consideration for the services he rendered the police, and therefore had an incentive to produce the information which he knew the police hoped to obtain. Just as Nichols had done, Lee obeyed instructions not to question respondent and to report to the police any statements made by the respondent in Lee's presence about the crime in question. And, like Nichols, Lee encouraged respondent to talk about his crime by conversing with him on the subject over the course of several days and by telling respondent that his exculpatory story would not convince anyone without more work. However, unlike the situation in *Henry,* a disturbing visit from respondent's brother, rather than a conversation with the informant, seems to have been the immediate catalyst for respondent's confession to Lee. While it might appear from this sequence of events that Lee's comment regarding respondent's story and his general willingness to converse with respondent about the crime were not the immediate causes of respondent's admission, I think that the deliberate-elicitation standard requires consideration of the entire course of government behavior. . . .

Problem 8-9. Christian Burial Speech

On the afternoon of December 24, 1968, 10-year-old Pamela Powers went with her family to the YMCA in Des Moines, Iowa, to watch a wrestling tournament in which her brother was participating. When she failed to return from a trip to the washroom, a search for her began; it was unsuccessful.

Robert Williams, who had recently escaped from a mental hospital, was a resident of the YMCA. Soon after the girl's disappearance Williams was seen in the YMCA lobby carrying some clothing and a large bundle wrapped in a blanket. As Williams placed the bundle into his car, a witness noticed a body under the blanket. Williams immediately drove away. His abandoned car was found the following day in Davenport, Iowa, roughly 160 miles east of Des Moines. A warrant was then issued in Des Moines for his arrest on a charge of abduction.

On the morning of December 26, a Des Moines lawyer named Henry McKnight went to the Des Moines police station and informed the officers present that he had just received a long-distance call from Williams and that he had advised Williams to turn himself in to the Davenport police. Williams did surrender that morning to the police in Davenport, and they booked him on the charge specified in the arrest warrant and gave him the warnings required by Miranda v. Arizona. The Davenport police then telephoned their counterparts in Des Moines to inform them that Williams had surrendered. McKnight, the lawyer, was still at the Des Moines police headquarters, and Williams spoke with McKnight on the telephone. McKnight advised Williams that Des Moines police officers would be driving to Davenport to pick him up, that the officers would not interrogate him or mistreat him, and that Williams was not to talk to the officers about Pamela Powers until after consulting with McKnight upon his return to Des Moines. As a result of these conversations, McKnight and the Des Moines police officials agreed that Detective Cleatus Leaming and a fellow officer would drive to Davenport to pick up Williams, that they would bring him directly back to Des Moines, and that they would not question him during the trip.

In the meantime Williams was arraigned before a judge in Davenport on the outstanding arrest warrant. The judge advised him of his *Miranda* rights and committed him to jail. Before leaving the courtroom, Williams conferred with a lawyer named Thomas Kelly, who advised him not to make any statements until consulting with McKnight back in Des Moines.

Soon after Detective Leaming and his fellow officer arrived in Davenport, they met with Williams and Kelly. Detective Leaming repeated the *Miranda* warnings, and told Williams: "We both know that you're being represented here by Mr. Kelly and you're being represented by Mr. McKnight in Des Moines, and I want you to remember this because we'll be visiting between here and Des Moines." Kelly reiterated to Detective Leaming that Williams was not to be questioned about the disappearance of Pamela Powers until after he had consulted with McKnight back in Des Moines. When Leaming expressed some reservations, Kelly firmly stated that the agreement with McKnight was to be carried out — that there was to be no interrogation of Williams during the journey to Des Moines. Kelly was denied permission to ride in the police car back to Des Moines with Williams and the two officers. The two detectives, with Williams in their charge, then set out on the 160-mile drive. Williams said several times during the trip that "when I get to Des Moines and see Mr. McKnight, I am going to tell you the whole story."

Detective Leaming knew that Williams was a former mental patient, and knew also that he was deeply religious. Leaming and Williams soon embarked on a conversation covering a variety of topics, including the subject of religion. Leaming addressed Williams as "Reverend." He then made this speech:

> I want to give you something to think about while we're traveling down the road. Number one, I want you to observe the weather conditions, it's raining, it's sleeting, it's freezing, driving is very treacherous, visibility is poor, it's going to be dark early this evening. They are predicting several inches of snow for tonight, and I feel that you yourself are the only person that knows where this little girl's body is, that you yourself have only been there once, and if you get a snow on top of it you yourself may be unable to find it. And, since we will be going right past the area on the way into Des Moines, I feel that we could stop and locate the body, that the parents of this little girl should be entitled to a Christian burial for the little girl who was snatched away from them on Christmas Eve and murdered. And I feel we should stop and locate it on the way in rather than waiting until morning and trying to come back out after a snow storm and possibly not being able to find it at all.

Williams asked Detective Leaming why he thought their route to Des Moines would be taking them past the girl's body, and Leaming responded that he knew the body was in the area of Mitchellville — a town they would be passing on the way to Des Moines. (In fact, Leaming did not know where the body was.) Leaming then added, "I do not want you to answer me. I don't want to discuss it any further. Just think about it as we're riding down the road."

As the car approached Grinnell, a town approximately 100 miles west of Davenport, Williams asked whether the police had found the victim's shoes. When Detective Leaming replied that he was unsure, Williams directed the officers to a service station where he said he had left the shoes; a search for them proved unsuccessful. As they continued toward Des Moines, Williams asked whether the police had found the blanket, and directed the officers to a rest area where he said he had disposed of the blanket. Nothing was found. The car continued toward Des Moines, and as it approached Mitchellville, Williams said that he would show the officers where the body was. He then directed the police to the body of Pamela Powers.

Williams was indicted for first-degree murder. Because a warrant had been issued for Williams' arrest, and because he had been arraigned and confined to jail, Williams' Sixth Amendment right to counsel attached. Before trial, his counsel moved to suppress all evidence resulting from any statements Williams had made during the automobile ride from Davenport to Des Moines. Should the judge grant the motion? Compare Brewer v. Williams, 430 U.S. 387 (1977); Yale Kamisar, Brewer v. Williams — A Hard Look at a Discomfiting Record, 66 Geo. L.J. 209 (1977).

Notes

1. *The Sixth Amendment right to counsel and "deliberately eliciting" a confession.* The Sixth Amendment to the U.S. Constitution provides for a right to counsel "in all criminal prosecutions." The U.S. Supreme Court, along with most states applying analogous state constitutional provisions, has held that Sixth Amendment counsel rights attach after the initiation of formal proceedings, whether by way of indictment, information, or initial arraignment.

In Brewer v. Williams, 430 U.S. 387 (1977), the case on which Problem 8-9 is based, the Court held that Detective Leaming violated that right by "deliberately eliciting" information from Williams while his counsel was absent, and that Williams had not waived his right to counsel: "It is true that Williams had been informed of and appeared to understand his right to counsel. But waiver requires not merely comprehension but relinquishment, and Williams's consistent reliance upon the advice of counsel in dealing with the authorities refutes any suggestion that he waived that right." How do the facts compare in the *Innis* case, reprinted in Part B, where the Court held that no interrogation occurred, and in *Williams,* where the Court concluded that the police deliberately elicited information? Are the Fifth and Sixth Amendment definitions of "interrogation" comparable?

In Michigan v. Jackson, 475 U.S. 625 (1986), the Court explained that Sixth Amendment Rights deserve at least as much protection as Fifth Amendment rights, and applied Edwards v. Arizona, 451 U.S. 477 (1981), to hold that government agents could not initiate a conversation with a defendant after the Sixth Amendment right to counsel had attached.

> [After] a formal accusation has been made — and a person who had previously been just a "suspect" has become an "accused" within the meaning of the Sixth Amendment — the constitutional right to the assistance of counsel is of such importance that the police may no longer employ techniques for eliciting information from an uncounseled defendant that might have been entirely proper at an earlier stage of their investigation. Thus, the surreptitious employment of a cellmate, or the electronic surveillance of conversations with third parties, may violate the defendant's Sixth Amendment right to counsel even though the same methods of investigation might have been permissible before arraignment or indictment. Far from undermining the *Edwards* rule, the difference between the legal basis for the rule applied in *Edwards* and the Sixth Amendment claim asserted in these cases actually provides additional support for the application of the rule in these circumstances.

The Court observed that "after the initiation of adversary judicial proceedings, the Sixth Amendment provides a right to counsel at a 'critical stage' even when there is no interrogation and no Fifth Amendment applicability." As with *Edwards,* however, the Court did not preclude a later confession where the defendant initiated a later conversation.

2. *Sixth Amendment right to counsel and cellmate confessions.* In Kuhlmann v. Wilson, the U.S. Supreme Court deferred to the factual findings of the trial court that

prisoner Benny Lee was not acting as a government interrogator when the government planted Lee in Wilson's cell. *Kuhlmann* is the Court's latest statement on the topic of whether government agents "deliberately elicit" a confession from a defendant whose Sixth Amendment rights have attached. The fact-driven bottom line in *Kuhlmann* and the Court's long silence on the issue since then suggests that the U.S. Supreme Court now leaves it to trial courts to sort out those cases. Why is there a different standard for assessing when government agents have violated defendants' Fifth Amendment and Sixth Amendment rights to counsel?

3. *Scope of the Sixth Amendment right to counsel for "other" offenses.* Can government agents interrogate a defendant about a crime other than an offense for which the government has initiated formal proceedings? In McNeil v. Wisconsin, 501 U.S. 171 (1991), the Court explained that "The Sixth Amendment right [to counsel] is offense specific. It cannot be invoked once for all future prosecutions, for it does not attach until a prosecution is commenced, that is, at or after the initiation of adversary judicial criminal proceedings—whether by way of formal charge, preliminary hearing, indictment, information, or arraignment." In Texas v. Cobb, 532 U.S. 162 (2001), the Court addressed the issue of what constituted the "same offense." Some state court and lower federal court decisions treated "factually related" crimes as the "same offense." The Supreme Court, however, held that the determination of whether a second offense was the "same offense" under the Sixth Amendment should be determined under the narrow standards applied under federal law to determine whether double jeopardy barred the filing of two separate charges for the "same offence." See Blockburger v. United States, 284 U.S. 299 (1932), discussed in Chapter 14. Thus, a second offense would not be considered the "same offense" and would allow subsequent interrogation when each of two statutory provisions "requires proof of a fact which the other does not."

F. *MIRANDA* CURES, IMPACTS, AND ALTERNATIVES

The decades-long debate over the wisdom of *Miranda* turns in part on how much of an impact it has on criminal investigations and prosecutions. The first part of this section considers whether a *Miranda* error can be fixed, thus lessening any harm to the prosecution from failure to give proper warnings. The second part considers evidence about the impact of *Miranda* on the criminal justice system. The final part considers whether there are alternatives to giving *Miranda* warnings that would encourage voluntary confessions.

1. *Cures and Remedies for* Miranda *Violations*

In the ordinary case, a *Miranda* violation will mean that the confession obtained as a result of the tainted interrogation will be inadmissible as evidence. But what about physical evidence or testimony of witnesses obtained as a result of the improper interrogation? Will this derivative evidence—the "fruit of the poisonous tree"—be admissible? There are a number of circumstances under which courts will admit evidence obtained after a *Miranda* violation, even if the improper interrogation was the "but for" cause of the police obtaining the evidence. As you read the following materials, try to sort out the various arguments in favor of ignoring the original violation of law.

■ STATE v. HOSIE VAN SMITH

834 S.W.2d 915 (Tenn. 1992)

ANDERSON, J.

The primary issue raised on this appeal is whether the defendant's confession, obtained after proper administration of *Miranda* warnings, is inadmissible at trial because a prior incriminating statement was obtained in violation of the Fifth Amendment of the United States Constitution and Article I, §9 of the Tennessee Constitution. The initial incriminating statement made by the defendant, Hosie Smith, before any *Miranda* warning was given to him was suppressed. A later confession was obtained after a search had revealed cocaine in Smith's possession and after the police had read Smith his *Miranda* rights. The admissibility of the confession was challenged on the grounds it was involuntary and tainted as the fruit of the first unwarned incriminating statement given in violation of the Federal and State Constitutions. [The trial court denied the motion, and the defendant was convicted.

Officers Mike Hannan and Terry Thomas of the Tennessee Highway Patrol stopped a speeding vehicle driven by Kellie Alisha Jones. When Jones was unable to find the vehicle's registration, Officer Hannan asked her to accompany him to his squad car while he wrote out a traffic citation.

While Jones went to the squad car, the passenger, Hosie Smith, looked in the glove compartment for the vehicle's registration. Officer Thomas, who was on the passenger's side of the car, asked Smith questions regarding ownership of the car and the couple's destination. After this brief conversation with Smith, Thomas returned to the squad car and sat in the back seat. While waiting for radio verification of Jones's license and the vehicle's registration, both officers continued to question Jones about the ownership of the car and her destination. When asked who her passenger was, Jones stated that it was her boyfriend, but she could only give the name "Pumpkin" when asked about his name.

Because Smith and Jones appeared to be extremely nervous, and had given inconsistent answers to the questions about their destination and the ownership of the car, the officers became suspicious and asked Jones if she was carrying any illegal items, weapons, or contraband. Jones denied knowledge of such cargo, and consented to a search of the car.

Officer Thomas re-approached the station wagon on the passenger side and asked Smith if there were any illegal items in the car. Smith denied knowledge of any such contraband. Thomas then told Smith that he had permission to look through the vehicle, and asked again about any illegal items in the car. Smith said, "Yes, it was probably a hot load." Thomas then asked, "By a hot load, do you mean cash, marijuana, or cocaine, one of the three?" Smith responded, "Probably." Thomas searched the car and found 22 pounds of pure cocaine in the locked glove compartment. At 6:25 P.M., the officers placed both Smith and Jones under arrest, read them their *Miranda* rights, and transported them to Highway Patrol Headquarters.]

At 9:45 P.M., Smith was questioned by Officer Lonnie Hood. Before he was questioned, Smith was read his *Miranda* rights again and signed a written waiver of those rights. During the course of the interrogation, Smith gave Officer Hood an incriminating account of his employment to drive the station wagon with Jones from Oklahoma City, Oklahoma, to Fayetteville, North Carolina. This statement was reduced to writing by Officer Hood and signed by Smith.

Following a suppression hearing, the trial court held that Smith's statements about the vehicle containing a "hot load" prior to his being Mirandized were inadmissible. The trial court held, however, that the cocaine was admissible at trial as the fruit of a valid consensual search, and that the later written confession signed by Smith was admissible. . . .

The dispositive issue in this case involves the admissibility of the confession given to Officer Hood and signed by Smith at the Highway Patrol Headquarters. . . . Smith argues that his waiver of rights and his statement to Officer Hood were not voluntary, because they were tainted by Officer Thomas' conduct in first questioning Smith on the side of the interstate without administering *Miranda* warnings.

The Fifth Amendment to the United States Constitution . . . provides that "no person . . . shall be compelled in any criminal case to be a witness against himself." The corresponding provision of the Tennessee Constitution provides "that in all criminal prosecutions, the accused . . . shall not be compelled to give evidence against himself." Tenn. Const. art. I, §9. Although these provisions are not identical, this Court has previously declined to hold that protection under the state constitution is broader than that of the federal constitution merely because the language of the two provisions is not the same. This observation, however, does not foreclose the possibility that the state constitutional provision might be applied more broadly than its federal counterpart, based upon considerations other than, and in addition to, the difference in terminology. . . .

In Oregon v. Elstad, 470 U.S. 298 (1985, a majority of the United States Supreme Court decided that, in a situation similar to that faced by the defendant in this case, a trial court must conclude that an initial confession obtained without prior warnings regarding the right against self-incrimination is inadmissible. The court went on to hold, however, that the presumption of compulsion attaching to an unwarned confession does not also apply to a subsequent confession obtained after administering *Miranda* warnings. In discussing the admissibility of such a second confession at trial, the court stated:

> Absent deliberately coercive or improper tactics in obtaining the initial statement, the mere fact that a suspect has made an unwarned admission does not warrant a presumption of compulsion. A subsequent administration of *Miranda* warnings to a suspect who has given a voluntary but unwarned statement ordinarily should suffice to remove the conditions that precluded admission of the earlier statement.

This holding by the United States Supreme Court represented a clear break with past precedent embracing the "cat out of the bag" theory espoused in United States v. Bayer, 331 U.S. 532 (1947). In *Bayer,* the court recognized:

> Of course, after an accused has once let the cat out of the bag by confessing, no matter what the inducement, he is never thereafter free of the psychological and practical disadvantages of having confessed. He can never get the cat back in the bag. The secret is out for good. In such a sense, a later confession always may be looked upon as fruit of the first.

See also Martin v. State, 440 S.W.2d 624 (Tenn. Crim. App. 1968). Even in *Bayer,* however, the United States Supreme Court refused to hold that an illegally-obtained confession would forever foreclose the possibility that a subsequent admissible confession could be elicited from the defendant. In fact, in that case, the court determined that the subsequent confession given six months after the defendant's first statement would not be held invalid. . . .

We believe that adherence to the spirit and principles of Article I, §9 of the Tennessee Constitution requires us to recognize, as a matter of Tennessee constitutional law, the inherent reasonableness of the underlying premise expressed in *Bayer* and *Martin.* Consequently, we dispute the rationale of the *Elstad* decision that, absent coercion in eliciting an initial confession, psychological pressures and other pressures flowing from that confession can never lead a defendant to give subsequent, involuntary, incriminating statements. . . .

Like the court in *Bayer,* however, we also refuse to hold that an initial, illegally-obtained confession forever bars the prosecution from obtaining a subsequent, admissible confession from the defendant. Rather, we hold that the provisions of Article I, §9 of the Tennessee Constitution necessitate that we recognize that extraction of an illegal, unwarned confession from a defendant raises a rebuttable presumption that a subsequent confession, even if preceded by proper *Miranda* warnings, is tainted by the initial illegality. That presumption may be overcome by the prosecution, however, if the State can establish "that the taint is so attenuated as to justify admission of the subsequent confession."

In each such case, the crucial inquiry for the courts becomes whether the events and circumstances surrounding and following the initial, illegal conduct of the law enforcement officers prevented the accused from subsequently (1) making a free and informed choice to waive the State constitutional right not to provide evidence against one's self, and (2) voluntarily confessing his involvement in the crime. In addressing these questions, courts should examine the following factors:

1. The use of coercive tactics to obtain the initial, illegal confession and the causal connection between the illegal conduct and the challenged, subsequent confession;
2. The temporal proximity of the prior and subsequent confessions;
3. The reading and explanation of *Miranda* rights to the defendant before the subsequent confession;
4. The circumstances occurring after the arrest and continuing up until the making of the subsequent confession including, but not limited to, the length of the detention and the deprivation of food, rest, and bathroom facilities;
5. The coerciveness of the atmosphere in which any questioning took place including, but not limited to, the place where the questioning occurred, the identity of the interrogators, the form of the questions, and the repeated or prolonged nature of the questioning;
6. The presence of intervening factors including, but not limited to, consultations with counsel or family members, or the opportunity to consult with counsel, if desired;
7. The psychological effect of having already confessed, and whether the defendant was advised that the prior confession may not be admissible at trial;

8. Whether the defendant initiated the conversation that led to the subsequent confession; and
9. The defendant's sobriety, education, intelligence level, and experience with the law, as such factors relate to the defendant's ability to understand the administered *Miranda* rights.

In ruling upon the admissibility of a subsequent confession following the determination that an initial, unwarned confession may not be introduced in the State's case-in-chief, no single factor listed above is determinative. Rather, a court must examine the totality of the circumstances surrounding the two confessions to determine whether the subsequent confession by the defendant can truly be termed a knowing and voluntary statement.

The facts of this case demonstrate that Smith's subsequent confession was given knowingly and voluntarily. No coercive tactics were employed by the law enforcement officials to elicit either the first or the second incriminating statement given by the defendant. More than three hours elapsed between the time Smith was arrested and first given his *Miranda* warnings and the time when he gave his second confession to the authorities. There is no evidence in the record that Smith was in any way mistreated during that time period or that he was prevented from contacting friends, family or legal counsel. Additionally, Smith had been advised of his *Miranda* rights twice before his second statement was given (once at the time of his arrest and again immediately before the second statement), both the interrogators and the place of interrogation changed from the first illegally-obtained confession, and there is no indication that Smith did not fully understand the rights explained to him. In fact, Smith acknowledged that he understood his rights and signed a written waiver of them. . . .

The only coercive influence apparent in this record is the fact that Smith was in police custody at the time of his statement and at all relevant times after his arrest. Although police custody is inherently coercive and compelling, if we were to hold this single factor sufficient to vitiate the voluntariness of a subsequent confession, an accused could never give a voluntary confession after arrest. We are unwilling to condone such a result because of our belief that "confessions remain a proper element in law enforcement." . . .

DROWOTA, J., concurring.

I would affirm but apply the rule announced by the United States Supreme Court in Oregon v. Elstad. . . . While the majority purports to adopt a presumption, apparently gleaned from Justice Brennan's dissent in *Elstad,* that an illegally obtained initial confession taints any subsequent confession, I submit that the majority does nothing more than examine the totality of the circumstances in order to determine whether Smith's post-*Miranda* statement was voluntarily made.

Further, the "psychological stress" component of the majority's presumption gives reason for pause: Were the majority to actually apply Justice Brennan's "cat out of the bag" presumption, it is difficult to imagine that Smith's post-*Miranda* statement would be found free of taint. Smith waived his *Miranda* rights a mere three hours after his initial statement, and at a time when he was burdened by the "psychological stress" of knowing the police found 10,000 grams (22 pounds) of 94 percent pure cocaine in his car. . . .

Notes

1. *Out-of-court statements obtained after earlier* Miranda *violations: majority position.* Unlike illegal searches and seizures, an unwarned interrogation will not necessarily require a later court to exclude all the evidence derived from the tainted statement. Although any statement made during an unwarned interrogation must not come into evidence, later statements of the suspect might still be admissible — even though the statements appear to be the "fruit of the poisonous tree." The federal position on the use of statements obtained after earlier tainted statements was established in Oregon v. Elstad, 470 U.S. 298 (1985). In that case, two deputy sheriffs investigating a burglary came to the home of a suspect, 18-year-old Michael Elstad, to execute an arrest warrant. Elstad's mother answered the door and led the officers to the suspect, who was in his bedroom at the time. The officers then took Elstad to the living room, where they asked if he knew the victims of the burglary. Elstad admitted that he had been involved in the burglary. The officers then took Elstad to the sheriff's headquarters. About an hour later, they advised him for the first time of his *Miranda* rights. Elstad waived his rights and confessed to the crime. The Supreme Court held that the state could use as evidence the confession obtained at the station but not the earlier confession obtained at Elstad's home. According to the Court, when the initial unwarned statement was given voluntarily,

> a careful and thorough administration of *Miranda* warnings serves to cure the condition that rendered the unwarned statement inadmissible. The warning conveys the relevant information and thereafter the suspect's choice whether to exercise his privilege to remain silent should ordinarily be viewed as an act of free will.

470 U.S. at 310.

A significant minority of states — around 15 — join Tennessee in rejecting the *Elstad* decision, placing a burden on the government to overcome a presumption of compulsion for subsequent confessions. See, e.g., Commonwealth v. Smith, 593 N.E.2d 1288 (Mass. 1992). A larger group of states follow the *Elstad* standard and allow introduction of the subsequent confession if it was made pursuant to proper warnings. In what types of cases might the test described in *Smith* produce results different from the *Elstad* standard? Was it significant in *Elstad* that the original unwarned questioning occurred in the suspect's home?

2. *Confession in open court. Smith* and *Elstad* address only out-of-court confessions made during a noncoercive interrogation that proceeds after proper warnings and waivers. Note that if a defendant makes an admission during testimony at trial, no inquiry is necessary to determine whether the effects of the earlier improper interrogation have attenuated. Why are in-court and out-of-court admissions treated differently? Are defendants more likely to be honest, or less coerced, in the courtroom setting? A number of state statutes have special rules for in-court confessions. See Tex. Code Crim. Proc. Ann. art. 38.22, §5.

3. *Use of statements for impeachment at trial.* Although state and federal courts exclude *Miranda*-tainted statements from the prosecution's case in chief, they allow the prosecution to use such statements (and the evidentiary fruit of those statements) to impeach a defendant's testimony at trial. See Oregon v. Hass, 420 U.S. 714 (1975); Harris v. New York, 401 U.S. 222 (1971). Again, not all states agree. See Commonwealth v. Triplett, 462 Pa. 244, 341 A.2d 62 (1975) (under Pennsylvania Constitution,

statement obtained in violation of an accused's *Miranda* rights cannot be used to impeach his trial testimony.

In light of these rulings, will police officers routinely violate *Miranda* after a suspect invokes the right to silence or to an attorney, simply to provide the prosecutor with potential impeachment evidence? See Richard Leo, The Impact of *Miranda* Revisited, 86 J. Crim. L. & Criminology 621 (1996) (in study of more than 180 interrogations, observing only one instance of interrogator pursuing questions in known violation of *Miranda*). In California and other states, some training material for prosecutors and police officers explicitly advocate that investigators continue an interrogation even after a suspect invokes *Miranda* rights. As Assistant District Attorney Devallis Rutledge of Orange County, California, puts it in a training video, "Can you [question a guy outside *Miranda*]? Sure you can. All of these cases have said there's legitimate uses that a *Miranda*-violative statement can be put to. The only use it can't be put to is to prove the person's guilt at trial." The California Peace Officers Legal Sourcebook, issued by the State Attorney General's office, makes the same point. See Jan Hoffman, Police Are Skirting Restraints to Get Confessions, New York Times, Mar. 29, 1998, at 1, 21; Charles Weisselberg, Saving *Miranda,* 84 Cornell L. Rev. 109 (1998) (collecting evidence of training that encourages interrogations outside *Miranda*).

Does the fact that investigators intentionally obtain "*Miranda*-violative statements" on a department-wide basis change the remedy that is constitutionally required? See People v. Peevy, 953 P.2d 1212 (Cal. 1998) (government can use statements for impeachment even if police intentionally questioned defendant in violation of *Miranda*).

4. *Harmless error.* There are some constitutional errors in a trial that an appellate court will consider "harmless" because the verdict likely would have remained the same even if the errors had not occurred. There are other errors that courts say can never be harmless. For a number of years after the *Miranda* decision, courts said that the introduction into evidence of a coerced confession qualified as one such error. This type of error was said to involve a right so basic to a fair trial that courts would not bother with a harmless-error inquiry. In Arizona v. Fulminante, 499 U.S. 279 (1991), however, the Supreme Court decided that the introduction of coerced confessions could be treated as a harmless error after all. We discuss this issue further in Chapter 20, dealing with appeals.

5. *Alternatives to exclusion.* The remedy for improper efforts to obtain confessions has been exclusion of the confession. If the confession was coerced (as opposed to a technical violation of the *Miranda* requirements), any evidentiary fruits of the confession are also inadmissible. Is some alternative remedy possible? Are damage suits, injunctions, or administrative sanctions workable alternatives?

Both federal and state law allow criminal suspects to sue police officers for the use of illegal interrogation techniques. Although there are some important barriers to recovery in both state and federal courts (as we saw in Chapter 6), plaintiffs sometimes can recover damages after they have been subjected to illegal interrogations, including *Miranda* violations and the use of physical deprivations. Would an intentional violation of *Miranda* make recovery easier in a civil suit? See California Attorneys for Criminal Justice v. Butts, 195 F.3d 1039 (9th Cir. 1999); Susan Klein, *Miranda* Deconstitutionalized: When the Self-Incrimination Clause and the Civil Rights Act Collide, 143 U. Pa. L. Rev. 417 (1994).

Problem 8-10. Inevitable Discovery

Elizabeth Reed, an attendant at a county landfill, died from a shotgun wound fired at close range as she was preparing to leave work. The killer left Reed's body hidden in some brush beside a dirt road, approximately 95 feet from the landfill office. The police soon began to focus their investigation on Kenneth DeShields, who had been seen that day driving Reed's car. They arrested him the morning after the murder.

Before any questioning began, DeShields requested an attorney and said that he did not wish to speak about the incident. However, the investigating officers persisted in their questions, and DeShields ultimately gave a series of statements. Although DeShields initially denied any knowledge of the murder, he eventually told the police that he had been with a man named "Blair" when Blair had killed Reed during an attempt to rob her. DeShields also said that after he and Blair had left the landfill, Blair had thrown a rake into a ditch and driven down a dirt road in the nearby woods to discard several items from the robbery. Detective Hudson then searched the dirt road that DeShields had described. He found an expended shotgun shell casing and the victim's wallet approximately 15 feet east of the dirt road and approximately 1,000 feet from the dump site.

At trial, the state did not introduce any of DeShields's postarrest statements into evidence. However, the shell casing and wallet were admitted into evidence, and an expert testified that the shell casing had been fired from DeShields's shotgun. The shell casing was the only direct evidence linking the killing to his shotgun. Two police officers testified that it was routine police practice to search the general area extensively in a homicide case and that this practice was followed in this case. By the time Hudson found the evidence, the police had already searched the landfill compound and several county roads that crisscrossed the area.

Did the trial court rule correctly in admitting the shell casing and wallet into evidence? Compare DeShields v. State, 534 A.2d 630 (Del. 1987).

Note

1. *Tainted leads to witnesses and physical evidence.* An improper interrogation might give the authorities information that can lead them to other witnesses or to physical evidence. In Michigan v. Tucker, 417 U.S. 433 (1974), the Supreme Court allowed the use of prosecution witnesses whose names had been obtained during an interrogation where proper *Miranda* warnings had not been given. While recognizing that a truly involuntary confession, obtained in violation of the due process clause, could be remedied only by complete exclusion of all evidentiary "fruits" of the confession, this was not such a case. The failure to give proper *Miranda* warnings was merely a violation of a "prophylactic" rule rather than a constitutional violation as such. For *Miranda* violations that do not create an involuntary (and thus unconstitutional) confession, the Court believed that exclusion of evidence would be too costly. While no state court has rejected this analysis explicitly, many seem to assume that any evidentiary "fruit" from a confession obtained in violation of *Miranda* must be excluded unless one of the three traditional exceptions to the "fruits" rule is present. Those exceptions, as you may recall from Chapter 6, are inevitable discovery,

independent source, and attenuation. For example, the Delaware Supreme Court in the case that is the basis for Problem 8-10 admitted the shell casing and wallet because standard crime scene search practices would have led to their discovery. Some jurisdictions limit the inevitable discovery exception by requiring the government to prove that the police did not act in bad faith to accelerate the discovery of the evidence. See State v. Phelps, 297 N.W.2d 769 (N.D. 1980).

2. *Systemwide Impacts*

Miranda has been criticized on both doctrinal and practical grounds. The practical critiques take many forms, but they boil down to the question of how many convictions are "lost" because *Miranda* warnings were given. Before reading the following study, it is worth thinking in the abstract about the challenge of measuring the impact of *Miranda.* The article illustrates recent efforts, 30 years after the decision, to study its continuing impact. Is it possible to reach a conclusion about the impact of *Miranda,* either 30 years ago or today? Can the benefits of *Miranda* be quantified?

■ POLICE INTERROGATION IN THE 1990S: AN EMPIRICAL STUDY OF THE EFFECTS OF *MIRANDA*

PAUL CASSELL AND BRET HAYMAN

43 UCLA L. Rev. 839 (1996)

[W]e undertook an empirical survey of confessions and their importance [in Salt Lake City, Utah]. We collected the basic data for the study by attending "screening" sessions held at the Salt Lake County District Attorney's office during a six-week period in the summer of 1994. Prosecutors in the District Attorney's Office screen all felony cases for prosecutive merit. . . . The screening session is a forty-five-minute interview by the prosecutor of the police officer concerning the evidence supporting the filing of charges. . . . There were 219 suspects in our sample. . . .

A. The Frequency of Questioning, Waivers, and Confessions

One important issue that has not been the subject of much empirical study is the frequency with which suspects are questioned. Not every person who is arrested will be questioned. In our sample, police questioned 79.0% of the suspects. This means that a surprisingly large percentage (21.0%) were not questioned.

[We also] collected information on why police failed to interrogate suspects (as reported by the officer at screening). [In] two cases (4.9% of the nonquestioning cases), the reason for not questioning was a belief that the suspect would invoke *Miranda.* In two other cases (4.9% of the nonquestioning cases), the police cited the fact that a suspect had an attorney as the obstacle to questioning, a reason that has a possible connection with *Miranda.* . . The most often-given reason for nonquestioning [accounting for 34.1% of the nonquestioning cases] was that a suspect's whereabouts was unknown at the time police screened the case. The second most common reason [26.8%] for failure to question was the officer's belief that the case against the suspect was overwhelming. . . .

One of the most important questions about the *Miranda* regime is how often suspects invoke their *Miranda* rights, preventing any police questioning. A suspect can claim *Miranda* rights in two ways. First, he can refuse at the start of an interview to waive his rights (including the right to remain silent and the right to counsel), thus precluding any interview. Second, even if he initially waives his rights, he can assert them at any point in the interview. If a suspect asserts *Miranda* rights, police questioning must stop. . . . Surprisingly very little information is available on such a fundamental subject. The previously published evidence . . . suggests that about 20% of all suspects invoke their *Miranda* rights.

We gathered data on how often and in what ways suspects asserted their *Miranda* rights. [Of] suspects given their *Miranda* rights, 83.7% waived them. Reflecting the practices of the local law enforcement agencies, virtually all of these waivers were verbal rather than written. At the same time, 16.3% invoked their rights. Of the twenty-one suspects who invoked their rights, nine invoked their right to an attorney (two even before *Miranda* warnings could be read), six invoked their right not to make a statement, and six either refused to execute a waiver or otherwise invoked their rights.

[F]ive suspects who initially waived their rights [3.9% of the total] changed their minds later and invoked their rights during the interview. Of these five suspects, three asked for an attorney during the interview (two after giving incriminating statements, one after giving a denial with an explanation), and two asserted their right to remain silent during the interview (one after giving a flat denial, one after giving a denial with an explanation). . . . If these three are added to suspects who invoked their rights initially, then a total of 18.6% of the suspects in our sample who were given *Miranda* rights invoked them before police succeeded in obtaining incriminating information. . . .

Perhaps the critical issue in the debate over *Miranda* is how often today suspects confess or otherwise make incriminating statements. Surprisingly little information is available on this subject, despite frequent definitive pronouncements that many suspects still confess.

[W]e divided the outcomes into "successful" and "unsuccessful" categories—looking at the results from law enforcement's point of view. The result of questioning was "successful" when the police: (1) obtained a written confession; (2) obtained a verbal confession; (3) obtained an incriminating statement; or (4) locked a suspect into a false alibi.

A written or verbal "confession" was "any substantial acknowledgment by the suspect that he or she committed the crime." Simply put, the suspect had to say in essence "I did it." . . . A "confession" could include statements in mitigation. . . .

Our next category was for "incriminating statements." Because this category is somewhat subjective and because its scope makes a critical difference in determining the scope of police success statistics, it is worth explaining in detail. An "incriminating statement" was "any statement that tends to establish guilt of the accused or from which with other facts guilt may be inferred or which tends to disprove some anticipated defense."

We found that such statements generally occurred in one of three situations. First, a suspect might give a statement that linked him to the crime or crime scene without admitting his guilt. For example, in an attempted homicide case the police asked the suspect if a certain car, known to have been involved in the crime, was his. He responded that it was, but denied any involvement in the crime. . . . A second

Table 4 — Results
(N = 219 overall; 173 for those questioned)

	No.	*Questioned Only* %	*Overall* %
Invoked rights	21	12.1	9.5
Successful	73	42.2	33.3 . . .
Unsuccessful	79	45.7	36.1 . . .
Not questioned	46	—	21.0
Total	219	100	100

kind of incriminating statement was a partial admission of guilt. For example, in one case involving a burglary, a suspect admitted being in the house unlawfully, but said he was there because of something the victim had done to his girlfriend, not to steal anything. . . .

Third, a suspect might make statements to the police that tended to call into question his truthfulness or make him appear suspicious. For example, in one case an officer suspected a car was stolen and pulled over the suspect. The officer asked the suspect certain questions concerning his license, registration, and his relationship to the car. The suspect was visibly shaken by the questions and gave stammering and sometimes contradictory answers. We classified these statements as "incriminating."

After confessions and incriminating statements, the final category of "successful" outcomes was for a suspect who was "locked into a false alibi." . . .

The number of incriminating statements and denials we found are shown in Table 4. Overall, 9.5% of the suspects invoked their rights, 33.3% were successfully questioned, 36.1% were questioned unsuccessfully, and 21.0% were not questioned. Because some might argue that only suspects who were in fact questioned should be included in determining a confession rate, we also report percentages for only those suspects who were questioned. As can also be seen in Table 4, of all police interviews, 12.1% produced an immediate invocation of *Miranda* rights, 42.2% were successful, and 45.7% were unsuccessful. It should also be noted that, however measured, our "success" rate is artificially inflated because of the point at which our sample was drawn. We sampled cases from screening sessions where police officers believed they had gathered sufficient evidence for prosecution. As a consequence, our sample excludes a significant number of cases that police thought were too weak to warrant prosecution — including cases that were too weak because of an unsuccessful outcome of police questioning. . . .

[We] also examined whether suspects for particular types of crimes were more likely to confess. The limited previous research on this issue, from studies conducted in the 1960s, suggests that suspects are less likely to confess to violent crimes than to property crimes. Our data trend in this direction; . . . police were less successful in interrogating suspects for crimes of violence than for property crimes, although the result is not statistically significant at the conventional . . . confidence level. . . .

Although our success rate is inflated, it is lower than success rates found in this country before *Miranda,* suggesting that *Miranda* has hampered law enforcement efforts to obtain incriminating statements. [The] available pre- and post-*Miranda* information on confession rates in this country . . . suggests that interrogations were successful, very roughly speaking, in about 55% to 60% of interrogations conducted before the *Miranda* decision. For example, the earliest academic study in this country reported confession rates of 88.1% and 58.1% in two cities in California in 1960.[149] Similarly, a 1961 survey in Detroit reported a 60.8% confession rate, which fell slightly to 58.0% in 1965. [These figures] avoid the problem of anticipatory implementation of *Miranda* in various jurisdictions. In particular, confession rates after June 1964 might be dampened by the Supreme Court's *Escobedo* decision, which led some police to adopt *Miranda*-style warnings even before the decision. Our 33.3% overall success rate (and even our 42.2% questioning success rate) is well below the 55%-60% estimated pre-*Miranda* rate and, therefore, is consistent with the hypothesis that *Miranda* has harmed the confession rate.

B. Questioning Inside and Outside the *Miranda* Regime

One question that has not been the subject of any substantial empirical research is the extent to which police questioning falls inside or outside the *Miranda* regime and whether this makes any difference to ultimate outcomes. . . .

The *Miranda* rules cover only "custodial" interrogation. Evidence suggests that police have adjusted to *Miranda* by shifting to noncustodial "interviews" to skirt *Miranda*'s requirements. In talking to police officers, the researchers found some anecdotal evidence supporting this view. In a few screenings, officers (mostly from one large department) referred to giving suspects a "*Beheler*" warning, as in "I gave him *Beheler*." This is a reference to the Supreme Court's decision in California v. Beheler, 463 U.S. 1121 (1983), which held that a suspect was not in custody when he "voluntarily agreed to accompany police to the station house [and] the police specifically told [him] that he was not under arrest." . . . On the other hand, in a few cases in our sample it appeared that officers Mirandized when not required to do so. . . .

To date, no one has quantified how often police interview in noncustodial settings. In our sample, 69.9% of the interviews were custodial while 30.1% were noncustodial. Of the noncustodial interviews, 40.3% were at the scene, 26.9% were field investigations, and 32.7% were arranged interviews (that is, interviews where police officers had previously contacted the suspects to set up an interview time).

Even if police are able to avoid *Miranda*'s requirements by conducting various noncustodial interviews, the question would remain whether such interviews are less effective in obtaining incriminating information. We found that police were less successful in noncustodial interviews [with a 30% success rate, compared to 56.9% in custodial interrogations].

Notes

1. *Number of attempted interrogations.* Would the *Miranda* decision be likely to affect the number of cases in which the police at least attempt an interrogation? Should a study of the impact of *Miranda* include cases in which the suspect was not

149. Edward Barrett, Jr., Police Practices and the Law — from Arrest to Release or Charge, 50 Cal. L. Rev. 11 (1962).

available for questioning? The Salt Lake City study did so. One prominent *Miranda*-era study — of the pseudonymous "Seaside City," California — concluded that officers failed to interrogate only 2 percent of the suspects "actually arrested and incarcerated." James Witt, Non-Coercive Interrogation and the Administration of Criminal Justice: The Impact of *Miranda* on Police Effectuality, 64 J. Crim. L. & Criminology 320 (1973).

2. *Number of waivers.* The most current studies have concluded that roughly 80 percent of all suspects waive their *Miranda* rights and make statements without counsel present. Some studies have found waiver rates in excess of 90 percent. See Paul Cassell, *Miranda*'s Social Costs: An Empirical Reassessment, 90 Nw. U. L. Rev. 387 (1996) (collecting studies of waiver rate). A study in Great Britain suggested that about 68 percent of suspects in 1991 requested legal advice, after receiving warnings similar to those in *Miranda.* David Brown, Tom Ellis, and Karen Larcombe, Changing the Code: Police Detention Under the Revised PACE Codes of Practice, Home Office Research and Planning Unit, London HMSO (1992). The tendency to waive the right to counsel or the right to silence is especially strong among suspects with no prior criminal convictions. Richard Leo, Inside the Interrogation Room, 86 J. Crim. L. & Criminology 266 (1996). Would the repeat offenders who tend more often to invoke their rights be more or less likely than the average offender to provide an incriminating statement in the absence of a warning? If so many suspects waive their rights, is that an indication of *Miranda*'s failure or success? See George Thomas, Is *Miranda* a Real-World Failure? A Plea for More (and Better) Empirical Evidence, 43 UCLA L. Rev. 821 (1996).

3. *Number of confessions or admissions.* The major concern of *Miranda*'s critics is that the warnings change the dynamic between the questioner and the suspect and reduce the number of successful interrogations, even when the suspect agrees to talk to the police. A number of empirical studies attempt to measure the "success rate" for interrogations immediately before and after the *Miranda* decision. A Pittsburgh study concluded that 48.5 percent of suspects confessed before *Miranda* while 32.3 percent confessed after *Miranda.* Richard Seeburger and Stanton Wettick, *Miranda* in Pittsburgh — A Statistical Analysis, 29 U. Pitt. L. Rev. 1 (1967). The "Seaside City" (California) study noted above pointed to a pre-*Miranda* confession rate of 68.9 percent, and a post-*Miranda* rate of 66.9 percent. This study included only suspects who were arrested and incarcerated; it excluded cases in which suspects were detained for questioning but never incarcerated. A study of interrogations in 1965-1966 in the District of Columbia found that suspects made "statements" (not necessarily incriminating) in 43 percent of cases pre-*Miranda* and 40 percent of cases post-*Miranda.* However, police had given suspects some warnings in some cases before *Miranda* and had complied with the required warnings unevenly after *Miranda.* Among the post-*Miranda* suspects who received no warnings about the right to silence or the right to counsel, 55 percent made "statements," as compared to 41 percent of the suspects who received some warning. See Richard Medalie, Leonard Zeitz, and Paul Alexander, Custodial Police Interrogation in Our Nation's Capital: The Attempt to Implement *Miranda,* 66 Mich. L. Rev. 1347 (1968). The Salt Lake City study, based on cases investigated in 1994, found a success rate of 33.3 percent overall and 42.2 percent of cases where questioning actually occurred. In contrast, a study of interrogations in three California cities in 1992-1993 concluded that 64 percent of all the observed interrogations produced a confession or incriminating admission. Richard Leo, Inside the Interrogation Room, 86 J. Crim. L. & Criminology 266 (1996).

One difficulty in studying this issue is defining what constitutes a "successful" interrogation. The studies all include outright confessions, in which the suspect tells the police that he committed the crime. Many also include some partially successful interrogations leading to "admissions": statements that police and prosecutors can use to prove one or more elements of the crime. Do you agree with the way Cassell and Hayman resolved this issue in the Salt Lake City study? A second difficulty in this debate comes from the (possibly) changing effects of *Miranda* over the 30-plus years since the decision appeared. Is it plausible to think that the confession rate "rebounded" after an initial drop, once police officers adjusted their practices to the new requirements and found the best ways to prevent lost confessions? A reporter who spent one year with homicide detectives in Baltimore concluded that the police are able to use the *Miranda* warnings to create an atmosphere of cooperation with at least some suspects. He observed cases in which the suspect's act of acknowledging an understanding of the rights, followed by a waiver of those rights, created some momentum for cooperation during the interrogation. David Simon, Homicide: A Year on the Killing Streets (1991). At the same time, early studies may have *understated* the current effects of *Miranda* because over the years the nature of *Miranda* rights have become more broadly known and understood.

Another difficulty in measuring the effects of *Miranda* on the confession rate is that the warnings and a request for waiving the rights might simultaneously discourage and encourage confessions. Some suspects will refuse to talk once they hear the warnings, while the process of explaining the *Miranda* rights and obtaining a waiver may create a more cooperative atmosphere and lead to more (or more damaging) admissions. George Thomas reviewed the available empirical studies and concluded that they are inconclusive, but still consistent with the view that *Miranda* helps as much as it hurts. Thomas, Plain Talk About the *Miranda* Empirical Debate: A "Steady-State" Theory of Confessions, 43 UCLA L. Rev. 933 (1996).

4. *Number of convictions.* Another measurement of *Miranda*'s effects might come from estimating its impact on the conviction rate. There are two methods of arriving at this number. First, one might compare the percentage of all suspects convicted of crimes in the same location immediately before and after the Court's decision, and presume that some or all of the change in conviction rates was attributable to *Miranda.* Using this method, the Pittsburgh study concluded that the conviction rate was unchanged after the *Miranda* decision. The Seaside City study found a 9 percent decline in the conviction rate (from 92 percent to 83 percent). Is there any problem with this method of estimating the decision's impact on convictions? Second, one might start with an estimate of the number of confessions lost and combine it with some estimate of the proportion of cases in which a confession is essential to obtain a conviction. Multiplying the lost confessions by the number of cases in which confessions are necessary results in a final estimate. A researcher might estimate the number of cases in which a confession is important by asking for the opinion of prosecutors and others involved in the case. She might also review the case files herself to imagine which cases might have ended differently if a confession were or were not available. Using these methods (or a combination of them), most studies have estimated that confessions are essential in 13 percent to 28 percent of all cases. See Paul Cassell, *Miranda*'s Social Costs, 90 Nw. U. L. Rev. 387 (1996) (summarizing studies and reaching average of 23.8 percent). In choosing which studies of this question are most reliable, what would you want to know?

5. *Number of reversals on appeal.* Yet another measure of *Miranda*'s effects is the number of convictions overturned on appeal because of *Miranda* violations. All the

evidence suggests that a trivial number of cases are lost on appeal because of *Miranda.* Karen Guy and Robert Huckabee, Going Free on a Technicality: Another Look at the Effect of the *Miranda* Decision on the Criminal Justice Process, 4 Crim. Just. Res. Bull. 1 (1988) (evidence excluded for *Miranda* violations in 0.51 percent of appealed cases); Peter Nardulli, The Societal Costs of the Exclusionary Rule Revisited, 1987 U. Ill. L. Rev. 223 (confessions suppressed in 0.04 percent of all cases). Why might this be the case when other measures of *Miranda*'s impact show evidence of a larger impact?

6. *Clearance rates.* An ideal measurement of *Miranda*'s costs over time (such as a reliable account of confession rates before *Miranda* and during the years since then) is not available. One indirect measurement of the effects is the "clearance rate," that is, the percentage of reported crimes that the police declare "solved." Those rates, which have been collected and reported since at least 1950, declined just after the *Miranda* decision and have remained at the lower levels since that time. Paul Cassell and Richard Fowles analyzed this data. After attempting to control for other possible explanations for the lower clearance rates, they conclude that "without *Miranda,* the number of crimes cleared would be substantially higher—by as much as 6.6-29.7% for robbery, 6.2-28.9% for burglary, 0.4-11.9% for larceny, and 12.8-45.4% for vehicle theft." Cassell and Fowles, Handcuffing the Cops? A Thirty-Year Perspective on *Miranda*'s Harmful Effects on Law Enforcement, 50 Stan. L. Rev. 1055, 1126 (1998). For what crimes would you expect *Miranda* to have the largest effect? Would you expect clearance rates to show more or less of an impact than confession rates? See John Donohue, Did *Miranda* Diminish Police Effectiveness?, 50 Stan. L. Rev. 1147 (1998); Floyd Feeney, Police Clearances: A Poor Way to Measure the Impact of *Miranda* on the Police, 32 Rutgers L.J. 1 (2000).

7. *Acceptable costs and benefits.* After resolving all the factual disputes about the actual effects of the *Miranda* decision, one is left with a different type of question: How much of the undesirable effect is too much? If the effects of *Miranda* described thus far could be considered the "costs" of the decision, are there any corresponding benefits? What are those benefits and how might one measure them and compare them to the costs?

3. *Alternatives to* Miranda

Miranda continues to be the subject of criticism, though law enforcement officers in particular have become more supportive of *Miranda* as they have made it part of their routine. Remember that the Court in *Miranda* expressly invited legislatures to find alternative methods for protecting the privilege against self-incrimination.

> It is impossible for us to foresee the potential alternatives for protecting the privilege which might be devised by Congress or the States in the exercise of their creative rule-making capacities. Therefore we cannot say that the Constitution necessarily requires adherence to any particular solution for the inherent compulsions of the interrogation process as it is presently conducted. Our decision in no way creates a constitutional straitjacket which will handicap sound efforts at reform, nor is it intended to have this effect. . . . Congress and the States are free to develop their own safeguards for the privilege, so long as they are fully as effective as those described above in informing accused persons of their right of silence and in affording a continuous opportunity to exercise it.

What are the alternatives to *Miranda?* The Court in Dickerson v. United States, 530 U.S. 428 (2000), struck down one such effort, a federal statute instructing judges to judge the admissibility of confessions only by the traditional standards of voluntariness. What sort of alternatives might succeed where the 1968 federal statute failed? See Michael Dorf and Barry Friedman, Shared Constitutional Interpretation, 2000 Sup. Ct. Rev. 61.

Perhaps a legislature could revise the *Miranda* warning to remove aspects most often criticized as obstacles to proper crime-solving techniques. Perhaps interrogations should occur before a judicial officer. Or perhaps a trial jury might later be told of any refusal to make a statement to the magistrate, or the refusal to make a statement to the judicial officer might be punishable as contempt of court. See Akhil Amar and Renee Lettow, Fifth Amendment First Principles: The Self-Incrimination Clause, 93 Mich. L. Rev. 857 (1995); Donald Dripps, Foreword: Against Police Interrogation—And the Privilege Against Self-Incrimination, 78 J. Crim. L. & Criminology 699 (1988). Consider the following approach to interrogations, made possible by technological advances.

■ TEXAS CODE OF CRIMINAL PROCEDURE ART. 38.22

Sec. 2. No written statement made by an accused as a result of custodial interrogation is admissible as evidence against him in any criminal proceeding unless it is shown on the face of the statement that:

(a) the accused, prior to making the statement, . . . received from the person to whom the statement is made a warning that:

(1) he has the right to remain silent and not make any statement at all and that any statement he makes may be used against him at his trial; (2) any statement he makes may be used as evidence against him in court; (3) he has the right to have a lawyer present to advise him prior to and during any questioning; (4) if he is unable to employ a lawyer, he has the right to have a lawyer appointed to advise him prior to and during any questioning; and (5) he has the right to terminate the interview at any time; and

(b) the accused, prior to and during the making of the statement, knowingly, intelligently, and voluntarily waived the rights set out in the warning prescribed by Subsection (a) of this section.

Sec. 3. (a) No oral or sign language statement of an accused made as a result of custodial interrogation shall be admissible against the accused in a criminal proceeding unless:

(1) an electronic recording, which may include motion picture, video tape, or other visual recording, is made of the statement; (2) prior to the statement but during the recording the accused is given the warning in Subsection (a) of Section 2 above and the accused knowingly, intelligently, and voluntarily waives any rights set out in the warning; (3) the recording device was capable of making an accurate recording, the operator was competent, and the recording is accurate and has not been altered; (4) all voices on the recording are identified; and (5) not later than the 20th day before the date of the proceeding, the attorney representing the defendant is provided with a true, complete, and accurate copy of all recordings of the defendant made under this article. . . .

(c) Subsection (a) of this section shall not apply to any statement which contains assertions of facts or circumstances that are found to be true and which conduce to establish the guilt of the accused, such as the finding of secreted or stolen property or the instrument with which he states the offense was committed. . . .

(e) The courts of this state shall strictly construe Subsection (a) of this section and may not interpret Subsection (a) as making admissible a statement unless all requirements of the subsection have been satisfied by the state, except that:

(1) only voices that are material are identified; and (2) the accused was given the warning in Subsection (a) of Section 2 above or its fully effective equivalent.

Sec. 4. When any statement, the admissibility of which is covered by this article, is sought to be used in connection with an official proceeding, any person who swears falsely to facts and circumstances which, if true, would render the statement admissible under this article is presumed to have acted with intent to deceive and with knowledge of the statement's meaning for the purpose of prosecution for aggravated perjury. . . . No person prosecuted under this subsection shall be eligible for probation.

Sec. 5. Nothing in this article precludes the admission of a statement made by the accused in open court at his trial, before a grand jury, or at an examining trial . . . , or of a statement that does not stem from custodial interrogation, or of a voluntary statement, whether or not the result of custodial interrogation, that has a bearing upon the credibility of the accused as a witness, or of any other statement that may be admissible under law.

■ DONALD STEPHAN v. STATE

711 P.2d 1156 (Alaska 1985)

BURKE, J.

More than five years ago, in Mallott v. State, 608 P.2d 737 (Alaska 1980), we informed Alaska law enforcement officials that "it is incumbent upon them to tape record, where feasible, any questioning [of criminal suspects,] and particularly that which occurs in a place of detention." This requirement (hereinafter the *Mallott* rule) was again noted in S.B. v. State, 614 P.2d 786 (Alaska 1980), with the observation that an electronic record of such interviews "will be a great aid" when courts are called upon to determine "the circumstances of a confession or other waiver of [a suspect's] *Miranda* rights." In a third case, McMahan v. State, 617 P.2d 494 (Alaska 1980), the recording requirement was repeated, with the further statement that "if *Miranda* rights are read to the defendant, this too should be recorded." Today, we hold that an unexcused failure to electronically record a custodial interrogation conducted in a place of detention violates a suspect's right to due process, under the Alaska Constitution, and that any statement thus obtained is generally inadmissible.[2]

2. We are not alone in recognizing the importance of recording custodial interrogations. See Hendricks v. Swenson, 456 F.2d 503 (8th Cir. 1972) (suggesting that videotapes of interrogations protect a defendant's rights and are a step forward in the search for truth); Ragan v. State, 642 S.W.2d 489 (Tex. Crim. App. 1982) (Tex. Code Crim. Proc. Ann. art. 38.22, §3 requiring that oral statements of the accused during custodial interrogations must be recorded in order to be admissible); Model Code of Pre-Arraignment Procedure §130.4 (Proposed Official Draft 1975) (requiring sound recordings of custodial interviews). . . .

The relevant facts in the two cases now before us are similar. Malcolm Scott Harris and Donald Stephan, petitioners, were arrested on unrelated criminal charges, taken to police stations and questioned by police officers. Harris was interrogated on two separate occasions; Stephan was interrogated only once. Both men made inculpatory statements. In each instance, a working audio or video recorder was in the room and was used during part, but not all, of the interrogation. The officers, in each case, offered no satisfactory excuse for their clear disregard of the *Mallott* rule.[3]

Prior to their respective trials, Harris and Stephan both moved to suppress confessions made during their interrogations. At the suppression hearings there was conflicting testimony about what occurred during the unrecorded portions of the interviews. Harris claimed that, in his first interrogation, he was not informed of his *Miranda* rights at the beginning of the session, that the questioning continued after he asserted his right to remain silent, and that the officer made threats and promises during the untaped portions. Stephan claimed that his ultimate confession was induced by promises of leniency and was obtained in the absence of an attorney, after he requested one. In both cases, the officers' testimony was to the contrary. Without a full recording to resolve the conflict, the superior court was required to evaluate the credibility of the witnesses and choose which version of the unrecorded events to believe. In each case, the court chose the police officers' recollections and determined that the confession was voluntary and, thus, admissible at trial. Harris and Stephan were ultimately found guilty and filed notices of appeal. . . .

In its decision, the court of appeals acknowledged: "The supreme court has clearly stated in three separate cases that the police are under a duty to record statements which suspects make where recording is feasible. That admonition cannot be ignored." The court, nevertheless, refused to adopt a general exclusionary rule, stating:

> We believe that the issue of what sanction is appropriate is best approached on a case by case basis. . . . Exactly what sanction, if any, to apply for the failure to record a defendant's statement in a given case is a decision which is best left to the sound discretion of the trial court. . . .

The court of appeals' refusal to adopt an exclusionary rule in these circumstances is perhaps due to failure on our part to adequately explain the full significance of our prior decisions. Electronic recording of suspect interrogations was described in those cases, rather ambiguously, as "part of a law enforcement agency's duty to preserve evidence." Today, we resolve that ambiguity. Such recording is a requirement of state due process when the interrogation occurs in a place of detention and recording is feasible.[11] We reach this conclusion because we are

3. One officer stated that it was "normal practice" to get the suspect's statement "laid out in the desired manner," and only then record the full, formal confession. Another officer explained that a suspect is more at ease and likely to talk without a tape recorder running.

11. Unif. R. Crim. P. 243 (Proposed Final Draft 1974) provides in pertinent part:

> The information of rights, any waiver thereof, and any questioning shall be recorded upon a sound recording device whenever feasible and in any case where questioning occurs at a place of detention.

While we assume that most law enforcement agencies will employ audio or video tape recordings as the most efficient and economical means of preserving the contents of such interviews, the use of alternative methods, such as the preparation of a verbatim transcript by a certified shorthand reporter, in lieu of an electronic device, would also satisfy the requirements of state due process. Thus, "electronic" recording is not a strict requirement.

convinced that recording, in such circumstances, is now a reasonable and necessary safeguard, essential to the adequate protection of the accused's right to counsel, his right against self incrimination and, ultimately, his right to a fair trial. . . . Thus, as we have done on previous occasions, we construe Alaska's constitutional provision, in this instance, as affording rights beyond those guaranteed by the United States Constitution.

In Municipality of Anchorage v. Serrano, 649 P.2d 256 (Alaska Ct. App. 1982), the Alaska Court of Appeals extended the state's duty to preserve evidence to include breath samples taken during the administration of a breathalyzer test. Given the importance of breath samples in cases involving a charge of driving while intoxicated, and the minimal cost and effort involved in obtaining them, the court of appeals explicitly held that the due process clause of the Alaska Constitution requires the state to gather and preserve a defendant's breath sample. The need to insure that the voluntariness of a confession can be confirmed by reference to an accurate and complete record is at least as important as the need to insure that the validity of breathalyzer test results can be independently tested. Given the relative ease with which such confirmation can be provided, by means of an electronic recording, we see no legitimate reason not to require it, at least to the extent mandated by this opinion. . . .

The contents of an interrogation are obviously material in determining the voluntariness of a confession. The state usually attempts to show voluntariness through the interrogating officer's testimony that the defendant's constitutional rights were protected. The defendant, on the other hand, often testifies to the contrary. The result, then, is a swearing match between the law enforcement official and the defendant, which the courts must resolve.

> The difficulty in depicting what transpires at such interrogations stems from the fact that in this country they have largely taken place incommunicado. . . . Interrogation still takes place in privacy. Privacy results in secrecy and this in turn results in a gap in our knowledge as to what in fact goes on in the interrogation rooms. [Miranda v. Arizona, 384 U.S. at 445, 448.]

Thus, we believe a recording requirement is justified, because a tape recording provides an objective means for evaluating what occurred during interrogation. . . .

In the absence of an accurate record, the accused may suffer an infringement upon his right to remain silent and to have counsel present during the interrogation. Also, his right to a fair trial may be violated, if an illegally obtained, and possibly false, confession is subsequently admitted. An electronic recording, thus, protects the defendant's constitutional rights, by providing an objective means for him to corroborate his testimony concerning the circumstances of the confession.

The recording of custodial interrogations is not, however, a measure intended to protect only the accused; a recording also protects the public's interest in honest and effective law enforcement, and the individual interests of those police officers wrongfully accused of improper tactics. A recording, in many cases, will aid law enforcement efforts, by confirming the content and the voluntariness of a confession, when a defendant changes his testimony or claims falsely that his constitutional rights were violated. In any case, a recording will help trial and appellate courts to ascertain the truth.

The concept of due process is not static; among other things, it must change to keep pace with new technological developments. For example, the gathering and preservation of breath samples was previously impractical. Now that this procedure is technologically feasible, many states require it, either as a matter of due process or by resort to reasoning akin to a due process analysis. The use of audio and video tapes is even more commonplace in today's society. The police already make use of recording devices in circumstances when it is to their advantage to do so. Examples would be the routine video recording of suspect behavior in drunk driving cases and, as was done in these cases, the recording of formal confessions. Furthermore, media reports indicate that many Alaska police officers have purchased their own recorders, carry them while on duty and regularly record conversations with suspects or witnesses, in order to protect themselves against false accusations. When a portable recorder has not been available, some officers have even used their patrol car radio to record conversations through the police dispatch center.

In both of the cases before us, the police were engaged in custodial interrogations of suspects in a place of detention. A working recording device was readily available, but was used to record only part of the questioning. Compliance with the recording rule is not unduly burdensome under these circumstances. Turning the recorder on a few minutes earlier entails minimal cost and effort. In return, less time, money and resources would have been consumed in resolving the disputes that arose over the events that occurred during the interrogations.

The only real reason advanced by police for their frequent failure to electronically record an entire interrogation is their claim that recordings tend to have a "chilling effect" on a suspect's willingness to talk. Given the fact that an accused has a constitutional right to remain silent, under both the state and federal constitutions, and that he must be clearly warned of that right prior to any custodial interrogation, this argument is not persuasive.[20]

In summary, the rule that we adopt today requires that custodial interrogations in a place of detention, including the giving of the accused's *Miranda* rights, must be electronically recorded. To satisfy this due process requirement, the recording must clearly indicate that it recounts the entire interview. Thus, explanations should be given at the beginning, the end and before and after any interruptions in the recording, so that courts are not left to speculate about what took place.

Since its announcement, the *Mallott* rule has always included a proviso, "when feasible." The failure to electronically record an entire custodial interrogation will, therefore, be considered a violation of the rule, and subject to exclusion, only if the failure is unexcused. Acceptable excuses might include an unavoidable power or equipment failure, or a situation where the suspect refuses to answer any questions if the conversation is being recorded. We need not anticipate all such possible excuses here, for courts must carefully scrutinize each situation on a case-by-case basis. Any time a full recording is not made, however, the state must persuade the trial court, by a preponderance of the evidence, that recording was not feasible under the circumstances, and in such cases the failure to record should be viewed with distrust.

[W]e adopt a general rule of exclusion. While other remedies may each have their merits, we believe an exclusionary rule will best protect the suspects' constitutional rights, provide clear direction to law enforcement agencies and lower courts, and preserve the integrity of our justice system.

20. Also relevant to this argument, perhaps, is the fact that, when the interrogation occurs in a place of detention and the suspect knows or has reason to know he is speaking to a police officer, there is no constitutional requirement that the suspect be informed that the interview is being recorded.

[L]aw enforcement agencies and lower courts have repeatedly failed to give due regard to the protections the *Mallott* rule is intended to provide, even though the rule was first announced over five years ago. We believe that a strong and certain remedy will have a considerable deterrent effect in future cases. Compliance imposes such minimal costs and burdens on law enforcement agencies that they will have little to gain from noncompliance. . . .

The imposition of sanctions against an individual officer will not necessarily solve what appears to be a systemic problem. Agency policy and operations must change, not simply individual behaviors. Once they are fully aware of the consequences of unexcused violations of the *Mallott* rule, we are confident that law enforcement agencies will establish effective procedures to implement the rule and provide adequate training for their personnel. Suppression of statements taken in violation of the rule will, therefore, deter continued disregard of its requirements by officers, agencies and courts.

Another purpose is also served by the rule that we now adopt. The integrity of our judicial system is subject to question whenever a court rules on the admissibility of a questionable confession, based solely upon the court's acceptance of the testimony of an interested party, whether it be the interrogating officer or the defendant. This is especially true when objective evidence of the circumstances surrounding the confession could have been preserved by the mere flip of a switch. Routine and systematic recording of custodial interrogations will provide such evidence, and avoid any suggestion that the court is biased in favor of either party.

Most importantly, an exclusionary rule furthers the protection of individual constitutional rights. Strong protection is needed to insure that a suspect's right to counsel, his privilege against self incrimination, and due process guarantees are protected. A confession is generally such conclusive evidence of guilt that a rule of exclusion is justified, when the state, without excuse, fails to preserve evidence of the interchange leading up to the formal statement. [E]xclusion of the defendant's statement is the only remedy which will correct the wrong that has been done and place the defendant in the same position he or she would have been in had the evidence been preserved and turned over in time for use at trial.

Thus, we conclude that exclusion is the appropriate remedy for an unexcused failure to electronically record an interrogation, when such recording is feasible. A general exclusionary rule is the only remedy that provides crystal clarity to law enforcement agencies, preserves judicial integrity, and adequately protects a suspect's constitutional rights. The necessity for this strong remedy remains, even when we consider society's interests in crime prevention and the apprehension of criminal offenders. Exclusion of reliable, yet unrecorded, statements will not occur frequently when compliance is widespread.[33]

Despite what we have said thus far, we recognize that nearly every rule must have its exceptions, and that exclusion of a defendant's statements in certain instances would be wholly unreasonable. A violation of the *Mallott* rule does not, therefore,

33. Caveat: We recognize that many custodial interrogations must take place in the field, where recording may not be feasible. Because of this, the rule that we announce today has limited application; it applies only to custodial interrogations conducted in a place of detention, such as a police station or jail, where it is reasonable to assume that recording equipment is available, or can be made available with little effort. In a future case, however, we may be persuaded to extend the application of this rule, particularly if it appears that law enforcement officials are engaging in bad faith efforts to circumvent the recording requirement set forth in this opinion.

require exclusion of the defendant's statements in all cases. Thus, the holding in this case does not bar the admission of statements obtained before a violation of the recording rule occurs. Where recording ceases for some impermissible reason, properly recorded statements made prior to the time recording stops may be admitted, even when the failure to record the balance of the interrogation is unexcused, since such prior statements could not be tainted by anything that occurred thereafter. Also, failure to record part of an interrogation does not bar the introduction of a defendant's recorded statements, if the unrecorded portion of the interrogation is, by all accounts, innocuous. In such cases, there is no reason to exclude the defendant's recorded statements, because no claim of material misconduct will be presented. See Alaska R. Crim. P. 47(a) (errors which do not affect substantial rights shall be disregarded). For the same reason, a defendant's unrecorded statement may be admitted if no testimony is presented that the statement is inaccurate or was obtained improperly, apart from violation of the *Mallott* rule.

Reversed and remanded for further proceedings, with orders that Harris' and Stephan's statements be suppressed.

Notes

1. *Videotaping as a constitutional requirement: majority position.* Only the Alaska Supreme Court has required that interrogations be videotaped as a constitutional matter. While the argument has been made in a number of jurisdictions, courts typically have not received it with any sympathy. See, e.g., Brashars v. Commonwealth, 25 S.W.3d 58 (Ky. 2000); State v. Gorton, 548 A.2d 419 (Vt. 1988) (suggesting that any recording requirement should come from the legislature). After *Stephan* was decided the Minnesota Supreme Court, relying on its supervisory authority, mandated recordings of "custodial interrogations" when they occur "at a place of detention." See State v. Scales, 518 N.W.2d 587, 592 (Minn. 1994). The *Scales* court wrote:

> We choose not to determine at this time whether under the Due Process Clause of the Minnesota Constitution a criminal suspect has a right to have his or her custodial interrogation recorded. Rather, in the exercise of our supervisory power to insure the fair administration of justice, we hold that all custodial interrogation including any information about rights, any waiver of those rights, and all questioning shall be electronically recorded where feasible and must be recorded when questioning occurs at a place of detention. If law enforcement officers fail to comply with this recording requirement, any statements the suspect makes in response to the interrogation may be suppressed at trial.

Other courts have indicated that recording will weigh strongly in favor of findings of voluntariness. See, e.g., State v. Grey, 907 P.2d 951 (Mont. 1995) ("[I]n the context of a custodial interrogation conducted at the station house or under other similarly controlled circumstances, the failure of the police officer to preserve some tangible record of his or her giving of the *Miranda* warning and the knowing, intelligent waiver by the detainee will be viewed with distrust in the judicial assessment of voluntariness under the totality of circumstances surrounding the confession or admission").

Was it appropriate for the Alaska Supreme Court to "warn" police and prosecutors about the possibility of a judicially mandated rule unless a recording rule was adopted voluntarily? Would a long history of *Miranda* and voluntariness violations in a particular state provide a justification for a state court to mandate a recording rule? Can constitutional remedies be supported by the failure of all other remedies to end or diminish serious constitutional violations? See People v. Cahan, reprinted in Chapter 6 (arguing that the exclusionary rule was necessary because no other remedy had worked to control police searches and seizures).

2. *Videotaping as a statutory requirement.* Texas is the lone state in which the legislature has implemented a statutory videotaping requirement. Indeed, Texas has extended the statutory requirement of videotaping to include persons arrested for DUI in all counties with a population greater than 25,000. Tex. Rev. Civ. Stat. Ann. art. 67011-1, §24; Texas Penal Code Ann. §19.05. (The remedy for failure to videotape persons arrested for DUI is not suppression but permission for the defendant to inform the jury of the failure to tape.) It may be easy to understand why other states have not been swayed by the Alaska decision in *Stephan* to mandate recording as a constitutional matter, but why have states been reluctant to mandate taping by statute? Why not videotape every interrogation and confession? Do police departments think use of videotapes will lead to fewer confessions? Do legislatures think that videotaping policies should be left to local police and prosecutors to implement? If you drafted a new law requiring that in general interrogations and confessions be videotaped, what requirements, exceptions, and limitations would you include?

3. *Police discretion to videotape interrogations and confessions.* A 1990 survey showed that about one-sixth of the 14,000 police and sheriffs' departments, and one-third of the 710 departments serving populations over 50,000, videotaped some interrogations or confessions. William Geller, Videotaping Interrogations and Confessions: NIJ Research in Brief, NCJ 139962 (1993). Given the prevalence of the technology and prominent recommendations for its use, videotaping of interrogations and confessions may now be even more likely to happen. The 1993 National Institute of Justice report by Geller found that videotape was used most often in homicide and rape investigations and for other serious crimes. The majority of jurisdictions that used videotape believed it had led to better preparation by detectives and better monitoring of detectives' work by supervisors; the tape was also used to train detectives. Sometimes a co-defendant will change his tune after viewing a videotape. By a ratio of 3 to 1, however, more agencies found suspects less willing to talk when videotape was used. Not surprisingly, the study found that videotaping led to fewer claims against police that they had coerced or intimidated a suspect or fabricated a confession. Prosecutors were generally more supportive of videotaping interrogations than were defense attorneys, who found videotapes harder to attack than written or audiotaped confessions. Detectives tended at first to disapprove of taping, but most jurisdictions found a strong shift among detectives in favor of taping once they had experience with its use.

4. *Limits of* Stephan. Should *Stephan* be applied to require recording of interrogations in noncustodial settings such as the scene of an arrest? Should the recording requirement extend to actions other than interrogation, such as sobriety tests of DUI suspects? See Swanson v. City of Juneau, 784 P.2d 678 (Alaska Ct. App. 1989) (rejecting extension of *Stephan* to sobriety tests of DUI suspects at police station). Should confessions be rejected if not all of the interrogation was recorded? See Young v. State, 743 P.2d 941 (Alaska Ct. App. 1987) (allowing partial recording when voluntariness of confession was evident from available portion and despite allegation of excessive promises in unrecorded portion).

5. *Taping: administrative issues.* Most police departments record interrogations openly or ask the subject about recording. Some police departments, however, use surreptitious recording equipment. Such practices reduce the chance that the use of video will discourage suspects from confessing (since they will not know they are being taped). What reasons might there be not to tape surreptitiously? See City of Juneau v. Quinto, 684 P.2d 127 (Alaska 1984) (admitting surreptitious tape when defendant knew or reasonably should have known that he was speaking to a police officer). Must police record the whole interrogation, or is it necessary to record only the defendant's confession and summary after interrogation? Suppose the interrogation takes seven hours but the summary only 30 minutes. Should the cost of the recording medium factor into the decision whether to videotape the entire confession? What about the cost of making transcripts? Does the emergence of technology that automatically makes a rough transcription of speech ironically make recording interrogations more functional? See State v. Barnett, 789 A.2d 629 (N.H. 2001) (under supervisory power, court requires any videotape of interrogation admitted into evidence to be complete). In some jurisdictions defense counsel are not given immediate access to recorded interrogations and confessions. Some prosecutors show defense counsel taped confessions but object to making copies. Other jurisdictions do not give defense counsel access to tapes until after indictment or for a period of time after the interrogation.

6. *Is videotaping an "alternative" to* Miranda? What would be the judicial response to fully videotaped but unwarned confessions in a jurisdiction whose legislature took the U.S. Supreme Court's invitation and passed a mandatory taping statute expressly to take the place of *Miranda* warnings in protecting each suspect's Fifth Amendment rights? Is there any reason not to videotape interrogations and confessions along with providing *Miranda* warnings? Would you expect foreign jurisdictions, without the constraints or protections of *Miranda,* to be more or less hesitant to adopt taping procedures? The 1991 Code of Practice for Interrogation in England requires that all interviews be recorded, wherever they occur, unless it is impracticable to do so. See Craig Bradley, The Emerging International Consensus as to Criminal Procedure Rules, 14 Mich. J. Intl. L. 171 (1993); M. McConville, P. Morrell, "Recording the Interrogation: Have the Police Got It Taped?", 1983 Crim. L.R. 159 (noting an increase after appearance of Code of Practice in spontaneous confessions allegedly spoken before the tape was running). For a summary of videotaping practices in Australia, see Wayne T. Westling and Vicki Waye, Videotaping Police Interrogations: Lessons From Australia, 25 Am. J. Crim. L. 493 (1998).

7. *Confessions, lies, & videotape.* Taping interrogations and confessions seems to solve a number of problems, such as reducing or eliminating the frequent claims by suspects that they were threatened or that they did not in fact confess or say what the police say they did. But does taping solve all issues from interrogations and confessions? Will tapes make all confessions look voluntary even when they have been compelled by forces not visible (or audible) on the tape? Won't taping create a whole new set of factual issues about whether the recording is complete? Is taping of interrogations and confessions a great reform for a past era?

Perhaps it is not the requirement of warnings but the content of the warnings that needs rethinking. Consider the following reform in Great Britain and its implications for the warnings offered suspects during investigations.

■ UNITED KINGDOM, CRIMINAL JUSTICE AND PUBLIC ORDER ACT OF 1994, §34

(1) Where, in any proceedings against a person for an offence, evidence is given that the accused . . . at any time before he was charged with the offence, on being questioned under caution by a constable trying to discover whether or by whom the offence had been committed, failed to mention any fact relied on in his defence in those proceedings . . . being a fact which in the circumstances existing at the time the accused could reasonably have been expected to mention when so questioned, charged or informed, as the case may be, subsection (2) below applies.

(2) Where this subsection applies . . . the court, in determining whether there is a case to answer; [or] the court or jury, in determining whether the accused is guilty of the offence charged, may draw such inferences from the failure as appear proper.

Notes

1. *Warnings in Great Britain and elsewhere in Europe.* Great Britain changed the law relating to the warnings that suspects must receive before interrogation. Under the old law (which goes back to the nineteenth century and was embodied in the Police and Criminal Evidence Act of 1984), suspects were told, "You do not have to say anything unless you wish to do so, but what you say may be given in evidence." The 1984 act (and the related Code of Practice promulgated by the government a year later) also required that the police inform suspects in custody that they have a right to consult an attorney before any interrogation, that the police make available a "duty solicitor" for suspects who want advice, and that the warnings be given both orally and in writing. How does the 1994 statute, reprinted above, change these practices?

Some form of warnings about the right to silence and the consequences of speaking (or not speaking) are now standard practice in many European nations. For instance, suspects in France are informed of the right to silence and to consult counsel during detention, but they are not entitled to have counsel present during interrogation. In Germany, police must inform suspects of the right to remain silent when they become the focus of an investigation. The warnings also inform suspects of their right to consult a defense attorney *prior* to interrogation, although there is no right to counsel during interrogation. If the suspect chooses to remain silent, police may continue to question the suspect. German courts prohibit the police from making affirmative misrepresentations during interrogations. See Christopher Slobogin, An Empirically Based Comparison of American and European Regulatory Approaches to Police Investigation, 22 Mich. J. Int'l L. 423, 442-45 (2001); Stephen C. Thaman, Miranda in Comparative Law, 45 St. L. U.L.J. 581 (2001); Criminal Procedure: A Worldwide Study (Craig M. Bradley ed. 1999).

2. *Warnings about silence.* Would the 1994 English statute be consistent with the Fifth Amendment to the U.S. Constitution? Would it have any effect on the everyday practices of criminal investigators? Should the Fifth Amendment also require a warning to a suspect that "silence cannot be used against you"?

IX

Identifications

Eyewitnesses to crime can provide some of the most convincing evidence to support a conviction. This is especially true when the physical evidence linking the defendant to the crime is thin, or when the offender is a stranger to others at the scene (as in many robbery cases). All too often, however, this important evidence turns out to be unreliable. How do legal institutions respond to the special value and risks of eyewitness identifications?

This chapter explores this question. Section A reviews some of the psychological literature detailing the risks of eyewitness identifications. Section B surveys the conditions that lead courts to exclude evidence coming from in-person identifications (both in the field and at the police station) and from identifications of photographs. Section C considers the remedies other than exclusion of evidence that are available to a defendant who believes that an identification procedure was unreliable.

A. RISKS OF MISTAKEN IDENTIFICATION

Eyewitnesses are wrong in a disturbing number of cases. One famous example involves the case of Ronald Cotton. One night in 1984, a man broke into the apartment of Jennifer Thompson, who was then a 22-year-old college student in Burlington, North Carolina. The intruder raped Thompson. When police received an anonymous tip in the case, they showed Thompson several photographs of potential suspects, and she picked the photograph of Ronald Cotton. Cotton was a plausible suspect, who had been convicted in 1980 of attempted rape and had recently been released from prison. Although there was no physical evidence linking Cotton to the crime, the jury convicted based on Thompson's confident identification of Cotton during the trial as the man who had raped her. The judge sentenced him to fifty years in prison. Eleven years later, lawyers for Cotton arranged for DNA tests on some of the physical evidence in the case. The tests conclusively established that Cotton was the wrong man. The evidence pointed instead to Bobby Poole — already convicted and serving a prison term for another sexual assault — and Poole later confessed to the rape of Thompson. One of Cotton's lawyers explained the jury's mistake this way: "It is incredibly powerful evidence, and jurors want to believe the victim. They identify with the victim and especially when there's really no motive for the victim to lie. It is very hard evidence to overcome." See Walter Goodman, A Case of Rape, Memory and DNA, N.Y. Times, Feb. 25, 1997, p. C16 (review of television news special featuring Cotton's case).

One famous example, of course, does not tell us how often the problem arises in criminal justice systems that produce millions of criminal convictions each year. How often does a mistaken identification lead to an erroneous conviction? Nobody really knows since we have no convincing way to identify all the wrongful convictions.

It is possible, however, to estimate the importance of mistaken identifications *relative to other causes* of the wrongful convictions we have learned about over the years. Over the last few years, the widespread availability of DNA testing has confirmed many examples of wrongful convictions. Far and away the most common cause of these errors is mistaken identifications by eyewitnesses. By some estimates, this problem caused about 90 percent of the erroneous convictions that DNA evidence has corrected. See Gary L. Wells, et al., Eyewitness Identification Procedures: Recommendations for Lineups and Photospreads, 22 Law & Human Behavior 603 (1998); Jim Dwyer, Peter Neufeld & Barry Scheck, Actual Innocence: Five Days to Execution and Other Dispatches From the Wrongly Convicted (2000). Another study of wrongful convictions, based on earlier cases (drawn heavily from the 1920s and 1930s), attributed about half of all mistaken convictions to eyewitness misidentifications. The next most common causes, perjury by witnesses and negligence by criminal justice officials, each accounted for only about 10 percent of the cases. See Arye Rattner, Convicted But Innocent: Wrongful Conviction and the Criminal Justice System, 12 Law & Hum. Behav. 283 (1988).

Psychologists have studied witness memory in great detail over the years. The following summary of psychological research may suggest some of the reasons why eyewitness identifications sometimes lead to erroneous convictions.

■ EXPERIENCING, REMEMBERING AND REPORTING EVENTS
RALPH NORMAN HABER AND LYN HABER

6 Psych. Pub. Pol. & L. 1057-1091 (2000)

[Consider] the following description of a bank robbery, drawn from actual cases. Several men entered a bank, tied up the only guard in the lobby, told the customers to lie down on the floor, and demanded that the tellers hand over all their money. The robbers then left. There were five tellers, two officers, one guard, and five customers in the bank at the time. When the police took their statements over the next hour, there was little consensus among the thirteen witnesses as to the number of robbers, what they looked like, what they did, the presence of weapons, or the duration of the robbery.

Video cameras in the bank recorded the robbery. Comparing these recordings to the descriptions provided by the witnesses, it was found that no single witness gave an accurate report of the sequence of events, nor did any single witness provide a consistently accurate description of any of the robbers. Further, in subsequent photo identification line-ups, half of the witnesses made serious errors: Four of the thirteen witnesses erroneously selected as a perpetrator one of the other people who had been in the bank at the time of the robbery (a teller or a customer), and three of the thirteen erroneously selected a photograph of someone who had not been there at all at the time. All seven of these witnesses asserted that they were sure they had correctly identified one of the robbers and that they were willing to so testify.

Law enforcement officials, lawyers, and memory experts treat this example as a common occurrence. . . . In contrast, the average person treats this example with incredulity. Most people (typical people, who might become members of a jury) expect an individual eyewitness's report to be accurate. . . .

The purpose of this article is to summarize the scientific evidence on the accuracy of eyewitness testimony, with specific attention to the factors that enhance or impair the likelihood of accuracy. Our hope in writing this article is that the information presented here will be made available to juries now, and incorporated into the law in the future.

Observing and Encoding Events into Memory

In this first section, we consider the factors that might lead witnesses to make and remember differing observations of the same event. . . .

Observational point of view. In the bank robbery described earlier, the customers forced to lie down on the floor had less opportunity to view from the front those robbers who approached the teller booths, whereas some of the tellers had frontal views. Therefore, those tellers should be able to give more detailed descriptions of the appearance of those robbers, and in the absence of other factors, those descriptions are more likely to be accurate. It is critical in evaluating a witness's statements about an event to be sure that the witness had a sufficient opportunity to view the event from a position consistent with the statements being given. . . . In addition to distance, lighting conditions, especially back lighting, reflections, and shadows impact the ability to see fine details. . . .

Allocation of Attention. Attention is memory's gatekeeper. At any moment your five senses are bombarded with vast amounts of external stimulation. [For] encoding to occur, you must attend to [stimulation] during the time it impinges on your senses. [The] deployment of attention has two consequences: it allows you to encode and retain memory of some aspects of what happens to you, and it allows the remainder to slip away and be lost forever.

[Y]ou can switch attention quickly. Any change in stimulation, such as a loud noise, or a movement off to the side, will cause you to orient your attention to it. That re-orientation allows you to encode sudden changes in what is happening, though at the expense of what you had been attending to just previously, which then stops being accessible for encoding into memory. When driving comfortably, it is possible to divide your attention so you can control the car while conversing with a passenger. However, a sudden squeal of brakes refocuses your attention exclusively on the emergency, and you cannot remember what your passenger said during that interval.

This focusing is not simply like moving your eyes. [W]hat you as an observer will encode about an event depends on where and how your attention is focused, not just where you happen to be looking. Most important, it is possible for events to occur directly in front of you, well within your range of seeing and hearing, and yet make no impact on your memory if you were attending to something else at the time. . . .

Bias in Attentional Focus. [F]requently, some aspect of an event causes an involuntary narrowing of attention to some particular detail, so much so that other parts of the event are not attended to at all, and therefore not encoded into memory. One area of great legal importance concerns the narrowing of attention that occurs for most witnesses when they detect the presence of a weapon. People focus their attention on the weapon so much that almost everything else that's happening goes unnoticed and therefore unremembered. . . . Specifically, scientific research on "weapon focus" has shown that, when a weapon is present, witnesses are far less able to remember distinctive features of the people present, including those of the person holding the weapon. Hence, a witness's chances of making a correct identification of a person are reduced if that person held a weapon.

It is equally likely that a narrowing of attention will occur, with its concomitant loss in encoding, whenever any component of the event is highly dramatic, frightening, violent, or distasteful to the witness. It should always be assumed that violence in any form narrows attention, and that which is outside the resultant narrowed attention is encoded less completely, if at all. . . .

Knowledge, Familiarity and Expertise With the Content of the Event. In the course of everyday life, you are highly familiar with aspects of your work, both inside your home and at your jobsite. If you work as a supermarket clerk, you are likely to be far more knowledgeable than most people about a wide range of edible products; if you are a car salesman you know a lot about the makes of cars. Within your own sphere, you are an expert. Bystander-witnesses are often required to testify about details of what they observed, such as the characteristics of a vehicle or a weapon. If the eyewitness has little knowledge of that class of objects, the witness's reports about the object are often incomplete or simply wrong. . . .

Similarly, lack of familiarity has been demonstrated in scientific experiments to lead to inaccurate identification of people. The adage that "all Asians look alike (to non-Asians)" is in fact mostly true. In experiments on cross-racial identification, in which the race of the criminal is different from that of the witness and the witness has few close interactions with people of that race, the witness cannot provide as many identifying features of the criminal he observed, thereby making it less likely that subsequent identifications will be accurate. . . .

Witness Expectations and Interpretation of the Event. Research has shown that the beliefs of the witness produce fundamental changes in the reports of what was observed. For example, one study [from 1947] concerned with racial prejudice asked subjects/witnesses to view a scene depicting two men in which one man held a knife: The witnesses were to describe the scene to other people who had not seen it. The two critical contents of the scene that were varied were whether both men were the same race and which one held the knife. When both men were of the same race, nearly all witnesses correctly described the critical element of who held the knife, as well as most of the details of dress and the position of the two men. However, if one man was Black and one White, most witnesses (Black and White alike) reported that the Black man held the knife even when it was held by the White man. Some witnesses who correctly described who held the knife incorrectly added that the White man was defending himself (there was nothing in either man's posture or position to suggest this conclusion). All of the witnesses stated that they believed that crimes were more likely to be committed by Blacks than by Whites. The results suggest that eyewitnesses sometimes encode and remember the event so as to be consistent with their beliefs rather than the way it actually happened. . . .

Remembering Events

Experts on memory research refer to a witness's first report of an observed event, when it is given after the event, as an independent memory. . . . A witness's independent memory report of an event is normally the most accurate description the witness will ever be able to produce. . . .

In normal life, your own independent memories often undergo influences that, in psychological parlance, "taint" them: You dress your stories up for your listeners who did not observe the events, and you discuss the events with other people who also observed them and you incorporate what they say as part of your memory. A tainted memory is not necessarily a false or inaccurate memory, but it is no longer your own, original, independent encoding of the event. It is a compendium of information and detail, some of which you yourself did not see or remember. In this respect, it is analogous to hearsay, and, for the same reasons that hearsay testimony is rarely admissible, testimony based on nonindependent memories should also be excluded from the courtroom. . . . In this section, we consider [some] factors that might cause eyewitnesses to change their memory and, therefore, their report of an event. . . .

The Inevitably Wrong Focus of Autobiographical Memory. . . . Typically, as an event unfolds, you as an observer are not thinking about describing the other people and their actions: you see the event in terms of how it affects you. The event has all of the properties of a story, with a beginning, middle, and end, and a sequence of actions with one or more actors. The most important actor — the protagonist in your story — is you. . . . As an example of how an eyewitness describes events from a personal point of view, consider one of the eyewitness accounts from a woman who was in the bank described above:

> I stopped at the bank to cash a check. I was putting the money in my purse when armed men ran into the bank, waved their guns at everyone and ordered me to lie down on the floor. One gigantic man, who looked like a football player, stepped over me and I was afraid he would take all of the money I just got. I was so scared he would hurt me. He went to the same teller who had just helped me, threatened her with his pistol, and stuffed what she handed him into his bag. After what seemed like hours of terror, all the robbers ran out. They didn't take my money.

This report has little helpful content for the policeman who wants to identify the robbers. The policeman asked her: How many robbers were there? Which ones had guns? What did each of the robbers look like? What were they wearing? What did each of the other robbers do? Every investigator and every interrogator forces the witness to switch from "What happened to you?" to "What happened in the bank?" Hence, almost immediately, the eyewitness is required to change from an autobiographical and psychological focus to an objective focus. This translation usually produces changes in the report, changes that may introduce inaccuracies about the physical reality.

The most typical and pervasive changes occur when the observer is asked about details that were not in her perspective or about links in the sequence that were not important to her at the time — details and links she did not notice, encode, or retain in memory. In trying to answer the interrogator's questions, the witness often adds content and details that "must have happened"— details not present in independent memory. . . .

Systematic Changes in the Content of Memory with Each Repetition. Unlike a video recording, which remains the same each time it is played, memory undergoes changes with rehearsal. [E]ach further repetition of the report produces predictable changes in the report. These predictable changes are, first, that many of the details drop out of the subsequent reports altogether and are never reported again and, second, that other details are altered or additions are made to fit more consistently with the overall description provided by the observer. . . . Further, not surprisingly, observers also are shown to alter their descriptions depending on the audience to whom they are speaking. . . .

These facts about alterations of memory produced by rehearsal are particularly relevant to testimony made by witnesses in court. By the time the witness reaches the stand and is questioned by counsel, she has told her story dozens of times. Often, the first time the story is told is to other observers or to the first new arrivals at the scene. That description, the closest one available from the independent memory of the observer, is usually unrecorded. The first recorded description, taken down by one of the officers at the scene, may already have undergone many changes after several prior rehearsals, each with its smoothings, rearrangements of facts, and attempts to be congruent with what has been learned from other witnesses. This is only the beginning of the rehearsals required of the witness. More than one policeman will demand a repetition; then come the investigators and the lawyers. . . .

Post-Event Information Can Create New (and Potentially) False Memories. The single most dramatic finding in recent memory research concerns changes in reports made by witnesses when other people give them information. Two insidious facts have emerged: First, witnesses are unaware that they have acquired new information from somebody else — the information is treated as if it were part of what they themselves originally observed; and second, witnesses usually are unaware that they have changed their report based on that new information. . . .

Consider some findings from recent research: (a) Embedding a false presupposition into a question (asking "Did the red car stop or run the light just before the crash?" when the car's color has not been previously specified) will often change the witness's subsequent testimony as to the color of the car; (b) varying the intensity of verbs in a question (asking "Did the car hit . . ., Did the car collide . . . Did the car smash . . . Did the car demolish . . .?") will often change the witness's subsequent testimony about the speed of the car; (c) showing a witness line-up pictures of people not involved in the observed event will often result in the witness subsequently choosing one of those innocent people as the criminal, even when the real criminal is present in the later line-up; (d) allowing the witness to overhear a new or different description about the event or about the persons involved will often lead the witness to include the divergent information in subsequent testimony. . . .

Why is it so easy for post-event information to become incorporated into memory? Research has shown that the main reason is that human beings do not have a particularly good memory for the sources of their knowledge about events. When you acquire information about an event from several sources, regardless of how accurate you are in remembering the information itself, you are less accurate about remembering from which source you acquired it. . . .

Encoding, Remembering, and Identifying Strangers

In the preceding sections, we have discussed memory processes without differentiating between memory of events and memory of people. An eyewitness is frequently required to identify an unfamiliar person who might have perpetrated a crime. Such identifications often comprise the only evidence against the defendant. In this section, we focus specifically on what is known about the accuracy of a witness's identification of unfamiliar people from memory. . . .

In a large number of controlled experiments, witnesses have been asked to observe a realistic enactment of a crime committed by a stranger and then to give descriptions of the criminal. Then, after differing periods of time, these witnesses have been asked to attempt to identify whether the perpetrator they observed is present in a line-up. The observation factors studied have included the type of event being observed, length of time of observation, distance and viewing conditions, amount of activity by the stranger, presence of a weapon, presence of frightening events, number of different strangers, amount of stress felt by the eyewitness, and post-event exposure to other people who had been present at the event or who talk to the eyewitness about the event.

[C]onsider identification accuracy for research line-ups that are constructed with the known perpetrator present. The first kind of accuracy of concern is whether the witness can discriminate between the true perpetrator and the remaining foils who are innocent of the crime. Based on a large number of experiments, about 75% of the time the perpetrator is correctly selected (true positive); the remaining 25% of the time the witness identifies someone who either was not present at the crime scene, or was a bystander at the scene, but not the criminal (false positive). If no weapon is present, no violence, no bystanders, no post-event contamination, and little delay, true-positive rates can approach 90% (with false-positive rates dropping to a low of about 10%). Conversely, if a weapon is present, the scene is violent, bystanders are present, post-event information is available, the witness feels great stress, and there is a long time delay between observation and identification, the true-positive rate for correct identification of the perpetrator drops well below 50%, with the false-positive rate exceeding 50%. These percentages just quoted are rough consensual estimates, based on the results of perhaps 100 experiments with line-ups. . . .

The fallibility of the eyewitness becomes even more evident when results of line-up research are considered in which the perpetrator is known not to be in the line-up. Now the correct response for the eyewitness is to say "no," none of the people in the line-up is the perpetrator. The results show that, on average, under normal observation conditions, eyewitnesses still say "yes" (that someone present is the perpetrator) about 60% of the time when the perpetrator is known to be absent! All of these "yes" responses are false positives: The eyewitness has identified an innocent person. Only under the most favorable observation conditions (as described in the previous section) is there some reduction in the false-positive rates (with the perpetrator absent). Even more seriously, "yes" responses are found to increase to a high of 90% (a 90% false-positive rate of identifying an innocent person incorrectly as the perpetrator who committed the crime) when the observation conditions are poor, and the eyewitness is led to believe that the perpetrator is present. . . .

We have presented an array of scientific research evidence showing that, by the time an eyewitness testifies in court, the identification and testimony offered may not accurately reflect either what actually happened, or what was originally observed. . . . The recent examples of DNA evidence being used to reverse convictions that had been originally based on only eyewitness identifications suggest that there are in fact many innocent people who have been wrongly convicted on the basis of erroneous eyewitness testimony. . . .

Notes

1. *Relative importance of different memory problems.* The psychological studies described above identify problems at the encoding, storage, and retrieval phases of memory that might affect the accuracy of an eyewitness identification. Which of the various problems a witness might encounter will have the largest impact on the memory? In one effort to answer this question, researchers performed a statistical analysis (known as a "meta-analysis") on the results of more than 190 studies of eyewitness performance. The analysis measured the relative effects of many different obstacles and aids to accurate memory. The authors concluded that "context reinstatement" was among the most important contributing factors to an accurate identification: For instance, if the target was placed in the same pose at the initial exposure and at the later time of recognition (or asked to wear a distinctive piece of clothing or speak words that the witness recalled from the original incident), the accuracy of the witness identifications increased. The other factors having the largest effect on witness accuracy include the distinctiveness of the target, exposure time, age of the witness, cross-racial identification, and amount of time elapsed between the original event and the recognition exercise. See Peter Shapiro and Steven Penrod, Meta-Analysis of Facial Identification Studies, 100 Psychological Bull. 139 (1986).

The psychological experiments described above test human memory, but they often take place in a setting different from what an actual crime victim might face. What might those differences be? Would they make a crime witness more or less likely than an experimental "subject" to give an accurate identification?

2. *Cross-racial identifications.* Unfortunately, there is some truth to the distasteful phrase, "They [people of another race] all look alike." Research studies for over thirty years have found an empirical basis for saying that people of one race find it more difficult to identify people of another race. A witness's difficulty in making such identifications seems to be tied to unfamiliarity: People who have more regular contact with those of another race have less difficulty making such identifications. The so-called "own-race bias" accounts for about 15 percent of the variation in the ability of witnesses to identify another person. See Christian A. Meissner and John C. Brigham, Eyewitness Identification: Thirty Years of Investigating the Own-Race Bias in Memory for Faces: A Meta-Analytic Review, 7 Psych. Pub. Pol. & L. 3 (2001).

3. *Individual recognition skills and witness certainty.* It is important to remember that these difficulties with memory address only trends and averages: Any individual witness might be affected less (or more) by such problems. Unfortunately, it is

difficult to determine whether a particular witness is above average or below average in her ability to identify a crime suspect. The age of a witness is one of the few consistently helpful indicators: Children tend to make less accurate identifications, mostly because they are substantially more suggestible than adults. See M. Bruck & S. J. Ceci, The Description of Children's Suggestibility, in Memory for Everyday and Emotional Events (Stein, Ornstein, Tversky, & Brainerd eds., 1997). Witnesses over 70 are less accurate when describing events that are especially unfamiliar, or those that unfold quickly with many distractions present. See Daniel Yarmey, The Elderly Witness, in Psychological Issues in Eyewitness Identification (Sporer, Malpass, and Koehnken eds., 1996).

One might be tempted to rely on the witness's level of certainty to identify the most "able" witnesses, i.e., the witness who says, "I'm absolutely sure it was him." But witness certainty, it turns out, is not a good measure of accuracy. As one summary of the psychological literature put it, "[T]he eyewitness accuracy-confidence relationship is weak under good laboratory conditions and functionally useless in forensically representative settings." Gary Wells and Donna Murray, Eyewitness Confidence, in Eyewitness Testimony: Psychological Perspectives 155 (Gary Wells and Elizabeth Loftus eds., 1984).

4. *Police officers as witnesses.* Sometimes the witness to a crime is a police officer, who may have special training in facial recognition techniques. Does the special training and experience of police officers increase their accuracy as eyewitnesses? The evidence on this question is equivocal. On the one hand, police officers (as well as untrained witnesses) tend to have more complete and accurate memories if they are able to anticipate an event and know that they will later need to recall it accurately. A police officer may be in a good position to anticipate the need for later recall. On the other hand, a number of studies have concluded that police officers and others with special training fare no better than other witnesses under realistic eyewitness conditions.

5. *Early forgetting.* Some of the earliest research in memory showed that more forgetting happens early. We forget very rapidly immediately after an event — usually within a few hours — but forgetting becomes more and more gradual as time passes. See Elizabeth Loftus, Eyewitness Testimony 21-83 (1979). What are the implications of this research for police work?

B. EXCLUSION OF IDENTIFICATION EVIDENCE

Witnesses identify potential suspects in several settings. The most formal identification procedures — and the easiest to subject to legal controls — occur in the police station. The "lineup" places a small group of persons before the witness; the witness is asked if any person in the lineup is the person who committed the crime. In another identification technique that often takes place in a police station, the witness reviews photographs of different persons to identify a suspect. Finally, there are "confrontations" or "showups," in which the police ask the witness to view the suspect alone. This sort of identification occurs most frequently in the field, near the crime scene, but it can also occur at the station.

Until the mid-1960s, the legal system relied on adversarial testing of evidence to control these identification procedures. If a "showup" produced unreliable evidence, defense counsel was expected to point this out. But in recent decades, federal and state constitutions (and to a lesser extent, statutes and court rules) have required the exclusion of some evidence obtained during identification procedures. The constitutional controls derive from (1) the right to counsel clauses and (2) the due process clauses of the federal and state constitutions. Courts have declared a select group of identification procedures invalid unless they take place with counsel for the defendant present. For a larger group of identification procedures, defendants make claims based on the due process clause, arguing that the identifications were too unreliable to be admitted as evidence. The following materials explore the right-to-counsel and due process limitations in several common settings.

1. Exclusion on Right to Counsel Grounds

The Sixth Amendment to the U.S. Constitution provides that "In all criminal prosecutions, the accused shall . . . have the Assistance of Counsel for his defence." Every state constitution except one (Virginia's) also provides explicitly for legal counsel in criminal cases. A number describe the point at which the right to counsel attaches by using phrases such as "appear" or "defend," as in New York's article I, section 6: "In any trial in any court whatever the party accused shall be allowed to appear and defend in person and with counsel. . . ." Others speak in terms of a right to be "heard" through counsel, as in New Hampshire's article 15: "Every subject shall have a right . . . to be fully heard in his defense, by himself, and counsel." In what way are these constitutional provisions relevant to police efforts to obtain eyewitness identifications of suspects?

■ UNITED STATES v. BILLY JOE WADE

388 U.S. 218 (1967)

BRENNAN, J.

The question here is whether courtroom identifications of an accused at trial are to be excluded from evidence because the accused was exhibited to the witnesses before trial at a post-indictment lineup conducted for identification purposes without notice to and in the absence of the accused's appointed counsel.

The federally insured bank in Eustace, Texas, was robbed on September 21, 1964. A man with a small strip of tape on each side of his face entered the bank, pointed a pistol at the female cashier and the vice president, the only persons in the bank at the time, and forced them to fill a pillowcase with the bank's money. [Wade was indicted for the robbery on March 23, 1965 and arrested on April 2. Counsel was appointed to represent him on April 26.] Fifteen days later an FBI agent, without notice to Wade's lawyer, arranged to have the two bank employees observe a lineup made up of Wade and five or six other prisoners and conducted in a courtroom of the local county courthouse. Each person in the line wore strips of tape such as allegedly worn by the robber and upon direction each said something like "put the money in the bag," the words allegedly uttered by the robber. Both bank employees identified Wade in the lineup as the bank robber.

At trial, the two employees, when asked on direct examination if the robber was in the courtroom, pointed to Wade. The prior lineup identification was then elicited from both employees on cross-examination. At the close of testimony, Wade's counsel moved for a judgment of acquittal or, alternatively, to strike the bank officials' courtroom identifications on the ground that conduct of the lineup, without notice to and in the absence of his appointed counsel, violated his . . . Sixth Amendment right to the assistance of counsel. The motion was denied, and Wade was convicted. . . .

The Framers of the Bill of Rights envisaged a broader role for counsel than under the practice then prevailing in England of merely advising his client in "matters of law," and eschewing any responsibility for "matters of fact." The constitutions in at least 11 of the 13 States expressly or impliedly abolished this distinction. . . .

When the Bill of Rights was adopted, there were no organized police forces as we know them today. The accused confronted the prosecutor and the witnesses against him, and the evidence was marshalled, largely at the trial itself. In contrast, today's law enforcement machinery involves critical confrontations of the accused by the prosecution at pretrial proceedings where the results might well settle the accused's fate and reduce the trial itself to a mere formality. In recognition of these realities of modern criminal prosecution, our cases have construed the Sixth Amendment guarantee to apply to "critical" stages of the proceedings. The guarantee reads: "In all criminal prosecutions, the accused shall enjoy the right . . . to have the Assistance of Counsel for his defence." The plain wording of this guarantee thus encompasses counsel's assistance whenever necessary to assure a meaningful "defence." . . . The presence of counsel at such critical confrontations, as at the trial itself, operates to assure that the accused's interests will be protected consistently with our adversary theory of criminal prosecution. . . .

The Government characterizes the lineup as a mere preparatory step in the gathering of the prosecution's evidence, not different — for Sixth Amendment purposes — from various other preparatory steps, such as systematized or scientific analyzing of the accused's fingerprints, blood sample, clothing, hair, and the like. We think there are differences which preclude such stages being characterized as critical stages at which the accused has the right to the presence of his counsel. Knowledge of the techniques of science and technology is sufficiently available, and the variables in techniques few enough, that the accused has the opportunity for a meaningful confrontation of the Government's case at trial through the ordinary processes of cross-examination of the Government's expert witnesses and the presentation of the evidence of his own experts. . . .

But the confrontation compelled by the State between the accused and the victim or witnesses to a crime to elicit identification evidence is peculiarly riddled with innumerable dangers and variable factors which might seriously, even crucially, derogate from a fair trial. The vagaries of eyewitness identification are well-known; the annals of criminal law are rife with instances of mistaken identification. . . . A major factor contributing to the high incidence of miscarriage of justice from mistaken identification has been the degree of suggestion inherent in the manner in which the prosecution presents the suspect to witnesses for pretrial identification. [I]t is a matter of common experience that, once a witness has picked out the accused at the lineup, he is not likely to go back on his word later on, so that in practice the issue of identity may (in the absence of other relevant evidence) for all practical purposes be determined there and then, before the trial.

[A]s is the case with secret interrogations, there is serious difficulty in depicting what transpires at lineups and other forms of identification confrontations. [T]he defense can seldom reconstruct the manner and mode of lineup identification for judge or jury at trial. Those participating in a lineup with the accused may often be police officers; in any event, the participants' names are rarely recorded or divulged at trial. The impediments to an objective observation are increased when the victim is the witness. Lineups are prevalent in rape and robbery prosecutions and present a particular hazard that a victim's understandable outrage may excite vengeful or spiteful motives. In any event, neither witnesses nor lineup participants are apt to be alert for conditions prejudicial to the suspect. . . . Improper influences may go undetected by a suspect, guilty or not, who experiences the emotional tension which we might expect in one being confronted with potential accusers. Even when he does observe abuse, if he has a criminal record he may be reluctant to take the stand and open up the admission of prior convictions. Moreover, any protestations by the suspect of the fairness of the lineup made at trial are likely to be in vain; the jury's choice is between the accused's unsupported version and that of the police officers present. In short, the accused's inability effectively to reconstruct at trial any unfairness that occurred at the lineup may deprive him of his only opportunity meaningfully to attack the credibility of the witness' courtroom identification. . . .

The potential for improper influence is illustrated by the circumstances, insofar as they appear, surrounding the prior identifications in the three cases we decide today. [The companion cases were Gilbert v. California, 388 U.S. 263 (1987), and Stovall v. Denno, 388 U.S. 293 (1981).] In the present case, the testimony of the identifying witnesses elicited on cross-examination revealed that those witnesses were taken to the courthouse and seated in the courtroom to await assembly of the lineup. The courtroom faced on a hallway observable to the witnesses through an open door. The cashier testified that she saw Wade "standing in the hall" within sight of an FBI agent. . . . The lineup in *Gilbert* was conducted in an auditorium in which some 100 witnesses to several alleged state and federal robberies charged to Gilbert made wholesale identifications of Gilbert as the robber in each other's presence, a procedure said to be fraught with dangers of suggestion. And the vice of suggestion created by the identification in *Stovall,* was the presentation to the witness of the suspect alone handcuffed to police officers. It is hard to imagine a situation more clearly conveying the suggestion to the witness that the one presented is believed guilty by the police. . . .

Insofar as the accused's conviction may rest on a courtroom identification in fact the fruit of a suspect pretrial identification which the accused is helpless to subject to effective scrutiny at trial, the accused is deprived of that right of cross-examination which is an essential safeguard to his right to confront the witnesses against him. . . . The trial which might determine the accused's fate may well not be that in the courtroom but that at the pretrial confrontation, with the State aligned against the accused, the witness the sole jury, and the accused unprotected against the overreaching, intentional or unintentional, and with little or no effective appeal from the judgment there rendered by the witness — "that's the man." . . .

No substantial countervailing policy considerations have been advanced against the requirement of the presence of counsel. Concern is expressed that the requirement will forestall prompt identifications and result in obstruction of the confrontations. As for the first, we note that in the two cases in which the right to counsel is today held to apply, counsel had already been appointed and no argument is made in either case that notice to counsel would have prejudicially delayed the confrontations. [L]aw enforcement may be assisted by preventing the infiltration of taint in the prosecution's identification evidence. That result cannot help the guilty avoid conviction but can only help assure that the right man has been brought to justice.[29]

Legislative or other regulations, such as those of local police departments, which eliminate the risks of abuse and unintentional suggestion at lineup proceedings and the impediments to meaningful confrontation at trial may also remove the basis for regarding the stage as "critical." But neither Congress nor the federal authorities have seen fit to provide a solution. What we hold today in no way creates a constitutional straitjacket which will handicap sound efforts at reform, nor is it intended to have this effect.

We come now to the question whether the denial of Wade's motion to strike the courtroom identification by the bank witnesses at trial because of the absence of his counsel at the lineup required . . . the grant of a new trial at which such evidence is to be excluded. We do not think this disposition can be justified without first giving the Government the opportunity to establish by clear and convincing evidence that the in-court identifications were based upon observations of the suspect other than the lineup identification. [T]he appropriate procedure to be followed is to vacate the conviction pending a hearing to determine whether the in-court identifications had an independent source, or whether, in any event, the introduction of the evidence was harmless error, and for the District Court to reinstate the conviction or order a new trial, as may be proper. . . .

WHITE, J., dissenting in part and concurring in part.

The Court has again propounded a broad constitutional rule barring use of a wide spectrum of relevant and probative evidence, solely because a step in its ascertainment or discovery occurs outside the presence of defense counsel. This was the approach of the Court in Miranda v. Arizona, 384 U.S. 436 (1966). I objected then to what I thought was an uncritical and doctrinaire approach without satisfactory factual foundation. I have much the same view of the present ruling and therefore dissent. . . .

The Court's opinion is far-reaching. . . . It matters not how well the witness knows the suspect, whether the witness is the suspect's mother, brother, or long-time associate, and no matter how long or well the witness observed the perpetrator at the scene of the crime. . . .

To find the lineup a "critical" stage of the proceeding and to exclude identifications made in the absence of counsel, the Court must [assume] that there is now no adequate source from which defense counsel can learn about the circumstances of the pretrial identification in order to place before the jury all of the considerations which should enter into an appraisal of courtroom identification evidence. But [I am not willing to assume] that the police and the witnesses will forget or prevaricate, that defense counsel will be unable to bring out the truth and that neither jury, judge, nor appellate court is a sufficient safeguard against unacceptable police conduct occurring at a pretrial identification procedure. I am unable to share the

29. Many other nations surround the lineup with safeguards against prejudice to the suspect. In England the suspect must be allowed the presence of his solicitor or a friend; Germany requires the presence of retained counsel; France forbids the confrontation of the suspect in the absence of his counsel; Spain, Mexico, and Italy provide detailed procedures prescribing the conditions under which confrontation must occur under the supervision of a judicial officer who sees to it that the proceedings are officially recorded to assure adequate scrutiny at trial.

Court's view of the willingness of the police and the ordinary citizen-witness to dissemble. . . .

Identifications frequently take place after arrest but before an indictment is returned or an information is filed. The police may have arrested a suspect on probable cause but may still have the wrong man. Both the suspect and the State have every interest in a prompt identification at that stage, the suspect in order to secure his immediate release and the State because prompt and early identification enhances accurate identification and because it must know whether it is on the right investigative track. Unavoidably, however, the absolute rule requiring the presence of counsel will cause significant delay and it may very well result in no pretrial identification at all. . . . Nor do I think the witnesses themselves can be ignored. They will now be required to be present at the convenience of counsel rather than their own. Many may be much less willing to participate if the identification stage is transformed into an adversary proceeding not under the control of a judge. . . .

Finally, I think the Court's new rule is vulnerable in terms of its own unimpeachable purpose of increasing the reliability of identification testimony. Law enforcement officers have the obligation to convict the guilty and to make sure they do not convict the innocent. . . . To this extent, our so-called adversary system is not adversary at all; nor should it be. But defense counsel has no comparable obligation to ascertain or present the truth. Our system assigns him a different mission. [A]s part of our modified adversary system and as part of the duty imposed on the most honorable defense counsel, we countenance or require conduct which in many instances has little, if any, relation to the search for truth. [Defense counsel] will not only observe what occurs and develop possibilities for later cross-examination but will hover over witnesses and begin their cross-examination then, menacing truthful factfinding as thoroughly as the Court fears the police now do. . . . In my view, the State is entitled to investigate and develop its case outside the presence of defense counsel. . . .

■ PEOPLE v. FREDDIE HAWKINS

435 N.E.2d 376 (N.Y. 1982)

GABRIELLI, J.

These four appeals present the common question whether a suspect has a right to counsel at an investigatory lineup. In each case, we are urged by the defendant to interpret our State Constitution as providing this right at lineups conducted before the commencement of formal adversarial proceedings against a defendant.

In People v. Laffosse, 79 A.D.2d 894 (1980), the defendant was convicted of robbery in the second degree for his part in the robbery of an off-duty police officer by three males. Laffosse was apprehended after the officer had selected his picture from a photo array. Once at the station house, the defendant was advised of his *Miranda* rights and he then agreed to talk to a detective. During the questioning he requested an attorney, but he and the police were unsuccessful in locating the particular attorney he desired; Laffosse then refused the offer of the police to procure a Legal Aid attorney to represent him. Shortly thereafter, he was informed that he was to be placed in a lineup. . . . Laffosse subsequently was identified at the lineup by his victim. [In a second case, a murder suspect requested counsel for the first time moments before a lineup. In the third case, the defendant Hawkins did not request an attorney prior to a lineup. In the fourth case, an assault victim selected the defendant from a photo array, and the defendant was placed in a lineup without notice to the attorney representing him on unrelated criminal charges.] Each lineup in these four cases was conducted before an accusatory instrument had been filed and before an adversary criminal proceeding had commenced. Suppression was denied in each case, and the subsequent convictions were later affirmed at the Appellate Division. We also affirm.

Initially, we observe that defendants present no cognizable claim under the United States Constitution to a right to counsel at their lineups, since these lineups occurred prior to the initiation of formal prosecutorial proceedings. See Kirby v. Illinois, 406 U.S. 682 (1972). The Supreme Court in United States v. Wade, 388 U.S. 218 (1967), held that a person accused of a crime by Federal or State officials is entitled under the Sixth and Fourteenth Amendments to have his attorney present at pretrial lineups. In Kirby v. Illinois, however, the court limited that holding and refused to extend this principle to provide a right to counsel at lineups held prior to the initiation of formal prosecutorial proceedings. In reaching this conclusion, the court observed that a person's Sixth and Fourteenth Amendment right to counsel attaches only at or after the time that adversary judicial proceedings have been initiated against him. The court went on to indicate that a formal charge, preliminary hearing, indictment, information or arraignment may mark the initiation of such adversary judicial proceedings. . . .

It follows, therefore, that the defendants in the four cases here presented to us had no right to counsel at their lineups by virtue of the United States Constitution. Each lineup occurred before the initiation of formal judicial proceedings and, accordingly, defendants' Sixth and Fourteenth Amendment right to counsel had not yet attached. . . . Nevertheless, defendants press their contention that the lineup identifications must be suppressed, arguing that our State Constitution should be so interpreted as providing a right to counsel at investigatory lineups.

On several occasions in the custodial interrogation context this court has extended the protections of counsel afforded to a defendant under our State Constitution beyond those afforded by the United States Constitution. The lifeblood of the New York rule is that once the right to counsel has indelibly attached, the defendant can effectively waive the protections of counsel only if counsel is present.

[The] New York rule has developed along two lines. In the first line, it has been held that a waiver of the protections of counsel by a person against whom formal criminal proceedings have been commenced is ineffective unless made in the presence of counsel. In the second line, it has been ruled that the nonwaivability rule is applicable to a suspect who is represented by an attorney. [The defendants claim that they, like suspects who are interrogated, have a right to counsel.]

The fundamental error in these arguments is that they misconstrue the nature of New York's counsel rule and ignore the reasons for its development. Much like the Supreme Court's decision in *Miranda,* our decisions developing the independent New York counsel rules have arisen simply out of a concern for protecting the individual during interrogations. This court has repeatedly stressed that absent the advice of an attorney, the average person, unschooled in legal intricacies, might very well unwittingly surrender his privilege against compulsory self incrimination when confronted with the coercive power of the State and its agents. Thus, our indelible right to counsel rule has developed to ensure that an individual's protection against self incrimination is not rendered illusory during pretrial interrogation.

Although we have found the assistance of counsel to be of importance during interrogations, . . . counsel plays a much more limited role at identification confrontations. During interrogations, counsel may take an active role on behalf of his client, both in advising a suspect on whether to remain silent and in counseling a suspect on whether to answer particular questions once the right to remain silent has been waived. In contrast, during a lineup counsel plays the relatively passive role of an observer. Counsel may not actively advise his client during the lineup itself. . . .

To be sure, the assistance of counsel is not completely valueless at investigatory lineups. But that is not the constitutional test of whether it is required. Nor does its value to a suspect provide the full practical and reasonable picture concerning its effect on the other side of the criminal process equation — law enforcement and protection of the community and, indeed, society itself. Before a right to counsel is extended to this investigatory stage, consideration must be given to the serious detriments that emanate from the sought-after requirement of counsel at investigatory lineups. A primary policy consideration is that lineups should be conducted as close in time to the occurrence of the incident under investigation as possible. First, the recollections of a witness may fade as time passes. Second, a prompt identification confrontation will benefit the suspect, both because it may diminish the possibility of a mistaken identification and, further, because it may also permit the release of an innocent suspect with a minimum of delay. Finally, prompt identification confrontations may assist the police in determining whether to continue their search of the vicinity of the crime. These necessary advantages often may be lost if the lineup is required to be delayed.

We conclude that the limited benefits provided by counsel at investigatory lineups are far outweighed by the policy considerations militating against requiring counsel at this stage of the investigatory process. The Constitution does not expressly or even impliedly require it. . . . The right to the assistance of counsel at corporeal identifications therefore arises only after the initiation of formal prosecutorial proceedings. After the accused has been formally charged by indictment, information or complaint, his Sixth and Fourteenth Amendment right to counsel will attach, and a lineup conducted without notice to and in the absence of his counsel will be held to violate that right. In contrast, the police have no obligation to secure counsel for a suspect who is merely being placed in an investigatory lineup, even when the suspect requests that counsel be provided.

Although we conclude that the State has no obligation to supply counsel at investigatory lineups, we have previously noted that if a suspect already has counsel, his attorney may not be excluded from the lineup proceedings. That does not mean, however, that the police must notify counsel of an impending investigatory lineup or that counsel is entitled to a lengthy adjournment at this stage of the investigatory process. In view of the limited benefits which counsel provides at this stage, the police need not suspend the lineup in anticipation of the arrival of counsel if this would cause unreasonable delay. Pertinent to this consideration is whether the delay would result in significant inconvenience to the witnesses or would undermine the substantial advantages of a prompt identification confrontation. It follows that since the defendants in each of the present appeals were placed in lineups prior to the initiation of formal prosecutorial proceedings, they were deprived of no rights guaranteed by our Federal or State Constitutions by the absence of counsel at this stage. . . .

MEYER, J., dissenting.

. . . Comment on the *Kirby* decision has made abundantly clear the illogic of its efforts to distinguish the Supreme Court's prior holding in United States v. Wade. [It is a decision that removes the protective effects of counsel's presence precisely when the danger of convicting an innocent defendant upon a mistaken identification is greatest.] Nor would we be blazing a new trail in refusing on State constitutional grounds to follow *Kirby*. Though the majority of State courts deciding the issue since *Kirby* was decided have followed its rule, notwithstanding its lack of logic . . ., other State courts have not felt so constrained. [The dissenting opinion then discussed decisions from Alaska, Michigan, New York, and Pennsylvania, which held that the right to counsel applies to any post-arrest lineup.] There is strong reason why we should do likewise and little of practical significance to justify the majority's conclusion.

The reason, of course, is the numerous instances in which innocent persons have been convicted on the basis of erroneous identification testimony. . . . Over 55 years ago Professor (later Justice) Felix Frankfurter pointed out that "The identification of strangers is proverbially untrustworthy. The hazards of such testimony are established by a formidable number of instances in the records of English and American trials." Felix Frankfurter, The Case of Sacco and Vanzetti (1927). Nor are such statements vague speculations; the documentation is exhaustive, explicit and vast. [A book by Edwin Borchard, entitled "Convicting the Innocent,"] dramatically illustrates the strength of the proof. Of 65 cases discussed by Professor Borchard in which innocent persons lost their lives or served prison terms, 29 were the result of mistaken eyewitness identifications. . . .

The dogma is that the role of counsel at a lineup is "passive," but this is true only in the relative sense that he cannot engage in the plenary activity that he would during a trial. That he can be much more than an observer who will later use the knowledge thus gained to cross-examine witnesses at the trial or himself bear witness at the trial to events at the lineup is evident from our recent decision in People v. Yut Wai Tom, 422 N.E.2d 556 (N.Y. 1981). There defense counsel, though he did not stay to observe the actual lineup, arranged for defendant to be placed in different positions in the separate lineups that were to occur, for the removal of the jackets of the stand-ins because defendant was without a jacket, for the witnesses to view the lineup separately and for the wording of the questions to be addressed to them, and advised the defendant to assume the same pose that the stand-ins did and not to allow himself to be conspicuous. [C]ounsel will reduce even unintentional biasing effects . . . by asking that witnesses be kept apart from one another both before and after lineups and that as to each witness a so-called blank lineup (without defendant in it) be held prior to that in which defendant appears, by making sure that disparities in size and physique are reduced and that none of the stand-ins are known to the witness, and by seeking, where law enforcement officials do not automatically do so, permission to have the procedure video taped. Moreover, although the officials in charge cannot be forced to accede to such requests, experience teaches that they often do, both because obviating objections to fairness more readily assures admissibility at trial of the resulting identification if there is one and because it is a necessary concomitant of every mistaken identification that the actual perpetrator remains free to commit new crimes. . . .

Until it has been demonstrated that the presence of counsel at a prearraignment lineup in Alaska, California, Michigan, Pennsylvania and Oklahoma has presented some real problems for law enforcement in those States, or that the New York situation is so different from theirs as to make their system unworkable here, there is nothing to weigh in the constitutional balance against requiring counsel except speculation. . . .

■ NEW YORK CITY POLICE DEPARTMENT, LEGAL BUREAU EYEWITNESS IDENTIFICATION PROCEDURES: LINEUPS

A. Prior to the lineup.

1. The suspect's rights:

a. He must be advised of his *Miranda* Warnings only if he is to be interrogated—whether before, during or after the "lineup."

b. He must be advised that he is going to be placed in a lineup so that his identity may be established concerning a particular crime or crimes.

c. There is no right to counsel at a lineup held prior to arraignment.

d. If the suspect requests a lawyer for the lineup he should be advised that he does not have a right to a lawyer.

e. If the suspect has a lawyer, and the lawyer requests to be present at the lineup, allow [the lawyer] a reasonable time to appear.

f. If the attorney cannot, or does not appear within a reasonable amount of time, the lineup can proceed without him being present.

2. The attorney:

a. If an attorney is present at the lineup site he must be allowed to view the lineup.

b. If the attorney for the suspect is present during the lineup, he shall be permitted to observe the manner in which the lineup is conducted. He may view the lineup in the room in which it is conducted, or, if he prefers, in a place in which he cannot be observed. . . .

c. The suspect's attorney shall not be permitted to talk to any of the witnesses participating in the identification of the suspect. He shall be free, however, to confer with his client. The attorney should not be permitted to hear the officer's interview of the witness after viewing the lineup.

d. If the attorney makes suggestions to improve the fairness of the lineup, the officer conducting the lineup should follow them if he deems the suggestions reasonable and practical.

e. The attorney should not be permitted to interfere with the conduct of the lineup but should be advised that all suggestions concerning the lineup should be addressed to the officer conducting the lineup.

3. The police officer conducting the lineup: . . .

b. He should see that the identifying witnesses are interviewed prior to the lineup. If there is more than one witness, they should be interviewed separately.

c. He should make a complete record of: the details of the procedure utilized; specific utterances required of any person in the lineup (e.g., speaking the words at the scene of the crime); any actions of persons in lineup required to facilitate identification (e.g., trying on a hat, stand up, turning sideways); all responses or statements made by viewing witnesses; names, addresses/commands of all persons present, including but not limited to suspects, victims, other witnesses, police officers, assistant district attorneys, or defense counsel. . . .

B. The lineup procedure.

Whether a lineup is to take place at a police facility or any other place of custody, the following procedure should be utilized (except in emergency situations and on-the-scene showups):

1. The suspect should be viewed with at least five other persons (fillers). No one can be used as a filler who may be known to any witness.

2. All persons in the lineup must be of the same race and sex.

3. All persons in the lineup should be about the same age, height and physical makeup, e.g., an obvious 16 year old could not be shown with adults; a suspect identified as having red hair cannot be shown with black haired persons; a suspect identified as having a scar on his face cannot be shown unless all persons in the lineup have some similar markings or all persons have a bandage or something similar covering the area.

4. All persons in the lineup should be similarly clothed. . . .

9. No person in the lineup may be asked to say or do anything in connection with the crime unless all are asked to do the same thing, e.g., say "This is a robbery" or "Put up your hands."

10. Neither directly nor indirectly should the officers conducting the lineup, in any manner, indicate who the suspect is, nor should they assist the witnesses in their attempts to identify the suspect, e.g., "Is this the guy?" or "How about the guy in the brown coat?"

11. Where there are two or more victims or witnesses, they must not be permitted to view the lineup at the same time, nor may they be permitted to speak to each other either before or during the lineups. . . .

12. No witness may be told that another witness did or did not make an identification of someone in the lineup. . . .

14. If the lineup is not videotaped, a Polaroid photograph should be taken of the lineup as viewed by the identifying witnesses. . . .

Notes

1. *Availability of counsel during in-person identifications: majority position.* The decisions in *Wade* and Gilbert v. California, 388 U.S. 263 (1967), gave a dramatic debut to the constitutional right to counsel for identification procedures. The Supreme Court spoke broadly of the unreliability of this type of evidence and of the need for defense counsel to help counter this problem. But five years later, in Kirby v. Illinois, 406 U.S. 682 (1972), the Court sharply limited the type of lineup procedures in which counsel would be required under the Constitution: The *Wade-Gilbert* rule applied only to lineups occurring "at or after the initiation of adversary judicial criminal proceedings." For purposes of the federal constitution, that point arrives as early as the pre-indictment "preliminary hearing" in which a magistrate determines if there is probable cause to bind the defendant over to the grand jury. Moore v. Illinois, 434 U.S. 220 (1977).

Most states (like New York in *Hawkins*) have adopted the *Kirby* rule to determine which identification procedures fall within the reach of the constitutional right to counsel. Fewer than a half dozen states extend the right to counsel to lineups occurring earlier in the process. In these states, counsel must be present at any postarrest in-person identification. See People v. Bustamante, 634 P.2d 927

(Cal. 1981); State v. Mitchell, 593 S.W.2d 280 (Tenn. 1980) (applies to all warranted arrests).

No state has applied the right to counsel to field confrontations or showups, in which the police bring the crime victim together with a single suspect near the time and place where the crime occurred. To require counsel in such a setting would amount to a constitutional ban on the use of evidence from a field confrontation. How much does the refusal of the legal system to require counsel at field interrogations diminish the counsel requirement of *Wade?*

2. *How much does counsel see?* If you were a lawyer, would you want to know where the witness had been in the station prior to the lineup? Whom she had seen? What route your client took to get to the station? Note the provision in the New York City police training materials stating that a lawyer may not be present during any post-lineup interview with a witness. In light of the importance of what the witness has to say immediately after the lineup, can a defense attorney be excluded from the interview? Is this consistent with the reasoning of *Wade?* The handful of cases that address this question generally uphold police efforts to exclude defense counsel from these conversations.

3. *The role of counsel in creating a record.* What should an attorney do at a lineup? Silently observe any suggestive police practices, or object to them? If the attorney takes an observer role, does he have to terminate representation of the defendant later in order to become a witness in the case? If the primary function of the defense counsel is to create a record for possible challenges to the use of the identification evidence at trial, could a state conduct a lineup without counsel present, so long as it is recorded? See Utah Code §77-8-4: "The entire lineup procedure shall be recorded, including all conversations between the witnesses and the conducting peace officers. The suspect shall have access to and may make copies of the record and any photographs taken of him or any other persons in connection with the lineup." In addition, Utah Code §77-8-2 provides suspects with a right to counsel during post-indictment lineups.

4. *Police rules as substitute for counsel? Wade* addressed the possibility of statutes or police regulations as a substitute for a right to counsel: "Legislative or other regulations, such as those of local police departments, which eliminate the risks of abuse and unintentional suggestion at lineup proceedings and the impediments to meaningful confrontation at trial may also remove the basis for regarding the stage as 'critical.'" Could a police department adopting regulations along the lines of the New York City procedures make an argument that the lineup is no longer a "critical" stage and therefore that the right to counsel does not apply? Are there any reasons to believe that police will not follow the procedures established by department's legal counsel? During the first few years after *Wade,* a number of police departments developed internal regulations governing lineup procedures. See Frank Read, Lawyers at Lineups: Constitutional Necessity or Avoidable Extravagance? 17 UCLA L. Rev. 339 (1969) (reprinting police department lineup policies issued in response to *Wade*). After a few years, police lineup rules received less attention. But interest in the subject revived in light of the use of DNA evidence to uncover cases of wrongful convictions. See Mark Hansen, Second Look at the Lineup: New Jersey Hopes to Net Fewer False Identifications, 87 A.B.A. J. 20 (Dec. 2001). Would you expect police lineup practices to become part of formal department policy, or to follow informal guidelines shared among individual officers?

5. *Best practices during lineups.* The extensive academic research on the subject of eyewitness testimony produced a long list of possible improvements to current police practices. The U.S. Department of Justice sponsored a Technical Working Group that published a set of recommended practices in 1999. See U.S. Department of Justice, Eyewitness Evidence: A Guide for Law Enforcement (Oct. 1999, NCJ 178240). The guidelines for lineups call for a minimum of four "fillers" (nonsuspects) per lineup. Investigators should select fillers who generally fit the witness's description of the perpetrator (rather than those who resemble the suspect), unless the description of the perpetrator "differs significantly from the appearance of the suspect." Witnesses should be told that the perpetrator may or may not be present in the lineup. Research indicates that this latter instruction greatly decreases the number of false positives.

However, the Department of Justice recommendations stop short of imposing two further requirements that find strong support in the academic research. It is clear that "blind presentations" of the lineup (that is, the officer conducting the lineup procedure does not know which participant is the suspect) improve the accuracy of witness identification. Officers who know the identity of the suspect can signal to the witness, either through words or subtle body language, which is the "correct" choice. A second technique involves "sequential" lineups, where the officer presents to the witness one person at a time, asking each time whether he or she is the perpetrator. Sequential lineups encourage witnesses to compare each person to their memory of the events, rather than asking which lineup participant (relatively speaking) most closely resembles the original description. What might prevent the Department of Justice from recommending these two techniques that so clearly contribute to more accurate identifications? See Gary L. Wells, Police Lineups: Data, Theory, and Policy, 7 Psychol. Pub. Pol'y & L. 791 (2001).

6. *Identifications compelled by the defense.* Sometimes the police present a witness with two lineups, and only one of them contains the suspect. If the witness refuses to identify a person from the "blank" lineup (with no suspect present), her credibility becomes much stronger. Can a defense lawyer force the police to conduct a blank lineup? Evans v. Superior Court, 522 P.2d 681 (Cal. 1974) (due process requires in some cases a defendant-compelled blank lineup); Gerald Lefcourt, The Blank Lineup: An Aid to the Defense, 14 Crim. L. Bull. 428 (1978). Can the defendant compel the victim to attend a blank lineup staged by the defense?

7. *The exclusion remedy.* If police fail to allow counsel to be present during identification when such presence is constitutionally required, then the judge must exclude at trial any evidence of the pretrial identification. In addition, any identification of the defendant by the witness *at trial* is excludable unless the prosecution can demonstrate that the witness's ability to recognize the defendant at trial has an "independent basis" apart from the tainted pretrial identification. Justice White's dissent in *Wade* predicted that trial identifications would rarely meet this standard, but one limited survey of case law in the years immediately after *Wade* found that courts still routinely allowed at-trial identifications. Joseph Quinn, In the Wake of *Wade:* The Dimensions of the Eyewitness Identification Cases, 42 U. Colo. L. Rev. 135 (1970) (citing six cases as illustrations of larger trend).

8. *Counsel at identification procedures in foreign practice.* Several legal systems outside the United States rely on counsel at formal identification procedures more heavily than the U.S. system does. For instance, in England and Wales, Code D of the Police and Criminal Evidence Act of 1984 provides for defense counsel at any

formal "identification parade." Case law in Israel provides that a suspect must be informed of the right to counsel during a lineup. See Eliahu Harnon and Alex Stein, Israel, in Criminal Procedure: A Worldwide Study (Bradley, ed. 1999). In civil law systems (said to be less "adversarial" than common law systems), would you expect defense counsel to take part in lineups?

2. *Exclusion on Due Process Grounds*

As we saw in the preceding subsection, federal and state constitutions generally require the presence of counsel only for lineups taking place after the initiation of adversary criminal proceedings (typically post-indictment lineups). This accounts for a small number of the identification procedures that take place. Are there any limitations — constitutional or otherwise — on the larger number of lineups and "field confrontations" that occur earlier in the investigative process?

For more than a generation, courts have insisted that due process will prevent the use of the least reliable identification procedures, regardless of the presence or absence of counsel. In Stovall v. Denno, 388 U.S. 293 (1967), decided the same day as United States v. Wade, the Supreme Court excluded evidence of a pretrial identification under the due process clause because the identification was unduly "suggestive." While investigating a stabbing case, the police entered the victim's hospital room with the suspect handcuffed to an officer, and asked the victim if the suspect was the person who had committed the crime. The Court held that this identification was "so unnecessarily suggestive and conducive to irreparable mistaken identification" that admission of the evidence would violate due process of law.

The Supreme Court appeared to shift its emphasis in two later cases, Neil v. Biggers, 409 U.S. 188 (1972), and Manson v. Brathwaite, 432 U.S. 98 (1977). While the Court had focused in *Stovall* on the suggestiveness of the identification procedures used, that was not enough to show a due process violation in *Biggers* or *Brathwaite.* Even though the police had used suggestive "showups" to identify suspects in those cases, the Court reasoned that a witness with an adequate memory of the original crime could reliably identify the criminal despite the suggestive procedure followed at the time of the identification. The Court went on to describe the factors it would consider, as part of the "totality of the circumstances," that could outweigh a suggestive identification procedure. Thus, the Court rejected a "per se" rule that would exclude all evidence obtained through unduly suggestive identification procedures, in favor of a "reliability test" that would allow some identification evidence to stand because other factors supported its accuracy. The following case describes this "totality" approach to identification evidence obtained at the police station and offers an alternative version of the legal standard.

■ STATE v. LIVIO ALPHONSO RAMIREZ

817 P.2d 774 (Utah 1991)

ZIMMERMAN, J.

. . . Shortly before one o'clock in the early morning hours of August 13, 1987, Kathy Davis was preparing to leave the Pizza Hut . . . where she was employed as manager. Her husband, John Davis, and her brother, Gerald Wilson, had come to visit her and accompany her home. As they left the building, they were accosted by a man wearing a white scarf across his face and carrying a metal pipe ("the pipe man"). He demanded that they give him the bank bag with the day's receipts. . . . Wilson attempted to grapple with the robber. The robber hit Wilson with the pipe and then told a second robber ("the gunman") that if Wilson moved again, the gunman should kill him.

This was the first indication that a second robber was present. [T]he gunman was crouched near the corner of the building, holding a gun. The man, who also wore a white scarf covering most of his face, held the gun on Wilson while Kathy and John went back into the building and brought the bank bag out to the robbers. Both robbers then fled. The victims reported the robbery to the police, who responded within a few minutes. The victims described the robbers to the police, but the descriptions were somewhat conflicting.

[A short time after the robbery, police officers apprehended Livio Ramirez, who had been walking with another man who fled at the sight of a police car. The officers concluded that Ramirez matched the description of the gunman in the Pizza Hut robbery. They searched Ramirez, and handcuffed him] to the fence by placing a second set of handcuffs through the fence and attaching them to the handcuffs Ramirez was wearing.

[T]he police drove Kathy Davis, John Davis, and Gerald Wilson to where Ramirez was detained to determine whether they could identify him as one of the robbers. When testifying later, the witnesses were confused as to . . . what the police told [them] about the person they were about to see, beyond a statement to the effect that the officers had found someone who matched the description of one of the robbers.

The identification showup then occurred under the following circumstances: It was approximately one o'clock in the morning. Ramirez, a dark-complexioned Apache Indian, was handcuffed to a chain link fence. He was the only suspect present and was surrounded by police officers. The police turned the headlights and spotlights from the police cars on Ramirez to provide enough light. The witnesses viewed Ramirez by looking at him from the back seat of a police car. Of the three witnesses, only Wilson identified Ramirez as the masked man with the gun; the other two witnesses were unable to identify him as one of the robbers. Following the identification, Ramirez was placed under arrest and was charged with the robbery. Prior to trial, the defense moved to suppress the out-of-court and in-court identifications by Wilson on grounds that the initial identification procedure gave rise to a substantial likelihood of irreparable misidentification and that the initial identification tainted subsequent identifications. [The trial court denied the motion.]

Article I, §7 of the Utah Constitution provides, "No person shall be deprived of life, liberty or property, without due process of law." Ramirez contends that he was denied due process when the prosecution was permitted to introduce the identification of him as the gunman. He argues that the circumstances surrounding the identification rendered it fatally unreliable. . . .

Under the federal constitution, the basic due process issue is whether the identification is sufficiently reliable to be admitted into evidence. See Neil v. Biggers, 409 U.S. 188 (1972). Until our decision in State v. Long, 721 P.2d 483 (Utah 1986), we had never suggested that the standard under article I, §7 of the Utah Constitution for determining whether an identification was admissible might diverge from the federal. . . . Our cases had simply applied the federal analytical model for determining the reliability, and hence the admissibility of the identification as that model had developed in the line of cases beginning with Stovall v. Denno and continuing through Neil v. Biggers.

[Under the federal standard, a court determining admissibility of identification evidence] is to consider "all the circumstances" surrounding the identification and appraise those circumstances in light of five factors which were identified by the United States Supreme Court in *Biggers* as important to a determination of the reliability of an identification. These factors are

> the opportunity of the witness to view the criminal at the time of the crime, the witness' degree of attention, the accuracy of the witness' prior description of the criminal, the level of certainty demonstrated by the witness at the confrontation, and the length of time between the crime and the confrontation. [409 U.S. at 199-200.]

If, after performing this analysis, the identification is found to be unreliable, it is not to be admitted.

In *Long*, we were presented with the question of the reliability of eyewitness identifications in the context of a claim that an instruction cautioning the jury about the fallibility of such identifications was required. . . . To answer the cautionary instruction claims presented in *Long*, we reviewed the scientific literature and concluded that it is replete with empirical studies documenting the unreliability of eyewitness identification. We further noted [that jurors are, for the most part, unaware of these problems.]

We next observed that in this area, courts and lawyers tend to "ignore the teachings of other disciplines, especially when they contradict long-accepted legal notions." As an example of such a lag between the assumptions embodied in the law and the findings of other disciplines, we . . . noted that "several of the criteria listed by the [*Biggers*] Court are based on assumptions that are flatly contradicted by well-respected and essentially unchallenged empirical studies." . . . Although the empirical research might justify excluding all such evidence, we rejected such a step as impracticable.

[The opinion in *Long* described the sort of cautionary instructions a trial judge should give a jury about identification testimony, and suggested that those same factors would be pertinent in determining whether admission of the evidence would constitute a violation of the state constitution's due process clause.]

[F]or purposes of determining the due process reliability of eyewitness identifications under article I, §7, we will not limit ourselves to an analytical model that merely copies the federal. We will require an in-depth appraisal of the identification's reliability along the lines laid out by *Long*, [and] we have no doubt that the more empirically based approach of *Long* will . . . meet or exceed in rigor the federal standard as expressed in *Biggers* and *Stovall*.

[In] *Long*, we gave the following listing of the pertinent factors by which reliability must be determined:

> (1) The opportunity of the witness to view the actor during the event; (2) the witness's degree of attention to the actor at the time of the event; (3) the witness's capacity to observe the event, including his or her physical and mental acuity; (4) whether the witness's identification was made spontaneously and remained consistent thereafter, or whether it was the product of suggestion; and (5) the nature of the event being observed and the likelihood that the witness would perceive, remember and relate it

> correctly. This last area includes such factors as whether the event was an ordinary one in the mind of the observer during the time it was observed, and whether the race of the actor was the same as the observer's. [721 P.2d at 493.]

Although the factors enumerated in *Long* are generally comparable to the *Biggers* factors, they [differ in several respects]. In *Biggers,* the Court listed as a factor "the level of certainty demonstrated by the witness at the confrontation." In *Long,* we criticized this factor [because it conflicted with the available scientific studies] and essentially rejected it as an indicator of an identification's reliability. Also, suggestibility is included in the fourth *Long* factor, with no comparable emphasis given to this element by *Biggers.*

We now consider the decision to admit the identification evidence in this case. The first factor to be considered in determining the reliability of the identification is the opportunity of the witness to view the actor during the event. Here, pertinent circumstances include the length of time the witness viewed the actor; the distance between the witness and the actor; whether the witness could view the actor's face; the lighting or lack of it; whether there were distracting noises or activity during the observation; and any other circumstances affecting the witness's opportunity to observe the actor.

In the present case, we find that statements by Wilson about the length of time he viewed the gunman varied from a "few seconds" or "a second" to "a minute" or longer. Wilson testified that the distance between himself and the gunman was about "ten feet," although testimony from another witness indicated that the distance was up to 30 feet. The three witnesses testified that the gunman was crouched near the end of the building, wearing a mask over the lower part of his face. None of the witnesses, including Wilson, were able to see his face during the robbery. Wilson testified that he could not see the gunman's eyes clearly but he "could see enough to know" and that the gunman had small eyes. Wilson testified at one time that there were no obstructions between him and the gunman and at another time that the pipe man was between him and the gunman. Wilson and the other witnesses generally described the lighting as good, but on occasion, they described it as poor and stated that the gunman was in a shadowy area.

The second reliability factor is Wilson's degree of attention to the gunman. Wilson was fully aware that a robbery was taking place. Even though the pipe man was still threatening and swinging the pipe at Wilson after Wilson saw the gunman, Wilson testified at the preliminary hearing that he did not look at the pipe man. Although at the time of the robbery Wilson's description of the pipe man was much more detailed than his description of the gunman, Wilson testified at trial that he stared at the gunman, trying to get a good description, and that he did not see the pipe man as clearly as he saw the gunman.

The third reliability factor is whether the witness had the capacity to observe the actor during the event. Here, relevant circumstances include whether the witness's capacity to observe was impaired by stress or fright at the time of the observation, by personal motivations, biases, or prejudices, by uncorrected visual defects, or by fatigue, injury, drugs, or alcohol.

In the present case, Wilson struggled with the pipe man, who hit Wilson in the stomach with the pipe once and nearly hit him a second time. Wilson was then threatened by a masked robber who was pointing a pistol at him; at the same time, the pipe man was still threatening to hit him with the pipe. Although the record does not describe the stress or fright that Wilson experienced, under the circumstances it is reasonable to assume that Wilson experienced a heightened degree of stress. . . . Aside from the late hour and the injury from the pipe blow, there is nothing in the record to indicate that Wilson was impaired by fatigue, injury, drugs, or alcohol.

The fourth reliability factor is whether the witness's identification was made spontaneously and remained consistent thereafter or whether it was a product of suggestion. Here, relevant circumstances include the length of time that passed between the witness's observation at the time of the event and the identification of defendant; the witness's mental capacity and state of mind at the time of the identification; the witness's exposure to opinions, descriptions, identifications, or other information from other sources; instances when the witness or other eyewitnesses to the event failed to identify defendant; instances when the witness or other eyewitnesses gave a description of the actor that is inconsistent with defendant; and the circumstances under which defendant was presented to the witness for identification.

The identification took place from 30 minutes to an hour after the crime, so the elapsed time was minimal. Aside from the normal agitation that would result from being robbed, nothing in the record indicates that Wilson's mental capacity and state of mind influenced his identification of Ramirez. At the time of the identification, Wilson was aware that at least one of the other two victims of the robbery had not identified Ramirez, but he was not otherwise exposed to other identifications or opinions. Neither of the other two victims of the robbery, including [John] Davis, who initially gave an equally detailed description of the gunman to the police, identified Ramirez as the gunman.

With regard to the consistency of the descriptions given by the witnesses, it is evident that the descriptions are somewhat confused. Wilson described the gunman as a male Mexican, five feet nine inches to six feet tall, wearing a blue sweater and Levi's, with a white scarf around the lower part of his face. He described the pipe man in more detail: male Mexican, 21 to 22 years old, five feet seven inches to five feet eight inches tall, 155 to 160 pounds, shaggy brown hair, brown eyes, wearing a blue sweater and Levi's and a white scarf over the lower part of his face, one front tooth missing, and a bald spot on the side of his head. . . . At the time of his arrest, Ramirez was wearing Levi's, a blue sweatshirt with paint spattered on the front but which may have been worn inside out, and a brown baseball cap. Ramirez also had readily visible tattoos on his arms. At the suppression hearing, Wilson stated positively that the gunman wore no hat, although he testified at trial that he was not sure whether the gunman wore a hat. Wilson did not mention any tattoos at the time of the robbery or at the suppression hearing but at trial, for the first time, asserted that he had seen tattoos on the gunman.

Finally, and most critically for purposes of this case, we address . . . whether the witness's identification was the product of suggestion. The identification took place on the street in the middle of the night. Ramirez, with dark complexion and long hair, was the only person at the showup who was not a police officer. He stood with his hands cuffed to a chain link fence behind his back. The headlights of several police cars were trained on him. The witnesses viewed him from the back seat of a police car. And while the remarks of the police officers prior to the showup were to the effect that they had apprehended someone who fit the description of one of the robbers may not of themselves be unnecessarily suggestive, they must be considered as part of the circumstances surrounding the identification.

Having considered all the factors, we find this to be an extremely close case. The blatant suggestiveness of the showup is troublesome and is compounded because none of the witnesses, including Wilson, ever saw the full face of the gunman. Furthermore, Wilson claimed to have identified Ramirez principally by his eyes, the only part of the gunman's face that any of the witnesses could have seen, but gave contradictory testimony about whether the gunman wore a hat, which would seem to affect a witness's view of the gunman's eyes. The differences in racial characteristics between Wilson and Ramirez raise additional questions about the identification, although because the identification was based principally on the eyes, physical size, and clothing, these racial factors may have been of relatively little importance.

The trial court apparently resolved the contradictions in the testimony in Wilson's favor and was persuaded that Wilson observed the gunman closely enough, including his eyes and clothing, to identify him less than an hour after the robbery. Considering the facts in the light most favorable to the trial court's decision and giving due deference to the trial judge's ability to appraise demeanor evidence, we cannot say that Wilson's testimony is legally insufficient when considered in light of the other circumstances to warrant a preliminary finding of reliability and, therefore, admissibility. This leads to the conclusion that the trial court did not err by admitting the identification in violation of Ramirez's right to due process of law under article I, §7 of the Utah Constitution. . . .

Problem 9-1. Prompting in a Lineup

Suppose that Kathy Davis, John Davis, and Gerald Wilson (the crime victims in *Ramirez*) had their first opportunity to identify a suspect during a lineup at the police station two days after the Pizza Hut robbery. Would the due process clause (federal or state) bar the introduction at trial of any evidence of the pretrial identification or an at-trial identification under the following circumstances?

(a) Before the lineup takes place, a police officer mentions to the witnesses that "we have arrested someone for this crime and have included that person in this lineup."

(b) During the lineup, John says (in the presence of Kathy and Gerald), "It's definitely the third guy — I can tell by his eyes." Kathy and Gerald agree that the third lineup participant was the gunman in the robbery.

(c) After the three witnesses have identified a lineup participant as the gunman, a detective says, "You picked out the guy we had arrested for the crime."

Problem 9-2. Wigs and Mustaches

At 9:00 P.M. on a June evening, Ronald Pang, his brother Roland Pang, and their friend Gerrold Kam were walking towards the lights of the 50th State Fair at the Aloha Stadium. A young Samoan male and a young Filipino male approached them from behind and asked for a cigarette. They replied that they did not have any, and continued to walk towards the well-lit intersection. The Samoan youth then put his right arm around Gerrold's shoulder and asked him if he had a car. Ronald, who was walking ahead of Roland and Gerrold, told the Samoan to leave Gerrold alone. The Samoan walked up to Ronald, pushed him against a fence, held a gun to his throat, and said, "Don't act smart or you're going to get it." The Filipino youth then told them to hand over their money and said that he had a "blade." Ronald gave his money to the Samoan youth, and Roland and Gerrold gave their money to the Filipino youth. The robbers also took watches from Roland and Gerrold. They ordered the three young men to leave without looking back, but Ronald turned and got another look at the Samoan's face as he walked away, this time with better lighting from the intersection up ahead.

When the Pang brothers reported the crime to the police, Ronald described the assailant as a Samoan male in his twenties, about five feet seven to eight inches tall, about 180 pounds, dark complexion, with a small Afro hairstyle. Roland described the assailant as a Samoan male, 19 years old, five feet nine inches tall, 160 pounds, dark complexion, with a small Afro hairstyle.

The police arrested Sooga Masaniai and took him to the police station for a lineup. The seven lineup participants were asked to approach the witness viewing box and say, "Don't act smart or you're going to get it." Masaniai was the only one of the seven lineup participants who met the description of a young Samoan male with a small Afro hairstyle. Three participants were wearing wigs and two had straight hair. The four participants who did not have mustaches wore false mustaches. There were significant height and weight differences among the participants in the lineup. At the time of the lineup, Masaniai was 18 years old, five feet six inches tall, and 160 pounds. Both Ronald and Roland viewed the lineup at the same time, but they were not allowed to speak with one another. Each identified Masaniai as one of the assailants. At the ensuing robbery trial, Masaniai moves to exclude the identification evidence. Should the trial judge grant the motion? Compare State v. Masaniai, 628 P.2d 1018 (Haw. 1981).

■ NEW YORK CITY POLICE DEPARTMENT, LEGAL BUREAU EYEWITNESS IDENTIFICATION PROCEDURES: SHOWUPS

A. The one-on-one display of a suspect to a victim is *generally prohibited* as being unnecessarily suggestive, *except:*

1. where it is conducted promptly on-the-scene; or,
2. where there is an emergency hospital situation (witness critically injured and likely to die). . . .

C. Showup Procedures — A police officer should consider the following factors when determining if a prompt on-the-scene showup is permissible:

1. The time elapsed since crime [was] committed. There is no set time limit. However, if more than a few hours have elapsed since the commission of the crime, a showup should *not* be employed. Usually, the apprehension of a suspect and return to the scene for viewing will be within minutes, not hours, of the crime. . . .

4. Showups should not be conducted at a stationhouse.
5. Manner in which suspect is displayed.
   a. Never tell the witness that the perpetrator has been "caught," and that the witness must view him for identification purposes.

b. If a witness becomes aware that a "suspect" is in custody, emphasize before the viewing that it is *only a suspect,* and that the witness must not assume it is the perpetrator before even viewing the suspect. . . .

D. Group Identifications

1. Occasions will arise where an officer will ask a witness if he can pick out the suspect from a group of persons not in police custody. [For example, an officer may ask the witness to] observe suspect among a group of individuals (unarranged confrontation). [An officer also might accompany] a witness to an area where suspect is likely to be with other persons, i.e., let witness watch person coming and going from suspect's place of employment, at a park, playground, etc. Procedures:

a. Allow witness to view area, with instructions to look carefully at people on street, in doorways or in stores, etc.

b. If police officer sees a possible suspect, he may draw witness' attention in that direction.

c. Avoid pointing out a single individual, or if necessary, do so in a nonsuggestive manner. Don't say, "That looks like him, doesn't it?"

E. There is no right to counsel at any showup procedure.

Notes

1. *Due process limits on suggestive identifications: majority position.* Virtually all jurisdictions have followed the federal position set out in the *Biggers* case and in Manson v. Brathwaite, 432 U.S. 98 (1977). When applying state constitutions to suggestive identifications, courts look to the totality of the circumstances, emphasizing the five factors listed in *Biggers* to determine the "reliability" of an identification despite suggestiveness in the identification procedure. A growing number of state courts, however, now de-emphasize the importance of witness certainty. See State v. McMorris, 570 N.W.2d 384 (Wis. 1997) (eyewitness certainty not relevant to reliability issue; courts split). Courts applying this test refuse to overturn convictions in the overwhelming majority of due process challenges to "suggestive" identifications, although there are exceptions.

Massachusetts employs a per se rule and excludes from evidence *any* identification produced by an unduly suggestive process. See Commonwealth v. Johnson, 650 N.E.2d 1257 (Mass. 1995). The *Johnson* court explained its decision as follows:

> [M]istaken identification is believed widely to be the primary cause of erroneous convictions. Compounding this problem is the tendency of juries to be unduly receptive to eyewitness evidence. We have stated that "the law has not taken the position that a jury can be relied on to discount the value of an identification by a proper appraisal of the unsatisfactory circumstances in which it may have been made." . . . The "reliability test" is unacceptable because it provides little or no protection from unnecessarily suggestive identification procedures, from mistaken identifications and, ultimately, from wrongful convictions.

Do you agree? Does the per se rule make a defendant better off than she would have been in the absence of any suggestive identification procedure at all?

2. *Unreliable measures of reliability.* The Utah court in *Ramirez* criticized the federal "reliability" factors from Neil v. Biggers, 409 U.S. 188 (1972), because they are inconsistent with "empirical" findings of psychologists studying eyewitness memory. One "reliability" factor said to be overrated is the level of certainty a witness displays: Many studies have suggested a very weak correlation, at best, between witness certainty and witness accuracy. A second questionable "reliability" factor is the amount of time a witness originally has to view the suspect. Although the amount of initial exposure is indeed related to the accuracy of memory, most people tend to overestimate the amount of time that elapsed during events that they witness. Did the Utah court respond adequately to these alleged problems with the federal "reliability" test? Is the court's modified test more empirically grounded? Will it lead to different results?

3. *Showups and lineups.* All other factors being equal, showups are thought to be more suggestive than lineups. Does the due process limitation on the use of identification evidence give police enough reason to avoid showups in favor of lineups whenever possible? Note that the New York City police policy allows showups in the field, but only those occurring within a "reasonable time" (ordinarily within a few hours) of the crime. What proportion of total identification procedures would you imagine occur in this setting? In light of the rapid deterioration of human memory, does the short time lapse between the crime and the identification make the showup, on balance, as reliable as a lineup occurring several hours, days, or weeks later? The recommended procedures for eyewitness evidence issued by the U.S. Department of Justice allow police officers to conduct a showup. Because of the "inherent suggestiveness" of the showup, the witness should be cautioned that the person may not be the perpetrator. According to the guidelines, if one witness identifies a suspect during a showup, the police should use other identification procedures for other witnesses.

4. *Statutory limits on lineups.* Very few jurisdictions have passed statutes or court rules addressing the use of identification procedures by police. An exception is Utah Code §77-8-3, which states in general terms that "[t]he peace officers conducting a lineup shall not attempt to influence the identification of any particular suspect." Was this statute relevant to *Ramirez?*

Why have legislatures and drafters of procedural rules remained silent on identification procedures when they have proven willing to address so many others? Their reluctance to address these questions cannot be explained by a lack of guidance or model legislation. Section 160.2 of the American Law Institute's Model Code of Pre-Arraignment Criminal Procedure provides as follows:

> (1) The identification of a suspect by having a witness view the suspect shall be from an array of several persons, a reasonable number of whom are similar in dress and appearance to the person to be identified, except such line-up or other array is not required [when a] law enforcement officer arranges a confrontation by a witness to a crime promptly following the commission of that crime, unless there is reason to believe that a line-up or other procedure is necessary to make the identification reliable. . . .
>
> (4) A witness shall not be allowed, except as part of a judicial proceeding, to participate in more than one identification procedure involving viewing the same suspect or representation of that suspect unless
>
> (a) a prior procedure was conducted at a time when the suspect was unknown or at large;

(b) the witness reasonably requests a subsequent procedure to resolve doubt;

(c) there are special circumstances such that there is reason to believe that a further procedure is necessary to produce a reliable identification; or

(d) counsel for the suspect requests a further identification procedure.

Section 160.1 of the Model Code also requires law enforcement agencies engaged in identification procedures to issue regulations designed to ensure that "identification procedures will be reasonably reliable" and that "an objective record is kept of any identification procedure." Does a statutory bar on multiple identifications, such as the one in section 160.2(4) of the Model Code, accomplish anything different from a due process analysis of multiple identifications?

5. *Detention for identification.* Do the police have the power to compel a person who is not currently in custody to participate in a lineup? Many states *do* address this question by statute and court-issued rules of procedure. See Model Code of Pre-Arraignment Criminal Procedure, art. 170. Nebraska Revised Statutes §29-3303 is typical. It authorizes a judge to order a person to submit to a lineup or some other identification procedure (such as fingerprinting). The order may issue upon a showing that (1) there is probable cause to believe that an offense has been committed; (2) identification procedures may contribute to the identification of the individual who committed the offense; and (3) the identified or described individual has refused, or will refuse, to participate voluntarily.

Such a court order is not necessary if a suspect is already in police custody. A few state rules and statutes allow the detention of persons for the purpose of participating in lineups or other identification procedures, even in the absence of probable cause to believe the detained person committed the crime. See State v. Rodriguez, 921 P.2d 643 (Ariz. 1996). Courts have approved of this practice even in the absence of a statute or rule authorizing it. See State v. Hall, 461 A.2d 1155 (N.J. 1983) (court can compel participation in lineup without probable cause). Are identification procedures are sufficiently similar to fingerprinting to allow a judicial order of detention based on less than probable cause? Note that detention for fingerprinting at the station house, based on less than probable cause, would likely be an unconstitutional "seizure" if it took place without a judicial order. See Davis v. Mississippi, 394 U.S. 721 (1969). In a state allowing the police to detain a suspect for identification purposes, should a defendant have a comparable power to obtain a court order forcing *another* suspect to attend a lineup? Should citizens generally have an obligation to take part in a lineup along with a suspect who physically resembles them? Would you willingly take part in a lineup? For modest compensation, say, $100?

■ ATTORNEY GENERAL GUIDELINES FOR PREPARING AND CONDUCTING PHOTO AND LIVE LINEUP IDENTIFICATION PROCEDURES

JOHN J. FARMER

Attorney General of New Jersey, April 18, 2001

I. Composing the Photo or Live Lineup

The following procedures will result in the composition of a photo or live lineup in which a suspect does not unduly stand out. An identification obtained through a lineup composed in this manner should minimize any risk of misidentification and have stronger evidentiary value than one obtained without these procedures.

A. In order to ensure that inadvertent verbal cues or body language do not impact on a witness, whenever practical, considering the time of day, day of the week, and other personnel conditions within the agency or department, the person conducting the photo or live lineup identification procedure should be someone other than the primary investigator assigned to the case. The Attorney General recognizes that in many departments, depending upon the size and other assignments of personnel, this may be impossible in a given case. In those cases where the primary investigating officer conducts the photo or live lineup identification procedure, he or she should be careful to avoid inadvertent signaling to the witness of the "correct" response.

B. The witness should be instructed prior to the photo or live lineup identification procedure that the perpetrator may not be among those in the photo array or live lineup and, therefore, they should not feel compelled to make an identification.

C. When possible, photo or live lineup identification procedures should be conducted sequentially, i.e., showing one photo or person at a time to the witness, rather than simultaneously.

D. In composing a photo or live lineup, the person administering the identification procedure should ensure that the lineup is comprised in such a manner that the suspect does not unduly stand out. However, complete uniformity of features is not required.

E. *Photo Lineup.* In composing a photo lineup, the lineup administrator or investigator should:

1. Include only one suspect in each identification procedure.
2. Select fillers (non-suspects) who generally fit the witness' description of the perpetrator. When there is a limited or inadequate description of the perpetrator provided by the witness, or when the description of the perpetrator differs significantly from the appearance of the suspect, fillers should resemble the suspect in significant features.
3. Select a photo that resembles the suspect's description or appearance at the time of the incident if multiple photos of the suspect are reasonably available to the investigator.
4. Include a minimum of five fillers (nonsuspects) per identification procedure.
5. Consider placing the suspect in different positions in each lineup when conducting more than one lineup for a case due to multiple witnesses.
6. Avoid reusing fillers in lineups shown to the same witness when showing a new suspect. . . .

9. Preserve the presentation order of the photo lineup. In addition, the photos themselves should be preserved in their original condition. . . .

II. Conducting the Identification Procedure . . .

B. *Sequential Photo Lineup.* When presenting a sequential photo lineup, the lineup administrator or investigator should:

1. Provide viewing instructions to the witness as outlined in subsection I B, above.

2. Provide the following additional viewing instructions to the witness:
   a. Individual photographs will be viewed one at a time.
   b. The photos are in random order.
   c. Take as much time as needed in making a decision about each photo before moving to the next one.
   d. All photos will be shown, even if an identification is made prior to viewing all photos; or the procedure will be stopped at the point of an identification (consistent with jurisdiction/departmental procedures).
3. Confirm that the witness understands the nature of the sequential procedure.
4. Present each photo to the witness separately, in a previously determined order, removing those previously shown.
5. Avoid saying anything to the witness that may influence the witness' selection.
6. If an identification is made, avoid reporting to the witness any information regarding the individual he or she has selected prior to obtaining the witness' statement of certainty.
7. Record any identification results and witness' statement of certainty. . . .
9. Instruct the witness not to discuss the identification procedure or its results with other witnesses involved in the case and discourage contact with the media.

Problem 9-3. Photo Lineups

On August 8, a man robbed the Fort Gratiot branch of the People's Bank in Port Huron, Michigan, of more than $22,000 (including approximately $600 in Canadian currency). Three bank tellers, the branch manager, and a customer witnessed the robbery and gave descriptions of the robber and his car to investigators. Bank teller Mary Kamendat described the robber as approximately 45 or 46 years old, almost six feet tall, weighing about 210 pounds, with dust or some other substance on his face. She also described him as needing a haircut. Another bank teller, Cindy Dortman, noticed that the robber was wearing a light-colored shirt, a baseball cap, dark sunglasses, and had longer hair than normal for a man of his age. She also described him as wearing flared jeans, with a chain hanging out of his pocket and his shirt pulled over his pants. She said that the robber had a "long, very distinguished" nose.

The bank's surveillance camera took photographs of the robber. After the local newspaper published two of the surveillance photographs a few days after the crime, the St. Clair County Sheriff's Department received several phone calls regarding the robbery. One caller identified Albin Kurylczyk as the man in the photographs. This information prompted a detective and an FBI agent to visit Kurylczyk at his home on August 17. At their request, Kurylczyk permitted the officers to search his house and his car, which was similar to the getaway car the eyewitnesses had described. He also agreed to accompany the investigators to the local police station for further interviews. Once there, he consented to be photographed. At that time, he was not represented by counsel, nor did he request an attorney.

On the same day, other deputies responded to a call from the bank. The bank tellers Dortman and Kamendat believed the robber had returned when a customer dressed like the robber entered the bank and attempted to exchange some

Canadian currency. The tellers detained him by delaying his transaction until the deputies arrived. However, after an investigation, the law enforcement authorities were satisfied that this customer was not the bank robber. He was not included in any of the identification procedures used later in the investigation.

Two days later, on August 19, a detective assembled an array of six photographs, including the photograph he had taken of Kurylczyk and one of another suspect. Kurylczyk was the only man in the photographic array dressed in clothing that matched the description of the eyewitnesses. In particular, his photo showed him wearing a chain attached to his belt and extending to a wallet in the rear pocket of his jeans. None of the others in the photographic lineup wore such a trucker's wallet. This same type of wallet was visible in the bank's surveillance photographs, as published in the local paper. In addition, Kurylczyk's photograph was taken from a closer distance, so that his image appeared larger than the others. Three of the men in the array had mustaches; Kurylczyk did not have a mustache, and none of the witnesses described the robber as having a mustache.

The detective showed the photo array to Kamendat and Dortman, and both identified Kurylczyk as the bank robber. As a result, the government charged him with the crime. Before trial, Kurylczyk moved to exclude the identification testimony of the eyewitnesses. First, he contended that he was entitled to the assistance of counsel during the photographic lineup. Second, he argued that the photographic lineup was impermissibly suggestive in violation of his Fourteenth Amendment right of due process. How should the trial court rule? Compare People v. Kurylczyk, 505 N.W.2d 528 (Mich. 1993).

Problem 9-4. Videotaped Lineups

At 2:20 A.M., a man entered a gas station and asked Roy Beals, the attendant, for permission to use the telephone. He was followed by a second man, holding what appeared to be a .45-caliber automatic pistol, and by a third man, whom Beals was unable to see. The three men robbed the gas station. Beals told police after the robbery that the gunman was approximately 5′6″ or 5′7″ tall, and wore a knee-length brown vinyl coat, with a fleecy lining and collar. From the loose fit of the coat, Beals assumed the man was thin. The man wore what appeared to be uniform pants and a security guard's cap, with a badge, and had a second badge pinned on his collar. The fleecy coat collar was turned up around the man's face, and the bill of his cap came down to his eyebrows. Beals was therefore able to observe only a portion of the man's face. From his observation, Beals could tell that the gunman was a black man and that he was not wearing glasses, but could not describe him further. He could not describe the man's hair or estimate his age.

The gunman told Beals to turn around, go into a back room, and lie face down on the floor. Following Beals into the back room, the gunman then asked where "the money" was. Beals answered that the money was in a locked box on a post outside. The man demanded a key, but Beals did not have one. At one point, the gunman struck him with the weapon he was carrying. The robbers were in the station for about five minutes, and Beals spent most of this time face down on the floor.

Later that same day, the police stopped a car containing four young black men, including Oscar McMillian. The four occupants of the car were taken into custody. At some point, the police staged a lineup, consisting of these four men, in connection with the investigation of an unrelated crime, a purse-snatching. The lineup was recorded on videotape with an audio recording of the men speaking. No attorney was present at this lineup.

Several days later, McMillian was charged with armed robbery. Soon thereafter, the police showed the videotaped lineup to Beals. McMillian was given no notice that Beals was to view the recorded lineup, and defense counsel was not present at the viewing. Based on the defendant's height, build, and voice, Beals identified McMillian as the gunman in the gas station robbery. Was it error to allow Beals to view the videotape without McMillian's attorney being present? Will the trial court allow Beals to identify McMillian at trial? Compare McMillian v. State, 265 N.W.2d 553 (Wis. 1978).

Notes

1. *Right to counsel for photographic identifications: majority position.* The identification techniques we have considered so far all involve a live encounter between the witness and a suspect. Rather than arranging an acceptable in-person encounter, it is often easier for police investigators to show pictures of potential suspects to a witness. Furthermore, pictures can be matched on more features. Are concerns about the reliability of the witness's identification different when investigators use photographs or other recorded images of a suspect? Do different types of legal regulation then become more or less feasible?

In United States v. Ash, 413 U.S. 300 (1973), the Court held that the federal Constitution does not require the presence of counsel at *any* photographic identification, whether it is conducted before or after the start of adversarial criminal proceedings. It reasoned that a photographic display, unlike an in-person lineup, does not involve a "trial-like confrontation" between the defendant and the witness. Thus, the presence of a lawyer is less important to a defendant whose picture is used in a photo array. Is this distinction convincing?

Most state courts have followed *Ash* and concluded that there is no right to counsel for photographic identifications. See Barone v. State, 866 P.2d 291 (Nev. 1993) (reversing a 1969 decision that had granted right to counsel for photo identification). A handful (less than a half dozen) do require the presence of defense counsel for at least some photo identifications. See People v. Kurylczyk, 505 N.W.2d 528 (Mich. 1993) (right to counsel applies to photo identifications conducted while suspect is in custody, even before indictment).

2. *Photographic identifications as a last resort.* Most states do not, as a matter of statute or constitutional law, require the police to prefer the use of live lineups over photo identifications. But see State v. Lopez, 886 P.2d 1105 (Utah 1994) (discourages police in Utah from using photo displays where lineups are practical). Some police department policies, however, discourage the use of photo identifications after investigators arrest the suspect; at that point, live lineups become the preferred method. Why would a police department adopt such a policy? Aren't photo arrays easier to align, preserve, and review? Shouldn't they be favored?

3. *Due process limits on photo identifications.* As with in-person identifications, the due process clause creates a second constitutional restraint on photographic identifications. If the photo array is unduly suggestive, *and* if the totality of the circumstances suggests that the improper identification procedure created an undue

risk of misidentification, the court will exclude at trial any evidence based on that tainted identification.

Many of the claims of unduly "suggestive" photo arrays derive from the fact that the picture of the defendant is taken when he is wearing prison clothing or displaying an identification number. If the other photos in the array do not have similar features, the witness has reason to select the suspect's picture. See Commonwealth v. Thornley, 546 N.E.2d 350 (Mass. 1989) (photographic array presented to witnesses who had already told police that the suspect was wearing glasses; defendant was the only subject pictured wearing glasses, making the array impermissibly suggestive). Another source of "suggestiveness" claims is the showing of multiple photo arrays to the witness when the suspect's picture appears in each of the arrays. Courts virtually always reject challenges based on these claims. See, e.g., State v. Rezk, 609 A.2d 391 (N.H. 1992) (approves an identification in second photo lineup when defendant was the only subject pictured also in first photo lineup and was the only person pictured in prison overalls).

4. *Departmental policies and photospreads.* The New Jersey Attorney General policy on photo identifications reprinted above is based in part on recommendations from the U.S. Department of Justice. What would motivate a law enforcement official to recommend procedures that are more specific than what the courts have required in constitutional litigation? The New Jersey policy differs from the DOJ policy in stating a preference for sequential lineups and "blind" presentations. What are the arguments against these two requirements?

5. *Whose pictures?* When the police have no suspect, they will sometimes ask the witness to review a large number of photos in the hopes that the perpetrator's picture will appear. Which pictures can the police show to a witness? Can the photos include only those who have been convicted of a crime similar to the one now at issue? Any arrested person? Any person at all? Suppose the police collect pictures of persons from one ethnic group, awaiting those occasions when a crime victim is attempting to identify, say, an Asian perpetrator? See San Jose Recorder, Jan. 31, 1996 (lawsuit settlement by the town of San Jose, California, paying $150,000 in damages to person who spent three months in jail after being identified by witness to armed robbery; witness selected photograph from mug book containing pictures only of Asians, many of whom — like plaintiff — had never been arrested or convicted). More recently, computer programs have enabled the police to create a digitized image based on the description by a witness, and to match that digitized image to photographs in existing databases such as arrest files or drivers' license pictures. Do you anticipate that state legislatures will place limits on the use of this software? See Bill Richards, Cops Nab Perps with Digitized Drawings and Databases, Wall Street Journal, Jan. 28, 1998 (600 police departments now use ImageWare program).

C. OTHER REMEDIES FOR IMPROPER IDENTIFICATION PROCEDURES

As we have seen, one remedy for improper pretrial identification procedures is the exclusion at trial of any evidence of the pretrial identification, along with the possible exclusion of any at-trial identification based on the earlier procedure. But the exclusion remedy is extreme. Recall that identifications tend to be important to the prosecution in cases charging very serious crimes such as rape and robbery. Perhaps for this reason, courts invoke the remedy in only a small number of cases. Whatever problems might be present with the identification procedure, courts have concluded most of the time that the improper identification method was a "harmless error" of sorts — that it did not cause the witness to make an improper identification.

In sum, the exclusion remedy is available to very few defendants who have legitimate complaints about improper identification procedures. Is there some way other than exclusion for these defendants to reduce the chances of an erroneous conviction?

The following case considers the need for a jury instruction that highlights the difficulties of cross-racial identifications. Do you believe that the arguments in favor of such an instruction are basically the same as those supporting instructions about identifications more generally, or is there something distinctively difficult about cross-racial identifications? Will jury instructions of the sort described in this opinion actually change juror conduct?

■ STATE v. McKINLEY CROMEDY

727 A.2d 457 (N.J. 1999)

COLEMAN, J.

This appeal involves a rape and robbery in which a cross-racial identification was made of defendant as the perpetrator seven months after the offenses occurred. The identification of the perpetrator was the critical issue throughout the trial. The trial court denied defendant's request to have the jury instructed concerning the cross-racial nature of the identification. . . . The novel issue presented is whether a cross-racial identification jury instruction should be required in certain cases before it is established that there is substantial agreement in the scientific community that cross-racial recognition impairment of eyewitnesses is significant enough to warrant a special jury instruction. Our study of the recommendations of a Court-appointed Task Force, judicial literature, and decisional law from other jurisdictions persuades us that there exists a reliable basis for a cross-racial identification charge. We hold that the trial court's failure to submit to the jury an instruction similar to the one requested by defendant requires a reversal of defendant's convictions.

On the night of August 28, 1992, D.S., a white female student then enrolled at Rutgers University in New Brunswick, was watching television in her basement apartment. While she was relaxing on the couch, an African-American male entered the brightly lit apartment and demanded money from D.S., claiming that he was wanted for murder and that he needed funds to get to New York. After D.S. told the intruder that she had no money, he spotted her purse, rifled through it, and removed money and credit cards.

The intruder then [demanded that she remain quiet and led her by the arm into the brightly lit kitchen. He sexually assaulted her.] Throughout the sexual assault, D.S. was facing the kitchen door with her eyes closed and hand over her mouth to avoid crying loudly. Once the assault was over, D.S. faced her attacker who, after threatening her again, turned around and left the apartment. At the time of the second threat, D.S. was standing approximately two feet away from her assailant. The attacker made no attempt to conceal his face at any time. D.S. immediately called the New Brunswick Police Department after the intruder left the apartment. . . .

D.S. described her assailant as an African-American male in his late 20s to early 30s, full-faced, about five feet five inches tall, with a medium build, mustache, and unkempt hair. She stated that the intruder was wearing a dirty gray button-down short-sleeved shirt, blue warm-up pants with white and red stripes, and a Giants logo on the left leg. . . . Three days later, a composite sketch was drawn by an artist with her assistance. The following day at police headquarters, D.S. was shown many slides and photographs, including a photograph of defendant, in an unsuccessful attempt to identify her assailant.

On April 7, 1993, almost eight months after the crimes were committed, D.S. saw an African-American male across the street from her who she thought was her attacker. She spotted the man while she was standing on the corner of a street in New Brunswick waiting for the light to change. As the two passed on the street, D.S. studied the individual's face and gait. Believing that the man was her attacker, D.S. ran home and telephoned the police, giving them a description of the man she had just seen. Defendant was picked up by the New Brunswick police and taken to headquarters almost immediately. Within fifteen minutes after seeing defendant on the street, D.S. viewed defendant in a "show-up" from behind a one-way mirror and immediately identified him as the man she had just seen on the street and as her attacker. Defendant was then arrested and, with his consent, saliva and blood samples were taken for scientific analysis. [The State Police Laboratory was unable to determine whether those samples matched the samples obtained from D.S. at the time of the crime.]

Because of the nature of the crimes, the races of the victim and defendant, and the inability of the victim to identify defendant from his photograph, and because defendant was not positively identified until almost eight months after the date of the offenses, defense counsel sought a cross-racial identification jury charge. The following language was proposed:

> [Y]ou know that the identifying witness is of a different race than the defendant. When a witness who is a member of one race identifies a member who is of another race we say there has been a cross-racial identification. You may consider, if you think it is appropriate to do so, whether the cross-racial nature of the identification has affected the accuracy of the witness's original perception and/or accuracy of a subsequent identification.

In support of that request, defendant cited the June 1992 New Jersey Supreme Court Task Force on Minority Concerns Final Report, 131 N.J.L.J. 1145 (1992) (Task Force Report).

The trial court denied the request because this Court had not yet adopted the Task Force Report and because there had been no expert testimony with respect to the issue of cross-racial identification. The trial court instead provided the jury with the Model Jury Charge on Identification. The jury convicted defendant of first-degree aggravated sexual assault. . . .

For more than forty years, empirical studies concerning the psychological factors affecting eyewitness cross-racial or cross-ethnic identifications have appeared with increasing frequency in professional literature of the behavioral and social sciences. People v. McDonald, 690 P.2d 709, 717-18 (Cal. 1984). [Studies] have concluded that eyewitnesses are superior at identifying persons of their own race and have difficulty identifying members of another race. See generally Gary Wells &

Elizabeth Loftus, Eyewitness Testimony: Psychological Perspectives 1 (1984); Elizabeth Loftus, Eyewitness Testimony (1979). This phenomenon has been dubbed the "own-race" effect or "own-race" bias. Its corollary is that eyewitnesses experience a "cross-racial impairment" when identifying members of another race. Studies have consistently shown that the "own-race effect" is strongest when white witnesses attempt to recognize black subjects.

Although researchers generally agree that some eyewitnesses exhibit an own-race bias, they disagree about the degree to which own-race bias affects identification. In one study, African-American and white "customers" browsed in a convenience store for a few minutes and then went to the register to pay. Researchers asked the convenience store clerks to identify the "customers" from a photo array. The white clerks were able to identify 53.2% of the white customers but only 40.4% of the African-American subjects. Stephanie Platz & Harmon Hosch, Cross-Racial/Ethnic Eyewitness Identification: A Field Study, 18 J. Applied Soc. Psychol. 972, 977-78 (1988). . . .

Many studies on cross-racial impairment involve subjects observing photographs for a few seconds. Because the subjects remembered the white faces more often than they recalled the African-American faces, researchers concluded that they were biased towards their own race. See Paul Barkowitz & John C. Brigham, Recognition of Faces: Own-Race Bias, Incentive, and Time Delay, 12 J. Applied Soc. Psychol. 255 (1982). Yet, there is disagreement over whether the results of some of the tests can be generalized to real-world situations in which a victim or witness confronts an assailant face-to-face and experiences the full range of emotions that accompany such a traumatic event.

The debate among researchers did not prevent the Supreme Court of the United States, in the famous school desegregation case of Brown v. Board of Education of Topeka, 347 U.S. 483, 494 n. 11 (1954), from using behavioral and social sciences to support legal conclusions without requiring that the methodology employed by those scientists have general acceptance in the scientific community. . . . Thus, Brown v. Board of Education is the prototypical example of an appellate court using modern social and behavioral sciences as legislative evidence to support its choice of a rule of law.

In United States v. Telfaire, 469 F.2d 552 (D.C. Cir. 1972), Chief Judge Bazelon urged in his concurring opinion that juries be charged on the pitfalls of cross-racial identification. He believed that the cross-racial nature of an identification could affect accuracy in the same way as proximity to the perpetrator and poor lighting conditions. He felt that a meaningful jury instruction would have to apprise jurors of that fact. . . . Judge Bazelon rejected the notion that instructions on interracial identifications "appeal to racial prejudice." Rather, he believed that an explicit jury instruction would safeguard against improper uses of race by the jury and would delineate the narrow context in which it is appropriate to consider racial differences. . . .

The Supreme Court of the United States has acknowledged that problems exist with eyewitness identifications in general and cross-racial identifications in particular. Manson v. Brathwaite, 432 U.S. 98 (1977). Although there have been no reported decisions in our own State addressing the propriety of requiring a cross-racial identification jury instruction, decisions have been rendered by courts in other jurisdictions. The majority of courts allowing cross-racial identification charges hold that the decision to provide the instruction is a matter within the trial judge's discretion. Omission of such a cautionary instruction has been held to be prejudicial error where identification is the critical or central issue in the case, there is no corroborating evidence, and the circumstances of the case raise doubts concerning the reliability of the identification. See United States v. Thompson, 31 M.J. 125 (C.M.A. 1990) (calling for cross-racial identification instruction when requested by counsel and when cross-racial identification is a "primary issue"); People v. Wright, 755 P.2d 1049 (Cal. 1988). . . .

Courts typically have refused the instruction where the eyewitness or victim had an adequate opportunity to observe the defendant, there was corroborating evidence bolstering the identification, and/or there was no evidence that race affected the identification. See Commonwealth v. Hyatt, 647 N.E.2d 1168 (Mass. 1995) (declining instruction in rape and robbery case where victim was terrorized for fifteen to twenty minutes in broad daylight and could see the attacker's face).

A number of courts have concluded that cross-racial identification simply is not an appropriate topic for jury instruction. See State v. Willis, 731 P.2d 287, 292-93 (Kan. 1987); People v. McDaniel, 630 N.Y.S.2d 112, 113 (N.Y. App. Div. 1995). Those courts have determined that the cross-racial instruction requires expert guidance, and that cross-examination and summation are adequate safeguards to highlight unreliable identifications. Other jurisdictions have denied the instruction, finding that the results of empirical studies on cross-racial identification are questionable. People v. Bias, 475 N.E.2d 253, 257 (Ill. App. Ct. 1985) (rejecting instruction in robbery case where eyewitness failed to describe key distinguishing facial features and gave inconsistent descriptions because empirical studies are not unanimous). One jurisdiction has even rejected cross-racial identification instructions as improper commentary on "the nature and quality" of the evidence. See State v. Hadrick, 523 A.2d 441, 444 (R.I. 1987) (rejecting such instruction in robbery case where victim viewed perpetrator for two to three minutes at close range during robbery and identified him from a line-up). . . .

It is well-established in this State that when identification is a critical issue in the case, the trial court is obligated to give the jury a discrete and specific instruction that provides appropriate guidelines to focus the jury's attention on how to analyze and consider the trustworthiness of eyewitness identification. State v. Green, 430 A.2d 914 (N.J. 1981). *Green* requires that as a part of an identification charge a trial court inform the jury that [it] should consider, among other things, "the capacity or the ability of the witness to make observations or perceptions . . . at the time and under all of the attendant circumstances for seeing that which he says he saw or that which he says he perceived with regard to his identification." What defendant sought through the requested charge in the present case was an instruction that informed the jury that it could consider the fact that the victim made a cross-racial identification as part of the "attendant circumstances" when evaluating the reliability of the eyewitness identification.

The Court-appointed Task Force discussed and debated the issue of the need for a cross-racial and cross-ethnic identification jury instruction for more than five years. That Task Force was comprised of an appellate judge, trial judges, lawyers representing both the prosecution and defense, social scientists, and ordinary citizens. . . . Task Force sessions were conducted in much the same way as legislative committees conduct hearings on proposed legislation. . . . Ultimately, in 1992 the Task Force submitted its final report to the Court in which it recommended, among other things, that the Court develop a special jury charge regarding the unreliability of cross-racial identifications.

The Court referred that recommendation to the Criminal Practice Committee. . . . The Criminal Practice Committee has submitted that proposed charge to the Model Jury Charge Committee for its review. That Committee is withholding further consideration of the proposed charge pending the Court's decision in the present case.

We reject the State's contention that we should not require a cross-racial identification charge before it has been demonstrated that there is substantial agreement in the relevant scientific community that cross-racial recognition impairment is significant enough to support the need for such a charge. This case does not concern the introduction of scientific evidence to attack the reliability of the eyewitness's identification. Defendant's requested jury instruction was not based upon any "scientific, technical, or other specialized knowledge" to assist the jury. N.J.R.E. 702. He relied instead on ordinary human experience and the legislative-type findings of the Task Force because the basis for his request did not involve a matter that was beyond the ken of the average juror.

[I]n a prosecution in which race by definition is a patent factor, race must be taken into account to assure a fair trial. At the same time, we recognize that unrestricted use of cross-racial identification instructions could be counter-productive. Consequently, care must be taken to insulate criminal trials from base appeals to racial prejudice. An appropriate jury instruction should carefully delineate the context in which the jury is permitted to consider racial differences. The simple fact pattern of a white victim of a violent crime at the hands of a black assailant would not automatically give rise to the need for a cross-racial identification charge. More is required.

A cross-racial instruction should be given only when, as in the present case, identification is a critical issue in the case, and an eyewitness's cross-racial identification is not corroborated by other evidence giving it independent reliability. Here, the eyewitness identification was critical; yet it was not corroborated by any forensic evidence or other eyewitness account. The circumstances of the case raise some doubt concerning the reliability of the victim's identification in that no positive identification was made for nearly eight months despite attempts within the first five days following the commission of the offenses. Under those circumstances, turning over to the jury the vital question of the reliability of that identification without acquainting the jury with the potential risks associated with such identifications could have affected the jurors' ability to evaluate the reliability of the identification. We conclude, therefore, that it was reversible error not to have given an instruction that informed the jury about the possible significance of the cross-racial identification factor, a factor the jury can observe in many cases with its own eyes, in determining the critical issue — the accuracy of the identification. . . .

Because of the widely held commonsense view that members of one race have greater difficulty in accurately identifying members of a different race, expert testimony on this issue would not assist a jury, and for that reason would be inadmissible. We request the Criminal Practice Committee and the Model Jury Charge Committee to revise the current charge on identification to include an appropriate statement on cross-racial eyewitness identification that is consistent with this opinion. . . .

Notes

1. *Jury instructions about eyewitness testimony: majority position.* Judicial instructions to the jury can remind jurors about the vagaries of human memory. Such instructions are sometimes called *Telfaire* instructions, after one of the first cases to approve of their use. See United States v. Telfaire, 469 F.2d 552 (D.C. Cir. 1972) (describing a suggested jury instruction). Most states leave it to the trial judge to decide whether to grant a defense request for such an instruction. About 30 states allow (but do not require) the trial judge to grant a request for such jury instructions. See People v. Wright, 729 P.2d 280 (Cal. 1987). Roughly 10 states do require jury instructions, at least when there is some special reason to question the identification. See State v. Dyle, 899 S.W.2d 607 (Tenn. 1995); cf. State v. Maestas, 984 P.2d 376 (Utah 1999) (failure to ask for cautionary instruction on eyewitness identification amounted to ineffective assistance). As the court in *Cromedy* discussed, there may be special reasons to instruct the jury on this issue when the prosecution depends on a cross-racial identification. However, a small but growing number of states prohibit the use of such instructions. See Graham v. Commonwealth, 250 Va. 79 (1995). If jury instructions provide enough specific information about the circumstances that tend to produce less reliable eyewitness testimony, are they an adequate replacement for exclusion? See Edith Greene, Eyewitness Testimony and the Use of Cautionary Instructions, 8 U. Bridgeport L. Rev. 15 (1987) (study of impact of standard jury instructions regarding eyewitness memory, concluding they do not improve juror performance).

2. *Admissibility of expert testimony on eyewitness memory.* Starting in the early 1980s, a few defendants asked courts to allow experts to testify about recurring problems with witness memory. At first, very few courts allowed those experts to testify. Since then, the trend has been toward allowing such testimony. The high state courts addressing this question fall into several different groups. Appellate courts in fewer than 10 states still instruct trial courts that such expert testimony is not admissible because it invades the province of the jury. See State v. Coley, 32 S.W.3d 831 (Tenn. 2000) (general expert testimony about reliability of eyewitness identification does not substantially assist the trier of fact and is therefore inadmissible). The largest group of appellate courts (over 30 states) now allow the trial court the discretion to admit or exclude the testimony. See People v. McDonald, 690 P.2d 709 (Cal. 1984) (admitted); Weatherred v. State, 15 S.W.3d 540 (Tex. Crim. App. 2000) (excluded); People v. Lee, 750 N.E.2d 63 (N.Y. 2001) (trial court must consider case by case); United States v. Smithers, 212 F.3d 306 (6th Cir. 2000) (collecting cases). Appellate courts in a few states say that the trial has discretion on expert testimony about eyewitness memory, but can admit such evidence only in specialized cases. There are still very few appellate courts that will overturn a trial court's decision to exclude such testimony as an abuse of discretion. Under what circumstances might a court conclude that such testimony is necessary to a fair trial?

3. *The experts on expert testimony.* Social scientists have concluded that there is a great need for expert testimony about eyewitness identifications. Studies of jurors have indicated (with the usual ambiguity of social science studies) that jurors (1) place great weight on eyewitness testimony as they deliberate and reach their verdicts and (2) often have misconceptions about the reliability of eyewitness testimony and the conditions that pose the greatest risks for misidentification. See Brian Cutler, Steven Penrod, and Hedy Dexter, Juror Sensitivity to Eyewitness Identification Evidence, 14 Law & Hum. Behav. 185 (1990) (study showing jurors remain unaffected

by factors that should influence accuracy of witness's memory); but cf. Rogers Elliott, B. Farrington, and H. Manheimer, Eyewitnesses Credible and Discredible, 18 J. Applied Soc. Psych. 1411 (1988) (recounts difficulty in replicating early studies showing that jurors rely heavily on eyewitness testimony). Social scientists are split on the question of whether expert testimony can correct juror misconceptions about eyewitness memory without affecting their overall willingness to believe eyewitness testimony. Compare Brian Cutler, Steven Penrod, and Hedy Dexter, The Eyewitness, the Expert Psychologist, and the Jury, 13 Law & Hum. Behav. 311 (1989); with E. B. Ebbesen and V. J. Konecni, Eyewitness Memory Research: Probative v. Prejudicial Value, 5 Expert Evidence 2-28 (1997) (prejudicial outweighs probative value).

4. *Expert testimony as a substitute for exclusion.* In light of the rare use of the exclusion remedy, is expert testimony a more effective method of preventing wrongful convictions? Is due process satisfied whenever the defense can counter any prosecution eyewitness testimony with expert testimony about human memory? Must the government pay for such experts to testify for indigent criminal defendants? See Espinosa v. State, 589 So. 2d 887 (Fla. 1991) (trial court did not abuse discretion in refusing to order state to pay for defense expert on eyewitness memory); State v. Broom, 533 N.E.2d 682 (Ohio 1988) (refusal to appoint eyewitness identification expert to aid in indigent's defense was no due process violation; defendant made no particularized showing of reasonable probability that such an expert would aid in his defense).

5. *Corroboration.* Would it make sense to exclude identification evidence—regardless of any violations of due process or right to counsel—unless there is independent evidence to corroborate the identification evidence? See Regina v. Turnbull, [1977] 1 Q.B. 224 (1976):

> When, in the judgment of the trial judge, the quality of the identifying evidence is poor, as for example when it depends solely on a fleeting glance or on a longer observation made in difficult conditions, [the] judge should then withdraw the case from the jury and direct an acquittal unless there is other evidence which goes to support the correctness of the identification. [For] example, X sees the accused snatch a woman's handbag; he gets only a fleeting glance of the thief's face as he runs off but he does see him entering a nearby house. [Although this is poor identification evidence, the judge need not withdraw the case from the jury] if there was evidence that the house into which the accused was alleged by X to have run was his father's.

6. *Prosecutors as the cure.* Is the ultimate remedy for weak identification evidence the power of the prosecutor not to pursue charges against a defendant? Do prosecutors have adequate incentives and ability to screen out cases with the most questionable eyewitness-identification evidence? When Samuel Gross studied the records available in a large number of misidentification cases, he reached the following conclusions:

> (1) More often than not, a misidentified defendant was originally suspected because of his appearance. (2) A misidentified defendant is more likely to be cleared before his case comes to trial than after. (3) If he is not exonerated before trial, a misidentified defendant will almost certainly go to trial rather than plead guilty, even in return for an attractive plea bargain. (4) A misidentified defendant who is convicted at trial may still be exonerated, but the chances decrease over time.

Gross, Loss of Innocence: Eyewitness Identification and Proof of Guilt, 16 J. Legal Stud. 395 (1987).

X

Complex Investigations

Most crime investigations last for a short time and involve the efforts of only a few law enforcement officers. Different procedural issues crop up when investigations last longer and involve more people. Complex investigations involve people working in different governmental institutions, using distinctive investigative techniques. In this chapter, we consider two central issues. In the first section, we consider whether the legal system places any limits on the government's choice and pursuit of targets. In the second section, we consider the power of the grand jury to investigate crimes and the legal and practical limits on that power.

A. SELECTION AND PURSUIT OF TARGETS

1. Selective Investigations

The typical crime investigation is reactive: It aims to collect evidence of a known and completed crime. What if an investigation focuses instead on a person when there is no evidence of wrongdoing, or on a specific area where crimes might be committed? Does the government ever have to justify its decision to investigate, so long as it does not conduct a "search" or "seizure"? In this section, we consider whether targets of investigations can object to the criteria that the government uses to select places or persons to investigate.

What criteria *should* government agents use — or not use — to focus attention on settings when there is not yet any evidence that a crime has taken place? The Environmental Protection Agency memorandum below represents one internal effort by an investigating body to select investigative targets. The following two cases identify the possible grounds for constitutional challenges to investigators' choices. In

Chapter 13, we will consider the distinct but related question of "selective prosecution": challenges to the decision of a prosecutor (as opposed to an investigator) to file criminal charges in some but not all similar cases when there is sufficient evidence of a crime.

■ U.S. ENVIRONMENTAL PROTECTION AGENCY MEMORANDUM

Subject: The Exercise of Investigative Discretion
From: Earl E. Devaney, Director, Office of Criminal Enforcement
To: All EPA Employees Working in or in Support of the Criminal Enforcement Program
Date: January 12, 1994

. . . In an effort to maximize our limited criminal resources, this guidance sets out the specific factors that distinguish cases meriting criminal investigation from those more appropriately pursued under administrative or civil judicial authorities.[2] . . . The Pollution Prosecution Act of 1990 recognized the importance of a strong national environmental criminal enforcement program and mandates additional resources necessary for the criminal program to fulfill its statutory mission. The sponsors of the Act recognized that EPA had long been in the posture of reacting to serious violations only after harm was done, primarily due to limited resources. Senator Joseph Lieberman (Conn.), one of the co-sponsors of the Act, explained that as a result of limited resources, "few cases are the product of reasoned or targeted focus on suspected wrongdoing." He also expressed his hope that with the Act's provision of additional Special Agents, "EPA would be able to bring cases that would have greater deterrent value than those currently being brought." . . .

The case selection process is designed to identify misconduct worthy of criminal investigation. The case selection process is not an effort to establish legal sufficiency for prosecution. Rather, the process by which potential cases are analyzed under the case selection criteria will serve as an affirmative indication that OCE has purposefully directed its investigative resources toward deserving cases.

This is not to suggest that all cases meeting the case selection criteria will proceed to prosecution. Indeed, the exercise of investigative discretion must be clearly distinguished from the exercise of prosecutorial discretion. The employment of OCE's investigative discretion to dedicate its investigative authority is, however, a critical precursor to the prosecutorial discretion later exercised by the Department of Justice.

At the conclusion of the case selection process, OCE should be able to articulate the basis of its decision to pursue a criminal investigation, based on the case selection criteria. Conversely, cases that do not ultimately meet the criteria to proceed criminally, should be systematically referred back to the Agency's civil enforcement office for appropriate administrative or civil judicial action, or to a state or local prosecutor.

2. This memorandum is intended only as internal guidance to EPA. It is not intended to, does not, and may not be relied upon to create a right or benefit, substantive or procedural, enforceable at law by a party to litigation with the United States, nor does this guidance in any way limit the lawful enforcement prerogatives, including administrative or civil enforcement actions, of the Department of Justice and the Environmental Protection Agency.

Case Selection Criteria

The criminal case selection process will be guided by two general measures—significant environmental harm and culpable conduct. . . .

The measure of significant environmental harm should be broadly construed to include the presence of actual harm, as well as the threat of significant harm, to the environment or human health. The following factors serve as indicators that a potential case will meet the measure of significant environmental harm.

> *Factor 1. Actual* harm will be demonstrated by an illegal discharge, release or emission that has an identifiable and significant harmful impact on human health or the environment. This measure will generally be self-evident at the time of case selection.
>
> *Factor 2.* The *threat* of significant harm to the environment or human health may be demonstrated by an actual or threatened discharge, release or emission. This factor may not be as readily evident, and must be assessed in light of all the facts available at the time of case selection.
>
> *Factor 3.* Failure to report an actual discharge, release or emission . . . will serve as an additional factor favoring criminal investigation. While the failure to report, alone, may be a criminal violation, our investigative resources should generally be targeted toward those cases in which the failure to report is coupled with actual or threatened environmental harm.
>
> *Factor 4.* When certain illegal conduct appears to represent a trend or common attitude within the regulated community, criminal investigation may provide a significant deterrent effect incommensurate with its singular environmental impact. While the single violation being considered may have a relatively insignificant impact on human health or the environment, such violations, if multiplied by the numbers in a cross-section of the regulated community, would result in significant environmental harm. . . .

The measure of culpable conduct is not *necessarily* an assessment of criminal intent, particularly since criminal intent will not always be readily evident at the time of case selection. Culpable conduct, however, may be indicated at the time of case selection by several factors.

> *Factor 1.* History of repeated violations. While a history of repeated violations is not a prerequisite to a criminal investigation, a potential target's compliance record should always be carefully examined. . . . Clearly, a history of repeated violations will enhance the government's capacity to prove that a violator was aware of environmental regulatory requirements, had actual notice of violations and then acted in deliberate disregard of those requirements.
>
> *Factor 2.* Deliberate misconduct resulting in violation. Although the environmental statutes do not require proof of specific intent, evidence, either direct or circumstantial, that a violation was deliberate will be a major factor indicating that criminal investigation is warranted.
>
> *Factor 3.* Concealment of misconduct or falsification of required records. In the arena of self-reporting, EPA must be able to rely on data received from the regulated community. If submitted data are false, EPA is prevented from effectively carrying out its mandate. Accordingly, conduct indicating the falsification of data will always serve as the basis for serious consideration to proceed with a criminal investigation.
>
> *Factor 4.* Tampering with monitoring or control equipment. The overt act of tampering with monitoring or control equipment leads to the certain production of false data that appears to be otherwise accurate. The consequent submission of false data threatens the basic integrity of EPA's data and, in turn, the scientific validity of EPA's

regulatory decisions. Such an assault on the regulatory infrastructure calls for the enforcement leverage of criminal investigation. . . .

The fundamental purpose of [case screening] is to consider criminal enforcement in the greater context of all available EPA enforcement and environmental response options, to do so early (at the time of each case opening) before extensive resources have been expended, and to identify, prioritize, and target the most egregious cases. . . . Full and effective implementation of these processes will achieve two important results: it will ensure that OCE's investigative resources are being directed properly and expended efficiently, and it will foreclose assertions that EPA's criminal program is imposing its powerful sanctions indiscriminately. . . .

■ AH SIN v. GEORGE WITTMAN

198 U.S. 500 (1905)

McKenna, J.

[Ah Sin filed a petition] alleging that he was a subject of the Emperor of China, and was restrained of his liberty by . . . the chief of police of the city and county of San Francisco, under a judgment of imprisonment rendered in the police court of said city for the violation of one of its ordinances. [Defendant was convicted under a city ordinance making it "unlawful for any person within the limits of the city and county of San Francisco to exhibit or expose to view in . . . any place built or protected in a manner to make it difficult of access or ingress to police officers when three or more persons are present, any cards, dice, dominoes, fan-tan table or layout, or any part of such layout, or any gambling implements whatsoever." The ordinance also made it unlawful to "visit or resort to" such a house or room, and provided for punishment upon conviction by a fine not to exceed five hundred dollars, or by imprisonment in the county jail for not more than six months, or both.]

Plaintiff in error avers "That said ordinance and the provisions thereof are enforced and executed by the said municipality of San Francisco, and said State of California, solely and exclusively against persons of the Chinese race, and not otherwise." The contention is that Chinese persons are thereby denied the equal protection of the law in violation of the Fourteenth Amendment of the Constitution of the United States. Yick Wo v. Hopkins, 118 U.S. 356 (1886), is cited to sustain the contention. . . . That case concerned the use of property for lawful and legitimate purposes. The case at bar is concerned with gambling, to suppress which is recognized as a proper exercise of governmental authority, and one which would have no incentive in race or class prejudice or administration in race or class discrimination. In the *Yick Wo* case there was not a mere allegation that the ordinance attacked was enforced against the Chinese only, but it was shown that not only the petitioner in that case, but two hundred of his countrymen, applied for licenses, and were refused, and that all the petitions of those not Chinese, with one exception, were granted. The averment in the case at bar is that the ordinance is enforced "solely and exclusively against persons of the Chinese race and not otherwise." There is no averment that the conditions and practices to which the ordinance was directed did not exist exclusively among the Chinese, or that there were other offenders against the ordinance than the Chinese as to whom it was not enforced. No latitude of intention should be indulged in a case like this. There should be certainty to every intent.

Plaintiff in error seeks to set aside a criminal law of the State, not on the ground that it is unconstitutional on its face, not that it is discriminatory in tendency and ultimate actual operation as the ordinance was which was passed on in the *Yick Wo* case, but that it was made so by the manner of its administration. This is a matter of proof, and no fact should be omitted to make it out completely, when the power of a Federal court is invoked to interfere with the course of criminal justice of a State. We think, therefore, the judgment of the Superior Court should be and it is hereby affirmed.

■ DENNIS BALUYUT v. SUPERIOR COURT

911 P.2d 1 (Cal. 1996)

BAXTER, J.

Petitioners below are defendants charged with violation of Penal Code section 647(a)[1] in the Municipal Court for the Santa Clara County Judicial District. They sought dismissal of the charges on the ground that the Mountain View police who arrested them engaged in a pattern of discriminatory arrest and prosecution of homosexuals under this statute, thereby denying them equal protection of the law. [The trial court denied the motion to dismiss.]

In support of their motion to dismiss, defendants presented ten arrest reports spanning a two-year period. The reports described decoy officers' arrests of men in and outside an adult bookstore in Mountain View for violations of section 647(a). The arrests involved a decoy officer who had engaged a person in small talk. [A]fter the person eventually made it clear that he was interested in a sexual encounter the officer suggested that the person accompany the officer to the officer's car. Once at the officer's car, the person was arrested for soliciting a lewd act to be performed in a public place. . . . Other evidence was offered that the modus operandi of the decoy officers was typical of a "cruising" pattern of homosexual men and that it invited homosexual men to make contact with the decoy officer.

Mountain View police records for the two years prior to the arrest of defendants were reviewed by the municipal court which also heard testimony about the decoy operation. The court concluded that the operation was focused solely on persons who had a proclivity to engage in homosexual conduct, [and that] it did so without any relationship to the alleged problems at that location for which the citizen complaint had been initially lodged.

Based on these factual conclusions, and applying this court's decision in Murgia v. Municipal Court, 540 P.2d 44 (Cal. 1975), the municipal court ruled that defendants had established there was improper selectivity — discrimination — in prosecution and that the discrimination had an invidious basis. It was unjustifiable, arbitrary, and without a rational relationship to legitimate law enforcement interests. Notwithstanding these conclusions and the court's belief that the complaints should be dismissed, the court felt bound by People v. Smith, 155 Cal. App. 3d 1103 (1984) to deny the motion to dismiss because defendants had not established that the Mountain View police had a specific intent to punish the defendants for their membership in a particular class. . . .

1. . . . Section 647: "Every person who commits any of the following acts is guilty of disorderly conduct, a misdemeanor: (a) Who solicits anyone to engage in or who engages in lewd or dissolute conduct in any public place or in any place open to the public or exposed to public view."

Although referred to for convenience as a "defense," a defendant's claim of discriminatory prosecution goes not to the nature of the charged offense, but to a defect of constitutional dimension in the initiation of the prosecution. The defect lies in the denial of equal protection to persons who are singled out for a prosecution that is "deliberately based upon an unjustifiable standard such as race, religion, or other arbitrary classification." When a defendant establishes the elements of discriminatory prosecution, the action must be dismissed even if a serious crime is charged unless the People establish a compelling reason for the selective enforcement.

Unequal treatment which results simply from laxity of enforcement or which reflects a nonarbitrary basis for selective enforcement of a statute does not deny equal protection and is not constitutionally prohibited discriminatory enforcement. However, the unlawful administration by state officers of a state statute that is fair on its face, which results in unequal application to persons who are entitled to be treated alike, denies equal protection if it is the product of intentional or purposeful discrimination.

In *Murgia* this court explained the showing necessary to establish discriminatory prosecution: "In order to establish a claim of discriminatory enforcement a defendant must demonstrate [1] that he has been deliberately singled out for prosecution on the basis of some invidious criterion, [and (2) that] the prosecution would not have been pursued except for the discriminatory design of the prosecuting authorities." The *Smith* court elaborated on these elements and in so doing appeared to hold that the defendant must show not only that an invidious discriminatory purpose underlies the prosecution, but also that this purpose is to punish the defendant for his membership in a particular class. . . .

Nothing in *Murgia* . . . or the controlling decisions of the United States Supreme Court supports the imposition of this additional burden on a defendant. Showing an intent to punish for membership in a group or class is not necessary to establish a violation of an individual's right to equal protection under the Fourteenth Amendment to the United States Constitution. There must be discrimination and that discrimination must be intentional and unjustified and thus "invidious" because it is unrelated to legitimate law enforcement objectives, but the intent need not be to "punish" the defendant for membership in a protected class or for the defendant's exercise of protected rights. . . .

Murgia arose in the context of a motion for discovery by defendants who claimed that they were being discriminatorily prosecuted under various statutes on the basis of their membership in or support of the United Farm Workers Union (UFW) and sought information relevant to that claim. Discovery had been denied on the ground that the evidence sought was irrelevant as defendants had violated the laws under which they were charged. [We held as follows:] "Neither the federal nor state Constitution countenances the singling out of an invidiously selected class for special prosecutorial treatment, whether that class consists of black or white, Jew or Catholic, Irishman or Japanese, United Farm Worker or Teamster. If an individual can show that he would not have been prosecuted except for such invidious discrimination against him, a basic constitutional principle has been violated, and such prosecution must collapse upon the sands of prejudice."

[*Murgia* recognized that] an equal protection violation does not arise whenever officials prosecute one and not [another] for the same act; instead, the equal protection guarantee simply prohibits prosecuting officials from purposefully and intentionally singling out individuals for disparate treatment on an invidiously discriminatory basis. [But the suggestion] that discriminatory enforcement is not established unless the defendant establishes that the law enforcement officers responsible had a specific intent to punish the defendants for their membership in a particular classification finds no support in [*Murgia*]. Rather, the purpose or intent that must be shown is simply intent to single out the group or a member of the group on the basis of that membership for prosecution that would not otherwise have taken place. When there is no legitimate law enforcement purpose for singling out those persons for prosecution, the prosecution is arbitrary and unjustified and thus results in invidious discrimination. . . .

Subsequent to *Murgia* and the United States Supreme Court decisions on which it relied, the high court again visited the question and reaffirmed the factors which establish a violation of a defendant's right to equal protection, noting that ordinary equal protection principles apply in assessing discriminatory prosecution claims. In Wayte v. United States, 470 U.S. 598 (1985), the court considered a "passive enforcement" policy under which the federal government prosecuted persons who failed to register for the draft. Under that policy the government prosecuted only persons who reported themselves as unwilling to register. Those who reported themselves were known by the government as likely to be persons who for moral or religious reasons were vocal opponents of the registration requirement. At the time the policy existed, the Selective Service system was unable to develop a more active enforcement system.

Wayte . . . was one of the first persons indicted under the passive enforcement policy. He claimed to be a victim of selective or discriminatory enforcement and asserted that the indictment violated his First Amendment rights. The district court dismissed the indictment, ruling that the government had not rebutted Wayte's prima facie case of selective prosecution. [The Supreme Court held, however, that the prosecution could go forward because Wayte had failed to show that the government focused its investigation on him because of his protest activities.]

The court held that even if the government's passive enforcement policy had a discriminatory effect, Wayte had not shown that the government intended that result. Although he had shown that the government was aware that the likely impact of its passive enforcement policy was prosecution of vocal objectors, a showing of "discriminatory purpose" required more. That showing is that the government selected the course of action "at least in part 'because of,' not merely 'in spite of,' its adverse effects upon an identifiable group." . . .

We are not free to adopt a narrower construction of the protection afforded by the equal protection clause of the Fourteenth Amendment than that enunciated by the United States Supreme Court. Requiring a defendant to show that the government had a specific intent to punish a person singled out as a member of a class for criminal prosecution finds no support in the controlling precedent of the United States Supreme Court cases. . . .

Problem 10-1. Selection of Participants

A Brockton police officer arrested Ann O'Connor for two violations of the city ordinance against prostitution. After being charged with these offenses, she filed a motion to dismiss the complaints, arguing that the police had engaged in improper selective enforcement of the prostitution laws. O'Connor claimed that no male was arrested with her on either charge, because it is the police department's policy and practice to arrest only prostitutes and not their clients.

The ordinance in question was amended three years prior to O'Connor's arrest, to apply both to the prostitute and the client:

> Any person who engages, agrees to engage, or offers to engage in sexual conduct with another person in return for a fee, or any person who pays, agrees to pay or offers to pay another person to engage in sexual conduct, or to agree to engage in sexual conduct with another natural person may be punished by imprisonment in a jail or house of correction for not more than one year, or by a fine of not more than five hundred dollars, or by both such fine and imprisonment.

One Brockton police detective testified at the motion hearing about the department's typical methods of surveillance of female suspects on certain streets in Brockton. The police officer typically would observe (1) females on the street waving at males in cars, (2) a female entering a vehicle and driving off with a male, (3) both returning after an interval, and then (4) a repetition of the process with a different male. The detective testified that, in such circumstances, "ordinarily" the police do not arrest the driver of the vehicle. In cases in which the officer follows the vehicle and discovers two passengers in the vehicle engaged in a sexual act, only the female is arrested.

The detective stated that the basic reason for the policy was that complaints from area citizens related "mainly to the girls," and that the women arrested are known to the police whereas the men are not. The department's arrest records for the previous year show that 36 of the 37 persons arrested for prostitution were female and that 23 of the 25 persons arrested for soliciting prostitution were female.

Will the court grant O'Connor's motion to dismiss? On the basis of a constitutional provision, or on some other basis? Compare Commonwealth v. An Unnamed Defendant, 492 N.E.2d 1184 (Mass. 1986) (constitutional violation for selective enforcement of prostitution laws) with City of Minneapolis v. Buschette, 240 N.W.2d 500 (Minn. 1976) (no constitutional violation).

Notes

1. *Discriminatory selection of investigative targets: majority position.* Courts in almost all jurisdictions agree about the basic steps to follow in resolving a constitutional challenge to an investigator's selection of a target. Under the equal protection clause of the federal Constitution, "no state shall" make any law denying persons "the equal protection of the laws." When criminal defendants have claimed that the government's "selective enforcement" of a law violates the equal protection clause, courts have asked the defendant to address several issues. First, the defendant must show that others similarly situated were treated differently (that is, the police did not make an arrest or follow up on a viable investigative lead). Second, the defendant must show that differences between the groups receiving different treatment are legally significant (for instance, different treatment of racial or gender groups). Finally (and this is the most difficult showing), a defendant must demonstrate that the government agents intentionally discriminated against the group — that is, they

chose the target *because of* the group membership, and not *in spite of* the group membership. See Wayte v. United States, 470 U.S. 598 (1985).

2. *Proving intent.* If the investigator's state of mind is critical to a claim of discriminatory investigation, how would a defendant get evidence of such a state of mind? As we will see in Chapter 13, courts have created a difficult standard for defendants to satisfy before they can obtain discovery on such questions. See United States v. Armstrong, 517 U.S. 456 (1996) (defendant must show that the government declined to prosecute similarly situated suspects of other races). What showings do the courts in *Ah Sin* and *Baluyut* require of a defendant challenging an alleged discriminatory investigation? Note the California court's use of the doctrine of "specific intent," drawn from substantive criminal law. Although the term is slippery, courts speaking of specific intent usually mean (a) an awareness of some specific circumstance surrounding the crime (e.g., knowledge that property is stolen, to be convicted of receiving stolen property), or (b) an intent to do some future act beyond the act that forms the basis for a crime (e.g., a specific intent to deprive the owner of property permanently, as an element of larceny). See Joshua Dressler, Understanding Criminal Law §10.06 (2d ed. 1995). Exactly what state of mind of the investigator does the California court in *Baluyut* require the defendant to prove?

3. *Public complaints as a selection criterion.* Is it adequate for the police to explain their enforcement policy by saying that they enforce certain laws only in situations when a citizen complains about a possible violation? In *Baluyut,* suppose all the complaints about violations of the public lewdness ordinance dealt with homosexual activity. Is there any danger in a police policy that ensures responsiveness to public concerns? Compare State v. Anonymous, 364 A.2d 244 (Conn. C.P. 1976) (invalidating police policy of enforcing Sunday "blue laws" only upon receiving a citizen complaint) with State v. Russell, 343 N.W.2d 36 (Minn. 1984) (denying challenge to police policy of concentrating enforcement efforts in burglary cases in one predominantly black precinct receiving most reports of burglary).

4. *Resources as a selection criterion.* Police departments and other criminal investigators, just like everyone else, must economize on a limited budget. Is the resource constraint, in the end, the best constraint on investigative decisions? Will budgetary considerations, like Adam Smith's invisible hand, lead investigators to direct their efforts to solve and prevent the greatest number of crimes that are of greatest concern to the community? Could the rules of legal ethics effectively supplement prosecutorial budgets by requiring prosecutors to advise criminal investigators to go forward only when the investigation is "proportional" to the suspected conduct? See Rory Little, Proportionality as an Ethical Precept for Prosecutors in Their Investigative Role, 68 Fordham L. Rev. 723 (1999).

For some special investigators resource questions essentially do not exist. So-called special prosecutors (formerly known in the federal system as the "independent counsel") are typically appointed to investigate politically sensitive cases in which the public might not trust the judgment of the ordinary prosecutors or investigators. Special prosecutors do not have to apportion a limited investigative budget over a large number of potential criminal cases. If there is no effective limit on the amount of time government agents can spend investigating a single person, do the legal and political systems have any workable way to prevent abuses of the investigative power? See Katy Harriger, Independent Justice: The Federal Special Prosecutor in American Politics (1992); Julie O'Sullivan, The Independent Counsel Statute: Bad Law, Bad Policy, 33 Am. Crim. L. Rev. 463 (1996).

5. *Written guidelines as the norm?* The investigative guidelines of the Environmental Protection Agency are unusual because they are written. Federal investigators put these policies in writing more often than state investigators, and they tend to appear in white-collar crime settings. See Federal Prosecution of Corporations, June 1999 *(http://www.usdoj.gov:80/criminal/fraud/policy/Chargingcorps.html)*. Nevertheless, law enforcement agencies routinely make decisions about how to allocate their resources. Some of these choices involve "proactive" efforts to uncover crimes that have not yet been committed or reported to the police. Is the guidance provided by the EPA memorandum on case selection better than the ad hoc, oral standards recounted in Problem 10-1? If so, what are the differences between them? Or are these policies all equally futile or misleading because discretion and arbitrariness in enforcement is inevitable?

2. *Entrapment Defenses*

Some crimes, such as prostitution, drug trafficking, or price fixing, involve voluntary transactions that are difficult for anyone other than the participants to observe. Sometimes government agents investigate such crimes through "undercover" operations, not revealing to their targets the fact that they are law enforcement officers. The undercover agent might pretend to participate in a crime as it takes place rather than inquiring after a crime has happened. The agent might also create the opportunity for some person to commit a crime under "simulated" conditions. How should judges, legislators, and enforcement officials respond to the dangers — and perhaps the necessity — of these enforcement techniques? When will a defendant escape a conviction because the government "entrapped" him? The case and statutes that follow take up the central question surrounding the entrapment doctrine: whether the defendant's state of mind, the activities of the government, or some combination of the two should be the key concept in resolving entrapment claims.

■ STATE v. ANNA LEE

640 A.2d 553 (Conn. 1994)

BORDEN, J.

The defendant, Anna Lee, was convicted after a jury trial of criminal attempt to possess more than one kilogram of marijuana with intent to sell by a person who is not drug-dependent. . . . During the summer of 1990, two confidential informants, Linda and Augustus Buckley, contacted Detective Daniel Losey of the organized crime division of the Fort Lauderdale, Florida, police department to inform him that the defendant, a resident of Connecticut, was interested in obtaining a large amount of marijuana for resale purposes. Posing as a drug supplier, Losey telephoned the defendant at her home in Connecticut to arrange a marijuana sale. In July and August, 1990, Losey and the defendant communicated frequently by telephone in connection with the potential sale. [Lee was arrested after she consummated the sale in Connecticut.]

The defendant's primary defense was entrapment under General Statutes §53a-15. The defendant, a fifty-five year old woman with no prior criminal record, testified that her son was currently incarcerated in Florida and that Augustus Buckley was in prison with him. She testified that Buckley had sent her crude, intimidating letters and that he had threatened her son's life. She further testified that Buckley had urged her to hire a private attorney to get her son out of jail and had offered to facilitate a drug deal in order to raise money for the attorney. She testified that Buckley had threatened her son's life if she failed to go through with the deal, and that he had offered to arrange for both a purchaser and seller of marijuana. It was in this context, she asserted, that she had agreed to purchase the drugs from Losey.

[Lee] claims that the Appellate Court improperly failed to recognize a defense of "objective" entrapment under Connecticut law, in addition to the statutory defense of "subjective" entrapment. We disagree, and affirm the Appellate Court's conclusion on this claim.

The subjective test of entrapment focuses on the disposition of the defendant to commit the crime of which he or she is accused.

> Government agents may not originate a criminal design, implant in an innocent person's mind the disposition to commit a criminal act, and then induce commission of the crime so that the Government may prosecute. [When the defense of entrapment is at issue], the prosecution must prove beyond a reasonable doubt that the defendant was disposed to commit the criminal act prior to first being approached by Government agents.

Jacobson v. United States, 503 U.S. 540 (1992). Thus, the subjective defense of entrapment succeeds only if the government, not the accused, is the source of the criminal design. The subjective defense fails if the accused is previously disposed to commit the crime, and the government merely facilitates or assists in the criminal scheme. Consequently, the subjective defense focuses attention on the disposition of the accused. . . .

The majority of states have adopted the subjective standard for the entrapment defense, either by statute or caselaw. [The court cites cases from Alabama, Louisiana, Maine, Ohio, Wisconsin, and Wyoming.] Furthermore, the United States Supreme Court has adopted the subjective standard for the federal courts. See, e.g., Jacobson v. United States; Hampton v. United States, 425 U.S. 484 (1976); United States v. Russell, 411 U.S. 423 (1973); Sherman v. United States, 356 U.S. 369 (1958); Sorrells v. United States, 287 U.S. 435 (1932).

The alternative test, adopted by some states, is the objective test. [The court cites cases from Alaska, California, Hawaii, Iowa, Michigan, New Mexico, North Dakota, Pennsylvania, and West Virginia.] Under this standard, entrapment exists if the government conduct was such that a reasonable person would have been induced to commit the crime. This standard necessarily focuses attention on the conduct of the government. "The conduct with which the defense of entrapment is concerned is the manufacturing of crime by law enforcement officials and their agents. . . . For the Government cannot be permitted to instigate the commission of a criminal offense in order to prosecute someone for committing it." United States v. Russell, 411 U.S. at 439 (Stewart, J., dissenting). . . . Under an objective standard, the disposition of the accused to commit the crime is irrelevant. . . .

The Connecticut legislature has chosen to adopt the subjective defense of entrapment. General Statutes §53a-15 provides:

> In any prosecution for an offense, it shall be a defense that the defendant engaged in the proscribed conduct because he was induced to do so by a public servant, or by a

> person acting in cooperation with a public servant, for the purpose of institution of criminal prosecution against the defendant, and that the defendant did not contemplate and would not otherwise have engaged in such conduct.

This statute codifies prior Connecticut caselaw, particularly State v. Marquardt, 89 A.2d 219 (Conn. 1952), and State v. Avery, 211 A.2d 165 (Conn. 1965). . . . Since its codification, §53a-15 has consistently been interpreted to impose a subjective standard.

As the subjective entrapment doctrine has been applied in Connecticut, the defendant has the initial responsibility to present sufficient evidence that the state induced him or her to commit the offense charged. Once that burden has been met, however, the burden shifts to the state to prove beyond a reasonable doubt that the defendant was predisposed to commit the offense.

The defendant now advocates adoption of a two-tiered approach to entrapment, modeled after the law of New Mexico. See, e.g., Baca v. State, 742 P.2d 1043 (N.M. 1987). The defendant proposes that the defense of entrapment be expanded to include cases in which the defendant was not predisposed to commit the crime or the police conduct exceeded the bounds of proper investigation. Thus, the defendant seeks to add a judicially created defense of objective entrapment to the statutory defense of subjective entrapment. Specifically, she proposes that, if the defense has been properly raised, the trial court should first evaluate the investigative actions of the police, and if they do not satisfy proper standards, dismiss the case. If this hurdle is passed, she proposes that the question should then be submitted to the jury with an instruction on subjective entrapment. The defendant contends that the saving clause of General Statutes §53a-4[17] and the court's inherent power to protect its own processes provide authority for judicial adoption of the proposed defense.

We decline the defendant's invitation so to amend our penal code. Although the defendant is correct that §53a-4 permits us to recognize principles of criminal liability and defenses in addition to those created by statute, we are not free to fashion a defense that would be inconsistent with a provision of the code. . . .

Adoption of an objective standard of entrapment would substantially abrogate the present provision of our penal code. Section 53a-15 specifically centers the defense around the disposition of the defendant rather than the conduct of the police. Under the statute, it is a defense that the defendant "was induced to [engage in proscribed conduct] by a public servant . . . and that the defendant did not contemplate and would not otherwise have engaged in such conduct." Under an objective test of entrapment, the defendant's disposition would become irrelevant. A person who was predisposed to commit the charged offense, and might have committed it regardless of the contribution of the police, would be entitled to acquittal solely because of police practices. This result plainly contravenes the intent of the statute, which provides that a defendant is entitled to an entrapment defense only if he or she would not otherwise have contemplated or engaged in the proscribed conduct.

The defendant's suggestion to bifurcate the defense into two portions, an objective test applied by the judge and a subjective test applied by the jury, does not

17. General Statutes §53a-4 provides: "The provisions of this chapter shall not be construed as precluding any court from recognizing other principles of criminal liability or other defenses not inconsistent with such provisions."

change this result.[19] The possibility that a defendant predisposed to commit a crime may be acquitted of that crime by the objective portion of the defense, makes the proposal inconsistent with the statutory defense. The judgment is affirmed.

BERDON, J., dissenting.

I agree with the defendant that we should adopt a defense of objective entrapment in addition to the statutory subjective defense. . . . The objective defense, recognized by some jurisdictions as the sole available defense, and in other jurisdictions in conjunction with the subjective defense, is established if the trial judge finds that the activities of government agents were objectively likely to instigate or create a criminal offense. The defense is available only in situations involving highly egregious police activity, and applies irrespective of the defendant's predisposition to commit the crime.

In order to put the issue in its proper perspective, the limited evidence that the trial court allowed the defendant to introduce should be reviewed. The defendant, Anna Lee, a fifty-five year old woman, had no previous criminal record. Her attorney described her as "slightly daffy" during final arguments before the jury. Her son Mario was imprisoned in Florida on a conviction of conspiracy to possess cocaine. During Mario's imprisonment, and while his case was on appeal, the defendant received letters from other inmates threatening her son's life. The defendant was deeply concerned about Mario's well-being, and in response to the threats she sent money orders and other items to inmates for her son's protection. . . . The defendant wanted to obtain the assistance of a private attorney in order to pursue her son's appeal, but had previously borrowed thousands of dollars [to pay] Mario's trial legal fees. . . .

It was in this context that Augustus Buckley, a government informant and fellow inmate of Mario's, telephoned the defendant. He told her that he was a friend of Mario's and urged her to obtain the services of a private appellate attorney for her son. When she explained her financial predicament to him, Buckley suggested a way to raise the necessary funds. He offered to arrange the delivery and sale to her of fifty pounds of high quality marijuana for $40,000, with the arrangement that his friends would purchase the marijuana from her at a substantial profit that she could in turn use to pay for Mario's legal expenses. . . .

Buckley informed Detective Daniel Losey of the Fort Lauderdale police department that the defendant had become interested in purchasing marijuana for resale. On July 23, 1990, Losey telephoned the defendant, claiming to be a drug dealer, and stated that he had been advised of her interest in purchasing marijuana. [Losey proposed a $150,000 sale, with a $3,000 down payment.] The defendant responded that "for the first time it's too big an amount."

[Losey also called Lee on July 24, August 2, and August 3, and offered to reduce the price, but they could not come to terms. During one of these calls, Lee mentioned that Buckley had threatened to kill her son, by saying to her, "I think your son's sentence will end very soon. We end his sentence very soon if you no go

19. The dissent's insistence that a court applied defense of objective entrapment . . . is necessary to protect our judicial processes, overlooks the fact that this defendant [was] permitted to subject her evidence of entrapment to the fact-finding processes of the jury. . . . Thus, the dissent's approach, besides adding a defense that is inconsistent with General Statutes §53a-15, would, in this case, substitute the court for the jury as fact finder regarding not only the conduct of the state, but also the predisposition of the defendant. . . .

through with the deal." Five days later, Losey called Lee again, and reached an agreement. A week later, Losey telephoned Lee to confirm the agreement; at first she said that she did not want to purchase the marijuana, believing that Losey and Buckley were "setting her up," but Losey convinced her that he was not a police officer. The next day Losey telephoned Lee for the seventh time, and she agreed to meet him in Connecticut to complete the transaction. Lee and Losey met as planned, and she was arrested immediately after drawing a check for $40,000 against her equity line of credit.]

This evidence demonstrates that entrapment is a potentially dangerous tool given to police to fight crime. This does not mean, of course, that the Government's use of undercover activity, strategy, or deception is necessarily unlawful. Indeed, many crimes, especially so-called victimless crimes, could not otherwise be detected. Thus, government agents may engage in conduct that is likely, when objectively considered, to afford a person ready and willing to commit the crime an opportunity to do so.

The allegations of fact in this case, however, reach a level that substantially deviates from acceptable police activity, painting a picture of outrageous police conduct that sickens the civilized mind and heart and cries out for the adoption of an objective entrapment defense. . . . I would hold that, in addition to the subjective defense of §53a-15 to be applied by the jury, this court should adopt a threshold objective defense decided by the court. . . .

The majority, however, states that we are prohibited from judicially adopting an objective defense by General Statutes §53a-4, the saving clause of our penal code. Section 53a-4 provides that the court may recognize "other principles of criminal liability or other defenses not inconsistent with" the provisions of the penal code. . . . The subjective and objective entrapment formulations, however, are quite separate and distinct. The subjective defense serves the purpose of protecting the innocent citizen from police manufacture of crime while the objective defense serves to protect the courts and the public at large from judicial sanction of outrageous police tactics. [Under the subjective defense, the] egregiousness of the police conduct is not at issue, as the subjective defense merely requires that the government agents induce the commission of the crime.

On the other hand, the objective defense, applied by the court, addresses egregious conduct of the police or other government agents; whether the defendant had a predisposition to commit the crime is irrelevant. [The focus of this approach is on whether the police conduct falls below standards, to which common feelings respond, for the proper use of governmental power. This determination is made by the trial judge, not the jury.][7]

In addition to serving different purposes, the objective and subjective defenses are activated by different factual situations. In particular, the objective defense is limited to egregious police practices such as those described by the defendant in

7. The defenses are also distinguished by the burden of proof. Once the defendant raises the subjective entrapment defense, the state bears the burden of disproving the defense beyond a reasonable doubt. General Statutes §53a-12. The defendant, however, bears the burden of proving the objective defense by a fair preponderance of the evidence. The drafters of Model Penal Code §2.13 explained the reasons for placing the burden of proving the objective defense on the defendant as follows: "Since it is not required that the defense of entrapment negative an element of the offense . . . it was believed appropriate to place the burden of proof on the defendant. [The defendant may] be analogized to a plaintiff who in seeking relief should be required to come forward with evidence in support of his claim and to establish its main elements by a preponderance of the proof. . . ."

the present case; this limitation ensures that adoption of the defense would not "substantially abrogate the present provision of our penal code" as the majority opines. In cases of legitimate police sting operations, the objective defense will have no application, although defendants in such cases will be entitled to present their subjective defense before the jury. Because the defenses address different concerns and apply in different types of factual situations, courts have held that the coexistence of the two standards presents no conflict. . . .

We are a civilized nation. The conduct alleged in this case on the part of the police and their agents, if true, is outrageous and inconsistent with common decency — it offends my sense of justice. . . . In the face of the conduct alleged by the defendant in this case, in the first instance when applying the objective defense, her predisposition or lack thereof should be irrelevant. . . .

■ MODEL PENAL CODE §2.13

American Law Institute (1962)

(1) A public law enforcement official or a person acting in cooperation with such an official perpetrates an entrapment if for the purpose of obtaining evidence of the commission of an offense, he induces or encourages another person to engage in conduct constituting such offense by either:

(a) making knowingly false representations designed to induce the belief that such conduct is not prohibited; or

(b) employing methods of persuasion or inducement that create a substantial risk that such an offense will be committed by persons other than those who are ready to commit it.

(2) Except as provided in Subsection (3) of this Section, a person prosecuted for an offense shall be acquitted if he proves by a preponderance of evidence that his conduct occurred in response to an entrapment. The issue of entrapment shall be tried by the Court in the absence of the jury.

(3) The defense afforded by this Section is unavailable when causing or threatening bodily injury is an element of the offense charged and the prosecution is based on conduct causing or threatening such injury to a person other than the person perpetrating the entrapment.

■ MISSOURI REVISED STATUTES §562.066

1. The commission of acts which would otherwise constitute an offense is not criminal if the actor engaged in the prescribed conduct because he was entrapped by a law enforcement officer or a person acting in cooperation with such an officer.

2. An "entrapment" is perpetuated if a law enforcement officer or a person acting in cooperation with such an officer, for the purpose of obtaining evidence of the commission of an offense, solicits, encourages or otherwise induces another person to engage in conduct when he was not ready and willing to engage in such conduct.

3. The relief afforded by subsection 1 is not available as to any crime which involves causing physical injury to or placing in danger of physical injury a person other than the person perpetrating the entrapment.

4. The defendant shall have the burden of injecting the issue of entrapment.

Notes

1. *Entrapment: majority position.* The Supreme Court first recognized an entrapment defense in Sorrells v. United States, 287 U.S. 435 (1932). In that case, a government agent posed as a tourist and befriended Sorrells. The agent asked Sorrells to get him some illegal liquor. At first, Sorrells declined. Eventually, however, Sorrells obtained a half-gallon of whiskey for the agent. The Supreme Court stated that improper entrapment occurs when "the criminal design originates with the officials of the Government, and they implant in the mind of an innocent person the disposition to commit the alleged offense and induce its commission in order that they may prosecute." The concurring opinions focused on the conduct of law enforcement personnel rather than on the predisposition of the defendant. The opinions in *Sorrells* were the origins of the "subjective" and "objective" approaches to entrapment. See also Sherman v. United States, 356 U.S. 369 (1958) (improper entrapment sets a "trap for the unwary innocent [rather than a] trap for the unwary criminal"); United States v. Russell, 411 U.S. 423 (1973) (also recognizing due process defense of "outrageous governmental conduct"). The *Sorrells* and *Sherman* cases were not constitutional rulings. The courts instead based the entrapment defense on the presumed intent of the legislators that had passed the criminal statutes involved. The courts reasoned that Congress did not mean to criminalize acts that were entirely the creations of government action.

Just under half the states follow the "subjective" test developed in the federal courts. Roughly 10-15 states apply the "objective" approach, both through statutes and judicial rulings. See People v. Barraza, 591 P.2d 947 (Cal. 1979). Another group of about 10 states purports to follow a "hybrid" approach, combining both subjective and objective elements. England v. State, 887 S.W.2d 902 (Tex. Crim. App. 1994); State v. Vallejos, 945 P.2d 957 (N.M. 1997). If you were a prosecutor, would you systematically prefer one test over the other or would you guess that each test will be favorable to you in some factual settings and not in others? More than half the states have statutes addressing the entrapment defense; section 2.13 of the Model Penal Code, which opts for the objective approach, has been influential. What might lead a legislature to adopt instead the subjective standard for entrapment? Could it be that those who are entrapped lack the criminal intent that the legislature was targeting when it defined the crime? If one reason to adopt an objective entrapment standard is to protect the integrity of the courts, should the legislatures attempt to address this question or should they leave it to the courts themselves?

2. *The pliability of subjective standards.* Under the "subjective" version of the entrapment defense, a defendant must demonstrate that the government "induced" him to commit the crime and that he was not "predisposed" to commit the crime. In Jacobson v. United States, 503 U.S. 540 (1992), the Supreme Court applied once again its subjective standard of entrapment. The opening words of the opinion tell the reader right away about the Court's view of the case:

> In February 1984, petitioner, a 56-year-old veteran-turned-farmer who supported his elderly father in Nebraska, ordered two magazines and a brochure from a California adult bookstore. The magazines . . . contained photographs of nude preteen and teenage boys. The contents of the magazines startled petitioner, who testified that he had expected to receive photographs of "young men 18 years or older." [P]ostal inspectors found petitioner's name on the mailing list of the California bookstore. . . . There

> followed over the next two and one half years, repeated efforts by two Government agencies, through five fictitious organizations and a bogus pen pal, to explore petitioner's willingness to break the new [child pornography] law by ordering sexually explicit photographs of children through the mail.

The Court explained that the evidence must demonstrate predisposition both prior to and independent of the government's acts. On the evidence presented, the Court found that neither Jacobson's prior behavior nor his response to the agencies' inducements was enough to establish predisposition. Does this mean that the government must have reasonable suspicion of wrongdoing before proceeding with a sting operation against a target? See Foster v. State, 13 P.3d 61 (Nev. 2000) (undercover police need not have grounds for believing that target is predisposed; overrules earlier case case requiring reasonable cause); Maura Whelan, Lead Us Not Into (Unwarranted) Temptation: A Proposal to Replace the Entrapment Defense with a Reasonable Suspicion Requirement, 133 U. Pa. L. Rev. 1193 (1985). Prior to *Jacobson,* most federal cases concluded that the defendant was predisposed to commit a crime. Paul Marcus surveyed the federal law immediately after *Jacobson* and concluded that the decision changed the application of the subjective entrapment defense. He argues that courts are now more likely to scrutinize the government's conduct as part of the determination whether the defendant was predisposed to commit the crime and are more likely to rule that the defendant established a successful entrapment defense. See Paul Marcus, Presenting, Back from the (Almost) Dead, the Entrapment Defense, 47 Fla. L. Rev. 205 (1996).

3. *Physical injury limitation.* Note that the Model Penal Code provision on entrapment makes the defense unavailable when the crime threatens violence to someone other than the government agent making the proposition. Why does the code make this exception? Does the threat of violence have any bearing on the defendant's predisposition? On the acceptability of the government's conduct? This statutory limitation appears in many state codes and is equally common in statutes adopting subjective and objective standards for entrapment. Ky. Rev. Stat. §505.010 (subjective standard); Utah Code Ann. §76-2-303 (objective standard). Would this exception cover drug trafficking cases?

4. *Burden of proof; judge or jury.* In the federal system, and in some other jurisdictions using the subjective test, the defendant must demonstrate a prima facie case for entrapment by proving that the government "induced" the crime. In some systems, the defendant has only the burden of producing some evidence on this issue, and in fewer than 10 states the defendant must prove "inducement" by a preponderance of the evidence. If the defendant meets the burden, the burden shifts to the prosecution to prove beyond a reasonable doubt that the defendant *was* predisposed to commit the crime. Statutes adopting the objective test, along with several of the statutes employing the subjective test, leave the burden on the defendant to prove all elements of entrapment by a preponderance of the evidence. Which party is in the better position to bring forward proof on the various questions relevant to an entrapment defense? Most of the time, entrapment is a question for the jury to resolve. This is true particularly in jurisdictions using the subjective standard for entrapment, since the defense often boils down to the credibility of the defendant's claim that she had no predisposition to commit the crime. (Of course, the judge can take the issue away from the jury if there is insufficient evidence on one side of the question.) In jurisdictions following the objective standard, it is more common to give the

factfinding responsibility to the judge, who may be better suited to control the behavior of investigators and protect the integrity of the court. Would defendants prefer judges or juries as the primary decision maker for their entrapment claims?

5. *Entrapment and trial strategy.* When a defendant raises the entrapment defense, it has some important consequences at trial. Perhaps most important is the effect on the usual rules of evidence. Once a defendant claims entrapment, the rules barring the introduction of evidence of a defendant's prior criminal conduct are suspended. That evidence becomes relevant to proving predisposition; it also may be relevant to the reasonableness of the government's actions if government agents knew about the conduct. Because of this change in the rules of evidence, many defense lawyers consider entrapment to be a high-risk defense. Raising entrapment also affects the instructions a trial jury could receive about possible defenses. In many jurisdictions, a defendant raising the defense of entrapment traditionally had to admit to the *conduct* constituting the offense (but not necessarily the requisite state of mind). See Davis v. State, 804 So. 2d 400 (Fla. 2001). This was true even though a defendant ordinarily is free to raise inconsistent defenses. Now in the federal courts, along with a majority of state courts ruling on the issue (roughly 15), the defendant is entitled to pursue an entrapment defense (and to have the jury instructed accordingly) in any case in which there is sufficient evidence, even if the defendant is pursuing inconsistent defenses. See Mathews v. United States, 485 U.S. 58 (1988) (allowing inconsistent defenses); People v. Butts, 533 N.E.2d 660 (N.Y. 1988) (defendant can deny involvement in narcotics sales and obtain instruction on entrapment if evidence is sufficient). Are these special trial rules for entrapment necessary because the defense would otherwise distort the truth-seeking function of criminal trials? Or are they simply indications that entrapment is a disfavored defense?

6. *Common law in an age of statutes.* The *Lee* court argued that the "saving clause" statute prevented it from adopting an objective entrapment defense; the dissent read the statute differently. Who got the better of the argument? Does a legislature have the power to prevent state courts from considering some defenses to criminal charges? See Guido Calabresi, A Common Law for the Age of Statutes (1982). Perhaps the answer to this question depends on whether the entrapment defense has a constitutional basis rather than being strictly a creation of the common law or a rule of statutory construction. See Munoz v. State, 629 So. 2d 90 (Fla. 1993) (entrapment statute adopted subjective test and attempted to overrule earlier cases using objective test; entrapment defense in state rested in part on state constitution, so legislature could not eliminate it).

Problem 10-2. Outrageous Government Conduct

During the summer of 1988, defendants Jerome Johnson, a New Jersey state trooper, and Wanda Bonet, Johnson's girlfriend, met a person who became their cocaine supplier. On one occasion, Johnson told his supplier, "I would like to rip off a drug dealer with a lot of cocaine and then I could turn around and sell it and make some money." Some months later, Johnson's supplier was arrested while delivering a large quantity of cocaine to an undercover agent of the Drug Enforcement Administration Task Force. The supplier decided to cooperate with law enforcement authorities by becoming an informant. He told DEA agents that Johnson was willing to "rip off" drugs from a drug dealer and then sell those drugs for money.

The federal agents and the New Jersey State Police jointly developed a plan to give Johnson the opportunity to steal drugs from a drug dealer and to sell those drugs. The plan contemplated that the informant would tell Johnson that he knew of an opportunity for Johnson to steal drugs from a drug courier and make a lot of money; that he, the informant, was acting as a broker for the sale of a kilogram of cocaine; that he had arranged for a "mule," a paid courier, to transport the drugs by car to a meeting place with a prospective buyer; and that the informant and the seller of the cocaine would be in a second car following the mule. According to the plan, Johnson, wearing his state trooper uniform, would pretend to make a traffic stop of the mule's car at a prearranged location and then would seize the cocaine. The seller of the cocaine, following in the car with the broker-informant, would see the seizure and chalk up the loss of the cocaine as a cost of doing business. Johnson then would meet the broker at Johnson's apartment and sell the cocaine to the mule for $5,000.

When the informant presented and explained the scheme to Johnson, he agreed to participate and added new elements to the plan. He requested $1,000 cash in advance, an unmarked car, and a portable flashing red light to use to make the traffic stop. Johnson also indicated he would change shifts so that he would be off-duty at the time of the stop. On December 22, 1988, the informant and a detective, acting as the mule, met with Johnson and Bonet in their Newark apartment. The parties reviewed and discussed the details of the plan. The next day Johnson stopped the mule as planned and seized one kilogram of cocaine. The informant and a special agent, posing as the seller, drove off. Johnson drove to his apartment, followed by the mule. On his arrival at approximately 12:05 P.M., Johnson was arrested.

Johnson was indicted for drug offenses and for crimes related to the abuse of his office. He moved to dismiss the indictment on two grounds. First, he argued that the sting involved such outrageous government conduct that it violated state due process standards. Second, he claimed that the sting violated the New Jersey statutory entrapment defense, N.J. Stat. Ann. §2C:2-12, which provides as follows:

> A public law enforcement official or a person engaged in cooperation with such an official or one acting as an agent of a public law enforcement official perpetrates an entrapment if for the purpose of obtaining evidence of the commission of an offense, he induces or encourages and, as a direct result, causes another person to engage in conduct constituting such offense by [e]mploying methods of persuasion or inducement which create a substantial risk that such an offense will be committed by persons other than those who are ready to commit it.

How would you rule? Compare State v. Johnson, 606 A.2d 315 (N.J. 1992).

■ CINCINNATI POLICE DIVISION PROCEDURE MANUAL §12.131 CONFIDENTIAL INFORMANT MANAGEMENT AND CONTROL

A. A person must meet three criteria to establish them as a CI: (1) the person is in a unique position to help the Division in a present or future investigation, (2) the person will not compromise Division interests or activities, (3) the person will accept the direction necessary to effectively use their services.

B. Precautions when dealing with CIs:

1. Never provide CIs with knowledge of police facilities, operations, activities, or personnel.

2. Two police officers must be capable of contacting a CI. Two officers will be present at all contact with CIs unless otherwise approved by a supervisor. [W]hen dealing with CIs of the opposite sex or homosexual CIs, two officers will always be present. [T]wo officers will always be present when paying CIs.

3. Immediately document initial debriefing contacts with CIs on the Confidential Informant Registration and Reliability Report.

4. Document all significant contacts with CIs on the Controlling District/Section/Unit Debriefing Report. Examples of significant contact are: (a) receiving information about criminals or criminal activity including information from phone conversations, (b) any compensation made to CIs, (c) any contact that results in an arrest or the execution of a search warrant. . . .

D. Undesirable CIs are those who (1) commit an act which could endanger the life or safety of a police officer, (2) reveal the identity of a police officer to suspects, or in any other way compromise an official investigation, (3) try to use the Division to further criminal goals, (4) provide false or misleading information to police officers, (5) engage in conduct that brings discredit or embarrassment upon the Division. . . .

L. Controlled Purchases Using Confidential Informants:

(1) Get permission from an immediate supervisor before making controlled purchases.

(2) When possible, use CIs to introduce police officers to make purchases.

(3) Use a concealed body transmitting device and/or recording devices on CIs whenever possible. Never destroy recordings before the conclusion of court proceedings, including appeals.

(4) Search all CIs before and after conducting a controlled purchase of drugs. The Strip Search Law does not apply to the voluntary search of CIs. . . .

(5) Currency used in controlled purchases: (a) photocopy and record serial numbers, (b) two officers will witness buy money given to CIs.

(6) When possible, use two or more officers for surveillance of CIs during controlled purchases.

Notes

1. *Outrageous conduct: majority position.* Most state and federal courts recognize, at least theoretically, a constitutional defense to criminal charges based on the overly aggressive tactics of government investigators. In some jurisdictions, it is called "due process entrapment," while in others (including the federal system) it is known as "outrageous governmental conduct." United States v. Russell, 411 U.S. 423 (1973). However, the defense rarely succeeds. There is no clear consensus among courts on the elements necessary to prove the defense, although many courts consider the four issues raised by the New Jersey Supreme Court in State v. Johnson, 606 A.2d 315 (N.J. 1992), the case on which Problem 10-2 was based.

> Relevant factors are (1) whether the government or the defendant was primarily responsible for creating and planning the crime, (2) whether the government or the defendant primarily controlled and directed the commission of the crime, (3) whether

> objectively viewed the methods used by the government to involve the defendant in the commission of the crime were unreasonable, and (4) whether the government had a legitimate law enforcement purpose in bringing about the crime. Although courts have used varying formulations of the primary factors governing due process entrapment, the factors most invoked center around two major recurrent concerns: the justification for the police in targeting and investigating the defendant as a criminal suspect; and the nature and extent of the government's actual involvement in bringing about the crime.

606 A.2d at 323. The defense commonly appears in drug cases because it would be difficult to prosecute many narcotics violations (which are often consensual transactions leaving behind little evidence and few willing witnesses) without undercover operations.

Most courts and commentators note that there is some overlap between the defenses of subjective entrapment, objective entrapment, and due process "outrageous conduct." See Michael Seidman, The Supreme Court, Entrapment, and Our Criminal Justice Dilemma, 1981 Sup. Ct. Rev. 111. The various tests all allow for some inquiry into both the predisposition of the defendant and the reasonableness of the government's conduct.

2. *Per se outrageous conduct.* Most courts declare that they will assess outrageous misconduct claims by weighing factors on a case-by-case basis. On occasion, a court will declare a particular government tactic, regardless of the other circumstances in the case, to be outrageous conduct per se. One court has declared the use of contingency fees for informants to be outrageous governmental conduct per se. See State v. Glosson, 462 So. 2d 1082 (Fla. 1985); but see State v. Florez, 636 A.2d 1040 (N.J. 1994) (court considers contingency fee for confidential informant a troubling tactic, but not enough standing alone to warrant dismissal of charges). Some courts have also placed controlling weight on the government's use of informants who have a close personal relationship with the defendants; a few others have dismissed charges based on use of force by government agents. See People v. Isaacson, 378 N.E.2d 78 (N.Y. 1978). For most courts, however, circumstances such as these would weigh heavily against an investigation but would not necessarily invalidate the government's effort. As a police investigator, would you rather see a court apply per se rules about investigations or evaluate them case-by-case?

Are undercover operations simply too corrosive to tolerate in an open and democratic society? Consider this description of the use of informants in Communist East Germany: "Of all aspects of the MfS [Ministry for State Security], the generation of an army of individuals, willing to report suspicious information about acquaintances, friends, and family roused the fiercest resentment—and fear. The end result was to turn citizens against one another and to create an atmosphere of debilitating apprehension." Nancy Travis Wolfe, Policing a Socialist Society: The German Democratic Republic 78 (1992).

3. *Confidential informant guidelines.* The use of a confidential informant raises special difficulty for law enforcement agencies because the government has less control over the actions of its agent. The problem is most pronounced when the informant participates in a crime while being paid by the government, as opposed to simply telling a police officer about past crimes. The Cincinnati police guidelines regarding confidential informants illustrate how executive branch agencies respond to these special concerns. What dangers were the drafters of the Cincinnati guidelines trying to prevent?

Although the amounts of money paid to informants are often small, some cases involve huge sums. See David Rosenzweig, Undercover Informant Got $2 Million for Aiding Drug Probe, Los Angeles Times, Jan. 30, 1999, at B1. In some money laundering or fraud cases, the compensation for the witness comes from commissions paid by banks or other participants in the criminal scheme. Should the amount of compensation be based on the amount of physical danger an informant faces, the amount of loss to crime victims, or the amount of gain to criminals?

4. *Undercover operations guidelines.* The Federal Bureau of Investigation has guidelines on undercover operations that involve government agents rather than informants. They address the selection of targets for sting operations and the methods used to carry them out. The guidelines require a field agent to obtain prior authorization for certain undercover operations, including those that will last more than six months, target public officials or the news media, or require government agents to engage in a felony. See S. Rep. No. 682, 97th Cong., 2d Sess. 536-552 (1982). Most large police departments also have policies that address undercover operations, especially for narcotics and vice officers. For instance, the narcotics division of the Dallas Police Department requires written approval for all "long-term undercover operations" (longer than one to two hours). The undercover officer works with a partner whenever possible; when the officer must work undercover alone, a partner is still assigned to maintain daily contact, "cover" the undercover officer during sales, and maintain records and chain of custody for all evidence. The policy also forbids the officer to consume any narcotic unless forced to do so "under threat of immediate bodily injury." Procedure 5010 (1995). If you were drafting police guidelines on the subject of undercover investigations, what criteria would you set out for selecting the targets of undercover investigations? If you were drafting a statute on the subject, as opposed to internal guidelines, would the content of the provisions change?

5. *Supervision by prosecutors.* Prosecutors are often involved in planning and executing undercover operations. Although prosecutors have absolute immunity from any tort suit for their "prosecutorial" decisions, that immunity does not extend to a prosecutor's actions when advising criminal investigators about an undercover operation. See Burns v. Reed, 500 U.S. 478 (1991) (granting qualified "good faith" immunity but not absolute immunity to prosecutors for participation in investigations). What are the potential tort claims that might arise against a prosecutor who is advising criminal investigators?

Problem 10-3. The Mayor

Federal prosecutors and FBI investigators became convinced in the early 1980s that Mayor Marion Barry of the District of Columbia was involved in various illegal activities. Over an eight-year period, federal law enforcement agencies carried out 10 separate investigations of potential illegal actions by Barry, including bribery, campaign finance fraud, prostitution, and drug use. A grand jury heard accusations from several of Barry's associates (some of them convicted for selling drugs) that the mayor had purchased and used cocaine, but Barry testified before the grand jury that he never used cocaine. None of these investigations resulted in any criminal charges.

In December 1988, district police were notified that Charles Lewis, a friend of Barry, had offered drugs to a maid at a downtown hotel. The detectives were on their way to Lewis's room but left the hotel when they learned that Barry was in the room with Lewis. That incident renewed the government's interest in the mayor's long-rumored drug use.

To create an opportunity for Barry to commit a crime, the government asked for help from a former intimate friend of Barry's, Rasheeda Moore. Moore was willing to cooperate because she was facing criminal charges herself. In January 1990, the government flew Moore to Washington from California and got her a room at the Vista International Hotel. They paid to have her hair styled. On January 18, three days before Barry planned to announce his plans to seek reelection, the agents asked Moore to invite the mayor to her hotel room.

When Barry met Moore in the hotel lobby, he was at first reluctant to go up to her room. She convinced him to accompany her to the room, along with a woman she described as her cousin, Wanda. Wanda was actually an FBI agent. Once in the room, Barry engaged Moore in small talk and drank cognac. Then Barry asked, "Can we make love before you leave, before you leave town?" Moore complained that Barry wasn't sufficiently romantic: "I can't just jump into it." Then she said, "So what are you going to do? Let's do something."

A few minutes later, Barry asked Moore about Wanda, who had left the room a few minutes earlier: "Your friend mess around?" Moore, taking the question as one about drugs, responded, "She has some, yeah, sometimes. . . . She toots [snorts cocaine] more than she'll do anything else." Soon afterward, Barry said, "I don't have anything. What about you?" A short time later, Wanda returned to the room with crack cocaine. Moore presented Barry with a pipe loaded with crack cocaine, and Barry paid for it. Then Barry looked at the pipe and said "How does this work? . . . I never done it before."

Moore replied, "That's what we used to do all the time, what are you talking about?" Barry, however, insisted that he had never "done that before." Moore then said, "Put it in there. . . . Let me give you a lighter." Barry replied "You do it," but Moore said "No, I'm not doing nothing." Each insisted several more times that the other light the pipe. Moore asked, "Are you chicken?"

Eventually Barry lit the crack pipe, put it to his mouth and inhaled twice. Almost immediately, the mayor picked up his jacket and started for the door, as Moore asked if he wanted to smoke more of the crack. "No. You're crazy," Barry responded. Barry then turned for the door, and law enforcement agents burst in from the adjoining room.

A medic told Barry that he had been exposed to a dangerous substance and asked whether the mayor wanted to go to the hospital. Barry said no. "Man, I should have followed my first instincts, I tell you," he said. Then D.C. Police Sergeant James Pawlik said, "I mean, we really didn't want this to happen."

"I didn't want it to happen, either," Barry replied. "I should, if I had followed my instincts tonight, I'd have been all right. I should have stayed downstairs. Bitch kept insisting coming up here." After complaining about the tightness of the handcuffs, Barry spoke further about Moore: "She was slick, though. I should have known better when she wouldn't do it first. I should have known something was up." He repeatedly muttered, "Damn bitch set me up."

Pawlik asked Barry if he hadn't expected to be caught in a sting sooner or later. "I don't know," Barry said. "I guess you all been checking on me for a long time, huh?" "Obviously," Pawlik responded. "Some day it's got to happen."

"I guess you all figured that I couldn't resist that lady," Barry said. As the agents prepared to lead Barry from the room, Pawlik said, "When it's all over, it'll be better for everybody." Barry responded, "You think so?"

The government brought charges against Barry for perjury (based on his testimony to the grand jury that he had never used cocaine) and for possession of cocaine (a misdemeanor). The FBI's guidelines on undercover operations state that sting operations should be directed toward obtaining evidence of serious crimes by major criminal figures. The same guidelines suggest that officers should ordinarily arrest a suspect immediately after taking possession of cocaine (or making a purchase) and before the suspect smokes or inhales the drug.

Why did the prosecutors decide to give Barry an opportunity to commit only a misdemeanor (possession of a small amount of crack cocaine)? What form of the entrapment defense (if any) would you advise Barry to pursue? What outcome would you predict?

Problem 10-4. Rolling Drunks

Because of many reports of thefts and robberies near the intersection of Wilikina Drive and Kamehameha Highway, the Honolulu Police Department decided to carry out a series of "drunk decoy" operations in the area. They repeated the operation on eleven occasions between November and March, resulting in the arrests of 19 individuals.

The victim of each of these thefts was a police officer feigning drunkenness. The officer lay on his side in a fetal position with a paper bag containing a beer bottle in his hand. A wallet protruded from his rear pants pocket, with bills sticking out. Several other officers stationed themselves nearby and waited for possible criminal activity.

Shortly after 11:00 P.M. during one of these operations, Lucy Powell walked by the disguised officer. She then turned back, approached the apparently vulnerable victim, and stole the wallet. Two officers who witnessed the theft sprang from cover and arrested Powell as she left the scene.

Does Powell have a viable entrapment defense? Hawaii has adopted by statute the "objective" approach to entrapment, using language much like that found in the Model Penal Code. Compare State v. Powell, 726 P.2d 266 (Haw. 1986).

B. THE INVESTIGATIVE GRAND JURY

Efforts by police officers to gather information about criminal suspects have occupied most of our attention thus far. The police are indeed the government agents who gather information in most criminal law enforcement. But in more complex investigations, other institutions such as grand juries and regulatory bodies, often acting under prosecutorial guidance, become important players in the effort to collect information that could lead to criminal charges.

Unlike police departments, which emerged in this country late in the nineteenth century, the grand jury is an ancient institution. It can trace its heritage at least as far back as twelfth-century England. The grand jury began as a body of citizens that the courts empowered to investigate criminal violations in the vicinity. Initially, the criminal charges that the grand jury issued were based on the personal knowledge of grand jurors. Only later did they acquire the power to call witnesses and to consider evidence that representatives of the Crown placed before them.

The grand jury thrived when first transplanted to England's American colonies. Each state entering the Union prior to the Civil War created grand juries and gave them broad powers to call witnesses and to gather documents. Later in the nineteenth century, voters grew less enthusiastic about the institution (especially in new states, such as Colorado and Nebraska) and passed constitutional provisions allowing the legislature to abolish the grand jury altogether. Although many of the newer states no longer *required* indictments as the method of initiating charges in serious criminal cases, they retained the grand jury as one method of investigating important cases, particularly those involving political corruption, where the independence of the police or prosecutor might be in question. Because of special investigative powers given to grand juries, prosecutors found it convenient to rely on them to gather evidence in cases, such as those involving conspiracies and documentary material, where routine police work could not produce enough evidence.

The grand jury is technically an arm of the court, and a judge supervises some of its activities. For instance, a judge hears any motions to quash a subpoena and will enforce a subpoena if a witness refuses to comply. The court instructs the grand jurors at the beginning of their term about their general responsibilities. Despite this supervisory power, the judge is generally not present during grand jury proceedings, and state and federal courts have proven reluctant to interfere in the affairs of the grand jury.

In this section, we consider issues relating to the special investigative powers of grand juries and similar governmental bodies to subpoena testimony and evidence. We postpone until Chapter 13 our discussion of the charging functions of the grand jury.

1. Grand Jury Secrecy

A witness who receives a subpoena to testify before a grand jury enters an unfamiliar room where the prosecuting attorney asks most of the questions, the grand jurors listen, and the stenographer records everything said. The witness usually knows very little about the grand jury's overall investigation or her place in that investigation. In this setting, most of the information flows in one direction. The grand jury can obtain a lot of information without revealing much of its investigative strategy.

Witnesses, however, often have legal counsel who can make the grand jury less intimidating. In the more ordinary criminal case, an attorney enters the scene only after the government already has gathered most of its evidence. But lawyers have the opportunity to become involved earlier in more complex investigations because of the long time period involved: A white-collar crime case will often take months, or even years to investigate. Lawyers also get involved earlier in the more complex cases because larger amounts of money are often at stake, and the targets of the investigation can afford to hire an attorney. As you read the statutes and notes below, consider the intricate game that occurs when counsel and sophisticated grand jury witnesses face off against prosecutors trying to get the most information from witnesses without revealing too much about the grand jury's investigation.

■ FEDERAL RULE OF CRIMINAL PROCEDURE 6

(d) (1) Attorneys for the government, the witness under examination, interpreters when needed and, for the purpose of taking the evidence, a stenographer or operator of a recording device may be present while the grand jury is in session.

(2) During deliberations and voting. No person other than the jurors, and any interpreter necessary to assist a juror who is hearing or speech impaired, may be present while the grand jury is deliberating or voting.

(e) (1) All proceedings, except when the grand jury is deliberating or voting, shall be recorded stenographically or by an electronic recording device. An unintentional failure of any recording to reproduce all or any portion of a proceeding shall not affect the validity of the prosecution. The recording or reporter's notes or any transcript prepared therefrom shall remain in the custody or control of the attorney for the government unless otherwise ordered by the court in a particular case.

(2) A grand juror, an interpreter, a stenographer, an operator of a recording device, a typist who transcribes recorded testimony, an attorney for the government, or any person [assisting the attorney for the government] shall not disclose matters occurring before the grand jury, except as otherwise provided for in these rules. No obligation of secrecy may be imposed on any person except in accordance with this rule. A knowing violation of Rule 6 may be punished as a contempt of court.

■ COLORADO REVISED STATUTES §16-5-204(d)

Any witness subpoenaed to appear and testify before a grand jury or to produce books, papers, documents, or other objects before such grand jury shall be entitled to assistance of counsel during any time that such witness is being questioned in the presence of such grand jury, and counsel may be present in the grand jury room with his client during such questioning. However, counsel for the witness shall be permitted only to counsel with the witness and shall not make objections, arguments, or address the grand jury. Such counsel may be retained by the witness or may, for any person financially unable to obtain adequate assistance, be appointed in the same manner as if that person were eligible for appointed counsel. An attorney present in the grand jury room shall take an oath of secrecy. If the court, at an in camera hearing, determines that counsel was disruptive, then the court may order counsel to remain outside the courtroom when advising his client. No attorney shall be permitted to provide counsel in the grand jury room to more than one witness in the same criminal investigation, except with the permission of the grand jury.

Problem 10-5. Selecting Witnesses

Janet Terreton has contacted the federal government with information about possible corruption in New Jersey's state and local governments. Terreton's former employer, Anderson Hagelman, is the sole proprietor of two companies that do business with various units of local governments in New Jersey. She alleges that Hagelman, and many other businesses selling goods and services to state and local governments, have bribed governmental contracting officials to obtain the government contracts. Terreton resigned from her management position in Hagelman's firm two months before contacting the government after a dispute over her retirement compensation. Terreton's information ultimately arrives in the office of the U.S. Attorney. As the government attorney assigned to this matter, how would you begin the investigation? Should you, or the agents working with you, attempt to interview any witnesses outside the presence of the grand jury?

Notes

1. *Grand jury secrecy.* The proceedings of grand juries traditionally are secret. The federal rules of criminal procedure, like the rules and statutes of most states, codify the traditional practice: Only the grand jurors, attorneys for the government, the witness, and (sometimes) a stenographer can be present in the room. Each of these parties except for the witness has an obligation not to disclose what happens in the grand jury room. A classic explanation for the secrecy of grand jury proceedings appears in United States v. Amazon Industrial Chemical Corp., 55 F.2d 254, 261 (D. Md. 1931):

> The reasons which lie behind the requirement of secrecy may be summarized as follows: (1) To prevent the escape of those whose indictment may be contemplated; (2) to insure the utmost freedom to the grand jury in its deliberations, and to prevent persons subject to indictment or their friends from importuning the grand jurors; (3) to prevent subornation of perjury or tampering with the witnesses who may testify before the grand jury and later appear at the trial of those indicted by it; (4) to encourage free and untrammeled disclosures by persons who have information with respect to the commission of crimes; (5) to protect the innocent accused who is exonerated from disclosure of the fact that he has been under investigation, and from the expense of standing trial where there was no probability of guilt.

About 20 states have statutes or court rules, like the Colorado statute reprinted above, that allow a grand jury witness to bring an attorney into the grand jury room. See also Fla. Stat. §§905.17(1), (2). Rules of evidence do not apply to grand jury proceedings, and the witness's attorney typically may not object to any questions. What, then, is the attorney's function? Will the presence of an attorney in the grand jury room influence the type of questions asked or the witnesses selected to testify?

2. *Makeup and selection of the grand jury.* At common law, a grand jury had anywhere between 12 and 23 members. Federal grand juries have 16 to 23 members, Fed. R. Crim. P. 6(a), and most state grand juries stay within the common-law size limits. See Alaska Stat. §12.40.020 (12 to 18 jurors); Utah Code Ann. §77-10a-4 (9 to 15 jurors). Some jurisdictions have grand juries that sit routinely, and the court impanels such a grand jury on its own initiative; elsewhere, the prosecutor requests the court to impanel a grand jury for some special purpose. The clerk of the court summons the potential grand jurors, typically (as in the federal system) from the list of registered voters. The judge may excuse some potential jurors if service would be particularly burdensome to them. See Sara Sun Beale et al., Grand Jury Law and Practice §§3:04, 3:05, 4:8 (2d ed. 1997). What sorts of document requests will an investigative body of this type tend to make? How might the grand jury's requests for testimony and documents change if the court assigned staff members or experts to advise the grand jurors?

3. *Witness debriefing.* Although attorneys for grand jury witnesses are not allowed in the grand jury room in a majority of American jurisdictions, they still obtain information about the grand jury's questions and the witness's answers by debriefing their clients immediately after the testimony. Many attorneys also encourage their clients to step outside the grand jury room periodically (perhaps after each question) for a consultation. See Sara Sun Beale et al., Grand Jury Law and Practice §6:28 (2d ed. 1997) (surveying statutory and common law protections for witnesses' ability to consult counsel outside grand jury room). Some attorneys attempt to debrief witnesses who are not their clients. Statutes and rules of criminal procedure typically impose an obligation of secrecy on the grand jurors and the government attorneys but not on grand jury witnesses. See Fed. R. Crim. P. 6(e)(2); Ill. Code Crim. Proc. §112-6. About a dozen states have statutes or rules that prevent a grand jury witness from discussing her testimony with anyone other than her attorney. See N.C. Gen. Stat. §§15A-623(e), (g). What would be the likely attitude of government attorneys about witness debriefing? Is there anything government attorneys can or should do about it? See In re Grand Jury Proceedings, 558 F. Supp. 532 (W.D. Va. 1983) (defense lawyers may debrief all witnesses, but government attorneys may request grand jury witnesses not to discuss their testimony with others).

4. *Warnings to grand jury witnesses: constitutional requirements.* The witness who receives a subpoena to testify before the grand jury can be held in contempt of court for failing to appear, even if the witness plans only to invoke the Fifth Amendment privilege. Despite this element of coercion, the Supreme Court has decided (along with the great majority of state courts) that prosecutors need not give *Miranda* warnings to grand jury witnesses. United States v. Mandujano, 425 U.S. 564 (1976); State v. Driscoll, 360 A.2d 857 (R.I. 1976). Would you require a warning only for those witnesses who become "targets" of a grand jury investigation? Again, most jurisdictions have not required such warnings as a constitutional matter. See United States v. Washington, 431 U.S. 181 (1977) (no warning of "target" status is required by federal Constitution); People v. J.H., 554 N.E.2d 961 (Ill. 1990) (same for Illinois constitution); but see People ex rel. Gallagher v. District Court, 601 P.2d 1380 (Colo. 1979) (Colorado constitution requires warnings).

5. *Nonconstitutional requirements of warnings.* Despite a lack of success on the constitutional front, witnesses still often receive various warnings before appearing in front of the grand jury. In the federal system, the U.S. Attorney's Manual requires prosecutors to inform witnesses of their right to silence, the fact that statements to the grand jury can be used against the witness, and the fact that those who have retained attorneys may consult with their attorneys outside the grand jury room. See §§9-11.151. The manual also requires prosecutors to inform grand jury witnesses (and some nonwitnesses) of their status as "targets" of the investigation. See §§9-11.151 to 155. What would be the remedy for a violation of this written prosecutorial policy? In a strong minority of states, statutes require the prosecutor to inform grand jury witnesses of their right to silence, especially when the witness is a target of the investigation. Ill. Rev. Stat. ch. 38, para. 112-4(b); Tex. Code Crim. Proc. art. 20.17. Some state statutes also require the state to notify subpoena recipients if they are targets of the investigation. See Ind. Code Ann. §35-34-2-5. Why would a potential witness want to know if he is a target of the investigation? Some state statutes provide certain advantages (such as the right to consult with counsel in the grand jury room) only to targets and not to other witnesses.

6. *Grand jury witnesses versus police interrogation.* The question of warnings for grand jury witnesses calls for a comparison between interrogation during grand jury proceedings and custodial interrogation in a police station. There are certain similarities in the two experiences: In both cases, the witness is confined against her will, and the questioning takes place in isolation and in an unfamiliar setting. The two forms of questioning are also different: A person in police custody can end all questioning by invoking the right to silence, while a grand jury witness has no general right to silence and can be imprisoned for contempt of court for refusing to answer questions (unless the answers would be self-incriminating). Can you think of other parallels and differences between the two forms of questioning? Who goes to the grand jury and who goes to the police station?

7. *The legal ethics of contacting represented persons.* There may be times when a prosecutor would prefer to speak to witnesses outside the grand jury room. Such an interview can save the witness the trouble of appearing at a specific time and place to testify, and it allows the prosecutor to screen out all but the most relevant inculpatory evidence from the grand jury. But if the witness is represented by counsel, can the prosecutor accomplish these purposes? Can the prosecutor (or an investigator working with the prosecuting attorney) interview the witness without the witness's attorney present? The Model Rule of Professional Conduct 4.2 has some bearing on this question: "In representing a client, a lawyer shall not communicate about the subject of the representation with a person the lawyer knows to be represented by another lawyer in the matter, unless the lawyer has the consent of the other lawyer or is authorized by law to do so."

In light of this ethical rule, will criminal suspects be able to protect themselves from interrogation by placing a lawyer on retainer and notifying the government of that fact? Would principles of federalism prevent a state bar association from bringing disciplinary proceedings against a federal prosecutor who directly contacted represented persons? In 1989, Attorney General Richard Thornburgh issued a memorandum declaring that the supremacy clause of the U.S. Constitution prevented the state judiciary and state licensing authorities from regulating the conduct of federal prosecutors. In 1994, Attorney General Janet Reno issued a set of regulations on the subject, allowing a government attorney to contact a represented party without the consent of the party's lawyer under defined circumstances. Such a communication could occur, for instance, if it was "made in the course of an investigation, whether undercover or overt, of additional, different, or ongoing criminal activity," or if the government attorney believed that the communication could "protect against the risk of injury or death." 28 C.F.R. §77.6 (1995). Were these regulations consistent with the Model Rules?

In 1998, Congress became interested in this dispute between the Department of Justice and state bar associations, and passed the "McDade Act," requiring attorneys from the Department of Justice to comply with ethical rules established by state bar authorities. 28 U.S.C. §530B. What incentive did the U.S. Congress have to ignore the lobbying efforts of the Department of Justice and to impose state ethical rules on federal attorneys? The Department amended its 1994 regulations regarding contacts with represented persons. In some respects, the earlier 1994 regulations contained protections for represented persons that were greater than those provided under the ethics rules of most states. In light of the fact that attorneys are often involved very early in federal criminal investigations, does Model Rule 4.2 place excessive limits on federal prosecutors to perform investigations that would be available to any state or local police department questioning the same suspects?

2. *Immunity for Witnesses*

Although the grand jury can ask for a very broad range of testimony and documents, there is still some evidence beyond its reach. For instance, a grand jury cannot obtain information protected by common law privileges, such as the attorney-client privilege. There is also an important constitutional limit on the statements that a grand jury may obtain from a witness. The Fifth Amendment to the U.S. Constitution, and analogous provisions in almost every state constitution (all but two), create a privilege against self-incrimination:

> No person . . . shall be compelled in any criminal case to be a witness against himself. . . . [U.S. Const., amend. 5]
>
> No subject shall be . . . compelled to accuse or furnish evidence against himself. [N.H. Const., pt. I, art. 15]

A witness who receives a subpoena to appear and testify before a grand jury (or before a magistrate, administrative agency, or congressional committee, as the case may be) can invoke this constitutional privilege and refuse to answer questions when the answers would incriminate the witness. But this does not end the matter for the witness. Once he has invoked the privilege against self-incrimination, the prosecutor has another option. She can ask a court to order the witness to testify despite the risk of self-incrimination; in exchange, the prosecutor promises that no government agent will use the "compelled" testimony to further a later criminal prosecution against the witness. This promise is known as "immunity."

The question of immunity offers a useful vantage point for studying the privilege against self-incrimination. Just as the nature of a contract can be understood by exploring remedies for breach of contract, so the nature of the privilege against self-incrimination becomes clear when one explores the nature of the immunity necessary to overcome that privilege. The following case explores exactly what sort of promises a prosecutor must make to an immunized witness. Although the case deals with witnesses at trial, the same constitutional reasoning would apply to the immunity offered to grand jury witnesses.

■ COMMONWEALTH v. PATRICIA SWINEHART

664 A.2d 957 (Pa. 1995)

CAPPY, J.

This case presents the question of whether the use and derivative use immunity provided in 42 Pa. C.S. §5947,[1] is consistent with the Pennsylvania constitutional privilege at Article I, Section 9, against compelled self-incrimination. For the

1. The pertinent portions of the immunity statute that are at issue provide: . . .

(c) Whenever a witness refuses, on the basis of his privilege against self-incrimination, to testify or provide other information in a [judicial proceeding, and the judge] communicates to the witness an immunity order, that witness may not refuse to testify based on his privilege against self-incrimination.

reasons that follow we find that use and derivative use immunity is consistent with the protection provided under our state constitution.

[After the murder of David Swinehart, authorities charged his nephew, Thomas DeBlase, with the crime. Preliminary rulings and interlocutory appeals delayed his trial for several years. In the meantime,] Patricia Swinehart, the wife of the decedent, was arrested and charged with the murder of her husband, and with being a co-conspirator of DeBlase. DeBlase was subpoenaed as a witness in the Patricia Swinehart trial and offered a grant of immunity pursuant to 42 Pa. C.S. §5947. DeBlase moved to quash the subpoena and objected to the grant of immunity. . . . The trial court refused to quash the subpoena, approved the grant of immunity to DeBlase, and then when DeBlase still refused to answer, found him to be in both civil and criminal contempt. [Without DeBlase's testimony, the trial of Patricia Swinehart resulted in an acquittal. This is DeBlase's appeal of his contempt conviction.]

DeBlase asserts that the Act, which grants an immunized witness use and derivative use immunity, offers insufficient safeguards in exchange for the considerable protection guaranteed under Article I, Section 9 of the Pennsylvania Constitution which the immunized witness is forced to forsake. DeBlase acknowledges that the United States Supreme Court has upheld use and derivative use immunity as sufficient protection under the Fifth Amendment to the United States Constitution in Kastigar v. United States, 406 U.S. 441 (1972). He argues, however, that the Pennsylvania Constitutional protection is broader and can only be satisfied by a grant of transactional immunity.[5]

[We] will begin our analysis with a review of the text of the constitutional provision at issue, the history of that provision as related through legislative enactments and prior decisions of this Court, related case law from our sister states, and finally, policy considerations which include matters unique to our Commonwealth.

Article I, Section 9 [says that] "In all criminal prosecutions the accused . . . cannot be compelled to give evidence against himself. . . . A comparison of the actual language in Article I, Section 9 and the Fifth Amendment does not reveal any major differences in the description of the privilege against self-incrimination within the two Constitutions. As the words themselves are not persuasive of either interpretation on the issue at bar, we turn to the prior decisions of this Court which interpreted the right against self-incrimination as contained within the Pennsylvania Constitution.

[It] was not until after the United States Supreme Court decision in Counselman v. Hitchcock, 142 U.S. 547 (1892), that this Court addressed the question of immunity in relation to the privilege against self-incrimination. In *Counselman,* the United States Supreme Court rejected a federal statute which conferred only use

(d) No testimony or other information compelled under an immunity order, or any information directly or indirectly derived from such testimony or other information, may be used against a witness in any criminal case, except that such information may be used . . . in a prosecution [for perjury or false swearing.]

5. Generally three types of immunity are recognized, although some scholars treat "use" and "use and derivative use" immunity as one and the same. "Use" immunity provides immunity only for the testimony actually given pursuant to the order compelling said testimony. "Use and derivative use" immunity enlarges the scope of the grant to cover any information or leads that were derived from the actual testimony given under compulsion. Thus, under either "use" or "use and derivative use" immunity a prosecution against the witness is not foreclosed; any prosecution must, however, arise from evidence unrelated to the information which is derived from the witness' own mouth. "Transactional" immunity is the most expansive, as it in essence provides complete amnesty to the witness for any transactions which are revealed in the course of the compelled testimony.

immunity as being an insufficient substitute for the privilege guaranteed under the Fifth Amendment. . . . The Court then went on to conclude that a statutory grant of immunity, in order to be valid as against the Fifth Amendment, "must afford absolute immunity against future prosecution for the offense to which the question relates." In the wake of *Counselman,* only those legislative grants of immunity which compelled testimony from a witness in exchange for transactional immunity were found to be valid.

Thus, from 1892 until 1978, Pennsylvania recognized only transactional immunity as a sufficient exchange for compelling a witness to forsake the privilege against self-incrimination. The courts in Pennsylvania followed the lead of the United States Supreme Court on this issue.

The Pennsylvania Legislature also adhered to the dictates of the United States Supreme Court when drafting legislation on the issue of immunity grants for witnesses. Prior to the 1978 revisions, which are at issue in this case, the immunity conferred under the Act was transactional immunity. This shift in the type of immunity authorized by the Act can easily be traced to the United States Supreme Court decision in Kastigar v. United States, 406 U.S. 441 (1972).

In *Kastigar,* the United States Supreme Court found use and derivative use immunity to adequately protect the privilege against compulsory self-incrimination contained within the Fifth Amendment. The Court reconsidered its opinion in *Counselman* and determined that although use immunity offers insufficient protection under the Fifth Amendment, transactional immunity offers greater protection than is necessary and thus concluded that use and derivative use immunity would thereafter be sufficient.

> [The] privilege has never been construed to mean that one who invokes it cannot subsequently be prosecuted. Its sole concern is to afford protection against being forced to give testimony leading to the infliction of penalties affixed to criminal acts. Immunity from the use of compelled testimony, as well as evidence derived directly and indirectly therefrom, affords this protection. It prohibits the prosecutorial authorities from using the compelled testimony in any respect, and it therefore insures that the testimony cannot lead to the infliction of criminal penalties on the witness.

This shift by the United States Supreme Court away from transactional immunity in favor of use and derivative use immunity was commented upon by this Court in [1975. Following the *Kastigar* decision and our 1975 decision commenting favorably on *Kastigar,*] the immunity statute was revised to its present form wherein transactional immunity was replaced with use and derivative use immunity. [It] is clear that Pennsylvania, for the most part, followed the lead of the United States Supreme Court. . . .

Turning to our sister states, we find that they are evenly split on the issue of whether their state constitutions afford protection against compulsory self-incrimination greater than the Fifth Amendment in the wake of *Kastigar.* The six states that have rejected *Kastigar* and found their constitutions to require transactional immunity are [Alaska, Hawaii, Massachusetts, Mississippi, Oregon, and South Carolina].[13]

13. Eleven jurisdictions provide for transactional immunity through legislation. [These include California, Idaho, Illinois, Maine, Michigan, Nevada, New Hampshire, Rhode Island, Utah, Washington, and West Virginia.]

In each of [these six states], the state courts, relying upon their constitutional self-incrimination clauses, rejected legislation that had been developed post-*Kastigar* replacing transactional immunity with use/derivative use immunity. South Carolina and Alaska found the protection of use/derivative use immunity to be too cumbersome to enforce, citing the practical problems in determining whether or not later prosecutions stemmed from the immunized testimony. Mississippi had the same practical reasons for rejecting *Kastigar* as South Carolina and Alaska. Mississippi more bluntly phrased the problem as being one of having to rely upon the good faith of the prosecutor in use/derivative use situations. . . . Oregon found the rationale of *Kastigar* unpersuasive and chose to remain consistent with their case law which had always followed the reasoning of *Counselman*. . . .

The six states which have found use and derivative use immunity consistent with the self-incrimination clauses in their state constitutions are [Arizona, Indiana, Maryland, New Jersey, New York, and Texas].[14] [These courts] accepted use and derivative use immunity grants as consistent with their state constitutions [because they] found the state constitutional privilege at issue to be coextensive with the Fifth Amendment.

In reviewing the relevant opinions and legislation from our sister states we find no clear preference among the jurisdictions. What appears most striking among the courts which reject use/derivative use immunity is the concern for the practical effect of separating out the information garnered from the compelled testimony when later prosecuting the individual. It is this fear that the individual will be condemned by his/her own words, even inadvertently, which caused South Carolina, Alaska, Mississippi, and to some extent, Oregon, to reject use/derivative use immunity as inconsistent with the protection from self-incrimination found within their state constitutions. . . . To complete our analysis of this issue we now turn to a consideration of policy concerns which would affect our conclusion.

This case involves the juxtaposition of the privilege against self-incrimination and the need to compel testimony. The inherent conflict between these two important concepts is the heart of this case. Each of these concepts carr[ies] historical baggage of considerable proportion. Our system of jurisprudence abhors the ancient star chamber inquisitions which forced a witness into "the cruel trilemma of self-accusation, perjury or contempt." On the other hand, of equal importance to our system of justice is the ancient adage that "the public has a right to every man's evidence." The concept of compelling a witness to testify has been recognized in Anglo-American jurisprudence since the Statute of Elizabeth, 5 Eliz. 1, c.9, §12 (1562). Immunizing a witness has always been a feature of Pennsylvania jurisprudence. The dilemma in balancing these competing concerns centers on the type of immunity which can best provide the public with the information to which it is entitled in order to ferret out criminal activity and at the same time protect the rights of the witness being forced to testify under compulsion.

In urging this Court to declare the present immunity statute unconstitutional, DeBlase places great emphasis on the fact that Pennsylvania has historically required transactional immunity as the only adequate safeguard for compelling a witness's

14. Eighteen jurisdictions have provided for use/derivative use immunity through legislation passed after *Kastigar*. [These include Arkansas, Colorado, Connecticut, Delaware, Florida, Georgia, Iowa, Kansas, Louisiana, Minnesota, Montana, Nebraska, New Mexico, North Carolina, North Dakota, South Dakota, Vermont, and Wisconsin.]

testimony in violation of the right against self-incrimination. As with most critics of use/derivative use immunity, DeBlase asserts that only transactional immunity can truly protect a witness from later being condemned by his own words. The strongest argument for rejecting use/derivative use immunity is what has been commonly referred to as the "web effect." . . .

In fact in the instant case DeBlase argues that if forced to testify against his co-conspirator he will forever be caught within the web and his ability to receive a fair trial forever tainted. Specifically, the untraceable effects of his immunized testimony will impact upon the selection of his jury, the presentation of a defense, the ability to utilize character witnesses and infringe upon his decision to testify in his own behalf. The practical consequences of rejecting transactional immunity and leaving a witness clothed in only the protection of use/derivative use immunity constitutes the most salient argument against the constitutionality of 42 Pa. C.S. §5947.

On the other hand, there is no dispute that immunization of a witness is a necessary, effective and ancient tool in law enforcement. As the United States Supreme Court stated in *Kastigar,* "many offenses are of such a character that the only persons capable of giving useful testimony are those implicated in the crime." The very nature of criminal conspiracies is what forces the Commonwealth into the Hobson's choice of having to grant one of the parties implicated in the criminal scheme immunity in order to uncover the entire criminal enterprise. Thus, in order to serve justice an accommodation must be made; however, that arrangement should not place the "witness" in a better position as to possible criminal prosecution than he had previously enjoyed. A grant of immunity should protect the witness from prosecution through his own words, yet it should not be so broad that the witness is forever free from suffering the just consequences of his actions, if his actions can be proven by means other than his own words.

Clearly, there are compelling "pros" and "cons" on the question of the right against self-incrimination versus the need to immunize the witness. However, to elevate the right against self-incrimination above the right of the public to every person's evidence would not achieve a proper balance of these competing interests. Transactional immunity offers complete amnesty to the witness, a measure of protection clearly greater than the privilege against self-incrimination. The practical consequences, otherwise known as the "web effect," created by immunizing a witness should not tip the balance so far in favor of the witness that the Commonwealth is only left with the option of granting complete amnesty to a witness in order to fully investigate criminal enterprises and serve the public need for justice. Use/derivative use immunity strikes a better balance between the need for law enforcement to ferret out criminality and the right of the witness to be free of self-incrimination.

In this case we find that Article I, Section 9 is, in fact, more expansive than the Fifth Amendment; it is not, however, so expansive that the privilege against self-incrimination would require greater protection than that provided within the Act. . . . Recognizing the serious practical concerns which almost always accompany a later prosecution of the immunized witness, we hold that in the later prosecution, the evidence offered by the Commonwealth shall be reviewed with the most careful scrutiny. That is, the Commonwealth must prove, of record, by the heightened standard of clear and convincing evidence, that the evidence upon which a subsequent prosecution is brought arose wholly from independent sources. Accordingly, . . . the decision of the Superior Court is affirmed and this matter is remanded to the trial court for further proceedings consistent with this opinion. . . .

Notes

1. *Transactional and use immunity: majority position.* As the *Swinehart* court indicates, "use/derivative use" immunity is sufficient to satisfy the federal constitution, while states are evenly divided over the type of immunity that prosecutors must offer to witnesses before a court will compel the witness to give self-incriminating testimony. State v. Ely, 708 A.2d 1332 (Vt. 1997) (adopts *Kastigar* under state constitution and discusses split among states). Note that more states resolve this question by statute than by a constitutional court ruling. But courts have sometimes ruled on state constitutional grounds that a legislature must choose transactional rather than use immunity. See State v. Thrift, 440 S.E.2d 341 (S.C. 1994). Between 1973 and 2000, prosecutors in the federal system requested immunity for an average of 3,579 witnesses per year, in an average of about 24,000 grand jury proceedings per year. U.S. Dept. of Justice, Sourcebook of Criminal Justice Statistics 408, 411 (2001).

2. *Simple use immunity.* The Supreme Court's *Kastigar* decision approved of "use/derivative use" immunity: Later prosecution of an immunized witness is possible, but only if the prosecution's case is not based on the witness's statements *or* on any investigative leads obtained from that testimony. But was the Court correct to insist on this form of immunity, instead of "simple" use immunity? Simple use immunity would prevent use of immunized testimony in a later prosecution, but it would leave the prosecution free to use evidence obtained from investigative leads created by the witness's compelled testimony. For instance, the judicially compelled testimony of a murder suspect could not be introduced at the suspect's trial, but the murder weapon found through leads obtained during compelled testimony might come into evidence. Simple use immunity was an acceptable form of overcoming the self-incrimination privilege in most states during the nineteenth century. See State ex rel. Hackley v. Kelly, 24 N.Y. 74 (1861). Courts in England today do not exclude the fruits of testimony compelled under an immunity order. Does this approach, which bars only the use of a witness's actual statements, make the most sense of the Fifth Amendment's language: "No person . . . shall be compelled . . . to be *a witness* against himself"? Would your attitude about simple use immunity be different if you were interpreting a state provision such as the one in Texas, "[T]he accused . . . shall not be compelled to give evidence against himself"? Tex. Const. art. I, §10. For a constitutional defense of simple use immunity, see Akhil Amar and Renee Lettow, Fifth Amendment First Principles: The Self-Incrimination Clause, 93 Mich. L. Rev. 857 (1995).

3. *The history of the privilege against self-incrimination.* What exactly does the privilege against self-incrimination — in a federal or state constitution — protect? Because an immunity order must substitute for the privilege against self-incrimination, it creates an occasion for addressing this question. What are the relevant sources for an answer? The precise words of the constitutional provision surely should have some role. What is the relevance of the *history* of the self-incrimination concept? See generally Richard Helmholtz et al., The Privilege Against Self-Incrimination: Its Origins and Development (1997).

The Latin maxim *nemo tenetur seipsum prodere* ("no one is obliged to accuse himself") originated in the medieval law of the Roman Catholic church: It confirmed that even though a believer had a duty to confess sins to a priest, that obligation did not extend to criminal proceedings. The concept first became prominent in England in the ecclesiastical courts which were investigating and prosecuting those who resisted Anglican religious practice and belief. Puritans and other nonconformists invoked the concept to prevent their investigation and prosecution by ecclesiastical courts. See Michael Macnair, The Early Development of the Privilege Against Self-Incrimination, 10 Oxford J. Legal Stud. 66 (1990). One of the most famous of these crusaders for religious toleration and civil liberties was John Lilburn (a leader in a movement known as the "Levellers"), who invoked the privilege against self-incrimination as a natural right in various pamphlets and at his trial for treason. Lilburn also gave a pragmatic defense of the privilege: The privilege was necessary because "most men once entrusted with authority . . . pervert the same to their own domination and to the prejudice of our Peace and Liberties." Lilburn, An Agreement of the Free People of England (1649).

Despite these early uses in ecclesiastical courts, an evidentiary privilege against the use of self-incriminating statements did not operate in the English common law criminal courts until late in the eighteenth century, when defense counsel first became widely available and it was possible for a defendant to offer a defense without testifying himself. See John Langbein, The Historical Origins of the Privilege Against Self-Incrimination at Common Law, 92 Mich. L. Rev. 1047 (1994).

The American drafters of constitutions in the late eighteenth century all included a privilege against self-incrimination as part of a cluster of rights designed to reinforce the importance of the jury in a criminal trial as the central guarantee against oppressive government. But as Eben Moglen argues, the new constitutional provision was not meant to alter existing practices, and those practices included widespread techniques to encourage an accused to testify. See Eben Moglen, Taking the Fifth: Reconsidering the Origins of the Constitutional Privilege Against Self-Incrimination, 92 Mich. L. Rev. 1086 (1994); cf. Katharine B. Hazlett, The Nineteenth Century Origins of the Fifth Amendment Privilege Against Self-Incrimination, 42 Am. J. Legal Hist. 235 (1998). Defendants in custody had to appear before a magistrate who would routinely question the defendant about his involvement in the alleged crime. If the defendant confessed, the confession could form the basis for a summary conviction before the magistrate (for lesser offenses) or could be introduced at a later trial. If the defendant refused to answer a magistrate's questions, that fact could be revealed at trial. Does this history point in the direction of transactional immunity, use/derivative use immunity, or simple use immunity? Does it point in any direction at all?

4. *The purpose of the privilege.* If the text and history leave some doubt about the proper scope of the privilege, should legislators (who draft immunity statutes) and judges (who apply them) engage in some form of moral or political philosophy to flesh out the meaning of the privilege that is most attractive, or one most in keeping with our governmental structure and traditions? David Dolinko summarized the philosophical support for the privilege as follows:

> The rationales for the privilege fall, very roughly, into two categories. Systemic rationales are policies their proponents believe to be crucial to our particular kind of criminal justice system. Individual rationales are principles claimed to be entailed by a proper understanding of human rights or by a proper respect for human dignity and individuality. Among systemic rationales are the suggestions that the privilege encourages third-party witnesses to appear and testify by removing the fear that they might be compelled to incriminate themselves and removes the temptation to employ short cuts to conviction that demean official integrity. Individual rationales include the arguments that compelled self-incrimination works an unacceptable cruelty or invasion of

> privacy, as well as the notion of respect for the inviolability of the human personality, and the belief that punishing an individual for silence or perjury when he has been placed in a position in which his natural instincts and personal interests dictate that he should lie is an intolerable invasion of his personal dignity.

Dolinko, Is There a Rationale for the Privilege Against Self-Incrimination? 33 UCLA L. Rev. 1063 (1986). The philosopher Jeremy Bentham criticized some of the leading arguments in favor of the privilege. He listed them as follows:

> 2. The old woman's reason. The essence of this reason is contained in the word *hard:* 'tis hard upon a man to be obliged to criminate himself. Hard it is upon a man, it must be confessed, to be obliged to do any thing that he does not like. That he should not much like to do what is meant by his criminating himself, is natural enough; for what it leads to, is, his being punished. [But] did it ever yet occur to a man to propose a general abolition of all punishment, with this hardship for a reason for it? . . .
>
> You know of such or such a paper; tell us where it may be found. A request thus simple, your tenderness shudders at the thoughts of putting to a man: his answer might lead to the execution of that justice, which you are looking out for pretences to defeat. This request, you abhor the thought of putting to him: but what you scruple not to do (and why should you scruple to do it?) is, to dispatch your emissaries in the dead of night to his house, to that house which you call his castle, to break it open, and seize the documents by force. . . .
>
> 3. The fox-hunter's reason. This consists in introducing upon the carpet of legal procedure the idea of *fairness,* in the sense in which the word is used by sportsmen. The fox is to have a fair chance for his life: he must have . . . leave to run a certain length of way, for the express purpose of giving him a chance for escape. . . . In the sporting code, these laws are rational, being obviously conducive to the professed end. Amusement is that end. [The] use of a fox is to be hunted; the use of a criminal is to be tried. . . .
>
> 4. Confounding interrogation with torture: with the application of physical suffering, till some act is done; in the present instance, till testimony is given to a particular effect required. [The] act of putting a question to a person whose station is that of defendant in a cause, is no more an act of torture than the putting the same question to him would be, if, instead of being a defendant, he were an extraneous witness. [If] any thing he says should be mendacious, he is liable to be punished for it. . . .
>
> 5. Reference to unpopular institutions. Whatever Titius did was wrong: but this is among the things that Titius did; therefore this is wrong: such is the logic from which this sophism is deduced. In the apartment in which the court called the Court of Star-chamber sat, the roof had stars in it for ornaments. [The] judges of this court conducted themselves very badly: therefore judges should not sit in a room that has had stars in the roof. [Using this reasoning, lawyers claim that the Star Chamber was a bad court because of its] abominable practice of asking questions, by the abominable attempt to penetrate to the bottom of a cause.

5 Bentham, Rationale of Judicial Evidence 230-243 (1827). Which of the possible rationales can best explain limitations on the applicability of the concept (i.e., its use to protect a person from criminal but not civil consequences of wrongdoing, or its application only to "testimony" and not other forms of compelled cooperation with a prosecution, such as participation in a lineup)? Which of the "principled" rationales described above might support transactional immunity?

5. *Prosecution based on independent sources.* As the *Swinehart* court indicates, the government might successfully prosecute an immunized witness for the crime

that is the subject of the testimony, but only under limited circumstances. The prosecutors must show that the evidence upon which a subsequent prosecution is brought "arose wholly from independent sources" and that they did not use the compelled testimony "in any respect." If you were a prosecutor in such a case, how would you attempt to prove that your evidence was based on "independent" sources? Consider this policy from the U.S. Department of Justice Criminal Resource Manual, §9-706:

> [P]rosecutors should take the following precautions in the case of a witness who may possibly be prosecuted for an offense about which the witness may be questioned during his/her compelled testimony: (1) Before the witness testifies, prepare for the file a signed and dated memorandum summarizing the existing evidence against the witness and the date(s) and source(s) of such evidence; (2) ensure that the witness's immunized testimony is recorded verbatim and thereafter maintained in a secure location to which access is documented; and (3) maintain a record of the date(s) and source(s) of any evidence relating to the witness obtained after the witness has testified pursuant to the immunity order.

How often will these procedures be feasible? How often will they suffice when the defendant raises a constitutional challenge to the prosecution?

6. *Effect of immunity in other jurisdictions.* If a state prosecutor immunizes a grand jury witness and compels self-incriminating testimony, what assurance does the witness have that federal prosecutors will not use the testimony as a basis for federal criminal charges? The Supreme Court has declared that the Fifth Amendment requires federal prosecutors to respect the immunity grants of state governments. Murphy v. Waterfront Commission, 378 U.S. 52 (1964). Does this ruling create a potential source of conflict between state and federal authorities? If so, how might the various actors respond to the conflict?

7. *Invoking the privilege based on potential future prosecutions.* Although the Fifth Amendment speaks of a privilege "in any criminal case," a person need not testify in a criminal courtroom to invoke the privilege. In fact, it is extraordinarily easy to invoke Fifth Amendment protections, because they apply to any legally compelled statements that *could* lead to the discovery of incriminating evidence, even though the statements themselves are not incriminating and are not introduced into evidence. Such statements would include grand jury testimony or testimony in a civil trial. For instance, in Ohio v. Reiner, 532 U.S. 17 (2001), the court held that a witness' denial of all culpability for a crime does not prevent the witness from validly claiming the Fifth Amendment privilege. The relevant test is whether the witness has "reasonable cause to apprehend danger" from a truthful answer. But cf. United States v. Balsys, 524 U.S. 666 (1998) (federal government issued administrative subpoena to determine whether Balsys lied in his immigration application about his activities during World War II; Balsys claimed that an answer to the questions might expose him to prosecution in foreign countries; Court holds that concern with foreign prosecution was not an adequate basis for invoking privilege).

3. Document Subpoenas

Documents are the stock in trade of an investigative grand jury. The grand jury obtains documents by issuing subpoenas to document holders, compelling them to appear before the grand jury with the documents in hand. In reality, the prosecutor who advises the grand jury draws up the subpoena duces tecum describing the documents the grand jury demands. The terms of the subpoena are often very broad, and courts and legislatures have placed few if any bounds on the document requests. There is no requirement for the grand jury to show probable cause or reasonable suspicion that the documents they request will contain evidence of a crime. Historically, the documents needed only to be relevant to some legitimate grand jury inquiry. In the following case, consider whether the Supreme Court places any limits on the documents a grand jury may request.

■ UNITED STATES v. R. ENTERPRISES, INC.

498 U.S. 292 (1991)

O'CONNOR, J.

This case requires the Court to decide what standards apply when a party seeks to avoid compliance with a subpoena duces tecum issued in connection with a grand jury investigation.

Since 1986, a federal grand jury sitting in the Eastern District of Virginia has been investigating allegations of interstate transportation of obscene materials. In early 1988, the grand jury issued a series of subpoenas to three companies — Model Magazine Distributors, Inc. (Model), R. Enterprises, Inc., and MFR Court Street Books, Inc. (MFR). Model is a New York distributor of sexually oriented paperback books, magazines, and videotapes. R. Enterprises, which distributes adult materials, and MFR, which sells books, magazines, and videotapes, are also based in New York. All three companies are wholly owned by Martin Rothstein. The grand jury subpoenas sought a variety of corporate books and records and, in Model's case, copies of 193 videotapes that Model had shipped to retailers in the Eastern District of Virginia. All three companies moved to quash the subpoenas, arguing that the subpoenas called for production of materials irrelevant to the grand jury's investigation and that the enforcement of the subpoenas would likely infringe their First Amendment rights. [The district court denied the motions.]

The grand jury occupies a unique role in our criminal justice system. It is an investigatory body charged with the responsibility of determining whether or not a crime has been committed. Unlike this Court, whose jurisdiction is predicated on a specific case or controversy, the grand jury can investigate merely on suspicion that the law is being violated, or even just because it wants assurance that it is not. The function of the grand jury is to inquire into all information that might possibly bear on its investigation until it has identified an offense or has satisfied itself that none has occurred. As a necessary consequence of its investigatory function, the grand jury paints with a broad brush. A grand jury investigation is not fully carried out until every available clue has been run down and all witnesses examined in every proper way to find if a crime has been committed. [The] Government cannot be required to justify the issuance of a grand jury subpoena by presenting evidence sufficient to establish probable cause because the very purpose of requesting the information is to ascertain whether probable cause exists.

[Any requirement that the government show probable cause or the relevance of a request in a grand jury subpoena] ignores that grand jury proceedings are subject to strict secrecy requirements. See Fed. R. Crim. P. 6(e). Requiring the

Government to explain in too much detail the particular reasons underlying a subpoena threatens to compromise the indispensable secrecy of grand jury proceedings. Broad disclosure also affords the targets of investigation far more information about the grand jury's internal workings than the Federal Rules of Criminal Procedure appear to contemplate.

The investigatory powers of the grand jury are nevertheless not unlimited. Grand juries are not licensed to engage in arbitrary fishing expeditions, nor may they select targets of investigation out of malice or an intent to harass. In this case, the focus of our inquiry is the limit imposed on a grand jury by Federal Rule of Criminal Procedure 17(c), which governs the issuance of subpoenas duces tecum in federal criminal proceedings. The Rule provides that "[the] court on motion made promptly may quash or modify the subpoena if compliance would be unreasonable or oppressive."

This standard is not self-explanatory. [What] is reasonable depends on the context. . . . In the grand jury context, the decision as to what offense will be charged is routinely not made until after the grand jury has concluded its investigation. One simply cannot know in advance whether information sought during the investigation will be relevant and admissible in a prosecution for a particular offense.

To the extent that Rule 17(c) imposes some reasonableness limitation on grand jury subpoenas, however, our task is to define it. In doing so, we recognize that a party to whom a grand jury subpoena is issued faces a difficult situation. As a rule, grand juries do not announce publicly the subjects of their investigations. A party who desires to challenge a grand jury subpoena thus may have no conception of the Government's purpose in seeking production of the requested information. Indeed, the party will often not know whether he or she is a primary target of the investigation or merely a peripheral witness. Absent even minimal information, the subpoena recipient is likely to find it exceedingly difficult to persuade a court that compliance would be unreasonable. . . .

Our task is to fashion an appropriate standard of reasonableness, one that gives due weight to the difficult position of subpoena recipients but does not impair the strong governmental interests in affording grand juries wide latitude, avoiding minitrials on peripheral matters, and preserving a necessary level of secrecy. We begin by reiterating that the law presumes, absent a strong showing to the contrary, that a grand jury acts within the legitimate scope of its authority. Consequently, a grand jury subpoena issued through normal channels is presumed to be reasonable, and the burden of showing unreasonableness must be on the recipient who seeks to avoid compliance. . . . Drawing on the principles articulated above, we conclude that where, as here, a subpoena is challenged on relevancy grounds, the motion to quash must be denied unless the district court determines that there is no reasonable possibility that the category of materials the Government seeks will produce information relevant to the general subject of the grand jury's investigation. . . .

It seems unlikely, of course, that a challenging party who does not know the general subject matter of the grand jury's investigation, no matter how valid that party's claim, will be able to make the necessary showing that compliance would be unreasonable. After all, a subpoena recipient cannot put his whole life before the court in order to show that there is no crime to be investigated. Consequently, a court may be justified in a case where unreasonableness is alleged in requiring the Government to reveal the general subject of the grand jury's investigation before requiring the challenging party to carry its burden of persuasion. We need not resolve this question in the present case, however, as there is no doubt that respondents knew the subject of the grand jury investigation pursuant to which the business records subpoenas were issued. . . .

Applying these principles in this case demonstrates that the District Court correctly denied respondents' motions to quash. It is undisputed that all three companies — Model, R. Enterprises, and MFR — are owned by the same person, that all do business in the same area, and that one of the three, Model, has shipped sexually explicit materials into the Eastern District of Virginia. The District Court could have concluded from these facts that there was a reasonable possibility that the business records of R. Enterprises and MFR would produce information relevant to the grand jury's investigation into the interstate transportation of obscene materials. Respondents' blanket denial of any connection to Virginia did not suffice to render the District Court's conclusion invalid. A grand jury need not accept on faith the self-serving assertions of those who may have committed criminal acts. Rather, it is entitled to determine for itself whether a crime has been committed. . . .

STEVENS, J., concurring in part and concurring in the judgment.

Federal Rule of Criminal Procedure 17(c) authorizes a federal district court to quash or modify a grand jury subpoena duces tecum "if compliance would be unreasonable or oppressive." This Rule requires the district court to balance the burden of compliance, on the one hand, against the governmental interest in obtaining the documents on the other. A more burdensome subpoena should be justified by a somewhat higher degree of probable relevance than a subpoena that imposes a minimal or nonexistent burden. Against the procedural history of this case, the Court has attempted to define the term "reasonable" in the abstract, looking only at the relevance side of the balance. Because I believe that this truncated approach to the Rule will neither provide adequate guidance to the district court nor place any meaningful constraint on the overzealous prosecutor, I add these comments.

The burden of establishing that compliance would be unreasonable or oppressive rests, of course, on the subpoenaed witness. . . . This showing might be made in various ways. Depending on the volume and location of the requested materials, the mere cost in terms of time, money, and effort of responding to a dragnet subpoena could satisfy the initial hurdle. Similarly, if a witness showed that compliance with the subpoena would intrude significantly on his privacy interests, or call for the disclosure of trade secrets or other confidential information, further inquiry would be required. Or, as in this case, the movant might demonstrate that compliance would have First Amendment implications.

The trial court need inquire into the relevance of subpoenaed materials only after the moving party has made this initial showing. And, as is true in the parallel context of pretrial civil discovery, a matter also committed to the sound discretion of the trial judge, the degree of need sufficient to justify denial of the motion to quash will vary to some extent with the burden of producing the requested information. For the reasons stated by the Court, in the grand jury context the law enforcement interest will almost always prevail, and the documents must be produced. I stress, however, that the Court's opinion should not be read to suggest that the deferential relevance standard the Court has formulated will govern decision in every case, no matter how intrusive or burdensome the request.

■ OHIO REVISED CODE §2939.12

When required by the grand jury, prosecuting attorney, or judge of the court of common pleas, the clerk of the court of common pleas shall issue subpoenas and other process to any county to bring witnesses to testify before such jury.

■ ARKANSAS STATUTES §16-43-212

(a) The prosecuting attorneys and their deputies may issue subpoenas in all criminal matters they are investigating and may administer oaths for the purpose of taking the testimony of witnesses subpoenaed before them. Such oath when administered by the prosecuting attorney or his deputy shall have the same effect as if administered by the foreman of the grand jury. . . .

(b) The subpoena provided for in subsection (a) of this section shall be served in the manner as provided by law and shall be returned, and a record made and kept, as provided by law for grand jury subpoenas. . . .

Notes

1. *Breadth of document subpoena.* As *R. Enterprises* states, a recipient of a grand jury subpoena can challenge both the breadth of the subpoena and the burden of compliance. The Supreme Court stated in Oklahoma Press Publishing Co. v. Walling, 327 U.S. 186 (1946), that an unreasonably indefinite or overbroad subpoena might violate the Fourth Amendment or perhaps due process; in many states, such a subpoena would also violate statutes or rules of procedure. Note that in *R. Enterprises,* Federal Rule of Criminal Procedure 17(c) placed the most pertinent limit on the range of documents requested: Compliance must not be "unreasonable or oppressive." What specific facts might convince a court that a particular subpoena is overbroad or too indefinite? Does the subject matter of the grand jury's investigation matter? How about the cost of collecting relevant documents? The proportion of a business's documents falling within the terms of the subpoena (as opposed to the absolute number of documents)?

2. *The justification needed for a subpoena.* The *R. Enterprises* court followed the majority position in concluding that the prosecution does not need to make any preliminary showing of the relevance of testimony or other evidence sought through a grand jury subpoena. The probable cause necessary to support a search warrant is not a prerequisite for a grand jury subpoena. As the Court reasoned in United States v. Dionisio, 410 U.S. 1 (1973), a subpoena is different from an arrest, or even a more limited "stop," because the subpoena is served like any other legal process and involves no stigma and no force. Although the recipient of a subpoena to testify before a grand jury might challenge it on relevance grounds, it is very difficult to succeed on such a claim, in light of the breadth of the grand jury's duties to investigate any violations of the criminal law. Again, the *R. Enterprises* court is typical in its willingness to allow the grand jury to obtain documents and testimony relevant to a broad range of *potentially* criminal conduct. A few jurisdictions have required a modest grand jury showing of relevance. A grand jury subpoena in these courts is enforceable only if the grand jury (or the prosecutor on behalf of the grand jury)

affirms that the testimony or documents it seeks will be relevant to a legitimate subject of inquiry. See In re Grand Jury Proceeding, Schofield I, 486 F.2d 85 (3d Cir. 1973); Robert Hawthorne, Inc. v. County Investigating Grand Jury, 412 A.2d 556 (Pa. 1980). Would this preliminary statement from the grand jury make it any easier for the subpoena recipient to show that the subpoena is not relevant to some possible investigation? Should the level of justification to support a grand jury subpoena turn on the type of document involved? See State v. Nelson, 941 P.2d 441 (Mont. 1997) (state constitution requires state to show probable cause to support investigative subpoena for discovery of medical records).

3. *The prosecutor and grand jury subpoenas.* The subpoenas requiring witnesses to appear before a grand jury are, strictly speaking, issued under the authority of the grand jury itself. In practice, however, the prosecutor coordinating the grand jury's investigation has virtually complete control over the subpoenas that issue. Some statutes, such as the Ohio statute above, give independent authority to the prosecutor to issue grand jury subpoenas. State v. Guido, 698 A.2d 729 (R.I. 1997) (prosecutor used subpoena to obtain document for delivery to State Attorney General, grand jury did not see it, information issued on basis of document; no abuse of grand jury power). Others give the prosecutor the power to subpoena a witness only if the grand jury approves of the request, either before or after the subpoena issues.

The Arkansas statute reprinted above is an unusual one, giving the prosecutor the subpoena power completely separate from the grand jury. See also Mich. Comp. Laws 767A.1 et seq. (empowers prosecutors to issue investigatory subpoenas; judge must find probable cause that felony has been committed and that the person subpoened "may have knowledge regarding the commission of the felony," before authorizing investigative subpoena); Oman v. State, 737 N.E.2d 1131 (Ind. 2000) (prosecutor acting without grand jury must get court approval to subpoena documents). In the many states where prosecutors have no such subpoena power, do they miss significant investigative opportunities? Must they conduct all their witness interviews in front of the grand jury? How do prosecutors ever speak in private with hostile witnesses during an investigation? Some states (fewer than a dozen) allow a magistrate to issue a subpoena to witnesses during an investigation, requiring the witness to appear before the magistrate rather than a grand jury. This system is sometimes called the "one-man grand jury." See Idaho Code §19-3004. Would you insist on secrecy in such proceedings, as in grand jury proceedings? Would you allow the witness to have counsel present during the testimony?

4. *Administrative subpoenas.* Many regulatory agencies have the power to issue subpoenas calling on recipients to testify or to submit documents to the agency. It can use that information for many purposes, including the creation of a case file that the agency can refer to prosecutors with a recommendation that they pursue criminal charges. The standards for judging the validity of administrative subpoenas are roughly the same as those described above for grand jury subpoenas. United States v. Powell, 379 U.S. 48, 57-58 (1964), described in these terms the constitutional prerequisites for a valid summons issued by the Internal Revenue Service:

> [The agency] must show that the investigation will be conducted pursuant to a legitimate purpose, that the inquiry may be relevant to the purpose, that the information sought is not already within the Commissioner's possession, and that the administrative steps required by the [Internal Revenue Code] have been followed — in particular, that the "Secretary or his delegate," after investigation, has determined the further examination to be necessary and has notified the taxpayer in writing to that effect.

These administrative subpoenas are issued by full-time governmental entities, staffed by experts in the relevant subject matter. How might the differences between grand juries and administrative agencies affect the sort of evidence that agencies might request and receive?

Problem 10-6. Subpoena Versus Search Warrant

After a violent clash at Stanford University between student antiwar protesters and local police officers, the district attorney's office opened a grand jury investigation to determine the identity of any students who assaulted the officers. Some of the students had assaulted the officers with sticks and clubs, and both students and officers were seriously injured. A few days after the grand jury started to hear testimony, a special edition of the *Stanford Daily,* a student newspaper, carried articles and photographs about the student protest and the violent events of that day. The photographs were the work of a staff photographer for the *Daily.* The police believed that the staff photographer might have taken additional pictures that would help identify the students who had assaulted the officers.

The day after the pictures were published, the district attorney's office secured a warrant to search the *Daily*'s offices for negatives, film, and pictures showing the events and occurrences at the protest. The warrant affidavit contained no allegation that members of the *Daily* staff were in any way involved in unlawful acts during the protest. Four police officers executed the search warrant later the same day. While staff members at the *Daily* looked on, the officers searched photographic laboratories, filing cabinets, desks, and wastepaper baskets. Some of the files they searched contained notes and correspondence. Some of the materials were confidential, although no staff member informed the officers of that fact. The search revealed only the photographs that had already been published in the *Daily,* and the police removed no materials from the *Daily*'s office.

The *Daily* and various members of its staff brought a civil action in federal court against the police officers who conducted the search, the chief of police, the district attorney and one of his deputies, and the judge who had issued the warrant. The complaint alleged that the search of the *Daily*'s office was a violation of the First, Fourth, and Fourteenth Amendments of the U.S. Constitution. Assuming there was probable cause to support the search warrant, how would you argue this case on behalf of the *Daily*? Compare Zurcher v. Stanford Daily, 436 U.S. 547 (1978).

Notes

1. *Subpoenas and search warrants.* A prosecutor advising a grand jury during an investigation may have the choice of obtaining documents through a subpoena or a search warrant. What considerations will help the prosecutor make the choice? As we have seen, a subpoena requires the government to show no reasonable suspicion or probable cause to believe that the subpoena will produce evidence of a crime, and it requires virtually no showing of relevance. A search warrant, of course, must be based on probable cause and must particularly describe the place to be searched and the things to be seized. Does a subpoena give the government a way to bypass all the ordinary restraints on searches and seizures? Is the deference to grand jury

requests a relic, or are grand jury investigations truly different from investigations that would require a search warrant? Which method is likely to produce more evidence? Which will be more intrusive and which will cost the recipient more to comply with? State and federal statutes make it a crime for a person to destroy or alter documents that have been subpoenaed by a grand jury. How might these statutes affect a prosecutor's choice about the timing, scope, and recipients of subpoenas?

2. *Searches and freedom of the press.* In Zurcher v. Stanford Daily, 436 U.S. 547 (1978), the Supreme Court considered the validity of a search warrant authorizing the search of a newspaper's offices for photographs of demonstrators who had injured several police officers. The Court concluded that the Constitution imposed no special requirements for "third party" searches: The probable cause necessary to obtain a warrant was sufficient justification for a search, even if the target of the search was a newspaper not itself involved in wrongdoing. Congress responded to this decision by passing the Privacy Protection Act of 1980, 42 U.S.C. §2000aa. The statute, recognizing the special threats to the constitutional freedom of the press that are involved with searches of newspaper offices, creates a presumption in favor of subpoenas rather than search warrants to obtain documents from publishers. It prevents all criminal law enforcement agents (both state and federal) from searching for or seizing any "work-product materials" possessed by a publisher or broadcaster, unless there is probable cause to believe that the publisher has committed a crime relating to the documents or that immediate seizure is necessary to prevent death or serious bodily injury. Is this statute sufficient to protect the special First Amendment concerns involved in the search of newspaper offices? Cf. Branzburg v. Hayes, 408 U.S. 665 (1972) (enforcing grand jury subpoena for testimony of news reporter despite claim of privilege for news sources). Department of Justice regulations establish a similar presumption in favor of subpoenas rather than search warrants for document searches in the offices of attorneys, physicians, and clergy. 28 C.F.R. §59.4(b). Those regulations (unlike the statute) apply only to searches by federal agents. Why treat these categories of document holders any differently from other third parties who hold possible evidence of a crime?

3. *Attorneys as subpoena and search targets.* Internal guidelines at the Department of Justice require special authorization before seeking a subpoena of an attorney to obtain information about that attorney's representation of a client. Before a federal prosecutor may request such a subpoena, the U.S. Attorneys' Manual §9-13.410 requires certification of the following: (1) information is not privileged, (2) information is reasonably necessary to complete investigation, (3) alternative sources of the information are not available, and (4) need for information outweighs "potential adverse effects" on attorney-client relationship. What sorts of harms might flow from issuing a subpoena to an attorney? One of the ABA Model Rules of Professional Conduct, Rule 3.8(f), at one time required a prosecutor to obtain judicial approval after an adversarial hearing before she could issue a grand jury subpoena to a lawyer. The rule has since been revised to remove the requirement of judicial approval, but ethics rules in a handful of states still retain it. Is the requirement consistent with the guidelines in the U.S. Attorneys' Manual?

Section 9-13.420 of the U.S. Attorney's Manual creates special rules for the use of search warrants to search the offices of attorneys who are suspects, subjects, or targets of a criminal investigation. The application may go forward only if there is a "strong need" for material and if alternatives (such as a subpoena) will not work because of a risk of destroyed documents. The rules call for the creation of a "privilege team" consisting of agents and lawyers not involved in the investigation, who must review seized documents to identify those containing possibly privileged information. The privilege team cannot reveal the contents of privileged documents to the investigating agents and attorneys. Why do the rules for search warrants not require a pre-search certification that it will not reach privileged documents?

4. *Negotiations over terms of compliance.* If your client receives a grand jury subpoena for documents, and you conclude that there is no viable constitutional basis for objecting to the subpoena, is there anything left to do except collect the documents and turn them over? Can you negotiate some less onerous form of compliance? What negotiating leverage do you have, if any?

■ UNITED STATES v. WEBSTER HUBBELL

530 U.S. 27 (2000)

STEVENS, J.

The two questions presented concern the scope of a witness' protection against compelled self-incrimination: (1) whether the Fifth Amendment privilege protects a witness from being compelled to disclose the existence of incriminating documents that the Government is unable to describe with reasonable particularity; and (2) if the witness produces such documents pursuant to a grant of immunity, whether 18 U.S.C. §6002 prevents the Government from using them to prepare criminal charges against him.[2]

This proceeding arises out of the second prosecution of respondent, Webster Hubbell, commenced by the Independent Counsel appointed in August 1994 to investigate possible violations of federal law relating to the Whitewater Development Corporation. The first prosecution was terminated pursuant to a plea bargain. In December 1994, respondent pleaded guilty to charges of mail fraud and tax evasion arising out of his billing practices as a member of an Arkansas law firm from 1989 to 1992, and was sentenced to 21 months in prison. In the plea agreement, respondent promised to provide the Independent Counsel with "full, complete, accurate, and truthful information" about matters relating to the Whitewater investigation.

The second prosecution resulted from the Independent Counsel's attempt to determine whether respondent had violated that promise. In October 1996, while respondent was incarcerated, the Independent Counsel served him with a subpoena *duces tecum* calling for the production of 11 categories of documents before a grand jury sitting in Little Rock, Arkansas. On November 19, he appeared before the grand jury and invoked his Fifth Amendment privilege against self-incrimination. In response to questioning by the prosecutor, respondent initially refused "to state whether there are documents within my possession, custody, or control responsive to the Subpoena." Thereafter, the prosecutor [obtained a court order] directing

2. Section 6002 provides: "Whenever a witness refuses, on the basis of his privilege against self-incrimination, to testify or provide other information in a proceeding before . . . a court or grand jury of the United States [and the presiding judge] communicates to the witness an order issued under this title, the witness may not refuse to comply with the order on the basis of his privilege against self-incrimination; but no testimony or other information compelled under the order (or any information directly or indirectly derived from such testimony or other information) may be used against the witness in any criminal case, except a prosecution for perjury, giving a false statement, or otherwise failing to comply with the order."

him to respond to the subpoena and granting him immunity "to the extent allowed by law." Respondent then produced 13,120 pages of documents and records and responded to a series of questions that established that those were all of the documents in his custody or control that were responsive to the commands in the subpoena, with the exception of a few documents he claimed were shielded by the attorney-client and attorney work-product privileges.

The contents of the documents produced by respondent provided the Independent Counsel with the information that led to this second prosecution. On April 30, 1998, a grand jury in the District of Columbia returned a 10-count indictment charging respondent with various tax-related crimes and mail and wire fraud. The District Court dismissed the indictment relying, in part, on the ground that the Independent Counsel's use of the subpoenaed documents violated §6002 because all of the evidence he would offer against respondent at trial derived either directly or indirectly from the testimonial aspects of respondent's immunized act of producing those documents. Noting that the Independent Counsel had admitted that he was not investigating tax-related issues when he issued the subpoena, and that he had "'learned about the unreported income and other crimes from studying the records' contents,'" the District Court characterized the subpoena as "the quintessential fishing expedition." The Court of Appeals vacated the judgment and remanded for further proceedings [because the District Court should have inquired about] the extent of the Government's independent knowledge of the documents' existence and authenticity, and of respondent's possession or control of them. . . .

It is useful to preface our analysis of the constitutional issue with a restatement of certain propositions that are not in dispute. The term "privilege against self-incrimination" is not an entirely accurate description of a person's constitutional protection against being "compelled in any criminal case to be a witness against himself."

The word "witness" in the constitutional text limits the relevant category of compelled incriminating communications to those that are "testimonial" in character. As Justice Holmes observed, there is a significant difference between the use of compulsion to extort communications from a defendant and compelling a person to engage in conduct that may be incriminating. Thus, even though the act may provide incriminating evidence, a criminal suspect may be compelled to put on a shirt, to provide a blood sample, or handwriting exemplar, or to make a recording of his voice. Schmerber v. California, 384 U.S. 757 (1966); Gilbert v. California, 388 U.S. 263 (1967); United States v. Wade, 388 U.S. 218 (1967). The act of exhibiting such physical characteristics is not the same as a sworn communication by a witness that relates either express or implied assertions of fact or belief. Similarly, the fact that incriminating evidence may be the byproduct of obedience to a regulatory requirement, such as filing an income tax return, maintaining required records, or reporting an accident, does not clothe such required conduct with the testimonial privilege. United States v. Sullivan, 274 U.S. 259 (1927); Shapiro v. United States, 355 U.S. 1 (1948); California v. Byers, 402 U.S. 424 (1971); Baltimore City Dept. of Social Servs. V. Bouknight, 493 U.S. 549 (1990) ("The Court has on several occasions recognized that the Fifth Amendment privilege may not be invoked to resist compliance with a regulatory regime constructed to effect the State's public purposes unrelated to the enforcement of its criminal laws").

More relevant to this case is the settled proposition that a person may be required to produce specific documents even though they contain incriminating assertions of fact or belief because the creation of those documents was not "compelled" within the meaning of the privilege. Our decision in Fisher v. United States, 425 U.S. 391 (1976), dealt with summonses issued by the Internal Revenue Service (IRS) seeking working papers used in the preparation of tax returns. Because the papers had been voluntarily prepared prior to the issuance of the summonses, they could not be "said to contain compelled testimonial evidence, either of the taxpayers or of anyone else." Accordingly, the taxpayer could not "avoid compliance with the subpoena merely by asserting that the item of evidence which he is required to produce contains incriminating writing, whether his own or that of someone else." It is clear, therefore, that respondent Hubbell could not avoid compliance with the subpoena served on him merely because the demanded documents contained incriminating evidence, whether written by others or voluntarily prepared by himself.

On the other hand, we have also made it clear that the act of producing documents in response to a subpoena may have a compelled testimonial aspect. We have held that "the act of production" itself may implicitly communicate "statements of fact." By "producing documents in compliance with a subpoena, the witness would admit that the papers existed, were in his possession or control, and were authentic." Doe v. United States, 487 U.S. 201, 209-210 (1988). Moreover, as was true in this case, when the custodian of documents responds to a subpoena, he may be compelled to take the witness stand and answer questions designed to determine whether he has produced everything demanded by the subpoena. The answers to those questions, as well as the act of production itself, may certainly communicate information about the existence, custody, and authenticity of the documents. Whether the constitutional privilege protects the answers to such questions, or protects the act of production itself, is a question that is distinct from the question whether the unprotected contents of the documents themselves are incriminating. . . .

The "compelled testimony" that is relevant in this case is not to be found in the contents of the documents produced in response to the subpoena. It is, rather, the testimony inherent in the act of producing those documents. The disagreement between the parties focuses entirely on the significance of that testimonial aspect.

The Government correctly emphasizes that the testimonial aspect of a response to a subpoena *duces tecum* does nothing more than establish the existence, authenticity, and custody of items that are produced. We assume that the Government is also entirely correct in its submission that it would not have to advert to respondent's act of production in order to prove the existence, authenticity, or custody of any documents that it might offer in evidence at a criminal trial; indeed, the Government disclaims any need to introduce any of the documents produced by respondent into evidence in order to prove the charges against him. It follows, according to the Government, that it has no intention of making improper "use" of respondent's compelled testimony. . . . But the fact that the Government intends no such use of the act of production leaves open the separate question whether it has already made "derivative use" of the testimonial aspect of that act in obtaining the indictment against respondent and in preparing its case for trial. It clearly has.

It is apparent from the text of the subpoena itself that the prosecutor needed respondent's assistance both to identify potential sources of information and to produce those sources. Given the breadth of the description of the 11 categories of documents called for by the subpoena, the collection and production of the materials demanded was tantamount to answering a series of interrogatories asking a witness to disclose the existence and location of particular documents fitting certain broad descriptions. The assembly of literally hundreds of pages of material in response to a request for "any and all documents reflecting, referring, or relating to any direct or indirect sources of money or other things of value received by or provided to" an individual or members of his family during a 3-year period, is the functional equivalent of the preparation of an answer to either a detailed written interrogatory or a series of oral questions at a discovery deposition. Entirely apart from the contents of the 13,120 pages of materials that respondent produced in this case, it is undeniable that providing a catalog of existing documents fitting within any of the 11 broadly worded subpoena categories could provide a prosecutor with a "lead to incriminating evidence," or "a link in the chain of evidence needed to prosecute."

Indeed, the record makes it clear that that is what happened in this case. The documents were produced before a grand jury sitting in the Eastern District of Arkansas in aid of the Independent Counsel's attempt to determine whether respondent had violated a commitment in his first plea agreement. The use of those sources of information eventually led to the return of an indictment by a grand jury sitting in the District of Columbia for offenses that apparently are unrelated to that plea agreement. What the District Court characterized as a "fishing expedition" did produce a fish, but not the one that the Independent Counsel expected to hook. It is abundantly clear that the testimonial aspect of respondent's act of producing subpoenaed documents was the first step in a chain of evidence that led to this prosecution. The documents did not magically appear in the prosecutor's office like "manna from heaven." They arrived there only after respondent asserted his constitutional privilege, received a grant of immunity, and — under the compulsion of the District Court's order — took the mental and physical steps necessary to provide the prosecutor with an accurate inventory of the many sources of potentially incriminating evidence sought by the subpoena. . . .

The assembly of those documents was like telling an inquisitor the combination to a wall safe, not like being forced to surrender the key to a strongbox. The Government's anemic view of respondent's act of production as a mere physical act that is principally nontestimonial in character and can be entirely divorced from its "implicit" testimonial aspect . . . simply fails to account for these realities. . . .

Kastigar v. United States, 406 U.S. 441 (1972), requires that respondent's motion to dismiss the indictment on immunity grounds be granted unless the Government proves that the evidence it used in obtaining the indictment and proposed to use at trial was derived from legitimate sources "wholly independent" of the testimonial aspect of respondent's immunized conduct in assembling and producing the documents described in the subpoena. The Government, however, does not claim that it could make such a showing. Rather, it contends that its prosecution of respondent must be considered proper unless someone — presumably respondent — shows that "there is some substantial relation between the compelled testimonial communications implicit in the act of production (as opposed to the act of production standing alone) and some aspect of the information used in the investigation or the evidence presented at trial." We could not accept this submission without repudiating the basis for our conclusion in *Kastigar* that the statutory guarantee of use and derivative-use immunity is as broad as the constitutional privilege itself. This we are not prepared to do. Accordingly, the indictment against respondent must be dismissed. . . .

THOMAS, J., concurring.

. . . I write separately to note that [the act of production] doctrine may be inconsistent with the original meaning of the Fifth Amendment's Self-Incrimination Clause. A substantial body of evidence suggests that the Fifth Amendment privilege protects against the compelled production not just of incriminating testimony, but of any incriminating evidence. In a future case, I would be willing to reconsider the scope and meaning of the Self-Incrimination Clause.

The Fifth Amendment provides that "[n]o person . . . shall be compelled in any criminal case to be a witness against himself." The key word at issue in this case is "witness." The Court's opinion, relying on prior cases, essentially defines "witness" as a person who provides testimony, and thus restricts the Fifth Amendment's ban to only those communications that are "testimonial" in character. None of this Court's cases, however, has undertaken an analysis of the meaning of the term at the time of the founding. A review of that period reveals substantial support for the view that the term "witness" meant a person who gives or furnishes evidence, a broader meaning than that which our case law currently ascribes to the term. If this is so, a person who responds to a subpoena *duces tecum* would be just as much a "witness" as a person who responds to a subpoena *ad testificandum*. . . .

Such a meaning of "witness" is consistent with, and may help explain, the history and framing of the Fifth Amendment. The 18th-century common-law privilege against self-incrimination protected against the compelled production of incriminating physical evidence such as papers and documents. And this Court has noted that, for generations before the framing, "one cardinal rule of the court of chancery [was] never to decree a discovery which might tend to convict the party of a crime." Boyd v. United States, 116 U.S. 616 (1886). . . .

Against this common-law backdrop, the privilege against self-incrimination was enshrined in the Virginia Declaration of Rights in 1776. That document provided that no one may "be compelled to give evidence against himself." Following Virginia's lead, seven of the other original States included specific provisions in their Constitutions granting a right against compulsion "to give evidence" or "to furnish evidence." And during ratification of the Federal Constitution, the four States that proposed bills of rights put forward draft proposals employing similar wording for a federal constitutional provision guaranteeing the right against compelled self-incrimination. Each of the proposals broadly sought to protect a citizen from being "compelled to give evidence against himself." . . . In response to such calls, James Madison penned the Fifth Amendment. In so doing, Madison substituted the phrase "to be a witness" for the proposed language "to give evidence" and "to furnish evidence." But it seems likely that Madison's phrasing was synonymous with that of the proposals. . . .

This Court has not always taken the approach to the Fifth Amendment that we follow today. The first case interpreting the Self-Incrimination Clause — Boyd v. United States — was decided, though not explicitly, in accordance with the understanding that "witness" means one who gives evidence. In *Boyd*, this Court unanimously held that the Fifth Amendment protects a defendant against compelled production of books and papers. And the Court linked its interpretation of the Fifth Amendment to the common-law understanding of the self-incrimination privilege.

But this Court's decision in Fisher v. United States rejected this understanding, permitting the Government to force a person to furnish incriminating physical evidence and protecting only the "testimonial" aspects of that transfer. In so doing, *Fisher* not only failed to examine the historical backdrop to the Fifth Amendment, it also required . . . a difficult parsing of the act of responding to a subpoena *duces tecum.*

Notes

1. *The contents of incriminating documents.* When a grand jury forces a witness to provide documents, including some that the witness created personally, is it forcing him to "witness" against himself? Should the privilege against self-incrimination apply to the contents of all documents a suspect creates? Under federal law, it is now clear that the contents of preexisting documents are not "testimonial" and therefore the privilege against self-incrimination cannot stop the grand jury from obtaining such documents. See Fisher v. United States, 425 U.S. 391 (1976). All the states addressing this question have followed the federal lead. Justice Thomas' opinion in *Hubbell* proposes to reopen this question. How much documentary evidence would be beyond the reach of a grand jury if the contents of documents were considered privileged when self-incriminating? If the government can force a person to turn over written statements that incriminate, does a privilege against oral testimony mean much at all?

2. *Act of production doctrine.* There is an exception to the *Fisher* rule regarding the contents of incriminating documents. Compliance with a subpoena is an implicit admission that the records requested in the subpoena exist, that they are in the possession or control of the subpoena recipient, and that they are authentic. The U.S. Supreme Court, along with all the state courts to address the issue, recognizes that the *act* of producing documents under a grand jury subpoena can give the government valuable information that might ultimately help convict the document holder of a crime. The contents of the documents, as opposed to the act of producing the documents, remains a valid source of evidence. Is this "act of production" any more "testimonial" than the contents of the documents? See United States v. Doe, 465 U.S. 605 (1984) (act of producing incriminating business records is itself testimonial self-incrimination); Braswell v. United States, 487 U.S. 99 (1988) (individual representative of legal entity must submit subpoenaed documents to grand jury, but prosecution may not use act of production evidence against individual).

United States v. Hubbell addressed a new wrinkle in this doctrine. Independent Counsel Kenneth Starr served Webster Hubbell (a former Department of Justice official and advisor to President Clinton) with a grand jury subpoena calling for the production of documents. The *Hubbell* Court went beyond its earlier cases holding that the "act of production" would qualify as self-incriminating testimony whenever the act of production communicated information about the documents' existence, custody, and authenticity. In this case, the prosecutor could show the existence, custody, and authenticity of the documents without Hubbell's help. However, the prosecutor did not appreciate the evidentiary value of the documents until Hubbell submitted them to the grand jury. Thus, he gave prosecutors "a link in the chain of evidence needed to prosecute."

3. *The "collective entity" doctrine.* The Supreme Court decided in Hale v. Henkel, 201 U.S. 43 (1906), that corporate entities do not hold any privilege against self-incrimination. State courts have also read state constitutions to deny self-incrimination privileges to corporations. The same result holds for labor unions, partnerships, and other unincorporated associations. The only exceptions to this rule occur

in a few states, where courts allow a legal entity dominated by one individual (or perhaps one family) to claim the privilege. Layman v. Webb, 350 P.2d 323 (Okla. Crim. App. 1960) (privilege against self-incrimination extends to partnership records of a family or similar personal partnership). Given that the law recognizes a corporation as a juridical "person" and will convict a corporation on criminal charges, don't corporations have the same interests as an individual in avoiding self-incrimination? Corporations do enjoy the protection of some other constitutional provisions, including the Fourth Amendment. If a corporation were to have a self-incrimination privilege, what sorts of evidence might become unavailable to the government?

4. *The "required records" doctrine.* There are many records the government requires persons and business entities to create and maintain, such as tax returns, health or safety records, and environmental compliance records. If the grand jury subpoenas such records, has it compelled a person to become a "witness" against herself, in violation of the federal or state constitutions? Generally, courts have declared that there is no self-incrimination problem with a subpoena for such "required records" unless the primary purpose of requiring the recordkeeping was enforcement of criminal laws. Compare Shapiro v. United States, 335 U.S. 1 (1948) (subpoena for pricing records of wholesale produce dealer acceptable) with Marchetti v. United States, 390 U.S. 39 (1968) (statute requires gamblers to register with government and pay occupational tax; subpoena for these documents violates self-incrimination privilege). How might a statute be drafted to avoid the difficulty encountered in *Marchetti?* Is there any practical difference between compelling someone to speak to the grand jury and compelling him to write the testimony down and then issuing a subpoena for the document?

5. *Other acts compelled by the grand jury.* Is a person serving as a "witness" against herself if the grand jury asks for a blood sample for testing? Handwriting exemplars? Are these actions any different from the act of producing documents? In Schmerber v. California, 384 U.S. 757 (1966) the Court held that there is no compelled self-incrimination when a grand jury orders a witness to provide a blood sample. Some states make an exception to the grand jury's broad subpoena power when it comes to the most intrusive grand jury requests for evidence. For instance, grand juries will sometimes subpoena witnesses and ask for fingerprints, hair samples, or voice exemplars. Compare Woolverton v. Multi-County Grand Jury, 859 P.2d 1112 (Okla. Crim. App. 1993) (requiring showing of probable cause to support request for blood samples, reasonable suspicion for palm prints) with United States v. Dionisio, 410 U.S. 1 (1973) (upholding subpoena for voice exemplar with no special government justification). Is there an argument for treating voice exemplars differently from palm prints? From blood samples?

PART TWO

EVALUATING CHARGES

XI

Defense Counsel

During the earliest phases of the criminal process, defense lawyers are rarely to be seen. But as the prosecution and police formulate and file charges against some suspects, and as the courts begin to process those charges, defense counsel become involved.

In this chapter, we introduce the various sources of law that make it possible for a criminal defendant to get a lawyer. We also consider the practical value of these legal entitlements to the ordinary criminal defendant. Does having an attorney really matter to defendants? What do defense lawyers do? Can you imagine a criminal justice system without them?

A. WHEN WILL COUNSEL BE PROVIDED?

Not every person charged with a crime consults a lawyer. The most common reason for a defendant to face charges alone, without a lawyer, is financial — defendants often cannot afford counsel. But our legal systems have not left matters there. The same government that pays the judge, the prosecutor, and the investigators will also (at least in some cases) pay for the defendant's lawyer.

The question that has persisted over many decades is when the state will pay for defense counsel and when it will not. Some cases involve charges that are not serious enough to require counsel; some proceedings are too early or late in the process to require counsel. This section reviews the law on (1) the types of charges necessary to invoke constitutional and statutory rights to counsel and (2) the points in criminal proceedings when a defendant can expect to consult with counsel.

1. *Types of Charges*

Constitutions have much to say about the availability of defense counsel. The Sixth Amendment to the federal constitution states that "In all criminal prosecutions, the accused shall enjoy the right . . . to have the assistance of counsel for his defence." Almost every state constitution has an equivalent provision.

The most important early decision regarding the Sixth Amendment right to counsel was Powell v. Alabama, 287 U.S. 45 (1932). The defendants were nine young black men who were accused of raping two young white women on a train near Scottsboro, Alabama. The case against the defendants attracted much local attention: Soldiers escorted the defendants to and from their proceedings to protect them from hostile mobs. None of the defendants was literate, and none was a resident of Alabama.

The defendants were divided into three groups for trial. The first trial began six days after indictment, and each of the three trials was completed within one day. Until the morning of the first trial, the court named no particular lawyer to represent the defendants. The trial judge instead appointed all the members of the Scottsboro bar "for the limited purpose of arraigning" the defendants. Some members of the bar consulted with the defendants in jail, but did nothing further. A colloquy on the morning of the trial left it unclear which attorney, if any, would represent the defendants at trial. An attorney sent from Tennessee by people concerned about the young men's situation was unprepared to serve as lead counsel, but members of the Scottsboro bar were quick to say they would "assist" the newly arrived lawyer. The juries found all the defendants guilty and imposed the death penalty upon each of them.

The Supreme Court concluded that appointment of a primary defense lawyer, at least under these circumstances, was a requirement of due process. The Court made some general observations about the value of legal counsel:

> The right to be heard would be, in many cases, of little avail if it did not comprehend the right to be heard by counsel. Even the intelligent and educated layman has small and sometimes no skill in the science of law. If charged with crime, he is incapable, generally, of determining for himself whether the indictment is good or bad. He is unfamiliar with the rules of evidence. Left without the aid of counsel he may be put on trial without a proper charge, and convicted upon incompetent evidence, or evidence irrelevant to the issue or otherwise inadmissible. He lacks both the skill and knowledge adequately to prepare his defense, even though he had a perfect one. He requires the guiding hand of counsel at every step in the proceedings against him. Without it, though he be not guilty, he faces the danger of conviction because he does not know how to establish his innocence.

287 U.S. at 68-69. The opinion also stressed some of the more compelling facts in the case:

> In the light . . . the ignorance and illiteracy of the defendants, their youth, the circumstances of public hostility, the imprisonment and the close surveillance of the defendants by the military forces, the fact that their friends and families were all in other states and communication with them [was] necessarily difficult, and above all that they stood in deadly peril of their lives, . . . the necessity of counsel was so vital and imperative that the failure of the trial court to make an effective appointment of counsel was . . . a denial of due process within the meaning of the Fourteenth Amendment.

> Whether this would be so in other criminal prosecutions, or under other circumstances, we need not determine. . . . In a case such as this, whatever may be the rule in other cases, the right to have counsel appointed, when necessary, is a logical corollary from the constitutional right to be heard by counsel.

287 U.S. at 71. The Scottsboro case became an international *cause célebre.* A crusading New York lawyer, Samuel Leibowitz, participated in the defense during the second trial, which also ended in the conviction of all defendants by an all-white jury. After the later convictions were overturned on appeal in the state system, the government agreed to a plea agreement allowing for the release of four defendants and prison terms for the other five. See James Goodman, Stories of Scottsboro (1994).

After a series of later Supreme Court cases considering the right to appointed counsel at trial, Betts v. Brady, 316 U.S. 455 (1942), settled on the "special circumstances" test to govern the appointment of counsel; that is, counsel would be constitutionally required only under "special circumstances," and not in every criminal case. Betts was indicted for robbery. Due to lack of funds, he was unable to employ counsel, and asked the judge to appoint counsel for him. The judge refused because the local practice was to appoint counsel only in prosecutions for murder and rape. Betts then pleaded not guilty and elected to be tried without a jury. Witnesses were summoned in his behalf. He cross-examined the State's witnesses and examined his own alibi witnesses. Betts did not take the witness stand. The judge found him guilty and sentenced him to eight years in prison. The Court concluded that due process did not require the appointment of counsel under these circumstances.

In the following case, the Supreme Court returned to the question of appointed counsel, this time giving a different answer.

■ CLARENCE EARL GIDEON v. LOUIE WAINWRIGHT

372 U.S. 335 (1963)

Black, J.

Petitioner was charged in a Florida state court with having broken and entered a poolroom with intent to commit a misdemeanor. This offense is a felony under Florida law. Appearing in court without funds and without a lawyer, petitioner asked the court to appoint counsel for him. [When the Court denied his request, Gideon objected: "The United States Supreme Court says I am entitled to be represented by Counsel."]

Put to trial before a jury, Gideon conducted his defense about as well as could be expected from a layman. He made an opening statement to the jury, cross-examined the State's witnesses, presented witnesses in his own defense, declined to testify himself, and made a short argument "emphasizing his innocence to the charge contained in the Information filed in this case." The jury returned a verdict of guilty, and petitioner was sentenced to serve five years in the state prison. [The state supreme court later denied habeas corpus relief.] Since 1942, when Betts v. Brady, 316 U.S. 455, was decided by a divided Court, the problem of a defendant's federal constitutional right to counsel in a state court has been a continuing source of controversy and litigation in both state and federal courts. To give this problem another review here, we granted certiorari. . .

The facts upon which Betts claimed that he had been unconstitutionally denied the right to have counsel appointed to assist him are strikingly like the facts upon which Gideon here bases his federal constitutional claim. Betts was indicted for robbery in a Maryland state court. On arraignment, . . . Betts was advised that it was not the practice in that county to appoint counsel for indigent defendants except in murder and rape cases. He then pleaded not guilty, had witnesses summoned, cross-examined the State's witnesses, examined his own, and chose not to testify himself. He was found guilty by the judge, sitting without a jury. [Upon review of the conviction, this Court] held that a refusal to appoint counsel for an indigent defendant charged with a felony did not necessarily violate the Due Process Clause of the Fourteenth Amendment. . . . The Court said: "Asserted denial [of due process] is to be tested by an appraisal of the totality of facts in a given case. That which may, in one setting, constitute a denial of fundamental fairness, shocking to the universal sense of justice, may, in other circumstances . . . fall short of such denial." [316 U.S. at 462.]

Treating due process as "a concept less rigid and more fluid than those envisaged in other specific and particular provisions of the Bill of Rights," the Court held that refusal to appoint counsel under the particular facts and circumstances in the *Betts* case was not so "offensive to the common and fundamental ideas of fairness" as to amount to a denial of due process. Since the facts and circumstances of the two cases are so nearly indistinguishable, we think the Betts v. Brady holding if left standing would require us to reject Gideon's claim that the Constitution guarantees him the assistance of counsel. Upon full reconsideration we conclude that Betts v. Brady should be overruled.

The Sixth Amendment provides, "In all criminal prosecutions, the accused shall enjoy the right . . . to have the Assistance of Counsel for his defence." We have construed this to mean that in federal courts counsel must be provided for defendants unable to employ counsel unless the right is competently and intelligently waived. [In *Betts,* the Court] set out and considered "relevant data on the subject . . . afforded by constitutional and statutory provisions subsisting in the colonies and the States prior to the inclusion of the Bill of Rights in the national Constitution, and in the constitutional, legislative, and judicial history of the States to the present date." On the basis of this historical data the Court concluded that appointment of counsel is not a fundamental right, essential to a fair trial, [and thus was not a due process requirement applicable to the States.]

We accept Betts v. Brady's assumption, based as it was on our prior cases, that a provision of the Bill of Rights which is "fundamental and essential to a fair trial" is made obligatory upon the States by the Fourteenth Amendment. We think the Court in *Betts* was wrong, however, in concluding that the Sixth Amendment's guarantee of counsel is not one of these fundamental rights. Ten years before Betts v. Brady, this Court, after full consideration of all the historical data examined in *Betts,* had unequivocally declared that "the right to the aid of counsel is of this fundamental character." Powell v. Alabama, 287 U.S. 45, 68 (1932). While the Court at the close of its *Powell* opinion did by its language, as this Court frequently does, limit its holding to the particular facts and circumstances of that case, its conclusions about the fundamental nature of the right to counsel are unmistakable. Several years later, in 1936, the Court reemphasized what it had said about the fundamental nature of the right to counsel in this language:

> We concluded that certain fundamental rights, safeguarded by the first eight amendments against federal action, were also safeguarded against state action by the due

> process of law clause of the Fourteenth Amendment, and among them the fundamental right of the accused to the aid of counsel in a criminal prosecution.

Grosjean v. American Press Co., 297 U.S. 233, 243-244 (1936). [Similar statements appear in several other decisions. In] deciding as it did — that "appointment of counsel is not a fundamental right, essential to a fair trial" — the Court in Betts v. Brady made an abrupt break with its own well-considered precedents. In returning to these old precedents, sounder we believe than the new, we but restore constitutional principles established to achieve a fair system of justice.

Not only these precedents but also reason and reflection require us to recognize that in our adversary system of criminal justice, any person haled into court, who is too poor to hire a lawyer, cannot be assured a fair trial unless counsel is provided for him. This seems to us to be an obvious truth. Governments, both state and federal, quite properly spend vast sums of money to establish machinery to try defendants accused of crime. Lawyers to prosecute are everywhere deemed essential to protect the public's interest in an orderly society. Similarly, there are few defendants charged with crime, few indeed, who fail to hire the best lawyers they can get to prepare and present their defenses. That government hires lawyers to prosecute and defendants who have the money hire lawyers to defend are the strongest indications of the widespread belief that lawyers in criminal courts are necessities, not luxuries. The right of one charged with crime to counsel may not be deemed fundamental and essential to fair trials in some countries, but it is in ours. From the very beginning, our state and national constitutions and laws have laid great emphasis on procedural and substantive safeguards designed to assure fair trials before impartial tribunals in which every defendant stands equal before the law. This noble ideal cannot be realized if the poor man charged with crime has to face his accusers without a lawyer to assist him. . . .

The Court in Betts v. Brady departed from the sound wisdom upon which the Court's holding in Powell v. Alabama rested. Florida, supported by two other States, has asked that Betts v. Brady be left intact. Twenty-two States, as friends of the Court, argue that *Betts* was "an anachronism when handed down" and that it should now be overruled. We agree. . . .

HARLAN, J., concurring.

I agree that Betts v. Brady should be overruled, but consider it entitled to a more respectful burial than has been accorded, at least on the part of those of us who were not on the Court when that case was decided. I cannot subscribe to the view that Betts v. Brady represented "an abrupt break with its own well-considered precedents." In 1932, in Powell v. Alabama, a capital case, this Court declared that under the particular facts there presented — "the ignorance and illiteracy of the defendants, their youth, the circumstances of public hostility . . . and above all that they stood in deadly peril of their lives" — the state court had a duty to assign counsel for the trial as a necessary requisite of due process of law. It is evident that these limiting facts were not added to the opinion as an afterthought; they were repeatedly emphasized, and were clearly regarded as important to the result.

Thus when this Court, a decade later, decided Betts v. Brady, it did no more than to admit of the possible existence of special circumstances in noncapital as well as capital trials, while at the same time insisting that such circumstances be shown in order to establish a denial of due process. The right to appointed counsel had been recognized as being considerably broader in federal prosecutions, but to have imposed these requirements on the States would indeed have been "an abrupt break" with the almost immediate past. . . .

The principles declared in *Powell* and in *Betts,* however, have had a troubled journey throughout the years that have followed first the one case and then the other. . . . In noncapital cases, the "special circumstances" rule has continued to exist in form while its substance has been substantially and steadily eroded. [Since 1950] there have been not a few cases in which special circumstances were found in little or nothing more than the "complexity" of the legal questions presented, although those questions were often of only routine difficulty. The Court has come to recognize, in other words, that the mere existence of a serious criminal charge constituted in itself special circumstances requiring the services of counsel at trial. In truth the Betts v. Brady rule is no longer a reality. This evolution, however, appears not to have been fully recognized by many state courts, in this instance charged with the front-line responsibility for the enforcement of constitutional rights. To continue a rule which is honored by this Court only with lip service is not a healthy thing and in the long run will do disservice to the federal system.

The special circumstances rule has been formally abandoned in capital cases, and the time has now come when it should be similarly abandoned in noncapital cases, at least as to offenses which, as the one involved here, carry the possibility of a substantial prison sentence. (Whether the rule should extend to all criminal cases need not now be decided.) This indeed does no more than to make explicit something that has long since been foreshadowed in our decisions. . . .

■ In re ADVISORY OPINION TO THE GOVERNOR (APPOINTED COUNSEL)

666 A.2d 813 (R.I. 1995)

WEISBERGER, C.J.

To His Excellency Lincoln Almond, Governor of the State of Rhode Island and Providence Plantations: We have received from Your Excellency a request seeking the advice of the justices of this Court in accordance with article X, section 3, of the Rhode Island Constitution on the following question of law:

> In view of the historical development of the law relating to the right of appointed counsel under the federal and state constitutions, and the more recent developments in federal case law, is the State of Rhode Island required by the Rhode Island Constitution to provide free counsel to indigents notwithstanding that the trial justice determines that no incarceration will be imposed?

The governor submitted this question to the Court in preparation for proposing to the legislature an annual operating budget for the state.] In response, we issued an order inviting briefs from various specified parties and all other interested parties. . . .

The Sixth Amendment to the United States Constitution mandates that "in all criminal prosecutions, the accused shall enjoy the right . . . to have the assistance of counsel for his defense." In 1963, the United States Supreme Court made this requirement applicable to the states via the Fourteenth Amendment in Gideon v. Wainwright, 372 U.S. 335.

The *Gideon* decision, however, did not reveal the contours of the right to counsel inasmuch as that holding was limited to facts that involved a felony conviction. The issue of the right to counsel was revisited in Argersinger v. Hamlin, 407 U.S. 25 (1972), in which the Supreme Court was asked to rule on whether indigent defendants facing misdemeanor charges are entitled to appointed counsel. The *Argersinger* Court concluded that the rationale of the *Gideon* decision "has relevance to any criminal trial, where an accused is deprived of his liberty." *Argersinger* went on to hold that any criminal prosecution resulting in the actual deprivation of an indigent defendant's liberty must be accompanied by the appointment of counsel for that defendant.

Although *Argersinger* did not specifically address the question of whether counsel must be appointed when no imprisonment will result, the Supreme Court did reach this issue seven years later, in Scott v. Illinois, 440 U.S. 367 (1979). Scott, an indigent defendant, was convicted of shoplifting and fined $50 after a trial in which he was not assisted by appointed counsel. In an opinion by Justice Rehnquist, the Court held that the right to appointed counsel under the Sixth and Fourteenth Amendments of the United States Constitution requires "only that no indigent criminal defendant be sentenced to a term of imprisonment unless the State has afforded him the right to assistance of appointed counsel in his defense."...

The Rhode Island constitutional analogue to the Sixth Amendment guarantee of the right to counsel is found in article I, section 10, of the Rhode Island Constitution. This section protects a defendant's right to assistance of counsel in terms almost identical to those of its federal counterpart: "In all criminal prosecutions, accused persons shall . . . have the assistance of counsel in their defense." In 1971, prior to the Supreme Court's rulings in *Argersinger* and *Scott,* this provision was interpreted in State v. Holliday, 280 A.2d 333 (R.I. 1971). In *Holliday,* this Court . . . construed article I, section 10, broadly to require appointment of counsel for indigent defendants charged with misdemeanors that carry a potential prison sentence in excess of six months, even if no imprisonment is actually imposed. . . . In *Holliday* this Court had no means of ascertaining the direction that the Supreme Court would take, and it is clear that our prognostication in *Holliday* was inaccurate. . . .

Although certain *amici* have argued that the protections afforded by the Federal Constitution establish only a minimum level of protection for criminal defendants, the decision to depart from minimum standards and to increase the level of protection should be made guardedly and should be supported by a principled rationale. We are presented with no such rationale here.

[The] balance achieved by the Supreme Court of the United States is as favorable to the perceived rights of defendants as should rationally be applied in criminal cases. We are unwilling to interpret article I, section [10] of the Rhode Island Constitution in such fashion as further to subordinate societal interests in effective prosecution of the guilty. . . . Moreover, this Court has recognized the validity of considering budgetary limitations in determining the extent of state-funded benefits for indigents. . . .

Certain of the *amici* would have this Court provide heightened constitutional protection to indigent criminal defendants who, although they may face no threat of imprisonment, may suffer such consequences as denial of public housing and loss of professional licenses. It is well settled, however, that the full panoply of due-process protections attaches only when loss of a fundamental liberty results from state action. . . . Although loss of a license or permit and denial of public housing are grave occurrences, they do not rise to the level of deprivation characterized by incarceration. An automobile driver, for instance, is not entitled to confer with counsel when asked to submit to a breathalyzer test, even though submission to or refusal of that test may result in loss of that driver's license, because there is no fundamental constitutional right to operate a motor vehicle. Therefore, we disagree with *amici* that counsel must be provided in a criminal proceeding simply because an indigent defendant may subsequently lose a comparable property right. . . .

We conclude that it is (1) within the authority of the General Assembly to determine that the public interest would be served by increasing appropriations to provide counsel in situations not constitutionally required and (2) not the province of this Court to impose upon the state obligations that have no constitutional or statutory basis. We therefore advise Your Excellency that the United States Supreme Court's interpretation of the Sixth Amendment as a guarantee of a criminal defendant's right to counsel only when imprisonment is actually imposed represents the appropriate standard that should be applied under article I, section 10, of the Rhode Island Constitution. In conclusion, therefore, we respond to Your Excellency's question in the negative.

MURRAY, J., dissenting.

I respectfully dissent. [T]his state has a proud history of affording its citizens the right to counsel and has specifically declined to follow the United States Supreme Court in limiting the provision of counsel to indigents. In 1941, long before Gideon v. Wainwright, 372 U.S. 335 (1963), Rhode Island established a public counsel system for accused felons. Thirty years later, before the United States Supreme Court decided Argersinger v. Hamlin, 407 U.S. 25 (1972), this court, in State v. Holliday, 280 A.2d 333 (R.I. 1971), extended the right to counsel for indigent defendants charged with serious misdemeanors which could subject them to an imposition of penalty in excess of six months' imprisonment. In 1987, after the Supreme Court decided Scott v. Illinois, 440 U.S. 367 (1979), we stated in State v. Moretti, 521 A.2d 1003 (R.I. 1987), and in State v. Medeiros, 535 A.2d 766 (R.I. 1987), that the Rhode Island Constitution provides a broader right to counsel than that provided under the Federal Constitution.

Specifically, we found in *Moretti* that "the confluence of the federal and the state guarantees is if an indigent Rhode Island criminal defendant faces a potential sentence of more than six months, Rhode Island constitutional law guarantees to a defendant appointed counsel, even if the trial justice predetermines that no prison sentence will be imposed. If the potential sentence is less than six months, federal constitutional law guarantees the defendant appointed counsel unless the trial justice predetermines that no prison sentence will be imposed." [Thus,] even after *Scott,* this court held that the Rhode Island Constitution afforded indigent defendants a higher degree of protection; that is, we have recognized the right of indigent persons to appointed counsel notwithstanding that the trial justice determines that no incarceration will be imposed.

As a final matter, it should be stressed that we should not attempt to peer into the minds of trial justices. By answering His Excellency's request in the negative, the majority's decision effectively reduces the range of discretion previously afforded to trial justices in misdemeanor cases. The majority would have each trial justice determine whether incarceration may be imposed at the initial stages of an action, regardless of any later developments that may require the trial justice to impose a sanction of imprisonment. It is noteworthy that the District Court judges have represented that such a result would profoundly affect the quality of justice which is administered in the trial courts. . . .

In 2002 the Supreme Court returned to the question of the types of cases triggering a right to appointed counsel for indigent defendants. The precise issue in the case may seem minor on first glance: must the state provide counsel where the judge gives the defendant a suspended sentence, but does not actually order a prison term? Hiding behind these fine lines, however, are large numbers of cases. As with *Gideon* and prior cases, decisions requiring the provision of counsel may impose substantial direct and indirect costs on the states. Of course, such monetary and policy costs must be lined up against the benefits of principles so fundamental as the right to counsel. Consider the balance between federal constitutional principle and practical considerations in the following case.

■ ALABAMA v. LeREED SHELTON

122 S.Ct. 1764 (U.S. 2002)

GINSBURG, J.

This case concerns the Sixth Amendment right of an indigent defendant charged with a misdemeanor punishable by imprisonment, fine, or both, to the assistance of court-appointed counsel. Two prior decisions control the Court's judgment. First, in Argersinger v. Hamlin, 407 U.S. 25 (1972), this Court held that defense counsel must be appointed in any criminal prosecution, whether classified as petty, misdemeanor, or felony, "that actually leads to imprisonment even for a brief period." Later, in Scott v. Illinois, 440 U.S. 367 (1979), the Court drew the line at "actual imprisonment," holding that counsel need not be appointed when the defendant is fined for the charged crime, but is not sentenced to a term of imprisonment.

Defendant-respondent LeReed Shelton, convicted of third-degree assault, was sentenced to a jail term of 30 days, which the trial court immediately suspended, placing Shelton on probation for two years. The question presented is whether the Sixth Amendment right to appointed counsel, as delineated in *Argersinger* and *Scott,* applies to a defendant in Shelton's situation. We hold that a suspended sentence that may "end up in the actual deprivation of a person's liberty" may not be imposed unless the defendant was accorded "the guiding hand of counsel" in the prosecution for the crime charged.

After representing himself at a bench trial in the District Court of Etowah County, Alabama, Shelton was convicted of third-degree assault, a class A misdemeanor carrying a maximum punishment of one year imprisonment and a $2000 fine. He invoked his right to a new trial before a jury in Circuit Court where he again appeared without a lawyer and was again convicted. The court repeatedly warned Shelton about the problems self-representation entailed but at no time offered him assistance of counsel at state expense.

The Circuit Court sentenced Shelton to serve 30 days in the county prison. As authorized by Alabama law, however, the court suspended that sentence and placed Shelton on two years' unsupervised probation, conditioned on his payment of court costs, a $500 fine, reparations of $25, and restitution in the amount of $516.69. Shelton appealed his conviction and sentence on Sixth Amendment grounds. . . .

Three positions are before us in this case. . . . Shelton argues that an indigent defendant may not receive a suspended sentence unless he is offered or waives the assistance of state-appointed counsel. Alabama now concedes that the Sixth Amendment bars *activation* of a suspended sentence for an uncounseled conviction, but maintains that the Constitution does not prohibit *imposition* of such a sentence as a method of effectuating probationary punishment. To assure full airing of the question presented, we invited an *amicus curiae* to argue in support of a third position, one Alabama has abandoned: Failure to appoint counsel to an indigent defendant does not bar the imposition of a suspended or probationary sentence upon conviction of a misdemeanor, even though the defendant might be incarcerated in the event probation is revoked.

In Gideon v. Wainwright, 372 U.S. 335 (1963), we held that the Sixth Amendment's guarantee of the right to state-appointed counsel, firmly established in federal-court proceedings in Johnson v. Zerbst, 304 U.S. 458 (1938), applies to state criminal prosecutions through the Fourteenth Amendment. We clarified the scope of that right in *Argersinger,* holding that an indigent defendant must be offered counsel in any misdemeanor case "that actually leads to imprisonment." Seven Terms later, *Scott* confirmed *Argersinger's* "delimitation." Although the governing statute in *Scott* authorized a jail sentence of up to one year, we held that the defendant had no right to state-appointed counsel because the sole sentence actually imposed on him was a $50 fine. . . .

Applying the "actual imprisonment" rule to the case before us, we take up first the question we asked *amicus* to address: Where the State provides no counsel to an indigent defendant, does the Sixth Amendment permit activation of a suspended sentence upon the defendant's violation of the terms of probation? We conclude that it does not. A suspended sentence is a prison term imposed for the offense of conviction. Once the prison term is triggered, the defendant is incarcerated not for the probation violation, but for the underlying offense. The uncounseled conviction at that point results in imprisonment; it "ends up in the actual deprivation of a person's liberty." This is precisely what the Sixth Amendment, as interpreted in *Argersinger* and *Scott,* does not allow.

Amicus resists this reasoning primarily on two grounds. First, he attempts to align this case with our decisions in Nichols v. United States, 511 U.S. 738 (1994), and Gagnon v. Scarpelli, 411 U.S. 778 (1973). We conclude that Shelton's case is not properly bracketed with those dispositions.

Nichols presented the question whether the Sixth Amendment barred consideration of a defendant's prior uncounseled misdemeanor conviction in determining his sentence for a subsequent felony offense. Nichols pleaded guilty to federal felony drug charges. Several years earlier, unrepresented by counsel, he was fined but not incarcerated for the state misdemeanor of driving under the influence (DUI). Including the DUI conviction in the federal Sentencing Guidelines calculation allowed the trial court to impose a sentence for the felony drug conviction 25 months longer than if the misdemeanor conviction had not been considered. We upheld this result, concluding that "an uncounseled misdemeanor conviction, valid under *Scott* because no prison term was imposed, is also valid when used to enhance punishment at a subsequent conviction." In *Gagnon,* the question was whether the defendant, who was placed on probation pursuant to a suspended sentence for armed robbery, had a due process right to representation by appointed counsel at a probation revocation hearing. We held that counsel was not invariably required in parole or probation revocation proceedings; we directed, instead, a "case-by-case approach" turning on the character of the issues involved.

Considered together, *amicus* contends, *Nichols* and *Gagnon* establish this principle: Sequential proceedings must be analyzed separately for Sixth Amendment purposes and only those proceedings "result[ing] in *immediate* actual imprisonment" trigger the right to state-appointed counsel. . . . *Gagnon* and *Nichols* do not stand for the broad proposition *amicus* would extract from them. The dispositive factor in those cases was not whether incarceration occurred immediately or only after some delay. Rather, the critical point was that the defendant had a recognized right to counsel when adjudicated guilty of the felony offense for which he was imprisoned. Unlike this case, in which revocation of probation would trigger a prison term imposed for a misdemeanor of which Shelton was found guilty without the aid of counsel, the sentences imposed in *Nichols* and *Gagnon* were for felony convictions—a federal drug conviction in *Nichols*, and a state armed robbery conviction in *Gagnon*—for which the right to counsel is unquestioned. Thus, neither *Nichols* nor *Gagnon* altered or diminished *Argersinger's* command that "no person may be imprisoned *for any offense* . . . unless he was represented by counsel at his trial.". . .

Amicus also contends that "practical considerations clearly weigh against" the extension of the Sixth Amendment appointed-counsel right to a defendant in Shelton's situation. He cites figures suggesting that although conditional sentences are commonly imposed, they are rarely activated. . . . *Amicus* observes that probation is "now a critical tool of law enforcement in low level cases." Even so, it does not follow that preservation of that tool warrants the reduction of the Sixth Amendment's domain. . . . *Amicus* does not describe the contours of the hearing that, he suggests, might precede revocation of a term of probation imposed on an uncounseled defendant. In Alabama, however, the character of the probation revocation hearing currently afforded is not in doubt. The proceeding is an "informal" one at which the defendant has no right to counsel, and the court no obligation to observe customary rules of evidence. More significant, the sole issue at the hearing—apart from determinations about the necessity of confinement—is whether the defendant breached the terms of probation. The validity or reliability of the underlying conviction is beyond attack.

We think it plain that a hearing so timed and structured cannot compensate for the absence of trial counsel, for it does not even address the key Sixth Amendment inquiry: whether the adjudication of guilt corresponding to the prison sentence is sufficiently reliable to permit incarceration. Deprived of counsel when tried, convicted, and sentenced, and unable to challenge the original judgment at a subsequent probation revocation hearing, a defendant in Shelton's circumstances faces incarceration on a conviction that has never been subjected to "the crucible of meaningful adversarial testing." The Sixth Amendment does not countenance this result.

In a variation on *amicus'* position, the dissent would limit review in this case to the question whether the *imposition* of Shelton's suspended sentence required appointment of counsel. . . . The dissent imagines a set of safeguards Alabama might provide at the probation revocation stage sufficient to cure its failure to appoint counsel prior to sentencing, including, perhaps, complete retrial of the misdemeanor violation with assistance of counsel. But there is no cause for speculation about Alabama's procedures; they are established by Alabama statute and decisional law, and they bear no resemblance to those the dissent invents in its effort to sanction the prospect of Shelton's imprisonment on an uncounseled conviction. . . .

Nor do we agree with *amicus* or the dissent that our holding will substantially limit the states' ability to impose probation or encumber them with a large, new burden. Most jurisdictions already provide a state-law right to appointed counsel more generous than that afforded by the Federal Constitution. All but 16 States, for example, would provide counsel to a defendant in Shelton's circumstances, either because he received a substantial fine or because state law authorized incarceration for the charged offense or provided for a maximum prison term of one year. There is thus scant reason to believe that a rule conditioning imposition of a suspended sentence on provision of appointed counsel would affect existing practice in the large majority of the States. And given the current commitment of most jurisdictions to affording court-appointed counsel to indigent misdemeanants while simultaneously preserving the option of probationary punishment, we do not share *amicus*' concern that other States may lack the capacity and resources to do the same.

Moreover, even if *amicus* is correct that "some courts and jurisdictions at least [can]not bear" the costs of the rule we confirm today, those States need not abandon probation or equivalent measures as viable forms of punishment. Although they may not attach probation to an imposed and suspended prison sentence, States unable or unwilling routinely to provide appointed counsel to misdemeanants in Shelton's situation are not without recourse to another option capable of yielding a similar result.

That option is pretrial probation, employed in some form by at least 23 States. Under such an arrangement, the prosecutor and defendant agree to the defendant's participation in a pretrial rehabilitation program,[11] which includes conditions typical of post-trial probation. The adjudication of guilt and imposition of sentence for the underlying offense then occur only if and when the defendant breaches those conditions.

Like the regime urged by *amicus,* this system reserves the appointed-counsel requirement for the "small percentage" of cases in which incarceration proves necessary thus allowing a State to "supervise a course of rehabilitation" without providing a lawyer every time it wishes to pursue such a course. Unlike *amicus*' position, however, pretrial probation also respects the constitutional imperative that "no person may be imprisoned for any offense . . . unless he was represented by counsel at his trial." . . .

SCALIA, J., dissenting.

In Argersinger v. Hamlin we held that "absent a knowing and intelligent waiver, *no person may be imprisoned* for any offense . . . unless he was represented by counsel at his trial." Although, we said, the "run of misdemeanors will not be affected" by this rule, "in those *that end up in the actual deprivation of a person's liberty,* the accused will receive the benefit" of appointed counsel. We affirmed this rule in *Scott v. Illinois,* drawing a bright line between imprisonment and the mere threat of imprisonment: "[T]he central premise of *Argersinger*— that actual imprisonment is a penalty different in kind from fines *or the mere threat of imprisonment*— is eminently sound

11. Because this device is conditioned on the defendant's consent, it does not raise the question whether imposition of probation alone so restrains a defendant's liberty as to require provision of appointed counsel.

and warrants adoption of *actual imprisonment* as the line defining the constitutional right to appointment of counsel." We have repeatedly emphasized actual imprisonment as the touchstone of entitlement to appointed counsel.

Today's decision ignores this long and consistent jurisprudence, extending the misdemeanor right to counsel to cases bearing the mere threat of imprisonment. Respondent's 30-day suspended sentence, and the accompanying 2-year term of probation, are invalidated for lack of appointed counsel even though respondent has not suffered, and may never suffer, a deprivation of liberty. The Court holds that the suspended sentence violates respondent's Sixth Amendment right to counsel because it "*may* end up in the actual deprivation of [respondent's] liberty," *if* he someday violates the terms of probation, *if* a court determines that the violation merits revocation of probation, and *if* the court determines that no other punishment will "adequately protect the community from further criminal activity" or "avoid depreciating the seriousness of the violation." And to all of these contingencies there must yet be added, before the Court's decision makes sense, an element of rank speculation. Should all these contingencies occur, the Court speculates, the Alabama Supreme Court would mechanically apply its decisional law applicable to routine probation revocation (which establishes procedures that the Court finds inadequate) rather than adopt special procedures for situations that raise constitutional questions in light of *Argersinger* and *Scott*. The Court has miraculously divined how the Alabama justices would resolve a constitutional question. . . .

In the future, *if and when* the State of Alabama seeks to imprison respondent on the previously suspended sentence, we can ask whether the procedural safeguards attending the imposition of that sentence comply with the Constitution. But that question is *not* before us now. . . .

Our prior opinions placed considerable weight on the practical consequences of expanding the right to appointed counsel beyond cases of actual imprisonment. Today, the Court gives this consideration the back of its hand. Its observation that all but 16 States already appoint counsel for defendants like respondent is interesting but quite irrelevant, since today's holding is not confined to *defendants like respondent*. Appointed counsel must henceforth be offered before *any* defendant can be awarded a suspended sentence, no matter how short. Only 24 States have announced a rule of this scope.[4] Thus, the Court's decision imposes a large, new burden on a majority of the States, including some of the poorest (*e.g.*, Alabama, Arkansas, and Mississippi). That burden consists not only of the cost of providing state-paid counsel in cases of such insignificance that even financially prosperous defendants sometimes forgo the expense of hired counsel; but also the cost of enabling courts and prosecutors to respond to the "over-lawyering" of minor cases. Nor should we discount the burden placed on the minority 24 States that currently provide counsel: that they keep their current disposition forever in place, however imprudent experience proves it to be.

4. Ten of the 34 States cited by the Court do not offer appointed counsel in all cases where a misdemeanor defendant might suffer a suspended sentence. Six States guarantee counsel only when the authorized penalty is *at least* three or six months' imprisonment. South Dakota does not provide counsel where the maximum permissible sentence is 30 days' imprisonment if "the court has concluded that [the defendant] will not be deprived of his liberty if he is convicted." . . . Misdemeanors punishable by less than six months' imprisonment may be a narrow category, but it may well include the vast majority of cases in which (precisely *because* of the minor nature of the offense) a suspended sentence is imposed. There is simply nothing to support the Court's belief that few offenders are prosecuted for crimes in which counsel is not already provided. . . .

Today's imposition upon the States finds justification neither in the text of the Constitution, nor in the settled practices of our people, nor in the prior jurisprudence of this Court. I respectfully dissent.

■ FLORIDA RULE OF CRIMINAL PROCEDURE 3.111

(a) A person entitled to appointment of counsel as provided herein shall have counsel appointed when the person is formally charged with an offense, or as soon as feasible after custodial restraint, or at the first appearance before a committing magistrate, whichever occurs earliest.

(b) (1) Counsel shall be provided to indigent persons in all prosecutions for offenses punishable by imprisonment (or by incarceration in a juvenile corrections institution) including appeals from the conviction thereof. Counsel does not have to be provided to an indigent person in a prosecution for a misdemeanor or violation of a municipal ordinance if the judge, before trial, files in the cause a statement in writing that the defendant will not be imprisoned if convicted.

(2) Counsel may be provided to indigent persons in all proceedings arising from the initiation of a criminal action against a defendant, including postconviction proceedings and appeals therefrom, extradition proceedings, mental competency proceedings, and other proceedings that are adversary in nature, regardless of the designation of the court in which they occur or the classification of the proceedings as civil or criminal.

(3) Counsel may be provided to a partially indigent person on request, provided that the person shall defray that portion of the cost of representation and the reasonable costs of investigation as he or she is able without substantial hardship to the person or the person's family, as directed by the court.

(4) "Indigent" shall mean a person who is unable to pay for the services of an attorney, including costs of investigation, without substantial hardship to the person or the person's family; "partially indigent" shall mean a person unable to pay more than a portion of the fee charged by an attorney, including costs of investigation, without substantial hardship to the person or the person's family.

■ VERMONT STATUTES TIT. 13, §§5231, 5201

§5231

A needy person who is being detained by a law enforcement officer without charge or judicial process, or who is charged with having committed or is being detained under a conviction of a serious crime, is entitled:

(1) To be represented by an attorney to the same extent as a person having his own counsel; and

(2) To be provided with the necessary services and facilities of representation. Any such necessary services and facilities of representation that exceed $1,500 per item must receive prior approval from the court after a hearing involving the parties. . . . This obligation and requirement to obtain prior court approval shall also be imposed in like manner upon the Attorney General or a State's Attorney prosecuting a violation of the law. . . .

§ 5201

In this chapter, the term . . . "Serious crime" includes: (A) A felony; (B) A misdemeanor the maximum penalty for which is a fine of more than $1,000 or any period of imprisonment unless the judge, at the arraignment but before the entry of a plea, determines and states on the record that he will not sentence the defendant to a fine of more than $1,000 or period of imprisonment if the defendant is convicted of the misdemeanor. . . .

Notes

1. *Constitutional right to appointed defense counsel in minor cases: majority position.* The Rhode Island advisory opinion reflects the overwhelming majority view in this country: Provision of counsel is constitutionally required for any defendant charged with a felony and for any defendant charged with a misdemeanor that results in actual imprisonment, even if less than six months. The decision in Scott v. Illinois, 440 U.S. 367 (1979), declared that only misdemeanors resulting in "actual imprisonment" would require appointed counsel. Prior to the *Scott* decision, more than 20 states provided counsel (by statute or under the federal or state constitution) for a broader range of misdemeanors, and not just those involving actual imprisonment. Today, fewer states go beyond the "actual imprisonment" rule as a matter of state constitutional law. See State v. Dowd, 478 A.2d 671 (Me. 1984) (accused receives counsel when facing charges that might result in prison term of more than six months or a fine of more than $500); Commonwealth v. Thomas, 507 A.2d 57 (Pa. 1986) (adopting actual imprisonment rule).

What explains this shift in constitutional rules over the years? Is it an example of the leading role the U.S. Supreme Court can play in constitutional interpretation? Does it exemplify what can happen when legal rules created in a system dealing with a relatively small number of cases are used in a system processing much larger numbers of cases? Is it significant that Rhode Island's governor requested an advisory opinion on the extent of the right to counsel when formulating the state budget?

What do the courts in *Gideon* and in the Rhode Island advisory opinion believe that lawyers do? Are attorneys indispensable to criminal justice, or an impediment to criminal justice, or both? Consider, in this connection, what happened to Clarence Gideon. After the Supreme Court reversed Gideon's conviction, an attorney defended Gideon at his retrial on the charges. He was acquitted. See Anthony Lewis, Gideon's Trumpet 223-238 (1964).

2. *Statutory right to appointed counsel in minor cases.* There is more variation among state statutes providing counsel than among state constitutional interpretations. Some states have statutes or rules that track the federal and state constitutional requirements. However, there is also a large group, represented by the Vermont statute above, that add to the list of crimes for which the state must provide counsel for indigent defendants. As the opinions in *Shelton* indicated, a number of state statutes provided counsel for defendants who receive a suspended sentence even before it became clear that the constitution requires defense lawyers in such cases. Some states also provide counsel for some cases involving large criminal fines.

Statutes providing for the appointment of defense counsel appeared early in the history of this country, and some covered a wide range of crimes. Many of the earliest statutes provided for appointed counsel in capital cases—which included a broader range of crimes at that time than it does today—but some (like a 1795 Act in New Jersey) required appointment in the case of any person tried upon an indictment. See Betts v. Brady, 316 U.S. 455, 470 n.28 (1942).

Perhaps the most important statutory provisions and rules on this subject are the ones (like the Florida rule above) giving a trial judge the *discretion* to appoint counsel in any criminal proceedings, regardless of the crime involved. The critical decisions here are funding decisions, which are often made at the local rather than state level. See Bureau of Justice Statistics, Indigent Defense Services in Large Counties, 1999 at 3 (Nov. 2000, NCJ 184932) (in largest 100 counties, 69 percent of funds for indigent defense comes from county or city government, 25 percent from state). Will a city provide enough money to fund attorneys for all those accused of violating its criminal ordinances? As a trial judge, can you identify any class of cases where you would not routinely appoint counsel even if the funds were available?

3. *Determination of indigence.* The trial court typically determines, in a hearing soon after charges are filed, whether or not the defendant qualifies as an indigent to receive state-provided counsel. The trial judge must consult factors listed in appellate opinions, statutes, or procedure rules, but those factors tend to be general enough to leave the trial judge with much discretion in deciding which defendants qualify. The judge often must consider such factors as the seriousness of the crime, the amount of bail bond required, the defendant's assets and debts, and the defendant's employment status. See Tenn. Code §40-14-202(c). The state might provide counsel and later attempt to collect the attorneys' fees from defendants who have more resources than they originally appeared to have. In the end, the great majority of felony defendants are indigents who receive public defenders or appointed counsel. By some estimates, more than three-quarters of all defendants charged with eligible crimes are provided with counsel. Bureau of Justice Statistics, Defense Counsel in Criminal Cases (Nov. 2000, NCJ 179023) (82 percent of felony defendants in state court represented by publicly financed counsel).

Why bother to distinguish between indigent and nonindigent defendants? Would the criminal justice system improve if the state offered to pay for an attorney (at state-determined rates) for any criminal defendant charged with an eligible crime—no questions asked about the defendant's ability to pay? Would this make the provision of defense counsel more like Social Security benefits, an entitlement with broad political support because it benefits a broad group?

4. *Distribution of offenses.* The decision about providing counsel to different classes of misdemeanants has serious consequences, not the least of them fiscal. If felonies rest at the top of a "pyramid" of criminal charges, the least serious misdemeanors are the charges at the broad bottom of the pyramid: In most systems, they are by far the most numerous charges. See Bureau of Justice Statistics, Prosecutors in State Courts, 2001 at 6 (May 2002, NCJ 193441) (prosecutors' offices close three times more misdemeanor cases than felony cases). As a result, choices about the appointment of counsel for the lowest-level charges will generally have the largest impact on the system for providing counsel. The federal system is atypical on this score, since only about a quarter of all charges filed in a given year are misdemeanors. Many states create special court systems to handle the lowest-level offenses, with names such as "misdemeanor court" or "district court."

5. *Constitutional sources of the right to counsel.* It is important to keep in mind the different constitutional sources for the right to counsel. In some settings

(a "criminal prosecution"), the Sixth Amendment requires counsel to be present. When it comes to police station interrogations, as we have seen in Chapter 8, the Fifth Amendment requires that a defendant be told about the right to have counsel present. In others (such as some postconviction proceedings), the due process clause requires counsel. In still other settings, the equal protection clause requires the state to provide counsel to all if it provides counsel to some. Recall also that most states have analogs to these federal constitutional provisions. What constitutional source was the basis for the *Gideon* decision?

What does the text of the Sixth Amendment suggest about the types of cases in which the state must provide counsel? On the one hand, the amendment does provide for a right to counsel "in *all* criminal prosecutions." Thus it would seem to cover any misdemeanor — even one not resulting in imprisonment. On the other hand, the Sixth Amendment was originally thought to address access to *retained* counsel, not defense counsel provided by the state. The Sixth Amendment right to counsel apparently was drafted as a repudiation of the common law of England, which prevented those accused of most felonies from relying upon retained counsel to conduct their defense at trial. Before the federal constitution was adopted, the constitutions of most states (including Maryland, Massachusetts, New Hampshire, New York, and Pennsylvania) granted the accused in criminal proceedings the right to retain counsel. When James Madison drafted the federal Bill of Rights, he drew upon existing provisions in various state constitutions. However, there is no extensive history to show the intentions of those who adopted the right to counsel embodied in the Sixth Amendment to the federal constitution.

6. *Incorporation.* Long before *Gideon,* the Supreme Court had declared that the Sixth Amendment required the government to appoint counsel for all criminal defendants in *federal* court. See Johnson v. Zerbst, 304 U.S. 458 (1938). The language of the Sixth Amendment and the rest of the Bill of Rights applied only to the federal government, not to the states. Thus, the *Gideon* Court had to resolve the larger question (given the relative sizes of the federal and state criminal systems) of whether the due process clause of the Fourteenth Amendment — which did apply to the states — "incorporated" the specific guarantees of the Bill of Rights.

The majority in *Gideon* argued that the *Betts* rule was an aberration and a departure from earlier cases dealing with the incorporation of the right to counsel; Justice John Marshall Harlan suggested instead that the *Betts* case was a plausible but impracticable extension of earlier cases. Who was right? Was the *Betts* approach simply not clear enough to provide predictable guidance, or was it faulty in some other respect?

The Supreme Court has decided that due process "selectively" incorporates some Bill of Rights guarantees. *Gideon* was an important development in this broader constitutional trend. While there has been debate over the years about the extent to which the framers and adopters of the Fourteenth Amendment intended to incorporate provisions of the Bill of Rights, the current consensus seems to be that the Court was substantially correct to incorporate most, if not all, of the provisions. See Michael Kent Curtis, No State Shall Abridge: The Fourteenth Amendment and the Bill of Rights (1986); Akhil Amar, The Bill of Rights and the Fourteenth Amendment, 101 Yale L.J. 1193 (1992).

7. *Actual imprisonment for later crimes.* A conviction for a misdemeanor that is not punished with a prison sentence might become relevant at a later time, during sentencing for some different crime. Can a sentencing judge use an earlier

uncounseled misdemeanor conviction to lengthen the prison term imposed for the later offense? In Nichols v. United States, 511 U.S. 738 (1994), the Supreme Court decided that a sentencing court may consider a defendant's previous uncounseled misdemeanor conviction in sentencing him for a subsequent offense. The opinion argued that the later sentencing decision does not convert the punishment for the original crime into a prison term, and that sentencing judges often rely on past conduct not proven in a criminal trial as a part of sentencing. Should the state provide counsel for *any* crime if a conviction for that crime will affect a person's liberty, whether now or later? Compare Brisson v. State, 955 P.2d 888 (Wyo. 1998) (rejects *Nichols;* use of prior uncounseled misdemeanor conviction to enhance later sentence is violation of state right to counsel); State v. Woodruff, 951 P.2d 605 (N.M. 1997) (adopts *Nichols* under state constitution).

Problem 11-1. Lawyers and Experts

Paul Husske was charged with rape. Part of the government's case against him was a DNA analysis of tissue obtained from the rape victim. Several months before trial, the defendant filed a motion asserting his indigence and requesting that the trial court appoint an expert, at the government's expense, to help him challenge the DNA evidence that the prosecution intended to use. Husske asserted that because DNA evidence is "of a highly technical nature," it is "difficult for a lawyer to challenge DNA evidence without expert assistance." He expressed concern about the use of DNA evidence because the state's laboratory in the Division of Forensic Science had a "well-known record" for incompetent or biased testing. He also attached an affidavit from a local attorney who had read extensively on the subject of DNA and who also asserted the need for expert assistance to test the reliability of such evidence. Even though the trial court denied the defendant's motion, the court appointed the local attorney as co-counsel to assist the defendant, because he was "the most knowledgeable member of the local bar in the area of forensic DNA application."

A researcher from the Division of Forensic Science and a faculty member from a nearby state university testified at trial for the government as expert witnesses on the subject of DNA analysis. The experts each testified that the defendant's DNA profile matched the profile of the individual who had attacked the victim. They said that the DNA analysis did not exclude the defendant as a contributor of the genetic material that the assailant left on the victim's body and clothing. They also stated that the statistical probability of randomly selecting a person unrelated to the defendant in the Caucasian population with the same DNA profile was 1 in 700,000.

Was the trial judge obliged to appoint an expert to assist defense counsel? Compare Husske v. Commonwealth, 476 S.E.2d 920 (Va. 1996).

Note

In Ake v. Oklahoma, 470 U.S. 68 (1985), the Supreme Court held that the due process and equal protection clauses (but not the Sixth Amendment) require a state to provide an indigent defendant with access to a psychiatrist if the defendant makes a preliminary showing that his sanity will be a "significant issue" at trial. Later litigation focused on the question of when an appointed expert is one of the "raw materials integral to building an effective defense." See Caldwell v. Mississippi, 472 U.S. 320 (1985) (trial court properly denied an indigent defendant's requests for the appointment of a criminal investigator, a fingerprint expert, and a ballistics expert). Most courts that have considered the appointment of a nonpsychiatric expert have held that state constitutions require the appointment of nonpsychiatric experts to indigent defendants where they make a "particularized" showing of the need for the assistance. See Harrison v. State, 644 N.E.2d 1243 (Ind. 1995) (no appointment of DNA expert required because evidence involved "precise, physical measurements and chemical testing," and no showing that state's evidence was less than precise); Rey v. State, 897 S.W.2d 333 (Tex. Crim. App. 1995) (requiring appointment of pathologist to assist in cross-examination of state pathologist regarding autopsy).

2. *Point in the Proceedings*

When does the constitutional right to counsel take effect? For typical crimes, it would probably be unworkable to provide counsel (or even to give notice of the right to counsel) as soon as a person becomes a suspect or interacts with the police. Consider, in this regard, the great variety of interactions between citizens and police. The right to counsel more plausibly could attach whenever a person is arrested, though no jurisdiction has found a right to counsel based simply on the fact of arrest. Perhaps no right to counsel should attach until a person appears in court and is asked to plead guilty or not guilty, or at some other point in the standard criminal process.

Courts trying to determine when the right to counsel attaches have concluded that different constitutional provisions create obligations arising at different points in the process. There are at least two distinct counsel rights — one based on the Sixth Amendment and its state analogs, the other based on the Fifth Amendment privilege against self-incrimination.

The Fifth Amendment right to counsel — a right derived from the inherently compulsory nature of custodial interrogation and from the need to protect against compulsory self-incrimination — was recognized in Miranda v. Arizona, 384 U.S. 436 (1966) (see Chapter 8). The Fifth Amendment right to counsel arises whenever the police conduct a custodial interrogation. Because interrogations usually occur before charging (since they are used to gather evidence), the Fifth Amendment right to counsel will often arise before any Sixth Amendment right to counsel.

The Sixth Amendment provides that "In all criminal prosecutions, the accused shall . . . have the assistance of counsel for his defense." The language raises the question: What is a "criminal prosecution"? One aspect of the right to counsel is largely settled and uniform. All jurisdictions, led by the U.S. Supreme Court, agree that the right to counsel attaches by the time of arraignment — a hearing in which the defendant typically is informed of the charges that have been filed and is asked to plead "guilty" or "not guilty." See Hamilton v. Alabama, 368 U.S. 52 (1961). In addition, the analysis of whether a Sixth Amendment right to counsel attaches turns on whether the procedure is considered a "critical stage" of the criminal process, taking place after the "initiation" of the adversarial judicial proceedings. We saw in Chapter 9 that the U.S. Supreme Court considers post-indictment lineups to be a "critical stage" of the criminal process. What is it that makes a police technique or judicial hearing a "critical stage"?

■ ALABAMA RULE OF CRIMINAL PROCEDURE 6.1(a)

A defendant shall be entitled to be represented by counsel in any criminal proceedings held pursuant to these rules and, if indigent, shall be entitled to have an attorney appointed to represent the defendant in all criminal proceedings in which representation by counsel is constitutionally required. The right to be represented shall include the right to consult in private with an attorney or the attorney's agent, as soon as feasible after a defendant is taken into custody, at reasonable times thereafter, and sufficiently in advance of a proceeding to allow adequate preparation therefor.

■ MISSOURI SUPREME COURT RULES 31.01, 31.02

31.01

Every person arrested and held in custody by any peace officer in any jail, police station or any other place, upon or without a warrant or other process for the alleged commission of a criminal offense, or upon suspicion thereof, shall promptly, upon request, be permitted to consult with counsel or other persons in his behalf, and, for such purpose, to use a telephone.

31.02

(a) In all criminal cases the defendant shall have the right to appear and defend in person and by counsel. If any person charged with an offense, the conviction of which would probably result in confinement, shall be without counsel upon his first appearance before a judge, it shall be the duty of the court to advise him of his right to counsel, and of the willingness of the court to appoint counsel to represent him if he is unable to employ counsel. Upon a showing of indigency, it shall be the duty of the court to appoint counsel to represent him. . . .

■ JOY FRIEDMAN v. COMMISSIONER OF PUBLIC SAFETY

473 N.W.2d 828 (Minn. 1991)

YETKA, J.

. . . On the evening of March 12, 1989, Joy Friedman was arrested by a Minneapolis police officer for DWI following her failure of a preliminary breath test. The officer took Friedman to the police station for an intoxilyzer test. They were forced to wait 25 minutes because the testing unit was in use. Friedman asked what her rights were and whether she could consult an attorney. The officer did not allow her to contact an attorney.

During the wait, another officer took Friedman into a video taping room. He questioned her on tape. The arresting officer read the implied consent advisory to Friedman. The advisory stated that Friedman's driver's license would be revoked for one year if she refused the chemical test for blood alcohol, that the refusal or the results of the test would be used against her at trial, and that she had a right to consult an attorney after testing. The officer read the advisory three times. Friedman told him that she didn't understand the advisory and that she had already been tested in the squad car. The police took Friedman's response as a refusal to be tested, and her driver's license was revoked for 1 year pursuant to Minn. Stat. §169.123, subd. 4. The issue before this court is: When does the right to counsel in a DWI proceeding attach?

The right to counsel is a long-established principle in this nation. Under the common law of England, those accused of felonies had no right to retain counsel. In 1695, Parliament enacted a statute which permitted those accused of treason to retain counsel, but for all other felonies, there was no such provision until 1836. Illogically, for minor offenses, including libel, perjury, battery, and conspiracy, counsel was permitted. Blackstone denounced the English rule as inhumane.

The American colonies rejected the harsh English rule. Even before the federal Constitution was adopted, the constitutions of Maryland, Massachusetts, New Hampshire, New York and Pennsylvania granted the accused in criminal proceedings the right to retain counsel. Delaware, North Carolina, South Carolina, Virginia, Connecticut, Georgia, and Rhode Island early in their history adopted constitutional or statutory provisions guaranteeing the right to counsel. When James Madison drafted the federal Bill of Rights, he drew upon existing provisions in various state constitutions. . . .

Minnesota has a long tradition of assuring the right to counsel. Article I, section 6 of the Minnesota Constitution requires that "in all criminal prosecutions the accused shall enjoy the right . . . to have the assistance of counsel in his defense." Minnesota Statutes §481.10, which has been the law in this state since 1887, provides: "All officers or persons having in their custody a person restrained of liberty upon any charge or cause alleged, except in cases where imminent danger of escape exists, shall admit any resident attorney retained by or in behalf of the person restrained, or whom the restrained person may desire to consult, to a private interview at the place of custody. . . ." In State v. Schabert, 15 N.W.2d 585 (Minn. 1944), we construed the statute and held that interrogation of an accused person was a "proceeding."

We turn now to our case law in the area of DWI proceedings. The [government] relies on State v. Palmer, 191 N.W.2d 188 (Minn. 1971), where we held that, under the Minnesota Constitution, the right to counsel does not extend to a DWI license revocation because of the civil or administrative nature of the proceeding. However, we subsequently questioned the validity of the "civil" label of the DWI license revocation proceeding in Prideaux v. State Dep't of Public Safety, 247 N.W.2d 385 (Minn. 1976). [We] articulated in *Prideaux* three reasons why the "civil" label was subject to question. First, a driver's license revocation for failure to submit to chemical testing is necessarily and inextricably intertwined with an undeniably criminal proceeding — namely, prosecution for driving while under the influence of an alcoholic beverage. Second, the revocation of a driver's license has, in most instances, the same impact as the traditional criminal sanctions of a fine and imprisonment. . . . Third, we noted that the choice of whether to submit to the chemical testing procedures is a very important one to the individual driver. A driver must make a critical and binding decision regarding chemical testing, a decision that will affect him or her in subsequent proceedings. Therefore, when asked to submit to a chemical test, a driver finds him- or herself at a "critical stage" in the DWI process. However, we did not have to reach the constitutional issues in *Prideaux,* finding instead that the Minnesota Legislature, pursuant to Minn. Stat. §481.10, did not intend a blanket denial of a right to counsel.

Subsequent to *Prideaux,* we reached the right-to-counsel issue in Nyflot v. Commissioner of Public Safety, 369 N.W.2d 512 (Minn. 1985). We held that the decision of whether to submit to chemical testing was not a "critical stage" in the pretrial investigation. Thus, no right to counsel attached at that point. However, *Nyflot* was decided under federal constitutional law. We must now confront directly whether Minnesota constitutional history dictates a different result. Because we do not find the *Nyflot* analysis persuasive under our constitution, we conclude that article I, section 6 requires that the right to counsel attaches at the chemical testing stage. . . .

As the United States Supreme Court explained in United States v. Ash, 413 U.S. 300 (1973), the . . . test for whether the defendant needed assistance of counsel is "whether the accused required aid in coping with legal problems or assistance in meeting his adversary." In defining what constitutes a "critical stage" in the proceeding, the Court held that it includes "those pretrial procedures that would impair defense on the merits if the accused is required to proceed without counsel." Gerstein v. Pugh, 420 U.S. 103 (1975). We adopt this broad definition as we now interpret the right to counsel set forth in the Minnesota Constitution. We believe that a driver who has been stopped for a possible DWI violation and has been asked to submit to a chemical test is at a "critical stage" in DWI proceedings, thus triggering the right to counsel.

The implied consent situation usually begins with a police officer requesting that the accused perform either a preliminary breath test or field sobriety test. Failure of either test can result in the issuance of a ticket or tab charge.[5] Though the police could issue a ticket at this initial confrontation, one is not usually issued until after the implied consent advisory has been recited and the chemical test performed (or not performed if the accused declines to submit).

It was at this point in the process that Friedman requested, and was denied, an opportunity to consult her lawyer. As the facts in this case indicate, she initially agreed to take the preliminary breath test, failed it, and was taken to the police station. She was in police custody and was questioned on video tape. She was told that she would be tested again. When she asked why she had to be tested again, the officer made no attempt to explain. Another officer then read the implied consent advisory. When Friedman expressed confusion about the advisory, requesting a consultation with her attorney, her confused response was deemed a refusal to take the test.

In the facts before this court, the driver was confused about the legal ramifications of her decision. As is often the case, the driver at this critical stage looked to the police for guidance. An attorney, not a police officer, is the appropriate source of legal advice. An attorney functions as an objective advisor who could explain the alternative choices. We think the Minnesota Constitution protects the individual's right to consult counsel when confronted with this decision. [O]ther courts have

5. The ticket or tab charge is the functional equivalent of a complaint. If the prosecution has not filed a complaint by the time of the defendant's first appearance in court under a gross misdemeanor DWI, the court administrator's office enters on the record a brief statement of the offense charged. . . .

taken a similar view, finding a state constitutional basis for expanding the right to counsel at the chemical testing stage of a DWI proceeding. See State v. Spencer, 750 P.2d 147 (Or. 1988). . . .

It is strange logic that concludes that there will be more drunk drivers on the road because a driver can consult counsel before taking a test rather than after taking it. If the objective of DWI prosecution is to get drunk drivers off the highways, into treatment, and on the way to sobriety, an attorney can play a very important role. A good lawyer is not only interested in protecting the client's legal rights, but also in the well-being, mental and physical health of the client. A lawyer has an affirmative duty to be a counselor to his client. See Minn. R. Prof. Conduct 2.1 (1985) ("In rendering advice, a lawyer may refer not only to law but to other considerations such as moral, economic, social and political factors, that may be relevant to the client's situation"). The lawyer may be able to persuade a problem drinker to seek treatment. The prosecution, on the other hand, may be concerned only with getting statistics and convictions. . . .

However, we also recognize that the evanescent nature of the evidence in DWI cases requires that the accused be given a limited amount of time in which to contact counsel. . . . The right to counsel will be considered vindicated if the person is provided with a telephone prior to testing and given a reasonable time to contact and talk with counsel. If counsel cannot be contacted within a reasonable time, the person may be required to make a decision regarding testing in the absence of counsel. . . .

COYNE, J., dissenting.

. . . The term "criminal prosecution" is a legal term of art [referring] not to the investigative, evidence-gathering phase of a proceeding, nor to all proceedings taking place after a suspect is arrested, but only to those proceedings which occur after the state has committed itself to prosecuting the suspect by formally charging the suspect with a crime. The right to counsel does not attach until the state has formally made the suspect a defendant, usually either by indictment or by filing a formal complaint or what in some jurisdictions is called an "information."

There is, moreover, a second prerequisite to the attachment of the constitutional right to counsel: the stage of the prosecution must be a "critical stage." The presence of one but not the other prerequisite is not enough. That a criminal prosecution has been formally commenced is not enough to invoke the right to counsel if the stage of the proceeding is not a "critical stage." On the other hand, the fact that the stage might otherwise be deemed a "critical stage" does not mean that the suspect has a constitutional right to counsel if the government has not yet formally commenced a criminal prosecution of that suspect. Thus, it has been held that before being formally charged, a suspect has no right to consult a lawyer before submitting to a search or the drawing of a blood sample or before appearing in a lineup.[2] Nor does a defendant formally charged have a right to counsel at a photographic display or when providing a handwriting exemplar because neither event is a "critical stage" of the prosecution.

2. A suspect has no right under these provisions to consult with an attorney as a prerequisite to giving consent to search, at least before he has been formally charged. Schneckloth v. Bustamonte, 412 U.S. 218 (1973). A suspect does not have a right to consult with counsel before deciding whether to comply with an order, lawful under the fourth and fifth amendments, to allow a trained technician to remove a blood sample as part of a precharge criminal investigation. Schmerber v. California, 384 U.S. 757 (1966). . . .

There is, of course, a "*Miranda* right to counsel" which a suspect who is in custody but who has not yet been formally charged may assert before being interrogated. Miranda v. Arizona, 384 U.S. 436 (1966). But the court-created *Miranda* right to counsel is not based on the sixth amendment; it is specifically designed to vindicate the fifth amendment privilege against self-incrimination. Furthermore, the defendant in the present case does not (nor could she) assert a *Miranda* right to counsel, which applies only to custodial interrogation and has nothing to do with whether an accused has a right to counsel before deciding whether to submit peaceably to a police search.

Based on this bedrock of recognized constitutional law, this court has heretofore resisted the temptation to declare that a person arrested for DWI has a constitutional right to consult counsel before deciding whether to submit to chemical testing. . . . In Prideaux v. State Dept. of Public Safety, 247 N.W.2d 385 (Minn. 1976), it was held that Minn. Stat. §481.10 gives a driver arrested for DWI a limited statutory right to consult counsel before deciding whether to submit to chemical testing. . . . In 1984, however, the legislature amended the [implied consent] advisory by inserting a new warning that Minnesota law "requires" the person to submit to testing and by adding a statement that "after submitting to testing" the driver has a right to consult with an attorney (and to have additional tests made by someone of the person's own choosing).

The effect of the 1984 amendment was tested in Nyflot v. Commissioner of Public Safety, 369 N.W.2d 512 (Minn. 1985). [This court] held that "a driver arrested for DWI has no right, statutory or constitutional, to consult with counsel before deciding whether to submit to chemical testing." [A] fair reading of the opinion, the two special concurrences, and the dissent in *Nyflot* demands recognition that this court fully understood at that time that it was specifically holding under both federal and state constitutions that there was no constitutional right to consult counsel before deciding whether to submit to chemical testing under the implied consent law. . . .

The Minnesota Rules of Criminal Procedure provide that "the complaint, tab charge and indictment are the only accusatory pleadings by which a prosecution may be initiated and upon which it may be based." Comment to Minn. R. Crim. P. 2. Accordingly, it seems clear to me that the court correctly determined in *Nyflot* that no "criminal prosecution" had been commenced at the time the officer invoked the provisions of the implied consent law and gave Ms. Nyflot the advisory and that, therefore, neither the right to counsel provided by the United States Constitution nor the right to counsel contained in the corresponding provision of the Minnesota Constitution, was activated. . . .

Finally, the majority refuses to recognize that it is according a drunk driving arrestee special treatment accorded no other criminal arrestee who is required to submit to a search. The majority justifies its position by declaring that it is more than just a search to require a person to submit to a breath test because . . . the evidence seized, i.e., the breath sample, is so incriminating that it is pointless for the defendant to insist on his or her right to trial. But, of course, the same can be said of many other types of evidence discovered and seized during lawful searches conducted in the investigation of other crimes. For example, if police arrest a murder suspect moments after the commission of the offense and swab the suspect's hands with a chemical substance in order to determine if the suspect recently fired a gun, no one would be heard to argue that the police had to let the defendant speak with counsel first. . . . What the majority has done, therefore, is to hold that under the Minnesota Constitution a drunk driving arrestee is entitled to special treatment, treatment that is not and has never been accorded by either the United States Constitution or the Minnesota Constitution to persons arrested for other kinds of offenses.

KEITH, C.J., dissenting.

. . . The DWI prosecution does not commence until the suspect appears in court and agrees to the tab-charging procedure, i.e., the in-court reading of a brief statement of the offense as a substitute for the complaint, or, if the defendant demands a complaint, until the complaint is issued. Minn. R. Crim. P. 4.02, subd. 5(3). The flaw in the majority's reasoning occurs in its statement that "the ticket or tab charge is the functional equivalent of a complaint." The tab charge is a substitute for a complaint in misdemeanor and gross misdemeanor DWI cases; the issuance of the ticket alongside the highway is not.

To the extent the majority places significance on its view that DWI proceedings are formally commenced upon the issuance of the ticket at the roadside, the majority creates contradictory rules for when the right to counsel attaches in felony and gross misdemeanor cases in contrast to misdemeanor and DWI cases. The state may initiate a prosecution by tab charge for misdemeanor offenses and for gross misdemeanor DWI offenses. Minn. R. Crim. P. 17.01. If ticketing a suspect for an offense that may be tab-charged triggers the attachment of the right to counsel under Minn. Const. art. I, §6, misdemeanor offenders and DWI offenders benefit from the right to counsel from the point of arrest. At the same time, defendants who are arrested for the most serious crimes do not have the right to counsel until they appear in court. I do not believe the federal or the Minnesota constitutions require this result. . . .

Problem 11-2. Psychiatric Examinations

Raymond Larsen was charged with murder in Illinois. He admitted that he killed the victim but relied on the affirmative defense of insanity at the time of the slaying. The state filed a written pretrial motion to require Larsen to submit to examination by a state-designated psychiatrist as provided by statute. The court appointed Dr. Robert Reifman, assistant director of the Psychiatric Institute of the Circuit Court of Cook County, to conduct an examination "on August 23, or on any date subsequent, necessary to complete such examination." The defendant's counsel did not receive notice of the location and time, or of the name of the psychiatrist, prior to the examination, which was conducted on August 24.

Based on the court-ordered psychiatric examination, Dr. Reifman testified for the state on rebuttal at trial. He opined that the defendant had an antisocial personality but did not suffer from a mental defect or disease and had substantial capacity to conform his conduct to the requirement of the law and to appreciate the criminality of his conduct. On appeal the defendant argues that the psychiatric examination was a "critical stage" of the proceedings and that he had the right to notice and presence of counsel. How would you rule? See People v. Larsen, 385 N.E.2d 679 (Ill. 1979).

Notes

1. *Critical stages before trial: majority position.* The federal constitutional right to counsel applies only after the initiation of an "adversarial proceeding," and only during a "critical stage" of those proceedings. The right extends to preliminary hearings

in which the government must demonstrate a prima facie case against the defendant, Coleman v. Alabama, 399 U.S. 1 (1970), because defense counsel at such a hearing can obtain discovery of the state's evidence, make a record for later impeachment of state witnesses at trial, and preserve defense witness testimony. However, the federal constitutional right to counsel does not begin with arrest, or even with a postarrest probable cause hearing required by Gerstein v. Pugh, 420 U.S. 103 (1975).

State constitutions are almost always interpreted to cover the same pretrial proceedings as the federal constitution. Typically, a state's rules of criminal procedure will track these constitutional boundaries and will provide for the appointment of legal counsel at the defendant's initial appearance before a magistrate, when the defendant is informed of the charges. The Missouri rule reprinted above is typical. According to a survey by Douglas Colbert, defense attorneys are usually not available when the judge makes the first determination of bail or pretrial detention at the initial appearance. Eight states provide counsel when a judge decides whether to order pretrial release or bail. Nineteen states provide no counsel at the time of bail, while the remaining 23 provide counsel only in urban centers. See Douglas Colbert, Thirty-Five Years After *Gideon*: The Illusory Right to Counsel, 1998 Ill. L. Rev. 1 (1998).

Some high state courts have read their state constitutions to provide for a right to counsel earlier than in the federal system. See Page v. State, 495 So. 2d 436 (Miss. 1986) (right to counsel attaches before arraignment, when proceedings reach "accusatory" stage); cf. McCarter v. State, 770 A.2d 195 (Md. 2001) (statute gives defendant right to counsel at initial appearance; not necessary to decide if initial appearance is "critical stage" for constitutional counsel right). You may also recall from Chapter 9 that a minority of states have concluded that a postarrest identification lineup or photo identification can qualify as a "critical stage" that triggers the right to counsel. See, e.g., People v. Jackson, 217 N.W.2d 22 (Mich. 1974) (photo lineup); Commonwealth v. Richman, 320 A.2d 351 (Pa. 1974) (lineup). Some states also conclude that it is a violation of the right to counsel to fail to inform a suspect during interrogation that his attorney is trying to make contact. See Haliburton v. State, 514 So. 2d 1088 (Fla. 1987). See Chapter 8.

2. *Defense counsel for DWI examinations: majority position.* Roughly 10 high state courts have granted a person arrested on DWI charges the right to consult with retained counsel before performing sobriety tests. See State v. Spencer, 750 P.2d 147 (Or. 1988). Does this position create a special rule for DWI defendants not applicable to most criminal defendants? Are DWI defendants as a class different from other criminal defendants? Will the lawyer be able to persuade a problem drinker to seek treatment?

3. *Handwriting and blood samples.* Under federal law, a defendant has no right to counsel when she produces a handwriting exemplar, even after issuance of a formal charge, because the taking of such an exemplar is not a "critical stage" of the proceedings. Gilbert v. California, 388 U.S. 263 (1967). Similarly, there is no federal constitutional right to consult with counsel before submitting to an order for the drawing of a blood sample. A few states disagree. See Roberts v. State, 458 P.2d 340 (Alaska 1969) (right to counsel during collection of handwriting samples).

4. *Are psychiatric examinations a "critical stage"?* Should there be a rule governing whether all psychiatric examinations are a critical stage in the proceedings, or should it depend on the use of the information gained by the examination? Courts in about a dozen states have concluded that there is a right to counsel during at least some psychiatric exams, and these opinions typically state that the examination

might be a "critical stage" in some cases but not in others. More than 20 states have declared that there is no constitutional right to counsel during any psychiatric exams. Should competency examinations be treated differently from examinations used to undermine potential defenses? Those used at sentencing? Those used to establish aggravating factors for a capital sentence? In Estelle v. Smith, 451 U.S. 454 (1981), the Supreme Court held that use of a psychiatrist's testimony at a capital sentencing proceeding based on a pretrial psychiatric examination at which defendant had not been represented by counsel violated defendant's Fifth Amendment rights against compulsory self-incrimination. What would a lawyer do at a psychiatric examination? Would a lawyer have a right to review a psychiatrist's questions before the examination?

5. *Right to counsel at sentencing.* The Sixth Amendment and its state constitutional analogs apply to sentencing hearings; the government must provide the defendant with an attorney at these hearings. Mempa v. Rhay, 389 U.S. 128 (1967); State v. Alspach, 554 N.W.2d 882 (Iowa 1996) (right to counsel at postconviction hearing to challenge amount of restitution). However, counsel is not required if the trial court sentences a defendant to probation and the state later attempts to convince the judge to revoke the defendant's probation (and send the defendant to prison) because she has violated the conditions of probation. Gagnon v. Scarpelli, 411 U.S. 778 (1973). If the end result is the same for the offender (a prison term), what is the constitutional distinction between sentencing hearings and probation revocation hearings?

6. *Right to counsel on appeal.* The criminal prosecution ends with a conviction and sentence. If the defendant appeals the case, the government is defending the judgment rather than "prosecuting" the case. As a result, courts say, the Sixth Amendment right to counsel does not apply to criminal appeals. The federal constitutional right to counsel on the first appeal as of right is based instead on both due process and equal protection principles. See Douglas v. California, 372 U.S. 353 (1963). The federal constitutional right does not extend to discretionary appeals. Ross v. Moffitt, 417 U.S. 600 (1974). The government also has no federal constitutional obligation to supply counsel for postconviction proceedings such as habeas corpus. See Murray v. Giarratano, 492 U.S. 1 (1989). Once again, state courts have by and large followed the federal lead when interpreting their own constitutional provisions. Nevertheless, many states do appoint counsel for at least some defendants during these postconviction proceedings. See, e.g., Mont. Code Ann. §§46-8-103, 46-8-104 ("Any court of record may assign counsel to defend any defendant, petitioner, or appellant in any postconviction criminal action or proceeding if he desires counsel and is unable to employ counsel").

7. *Conditions of consultation.* For defendants held in custody, the government has great control over the physical setting where the defense lawyer and client meet and talk. Usually this occurs in special visitation areas in a jail, where the conversation between lawyer and client remains confidential and unmonitored.

After the terrorist attacks of September 2001, the U.S. Department of Justice announced a new policy allowing the government to monitor these conversations in exceptional cases. The monitoring will be conducted without a court order whenever the Attorney General certifies that "reasonable suspicion exists to believe that an inmate may use communications with attorneys or their agents to facilitate acts of terrorism." The Department says that it will notify inmates and their attorneys about their plans to listen in on the conversations; it will assign a special "taint team" to perform the monitoring and the teams will not disclose what they hear to the prosecutors working on the case. 66 Fed. Reg. 55062-01(Oct. 31, 2001); George Lardner Jr., U.S. Will Monitor Calls to Lawyers; Rule on Detainees Called "Terrifying," Wash. Post, A1, Nov. 9, 2001. How would a client react to news that a taint team from the Department of Justice will listen to conversations with the defense attorney? How would you construct an argument that this eavesdropping violates the right to counsel?

B. SELECTION AND REJECTION OF COUNSEL

Although the government may have an obligation to offer an attorney to most criminal defendants, not all defendants accept the offer. Some will insist on representing themselves, while others will be unhappy with the assigned lawyer and will ask for some other attorney. Which legal institutions must respond to these sorts of requests?

The U.S. Supreme Court, for one, has declared a general principle that the Sixth Amendment right to counsel includes a right to self-representation. In Faretta v. California, 422 U.S. 806 (1975), the Court pointed to historical practices giving the defendant power to waive counsel. The Sixth Amendment made the assistance of counsel "an aid to a willing defendant — not an organ of the State interposed between an unwilling defendant and his right to defend himself personally."

The right to self-representation, however, is far different from what most defendants might prefer: the right to select the attorney who will be appointed to represent them. Most defendants who choose to represent themselves do so after a frustrating experience with an attorney assigned to their case (or an attorney assigned to some earlier case). But it is clear that poor defendants do not have the legal right to select which attorney will represent them. Courts do not grant indigent defendants such a power, nor do most managers of public defender organizations. The decision about self-representation, then, is part of a broader negotiation between the defendant, the judge, the former attorney, and a prospective new attorney about who will represent the defendant. What interests will each of these parties bring to the negotiation?

■ STATE v. JOSEPH SPENCER

519 N.W.2d 357 (Iowa 1994)

McGiverin, C.J.

The question presented here is whether a criminal defendant suffered a violation of his sixth amendment right to self-representation when the district court appointed counsel for him over his objection. . . . On July 18, 1990, Monona County Sheriff Dennis Smith went to Joseph Spencer's rural home to investigate complaints that Spencer was discharging firearms on his property. Sheriff Smith [observed marijuana growing in Spencer's garden, obtained a search warrant, and seized marijuana plants, cocaine, and firearms from the house]. On August 20, trial informations were filed charging Spencer with possession of marijuana with intent to manufacture, unauthorized possession of firearms, possession of cocaine, and possession of marijuana. . . .

Defendant Spencer retained a private attorney, Richard Mock of Onawa, to represent him and pleaded not guilty. Attorney Mock filed a motion to suppress drugs and weapons seized during the execution of the search warrant. After an evidentiary hearing, the district court overruled the motion.

A trial date was set. On May 17, 1991, a few days before trial, attorney Mock moved to withdraw from his representation of defendant Spencer. During the hearing on that motion, the question arose as to who would represent defendant at trial. Defendant Spencer told the court he wished to represent himself but admitted he did not know legal procedures or how to object to improper evidence. After a lengthy colloquy, the district court stated, "As far as I'm concerned, although he indicates he wants to do it himself, I don't see that he's competent and qualified to do it himself." The district court then appointed attorney Richard McCoy of Sioux City to represent Spencer. The case was continued and went to trial about one year later. Attorney McCoy fully represented defendant prior to and during the trial. Spencer was found guilty by a jury and was sentenced on the four charges. Spencer appealed, contending through new counsel that the district court denied his right to self-representation. [He] contends that the district court forced counsel upon him, contrary to his rights under the sixth amendment of the federal constitution. . . .

The sixth amendment provides that an accused "shall enjoy the right . . . to have the assistance of counsel for his defence." The fourteenth amendment of the federal constitution extends this right to state prosecutions. In Faretta v. California, 422 U.S. 806 (1975), the Supreme Court held that the right to self-representation to make one's own defense is necessarily implied by the structure of the Sixth Amendment. However, the Supreme Court also recognized an important limitation on that right: Although the defendant may elect to represent himself (usually to his detriment), the trial court "may — even over objection by the accused — appoint a 'standby counsel' to aid the accused if and when the accused requests help, and to be available to represent the accused in the event that termination of the defendant's self-representation is necessary." Such an appointment serves "to relieve the judge of the need to explain and enforce basic rules of courtroom protocol or to assist the defendant in overcoming routine obstacles that stand in the way of the defendant's achievement of his own clearly indicated goals." McKaskle v. Wiggins, 465 U.S. 168 (1984). . . .

Moreover, a defendant waives his right to self-representation unless he asserts that right by "knowingly and intelligently forgoing his right to counsel." This waiver may occur despite the defendant's statement that he wishes to represent himself if he makes that statement merely out of brief frustration with the trial court's decision regarding counsel and not as a clear and unequivocal assertion of his constitutional rights. In addition, a waiver [of the right to self-representation] may be found if it reasonably appears to the court that defendant has abandoned his initial request to represent himself.

We believe that the trial court did not err in appointing an attorney for Spencer. The intent behind the appointment, from the comments of both the court and Mock, defendant's withdrawing attorney, was to provide Spencer with "standby counsel" as envisioned in *Faretta* and *McKaskle.* The following comments were made at the hearing on attorney Mock's application to withdraw:

The Court: Well, I don't think that you're [the defendant] in the position of being able to defend yourself. And the least I would do is have somebody appointed to sit and be available as your counsel. But, frankly, I'm not going to put the court in the position whereby you defend yourself and then it's reversed if there is a conviction, just because there was no attorney present. It's as simple as that. Now, do you have any other person in mind?

The Defendant: No, sir . . .

The Court: Well, what familiarity do you have with the legal system?

The Defendant: I don't have any, Your Honor. . . .

The Court: An ordinary citizen can defend himself, but frankly an ordinary citizen is going to have a little difficulty following the procedures, making the proper objections and defending his own interests, unless he's familiar with the procedure in court. That's the problem I have. If you think you can do that, that's one thing; otherwise, what will happen is, if there is a conviction, it will be appealed and they will say you should have had somebody here to protect your rights.

The court thus properly appointed attorney McCoy over defendant's objection. If defendant had wished to treat this appointed attorney as standby counsel, he could have done so. The record here, however, evinces Spencer's initial desire to be represented by counsel (in employing attorney Mock), leading us to conclude that even if he wished to proceed pro se at the time of the withdrawal hearing, he waived and abandoned that right by acquiescing to attorney McCoy's full representation of his case for the following year leading up to and during the jury trial. . . .

Spencer's request for self-representation came out of frustration rather than a distinct and unequivocal request for that constitutional right. When Spencer was first charged in August 1990, he hired a private attorney (Richard Mock). Spencer worked with him until his motion to suppress evidence was overruled. Then, in May 1991, Mock moved to withdraw. Defendant was exasperated and did not want to pay for another attorney. Yet he willingly accepted attorney McCoy's name and address from the court and clearly relied on McCoy's representation during the following year and throughout trial. Spencer never attempted to try the jury case himself with McCoy as standby counsel. He never again raised the self-representation issue in the trial court. . . . Finally, defendant Spencer has pointed to nothing that he would have done differently had he represented himself at trial, nor has he demonstrated any way in which attorney McCoy denied him "a fair chance to present his case in his own way." *McKaskle*, 465 U.S. at 177. . . .

We believe that the trial court's appointment of attorney McCoy to be available as standby counsel satisfied Spencer's request to represent himself but ensured that Spencer's other rights were protected as well. By his later acts Spencer waived and abandoned any right to self-representation that he may have had. . . .

LAVORATO, J., dissenting.

In a state criminal trial, a defendant has a Sixth and Fourteenth Amendment right under the federal Constitution to self-representation. Faretta v. California, 422 U.S. 806 (1975). Before the right attaches, the defendant must voluntarily elect to proceed without counsel by "knowingly and intelligently" waiving his Sixth Amendment right to counsel. In addition, the defendant's request to proceed without counsel must be "clear and unequivocal." Before a trial court accepts the request, the court must make the defendant aware of the dangers and disadvantages of self-representation, so that the record will establish that "he knows what he is doing and his choice is made with eyes open." *Faretta*, 422 U.S. at 835. A trial court may not bar a defendant from proceeding without counsel even though the defendant is not technically competent in the law. The defendant must only be competent to make the choice to proceed without counsel. . . .

I easily infer from the record that Spencer is above average in intelligence. He has college training in electronics and math. His work experience included several years in the Air Force. He also worked as an electronics technician at General Dynamics. . . .

Unlike the majority, I believe the following colloquy between the court and Spencer shows that (1) Spencer made a clear and unequivocal request — not once, but several times — to proceed without counsel, (2) his request was knowingly and intelligently made, and (3) the trial court understood Spencer was making a clear and unequivocal request to proceed without counsel: . . .

The Court: . . . Do you want to get another attorney or do you want to go to trial tomorrow with him?

The Defendant: I feel I would be better off defending myself, Your Honor. He doesn't want to listen to what I'm telling him. . . . I'll have to go pro — I'll have to defend myself.

The Court: Before I would let you do that, I would appoint somebody. If your status is as it appears to be, that you have property, those will be assessed — the fees of whoever is appointed will be assessed against that.

The Defendant: I don't see how you can force me to do that, Your Honor.

The Court: Well, I don't think that you're in the position of being able to defend yourself. And the least I would do is have somebody appointed to sit and be available as your counsel. But, frankly, I'm not going to put the court in the position whereby you defend yourself and then it's reversed if there is a conviction, just because there was no attorney present. It's as simple as that. [W]hat familiarity do you have with the legal system?

The Defendant: I don't have any, Your Honor. Shouldn't make the legal system that way where I can't defend myself. I'm the one that's familiar with the case. I'm the one that's arrested. I know what my best interest is.

The Court: Well, if I understand your complaint, [Mr. Mock] wanted to plead it and you wanted to fight it. Now, the question is, how are you going to fight it in the courtroom? My problem with it is that I don't want you to sit in the courtroom not being prepared for the procedures and end up with a verdict against you because you weren't familiar with the procedures. Do you understand what I'm saying?

The Defendant: I understand what you're saying, but I don't understand why you make them that way.

The Court: Why do we make what that way?

The Defendant: Court procedures that way. Ordinary citizen can't come in and defend himself. . . .

The Court: Okay. During the interim, the court has attempted to contact an attorney to represent the defendant in this case. I have contacted Richard McCoy in Sioux City. He practices in criminal court and he's . . . tried a lot of cases and I feel that he's a good attorney. He's indicated that he would be willing to take your case. . . . Does that meet with your approval?

The Defendant: Doesn't meet with my approval, Your Honor, but if you're going to force it on me, I'm going to have to take it. . . .

The Prosecutor: The appointment of Mr. McCoy is pursuant to [section] 815.10(2) then?

The Court: That's right. And I can appreciate that it says, ". . . if a person desires legal assistance and is not indigent." As far as I'm concerned, although he indicates he wants to do it himself, I don't see that he's competent and qualified to do it himself. There should be somebody there. And on that basis, [the] court interprets that section to apply. . . .

Spencer captured the essence of *Faretta* when he insisted that we "shouldn't make the legal system that way where I can't defend myself. I'm the one that's familiar with the case. I'm the one that's arrested. I know what my best interest is." On this point, *Faretta* eloquently says:

> . . . To force a lawyer on a defendant can only lead him to believe that the law contrives against him. Moreover, it is not inconceivable that in some rare instances, the defendant might in fact present his case more effectively by conducting his own defense. Personal liberties are not rooted in the law of averages. The right to defend is personal. [Although the defendant] may conduct his own defense ultimately to his own detriment, his choice must be honored out of "that respect for the individual which is the lifeblood of the law."

The majority . . . attempts to finesse the trial court's denial of Spencer's request to defend himself by simply characterizing the court's actions as appointment of standby counsel. [However, the] role of standby counsel is limited to assisting a pro se defendant when such defendant wants assistance. A pro se defendant has the right to control the case the defendant chooses to present to the jury. That means a trial court must permit the pro se defendant to control the organization and content of the defense, to make motions, to argue points of law, to participate in voir dire, to question witnesses, and to address the court and jury at appropriate points in the trial. . . . If the trial court permits standby counsel to participate in the defense over the defendant's objections, such participation effectively allows counsel to make or substantially interfere with any significant tactical decisions, or to control questioning of witnesses, or to speak instead of the defendant on any matter of importance. Such interference is a denial of the pro se defendant's right to self-representation. . . .

These stringent limitations were recently spelled out in McKaskle v. Wiggins, 465 U.S. 168 (1984), the first case in which the Supreme Court has described the role of standby counsel. Because the role of standby counsel is severely restricted, trial courts contemplating appointment of standby counsel should — at a minimum — explain the limitations I have sketched out above from *McKaskle.* The reason is obvious: if the right to self-representation is to mean anything, a defendant who is appointed standby counsel should know how far the defendant can go in defending himself or herself without interference.

Here the trial court should have granted Spencer's request to defend himself. If the court was still concerned, the court should have then explicitly told Spencer he was appointing standby counsel and should have explained the limitations on standby counsel's role. Although above average in intelligence, Spencer is still a layperson untrained in the intricacies of criminal law. . . . After the colloquy between the court and himself, Spencer could only have had one thought: appointed counsel was being forced upon him and he was not going to be allowed to defend himself. . . .

At English common law the insistence upon a right of self-representation was the rule, rather than the exception. It is ironic that in the long history of British criminal jurisprudence there was only one tribunal that ever adopted the practice of forcing counsel upon an unwilling criminal defendant. That tribunal was the Star Chamber, a tribunal that for centuries symbolized the disregard of basic human rights. And the insistence upon a right to self-representation was, if anything, more fervent in the American colonies than at English common law. As *Faretta* points out, [the] "value of state-appointed counsel was not unappreciated by the Founders, yet the notion of compulsory counsel was utterly foreign to them. And whatever else may be said of those who wrote the Bill of Rights, surely there can be no doubt that they understood the inestimable worth of free choice." In sum, I would hold that the trial court denied Spencer the right to represent himself. I would therefore reverse and remand for a new trial.

Notes

1. *Knowing and voluntary waiver of counsel: majority position.* Once the right to counsel has attached, the defendant can waive that right, but only if the choice is "knowing and voluntary." Johnson v. Zerbst, 304 U.S. 458 (1938). In Faretta v. California, 422 U.S. 806 (1975), the Supreme Court declared that the right to "assistance" of counsel logically implied a defendant's right to represent herself at trial without counsel. How does this square with the Court's observation in *Gideon* that a lawyer is a "necessity, not a luxury"?

As *Spencer* indicates, there is no simple answer to the question of how a trial court will determine that the defendant's request is a knowing and voluntary waiver of the right to counsel. Typically, courts say that the defendant can waive counsel and invoke the *Faretta* right to self-representation only if (1) the trial court informs the defendant about the dangers of such a strategy, or (2) it otherwise appears from the record that the defendant understood the dangers. See People v. Adkins, 551 N.W.2d 108 (Mich. 1996) (waiver of counsel requires an unequivocal request by defendant, offer by trial court to appoint counsel, explanation of dangers of self-representation and the punishment for the crime charged, and a finding that self-representation will not disrupt trial). Courts often say that a waiver hearing expressly addressing the disadvantages of a pro se defense is much preferred but not absolutely necessary. The ultimate test, they say, is not the trial court's express advice but the defendant's understanding.

Defendants who represent themselves sometimes claim after conviction that the trial judge did not adequately warn them about the perils of acting as their own counsel. What kinds of warnings should judges give? State v. Cornell, 878 P.2d 1352 (Ariz. 1994) (no reversible error where court did not warn defendant that self-representation would undermine his planned insanity defense). Should courts, legislatures, or drafters of procedural rules design the standard *Faretta* warnings? See Benchbook for United States District Judges, 1.02 (4th ed. 2000); People v. Arguello, 772 P.2d 87 (Colo. 1989) (model inquiry); Michigan Court Rules 6.005(D) and (E) (court must advise the defendant of the charge, the maximum possible prison sentence for the offense, any mandatory minimum sentence required by law, and the risk involved in self-representation).

2. *Standby counsel.* Often a judge will respond to a request for self-representation by appointing "standby counsel." Even if the standby counsel gives the defendant unwelcome advice and direction, a conviction can be upheld. See McKaskle v. Wiggins, 465 U.S. 168 (1984) (appointment of standby counsel does not violate self-representation right unless counsel interferes with substantial tactical decisions of defendant). Is the obligation of the trial judge to warn the defendant about the dangers of self-representation lower when the defendant's lawyer accepts "standby counsel" status at the time defendant asks to represent herself? See State v. Layton, 432 S.E.2d 740 (W. Va. 1993) (allowing less extensive warning about self-representation when standby counsel played relatively active role at trial); Anne Bowen Poulin, The Role of Standby Counsel in Criminal Cases: In the Twilight Zone of the Criminal Justice System, 75 N.Y.U. L. Rev. 676 (2000). Can courts *limit* the extent to which standby counsel can be involved? Commonwealth v. Molino, 580 N.E.2d 383 (Mass. 1991) (upholds trial court decision to limit standby counsel to answering requests for advice from defendant).

3. *Imposing counsel.* In *Spencer,* what could the defendant have said to the trial judge to convince the appellate court that he had tried to exercise his right to represent himself? If trial judges can appoint counsel over requests like Spencer's, how vibrant is the right to self-representation? See State v. Colt, 843 P.2d 747 (Mont. 1992) (trial judge directs standby counsel to take over cross-examination after repeated courtroom errors by the defendant). Have state courts in effect overruled *Faretta?* Which constituency, if any, keeps *Faretta* rights alive? If you were a prosecutor, would you argue on behalf of defendants who want to represent themselves? If lawyers are essential to justice, shouldn't *Faretta* be reversed?

In Martinez v. Court of Appeal of California, 528 U.S. 152 (2000), the Supreme Court refused to extend the *Faretta* right of self-representation to a direct appeal. The appellate courts may properly appoint counsel for the appellant, even if the appellant objects. Are trial judges better able than appellate judges to manage the difficulties presented by defendants who represent themselves? Are a defendant's interests in self-representation stronger at trial than during an appeal?

4. *Competence to waive the right to counsel.* Some defendants are not competent to make a "knowing and voluntary waiver" of the right to counsel. In Godinez v. Moran, 509 U.S. 389 (1993), the Supreme Court held that the due process clause does not require a higher standard to assess whether a defendant is competent to waive counsel or plead guilty than is used to assess competency to stand trial. See also State v. Day, 661 A.2d 539 (Conn. 1995). Is there any reason to employ different standards for competence to stand trial and for waiver of counsel?

5. *Performance standards for pro se counsel.* In practice, trial courts appear to give some leeway to lay lawyers, but appellate cases consistently hold that the ordinary standards of practice and evidence are to be applied to defendants who appear pro se. See Commonwealth v. Jackson, 647 N.E.2d 401 (Mass. 1995). Should judges assist pro se litigants in questioning witnesses? Should judges give pro se litigants miniature "lessons" in trial procedure and the rules of evidence?

6. *Selection of appointed counsel.* Defendants who retain their own lawyers may retain any lawyer they can afford who will agree to take the case (assuming the lawyer has no conflict of interest). This ability of the client to choose a particular lawyer helps to create a cooperative relationship. The lawyer is urged to "establish a relationship of trust and confidence with the accused." ABA Standards for Criminal Justice 4-3.1 (1980). An indigent defendant, however, may not choose his appointed

counsel. In the homely phrase of the Nebraska trial judge in State v. Green, 471 N.W.2d 402 (Neb. 1991), "beggars can't be choosey." This is a fair, if blunt, statement of the law in almost every jurisdiction. See Morris v. Slappy, 461 U.S. 1 (1983) (upholds trial court's refusal to grant continuance necessary to allow original counsel to represent defendant; trial proceeded with new appointed counsel). Does this rule suggest we are committed to providing counsel only in the most minimal sense to indigent defendants? If you were a supervisor in a public defender's office, would you institute a rule that allowed clients to take part in the choice of their lawyers?

Should a judge appointing defense counsel place any weight on a defendant's request to work with an attorney with specific qualities? Consider this possible conversation between a lawyer and client:

> "I want a Black lawyer to represent me." These are the first words you hear after you introduce yourself to your new client. . . . You are white. He is Black. You answer that you are an experienced criminal lawyer and will represent him to the best of your ability, regardless of his or your race. He responds that he too is experienced with the criminal justice system — a system that targets Black men, like himself, for prosecution far more than whites, that sentences Black men to prison more frequently and for a longer duration than whites, and that fails to acknowledge or address the role that race and racism play in the development, enforcement, and execution of the criminal laws established by "the system." . . . He explains that an African-American lawyer will be better able to understand and appreciate the circumstances that resulted in the bringing of these charges and that he, the client, can trust a Black lawyer more than a white one.

Kenneth P. Troccoli, "I Want a Black Lawyer to Represent Me": Addressing a Black Defendant's Concerns With Being Assigned a White Court-Appointed Lawyer, 20 Law and Inequality: A Journal of Theory and Practice 1 (Winter 2002). See also Marcus T. Boccaccini, Marcus T. and Stanley L. Brodsky, Characteristics of the Ideal Criminal Defense Attorney from the Client's Perspective: Empirical Findings and Implications for Legal Practice, 25 Law & Psychol. Rev. 81, 116 (2001) (client survey lists the following, in descending order, as most desired attorney characteristics: advocates for client's interest, works hard, keeps client informed, cares about the client, honest, gets favorable outcome, "would not do whatever prosecution says," listens to client, spends time with client before court date).

7. *Law students as counsel.* Almost every state allows some law students to participate in the defense of criminal cases. Statutes and court rules typically allow law students to represent indigent criminal defendants, so long as the defendant is informed that the representative is a law student and consents to the representation and a licensed attorney supervises the student's efforts. See Fla. R. Crim. P. 11-1.2(b); Miss. Code Ann. §73-3-207. What would you say to a defendant to convince her to allow a law student to "practice" on her case?

C. ADEQUACY OF COUNSEL

Constitutions and other laws not only govern the availability of a lawyer; they also address the quality of the legal representation that the attorney must give the client. So long as lawyers make mistakes, courts and other legal institutions must decide whether the client will be the one who pays. The next case lays down a legal standard now followed almost uniformly by courts trying to determine whether an attorney has provided a client with the "effective assistance of counsel" necessary for a constitutionally acceptable criminal conviction.

■ CHARLES STRICKLAND v. DAVID WASHINGTON

466 U.S. 668 (1984)

O'CONNOR, J.

This case requires us to consider the proper standards for judging a criminal defendant's contention that the Constitution requires a conviction or death sentence to be set aside because counsel's assistance at the trial or sentencing was ineffective.

During a 10-day period in September 1976, respondent planned and committed three groups of crimes, which included three brutal stabbing murders, torture, kidnapping, severe assaults, attempted murders, attempted extortion, and theft. After his two accomplices were arrested, respondent surrendered to police and voluntarily gave a lengthy statement confessing to the third of the criminal episodes. The State of Florida indicted respondent for kidnapping and murder and appointed an experienced criminal lawyer to represent him.

Counsel actively pursued pretrial motions and discovery. He cut his efforts short, however, and he experienced a sense of hopelessness about the case, when he learned that, against his specific advice, respondent had also confessed to the first two murders. [Respondent also acted against counsel's advice in pleading guilty to all charges, and waiving the right to an advisory jury at his capital sentencing hearing.]

In preparing for the sentencing hearing, counsel spoke with respondent about his background. He also spoke on the telephone with respondent's wife and mother, though he did not follow up on the one unsuccessful effort to meet with them. He did not otherwise seek out character witnesses for respondent. Nor did he request a psychiatric examination, since his conversations with his client gave no indication that respondent had psychological problems. [To establish his claim of "emotional stress" as a "mitigating factor" against a death sentence, counsel decided to rely on the defendant's statements at the guilty plea colloquy about his emotional state, and not to introduce further evidence on the question. By foregoing the opportunity to present new evidence on these subjects, counsel prevented the State from cross-examining respondent on his claim and from putting on psychiatric evidence of its own.]

Counsel also excluded from the sentencing hearing other evidence he thought was potentially damaging. He successfully moved to exclude respondent's "rap sheet." Because he judged that a presentence report might prove more detrimental than helpful, as it would have included respondent's criminal history and thereby would have undermined the claim of no significant history of criminal activity, he did not request that one be prepared.

[Because the sentencing judge had a reputation as a person who thought it important for a convicted defendant to own up to his crime, counsel argued at sentencing that Washington's remorse and acceptance of responsibility justified sparing him from the death penalty. Counsel also argued that respondent had no history of criminal activity and that respondent committed the crimes under extreme mental or emotional disturbance, thus coming within the statutory list of mitigating circumstances. The trial judge found numerous aggravating circumstances and no significant mitigating circumstances, and sentenced respondent to death on each of the three counts of murder.]

Respondent subsequently sought collateral relief in state court on numerous grounds, among them that counsel had rendered ineffective assistance at the sentencing proceeding. Respondent challenged counsel's assistance in six respects. He asserted that counsel was ineffective because he failed to move for a continuance to prepare for sentencing, to request a psychiatric report, to investigate and present character witnesses, to seek a presentence investigation report, to present meaningful arguments to the sentencing judge, and to investigate the medical examiner's reports [about the condition of the victims' bodies] or cross-examine the medical experts. [The state trial court, the state appellate courts, and the federal district court all refused to find ineffective assistance of counsel, and therefore refused to grant postconviction relief. The federal appeals court announced a new legal standard for claims of ineffective assistance of counsel and remanded the case for further fact-finding under the new standards. This appeal followed.]

In a long line of cases that includes Powell v. Alabama, 287 U.S. 45 (1932) . . . and Gideon v. Wainwright, 372 U.S. 335 (1963), this Court has recognized that the Sixth Amendment right to counsel exists, and is needed, in order to protect the fundamental right to a fair trial [in the adversary system. It has also] recognized that the right to counsel is the right to the effective assistance of counsel. . . .

The Court has not elaborated on the meaning of the constitutional requirement of effective assistance in [cases] presenting claims of "actual ineffectiveness." In giving meaning to the requirement, however, we must take its purpose — to ensure a fair trial — as the guide. The benchmark for judging any claim of ineffectiveness must be whether counsel's conduct so undermined the proper functioning of the adversarial process that the trial cannot be relied on as having produced a just result. . . .

A convicted defendant's claim that counsel's assistance was so defective as to require reversal of a conviction or death sentence has two components. First, the defendant must show that counsel's performance was deficient. This requires showing that counsel made errors so serious that counsel was not functioning as the "counsel" guaranteed the defendant by the Sixth Amendment. Second, the defendant must show that the deficient performance prejudiced the defense. This requires showing that counsel's errors were so serious as to deprive the defendant of a fair trial, a trial whose result is reliable. Unless a defendant makes both showings, it cannot be said that the conviction or death sentence resulted from a breakdown in the adversary process that renders the result unreliable. . . .

When a convicted defendant complains of the ineffectiveness of counsel's assistance, the defendant must show that counsel's representation fell below an objective standard of reasonableness. More specific guidelines are not appropriate. The Sixth Amendment refers simply to "counsel," not specifying particular requirements of effective assistance. It relies instead on the legal profession's maintenance of standards sufficient to justify the law's presumption that counsel will fulfill the role in the adversary process that the Amendment envisions. The proper measure of attorney performance remains simply reasonableness under prevailing professional norms.

Representation of a criminal defendant entails certain basic duties. Counsel's function is to assist the defendant, and hence counsel owes the client a duty of loyalty, a duty to avoid conflicts of interest. Cuyler v. Sullivan, 446 U.S. 335 (1980). From counsel's function as assistant to the defendant derive the overarching duty to advocate the defendant's cause and the more particular duties to consult with the defendant on important decisions and to keep the defendant informed of important developments in the course of the prosecution. Counsel also has a duty to bring to bear such skill and knowledge as will render the trial a reliable adversarial testing process.

These basic duties neither exhaustively define the obligations of counsel nor form a checklist for judicial evaluation of attorney performance. In any case presenting an ineffectiveness claim, the performance inquiry must be whether counsel's assistance was reasonable considering all the circumstances. Prevailing norms of practice as reflected in American Bar Association standards and the like, e.g., ABA Standards for Criminal Justice 4-1.1 to 4-8.6 (2d ed. 1980), are guides to determining what is reasonable, but they are only guides. No particular set of detailed rules for counsel's conduct can satisfactorily take account of the variety of circumstances faced by defense counsel or the range of legitimate decisions regarding how best to represent a criminal defendant. Any such set of rules would interfere with the constitutionally protected independence of counsel and restrict the wide latitude counsel must have in making tactical decisions. Indeed, the existence of detailed guidelines for representation could distract counsel from the overriding mission of vigorous advocacy of the defendant's cause. Moreover, the purpose of the effective assistance guarantee of the Sixth Amendment is not to improve the quality of legal representation, although that is a goal of considerable importance to the legal system. The purpose is simply to ensure that criminal defendants receive a fair trial.

Judicial scrutiny of counsel's performance must be highly deferential. It is all too tempting for a defendant to second-guess counsel's assistance after conviction or adverse sentence, and it is all too easy for a court, examining counsel's defense after it has proved unsuccessful, to conclude that a particular act or omission of counsel was unreasonable. A fair assessment of attorney performance requires that every effort be made to eliminate the distorting effects of hindsight, to reconstruct the circumstances of counsel's challenged conduct, and to evaluate the conduct from counsel's perspective at the time. Because of the difficulties inherent in making the evaluation, a court must indulge a strong presumption that counsel's conduct falls within the wide range of reasonable professional assistance; that is, the defendant must overcome the presumption that, under the circumstances, the challenged action might be considered sound trial strategy. There are countless ways to provide effective assistance in any given case. Even the best criminal defense attorneys would not defend a particular client in the same way.

The availability of intrusive post-trial inquiry into attorney performance or of detailed guidelines for its evaluation would encourage the proliferation of ineffectiveness challenges. Criminal trials resolved unfavorably to the defendant would increasingly come to be followed by a second trial, this one of counsel's unsuccessful defense. Counsel's performance and even willingness to serve could be adversely affected. . . .

An error by counsel, even if professionally unreasonable, does not warrant setting aside the judgment of a criminal proceeding if the error had no effect on the judgment. The purpose of the Sixth Amendment guarantee of counsel is to ensure that a defendant has the assistance necessary to justify reliance on the outcome of the proceeding. Accordingly, any deficiencies in counsel's performance must be prejudicial to the defense in order to constitute ineffective assistance under the Constitution.

In certain Sixth Amendment contexts, prejudice is presumed. Actual or constructive denial of the assistance of counsel altogether is legally presumed to result in prejudice. So are various kinds of state interference with counsel's assistance. Prejudice in these circumstances is so likely that case-by-case inquiry into prejudice is not worth the cost. Moreover, such circumstances involve impairments of the

Sixth Amendment right that are easy to identify and, for that reason and because the prosecution is directly responsible, easy for the government to prevent.

One type of actual ineffectiveness claim warrants a similar, though more limited, presumption of prejudice. In Cuyler v. Sullivan, 446 U.S. 335 (1980), the Court held that prejudice is presumed when counsel is burdened by an actual conflict of interest. In those circumstances, counsel breaches the duty of loyalty, perhaps the most basic of counsel's duties. Moreover, it is difficult to measure the precise effect on the defense of representation corrupted by conflicting interests. Given the obligation of counsel to avoid conflicts of interest and the ability of trial courts to make early inquiry in certain situations likely to give rise to conflicts, it is reasonable for the criminal justice system to maintain a fairly rigid rule of presumed prejudice for conflicts of interest. . . .

Conflict of interest claims aside, actual ineffectiveness claims alleging a deficiency in attorney performance are subject to a general requirement that the defendant affirmatively prove prejudice . . . It is not enough for the defendant to show that the errors had some conceivable effect on the outcome of the proceeding. Virtually every act or omission of counsel would meet that test, and not every error that conceivably could have influenced the outcome undermines the reliability of the result of the proceeding. . . .

On the other hand, we believe that a defendant need not show that counsel's deficient conduct more likely than not altered the outcome in the case. [The "more likely than not altered the outcome" test, which is used to decide whether to grant a new trial based on new evidence,] is not an apt source from which to draw a prejudice standard for ineffectiveness claims. The high standard for newly discovered evidence claims presupposes that all the essential elements of a presumptively accurate and fair proceeding were present in the proceeding whose result is challenged. An ineffective assistance claim asserts the absence of one of the crucial assurances that the result of the proceeding is reliable, so finality concerns are somewhat weaker and the appropriate standard of prejudice should be somewhat lower. The result of a proceeding can be rendered unreliable, and hence the proceeding itself unfair, even if the errors of counsel cannot be shown by a preponderance of the evidence to have determined the outcome.

Accordingly, the appropriate test for prejudice finds its roots in the test for materiality of exculpatory information not disclosed to the defense by the prosecution, and in the test for materiality of testimony made unavailable to the defense by Government deportation of a witness. The defendant must show that there is a reasonable probability that, but for counsel's unprofessional errors, the result of the proceeding would have been different. A reasonable probability is a probability sufficient to undermine confidence in the outcome. . . .

Although we have discussed the performance component of an ineffectiveness claim prior to the prejudice component, there is no reason for a court deciding an ineffective assistance claim to approach the inquiry in the same order or even to address both components of the inquiry if the defendant makes an insufficient showing on one. In particular, a court need not determine whether counsel's performance was deficient before examining the prejudice suffered by the defendant as a result of the alleged deficiencies. The object of an ineffectiveness claim is not to grade counsel's performance. If it is easier to dispose of an ineffectiveness claim on the ground of lack of sufficient prejudice, which we expect will often be so, that course should be followed. . . .

Having articulated general standards for judging ineffectiveness claims, we think it useful to apply those standards to the facts of this case in order to illustrate the meaning of the general principles . . . With respect to the performance component, the record shows that respondent's counsel made a strategic choice to argue for the extreme emotional distress mitigating circumstance and to rely as fully as possible on respondent's acceptance of responsibility for his crimes. . . . The trial judge's views on the importance of owning up to one's crimes were well known to counsel. The aggravating circumstances were utterly overwhelming. Trial counsel could reasonably surmise from his conversations with respondent that character and psychological evidence would be of little help. Respondent had already been able to mention at the plea colloquy the substance of what there was to know about his financial and emotional troubles. Restricting testimony on respondent's character to what had come in at the plea colloquy ensured that contrary character and psychological evidence and respondent's criminal history, which counsel had successfully moved to exclude, would not come in. On these facts, there can be little question, even without application of the presumption of adequate performance, that trial counsel's defense, though unsuccessful, was the result of reasonable professional judgment.

With respect to the prejudice component, the lack of merit of respondent's claim is even more stark. The evidence that respondent says his trial counsel should have offered at the sentencing hearing would barely have altered the sentencing profile presented to the sentencing judge. [At] most this evidence shows that numerous people who knew respondent thought he was generally a good person and that a psychiatrist and a psychologist believed he was under considerable emotional stress that did not rise to the level of extreme disturbance. Given the overwhelming aggravating factors, there is no reasonable probability that the omitted evidence would have changed the conclusion that the aggravating circumstances outweighed the mitigating circumstances and, hence, the sentence imposed. Indeed, admission of the evidence respondent now offers might even have been harmful to his case: his "rap sheet" would probably have been admitted into evidence, and the psychological reports would have directly contradicted respondent's claim that the mitigating circumstance of extreme emotional disturbance applied to his case.

[R]espondent has made no showing that the justice of his sentence was rendered unreliable by a breakdown in the adversary process caused by deficiencies in counsel's assistance. . . .

MARSHALL, J., dissenting.

[S]tate and lower federal courts have developed standards for distinguishing effective from inadequate assistance. Today, for the first time, this Court attempts to synthesize and clarify those standards. For the most part, the majority's efforts are unhelpful. . . .

My objection to the performance standard adopted by the Court is that it is so malleable that, in practice, it will either have no grip at all or will yield excessive variation in the manner in which the Sixth Amendment is interpreted and applied by different courts. To tell lawyers and the lower courts that counsel for a criminal defendant must behave "reasonably" . . . is to tell them almost nothing. In essence, the majority has instructed judges called upon to assess claims of ineffective assistance of counsel to advert to their own intuitions regarding what constitutes "professional" representation, and has discouraged them from trying to develop more detailed standards governing the performance of defense counsel. In my view, the Court has thereby not only abdicated its own responsibility to interpret the Constitution, but also impaired the ability of the lower courts to exercise theirs.

The debilitating ambiguity of an "objective standard of reasonableness" in this context is illustrated by the majority's failure to address important issues concerning the quality of representation mandated by the Constitution. . . . Is a "reasonably competent attorney" a reasonably competent adequately paid retained lawyer or a reasonably competent appointed attorney? It is also a fact that the quality of representation available to ordinary defendants in different parts of the country varies significantly. Should the standard of performance mandated by the Sixth Amendment vary by locale? The majority offers no clues as to the proper responses to these questions. . . .

I agree that counsel must be afforded wide latitude when making tactical decisions regarding trial strategy, but many aspects of the job of a criminal defense attorney are more amenable to judicial oversight. For example, much of the work involved in preparing for a trial, applying for bail, conferring with one's client, making timely objections to significant, arguably erroneous rulings of the trial judge, and filing a notice of appeal if there are colorable grounds therefor could profitably be made the subject of uniform standards.

I object to the prejudice standard adopted by the Court for two independent reasons. First, it is often very difficult to tell whether a defendant convicted after a trial in which he was ineffectively represented would have fared better if his lawyer had been competent. Seemingly impregnable cases can sometimes be dismantled by good defense counsel. On the basis of a cold record, it may be impossible for a reviewing court confidently to ascertain how the government's evidence and arguments would have stood up against rebuttal and cross-examination by a shrewd, well-prepared lawyer. The difficulties of estimating prejudice after the fact are exacerbated by the possibility that evidence of injury to the defendant may be missing from the record precisely because of the incompetence of defense counsel. . . .

Second and more fundamentally, the assumption on which the Court's holding rests is that the only purpose of the constitutional guarantee of effective assistance of counsel is to reduce the chance that innocent persons will be convicted. In my view, the guarantee also functions to ensure that convictions are obtained only through fundamentally fair procedures. The majority contends that the Sixth Amendment is not violated when a manifestly guilty defendant is convicted after a trial in which he was represented by a manifestly ineffective attorney. I cannot agree. Every defendant is entitled to a trial in which his interests are vigorously and conscientiously advocated by an able lawyer. [I would hold] that a showing that the performance of a defendant's lawyer departed from constitutionally prescribed standards requires a new trial regardless of whether the defendant suffered demonstrable prejudice thereby.

[I must also] dissent from the majority's disposition of the case before us. It is undisputed that respondent's trial counsel made virtually no investigation of the possibility of obtaining testimony from respondent's relatives, friends, or former employers pertaining to respondent's character or background. Had counsel done so, he would have found several persons willing and able to testify that, in their experience, respondent was a responsible, nonviolent man, devoted to his family, and active in the affairs of his church. . . . Had this evidence been admitted, respondent argues, his chances of obtaining a life sentence would have been significantly better. . . .

The State makes a colorable — though in my view not compelling — argument that defense counsel in this case might have made a reasonable "strategic" decision not to present such evidence at the sentencing hearing on the assumption that an unadorned acknowledgment of respondent's responsibility for his crimes would be more likely to appeal to the trial judge, who was reputed to respect persons who accepted responsibility for their actions. But however justifiable such a choice might have been after counsel had fairly assessed the potential strength of the mitigating evidence available to him, counsel's failure to make any significant effort to find out what evidence might be garnered from respondent's relatives and acquaintances surely cannot be described as "reasonable." . . . If counsel had investigated [and presented the available mitigating evidence], there is a significant chance that respondent would have been given a life sentence. . . .

Ineffective assistance of counsel claims are especially common in capital cases where the law is complex, and where errors can arise both at the guilt/innocence and sentencing stages of the trial. Typically, such claims arise on collateral review.

Sometimes ineffective assistance claims turn on a single act (or failure to act) by counsel, but often these claims take the form of a list, where the defendant claims that counsel's errors — individually and collectively — violated the standards of *Strickland.* Consider how the court in the following case assesses, for each of the defendant's multiple claims, whether the evidence shows unreasonable "performance" ("that counsel made errors so serious that counsel was not functioning as the 'counsel' guaranteed the defendant by the Sixth Amendment") or "prejudice" ("a reasonable probability that, but for counsel's unprofessional errors, the result of the proceeding would have been different").

■ MICHAEL BRUNO v. STATE

807 So.2d 55 (Fla. 2001)

PER CURIAM

Michael J. Bruno, under sentence of death, appeals the denial of relief following an evidentiary hearing on his first motion filed pursuant to Florida Rule of Criminal Procedure 3.850*. . . . For the reasons expressed below, we affirm the denial of relief. . . .

On August 8, 1986, appellant Michael Bruno and his fifteen-year-old son, Michael Jr., were in the apartment of a friend, Lionel Merlano, when Bruno beat Merlano with a crowbar. Bruno then sent Michael Jr. elsewhere in the apartment to fetch a handgun and, when the boy returned with a gun, Bruno shot Merlano twice in the head. Bruno was arrested several days later and gave a taped statement wherein he at first denied any knowledge of the murder but then later admitted committing the crime, claiming it was self-defense. Michael Jr. also gave a full tatement to police. Prior to being arrested, Bruno made numerous inculpatory statements to friends concerning both his plan to commit the murder and the

* Fla. R. Cr. Pro. 3.850 is the statutory section providing for collateral review. — EDS.

commission of the crime itself. Police found the gun in a canal where a friend, Jody Spalding, saw Bruno throw it.

Bruno was charged with first-degree murder and robbery (he stole a stereo from the apartment after the murder) and his strategy at trial was to raise a reasonable doubt in jurors' minds by claiming that Jody Spalding was the killer. He was convicted as charged, and the judge followed the jury's eight-to-four vote and imposed a sentence of death based on three aggravating circumstances and no mitigating circumstances. This Court affirmed. Bruno filed the present rule 3.850 motion and the trial court conducted an evidentiary hearing at which Bruno presented six witnesses and the State presented one witness. The trial court denied the motion. Bruno appeals. . . .

Bruno argues that the trial court erred in denying his postconviction claims concerning alleged ineffective assistance of counsel. The test to be applied by the trial court when evaluating an ineffectiveness claim is two-pronged: The defendant must show both that trial counsel's performance was deficient and that the defendant was prejudiced by the deficiency. The standard of review for a trial court's ruling on an ineffectiveness claim also is two-pronged: The appellate court must defer to the trial court's findings on factual issues but must review the court's ultimate conclusions on the deficiency and prejudice prongs de novo.

In his brief before this Court, Bruno asserts several instances of ineffectiveness. . . . In subclaim two, Bruno contends that defense counsel was ineffective during the trial due to alcohol and drug impairments. Bruno points to the previous hospitalization of trial counsel for drug and alcohol use. Private counsel was retained in August 1986 to represent Bruno. Over the next few months, counsel developed a drinking problem and, when he was drinking, would occasionally use cocaine. He enrolled in Alcoholics Anonymous on October 15, 1986, and remained alcohol and drug free from then until March 1987, when he began drinking again but not using cocaine. He admitted himself into a hospital on March 15, 1987, for his drinking problem, remained hospitalized for twenty-eight days, and subsequently remained alcohol- and drug-free. After being released, counsel apprised both Bruno and the court of his problem and offered to withdraw, but Bruno asked him to continue as counsel. The trial, which originally had been set for March 30, 1987, was rescheduled for August 5, 1987, and began on that date. Counsel testified at the evidentiary hearing below that he never was under the influence of alcohol or drugs while working on this case. The trial court concluded that Bruno "failed to meet his burden of demonstrating how [counsel's] drug and alcohol usage prior to trial rendered ineffective his legal representation to the Defendant and how such conduct prejudiced the Defendant." We agree.

In subclaim three, . . . Bruno argues that defense counsel repeatedly divulged confidential and damaging information to the trial court. [One] example of the alleged conflict of interest relates to comments made by defense counsel during the penalty phase. The comments were made in response to Dr. Stillman's testimony that Bruno was insane at the time of the offense. Shortly after Dr. Stillman's testimony, defense counsel requested a side-bar conference and told the trial court that he was surprised by the testimony, as Dr. Stillman had previously informed defense counsel that Bruno was sane at the time of the offense. At the evidentiary hearing below, defense counsel explained that he conveyed his surprise to the court in order to justify his subsequent motion for an additional psychological examination. [The trial court found that the defense attorney's] "statements to the Trial Judge were made as a justification for his seeking leave of court to file a belated notice of intent to rely on an insanity defense. . . . The Defendant has failed to show that he was prejudiced by [defense counsel]'s statements to the trial judge." Ultimately, the trial court concluded that Bruno failed both prongs of the *Strickland* test. We agree.

In subclaim four, Bruno argues that counsel was ineffective because he failed to present a defense of voluntary intoxication. At the evidentiary hearing below, defense counsel testified that Bruno adamantly refused the presentation of a voluntary intoxication defense. In rejecting this claim, the trial court stated that "[t]he decision not to present the affirmative defense of 'voluntary intoxication' was based on a strategy decision which was motivated by the Defendant's conscious decision, rather than a result of [counsel's] legal incompetency." We agree with the trial court that Bruno has failed to satisfy the first prong of the *Strickland* test.

In subclaim five, Bruno asserts that counsel negligently failed to move to suppress Bruno's initial statement to the police. . . . Bruno was first interrogated by the police on August 12, 1986. Bruno alleges that he was not given *Miranda* warnings at this time. During the interrogation, Bruno told the police that he knew the victim and had previously consumed a few beers with the victim at the victim's apartment, which was located in the Candlewood apartment complex. Bruno told the police that, the weekend the crime was committed, he was working on Jody Spalding's car, with the exception of going to the Candlewood apartment complex to obtain a receipt for a refrigerator. . . . Bruno claims that this statement provided the police with additional evidence, as it contradicted the later statement in which Bruno claimed that he killed the victim in self-defense, it contradicted other testimony about his whereabouts in the days following the killing, and shows guilty knowledge. . . . The trial court concluded that Bruno failed to meet the second prong of the *Strickland* test. We agree. . . .

In subclaim ten, Bruno argues that counsel was ineffective in failing to investigate and present available mitigation. The trial court rejected this claim as follows:

> The testimony and exhibits presented at the evidentiary hearing reflect that the Defendant's mis-information to, and his failure to fully cooperate with [counsel] in the preparation of his defense, prevented [counsel] from initially obtaining information relating to the Defendant's previous hospitalization at Pilgrim State Hospital. . . . Dr. Stillman's trial testimony . . . acquainted the jury with the Defendant's extensive emotional and drug history, and drug use at the time of the murder. The Defendant's parents testified that Mr. Bruno had tried to commit suicide, and was briefly hospitalized until his sister had him released. The fact that there could have been a more detailed presentation of these circumstances does not establish that defense counsel's performance was deficient. Defense counsel cannot be faulted for failing to investigate background information, which he had no reason to suspect existed.

We agree. The trial court noted that Bruno's failure to cooperate with counsel prevented counsel from initially obtaining relevant information pertaining to the penalty phase. Despite this obstacle, counsel still presented evidence concerning several potential mitigating circumstances: Bruno's extensive emotional and drug history, Bruno's drug use at the time of the murder, Dr. Stillman's testimony that Bruno had organic brain damage as a result of his drug use, and testimony that Bruno had attempted suicide and was briefly hospitalized. . . . Counsel's performance in this case may not have been perfect, but it did not fall below the required standard. [Even] assuming that counsel's performance was deficient, we agree with the trial court that Bruno has failed to satisfy the second prong of the *Strickland* test. . . .

Bruno claims that counsel was ineffective in failing to provide Dr. Stillman with sufficient background information. Bruno argues that counsel's neglect prevented Dr. Stillman from sufficiently assessing Bruno's competence to stand trial and potential mitigating circumstances.

Prior to trial, Dr. Stillman was appointed to evaluate whether Bruno was insane at the time of the offense or incompetent to stand trial. The record reveals that Dr. Stillman informed defense counsel on two separate occasions that he did not believe that Bruno was either insane at the time of the offense or incompetent to stand trial. Subsequently, Dr. Stillman was called as a defense witness during the penalty phase. In preparing for this testimony, Dr. Stillman interviewed, for the first time, members of Bruno's family and a jail nurse who had contact with Bruno. These meetings occurred within two days of Dr. Stillman's testimony. During the State's cross-examination, Dr. Stillman opined that he believed that Bruno was insane at the time of the offense. Dr. Stillman testified that despite his previous determinations that Bruno was not insane, he still had a suspicion, and that this suspicion was confirmed upon meeting with members of Bruno's family and the nurse. . . . The trial court below rejected this claim as follows:

> Since Dr. Stillman is dead, there is no way for the court to ascertain what factors he considered, or did not consider, in the way of background material on the Defendant. . . . Dr. Stillman interviewed the defendant twice for a total of two and a half hours. He . . . spoke with the defendant's sister and parents, [and] was aware of the Defendant's extensive drug usage, and his stay at Pilgrim State hospital. . . . The fact that the defendant and his family withheld information from [counsel] does not render [counsel's] performance deficient.

We agree. As far as Dr. Stillman's penalty phase testimony, it is clear from the record that Dr. Stillman had been provided with all necessary information at the time of his testimony. In regards to whether Bruno was competent to stand trial or insane at the time of the offense, we find no negligence on the part of defense counsel. Defense counsel asked Dr. Stillman to evaluate Bruno prior to trial. Dr. Stillman rendered an opinion, on two separate occasions, that Bruno was neither incompetent to stand trial nor insane at the time of the offense. Bruno has not established that Dr. Stillman told defense counsel that he needed more information in order to form this opinion. [We] find no merit to this claim. . . .

Based on the foregoing, we affirm the trial court's denial of Bruno's motion for postconviction relief. . . .

Anstead, J., concurring in part and dissenting in part.

. . . While I agree with the majority's analysis and rejection of claims of error as to eight of [the ineffective assistance] claims, it appears that two of Bruno's claims present valid instances of ineffectiveness. They include: (1) the improper and prejudicial disclosure of confidential information by counsel; and (2) counsel's critical failure to investigate and present mitigating evidence on behalf of the defendant to the sentencing jury and judge.

Bruno argues that his trial counsel substantially prejudiced the outcome of his penalty phase proceedings when trial counsel divulged confidential and damaging information to the trial court by informing the court during the penalty phase that he was completely surprised by Dr. Stillman's testimony that Bruno was "insane" at the time of the offense. After Stillman made the surprise disclosure that he believed Bruno was insane at the time of the crime, defense counsel approached both the court and the prosecutor and told them that Stillman had personally assured him many times just the opposite — that Bruno was "totally competent." Critically, the prosecutor later used this assurance during closing argument to completely impeach Stillman's testimony, and the sentencing court subsequently rejected Stillman's penalty phase testimony *in toto.* Bruno claims that his lawyer was ineffective because counsel's disclosures completely discredited Bruno's most important mitigation witness and his only expert witness, thereby conceding away virtually his entire case for mitigation. . . .

During direct examination, Stillman actually testified to the existence of some mitigation. According to Stillman, Bruno suffered from a passive-aggressive personality, and he also exhibited signs of a schizophrenic-type disorder when he was under the influence of drugs. . . . Stillman testified that Bruno started using L.S.D. and marijuana when he was married and that his drug abuse progressively worsened over the years. When his wife left him, he tried to kill himself by taking Quaaludes and by attempting to drown himself in the ocean. Further, Stillman testified that Bruno had been using an ounce of cocaine every day for weeks prior to the offense.

However, during cross-examination, Stillman proclaimed for the first time that he believed Bruno was insane at the time of the murder. He claimed that at the prior times he had evaluated the defendant, he suspected that Bruno may have been insane at the time of the offense but the lack of corroborating evidence prevented him from reaching such a conclusion. Stillman testified that he received the corroborating evidence just a few days before trial, when he discussed Bruno with his parents and sister . . . and a nurse who worked with Bruno at the jail. . . .

In an apparent panic, trial counsel reacted to Stillman's revelation by immediately disclosing to the court two confidential letters to trial counsel in which Stillman had opined that Bruno was competent to stand trial and was not insane. Trial counsel told the court that he thought he was duty bound to bring this patent inconsistency in Stillman's evaluations to the trial court's attention.

At the evidentiary hearing in the 3.850 proceeding, trial counsel sought to justify his breach of confidence by claiming that he acted in order to justify his subsequent motion for an additional psychological examination. However, the record directly refutes this assertion. In the actual motion for psychiatric evaluation, which was filed after the jury's recommendation for death but prior to the trial court's sentencing, trial counsel made absolutely no reference to the fact that Stillman had changed his opinion concerning Bruno's sanity. Rather, the motion . . . alleges that trial counsel and Stillman were unaware of Bruno's psychological history until trial counsel talked with Bruno's sister and learned about Bruno's history of drug use, attempted suicide, and hospitalization for mental problems.

Thus, trial counsel's stated tactical reason for disclosing this obviously damaging and confidential information to the court is not supported by the record. Rather, trial counsel's reason for disclosing this confidential information appears to have been prompted more by counsel's interest in maintaining his own credibility with the court and demonstrating that he had not been negligent in failing to present an insanity defense during the guilt phase, than by an interest in securing a future psychiatric examination for his client.

In Douglas v. Wainwright, 714 F.2d 1532 (11th Cir.1983), the Eleventh Circuit noted that "the most egregious examples of ineffectiveness do not always arise because of what counsel did *not* do, but from what he *did* do — or say." In *Douglas,* the Eleventh Circuit reasoned that counsel's deficient conduct undoubtedly prejudiced the defendant because based on counsel's comments during the penalty phase, the trial court concluded there was no mitigating evidence to present on the defendant's behalf. Similarly, in Blanco v. Singletary, 943 F.2d 1477 (11th Cir.1991), the trial attorneys volunteered inappropriate information to the trial court concerning the fact that they did not have any mitigating evidence to present and that none of the defendant's friends or family members would agree to testify on his behalf. As in *Douglas,* the defense in *Blanco* did not present any mitigating evidence during the trial. Relying on *Douglas,* the Eleventh Circuit held that counsel's errors did not fall within the range of competent performance expected in criminal cases.

Unlike *Blanco* and *Douglas,* trial counsel in the instant case did present some mitigating evidence. . . . However, trial counsel's improper disclosure to the trial court that Stillman had earlier consistently opined that Bruno was sane highlighted a serious inconsistency in Stillman's professional opinion, which, when explored, completely undermined the expert's credibility to the jury and the court. . . .

The only other witnesses trial counsel presented were Bruno's parents, who provided marginal evidence of mitigation. At the close of all the evidence, the jury recommended death by a vote of eight to four and the court imposed death, *finding no mitigating circumstances.* Because the trial court in this case ultimately rejected Stillman's testimony and found no mitigating evidence, counsel's error in revealing damaging, confidential information to the trial court against his most important witness clearly affected the jury's and the trial court's evaluation of the evidence and the outcome of the case.

Bruno further claims that counsel was manifestly ineffective in his more or less complete failure to investigate and present evidence of the abundant mitigating evidence that actually existed of Bruno's troubled history of mental problems and drug abuse. [T]he trial court allowed no break between the finding of guilt by the jury and the penalty phase of the trial; indeed, the penalty phase began the very next morning. Trial counsel acceded to this procedure.

[The defense attorney did call] Bruno's parents to testify. Bruno's mother described Bruno as he was as a young man, claiming that he was "good boy." However, she testified that after he left home and got married, he changed drastically. He started wearing his hair long (in a mohawk), tattooed his body, and started hanging around with a motorcycle group and bands. She testified that after his marriage ended he went "berserk," lost the desire to live and attempted to commit suicide by drowning himself and overdosing on drugs. . . .

Critically, however, at the end of her testimony, when trial counsel asked her whether she had anything to say to the jury about the possible punishment her son should receive, Bruno's mother declared: "All I can say is that I don't have much time, neither does my husband. But if that's your wish [i.e., the imposition of the punishment of death] and you think you are doing right, God bless you. But other than that I don't know what to say. I just feel sorry for my husband, but if a child does something wrong, he should be punished. That is my belief." [U]nlike Bruno's mother, Bruno's father testified that he did not believe that Bruno deserved the death penalty. . . .

On direct examination during the penalty phase, counsel did not elicit a single affirmative opinion from Stillman concerning the applicability of mitigators to this crime. Counsel was apparently unaware of his obligation to do so. Importantly, the record reflects that Dr. Stillman was appointed by the court *only* to assess Bruno's sanity and competency for guilt phase purposes, and not to evaluate Bruno and his background to determine the existence of mitigation for penalty phase purposes. . . . Counsel never sought a mental health evaluation of his client for mitigation purposes, an evaluation that is fundamental in defending against the death penalty.

Further, the record reflects that although trial counsel presented Bruno's parents and Dr. Stillman as witnesses at the penalty phase, counsel did nothing to prepare these witnesses for testifying and, most tellingly, was unaware of the content of their testimony beforehand, especially regarding the opinion of Bruno's mother that he must accept his punishment. . . . At the time of the penalty phase, counsel did not even know who comprised the members of Bruno's immediate family — he did not know of the existence of Bruno's younger sister, who held key mental health information concerning him. . . .

The postconviction record reveals that copious mitigation actually existed in this case. . . . Bruno has a life-long and extensive record of drug abuse beginning with sniffing glue and lacquer thinner at ages eleven to thirteen. At the postconviction evidentiary hearing, Bruno called . . . Dr. Dee, a neuropsychologist. . . . Dr. Dee testified that Bruno suffers from organic brain syndrome as a result of his continuous, heavy, chronic drug use, which included cocaine, LSD, and marijuana. The most significant injury to his brain is manifested by impaired memory, increased impulsivity, difficulty in impulse control, deteriorated work performance, and inability to hold a job. According to Dr. Dee, at the time of the murder, Bruno was under the influence of extreme mental or emotional disturbance due to cerebral damage and drug usage.

Dr. Dee testified that according to Bruno's son Michael, on the day of the murder, Bruno free-based cocaine mid-day and used it continuously throughout the day until he and his son left for the victim's apartment. Bruno had also taken three purple micro-dots of LSD and eight or nine Quaaludes. Dr. Dee also testified that Bruno's ability to appreciate the criminality of his conduct or conform his conduct to the requirements of the law was substantially impaired, also due to his cerebral impairment and intoxication. As for nonstatutory mitigation, Dr. Dee testified that Bruno and his siblings were physically beaten and abused by their mother as young children. This finding, based on accounts from Bruno's family members, differ significantly from Bruno's mother's testimony during the penalty phase proceedings that Bruno grew up in a happy home. . . .

Bruno has clearly demonstrated deficient performance by his counsel which prejudiced the outcome of the penalty phase of the proceedings. [T]he jury recommended death by a vote of eight to four, four votes for life even without the substantial mitigation we now know existed all the time. In the words of the United States Supreme Court in *Strickland,* it is apparent that confidence in the outcome of Bruno's penalty phase proceeding has been substantially undermined by counsel's neglect and lack of preparation.

Problem 11-3. *Cronic* Errors

Joe Elton Nixon was convicted of first-degree murder, kidnapping, robbery, and arson; the court sentenced him to death. Nixon's trial counsel made the following remarks during his opening statement in the guilt phase:

> In this case, there will be no question that Jeannie [sic] Bickner died a horrible, horrible death. In fact, that horrible tragedy will be proved to your satisfaction beyond any

> reasonable doubt. In this case, there won't be any question, none whatsoever, that my client, Joe Elton Nixon, caused Jeannie [sic] Bickner's death. This case is about the death of Joe Elton Nixon and whether it should occur within the next few years by electrocution or maybe its natural expiration after a lifetime of confinement.

During his closing argument, Nixon's counsel said:

> Ladies and gentlemen of the jury, I wish I could stand before you and argue that what happened wasn't caused by Mr. Nixon, but we all know better. I know what you will decide will be unanimous. You will decide that the State of Florida, through Mr. Hankinson and Mr. Guarisco, has proved beyond a reasonable doubt each and every element of the crimes charged, first-degree premeditated murder, kidnapping, robbery, and arson.

Nixon filed a motion for collateral review, claiming that his trial counsel was ineffective during the guilt phase of the trial. Nixon argues that these comments were the equivalent of a guilty plea by his attorney. He claims that he did not give his attorney consent to enter a guilty plea or to admit guilt as part of a trial strategy.

Nixon argues that counsel's conduct in this case amounted to *per se* ineffective assistance of counsel, and that the proper test for assessing counsel arises under United States v. Cronic, 466 U.S. 648 (1984), rather than Strickland v. Washington. In *Cronic,* decided the same day as *Strickland,* the Supreme Court created an exception to the *Strickland* standard for ineffective assistance of counsel and acknowledged that certain circumstances are so egregiously prejudicial that ineffective assistance of counsel will be presumed. In *Cronic,* the Supreme Court stated:

> [There are] circumstances that are so likely to prejudice the accused that the cost of litigating their effect in a particular case is unjustified. Most obvious, of course, is the complete denial of counsel. [A] trial is unfair if the accused is denied counsel at a critical stage of his trial. Similarly, if counsel entirely fails to subject the prosecution's case to meaningful adversarial testing, then there has been a denial of Sixth Amendment rights that makes the adversary process itself presumptively unreliable.

How would you rule on Nixon's motion? Compare Nixon v. Singletary, 758 So. 2d 618 (Fla. 2000).

Notes

1. *The test for ineffective assistance of counsel: majority position.* The *Strickland* opinion was the Supreme Court's first substantial effort to define the quality of representation required by the Sixth Amendment. In *Strickland,* the court announced its two-part standard: (1) counsel's performance must be "reasonably effective" and cannot fall below an "objective standard" of reasonableness, and (2) the defendant must show a "reasonable probability" that the outcome in the proceedings changed because of the attorney's deficient performance. The *Strickland* opinion has been enormously influential, with states overwhelmingly adopting its framework under state constitutions. Why did it take until 1984 (almost 200 years) to get a square decision from the U.S. Supreme Court on standards of attorney competence? Note that the Court did not explicitly require access to counsel as an element of due

process in state criminal trials until Powell v. Alabama, 287 U.S. 45 (1932), and it was not until Gideon v. Wainwright, 372 U.S. 335 (1963), that state-provided attorneys became the rule rather than the exception. Why might these events be useful or necessary for the development of a constitutional standard for effective counsel?

State courts and lower federal courts were developing their own approaches to claims of ineffective assistance before the *Strickland* decision in 1984. The earliest standard declared that counsel would be ineffective in the constitutional sense only if the lawyer's performance converted the trial into a "farce and mockery" or a "sham trial." See Diggs v. Welch, 148 F.2d 667 (D.C. Cir. 1945); Anderson v. Peyton, 167 S.E.2d 111 (Va. 1969). By the late 1970s just under 20 states took this approach. See William Erickson, Standards of Competency for Defense Counsel in a Criminal Case, 17 Am. Crim. L. Rev. 233 (1979).

Before *Strickland,* another group of about 20 states used more general (and arguably more pro-defense) language to describe the standard for judging ineffective assistance. These courts spoke of the need for attorneys to demonstrate "reasonable competence" in light of the typical conduct of other attorneys faced with the same situation. See People v. Blalock, 592 P.2d 406 (Colo. 1979). Finally, a smaller group of states elaborated on this general "reasonable competence" by pointing to specific "checklists" of tasks for counsel. The checklists gave more precise meaning to the general phrases in certain settings. Very often, the ABA Defense Function Standards (approved between 1968 and 1973) were one source of these checklists, although some of the standards also developed in common law fashion. See People v. Pope, 590 P.2d 859 (Cal. 1979); Rodgers v. State, 567 S.W.2d 634 (Mo. 1978). State courts also differed from one another on the question of the level of prejudice that the defendant had to show. The possibilities ranged from a stringent "outcome determinative" test, or a "reasonable probability" that counsel's error affected the outcome, to an automatic reversal rule.

In *Strickland,* Justice O'Connor describes the effectiveness standard as an "objective" standard. What makes a standard "objective" or "subjective"? The majority also rules out strategic decisions as a basis for a finding of ineffectiveness. How should a court determine whether a decision is "strategic"? Is this an objective test? Why does the court create a "strong presumption" of sound lawyering? Is that an objective standard?

2. *Measuring prejudice.* The prejudice standard under *Strickland,* requiring a "reasonable probability" of a different outcome absent attorney error, calls for a counterfactual inquiry into what the outcome would have been in a hypothetical trial without attorney error. Is the prejudice standard too restrictive or too liberal? Should a court insist on reaching the difficult and counterfactual prejudice issue only after finding substandard attorney performance? The bulk of the appellate cases on ineffective assistance (and it is indeed a bulky body of cases) turn on prejudice rather than ineffectiveness. Although the *likelihood* of prejudice is central to this litigation, the *amount* of prejudice is not. See Glover v. United States, 531 U.S. 198 (2001) (increase in prison sentence due to inadequate performance by attorney does not have to meet any particular "significance" threshold to qualify as potential prejudice).

3. *Measuring performance.* The defendant has the burden of proving unreasonable performance, by a preponderance of the evidence. The most straightforward cases of substandard performance involve an attorney's failure to consult a client (or failure to follow client instructions) over the basic direction of the litigation, such as

a decision whether to file a notice of appeal, or a decision to concede guilt and concentrate on the sentencing phase of a capital case. See Nixon v. Singletary, 758 So. 2d 618 (Fla. 2000) (attorney concedes guilt at trial); Roe v. Flores-Ortega, 528 U.S. 470 (2000) (ineffectiveness often present but not presumed when counsel fails to consult client about appeal and misses deadline for filing notice of appeal).

The more common and more difficult claims about attorney performance involve questionable choices about trial preparation and presentation of evidence. Does the legal standard in *Strickland* prevent a finding of unreasonable performance in any case where the attorney (or an appellate court) can construct a *post hoc* justification for the choice? When a defendant complains about a large collection of attorney decisions, does the standard require a court to consider them one at a time, or can the court consider the collective impact of many borderline attorney choices?

With sad regularity, attorneys are accused of sleeping, being drunk or drugged, or otherwise being physically unable to present an effective defense. Most courts have held that such impairments do not deny defendants of effective counsel without specific proof about faulty legal decisions caused by the impairment. See, e.g., McFarland v. Texas, 928 S.W.2d 482 (Tex. Crim. App. 1996) (72-year-old lawyer who said he "customarily take[s] a short nap in the afternoon" held not to be ineffective assistance where napping might have been a "strategic" move to generate jury sympathy and where co-counsel remained awake). Are attorneys impaired if they do not know the most basic law governing the case? Should courts give experienced attorneys a stronger presumption of reasonable performance than newer attorneys?

4. *Structural ineffectiveness and presumed prejudice.* In a few settings, the trial might occur in a setting so likely to produce error that prejudice can be presumed; no attorney is likely to provide adequate defense in these settings. Examples of "structural" ineffectiveness appear in conflict of interest cases, in which an attorney represents multiple clients and runs the risk of harming one client while furthering the interests of the other. If defense counsel raises at trial the issue of potential conflict of interest, and the trial court fails to appoint new counsel or to hold a hearing to determine the risk of a conflict, prejudice is presumed. Holloway v. Arkansas, 435 U.S. 475 (1978); Lettley v. State, 746 A.2d 392 (Md. 2000) (presumed prejudice where attorney represented two clients, second client admitted guilt in crime for which first client was being tried). If the defendant raises the issue after trial, she must prove that there was an "actual conflict of interest" that "adversely affected" her lawyer's performance, but there is no need to prove that the adverse effects on lawyer performance changed the outcome at trial. See Cuyler v. Sullivan, 446 U.S. 335 (1980); but see Mickens v. Taylor, 122 S. Ct. 1227 (2002) (defendant must show prejudice where defense lawyer had *potential* conflict of interest based on former representation of murder victim in juvenile proceedings).

Structural ineffectiveness (and the presumption of prejudice) is more difficult to establish in other settings. In United States v. Cronic, 466 U.S. 648 (1984), a companion case to *Strickland,* the Court rejected a presumption of ineffectiveness when an inexperienced lawyer was appointed shortly before a complex case. However, the court noted that such a presumption could be found "if the accused is denied counsel at a critical stage of his trial," or "if counsel entirely fails to subject the prosecution's case to meaningful adversarial testing." See, e.g., State v. Smith, 558 N.W.2d 379 (Wis. 1997) (prejudice presumed, counsel failed to object to prosecutor's substantial breach of plea agreement); Bell v. Cone, 122 S.Ct. 1843 (2002) (*Cronic* presumption does not apply when client's complaint goes to specific aspects of counsel's performance — failing to present mitigating evidence and waiving closing argument).

5. *Pervasiveness of ineffective counsel claims.* A claim of ineffective assistance of counsel may be one of the most common legal challenges to criminal convictions. Perhaps this is so because virtually any pretrial or trial error can be framed as ineffective assistance. If the lawyer failed to correct the error — even if the error itself is not of constitutional or otherwise sufficient magnitude — it is possible to question that lawyer's effectiveness on direct appeal or during a collateral attack on the conviction.

How common is it for defendants to obtain reversals of their convictions on effectiveness grounds? Richard Klein analyzed about 4,000 appellate decisions in state and federal court between 1970 and 1983 that raised ineffective assistance of counsel claims; he concluded that the court found ineffective assistance in about 3.9 percent of the cases. Richard Klein, The Emperor *Gideon* Has No Clothes: The Empty Promise of the Constitutional Right to Effective Assistance of Counsel, 13 Hastings Const. L.Q. 625 (1986). In an analysis of cases decided after 1984 (after *Strickland*), would you expect this "success" rate to go up or down?

6. *Public and private incompetence.* Should the judicial standards for ineffective assistance of counsel be the same for public defenders and private attorneys practicing criminal defense? There was a time when courts in some jurisdictions used different standards for publicly provided and privately retained defense counsel, applying a less demanding standard when reviewing the work of privately retained counsel because the work of such an attorney was not considered "state action." See People v. Stevens, 53 P.2d 133 (Cal. 1935). However, in Cuyler v. Sullivan, 446 U.S. 335, 344-345 (1980), the Supreme Court rejected the idea that private attorneys are to be judged by some lesser standard of constitutional scrutiny: "Since the State's conduct of a criminal trial itself implicates the State in the defendant's conviction, we see no basis for drawing a distinction between retained and appointed counsel that would deny equal justice to defendants who must choose their own lawyers." Although it is clear that retained attorneys cannot be scrutinized less carefully than appointed counsel, could they be scrutinized *more* carefully? On average, which type of attorney do you suppose would be more effective? Does your answer change for different types of criminal cases? See Bureau of Justice Statistics, Defense Counsel in Criminal Cases (Nov. 2000, NCJ 179023) (in both federal and state courts, conviction rates were the same for defendants represented by publicly and privately financed counsel; pretrial release less common for state court defendants with public counsel; state defendants with public counsel sentenced more often to prison or jail but for shorter terms than those with private lawyers).

7. *Does quality of counsel matter?* By focusing on the effectiveness of lawyers, do we lose sight of more important questions about the *contents* of procedural rules that the lawyers must use? If you are convinced that the law of criminal procedure is designed first and foremost to produce convictions efficiently, would you conclude that lawyers (regardless of their effectiveness) will rarely have any procedural claims available that could prevent a conviction from happening? Conversely, if you are convinced that the law of criminal procedure focuses more on police shortcomings than on a defendant's guilt or innocence, would you conclude that judges will find a way to review police conduct, whether or not a lawyer raises the claim in a timely and effective manner?

■ AMERICAN BAR ASSOCIATION DEFENSE FUNCTION STANDARDS (3d ed. 1993)

Standard 4-3.6 Prompt Action to Protect the Accused

Many important rights of the accused can be protected and preserved only by prompt legal action. Defense counsel should inform the accused of his or her rights at the earliest opportunity and take all necessary action to vindicate those rights. Defense counsel should consider all procedural steps which in good faith may be taken, including, for example, motions seeking pretrial release of the accused, obtaining psychiatric examination of the accused when a need appears, moving for change of venue or continuance, moving to suppress illegally obtained evidence, moving for severance from jointly charged defendants, and seeking dismissal of charges.

Standard 4-4.1 Duty to Investigate

(a) Defense counsel should conduct a prompt investigation of the circumstances of the case and explore all avenues leading to facts relevant to the merits of the case and the penalty in the event of conviction. The investigation should include efforts to secure information in the possession of the prosecution and law enforcement authorities. The duty to investigate exists regardless of the accused's admissions or statements to defense counsel of facts constituting guilt or the accused's stated desire to plead guilty. . . .

Standard 4-6.1 Duty to Explore Disposition Without Trial

(a) Whenever the law, nature, and circumstances of the case permit, defense counsel should explore the possibility of an early diversion from the criminal process through the use of other community agencies.

(b) Defense counsel may engage in plea discussions with the prosecutor. Under no circumstances should defense counsel recommend to a defendant acceptance of a plea unless appropriate investigation and study of the case has been completed, including an analysis of controlling law and the evidence likely to be introduced at trial.

■ RULE 33, COURT OF COMMON PLEAS CUYAHOGA COUNTY, OHIO

No attorney will be assigned to defend any indigent person in a criminal case unless his or her name appears on the applicable list of approved trial counsel. . . . The approved trial counsel list shall remain in effect for a period of two years. . . . Counsel whose name appears on the approved trial counsel list shall file an application for renewal to serve as appointed counsel in order to remain on the approved trial counsel list. . . . The following experience qualifications shall be a prima facie basis for the inclusion of a lawyer on the lists designated below:

(A) Assigned counsel for murder cases (including charges of murder, aggravated murder and aggravated murder with specifications).

(1) Trial counsel in a prior murder trial; or

(2) Trial counsel in four first degree felony jury trials; or

(3) Trial counsel in any ten felony or civil jury trials;

(4) No lawyer may appear on the list for murder cases unless he is also listed as counsel for major felony cases described below.

(B) Assigned counsel for major felony cases (first, second and third degree felonies).

(1) Trial counsel in two previous major felony jury trials (first, second or third degree felonies); or

(2) Trial counsel in any four previous criminal jury trials; or

(3) Trial counsel in any previous six criminal or civil jury trials; or

(4) Trial counsel in any two criminal jury trials plus assistant trial counsel in any two criminal jury trials.

(C) Assigned counsel for fourth degree felony cases.

(1) Trial counsel in any previous criminal or civil jury trial; or

(2) Assistant counsel in any two civil or criminal jury trials. . . .

To assist attorneys in obtaining trial experience in criminal cases, and for the purposes of obtaining experience necessary for inclusion on one of the above lists, this Court will cooperate with programs organized by local bar associations in which interested attorneys may be assigned as assistant trial counsel on a non-fee basis in cooperation with regularly retained or assigned counsel in criminal case trials in this county, under the supervision of the trial judge. . . .

The office of the Cuyahoga County Public Defender shall be assigned no less than 35 percent defendants in each category of cases described above for which counsel are selected for indigent defendants. The assigned Public Defender, before being assigned to represent an indigent defendant, shall also meet the established criteria. . . .

Problem 11-4. More Objective Competence Standards

Assume that you are chief counsel to the senate rules committee in a state where the legislature promulgates rules of criminal procedure. The chair of the committee, with the support of the chief justice of the state supreme court, has asked you to draft specific competence standards for the pretrial process. In particular, you are directed to research and draft standards providing guidance on the following three questions:

- How soon must attorneys see a new client?
- How much time must attorneys have, at a minimum, to prepare for plea negotiations?
- What obligations, if any, should counsel have with respect to researching alibi or character witnesses?

How specific can such rules be without interfering with effective defense in some cases? Do nonbinding guidelines accomplish anything? Would you recommend ultimate adoption of these types of rules, or would you encourage the committee and the courts to rely on the *Strickland* standards without additional guidance?

Notes

1. *Rules and standards.* The majority in *Strickland* said that "specific guidelines are not appropriate." Was Justice O'Connor correct in concluding that courts should not specify what is adequate representation of a criminal defendant? What is the significance of the fact that a few states had begun to announce specific expectations for defense counsel to meet? Is any institution other than the judiciary more capable of specifying the standards for effective assistance of counsel, or is lawyering an activity that simply cannot be reduced to enforceable standards?

2. *Performance standards versus experience standards.* The Cuyahoga County rules take a fairly typical approach to the problem of attorney competence: Like the court rules in many other local jurisdictions, these rules focus on the prior experience of attorneys rather than specifying the tasks a competent attorney should perform. Are the approaches embodied in the ABA Standards and the Cuyahoga County standards compatible? Were both standards drafted based on the same goals or assumptions? Should jurisdictions focus on the qualifications of counsel in the absence of clear performance standards? Do prospective standards for appointment prevent incompetent representation better than retrospective claims by disgruntled clients?

3. *Consequences for attorneys.* If substandard work by criminal defense counsel injures a client, can the client sue for malpractice? While malpractice suits in criminal cases are possible, they face more obstacles than civil malpractice claims. For suits against publicly financed attorneys, sovereign immunity and various official immunities block the suit unless state law waives those defenses. Often state law allows criminal defendants to bring malpractice suits only if they can prove they were actually innocent; it is not enough to claim that the attorney caused an overly severe sentence. See Meredith J. Duncan, The (So-Called) Liability of Criminal Defense Attorneys: A System in Need of Reform, 2002 BYU L. Rev. 1-52; Schreiber v. Rowe, 814 So. 2d 396 (Fla. 2002) (public defenders cannot assert judicial immunity in malpractice cases, but former defendant must prove actual innocence to maintain suit). Compare malpractice suits to an alternative form of accountability for attorneys, embodied in Rule 13 of the Rules of the Supreme Court of the State of Hawaii. Under Rule 13, after a conviction has been overturned because of ineffective assistance of counsel, the Supreme Court appoints a special master who can recommend "corrective action" against the attorney such as remedial education, suspension of the attorney's license to practice law, and referral to the state legal ethics authorities.

D. SYSTEMS FOR PROVIDING COUNSEL

We have surveyed the legal standards designed to ensure that individual defense counsel will provide effective assistance of counsel. The methods the government uses to fund and deliver legal services to the indigent also have a powerful effect on the performance of the defense counsel in individual cases. What institutions and sources of law shape entire systems for providing counsel?

The first method of providing defense counsel to indigent defendants in this country was the appointment of a private attorney to the case. The attorney might have handled the case as an unpaid volunteer or might have received some small compensation from the government. Early in the twentieth century, however, organizations of full-time defense attorneys began to spring up in major urban areas.

The first appeared in Los Angeles in 1914. Supporters of these "defender organizations" (public agencies and private charitable groups) hoped that they would provide criminal defense at less expense to the public and would avoid the distracting and needlessly confrontational style of the "shyster" lawyers who often accepted court appointments. As one prominent defense attorney put it, the publicly accountable defense attorney could join forces with the prosecutor to see that "no innocent man may suffer or guilty man escape." Mayer Goldman, The Need for a Public Defender, 8 J. Crim. L. & Criminology 273 (1917-1918).

These historical origins are still visible in our current systems for providing defense counsel to the indigent. Most places still use more than one method of providing defense counsel, but the "organizational" defenders have become the most important piece of the puzzle. Those who create and fund the defender organizations hope to control the costs of providing adequate criminal defense and to do so without compromising either the fairness or the efficiency of the criminal justice system. As you read the following materials, think about how to determine the proper goals of a system for delivering criminal defense services. Do the different systems provide defense counsel with different incentives to handle criminal cases in particular ways, such as choosing between plea bargains and trials?

■ INDIGENT DEFENSE
STEVEN SMITH AND CAROL DEFRANCES

NCJ-158909 (February 1996)

Court-appointed legal representation for indigent criminal defendants plays a critical role in the Nation's criminal justice system. In 1991 about three-quarters of State prison inmates and half of Federal prison inmates reported that they had a court-appointed lawyer to represent them for the offense for which they were serving time. In 1989, nearly 80 percent of local jail inmates indicated that they were assigned an attorney to represent them for the charges on which they were being held. . . .

TYPES OF DELIVERY SYSTEMS

Although the U.S. Supreme Court has mandated that the States must provide counsel for indigents accused of crime, the implementation of how such services are to be provided has not been specified. The States have devised various systems, rules for organizing, and funding mechanisms for indigent defense programs. As a consequence, each State has adopted its own approach for providing counsel for poor defendants. Three systems have emerged throughout the country as the primary means to provide defense services for indigent defendants.

Public defender programs are public or private nonprofit organizations with full- or part-time salaried staff. Local public defenders operate autonomously and do not have a central administrator. By contrast, under a statewide system, an individual appointed by the governor, a commission, council, or board is charged with developing and maintaining a system of representation for each county of the State. In 30 States a public defender system is the primary method used to provide indigent counsel for criminal defendants. . . .

Assigned counsel systems involve the appointment by the courts of private attorneys as needed from a list of available attorneys. Assigned counsel systems consist of two types. Ad hoc assigned counsel systems are those in which individual private attorneys are appointed by an individual judge to provide representation on a case-by-case basis. Coordinated assigned counsel systems employ an administrator to oversee the appointment of counsel and to develop a set of standards and guidelines for program administration.

Contract attorney systems involve governmental units that reach agreements with private attorneys, bar associations, or private law firms to provide indigent services for a specified dollar amount and for a specified time period. . . .

The Federal justice system provides indigent defense to eligible defendants through the Federal Defender Services, community defender organizations, and private attorneys as established by the Criminal Justice Act of 1964, as amended.

Use of Different Types of Counsel for Indigent Defense

Traditionally, assigned counsel systems and public defenders have been the primary means to provide legal representation to the poor. In 1992, 64% of State court prosecutors' offices nationwide reported a public defender program in their jurisdiction and 58% indicated an assigned counsel system. In 1992, 25% of prosecutors' offices indicated that their district contracted with law firms, private attorneys, or local bar associations to provide services to indigent offenders. . . . A majority of prosecutors' offices (59%) reported only one method was used in their jurisdiction to provide services to poor offenders.

Among all prosecutorial districts, a public defender program was used exclusively in 28%, an assigned counsel system in 23%, and a contract attorney system in 8%. Forty-one percent of the prosecutors' offices reported a combination of methods were used in their jurisdiction. The most prevalent was a combination of an assigned counsel system and a public defender program reported by 23% of the offices. In the Nation's 75 largest counties, 43% of the State court prosecutors' offices reported both an assigned counsel system and a public defender program operating in their jurisdiction. . . .

Type of Legal Representation Reported by Prison and Jail Inmates

Ninety-seven percent of inmates in State correctional facilities reported that they had an attorney to represent them for the offense for which they were incarcerated. Seventy-six percent of those who had an attorney were represented by a public defender or assigned counsel. Counsel assigned by the court may include legal representation provided by a public agency or by private attorneys whom the court pays.

Among those represented by counsel, 79% of black State prison inmates reported they had been represented by an assigned attorney. Among white State prison inmates, 73% said they had been represented by an assigned attorney. Among State prison inmates incarcerated for property offenses, 85% had an assigned counsel; for violent offenses, 74%; and for drug offenses, 70%.

Ninety-nine percent of Federal inmates reported that they were represented by counsel. Forty-three percent of those who had an attorney hired private counsel. Nearly 50% of white Federal inmates hired private counsel, as did 33% of black Federal inmates. Almost two-thirds of black Federal inmates were assigned counsel by the court. Overall, among those Federal inmates serving time for violent offenses, 72% had court assigned counsel; for property offenses, 53%; and for drug offenses, 48%.

Eighty-three percent of jail inmates said they had a lawyer to represent them for the offense for which they were being held. Among those who had legal representation, about three-fourths had assigned counsel. About three-fourths of those in jail for a drug or violent offense relied on assigned counsel. Among those charged with property offenses, 85% had assigned counsel. About two-thirds of those jail inmates with hired counsel said they first met with their attorney either before admission or during the first week after admission.

■ STATE v. LEONARD PEART

621 So. 2d 780 (La. 1993)

Calogero, C.J.

In this case we assess a multifaceted ruling made by the trial judge in Section E of Orleans Parish Criminal District Court. Based on his examination of the defense services being provided to indigent defendants in that section of court, the trial judge ruled that LSA-R.S. 15:145, 15:146 and 15:304, as well as "the system for securing and compensating qualified counsel" as a whole are "unconstitutional as applied in the City of New Orleans." He also specifically ordered that the legislature provide funding for improved indigent defense services and ordered a reduction in the case loads of those attorneys representing indigent defendants in his court. Because we find that the statutes are not unconstitutional and that the remedies ordered are inappropriate at this time, we reverse the trial court's rulings.

We nonetheless also find, based on the record developed in the trial court, that the services being provided to indigent defendants in Section E of Orleans Criminal District Court do not in all cases meet constitutionally mandated standards for effective assistance of counsel. Because we find that the provision of indigent defense services in Section E is in many respects so lacking that defendants who must depend on it are not likely to receive the reasonably effective assistance of counsel the constitution guarantees, we remand this case to the trial court and instruct the judge of Section E of Criminal District Court, when hearing Leonard Peart's case and others in which similar claims are asserted by indigent defendants pre-trial, to hold individual hearings for each defendant and apply a rebuttable presumption that indigents are not receiving assistance of counsel sufficiently effective to meet constitutionally required standards. If the trial judge, applying this presumption and weighing all evidence presented, finds that Leonard Peart or any other defendant in Section E is not likely receiving reasonably effective assistance of counsel, then he shall not permit the trial of such cases to be conducted.

Louisiana Const. art. 1 sec. 13 guarantees a number of rights to persons accused of a crime. One of those "Rights of the Accused" is the right to assistance of counsel "at each stage of the proceedings." . . . In addition, art. 1 sec. 13 requires that the legislature "shall provide for a uniform system for securing and compensating qualified counsel for indigents."

The legislature has [established] Louisiana's indigent defender system. LSA-R.S. 15:144 creates Indigent Defender Boards to oversee indigent defense operations in each judicial district. . . . LSA-R.S. 15:146 sets up a mechanism for local funding of individual districts' indigent defender systems. LSA-R.S. 15:304 is a general statute which requires all parishes and the city of New Orleans to pay "all expenses . . . whatever attending criminal proceedings. . . ."[2]

Leonard Peart was charged with armed robbery, aggravated rape, aggravated burglary, attempted armed robbery, and first degree murder. He is indigent.

In New Orleans, the Indigent Defender Board ("IDB") has created the Orleans Indigent Defender Program ("OIDP"). OIDP operates under a public defender model. The trial court appointed Rick Teissier, one of the two OIDP attorneys assigned to Section E, to defend Peart against all the above charges except first degree murder.

. . . At the time of his appointment, Teissier was handling 70 active felony cases. His clients are routinely incarcerated 30 to 70 days before he meets with them. In the period between January 1 and August 1, 1991, Teissier represented 418 defendants. Of these, he entered 130 guilty pleas at arraignment. He had at least one serious case set for trial for every trial date during that period. OIDP has only enough funds to hire three investigators. They are responsible for rendering assistance in more than 7,000 cases per year in the ten sections of Criminal District Court, plus cases in Juvenile Court, Traffic Court, and Magistrates' Court. In a routine case Teissier receives no investigative support at all. There are no funds for expert witnesses. OIDP's library is inadequate.

The court found that Teissier was not able to provide his clients with reasonably effective assistance of counsel because of the conditions affecting his work, primarily the large number of cases assigned to him. The court further ruled that "the system of securing and compensating qualified counsel for indigents" in LSA-R.S. 15:145, 15:146 and 15:304 was "unconstitutional as applied in the City of New Orleans" because it does not provide adequate funding for indigent defense and because it places the burden of funding indigent defense on the city of New Orleans. The trial judge ordered short and long term relief. In the short term, he ordered Teissier's case load reduced; ordered the legislature to provide funding for an improved library and for an investigator for Teissier; and announced his intention to appoint members of the bar to represent indigents in his court. For the long term, he ordered that the legislature provide funds to OIDP to pay additional attorneys, secretaries, paralegals, law clerks, investigators, and expert witnesses.

The State appealed Judge Johnson's ruling. [While the appeal of this ruling was pending, Peart was tried and acquitted of armed robbery.] In a second trial, in which he was represented by other counsel, he was acquitted on the murder charge. He is awaiting trial on the aggravated rape charge. Teissier again represents him.[5] . . .

We begin with the proposition that because there is no precise definition of reasonably effective assistance of counsel, any inquiry into the effectiveness of counsel

2. [Indigent Defender Boards] choose between public defender, contract attorney, and assigned counsel models, or may use a combination of these models. LSA-R.S. 15:146 sets up a mechanism for local funding of individual districts' indigent defender systems. This provision, unique in the United States, creates a system whereby almost all of the funds for indigent defense come from criminal violation assessments [in] an amount ranging from $17.50 to $25.00 for each violation. Parking violations are excepted. . . .

5. Ironically, the trial court judgment indicates that at the time of the judgment Peart himself was receiving the effective assistance of counsel guaranteed him by the constitution. As the trial judge wrote, "each of Mr. Teissier's clients is entitled to the same kind of defense Leonard Peart is receiving." That Peart himself could receive effective assistance, while Teissier's other clients do not, reflects the fact that indigent defenders must select certain clients to whom they give more attention than they give to others. . . . We therefore anticipate, although we do not decide, that the State may well be able to rebut the presumption of ineffectiveness in the pending rape case against Peart.

must necessarily be individualized and fact-driven. In different contexts, Louisiana courts have found a wide variety of attorneys' failings to constitute ineffective assistance. These courts [have determined] whether an individual defendant has been provided with reasonably effective assistance, and no general finding by the trial court regarding a given lawyer's handling of other cases, or workload generally, can answer that very specific question as to an individual defendant and the defense being furnished him. . . . Each defendant who raises a serious question regarding the effectiveness of his representation is entitled to a ruling. The trial judge who conducts the pre-trial hearing may consolidate proceedings and take some general evidence, but he must make a particularized finding about and issue an independent judgment regarding each defendant. . . .

Although we find that a trial judge reviewing a defendant's pre-trial claim that he is receiving ineffective assistance of counsel must undertake an individualized inquiry and issue an independent judgment regarding each defendant, this Court, in order adequately to review the record and judgment now before us, must make some global findings about the state of indigent defense in Section E of Orleans Criminal District Court.

[T]he language of La. Const. art. 1 sec. 13 is unequivocal: "At each stage of the proceedings, every person is entitled to the assistance of counsel . . . appointed by the court if he is indigent and charged with a crime punishable by imprisonment." That assistance must be reasonably effective. Article 1 sec. 13 also provides that "the legislature shall provide for a uniform system for securing and compensating qualified counsel for indigents." As noted above, the legislature has enacted statutes responsive to these constitutional requirements.

However, we cannot say that the system these statutes have put in place invariably — or, in Section E, even regularly — affords indigent defendants reasonably effective assistance of counsel. We take reasonably effective assistance of counsel to mean that the lawyer not only possesses adequate skill and knowledge, but also that he has the time and resources to apply his skill and knowledge to the task of defending each of his individual clients.

[This] system has resulted in wide variations in levels of funding, both between different IDB's and within the same IDB over time. The general pattern has been one of chronic underfunding of indigent defense programs in most areas of the state. The system is so underfunded that [one recent study committee, appointed by the state judiciary, concluded that] there is a "desperate need to double the budget for indigent defense in Louisiana in the next two years." The unique system which funds indigent defense through criminal violation assessments, mostly traffic tickets, is an unstable and unpredictable approach.[10] . . .

The conditions in Section E should be contrasted with the American Bar Association Standards for Criminal Justice (1991). These conditions routinely violate the standards on workload (Std. 4-1.3(e)) ("defense counsel should not carry a workload that, by reason of its excessive size, interferes with the rendering of quality representation"); initial provision of counsel (Std. 5-6.1) (counsel should be provided to the accused . . . at appearance before a committing magistrate, or when criminal charges are filed, whichever occurs earliest"); investigation (Std. 4-4.1) ("defense

10. Examples of the approach's unpredictability abound. One particularly stark example: when the City of East Baton Rouge ran out of pre-printed traffic tickets in the first half of 1990, the indigent defender program's sole source of income was suspended while more tickets were being printed.

counsel should conduct a prompt investigation of the circumstances of the case and explore all avenues leading to facts relevant to the merits of the case"); and others. We know from experience that no attorney can prepare for one felony trial per day, especially if he has little or no investigative, paralegal, or clerical assistance. As the trial judge put it, "not even a lawyer with an S on his chest could effectively handle this docket." We agree. Many indigent defendants in Section E are provided with counsel who can perform only pro forma, especially at early stages of the proceedings. . . . In light of the unchallenged evidence in the record, we find that because of the excessive caseloads and the insufficient support with which their attorneys must work, indigent defendants in Section E are generally not provided with the effective assistance of counsel the constitution requires.

Having found that indigent defendants in Section E cannot all be receiving effective assistance of counsel, we must decide what remedy this Court should impose.

Louisiana is not the only state to have faced a crisis in its indigent defense system. Over the last decade, numerous states have addressed problems like those Louisiana faces. In some states, legislatures have on their own initiative improved provision of indigent defense services. For example, in 1989 alone the legislatures of New Mexico, Missouri and Kentucky provided for large increases in the budgets of their statewide public defender offices; the Tennessee and Georgia legislatures established new statewide public defender offices. In other states, litigation challenging the adequacy of defense services has resulted in systemic changes. [The court cited cases from Arkansas, Florida, Kansas, New Hampshire, and Oklahoma.]

We have before us numerous recommendations for reform of Louisiana's IDB system. [*Amici* and academic commentators offer the following suggestions: (1) create a statewide indigent defender board to plan, oversee, and coordinate the delivery of indigent defense services throughout the state; (2) appoint a chief public defender to carry out the policies of the IDB; (3) increase the amount of general state revenues devoted to indigent defense; (4) mandate that the criminal violation assessment be raised to $25 in every parish; (5) appoint a special master to oversee use of these funds; and (6) issue a structural injunction to require the state legislature to raise money to bring the system into compliance with constitutional requirements.]

By virtue of this Court's constitutional position as the final arbiter of the meaning of the state constitution and laws, we have a duty to interpret and apply the constitution. In addition, the constitution endows this Court with general supervisory jurisdiction over all other courts. . . . Acting pursuant to the established sources of authority noted above, . . . we find that a rebuttable presumption arises that indigents in Section E are receiving assistance of counsel not sufficiently effective to meet constitutionally required standards. See State v. Smith, 681 P.2d 1374 (Ariz. 1984). This presumption is to apply prospectively only; it is to apply to those defendants who were represented by attorney Teissier when he filed the original "Motion for Relief" who have not yet gone to trial; and it will be applicable to all indigent defendants in Section E who have OIDP attorneys appointed to represent them hereafter, so long as there are no changes in the workload and other conditions under which OIDP assigned defense counsel provide legal services in Section E. If legislative action is not forthcoming and indigent defense reform does not take place, this Court, in the exercise of its constitutional and inherent power and supervisory jurisdiction, may find it necessary to employ the more intrusive and specific measures it has thus far avoided to ensure that indigent defendants receive reasonably effective assistance of counsel. We decline at this time to undertake these more intrusive and specific measures because this Court should not lightly tread in the affairs of other branches of government and because the legislature ought to assess such measures in the first instance.

We remand this case to the district court for retrial of the motion filed on behalf of Peart. . . . We instruct the judge of Section E, when trying Leonard Peart's motion and any others which may be filed, to hold individual hearings for each such moving defendant and, in the absence of significant improvement in the provision of indigent defense services to defendants in Section E, to apply a rebuttable presumption that such indigents are not receiving assistance of counsel effective enough to meet constitutionally required standards. If the court, applying this presumption and weighing all evidence presented, finds that Leonard Peart or any other defendant in Section E is not receiving the reasonably effective assistance of counsel the constitution requires, and the court finds itself unable to order any other relief which would remedy the situation, then the court shall not permit the prosecution to go forward until the defendant is provided with reasonably effective assistance of counsel. . . . Reversed and remanded.

Dennis, J., dissenting.

[T]he majority, without articulating constitutional principles or legal assistance guidelines, sweepingly creates a presumption that indigent defense services in Section E are ineffective and invites the trial judge to halt trials until the presumption has been overcome by the state. Evidently, my colleagues intend to offer up Section E as a lamb for burnt offering, hoping that an all-knowing, benevolent deity will miraculously cure the ills of the indigent defense system in that section and perhaps elsewhere. I respectfully decline to join the majority's decision because it does not realistically and thoroughly address or attempt to remedy the systemic constitutional deficiencies affecting the provision of indigent defense services in Orleans and perhaps other parishes. . . .

The Legislature and the Executive branch of Louisiana have a duty to correct the constitutional deficiencies in the system. However, without a clear explanation by this court of the controlling constitutional principles and standards, the legislature cannot know exactly what is required to bring the indigent defender system into constitutional alignment; and it is unlikely that the legislature will be inspired or impelled to take satisfactory action without adequate guidance from this court. . . .

This court should establish standards by setting limits on the number of cases handled by indigent defense attorneys, by requiring a minimum number of investigators to be assigned to each defender, and by requiring specified support resources for each attorney. If a defendant demonstrates future error due to funding and resource deficiencies, the courts should be instructed to view the harm as state-imposed error, which would require reversal of the conviction unless the state demonstrates that the error was harmless.

In State v. Smith, 681 P.2d 1374 (Ariz. 1984), the Arizona Supreme Court found that a county's bid system failed to consider such factors in awarding criminal defense contracts. Holding that this failure created an inference that the system produced inadequate representation, the court required the county to follow a series of guidelines in order to maintain a contract defense system. The county's failure to comply would result in the automatic reversal of any conviction obtained under the system and appealed by the defendant, unless the state could demonstrate that the error was harmless. The decision prompted the county to begin paying appointed counsel on an hourly basis, increasing the county's expenditure on defense services and improving the quality of representation.

The majority has created a *Smith*-type presumption but has failed to set forth any standards to give the legislative and executive branches guidance in bringing the system into constitutional compliance. Furthermore, the majority has adopted a per se rule that would allow the trial court to prevent criminal trials in Section E until the defense counsel system is in compliance with the constitution. In my opinion, the per se rule may be too drastic at this time. Utilizing the *Smith*-type harmless error standard alone would be appropriate and would ensure that the criminal justice system continues to operate while the state attempts to comply with the constitutional requirements. . . .

■ STATE v. DELBERT LYNCH

796 P.2d 1150 (Okla. 1990)

KAUGER, J.

In these cases of first impression, we are asked to decide whether the trial court erred in declaring 21 O.S. Supp. 1985 §701.14 unconstitutional because court appointed counsel were forced to represent indigent defendants without the assurance of receiving adequate, speedy, and certain compensation for such representation. We find that: 1) Although the statute is not facially unconstitutional, it is unconstitutional in application; 2) The present system presses lawyers into service without affording a post-appointment opportunity to show cause why they should not be forced to accept the appointment; and 3) The statute provides an arbitrary and unreasonable rate of compensation for lawyers which may result in an unconstitutional taking of private property depending on the facts of each case. While we recognize the responsibility of members of the Oklahoma bar to assist in the provision of legal representation to indigent defendants, we find that in some instances the arbitrary and unreasonable statutory scheme contravenes the due process clause of the Okla. Const. art. 2, §7. . . .

Two Seminole County lawyers, Jack Mattingly and Rob Pyron, were appointed by the district court to represent Delbert Lynch, an indigent who had been charged with first degree murder. Although the State had sought the death penalty, after a complicated trial, which began on August 21, 1989, and ended on August 31, 1989, the jury rendered a guilty verdict and gave Lynch a life sentence. Following Lynch's sentencing on September 6, 1989, the lawyers petitioned the court for fees and expenses.

At the hearing on counsel fees, Mattingly testified that he had spent 169 hours on the case, and incurred $173.03 in out of pocket expenses, requesting a $17,073.03 fee. Pyron's testimony was that he had expended 109.55 hours on Lynch's behalf, and he sought a $10,995.00 fee. Mattingly submitted a statement documenting his hourly overhead rate for 1986, 1987, 1988 which ranged from $45.80 to $53.53 — averaging $50.88. Pyron submitted his overhead figures for 1988, reflecting an average hourly rate of $48.00. Had the two lawyers split the maximum statutory fee of $3,200, Mattingly would have received $9.47 per hour, with Pyron receiving $14.61 per hour. Based on these computations, Mattingly would lose $41.41 and Pyron would lose $33.39 in overhead expenses for every hour that they worked on the defense. These figures do not reflect any compensation for the attorneys' services. The trial court approved the requested fees, finding that the $3,200 restriction on attorney fees was unconstitutional. . . .

The parties do not dispute that Oklahoma is required to provide attorneys for indigent defendants who are charged in Oklahoma courts with felonies, certain misdemeanors, competency to stand trial, contempt proceedings, and guardianship matters, or that the State of Oklahoma has attempted to provide such representation. The basic concern is not with the constitutional requirements of the Okla. Const. art. 2, §20, or the public policy which requires representation of indigent defendants; but, rather, with the practical application of the public policy and its impairment of constitutionally guaranteed private property rights. The State asserts that compensation should only exceed the statutory limit when extraordinary circumstances are shown as established in Bias v. State, 568 P.2d 1269 (Okla. 1977), and that an unconstitutional taking does not occur when a court-appointed attorney is required to represent indigent defendants.

The Okla. Const. art. 2, §7 provides that "No person shall be deprived of life, liberty, or property without due process of law." The lawyers contend that under this constitutional provision mandatory representation without just compensation is unconstitutional. The Oklahoma Constitution . . . also requires that competent counsel be provided for indigent defendants. [A] criminal defendant has a fundamental right to the reasonably effective assistance of counsel, regardless of whether counsel is appointed or retained. This means a lawyer must render the same obligations of loyalty, confidentiality, and competence to a court-appointed client as a retained client would receive. Oklahoma has fulfilled the constitutional requirement of competent counsel by utilizing public defenders' offices, voluntary pools, and court appointments. In order for the system to work, a balance must be maintained between the lawyer's [professional obligations], an indigent's fundamental right to counsel, and the avoidance of state action tantamount to confiscation of a lawyer's practice.

To achieve an appropriate balance of constitutional interests the rights of both the indigent defendant and the lawyer must be protected. Here, the constitutional right of the indigent to counsel is not at issue — the due process rights of appointed counsel for indigent defendants are. Although it is obvious that while Oklahoma's statutorily mandated cap may not be facially defective, and that in some instances payment of the statutory fee might even be an excessive rate of compensation, there is a substantial probability that it will be defective in application. Here, it is apparent that the maximum statutory fee is inadequate to compensate the lawyers who represented Lynch.[13]

In Bias v. State, a lawyer had been compelled both to subsidize indigent representation and to forsake his regular law practice during the representation of the indigent defendant. The *Bias* Court recognized that such circumstances may constitute a taking of private property without compensation. In order to harmonize conflicting interests, the Court authorized payment in excess of the statutorily prescribed norms for extraordinary expenditures of time and expense. . . .

13. The maximum statutory fee set by the legislature is: 1) in capital cases, $200 for services rendered before the preliminary hearing, $500 for services rendered during the preliminary hearing, $2,500 for services rendered from the time the defendant is bound over until final disposition in the trial court; 2) in other criminal cases, the fee is not to exceed $500; 3) in juvenile and guardianship cases, the fee is not to exceed $100 in a preliminary hearing, $500 if the cause goes to trial and $100 for post-disposition hearings. . . .

Clearly, there is a substantial risk of the erroneous deprivation of property rights under the current appointment system. A lawyer's skills and services are his/her only means of livelihood. The taking thereof, without adequate compensation, is analogous to taking the goods of merchants or requiring free services of architects, engineers, accountants, physicians, nurses or of one of the 34 other occupations or professions in this state which require a person to be licensed before practicing the occupation or profession. None of the licensing statutes require that the members of those professions donate their skills and services to the public. We know that many of these professionals do so. We also know that it would be unusual for the various licensing boards to force their licensees to proffer their services to indigents or to offer cut-rate prices on haircuts, perms, embalming, dentures, or surgeries. . . .

Nevertheless, we also recognize that a lawyer's calling is different from that of other licensed professions. We are a government of laws and not of men and women. At the foundation of this republic is the respect for enforcement of the law in a neutral way. The services of competent counsel are necessary to insure that our system of justice functions smoothly, that justice is dispensed even handedly, and that the rights and interests of indigent defendants are safeguarded in a truly adversarial forum. A lawyer is weighted with responsibility which is uncommon to the ordinary professional, and as a member of the integrated bar, an Oklahoma lawyer has a duty to the oath of office, to the Courts, to his/her clients, and to the public at large to be more than a tradesperson.

Procedural due process of law requires adequate notice, a realistic opportunity to appear at a hearing, and the right to participate in a meaningful manner before one's rights are irretrievably altered. We find that in order to provide safeguards which will bring the system into compliance with due process, trial courts must proffer a post-appointment opportunity for the lawyer to appear and to show cause without penalty, why he/she should not be appointed to represent an indigent defendant. [This is] in accord with the Model Rules of Professional Conduct, 5 O.S. Supp. 1988 Ch.1, App. 3-A, Rule 6.2 and the committee comments thereto, which provide that a lawyer may refuse an appointment for the representation of an indigent upon a showing of good cause.

We find that good cause consists of, but is not limited to the following factors: 1) the lawyer is not qualified to provide competent representation; 2) the representation will result in a conflict of interest; and 3) the case is so repugnant to the lawyer that it would impair either the attorney-client relationship or the lawyer's ability to represent the client. Title 5 O.S. Supp. 1988 Ch. 1, App. 3-A, Rule 6.2. We also find that Rule 1.16 of the Model Rules of Professional Conduct, 5 O.S. Supp. 1988 Ch. 1, App. 3-A, is applicable to all client representation, and that it should be construed with the "good cause" factors. This rule provides that a lawyer may refuse to represent a client if: 1) the representation would violate the Rules of Professional Conduct or other law; 2) the lawyer's physical or mental condition materially impairs the lawyer's representation of the client; 3) the client persists in conduct involving the lawyer's service which the lawyer believes is criminal or fraudulent; 4) the client has used the lawyer's services to perpetrate a crime or fraud; or 5) the client discharges the lawyer. . . .

For all practical purposes [Oklahoma statutes] exempt attorneys in counties which have public defenders' offices from representing indigent defendants in state courts. Lawyers in these counties are subject to appointment only when a conflict of interest arises in the public defender's office. Currently, these attorneys are neither faced with impending financial disaster nor forced to ignore their practice in order to provide effective counsel for an indigent. Except in rare circumstances, these attorneys have been granted an "immunity" by the legislature. . . . Because lawyers who practice in certain counties are immunized from the representation of indigent defendants, not all Oklahoma lawyers are treated equally. [D]iscrimination between attorneys who may be forced to represent indigent defendants based solely on the population of the county in which they practice law is unconstitutional under any level of scrutiny. . . .

We applaud individual attorneys or associations of attorneys who volunteer to provide either pro bono legal representation or representation of indigent defendants at rates which may be drastically under the market value of the lawyers' skills and services. It reflects pride in the practice of law, and it exemplifies the best of many virtues found in the practicing bar. The provision of legal services to indigents is one of the responsibilities assumed by the legal profession, and personal involvement in the problems of the disadvantaged can be one of the most rewarding experiences in the life of a lawyer.

Every lawyer, regardless of professional prominence or professional workload, should find time to participate in or otherwise support the provision of legal services to the disadvantaged. We strongly urge the continuation of these services. We believe that attorneys would voluntarily donate their skills and services were they not unduly burdened with compulsory appointments. We also believe that Oklahoma lawyers will form local, county, district, and intrastate voluntary pools to assume this responsibility and to relieve lawyers who practice in counties with few lawyers from an unfair court-imposed case load. We also recognize that at this time voluntary services are insufficient to accommodate the right of indigent citizens to the effective assistance of counsel where that right is implicated.

[The State] has an obligation to pay appointed lawyers sums which will fairly compensate the lawyer, not at the top rate which a lawyer might charge, but at a rate which is not confiscatory, after considering overhead and expenses. The basis of the amount to be paid for services must not vary with each judge; rather there must be a statewide basis or scale for ascertaining a reasonable hourly rate in order to avoid the enactment of a proscribed special law.

Although we invite legislative attention to this problem, in the interim, we must establish guides which will apply uniformly without either violating due process rights or granting constitutional immunities. *Bias* provided some relief to Oklahoma lawyers; however, it did not address the constitutional infirmities which are squarely presented here. Therefore, in order to correct the defects which render the present statutory scheme unconstitutional, we must build on the foundation which was laid in *Bias*. We find that the most even handed approach in setting fees is to tie the hourly rate of the counsel appointed for the indigent defendant to the hourly rate of the prosecutor/district attorney and the public defenders.

[A]ll district attorneys receive the same salary—$56,180 per year or $29.26 per hour. We find that the trial court may award the attorney from $14.63 to $29.26 based on the attorney's qualifications. This range is tied to the salary range paid to assistant district attorneys and the district attorneys. (As a matter of course, when the district attorneys' and public defenders' salaries are raised by the Legislature so, too, would the hourly rate of compensation for defense counsel.) The overhead and the litigation expense of the district attorney are furnished by the state. In order to place the counsel for the defense on an equal footing with counsel for the prosecution, provision must be made for compensation of defense counsel's reasonable overhead and out of pocket expenses.

However, before the lawyer can be compensated for overhead, the percentage of reasonable hourly overhead rate directly attributable to the case in controversy, and the amount of out-of-pocket expenses incurred, must be presented to the trial court. . . . To receive payment for the reasonable overhead, attorney fees, and out of pocket expenses charged to the case, the lawyer must present accurate itemizations of overhead expenditures, time sheets, and invoices to support the number of hours reasonably spent on the defense.

Mattingly and Pyron have complied with the guidelines we are establishing. Were this not so, we would remand for further proceedings. We find that they are seasoned lawyers who should be paid an hourly rate of $29.26 per hour; that the average overhead rate and out of pocket expenses presented are reasonable; and that the lawyers spent the time alleged in the pursuit of Lynch's defense.

[T]he provision of counsel for indigent defendants, and the compensation of such counsel also lie within the Legislative sphere, and its consideration of the myriad problems presented is invited. This is an important area, which the Legislature should act to address. Nevertheless, until such time as the Legislature considers these matters . . . these guidelines shall become effective [immediately] in all cases in which the State of Oklahoma is required to provide assistance of counsel, insofar as the appointment of counsel and the implementation of post-appointment show cause hearings are concerned. [R]ecovery of attorney fees under the new guidelines will not be effective in non-capital cases until August 24, 1992, to allow the Legislature to address the problem, and to enact corrective legislation.

SIMMS, J., dissenting.

Under our system of criminal jurisprudence, a licensed attorney finds himself in a very unique position. That lawyer is an officer of the court. And as such, is bound to render service when required by his or her appointment to represent an indigent defendant. However, he is not [an] "officer" within the ordinary meaning of that term. An attorney is not in the same category as marshals, bailiffs, court clerks or judges. A lawyer is engaged in a private profession, important though it be to our system of justice. [B]ecause of this unique relationship a lawyer enjoys with our system of criminal justice, fulfilling his legally recognized duty to render services when required by an appointment to represent an indigent defendant, cannot to me, be described in most instances in terms of a taking of his "property" without due process of law. . . .

We should direct the Legislature's attention to the Criminal Justice Act which the Congress of the United States enacted, titled "Adequate Representation of Defendants." . . . The federal act further provides for a uniform hourly rate for time expended in court or before a magistrate and a uniform hourly rate for time expended out of court. I would submit that enactment of a state statute closely paralleling [the federal act] might be a simple and direct answer to the problems raised by the majority opinion in this case. We should emphasize that the solutions to these problems are within the expertise and proper power of the Legislature and not this Court.

OPALA, V.C.J., concurring in part and dissenting in part.

. . . I join in concluding that the regime of assigning lawyers for criminal defense work in counties which are without public defender services is tainted by a constitutional infirmity. I recede from the court's interim institutional design that is to govern until the legislature overhauls the system. In my view, the whole scheme is affected by a fatal and incurable flaw. It saddles the judiciary with the responsibility of operating defense services in 75 counties — a function properly to be performed by the executive department. Until the legislature establishes a professionally independent statewide public defender system within the executive department, I would, merely as a stopgap measure, (1) develop guidelines that would equalize, on a statewide basis, the Bar's burden for providing defense services in those 75 counties and (2) call upon the Oklahoma Bar Association [hereafter called the Bar] to manage a statewide service pool of qualified lawyers for deployment in criminal as well as other mandated public-service work. . . .

The law must insulate from anyone's interference — judicial, legislative or executive — all aspects of a public defender's attorney/client relationship. The litigation-related strategy choices, as well as any other facet of professional decision-making in the conduct of a person's defense, must be beyond the pale of outsiders' meddling. Nevertheless, the essence of the service to be provided is correctly characterized as extraneous to the judicial or legislative function and akin to that of the executive. It is the executive's responsibility to seek reversal-proof convictions in judicial tribunals properly constituted to administer that standard of adjudicative process which conforms to the dictates of our fundamental law. In short, in the aftermath of *Gideon* and its progeny, defense, as much as prosecution, is an essential component of government service for the enforcement of criminal laws. . . .

■ AMERICAN BAR ASSOCIATION MODEL RULE OF PROFESSIONAL CONDUCT 1.5(D)

A lawyer shall not enter into an arrangement for, charge, or collect . . . a contingent fee for representing a defendant in a criminal case.

Problem 11-5. Flat Fees for Service

From 1967 to 1988, the Detroit Recorder's Court used an "event based" fee system to compensate counsel assigned to represent indigent criminal defendants. Under this system, a separate fee was paid for pre-preliminary examination jail visits, preliminary examinations, two post-preliminary examination jail visits, investigation and trial preparation, written motions filed and heard, calendar conferences, arraignments on the information, final conferences, evidentiary hearings, pleas, and forensic hearings. The system also provided compensation for each day of trial necessary to dispose of any particular case, and for counsel appearances in court for sentencing of the defendant.

In an effort to reduce jail overcrowding, a jail oversight committee studied the Recorder's Court and found a direct correlation between jail bed demand and the length of the criminal docket. The committee concluded that a substantial savings in jail bed demand could be recognized by reducing the time between a defendant's arrest and the ultimate disposition of the case. The committee was concerned that the event-based system gave assigned counsel an incentive to prolong final disposition of cases to earn a larger fee.

The committee asked the clerk of the Detroit Recorder's Court to devise a compensation system that would promote docket efficiency without reducing the overall level of compensation paid to assigned counsel. A statistical analysis revealed that attorneys tended to perform more "events" for clients who faced charges punishable by longer prison terms. The clerk grouped all assigned cases for the previous two years by potential maximum sentence and averaged the fees paid in each group of cases. The clerk then proposed a fee system that would pay attorneys a flat fee for representing a defendant, regardless of the number of "events" the attorney performed. Assigned counsel would be entitled to the full fee, regardless of whether the case is dismissed at the preliminary examination, the defendant pleads guilty at the arraignment on the information, or the case is ultimately disposed of after a jury trial. The flat fee would vary for different types of offenses and would reflect the average fees paid for defending such cases under the old system. The fixed rates would range from $475 for a 24-month maximum crime to $1,400 for a first-degree murder case.

The local court adopted the fixed fee system, and it succeeded in speeding up the docket. By shortening the time between arrest and disposition, the system alleviated some of the pressure for more jail space. A lawyer could earn $100 an hour for a guilty plea, typically three to four hours of work. If she went to trial the earnings could be $15 an hour or less. Prosecutors also noted a decrease in the number of "frivolous" defense motions and increased pressure from the defense bar for the prosecutor to dismiss weak cases at an earlier stage.

The fee system permits assigned counsel to petition the chief judge of the Recorder's Court for payment of extraordinary fees in cases requiring above-average effort. However, undercompensated attorneys have hesitated to petition for extraordinary fees, believing that such requests either would prove futile or perhaps even adversely affect their prospects of receiving future assignments. While more than 3,000 indigent criminal defense assignments were made in the Court during 1989, only 29 petitions were filed for extraordinary fees, of which 23 were granted, totaling $11,175. This is approximately 1.6 percent of the total indigent attorney fees paid for that year.

In Michigan, assigned counsel have a statutory right to compensation for providing criminal defense services to the indigent. The controlling statute provides that the chief judge "shall appoint" an attorney "to conduct the accused's examination and to conduct the accused's defense." The appointed attorney appointed "shall be entitled to receive from the county treasurer, on the certificate of the chief judge that the services have been rendered, the amount which the chief judge considers to be reasonable compensation for the services performed." Mich. Comp. Laws § 775.16. Does the fixed fee system provide assigned counsel "reasonable compensation for the services performed"? Does it violate indigent defendants' right to effective assistance of counsel? Compare Recorder's Court Bar Assoc. v. Wayne Circuit Court, 503 N.W.2d 885 (Mich. 1993).

Problem 11-6. The Neighborhood Defender

The Neighborhood Defender Service (NDS) of Harlem created a new method of organizing public defense resources. The differences between NDS and the more typical public defender's office were manifest in the outreach efforts of the office, the range of legal services offered to clients, and the assignment of staff to clients.

Rather than placing its offices in one location near the courthouse, NDS placed several offices around the community to make the organization more visible and available to its clients. The service also placed posters, business cards, and other outreach devices in the community so that people in the neighborhood would be familiar with the service before they or their family members needed legal representation in a criminal matter. NDS hoped that this would help attorneys establish a relationship with their clients earlier in the criminal process and would give clients more reason to trust and cooperate with their attorneys.

NDS also shifted its focus from trial to the early stages of cases (sometimes even before arrest), emphasizing investigation and early resolution of charges. Through mediation, attorneys in NDS could sometimes resolve conflicts between victims and defendants, leading the victim to ask the prosecutor to drop charges. The service also continued to advise clients after conviction, to avoid problems during probation or parole. On occasion, NDS would represent clients or their family members in civil matters closely connected to a criminal charge (for instance, possible eviction from public housing based on drug trafficking charges).

As for assignment of staff to the clients, NDS moved away from the typical arrangement of placing one attorney alone in charge of a proportional share of cases the office receives. Each NDS client is represented by a team, consisting of a lead attorney, secondary attorneys, community workers, an investigator, and an administrative assistant. Each NDS attorney is assigned to more total cases than he would handle alone under the traditional arrangement, but the attorneys share the workload on each of the cases. If a client ever has a second case, the same team handles the client's case again. The strategy is to assign more tasks to nonlawyers and to ensure continuity of representation over time and more widespread responsibility for making early progress on the cases.

Is this organizational model for public defender services likely to work in many different communities? If not, what are the conditions necessary for a neighborhood defender service to succeed? See National Inst. of Justice, Public Defenders in the Neighborhood: A Harlem Law Office Stresses Teamwork, Early Investigation, NCJ 163061 (1997).

Notes

1. *Local variety in indigent defense systems.* As the materials above indicate, jurisdictions have created several different systems for providing defense counsel to indigent criminal defendants. Although public defender services are the exclusive method of providing defense counsel in less than a third of all jurisdictions, they tend to be used in the largest jurisdictions, meaning that the majority of criminal defendants in this country receive their attorney through a public defender's office. Bureau of Justice Statistics, Indigent Defense Services in Large Counties, 1999 at Table 7 (Nov. 2000, NCJ 184932) (82 percent of cases in 100 largest counties handled through public defender programs). The federal system continues to rely on different systems from district to district. This local variation in the federal system is the legacy of one of the great justice reform reports in U.S. history, the Report of the Attorney General's Committee on Poverty and the Administration of Federal Criminal Justice (1963), known after its chair as the "Allen Report." The Allen Report

led to the federal Criminal Justice Act of 1964, which provided a framework for funding indigent defense in the federal system.

In most states, local governments choose and finance systems of indigent defense. A growing group of states — currently over 20 of them — fund and operate statewide indigent defender services with full authority to provide legal services. See Bureau of Justice Statistics, State-Funded Indigent Defense Services, 1999 (2001, NCJ 188464). Other states create a statewide commission to provide uniform policies and training for public defenders but leave the choice and funding of systems to the local government. Still another group of 10 to 15 states use county and regional commissions to direct the work of local public defender programs within a single judicial district. See Robert Spangenberg and Marea Beeman, Indigent Defense Systems in the United States, 58 Law & Contemp. Probs. 31 (Winter 1995). There is more statewide uniformity for police practices and trial procedures (through state statutes, constitutional rulings, and procedural rules) than for the provision of defense counsel. Why have the local governments rather than the state governments become the focal point for choices about defense counsel?

2. *Legal challenges to public defender systems.* On those relatively rare occasions when defendants challenge the overall effectiveness of a public defender program, the caseload of the attorneys is always a key variable. See In re Order on Prosecution of Criminal Appeals by the Tenth Judicial Circuit Public Defender, 561 So. 2d 1130 (Fla. 1990) (backlog of appellate cases assigned to public defenders supports habeas corpus relief for indigent appellants unless new funds appropriated within 60 days); John Gibeaut, Defense Warnings, ABA Journal, Dec. 2001, at 35 (describing litigation over caseloads for indigent defense in Quitman County, Mississippi; Pittsburgh; Connecticut; Coweta County, Georgia).

The ABA standards recommend annual caseloads of no more than 150 non-capital felonies per attorney, 400 misdemeanors, 200 juvenile cases or 25 appeals. ABA Standards for Criminal Justice, Providing Defense Services §5-5.3 cmt. (3d ed. 1992). How do these standards compare to the workload of Rick Teissier, the defense attorney in *Peart?* Several states have statutes directing public defenders not to accept additional cases if the heavier caseload prevents them from providing effective representation. A handful of states have statutes adopting specific annual caseload caps for public defender programs. See N.H. Rev. Stat. §604-B:6; Wash. Rev. Code §10.101.030; Wis. Stat. §977.08(5)(bn).

3. *Legal challenges to appointed counsel systems.* Almost all jurisdictions rely on volunteer attorneys to represent some indigent defendants. Sometimes these attorneys take cases when the public defender organization has a conflict of interest; in other places, the court appoints attorneys for all cases from a list of volunteers. The amount of compensation varies. A volunteer attorney can ordinarily expect some compensation for "overhead" expenses and some reduced compensation for her time. But payment in some systems is discretionary, and the lawyers on the list do not have complete freedom to accept or refuse appointments from the court, depending on schedule and income needs. In a companion case to *Peart,* the Louisiana court in State v. Clark, 624 So. 2d 422 (La. 1993), upheld a contempt finding against an attorney who had refused to accept an appointment to represent a criminal defendant. The attorney, who had placed himself on the volunteer list, had been appointed to five felony cases over a four-month period; he refused to represent the fifth defendant because his private practice was suffering from neglect.

The Louisiana court said that attorneys must represent indigents unless a court decides that the appointment is "unreasonable and oppressive," and that these circumstances were not enough to meet the standard.

Lawyers raising constitutional challenges to the adequacy of payments for their work as appointed or contract counsel in individual criminal cases have found modest but consistent success. Courts often recognize that lawyers can be asked to perform enough services for so little compensation that a due process or takings clause violation occurs. See Arnold v. Kemp, 813 S.W.2d 770 (Ark. 1991); Jewell v. Maynard, 383 S.E.2d 536 (W. Va. 1989) (when caseload attributable to court appointments occupies substantial amount of attorney's time, or when attorney's costs and out-of-pocket expenses from representing indigent persons charged with crime reduce substantially the attorney's net income from private practice, requirement of court-appointed service is confiscatory and unconstitutional). The challenge could also be based on a violation of the client's constitutional right to counsel or on violations of the ethical obligations of attorneys.

Broad-based challenges to appointment systems do not occur routinely. A few systemic lawsuits have produced more funding and better organization for appointed counsel systems, including recent litigation in New York City. See Daniel Wise and Tom Perrotta, New Hourly Rates Set for Court-Appointed Lawyers, N.Y. Law Journal, May 6, 2002 (judge issues preliminary injunction raising hourly rate for appointed lawyers from 40 to 90 dollars per hour). More often, however, courts conclude that the level of compensation at issue, while perhaps in need of an increase, does not create a constitutional problem. See Lewis v. Iowa District Court for Des Moines County, 555 N.W.2d 216 (Iowa 1996). What might explain the small amount of litigation over a subject as volatile as compensation for appointed attorneys? Do lawyers simply decline to participate in the appointment system (when the choice is theirs) rather than litigate over the adequacy of the compensation?

4. *Challenges to contract attorney systems: majority position.* In contract attorney programs, the government (typically at the county level) agrees with a private law firm, bar association, or nonprofit organization to provide indigent defense. The contract may cover all criminal cases or specific classes of cases (such as all juvenile cases or adult cases in which the public defender's office has a conflict of interest). These contracts become especially attractive in jurisdictions where the costs of appointed attorneys has increased. For instance, Oklahoma turned to lowest-bidder contract providers after the *Lynch* case was decided.

The method of pricing the services is the difficult issue. Some jurisdictions use a fixed price contract, in which the provider agrees to perform defense services at the stated price, regardless of the number of cases that actually arise. Although this method of setting the contract amount is relatively common, it has only rarely been challenged on constitutional grounds. In State v. Smith, 681 P.2d 1374 (Ariz. 1984), a defendant convicted of burglary argued that he was denied effective assistance of counsel because of his attorney's "shocking, staggering and unworkable" caseload, which was the product of a fixed price contract. The county had granted the contract to the lowest bidder, but the contract did not allow for support costs such as investigators, paralegals, and secretaries and did not consider the experience or competence of the attorney. Smith's attorney handled a "part time" caseload of 149 felonies, 160 misdemeanors, 21 juvenile cases, and 33 other cases in the year Smith was convicted, in addition to a private civil practice. The court therefore found that the bid system violated the rights of defendants to due process and the right to counsel. Would a government avoid these problems by entering a contract that pays a fixed fee per case?

The American Bar Association's Criminal Justice Standards discourage local governments from awarding an indigent-services contract based on a fixed price for a time period. The standards recommend that contracts include detailed information about minimum attorney qualifications, attorney workloads, use of support services, and so forth. ABA Standards for Criminal Justice, Providing Defense Services §5-3.3(b) (3d ed. 1992). The well-regarded system in Oregon asks potential contractors to submit information on caseloads, areas of coverage (including geographic limits and types of cases), level of services, staffing plans, and the applicants' experience and qualifications. Spangenberg Group, Contracting for Indigent Defense Services: A Special Report (2000, NCJ 181160). Will a contracting government be able to follow these standards and still obtain the predictability of legal expenses so necessary to government budgeting and administration?

5. *Remedies.* The most vexing question in much of the litigation challenging systems for providing defense counsel is the question of remedy. If an attorney is placed in a situation in which effective assistance is difficult or impossible for her to provide, what should the court do? Overturn individual convictions of those who challenge the effectiveness of their attorneys? Order the legislature to provide additional funding? Mandate a minimally acceptable caseload or fee schedule? After *Peart* was decided, the Louisiana legislature created the Louisiana Indigent Defender Board and gave it a $10 million budget to use for studying problems with indigent defense in the state and for granting operating funds in trouble areas, such as appointment of defense experts in particular cases. The legislature later cut the budget to $5 million, at a time when defense of capital cases was becoming a larger concern for the board. Does this aftermath of the *Peart* litigation tell you anything about the remedies a court should impose?

6. *Incentives for aggressive representation.* Which system — public defender organizations, appointed counsel, or contract attorneys — provides an acceptable defense for the least amount of money? The best defense for an acceptable amount of money? There is no single answer to these questions. Ontario, Canada, has an extremely well-funded public defender agency; it spent about $1,246 per matter in 1991. In Los Angeles, it costs an average of $683 for a public defender to defend a felony case, while it takes a court-appointed attorney an average of $2,914. See American Lawyer, Jan.-Feb. 1993, at 64, 83. In the end, the cost of any of these systems will depend on what the public believes should be the "normal" method of defending a case. One often hears the assertion that defender organizations are funded at a level that compels the attorneys to urge their clients to plead guilty in most cases. For instance, one public defender explained why some innocent defendants plead guilty: "[W]e don't have enough resources, and . . . the system is geared toward putting people away as efficiently as possible." American Lawyer, Jan.-Feb. 1993, at 72. See Michael McConville and Chester Mirsky, Criminal Defense of the Poor in New York City, 15 N.Y.U. Rev. L. & Soc. Change 581 (1986-1987). Is it inevitable that defense attorneys who regularly accept money from the government will, in the long run, moderate their demands on prosecutors, police, and judges?

Some believe that "organizational" defenders are more cost-efficient because they represent many defendants at once and work in criminal justice full time. Thus, legislatures tend to create public defender programs because of potential cost savings. Are public defenders more efficient than appointed counsel, or do they choose certain cases and issues to pursue aggressively while allowing the other cases and clients to suffer from neglect? Is this what the public defender from Louisiana did in *Peart*? Would an appointed attorney be better able to represent each client more thoroughly, without trading off one client's needs against those of another? Are attorneys who spend all their time representing criminal defendants in the best position to bring systemwide challenges to the practices of police, prosecutors, or judges?

7. *Funding parity*. If popular support for prosecution of crimes is higher than the support for funding criminal defense, is the answer to require parity of funding between prosecution and defense? How would you accomplish this most effectively—through a constitutional ruling, a statute, or a local ordinance?

There is little doubt that the total resources available for the investigation and prosecution of crime are greater than those available for defending against criminal charges. See David Luban, Are Criminal Defenders Different? 91 Mich. L. Rev. 1729 (1993) (resources for prosecution versus public and private defense counsel may be at roughly comparable levels, but only when ignoring prosecutorial access to police and forensic expert support). The imbalance in resources has arguably become more pronounced over the past two decades, as governments have increased the size of police, prosecutorial, and judicial staffs without comparably increasing defense counsel funding. As prosecutions and convictions have risen faster than the number of defense attorneys, defense caseloads have risen faster than prosecution caseloads.

If it is true that prosecutors and police combined receive more resources than defense counsel, is that a problem? Perhaps one might respond that prosecutors have more funding because they perform a wider range of functions than defense counsel. For instance, they make screening decisions on cases that are never charged. Alternatively, one might ask whether the increased demands on defense counsel really translate into worse outcomes for clients. One study of nine jurisdictions, conducted in 1992 for the National Center for State Courts, concluded that publicly provided attorneys produced outcomes similar to privately retained defense counsel. Private and publicly funded attorneys produced no significant difference in rates of convictions or length of sentences. Privately retained counsel obtained slightly better results in avoiding incarceration for their clients. Roger Hanson, Brian Ostrom, William Hewitt, and Christopher Lomvardias, Indigent Defenders Get the Job Done and Done Well (National Center for State Courts, 1992). Is there any basis for arguing that defense counsel should be funded on a level comparable to the prosecution if there is no demonstrable effect on the outcomes for defendants?

Apart from the question of funding for entire offices, is there any justification for paying individual prosecutors a higher salary than individual defense attorneys? See Ariz. Stat. §11-582 (public defender salary to be at least 70 percent of prosecutor salary); Tenn. Code §16-2-518 ("any increase in local funding for positions or office expense for the district attorney general shall be accompanied by an increase in funding of 75 percent of the increase in funding to the office of the public defender in such district"). For an effort to contrast the "ex post" evaluation of a lawyer's performance under *Strickland* with an "ex ante" evaluation of the resources available to prosecution and defense, see Donald Dripps, Ineffective Assistance of Counsel: The Case for an Ex Ante Parity Standard, 88 J. Crim. L. & Criminology 242-308 (1997); cf. Albert Alschuler, Personal Failure, Institutional Failure, and the Sixth Amendment, 14 N.Y.U. Rev. L. & Soc. Change 149 (1986).

8. *Contingent fees*. Would private defense attorneys be more willing to represent criminal defendants if they could make contingent fee arrangements with their

clients, calling for different levels of compensation depending on the outcome of the proceedings? The ABA standard reprinted above, barring the use of contingent fees in criminal cases, reflects the law of all the states. Why are contingent fees prohibited in criminal cases when they have been such an effective method (some might say too effective) for providing counsel to civil litigants? For further reading, see Pamela Karlan, Contingent Fees and Criminal Cases, 93 Colum. L. Rev. 595 (1993).

E. THE ETHICS OF DEFENDING CRIMINALS

If you are a defense lawyer, you may often hear the question, "how can you defend those people?" Should all lawyers be required to defend criminals, regardless of the crime of which the defendant is accused or the lawyer's view of the defendant's guilt? The following selections represent a range of time-honored answers to this question. As you read them, try to come up with a short phrase to describe the position suggested in each passage. Which of the positions reflects the current mainstream of thought among American lawyers? Among law students? What are the institutional and ethical implications of each position?

■ SPEECHES OF LORD ERSKINE

(James High ed., 1876)

In every place where business or pleasure collects the public together, day after day, my name and character have been the topics of injurious reflection.* And for what? Only for not having shrunk from the discharge of a duty which no personal advantage recommended, but which a thousand difficulties repelled. Little indeed did they know me, who thought that such calumnies would influence my conduct. I will forever, at all hazards assert the dignity, independence and integrity of the English Bar, without which impartial justice, the most valuable part of the English Constitution, can have no existence. From the moment that any advocate can be permitted to say that he will or will not stand between the Crown and the subject arraigned in the court where he daily sits to practice, from that moment the liberties of England are at an end. If the advocate refuses to defend, from what he may think of the charge or of the defense, he assumes the character of the judge; nay he assumes it before the hour of judgment; and in proportion to his rank and reputation puts the heavy influence of perhaps a mistaken opinion into the scale against the accused in whose favor the benevolent principles of English law makes all presumptions. . . .

■ THE AMERICAN LAWYER JOHN DOS PASSOS

158 (1907)

I do not place the right of the lawyer to defend a client when he believes him to be guilty upon the ground that he cannot know that his client is guilty until his

* Lord Erskine was defense counsel for Thomas Paine, the influential pamphleteer.—EDS.

guilt has been officially and finally declared by a court and jury, because he often does know, in the sense that he has a moral conviction of the guilt of his client which he has derived through the ordinary channels of information. I place the right of the lawyer upon the ground that he is an officer of the law, and that it is his *duty* to see that the forms of law are carried out, quite irrespective of individual knowledge.

■ AMERICAN BAR ASSOCIATION AND ASSOCIATION OF AMERICAN LAW SCHOOLS PROFESSIONAL RESPONSIBILITY: REPORT OF THE JOINT CONFERENCE (1958)

The Joint Conference on Professional Responsibility* was established in 1952 by the American Bar Association and the Association of American Law Schools. [T]hose who had attempted to teach ethical principles to law students found that the students were uneasy about the adversary system, some thinking of it as an unwholesome compromise with the combativeness of human nature, others vaguely approving of it but disturbed by their inability to articulate its proper limits. . . . Confronted by the layman's charge that he is nothing but a hired brain and voice, the lawyer often finds it difficult to convey an insight into the value of the adversary system. . . . Accordingly, it was decided that the first need was for a reasoned statement of the lawyer's responsibilities, set in the context of the adversary system. . . .

The Lawyer's Role as Advocate in Open Court

The lawyer appearing as an advocate before a tribunal presents, as persuasively as he can, the facts and the law of the case as seen from the standpoint of his client's interest. . . . In a very real sense it may be said that the integrity of the adjudicative process itself depends upon the participation of the advocate. This becomes apparent when we contemplate the nature of the task assumed by any arbiter who attempts to decide a dispute without the aid of partisan advocacy.

Such an arbiter must undertake, not only the role of judge, but that of representative for both of the litigants. Each of these roles must be played to the full without being muted by qualifications derived from the others. When he is developing for each side the most effective statement of its case, the arbiter must put aside his neutrality and permit himself to be moved by a sympathetic identification. . . . When he resumes his neutral position, he must be able to view with distrust the fruits of this identification and be ready to reject the products of his own best mental efforts. The difficulties of this undertaking are obvious. If it is true that a man in his time must play many parts, it is scarcely given to him to play them all at once.

It is small wonder, then, that failure generally attends the attempt to dispense with the distinct roles traditionally implied in adjudication. What generally occurs in practice is that at some early point a familiar pattern will seem to emerge from the evidence; an accustomed label is waiting for the case and, without further proofs, this label is promptly assigned to it. [W]hat starts as a preliminary diagnosis

* The conference was chaired by Lon Fuller and John Randall.—Eds.

designed to direct the inquiry tends, quickly and imperceptibly, to become a fixed conclusion, as all that confirms the diagnosis makes a strong imprint on the mind, while all that runs counter to it is received with diverted attention.

An adversary presentation seems the only effective means for combating this natural human tendency to judge too swiftly in terms of the familiar that which is not yet fully known. The arguments of counsel hold the case, as it were, in suspension between two opposing interpretations of it. While the proper classification of the case is thus kept unresolved, there is time to explore all of its peculiarities and nuances. . . .

Viewed in this light, the role of the lawyer as a partisan advocate appears not as a regrettable necessity, but as an indispensable part of a larger ordering of affairs. The institution of advocacy is not a concession to the frailties of human nature, but an expression of human insight in the design of a social framework within which man's capacity for impartial judgment can attain its fullest realization. . . .

The Representation of Unpopular Causes

One of the highest services the lawyer can render to society is to appear in court on behalf of clients whose causes are in disfavor with the general public. . . . Where a cause is in disfavor because of a misunderstanding by the public, the service of the lawyer representing it is obvious, since he helps to remove an obloquy unjustly attaching to his client's position. But the lawyer renders an equally important, though less readily understood, service where the unfavorable public opinion of the client's cause is in fact justified. It is essential for a sound and wholesome development of public opinion that the disfavored cause have its full day in court, which includes, of necessity, representation by competent counsel. Where this does not occur, a fear arises that perhaps more might have been said for the losing side and suspicion is cast on the decision reached. Thus, confidence in the fundamental processes of government is diminished.

The extent to which the individual lawyer should feel himself bound to undertake the representation of unpopular causes must remain a matter for individual conscience. The legal profession as a whole, however, has a clear moral obligation with respect to this problem. . . . No member of the Bar should indulge in public criticism of another lawyer because he has undertaken the representation of causes in general disfavor. Every member of the profession should, on the contrary, do what he can to promote a public understanding of the service rendered by the advocate in such situations. . . .

These are problems each lawyer must solve in his own way. But in solving them he will remember, with Whitehead, that moral education cannot be complete without the habitual vision of greatness. And he will recall the concluding words of a famous essay by Holmes:

> Happiness, I am sure from having known many successful men, cannot be won simply by being counsel for great corporations and having an income of fifty thousand dollars. An intellect great enough to win the prize needs other food besides success. The remoter and more general aspects of the law are those which give it universal interest. It is through them that you not only become a great master in your calling, but connect your subject with the universe and catch an echo of the infinite, a glimpse of its unfathomable process, a hint of the universal law.

■ DEFENDING GUILTY PEOPLE JOHN KAPLAN

7 U. Bridgeport L. Rev. 223 (1986)

I would like to address an often asked, many times answered, but still extremely complex question: Why would lawyers want to defend guilty people? I will try to do so by examining first a somewhat different issue: Why should society as a whole want guilty people to be represented by lawyers? . . . The first means of approach is to ask two related questions: "Why do we want lawyers to represent criminal defendants at all?" and, second, "How does this rationale change in the case when we know that the defendant is guilty?". . .

The first of the questions seems simple, but there are three quite different reasons why we wish those accused of crimes to be defended by lawyers. The most obvious reason is that defense lawyers improve the accuracy of the fact-finding process in which they are engaged. Many people may dispute this, since over the years the adversary system has played, at best, to mixed reviews. . . . Often it was said that a system where each of the two sides was trying to put something over on the decision maker was a crazy method of deciding important questions. . . .

The second major reason why we want defendants in criminal cases to be defended by counsel is much more complex. [T]he basic idea is that one major characteristic of the due process model of criminal litigation is the use of the criminal process to check and regulate its own institutions. Thus, in a particular case, the defendant's lawyer will litigate much more than whether the defendant has violated a particular law with the appropriate state of mind. The lawyer also will be making sure that the arms of the state have complied with the many legal rules which bind them. . . .

The third major reason for providing an attorney for those accused of crimes involves the symbolic statement that it makes about us and our society; it is a multi-faceted statement. It says that we are a compassionate people and that in our society even the worst off (and it is hard to think of any who, as a class, are worse off than those accused of crimes) are entitled to have one person in their corner to help them. It underlines the value we place upon equality, because though lawyers vary considerably in their ability to manipulate our complex system of jury trials, their variation is far less than that among criminal defendants. [Our] trial system makes the statement that in our society the individual has rights against the state which can actually be enforced through the legal system. . . .

Next we move to the second question — which of these three reasons for having the defendant represented by an attorney no longer applies when we know that the defendant is guilty. [It] seems that only the first reason, improving the accuracy of the fact-finding process, loses its force. Of course, when the defendant is by hypothesis guilty, we need not worry about the accuracy of the process by which this is determined.

With respect to the second reason, checking the operation of the institutions of the criminal law, most of the checks are expected to apply where the accused is guilty of the crimes charged. . . . There is a thin line between arguing that a defendant is innocent — a matter that goes to fact-finding — and arguing that the police and prosecutors improperly brought the case on insufficient evidence — a matter involving the checking function.

The closeness of these two functions at this point is also seen when we adopt a dynamic, rather than a static, view of the criminal process. We must remember that when prosecutors and police do their jobs well, they do so in part because of the discipline imposed upon them by the fact that they will have to prove their case against a defendant represented by a lawyer. If that should cease, it may be impossible to guarantee that the police and prosecutors will continue at the same level of competence, energy, and integrity. The perhaps apocryphal example of a mountain village may be instructive: it is said that the town fathers took down the "dangerous curve ahead" sign because no one had gone off the road there. They had therefore concluded that the curve was no longer dangerous.

The fact that innocent defendants may benefit from some applications of the checking function, such as those related to the strength of the prosecution's case, might lead to the argument that at least as to these applications, the checking function should not be applied where the defendant is guilty. So far as the checking function is concerned, a defense lawyer is unnecessary in those cases where we know that the defendant is guilty. If enough innocent defendants went to trial so that we could perform the checking function adequately in their cases, why should a lawyer do so on behalf of one who is guilty? The problem . . . is that our criminal justice system is so heavily structured to produce guilty pleas that there may not be enough innocent defendants going to trial to raise the inadequacies of the police and prosecutorial screening in their cases. . . .

Similarly, the third major reason for having attorneys represent criminal defendants is not affected by whether the defendant is guilty. Indeed, the symbolic value of having an attorney represent a defendant may even be increased when we know the accused is guilty. The statement, then, becomes that much louder that the rights of those defendants whose guilt has not been officially and fairly determined are so fixed and important that, even if we knew they were guilty, these rights would remain. . . .

The last question we need to ask is, "Why would anyone want to make a living this way?" The answer to that question involves a very different kind of discourse, but my answer is simple. The question should not be asked. It is important to remember that, for one reason or another, criminal lawyers want to defend criminal defendants. Their taste may be as baffling to us as is the proctologist's, but we need both and should not try to dissuade either from pursuing his or her profession. Instead, we ought to encourage both because, whether they realize it or not — or even care — they are doing exactly what we want them to do.

IS A LAWYER BOUND TO SUPPORT AN UNJUST CAUSE? A PROBLEM OF ETHICS
AARON CUTLER
300-302 (1952)

The layman's question which has most tormented the lawyer over the years is: "How can you honestly stand up and defend a man you know to be guilty?" [A]dvocates enjoy reciting the following colloquy attributed to Samuel Johnson by his famous biographer, James Boswell:

Boswell: But what do you think of supporting a cause which you know to be bad?
Johnson: Sir, you do not know it to be good or bad till the Judge determines it. You are to state facts clearly; so that your thinking, or what you call knowing, a cause

to be bad must be from reasoning, must be from supposing your arguments to be weak and inconclusive. But Sir, that is not enough. An argument which does not convince yourself may convince the judge to whom you urge it; and if it does convince him, why then, sir, you are wrong and he is right. . . .

Boswell: But, Sir, does not affecting a warmth when you have no warmth, and appearing to be clearly of one opinion when you are in reality of another opinion, does not such dissimulation impair one's honesty? Is there not some danger that a lawyer may put on the same mask in common life in the intercourse with his friends?

Johnson: Why, no, Sir. Everybody knows you are paid for affecting warmth for your client, and it is therefore properly no dissimulation: the moment you come from the Bar you resume your usual behaviour. Sir, a man will no more carry the artifice of the Bar into the common intercourse of society, than a man who is paid for tumbling upon his hands will continue to tumble on his hands when he should walk upon his feet. . . .

Such an attitude we submit entirely overlooks the bifurcated roles of a lawyer. The duty is not simply one which he owes his client. Just as important is the duty which the lawyer owes the court and society. Great as is his loyalty to the client, even greater is his sacred obligation as an officer of the court. He cannot ethically, and should not by preference, present to the court assertions he knows to be false. . . .

It is only when a lawyer really believes his client is innocent that he should undertake to defend him. All our democratic safeguards are thrown about a person accused of a crime so that no innocent man may suffer. Guilty defendants, though they are entitled to be defended sincerely and hopefully, should not be entitled to the presentation of false testimony and insincere statements by counsel.

It is too glibly said a lawyer should not judge his own client and that the court's province would thus be invaded. In more than 90 percent of all criminal cases a lawyer knows when his client is guilty or not guilty. The facts usually stand out with glaring and startling simplicity.

If a lawyer knows his client to be guilty, it is his duty in such case to set out the extenuating facts and plead for mercy in which the lawyer sincerely believes. In the infrequent number of cases where there is doubt of the client's guilt and the lawyer sincerely believes his client is innocent, he of course should plead his client's cause to the best of his ability.

In civil cases, the area of doubt is undoubtedly considerably greater. At a guess, only one-third [of] the cases presented to a lawyer are pure black or pure white. In only one-third of the cases does the lawyer indubitably know his client is wrong or right. In the other two-thirds gray is the predominant color. It is the duty of the advocate to appraise the client's cause in his favor, after giving due consideration to the facts on the other side. In such a case, it is of course the duty of the advocate to present his client's case to the best of his ability. . . .

A lawyer should worship truth and fact. He should unhesitatingly cast out the evil spirits of specious reasoning, of doubtful claims, of incredible or improbable premises. Truly, the best persuader is one who has first really persuaded himself after a careful analysis of the facts that he is on the right side. Some assert that lawyers must be actors. That is only partially true. An actor can portray abysmal grief or ecstatic happiness without having any such corresponding feeling in his own heart. A young actor can well portray the tragedy of King Lear, though his face is unwrinkled and unmarred after his make-up is removed. [But the] true lawyer can only be persuasive when he honestly believes he is right. . . .

Whatever the situation was in Johnson's day, there should be no artifice at the Bar. Nor should a man "resume his usual behaviour" the moment he comes from the Bar. The lawyer's usual behavior both in his office, and at the Bar and in Society, should be that of a man of probity, integrity and absolute dependability.

The argument that a lawyer should be a mouthpiece for his client, indelicate as that connotation may be, is specious and only logical to a limited extent. A lawyer should not be merely a mechanical apparatus reproducing the words and thoughts and alibis of his client, no matter how insincere or dishonest. Rather the lawyer should refuse to speak those words as a mouthpiece, unless the utterances of his client are filtered and purified by truth and sincerity. . . .

■ LETTER FROM WILLIAM TOWNSEND

4 N.Y. L. Rev. 173 (1926)

To William H. Townsend, of the Lexington, Kentucky, bar, writing for the February American Bar Association Journal, we are indebted for some interesting light upon Abraham Lincoln's views. . . . Mr. Townsend writes:

> Lincoln was regarded as a really formidable antagonist only when he was thoroughly convinced of the justice of his cause. He seemed utterly incapable of that professional partisanship that enlisted the best efforts of his colleagues at the bar, regardless of the side they were on. He would never argue a case before a jury when he believed he was wrong. His associate, Henry C. Whitney, says of him in this respect: "No man was stronger than he when on the right side, and no man weaker than he when on the opposite. A knowledge of this fact gave him additional strength before a court or a jury."
>
> Leonard Swett (one of Lincoln's closest friends) and Lincoln were once defending a man charged with murder, and, after all the evidence was in, Lincoln believed their man was guilty. "You speak to the jury," he said to Swett, "if I say a word they will see from my face that the man is guilty and convict him."
>
> In another murder case, the circumstantial evidence of guilt seemed almost conclusive and, when Lincoln, who had never wavered in his masterly defense, arose to address the jury, he frankly conceded that the testimony for the State was exceedingly strong. He said, in his slow, drawling way, that he had thought a great deal about the case and that the guilt of his client seemed probable. "But I am not sure," he said as his honest gray eyes looked the jury squarely in the face, "are you?" It was an application of the rule of reasonable doubt which secured an acquittal.

From the foregoing it would seem that Lincoln had no scruple against effort to acquit a guilty client, only that he preferred that associate counsel should do the summing up. In the other example Lincoln invoked the rule of reasonable doubt artfully and dramatically and the client whose guilt Lincoln conceded to be probable, was cleared of the crime.

Notes

1. *The line between obligation and excuse.* In England the question appears to be not whether lawyers should choose to represent those who are guilty but whether

any advocate can or should ever refuse to represent a defendant. A barrister cannot refuse to take a case, whether to act as an advocate or to advise, "unless the barrister is professionally committed already, has not been offered a proper fee, is professionally embarrassed by a prior conflict of interest or lacks sufficient experience or competence to handle the matter." Anthony Thornton, Responsibility and Ethics of the English Bar, in Legal Ethics and Professional Responsibility 68 (Ross Cranston ed., 1995). In the United States, lawyers can choose whether to take a case and then are asked to defend this choice. Is the English practice the best way, in the end, to reduce public criticism of criminal defense work?

The ethics of defending criminals, the related question of the proper ethical boundaries in prosecuting criminals, and the more general question of the proper ethical boundaries for criminal defense lawyers make the subject an extensive and complex debate. For just a few examples, consider Barbara Babcock, Defending the Guilty, 32 Clev. St. L. Rev. 175 (1983-1984); and Abbe Smith, Defending Defending: The Case for Unmitigated Zeal on Behalf of People Who Do Terrible Things, 28 Hofstra L. Rev. 925 (2000). These questions occupy the attention of attorneys in criminal practice, and not just legal ethicists. See Lisa J. McIntyre, The Public Defender: The Practice of Law in the Shadows of Repute 139-170 (1987) (based on interviews with public defenders in Cook County, Illinois).

2. *Asking the question.* Some of the justifications for representing potentially guilty defendants depend on the possibility (however slim) that a client could be innocent of the charges. If a defense lawyer learns that a particular client did indeed commit the crime as charged, what justifications remain for going forward with the case? Should a defense lawyer ever ask a client, "Are you guilty?" Experienced lawyers give different answers to this question. Some insist on asking their clients, because they believe they cannot prepare a good defense unless they know "the whole truth." Others do not ask, because they believe the answer would be irrelevant to the defense.

During the 1997 trial of Timothy McVeigh, who was ultimately convicted of bombing a federal courthouse in Oklahoma City and killing hundreds of people, reports circulated that McVeigh had confessed to his lawyers. The lead defense attorney, Stephen Jones, appeared on a nationally televised talk show to discuss the case with the viewers:

Oklahoma Caller: Yes, Mr. Jones, assuming McVeigh told you he was guilty, and assuming you got him off, how can you live with yourself morally the rest of your life?

Jones: Well, I think that's a fair question. . . . I'm not a judge. I'm a defense lawyer. I don't ask a client whether they're guilty. I ask them to tell me what happened. And then I compare what they tell me with what the evidence is. It's the prosecution's job to prosecute him, the jury's job to judge the facts, my job to represent him. . . . I don't have trouble sleeping at night. I have confidence in the system.

CNN Larry King Live, March 17, 1997 (Transcript #97031700V22). How might the Oklahoma caller respond to Jones's answer?

3. *Ethical deliberation for lawyers.* Even if a theory supporting the strong defense of criminal defendants, including those clients a lawyer believes to be guilty, provides general justification for an individual lawyer to defend criminals, these theories

hardly answer the difficult questions that arise in actually defending clients. There are more than a few difficult questions of application. What ought a defense attorney to do if she believes her client is lying? What ought a defense attorney to do if she obtains possible relevant evidence (say, a gun)? Is it appropriate for a defense attorney to use procedural tactics or create scheduling conflicts to increase the chance that the state's case will weaken and that the memory of witnesses will fade? Some of these questions will receive further attention in later chapters. Each deserves considered reflection by a lawyer before the moment of decision. As Monroe Freedman explains: "In making a series of ethical decisions, we create a kind of moral profile of ourselves. You should be conscious, therefore, of how your own decisions on issues of lawyers' ethics establish your moral priorities and thereby define your own moral profile. In understanding lawyers' ethics, you may come to better understand your moral values, and yourself." Freedman, Understanding Lawyers' Ethics (1990).

[illegible]

XII

Pretrial Release and Detention

Not long after the police arrest a suspect, the government must decide what charges (if any) to file against the suspect. More or less contemporaneously with the preliminary charging decision, the court must decide whether to release the suspect from custody. Questions about charging and release arise, sometimes repeatedly, in a group of preliminary proceedings that differ in title and in detail from jurisdiction to jurisdiction. This chapter explores the decision whether to release or detain a suspect, and Chapter 13 considers the related decision of what charges to file.

For many suspects, the release decision is resolved at the police station, without any appearance before a judicial officer. Most jurisdictions allow "station-house bail" for minor crimes: An administrative official within the law enforcement agency (or perhaps an administrative employee of the courts) releases the suspect by following routine requirements. For instance, the suspect might make a written promise to appear at later proceedings or might pay a modest amount of money "bail" that would be forfeited upon a failure to appear.

Release decisions may also occur a few hours later, when the suspect appears before a judge or magistrate. This "initial appearance" before a judicial officer combines several functions: (1) a determination of whether the government had probable cause to support an arrest of the suspect, (2) an inquiry into whether it will be necessary to assign defense counsel to the case, and (3) the decision whether to release the suspect. The release decision might be the first determination of a bail amount (or other conditions of release), or it might involve an adjustment of a bail amount set earlier.

Finally, the release decision can occur at a later proceeding, when a judge reconsiders the bail amount or other conditions of release. The later proceeding might be a "preliminary hearing," when a judge also determines whether there is enough evidence to hold the defendant for trial; the later proceeding might also be a "bail hearing," devoted exclusively to the question of release or detention. Defense counsel could be involved at the earliest judicial determination of bail amounts, but usually counsel has little opportunity to become familiar with the defendant's circumstances and to make an effective argument at that point. Only when the court revisits the release decision (often several days after the arrest) can defense counsel develop and present relevant facts.

The release decision has changed dramatically over the past few generations, and it is still in flux. Section A below highlights the reform movement, begun more than 40 years ago and still a vibrant part of federal and state law, to make it easier for defendants to gain release from custody before trial. The section also describes the factors that influence the release decision and the institutions most responsible for making that choice. Section B then traces a more recent movement — in part a reaction to the first reform — to expand the state's power to detain some defendants until the time of trial in an effort to protect the public from further crimes the defendant might commit.

A. PRETRIAL RELEASE

1. *Method of Release*

Bail procedures have been the subject of extensive social science research. The researchers' interest in bail stems from the pervasiveness of bail determinations, the relative ease of quantifying bail determinations, and the moral problems raised by detaining those who have not yet been tried (and are, therefore, presumptively innocent) and releasing those who threaten additional harm. A classic illustration of the use of social science as an engine of reform is the Manhattan Bail Project conducted by the Vera Institute of Justice. In reading the following account of the bail experiment, consider the project's origin, implementation (including the essential role played by law students), and effects.

■ FAIR TREATMENT FOR THE INDIGENT: THE MANHATTAN BAIL PROJECT VERA INSTITUTE OF JUSTICE

Ten-Year Report 1961-1971 (May 1972)

There are many penalties imposed upon an accused person who is detained in jail because he is too poor to post bail. [T]he detainee is more apt to be convicted than if he were free on bail; and, if convicted, he is more apt to receive a tougher sentence. [Detainees] lose income while they are away from their jobs, and suffer dislocation and sometimes even permanent rupture in their family lives. They frequently suffer social stigmatization and loss of self respect because of their confinement — even though they have not been convicted of anything and must be presumed innocent, and may eventually be acquitted. . . .

In a large city like New York, these people can also expect to be detained in jails where conditions are comparable to maximum security prisons. . . . Meanwhile, detained persons' defense preparations suffer as it is difficult or impossible for them to consult with attorneys, communicate with family or friends, locate witnesses, or gather evidence.

The Origins and Evolution of Bail

The concept of bail has a long history and deep roots in English and American law. In medieval England, the custom grew out of the need to free untried prisoners from disease-ridden jails while they were waiting for the delayed trials conducted by traveling justices. Prisoners were bailed, or delivered, to reputable third parties of their own choosing who accepted responsibility for assuring their appearance at trial. If the accused did not appear, the bailor would stand in his place.

Eventually it became the practice for property owners who accepted responsibility for accused persons to forfeit money when their charges failed to appear for trial. From this grew the modern practice of posting a money bond through a commercial bondsman who receives a cash premium for his service, and usually demands some collateral as well. In the event of non-appearance the bond is forfeited, after a grace period of a number of days during which the bondsman may produce the accused in court.

The Constitution of the United States did not specifically grant the right to bail, although the Eighth Amendment stipulated that "excessive bail shall not be required." The Judiciary Act of 1789 and subsequent statutes in all but seven of the states did require admission to bail, however, in all non-capital cases. . . .

The emergence of the bondsman as a commercial adjunct to the processes of American criminal justice brought with it certain advantages — he was added to the agencies seeking to enforce court appearance, for example — but it also brought serious drawbacks. Abuses tended to creep into the system, such as collusive ties some bondsmen developed with police, lawyers, court officials and also with organized crime. But more important, the central determinant in whether an accused person would go free on bail pending trial became the decision of a businessman who was interested not in the evenhanded application of justice, but in profit . . . .

Real reform was indeed possible. . . . This was the idea of encouraging judges to release far more accused persons on their honor pending trial, and providing the judges with verified information about the accused on which such releases could be based. It was an obvious, but . . . daring idea: find out who can be trusted, and trust them to appear for trial.

What was needed was a carefully designed project that would . . . develop information about defendants which would enable the courts to grant release to good risks. . . . A project based on these concepts quickly took form:

1. Indigent defendants awaiting arraignment in Manhattan's criminal courts would be questioned by Vera staff interviewers to determine how deep their community roots were and thus whether they could be relied upon to return to court for trial if they were released without bail.
2. The test of indigency would be representation by a Legal Aid lawyer.
3. Questioners would develop information about the defendant's length of residence in the city, his family ties, and his employment situation.
4. Responses of the defendant would be verified immediately in personal or telephone interviews with family, friends, and employers.

5. When verified information indicated that an individual was trustworthy and could be depended on to return for trial, the Vera staff member would appear at arraignment and recommend to the judge that the accused be released on his own recognizance (R.O.R. or pretrial parole) pending trial.

A Demonstration Project Is Set Up

It was anticipated that such a simple but radical change in generally accepted procedures would meet opposition from those accustomed to the old ways or fearful of the new, and so the entire project was devised as a demonstration — an experiment to see whether people would return for trial if released without bail and, in general, how their cases compared with the cases of those not granted release as well as those released on bail. . . .

The experiment was scheduled to begin in the fall of 1961 in the arraignment part of the Manhattan Magistrate's Felony Court. [S]tudents from the School of Law at New York University were recruited as Vera staff interviewers and received a period of training during which they learned how the arraignment court functioned. The Law School agreed to give the students credit for their Vera work in conjunction with a University seminar on legal problems of the indigent. The entire experience was thought to be an important introduction to the criminal justice process for the aspiring young lawyer. . . .

On October 16, 1961 after months of detailed planning, the Manhattan Bail Project began operations. Specifics attending the launching were carefully arranged:

1. No publicity was given the inauguration of the venture, on grounds that it would be most effective as a demonstration to the community if the results could later speak for themselves. . . .
2. The answers sought through the project were limited and precise: (a) Would judges release more defendants on their own recognizance if they were given verified information about the defendants than they would without such information? (b) Would released defendants return for trial at the same rate as those released on bail? (c) How would the cases of released defendants compare with a control group not recommended for release, both in convictions and in sentencing? . . .
4. All magistrates who would be sitting in court during the project were visited personally by Vera staff members prior to its initiation so that they would understand fully what was happening and why.
5. Since a primary function of the project was to demonstrate to the public and to those within the criminal justice system that pretrial parole was a device that could serve the public's interest as well as the defendant's, some offenders were excluded at the outset from the experiment. These were homicide, forcible rape, sodomy involving a minor, corrupting the morals of a child, and carnal abuse — crimes that were all thought to be too sensitive and controversial to be associated with a release program; narcotics offenses, because of special medical problems and . . . a greater risk of flight; and assault on a police officer, where intervention by Vera might, it was feared, arouse police hostility.

6. Comprehensive follow-up procedures were devised to be sure that released defendants knew when they were expected in court for further appearances in connection with their trials. These procedures included mailed reminders, telephone calls, visits at home or work, and special notifications in the defendant's language, if he did not speak English.

[The] law students began their interviews in the detention pens in the arraignment court. At first, they were asked to make subjective evaluations of the defendant's eligibility for pretrial parole after they had verified their community ties. It was discovered, however, that pressures were developing that caused some interviewers to withhold recommendations for release in cases where it was probably justified. To relieve the individual of these pressures and of the personal responsibility that, in part, created them, a weighted system of points was developed and the sole determinant as to whether or not a defendant would be recommended for release without bail was his achieving a point score of five or above. This development of a set of objective criteria on which to base release recommendations proved to be an important innovation. . . .

POINT SCORING SYSTEM
MANHATTAN BAIL PROJECT

To be recommended, defendant needs [a] New York area address where he can be reached and [a] total of five points from the following categories—

Prior Record

1 No convictions.
0 One misdemeanor conviction.
−1 Two misdemeanor or one felony conviction.
−2 Three or more misdemeanors or two or more felony convictions.

Family Ties (in New York area)

3 Lives in established family home AND visits other family members (immediate family only).
2 Lives in established family home (immediate family).
1 Visits others of immediate family.

Employment or School

3 Present job one year or more, steadily.
2 Present job 4 months. . . .
1 Has present job which is still available,
or Unemployed 3 months or less and 9 months or more steady prior job,
or Unemployment Compensation,
or Welfare.
3 Presently in school, attending regularly.
2 Out of school less than 6 months but employed or in training.
1 Out of school 3 months or less, unemployed and not in training.

Residence (in New York area steadily)

3 One year at present residence.
2 One year at present [and] last prior residence or 6 months at present residence.
1 Six months at present and last prior residence
or in New York City 5 years or more.

Discretion

+1 Positive, over 65, attending hospital, appeared on some previous case.
0 Negative — intoxicated — intention to leave jurisdiction.

Comparing the Experimental and the Control Groups

. . . Vera was especially anxious to compare the experiences of those who had been recommended for release with the experiences of the control group, a statistically identical group for which recommendations had not been made to the judges. It found that 59 percent of its pretrial parole recommendations were followed by the court and that only 16 percent of the control group was released without bail by the judges acting on their own. Judges were clearly basing their actions on the availability of reliable information about the defendants. More significantly, *60 percent of those released pending trial during the first year eventually were acquitted or had their case dismissed, compared with only 23 percent of the control group. And only 16 percent of the released defendants who were convicted were sentenced to prison, where 96 percent of those convicted in the control group received prison sentences.* Unquestionably, detention was resulting in a higher rate of convictions and in far more punitive dispositions. At the end of the second year, the control group was dropped. . . .

Modifications in Project Procedures

Further innovations came in the third year of the project. An important one was that the number of offenses that had been excluded for political reasons was sharply reduced to include only homicide and certain narcotics offenses. Also, the indigency requirement was dropped. It was felt that bail costs should not be imposed on a defendant merely because he had funds; the test for those with money, as well as for those without, should be the same: will the accused return to court for trial? . . .

Meanwhile, in 1963, two developments suggested that a large potential existed for applying new concepts of bail reform outside of New York City. One of these was the strong interest expressed by the United States Department of Justice in helping to sponsor a national conference on bail. The other was the speed with which civic leaders in Des Moines, Iowa, learned from the news media of the Vera experiment, decided to investigate the possibility of a bail project in Des Moines, then designed and adopted such a project.

[T]he Bail Reform Act of 1966 [was] signed into law by President Lyndon B. Johnson on June 22, 1966 — the first change in federal bail law since the Judiciary Act of 1789. [The] Act seemed a fitting climax to the effort begun just five years earlier. The Act stipulated that persons should not be detained needlessly in the federal courts to face trial, to testify, or to await an appeal; that release should be granted in non-capital cases where there is reasonable assurance the individual will reappear when required; that the courts should make use of a variety of release options, depending on the circumstances (for example, release in custody of a third party, or with cash deposit, or bail, or with restricted movements); and that information should be developed about the individual on which intelligent selection of alternatives could be based. The Act guaranteed the right to judicial review of release conditions, and also the right to appeal.

[I]n the fall of 1964, the New York City Office of Probation took over the administration of the Vera project. . . . During the three years [of the Bail Project] 3,505 defendants had been released on their own recognizance following the recommendations of Vera staff members, out of a total of some 10,000 defendants who had been interviewed. *Only 56 of these parolees, or 1.6 percent of the total, willfully failed to appear in court for trial. During the same period, three percent of those released on bail failed to appear, or nearly twice as many as had been released without bail.* The figures strongly suggested that bail was not as effective a guarantee of court appearance as was release on verified information.

Over the thirty-five months, a little less than half— 48 percent— of those released through the Vera project were acquitted or had their cases dismissed, while the remaining 52 percent were found guilty. Of those found guilty, 70 percent received suspended sentences, 10 percent were given jail terms, and 20 percent were given the alternative of a fine or jail sentence.

During the Vera operation, staff recommendations became increasingly liberal as experience established that more and more persons could be released safely on their assurances that they would return for trial. Also judicial acceptance of the recommendations rose sharply. At the outset, Vera urged release for 28 percent of the defendants interviewed, while two and a half years later the figure was 65 percent. Judges were following Vera's advice 55 percent of the time in 1961, and 70 percent of the time in 1964. . . .

■ ALABAMA RULES OF CRIMINAL PROCEDURE 7.2, 7.3

Rule 7.2

(a) Any defendant charged with an offense bailable as a matter of right may be released pending or during trial on his or her personal recognizance or on an appearance bond unless the court or magistrate determines that such a release will not reasonably assure the defendant's appearance as required, or that the defendant's being at large will pose a real and present danger to others or to the public at large. If such a determination is made, the court may impose the least onerous condition or conditions contained in Rule 7.3(b) that will reasonably assure the defendant's appearance or that will eliminate or minimize the risk of harm to others or to the public at large. In making such a determination, the court may take into account the following:

(1) The age, background and family ties, relationships and circumstances of the defendant.

(2) The defendant's reputation, character, and health.

(3) The defendant's prior criminal record, including prior releases on recognizance or on secured appearance bonds, and other pending cases.

(4) The identity of responsible members of the community who will vouch for the defendant's reliability.

(5) Violence or lack of violence in the alleged commission of the offense.

(6) The nature of the offense charged, the apparent probability of conviction, and the likely sentence, insofar as these factors are relevant to the risk of nonappearance . . . .

(11) Residence of the defendant, including consideration of real property ownership, and length of residence in his or her place of domicile.

(12) In cases where the defendant is charged with a drug offense, evidence of selling or pusher activity should indicate a substantial increase in the amount of bond.

(13) Consideration of the defendant's employment status and history, the location of defendant's employment, e.g., whether employed in the county where the alleged offense occurred, and the defendant's financial condition. . . .

Rule 7.3

(a) Every order of release under this rule shall contain the conditions that the defendant:

(1) Appear to answer and to submit to the orders and process of the court having jurisdiction of the case;

(2) Refrain from committing any criminal offense;

(3) Not depart from the state without leave of court; and

(4) Promptly notify the court of any change of address.

(b) An order of release may include any one or more of the following conditions reasonably necessary to secure a defendant's appearance:

(1) Execution of an appearance bond in an amount specified by the court, either with or without requiring that the defendant deposit with the clerk security in an amount as required by the court;

(2) Execution of a secured appearance bond;

(3) Placing the defendant in the custody of a designated person or organization agreeing to supervise the defendant;

(4) Restrictions on the defendant's travel, associations, or place of abode during the period of release;

(5) Return to custody after specified hours; or

(6) Any other conditions which the court deems reasonably necessary.

■ PRETRIAL RELEASE OF FELONY DEFENDANTS, 1992 BRIAN REAVES AND JACOB PEREZ

Bureau of Justice Statistics, NCJ-148818 (November 1994)

An estimated 63 percent of the defendants who had State felony charges filed against them in the Nation's 75 most populous counties during May 1992 were released by the court prior to the disposition of their case. . . .

Nonfinancial Release. Among the 63 percent of felony defendants in the 75 largest counties who were released prior to case disposition, about 3 in 5 were released on nonfinancial terms that required no posting of bail. . . . Release on recognizance [ROR], granted to 24 percent of all defendants and to 38 percent of all released defendants, was the most common type of pretrial release. . . . Approximately 13 percent of all pretrial releases in the 75 largest counties (23 percent of nonfinancial releases) were on conditional release. About a fourth of conditional releases included an unsecured bail amount to be forfeited should the defendant fail to appear in court as scheduled. About two-thirds of conditional releases included an agreement by the defendant to maintain regular contact with a pretrial program through telephone calls and/or personal visits. Fifteen percent of conditional releases involved regular drug monitoring or treatment, and 6 percent included a third party custody agreement. . . .

Financial Release. Overall, about 2 in 5 defendants released before case disposition received that release through financial terms involving a surety, full cash, deposit, or property bond. Deposit, full cash, and property bonds are posted directly with the court, while surety bonds involve the services of a bail bond company. [To be released on full cash or property bond, defendants] must post the full bail amount in cash or collateral. . . . The cash or property is forfeited if the defendants do not appear in court as required. Typically, a defendant must provide 10 percent of the full bail amount to be released on deposit or surety bond. Either the defendant (deposit bond) or the bail bond company (surety bond) are liable to the court for the full bail amount if the defendant does not appear in court as required. Release on surety bond, the second most common type of pretrial release for felony defendants, was used in 54 percent of all financial releases and in 21 percent of all pretrial releases. . . .

Factors Affecting Probability of Release

Overall, 37 percent of the felony defendants included in the [sample] were detained until the court disposed of their case, roughly the same percentage as in [earlier] studies for 1988 (34 percent) and 1990 (35 percent). Five out of six detainees from the 1992 study had a bail amount set but did not post the money required to secure release. The remainder, representing 17 percent of detained defendants and 6 percent of all defendants, were ordered held without bail.

While denial of bail provides the court with an absolute assurance that a defendant will not be released prior to case disposition, the [data] also show that when a defendant is required to post bail, the probability of release decreases as bail amounts increase. When bail was set at $20,000 or more, 18 percent of the defendants were eventually released. When the bail amount was between $10,000 and $19,999, 38 percent of the defendants secured release; from $2,500 to $9,999, 52 percent of the defendants; and under $2,500, 66 percent. The effect of bail amount on the likelihood of a defendant's being released varied according to the type of arrest charge. For example, when the bail amount was set at $20,000 or more, drug defendants (29 percent) secured release more often than defendants charged with a public-order offense (18 percent), violent offense (17 percent), or property offense (11 percent). . . .

Seriousness of Offense. The [data] indicate that defendants charged with murder were the least likely of all felony defendants to be released prior to case disposition (24 percent). While about a fourth of murder defendants were released, about half of defendants charged with rape, robbery, or burglary were released, as were about two-thirds of assault, theft, or drug trafficking defendants. Murder defendants had the lowest release rate, mainly because they were the most likely to be denied bail or to have a high bail amount. Forty percent of murder defendants were denied bail, compared to 9 percent or less for other defendants. . . .

Criminal Justice Status. The [data] indicate that a defendant's criminal justice status at the time of arrest is also related to the probability of pretrial release. Among felony defendants without an active criminal justice status at the time of arrest, 72 percent were released before case disposition. In contrast, just 32 percent of defendants on parole and 44 percent of defendants on probation at the time of the current arrest were released. Among defendants who were already on pretrial release for a pending case when arrested, 56 percent were released pending disposition of the current charge. . . .

Court Appearance History. The court is also likely to consider a defendant's court appearance history when setting bail and the terms of release for the current felony charge. . . . Among defendants who made all scheduled court appearances related to prior arrests, 57 percent were released prior to disposition of the current case. The probability of release was somewhat lower for defendants who had failed to appear in court previously (51 percent). . . .

Prior Conviction Record. Defendants with more than one prior conviction or with a felony conviction record were less likely than other defendants to await disposition of their case outside jail. Just under half were released prior to case disposition. About 3 in 5 defendants with a single prior conviction or only misdemeanor convictions were able to obtain release, while 4 in 5 defendants with no prior convictions were released. About 10 percent of defendants who had a prior felony conviction were denied bail, compared to 3 percent of other defendants.

Time from Arrest to Pretrial Release

Fifty-two percent of all pretrial releases occurred either on the day of arrest or on the following day, [77 percent occurred within 1 week,] and 91 percent occurred within 1 month of arrest. The time from arrest to release varied by factors that included the type of release conditions imposed, the bail amount set (if any), and the type of arrest charge. . . .

Misconduct by Defendants Placed on Pretrial Release

Failure To Appear In Court. A primary goal of any pretrial release decision by the court is to ensure the defendant's appearance in court as scheduled. Among those felony defendants who were released prior to case disposition, 3 out of 4 made all scheduled court appearances. A bench warrant was issued for the arrest of the remaining 25 percent because they had missed one or more court dates. Two-thirds of these defendants had been returned to the court by the end of the 1-year study period [some of them voluntarily], while a third of them, 8 percent of all released defendants, remained fugitives. . . .

Rearrest for a New Offense. In addition to considering the likelihood that a released defendant may not return for scheduled court appearances, courts in most States also assess the risk of crimes being committed by a defendant who is not held in jail. Rearrest data collected during the 1-year study indicated that 14 percent of released defendants were rearrested for an offense allegedly committed while on pretrial release. . . . Released defendants with 10 or more prior convictions had a rearrest rate of 38 percent, 4 times that of defendants who had no prior convictions (9 percent). . . . For rearrested defendants, the median time from pretrial release to the alleged commission of a new offense was 48 days. . . .

Notes

1. *Statutory fruits of 1960s bail reform: majority view.* The thrust of efforts to change the bail system in the 1950s and 1960s was to increase the use of nonfinancial techniques such as release on recognizance (ROR) and to standardize the criteria used

for release decisions as a way of preventing the wealth of defendants from dominating the release decision. See Daniel Freed and Patricia Wald, Bail in the United States (1964). The efforts bore fruit in the 1966 Federal Bail Reform Act, 18 U.S.C. §3146(b). Unlike the federal statute at work until that time, which gave essentially no guidance to the judge on release and bail decisions, the 1966 statute required courts to consider standard criteria in reaching their decisions. The statutory factors included "(1) the nature of the offense charged; (2) the weight of the evidence against the accused; (3) the accused's family ties; (4) employment; (5) financial resources; (6) character; (7) mental health; (8) the length of residence in the community; (9) a record of convictions; and (10) a record of failure to appear at court appearances or of flight to avoid prosecution." The ABA Standards on Criminal Justice, Pretrial Release (1968), also embodied many of the aspirations of critics of the money bail system. Both the 1966 Bail Reform Act and the ABA standards influenced state legislatures to revise their criteria for making release decisions, and most states have a similar (though not identical) list of factors. See, e.g., Cal. Penal Code §1275. Around 10 jurisdictions have statutes without lists of factors and leave the determination to the discretion of the judge or magistrate. See, e.g., Mass. Gen. L. ch. 276, §57. A similar number of states include only a very short list of factors. See, e.g., Fla. Stat. §903.03. State rules based on the ABA standards or the 1966 federal statute explicitly make ROR the presumptive outcome for defendants.

This era of federal and state legislation, together with changes in local practices, resulted in higher numbers of defendants being released before trial or guilty plea. While it was common earlier in the century for a state to release fewer than one-third of all defendants, it is now more common to release close to two-thirds of defendants. In large urban areas in 1998, 64 percent of felony defendants were released before trial. Just under half of all released defendants faced no financial conditions such as bail. See Bureau of Justice Statistics, Felony Defendants in Large Urban Counties, 1998, at 16-19 (2001, NCJ 187232). Would this change in practice have occurred without changes in the federal and state statutes?

2. *Rates of failure to appear.* The average rate of failure to appear based on nationwide data in 1992 was about 25 percent, with jurisdictions varying between 2 percent and 56 percent. See John Clark and D. Alan Henry, The Pretrial Release Decision, 81 Judicature 76, 77 (Sept.-Oct. 1997). These statistics, however, include "technical defaults" where defendants miss the initial court date but come voluntarily at a later time for rescheduled hearings or trials. See Wayne Thomas, Bail Reform in America (1976). The FTA rate typically improves when a jurisdiction establishes a system of notification and supervision of those who are released before trial. Who should notify the defendant of the upcoming proceeding, and what form should the notice take?

3. *Bond dealers and bounty hunters.* In jurisdictions requiring payment of the full amount of money bail prior to release, many defendants rely on the services of bail bond dealers. Indeed, surety bonds remain the most common form of financial release. The bond dealer makes the required payment to the court in the form of a bond obligating the dealer to pay the amount of the bail if the defendant does not appear for court proceedings. The dealer charges the defendant a nonrefundable fee, often around 10 percent of the total bond amount, although it varies with the dealer's assessment of the risk that a particular defendant will flee. See State v. Brooks, 604 N.W.2d 345 (Minn. 2000) (state constitution requires availability of bond rather than "cash bail" requiring defendant to deposit entire bail amount in cash).

About half of the states grant express authority to the dealer and their agents—often called "bounty hunters"—to arrest a defendant who tries to flee. See Ala. Code §15-13-117. Nineteenth-century authority confirms the substantial powers of bond dealers and bounty hunters, which in some respects exceeds that of government agents trying to recapture a fugitive. Reese v. United States, 76 U.S. 13 (1869); Taylor v. Taintor, 83 U.S. 366 (1872). This authority creates a potential for rough practices—and for adventures that have occasionally become the subject of front-page stories and the plot lines for movies, classic and otherwise.

4. *Abolition of surety bonds.* Critics of the surety bond system argue that it fosters violence and leaves defendants with no financial incentive to appear in court after their release. Jurisdictions have taken a number of steps to reduce the importance of bond dealers. A handful of states have directly outlawed the offering of surety bonds. Stephens v. Bonding Association of Kentucky, 538 S.W.2d 580 (Ky. 1976); Wis. Stat. §969.12. Around 20 states have made the surety bond less attractive to defendants by using "deposit" bonds, allowing defendants themselves to deposit a portion of their bail—usually 10 percent—comparable to the rates charged by sureties. See, e.g., Cal. Penal Code §1295; Ohio R. Crim. P. 46; Or. Rev. Stat. §135.265. Because the cash deposit to the state is refundable and the fee to the bond dealer is not, defendants have little reason to call on the dealer. The state can also profit from the use of cash bail because courts often do not collect bonds from sureties when the defendant fails to appear. Given all these advantages of cash bail, why does the surety bond system remain the most common form of financial release? See also Commonwealth v. Ray, 755 N.E.2d 1259 (Mass. 2001) (under bail statute, judge may properly set alternative bails for pretrial release: surety company bond, or ten percent of that amount in cash, equivalent to maximum nonrefundable premium required to purchase surety bond).

Consider this alternative to bond dealers. Jails can now install an interactive kiosk allowing detainees to use a credit card to make bail. For relatively minor crimes with bails under $5,000, the necessary amount falls with the limit that many people carry on their credit cards. If the defendants do appear for their hearings, the county refunds the bail amount to the defendant's credit card account; the fees for the transaction are far lower than the 10 percent typically charged by bond dealers. Julie N. Lynem, Bonds Agents Fight New Jail Bail Machine; Device Could Help Clear Out Packed Cells in Santa Clara, San Francisco Chronicle, Dec. 2, 1998 at A13.

5. *Nonfinancial release conditions.* A defendant's pretrial release might be conditioned not on payment of bail but on performance of certain nonfinancial conditions. The most common nonfinancial release condition is a requirement that the defendant maintain regular contact with a pretrial program. It is also common for the judge to insist that the defendant avoid any contact with the victim of the alleged crime. An increasingly common condition of release is regular drug monitoring or treatment. See Kan. Stat. §22-2802 (drug testing limited to those charged with felonies); La. Code Crim. Proc. art. 336. Testing positive for some drugs (particularly cocaine) is a predictor, according to some studies, of a higher rate of nonappearance and arrests for crimes committed after release. Peggy Tobolowsky and James Quinn, Drug-Related Behavior as a Predictor of Defendant Pretrial Misconduct, 25 Tex. Tech L. Rev. 1019 (1994). If positive drug tests are not predictive of a failure to appear, should the tests still be administered? What is the rationale for requiring drug treatment? Another increasingly common nonfinancial condition of release is the use of electronic monitoring. An electronic device attached to the defendant's

person (often a wrist or an ankle bracelet) allows the government to monitor his proximity to home or to some other location. Should electronic monitoring be used primarily for those who receive ROR or for those who would otherwise remain in jail?

6. *Racial and gender bias in release and bail decisions.* Evidence periodically surfaces to suggest that black and Hispanic defendants receive less favorable bail and release decisions than white defendants. One study of bail practices in Connecticut by Professors Ian Ayres and Joel Waldfogel revealed that bond dealers charged lower bond rates to black and Hispanic defendants than to white defendants, suggesting that judges set the bail amounts for black and Hispanic defendants higher than the real risk of flight. The "competitive market"— in the form of the bond dealers — thus was able to discount the rate for minority defendants and still make a profit. Ian Ayres and Joel Waldfogel, A Market Test for Race Discrimination in Bail Setting, 46 Stan. L. Rev. 987 (1994). Studies have also consistently indicated that female defendants are more likely than male defendants to obtain pretrial release and to receive nonfinancial conditions of release. Why might a judge make more "lenient" release decisions for female defendants? See Ellen Steury and Nancy Frank, Gender Bias and Pretrial Release: More Pieces of the Puzzle, 18 J. Crim. Justice 417 (1990) (finding most of differential treatment for women explained by seriousness of offense and prior record).

7. *Effects of pretrial release on acquittal rates.* Bail researchers have long believed that a defendant's odds of acquittal at trial go down if the defendant fails to obtain pretrial release. They reason that a defendant who remains in jail is less able to locate witnesses and otherwise prepare a defense. Caleb Foote's study of bail practices in Philadelphia in the 1950s observed that 67 percent of the defendants charged with violent crimes were acquitted if they were released before trial, while only 25 percent of jailed defendants were acquitted. Caleb Foote, Compelling Appearance in Court: Administration of Bail in Philadelphia, 102 U. Pa. L. Rev. 1031 (1954). A number of later studies found a causal relationship (and not just a statistical association) between pretrial release and acquittal rates. However, the trend (not uniform) among more recent studies is to conclude that pretrial release is correlated with — but does not necessarily cause — high acquittal rates. For instance, the seriousness of a charge is a factor both in making release less likely and in making conviction more likely because (among other reasons) prosecution witnesses are more likely to show up. See Gerald Wheeler and Carol Wheeler, Bail Reform in the 1980s: A Response to the Critics, 18 Crim. L. Bull. 228 (1982).

8. *Effects of pretrial release on sentences.* There is stronger evidence of a causal linkage between the pretrial release decision and the choice of punishment after a conviction. The best evidence indicates that defendants not released before their conviction are more likely to receive prison sentences than those who are released. For instance, one analysis of the New York City data produced in the Vera Institute study found that 64 percent of persons detained received prison sentences, compared to only 17 percent of those released before disposition of the charges. See Anne Rankin, The Effect of Pretrial Detention, 39 N.Y.U. L. Rev. 641 (1964). See also Stevens Clark, Jean Freeman, and Gary Koch, Bail Risk: A Multivariate Analysis, 5 J. Legal Stud. 341 (1976) (study of Charlotte, North Carolina).

9. *Length of time before release.* About half of all defendants released are able to leave the jail within one day. Eighty percent of defendants who are released leave custody within one week; 94 percent leave within one month. Bureau of Justice

Statistics, Felony Defendants in Large Urban Counties, 1998, at 19 (2001, NCJ 187232) (54 percent of all defendants). What is likely to change between Day 2 and Day 31 of confinement that convinces so many judges to release more defendants?

2. *Who Sets Bail?*

We have seen examples of jurisdictions willing to reduce traditional bail amounts or to set nonfinancial conditions of release, and we have considered the multiple criteria that determine which conditions will be imposed. Which institution or decisionmaker is best positioned to choose among the expanded options for release in an individual case? To what degree should bail and release decisions be structured?

The earliest available point of release, "station-house bail," often occurs when officers use a "bail schedule," a listing of the presumptive amount of bail to require from various types of offenders. Most often, the presumptive bail is linked to the criminal charge a defendant is facing. For example, a recent Los Angeles County bail schedule made $60,000 the presumptive bail amount for voluntary manslaughter; for kidnapping for ransom, $500,000; and for bookmaking, $2,500. Along with the list of factors and rules reprinted above, Alabama provides a recommended set of bail ranges "as a general guide . . . in setting bail" and states that "courts should exercise discretion in setting bail above or below the scheduled amounts." Ala. R. Crim. P. 7.2. The recommended ranges in Alabama are as follows:

FELONIES

Capital felony	$10,000 to No Bail Allowed,
Murder	$5,000 to $50,000,
Class A felony	$3,000 to $30,000,
Class B felony	$2,000 to $20,000,
Class C felony	$1,000 to $10,000,
Drug trafficking	$3,000 to $1,000,000,

MISDEMEANORS (NOT INCLUDED ELSEWHERE IN THE SCHEDULE)

Class A misdemeanor	$300 to $3,000,
Class B misdemeanor	$100 to $1,000,
Class C misdemeanor	$50 to $500,
Violation	$50 to $500,

MUNICIPAL ORDINANCE VIOLATIONS $100 to $1,000,

TRAFFIC-RELATED OFFENSES

DUI	$300 to $5,000,
Reckless driving	$100 to $300,
Speeding	$50 to $100,
Other traffic violations	$50 to $100,

The following case considers a trial court's efforts to reform bail practices by eliminating access to administrative bail for domestic violence offenders.

■ DONALD WESTERMAN v. CHRISTINE CARY

885 P.2d 827 (Wash. 1994)

MADSEN, J.

This case revolves around the Spokane County District Court's issuance of a general order providing that domestic violence offenders be detained in custody pending their first appearance in court. Under the previous bail schedule provision, such offenders would be eligible for release on bail preset by the court. . . .

On October 14, 1992, Spokane County's then-presiding District Court Judge, Christine Cary, issued a general order entitled "Domestic Violence Offense—Mandatory Court Appearance—No Bail." The Order provides: "Any person arrested for a crime classified under Section 10.99 of the Revised Code of Washington as Domestic Violence shall be held in jail without bail pending their first appearance. [This order] shall apply to all offenses listed under Section 10.99 . . . irrespective of their classification as a Felony, Gross Misdemeanor, or Misdemeanor." By requiring that bail be set at the first appearance, the District Court sought to amend the County's bail schedule and pretrial release procedures to conform with the Washington State Supreme Court's amendment of CrRLJ 3.2.* Under the previous procedure, jail personnel were allowed to determine bail according to a preset bail schedule and grant release prior to an individualized judicial determination or a preliminary court appearance. The District Court issued the Order as the first of a number of changes intended to bring the court's procedures into conformance with CrRLJ 3.2. The Order does not specify the length of detention; however, CrRLJ 3.2.1(d)(1) requires that an accused "detained in jail must be brought before a court of limited jurisdiction as soon as practicable after the detention is commenced, but in any event before the close of business on the next court day." An on-call judge was available under the Order to set bail prior to the preliminary appearance in appropriate cases.

On October 15, 1992, Prosecutor Brockett advised Sheriff Larry Erickson to disregard the Order because he believed it would violate arrestees' constitutional right to bail and would expose the County to liability. . . . The District Court then asked Prosecutor Brockett for a brief outlining his concerns with the legality of the Order. Brockett refused, suggesting instead that the District Court write a brief justifying its position to him. [T]he Spokane County public defender's office [supported by *amicus curiae,* the Washington Defender Association (WDA),] filed an emergency application for writ of review and for immediate stay of the Order in superior court. The public defender's office argued that the Order was unconstitutional and was not adopted in accordance with procedures required by the court's own local rules. [*A*]*micus curiae,* the Young Women's Christian Association (YWCA), filed a memorandum of authorities in support of the Order. [During the litigation], the new District Court Presiding Judge, Salvatore Cozza, issued General Bail Order [02-93] containing a new bail schedule . . . providing that misdemeanor domestic violence and harassment probable cause arrestees are to be held in jail pending their first court

* The current version of Rule 3.2(a) of the Criminal rules for Courts of Limited Jurisdiction (CrRLJ) provides: "A court of limited jurisdiction may adopt a bail schedule for persons who have been arrested on probable cause but have not yet made a preliminary appearance before a judicial officer. With the exception of [certain traffic offenses], the adoption of such a schedule or whether to adopt a schedule, is in the discretion of each court of limited jurisdiction . . ."—EDS.

appearance absent a contrary judicial order. [The trial court ruled that the bail order was constitutional.]

Unlike the federal constitution, Washington's constitution has a specific provision creating a right to bail. Article 1, section 20 of the Washington Constitution provides that "all persons charged with crime shall be bailable by sufficient sureties, except for capital offenses when the proof is evident, or the presumption great." The issue presented in this case is the point at which the right to bail attaches. Westerman contends that the right attaches immediately following arrest. WDA argues that the right attaches within a reasonable time following the incidents of arrest. The District Court and the YWCA argue that the right does not attach until a judicial determination can be made. . . .

Westerman argues that the "charged" language is determinative. While the provision uses the language "charged with crime," we find that this language was not intended to trigger the point at which the right attaches. Rather, the phrase "charged with crime" only modifies the word "persons." This is evidenced by the fact that the drafters changed the language of the proposed section 20 which previously had said "all prisoners" to the current language of "all persons charged with crime." The reason for the substituted language was not articulated; however, it is significant that one was merely substituted for the other. Because the phrase "charged with crime" modifies "persons," we conclude that the framers [in 1889] chose this language to describe the status of persons entitled to bail rather than the time of entitlement. Furthermore, the time of charging makes little practical sense as the triggering point for the right given the context in which the question of bail arises. When an arrest is made pursuant to a warrant, charges will have been filed and the judge issuing the warrant will determine probable cause and set bail. However, when an arrest is made without a warrant, charges may or may not be filed prior to a preliminary court appearance which must be held by the next judicial day, or in any event, within 48 hours. CrRLJ 3.2.1; see also County of Riverside v. McLaughlin, 500 U.S. 44 (1991). Charges may not be filed for up to 72 hours (not including Saturdays, Sundays, or holidays) after the arrest. CrRLJ 3.2.1(f); CrR 3.2B(c). This may be hours after the accused's preliminary appearance where bail or release could have been determined.

While we reject the time of charging as the triggering point, the language of the provision alone provides no clear answer. We must then look to the context in which the provision arose to determine the drafters' intent. . . . At the time the constitution was adopted, the Code of 1881 provided that bail could be granted only by judges and the amount set on a case-by-case basis. Section 778 of the Code of 1881 is similar to the adopted version of Const. art. 1, §20 and reads:

> Every person charged with an offense except that of murder in the first degree, where the proof is evident or the presumption great, may be bailed by sufficient sureties . . .: Provided, That all persons accused of crime in any court of this Territory, whether by indictment or otherwise, shall be admitted to bail *by the court,* where the same is pending, . . . and the bail bond in such cases shall be reasonable and at the sound discretion of the court.

(Italics ours). . . . Today, bail and release remain judicial functions. Bail schedules have been recently developed by many counties to allow earlier release. However, these bail schedules are developed and maintained by each county's judiciary. In short, the fixing of bail and the release from custody traditionally has been, and we think is, a function of the judicial branch of government, unless otherwise directed and mandated by unequivocal constitutional provisions to the contrary.

This court has encouraged the giving of bail in proper instances because the State is relieved of the burden of keeping the accused and the innocent are set free. However, we have never mandated bail schedules; this is a choice best left to the counties. Moreover, we have established detailed procedures which require judicial determinations of bail or release to be made no later than the preliminary appearance stage. Even where bail or release has been actuated under a bail schedule, our rules provide that the individual case must be reviewed by a judge at this initial appearance. See CrR 3.2; CrRLJ 3.2. The primary purposes of the preliminary appearance are a judicial determination of probable cause and judicial review of the conditions of release. The preliminary appearance must be held "as soon as practicable after the detention is commenced, . . . but in any event before the close of business on the next judicial day." CrR 3.2B; CrRLJ 3.2.1. When combining a probable cause determination, this must be accomplished within 48 hours. County of Riverside v. McLaughlin, 500 U.S. 44 (1991).

Considering the history and case law regarding bail, as well as relevant court rules, we find that detention without bail pending a speedy judicial determination does not violate Const. art. 1, §20. Under the current system where bail must be determined at the preliminary appearance, the right is sufficiently protected. We decline to extend the right to bail beyond what it has traditionally been: the right to a judicial determination of reasonable bail or release. We conclude, however, that such a determination must be made as soon as possible, no later than the probable cause determination, and, as with probable cause, may be determined by a judge prior to the preliminary hearing. Our decision today is not intended to foreclose the use of bail schedules, but rather to leave the choice to counties, balancing the flexibility that the county courts need with the interests of those detained.

Our result is further supported by the results of other states who have upheld similar . . . provisions against challenge. [The court cited decisions from Rhode Island, California, Oklahoma, and Alaska]. We thus find the Order constitutional under Const. art. 1, §20 to the extent it conforms with this opinion. . . .

Westerman argues that the Order violates state and federal substantive due process. [An] individual's liberty interest is important and fundamental. A government action affecting this fundamental right is constitutional only if it furthers compelling state interests and is narrowly drawn to serve those interests.

The government has compelling interests in preventing crime and ensuring that those accused of crimes are available for trial and to serve their sentences if convicted. The Fourth Amendment permits limited restraint on the liberty of an arrestee. It is well recognized that a police officer may detain an individual without a warrant if the officer has probable cause to believe that the arrestee committed an offense. Gerstein v. Pugh, 420 U.S. 103 (1975). To justify further pretrial detention, a fair and reliable determination of probable cause must be made by a judicial officer promptly following the arrest. The Supreme Court later elaborated on *Gerstein* by requiring that the determination of probable cause must be made within 48 hours and cannot be delayed unreasonably. County of Riverside v. McLaughlin, 500 U.S. 44 (1991). [R]estrictions on liberty that comply with the Fourth Amendment and which do not constitute impermissible punishment do not violate substantive due process.

Given the limited nature of the detention and the legitimate reasons behind the Order, we do not find that the Order violates substantive due process. Under our ruling today, the Order imposes no more significant restraint on liberty than that allowed by the Fourth Amendment under *Gerstein* and *County of Riverside* because the probable cause and release hearing must be held within 48 hours of detention. After the preliminary appearance, release must be given to those arrestees. Furthermore, the District Court did not promulgate the Order for the purposes of punishing domestic violence arrestees. The District Court only sought to insure individualized judicial determinations of bail and conditions of release in domestic violence cases. . . .

Notes

1. *Rules and discretion in bail: majority view.* Most systems leave substantial discretion in the hands of judges in setting bail amounts. Many jurisdictions rely on bail schedules set at local levels, such as the Spokane bail schedule proposed in *Westerman* under general state rulemaking authority. See, e.g., Mont. Code §46-9-302 ("A judge may establish and post a schedule of bail for offenses over which the judge has original jurisdiction"). Tennessee allows magistrates substantial discretion but imposes statewide caps on bail amounts based on the nature of the offense. See Tenn. Code §40-11-105. A few states such as Alabama (printed above), Kentucky, and Utah have more specific statewide bail schedules.

The *Westerman* decision is not alone in revealing clashes between different actors over proper bail policies for domestic assault arrests. In Pelekai v. White, 861 P.2d 1205 (Haw. 1993), the senior judge of the Honolulu Family Court issued an order raising bail in domestic assault cases from the prior police department practice of $50 to between $500 and $900 depending on the prior record and threat posed by the accused. The Hawaii Supreme Court struck down the guidelines, holding that they eliminated the discretionary power given to judges or to the police department by Haw. Rev. Stat. §804-9, which provided that the "amount of bail rests in the discretion of the justice or judge or the officers [setting bail]; but should be so determined as not to suffer the wealthy to escape by the payment of a pecuniary penalty, nor to render the privilege useless to the poor." Nor is domestic assault the only crime for which judges have tried to alter bail practices. See City of Fargo v. Stutlien, 505 N.W.2d 738 (N.D. 1993) (rejecting district court rule providing minimum 12-hour detention for DUI arrestees who refuse blood-alcohol test). Bail decisions have become both more and less regulated with the use of bail schedules, and with the addition, often by statute, of new types of pretrial release terms such as lower bail amounts paid by the defendant directly to the court, supervised release, and electronic monitoring. Are specific bail guidelines useful? Who should develop guidelines?

2. *Appellate court controls on bail.* There are constitutional limits on the amount of bail a trial court can set. According to Stack v. Boyle, 342 U.S. 1 (1951), the "excessive bail" clause of the Eighth Amendment prevents a trial court from setting bail "higher than an amount reasonably calculated to fulfill the purpose" of ensuring the accused's presence at trial. A slight majority of states have an even stronger constitutional provision guaranteeing a right to bail. Do these constitutional provisions suggest that the appellate courts are the institution with the ultimate authority in setting bail? Should appellate courts actively review bail determinations? What impact would bail guidelines have on appellate review of individual cases?

3. *Bail, race, and wealth.* Would evidence of discriminatory bail practices support use of bail schedules? Recall that the 1994 study by Professors Ayres and Waldfogel offered evidence of such discrimination. Would factors in bail schedules need to be tested to make sure they did not incorporate a racial bias? If wealth is a significant predictor of likelihood of appearance, then which principle should govern: using accurate appearance rules or avoiding wealth-based discrimination?

4. *Consultation with victims.* All 50 states have passed statutes offering protections to victims during the criminal justice process, and about 30 have given some of these protections constitutional status. These provisions all require authorities to provide information to victims, such as explaining the possibility of pretrial release, notifying victims after a suspect is arrested, and notifying victims about the time and place of release hearings. See, e.g., Cal.Penal Code §4024.4 (granting power to local governments to contract for victim notification). About half of the states require that victims be notified of a suspect's release, and the terms of release, including the amount of any bail, though many states require the victim to make a written request for such information. See, e.g., Iowa Code §910A.6. Some states limit notice provisions to victims of specified crimes such as stalking, sex offenses, or domestic assault. See, e.g., Ga. Code §16-5-93 (stalking); Ky. Rev. Stat. §431.064 (assault, sexual offenses, and violations of protective orders). A few "victims' rights" provisions indicate that the judge should consider the concerns of the victim of the alleged crime when determining the conditions to place upon the defendant during pretrial release. Tenn. Code Ann. §40-11-150 (domestic assault); Texas Code Crim. Proc. art. 56.02 ("A victim, guardian of a victim, or close relative of a deceased victim is entitled to the following rights within the criminal justice system: . . . (2) the right to have the magistrate take the safety of the victim or his family into consideration as an element in fixing the amount of bail for the accused"). A few states allow the victim to have some input prior to the bail decision. See, e.g., Mo. Const. art. I, §32 ("Crime victims . . . shall have the following rights, as defined by law: . . . (2) Upon request of the victim, the right to be informed of and heard at . . . bail hearings, . . . unless in the determination of the court the interests of justice require otherwise"). Are such provisions likely to change the release decisions that judges make? Are they consistent with the practice of station-house bail?

The implementation and effects of these laws have been uneven. According to a 1995 survey, over 60 percent of crime victims living in states with "strong" legal protections for victims were notified about the dates for bond hearings for the defendants, while about 40 percent of crime victims living in states with weaker legal provisions received this information. About 40 percent of victims in the strong states made a recommendation to the court at the bond hearing; about 25 percent in the weak states did. See Dean Kilpatrick, et al., The Rights of Crime Victims—Does Legal Protection Make a Difference? (Research in Brief) (NCJ 173839, Dec. 1998).

5. *Prosecutors and bail.* Statutes and rules tell judges what they should consider in their bail and pretrial release decisions. What factors actually influence judges the most? Judges are less likely to release a defendant already on parole or probation at the time of the current charges; the same is true for defendants with prior arrests or convictions, and those currently charged with violent offenses. In particular, only 13 percent of murder defendants are released before trial. Bureau of Justice Statistics, Felony Defendants in Large Urban Counties, 1998, at 16, 20 (2001, NCJ 187232).

Some observers of bail practices contend that the recommendation of the prosecutor is the single most influential variable as judges make bail and release decisions. A study of San Diego judges reached this conclusion. When researchers presented the judges with several hypothetical case files and asked them to set bail, the local ties of the defendant was the most important variable. However, when observers watched judges decide actual cases, the recommendation of the prosecutor became the most important variable in setting bail amounts — more important than severity of the crime, prior record, defense attorney recommendation, or local ties. The prosecutors, for their part, were most heavily influenced by the severity of the crime and (to a lesser extent) the defendant's local ties. See Ebbe Ebbeson and Vladimir Konecni, Decision Making and Information Integration in the Courts: The Setting of Bail, 32 J. Personality & Soc. Psychol. 805 (1975). Why did the researchers observe judges in the courtroom in addition to asking them about simulated case files?

B. PRETRIAL DETENTION

Until the 1980s, a substantial majority of state constitutions guaranteed a right to bail except in capital cases. Earlier in our history, the capital case exception applied to a large number of defendants because a wide range of crimes (from murder to burglary) were punishable by death. Once capital punishment became available only for a subset of murders, however, the state constitutional right to bail extended to a much larger group — indeed, to most criminal defendants.

These constitutional provisions never meant that all defendants were released before trial. A judge could, consistent with these constitutional provisions, deny bail altogether or set bail in prohibitively high amounts when necessary to ensure a defendant's appearance at trial or to prevent the defendant from threatening witnesses or otherwise undermining the integrity of the judicial process. These hard-to-identify practices blunted the practical impact of the constitutional provisions and statutes declaring in broad terms the "right to bail."

However, the success of the bail reform movement of the 1960s and 1970s in decreasing the use of money bail and increasing the number of defendants released before trial gave new visibility and urgency to an old question: What are the purposes of pretrial release and detention? Should systems refuse to release a defendant before trial only when necessary to preserve the integrity of the judicial process? Or could a judge deny bail altogether if necessary to serve different purposes, such as protecting the public from further wrongdoing by the defendant before trial?

In 1970, only four years after the 1966 Bail Reform Act, Congress passed a controversial pretrial detention law for the District of Columbia that allowed detention on the basis of the threat of additional criminal acts by the defendant before trial. In 1984 Congress declared, in a new Bail Reform Act, that prevention of future wrongdoing was indeed a proper basis for detaining a defendant in custody before trial. That declaration gave momentum to a movement that has now become the law in over half the states.

■ U.S. CONSTITUTION AMENDMENT VIII

Excessive bail shall not be required, nor excessive fines imposed, nor cruel and unusual punishments inflicted.

■ TENNESSEE CONSTITUTION ART. I, §§15, 16

15. That all prisoners shall be bailable by sufficient sureties, unless for capital offences, when the proof is evident or the presumption great. And the privilege of the writ of habeas corpus shall not be suspended, unless when in case of rebellion or invasion the public safety may require it.

16. That excessive bail shall not be required, nor excessive fines imposed, nor cruel and unusual punishments inflicted.

■ 18 U.S.C. §3142(e), (f)

(e) If, after a hearing pursuant to the provisions of subsection (f) of this section, the judicial officer finds that no condition or combination of conditions will reasonably assure the appearance of the person as required and the safety of any other person and the community, such judicial officer shall order the detention of the person before trial. In a case described in subsection (f)(1) of this section, a rebuttable presumption arises that no condition or combination of conditions will reasonably assure the safety of any other person and the community if such judicial officer finds that—

(1) the person has been convicted of a Federal offense that is described in subsection (f)(1) of this section, or [a similar] State or local offense . . . ;

(2) the offense described in paragraph (1) of this subsection was committed while the person was on release pending trial for a Federal, State, or local offense; and

(3) a period of not more than five years has elapsed since the date of conviction, or the release of the person from imprisonment, for the offense described in paragraph (1) of this subsection, whichever is later.

Subject to rebuttal by the person, it shall be presumed that no condition or combination of conditions will reasonably assure the appearance of the person as required and the safety of the community if the judicial officer finds that there is probable cause to believe that the person committed an offense for which a maximum term of imprisonment of ten years or more is prescribed in the [federal laws proscribing drug trafficking and crimes of violence].

(f) The judicial officer shall hold a hearing to determine whether any condition or combination of conditions . . . will reasonably assure the appearance of the person as required and the safety of any other person and the community—

(1) upon motion of the attorney for the Government, in a case that involves—(A) a crime of violence; (B) an offense for which the maximum sentence is life imprisonment or death; (C) an offense for which a maximum term of imprisonment of ten years or more is prescribed in the [federal drug trafficking laws]; (D) any felony if the person has been convicted of two or more offenses described in subparagraphs (A) through (C) of this paragraph, or two or more [similar] State or local offenses . . . , or a combination of such offenses; or

(2) Upon motion of the attorney for the Government or upon the judicial officer's own motion, in a case that involves—(A) a serious risk that the person will flee; or (B) a serious risk that the person will obstruct or attempt to obstruct justice, or threaten, injure, or intimidate, or attempt to threaten, injure, or intimidate, a prospective witness or juror. . . .

The facts the judicial officer uses to support a finding pursuant to subsection (e) that no condition or combination of conditions will reasonably assure the safety of any other person and the community shall be supported by clear and convincing evidence. . . .

■ UNITED STATES v. ANTHONY SALERNO

481 U.S. 739 (1987)

REHNQUIST, C.J.

The Bail Reform Act of 1984 allows a federal court to detain an arrestee pending trial if the Government demonstrates by clear and convincing evidence after an adversary hearing that no release conditions "will reasonably assure . . . the safety of any other person and the community." . . . We hold that, as against the facial attack mounted by these respondents, the Act fully comports with constitutional requirements. . . .

Responding to "the alarming problem of crimes committed by persons on release," S. Rep. No. 98-225, p.3 (1983), Congress formulated the Bail Reform Act of 1984, 18 U.S.C. §3141 et seq., as the solution to a bail crisis in the federal courts. The Act represents the National Legislature's considered response to numerous perceived deficiencies in the federal bail process. By providing for sweeping changes in both the way federal courts consider bail applications and the circumstances under which bail is granted, Congress hoped to give the courts adequate authority to make release decisions that give appropriate recognition to the danger a person may pose to others if released.

To this end, §3141(a) of the Act requires a judicial officer to determine whether an arrestee shall be detained. Section 3142(e) provides that "if, after a hearing pursuant to the provisions of subsection (f), the judicial officer finds that no condition or combination of conditions will reasonably assure the appearance of the person as required and the safety of any other person and the community, he shall order the detention of the person prior to trial." . . . If the judicial officer finds that no conditions of pretrial release can reasonably assure the safety of other persons and the community, he must state his findings of fact in writing, §3142(i), and support his conclusion with "clear and convincing evidence," §3142(f).

The judicial officer is not given unbridled discretion in making the detention determination. Congress has specified the considerations relevant to that decision. These factors include the nature and seriousness of the charges, the substantiality of the Government's evidence against the arrestee, the arrestee's background and characteristics, and the nature and seriousness of the danger posed by the suspect's release. §3142(g). Should a judicial officer order detention, the detainee is entitled to expedited appellate review of the detention order. §§3145(b), (c).

Respondents Anthony Salerno and Vincent Cafaro were arrested on March 21, 1986, after being charged in a 29-count indictment alleging various Racketeer Influenced and Corrupt Organizations Act (RICO) violations, mail and wire fraud offenses, extortion, and various criminal gambling violations. The RICO counts alleged 35 acts of racketeering activity, including fraud, extortion, gambling, and conspiracy to commit murder. At respondents' arraignment, the Government moved to have Salerno and Cafaro detained pursuant to §3142(e), on the ground that no condition of release would assure the safety of the community or any person. The District Court held a hearing at which the Government made a detailed proffer of evidence. The Government's case showed that Salerno was the "boss" of the Genovese crime family of La Cosa Nostra and that Cafaro was a "captain" in the Genovese family. According to the Government's proffer, based in large part on conversations intercepted by a court-ordered wiretap, the two respondents had participated in wide-ranging conspiracies to aid their illegitimate enterprises through violent means. The Government also offered the testimony of two of its trial witnesses, who would assert that Salerno personally participated in two murder conspiracies. Salerno opposed the motion for detention, challenging the credibility of the Government's witnesses. He offered the testimony of several character witnesses as well as a letter from his doctor stating that he was suffering from a serious medical condition. Cafaro presented no evidence at the hearing, but instead characterized the wiretap conversations as merely "tough talk."

The District Court granted the Government's detention motion, concluding that the Government had established by clear and convincing evidence that no condition or combination of conditions of release would ensure the safety of the community or any person. . . . Respondents appealed, contending that to the extent that the Bail Reform Act permits pretrial detention on the ground that the arrestee is likely to commit future crimes, it is unconstitutional on its face. . . . A facial challenge to a legislative Act is, of course, the most difficult challenge to mount successfully, since the challenger must establish that no set of circumstances exists under which the Act would be valid. . . . We think respondents have failed to shoulder their heavy burden to demonstrate that the Act is "facially" unconstitutional.

Respondents present two grounds for invalidating the Bail Reform Act's provisions permitting pretrial detention on the basis of future dangerousness. First, they [argue] that the Act exceeds the limitations placed upon the Federal Government by the Due Process Clause of the Fifth Amendment. Second, they contend that the Act contravenes the Eighth Amendment's proscription against excessive bail. We treat these contentions in turn.

The Due Process Clause of the Fifth Amendment provides that "No person shall . . . be deprived of life, liberty, or property, without due process of law. . . ." Respondents first argue that the Act violates substantive due process because the pretrial detention it authorizes constitutes impermissible punishment before trial. The Government, however, has never argued that pretrial detention could be upheld if it were "punishment." The Court of Appeals assumed that pretrial detention under the Bail Reform Act is regulatory, not penal, and we agree that it is. . . .

To determine whether a restriction on liberty constitutes impermissible punishment or permissible regulation, we first look to legislative intent. Unless Congress expressly intended to impose punitive restrictions, the punitive/regulatory distinction turns on whether an alternative purpose to which the restriction may rationally be connected is assignable for it, and whether it appears excessive in relation to the alternative purpose assigned to it.

We conclude that the detention imposed by the Act falls on the regulatory side of the dichotomy. The legislative history of the Bail Reform Act clearly indicates that Congress did not formulate the pretrial detention provisions as punishment for dangerous individuals. Congress instead perceived pretrial detention as a potential solution to a pressing societal problem. There is no doubt that preventing danger to the community is a legitimate regulatory goal.

Nor are the incidents of pretrial detention excessive in relation to the regulatory goal Congress sought to achieve. The Bail Reform Act carefully limits the circumstances under which detention may be sought to the most serious of crimes.

See 18 U.S.C. §3142(f) (detention hearings available if case involves crimes of violence, offenses for which the sentence is life imprisonment or death, serious drug offenses, or certain repeat offenders). The arrestee is entitled to a prompt detention hearing, and the maximum length of pretrial detention is limited by the stringent time limitations of the Speedy Trial Act. Moreover, . . . the conditions of confinement envisioned by the Act appear to reflect the regulatory purposes relied upon by the Government. [T]he statute at issue here requires that detainees be housed in a facility "separate, to the extent practicable, from persons awaiting or serving sentences or being held in custody pending appeal." 18 U.S.C. §3142(i)(2). We conclude, therefore, that the pretrial detention contemplated by the Bail Reform Act is regulatory in nature, and does not constitute punishment before trial in violation of the Due Process Clause.

[T]he Government's regulatory interest in community safety can, in appropriate circumstances, outweigh an individual's liberty interest. For example, in times of war or insurrection, when society's interest is at its peak, the Government may detain individuals whom the Government believes to be dangerous. See Ludecke v. Watkins, 335 U.S. 160 (1948) (approving unreviewable executive power to detain enemy aliens in time of war); Moyer v. Peabody, 212 U.S. 78 (1909) (rejecting due process claim of individual jailed without probable cause by Governor in time of insurrection). Even outside the exigencies of war, we have found that sufficiently compelling governmental interests can justify detention of dangerous persons. Thus, we have found no absolute constitutional barrier to detention of potentially dangerous resident aliens pending deportation proceedings. Carlson v. Landon, 342 U.S. 524 (1952). We have also held that the government may detain mentally unstable individuals who present a danger to the public, Addington v. Texas, 441 U.S. 418 (1979), and dangerous defendants who become incompetent to stand trial, Jackson v. Indiana, 406 U.S. 715 (1972). We have approved of postarrest regulatory detention of juveniles when they present a continuing danger to the community. Schall v. Martin, 467 U.S. 253 (1984). Even competent adults may face substantial liberty restrictions as a result of the operation of our criminal justice system. If the police suspect an individual of a crime, they may arrest and hold him until a neutral magistrate determines whether probable cause exists. Gerstein v. Pugh, 420 U.S. 103 (1975). Finally, . . . an arrestee may be incarcerated until trial if he presents a risk of flight . . . or a danger to witnesses.

Respondents characterize all of these cases as exceptions to the "general rule" of substantive due process that the government may not detain a person prior to a judgment of guilt in a criminal trial. Such a "general rule" may freely be conceded, but we think that these cases show a sufficient number of exceptions to the rule that the congressional action challenged here can hardly be characterized as totally novel. Given the well-established authority of the government, in special circumstances, to restrain individuals' liberty prior to or even without criminal trial and conviction, we think that the present statute providing for pretrial detention on the basis of dangerousness must be evaluated in precisely the same manner that we evaluated the laws in the cases discussed above.

The government's interest in preventing crime by arrestees is both legitimate and compelling. In *Schall*, we recognized the strength of the State's interest in preventing juvenile crime. This general concern with crime prevention is no less compelling when the suspects are adults. . . . The Bail Reform Act of 1984 responds to an even more particularized governmental interest than the interest we sustained in *Schall*. The statute we upheld in *Schall* permitted pretrial detention of any juvenile arrested on any charge after a showing that the individual might commit some undefined further crimes. The Bail Reform Act, in contrast . . . operates only on individuals who have been arrested for a specific category of extremely serious offenses. Congress specifically found that these individuals are far more likely to be responsible for dangerous acts in the community after arrest. Nor is the Act by any means a scattershot attempt to incapacitate those who are merely suspected of these serious crimes. The Government must first of all demonstrate probable cause to believe that the charged crime has been committed by the arrestee, but that is not enough. In a full-blown adversary hearing, the Government must convince a neutral decisionmaker by clear and convincing evidence that no conditions of release can reasonably assure the safety of the community or any person. While the Government's general interest in preventing crime is compelling, even this interest is heightened when the Government musters convincing proof that the arrestee, already indicted or held to answer for a serious crime, presents a demonstrable danger to the community. Under these narrow circumstances, society's interest in crime prevention is at its greatest.

On the other side of the scale, of course, is the individual's strong interest in liberty. We do not minimize the importance and fundamental nature of this right. But, as our cases hold, this right may, in circumstances where the Government's interest is sufficiently weighty, be subordinated to the greater needs of society. We think that Congress' careful delineation of the circumstances under which detention will be permitted satisfies this standard. When the Government proves by clear and convincing evidence that an arrestee presents an identified and articulable threat to an individual or the community, we believe that, consistent with the Due Process Clause, a court may disable the arrestee from executing that threat. . . .

Respondents also contend that the Bail Reform Act violates the Excessive Bail Clause of the Eighth Amendment. . . . The Eighth Amendment addresses pretrial release by providing merely that "excessive bail shall not be required." This Clause, of course, says nothing about whether bail shall be available at all. Respondents nevertheless contend that this Clause grants them a right to bail calculated solely upon considerations of flight. They rely on Stack v. Boyle, 342 U.S. 1, 5 (1951), in which the Court stated that "bail set at a figure higher than an amount reasonably calculated [to ensure the defendant's presence at trial] is 'excessive' under the Eighth Amendment." In respondents' view, since the Bail Reform Act allows a court essentially to set bail at an infinite amount for reasons not related to the risk of flight, it violates the Excessive Bail Clause. Respondents concede that the right to bail they have discovered in the Eighth Amendment is not absolute. A court may, for example, refuse bail in capital cases. [A] court may [also] refuse bail when the defendant presents a threat to the judicial process by intimidating witnesses. Respondents characterize these exceptions as consistent with what they claim to be the sole purpose of bail — to ensure the integrity of the judicial process.

While we agree that a primary function of bail is to safeguard the courts' role in adjudicating the guilt or innocence of defendants, we reject the proposition that the Eighth Amendment categorically prohibits the government from pursuing other admittedly compelling interests through regulation of pretrial release. The above-quoted dictum in Stack v. Boyle is far too slender a reed on which to rest this argument. [T]he statute before the Court in that case in fact allowed the defendants to be bailed. Thus, the Court had to determine only whether bail, admittedly available in that case, was excessive if set at a sum greater than that necessary to ensure the arrestees' presence at trial.

The holding of *Stack* is illuminated by the Court's holding just four months later in Carlson v. Landon, 342 U.S. 524 (1952). In that case, remarkably similar to the present action, the detainees had been arrested and held without bail pending a determination of deportability. The Attorney General refused to release the individuals, "on the ground that there was reasonable cause to believe that [their] release would be prejudicial to the public interest and would endanger the welfare and safety of the United States." The detainees brought the same challenge that respondents bring to us today: the Eighth Amendment required them to be admitted to bail. The Court squarely rejected this proposition:

> The bail clause was lifted with slight changes from the English Bill of Rights Act. In England that clause has never been thought to accord a right to bail in all cases, but merely to provide that bail shall not be excessive in those cases where it is proper to grant bail. When this clause was carried over into our Bill of Rights, nothing was said that indicated any different concept. [342 U.S. at 545.]

Nothing in the text of the Bail Clause limits permissible Government considerations solely to questions of flight. The only arguable substantive limitation of the Bail Clause is that the Government's proposed conditions of release or detention not be "excessive" in light of the perceived evil. Of course, to determine whether the Government's response is excessive, we must compare that response against the interest the Government seeks to protect by means of that response. Thus, when the Government has admitted that its only interest is in preventing flight, bail must be set by a court at a sum designed to ensure that goal, and no more. We believe that when Congress has mandated detention on the basis of a compelling interest other than prevention of flight, as it has here, the Eighth Amendment does not require release on bail.

In our society liberty is the norm, and detention prior to trial or without trial is the carefully limited exception. We hold that the provisions for pretrial detention in the Bail Reform Act of 1984 fall within that carefully limited exception. The Act authorizes the detention prior to trial of arrestees charged with serious felonies who are found after an adversary hearing to pose a threat to the safety of individuals or to the community which no condition of release can dispel. The numerous procedural safeguards detailed above must attend this adversary hearing. We are unwilling to say that this congressional determination, based as it is upon that primary concern of every government — a concern for the safety and indeed the lives of its citizens — on its face violates either the Due Process Clause of the Fifth Amendment or the Excessive Bail Clause of the Eighth Amendment. The judgment of the Court of Appeals is therefore reversed.

MARSHALL, J., dissenting.

This case brings before the Court for the first time a statute in which Congress declares that a person innocent of any crime may be jailed indefinitely, pending the trial of allegations which are legally presumed to be untrue, if the Government shows to the satisfaction of a judge that the accused is likely to commit crimes, unrelated to the pending charges, at any time in the future. Such statutes, consistent with the usages of tyranny and the excesses of what bitter experience teaches us to call the police state, have long been thought incompatible with the fundamental human rights protected by our Constitution.

[In connection with the Due Process challenge,] the majority concludes that the Act is a regulatory rather than a punitive measure. The ease with which the conclusion is reached suggests the worthlessness of the achievement. . . . Let us apply the majority's reasoning to a similar, hypothetical case. After investigation, Congress determines (not unrealistically) that a large proportion of violent crime is perpetrated by persons who are unemployed. It also determines, equally reasonably, that much violent crime is committed at night. From amongst the panoply of "potential solutions," Congress chooses a statute which permits, after judicial proceedings, the imposition of a dusk-to-dawn curfew on anyone who is unemployed. Since this is not a measure enacted for the purpose of punishing the unemployed, and since the majority finds that preventing danger to the community is a legitimate regulatory goal, the curfew statute would, according to the majority's analysis, be a mere "regulatory" detention statute, entirely compatible with the substantive components of the Due Process Clause.

The absurdity of this conclusion arises, of course, from the majority's cramped concept of substantive due process. The majority proceeds as though the only substantive right protected by the Due Process Clause is a right to be free from punishment before conviction. The majority's technique for infringing this right is simple: merely redefine any measure which is claimed to be punishment as "regulation," and, magically, the Constitution no longer prohibits its imposition. Because . . . the Due Process Clause protects other substantive rights which are infringed by this legislation, the majority's argument is merely an exercise in obfuscation.

The logic of the majority's Eighth Amendment analysis is equally unsatisfactory. [The majority] declares, as if it were undeniable, that: "this Clause, of course, says nothing about whether bail shall be available at all." If excessive bail is imposed the defendant stays in jail. The same result is achieved if bail is denied altogether. Whether the magistrate sets bail at $1 billion or refuses to set bail at all, the consequences are indistinguishable. It would be mere sophistry to suggest that the Eighth Amendment protects against the former decision, and not the latter. Indeed, such a result would lead to the conclusion that there was no need for Congress to pass a preventive detention measure of any kind; every federal magistrate and district judge could simply refuse, despite the absence of any evidence of risk of flight or danger to the community, to set bail. . . .

The essence of this case may be found, ironically enough, in a provision of the Act to which the majority does not refer. Title 18 U.S.C. §3142(j) provides that "nothing in this section shall be construed as modifying or limiting the presumption of innocence." But the very pith and purpose of this statute is an abhorrent limitation of the presumption of innocence. . . .

The statute does not authorize the Government to imprison anyone it has evidence is dangerous; indictment is necessary. But let us suppose that a defendant is indicted and the Government shows by clear and convincing evidence that he is dangerous and should be detained pending a trial, at which trial the defendant is acquitted. May the Government continue to hold the defendant in detention based upon its showing that he is dangerous? The answer cannot be yes, for that would allow the Government to imprison someone for uncommitted crimes based upon "proof" not beyond a reasonable doubt. The result must therefore be that once the indictment has failed, detention cannot continue. But our fundamental principles of justice declare that the defendant is as innocent on the day before his trial as he is on the morning after his acquittal. Under this statute an untried indictment somehow acts to permit a detention, based on other charges, which after an acquittal would be unconstitutional. The conclusion is inescapable that the indictment has been turned into evidence, if not that the defendant is guilty of the crime charged, then that left to his own devices he will soon be guilty of something else. . . .

The finding of probable cause conveys power to try, and the power to try imports of necessity the power to assure that the processes of justice will not be evaded or obstructed. [Detention under] this statute bears no relation to the Government's power to try charges supported by a finding of probable cause, and thus the interests it serves are outside the scope of interests which may be considered in weighing the excessiveness of bail under the Eighth Amendment. . . .

Throughout the world today there are men, women, and children interned indefinitely, awaiting trials which may never come or which may be a mockery of the word, because their governments believe them to be "dangerous." Our Constitution, whose construction began two centuries ago, can shelter us forever from the evils of such unchecked power. Over 200 years it has slowly, through our efforts, grown more durable, more expansive, and more just. But it cannot protect us if we lack the courage, and the self-restraint, to protect ourselves. Today a majority of the Court applies itself to an ominous exercise in demolition. Theirs is truly a decision which will go forth without authority, and come back without respect. I dissent.

STEVENS, J., dissenting.

There may be times when the Government's interest in protecting the safety of the community will justify the brief detention of a person who has not committed any crime. [I]t is indeed difficult to accept the proposition that the Government is without power to detain a person when it is a virtual certainty that he or she would otherwise kill a group of innocent people in the immediate future. Similarly, I am unwilling to decide today that the police may never impose a limited curfew during a time of crisis. These questions are obviously not presented in this case, but they lurk in the background and preclude me from answering the question that is presented in as broad a manner as Justice Marshall has. Nonetheless, I firmly agree with Justice Marshall that the provision of the Bail Reform Act allowing pretrial detention on the basis of future dangerousness is unconstitutional. Whatever the answers are to the questions I have mentioned, it is clear to me that a pending indictment may not be given any weight in evaluating an individual's risk to the community or the need for immediate detention.

If the evidence of imminent danger is strong enough to warrant emergency detention, it should support that preventive measure regardless of whether the person has been charged, convicted, or acquitted of some other offense. In this case, for example, it is unrealistic to assume that the danger to the community that was present when respondents were at large did not justify their detention before they were indicted, but did require that measure the moment that the grand jury found probable cause to believe they had committed crimes in the past. It is equally unrealistic to assume that the danger will vanish if a jury happens to acquit them. . . .

■ NEW MEXICO CONSTITUTION ART. II, §13

All persons shall before conviction be bailable by sufficient sureties, except for capital offenses when the proof is evident or the presumption great and in situations in which bail is specifically prohibited by this section. Excessive bail shall not be required, nor excessive fines imposed, nor cruel and unusual punishment inflicted.

Bail may be denied by the district court for a period of sixty days after the incarceration of the defendant by an order entered within seven days after the incarceration, in the following instances:

A. the defendant is accused of a felony and has previously been convicted of two or more felonies, within the state, which felonies did not arise from the same transaction or a common transaction with the case at bar;

B. the defendant is accused of a felony involving the use of a deadly weapon and has a prior felony conviction, within the state.

The period for incarceration without bail may be extended by any period of time by which trial is delayed by a motion for a continuance made by or on behalf of the defendant. . . .

■ VIRGINIA CODE §19.2-120

. . . A. A person who is held in custody pending trial or hearing for an offense, civil or criminal contempt, or otherwise shall be admitted to bail by a judicial officer, unless there is probable cause to believe that:

1. He will not appear for trial or hearing or at such other time and place as may be directed, or

2. His liberty will constitute an unreasonable danger to himself or the public.

B. The judicial officer shall presume, subject to rebuttal, that no condition or combination of conditions will reasonably assure the appearance of the person or the safety of the public if the person is currently charged with:

1. An act of violence as defined in [this code];

2. An offense for which the maximum sentence is life imprisonment or death;

3. A violation . . . involving a Schedule I or II controlled substance if (i) the maximum term of imprisonment is ten years or more and the person was previously convicted of a like offense or (ii) the person was previously convicted as a "drug kingpin" as defined in [this code];

4. A violation . . . which relates to a firearm and provides for a minimum, mandatory sentence;

5. Any felony, if the person has been convicted of two or more offenses described in subdivision 1 or 2 . . .;

6. Any felony committed while the person is on release pending trial for a prior felony under federal or state law or on release pending imposition or execution of sentence or appeal of sentence or conviction;

7. [Felony sexual assault] and the person had previously been convicted of [felony sexual assault] and the judicial officer finds probable cause to believe that the person who is currently charged with one of these offenses committed the offense charged; or

8. A violation of [the statutes prohibiting acts of terrorism or acts of bioterrorism against agricultural crops or animals].

C. The court shall consider the following factors and such others as it deems appropriate in determining, for the purpose of rebuttal of the presumption against bail described in subsection B, whether there are conditions of release that will reasonably assure the appearance of the person as required and the safety of the public:

1. The nature and circumstances of the offense charged;
2. The history and characteristics of the person, including his character, physical and mental condition, family ties, employment, financial resources, length of residence in the community, community ties, past conduct, history relating to drug or alcohol abuse, criminal history, and record concerning appearance at court proceedings; and
3. The nature and seriousness of the danger to any person or the community that would be posed by the person's release.

Notes

1. *Preventive detention: majority position.* Like the federal system, about half the states authorize courts to detain defendants before trial for the purpose of preventing the commission of new crimes ("preventive detention"). See, e.g., Mass. Gen. L. ch. 276, §58A. On the other hand, about 25 states have constitutional provisions that, like Tennessee, guarantee the right to bail except in capital cases. Detention based on risk of future crime is often distinguished from detention based on fear of flight or threat to witnesses. Do the categories of fear of flight or threat to witnesses overlap with risk of future crime? Among states that authorize detention, the details of their statutes and constitutions vary substantially. A handful create a presumption against bail, but most allow detention in the discretion of the court. Some states limit preventive detention to "serious crimes"; others limit detention to offenders with specific combinations of prior record and sufficiently serious current charges. A handful of states have enacted limits on the maximum time a defendant may be detained to prevent crimes. See, e.g., Mass. Gen. L. ch. 276, §58A (90 days); Wis. Stat. §969.035 (60 days). Why have so many states continued to reject preventive detention laws over the more than 15 years since passage of the federal Bail Reform Act and the decision of the Supreme Court in *Salerno*? Are other states likely, over time, to make the statutory and constitutional changes necessary to allow preventive detention? Some state constitutional provisions that seemed to bar the use of preventive detention have either been amended by the voters (e.g., Ohio Const. art. I, §9 was amended in 1997) or read restrictively to avoid any inconsistency with a new preventive detention statute. See State v. Ayala, 610 A.2d 1162 (Conn. 1992); Mo. Rev. Stat. §544.457 (allowing preventive detention "notwithstanding" constitutional guarantee of bail).

2. *Presumption of innocence.* The justices in *Salerno* disagreed about the meaning of the presumption of innocence. A critic of the majority opinion might draw a comparison to the following passage from Lewis Carroll's *Through the Looking Glass,* where the Queen and Alice discuss the consequences of having a memory that works both ways:

> "I'm sure mine only works one way," Alice remarked. "I can't remember things before they happen."
>
> "It's a poor sort of memory that only works backward," the Queen remarked.
>
> "What sort of things do you remember best?" Alice ventured to ask.
>
> "Oh, things that happened the week after next," the Queen replied in a careless tone.
>
> "For instance, now," she went on, sticking a large piece of plaster on her finger

as she spoke, "there's the King's Messenger. He's in prison now, being punished: and the trial doesn't even begin till next Wednesday: and of course the crime comes last of all."

"Suppose he never commits the crime?" said Alice.

"That would be all the better, wouldn't it?" the Queen said, as she bound the plaster round her finger with a bit of ribbon.

Alice felt there was no denying that. "Of course it would be all the better," she said: "but it wouldn't be all the better his being punished."

"You're wrong there, at any rate," said the Queen: "Were you ever punished?"

"Only for faults," said Alice.

"And you were all the better for it, I know!" the Queen said triumphantly.

"Yes, but then I had done the things I was punished for," said Alice: "that makes all the difference."

"But if you hadn't done them," the Queen said, "that would have been better still; better, and better, and better!" . . .

Alice was just beginning to say, "There's a mistake somewhere —," when the Queen began screaming, so loud that she had to leave the sentence unfinished. "Oh, oh, oh!" shouted the Queen, shaking her hand about as if she wanted to shake it off. "My finger's bleeding! Oh, oh, oh, oh!" . . .

"What is the matter?" she said, as soon as there was a chance of making herself heard.

"Have you pricked your finger?"

"I haven't pricked it yet," the Queen said, "but I soon shall — oh, oh, oh!"

Is this the message of the *Salerno* opinion? If not, in what sense can we say that *Salerno* respects the presumption of innocence?

3. *Limitation to serious felonies and repeat offenders.* Most of the states passing new statutory or constitutional provisions to allow preventive detention have limited its use to criminal defendants who are accused of committing a select group of serious or violent felonies. See Mendonza v. Commonwealth, 673 N.E.2d 22 (Mass. 1996) (upholding revised statute under federal and state constitutions; statute applies to felonies involving the use, or threatened use, of violence or abuse, or the violation of protective orders); Aime v. Commonwealth, 611 N.E.2d 204 (Mass. 1993) (striking down preventive detention law on federal grounds because of wide range of crimes covered; court distinguishes *Salerno*). Some, like the New Mexico constitutional provision above, apply only to those accused of a felony who have also been convicted of one or more felonies in the past. See also Colo. Const. art. II, §19 (new bail denied to those accused of committing violent crime while on prior bail, parole, or probation for previous charges of violent crime). Do both the "serious crime" and "repeat offender" limitations serve the same purpose? Another variety of selective detention statutes applies only to defendants accused of a particularly high-priority crime, such as stalking or domestic violence. See Alaska Stat. §12.30.025; Ill. Rev. Stat. ch. 725, para. 5/110-4. Do these provisions raise any concerns different from a provision focusing on all serious felonies?

4. *Presumptions based on crime charged.* Some of the preventive detention measures go further than authorizing the trial court to detain a defendant when necessary to protect the community: They instruct the judge that detention is presumed when a defendant is charged with committing designated crimes of drugs and violence. The Virginia statute above is an example. Are these statutes the modern equivalent of the old "capital punishment" exception in the typical constitutional bail provision? Or did the capital punishment exception serve more traditional purposes, such as preventing the defendant from fleeing upon his or her release?

5. *How many defendants are detained?* The number of defendants detained in the federal system is creeping upward. While 29 percent of the federal defendants in 1992 were detained without bail, the number had reached 55 percent by 1999. Bureau of Justice Statistics, Sourcebook of Criminal Justice Statistics 2000, table 5.12 (2001). As for the state systems, in large counties in 1998, 36 percent of defendants were detained until case disposition. These national average statistics obscure some real differences among jurisdictions.

What is the proper practical balance between the 1960s reform encouraging presumptive release and the 1980s reform encouraging open detention for those who threaten harm? Does detention until trial of almost one-third of those charged with felonies in the federal system seem too high? Does the federal system reflect the victory of candor? Is open preventive detention preferable to continued sub-rosa detention through unrealistically high bail requirements in states where there is no legal authority to detain defendants for the purpose of protecting the public from the commission of additional crimes?

6. *Compensation for wrongful detention.* Should the government compensate people who are detained under the Bail Reform Act or analogous state statutes and are later found at trial to be not guilty? See Masson v. Netherlands, 22 EHRR 491 (1996) (European Court of Human Rights reviewing domestic law that allows civil court, after a failure to convict a suspect in criminal proceedings, to grant compensation at expense of the state for damage suffered as a result of wrongful pretrial detention).

7. *Detention after completion of sentence.* States are now using post-sentence detention to extend their control over some persons convicted of sex offenses. Statutes passed since the mid-1990s authorize the government to request continued detention of convicted sex offenders after they have completed their sentences. These statutes typically require the government to demonstrate, on a year-to-year basis, that the offender remains "dangerous." The Supreme Court has upheld statutes against challenges based on the due process, ex post facto, and double jeopardy clause of the federal constitution. Kansas v. Hendricks, 521 U.S. 346 (1997). Employing the same distinction that it used in *Salerno,* the court said that this detention was "regulatory" rather than "punitive." See also Kansas v. Crane, 534 U.S. 407 (2002) (constitution does not require judicial finding of total or complete lack of control to support regulatory detention of sexual offender, but Constitution does require a showing that person does lack some control over his or her behavior).

8. *The revenge of social science.* Social science studies were the driving force behind legal changes to make pretrial release easier and less dependent on money bail. Similarly, social science figured prominently in the movement to expand the power of judges to detain defendants before trial. These studies focused on the number of defendants released before trial who were soon rearrested for committing additional crimes. In 1998, for example, 16 percent of released defendants were rearrested for a new offense allegedly committed while their original case was pending.

Over the past generation, we have reduced the number of people who are detained and have changed the acceptable reasons for detaining persons, allowing the detention of some defendants who at one time would have been released on bail. Do we now have it just about right? Are we now detaining the right people? Does this trend reflect a shift in the fundamental basis for the criminal law, punishing criminal propensities rather than criminal acts? See Paul H. Robinson, Punishing

Dangerousness: Cloaking Preventive Detention as Criminal Justice, 114 Harv. L. Rev. 1429 (2001).

After the terrorist attacks of September 11, 2001, the federal government detained several groups of people as part of the effort to investigate the previous attacks and to prevent future terrorist crimes. First, the government detained a large number of noncitizens from Arab nations, present within the United States, on the basis of potential immigration violations such as expired student visas. Under the immigration laws, the government incarcerated these noncitizens for several months with limited access to counsel, while government agents investigated their potential immigration violations, along with their potential involvement in terrorist activities. The government has not released the precise number and identity of these detainees; estimates range from 1,200 to 2,000 persons. Many of these detainees were ultimately deported for their immigration violations, and a few were charged with crimes (although none were charged with crimes directly connected to terrorism). The government also declared that the immigration proceedings related to these people were closed to the public, and no individualized showing was needed to establish that secrecy was necessary in each particular case.

Second, the government detained dozens of people in the United States as "material witnesses" who might have information relating to the attacks. The traditional use of the federal material witness statute was to hold reluctant or fearful witnesses for a short time (typically a few days) to obtain their grand jury testimony. During this investigation, FBI agents obtained judicial approval for warrants allowing them to detain material witnesses, and then held them for several months; only about half the witnesses ever testified before a grand jury.

Third, the United States military captured men during fighting in Afghanistan, and transported several hundred of them to a military detention facility in Cuba. These men were held for questioning without criminal charges and without access to counsel. One of them, Feroz Ali Abbasi, was a British national who challenged his detention in the British courts on the basis of international law. The following opinion responds to his claim. To what extent do the limits on detention in the United States track the requirements of international justice as described in this opinion?

Is it possible to maintain a distinction between detention for criminal purposes and detention for military purposes? As you think about this question, imagine that some additional terrorist atrocity is committed, perhaps by a group based in China. If investigators detained a large number of suspects of Chinese origins, what limits would apply to that detention?

■ FEROZ ABBASI v. SECRETARY OF STATE

2002 EWCA Civ. 1598 (Court of Appeal, Civil Division, 2002)

LORD PHILLIPS:

. . . 1. Feroz Ali Abbasi . . . is a British national. He was captured by United States forces in Afghanistan. In January 2002 he was transported to Guantanamo Bay in Cuba, a naval base on territory held by the United States on long lease pursuant to a treaty with Cuba. By the time of the hearing before us he had been held captive for eight months without access to a court or any other form of tribunal or even to a lawyer. These proceedings, brought on his behalf by his mother . . . , are founded on the contention that one of his fundamental human rights, the right not to be arbitrarily detained, is being infringed. They seek, by judicial review, to compel the Foreign Office to make representations on his behalf to the United States Government or to take other appropriate action or at least to give an explanation as to why this has not been done. . . .

5. The government was able to obtain permission from the United States Government to visit detainees at Guantanamo Bay on three occasions, between 19 and 20 January, between 26 February and 1 March and between 27 and 31 May. These visits were conducted by officials of the Foreign and Commonwealth Office and members of the security services. The former were able to assure themselves that the British prisoners, including Mr. Abbasi, were being well treated and appeared in good physical health. By the time of the third visit, facilities had been purpose built to house detainees. Each was held in an individual cell with air ventilation, a washbasin and a toilet. It is not suggested by the claimants that Mr. Abbasi is not being treated humanely. . . .

8. In or about February 2002 the claimants initiated habeas corpus proceedings in the District Court of Columbia. [R]ulings in proceedings brought by other detainees in a similar position demonstrate that Mr. Abbasi's proceedings have, at present, no prospect of success.

9. On 2 July 2002 the First Secretary at the American Embassy in London wrote to solicitors acting for the claimants in the following terms:

> The United States Government believes that individuals detained at Guantanamo are enemy combatants, captured in connection with an on-going armed conflict. They are held in that capacity under the control of U.S. military authorities. Enemy combatants pose a serious threat to the United States and its coalition partners.
>
> Detainees are being held in accordance with the laws and customs of war, which permit the United States to hold enemy combatants at least for the duration of hostilities. I can assure you that the United States is treating these individuals humanely and in a manner consistent with the principles of the Third Geneva Convention 1949. Representatives of the International Committee of the Red Cross are at Guantanamo Bay and meet with detainees individually and privately.
>
> Under international humanitarian law, captured enemy combatants have no right of access to counsel or the courts to challenge their detention. If and when a detainee is charged with a crime, he would have the right to counsel and fundamental procedural safeguards.

10. The Third Geneva Convention 1949 relates to Prisoners of War. The United States has not, however, accepted that prisoners held at Guantanamo have the status of prisoners of war. The position of the United States is made plain in the following passage of a statement made by the United States Press Secretary on 2 February 2002:

> Taliban detainees are not entitled to POW status. [They] have not conducted their operations in accordance with the laws and customs of war, [and] al Qaeda is an international terrorist group and cannot be considered a state party to the Geneva Convention. Its members, therefore, are not covered by the Geneva Convention, and are not entitled to POW status under the treaty. . . .

11. Mr. Abbasi is, as we understand the position, detained pursuant to the executive authority entrusted to the President as Commander in Chief of the US

Military. It is not clear whether he is detained pursuant to a Military Order issued by the United States President on 13 November 2001 relating to "Detention, treatment, and trial of certain non-citizens in the war against terrorism". . . . The Order stipulates that it applies to any individual who is not a citizen of the United States with respect to whom the President has determined in writing that there is reason to believe (1) that such individual is a member of al-Qaeda or (2) that he was engaged in international terrorism, or (3) that it is in the interests of the United States that he should be subject to the order. The order provides that any such individual will be detained at an appropriate location and treated humanely. It provides that any individual "when tried" will be tried by a military tribunal, and contains extensive provisions relating to such trial. It further provides:

> With respect to any individual subject to this order . . . the individual shall not be privileged to seek any remedy or maintain any proceeding, directly or indirectly, or to have any such remedy or proceeding sought on the individual's behalf, in (i) any court of the United States, or any State thereof, (ii) any court of any foreign nation, or (iii) any international tribunal.

There is no indication whether Mr. Abbasi is going to be tried and thus whether the Order applies to him.

12. On 19 February 2002 three prisoners detained at Guantanamo Bay, two British and one Australian, commenced a civil action in the District Court of Columbia . . . in which they petitioned for a writ of habeas corpus. . . . After hearing argument the Court ruled that the military base at Guantanamo Bay was outside the sovereign territory of the United States and that, in consequence of this fact and the fact that the claimants were aliens, the Court had no jurisdiction to entertain their claims. The position would have been different had they been American subjects.

13. In so holding, the District Court purported to follow a majority decision of the Supreme Court in Eisentrager v. Forrestal, 174 F.2d 961 (D.C. Cir. 1949). That case concerned German citizens who had been convicted of espionage by a United States military commission after the surrender of Germany at the end of the Second World War and repatriated to Landsberg Prison in Germany to serve their sentences. The prison was under the control of the United States army. The prisoners petitioned for writs of habeas corpus. Giving the decision of the majority, Justice Robert Jackson held that a court was unable to extend the writ of habeas corpus to aliens held outside the territory of the United States. He distinguished between aliens and citizens, observing that "citizenship as a head of jurisdiction and a ground of protection was old when Paul invoked it in his appeal to Caesar". . . .

18. There have been widespread expressions of concern, both within and outside the United States, in respect of the stand taken by the United States government. . . . On 16 January 2002 the United Nations High Commissioner for Human Rights issued a statement which included the following assertions

> All persons detained in this context are entitled to the protection of international human rights law and humanitarian law, in particular the relevant provisions of the International Covenant on Civil and Political Rights (ICCPR) and the Geneva Conventions of 1949. The legal status of the detainees, and their entitlement to prisoner-of-war (POW) status, if disputed, must be determined by a competent tribunal, in accordance with the provisions of Article 5 of the Third Geneva Convention.

19. Submissions made in [by the United States in other cases] seem . . . to entail that the decision of the military as to who is an enemy combatant is almost unchallengeable. Furthermore, whereas in a conventional war prisoners of war have to be released at the end of hostilities, there is the possibility that, by denying the detainees captured during the war against terrorism the status of prisoners of war, their detention may be indefinite. . . .

21. The Inter-American Commission on Human Rights is an organ of the Organisation of American States, of which the United States is a member. By letter dated 12 March 2001 the Commission requested that the United States: "take the urgent measures necessary to have the legal status of the detainees at Guantanamo Bay determined by a competent Tribunal." The United States response was delivered under cover of a letter dated 11 April, the letter stating:

> The United States wishes to inform the Commission that the legal status of the detainees is clear, that the Commission does not have jurisdictional competence to apply international humanitarian law, that the precautionary measures are neither necessary nor appropriate in this case, and that the Commission lacks authority to request precautionary measures of the United States. . . .

25. [Mr. Blake, the attorney for the claimant, had] great difficulty in advancing his claim to relief in a form which could readily be transposed into an order of the court. The essence of his submissions was that Mr. Abbasi was subject to a violation by the United States of one of his fundamental human rights and that, in these circumstances, the Foreign Secretary owed him a duty under English public law to take positive steps to redress the position, or at least to give a reasoned response to his request for assistance. . . .

58. . . . If the decision of the District Court of Columbia accurately represents the law of the United States, then the United States executive is detaining Mr. Abbasi on territory over which it has total control in circumstances where Mr. Abbasi can make no challenge to his detention before any court or tribunal. How long this state of affairs continues is within the sole control of the United States executive. Mr. Blake contends that this constitutes arbitrary detention contrary to the fundamental norms of international law. It is not the fact that Mr. Abbasi is detained on which Mr. Blake relies — it is the fact that Mr. Abbasi has no means of challenging the legality of his detention. It is this predicament which, so Mr. Blake contends, gives rise to a duty on the part of the Foreign Secretary to come to Mr. Abbasi's assistance. . . .

59. The United Kingdom and the United States share a great legal tradition, founded in the English common law. One of the cornerstones of that tradition is the ancient writ of habeas corpus, recognised at least by the time of Edward I, and developed by the 17th Century into "the most efficient protection yet developed for the liberty of the subject". . . .

60. The underlying principle, fundamental in English law, is that every imprisonment is prima facie unlawful, and that no member of the executive can interfere with the liberty . . . of a British subject except on the condition that he can support the legality of his action before a court of justice. This principle applies to every person, British citizen or not, who finds himself within the jurisdiction of the court. . . . It applies in war as in peace; in Lord Atkin's words (written in one of the darkest periods of the last war): "In this country, amid the clash of arms, the laws are not silent. They may be changed, but they speak the same language in war as in peace." . . .

As one would expect, endorsement of this common tradition is no less strong in the United States. . . . The recognition of this basic protection in both English and American law long pre-dates the adoption of the same principle as a fundamental part of international human rights law. . . .

64. For these reasons we do not find it possible to approach this claim for judicial review other than on the basis that, in apparent contravention of fundamental principles recognised by both jurisdictions and by international law, Mr. Abbasi is at present arbitrarily detained in a "legal black-hole."

65. That is not to say that his detention as an alleged "enemy combatant" may not be justified. This court has very recently had occasion to consider the legitimacy of legislation that empowers the Secretary of State to detain within this jurisdiction aliens who are suspected of being international terrorists—*A, X and Y and Others v. Secretary of State for the Home Department* [2002] EWCA Civ 1502. We would endorse the summary of the position under international law of Brooke LJ:

> What emerges from the efforts of the international community to introduce orderly arrangements for controlling the power of detention of non-nationals is a distinct movement away from the doctrine of the inherent power of the state to control the treatment of non-nationals within its borders as it will towards a regime, founded on modern international human rights norms, which is infused by the principle that any measures that are restrictive of liberty, whether they relate to nationals or non-nationals, must be such as are prescribed by law and necessary in a democratic society. The state's power to detain must be related to a recognised object and purpose, and there must be a reasonable relationship of proportionality between the end and the means. On the other hand, both customary international law and the international treaties by which this country is bound expressly reserve the power of a state in time of war or similar public emergency to detain aliens on grounds of national security when it would not necessarily detain its own nationals on those grounds.

These comments can be applied with equal force to those suspected of having taken part in military operations involving terrorist organisations.

66. What appears to us to be objectionable is that Mr. Abbasi should be subject to indefinite detention in territory over which the United States has exclusive control with no opportunity to challenge the legitimacy of his detention before any court or tribunal. . . .

67. It is clear that there can be no direct remedy in this court. The United States Government is not before the court, and no order of this court would be binding upon it. Conversely, the United Kingdom Government, which, through the Secretaries of State is the respondent to these proceedings, has no direct responsibility for the detention. Nor is it suggested that it has any enforceable right, or even standing, before any domestic or international tribunal to represent the rights of the applicant, or compel access to a court. . . .

XII

Charging

Soon after arrest, suspects learn why they have been detained. Most often, this occurs when the arresting officer files a form (sometimes called a complaint, sometimes an investigation report) indicating the charges to be filed against the arrestee. Those charges are subject to change at many points later in the process. A prosecutor ordinarily decides whether to accept the police officer's proposed charge and files that charge or another at an initial appearance before a judicial officer, a hearing that is given various names in different jurisdictions. This hearing takes place within a short period (typically 48 hours, or some other time defined by rule or statute). The charges can also change at a later hearing, sometimes known as a preliminary examination, or at an arraignment, when the defendant indicates how he will plead. Charges can also be dismissed later in the process.

You might think of the charging process as a set of screens following investigation: Various government institutions help decide which persons in custody will become criminal defendants and which charges they will face. The arresting police officer and the officer's supervisor have some input into the charging decision. Prosecuting attorneys usually have the most important voice in determining whether to charge and what charges to select; criminal codes commonly give the prosecutor more than one legally viable option in a particular case. The prosecutor might follow personal criteria, policies and principles established for the office, or (less frequently) statutes dictating the charging decision. Courts are usually less involved in the charging decision than in most other procedural choices. Much of the time, courts review charging decisions only to confirm that there is a minimal amount of evidence supporting the charge, enough to justify "binding over" the case for trial. Grand juries are another special institution designed in part to determine whether there is probable cause to charge defendants, especially in more serious cases.

Because the prosecutor's choices dominate the charging phase, we concentrate in this chapter on unfamiliar sources of law. As you survey the charging process, ask whether the various executive branch guidelines and practices at work here are comparable in any way — in origins, function, evolution, and so on — to the way legislatures and courts craft rules.

A. POLICE SCREENING

Should police officers make an independent judgment about whether to file charges for every crime that might be charged? Should police departments set up internal mechanisms to review arrests before submitting a file or report to prosecutors? On what grounds might a police supervisor reject a charge when the facts appear to satisfy the elements of the crime?

Police screening of charges is largely hidden in the modern, big-city criminal process. Hints about the extent of police screening can be seen in occasional studies of "clearance rates" and case "attrition." Clearance rates refer to the percentage of complaints made to police that are solved in some fashion. Attrition is the term describing how initial complaints drop out of the criminal process and why only a relatively small percentage of complaints end with convictions.

The amount of case attrition in a system depends on the interaction between police and prosecutors. Where the police and prosecutors have different ideas about which cases are worthwhile, many cases that the police assemble will fall out of the system, some sooner and some later. Police screening represents an effort to anticipate how the prosecutor will evaluate the case.

In practice, the types of interaction between police and prosecutors during the screening of cases can vary a great deal. According to one influential study attempting to measure the quality of prosecutors' offices, the arrangement between police and prosecutors depends as much on legal culture as on the legal authority to make charging decisions:

> In Buffalo, New York . . . the police arrest the defendant, take him before the committing magistrate where his bond is set, the complaint filed, defense counsel appointed, if necessary, and the case set for preliminary hearing. It is only prior to the preliminary hearing that the prosecutor is made aware of the case and the files are sent to him. Thus, the preliminary hearing provides the first opportunity for case review and witness interviews. The result is to place the prosecutor in a reactive position since he does not exercise the charging function which controls the intake into the system. . . .
>
> It is sometimes difficult to change the external conditions that create a transfer [of control to some other institution]. For example, in Buffalo, police arrestees are processed at the precinct level, not at a centrally located facility. This fragmentation coupled with a strong tradition of police filing charges has supported the transfer [of initial charging authority to police]. In other cities, such as Philadelphia, attempts have been made to overcome the absence of centralized booking. In one experiment, assistant prosecutors were stationed at the police precincts. But the problems resulting from irregularly occurring work, isolation from the main office and the attorney's subsequent role identification with the police function, all worked against its success. [A]s long as arrests are booked at scattered precincts, the opportunity for the prosecutor to intervene before the charge is filed in court is severely diminished.

Joan Jacoby, Basic Issues in Prosecution and Public Defender Performance 25-30 (1982). In the following police department rules, what differences do you see in the working relationships between police and prosecutors leading to a charging decision?

■ PHILADELPHIA POLICE DEPARTMENT DIRECTIVE 50 SUBJECT: INVESTIGATION AND CHARGING PROCEDURE

I. Policy

A. All adults arrested for a felony or misdemeanor offense will be investigated, processed and charged in accordance with the procedures outlined in this directive. . . .

C. The Complaint Fact Sheet (CFS) will serve as the police report for the District Attorney's Charging Unit (DACU). Prior to slating a defendant, the DACU should receive the CFS from the investigating unit to clarify certain facts or to supply needed information. . . .

E. The Criminal Complaint will be prepared and delivered to the Arraignment Court by the DACU.

II. Investigating Unit Procedure

A. The assigned investigator will prepare the following forms:

1. Arrest Report
2. Hearing Sheet
3. Investigator's Aid to Interview
4. Complaint Fact Sheet. . . .
5. Investigation Report

B. The assigned investigator will ensure that:

1. When charging a suspect with a misdemeanor or felony offense, appropriate summary offenses are included in the Arrest Reports and Complaint Fact Sheet. Substantiated facts and testimony will be included in these reports to support all charges listed. . . .

3. The CFS is promptly submitted to the unit supervisor for review. . . .

4. In division/units electronically equipped with a facsimile transceiver, the CFS will be transmitted to the DACU immediately after review and approval by the supervisor. . . .

C. The investigating unit supervisor will ensure that:

1. The Complaint Fact Sheet is properly prepared and the charges are appropriate for the facts and testimony as listed on the CFS.

2. Review and approve CFS.

3. The CFS is promptly transmitted to the DACU if electronically equipped to do so. . . .

6. When any charges are modified or disapproved by the DACU, attach the Record of Declination form (when received) to the CFS . . . , and submit to the commanding officer for review. . . .

D. Commanding Director of the Investigating Unit will [r]eview all modified and disapproved CFS and compare with submitted [CFS] for consistency [and forward] a memorandum through the chain of command describing any case where modification or disapproval appears to be totally unjustified or inconsistent with previous DACU decisions and policies.

■ HOUSTON POLICE DEPARTMENT GENERAL ORDER 500-7

Effective law enforcement requires cooperation between police officers and members of the district attorney's office. It is the purpose of this General Order to establish procedural guidelines for officers to use when consulting with the district attorney's office regarding the filing of charges.

1. Consultation with an Assistant District Attorney

Before using the computer terminal to file any charges with the district attorney's office, the officer filing the charges must speak with an assistant district attorney to ensure that the charges will be accepted. During the consultation, the officer shall provide the elements of the offense, sufficient details to show that probable cause existed to arrest the person and evidence that the person being charged did in fact commit the offense. These probable cause details should be included in the charges filed via the [computer]. It is important that an adequate probable-cause statement be contained in the warrant because this is sometimes the only information available to the assistant district attorney when the defendant is arraigned before a magistrate during a probable-cause hearing.

An assistant district attorney also will be consulted before the simultaneous filing of both county *and* municipal charges against *one* suspect if these charges are based on the same set of circumstances or the same criminal action. This consultation eliminates the possibility of a case being dismissed because of noncompliance with the Speedy Trial Act or because of violations of legal restraints against placing a defendant in double jeopardy.

Whenever an officer is unsure of the elements of a particular case, he shall discuss the matter with his immediate supervisor or contact the district attorney's office. Under no circumstances will a lesser charge be filed merely as a matter of convenience. For example, a charge of public intoxication will not be filed if the actual offense was driving while intoxicated. Appropriate charges shall be filed according to the elements of the offense.

2. Rejection of Charges by Assistant District Attorneys

If an officer tries to file charges through the district attorney's intake office and these charges are rejected, he will include the following information in his original or supplemental offense report: a) Time and date the officer spoke with the assistant district attorney about filing charges in the case; b) Name of the assistant district attorney who rejected the charges; [and] c) Reasons given by the assistant district attorney for rejecting the charges.

If the charges are rejected because of alleged mishandling by an officer, the officer will refer the case to his supervisor for review. If the supervisor does find mishandling on the part of the officer, he shall instruct the officer on policy and proper procedures, to avert recurrences. . . .

Notes

1. *Police screening.* Police departments have many different approaches to screening cases. Many departments do not openly acknowledge that officers screen cases *after* arrest, even though almost all police officials recognize the substantial discretion of police officers in making arrest decisions. See Chapter 5. Some departments train officers to select certain kinds of charges from among different possible charges. Other departments institute a formal screening process, either at the scene of an arrest or as part of the booking process at jail. This screening can take the form of review by a supervisor or by an officer trained to examine the facts of cases and the charges filed. Many departments establish methods of pretransfer review by prosecutors. Under the Philadelphia and Houston police department policies reprinted above, how early do prosecutors review the charges? Which system gives the police greater control over the selection of initial charges?

2. *Police courts.* For most of this century many larger cities utilized what were known as "police courts." These courts of limited jurisdiction heard charges brought by police for violations and sometimes for more serious offenses. Police courts were sometimes located at police headquarters. Officers would act not only as witnesses but also, in effect, as the prosecutor, making police decisions the only charging "screen." In Atlanta, the police court was not abolished until the mid-1970s, when prosecutors and then public defense appeared on the scene. The Atlanta Municipal Court — the successor to the police court — did not physically leave Atlanta police headquarters until the early 1990s. Fewer than 10 states still provide statutory authority for police courts. See, e.g., Wyo. Stat. §5-6-207; Andrew Horwitz, Taking the Cop Out of Copping a Plea: Eradicating Police Prosecution of Criminal Cases, 40 Ariz. L. Rev. 1305 (1998).

Police courts offered a highly tempered form of justice. They resolved cases quickly, but they collapsed in the face of new requirements for counsel and enforcement of rights to a trial by jury. Some hint of how police courts operated — and some suggestion of why they have largely disappeared — comes from reading the brief U.S. Supreme Court decision in Thompson v. Louisville, 362 U.S. 199 (1960). Sam Thompson, who committed the grave offense of dancing by himself one evening in a café after eating macaroni and drinking beer, was convicted in the Louisville police court of disorderly conduct and loitering and fined $10 on each charge. The Supreme Court reversed the conviction, in an opinion by Justice Black, noting that "although the fines here are small, the due process questions presented are substantial." The court observed that there was "no semblance of evidence" supporting either charge, and found it a "violation of due process to convict and punish a man without evidence of his guilt." What kind of court could convict a person on the basis of no evidence at all? What are the minimum procedural elements of a just criminal justice system?

3. *Police cautions in England.* Because the police in England make the initial decision whether to prosecute a criminal case, a practice has grown up (without a statutory basis) known as a "police caution." The caution is a warning to an arrested person, delivered by a senior police officer. If the person accepts the caution, the police

agree not to refer the case to the Crown Prosecution Service. The caution becomes part of the offender's prior record. The Home Secretary has issued "National Standards for Cautioning" to guide police decisions in this area. See Home Office Circular 18/1994, The Cautioning of Offenders; Andrew Ashworth, The Criminal Process (2d ed. 1998). Does the consent of the suspect (when he accepts a caution) make the caution fundamentally different from a conviction in police court?

4. *Screening and "the tank."* Police departments exercising a screening function may release a person under arrest before the time for an initial appearance. In the meantime, arrestees can spend one or two nights in the local jail or holding facility before release. What circumstances might properly lead a police department to arrest and then release a person without filing formal charges? Are the police effectively given the power to punish citizens for short periods of time without prosecutorial or judicial supervision? Should prosecutors review all arrests, even when the police department does not believe charges should be pursued?

B. PROSECUTORIAL SCREENING

Prosecutors (who go by various names, such as "district attorneys," "county attorneys," "state's attorneys," or simply "prosecuting attorneys") have the most to say about whether to file charges against a suspect and which charges to select. Granted, they react to an initial charge proposed by the police, and they may have to convince a judge or a grand jury that there is enough evidence to justify going forward with a prosecution. But in the end, the prosecutor can overrule police charging decisions without interference, and judges and grand juries only rarely refuse to go forward with the prosecutor's charging decisions.

The prosecutor's broad charging discretion has a long history in the common law, both in England and in the United States. Judges today explain their reluctance to become involved in charging decisions on three grounds: (1) under the separation of powers doctrine, the executive branch has the responsibility to enforce the criminal law; (2) judges are poorly situated to make judgments about allocation of limited prosecutorial resources; and (3) overbroad provisions in criminal codes require selection from among the possible charges that could be filed.

The charging decision is subject to some limits. The constraining rules come primarily from prosecutorial office policies, but they also appear at times in statutes and in a few judicial decisions. Even when charging decisions are not subject to such limits, external influences make them somewhat patterned and predictable. What considerations — both legal and otherwise — direct this prosecutorial decision?

1. Declination and Diversion

The initial question that a prosecutor faces is whether to file criminal charges at all. Many times when the police believe a person has committed a crime, the prosecutor "declines" to file charges. Prosecutors can also "divert" charges from the criminal process by suspending any decision about filing criminal charges while the potential defendant completes some agreed-upon rehabilitative or restitution program. If the person carries out the agreement, the prosecutor declines to file charges (or drops existing charges). If the defendant does not meet the conditions, the prosecutor goes forward with the charges. Are the legal and practical controls on declination and diversion decisions likely to be the same?

a. Declination Policies

Declinations are typically based on a prosecutor's ad hoc discretionary decision that the pursuit of criminal charges is not a good use of the limited resources of the office or is not a proper use of the criminal sanction. Sometimes, however, these discretionary decisions will develop into a pattern which may become formalized in internal office policies or rules. Chief prosecutors will at times create declination policies to control the decisions of the attorneys in the office. On rare occasions, statutes or judicial rulings require the creation of general policies to govern declinations.

The Justice Department produced the following document in response to two critical reports from the General Accounting Office, a research arm of Congress. The most controversial of those reports was titled, "U.S. Attorneys Do Not Prosecute Many Suspected Violators of Federal Law" (February 27, 1978). Does the following report answer the evident concerns of the GAO?

■ U.S. DEPARTMENT OF JUSTICE UNITED STATES ATTORNEYS' WRITTEN GUIDELINES FOR THE DECLINATION OF ALLEGED VIOLATIONS OF FEDERAL CRIMINAL LAWS

A Report to the United States Congress (November 1979)

This report examines the written guidelines issued by various United States Attorneys concerning the types of alleged violations of federal criminal laws they will normally decline to prosecute. . . . They are promulgated by United States Attorneys, with the Department's knowledge and encouragement, as a means of formalizing and crystallizing prosecutorial priorities, thereby increasing the effectiveness of limited prosecutorial and investigative resources. Written guidelines represent United States Attorneys' attempts to respond to local demands and circumstances within the context of national law enforcement priorities. They are typically formulated after consideration of Department policies and consultation with federal investigative agencies. . . .

Although written declination guidelines are sometimes referred to as "blanket" declinations, they are, either explicitly or implicitly, made subject to the caveat that unusual or aggravating circumstances should always be considered before any complaint is declined. Decisions to decline cases pursuant to written guidelines are also typically subject to reconsideration, for example, if matters are referred to state and local prosecutors and declined or not pursued by them. In addition, alleged offenses that would otherwise be subject to the guidelines may be prosecuted in clusters at a later date if enough similar offenses accumulate and prosecution would have a significant deterrent impact.

Written declination guidelines are applied with varying degrees of frequency to different categories of federal criminal offenses. [They] are usually expressed in terms of the amount of money or value of property involved, whether the offense appears to be connected with other criminal activity, or other similar factors. The ranges and distributions of declination "cut-off points" vary across districts. For some offenses, the declination cut-off points of the various districts congregate around similar values and factors, while for others, the declination guidelines show considerable variation among districts. . . . Of the 94 United States Attorneys' offices, 83 reported written declination guidelines in some form. The remaining 11 offices reported that they did not have written guidelines, but instead made all declination decisions on a case-by-case basis.

[D]eclination policies are a crucial part of the investigative and prosecutorial system. Investigators and prosecutors alike rely upon such policies to help channel limited law enforcement resources toward their most productive uses. Indeed, since law enforcement resources are limited, it is clearly impossible to investigate and prosecute every alleged criminal violation. Some priorities are required to reduce wastage and to increase the effective deployment of scarce investigative and prosecutorial time and effort. . .

Written Declination Guidelines Currently in Use by United States Attorneys

The specific written declination guidelines supplied by U.S. Attorneys were applicable to 42 categories of criminal offenses. [F]or a number of categories of offenses, only a few districts have written declination guidelines. For other types of offenses, written guidelines are very frequently in force. The following 11 categories of offenses are the ones most frequently made subject to written guidelines by U.S. Attorneys:

Categories of Criminal Offenses Most Frequently Subject to Written Declination Guidelines

Category of Offense	Number of Districts with Written Declination Policies
1. Theft from Interstate Shipment	61
2. Interstate Transportation of Stolen Property	51
3. Bank Fraud and Embezzlement	51
4. Forgery of U.S. Treasury Checks	51
5. Theft of Government Property	48
6. Dyer Act: Interstate Transportation of a Stolen Vehicle	45
7. Crimes on Government Reservations	36
8. Bank Robbery and Related Offenses	33
9. Fraud Against the Government	28
10. Drug Offenses	24
11. Immigration and Naturalization — Illegal Aliens	24

A review of the written declination policies for various offenses indicates a number of general characteristics:

- Written guidelines are typically categorized by the type of criminal offense or the statutory provisions involved. . . .

- Written guidelines are more prevalent for non-violent criminal offenses, though some exist for violent crimes.
- Written guidelines are usually expressed in terms of the gravity of the alleged offense, the history and circumstances of the defendant involved, and the connection of the alleged offense to a pattern of illegal activity.
- Other frequently mentioned declination determining factors include the sufficiency and strength of the Government's evidence and the availability of alternatives to federal prosecution.

The most frequently used measurement of the gravity of the offense is the value of property or loss involved. Using Theft from Interstate Shipment as an example, the value of property involved is used by 52 of 61 districts as a declination-determining factor. . . . Written declination guidelines [use varying] ranges and distributions of declination cut-off points (e.g., monetary value, quantity of drugs) from district to district and from offense to offense. The variation among districts is illustrated again by the policies with respect to Theft from Interstate Shipment. [T]he range of declination cut-off points goes from $100 to $5,000 in property value, with many districts clustered around $500 (15 districts), $1,000 (11 districts), and $5,000 (10 districts). The declination cut-off points for other offenses are differently distributed across ranges of differing size. . . .

■ STATEMENT OF ASSISTANT ATTORNEY GENERAL PHILIP HEYMANN

Before the Committee on the Judiciary of the United States Senate (April 23, 1980)

Winning convictions is only half of a prosecutor's job. Equally vital is to sort out which cases to prosecute and which to decline.

Declinations are the rule, not the exception. Of 171,000 criminal matters referred to federal prosecutors in Fiscal Year 1976, 108,000 were declined — a declination rate of 63 percent. Many other uncounted declinations are made by the investigative agencies, in accord with guidelines agreed on with federal prosecutors.

Cases are declined for a variety of reasons. The first is scarcity of resources; the federal system cannot handle every allegation of a federal criminal violation generated in a country of 200 million people. We try to make our resources have the most effect by selecting areas where deterrence is especially important, where the federal interest is the greatest, cases of the greatest culpability and cases where we have a good chance of winning. To conserve resources, we will often defer to state and local prosecution, or in appropriate cases of lesser culpability, to administrative discipline by a suspect's employer or professional association.

The more important reason for declining is lack of merit in the prosecution. Often, upon investigation, we discover that there simply is no evidence supporting the initial allegation. In other cases the available evidence turns out to be weak; there is a vast difference between making an allegation and mustering sufficient proof to convince 12 jurors beyond a reasonable doubt. Declining a weak case is part of the prosecutor's duty of fairness, for the burdens of indictment and trial were never intended to be a form of curbstone punishment to be used without a reasonable chance of securing a conviction. Declining weak cases is also important because too many losses at trial would seriously weaken the credibility of the Department's future prosecutions. . . .

Judging what is a weak case is partly a technical evaluation of the evidence—what witnesses are likely to be available, what they will testify to and with what credibility. It is also a matter of gauging whether the jury is likely to be impressed by the wrongfulness of the defendant's conduct. The phenomenon of jury nullification is not unknown in the federal system and elements of a crime such as "corrupt intent" provide another way for jurors to act on their assessment of the wrongfulness of conduct. . . .

It is important to have public support and understanding of this part of the job of prosecutors and investigators. . . . Without pubic understanding of the declination function, the temptation always will be to prolong investigations that deserve to be closed, to reveal information that should be kept a confidential part of the investigative process, even to charge and prosecute where no indictment deserves to be brought.

[T]here are a number of common reasons why the declination function may have been misunderstood. First, that declinations are so common an occurrence in law enforcement is a fact frankly unfamiliar to many citizens, legislators and writers. For instance, when GAO published a study two years ago describing the 63 percent declination rate common to federal prosecutors, several Committees in the House and Senate issued a request for a study of "recommendations for improving the percentage of such [criminal] complaints which are prosecuted by the Department."

Second, it can be hard to keep in clear view the difference between scandalous behavior and criminal behavior, and the difference between suspecting criminal behavior and proving it—particularly when a matter is being discussed in the non-technical confines of a journal or newspaper. When we pursue an investigation, often we find that the suspect behaved badly, may even have acted like a scoundrel, and yet has not committed a federal criminal violation. . . . Sometimes we end up at the conclusion of an investigation strongly suspecting that a person is guilty of a criminal offense, but unable to assemble adequate admissible evidence. Keeping these distinctions in mind is essential in understanding that a declination does not amount to approval or condoning of the examined behavior.

Another cause of potential misunderstanding is that we can't talk very much about our declinations. Investigative information is generally to be presented in court or not at all. By law we can't make grand jury information public, and by ethical practice, to protect privacy, we generally refrain from disclosing other investigative information except in the confines of an indictment and trial or in response to oversight requests from the Congress on closed cases. Certainly, as an agency following the rule of law, we have no business broadcasting our "suspicions" or "hunches" about guilt. So the public is often not given any detailed information on the reason for a declination; they simply learn that an investigation of an obvious scoundrel has been closed. This may contribute to suspicion that the real reason for the declination is political. . . .

I do not make light of the public's responsibility for scrutinizing the actions of law enforcement and prosecutorial agencies. That is a very strong long-term safeguard against abuse. But at the same time, we must avoid creating a system in which the only incentive is to prosecute, no matter how weak or nonexistent the case. . . . When we decline to prosecute unmeritorious cases, it is as much a part of a system of justice as when we prosecute the guilty.

■ REVISED CODE OF WASHINGTON §9.94A.411(1)

STANDARD

A prosecuting attorney may decline to prosecute, even though technically sufficient evidence to prosecute exists, in situations where prosecution would serve no public purpose, would defeat the underlying purpose of the law in question or would result in decreased respect for the law.

GUIDELINE/COMMENTARY

. . . The following are examples of reasons not to prosecute which could satisfy the standard.

(a) Contrary to Legislative Intent — It may be proper to decline to charge where the application of criminal sanctions would be clearly contrary to the intent of the legislature in enacting the particular statute.

(b) Antiquated Statute — It may be proper to decline to charge where the statute in question is antiquated in that: (i) it has not been enforced for many years; and (ii) most members of society act as if it were no longer in existence; and (iii) it serves no deterrent or protective purpose in today's society; and (iv) the statute has not been recently reconsidered by the legislature. This reason is not to be construed as the basis for declining cases because the law in question is unpopular or because it is difficult to enforce.

(c) De Minimus Violation — It may be proper to decline to charge where the violation of law is only technical or insubstantial and where no public interest or deterrent purpose would be served by prosecution.

(d) Confinement on Other Charges — It may be proper to decline to charge because the accused has been sentenced on another charge to a lengthy period of confinement; and (i) conviction of the new offense would not merit any additional direct or collateral punishment; (ii) the new offense is either a misdemeanor or a felony which is not particularly aggravated; and (iii) conviction of the new offense would not serve any significant deterrent purpose.

(e) Pending Conviction on Another Charge — It may be proper to decline to charge because the accused is facing a pending prosecution in the same or another county; and (i) conviction of the new offense would not merit any additional direct or collateral punishment; (ii) conviction in the pending prosecution is imminent; (iii) the new offense is either a misdemeanor or a felony which is not particularly aggravated; and (iv) conviction of the new offense would not serve any significant deterrent purpose.

(f) High Disproportionate Cost of Prosecution — It may be proper to decline to charge where the cost of locating or transporting, or the burden on, prosecution witnesses is highly disproportionate to the importance of prosecuting the offense in question. This reason should be limited to minor cases and should not be relied upon in serious cases.

(g) Improper Motives of Complainant — It may be proper to decline charges because the motives of the complainant are improper and prosecution would serve no public purpose, would defeat the underlying purpose of the law in question or would result in decreased respect for the law.

(h) Immunity — It may be proper to decline to charge where immunity is to be given to an accused in order to prosecute another where the accused's information or testimony will reasonably lead to the conviction of others who are responsible for more serious criminal conduct or who represent a greater danger to the public interest.

(i) Victim Request — It may be proper to decline to charge because the victim requests that no criminal charges be filed and the case involves the following crimes or situations: (i) assault cases where the victim has suffered little or no injury; (ii) crimes against property, not involving violence, where no major loss was suffered; (iii) where doing so would not jeopardize the safety of society. Care should be taken to insure that the victim's request is freely made and is not the product of threats or pressure by the accused. . . . The prosecutor is encouraged to notify the victim, when practical, and the law enforcement personnel, of the decision not to prosecute.

Notes

1. *Number of declinations.* The precise number of criminal matters that are declined for prosecution each year is hard to pin down. In the federal system, where the best data are available, U.S. Attorneys' offices decline to prosecute a large proportion of criminal matters they receive. In 1999, federal prosecutors filed charges in district court in 60 percent of the "criminal matters" referred to them for investigation or prosecution. They declined to prosecute 27 percent of the matters and referred 13 percent of the suspects to federal magistrates (who handle misdemeanors and charges that are ultimately dismissed and prosecuted instead in state court). Bureau of Justice Statistics, Compendium of Federal Justice Statistics, 1999 table 2.2, NCJ-186179 (April 2001). This estimate of the number of declinations did not include minor matters which occupied less than one hour of a prosecutor's time. If these were included in the overall base of cases, the percentage of declinations would rise sharply. For instance, in a classic 1980 study of declinations in the federal system, Richard Frase calculated that U.S. Attorneys nationwide filed criminal cases in 20 percent to 23.4 percent of the "criminal matters received" during 1974-1978. The district Frase studied most closely, the Northern District of Illinois, prosecuted about 17 percent of all matters received and 21 percent of all suspects. See Richard Frase, The Decision to File Federal Criminal Charges: A Quantitative Study of Prosecutorial Discretion, 47 U. Chi. L. Rev. 246 (1980).

The level of declinations varies a good deal depending on the offense involved. In 1999, federal prosecutors declined to file charges in 21 percent of the robbery cases they received, 17 percent of the drug cases received, 46 percent of the fraud cases, 3 percent of the immigration cases, and 93 percent of the civil rights cases.

The number of declinations in the typical state system also makes up a significant proportion of the criminal matters that a prosecutor's office handles. Among felony defendants in large urban counties in 1998, charges were dismissed for 27 percent of all defendants initially charged with a felony. Bureau of Justice Statistics, Felony Defendants in Large Urban Counties, 1998, at table 23, NCJ-187232 (November 2001). Of course, the dismissal rate does not capture the total number of *arrests* declined for prosecution. Earlier studies have estimated that more than 40 percent of all felony arrests are declined for prosecution, while a similarly large group of felony arrestees are ultimately charged with misdemeanors. See Vera Institute of Justice, Felony Arrests: Their Prosecution and Disposition in New York City's

Courts (Malcolm Feeley ed., rev. ed. 1980). See also Donald McIntyre and David Lippmann, Prosecutors and Early Disposition of Felony Cases, 56 A.B.A. J. 1154 (1970) (estimating for Los Angeles a declination rate of 50 percent of felony arrests; 30 percent in Detroit; 25 percent in Houston; virtually no declinations reported in Chicago, Brooklyn, or Baltimore, but prosecutors in each of these cities screen out large proportion of arrests at preliminary judicial hearing).

2. *Reasons for declinations.* The reasons why individual prosecutors decline to file charges are even more elusive than the number of declinations they make. Over the years, several scholars, commissions, and associations have described some common reasons for individual prosecutors to choose not to file criminal charges in a particular case. Frank Miller offered one such typology of reasons *why* prosecutors decline charges, listing attitude of victim, cost to the system, undue harm to the suspect, adequacy of alternative procedures, and willingness of suspect to cooperate in achieving other enforcement goals. See Miller, Prosecution: The Decision to Charge a Suspect with a Crime (1969). The National District Attorneys Association, in its National Prosecution Standards, §42.3 (2d ed. 1991), lists several possible grounds for a prosecutor to decline a criminal case, including "doubt as to the accused's guilt," "possible improper motives of a victim or witness," "undue hardship caused to the accused," "the expressed desire of an accused to release potential civil claims against victims, witnesses, law enforcement agencies and their personnel, and the prosecutor and his personnel," and "any mitigating circumstances." How do these reasons compare to those in the Washington statute reprinted above?

How often do prosecutors actually rely on these plausible reasons for declination? In 1999, federal prosecutors gave the following reasons for their declinations: no crime committed (22 percent of the declinations), matter handled in other prosecutions (21 percent), pretrial diversion (2.5 percent), weak evidence (21 percent), minimal federal interest (4 percent), U.S. Attorney policy (5 percent), lack of resources (4 percent), and several others. Richard Frase reviewed screening documents for one U.S. Attorney's office that required the prosecutor to specify a reason for declining a prosecution. He found that the most common explanations for declining to prosecute on federal charges were the availability of state prosecution (26 percent) and insufficient evidence (10 percent). Once again, data for state systems are sketchier. One older study pointed to insufficient evidence connecting the suspect to the alleged crime as the leading reason for rejections of felony charges in Los Angeles County. Peter Greenwood et al., Prosecution of Adult Felony Defendants in Los Angeles County: A Policy Perspective 66-68 (1973) (overall rejection rate of 45 percent of complaints).

3. *Declination policies versus ad hoc judgments.* Although most declination decisions fall within the discretion of the individual prosecutor, many offices develop written policies to govern the declination decision for at least some types of cases. For example, federal prosecutors in Southern California have determined, in evaluating possible immigration crimes, that "criminal charges shall not be filed in cases where the defendant makes an unaggravated illegal entry and has no prior criminal record." What do you suppose would be the purpose of such a policy? The U.S. Department of Justice also has written guidelines to govern the charging of corporate entities. The National District Attorneys Association, in its National Prosecution Standards (2d ed. 1991), declares that "The decision to initiate or pursue criminal charges should be within the discretion of the prosecutor . . . and whether the screening takes place before or after formal charging, it should be pursuant to the

prosecutor's established guidelines." In speaking of "discretion" and "guidelines," is this Standard sending an inconsistent message? The Washington statute reprinted above is one of the few legislative efforts to establish criteria for declination decisions. Is a legislature likely to produce declination guidelines that look different from guidelines that a prosecutor's office develops for its own use? What do you imagine is the attitude of Washington prosecutors about the declination statute? The same Washington statute provides that "crimes against persons will be filed if sufficient admissible evidence exists, which, when considered with the most plausible, reasonably foreseeable defense that could be raised under the evidence, would justify conviction by a reasonable and objective fact-finder." See Wash. Rev. Stat. 9.94A.411(2). How can this provision be reconciled with the declination provision printed in text?

4. *Judicial review of declinations and decisions to file charges.* Judges might overturn a prosecutor's decision to file charges or not to file charges, but only in rare circumstances. See State v. Foss, 556 N.W.2d 540 (Minn. 1996) (acknowledging power of trial court to stay adjudication of guilt over prosecutor's objection in "special circumstances"; such circumstances existed in earlier case involving consensual sex with 14-year-old when victim and her mother did not desire criminal prosecution, but no special circumstances exist in typical misdemeanor assault case). Although a strong minority of states have statutes explicitly authorizing a judge to order a prosecutor to file and prosecute criminal charges, judges have interpreted these statutes to allow judicial review only under very deferential standards of review. See Colo. Rev. Stat. §16-5-209 (judge may order prosecution if refusal to prosecute was "arbitrary or capricious and without reasonable excuse"); Tooley v. District Court, 549 P.2d 772 (Colo. 1976) (court may not reverse prosecutor's decision absent "clear and convincing evidence" that the decision was arbitrary or capricious). Legislatures have been more willing to give judges power to review a prosecutor's *refusal* to prosecute than a prosecutor's decision to *file* charges. Why?

5. *Public reasons.* Most larger prosecutors' offices require the prosecutor who declines to file charges to give reasons in some written form in the case file. What purposes might the requirement of written reasons serve? If, as chief prosecutor, you supervised an office that had an explicit declination policy, would you reveal to the public the terms of your policy? A few states (but a growing number) have statutes requiring a prosecutor to explain in writing each refusal to prosecute a case. See Mich. Stat. §767.41; Neb. Rev. Stat. §29-1606; Pa. R. Crim. P. 133(b)(2).

6. *Enforceable reasons.* If an individual prosecutor appears to be violating a known office policy by filing criminal charges when the policy calls for declination, can the defendant convince a court to enforce the policy? See United States v. Caceres, 440 U.S. 741 (1979) (defendant may not enforce internal rules of law enforcement agency, such as IRS rule requiring internal approval before eavesdropping). Would the result depend on whether the policy includes an explicit disclaimer that it does not create any enforceable rights? On whether it is written? Are written policies a meaningful limit on prosecutorial choices if defendants cannot enforce them? See Kenneth Culp Davis, Discretionary Justice (1969); Gerard E. Lynch, Our Administrative System of Criminal Justice, 66 Fordham L. Rev. 2117 (1998).

7. *Consultation before charging.* A declination policy is only one method of discouraging the use of criminal charges for specific types of cases. Prosecutors' offices will sometimes adopt policies requiring the "line" prosecutors to consult with

supervisors or others in the office with special expertise before filing criminal charges under certain statutes. See U.S. Attorneys' Manual §9-2.400 (requiring line prosecutor to consult with supervisors before filing charges against member of news media or for desecration of flag, draft evasion, obscenity, RICO, and other offenses). Is it possible to predict which offenses are most likely to be singled out for a prior consultation requirement?

8. *Dismissals after charges are filed.* At English common law, the power of the prosecutor to dismiss a charge — to enter a plea of *nolle prosequi*— was every bit as broad as the discretion to file charges initially. An illustration of this power appears in the following conversation between an advocate, Lacy, and Chief Justice John Holt in seventeenth-century England. Lacy asked the chief justice to dismiss seditious libel charges against other members of his religious sect:

Lacy: I come to you, a prophet from the Lord God, who has sent me to thee, and would have thee grant a nolle prosequi for John Atkins, His servant, whom thou hast cast into prison.

Chief Justice Holt: Thou art a false prophet, and a lying knave. If the Lord God had sent thee, it would have been to the attorney general, for He knows that it belongeth not to the Chief Justice to grant a nolle prosequi; but I, as Chief Justice, can grant a warrant to commit thee to bear him company.

See 2 Francis Wharton, A Treatise on Criminal Procedure §1310 (10th ed. 1918). This common-law rule on dismissals took hold in the United States and was especially useful in systems that allowed private prosecutors to file charges without consulting the public prosecutor. Today, however, a strong majority of jurisdictions (more than 30) give prosecutors less control over dismissals than over the initial decision whether to charge. They require the prosecutor to state reasons and obtain the leave of the court before dismissing charges. See Tenn. Code §40-2101; Fed. R. Crim. P. 48(a) (indictment, information or complaint can be dismissed "with leave of court"). For reasons you can well imagine, judges rarely deny a prosecutor's motion to dismiss charges.

9. *Prosecutorial policy and office size.* The size and structure of the prosecutor's office determines to some extent whether explicit declination policies will be in place and what topics the policies will address. As of 2001, the chief prosecutors in 47 of the 50 states were elected locally, most for four-year terms. Full-time prosecutors' offices in jurisdictions with large populations (one million persons or more) had a median of 151 assistant prosecutors; nationwide, the median prosecutor's office employed eight assistant prosecutors. Bureau of Justice Statistics, Prosecutors in State Courts, 2001, NCJ-193441 (May 2002). Prosecutors in the state system are decentralized to a great extent. In a few states, however, the state attorney general has some supervisory control over local prosecutorial decisions. See Conn. Gen. Stat. Ann. §§51-275 to 51-277. What effects will a decentralized structure have on the declination policies to be adopted or followed in prosecutors' offices?

b. Diversion of Defendants

Prosecutors file charges in some cases and decline to charge in others, but they have other options as well. The prosecutor may, for example, "divert" the suspect from the criminal justice system into an alternative program for rehabilitation and restitution. Diversion occurs in some states before charges are ever filed: The prosecutor agrees to withhold any criminal charges, provided the suspect successfully completes the designated program or other conditions that the prosecutor specifies. Diversion can also take place after charges are filed, in which case the prosecution is suspended while the defendant completes the diversion program. If the defendant succeeds, the prosecutor dismisses the criminal charges. The archetypal "diversion" case involves a first-time offender who has committed a nonviolent crime. Some diversion programs explicitly focus on classes of offenders, such as nonviolent drug offenders.

As you read the following materials, consider whether the prosecutor is properly situated to identify "good" cases for diversion and to set the proper conditions for a successful diversion program. Will a prosecutor systematically place requirements on a defendant that a judge at sentencing would not? Will defendants respond differently to diversion programs than they would to requirements imposed at sentencing after a conviction?

■ MONTANA CODE §46-16-130

(1) (a) Prior to the filing of a charge, the prosecutor and a defendant who has counsel or who has voluntarily waived counsel may agree to the deferral of a prosecution for a specified period of time based on one or more of the following conditions:

(i) that the defendant may not commit any offense;

(ii) that the defendant may not engage in specified activities, conduct, and associations bearing a relationship to the conduct upon which the charge against the defendant is based;

(iii) that the defendant shall participate in a supervised rehabilitation program, which may include treatment, counseling, training, or education;

(iv) that the defendant shall make restitution in a specified manner for harm or loss caused by the offense; or

(v) any other reasonable conditions.

(b) The agreement must be in writing, must be signed by the parties, and must state that the defendant waives the right to speedy trial for the period of deferral. The agreement may include stipulations concerning the admissibility of evidence, specified testimony, or dispositions if the deferral of the prosecution is terminated and there is a trial on the charge.

(c) The prosecution must be deferred for the period specified in the agreement unless there has been a violation of its terms.

(d) The agreement must be terminated and the prosecution automatically dismissed with prejudice upon expiration and compliance with the terms of the agreement. . . .

(3) After a charge has been filed, a deferral of prosecution may be entered into only with the approval of the court.

(4) A prosecution for a violation of [laws that prohibit driving while impaired] may not be deferred.

Montana Commission on Criminal Procedure: Comments

A provision regulating pretrial diversion, sometimes called deferred prosecution, is new to Montana, although the practice has been statutorily recognized since at least 1979. The Commission believed a pretrial diversion provision was necessary because prosecutors have long employed diversion on an informal, individual basis by deferring prosecution if, for example, the accused agreed to undergo rehabilitative treatment. Since the President's Commission on Law Enforcement and Administration of Justice recommended such programs in its 1967 report, many states have formalized diversion by statute or court rule. Pretrial diversionary programs are premised on the belief that it is not always necessary and, in fact, may often be detrimental to pursue formal courtroom prosecution for every criminal violation. In most situations, the criminal prosecution is suspended subject to the defendant's consent to treatment, rehabilitation, restitution, or other noncriminal or nonpunitive alternatives.

The statute contemplates that the decision to divert lies with the prosecutor in an exercise of his powers and is not ordinarily subject to judicial review. This conforms with existing practice in that several Montana County Attorneys conduct formal diversion programs, yet no Montana case has been found that discusses the practice. However, some litigation has occurred in other jurisdictions. . . .

■ STATE v. WALLACE BAYNES

690 A.2d 594 (N.J. 1997)

Garibaldi, J.

The Court again addresses whether a trial court correctly reversed a prosecutor's rejection of a defendant's admission into a Pretrial Intervention (PTI) Program. In particular, we must determine whether the Monmouth County prosecutor's decision, based on his stated policy of denying admission into PTI to any defendant charged with possession of a controlled dangerous substance within 1,000 feet of a school zone, constitutes a "patent and gross abuse of discretion."

The facts of this case are undisputed. On September 28, 1994, at approximately 5:30 P.M., defendant, Wallace Baynes, purchased .44 grams of heroin from Jose Morales. The purchase was made outside of the Rainbow Liquor Store, [which was under police surveillance at the time.] The location of the purchase occurred approximately 900 feet from the Garfield Primary School. Baynes was arrested and subsequently indicted [for possession of heroin within 1,000 feet of a school zone]. Drug possession is a third-degree crime.

Defendant claims that he purchased the heroin because he was having difficulty dealing with the serious illness of his mother, who has since passed away. At the time of his application for admission into the Monmouth County Pretrial Intervention Program, defendant was a 43-year-old gainfully employed father of one, residing with and supporting his elderly mother and his 17-year-old son. He had completed two years of college. According to defendant, he had been employed by the same employer for the previous nine years. . . .

The Director of the PTI program accepted Baynes's application for admission. Further, the head of the narcotics team that arrested Baynes did not object to Baynes's diversion. The prosecutor, however, advised Baynes in an April 27, 1995, memorandum that his PTI application was rejected because of that prosecutor's acknowledged policy to deny PTI admission to defendants charged with "school zone offenses," including those involving possession of controlled dangerous substances (CDS) for personal use.

On June 23, 1995, a hearing was held before the trial court for reconsideration of the prosecutor's decision. In reversing the prosecutor's decision and referring the matter back to the prosecutor for reconsideration, the court observed that "the prosecutor [had failed] to consider all the relevant factors" in this case. The decision to refer the matter back to the prosecutor follows our past decisions, finding remand to the prosecutor useful where "the prosecutorial decision was based upon a consideration of inappropriate factors or not premised upon a consideration of all relevant factors. . . ." State v. Bender, 402 A.2d 217 (N.J. 1979).

In a letter to the trial court, the prosecutor advised the court that he had reviewed all the information again and continued to oppose defendant's diversion into PTI. After a second hearing appealing that decision, the trial court ordered Baynes's admission into the PTI program over the prosecutor's objection, stating that [the prosecutor's decision was] "so clearly unreasonable that it shocks the judicial conscience, subverts the goals of PTI, and constitutes a clear error of judgment because it could not have reasonably been made upon a fair weighing of all relevant factors." . . .

PTI is a diversionary program through which certain offenders are able to avoid criminal prosecution by receiving early rehabilitative services expected to deter future criminal behavior. [The Supreme Court initially established PTI by Rule 3:28 in 1970, creating] the vocational-service pretrial intervention program operated by the Newark Defendants Employment Project. By October 1976, the Court had approved programs for 12 counties. In 1979, the Legislature authorized a state-wide PTI program as part of the Criminal Code of Justice. The Code provisions generally mirrored the procedures and guidelines previously established under Rule 3:28.

Admission into PTI is based on a recommendation by the criminal division manager, as Director of the PTI Program, with the consent of the prosecutor. The Court has provided criteria for making PTI decisions in its Guidelines for Operation of Pretrial Intervention. Guidelines 1, 2, 3, and 8 are particularly relevant to this case. Guideline 1 sets forth the purposes of PTI:

> (1) to enable defendants to avoid ordinary prosecution by receiving early rehabilitative services expected to deter future criminal behavior; (2) to provide defendants who might be harmed by the imposition of criminal sanctions with an alternative to prosecution expected to deter criminal conduct; (3) to avoid burdensome prosecutions for "victimless" offenses; (4) to relieve overburdened criminal calendars so that resources can be expended on more serious criminal matters; and (5) to deter future criminal behavior of PTI participants.

Guideline 2 provides that "[a]ny defendant accused of crime shall be eligible for admission into a PTI program." Thus, . . . PTI decisions are primarily individualistic in nature and a prosecutor must consider an individual defendant's features that bear on his or her amenability to rehabilitation.

Guideline 3 refers to and supplements N.J.S.A. 2C:43-12(e), which presents 17 criteria that prosecutors and criminal division managers are to consider in formulating their PTI recommendation. Guideline 3(i) clarifies how "the nature of the offense" is to be used in assessing a defendant's PTI eligibility. That guideline explains that although all defendants are eligible for enrollment in a PTI program, the nature of the crime is only one factor to be considered. Moreover, Guideline 3(i) states that there is a presumption against acceptance into a program when "the crime was (1) part of organized criminal activity; or (2) part of a continuing criminal business or enterprise; or (3) deliberately committed with violence or threat of violence against another person; or (4) a breach of the public trust." A presumption against acceptance into a PTI program also exists when the defendant is "charged with a first or second degree offense or sale or dispensing of Schedule I or II narcotic drugs [and is] not drug dependent." Finally, Guideline 8 requires a judge, prosecutor, or criminal division manager, making a PTI decision, to provide the defendant with a statement of reasons justifying the decision, as well as demonstrating that all of the facts have been considered. That statement may not simply parrot the language of relevant statutes, rules, and guidelines. Additionally, the statement cannot be vague; it must be sufficiently specific to provide the defendant with an opportunity to demonstrate that the reasons are unfounded.

The decision to divert a defendant from criminal prosecution implicates both judicial and prosecutorial functions. . . . Judicial review of the prosecutor's PTI decision is strictly limited, but necessary because "PTI involves far more than merely an exercise of the charging function." State v. Leonardis, 375 A.2d 607 (N.J. 1977). "It is one thing not to charge and let the accused go totally free, but it may be quite another to withhold a charge, and hence not to invoke the jurisdiction of the court system, on condition that an uncharged, untried, unconvicted person submit to a correctional program."

[Our expectation is] that a prosecutor's decision to reject a PTI applicant will rarely be overturned. A prosecutor's decision is to be afforded great deference. In fact, the level of deference which is required is so high that it has been categorized as "enhanced deference" or "extra deference." Absent evidence to the contrary, a reviewing court must assume that all relevant factors were considered by the prosecutor's office. That presumption makes it difficult to reverse a prosecutor's decision. A reviewing court may order a defendant into PTI over the prosecutor's objection, only if the defendant can clearly and convincingly establish that the prosecutor's refusal to sanction admission into the program was based on a patent and gross abuse of discretion. In State v. Bender, 402 A.2d 217, 222 (N.J. 1979), the Court defined the "patent and gross abuse of discretion" standard:

> Ordinarily, an abuse of discretion will be manifest if defendant can show that a prosecutorial veto (a) was not premised upon a consideration of all relevant factors, (b) was based upon a consideration of irrelevant or inappropriate factors, or (c) amounted to a clear error in judgment. In order for such an abuse of discretion to rise to the level of "patent and gross," it must further be shown that the prosecutorial error complained of will clearly subvert the goals underlying Pretrial Intervention. . . .

In this case, the prosecutor's rejection of Baynes's PTI application falls under categories (a) and (c), as set forth in *Bender*. First, the prosecutor's rejection in this case was not based on all of the relevant factors. After the initial remand for reconsideration by the trial court, the prosecutor claimed to have considered all of the relevant factors. We do not doubt his veracity, in the sense that he re-read the application and the police report. He could not, however, have considered all relevant factors, because the per se rule under which he made his decision had effectively denied Baynes's application from the moment Baynes was charged with possession of CDS in a school zone.

By their nature, per se rules require prosecutors to disregard relevant factors, contrary to the guidelines, and when a defendant demonstrates that a prosecutor has relied on such a rule, the presumption that the prosecutor has considered all relevant facts is overcome. As a result, the June 23, 1995, memorandum denying Baynes's application was merely an impermissible "parrot-like" recitation of the language of relevant statutes, rules, and guidelines.

The State correctly points out that prosecutors may rely on the nature of the offense, in "appropriate circumstances," as the sole basis for making PTI decisions. Although caselaw supports the proposition that certain offensive conduct can outweigh all other factors considered, no court has indicated that possession of CDS for personal use is an "appropriate circumstance" that alone can justify denying PTI.

Where courts have found a prosecutor's reliance on the nature of the offense charged to be an appropriate basis for a PTI decision, the crime was of a more serious nature than possession of CDS for personal use. In State v. Wallace, 684 A.2d 1355 (N.J. 1996), for example, . . . Wallace had entered his former girlfriend's house with a loaded gun and threatened to kill her. He was charged with second-degree possession of a firearm for an unlawful purpose and third-degree making of terroristic threats. In supporting her decision, . . . the prosecutor primarily relied on a prosecutorial guideline that discourages PTI for those defendants charged with either first- or second-degree offenses [or criminal acts committed with violence].

Under the caselaw of this jurisdiction, it is, therefore, appropriate for prosecutors to base their rejections solely on the nature of an offense for which the Guidelines express a presumption against admission. . . . Our prior opinions indicate that possession of CDS for personal consumption does not fall into [this category].

In addition to satisfying the first category of abuse of discretion set forth in *Bender,* the prosecutor's veto also fulfills the third, i.e. it was a "clear error in judgment." A prosecutor will be found to have made a "clear error in judgment," when the decision was premised on appropriate factors and rationally explained but is contrary to the predominate views of others responsible for the administration of justice. Although a reviewing court cannot substitute its own judgment for that of the prosecutor, others responsible for the administration of justice in New Jersey hold contrary views of how first-time offenders charged with possession of drugs for personal use should, as a class, be treated.

The 1987 Comprehensive Drug Reform Act simply does not indicate the intent prescribed to it by the Monmouth County prosecutor. [T]he Legislature created a new crime, covering possession with intent to distribute or actual distribution of drugs in a school zone. Under that section, proof that the offensive conduct occurred within a school zone is an element of the offense, and if the defendant is found guilty a jail term must be imposed as well as a minimum term. The penalty structure for this type of offense is similar to that for second-degree offenses for which admission to PTI is presumptively unavailable.

Possession of CDS in a school zone, on the other hand, is not a separate crime. Rather, it is a sentencing factor that requires the court to impose 100 hours of community service as a condition of probation if the defendant is not given a prison term. . . .

The Monmouth County Prosecutor's Office is the only prosecutor's office in the State to have adopted the policy that a simple possession offense makes a defendant ineligible for admission into PTI. Nor has the Attorney General adopted such a policy. [A 1997 Directive from the Attorney General] prohibits a prosecutor from consenting to PTI for a person charged with simple possession of drugs within 1,000 feet of school property unless, as a condition of PTI, the defendant serves not less than 100 hours of community service and pays a Drug Enforcement and Demand Reduction penalty. . . . Clearly, that policy is inconsistent with the Monmouth County prosecutor's policy of excluding from PTI all defendants charged with simple possession of drugs in a school zone. In fact, early diversion programs were begun in many jurisdictions in order to cope with both the non-addict first offender and the drug-dependent defendant.

As a first-time offender charged with a non-violent, third-degree offense, Baynes is eligible for diversion into the PTI program. By abandoning his discretion in favor of a per se rule, the prosecutor made a decision unsupported by the legislative purpose behind both the PTI Statute and the Comprehensive Drug Reform Act, by the Guidelines, and by caselaw. Thus, the rejection of Baynes's PTI application was an abuse of discretion under two of the three categories of the *Bender* test. . . .

■ OFFICE OF THE DISTRICT ATTORNEY ORLEANS PARISH, LOUISIANA DIVERSIONARY PROGRAM

The Orleans Parish District Attorney's Office first began a Diversionary Program in 1973 for first-time, non-violent offenders. . . . The program offers a constructive alternative to prosecution. The DA defers prosecution of eligible persons shortly after arrest. Upon successful completion of program conditions, the charge is dismissed. It permits the accused to voluntarily enter a course of treatment that will address the individual factors producing the criminal behavior. This option is offered prior to the acceptance of any formal charges. However, only cases which would be accepted for prosecution are eligible. Arresting officers and victims are contacted to discuss the program referral.

Individuals arrested for simple possession of a controlled substance comprise the majority of the caseload. Others, however, are in the program due to arrests for general crimes, such as theft. In all cases, the participant is harmfully involved in the use of alcohol or other mood-altering drugs.

The program seeks to enhance public safety, reduce criminal recidivism, reduce the demand for drugs, alleviate overburdened court dockets, and provide close case monitoring including drug testing and individually-tailored treatment plans. These benefits are achieved through smaller caseloads than normal probation services as well as collaboration with community resources for a comprehensive approach. This includes substance abuse, mental health, and educational assistance. The social and health care costs directly related to criminal activity are reduced through this intervention. The Diversionary Program is cost effective by freeing up scarce resources for the more dangerous offender and utilizing the cost benefits of treatment. It is designed to reduce the risk of continued progression into a criminal lifestyle and steer individuals toward more productive goals. The benefits directly affect not only program participants but their families and the community at large.

Eligibility Criteria

The program is offered to individuals who:

- are first-time arrestees of state misdemeanor or felony statutes (no prior convictions and no significant arrest history including any prior acts of violence).
- have not been arrested for a violent crime, drug distribution, illegal carrying or use of a weapon, or heroin possession.
- abuse substances (alcohol, illicit drugs, or prescription medications).
- are willing to accept professional treatment recommendations.
- are a resident of the greater New Orleans area.
- are aged 17 or older.
- acknowledge their wrongdoing.

Program Requirements

- Regular meetings with Diversionary Program Case Managers-Counselors.
- Abstinence from all mood-altering substances (unless prescribed by a physician).
- Periodic hair tests for illicit drugs; daily telephone contacts for random urine testing.
- Family involvement.
- Compliance to treatment recommendations from local substance abuse treatment providers (such as drug education, out-patient, in-patient, or longer-term residential treatment).
- Attendance at 12-step groups, if appropriate.
- Referrals to other support services for educational and vocational needs, mental health care, medical services, housing, etc.
- Payment of a sliding scale program fee and drug testing costs.
- Payment of restitution in full to victims for property crimes.
- Minimum program length of 3 months for misdemeanor charges and 6 months for felony charges.

Initial violations of program conditions result in a program extension and intensified treatment. Continued violations or re-arrest result in unsuccessful termination. Prosecution of the deferred charges occurs when a person violates out of the program. . . .

Notes

1. *Prevalence of diversion.* Diversion of arrestees is not as common as the outright rejection of criminal charges or the filing of felony charges. Prosecutors are most likely to offer diversion to suspects who face misdemeanor charges. Less than 5 percent of all felony arrestees in the largest urban counties in 1998 took part in diversion

or "deferred adjudication" programs. Bureau of Justice Statistics, Felony Defendants in Large Urban Counties, 1998, NCJ-187232 (November 2001). Federal diversion programs are small: About 1,500 suspects were handled through pretrial diversion in 1999 (compared to more than 60,000 cases prosecuted and 30,000 cases declined).

2. *Authority for diversion.* Prosecutors do not always have clear legal authority to take part in diversion programs. In some states, programs have statewide statutory authority (illustrated by the Montana statute reprinted above). Elsewhere, judges establish and supervise diversion programs (as in the New Jersey program described in *Baynes*). In a few jurisdictions, prosecutors send offenders into diversion programs without any explicit statutory authority to do so. Combinations of these situations are also possible: A statute might authorize diversion of offenders only after the filing of charges, yet the prosecutor may decide unilaterally to send some offenders into diversion programs before filing charges. Did the origins of the New Jersey program in the judicial branch influence the outcome or analysis in *Baynes*? Would the source of authority affect the level of funding for the program or the prosecutor's control over the conditions that program participants must meet?

3. *Who decides who enters the program?* State statutes dealing with pretrial diversion programs most often empower judges to approve of prosecutorial recommendations of individual offenders. Yet, as the New Jersey court in *Baynes* recognized, in practice prosecutors decide which defendants or suspects will enter a pretrial diversion program, and a court will give great deference to the prosecutor's decision. Indeed, in many states courts refuse to review the prosecutor's decision on whether to offer diversion to a suspect unless the prosecutor relies on unconstitutional grounds such as race. Cleveland v. State, 417 So. 2d 653 (Fla. 1982) (decision on pretrial intervention is prosecutorial rather than judicial in nature and is not subject to judicial review; review of arbitrary decisions allowed in other jurisdictions because statute explicitly authorizes review). Statutes in about a dozen states give prosecutors complete control over who may enter pretrial diversion programs. Prosecutors' offices sometimes create policies to govern eligibility for diversion, at least for some types of cases.

Legislatures also create some preconditions for defendants or suspects to participate in pretrial diversion programs. See, e.g., Ind. Code §33-14-1-7 (prosecutor "may" withhold prosecution against a person charged with a misdemeanor if person agrees to listed conditions of pretrial diversion program); Utah Code §77-36-2.7 (court may not approve diversion for domestic violence defendants but may hold guilty plea in abeyance during treatment program). If the prosecutor and the suspect disagree about the proper interpretation of the statute defining eligibility requirements, can a court review the prosecutor's decision based on its independent interpretation of the statute? Or must it defer to the prosecutor's reading of the statute?

4. *Who decides whether the defendant has completed the program?* Suppose a defendant believes she has fulfilled all the conditions of the diversion program but the prosecutor disagrees and files criminal charges. Will a court review the prosecutor's conclusion that the defendant failed to complete the program? Is there any reason to treat this question differently from the question of who will enter a diversion program? Among states with statutes addressing this question, the majority require court approval for a decision to remove an offender from a diversion program, but some (fewer than 10) have statutes granting this decision exclusively to the prosecutor. See Fla. Stat. §948.08. Compare State ex rel. Harmon v. Blanding, 644 P.2d 1082 (Or. 1982) (criminal defendant is not entitled to full hearing on issue of

whether he had violated his diversion agreement but only to limited hearing on issue of whether reasonable basis existed for district attorney's finding) with State v. Hancich, 513 A.2d 638 (Conn. 1986) (once defendant was admitted to pretrial alcohol-education program following her first arrest for driving under the influence, she could not be removed unless court made independent determination that she had lost her eligibility or that she had not completed program successfully). What circumstances might enable a court to make an independent judgment about the defendant's success or failure in the program?

5. *Statement of reasons.* A few diversion programs require the prosecutor to provide an applicant to the program with written notice of rejection, along with the reasons for the rejection. The statement of reasons facilitates judicial review of the prosecutor's decision and is thought to help the courts identify arbitrary and abusive denials by the prosecutor. See State v. Herron, 767 S.W.2d 151 (Tenn. 1989). However, fewer than 10 states have a statewide legal requirement that the prosecutor give written reasons. Why do most states refuse to require a statement of reasons from the prosecutor? Have they concluded that such statements are pointless?

6. *Suspended charges vs. suspended sentences vs. probationary sentences.* Cases considered for diversion might be handled in various ways, including holding charges in abeyance during treatment, suspending an imposed sentence, or mandating probation. In each case, the primary goal may be treatment of the person rather than punishment. For example, voters in California in 2000 passed Proposition 36, which places all convicted nonviolent drug offenders in treatment, but which repealed a deferred entry of judgment program for narcotics and drug abuse statutes. See 2000 California Op. Atty. Gen. 207. Other emerging reform efforts include creation of entirely distinct courts with "therapeutic" purposes. See, e.g., Teresa W. Carns, Michael G. Hotchkin & Elaine M. Andrews, Therapeutic Justice in Alaska's Courts, 19 Alaska L. Rev. 1 (2002) (discussing the concept and use of "wellness court," drug courts, mental health court, and therapeutic justice courts); Peggy F. Hora, William G. Schma & John T. A. Rosenthal, Therapeutic Jurisprudence and the Drug Treatment Court Movement: Revolutionizing The Criminal Justice System's Response to Drug Abuse and Crime in America, 74 Notre Dame L. Rev. 439 (1999). What are the legal, institutional and policy advantages to diverting a person out of the criminal justice system rather than using the power and control over citizens that the criminal justice system authorizes?

2. *Encouraging or Mandating Criminal Charges*

Should prosecutors pursue every crime brought to them? Could they? Are there instances in which the substantial discretion typically granted to prosecutors in the United States should be limited or removed?

Many jurisdictions have restricted the power of prosecutors to decline or divert domestic assault cases, because these cases present distinctive challenges for prosecutors. "No drop" prosecutorial policies combine with other system-wide policy initiatives regarding domestic assaults, including mandatory arrest policies (considered in Chapter 5), detention policies (considered in Chapter 12), and sentencing policies.

Many courts in the U.S. have appointed groups of lawyers to explore these specialized issues. One such group, the Missouri Task Force on Gender and Justice

(1993), noted that domestic violence is surprisingly widespread: "Domestic violence is found at all socio-economic levels, in all racial and age groups, and among people with all degrees of education. National statistics show that three million to four million American women are battered each year by their husbands or partners." Victims of abuse are often reluctant to testify in criminal cases against their partners, and prefer that prosecutors drop the charges. The Missouri Task Force describes the following psychological pattern that applies to many victims of domestic violence:

> [An] abusive relationship is characterized by a cycle of violence containing three phases. During Stage One, tension builds; although the victim is compliant and on good behavior, the batterer exercises increased tension, threats, and control. When the tension reaches a plateau, the relationship enters Stage Two. The batterer becomes unpredictable, highly abusive, and claims a loss of control. The victim feels helpless and trapped and is highly traumatized. After an acute episode of battering comes the remorsefulness of Stage Three, when the batterer is apologetic and attentive, promises to change, and manipulates the victim, causing her to feel guilty and responsible for the behavior of the batterer, yet making her want to believe his insistence that he will change. When tension begins again, the relationship reenters Stage One. Over time, the tension building stages occur more frequently, the battering becomes more acute, and the contrition stage shortens.

Victim advocates report that an abused woman will return to her partner an average of six times before she leaves permanently. A battered spouse is often isolated, having few friends or sources of support. She also might find the criminal process to be daunting and frustrating, particularly if the prosecutor fails to file serious charges in the case or delays its progress. A prosecutor's office can address some of these problems by adopting a "no drop" policy, mandating prosecution for all domestic violence cases filed. Such a policy takes the victim "off the hook" and insulates her from pressure to drop the case, coming from her partner, family and friends. These policies also emphasize that society at large has an interest in deterring domestic violence. Domestic violence can lead to murder or to injuries that require medical treatment. Children growing up in violent families are more likely to suffer from alcohol or drug abuse, and are more likely to commit violent crimes themselves later in life.

The materials that follow offer several different responses to the special problems of domestic violence. The provisions from Italy, Germany, and West Virginia that close this unit place the issue of mandatory prosecution into a more general context.

■ FLORIDA STATUTES §741.2901

(1) Each state attorney shall develop special units or assign prosecutors to specialize in the prosecution of domestic violence cases, but such specialization need not be an exclusive area of duty assignment. These prosecutors, specializing in domestic violence cases, and their support staff shall receive training in domestic violence issues.

(2) It is the intent of the Legislature that domestic violence be treated as a criminal act rather than a private matter. . . . The state attorney in each circuit shall adopt a pro-prosecution policy for acts of domestic violence. . . . The filing,

nonfiling, or diversion of criminal charges, and the prosecution of violations of injunctions for protection against domestic violence by the state attorney, shall be determined by these specialized prosecutors over the objection of the victim, if necessary. . . .

■ WISCONSIN STATUTES §968.075

(7) Each district attorney's office shall develop, adopt and implement written policies encouraging the prosecution of domestic abuse offenses. The policies shall include, but not be limited to, the following:

(a) A policy indicating that a prosecutor's decision not to prosecute a domestic abuse incident should not be based:

1. Solely upon the absence of visible indications of injury or impairment;
2. Upon the victim's consent to any subsequent prosecution of the other person involved in the incident; or
3. Upon the relationship of the persons involved in the incident.

(b) A policy indicating that when any domestic abuse incident is reported to the district attorney's office, including a report [police officers are required by law to submit after responding to a domestic abuse incident], a charging decision by the district attorney should, absent extraordinary circumstances, be made not later than two weeks after the district attorney has received notice of the incident. . . .

(9) Each district attorney shall submit an annual report to the department of justice listing [t]he number of arrests for domestic abuse incidents in his or her county as compiled and furnished by the law enforcement agencies within the county [and the] number of subsequent prosecutions and convictions of the persons arrested for domestic abuse incidents. . . .

■ PROSECUTION GUIDELINES FOR DULUTH, MINNESOTA

The prosecution guidelines of the Duluth City Attorney's Office were first conceived in 1982. The current guidelines are a result of revisions made in 1989. The guidelines were developed through extensive meetings and discussions between prosecutors in the criminal division of the City Attorney's Office and staff persons of the Domestic Abuse Intervention Project (DAIP). The guidelines are used consistently by prosecutors in Duluth in the prosecution of domestic abuse cases.

These guidelines provide a framework upon which to base decisions. They do not make up a specific set of absolute procedures to fit the myriad possibilities these cases present. The prosecution goals stated below sometimes come into conflict and need to be balanced, based on the circumstances of each case. Because of the complex nature of victims' reluctance to testify against abusers, the prosecutor should not be motivated by a desire to punish the victim in effectuating the goals of this policy.

The goals of prosecution in domestic abuse cases are: 1) to protect the victim from additional acts of violence committed by the defendant, 2) to deter the defendant from committing continued acts of violence against others in the community, [and] 3) to create a general deterrence to battering in the community. In the prosecution of cases, the prosecutor will assist in maximizing the ability of the court to place controls on the abuser and in deterring continued use of violence by following these guidelines:

1) The prosecutor will seek to obtain convictions as an optimum result and will avoid entering into conditional deferrals, except where supported by statute, ordinance, case law, the Minnesota Rules of Criminal Procedure, and rules of conduct for prosecutors.
2) The prosecutor will attempt to proceed with these cases with as few continuances as possible to increase the likelihood of a conviction and to decrease the abuser's opportunity to pressure the victim and to continue to commit violent acts against her/him.
3) Whenever possible, the prosecutor and law enforcement officials will sign the complaint.
4) The prosecutor will subpoena the victim to shield her/him from pressure from the abuser or other parties who do not want the victim to participate in the case as a witness.
5) The prosecutor will approach plea agreements with the intent of expediting the goals of the prosecution, especially that of protecting the victim. Plea agreements will not be used to reduce the prosecutor's case load or the court's calendar. . . .
6) To ensure that victims have access to advocacy, the prosecutor will make a reasonable effort to provide information to the shelter . . . regarding cases charged in which no arrest procedure occurred. . . .
8) The prosecutor will review police investigation reports submitted by the police department in cases which did not result in an arrest but in which police officers believe that prosecution is warranted. . . .
9) The prosecutor shall make available to the shelter and the DAIP information regarding the disposition of all cases and actions taken on police investigation reports. . . .

■ ITALIAN CONSTITUTION ART. 112

The public prosecutor has the duty to exercise criminal proceedings.

■ GERMAN CODE OF CRIMINAL PROCEDURE 152(2)

[The public prosecutor] is required . . . to take action against all judicially punishable . . . acts, to the extent that there is a sufficient factual basis. [Translator: John Langbein]

■ WEST VIRGINIA CODE §7-4-1

It shall be the duty of the prosecuting attorney to attend to the criminal business of the State in the county in which he is elected and qualified, and when he has information of the violation of any penal law committed within such county, he shall institute and prosecute all necessary and proper proceedings against the offender, and may in such case issue or cause to be issued a summons for any witness he may deem material. . . .

Notes

1. *Discretion in filing charges: majority position.* At common law, each local prosecutor had complete discretion to refuse to file charges or to dismiss charges after they had been filed. See Wilson v. Renfroe, 91 So. 2d 857 (Fla. 1956). This remains the dominant position for most crimes in almost all jurisdictions, but there are three exceptions to this general rule. First, for some crimes (including domestic assault and weapons charges) some jurisdictions have implemented mandatory prosecution policies. See Daniel C. Richman, "Project Exile" and the Allocation of Federal Law Enforcement Authority, 43 Ariz. L. Rev. 369 (2001). Second, a few jurisdictions have statutes suggesting that prosecutors have an obligation to prosecute crimes for which they believe probable cause exists. See, e.g., Ala. Code §12-17-184. Third, some jurisdictions provide the state attorney general with varying degrees of supervisory power over all local prosecutors. See Conn. Gen. Stat. §§51-275 to 51-277; Del. Code Ann. tit. 29, §2502.

2. *No-drop policies for domestic abuse cases.* A number of jurisdictions have adopted policies limiting the discretion of prosecutors to decline or dismiss domestic assault and abuse cases, illustrated by the Duluth, Minnesota, policy. It is difficult to count such provisions since, like most executive branch policies, they are often not published and are otherwise difficult to obtain. In addition to Florida and Wisconsin, the Minnesota and Utah legislatures have enacted laws encouraging or requiring the development of plans and policies to increase prosecutions and convictions in domestic abuse cases. Congress has encouraged the development of no-drop policies in the Child Abuse, Domestic Violence, Adoption and Family Services Act of 1992, 42 U.S.C. §10415. Many jurisdictions, however, have implemented written or unwritten guidelines about domestic abuse cases in the absence of specific legislative guidance. A growing group of state attorneys general (for instance, in New Jersey and North Carolina) have adopted statewide policies discouraging local prosecutors from dropping domestic violence charges. Policies like the one set out in the Florida statute, encouraging the prosecutor to proceed over the victim's objections, are known as "hard no-drop" policies; the more common policies, focusing on victim support and encouragement, are known as "soft no-drop" policies. Other approaches require the prosecutor to consult with the victim or with other individuals or agencies before dismissing a prosecution. Should the decision be left to the police, or should it depend on the victim's willingness to make an initial complaint?

3. *Assessing no-drop policies: costs, benefits, and options.* Advocates of no-drop policies for domestic violence cases start with the observation that the rate of prosecution for domestic violence complaints remains lower than the rate of prosecution for other types of complaints. In some communities, less than 10 percent of the misdemeanor complaints are prosecuted. See Jeffrey Fagan, Cessation from Family Violence: Deterrence and Dissuasion, 11 Crime and Justice: An Annual Review of Research 377 (Lloyd Ohlin and Michael Tonry eds., 1989). Research indicates that no-drop policies do reduce the number of domestic abuse cases dismissed or diverted, although the most comprehensive studies on this question indicate that the

effect is rather small. See Angela Corsilles, No-Drop Policies in the Prosecution of Domestic Violence Cases: Guarantee to Action or Dangerous Solution? 63 Fordham L. Rev. 853 (1994). A study of the Duluth policies set out above showed a substantial reduction in dismissals in domestic abuse cases. Mary Asmus, Tineke Ritmeester, and Ellen Pence, Prosecuting Domestic Abuse Cases in Duluth: Developing Effective Prosecution Strategies from Understanding the Dynamics of Abusive Relationships, 15 Hamline L. Rev. 115 (1991). The impact of no-drop policies on public behavior has not been well established, but some partial evidence has emerged. Hard no-drop policies appeared to have a substantial impact on domestic homicides in San Diego. Casey Gwinn and Anne O'Dell, Stopping the Violence: The Role of the Police Officer and the Prosecutor, 20 W. St. U. L. Rev. 297 (1993). What is the impact of no-drop policies on the victim? Is the victim "re-victimized" if she is forced, under threat of jail or other sanctions, to testify? Will no-drop policies encourage more women who have been abused to call police or prosecutors, or will they discourage calls for fear that the victim will again lose control of her situation? See Meg Obenauf, The Isolation Abyss: A Case Against Mandatory Prosecution, 9 UCLA Women's L.J. 263 (1999).

The relationship between no-drop policies and shall-arrest policies is not yet well understood. According to one analysis of arrest and prosecution records in domestic violence cases in Ann Arbor and Ypsilanti, Michigan, a shall-arrest policy leads to more frequent dismissal of charges and to more frequent acquittals after trial. Andrea Lyon, Be Careful What You Wish For: An Examination of Arrest and Prosecution Patterns of Domestic Violence Cases in Two Cities in Michigan, 5 Mich. J. Gender & L. 253 (1999). The same study found that the police arrested women in 12 percent of the cases. If the police had been called to that residence before, they were more likely to arrest a woman — possibly a form of retaliation against women for staying in an abusive situation.

4. *Prosecutorial ethics and defendants.* No-drop statutes and rules emphasize the fact that prosecutors represent not only the victim but society as well. Prosecutors also have obligations to defendants, including a duty to clear quickly any defendants who are falsely accused. See National District Attorneys Association, National Prosecution Standards §§42, 43 (2d ed. 1991). Do no-drop policies conflict with the prosecutor's ethical obligations to defendants?

5. *Case "attrition."* Arguments for no-drop prosecution policies have been bolstered by statistics suggesting that the substantial majority of domestic abuse cases — often in the range of 50 to 80 percent — are dismissed. The phenomenon of cases "falling out" of the criminal process is commonly referred to as case "attrition." One possible reaction to the level of case attrition is to claim that police and prosecutors are failing in their obligation to protect the public. What are other possible implications of case attritions? A famous study conducted in the 1970s closely examined case attrition for felony cases in New York City. Vera Institute of Justice, Felony Arrests: Their Prosecution and Disposition in New York City's Courts (Malcolm Feeley ed., rev. ed. 1980). It found an unexpectedly high level of prior relationships throughout felony crime categories, and it attributed the bulk of case attrition to the relationships between the parties involved.

> [Criminal] conduct is often the explosive spillover from ruptured personal relations among neighbors, friends and former spouses. Cases in which the victim and defendant were known to each other constituted 83 percent of rape arrests, 69 percent of assault

> arrests, 36 percent of robbery arrests, and 39 percent of burglary arrests. The reluctance of the complainants in these cases to pursue prosecution (often because they were reconciled with the defendants or in some cases because they feared the defendants) accounted for a larger portion of the high dismissal rate than any other factor.

Does this study suggest that the problems with domestic abuse victims as reliable complainants are commonplace for other crimes? Does this study reveal reasons to hesitate in implementing a no-drop policy for domestic abuse cases, or does it offer a reason to consider no-drop policies for at least some other crimes? From another perspective, is there a proper ratio of convictions to complaints (or arrests) for most types of crimes?

6. *Specialized units in prosecutors' offices.* Although the criminal code might give prosecutors huge amounts of discretion over whether to file criminal charges, the legislature or the chief prosecutor might structure the prosecutor's office in ways that will encourage the filing of some criminal charges and discourage the filing of others. For instance, the office might have specialized units, whose work is easy to monitor. Line items in budgets give strong incentives to pursue certain charges. Some investigative techniques or charging decisions require special authorization from those high in the prosecutorial hierarchy. As Professor Daniel Richman points out, these office structures operate as predictable limits on the reach of substantive criminal law, even when those criminal laws are drafted very broadly and delegate nominally large powers to the prosecutor. Richman, Federal Criminal Law, Congressional Delegation, and Enforcement Discretion, 46 UCLA L. Rev. 757 (1999).

7. *Discretion in charging in civil law systems.* The civil law tradition that prevails in most of the legal systems of the world nominally denies the prosecutor discretion in charging. Studies of such systems — especially the Italian, German, and French systems, which have received relatively close examination — suggest that in fact prosecutors exercise a substantial degree of discretion in charging. See, e.g., Marco Fabri, Theory versus Practice of Italian Criminal Justice Reform, 77 Judicature 211 (January-February 1994); Abraham Goldstein and Martin Marcus, The Myth of Judicial Supervision in Three "Inquisitorial" Systems: France, Italy and Germany, 87 Yale L.J. 240 (1977); cf. John Langbein and Lloyd Weinreb, Continental Criminal Procedure: "Myth" and Reality, 87 Yale L.J. 1549 (1978). See also Mark West, Prosecution Review Commissions: Japan's Answer to the Problem of Prosecutorial Discretion, 92 Colum. L. Rev. 684 (1992) (finding that Japanese prosecutors have conviction rates of close to 100 percent because of selectivity in bringing charges).

8. *Mandatory charging statutes in the United States.* The West Virginia Code creates what seems to be a nondiscretionary charging obligation, in sync with the provisions from Italy and Germany. However, prosecutors retain substantial discretion in West Virginia despite the mandatory language of the statute. See State ex rel. Bailey v. Facemire, 413 S.E.2d 183 (W. Va. 1991). The Colorado Criminal Code permits a person to challenge the district attorney's decision not to charge, but the Colorado Supreme Court has warned that the statute does not permit a judge to substitute her judgment for that of the prosecutor. Colo. Rev. Stat. §16-5-209. The court must find that the "district attorney's decision was arbitrary or capricious and without reasonable excuse" before the court will step in. Landis v. Farish, 674 P.2d 957, 958 (Colo. 1984). Why are courts so hesitant in both civil and common law systems to review and enforce mandatory charging provisions? Do the realities of justice systems or human nature make mandatory charging provisions unlikely to succeed?

3. *Private Prosecution*

If prosecutors won't prosecute, perhaps an aggrieved citizen will. Indeed, there is a long tradition of private rather than public prosecution. Public prosecutors—like many of the institutions of criminal justice, including police and public defense counsel—are a modern invention. An older tradition, which saw tort and crime more closely linked, required private parties to bring criminal actions against alleged wrongdoers. Throughout much of the eighteenth and nineteenth centuries, it was common for private citizens to bring complaints to a grand jury or a magistrate, *and* to hire private attorneys to assist the public prosecutor or to prosecute the criminal case alone. Only at the turn of the twentieth century did the public prosecutor become the primary method for initiating criminal charges.

Remnants of true private prosecution exist still in United States law. The "victim's rights" concept has strengthened the accountability of public prosecutors to victims of crime. Prosecutors also reflect the political priorities of the voters or the Executive who appoints them, and the Legislature which funds them.

As traditional and well recognized as interest group politics may be, the link between private preferences and public prosecution is not widely recognized. Consider the legal and policy dimensions of the modern forms of private prosecution described in the following statute, case and problem.

■ WISCONSIN STATUTES §968.02

(1) Except as otherwise provided in this section, a complaint charging a person with an offense shall be issued only by a district attorney of the county where the crime is alleged to have been committed. A complaint is issued when it is approved for filing for the district attorney. . . .

(3) If a district attorney refuses or is unavailable to issue a complaint, a circuit judge may permit the filing of a complaint, if the judge finds there is probable cause to believe that the person to be charged has committed an offense after conducting a hearing. If the district attorney has refused to issue a complaint, he or she shall be informed of the hearing and may attend. The hearing shall be ex parte without the right of cross-examination.

■ STATE v. DONALD CULBREATH

30 S.W.3d 309 (Tenn. 2000)

ANDERSON, C.J.

We granted this appeal to determine whether the trial court abused its discretion by disqualifying a District Attorney General and his staff due to the use of a private attorney to assist the prosecution where the private attorney received substantial compensation from a private, special interest group. . . . We agree that the prosecution's appointment and use of a private attorney who received substantial compensation from a private, special interest group created a conflict of interest and an appearance of impropriety that required disqualification of the District Attorney General's office. [The] prosecutor's use of the private attorney under the circumstances of this case violated the defendants' right to due process under the Tennessee Constitution and required dismissal of the indictments. . . .

In December of 1995, Larry Parrish, an attorney in Memphis, Tennessee, was approached by the executive director of an organization known as the Citizens for Community Values, Inc., ("CCV"), who asked him to meet with two Shelby County assistant district attorneys, Amy Weirich and Jennifer Nichols, regarding the prosecution of obscenity cases. Parrish, a former Assistant United States Attorney, was experienced in the prosecution of obscenity cases.

Parrish met with Weirich and Nichols for three hours. When they asked for his help, Parrish replied, "I haven't been asked." On the following day, then-Shelby County District Attorney John Pierotti contacted Parrish and requested his assistance. Pierotti told Parrish that his office could not pay for Parrish's services but could reimburse expenses. When Parrish asked if he could be compensated by outside sources, Pierotti agreed. According to Parrish, "that's how it got started."

Thereafter, Parrish conducted an extensive investigation into sexually-oriented businesses in Shelby County, Tennessee, with the assistance of two assistant district attorneys, an investigator from the District Attorney General's office, and investigators from the Tennessee Bureau of Investigation and the Department of Revenue. Parrish met with these employees in his law firm office on a daily basis for several months. Beginning in January of 1996, the group's investigation consisted of conducting surveillance of sexually-oriented establishments and taking statements from a large number of witnesses. Although Parrish testified that it was "understood" that General Pierotti had the ultimate decision-making authority, there were no procedures or guidelines establishing Parrish's specific duties or Pierotti's oversight.

The initial agreement called for the District Attorney General's office to pay for expenses incurred during the investigation, but Parrish began to pay expenses from contributions by CCV and numerous members of the community. Parrish testified that CCV received a monthly statement itemizing his time and expenses, just as any other client. Parrish's expenses included the use of court reporters to take statements, a TV/VCR, copying and courier expenses, video monitors, special telephone lines, and various office supplies and equipment. The expenses were paid from CCV contributions. . . .

On July 11, 1996, Parrish was "appointed" as a "Special Assistant District Attorney" by General Pierotti and was administered an oath of office for the first time. On the same day, a civil nuisance suit seeking injunctive relief against several sexually-oriented businesses was filed in Shelby County Chancery Court. The civil complaint was signed by Parrish as "Special Assistant District Attorney General," District Attorney General Pierotti, and two assistant district attorneys. At Pierotti's request, Parrish was appointed as additional counsel in matters relating to the civil cases in chancery court by Governor Don Sundquist on August 30, 1996. The letter of appointment noted that Parrish would not be compensated by the State, that Parrish would disclose the amount and source of any compensation received, that such information was a matter of public record, and that Parrish was under the direct supervision of General Pierotti.

When Pierotti resigned, effective November 1, 1996, his successor, William Gibbons, continued to work with Parrish in the investigation and prosecution of sexually-oriented businesses. In addition to the civil nuisance suit already filed in chancery court, Gibbons sought criminal indictments from the grand jury. In December of 1996, the grand jury returned an 18-count indictment against the defendant, Donald L. Culbreath, [including ten counts of promoting prostitution, six counts of prostitution, and two counts of public indecency].

The trial court found that over a 19-month period, Parrish received $410,931.87 for his services from CCV and other private contributors between December of 1995 and July of 1997. Of this amount, Parrish's expenses exceeded $100,000. The trial court found that Parrish's substantial involvement in the prosecution of these cases and his "enormous" compensation from a private, special interest group created a conflict of interest that required Parrish's disqualification. . . .

In determining whether to disqualify a prosecutor in a criminal case, the trial court must determine whether there is an actual conflict of interest, which includes any circumstances in which an attorney cannot exercise his or her independent professional judgment free of "compromising interests and loyalties." See Tenn. R. Sup. Ct. 8, EC 5-1. If there is no actual conflict of interest, the court must nonetheless consider whether conduct has created an appearance of impropriety. See Tenn. R. Sup. Ct. 8, EC 9-1, 9-6. If disqualification is required under either theory, the trial court must also determine whether the conflict of interest or appearance of impropriety requires disqualification of the entire District Attorney General's office. The determination of whether to disqualify the office of the District Attorney General in a criminal case rests within the discretion of the trial court. . . .

A District Attorney General is an elected constitutional officer whose function is to prosecute criminal offenses in his or her circuit or district. Tenn. Const. art. VI, §5. The District Attorney General "[s]hall prosecute in the courts of the district all violations of the state criminal statutes and perform all prosecutorial functions attendant thereto. . . ." Tenn. Code Ann. §8-7-103(1). . . .

The proper role of the prosecutor in our criminal justice system has been addressed on numerous occasions by various courts and ethical rules. As early as 1816, the Tennessee Supreme Court said that a prosecutor

> is to judge between the people and the government; he is to be the safeguard of the one and the advocate of the rights of the other; he ought not to suffer the innocent to be oppressed or vexatiously harassed any more than those who deserve prosecution to escape; he is to pursue guilt; he is to protect innocence; he is to judge of circumstances, and, according to their true complexion, to combine the public welfare and the safety of the citizens, preserving both and not impairing either.

Foute v. State, 4 Tenn. (3 Haywood) 98 (1816). The United States Supreme Court has said that a prosecutor:

> is the representative not of an ordinary party to a controversy, but of a sovereignty whose obligation to govern impartially is as compelling as its obligation to govern at all; and whose interest, therefore, in a criminal prosecution is not that it shall win a case, but that justice shall be done. As such, he is in a peculiar and very definite sense the servant of the law the twofold aim of which is that guilt shall not escape or innocence suffer. He may prosecute with earnestness and vigor — indeed, he should do so. But, while he may strike hard blows, he is not at liberty to strike foul ones.

Berger v. United States, 295 U.S. 78 (1935).

These principles are likewise embodied within the ethical considerations of the Model Code of Professional Responsibility governing the conduct of prosecutors:

> The responsibility of a public prosecutor differs from that of the usual advocate; his duty is to seek justice, not merely to convict. This special duty exists because: (1) the

prosecutor represents the sovereign and therefore should use restraint in the discretionary exercise of governmental powers, such as in the selection of cases to prosecute; (2) during trial the prosecutor is not only an advocate but also may make decisions normally made by an individual client, and those affecting the public interest should be fair to all; and (3) in our system of criminal justice the accused is to be given the benefit of all reasonable doubts.

Tenn. R. Sup. Ct. 8, EC 7-13; see ABA Standards for Criminal Justice, Standard 3-1.1(c) (1979) ("[T]he duty of the prosecutor is to seek justice, not merely to convict"). The Model Code also discusses the differences in the role of the prosecutor from that of the private attorney:

> With respect to evidence and witnesses, the prosecutor has responsibilities different from those of a lawyer in private practice; the prosecutor should make timely disclosure to the defense of available evidence, known to the prosecutor, that tends to negate the guilt of the accused, mitigate the degree of the offense, or reduce the punishment. Further, a prosecutor should not intentionally avoid pursuit of evidence merely because the prosecutor believes it will damage the prosecutor's case or aid the accused. [Tenn. R. Sup. Ct. 8, EC 7-13].

In short, public prosecutors hold a unique office in our criminal justice system. [P]rosecutors are expected to be impartial in the sense that they must seek the truth and not merely obtain convictions. They are also to be impartial in the sense that charging decisions should be based upon the evidence, without discrimination or bias for or against any groups or individuals. Yet, at the same time, they are expected to prosecute criminal offenses with zeal and vigor within the bounds of the law and professional conduct.

Under English common law, the criminal justice system required the victim of a criminal offense, or the victim's family, to initiate and pursue criminal proceedings. Although the development and role of the public prosecutor in the United States over the past several centuries has largely supplanted the English common law in this regard, many jurisdictions still allow a private attorney to be retained or appointed to assist in the prosecution of a criminal case.

Numerous courts and commentators have recognized, however, that the use of a private attorney in the prosecution of a criminal case may present ethical dilemmas, including conflicts of interest. The private attorney must comply with the standards and ethical responsibilities for a public prosecutor — to not merely seek convictions but also to pursue justice. At the same time, however, the private attorney's ethical duty "both to client and to the legal system, is to represent the client zealously within the bounds of the law, which include Disciplinary Rules and enforceable professional regulations." Tenn. R. Sup. Ct. 8, EC 7-1.

In Tennessee, there are two statutes pertaining to the prosecutor's use of additional counsel. One, which the parties agree is not applicable in this case, permits the victim of a crime or the victim's family to retain an attorney to assist in the trial of a criminal case under the supervision of the District Attorney General. Tenn. Code Ann. §8-7-401. The second, which the parties contend is applicable here, provides for the employment of additional counsel:

> [W]here the interest of the state requires . . . additional counsel to the attorney general and reporter or district attorney general, the governor shall employ such counsel, who

> shall be paid such compensation for services as the governor, secretary of state, and attorney general and reporter may deem just, the same to be paid out of any money in the treasury not otherwise appropriated. [Tenn. Code Ann. §8-6-106.]

Although the statutory provisions in Tennessee, similar to the laws in other jurisdictions, purport to address the potential conflicts by requiring that the private attorney work under the supervision of the District Attorney or be compensated by the state, they do not foreclose the risk that a conflict of interest, or appearance of such a conflict, may exist under the circumstances of a particular case. For example, there is a conflict of interest whenever an attorney is retained to assist the prosecution and acquires a direct financial interest in the proceeding. Moreover, an actual conflict or an apparent conflict may exist anytime a lawyer cannot exercise his or her independent professional judgment free of "compromising influences and loyalties." Tenn. R. Sup. Ct. 8, EC 5-1. Accordingly, a court must review the facts and circumstances of each case with these standards in mind.

In this case, Parrish's involvement began without any formal appointment by the Governor and no oath of office, and it continued in this manner for eight months from December of 1995 to July 1996. Parrish was compensated for his services by a private, special interest group that he billed each month. During this time, Parrish spearheaded a comprehensive investigation with a "staff" that included two assistant district attorneys and three investigators. There was no specific agreement or arrangement as to Parrish's role, the extent of his participation, or the extent of District Attorney General Pierotti's supervision — for all practical purposes, there appeared to be little supervision or control by Pierotti. . . .

Although General Pierotti purportedly appointed Parrish as a special prosecutor on the same day the [civil nuisance] suit was filed, there was (and is) no constitutional or statutory authority for such an appointment to be made. Moreover, although Parrish was later appointed as additional counsel by the Governor, there was (and is) no legal authority allowing Parrish to be compensated on an hourly basis by a private, special interest group. . . .

Parrish had an actual conflict of interest under the circumstances of this case. He was privately compensated by a special interest group and thus owed a duty of loyalty to that group; at the same time, he was serving in the role of public prosecutor and owed the duty of loyalty attendant to that office. Moreover, because Parrish was compensated on an hourly basis, the reality is that he acquired a direct financial interest in the duration and scope of the ongoing prosecution. . . .

The State contends that there was no conflict of interest because Parrish and the prosecution had the same interest — eradicating sexually-oriented businesses. The prosecutor's discretion about whom to prosecute and to what extent they should be prosecuted, however, is vast and to a large degree, not subject to meaningful review. Moreover, as the United States Supreme Court has recognized, the prosecutor's discretion goes beyond initial charging decisions:

> A prosecutor exercises considerable discretion in matters such as the determination of which persons should be targets of investigation, what methods of investigation should be used, what information will be sought as evidence, which persons should be charged with what offenses, which persons should be utilized as witnesses, whether to enter into plea bargains and the terms on which they will be established, and whether any individuals should be granted immunity. . . .

Young v. United States ex rel. Vuitton et Fils S.A., 481 U.S. 787, 807 (1987). [T]he foundation for the exercise of the vast prosecutorial discretion is freedom from conflict of interest and fidelity to the public interest.

Finally, we agree that the trial court did not abuse its discretion in disqualifying the District Attorney General's staff based on the appearance of impropriety created by Parrish's conflict of interest. [T]he record supports the trial court's finding that Parrish played a substantial role in the prosecution. . . . Despite Parrish's extensive contact with the office of the District Attorney General, including daily working involvement with two assistant district attorneys and several investigators, there were no guidelines as to Parrish's duties and no efforts to screen Parrish from other members of the District Attorney General's office. Both [Pierotti and Gibbons] knew that Parrish was being compensated by a private, special interest group. Moreover, the trial court found that on one occasion, Pierotti, Gibbons, and Parrish attended a fund-raiser which "stressed the necessity to continue on with the prosecution of criminal activity in topless clubs and the need for continued donations to pursue these goals." . . .

Here, the private attorney's conflict of interest tainted the entire prosecution of the case well before the charges were presented to the grand jury. Accordingly, we conclude that the proceedings were inherently improper and that dismissal of the indictments is the appropriate remedy to redress the constitutional error. . . .

Problem 13-1. Private Money, Public Prosecutions

The Massachusetts legislature created the Insurance Fraud Bureau (IFB), to investigate charges of fraudulent insurance transactions and to refer any violation of law regarding insurance fraud to the appropriate prosecutor. The IFB is governed by a board of fifteen members, five each from the governing committees of two insurance rating bureaus (one for auto insurance and the other for workers' compensation insurance) and five public officials, including the Commissioner of Insurance and the Commissioner of the Department of Industrial Accidents.

According to the statute, every insurer "having reason to believe that an insurance transaction may be fraudulent" must report its suspicions to the IFB. The IFB must review each report and may investigate further. Whenever the IFB's executive director is satisfied that a material fraud or intentional misrepresentation has been committed in an insurance transaction, he must "refer the matter to the attorney general, the appropriate district attorney or the United States attorney, and to appropriate licensing agencies." A person convicted of any law concerning insurance fraud, following an IFB referral for prosecution, "shall be ordered to make restitution to the insurer for any financial loss sustained as a result of such violation."

The IFB receives reports of suspected insurance fraud from a variety of sources. During the IFB's first seven years, slightly more than half of these reports came from insurance companies. Other reports come from government agencies, professional organizations, and the public. Of the more than 12,800 reports received in those seven years, more than 5,000 were accepted for investigation, 64 percent of which were from insurance companies.

The Commissioner of Insurance must cover the IFB's investigation costs through annual assessments against the two insurance rating bureaus, which are themselves funded by insurance companies operating in the state. For fiscal year

1999, the appropriation from the general fund for the investigation and prosecution of automobile insurance fraud was $270,871, and the assessment against the auto insurance rating bureau was $250,000. In that same year, the legislative appropriation for the investigation and prosecution of workers' compensation fraud was $463,159 and the assessment against workers' compensation rating board was $250,000.

The commissioner must also collect from the rating bureaus enough money to cover funds spent for fringe benefits "attributable to personnel costs of the attorney general's office related to the purposes" of the program. Under this law, the Attorney General uses the assessments to hire 13 assistant attorneys general, six for automobile insurance fraud matters and seven for workers' compensation insurance fraud matters.

James Ellis and Nicholas Ellis were partners in a law firm that represented plaintiffs in workers' compensation and personal injury cases. Along with other associates, employees and clients, they were charged with insurance fraud and related offenses. Both defendants moved to dismiss the indictments based on the partiality of the attorneys prosecuting the cases. They challenged the constitutionality of the statutorily funding scheme.

The state argued in reply that routine cooperation from a victim of a crime is often necessary and should be encouraged. Victims of commercial or corporate crimes may assist the prosecution by collecting and organizing necessary information and may properly hire private investigators for external investigation of suspected crimes. In addition, the state noted that assessments are made industry-wide, rather than on one particular victim corporation, and are spent on investigation and prosecution of automobile and workers' compensation insurance fraud generally, rather than for the particular benefit of any one victim. How would you rule on the motion to dismiss? Compare Commonwealth v. Ellis, 708 N.E. 2d 644 (Mass. 1999).

Notes

1. *Private filing of complaints.* Is it possible to encourage the filing of criminal charges by giving the power to file a criminal complaint directly to an aggrieved citizen, allowing the citizen to bypass the public prosecutor? Most states give the public prosecutor exclusive authority to file criminal complaints. See Cal. Govt. Code §26500 ("The public prosecutor shall attend the courts, and within his or her discretion shall initiate and conduct on behalf of the people all prosecutions"). The same is true in the federal system. The court in Harman v. Frye, 425 S.E.2d 566 (W. Va. 1992), considered criminal complaints for battery that two participants in a fight filed against each other. The opinion summarized the reasons why most states have required the public prosecutor to approve of the filing of any criminal charges:

> [Problems] have resulted from allowing citizens to file criminal complaints before a magistrate without the approval of the prosecuting attorney or law enforcement officers. First, citizens can misuse the right to file a criminal complaint before a magistrate by exaggerating the facts or omitting relevant facts they disclose to the magistrate so as to transform a noncriminal dispute into a crime. The magistrate, who must remain neutral, is not in the same position as the prosecuting attorney or law enforcement officers to ascertain whether all of the relevant facts have been disclosed accurately. . . . When citizens file criminal complaints before the magistrate which later prove to be

> frivolous, retaliatory or unfounded, the prosecuting attorney is required to take the time to investigate the complaint before moving a nolle pros to dismiss. . . . Moreover, additional time and expense are also incurred when either the public defender or an attorney-at-law must be appointed to represent indigent persons against whom frivolous, retaliatory or unfounded charges have been filed. . . . Finally, private citizens have not undergone the same professional training as prosecuting attorneys or law enforcement officers nor are they subject to the same rules of professional conduct and discipline which are imposed on prosecuting attorneys and law enforcement officers.

In a few states, statutes authorize citizens to file criminal complaints even when the prosecutor has declined to do so. Most of these statutes (like the Wisconsin statute reprinted above) allow the private complaint to occur only after the public prosecutor has affirmatively decided not to file charges, and they require the citizen to obtain approval for the charges from a judge or grand jury. A few of the statutes apply only to particular crimes, such as domestic violence or issuance of a worthless check. See W. Va. Code §§48.2A-4(a), 61-3-39a. Can the public prosecutor prevent any abuses of private complaints simply by dismissing charges once they are filed? If the prosecutor retains the power to dismiss charges filed by a private citizen, has the mechanism accomplished anything other than creating more recordkeeping?

2. *The historical roots of private prosecution of criminal cases.* By the turn of the twentieth century the public prosecutor became the primary method for initiating criminal charges. Private prosecutions became the exception rather than the rule as public prosecutors became more professionalized and independent of the courts, professional police departments became more common in metropolitan areas, and acquittal rates rose for privately initiated complaints. See Allan Steinberg, The Transformation of Criminal Justice: Philadelphia, 1800-1880 (1989); Michael McConville and Chester Mirsky, The Rise of Guilty Pleas: New York, 1800-1865, 22 J. Law & Soc'y 443 (1995). This transformation was part of a larger formalization of the entire criminal process, starting in the English courts for felony cases in the 1730s. See John Langbein, The Prosecutorial Origins of Defense Counsel in the Eighteenth Century: The Appearance of Solicitors, 58 Cambridge L.J. 314 (1999) (courts allowed participation of defense counsel to counter increasing influence of solicitors in investigating and preparing witnesses).

Traces of the older private prosecution system remain visible today, and are gaining renewed attention as a method of empowering the victims of crime. More than half the states still have statutes or constitutional provisions that allow private counsel, retained by a crime victim, to participate in criminal proceedings. In most jurisdictions, the private prosecutor may only assist the prosecutor, while in a few the private prosecutor has more authority to direct the criminal proceedings. See, e.g., Pa. Stat. tit. 16, §1409 (the court may "direct any private counsel employed by [a complainant] to conduct the entire proceeding"). Are private prosecutions of crime an effective way to supplement the limited resources of a public prosecutor, much as we rely on "private attorneys general" to help enforce some civil statutes? What if private prosecutions could only result in non-prison sentences?

3. *Private financial aid to public prosecution.* What is wrong with private parties funding public prosecutions so long as the public prosecutor makes the decisions? In Commonwealth v. Ellis, 708 N.E. 2d 644 (Mass. 1999), which provides the basis for Problem 13-1, the Massachusetts Supreme Court upheld the statutory industry

funding scheme for insurance and fraud prosecutions, finding no appearance of conflict. The court observed:

> If we were confronted with a challenge to an arrangement between insurers and the Attorney General of the sort involved here that was not endorsed by statute, the appearance of the possibility of improper influence would be far clearer. Although statutory endorsement of an unconstitutional plan cannot make it constitutional, where the question is whether the appearance of an arrangement may support a determination of unconstitutionality, the fact that the Legislature has endorsed the plan, has supervisory authority over it, and appropriates funds for it substantially changes appearances.

Can you distinguish the outcomes in *Culbreath* and *Ellis?* See also Hambarian v. Superior Court, 44 P.3d 102 (Cal. 2002) (prosecutor's office need not be removed despite use of accountant paid by victim). Do *Culbreath* and *Ellis* suggest a resurgence of private prosecution? A prosecutor who is paid by a private interest but is working under the direction of a public prosecutor can be said to serve two (or more) clients. One client might be considered the private funding source. Who is the other client? Do these clients have conflicting interests?

4. *Victim notice and consultation regarding charges.* Crime legislation over the past generation has given victims of alleged crimes more input into prosecutorial decisions. Almost all states now have passed statutes or constitutional provisions that focus on the prosecutor's power to resolve criminal charges through plea agreements or other methods. Most, however, do not give the victim any right to "consult" with the prosecutor about the charges. They simply instruct the prosecutor to inform the victim about the charges to be filed or about the decision not to file charges. See Ariz. Stat. §13-4408 (prosecutor to give victim notice of the charge against defendant and concise statement of procedural steps in criminal prosecution, and to inform victim of decision to decline prosecution, with reasons for declination). Are these "notice" and "consultation" statutes an inevitable response to the abandonment of private prosecutions? Is the victim, in a functional if not literal sense, the client of the prosecuting attorney? Cf. Gina Cappello, Women's Groups Can Oversee Sex Cases, N.Y. Times, March 21, 2000 (Philadelphia police allow women's organizations to help evaluate and classify sexual assault complaints; response to revelations that department mislabeled rapes as less violent offenses to make city seem safer).

5. *Special prosecutors.* Almost all states have statutes empowering a judge (or a prosecuting attorney) to appoint a "special prosecutor" to file and prosecute criminal charges. The court appoints the special prosecutor when the district attorney "refuses to act" or "neglects" to perform a duty. See Ala. Code §12-17-186; Tenn. Const. art. 6, §5 ("In all cases where the Attorney for any district fails or refuses to attend and prosecute according to law, the Court shall have power to appoint an Attorney pro tempore"). Courts will also order the use of a special prosecutor when the prosecuting attorney has a conflict of interest regarding a suspect, a complainant, or some other person involved in a potential criminal case. See Young v. United States ex rel. Vuitton et Fils S.A., 481 U.S. 787 (1987) (district courts have authority under Rule 42(b) to appoint private attorney to prosecute contempt case, but should do so only after requesting public prosecutor to initiate case). If an independent official who decides whether to file criminal charges does not operate

within a limited budget and does not compare the current case to all other potential criminal cases that an office might prosecute, will the quality of the prosecutorial decision improve? Are budget constraints a necessary evil, or are they the essence of prosecutorial accountability?

4. *Selection of Charges and System*

Up to this point, we have focused on prosecutorial choices that would place a suspect either "in" or "out" of the criminal justice system. But prosecutors also make important choices about each criminal defendant who will be charged. For one thing, the prosecutor selects among a range of criminal charges that could apply to the case. For another, prosecutors might select which judicial system (state or federal, juvenile or adult) will adjudicate the charges.

a. Selection Among Charges

■ U.S. DEPARTMENT OF JUSTICE PRINCIPLES OF FEDERAL PROSECUTION

(1980)

SELECTING CHARGES

1. Except as hereafter provided, the attorney for the government should charge, or should recommend that the grand jury charge, the most serious offense that is consistent with the nature of the defendant's conduct, and that is likely to result in a sustainable conviction.

2. Except as hereafter provided, the attorney for the government should also charge, or recommend that the grand jury charge, other offenses only when, in his judgment, additional charges:

(a) are necessary to ensure that the information or indictment: (i) adequately reflects the nature and extent of the criminal conduct involved; and (ii) provides the basis for an appropriate sentence under all the circumstances of the case; or

(b) will significantly enhance the strength of the government's case against the defendant or a codefendant.

3. The attorney for the government may file or recommend a charge or charges without regard to the provisions of paragraphs 1 and 2, if such charge or charges are the subject of a pre-charge plea agreement. . . .

■ MINNESOTA STATUTES §388.051

(1) The county attorney shall [p]rosecute felonies, including the drawing of indictments found by the grand jury, and, to the extent prescribed by law, gross misdemeanors, misdemeanors, petty misdemeanors, and violations of municipal ordinances, charter provisions and rules or regulations. . . .

(3) [E]ach county attorney shall adopt written guidelines governing the county attorney's charging . . . policies and practices. The guidelines shall address,

but need not be limited to, the . . . factors that are considered in making charging decisions. . . .

■ STATE v. TANYA CASKEY

539 N.W.2d 176 (Iowa 1995)

PER CURIAM.

Tanya Janean Caskey appeals from her conviction, following a bench trial, for neglect of a dependent person, a class "C" felony, in violation of Iowa Code section 726.3 (1993). Caskey contends she was convicted under the wrong statute. We affirm.

The district court found Caskey guilty of neglect of a dependent person based on evidence that she had driven while intoxicated with her children, Dani, age three, and Sara, age eight, in the car. Caskey argues she should have been charged under section 726.6 for child endangerment which would be an aggravated misdemeanor in her case because the children did not suffer serious injury. See Iowa Code §726.6(3).* She claims her behavior did not warrant a class "C" felony classification. Caskey asserts the language and historical analysis of the neglect or abandonment of dependent person statute reveal the legislature did not intend for the statute to encompass a caretaker driving a motor vehicle while intoxicated.

In considering statutory questions our review is to correct errors of law. When a statute's terms are unambiguous and its meaning plain, there is no need to apply principles of statutory construction. We need only look at the plain and rational meaning of the precise language. Iowa Code section 726.3 provides:

> A person who is the father, mother, or some other person having custody of a child, or of any other person who by reason of mental or physical disability is not able to care for the person's self, who knowingly or recklessly exposes such person to a hazard or danger against which such person cannot reasonably be expected to protect such person's self or who deserts or abandons such person, knowing or having reason to believe that the person will be exposed to such hazard or danger, commits a class "C" felony.

According to the expert testimony, Caskey exposed her children to 50 to 100 times greater risk of injury or fatality from a car crash by her hazardous driving while intoxicated. This behavior clearly comes within the plain and rational meaning of the language in section 726.3. We thus do not need to look beyond the plain language to the legislative history of this section. . . .

"The fact that two statutes provide different criminal penalties for essentially the same conduct is no justification for taking liberties with unequivocal statutory language." State v. Perry, 440 N.W.2d 389 (Iowa 1989). Moreover, contrary to Caskey's

* Iowa Code §726.6 provides as follows:

1. A person who is the parent, guardian, or person having custody or control over a child or a mentally or physically handicapped minor under the age of eighteen, commits child endangerment when the person [k]nowingly acts in a manner that creates a substantial risk to a child or minor's physical, mental or emotional health or safety. . . .
2. A person who commits child endangerment resulting in serious injury to a child or minor is guilty of a class "C" felony.
3. A person who commits child endangerment not resulting in serious injury to a child or minor is guilty of an aggravated misdemeanor.

—EDS.

argument, driving her car with the children in it while she was intoxicated was neglectful of her natural and legal duty to not expose them to the hazard of injury or death. Such a serious neglect of duty warrants a class "C" felony classification. Finally, Caskey does not claim the child endangerment section is inconsistent with the neglect of a dependent person section. When two statutory provisions are reconcilable, the prosecutor has discretion to choose what charges to file. State v. Peters, 525 N.W.2d 854 (Iowa 1994).

We find no abuse of prosecutorial discretion in charging Caskey with neglect of a dependent child. According to the plain and rational meaning of that statute's language, there was sufficient evidence to support Caskey's conviction. We thus affirm the district court judgment.

In 1988, the Florida legislature revised the state's "habitual offender" statute. Under the new statute, a prosecutor's decision to charge an eligible defendant as a habitual offender translated into longer prison sentences. Within a few years, defendants and others began to complain that prosecutors were using their new charging power in an arbitrary and discriminatory manner. Legislative committees asked for a study of the use of the habitual offender statute. The study, completed in 1992, concluded as follows:

> [First, in] most circuits, and certainly on a statewide basis, the statute has not been limited to use against the very worst offenders but has been applied more frequently to the less serious offenders. . . . Second, the circuit in which an offender is prosecuted is of enormous importance to the risk of habitualization. This means that for the roughly one third of all guilty adjudications who are eligible for habitualization, Florida does not have a single statewide system of reasonably uniform sentencing. For this group of offenders . . . there are effectively 20 separate sentencing systems that vary widely in their treatment of offenders eligible for habitualization.
>
> Third, in all but two circuits [those encompassing Miami and Sarasota], the habitual offender sanctions are much more likely to be used against black offenders than non-black offenders, even after adjusting for prior record, the nature of the current offense and a variety of other factors that might have a bearing on the decision to habitualize. It was also found that, on a statewide basis, prosecutors were much more likely to use the statute against male offenders than similarly situated female offenders. . . .

After receiving this report, several state legislators called for revisions to the statute that would restrict or remove the prosecutor's power to decide when to charge an offender as a habitual felon. Consider the following statement that a group of prosecutors in the state made in this volatile context.

■ FLORIDA PROSECUTING ATTORNEYS' ASSOCIATION STATEMENT CONCERNING IMPLEMENTING OF HABITUAL OFFENDER LAWS

(1993)

The Florida Prosecuting Attorneys' Association desires to provide continuing effective protection to the public from habitual offenders by discouraging the legislature from the total elimination of habitual offender laws and minimum mandatory sentence laws through the voluntary adoption by the State Attorneys of implementation criteria for use of habitual offender laws.

To fulfill this desire, the State Attorneys of the State of Florida adopt the criteria set forth below for the implementation of the habitual offender laws of Florida in their respective circuits to be utilized whenever such utilization would not result in the interference with the proper and fair administration of the duties of a State Attorney, as shall be determined by the respective State Attorney. Recognizing that there will be cases which would justify habitual offender treatment which will not meet these criteria, such cases shall have the reasons set forth in writing and signed by the designated Assistant State Attorney(s), and the State Attorneys filing such cases shall notify this Organization's President of such filings.

I. Habitual Violent Felony Offenders

A. Charged offense must be a second degree felony or higher . . ., AND
B. Charged offense must be an enumerated violent felony, AND
C. Defendant must have at least one prior conviction for an enumerated violent felony, AND
D. The felony for which the defendant is to be sentenced was committed within five years of the date of the conviction for the last enumerated violent felony or within five years of the defendant's release, on parole or otherwise, from a prison sentence or other commitment imposed as a result of the prior enumerated felony conviction.

II. Habitual Felony Offenders

A. *Violent Offenses:* Defendants charged with a second degree or higher enumerated violent felony . . . must have at least two prior felony convictions of any type.
B. *Second Degree Felonies (Excluding Sale or Purchase of or Trafficking in Controlled Substances and Burglary Cases):* Defendants charged with a non-violent, second degree or higher offense (excluding Sale or Purchase of or Trafficking in a Controlled Substance and Burglary) must have at least three prior felony convictions of any type, or two prior enumerated violent felony convictions.
C. *Second Degree Burglary:* Defendants charged with a second degree or higher Burglary must have at least two prior felony convictions of any type.
D. *Sale of or Trafficking in Controlled Substances:* Defendants charged with a second degree or higher sale of or trafficking in a Controlled Substance (including attempts and conspiracies of a second degree or higher) must have at least two prior felony convictions for sale of or trafficking in Controlled Substances (including attempts or conspiracies but not including Counterfeit Drugs); OR two prior enumerated violent felony convictions; OR one sale or trafficking in a Controlled Substance (including attempts and conspiracies but not including Counterfeit Drugs) conviction and one enumerated violent felony conviction.
E. *Third Degree Felonies:* Defendants charged with third degree felonies shall receive habitual offender sanctions only if they meet one of the following criteria:
   1. The defendant is charged with: Aggravated Assault, OR Aggravated Stalking, OR Attempted Sexual Battery (victim 12 or older, no physical force),

OR Battery on a Law Enforcement Officer, OR Child Abuse, OR Felony DUI, OR Resisting Arrest with Violence, OR . . . Vehicular Homicide, AND the defendant has at least four prior felony convictions of any type, or two prior enumerated violent convictions; OR

2. The defendant is charged with Burglary of a Structure AND the defendant has at least two prior felony convictions, one of which is a Burglary of a Dwelling or Structure; OR
3. The defendant is charged with Grand Theft of a Motor Vehicle AND the defendant has at least four prior felony convictions, three of which must be for Grand Theft of a Motor Vehicle. . . .

Problem 13-2. Available Charges

On the evening of January 9, Ida County deputy sheriff Randy Brown was on patrol in Ida Grove. He observed three snowmobiles traveling on a downtown sidewalk and then on the streets in a careless and reckless manner. Once Brown began pursuit, the trio split up. With the aid of another deputy, Brown eventually stopped and arrested Mitch Peters.

At the time of arrest, Peters had a strong odor of alcohol on his breath. The deputies took him to the Ida County sheriff's office, where they administered sobriety tests. Peters failed the horizontal gaze nystagmus test and the preliminary breath test, registering above .10. Peters was charged with operating a motor vehicle while intoxicated, second offense, under Iowa Code §321J.2, which provides as follows:

> A person commits the offense of operating while intoxicated if the person operates a motor vehicle in this state [w]hile under the influence of an alcoholic beverage or other drug or a combination of such substances, [or while] having an alcohol concentration . . . of .10 or more.

Peters objects to the charge, claiming that he could be prosecuted only under section 321G.13(3), which provides as follows: "A person shall not drive or operate an all-terrain vehicle or snowmobile [w]hile under the influence of intoxicating liquor or narcotics or habit-forming drugs." This statute carries a lesser punishment than §321J.2. The trial court rejected Peters's claim. After conviction Peters appealed, claiming that §321J.2 did not apply to his conduct. How would you rule? Compare State v. Peters, 525 N.W.2d 854 (Iowa 1994); People v. Rogers, 475 N.W.2d 717 (Mich. 1991).

Notes

1. *Selection among charges: majority view.* According to judges in the United States, prosecutors may select among all applicable statutes in deciding what charges to bring, with no outside interference. The occasional claim by defendants that one crime better fits the offense and offender than another always fails. See United States v. Batchelder, 442 U.S. 114 (1979) (statutes with overlapping or identical elements and different penalties do not violate due process, equal protection, or separation of powers doctrines by granting prosecutor charging discretion). Many courts apply a technique of statutory interpretation or "rule of construction" referred to

by its Latin name, *in pari materia,* which leads courts to presume that all related statutes make up a single, coherent statutory scheme, regardless of when they were enacted. Courts often work hard to treat statutes that at first appear to be general and specific instances of the same offense as separate crimes subject to the prosecutor's discretion.

2. *Structuring the charging discretion.* Does the absence of judicial regulation of selection among available charges create the need for detailed charging guidelines? What institutions could develop charging policies? Should legislatures draft policies or should they follow the Minnesota legislature's approach, simply directing that each prosecutor draft charging policies?

Consider again the Justice Department's Principles of Federal Prosecution. Do they give any surprising or meaningful direction to a prosecutor making a charging decision? The National District Attorneys Association lists the following among the appropriate factors for a prosecutor to consider in selecting charges: "the probability of conviction," "the willingness of the offender to cooperate with law enforcement," "possible improper motives of a victim or witness," "excessive cost of prosecution in relation to the seriousness of the offense," "recommendations of the involved law enforcement agency," and "any mitigating circumstances." National Prosecution Standards §43.6 (2d ed. 1991). Does this list differ in emphasis or in particulars from the federal standards? If prosecutors develop written charging policies on their own initiative, should the policies be made public? Should prosecutors be rewarded for obtaining convictions on whatever charges they initially file? See Tracey Meares, Rewards for Good Behavior: Influencing Prosecutorial Discretion and Conduct with Financial Incentives, 64 Fordham L. Rev. 851 (1995).

3. *Charges of overcharging.* Defense attorneys and many observers of the criminal justice system claim that prosecutors routinely "overcharge" cases in anticipation of plea bargain negotiations. Standard 3-3.9 of the ABA Standards for Criminal Justice (3d ed. 1993) advises prosecutors against bringing charges greater than necessary "to reflect the gravity of the offense" or charges where there is not "sufficient admissible evidence to support a conviction." How can we know when prosecutors are "overcharging" for strategic reasons? If it is difficult to prove that an abuse is taking place at all, is there any hope of reducing the amount of any abuse?

4. *Statutory limits on multiple convictions.* About a half-dozen states have statutes that approach the question of charge selection at the "back end" of convictions rather than the "front end" of charges. These statutes limit the number of convictions that can result from overlapping charges. Consider Mo. Ann. Stat. §556.041:

> When the same conduct of a person may establish the commission of more than one offense he may be prosecuted for each such offense. He may not, however, be convicted of more than one offense if [t]he offenses differ only in that one is defined to prohibit a designated kind of conduct generally and the other to prohibit a specific instance of such conduct. . . .

But cf. Ill. Ann. Stat. ch. 720, para. 5/3-3 ("When the same conduct of a defendant may establish the commission of more than one offense, the defendant may be prosecuted for each such offense"). Is a statute directed to the trial judge who enters final judgment more likely to produce consistent punishment for similar conduct than any effort to influence the charging decision more directly?

5. *Criminal code reform.* Would a well-drafted criminal code reduce concerns about consistent and fair charging? See Paul Robinson, Are Criminal Codes Irrele-

vant? 68 S. Cal. L. Rev. 159 (1994). Are there fewer overlaps and conflicts between statutes in states with a uniform criminal code? The majority of states revised their criminal codes in the decades following the promulgation of the path breaking Model Penal Code by the American Law Institute in 1962. Criminal codes before reform often include hundreds or, in some cases, thousands of separate crimes. The most prominent examples of jurisdictions that have failed to reform their codes — and in both cases the codes are complex and jumbled — are the federal system and California. See Ronald Gainer, Report to the Attorney General on Federal Criminal Code Reform, 1 Crim. L.F. 99 (1989). Whenever there is an apparent conflict between two statutory provisions, should the courts (or the lawyers) notify the appropriate legislative committees? Consider again the overlapping statutes in the *Caskey* case from Iowa and the two statutes described in Problem 13-2. Why do you suppose the state legislatures passed these overlapping statutes? Was it an oversight that could be rationalized through criminal code reform?

b. Selection of System

The absolute number of juveniles arrested and prosecuted for criminal offenses has grown over the last generation. Most of the crimes committed by defendants under 18 years old are handled in specialized juvenile courts as "delinquency" cases. Juvenile courts handled more than 1.8 million delinquency cases in 1996 (up from 1.25 million in 1993); juveniles made up 17 percent of all arrestees in 1999. See *http://ojjdp.ncjrs.org/ojstatbb/* (statistical briefing book for juvenile justice).

Juvenile courts (which go by various names, such as "Family Court") operate differently from the adult criminal justice system. Their informal processes, which are considered civil rather than criminal proceedings, are designed to emphasize rehabilitation and avoid the stigma associated with adult criminal punishment. The juvenile justice system loses its authority over offenders when they reach age 18 or 21.

While most juvenile offenders have their cases adjudicated in the juvenile system, some are transferred to the adult criminal justice system. Fewer than 5 percent of all adjudicated juvenile cases transfer into the adult system. States have created a variety of mechanisms and presumptions to direct juvenile offenders into one system or the other. As with other charging decisions, the prosecutor is the key decisionmaker over this transfer decision, while the legislature also sets some important parameters. Do the limitations on the prosecutor's choice between systems differ from the limits on other prosecutorial charging decisions?

■ JUVENILE TRANSFERS TO CRIMINAL COURT IN THE 1990'S: LESSONS LEARNED FROM FOUR STUDIES HOWARD N. SNYDER, MELISSA SICKMUND, & EILEEN POE-YAMAGATA

National Center for Juvenile Justice (August 2000)

Juveniles may be prosecuted in criminal court under certain circumstances, and State law determines the conditions under which youth charged with a criminal law violation can be processed in the criminal, rather than the juvenile, justice system. The legal mechanisms for "transferring" juveniles from the juvenile to the criminal justice system differ from State to State. . . . These mechanisms, while having different labels across the States, fall into three general categories, according to who makes the transfer decision. The three mechanisms are judicial waiver, statutory exclusion, and concurrent jurisdiction; the decisionmakers are, respectively, the juvenile court judge, the legislature, and the prosecutor.

Judicial waiver (the juvenile court judge). In judicial waivers, a hearing is held in juvenile court, typically in response to the prosecutor's request that the juvenile court judge "waive" the juvenile court's jurisdiction over the matter and transfer the juvenile to criminal court for trial in the "adult" system. Most State statutes limit judicial waiver by age and offense criteria and by "lack of amenability to treatment" criteria. States often limit waiver to older youth or to youth who have committed certain serious offenses. Amenability determinations are typically based on a juvenile's offense history and previous dispositional outcomes but may also include psychological assessments. Under many State statutes, a court making an amenability determination must also consider the availability of dispositional alternatives for treating the juvenile, the time available for sanctions (for older juveniles), public safety, and the best interests of the child. Judicial waiver provisions vary in the degree of flexibility they allow the court in decisionmaking. Some provisions make the waiver decision entirely discretionary. Others establish a presumption in favor of waiver or specify circumstances under which waiver is mandatory.

Regardless of the degree of flexibility accorded to the court, the waiver process must adhere to certain constitutional principles of fairness. The U.S. Supreme Court, in Kent v. United States (1966), held that juvenile courts must provide "the essentials of due process" when transferring juveniles to criminal court. In 1996, approximately 10,000 cases — or 1.6 percent of all formally processed delinquency cases disposed in juvenile courts that year — were judicially waived to criminal court.

Statutory exclusion (the legislature). In a growing number of States, legislatures have statutorily excluded certain young offenders from juvenile court jurisdiction based on age and/or offense criteria. Perhaps the broadest such exclusion occurs in States that have defined the upper age of juvenile court jurisdiction as 15 or 16 and thus excluded large numbers of youth under age 18 from the juvenile justice system. NCJJ has estimated that (assuming such age-excluded youth are referred to criminal court at rates similar to those at which their juvenile counterparts are referred to juvenile court) as many as 218,000 cases involving youth under age 18 were tried in criminal court in 1996 as a result of State laws that defined them as adults solely on the basis of age. Whether juvenile and criminal court referral rates are in fact similar is not known. If they are not, or if the most minor incidents referred to juvenile court are never prosecuted in criminal court, the estimated number of age-excluded youth would be lower.

Many States also exclude certain individuals charged with serious offenses from juvenile court jurisdiction. Such exclusions are typically limited to older youth. The offenses most often targeted for exclusion are capital and other murders and violent offenses; however, an increasing number of States are excluding additional felony offenses. No national data exist on the number or characteristics of cases excluded by statute from juvenile court jurisdiction.

Concurrent jurisdiction (the prosecutor). Under this transfer option, State statutes give prosecutors the discretion to file certain cases in either juvenile or criminal court because original jurisdiction is shared by both courts. State concurrent jurisdiction provisions, like other transfer provisions, typically are limited by age and offense criteria.

Prosecutorial transfer, unlike judicial waiver, is not subject to judicial review and is not required to meet the due process requirements established in *Kent.* According to some State appellate courts, prosecutorial transfer is an "executive function" equivalent to routine charging decisions. Some States, however, have developed guidelines for prosecutors to follow in "direct filing" cases. No national data exist on the number or characteristics of the cases that prosecutors exclude or have the discretion to exclude from juvenile court jurisdiction.

State legislation delineates the conditions under which individuals charged with a violation of the law (and whose age places them under the original jurisdiction of the juvenile court) may or must be processed in the adult criminal system. Historically, the majority of States have relied on judicial waiver as the mechanism for transferring juveniles to criminal court. For many years, all States except Nebraska, New York, and, more recently, New Mexico have had statutory provisions that allow juvenile court judges to waive the juvenile court's jurisdiction over certain cases and transfer them to criminal court for prosecution. Statutory exclusion and concurrent jurisdiction provisions have been relatively less common, but the number of States in which these options exist is growing. Between the 1992 and 1997 legislative sessions, 45 States expanded their statutory provisions governing the transfer of juveniles to criminal court. Generally, States have done so by adding statutory exclusion provisions, lowering minimum ages, adding eligible offenses, or making judicial waiver presumptive. As of the end of 1997, legislatures in 28 States had statutorily excluded from juvenile court jurisdiction cases involving certain offenses and certain age youth, and, in 15 States, prosecutors had the discretion to file certain cases in criminal court.

Nearly all States rely on a combination of transfer provisions to move juveniles to the criminal system. As of the end of 1997, the most common combination (18 States) was judicial waiver together with statutory exclusion. Relying on judicial waiver alone was the second most common transfer arrangement (16 States). . . .

Prior Research on Transfer

Research on transfers in the 1970's through the middle 1980's . . . found that although transfer to criminal court was intended for the most serious juvenile offenders, many transferred juveniles were not violent offenders, but repeat property offenders. In addition, studies found that transferred youth often were handled more leniently in criminal court than they would have been in juvenile court — arguably because they were appearing in criminal court for the first time at a relatively young age and with a relatively short offending history. . . .

Other studies, by contrast, have found that criminal courts were more likely than juvenile courts to incarcerate offenders. Fagan (1991), for example, compared juvenile and criminal court handling in 1981 and 1982 of 15- and 16-year-old felony offenders in similar counties in New York (where they are excluded from juvenile court) and New Jersey (where they are not). The study found that criminal court sanctions in New York were twice as likely to include incarceration as juvenile court sanctions in New Jersey. In a followup study of more recent cases (1986-87), however, Fagan (1995) found the reverse (at least for robbery cases). . . .

Recidivism rates of juveniles transferred to criminal court and juveniles retained in juvenile court have also been compared to assess the ultimate impact of transfer. For example, Fagan's 1991 analysis of felony burglary and robbery cases found that the likelihood of rearrest and reincarceration, as described earlier, did not differ among youth charged with burglary. Among juveniles charged with robbery, however, those handled in juvenile court in New Jersey were significantly less likely to be rearrested and reincarcerated than those handled in criminal court in New York. . . .

The difficulty with much of the research concerning the effect of transfer is that observed differences in case handling and outcomes may result from differences in the seriousness of the cases ultimately handled in juvenile and criminal courts. The underlying assumption is that transfer is reserved for the most serious cases. Because the very rationale for transfer is to allow courts to impose potentially harsher penalties on the most serious juvenile offenders, one would expect cases handled in criminal court to be more serious than those remaining in juvenile court. However, with numerous studies finding large proportions of relatively less serious cases (e.g., property cases) among transferred cases, it remains uncertain what case characteristics trigger a decision to transfer.

[Recent studies of juvenile justice in South Carolina, Utah, and Pennsylvania provide more current findings on these questions.]

Findings: What Criteria Are Used in the Transfer Decision?

Although there is a general sense that transfer should be reserved for the most serious juvenile cases, numerous studies have shown that a significant proportion of transfers seem to fall outside that category, calling into question the decisionmaking of the juvenile court judges and/or prosecutors who control transfer decisions. Other than the general seriousness of an offense, what characteristics make a case more likely to result in transfer? For example, does the likelihood of transfer vary with the seriousness of a victim's injury, the use of weapons (especially firearms), the presence of gang motivation in the underlying incident, or a juvenile's history of substance abuse or prior offending? Are there interactions between these characteristics?

Judges concurred with most waiver requests made by prosecutors (solicitors) in South Carolina and Utah. Two factors distinguished cases that were waived from those that were not: the extent of a juvenile's court history and the seriousness of his or her offense. . . . In South Carolina, offense seriousness was . . . a key determinant in the waiver decision. Regardless of a youth's court history, cases involving serious person offenses were more likely to be approved for waiver than other types of cases. Although the seriousness of the offense category alone was not as key in Utah as it was in South Carolina, the juvenile court in Utah was also quite consistent in its waiver decisionmaking. Characteristics of the crime incident were important in decisions to waive in Utah. Waiver was most likely to be granted in cases involving serious person offenders who used weapons and seriously injured someone, regardless of the offenders' court history. Even first-time offenders in Utah were waived if they seriously injured their victim. For other types of cases, the court looked to a youth's court history to decide whether to waive the matter to criminal court. In these cases, youth with long histories were more likely to be waived than those with shorter histories.

Findings: Did the Nature of Transfer Decisionmaking Change During the 1980's and 1990's Over and Above Changes in Legislation?

In the past several years, many States have passed legislation that makes it easier to transfer juveniles to criminal court. Has there been any change, however, in the nature of transferred cases and/or decision criteria in jurisdictions where transfer provisions did not change? In other words, did the transfer process change even where there was no change in State statutes?

A youth referred to juvenile court in Pennsylvania for a delinquency offense in 1994 was far more likely to be judicially waived to criminal court than a youth referred in 1986. The large increase in the likelihood of waiver does not appear to be related to a change in transfer legislation, the growth of the juvenile population, or a change in the overall number of juvenile arrests. Between 1986 and 1994, the 84-percent growth in judicial waivers was greater even than the 32-percent increase in juvenile arrests for violent crimes. . . .

The growth of waiver in Pennsylvania was greatly affected by the waiver of a much larger number of juveniles charged with drug offenses — in fact, about 40 percent of the overall increase in the number of waivers between 1986 and 1994 can be attributed to these youth. . . . Another important difference between the 1986 and the 1994 waiver groups was that juveniles waived in 1994 had less serious court histories than juveniles waived in 1986. . . .

Findings: What Was the Impact of New Legislation That Excludes Additional Offenders from Juvenile Court Jurisdiction?

Of those States that have passed laws that make it easier to try juveniles in criminal court, the most common change was the enactment or expansion of statutory exclusion provisions. Legislatures responded to public outcry regarding "failures" of the juvenile justice system and proposed exclusion as at least a partial solution. The phrase "Do the adult crime, do the adult time" became a cliché. The efficacy of exclusion provisions, however, was not well established. Were more or different juveniles tried in the criminal system in jurisdictions that had enacted new statutory exclusion provisions? Did excluded juveniles receive harsher sanctions under new exclusion provisions than they would have received under prior judicial waiver provisions?

In many ways, implementation of Pennsylvania's 1996 exclusion law mimicked the State's judicial waiver process in previous years. Under the statute, when a case is not dismissed at the preliminary hearing, the criminal court judge's decision to keep the case in criminal court or to decertify it to juvenile court must be based on the same factors that a juvenile court judge uses to decide whether a youth should be waived to criminal court: the youth's age, prior referrals to juvenile court, and amenability to treatment.

The juvenile courts in the three Pennsylvania study counties judicially waived 277 youth in 1995. In the transition year of 1996, when the State's exclusion law took effect, the number of waivers dropped to 157 — a decrease of 120 youth. Of the 473 youth excluded from juvenile court jurisdiction in these counties in 1996, a total of 109 were convicted in criminal court. Assuming that cases still open in criminal court at the end of the study period resulted in the same proportion of convictions and dismissals, approximately 135 of the 473 excluded youth eventually would have been convicted in criminal court. The drop in the number of waived youth between 1995 and 1996 — 120 — is close to the number of excluded youth convicted in criminal court when all cases are closed — 135. These numbers suggest that the ultimate impact of Pennsylvania's 1996 exclusion legislation was to retain in criminal court those cases that the juvenile court would have judicially waived had it been given the opportunity. Consequently, regardless of the transfer path in Pennsylvania — judicial waiver or legislative exclusion — about the same number of youth were sentenced to an adult correctional facility.

Therefore, considering only case outcomes, the impact of Pennsylvania's new exclusion statute was negligible. The statute, however, increased the processing time for cases eventually handled within the juvenile justice system and placed an additional burden on local jails and the criminal courts. . . .

Findings from the project's four transfer studies can be summarized as follows:

Juvenile court judges largely concur with prosecutors as to which juveniles should be transferred to criminal court. These studies show that the juvenile court supports the prosecutor's request for transfer in approximately four out of five cases — indicating that these two key decisionmakers generally agree about who should be waived and who should not. Anecdotal evidence from the Utah study, in fact, indicates that in many cases in which a waiver petition was denied, the denial was based on a prosecutor's recommendation to withdraw the petition (following a plea bargaining agreement). It may be that the high proportion of judicial approval of waiver requests indicates that prosecutors are able to gauge which cases juvenile court judges will agree to waive and request waivers in only those cases. However, the study of exclusions in Pennsylvania implies that criminal court judges agree with juvenile court judges as to which youth should receive criminal court sanctions. . . .

Waiver decisions adjust to changing practice. The studies reveal that judges continued to waive those juveniles who failed in custody, even when custody occurred at an early stage in a youth's court career. It appears at first that between the mid-1980's and mid-1990's, waiver in Pennsylvania was modified by the public's concerns about a "new breed" of juvenile offender.

In response to these concerns, more and more youth with shorter juvenile court careers were waived. Unlike the earlier waiver group, a smaller proportion of the more recent waiver group in Pennsylvania had previously been placed on probation (51 percent of 1994 group versus 65 percent of 1986 group). However, approximately the same proportion (about 60 percent) of the youth waived in 1994 (who had shorter court careers) had been placed in custody at least once prior to the waiver incident. Thus, rather than changing the waiver decision criteria, the juvenile court [became] more likely to place juveniles in a facility without first trying probation. Recidivism after residential placement continued to be a key factor in the waiver decision.

The system adapts to large changes in structure. The structure of transfer decisions has changed in response to the public's concern over the increase in juvenile violence. Data in these studies confirm that the decisionmaking process will adapt to changing legal conditions and social pressure. For example, the study of the implementation of Pennsylvania's exclusion law found that even though the justice system adopted the State's new set of rules and followed new paths, case processing resulted in the same outcomes that would have occurred if the rules had not changed. There had been an expectation that the changed statutory exclusion provision would result in many, many more juveniles being tried in criminal court and in many of these youth ending up incarcerated in adult correctional facilities. However, Pennsylvania's exclusion legislation has had little overall impact on either the number of juveniles handled in criminal court or the proportion incarcerated in adult correctional facilities.

There was also an underlying assumption that transfer decisionmaking by juvenile court judges in Pennsylvania tended to favor juveniles and that decisionmaking by criminal court judges under the new provisions would be different. However, this study found that, in Pennsylvania, the decisionmaking process followed by criminal court judges regarding decertification was much the same as that followed by juvenile court judges regarding waiver. . . .

■ KRISTY MADDOX v. STATE

931 S.W.2d 438 (Ark. 1996)

BROWN, J.

This is a juvenile-transfer case. On October 16, 1995, an information was filed charging appellant Kristy Maddox with criminal mischief in the first degree, a Class C felony. She was accused of intentionally throwing a Mountain Dew bottle from a moving vehicle and striking the victim's automobile, causing damage in excess of $500. Maddox, who was 17 years old at the time of the alleged incident, and who turned 18 on February 4, 1996, moved to have the charge transferred to juvenile court. Her motion was denied. She now appeals that denial.

Only two witnesses testified at the juvenile-transfer hearing. Pamela Maddox, the appellant's mother, related to the court that at the time of the hearing, Maddox was living with her and assisting around the house by doing chores and taking care of her younger siblings. She testified that Maddox was not currently in high school, but that she was working on her G.E.D. and planned to attend college in the Fall. She stated that she had a good relationship with her daughter, but that she did have to call the police on one occasion for an undisclosed "family disturbance." She and the prosecutor agreed that Maddox had no prior criminal history.

Sherry Lynn Kinnamon, the victim, was called as a witness by the prosecution. She testified that on April 20, 1995, she was driving her grandparents from Huntsville to the VA Hospital in Fayetteville when she noticed a red pick-up truck following very closely behind her. She stated that she tapped her brakes a few times to get the driver's attention and slowed so that the truck could pass, but that the driver would not do so. Even when given a straight stretch of road with no cars approaching, the driver of the truck would not pass her. She explained that the driver instead pulled alongside her car several times, and that the driver and two passengers would simply look at her, then drop back behind her car, where they made obscene gestures. She stated that she slowed her car to two miles an hour so that the truck would pass, but that it again would not. Finally, she accelerated, and the truck pulled alongside her car. Maddox hung out of the window on the passenger's side of the truck, held by her belt loops. She was holding a full glass bottle of Mountain Dew, and she and the other occupants of the truck were yelling obscenities at Kinnamon. Kinnamon testified that Maddox then intentionally threw the glass bottle at her car. It dented the front of the hood and cracked the windshield. Kinnamon said that after she regained her composure, she pursued the truck and got its license plate number. No one was injured, but she estimated that the damage to her car was about $800.

The trial court denied the motion to transfer after determining that Maddox's intentional throwing of the Mountain Dew bottle at Kinnamon's car was not only a serious act but a violent one. The court emphasized the harassing nature of the episode and referred to an incident in Oklahoma where a person was killed because an object had been thrown at his vehicle. The court noted that Maddox had no prior criminal record and mentioned that there had been no evidence introduced, one way or the other, with regard to her prospects for rehabilitation.

Maddox claims in her appeal that the trial court clearly erred in retaining jurisdiction of this matter. The Arkansas Juvenile Code provides that the circuit court shall consider the following factors in determining whether to retain jurisdiction or transfer a case to juvenile court: 1) The seriousness of the offense, and whether violence was employed by the juvenile in the commission of the offense; 2) Whether the offense is part of a repetitive pattern of adjudicated offenses which would lead to the determination that the juvenile is beyond rehabilitation under existing rehabilitation programs, as evidenced by past efforts to treat and rehabilitate the juvenile and the response to such efforts; and 3) The prior history, character traits, mental maturity, and any other factor which reflects upon the juvenile's prospects for rehabilitation. Ark. Code §9-27-318(e). The decision to retain jurisdiction must be supported by clear and convincing evidence. Ark. Code §9-27-318(f). In making its decision, the trial court need not give equal weight to each of the statutory factors. Furthermore, the trial court's denial of a motion to transfer will be reversed only if its ruling was clearly erroneous.

Maddox asserts a twofold challenge to the denial of her motion to transfer. She first urges that the trial court did not recognize the relevance of her mother's testimony and emphasizes that her mother presented sufficient evidence of her character traits to support a positive finding on the issue of her prospects for rehabilitation. She further argues that the charge of criminal mischief is a crime against property which the trial court improperly characterized as "violent" in order to keep the matter in circuit court.

The State responds that criminal mischief is a Class C felony that satisfies the seriousness criterion for purposes of section 9-27-318(e) and that violence was employed in the commission of this offense. The State also questions whether the mother's testimony was really relevant to the criterion of rehabilitation, when there was no showing that Maddox was remorseful or willing to accept responsibility for her actions. Finally, the State contends that the fact Maddox was 18 at the time of her hearing is sufficient, standing alone, to affirm the trial court's ruling.

In recent years, this court has fashioned the following rule in juvenile-transfer cases: The use of violence in the commission of a serious offense is a factor sufficient in and of itself for a circuit court to retain jurisdiction of a juvenile's case, but the commission of a serious offense without the use of violence is not sufficient grounds to deny the transfer. Sebastian v. State, 885 S.W.2d 882 (Ark. 1994). In Green v. State, 916 S.W.2d 756 (Ark. 1996), this court noted that manslaughter, a Class C felony, was a serious offense: "No doubt the offense charged is serious. Manslaughter is a Class C felony. If [the appellant] were convicted he would be sentenced to imprisonment for not less than three nor more than ten years." Criminal mischief in the first degree is also a Class C felony, and it satisfies the seriousness requirement.

The question we next address is whether the trial court was correct in its finding that Maddox committed a violent act. We agree with the trial court that she did. This is not a case where a juvenile merely committed a crime against property such as we had in Pennington v. State, 807 S.W.2d 660 (1991). In *Pennington,* two 17-year-olds broke about 30 tombstones in a cemetery and were charged with criminal mischief. The circuit court refused to transfer the cases to juvenile court, and we reversed on the basis that the trial court gave too much deference to the prosecutor, after the court acknowledged that violence was not embraced in the young men's actions.

In the instant case, the trial court noted that these facts would likely support an aggravated assault charge as well as a charge of criminal mischief. This court has observed that the crime of aggravated assault is not only serious, but that no violence beyond that necessary to commit aggravated assault is necessary to meet the requirement under Ark. Code §9-27-318(e)(1). We conclude that a violent act lies at the core of the alleged crime in the instant case — the willful throwing of a glass bottle at a moving vehicle containing three passengers, as testified to by Kinnamon. These facts are sufficient to sustain a refusal to transfer in our judgment.

There is, too, the fact that Maddox has now turned 18. Young people over age 18 can no longer be committed to the Division of Youth Services for rehabilitation unless they are already committed at the time they turn 18. The fact that Maddox cannot now be committed to the Division of Youth Services is highly relevant to her prospects for rehabilitation as a juvenile and is a factor that this court considers important in reviewing a trial court's denial of a motion to transfer. This circumstance lends additional support to an affirmance.

ROAF, A.J., dissenting.*

In 1989, the Arkansas General Assembly enacted . . . the Arkansas Juvenile Code of 1989. A declaration of purpose for this legislation is found at Ark. Code §9-27-302. It is important in the context of this appeal and warrants our reconsideration:

> This subchapter shall be liberally construed to the end that its purposes may be carried out:
>
> (1) To assure that all juveniles brought to the attention of the courts receive the guidance, care and control, preferably in each juvenile's own home, which will best serve the emotional, mental, and physical welfare of the juvenile and the best interests of the state;
>
> (2) To preserve and strengthen the juvenile's family ties whenever possible, removing him from the custody of his parents only when his welfare or the safety and protection of the public cannot adequately be safeguarded without such removal; . . .
>
> (3) To protect society more effectively by substituting for retributive punishment, whenever possible, methods of offender rehabilitation and rehabilitative restitution, recognizing that the application of sanctions which are consistent with the seriousness of the offense is appropriate in all cases;
>
> (4) To provide means through which the provisions of this subchapter are executed and enforced and in which the parties are assured a fair hearing and their constitutional and other legal rights recognized and enforced.

Since 1991, this court has been called upon numerous times to interpret the provisions of the juvenile code dealing with how we treat youth who are charged with criminal offenses. The General Assembly has in turn had the opportunity on several occasions to react to our holdings. I submit that this court and the General Assembly have so woefully failed to consider a significant portion of the stated purposes underpinning the juvenile code that this language has become meaningless.

We have neither liberally construed the statute to the benefit of the emotional, mental, and physical welfare of the juveniles, nor even for the best interests of the state. We have failed to insure that methods of rehabilitation and restitution are

* Associate Justice Roaf incorporated by reference here the dissenting opinion from another case, Butler v. State, 922 S.W.2d 685 (Ark. 1996). — EDS.

substituted wherever possible, for retributive punishment, and we have surely failed to provide that juveniles are assured fair hearings and that their constitutional and other rights provided by this statute are uniformly recognized and enforced. We share this responsibility equally with our elected state representatives.

Today, we once again affirm a trial court's refusal to transfer a criminal case involving a juvenile to juvenile court. The trial court's ruling, and our affirmance, were foregone conclusions because of the prior holdings of this court, because of the weight of stare decisis, and because of the legislature's failure to revisit this legislation in light of our holdings. Children between the ages of 14 and 17 years are paying the price for our failures. We cannot even take comfort in the notion that the best interests of the state are being served, for many of these juveniles will return to our midst as adults, and the opportunity to use our best efforts to rehabilitate, guide and care for them will have been lost.

The landmark case which has led us down this path is, of course, Walker v. State, 803 S.W.2d 502 (Ark. 1991). In *Walker*, by a 4 to 3 decision, this court reached several significant holdings which have been repeatedly reavowed and reaffirmed since *Walker*— that a juvenile movant has the burden of proof when seeking to transfer a case from circuit court to juvenile court — that the trial court need not give equal weight to the three factors that the statute directs it to consider in determining whether to transfer a case — that the prosecutor is not even required to introduce proof on each of the three factors that the trial court is directed to consider — that the criminal information alone can provide a sufficient basis for the denial of a transfer to juvenile court — that a trial court does not have to make findings of fact or provide a rationale for its decision in a juvenile transfer proceeding. We have also held that juveniles "ultimately" charged and tried in circuit court are subject to the procedures prescribed for adults, and are not afforded the protections provided by the juvenile code, such as the requirement of parental consent to a waiver of right to counsel.

I am not unmindful of the fact that since 1991, the general assembly has twice amended Ark. Code §9-27-318, which deals with waiver and transfer to circuit court, each time to the detriment of juvenile defendants. However, they have not seen fit to amend the stated purposes for the juvenile code. I suggest that they do so at the next opportunity. Until then, our decisions and their inaction are in direct conflict with these purposes. I dissent.

Notes

1. *Choice of system for juvenile offenders: majority position.* The choice between the adult and juvenile systems is cluttered with various starting presumptions, shifting burdens of proof or persuasion, and opportunities to reconsider the choice of systems. In the end, the statutes in almost every state (along with the federal juvenile system) initially assign the great majority of juveniles to the juvenile court, and then allow a judge in the juvenile court to "waive" jurisdiction after an investigation, a hearing, and a statement of reasons by the court. See Kent v. United States, 383 U.S. 541 (1966). About 15 states give prosecutors the power in some cases to select between the adult and juvenile systems when there is "concurrent" jurisdiction (ordinarily for the most serious offenses and the oldest juveniles). Most states initially place into the adult system the oldest juveniles who commit the most serious crimes,

and place into the juvenile system (at least initially) the youngest juveniles and those who commit the least serious crimes. Franklin Zimring's major study suggests that, despite major changes in the laws dealing with the assignment of juveniles to the adult criminal justice system, the legal changes have made little difference in the numbers of juvenile cases actually resolved in the adult system. See Zimring, American Youth Violence (1998).

Where the law gives the prosecutor the initial choice of systems, that decision is usually subject to judicial review, and the burden of proof usually falls on the party seeking to transfer the case (that is, the juvenile attempting to move into the juvenile court). In Arkansas, as we saw in the *Maddox* case, the trial court in the adult system may retain jurisdiction if there is "clear and convincing evidence" that the juvenile should be tried as an adult. In many other states, such as North Dakota, the trial court in the adult system retains jurisdiction if there are "reasonable grounds" (in essence, probable cause) to believe that the juvenile committed the crime as charged and would not be "amenable to rehabilitation" in the juvenile system. See In the Interest of A.E., 559 N.W.2d 215 (N.D. 1997). Does *Maddox* convince you that the statutory requirement of judicial review makes little difference in transfer cases?

In 1998, about three percent of all felony defendants in the nation's 75 largest counties were juveniles. Two-thirds of the juveniles transferred to criminal court were charged with a violent offense; 59 percent of the juveniles transferred were convicted of a felony. In the 75 largest counties in 1994, almost two percent of juveniles older than age 14 were transferred to adult criminal courts by judicial waiver. See Bureau of Justice Statistics, Juvenile Felony Defendants in Criminal Courts (Sept. 1998, NCJ 165815).

2. *Constitutional challenges to charging of juveniles.* Juveniles in several states have challenged the constitutionality of statutes that mandate the choice of the adult system for some cases or that give prosecutors the discretion to file charges in the adult system. These challenges are based on many different clauses in state constitutions, most frequently due process and equal protection clauses. More often than not, the challenges have failed. See Manduley v. Superior Court, 41 P.3d 3 (Cal. 2002) (upholds constitutionality of system allowing prosecutor to choose juvenile versus adult system for certain defendants); but see State v. Mohi, 901 P.2d 991 (Utah 1995) (strikes down statute for excessive prosecutorial discretion; concludes that statutes in other states limit more severely the class of juveniles subject to transfer by prosecutor, or list criteria for eligible juveniles).

Juveniles have also found very limited success in challenging the procedures used at a judicial hearing to determine whether to transfer a case from one system to another, and in challenging the complete absence of such a judicial hearing. See In re Boot, 925 P.2d 964 (Wash. 1996) (statute giving exclusive original jurisdiction over juveniles charged with specified crimes to adult criminal court does not permit hearing on juvenile court jurisdiction; assignment to adult court without declination hearing does not violate procedural or substantive due process or equal protection); but see Hughes v. State, 653 A.2d 241 (Del. 1994) (statute's elimination of judicial investigation into factual basis of felony charge against child who reaches age of 18 while pending trial violates constitutional guarantees of due process and equal protection).

3. *Right to counsel in juvenile delinquency proceedings.* The right to retained counsel in delinquency proceedings was made a federal constitutional requirement in In re Gault, 387 U.S. 1 (1967). Because counsel is not appointed or is often waived,

less than half of all juveniles are represented by legal counsel in their delinquency proceedings. Barry Feld, Criminalizing the American Juvenile Court 222 (1993). Statutes in many states have created systems for appointing counsel for at least some juvenile proceedings. Roughly 10 states have mandatory appointment statutes; about half the states make appointment of counsel discretionary. See Tory Caeti, Craig Hemmens, and Velmer Burton, Jr., Juvenile Right to Counsel: A National Comparison of State Legal Codes, 23 Am. J. Crim. L. 611 (1996). Jury trials are not available in the juvenile system even when they would be required for comparable charges in the adult system. In situations where transfer into the adult criminal courts means that the state will appoint an attorney and provide a jury, will a juvenile welcome the transfer?

4. *Consequences at later sentencing.* In more than 40 states, adjudications in the juvenile system can be used years later to increase a sentence imposed in adult court for some later criminal offense. Adult criminal defendants have challenged this use of their juvenile adjudications, arguing that the lack of procedural safeguards in the juvenile system (such as absence of a jury trial or appointed counsel) should bar the use of the juvenile adjudication as a "prior conviction." Some courts have accepted this argument for cases in which the juvenile was not represented by counsel.

5. *Abolition of juvenile court?* The first juvenile court was created in Chicago after the Illinois legislature passed the Illinois Juvenile Court Act of 1899. By 1925, 46 states, 3 territories and the District of Columbia had separate juvenile courts. See Robert E. Shepherd, The Juvenile Court at 100 Years: A Look Back, Juvenile Justice, Vol 6, No. 2, p.13 (OJJDP, Dec. 1999). About twenty states have created "family courts" with broader jurisdiction to handle the full range of criminal and civil issues involving children. Now, 100 years after their creation, juvenile courts are under attack. Are children who commit crimes better served by having a separate system for adjudicating their crimes and imposing sentences? Or would they be better off in a single criminal justice system, perhaps with special allowances made for their age? What conditions are necessary for a successful separate juvenile system?

6. *Disparate racial impact in juvenile justice.* A report funded by the U.S. Department of Justice and several private foundations documented some major disparities in the treatment of white and black defendants in the juvenile justice system. Some of the findings of the report are as follows:

> It is clear that minority youth are more likely than others to come into contact with the juvenile justice system. Research suggests that this disparity is most pronounced at the beginning stages of involvement with the juvenile justice system. When racial/ethnic differences are found, they tend to accumulate as youth are processed through the system. . . .
>
> - In 1998, African American youth were overrepresented as a proportion of arrests in 26 of 29 offense categories documented by the FBI.
> - In 1997, the majority of cases referred to juvenile court involved White youth. Minority youth were overrepresented in the referral cohort. . . . While White youth comprised 66 percent of the juvenile court referral population they comprised 53 percent of the detained population. In contrast, African American youths made up 31 percent of the referral population and 44 percent of the detained population. . . .
> - For offenses against persons, White youth were 57 percent of cases petitioned but only 45 percent of cases waived to adult court. African American youth charged with similar offenses were 40 percent of the cases petitioned but rose to 50 percent of

cases waived to adult court. Similarly, in drug cases, White youth were 59 percent of cases petitioned but only 35 percent of cases waived to adult court. . . .

- In 1993, when controlling for current offense and prior admissions, incarceration rates to state public facilities were higher for African American and Latino youth than White youth. . . . African American youth were confined on average for 61 days more than White youth, and Latino youth were confined 112 days more than white youth.

Eileen Poe-Yamagata & Michael Jones, And Justice for Some (Building Blocks for Youth, 2000). The racial disparities described in the report are larger than disparities found in some studies of the adult criminal justice system. As a legislator, how would you respond to this study? Would you argue to transfer fewer juveniles into the adult system (even though the racial disparities in the adult system might be smaller overall)? To make the juvenile system less discretionary?

Another critical choice of system for many serious cases is between state and federal court, or between different state courts. For large classes of drug and firearm cases, for example, there is overlapping state and federal jurisdiction. Consider the following problem.

Problem 13-3. Federal Day

In Manhattan, federal prosecutors have developed a program known as "Federal Day." One day each week chosen at random, all drug arrests obtained by state and local police agencies are processed in federal court, where sentences for drug crimes are much higher than they are in the state courts. Prosecutors say that the program is designed to help the overwhelmed state courts and to deter criminal activity by imposing the stiffer sentences. Since 1983 there have been between 100 and 200 federal indictments per year in cases that the local police have developed. For instance, 231 cases went to federal district court under the Federal Day program between January 1984 and May 1986. During that same period, New York police made 5,837 felony narcotics arrests. Of the 5,606 cases sent to the state prosecutor in Manhattan, 1,172 resulted in state felony indictments. A total of 1,043 other cases were reduced to state misdemeanors.

A U.S. Senator has heard about the Federal Day program and plans to introduce legislation requiring all U.S. Attorneys' offices to institute such programs. Would you advise the U.S. Attorney for Manhattan to continue the program? Under what conditions? Do you believe that those who support the Manhattan policy will also support the proposed legislation, and vice versa? What are the prospects for its passage? Compare Katherine Bishop, Mandatory Sentences in Drug Cases: Is the Law Defeating Its Purpose? N.Y. Times, June 8, 1990, at B16. See also Sara Sun Beale, Federalizing Hate Crimes: Symbolic Politics, Expressive Law, or Tool for Criminal Enforcement? 80 Boston Univ. L. Rev. 1227 (2000); Kathleen Brickey, Criminal Mischief: The Federalization of American Criminal Law, 46 Hastings L.J. 1135 (1995).

Note

The federalization trend. The federal government has been exerting more authority and money on criminal matters during the last few decades than at any previous point in the nation's history. The 1999 report of the American Bar Association's Task Force on Federalization of Criminal Law documents various aspects of this growth. Federal crime legislation has become more common: "more than forty percent of the federal criminal provisions enacted since the Civil War have been enacted since 1970." The number of federal investigators and prosecutors has expanded along with the number of available federal crimes. The types of cases making up the federal criminal docket have also shifted in recent decades. Federal theft and forgery cases have become less common; the number of federal fraud cases have increased. Narcotics offenses have increased more than any other category (18 percent of the caseload in 1977 and 36 percent in 1997). The report lists some negative consequences of federalization: "diminution of the stature of the state courts in the perception of citizens" and "disparate results for the same conduct." What would be a legitimate basis for extending federal law to criminalize additional conduct? Would the same arguments support a new emphasis in enforcing existing federal laws? See Michael A. Simons, Prosecutorial Discretion and Prosecution Guidelines: A Case Study in Controlling Federalization, 75 N.Y.U. L. Rev. 893 (2000).

5. *Selective Prosecution*

For each of the prosecutorial charging decisions considered in this chapter, judges mostly refuse to second-guess the exercise of charging discretion. A prosecutor might make very different charging decisions in two similar cases and will not have to explain those choices. In all of these cases, however, judges asked to review the prosecutor's decision point out that if a prosecutor bases the charging decision on some constitutionally suspect grounds — such as the defendant's race or gender — the court stands willing to step in. Similarly, the prosecutor cannot file a charge as a way of punishing a defendant for taking constitutionally protected action, such as exercising free speech or insisting on a jury trial. Thus, a prosecutor can have many different reasons for a charging decision, but she cannot rely on a limited set of constitutionally improper reasons. How is a defendant to know the prosecutor's reason for a particular charging decision?

■ UNITED STATES v. CHRISTOPHER ARMSTRONG

517 U.S. 456 (1996)

REHNQUIST, C.J.

In this case, we consider the showing necessary for a defendant to be entitled to discovery on a claim that the prosecuting attorney singled him out for prosecution on the basis of his race. We conclude that respondents failed to satisfy the threshold showing: They failed to show that the Government declined to prosecute similarly situated suspects of other races.

In April 1992, respondents were indicted in the United States District Court for the Central District of California on charges of conspiring to possess with intent to distribute more than 50 grams of cocaine base (crack) and conspiring to distribute the same, [and federal firearms offenses]. In response to the indictment, respondents filed a motion for discovery or for dismissal of the indictment, alleging that they were selected for federal prosecution because they are black. In support of their motion, they offered only an affidavit by a "Paralegal Specialist," employed by the

Office of the Federal Public Defender representing one of the respondents. The only allegation in the affidavit was that, in every one of the 24 [narcotics] cases closed by the office during 1991, the defendant was black. Accompanying the affidavit was a "study" listing the 24 defendants, their race, whether they were prosecuted for dealing cocaine as well as crack, and the status of each case.

The Government opposed the discovery motion, arguing, among other things, that there was no evidence or allegation "that the Government has acted unfairly or has prosecuted non-black defendants or failed to prosecute them." The District Court granted the motion. It ordered the Government (1) to provide a list of all cases from the last three years in which the Government charged both cocaine and firearms offenses, (2) to identify the race of the defendants in those cases, (3) to identify what levels of law enforcement were involved in the investigations of those cases, and (4) to explain its criteria for deciding to prosecute those defendants for federal cocaine offenses.

The Government moved for reconsideration of the District Court's discovery order. With this motion it submitted affidavits and other evidence to explain why it had chosen to prosecute respondents and why respondents' study did not support the inference that the Government was singling out blacks for cocaine prosecution. The federal and local agents participating in the case alleged in affidavits that race played no role in their investigation. An Assistant United States Attorney explained in an affidavit that the decision to prosecute met the general criteria for prosecution, because

> there was over 100 grams of cocaine base involved, over twice the threshold necessary for a ten year mandatory minimum sentence; there were multiple sales involving multiple defendants, thereby indicating a fairly substantial crack cocaine ring; . . . there were multiple federal firearms violations intertwined with the narcotics trafficking; the overall evidence in the case was extremely strong, including audio and videotapes of defendants; . . . and several of the defendants had criminal histories including narcotics and firearms violations.

The Government also submitted sections of a published 1989 Drug Enforcement Administration report which concluded that "[l]arge-scale, interstate trafficking networks controlled by Jamaicans, Haitians and Black street gangs dominate the manufacture and distribution of crack." In response, one of respondents' attorneys submitted an affidavit alleging that an intake coordinator at a drug treatment center had told her that there are "an equal number of caucasian users and dealers to minority users and dealers." Respondents also submitted an affidavit from a criminal defense attorney alleging that in his experience many nonblacks are prosecuted in state court for crack offenses. . . . The District Court denied the motion for reconsideration. When the Government indicated it would not comply with the court's discovery order, the court dismissed the case. [The Court of Appeals affirmed the order.]

A selective-prosecution claim is not a defense on the merits to the criminal charge itself, but an independent assertion that the prosecutor has brought the charge for reasons forbidden by the Constitution. Our cases delineating the necessary elements to prove a claim of selective prosecution have taken great pains to explain that the standard is a demanding one. These cases afford a "background presumption" that the showing necessary to obtain discovery should itself be a significant barrier to the litigation of insubstantial claims.

A selective-prosecution claim asks a court to exercise judicial power over a "special province" of the Executive. The Attorney General and United States Attorneys retain "broad discretion" to enforce the Nation's criminal laws. Wayte v. United States, 470 U.S. 598 (1985). They have this latitude because they are designated by statute as the President's delegates to help him discharge his constitutional responsibility to "take Care that the Laws be faithfully executed." U.S. Const., Art. II, §3. . . .

Of course, a prosecutor's discretion is subject to constitutional constraints. One of these constraints, imposed by the equal protection component of the Due Process Clause of the Fifth Amendment, is that the decision whether to prosecute may not be based on "an unjustifiable standard such as race, religion, or other arbitrary classification," Oyler v. Boles, 368 U.S. 448, 456 (1962). A defendant may demonstrate that the administration of a criminal law is "directed so exclusively against a particular class of persons . . . with a mind so unequal and oppressive" that the system of prosecution amounts to "a practical denial" of equal protection of the law. Yick Wo v. Hopkins, 118 U.S. 356, 373 (1886).

In order to dispel the presumption that a prosecutor has not violated equal protection, a criminal defendant must present clear evidence to the contrary. We explained in *Wayte* why courts are "properly hesitant to examine the decision whether to prosecute." Judicial deference to the decisions of these executive officers rests in part on an assessment of the relative competence of prosecutors and courts. "Such factors as the strength of the case, the prosecution's general deterrence value, the Government's enforcement priorities, and the case's relationship to the Government's overall enforcement plan are not readily susceptible to the kind of analysis the courts are competent to undertake." It also stems from a concern not to unnecessarily impair the performance of a core executive constitutional function. "Examining the basis of a prosecution delays the criminal proceeding, threatens to chill law enforcement by subjecting the prosecutor's motives and decisionmaking to outside inquiry, and may undermine prosecutorial effectiveness by revealing the Government's enforcement policy."

The requirements for a selective-prosecution claim draw on ordinary equal protection standards. The claimant must demonstrate that the federal prosecutorial policy had a discriminatory effect and that it was motivated by a discriminatory purpose. To establish a discriminatory effect in a race case, the claimant must show that similarly situated individuals of a different race were not prosecuted. This requirement has been established in our case law since Ah Sin v. Wittman, 198 U.S. 500 (1905). Ah Sin, a subject of China, petitioned a California state court for a writ of habeas corpus, seeking discharge from imprisonment under a San Francisco county ordinance prohibiting persons from setting up gambling tables in rooms barricaded to stop police from entering. He alleged in his habeas petition "that the ordinance is enforced solely and exclusively against persons of the Chinese race and not otherwise." We rejected his contention that this averment made out a claim under the Equal Protection Clause, because it did not allege "that the conditions and practices to which the ordinance was directed did not exist exclusively among the Chinese, or that there were other offenders against the ordinance than the Chinese as to whom it was not enforced."

The similarly situated requirement does not make a selective-prosecution claim impossible to prove. Twenty years before *Ah Sin,* we invalidated an ordinance, also adopted by San Francisco, that prohibited the operation of laundries in wooden buildings. *Yick Wo,* 118 U.S. at 374. The plaintiff in error successfully demonstrated that the ordinance was applied against Chinese nationals but not against other laundry-shop operators. The authorities had denied the applications of 200 Chinese subjects for permits to operate shops in wooden buildings, but granted the applications of 80 individuals who were not Chinese subjects to operate laundries in wooden buildings "under similar conditions." . . .

Having reviewed the requirements to prove a selective-prosecution claim, we turn to the showing necessary to obtain discovery in support of such a claim. If discovery is ordered, the Government must assemble from its own files documents which might corroborate or refute the defendant's claim. Discovery thus imposes many of the costs present when the Government must respond to a prima facie case of selective prosecution. It will divert prosecutors' resources and may disclose the Government's prosecutorial strategy. The justifications for a rigorous standard for the elements of a selective-prosecution claim thus require a correspondingly rigorous standard for discovery in aid of such a claim.

The parties [describe] the requisite showing to establish entitlement to discovery . . . with a variety of phrases, like "colorable basis," "substantial threshold showing," "substantial and concrete basis," or "reasonable likelihood." However, the many labels for this showing conceal the degree of consensus about the evidence necessary to meet it. The Courts of Appeals require some evidence tending to show the existence of the essential elements of the defense, discriminatory effect and discriminatory intent.

In this case we consider what evidence constitutes "some evidence tending to show the existence" of the discriminatory effect element. . . . The vast majority of the Courts of Appeals require the defendant to produce some evidence that similarly situated defendants of other races could have been prosecuted, but were not, and this requirement is consistent with our equal protection case law.[3]

The Court of Appeals [in this case] reached its decision in part because it started "with the presumption that people of all races commit all types of crimes — not with the premise that any type of crime is the exclusive province of any particular racial or ethnic group." It cited no authority for this proposition, which seems contradicted by the most recent statistics of the United States Sentencing Commission. Those statistics show that: More than 90 percent of the persons sentenced in 1994 for crack cocaine trafficking were black, 93.4 percent of convicted LSD dealers were white, and 91 percent of those convicted for pornography or prostitution were white. Presumptions at war with presumably reliable statistics have no proper place in the analysis of this issue.

The Court of Appeals also expressed concern about the "evidentiary obstacles defendants face." But . . . if the claim of selective prosecution were well founded, it should not have been an insuperable task to prove that persons of other races were being treated differently than respondents. For instance, respondents could have investigated whether similarly situated persons of other races were prosecuted by the State of California, were known to federal law enforcement officers, but were not prosecuted in federal court. We think the required threshold — a credible showing of different treatment of similarly situated persons — adequately balances the Government's interest in vigorous prosecution and the defendant's interest in avoiding selective prosecution.

3. We reserve the question whether a defendant must satisfy the similarly situated requirement in a case involving direct admissions by prosecutors of discriminatory purpose.

In the case before us, respondents' "study" did not constitute some evidence tending to show the existence of the essential elements of a selective-prosecution claim. The study failed to identify individuals who were not black, could have been prosecuted for the offenses for which respondents were charged, but were not so prosecuted. This omission was not remedied by respondents' evidence in opposition to the Government's motion for reconsideration. . . . Respondents' affidavits, which recounted one attorney's conversation with a drug treatment center employee and the experience of another attorney defending drug prosecutions in state court, recounted hearsay and reported personal conclusions based on anecdotal evidence. The judgment of the Court of Appeals is therefore reversed, and the case is remanded for proceedings consistent with this opinion. It is so ordered.

STEVENS, J., dissenting.

Federal prosecutors are respected members of a respected profession. Despite an occasional misstep, the excellence of their work abundantly justifies the presumption that they have properly discharged their official duties. Nevertheless, the possibility that political or racial animosity may infect a decision to institute criminal proceedings cannot be ignored. For that reason, it has long been settled that the prosecutor's broad discretion to determine when criminal charges should be filed is not completely unbridled. . . .

The Court correctly concludes that in this case the facts presented to the District Court in support of respondents' claim that they had been singled out for prosecution because of their race were not sufficient to prove that defense. Moreover, I agree with the Court that their showing was not strong enough to give them a right to discovery, either under Rule 16 or under the District Court's inherent power to order discovery in appropriate circumstances. [H]owever, I am persuaded that the District Judge did not abuse her discretion when she concluded that the factual showing was sufficiently disturbing to require some response from the United States Attorney's Office. Perhaps the discovery order was broader than necessary, but I cannot agree with the Court's apparent conclusion that no inquiry was permissible.

The District Judge's order should be evaluated in light of three circumstances that underscore the need for judicial vigilance over certain types of drug prosecutions. First, the Anti-Drug Abuse Act of 1986 and subsequent legislation established a regime of extremely high penalties for the possession and distribution of so-called "crack" cocaine. Those provisions treat one gram of crack as the equivalent of 100 grams of powder cocaine. The distribution of 50 grams of crack is thus punishable by the same mandatory minimum sentence of 10 years in prison that applies to the distribution of 5,000 grams of powder cocaine. . . . Second, the disparity between the treatment of crack cocaine and powder cocaine is matched by the disparity between the severity of the punishment imposed by federal law and that imposed by state law for the same conduct. For a variety of reasons, often including the absence of mandatory minimums, the existence of parole, and lower baseline penalties, terms of imprisonment for drug offenses tend to be substantially lower in state systems than in the federal system. The difference is especially marked in the case of crack offenses. . . . Finally, it is undisputed that the brunt of the elevated federal penalties falls heavily on blacks. While 65 percent of the persons who have used crack are white, in 1993 they represented only 4 percent of the federal offenders convicted of trafficking in crack. Eighty-eight percent of such defendants were black. . . . Those figures represent a major threat to the integrity of federal sentencing reform, whose main purpose was the elimination of disparity (especially racial) in sentencing. . . .

The extraordinary severity of the imposed penalties and the troubling racial patterns of enforcement give rise to a special concern about the fairness of charging practices for crack offenses. Evidence tending to prove that black defendants charged with distribution of crack in the Central District of California are prosecuted in federal court, whereas members of other races charged with similar offenses are prosecuted in state court, warrants close scrutiny by the federal judges in that District. In my view, the District Judge, who has sat on both the federal and the state benches in Los Angeles, acted well within her discretion to call for the development of facts that would demonstrate what standards, if any, governed the choice of forum where similarly situated offenders are prosecuted. . . .

The majority discounts the probative value of the [defendant's] affidavits, claiming that they recounted "hearsay" and reported "personal conclusions based on anecdotal evidence." But [i]t was certainly within the District Court's discretion to credit the affidavits of two members of the bar of that Court, at least one of whom had presumably acquired a reputation by his frequent appearances there, and both of whose statements were made on pains of perjury. The criticism that the affidavits were based on "anecdotal evidence" is also unpersuasive. I thought it was agreed that defendants do not need to prepare sophisticated statistical studies in order to receive mere discovery in cases like this one. . . .

Even if respondents failed to carry their burden of showing that there were individuals who were not black but who could have been prosecuted in federal court for the same offenses, it does not follow that the District Court abused its discretion in ordering discovery. There can be no doubt that such individuals exist, and indeed the Government has never denied the same. In those circumstances, I fail to see why the District Court was unable to take judicial notice of this obvious fact and demand information from the Government's files to support or refute respondents' evidence. The presumption that some whites are prosecuted in state court is not "contradicted" by the statistics the majority cites, which show only that high percentages of blacks are convicted of certain federal crimes, while high percentages of whites are convicted of other federal crimes. Those figures are entirely consistent with the allegation of selective prosecution. The relevant comparison, rather, would be with the percentages of blacks and whites who commit those crimes. But, as discussed above, in the case of crack far greater numbers of whites are believed guilty of using the substance. The District Court, therefore, was entitled to find the evidence before her significant and to require some explanation from the Government.[6] I therefore respectfully dissent. . . .

Notes

1. *Selective prosecution: majority position.* The U.S. Supreme Court has made it clear from time to time that it is possible, at least in theory, for a court to overturn a

6. Also telling was the Government's response to respondents' evidentiary showing. It submitted a list of more than 3,500 defendants who had been charged with federal narcotics violations over the previous 3 years. It also offered the names of 11 nonblack defendants whom it had prosecuted for crack offenses. All 11, however, were members of other racial or ethnic minorities. . . .

prosecutor's charging decision when it is based on a constitutionally impermissible ground such as race, religion, or sex. A defendant who makes such a claim must establish that (a) the prosecutor made different charging decisions for similarly situated suspects (a discriminatory effect), and (b) the prosecutor intentionally made the decision on the basis of an "arbitrary" classification (a discriminatory intent). Arbitrary classifications would include "suspect classes" under equal protection doctrine and those exercising their constitutional liberties such as freedom of speech or religion. See Oyler v. Boles, 368 U.S. 448 (1962); Wayte v. United States, 470 U.S. 598 (1985). The *Wayte* decision made it clear that the government must choose the defendant for prosecution "because of" and not "despite" the protected conduct or status of the defendant. In that case, the government had prosecuted for draft evasion a person who had publicly criticized the military draft. The government had chosen to prosecute the case under a "passive enforcement" policy, in which the government filed charges only when told about a person's refusal to register for the draft and only when the person refused to comply with the law after a specific request. The government carried out this policy in Wayte's case, despite (and not because of) his speech criticizing the draft. This basic federal framework for analyzing constitutional challenges to discriminatory charging policies has also been very influential in state courts. See, e.g., Salaiscooper v. Eighth Judicial District Court ex rel. County of Clark, 34 P.3d 509 (Nev. 2001) (disparate treatment of prostitutes and customers is not discrimination on basis of sex); State v. Muetze, 534 N.W.2d 55 (S.D. 1995) (no proof that non-Native Americans who were not charged were similarly situated).

2. *Discovery to support selective prosecution claims.* According to the opinion in *Armstrong,* a court hearing a claim of selective prosecution may grant discovery to the defendant if there is "some evidence" to support each of the elements of the claim. Do you agree with the court that the defendants in *Armstrong* failed to produce "some evidence"?

What sort of evidence is likely to be available to support a selective prosecution claim? To show disparate treatment, a defendant must prove that he is "similarly situated" to a pool of other suspects who were not prosecuted. Those who are similarly situated would have committed basically the same act as the defendant. Further, there could be no significant difference in the harm caused by these similar acts, and prosecution of one case could not be significantly less costly or difficult than the others. Where can a defendant get information about this pool of unprosecuted suspects?

Will it ever be possible to prove disparate impact in those prosecutorial offices (the overwhelming majority) in which the prosecuting attorneys keep no records of the cases they decline to charge or of the reasons for the declination? Very few courts have reversed convictions on selective prosecution grounds, and no Supreme Court opinions have done so on racial grounds except for Yick Wo v. Hopkins, 118 U.S. 356 (1886). Does this pattern prove anything? What did the claimants in *Yick Wo* do that claimants today might emulate?

3. *Racial patterns in charging.* It is clear that racial minorities are charged with crimes at a rate disproportionate to their numbers. But is the rate higher after accounting for different levels of participation in crime? Criminologists addressing this question have studied records of large numbers of cases using statistical techniques (especially "regression" analysis) to compare similar cases and sort out racial and nonracial influences over charging decisions. For instance, one study by

Richard Berk analyzed the correlation between race and crack cocaine charging practices in Los Angeles between 1990 and 1992. The study indicates that the U.S. Attorney prosecuted black offenders at a higher rate than comparable white offenders. Richard Berk and Alec Campbell, Preliminary Data on Race and Crack Charging Practices in Los Angeles, 6 Fed. Sentencing Rep. 36 (1993). See also Cassia Spohn, John Gruhl, and Susan Welch, The Impact of the Ethnicity and Gender of Defendants on the Decision to Reject or Dismiss Felony Charges, 25 Criminology 175 (1987) (study of 33,000 felony cases between 1977 and 1980 to determine whether racial bias influenced prosecutor's decisions to decline felony charges; declinations occur more frequently for white suspects after controlling for age, criminal record, and seriousness of offense); Developments in the Law—Race and the Criminal Process, 101 Harv. L. Rev. 1520 (1988) (summarizing other studies). Does any of this analysis support the conclusion that selective prosecution doctrine fails to control biased prosecution? If racial discrimination in charging is indeed widespread, is it unrealistic to ask a defendant to make a prediscovery showing?

4. *Racial discrimination and written charging policies.* Do charging policies reduce the likelihood that individual prosecutors will consider race as a factor in charging decisions? As we saw earlier in this chapter, the state of Washington has passed a statute instructing prosecutors on the general factors to consider when making a charging decision. A 1994 study of King County, Washington (where written office policies supplement the state statutes) attempted to determine whether race influenced the charging decisions of prosecutors. See Larry Michael Fehr, Racial and Ethnic Disparities in Prosecution and Sentencing: Empirical Research of the Washington State Minority and Justice Commission, 32 Gonz. L. Rev. 577 (1996/97). The study found that white defendants were charged in 60 percent of the cases referred to prosecutors, while black defendants were charged in 65 percent. The researchers could explain only part of this difference based on legally relevant factors, such as the type of crime involved.

5. *Prosecutorial vindictiveness.* If all criminal defendants were to insist on exercising all of their constitutional and statutory procedural rights, they could make life difficult for a prosecutor. Can a prosecutor charge defendants more severely if they insist on a jury trial, an appeal, or some other procedural right? In Blackledge v. Perry, 417 U.S. 21 (1974), a defendant was initially charged in state district court with misdemeanor assault. After conviction, he requested a trial de novo on the charges in state superior court, and the prosecutor changed the charges to felony assault. The Supreme Court concluded that a prosecutor in such a situation would have an incentive to "retaliate" against the defendant for taking an action that the prosecutor finds inconvenient. Thus, the prosecutor would have to demonstrate on the record that the change in charges was based on some factor other than the defendant's exercise of procedural rights. The limit on "prosecutorial vindictiveness" set out in Blackledge v. Perry does not apply, however, to a prosecutor's *pretrial* decision to add or reduce charges based on a defendant's willingness to waive procedural rights. See United States v. Goodwin, 457 U.S. 368 (1982) (no presumption of vindictiveness where prosecutor changes misdemeanor charges to felony after defendant requests jury trial); Peter J. Henning, Prosecutorial Misconduct and Constitutional Remedies, 77 Wash. U. L.Q. 713 (1999). Is this distinction a meaningful one?

6. *Prosecution in the sunshine.* Would prosecutors benefit or lose more from the collection and publication of data on the race of every defendant and victim for every criminal matter the office encounters? If a chief prosecutor were to carry out

this policy (either voluntarily or pursuant to a statute), would she want to show the data broken down by type of crime and by the action the office chose to pursue? If you believe prosecutors would resist the collection and publication of such data, what arguments might they raise against this proposal? What if the legislature were willing to provide funds for any extra personnel needed to collect and analyze the data? See Angela J. Davis, Prosecution and Race: The Power and Privilege of Discretion, 67 Fordham L. Rev. 13 (1998) (proposing a requirement that prosecutors publish "racial impact studies").

C. GRAND JURY AND JUDICIAL SCREENING

"The grand jury would indict a hamburger."
— Traditional courthouse wisdom

Pretrial judicial hearings that go by names such as "initial appearance" and "preliminary examination" serve multiple functions. At the initial appearance, the magistrate informs the defendant about the nature of the charges, the right to remain silent, the right to appointed counsel, and other features of the criminal process. An initial appearance also gives the magistrate an occasion to assign counsel to indigent defendants (or at least to ascertain whether a defendant is eligible for appointed counsel) and to set bail or other conditions of pretrial release.

For our present purposes, we will focus on the ability of judges in these pretrial hearings to screen out charges without enough factual support. If the prosecutor, in the adversarial "preliminary examination," is not able to produce evidence showing probable cause to believe that the defendant committed the crime as charged, then the charges are dismissed and the defendant released. If probable cause is present, the magistrate will "bind over" the defendant for arraignment and trial in a court with jurisdiction to try the offense.

There are alternatives to the use of the preliminary judicial hearing as the initial filter in the accusatory process. The charges in most criminal cases are contained in a charging document known as an "information," which the prosecutor can file after judicial screening at the preliminary hearing, without consulting a grand jury. But in just under half of the states, a defendant can insist that the prosecutor seek the permission of a grand jury before filing felony charges. If the grand jury agrees with the prosecutor's request to charge an individual, the charges appear in a grand jury "indictment." In Chapter 10 we studied the role of the grand jury in investigating crimes — the grand jury as a "sword." Now we consider the grand jury's function as a "shield" against unfounded prosecutions, and the interaction between the grand jury and the judicial "preliminary examination" as screening devices.

The traditional image of the grand jury as a shield might be misleading. By all accounts, grand juries indict in virtually all cases when a prosecutor requests the indictment. There are several possible reasons for this, all built into the structure of the grand jury. See Andrew Leipold, Why Grand Juries Do Not (and Cannot) Protect the Accused, 80 Cornell L. Rev. 260 (1995). First, the grand jury's review standard is quite low: It must determine only whether there is probable cause to believe that the accused has committed the crime that the prosecutor has specified. Second, the grand jury proceedings are not adversarial. Only the prosecutor presents evidence to the grand jury, and he has no obligation (in most states) to present any exculpatory evidence. In most jurisdictions, no representatives of the grand jury witnesses or targets are even present in the grand jury room during testimony or deliberations.

■ NEW YORK CONSTITUTION ART. I, §6

No person shall be held to answer for a capital or otherwise infamous crime . . . unless on indictment of a grand jury, except that a person held for the action of a grand jury upon a charge for such an offense, other than one punishable by death or life imprisonment, with the consent of the district attorney, may waive indictment by a grand jury and consent to be prosecuted on an information filed by the district attorney; such waiver shall be evidenced by written instrument signed by the defendant in open court in the presence of his or her counsel. . . .

The power of grand juries to inquire into the wilful misconduct in office of public officers, and to find indictments or to direct the filing of informations in connection with such inquiries, shall never be suspended or impaired by law. . . .

■ ILLINOIS ANNOTATED STATUTES CH. 725, PARA. 5/111-2

(a) All prosecutions of felonies shall be by information or by indictment. No prosecution may be pursued by information unless a preliminary hearing has been held or waived . . . and at that hearing probable cause to believe the defendant committed an offense was found. . . .

(b) All other prosecutions may be by indictment, information or complaint. . . .

(f) Where the prosecution of a felony is by information or complaint after preliminary hearing, or after a waiver of preliminary hearing in accordance with paragraph (a) of this Section, such prosecution may be for all offenses, arising from the same transaction or conduct of a defendant even though the complaint or complaints filed at the preliminary hearing charged only one or some of the offenses arising from that transaction or conduct.

■ STATE v. ERIC EDMONSON

743 P.2d 459 (Idaho 1987)

DONALDSON, J.

Eric Roy Edmonson was indicted by a grand jury in Latah County on the following charges: racketeering; grand theft; conspiracy to engage in racketeering; conspiracy to engage in grand theft; and the falsification of corporate books and records. Edmonson filed a barrage of motions raising a number of constitutional and procedural arguments alleging error in the grand jury indictment and requesting the indictment be set aside. After a hearing, the district court issued an opinion denying the motions. . . .

On appeal Edmonson [argues that] dismissal of the indictment is required [due to the] prosecutor's use of the grand jury to indict was not based on any systematic set of criteria and therefore violates the Equal Protection Clause of the Idaho Constitution. . . . We reject all of Edmonson's contentions and affirm the trial court's findings. . . .

Edmonson contends that the use of a grand jury in this case deprived him of the equal protection of the laws in violation of art. 1, §2 of the Idaho Constitution. [He] argues that the system used in Idaho allowing the prosecutor unfettered discretion to initiate criminal proceedings by indictment or information without regard to any systematic or coherent policy violates a defendant's right to equal protection. Here, two other co-defendants were charged by information rather than by indictment. Since the prosecutor did not have any systematic coherent policy to decide when to proceed by indictment or information, but rather arbitrarily made that decision, Edmonson contends that he was denied the same rights as his co-defendants, namely the right to a preliminary hearing.

Article 1, §8 of the Idaho Constitution provides:

> No person shall be held to answer for any felony or criminal offense of any grade, unless on presentment or indictment of a grand jury or on information of the public prosecutor, after a commitment by a magistrate . . . ; provided [that] after a charge has been ignored by a grand jury, no person shall be held to answer, or for trial therefor, upon information of the public prosecutor.

Thus, the prosecutor can use either a grand jury proceeding or a preliminary hearing before an impartial magistrate to initiate criminal proceedings. However, the rights afforded the accused in these proceedings are different. A proceeding initiated by information entitles the accused the right to a preliminary hearing before an impartial magistrate to determine whether a crime has been committed and whether there is probable cause to believe that the accused committed it. The accused has the right to assistance of counsel, the right to produce evidence, and the right to cross-examine adverse witnesses. These procedures allow an accused to contest the prosecutor's evidence and the right to a finding of probable cause by an impartial and detached judicial officer.

In contrast, an indictment by a grand jury does not afford the accused a right to a preliminary hearing. Only the prosecutor and witnesses under examination may be present during the grand jury proceeding. Further, the grand jury is not bound to hear evidence presented by the defendant; however, it is required to weigh all evidence submitted to it, and can require additional evidence when necessary.

Edmonson relies on a series of Oregon cases starting with State v. Clark, 630 P.2d 810 (Or. 1981), continuing with State v. Edmonson, 630 P.2d 822 (Or. 1981), and State v. Freeland, 667 P.2d 509 (Or. 1983), to support his argument that a prosecutor must afford all similarly situated defendants equal treatment of the laws. In [these cases], the defendants were charged by indictment and not afforded a preliminary hearing. They . . . argued that a denial of a preliminary hearing violated their rights to equal protection of the laws because other potential defendants charged with the same crime could be charged by an information and allowed a preliminary hearing. The Oregon Supreme Court rejected this contention, noting that its constitution provides for alternative charging methods (information with a preliminary hearing or indictment without one) which are capable of valid administration. However, the court held that a choice between indictment and information must "rest on meaningful criteria that indeed make the privileges of a preliminary hearing equally available to all persons similarly situated. . . ." In other words, the equal protection clause of the Oregon constitution prevents the prosecutor from arbitrarily choosing to proceed by indictment or information, but instead, requires the choice be made on a coherent, systematic basis. . . .

Edmonson urges us to adopt the reasoning of the Oregon Supreme Court. We refuse to do so. . . . In this case, we have two constitutional provisions that need to be construed together. Art. 1, §8 allows for alternative charging procedures which are of equal dignity. Art. 1, §2 guarantees equal rights, privileges and immunities to all persons within the state. The appellant argues that art. 1, §2 is a limitation of art. 1, §8. [Constitutional provisions, like statutes,] must be construed, if at all possible, consistently and harmoniously. Either of the two alternative charging procedures can be used, but will be subject to an equal protection analysis. . . .

First we note that the United States Supreme Court has held that a state's refusal to afford a criminal defendant a preliminary hearing does not violate the fourteenth amendment through the fifth amendment. Lem Woon v. Oregon, 229 U.S. 586 (1913). In a slightly different context (whether a person arrested and held for trial is entitled to a judicial determination of probable cause for detention), the Supreme Court also has held [that cross-examination and rules of evidence are not constitutionally required during a preliminary hearing]. As the Court stated in Gerstein v. Pugh, 420 U.S. 103, 121-122 (1975):

> The use of an informal procedure is justified not only by the lesser consequences of a probable cause determination but also by the nature of the determination itself. It does not require the fine resolution of conflicting evidence that a reasonable-doubt or even a preponderance standard demands, and credibility determinations are seldom crucial in deciding whether the evidence supports a reasonable belief in guilt. . . .

Even an informal procedure in which an accused is not given the right to contest the state's evidence, or even put on his own evidence is not per se constitutionally infirm. . . .

The grand jury is an accusing body and not a trial court. Its functions are investigative and charging. The purpose of both a grand jury proceeding and a preliminary hearing is to determine probable cause. Any advantage that a preliminary hearing affords a defendant is purely incidental to that purpose. The independent grand jury's function would be duplicated by requiring a subsequent preliminary hearing.

Professors LaFave and Israel have discussed prosecutorial discretion and noted many valid reasons why a prosecutor may choose to proceed by either alternative:

> . . . The tradition in most information jurisdictions is to prosecute by information in all but a very small group of cases that require the grand jury's investigative authority. . . . In most information states, when a prosecutor uses the indictment process his basic objective is not to avoid the preliminary hearing, but to utilize some other feature of the indictment process. . . . But prosecutors in other information jurisdictions have been known to use the indictment alternative in certain cases mainly because they want to avoid the preliminary hearing. Grounds typically advanced for avoiding the hearing in those cases, notwithstanding the prosecutor's usual preference for prosecution by information, include: (1) the desire to save time where the preliminary hearing would be protracted due to the number of exhibits or witnesses or the number of separate hearings that would have to be held for separate defendants (the grand jury could save time in such situations due to the absence of cross-examination, less stringent application of

> evidentiary rules, and its capacity to consider a series of related cases in a single presentation); (2) the desire to preclude the defense discovery inherent in a preliminary hearing, particularly where a key witness is an informer whose identity should be shielded until trial; and (3) the desire to limit the number of times that a particular complainant (e.g., a victim of a sex offense) will be required to give testimony in public. [Wayne LaFave and Jerold Israel, Criminal Procedure §14.2 (1984).]

There are a number of other factors which may influence the prosecutor's choice of indictment or information. Uncertainty of the law, credibility of witnesses, the winds of public opinion, the nature of the offense, publicity surrounding the crime and the resources of investigation are just some of these factors. We accept the above reasoning as persuasive and hold that a prosecutor may proceed by either alternative — indictment or information. . . .

Edmonson has not shown, nor even contended discriminatory intent by the prosecutor in respect to the charging selection. The prosecutor did choose to allow similarly situated defendants a preliminary hearing, but without more evidence of a deliberate and intentional plan to discriminate, we cannot conclude that the equal protection clause was violated. . . .

BISTLINE, J., dissenting.

[In] territorial days, all prosecutions after commitment were by grand jury indictment. There was no alternative provision for prosecution upon a prosecutor's information. . . . To prosecution under indictment the Constitutional Convention, after considerable debate, added that a committed defendant could also be charged and tried in district court by a prosecutor's information. . . . Although art. 1, §8 of the Idaho Constitution is not identical to art. 1, §8 of the 1879 California Constitution, it is virtually the same. Both provisions allow for prosecution of offenses by information of the public prosecutor, or by indictment. Mr. Standrod of Oneida County in speaking for the use of an information, as an alternative to an indictment, after first expounding on the paucity of crime and the cost to the counties of grand juries, specifically referred the Convention to what he called the California success: "and in California, that great state, where the survival of the fittest is a maxim that has been put into practical use, instead of theory, they have adopted this plan and the prosecutions of this state have been successful and they are conducted under a section of this kind."

[The California Supreme Court has recently interpreted this analogous constitutional provision in Hawkins v. Superior Court, 586 P.2d 916 (Cal. 1978). That court concluded] that an accused is denied equal protection of the law when prosecuted by indictment and deprived of a preliminary hearing and the concomitant rights which attach when prosecution is by information:

> The defendant accused by information immediately becomes entitled to an impressive array of procedural rights, including a preliminary hearing before a neutral and legally knowledgeable magistrate, representation by retained or appointed counsel, the confrontation and cross-examination of hostile witnesses, and the opportunity to personally appear and affirmatively present exculpatory evidence. In vivid contrast, the indictment procedure omits all the above safeguards: the defendant has no right to appear or be represented by counsel, and consequently may not confront and cross-examine the witnesses against him, object to evidence introduced by the prosecutor, make legal arguments, or present evidence to explain or contradict the charge. . . .

> It cannot be seriously argued that an indicted defendant enjoys a comparable opportunity to discover the state's case and develop evidence because he later obtains a transcript of grand jury proceedings. Such a transcript will invariably reflect only what the prosecuting attorney permits it to reflect; it is certainly no substitute for the possibility of developing further evidence through a probing cross-examination of prosecution witnesses — a possibility foreclosed with the denial of an adversarial proceeding. There is no other effective means for the defense to compel the cooperation of a hostile witness.
>
> [C]urrent indictment procedures create what can only be characterized as a prosecutor's Eden: he decides what evidence will be heard, how it is to be presented, and then advises the grand jury on its admissibility and legal significance. In sharp contrast are information procedures. . . . Yet the prosecuting attorney is free in his completely unfettered discretion to choose which defendants will be charged by indictment rather than information and consequently which catalogue of rights, widely disparate though they may be, a defendant will receive. He may act out of what he believes to be proper law enforcement motives, or he may act whimsically; no case law or statutory guidelines exist to circumscribe his discretion. [586 P.2d at 917-921.]

. . . In days not too long ago, accused defendants were taken to preliminary hearings, and, if indigent, had no representation. Only on going to trial was counsel appointed for the indigent accused, who often waived the right. I cannot remember of a case where, prior to trial, the district court ever denied appointed counsel's motion to turn back the clock and give the defendant a preliminary hearing. In fact, personally, I can remember clients of mine who were allowed that right. Everyone involved seemed to be interested in seeing that justice was served. . . . Then, too, think of the cost — not much. At a preliminary hearing, the prosecutor need not put his entire case, but only so much as will result in the defendant being held to answer. . . .

Notes

1. *Which crimes require an indictment?* In almost half the states, a grand jury indictment rather than a prosecutor's information is necessary for at least some charges. In some of these jurisdictions, such as New York, the constitution requires a grand jury indictment; in other "indictment" states, the state constitution allows the legislature to decide which if any crimes must be charged through grand jury indictment. For the most part, the "indictment" states have retained the traditional requirement embodied in the Fifth Amendment to the federal constitution: Indictment must occur in all capital and "infamous" crimes — that is, felonies. A few require indictments only for crimes punishable by death or life imprisonment. The grand jury requirement is one of the few provisions of the federal Bill of Rights that has not been "incorporated" against the states through the due process clause of the Fourteenth Amendment. Hurtado v. California, 110 U.S. 516 (1884).

In most states and for most charges, the grand jury is optional. Prosecutors can decide whether to proceed under an information or a grand jury indictment (as in Illinois, under the statute reprinted above). Indictments have become one weapon in the prosecutor's arsenal of ways to investigate and charge crimes. Prosecutors often use grand juries to charge politically sensitive crimes (to share responsibility for the charging decision) or to charge crimes that come to light as the result of grand jury investigations.

2. *Grand jury versus preliminary examinations.* The Idaho court in *Edmonson* reflects the majority view that there is no constitutional right to a preliminary hearing once a prosecutor has decided to seek an indictment. See People v. Glass, 627 N.W.2d 261 (Mich. 2001) (overruling earlier case granting right to preliminary examination to all defendants, including indictees). Further, there is no federal constitutional requirement that either a judge or a grand jury determine whether probable cause supports the criminal charges filed against a defendant. Lem Woon v. Oregon, 229 U.S. 586 (1913) (upholding statute providing for no preliminary examination after information). All states have statutes offering at least some defendants a determination of probable cause underlying the charges, whether the determination comes from a judge in a preliminary hearing or from a grand jury indictment. A few states provide, as an alternative charging method, for "direct filing" of charges by the prosecutor without testing in a preliminary hearing or indictment. These states usually allow the defendant to file a motion to dismiss the charges after discovery is complete.

The statutes and constitutions providing for adversary preliminary hearings typically apply only when the prosecutor has *chosen* to proceed by information rather than indictment. See Cal. Const. art. 1, §14.1. In the federal system, once a prosecutor obtains an indictment the defendant cannot insist on a preliminary hearing. 18 U.S.C. §3060. A few states do require an adversary preliminary hearing (even after a grand jury indicts the defendant) and a few others require some showing that the prosecutor had satisfactory reasons for choosing indictments in some cases and informations in others. People v. Duncan, 201 N.W.2d 629 (Mich. 1972); State v. Freeland, 667 P.2d 509 (Or. 1983). The practical value of an adversarial preliminary hearing for a defendant is the chance to preview the prosecution's witnesses and evidence.

3. *Waiver of indictment.* In the jurisdictions requiring indictment for some crimes, defendants often waive their right to indictment and proceed without any grand jury or judicial screening of the charges. Are there times when the legal system might prevent defendants from waiving the right to indictment? See N.Y. Crim. Proc. Law §195.20(a) (waiver must be written, executed in open court in presence of counsel); Pa. R. Crim. P. 215(a) (waiver allowed except for offenses punishable by death or life imprisonment).

4. *Nonadversarial proceedings.* Time and again, judicial opinions point out that grand jury proceedings are not adversarial and are not a "mini-trial." Truer words have never been spoken. To begin with, the grand jury's task is far different from that of a trial jury: The grand jury need only decide whether the prosecutor has demonstrated probable cause to believe that the defendant committed the crime charged. In most jurisdictions, only the prosecutor presents testimony and documents to the grand jury, and none of it is subject to cross-examination or the rules of evidence. Costello v. United States, 350 U.S. 359 (1956). In a strong minority of states, attorneys for some grand jury witnesses may observe the testimony of their clients, but the attorneys may not question the witness or make any statements to the grand jury. See, e.g., Ill. Ann. Stat. ch. 725, para. 5/112-4.1.

In most systems, the prosecutor has no obligation to present exculpatory evidence, United States v. Williams, 504 U.S. 36 (1992), although support for this traditional position is eroding. More than a dozen states have statutes or judicial rulings that require the prosecutor to present exculpatory evidence under some circumstances. See People v. Lancaster, 503 N.E.2d 990 (N.Y. 1986). Prosecutorial policies also sometimes recognize the obligation of a prosecutor to present exculpatory evidence that would lead the grand jury to refuse to indict. See U.S. Attorneys' Manual §9-11.233; see also ABA Standards for Criminal Justice, Prosecution Function Standard 3-3.6(b) ("No prosecutor should knowingly fail to disclose to the grand jury evidence which tends to negate guilt or mitigate the offense"). Sometimes the target of a grand jury investigation must have notice and an opportunity to testify before the grand jury can indict. See Sheriff of Humboldt County v. Marcum, 783 P.2d 1389 (Nev. 1989).

Most traditional nonadversarial practices trace their roots to the earliest English grand juries in the twelfth century. See Richard Younger, The People's Panel (1963). Does this nonadversarial process serve any useful purpose now? Does the high rate of guilty pleas in modern criminal justice systems make these practices more questionable than they once may have been?

5. *Judicial review of indictments.* As you might imagine based on the other materials in this chapter, judicial dismissal of charges contained in an indictment is a rare event. Only about 10 states even authorize courts to inquire into the sufficiency of the evidence to support an indictment. See, e.g., Colo. Rev. Stat. §16-5-204(4)(k). Challenges based on prosecutorial misconduct are only slightly more successful as a basis for dismissal of an indictment.

Assuming that a court is willing to review an indictment, will there be a record of the proceedings sufficient to allow judicial review? Statutes and rules of procedure in the federal system and in a majority of the states require recording of at least the testimony that a grand jury hears, and a strong minority also require recording of other statements made to the grand jury, such as the commentary of the prosecutor. Virtually nowhere are the deliberations and votes of the grand jury recorded.

6. *Timing of initial appearance and preliminary hearing.* The federal constitution requires that the initial determination of probable cause to support an *arrest* (but not to support the charges) occur within 48 hours of the arrest. County of Riverside v. McLaughlin, 500 U.S. 44 (1991) (delay longer than 48 hours presumptively unreasonable). Some states have rules calling for such a hearing in even less time, but most simply require a hearing within a "reasonable" time. As for the determination of whether there is probable cause to support the crimes charged, the hearing usually takes place within 10 to 20 days of the initial appearance if the defendant does not waive the hearing or if the grand jury does not return an indictment in the meantime.

If traditional grand juries provide defendants little protection, are there changes to the institution that might make the grand jury a more independent screen against unreasonable prosecution? Consider the following Hawaiian reform.

Consider, too, the mechanism of reform. Express constitutional reform of the federal system has been relatively rare, and amendments have reflected fundamental social and political changes (e.g. the Thirteenth, Fourteenth, Fifteenth, and Eighteenth Amendments). This is not the story in the states, where a 1987 account found 5,198 amendments to state constitutions (5,083 approved by voters in 49 states, out of 8,279 amendments submitted to them). See Janice C. May, Constitutional Amendment and Revision Revisited, Publius: The Journal of Federalism, 153 (Winter 1987) (finding the average number of amendments adopted per state to be 103.9).

■ STATE v. GABRIEL KAHLBAUN

638 P.2d 309 (Haw. 1981)

OGATA, J.

[T]he indictment against defendant-appellee, Gabriel Kahlbaun, was dismissed for lack of independent grand jury counsel as provided for under Article I, Section 11 of the Hawaii State Constitution. The question presented for our consideration is whether Article I, Section 11 of the Hawaii Constitution requires the physical presence of the independent grand jury counsel throughout the grand jury proceeding. . . .

On June 6, 1980, the statutory provisions implementing Article I, Section 11 were enacted into law. David Fong and retired Judge Masato Doi were appointed by the chief justice as independent grand jury counsel on June 19, 1980. Thereafter, on June 25, 1980, the independent counsel were sworn in and introduced to the members of the Oahu Grand Jury. A supplemental charge was then given to the grand jurors by the supervising circuit court judge, informing them of the role of the independent grand jury counsel.[1] . . .

As a matter of practice, the grand jurors were also informed that if they needed to consult with the independent grand jury counsel, the grand jurors were to call the Criminal Assignments Office of the First Circuit Court. Then, in turn, the assignments office clerk would contact the independent counsel, on a beeper, to come and consult with the grand jury.

Appellee was indicted by the Oahu Grand Jury on August 20, 1980, for burglary in the first degree. . . . Independent counsel David Fong was responsible for advising the grand jury on this date. The record indicates that Fong informally noted his appearance to the grand jury prior to the start of the grand jury proceeding. However, Fong was not present during the presentation of evidence in the instant case. And in this particular case, the grand jurors did not direct any questions of law to the independent grand jury counsel. On October 20, 1980, appellee filed a motion to dismiss indictment alleging . . . that the absence of the grand jury counsel during the grand jury proceeding requires the dismissal of the instant indictment. . . .

Article I, Section 11 of the Hawaii State Constitution reads:

> Whenever a grand jury is impaneled, there shall be an independent counsel as appointed by law to advise the members of the grand jury regarding matters brought before it. Independent counsel shall be selected from among those persons licensed to practice law by the supreme court of the State and shall not be a public employee. The term and compensation for independent counsel shall be as provided by law.

This provision is unique in American jurisprudence for there is no comparable provision in either the federal or other state constitutions. [I]n State v. Hehr, 633 P.2d 545, 546-547 (Haw. 1981), we held that Article I, Section 11 did not create a substantive right for the accused. We stated:

> Although this constitutional provision provides indirect benefits to the accused, the independent counsel's role is not to serve as an advocate on the accused's behalf. Rather,

1. The supplemental charge read in pertinent part: . . . "The grand jury counsel shall serve as independent legal counsel to the grand jury, to be at the disposal of the grand jury during its proceedings in obtaining appropriate advice on matters of law sought by the grand jury, conduct legal research, and provide appropriate answers. [Y]ou are not to seek or obtain advice on matters of law from the prosecution. . . ."

> Article I, Section 11 was established to ensure an independent grand jury and to relieve the prosecutor of the conflicting burdens of presenting evidence in support of the indictment and advising the grand jury on matters of law.

Given [this prior interpretation] of Article I, Section 11, we are also mindful of the rules of construction relating to constitutional provisions. The fundamental principle in construing a constitutional provision is to give effect to the intention of the framers and the people adopting it. This intent is to be found in the instrument itself. When the text of a constitutional provision is not ambiguous, the court, in construing it, is not at liberty to search for its meaning beyond the instrument. However, if the text is ambiguous, extrinsic aids may be examined to determine the intent of the framers and the people adopting the proposed amendment. . . .

The language of Article I, Section 11, does not clearly express the intent of the framers on the issue of whether the independent grand jury counsel must be physically present at all times during the grand jury proceeding. The Constitution only requires that the independent counsel advise the grand jury. The function of advising the grand jury on matters of law still can be accomplished without counsel having to be physically present throughout the grand jury proceeding. . . . Using this term in its ordinary sense, "advise" does not indicate or suggest that a physical presence is required. Advice can come in many forms, but physical presence is not a prerequisite. Given this ambiguity, it is necessary to examine extrinsic aids in order to ascertain the meaning of Article I, §11 of the Hawaii Constitution.

Another established rule of construction is that a court may look to the object sought to be accomplished and the evils sought to be remedied by the amendment, along with the history of the times and the state of being when the constitutional provision was adopted. In addition, we can also look to the understanding of the voters who adopted the constitutional provisions, and the legislative implementation of the constitutional amendment.

It is important to remember the role the grand jury plays in the criminal justice system. The grand jury functions as a barrier to reckless or unfounded charges and serves as a "shield against arbitrary or oppressive action, by insuring that serious criminal accusations will be brought only upon the considered judgment of a representative body of citizens acting under oath and under judicial instruction and guidance." United States v. Mandujano, 425 U.S. 564 (1976); State v. Pacific Concrete and Rock Co., 560 P.2d 1309 (Haw. 1977). . . . The grand jury system provides additional benefits which were aptly stated in Standing Committee Report No. 69, at 673, 3d Hawaii Constitutional Convention (1978):

> [T]he grand jury does have some positive aspects. In certain cases, such as sex crimes or those involving a youthful victim, it protects the victim against being cross-examined at the preliminary hearing level and at trial. Fears were expressed that undergoing cross-examination twice would be hard on those witnesses and may discourage them from acting as witnesses. . . .

However, in recent years, the grand jury system has come under severe criticism. Rather than being a shield to unfounded charges as intended, critics charge that the grand jury has become a rubber stamp of the prosecuting attorney. These criticisms were not unfounded; thus, a substantial movement developed to abolish the grand jury in total. Instead of completely abolishing the grand jury system in Hawaii, the 1978 Constitutional Convention sought to cure some of the ills by proposing the concept of the independent grand jury counsel. This proposal sought to relieve the prosecutor of the conflicting roles of advising the grand jury and presenting sufficient evidence to sustain an indictment. Ultimately, this measure would ensure the independence of the grand jury from the domination of the prosecutor. . . .

Our examination of the convention debates, proceedings and committee reports reveals that the intent of the framers of the constitutional convention in adopting the independent grand jury counsel provision was to ensure an independent grand jury. The concern of the delegates was evidenced in Standing Committee Report No. 69, at 673, where it was expressed:

> . . . In order to counter the dominance of the prosecutor, the independent grand jury counsel was proposed to remedy the situation. The independent grand jury counsel's role was envisioned by some delegates as follows: The role of counsel will be to advise the grand jury and not the witness or the prosecutor. Until now the prosecutor has served as the legal adviser to the grand jury, but there seems to be a conflict between presenting evidence to a grand jury in the hope that they will return an indictment and being their legal adviser. Independent legal counsel will be available to advise the grand jury on any appropriate matter. Your Committee believes that the parameters of the role of the independent counsel will be determined by the grand jury, but if his role is to be effective counsel should advise the grand jury whenever it is appropriate rather than when asked.

In the above-cited passage from Standing Committee Report No. 69, it indicates that the framers of the amendment wanted the independent grand jury counsel to be available to advise the grand jury. By definition, *available* means "that is accessible or may be obtained." Webster's Third International Dictionary. Given this definition, physical presence is not a necessary condition to availability. Thus, it further appears that the framers did not intend for the independent grand jury counsel to be physically present throughout the grand jury proceeding.

We also find it necessary to look to the understanding of the voters who adopted the constitutional provision. The 1978 Constitutional Convention provided to each voter an informational booklet which summarized each proposed amendment. These summaries fairly and sufficiently advised voters of the substance and effect of the proposed amendment. The summary for Article I, Section 11 reads as follows: "If adopted, this amendment provides . . . an independent lawyer to advise the grand jury . . . and requires that the legislature set their pay and how long they shall work." In this clear expression of their intent, the framers did not specifically require nor did they intend for the independent grand jury counsel to be physically present throughout the grand jury proceeding. . . . The independent grand jury counsel was established to advise the grand jury.

The legislative construction of Article I, Section 11 rendered a similar conclusion. The legislature enacted HRS §612-57, to implement Article I, Section 11 of the Hawaii Constitution. . . . That statute reads in pertinent part:

> The grand jury counsel may be present during the grand jury proceeding but shall not participate in the questioning of witnesses or the prosecution. The grand jury counsel's function shall be to receive inquiries on matters of law sought by the grand jury, conduct legal research, and provide appropriate answers.

By using the non-mandatory language, "may be present," the legislature found that the physical presence of the independent grand jury counsel throughout the grand jury proceeding was unnecessary and was not the intent of the framers of the 1978 Constitutional Convention.

A legislative construction implementing a constitutional amendment cannot produce an absurd result or be inconsistent with the purposes and policies of the amendment. However, when a legislative construction of a constitutional amendment is reasonable, courts will normally follow the legislative construction. We think that the legislative construction of Article I, Section 11 does not produce an absurd result nor is inconsistent with the purposes underlying the amendment. Therefore, we find that the legislative construction of Article I, Section 11 is reasonable and choose to follow such a construction.

Moreover, . . . the amendment has improved the situation that existed in the grand jury prior to the enactment of the amendment. Being that the independent grand jury counsel advises the grand jury on matters of law, the absence of the counsel does not revert the grand jury proceeding to its pre-amendment status. The independent counsel must still be consulted with by the grand jury if they have questions of law. . . .

We have held that the absence of the independent grand jury counsel from the grand jury proceeding must be shown to be prejudicial to the accused in order to invalidate the indictment. . . . The bare allegation of the absence of the independent grand jury counsel from the grand jury proceeding, without more, is insufficient to establish prejudice. Moreover, the record reveals that for the instant case the grand jury did not seek the advice of the independent grand jury counsel. The record also shows that the independent counsel was available to render advice to the grand jury. Therefore, based on this record, we find that the absence of the independent grand jury counsel was not prejudicial.

Although we found that the constitution does not mandate the physical presence of the independent grand jury counsel throughout the grand jury proceeding, and that appellee was not prejudiced by such an absence, we find it appropriate to express further views on the independent grand jury counsel.

In addition to advising the grand jurors on questions of law when asked, at the outset of each grand jury session, the independent counsel, on the record, must note his/her presence and instruct the grand jurors on the procedures to summon the counsel for consultation. By this act, a record will be available which shows the court that the independent counsel was present before the grand jury; that the independent counsel was available to advise the grand jury; and that the grand jurors knew the procedures to consult with their counsel.

Additionally, the independent grand jury counsel should be in close proximity to the grand jury. We do not mean that the independent grand jury counsel may return to his/her law office while awaiting to be summoned by the grand jury. Preferably, the independent counsel should be in a separate room, next to the grand jury. But at the very least, the independent counsel should be in the same building that the grand jury meets. Of course, the independent grand jury counsel is not prohibited from being in the grand jury room if desired. We impose this proximity requirement so that the independent grand jury counsel will be readily available to the grand jury and that delays will be kept to a minimum.

With these additional requirements, we believe that the independent grand jury counsel will be effective in insuring an independent grand jury. . . .

Notes

1. *Staff for grand jury.* As *Kahlbaun* indicates, Hawaii is in the minority in providing independent legal counsel for the grand jury. Fewer than 10 states have statutes authorizing support staff for grand juries, such as legal counsel, accountants, or detectives. See Kan. Stat. §22-3006. More frequently, statutes authorize the prosecutor to attend the sessions of the grand jury (except during deliberations and voting), to examine witnesses, and to provide legal advice to the grand jury. Fla. Stat. §905.19. The supervising judge for the grand jury is also available to provide legal advice, although the grand jury rarely requests advice from the judge. But other sources of staff support for the grand jury have not developed in most places. When grand juries attempted at the turn of the century to analyze information about government operations — say, an audit of the county books — the courts routinely denied the grand juries any power to hire their own accountants or detectives. Stone v. Bell, 129 P. 458 (Nev. 1912). When the grand jury lost confidence in the district attorney and sought legal counsel elsewhere, the supervising courts blocked the effort. Woody v. Peairs, 170 P. 660 (Cal. Ct. App. 1917). While private prosecutors appeared before grand juries in the nineteenth century, at the turn of the century courts began to exclude them from the grand jury proceedings. Hartgraves v. State, 114 P. 343 (Okla. 1911).

Consider this lack of support staff against the background of a growing bureaucracy attached to virtually every other governmental institution early in the twentieth century. Grand jurors were no longer personally aware of crimes committed or conditions to investigate, as they once were. They were without the increasingly specialized auditing and management skills necessary to investigate crimes or to monitor government. Given the complexity of governance, what institution of government could survive without support staff? Could Congress or the president perform their duties without the benefit of their own counsel?

2. *State constitutional interpretation.* Do the methods used by the Hawaiian Supreme Court to interpret Art. I, §11 look the like methods typically used by the U.S. Supreme Court to interpret the federal constitution? In what ways does constitutional interpretation change when many of the drafters are enacters (here voters) are still very much alive, and part of constitutional debate? Does a shorter time frame provide stronger arguments for "originalism" as the primary theory of constitutional interpretation? Does the ability to actually amend the constitution provide arguments for originalism or some other interpretative theory?

3. *Grand jury reports.* Just as prosecutors will decline to file charges in many cases, grand juries sometimes investigate crimes and then decide not to indict. These grand juries sometimes write "reports" criticizing the targets of the grand jury's investigation, even though the grand jury issued no indictment or "presentment" (criminal charges which the prosecutor did not request). Should "reports" be issued as standard practice whenever a grand jury conducts an investigation? Should reports be used to encourage or set prosecutorial policies for prosecutors as opposed to making judgments in particular cases?

Grand jury reports can serve many purposes. Some state statutes encourage the use of grand jury reports to examine issues of public health and welfare. See Nev. Rev. Stat. Ann. §172.267. In some jurisdictions the prosecutors ask grand juries to determine whether a class of offense or a type of offender should be prosecuted. For example, a grand jury might give guidance on the prosecution of those who rent pornographic videos or the searching of rental records. An instruction from the grand jury not to prosecute may help shield a local (and usually elected) prosecutor from criticism.

The critical issue, both in jurisdictions that encourage grand jury reports and those that discourage them, is whether the grand jury uses its report power to harm the reputation of individuals without going so far as to charge them with any crime. Some states guard against this danger by insisting that a grand jury issue a report only in conjunction with criminal charges; others hold that the report cannot name any private individuals, and a few prevent the report from naming even public officials. Ex parte Simpson, 664 S.W.2d 872, 873 (Ark. 1984) (person mentioned in grand jury report has no right to cross-examine accusers; report is a state publication that carries aura of approval by judge who accepted it, and press has no way to look behind it to determine its fairness or accuracy).

Grand jury reports offer a way for lay citizens to participate in the court system and in criminal justice. Should we preserve or expand the tradition of reports as a way to increase the influence of one of the few truly democratic institutions in American criminal justice?

XIV

Jeopardy and Joinder

Chapter 13 addressed the legal forces at work when a prosecutor chooses whether to charge a suspect and which charges to select. We concentrate now on those cases in which the prosecutor could file multiple charges. When several related criminal incidents happen, a prosecutor might file a single count or multiple counts in a single prosecution against one or more defendants, or she might instead file separate criminal cases.

Several sources of law shape the prosecutor's grouping of multiple charges. First, the constitutional bar against "double jeopardy," embodied in the Fifth Amendment of the U.S. Constitution and in most state constitutions, puts some pressure on the prosecutor to include more charges and more conduct within a single prosecution, because double jeopardy might bar any later attempt to pursue the related charges. Section A considers double jeopardy issues.

Prosecutors must also consider statutes and procedural rules on the conceptually related concepts of "joinder" and "severance" of charges and defendants. These rules define both the maximum and minimum range of charges that a prosecutor can join together into a single proceeding. Under the joinder and severance rules, both the prosecutor and the trial court decide whether to include or exclude charges or defendants in a single proceeding. Section B explores these rules.

A. DOUBLE JEOPARDY

A prosecutor must plan for the future when filing charges. If she chooses not to combine related charges in an initial set of proceedings and instead files some of the charges later, there is a risk that the court will bar the later charges. As mentioned above, the legal basis for this decision is the double jeopardy clause of the federal constitution and of most state constitutions. The Fifth Amendment to the federal constitution provides: "No person shall . . . be subject for the same offence to be twice put in jeopardy of life or limb. . . ."

Double jeopardy, it is often said, protects criminal defendants from (1) a second prosecution after acquittal, (2) a second prosecution after conviction, and (3) multiple punishments for the same offense within the same proceeding. The materials in this part touch on some prominent double jeopardy issues that flow from the charging decision. First, we consider a controversial and revealing limitation on the operation of the double jeopardy principle — the "dual sovereignty" exception. Second, we consider which charges in a later proceeding amount to the "same offence" that was charged in a prior proceeding.

1. Multiple Sovereigns

Federal and state governments have overlapping responsibilities for enforcing criminal laws. Many economic and other activities cross state lines, and the criminal codes of most states and the federal government now reach much of the same conduct. Often a person who engages in criminal behavior could face charges in two states, or in both state and federal systems.

The overlap between the federal and state criminal laws is a recurring issue for double jeopardy purposes. In United States v. Lanza, 260 U.S. 377 (1922), several defendants were convicted under state law in Washington for manufacturing, transporting, and possessing liquor and were fined $750 each. When the federal government also brought criminal charges under the National Prohibition Act, Lanza raised a double jeopardy objection to the federal prosecution. He noted that the Eighteenth Amendment, prohibiting the manufacture, sale, or transportation of intoxicating liquors, gave both Congress and the states "concurrent power to enforce" the prohibition. According to Lanza, the state and the federal criminal statutes were punishing the "same offense" because they each derived from the same constitutional authority.

The Court rejected this argument and embraced instead the doctrine known as the "dual sovereign" exception to double jeopardy:

> We have here two sovereignties, deriving power from different sources, capable of dealing with the same subject-matter within the same territory. Each may, without interference by the other, enact laws to secure prohibition. . . . . Each government in determining what shall be an offense against its peace and dignity is exercising its own sovereignty, not that of the other.

260 U.S. at 382.

The following materials trace the continuing vitality of the "dual sovereign" doctrine during a time when the overlap between federal and state criminal laws has grown larger.

■ ALFONSE BARTKUS v. ILLINOIS
359 U.S. 121 (1959)

FRANKFURTER, J.

Petitioner was tried in the Federal District Court for the Northern District of Illinois on December 18, 1953, for robbery of a federally insured savings and loan association, the General Savings and Loan Association of Cicero, Illinois, in violation of 18 U.S.C. §2113. The case was tried to a jury and resulted in an acquittal. On January 8, 1954, an Illinois grand jury indicted Bartkus. The facts recited in the Illinois indictment were substantially identical to those contained in the prior federal indictment. The Illinois indictment charged that these facts constituted a violation of [the Illinois robbery statute. Bartkus entered a plea of autrefois acquit, which the trial court rejected. Bartkus was tried, convicted, and sentenced to life imprisonment.]

The state and federal prosecutions were separately conducted. It is true that the agent of the Federal Bureau of Investigation who had conducted the investigation on behalf of the Federal Government turned over to the Illinois prosecuting officials all the evidence he had gathered against the petitioner. Concededly, some of that evidence had been gathered after acquittal in the federal court. The only other connection between the two trials is to be found in a suggestion that the federal sentencing of the accomplices who testified against petitioner in both trials was purposely continued by the federal court until after they testified in the state trial. The record establishes that the prosecution was undertaken by state prosecuting officials within their discretionary responsibility. . . . It establishes also that federal officials acted in cooperation with state authorities, as is the conventional practice between the two sets of prosecutors throughout the country. It does not support the claim that the State of Illinois in bringing its prosecution was merely a tool of the federal authorities, who thereby avoided the prohibition of the Fifth Amendment against a retrial of a federal prosecution after an acquittal. It does not sustain a conclusion that the state prosecution was a sham and a cover for a federal prosecution. . . . Since the new prosecution was by Illinois, and not by the Federal Government, the claim of unconstitutionality must rest upon the Due Process Clause of the Fourteenth Amendment. . . .

Time and again this Court has attempted by general phrases not to define but to indicate the purport of due process and to adumbrate the continuing adjudicatory process in its application. The statement by Mr. Justice Cardozo in Palko v. Connecticut, 302 U.S. 319, 324-325 (1937), has especially commended itself and been frequently cited in later opinions. Referring to specific situations, he wrote:

> In these and other situations immunities that are valid as against the federal government by force of the specific pledges of particular amendments have been found to be implicit in the concept of ordered liberty, and thus, through the Fourteenth Amendment, become valid as against the states.

[H]e suggested that [due process] prohibited to the States only those practices "repugnant to the conscience of mankind." In applying these phrases in *Palko,* the Court ruled that, while at some point the cruelty of harassment by multiple prosecutions by a State would offend due process, the specific limitation imposed on the Federal Government by the Double Jeopardy Clause of the Fifth Amendment did not bind the States. [*Palko* sustained a first degree murder conviction returned in a second trial after an appeal by the State from an acquittal of first degree murder.]

The Fifth Amendment's proscription of double jeopardy has been invoked and rejected in over twenty cases of real or hypothetical successive state and federal prosecution cases before this Court. While United States v. Lanza, 260 U.S. 377 (1922), was the first case in which we squarely held valid a federal prosecution arising out of the same facts which had been the basis of a state conviction, the validity of such a prosecution by the Federal Government has not been questioned by this Court since the opinion in Fox v. Ohio, 46 U.S. 410 (1847), more than one hundred years ago.

In Fox v. Ohio, argument was made to the Supreme Court that an Ohio conviction for uttering counterfeit money was invalid. This assertion of invalidity was based in large part upon the argument that since Congress had imposed federal sanctions for the counterfeiting of money, a failure to find that the Supremacy Clause precluded the States from punishing related conduct would expose an individual to double punishment. Mr. Justice Daniel, writing for the Court (with Mr. Justice McLean dissenting), recognized as true that there was a possibility of double punishment, but denied that from this flowed a finding of pre-emption, concluding instead that both the Federal and State Governments retained the power to impose criminal sanctions, the United States because of its interest in protecting the purity of its currency, the States because of their interest in protecting their citizens against fraud. . . .

The experience of state courts in dealing with successive prosecutions by different governments is obviously also relevant in considering whether or not the Illinois prosecution of Bartkus violated due process of law. Of the twenty-eight States which have considered the validity of successive state and federal prosecutions as against a challenge of violation of either a state constitutional double-jeopardy provision or a common-law evidentiary rule of autrefois acquit and autrefois convict, twenty-seven have refused to rule that the second prosecution was or would be barred. These States were not bound to follow this Court and its interpretation of the Fifth Amendment. The rules, constitutional, statutory, or common law which bound them, drew upon the same experience as did the Fifth Amendment, but were and are of separate and independent authority. . . .

With this body of precedent as irrefutable evidence that state and federal courts have for years refused to bar a second trial even though there had been a prior trial by another government for a similar offense, it would be disregard of a long, unbroken, unquestioned course of impressive adjudication for the Court now to rule that due process compels such a bar. A practical justification for rejecting such a reading of due process also commends itself in aid of this interpretation of the Fourteenth Amendment. In Screws v. United States, 325 U.S. 91 (1945), defendants were tried and convicted in a federal court under federal statutes with maximum sentences of a year and two years respectively. But the state crime there involved was a capital offense. Were the federal prosecution of a comparatively minor offense to prevent state prosecution of so grave an infraction of state law, the result would be a shocking and untoward deprivation of the historic right and obligation of the States to maintain peace and order within their confines. It would be in derogation of our federal system to displace the reserved power of States over state offenses by reason of prosecution of minor federal offenses by federal authorities beyond the control of the States.[25] . . .

The entire history of litigation and contention over the question of the imposition of a bar to a second prosecution by a government other than the one first prosecuting is a manifestation of the evolutionary unfolding of law. Today a number of States have statutes which bar a second prosecution if the defendant has been once

25. Illinois had an additional and unique interest in Bartkus beyond the commission of this particular crime. If Bartkus was guilty of the crime charged he would be an habitual offender in Illinois and subject to life imprisonment. The Illinois court sentenced Bartkus to life imprisonment on this ground.

tried by another government for a similar offense. A study of the cases under the New York statute, which is typical of these laws, demonstrates that the task of determining when the federal and state statutes are so much alike that a prosecution under the former bars a prosecution under the latter is a difficult one. [E]xperience such as that of New York may give aid to Congress in its consideration of adoption of similar provisions in individual federal criminal statutes or in the federal criminal code.

Precedent, experience, and reason alike support the conclusion that Alfonse Bartkus has not been deprived of due process of law by the State of Illinois. Affirmed.

BLACK, J., dissenting.

. . . The Court's holding further limits our already weakened constitutional guarantees against double prosecutions. United States v. Lanza, decided in 1922, allowed federal conviction and punishment of a man who had been previously convicted and punished for the identical acts by one of our States. Today, for the first time in its history, this Court upholds the state conviction of a defendant who had been acquitted of the same offense in the federal courts. . . . Palko v. Connecticut, 302 U.S. 319 (1937), expressly left open the question of whether "the state [could be] permitted after a trial free from error to try the accused over again." That question is substantially before us today.

Fear and abhorrence of governmental power to try people twice for the same conduct is one of the oldest ideas found in western civilization. Its roots run deep into Greek and Roman times. Even in the Dark Ages, when so many other principles of justice were lost, the idea that one trial and one punishment were enough remained alive through the canon law and the teachings of the early Christian writers. By the thirteenth century it seems to have been firmly established in England, where it came to be considered as a "universal maxim of the common law." [S]ome writers have explained the opposition to double prosecutions by emphasizing the injustice inherent in two punishments for the same act, and others have stressed the dangers to the innocent from allowing the full power of the state to be brought against them in two trials. . . .

The Court apparently takes the position that a second trial for the same act is somehow less offensive if one of the trials is conducted by the Federal Government and the other by a State. Looked at from the standpoint of the individual who is being prosecuted, this notion is too subtle for me to grasp. If double punishment is what is feared, it hurts no less for two "Sovereigns" to inflict it than for one. If danger to the innocent is emphasized, that danger is surely no less when the power of State and Federal Governments is brought to bear on one man in two trials, than when one of these "Sovereigns" proceeds alone. In each case, inescapably, a man is forced to face danger twice for the same conduct.

The Court, without denying the almost universal abhorrence of such double prosecutions, nevertheless justifies the practice here in the name of "federalism." This, it seems to me, is a misuse and desecration of the concept. Our Federal Union was conceived and created "to establish Justice" and to "secure the Blessings of Liberty," not to destroy any of the bulwarks on which both freedom and justice depend. We should, therefore, be suspicious of any supposed "requirements" of "federalism" which result in obliterating ancient safeguards. I have been shown nothing in the history of our Union, in the writings of its Founders, or elsewhere, to indicate that individual rights deemed essential by both State and Nation were to be lost through the combined operations of the two governments. . . .

The Court's argument also ignores the fact that our Constitution allocates power between local and federal governments in such a way that the basic rights of each can be protected without double trials. The Federal Government is given power to act in limited areas only, but in matters properly within its scope it is supreme. It can retain exclusive control of such matters, or grant the States concurrent power on its own terms.

[T]his practice, which for some 150 years was considered so undesirable that the Court must strain to find examples, is now likely to become a commonplace. For, after today, who will be able to blame a conscientious prosecutor for failing to accept a jury verdict of acquittal when he believes a defendant guilty and knows that a second try is available in another jurisdiction and that such a second try is approved by the Highest Court in the Land? Inevitably, the victims of such double prosecutions will most often be the poor and the weak in our society, individuals without friends in high places who can influence prosecutors not to try them again. The power to try a second time will be used, as have all similar procedures, to make scapegoats of helpless, political, religious, or racial minorities and those who differ, who do not conform and who resist tyranny.

There are some countries that allow the dangerous practice of trying people twice. [Such practices] are not hard to find in lands torn by revolution or crushed by dictatorship. I had thought that our constitutional protections embodied in the Double Jeopardy and Due Process Clauses would have barred any such things happening here. Unfortunately, [today's decision causes] me to fear that in an important number of cases it can happen here. I would reverse.

BRENNAN, J., dissenting.

Bartkus was tried and acquitted in a Federal District Court of robbing a federally insured savings and loan association in Cicero, Illinois. He was indicted for the same robbery by the State of Illinois less than three weeks later, and subsequently convicted and sentenced to life imprisonment. The single issue in dispute at both trials was whether Bartkus was the third participant in the robbery along with two self-confessed perpetrators of the crime.

The Government's case against Bartkus on the federal trial rested primarily upon the testimony of two of the robbers, Joseph Cosentino and James Brindis, who confessed their part in the crime and testified that Bartkus was their confederate. The defense was that Bartkus was getting a haircut in a barber shop several miles away at the time the robbery was committed. The owner of the barber shop, his son and other witnesses placed Bartkus in the shop at the time. The federal jury in acquitting Bartkus apparently believed the alibi witnesses and not Cosentino and Brindis.

The federal authorities were highly displeased with the jury's resolution of the conflicting testimony, and the trial judge sharply upbraided the jury for its verdict. The federal authorities obviously decided immediately after the trial to make a second try at convicting Bartkus, and since the federal courthouse was barred to them by the Fifth Amendment, they turned to a state prosecution for that purpose. It is clear that federal officers solicited the state indictment, arranged to assure the attendance of key witnesses, unearthed additional evidence to discredit Bartkus and one of his alibi witnesses, and in general prepared and guided the state prosecution. . . .

I think that the record before us shows that the extent of participation of the federal authorities here [made] this state prosecution [into] a second federal prosecution of Bartkus. The federal jury acquitted Bartkus late in December 1953. Early in January 1954 the Assistant United States Attorney who prosecuted the federal case summoned Cosentino to his office. Present also were the FBI agent who had investigated the robbery and the Assistant State's Attorney for Cook County who later prosecuted the state case. The Assistant State's Attorney said to Cosentino, "Look, we are going to get an indictment in the state court against Bartkus, will you testify against him?" Cosentino agreed that he would. Later Brindis also agreed to testify. Although they pleaded guilty to the federal robbery charge in August 1953, the Federal District Court postponed their sentencing until after they testified against Bartkus at the state trial, which was not held until April 1954. . . . Both Cosentino and Brindis were also released on bail pending the state trial, Brindis on his own recognizance.

In January, also, an FBI agent who had been active in the federal prosecution purposefully set about strengthening the proofs which had not sufficed to convict Bartkus on the federal trial. . . . He uncovered a new witness against Bartkus, one Grant Pursel. . . . The first time that Pursel had any contact whatsoever with a state official connected with the case was the morning that he testified. . . .

Given the fact that there must always be state officials involved in a state prosecution, I cannot see how there can be more complete federal participation in a state prosecution than there was in this case. I see no escape from the conclusion that this particular state trial was in actuality a second federal prosecution — a second federal try at Bartkus in the guise of a state prosecution. If this state conviction is not overturned, then, as a practical matter, there will be no restraints on the use of state machinery by federal officers to bring what is in effect a second federal prosecution. . . .

Of course, cooperation between federal and state authorities in criminal law enforcement is to be desired and encouraged, for cooperative federalism in this field can indeed profit the Nation and the States in improving methods for carrying out the endless fight against crime. But the normal and healthy situation consists of state and federal officers cooperating to apprehend lawbreakers and present the strongest case against them at a single trial, be it state or federal. . . .

■ U.S. ATTORNEYS' MANUAL §9-2.031 DUAL PROSECUTION AND SUCCESSIVE PROSECUTION POLICY (*PETITE* POLICY)

A. *Statement of Policy:* This policy establishes guidelines for the exercise of discretion by appropriate officers of the Department of Justice in determining whether to bring a federal prosecution based on substantially the same act(s) or transactions involved in a prior state or federal proceeding. See Rinaldi v. United States, 434 U.S. 22, 27, (1977); Petite v. United States, 361 U.S. 529 (1960). Although there is no general statutory bar to a federal prosecution where the defendant's conduct already has formed the basis for a state prosecution, Congress expressly has provided that, as to certain offenses, a state judgment of conviction or acquittal on the merits shall be a bar to any subsequent federal prosecution for the same act or acts. See 18 U.S.C. §§659 [interstate or foreign shipments by carrier], 660 [embezzling carrier's funds derived from commerce], 2101 [travel in interstate commerce to incite a riot].

The purpose of this policy is to vindicate substantial federal interests through appropriate federal prosecutions, to protect persons charged with criminal conduct from the burdens associated with multiple prosecutions and punishments for substantially the same act(s) or transaction(s), to promote efficient utilization of Department resources, and to promote coordination and cooperation between federal and state prosecutors.

This policy precludes the initiation or continuation of a federal prosecution, following a prior state or federal prosecution based on substantially the same act(s) or transaction(s) unless three substantive prerequisites are satisfied: first, the matter must involve a substantial federal interest; second, the prior prosecution must have left that interest demonstrably unvindicated; and third, applying the same test that is applicable to all federal prosecutions, the government must believe that the defendant's conduct constitutes a federal offense, and that the admissible evidence probably will be sufficient to obtain and sustain a conviction by an unbiased trier of fact. In addition, there is a procedural prerequisite to be satisfied, that is, the prosecution must be approved by the appropriate Assistant Attorney General. . . .

In order to insure the most efficient use of law enforcement resources, whenever a matter involves overlapping federal and state jurisdiction, federal prosecutors should, as soon as possible, consult with their state counterparts to determine the most appropriate single forum in which to proceed to satisfy the substantial federal and state interests involved, and, if possible, to resolve all criminal liability for the acts in question.

B. Types of Prosecution to Which This Policy Applies: [T]his policy applies whenever the contemplated federal prosecution is based on substantially the same act(s) or transaction(s) involved in a prior state or federal prosecution. This policy constitutes an exercise of the Department's prosecutorial discretion, and applies even where a prior state prosecution would not legally bar a subsequent federal prosecution under the Double Jeopardy Clause because of the doctrine of dual sovereignty (see Abbate v. United States, 359 U.S. 187 (1959)), or a prior prosecution would not legally bar a subsequent state or federal prosecution under the Double Jeopardy Clause because each offense requires proof of an element not contained in the other. See United States v. Dixon, 509 U.S. 688 (1993); Blockburger v. United States, 284 U.S. 299 (1932).

This policy does not apply, and thus prior approval is not required, where the prior prosecution involved only a minor part of the contemplated federal charges. For example, a federal conspiracy or RICO prosecution may allege overt acts or predicate offenses previously prosecuted as long as those acts or offenses do not represent substantially the whole of the contemplated federal charge, and, in a RICO prosecution, as long as there are a sufficient number of predicate offenses to sustain the RICO charge if the previously prosecuted offenses were excluded. . . .

D. Substantive Prerequisites for Approval of a Prosecution Governed by This Policy. As previously stated there are three substantive prerequisites that must be met before approval will be granted for the initiation or a continuation of a prosecution governed by this policy.

The first substantive prerequisite is that the matter must involve a substantial federal interest. This determination will be made on a case-by-case basis, applying the considerations applicable to all federal prosecutions. See Principles of Federal Prosecution, USAM 9-27.230. Matters that come within the national investigative or prosecutorial priorities established by the Department are more likely than others to satisfy this requirement.

The second substantive prerequisite is that the prior prosecution must have left that substantial federal interest demonstrably unvindicated. In general, the Department will presume that a prior prosecution, regardless of result, has vindicated the relevant federal interest. That presumption, however, may be overcome when there are factors suggesting an unvindicated federal interest.

The presumption may be overcome when a conviction was not achieved because of the following sorts of factors: first, incompetence, corruption, intimidation, or undue influence; second, court or jury nullification in clear disregard of the evidence or the law; third, the unavailability of significant evidence, either because it was not timely discovered or known by the prosecution, or because it was kept from the trier of fact's consideration because of an erroneous interpretation of the law; fourth, the failure in a prior state prosecution to prove an element of a state offense that is not an element of the contemplated federal offense; and fifth, the exclusion of charges in a prior federal prosecution out of concern for fairness to other defendants, or for significant resource considerations that favored separate federal prosecutions.

The presumption may be overcome even when a conviction was achieved in the prior prosecution in the following circumstances: first, if the prior sentence was manifestly inadequate in light of the federal interest involved and a substantially enhanced sentence — including forfeiture and restitution as well as imprisonment and fines — is available through the contemplated federal prosecution, or second, if the choice of charges, or the determination of guilt, or the severity of sentence in the prior prosecution was affected by the sorts of factors listed in the previous paragraph. An example might be a case in which the charges in the initial prosecution trivialized the seriousness of the contemplated federal offense, for example, a state prosecution for assault and battery in a case involving the murder of a federal official.

The presumption also may be overcome, irrespective of the result in a prior state prosecution, in those rare cases where the following three conditions are met: first, the alleged violation involves a compelling federal interest, particularly one implicating an enduring national priority; second, the alleged violation involves egregious conduct, including that which threatens or causes loss of life, severe economic or physical harm, or the impairment of the functioning of an agency of the federal government or the due administration of justice; and third, the result in the prior prosecution was manifestly inadequate in light of the federal interest involved.

The third substantive prerequisite is that the government must believe that the defendant's conduct constitutes a federal offense, and that the admissible evidence probably will be sufficient to obtain and sustain a conviction by an unbiased trier of fact. This is the same test applied to all federal prosecutions. See Principles of Federal Prosecution, USAM 9-27.200 et seq. . . .

E. Procedural Prerequisite for Bringing a Prosecution Governed by This Policy. Whenever a substantial question arises as to whether this policy applies to a prosecution, the matter should be submitted to the appropriate Assistant Attorney General for resolution. Prior approval from the appropriate Assistant Attorney General must be obtained before bringing a prosecution governed by this policy. The United States will move to dismiss any prosecution governed by this policy in which prior approval was not obtained, unless the Assistant Attorney General retroactively approves it on the following grounds: first, that there unusual or overriding circumstances justifying retroactive approval, and second, that the prosecution would have been approved had approval been sought in a timely fashion. Appropriate administrative action may be initiated against prosecutors who violate this policy.

F. . . . No Substantive or Procedural Rights Created. This policy has been promulgated solely for the purpose of internal Department of Justice guidance. It is not intended to, does not, and may not be relied upon to create any rights, substantive or procedural, that are enforceable at law by any party in any matter, civil or criminal, nor does it place any limitations on otherwise lawful litigative prerogatives of the Department of Justice.

■ NEW JERSEY STATUTES §2C:1-11

When conduct constitutes an offense within the concurrent jurisdiction of this State and of the United States, a prosecution in the District Court of the United States is a bar to a subsequent prosecution in this State under the following circumstances:

a. The first prosecution resulted in an acquittal or in a conviction, or in an improper termination . . . and the subsequent prosecution is based on the same conduct, unless (1) the offense of which the defendant was formerly convicted or acquitted and the offense for which he is subsequently prosecuted each requires proof of a fact not required by the other and the law defining each of such offenses is intended to prevent a substantially different harm or evil or (2) the offense for which the defendant is subsequently prosecuted is intended to prevent a substantially more serious harm or evil than the offense of which he was formerly convicted or acquitted or (3) the second offense was not consummated when the former trial began; or

b. The former prosecution was terminated, after the information was filed or the indictment found, by an acquittal or by a final order or judgment for the defendant which has not been set aside, reversed or vacated and which acquittal, final order or judgment necessarily required a determination inconsistent with a fact which must be established for conviction of the offense of which the defendant is subsequently prosecuted.

■ OHIO REVISED CODE §2925.50

If a violation of this chapter is a violation of the federal drug abuse control laws . . . a conviction or acquittal under the federal drug abuse control laws for the same act is a bar to prosecution in this state.

Problem 14-1. Rodney King's Attackers

Rodney King was driving while intoxicated on a major freeway in Los Angeles. California Highway Patrol officers spotted King driving more than 80 miles per hour and decided to follow him with red lights and sirens activated. They ordered him by loudspeaker to pull over, but he continued to drive. Los Angeles Police Department officers joined in the pursuit, including Officer Laurence Powell. King left the freeway and eventually stopped at an entrance to a recreation area. LAPD Sergeant Stacey Koon arrived at the scene and took charge.

The officers ordered King and his two passengers to exit the car and to lie face down on the pavement with legs spread and arms behind their backs. King's two friends complied. King got out of the car but put his hands on the hood of the car rather than lying down. The officers again ordered King to assume a prone position. King got on his hands and knees but did not lie down. Several officers tried to force King down and to handcuff him, but King resisted, so the officers retreated. Koon then fired taser darts (designed to stun a combative suspect) into King.

King rose from the ground and stepped toward Officer Powell. Powell used his baton to strike King on the side of his head. King fell to the ground. King attempted to rise, but Powell and another officer each struck him with their batons to prevent him from doing so. For about one minute after this point, several officers struck King more than 50 times with their batons and kicked or stepped on him. King remained on the ground. He was eventually hospitalized for facial fractures, a broken leg, and other injuries.

A bystander captured most of the events on videotape, and it was broadcast right away on the local and national media. Within one week of the beating, Los Angeles District Attorney Ira Reiner sought charges against the officers for excessive use of force. The Los Angeles County grand jury returned an indictment.

When the trial judge in Los Angeles County refused to grant the defendants' motion to change venue, they appealed and the ruling was overturned. The case was then reassigned to a different court, in suburban Ventura County. The district attorney's office did not appeal the intermediate appellate court's decision to transfer venue, nor did it challenge the selection of Ventura County as the new venue site. Trial commenced in Simi Valley before a predominantly white jury, containing no African American jurors; King was an African American. The prosecution's case at trial relied heavily on the videotape. The prosecution did not call an expert on the use of force by police until the rebuttal phase of the trial. The prosecutors also did not present any civilian witnesses to the beating. Rodney King did not testify in the case because of his prior criminal background and his inconsistent prior statements about the beating.

The state court jury acquitted all the officers of the excessive force and assault charges. Following the verdict, riots erupted in Los Angeles; at least 45 people were killed and more than 5,000 buildings were destroyed. Political and community leaders in Los Angeles asked for a federal prosecution of the officers. The President announced on television that he was surprised by the verdict and that the federal authorities would renew their investigation of the matter.

Federal prosecutors could charge the officers under 18 U.S.C. §242 with willfully violating the civil rights of Rodney King. Section 242 provides in pertinent part:

> Whoever, under color of any law . . . willfully subjects any inhabitant of any State . . . to the deprivation of any rights, privileges, or immunities secured or protected by the Constitution or laws of the United States [shall] if bodily injury results . . . be fined under this title or imprisoned not more than ten years, or both. . . .

A provision of the California constitution and a California statute both prohibit a state prosecution if the federal government has already prosecuted the defendant for the "same offense." Cal. Const. art I, §15; Cal. Penal Code §§656, 793-794. As U.S.

Attorney for the Southern District of California, would you file charges against the officers? What legal considerations would be relevant to your choice? What other considerations? Compare Laurie Levenson, The Future of State and Federal Civil Rights Prosecutions: The Lessons of the Rodney King Trial, 41 UCLA L. Rev. 509 (1994); Powell v. Superior Court, 283 Cal. Rptr. 777 (Ct. App. 1991) (venue); United States v. Powell, 34 F.3d 1416 (9th Cir. 1994); Koon v. United States, 518 U.S. 81 (1996) (sentencing).

Notes

1. *Double jeopardy and dual sovereigns: majority position.* The substantial majority of states follow the U.S. Supreme Court and hold that the constitutional double jeopardy bar does not prohibit a second prosecution by a different sovereign, even for an offense defined by identical elements that would be considered the "same offence" within one jurisdiction. See State v. Franklin, 735 P.2d 34 (Utah 1987) (avowed racist killed two black men who were jogging in park with two white women; federal conviction for civil rights crime does not bar state murder trial under state statute or constitution). A few states have extended their constitutional double jeopardy provisions to bar a second prosecution for the same offense — or sometimes a similar offense — if it has been prosecuted in another jurisdiction. State v. Hogg, 385 A.2d 844 (N.H. 1978); People v. Cooper, 247 N.W.2d 866 (Mich. 1976) (balancing test to determine whether subsequent prosecution allowed).

2. *Dual sovereign statutes.* In contrast to the narrow constitutional rulings, around fifteen states reject the dual sovereignty doctrine by statute. See, e.g., Cal. Penal Code §656 ("Whenever on the trial of an accused person it appears that upon a criminal prosecution under the laws of another State, Government, or country, founded upon the act or omission in respect to which he is on trial, he has been acquitted or convicted, it is a sufficient defense"). Most statutory limits on second prosecutions are limited to particular categories of offenses, such as the Ohio statute relating to drug offenses. Typically, these statutes are based on either the Uniform Narcotic Drug Act or the Uniform Controlled Substances Act. Unif. Narcotic Drug Act 21, 9B U.L.A. 284 (1958); Unif. Controlled Substances Act 418, 9 U.L.A. 596 (1990). See State v. Hansen, 627 N.W.2d 195 (Wis. 2001) (state statute applicable to controlled substance offenses bars prosecution of defendant by state officials for offenses arising out of the same conduct for which the defendant has been federally prosecuted). Why might legislatures restrict statutory double jeopardy provisions to specified types of crimes? The statutes are intended to prevent the unfairness of multiple prosecutions and to avoid the unnecessary use of state resources to prosecute cases already adequately prosecuted in federal courts. They often provide for exceptions when a reprosecution serves a different purpose or addresses a different evil from the earlier prosecution. See Ga. Code Ann. §16-1-8(c) (barring reprosecution except to prevent a "substantially more serious" or different harm or evil).

3. *Silver platters and dual sovereigns.* When more than one system can prosecute a criminal case, choice of law questions will crop up. For instance, which system's rules will be used to evaluate the work of the government agents who collected the evidence? Will the agents of one sovereign, acting in violation of the rules of their own government, be able to offer any evidence they obtain on a "silver platter" to prosecutors in another jurisdiction? When the federal constitution creates the

obligations for the government agents, the answer is clear: No court (state or federal) may rely on evidence obtained by any state or federal agents in violation of the federal constitution. But what happens when the states have different rules from the federal government? If a state has its own rules (constitutional or statutory) to control government agents, and its agents violate those rules and offer the tainted evidence to federal prosecutors, the federal courts will admit the evidence. See United States v. Wright, 16 F.3d 1429 (6th Cir. 1994). State courts also accept evidence from government agents in another jurisdiction that violate the rules of that other jurisdiction. See Burge v. State, 443 S.W.2d 720 (Tex. Crim. App. 1969). Should a prosecutorial office policy dealing with prosecutions by multiple jurisdictions also address the use of evidence obtained in violation of law in another jurisdiction?

4. *Creation of the federal* Petite *policy.* Some jurisdictions that do not have constitutional or statutory limitations on filing cases already prosecuted in another jurisdiction nonetheless have *internal* prosecutorial rules or guidelines limiting successive prosecutions. The best-known illustration is the federal *Petite* policy. One week after the decision in *Bartkus,* which made it clear that the "dual sovereign" exception to the constitutional doctrine of double jeopardy would allow both state and federal prosecutions of the same crime, the Department of Justice issued a policy limiting federal prosecution after a state prosecution. The policy allows a federal prosecution following a state prosecution only when necessary to advance compelling interests of federal law enforcement. The policy later took its name from Petite v. United States, 361 U.S. 529 (1960), in which the Court noted with approval the existence of the policy. It was designed to limit successive prosecutions for the same offense to situations involving distinct federal and state interests. In announcing the policy, Attorney General William Rogers stated:

> We should continue to make every effort to cooperate with state and local authorities to the end that the trial occur in the jurisdiction, whether it be state or federal, where the public interest is best served. If this be determined accurately, and is followed by efficient and intelligent cooperation of state and federal law enforcement authorities, then consideration of a second prosecution very seldom should arise.

Dept. of Justice Press Release, Apr. 6, 1959, at 3. The policy creates internal guidance only and does not create any rights that a defendant can enforce in court. See United States v. Snell, 592 F.2d 1083 (9th Cir. 1979). Are such policies properly considered "law"?

5. *Double jeopardy, extradition, and international law.* The law in some other nations clearly rejects any dual sovereignty exception. As global legal regimes emerge, should double jeopardy principles bar multiple prosecutions by different countries? Is the principle barring double jeopardy an essential element of human rights? A partial answer to this question may be worked out on a bilateral basis as part of extradition treaties, for if a country cannot obtain control over the defendant, it is difficult to conduct a trial or to punish a person. Even in the domestic U.S. context, one state's refusal to extradite a suspect could limit the capacity of another state to try that person regardless of the double jeopardy law in either jurisdiction. The possibility of such conflicts, however, has been reduced through the Interstate Agreement on Detainers, which provides a regular method of processing criminal charges filed by more than one state. The IAD is an interstate compact that most state legislatures have adopted. See Calif. Penal Code §1389. It allows prosecutors to

notify officials holding a criminal defendant in an out-of-state facility that the state wishes to pursue criminal charges against the defendant; such notice is called a "detainer." The IAD also allows the defendant to request that the state issuing the detainer dispose of the charges promptly.

2. *"Same Offence"*

The limitations on double jeopardy apply only when a person is placed twice in jeopardy for the "same offence." Determining whether a second offense is the "same" offense raises difficult challenges. First, many criminal codes include hundreds or even thousands of crimes with overlapping elements, aimed at punishing similar harms. The federal code, for example, includes more than 3,000 separate offenses. Because of the intricacy (to use a kind label) of most criminal codes, courts have conceded that charges need not be brought twice under precisely the same statute in order to conclude that the prosecution is for the same offense. How to determine whether charges under different code provisions should be considered the same offense is the topic of this subsection.

The Supreme Court has tried several approaches to the problem of distinguishing similar and different offenses. In Blockburger v. United States, 284 U.S. 299 (1932), the defendant was convicted of three counts of violating the Harrison Narcotics Act based on the sale of small amounts of morphine hydrochloride. One of the counts of conviction charged a sale of eight grains of the drug not from the original stamped package; another count alleged that the same sale was not made according to a written order of the purchaser, as required by the statute. The court sentenced Blockburger to five years in prison and imposed a fine of $2,000 upon each count, the terms of imprisonment to run consecutively. Blockburger asserted that these two counts constituted one offense for which only a single penalty could be imposed. The Court disagreed, holding that "where the same act or transaction constitutes a violation of two distinct statutory provisions, the test to be applied to determine whether there are two offenses or only one is whether each provision requires proof of an additional fact which the other does not." 284 U.S. at 304.

The *Blockburger* test was criticized because the government could so easily obtain multiple convictions based on the same conduct, but it remained the applicable standard in federal courts and in most state courts until 1990, when the Court decided Grady v. Corbin, 495 U.S. 508 (1990). Thomas Corbin drove his car across the center line while intoxicated, killing Brenda Dirago and injuring her husband, Daniel. Corbin was charged with two misdemeanors, driving while intoxicated and failing to keep right of the median. He pleaded guilty and was punished with a $350 fine, a $10 surcharge, and a six-month license revocation. Two months later a grand jury indicted Corbin for reckless manslaughter, second-degree vehicular manslaughter, and criminally negligent homicide for causing the death of Brenda Dirago, third-degree reckless assault for causing physical injury to Daniel Dirago, and driving while intoxicated. The bill of particulars supporting the indictment alleged that Corbin operated a motor vehicle on a public highway in an intoxicated condition, failed to keep right of the median, and drove approximately 45 to 50 miles per hour in heavy rain, "a speed too fast for the weather and road conditions then pending." Corbin challenged the indictment as a violation of double jeopardy. The Court agreed, and added a "same conduct" test on top of the *Blockburger* "same elements" test for those cases when the government pursues successive prosecutions:

> If *Blockburger* constituted the entire double jeopardy inquiry in the context of successive prosecutions, the State could try Corbin in four consecutive trials: for failure to keep right of the median, for driving while intoxicated, for assault, and for homicide. The State could improve its presentation of proof with each trial, assessing which witnesses gave the most persuasive testimony, which documents had the greatest impact, and which opening and closing arguments most persuaded the jurors. Corbin would be forced either to contest each of these trials or to plead guilty to avoid the harassment and expense.
>
> Thus, a subsequent prosecution must do more than merely survive the *Blockburger* test. [T]he Double Jeopardy Clause bars any subsequent prosecution in which the government, to establish an essential element of an offense charged in that prosecution, will prove conduct that constitutes an offense for which the defendant has already been prosecuted. This is not an "actual evidence" or "same evidence" test. The critical inquiry is what conduct the State will prove, not the evidence the State will use to prove that conduct. [T]he presentation of specific evidence in one trial does not forever prevent the government from introducing that same evidence in a subsequent proceeding. [495 U.S. at 520-521.]

Applying the new standard, the Court held that the double jeopardy clause barred the second prosecution because "the State has admitted that it will prove the entirety of the conduct for which Corbin was convicted — driving while intoxicated and failing to keep right of the median — to establish essential elements of the homicide and assault offenses."

Three years later, the Court overruled *Grady* and reinstated the "same elements" test as the basic way to identify double jeopardy violations in United States v. Dixon, 509 U.S. 688 (1993). The complex facts in *Dixon* concerned two cases in which contempt judgments — in one case for violation of a condition of release, and in the other for violation of civil protection orders — were entered before each defendant was prosecuted for the offenses underlying the contempt violation.

> We have concluded . . . that *Grady* must be overruled. Unlike *Blockburger* analysis, whose definition of what prevents two crimes from being the "same offence," has deep historical roots and has been accepted in numerous precedents of this Court, *Grady* lacks constitutional roots. The "same-conduct" rule it announced is wholly inconsistent with earlier Supreme Court precedent and with the clear common-law understanding of double jeopardy. . . . *Grady* was not only wrong in principle; it has already proved unstable in application. [W]e think it time to acknowledge what is now, three years after *Grady*, compellingly clear: the case was a mistake.

509 U.S. at 704, 709, 711. The first of the following two cases shows the *Blockburger* test at work. The second case discusses the choices among different tests for the "same offense" and illustrates the response of state courts to the leadership of the U.S. Supreme Court in this difficult area.

■ ROBERT TAYLOR v. COMMONWEALTH

995 S.W.2d 355 (Ky. 1999)

COOPER, J.

. . . On the afternoon of October 9, 1996, Appellant, then seventeen years of age, his girlfriend, Lucy Cotton, and Cotton's infant son had attended the Daniel Boone

Festival and were traveling through rural Knox County in a 1985 Buick owned by Cotton's mother. They had with them a .22 rifle, a .38 Derringer handgun, and two shotguns. When the vehicle stalled, Appellant sought assistance from Herman McCreary, who lived nearby. McCreary agreed to help and drove his 1984 Ford pickup truck to the location of the stalled vehicle. Upon arrival, he observed Cotton sitting in the passenger seat of the Buick holding a child in her lap. Several attempts to jump-start the Buick failed. According to Cotton, Appellant told her, "If it don't start this time, I'm gonna take his truck," and armed himself with the .22 rifle and the .38 handgun. According to Appellant, Cotton pointed the .38 handgun at him and threatened to shoot him if he did not steal McCreary's truck.

When a final attempt to jump-start the Buick was unsuccessful, Appellant got out of the vehicle, pointed the .22 rifle at McCreary, and ordered him to lie on the ground. When McCreary complied, Appellant fired a round from the rifle into the ground near McCreary's head. According to Cotton, Appellant then struck McCreary in the head with the stock of the rifle. McCreary temporarily lost consciousness. Upon regaining consciousness, McCreary experienced dizziness and noticed blood coming from the left side of his head. Appellant then told McCreary to get into the ditch beside the road or he would "blow his head off." McCreary again complied, whereupon Appellant, Cotton and the child departed the scene in McCreary's truck. McCreary walked to a neighbor's house and called the police. [Taylor and Cotton were later apprehended and Taylor was convicted of assault in second degree, robbery in first degree, and possession of handgun by a minor. Taylor] asserts that his convictions violated the constitutional proscription against double jeopardy. U.S. Const. amend. V; Ky. Const. §13.

In Commonwealth v. Burge, 947 S.W.2d 805, 809-11 (1997), we reinstated the "*Blockburger* rule," Blockburger v. United States, 284 U.S. 299 (1932), as incorporated in KRS §505.020, as the sole basis for determining whether multiple convictions arising out of a single course of conduct constitutes double jeopardy. The test in this case is not whether all three convictions were premised upon the use or possession of a firearm, or whether both the assault and the robbery occurred in the course of a single transaction. "[W]here the same act or transaction constitutes a violation of two distinct statutory provisions, the test to be applied to determine whether there are two offenses or only one is whether each provision requires proof of an additional fact which the other does not." Blockburger v. United States, 284 U.S. 299, 304 (1932).

KRS §515.020(1) defines robbery in the first degree as follows:

> A person is guilty of robbery in the first degree when, in the course of committing a theft, he uses or threatens the immediate use of physical force upon another person with intent to accomplish the theft and when he:
>
> (a) Causes physical injury to any person who is not a participant in the crime; or
>
> (b) Is armed with a deadly weapon; or
>
> (c) Uses or threatens the use of a dangerous instrument upon any person who is not a participant in the crime.

The first paragraph of the statute sets forth three elements which must be proven in any robbery case, viz: (1) In the course of committing a theft, (2) the defendant used or threatened the immediate use of physical force upon another person (3) with the intent to accomplish the theft. Subsections (a), (b), and (c) of the statute then describe three separate and distinct factual situations, any one of which could constitute the fourth element of the offense. The indictment of Appellant for robbery in the first degree in this case charged that he committed the offense "by being armed with a deadly weapon." The jury was instructed that it could convict Appellant of robbery in the first degree only if it believed beyond a reasonable doubt that "when he did so, he was armed with a .22 rifle." Thus, both the indictment and the instruction were predicated upon a violation of KRS 515.020(1)(b). Neither the indictment nor the instruction required Appellant to have caused a physical injury to McCreary or to have used or threatened the use of a dangerous instrument upon McCreary.

KRS 508.020(1) defines assault in the second degree as follows:

> A person is guilty of assault in the second degree when:
> (a) He intentionally causes serious physical injury to another person; or
> (b) He intentionally causes physical injury to another person by means of a deadly weapon or a dangerous instrument; or
> (c) He wantonly causes serious physical injury to another person by means of a deadly weapon or a dangerous instrument.

The statute sets forth three alternative factual situations by which the offense can be committed. Although the indictment charged Appellant with having committed the offense "by striking Herman McCreary with a pistol," the jury instruction conformed to the testimony of Lucy Cotton, who provided the only evidence with respect to this offense:

> You will find the defendant guilty under this instruction if, and only if, you believe from the evidence beyond a reasonable doubt all of the following: (a) that in this county on or about October 9, 1996 and before the finding of the indictment herein, he inflicted an injury upon Herman McCreary by striking him with a .22 rifle, a deadly weapon; AND (b) that in so doing, the defendant intentionally caused physical injury to Herman McCreary.[1]

Thus, conviction of either the assault or the robbery of McCreary required proof of an element not required to prove the other. The conviction of robbery required proof of a theft, which was not required to convict of assault. The conviction of assault required proof of a physical injury to McCreary, whereas the conviction of robbery required proof only that Appellant used or threatened the use of physical force upon McCreary while armed with a .22 rifle. . . .

STUMBO, J., dissenting.

Respectfully, I must dissent. I believe Appellant's convictions for both assault and robbery violated the prohibition against double jeopardy. . . . As written, the indictment did not violate the double jeopardy prohibition. The indictment charged Appellant with "Assault in the Second Degree by striking Herman McCreary with a pistol" and "Robbery in the First Degree by being armed with a deadly weapon while in the course of committing a theft of Herman McCreary." Clearly, these offenses

1. Appellant did not object to the variance of this instruction from the language of the indictment. The indictment described the weapon used to inflict the injury as a pistol, whereas the instruction described the weapon as a .22 rifle. Generally, instructions should be based on the evidence introduced at trial, and any variance between the language of the indictment and the language of the instruction is not deemed prejudicial unless the defendant was misled.

arise from two distinct statutes. As charged, each would have required proof of a fact which the other did not. For the assault, the prosecution would have had to prove that Appellant struck McCreary with the .38 pistol causing a physical injury. For the robbery, the prosecution would have had to prove Appellant used or threatened to use physical force on McCreary while armed with a deadly weapon (presumably the .22 rifle) during the course of the theft of his truck.

In the end, however, the prosecution was unable to maintain this logically sound but practically impossible distinction. By the time the jury was instructed, the assault had merged into the robbery so that one was clearly included within the other. This is so because the jury instruction on second-degree assault required the jury to find the offense was accomplished "by striking him with a .22 rifle, a deadly weapon." The jury instruction on first-degree robbery required the jury to find Appellant "used or threatened the immediate use of physical force upon Herman McCreary; AND (c) that when he did so, he was armed with a .22 rifle." This melding of the charges allowed the jury to consider any assault with the .22 rifle during the incident as an element of the robbery and thus made the assault charge a lesser included offense of the robbery charge. Appellant may be convicted of only one of these offenses without violating the prohibition against double jeopardy. Therefore, I would vacate the conviction on the lesser charge of assault in the second degree.

■ STATE v. JAMES LESSARY

865 P.2d 150 (Haw. 1994)

KLEIN, J.

James Easter Lessary was charged with [Abuse of a Family Member, Unlawful Imprisonment, and Terroristic Threatening]. After Lessary was found guilty of the Abuse charge in family court, the circuit court dismissed the Unlawful Imprisonment and Terroristic Threatening charges on double jeopardy grounds. . . . For the reasons set forth below, we affirm in part and reverse in part.

The alleged criminal episode began on the morning of April 4, 1991, when Lessary drove to the place of work of his estranged wife. . . . Upon arrival, Lessary got out of his jeep, walked into the office, grabbed her by the head and hair, and threw her against a wall. A co-worker, hearing the commotion, intervened between Lessary and the victim. Lessary backed off slightly, but when the victim refused to leave with him, he picked up a pair of scissors and, wielding them like a knife, pointed them towards the victim and her co-worker. Lessary, who said he "just wanted to talk to her," grabbed the victim by the front of her shirt and, while holding the scissors in his free hand, dragged her from the office to his jeep. When she refused to enter the jeep, Lessary pointed the scissors at her stomach and told her that he would stab her if she continued to refuse. After they were both in the jeep, he sped away and threw the scissors out the window shortly thereafter. Lessary drove them to a canefield where they talked together for several hours. Lessary eventually decided to surrender and allowed the victim to drive them out of the canefield.

On April 5, 1991, Lessary was charged by complaint in district court with Terroristic Threatening and [Unlawful Imprisonment]. On the same day, Lessary was charged by complaint in family court with Abuse. At the April 29, 1991 family court arraignment and plea hearing, Lessary pled "no contest" to the Abuse charge in exchange for the State recommending a sentence of five days incarceration on the

Abuse charge and dismissing a pending contempt of court charge [based on a failure to appear for the family court arraignment]. In response to the family court's inquiry concerning the facts supporting the Abuse charge, the prosecutor responded as follows:

> The defendant was reported to have gone to the victim's job site within the office and had thrown her against the wall, your Honor. The defendant then dragged [the victim] out of the office into his vehicle. Injuries included redness to the victim's left ear from being thrown against the wall and pain to the right hamstring area and right elbow from being dragged to his car.

Based on these representations, the court found Lessary guilty of Abuse and sentenced him to five days incarceration and one year probation. [Lessary then moved to dismiss the Terroristic Threatening and Unlawful Imprisonment charges on double jeopardy grounds. The trial court granted the motion. The trial court's dismissal was based on its reading of Grady v. Corbin, 495 U.S. 508 (1990). However,] the United States Supreme Court subsequently overruled *Grady* and reinstated the "same elements" test that was first set forth in Blockburger v. United States, 284 U.S. 299 (1932), as the sole test under the double jeopardy clause of the United States Constitution. United States v. Dixon, 509 U.S. 688 (1993). According to *Blockburger*, . . . "the test to be applied to determine whether there are two offenses or only one, is whether each requires proof of a fact which the other does not." 284 U.S. at 304.

Lessary concedes that under the "same elements" test, the prosecution of the Unlawful Imprisonment and Terroristic Threatening offenses is not barred.[8] . . . Lessary urges us nonetheless to affirm the dismissal of the charges on independent state constitutional grounds. Article I, section 10 of the Hawaii Constitution provides in pertinent part: "No person shall . . . be subject for the same offense to be twice put in jeopardy." Although this language is virtually identical to the double jeopardy clause of the United States Constitution, we are not bound to give provisions of the Hawaii Constitution the same interpretations as those given under the United States Constitution. . . .

In *Blockburger*, the Supreme Court addressed the applicability of the double jeopardy clause in the context of a single prosecution for multiple offenses. The Court ruled that the double jeopardy clause protects individuals from receiving multiple punishments for the "same offense," even in a single prosecution, and created the "same elements" test to implement that protection.

Protection against multiple punishments, however, is not the only protection that the double jeopardy clause provides. "It protects against a second prosecution for the same offense after acquittal. It protects against a second prosecution for the same offense after conviction. And it protects against multiple punishments for the same offense." North Carolina v. Pearce, 395 U.S. 711 (1969). *Blockburger* and its progeny focused almost exclusively on whether the legislature intended to allow the imposition of multiple punishments for the commission of a particular act. See, e.g., Missouri v. Hunter, 459 U.S. 359 (1983). . . .

8. Abuse requires proof of physical abuse; Unlawful Imprisonment and Terroristic Threatening do not. Unlawful Imprisonment requires proof of restraint; Abuse and Terroristic Threatening do not. Terroristic Threatening requires proof of a threat to cause bodily injury; Abuse and Unlawful Imprisonment do not. Thus, Abuse, Unlawful Imprisonment, and Terroristic Threatening are all "different" offenses under the double jeopardy clause of the United States Constitution.

Because of its focus on the statutory definitions of offenses, however, the "same elements" test does not prevent the government from initiating multiple prosecutions against an individual based on a single act as long as the subsequent prosecutions are for offenses with "different" elements. In *Grady,* the United States Supreme Court recognized the dangers inherent in allowing the government to pursue multiple prosecutions against an individual. The Court described the dangers as follows:

> [T]he State with all its resources and power should not be allowed to make repeated attempts to convict an individual for an alleged offense, thereby subjecting him to embarrassment, expense and ordeal and compelling him to live in a continuing state of anxiety and insecurity. . . . Multiple prosecutions also give the State an opportunity to rehearse its presentation of proof, thus increasing the risk of an erroneous conviction for one or more of the offenses charged. Even when a State can bring multiple charges against an individual under *Blockburger,* a tremendous additional burden is placed on that defendant if he must face each of the charges in a separate proceeding. [495 U.S. at 518.]

[The decision in United States v. Dixon, 509 U.S. 688 (1993), overruled *Grady* and reestablished the "same elements" test as the sole protection against double jeopardy.] The State urges us to follow *Dixon* and argues that any test more restrictive than the "same elements" test would contravene the public policy of having different courts handle different offenses (e.g., traffic court for traffic violations, juvenile court for offenses committed by minors, and family court for intra-family offenses committed by adults). In "instances of successive prosecutions," however, "the interests of the defendant are of *paramount* concern." *Dixon,* 509 U.S. at 724 (White, J., concurring in part and dissenting in part) (emphasis in original). We do not believe that the State's interest in prosecuting different offenses in different courts outweighs a defendant's "paramount" interest in being free from vexatious multiple prosecutions. Moreover, the State should not be allowed to circumvent the constitutional prohibition against double jeopardy by creating a variety of courts, each having limited jurisdiction, in which to bring successive prosecutions that could not otherwise be pursued.

Thus, we are not persuaded by the State's argument and agree with the majority in *Grady* and the "dissenters" in *Dixon* that individuals should be protected against multiple prosecutions even when multiple punishments are permissible under the "same elements" test. Therefore, we conclude that the interpretation given to the double jeopardy clause by the United States Supreme Court in *Dixon* does not adequately protect individuals from being "subject for the same offense to be twice put in jeopardy."

Having concluded that the protections afforded under the United States Constitution are inadequate, we must determine what further protections are required by the Hawaii Constitution. The protections must ensure that individuals are not subjected to multiple prosecutions for a single act. The "same conduct" test set forth by the United States Supreme Court in *Grady* attempted to provide those protections. The Court there held that

> the Double Jeopardy Clause bars any subsequent prosecution in which the government, to establish an essential element of an offense charged in that prosecution, will prove conduct that constitutes an offense for which the defendant has already been prosecuted. [495 U.S. at 521.]

Lessary urges us to extend the protections of the Hawaii Constitution even further than the *Grady* rule and adopt the "same episode" test. Under the "same episode" test, all offenses "that grow out of a single criminal act, occurrence, episode, or transaction" would be considered the "same offense" for purposes of determining whether the guarantee against being "subject for the same offense to be twice put in jeopardy" bars a second prosecution. See Ashe v. Swenson, 397 U.S. 436 (1970) (Brennan, J., concurring). Under that test, once an individual has been prosecuted for one offense, that individual cannot be later prosecuted for any other offense committed during the same episode, even if the offenses were committed by distinct acts. For example, if an individual kidnapped, then raped, and finally murdered another person, and was initially prosecuted for the kidnapping offense alone, the "same episode" test would preclude any subsequent prosecution for the rape or murder. We do not believe this is the result intended by the double jeopardy clause. The double jeopardy clause should protect an individual from being twice put in jeopardy for a single act; it should not protect an individual from separate prosecutions for separate acts. Therefore, we hold that the double jeopardy clause of the Hawaii Constitution does not require the application of the "same episode" test.[12] The "same conduct" test as set forth in *Grady,* on the other hand, protects individuals from multiple prosecutions for the same act without unnecessarily restricting the ability of the State to prosecute individuals who perform separate acts that independently constitute separate offenses. . . .

We now address the application of the "same conduct" test to the offenses at issue in the instant case. Because the State concedes that prosecution of the Unlawful Imprisonment charge is barred by the "same conduct" test, the only remaining issue is whether prosecution of the Terroristic Threatening charge is also barred.[13]

Under the "same conduct" test, prosecution of the Terroristic Threatening charge is barred if the State, to establish the conduct element of Terroristic Threatening, will prove acts of the defendant on which the State relied to prove the conduct element of the Abuse offense for which Lessary had already been prosecuted. The conduct element of Abuse is physically abusing a family or household member. In the Abuse prosecution, Lessary's acts of throwing the victim against the office wall and dragging her from the office to his jeep were used to prove that Lessary physically abused the victim. The State cannot use those acts to prove the conduct element of Terroristic Threatening. The conduct element of Terroristic Threatening is threatening to cause bodily injury to another person. The State contends that it will rely on different acts, namely Lessary's act of brandishing the scissors towards the victim and her co-worker in the office and his acts of pointing the scissors at the victim's stomach and telling her that he would stab her if she refused to enter his jeep, to prove that Lessary threatened to cause bodily injury.

12. In most cases, however, the Hawaii legislature has mandated the joinder of all offenses "arising from the same episode." HRS §701-109(2) provides in pertinent part:

> Except [when the judge orders separate trials], a defendant shall not be subject to separate trials for multiple offenses based on the same conduct or arising from the same episode, if such offenses are known to the appropriate prosecuting officer at the time of the commencement of the first trial and are within the jurisdiction of a single court.

The prosecution of the Unlawful Imprisonment and Terroristic Threatening charges in the instant case is not barred by this statute because those charges and the Abuse charge were not within the jurisdiction of a single court.

13. The conduct element of Unlawful Imprisonment is restraining another person. The State concedes that in order to prove that Lessary restrained the victim, it would have to prove either that Lessary threw her against the office wall or that he dragged her to his jeep. Those acts had been used to prove the conduct element of the Abuse charge in the earlier prosecution. Therefore, under the "same conduct" test, prosecution of the Unlawful Imprisonment charge is barred.

Lessary argues that because the alleged threats were so closely intertwined with the acts of abuse, they constituted the "same conduct." Lessary, however, is confusing the "same conduct" test with the "same episode" test. We have held that the test for determining the singleness of a criminal episode should be based on whether the alleged conduct was so closely related in time, place and circumstances that a complete account of one charge cannot be related without referring to details of the other charge. Although we agree that the Terroristic Threatening and Abuse charges arose from the same episode, as discussed above, the Hawaii Constitution does not require application of the "same episode" test. Because the conduct element of the Terroristic Threatening charge can be established by proof of acts independent of the acts alleged in the Abuse prosecution, the two offenses are not based on the "same conduct." Therefore, the prosecution of the Terroristic Threatening charge is not barred by the double jeopardy clause of the Hawaii Constitution. . . .

■ NEW YORK CRIMINAL PROCEDURE LAW §40.20

1. A person may not be twice prosecuted for the same offense.

2. A person may not be separately prosecuted for two offenses based upon the same act or criminal transaction unless:

(a) The offenses as defined have substantially different elements and the acts establishing one offense are in the main clearly distinguishable from those establishing the other; or

(b) Each of the offenses as defined contains an element which is not an element of the other, and the statutory provisions defining such offenses are designed to prevent very different kinds of harm or evil; or

(c) One of such offenses consists of criminal possession of contraband matter and the other offense is one involving the use of such contraband matter, other than a sale thereof; or

(d) One of the offenses is assault or some other offense resulting in physical injury to a person, and the other offense is one of homicide based upon the death of such person from the same physical injury, and such death occurs after a prosecution for the assault or other non-homicide offense; or

(e) Each offense involves death, injury, loss or other consequence to a different victim; or

(f) One of the offenses consists of a violation of a statutory provision of another jurisdiction, which offense has been prosecuted in such other jurisdiction and has there been terminated by a court order expressly founded upon insufficiency of evidence to establish some element of such offense which is not an element of the other offense, defined by the laws of this state; or

(g) The present prosecution is for a consummated result offense . . . which occurred in this state and the offense was the result of a conspiracy, facilitation or solicitation prosecuted in another state. . . .

Notes

1. *Determining whether two charges are for the "same offence": majority position.* The Supreme Court's decision in United States v. Dixon, 509 U.S. 688 (1993),

reestablished the "same elements" test of Blockburger v. United States, 284 U.S. 299 (1932). Under this test, if the two offenses *each* have at least one distinct "element," they are not treated as the same offense. Hence, multiple trials or multiple punishments based on these offenses do not violate the protection against double jeopardy.

About 30 state courts follow *Dixon* and have adopted (or readopted) the *Blockburger* "same elements" test under state law. See, e.g., State v. Alvarez, 778 A.2d 938 (Conn. 2001); City of Fargo v. Hector, 534 N.W.2d 821 (N.D. 1995). About 10 jurisdictions, like the Hawaii Supreme Court in *Lessary,* have interpreted their state constitutions to employ the *Grady* "same conduct" test (or the closely related "same evidence" test) in addition to the *Blockburger* analysis as a limit on multiple prosecutions. A smaller group of states (about a half dozen) apply a test that places even stronger limits on government attempts to bring multiple prosecutions: the "same transaction" test (also called the "same episode" or "same incident" test) suggested by Justice Brennan in his concurring opinion in Ashe v. Swenson, 397 U.S. 436 (1970). See, e.g., People v. Harding, 506 N.W.2d 482 (Mich. 1993); State v. Farley, 725 P.2d 359 (Or. 1986). Around 15 states have adopted statutory tests for whether a second charge is for the "same offense"; some statutes mirror the *Blockburger* test, Fla. Stat. §775.021(4)(a), while others add a "same facts" or "same conduct" test.

There is no shortage of suggestions in the academic literature for reworking this doctrine from the ground up. See Akhil Amar, Double Jeopardy Law Made Simple, 106 Yale L.J. 1807 (1997) (suggests due process rather than double jeopardy as remedy for vexatious litigation); George Thomas, A Blameworthy Act Approach to the Double Jeopardy Same Offense Problem, 83 Cal. L. Rev. 1027, 1041-1049 (1995) (looks to blameworthiness rather than *Blockburger* as best indicator of legislative intent as to multiple punishment and trials). Consider this critique of the doctrine by Justice Breyer: "[T]he simple-sounding *Blockburger* test has proved extraordinarily difficult to administer in practice. Judges, lawyers, and law professors often disagree about how to apply it. [The *Blockburger* test is] "the criminal law equivalent of Milton's 'Serbonian Bog . . . Where Armies whole have sunk.'" Texas v. Cobb, 532 U.S. 162 (2001). Exactly how do the Kentucky Justices in *Taylor* disagree on the application of *Blockburger?*

2. *Punishment for greater and lesser included offenses.* A lesser included offense is one that is necessarily included within the statutory elements of another offense. Thus, if Crime 1 has elements A and B, it is a lesser included offense for Crime 2, with elements A, B, and C. In a straightforward application of the *Blockburger* test, a prosecution for either Crime 1 or Crime 2 would prevent a later prosecution or punishment for the second crime. An exception to this bar would allow a prosecution for Crime 2 after a prosecution for Crime 1, if the additional element C had not yet occurred at the time of the Crime 1 prosecution (for instance, if an assault victim dies after the trial for assault goes forward). See Brown v. Ohio, 432 U.S. 161, 169 n.7 (1977).

But the courts have gone beyond this literal understanding of lesser included offenses. Both federal and state courts declare that double jeopardy limits for the "same offense" also apply to "a species of lesser included offense." In Harris v. Oklahoma, 433 U.S. 682 (1977), the court held that a conviction for felony murder barred a later trial of the defendant for the underlying robbery. Strictly speaking, the robbery and felony murder statutes pass the *Blockburger* test: Felony murder requires proof of a killing (robbery does not), and robbery requires proof of forcible taking of property (which felony murder does not necessarily require). But the court was willing to treat robbery and felony murder as the "same offense" because in the *case at hand,* the prosecution was relying on forcible taking of property to establish the predicate felony for felony murder. See also United States v. Dixon, 509 U.S. 688, 697-700 (1993) (criminal contempt of court for violation of judicial order not to commit "any criminal offense" and possession of cocaine with intent to distribute are the same offense); People v. Wood, 742 N.E.2d 114 (N.Y. 2000) (multiple contempt convictions in different courts for same acts violate double jeopardy; defendant made late-night hang-up calls, violated no-contact orders issued by criminal court and family court). On the other hand, the same logic does not seem to apply to conspiracy or "continuing criminal enterprise" crimes. See United States v. Felix, 503 U.S. 378, 387-392 (1992) (conspiracy to manufacture narcotics is not same offense as manufacturing narcotics); Garrett v. United States, 471 U.S. 773, 777-786 (1985) (distribution of marijuana is not same offense as conducting a continuing criminal enterprise to distribute marijuana).

3. *The "multiple punishment" prong of double jeopardy.* Unlike the relatively clear rule against multiple *prosecutions* for the same offense, there are looser limits when the prosecutor files multiple charges in a *single proceeding,* and the defendant claims that the charges are actually an attempt to impose multiple punishments for what is really a single offense. In this setting, the legislature sets the constraints on the prosecutor. In Missouri v. Hunter, 459 U.S. 359 (1983), the Supreme Court held that "the Double Jeopardy Clause does no more than prevent the sentencing court from prescribing greater punishment than the legislature intended."

Most states follow Missouri v. Hunter and hold that in the context of a single prosecution, the *Blockburger* test (or an alternative test) only helps determine whether the legislature intended to allow separate convictions and punishments for a single criminal episode or event. See, e.g., State v. Adel, 965 P.2d 1072 (Wash. 1998). The courts reason that the legislature can select from a wide range of punishments for any particular offense. Other states have rejected the majority rule and have applied state law to limit cumulative punishments regardless of the legislature's intent. See, e.g., Ingram v. Commonwealth, 801 S.W.2d 321 (Ky. 1990). In one especially difficult area, states are split on whether punishment is acceptable for both felony murder and the underlying felony when they are tried together. See, e.g., Todd v. State, 917 P.2d 674 (Alaska 1996) (allowing multiple punishment); cf. Boulies v. People, 770 P.2d 1274 (Colo. 1989) (state merger rule barring multiple punishment).

What reasons might justify the different treatment of "multiple proceedings" on the one hand, and "multiple punishment" for the same conduct in a single proceeding on the other hand? Does this distinction make sense? See Nancy King, Portioning Punishment: Constitutional Limits on Successive and Excessive Penalties, 144 U. Pa. L. Rev. 101 (1995) (points to illogic of cases allowing multiple punishments in a single trial but not in successive trials; argues for limiting Eighth Amendment to a remedy for excessive punishments imposed in multiple proceedings).

4. *When do double jeopardy claims arise?* Double jeopardy claims can arise at a variety of points in the criminal justice process. A defendant can raise double jeopardy claims as soon as she is charged with multiple counts in a single proceeding. A defendant might challenge even a single count, claiming that jeopardy already attached at an earlier proceeding. Double jeopardy "attaches" at an initial trial when the jury is sworn in (for jury trials) or when the first witness is sworn in (for a bench trial) or when the court accepts a guilty plea. The defendant might raise a double jeopardy challenge at the time of sentencing, claiming that the state has requested

multiple punishments for the same offense. Double jeopardy challenges might also arise when the state attempts to impose some civil penalties before or after adjudicating the criminal charges.

It is important to recognize that double jeopardy influences the work of all three branches of government. Double jeopardy rules have a substantial impact on what kinds of charges the prosecution chooses to file. Principles of prior jeopardy may also shape the actions of judges at sentencing, when the judge can group together charges to produce a single sentence lower than what technically could be imposed for each separate conviction. Finally, legislators will have a powerful effect on the grouping of crimes when they define the elements of different crimes. Ultimately, are double jeopardy principles anything more than instructions to legislatures to draft cleanly?

5. *States without double jeopardy provisions.* Five states have no double jeopardy provisions in their constitutions. Each has incorporated double jeopardy principles but through different conceptual doorways. Connecticut imports double jeopardy though its due process clause. See, e.g., State v. Nixon, 651 A.2d 1264 (Conn. 1995). Maryland, Massachusetts, and North Carolina rely on the common law as the source for their double jeopardy rules. See, e.g., Berry v. Commonwealth, 473 N.E.2d 1115 (Mass. 1985). Vermont courts have simply adopted federal double jeopardy standards. See In re Dunkerley, 376 A.2d 43 (Vt. 1977).

6. *Consistency and respect.* What principles of decision making underlie the Supreme Court's boomerang from *Grady* (1990) to *Dixon* (1993)? It is arguable that *Grady* and *Dixon* both reveal substantial departures from established rules (*Grady* from *Blockburger,* and *Dixon* from *Grady*). All courts offer words of respect for stare decisis. Should courts have a different stare decisis rule with respect to constitutional and nonconstitutional decisions? Should all constitutional decisions have a natural life span? Should readers discount all constitutional decisions by the age of the justices and the number of justices who decided the case who are still active — a kind of actuarial jurisprudence? Are constitutions nothing more than the sum of the personal views of those who interpret and enforce them?

Problem 14-2. Multiplicity

On December 11, 1989, Ronald Gardner, Cato Peterson, Amir Wilson, and Aaron Banks were traveling in a white Cougar automobile from Detroit to Muskegon. Muskegon County Sheriff Deputy Al VanHemert received a tip from a confidential informant that Aaron Banks and several other persons would be transporting crack cocaine to a Muskegon Heights neighborhood that afternoon. Two deputies executed a legal stop and search of the vehicle. They seized 222 grams of crack cocaine and arrested the occupants of the car.

Ronald Gardner, Cato Peterson, and Amir Wilson each made statements to the officers. Gardner said that Ricky Franklin paid him two hundred dollars to drive Peterson, Wilson, and Banks to the Muskegon Heights area. He admitted that he had previously transported sellers and drugs to that area. Gardner also stated he had picked up money at the home of "Miss Louise" in Muskegon and transported the cash back to Detroit. He stated that cocaine was sometimes transported in the spare tire in the trunk. Gardner called Franklin the head of the organization, while Banks was the boss of the Muskegon portion of the operation.

Peterson stated to the officers that he was traveling to Muskegon to sell crack cocaine, that this was his second trip to Muskegon, and that Franklin was the head of the organization.

Wilson also made a statement to the Muskegon authorities after his arrest. He stated that he sold crack cocaine for Ricky Franklin and that he had sold drugs on three previous trips to Muskegon. He stated that Banks would stay at Miss Louise's house and dispense the crack baggies to the sellers there. The cocaine was transported in the spare tire in the trunk. Robert Johnson was also involved in the sale of cocaine.

On June 6, 1990, Amir Wilson was convicted by a Muskegon County jury of possession with intent to deliver and conspiracy to deliver between 50 and 225 grams of cocaine. On July 3, 1990, Wilson was sentenced to two concurrent prison terms of eight to twenty years.

On July 5, 1990, police arrested Gerald Hill in Southfield (in Oakland County, near Muskegon County) for possession with intent to deliver between 225 and 649 grams of cocaine. Southfield police made the arrest after a routine traffic stop of the vehicle in which Hill and Ricky Franklin were passengers. The police allowed Hill to go into a store across the street from where the vehicle was stopped. After Hill left the area, store employees alerted police officers that they had found cocaine in a jacket behind the store. The Muskegon and Oakland County Sheriff Departments joined efforts to investigate the "Franklin organization."

In December 1990, an Oakland County grand jury indicted Wilson, Banks, Hill, Johnson, and another individual, Terrence Moore, on charges of conspiring from October 1988 to December 1990 to possess with intent to deliver over 650 grams of cocaine. Wilson moved to set aside the indictment on the basis of a violation of double jeopardy. Should the trial judge in Oakland County grant the motion? Compare People v. Wilson, 563 N.W.2d 44 (Mich. 1997).

Notes

1. *Multiplicity: majority view.* At what point does the commission of one offense end and the commission of a second offense begin? This can be a very difficult question with criminal acts that occur in several locations (such as drug sales), through multiple events (such as conspiracies based on a series of conversations), or over extended periods of time. All jurisdictions must face claims that multiple, identical charges are applied to what is only a single event. In fact, in *Blockburger* itself the defendant claimed that two drug sales on successive days constituted one offense. Shortly after delivery of the drug that was the subject of the first sale, the purchaser paid for an additional quantity to be delivered the next day. The defendant argued that these two sales to the same purchaser, with no substantial interval of time between the delivery of the drug in the first transaction and the payment for the second quantity sold, constituted a single continuing offense. 284 U.S. at 301. The Court rejected the claim: "The Narcotic Act does not create the offense of engaging in the business of selling the forbidden drugs, but penalizes any sale made. . . . Each of several successive sales constitutes a distinct offense, however closely they may follow each other." 284 U.S. at 302.

Some courts refer to the issue of dividing one offender's behavior into distinct offenses as the problem of "multiplicity." See, e.g., State v. Smith, 864 P.2d 709

(Kan. 1993). Though not all jurisdictions use the term, the question of multiplicity is common to all jurisdictions. To what extent does application of the *Blockburger* test answer the question of how many different crimes can be charged? Beyond the scope of *Blockburger,* what principles should govern?

2. *The special problem of conspiracies.* The puzzle of determining how many separate charges are possible is especially difficult in the context of conspiracies — especially drug conspiracies — which tend to take place over time and space and to involve multiple participants. To determine whether criminal conduct amounted to one conspiracy or two, courts consult the "totality of the circumstances," with special emphasis on 1) the time of the conduct, 2) the persons acting as coconspirators, 3) the overlap among the statutory offenses charged in the indictments, 4) the overt acts charged by the government or any other description of the offenses charged that indicate the nature and scope of the activity that the government sought to punish in each case, and 5) places where the events alleged as part of the conspiracy took place. The procedural difficulties regarding the parsing of conspiracies reflect the substantive battles over the scope of conspiracy law. See Paul Marcus, Criminal Conspiracy Law: Time to Turn Back from an Ever Expanding, Ever More Troubling Area, 1 Wm. & Mary Bill of Rights J. 1 (1992); William Theis, The Double Jeopardy Defense and Multiple Prosecutions for Conspiracy, 49 SMU L. Rev. 269 (1996).

3. Collateral Estoppel

The common-law doctrine of collateral estoppel raises a question related to double jeopardy: When has an issue or a fact been resolved in one proceeding in a way that will bind the parties in later disputes? The doctrine of collateral estoppel has reached constitutional status in the criminal context. Collateral estoppel is obviously a cousin to double jeopardy, but how closely is it related? In what ways are the doctrines different?

■ AVERY FERRELL v. STATE

567 A.2d 937 (Md. 1990)

ELDRIDGE, J.

This criminal case involves the applicability of the doctrine of collateral estoppel where a defendant was acquitted on one count of a two-count charging document, where the jury was unable to agree on the other count, where the disputed issue under both counts was the same, and where the defendant was subsequently retried for the offense on which the jury had previously been unable to agree.

The pertinent facts, as disclosed by the prosecution's evidence, are as follows. On the morning of April 10, 1985, three women and a school girl were robbed at gunpoint by a lone man carrying a handgun and wearing a ski mask, a blue hooded sweatshirt, a long gray coat and tennis shoes. During the course of the robbery, one of the victims attempted to flee the scene at which time the robber fired a shot from the handgun and grabbed the fleeing victim's pocketbook. As the robber fled the scene, he was followed a short distance by one of the victims who later testified that she observed the robber changing clothes as he was running away.

The police were called, arrived on the scene immediately, and began searching for the robber in a nearby apartment development. One of the officers testified that he observed the defendant, Avery Ferrell, emerging from an apartment building wearing a blue-gray suit, hard shoes, and carrying a gray coat and a shopping bag. As the officer approached him, Ferrell began to walk away at an increasingly brisk pace. According to the officer's testimony, Ferrell dropped the shopping bag and ran behind a building. The officer then observed Ferrell entering a different apartment building and relayed that information to another officer at the scene who arrested Ferrell. When Ferrell was apprehended, he was carrying a three-quarter length gray coat which was identified by one of the victims as looking like the coat the robber wore. None of the victims, however, was able to identify Ferrell as the masked robber. The shopping bag was recovered and found to contain the articles stolen from the victims, along with a handgun containing five live rounds with one spent cartridge, and a ski mask.

The State's Attorney filed four criminal informations against Ferrell, each relating to one of the victims, and each charging the following [eight counts: robbery with a deadly weapon, attempted robbery with a deadly weapon, robbery, assault with intent to rob, assault, theft of less than $300, use of a handgun in the commission of a felony or crime of violence, and unlawful carrying of a handgun]. A fifth information charged Ferrell with assault with intent to murder one of the victims.

Ferrell has since stood trial four times in the Circuit Court for Baltimore City. At the first trial on the above-described charges, the jury returned a verdict of not guilty of assault with intent to murder and guilty of the other charges. . . . Ferrell moved for a new trial, and the motion was granted [on the ground that the jury's verdicts were not unanimous]. The second trial resulted in a hung jury on all charges submitted to the jury. At the third trial, the State desired that only the charges of armed robbery and use of a handgun in the commission of a felony or crime of violence would be submitted to the jury. The jury found Ferrell not guilty of using a handgun in the commission of a felony or crime of violence, but the jury was unable to reach a verdict as to armed robbery. Once again a mistrial was declared.

The State decided to bring Ferrell to trial a fourth time for armed robbery. Prior to the fourth trial, Ferrell moved to have the armed robbery counts dismissed on the grounds of collateral estoppel and double jeopardy. Ferrell argued that, as the only issue before the jury at the third trial on both the handgun counts and the armed robbery counts was the identity of the robber, his acquittal on the handgun charges necessarily determined the identity issue in his favor, thus precluding the State from relitigating that issue. The trial judge denied the motion. While finding that only one person was accused of robbery with a handgun, and that the disputed issue at the third trial was whether the defendant was that person, the trial judge took the position that the jury's acquittal on the handgun charges could have been based on some theory other than a determination that the defendant was not the armed robber. At one point the trial judge stated: "How do you know they [the jurors] didn't feel that the gun wasn't used in the robbery, even though there was a gun? I mean, I can't speculate on what the jury determined."

The trial proceeded, and Ferrell was convicted. He was given two fifteen year sentences on two of the armed robbery counts, to be served concurrently, and two ten year sentences on the two remaining counts, to be served consecutively to the fifteen year term and consecutively to each other, for a total of thirty-five years imprisonment. . . .

Both the Fifth Amendment to the United States Constitution and Maryland common law provide that no person shall be put in jeopardy twice for the same offense. Moreover, under both the Fifth Amendment and Maryland common law, it is established that the doctrine of collateral estoppel is embodied in the double jeopardy prohibition. Ashe v. Swenson, 397 U.S. 436 (1970); Robinson v. State, 517 A.2d 94 (Md. 1986).

In Ashe v. Swenson the defendant was charged with the robbery of one of six poker players who had been robbed by three or four armed men. The only contested issue in the case was whether the defendant was one of the robbers. At the end of the trial, the jury found the defendant not guilty. Six weeks later, the defendant was brought to trial and convicted for the robbery of one of the other poker players. The United States Supreme Court reversed the conviction, stating [that] "when an issue of ultimate fact has once been determined by a valid and final judgment, that issue cannot again be litigated between the same parties in any future lawsuit."

In Powers v. State, 401 A.2d 1031 (Md. 1978), this Court applied the principles of Ashe v. Swenson and its progeny to circumstances similar to those in the case at bar. In *Powers,* the defendant was charged with the armed robbery of two victims, and the attempted armed robbery of a third victim, all at the same time and place. Unlike the facts of Ashe v. Swenson, all of the charges against Powers were tried at a single trial. A jury acquitted Powers of charges relating to two of the victims but could not agree on the charge relating to the third victim. When the State decided to retry Powers on the armed robbery charge relating to the third victim, Powers filed a motion to dismiss on the ground of collateral estoppel. The trial court denied the motion, but this Court reversed.

The Court in *Powers* held "that the doctrine of collateral estoppel applies after a jury, at a single trial, acquits on one count of a multicount indictment and is unable to agree upon a verdict on a related count of the same indictment involving a common issue of ultimate fact, which if found in favor of an accused would establish his innocence on both counts." We reasoned that, even though under Maryland common law a mistrial is equivalent to no trial at all, is not a final determination, and resolves no issue, we could not ignore the fact that in the same trial a final determination of the common issue of ultimate fact had indeed been made on a related count and had been decided in the defendant's favor. . . . The only disputed issue before the jury in *Powers* was whether Powers had been one of the robbers. . . .

There is a difference between *Powers* and the instant case. *Powers* involved separate victims and essentially identical offenses, with the retrial concerning the same offense but a different victim than the ones to whom the earlier acquittals related. The case at bar involves separate victims and offenses which are separate but deemed the same under the required evidence test, and the retrial relates to the same victims but a different offense than that which was the subject of the acquittal at the earlier trial. Nevertheless, the critical questions in applying collateral estoppel are not whether the victim is the same or whether each offense is the same. The important questions are whether the offense for which the defendant was earlier acquitted, and the offense for which he is being retried, each involved a common issue of ultimate fact, and whether that issue was resolved in the defendant's favor at the earlier trial.

[T]he trial judge, although finding that the only issue at the third trial in this case was the identity of the lone robber who used an operative handgun, nevertheless speculated that the jury's acquittal on the handgun charge could have been based on some theory conjured up by the jury and having nothing to do with the identity of the armed robber. The [intermediate appellate court], on the other hand, purported to find some indication in the record that the jury at the third trial might have grounded its verdict on a finding that the defendant was an accomplice in the robbery as opposed to being the actual robber. Neither the trial court's nor the Court of Special Appeals' position is tenable in light of the case law and the record here.

In Ashe v. Swenson the Supreme Court stated that the "decisions have made clear that the rule of collateral estoppel in criminal cases is not to be applied with the hypertechnical and archaic approach of a 19th century pleading book, but with realism and rationality. [T]his approach requires a court to examine the record of a prior proceeding, taking into account the pleadings, evidence, charge, and other relevant matter, and conclude whether a rational jury could have grounded its verdict upon an issue other than that which the defendant seeks to foreclose from consideration." 397 U.S. at 444. In Simpson v. Florida, 403 U.S. 384 (1971), the Court indicated that collateral estoppel precluded a retrial following an acquittal where the "sole disputed issue at each of [petitioner's] trials" was the same, namely petitioner's identity as a perpetrator of the armed robbery.

Consequently, in determining whether the State at a subsequent trial is attempting to relitigate an issue which was resolved in the defendant's favor at an earlier trial, a court must realistically look at the record of the earlier trial, including the pleadings, the evidence, the prosecution's theory, the disputed issues, and the jury instructions. A court should not, as did the trial court in the instant case, ignore the evidence and disputed issues at the earlier trial and speculate that the jury's acquittal might have been based on a theory having nothing to do with the evidence and issues presented to the jury. . . .

The record in this case is devoid of any indication that the jury at the third trial could have rationally based its acquittal on the handgun charges upon the accomplice theory suggested by the Court of Special Appeals or upon any issue other than the identity of the lone robber. Nowhere in the evidence is there a suggestion of an accomplice. Indeed, the State throughout all of the trials established that there was only one robber. All testimony and other evidence put on by the State were designed to convince the jury that the defendant Ferrell was the man who robbed the four victims with a handgun and fired the gun at one of the victims. The only theory posited throughout was that there had been one gun and one robber, and that Ferrell was the robber. In fact, the State's attorney said in his closing argument at the fourth trial that there is no dispute as to whether an armed robbery took place. "The dispute . . . becomes whether or not this defendant Avery Vincent Ferrell was the young man who on that morning wore this mask pulled down over his face and wore this gray coat" to rob the four victims. The record discloses that during the third trial the State maintained the same theory of the case as in the fourth trial. Ferrell's only disagreement with the State's theory was that he was not the lone armed robber.

During the hearing on Ferrell's motion to dismiss prior to the fourth trial, the trial judge, who also presided over the third trial, stated the issue at the third trial as follows: "[W]e all agree one person is accused of doing it, and one person is accused of doing it with the use of a handgun, and the defendant says I am not that person. . . ." The prosecution at no point disagreed with the trial court's statements concerning the case and the issue. . . .

Ferrell was tied to this crime because of the long gray coat he was carrying when he was arrested and testimony that he was seen with the shopping bag containing the stolen goods. There was never a positive identification made of the robber by the victims. Furthermore, when he was arrested Ferrell was dressed nothing like the robber. The State attempted to explain this discrepancy through the testimony of one of the victims who saw the robber changing clothes as he fled the scene. In closing argument, the State went to great lengths to tie all of this circumstantial evidence to Ferrell in an attempt to persuade the jury that Ferrell was indeed the man who terrorized the four victims with a gun. Finally, the jury was never given an accomplice instruction at either the third trial or the fourth trial. The State's argument . . . that the acquittal on the handgun charges might reasonably have been based on a jury finding that Ferrell was an accomplice, instead of the person wielding the handgun, is totally contrary to the record in this case. [T]he acquittal on the handgun charge resolved [the] identity issue in Ferrell's favor and precluded the State from relitigating the issue.

Alternatively, the State argues that we should overrule Powers v. State. The State contends that *Powers* was wrongly decided and that collateral estoppel should not prevent a retrial on a count of an indictment where the jury had been unable to agree, but where the jury had acquitted on another count of the indictment having a common issue of ultimate fact which, if found in the defendant's favor, would establish his innocence on both of the counts. . . .

The principal arguments that have been made against applying collateral estoppel in this situation have involved reliance upon the rule that inconsistent jury verdicts ordinarily are tolerated. This reliance is misplaced for two reasons. First, as this Court pointed out in *Powers,* there is no inconsistency between an acquittal on one count and no verdict on another count. The Court there stated:

> In our view, there can be no inconsistency in a jury's findings of fact when it acquits on one count and is unable to agree on another count having a common issue of ultimate fact, which if found in favor of an accused would establish his innocence on both counts. In Maryland, a mistrial is equivalent to no trial at all. It is not a final determination and decides no question of fact. Accordingly, a jury's failure to agree, which results in a mistrial, does not establish any facts, and thus cannot establish facts inconsistent with those established by its verdicts of acquittal. [401 A.2d at 1040.]

Second, even if the jury's failure to agree on one count is viewed as inconsistent with an acquittal on another count of a multicount indictment where the disputed issue under both counts was the same, the rule that inconsistent jury verdicts are allowed has no application to the situation in *Powers* and in the present case. The rule concerning inconsistent jury verdicts . . . relates to inconsistency at the same trial, and has no application to successive trials. The rule does not authorize a second trial on an issue which has been resolved against the prosecution.

[As the Supreme Court noted] in United States v. Powell, 469 U.S. 57 (1984), inconsistent verdicts in the context of a single jury trial are tolerated for certain policy reasons even though they represent "jury irrationality," whereas "principles of collateral estoppel . . . are predicated on the assumption that the jury acted rationally and found certain facts in reaching its verdict. . . ." When it comes to the prosecution's attempted relitigation at a second trial, of an issue resolved in the defendant's favor by an acquittal at an earlier trial, collateral estoppel and the assumption of jury rationality is applicable. . . .

Another argument made against applying collateral estoppel in the circumstances of the case at bar, is that the earlier jury, because it was hung on certain counts involving the common issue of ultimate fact, did not resolve that issue in the defendant's favor. In other words, by focusing exclusively on the count or counts where the jury was unable to agree, there may be some force in the contention that the jury did not decide the critical issue in the defendant's favor. Nevertheless . . . principles of collateral estoppel require that the focus be upon the jury's earlier acquittal, with that acquittal being viewed as a rational resolution of the underlying facts. . . .

The State in the present case also invokes the settled rule that the double jeopardy prohibition ordinarily does not preclude a retrial following the declaration of a mistrial because the jury was unable to agree. See United States v. Perez, 9 Wheat. 579 (1824); Wooten-Bey v. State, 520 A.2d 1090 (Md. 1987). Those cases, and others like them, did not involve a collateral estoppel bar because of an acquittal at the earlier trial on a count having a common issue of ultimate fact with the count on which the jury was hung and which is the subject of the second prosecution. In the instant case, if the jury had not acquitted the defendant of the handgun charges, or if the handgun charges had not involved the same disputed issue as the armed robbery charges, the above-cited cases would be fully applicable and a retrial on the armed robbery charges would not be precluded by double jeopardy principles. Nothing in the above-cited cases, however, supports the view that the State is entitled to relitigate the facts or issues resolved against it by a previous acquittal.

[T]he overwhelming majority of cases take the position that the principles of collateral estoppel are applicable to the situation presented in Powers v. State and in the case at bar. [The court cited federal circuit cases and decisions from California and Pennsylvania, and noted a minority position in New Jersey.] In light of this authority, and the reasons underlying the holding in Powers v. State, we adhere to that holding.

The State in this case had more than "'one full and fair opportunity to convict'" the defendant Ferrell of robbery with a handgun. After three trials, a jury acquitted Ferrell of committing robbery with a handgun. Consequently, the State should not have been permitted to relitigate this issue at a fourth trial.

McAuliffe, J., dissenting.

[T]he record that Ferrell presents for this Court's consideration is insufficient to show much of anything about what occurred at the third trial. [W]hatever the jurors in the third trial might have decided, we can be sure they did not decide that Ferrell was not the robber. Had they decided that, they would have found Ferrell not guilty of the robbery as well. It is absolutely illogical to conclude that the same jurors who unanimously found that Ferrell was not the man who robbed these victims with a handgun would be unable to reach a verdict on the robbery count.

The majority apparently holds that because the State is unable to demonstrate exactly why the jury reached the conclusion it did, the defendant must prevail. That, I suggest, is not a proper application of the principles of collateral estoppel. The Supreme Court has said that the relevant inquiry is "whether a rational jury could have grounded its verdict upon an issue other than that which the defendant seeks to foreclose from consideration." Ashe v. Swenson, 397 U.S. at 444. The Court cautioned that the inquiry must be approached "with realism and rationality," and "must be set in a practical frame and viewed with an eye to all the circumstances of the proceedings." The only practical and rational conclusion that I can reach upon consideration of all the known circumstances of the third trial is that the jury could not have concluded that which Ferrell argues it must have concluded.

I cannot be certain why the jury found as it did on the charge of use of a handgun in the commission of a felony or a crime of violence. It may have erroneously concluded that the defendant did not "use" the handgun because no one was shot. It may have felt that the State had not proven the gun involved was a "handgun" within the meaning of our statute. One cannot say, without speculating, why the jury reached the verdict it did. One can say, however, with confidence, that the jury did not reach that verdict because they found the defendant was not involved. I would affirm the conviction.

Notes

1. *Collateral estoppel: majority position.* As the Maryland court in *Ferrell* indicated, the U.S. Supreme Court declared in Ashe v. Swenson, 397 U.S. 436 (1970), that the federal guarantee against double jeopardy includes the concept of collateral estoppel: "when an issue of ultimate fact has once been determined by a valid and final judgment, that issue cannot again be litigated between the same parties in any future lawsuit." There are several limitations, however, that prevent collateral estoppel from having an impact in a wide range of cases. First, the doctrine typically does not apply to matters resolved by guilty plea. Federal and state courts agree that collateral estoppel applies only after an "adjudication on the merits after full trial." Ohio v. Johnson, 467 U.S. 493, 500 (1984). Second, as *Ferrell* illustrates, it is often difficult, based on a jury's general verdict, to determine exactly what factual findings were the basis for a jury's acquittal. This problem is commonplace because defendants are prone to give the jury more than one possible theory for an acquittal. Would the use of special interrogatories to the jury (to be completed only after the jury has delivered its general verdict) make the collateral estoppel doctrine a more meaningful limitation on multiple criminal trials?

2. *Collateral estoppel against defendants.* Although collateral estoppel binds the government, most courts say that the doctrine is asymmetrical; that is, it does not bind defendants. If a fact finder determines some fact against a defendant in one criminal proceeding, the defendant may still ask a fact finder in some later criminal case to find that same fact in his favor. For instance, in People v. Goss, 521 N.W.2d 312 (Mich. 1994), the defendant was convicted during a first trial of armed robbery and felony murder. Appellate courts affirmed the robbery conviction, but overturned the felony murder conviction because of improper jury instructions. On retrial for felony murder, the government asked the trial court to prevent the defendant from relitigating the underlying charge of armed robbery, and sought an instruction to the jury that Goss had already been found guilty of armed robbery. The Michigan Supreme Court held that collateral estoppel could not operate against a defendant in this setting. Some of the Justices believed that such a use of the doctrine would violate the right to a jury trial; others called it a violation of the presumption of innocence. However, there are also a few cases applying collateral estoppel against defendants. See Hernandez-Uribe v. United States, 515 F.2d 20 (8th Cir. 1975) (after conviction and deportation for illegal entry into United States, defendant reenters and is charged again; defendant's alien status is established by collateral estoppel); People v. Majado, 70 P.2d 1015 (Cal. 1937) (conviction for failure to support child; in later criminal charges for another period of failure to support child, previous conviction estops relitigation of issue of paternity). Can you reconcile cases like *Majado* and *Goss*?

3. *Collateral estoppel and administrative findings.* Can a finding of fact made in an administrative or civil proceeding be the basis for collateral estoppel in a later criminal proceeding? For instance, if a defendant in license revocation proceedings convinces the fact finder that some critical factual element of drunken driving charges is missing, does that finding bar a later criminal prosecution for driving while impaired? Does it matter that the two proceedings operate under two different standards of proof (preponderance of the evidence in the administrative proceedings, and beyond a reasonable doubt in the criminal proceedings)? In State v. Miller, 459 S.E.2d 114 (W. Va. 1995) a state hospital nurse was convicted of battery after slapping a patient. The state hospital also attempted to terminate her employment and defended its decision during administrative proceedings before a state employee grievance board. Because the hospital failed to demonstrate grounds for termination before the grievance board, Miller argued that the battery charges were collaterally estopped. The court held that collateral estoppel did not apply because there were several possible grounds for the grievance board decision not to terminate the defendant's employment and there was no "privity" between the state agency that sought to terminate her employment and the prosecutor's office.

In Dowling v. United States, 493 U.S. 342 (1990), the Court held that the defendant's acquittal on robbery charges did not bar later use of testimony from a key witness from the first trial in a second criminal trial for a similar robbery charge against the same defendant. The Court allowed the testimony because the standard for admissibility of evidence was whether the second jury "could reasonably conclude" that the defendant committed the first robbery — a standard lower than the one applied by the first jury that acquitted the defendant. Does *Dowling* eviscerate collateral estoppel?

4. *Collateral estoppel and dual sovereigns.* It is common to find the collateral estoppel principle embodied in state statutes barring or limiting multiple prosecutions. Around 10 states have statutes recognizing collateral estoppel based on adverse factual findings made in criminal proceedings in another jurisdiction. See Colo. Rev. Stat. §18-1-303(1)(b). Recall that the common-law doctrine of collateral estoppel required "mutuality of parties"— that is, the same two parties had to be involved in both the original proceedings and the later relitigation of the same factual issue. Is there any reason to insist on "mutuality of parties" when it comes to dual sovereigns prosecuting the same person for crimes based on the same factual premise? In other words, should one government's loss in a criminal trial prevent another government from relitigating the same factual issue? Now consider mutuality of parties when it comes to defendants. Should a government victory against one criminal defendant prevent another defendant at another criminal trial from relitigating the resolved factual question?

B. JOINDER

Constitutional and statutory double jeopardy rules require prosecutors to choose carefully when grouping together the potential charges to be brought against a defendant. We now look at some doctrinal cousins to double jeopardy: the statutory and court rules that govern "joinder" and "severance" of potentially related charges. As you read the following materials, consider to what extent the joinder and severance rules further interests different from the constitutional or statutory bar on double jeopardy.

The most common joinder rules (exemplified by Rule 8 of the Federal Rules of Criminal Procedure) are known as "permissive" joinder rules. They define the outer boundaries of the prosecutor's power to join charges together for a single trial, that is, the *maximum* range of charges that can be grouped together. These rules address both the joinder of separate offenses filed against a single defendant and joinder of multiple defendants in a single trial. Some states also have "compulsory" or "mandatory" joinder rules. These rules identify the *minimum* range of charges that the prosecutor must group together for a single trial. Like the doctrines of double jeopardy and collateral estoppel, these compulsory joinder rules require dismissal of charges if they should have been tried in an earlier proceeding dealing with related charges. Rules on "severance" address the power of the court to override a prosecutor's joinder decisions and order separate trials for charges that were otherwise properly joined.

The joinder rules may on first inspection seem dry and technical. But joinder and severance rules are enormously important to defendants and prosecutors because they define the scope of each trial and determine whether more than one trial may take place. Decisions on joinder and severance can give prosecutors or defendants enormous strategic advantage and are therefore often strongly argued. The issues appeal to lawyers who enjoy puzzles.

1. *Discretionary Joinder and Severance of Offenses*

When a prosecutor files multiple charges against a defendant, the charges usually fall within the minimum and maximum range of charges that a prosecutor has the power to group together in a single case. If the prosecutor fails to join the charges and the defendant wishes to resolve them in one trial, the court has the discretion to join the charges even though the prosecutor did not file them together. The parties can also urge the trial court to sever the joined charges as a discretionary matter to avoid prejudice. These cases call for the use of lawyerly skills, including close reading and attention to trial strategies. Review the federal rules and Vermont rules reprinted below, then read the following case. Would the outcome of the case change under the Vermont rules?

■ FEDERAL RULE OF CRIMINAL PROCEDURE 8(a)

The indictment or information may charge a defendant in separate counts with two or more offenses if the offenses charged — whether felonies or misdemeanors or both — are of the same or similar character, or are based on the same act or transaction, or are connected with or constitute parts of a common scheme or plan.

■ FEDERAL RULE OF CRIMINAL PROCEDURE 13

The court may order that separate cases be tried together as though brought in a single indictment or information if all offenses . . . could have been joined in a single indictment or information.

■ FEDERAL RULE OF CRIMINAL PROCEDURE 14

(a) If the joinder of offenses or defendants in an indictment, an information, or a consolidation for trial appears to prejudice a defendant or the government, the court may order separate trials of counts, sever the defendants' trials, or provide any other relief that justice requires.

(b) Defendant's Statements. Before ruling on a defendant's motion to sever, the court may order an attorney for the government to deliver to the court for in camera inspection any defendant's statement that the government intends to use as evidence.

■ VERMONT RULE OF CRIMINAL PROCEDURE 8(a)

Two or more offenses may be joined in one information or indictment, with each offense stated in a separate count, when the offenses, whether felonies or misdemeanors or both,

(1) are of the same or similar character, even if not part of a single scheme or plan; or

(2) are based on the same conduct or on a series of acts connected together or constituting parts of a single scheme or plan.

■ VERMONT RULE OF CRIMINAL PROCEDURE 14

(a) The court may order a severance of offenses or defendants before trial if a severance could be obtained on motion of a defendant or the prosecution under subdivision (b) of this rule.

(b)(1) Severance of Offenses.

(A) Whenever two or more offenses have been joined for trial solely on the ground that they are of the same or similar character, the defendant shall have a right to a severance of the offenses.

(B) The court, on application of the prosecuting attorney, or on application of the defendant other than under subparagraph (A), shall grant a severance of offenses whenever,

(i) if before trial, it is deemed appropriate to promote a fair determination of the defendant's guilt or innocence of each offense; or

(ii) if during trial upon consent of the defendant, or upon a finding of manifest necessity, it is deemed necessary to achieve a fair determination of the defendant's guilt or innocence of each offense.

VERMONT REPORTER'S NOTES

[Rule 8] is taken from ABA Minimum Standards (Joinder and Severance) §§1.1, 1.2, and is similar to Federal Rule 8. Rule 8(a) permits joinder of offenses either because they are of similar character though factually unrelated or because they are factually related. Note that each offense must be pleaded in a separate count. . . . Under the federal rule the phrase "same character" adopted for Rule 8(a)(1) has been ordinarily held to mean the same crime committed against distinct objects upon distinct occasions. Although joinder of similar offenses has been criticized as tending to prejudice the defendant through its cumulative effect, the ABA recommends the provision, because it may actually work to the defendant's advantage in preventing multiple trials and facilitating concurrent sentencing. Prejudice will be avoided because under Rule 14(b)(1)(A) defendant has an absolute right to severance of such offenses for trial. ABA Minimum Standards §1.1(a), Commentary. . . .

Rule 8(a)(2) is, of course, a rule of permissive joinder. As a practical matter, if the same facts are centrally involved in two offenses, joinder is virtually compelled. Otherwise, acquittal of the defendant upon one offense will bar prosecution for the second offense by virtue of the Fifth Amendment's Double Jeopardy Clause, which includes the principles of collateral estoppel. Ashe v. Swenson, 397 U.S. 436 (1970).

[Rule 14] is based on ABA Minimum Standards (Joinder and Severance) §§2.1-2.4, 3.1, with variations reflecting Vermont practice. It is similar in effect to the more complicated provisions of Federal Rule 14. Note that Rule 14 is a grant of discretion to sever a joinder otherwise proper under Rule 8 in the interests of fairness or to avoid prejudice. If a joinder is improper under Rule 8, a severance must be granted or it is reversible error. Rule 14(a) is based on ABA Minimum Standards §3.1(b). A power in the court to sever on its own motion, like the comparable power to join under Rule 13(a), is necessary to allow the court to carry out its responsibilities for the orderly conduct of the trial. The federal courts have recognized a power in the court to act on its own motion under Federal Rule 14. . . . Rule 14(b)(1), dealing with severance of offenses, is taken from ABA Minimum Standards §2.2. Subparagraph (A), conferring an absolute right of severance where offenses have been joined solely by virtue of Rule 8(a)(1) because they are of the same or similar character, is a necessary protection for defendants against what would otherwise be potential prejudice in such joinders. That prejudice may consist in the defendant's fear of testifying in his own behalf on one count because of the effect of such testimony on the other count, or in the danger that proof of one count will have prejudicial effect on the other count as inadmissible evidence of another crime. In requiring severance in these circumstances the rule is stricter than Federal Rule 14, although individual decisions under the latter rule have allowed severance for similar purposes. The rule is stricter than prior Vermont practice, which gave the court discretion as to severance even where unrelated offenses were involved. See State v. Dopp, 255 A.2d 186 (Vt. 1969). Severance of offenses joined under Rule 8(a)(2) as arising from the same or connected conduct or a single scheme is available to either party under Rule 14(b)(1)(A) when necessary in the interests of fair trial. . . .

■ DAMIAN LONG v. UNITED STATES

687 A.2d 1331 (D.C. 1996)

FERREN, J.

A jury found appellant, Damian Long, guilty of assault with intent to rob three victims while armed on September 8, 1992, at about 10:30 P.M., at 12th and Orren Streets, N.E. He also was found guilty of attempted robbery while armed and felony murder while armed of another victim several minutes later on Trinidad Avenue, N.E., a block away from the first crime. Long contends . . . the trial court erroneously joined the Orren Street and Trinidad Avenue offenses for trial and then abused its discretion in denying the defense motion for severance. . . . We affirm in part, reverse in part, and remand for reconsideration of Long's severance motion.

[Around 5:30 to 6:00 P.M. on September 8], appellant Long left the apartment of Scholethia Monk, located at Holbrook Terrace, N.E., where he had been spending time with Ms. Monk, her brother (David), and Kimberly Bridgeford. Long was dressed in a black suede jacket with fringe, a black shirt, black jeans, black boots, and a black silk-stocking skull cap. The Holbrook Terrace apartment was only a few blocks from the area where the Orren Street and Trinidad Avenue incidents at issue here took place.

Several hours later, at about 10:30 P.M., a man dressed in a black fringed jacket, black pants, and black shoes — later identified as Damian Long — approached the three Orren Street victims, Sabrina Fox, Carla Davis, and Guy Foster, who were standing in the street on the driver's side of the car that was parked against the curb in front of Fox's home. They were attempting to open the door and window of the car with a coat hanger because they had inadvertently locked the keys inside. Long crossed over to them from the opposite side of the street, pointed a revolver at them, and said something to the two women that sounded like "get the fuck out of here." He then pressed the pistol against Foster's head and demanded his money. When Foster protested that he had none, Long put his hand in Foster's pants pockets and satisfied himself that this was true. Long then ordered Foster to crawl under the car, and Long walked away in the direction of Trinidad Avenue.

Fox and Davis had fled in the same direction. They feared that their assailant was following them, so they hid in an alleyway a few blocks away from where the car was parked. Fox and Davis then heard gunshots and unsuccessfully tried to flag down a passing police cruiser. They hailed a taxi and went to a nearby police precinct where they told their story and gave a description of the perpetrator.

In the meantime, Fox's mother, Penelope Boyd-Fox, who had witnessed the assault on the three from the porch of her home on Orren Street, had immediately telephoned "911" for help. While she was still on the phone to the police department emergency number, she heard gunshots nearby. At about the same time, Foster came out from under the car and fled to his home on Orren Street. He telephoned the police to report the crime. While on the phone with the police, he heard gunshots and reported that as well.

Deborah Alford . . . was sitting on her front porch [on Trinidad Avenue] with several family members at approximately 10:30 P.M. the same night. A few minutes earlier, she had seen [her neighbor Louis Johnson] park his Suzuki sports vehicle on the street and enter his home several doors away. Apparently returning home from work, Johnson had been wearing his Army uniform. Shortly thereafter, Alford saw Johnson walking from his home, dressed in his bathrobe, and returning to his Suzuki. At this moment, Alford saw a man dressed in a black jacket ("I didn't know it had suede fringes on it"), black pants, and a black skull cap walking in Trinidad Street alongside the parked cars. Alford saw the man in black, after he had passed by Johnson, take out a pistol from his jacket and turn back toward Johnson as Johnson put the keys into the car's doorlock. Alford next saw the man in black and her neighbor "tussling." Frightened by the sight of the pistol, she and the others fled into their home. A few seconds later, Alford heard a series of gunshots. Johnson was later pronounced dead of gunshot wounds.

Kimberly Bridgeford testified that at around 5:00 P.M. on September 8, 1992, she and her boyfriend, David Monk, had gone with Damian Long to David's sister's,

Scholethia Monk's, apartment on Holbrook Terrace. After awhile, Long left the apartment and, shortly thereafter, Bridgeford and David Monk left to go to the store. On the way to the store, Bridgeford heard gunshots, saw an ambulance, and walked by the Trinidad Avenue murder scene where she saw Johnson lying on the street with blood all over him. Bridgeford and David Monk then returned to the Holbrook Terrace apartment and found Long on the front porch. Long told Bridgeford that he had "shot a man on Trinidad Avenue because the man tried to rob him with a knife."

Scholethia Monk testified that Long returned later to her Holbrook Terrace apartment on September 8, 1992 "panicking and sweating." Long had told Monk that "two dudes" had tried to rob him on Trinidad Avenue and that he had just shot one of them. There was blood on Long's face, he no longer wore a skull cap, and he was carrying a pistol. Long put the gun under a couch. Monk told Long to get his pistol out of her apartment. He then wrapped it in a plastic bag and took it outside. Ten days later, the police recovered a gun from under the seat of the car where Long's close friend, Monk's brother, had been sitting just before they found the gun. A ballistics expert was "positive" that a bullet recovered from the scene of the murder on Trinidad Avenue had been fired by that pistol.

Homicide detective Willie Toland investigated the Trinidad Avenue case. When he arrived at the scene, he noticed a black skull cap seven feet from the place where Johnson had been shot, and Johnson's keys were still in the Suzuki's passenger door lock. As Toland investigated the crime scene, Foster arrived and informed Toland of what had happened earlier on Orren Street. Toland spoke with Davis and Fox later the same night and a few days later conducted a video lineup in which they identified Long as their attacker. . . .

Long's argument, raised before trial and renewed at the end of the government's case, [is] that the Orren Street and Trinidad Avenue charges had been improperly joined for trial. Specifically, Long protested joinder because the offenses were "not similar offenses[, nor] offenses committed in a single act or transaction, nor a series of offenses that [we]re sufficiently connected to each other."

Super. Ct. Crim. R. 8(a) provides for joinder of offenses when the offenses charged "are of the same or similar character or are based on the same act or transaction or on two or more acts or transactions connected together or constituting parts of a common scheme or plan." We review the trial court's joinder decision de novo.

The government urges that joinder was proper because the Orren Street offenses had been "connected together" with the Trinidad Avenue offenses in the sense that proof of the Orren Street offenses "constitut[ed] a substantial portion of the proof" of the Trinidad Avenue offenses. The facts, however, do not support the government's argument. None of the witnesses to the Orren Street incident saw the Trinidad Avenue incident, and neither crime depended on the other for its furtherance or success.

The government also argues that the Orren Street and Trinidad Avenue offenses had been properly joined as part of a "common scheme or plan," because Long had been "walking the neighborhood in search of people to rob." We have previously rejected such an argument when considering joinder of defendants under Super. Ct. Crim. R. 8(b), and we reject the argument in this context as well. See Jackson v. United States, 623 A.2d 571 (D.C. 1993) ("The goal of obtaining property from others, here money and guns, was too general for joinder of offenses under Rule 8(b).").

The government contends, finally, that the Orren Street offenses were similar in character to the Trinidad Avenue offenses, and we agree. The "similarity of offenses [under Rule 8(a)] is determined by the content of the indictment"; it is not dependent on whether evidence of one crime would be admissible in the trial of the other. In this case . . . the two crimes, as charged, "both involved armed robberies which were closely related in time and place." Accordingly, it cannot plausibly be maintained that they are insufficiently similar to one another to warrant initial joinder under Rule 8(a). We must conclude that the two sets of offenses were properly joined.

Long contends the trial court erred nonetheless in denying his severance motion under Super. Ct. Crim. R. 14. He says the Orren Street offenses should have been severed from the Trinidad Avenue charges because the evidence of each would be inadmissible in a separate trial of the other. Long adds he was further prejudiced because he was "precluded from presenting separate defenses" to each group of charges.[4]

We have noted that

> [e]ven when offenses are properly joined, it is within the trial court's discretion to sever counts and order separate trials if the defendant would be prejudiced by joinder. Our standard of review of such rulings is abuse of discretion, and appellant must make a showing of compelling prejudice to show such error. Of course, there is a potential for prejudice whenever similar, but unrelated offenses are charged. However, the requisite prejudicial effect for a severance will not be found where the evidence [1] can be kept separate and distinct at trial or [2] is mutually admissible at separate trials. [Cox v. United States, 498 A.2d 231, 235 (D.C. 1985).]

Because the incidents were not tried separately and distinctly,[5] resolution of the severance issue turns on mutual admissibility: whether the evidence of each joined offense would be admissible at a separate trial of the other. The first sentence of Super. Ct. Crim. R. 14 provides:

> [If] it appears that a defendant or the government is prejudiced by a joinder of offenses or of defendants in an indictment or information or by such joinder for trial together, the Court may order an election or separate trials of counts, grant a severance of defendants or provide whatever other relief justice requires.

In response to Long's contention, the government argues that the severance motion was properly denied because evidence of each group of offenses would have

4. Long apparently wanted to present a misidentification defense as to Orren Street and to claim self-defense at Trinidad Avenue, but realistically separate defenses appeared to be possible only if the offenses were tried separately. . . .

5. The evidence as to each offense was not "kept separate and distinct such that it would not be amalgamated in the jury's mind into a single inculpatory mass." Although the prosecutor attempted to structure the trial to separate the incidents, calling first the Orren Street witnesses and then the Trinidad Avenue witnesses, the evidence of the two crimes was closely tied together by some of the witnesses whose testimony pertained to both crimes, e.g., Scholethia Monk, Kimberly Bridgeford, and the homicide investigator, Willie Toland. Moreover, the government's closing argument also brought together evidence of the two crimes. Finally, the strong identification evidence and intent-to-rob evidence from the Orren Street incident served to supply identification and motive evidence for the Trinidad Avenue incident, so there was a substantial likelihood that the jury would cumulate the evidence. Accordingly, we cannot uphold the denial of severance based on the "separate and distinct"— sometimes known as the "simple and distinct"— theory.

been admissible in a separate trial of the other "to explain the immediate circumstances surrounding the offense charged." Technically speaking, such evidence "is not other crimes evidence because it is too intimately entangled with the charged criminal conduct."[6] Alternatively, the government argues that the evidence of each incident would be admissible in a trial of the other as "other crimes" evidence tending to prove "identity."[7]

Commonly, the question is whether uncharged criminal conduct shall be admitted in a trial of the charged crime, but in this case the question is the admissibility of a charged crime in the trial of another charged crime. If each would be admissible in the other, then there would be no reason why the two should not be tried together; but, if one or both would not meet the test for admissibility in the other, then severance is required. . . .

In this case, Long presented a misidentification defense at trial. Thus, identity was a contested issue. . . . We therefore believe it appropriate to scrutinize the evidence of each incident, as it bears on proving identity of the assailant in the other. . . . The Orren Street evidence informed the jury that, at about 10:30 P.M., on September 8, 1992, a man identified as Damian Long, dressed entirely in black (including a fringe jacket and skull cap) and carrying a gun, had . . . attempted a robbery at gunpoint. After the assault, the witnesses saw Long headed toward nearby Trinidad Avenue. They heard gunshots soon thereafter.

As for Trinidad Avenue, earlier on the same day at about 5:30 to 6:00 P.M., Scholethia Monk and Kimberly Bridgeford saw Long, dressed entirely in black (including a fringe jacket and skull cap), leave Monk's apartment. Bridgeford saw Long depart in the direction of Trinidad Avenue. Later that evening shortly after 10:30 P.M., Deborah Alford, from her front porch on Trinidad Avenue, saw a man dressed in a black jacket (she did not notice fringe on it), black pants, and a black skull cap walk past her neighbor, Louis Johnson, who was standing next to his car. . . . Alford never identified the assailant. Both Monk and Bridgeford, however, witnessed Long's return to Monk's apartment "panicking and sweating," admitting he had "shot a man on Trinidad Avenue because the man tried to rob him with a knife." Long had blood on his face and was carrying a pistol. His skull cap was missing. The police later found a black skull cap seven feet from where Johnson had been shot. Monk's apartment on Holbrook Terrace was but a few blocks away from where the offenses occurred on Orren Street and Trinidad Avenue.

We believe that the testimony of the Orren Street witnesses, Davis and Fox (who identified Long as a would-be robber), that they saw Long heading in the direction of Trinidad Avenue nearby, and then heard gunshots — all around 10:30 P.M., on September 8, 1992 — provided powerful evidence of the Trinidad Avenue assailant's identity. Indeed, this evidence was particularly significant for the Trinidad Avenue

6. The trial court accepted the government's . . . theory in denying Long's renewed motion to sever: "[T]his matter is so inextricably intertwined each with each other that there is no way the Government can separate it all and make sense of the whole matter. They absolutely need for identification purposes, if for nothing else, they absolutely have to have these cases tried together, they should be tried together temporally. And by temporally, I mean both time and place they are as connected as can be." Recently our en banc court discerned three subcategories of evidence embraced by [the] "immediate circumstances" rationale: such evidence (1) is direct and substantial proof of the charged crime, (2) is closely intertwined with the evidence of the charged crime, or (3) is necessary to place the charged crime in an understandable context.

7. . . . . "[O]ther crimes" evidence is admissible only if [it is introduced to show] motive, intent, absence of mistake or accident, common scheme or plan, or identity as reflected in Fed. R. Evid. 404(b).

prosecution, when coupled with Monk's and Bridgeford's testimony about Long's admission that he had shot a man on Trinidad Avenue, because the only person who saw the assailant approach Johnson, Deborah Alford, was unable to identify Johnson's killer (although Alford provided a description consistent with Fox's, Davis's, Monk's, and Bridgeford's description of Long). The Orren Street evidence also revealed the assailant's possible motive for approaching Johnson on Trinidad Avenue (robbery).

We also recognize that the Trinidad Avenue evidence was probative of the identity of the Orren Street attacker. Alford's description of an unidentified, black-jacketed, gun-carrying assailant on Trinidad Avenue, combined with the Monk/Bridgeford testimony that Damian Long had come to Monk's apartment with a gun, "panicking and sweating," tended to identify Long as the Orren Street assailant dressed in black seen heading toward Trinidad Avenue just before shots were fired around 10:30 P.M. The fact that Monk testified that Long's skull cap was missing when he returned to her apartment, coupled with the police officer's finding a skull cap on Trinidad Avenue, adds to Long's connection with the Orren Street attack by a man wearing a black skull cap.

Accordingly, without regard to the required probative value/prejudicial impact analysis, we can say that the Orren Street and Trinidad Avenue offenses [would be mutually admissible] in separate trials (and thus would not be joined prejudicially if prosecuted in a joint trial).

We turn to the ruling on probative value/prejudicial impact. The motions judge said, "I don't see prejudice under [Super. Ct. Civ. R.] 14 that would justify severance." The trial judge, in considering the renewed severance motion at trial, referred to the motions judge's ruling and then added his own belief that [a joint trial was permissible] because the cases were "inextricably intertwined."

The trial judge, therefore, said not a word about probative value relative to prejudice. That was unfortunate. At least as to admissibility of Trinidad Avenue evidence in an Orren Street trial, we see a serious question whether probative value outweighs prejudicial impact. Monk and Bridgeford identified the man — Damian Long — whom Alford apparently had seen accosting Johnson: a man fitting the description of the person who had attempted the robbery only blocks away on Orren Street minutes earlier. This identification evidence from Trinidad Avenue, however, was cumulative of — and of far less probative value than — the direct eyewitness testimony from Fox and Davis . . . that Long was the would-be bandit on Orren Street. Furthermore, this weaker identification evidence includes the powerfully prejudicial testimony that Long had committed a murder, not merely an assault, on Trinidad Avenue.

The trial judge, after a pretrial severance motion has been denied, has a continuing obligation to grant a severance if undue prejudice arises as a result of joinder at any time during trial. The trial judge recognized this obligation: "the Court of Appeals seems to indicate that I have to listen [to severance motions] again and again and again and again." Here, however, in denying the renewed severance motion, the trial judge, for his prejudice analysis, merely referred to the ruling of the motions judge, who did not "see prejudice" from a pretrial perspective. . . .

The probative/prejudicial analysis is a discretionary evaluation which an appellate court cannot undertake itself when the trial court fails to do so unless it is clear from the record, as a matter of law, that the trial court had "but one option." In this case, admissibility of the Trinidad Avenue murder evidence in an Orren Street trial appears to be a more difficult discretionary call than admissibility of the Orren Street assault in a Trinidad Avenue trial, but as to either case we find no sound basis on the record for this court to take over the trial court's function by ruling on probative value/prejudicial impact.

We, therefore, must remand the case for the trial judge to make a probative/prejudicial ruling for each case and thus to rule once again on the severance motion — including consideration of Long's contention that he was prejudiced by his inability, in a single trial, to present separate defenses (Orren Street, misidentification; Trinidad Avenue, self-defense). The judge shall order a new trial of the Orren Street prosecution if he concludes that the murder evidence from Trinidad Avenue should have been omitted from the Orren Street trial. Otherwise, the Orren Street convictions . . . shall stand, without prejudice to Long's right to appeal the severance ruling on remand.[17] Similarly, the judge shall make a probative/prejudice ruling on admissibility of Orren Street evidence in the Trinidad Avenue trial, and also shall rule on Long's claim of prejudice from his practical inability to claim self-defense for Trinidad Avenue at a joint trial. The judge shall order a new trial, or not, as indicated. Absent a new trial order, the Trinidad Avenue conviction shall stand, subject to Long's right of appeal of that severance ruling. . . .

Problem 14-3. Compulsory Joinder

Matthew Hensley was involved in a bar fight in Kanawha County, West Virginia on November 16, 1991. Ambulances arrived at the scene took several people from the bar to a local hospital. Hensley and four other people were arrested at the scene and were immediately charged in magistrate court with public intoxication and destruction of property, both misdemeanors. On November 21, one of the victims of the fight, Barbara Lane, provided a statement to a detective with the Sheriff's Department regarding injuries she suffered during the fight. Lane told the detective that Hensley threw a cue ball, hitting her in her left eye, causing bone fractures and resulting in plastic and reconstructive surgery. However, no additional charges were brought against Hensley prior to his trial in magistrate court on March 13, 1992. He was acquitted of both misdemeanors following the trial in magistrate court.

17. We have indicated that other crimes evidence on occasion should be tailored to minimize prejudice. Theoretically, it would be possible to sanitize the Trinidad Avenue evidence for a separate Orren Street trial. In such a trial, the Trinidad Avenue identification testimony would have to be trimmed to leave out reference to a murder, and Deborah Alford would be limited to testifying that an unidentifiable man in black had accosted Johnson with a gun at about 10:30 P.M. Scholethia Monk and Kimberly Bridgeford would be limited to saying that Long — dressed in black — had returned to the apartment shortly after 10:30 P.M., admitting he had just assaulted someone on Trinidad Avenue. The police could then testify about finding a black skull cap on Trinidad Avenue nearby.

The trial court will have to decide, as part of the required probative value/prejudicial impact analysis, (1) whether the preferred approach would be admission of sanitized Trinidad Avenue evidence in a separate Orren Street trial, in order to keep prejudicial homicide evidence from that jury, or (2) whether, because (a) the Fox/Davis identification evidence was strong, (b) the Monk/Bridgeford testimony could be limited to identification of Long as the man who returned "panicking and sweating" at about 10:30 P.M., (c) the murder evidence was highly prejudicial, and (d) because sanitizing the evidence would be complicated, the Trinidad Avenue murder evidence should be kept out of the Orren Street trial altogether, or (3) whether sanitizing the Trinidad Avenue evidence would not work, and the probative value of that evidence outweighs prejudice. If either of the first two instances applies, the court should grant the severance motion; in the third, the court should deny it.

The Sheriff's Department did not tell the prosecutor's office about the nature of Lane's injuries until January 1994, over two years after the bar fight and nearly two years after the acquittal in magistrate court. Soon after learning about the severity of Lane's injuries, the prosecutor charged Hensley with malicious assault, a felony. Hensley moved to dismiss the indictment under Rule 8(a) of the West Virginia Rules of Criminal Procedure based on the failure of the State to join the felony charge with the misdemeanor charges prior to the trial in magistrate court in March 1992.

Rule 8(a) of West Virginia Rules of Criminal Procedure provides:

> Joinder of Offenses.—Two or more offenses may be charged in the same indictment or information in a separate count for each offense if the offenses charged, whether felonies or misdemeanors or both, are of the same or similar character. All offenses based on the same act or transaction or on two or more acts or transactions connected together or constituting parts of a common scheme or plan shall be charged in the same indictment or information in a separate count for each offense, whether felonies or misdemeanors or both.

West Virginia courts have developed several exceptions to the application of the rule despite the absence of explicit language within the rule. The first exception is that all offenses, even though based on the same act or transaction or constituting parts of a common scheme or plan, must have occurred in the same jurisdiction before there is a compulsion to charge all offenses in the same charging documents. The second exception applies when the prosecuting attorney does not know and has no reason to know about all the offenses. The third exception happens when the prosecuting attorney had no opportunity to attend the proceeding where the first offense is presented. See Cline v. Murensky, 322 S.E.2d 702 (W. Va. 1984) (two people involved in bar fight were charged and pled guilty in magistrate court to misdemeanor offense of brandishing weapon, all within few hours of fight; both were later indicted in Circuit Court for carrying weapon without license, state not precluded because prosecutor did not have opportunity to attend magistrate court's hearing).

If you were the trial judge in Hensley's felony case, what issues would you ask the parties to address during the hearing on the motion to dismiss? How would you expect to rule? Would your ruling change if the felony charges were already pending in Circuit Court at the time of the acquittal in magistrate court? Would the outcome change if West Virginia had adopted a rule identical to Federal Rule of Criminal Procedure 8(a)? Compare State ex rel. Forbes v. Canady, 475 S.E.2d 37 (W.Va. 1996)

Problem 14-4. Protective Order

Aurelio Chenique-Puey and Susan Lane cohabited from 1983 until 1987, and they had a daughter in 1986. After their separation in 1987, Chenique-Puey harassed Lee by banging on the door and windows of her New Jersey home, and by threatening to kill her. Lane obtained a domestic violence restraining order, which prohibited Chenique-Puey from "returning to the scene of the domestic violence" and "from having any contact with the plaintiff or harassing plaintiff or plaintiff's relatives in any way." It also curtailed his child-visitation rights.

Chenique-Puey was convicted and imprisoned on unrelated charges, so Lane did not have any further contact with him until 1991. Five days after his release from prison, Chenique-Puey came to Lane's apartment to see his daughter. At the time,

Lane was watching a football game on television with two of her children and her boyfriend, John Clifford. Lane refused to admit Chenique-Puey and told him to leave. The parties disagree about what happened at that point. According to Lane, Chenique-Puey taunted Clifford through an open rear window. He reached his arm through the window bars and waved a knife at them. After failing to provoke Clifford, Chenique-Puey threatened to return to the apartment with a shotgun and kill the couple.

Chenique-Puey claimed that he went to the open rear window with his companions, Pedro and Marisa Mondo, and looked inside the apartment. Lane told them that she would not let them in and that they should leave. Chenique-Puey then told Lane that he would return on another day and they left. He says that there was no knife and that he made no threats to Lane and Clifford.

When Chenique-Puey and his companions left the premises, Lane called the police and filed a criminal complaint against him. He was indicted on charges of third-degree terroristic threats and fourth-degree contempt of a judicial restraining order. At the start of trial, the defendant moved for a severance of the contempt charge. He argued that joinder of this offense would prejudice him because evidence of the restraining order would convince the jury that he had in fact made the alleged terroristic threats against Lee.

In New Jersey, joinder of offenses is governed by Rule 3:7-6, which provides that two or more offenses may be charged together if they are "of the same or similar character or are based on the same act or transaction or on two or more acts or transactions connected together or constituting parts of a common scheme or plan." Mandatory joinder under Rule 3:15-1(b) is required when multiple criminal offenses charged are "based on the same conduct or arise from the same episode." Rule 3:15-2(b) vests a trial court with discretion to order separate trials if a defendant or the State is "prejudiced" by permissive or mandatory joinder of offenses.

To convict a defendant of the fourth-degree crime of contempt of a domestic violence restraining order, the State must prove that (1) a restraining order was issued under the act, (2) the defendant violated the order, (3) the defendant acted purposely or knowingly, and (4) the conduct that constituted the violation also constituted a crime or disorderly persons offense. The crime of terroristic threats in the third degree occurs if a person "threatens to kill another with purpose to put him in imminent fear of death under circumstances reasonably causing the victim to believe the immediacy of the threat and the likelihood that it will be carried out."

As a trial court judge, would you grant the motion to sever the offenses? Would you grant other relief? As an appellate court judge, would you reverse a trial court that had refused to grant the severance? Compare State v. Chenique-Puey, 678 A.2d 694 (N.J. 1996).

Notes

1. *Permissive joinder of offenses: majority view.* The rules governing joinder and severance work together to define the permissible bounds for single prosecutions and the extent of allowable judicial discretion. A slight majority of states track the federal rule on permissive joinder and allow prosecutors or judges to join offenses for trial, whether they are "related" charges ("based on the same act or transaction or on two or more acts or transactions connected together or constituting parts of a

common scheme or plan") or similar but "unrelated" charges (having the "same or similar character"). A significant minority of states authorize joinder only for "related" offenses utilizing a variety of formulations. See, e.g., Fla. R. Crim. P. 3.150; Ill. Ann. Stat. ch. 725, para. 5/111-4; Pa. R. Crim. P. 228. Given that "related" offenses can include two or more acts "connected together or constituting parts of a common scheme or plan," will the results of this rule be much different from the results of a rule allowing joinder of acts with the "same or similar character"?

2. *Severance of offenses: majority view.* A majority of states have separate provisions governing severance. A group of about seven states (represented by the Vermont rule reprinted above) follow the recommendations of the ABA Standards for Criminal Justice by giving the defendant the absolute right to sever "unrelated but similar" offenses. This approach bars the joinder of the unrelated but similar offenses unless the defendant consents. See, e.g., Mich. R. Crim. P. 6.121; Tenn. R. Crim. P. 8(b), 14. What reasons might lead a defendant to accept joinder of unrelated but similar offenses? Most states with severance provisions require severance upon a finding of prejudice, or if necessary to promote a "fair determination of innocence or guilt." A few authorize severance in the "interests of justice."

Under what circumstances might a single trial of properly joined offenses create prejudice for the government? The *Long* decision from the District of Columbia reviews the most important sources of prejudice to defendants. First, a defendant might want to pursue separate and inconsistent defenses to the different charges. Was Long asking for the opportunity to mislead two different juries? A second common source of prejudice to defendants from a joint trial of separate offenses involves "other crimes" evidence. The rules of evidence limit the prosecutor's ability to introduce evidence of one crime during the trial of another crime, because the jury might infer that a person who committed one crime is more likely to have committed a second crime. Joinder of offenses might allow a prosecutor to overcome this evidentiary rule; thus, severance is often granted when a court determines that the rules of evidence would exclude evidence of one charge in a separate trial of the other charge. Federal Rule of Evidence 404(b) governs such questions in the federal system. Evidence of "other crimes" is admissible to show a defendant's motive, intent, absence of mistake or accident, common scheme or plan, or identity, but not her propensity to commit a crime. Even when the rules of evidence might exclude evidence of one crime during a separate trial for the other crime, the charges can still be joined if the evidence remains "simple and distinct" at trial. See United States v. Lotsch, 102 F.2d 35 (2d Cir. 1939) (Hand, J.) ("Here we can see no prejudice from the joining of the three charges: The evidence to each was short and simple; there was no reasonable ground for thinking that the jury would not keep separate what was relevant to each"). "Simple and distinct" (or "separate and distinct") refers both to the content of the evidence and to the method the prosecution uses to present it. If witnesses for one crime are presented together, followed by a different set of witnesses for the other crime, the evidence is more likely to be considered "simple and distinct."

3. *Appellate review of joinder and severance decisions.* Appellate courts rarely overturn a trial court's joinder and severance decisions. The standard of review in virtually all jurisdictions is "abuse of discretion." Did the trial court in *Long* abuse its discretion? Given that most joinder and severance decisions are resolved before trial and are based on the charges in the indictment or information rather than testimony of witnesses at trial, are trial courts really better situated to resolve these claims than an appellate court?

4. *Per se severance rules.* Consider Problem 14-4. Is it possible or desirable to develop per se severance rules — that is, rules *requiring* a trial court to exercise its discretion under certain circumstances to sever charges that were properly joined? Are there any advantages to a per se rule in the context of severance decisions?

5. *Insufficient proof at trial.* Although challenges to compulsory joinder and misjoinder are generally resolved in a pretrial motion, sometimes the prosecution's evidence presented at trial will reveal that the offenses are not as closely related as they first appeared. Can the defendant obtain a declaration of misjoinder at the close of the prosecution's evidence? The Supreme Court in Schaffer v. United States, 362 U.S. 511 (1960), said that a defendant may not obtain a misjoinder during trial but must instead show that some specific prejudice required the judge to grant a discretionary severance of charges. Misjoinder, which does not depend on any showing of prejudice, must be determined only from the allegations in the indictment or information.

6. *Mandatory joinder: majority position.* About 10 states have adopted a "mandatory" or "compulsory" joinder requirement, either by statute, procedural rule, or judicial ruling. See Colo. R. Crim. P. 8(a); N.Y. Crim. Proc. Law §40.40 ("Where two or more offenses are joinable in a single accusatory instrument against a person by reason of being based upon the same criminal transaction . . . such person may not . . . be separately prosecuted for such offenses"); Pa. R. Crim. P. 105(b). A larger group of states, following the federal approach embodied in Fed. R. Crim. P. 8(a), maintain a "permissive" joinder rule, which defines the maximum range of charges that the prosecutor can bring together in the same trial but does not speak to any minimum range of charges that the prosecutor must join together. Note that in a permissive joinder jurisdiction, double jeopardy principles and the related doctrine of collateral estoppel still define a minimum range of charges that must be resolved in a single criminal proceeding. Thus, the mandatory joinder jurisdictions have supplemented double jeopardy and collateral estoppel principles.

7. *Misjoinder.* The converse of mandatory joinder is "misjoinder." When a defendant believes that a prosecutor has grouped together more charges than the permissive joinder rules will allow, she can request the trial court to declare misjoinder. The remedy is separate trials, not dismissal of the charges. Misjoinder can occur in any jurisdiction, whether it has a permissive or compulsory joinder rule, because all jurisdictions define the maximum range of charges that may be grouped together. But not all jurisdictions declare the same maximum. Some follow the model of Fed. R. Crim. P. 8(a), allowing joinder of offenses based on (1) acts that are of the same or similar character or (2) the "same act or transaction" or (3) two or more acts or transactions connected together or constituting parts of a common scheme or plan. Another group of states do not include the first ground for joinder, acts of the "same or similar character." Can you imagine a class of cases in which this first ground for joinder would make a difference in the outcome on a motion to declare misjoinder, or do you expect the different formulations to produce essentially the same results?

2. *Joint Trials of Defendants*

The joinder and severance questions we have considered thus far all deal with multiple offenses and an individual defendant. Related questions arise when prosecutors charge two or more defendants with committing essentially the same crime. Under what circumstances will the co-defendants receive separate trials?

The key phrases in procedural rules such as the ones reprinted below are framed generally and require further elaboration by courts presented with recurring factual situations. Cases have generally held that a defendant should obtain severance from a co-defendant when (1) evidence admitted against one defendant is facially incriminating to the other defendant, such as a prior statement of one co-defendant that incriminates the other co-defendant; (2) evidence admitted against one defendant influences the jury so strongly that it has a harmful "rub-off effect" on the other defendant; (3) there is a significant disparity in the amount of evidence introduced against each of the two defendants; or (4) co-defendants present defenses that are so antagonistic that they are mutually exclusive.

Only clear examples of these types of prejudice will convince an appellate court to reverse a trial court's decision to require a joint trial. For instance, to determine if a "rub off" problem exists, the court must ask whether the jury can keep separate the evidence that is relevant to each defendant and render a fair and impartial verdict as to each. Even in some cases where such prejudicial factors are strong enough to warrant a severance, courts sometimes decide that curative jury instructions can remove any risk of prejudice that might result from a joint trial.

■ FEDERAL RULE OF CRIMINAL PROCEDURE 8(b)

The indictment or information may charge two or more defendants if they are alleged to have participated in the same act or transaction, or in the same series of acts or transactions, constituting an offense or offenses. The defendants may be charged in one or more counts together or separately. All defendants need not be charged in each count.

■ VERMONT RULE OF CRIMINAL PROCEDURE 8(b)

Two or more defendants may be joined in the same information or indictment:

(1) when each of the defendants is charged with accountability for each offense included;

(2) when each of the defendants is charged with conspiracy and some of the defendants are also charged with one or more offenses alleged to be in furtherance of the conspiracy; or

(3) when, even if conspiracy is not charged and all of the defendants are not charged in each count, it is alleged that the several offenses charged

(A) were part of a common scheme or plan; or

(B) were so closely connected in respect to time, place, and occasion that it would be difficult to separate proof of one charge from proof of others.

■ VERMONT RULE OF CRIMINAL PROCEDURE 14(b)(2)

Whenever two or more defendants have been joined together in the same information or indictment,

(A) On motion of the prosecuting attorney or a defendant before trial, the court shall grant severance of one or more defendants if the court finds that they are not joinable under Rule 8(b)(2).

(B) On motion of the prosecuting attorney before trial, other than under subparagraph (A) of this paragraph, the court shall grant severance of one or more defendants if the court finds that there is no reasonable likelihood of prejudice to any defendant. On motion of the prosecuting attorney during trial, the court shall grant severance of one or more defendants only with the consent of the defendant or defendants to be severed or upon a finding of manifest necessity.

(C) On motion of a defendant for severance because an out-of-court statement of a codefendant makes reference to, but is not admissible against, the moving defendant, the court shall determine whether the prosecution intends to offer the statement in evidence as part of its case in chief. If so, the court shall require the prosecuting attorney to elect one of the following courses:

(i) a joint trial at which the statement is not admitted into evidence:

(ii) a joint trial at which the statement is admitted into evidence only after all references to the moving defendant have been deleted, provided that the court finds that the statement, with the references deleted, will not prejudice the moving defendant; or

(iii) severance of the moving defendant.

(D) On motion of a defendant other than under subparagraph (A) or (C) of this paragraph, the court shall grant severance of the moving defendant unless the court finds that there is no reasonable likelihood that that defendant would be prejudiced by a joint trial.

(E) In determining whether there is no reasonable likelihood that a defendant would be prejudiced, the court shall consider among other factors whether, in view of the number of offenses and defendants charged and the complexity of the evidence to be offered, the trier of fact will be able to distinguish the evidence and apply the law intelligently as to each offense and as to each defendant.

(F) The court may, at any time, grant severance of one or more defendants with the consent of the prosecution and the defendant or defendants to be severed.

Vermont Reporter's Notes—1995 Amendment

Rule 14(b)(2) is amended to eliminate the absolute right of severance for a defendant in a felony case and to provide guidelines under which a motion for severance of defendants is to be considered. Under the prior rule, in misdemeanor cases severance or whatever other relief justice required was to be granted when either a defendant or the State was prejudiced by joinder. The amended rule applies to both felonies and misdemeanors. The amendment is based on ABA Standard 13-3.2. The purposes of the amendment are to give the court flexibility and to strike a proper balance between avoidance of multiple trials for victims and the right of defendants to a fair trial. . . .

When two or more defendants have been joined, the first issue for determination is whether the joinder is proper under the terms of that rule. Amended Rule 14(b)(2)(A) requires the court to grant a pretrial request by either prosecution or defense for severance on grounds of misjoinder, regardless of whether there is prejudice. If a defect in joinder appears during trial, a severance on that ground is to be considered in accordance with the standards of subparagraphs (B) and (D).

Under Rule 14(b)(2)(B), even if joinder is proper pursuant to Rule 8(b), the prosecutor will be granted a severance on motion before trial if the court finds "no reasonable likelihood" that any defendant would be prejudiced by the severance. . . . On an appropriate motion by a defendant under Rule 14(b)(2)(C), the court must determine whether Bruton v. United States, 391 U.S. 123 (1968), affects the severance decision. Under *Bruton,* the trial court must protect the confrontation rights of a nonconfessing defendant where a codefendant has confessed and that confession is admissible only against the confessing defendant. Rule 14(b)(2)(C)(i)-(iii) set out the options which must be followed for compliance with *Bruton*. . . .

If a defendant moves for severance before trial on grounds other than misjoinder or the potential use of a codefendant's confession, the court under Rule 14(b)(2)(D) is to sever the moving defendant unless it finds that there is no reasonable likelihood of prejudice to that defendant from the joinder. The standard for determining prejudice is set forth in Rule 14(b)(2)(E). That standard departs from the formulation, "fair determination of guilt or innocence," found in ABA Standard 13-3.2(b)(i), (ii). In deciding the question, the court is to consider "prejudice" in terms of the impact of the challenged joinder on each defendant's right to a fair trial where the prosecution makes the motion and on the moving defendant's fair trial right where a defendant makes the motion. [T]here is a reasonable likelihood of prejudice where the jury might consider evidence against one defendant that is properly offered only against a codefendant, either on the merits or as to character or credibility. Where the evidence against both defendants is substantially similar, however, they may be tried jointly in the absence of other factors giving rise to a reasonable likelihood of prejudice. . . .

Problem 14-5. Antagonistic Brothers

Brothers Durid and Kafan Hana were arrested following a controlled narcotics purchase in January 1988 that took place at the Sterling Heights home in which the brothers lived with their parents and siblings. The drug transaction arose out of a conversation between James Hornburger and Raed Alsarih at the Sterling Heights High School where they were students. Hornburger approached Alsarih about obtaining twelve ounces of cocaine for Stephen Putnam, who happened to be an undercover narcotics police officer. Alsarih agreed to the transaction after contacting Kafan. Hornburger, Putnam, and Alsarih drove to Kafan's home. Alsarih went to the door and spoke with Durid, who contacted Kafan by beeper and reported that Kafan would be back in 15 minutes. When the purchasers returned to the house later that evening, they saw Kafan drive up and Alsarih and Kafan went into the house together.

According to Alsarih, testifying pursuant to a plea bargain, he went with Kafan to a back bedroom where Durid was sleeping. Durid awoke when Kafan turned on the light. While Kafan opened a safe, Durid asked Alsarih whether the person outside was a police officer and whether Alsarih had dealt with him before. Kafan removed a plastic bag from the safe, mixed it with the contents from some other bags and gave it to Alsarih. They returned to the front of the house, and Kafan watched while Alsarih went out to Putnam's car. Durid was watching from the living room window. Alsarih then got in the back seat and gave the bag of cocaine to Putnam. Putnam signaled to a surveillance team, which moved in and arrested Hornburger, Alsarih, Kafan, and Durid. A subsequent search of the home, pursuant to a search warrant, disclosed that the safe contained three kilograms of cocaine, miscellaneous jewelry and papers, a telephone recorder, and a telephone beeper. Both Kafan and Durid initially denied knowing the combination to the safe. However, Kafan later supplied the combination, and Durid admitted that the safe was his.

Both Durid and Kafan filed pretrial motions for separate trials. Michigan Court Rule 6.121 provides for permissive joinder and conditional severance:

(A) Permissive Joinder. An information or indictment may charge two or more defendants with the same offense. [T]wo or more informations or indictments against different defendants may be consolidated for a single trial whenever the defendants could be charged in the same information or indictment under this rule. . . .

(C) Right of Severance; Related Offenses. On a defendant's motion, the court must sever the trial of defendants on related offenses on a showing that severance is necessary to avoid prejudice to substantial rights of the defendants.

(D) Discretionary Severance. On the motion of any party, the court may sever the trial of defendants on the ground that severance is appropriate to promote fairness to the parties and a fair determination of the guilt or innocence of one or more of the defendants. Relevant factors include the timeliness of the motion, the drain on the parties' resources, the potential for confusion or prejudice stemming from either the number of defendants or the complexity or nature of the evidence, the convenience of the witnesses, and the parties' readiness for trial. . . .

In a supporting affidavit, Durid's counsel explained the results of a meeting with Kafan's attorneys:

> At said meeting affiant was advised by both counsel that the defense theory of the above case was that evidence would show that the controlled substances seized from 3105 Metropolitan Parkway were the property of, or possessed by, Durid Bajhat Hana and not by Kafan Hana. Given the fact that Durid Bajhat Hana's theory of the case is that the controlled substances seized from 3105 Metropolitan Parkway were the property of, or possessed by, Kafan Hana, and not by Durid Bajhat Hana, Durid Bajhat Hana will be compelled to act, for all practical purpose, as an assistant prosecutor as to Kafan Hana.

The trial court heard argument on the motions. Durid's attorney argued that "the two defenses could not be more antagonistic. Two people are pointing the finger at each other and the case is clear that severance must be granted." The prosecutor argued that it took more than "a mere allegation of pointing fingers at one another" to warrant separate trials. The trial court denied the motion.

The brothers were tried jointly before a jury in February 1989. Durid was tried on an aiding and abetting theory. In his opening statement, Kafan's attorney told jurors that their deliberations necessarily pitted brother against brother. During closing argument, Durid's attorney similarly described the defense postures as "brother pitted against brother." In closing arguments, Kafan's attorney disputed the theory that his client had control over the three kilograms of cocaine seized from the safe:

> We know he used the Cadillac, we know he used the house, we know he used the safe, but we know he didn't own the Cadillac and own the house and own the safe. Everybody who has ever shared a locker in school or anybody who's ever shared an apartment, everybody who's ever lived in a rooming house and had to share a bathroom knows that you can share special areas and have absolutely no right to control something that belongs to somebody else.

The prosecutor pointed out the conflict during rebuttal closing argument when she noted: "That's real convenient for these two boys to sit here and say that the drugs belonged to one another." This remark was stricken. The prosecutor later stated:

> The position that Durid Hana and Kafan Hana took in this trial is saying that the drugs did not belong to them, but they were in their bedroom and they were in a safe that they both had access to, and if you believe both Durid Hana and Kafan Hana, the good fairy must have delivered the drugs and locked them in the safe. It's not reasonable to believe that they did not know that they were there. Someone put those drugs in that safe, and if you look at all of the evidence that occurred that night, it is reasonable to believe that both of them knew it. . . .

The prosecutor further explained in closing argument: "As to Durid Hana, it is the People's theory that Durid aided his brother in the delivery of cocaine in the sum of 225 to 649 grams of cocaine, that he provided support, advice and encouragement and took an active role in that delivery. It is further alleged that Durid Hana knew that the cocaine was being stored in that safe and that he had dominion and control over the contents of what was kept in that safe, as did his brother Kafan Hana." Neither Durid nor his brother testified. Durid and Kafan were both convicted of possession of more than 650 grams of cocaine and delivery of more than 225, but less than 650, grams of cocaine.

Durid appeals, alleging that the trial court erred in denying his motion for a separate trial given the antagonistic defenses of the two brothers. He argues that the events at trial support his claim of antagonistic defenses. How would you rule? Compare People v. Hana, 524 N.W.2d 682 (Mich. 1994).

Notes

1. *Joinder of defendants: majority view.* Joint trials account for almost one-third of all federal criminal trials, a rate much higher than in most state systems. As a result, the federal courts have dealt extensively with severance issues. See Richardson v. Marsh, 481 U.S. 200 (1987). In general, the federal courts have shown a strong preference for joint trials. This preference has become even more pronounced in recent years, and severance requests in the federal courts are now routinely denied. A majority of states leave decisions on the joinder and severance of trials for multiple defendants to the discretion of the trial judge. Defendants in these jurisdictions find courts generally unreceptive when they request separate trials based on the special legal and practical difficulties of defending against conspiracy charges. As the reporter's notes to Vermont Rule 14(b)(2) indicate, Vermont had a mandatory severance rule but amended it in 1995, in line with the dominant view, allowing the trial judge some discretion over whether to order joint trials. See Kan. Stat. §22-3204. A significant minority of states, including Vermont, provide more detailed rules to guide courts in assessing out-of-court statements by co-defendants. See, e.g., Fla. R. Crim. P. 3.152(b).

2. *Remedies short of severance.* Courts take several approaches short of severing trials to deal with conflicts among co-defendants. The most common is simply to issue cautionary instructions to the jury before it retires to consider the case.

Sometimes the judge also instructs the jury at the beginning of the trial or when particular evidence is presented. Occasionally courts will bar the use of evidence that would be admissible at a trial of a co-defendant tried separately. A more complex option, which has been tried in a number of states, is the use of "dual" juries to hear the same case. Each jury considers the charges against one defendant. The court will excuse one of the juries when evidence is presented against one defendant that could not be presented against the other. For a general discussion of "mega-trials" in the federal courts, see James Jacobs et al., Busting the Mob: United States v. Cosa Nostra (1994).

PART THREE

RESOLVING GUILT AND INNOCENCE

XV

Discovery and Speedy Trial

Parties must prepare for trial if the process is to create justice. The most critical task for the attorney preparing for trial is to gather information about the events in question. Much of the best information is in the hands of the other party. The rules of discovery govern how and when the parties exchange information that may be relevant in resolving the charges, whether through trial or guilty plea. These rules are grounded in constitutions, statutes, court rules, and local policies and practices.

Adequate preparation takes time. But all the while, the defendant must live with the shame of accusation and the inconvenience and expense of preparing for trial. For defendants who are detained, the period before trial can destroy employment and personal relationships. Many defendants, and especially those in detention, want a "speedy" trial. In this chapter, we review the tools for discovering information and the many sources of law that give parties the ability, and the incentive, to speed up or slow down the trial date.

A. DISCOVERY

In all litigation, there are rules about exchanging information among the parties and gathering information from nonparties. What the parties learn during discovery determines in large part the evidence they will have at their disposal at trial. Even more important for most defendants, discovery allows them to estimate their chances of success at trial and to enter plea bargain negotiations with that information in mind.

Two sets of interrelated questions dominate the law of discovery in criminal cases. First, discovery rules must resolve whether shared information or independent information is the norm. The answer to this question reflects the expected relationship among prosecutors, judges, and defense attorneys. Less exchange of information reflects a more adversarial and independent model, where each side develops its own evidence; more exchange reflects a more cooperative model of litigation, with the court taking a stronger role in coordinating a collective search for truth. When describing the criminal discovery process on this score, it may be helpful to draw a comparison to discovery in civil litigation. It is commonplace to hear that criminal discovery is less extensive than civil discovery. Is this claim accurate today? If so, will it remain true in the future? As you read and discuss the materials in this section, try to draw comparisons to civil discovery techniques and to identify trends over time toward more or less extensive criminal discovery.

The second set of questions deals with the symmetry of discovery. Will prosecution and defense have an equal ability to obtain information from the opposing side? In a system with other asymmetries built into it (such as the "beyond a reasonable doubt" standard of proof, the privilege against self-incrimination, and the government's funding of prosecutors and investigators), are asymmetrical discovery rights necessary or desirable?

1. Prosecution Disclosures

A defense attorney with enough time, ingenuity, and resources could learn much about the government's evidence in a criminal case. Rules of procedure and statutes in most jurisdictions set out the obligations of the prosecution to disclose some of the incriminating evidence against the accused, but only after the defendant requests it. Local court rules sometimes supplement the statewide rules.

Despite these discovery rules, however, the defense attorney frequently knows much less than the prosecutor about the case at the time of plea bargaining or trial. Some of the functional limits on discovery are built into the rules themselves, and others are a function of the defense attorney's limited time and resources.

The criminal discovery rules show remarkable variety from jurisdiction to jurisdiction. Federal Rule of Criminal Procedure 16 and the North Carolina statute reprinted below are typical of the more restrictive rules, which give the defendant access to only a handful of documents and tangible objects before trial. Most states go beyond these limited categories to allow defense discovery of a wider range of prosecution information. The ABA Standards for Criminal Justice have been an influential model for those states moving in the direction of wider discovery. The New Jersey rule reprinted below illustrates the greater scope of documents and other information that some states consider essential to the preparation of a defense.

Use the following problem as a setting for applying the New Jersey and North Carolina statutes. Under each of these approaches to criminal discovery, what information gets exchanged, and what types of evidence go unmentioned? How will a plea negotiation or a trial progress if the defense lawyer does not have access to such information before trial? Can defense counsel develop the same information through different avenues?

Problem 15-1. Exchanging Words

Two groups in a bar were arguing one night. One group, which included Wayne Galvan, left shortly before the bar closed, while the other group, which included

Perry Sutton, waited inside a few minutes longer, hoping to avoid any contact outside with the other group. When Sutton and his friends went outside, Galvan and his friends appeared from around the corner and started taunting Sutton's group. Soon the two groups were involved in a heated argument. In the midst of the noise and confusion, Galvan drew a small handgun and fired two shots, while standing less than five feet from Sutton. The second shot killed Sutton. Galvan ran away. Several of Sutton's friends knew Galvan by name and identified him to police officers. The officers later arrested Galvan at his cousin's home, where they also found a small handgun.

You have been appointed to represent Galvan. During his initial conversation with you, Galvan claimed that he meant to frighten Sutton and his friends by firing his handgun into the air, but that he did not intend to harm Sutton. Galvan said that he had discussed the incident with two other detainees in the county jail.

You have obtained from your client the names and addresses of some of his friends who were present that evening. During telephone conversations with two of those friends, you learn that one was interviewed within a week of the shooting by a police officer and an attorney from the district attorney's office, both of whom were taking notes. The second was interviewed by a police officer alone, and the officer did not take any notes. You learned from Galvan's friends the name of one of Sutton's friends who was present on the night of the shooting, but that person refuses to talk to you.

Galvan has authorized you to engage in plea negotiations. What sort of discovery will you request before plea negotiations begin? Consider each of the following categories of potentially useful information:

- Any statements that Galvan made to police officers, prosecutors, his friends, or members of the rival group. Does it matter whether the statements have been recorded in a document?
- Any statements that members of the rival group made to police or prosecutors about what they saw or heard that night. Can you insist that the police tell you what they know about the background and reliability of these witnesses?
- Any statements that members of Galvan's group made to the police or prosecutors. Can the prosecutors gain discovery of these statements? Is there anything you can or should do to prepare these potential defense witnesses for an interview with the police or cross-examination at trial by the prosecutor?
- Any ballistics or other scientific tests performed on the gun, along with any medical examinations performed on Sutton.

Anticipate how the prosecutors might respond if the relevant discovery rules are similar to those in North Carolina. Then compare the government's response if the rules look like those in New Jersey. Would any of the evidence you might obtain through requests under these discovery rules dramatically change the course of the plea negotiations?

Think also about the timing of discovery. Suppose you are assigned to the case at the arraignment, less than a month after the charges are filed. The median time it takes to process felony cases in the state is 80 days (roughly the national median time), although a few cases last a good deal longer. About ten percent of the felony cases require more than a year to resolve.

Finally, consider the investigative resources at your disposal. You work full time as a defense attorney, and you represent about 150 felony defendants per year (the maximum workload prescribed in the ABA Standards on Criminal Justice, but lighter than the load many defense attorneys actually carry). Your office employs a former police detective as an investigator, but seven other criminal defense attorneys in your office share the services of this investigator. In light of these resource constraints and the legal rules described below, what would be your strategy for obtaining the types of information listed above?

■ NORTH CAROLINA GENERAL STATUTES §15A-903

(a) Upon motion of a defendant, the court must order the prosecutor:

(1) To permit the defendant to inspect and copy or photograph any relevant written or recorded statements made by the defendant, or copies thereof, within the possession, custody, or control of the State the existence of which is known or by the exercise of due diligence may become known to the prosecutor; and

(2) To divulge, in written or recorded form, the substance of any oral statement relevant to the subject matter of the case made by the defendant, regardless of to whom the statement was made, within the possession, custody or control of the State, the existence of which is known to the prosecutor or becomes known to him prior to or during the course of trial; except that disclosure of such a statement is not required if it was made to an informant whose identity is a prosecution secret and who will not testify for the prosecution, and if the statement is not exculpatory. . . . If disclosure of the substance of defendant's oral statement to an informant whose identity is or was a prosecution secret is withheld, the informant must not testify for the prosecution at trial.

(b) Upon motion of a defendant, the court must order the prosecutor:

(1) To permit the defendant to inspect and copy or photograph any written or recorded statement of a codefendant which the State intends to offer in evidence at their joint trial; and

(2) To divulge, in written or recorded form, the substance of any oral statement made by a codefendant which the State intends to offer in evidence at their joint trial.

(c) Upon motion of the defendant, the court must order the State to furnish to the defendant a copy of his prior criminal record, if any, as is available to the prosecutor.

(d) Upon motion of the defendant, the court must order the prosecutor to permit the defendant to inspect and copy or photograph books, papers, documents, photographs, motion pictures, mechanical or electronic recordings, buildings and places, or any other crime scene, tangible objects, or copies or portions thereof which are within the possession, custody, or control of the State and which are material to the preparation of his defense, are intended for use by the State as evidence at the trial, or were obtained from or belong to the defendant.

(e) Upon motion of a defendant, the court must order the prosecutor to provide a copy of or to permit the defendant to inspect and copy or photograph results or reports of physical or mental examinations or of tests, measurements or experiments made in connection with the case, or copies thereof. . . . In addition, upon motion of a defendant, the court must order the prosecutor to permit the defendant to inspect, examine, and test, subject to appropriate safeguards, any physical evidence, or a sample of it, available to the prosecutor if the State intends to offer the evidence, or tests or experiments made in connection with the evidence, as an exhibit or evidence in the case.

(f) (1) In any criminal prosecution brought by the State, no statement or report in the possession of the State that was made by a State witness or prospective State witness, other than the defendant, shall be the subject of subpoena, discovery, or inspection until that witness has testified on direct examination in the trial of the case.

(2) After a witness called by the State has testified on direct examination, the court shall, on motion of the defendant, order the State to produce any statement of the witness in the possession of the State that relates to the subject matter as to which the witness has testified. If the entire contents of that statement relate to the subject matter of the testimony of the witness, the court shall order it to be delivered directly to the defendant for his examination and use. . . .

(5) The term "statement," as used in subdivision (2) . . . in relation to any witness called by the State means

a. A written statement made by the witness and signed or otherwise adopted or approved by him;

b. A stenographic, mechanical, electrical, or other recording, or a transcription thereof, that is a substantially verbatim recital or an oral statement made by the witness and recorded contemporaneously with the making of the oral statements.

(g) The defendant shall have the right to obtain a copy of DNA laboratory reports provided to the district attorney revealing that there was a DNA match to the defendant that was derived from a CODIS match during a comparison search involving the defendant' s DNA sample. . . .

■ NEW JERSEY COURT RULE 3:13-3

(a) Where the prosecutor has made a pre-indictment plea offer, the prosecutor shall upon request permit defense counsel to inspect and copy or photograph any relevant material which would be discoverable following an indictment pursuant to section (b) or (c).

(b) A copy of the prosecutor's discovery shall be delivered to the criminal division manager's office, or shall be available at the prosecutor's office, within 14 days of the return or unsealing of the indictment. . . . A defendant who does not seek discovery from the State shall so notify the criminal division manager's office and the prosecutor, and the defendant need not provide discovery to the State [except as] otherwise required by law. . . .

(c) The prosecutor shall permit defendant to inspect and copy or photograph the following relevant material if not given as part of the discovery package under section (b):

(1) books, tangible objects, papers or documents obtained from or belonging to the defendant;

(2) records of statements or confessions, signed or unsigned, by the defendant or copies thereof, and a summary of any admissions or declarations against penal interest made by the defendant that are known to the prosecution but not recorded;

(3) results or reports of physical or mental examinations and of scientific tests or experiments made in connection with the matter or copies thereof, which are within the possession, custody or control of the prosecutor;

(4) reports or records of prior convictions of the defendant;

(5) books, papers, documents, or copies thereof, or tangible objects, buildings or places which are within the possession, custody or control of the prosecutor;

(6) names and addresses of any persons whom the prosecutor knows to have relevant evidence or information including a designation by the prosecutor as to which of those persons may be called as witnesses;

(7) record of statements, signed or unsigned, by such persons or by co-defendants which are within the possession, custody or control of the prosecutor and any relevant record of prior conviction of such persons;

(8) police reports which are within the possession, custody, or control of the prosecutor;

(9) names and addresses of each person whom the prosecutor expects to call to trial as an expert witness, the expert's qualifications, the subject matter on which the expert is expected to testify, a copy of the report, if any, of such expert witness, or if no report is prepared, a statement of the facts and opinions to which the expert is expected to testify and a summary of the grounds for each opinion. . . .

Notes

1. *Defendant and co-defendant statements.* Discovery rules in all jurisdictions allow defense counsel at least some access to the government's evidence regarding statements that the defendant made about the alleged crime. This does not mean, however, that the government must turn over all statements by a defendant. Under Fed. R. Crim. P. 16(a)(1)(A), the defense may obtain "written or recorded" statements of a defendant and written evidence of "oral statements" made by a defendant in response to interrogation by a known government agent. The ABA Standard for Criminal Justice, Discovery 11-2.1(a)(i) (3d ed. 1996) calls for the prosecutor to disclose "all written and oral statements of the defendant or any co-defendant," along with any documents "relating to the acquisition of such statements." See also Fla. R. Crim. P. 3.220(b)(1)(C). What sorts of statements does the ABA standard cover that the Federal Rule does not? Does a defense attorney really need to obtain such statements from the government when he could simply ask his client about any statements he made? How would he use documents "relating to the acquisition" of a defendant's statement?

Note that Rule 16 makes no provision for the discovery of co-defendant's statements. Cf. Fla. R. Crim. P. 3.220(b)(1)(D) (discovery of "any written or recorded statements and the substance of any oral statements made by a codefendant if the trial is to be a joint one"). When might defense counsel use such a statement? Does defense counsel have an alternative method of preparing for any co-defendant statements that might be used at trial?

2. *Prosecution expert witnesses.* Criminal discovery rules, like their civil counterparts, recognize the special challenges of preparing for the trial testimony of expert witnesses. Fed. R. Crim. P. 16(a)(1)(E) calls for disclosure of a "written summary of testimony the government intends to use" from experts in its case in chief, which

includes the expert's opinions, the bases and the reasons for the opinions, and the expert's qualifications. Once again, many states give the defense more information, by including disclosure of the reports or statements of any experts (such as the results of tests) made "in connection with" a particular case, whether or not the government plans to call the expert at trial. Fla. R. Crim. P. 3.220(b)(1)(J). The rules typically impose on both parties the same obligations of disclosure about their experts.

3. *Nonexpert witnesses and potential witnesses.* Perhaps the greatest variety in discovery rules involves information about nonexpert witnesses and potential witnesses. Federal Rule of Criminal Procedure 26.2 provides for disclosure at trial by both the prosecution and defense of written "statements" of any witnesses other than the defendant. The Jencks Act, 18 U.S.C. §3500, requires the prosecution alone to disclose witness statements after direct examination at trial. Rule 26.2 largely supplants the Jencks Act by extending to both parties the obligations that applied only to prosecution witnesses under the statute. The only statements that qualify for disclosure under Rule 26.2 are written statements "adopted" or signed by the witness, or a "substantially verbatim transcription" of the witness's oral statement, which would usually not include a government agent's notes of an interview. The Rule does not require any disclosure until *after* the witness has testified on direct examination at trial. Any disclosure of witness statements before trial (or before entry of a guilty plea) results from negotiations between the parties. See Ellen S. Podgor, The Ethics and Professionalism of Prosecutors in Discretionary Decisions, 68 Fordham L. Rev. 1511 (2000). Some states, such as North Carolina and Texas, are silent about pretrial discovery of witness statements. See Tex. Code Crim. Proc. art. 39.14. What impact would this timing question have on the course of plea negotiations?

Discovery rules in other jurisdictions treat information about potential witnesses as a matter that the defense cannot develop alone before trial. The rules commonly require the government to give the defense — before trial — the names and addresses of its witnesses and other persons who have knowledge of the events surrounding the alleged crime. See Fla. R. Crim. P. 3.220(b)(1)(A); National District Attorneys Association, National Prosecution Standards 53.2(a) (2d ed. 1991) (covering prosecution witnesses but not potential witnesses). The rules also oblige the government to provide the defense with potential impeachment material, such as the prior criminal record of any witnesses or the nature of any cooperation agreement between the government and the witness. The rules also typically extend to any written summaries of witness statements, even if the statements are not "adopted" or "verbatim." See ABA Standard 11-2.1(a)(ii); Fla. R. Crim. P. 3.220(b)(1)(B). Is all of this discovery about witnesses necessary? Once a defense attorney has the name and address of a potential witness, can she obtain statements from the witness on equal terms with the government?

When prosecuting attorneys take the statements of witnesses, the "work-product" doctrine comes into play. In its original form as a common law doctrine developed in civil cases, the work-product doctrine limits a party trying to obtain any material reflecting the "work product" of the opponent's attorney. Facts developed in anticipation of litigation are discoverable only after showing a "substantial need" for the information, that is, that the requesting party cannot obtain the facts elsewhere without "undue hardship." The attorney's opinions and strategies remain beyond the reach of discovery. See Hickman v. Taylor, 329 U.S. 495 (1947). In the criminal context, discovery rules usually grant to the prosecutor a truncated form of the work-product privilege. The defendant may obtain witness statements that are otherwise discoverable, even if the prosecutor was involved in obtaining the statement, and the defendant does not have to show any special need for the statement. Any of the prosecutor's mental impressions, theories, or strategies appearing in the statement, however, are typically protected from discovery. Should the work-product doctrine apply at all to a criminal prosecutor? Does the prosecutor have different needs and obligations than a civil litigant when it comes to disclosure?

4. *Open file policies.* A few jurisdictions (such as New Jersey, as indicated in the provisions reprinted above) have embraced "open file" discovery—rules that require the prosecutor to keep any written records about the case completely open to the defense attorney. While such a position is unusual to find in statewide statutes or rules, it is commonplace to find individual prosecutors' offices that have committed themselves to open file discovery. Why would prosecutors create discovery rules that go well beyond the requirements of the applicable law? Does it save them the trouble of sorting through documents to comply with discovery requests? Keep in mind that prosecutors adopting an open file policy still must identify material exculpatory evidence for defense attorneys and offer such information to the defense, even if there is no specific request for it. See State v. Adam, 896 P.2d 1022 (Kan. 1995). Does an open file policy best achieve the discovery objectives identified by the National District Attorneys Association: "to provide information for informed pleas, expedite trials, minimize surprise, afford the opportunity for effective cross-examination, meet the requirements of due process, and otherwise serve the interests of justice"? National Prosecution Standards 52.1 (2d ed. 1991). Can a prosecutor's office count on the limited time available to a defense attorney in most smaller cases to minimize the impact of an open file policy? Cf. ABA Standard 11-1.2 (discovery "may be more limited" in cases involving minor offenses).

5. *Writings already in existence.* Even with open file policies, the emphasis is on written materials rather than the knowledge of the people who provide or analyze the evidence. Is this why the federal system, with its first-class capacity for developing written evidence and keeping records, has more restrictive discovery rules than most jurisdictions? Note that most of the discovery provisions described above require the prosecution to hand over existing documents, but they do not oblige the prosecutor to create or compile information (which is more common under civil discovery rules). There are a few exceptions to this pattern: Some discovery rules call on the prosecutor to commit to writing any known oral statement of the defendant, and to summarize information about expert witnesses. Given that criminal justice systems rely so heavily on guilty pleas rather than development of the facts during a trial, should the systems move in the direction of forcing the parties to summarize evidence before trial?

6. *Depositions.* Depositions of witnesses and other third parties, the lifeblood of civil discovery, does not hold an important place in criminal discovery. In the federal system and in most states, depositions are available only to preserve the testimony of a witness who is unlikely to be available at trial. A few states, however, have begun to make it easier to obtain depositions and to use them in criminal proceedings. These are sometimes called "discovery" depositions, as opposed to depositions used to preserve testimony. See Fla. R. Crim. P. 3.220(h). Why have criminal discovery innovators focused their attention on the available documents rather than the deposition or written interrogatory?

Despite the rarity of criminal depositions in most jurisdictions, the parties do interview witnesses before trial. Does this voluntary system of gathering evidence give the parties equal access to information? See ABA Standard 11-6.3 (neither prosecutor nor defense should advise persons other than defendant to refrain from speaking with counsel for opposing side).

7. *Remedies.* Discovery rules typically leave courts with a great deal of discretion in selecting a remedy for a violation of the law. The most common remedies are continuances (to allow the party time to develop a response to the evidence) and exclusion of the evidence that the party should have disclosed (particularly where the aggrieved party can show some prejudice flowing from the discovery violation). Trial courts have also dismissed charges for more serious discovery violations by a prosecutor. State ex rel. Rusen v. Hill, 454 S.E.2d 427 (W. Va. 1994). If an appellate court decides that a discovery violation occurred, it can reverse the conviction if the defendant shows prejudice. Contempt citations against the attorney or later disciplinary proceedings by the state bar are also possibilities.

8. *Discovery by any other name.* The rules of pretrial discovery are not the defendant's only method of finding out about the government's evidence. The preliminary hearing, where the government establishes probable cause to support the charges in the case, often gives defense counsel a glimpse of the government's theory of the case. Defendants will also on occasion request a "bill of particulars," a document that supplements the indictment or information when necessary to give proper notice to the defendant of the charges he must defend against.

Problem 15-2. Discovery from Victims

Joan Simms is charged with aggravated assault. The state of Arizona alleges that she used a knife to injure her husband, Daniel McPhee. According to Simms, McPhee received psychiatric treatment over the years for a multiple personality disorder. She claims that McPhee abused her emotionally and physically during their marriage, and at the time of the assault, he was manifesting one of his "violent personalities." Simms called 911 at 3:34 A.M. on the date of the alleged assault, asking for help because her husband was beating her and threatening her with a knife. When the police arrived at the home, they found McPhee bleeding from a stomach wound. She said that she had used the knife in self-defense.

Simms filed two discovery motions. The first motion asked the trial judge to compel the victim/husband to make available to the defense "all of his past and present medical records from any institution in any jurisdiction." The records might support defense allegations that the victim is a violent and psychotic individual who has been treated for multiple personality disorder for at least 12 years in the nearby state hospital and by a number of local psychiatrists. The second motion asked for an order compelling McPhee to submit to a deposition.

The state opposes both motions. It argues that the physician-patient privilege protects the treatment documents, even though McPhee may have waived this privilege for some of the documents because he provided them to the prosecuting attorneys. In addition, the government argues that the Arizona Constitution, art. II, §2.1, bars these two discovery requests: "A victim of crime has a right [to] refuse an interview, deposition, or other discovery request by the defendant, the defendant's attorney, or other person acting on behalf of the defendant [and to] be informed of victims' constitutional rights." Under the Arizona Rules of Criminal Procedure, the state is required to provide the defendant with all materials or information that tend to mitigate or negate the defendant's guilt or that tend to reduce his punishment. The Rules also provide for depositions of key witnesses in criminal cases. Will the trial court grant the two motions? Compare State ex rel. Romley v. Superior Court, 836 P.2d 445 (Ariz. Ct. App. 1992); State v. Warner, 812 P.2d 1079 (Ariz. Ct. App. 1990).

Under the criminal discovery rules, the defense lawyer must ask before receiving material from the government. But the prosecutor's duty sometimes goes beyond responding to valid defense requests for discovery. There are several types of information that the law requires the prosecution to disclose to the defense, even if the defense lawyer never asks for the information.

One disclosure duty that courts place on prosecutors involves perjured testimony of government witnesses. If the prosecutor knows or should know that government witnesses are presenting false testimony or evidence, due process requires the prosecutor to disclose this fact to the defendant and to the court. A conviction must be set aside if there is any reasonable likelihood that the false testimony could have affected the judgment of the jury. See Mooney v. Holohan, 294 U.S. 103 (1935); Napue v. Illinois, 360 U.S. 264 (1959).

A second constitutional duty to disclose derives from Brady v. Maryland, 373 U.S. 83 (1963). In that case, a defense attorney in a murder case asked to review all the extrajudicial statements of a coconspirator, but the prosecutor withheld a statement in which the coconspirator admitted to shooting the victim. The Supreme Court ruled that the constitution's due process clause requires the prosecution to disclose "evidence favorable to an accused" if that evidence is "material either to guilt or to punishment." The Court expanded this disclosure duty in United States v. Agurs, 427 U.S. 97 (1976). The obligation to disclose all material evidence favorable to the accused, the Court said, applies even when the defendant makes only a general request for exculpatory material or makes no request for material at all.

Litigation over *Brady* issues remains quite common. Courts struggle to identify which prosecutorial failures to disclose are important enough to justify overturning a conviction. This difficult question necessarily calls for the court to speculate: What would have happened if the prosecutor had disclosed the material? How certain does the reviewing court have to be?

■ RAULAND GRUBE v. STATE

995 P.2d 794 (Idaho 2000)

WALTERS, J.

This is an appeal from the denial of a post-conviction relief application filed with regard to Rauland Grube's conviction for first-degree murder in the 1983 death of Amy Hossner in Ashton, Idaho. The order denying relief is affirmed.

Amy Hossner was murdered while she slept in her bedroom in the basement of her parent's home in the early morning hours of June 4, 1983. She was killed by a single shotgun blast through a window above her bed. Rauland Grube was tried for the crime in October of 1991, after information came to light placing Grube at Amy Hossner's house on the night of the murder. Brenda Fredricksen Briggs, a witness who did not come forward until 1991, testified at trial that shortly after the murder, Grube had approached her and told her that he had a crush on Amy and had spoken to Amy through her bedroom window the night Amy was murdered. Briggs also testified Grube told her that when Amy failed to meet him several hours later, he went back to her house and looked in the window, whereupon he told Briggs that he had "never seen so much blood in his life." Although Grube did not testify, a tape-recorded interview of Grube which had been conducted by the police in 1991 was played for the jury, in which Grube said that the story he had told Briggs was a lie. There was testimony relating to the various tests performed by firearms experts on Grube's weapon, a shotgun, both in 1983 and in 1991. The jury found Grube guilty of first-degree murder in the death of Amy Hossner, and he was sentenced to life imprisonment without the possibility of parole. . . .

In 1994, while Grube's appeal from the judgment of conviction was pending, Lynn Gifford approached defense counsel. Gifford indicated that he was the person who had first told Grube that Amy Hossner had been murdered, and that although he had been interviewed by the police in 1991, he had not been called to testify at Grube's trial. In their conversation with Gifford, defense counsel learned information (1) that Grube had reacted with genuine surprise and sadness to the news of Amy Hossner's death, and (2) that Gifford had reported seeing Ashton police officer Stephen Brood — an early suspect in this crime — driving a police car within a few blocks of Amy Hossner's house at approximately 2:30 A.M. on the night of the murder. This information had been communicated to the police investigator in 1991 but was never disclosed by the state to the defense, prompting counsel to seek post-conviction relief on Grube's behalf from the district court.

In his application for post-conviction relief, Grube asserted that he was entitled to a new trial because he had been denied due process by the state's failure to disclose exculpatory information contained in Gifford's interview with the investigator in 1991. The Gifford information led defense counsel to discover that Ashton police logs recording activity the night of the murder appeared to have been altered. [The] district court conducted an evidentiary hearing on the application. According to the state, the police logs in question could not be located and were unavailable for the defense to [determine] whether they corroborated Gifford's story and supported an investigator's testimony that Chief of Police Sebek, the only other Ashton police officer, had gone home before midnight the night that the murder took place. Just days before the scheduled post-conviction hearing, the police logs were found, necessitating a continuance to allow examination of the logs by forensic experts.

The district court denied Grube any relief on his post-conviction application. The district court [found] that even if it were proven that Officer Brood had written on the log of June 3, 1983, such evidence does little more than prove that he had access to the logs and does not provide any solid footing to conclude that Officer Brood may have murdered Amy Hossner or had access to the police vehicle on that date. [The court also found] that Gifford's conclusions regarding Grube's reactions upon learning of Amy Hossner's murder would not be admissible over an appropriate objection. . . .

Grube contends that the state withheld evidence favorable to him upon a discovery request by the defense. Only after the trial did Grube learn [about] information that contradicted the testimony of the state's primary witness against Grube, put into question the alibi of the other suspect (Brood), and supported Grube's theory of defense that someone else had killed Amy Hossner. This evidence, commonly referred to as *Brady* material, is required to be disclosed if the police or prosecutor possessed the evidence.

Under Brady v. Maryland, 373 U.S. 83 (1963), the prosecution is bound to disclose to the defense all exculpatory evidence known to the state or in its possession. The duty to disclose encompasses impeachment evidence as well as exculpatory evidence. United States v. Bagley, 473 U.S. 667 (1985). In the situation where a general request for *Brady* materials is made and when the exculpatory information in the possession of the prosecutor may be unknown to the defense, the reviewing court must look to the whole record and determine whether "the omitted evidence creates a reasonable doubt that did not otherwise exist." United States v. Agurs, 427 U.S. 97 (1976). "If there is no reasonable doubt about guilt whether or not the additional evidence is considered, there is no justification for a new trial. On the other hand, if the verdict is already of questionable validity, additional evidence of relatively minor importance might be sufficient to create a reasonable doubt."

Suppression by the prosecution of evidence favorable to an accused upon request violates due process where the evidence is material either to guilt or to punishment, irrespective of the good faith or bad faith of the prosecution. Evidence is material if there is a reasonable probability that, had the evidence been disclosed to the defense, the result of the proceeding would have been different. A reasonable probability is a probability sufficient to undermine confidence in the outcome. As the Supreme Court elaborated in Kyles v. Whitley, 514 U.S. 419 (1995), "the question is not whether the defendant would more likely than not have received a different verdict with the evidence, but whether in its absence he received a fair trial, understood as a trial resulting in a verdict worthy of confidence."

In a recent decision, the United States Supreme Court further explained the holding of *Kyles,* stating that "the materiality inquiry is not just a matter of determining whether, after discounting the inculpatory evidence in light of the undisclosed evidence, the remaining evidence is sufficient to support the jury's conclusions. Rather, the question is whether the favorable evidence could reasonably be taken to put the whole case in such a different light as to undermine confidence in the verdict." Strickler v. Greene, 527 U.S. 263 (1999). Therefore, we examine the withheld evidence in Grube's case to determine whether it substantially undermined confidence in the outcome of the jury's verdict, thus entitling Grube to a reversal of his conviction and a new trial.

Lynn Gifford testified . . . that he learned of the murder the following morning at a convenience store in Ashton where he went on his break from the potato warehouse where he and Grube worked. When he returned to work, he told Grube and others of the murder that had taken place the night before. Gifford testified that Grube fell to his knees, exclaiming "Oh, God!" and that he appeared to be sincerely upset and sad upon learning of Amy's death. Gifford then testified that Grube left work, feeling sick, and went home thereafter. In addition to this information, Gifford testified that he had also told the state investigator in 1991 that, on the night of the murder, he had seen Steven Brood pass by in the police vehicle between 2:00 and 2:30 A.M. He testified that the investigator did not want to hear about Officer Brood, only about Rauland Grube.

Grube argues that the district court erred when it found that the contents of the Gifford interview were only marginally relevant, did not impeach the testimony of any witness critical to the state's case, and did not undermine confidence in the jury's verdict. Grube contends that Gifford's testimony about Grube's reaction to the news of Amy Hossner's death would have provided the defense with evidence to rebut Brenda Fredericksen Briggs' testimony at trial which suggested that Grube had been with Amy the night of the murder and had personal knowledge that she had been killed.

The information contained in the statement from Gifford that was withheld from Grube was information which the jury had already heard when the tape of Grube's interview with the police was played during the trial. On the tape, Grube indicated that it was Gifford who had told him about the murder and that the news had made him sick such that he did not return to work after his break. For Gifford to testify to these same observations would present cumulative evidence. When nondisclosed evidence is merely cumulative of other evidence, no *Brady* violation occurs. This evidence from Gifford, had it been disclosed, would not have led to a different result and would not have cast the entire case in such a different light as to undermine confidence in the verdict.

Grube argues that the Gifford evidence relating to Officer Brood's whereabouts at the approximate time of the murder suggested that Brood may have committed the murder. Grube claims that the withheld evidence was material because it undermined the testimony of the state's "Brood alibi" witness (Investigator Watts) who testified that Brood reported spending the night of the murder at his girlfriend's house in Ashton until 1:00 A.M., after which he went home and stayed there the rest of the night. The evidence also called into question the police logs from the night of the murder, which appeared to have been altered and which supported the defense theory that Brood had committed the murder and that his involvement was being covered up.

This information was explored at the hearing on the post-conviction application. Gifford gave details about seeing Officer Brood on the night of the murder. He indicated that he was sixteen years old in June of 1983. He related that he was in his car with a friend, visiting with two other friends in another car, in the parking lot of the REA store across from the Circle K in Ashton between 2:00 and 2:30 A.M. when he noticed a police vehicle approach from the west on Idaho Street, then turn north on Seventh Street. Gifford testified that when the police car stopped at the stop sign, Gifford could see that it was Officer Brood in the vehicle which was lit by the street light. The officer looked at the cars with the teens, then left and was not seen again that night which, according to Gifford, was unusual because the police usually stayed around until the teenagers dispersed and went home. Gifford testified that he had no doubt that it was Officer Brood in the police car, whom he not only saw and recognized but who, in terms of physical size was a much smaller man than Chief Sebek, the only other policeman on the Ashton police force.

Chief Sebek testified in the post-conviction proceeding that he, not Officer Brood, was on duty the night of the murder and . . . that he had filled out the log sheets at the police station showing that he was the officer on duty and that his shift ended at 2:30 A.M. Chief Sebek also related that he had written a traffic ticket at 1:59 A.M., again showing that he, not Officer Brood, was on duty and patrolling in the town's only police car.

The district court concluded that the information from Gifford, which the court found had been suppressed by the state, was not material in view of the other evidence upon which Grube was convicted. Even if believed, Gifford's observations only established that Officer Brood was out later the night of the murder than he claimed and that he and Chief Sebek either were mistaken or lied about their activities that night. Although the defense argued that the jury could have inferred from Gifford's testimony that Officer Brood was involved in the murder, the testimony does not exonerate Grube. Gifford's testimony does not significantly impeach the truthfulness of any prosecution witness who provided incriminating evidence against Grube at his trial, nor does it impair the incriminating quality of such testimony. Gifford's testimony did not contradict the physical evidence of tool marks on Grube's gun and the window through which the fatal shot was fired or the pellets in Amy's body that came from the same batch as the unfired shells that were found in Grube's possession. Those items of evidence do not change regardless of Gifford's version of the events and any records shown in the police logs. Nor does the Gifford testimony weaken the overall case against Grube, which included testimony from a parade of witnesses about Grube's obsession with Amy Hossner and statements made by Grube that Amy had rearranged the furniture in her bedroom and that the shooter never meant to kill her. The evidence from Gifford, which was withheld, does not as a matter of law raise a reasonable doubt as to Grube's guilt that did not otherwise exist in the evidence presented at Grube's trial, which compels us to uphold the district court's ruling on materiality. Accordingly, the nondisclosure of the Gifford testimony, because it was not material and would not have changed the outcome of the trial, does not entitle Grube to post-conviction relief for the alleged *Brady* violation.

Until the Gifford testimony was developed, the relevance of the police logs for the night of Amy Hossner's murder was not readily apparent. The logs were examined to verify which officer was on duty and which officer had filled in the daily log and could have been used to argue to the jury that not only did Officer Brood commit the murder, but he was involved in a coverup to hide his involvement. The state argues that only the testimony of the forensic expert who examined the police logs, not the logs themselves, could be considered exculpatory. Since the expert testimony that related to the police logs was not in the possession of the prosecution, the state properly asserts that such evidence could not be deemed withheld or in any way suppressed by the state in contravention of *Brady* principles. . . .

Lynn Gifford's interview with the state investigator in 1991 was improperly withheld by the state in response to the defense's request for exculpatory information under *Brady*. The withheld evidence, however, does not raise a reasonable doubt about Grube's guilt that did not previously exist. . . . Therefore, the district court properly concluded that Grube was not entitled to relief under the standards applicable to undisclosed evidence. . . .

KIDWELL, J., dissenting.

Upon review of withheld evidence, doctored police logs, evidence that suspiciously appeared after several years, and the absence of convincing direct proof, my confidence in the original jury verdict has been undermined. Mr. Grube did not receive the fair trial to which he is entitled under our constitutional system. Therefore I respectfully dissent.

It should be noted at the outset that the evidence at trial linking Grube to Amy's shooting was scant. The prosecution's case rested on two grounds. First, the prosecution showed that Grube, who had some psychological problems, obsessed about Amy for years *after* her death.[2] Second, the prosecution attempted to link Grube's

2. The prosecution introduced evidence that Amy had, for several months before her death, received strange and distressing phone calls from a man. The prosecution failed to show, however, that Grube made these calls. Indeed, Briggs testified that Amy had told her, in the months before her death,

shotgun to the scene of the shooting. It attempted to make this link by demonstrating that Grube's shotgun had contacted the trim around Amy's window and by showing that the shot pattern produced by Grube's gun was consistent with the shot pattern on Amy.

Key to the prosecution's case was evidence that Grube's shotgun had scraped against the aluminum trim of Amy's window frame. Both the transfers on the gun barrel and the tool marks on the window trim were obvious to every person who examined the evidence in 1991. Investigators had removed the window trim from the Hossners' house late in 1983. The trim was sent to Edward Peterson, a firearms expert at the Bureau of Alcohol, Tobacco, and Firearms (ATF), in November 1983. In 1983, several persons had noticed that the trim had a dent in it. *For eight years, however, none of the city, county, state, or federal investigators working on the Hossner case noticed either the tool marks on the aluminum trim or the aluminum and paint transfers on Grube's shotgun.* Mysteriously, investigators discovered these marks only in 1991 after Briggs's statements to police made Grube a suspect again.

The defense's theory was the police manufactured this evidence sometime after 1983 to pin the blame on Grube and exonerate Steven Brood, an Ashton police officer and an original suspect. Abundant evidence supported this theory:

- In 1983 or 1984, Idaho investigators specifically requested that ATF firearms expert Peterson inspect the suspect guns for brown paint residue. In reply, Peterson told State investigator Jim Mason that he did not find any brown paint on the barrels of any of the suspect guns.
- Peterson examined Grube's shotgun again after the aluminum and paint marks were found in 1991. He testified that he could not reproduce the tool marks by recoil, that the shotgun would have to pivot in an extremely unusual pattern on recoil to receive the transfer, and that he could reproduce the marks on the shotgun only by mechanically scraping the gun barrel with the window trim.
- Ashton Police Chief Sebek testified that he did not see the tool marks on the window frame trim until 1991. He "couldn't believe that [he] didn't see them before." He was surprised to see the tool marks at Grube's preliminary hearing because they looked fresh and he'd never seen them before. Sebek conceded that tool marks on the trim were not visible in pictures taken in 1983. . . .
- Burt Bates, the lead investigator for Fremont County, did not notice any unusual marks, dents, or scratches on Grube's gun when police took possession of the gun in 1983. At that time, he noticed the dent in the window trim, and a place where brown paint was scraped off the trim, but he first saw tool marks in the window trim in 1991. . . .

In addition, the evidence linking the shot pattern of Grube's gun to the shot pattern at the scene was inconclusive at best. The shot that killed Amy went through two panes of glass and a curtain. In 1983, ATF firearms expert Peterson test-fired Grube's shotgun and the two shotguns of Brood. Peterson conducted the test firings

---

that a guy named Jack was calling her on the telephone and scaring her. It is undisputed that Amy and Grube attended the same church and knew each other. Mrs. Hossner testified that Grube made four to six "pointless" phone calls to her in the six months before Amy's death, but he did not mention Amy during these calls. It is difficult to understand why Grube identified himself to Mrs. Hossner if he was concealing his identity from Amy.

through two panes of glass and a curtain. When Peterson compared the shot patterns from his test firings to the pattern in Amy's room, he eliminated Grube's shotgun as the murder weapon but could not eliminate Brood's two guns. When the State began reinvestigating Grube in 1991, its firearms examiner conducted four series of test firings, again using intervening objects. Peterson opined that the State's first three tests were consistent with the results of his own 1983 test firing. On the basis of the State's fourth test on deer necks, conducted *during* the trial, Peterson stated that he could not eliminate Grube's gun, but he emphasized that the pattern differed from the shot pattern on the victim and another test shot was needed. Even though Peterson had testified for the State, the prosecution brought in an FBI firearms expert, Gerald Wilkes, to refute Peterson's equivocal testimony. Wilkes opined that it was not possible to reproduce shot patterns through intervening objects . . . and stated that the shot pattern from his own test firing had "no relevance to the Defendant."

No evidence placed Grube near the scene on the night of the shooting. One neighbor testified to hearing a shotgun blast at 4:24 A.M. the morning of the shooting, followed within a few minutes by a souped-up vehicle starting up and driving off. The prosecution did not attempt to link Grube to any vehicle. Although the State provided some evidence that Grube sometimes walked around town late in the evening, it provided no evidence of Grube ever driving. Grube introduced abundant testimony that he had no access to any vehicles and that none of the family vehicles were "souped-up." No one saw Grube either walking or driving on the night of the shooting. In addition, Grube presented three witnesses who testified that he was in his room, along with his two brothers, from 11:00 P.M. on the night before the shooting until 7:00 A.M. the following morning, and that it was extremely difficult to sneak out of the house unnoticed by his father and brothers.

Further, fingerprint evidence tended to exonerate Grube. On the night of the shooting, electricity in the Hossners' house (but not elsewhere in the neighborhood) was off for forty-five minutes. The electrical box for the Hossners' house was directly outside Amy's window. Seven fingerprints were lifted from the electrical box. Six prints were from persons involved in the investigation, but one suspicious partial print was on the edge of the electrical box. Testifying for the State, fingerprint expert Robert Kerchusky testified that the print was negative as to Grube.

Here, the State withheld evidence that its investigator, Scott Birch, had interviewed Lynn Gifford, who had impeaching and exculpatory information. Gifford impeached the testimony of Brenda Fredrickson Briggs, the witness whose testimony placed Grube outside Amy's bedroom shortly after the shooting. . . . Gifford's testimony also cast serious doubt on Brood's alibi. . . . Gifford noted that Brood departed from his usual late-night routine in dealing with juveniles. He emphasized that he knew both of Ashton's police officers well by sight and that he had clearly recognized the officer in the patrol car as being Brood. As a direct result of Gifford's testimony, defense counsel reexamined prosecution documents. This led to the discovery that police logs for the night of the shooting had been altered. . . .

The duty to disclose encompasses impeachment as well as exculpatory evidence, and evidence known only to police as well as that known by prosecutors. Strickler v. Greene, 527 U.S. 263 (1999). The U.S. Supreme Court recently clarified:

> There are three components of a true *Brady* violation: The evidence at issue must be favorable to the accused, either because it is exculpatory, or because it is impeaching;

that evidence must have been suppressed by the State, either willfully or inadvertently; and prejudice must have ensued.

To show prejudice, it is not enough to show that it made a defendant's conviction more likely than if the withheld evidence had been used, or that "discrediting a witness's testimony might have changed the outcome of the trial." The question is not whether the defendant would more likely than not have received a different verdict with the evidence, but whether in its absence he received a fair trial, understood as a trial resulting in a verdict worthy of confidence. . . .

In conclusion, it is my opinion that Rauland Grube was convicted of murder based on possibly doctored physical evidence, on inconclusive test-firing evidence, and on evidence that Grube had an unhealthy obsession with Amy after her death. Gifford's direct evidence impeached several key prosecution witnesses, put another suspect, who was a policeman, near the murder scene, and led to the discovery that the police logs for the night of the shooting had been doctored. The possibility that police lied on the witness stand and doctored the police logs undermines the validity of the physical evidence linking Grube to the shooting. Combined with the weakness of the other evidence presented in the trial, this is enough to undermine confidence in the original verdict. Therefore, the State's suppression of the Gifford evidence meets *Strickler*'s prejudice prong, and the case should be sent back to give Mr. Grube a fair trial.

■ HAWAII PENAL PROCEDURE RULE 16

(b) Disclosure by the Prosecution.

(1) Disclosure of Matters Within Prosecution's Possession. The prosecutor shall disclose to the defendant or the defendant's attorney the following material and information within the prosecutor's possession or control: . . . (vii) any material or information which tends to negate the guilt of the defendant as to the offense charged or would tend to reduce the defendant's punishment therefor.

(2) Disclosure of Matters Not Within Prosecution's Possession. Upon written request of defense counsel and specific designation by defense counsel of material or information which would be discoverable if in the possession or control of the prosecutor and which is in the possession or control of other governmental personnel, the prosecutor shall use diligent good faith efforts to cause such material or information to be made available to defense counsel; and if the prosecutor's efforts are unsuccessful the court shall issue suitable subpoenas or orders to cause such material or information to be made available to defense counsel. . . .

(d) Discretionary Disclosure. Upon a showing of materiality and if the request is reasonable, the court in its discretion may require disclosure as provided for in this Rule 16 in cases other than those in which the defendant is charged with a felony, but not in cases involving violations.

(e) Regulation of Discovery.

(1) Performance of Obligations. Except for matters which are to be specifically designated in writing by defense counsel under this rule, the prosecution shall disclose all materials subject to disclosure pursuant to subsection (b)(1) of this rule to the defendant or the defendant's attorney within ten calendar days following arraignment and plea of the defendant. The parties may perform their

obligations of disclosure in any manner mutually agreeable to the parties or by notifying the attorney for the other party that material and information, described in general terms, may be inspected, obtained, tested, copied or photographed at specified reasonable times and places.

(2) Continuing Duty of Disclose. If subsequent to compliance with these rules or orders entered pursuant to these rules, a party discovers additional material or information which would have been subject to disclosure pursuant to this Rule 16, that party shall promptly disclose the additional material or information, and if the additional material or information is discovered during trial, the court shall be notified.

■ UTAH CRIMINAL PROCEDURE RULE 16

(a) Except as otherwise provided, the prosecutor shall disclose to the defense upon request the following material or information of which he has knowledge: . . . (4) evidence known to the prosecutor that tends to negate the guilt of the accused, mitigate the guilt of the defendant, or mitigate the degree of the offense for reduced punishment. . . .

(b) The prosecutor shall make all disclosures as soon as practicable following the filing of charges and before the defendant is required to plead. The prosecutor has a continuing duty to make disclosure.

Notes

1. *Evidence favorable to the accused: majority position.* The Supreme Court decision in Brady v. Maryland, 373 U.S. 83 (1963), remains central to discovery practice in American criminal justice. Because the disclosure duty described in *Brady* is a requirement of federal due process, it applies in every criminal case unless the defendant expressly waives the disclosure. As illustrated by the Hawaii and Utah rules reprinted above, over 40 states have passed rules or statutes codifying the *Brady* disclosure requirement, although many of these rules and statutes (unlike the constitutional requirement) only take effect after a request from the defense. See Ohio R. Crim. P. 16(A) (disclosure upon defendant's request).

Defendants often win *Brady* claims that are appealed in the state courts, at least when those claims are the focus of the appeal (as opposed to one in a laundry list of claims, especially in capital cases). Sometimes defendants win in cases where the *Brady* evidence is far weaker than in *Grube.* See, e.g., State v. Higgins, 788 So. 2d 238 (Fla. 2001) (prosecutors failed to turn over a statement by a minor witness that a prosecution witness might herself have been seen driving the victim's vehicle). But *Brady* claims appear to be appealed infrequently, so the relative success of defendants in this context says little if anything about the nature of *Brady* claims and discovery practice in the mine run of cases.

2. *Exculpatory or impeachment evidence in government hands.* The defendant who seeks dismissal of charges because of a *Brady* violation need not show bad faith by the prosecutor. The prosecutor does not even have to know about the evidence that must be disclosed: Evidence in the hands of government agents (such as criminal investigators) who regularly report to the prosecutor can be the basis for a *Brady*

violation because the prosecutor has a duty to inquire about such information. See Kyles v. Whitley, 514 U.S. 419 (1995); Commonwealth v. Burke, 781 A.2d 1136 (Pa. 2001) (obligation extends to exculpatory evidence in files of police agencies of the same government bringing the prosecution); Stanley Z. Fisher, The Prosecutor's Ethical Duty to Seek Exculpatory Evidence in Police Hands: Lessons from England, 68 Fordham L. Rev. 1379 (2000) (police in England must comply with specific legislation requiring record keeping and regular notification of prosecutors about exculpatory evidence; prosecutors and police in U.S. left to make their own arrangements for tracking exculpatory evidence).

Does "exculpatory" material only include evidence that could be admitted at trial? Suppose a prosecutor learns about facts to suggest that the key evidence in a case was obtained through an illegal search. Must the prosecutor disclose the facts about the search under *Brady?* Compare People v. Jones, 375 N.E.2d 41 (N.Y. 1978) (*Brady* does not require disclosure of fact that prosecution witness died).

3. *Materiality of exculpatory evidence.* The major limit on the *Brady* disclosure duty is the requirement that the undisclosed evidence be "material" to the defense. Under federal law, all *Brady* violations share a uniform materiality standard: The defendant must show a "reasonable probability" that the verdict would have been different if the prosecution had disclosed the exculpatory evidence. State courts have split over the proper materiality standard. See Strickler v. Greene, 527 U.S. 263 (1999) (prosecutors failed to disclose materials casting doubt on testimony of an eyewitness to alleged crime; because of evidence of guilt independent of eyewitness testimony, failure to disclose did not create a "reasonable probability" of different outcome at trial). How might you apply this standard in the context of guilty pleas?

About 30 states have adopted the federal "uniform" standard, but a strong minority (including New York) have granted defendants a more favorable materiality standard in cases where the defense makes specific requests for the information. People v. Vilardi, 555 N.E.2d 915 (N.Y. 1990); Roberts v. State, 881 P.2d 1 (Nev. 1994) (collecting cases). Does a specific request for discovery from the defense change the legitimate expectations of both parties? Is "materiality" linked to party expectations? Note also that many state rules of criminal procedure (like the Utah rule reprinted above), include something similar to the *Brady* disclosure duty without including any materiality requirement; most of these rules, however, depend on a request from the defense.

Who should carry the burden of proof on the question of whether the withheld evidence was material? On questions of ineffective assistance of counsel under Strickland v. Washington, 466 U.S. 668 (1984), the defense carries the burden of showing prejudice; the prosecution carries the burden of proving that errors were "harmless" in most other settings. Because a failure to disclose under *Brady* is more within the control of the prosecution than ineffective assistance of counsel, does this mean that the burden should rest with the government? Surprisingly few courts have addressed this question directly. Most (but not all) courts simply assume without discussion that the burden lies on the defendant. See State v. Anderson, 410 N.W.2d 231 (Iowa 1987) (places burden on defendant); State v. Williamson, 562 A.2d 470 (Conn. 1987) (burden on government).

4. Brady *and plea bargaining.* While *Brady* information might affect the outcome at trial, it could also affect the negotiating strength of the defendant during plea bargaining. Given the dominance of guilty pleas and plea bargaining in American criminal justice, it is critical to know whether a defendant can challenge the validity

of a guilty plea if she discovers later that the prosecutor failed to disclose *Brady* material. A few states have statutes or rules that explicitly link the prosecutor's disclosure obligation to a defendant's not-guilty plea at arraignment. See N.H. Super. Ct. R. 98 (prosecutor to disclose exculpatory material within 30 days from a not-guilty plea). The U.S. Supreme Court has never addressed this question, and the state courts and lower federal courts are split. See Gibson v. State, 514 S.E.2d 320, 324 (S.C. 1999) (*Brady* violation automatically renders plea invalid); State v. Martin, 495 A.2d 1028 (Conn. 1985) (*Brady* claim barred by guilty plea). See generally, Corinna Barrett Lain, Accuracy Where It Matters: Brady v. Maryland in the Plea Bargaining Context, 80 Wash. U. L.Q. 1 (2002); Kevin C. McMunigal, Disclosure and Accuracy in the Guilty Plea Process, 40 Hastings L.J. 957 (1989).

5. *Access to confidential information.* Who decides whether information in the possession of the government is exculpatory and material and therefore subject to disclosure? If the prosecutor is not to make the decision alone, can the judge rule on the question without an adversarial hearing and input from both sides? At least when the information that the defense seeks is confidential under some other provision of law, the judge (under federal law) can make the discovery ruling without an adversarial hearing. The Court in Pennsylvania v. Ritchie, 480 U.S. 39 (1987), approved of an in camera review of the confidential files of the state child welfare department to determine the exculpatory and material nature of any information in them. Again, a strong minority of the states addressing this question have struck out on their own path. See Commonwealth v. Lloyd, 567 A.2d 1357 (Pa. 1989) (requiring access to psychotherapeutic files of victim). Does the judge need input from defense counsel to determine whether evidence is exculpatory and material? Can a judge effectively protect confidential information by preventing its disclosure at trial?

6. *Preservation of evidence.* It is often said that the duty to disclose evidence would be meaningless if the prosecutor were free to destroy evidence. Is this true? The Supreme Court has addressed the government's obligation, under the due process clause, to preserve some types of evidence. In California v. Trombetta, 467 U.S. 479 (1984), two defendants accused of drunken driving submitted to breath analysis tests, and the tests showed a blood-alcohol concentration high enough to presume intoxication. Each defendant tried to suppress the test results because the police (who were following their standard procedure) failed to preserve the breath samples. The Supreme Court rejected the defendants' arguments because the police discarded the samples "in good faith and in accord with normal practice." The *Trombetta* court also observed that the chances were slim that the defendants could have exposed inaccuracies in the breath analysis test, and a state's constitutional duty to preserve evidence can be applied only to "evidence that might be expected to play a significant role in the suspect's case."

In Arizona v. Youngblood, 488 U.S. 51 (1988), the police failed to preserve semen samples from the victim's body and clothing. The defendant accused of child molestation and sexual assault argued that he could have performed tests on the samples that might have established his defense of mistaken identity. However, the Supreme Court noted that the state did not attempt to use the materials in its own case in chief, and it limited the government's duty to preserve evidence as follows:

> [R]equiring a defendant to show bad faith on the part of the police both limits the extent of the police's obligation to preserve evidence to reasonable bounds and confines it to that class of cases where the interests of justice most clearly require it, i.e., those

> cases in which the police themselves by their conduct indicate that the evidence could form a basis for exonerating the defendant. We therefore hold that unless a criminal defendant can show bad faith on the part of the police, failure to preserve potentially useful evidence does not constitute a denial of due process of law.

Once again, there is dissension among state courts on an important aspect of this discovery issue. Most states directly addressing the question have accepted the holding in *Youngblood.* About a dozen states, however, have declared that bad faith is not a necessary part of the defendant's showing because the destruction of evidence often reflects some negligence by the government and because the evidence could sometimes be crucial to the defense. In State v. Morales, 657 A.2d 585 (Conn. 1995), the court held that a trial judge, in determining what consequences should flow from the government's breach of its duty, should consider (1) the degree of negligence or bad faith involved, (2) the importance of the missing evidence in light of the remaining evidence, and (3) the sufficiency of the other evidence to sustain the conviction. See also State v. Ferguson, 2 S.W.3d 912 (Tenn. 1999). Why do state courts seem so willing to part ways with the Supreme Court on constitutional questions involving discovery? Do the state courts take more responsibility for their own litigation management, in light of the state's needs and practices?

The preservation of evidence has made a critical difference in more cases lately as DNA testing procedures become available. These tests make it possible to reevaluate the convictions of some defendants in cases (such as rape and murder cases) where blood or other biological material from the perpetrator is available at the crime scene or from the victim. The incentive to test this material and to match it to the convicted defendant is very strong in capital cases, and a few capital defendants have been released on the basis of DNA test information. See Roger Parloff, Gone But Not Forgotten, The American Lawyer, Jan./Feb. 1999 (discussing ruling by Virginia courts allowing prosecutors to destroy evidence of executed defendant prior to DNA testing).

7. *Disclosing false testimony.* Over the years, the U.S. Supreme Court has said that prosecutors must correct any false testimony presented by prosecution witnesses at trial. See Alcorta v. Texas, 355 U.S. 28 (1957). This can include false statements about any lenient treatment the witness expects to receive from the government as a result of cooperating as a witness. See Giglio v. United States, 405 U.S. 150 (1972) (reversal required when witness denied any arrangement for lenient treatment; promise came from another prosecutor, unknown to government attorney at trial). The test for materiality under *Giglio* is whether there is a "reasonable probability" that the false evidence may have affected the judgment of the jury. Even if the prosecution does not lie on the witness stand about any promise of leniency, the existence of such deals with witnesses typically qualifies as *Brady* material. See State v. Bowie, 813 So. 2d 377 (La. 2002).

8. *The extent of disclosure violations.* How often do prosecutors and defense attorneys fail to disclose the information that they should to the opposing party? Periodic newspaper reports on "prosecutorial misconduct" focus on discovery violations; they suggest (inconclusively) that discovery violations by prosecutors occur regularly. The *Chicago Tribune* conducted an ambitious analysis of nationwide court records in 1999. It found records of 381 reversals of homicide cases since 1963, due to prosecutors concealing exculpatory evidence or using false evidence at trial. While this was an extremely small percentage of the homicide convictions during this time, the

report notes that such violations are difficult to document and rarely lead to reversals of a conviction. See Ken Armstrong and Maurice Possley, The Verdict: Dishonor, Chicago Tribune, Jan. 8, 1999; see also Cris Carmody, The *Brady* Rule: Is It Working? National L.J., May 17, 1993, at 30.

Prosecutors' offices sometimes evaluate the performance of their own attorneys and create systems to sanction wrongdoers and to train less experienced attorneys to avoid discovery violations. One such mechanism is the Office for Professional Responsibility (OPR) within the U.S. Department of Justice. A spate of news reports has argued that OPR has been ineffective in countering a "win at all costs" mentality among federal prosecutors. See Special Report: OPR in Transition, 4 No. 1 DOJ Alert 3 (Jan. 3-17, 1994); Jim McGee, Prosecutor Oversight Is Often Hidden from Sight, Washington Post, Jan. 15, 1993, at A1. How would you measure in a reliable way whether prosecutors are now committing more discovery violations than in the past? If such a trend were proven, could it be traced to the number of new prosecutors hired in a given time period?

9. *Remedies for prosecutorial disclosure violations.* As we have seen, courts might reverse criminal convictions if the prosecutor fails to disclose material information when required by law. Will the state bar authorities also sanction prosecutors who violate their legal obligations to disclose information, even when the evidence is not material? Examples of disciplinary proceedings against prosecutors for discovery violations do get reported from time to time. See Disciplinary Counsel v. Jones, 613 N.E. 2d 178 (Ohio 1993) (prosecutor's failure to turn over two exhibits tending to establish defendant's self-defense argument resulted in prosecutor's suspension from practice for six months). However, state bar authorities discipline criminal prosecutors far less often than they discipline private attorneys. One survey of state bar records revealed that criminal attorneys (both prosecutors and defense attorneys) are sanctioned far less often than attorneys in civil practice, and that discipline rarely occurs after a "first offense." See Fred C. Zacharias, The Professional Discipline of Prosecutors, 79 N.C. L. Rev. 721 (2001). What might explain the relatively infrequent disciplinary actions against criminal prosecutors?

Problem 15-3. Preserving Evidence

Kanju Osakalumi and several other residents of New York City traveled to the home of Allison Charlton in Bluefield, West Virginia, bringing with them an assortment of drugs and firearms. On the afternoon of June 14, 1991, one of the persons from New York City, Chandel Fleetwood, died from a single gunshot wound to the head, fired from his own revolver. Osakalumi and others who were present took the body to a wooded area approximately one mile away. They also disposed of the victim's revolver and a bloodied cushion from the couch where the victim had been sitting. The following day, Osakalumi and his friends returned to New York City.

Officers from the Bluefield Police Department soon began hearing rumors that someone had been shot at the Charlton home. In January 1992, about seven months after Fleetwood's death, two detectives visited the home. Upon observing a stained couch, the detectives took samples from it and from the carpet surrounding it. Approximately two months later, police officers returned to the Charlton home, and inspected the couch again. This time, they discovered a bullet hole in it. Detective Ted Jones inserted a writing pen into the bullet hole to determine the trajectory of the bullet. He extracted a badly deformed bullet as well as some hair and bone fragments. The officers confiscated the couch and stored it at the police department.

The couch gave off an unpleasant odor and was both a fire and health hazard. As a result, the police (with the consent of the prosecutor's office) soon disposed of the couch at the county landfill. The police did not measure either the proportions of the couch, the location of the bullet hole in the couch, or the trajectory of the bullet. Neither did they photograph the couch or the bullet hole.

In May 1993, almost two years after Fleetwood's death, a passerby discovered his skeletal remains in the woods. After the Bluefield police completed their investigation, Osakalumi was arrested in New York. He claimed that Fleetwood was under the influence of marijuana when he loaded one round of ammunition into his own revolver, spun the cylinder, put it to his own head and shot himself. Osakalumi said that he and the others in the house panicked and disposed of the body and the revolver in a nearby wooded area.

The only evidence that Fleetwood had been murdered was the trial testimony of Dr. Irvin Sopher, medical examiner for the state of West Virginia. Dr. Sopher testified that in March 1992, approximately nine months after Fleetwood's death but approximately 14 months before his body was found, Detective Ted Jones delivered to him the bullet, blood samples, and bone fragments. In addition, Detective Jones drew for Dr. Sopher a diagram of the couch, along with the location of the bullet hole and the position of the bullet when officers found it.

Although Jones's diagram of the couch was lost, Dr. Sopher drew Detective Jones's couch diagram from memory at trial. Dr. Sopher testified that based upon examination of the skull and the purported right-to-left, straight-line trajectory of the bullet through the couch, the manner of Fleetwood's death was homicide. Dr. Sopher testified that he came to this conclusion when he lined up the trajectory of the bullet through the skull with the right-to-left path of the bullet through the couch, as drawn by Detective Jones. Dr. Sopher determined that Fleetwood was held down on the couch and was shot through the head, with the bullet traveling in a straight line.

The jury convicted Osakalumi of first-degree murder. On appeal he claims that the trial court erred when it allowed Dr. Sopher to testify based on the condition of the couch. As the appellate court judge, how do you rule? Compare State v. Osakalumi, 461 S.E.2d 504 (W. Va. 1995).

2. *Defense Disclosures*

The trend over the past several decades has been toward broader criminal discovery rights for both the defense and the prosecution. The most potent arguments against expanding discovery at each juncture have pointed to some necessary limits on defense disclosures. There may be constitutional difficulties in forcing a defendant to disclose certain information to the prosecution. Among other things, forced disclosure might be considered self-incrimination in violation of the constitutional privilege. Faced with this sort of barrier, prosecutors have resisted the general expansion of criminal discovery on the basis of litigation fairness. If the defendant does not have to disclose evidence, prosecutors argue, then neither should they.

In the end, the arguments for limiting criminal discovery have lost more often than they have won — in part because the constitutional problems with compelling the defendant to disclose evidence have turned out to be surprisingly small. Where the Constitution has created no barrier, both defense and prosecution disclosures have increased.

If the Constitution will stop only a few types of defense disclosures, what are other possible grounds for evaluating discovery innovations? Are there some types of information that the prosecution will not develop if the defendant does not provide it? What, if anything, do we gain from a truly adversarial system of developing and presenting evidence?

■ PENNSYLVANIA RULE OF CRIMINAL PROCEDURE 573(C)

(1) Mandatory.

(a) A defendant who intends to offer the defense of alibi at trial shall [file a notice before trial] specifying intention to claim such defense. Such notice shall contain specific information as to the place or places where the defendant claims to have been at the time of the alleged offense and the names and addresses of witnesses whom the defendant intends to call in support of such claim.

(b) A defendant who intends to offer at trial the defense of insanity, or a claim of mental infirmity, shall [file a notice before trial] specifying intention to claim such defense. Such notice shall contain specific available information as to the nature and extent of the alleged insanity or claim of mental infirmity, the period of time which the defendant allegedly suffered from such insanity or mental infirmity, and the names and addresses of witnesses, expert or otherwise, whom the defendant intends to call at trial to establish such defense.

(c) Within 7 days after service of such notice of alibi defense or of insanity or claim of mental infirmity defense, or within such other time as allowed by the court upon cause shown, the attorney for the Commonwealth shall disclose to the defendant the names and addresses of all persons the Commonwealth intends to call as witnesses to disprove or discredit the defendant's claim of alibi or of insanity or mental infirmity. . . .

(2) Discretionary with the Court.

(a) In all court cases, if the Commonwealth files a motion for pretrial discovery, upon a showing of materiality to the preparation of the Commonwealth's case and that the request is reasonable, the court may order the defendant, subject to the defendant's rights against compulsory self- incrimination, to allow the attorney for the Commonwealth to inspect and copy or photograph any of the following requested items:

(i) results or reports of physical or mental examinations, and of scientific tests or experiments made in connection with the particular case, or copies thereof, within the possession or control of the defendant, that the defendant intends to introduce as evidence in chief, or were prepared by a witness whom the defendant intends to call at the trial, when results or reports relate to the testimony of that witness, provided the defendant has requested and received discovery [of comparable material from the Commonwealth]; and

(ii) the names and addresses of eyewitnesses whom the defendant intends to call in its case in chief, provided that the defendant has previously requested and received discovery [of comparable material from the Commonwealth].

(b) If an expert whom the defendant intends to call in any proceeding has not prepared a report of examination or tests, the court, upon motion, may order that the expert prepare and the defendant disclose a report stating the subject matter on which the expert is expected to testify; the substance of the facts to which the expert is expected to testify; and a summary of the expert's opinions and the grounds for each opinion.

■ STATE v. JOHN LUCIOUS

518 S.E.2d 677 (Ga. 1999)

HUNSTEIN, J.

The State is seeking imposition of the death penalty against John R. Lucious for the murder of Mohammad A. Aftab in Clayton County. Lucious was indicted on charges of malice murder, two counts of felony murder, possession of a firearm during the commission of a felony, and misdemeanor possession of marijuana in connection with the alleged 1996 murder and armed robbery. During pretrial proceedings, the State refused to open its file except to the extent mandated by the Georgia and United States Constitutions because Lucious elected not to participate in Georgia's Criminal Procedure Discovery Act, OCGA §17-16-1 et seq. Lucious filed an omnibus motion seeking an order of the trial court declaring the Act unconstitutional. The trial court denied the motion but granted Lucious the unilateral right to discover specific material, including the State's trial witness list, scientific reports, and scientific work product. [The] State filed an application to appeal asserting that Lucious was not entitled to the pretrial discovery information granted by the trial court because of his election not to participate in the Act.

Prior to passage of the Act, there was no comprehensive Georgia statute or rule of law which governed discovery in criminal cases. Enacted in 1994, the Act [provides] for the "comprehensive regulation of discovery and inspection in criminal cases [and repeals] conflicting laws." . . . Ga. L. 1994, pp.1895-1896. The Act, which applies only to those cases in which the defendant elects by written notice to have it apply, broadens discovery in felony cases by imposing corresponding discovery obligations upon both the defendant and the State. For example, the Act requires the State and the defendant to disclose, inter alia, the identities and addresses of all persons they intend to call as witnesses at trial, relevant written or recorded statements of all witnesses, and scientific reports, physical or mental reports, and other evidence intended for use at trial or evidence obtained from or that belongs to the defendant regardless of whether the State intends to use such evidence at trial. The Act also [provides] for discovery of a custodial statement and [requires] notice of an intent to offer an alibi defense and a list of witnesses to be offered to rebut the defense of alibi. These provisions reveal that the Act provides a comprehensive scheme of reciprocal discovery in criminal felony cases. . . .

Lucious contends the Act's discovery provisions violate his right to due process under the United States and Georgia Constitutions. We disagree. In Wardius v. Oregon, 412 U.S. 470 (1973), the Supreme Court held that under the due process clause a defendant cannot be compelled to disclose to the State evidence or witnesses to be offered in support of an alibi defense absent reciprocal discovery of the State's rebuttal witnesses. The *Wardius* Court reviewed its earlier decision in Williams v. Florida, 399 U.S. 78 (1970), which upheld Florida's notice-of-alibi statute because such statute provided reciprocal discovery, and stated:

> [a]lthough the Due Process Clause has little to say regarding the amount of discovery which the parties must be afforded, it does speak to the balance of forces between the accused and his accuser. The Williams Court was therefore careful to note that "Florida law provides for liberal discovery by the defendant against the State, and [Florida's] notice-of-alibi rule is itself carefully hedged with reciprocal duties requiring state disclosure to the defendant." . . . We do not suggest that the Due Process Clause of its own force requires [a state] to adopt [reciprocal discovery] provisions. But we do hold that in the absence of a strong showing of state interests to the contrary, discovery must be a two-way street. [412 U.S. at 474-75.]

The Court in *Wardius* thus articulated a due process requirement of reciprocity in criminal discovery statutes in the absence of a strong state interest to the contrary. This same requirement has been held to apply under the due process clause of the Georgia Constitution. See Rower v. State, 443 S.E.2d 839 (Ga. 1994) (to satisfy due process, discovery practices in criminal cases must provide a balance of forces between the defendant and the State). Applying this due process standard to the Act, we find that the Act furthers legitimate State interests by establishing a closely symmetrical scheme of discovery in criminal cases that maximizes the presentation of reliable evidence, minimizes the risk that a judgment will be predicated on incomplete or misleading evidence, and fosters fairness and efficiency in criminal proceedings. Because the Act provides for reciprocal discovery in criminal felony cases with any imbalance favoring the defendant, the Act does not violate the due process clause of the United States or Georgia Constitutions.

Nor do the Act's discovery provisions violate Lucious's right to confrontation. The right to confrontation is a "trial right," guaranteeing a defendant the ability to confront and question adverse witnesses at trial. See Pennsylvania v. Ritchie, 480 U.S. 39, 52-53 (1987). As a trial right, it "does not include the power to require the pretrial disclosure of any and all information that might be useful in contradicting unfavorable testimony," id. at 53, and does not guarantee "cross-examination that is effective in whatever way, and to whatever extent, the defense might wish." Delaware v. Fensterer, 474 U.S. 15, 20 (1985). Because the confrontation clause guarantees only the right to confront and cross-examine those individuals called to testify against a defendant at trial and the pretrial discovery provisions of the Act do not implicate or infringe upon such right, we find no merit to this argument.

[Lucious argues further] that the Act's reciprocal discovery provisions violate his right to effective representation of counsel by denying him the benefit of defense counsel's judgment of whether and when to reveal aspects of his case to the State. The Act simply requires disclosure of witnesses and evidence a defendant intends to introduce at trial as part of a reciprocal discovery process. The United States Supreme Court has affirmed the right of states to experiment with systems of broad discovery designed to aid in the administration of justice and to enhance the fairness of the adversary system. That the Act provides for discovery before trial rather than after a witness has testified is of no constitutional significance. See United States v. Nobles, 422 U.S. 225, 241 (1975) ("[t]he Sixth Amendment does not confer the right to present testimony free from the legitimate demands of the adversarial system").

Because there is no general constitutional right to discovery in a criminal case, the election not to invoke the discovery provisions of the Act necessarily entitles a defendant to only that discovery specifically afforded by the Georgia and United

States Constitutions, statutory exceptions to the Act, and non-conflicting rules of court. This panoply of discovery rights exists separately from the Act and provides abundant discovery opportunities for all criminal defendants, including death penalty defendants, who elect not to have the Act apply to their case. We therefore find that the trial court erred in granting Lucious those discovery rights identified below which are not guaranteed under the United States or Georgia Constitutions or otherwise provided for by statute or court rule.

Specifically, the trial court erred by holding that a defendant who chooses not to participate in the Act is entitled to discover all of the State's scientific reports. In a broadly-worded order the trial court directed the State to produce its Georgia Bureau of Investigation "Crime Lab reports and any and all other scientific reports." A defendant's right to discover scientific reports is a procedural right derived from former OCGA §17-7-211, a statute expressly repealed by passage of the Act. Procedural rights which flow from a repealed criminal discovery statute can be eliminated. In order to obtain discovery of scientific reports, therefore, a defendant must elect to proceed under the provisions of the Act.

For the same reasons, we find the trial court erred in holding that a defendant who chooses not to opt into the Act is entitled to discover all of the State's scientific work product. The trial court's order provides that the State must produce "any and all . . . memos, notes, graphs, computer print-outs, photographs, and other data that the State's experts will rely on to support their testimony during direct examination." To the extent such information may be discoverable in felony criminal cases, its production is now governed by the Act and a defendant is entitled to this information only if he invokes the Act. Because the right to subpoena work product was derived from former OCGA §17-7-211 and is not a substantive right apart from the discovery provisions of the Act, [defendants may not] unilaterally obtain evidence of scientific work product.

The trial court also erred in holding that Lucious was entitled to the witness list provided by Uniform Superior Court Rule 30.3. Rule 30.3 provides that upon request of defense counsel, the State shall furnish the addresses and telephone numbers of trial witnesses known to the State. The Legislature intended, in enacting the Act, to amend the criminal discovery procedures and to provide certain criminal defendants the opportunity to discover information well in excess of that mandated by either the United States or Georgia Constitutions, including the opportunity to receive from the State a continuing list of trial witnesses and related information. Under the Act, a defendant is entitled to a trial witness list and information concerning trial witnesses only if he chooses to have the Act apply, thereby agreeing to the reciprocal discovery provisions of the Act. Because Rule 30.3 conflicts with OCGA §§17-16-3 and 17-16-8 in that it requires the State to furnish a trial witness list without imposing reciprocal discovery obligations upon the defendant, we find the Rule to be unenforceable. Rule 30.3 must yield to the substantive law contained in these statutes.

Although Lucious did not choose to have the Act apply to his case and, therefore, is not entitled to a list of trial witnesses pursuant to Rule 30.3, Lucious remains entitled to a list of witnesses who appeared before the grand jury and upon whose testimony the charges against him are founded. See Ga. Const., Art. I, Sec. I, Par. XIV; Evans v. State, 150 S.E.2d 240 (Ga. 1966).

Finally, we find the Act is inapplicable to presentence hearings. Discovery in presentence hearings in both capital or non-capital cases remains governed by OCGA

§17-10-2, which was not among the various discovery statutes related to felony cases specifically repealed or amended by the enactment of the Act.

FLETCHER, P.J., concurring in part and dissenting in part.

Because the majority opinion interprets the discovery act as repealing by implication the defendant's right to the state's trial witness lists, scientific reports, and scientific work product, I dissent [from that portion of the opinion].

The majority construes too narrowly the constitutional requirement that the defendant shall be furnished "a list of witnesses on whose testimony such charge is founded." In Sutton v. State, 228 S.E.2d 820 (Ga. 1976), we held that the constitutional right to be furnished a list of witnesses "is the right, on demand, to be furnished by the district attorney's office, prior to arraignment, with the list of witnesses who will testify for the state on the trial."

As a matter of due process and fundamental fairness, I would continue to interpret the constitutional provision as requiring the state to provide a list of its trial witnesses despite the repeal of the statute. The requirement enables the defendant to prepare a defense by interviewing potential trial witnesses; it aids judicial economy by requiring defense counsel to investigate and interview the witnesses before trial, thus avoiding the need for a continuance; and it places no undue burden on the prosecutor, as shown by the attorney general office's practice of furnishing a list of potential trial witnesses in all criminal cases.

Even in the absence of a constitutional right, the better policy and practice is for prosecutors to furnish a list of potential trial witnesses to avoid unfair surprise and make trials more efficient. The discovery act repealed former OCGA §17-7-110, which required disclosure of witness lists and the indictment, but reenacted that provision to apply in misdemeanor cases. Because persons charged with less serious offenses are entitled to the names of trial witnesses, persons charged with felonies should receive the same information from the state.

The due process clause of the United States Constitution guarantees a defendant the right to an independent examination of critical evidence. Depending on the case, this right may include the state's scientific reports and data on which its experts will rely at trial. Despite the majority's unsupported assertion, the repeal of OCGA §17-7-211 cannot eliminate the defendant's due process right to scientific reports and work product when they are critical evidence. Any doubts about the importance of the evidence should weigh in favor of disclosure towards the defendant.

Both the Georgia Attorney General and the Georgia Association of Criminal Defense Lawyers agree that a defendant preparing for trial is entitled to a significant amount of information under the United States Constitution and the Georgia Constitution, statutes, court rules, and court decisions. Specifically, they agree that a defendant is entitled to the following:

1. Exculpatory material as set forth in Brady v. Maryland, 373 U.S. 83 (1963).
2. Evidence of an understanding, agreement, or promise of leniency under Giglio v. United States, 405 U.S. 150 (1972), and Patillo v. State, 368 S.E.2d 493 (Ga. 1988).
3. Evidence in aggravation that the state intends to rely on at presentence hearings and victim impact evidence under OCGA §17-10-1.2 and Livingston v. State, 444 S.E.2d 748 (Ga. 1994).
4. Independent examination of critical evidence under the due process clause of the United States Constitution.

5. Materials used by a witness to refresh memory as set forth in Sterling v. State, 477 S.E.2d 807 (Ga. 1996), and Johnson v. State, 383 S.E.2d 118 (Ga. 1989).
6. Notice of state's intent to introduce evidence of similar transactions that do not involve prior difficulties between the defendant and victim under Uniform Superior Court Rule 31.3 and Wall v. State, 500 S.E.2d 904 (Ga. 1998).
7. Certain information from the Georgia Crime Information Center under OCGA §35-3-34.
8. Notice of the state's intention to rebut evidence of specific acts of violence by the victim against third persons under Chandler v. State, 405 S.E.2d 669 (Ga. 1991), and Uniform Superior Court Rule 31.6.
9. Pre-trial examination of known handwriting samples under OCGA §24-7-7.
10. Disclosure of the name of an informant in certain circumstances under Roviaro v. United States, 353 U.S. 53 (1957), and Wilson v. State, 433 S.E.2d 703 (Ga. App. 1993).
11. Examination of any report prepared under OCGA §17-4-20.1 about an act of family violence for which the defendant has been arrested.
12. Presentation of evidence at a court proceeding by way of a notice to produce, if the matter would be admissible and the defendant needs it for use as evidence on his own behalf.
13. Access to records under the Open Records Act, OCGA §50-18-70.

These rights remain available despite a defendant's decision not to have the criminal discovery statute apply. . . .

Notes

1. *Reciprocal discovery: majority position.* The trend in American jurisdictions is toward increasingly reciprocal discovery. These statutes usually survive constitutional challenges. See State v. Brown, 940 P.2d 546 (Wash. 1997). However, the full "two-way street" form of discovery is more rare. Some courts have struck down the most ambitious efforts to create reciprocal discovery, particularly those requiring the defendant to reveal information about potential witnesses that she does *not* plan to call at trial. See Binegar v. District Court, 915 P.2d 889 (Nev. 1996). The Georgia decision in *Lucious* is typical in focusing on whether the material that the defense must disclose under the statute would be disclosed later at trial. See also Izazaga v. Superior Court, 815 P.2d 304 (Cal. 1991) (upholding California's redrafted discovery provisions). The most common constitutional objections are based on the self-incrimination privilege, the right to cross-examination, the right to effective assistance of counsel, and due process.

Discovery rules in most state regulate specialized defenses such as alibis, self-defense, or insanity. The Supreme Court has upheld the constitutionality of such statutes in Williams v. Florida, 399 U.S. 78 (1970). The defenses must be reciprocal: The Supreme Court has struck down a statute that required the defense to provide notice of an alibi defense without requiring the prosecution to disclose its alibi-rebuttal witnesses. Wardius v. Oregon, 412 U.S. 470 (1973). Why are alibi, self-defense, and insanity the three types of defense evidence that appear most often in the statutes and rules regarding disclosure? At least two of these defenses (alibi and insanity) require the development of evidence unrelated to the events of the alleged crime. But why should the government obtain special notice about self-defense? And once the government knows that a defendant plans to pursue an insanity defense, why should the government have access to defense experts? Can't the prosecution hire its own experts?

2. *Consensual discovery*. Statutes in many states finesse the constitutional questions involved in compelling defendant disclosures by giving the defendant the choice of opting out of extensive discovery. Only if the defendant obtains full discovery rights against the government must she also comply with the disclosure duties. Note that the Pennsylvania rule, reprinted above, has defense disclosure provisions that are triggered by a defense request for discovery from the prosecution, and the *Lucious* court mentioned the consent feature of the Georgia statute. Does a defendant "waive" objections to disclosure in the same sense that he or she can "waive" the right to trial or to an appointed attorney? Does consensual discovery protect a true adversarial option?

3. *Work-product doctrine in criminal cases.* Recall that discovery rules usually include a privilege, developed at common law, for the "work product" of attorneys and their agents. The privilege limits the disclosures of both defense and prosecution. The U.S. Supreme Court recognized the work-product doctrine in Hickman v. Taylor, 329 U.S. 495 (1947), establishing a qualified privilege for certain materials prepared by an attorney in anticipation of litigation. The Court explained the decision as follows:

> Historically, a lawyer is an officer of the court and is bound to work for the advancement of justice while faithfully protecting the rightful interests of his clients. In performing his various duties, however, it is essential that a lawyer work with a certain degree of privacy, free from unnecessary intrusion by opposing parties and their counsel. Proper preparation of a client's case demands that he assemble information, sift what he considers to be the relevant from the irrelevant facts, prepare his legal theories and plan his strategy without undue and needless interference. . . . This work is reflected, of course, in interviews, statements, memoranda, correspondence, briefs, mental impressions, personal beliefs, and countless other tangible and intangible ways — aptly though roughly termed . . . as the [w]ork product of the lawyer. Were such materials open to opposing counsel on mere demand, much of what is now put down in writing would remain unwritten. An attorney's thoughts, heretofore inviolate, would not be his own. Inefficiency, unfairness and sharp practices would inevitably develop in the giving of legal advice and in the preparation of cases for trial. The effect on the legal profession would be demoralizing. And the interests of the clients and the cause of justice would be poorly served.

329 U.S. at 510-511. There are two levels of "work-product" protections. An "absolute" privilege attaches to any mental impressions, conclusions, opinions or legal theories of an attorney; that is, any document containing such material must be redacted to remove it before disclosure to another party. On the other hand, a "qualified" privilege attaches to other materials created "in anticipation of litigation." An opposing party can obtain this material if there is a strong enough reason for the disclosure. See State v. Chagnon, 662 A.2d 944 (N.H. 1995) (rejects traditional civil requirements of "substantial need" and "unavailability from other sources" as prerequisites for obtaining qualified work-product material; in criminal litigation, work product subject only to discretion of trial court). Is a state that has embraced broad defense disclosures likely to weaken the work-product doctrine?

Is the work-product privilege based on a view of an independent and adversarial development of information that is incompatible with extensive discovery?

4. *Remedies for defense discovery violations.* When the defense attorney violates discovery obligations, what price should the client pay? It is possible for a trial judge to prevent the defendant from using a witness if the defense lawyer fails to disclose the required information about that witness to the prosecution. See Taylor v. Illinois, 484 U.S. 400 (1988) (defense counsel deliberately withheld name of witness from prosecutor; trial court may preclude that witness from testifying); Coleman v. State, 749 So. 2d 1003 (Miss. 1999) (exclusion of alibi witness was appropriate sanction for delay in notifying prosecution and failure to disclose address of witness). Should sanctions for these violations be left instead to disciplinary proceedings brought against the attorney?

5. *Effective advocacy and reciprocal discovery.* Which of the following sorts of information would an advocate most want to withhold from the other party before trial: information about fact witnesses, expert witnesses, or documents? Do the discovery rules in criminal cases provide the most protection to information that requires the most effort to develop? Or do they protect the information that will have the most impact at trial? Or is the objective instead to require disclosure of information precisely *because* it is likely to have an impact at trial or *because* it is difficult to develop? Discovery rules that restrict independent development of evidence to peripheral issues make a profound statement about the adversary system. For instance, in Germany, the judge and the defense attorney have full access to the prosecution file, but the defense has no corresponding duty to disclose its information to the court or the prosecution. Do our discovery rules now declare that an adversarial development of evidence is more likely to obscure truth than to further it? As you evaluate the rules of criminal discovery, try to anticipate how lawyers in the adversarial tradition will react to rules that attempt to shift that tradition toward reciprocal discovery.

3. *Discovery Ethics*

During discovery, defense attorneys could face one of the classic puzzles of legal ethics. If a client gives her lawyer incriminating physical evidence, what are the lawyer's obligations? Do the obligations change if the material comes from a third party? If the client or a third party tells the lawyer about the location of such material? Finally, does defense counsel have an affirmative ethical obligation to seek out incriminating evidence?

■ MICHAEL HITCH v. PIMA COUNTY SUPERIOR COURT

708 P.2d 72 (Ariz. 1985)

Cameron, J.

This is a special action brought by defendant from an order of the trial court compelling defendant's attorney to deliver potentially inculpatory, physical evidence to the state and requiring that the attorney withdraw from representation. . . . We must decide three questions:

1. Does a defense attorney have an obligation to turn over to the state potentially inculpatory, physical evidence obtained from a third party?

2. If so, in what manner may this be done?
3. Must he then withdraw as attorney for the defendant?

The essential facts are not in dispute. Defendant was indicted for first degree murder and is currently awaiting trial on that charge. In the course of their investigation, the police interviewed defendant's girlfriend, Diane Heaton, who told them that the victim was in possession of a certain wristwatch shortly before his death. Subsequently, an investigator for the Pima County Public Defender's Office contacted Ms. Heaton and she informed him that she had found a wristwatch in defendant's suit jacket. She also stated that she did not want to turn the evidence over to the police. The investigator contacted defendant's attorney who told him to take possession of the watch and bring it to the attorney's office. The attorney indicated that he did this for two reasons. First, he wanted to examine the watch to determine whether it was the same one that Ms. Heaton had described to the police. Second, he was afraid that she might destroy or conceal the evidence. Shortly thereafter, defendant informed the police that he had taken a watch from the victim. The police were, however, unaware of the location of that watch.

On 11 June 1984, defendant's attorney filed a petition with the Ethics Committee of the Arizona State Bar, requesting an opinion concerning his duties with respect to the wristwatch. The Ethics Committee informed the attorney that he had a legal obligation to turn over the watch to the state and that he also might be compelled to testify as to the original location and source of the evidence. Opinion No. 85-4 (14 March 1985).

Defendant's attorney informed the Respondent Judge of the Committee's decision. Judge Veliz ordered that the watch be turned over to the state and that the attorney withdraw from the case. He also stayed the order to allow the filing of this petition for special action. . . .

We have previously held that an attorney need not turn over physical evidence obtained from his client if the evidence was such that it could not be obtained from the client against the client's will, State v. Superior Court, 625 P.2d 316 (Ariz. 1981). We have not, however, ruled as to physical evidence obtained from a third party. As to this question, cases from other jurisdictions are few in number. . . .

The Alaska Supreme Court was confronted with a case in which the defendant's attorney in a kidnapping case had received from a third party written plans for the kidnapping drawn by the client. In reviewing whether counsel violated defendant's right to adequate representation by making the existence of the plans known to the state, the court stated:

> [A] criminal defense attorney has an obligation to turn over to the prosecution physical evidence which comes into his possession, especially where the evidence comes into the attorney's possession through acts of a third party who is neither a client of the attorney nor an agent of a client. After turning over such evidence, an attorney may have either a right or a duty to remain silent as to the circumstances under which he obtained such evidence. . . . Morrell v. State, 575 P.2d 1200 (Alaska 1978).

[The *Morrell* court] relied on dictum from State v. Olwell, 394 P.2d 681 (Wash. 1964), in finding that counsel had acted properly. In *Olwell,* defense counsel was served with a subpoena duces tecum in which he was asked to produce, at a coroner's inquest, all knives in his possession and control relating to the defendant.

The attorney refused to indicate whether or not he was in possession of these knives, arguing that to do so would violate the confidential relationship of attorney and client. The Washington Supreme Court found that the subpoena was defective on its face because it required the attorney to reveal information given to him in the course of discussions with his client. The court stated, however:

> The attorney should not be a depository for criminal evidence . . . which in itself has little, if any, material value for the purposes of aiding counsel in the preparation of the defense of his client's case. Such evidence given the attorney during legal consultation for information purposes and used by the attorney in preparing the defense of his client's case, whether or not the case ever goes to trial, could clearly be withheld for a reasonable period of time. It follows that the attorney, after a reasonable period, should, as an officer of the court, on his own motion turn the same over to the prosecution. [394 P.2d at 684-685.]

Of course, if the physical evidence is contraband, the attorney may be required to turn over the property even if he obtained that evidence from his client. For example, in a case where the attorney obtained from his client the money taken in a bank robbery and a sawed-off shotgun used in the crime, the attorney was required to turn the property over to the state. In re Ryder, 381 F.2d 713 (4th Cir. 1967).

At issue is the conflict between a defense attorney's obligation to his client and to the court. As the Preamble to the Rules of Professional Conduct notes, a lawyer is both "a representative of [his] clients, an officer of the legal system and a public citizen having special responsibility for the quality of justice." As a representative of his client, a lawyer must act as a zealous advocate, demonstrating loyalty to his client and giving him the best legal advice possible within the bounds of the law. As part of this zealous representation, the lawyer is admonished not to reveal information relating to representation of his client. ER 1.6. The Comment to ER 1.6 states:

> . . . The confidentiality rule applies not merely to matters communicated in confidence by the client but also to all information relating to the representation, whatever its source. A lawyer may not disclose such information except as authorized or required by the Rules of Professional Conduct or other law.[2]

Because clients are aware that their lawyers will not repeat their communications, they feel that they may make both full and honest disclosure. Trial counsel is thus better able to evaluate the situation and prepare a proper defense. . . .

We note also that the lawyer's role as a zealous advocate is an important one, not only for the client but for the administration of justice. We have chosen an adversary system of justice in which, in theory, the state and the defendant meet as equals. . . . In order to close the gap between theory and practice and thereby ensure that the system is working properly, a defendant must have an attorney who will fight against the powerful resources of the state. It is only when this occurs that we

2. [S]ee also ER 3.4 ("A lawyer shall not: (a) unlawfully . . . alter, destroy or conceal a document or other material having potential evidentiary value. . . ."). The Arizona Bar Ethics Committee opinion focused on A.R.S. §13-2809, Tampering with Physical Evidence, and §13-2510, et seq., Hindering Prosecution, and stated that these two sections created a legal obligation of disclosure. We do not agree. Both statutes require an intent to make unavailable certain evidence for prosecution. In this case, however, the attorney was not acting to impede prosecution but rather to preserve evidence. If he were acting otherwise he would not retain the evidence and then request advice as to what to do with it but would destroy it, preventing the state from being able to obtain it through normal discovery channels.

can be assured that the system is functioning properly and only the guilty are convicted.

Balanced against the attorney's obligation to his client is the attorney's obligation as an officer of the court, which requires him [to aid] in determining truth whenever possible. Both sides must have equal access to the relevant information. As the American Bar Association had noted: "[w]here the necessary evaluation and preparation are foreclosed by lack of information, the trial becomes a pursuit of truth and justice only by chance rather than by design, and generates a diminished respect for the criminal justice system, the judiciary and the attorney participants." II ABA Standards for Criminal Justice, comment to Standard 11-1.1(a) (2d ed. 1982). Thus, in order to aid the truth determining process an attorney must refrain from impeding the flow of information to the state. The defendant's attorney can neither assist nor obstruct the prosecution in its efforts to discover evidence.

Defendant asks us, in balancing these competing interests, to hold that there is "no affirmative duty on the part of defense counsel to disclose possible inculpatory evidence obtained by counsel during the course of his representation of the client." Defendant maintains that to hold otherwise would cause irreparable harm to the attorney-client relationship. The National Legal Aid and Defender Association in its amicus brief agrees with defendant that there should be no "absolute affirmative duty rule" requiring defendant's attorney to routinely disclose all physical evidence discovered during investigation of a case. The National Legal Aid and Defender Association suggests that we adopt the "Ethical Standard to Guide [A Lawyer] Who Receives Physical Evidence Implicating His Client in Criminal Conduct," proposed by the Criminal Justice Section's Ethics Committee. This standard reads as follows:

> (a) A lawyer who receives a physical item under circumstances implicating a client in criminal conduct shall disclose the location of or shall deliver that item to law enforcement authorities only: (1) if such is required by law or court order, or (2) as provided in paragraph (d).
>
> (b) Unless required to disclose, the lawyer shall return the item to the source from whom the lawyer receives it, as provided in paragraphs (c) and (d). In returning the item to the source, the lawyer shall advise the source of the legal consequences pertaining to possession or destruction of the item.
>
> (c) A lawyer may receive the item for a period of time during which the lawyer: (1) intends to return it to the owner; (2) reasonably fears that return of the item to the source will result in destruction of the item; (3) reasonably fears that return of the item to the source will result in physical harm to anyone; (4) intends to test, examine, inspect or use the item in any way as part of the lawyer's representation of the client; or (5) cannot return it to the source. If the lawyer retains the item, the lawyer shall do so in a manner that does not impede the lawful ability of law enforcement to obtain the item.
>
> (d) If the item received is contraband, or if in the lawyer's judgment the lawyer cannot retain the item in a way that does not pose an unreasonable risk of physical harm to anyone, the lawyer shall disclose the location of or shall deliver the item to law enforcement authorities.
>
> (e) If the lawyer discloses the location of or delivers the item to law enforcement authorities under paragraphs (a) or (d), or to a third party under paragraph (c)(1), the lawyer shall do so in the way best designed to protect the client's interest.

We agree with defendant that any requirement that the defendant's attorney turn over to the prosecutor physical evidence which may aid in the conviction of the defendant may harm the attorney-client relationship. We do not believe, however, that this reason, by itself, is sufficient to avoid disclosure. [We] feel that the potential damage to the adversary system is greater, and in need of greater protection, than the attorney-client relationship. We do not wish to create a situation in which counsel is made a repository for physical evidence — a serious and inevitable problem once clients become aware that evidence given to their attorneys, even by friends, may never be turned over to the state.

We, therefore, adopt essentially the ethical standard proposed by the Ethics Committee of the Section on Criminal Justice of the American Bar Association with regards to inculpatory evidence delivered to the attorney by a third party. Our holding is as follows: first, if the attorney reasonably believes that evidence will not be destroyed, he may return it to the source, explaining the laws on concealment and destruction. Second, if the attorney has reasonable grounds to believe that the evidence might be destroyed, or if his client consents, he may turn the physical evidence over to the prosecution. Applying this test to the instant facts, the trial court was correct in ordering the wristwatch to be turned over to the state.

Having decided that the evidence must be turned over to the prosecution, we must determine how this can best be done without further prejudice to the defendant. The Ethics Committee's proposed standards provide that when this is done "the lawyer shall do so in [a] way best designed to protect the client's interest." Amicus National Legal Aid and Defender Association suggests that if the lawyer decides to disclose the item he should do so by delivering the evidence to an agent who would then deliver it to the police without disclosing the source of the item or the case involved. Defendant, however, suggests that . . . this Court adopt a system whereby an attorney could anonymously deliver evidence to State Bar counsel, or presidents of local county bar associations, in a sealed package which indicates that it is being delivered due to the affirmative disclosure requirement.

We disagree with both suggestions. Not all items have evidentiary significance in and of themselves. In this case, for instance, the watch is not inculpatory per se; rather, it is the fact that the watch was found in defendant's jacket that makes the watch material evidence. By returning the watch anonymously to the police, this significance is lost. Assuming investigating officials are even able to determine to what case the evidence belongs, they may never be able to reconstruct where it was originally discovered or under what circumstances. Cf. People v. Meredith, 631 P.2d 46 (Cal. 1981) ("it is as if . . . the wallet in this case bore a tag bearing the words 'located in the trash can by Scott's residence,' and the defense, by taking the wallet, destroyed this tag.").

We believe it is simpler and more direct for defendant's attorney to turn the matter over to the state as long as it is understood that the prosecutor may not mention in front of the jury the fact that the evidence came from the defendant or his attorney. . . . If a defendant is willing to enter a stipulation concerning the chain of possession, location or condition of the evidence, then the evidence may be admitted without the jury becoming aware of the source of the evidence. Under these circumstances, the attorney need not be called as a witness.

Under these procedures, the attorney need not withdraw as counsel. If the attorneys can stipulate as to the chain of possession and no reference is made to the fact that the defendant's attorney turned the matter over to the prosecution, then there is no need for the attorney to withdraw as counsel for the defendant. There may be some cases where the client will believe that his attorney no longer has his best interest in mind. In such a case, it may be wise for the attorney to ask to withdraw.

Such request should be liberally granted by the court. Where, however, the client does not object, there is no need for the attorney to withdraw from the case.

As to the instant case, we find that defense counsel was forced to take possession of the evidence because of a reasonable fear that to do otherwise would result in its destruction. Because the source was a nonclient, and because he had reason to believe that the witness (source) would conceal or destroy the evidence, the attorney had an obligation to disclose the item and its source to the prosecution. The order requiring disclosure is affirmed and the order requiring defendant's attorney to withdraw is reversed. . . .

FELDMAN, J., dissenting.

I dissent both because I disagree with some of the majority's conclusions and because I fear that the court's opinion leaves many unanswered questions. [T]he opinion of the court affects vital areas of practice with which prosecutors and defense counsel must deal on a day-to-day basis. . . .

The court fails to consider the full scope of the role of defense counsel. The opinion indicates that defense counsel acts both as an advocate for the defendant and an officer of the court. I believe that the role of defense counsel has an even more profound dimension. The adversary feature of the criminal justice system evolved as a control on governmental absolutism and is, therefore, a fundamental component of political liberty. . . .

In my view, therefore, defense counsel should never be put in the position of helping the government prove its case. Of course, counsel may not mislead, tamper with evidence, lie or promote such acts. To do so would violate his duty as an officer of a court which seeks to ascertain the truth. On the other hand, because defense counsel is neither an assistant to nor an investigator for the prosecutor, his function is neither to gather nor preserve inculpatory evidence for the prosecution. If he engages in such conduct, how can he then put the government to its proof? How can he be a zealous advocate for the defendant when at the same time he is likely to make himself a star witness for the prosecution?

I am led to the inevitable conclusion that defense counsel has no obligation to take possession of inculpatory evidence from third parties. Further, caution and common sense dictate that as a general rule he should never actively seek to obtain such evidence and should refuse possession even if it is offered to him. His guiding principle should be to leave things as they are found. If counsel has reasonable grounds to believe that evidence is in danger of being tampered with or destroyed by a third party, his obligations are satisfied by cautioning that person against such conduct. The majority opinion is ambiguous on this issue, but I believe that we should make it clear to the defense bar that the general rule to be followed in connection with inculpatory evidence is "hands off." Of course, there are limited exceptions to that general rule. The defense lawyer is justified in obtaining possession of evidence where necessary to test, examine or inspect that evidence in order to determine whether it is exculpatory. . . .

Although the court purports "essentially" to adopt the standard [of the ABA Ethics Committee], I believe it misconstrues it. [T]he standard would instruct us as follows in the present case: if defense counsel had a legitimate reason to obtain the evidence, such as examination or testing, then it was proper to receive it from the third person who had possession. When so received, it was proper for defense counsel to retain the item while he examined it or had it tested. When he had finished with it and had discovered that he would not need it for trial, it was his duty to return it to the source with instructions as to the consequences of tampering or destruction. If he had a good faith belief that return to the source would result in damage to or destruction of the evidence, then it was his duty to retain the evidence in his possession "in a manner that [did] not impede the lawful ability of law enforcement to obtain the item."

Thus, I believe the majority is incorrect in holding that defense counsel should turn the evidence over to the prosecution. This holding has not only made defense counsel an assistant to the prosecutor's investigator but also an important witness for the prosecution. The future consequences of such a confusion of roles is bound to damage a system which, despite what we are told during periods of hysteria, has survived the test of time.

Notes

1. *Ethical obligations to turn over physical evidence.* The rules about a defense lawyer's obligations to disclose physical evidence are largely uniform. If a defense lawyer receives incriminating *testimony* from a client, the attorney-client privilege and the self-incrimination clause combine to prevent the attorney from revealing that information to the government. But if the defense lawyer receives incriminating *physical* evidence, the outcome is different. Discovery rules do not address this question. Instead, Rule 3.4 of the Model Rules of Professional Conduct, adopted as law in many states, provides the starting point for analyzing the attorney's duties:

> A lawyer shall not . . . unlawfully obstruct another party's access to evidence or unlawfully alter, destroy or conceal a document or other material having potential evidentiary value. A lawyer shall not counsel or assist another person to do any such act.

Hence, the key question is whether a lawyer's act is an "unlawful" obstruction of access or tampering with evidence. Most states have statutes that prohibit obstruction of investigations or tampering with evidence. In some places, an investigation must be pending before the destruction or concealment of potential evidence becomes unlawful, while elsewhere the intent to prevent detection of a crime is the critical element, regardless of the timing of the destruction or concealment. The courts addressing these situations have held that the attorney who takes possession of contraband relevant to a criminal investigation against a client must ordinarily give the evidence to the government. The attorney can return the evidence to its original location only if the return of the evidence does not create a risk that the evidence will be concealed or altered. See Rubin v. State, 602 A.2d 677 (Md. 1992). Do the standards suggested in *Hitch* by the National Legal Aid and Defender Association do a better job of balancing the need for both vigorous advocacy and the ultimate determination of truth? What are the practical effects on defense counsel of the current rules? What would you say to your client or a third party about incriminating physical evidence? When would you say it? Appellate cases involving the ethical obligations of counsel during criminal discovery are relatively rare, though logic suggests that the issues involved arise frequently. Why might case law on these topics be so uncommon?

2. *Source and type of evidence.* Does it matter that the watch in *Hitch* was not contraband (that is, it was not illegal for anyone to possess the watch)? Does it matter

that the attorney learned of the location of the wristwatch from a third party rather than from the client? Can the prosecutor reveal to the jury that defense counsel was the source of the watch when it comes into evidence at trial? See State v. Olwell, 394 P.2d 681 (Wash. 1964) (if client provides defense counsel with evidence that must be given to government, attorney-client privilege prevents prosecutor from informing jury about source of evidence). Can the prosecutor call the defendant's *former* lawyer to testify about the source of the evidence? See State v. Green, 493 So. 2d 1178 (La. 1986).

3. *Ethics rules and prosecutorial disclosures.* Rules of ethics often recognize a distinctive set of duties for prosecuting attorneys. How might these rules be relevant during the discovery process? Consider the following passage from Rule 8 of the Supreme Court of Tennessee, EC 7-13:

> The responsibility of a public prosecutor differs from that of the usual advocate; the public prosecutor's duty is to seek justice, not merely to convict. . . . With respect to evidence and witnesses, the prosecutor has responsibilities different from those of a lawyer in private practice; the prosecutor should make timely disclosure to the defense of available evidence, known to the prosecutor, that tends to negate the guilt of the accused, mitigate the degree of the offense, or reduce the punishment. Further, a prosecutor should not intentionally avoid pursuit of evidence merely because the prosecutor believes it will damage the prosecutor's case or aid the accused.

B. SPEEDY TRIAL PREPARATION

An old bromide reminds us that "justice delayed is justice denied." This can be true both for the prosecution and the defense in criminal cases. If preparations for trial last too long, the evidence becomes less reliable for both sides. The uncertainty about the criminal charges may harm the defendant's reputation and can make it difficult for the defendants and the victims of the alleged crime to move ahead with their lives. The need for speedy resolution of criminal charges has been mentioned in some of the earliest documents in our legal tradition, including the Magna Carta of 1215, which states, "we will not deny or defer to any man either justice or right."

The right to a speedy trial appears in constitutional provisions, both state and federal. The Sixth Amendment guarantees a "speedy and public trial," and most states have similar provisions. The federal and state due process clauses prevent some extreme forms of delay. Recent constitutional amendments recognizing the rights of victims of crime have declared that victims, too, have a right to a speedy trial. Many state and federal statutes also hurry the criminal process along. These include statutes of limitation (requiring charges to be filed within a limited time from the events in question) and speedy trial acts (requiring the parties and the courts to bring the matter to trial within a specified period from the start of the process).

Despite all this emphasis on speed, another bromide reminds us that "haste makes waste." Both prosecution and defense have some reasons to slow down the process. Some of their reasons may be less than noble. If testimony is going to damage one side or another, a witness's fading memory may make the testimony less convincing and more susceptible to attack. If a defendant remains in custody before trial, a prosecutor may not be so anxious to risk an acquittal that would release the defendant from custody; a defendant not in custody may want to delay the day of reckoning. But other reasons for delay are surely necessary, even praiseworthy, including a desire to complete the discovery processes examined in the previous section.

1. *Pre-accusation Delay*

Once a crime occurs and an investigation begins, the matter typically becomes the basis for criminal charges or is declined for criminal charges within a matter of days. Among the handful of matters that take more time, a small proportion can remain active for many months or years after the events take place. This is the first delay in the criminal process that suspects, victims, witnesses, and the general public encounter. What legal principles and institutions are available to limit the amount of time that can pass between the commission of a crime and the filing of criminal charges? Once a state legislature has passed a statute of limitations, is any further limitation necessary to avoid delays that might create hardship or unreliable outcomes?

■ NEW YORK CRIMINAL PROCEDURE LAW §30.10

1. A criminal action must be commenced within the period of limitation prescribed in the ensuing subdivisions of this section.

2. Except as otherwise provided in subdivision three:

(a) A prosecution for a class A felony may be commenced at any time;

(b) A prosecution for any other felony must be commenced within five years after the commission thereof;

(c) A prosecution for a misdemeanor must be commenced within two years after the commission thereof;

(d) A prosecution for a petty offense must be commenced within one year after the commission thereof.

3. Notwithstanding the provisions of subdivision two, the periods of limitation for the commencement of criminal actions are extended as follows in the indicated circumstances:

(a) A prosecution for larceny committed by a person in violation of a fiduciary duty may be commenced within one year after the facts constituting such offense are discovered or, in the exercise of reasonable diligence, should have been discovered by the aggrieved party or by a person under a legal duty to represent him who is not himself implicated in the commission of the offense. . . .

(f) For purposes of a prosecution involving a sexual offense . . . committed against a child less than 18 years of age, . . . the period of limitation shall not begin to run until the child has reached the age of 18 or the offense is reported to a law enforcement agency. . . .

4. In calculating the time limitation applicable to commencement of a criminal action, the following periods shall not be included:

(a) Any period following the commission of the offense during which (i) the defendant was continuously outside this state or (ii) the whereabouts of the defendant were continuously unknown and continuously unascertainable by the exercise of reasonable diligence. However, in no event shall the period of limitation be extended by more than five years beyond the period otherwise applicable under subdivision two.

(b) When a prosecution for an offense is lawfully commenced within the prescribed period of limitation therefor, and when an accusatory instrument upon which such prosecution is based is subsequently dismissed by an authorized court under directions or circumstances permitting the lodging of another charge for the same offense or an offense based on the same conduct, the period extending from the commencement of the thus defeated prosecution to the dismissal of the accusatory instrument does not constitute a part of the period of limitation applicable to commencement of prosecution by a new charge.

■ STATE v. SHANE TROMPETER

555 N.W.2d 468 (Iowa 1996)

HARRIS, J.

The State waited nearly three years, waited deliberately for the defendant's 18th birthday, to file this felony case. The district court correctly dismissed it because the long delay violated defendant's due process rights.

In July 1993 defendant Shane Trompeter, who was then 16 years old, was found to have committed a third-degree sexual assault. In September 1993 he was adjudicated delinquent and was eventually placed in a Sioux City facility for delinquent youth. Trompeter was released from the facility on June 26, 1995, due to his upcoming 18th birthday and the consequent termination of juvenile court jurisdiction over him. The next day, Trompeter's 18th birthday, the State filed a trial information charging him with second-degree sexual abuse, alleged to have been committed on August 10, 1992. Second-degree sexual abuse is a class B felony. It calls for imprisonment of not to exceed 25 years.

Trompeter filed a motion to dismiss the charge alleging, among other things, the pre-accusatorial delay violated his due process rights under the Fourteenth Amendment of the United States Constitution. At the motion hearing the assistant county attorney, Richard Meyer, conceded that the State was aware of the August 10, 1992, incident at the time of the September 1993 delinquency adjudication. He stated that, during the prehearing negotiations, he had proposed to Trompeter's attorney that, if Trompeter pled guilty to third-degree sexual assault, the State would not seek to prosecute the August 10, 1992, incident. This offer was rejected.

Meyer testified he did not file the charge relating to the August 10, 1992, incident at the 1993 delinquency hearing because "it was my understanding that [Trompeter] was going into various sexual offender, sexual deviation behavior treatment programs and I thought the matter was being taken care of." Meyer was satisfied at the time to have Trompeter "handled by the juvenile court authorities." He only decided later to charge Trompeter for the August 10, 1992 incident when he learned that Trompeter had [not successfully completed his treatment program, and psychiatric professionals predicted that he would re-offend.]

The district court granted Trompeter's motion to dismiss the criminal charge brought on June 27, 1995. The court found the State actions in "offering to plea bargain the charge away, then holding it over the defendant's head for three years, then charging him on his 18th birthday" constituted "unjustifiable government conduct" or was based on an "illegitimate prosecutorial motive," and a violation of Trompeter's due process rights. . . .

A claim of pre-accusatorial delay in violation of due process is distinct from a statute-of-limitations claim. The applicable statute of limitations has not run here, but Trompeter can nevertheless assert the claim that the pre-accusatorial delay violated his right to due process. See State v. Lange, 531 N.W.2d 108 (Iowa 1995). Our cases are in accord with federal authority. United States v. Lovasco, 431 U.S. 783 (1977).

There is no constitutional right to be arrested and charged at the precise moment probable cause comes into existence. But if the government delays filing charges to intentionally "gain [a] tactical advantage over the accused," the defendant's due process rights are implicated. United States v. Marion, 404 U.S. 307 (1971). To prove a pre-accusatorial delay violated due process, the defendant must show: (1) the delay was unreasonable; and (2) the defendant's defense was thereby prejudiced. A defendant must prove both of these elements to prevail. Prejudice to the defendant must be actual; the defendant cannot rely on mere general claims of prejudice. The length of the delay, and any valid reason for it, must be balanced against the resulting prejudice against the defendant.

The first element of the pre-accusatorial due process test requires a showing of unreasonable delay in filing charges. This involves a consideration of both the length of the delay and the State's reason for it. We think that as the delay becomes longer it requires correspondingly better reasons to justify it. Many legitimate reasons might justify a delay in bringing criminal charges. One obvious example would be time required for further investigation into the crime. Other reasons listed by the United States Supreme Court in *Lovasco* included:

> (i) The prosecutor's reasonable doubt that the accused is in fact guilty; (ii) the extent of the harm caused by the offense; (iii) the disproportion of the authorized punishment in relation to the particular offense or the offender; (iv) possible improper motives of a complainant; (v) reluctance of the victim to testify; (vi) cooperation of the accused in the apprehension or conviction of others; (vii) availability and likelihood of prosecution by another jurisdiction. [431 U.S. at 794.]

One motive for delay rejected as unjustified by the United States Supreme Court in *Lovasco* was a prosecutor's "wish to hold a 'club' over the defendant." Another illegitimate motive noted in *Lovasco* was to "postpone the beginning of defense investigation."

No Iowa case has held the State used an illegitimate motive in delaying the prosecution and therefore created an unreasonable delay in violation of due process. We have however warned that, "had defendant established that the pre-indictment delay was occasioned solely to avoid the possibility of concurrent sentencing, we would not condone such a late prosecution." State v. Sunclades, 305 N.W.2d 491 (Iowa 1981). . . . Many other courts have held that a delay to avoid the possibility of concurrent sentencing is not a legitimate reason for delay. [The court cites U.S. Supreme Court and lower federal court decisions and cases from North Carolina and West Virginia.] Because the prosecutor's plan imposed what was in effect consecutive sentences for Trompeter's two juvenile crimes, the prosecutor's excuse must be rejected as a legitimate reason for the delay.

The plan is also rejected as a legitimate reason for delay because it is out of plumb with our statutory scheme for juvenile justice. A juvenile court acquiring jurisdiction over a youth is ordinarily expected to undertake the juvenile's supervision with a view to all existing circumstances. Notwithstanding Trompeter's refusal to plead guilty to the present charge, the older of the two assault charges then pending, we assume the juvenile judge assessed its existence in choosing the Sioux City facility. Primacy of juvenile court over adult criminal court in such matters is clearly spelled out by statute. Iowa Code §232.8(1)(a) ("juvenile court . . . has exclusive original jurisdiction in proceedings concerning an adult who is alleged to have committed a delinquent act prior to having become an adult, and who has been transferred to the jurisdiction of juvenile court. . . ."). We conclude the delay here was unreasonable.

Without doubt Trompeter was prejudiced by the delay. Prejudice was indeed the stated reason for the delay. The delay was admittedly undertaken so that the full force of adult criminal court could later be brought to bear on a 16 year old, who — but for the delay — would experience only juvenile court. It seems unnecessary to detail the myriad advantages a youth under juvenile court jurisdiction enjoys over a youth facing a charge in adult criminal court.

Trompeter clearly established both elements in his due process claim. The trial court was correct in so holding.

Problem 15-4. Child Victims

Gilbert Vernier is a 69-year-old grandfather. In July 1984, M.E., then seven years old, supported by her sister, J.V., informed their mother, "Grandpa touched me in a bad way." The Wyoming Department of Family Services and the county sheriff's department investigated the claim. Two interviews of the victim and her sister were recorded on audiotape. A lieutenant in the sheriff's department who was present during the interview transcribed the second tape. No charges were filed at that time.

Ten years later, in 1994, another granddaughter, L.L., reported to the sheriff's department that in 1977 Vernier had molested her when she was nine years old and was living with her grandparents. Two weeks after L.L. made this report, M.E. again informed the sheriff's department that Vernier had sexually assaulted her in 1984. J.V. corroborated M.E.'s statements, recalling that Vernier routinely took M.E. into a locked bedroom. During the same time frame in 1994, other evidence emerged about sexual abuse perpetrated by Vernier. D.H. and D.P., Vernier's daughters, recounted repeated sexual abuse and rape by their father when D.H. was between the ages of 12 and 16 and D.P. between the ages of 8 and 13.

Following the 1994 investigation, the state charged Vernier with two counts of indecent liberties and one count of second-degree sexual assault based on the alleged incidents in 1984. At his arraignment, Vernier entered a plea of not guilty and filed a motion to dismiss, claiming the state intentionally had delayed filing charges. Although Wyoming has no statute of limitations for prosecuting crimes, Vernier claimed that the delay violated his due process rights. He argued that the 10-year delay impaired his efforts to defend himself against the charges. During that time, the government lost the two 1984 audiotapes of conversations between M.E. and investigators. The transcript of the second tape still exists, however, along with the deputy's notes reflecting her own observations about the interview. Vernier also argued that in 1984 he might have recalled an alibi that would have been helpful.

The district court denied the motion. How would you rule on appeal? How would you respond if Vernier asks your court to create a specific limitations period for crimes in the absence of a statute of limitations, either as a matter of constitutional law or as an exercise of the court's "supervisory" power over the state's criminal justice system? Compare Vernier v. State, 909 P.2d 1344 (Wyo. 1996).

Notes

1. *Pre-accusation delay: majority position.* All state courts have interpreted the due process provisions of their state constitutions to limit a few types of pre-accusation delay, applying the test that the U.S. Supreme Court created in United States v. Lovasco, 431 U.S. 783 (1977). A defendant raising a constitutional objection to a delay between the date of an alleged crime and the time of the indictment or information must show (1) the prejudice that the delay caused for the defense and (2) the reason for the delay. There are two basic approaches in the state courts on the burden of proving these elements. One group requires the defendant to prove both prejudice and an intentional prosecutorial delay to achieve a tactical advantage. See State v. Lacy, 929 P.2d 1288 (Ariz. 1996). A roughly equal number of states give the defendant the initial burden of proving prejudice and then require the government to prove a valid reason for the delay. See State v. Brazell, 480 S.E.2d 64 (S.C. 1997). In states that have passed statutes of limitations (as almost all states have), does the *Lovasco* analysis enable the courts to identify correctly the "stale" cases that the statute of limitations does not reach? Or does the constitutional analysis merely make the law less predictable, without systematically improving on the statutory limits?

2. *Reasons for delay.* The *Lovasco* Court declared categorically that there can be no due process violation if "good-faith investigative delay" is responsible for the timing of the charges. Courts also say that a delay created solely to gain a "tactical advantage" for the prosecution does create a due process problem. The longer the delay, the more willing courts are to find an improper reason for it.

The central question in the pre-accusation delay cases seems to be the good faith of the prosecutor. Compare this interpretation of the requirements of due process with the more general judicial reluctance to become involved in the prosecutor's charging decision in ordinary cases. See Chapter 13. Will an inquiry into the prosecutor's state of mind regarding a delay lead to more judicial scrutiny of prosecutorial charging decisions than traditional doctrine has allowed? In other words, is the test for pre-accusation delay more intrusive than the test for selective prosecution? Did the prosecutors in *Trompeter* and in Problem 15-4 delay charges for different reasons, or did they each just change their minds about criminal charges?

Problem 15-4 illustrates one reason for delay: Crime victims in some cases—notably for intrafamily sexual assaults on children—do not make allegations for many years after the incidents. Should special constitutional rules apply to such cases? See State v. Gray, 917 S.W.2d 668 (Tenn. 1996) (dismissal of charges of sexual abuse brought 42 years after incident involving nine-year-old girl). Specialized statutes of limitation in many states address this type of case (as does the New York statute above).

3. *Source of constitutional protections.* Although the federal constitution and most state constitutions provide specifically for a "speedy trial," these provisions do not apply to delays that occur before criminal charges are filed. The U.S. Supreme Court took the lead on this question in United States v. Marion, 404 U.S. 307 (1971). A review of the text and history of the Sixth Amendment's speedy trial clause (which

speaks of a speedy trial for the "accused") convinced the Court that only "a formal indictment or information or else the actual restraints imposed by arrest and holding to answer a criminal charge" would trigger the protections of the speedy trial clause. See also United States v. MacDonald, 456 U.S. 1 (1982) (no speedy trial protection for period between dismissal of first charges and second indictment). As you read further materials in this chapter and encounter cases decided under the Sixth Amendment or analogous state constitutional clauses, consider whether the due process cases dealing with pre-accusation delay would be decided differently if they were analyzed under the more specific constitutional language requiring a "speedy trial."

4. *Statutes of limitation.* The Court in United States v. Marion noted that statutes of limitation provide "the primary guarantee against bringing overly stale criminal charges." The New York statute above is typical in several respects. First, it provides longer limitation periods for more serious crimes. Second, it creates special rules for marking the beginning of the limitation period for certain crimes unlikely to be detected or reported immediately. The statute leaves it for judges to answer the difficult question of when a continuing crime, such as conspiracy, is "committed" in the sense necessary to trigger the statute. Finally, the statute defines certain events that can "toll" (i.e., suspend) the statute after it has begun to run. Should the drafters of the New York statute have included a provision that would allow judges to create additional "tolling" rules "in the interest of justice"?

Should statutes of limitation influence a court ruling on a constitutional challenge to pre-accusation delay? More specifically, if a statute gives extra latitude to a prosecutor in some cases (such as the Iowa statute of limitations dealing with juvenile offenders, relevant in *Trompeter* above), should that lead a court to give prosecutors extra latitude for delay under the due process clause? Or should the due process protections be strongest when legislatures have provided less statutory protection against delay?

5. *Abolition of statutes of limitation.* Although most jurisdictions in the United States have statutes of limitations, they are not universal. Three states (South Carolina, Kentucky, and Wyoming) do not have a general statute of limitations; the same is true for many other nations, such as England. State legislatures in recent years have also proved willing to create exceptions to these time bars. Do statutes of limitations still serve a useful function? One purpose of a statute of limitations is to prevent the deterioration of reliable evidence over time (for instance, the memories of witnesses might become less reliable as time goes by). Some special cases (for instance, when the prosecution proves the case through scientific evidence such as the DNA found in biological material at the crime scene) do not deteriorate over time. In such cases, should prosecutors be able to suspend the statute of limitations by charging a defendant who is identified only by his or her DNA profile? Perhaps the rationale for a statute of limitations is based on something other than deterioration of evidence. Should we keep statutes of limitations because criminals tend to be more short-sighted than the general public, and the deterrent power of criminal charges is lost if the case is not filed relatively quickly? See Yair Listokin, Efficient Time Bars: A New Rationale for the Existence of Statutes of Limitations in Criminal Law, 31 Journal Leg. Stud. 99 (2002) (because potential criminals tend to discount the future at higher rates than society, punishing crimes long after they are committed will have only a nominal deterrent effect, while they may cost society substantial sums).

2. *Speedy Trial After Accusation*

Once the prosecution obtains an indictment or files an information against a defendant, a wider array of legal provisions becomes available to move the process along. The Sixth Amendment grants to "the accused" the right to a "speedy and public trial." Analogous state constitutional clauses announce such rights in similarly general terms. The federal Speedy Trial Act creates a more specific obligation for the government to process all criminal trials within 70 days of the indictment or information, although it provides several ways to exclude days from the tally. Most states have statutes limiting the time between an accusation and the start of trial (or entry of a guilty plea). Statutes and judicial orders also allocate judicial resources to keep criminal dockets moving.

The deadlines become relevant in a great number of cases. In large urban jurisdictions in 1998, the median time it took to adjudicate a felony case was 79 days. Just over half the cases were adjudicated within three months. Ten percent of the felony cases were still unresolved after a year had passed since the arrest. See Bureau of Justice Statistics, Felony Defendants in Large Urban Counties, 1998, at tbl. 22 (2001) (NCJ 187232).

As you read the materials in this section, pay particular attention to the interaction among the constitutions, statutes, and other legal provisions that relate to speedy preparation for trial. Do these provisions operate differently? If so, are they different because they are framed in different language (some general and some specific), or because they seek different objectives? Note that the constitutional provisions described above are framed in terms of the defendant's rights. But victims of crime and the public at large also are interested in prompt resolution of charges against criminal defendants. A few constitutional provisions and many statutes recognize the interests of crime victims and the public in requiring the parties to prepare quickly for trial. Whose interests triumph when the defendant's interest and the public's interest in timely resolution of cases conflict?

From its earliest opportunity, the U.S. Supreme Court has insisted that the constitutional guarantee of a "speedy" trial is a "necessarily relative" concept. See Beavers v. Haubert, 198 U.S. 77 (1905). The same length of time between accusation and resolution of criminal charges might be acceptable in one case and unacceptable in another, depending on the prosecutor's reasons, the harm that the defendant suffered, and other circumstances. In Barker v. Wingo, 407 U.S. 514 (1972), the Court settled on four circumstances that every court must consider when resolving a claim that the government has violated a defendant's constitutional right to a speedy trial. As you read the following exercise in applying the four-part *Barker* standard, consider how the four factors interact and ask whether some pertinent questions have now been placed out of view.

■ STATE v. DAVID MAGNUSEN

646 So. 2d 1275 (Miss. 1994)

SMITH, J.

David Eugene Magnusen, charged with rape, aggravated assault, two counts of robbery and two counts of burglary of an inhabited dwelling, was incarcerated in the Harrison County Jail for 15 months without being tried. The charges lodged against him were dismissed by the Circuit Court for the State's failure to grant a constitutionally guaranteed speedy trial. The State of Mississippi . . . requests that this Court find that the trial judge erred in dismissing all charges against Magnusen. . . . After careful consideration in a close case, we must reverse and remand and require Magnusen to stand trial.

On December 14, 1990, two indictments were returned against 19-year-old David Magnusen charging him in multiple counts with [committing burglaries, robberies, assaults, and a rape on May 11 and 19, 1990. Magnusen was arrested on May 30, 1990.] On June 12, 1990, Danny Holloway, a detective with the Gulfport Police Department, requested the performance of a rape protocol on 12 articles of evidence he delivered to the Mississippi Crime Laboratory (hereinafter "crime lab") in Gulfport. Fifteen months later, on August 22, 1991, only a hair comparison analysis had been completed by the crime lab. None of the serological work requested by Holloway had been performed. The results of the hair analysis linked Magnusen to the rape of Evelyn Verchinski, who had identified Magnusen as her assailant in a police showup conducted on May 30, 1990.

Holloway waited four months for the rest of the test results before submitting the files to the district attorney's office on October 8, 1990. The district attorney's office, in turn, waited another seven weeks until November 30, 1990, before presenting the cases to the Grand Jury. Indictments were finally returned on December 14, 1990, six and one-half months following the defendant's arrest. There was a delay in setting Magnusen's arraignment because of inadvertence in the court administrator's office. On the day the arraignment was set, Magnusen was without counsel, his lawyer having been permitted by the trial court to withdraw from the case the previous week.

[Debra Butler, a forensic serologist with the Mississippi Crime Laboratory,] was the only serologist for a 15 county area on the Mississippi Gulf Coast. The exhibits in question were received at the Gulfport office and sent to Jackson for hair and fiber comparison. The specimens were then returned to the Gulfport laboratory for a serological analysis. According to Butler, it would take 80 man hours to test the exhibits submitted in this case. There is no statutory provision for the state to contract with private laboratories to perform their work.

The State argues vigorously that the trial judge erred in finding as a fact and concluding as a matter of law that the State violated Magnusen's constitutional right, as opposed to his statutory right, to a speedy trial when a period of 449 days elapsed between his arrest [on May 30, 1990, and the August 22, 1991,] hearing adjudicating Magnusen's motion to dismiss the multiple charges. . . . Magnusen's constitutional right to a speedy trial attached [when] he was arrested. . . . In Noe v. State, 616 So. 2d 298 (Miss. 1993), we . . . stated:

> When a defendant's constitutional right to a speedy trial is at issue, the balancing test set out in Barker v. Wingo, 407 U.S. 514 (1972), is applicable. The factors to consider are: (1) the length of the delay; (2) the reason for the delay; (3) whether the defendant has asserted his right to a speedy trial; and (4) whether the defendant was prejudiced by the delay.

This Court recognized in Beavers v. State, 498 So. 2d 788, 790 (Miss. 1986):

> No mathematical formula exists according to which the *Barker* weighing and balancing process must be performed. The weight to be given each factor necessarily turns on the

> quality of evidence available on each and, in the absence of evidence, identification of the party with the risk of nonpersuasion. In the end, no one factor is dispositive. The totality of the circumstances must be considered.

We are mindful indeed that no one factor is dispositive of the question. Nor is the balancing process restricted to the *Barker* factors to the exclusion of any other relevant circumstances. . . . We turn now to an analysis of the four *Barker* factors. The trial judge applied the correct legal standard in the form of the traditional four pronged balancing test but reached, in our opinion, an inappropriate result.

(1) Length of the Delay

The delay between arrest and trial was 449 days (approximately 15 months). The trial judge found that a delay of 449 days was sufficient to require the State to show that such delay necessitated a review of the remaining *Barker* factors. We agree.

In Smith v. State, 550 So. 2d 406 (Miss. 1989), this Court held "that any delay of eight months or longer is presumptively prejudicial." However, this factor, alone, is insufficient for reversal, but requires a close examination of the remaining factors. . . . "While such presumptive prejudice cannot alone carry a Sixth Amendment claim without regard to the other *Barker* criteria . . . it is part of the mix of relevant facts, and its importance increases with the length of the delay." Doggett v. United States, 505 U.S. 647 (1992).

The length of the delay not attributable to Magnusen or his lawyer or to the lower court is around 300 days . . . which, under the facts and circumstances in this case, is not an excessive or inordinate delay. In [five prior speedy trial cases decided in this court], each defendant, in the wake of a *Barker* analysis, was discharged following delays of 370, 423, 480, 298, and 566 days, respectively. We give Magnusen the benefit of any doubt. This factor favors the defendant, necessitating scrutiny of the case as to the remaining *Barker* factors.

(2) Reason for the Delay

The reason for delay included chronic congestion of trial docket; unavailability of evidence potentially material to the State's case as well as potentially exculpatory; heavy case load; understaffing and negligence of the crime laboratory; incarceration on other charges after bond was revoked; substitution of defense counsel; three continuances; unheard motions filed by the defense; and unavailability of judge at the time the trial was scheduled. This factor, viewed in its three part totality, favors the State, although slightly. At the very least, it weighs equally against the State and the defendant.

In the *Barker* case, the Supreme Court of the United States asserted:

> [D]ifferent weights should be assigned to different reasons. A deliberate attempt to delay the trial in order to hamper the defense should be weighed heavily against the government. A more neutral reason such as negligence or overcrowded courts should be weighed less heavily but nevertheless should be considered since the ultimate responsibility for such circumstances must rest with the government rather than with the defendant. Finally, a valid reason, such as a missing witness, should serve to justify appropriate delay.

In the case at bar, 198 days or 6½ months elapsed between arrest and indictment, 104 days or 3½ months intervened between indictment and arraignment, and there were 147 days or 5 months intervening between arraignment and the hearing on the motion to dismiss the charges. . . .

The most critical period of delay is the 198 day preindictment delay between Magnusen's arrest on May 30 and his indictment on December 14, 1990. We weigh this portion of the delay against the State but not heavily. The trial judge found as a fact that both the Gulfport Police Department and the district attorney's office "had done their job." He found that the fault lay with the neglect of the crime lab, one of many tentacles of the State. It is unclear from the testimony of Debra Butler whether this neglect was excusable or without just cause. The delay certainly was not intentional. What is clear is that from June 14, 1990, to November 30, 1990, a period of approximately 5½ months, the district attorney's office awaited the results of the laboratory testing before presenting the case to the grand jury. [T]he results of the serology tests could have just as easily been exculpatory as not.

On the other side of the coin, a blood specimen taken from the victim in May of 1990 was allowed to putrefy before it was tested, thereby necessitating a requirement for a new specimen. Negligence causing delay should be weighed against the State but not heavily. An additional observation is that [Magnusen also faced charges of "unlawful touching for lustful purposes," based on events in February 1989, predating the alleged offenses in this case. Although Magnusen was originally released on bond for the 1989 fondling charges, the bond was revoked on August 10, 1990. Thus, Magnusen would have been in jail on the "unlawful touching" charges during part of this period even if he had not been incarcerated on the charges at issue in this case]. It was not until December 21, 1990, a period of 133 days [from the time that bond was revoked], that the fondling indictments were dismissed because [the crime applied only to those at least 18 years old, and Magnusen was 17 at the time of the alleged offense].

In the final analysis, the official neglect of an understaffed and overworked crime lab gives this portion of the delay to the defendant but barely. . . .

We weigh [the 104 day delay from indictment to arraignment] equally because of [Magnusen's decision to substitute counsel in March 1991, a few weeks before the scheduled date of the arraignment]. Magnusen's two cases had not been set for arraignment any sooner because of inadvertence of the court administrator. Moreover, the testimony reflects that a 3½ month delay from indictment to arraignment is not an unusual length of time. Finally, the State was under a continuing duty to disclose by virtue of the defendant's discovery request for crime lab results, filed February 1, 1991.

The bulk of [the 147 day delay between the March 28, 1991, arraignment and the motion to dismiss on August 22, 1991] is attributed to the defendant who was without counsel near the day of arraignment because his lawyer had been permitted to withdraw on April 1, 1991. A congested trial docket and three continuances also contributed to this portion of the delay which weighs heavily against Magnusen.

First, within the context of our [statutory] 270 day rule and the defendant's statutory right, as opposed to his constitutional right, to a speedy trial, docket congestion has been held to constitute good cause for delay. While a crowded docket will not automatically suffice to establish good cause, the specific facts of the case may give rise to good cause. The same rationale should apply when the defendant's constitutional right to a speedy trial, as opposed to his statutory right, is at issue.

Second, during the period from April 15, 1991, to August 16, 1991, a total of three continuances were granted on motion of either the court, the defendant, or both. The reasons for the continuances were, at least in part, a crowded docket, the unavailability of the circuit judge who was engaged in trial elsewhere, and the defendant's motion for an omnibus hearing filed on June 3, 1991, the day the case was set for trial. [The motion included a request for discovery of any lab reports and a request for a speedy trial.] The first continuance was granted on April 15, 1991, upon motion of the circuit judge who was engaged in trial elsewhere. The second continuance was granted on June 3, 1991, upon motion of both the court and the defendant because the defendant filed a motion for an omnibus hearing the day of trial. Trial was reset for August 12, 1991. The third continuance was granted August 16, 1991, upon motion of the circuit judge who again was engaged in trial elsewhere. Trial was reset for August 26, 1991. A delay of 129 days between April 15, 1991, and August 22, 1991 (the day the charges were dismissed), was a by-product of continuances granted because of (1) a congested trial docket and (2) the defendant's motion for an omnibus hearing.

Delays caused by overcrowded dockets are not to be weighed heavily against the State. Continuances granted to the defendant toll the running of our speedy trial statute and should not be counted against the State. Again, the same rationale should apply when a defendant's constitutional right . . . to a speedy trial is at issue. Accordingly, over 100 days during the period from April 15, 1991 to August 22, 1991 should be deducted from the total number of days sandwiched between Magnusen's arrest and trial. Thus, the length of the delay not attributable to either the defendant or his lawyer is approximately 300 days or ten months.

(3) Assertion of Right

Magnusen asserted his constitutional right to a speedy trial in a multi-faceted motion filed February 1, 1991, by attorney Davis; again in a multi-faceted motion filed August 7, 1991, by attorney Woods; and again on August 20, 1991, in the Motion to Dismiss charges filed by attorney Woods. . . . Buried in the midst of a four page, eleven paragraph document filed February 1, 1991, by attorney Davis and styled simply "Motions," is a three line statement found under paragraph VII in which Magnusen "asserts his right to a speedy, public trial by jury as guaranteed under the 6th Amendment. . . ."

The State, of course, bears the burden of bringing an accused to trial in a speedy manner. Although the defendant has neither a duty nor an obligation to bring himself to trial, points are placed on his side of the ledger when, as here, he has made a demand for a speedy trial.

This factor favors the defendant, but only slightly. This is because the bulk of the delay from February 1, 1991, when Magnusen first asserted his right to a speedy trial, to August 22, 1991, when the charges were dismissed, can reasonably be charged to the defendant while the reasons for other portions of the delay are, at best, neutral. Moreover, certain actions by defense counsel were in derogation of Magnusen's assertion of his right to a speedy trial.

Immediately after asserting his right to a speedy trial by and through attorney Davis [on February 1, 1991], Magnusen retained a new lawyer, Cecil Woods, Jr. [Woods himself withdrew from the case but was reappointed on April 8, the date the arraignment took place.] On April 15, 1991, the lower court, on its own motion, entered a continuance because the circuit judge was engaged in trial elsewhere. On June 3, 1991, the State was again prepared to go to trial without the crime laboratory results. Magnusen, by and through attorney Woods, filed a motion for an omnibus hearing which was set but never held due to a death in defense counsel's family. On a later date, due to the engagement of the circuit judge in a capital murder case, once again the omnibus hearing although set, was not conducted. In addition to this, Magnusen filed motions which he never set for hearing. The multi-faceted motions filed on February 1, 1991, and August 7, 1991, were never set for hearing by the defendant. Such, in our opinion, detracts from the assertion of his right to a speedy trial.

The record reflects the State was ready, willing and able to go to trial on four separate occasions, April 8, June 3, August 12, and August 16, 1991, but was prevented from doing so by circumstances clearly not the fault of the State. We weigh this *Barker* factor in favor of Magnusen, but barely.

(4) Prejudice to the Defendant

No actual prejudice to Magnusen was demonstrated by the delay. . . . The only prejudice articulated by the trial judge in his written order was that the defendant "lost his freedom" on the date of the arrest on charges which had gone untried for over a year. Although Magnusen testified at the evidentiary hearing, no claim of prejudice was made at that time. The only such inference appears in Magnusen's motion to dismiss filed on August 20, 1991. Therein, blatant allegations are made that witnesses may not be available and apparently the memories of those witnesses who are available have faded. . . . This prong of the *Barker* analysis was discussed as follows:

> A fourth factor is prejudice to the defendant. Prejudice of course, should be assessed in the light of the interests of defendants which the speedy trial right was designed to protect. This Court has identified three such interests: (i) to prevent oppressive pretrial incarceration; (ii) to minimize anxiety and concern of the accused; and (iii) to limit the possibility that the defense will be impaired. Of these, the most serious is the last, because the inability of a defendant adequately to prepare his case skews the fairness of the entire system. If witnesses die or disappear during a delay, the prejudice is obvious. There is also prejudice if defense witnesses are unable to recall accurately events of the distant past. Loss of memory, however, is not always reflected in the record because what has been forgotten can rarely be shown. [407 U.S. at 532.]

As for the first interest, Magnusen was incarcerated from May 30, 1990, until the charges were dismissed on August 22, 1991, a period of almost 450 days. A healthy number of days, however, should be weighed against the defendant. The 147 day time frame between March 28, 1991, and August 22, 1991, is weighed more heavily against Magnusen than against the State. The remaining ten month period of incarceration is the same period of incarceration found in the *Barker* case where the Supreme Court of the United States held that Barker was not denied his right to a speedy trial. . . .

No proof was offered by the defendant that his employment or family life was disrupted or his financial resources drained or his associations curtailed; to the contrary, . . . Magnusen was single and unemployed. Although Magnusen was incarcerated from the time of his arrest to dismissal of the charges, we cannot categorize his pretrial incarceration as particularly "oppressive."

The second interest protected by the constitutional right to a speedy trial is minimizing anxiety and concern. There was no proof during the hearing that Magnusen suffered an extraordinary, or even an ordinary, amount of anxiety and concern over this particular case. There were several serious charges pending against him, including two fondling charges. While Magnusen may have had a right to be anxious and concerned, not all of his woes and tribulations were a product of the charges . . . in this case.

The third interest protected by the constitutional right to a speedy trial is that of minimizing the possibility that the defense of the accused will be impaired. There has been no allegation that the defense was impaired because of a loss of witnesses or their memories. In short, there has been no demonstration of actual prejudice to Magnusen in preparing for the defense of his case. Although the delay in this case is presumptively prejudicial, we will not infer prejudice to the defense out of the "clear blue."

In the final analysis, where, as here, the delay is neither intentional nor egregiously protracted, and where, as here, there is an absence of prejudice, we find this factor favoring the State.

On balance, an analysis of the *Barker* factors, when considered together with other relevant circumstances, favors the State, but not heavily. . . . The trial court paid insufficient attention to the various distinct periods of delay in reaching its conclusion. Additionally, the trial court erroneously required that the delay be for "good and sufficient cause" rather than whether the reason weighed "heavily," "lightly" or "not at all." [The trial judge] placed too much weight on the negligence of the crime lab and failed to properly focus on the various distinct periods of delay in reaching his conclusion. The judgment of the trial court is reversed and the matter is remanded for Magnusen to stand trial on all charges.

SULLIVAN, J., dissenting.

. . . The majority opinion rests on the faulty premise that the trial court decided this issue using the wrong legal standard. . . . True, the trial court considered whether the state showed "good and sufficient cause" for the delay; however, the trial court did so in conjunction with its determination of how much weight to accord the justification offered. The trial court correctly relied on State v. Ferguson, 576 So. 2d 1252 (Miss. 1991), for the proposition that once the delay has been determined to be presumptively prejudicial, "the burden shifts to the prosecution to produce evidence justifying the delay and to persuade the trier of fact of the legitimacy of these reasons." This Court also stated in *Ferguson* that "where the accused has not caused the delay, and where the prosecution has failed to show good cause therefor, this factor [reason for the delay] weighs in favor of the accused." . . .

Justice Smith correctly acknowledges the fact that the length of delay in this case warrants examination of the remaining *Barker* factors. It is with Justice Smith's reasoning beginning with the second constitutional speedy trial factor, "reason for the delay," that I must disagree. The trial court found that the cause of the delay "certainly cannot be attributable to the defendant." We cannot find to the contrary short of concluding that the lower court was manifestly wrong in making this finding. Instead, the majority simply reexamines the record, splits the 455 day delay into different periods of delay, argues that the court applied the wrong legal standard, and somehow reaches the conclusion that the cause of delay weighs against Magnusen, or, "at the very least, it weighs equally against the State and the defendant." . . .

I furthermore disagree with Justice Smith's implication that docket congestion should be considered good cause to the extent that the constitutional speedy trial clock should be deemed to have stopped running during those periods of delay. The *Barker* Court stated: "Overcrowded courts should be weighed less heavily but nevertheless should be considered since the ultimate responsibility for such circumstances must rest with the government rather than with the defendant."

[Magnusen] made his first speedy trial demand on February 1, 1991, shortly after the indictment was returned against him, after a period of delay attributable to the state because of the negligence of the state crime lab. He did not knowingly delay in making his demand. . . . Today's decision does not, in my opinion, place the proper importance on Magnusen's assertion of his right. Moreover, the inference that the prosecution should not be held to have been aware of the speedy trial demand because it was buried in a lengthy motion is not persuasive. Magnusen clearly asserted his right. . . .

Because the first three factors weigh in Magnusen's favor, it is not necessary to examine the fourth *Barker* factor, prejudice to the defendant. Nonetheless, the trial court weighed this factor in Magnusen's favor. The court stated:

> I know of nothing that is more prejudicial to anyone than to be confined for a period of 447 days without the benefit of a trial. It's somewhat likened to getting the cart before the horse, because once again, the State does carry the burden of proving a person's guilt, not assuming the person's guilt.

First, when a presumption of prejudice has been established, as it was in this case, a defendant is not responsible for proving prejudice. That is, the prosecution is responsible for rebutting the presumption that the defendant has suffered prejudice as a result of the delay. . . .

The majority correctly points out the fact that in *Barker*, the Court found that the defendant did not suffer oppressive pretrial incarceration for a period of time similar in length to that Magnusen spent in jail prior to trial through no fault of his own. In *Barker*, however, the Court took specific notice of the fact that *Barker* did not want to be tried—he allowed the state to continue his case 16 times without objection. Here, as mentioned earlier, Magnusen filed his speedy trial demand approximately six weeks after he was indicted—Barker waited approximately three and one-half years. The *Barker* Court's reasoning regarding the defendant's desire to be tried, and how that desire relates to the question of whether the defendant suffered oppressive pretrial incarceration, favors Magnusen. . . .

I believe today's decision fails to give the proper deference to the findings and conclusions of the trial judge who served as a part of the proceedings against this defendant from their inception, and throughout, until the charges were dismissed against him. The majority admits that this is a close case, and as such, we should affirm the lower court's decision. The trial court applied the correct legal standard and reached the correct result. Because I believe we cannot reverse this case on the record before us, I respectfully dissent.

Notes

1. *Constitutional speedy trial rights: majority position.* The Supreme Court has incorporated the "speedy trial" clause of the Sixth Amendment as a component of

the Fourteenth Amendment's due process clause that applies to the states. Klopfer v. North Carolina, 386 U.S. 213 (1967). In addition, virtually all states have used the four-part test from Barker v. Wingo, 407 U.S. 514 (1972), to determine the speedy trial rights of defendants under their state constitutions. As illustrated in the *Magnusen* case from Mississippi, the analysis of constitutional speedy trial claims often requires courts to answer a series of questions, assigning responsibility for each period of delay. The first *Barker* factor (the length of the delay) is a necessary threshold. Only when the delay becomes long enough will the court analyze the other factors. Although the exact length of time necessary is a question for common-law development, a delay of just under one year is usually sufficient to obtain a full review of the four factors. Once the full inquiry takes place, often the most important factor is whether the defendant has been prejudiced.

2. *Ranking reasons for delay.* Courts in most jurisdictions have followed the *Barker* Court's suggestion that a "deliberate attempt to delay the trial in order to hamper the defense" is weighed heavily against the government, while a "valid reason" such as a missing witness would justify some delay. Reasons such as prosecutorial negligence or lack of resources will count against the government, but not heavily. Does it make sense to make defendants bear the cost of inadequate court funding? Does a similar ranking system apply to a defendant's reasons for contributing to the delay? Will the defendant's actions only be weighed "heavily" against her claim if she has made a deliberate attempt to hamper the prosecution through delay? Did the *Magnusen* court place different weights on different actions of the defendant?

3. *Requests and waivers.* Before *Barker,* a number of states followed the "demand waiver" rule, which assumed that a defendant who did not request a speedy trial had waived the right. Even though a request for speedy trial is no longer strictly necessary to make a constitutional claim, a defendant can increase the chances of showing a violation if she asserts the right early in the process. Conversely, it is possible for a defendant to waive speedy trial rights explicitly. What if defense counsel waives speedy trial rights without consulting the client? Is this one of those rights (such as waiver of a jury trial) that a client should have to waive personally?

4. *Prejudice.* The *Barker* Court listed three types of prejudice that a speedy trial could avoid: (a) "oppressive pretrial incarceration"; (b) "anxiety and concern of the accused"; and (c) "the possibility that the defense will be impaired." Courts routinely say that the third type of prejudice, which can include disappearance of witnesses or loss of memory, is the most serious. If there is a statistical relationship between pretrial detention and conviction for the charged crime, is it plausible to argue that any prejudice of the first type (pretrial detention) also must count as prejudice of the third type (impairment of defense)? Does it matter what grounds the government has for holding the defendant? Speedy trial rights extend to persons imprisoned for other offenses. See Smith v. Hooey, 393 U.S. 374 (1969). Will incarceration for another offense weigh less heavily in favor of the defendant than incarceration only for the current charges? There are cases in which the other *Barker* factors create such a strong showing for the defendant that the court will presume prejudice. According to Doggett v. United States, 505 U.S. 647 (1992), the presumption of prejudice strengthens over time. The eight-year delay between indictment and arrest in *Doggett* was a product of the defendant's choice to leave the country (unaware that he was under indictment) and the government's negligence in pursuing him. The Court was willing to presume that such a lengthy delay would impair the defense. But see People v. Martinez, 996 P.2d 32 (Cal. 2000) (refuses to adopt federal rule that

defendant need not show specific prejudice if delay is sufficiently long; defendant must always show prejudice under state law).

5. *Remedy.* What should a court do if it is convinced that the government has violated a defendant's constitutional speedy trial rights? According to Strunk v. United States, 412 U.S. 434 (1973), dismissal of the charges with prejudice is the only proper remedy for a violation of the Sixth Amendment speedy trial right. State courts by and large have interpreted their own constitutions the same way. Can you imagine any alternative remedies that would effectively prevent delay without losing convictions of guilty persons? How about a reduction of sentence to reflect the amount of improper delay? What about money damages for improper pretrial incarceration or prolonged anxiety? If these alternatives had been available to the Mississippi court in *Magnusen,* would it have been more willing to find a constitutional violation? See Anthony Amsterdam, Speedy Criminal Trial: Rights and Remedies, 27 Stan. L. Rev. 525 (1975). Should a court be able to select a nondismissal remedy only for particular kinds of prejudice (such as anxiety or loss of reputation) but not for others (such as impairment of defense)? See Akhil Amar, The Constitution and Criminal Procedure: First Principles 96-116 (1997).

6. *Victim's right to speedy trial.* Over the past generation, state constitutional amendments and statutes have recognized some of the interests and procedural rights of victims of alleged crimes. A majority of states now have statutory or constitutional provisions requiring the trial court to consider the interests of crime victims (especially youthful or elderly victims) when responding to requests for continuances. A few states declare more generally that victims have a right to a speedy trial. Take, for instance, Utah Code §77-38-7:

> (1) In determining a date for any criminal trial or other important criminal or juvenile justice hearing, the court shall consider the interests of the victim of a crime to a speedy resolution of the charges under the same standards that govern a defendant's or minor's right to a speedy trial. . . .
>
> (3) (a) In ruling on any motion by a defendant or minor to continue a previously established trial or other important criminal or juvenile justice hearing, the court shall inquire into the circumstances requiring the delay and consider the interests of the victim of a crime to a speedy disposition of the case. . . .

What assurance does a crime victim have that a trial court will carry out these directives? Is the statute enforceable on appeal?

Almost all states now have statutes or procedural rules that oblige the government to complete criminal trials promptly. These "speedy trial acts" show some important differences from one another. First, these statutes and rules differ in how specifically they define the time period that may elapse between accusation and the start of trial. Most, like the federal Speedy Trial Act, give the state a specific number of days (70 days in the federal system) to process the case. Within the group of states that specify the time period, many allow more days to bring to trial a defendant who is not in custody than one who is in custody. See Ill. Ann. Stat. ch. 725, para. 5/103-5 (120 days for defendants in custody, 160 days for defendants released pretrial). A smaller group of states do not specify a number of days at all, but simply require the trial to take place within a "reasonable" time. Mich. R. Crim. P. 6.004 (provides that the "defendant and the people are entitled to a speedy trial and to a speedy resolution of all matters before the court," but states no specific time period for trial of charges against defendants not in custody).

Second, the statutes differ from one another in the methods available to extend the number of days the parties may use to prepare for trial. Some, like the federal statute, exhaustively list the events that can add time to the available days; a number of statutes allow the trial court to extend the time period for "good cause" (or on some other generally phrased grounds). Third, the statutes differ from one another in the remedies they provide for violations. The federal statute is typical of one group, giving the trial judge considerable discretion to choose whether to dismiss the charges with or without prejudice. Other statutes make it clear that one form of dismissal or the other is strongly preferred or required.

Can you identify a combination of features described above that is likely to have the most effect on the amount of time available to prepare a case for trial? The least effect? As you reflect on these statutes, keep a close eye on the interaction between rights and remedies. Is there a relationship between the clarity of the speedy trial obligations that the government faces and the stringency of the remedy for violations? Do these statutes "codify" the constitutional analysis or do they pursue different objectives, using different means?

■ 18 U.S.C. §3161

(c) (1) In any case in which a plea of not guilty is entered, the trial of a defendant charged in an information or indictment with the commission of an offense shall commence within 70 days from the filing date (and making public) of the information or indictment, or from the date the defendant has appeared before a judicial officer of the court in which such charge is pending, whichever date last occurs. . . .

(h) The following periods of delay shall be excluded in computing the time within which an information or an indictment must be filed, or in computing the time within which the trial of any such offense must commence:

(1) Any period of delay resulting from other proceedings concerning the defendant. . . .

(2) Any period of delay during which prosecution is deferred by the attorney for the Government pursuant to written agreement with the defendant, with the approval of the court, for the purpose of allowing the defendant to demonstrate his good conduct.

(3) . . . Any period of delay resulting from the absence or unavailability of the defendant or an essential witness. . . .

(6) If the information or indictment is dismissed upon motion of the attorney for the Government and thereafter a charge is filed against the defendant for the same offense, or any offense required to be joined with that offense, any period of delay from the date the charge was dismissed to the date the time limitation would commence to run as to the subsequent charge had there been no previous charge.

(7) A reasonable period of delay when the defendant is joined for trial with a codefendant as to whom the time for trial has not run and no motion for severance has been granted.

(8) (A) Any period of delay resulting from a continuance granted by any judge on his own motion or at the request of the defendant or his counsel or at

the request of the attorney for the Government, if the judge granted such continuance on the basis of [findings on the record] that the ends of justice served by taking such action outweigh the best interest of the public and the defendant in a speedy trial. . . .

(B) The factors, among others, which a judge shall consider in determining whether to grant a continuance under subparagraph (A) of this paragraph in any case are as follows:

(i) Whether the failure to grant such a continuance in the proceeding would be likely to make a continuation of such proceeding impossible, or result in a miscarriage of justice.

(ii) Whether the case is so unusual or so complex, due to the number of defendants, the nature of the prosecution, or the existence of novel questions of fact or law, that it is unreasonable to expect adequate preparation for pretrial proceedings or for the trial itself within the time limits established by this section. . . .

(iv) Whether the failure to grant such a continuance in a case which, taken as a whole, is not so unusual or so complex as to fall within clause (ii), would deny the defendant reasonable time to obtain counsel, would unreasonably deny the defendant or the Government continuity of counsel, or would deny counsel for the defendant or the attorney for the Government the reasonable time necessary for effective preparation, taking into account the exercise of due diligence.

(C) No continuance under subparagraph (A) of this paragraph shall be granted because of general congestion of the court's calendar, or lack of diligent preparation or failure to obtain available witnesses on the part of the attorney for the Government. . . .

■ 18 U.S.C. §3162

(a)(2) If a defendant is not brought to trial within the time limit required by section 3161(c) as extended by section 3161(h), the information or indictment shall be dismissed on motion of the defendant. The defendant shall have the burden of proof of supporting such motion but the Government shall have the burden of going forward with the evidence in connection with any exclusion of time under subparagraph 3161(h)(3). In determining whether to dismiss the case with or without prejudice, the court shall consider, among others, each of the following factors: the seriousness of the offense; the facts and circumstances of the case which led to the dismissal; and the impact of a reprosecution on the administration of this chapter and on the administration of justice. . . .

■ CALIFORNIA PENAL CODE §1382

(a) The court, unless good cause to the contrary is shown, shall order the action to be dismissed in the following cases: . . .

(2) In a felony case, when a defendant is not brought to trial within 60 days of the defendant's arraignment on an indictment or information, or reinstatement of criminal proceedings. . . . However, an action shall not be dismissed

under this paragraph if [the] defendant requests or consents to the setting of a trial date beyond the 60-day period. . . .

(c) If the defendant is not represented by counsel, the defendant shall not be deemed under this section to have consented to the date for the defendant's trial unless the court has explained to the defendant his or her rights under this section and the effect of his or her consent.

■ CALIFORNIA PENAL CODE §1387

(a) An order terminating an action pursuant to [section 1382] is a bar to any other prosecution for the same offense if it is a felony or if it is a misdemeanor charged together with a felony and the action has been previously terminated pursuant to [section 1382], or if it is a misdemeanor not charged together with a felony, except in those [cases in which] the judge or magistrate finds any of the following:

(1) That substantial new evidence has been discovered by the prosecution which would not have been known through the exercise of due diligence at, or prior to, the time of termination of the action.

(2) That the termination of the action was the result of the direct intimidation of a material witness, as shown by a preponderance of the evidence. . . .

(b) Notwithstanding subdivision (a), an order terminating an action pursuant to this chapter is not a bar to another prosecution for the same offense if it is . . . an offense based on an act of domestic violence, . . . and the termination of the action was the result of the failure to appear by the complaining witness, who had been personally subpoenaed. This subdivision shall apply only within six months of the original dismissal of the action, and may be invoked only once in each action. . . .

Problem 15-5. Whose Delay?

Michael Mayo was arrested in Illinois on February 3, 1998, and was charged the next day with two counts of aggravated criminal sexual assault. Mayo remained in custody and was never released on bond. On March 11, the trial court appointed a public defender to represent Mayo. The public defender entered a not-guilty plea on Mayo's behalf.

On July 1, Mayo's attorney demanded a trial; Mayo himself expressed his wish for the trial to begin quickly, but also said that he wanted to dismiss the public defender and to represent himself. The trial judge warned Mayo about the perils of self-representation, but allowed the public defender to withdraw and continued the case to July 9, on Mayo's request, so that he could answer the State's discovery motion.

On July 9, Mayo appeared in court without an answer to the State's discovery motion. He said that he needed some help and told the court and public defender that he could not represent himself. Based on Mayo's change of attitude, the trial judge reappointed the public defender. After a few status dates, Mayo appeared in court on November 30, this time with a different public defender assigned to the case. Mayo told the court that he wanted trial to be set. The public defender responded that if Mayo wanted to demand trial, he could try the case himself. The judge asked Mayo if he wanted to represent himself or have an attorney. Mayo said "I want an attorney." However, after the public defender and State's Attorney began to discuss a continuance date of December 21, 1998, Mayo interrupted the conversation as follows:

Mayo: I would like to take back my—I'm ready at this time. I don't need her help. She is not helping me.

Public Defender: I just got on the case. I'd like the record to reflect I got on the case two weeks ago and spoke to his wife.

The Court: Be back on December 21st. If you still want to represent yourself we'll go back at that time and you'll go to trial by yourself. I don't suggest it because I think it's—

Mayo: When this woman talked to my wife, she gave the impression that she is not working on my behalf. She told my wife she already finds no reason to be here. What is she doing for me if she is telling my wife that she shouldn't be here on my behalf?

Public Defender: I didn't tell her that.

Mayo: Ask my wife right there.

Public Defender: I don't want to get in the middle of this. If you want to get a private attorney or do this yourself you can.

Mayo appeared in court on December 21, with a different public defender than the one he had on November 30. Mayo informed the court that he wanted to go to trial and represent himself. The trial court did not dismiss the public defender. The judge stated that he was going to hold the case over until December 23, so that Mayo could discuss representing himself with the public defender who represented him on November 30. If Mayo continued in his wish to represent himself at that time, he could do so then. Mayo again stated that he had made his decision and that he wanted to represent himself. The trial court still held the matter over until December 23, 1998. The State's Attorney asked if Mayo was going to answer its discovery motion to which the trial court responded, "he will or he's not calling any witnesses."

On December 23, Mayo again demanded trial, stating his wish to represent himself. The trial court then dismissed the public defender and Mayo represented himself from that point forward. On February 18, 1999, Mayo moved to dismiss the charges on speedy-trial grounds. The court denied the motion on March 29. The trial commenced on April 12, and the jury found Mayo guilty of two counts of aggravated criminal sexual assault. The court sentenced defendant to eight years' imprisonment for each count of aggravated criminal sexual assault, to run consecutively.

On appeal, Mayo argues that his convictions should be reversed because the speedy trial act was violated. The Illinois speedy trial act, appearing at 725 ILCS 5/103-5(a), provides: "Every person in custody in this State for an alleged offense shall be tried by the court having jurisdiction within 120 days from the date he was taken into custody unless delay is occasioned by the defendant." The relevant period is 160 days from the date of arrest for defendants who were released from custody before trial.

In this case, over a year passed between Mayo's arrest and the start of his trial. Both parties agree, however, that at least 114 days of the delay should be attributed to the State. The parties only disagree about the responsibility for an additional 21 days of delay, falling between November 30 and December 21. According to case law in Illinois, each delay must be reviewed individually and attributed to the party who causes it. Any delay found to be occasioned by the defendant tolls the applicable statutory period. When a defense attorney requests a continuance on behalf of a defendant, any delay caused by that continuance will be attributed to the defendant. However, a defendant cannot be bound by his attorney's actions when he clearly and convincingly attempted to assert his right to discharge his attorney and proceed to an immediate trial.

Was there a violation of the Illinois Speedy Trial Act? If these proceedings had occurred in federal court, would the relevant 21-day period be counted against the 70-day limit of the federal statute? Do the Illinois and federal statute turn on different factual inquiries? Compare People v. Mayo, 764 N.E.2d 525 (Ill. 2002).

Notes

1. *Speedy trial statutes and the federal constitution.* Almost all states have statutes or court rules addressing speedy trial preparation. Some of these statutes are intended to implement the constitutional speedy trial right, while others serve the additional purpose of clearing court dockets. Do these provisions add a new dimension to the constitutional analysis simply because they are more specific than a general right to a "speedy trial"? In the minority of states where statutes or rules use general language (such as a statutory bar against "unreasonable delay"), does the statute or rule add anything at all to the constitutional inquiry? Why would drafters of rules or statutes bother to pass a provision without specific time limits?

2. *Time allowed for preparation.* Speedy trial statutes select many different time periods to allow the parties to prepare for trial. The federal statute's 70-day limit is one of the shorter periods; some state statutes allow periods longer than six months. Most have tighter time limits for defendants in custody than for those who have been released before trial. It is also customary for these statutes to provide longer time limits for felonies than for misdemeanors, and some create even finer distinctions between the more serious and less serious offenses. See Ohio Rev. Stat. §2945.71. The statutes list several events that can start the speedy trial "clock." Under the federal statute, an arrest starts a time period that must end within 30 days in an indictment or information, while the indictment or information starts the 70-day countdown to the trial. Under most of the state statutes, an indictment or information starts the clock for felonies, and the filing of a complaint begins the period for misdemeanors. Trials that end in mistrials or in convictions reversed on appeal have their own specialized timing rules.

If you were drafting a speedy trial statute, would you anticipate the ways that the parties might try to manipulate the time periods? For instance, would you address the defendant's ability to enter a plea agreement and withdraw it near the arrival of the statutorily designated number of days from the filing of the charge? How would you respond to the prosecutor's power to enter a nolle prosequi as the deadline nears and to refile charges when the case is ready to try?

3. *Minimum time required for preparation.* What are the narrowest time boundaries a system could set without being unconstitutional? Under the federal statute, a trial cannot commence "less than 30 days from the date on which the defendant first appears through counsel" unless the defendant consents to a quicker deadline. 18 U.S.C. §3161(c)(2). A minority of states have statutes setting a minimum time period for trial preparation. This question ordinarily arises as a constitutional challenge (based on due process or the right to counsel) to a trial court's refusal to

grant a defense motion for a continuance; appellate courts almost always defer to the trial court's discretion on this question. See State v. Jones, 467 S.E.2d 12 (N.C. 1996). Should states aim for the fastest possible trials consistent with due process?

4. *Excluded time periods.* One major difference among speedy trial statutes appears in the method of identifying "excluded" days, those that do not count toward the speedy trial deadline. Most jurisdictions, represented by the federal statute reprinted above, list the particular events that can be excluded from the speedy trial countdown. A minority of states, represented by the California statute above, do not specify the grounds for excluding days, instead allowing judges to determine in a particular case whether "good cause" exists to allow an exclusion. Some statutes, like the Illinois provision quoted above, state simply that any delay "caused" by the defendant is excluded from the countdown. Consult the federal statute again, giving particular attention to section 3161(h)(8). Does this provision convert the statute's itemized list into a less predictable standard? Is it inevitable that an itemized list of grounds for excluding days will include reasons such as these? How would a judge in California respond to a claim that "court congestion" is a "good cause" for a delay beyond the statutory limits? See People v. Johnson, 606 P.2d 738 (Cal. 1980) (ordinary congestion arising from inadequate resources is not good cause, but congestion arising from extraordinary and nonrecurring circumstances can be good cause).

5. *Sanctions for violations of statutes.* Another major difference among speedy trial statutes is the remedy they require or encourage for statutory violations. As you saw in the federal statute reprinted above, dismissal without prejudice is the preferred remedy under some speedy trial statutes. United States v. Taylor, 487 U.S. 326 (1988) (overturning trial court decision to dismiss with prejudice for Speedy Trial Act violation); State v. Clovis, 864 P.2d 687 (Kan. 1993) (government successfully showed a "necessity" for dismissing and refiling charges). Is dismissal without prejudice a toothless remedy? Consult again the New York statute of limitations reprinted at the beginning of this section and consider whether such provisions make the dismissal without prejudice remedy more effective. It is more common to find speedy trial statutes or rules of procedure that make dismissal with prejudice the preferred remedy. See Neb. Stat. §29-1208. Does the California statute reprinted above make dismissal with prejudice the preferred remedy?

Is the dismissal remedy for speedy trial violation similar to the exclusionary rule for unconstitutional searches and seizures because it rewards some guilty defendants out of proportion to the wrong that the state has committed? Would monetary damages be a better remedy, at least for defendants who make no showing that the delay impaired their defense? A Massachusetts statute offers compensation to some defendants whose cases are delayed beyond the statutory limits. See Commonwealth v. Bunting, 518 N.E.2d 1159 (Mass. 1988) (in action to recover damages for statutory speedy trial delays, state can still litigate question of whether defendant consented to delays, even after dismissal of criminal charges on speedy trial grounds).

6. *Prioritizing cases.* Speedy trial statutes give priority to criminal matters over civil matters; among criminal matters, they give priority to felonies and cases involving defendants who are detained before trial. See Cal. Penal Code §1048. In a world where ordinary civil litigation must wait in line behind criminal cases, does this give every segment of society a concrete interest in speedy trials? Is this what courts mean when they speak of the "public's interest" in speedy trials?

XVI

Pleas and Bargains

In criminal courts in this country, guilty pleas before trial occur far more often than verdicts after trial. In large urban counties in 1998, 9 of 10 felony defendants resolved their criminal charges through a guilty plea rather than a trial. Only murder charges produced trials in more than 10 percent of the cases; the rate of guilty pleas was even higher than 90 percent for misdemeanor charges. In the federal system in 2000, 95 percent of all convictions resulted from pleas of guilty or nolo contendere rather than trials. Most of the time, in most places in this country, the overwhelming majority of criminal charges are resolved through guilty pleas.

Why do we see so few criminal trials? Plea bargains are the short — and incomplete — answer. A large proportion of felony defendants enter pleas of guilty only after they have reached an agreement with the prosecutor, obliging the prosecutor to make some concessions. Perhaps the prosecutor will agree to dismiss some pending charges or to reduce the pending charge to something less serious (this is known as a "charge bargain"). Or perhaps the prosecutor will agree to recommend a particular sentence or to refrain from making certain recommendations (a "sentence" bargain). Other agreement terms are possible, such as a promise not to file charges against third parties.

But plea agreements are not the only explanation for guilty pleas. Some defendants plead guilty as charged without extracting any promises at all from the prosecutor (an "open" plea). These defendants (and their attorneys) know that judges tend to impose less severe sentences on offenders who plead guilty, compared to those who go to trial. This "plea discount" is a reality in virtually every court, but it is rare to find formal acknowledgment of the practice in case law, statutes, or procedural rules.

Anyone who wants to understand American criminal justice must study both guilty pleas and plea bargains. The numbers suggest that these topics are more fundamental than criminal trials. Of course, it may be that plea bargaining takes place in the "shadow" of criminal trials, so that the terms of any agreement reflect the parties' predictions about what *would* have happened at a trial. But it is also possible that some types of cases are resolved by guilty pleas so often that the rules of trial have little importance, while the trials that do occur represent some different universe of cases.

The materials in this chapter survey the boundaries that our legal institutions place on the practice of plea bargaining. We begin within those boundaries, examining some of the typical topics for bargaining and the ordinary motives of parties who enter plea agreements. We then move to the boundaries, looking at the types of bargains that the negotiating parties are willing to accept but the legal system as a whole rejects. Categorical constraints on plea bargains come from legislatures, the executive branch, and (less frequently) judges. As always, we will consider whether these different institutions create distinctive answers to the puzzle of what makes a fair plea bargain. Running throughout the chapter is a question about the controlling substantive principles: Does the common law of contracts provide the necessary guidance for determining which plea agreements are enforceable and which are not? Finally, the chapter closes with a discussion of the largest questions about plea bargaining: Is the practice inevitable, and is it desirable?

A. BARGAIN ABOUT WHAT?

Every defendant who pleads guilty gives up the right to a jury trial, and the concomitant rights to be represented by counsel, compel witnesses to testify, and confront adverse witnesses. Why would a defendant waive these key rights — essentially those guaranteed by the Fifth and Sixth Amendments to the federal constitution and their state analogues — along with the chance of an acquittal? And why would prosecutors be willing to bargain away the chance of a conviction in court, with the public affirmation of justice and the publicity that go along with it? The materials in this section explore the objectives of the prosecution and defense as they bargain over a possible plea of guilty. This section also pursues a second theme: Are there some terms that are implicit in every plea bargain? Are there some terms that our legal system will not allow the parties to negotiate?

■ FEDERAL RULE OF CRIMINAL PROCEDURE 11(a), (c)

(a) (1) A defendant may plead not guilty, guilty, or (with the court's consent) nolo contendere.

(2) With the consent of the court and the government, a defendant may enter a conditional plea of guilty or nolo contendere, reserving in writing the right to have an appellate court review an adverse determination of a specified pretrial motion. A defendant who prevails on appeal may then withdraw the plea.

(3) Before accepting a plea of nolo contendere, the court must consider the parties' views and the public interest in the effective administration of justice.

(4) If a defendant refuses to enter a plea or if a defendant organization fails to appear, the court must enter a plea of not guilty.

(c) (1) An attorney for the government and the defendant's attorney, or the defendant when proceeding pro se, may discuss and reach a plea agreement. The court must not participate in these discussions. If the defendant pleads guilty or nolo contendere to either a charged offense or a lesser or related offense, the plea agreement may specify that an attorney for the government will:

(A) not bring, or will move to dismiss, other charges;

(B) recommend, or agree not to oppose the defendant's request, that a particular sentence or sentencing range is appropriate or that a particular provision of the Sentencing Guidelines, or policy statement, or sentencing factor does or does not apply (such a recommendation or request does not bind the court); or

(C) agree that a specific sentence or sentencing range is the appropriate disposition of the case, or that a particular provision of the Sentencing Guidelines, or policy statement, or sentencing factor does or does not apply (such a recommendation or request binds the court once the court accepts the plea agreement).

(2) The parties must disclose the plea agreement in open court when the plea is offered, unless the court for good cause allows the parties to disclose the plea agreement in camera.

(3) (A) To the extent the plea agreement is of the type specified in Rule 11(c)(1)(A) or (C), the court may accept the agreement, reject it, or defer a decision until the court has reviewed the presentence report.

(B) To the extent the plea agreement is of the type specified in Rule 11(c)(1)(B), the court must advise the defendant that the defendant has no right to withdraw the plea if the court does not follow the recommendation or request.

■ PEOPLE v. GREGORY LUMZY

730 N.E.2d 20 (Ill. 2000)

HEIPLE, J.

. . . On June 10, 1997, defendant was charged with the offenses of aggravated battery and robbery. On June 23, 1997, defendant pled guilty to robbery in exchange for the State's dismissal of the aggravated battery charge. The circuit court of Lee County sentenced defendant to seven years in prison.

On August 1, 1997 defendant's attorney filed a motion to reconsider defendant's sentence. Defendant did not move to withdraw his guilty plea. The trial court denied defendant's motion and defendant filed a notice of appeal. . . .

The State argued that defendant's plea was a "negotiated plea" because the State had agreed to drop the aggravated battery charge in exchange for defendant's guilty plea. Accordingly, under the rationale of People v. Evans, 673 N.E.2d 244 (Ill. 1996), defendant could not ask the court to reconsider the length of his sentence without having first filed a motion to withdraw his guilty plea. The appellate court, with one justice dissenting, held that defendant could properly challenge the length of his sentence even though he had not filed a motion to withdraw his guilty plea. . . .

In *Evans,* this court held that . . . in a challenge to a sentence entered pursuant to a negotiated plea agreement, the defendant must (1) move to withdraw the guilty plea and vacate the judgment, and (2) show that the granting of the motion is necessary to correct a manifest injustice. While that terminology used in *Evans* was perfectly appropriate and adequate to dispose of the issue before the court in that case, it did not, nor did it purport to, address every conceivable type of plea agreement.

As Justice Freeman correctly observed in his special concurrence in People v. Linder, 708 N.E.2d 1169 (Ill. 1999), "not all 'negotiated' pleas are the same." Indeed, there are at least four distinct plea scenarios which can occur when a defendant decides to enter a plea of guilty. First, a defendant may simply enter a "blind," or "open," plea without any inducement from the State. In such a case, both the defendant and the State may argue for any sentence permitted by law. Likewise, the trial court in such a case exercises its full discretion and selects the defendant's sentence from the range provided by the relevant statute. . . .

At the other extreme, a defendant may enter a fully negotiated plea under which he agrees to plead guilty in exchange for a specific sentencing recommendation by the State. This was the fact pattern addressed in *Evans*. In that case, two defendants had each pled guilty pursuant to plea agreements under which the State agreed to drop other pending charges and to recommend a specific sentence. The trial courts accepted the plea agreements and entered judgment thereon. Subsequently, however, each defendant sought to reduce his respective sentence by filing a motion for sentence reconsideration. After those motions were denied, the defendants filed appeals arguing that their sentences were excessive.

Relying primarily on contract-law principles, this court in *Evans* rejected the defendants' attempts to reduce the sentences to which they had agreed as part of their plea bargains without first moving to withdraw their guilty pleas. This court recognized that a contrary rule would permit defendants to hold the State to its side of the bargain, by eliminating the possibility of convictions on the dropped charges or sentences in excess of the agreed-upon recommendation, while reneging on the agreement by trying to unilaterally reduce the sentences to which they had agreed.

This court considered a slightly different type of plea agreement in People v. Linder, 708 N.E.2d 1169 (Ill. 1999). In that case, we considered the consolidated appeals of two defendants who pled guilty pursuant to agreements under which the State agreed to drop other pending charges and to recommend a sentence not to exceed an agreed-upon cap. Under this third type of plea bargain, the State's ability to argue for the full range of penalties provided for in the Unified Code of Corrections was constrained by the terms of its agreements with the defendants. After the trial judges in *Linder* accepted the defendants' guilty pleas and imposed sentences within the caps, both defendants sought on appeal to challenge the sentences imposed upon them as excessive. Once again relying upon the contract-law principles described in *Evans*, this court held that such appeals were improper where the defendants had not moved to withdraw their guilty pleas. . . . Accordingly, this court held that it would be fundamentally unfair to permit defendants to unilaterally modify their sides of the plea bargains while simultaneously holding the State to its side of the bargain.

The instant case involves a fourth type of guilty plea which is fundamentally different from the pleas this court considered in *Evans* and *Linder*. Here, as in *Evans* and *Linder*, the State agreed to drop certain charges against defendant in exchange for defendant's plea of guilty to another charge. In stark contrast to the facts of *Evans* and *Linder*, however, the plea bargain in the instant case was utterly silent as to the sentence which defendant would receive. In this case, therefore, both the State and the defendant were free to argue for any sentence provided for in the Unified Code of Corrections. Likewise, the trial court was able to exercise its full discretion in selecting any sentence permitted by law.

Accordingly, where the record is clear that *absolutely no agreement existed* between the parties as to defendant's sentence, defendant manifestly cannot be breaching such a nonexistent agreement by arguing that the sentence which the court imposed was excessive. For the reasons stated above, the judgment of the appellate court . . . is affirmed.

FREEMAN, J., specially concurring.

[T]he State argues that, by reducing the charges, the State did make a sentencing concession because the sentence would have been greater had the aggravated battery charge not been dropped. I disagree. [A]n agreement by the State to reduce or dismiss charges against a defendant in exchange for the defendant's plea to the reduced or remaining charges, which has the effect of reducing the sentencing range or the number of sentences a defendant could face, does not constitute an implicit agreement as to sentence. By agreeing to drop a charge, the State has made only the concession of forgoing its right to establish defendant's guilt of that charge. To imply a sentencing concession on the part of the State in this circumstance would require this court to presume that defendant was, in fact, guilty of the charge. Such a presumption would, of course, fly in the face of the presumption of innocence that exists in our criminal justice system.

The rule enunciated in *Evans* focused on returning the parties to their status quo. When a defendant pleads guilty solely in return for the dismissal of charges, the State and defendant receive just what they bargained for, *i.e.*, a guilty plea in exchange for dismissing charges. The parties have not agreed as to the length of the sentence, which is left to the circuit court's full discretion. Thus, no part of the bargain would be undermined by allowing defendant to seek reconsideration of the sentence decided by the circuit court alone. [W]e should avoid a bright-line rule that places meaningless procedural obstacles in the path of an appeal. For these reasons and those expressed in the court's opinion, I concur in today's holding.

BILANDIC, J., dissenting.

. . . This court in People v. Evans, 673 N.E.2d 244 (Ill. 1996), interpreted Supreme Court Rule 604(d), which provides that a defendant may not appeal from a judgment entered upon a plea of guilty unless the defendant timely "files in the trial court a motion to reconsider the sentence, if only the sentence is being challenged, or, if the plea is being challenged, a motion to withdraw his plea of guilty and vacate the judgment." This court held that the motion-for-sentence-reconsideration provisions of Rule 604(d) apply only to "open," as opposed to "negotiated," guilty pleas. We defined an open guilty plea as one in which a defendant pleads guilty "without receiving *any* promises from the State in return." (Emphasis added.) Accordingly, we concluded that, following the entry of judgment on a negotiated guilty plea, a defendant must move to withdraw the guilty plea and vacate the judgment, even if the defendant wants to challenge only his sentence.

Evans explained that allowing a defendant to challenge only his sentence following the entry of judgment on a negotiated guilty plea would violate basic contract law principles. In such a circumstance, the defendant is attempting to hold the State to its part of the bargain while unilaterally reneging on or modifying the terms that the defendant had previously agreed to accept. For example, the defendants in *Evans* agreed to plead guilty and, in exchange, the State promised to dismiss other charges and recommend a specific sentence. . . .

Subsequently, in People v. Linder, 708 N.E.2d 1169 (Ill. 1999), this court determined that the holding in *Evans* applies to plea agreements in which the defendant agrees to plead guilty in exchange for the State's promises to dismiss other charges and to recommend a cap on the length of the defendant's sentence. We reasoned that, by agreeing to plead guilty in exchange for the sentencing cap, the defendant is effectively agreeing not to challenge a sentence imposed below the cap.

In this case, defendant was charged with robbery, a Class 2 felony, and aggravated battery, a Class 3 felony. At a hearing, the circuit court advised defendant of the charges against him and that he faced possible prison sentences of three to seven years for the robbery, and two to five years for the aggravated battery. The circuit court further advised defendant that he could receive extended prison terms and therefore be sentenced to prison terms of 14 and 10 years, respectively. Defendant and the State ultimately reached a plea agreement. Defendant agreed to plead guilty to robbery in exchange for the State's promise to dismiss the aggravated battery charge against defendant. The parties presented the plea agreement to the circuit court. The circuit court again advised defendant that he could be sentenced to a maximum of 14 years' imprisonment for the robbery. The circuit court accepted the plea agreement and, following defendant's guilty plea to robbery, sentenced defendant to seven years in prison.

Defendant's plea agreement is negotiated within the meaning of *Evans*. Defendant pled guilty in exchange for the State's promise to dismiss the aggravated battery charge against him. Because defendant obtained the State's promise to dismiss this charge, the prison sentence that defendant could have expected to receive was reduced from 12 years to 7 years if extended sentences were not imposed, and from 24 years to 14 years if extended sentences were imposed. The plea agreement that the parties negotiated, therefore, provided defendant the valuable benefit of a less severe sentence than he could have received had he been convicted of both robbery and aggravated battery.

Moreover, by pleading guilty to robbery in exchange for the State's promise to dismiss the aggravated battery charge, defendant, in effect, agreed that a sentence within the statutory range for robbery was appropriate. Defendant was in fact sentenced to seven years in prison for the robbery—a sentence within the statutory range.

Allowing defendant to modify unilaterally this plea agreement while holding the State to the terms of the agreement will discourage prosecutors from entering into plea agreements. . . . I therefore respectfully dissent.

Problem 16-1. Waiving Right to Appeal a Sentence

The United States Attorney for your district adopted a policy to encourage defendants to waive the right to appeal. The new office policy states that any plea agreements with federal criminal defendants must include the following language:

> The defendant is aware that Title 18, United States Code, Section 3742 affords a defendant the right to appeal the sentence imposed. Acknowledging this, the defendant knowingly waives the right to appeal any sentence within the maximum provided in the statute(s) of conviction (or the manner in which that sentence was determined) on the grounds set forth in Title 18, United States Code, Section 3742 or on any ground

> whatever, in exchange for the concessions made by the United States in this plea agreement. The defendant also waives his right to challenge his sentence or the manner in which it was determined in any collateral attack....

Any proposed plea agreements that do not include this language must receive approval from a supervisory committee, and the committee will grant these "exceptions" only under "extraordinary circumstances." The policy calls on prosecutors to negotiate for the government to retain its right to appeal any legal error in the application of the federal sentencing guidelines.

The policy recognizes that a sentencing appeal waiver provision does not waive all claims on appeal. The federal courts of appeals have held that appellate review of some claims cannot be waived, such as a defendant's claim that he was denied the effective assistance of counsel at sentencing, that he was sentenced on the basis of his race, or that his sentence exceeded the statutory maximum. The memo also warns that prosecutors must not use the appeal waiver provision "to promote circumvention of the sentencing guidelines."

You are the director of the office of the Federal Public Defender in this district. How will you respond to the new bargaining policy of the federal prosecutors? How do you predict this new policy will be received by the courts? Can you predict whether the policy will be difficult for the prosecutors to implement in particular types of cases? Develop some alternative bargaining strategies for the public defenders in your office to pursue. See United States v. Guevara, 941 F.2d 1299 (4th Cir. 1991); Memo from John Keeney, Acting Assistant Attorney General, October 4, 1995.

Problem 16-2. Dealing Away Double Jeopardy

The state of Florida charged Juan Novaton with multiple offenses arising from two separate incidents in the same year. Because he had two prior felony convictions, Novaton faced the possibility of being treated as a habitual violent felony offender and a probable sentence of life in prison without parole. Recognizing this possibility, Novaton entered into a plea bargain. The state agreed to give up the possibility of securing the usual sentence of life without parole for a habitual violent offender, while Novaton agreed to plead guilty to all of the charges and to accept concurrent sentences totaling 50 years, subject to a 15-year mandatory minimum requirement. As a result of this plea bargain, Novaton was adjudicated guilty and sentenced for burglary, robbery, and aggravated battery with a firearm and, in addition, was adjudicated guilty and sentenced for two separate crimes of possessing a firearm in the commission of the same felonies. Florida law would bar these latter two convictions and sentences under state double jeopardy principles. Can the court accept the plea agreement between Novaton and the prosecutor? Compare Novaton v. State, 634 So. 2d 607 (Fla. 1994); Daniel C. Richman, Bargaining About Future Jeopardy, 49 Vand. L. Rev. 1181 (1996).

Notes

1. *Common types of bargains.* Prosecutors and defendants are allowed to bargain over a wide variety of topics. What do prosecutors typically offer during plea

negotiations? Under a "charge bargain" (see Federal Rule 11(c)(1)(A) above), the prosecutor agrees to reduce charges or to drop some counts entirely. The prosecutor might also agree not to file charges in the future against the defendant or some third party based on the events in question. Under a "sentence bargain" (see Rule 11(c)(1)(B) above), a prosecutor agrees to ask the sentencing judge for a certain outcome, or to refrain from asking for a certain outcome, or to make no sentencing recommendation at all. See ABA Standards for Criminal Justice, Prosecution Function 3-4.2(a) (prosecutor "should not make any promise or commitment assuring a defendant or defense counsel that a court will impose a specific sentence or a suspension of sentence; a prosecutor may properly advise the defense what position will be taken concerning disposition").

What does a defendant typically offer? The most important and obvious benefit the defendant can offer is to waive the trial and all its accompanying procedural protections, such as the right to confront witnesses. The waiver of a trial saves the government the expense of preparing and conducting a trial, along with the uncertainty about the outcome at trial. See Commonwealth v. Stagner, 3 S.W.3d 738 (Ky. 1999) (allowing defendant to plead guilty while jury is deliberating; some other jurisdictions prevent guilty pleas after the jury receives case because bargain no longer serves public function of clearing docket). A defendant can also offer to cooperate during investigations of other defendants and other crimes.

There are several ways for a defendant to give up some procedural options while preserving others. The "conditional plea" (see Rule 11(a) above) allows the defendant to plead guilty while reserving the right to appeal on a defined pretrial issue, such as the voluntariness of a confession. If the defendant succeeds on appeal, the guilty plea can be withdrawn. Although it is used less often than the conditional plea, the "slow plea" is another way for a defendant to preserve some options while waiving others. Under a slow plea, the defendant and the prosecution stipulate to the existence of some facts, and then go forward with an abbreviated bench trial to resolve the remaining factual and legal issues. See State v. Mierz, 901 P.2d 286 (Wash. 1995).

Finally, a defendant might offer a plea of nolo contendere rather than a plea of guilty. A plea of nolo contendere (meaning "I will not contest" the charges) allows the court to impose criminal sanctions, just as a guilty plea would, but the nolo plea cannot be used against the defendant in any later civil litigation as an admission of guilt. The court (and in some jurisdictions, the prosecutor) must agree before a defendant enters a nolo plea rather than a guilty plea.

2. *Why plead guilty? Plea discounts.* Defendants considering a guilty plea surely know the conventional wisdom that those who plead guilty receive less severe sentences than those who are convicted after a trial. The size of the so-called plea discount varies from place to place, and it is difficult to measure because where the plea discount is most effective (not necessarily where it is most generous) it results in very few trials as a point of comparison. One estimate placed the discount in the federal system at about 30 to 40 percent of the typical sentence imposed on those convicted after trial. See U.S. Sentencing Commission, Supplemental Report on the Initial Sentencing Guidelines and Policy Statements 48 (1987); David Brereton and Jonathan Casper, Does It Pay to Plead Guilty? Differential Sentencing and the Functioning of Criminal Courts, 16 L. & Socy. Rev. 45 (1981-1982). Many consider the fact of a plea bargain to be an illegitimate basis for sentencing some offenders less severely than others. See ABA Standards for Criminal Justice,

Prosecution Function 14-1.8 (guilty plea alone is not sufficient grounds for leniency in sentence).

Would a legislature improve the certainty and honesty of criminal justice by specifying the proper size for a plea discount? The Italian criminal code offers an example of such an explicit plea discount. It provides for a one-third reduction in applicable sentence after guilty plea, provided that maximum sentence does not exceed two years and for an "abbreviated trial" with one-third reduction in applicable sentence upon conviction, available for more serious charges. See Codice di procedura penale art. 442, 444; Nicola Boari and Gianluca Fiorentini, An Economic Analysis of Plea Bargaining: The Incentives of the Parties in a Mixed Penal System, 21 Int'l Rev. L. & Econ. 213 (2001) (five years after 1989 revisions to Italian code, only 8 percent of cases are disposed of through new accusatorial proceedings).

Could the courts improve on the current implicit plea discount by allowing defendants who plead guilty to select the sentencing judge? See Inger Sandal, Plead Guilty, Pick Sentencing Judge, Ariz. Daily Star, October 29, 1999 (describing such a policy operating in Pima County, Arizona for defendants who plead guilty within 25 days of arraignment; defense attorney and former judge calls system a "prosecutor's delight" because guilty plea decision occurs before defense attorney receives police report).

3. *Presumed good faith in bargaining.* Courts in the United States, since at least the middle of the twentieth century, have generally presumed that plea bargaining is both an appropriate and necessary part of the criminal justice system. As the U.S. Supreme Court put it in Santobello v. New York, 404 U.S. 257 (1971), plea bargaining is "not only an essential part of the process but a highly desirable part for many reasons." The courts have also presumed, except in extraordinary cases, that a prosecutor who negotiates a plea bargain does so for proper reasons (such as faster disposition of cases and elimination of uncertainty) and not improper ones (such as obtaining convictions of innocent defendants). For instance, the Supreme Court has rejected claims that a prosecutor acted "vindictively" and contrary to due process by increasing the charges against a defendant who rejected an initial offer of a plea bargain. Bordenkircher v. Hayes, 434 U.S. 357 (1978). What sort of prosecutorial motives for entering plea negotiations might be improper ones? Is it possible for courts to identify such cases?

4. *Waiver of appeal.* Most state and federal courts have concluded that a defendant may explicitly waive the right to appeal a conviction as part of a plea agreement. See State v. Hinners, 471 N.W.2d 841 (Iowa 1991); People v. Seaberg, 541 N.E.2d 1022 (N.Y. 1989). A few courts maintain that public policy forbids prosecutors from insulating themselves from review by bargaining away a defendant's appeal rights. Cf. State v. Ethington, 592 P.2d 768 (Ariz. 1979) (defendant can appeal conviction, notwithstanding agreement not to appeal). Is it necessary for a defendant to waive the right to appeal explicitly, or does it go without saying that a defendant who pleads guilty will not attack the conviction on appeal? If a defendant wants to appeal some aspect of a conviction based on a guilty plea, should she explicitly condition the guilty plea on the outcome of the planned appeal? How might we decide what must be explicit in a plea agreement, and what will be implied? Does it depend on what the parties are likely to have contemplated, even if they did not address the issue in so many words? See Peter Westen, Away from Waiver: A Rationale for the Forfeiture of Constitutional Rights in Criminal Procedure, 75 Mich. L. Rev. 1214 (1977).

Consider the effect of this Michigan statute, enacted in 1999, on the decision to plead guilty:

> (1) Except as provided [below], a defendant who pleads guilty . . . shall not have appellate counsel appointed for review of the defendant's conviction or sentence.
>
> (2) The trial court shall appoint appellate counsel for an indigent defendant who pleads guilty . . . if any of the following apply:
>
> (a) The prosecuting attorney seeks leave to appeal.
>
> (b) The defendant's sentence exceeds the upper limit of the minimum sentence range of the applicable sentencing guidelines.
>
> (c) The court of appeals or the supreme court grants the defendant's application for leave to appeal.
>
> (d) The defendant seeks leave to appeal a conditional plea. . . .

Mich. Comp. Laws §770.3a. How would a challenge to this statute differ from a challenge to a prosecutor's policy to seek waivers of appeal?

5. *Forfeiture of claims.* In some contexts, a guilty plea will lead a court to conclude that the defendant forfeited a legal challenge, even though the defendant did not knowingly and intelligently relinquish a known right. This "forfeiture" (as opposed to "waiver") of claims occurs most often when a defendant raises a claim in collateral proceedings such as habeas corpus, which take place after the direct appeal. A guilty plea will automatically bar most postconviction collateral challenges to the conviction based on events occurring before the entry of the plea. See United States v. Broce, 488 U.S. 563 (1989) (guilty plea bars later double jeopardy claim when further evidence is necessary to determine whether one conspiracy or two were present); Tollett v. Henderson, 411 U.S. 258 (1973) (forfeiture of claim of racial discrimination in grand jury selection); McMann v. Richardson, 397 U.S. 759 (1970) (forfeiture of claims regarding jury exposure to coerced confessions). For some exceptional claims, however, a defendant can raise the issue on collateral attack. See Menna v. New York, 423 U.S. 61 (1975) (allowing habeas petitioner to raise double jeopardy claim despite guilty plea); Blackledge v. Perry, 417 U.S. 21 (1974) (allowing petitioner for habeas corpus to raise claim of vindictive prosecutorial charging decision). The Supreme Court in *Blackledge* explained that these exceptional claims are not forfeited, despite the guilty plea, because they go to "the very power of the State" to charge the defendant. The claims that are forfeited after a guilty plea are those that would have been cured (absent the guilty plea) by recharging or retrying the case.

6. *Nonwaivable claims.* There are a few types of legal challenges to a conviction that some courts say a defendant may not waive, even if the waiver appears explicitly in a plea agreement. Courts have taken this position on constitutional speedy trial rights, People v. Callahan, 604 N.E.2d 108 (N.Y. 1992), and for sentences more severe than the statutory maximum allowable sentence, Lanier v. State, 635 So. 2d 813 (Miss. 1994). Courts are split on whether the parties can agree to a sentence outside the statutorily authorized range of punishments; often they enforce illegal sentences falling below the authorized range of punishments but not illegal sentences set above the authorized range. Ex parte Johnson, 669 So. 2d 205 (Ala. 1995) (enforces prosecutor's agreement to two-year prison term, even though prosecutor failed to account for sentencing enhancements requiring additional minimum sentences); but see Patterson v. State, 660 So. 2d 966 (Miss. 1995) (holding plea bargain to life without possibility of parole invalid because no statute authorizes such a sentence for murder).

When defendants attempt to raise challenges that they waived in plea agreements, claiming that the agreement is unenforceable, it is far more common for courts to refuse to hear the challenge. Courts allow defendants to bargain away rights of all sorts. See United States v. Mezzanatto, 513 U.S. 196 (1995) (allowing defendant to waive protections of Rule 11(e)(6), which prevented later introduction into evidence of statements made during plea negotiations); People v. Stevens, 610 N.W.2d 881 (Mich. 2000) (statements made during plea negotiations are admissible in prosecution's case-in-chief); Cowan v. Superior Court, 926 P.2d 438 (Cal. 1996) (allowing waiver of statute of limitations); People v. Allen, 658 N.E.2d 1012 (N.Y. 1995) (allowing waiver of double jeopardy); Joseph A. Colquitt, Ad Hoc Plea Bargaining, 75 Tul. L. Rev. 695 (2001).

Is there any pattern that separates the waivable from the nonwaivable rights? Are the waivable rights the least important ones? See Nancy J. King, Priceless Process, 47 UCLA L. Rev. 113 (1999) (notes evolution of law in direction of more waiver allowed; argues for keeping as non-waivable rights only constitutional claims with impact on third parties, since legislature can decide whether to protect statutory rights from waiver). Should courts allow defendants to waive their right to effective assistance of counsel?

B. CATEGORICAL RESTRICTIONS ON BARGAINING

As we have seen, both the prosecution and the defense have reasons to make concessions during plea negotiations, leading to guilty pleas, and there are few categorical restrictions on topics for bargaining. But the parties do not act alone in reaching or enforcing agreements. Because the parties are negotiating about criminal punishments, many different people and institutions have an interest in the outcome. Increasingly, there are times when government officials will not approve the "deal" that the parties have reached. Officials may sometimes refuse to enforce the deal, or they may take measures to prevent similar deals in the future. In short, various actors remove terms from the bargaining table. In this section, we survey the limits that legislatures, prosecutorial supervisors, and judges have placed on the terms available to the negotiating parties during plea bargaining. As you read this material, note the precise subset of cases that these institutions target as unacceptable bargains. In what ways do the unacceptable bargains differ from the acceptable ones? Consider as well the ways that these institutions have developed distinctive approaches to plea bargaining limits.

1. *Legislative Limits*

Until recently, legislatures did not explicitly limit the power of the prosecution and defense to enter plea agreements. Even now, it is unusual to find a statute that addresses the topic of plea agreements directly, except to authorize the prosecuting attorney in general terms to enter such agreements. It is common to find statutes setting out the procedures necessary to ensure that a defendant enters a guilty plea knowingly and voluntarily, but these procedures apply both to negotiated pleas and non-negotiated (or "open") pleas.

Yet, in many jurisdictions, statutes have profound — even if indirect — effects on plea bargaining. Most states have at least some statutes that specify mandatory minimum penalties for certain crimes. The statutes do not require the prosecutor to charge the crime in question whenever there is sufficient evidence, and they do not stop the prosecutor from reducing or dismissing charges when this crime occurs. Nevertheless, these statutes do influence bargaining, for once the prosecutor obtains a conviction for the designated crime, the prosecutor has limited influence over the sentence and the judge has fewer sentencing options.

In addition to these sentencing statutes, some state legislatures have begun to address more directly the prosecutor's power to negotiate over charges and sentences. Three examples follow. In what ways do the statutes represent different strategies for limiting plea bargains? Which strategies are likely to have the most impact on actual charging and negotiating practices?

■ CALIFORNIA PENAL CODE §1192.7

(a) Plea bargaining in any case in which the indictment or information charges any serious felony, any felony in which it is alleged that a firearm was personally used by the defendant, or any offense of driving while under the influence of alcohol, drugs, narcotics, or any other intoxicating substance, or any combination thereof, is prohibited, unless there is insufficient evidence to prove the people's case, or testimony of a material witness cannot be obtained, or a reduction or dismissal would not result in a substantial change in sentence.

(b) As used in this section "plea bargaining" means any bargaining, negotiation, or discussion between a criminal defendant, or his or her counsel, and a prosecuting attorney or judge, whereby the defendant agrees to plead guilty or nolo contendere, in exchange for any promises, commitments, concessions, assurances, or consideration by the prosecuting attorney or judge relating to any charge against the defendant or to the sentencing of the defendant.

(c) As used in this section, "serious felony" means any of the following: (1) Murder or voluntary manslaughter; (2) mayhem; (3) rape; (4) sodomy by force, violence, duress, menace, threat of great bodily injury, or fear of immediate and unlawful bodily injury on the victim or another person; (5) oral copulation by force, violence, duress, menace, threat of great bodily injury, or fear of immediate and unlawful bodily injury on the victim or another person; (6) lewd or lascivious act on a child under the age of 14 years; (7) any felony punishable by death or imprisonment in the state prison for life; (8) any felony in which the defendant personally inflicts great bodily injury on any person, other than an accomplice, or any felony in which the defendant personally uses a firearm; (9) attempted murder; (10) assault with intent to commit rape or robbery; (11) assault with a deadly weapon or instrument on a peace officer; (12) assault by a life prisoner on a noninmate; (13) assault with a deadly weapon by an inmate; (14) arson; (15) exploding a destructive device or any explosive with intent to injure; (16) exploding a destructive device or any explosive causing bodily injury, great bodily injury, or mayhem; (17) exploding a destructive device or any explosive with intent to murder; (18) any burglary of the first degree; (19) robbery or bank robbery; (20) kidnapping; . . . (23) any felony in which the defendant personally used a dangerous or deadly weapon; (24) selling, furnishing, administering, giving, or offering to sell, furnish, administer, or give to a minor any heroin, cocaine, phencyclidine (PCP), or any methamphetamine-related drug, . . . (26) grand theft involving a firearm; (27) carjacking; . . . (31) assault with a deadly weapon, firearm, machinegun, assault weapon, or semiautomatic firearm or assault on a peace officer or firefighter . . . (32) assault with a deadly weapon against a public transit employee, custodial officer, or school employee . . . (33) discharge of a firearm at an inhabited dwelling, vehicle, or aircraft . . . (37) intimidation of victims or witnesses . . . (38) terrorist threats . . . ; and (41) any conspiracy to commit an offense described in this subdivision.

■ NEW YORK CRIMINAL PROCEDURE LAW §220.10

The only kinds of pleas which may be entered to an indictment are those specified in this section:

1. The defendant may as a matter of right enter a plea of "not guilty" to the indictment.

2. Except as provided in subdivision five, the defendant may as a matter of right enter a plea of "guilty" to the entire indictment.

3. Except as provided in subdivision five, where the indictment charges but one crime, the defendant may, with both the permission of the court and the consent of the people, enter a plea of guilty of a lesser included offense. . . .

4. Except as provided in subdivision five, where the indictment charges two or more offenses in separate counts, the defendant may, with both the permission of the court and the consent of the people, enter a plea of:

(a) Guilty of one or more but not all of the offenses charged; or

(b) Guilty of a lesser included offense with respect to any or all of the offenses charged; or

(c) Guilty of any combination of offenses charged and lesser offenses included within other offenses charged.

5. (a) (i) Where the indictment charges one of the class A-I felonies . . . or the attempt to commit any such class A-I felony, then any plea of guilty entered pursuant to subdivision three or four must be or must include at least a plea of guilty of class A-II felony. . . .

(ii) Where the indictment charges one of the class A-II felonies . . . or the attempt to commit any such class A-II felony, then any plea of guilty entered pursuant to subdivision three or four must be or must include at least a plea of guilty of class B felony.

(iii) Where the indictment charges one of the class B felonies . . . then any plea of guilty entered pursuant to subdivision three or four must be or must include at least a plea of guilty of a class D felony.

■ REVISED CODE OF WASHINGTON §§9.94A.450, 9.94A.460

§9.94A.450

(1) Except as provided in subsection (2) of this section, a defendant will normally be expected to plead guilty to the charge or charges which adequately describe the nature of his or her criminal conduct or go to trial.

(2) In certain circumstances, a plea agreement with a defendant in exchange for a plea of guilty to a charge or charges that may not fully describe the nature of his or her criminal conduct may be necessary and in the public interest. Such situations may include the following:

(a) Evidentiary problems which make conviction on the original charges doubtful;

(b) The defendant's willingness to cooperate in the investigation or prosecution of others whose criminal conduct is more serious or represents a greater public threat;

(c) A request by the victim when it is not the result of pressure from the defendant;

(d) The discovery of facts which mitigate the seriousness of the defendant's conduct;

(e) The correction of errors in the initial charging decision;

(f) The defendant's history with respect to criminal activity;

(g) The nature and seriousness of the offense or offenses charged;

(h) The probable effect on witnesses.

§9.94A.460

The prosecutor may reach an agreement regarding sentence recommendations. The prosecutor shall not agree to withhold relevant information from the court concerning the plea agreement.

Notes

1. *Codifying plea considerations.* The Washington statute lists several considerations that prosecutors traditionally describe as reasons to reduce charges or to recommend a lesser sentence as part of a plea bargain. The National District Attorneys Association lists similar factors for a prosecutor to consider before negotiating a plea agreement, including the following: "the nature of the offense(s)"; "age, background, and criminal history of the defendant"; "sufficiency of admissible evidence to support a verdict"; "undue hardship caused to the defendant"; "possible deterrent value of prosecution"; "age of the case"; "willingness of the defendant to waive (release) his right to pursue potential civil causes of action arising from his arrest"; and "availability and willingness [of witnesses] to testify." National Prosecution Standards 68.1 (2d ed. 1991). A few other states have similar statutes. See Oregon Code §135.415 (nonexclusive list of criteria the prosecutor may consider in making plea agreements). Would the passage of such a statute alter any practices in a prosecutor's office? What would motivate a legislature to pass such a statute?

2. *Particular charges.* In recent years, it has become more common for legislatures to instruct prosecutors not to dismiss or reduce charges for specific crimes. As you might imagine, the crimes involved are usually those that have become high priorities for the public. See Nev. Rev. Stat. §§483.560, 484.3792 (prosecutor may not dismiss charges for driving with suspended or revoked license, or for drunk driving offenses, unless there is no probable cause to support charge). Cf. Miss. Stat. §43-21-555 (no plea bargaining in youth court).

3. *Size of discount.* The New York statute does not bar plea bargains for any particular crimes. Rather, it defines the maximum reduction in charges and authorized sentences that the prosecutor may offer. A statute specifying the size of the discounts a prosecutor can offer may create a very visible incentive to plead guilty. For instance, in Corbitt v. New Jersey, 439 U.S. 212 (1978), the Supreme Court upheld the constitutionality of a statute that required a mandatory term of life imprisonment for a conviction after trial; the same statute allowed either a life term or a 30-year term for a conviction under the statute based on a guilty or nolo plea. Compare United States v. Jackson, 390 U.S. 570 (1968) (overturning statute as undue burden on right to jury trial where death penalty is authorized only for defendants who go to trial); Shumpert v. Department of Highways, 409 S.E.2d 771 (S.C. 1991) (statute reducing period of driver's license suspension for those pleading guilty of drunk driving offenses is overturned as burden on trial rights).

4. *Exceptions under the California statute.* Section 1192.7 of the California Penal Code became law as a result of a voter referendum in 1982. Other provisions of the "victims' rights" referendum included greater admissibility of evidence of a defendant's prior convictions and increased penalties for repeat felony offenders. The plea bargain limitations for "serious felonies," however, never reduced the number of cases resolved through guilty pleas and plea negotiations in California. One study of California plea bargaining concluded that the statutory ban never reduced the use of guilty pleas because §1192.7 applied only to cases in superior court. Since virtually all serious felonies are charged initially in municipal court and transferred to superior court only after the preliminary examination, the prosecution and defense can negotiate a plea bargain in almost any case during the first few days after the filing of the charge, before any preliminary examination and before much discovery has taken place. See Candace McCoy, Politics and Plea Bargaining: Victims' Rights in California (1993). Even if the bar on plea negotiations were to apply to all court systems, how many dismissals and reductions of charges would it prevent? Consider the exceptions in subsection (a), allowing plea bargaining when there is "insufficient evidence" or when a material witness is not available, or when no substantial reduction in sentence would result. How many cases would fall within this subsection, and who would determine the breadth of coverage for this statutory language?

2. *Judicial Rules*

Judges are pulled in two directions when it comes to plea bargains. On the one hand, plea bargaining appears to be an extension of the prosecutor's charging decision, and judges are reluctant to become involved in charging decisions. See Chapter 13. On the other hand, plea bargaining is a key determinant in sentencing, and judges have customarily considered sentencing to be a judicial function. As a result, judges usually accept the practice of negotiated guilty pleas and allow prosecutors to dismiss or reduce charges. But they resist more strenuously when plea bargaining takes the form of a sentence bargain.

What form does judicial resistance to sentence bargains take? It is rare to find judges creating rules of criminal procedure or making other general pronouncements that place whole categories of agreements out of bounds. But they do frequently insist on the power, in individual cases, to make an independent judgment about any sentence that the parties might have selected under their agreement. This means that judges have been especially skeptical about agreements that give the judge only one sentencing option (the one that the prosecution and the defense have negotiated) and allow the defendant to withdraw the plea if the judge does not enter the sentence specified in the agreement. See Fed. R. Crim. P. 11(c)(1)(C) (parties may "agree that a specific sentence is the appropriate disposition of the case"). The following case indicates when judges are likely (or unlikely) to limit or scrutinize entire classes of plea bargains. Later in this chapter (in section C), we consider the role of the judge during plea negotiations in individual cases.

■ RAYMOND ESPINOZA v. HON. GREGORY MARTIN

894 P.2d 688 (Ariz. 1995)

CORCORAN, J.

Petitioner Raymond Espinoza, a criminal defendant in Maricopa County, challenges the policy adopted by a group of Maricopa County Superior Court judges of summarily rejecting all plea agreements containing stipulated sentences. . . .

The criminal divisions of the Maricopa County Superior Court are divided into four groups designated as quadrants A through D. Quadrant B [consists] of 5 judges. [T]he quadrant B judges issued a memorandum detailing a new plea agreement policy that was scheduled to take effect on January 25, 1993. The policy stated that quadrant B judges would no longer accept any plea agreements containing stipulated sentences because sentencing "is a judicial function which should not be subjected to limitations which are imposed by the parties, but are not required by law." . . . The relevant section of that policy reads as follows:

> 1. Plea agreements may stipulate to "probation," or "department of corrections" [DOC] for felonies, or "county jail" for misdemeanors. Agreements may not stipulate to any term of years (other than lifetime probation in dangerous crimes against children) or to any non-mandatory terms and conditions of probation . . . , or to sentences running concurrently or consecutively. . . .

The only 2 exceptions to the quadrant B policy are as follows:

> 2. Exceptions will be made for legitimate cooperation agreements. If the state wishes to make stipulated sentencing concessions in exchange for information, testimony or cooperation from a defendant, that fact should be made known to the judge in an appropriate manner prior to the change of plea. . .
>
> 4. Stipulations in capital murder cases to life imprisonment are viewed by the judges as charging concessions and not true sentencing stipulations. Therefore, such stipulations are unaffected by the policy.

On June 2, 1993, Espinoza was indicted on one count of offering to sell narcotic drugs and one count of misconduct involving weapons. At his arraignment, the case was assigned to respondent, quadrant B Judge Gregory Martin. On August 11, 1993, Espinoza appeared before Judge Martin in chambers to enter a plea of guilty to both counts pursuant to a plea agreement, which stipulated that the sentences would run concurrently with each other and with an unrelated probation revocation. Judge

Martin summarily rejected Espinoza's plea agreement because the stipulation to concurrent sentences violated the quadrant B policy. . . .

Rule 17.4, Arizona Rules of Criminal Procedure, governs plea negotiations and agreements. This court has stated that "the rules [of criminal procedure] recognize that properly negotiated plea agreements . . . are an essential part of the criminal process and can enhance judicial economy, protect the resources of the State, and serve the ends of justice for the defendant, the State and the victim." State v. Superior Court, 611 P.2d 928 (Ariz. 1980).

This case turns on the meaning of rule 17.4(a), which reads as follows: "The parties may negotiate concerning, and reach an agreement on, any aspect of the disposition of the case. The court shall not participate in any such negotiation." The plain language of rule 17.4(a) gives the parties the right to negotiate and reach agreement on "any aspect of the disposition of the case." This means that the State and the defendant may bargain both as to the plea of guilty and as to the sentence to be imposed.

Although rule 17.4(a) allows the parties to negotiate plea agreements, including sentences, rule 17.4 also grants trial courts considerable discretion in deciding whether to accept or reject such agreements. Rule 17.4(d) provides in part:

> After making such determinations [of the accuracy of the agreement and the voluntariness and intelligence of the plea] and considering the victim's view, if provided, the court shall either accept or reject the tendered negotiated plea.*

Furthermore, even if a trial court accepts a plea agreement, it is not bound by negotiated provisions regarding the sentence or the terms of probation if a review of the presentence report reveals the inadequacy of those provisions.

In order to ensure that agreements negotiated pursuant to rule 17.4(a) have some meaningful effect, we interpret rule 17.4 as guaranteeing the parties the right to present their negotiated agreement to a judge, to have the judge consider the merits of that agreement in light of the circumstances of the case, and to have the judge exercise his or her discretion with regard to the agreement. Instead of hampering judicial sentencing discretion, the current version of rule 17.4, taken as a whole, contemplates the exercise of judicial discretion when determining whether to accept or reject each particular plea agreement. In exercising that discretion, the trial court must review the plea agreement to see if the ends of justice and the protection of the public are being served by such agreement. . . .

After giving full consideration to the appropriateness of a plea agreement, the trial court has the discretion to either accept or reject the entire plea agreement, or to accept the agreement and later reject the sentencing provisions if deemed inappropriate after further inquiry. Therefore, there [is no need] to try to further enhance judicial sentencing discretion by approving a policy that limited the parties' right to negotiate. . . .

* Rule 17.4(d) continues as follows: "The court shall not be bound by any provision in the plea agreement regarding the sentence or the term and conditions of probation to be imposed, if, after accepting the agreement and reviewing a presentence report, it rejects the provision as inappropriate." Section (e) states as follows: "If an agreement or any provision thereof is rejected by the court, it shall give the defendant an opportunity to withdraw his or her plea, advising the defendant that if he or she permits the plea to stand, the disposition of the case may be less favorable to him or her than that contemplated by the agreement."—Eds.

Espinoza agreed to plead guilty to two charges: attempting to knowingly sell a narcotic drug and knowingly possessing a deadly weapon during the commission of a felony. In exchange, the parties agreed that the sentences imposed on both charges would be served concurrently, and that those sentences would also be concurrent with a probation revocation. . . . Judge Martin did not consider the particular circumstances of the case and made no findings regarding the appropriateness of the negotiated sentence. Instead, the presence of a stipulated sentence in the agreement triggered the quadrant B policy and precluded any individualized exercise of discretion. Absent the quadrant B policy, Judge Martin could have weighed the merits of the plea agreement and accepted it, rejected it entirely, or rejected the sentencing provisions as inappropriate once he had reviewed the presentence report. This is the type of discretion contemplated by rule 17.4, and trial courts are obligated to exercise it.

[G]roups of judges may not implement policies to automatically reject all such plea agreements without considering whether a stipulated sentence is appropriate in light of the circumstances of the case. Our holding applies equally to the actions of individual judges. [A trial judge may not] automatically reject a plea agreement without individualized consideration because it contains a stipulated sentence. . . .

FELDMAN, C.J., specially concurring.

I fully concur in the majority opinion. Two comments in Justice Martone's dissent, however, require a response from the Chief Justice.

Because the dissent departs from the issue before us to castigate the court for failing to adopt the petition to amend Ariz. R. Crim. Proc. 17.4, it is appropriate to explain why we did not adopt that proposal. The dissent makes much of the number of comments favoring the petition, but, as is often the case, the numbers do not paint an accurate picture. Other than judges, only three writers, none of whom is a practicing lawyer, supported the rule change. The dissent fails to mention that, in fact, several judges opposed the change and that the comments of representatives of the lawyers who would have had to practice under the proposed rule were unanimously unfavorable. The prosecutors opposed it on the grounds that it was contrary to the interests of victims and the public, and the defense bar opposed it on the grounds that it would significantly hinder their attempts to obtain fair treatment for their clients under a mandatory sentencing regime. . . .

This debate is, of course, a non-issue in this case. Those readers who desire an in-depth review, however, should peruse the comment to the petition to amend Rule 17.4 filed by Judge Ronald Reinstein, Presiding Criminal Judge of the Maricopa County Superior Court. [I] quote here one paragraph of that comment:

> While some have argued that sentencing stipulations are regularly crafted by inexperienced young attorneys, and judges are best suited to determine in the first instance what an appropriate disposition in a case should be, the fact is that most of the more significant and sensitive cases in the justice system are handled by experienced prosecutors and defense attorneys who have lived and breathed these cases for months. The sentencing judge on the other hand more than likely only reviews the presentence report the night before sentencing. Many of those judges, while perhaps experienced in life and the law, at least in the beginning of their judicial careers or their assignment to the criminal bench, have no experience at all in criminal sentencing. We are not all anointed with mystical and instant wisdom when we don our judicial robes.

Some may believe that we should damn the torpedoes and go forward with a rule opposed by all who would have to practice under it, but I disagree. Although we may empathize with the judges who seek to regain some of the discretion taken from them by mandatory sentencing, we must listen to those who would have had to practice under the changed rule. [I]t would be an abuse of power to impose the rule until it was first tried with a group willing to experiment. . . .

ZLAKET, J., dissenting.

The majority concedes that judges are empowered to reject plea agreements. I am of the additional opinion that they should be permitted to summarily reject those containing stipulated sentences for that reason alone, without having to go through the charade of considering each case individually. My hope is that most judges would not routinely follow such a course of action, at least until we can be sure it causes no damage to the plea-bargaining process that constitutes an integral part of our criminal justice system. Nevertheless, arriving at a general principle applicable to a class of plea agreements, after full consideration of the issue, seems to me more honest, more efficient, and every bit as thoughtful as pondering each agreement individually before rejecting it. . . .

I believe the court's ruling today not only threatens [judicial] candor but also reinforces the purely ministerial role about which [judges have] so vehemently and properly complained. Sentencing is, or at least should be, a judicial function. Regrettably, mandatory sentencing schemes have eliminated a great deal of judicial discretion in such matters. I prefer not to support a rule interpretation that potentially contributes to further erosion of this authority, especially where it is unnecessary to resolve the pending case.

MARTONE, J., dissenting.

I dissent. I would support the efforts of five trial judges to improve our criminal justice system. . . . The quadrant B policy was not in conflict with Rule 17.4. While Rule 17.4(a) allows the parties to agree on the disposition of a case, Rule 17.4(d) allows the court to "either accept or reject the tendered negotiated plea." Even after acceptance, the court may reject sentencing stipulations. Rule 17.4(d). If, after looking at the document, a judge is opposed to any part of the plea, he or she may summarily reject it. And that is precisely what Judge Martin did here. That he and other judges agreed to exercise their rights under Rule 17.4(d) does not make his decision conflict with the rule. Indeed, their agreement is collectively supportive of the rule. No one forced Judge Martin to participate in the policy. He was free to accept or reject it, altogether or in a specific case. He accepted it because he thought it was a good idea. The quadrant B policy was not binding on any judge who did not want to be bound by it.

[T]he Superior Court in Maricopa County has petitioned to amend Rule 17.4 to prohibit sentencing stipulations and the majority rejected it. See In Re Rule 17.4, Rules of Criminal Procedure, R-94-0007.* We are considering an experiment with the proposed amendment, but the majority rejected Maricopa County's request to participate in it.

* [This note is asterisked in the original dissenting opinion.] Of the approximately 60 comments received, over 40 were in favor of prohibiting sentencing agreements. . . . The majority is persuaded by the opposition of institutional bar groups. It is natural enough for lawyers to not want to surrender their sentencing power to judges. But if judges, and not lawyers, ought to possess the power to sentence, the reluctance of lawyers to transfer that power ought not carry the day. . . .

I believe that this court should be in the business of rewarding creative efforts that arise elsewhere in the system. We have not been at the forefront of reform in the criminal justice system. . . . The trial judges are trying new ideas as we approach the next millennium. We should support them.

Problem 16-3. Bargaining Ban in a Lower Court

The trial courts in New Jersey include superior courts, which are the courts of general jurisdiction, and municipal courts, which are courts of limited jurisdiction to try lesser criminal offenses. In 1974, the New Jersey Supreme Court passed a rule prohibiting all plea bargaining in municipal courts in the state.

In passing this rule, the court expressed the concern that plea bargaining might be abused in municipal court because of the part-time nature of the personnel in many municipal courts and the informal nature of the proceedings. For instance, municipal courts are not required to maintain stenographic records or audio recordings of proceedings and most municipal courts do not have a prosecutor or a public defender assigned full time to the court. In the view of the Supreme Court, this structure left the municipal courts vulnerable to allegations of improper "back room deals."

For several years, the Supreme Court maintained its rule on plea bargaining and emphasized that the ban was particularly important in drunken-driving offenses. In 1983, Chief Justice Robert Wilentz issued a reminder to judges on assignment in municipal courts that "without in any way affecting the generality of the plea bargaining prohibition, I suggest that you emphasize the particular importance of not allowing plea bargaining in drunken driving cases."

In 1988, the Supreme Court Task Force on the Improvement of Municipal Courts recommended the authorization of plea bargaining in the municipal courts, giving the following reasons:

> The existence of a regulated plea agreement process is essential to serve both the ends of justice and the effective response to burgeoning municipal court caseloads. It will foster increases in the productivity and professionalism of the municipal court bench, administrators, clerks and staff. The process provides for the certainty and fairness of punishment to better protect the rights of the defendants, victims and the interests of society.
>
> The municipal courts have a volume of cases in excess of 6 million that must be processed and resolved in an expeditious and summary manner. The Committee has been advised and is of the opinion that unless plea agreements are permitted in the carefully defined fashion being proposed, they will certainly take place in an unregulated fashion. Certainly, in the absence of some form of expeditious disposition, these courts would not be able to cope with their heavy calendars given the part-time nature of the courts and the part-time nature of the judges, most of whom have full-time law practices.

The committee, while acknowledging the feasibility of plea bargaining in general in the municipal courts, determined that drunken-driving offenses posed special problems. It noted the extraordinary emotional and fiscal costs of drunken driving, and "the public's concern that the process of plea bargaining, as applied to alcohol and drug offenses, might undermine the deterrent thrust of New Jersey's tough laws in these areas." Accordingly, the committee's report recommended that while the ban on municipal court plea bargaining should be lifted, the prohibition on plea agreements in drunken-driving offenses should continue.

In 1990, the court instituted a regulated system of plea agreements in municipal courts. It allowed plea bargaining pursuant to New Jersey Court Rule 7:4-8. The guidelines that the court issued with the court rules specified that their purpose was "to allow for flexibility in the definitions and exclusions relating to the plea agreement process as that process evolves and certain offenses come to demand lesser or greater scrutiny." Guideline 4 adopted the recommendation of the committee that plea bargaining not be allowed in drunken-driving cases.

As a member of the New Jersey Supreme Court, how would you respond to the recommendations of the committee? What more would you like to know about the municipal courts and their caseloads before you decide? Compare State v. Hessen, 678 A.2d 1082 (N.J. 1996).

Notes

1. *Individualized rejection of plea agreements.* Statutes and rules give judges the opportunity to approve or disapprove plea agreements. The court must decide whether to accept or reject the defendant's plea of guilty; if the plea grows out of an objectionable plea agreement, the court can simply refuse to accept the guilty plea. Further, rules and statutes in more than 30 states require prosecutors to obtain the consent of the court to dismiss a charge. But does the court need any justification, or any particular type of justification, to reject a guilty plea based on a plea agreement or to refuse to dismiss a charge? Almost all appellate courts allow trial courts to reject guilty pleas or dismissals of charges without any serious review of the judge's reasons for refusing. A few cases, however, have held that a trial judge must state reasons for rejecting a guilty plea; the judge may refuse the guilty plea or the dismissal of charges only if the prosecutor has abused his discretion by failing to consider facts important to the public interest in the case. Sandy v. District Court, 935 P.2d 1148 (Nev. 1997); United States v. Ammidown, 497 F.2d 615 (D.C. Cir. 1973). Limits on the judicial power to reject guilty pleas are based on separation of powers concepts and on judges' limited knowledge both about the relative strengths of individual cases and about the most efficient allocation of prosecutorial resources. Would you expect such limits on judicial power to apply equally to charging agreements and sentencing agreements?

2. *Stipulated sentences.* As described in the *Espinoza* case from Arizona, the state supreme court had considered (and rejected) an amendment to the guilty plea rules dealing with "stipulated sentences," and the trial judges of quadrant B created their own rule about stipulated sentences. What exactly can a trial judge do when the parties present a stipulated or "negotiated" sentence? The details vary from place to place. As with the federal rules, most jurisdictions allow the parties to choose the type of agreement they will present to the judge: They can agree either to recommend a sentence (leaving the judge free to accept or reject the recommendation) or to offer the judge only a stipulated sentence that the judge must simply accept or reject as a package with the guilty plea. A few states recognize only the "binding" form of sentencing agreements. See People v. Killebrew, 330 N.W.2d 834 (Mich. 1982) (when judge plans to impose sentence that exceeds sentence recommendation or agreement, defendant may withdraw guilty plea). Other states have statutes or rules to preserve the judge's power, in all cases, to accept a guilty plea but still depart from the sentence the parties recommend. See State v. Strecker, 883 P.2d 841 (Mont. 1994). English law permits plea bargaining but not negotiated sentences. See R. v. Turner (F.R.) [1970] 2 Q.B. 321, 54 Crim. App. 352 (guidelines for plea bargaining).

Even though most criminal procedure rules allow the parties to stipulate to a particular sentence, stipulated sentences are far less common in practice than charge bargains or nonbinding sentencing recommendations. Many judges declare that they will not accept "binding" sentence recommendations, even though the relevant rules of procedure authorize such agreements. Why does this pattern emerge in most places? Did the trial judges in Maricopa County need to create a common policy for the jurisdiction?

3. *Disfavored classes of agreements.* What was it about plea negotiations in the municipal courts (described in Problem 16-3) that made such practices a special concern to the New Jersey courts? See State v. Hessen, 678 A.2d 1082 (N.J. 1996). What features of drunken-driving cases created the need for special treatment? Were any of these features present in the types of plea bargains that the trial courts tried to ban in the *Espinoza* case from Arizona? Is there any explanation for the different outcomes in these cases, a ban on a category of plea bargains upheld in one case but not the other? Cf. State v. Hager, 630 N.W.2d 828 (Iowa 2001) (despite trial court rule forbidding plea bargains on day of trial, abuse of discretion not to consider plea entered on day of trial).

One type of agreement that courts have rejected categorically is known as the "consistency" agreement, in which a defendant receives charging concessions in exchange for an agreement to testify against another defendant and to testify consistently with past statements that the defendant has made. See State v. Fisher, 859 P.2d 179 (Ariz. 1993). Why are judges in most jurisdictions willing to ban this type of agreement when they allow the parties to negotiate over so many other potential terms of agreement?

4. *Prosecutor's objection to guilty plea and sentence.* We have considered the situation in which the judge objects to a sentence that the parties have negotiated. Can a judge side with a defendant against a prosecutor and accept a guilty plea (and impose a sentence or dismiss a charge) over the prosecutor's objection? Most courts have given the prosecutor the power to block a guilty plea if the judge plans to dismiss charges or impose a sentence below what the plea agreement specifies. See State v. Vasquez-Aerreola, 940 S.W.2d 451 (Ark. 1997) (court may not dismiss charge of gang activity and accept guilty plea on other charges over prosecutor's objection); People v. Siebert, 537 N.W.2d 891 (Mich. 1995) (court may not accept a plea bargain containing a sentence agreement but impose a lower sentence than that agreed to; in such a case, prosecutor must be given opportunity to withdraw from agreement). Nonetheless, a few courts insist, at least for sentence bargains, that the prosecutor cannot prevent the judge from selecting the sentence to impose. See State v. Warren, 558 A.2d 1312 (N.J. 1989) (prohibits use of plea agreements in which prosecutor reserves right to withdraw from plea agreement if court-imposed sentence is more lenient than one agreed to by parties or recommended to court by prosecutor).

3. *Prosecutorial Guidelines*

Decisions whether to offer or accept plea bargains, like decisions about charging a suspect, are often governed by executive branch policies. These policies vary in their level of detail; in many smaller offices, prosecutors follow consistent plea practices that may reflect unwritten (but explicit) guidelines, or they may simply reflect shared office culture and experience. Sometimes prosecutors develop formal plea review standards, describing substantively the types of bargains that are acceptable. Other times they create procedural review mechanisms, such as supervisory review or committee review of possible plea bargains. These guidelines or procedures might apply only for identified types of cases, such as those involving drugs or those likely to be controversial.

Federal prosecutors, under the central control of the U.S. Attorney General, have developed a detailed set of written plea bargaining policies. In addition to the nationwide guidelines set out below, many of the U.S. Attorneys' offices in the 92 federal districts around the country have developed additional guidance to reflect the distinctive caseloads, resources, and other factors in each district.

The federal executive branch plea policies that follow were created against a background of major changes in sentencing law. At the time of the 1980 policy printed below, the federal system (and all but a handful of state systems) still had an "indeterminate" sentencing system. Under indeterminate sentencing systems the legislature defined most crimes to include a wide range of possible sentences, sometimes covering (for a single crime) everything from nonprison sanctions, such as fines or probation, to long prison terms. In theory, huge discretion was left to the sentencing judge to set terms within the statutorily authorized range. The actual sentence to be served was often determined through "back-end" review by parole boards once the offender had spent a minimum required portion of the judicially imposed term in prison. In such systems, the charge might have only a modest binding effect on the sentence a judge could impose or the time a defendant would actually serve. In practice, however, the processing of many cases by the same "working group" of attorneys and judges within the criminal court culture would lead to very firm expectations or "prices" for various crimes. See Milton Heumann, Plea Bargaining: The Experiences of Prosecutors, Judges, and Defense Attorneys (1978).

Since the early 1980s the federal system and almost half of the states have shifted to a more rule-bound sentencing process known as "guideline" or "structured" sentencing. The basic elements of the new federal system as it relates to plea bargains are described after the 1980 policy statement. Remember as you read these policies that the Federal Rules of Criminal Procedure authorize three kinds of pleas: (1) agreements to enter a guilty plea to one or more charges in return for dismissal of other charges (a "charge" bargain under Rule 11(c)(1)(A)); (2) agreements to recommend a sentence in exchange for a guilty plea, subject to the judge's power to select the final sentence after accepting the guilty plea (a "sentence" bargain under Rule 11(c)(1)(B)); and (3) an agreement to a particular sentence in exchange for a guilty plea (a stipulated sentence plea under Rule 11(c)(1)(C)).

■ U.S. DEPARTMENT OF JUSTICE PRINCIPLES OF FEDERAL PROSECUTION

(1980)

ENTERING INTO PLEA AGREEMENTS

1. The attorney for the government may, in an appropriate case, enter into an agreement with a defendant that, upon the defendant's plea of guilty or nolo contendere to a charged offense or to a lesser or related offense, he will move for

dismissal of other charges, take a certain position with respect to the sentence to be imposed, or take other action.

2. In determining whether it would be appropriate to enter into a plea agreement, the attorney for the government should weigh all relevant considerations, including:

(a) the defendant's willingness to cooperate in the investigation or prosecution of others;

(b) the defendant's history with respect to criminal activity;

(c) the nature and seriousness of the offense or offenses charged;

(d) the defendant's remorse or contrition and his willingness to assume responsibility for his conduct;

(e) the desirability of prompt and certain disposition of the case;

(f) the likelihood of obtaining a conviction at trial;

(g) the probable effect on witnesses;

(h) the probable sentence or other consequences if the defendant is convicted;

(i) the public interest in having the case tried rather than disposed of by a guilty plea;

(j) the expense of trial and appeal; and

(k) the need to avoid delay in the disposition of other pending cases.

Comment: . . . The provision is not intended to suggest the desirability or lack of desirability of a plea agreement in any particular case or to be construed as a reflection on the merits of any plea agreement that actually may be reached; its purpose is solely to assist attorneys for the government in exercising their judgment as to whether some sort of plea agreement would be appropriate in a particular case. Government attorneys should consult the investigating agency involved in any case in which it would be helpful to have its views concerning the relevance of particular factors or the weight they deserve. . . .

A plea disposition in one case may facilitate the prompt disposition of other cases, including cases in which prosecution might otherwise be declined. This may occur simply because prosecutorial, judicial, or defense resources will become available for use in other cases, or because a plea by one of several defendants may have a "domino effect," leading to pleas by other defendants. In weighing the importance of these possible consequences, the attorney for the government should consider the state of the criminal docket and the speedy trial requirements in the district, the desirability of handling a larger volume of criminal cases, and the workloads of prosecutors, judges, and defense attorneys in the district.

3. If a prosecution is to be concluded pursuant to a plea agreement, the defendant should be required to plead to a charge or charges:

(a) that bears a reasonable relationship to the nature and extent of his criminal conduct;

(b) that has an adequate factual basis;

(c) that makes likely the imposition of an appropriate sentence under all the circumstances of the case; and

(d) that does not adversely affect the investigation or prosecution of others.

Comment: [T]he considerations that should be taken into account in selecting the charge or charges to which a defendant should be required to plead guilty . . . are essentially the same as those governing the selection of charges to be included in the original indictment or information.

(a) Relationship to criminal conduct — The charge or charges to which a defendant pleads guilty should bear a reasonable relationship to the defendant's criminal conduct, both in nature and in scope. . . . In many cases, this will probably require that the defendant plead to the most serious offense charged. . . . The requirement that a defendant plead to a charge that bears a reasonable relationship to the nature and extent of his criminal conduct is not inflexible. There may be situations involving cooperating defendants in which [lesser charges may be appropriate].

(b) Factual basis — The attorney for the government should also bear in mind the legal requirement that there be a factual basis for the charge or charges to which a guilty plea is entered. This requirement is intended to assure against conviction after a guilty plea of a person who is not in fact guilty. . . .

(c) Basis for sentencing — [T]he prosecutor should take care to avoid a "charge agreement" that would unduly restrict the court's sentencing authority. [I]f restitution is appropriate under the circumstances of the case, a sufficient number of counts should be retained under the agreement to provide a basis for an adequate restitution order. . . .

(d) Effect on other cases — . . . Among the possible adverse consequences to be avoided are the negative jury appeal that may result when relatively less culpable defendants are tried in the absence of a more culpable defendant or when a principal prosecution witness appears to be equally culpable as the defendants but has been permitted to plead to a significantly less serious offense. . . .

5. If a prosecution is to be terminated pursuant to a plea agreement, the attorney for the government should ensure that the case file contains a record of the agreed disposition, signed or initialed by the defendant or his attorney. . . .

In the Sentencing Reform Act of 1984, Congress designed a radically new sentencing system. In place of the indeterminate sentencing system that allowed judges to choose sentences from a broad range of available outcomes, Congress created a new agency — the United States Sentencing Commission — to draft detailed sentencing guidelines. The U.S. Sentencing Commission, following general statutory guidance, produced a lengthy set of guidelines in 1987. The guidelines direct federal judges in most cases to impose sentences from a much narrower range than before.

Under the sentencing guidelines, the trial judge calculates an "offense level" (ranging on a scale from 1 to 43) to measure the seriousness of the offense, and a "criminal history category" (ranging on a scale from 1 to 6) to account for the offender's prior criminal convictions. To combine these scores, the guidelines create a grid, placing the offense levels on a vertical axis, and the criminal history categories on the horizontal axis. Each combination of the two scores corresponds to one of the 258 boxes in the grid, and each box contains a presumptive sentencing range (expressed as months of imprisonment, such as 51-63 months) for that particular offense level and criminal history score.

The guidelines begin with a "base offense level" for each crime and instruct the judge to adjust that number up or down, in specified amounts, based on specific characteristics of the case. These factors focus mostly on offense information, such as the amount of drugs sold, whether the offender used a gun, or whether the offender played a leading or minor role in a multi-person offense. Because these particular factual findings can have such a clear impact on the sentence, the guidelines have spawned a new kind of bargaining — "fact bargaining" — in which the parties agree to the presence or absence of these relevant sentencing facts in a given case.

The offense levels are based not only on the elements of the offenses charged but also on other activities of the defendant (called "relevant conduct") that are related to the charged offense. Relevant conduct can include uncharged behavior, behavior underlying dismissed charges, and even behavior underlying prior acquittals. For instance, the government might charge a defendant with participating in one sale of a small amount of narcotics, although there is evidence that he participated in larger, related sales. The sentencing judge can consider both the sale that formed the basis for the charge and the uncharged sales in setting the sentence for the crime of conviction. Thus, dismissing charges ("charge bargains") are less likely to have an impact on the ultimate sentence because the sentencing guidelines instruct the judge to consider the underlying conduct regardless of the charges.

Once the judge determines the designated sentencing range under the guidelines, she must also decide whether to "depart" up or down from the narrow range of sentences specified under the guidelines. A sentencing court departing from the guidelines can be overturned on appeal if the ground for departure is not acceptable under the standard of 18 U.S.C. §3553(b) (part of the Sentencing Reform Act). Under that statute, departures may occur only in unusual cases, when "there exists an aggravating or mitigating circumstance of a kind, or to a degree, not adequately taken into consideration by the Sentencing Commission in formulating the guidelines." By far the most common ground for departures is the defendant's cooperation with the government in prosecuting other offenders — known as "substantial assistance." Before a defendant can get credit for substantial assistance, the prosecutor must present a special motion to the court.

What did the Sentencing Commission do about plea bargains, which account for roughly 90 percent of all convictions in the federal system, just as they do in most state systems? When the Sentencing Commission created its initial set of guidelines, it included a "policy statement" about plea agreements. At the time, it was generally assumed that policy statements had less binding effect than the guidelines themselves, although later events have all but erased this distinction. What was the commission trying to accomplish with regard to plea agreements?

■ 28 U.S.C. §994(a)(2)(E)

The Commission . . . shall promulgate . . . general policy statements regarding application of the guidelines or any other aspect of sentencing or sentence implementation . . . including the appropriate use of . . . the authority granted under Rule 11(c)(2) of the Federal Rules of Criminal Procedure to accept or reject a plea agreement. . . .

■ U.S. SENTENCING GUIDELINES §§6B1.2, 6B1.4 (POLICY STATEMENTS)

§6B1.2

(a) In the case of a plea agreement that includes the dismissal of any charges or an agreement not to pursue potential charges [under Rule 11(c)(1)(A)], the court may accept the agreement if the court determines, for reasons stated on the record, that the remaining charges adequately reflect the seriousness of the actual offense behavior and that accepting the agreement will not undermine the statutory purposes of sentencing or the sentencing guidelines. Provided, that a plea agreement that includes the dismissal of a charge or a plea agreement not to pursue a potential charge shall not preclude the conduct underlying such charge from being considered under the provisions of §1B1.3 (Relevant Conduct) in connection with the count(s) of which the defendant is convicted.

(b) In the case of a plea agreement that includes a nonbinding recommendation [under Rule 11(c)(1)(B)], the court may accept the recommendation if the court is satisfied either that: (1) the recommended sentence is within the applicable guideline range; or (2) the recommended sentence departs from the applicable guideline range for justifiable reasons.

(c) In the case of a plea agreement that includes a specific sentence [under Rule 11(c)(1)(C)], the court may accept the agreement if the court is satisfied either that: (1) the agreed sentence is within the applicable guideline range; or (2) the agreed sentence departs from the applicable guideline range for justifiable reasons.

§6B1.4

(a) A plea agreement may be accompanied by a written stipulation of facts relevant to sentencing. [S]tipulations shall: (1) set forth the relevant facts and circumstances of the actual offense conduct and offender characteristics; (2) not contain misleading facts; and (3) set forth with meaningful specificity the reasons why the sentencing range resulting from the proposed agreement is appropriate.

(b) To the extent that the parties disagree about any facts relevant to sentencing, the stipulation shall identify the facts that are in dispute. . . .

(d) The court is not bound by the stipulation, but may with the aid of the presentence report, determine the facts relevant to sentencing.

The U.S. Department of Justice realized that this new system of guideline sentencing was complicated. Thus, it issued special guidance to prosecutors that appeared simultaneously with the guidelines. Is this internal guidance to prosecutors consistent with the statute and with the policy statements? What changes does it make to the 1980 Principles of Federal Prosecution?

■ PROSECUTORS' HANDBOOK ON SENTENCING GUIDELINES ("THE REDBOOK")

William Weld, Assistant Attorney General (1987)

[T]he validity and use of the Commission's policy statements by prosecutors should depend upon whether the agreement reflects charge bargaining or sentence bargaining under [Rule 11(c)].

Sentence Bargaining

A significant problem with the Commission's policy statements on plea bargains which include a specific sentence under [Rule 11(c)(1)(B) and (C)], §6B1.2(b) and (c), is that the standard they set forth for acceptance or rejection of a sentence that departs from the guidelines appears to be of doubtful validity under the Sentencing Reform Act (SRA). The standard for departure from the guidelines is set forth in the Act and requires a finding that an aggravating or mitigating circumstance exists that was not adequately taken into consideration by the Commission in formulating the guidelines. Yet the Commission's policy statements relating to sentence bargains authorize departure "for justifiable reasons." We do not believe it is possible to argue that the Commission has not adequately taken into consideration the value of a plea agreement as a mitigating factor so as to support a departure. . . . We recognize, nonetheless, that many judges might be tempted to take a realistic approach; a sentence outside the guidelines in the context of a plea agreement is unlikely to result in an appeal of the sentence. Therefore, if urged to accept a plea agreement that departs from the guidelines, they will follow the policy statements despite their questionable basis.

Nevertheless, the Criminal Division has concluded that the apparent authority for a judge to depart from the guidelines pursuant to the Commission's policy statements, §6B1.2(b) and (c), for plea agreements involving a particular sentence under [Rule 11(c)(1)(B) and (C)] is at variance with the more restrictive departure language of [the statute] and that, consequently, these policy statements should not be used as a basis for recommending a sentence that departs from the guidelines. [P]rosecutors should not recommend or agree to a lower-than-guideline sentence merely on the basis of a plea agreement. They may, however, recommend or agree to a sentence at the low end of an applicable sentencing range [within the guidelines].

In addition to the above-described legitimate guideline reductions that may be used in sentence-type negotiations, a departure from the guidelines may be warranted and may be included in the recommended or agreed-upon sentence if the [statutory] standard . . . is met. That is, a mitigating circumstance must exist (other than the reaching of a plea agreement) that was not adequately taken into consideration by the Commission in formulating the guidelines and that should result in a sentence different from that described. Moreover, a departure from the guidelines may also be reflected in a plea agreement if the defendant provided substantial assistance in the investigation or prosecution of another person who has committed an offense. . . . Therefore, even though plea-bargained sentences must accord with the law and the guidelines, there is considerable room for negotiating.

The basic reason for rejecting the Commission's policy statements on sentence bargains and treating sentences which are the subject of a sentence bargain in the same manner as sentences which result from conviction after trial is that any other result could seriously thwart the purpose of the SRA to reduce unwarranted disparity in sentencing [among defendants with similar records who have been found guilty of similar criminal conduct]. Congress could not have expressed the concerns reflected in the SRA and the legislative history with unwarranted disparity and uncertainty in sentencing but have intended the reforms enacted to be limited to the small percentage of cases that go to trial. The legislative history of the SRA indeed indicates that Congress was concerned with the potential shift of discretion in sentencing from the court to the prosecutor through plea agreements and the unwarranted disparity that could result. . . .

Charge Bargaining

The policy statement on charge bargaining addresses agreements that include the dismissal of any charges under [Rule 11(c)(1)(A)] or an agreement not to pursue potential charges. It authorizes the court to accept such an agreement if it determines, "for reasons stated on the record, that the remaining charges adequately reflect the seriousness of the actual offense behavior and that accepting the agreement will not undermine the statutory purposes of sentencing." §6B1.2(a). The requirement that the "remaining charges adequately reflect the seriousness of the actual offense behavior" in charge bargaining is important since the charge of conviction itself is the most significant factor in establishing the guideline sentence. . . .

Although Congress intended that courts exercise "meaningful" review of charge reduction plea agreements, it is our view that moderately greater flexibility legally can and does attach to charge bargains than to sentence bargains. While, as indicated previously, the Commission's quite liberal policy statements on sentence bargaining appear to be inconsistent with the controlling (and stricter) statutory departure standard, the statutory departure standard is not applicable in the charge-bargain context. . . .

Nevertheless, in order to fulfill the objectives of the Sentencing Reform Act prosecutors should conduct charge bargaining in a manner consistent with the direction in the applicable policy statement, §6B1.2(a), i.e., subject to the policy statement's instruction that the "remaining charges [should] adequately reflect the seriousness of the actual offense behavior" and that the agreement not undermine the statutory purposes of sentencing. In our view, this translates into a requirement that readily provable serious charges should not be bargained away. The sole legitimate ground for agreeing not to pursue a charge that is relevant under the guidelines to assure that the sentence will reflect the seriousness of the defendant's "offense behavior" is the existence of real doubt as to the ultimate provability of the charge.

Concomitantly, however, the prosecutor is in the best position to assess the strength of the government's case and enjoys broad discretion in making judgments as to which charges are most likely to result in conviction on the basis of the available evidence. For this reason, the prosecutor entering into a charge bargain may enjoy a degree of latitude that is not present when the plea bargain addresses only sentencing aspects. . . .

It is appropriate that the sentence for an offender who agrees to plead guilty to relatively few charges should be different from the sentence for an offender convicted of many charges since guilt has not been determined as to the dismissed charges. At the same time, however, sentence bargaining should not result in a vastly different sentence as compared to a sentence following trial. . . .

The overriding principle governing the conduct of plea negotiations is that plea agreements should not be used to circumvent the guidelines. This principle is in accordance with the policies set forth in the Principles of Federal Prosecution. . . . For example, charges should not be filed simply to exert leverage to induce a plea. Rather, the prosecutor should charge the most serious offense consistent with the defendant's provable conduct. . . .

A subsidiary but nonetheless important issue concerns so-called "fact" bargaining or stipulations. [The policy statement §6B1.4] attaches certain conditions to such stipulations. The most important condition, with which the Department concurs, is that stipulations shall "not contain misleading facts." Otherwise, the basic purpose of the SRA to reduce unwarranted sentence disparity will be undermined. Thus, if the defendant can clearly be proved to have used a weapon or committed an assault in the course of the offense, the prosecutor may not stipulate, as part of a plea agreement designed to produce a lower sentence, that no weapon was used or assault committed. If, on the other hand, certain facts surrounding the offense are not clear, e.g., the extent of the loss or injury resulting from the defendant's fraud, the prosecutor is at liberty to stipulate that no loss or injury beyond that clearly provable existed. Prosecutors may not, however, instruct investigators not to pursue leads, or make less than ordinary efforts to ascertain facts, simply to be in a position to say that they are unable clearly to prove a sentencing fact and thereby increase the latitude for bargaining. . . . Subject to the above constraints, however, the Department encourages the use of stipulations accompanying plea agreements to the extent practicable. . . .

After the first few months of practice under the new sentencing and plea bargaining rules, officials in the Department of Justice believed that federal prosecutors in the field were not adhering closely enough to the department's plea bargaining policies. The following revision of the policy represents an effort to increase compliance with the plea practices that the leadership of the department wanted. What elements of the policy did the revisers focus on? What were the likely effects of the revisions?

■ PLEA POLICY FOR FEDERAL PROSECUTORS ("THORNBURGH BLUESHEET")

Richard Thornburgh, Attorney General (1989)

Whether bargaining takes place before or after indictment, the Department policy is the same: any departure from the guidelines should be openly identified rather than hidden between the lines of a plea agreement. It is inevitable that in some cases it will be difficult for anyone other than the prosecutor and the defendant to know whether, prior to indictment, the prosecutor bargained in conformity with the Department's policy. The Department will monitor, together with the Sentencing Commission, plea bargaining, and the Department will expect plea bargains to support, not undermine, the guidelines. . . .

Should a prosecutor determine in good faith after indictment that, as a result of a change in the evidence or for another reason (e.g., a need has arisen to protect the identity of a particular witness until he testifies against a more significant defendant), a charge is not readily provable or that an indictment exaggerates the seriousness of an offense or offenses, a plea bargain may reflect the prosecutor's reassessment. There should be a record, however, in a case in which charges originally brought are dropped. . . .

Department policy requires honesty in sentencing; federal prosecutors are expected to identify for U.S. District Courts departures when they agree to support them. For example, it would be improper for a prosecutor to agree that a departure is in order, but to conceal the agreement in a charge bargain that is presented to a court as a fait accompli so that there is neither a record of nor judicial review of the departure. . . .

The basic policy is that charges are not to be bargained away or dropped, unless the prosecutor has a good faith doubt as to the government's ability readily to prove a charge for legal or evidentiary reasons. It would serve no purpose here to seek to further define "readily provable." The policy is to bring cases that the government should win if there were a trial. There are, however, two exceptions.

First, if the applicable guideline range from which a sentence may be imposed would be unaffected, readily provable charges may be dismissed or dropped as part of a plea bargain. . . . Second, federal prosecutors may drop readily provable charges with the specific approval of the United States Attorney or designated supervisory level official for reasons set forth in the file of the case. This exception recognizes that the aims of the Sentencing Reform Act must be sought without ignoring other, critical aspects of the federal criminal justice system. For example, approval to drop charges in a particular case might be given because the United States Attorney's office is particularly overburdened, the case would be time-consuming to try, and proceeding to trial would significantly reduce the total number of cases disposed of by the office. . . .

The Department's policy is only to stipulate to facts that accurately represent the defendant's conduct. If a prosecutor wishes to support a departure from the guidelines, he or she should candidly do so and not stipulate to facts that are untrue. Stipulations to untrue facts are unethical. If a prosecutor has insufficient facts to contest a defendant's effort to seek a downward departure or to claim an adjustment, the prosecutor can say so. If the presentence report states facts that are inconsistent with a stipulation in which a prosecutor has joined, it is desirable for the prosecutor to object to the report or to add a statement explaining the prosecutor's understanding of the facts or the reason for the stipulation. . . .

In most felony cases, plea agreements should be in writing. If they are not in writing, they always should be formally stated on the record. Written agreements will facilitate efforts by the Department and the Sentencing Commission to monitor compliance by federal prosecutors with Department policies and the guidelines. . . .

After almost three more years of experience with the new system, officials in the Department of Justice remained unsatisfied with the plea bargaining practices of its attorneys in the field. In the following 1992 revision of the plea bargaining policy, the department moved away from an emphasis on describing the types of bargains that are acceptable, and instead strengthened the procedural review process for plea agreements. What are the likely effects of these changes?

■ DEPARTMENT OF JUSTICE POLICIES ("TERWILLIGER BLUESHEET")

George Terwilliger, Assistant Attorney General (1992)

This bluesheet is a clarification of [the procedures for plea bargaining described in Attorney General Thornburgh's memorandum of March 13, 1989]. The following procedures shall be adopted as to all pleas of guilty:

All negotiated plea agreements to felonies or misdemeanors negotiated from felonies shall be in writing and filed with the court. Thus any time a defendant enters into a negotiated plea, that fact and the conditions thereof will be memorialized and a copy of the plea agreement maintained in the office case file or elsewhere.

There shall be within each office a formal system for approval of negotiated pleas. The approval authority shall be vested in at least a supervisory criminal Assistant United States Attorney, or a supervisory attorney of a litigating division in the Department of Justice, who will have the responsibility of assessing the appropriateness of the plea agreement under the policies of the Department of Justice pertaining to pleas, including those set forth in the Thornburgh Memo. Where certain predictable fact situations arise with great frequency and are given identical treatment, the approval requirement may be met by a written instruction from the appropriate supervisor which describes with particularity the standard plea procedure to be followed, so long as that procedure is otherwise within Departmental guidelines. An example would be a border district which routinely deals with a high volume of illegal alien cases daily.

The plea approval process will be part of the office evaluation procedure. . . .

After the 1992 elections, the Clinton administration appointed new leadership to the Department of Justice. The following memorandum represented the first major pronouncement of the administration on plea bargaining policies. What prior statements does it hearken back to? What, if anything, is new in the policy?

■ CHARGING AND PLEA DECISIONS ("RENO BLUESHEET")

Janet Reno, Attorney General (1993)

As first stated in the preface to the original 1980 edition of the Principles of Federal Prosecution, "they have been cast in general terms with a view to providing guidance rather than to mandating results. The intent is to assure regularity without regimentation, to prevent unwarranted disparity without sacrificing flexibility."

It should be emphasized that charging decisions and plea agreements should reflect adherence to the Sentencing Guidelines. However, a faithful and honest application of the Sentencing Guidelines is not incompatible with selecting charges or entering into plea agreements on the basis of an individualized assessment of the extent to which particular charges fit the specific circumstances of the case, are consistent with the purposes of the federal criminal code, and maximize the impact of federal resources on crime. Thus, for example, in determining "the most serious offense that is consistent with the nature of the defendant's conduct, that is likely to result in a sustainable conviction," it is appropriate that the attorney for the government consider, inter alia, such factors as the sentencing guideline range yielded by the charge, whether the penalty yielded by such sentencing range (or potential mandatory minimum charge, if applicable) is proportional to the seriousness of the defendant's conduct, and whether the charge achieves such purposes of the criminal law as punishment, protection of the public, specific and general deterrence, and rehabilitation. Note that these factors may also be considered by the attorney for the government when entering into the plea agreements.

To ensure consistency and accountability, charging and plea agreement decisions must be made at an appropriate level of responsibility and documented with an appropriate record of the factors applied.

Notes

1. *Prosecutorial discretion and control.* How would you describe these policies in terms of the degree of control each policy exerts over federal prosecutorial plea practices? Do all of these policies move toward increasing control over individual prosecutorial decisions? For further background on the creation of these federal policies, see David Robinson, The Decline and Potential Collapse of Federal Guideline Sentencing, 74 Wash. U. L.Q. 881 (1996). Are executive plea bargaining policies a good idea? What problems could they solve? What problems might they create?

2. *Policies and practice.* Do "line" attorneys follow directives from their boss? The most complete studies of federal plea practices during the early implementation of the guidelines concluded that prosecutors manipulated the guidelines in 20-35 percent of all cases. Stephen Schulhofer and Ilene Nagel, A Tale of Three Cities: An Empirical Study of Charging and Bargaining Practice Under the Federal Sentencing Guidelines, 66 S. Cal. L. Rev. 501 (1992). Sentencing Commission studies found charge manipulation in 17 percent of all cases and 26 percent of drug cases. U.S. Sentencing Commission, The Federal Sentencing Guidelines: A Report on the Operation of the Guidelines System and Short-Term Impacts on Disparity in Sentencing, Use of Incarceration, and Prosecutorial Discretion and Plea Bargaining, Executive Summary 31-54 (December 1991). Why might line attorneys not follow plea guidelines? Why might different U.S. Attorneys' offices develop different patterns of plea bargaining?

3. *Policies and principles.* In response to the Reno Bluesheet, on January 13, 1994, Senator Orrin Hatch (R-Utah), the ranking minority member on the Judiciary Committee, sent Attorney General Janet Reno a letter that stated as follows:

> I want to express my strong opposition to a recent directive you issued to United States Attorneys. This directive reverses the Department of Justice's policy that prosecutors must charge the most serious, readily provable offense or offenses consistent with the defendant's conduct. The Department's new policy now permits prosecutors to make independent decisions about whether a prescribed guideline sentence or mandatory minimum charge is not "proportional to the seriousness of the defendant's conduct." In other words, this new policy increases the potential for the unwarranted softening of sentences for violent offenders. . . .
>
> While I support a review of charging practices to insure that prosecutors are not engaging in inappropriate conduct, I do not support the Department's announcement to drug traffickers and violent criminals that certain illegal conduct may not be charged because a Department employee may find the prescribed punishment too severe. If the Administration believes that existing sentences for drug cases and violent criminals are too severe, then it should seek to change the law or the relevant sentencing guidelines — not ignore them. I strongly urge you to reconsider your action in this matter.

Reno responded on March 8, 1994:

> I write in response to your recent letter regarding the charging policy of the Department of Justice and the directive which was issued to United States Attorneys. Let me reiterate, as set forth in the clarifying bluesheet to which you allude, that it remains the directive of the Department of Justice that prosecutors charge the most serious offense that is consistent with the nature of the defendant's conduct, that is likely to result in a sustainable conviction; that prosecutors adhere to the Sentencing Guidelines; and that charging and plea agreements be made at an appropriate level of responsibility with

> appropriate documentation. In short, contrary to what you suggest, individual prosecutors are not free to follow their own lights or to ignore legislative directives. . . . We are steadfast in our opposition to unwarranted softening of sentences for violent offenders or drug traffickers. . . . You note your support for such efforts, and we look forward to working with you.

What impact should this correspondence have on how assistant U.S. Attorneys apply the Reno Bluesheet? Can they now enter sentencing agreements that request a sentence outside the guideline range even when a "departure" might not be justified under the statute? What is likely to occur in such cases?

4. *Written and unwritten guidance.* A striking feature of the plea bargaining policies in the federal system is the fact that they are written. Many other prosecutors' offices in state systems have pursued goals similar to those of the Department of Justice in creating its plea policies. They hope to maintain adequate control over prosecutors in the field and to send appropriate public signals about sentencing and plea bargaining. See Richard Kuh, Plea Bargaining: Guidelines for the Manhattan District Attorney's Office, 11 Crim. L. Bull. 48 (1975) ("unless all of us here follow like principles in plea bargaining, the quality of justice administered by this office will vary from Assistant to Assistant"). Nonetheless, within the state systems, such policies are rarely written, even when they are explicit. Why might a supervising prosecutor choose to keep such a critical office policy unwritten? See William Pizzi, Understanding Prosecutorial Discretion in the United States: The Limits of Comparative Criminal Procedure as an Instrument of Reform, 54 Ohio St. L.J. 1325 (1993) (discussing reasons that offices keep their plea bargaining policies informal and unwritten, including ill effects on deterrent value of criminal law, unfavorable public impressions of perceived lenient policies, need for flexibility in unusual cases, need to avoid judicial review of prosecutorial decisions); but compare Kim Banks Mayer, Applying Open Records Policy to Wisconsin District Attorneys: Can Charging Guidelines Promote Public Awareness? 1996 Wis. L. Rev. 295 (giving examples of prosecutorial charging and plea bargaining guidelines made public with no apparent ill effects; arguing generally for public availability of policies). Is there any reason not to create a written office policy, given that all plea agreements in individual cases will become a matter of public record?

5. *Sentencing guidelines and the shift to charge bargains.* A large number of states have changed their sentencing laws over the past few decades to reduce the discretion of judges in selecting a sentence and to restrict the discretion of corrections or parole officials in releasing offenders before the end of their announced sentences. These more "determinate" sentencing systems make the selection of the criminal charge more important than it was under more discretionary sentencing systems. Unlike the federal system, state guideline systems reject the use of uncharged conduct when setting a sentence. As a result, prosecutors and defendants in these jurisdictions have shifted away from sentence bargains toward charge bargains and "fact" bargains. In Minnesota, which adopted a more determinate sentencing guideline system in 1980, studies focusing on the first few years of practice under the new laws revealed an increase in charge negotiations and a decrease in sentence negotiations. Terance Miethe, Charging and Plea Bargaining Practices Under Determinate Sentencing: An Investigation of the Hydraulic Displacement of Discretion, 78 J. Crim. L. & Criminology 155 (1987) (describing earlier studies).

The federal plea bargaining policies reprinted above apply to U.S. Attorneys' Offices throughout the country. While these offices still have a great deal of independence, and vary from one another in their plea bargaining practices, they are still subject to more centralized control than the various prosecutors' offices located throughout a given state. Since prosecutors often create plea bargaining policies for their own offices, shouldn't there be great variety in plea bargaining practices among the different prosecutors within a state? Or are there institutions or incentives that produce similar prosecutorial plea policies throughout a state or even across different states?

■ STATE v. REYNALDO LAGARES

601 A.2d 698 (N.J. 1992)

GARIBALDI, J.

This appeal concerns the constitutionality of N.J.S.A. 2C:43-6f (Section 6f), the repeat-offender-sentencing provision of the Comprehensive Drug Reform Act of 1986, which permits imposition of an extended term of imprisonment with a minimum term on defendants convicted of drug-related offenses who have previously been convicted of similar crimes. Whether an extended term is imposed depends on the prosecutor because Section 6f takes effect only on his or her application. However, the statute sets forth no guidelines to govern the prosecutor's discretion nor does it require the prosecutor to set forth reasons for making a Section 6f motion. Finally, the statute does not provide for judicial review of the prosecutor's decision to seek an enhanced punishment. Once the prosecutor invokes the statute and establishes the existence of a prior conviction, the court's role is limited to determining the term of years within the extended-term range to be imposed. . . .

A jury convicted defendant, Reynaldo Lagares, of possession of a controlled dangerous substance; possession of a controlled dangerous substance with intent to distribute; and distribution of a controlled dangerous substance. The convictions arose from defendant's sale of cocaine on a single occasion to an undercover police officer. Based on defendant's 1982 convictions for possession of marijuana and possession of marijuana with intent to distribute, the State moved for an extended term of imprisonment pursuant to N.J.S.A. 2C:43-6f. The statute states in pertinent part that

> [a] person convicted of manufacturing, distributing, dispensing or possessing with intent to distribute any dangerous substance . . . who has been previously convicted of manufacturing, distributing, dispensing or possessing with intent to distribute a controlled dangerous substance . . . shall upon application of the prosecuting attorney be sentenced by the court to an extended term . . . notwithstanding that extended terms are ordinarily discretionary with the court. . . .

At the sentencing hearing, the court explained that it had no discretion to impose a term less than an extended term of imprisonment or to forgo ordering a period of parole ineligibility. . . . Without enhancement, defendant's convictions would have carried a sentence in the range of three to five years with a presumptive four-year term. A parole ineligibility period would have been within the sentencing court's discretion. [However, the defendant] was sentenced to seven years imprisonment with a three-year parole disqualifier. . . . On appeal defendant challenged the sentencing provision by arguing that it violated the separation-of-powers doctrine by vesting in the prosecutor unbridled and unreviewable discretion over sentencing. . . .

As a general principle, the punishment of criminal defendants does not fit neatly within a single branch of government. The Legislature defines crimes and establishes the appropriate punishment for their commission. That power includes the ability to enact mandatory-sentencing statutes that eliminate any opportunity for a lesser punishment. The prosecutor, a member of the executive branch, determines the extent of a defendant's sentencing exposure when deciding what charges will be brought. Moreover, the executive branch has the constitutional authority to administer a parole system that may end incarceration prior to the expiration of a judicially-imposed base term of imprisonment. N.J. Const. art. V, §II, para. 2. Finally, the Constitution grants the Governor unreviewable power to pardon offenders and to commute judicially-imposed sentences. N.J. Const. art. V, §II, para. 1.

Although sentencing discretion is shared to some extent among the three branches of government, the determination of the sentence is committed to the discretion of the judiciary. Even when the State and a defendant have entered into a plea agreement, a court in discharging its sentencing duties may not simply accept the arrangement without reviewing its factual support and the circumstances surrounding its formation.

In only a few instances has the Legislature limited that discretion. See N.J.S.A. 2C:43-6c (the Graves Act); N.J.S.A. 2C:14-6 (repeat sex offenders). Under those statutes, however, the court automatically imposes a mandatory sentence after a conviction for a qualifying offense, without regard to prosecutorial consent. Section 6f is substantively different from those statutes. Section 6f permits leniency in some circumstances, but only those in which the prosecutor consents. The infirmity in Section 6f is the prosecutor's sole discretion to select, without standards and without being subject to the court's review, which defendants will receive an increased sentence or enjoy favorable treatment.

Where the Legislature has permitted the executive to select defendants for enhanced punishment or favorable treatment, this Court has generally required that decision-making be carried out in a fashion that limits potential arbitrariness. In addition, we have required that the judiciary retain the power to review prosecutorial decisions to avoid abuses of discretion. We continue that approach today. . . .

Recently, in State v. Warren, 558 A.2d 1312 (N.J. 1989), we prohibited use of "negotiated sentence" plea agreements, in which the prosecutor reserves the right to withdraw from a plea agreement and compel the defendant to go to trial if the court-imposed sentence is more lenient than the one agreed to by the parties or recommended to the court by the prosecutor. Noting that "we cannot overstress the significance of the judicial responsibility in imposing sentence," we invalidated such agreements. . . .

In addition, we cautioned that such unlimited prosecutorial discretion would be inimical to the important goals of uniformity. Individual prosecutors with distinctive perceptions of the gravity of particular offenses and offenders, and responsive to a very different constituency from that of the judiciary, would add undue variability, inevitable inconsistency, and greater disparity to the sentencing process. Hence, separate prosecutorial discretion cannot be superimposed on the court's sentencing discretion.

The Section 6f extended-term provision gives the prosecutor more discretion than did the negotiated-sentence agreements we rejected in *Warren*. In *Warren,* the trial court, although faced with the prospect of risking trial of defendant, had nonetheless been free to reject the plea agreement in its entirety. However, once a prosecutor applies for an extended sentence under Section 6f and establishes a prior conviction, the sentencing judge has no discretion to reject the enhanced sentence. Such unfettered discretion exceeds the permitted "prosecutorial influence on the sentencing determination" that we addressed in *Warren*.

Without standards the prosecutorial decision-making process remains unguided, and the danger of uneven application of enhanced sentences increases significantly. Such results upset the principal goal of the Code of Criminal Justice to insure sentencing uniformity. As currently written, therefore, Section 6f, with its lack of any guidelines and absence of any avenue for effective judicial review, would be unconstitutional.

[I]t is the duty of the Court to [interpret the statute] to render it constitutional if it is reasonably susceptible to such interpretation. Rather than striking down Section 6f, we construe it in a manner that upholds its constitutionality. We are certain that the Legislature would prefer the statute to survive as construed. Accordingly, we interpret the statute to require that guidelines be adopted to assist prosecutorial decision-making with respect to applications for enhanced sentences under N.J.S.A. 2C:43-6f. Those guidelines should reflect the legislative intent to make extended sentencing of repeat drug offenders the norm rather than the exception. However, prosecutors should remember that the Legislature did not mandate extended sentences, recognizing that in certain circumstances enhanced punishment may be unwarranted.

Because we are not familiar with all of the factors that law-enforcement agencies might consider significant in determining whether a defendant should be exempted from an extended sentence, we request that the Attorney General, in consultation with the various county prosecutors, adopt guidelines for use throughout the state. Such guidelines will promote uniformity and provide a means for prosecutors to avoid arbitrary or abusive exercises of discretionary power. Moreover, to permit effective review of prosecutorial sentencing decisions, prosecutors must state on the trial court record the reasons for seeking an extended sentence. Such a statement will provide for effective judicial review and will help to insure that prosecutors follow the guidelines in each case.

Finally, we find that the Legislature did not intend to circumvent the judiciary's power to protect defendants from arbitrary application of enhanced sentences. To protect against such arbitrary action, an extended term may be denied or vacated where defendant has established that the prosecutor's decision to seek the enhanced sentence was an arbitrary and capricious exercise of prosecutorial discretion.

We emphasize that the burden on defendant to prove that a prosecutor's decision to deny leniency constituted an arbitrary and capricious exercise of discretion is heavy. Defendants will have to do more than merely make general conclusory statements that a prosecutorial determination was abusive. . . . We remand the matter to the trial court for further proceedings consistent with this opinion.

Problem 16-4. Statewide Bargaining Guidelines

Within a few months of the New Jersey Supreme Court's decision in *Lagares*, the State Attorney General issued a directive to all county prosecutors that contained guidelines "governing the State's decision to apply for an extended term under N.J.S. 2C:43-6f." These guidelines require the prosecutor to determine, for all defendants charged with a crime enumerated in Section 6f, the individual's prior criminal record and eligibility for the extended term. While recognizing that extended-term sentencing should be the "norm rather than the exception," the guidelines state that the following factors constitute a basis for waiving the extended term:

> 1. The prior conviction relied upon to establish the defendant's eligibility for an extended term was based on a plea or trial at which the defendant did not have the benefit of counsel, or did not effectively waive the right to counsel; or
> 2. The State determines that waiver is essential to assure the defendant's cooperation with the prosecution; or
> 3. The State determines that waiver is appropriate based on an assessment of the proofs available to sustain a conviction against the defendant for the present offense; or
> 4. The State determines that the defendant's prior adult and juvenile record includes only convictions that are extremely remote and, if so, that there is no reason to believe that the defendant at any time derived a substantial source of income from criminal activity; or
> 5. The State determines that waiver is appropriate based upon the existence of compelling extraordinary circumstances, including an assessment of the seriousness of the present offense and the predicate offense(s), and consideration of the nature and amount of controlled and dangerous substance involved.

If you represent the defendant in a case in which the prosecutor relies on these guidelines and refuses to negotiate about the enhanced sentence request, what arguments can you make to establish that these guidelines do not fulfill the New Jersey Supreme Court's objectives in *Lagares*?

Notes

1. *Uniformity in guidelines.* The New Jersey decision in *Lagares* is unusual; courts do not often order prosecutors to create statewide policies on questions of plea bargaining or requests for sentencing enhancements. Prosecutors themselves do not often create statewide guidelines for such matters, either. Instead, it is more common to find policies about plea bargaining and related matters set at the local office level. See Pamela Utz, Settling the Facts (1978) (comparing practices in California jurisdictions).

How are prosecutors likely to respond to a judicial requirement that they create statewide guidelines? Were the New Jersey guidelines discussed in Problem 16-4 a predictable response to the state supreme court's mandate? Is there such a thing as too much uniformity from office to office? Within a single office? See State v. Pettitt, 609 P.2d 1364 (Wash. 1980) (striking down prosecutor's office policy mandating the filing of habitual criminal complaints against any defendant who had three or more prior felonies as abuse of discretion where policy resulted in mandatory life sentence for a defendant with three nonviolent property crimes).

The New Jersey court's opinion in *Lagares* did not explicitly require or prohibit any plea bargaining practices; it dealt instead with the prosecutor's decision whether to request a mandatory sentencing enhancement. However, the sentencing enhancement decision and negotiations for a plea agreement are linked. Many plea negotiations take place before the prosecutor has even filed charges, and the bargaining centers on the charges that the prosecutor will ultimately bring. Similarly, when the prosecutor has the power to request and receive an automatic sentencing enhancement, plea negotiations will include this topic. By requiring prosecutors statewide to create guidelines to govern the decision whether to request a sentencing enhancement, did the New Jersey court take any real plea bargaining discretion away from prosecutors in the field?

2. *Priority crimes.* Prosecutorial office policies on plea bargaining often restrict the power of the individual prosecutor to negotiate terms for a select group of high-priority crimes. While the line prosecutors remain free to reach plea agreements in less serious cases (which are by far the most numerous), the guidelines prohibit dismissal of charges or sentencing concessions in cases involving violent crimes such as murder, rape, or armed robbery. Alternatively, in such cases the guidelines may require special justifications for plea agreements or may limit the acceptable bargaining outcomes. See U.S. Department of Justice, Plea Bargaining: Critical Issues and Common Practices (1985). How do supervising prosecutors choose the priority crimes that will be subject to these special bargaining limitations? Do they take their cues from crime legislation and limit bargaining whenever the legislature has emphasized the importance of a crime by enhancing its penalty? See Milton Heumann and Colin Loftin, Mandatory Sentencing and the Abolition of Plea Bargaining: The Michigan Felony Firearm Statute, 13 L. & Socy. Rev. 393 (1979) (evaluating mandatory-minimum-sentence statute for firearms cases, and contemporaneous county prosecutor's no-plea-bargaining policy for crimes charged under the statute).

New Jersey offers a prominent example of crime-specific statewide guidelines. In the Comprehensive Drug Reform Act of 1986, the legislature imposed mandatory minimum sentences on those convicted of various drug crimes; the same statute gave the prosecutor the power to waive the mandatory prison term. Without the prosecutor's waiver, the sentencing judge had no power to reduce the sentence below the statutory minimum. In State v. Vasquez, 609 A.2d 29 (N.J. 1992), the court required the State Attorney General to create prosecutorial guidelines for these waivers of mandatory sentencing enhancements in narcotics cases. The Attorney General responded promptly. The 1992 policy stated that the mandatory minimum sentence would be considered the "normal" sentence, and any waiver would have to be explained in writing. These statewide guidelines instructed county prosecutors to give more specific direction to line prosecutors: "each county prosecutor shall adopt and implement a written policy governing plea and post-trial agreements and discretionary decisions utilizing these guidelines as a model." The guidelines specified minimum requirements for such standardized plea offers for typical cases. All plea agreements must provide for "a term of incarceration," and plea offers to a defendant charged with distributing narcotics on school property must provide for at least three years' imprisonment. A prosecutor in a particular case could negotiate a plea agreement below or above the "standardized" plea agreement that the county prosecutor has adopted, but only after considering several potential bases for "upward or downward departures" from the standard agreement. What grounds do you suppose these guidelines list as proper bases for upward or downward departures? See State v. Shaw, 618 A.2d 294 (N.J. 1993).

3. *Internal review.* One common prosecutorial policy on plea bargaining is procedural rather than substantive. Instead of banning plea bargains for some crimes or limiting the outcomes that a prosecutor can accept in certain cases, these policies simply require the line prosecutor to obtain approval from a supervisor (or some committee of supervisors) before entering a plea agreement. See Richard Kuh, Plea Bargaining: Guidelines for the Manhattan District Attorney's Office, 11 Crim. L. Bull. 48 (1975) (supervisor review for proposed agreements reducing charges to extent greater than ordinarily allowed under office policy); Mario Merola, Modern Prosecutorial Techniques, 16 Crim. L. Bull. 232, 237-38, 251-55 (1980). What criteria will the reviewing attorneys use under such a policy?

4. *Victim Consultation*

Many prosecutors feel obliged to inform crime victims about their efforts to negotiate a guilty plea. But only recently have legal provisions and institutions reinforced this sense of obligation. Over the past 10-20 years, a majority of states have enacted statutes and constitutional provisions requiring prosecutors to inform or consult the victims of alleged crimes about any plea agreements in their case. These laws differ in the type of information the victim and the prosecutor must exchange and in the timing of the exchange. But they share the assumption that the involvement of a crime victim will change the outcomes in at least some plea negotiations. Is the effect of the victim's involvement in plea negotiations predictable? Will the timing of the victim's involvement make a difference in many plea negotiations?

■ MAINE REVISED STATUTES TIT. 15, §812; TIT. 17-A, §§1172, 1173

Title 15, §812

1. The Legislature finds that there is citizen dissatisfaction with plea bargaining which has resulted in some criticism of the criminal justice process. The Legislature further finds that part of the dissatisfaction is caused because victims of crimes and law enforcement officers who respond to those crimes have no subsequent contact with the cases as they proceed through the courts for judicial disposition. Victims and law enforcement officers are many times not informed by prosecutors of plea agreements which are to be submitted to the court for approval or rejection. . . . It is the intent of this section to alleviate these expressions of citizen dissatisfaction and to promote greater understanding by prosecutors of citizens' valid concerns. This is most likely to be accomplished by citizens and law enforcement officers being informed of the results of plea negotiations before they are submitted to the courts. This notification will in no way affect the authority of the judge to accept, reject or modify the terms of the plea agreement.

2. Before submitting a negotiated plea to the court, the attorney for the State shall advise the relevant law enforcement officers of the details of the plea agreement

reached in any prosecution where the defendant was originally charged with murder, a Class A, B or C crime or [an assault crime, sex offense, or kidnapping,] and shall advise victims of their rights under Title 17-A, section 1173.

Title 17-A, §1172

1. When practicable, the attorney for the State shall make a good faith effort to inform each victim of a crime of the following: A) the details of a plea agreement before it is submitted to the court; B) the right to comment on the plea agreement pursuant to section 1173; C) the time and place of the trial; D) the time and place of sentencing; and E) the right to participate at sentencing. . . .

Title 17-A, §1173

When a plea agreement is submitted to the court . . . , the attorney for the State shall disclose to the court any and all attempts made to notify each victim of the plea agreement and any objection to the plea agreement by a victim. A victim who is present in court at the submission of the plea may address the court at that time.

■ STATE v. MICHAEL McDONNELL

837 P.2d 941 (Or. 1992)

Van Hoosmissen, J.

. . . In 1984, defendant was charged with the aggravated murder of Joey Keever after defendant had escaped from a state penal or correctional facility. . . . At his trial in 1988, defendant stipulated that he caused Keever's death by cutting her with a knife. His defense was that he did so while in a drug-induced psychosis and that, while he was in that condition, he was unable to form the intent necessary to commit the crime of aggravated murder and that, therefore, he was guilty only of the crime of manslaughter. . . . After a jury trial, defendant was found guilty of aggravated murder. In a separate sentencing hearing, [the jury and judge sentenced the defendant to death].

William Lasswell was the Douglas County District Attorney when Oregon voters reinstated the death penalty in 1984 and when defendant murdered Keever later that same year. At the time of this murder and at the time defense counsel proposed a plea offer to the district attorney's office, Lasswell's view was that, once a defendant was indicted for aggravated murder, plea bargaining was not permitted. . . .

The criminal investigation was assigned to Charles Lee, Lasswell's Chief Deputy, shortly after the murder was committed. . . . Lee intended to try the case as a death penalty case, and he communicated that decision to defense counsel. Lee testified that the policy of the Douglas County District Attorney's office concerning aggravated murder cases was that "there wouldn't be plea bargaining to life in death penalty cases."

[In] 1986, a few days before the trial of this case was scheduled to begin, the trial court declared unconstitutional that portion of the aggravated murder statute that punished as aggravated murder an intentional murder that was committed by one who was an escapee. The state appealed that ruling, and Lasswell felt that the appeal could delay the case at least one year. . . .

Following the trial court's ruling, the defense lawyers approached Lasswell regarding a plea. The lawyers proposed that defendant would plead guilty to aggravated murder, the state would then decline to present any evidence at the penalty phase, and defendant "would accept a life sentence." At the end of the meeting, Lasswell advised defense counsel that he would need to discuss the defense proposal with Lee and with the victim's parents.

Before that meeting with the defense lawyers, Lasswell had had a number of contacts with the victim's parents, primarily with the victim's mother. Lasswell felt that the victim's mother "was just overwhelmed with emotions involving her daughter's death." Lasswell also knew that at one time the victim's father was stalking the streets with a gun. As a result of his contacts with the victim's parents, Lasswell "was very concerned about [their] emotional health and their welfare so [he] thought it important to present to them this offer. . . ."

Lasswell's assessment of the proposed plea agreement was almost exclusively based on his concern for the victim's parents' emotional health and welfare. He was concerned that they "wouldn't make it through another year." Had the victim's parents told Lasswell that they could "not take another year," then Lasswell "would have told [Chief Deputy] Lee that it was [Lasswell's] recommendation that we accept that plea bargain." Lasswell's willingness to consider a plea "was based solely on [his] concern for the welfare [of the victim's parents]." Although Lasswell also had a concern about the delay that would be caused by an appeal of the trial court's ruling and the potential that evidence or witnesses might become unavailable while the appeal was pending, that consideration was "a very, very minor one." . . .

The victim's parents rejected the plea proposal. The victim's father "was offended" that Lasswell was considering the family's welfare. He told Lasswell that "both he and his wife wanted to go ahead with the case even though it was going to take at least another year." The position of the family was relayed to the defendant's lawyers.

Lasswell's dispositive reliance on the victim's family's wishes at that time led to our reversal and remand in State v. McDonnell, 794 P.2d 780 (Or. 1990). [McDonnell argued in that appeal that the district attorney had abdicated his statutory role in the plea discussion process. The statute in question, ORS 135.415, provided that the district attorney "may take into account" several listed considerations when "determining whether to engage in plea discussions." Because the statute placed the decision whether to enter a plea agreement in the hands of the district attorney, the court found a statutory violation because "the victim's parents' wishes were the controlling factor in the district attorney's decision not to accept defendant's plea offer." Accordingly, the court remanded the case to the trial court "for an evidentiary hearing to determine how the district attorney would have exercised his judgment and discretion on the basis of proper criteria and the facts that existed at the time he declined to enter into the plea agreement." If the trial court were to find that the district attorney would have accepted a negotiated plea after giving proper weight to the victims' wishes, the defendant would be allowed to plead guilty with a stipulated sentence of life imprisonment.]

On remand the trial court had to determine what Lasswell's decision would have been had it been based on appropriate considerations. During the remand hearing, . . . Lasswell testified:

> It's obvious that if this — if that plea had been accepted, the docket would have been cleared of that case, a month or two months, so other cases could have been tried. It is

true that by an acknowledgment of guilt, it would have been . . . an acknowledgment of responsibility and that's supposed to be one of the considerations in potential rehabilitation somewhat and also some finality as far as the community in identifying a particular person as a wrongdoer. And the fact that he appeared to be, under a plea offer, to spend at least twenty years of confinement, a substantial . . . measure of safety to the community. [But this] was an outrageous act against the community and that the people of Oregon had clearly expressed themselves how they wished their law enforcement officials, including myself, to react to this kind of situation. That the only appropriate method of proceeding was . . . to go ahead with the death penalty. So . . . there would have been some reasons for making a plea bargain separate from the [victim's parents'] feelings but . . . there was never any question in my mind about what we should do, going ahead. . . .

In other words, the only impact that consideration of the family's preference was going to have was in defendant's favor. And it was simply because the victim's parents did not ask for that consideration that the district attorney had no other reason not to proceed to trial. Thus, in the absence of that intervening consideration — removing it from Lasswell's decision-making process — the case would have proceeded just as it did. The trial court found that Lasswell would have considered a number of proper criteria and that, on the basis of those criteria, he would not have offered defendant a life sentence. . . .

Defendant does not challenge the accuracy of any of the trial court's findings on remand. [Instead, he argues that the prosecutor's ad hoc decision not to enter a plea agreement violated article I, section 20, of the Oregon Constitution,* and the Equal Protection Clause of the Fourteenth Amendment to the Constitution of the United States. McDonnell] attacks the district attorney's decision to deny the plea offer on the ground that it "was purely haphazard and not a part of a coherent, systematic policy." According to defendant, the decision was haphazard for two reasons: "There were no particular standards concerning when a plea bargain should be offered in any given case" and "[t]he decision whether to extend a plea offer was left up to each individual deputy." . . .

Defendant misreads the record. Both Lasswell and Lee testified that at the time defendant proposed his plea offer the policy of the office was that there would be no plea bargaining once a defendant was charged with aggravated murder. Lee and Lasswell made the decision to charge defendant with aggravated murder because the facts of the case fit one of the aggravated murder categories — murder after escaping — and because the facts of the case were strong. The factors on which the prosecutors relied in charging defendant with aggravated murder were permissible. The prosecution's "no-plea-bargaining" policy was based at least in part on both Lee's and Lasswell's interpretation that, under former ORS 163.150, it was impermissible to plea bargain in capital murder cases. . . .

Generally, a decision by the district attorney whether or not to engage in plea negotiations is subject to judicial scrutiny. In deciding whether to offer a plea bargain to a defendant, a district attorney must exercise discretion in a manner that adheres to sufficiently consistent standards to represent a coherent, systematic policy. A rational no-plea-bargaining policy, consistently applied, is permissible. Here, the decision

* Article I, section 20, provides as follows: "No law shall be passed granting to any citizen or class of citizens privileges, or immunities, which, upon the same terms, shall not equally belong to all citizens." — Eds.

not to plea bargain in aggravated murder cases was based on rational and proper grounds, including a "[g]enuine legal question as to the lawfulness or unlawfulness of bargaining certain offenses." . . . In light of the record on remand, we conclude that the district attorney's decision not to enter into a plea bargain was constitutionally permissible. Defendant, therefore, has not established a factual predicate for asserting any alleged violation of Article I, section 20, of the Oregon Constitution. . . .

Notes

1. *Informing victims of plea agreements: majority position.* A majority of states now have statutes or constitutional provisions dealing with the rights of crime victims in the criminal process. Virtually all of these laws address plea bargains. The most common type of provision requires the prosecutor, when feasible, to inform a victim that the prosecutor plans to recommend that a court accept a guilty plea based on a plea agreement. The statutes also typically instruct the prosecutor to inform the victim of the time and place for the plea hearing. See Sarah Welling, Victim Participation in Plea Bargains, 65 Wash. U. L.Q. 301 (1987). Does a law requiring notice about a public document (the plea agreement) and a public hearing (the plea hearing) give crime victims anything of practical value? Would the notice requirement have a different effect if it were to apply before the prosecutor finalizes any plea negotiations? Does a notice requirement remain ineffective until the legislature authorizes funds to hire extra prosecutorial staff members to provide support to victims?

A smaller number of statutes require the prosecution to "consult" with the victim before recommending a plea agreement. See Ind. Code §35-335-3.5; W. Va. Code §61-11A-6(a)(5)(C). A few laws also authorize the victim to make a statement to the court during the plea hearing or require the prosecutor to inform the court about the victim's views on any proposed plea agreement. R.I. Gen. Laws §§12-28-3(14), 12-28-4.1. What might the victim say to the prosecutor or the judge that would provide new information relevant to the case?

2. *Responsiveness to victims.* In its 1990 decision in the *McDonnell* case from Oregon, the appellate court ruled that an exclusive reliance on a victim's views violated a statutory requirement placing the authority to charge and enter plea agreements in the hands of the prosecutor. Did the state supreme court decision in 1992 overrule that reading of the statute? Are prosecutors now free to give controlling weight to the views of victims?

The victims' rights laws described above all assume the validity of a prosecutor's partial reliance on the wishes of crime victims. When defendants raise constitutional and other legal challenges to prosecutorial decisions based partly on the views of victims, courts have upheld the decisions. See Commonwealth v. Latimore, 667 N.E.2d 818 (Mass. 1996) (district attorney's decision not to accept defendant's offer of guilty plea to lesser offense, based in part on victim's family's desire to pursue murder conviction, was not prosecutorial misconduct). Would you predict the same result if a statute explicitly provided the victim with controlling authority — a "veto" power over any proposed plea agreement? What if a prosecutor adopted such a policy in the absence of a statute? Does the legitimacy of the victim's input change if he has filed a civil suit to recover monetary damages from the defendant? See N.D. Cent. Code §§29-01-16 and 29-01-17 (provides for "compromise" of a misdemeanor; victim accepts civil settlement, and there is no criminal conviction).

3. *The impact of victims' rights laws.* All 50 states have some statutory protections for the rights of victims during the criminal process, and about 30 states have amended their constitutions to provide for such rights. But some states have stronger requirements than others. Does the type of law at work in a state influence the way that government officials deal with the victim of an alleged crime? Does a stronger law change the likely reaction of the victim? A 1998 survey suggests that stronger victim protection laws do translate into some noteworthy differences in practice. For instance, victims in "strong-protection states" are more likely to learn about sentencing or parole hearings than victims in "weak-protection states." However, the strength of the victim protection laws did *not* affect the number of victims who learned about plea negotiations or a decision to dismiss charges. See Dean Kilpatrick, David Beatty, and Susan Smith Howley, The Rights of Crime Victims — Does Legal Protection Make a Difference? (Research in Brief) (Dec. 1998, NCJ 173839). What barriers might stand in the way of notifying victims about the progress of plea negotiations? Cf. Susan Bandes, Victim Standing, 1999 Utah L. Rev. 331 (the sorts of victim initiatives that have succeeded have been those that advance the prosecution's agenda, while preserving the prosecution's complete freedom from third party interference).

C. VALIDITY OF INDIVIDUAL PLEA BARGAINS

Most of the statutes and judicial opinions on the subject of guilty pleas do not address plea bargaining as an institution. Instead, they focus on the validity of the guilty plea in an individual case. There are three essential ingredients for a valid plea of guilty, whether the plea is "open" or "negotiated": The plea must reflect a knowing waiver of trial rights, the defendant must waive those rights voluntarily, and there must be an adequate "factual basis" to support the charges to which the defendant pleads guilty.

1. Lack of Knowledge

A defendant who pleads guilty must know about the nature of the charges and some of the consequences of waiving the right to trial and accepting a conviction. In essence, the defendant must see two future paths. Down one path, she must visualize the events likely to occur at a trial and after a possible conviction; down another path, she must picture the events likely to occur after a conviction based on a plea of guilty. But predicting the future is no easy task. Courts do not require that a defendant know every single consequence of pleading guilty; the challenge is to select *which* consequences a defendant must understand before entering a valid plea of guilty.

The rules of criminal procedure give the trial judge the primary responsibility for ensuring that defendants understand the consequences of waiving trial and pleading guilty. This judicial responsibility is also grounded in the federal constitution. In Boykin v. Alabama, 395 U.S. 238 (1969), the Supreme Court declared that guilty pleas will not be constitutionally valid unless the record affirmatively shows that defendants understand their privilege against self-incrimination, their right to trial by jury, and their right to confront their accusers. During a *Boykin* hearing, the judge asks the defendant a routine set of questions about these rights and other matters before the court will accept a plea of guilty or nolo contendere.

■ FEDERAL RULE OF CRIMINAL PROCEDURE 11(b)

(1) Before the court accepts a plea of guilty or nolo contendere, the defendant may be placed under oath, and the court must address the defendant personally in open court. During this address, the court must inform the defendant of, and determine that the defendant understands, the following:

(A) the government's right, in a prosecution for perjury or false statement, to use against the defendant any statement that the defendant gives under oath;

(B) the right to plead not guilty, or having already so pleaded, to persist in that plea;

(C) the right to a jury trial;

(D) the right to be represented by counsel — and if necessary have the court appoint counsel — at trial and at every other stage of the proceeding;

(E) the right at trial to confront and cross-examine adverse witnesses, to be protected from compelled self-incrimination, to testify and present evidence, and to compel the attendance of witnesses;

(F) the defendant's waiver of these trial rights if the court accepts a plea of guilty or nolo contendere;

(G) the nature of each charge to which the defendant is pleading;

(H) any maximum possible penalty, including imprisonment, fine, and term of supervised release;

(I) any mandatory minimum penalty;

(J) any applicable forfeiture;

(K) the court's authority to order restitution;

(L) the court's obligation to impose a special assessment;

(M) the court's obligation to apply the Sentencing Guidelines, and the court's discretion to depart from those guidelines under some circumstances; and

(N) the terms of any plea-agreement provision waiving the right to appeal or to collaterally attack the sentence.

■ STATE v. DONALD ROSS

916 P.2d 405 (Wash. 1996)

DOLLIVER, J.

Defendant Donald Ross has moved to withdraw his guilty plea as involuntary on the basis he was never informed a mandatory 12-month community placement would follow his prison sentence. We hold mandatory community placement constitutes a direct consequence of a guilty plea and failure to so inform a defendant renders that plea invalid. The trial court erred by denying Defendant's motion to withdraw his guilty plea. . . .

On November 6, 1991, Defendant pleaded guilty to three counts of second degree child rape committed against his former step-daughter prior to July 1, 1990. Those offenses carried a maximum sentence of 10 years and a $20,000 fine, a minimum sentence for Defendant's criminal history of 67 months, and a mandatory 12-month community placement. The parties do not dispute Defendant did not receive an explicit warning of his mandatory one-year community placement term prior to entering his plea. . . . Defendant received the maximum 89-month sentence within his sentencing range plus the mandatory one-year community placement. In addition to the standard community placement conditions, the court adopted special conditions recommended by the presentence investigator: no contact with the victim; no contact with females under 16 years old; Department of Corrections' approval of residence location and living arrangements; and urinalysis and polygraph at the will of his community corrections officer. Defendant subsequently moved the trial court to withdraw his guilty plea as involuntary. The trial court denied withdrawal, concluding [that] the omission of the mandatory 12-month community placement represented merely a collateral consequence of his plea insufficient for withdrawal. . . .

Due process requires an affirmative showing that a defendant entered a guilty plea intelligently and voluntarily. Beyond this constitutional minimum, CrR 4.2 details further safeguards on the voluntariness of pleas:

> The court shall not accept a plea of guilty, without first determining that it is made voluntarily, competently and with an understanding of the nature of the charge and the consequences of the plea. The court shall not enter a judgment upon a plea of guilty unless it is satisfied that there is a factual basis for the plea.

Here the question concerns whether Defendant understood the consequences of his plea. A defendant need not be informed of all possible consequences of a plea but rather only direct consequences. The court has distinguished direct from collateral consequences by whether the result represents a definite, immediate and largely automatic effect on the range of the defendant's punishment. Mandatory community placement produces a definite, immediate and automatic effect on a defendant's range of punishment. We reject the State's contention that the possibility of an overlap between a community placement term and any community custody imposed in lieu of earned early release renders community placement indefinite. That community custody in lieu of earned early release reduces a defendant's total confinement time but is uncertain at sentencing is irrelevant to the certainty of community placement. A defendant will definitely serve a full 12 months of mandatory community placement. Only the composition of community placement is uncertain at sentencing.

We also refute the State's argument that community placement is not immediate because the term begins upon the completion of confinement or transfer to community custody in lieu of earned early release credit instead of immediately upon sentencing. Immediacy does not necessitate the community placement itself occur immediately upon sentencing. Rather, as this court has repeatedly articulated, it is the "effect on the range of defendant's punishment" that must be immediate. State v. Ward, 869 P.2d 1062 (Wash. 1994). In contrast are sentencing conditions where any effect on punishment flows not from the guilty plea itself but from additional proceedings and thus cannot qualify as immediate. State v. Olivas, 856 P.2d 1076 (Wash. 1993) (mandatory DNA testing); State v. Barton, 609 P.2d 1353 (Wash. 1980) (discretionary habitual criminal proceeding); In re Ness, 855 P.2d 1191 (Wash. 1993) (federal sentence restricting possession of firearms); In re Peters, 750

P.2d 643 (Wash. 1988) (deportation). Community placement, on the other hand, affects the punishment flowing immediately from the guilty plea. . . .

Despite our categorization of mandatory community placement as a direct consequence, the State asserts Defendant received adequate sentencing information to uphold his plea as voluntary and intelligent. . . . There is no dispute the record lacks any evidence Defendant was advised of the specific consequence of community placement. The State describes Defendant's plea as voluntary because he knew of the maximum sentence of 10 years for his crime and the court's discretion to reject the plea agreement's sentencing recommendation. As the State points out, Defendant's actual total sentence of 101 months, 89 months in prison plus one year in community placement, fell short of that possible 120-month statutory maximum.

Defendant's knowledge of his maximum prison sentence was insufficient to assure his understanding of the direct consequence of community placement. The plea to which Defendant agreed was not the plea the State now seeks to enforce. Defendant signed a plea agreement believing the State was recommending a total sentence of 89 months, not 101 months. More significantly, mandatory community placement enhanced Defendant's minimum sentence and altered the standard of punishment applicable. Although Defendant knew the State's recommendation did not bind the trial court, he claims he would not have agreed to such a plea. Without evidence of an explicit explanation of mandatory community placement, we must conclude Defendant was unable to enter an intelligent, voluntary plea. . . .

■ UNITED STATES v. ANGELA RUIZ

536 U.S. 622 (2002)

BREYER, J.

In this case we primarily consider whether the Fifth and Sixth Amendments require federal prosecutors, before entering into a binding plea agreement with a criminal defendant, to disclose "impeachment information relating to any informants or other witnesses." We hold that the Constitution does not require that disclosure.

After immigration agents found 30 kilograms of marijuana in Angela Ruiz's luggage, federal prosecutors offered her what is known in the Southern District of California as a "fast track" plea bargain. That bargain — standard in that district — asks a defendant to waive indictment, trial, and an appeal. In return, the Government agrees to recommend to the sentencing judge a two-level departure downward from the otherwise applicable United States Sentencing Guidelines sentence. In Ruiz's case, a two-level departure downward would have shortened the ordinary Guidelines-specified 18-to-24-month sentencing range by 6 months, to 12-to-18 months.

The prosecutors' proposed plea agreement contains a set of detailed terms. Among other things, it specifies that "any [known] information establishing the factual innocence of the defendant" has been turned over to the defendant, and it acknowledges the Government's "continuing duty to provide such information." At the same time it requires that the defendant waive the right to receive "impeachment information relating to any informants or other witnesses" as well as the right to receive information supporting any affirmative defense the defendant raises if the case goes to trial. Because Ruiz would not agree to this last-mentioned waiver, the prosecutors withdrew their bargaining offer. The Government then indicted Ruiz for unlawful drug possession. And despite the absence of any agreement, Ruiz ultimately pleaded guilty.

At sentencing, Ruiz asked the judge to grant her the same two-level downward departure that the Government would have recommended had she accepted the "fast track" agreement. The Government opposed her request, and the District Court denied it, imposing a standard Guideline sentence instead. . . .

The Ninth Circuit vacated the District Court's sentencing determination. The Ninth Circuit pointed out that the Constitution requires prosecutors to make certain impeachment information available to a defendant before trial. It decided that this obligation entitles defendants to receive that same information before they enter into a plea agreement. The Ninth Circuit also decided that the Constitution prohibits defendants from waiving their right to that information. And it held that the prosecutors' standard "fast track" plea agreement was unlawful because it insisted upon that waiver. . . .

The constitutional question concerns a federal criminal defendant's waiver of the right to receive from prosecutors exculpatory impeachment material — a right that the Constitution provides as part of its basic "fair trial" guarantee. See U.S. Const., Amdts. 5, 6. See also Brady v. Maryland, 373 U.S. 83 (1963) (Due process requires prosecutors to avoid "an unfair trial" by making available "upon request" evidence "favorable to an accused" where the evidence is "material either to guilt or to punishment").

When a defendant pleads guilty he or she, of course, forgoes not only a fair trial, but also other accompanying constitutional guarantees. Boykin v. Alabama, 395 U.S. 238 (1969) (pleading guilty implicates the Fifth Amendment privilege against self-incrimination, the Sixth Amendment right to confront one's accusers, and the Sixth Amendment right to trial by jury). Given the seriousness of the matter, the Constitution insists, among other things, that the defendant enter a guilty plea that is "voluntary" and that the defendant must make related waivers knowingly, intelligently, and "with sufficient awareness of the relevant circumstances and likely consequences." *Brady,* at 742, 748. . . . We must decide whether the Constitution requires that preguilty plea disclosure of impeachment information. We conclude that it does not.

First, impeachment information is special in relation to the fairness of a trial, not in respect to whether a plea is voluntary ("knowing," "intelligent," and sufficiently "aware"). Of course, the more information the defendant has, the more aware he is of the likely consequences of a plea, waiver, or decision, and the wiser that decision will likely be. But the Constitution does not require the prosecutor to share all useful information with the defendant. Weatherford v. Bursey, 429 U.S. 545 (1977) ("There is no general constitutional right to discovery in a criminal case"). And the law ordinarily considers a waiver knowing, intelligent, and sufficiently aware if the defendant fully understands the nature of the right and how it would likely apply in general in the circumstances — even though the defendant may not know the specific detailed consequences of invoking it. A defendant, for example, may waive his right to remain silent, his right to a jury trial, or his right to counsel even if the defendant does not know the specific questions the authorities intend to ask, who will likely serve on the jury, or the particular lawyer the State might otherwise provide.

It is particularly difficult to characterize impeachment information as critical information of which the defendant must always be aware prior to pleading guilty given the random way in which such information may, or may not, help a particular defendant. The degree of help that impeachment information can provide will depend upon the defendant's own independent knowledge of the prosecution's potential case — a matter that the Constitution does not require prosecutors to disclose.

Second, . . . this Court has found that the Constitution, in respect to a defendant's awareness of relevant circumstances, does not require complete knowledge of the relevant circumstances, but permits a court to accept a guilty plea, with its accompanying waiver of various constitutional rights, despite various forms of misapprehension under which a defendant might labor. See Brady v. United States, 397 U.S., at 757 (defendant "misapprehended the quality of the State's case" [and] "the likely penalties"; defendant failed to "anticipate a change in the law regarding" relevant "punishments"); McMann v. Richardson, 397 U.S. 759, 770 (1970) (counsel "misjudged the admissibility" of a "confession"); United States v. Broce, 488 U.S. 563, 573 (1989) (counsel failed to point out a potential defense); Tollett v. Henderson, 411 U.S. 258 (1973) (counsel failed to find a potential constitutional infirmity in grand jury proceedings). It is difficult to distinguish, in terms of importance, (1) a defendant's ignorance of grounds for impeachment of potential witnesses at a possible future trial from (2) the varying forms of ignorance at issue in these cases.

Third, due process considerations, the very considerations that led this Court to find trial-related rights to exculpatory and impeachment information in *Brady* . . . argue against the existence of the "right" that the Ninth Circuit found here. This Court has said that due process considerations include not only (1) the nature of the private interest at stake, but also (2) the value of the additional safeguard, and (3) the adverse impact of the requirement upon the Government's interests. [A]s the proposed plea agreement at issue here specifies, the Government will provide "any information establishing the factual innocence of the defendant." . . . That fact, along with other guilty-plea safeguards, see Fed. Rule Crim. Proc. 11, diminishes the force of Ruiz's concern that, in the absence of impeachment information, innocent individuals, accused of crimes, will plead guilty.

At the same time, a constitutional obligation to provide impeachment information during plea bargaining, prior to entry of a guilty plea, could seriously interfere with the Government's interest in securing those guilty pleas that are factually justified, desired by defendants, and help to secure the efficient administration of justice. The Ninth Circuit's rule risks premature disclosure of Government witness information, which, the Government tells us, could "disrupt ongoing investigations" and expose prospective witnesses to serious harm. And the careful tailoring that characterizes most legal Government witness disclosure requirements suggests recognition by both Congress and the Federal Rules Committees that such concerns are valid. See, e.g., 18 U.S.C. §3432 (witness list disclosure required in capital cases three days before trial with exceptions); §3500 (Government witness statements ordinarily subject to discovery only after testimony given); Fed. Rule Crim. Proc. 16(a)(2) (embodies limitations of 18 U.S.C. §3500). Compare 156 F.R.D. 460 (1994) (congressional proposal to significantly broaden §3500) with 167 F.R.D. 221 (judicial conference opposing congressional proposal).

Consequently, the Ninth Circuit's requirement could force the Government to abandon its general practice of not disclosing to a defendant pleading guilty information that would reveal the identities of cooperating informants, undercover investigators, or other prospective witnesses. It could require the Government to devote substantially more resources to trial preparation prior to plea bargaining, thereby depriving the plea-bargaining process of its main resource-saving advantages. Or it could lead the Government instead to abandon its heavy reliance upon plea bargaining in a vast number — 90 percent or more — of federal criminal cases. We cannot say that the Constitution's due process requirement demands so radical a change in the criminal justice process in order to achieve so comparatively small a constitutional benefit.

These considerations, taken together, lead us to conclude that the Constitution does not require the Government to disclose material impeachment evidence prior to entering a plea agreement with a criminal defendant.

In addition, we note that the "fast track" plea agreement requires a defendant to waive her right to receive information the Government has regarding any "affirmative defense" she raises at trial. We do not believe the Constitution here requires provision of this information to the defendant prior to plea bargaining — for most (though not all) of the reasons previously stated. That is to say, in the context of this agreement, the need for this information is more closely related to the fairness of a trial than to the voluntariness of the plea; the value in terms of the defendant's added awareness of relevant circumstances is ordinarily limited; yet the added burden imposed upon the Government by requiring its provision well in advance of trial (often before trial preparation begins) can be serious, thereby significantly interfering with the administration of the plea bargaining process. . . .

THOMAS, J. concurring.

I agree with the Court that the Constitution does not require the Government to disclose either affirmative defense information or impeachment information relating to informants or other witnesses before entering into a binding plea agreement with a criminal defendant. The Court, however, suggests that the constitutional analysis turns in some part on the "degree of help" such information would provide to the defendant at the plea stage, a distinction that is neither necessary nor accurate. To the extent that the Court is implicitly drawing a line based on a flawed characterization about the usefulness of certain types of information, I can only concur in the judgment. The principle supporting *Brady* was "avoidance of an unfair trial to the accused." That concern is not implicated at the plea stage regardless.

Notes

1. *Knowledge of nature of charges.* The federal constitution requires a defendant to understand the nature of the charges before pleading guilty to them. Although defense counsel usually explains the elements of the offense to the client, the judge ordinarily must confirm that the defendant understands what he was told. In Henderson v. Morgan, 426 U.S. 637 (1976), a defendant with below-average intelligence pleaded guilty to second-degree murder while insisting that he "meant no harm" to the victim. Because the judge during the plea colloquy did not explain to the defendant that intent was a "critical" element of the crime, the Court overturned the conviction, even though there was overwhelming evidence of the defendant's guilt. The *Henderson* decision, however, does not require the judge to explain every element of every crime to every defendant. The constitutional requirement applies only to "critical" elements of the offense, and where there is room to doubt what a defendant knows, courts will presume that defense counsel has explained the elements of the offense to the client. See Marshall v. Lonberger, 459 U.S. 422 (1983)

(defendant represented by counsel presumed to know that attempted murder requires proof of intent to kill).

2. *Knowledge of direct penal consequences.* The Washington court in *Ross* stated the general rule about knowledge of the consequences of a guilty plea: A defendant must understand the "direct" consequences of the conviction but not the "collateral" consequences. A rich case law has developed in an effort to sort out direct from collateral consequences. Direct consequences include the maximum sentence authorized and some information about the prison term a defendant should expect. State v. Domian, 668 A.2d 1333 (Conn. 1996) (no need to inform defendant of 10-year mandatory minimum sentence when judge stated at plea hearing his intention to impose 10-year term). Most courts also conclude that any substantial restitution payments would be a direct consequence. State v. Wolff, 438 N.W.2d 199 (S.D. 1989). Possible deportation of a resident alien after completion of a prison term is usually treated as a collateral consequence that a defendant need not know before entering a valid guilty plea. People v. Ford, 657 N.E.2d 265 (N.Y. 1995). Eligibility for parole also tends to fall into the "collateral" category. People v. Barella, 975 P.2d 37 (Cal. 1999) (defendant need not be told about limited good time credits available); State v. Andrews, 752 A.2d 49 (Conn. 2000) (lack of knowledge that conviction would make defendant ineligible for parole did not render plea involuntary). Requirements that sex offenders register with law enforcement officers near their residence after the completion of any prison term are also considered collateral. See Johnson v. State, 922 P.2d 1384 (Wyo. 1996) (sex offender registration is regulatory rather than punitive). The *Ross* decision states that direct consequences are definite, immediate, and largely automatic effects on punishment. How did the state argue that mandatory community placement was not a direct consequence?

3. *Guilty pleas and incompetent lawyers.* A defendant who pleads guilty must be represented by counsel or must waive the right to counsel. Moore v. Michigan, 355 U.S. 155 (1957). Furthermore, if a lawyer gives constitutionally inadequate representation that causes a defendant to enter a guilty plea, the defendant may later withdraw the plea. But this does not mean that any faulty legal advice will invalidate a plea. In Brady v. United States, 397 U.S. 742 (1970), counsel gave the defendant incorrect but competent advice about the constitutionality of the death penalty statute at issue in the case; the incorrect advice of counsel was not sufficient reason to invalidate the defendant's "knowing" waiver of trial rights. See In re Resendiz, 19 P.3d 1171 (Cal. 2001) (mistaken advice about immigration consequences can support claim of ineffective assistance); Gabriel J. Chin and Richard W. Holmes, Jr., Effective Assistance of Counsel and the Consequences of Guilty Pleas, 87 Cornell L. Rev. 697 (2002) (ABA Standards for Criminal Justice and other lawyering guidelines require defense lawyers to consider collateral consequences; failure to inform client of collateral matters should in some cases constitute ineffective assistance).

4. *Guilty pleas before discovery.* If defendants must know about the nature of the charges and the direct consequences of a guilty plea, must they also know about the basic facts the prosecutor could present against them at trial? The Supreme Court's decision in *Ruiz* is typical in its refusal to declare a per se rule against bargaining away discovery rights. A few courts, however, have concluded that in some cases, accepting a guilty plea based on a plea agreement that prevents the defendant from engaging in discovery violates due process. See State v. Draper, 784 P.2d 259 (Ariz. 1989) (due process and right to counsel sometimes may prohibit plea agreement conditioned on defendant not interviewing victim of alleged crime; remand to determine defendant's access to state's evidence through other witnesses). Can you

identify circumstances in which a defendant could make a "knowing" waiver of the right to a jury trial without taking advantage of a discovery right? The *Ruiz* court found it significant that the condition relating to discovery was non-mandatory because the defendant could choose to go forward with discovery and forgo the plea agreement. Are there any terms that prosecutors simply may not offer because they prevent the defendant from making a knowing waiver?

5. *Professional obligations during plea negotiations.* Several sources of law address the information that attorneys for the prosecution and defense reveal to each other and to the defendant during plea negotiations. First, ethics rules and aspirational standards instruct a defense lawyer to inform the defendant about the terms of any proposed plea agreement because the client must decide what plea to enter. See ABA Model Rule of Professional Conduct 4.1; ABA Standards for Criminal Justice, Defense Function 4-6.2(a), (b); see also People v. Whitfield, 239 N.E.2d 850 (Ill. 1968) (overturning conviction after trial because defense counsel failed to communicate plea bargain offer to client). These ethics rules and aspirational standards state that it is unprofessional conduct for an attorney (prosecution or defense) to knowingly make false statements during plea negotiations. ABA Model Rule 4.1 (lawyer shall not knowingly make a false statement of material fact or law to a third person); ABA Standards 3-4.1(c), 4-6.2. To what extent do discovery rules provide for disclosure of information before the entry of a guilty plea? Do professional obligations require greater or earlier disclosures than those required under the rules of discovery? See State v. Gibson, 514 S.E.2d 320 (S.C. 1999) (prosecutor's failure to disclose *Brady* information can undermine voluntariness of guilty plea).

6. *Hearing procedures.* The decision in Boykin v. Alabama, 395 U.S. 238 (1969), gave a constitutional foundation to some of the information a defendant must know before entering a guilty plea. The record must show the defendant's awareness of three major constitutional rights waived through entry of a guilty plea: the privilege against self-incrimination, the right to jury trial, and the right to confront adverse witnesses. In addition to these constitutional requirements, many rules of procedure have added requirements such as knowledge regarding the nature of the charges, the direct consequences of a conviction, and the factual basis for the charge. Trial courts engage in lengthy (and elaborately scripted) "plea colloquies" to create a record establishing that a defendant knows what is necessary before pleading guilty. What happens if the trial court fails to cover one of the necessary questions, and thereby violates a rule of procedure? Fed. R. Crim. P. 11(h) allows a federal court to uphold a plea if the violation of the rule's requirements was "harmless error." A Supreme Court case decided before the drafting of current Rule 11(h), McCarthy v. United States, 394 U.S. 459 (1969), held that a guilty plea is per se invalid if the trial court fails to ask the questions required by the rule. How does an appellate court distinguish the important violations of the procedural rules at a plea hearing from the harmless violations?

2. *Involuntary Pleas*

Time and again, procedural rules and judicial opinions say that a plea of guilty or nolo contendere must be "voluntary." The question of voluntariness raises a familiar theme in criminal procedure: In what sense can we say that a defendant *chooses* to waive procedural advantages such as a right to jury trial? Surely a defendant is choosing among unpleasant options when she decides to plead guilty. Is it possible for the government to restrict the defendant's options in such a way that the defendant's decision to plead guilty is no longer a "choice" in any meaningful sense? In this section, we consider three settings in which defendants have repeatedly claimed that their decision to plead guilty was not truly voluntary.

a. *Alford* Pleas

A defendant who pleads guilty stands ready to accept punishment for the crime as charged. Is this decision coerced if the defendant insists that he did not commit the crime?

■ FEDERAL RULE OF CRIMINAL PROCEDURE 11(b)

(2) Before accepting a plea of guilty or nolo contendere, the court must address the defendant personally in open court and determine that the plea is voluntary and did not result from force, threats, or promises (other than promises in a plea agreement).

(3) Before entering judgment on a guilty plea, the court must determine that there is a factual basis for the plea.

■ NORTH CAROLINA v. HENRY ALFORD

400 U.S. 25 (1970)

WHITE, J.

On December 2, 1963, Alford was indicted for first-degree murder, a capital offense under North Carolina law. The court appointed an attorney to represent him, and this attorney questioned all but one of the various witnesses who appellee said would substantiate his claim of innocence. The witnesses, however, did not support Alford's story but gave statements that strongly indicated his guilt. Faced with strong evidence of guilt and no substantial evidentiary support for the claim of innocence, Alford's attorney recommended that he plead guilty, but left the ultimate decision to Alford himself. The prosecutor agreed to accept a plea of guilty to a charge of second-degree murder, and on December 10, 1963, Alford pleaded guilty to the reduced charge.

Before the plea was finally accepted by the trial court, the court heard the sworn testimony of a police officer who summarized the State's case. Two other witnesses besides Alford were also heard. Although there was no eyewitness to the crime, the testimony indicated that shortly before the killing Alford took his gun from his house, stated his intention to kill the victim, and returned home with the declaration that he had carried out the killing. After the summary presentation of the State's case, Alford took the stand and testified that he had not committed the murder but that he was pleading guilty because he faced the threat of the death penalty if he did not do so.[2] In response to the questions of his counsel, he acknowledged

---

2. After giving his version of the events of the night of the murder, Alford stated: "I pleaded guilty on second degree murder because they said there is too much evidence, but I ain't shot no man, but I take the fault for the other man. We never had an argument in our life and I just pleaded guilty because

that his counsel had informed him of the difference between second- and first-degree murder and of his rights in case he chose to go to trial. The trial court then asked appellee if, in light of his denial of guilt, he still desired to plead guilty to second-degree murder and appellee answered, "Yes, sir. I plead guilty on — from the circumstances that he [Alford's attorney] told me." After eliciting information about Alford's prior criminal record, which was a long one, the trial court sentenced him to 30 years' imprisonment, the maximum penalty for second-degree murder. [Alford sought postconviction relief, first in the state court, and later in federal habeas corpus proceedings.]

We held in Brady v. United States, 397 U.S. 742 (1970), that a plea of guilty which would not have been entered except for the defendant's desire to avoid a possible death penalty and to limit the maximum penalty to life imprisonment or a term of years was not for that reason compelled within the meaning of the Fifth Amendment. . . . The standard was and remains whether the plea represents a voluntary and intelligent choice among the alternative courses of action open to the defendant. That he would not have pleaded except for the opportunity to limit the possible penalty does not necessarily demonstrate that the plea of guilty was not the product of a free and rational choice, especially where the defendant was represented by competent counsel whose advice was that the plea would be to the defendant's advantage. . . .

Ordinarily, a judgment of conviction resting on a plea of guilty is justified by the defendant's admission that he committed the crime charged against him and his consent that judgment be entered without a trial of any kind. The plea usually subsumes both elements, and justifiably so, even though there is no separate, express admission by the defendant that he committed the particular acts claimed to constitute the crime charged in the indictment. Here Alford entered his plea but accompanied it with the statement that he had not shot the victim. If Alford's statements were to be credited as sincere assertions of his innocence, there obviously existed a factual and legal dispute between him and the State. Without more, it might be argued that the conviction entered on his guilty plea was invalid, since his assertion of innocence negatived any admission of guilt. . . .

In addition to Alford's statement, however, the court had heard an account of the events on the night of the murder, including information from Alford's acquaintances that he had departed from his home with his gun stating his intention to kill and that he had later declared that he had carried out his intention. Nor had Alford wavered in his desire to have the trial court determine his guilt without a jury trial. Although denying the charge against him, he nevertheless preferred the dispute between him and the State to be settled by the judge in the context of a guilty plea proceeding rather than by a formal trial. Thereupon, with the State's telling evidence and Alford's denial before it, the trial court proceeded to convict and sentence Alford for second-degree murder.

State and lower federal courts are divided upon whether a guilty plea can be accepted when it is accompanied by protestations of innocence and hence contains only a waiver of trial but no admission of guilt. Some courts, giving expression to the principle that "our law only authorizes a conviction where guilt is shown,"

---

they said if I didn't they would gas me for it, and that is all." [Alford later described his decision as follows:] "I'm still pleading that you all got me to plead guilty. I plead the other way, circumstantial evidence. . . . You told me to plead guilty, right. I don't — I'm not guilty but I plead guilty."

Harris v. State, 172 S.W. 975 (Tex. 1915), require that trial judges reject such pleas. [The court cited cases from Michigan, New Jersey, New Mexico, and Washington along with lower federal court cases.] But others have concluded that they should not . . . force any defense on a defendant in a criminal case . . . particularly when advancement of the defense might "end in disaster. . . ." Tremblay v. Overholser, 199 F. Supp. 569 (D.D.C. 1961). They have argued that, since [guilt is at times uncertain, an accused who believes in his own innocence] might reasonably conclude a jury would be convinced of his guilt and that he would fare better in the sentence by pleading guilty. [The court cited cases from Idaho, Illinois, Iowa, Minnesota, Pennsylvania, and several lower federal courts.]

This Court has not confronted this precise issue, but prior decisions do yield relevant principles. . . . The issue in Hudson v. United States, 272 U.S. 451 (1926), was whether a federal court has power to impose a prison sentence after accepting a plea of nolo contendere, a plea by which a defendant does not expressly admit his guilt, but nonetheless waives his right to a trial and authorizes the court for purposes of the case to treat him as if he were guilty. The Court held that a trial court does have such power, and . . . the federal courts have uniformly followed this rule, even in cases involving moral turpitude. Implicit in the nolo contendere cases is a recognition that the Constitution does not bar imposition of a prison sentence upon an accused who is unwilling expressly to admit his guilt but who, faced with grim alternatives, is willing to waive his trial and accept the sentence. These cases would be directly in point if Alford had simply insisted on his plea but refused to admit the crime. The fact that his plea was denominated a plea of guilty rather than a plea of nolo contendere is of no constitutional significance with respect to the issue now before us, for the Constitution is concerned with the practical consequences, not the formal categorizations, of state law. . . .

Nor can we perceive any material difference between a plea that refuses to admit commission of the criminal act and a plea containing a protestation of innocence when, as in the instant case, a defendant intelligently concludes that his interests require entry of a guilty plea and the record before the judge contains strong evidence of actual guilt. Here the State had a strong case of first-degree murder against Alford. Whether he realized or disbelieved his guilt, he insisted on his plea because in his view he had absolutely nothing to gain by a trial and much to gain by pleading. . . . In view of the strong factual basis for the plea demonstrated by the State and Alford's clearly expressed desire to enter it despite his professed belief in his innocence, we hold that the trial judge did not commit constitutional error in accepting it.[11] . . .

Alford now argues in effect that the State should not have allowed him this choice but should have insisted on proving him guilty of murder in the first degree. The States in their wisdom may take this course by statute or otherwise and may prohibit the practice of accepting pleas to lesser included offenses under any circumstances. But this is not the mandate of the Fourteenth Amendment and the Bill of Rights. The prohibitions against involuntary or unintelligent pleas should not be relaxed, but neither should an exercise in arid logic render those constitutional guarantees counterproductive and put in jeopardy the very human values they were meant to preserve. . . .

11. Our holding does not mean that a trial judge must accept every constitutionally valid guilty plea merely because a defendant wishes so to plead. A criminal defendant does not have an absolute right under the Constitution to have his guilty plea accepted by the court, although the States may by statute or otherwise confer such a right. . . .

Notes*

1. *Guilty pleas by defendants claiming innocence: majority position.* Although there was once a real dispute among state courts about the constitutionality of accepting guilty pleas from defendants who maintained their innocence, that dispute is now largely resolved. A substantial majority of states follow the lead of the U.S. Supreme Court and allow a defendant to plead guilty, despite claims of innocence, so long as the prosecution establishes a strong factual basis to support the conviction. See People v. Canino, 508 P.2d 1273 (Colo. 1973). Fewer than a half-dozen states prevent trial judges from accepting *Alford* pleas. See Ross v. State, 456 N.E.2d 420 (Ind. 1983).

The live question in connection with *Alford* pleas is whether the trial judge has discretion to *reject* an *Alford* plea. The Supreme Court (in footnote 11) suggested that an individual trial judge, or a state court system as a whole through its rules of procedure, might refuse to accept such guilty pleas. Many individual judges do refuse to accept *Alford* pleas, and the majority of appellate courts uphold their discretion to do so. See Albert Alschuler, The Defense Attorney's Role in Plea Bargaining, 84 Yale L.J. 1179 (1975). If a state system decides not to prohibit *Alford* pleas, should it place controls on the power of the trial judge to refuse to accept such pleas? Would this step ensure the equal treatment of defendants and prevent litigants from shopping for judges? See ABA Standards for Criminal Justice, Pleas of Guilty 14-1.6 (defendant's offer to plead guilty should not be refused "solely" because defendant refuses to admit culpability). What reasons might a judge give to refuse an offer of an *Alford* plea in a specific case, apart from a general ban on such pleas?

2. Alford *pleas and free will.* If a defendant is *not* coerced when she pleads guilty while insisting that she is innocent, who *is* coerced into pleading guilty? Defendants who offer an *Alford* plea have a very limited set of options. We can presume that defendants prefer to have the option of entering an *Alford* plea rather than face the expense or publicity of a trial, along with the risk of a more severe sentence after trial. Are there reasons why the public should deny this option to the bargaining parties?

As you might expect, a defendant who enters any guilty plea must be mentally competent; otherwise, the court cannot consider the plea to be knowing and voluntary. See Godinez v. Moran, 509 U.S. 389 (1993) (same competence standard used for entry of guilty plea and capacity to stand trial); State v. Engelmann, 541 N.W.2d 96 (S.D. 1995) (allows withdrawal of *Alford* plea based on lack of mental competence at arraignment).

3. Alford *pleas and the truth.* If trials always uncovered the truth about the events surrounding alleged crimes, would there be any reason to allow *Alford* pleas? Is a system that accepts such pleas implicitly admitting that trials often fail to uncover the truth and that an innocent defendant might be justifiably concerned about an erroneous conviction after trial? Are *Alford* pleas even less reliable measures of truth than a criminal trial? The factual basis for an *Alford* plea must come from sources other than the statements of the defendant. Most courts say that it is not necessary that the factual basis establish guilt beyond a reasonable doubt. The Supreme Court's opinion in *Alford* called the factual basis in that case "strong" and "overwhelming"; state courts have suggested several formulations to describe the necessary level of proof. Clewley v. State, 288 A.2d 468 (Me. 1972) (not unreasonable to conclude guilt); Re Guilty Plea Cases, 235 N.W.2d 132, 145 (Mich. 1975) (might have been convicted at trial); State v. Hagemann, 326 N.W.2d 861 (N.D. 1982)

("strong" proof of guilt). Would the "beyond a reasonable doubt" standard seriously reduce the number of *Alford* pleas accepted? See Ala. Code §15-15-23 (adopting beyond-reasonable-doubt standard for acceptance of guilty pleas); Richard Uviller, Pleading Guilty: A Critique of Four Models, 41 Law & Contemp. Probs. 102 (1977) (clear and convincing evidence). It is also possible to view an *Alford* plea as the most honest route available in a system in which some defendants want to avoid a trial even though they believe in their own innocence. When a state bans *Alford* pleas, does it invite defendants to lie to their attorneys and to the court?

Problem 16-5. An Offer You Can't Refuse

Joan Capriccioso worked as a waitress at a diner in Staten Island, where she met Philip Fiumefreddo. After a two-month courtship, the two were married; she was then 39 and he was 68. Throughout four years of marriage to Philip, Joan often complained to acquaintances about him, saying that she wished him dead.

Eventually, Joan's father Salvatore Capriccioso withdrew $3,200 from the bank and gave it to Joseph Gurrieri, with the understanding that Gurrieri would arrange for the murder of Philip Fiumefreddo. Gurrieri hired Christopher Munroe to kill Fiumefreddo for $1,000. Munroe went to the Fiumefreddo residence at 6:30 A.M. Joan let him in. After offering to fix breakfast for him, she told Munroe to make the house look burglarized, gave him a pillow, and instructed him to use it to kill her husband, who was still sleeping. She then left for work. Munroe suffocated Philip with the pillow as he slept.

Becoming increasingly distressed about the murder, Gurrieri went to the police and confessed. Joan Fiumefreddo and her father were indicted for second degree murder, second degree conspiracy, and second degree solicitation. On the same day, Munroe and Gurrieri were indicted for various crimes in connection with the killing; these latter two defendants soon pleaded guilty to the charges. On the day jury selection was scheduled to begin, Fiumefreddo and her attorney John Collins met for over an hour with the trial judge, her father, his attorney Joseph Lamattina, and the prosecutor. Immediately following this discussion, Collins told the court: "My client is now prepared to plead with only one promise having been made by me. That promise is with her pleading to this top count that the Court would sentence her to 18 years to life." Lamattina stated that Salvatore Capriccioso was prepared to plead guilty to second degree conspiracy in exchange for a sentence promise of one to three years.

Nine days after the plea colloquy, defendant made a motion pro se to withdraw her guilty plea. In the accompanying affidavit she stated that

> while I acknowledge that the Court advised me that I had certain rights, I nevertheless did not then, nor do I now realize the full consequences of my plea of guilty. I am not guilty of the offenses to which I pleaded guilty. I pleaded guilty with the promise that I would be sentenced to 18 to life and co-defendant's sentence would be lighter if the defendant pleads guilty to second degree murder.

The judge denied the motion to withdraw her plea, and sentenced her and her father to the agreed-upon terms of imprisonment. Was Fiumefreddo's guilty plea voluntary? Compare People v. Fiumefreddo, 626 N.E.2d 646 (N.Y. 1993).

Notes

1. *"Package" deals.* Can the prosecutor increase the cost of the trial by threatening to prosecute third parties, such as family members of the defendant? Courts have not announced any outright bans of "package deals" or "connected pleas," but they review them with some suspicion. What should a defendant emphasize to convince a court that her particular "package deal" produced an involuntary plea? How will the defendant obtain the evidence necessary to make this showing? Does the fact that a defendant's sentence is near the minimum available sentence help or hurt her claim that the plea was involuntary? See State v. Danh, 516 N.W.2d 539 (Minn. 1994) (requiring contingent terms of package-deal guilty plea to be explained on the record to trial court to allow assessment of voluntariness). Does the difficulty with package deals come from the defendant's reduced capacity to make decisions (because the package deal offers the defendant options that cannot be compared in a rational manner) or from the public's unease about using family or other intimate bonds to gain a litigation advantage?

2. *Coercive overcharging.* A prosecutor can make the decision to go to trial very costly, through a combination of serious charges and an attractive plea agreement. These decisions, however, will usually not provoke a court to rule that the defendant's guilty plea was involuntary. In Brady v. United States, 397 U.S. 742 (1970), the fact that the defendant believed that a decision to go to trial would expose him to a possible death penalty was not enough to invalidate the guilty plea. Nonetheless, some statutes and aspirational standards instruct the prosecutor not to "overcharge." Take, for instance, a North Carolina statute, N.C. Gen. Stat. §15A-1021(b), which forbids state agents from placing "improper pressure" on a defendant to plead guilty. According to the drafters' commentary, the statute (based on the American Law Institute's Model Code of Pre-Arraignment Procedure) was meant to prevent the prosecutor from filing charges not supported by provable facts or charges not ordinarily filed based on the conduct in question. See also ABA Standards for Criminal Justice, Prosecution Function 3-3.9(f) (prosecutor should not bring charges greater than "can reasonably be supported with evidence at trial" or greater than necessary to reflect gravity of offense).

3. *Civil consequences.* Do the prosecutor's proposed bargain terms become coercive when they move beyond matters of criminal charges and sentences to include civil consequences, matters that other legal institutions ordinarily decide? State courts have not expressed any special concern about such agreements. See Gustine v. State, 480 S.E.2d 444 (S.C. 1997) (prosecutor offers plea agreement on child sex-abuse charges contingent on defendant's giving up parental rights to stepdaughter; court does not declare parental rights term coercive as a matter of law but calls for case-by-case inquiry into knowing and voluntary nature of guilty plea). Is it wise to assume that criminal consequences are the most serious problems facing a defendant?

b. Judicial Overinvolvement

Earlier in this chapter we considered judicial efforts to place limits on the institution of plea bargaining, and the individual judge's responsibility during a plea hearing to confirm and document that the defendant is entering the guilty plea knowingly and voluntarily. But what is the individual judge's role prior to the guilty plea? Rules of procedure paint very different portraits of the judge's involvement in plea negotiations. Some rules, such as Pa. R. Crim. P. 319(b)(1), state that the trial judge "shall not participate in the plea negotiations preceding an agreement." See also Fed. R. Crim. P. 11(c)(1) ("The court shall not participate in any such discussions"). Others do not tell the judge what to do during the negotiations. Rules and statutes in a few states authorize the trial judge to take part in negotiations. See N.C. Gen. Stat. §15A-1021(a) ("The trial judge may participate in the discussions"). Do these rules reflect profound differences in practice, or do they reflect an ambiguity about what qualifies as judicial "participation" in the plea negotiations?

■ STATE v. LANDOUR BOUIE

817 So. 2d 48 (La. 2002)

CALOGERO, C.J.

We granted this writ application to determine whether the district court abused its discretion in not allowing the defendant to withdraw his plea of guilty, given that the trial judge had previously interjected his own opinions into the plea negotiations as to whether the defendant would be acquitted or found guilty. . . .

The state charged the defendant and his co-defendant, Cornelius Johnson, with attempted second degree murder. . . . The charge arose out of the shooting of Eddie Hughes, who had intervened in an attempt by [Bouie] and Johnson to secure the services of a prostitute doing business near Hughes's home. Using a rifle that [Johnson] retrieved from [Bouie's] house, where the two men had driven after the initial dispute with Hughes, Johnson confronted Hughes on the street outside his home and fired a bullet that struck the victim in the throat, severing his spinal column. The victim survived. . . .

From the outset, the defendant indicated that he wanted to go to trial, and throughout the discussions, he consistently indicated that he believed he was innocent of the charge of attempted second degree murder. . . . At the outset of the day set for trial, the defendant, represented by appointed counsel, stated that he understood that he was going to trial, and asserted that he *wanted* to go to trial. Immediately, the trial judge told the defendant that he was being tried for attempted second degree murder and that "if you go to trial, the penalty for that charge is fifty years at hard labor." The trial judge followed up by telling the defendant that, because he had been on probation at the time of the offense, he could be found guilty of being a second felony offender and receive a sentence of up to 100 years. But if he pleaded guilty, . . . and if the state filed a multiple offender bill, the trial judge would give the defendant the minimum twenty-five years at hard labor, or as low as ten years if the state did not file the multiple offender bill.

When the defendant was asked if this information helped him to make up his mind, the defendant responded affirmatively, but he also asserted, "Your Honor — uh — I'm just going you know, I haven't did anything." The trial judge quickly responded with his view on the certainty that the defendant would be convicted if he chose to go to trial: . . .

COURT: You may be able to be found not guilty. . . . But I can tell you this, all of the years that I've been either a prosecutor or a judge, I don't think I've ever seen more than one or two people who went to trial found not guilty. The D.A. knows what they're doing when they try somebody, generally, and the jury seems to believe them, generally. And the odds are not in your favor of going to trial and winning a case. Do you understand that? Do you?

BOUIE: Yes, sir.

COURT: And when I say all the years I've been doing that, that's been since 1981, so how long is that? Sixteen years I've been doing this, either a judge or an assistant district attorney and I think I've found two people found not guilty—uh—seen two people found not guilty in felony trials. Now, if you go to trial, I'm telling you the odds are against you winning. Do you understand that?

BOUIE: Yes, sir.

COURT: All right, then if you lose, then you're looking at the hundred years. . . . If you plead guilty, you're looking at no more than twenty-five and maybe as low as ten. Do you understand that?

BOUIE: Yes, sir.

At this point, the defendant was allowed to confer with his counsel and the matter of his co-defendant was taken up by the trial judge. Johnson, too, expressed indecision and questioned the state's version of the facts, but, after discussions with the trial judge, in which the judge offered the same deal and stated that a hundred-year sentence meant that Johnson would die in prison, Johnson eventually entered a plea of guilty as charged in return for a sentencing commitment by the court of twenty-five years imprisonment at hard labor, the minimum term for a second offender convicted of attempted murder and sentenced as a multiple offender. In its recitation of the case, the state indicated that Johnson had given a video-taped statement in which he stated that the defendant had encouraged him to retrieve the weapon and to shoot the victim. According to the state, Johnson said that, on the way back to the scene, the two men had struck a bargain in which the defendant agreed to drive the getaway car and Johnson vowed to shoot the victim. Johnson, in court, disagreed with the state's recitation, but he conceded that there had been a shooting and that what the state had said had basically happened "in so many ways."

After Johnson's plea was completed, the defendant returned to court. [The] defendant was asked what he thought he was facing and he replied, "Whew, um, I really don't know." Expressing some frustration, "All right, that's why I keep trying to explain it to you," the trial judge reiterated that the defendant was charged with attempted second degree murder, which carries a sentence of up to 50 years at hard labor, that a jury was waiting upstairs and would return a verdict in a few days if he elected to go to trial that day, that the defendant in fact had a prior felony conviction, and that the sentence would be up to 100 years at hard labor as a second felony offender if he went to trial, but only 25 years if he pleaded guilty. After conferring with his attorney, the defendant agreed to plead guilty, and the *Boykin* examination commenced. See Boykin v. Alabama, 395 U.S. 238 (1969).

During the colloquy, the trial judge gave a similar response anytime the defendant vacillated. When the defendant indicated that he thought he had been promised 10 years, the trial judge responded that it was only if the state chose not to file a multiple offender bill would he impose a sentence between 10 and 25 years at hard labor. The trial judge then asked if the defendant wanted to plead guilty. When he received no response, the trial judge stated that if not, "we've got the people waiting upstairs to get the trial started." The defendant responded, "I—whew, um—." The trial judge again asked if the defendant wanted to finish the guilty plea and if he understood what was happening. The defendant said he did "in a way" and expressed doubt about the evidence against him. The trial judge then explained the law of principals, using the getaway driver of an armed robbery as an example. The trial judge [said that if the jury concluded that Bouie] provided a gun to Johnson, drove him back to the scene, and encouraged him to shoot the victim, then the defendant would be as guilty as if he had shot the victim.

The trial judge then had the state repeat its case against the defendant for the record. Unlike his co-defendant Johnson, the defendant expressed considerable doubt that he was guilty of any crime for transporting Johnson back and forth from the scene of the shooting. In his own statement to the police, the defendant had acknowledged only that he had been on the scene with Johnson to pick up a prostitute, that after the initial confrontation with the victim he had driven Johnson back to his (the defendant's) house where Johnson retrieved a rifle that he (Johnson) had hidden there earlier that evening, and that he (the defendant) had then returned with Johnson to the scene to "turn a trick" with the prostitute. The defendant had denied in his statement that he knew beforehand that Johnson would shoot the victim and he continued to insist in court that the two men had gone back "to see . . . where the trick was. [Johnson] got out the car and the only thing I heard was a shot. . . ." [After Bouie observed that "everything is pointing at me," the trial judge returned to the question of a guilty plea]:

COURT: Do you think it's in your best interest at this point to go ahead and accept a guilty plea and get the lesser years that you've been offered rather than running the risk of going to trial and getting the Habitual Act charged against you and getting, maybe, up to a hundred years?

BOUIE: (no answer)

COURT: Do you think this guilty plea today, right now, is better than doing that? In other words, this is in your best interest at this point.

BOUIE: It seems like, Your Honor.

The trial court then accepted the defendant's guilty plea.[2] However, after the state filed a multiple offender bill, but before sentencing, the defendant moved to withdraw his plea, alleging that he had been under "extreme emotional stress" when he entered the plea. At the hearing on the motion, the defendant testified that the court had, in effect, stampeded him into pleading guilty, not simply by the sentencing offer of 25 years imprisonment at hard labor but also by informing him, in effect, that "if I take you to trial, I was not going to win in your courtroom. You was going to give me fifty to a hundred years. So I feel as though I wasn't going to win no matter what." On the basis of that testimony, the attorney representing the defendant asked the court at the close of the hearing, "You saw [two acquittals] in nearly a twenty-year period. . . . How is he going to knowingly and intentionally plead guilty after he hears that, Your Honor?"

2. Notably, the trial judge never explained to the defendant that, to prove him guilty of attempted second degree murder, the state was required to prove that the defendant, even as a principal, had possessed the requisite specific intent to kill the victim. Consequently, whether a jury accepting the defendant's story as true could have rationally found the requisite specific intent proved beyond a reasonable doubt appears less certain than the trial judge advocated.

The trial judge denied the motion on grounds that it had spent over an hour and a half with the defendant in a painstaking effort to persuade him that a guilty plea was in his best interests "because he probably would have gotten convicted and been sentenced to fifty to a hundred years. [Instead] of doing that, I gave him twenty-five, and, certainly . . . that was in his best interest." The court . . . sentenced him to the promised term of 25 years imprisonment at hard labor. . . .

A trial judge has broad discretion in ruling on a defendant's motion to withdraw his guilty plea before sentencing. La. Code Crim. Proc. art. 559. When circumstances indicate that the plea was constitutionally invalid, the trial judge should allow the defendant to withdraw his plea. . . . However, as a general rule, an otherwise valid plea of guilty is not rendered involuntary merely because it was entered to limit the possible maximum penalty to less than that authorized by law for the crime charged.

[The] defendant contends that the nature and extent of the district court judge's participation in the plea agreement had a coercive effect on his decision to plead guilty. While this court has not directly addressed the issue of a judge's participation in negotiating a plea agreement, in State v. Chalaire, 375 So. 2d 107, fn.2 (La. 1979), albeit in dicta, we stated: "Although not objected to in this appeal, the judge's active participation in the plea negotiations evokes our concern. The ABA Standards recommend that the trial judge should not be involved with plea discussions before the parties have reached an agreement. ABA Standards, The Function of the Trial Judge §4.1 (Approved Draft 1972); accord, Fed. R. Crim. P. [11(c)(1)]." As we noted in *Chalaire,* the reasons for proscribing judicial participation in plea negotiations, according to the ABA Standards Commentary, are:

> (1) judicial participation in the discussions can create the impression in the mind of the defendant that he would not receive a fair trial were he to go to trial before this judge; (2) judicial participation in the discussions makes it difficult for the judge objectively to determine the voluntariness of the plea when it is offered; (3) judicial participation to the extent of promising a certain sentence is inconsistent with the theory behind the use of the presentence investigation report; and (4) the risk of not going along with the disposition apparently desired by the judge may seem so great to the defendant that he will be induced to plead guilty even if innocent. ABA Standards, Pleas of Guilty §3.3(a) Commentary 73 (Approved Draft 1968).

On the other hand, we also pointed out that . . . removal of the judge from the bargaining process usually places the sentencing prerogative in the district attorney's office. [We] concluded that . . . "any judge who directly participates in plea discussions should take extreme care to avoid the dangers described in the ABA commentary."

In our decision today, we do not adopt a rule absolutely prohibiting the participation of Louisiana trial judges in plea negotiations, such as that provided by the Federal Rules of Criminal Procedure [11(c)(1)] ("The court shall not participate in any such discussions"). Instead, we find that the interjection of the trial judge's personal knowledge and opinion in the plea discussions under the circumstances of this case did, or probably did, have a coercive effect on this particular defendant's decision that a guilty plea was in his best interest.

In the present case, the trial judge's explanations of the penalties the defendant faced if he went to trial and if he were convicted by a jury, and of the trial judge's discretion to impose greater penalties after conviction than offered in the course of plea negotiations, were not inherently coercive because the advice concerned information that an accused ought to possess to enter a knowing and intelligent guilty plea. Furthermore, the court's explanation of the law of principals under La. Rev. Stat. 14:24, which would form the basis of any verdict rendered by a jury, also served the same end.

However, when the trial judge coupled those lengthy explanations with his personal view that the result of a jury trial was all but a foregone conclusion, he went beyond simply facilitating the entry of a knowing and voluntary guilty plea. The trial judge's discussion of the chances of an acquittal at a jury trial conveyed the court's personal experience over the years in unrelated cases and its confidence in the soundness of the exercise of the charging discretion of the District Attorney's Office. No matter how benign the judge's intent, and no matter how solicitous of the defendant's interests, the trial judge clearly conveyed his opinion that this particular defendant had no realistic choice other than to plead guilty or face penalties ranging from two to four times as great as the court offered. Aside from the question of its reliability, such a message was inherently coercive because it came from the court, not from the prosecutor. . . . See Standley v. Warden, 990 P.2d 983, 985 (Nev. 1999) ("Appellant had good reason to fear offending the judge if he declined [the plea offer] because the same judge would have presided over the trial and, if the trial resulted in a conviction, the judge would have determined the appropriate sentence"). The defendant here voiced those concerns in his own words at the hearing on his motion to withdraw his guilty plea when he explained to the court that he took the sentencing offer because, "You told me, if I take you to trial, I'm not going to win in your courtroom."

We recognize that a defendant may enter a voluntary guilty plea even while he continues to protest his innocence. North Carolina v. Alford, 400 U.S. 25 (1970). . . . However, *Alford* presupposes that the defendant "must be permitted to judge for himself in this respect." Therefore, whether the offered plea agreement was in fact in the defendant's best interest was not for the court to decide, but for the defendant to determine with the advice of his counsel.

We concede that a fine line may at times separate a trial judge's attempts to insure that the defendant understands that a guilty plea might serve his best interest and the overbearing of a defendant's will to reach a result the court, with the best of intentions, deems appropriate. However, we find that the trial judge in this case, by stating his personal views on the virtual certainty that the defendant would be convicted by a jury, as well as on the prospect of a sentence much greater than that offered, when this judge would be determining the sentence to be imposed following the guilty verdict, overstepped his bounds and acted as more of an advocate than as a neutral arbiter of the criminal prosecution. We conclude that the defendant's guilty plea under these circumstances was not knowingly and voluntarily entered, such that the district court abused its discretion in not granting the defendant's motion to withdraw the guilty plea. . . .

WEIMER, J., dissenting.

. . . I do not believe the statements were sufficient to coerce the defendant or unreasonably persuade him to plead guilty. It has not been alleged that anything the trial court stated was inaccurate. . . . It should be noted that defendant's admitted behavior in the events surrounding the shooting subjected him to a risk of conviction. This risk of conviction was amplified when the statement of his co-defendant, which implicated the defendant, was considered. . . .

Certainly, the trial court can and must inform the defendant of the consequences of his plea. However, in doing so, the court must avoid the impression of coercing or persuading the defendant to plead guilty. Despite the defendant's allegations, I believe the court succeeded in avoiding that impression.

Notes

1. *Legal limits on judicial participation in plea negotiations.* States have addressed the role of the judge during plea negotiations through statutes, rules of criminal procedure, rules of judicial ethics, and in judicial opinions interpreting constitutional provisions. More than half of the states instruct the judge not to "participate" in the plea discussions, the position embodied in the Federal Rules of Criminal Procedure. See People v. Collins, 27 P.3d 726 (Cal. 2001) (judge's promise of "some benefit" for giving up jury trial right rendered guilty plea involuntary); State v. Wakefield, 925 P.2d 183 (Wash. 1996); Colo. Rev. Stat. §16-7-302; Ga. Unif. Super. Ct. R. 33.5(a); Mass. R. Crim. P. 12(b) (reporter's notes). Does this mean that the judges cannot even be present as an observer during such discussions?

Another group of states discourages judges from participating in plea negotiations but does not prohibit it. Judicial opinions in these states suggest that judicial participation in negotiations, while not the best practice, is not a reason to invalidate a conviction on constitutional or other grounds. State v. Niblack, 596 A.2d 407 (Conn. 1991); State v. Ditter, 441 N.W.2d 622 (Neb. 1989). A small but growing number of states (now over a dozen) have rules or statutes that do not discourage judicial participation, and some even authorize judges to take part. See Mont. Code §46-12-211; N.C. Gen. Stat. §15A-1021(a). Some of the laws authorizing judges to participate extend only to limited types of participation. For instance, some states allow judges to take part only when the parties extend an invitation. People v. Cobbs, 505 N.W.2d 208 (Mich. 1993). Others limit the judge to commenting on the acceptability of charges and sentences that the parties themselves propose. See Ill. Sup. Ct. R. 402(d); State v. Warner, 762 So. 2d 507, 514 (Fla. 2000) (once invited by parties, court may actively discuss potential sentences and comment on proposed plea agreements). Do these limits identify the judicial practices with the most potential for making a guilty plea involuntary?

The ABA Standards for Criminal Justice, Pleas of Guilty 14-3.3, have embodied over the years an ambivalence about judicial involvement in plea discussions. The original 1968 version of Standard 14-3.3 completely barred judicial participation in plea negotiations. The 1980 edition of the Standards established a more active role for judges as a participant in plea negotiations. The parties could request to meet with the judge to discuss a plea agreement, and the judge could "serve as a moderator in listening to their respective presentations" and could "indicate what charge or sentence concessions would be acceptable." On the other hand, "the judge should never through word or demeanor, either directly or indirectly, communicate to the defendant or defense counsel that a plea agreement should be accepted or that a guilty plea should be entered." The 1997 edition of the Standards set out a more limited role for the judge: "a judge may be presented with a proposed plea agreement negotiated by the parties and may indicate whether the court would accept the terms as proposed and, if relevant, indicate what sentence would be imposed."

2. *Judicial involvement in practice.* Judges do participate in plea negotiations. As the variety of legal rules on the subject suggests, the practice varies from place to place. One study from the late 1970s concluded that about a third of judges in felony and misdemeanor courts nationwide attended plea negotiations. Most of the judges attending the negotiations "reviewed" recommendations by the parties, while a few judges made their own recommendations to the parties. These nationwide figures concealed some variety among different jurisdictions. Judges in states with rules clearly barring their participation in plea bargaining were much less likely to attend the negotiations than judges in other states. John Paul Ryan and James Alfini, Trial Judges' Participation in Plea Bargaining: An Empirical Perspective, 13 L. & Socy. Rev. 479 (1979). See also Allen Anderson, Judicial Participation in the Plea Negotiation Process: Some Frequencies and Disposing Factors, 10 Hamline J. Pub. L. & Poly. 39 (1990).

3. *Judicial neutrality and plea negotiations.* Critics of judicial participation in plea negotiations have argued that a judge who proposes or ratifies the terms of a plea agreement cannot properly perform judicial duties later in the case. For instance, they say, such a judge cannot properly decide at the plea hearing whether the defendant is entering the guilty plea voluntarily. If the defendant rejects a proposed offer, it may be difficult for the negotiating judge to preside at the trial. The participating judge may also find it difficult at sentencing to give proper consideration to a presentence investigation that recommends some sentence different from the negotiated recommendation. See Kathleen Gallagher, Judicial Participation in Plea Bargaining: A Search for New Standards, 9 Harv. C.R.-C.L. L. Rev. 29 (1974). Are these concerns realistic? Are there ways to avoid these problems in systems that permit judges to participate in plea discussions? Should rules require different judges for the plea and the trial?

4. *Judicial coercion and plea negotiations.* The most common objection to judicial participation in plea discussions is that the judge will coerce the defendant into accepting a plea agreement. While the prosecutor does not hold ultimate authority to impose a sentence in most cases, the judge can say with certainty what sentence she will impose after trial or after a guilty plea. If the judge indicates that a particular outcome is a "good deal," does the defendant have much hope for a better outcome? One might conclude alternatively that judges who participate in plea discussions merely give the defendant more accurate and complete information about what will occur at sentencing. Their presence might prevent prosecutors from misrepresenting local sentencing practices or from proposing unreasonable outcomes. Albert Alschuler, The Trial Judge's Role in Plea Bargaining (pt. 1), 76 Colum. L. Rev. 1059 (1976). For reasons such as these, a law reform commission in Great Britain has called for a return to the practice of "sentence canvassing," in which a judge can tell a defendant in private the most severe sentence he might expect after a guilty plea. The courts in Great Britain have put a stop to this traditional practice. Report of the Royal Commission on Criminal Justice 112-13 (1993) (Runciman Commission).

How does judicial participation in plea negotiations compare to other sources of coercion to plead guilty? If a defendant can voluntarily plead guilty while claiming innocence, and can voluntarily plead guilty when the prosecutor plans to seek more severe sanctions against the defendant's family members unless they all enter guilty pleas, why object to a judge who tells the defendant the going rate for an offense?

D. MAKING AND BREAKING BARGAINS

The law of plea bargains is often described by analogy to the law of contract. Sometimes the reference is casual, since contracts and plea bargains both involve enforceable agreements. But sometimes the reference is more formal: In both areas courts must decide (for purposes of enforcing rights) when an agreement is made, what terms the agreement includes, whether a breach has occurred, and the appropriate remedies. This section considers the contractual dimensions of bargains.

One difference sometimes noted between contract law and plea bargain law is that a contract is said to be complete when two private parties reach an agreement supported by consideration, but a plea bargain is said to require the approval of a third party — the court — to become enforceable. Do plea bargains always require court certification to be enforceable?

The basic federal law for deciding when a bargain is made comes from the U.S. Supreme Court decisions in Santobello v. New York, 404 U.S. 257 (1971), and Mabry v. Johnson, 467 U.S. 504 (1984). In *Santobello,* the Supreme Court stated:

> When a defendant pleads guilty to a crime, he waives significant rights, including the right to a jury trial, the right to confront his accusers, the right to present witnesses in his defense, the right to remain silent, and the right to have the charges against him proved beyond a reasonable doubt. If the guilty plea is part of a plea bargain, the State is obligated to comply with any promises it makes: [W]hen a plea rests in any significant degree on a promise or agreement of the prosecutor, so that it can be said to be part of the inducement or consideration, such promise must be fulfilled.

404 U.S. at 262. The Court did not clearly identify the constitutional basis for this decision, which gave powerful support to a contractual view of plea bargains. In *Mabry,* the Court explained that the enforceability of bargains was guaranteed by the due process clause, but that a plea was not binding until it was entered and accepted by a court: Until that point the plea bargain was a "mere executory agreement" without "constitutional significance." In general, therefore, a prosecutor can withdraw an offer any time before the formal plea is accepted by the court. A majority of state courts have adopted this framework. A few states reject *Mabry* and hold the government to its bargains. In Ex parte Yarber, 437 So. 2d 1330, 1334 (Ala. 1983), the Supreme Court of Alabama explained:

> Employing contract law by way of analogy, we cannot conclude that a plea agreement is unenforceable merely because it is tentative in the sense that it is subject to the trial court's approval. The mere fact that a contract is subject, in effect, to the approval of a third-party, does not, by itself, render it unenforceable. For example, a contract for the purchase of realty is not rendered unenforceable because it is subject to the release and approval of the seller's contemplated mortgage. . . . If we allow the state to dishonor at will the agreements it enters into, the result could only serve to weaken the plea negotiating system. Such a result also is inconsistent with the "honesty and integrity" encouraged by [the] Alabama Code of Professional Responsibility.

What is the likely practical effect of making prosecutors stand by their bargains?

In most courts, a plea agreement may also be binding if, before entry of the formal guilty plea, the defendant acts in detrimental reliance on the bargain. It is often difficult, however, to determine whether there has been detrimental reliance.

For example, in People v. Navarroli, 521 N.E.2d 891 (Ill. 1988), a state trial court had found that there had been an agreement between the defendant and the state and that the defendant had provided information to agents about other suspects. The Supreme Court of Illinois found that the defendant had not detrimentally relied on the bargain because he had provided information only about other people and not about himself (the latter might have implicated the privilege against self-incrimination or the right to counsel). Does detrimental reliance require some harm to the defendant, some benefit to the government, or both?

Once it becomes clear that the parties have indeed reached a binding plea agreement, breaches of that agreement have consequences. The principal case raises an important question: Are other state agents bound by a plea agreement between the prosecutor and the defendant? The problem following the case flags another difficult and central question: Who determines whether an agreement has been breached? The issue of proper remedies for breach is discussed in a second problem. For each of these critical questions about the nature of plea bargains, consider the extent to which contract law provides an analogy for the law of plea bargains. Where are there differences? Why do they exist?

■ STATE v. LIBRADO SANCHEZ

46 P.3d 774 (Wash. 2002)

Bridge, J.

We decide whether in each of these consolidated cases, the petitioner should be permitted to withdraw his plea of guilty because he entered it in exchange for a promise from the prosecutor to recommend a particular sentence to the sentencing judge. At the sentencing hearing, a person other than the prosecutor recommended a longer sentence than had been agreed to in the plea agreement. We hold that since neither of these people, Sanchez's investigating officer (IO) nor Harris's community corrections officer (CCO), was a party to the plea agreement, no breach of the plea agreement occurred. . . .

In 1991, Sanchez, who was 21 years old at the time, served as youth pastor to the church attended by 12-year-old CG and her family. In February or March of 1991, Sanchez kissed CG after they attended a movie together. For about eight months, the sexual contacts escalated, first to masturbation and oral sex, and eventually to two instances of penile-vaginal intercourse. The relationship terminated after CG's father saw Sanchez kissing her. CG disclosed the sexual contacts to her parents when she was 16, but did not report them to the police until October 10, 1997, when she was 19. In January 1998, Sanchez was arrested and ultimately charged. He then agreed to plead guilty to three counts of child molestation in the second degree and entered pleas accordingly. Pursuant to the plea agreement, the prosecutor agreed to make no sentencing recommendation at the sentencing hearing.

Prior to sentencing, Dr. Jerry Miller evaluated Sanchez for a Special Sex Offender Sentencing Alternative (SSOSA). Dr. Miller diagnosed Sanchez as suffering from sexual arousal to children, referring to a pattern of sexual contacts with younger children beginning when Sanchez was seven years old. Dr. Miller recommended that the judge impose a SSOSA sentence, stating his opinion that Sanchez would be amenable to treatment and was at a low risk to reoffend. Denise Hollenbeck, the CCO from the Department of Corrections, prepared a presentence report recommending a 75-month sentence, to be partially suspended under a SSOSA.

At the sentencing hearing, the prosecutor made no sentencing recommendation. He then advised the judge that CG, her parents, and Sergeant Dave Ruffin, the IO, wished to make statements to the court. The victim and her parents argued against a SSOSA on the grounds that the child had been severely traumatized, Sanchez had violated a position of trust to commit the crime, and indications of deceit in the report suggested a likelihood of reoffending. Sergeant Ruffin also argued against a SSOSA. In his opinion, Sanchez's acts "violated everything, the trust and what religion stood for," and were "as bad as if somebody drug someone in the bushes and violently raped them." Ruffin stated his belief that Sanchez had lied to Dr. Miller to get a SSOSA recommendation, and said that the judge should not give a SSOSA sentence. The judge then imposed a sentence, within the standard range, of 70 months in prison, stating that he did not believe a SSOSA was appropriate absent a perversion. . . .

Between October and December 1997, Mark Harris, who was in his mid-forties, performed oral sex on his 14-year-old nephew BJ on three or four different occasions. In December 1997, when BJ's parents became suspicious, they broke off the relationship between Mark and BJ. A year later, BJ informed his mother of what had happened. Harris was arrested on January 21, 1999. He was initially charged with third degree rape of a child. On May 13, 1999, as a result of a plea agreement, he entered a plea of guilty to an amended charge of communicating with a minor for immoral purposes. The prosecutor agreed to recommend a 29-month sentence, which was at the high end of the standard range. The standard range sentence was 22 to 29 months.

Pursuant to the plea agreement, the prosecutor recommended a 29-month sentence at the sentencing hearing. The CCO recommended an exceptional sentence of 60 months in his presentence report and spoke in support of that recommendation at the sentencing hearing. The court found the aggravating circumstances suggested by the CCO applicable, and sentenced Harris to 60 months. . . .

In each of these cases the prosecutor made the recommendation at sentencing to which he agreed in the plea agreement. The petitioners do not allege that the prosecutors breached the agreement by their own words or conduct. Rather, the issue presented is whether the recommendations made by others to the judge at the sentencing hearing breached the agreement. In effect, the petitioners claim that a plea agreement binds not only the individual prosecutor but also any other employee of the State of Washington or, indeed, in the case of the IO in Sanchez any government employee, even one in a separate department.

A plea agreement is like a contract and is analyzed according to contract principles. Petitioners point out that the caption in criminal cases is "State v. . . ." and they refer to courts' habit of using the terms "state" and "prosecutor" interchangeably. They also cite to RCW 36.27.005, which provides that prosecuting attorneys "appear for and *represent the state*" and RCW 36.27.020(4), stating that the prosecuting attorney shall prosecute "all criminal and civil actions in which *the state or the county may be a party.*" (Emphasis added.) The petitioners assert that because a contract binds not only the party to the contract, but also the party he or she represents and that party's agents, the plea agreement binds all "agents" of the state.

The State responds that the duty is restricted to the prosecutor, and that plea agreements are made not between the "state" and the defendant, but between the prosecutor and the defense attorney (or defendant if acting pro se). Thus, the State asserts that the agreements did not bind either Sanchez's IO or Harris's CCO.

We have previously held that "the prosecutor and the defendant are the only parties to a plea agreement." State v. Wakefield, 925 P.2d 183 (Wash. 1996). The statutes governing the plea bargaining process are in accord with this holding. Former RCW 9.94A.080 ("The prosecutor and the attorney for the defendant, or the defendant when acting pro se, may engage in discussions with a view toward reaching [a plea] agreement"). . . . Conversely, when the police enter into an agreement with the defendant but do not make the prosecutor a party, the prosecutor is not bound by its terms. Because the prosecutor and the defendant are the only parties to a plea agreement, we find the agency analysis argued by the petitioners inappropriate. Instead, whether a government employee other than the prosecutor is bound by the agreement depends not on the employee's role vis-à-vis the prosecutor, but on the employee's role vis-à-vis the sentencing court. Thus, for example, the Court of Appeals has previously held that because juvenile court probation counselors are employees of the court, they are not bound by the terms of the plea agreement. State v. Poupart, 773 P.2d 893 (Wash. App. 1989). In contrast, a parole officer who has no statutory role in the sentencing hearing and whose input was not requested by the trial court is bound by the plea agreement because he or she is acting on behalf of the prosecutor rather than the court. State v. Sledge, 947 P.2d 1199 (Wash. 1997). . . .

Unlike the probation counselors in *Poupart,* neither Sanchez's IO nor Harris's CCO is an employee of the court. Unlike the parole officer in *Sledge,* both Sanchez's IO and Harris's CCO have a statutory role in sentencing. And unlike the parole officer in *Sledge,* the sentencing court in *Harris* requested the CCO's input. . . .

Florida alone has determined that a prosecutor's plea bargain binds all state agents. Lee v. State, 501 So. 2d 591 (Fla.1987). This is similar to the position of federal courts, which have held that absent an express limitation on the government's obligations, a plea agreement entered on behalf of the government by one assistant attorney general (AAG) binds another AAG because "the federal prosecutor's office is an entity and as such it is the spokesman for the Government." Giglio v. United States, 405 U.S. 150 (1972). Here, the petitioners go further and claim not that one prosecutor binds another prosecutor but that a prosecutor's agreement binds other persons, including at least one, Sanchez's IO, who [was employed by the Moses Lake Police Department, and is not] a state employee. We cannot agree.

The statutory role of Sanchez's IO is outlined in former RCW 9.94A.110. An IO is listed as a person whose arguments the court *must* allow: "The court *shall* . . . allow arguments from the prosecutor, the defense counsel, the offender, the victim, the survivor of the victim, or a representative of the victim or survivor, *and an investigative law enforcement officer* as to the sentence to be imposed." . . .

Sanchez asserts that when a prosecutor enters a plea bargain knowing that another government employee will present the sentencing judge with strong reasons to impose a harsher sentence, there is an appearance of unfairness. However, . . . the IO, an independent official, was not involved in the plea agreement. . . .

Furthermore, a prosecutor does not control the actions of an IO. Despite the dissent's contention that former RCW 9.94A.440 allows prosecutors to "direct the activities of law enforcement," former RCW 9.94A.440(2)(b) merely requires a prosecutor to ensure that the investigating officer's evidence is sufficient to support a decision to prosecute. Moreover, unlike a prosecutor's obligation to inform victims of a proposed plea agreement, a prosecutor need not even discuss the proposed plea agreement with an IO. . . . We therefore hold that Sanchez's IO did not have a duty to abide by Sanchez's plea agreement with the county prosecutor, and therefore, his plea agreement was not breached by Sergeant Ruffin's testimony at the sentencing hearing.

The statutory duty imposed on a CCO is to produce a presentence report pursuant to court order, though the statute does not specifically mention him/her as a person whose arguments must be allowed at the sentencing hearing: "[T]he court shall, at the time of plea or conviction, order the department to complete a presentence report before imposing a sentence upon a defendant who has been convicted of a felony sexual offense." . . . Former RCW 9.94A.110. [This statute specifies] a minimum amount of information which, if available and offered, must be considered in sentencing. [The] court may rely on any information in the presentence report, unless it is the subject of an objection. . . . By statute, the CCO has an independent duty of investigation and recommendation in these cases. The CCO is not part of the prosecution team. The CCO was not involved in the preparation of, nor the promises made in, the plea agreement. In these circumstances, we hold that a CCO cannot be bound by the plea agreement. . . .

CHAMBERS, J., concurring in part and dissenting in part.

. . . While the community corrections officer in *Harris* functioned as an agent of the *court*, the investigating officer in *Sanchez* functions as the investigating arm of the *prosecutor*. Under Washington law, the prosecutor has the duty and the power to ensure that a thorough factual investigation has been conducted before a decision to prosecute is made. This is for the pragmatic reason that a prosecuting attorney is dependent upon law enforcement agencies to conduct the necessary factual investigation which must precede the decision to prosecute. It is the prosecutor who is empowered to enter into plea agreements and to make sentence recommendations. Investigating officers are so integral to the prosecutorial effort that to permit the investigating officer to undercut a plea agreement would, in effect, countenance the State's breach of promise in violation of *Santobello*. The prosecutor is obligated to comply with plea bargain promises, and the prosecutor's investigating officers may not undercut those promises by making inconsistent recommendations. . . . A prosecutor may not undercut a plea agreement directly or by words or conduct. Nor may he do so by proxy. . . .

MADSEN, J., dissenting.

I agree with the majority that the Investigating Officer (IO) in Sanchez's case has a statutory role in a sentencing hearing. I disagree, however, with the majority's conclusion that Investigating Officers and Community Corrections Officers (CCO) are entitled to make sentencing recommendations which undermine a plea agreement negotiated by the defendant and the prosecutor as the representative of the State of Washington. Basic agency principles and simple fairness require that they be bound to a prosecutor's plea agreement. . . .

Because plea agreements are based in contract law, the pivotal issue is whether IOs and CCOs are agents of the state, or independent agents of the court. The majority declines to analyze the question of agency and instead resolves the question by looking only at the statutory role each plays in sentencing.[1] . . . The authority of a Washington prosecuting attorney to act as an agent of the state of Washington is well established. The language of our state constitution directs that "all prosecutions shall be conducted . . . by [the State of Washington's] authority." Constitution article IV, section 27. . . . Statutes also dictate that the prosecuting attorney represents the State as well as the county. RCW 36.27.005 provides that "[p]rosecuting attorneys are attorneys authorized by law to appear for and represent the state and the counties thereof in actions and proceedings before the courts and judicial officers."

Based on the statutory duty placed on prosecutors by the Legislature to direct the activities of law enforcement, and the fact that the prosecuting attorney represents the State as well as the county, I would hold that the IO was bound by the plea agreement struck by the prosecuting attorney in *Sanchez*. Additionally, since case law establishes that the CCO is an agent of the State and the Constitution and state statutes dictate that the prosecuting attorney represents the State in criminal prosecutions, I would also hold that the CCO's recommendation undercutting the prosecutor's bargain requires reversal in *Harris*. . . .

Due process requires a prosecutor to adhere to the terms of the plea agreement. State v. Miller, 756 P.2d 122 (Wash. 1988) (holding that because a breach of plea agreement implicates fundamental principles of due process, the terms of a plea agreement override an otherwise contradictory statute). If a prosecutor cannot, per the plea agreement, make a contrary argument, it follows that IOs and CCOs are bound to the same due process limitations. . . .

To allow CCOs and IOs to present arguments to the sentencing judge, in any form, which contradict another state agency's contract not only appears unfair, but is unfair. It renders the prosecution's agreement meaningless, disintegrates the fabric of our criminal justice system, and will deter future plea agreements. In my view, IOs and CCOs are bound to prosecutorial plea agreements and, as a result, I respectfully dissent.

Problem 16-6. Breaking Bargains

On the afternoon of June 5, 1978, Floyd Jensen was robbed and murdered in his gasoline service station in Caledonia, Wisconsin. Shortly after the murder-robbery, Alan Rivest surrendered to police. Rivest, in a statement given to the police, admitted participating in the robbery of the gas station owner, but denied any involvement in his subsequent murder. Rivest indicated in his statement that Edward Rodriguez, his accomplice, repeatedly stabbed Jensen during the robbery; Rivest said that he did not participate in the murder and that he fled the gas station before Rodriguez but after the stabbing. Later that same evening, Rivest signed a sworn statement dictated to the police in which he repeated his earlier statement and denied any involvement in the stabbing of Floyd Jensen. Rivest, a minor, was initially charged with delinquency for the murder and armed robbery of Floyd Jensen in the

1. The majority repeatedly makes the point that the only parties to the plea agreement are the prosecuting attorney and the defendant — that neither an investigating officer nor a community corrections officer is involved in the negotiations or a party to the agreement. The majority apparently thinks this renders the agency question irrelevant. However, the question who is a party to the contract simply does not answer the question of who is bound by the agreement under agency principles.

juvenile court and was waived into adult court on August 1. Based on Rivest's prior statements and his investigation, Assistant District Attorney Finley charged Rivest only with the crime of armed robbery on August 3.

On September 25, Rivest took a private polygraph examination which showed that he was truthful in his denial of any participation in the stabbing of Floyd Jensen. Subsequent negotiations between Rivest, his attorney, and the Assistant District Attorney Finley produced a plea agreement. In the plea agreement, Rivest agreed to (1) plead guilty to a charge of robbery; (2) testify against Rodriguez whenever requested; and (3) pass a second polygraph examination conducted by a party chosen by the district attorney. The second polygraph examination indicated that Rivest was unaware that an assault was to be perpetrated on Jensen, and did not participate in stabbing Jensen. At a hearing on February 6, 1979, the plea agreement entered into between Rivest and the assistant district attorney was placed on the record and Rivest pled guilty to the crime of robbery, reduced from armed robbery. Rivest was sentenced to six years in prison.

On February 19, Rivest testified at the preliminary hearing of Edward Rodriguez. At the hearing, Rivest testified that he never got near Jensen nor did he come in physical contact with him. He also testified that he ran "straight out across the street" shortly after Rodriguez stabbed Jensen.

After Rivest's testimony at the preliminary hearing, the district attorney, Dennis Barry, while preparing the Rodriguez murder file, reviewed evidence that he believed directly contradicted both Rivest's initial statements to the police and his testimony at the preliminary hearing. This evidence established that there was a three to five minute delay between the time Jensen's body was discovered and the time that witnesses saw Rivest and Rodriguez flee the scene together. The evidence also proved that a "herringbone pattern" on the forehead of the victim matched the "herringbone pattern" on Rivest's shoes, but not Rodriguez's shoes. Finally, a State Crime Lab report indicated that the large bloodstains present on Rivest's pants and undershorts matched the blood type and factors of Floyd Jensen.

District Attorney Barry interviewed Rivest and confronted him with this evidence. At that interview, Rivest admitted leaving the gas station by a different door than the one he had originally testified about. However, Rivest offered no explanations for the presence of his shoe print on the deceased's head nor the presence of the deceased's blood on his clothing and he continued to repeat his original account of the stabbing. District Attorney Barry concluded after the interview that Rivest's account of the circumstances surrounding the stabbing was untrue, and that his prior testimony was false and thus, he breached the plea agreement. Based on this evidence, District Attorney Barry decided not to present Rivest's testimony at the Rodriguez trial.

The state filed first-degree murder charges against Rivest and then filed a motion before Judge Harvey to vacate the plea agreement and guilty plea. Judge Harvey entered an order setting aside the plea agreement and guilty plea and authorized the state to continue the prosecution of the murder complaint. The court held that Rivest had fraudulently induced the state to enter into the plea agreement through his false and misleading statements and had materially breached the agreement by giving false testimony at Rodriguez's preliminary hearing. Rivest appeals, arguing that his inconsistent testimony did not provide evidence beyond a reasonable doubt that he had committed perjury, and that even if he did, his actions were not a sufficient (or "material") breach of the plea agreement that would justify vacation of the agreement. How would you rule? Compare State v. Rivest, 316 N.W.2d 395 (Wis. 1982).

Notes

1. *Who is bound by plea agreements: majority position.* As the court in *Sanchez* notes, a number of states have found that the plea agreement binds only the defendant and the prosecutor, but not other state agents. Florida clearly rejects this position:

> Under Florida Rule of Criminal Procedure 3.171, the prosecuting attorney represents the state in all plea negotiations. [Once] a plea bargain based on a prosecutor's promise that the state will recommend a certain sentence is struck, basic fairness mandates that no agent of the state make any utterance that would tend to compromise the effectiveness of the state's recommendation. [It] matters not whether the recommendation contrary to the agreement is made in open court or whether, as here, it is contained in a PSI report. The crucial factor is that a recommendation contrary to the state's agreement came to the sentencing court's attention. Regardless of how a recommendation counter to that bargained for is communicated to the trial court, once the court is apprised of this inconsistent position, the persuasive effect of the bargained for recommendation is lost.

Lee v. State, 501 So. 2d 591, 593 (Fla. 1987). Sometimes the question is not whether other government agents are bound by a plea agreement, but whether another agency is precluded from taking additional civil action against a defendant after plea. See, e.g., Dickerson v. Kansas Dept. of Revenue, 841 P.2d 466 (Kan. 1992) (plea agreement collaterally estopped state revenue collection of drug tax).

Federal courts also hold that a plea agreement by the United States Attorney binds other agents of the federal government. See Giglio v. United States, 405 U.S. 150, 154 (1972) ("A promise made by one [government] attorney must be attributed . . . to the Government"); Margali-Olvera v. I.N.S., 43 F.3d 345 (8th Cir. 1994) (plea agreement by U.S. Attorney bound I.N.S.). Is this because the federal system is a unitary system under the direction of the Attorney General? Which way should that logic cut in the states? Within a particular county? Can one county's district attorney bind another county's district attorney? See Zebe v. State, 929 P.2d 927 (Nev. 1996) (holding that a second Nevada county was not bound by a plea to which it did not consent). Can the prosecutor of one state bind a prosecutor in another state (is this simply another way of asking whether double jeopardy or joinder rules apply)? Courts usually hold that one state cannot bind another. How can a defendant, as part of a plea bargain, protect against prosecution by multiple sovereigns?

2. *Assessing breach of plea bargains: majority position.* Plea bargains can be broken by the defendant, the prosecution, the court, or through an unanticipated change of circumstances that makes performance of the bargain impossible. The law regarding broken bargains might at first seem to be just a question of remedy; indeed, the question of available remedies will often shape a party's decision to breach a plea bargain. As with other kinds of contracts, if the cost of breaking the contract is lower than the cost of abiding by it, a person will often choose to breach.

Sometimes the parties disagree about whether the plea bargain has been breached at all. This often occurs when a defendant receives a stiff sentence and claims that the prosecution violated an agreement to recommend no sentence at all. When a prosecutor introduces elements of the defendant's prior record or otherwise implies that a higher sentence might be appropriate, the defendant may call this a breach of the agreement. Another common illustration occurs when the defendant agrees, as part of the plea bargain, to provide "complete" cooperation, or to testify against other parties, and the prosecution later alleges some inadequacy in the defendant's performance. Here, the defendant will claim performance, or substantial performance, and look to enforce the benefit of the bargain. What standard should a court apply to determine whether a party has fulfilled the terms of the agreement?

If the parties disagree about whether breach has occurred, the trial court will hold a hearing to determine relevant facts. Trial courts often treat the assessment of whether breach has occurred as a question of fact, without expressly reflecting on the standards to apply. When a party appeals the trial court's decision, however, an appellate court must decide whether breach is a question of fact, a question of law, or a mixed question of law and fact. State courts are divided on the proper standard to apply. Most treat the facts underlying the claim of breach as a factual matter for the trial judge, subject only to review for abuse of discretion. But some appellate courts have treated the question of whether particular facts are indeed breach or substantial compliance with a plea bargain as a question of law, subject to de novo appellate review. Courts more often find breach by defendants in failing to disclose all information than by prosecutors in failing to support a particular sentence recommendation. See, e.g., United States v. Benchimol, 471 U.S. 453 (1985) (prosecutor carried out agreement to recommend probation by saying agreement was accurate; there was no express agreement to be enthusiastic or to give reasons supporting probation); but see State v. Adams, 879 P.2d 513 (Haw. 1994) (government breached agreement to stand silent by providing probation officer with access to prosecution files).

Should prosecutors ever agree to support a particular sentence "with enthusiasm"? Could the prosecutor in Problem 16-6 have maintained full control over the plea by delaying Rivest's guilty plea hearing until after Rodriguez's preliminary hearing?

3. *Construing ambiguities.* How long would plea agreements become if they took account of all possible future events relevant to the bargain? All reasonably possible (if unlikely) events? Which side should get the benefit of ambiguous language? Should ambiguous terms be handled differently from events for which no term was drafted? See, e.g., State v. Wills, 765 P.2d 1114 (Kan. 1988) (ambiguity in agreement construed to favor defendant); State v. Bergman, 600 N.W.2d 311 (Iowa 1999) (prosecutor could not claim breach where defendant "did everything" under a cooperation agreement but was then charged before sentencing with possession of marijuana).

Often the parties will agree that a bargain has been broken, or the breach (such as defendant's failure to testify or the government's failure to dismiss charges) will be obvious. In such cases, the main issue is the appropriate remedy.

When one party breaches a contract, what remedies are available? A standard remedy for breach of a contract is money damages. Perhaps the state or the defendant should pay money damages for breaching a plea bargain, but this remedy has not been seriously considered. Instead, the typical remedies for breach of a plea bargain are either rescission or specific enforcement of the original bargain. Should the party against whom a breach has occurred get to choose the remedy?

Problem 16-7. Remedies for Broken Bargains

Following his arrest in 1999 in Billings, Montana, Daniel Munoz entered a pretrial agreement with the State. The State agreed to recommend that Munoz receive a three-year sentence in exchange for his voluntary plea of guilty to one count of sexual assault. On January 13, 2000, the court accepted Munoz's guilty plea and ordered a presentence investigation.

At a March 28 sentencing hearing, the prosecutor urged the court to adopt the five-year sentence recommended by Munoz's probation officer, who conducted the presentence investigation and issued a report. In addition to recommending the five-year sentence, the probation officer testified at the hearing that community supervision presented too much of a risk. Therefore, the officer recommended that all sex-offender treatment should be completed in prison.

The District Court sentenced Munoz to the recommended five-year sentence. On April 27, Munoz filed a motion to withdraw his guilty plea and a motion for a new trial. The State conceded that it breached the plea agreement. However, the State also contended that the sentencing court, not the defendant, possesses the right to choose the appropriate remedy, and argued that under the circumstances here specific performance of the plea agreement would be appropriate: Munoz should receive a new sentencing hearing before a new judge and the State would then in good faith recommend the three-year sentence pursuant to the plea agreement.

The trial court ordered specific performance, and Munoz appealed, arguing that he was entitled to withdraw his guilty plea and proceed to trial due to the State's breach of the plea agreement. The Montana Supreme Court set the stage for its decision as follows:

> Generally, when the State breaches a plea bargain agreement, one of two equitable remedies is available to safeguard a defendant's due process rights. This notion of an equitable "remedy" for a "breach" is unquestionably guided by general principles of contract law. Even so where a defendant's due process rights are concerned a "strict contract characterization" of a plea bargain may give way to a "reasonable expectations" standard.
>
> The first equitable remedy identified by the court in Santobello v. New York, 404 U.S. 257 (1971), is "specific performance" by the government. To safeguard a defendant's due process rights, circumstances may require the State uphold its end of the bargain, and, before a new sentencing judge, comply with the terms and conditions of the plea agreement by recommending a specific sentence, moving for the dismissal of other charges, or simply not opposing the defendant's requested sentence.
>
> The second equitable remedy is "rescission." Circumstances may require that a defendant be allowed to withdraw his or her guilty plea and then face trial on the original charges as if the plea agreement had never been entered—which also means that the defendant's "performance" is returned; i.e., his or her constitutional rights that were waived by the guilty plea are thereafter reinstated.

The Court in *Santobello* left the choice of remedy "to the discretion of the state court." Three general positions have emerged in state and federal courts since

Santobello. Some courts give the trial court authority to choose a remedy in each case. Other jurisdictions instruct trial judges to give deference to the defendant's choice of remedies, while some allow the defendant total discretion to choose between those remedies. What should Montana decide? See State v. Munoz, 23 P.3d 922 (Mont. 2001).

Notes

1. *Remedies for breach: majority position.* There are two standard remedies for breaches of plea agreements: rescission, in which the parties return to their positions before the agreement, and specific enforcement, in which the court orders government officials to carry out the terms of the agreement. State and federal courts split on whether the aggrieved party is allowed to select the remedy. In oft-quoted language, the U.S. Supreme Court in Santobello v. New York, 404 U.S. 257 (1971), stated that "when a plea rests in any significant degree on a promise or agreement of the prosecutor, so that it can be said to be part of the inducement or consideration, such promise must be fulfilled." Most courts have not interpreted this language to mean that defendants will always get specific enforcement of the bargain. The Court in *Santobello* left the choice of remedy to state courts, and most state courts follow what is commonly referred to as the "discretion of the court" rule. See State v. King, 576 N.W.2d 369 (Iowa 1998). Federal courts follow the "discretion of the court" rule, although some federal courts have expressed a preference for specific performance. See United States v. Clark, 55 F.3d 9 (1st Cir. 1995) (preference for specific performance before a different judge). A second position in some state and federal courts is a twist on the "discretion of the court theme" where courts suggest that the defendant's views should receive some special deference. See Roye v. United States, 772 A.2d 837 (D.C. Ct. App. 2001). What difference do rules make that "encourage" deference within the framework of acknowledged discretion? A few states allow the defendant to select the remedy, absent special circumstances. See State v. Miller, 756 P.2d 122 (Wash. 1988) ("We hold now that the defendant's choice of remedy controls, unless there are compelling reasons not to allow that remedy"). Some states apply a multifactor test to select between rescission and specific enforcement. See Citti v. State, 807 P.2d 724, 726-727 (Nev. 1991):

> The goal in providing a remedy for breach of the [plea] bargain is to redress the harm caused by the violation without prejudicing either party or curtailing the normal sentencing discretion of the trial judge. The remedy chosen will vary depending on the circumstances of each case. Factors to be considered include who broke the bargain and whether the violation was deliberate or inadvertent, whether circumstances have changed between entry of the plea and the time of sentencing, and whether additional information has been obtained that, if not considered, would constrain the court to a disposition that it determines to be inappropriate. . . . Courts find withdrawal of the plea to be the appropriate remedy when specifically enforcing the bargain would have limited the judge's sentencing discretion in light of the development of additional information or changed circumstances between acceptance of the plea and sentencing. Specific enforcement is appropriate when it will implement the reasonable expectations of the parties without binding the trial judge to a disposition that he or she considers unsuitable under all the circumstances. [Quoting People v. Mancheno, 654 P.2d 211 (Cal. 1982).]

See generally Peter Westen and David Westin, A Constitutional Law of Remedies for Broken Plea Bargains, 66 Cal. L. Rev. 471 (1978). Is specific performance an available remedy when a *defendant* breaches a plea agreement? Does your answer to this question affect your view of the ordinary remedy when the government breaches?

2. *Planning for breach.* Plea agreements sometimes include terms that account for various kinds of possible breach or other barriers to completion of the plea agreement (e.g. an agreement about how another jurisdiction will act, even though the sentencing jurisdiction has no power to compel that result). Who should bear the "cost" of failing to anticipate any particular kind of development? Is the general rule that ambiguous statutes will be interpreted to favor the criminal defendant (the so-called rule of lenity) relevant to interpretation and enforcement of plea agreements? Would you advise prosecutors systematically to alter the terms of their plea agreements in the future to address various issues of breach and remedy, akin to a large commercial contract that specifies procedural and substantive terms in case of breach? If so, will plea agreements be hundreds of pages long?

E. THE FUTURE OF BARGAINING

Is plea bargaining bad or good? If courts and executive branch policies actually do "regulate" plea bargaining — as the materials in this chapter suggest — are those regulations effective at limiting the undesirable aspects of plea bargaining? Should we ban plea bargaining altogether?

1. Legitimacy of Bargaining

Many scholars, judges, and lawyers believe that plea bargaining is inevitable. They say that the use of other processes (especially trials) to decide guilt or innocence would at best be hugely expensive and at worst cause a meltdown of the justice system. But before we consider whether it is feasible to ban plea bargaining, we need to know whether an attempted ban would be worth the effort. Is plea bargaining legitimate? Would we keep it in an ideal world?

■ IMPLEMENTING THE CRIMINAL DEFENDANT'S RIGHT TO TRIAL: ALTERNATIVES TO THE PLEA BARGAINING SYSTEM
ALBERT ALSCHULER
50 U. Chi. L. Rev. 931 (1983)

. . . Plea bargaining makes a substantial part of an offender's sentence depend, not upon what he did or his personal characteristics, but upon a tactical decision irrelevant to any proper objective of criminal proceedings. In contested cases, it substitutes a regime of split-the-difference for a judicial determination of guilt or innocence and elevates a concept of partial guilt above the requirement that criminal responsibility be established beyond a reasonable doubt. This practice also deprecates the value of human liberty and the purposes of the criminal sanction by treating these things as commodities to be traded for economic savings — savings that, when measured against common social expenditures, usually seem minor.

Plea bargaining leads lawyers to view themselves as judges and administrators rather than as advocates; it subjects them to serious financial and other temptations to disregard their clients' interests; and it diminishes the confidence in attorney-client relationships that can give dignity and purpose to the legal profession and that is essential to the defendant's sense of fair treatment. In addition, this practice makes figureheads of court officials who typically prepare elaborate presentence reports only after the effective determination of sentence through prosecutorial negotiations. Indeed, it tends to make figureheads of judges, whose power over the administration of criminal justice has largely been transferred to people of less experience, who commonly lack the information that judges could secure, whose temperaments have been shaped by their partisan duties, and who have not been charged by the electorate with the important responsibilities that they have assumed. Moreover, plea bargaining perverts both the initial prosecutorial formulation of criminal charges and, as defendants plead guilty to crimes less serious than those that they apparently committed, the final judicial labeling of offenses.

The negotiation process encourages defendants to believe that they have, [in the words of a Chicago defense attorney], "sold a commodity and . . ., in a sense, gotten away with something." It sometimes promotes perceptions of corruption. It has led the Supreme Court to a hypocritical disregard of its usual standards of waiver in judging the most pervasive waiver that our criminal justice system permits. The practice of plea bargaining is inconsistent with the principle that a decent society should want to hear what an accused person might say in his defense — and with constitutional guarantees that embody this principle and other professed ideals for the resolution of criminal disputes. Moreover, plea bargaining has undercut the goals of legal doctrines as diverse as the fourth amendment exclusionary rule, the insanity defense, the right of confrontation, the defendant's right to attend criminal proceedings, and the recently announced right of the press and the public to observe the administration of criminal justice. This easy instrument of accommodation has frustrated both attempts at sentencing reform and some of the most important objectives of the due process revolution.

Plea bargaining provides extraordinary opportunities for lazy lawyers whose primary goal is to cut corners and to get on to the next case; it increases the likelihood of favoritism and personal influence; it conceals other abuses; it maximizes the dangers of representation by inexperienced attorneys who are not fully versed in an essentially secret system of justice; it promotes inequalities; it sometimes results in unwarranted leniency; it merges the tasks of adjudication, sentencing, and administration into a single amorphous judgment to the detriment of all three; it treats almost every legal right as a bargaining chip to be traded for a discount in sentence; and it almost certainly increases the number of innocent defendants who are convicted. In short, an effort to describe comprehensively the evils that plea bargaining has wrought requires an extensive tour of the criminal justice system. . . .

At the end of a long investigation of plea bargaining, I confess to some bafflement concerning the insistence of most lawyers and judges that plea bargaining is inevitable and desirable. Perhaps I am wrong in thinking that a few simple precepts of criminal justice should command the unqualified support of fair-minded people:

- that it is important to hear what someone may be able to say in his defense before convicting him of crime;
- that, when he denies his guilt, it is also important to try to determine on the basis of all the evidence whether he is guilty;

- that it is wrong to punish a person, not for what he did, but for asking that the evidence be heard (and wrong deliberately to turn his sentence in significant part on his strategies rather than on his crime);
- and, finally, that it is wrong to alibi departures from these precepts by saying that we do not have the time and money to listen, that most defendants are guilty anyway, that trials are not perfect, that it is all an inevitable product of organizational interaction among stable courtroom work groups, and that any effort to listen would merely drive our failure to listen underground.

From my viewpoint, it is difficult to understand why these precepts are controversial; what is more, I do not understand why the legal profession, far from according them special reverence, apparently values them less than the public in general does. Daniel Webster thought it a matter of definition that "law" would hear before it condemned, proceed upon inquiry, and render judgment only after trial. Apparently the legal profession has lost sight of Webster's kind of law. . . .

■ PLEA BARGAINING AS COMPROMISE
FRANK EASTERBROOK

101 Yale L.J. 1969 (1992)

Is plea bargaining good or bad? Should we keep it or kick it? . . .

The analogy between plea bargains and contracts is far from perfect. Courts use contract as an analogy when addressing claims for the enforcement of plea bargains, excuses for nonperformance, or remedies for their breach. But plea bargains do not fit comfortably all aspects of either the legal or the economic model. Courts refuse to enforce promises to plead guilty in the future, although the enforcement of executory contracts is a principal mission of contract law.

On the economic side, plea bargains do not represent Pareto improvements. Instead of engaging in trades that make at least one person better off and no one worse off, the parties dicker about how much worse off one side will be. In markets persons can borrow to take advantage of good deals or withdraw from the market, wait for a better offer, and lend their assets for a price in the interim. By contrast, both sides to a plea bargain operate under strict budget constraints, and they cannot bide their time. They bargain as bilateral monopolists (defendants can't shop in competitive markets for prosecutors) in the shadow of legal rules that work suspiciously like price controls. Judges, who do not join the bargaining, set the prices, increasingly by reference to a table of punishments that looks like something the Office of Price Administration would have promulgated. Plea bargaining is to the sentencing guidelines as black markets are to price controls.

Black markets are better than no markets. Plea bargains are preferable to mandatory litigation — not because the analogy to contract is overpowering, but because compromise is better than conflict. Settlements of civil cases make both sides better off; settlements of criminal cases do so too. Defendants have many procedural and substantive rights. By pleading guilty, they sell these rights to the prosecutor, receiving concessions they esteem more highly than the rights surrendered. Rights that may be sold are more valuable than rights that must be consumed, just as money (which may be used to buy housing, clothing, or food) is more valuable to a poor person than an opportunity to live in public housing.

Defendants can use or exchange their rights, whichever makes them better off. So plea bargaining helps defendants. Forcing them to use their rights at trial means compelling them to take the risk of conviction or acquittal; risk-averse persons prefer a certain but small punishment to a chancy but large one. Defendants also get the process over sooner, and solvent ones save the expense of trial. Compromise also benefits prosecutors and society at large. In purchasing procedural entitlements with lower sentences, prosecutors buy that most valuable commodity, Time. With time they can prosecute more criminals. When [eighty] percent of defendants plead guilty, a given prosecutorial staff obtains five times the number of convictions it could achieve if all went to trial. Even so, prosecutors must throw back the small fish. The ratio of prosecutions (and convictions) to crimes would be extremely low if compromises were forbidden. Sentences could not be raised high enough to maintain deterrence, especially not when both economics and principles of desert call for proportionality between crime and punishment.

True, defense lawyers and prosecutors are imperfect agents of their principals. Of what agents is this not true? Real estate agents? Corporate managers? Agency costs are endemic and do not justify abandoning consensual transactions. . . . Monitoring the performance of agents is difficult, and serious monitoring means substantially increasing the time and number of lawyers devoted to each case. Critics of plea bargaining commit the Nirvana Fallacy, comparing an imperfect reality to a perfection achievable only in imaginary systems. . . .

Why should we interfere with compromises of litigation? If the accused is entitled to a trial at which all his rights are honored and the sentence is appropriate to the crime, yet prefers compromise, who are we to disagree? . . . Why is liberty too important to be left to the defendant whose life is at stake? Should we not say instead that liberty is too important to deny effect to the defendant's choice?

Every day people choose where (if at all) to obtain an education, what occupation to pursue, whom to marry, whether to bear children, and how to raise them. Often they choose in ignorance — not simply because they do not know whether Yale offers a better education than the University of Southern Mississippi, but also because they do not know what the future holds. Technological changes or fluctuations in trade with foreign nations will make some educations obsolete and raise the value of others. People may, without the approval of regulators, climb mountains, plummet down slopes at eighty miles per hour on waxed boards, fail to exercise, eat fatty foods, smoke cigarettes, skip physical checkups, anesthetize their minds by watching television rather than reading books, and destroy their hearing by listening to rock music at high volumes. Sometimes courts say that the Constitution protects the right to make these choices, precisely because they are so important. . . .

Courts give effect not only to life-and-death choices actually made but also to elections by inaction. When a defendant's lawyer fails to make an important motion or omits an essential line of argument, we treat the omission as a forfeiture. How bizarre for a legal system that routinely puts persons in jail for twenty years following their agents' oversight to deny them the right to compromise the same dispute, advertently, for half as much loss of liberty. . . .

Curtailing the discount for pleading guilty has been justified in the name of equality. Yet the greatest disparity in sentencing is between those convicted at trial and those not prosecuted. A reduction in the number of convictions attributable to a decline in the number of pleas would dramatically increase the effective disparity in the treatment of persons suspected of crime. . . .

Plea bargains are compromises. Autonomy and efficiency support them. "Imperfections" in bargaining reflect the imperfections of an anticipated trial. To improve plea bargaining, improve the process for deciding cases on the merits. When we deem that process adequate, there will be no reason to prevent the person most affected by the criminal process from improving his situation through compromise.

Notes

1. *Plea bargains: contract or charade?* Some scholars have accepted the essentially contractual nature of plea bargaining, and have suggested that the problem with plea bargaining law is that it does not take the contracting analogy seriously enough. Robert Scott and William Stuntz, for example, focus on the risk of convicting an innocent defendant, arguing that "by following appropriate contract models, one can devise different rules that reduce the harm to innocent defendants and meanwhile reduce transaction costs and inefficiency for everyone else." Scott and Stuntz, Plea Bargaining as Contract, 101 Yale L.J. 1909 (1992). Critics of plea bargaining, such as Professor Stephen Schulhofer, have rejected the notion that plea bargains are fair simply because the defendant agreed to the terms and because the agreement puts the defendant in a better position than if the defendant went to trial. Schulhofer, Plea Bargaining as Disaster, 101 Yale L.J. 1979 (1992). Schulhofer and other critics focus on the public interest in criminal justice that the contract model obscures. Does plea bargaining undermine public confidence in the criminal justice system? Stanley Cohen and Anthony Doob, Public Attitudes to Plea Bargaining, 32 Crim. L.Q. 85 (1989-1990) (1988 survey found that more than two-thirds of Canadians disapprove of plea bargaining). What is Judge Easterbrook's attitude toward the use of contract law to explain plea bargaining? Does he take account of the public interest arguments? Does Professor Alschuler account for the contractarian argument that plea bargains are the fairest (most preferable) means for the defendant to address criminal charges, except in very limited circumstances? Would the fairness of plea bargaining be cast into doubt if there were no trials at all? See Malcolm Feeley, The Process Is the Punishment (1979) (of 1,640 misdemeanor cases, not one defendant requested jury trial). Is there such a thing as a "natural" rate of trials?

2. *The public interest in trials.* Judge Easterbrook treats plea bargains as the best way to honor the rights of the defendant, including the right to autonomy — to determine one's own destiny. But do not offenders forgo any such right when they commit a crime? Do criminal defendants have a constitutional right to bargain? Why should society care about giving free choice to a person who has acted in a way that denies rights (life, health, autonomy, ownership, and so forth) to others? Might the public have a greater interest in public trials than in more convictions? Might the public have an interest in convictions and sentences as close as possible to conceptions of what "really" happened, whether the conviction and sentence follow a trial or a nonbargained guilty plea?

3. *Bargaining and bribery.* Sometimes the government will enter a plea bargain with a defendant in exchange for the defendant's cooperation in other criminal investigations, including testimony against other criminal defendants. Does this sort of plea bargain amount to bribing a witness? Courts never took such an argument seriously until a panel of the U.S. Court of Appeals for the Tenth Circuit reversed a money laundering conviction on the ground that the government had bribed the cooperating witness. A few months later, the en banc court changed direction and

upheld the conviction. The "anti-gratuity statute," 18 U.S.C. §201(c)(2), declares that whoever "directly or indirectly, gives, offers, or promises anything of value to any person, for or because of the testimony under oath or affirmation given or to be given by such person" has committed a crime. The en banc court read the word "whoever" to exclude prosecuting attorneys acting within the normal course of their authority. Any other result, the court said, would be a "a radical departure from the ingrained legal culture of our criminal justice system." United States v. Singleton, 165 F.3d 1297 (10th Cir. 1999) (en banc). What would be the effects if prosecutors stopped promising to enter lenient plea agreements with cooperative witnesses? Try to formulate alternatives that prosecutors might adopt to obtain cooperation from witnesses who were involved in alleged crimes.

2. *Efforts to Ban Bargaining*

Courts and commentators occasionally refer to plea bargaining as eternal and inevitable. It may be inevitable, though it is surely not eternal. Research suggests that plea bargaining was forbidden (at least formally) in the first two-thirds of the nineteenth century, and emerged in the last third of that century, becoming institutionalized and widespread in the twentieth century. See Lawrence Friedman, Plea Bargaining in Historical Perspective, 13 Law & Socy. Rev. 247 (1979); Albert Alschuler, Plea Bargaining and Its History, 13 Law & Socy. Rev. 211 (1979).

Professor George Fisher, through careful study of the origins of plea bargaining in nineteenth-century Massachusetts, revealed how plea bargaining first thrived for crimes that gave judges little choice over sentences (and therefore gave added importance to the prosecutor's choice of charges). Bargaining also became more attractive to prosecutors after the appearance of probation as a sentencing option. Judges became more amenable to plea bargaining after a flood of railroad tort suits created civil docket pressures. Fisher, Plea Bargaining's Triumph, 109 Yale L.J. 857 (2000).

Do the following cases indicate that plea bargaining was banned in fact, or do they instead imply a ban in law but a reality of underground bargains? As a historian, how would you determine which of the two stories — true bans, or de jure bans combined with de facto bargains — was closer to the truth?

■ COMMONWEALTH v. JOHN BATTIS

1 Mass. 95 (1804)

The Court will not direct an immediate entry of the plea of guilty to an indictment for a capital crime, but will give a reasonable time to the prisoner to consider the same, that he may, if he think proper, retract his plea.

The defendant, John Battis, a Negro of about twenty years of age, was indicted for the murder of one Salome Talbot, a white girl of the age of thirteen years, on the twenty-eighth day of June last. The indictment contained three counts. The 1st count charged the killing to have been with a stone, with which he beat and broke her skull, and etc. The 2d stated that the killing was by drowning; and the 3d charged the killing to have been by beating and breaking her skull with a stone, and throwing her body into the water, and suffocating and drowning. There was another indictment against the prisoner for committing a rape on the body of the said Salome, on the same day on which the murder was charged to have been committed.

On the second day of the term, in the forenoon, the prisoner was set to the bar, and had both indictments read to him, and pleaded guilty to each. The Court informed him of the consequence of his plea, and that he was under no legal or moral obligation to plead guilty; but that he had a right to deny the several charges, and put the government to the proof of them. He would not retract his pleas; whereupon the Court told him that they would allow him a reasonable time to consider of what had been said to him: and remanded him to prison. They directed the clerk not to record his pleas, at present.

In the afternoon of the same day, the prisoner was again set to the bar, and the indictment for murder was once more read to him; he again pleaded guilty. Upon which the Court examined, under oath, the sheriff, the jailer, and the justice (before whom the examination of the prisoner was had previous to his commitment) as to the sanity of the prisoner; and whether there had not been tampering with him, either by promises, persuasions, or hopes of pardon, if he would plead guilty. On a very full inquiry, nothing of that kind appearing, the prisoner was again remanded, and the clerk directed to record the plea on both indictments.

On the last day of the term, the prisoner was brought to the bar, and the Attorney-general (Sullivan) moved for sentence; which the chief justice delivered in solemn, affecting, and impressive address to the prisoner. The sentence was entered on the indictment for the rape. He has since been executed.

■ GEORGE EDWARDS v. PEOPLE

39 Mich. 760 (1878)

CAMPBELL, C.J.

Plaintiff in error was informed against on a charge of larceny, in the daytime, from a shop, of a gold watch of the value of twenty-five dollars. The information was sworn to on the 25th of June, averring the offense on the 11th. On the same 25th day of June the prisoner was arraigned, pleaded guilty and was sentenced to the Ionia house of correction for three years. . . . The error relied on to reverse the judgment is that the court did not make the proper investigation before proceeding to sentence the prisoner, to ascertain whether he ought not to have been put on trial.

It has always been customary, and is according to many authorities essential before sentence to inquire of the prisoner whether he has anything to say why sentence should not be pronounced against him; and that it is generally said should appear of record. . . .

The Legislature of 1875, having in some way had their attention called to serious abuses caused by procuring prisoners to plead guilty when a fair trial might show they were not guilty, or might show other facts important to be known, passed a very plain and significant statute designed for the protection of prisoners and of the public. It was thereby enacted as follows:

> That whenever any person shall plead guilty to an information filed against him in any circuit court, it shall be the duty of the judge of such court, before pronouncing judgment or sentence upon such plea, to become satisfied, after such investigation as he may deem necessary for that purpose, respecting the nature of the case, and the circumstances of such plea, that said plea was made freely, with full knowledge of the nature of the accusation, and without undue influence. And whenever said judge shall have reason to doubt the truth of such plea of guilty, it shall be his duty to vacate the

same, direct a plea of not guilty to be entered, and order a trial of the issue thus formed. . . .

It is contrary to public policy to have any one imprisoned who is not clearly guilty of the precise crime charged against him, and thus equally contrary to policy and justice to punish any one without some regard to the circumstances of the case. By confining this statute to information and not extending it to indictments, it is easy to see that the Legislature thought there was danger that prosecuting attorneys, either to save themselves trouble, to save money to the county, or to serve some other improper purpose, would procure prisoners to plead guilty by assurances they have not power to make of influence in lowering the sentence, or by bringing some other unjust influence to bear on them. It is to be presumed they had evidence before them of serious abuses under the information system which in their judgment required checking by stringent measures.

Every one familiar with the course of criminal justice knows that those officers exercise very extensive and dangerous powers, that in the hands of an arbitrary or corrupt man are capable of great abuse. And unless the general impression is wrong, great abuses have been practiced by this very device of inveigling prisoners into confessions of guilt which could not be lawfully made out against them, and deceiving them concerning the precise character of the charges which they are led to confess. And it has also happened, as is generally believed, that by receiving a plea of guilty from a person whose offense is not aggravated, worse criminals who have used him for their purposes remain unpunished, because the facts which would convict them have not been brought out.

This statute not only requires the judge to examine carefully into the facts of the case, which can require no less than a search into the depositions if they have been returned or similar evidence if they have not been taken, but also compels him to examine the prisoner himself concerning the circumstances which induced him to plead guilty. It is evident that for this purpose it would be highly improper to take any thing on the statement of the prosecuting attorney, or to allow him to be present at the examination of the prisoner. . . . It could not have been contemplated that this should be done during the routine business of court and in presence of all the officers of justice and the prosecutor.

Without deciding that the absence from the record of a recital of such investigation must in all cases void the validity of a sentence on such plea, we have no hesitation in saying that the record ought to show the fact, and unless it does so, must show at least a reasonable delay between plea and sentence which may justify some presumption that this duty has been performed. . . .

Being of opinion that the record before us furnishes presumptive evidence at least that the statute was disregarded, we feel compelled to reverse the judgment. It is to be hoped that some express provision of law will require the record to note what is done in these cases. The statute is a wholesome one, but in the evident want to care in carrying it out we do not feel warranted in holding that a failure to note the fact on the record is conclusive. It is too important a matter to be left without some more positive direction concerning its appearance on the court journals. Judgment must be reversed, and the prisoner discharged.

Plea bargaining bans are not only part of history. Bans have also appeared from time to time in modern criminal justice. The following article describes several bans on plea bargains, along with other efforts by prosecutors to limit their reliance on plea negotiations. Before reading this article, consider what you would expect to happen when legal systems try to ban plea bargaining. Does the account of New Orleans practices confirm or challenge your expectations?

■ THE SCREENING/BARGAINING TRADEOFF RONALD WRIGHT & MARC MILLER

55 Stanford L. Rev. 29 (2002)

When it comes to plea bargaining, we have created a false dilemma. . . . Scholars, judges, prosecutors, defense lawyers, and politicians have offered only two basic responses to the fact that guilt is mostly resolved through negotiated guilty pleas: They take it or they leave it.

Some take the system more or less as it is. They accept negotiated pleas in the ordinary course of events, either because such a system produces good results or because it is inevitable. They might identify some exceptional cases that create an intolerable risk of convicting innocent defendants, or unusual cases where there are special reasons to doubt the knowing and voluntary nature of the defendant's plea. These special cases might call for some regulation. But the mine run of cases, in this view, must be resolved with a heavy dose of plea bargains and a sprinkling of trials.

Then there are those who leave it, arguing that our system's reliance on negotiated guilty pleas is fundamentally mistaken. Some call for a complete ban on negotiated guilty pleas. Others, doubting that an outright ban is feasible, still encourage a clear shift to more short trials to resolve criminal charges. Restoring the criminal trial to its rightful place at the center of criminal justice might require major changes in public spending, and it might take a lifetime, but these critics say the monstrosity of the current system demands such a change.

This dilemma about plea bargaining — take it or leave it — is a false one. It is based on a false dichotomy. It errs in assuming that criminal trials are the only alternative to plea bargains. In this erroneous view, fewer plea bargains lead inexorably to more trials; indeed, the whole point in limiting plea bargains is to produce more trials.

This paper offers a different choice, and points to prosecutorial "screening" as the principal alternative to plea bargains. Of course all prosecutors "screen" when they make any charging decision. By prosecutorial screening we mean a far more structured and reasoned charge selection process than is typical in most prosecutors' offices in this country. The prosecutorial screening system we describe has four interrelated features, all internal to the prosecutor's office: early assessment, reasoned selection, barriers to bargains, and enforcement.

First, the prosecutor's office must make an early and careful assessment of each case, and demand that police and investigators provide sufficient information before the initial charge is filed. Second, the prosecutor's office must file only appropriate charges. Which charges are "appropriate" is determined by several factors. A prosecutor should only file charges that the office would generally want to result in a criminal conviction and sanction. In addition, appropriate charges must reflect reasonably accurately what actually occurred. They are charges that the prosecutor can very likely prove in court. Third, and critically, the office must severely restrict all plea bargaining, and most especially charge bargains. Prosecutors should also recognize explicitly that the screening process is the mechanism that makes such restrictions possible. Fourth, the kind of prosecutorial screening we advocate must include sufficient training, oversight, and other internal enforcement mechanisms to ensure reasonable uniformity in charging and relatively few changes to charges after they have been filed. If prosecutors treat hard screening decisions as the primary alternative to plea bargaining, they can produce changes in current criminal practice that would be fundamental, attractive, and viable. . . .

Traditional Alternatives to Plea Bargaining

. . . For those who wish to establish that plea bargaining is an inevitable and irrepressible force in American criminal justice, Philadelphia is a problem. The city has long operated a system that relies more on short bench trials than on pleas of guilty. A number of scholars conducted case studies in Philadelphia (and a few other cities with high rates of bench trials) and concluded that the trials in those cities were not truly adversarial trials. Instead, they were "slow pleas" of guilt. The brief trials allowed the defendant to present evidence about the circumstances of the case, not to obtain an acquittal, but to influence the judge at sentencing.

Stephen Schulhofer visited the Philadelphia courts and took away a different impression. [He] observed a large number of bench trials in the city and concluded that they were genuinely adversarial proceedings where defendants retained many of the constitutional protections sacrificed during plea bargaining. Schulhofer called for other jurisdictions to follow Philadelphia's lead and to treat short trials as a viable alternative to plea bargaining. . . .

Explicit efforts to shorten trials have not been the preferred technique among American prosecutors who want to limit the reach of negotiated pleas. Instead, the handful of prosecutors who aspire to "ban" plea bargaining — either for targeted crimes or for the entire criminal docket — have issued strong ukases against bargaining, enforced by more rigorous screening and modest staffing increases, as their most workable solution. . . .

Among the most famous American plea bargaining bans occurred in Alaska during the 1970s and 1980s. In 1975, state Attorney General Avrum Gross declared that prosecutors would no longer engage in charge bargaining or sentence bargaining. Attorney General Gross hoped to restore public confidence in the system, increase the number of trials, improve the litigation skills of prosecutors, and return prosecutors to their traditional roles of evaluating evidence and trying cases instead of negotiating.

Major studies in 1978 and 1991 evaluated the impact of the Alaska plea ban. By all accounts, both charge bargaining and sentence bargaining became rare events during the first ten years of the policy. During the late 1980s, charge bargains reappeared, but prosecutors continued to avoid sentence bargains. For a few years, the trial rate increased modestly. Seven percent of charged cases went to trial before the ban, and the rate moved to 10% before returning to 7% by the end of the 1980s.

Since the cases were not ending in negotiated pleas or trials, what was happening to them? The answer was a combination of aggressive screening and open guilty pleas. Before the ban, prosecutors in Fairbanks refused to prosecute about 4% of the felonies referred to them by the police or other investigators. After the ban, the proportion of felonies that prosecutors declined to prosecute increased to about 44%. A large portion of the case load (about 23%) was disposed of through open pleas of guilt. This was part of the Attorney General's thinking when he created the plea ban. More careful selection of cases would make it possible to stick with the initial charges, even in front of a judge or jury.

The Alaska experience received lackluster academic reviews. Some implied that the failure to increase trials proved that unseen bargains were still driving the system, and explained the high number of open guilty pleas. Others pointed to the reappearance of charge bargaining after ten years, and suggested that it is futile to place controls on the quintessential prosecutorial decision of charge selection. Some implied that Alaska was too unusual a jurisdiction to offer any guidance to prosecutors in most major American cities. However, other jurisdictions scattered around the country have duplicated pieces of the Alaska experience over the years. Some prosecutors in other locales have picked out priority crimes like homicide and banned plea bargains for those cases.[53] Some of the bans target particular forms of bargaining rather than particular crimes.[54] The reaction to these experiences, like the reaction to the Alaska plea ban, has been subdued. If these prosecutors were not increasing their trial rates, the critics found the effort unimportant.

These experiences do not mean that any ban on charge reductions will produce small trial increases and large numbers of open guilty pleas. If prosecutors do not change their screening principles to insist on more declinations of cases referred to the office, the dispositions shift in other directions. In El Paso County, Texas during the 1980s, the chief prosecutor announced an end to all plea bargaining in burglary cases. There was no organized effort to change the screening of such cases, and the number of trials increased enough to create a serious backlog of untried cases. Partial bans on plea bargaining appear regularly around the country. Most prosecutors today who plan to restrict plea negotiations focus on priority crimes, such as homicide or sex crimes. Some of the bans are limited to particular courts or phases of litigation, such as the statutory ban on plea bargains for most serious felonies in Superior Court in California, or the ban on plea bargaining in the Supreme Court in the Bronx in the mid-1990s.

When plea bans are limited to a particular court (such as the highest trial court), the effects are usually minimal because the bargainers simply move to a different (typically earlier) point in the process. Plea bans exist today, but we know little about their effects on case dispositions and sentences. The attention of academic

53. In the 1970s, the prosecutor in Maricopa County (Phoenix), Arizona barred plea bargains in cases involving designated crimes such as drug sales, homicide, robbery, burglary, assault with a deadly weapon, and sexual misconduct. The policy did not increase trial rates for these crimes because more defendants pled guilty as charged. Moise Berger, *The Case Against Plea Bargaining,* 62 A.B.A. J. 621 (1976). Similar reports came after prosecutors in Multnomah County, Oregon and Black Hawk County, Iowa banned plea bargaining for selected crimes during the early 1970s. Note, The Elimination of Plea Bargaining in Black Hawk County: A Case Study, 60 Iowa L. Rev. 1053 (1975). . . .

54. In an example of one such effort to discourage some forms of bargaining, the District Attorney for Manhattan in the mid-1970s prohibited his attorneys from recommending sentences and established (and published!) a 1974 memorandum suggesting specific charge discounts to offer in exchange for guilty pleas. Richard H. Kuh, Plea Bargaining: Guidelines for the Manhattan District Attorney's Office, 11 Crim. L. Bull. 48 (1975). Thomas Church documented the efforts of a county in a Midwestern state during the early 1970s to eliminate charge bargaining in drug sale cases. Thomas Church, Jr., Plea Bargains, Concessions and the Courts: Analysis of a Quasi-Experiment, 10 Law & Soc'y Rev. 377 (1976). The prosecutor left sentence bargaining in place, and the proportion of the cases resolved through defendants pleading guilty as charged increased from 17 to 90% between 1972 and 1974. In Church's view, the county's experience demonstrated the inevitability of plea bargaining. But his interviewees believed that the concessions the defendants were promised after the ban were far less reliable and valuable than the concessions they negotiated before the ban.

observers has strayed to other areas, even as prosecutors keep innovating. . . . Thirty years of scholarship has missed a fundamental perspective on plea bargaining: there are in fact many alternative points of comparison when assessing the wisdom and necessity of plea bargains. . . .

The Screening/Bargaining Tradeoff in Practice: NODA Data

A chief prosecutor attempting to change plea practices faces both administrative and political hurdles. Will her proposed policy actually change the use of negotiated guilty pleas? If so, can the office sustain it over the long haul? We do not believe that plea bargaining is inevitable, but plea bargaining surely is pervasive and deeply entrenched. Any effort to limit plea bargaining must confront the habits and relationships of prosecutors and defense attorneys.

Reform efforts emerging voluntarily from within one criminal justice institution may have a greater chance to succeed than reforms imposed externally. A single institution can set up review and reward systems, allowing for more supervision — and, we believe, more consistency — than external constraints can provide. Among the many virtues we see in the screening/bargaining tradeoff described in this paper is the authority of a chief prosecutor, acting alone, to set this change in motion.

What should we expect to happen when a prosecutor decides to shift the screening/bargaining tradeoff in the direction of screening? As for changes in case processing, the most direct effect should be measurable: fewer plea bargains. The kinds of plea bargains that are easiest to track are charge reductions after cases are filed. A jurisdiction with hard screening practices should produce fewer and smaller charge reductions than jurisdictions with weaker screening practices.

[We can] test the plausibility of the screening/bargaining tradeoff using previously unstudied and unreported data about one major urban prosecutor's office: the New Orleans District Attorney's Office, or NODA. This data exists because the District Attorney for Orleans Parish, Harry Connick, has remained committed to principled screening throughout his long term in office. . . .

Harry Connick was elected as the District Attorney for Orleans Parish in 1974. He has remained in that office for the past twenty-eight years. Connick first ran for office in 1969 against incumbent Jim Garrison, the flamboyant District Attorney made famous in the film JFK. His first unsuccessful campaign did not focus on plea bargaining. He promised faster prosecution and better tracking of defendants who failed to appear for trial. His 1973 campaign began with a similar emphasis on swift prosecution. As the campaign wore on, however, Connick's speeches began to feature attacks on plea bargaining. . . .

Connick told voters that widespread plea bargaining was wrong; years later, he explained that victims were right to resent it when cases were bargained away simply because of a "lazy" prosecutor. He promised to eliminate "baseless" plea bargaining and to hire full-time prosecutors who would not use plea bargains just to move cases from the docket.

As in other American cities, the criminal courts in New Orleans deal with enormous volume. In the face of this large urban caseload, Connick needed a strategy to carry out his campaign statements about plea bargaining. During the weeks between his election victory and taking office, he started speaking publicly about a plan with two central components. First, Connick planned to devote expertise and resources to screening. He proposed a screening procedure that "would weed out those cases really not worthy of being on the criminal docket, so more courtroom emphasis can be devoted to the violent offender." Second, he instructed his prosecutors not to engage in plea bargaining — particularly charge bargaining — except under very limited circumstances. . . .

The distinctiveness of the screening process in the NODA office is apparent from a closer examination of the path each new case takes through the system. Police officers develop a case folder after they complete an investigation and file charges with the magistrate. The first stop for the case folder in the NODA office is the Magistrate Section, where the least experienced assistants work. They typically have logged six months or fewer on the job. The ADA from the Magistrate Section appears for the state at the first appearance and bail hearing before the magistrate. A public defender is also present for the first appearance, but the case is reassigned immediately after the hearing and there is typically no further defense presence or participation in the case until after the DA files an information or obtains an indictment.

After any proceedings in the Magistrate Division, the folder moves to the Screening Section of the NODA office. Connick devotes extraordinary resources to this operation. For instance, in the late 1990s, about fifteen of the eighty-five attorneys in the office worked in Screening. . . . All attorneys in the Screening Section served previously (usually a couple of years) in the Trial Section. This level of experience comes at a premium in New Orleans, where the turnover among prosecuting attorneys is quite high. The average tenure of an ADA in the NODA office is around two years.

Within the Screening Section, designated cases such as homicide or rape get assigned to screeners with special expertise. Drug cases and a few other high-volume cases go to a subgroup known as Expedited Screening. Ordinary cases go to the Screening Attorney on duty for that day. The screener reviews the investigation file, speaks to all the key witnesses and the victims (often by telephone, but sometimes in person), and generally gauges the strength of the case. If the police report neglects to mention a factual issue that is likely to arise at trial, the screening attorney will speak directly with the police officer to resolve it. There is a powerful office expectation that the Screening Attorney will make a decision within ten days of receiving the folder.

NODA instituted a variety of measures to ensure reasonable uniformity in screening decisions. Connick committed his screening principles to writing in an office policy manual. The general office policy is to charge the most serious crime the facts will support at trial. The policy does not, on its face, allow individual prosecutors to consider for themselves the equities in the case when selecting the charge. By the same token, however, Connick insists that overcharging is unacceptable, because the charges chosen for the information will stay in place through the trial. If screening prosecutors overcharge cases too often, the Chief of the Trial Section might send the screening attorney back into the courtroom on at least one of those overcharged matters to "get his teeth kicked in."

Supervisors review all refusals to charge. Attorneys say they often compare notes, especially in early morning discussions, and this helps to educate and develop shared charging norms in the office. Office policy discourages refusal for select categories of crimes, notably domestic violence cases. For the most serious crimes, including rape and homicide, the office conducts "charge conferences" with senior prosecutors and police present to discuss the facts and potential charges.

Neither Connick nor any attorneys in his office claim to have abolished plea bargaining entirely from the New Orleans system. Prosecutors in the office acknowledge that sometimes new information appears and changes the value of a case. Witnesses leave town, victims decide not to testify, new witnesses appear, and investigators find new evidence. On occasion, the screening attorney makes a bad judgment and overcharges, and a plea could save the case.

Nevertheless, office policy tries to keep these changes in charges to a minimum. A supervisor must approve any decision to drop or change charges after the information is filed. The attorney requesting the change must complete a special form naming the screening and trial attorneys, and explaining the reason for the decision, drawing from a list of acceptable reasons. The ADAs believe there is a "stigma" involved in reducing charges, however strong the reasons for a reduction might be.

Attorneys from the NODA office believe that they decline to prosecute an exceptional number of cases. They view this as a necessary part of training police officers to investigate more thoroughly. The relatively high rate of declination also created a political challenge for Connick over the years. During each of his reelection campaigns — in 1978, 1984, 1990, and 1996 — Connick's challengers criticized the number of cases that the NODA office declined to prosecute. As his opponent Morris Reed put it in many public debates, "the PD arrests them and the DA turns them loose." Connick had several replies. Poor police work made declinations necessary. Further, he pointed to specific examples of how his office dealt severely with defendants once they were charged. Connick also explicitly linked his screening policies to his plea bargaining policies: Tough screening, he said, made it possible to keep plea bargaining at low levels.

Connick drew on case data to make specific claims about low rates of plea bargaining in the office: He asserted that plea bargaining in Jim Garrison's day reached 60 to 70%, but fell to 7 or 8% of all cases filed under his office policy. He also routinely mentioned the high number of trials in New Orleans compared to other Louisiana jurisdictions. In addition, Connick pointed to his routine use of the habitual felon law to enhance sentences. By the end of each of the four reelection campaigns, Connick convinced the voters that it was possible both to decline many cases and to run a tough prosecutor's office at the same time. . . .

The data mostly support District Attorney Harry Connick's claims to have implemented a screening/bargaining tradeoff over the last thirty years. Several kinds of information bolster that judgment, but the most substantial and useful by far is the data that Connick has kept to assist in his administration of the office. New Orleans shows that the screening/bargaining tradeoff does not necessarily lead to a disabling number of trials. The office also shows that a committed prosecutor can implement the screening/bargaining tradeoff even without the conscious support of other actors in the system. . . . Plea bargaining's triumph, and the cynical products of that triumph, are simply not as absolute as a century of practice and study suggest.

Notes

1. *The isolated popularity of bans.* Though a minor theme in current criminal justice debates, bans on plea bargaining occasionally become a topic of public concern, and they remain a subject of intense scholarly interest. Jurisdictions other than

Alaska have experimented with formal plea bans, though none have been statewide; most are implemented by a single prosecutor with a particular vision for improving the criminal justice system. Other modern efforts to abolish plea bargaining include a ban in El Paso, Texas; a Detroit ban on bargaining in felony firearm cases; another effort in Michigan to abolish charge bargaining in drug trafficking cases; and a judge-imposed ban in Superior Court in New Hampshire. See Amy Fixsen, Plea Bargaining: The New Hampshire "Ban," 9 New Eng. J. Crim. & Civ. Confinement 387 (1983); Robert Weninger, The Abolition of Plea Bargaining: A Case Study of El Paso County, Texas, 35 UCLA L. Rev. 265 (1987); see generally 13 Law & Socy. Rev. (1979). A recent effort in the Bronx District Attorney's office banned bargains in felony cases after indictment. See Kenneth Jost, Critics Blast New York Plea Ban, 9 CQ Researcher No. 6, at 124 (Feb. 12, 1999). Which aspect of plea bargaining do these reforms target? Is selective restriction on bargaining preferable to a total ban?

2. *Alternatives to plea bargaining.* If bargains are banned, what takes their place? The Alaska and New Orleans experiences suggest that guilty plea rates may remain quite high even in the absence of bargains. Why might this be so? Professor Schulhofer and others have argued that it is possible to offer meaningful trials in place of bargains, including greater use of bench rather than jury trials. See Stephen Schulhofer, Is Plea Bargaining Inevitable? 97 Harv. L. Rev. 1037 (1984) (discussing use of short trials in Philadelphia). In an article excerpted at the beginning of this section, Professor Alschuler makes a particularly eloquent argument in favor of offering some kind of trial over any kind of bargain: "In providing elaborate trials to a minority of defendants while pressing all others to abandon their right to trial, our nation allocates its existing resources about as sensibly as a nation that attempted to solve its transportation problem by giving Cadillacs to ten percent of the population while requiring everyone else to travel by foot. [L]ess would be more. . . ." Does the New Orleans District Attorney offer defendants, as a group, less procedural protection or less favorable outcomes than they might receive in a jurisdiction that negotiates more routinely for reduced charges?

3. *The inevitability of plea bargaining reconsidered.* The Alaska experience suggests that in some jurisdictions, at least, it is possible to have not only a formal plea ban, but one that causes substantial changes in the behavior of the key actors. But even in Alaska pressures led, over the course of a decade, to decay in the original stark vision of a land without bargains. Are bans likely to be effective only for a short time? Are plea bargains an inevitable answer to pressures within the justice system (whether political, legal, social, or economic)? See generally Milton Heumann, Plea Bargaining: The Experiences of Prosecutors, Judges, and Defense Attorneys (1978). Can individual lawyers or judges "ban" bargaining? For a ban to work, does there need to be a more proportional and modest system of punishments? Is plea bargaining a necessity or virtue in highly punitive times? In other words, does a world with no plea bargaining require penalties that judges and prosecutors are actually comfortable enforcing?

XVII

Decisionmakers at Trial

More than 90 percent of all criminal charges are resolved through plea bargains and guilty pleas, leaving less than 10 percent that go to trial. Looking at trials from this vantage point, however, obscures four important points. First, for some kinds of offenses and offenders, the trial rate is considerably higher. For example, in 1998 in state courts, about 45 percent of murder convictions and 20 percent of rape convictions were obtained through trial. Generally, trial rates for violent offenses against persons are higher than for property, drug, and weapons offenses.

Second, 10 percent of all charges may seem small compared to the proportion of charges settled through plea bargains, but there are still a large number of criminal trials in most U.S. jurisdictions. In 1998, for example, there were over 927,000 felony convictions in state courts. While 872,000 convictions (94 percent) were obtained through guilty pleas, there were still over 56,000 felony trials. A small change in the plea rate can have a major impact on the number of trials and the operation of court systems.

Third, there is not just one kind of trial. Public perception often seems to be shaped by long, high-profile trials. But in fact, most trials are short. In 2000, for example, of the 6,746 federal criminal trials, 48 percent were completed in a single day, 17 percent lasted two days, and 12 percent took three days. Thus, more than three-quarters of federal criminal trials were completed in three days or less. In contrast, 4 percent of the criminal trials lasted 10 days or longer. About half of state felony trials are handled by judges sitting without a jury. Judges try a much higher percentage of misdemeanor trials, though the rate varies enormously among the states and the proportion of the roughly 12 million misdemeanors each year that go to trial is difficult to determine.

Finally, plea bargaining practices do not develop in a vacuum: They reflect to some degree the availability, benefits, and costs of trials. For example, when sanctions imposed after trials start to resemble sanctions imposed after guilty pleas, more defendants are likely to go to trial since there is always some chance that the government will fail to prove the case or that a jury or judge will find the defendant not guilty for some other reason.

A useful perspective for studying the U.S. trial system is to consider not only the substantial variety within the United States but the very different processes used in other countries. For example, the paradigm decisionmaker in U.S. criminal trials — the criminal jury — is virtually unknown in some other lands. Other countries employ institutions not familiar in the United States, such as multijudge panels in criminal cases. In Germany lone judges try minor offenses, but more serious offenses are tried before panels made up of "professional" and "lay" judges.

The fact that other places conduct trials in other ways serves as a reminder that the U.S. justice system involves choices. One fundamental question about U.S. criminal trials is why they are relatively rare, compared to plea bargains, and whether that is a good or bad thing. If public criminal trials are preferred to private (and regulated) bargains, will different rules produce more trials?

This chapter examines different decisionmakers at trial. The first section examines the choice between jury and judge trials. The second and third sections study the procedures for selecting jurors and guiding juries as they perform their function. The final section considers the role of a decisionmaker in a larger sense — the public — in watching, reviewing, and judging criminal trials.

A. JUDGE OR JURY?

Perhaps the most distinctive feature of American criminal trials is the criminal jury. While studying these materials and the law related to juries, you should also sit as a judge, assessing the continuing vitality and relevance of this complicated and expensive institution. Consider whether the original assumptions and justifications for the criminal jury remain true today, or whether some other institution (perhaps judges) or some other form (perhaps smaller juries or juries that can convict on a majority vote) would be more appropriate.

1. *Availability of Jury Trial*

The Sixth Amendment provides in part: "In all criminal prosecutions, the accused shall enjoy the right to a speedy and public trial, by an impartial jury." The U.S. Supreme Court determined in Duncan v. Louisiana, 391 U.S. 145 (1968), that this fundamental right applies to the states through the due process clause of the Fourteenth Amendment. Despite the absolute language of the amendment ("*all* criminal prosecutions"), the right is not absolute; the constitutional guaranty of a jury trial does not cover "petty offenses." The *Duncan* Court explained that jury trials were not available historically for petty crimes and that nonjury trials are faster and less expensive than jury trials.

The question of which crimes qualify as "petty" crimes has enormous practical consequences because the largest number of cases in American criminal justice systems involve less serious (but not necessarily "petty") crimes. The Court in Baldwin v. New York, 399 U.S. 66 (1970), relied on the history of the Sixth Amendment in concluding that it was meant to protect jury trials only in cases that were triable by a jury at common law. In later cases, it has become clear that a "serious" offense covered by the federal right to jury trial must be punishable by a prison term of more than six months. In Blanton v. City of North Las Vegas, 489 U.S. 538, 541-542 (1989), the Court stated the test as follows:

> In determining whether a particular offense should be categorized as "petty," our early decisions focused on the nature of the offense and on whether it was triable by a jury at common law. In recent years, however, we have sought more objective indications of the seriousness with which society regards the offense. We have found the most relevant such criteria in the severity of the maximum authorized penalty. . . . In using the word "penalty," we do not refer solely to the maximum prison term authorized for a particular offense. A legislature's view of the seriousness of an offense also is reflected in the other penalties that it attaches to the offense. . . . Primary emphasis, however, must be placed on the maximum authorized period of incarceration.

The Court in *Blanton* held that a charge under Nevada's DUI statute, which had a maximum authorized prison term of six months as well as other possible penalties (including fines and wearing distinctive clothing to identify the offender as a convicted drunk driver), was not "constitutionally serious." In United States v. Nachtigal, 507 U.S. 1 (1993), the Court reiterated that "offenses for which the maximum period of incarceration is six months or less are presumptively 'petty.' . . . A defendant can overcome this presumption, and become entitled to a jury trial, only by showing that the additional mix of penalties, viewed together with the maximum prison term, are so severe that the legislature clearly determined that the offense is a 'serious' one." In *Nachtigal,* the Court held that a DUI charge with a maximum penalty of six months' imprisonment, a $5,000 fine, a five-year term of probation, and several other penalties, was not constitutionally serious.

Most state constitutions, like the federal constitution, protect the right to a jury trial. State courts interpreting these provisions have most often determined, like the U.S. Supreme Court, that the right to a jury trial applies only to "serious" offenses. However, most state courts have chosen a different line of demarcation between serious and petty offenses. State legislatures have also passed statutes guaranteeing a jury trial in a wider range of cases than the state or federal constitutions require. The majority and dissenting opinions in the following case offer two very different and archetypal approaches to the question of when a case is serious enough to warrant a jury trial.

■ STATE v. KENT BOWERS

498 N.W.2d 202 (S.D. 1993)

MILLER, C.J.

. . . On April 12, 1990, a large group of people, which included [Kent Bowers and four other appellants], gathered at the Women's Medical Clinic in Sioux Falls, South Dakota, to protest against abortions taking place there and to dissuade patients from entering the clinic to obtain an abortion. Prior to this protest, the organizers had met with police in hopes of keeping their protest peaceful. The protest consisted of praying, singing and reading the bible. The protesters congregated on the parking lot and lawn of the clinic and blocked the south and east doors into the clinic. Although the protesters made no threats and induced no violence, they obstructed at least one person's access to the clinic.

The police were called to the clinic. Anticipating a violent protest, they called in seventy-seven officers, including twenty-one off-duty officers. . . . An officer, using a bull horn to amplify his voice, read a statement to the protesters ordering them to leave the clinic's property. [P]rotesters crossed the police barrier to go back onto clinic property and to resume blocking the south and east doors of the clinic. The police then began to arrest protesters. . . . The arrested protesters were charged with one count of unlawful occupancy of property in violation of [a state misdemeanor statute] and one count of disorderly assembly in violation of [a Sioux Falls ordinance].

The protesters requested jury trials. . . . The magistrate judge denied the motions for jury trials, assuring the protesters that he would impose no jail sentences in the event they were found guilty. . . . The protesters were found guilty on both counts. The magistrate judge then imposed fines and jail sentences which included seven to fourteen days jail time which was suspended on the condition of no like offenses for one year. [On appeal, the] circuit judge affirmed the convictions but modified the sentences imposed by deleting the suspended jail time. This appeal followed.

The United States Constitution provides in part: "In all criminal prosecutions, the accused shall enjoy the right to a speedy and public trial, by an impartial jury of the State and district wherein the crime shall have been committed." U.S. Const. Amend. VI. This right, however, does not extend to crimes which carry a possible jail penalty of only six months' imprisonment. Baldwin v. New York, 399 U.S. 66 (1970).

The South Dakota Constitution provides in part: "In all criminal prosecutions the accused shall have the right to . . . a speedy public trial by an impartial jury of the county or district in which the offense is alleged to have been committed." S.D. Const. Art. VI, §7; SDCL 23A-16-3. In State v. Wikle, 291 N.W.2d 792 (S.D. 1980), this court explained that the right to a jury trial extends to a criminal prosecution for which there could be imposed "a direct penalty of incarceration for any period of time." In 1984, this court modified *Wikle* when we held "a court may deny a jury trial request in a criminal prosecution when the court assures the defendant at the time of request that no jail sentence will be imposed. This is, of course, limited to prosecution of offenses with maximum authorized jail sentences of less than six months." State v. Auen, 342 N.W.2d 236 (S.D. 1984). Appellants argue that the magistrate judge erred because the sentences imposed on them are beyond the scope of *Auen*.

Violators of either the state law, a Class 2 misdemeanor, or the municipal ordinance here at issue could, at the time of the alleged offenses, be punished by a maximum of thirty days in a county jail, a $100 fine, or both. When the magistrate judge was presented with the requests for jury trials, he noted that although he has granted jury trials in petty theft cases, he would not grant appellants jury trials. The magistrate judge assured appellants he would impose no jail sentences in the event they were found guilty. Nevertheless, after the trial the magistrate judge imposed suspended jail sentences as well as fines. The magistrate judge then placed appellants on probation for one year. . . .

On appeal, the circuit court noted that as the magistrate court "denied the jury trial upon this assurance [of no jail sentence], a final judgment entered imposing a suspended seven days in the county jail was contrary to the assurance of the court." The circuit court then modified the sentences imposed and deleted the portions of the judgments which imposed jail time. We agree with the circuit court judge that the magistrate judge improperly imposed a one-year probation with suspended jail sentences. . . . The circuit court's subsequent judgment cured the magistrate judge's improper sentencing.

We note further that appellants were not denied their Sixth Amendment right to a jury trial by being placed on probation for one year. No jail sentence remains which can be imposed on appellants even in the event that their suspended sentences are revoked. Of that part of the sentence which remained after the circuit court's judgment, not "one day of the defendant's freedom was involved . . . but only his pocketbook." *Wikle,* 291 N.W.2d at 795 (Henderson, J., concurring specially). Appellants were not improperly denied a jury trial. . . . Affirmed.

HENDERSON, J., concurring in part, dissenting in part.

. . . In the case before us, appellants were charged with disorderly assembly and unlawful occupancy of property. Whereas both offenses carry a maximum jail time of six months, the magistrate trial judge denied the request for a jury trial: "I'm not, first of all, going to open up the Pandora's box of giving trials to every Class 2 offense. I have done that in petty theft cases because no one wants to be a thief, but otherwise I'm not going to open up that box . . . so the request for a jury trial will be denied."

Attempting to follow *Auen,* the magistrate trial court assured the appellants that they would receive no jail sentence. Nevertheless, after the trial, the magistrate court imposed suspended sentences, community service, fines and probation. Although the circuit court eliminated the suspended sentences . . . , the one-year probation remained intact.

Both the magistrate court and circuit court erred in denying appellants a jury trial based upon the crime being a petty offense with no jail time. The first problem is defining "petty." Although the meaning and scope of petty crimes are not statutorily defined, the Court announced a formula in *Wikle* to distinguish the two. Courts must look to the maximum punishment and the nature of the offense, consider the common law background of the offense, determine if society views the offense with sufficient opprobrium, and consider the consequences of conviction.

Furthermore, Baldwin v. New York, 399 U.S. 66 (1970), does not hold that offenses which carry a maximum punishment of six months or less are automatically petty offenses. Rather, when deciding if an offense is "petty," the U.S. Supreme Court seeks out objective criteria reflecting the seriousness with which society regards the offense, and "we have found the most relevant such criteria in the severity of the maximum authorized penalty." Attempting to heed to that holding, this state broadly defines a "petty crime" as an offense that carries a maximum jail time of six months or less. *Auen.* What happened to our "eternal vigilance" here — as commanded by Thomas Jefferson, as being "the price of liberty"?

Under *Baldwin,* we are supposed to be looking at the maximum penalty, not simply jail time. Had appellants been charged with the state law version of disorderly assembly, rather than the city version, they would have violated a Class 1 misdemeanor with a maximum incarceration of one year. Thus, under state law, the court could not deny the appellants their mandatory and constitutionally guaranteed jury trial. Admittedly, these appellants were not charged with the state version. However, the inequity is obvious: Prosecutors can deftly deny a defendant a jury trial by simply charging him with the city version of a crime.

Granted, police and prosecutors may arrest and charge at their own discretion. But in Sioux Falls, a person can be denied a jury trial if the city officials believe the actions are petty, even though the state categorizes the actions as serious or when the judge decides not to "open up the Pandora's box," or when the prosecutor, as he stated during the motion hearing, does not want the appellants to use "the Court system as a forum by which to politicize their beliefs."

Despite the majority's labeling it as such, this protest was anything but petty. Before the protests began, organizers met with the police in hopes of keeping their assembly peaceful. Anticipating problems, the police, on the other hand, called in 21 off-duty officers, sent 77 officers to the protest, rented buses, brought video cameras, instituted new methods for arresting and identifying arrestees who might not be carrying identification. This was all set up in advance at an expense of nearly $5,000. Police Captain Gerald Kiesacker stated that he had anticipated more violence and more resistance than at previous similar demonstrations. Consider: The press was given its own observation area during the arrests. Petty? Baloney! . . .

Additionally, placing appellants on a one-year probation without benefit of a jury trial also denied them their Sixth Amendment rights. . . . Probation is an alternative to confinement where the defendant is under the control of the trial court in a manner designed to avoid incarceration. Public protection is provided through the ability of the trial court to revoke probation and impose a sentence should the defendant violate the terms of the probation. . . .

Thus, appellants were subject to a one-year punishment, a violation of which could subject them to jail time. Furthermore, though they may not be incarcerated, their actions are still under the disciplinary eye of the trial court. Appellants Dorr and Ellenbecker took jail time in lieu of the fine. . . . Today's holding permits a penalty beyond [the] six-month boundary. Probation, in itself, involves the freedom of a defendant. Even under the logic of *Baldwin* and *Auen,* the defendant escapes the grasp of the State within six months. Is not the purpose of the courts to protect, not chisel away, the rights of the accused? . . .

When the shadows are cast upon my judicial mantel, I am comforted with the conviction that I stood for jury trials and not against them. As Teddy Roosevelt once expressed: "I shall not join those weak and timid souls who know neither victory nor defeat." I have fought the good fight. Under the Statist's muskets, I have again fallen. So what. "Woe unto you, when all men shall speak well of you!" [Luke 6:26]. And so it may be said of these appellants.

■ MARYLAND COURTS AND JUDICIAL PROCEEDINGS CODE §12-401

(d) A defendant who has been found guilty of a municipal infraction . . . or a Code violation . . . may appeal from the final judgment entered in the District Court. . . .

(f) [In any criminal case, including a] case in which sentence has been imposed or suspended following a plea of nolo contendere or guilty, and an appeal in a municipal infraction or Code violation case, an appeal shall be tried de novo [in the trial court of original jurisdiction for felonies, the Circuit Court].

(g) In a criminal appeal that is tried de novo, there is no right to a jury trial unless the offense charged is subject to a penalty of imprisonment or unless there is a constitutional right to a jury trial for that offense.

Notes

1. *Jury trials and petty offenses under state constitutions: majority position.* Virtually all state constitutions guarantee the right to a jury trial, often by stating that the right "shall remain inviolate." Does this language suggest an effort to preserve a right in its limited historical form rather than an effort to declare a more extensive right based in natural law? Most state courts have concluded that the state constitution does not require a jury trial for all offenses, but only for "serious" (as opposed to "petty") offenses. However, most state courts disagree with the federal constitutional definition of a "petty" crime. The federal courts look primarily to the length of imprisonment imposed as an "objective" measure of a crime's seriousness for purposes of a jury trial. A crime whose punishment is more than six months' imprisonment is "presumptively" serious; any crime that is punished by a shorter term of imprisonment is very difficult to establish as "serious" under the Sixth Amendment, even when coupled with substantial fines and other penalties. Some state courts agree with this approach. See, e.g., State v. Smith, 672 P.2d 631 (Nev. 1983) (no jury trial for six-month prison term authorized for drunken-driving offense). A larger group of states adopt the federal methodology (focusing on the length of the prison term) but conclude that some shorter period of potential or actual imprisonment is enough to trigger the right to a jury trial. The majority opinion in *Bowers* offers an example of this approach. See also State v. Lindsey, 883 P.2d 83 (Haw. 1994) (30 days). Many states declare that any defendant facing the possibility of incarceration is entitled to a jury trial. See Opinion of the Justices (DWI Jury Trials), 608 A.2d 202 (N.H. 1992); State v. Dusina, 764 S.W.2d 766 (Tenn. 1989).

A substantial number of state courts reject the federal methodology for determining the scope of the right to a jury trial. Some of these courts continue to insist that jury trials are available only for the most serious crimes, but they give great weight to factors other than the length of potential or actual incarceration in deciding which crimes are serious. The dissenting opinion in *Bowers* illustrates this approach. See also Fisher v. State, 504 A.2d 626 (Md. 1986) (considers historical treatment of offense, "infamous" nature of offense, maximum authorized sentence, and place of incarceration). Other courts inquire about the "punitive" nature of the fines imposed. A number of courts turn to history to determine whether the offense is analogous to some crime that was tried by jury at the time the federal constitution was adopted. Medlock v. 1985 Ford F-150 Pick Up, 417 S.E.2d 85 (S.C. 1992). Are judicial decisions that look beyond the statutory length of authorized incarceration giving less authority to the legislature? State courts in more than 10 states have declared that the state constitution requires jury trials for all "offenses." The only exceptions involve crimes with trivial punishments or other characteristics that make them criminal offenses in name only. See Mitchell v. Superior Court, 783 P.2d 731 (Cal. 1989) (en banc) (jury trial for all misdemeanors and felonies and all infractions punishable by imprisonment); State v. Anton, 463 A.2d 703 (Me. 1983). If you were a state legislator hoping to draft a new criminal statute, would you prefer your state courts to use one of these constitutional approaches over the others?

2. *Statutory right to jury trials.* It is common to find state statutes that extend the right to a jury trial to a broader range of cases than the federal or state constitution requires. Some statutes provide a jury trial for a particular offense without declaring any general rule about the availability of jury trials. Others declare generally the minimum lengths of incarceration or minimum fine amounts that will create a right

to a jury. See Neahring v. State, 804 P.2d 1142 (Okla. Crim. App. 1991) (jury trial for charge of running stop sign; statute provides jury trial for any offense punishable by $20 fine); Ohio Rev. Code §2945.17 (jury trial for any offense punishable by a fine exceeding $100); Ill. Ann. Stat. ch. 725, para. 103-6 (jury trial for "[e]very person accused of an offense"); see also ABA Standards for Criminal Justice, Trial by Jury 15-1.1(a) (3d ed. 1996) (jury trial should be available in prosecutions in which confinement in jail or prison may be imposed). Another type of statute grants a right to jury trial for less serious cases but places conditions on the exercise of the right, such as the payment of a fee. See Colo. Stat. §16-10-109 (granting jury trial for petty offenses, provided defendant pays $25 fee). A common form of this "conditional" statutory right to a jury trial appears in two-tiered court systems; the Maryland statute offers an example. These laws provide for jury trials in all cases falling within the jurisdiction of a felony-level trial court, and allow any defendant in a case initially charged and tried in the misdemeanor-level trial court to appeal the case for a trial de novo (before a jury) in the felony-level court. This system, in effect, gives even those charged with misdemeanors a statutory right to a jury trial, but only for those who persist in an appeal from the misdemeanor court. See, e.g., Ark. Code §16-17-703. Do such "conditional" systems effectively deny the right to a jury trial to those defendants without the resources or persistence to jump through the proper hoops before receiving a jury? See Ludwig v. Massachusetts, 427 U.S. 618 (1976) (upholding against due process challenge a two-tier system with de novo jury trial for those convicted of minor crimes in lower-level court).

3. *Combining petty offenses.* Will a defendant receive a jury trial if she faces several "petty" charges, where convictions on the multiple counts would authorize the judge to impose a sentence longer than six months? In Lewis v. United States, 518 U.S. 322 (1996), the Court held that a defendant who is prosecuted in a single proceeding for multiple petty offenses does not have a Sixth Amendment right to a jury trial. Lewis was charged with two counts of obstructing the mail, each charge carrying a maximum authorized prison sentence of six months. The Court concluded that Congress, by setting the maximum prison term at six months, had categorized the offense as petty. Congress's judgment, and not the punishment imposed in a particular case, determines the seriousness of an offense under the Sixth Amendment. See also People v. Foy, 673 N.E.2d 589 (N.Y. 1996). Criminal contempt charges have received a more complex treatment. Traditionally, state law empowers a judge to punish acts in contempt of court, without defining the maximum authorized punishment. According to Codispoti v. Pennsylvania, 418 U.S. 506 (1974), a jury trial is necessary in multiple contempt proceedings when the combined sentence for all acts of contempt exceeds six months. How might you reconcile *Codispoti* and *Lewis*?

4. *Trial at option of prosecutor or judge.* As the *Bowers* case from South Dakota illustrates, judges in most courts can avoid a jury trial for some crimes that authorize prison or jail sentences if they commit before the trial not to incarcerate the defendants after conviction. The trial court in *Bowers* made such a promise but imposed a "suspended" prison term, which the offender does not serve unless he fails to complete the nonprison components of a sentence, such as payment of a fine. Should courts consider suspended sentences as incarceration for purposes of the right to a jury trial? Is it appropriate to allow trial judges to "override" the legislature's decision to make a crime eligible for jury trials?

Prosecutors also have much to say about the availability of a jury trial. The prosecutor can charge a defendant with multiple counts of a petty offense rather than a more serious one, or charge the lesser of two alternative offenses if the more serious offense triggers a jury trial. See City of Casper v. Fletcher, 916 P.2d 473 (Wyo. 1996) (prosecutor in battery case could choose between municipal ordinance, for which jury trial did not attach, and state statute that would qualify for jury trial). Is there any problem with the prosecutor initially filing the more serious charge, and revising the charge to some lesser crime (a non-jury trial offense) only for defendants who insist on a jury trial?

2. *Waiver of Jury Trial*

The seemingly simple question of how many trials are resolved by juries and how many by judges is surprisingly difficult to answer because of the lack of uniform records and lack of interest in low-level cases. In 1998, about 45 percent of the felony trials in state courts were bench trials rather than jury trials. But this overall rate of felony bench trials hides real differences among types of crimes and among jurisdictions. Juries are much more likely to try violent offenses, and judges are more likely to try drug offenses. In the federal system in 1999, about 25 percent of criminal trials were bench trials. Fewer than 10 percent of the felony trials are before the bench in some states (such as Alaska and New Jersey), while more than two-thirds of the trials are before the bench in other states (such as Virginia). See Sean Doran, John Jackson, and Michael Seigel, Rethinking Adversariness in Nonjury Criminal Trials, 23 Am. J. Crim. L. 1 (1995). Note that these figures deal only with felony trials. A much smaller proportion of misdemeanor cases are tried before juries in most places. See Neil Vidmar, Sara Sun Beale, Mary Rose, and Laura Donnelly, Should We Rush to Reform the Criminal Jury? Consider Conviction Rate Data, 80 Judicature 286 (1997) (2.6 percent of misdemeanor dispositions by jury trial in North Carolina superior courts).

The number of bench trials taking place each year is not simply a product of the legal rules that entitle some defendants and not others to a jury trial. Many defendants who could insist on a trial by jury instead waive the right and proceed to a bench trial with the judge as the sole fact finder. Sometimes the waiver of a jury trial will be welcome news to the government and to the public since jury trials are expensive and difficult to administer. Judges may even encourage some defendants to waive jury trials, perhaps by discounting the sentence in cases tried to the bench. However, there are times when the prosecutor or the judge will not share the defendant's desire to bypass the jury. In felony cases juries appear to convict at substantially higher rates than judges, though judges have a higher conviction rate for misdemeanors. See Kenneth Klein, Unpacking the Jury Box, 47 Hastings L.J. 1325 (1996). The defendant may believe the judge will better understand a complex defense or will react with more restraint to an abhorrent crime. What interests might lead a judge or a prosecutor to resist a defendant's waiver in such cases? Should defendants have a right to choose between jury and bench trials?

■ STATE v. ROBERT DUNNE

590 A.2d 1144 (N.J. 1991)

O'HERN, J.

A jury has convicted defendant of a bizarre murder that occurred in the South Mountain Reservation in 1986. The principal ground of appeal before us is that defendant was improperly denied the right to have the charges tried by a judge and not a jury. We hold that there is no unilateral right to a non-jury trial in such circumstances and that the trial court did not abuse its discretion in determining that the issues were properly to be decided by a jury.

[Dunne confessed to killing a stranger, who was sunbathing in a public area, by stabbing him in the chest.] Defendant anticipated raising an insanity defense at trial that would require testimony on the abnormal homosexual fantasies that may have moved defendant to attack the victim. Fearing adverse jury reaction to that defense, defendant made a pretrial motion for a non-jury trial. The trial court denied that motion. At trial, defendant raised the insanity defense, having indicated to his testifying physician that he had heard vague and indistinct voices telling him to "do it." The doctor testified that defendant suffered from paranoid schizophrenia. In the opinion of the doctor, defendant, on the morning of [the murder], became acutely psychotic and lost touch with reality. For unexplained reasons, defendant's persistent fantasies of homosexual gratification and aggression blended with reality, resulting in the attack. The doctor believed that defendant did not know that what he was doing was wrong.

The jury convicted defendant of murder. During deliberations the jury requested two read-backs of the psychiatric testimony offered by defendant, and asked the court for the legal definition of insanity. The jury also asked if it could return a verdict with a recommendation and if defendant would receive proper treatment and medication without regard to its verdict. Following the conviction, the court sentenced defendant to thirty years' imprisonment. . . .

As noted, the principal point raised in defendant's appeal is that the trial court erred in denying defendant's motion for a bench trial. . . . Defendant based his request for a non-jury trial on two grounds. First, defendant suggested that the jury would be prejudiced against him by the psychiatric testimony that was to be presented on the defense of insanity. He submitted that the jury "when encountering a really terrible killing which occurred in a public place for no apparent reason . . . may well feel that letting Mr. Dunne off on psychiatric grounds is not adequate, is dangerous, is risky, and goes against their moral beliefs." Second, he argued that because the defense would be presenting medical evidence that would reveal that defendant had violent and abnormal homosexual fantasies, the jury's evaluation of the testimony on the insanity defense would become tainted and biased against him.

Defendant argued that a jury waiver was appropriate because the court would be in a better position to evaluate the psychiatric testimony and the insanity defense without any of the anticipated biases of the jury. The trial court denied the motion to waive the jury, ruling that "this is the kind of case that is appropriate to have the community decide the case. . . . I see no compelling reasons why the case should go non-jury." The court further noted that the proposed jury voir dire would sufficiently screen out jurors who would be prejudiced against defendant.

We deal first with the question of whether defendant had a unilateral or absolute right to demand a non-jury trial, and then with the question of whether the trial court abused its discretion in not granting a non-jury trial.

Over sixty years ago, in Patton v. United States, 281 U.S. 276 (1930), Justice Sutherland set forth the guiding principles that dictate the disposition of this case. In *Patton,* a defendant in a prohibition bribery trial had consented in open court that his trial should continue with only eleven jurors, following the removal of one juror who had become seriously ill. The eleven remaining jurors found him guilty.

[The Supreme Court, after a review of the history of Article III, §2, clause 3 and the Sixth Amendment of the federal constitution], concluded that "it is reasonable to conclude that the framers of the Constitution simply were intent upon preserving the right of trial by jury primarily for the protection of the accused." The Court [held] that "article III, §2, is not jurisdictional, but was meant to confer a right upon the accused which he may forego at his election. To deny his power to do so is to convert a privilege into an imperative requirement." [The opinion included these] principles that remain of enduring guidance.

> Not only must the right of the accused to a trial by a constitutional jury be jealously preserved, but the maintenance of the jury as a factfinding body in criminal cases is of such importance and has such a place in our traditions, that, before any waiver can become effective, the consent of government counsel and the sanction of the court must be had, in addition to the express and intelligent consent of the defendant. And the duty of the trial court in that regard is not to be discharged as a mere matter of rote, but with sound and advised discretion, with an eye to avoid unreasonable or undue departures from the mode of trial or from any of the essential elements thereof, and with a caution increasing in degree as the offenses dealt with increase in gravity. [281 U.S. at 312-313.]

Consistent with those principles, Rule 23(a) of the later enacted Federal Rules of Criminal Procedure provides that "[c]ases required to be tried by jury shall be so tried unless the defendant waives a jury trial in writing with the approval of the court and the consent of the government."

In Singer v. United States, 380 U.S. 24 (1965), the defendant challenged the constitutionality of Rule 23(a), arguing that the United States Constitution "gives a defendant in a federal criminal case the right to waive a jury trial whenever he believes such action to be in his best interest, regardless of whether the prosecution and the court are willing to acquiesce in the waiver." Singer was charged with mail fraud. He offered to waive a jury in order to shorten the trial. Even though the trial court was willing to approve the waiver, the prosecution refused to consent. After reviewing English and American history surrounding the waiver of a jury trial, the Supreme Court concluded:

> A defendant's only constitutional right concerning the method of trial is to an impartial trial by jury. We find no constitutional impediment to conditioning a waiver of this right on the consent of the prosecuting attorney and the trial judge when, if either refuses to consent, the result is simply that the defendant is subject to an impartial trial by jury — the very thing that the Constitution guarantees him. [380 U.S. at 36.]

Limiting its decision to the facts, however, the *Singer* Court suggested an exception to the rule by pointing out that because the petitioner had requested the waiver only to save court time, it need not determine "whether there might be some circumstances where a defendant's reasons for wanting to be tried by a judge alone are so compelling that the Government's insistence on trial by jury would result in the denial to a defendant of an impartial trial." Absent proof of such special circumstances, federal constitutional doctrine remains the same, that there is no federal constitutional right to trial by a judge alone.

The question arises, then, whether we should interpret our New Jersey constitutional provision for trial by jury in any significantly different manner. See N.J. Const. of 1947 art. I, §§9, 10. We are unable to find any significant constitutional preference in New Jersey's history or tradition for a different result. New Jersey's consistent tradition has been that every right and privilege secured by our State Constitution belongs to each citizen, "as a personal right." That tradition includes, specifically, the guarantee that "the accused shall have the right to a speedy and public trial by an impartial jury," N.J. Const. of 1947 art. I, §10, and "so far as [the] right to a trial by jury is concerned, [a defendant] may waive it." Our courts found, as did the United States Supreme Court, that there is no constitutional impediment to the exercise of jurisdiction to try criminal causes without a jury. In Edwards v. State, 45 N.J.L. 419 (1883), the [court held that the right to a jury trial was] personal to the defendant and could be waived. [Nothing] in New Jersey's history or tradition suggests any implied correlative right on the part of a defendant to demand trial by a judge and not by jury.

The remaining question is whether the trial court abused its discretion in denying defendant's request for a non-jury trial. Rule 1:8-1(a) is the provision in our Rules that deals with non-jury trials in criminal cases. Like the federal rule, our state Rule mandates that the defendant must first obtain the approval of the trial court in order to waive the right to a jury trial. Our Rule differs from the federal rule in that except in capital cases . . . our Rule does not require the approval of the prosecutor; it merely requires notice to the prosecutor that the defendant has waived the right. The 1969 Revision of our Rules changed criminal practice by eliminating the State's consent as a prerequisite to the defendant's waiver of a jury trial.

[T]he ability to waive a constitutional right does not ordinarily carry with it the right to insist on the opposite of that right. For example, although able to waive the right to a public trial, a defendant cannot compel a private trial. . . .

Thus, although we agree . . . that the denial of a request for a non-jury trial cannot be a reflexive reaction and must be based on "an exercise of discretion by the trial court based on its consideration of the circumstances of the case," neither the Constitution nor the Rules of the Court tilt in favor of a non-jury trial. Rather, we believe that the more serious the crime, the greater the "gravity" of the offense, the greater the burden on the defendant to show why there should be a non-jury trial.

[The trial] court must consider the competing factors that argue for or against jury trial. One of the most important factors to consider is the judiciary's obligation to legitimately preserve public confidence in the administration of justice. . . . Public confidence in a criminal verdict is best sustained by a jury finding. And when we speak of the appearance of justice, we are not trying to avoid judicial responsibility to ensure the actuality of justice. We always expect judges to be made of sterner stuff . . . and never to fear public clamor over any decision. . . .

A court must always ensure . . . that denying a defendant's request for non-jury trial never denies the defendant a fair trial. But the validity of a claim of unfairness is better shown after voir dire of prospective jurors. . . . In this case, the trial court formulated questionnaires, after consultation with counsel, to be submitted to the jury in the voir dire process. Jurors must have reassured the court that they could follow the law because defendant did not renew his motion for a non-jury trial after the jury-selection process. . . .

Other factors that will tip the scale will be the position of the State, the anticipated duration and complexity of the State's presentation of the evidence, the amenability of the issues to jury resolution, the existence of a highly-charged emotional atmosphere (this may work both ways . . .), the presence of particularly-technical matters that are interwoven with fact, and the anticipated need for numerous rulings on the admissibility or inadmissibility of evidence. The sources of principled decision-making will remain rooted in a statement of reasons that will accompany the decision. This statement of reasons will give structure to the trial court's discretionary judgment and will soundly guide appellate review. . . .

We would never deprive the defendant of a fair trial in order to maintain public confidence, and on those occasions when fairness requires a waiver, obviously it must be granted. Having said that, we must never forget, as we have stated so often, the importance of maintaining the public's confidence in our criminal-justice system. Trial by jury, for reasons rooted in our history and tradition, is one of the foundations of that confidence. It is a foundation not simply because of trust in the common man, trust in the verdict of one's peers, but because it has proven itself as the best vehicle for attaining justice. We surrender to no clamor when we protect trial by jury; we simply accept the wisdom of the ages and benefit from the experience of thousands of judges over hundreds of years who continue to marvel at the consistent soundness of jury verdicts. . . .

HANDLER, J., dissenting.

The defendant is a homosexual suffering from a serious psychosis, a symptom of which was a sexual fantasy in which he would stab or strangle a man and then sodomize the corpse. Tragically, defendant attempted to act out his psychotic fantasy. He was driving to work one morning when he saw a young man sunbathing. Defendant stopped his car, approached the man, and after a brief exchange of words, stabbed him in the chest. . . .

In State v. Belton, 286 A.2d 78 (N.J. 1972), this Court upheld Rule 1:8-1 against a constitutional challenge to the restriction conditioning defendant's waiver of a jury trial on court approval. The Court, now, however, construes the Rule so that a defendant cannot waive a trial by jury except in the most extraordinary circumstances, which the Court neither explains nor illustrates. . . .

One is hard pressed to find within the Court's opinion sound or persuasive considerations that support its determination to make it so hard for a criminal defendant to obtain a trial without a jury. The majority relies heavily on federal law. I believe it misperceives and misapplies that law. The Court, focusing on Patton v. United States, 281 U.S. 276 (1930), . . . seems oblivious to *Patton*'s holding that the constitutional right to a trial by jury "was meant to confer a right upon the accused which he may forgo at his election," that "the right of trial by jury [is] primarily for the protection of the accused," and that the framers did not intend to establish the jury in criminal trials as an "integral and inseparable part of the court." . . .

The approaches of the various states are so diverse they provide no clear direction. Some states require that a defendant's motion to waive jury trial be granted if the waiver is made knowingly and intelligently and for more than merely tactical reasons. E.g., State v. Duchin, 190 N.E.2d 17 (N.Y. 1963). Other states give the trial judge broad discretion in determining whether to grant a defendant's motion to waive a jury. E.g., State v. Bleyl, 435 A.2d 1349 (Me. 1981). Still other jurisdictions require approval of both the judge and the prosecution. E.g., Cal. Const. art. 1, §16; Mich. R. Crim. P. 6.401. Ten states, including New Jersey, provide either by constitutional provision, statute, or court rule that a criminal defendant may waive trial by jury with consent of the trial court. E.g., Mass. R. Crim. Proc. 19(a); N.Y. Const. art. 1, §2; Penn. R. Crim. Proc. 1101. . . . The supreme courts of two states have held that a criminal defendant may never waive trial by jury in a felony case. State v. Scalise,

309 P.2d 1010 (Mont. 1957); State v. Underwood, 195 S.E.2d 489 (N.C. 1973). Several states, the statutes of which do not explicitly condition waiver on the consent of the court or prosecutor, have interpreted those statutes to give criminal defendants an absolute right to waive a jury trial (provided the waiver is knowing and intelligent). E.g., Garcia v. People, 615 P.2d 698 (Colo. 1980); State v. Lawrence, 344 N.W.2d 227 (Iowa 1984). Most of the states that, like New Jersey, condition a defendant's waiver of a jury trial on consent of the trial court, give the trial courts wide latitude in determining whether to accept a defendant's request for waiver. [The dissent cites Minnesota and Missouri cases.]

Under the sixth amendment of the United States Constitution, trial by jury is a right specifically bestowed upon "the accused." Under our state constitution, trial by jury is provided for in article I, which enumerates the "Rights and Privileges" of citizens. Paragraph 10, entitled "Rights of persons accused of crime," specifies trial by jury as a right belonging to the "accused." . . .

Given that trial by jury is a right belonging to the defendant, the burden of the argument would seem to be on the proponents of limiting a defendant's ability to waive that right. Most of the arguments in favor of curtailing a defendant's ability to waive a jury trial, such as "community expectations," "equal treatment of prosecution and defendant," and "preservation of the role of the jury," are imprecise and insubstantial. . . .

Public expectations are often at odds with the procedural protections accorded criminal defendants. The community's criticism or disapproval, like the community's expectations, should not be used as a gauge for determining the protections available to criminal defendants. . . . Constitutional rights . . . are meant to protect the accused, not to promote relations between the judiciary and the public. . . .

Notes

1. *Waiver of jury trial: majority position.* Almost all jurisdictions allow a defendant to waive the right to a jury trial; more than 30 states, however, allow the judge to *deny* the defendant's request for a bench trial. N.Y. Crim. Proc. Law §320.10; Or. Rev. Stat. §136.001(2). About 10 states give the defendant the unilateral power to select a bench trial over a jury trial. See, e.g., Iowa R. Crim. P. 16(1). North Carolina stands alone in forbidding jury waiver through an explicit constitutional text. N.C. Const. art. I, §24 ("No person shall be convicted of any crime but by the unanimous verdict of a jury in open court"). About 25 states and the federal courts also empower the prosecutor to block the defendant's choice of a bench trial. Fed. R. Crim. P. 23(a); Cal. Const. art. I, §6 ("consent of both parties"); Fla. R. Crim. P. 3.260; see also ABA Standards for Criminal Justice, Trial by Jury 15-1.2 (3d ed. 1996) (waiver must be "with the consent of the prosecutor"). Until the early twentieth century, very few states gave defendants facing felony charges the option to waive jury trial for bench trial; amendments to the rules allowing waiver of jury trial occurred at the same time that plea bargaining began to dominate criminal practice in the United States. Is there any connection between these developments? See George Fisher, Plea Bargaining's Triumph: A History of Plea Bargaining in America (2003).

Like the U.S. Supreme Court in Singer v. United States, 380 U.S. 24 (1965), most state courts have rejected constitutional challenges to rules and statutes that require the consent of the prosecution and the court before a waiver takes effect. People

v. Kirby, 487 N.W.2d 404 (Mich. 1992); but see State v. Baker, 976 P.2d 1132 (Ore. 1999) (statute granting the prosecution right to insist on jury trial despite defendant's waiver violates the waiver provision of Oregon Constitution's jury trial guarantee). In jurisdictions that permit the court to deny a defendant's request for a bench trial, the rules (or the judicial opinions interpreting those rules) often say that a trial court has discretion to deny such a request, and an appellate court can review that decision for an abuse of discretion. What circumstances might amount to an abuse of discretion? What reasons did the trial court in *Dunne* give for denying the defense request? The New Jersey decision in *Dunne* discusses the interests of both the accused and the general public in trying a case before a jury. What is relevant in deciding exactly who has a right to a jury trial? Is the constitutional text dispositive?

2. *Written and informed waiver.* Procedural rules and statutes typically require a defendant to waive the right to a jury trial in writing; sometimes they also allow the waiver to take place on the record in open court. See Or. Rev. Stat. 136.001(2) (requires written waiver). What purpose does a written waiver serve? What information should a defendant have before making a choice about waiver? The same information that a defendant receives when pleading guilty?

3. *Law-trained judges.* Most state court systems have different levels of trial courts, with "limited jurisdiction" courts to try misdemeanors and other minor offenses in the first instance, and "general jurisdiction" courts to try all felonies and (sometimes) the cases of defendants who appeal a conviction from the limited jurisdiction court. Judges in the general jurisdiction courts virtually always have legal training. However, a number of judges in limited jurisdiction courts do not have legal training. Courts have usually turned aside due process challenges to this arrangement, but the opinions often rely on the fact that cases tried before a nonlawyer judge will ultimately receive meaningful review by a law-trained judge. See North v. Russell, 427 U.S. 328 (1976); Amrein v. State, 836 P.2d 862 (Wyo. 1992); but see Gordon v. Justice Court for Yuba, 525 P.2d 72 (Cal. 1974) (criminal trials before nonlawyer judges violate due process). What differences would you expect in the arguments that lawyers make to nonlawyer judges?

4. *Waiver of full-size jury.* Most states require a 12-person jury for felonies where the defendant gets a jury. They also, however, allow defendants to waive the right to a 12-person jury and be tried by a lesser number. Hatch v. State, 958 S.W.2d 813 (Tex. Crim. App. 1997). Standards for waiver of juries often include a requirement that the waiver be made personally by the defendant in open court, in writing, or both. See, e.g., In re Hansen, 881 P.2d 979 (Wash. 1994) (waiver of 12-person jury down to 10 must be in writing, personal waiver by defendant rather than by lawyer); but see Blair v. State, 698 So. 2d 1210 (Fla. 1997) (explanation to defendant from defense counsel during trial sufficient to support waiver of six-person jury down to five; no on-the-record inquiry from judge necessary).

5. *Other decisionmakers.* Many other countries involve citizens on panels resembling juries to decide criminal cases. See Neil Vidmar, World Jury Systems (2000). But the details vary in important ways. Some foreign legal systems utilize decisionmakers other than lone judges or juries. Consider, for example, the use of multimember panels in Germany to try serious offenses. The panels are made up of three "professional" and two "lay" judges. See William Pizzi and Walter Perron, Crime Victims in German Courtrooms: A Comparative Perspective on American Problems, 32 Stan. J. Intl. L. 37 (1996). Some parties in the United States hire a "private"

judge — an arbitrator who mediates a settlement between the defendant and the crime victim, as part of a pretrial "diversion" program. What conditions would allow the use of alternative judges to flourish? History has given us judges and juries, but times and technologies change. What new forms of trial can you imagine?

B. SELECTION OF JURORS

Jury members are selected in two stages. The first stage involves the selection of the "venire" — the pool of potential jurors. Early in American history, only adult white males who owned a certain amount of property were eligible to serve on a jury. Over time, eligibility for service expanded in steps, first covering white males without property and eventually reaching all adults. As legal eligibility for jury service expanded, however, the actual methods for selecting the jury venire did not keep pace. Under the "key man" selection system used in many states, public officials or prominent citizens served as jury commissioners (the "key men") to nominate potential jurors. Not surprisingly, their nominations did not reflect a demographic cross section of the eligible jurors in the community.

The Supreme Court periodically has decided cases requiring the states to change their selection processes to produce venires that better represent the community. In the first case to deal with the question, Strauder v. West Virginia, 100 U.S. 303 (1880), the Court sustained an equal protection challenge to a statute excluding blacks from the jury venire. In Norris v. Alabama, 294 U.S. 587 (1935), the Court quashed an indictment because blacks were excluded *in fact* from serving on grand juries in the jurisdiction, even though they were legally eligible to participate. In later cases, the Court did not require the defendant to show complete exclusion of a racial group from jury service: A substantial disparity between the racial mix of the county's population and the racial mix of the venire, together with an explanation of how the jury selection process had created this outcome, would be enough to establish a prima facie case of discrimination. The government would then have to rebut the presumption of discrimination. See Turner v. Fouche, 396 U.S. 346 (1970) (underrepresentation of African Americans); Castaneda v. Partida, 430 U.S. 482 (1977) (underrepresentation of Mexican Americans).

The Supreme Court has also recognized a defendant's right to challenge the process of creating the venire in the Sixth Amendment's promise of an "impartial jury." In Taylor v. Louisiana, 419 U.S. 522 (1975), the Court held that a Louisiana law placing on the venire only those women who affirmatively requested jury duty violated the Sixth Amendment's requirement that the jury represent a "fair cross section" of the community. Duren v. Missouri, 439 U.S. 357 (1979), summarized the current test followed in both federal and state courts for challenging a venire under the Sixth Amendment and its analogs. The defendant must show that (1) the group allegedly excluded is a "distinctive" group in the community, (2) the representation of this group in venires is not reasonable in relation to the number of such persons in the community, and (3) this underrepresentation is a result of "systematic" exclusion of the group (not necessarily intentional discrimination) in the jury selection process. At that point, the burden of proof shifts to the government to show a "significant state interest" that justifies use of the method that systematically excludes a group. Courts have determined the distinctiveness of groups that are "cognizable" under the Sixth Amendment by looking to the shared attitudes and experiences of the group. By and large, this has meant that racial groups and gender are considered distinctive, while age groups (such as 18- to 24-year-olds) are not. See State v. Pelican, 580 A.2d 942 (Vt. 1990); Vikram Amar, Jury Service as Political Participation Akin to Voting, 80 Cornell L. Rev. 203 (1995) (arguing that "distinctive" groups for jury service should be defined by reference to constitutional grants of suffrage, including age groups).

1. Voir Dire

A second stage of juror selection takes place for each case. From among a large pool of prospective jurors at the courthouse on a given day, a random group will be called to a particular courtroom for a specific case. An initial group of jurors are seated in the jury box, and then the judge and lawyers determine which individuals will serve on the jury for that case. There are two ways to remove a potential juror from the box. First, there are removals "for cause": The judge removes from the panel any jurors who are not qualified to serve or are not capable of performing their duties. Second, the attorneys may remove a limited number of qualified jurors through "peremptory" challenges.

Each of these methods of removing potential jurors requires the judge and the attorneys to learn something about the attitudes and experiences of the individual jurors. Jurors are questioned in a process known as *voir dire* ("to speak the truth," or, more literally, "to see to say"). In most jurisdictions, statutes and rules of procedure allow both the judge and the attorneys to formulate the questions; often the judge asks questions proposed by counsel, but sometimes the attorneys query potential jurors directly. Fewer than 10 states allow the attorneys to conduct all the questioning. Some questions are directed to the jurors as a group, while follow-up questions with individual jurors are typical in most places. Regardless of the voir dire process described in statutes or procedure rules, the trial judge commonly retains discretion to alter the voir dire process in individual cases. The greatest authority of the trial judge relates to the content of the questions asked on voir dire. In the interest of saving time and preventing the attorneys from arguing their cases to the jury before the trial begins, judges will often prevent attorneys on both sides from asking some particular questions. Some of the most difficult challenges to judicial supervision of voir dire involve possible racial prejudice among the jurors.

■ ANDREW HILL v. STATE

661 A.2d 1164 (Md. 1995)

BELL, J.

This case requires that we revisit the issue of when, and define the circumstances under which, at the request of the defendant, voir dire in a criminal case must include a question regarding racial bias or prejudice. In line with what this Court consistently has held to be the overarching purpose of the voir dire examination — "to ascertain the existence of cause for disqualification . . ." — we shall hold that under the circumstances of the case sub judice, the trial court should have inquired, as requested, into the venire's racial bias. . . .

The State's only witness at trial was Barron Burch, a Baltimore City police officer. He testified that, while on armed robbery detail, he responded to the 2100 block of Booth Street, in answer to a call for a black male, wearing a black jacket and blue jeans, armed with a gun. When he arrived at that location, Officer Burch stated that he saw Andrew Hill, the petitioner. Observing that he matched the description he had been given, the officer approached the petitioner, placed him against the police cruiser Officer Burch was driving, and conducted a pat down search of the petitioner's clothing. He did not [discover a gun, but he did notice] that the petitioner was holding a box, inscribed with the word, "Dominoes." Despite the petitioner's express confirmation that the box did, indeed, contain Dominoes, Officer Burch took the box from the petitioner, opened it, and recovered 14 vials of cocaine.

The petitioner was charged with cocaine possession offenses. He elected to be tried by a jury. The petitioner being African-American and Officer Burch Caucasian, the petitioner requested the Circuit Court for Baltimore City to propound the following question during the voir dire examination of the venire:

> You have taken note, the defendant is African/American. Both sides to this case, and certainly the court want to make it abundantly clear to you that the racial background of the defendant is not to be considered against him in any way. It is imperative that the defendant be judged only upon the evidence or lack of evidence, without any regard whatever to whether he is African/American or white. If there is in your background any experience, or attitude, or predisposition, or bias, or prejudice, or thought that will make it more difficult for you to render a verdict in favor of this defendant because of his race, then I ask that you raise your hand.

The trial court refused to ask the question. It did ask, however, whether any member of the jury panel "knew of anything that would keep her or him from giving a fair and impartial verdict," and "whether any member knew of any reason why he or she should not serve on the jury." The jury having returned a guilty verdict as to both the possession and possession with intent to distribute cocaine charges, the petitioner, relying on the voir dire issue, among others, filed an appeal.

[In] Maryland, the principles governing jury voir dire are well settled. Of course, the nature and extent of the voir dire procedure, as well as the form of the questions propounded, are matters that lie initially within the discretion of the trial judge. [Informing] the trial court's exercise of discretion regarding the conduct of the voir dire, is a single, primary, and overriding principle or purpose: to ascertain the existence of cause for disqualification. This is consistent with the fundamental tenet underlying the trial by jury that each juror, as far as possible, be impartial and unbiased. Thus, the purpose of the voir dire examination is to exclude from the venire those potential jurors for whom there exists cause for disqualification, so that the jury that remains is capable of deciding the matter before it based solely upon the facts presented, uninfluenced by any extraneous considerations.

[Where] a defendant's proposed voir dire questions concern a specific cause for disqualification, he or she has "a right to have [those] questions propounded to prospective jurors. . . ." That "right" to examine prospective jurors to determine whether any cause exists for disqualification is guaranteed by Article 21 of the Maryland Declaration of Rights.* And the proper focus of the voir dire examination

* Article 21 provides in relevant part: "[I]n all criminal prosecutions, every man hath a right . . . to a speedy trial by an impartial jury, without whose unanimous consent he ought not to be found guilty."—EDS.

is the venireperson's state of mind and the existence of bias, prejudice, or preconception, i.e., "a mental state that gives rise to cause for disqualification. . . ."

In Davis v. State, 633 A.2d 867 (Md. 1993), we quite recently identified yet again areas of inquiry which, if reasonably related to the case at hand, are mandatory subjects of the voir dire examination. Because "[t]hese areas entail potential biases or predispositions that prospective jurors may hold which, if present, would hinder their ability to objectively resolve the matter before them," we concluded that the trial court must question the prospective jurors about them. Among the areas of inquiry is prospective jurors' possible racial bias. . . . Racial prejudice and bias has not been eradicated even as of today. And, as *Davis* recognized, a prospective juror who is prejudiced or biased based on race would be unable objectively to decide a matter in which a person of that race is a party.

In this case, the petitioner is an African-American on trial for a drug possession crime, whose guilt or innocence must be determined by the jury. We hold that he was entitled to have questions propounded to the venire on its voir dire concerning this possible prejudice or racial bias. The trial court's failure to propound such a question was an abuse of discretion.

We are aware, of course, that the Supreme Court of the United States has held that "there is no per se constitutional rule . . . requiring inquiry as to racial prejudice" based solely on an alleged criminal confrontation between an African-American assailant and a white victim. Ristaino v. Ross, 424 U.S. 589 (1976). That Court determined that the constitutional necessity to question prospective jurors concerning their racial or ethnic bias arises only when "special circumstances," of the kind reflected in Ham v. South Carolina, 409 U.S. 524 (1973), are present.

In *Ham,* the African-American civil rights activist, who was charged with a drug offense, defended on the basis that the police framed him in retaliation for his active, and widely known civil rights activities. Noting that "Ham's reputation as a civil rights activist and the defense he interposed were likely to intensify any prejudice that individual members of the jury might harbor," the *Ristaino* Court concluded that "racial issues . . . were inextricably bound up with the conduct of the trial" and that gave rise to the consequent need for voir dire "questioning specifically directed to racial prejudice" to assure the empanelling of an impartial jury.* In Rosales-Lopez v. United States, 451 U.S. 182, 189 (1981), the Court explained the *Ristaino* holding as follows:

> Only when there are more substantial indications of the likelihood of racial or ethnic prejudice [than an interracial confrontation] affecting the jurors in a particular case does the trial court's denial of a defendant's request to examine the juror's ability to deal impartially with this subject amount to an unconstitutional abuse of discretion.

In [*Rosales-Lopez*], the Supreme Court characterized the racial discrimination issue as one involving a conflict affecting the appearance of justice. Acting pursuant to its supervisory authority over the federal courts, the Court acknowledged, as it

* In Ristaino v. Ross, 424 U.S. 589 (1976), James Ross was tried in a Massachusetts court with two other black men for armed robbery and assault. The victim of the alleged crimes was a white man employed as a uniformed security guard. Under a state statute, the court was required during voir dire to inquire generally into prejudice. Ross asked the judge to question the prospective jurors specifically about racial prejudice. The judge refused to ask the more specific question. The Supreme Court held that a specific inquiry was not required in this case, based on the "mere fact that the victim of the crimes alleged was a white man and the defendants were Negroes."—EDS.

previously had done in *Ristaino,* that "it is usually best to allow the defendant to resolve this conflict by making the determination of whether or not he would prefer to have the inquiry into racial or ethnic prejudice pursued." . . .

In Bowie v. State, 595 A.2d 448 (Md. 1991), we held that, where the defendant and the victim are of different races and the case involves the violent victimization of other persons, inquiry into juror racial bias is required. This is the first occasion that we have had to address the situation where voir dire into racial or ethnic bias was requested in a case which did not involve interracial violence. We agree with the Supreme Court that determining an appropriate nonconstitutional standard involves resolution of a conflict concerning the appearance of justice. Also like that Court, we agree that how the conflict is to be resolved ordinarily should be determined by the defendant. Unlike that Court, however, we strike a different balance when the trial court does not defer to the defendant's preferred resolution.

In Aldridge v. United States, 283 U.S. 308, 314-315 (1931),* in which an African-American was tried for the murder of a white police officer, the Court explained why it was proper for the venire to be questioned with regard to racial prejudice:

> The argument is advanced on behalf of the government that it would be detrimental to the administration of the law in the courts of the United States to allow questions to jurors as to racial or religious prejudices. We think that it would be far more injurious to permit it to be thought that persons entertaining a disqualifying prejudice were allowed to serve as jurors and that inquiries designed to elicit the fact of disqualification were barred. No surer way could be devised to bring the processes of justice into disrepute. . . .

While we have not heretofore embraced, in total, the *Aldridge* analysis, we do so now. We hold, as a matter of Maryland nonconstitutional criminal law, that the refusal to ask a voir dire question on racial or ethnic bias or prejudice under the circumstances of this case constituted reversible error. . . .

■ COMMONWEALTH v. BRIAN GLASPY

616 A.2d 1359 (Pa. 1992)

NIX, C.J.

Appellants Brian Glaspy and Victor Jackson were, at the time of the incident, black students enrolled in the Johnstown Campus of the University of Pittsburgh. They have been found by a jury to be guilty of Rape [and related charges].

The factual matrix out of which this matter arises is as follows. Appellants attended a small party in one of the dormitory suites on the night of March 23, 1987. The victim was also a student at the time and was in attendance. On the night in question, the party was being held in a mutual friend's dormitory suite.

What happened next at the party is the basis of this appeal. The appellants have testified and continue to allege that what occurred that night was consensual sexual activity between Jackson and the victim, with Glaspy participating only to the extent of rubbing up against the victim while she danced and had sexual relations with Jackson. The victim's testimony was that Glaspy held her while Jackson removed

* *Aldridge* involved a conviction under federal law and did not involve a constitutional requirement imposed on the states under the due process clause — EDS.

her clothes and performed various sexual acts on her, and that Glaspy also penetrated her anally. The issue of the victim's consent was heatedly challenged at trial and various witnesses testified as to their own perceptions of her consent or lack thereof. The jury accepted the victim's allegations and convicted the appellants on all counts.

During the empanelling of the jury, defense counsel moved for individual voir dire to be conducted for all the jurors to explore any racial prejudices that the jurors may harbor. Defense counsel characterized this case as a "racially sensitive" case requiring heightened scrutiny of the jurors. The trial court denied the initial request for individual voir dire. During the questioning by the court, one prospective juror stated that he would not be able to render a fair verdict because of the race of the defendants. Defense counsel renewed the motion for individual voir dire and the trial judge again denied defense counsel's motion for individual voir dire. . . .

Appellants Glaspy and Jackson argue that the trial court incorrectly disallowed individual voir dire questioning about any particular racial prejudices. Appellants concede that it is within the trial court's discretion to conduct individual voir dire, but cite Commonwealth v. Christian, 389 A.2d 545 (Pa. 1978), as requiring individual voir dire when the court is faced with a racially sensitive case. Appellee responds that the only racial element in this case is that the co-defendants are black and the victim is white. Appellee relies on Commonwealth v. Richardson, 473 A.2d 1361 (Pa. 1984), to support its position that the bare fact that the victim is white and the assailants are black does not render this a racially sensitive case. For the reasons that follow, we agree with the appellants and hold that defense counsel should have been allowed to conduct individual voir dire. . . .

In Commonwealth v. Richardson, 473 A.2d 1361 (Pa. 1984), this Court reversed the Superior Court's order granting a new trial to a black defendant accused of raping a white victim and who was not allowed to question the jurors on potential racial bias. The majority of this Court stated that "[b]y posing such questions, however, the trial court would have risked creating racial issues in a case where such issues would not otherwise have existed." In this case, a prospective juror admitted during group voir dire that he could not render a fair verdict due to racial considerations. At that point the racial issue existed, and it was necessary for the trial court to allow counsel to examine the remaining jurors individually to ascertain whether any juror harbored any racial prejudices or biases that would affect that juror's ability to render a fair verdict. Thus, this case is distinguishable from *Richardson*.

We are not holding here that this jury was racially motivated. However, because the members of the jury were not examined individually, we cannot state that the jury was free of any prejudice that might have affected its judgment. As this writer stated previously, "[t]his type of situation requires that counsel be allowed to ascertain, of prospective jurors, whether personal deep seated biases would influence such a judgment. Often such predilections are consciously not evident even to the one possessing them and cannot be uncovered by the general question permitted in this case." *Richardson* (Nix, C.J., dissenting). In this case, counsel should have been allowed to question jurors individually in order to uncover any deep seated prejudices they might harbor. The failure of the trial judge to allow counsel to conduct individual voir dire was an abuse of his discretion. Therefore, unable to conclude that the voir dire in this case ensured the defendants a fair and impartial jury, we are constrained to grant a new trial to the defendants. The judgments of sentence are vacated and the appellants are granted a new trial.

CAPPY, J., concurring.

I join in the majority opinion and write separately to state that I would go further and specifically overrule Commonwealth v. Richardson as it applies to any case involving allegations of sexual misconduct where the parties are of different races — especially where the victim is white and the assailants are African-American. In my view, to conclude that allegations of rape or other sexual misconduct involving black males and white females is not racially sensitive per se, is to close your eyes to reality.

LARSEN, J., dissenting.

. . . The Rules of Criminal Procedure specifically provide that, in all non-capital cases, the trial judge shall select the method of voir dire — either individual voir dire or, in the alternative, group voir dire. Pa. R. Crim. P. 1106(e). In my view, group voir dire was sufficient to expose any racial inclinations or biases of the jury in the case herein. The fact that a prospective juror admitted during group voir dire that he was racially biased demonstrates that group voir dire was effective in ensuring a fair and impartial jury in this case. . . .

By holding that the trial court abused its discretion, the majority opinion creates an anomalous situation. In effect, the majority holds that, if group voir dire is effective in achieving its goal of ferreting out racial biases or inclinations, then group voir dire is not appropriate and the alternative method, individual voir dire, must be utilized. Whereas, if there is no evidence that group voir dire was effective (e.g., if none of the prospective jurors admitted racial bias), then group voir dire is proper.

The Rules of Criminal Procedure provide for alternative methods of voir dire at the discretion of the trial court. If the desired result is to remove that discretion from the trial judge and abolish group voir dire, the proper method to reach that result is to amend the Rules of Criminal Procedure — not to manipulate the facts in order to create situations, such as this, in which the trial court really has no choice. . . .

PAPADAKOS, J., dissenting.

I dissent since I perceive that the Chief Justice . . . seeks to establish a per se rule that, henceforth, in any racially mixed criminal proceeding, the trial judge is best advised to forego discretion and conduct individual voir dire to ferret out any deep seated racial biases of the individual venirepersons. . . .

In Commonwealth v. Richardson we decided that individual voir dire in non-capital cases would be appropriate where the defense could demonstrate that "membership in a certain group or minority would be emphasized by the evidence presented at trial," thus making the case "race-sensitive." The essential facts in this case with respect to the potential bias of a jury are the same as in *Richardson*. The defendants are black and the victim is white and the defendants assert the defense of consensual intercourse. The Chief Justice attempts to embellish these essential facts by adding that one juror admitted during voir dire that he would be unable to render a fair verdict due to racial bias. [The Chief Justice does not explain why "at that point the racial issue existed" or why, if it did exist, it was not removed by the removal of that venireman from the panel and a request made to the remaining panel if anyone had the same problem.]

Would the Chief Justice require individual voir dire if a venireman stood up in a case involving an assault upon a police officer and said that I can not judge this case fairly because I don't trust policemen or I am partial to policemen? Would the Chief Justice require individual voir dire in any case in which a venireman stood up and professed a prejudice against any of the parties or the prosecutors, etc., etc., etc.?

The Chief Justice's concern for the avoidance of racial sensitivity in our criminal cases is laudable but misplaced in this case. Racial sensitivity is not created by the mere fact that a defendant is black, a victim is white, or that the defendant is charged with rape and the defense is that the intercourse was consensual. . . .

Problem 17-1. Defendant Bias and Voir Dire

In January 1992, the decomposed body of Delores Jackson, a black female, was found in a wooded area in Riceland County, South Carolina. The pathologist determined that she died from a blow to the head from a blunt instrument. After the media publicized the discovery of the body, several witnesses reported to the authorities that Charles Cason had admitted killing a black woman in October of the previous year. Further investigation led police to other witnesses, who said that Cason had been drinking on the day of the alleged murder. He was angry because his sister-in-law failed to pick him up at work as promised. Jackson jeered at Cason on the bus ride home and during their walk down Decker Boulevard towards their respective homes. Cason's neighbors told police that he had in his possession some of Jackson's personal effects after she disappeared, suggesting a robbery. Two witnesses said that Cason admitted several days later that he killed Jackson, using exceptionally crude language to describe the victim: "I killed a nigger bitch."

Prior to trial, defense counsel requested a specific voir dire to ascertain racial bias on the part of the jury. They requested the specific voir dire because two prosecution witnesses planned to testify at trial about Cason's description of the victim. The prosecutors objected to the voir dire question; they said that they planned to use Cason's pejorative words to show his state of mind and not to show that race was a motive for the crime.

The trial judge refused defense counsel's request for the specific voir dire question about race. Rather, the trial judge asked a general question as to bias or prejudice. The trial judge explained that a specific question related to race is required only when there are "special circumstances creating a constitutionally significant likelihood that, absent questioning about racial prejudice, the jurors would not be indifferent in the matter."

S.C. Code Ann. §14-7-1020 provides in pertinent part as follows:

> The court shall, on motion of either party in the suit, examine on oath any person who is called as a juror therein to know whether he . . . has any interest in the case, has expressed or formed any opinion or is sensible of any bias or prejudice therein. . . . If it appears to the court that the juror is not indifferent in the cause, he shall be placed aside as to the trial of that cause and another shall be called.

The jury convicted, and Cason appealed. How would you rule? Compare State v. Cason, 454 S.E.2d 888 (S.C. 1995).

Notes

1. *Racial bias questions on voir dire: majority position.* As the Maryland opinion in *Hill* indicates, the federal constitution requires the judge to ask specific voir dire questions about racial prejudice only when "special circumstances" in the case create

a "reasonable possibility" that the jury will be influenced by racial prejudice. Virtually all state courts now agree on this general principle, saying that some "special circumstances" must be present before a trial court is obliged to ask racial prejudice questions on voir dire. See State v. Taylor, 423 A.2d 1174 (R.I. 1980). What did the *Hill* court hold about the necessary "circumstances"? Older decisions more often declared in general terms a defendant's right to insist on questions about racial prejudice. See Pinder v State, 8 So. 837 (Fla. 1891) (requiring questions on racial prejudice in murder case because such information is of "most vital import" to defendant); Spillers v. State, 436 P.2d 18 (Nev. 1968). While the state may not select an unrepresentative jury venire, the U.S. Supreme Court has repeatedly stressed that there is no right to a particular racial composition on a petit (trial) jury. See Virginia v. Rives, 100 U.S. 313 (1880). If an impartial jury requires a representative venire, why should it not also require a representative group of jurors actually chosen to serve at trial?

Most state courts say that special circumstances must amount to more than the fact that the defendant and the victim (or the arresting officer) are of different races. See Commonwealth v. Moffett, 418 N.E.2d 585 (Mass. 1981). But beyond this, there is little agreement about what qualifies as a "special" circumstance. State courts are split over whether charges of a "violent" crime are enough to invoke racial prejudice questions. Some conclude that a violent crime is enough, but others require some more specific showing. People v. Peeples, 616 N.E.2d 294 (Ill. 1993) (murder, no questions required); State v. Hightower, 680 A.2d 649 (N.J. 1996) (murder, questions required). Rape cases present some of the most compelling cases for questions about racial prejudice. In such cases, courts have concluded more often than not (like the Pennsylvania court in *Glaspy*) that racial prejudice questions were necessary in the case at hand, even if a blanket rule was not necessary. Commonwealth v. Sanders, 421 N.E.2d 436 (Mass. 1981) (questions required in interracial rape cases); but see State v. Jones, 233 S.E.2d 287 (S.C. 1977) (no specific questions required). Why have so few courts adopted a per se rule allowing the parties to insist on specific voir dire questioning about racial prejudice in any criminal case? Do such questions cause any harm? Do the questions create racial tensions or stereotyping where they would not otherwise appear? Do they allow a party to begin arguing a case before the evidence is introduced, by casting a case in racial terms? See Sheri Johnson, Racial Imagery in Criminal Cases, 67 Tul. L. Rev. 1739 (1993).

2. *Voir dire questions on other matters.* The trial court has substantial discretion over the content of voir dire questions regarding questions other than race. However, if the particular circumstances of a case make it reasonably likely that some potential jurors will not be able to render an impartial verdict, the court will inquire into those subjects if the parties request it. See State v. Thomas, 798 A.2d 566 (Md. 2002) (trial court may not refuse voir dire about attitudes toward crime charged; judge refused to ask venirepersons whether they had any "strong feelings regarding violations of the narcotics laws"). For instance, when a case has received media attention before trial, the judge asks specific questions about the juror's familiarity with the news coverage. Again, however, the trial court has broad discretion to decide how many questions to ask and whether to question jurors individually or as a group. See Mu'Min v. Virginia, 500 U.S. 415 (1991) (despite substantial publicity in the local news media about crime, trial judge properly denied motion for individual voir dire relating to content of news items that potential jurors might have seen or read; judge queried prospective jurors as a group, asking four separate questions about effect of pretrial publicity without asking about content of the publicity).

3. *Follow-up questions.* When a trial court allows specific questioning about juror prejudices — racial or otherwise — but limits it to one or two questions directed to the group of jurors as a whole, appellate courts are especially reluctant to rule that the trial court abused its discretion. See State v. Windsor, 316 N.W.2d 684 (Iowa 1982); but see State v. Tucker, 629 A.2d 1067 (Conn. 1993) (court should allow wide latitude to counsel in inquiring into possible prejudice of jurors whose preliminary responses to voir dire may indicate prejudice). If you were representing a defendant and the judge allowed only a single question about juror prejudice, would you use the question? How much success would counsel have in discovering racial prejudice through sharply limited questioning?

4. *Investigating venire members.* In the few cases in which the parties are able to spend lots of time and resources, they may decide to investigate the background of jury venire members prior to any voir dire questions. The parties also might hire jury consultants to assist in the selection of jurors. Part of the background investigation of the jurors involves a search for any record of prior criminal convictions or arrests. How might you argue as defense counsel that the government must share any information about prior criminal records of panel members? See State v. Bessenecker, 404 N.W.2d 134 (Iowa 1987) (prosecution must obtain court order before using arrest record of prospective juror, and defense counsel must have access to same report); Losavio v. Mayber, 496 P.2d 1032 (Colo. 1972) (granting public defender access to arrest records of prospective jurors when prosecution routinely obtained such information).

2. *Dismissal for Cause*

Recall that there are two methods to remove potential jurors from the panel: dismissal of any unqualified jurors "for cause," and dismissal of a limited number of qualified jurors based on "peremptory challenges" by the parties. We now consider the first of these methods of removal.

A potential juror might be unqualified to serve in any cases at all: For instance, the juror might be unable to understand English or might be a felon ineligible for jury duty. The juror might also be qualified to serve in some cases but not in others, as when a juror is closely related to the defendant or the alleged victim. More generally, the judge must dismiss a juror for cause whenever it appears that the juror cannot keep an open mind about the evidence and apply the relevant law. All these standards are straightforward, but they play out in a complex setting. Many jurors would prefer to avoid lengthy jury duty; the judge would prefer to seat the jury as quickly as possible without excusing many potential jurors; and the parties would prefer to convince the judge to remove unsympathetic jurors from the panel rather than using limited peremptory challenges. Everyone concerned must predict the jurors' future behavior based on brief answers to questions that are continually being rephrased. This subtle struggle calls for skills of perception and careful expression.

■ TEXAS CODE OF CRIMINAL PROCEDURE ART. 35.16

(a) A challenge for cause is an objection made to a particular juror, alleging some fact which renders him incapable or unfit to serve on the jury. A challenge for cause may be made by either the state or the defense for any one of the following reasons:

1. That he is not a qualified voter in the state and county under the Constitution and laws of the state; provided, however, the failure to register to vote shall not be a disqualification;

2. That he has been convicted of theft or any felony;

3. That he is under indictment or other legal accusation for theft or any felony;

4. That he is insane;

5. That he has such defect in the organs of feeling or hearing, or such bodily or mental defect or disease as to render him unfit for jury service . . . ;

6. That he is a witness in the case;

7. That he served on the grand jury which found the indictment;

8. That he served on a petit jury in a former trial of the same case;

9. That he has a bias or prejudice in favor of or against the defendant;

10. That from hearsay, or otherwise, there is established in the mind of the juror such a conclusion as to the guilt or innocence of the defendant as would influence him in his action in finding a verdict. To ascertain whether this cause of challenge exists, the juror shall first be asked whether, in his opinion, the conclusion so established will influence his verdict. If he answers in the affirmative, he shall be discharged without further interrogation by either party or the court. If he answers in the negative, he shall be further examined as to how his conclusion was formed, and the extent to which it will affect his action; and . . . if the juror states that he feels able, notwithstanding such opinion, to render an impartial verdict upon the law and the evidence, the court, if satisfied that he is impartial and will render such verdict, may, in its discretion, admit him as competent to serve in such case. If the court, in its discretion, is not satisfied that he is impartial, the juror shall be discharged;

11. That he cannot read or write.

No juror shall be impaneled when it appears that he is subject to the second, third or fourth grounds of challenge for cause set forth above, although both parties may consent. All other grounds for challenge may be waived by the party or parties in whose favor such grounds of challenge exist. . . .

(b) A challenge for cause may be made by the State for any of the following reasons:

1. That the juror has conscientious scruples in regard to the infliction of the punishment of death for crime, in a capital case, where the State is seeking the death penalty;

2. That he is related within the third degree of consanguinity or affinity [to the defendant]; and

3. That he has a bias or prejudice against any phase of the law upon which the State is entitled to rely for conviction or punishment.

(c) A challenge for cause may be made by the defense for any of the following reasons:

1. That he is related within the third degree of consanguinity or affinity . . . to the person injured by the commission of the offense, or to any prosecutor in the case; and

2. That he has a bias or prejudice against any of the law applicable to the case upon which the defense is entitled to rely, either as a defense to some phase of the

offense for which the defendant is being prosecuted or as a mitigation thereof or of the punishment therefor.

■ STATE v. BOBBY RAY HIGHTOWER

417 S.E.2d 237 (N.C. 1992)

WEBB, J.

The defendant . . . contends it was error not to allow a challenge for cause to a juror. The defendant . . . peremptorily challenged the juror. He then exhausted his peremptory challenges and renewed his challenge for cause to the juror, which was denied. During the selection of the jury the following colloquy occurred:

Mr. Lind: . . . Bobby very well may not take the witness stand. We may not present any evidence. Now, do you feel like if he didn't take the witness stand, do you feel like that might affect your ability to give him a completely fair and impartial trial because you might feel like you want to hear both sides before you could decide the case?

Juror Browning: Yes, I would like to hear both sides, but—

Mr. Lind: Well, if he—that's why I'm asking this now. There's a good chance that he probably will not testify. So, knowing that, do you feel like you could—that that would affect your ability to give him a fair and impartial trial?

Juror Browning: Yes. . . .

The Court: All right, Mr. Browning, as you may have heard me say earlier, under our law, the defendant is presumed to be innocent. He's not required to prove his innocence, and our law and the Constitution gives him the right not to testify if he so elects, and the law also says that that decision, if he should make that, not to testify, is not to be held against him, and that you, as a juror, are not to consider his silence in any way in your deliberations. Now, I don't care whether you agree with that law or disagree with it, or whether you don't like it or do like it. . . . My question is, could you follow that law whether you like it or not?

Juror Browning: I'm just trying to think and give you a fair answer.

The Court: I know that's a difficult question. . . . The bottom line is, can you follow the law as I explain it to you and not as you might like it to be or think it ought to be?

Juror Browning: Yeah, I could follow it, if it's the law.

The Court: And if I tell you that the law says that you're not to use, or consider in any way, the defendant's silence against him in your deliberations, you could do that, is that what you're saying?

Juror Browning: I still feel like it might stick in the back of my mind, even though I—you know, I'll try to discount it, but I—

The Court: But you would make every effort to follow the law?

Juror Browning: Right.

The Court: And you think you could follow the law?

Juror Browning: Yes.

The Court: You just have some reservation about whether or not that would stick in the back of your mind?

Juror Browning: Right . . .

Mr. Lind: . . . Despite your best efforts to try to follow that Judge's instructions, that would still be in your mind, . . . and you would have some severe concerns that it might affect your ability to give him a fair trial, correct?

Juror Browning: Right . . .

The Court: You would make every effort whatsoever to follow the law, whether you agree with it or not, would you not?

Juror Browning: Yes, right.

The Court: I'm going to DENY the challenge for cause.

N.C.G.S. §15A-1212 provides in part:

> A challenge for cause to an individual juror may be made by any party on the ground that the juror: . . . (8) As a matter of conscience, regardless of the facts and circumstances, would be unable to render a verdict with respect to the charge in accordance with the law of North Carolina. (9) For any other cause is unable to render a fair and impartial verdict. . . .

The defendant's challenge for cause should have been allowed under both section (8) and (9) of N.C.G.S. §15A-1212. . . . We can only conclude from the questioning of this juror that he would try to be fair to the defendant but might have trouble doing so if the defendant did not testify. In this case the defendant did not testify.

We have said that the granting of a challenge for cause of a juror is within the discretion of the judge. Nevertheless, in a case such as this one, in which a juror's answers show that he could not follow the law as given to him by the judge in his instructions to the jury, it is error not to excuse such a juror. It was error for the court not to allow the challenge for cause to Juror Browning in this case. . . .

MEYER, J., dissenting.

I do not agree with the majority that the trial court erred in denying defendant's challenge for cause of prospective juror Browning. . . . Until today, it has been well established that "[t]he question of the competency of jurors is a matter within the trial judge's discretion" and that the trial judge's ruling on a challenge for cause may be reversed only upon a showing of abuse of discretion. Although not explicitly delineated in our prior opinions, the reason for giving such great deference to a trial judge's ruling on a challenge for cause is clearly grounded upon the fact that the trial judge, as opposed to an appellate court, is in a much better position to decide whether a prospective juror will be fair, impartial, and able to render a decision based upon the laws of our state.

A trial judge is not required to remove from the panel every potential juror whose initial voir dire testimony supports a challenge for cause pursuant to N.C.G.S. §15A-1212. . . . If, in the trial judge's opinion, the prospective juror credibly maintains that he will be able to set aside any bias he may have and render a fair and impartial verdict based on the evidence presented at trial, then it is not error for the court to deny defendant's motion to remove [the] juror for cause.

. . . In State v. Cummings, 389 S.E.2d 66 (N.C. 1990), the initial voir dire examination of juror Walters showed that "Walters was a close friend and supporter of state's witness, Sheriff Barrington, had knowledge of the case based upon newspaper and television coverage and could potentially be biased against defendant if he elected to offer no evidence at trial." Despite the potential bias of Walters, we held that the trial judge did not abuse his discretion in denying the defendant's challenge for cause because the juror subsequently stated that he could set aside his preconceived opinions as to defendant's guilt or innocence and decide the case based upon the evidence presented at trial.

[In this case, after] carefully examining and clarifying Browning's responses, the trial judge determined that Browning could remain fair and impartial and render a verdict based on the evidence presented at defendant's trial. Having observed the demeanor of Browning and having heard the questions propounded to Browning, the trial judge was in a much better position than are we to determine the meaning of Browning's ambiguous responses and to assess Browning's ability to perform his duties as a juror. . . . Browning repeatedly stated that he could follow the law as he was instructed by the court. From this, one can only conclude that the trial judge's decision to deny the challenge for cause was amply supported by reason and was therefore a proper exercise of the trial judge's discretion. . . .

Notes

1. *Dismissals for cause: majority position.* The judge must confirm that each of the potential jurors meets the general requirements for service, such as residency and literacy requirements. At that point, the judge evaluates possible sources of bias against the defendant or against the government. The most common source of potential bias is a personal relationship between the juror and some person connected with the case, such as one of the attorneys. The judge also inquires into the prior experiences of the jurors; for instance, the judge might ask if a juror has been a victim of a crime. This ground leads to disqualification less often than do personal relationships. A juror who has learned before trial about the events that will be disputed at trial will receive special scrutiny. Although prior knowledge of the case alone does not disqualify a juror, a judge will sometimes conclude that the juror who has already learned about the events in question will be unable to keep an open mind and base a verdict only on the evidence presented at trial. Even if the judge allows the juror to remain on the panel, one of the parties will almost always remove the knowledgeable juror with a peremptory challenge. Does this special scrutiny of jurors who are aware of the relevant events systematically remove the most informed and intelligent candidates from the jury? Or is this a concern only in cases receiving unusual pretrial publicity?

2. *Excused for hardship.* The judge will at times "excuse" jurors who are qualified in general and who have no particular reason to favor one party or another. Statutes and procedural rules often specify that the judge may exempt jurors for "undue hardship" or "extreme inconvenience." Jurors themselves frequently raise this issue with the judge by describing the financial hardship of jury duty. See Sudler v. State, 611 A.2d 945 (Del. 1992) (trial court's excusal of five jurors based on their unavailability after holiday weekend violated defendant's right to jury trial). H. L. Mencken, the American journalist of the early twentieth century, defined a jury with this dynamic in mind: "Jury—A group of twelve men who, having lied to the judge about their hearing, health, and business engagements, have failed to fool him." What

behavior might one expect from a juror who faces unusual hardships while serving on a jury? Would the juror predictably favor the prosecution or the defense?

The judge's decision about whether to excuse a juror for hardships interacts with rules about the length of service expected of jurors and the sanctions for citizens who do not appear for jury duty. How do you suppose a judge would react to a juror asking for a hardship excuse in a system requiring 10 days of service from jurors, and where only 5 percent of all citizens who are summoned actually appear for jury duty? Would the judge's response to the hardship request change in a "one day or one trial" system? Under the "one day or one trial" system, prospective jurors serve in a maximum of one trial and complete their service after one day if they are not chosen for a trial.

3. *Dismissals for cause in death penalty cases.* Special problems arise during voir dire in cases in which the prosecutor plans to seek the death penalty. Many jurors have pronounced views about the use of capital punishment, and those who strongly favor or oppose its use may still serve on the jury if they remain able to apply the law that dictates the cases eligible for the death penalty. However, if a juror declares that he would always vote to impose the death penalty, or to recommend against the death penalty, then he will be excluded for cause. See Witherspoon v. Illinois, 391 U.S. 510 (1968). If you were a prosecutor and a juror declares that she believes in the biblical injunction "an eye for an eye," what follow-up questions would you ask?

4. *Recusal of judges.* Just as jurors can be excluded when they are unable to find the facts impartially, a judge presiding at a trial may be removed from a case if she is not able to preside impartially. A party who questions the judge's impartiality may request that the judge "recuse" herself from the case. Statutes typically list some specific grounds for mandatory recusal, along with an instruction that the judge recuse herself whenever her "impartiality might reasonably be questioned." See 28 U.S.C. §455 (lists personal knowledge of disputed facts, family relationship with a party or attorney, and financial interest in outcome among the grounds for recusal). Another federal statute, 28 U.S.C. §144, allows a party to file an affidavit that the judge has a personal bias against him, supported by the reasons for that belief and a certificate that the affidavit is filed in good faith. Once the party has filed the affidavit, the judge must be removed from the case. A party can file only one such affidavit in any case. Is this affidavit a removal of the judge for cause, or is it the equivalent of a peremptory challenge? See Liteky v. United States, 510 U.S. 540 (1994) (recusal and removal statutes require "extrajudicial source" of bias; bias allegations cannot be sustained solely on rulings by judge or information judge received during judicial proceedings). These statutory standards give specific content to the constitutional requirement that judges be impartial. See Withrow v. Larkin, 421 U.S. 35 (1975) (judge may preside at trial despite ruling on pretrial matters such as warrant); Tumey v. Ohio, 273 U.S. 510 (1927) (due process requires recusal of judge who has direct pecuniary interest in outcome of case).

3. Peremptory Challenges

In addition to removal of jurors for cause, all states allow the parties to "strike" additional jurors without any initial requirement of a reason or explanation. Such strikes are called "peremptory challenges." The following Idaho statute sets out the traditional definition: "A peremptory challenge . . . is an objection to a juror for which no reason need be given, but upon which the court must exclude him." Idaho Stat. §19-2015.

States usually allow a specific number of peremptory challenges, ranging from 2 to 20 or more. In some states, the parties have equal numbers of peremptories, while elsewhere the defense may excuse more jurors than the prosecution.

The procedures for exercising peremptory challenges vary enormously. Statutes and court rules describe the order in which peremptories must be exercised, often establishing a back-and-forth pattern between defense and prosecution. Challenges in some jurisdictions are made in the presence of jurors; in some jurisdictions challenges must be made in writing. Generally, to preserve a challenge about jury selection on appeal, a party must exhaust all peremptory challenges. The use of objections for cause and peremptory challenges involves an intense mix of law and trial strategy.

Why allow peremptory challenges? A number of theories have been advanced. Consider the following explanation of the functions of peremptory challenges.

> The peremptory challenge has traditionally served two principal functions. First, the peremptory challenge provides a margin of protection for challenges for cause. [The] difficulties of developing information about bias, together with the risk of error in adjudicating claims of bias, combine to make the peremptory challenge an essential fallback for use when a challenge for cause is rejected. . . . This device has the advantage of saving the time of attorneys, jurors, and the court that would otherwise be spent in probing the true extent, if any, of the bias of potential jurors. . . .
>
> The second principal function of the peremptory challenge is to provide the parties with an opportunity to participate in the construction of the decision-making body, thereby enlisting their confidence in its decision. To fulfill this function, the peremptory challenge gives the parties the power to exclude jurors who are indisputably free of bias, merely because the parties would prefer to be judged by others instead. (Indeed, the preference of the parties may well be not for unbiased jurors but for favorably biased ones.) [This power] permits the parties to select jurors not only for their freedom from bias, but also for such affirmative qualities as the parties may value.
>
> This aspect of jury selection does not enhance the competence of the jury, because by hypothesis it involves the exclusion of unbiased jurors, and therefore it does not improve the accuracy of factfinding. Instead, it enhances the acceptability of the jury to the parties, without in any way impairing the competence of the jury, and therefore it enhances the acceptability of the verdict.

Barbara Underwood, Ending Race Discrimination in Jury Selection: Whose Right Is It, Anyway? 92 Colum. L. Rev. 725 (1992).

It may be helpful to think about a range of potential jurors, some of whom are biased for the prosecution, and others for the defense; indeed it may be helpful to picture the array of jurors along a bell curve (without making any necessary assumptions about the shape of the curve). Some of those biased jurors (and perhaps some unbiased jurors) will be dismissed by the court for "cause," either on the decision of the court or the motion of counsel. But some jurors in the middle of the bell curve will remain who the lawyers believe are likely to favor one side or the other. In theory, peremptory challenges allow the parties to shape a fair jury for their perspective, which may mean both avoiding antagonistic jurors and finding sympathetic ones.

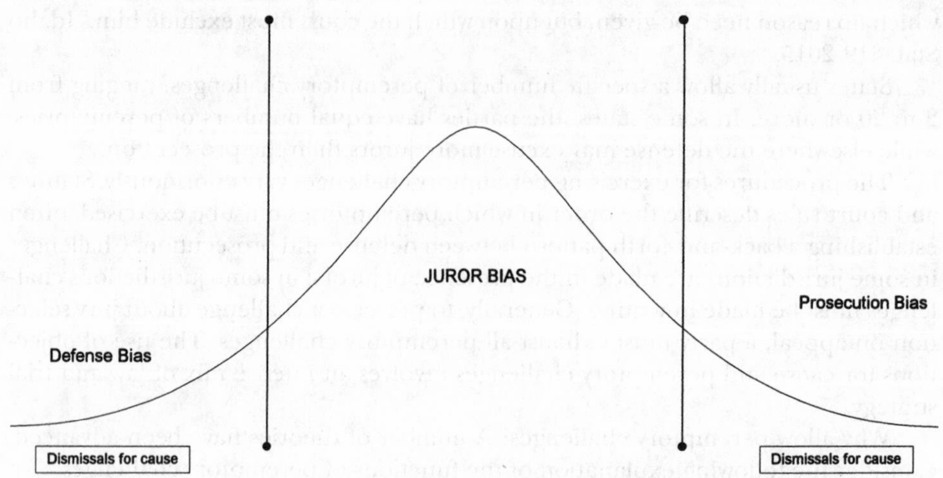

Should peremptory challenges be allowed on any basis? Should lawyers ever be required to explain why they struck a particular juror? Until fairly recent times, these questions had relatively clear answers: peremptory strikes were just that, with no explanation required. Only if prosecutors engaged in a pattern of peremptory strikes across several cases that revealed racial discrimination would a review of those peremptory decisions be allowed. Strauder v. West Virginia, 100 U.S. 303 (1880); Swain v. Alabama, 380 U.S. 202 (1965). In 1978 California became the first state to prohibit race-based peremptory challenges in individual cases as a matter of state constitutional law, People v. Wheeler, 583 P.2d 748 (Cal. 1978). Massachusetts took a similar position in 1979, Commonwealth v. Soares, 387 N.E.2d 499 (Mass. 1979), as did Florida in 1984, State v. Neil, 457 So. 2d 481 (Fla. 1984). In 1986, the U.S. Supreme Court addressed the claim that the federal constitution prohibited race-based peremptory challenges in Batson v. Kentucky.

■ JAMES BATSON v. KENTUCKY

476 U.S. 79 (1986)

POWELL, J.

This case requires us to reexamine that portion of Swain v. Alabama, 380 U.S. 202 (1965), concerning the evidentiary burden placed on a criminal defendant who claims that he has been denied equal protection through the State's use of peremptory challenges to exclude members of his race from the petit jury.

Petitioner, a black man, was indicted in Kentucky on charges of second-degree burglary and receipt of stolen goods. On the first day of trial in Jefferson Circuit Court, the judge conducted voir dire examination of the venire, excused certain jurors for cause, and permitted the parties to exercise peremptory challenges. The prosecutor used his peremptory challenges to strike all four black persons on the venire, and a jury composed only of white persons was selected. Defense counsel moved to discharge the jury before it was sworn on the ground that the prosecutor's removal of the black veniremen violated petitioner's rights under the Sixth and Fourteenth Amendments to a jury drawn from a cross section of the community, and under the Fourteenth Amendment to equal protection of the laws. Counsel requested a hearing on his motion. Without expressly ruling on the request for a hearing, the trial judge observed that the parties were entitled to use their peremptory challenges to "strike anybody they want to." The judge then denied petitioner's motion, reasoning that the cross-section requirement applies only to selection of the venire and not to selection of the petit jury itself. The jury convicted petitioner on both counts. . . .

In Swain v. Alabama, this Court recognized that a "State's purposeful or deliberate denial to Negroes on account of race of participation as jurors in the administration of justice violates the Equal Protection Clause." This principle has been "consistently and repeatedly" reaffirmed, in numerous decisions of this Court both preceding and following *Swain*. We reaffirm the principle today.

More than a century ago, the Court decided that the State denies a black defendant equal protection of the laws when it puts him on trial before a jury from which members of his race have been purposefully excluded. Strauder v. West Virginia, 100 U.S. 303 (1880). That decision laid the foundation for the Court's unceasing efforts to eradicate racial discrimination in the procedures used to select the venire from which individual jurors are drawn.

[A] defendant has no right to a petit jury composed in whole or in part of persons of his own race. . . . But the defendant does have the right to be tried by a jury whose members are selected pursuant to nondiscriminatory criteria. The Equal Protection Clause guarantees the defendant that the State will not exclude members of his race from the jury venire on account of race, or on the false assumption that members of his race as a group are not qualified to serve as jurors.

Purposeful racial discrimination in selection of the venire violates a defendant's right to equal protection because it denies him the protection that a trial by jury is intended to secure. "The very idea of a jury is a body . . . composed of the peers or equals of the person whose rights it is selected or summoned to determine; that is, of his neighbors, fellows, associates, persons having the same legal status in society as that which he holds." *Strauder*. . . .

The harm from discriminatory jury selection extends beyond that inflicted on the defendant and the excluded juror to touch the entire community. Selection procedures that purposefully exclude black persons from juries undermine public confidence in the fairness of our system of justice. . . .

In *Strauder*, the Court invalidated a state statute that provided that only white men could serve as jurors. We can be confident that no State now has such a law. The Constitution requires, however, that we look beyond the face of the statute defining juror qualifications and also consider challenged selection practices to afford protection against action of the State through its administrative officers in effecting the prohibited discrimination. Thus, the Court has found a denial of equal protection where the procedures implementing a neutral statute operated to exclude persons from the venire on racial grounds, and has made clear that the Constitution prohibits all forms of purposeful racial discrimination in selection of jurors. . . .

Accordingly, the component of the jury selection process at issue here, the State's privilege to strike individual jurors through peremptory challenges, is subject to the commands of the Equal Protection Clause. Although a prosecutor ordinarily is entitled to exercise permitted peremptory challenges for any reason at all, as long as that reason is related to his view concerning the outcome of the case to be tried, the Equal Protection Clause forbids the prosecutor to challenge potential jurors solely on account of their race or on the assumption that black jurors as a group will be unable impartially to consider the State's case against a black defendant.

The principles announced in *Strauder* never have been questioned in any subsequent decision of this Court. Rather, the Court has been called upon repeatedly to review the application of those principles to particular facts. A recurring question in these cases, as in any case alleging a violation of the Equal Protection Clause, was whether the defendant had met his burden of proving purposeful discrimination on the part of the State. That question also was at the heart of the portion of Swain v. Alabama we reexamine today. . . .

The record in *Swain* showed that the prosecutor had used the State's peremptory challenges to strike the six black persons included on the petit jury venire. While rejecting the defendant's claim for failure to prove purposeful discrimination, the Court nonetheless indicated that the Equal Protection Clause placed some limits on the State's exercise of peremptory challenges.

The Court sought to accommodate the prosecutor's historical privilege of peremptory challenge free of judicial control, and the constitutional prohibition on exclusion of persons from jury service on account of race. While the Constitution does not confer a right to peremptory challenges, those challenges traditionally have been viewed as one means of assuring the selection of a qualified and unbiased jury. To preserve the peremptory nature of the prosecutor's challenge, the Court in *Swain* declined to scrutinize his actions in a particular case by relying on a presumption that he properly exercised the State's challenges.

[On the other hand, it] was impermissible for a prosecutor to use his challenges to exclude blacks from the jury "for reasons wholly unrelated to the outcome of the particular case on trial" or to deny to blacks "the same right and opportunity to participate in the administration of justice enjoyed by the white population." [A]n inference of purposeful discrimination would be raised on evidence that a prosecutor, "in case after case, whatever the circumstances, whatever the crime and whoever the defendant or the victim may be, is responsible for the removal of Negroes who have been selected as qualified jurors by the jury commissioners and who have survived challenges for cause, with the result that no Negroes ever serve on petit juries." Evidence offered by the defendant in *Swain* did not meet that standard. . . .

A number of lower courts following the teaching of *Swain* reasoned that proof of repeated striking of blacks over a number of cases was necessary to establish a violation of the Equal Protection Clause. Since this interpretation of *Swain* has placed on defendants a crippling burden of proof, prosecutors' peremptory challenges are now largely immune from constitutional scrutiny. For reasons that follow, we reject this evidentiary formulation as inconsistent with standards that have been developed since *Swain* for assessing a prima facie case under the Equal Protection Clause.

Since the decision in *Swain,* we have explained that [c]ircumstantial evidence of invidious intent may include proof of disproportionate impact. . . . Moreover, since *Swain,* we have recognized that . . . a defendant may make a prima facie showing of purposeful racial discrimination in selection of the venire by relying solely on the facts concerning its selection in his case. . . . A single invidiously discriminatory governmental act is not "immunized by the absence of such discrimination in the making of other comparable decisions." For evidentiary requirements to dictate that several must suffer discrimination before one could object would be inconsistent with the promise of equal protection to all.

[A] defendant may establish a prima facie case of purposeful discrimination in selection of the petit jury solely on evidence concerning the prosecutor's exercise of peremptory challenges at the defendant's trial. To establish such a case, the defendant first must show that he is a member of a cognizable racial group, and that the prosecutor has exercised peremptory challenges to remove from the venire members of the defendant's race. Second, the defendant is entitled to rely on the fact, as to which there can be no dispute, that peremptory challenges constitute a jury selection practice that permits those to discriminate who are of a mind to discriminate. Finally, the defendant must show that these facts and any other relevant circumstances raise an inference that the prosecutor used that practice to exclude the veniremen from the petit jury on account of their race. This combination of factors in the empanelling of the petit jury, as in the selection of the venire, raises the necessary inference of purposeful discrimination.

In deciding whether the defendant has made the requisite showing, the trial court should consider all relevant circumstances. For example, a "pattern" of strikes against black jurors included in the particular venire might give rise to an inference of discrimination. Similarly, the prosecutor's questions and statements during voir dire examination and in exercising his challenges may support or refute an inference of discriminatory purpose. These examples are merely illustrative. We have confidence that trial judges, experienced in supervising voir dire, will be able to decide if the circumstances concerning the prosecutor's use of peremptory challenges creates a prima facie case of discrimination against black jurors.

Once the defendant makes a prima facie showing, the burden shifts to the State to come forward with a neutral explanation for challenging black jurors. Though this requirement imposes a limitation in some cases on the full peremptory character of the historic challenge, we emphasize that the prosecutor's explanation need not rise to the level justifying exercise of a challenge for cause. But the prosecutor may not rebut the defendant's prima facie case of discrimination by stating merely that he challenged jurors of the defendant's race on the assumption — or his intuitive judgment — that they would be partial to the defendant because of their shared race. Just as the Equal Protection Clause forbids the States to exclude black persons from the venire on the assumption that blacks as a group are unqualified to serve as jurors, so it forbids the States to strike black veniremen on the assumption that they will be biased in a particular case simply because the defendant is black. The core guarantee of equal protection, ensuring citizens that their State will not discriminate on account of race, would be meaningless were we to approve the exclusion of jurors on the basis of such assumptions, which arise solely from the jurors' race. Nor may the prosecutor rebut the defendant's case merely by denying that he had a discriminatory motive or affirming his good faith in making individual selections. . . . The prosecutor therefore must articulate a neutral explanation related to the particular case to be tried. The trial court then will have the duty to determine if the defendant has established purposeful discrimination.

[We] do not agree that our decision today will undermine the contribution the challenge generally makes to the administration of justice. The reality of practice, amply reflected in many state- and federal-court opinions, shows that the challenge may be, and unfortunately at times has been, used to discriminate against black jurors. By requiring trial courts to be sensitive to the racially discriminatory use of peremptory challenges, our decision enforces the mandate of equal protection and furthers the ends of justice. In view of the heterogeneous population of our Nation, public respect for our criminal justice system and the rule of law will be strengthened if we ensure that no citizen is disqualified from jury service because of his race. . . .

MARSHALL, J., concurring.

I join Justice Powell's eloquent opinion for the Court, which takes a historic step toward eliminating the shameful practice of racial discrimination in the selection of juries. . . . I nonetheless write separately to express my views. The decision today will not end the racial discrimination that peremptories inject into the jury-selection process. That goal can be accomplished only by eliminating peremptory challenges entirely. . . .

Merely allowing defendants the opportunity to challenge the racially discriminatory use of peremptory challenges in individual cases will not end the illegitimate use of the peremptory challenge. . . . First, defendants cannot attack the discriminatory use of peremptory challenges at all unless the challenges are so flagrant as to establish a prima facie case. This means . . . that where only one or two black jurors survive the challenges for cause, the prosecutor need have no compunction about striking them from the jury because of their race. See Commonwealth v. Robinson, 415 N.E.2d 805 (Mass. 1981) (no prima facie case of discrimination where defendant is black, prospective jurors include three blacks and one Puerto Rican, and prosecutor excludes one for cause and strikes the remainder peremptorily, producing all-white jury). Prosecutors are left free to discriminate against blacks in jury selection provided that they hold that discrimination to an "acceptable" level.

Second, when a defendant can establish a prima facie case, trial courts face the difficult burden of assessing prosecutors' motives. Any prosecutor can easily assert facially neutral reasons for striking a juror, and trial courts are ill equipped to second-guess those reasons. How is the court to treat a prosecutor's statement that he struck a juror because the juror had a son about the same age as defendant, or seemed uncommunicative, or "never cracked a smile"? . . .

Nor is outright prevarication by prosecutors the only danger here. . . . A prosecutor's own conscious or unconscious racism may lead him easily to the conclusion that a prospective black juror is "sullen," or "distant," a characterization that would not have come to his mind if a white juror had acted identically. A judge's own conscious or unconscious racism may lead him to accept such an explanation as well supported. . . .

Some authors have suggested that the courts should ban prosecutors' peremptories entirely, but should zealously guard the defendant's peremptory as essential to the fairness of trial by jury. . . . I would not find that an acceptable solution. Our criminal justice system "requires not only freedom from any bias against the accused, but also from any prejudice against his prosecution. Between him and the state the scales are to be evenly held." Hayes v. Missouri, 120 U.S. 68 (1887). We can maintain that balance, not by permitting both prosecutor and defendant to engage in racial discrimination in jury selection, but by banning the use of peremptory challenges by prosecutors and by allowing the States to eliminate the defendant's peremptories as well. . . .

BURGER, C.J., dissenting.

Today the Court sets aside the peremptory challenge, a procedure which has been part of the common law for many centuries and part of our jury system for nearly 200 years. . . . The peremptory challenge has been in use without scrutiny into its basis for nearly as long as juries have existed. "It was in use amongst the Romans in criminal cases, and the Lex Servilia (B.C. 104) enacted that the accuser and the accused should severally propose one hundred judices, and that each might reject fifty from the list of the other, so that one hundred would remain to try the alleged crime." W. Forsyth, History of Trial by Jury 175 (1852). . . .

Permitting unexplained peremptories has long been regarded as a means to strengthen our jury system. . . . One commentator has recognized:

> The peremptory, made without giving any reason, avoids trafficking in the core of truth in most common stereotypes. . . . Common human experience, common sense, psychosociological studies, and public opinion polls tell us that it is likely that certain classes of people statistically have predispositions that would make them inappropriate jurors for particular kinds of cases. But to allow this knowledge to be expressed in the evaluative terms necessary for challenges for cause would undercut our desire for a society in which all people are judged as individuals and in which each is held reasonable and open to compromise. . . . Instead we have evolved in the peremptory challenge a system that allows the covert expression of what we dare not say but know is true more often than not.

Babcock, Voir Dire: Preserving "Its Wonderful Power," 27 Stan. L. Rev. 545 (1975). . . . A moment's reflection quickly reveals the vast differences between the racial exclusions involved in *Strauder* and the allegations before us today:

> [E]xcluding a particular cognizable group from all venire pools is stigmatizing and discriminatory in several interrelated ways that the peremptory challenge is not. The former singles out the excluded group, while individuals of all groups are equally subject to peremptory challenge on any basis, including their group affiliation. Further, venire-pool exclusion bespeaks a priori across-the-board total unfitness, while peremptory-strike exclusion merely suggests potential partiality in a particular isolated case. . . . To suggest that a particular race is unfit to judge in any case necessarily is racially insulting. To suggest that each race may have its own special concerns, or even may tend to favor its own, is not.

United States v. Leslie, 783 F.2d 541 (5th Cir. 1986) (en banc). Unwilling to rest solely on jury venire cases such as *Strauder,* the Court also invokes general equal protection principles in support of its holding. [However,] in making peremptory challenges, both the prosecutor and defense attorney necessarily act on only limited information or hunch. The process cannot be indicted on the sole basis that such decisions are made on the basis of assumption or intuitive judgment. As a result, unadulterated equal protection analysis is simply inapplicable to peremptory challenges exercised in any particular case. A clause that requires a minimum "rationality" in government actions has no application to "an arbitrary and capricious right." *Swain.*

[I]f conventional equal protection principles apply, then presumably defendants could object to exclusions on the basis of not only race, but also sex, age, religious or political affiliation, mental capacity, number of children, living arrangements, and employment in a particular industry or profession. In short, it is quite probable that every peremptory challenge could be objected to on the basis that, because it excluded a venireman who had some characteristic not shared by the remaining members of the venire, it constituted a "classification" subject to equal protection scrutiny. . . .

Our system permits two types of challenges: challenges for cause and peremptory challenges. Challenges for cause obviously have to be explained; by definition, peremptory challenges do not. . . . Analytically, there is no middle ground: A challenge either has to be explained or it does not. It is readily apparent, then, that to permit inquiry into the basis for a peremptory challenge would force the peremptory challenge to collapse into the challenge for cause. . . .

A "clear and reasonably specific" explanation of "legitimate reasons" for exercising the challenge will be difficult to distinguish from a challenge for cause. Anything short of a challenge for cause may well be seen as an "arbitrary and capricious" challenge, to use Blackstone's characterization of the peremptory. Apparently the Court envisions permissible challenges short of a challenge for cause that are just a little bit arbitrary — but not too much. While our trial judges are experienced in supervising voir dire, they have no experience in administering rules like this.

[One] painful paradox of the Court's holding is that it is likely to interject racial matters back into the jury selection process, contrary to the general thrust of a long line of Court decisions and the notion of our country as a "melting pot." . . . Today we mark the return of racial differentiation as the Court accepts a positive evil for a perceived one. Prosecutors and defense attorneys alike will build records in support of their claims that peremptory challenges have been exercised in a racially discriminatory fashion by asking jurors to state their racial background and national origin for the record, despite the fact that such questions may be offensive to some jurors and thus are not ordinarily asked on voir dire. . . .

REHNQUIST, J., dissenting.

. . . In my view, there is simply nothing "unequal" about the State's using its peremptory challenges to strike blacks from the jury in cases involving black defendants, so long as such challenges are also used to exclude whites in cases involving white defendants, Hispanics in cases involving Hispanic defendants, Asians in cases involving Asian defendants, and so on. This case-specific use of peremptory challenges by the State does not single out blacks, or members of any other race for that matter, for discriminatory treatment. Such use of peremptories is at best based upon seat-of-the-pants instincts, which are undoubtedly crudely stereotypical and may in many cases be hopelessly mistaken. But as long as they are applied across-the-board to jurors of all races and nationalities, I do not see — and the Court most certainly has not explained — how their use violates the Equal Protection Clause. [G]iven the need for reasonable limitations on the time devoted to voir dire, the use of such "proxies" by both the State and the defendant may be extremely useful in eliminating from the jury persons who might be biased in one way or another. . . .

■ RODNEY LINGO v. STATE

437 S.E.2d 463 (Ga. 1993)

HUNT, P.J.

Rodney Dwayne Lingo was convicted of murder, theft by taking of a motor vehicle, and armed robbery. He was indicted for but found not guilty of rape. The state unsuccessfully sought a death sentence. Lingo received a life sentence for murder, a consecutive life sentence for armed robbery, and a consecutive 20-year sentence for theft by taking.

At the time the victim, Tracy Plank, was killed, Lingo was living with a friend or acquaintance of the victim, Teresa Cooper. The evidence showed that on the evening of November 4, 1985, the victim and Lingo left the home of a mutual friend together in the victim's car. Several hours later, Lingo was seen driving the victim's car alone. The next day, Lingo was seen wearing the victim's jacket and trying to sell parts of the victim's car. The victim's body was found in a roadside wooded area about five days later. She had been shot twice in the head with a gun belonging to Lingo. In statements given to the police, Lingo claims that another friend, who was riding around with him and the victim, was the one who actually shot the victim. In subsequent statements, Lingo implicates two other, different people with pulling the trigger. . . .

Lingo, who is black, contests the trial court's ruling that the reasons given by the prosecutor for the exercise of his peremptory strikes were adequate under Batson v. Kentucky, 476 U.S. 79 (1986), and its progeny. We find that notwithstanding the prima facie inference of racial discrimination, the record supports the trial court's findings that the prosecutor's reasons for his strikes were racially neutral, and shows that the prosecutor was able to overcome the prima facie case.

The venire was made up of 50 qualified jurors, and the petit jury was selected from the first 47 jurors called. Of those 47 jurors, 34 were white and 13 were black. The state exercised its ten peremptory strikes against the first ten black venire members called. After the state had exhausted its peremptory strikes, two black jurors were added to the petit jury by the defense. The state then used its only peremptory strike for alternate jurors on the first black potential alternate juror to be called. The record does not indicate the race of the three qualified jurors who remained after the jury was empanelled. Therefore, at least 13 and no more than 16 of the 50 qualified jurors were black (26 percent to 32 percent), and 2 of the 12 jurors who served were black (16.7 percent). The prosecutor exercised 100 percent of his peremptory strikes to exclude black jurors and did not accept any of the black jurors called before he exhausted his strikes.

This overwhelming pattern of strikes establishes a prima facie inference of racial discrimination. Ford v. State, 423 S.E.2d 245 (Ga. 1992). To overcome this inference of discrimination, the prosecutor must present concrete, tangible, race-neutral and neutrally-applied reasons for the strikes exercised against black venire members. The greater the disparity between the percentage of black jurors in the venire and the percentage of strikes exercised by the state against black jurors, the more likely it becomes that racial bias underlies the exercise of the peremptory challenges, and the greater the scrutiny the trial court must apply to the prosecutor's proffered explanations. . . .

Thus, we must review the prosecutor's stated reasons for his strikes to determine whether they overcame the defendant's prima facie case of discrimination. In so doing, we must give the trial court's factual findings great deference. We may only disregard those findings if they are clearly erroneous. Of course, we may still disagree with the trial court's conclusions based on those findings and where there is a strong prima facie case, as here, we must carefully scrutinize those conclusions. We review each of the prosecutor's strikes as follows:

(1) The prosecutor gave as his reasons in support of his first strike, which was against a black woman, the fact that the woman was "indecisive" about the death penalty, and preferred a life sentence, and that she had a hearing problem. . . .

(2) The prosecutor's reasons for his second strike, against a black man, were that he was strongly opposed to the death penalty, and had a DUI conviction. . . .

(3) The prosecutor's reasons for his third strike, against a black woman, were that she was hesitant about the death penalty, and initially stated she would not stand

up and affirm a verdict of death and the death penalty, and that she was familiar with the case and a witness in the case. . . .

(4) The prosecutor gave as his reasons for his fourth strike, against a black woman, the fact that she was opposed to the death penalty, and knew a witness in the case. . . .

(5) The prosecutor's reason in support of his fifth strike, against a black man, was that the juror made it very clear he did not want to serve, that the prosecutor was concerned the juror would be preoccupied with his financial problems, and that the prosecutor had difficulty in getting the juror to respond or pay attention to his questions. The trial court found these reasons to be race-neutral, specifically recalling that the juror could not keep still during the voir dire, and, itself, questioning whether "from his demeanor" this juror was "competent to handle this type of situation."

(6) The prosecutor's reasons in support of his sixth strike, also against a black man, were that the juror was opposed to the death penalty, and was familiar with the defendant and with a witness. . . .

(7) The prosecutor's reasons in support of his seventh strike, against a black woman, were that she was very opposed to the death penalty, and that if she served, the prosecutor was concerned she would be preoccupied with a sick child at home. The trial court . . . noted his recollection that the juror clearly did not want to be there, and someone had to be sent to get her for jury duty.

(8) The prosecutor's reasons for his eighth strike, against a black man, were that he was initially hostile in his responses, and this juror and the prosecutor "got off on the wrong foot at the very start." The prosecutor also gave as reasons the fact that the juror's criminal justice degree might affect his objectivity, and that the juror had testified as a character witness on behalf of a defendant in a prior case. The trial court, in accepting the prosecutor's reasons as race-neutral, specifically recalled this juror's responses as belligerent.

(9) The prosecutor's reasons for his ninth strike, against a black woman, were that she knew a witness in the case, could not give her sentence if polled, and that she had a conviction for shoplifting. . . .

(10) The prosecutor gave as his reason for his tenth strike, against a black man, that the juror had a prior conviction, and had indicated on the jury questionnaire that he had a "bad check problem." . . .

(11) Finally, the prosecutor gave as his reasons for striking an alternate juror, a black woman, the fact that she was opposed to the death penalty, as well as the fact that she was a teacher and school was to start the following Monday. . . .

The record supports the trial court's findings that the reasons given by the prosecutor were not racially motivated, and demonstrates that the prosecutor was able to overcome the very strong prima facie inference of racial discrimination.

The dissent correctly cites Strozier v. Clark, 424 S.E.2d 368 (Ga. Ct. App. 1992), a recent Court of Appeals case, for the rule that where racially-neutral and neutrally-applied reasons are given for a strike, the simultaneous existence of any racially motivated explanation results in a *Batson* violation.[4] However, the dissent would misap-

4. . . . *Strozier* stands for the proposition that where it can be determined that the racially-neutral explanation is, in fact, pretextual since there is a racially motivated reason that can be independently determined, the jury selection process is invalid under *Batson*. *Strozier* does not hold that where one racially-neutral reason is given for striking a juror, any additional reason, not also used against a juror of another race, is per se racially motivated. The cases cited by *Strozier* illustrate that there must be some indication that the "additional reason" is, in fact, racially motivated. In Moore v. State, 811 S.W.2d 197 (Tex. Ct. App.

ply this rule by creating a presumption that any reason for striking a black juror, not also used against a white juror — regardless of other reasons for striking a black juror — is per se racially motivated. This is not what *Batson* or *Strozier* hold, or even imply. Rather, there is a *Batson* violation only where the prosecutor's explanation is determined to be racially motivated. Where there are multiple reasons for striking a juror, white or black, it cannot be presumed that a reason applied to one juror, of one race, but not applied to another juror, of another race, is racially motivated.

Of course we are required, in a strong prima facie case such as here, to carefully examine the prosecutor's remaining reasons, to determine if there is an underlying racial motive. And, where a reason is given against a black juror, not also used against a white juror, the reason is particularly suspect. However, we are not authorized to create an inference of discrimination where none is apparent, and where none has been found by the trial court, to whose findings we must give great deference. . . . While we are required to carefully review the record in a case involving a *Batson* challenge, especially where a strong prima facie case is made, we are still required to give the trial court's findings "great deference," and we are not authorized to ignore them. Here, the trial court's findings are not clearly erroneous. . . . Judgment affirmed.

SEARS-COLLINS, J., dissenting.

When it comes to grappling with racial issues in the criminal justice system today, often white Americans find one reality while African-Americans see another. This perception gap is evident in the majority's affirmance of Rodney Dwayne Lingo's conviction. As I cannot ignore the race-based innuendo and subtle stereotyping used to exclude people of color from Lingo's jury, I must dissent.

The prosecutor exercised 100 percent of his peremptory strikes to exclude the first ten black jurors called from the venire. He was content with none of the African-American jurors called before he exhausted his strikes. This is an "overwhelming pattern" of strikes, as recognized by the majority, and establishes a powerful prima facie inference of racial discrimination. It is up to the prosecutor to present "concrete, tangible, race-neutral and neutrally-applied" reasons for the strikes exercised against black venire members. Ford v. State. In deciding whether the reasons given by the prosecutor were "neutrally applied," we consider whether the reasons given could apply equally to white jurors who were not struck by the prosecutor. "A prosecutor's failure to explain the apparently disparate treatment of similarly situated white and black jurors . . . diminishes the force of his explanation for striking a black juror." Ford v. State.

Even if racially-neutral and neutrally-applied reasons are given, the simultaneous existence of any racially motivated explanation "vitiates the legitimacy of the

1991), the prosecutor stated that she struck one juror, in part, because that juror was a member of a minority club. Of course, this was not a racially-neutral reason, notwithstanding that the prosecutor also gave, as a reason for striking this juror, that the juror was hesitant to impose a life sentence. In State v. Tomlin, 384 S.E.2d 707 (S.C. 1989) the prosecutor gave the racially-neutral reason for striking a juror as the fact that the juror was unemployed, but also stated that the juror "shucked and jived." In *Strozier* itself, the prosecutor, in addition to stating the apparently neutral reason of the juror's age as his reason for striking her, also gave his completely unsupported opinion that the juror was dishonest in her answer to questions, an opinion he stated was based on an experience the prosecutor had previously, with other jurors, in an unrelated case. Thus, . . . it is apparent that the "additional reasons," in themselves, were racially motivated and, accordingly, rendered the selection process invalid under *Batson*.

entire (jury selection) procedure." Strozier v. Clark, 424 S.E.2d 368 (Ga. Ct. App. 1992). . . .

The prosecutor explained that one potential black juror was struck because: he was "touchy" about one of the prosecutor's first questions and "hostile from there on"; he had previously testified in a trial as a character witness; and he had taken some criminal justice classes. The voir dire examination of this juror is set forth . . . as follows:

Q: Mr. Cothran, [this] is a potential death penalty case, and because of that I have to begin by asking you this question: Are you so conscientiously opposed to capital punishment that you would not vote for the death penalty under any circumstances?
A: No.
Q: Okay. . . . In a death penalty case, what happens is, and you may already be aware of this — you're a criminal justice major; you've taken some courses in criminal justice; is that right?
A: How was that revealed to you, sir? Was I supposed to answer that?
Q: Well, that's fine, but you put it on your questionnaire.
A: Oh, okay. I have forgot I put it down there, but I have taken some courses.
Q: So you already know this, . . . but in a death penalty case what happens is that trial is divided into two parts. The first part is called a guilt-innocence phase. [I]f and only if in phase one they find the defendant guilty of murder, then they move into phase two which we call the sentencing phase. . . . You understand that . . . the Court would authorize you to consider the death penalty as a sentence, but you'd also be obligated to consider life as a sentence? Now, would you be able to consider both of those options?
A: Yes.
Q: Okay. . . . if the Court charges you that proof beyond a reasonable doubt is not proof beyond all doubt, but is simply proof to a moral and a reasonable certainty, would you follow that charge?
A: If within myself, with the evidence that I have heard and able to reach an agreement within myself, then I would follow that.
Mr. Lukemire: Thank you.

With respect to this juror, the trial court stated:

> As far as Mr. Cothran was concerned, that one got very close to the line, but I do recall when he did make the response concerning the criminal justice degree that it definitely, just from an oral response, I was not looking at him, it caught my attention that he did seem to be belligerent, and I will be very candid about this, had there been no blacks on this jury, the court would have had real trouble with not possibly finding there might have been some type of pattern, just with [this juror].

Contrary to the trial court's statement, however, the fact that two black jurors were added to the jury after the prosecutor had exhausted his peremptory strikes is irrelevant to the inquiry of whether this juror was struck because of racial bias and does not eliminate the obvious racial discrimination in the prosecutor's strike against this juror. Moreover, the trial court's statement indicates that but for this irrelevancy it would have found racial bias in the striking of this juror. Furthermore, the above portion of the record reveals that other than being initially surprised by the prosecutor's knowledge of information the juror had provided on his juror questionnaire, the juror showed no indication of being "hostile" towards the prosecutor. Even giving great deference to the trial court, I still cannot believe that a white juror who gave exactly the same responses to the voir dire questions that this juror gave would have been labeled "hostile" and "belligerent." The hostility and belligerence found so readily by the prosecutor and the trial judge from this juror's one response evoke stereotypical images of the angry black man, who, at the slightest provocation and at even the faintest appearance of challenging the status quo will be tagged "hostile" or "belligerent."

The prosecutor further explained that he excluded this juror because he had served as a character witness in another proceeding. This reason was not neutrally applied, however, because the prosecutor accepted without complaint a white juror who had previously testified in a trial as a character witness. The prosecutor also explained that he did not want this juror on the panel because he had taken criminal justice classes. While a juror's legal background often justifies a strike, in this case the prosecutor asked the juror not one question as to whether the juror would be influenced by the classes he had taken, and when asked specifically whether he could follow the charge of the court the juror responded that he could do so.

To conclude, even assuming that the fact that the juror had taken some criminal justice classes was a non-racially motivated reason for striking this juror, both the prosecutor's application of the racial stereotype of the "hostile black male" and his failure to neutrally apply his other reason for striking this juror force me to conclude that improper racial motives played a role in the prosecutor's striking the juror.

The prosecutor explained that he struck one prospective juror, who was young, black, unemployed, and lived with his unemployed girlfriend and her three children, because he "made it very clear he did not want to be here" due to his financial problems, and might not be able to concentrate. When asked if he would have problems with service, this juror responded as follows: ". . . It's going to cause me a heap of problems. See, I've got a heap — I've got bills all the way up to my neck to pay. . . . I can't keep running down here and all because my girlfriend ain't working, and it's kind of hard on me. I can't go."

The record reveals that when asked, the juror stated that he would not have a problem focusing his attention on the trial. Moreover, the prosecutor accepted a white juror who was unemployed, and at least three other white jurors with whom the prosecutor was content stated specifically that jury service would be inconvenient or would pose a financial hardship for them. Compare the explanation given by one of the white jurors who expressed a problem with service on financial grounds:

> . . . I work for General Telephone, and if I don't work, I don't get paid, you know. I have no sick leave, no vacation leave, and I support my family, and it's, you know — you know, I know I have a civil duty to be here, but it's hard to make a living on . . . the money we receive.

While the white juror may have been better able to articulate his position, he made it no less clear that he did not want to be there. Yet the prosecutor accepted the white juror.

I would find on the basis of either of the above jurors alone that the prosecutor failed to overcome the powerful prima facie case of racial discrimination. In rebuffing the *Batson* challenge, the majority stresses the *Batson* edict that the trial court is to be afforded "great deference." I do not believe that "great deference" means ignoring blatant discrimination. . . .

With respect to seven of the black jurors struck by the prosecutor (including a prospective alternate juror), the prosecutor explained that the jurors had some aversion to the death penalty. The record reveals that one of the black jurors struck for this reason repeatedly indicated she was willing to impose a death sentence if warranted by the circumstances, and two others were hesitant about the death penalty, but said that they could consider it as a form of punishment after hearing the evidence. However, in ruling in the state's favor on the defendant's *Batson* motion, the trial court stated his recollection that while both black and white jurors expressed hesitancy about the death penalty, the black jurors struck for that reason were more adamant against the death penalty than were the white jurors. Even if we defer to the trial court's decision that this is a race-neutral reason, the fact remains that included among the prosecutor's reasons for striking those jurors were other reasons that were not well-founded in the record or were not neutrally applied among the black and white jurors. For example, the prosecutor reasoned that one potential juror would not be able to state her decision when polled in court. The record reveals, however, that the juror initially misunderstood the prosecutor's question; when it was clarified, she said that she would be able to give her decision when polled. Also, the prosecutor stated that one black prospective juror was struck because the juror had a hearing problem. While the prosecutor said that the juror had a hearing problem, the record indicates that the juror never claimed to have a hearing problem, and the state had no objection to a white juror who told the prosecutor twice during voir dire that he had a hearing problem.

The prosecutor stated that four black jurors were struck, among other reasons, because they knew witnesses. The record reveals that the state accepted six white jurors who also knew witnesses. Two of the four black jurors struck for this reason indicated they knew witnesses by sight but did not have personal relationships with those witnesses. Among the white jurors accepted by the state who knew witnesses, however, one played cards with two witnesses, while another had lived in the same neighborhood and belonged to the same church as a witness. . . .

The majority states that I would apply Strozier v. Clark to "create a presumption that any reason for striking a black juror, not also used against a white juror — regardless of other reasons for striking a black juror — is, per se racially motivated." That is not correct. To the contrary, as the majority itself notes, the inference of discrimination in this case is created by the prima facie case, which the prosecutor carries the burden of overcoming. I would apply to this case the rule established by this court that where there is a strong prima facie case, the prosecutor's reason for his strikes must be neutrally applied. Moreover, contrary to the implication in the majority, I do not say that any one non-neutrally applied reason renders the jury selection invalid, but that when inequity in application so permeates the process, the fact that a race-neutral reason was also given cannot . . . remedy the discrimination. The majority opinion does not refute the *Strozier* rule, but implies that it should not apply in this case because the "bad" reasons in *Strozier* were facially race-based or pretextual, whereas in this case it is necessary to look at all of the reasons given by the prosecutor to discern the overriding racial foundation for the strikes. I believe that this is a dangerous distinction without a difference, as subtle racial discrimination is just as damaging, if not more so, as overt racial discrimination.

We stand at the edge of the 21st century and many people of color in this country are still not free from insidious racial discrimination such as that manifested in this case. The constitutions of the United States and of Georgia demand the total, uncompromising racial neutrality of the jury selection process to ensure every American's right to fully participate, and Rodney Dwayne Lingo did not receive that neutrality. My candor in this dissent may lead some to believe that I am "hostile." I am not. I am, however, fully committed to the promise of the U.S. and Georgia Constitutions to afford their rights and privileges to all citizens.

Notes

1. *Number and theory of peremptory challenges: majority view.* States generally allow the most peremptory challenges in capital cases and the least in misdemeanor cases. In capital cases the number of challenges allowed varies between 4 (in Virginia) and 25 (in Connecticut), with the majority of capital states allowing between 12 and 20. Some of these states grant the defense more challenges than the prosecution. For felonies, states allow between 3 (Hawaii and New Hampshire) and 20 (New Jersey) peremptory challenges, with about a third of states allowing 6 challenges. As with capital cases, a significant minority of states provide the prosecution with fewer possible challenges than the defense. For misdemeanor jury trials, the number of peremptory challenges allowed ranges between 2 (Missouri) and 10 (California and New Jersey), with almost half the states allowing 3 possible challenges. Bureau of Justice Statistics, State Court Organization 1998, at tbl. 41 (June 2000, NCJ 178932). Peremptory challenges were allowed in the Judiciary Act of 1790 for treason and felonies punishable by death. In felony cases the federal system currently allows 10 strikes for the defense but only 6 for the prosecution. Fed. R. Crim. P. 24. In 1993, about 20 percent of all potential federal jurors were excluded through peremptory challenge. Under what theory are far greater numbers of challenges allowed in more serious cases? What differences explain the wide range in the numbers of peremptory challenges allowed in capital and serious felony cases?

In multidefendant trials some states allow each defendant to exercise an individual allotment of peremptory challenges. See, e.g., Wyo. Stat. §711.103 ("The number of peremptory challenges allowed to the prosecution shall be multiplied by the number of defendants on trial in each case. Each defendant shall be allowed separate peremptory challenges"). Those states typically provide the prosecution with proportionately greater number of challenges as well. Some states limit the total number of peremptories in multidefendant trials and require defendants to use fewer than if they were tried separately. See, e.g., Cal. Code Crim. Proc. §231(a) ("When two or more defendants are jointly tried, their challenges shall be exercised jointly, but each defendant shall also be entitled to five additional challenges which may be exercised separately, and the people shall also be entitled to additional challenges equal to the number of all the additional separate challenges allowed the defendants"). What theory of peremptory challenges supports limits on total peremptory challenges regardless of the number of defendants? What theory allows each defendant a separate allotment of peremptory challenges? Theories explaining peremptory challenges rely on often unstated assumptions. It is useful to articulate these assumptions and consider how you might test them. For example, if the goal of peremptories is thought to be the elimination of biased jurors, can jurors be tested for bias? See Hans Zeisel and Shari Diamond, The Effect of Peremptory Challenges on Jury and Verdict: An Experiment in a Federal District Court, 30 Stan. L. Rev. 491 (1978). If the goal of peremptories is to provide defendants with greater confidence in the fairness of the system, can this be tested? What other benefits might peremptories provide?

2. *Racial discrimination in peremptory challenges. Batson* has generated an enormous volume of state and federal case law as courts have wrestled with numerous claims of discrimination and pretext. *Batson* has also produced a large volume of commentary, with observers variously applauding the decision or criticizing it for not going far enough, for being unworkable, or for undermining an essential component of adversary trials. See, e.g., Barbara Underwood, Ending Race Discrimination in Jury Selection: Whose Right Is It, Anyway? 92 Colum. L. Rev. 725 (1992); Albert Alschuler, The Supreme Court and the Jury: Voir Dire, Peremptory Challenges, and the Review of Jury Verdicts, 56 U. Chi. L. Rev. 153 (1989). Some state legislatures have tried to clarify the law by codified the right recognized in *Batson.* See, e.g., Tex. Code Crim. Proc. art. 35.261; La. Code Crim. Proc. art. 795.

3. *Making a* Batson *claim.* Many difficult legal and strategic questions arise under *Batson.* However, it is not legal but factual and strategic decisions that dominate day-to-day jury practice. The court in *Batson* sketched the basic procedure, which largely mirrors federal discrimination claims made under Title VII: First, the defendant must establish a prima facie case of intentional discrimination; second, the prosecutor must offer a neutral explanation for why it struck black jurors; finally, the trial court determines whether or not there has been "purposeful discrimination." In 1995 the Supreme Court, in the case of Purkett v. Elem, 514 U.S. 765 (1995), strengthened the analogy between *Batson* claims and claims made under Title VII when it held that the government's burden at the second stage is merely a burden of production that can be satisfied by virtually any race-neutral explanation, and that it is the defendant who carries the burden of persuasion that purposeful discrimination has in fact occurred. Some states and federal courts have developed additional rules to guide litigants and the courts at each of the stages of a *Batson* claim. For example, in a widely cited decision, the Alabama Supreme Court identified factors to help decide when a defendant has made a sufficient prima facie case. Ex parte Branch, 526 So. 2d 609, 622-623 (Ala. 1987):

> In determining whether there is a prima facie case, the court is to consider "all relevant circumstances" which could lead to an inference of discrimination. The following are illustrative of the types of evidence that can be used to raise the inference of discrimination:
>
> 1. Evidence that the "jurors in question share[d] only this one characteristic — their membership in the group — that in all other respects they [were] as heterogeneous as the community as a whole." For instance "it may be significant that the persons challenged, although all black, include both men and women and are a variety of ages, occupations, and social or economic conditions," indicating that race was the deciding factor.
>
> 2. A pattern of strikes against black jurors on the particular venire; e.g., 4 of 6 peremptory challenges were used to strike black jurors.
>
> 3. The past conduct of the state's attorney in using peremptory challenges to strike all blacks from the jury venire.
>
> 4. The type and manner of the state's attorney's questions and statements during voir dire, including nothing more than desultory voir dire.

5. The type and manner of questions directed to the challenged juror, including a lack of questions, or a lack of meaningful questions.

6. Disparate treatment of members of the jury venire with the same characteristics, or who answer a question in the same or similar manner; e.g., . . . a black elementary school teacher was struck as being potentially too liberal because of his job, but a white elementary school teacher was not challenged.

7. Disparate examination of members of the venire; e.g., . . . a question designed to provoke a certain response that is likely to disqualify a juror was asked to black jurors, but not to white jurors.

8. Circumstantial evidence of intent may be proven by disparate impact where all or most of the challenges were used to strike blacks from the jury.

9. The state used peremptory challenges to dismiss all or most black jurors.

Trial courts are relatively amenable to hearing *Batson* challenges — in other words, recognizing that a prima facie case has been made — but find purposeful discrimination and grant relief much less often. See Kenneth Melilli, *Batson* in Practice: What We Have Learned About *Batson* and Peremptory Challenges, 71 Notre Dame L. Rev. 447 (1996). Professor Melilli studied all published *Batson* decisions in state and federal court between April 1986 and December 1993. He found that about 60 percent of prima facie claims were recognized by the court but that only about 20 percent of *Batson* claims resulted in a finding of discriminatory peremptory strikes.

4. *Pretext and truth.* The *Lingo* case illustrates both the established dynamic for *Batson* claims and the difficulty, for both trial and appellate courts, in assessing whether intentional discrimination has occurred. The key element of *Batson* battles are the explanations given by the prosecutor for striking one or more jurors. While courts hesitate to find a prima facie case when only a single juror strike is identified by the defendant as discriminatory, the decisions of trial and appellate courts often turn on the reasons given by the prosecutor for only one or two jurors, as in *Lingo.* Especially after Purkett v. Elem, prosecutors often find it easy to offer some race-neutral explanation for every juror: The difficult questions are whether the explanation, if honest, is sufficient and whether the explanation in each case is the "true" reason for a strike or is a pretext for striking a juror on the basis of race. See Mackintrush v. State, 978 S.W.2d 293 (Ark. 1998) (after second stage, when race-neutral explanation is given for prima facie pattern, court must accept that explanation unless challenger brings in additional evidence calling that explanation into doubt).

Many of the reasons prosecutors offer for strikes are generally accepted by trial courts and receive little examination on appellate review. *Lingo* provides several illustrations, including opposition to the death penalty (especially in death penalty cases), prior criminal record on the part of the juror, relationship or acquaintance with a witness, and involvement in prior court proceedings. Are there particular kinds of explanations that should not be allowed because trial courts cannot easily assess whether they are the real reason? Which of the following reasons given by prosecutors for striking jurors seem most likely to be true, and which seem to be a pretext? Does the difficulty of this judgment reveal the flaws or virtues of the *Batson* approach?

- appearance, e.g., shoulder-length, curly, unkempt hair, along with a mustache and a goatee-type beard (Purkett v. Elem); overweight; "a young, pretty woman" who might be "attracted to defendant or defense counsel"
- religious affiliation

- marital status
- education
- employment
- unemployment, e.g., "unemployed people are less likely to be sympathetic to the prosecution"
- age, e.g., "every juror below the age of thirty because . . . from my experience as a prosecutor and defense lawyer . . . older jurors are generally more likely to be prosecution minded or favorable to the prosecution"
- disability
- economic status
- sexual orientation
- place of residence, e.g., "high crime area"
- habits, e.g., "excessively verbal"; "loner"; "inattentive"
- fortuitous links: juror has same last name as defense lawyer

Most courts reject simple "gut feelings" or "hunches" as a reason to strike a juror, though it is sometimes difficult to distinguish gut feelings from the reasons that are offered. Is it possible to categorize explanations for strikes and to provide different standards of review to different types of explanations? If not, is the whole *Batson* scheme unworkable? Can't any bright lawyer with sufficient knowledge and planning always find a defensible reason to strike any juror? See Robin Charlow, Tolerating Deception and Discrimination After *Batson,* 50 Stan. L. Rev. 9 (1997); Andrew D. Leipold, Constitutionalizing Jury Selection in Criminal Cases: A Critical Evaluation, 86 Geo. L.J. 945 (1998); Michael Raphael and Edward Ungvarsky, Excuses, Excuses: Neutral Explanations Under *Batson v. Kentucky,* 27 U. Mich. J.L. Ref. 229 (1993).

5. *Race and decision making.* Did the Court in *Batson* assume that the race of the juror will systematically lead to different judgments? Is such a belief necessary to justify the decision? Professor Sheri Lynn Johnson critiqued the available research in 1985 and reached the following conclusions:

> Laboratory findings concerning the influence of race on white subjects' perception of criminal defendants are quite consistent. More than a dozen mock jury studies provide support for the hypothesis that racial bias affects the determination of guilt. . . . Nine very recent experiments find that the race of the defendant significantly and directly affects the determination of guilt. White subjects in all of these studies were more likely to find a minority-race defendant guilty than they were to find an identically situated white defendant guilty. Four studies find a significant interaction between the race of the defendant, guilt attribution, and some third variable. The one study that did not find any differences based on the race of the defendant may be reconciled with these findings based upon a careful analysis of its methodology.

Johnson, Black Innocence and the White Jury, 83 Mich. L. Rev. 1611, 1625-1626 (1985).

The *Batson* dissenters worried that allowing a discrimination claim for racial bias in peremptory challenges would require courts to recognize similar claims for peremptory challenges based on gender bias or other kinds of discrimination. The Supreme Court recognized the possibility of *Batson* claims on the basis of strikes against Latinos in Hernandez v. New York, 500 U.S. 352 (1991). In J.E.B. v. Alabama ex rel. T.B., 511 U.S. 127 (1994), the Court did extend *Batson* to cover peremptory challenges based on gender bias, holding that "gender, like race, is an unconstitutional proxy for juror competence and impartiality." State courts and lower federal courts have wrestled with the application of the *Batson* framework to claims of discrimination against other groups.

Problem 17-2. Extending *Batson*

Defendant Edward Lee Davis, an African American man, was charged with aggravated robbery. No jurors were struck for cause during the jury selection. The defense, however, exercised four of its five peremptory strikes, while the state used one of its three. When the state used the one peremptory to strike a black man from the jury panel, defense counsel objected and asked for a race-neutral explanation. The prosecutor, in response, stated for the record that the prospective juror would have been a very good juror for the state and that race had nothing to do with her decision to strike. She explained:

> However, it was highly significant to the State that the man was a Jehovah's Witness. I have a great deal of familiarity with the sect of Jehovah's Witness. I would never, if I had a peremptory challenge left, fail to strike a Jehovah's Witness from my jury. In my experience that faith is very integral to their daily life in many ways. At least three times a week he goes to church for separate meetings. The Jehovah's Witness faith is of a mind the higher powers will take care of all things necessary. In my experience Jehovah's Witnesses are reluctant to exercise authority over their fellow human beings in this Court House.

The prosecutor concluded her statement by saying she did not feel it appropriate "to pry" into this matter with the juror because there was no need to do so when exercising a peremptory on race-neutral grounds. Defense counsel had nothing further to add, and the trial judge ruled the peremptory strike would stand.

The defendant concedes the state's peremptory was exercised for race-neutral reasons but contends that the race-neutral explanation offered by the state is constitutionally impermissible as religious discrimination. How would you rule on appeal? See State v. Davis, 504 N.W.2d 767 (Minn. 1993).

Notes

1. *Extending* Batson *claims to other groups: majority view.* The U.S. Supreme Court has extended the coverage of *Batson* in a line of cases. A prima facie case of racial discrimination arises when a party uses peremptory strikes to exclude Latinos from the jury. Hernandez v. New York, 500 U.S. 352 (1991); State v. Alen, 616 So. 2d 452 (Fla. 1993) (recognizing *Batson* claims for Hispanics). The Court applied the *Batson* framework to claims of gender discrimination in J.E.B. v. Alabama ex rel. T.B., 511 U.S. 127 (1994). State courts continue to wrestle with the application of *Batson* and analogous state decisions to nonracial challenges. For example, states are divided on whether to extend *Batson* to claims based on religious orientation. See Casarez v.

State, 913 S.W.2d 468 (Tex. Crim. App. 1994) (allowing peremptory challenges based on religious orientation); State v. Hodge, 726 A.2d 531 (Conn. 1999). The battle over the extension of *Batson* does not extend only to groups subject to heightened standards of review under equal protection analysis. See, e.g., Commonwealth v. Carleton, 641 N.E.2d 1057 (Mass. 1994) (applying *Batson* to prosecutor's effort to strike all jurors with Irish-sounding names).

2. *Extending* Batson *to other proceedings and parties.* The federal and state courts have also extended the Batson limits on peremptory challenges to parties other than the prosecutor and to proceedings other than a criminal trial. In Powers v. Ohio, 499 U.S. 400 (1991), the Court held that any litigant, regardless of race, could raise a claim of racially discriminatory peremptory challenges. In Edmonson v. Leesville Concrete Co., Inc., 500 U.S. 614 (1991), the Court extended the prohibition against race-based strikes to civil trials. A year after *Edmonson,* the Court accepted challenges by prosecutors to race-based peremptory strikes by defendants in Georgia v. McCollum, 505 U.S. 42 (1992). While *Batson* claims can be made now in civil or criminal cases, and by defendants or prosecutors, criminal defendants made about 90 percent of *Batson* claims from 1991 to 1993 in state and federal courts. See Kenneth Melilli, *Batson* in Practice: What We Have Learned About *Batson* and Peremptory Challenges, 71 Notre Dame L. Rev. 447 (1996).

3. *Does* Batson *kill peremptories?* Some observers have argued that *Batson* and its progeny essentially eliminate the function of peremptory challenges. Barbara Underwood responds:

> Critics of the rule against race-based peremptory challenges, both before and after it was announced by the Supreme Court, have suggested that under such a rule nothing — or nothing valuable — remains of the peremptory challenge. . . . The claim that the rule is in hopeless conflict with the challenge is frequently linked to the suggestion that the ban on jury discrimination must inevitably expand to prohibit not only jury selection based on race, but also jury selection based on religion, national origin, gender, language, disability, age, occupation, political party, and a host of other categories. The relationship between the two points is clear: the longer the list of prohibited categories, the less room there is for a lawful challenge other than a challenge for cause. . . .
>
> If occupational groups are not protected by the *Batson* ban, then generalizations about people based on their occupations provide a rational nonracial reason for a challenge. The same can be said of generalizations based on membership in any other unprotected group. These generalizations might be supported by survey data or social science evidence of some kind, or they might be supported by the experiences of a particular attorney or group of attorneys. . . . The validity of this kind of challenge depends on what groups are protected by the ban on jury discrimination. For this kind of challenge involves precisely the same kind of generalization that *Batson* rightly outlaws when race is involved. . . .

Underwood, Ending Race Discrimination in Jury Selection: Whose Right Is It, Anyway? 92 Colum. L. Rev. 725 (1992). Peremptory challenges continue to play a central role in criminal trials, but should they be retained? A number of commentators have joined Justice Thurgood Marshall and advocated the abolition of peremptories, usually joined with a proposal for broader standards for removal of jurors for cause. See, e.g., Albert Alschuler, The Supreme Court and the Jury: Voir Dire, Peremptory Challenges, and the Review of Jury Verdicts, 56 U. Chi. L. Rev. 153

(1991); Raymond Broderick, Why the Peremptory Challenge Should Be Abolished, 65 Temple L. Rev. 369 (1992). Consider the observations of Justice Stephen Zappala of the Pennsylvania Supreme Court in Commonwealth v. Dinwiddie, 601 A.2d 1216, 1222-1223 (Pa. 1992):

> [We] are headed for much contentious litigation over questions germane not to the guilt or innocence of the accused, but to the fairness, or apparent fairness, of the process by which guilt or innocence is determined. The questions, moreover, would seem to be inherently unanswerable; if the traditional purpose of peremptory challenges is to eliminate "irrational . . . suspicions and antagonisms," Swain v. Alabama, 380 U.S. at 224, how can the courts demand rational explanations for their use? Instead of pushing our courts into the morass of trying to judge between explanations for the irrational, perhaps the entire process would be better served by abandoning the use of peremptory challenges altogether, trying cases before the first group of twelve jurors randomly chosen from the venire, and allowing only challenges for cause.

4. *Remedies for* Batson *violations.* One of the many complicated questions courts have tried to answer in the wake of *Batson* is the question of the proper remedy. Should the judge start with a fresh venire, or reseat the improperly excluded jurors, or reseat all jurors excluded after the first improper peremptory strike? Some jurisdictions require trial courts, as a general rule, to disallow the strike and reseat the improperly stricken juror. A few states require the trial court to conduct jury selection from a newly convened venire. Most courts, however, have allowed the trial judge to choose among available remedies, without designating a preferred or required remedy. See Jefferson v. State, 595 So. 2d 38 (Fla. 1992); People v. Willis, 43 P.3d 130 (Cal. 2002). If the preferred remedy for a *Batson* violation is dismissal of the initial panel and selection of the jury from a fresh venire, would the parties ever have an incentive to create a deliberate *Batson* violation? Which remedy is most consistent with the view that the jury is primarily a method of ensuring a fair trial? Which is most consistent with the view that the jury serves important functions for the jurors themselves and for the public at large? See Eric Muller, Solving the *Batson* Paradox: Harmless Error, Jury Representation, and the Sixth Amendment, 106 Yale L.J. 93 (1996). States have multifarious rules for the order of questioning and for the timing of the announcements about peremptory strikes. These rules have some bearing on the proper remedy for a *Batson* violation. Does it matter if the parties announce their peremptory decisions in the presence of some or all of the jurors or the remaining members of the venire pool?

5. *Peremptory challenges to judges.* What can be done if a party believes a judge is biased? Most jurisdictions typically allow parties to challenge judges for cause. In addition, about 20 states allow defendants to have one automatic strike — a kind of peremptory challenge — to the trial judge. See, e.g., Ill. Rev. Stat. ch. 38, para. 114-5(a); Minn. Stat. §487.40. Some statutes that appear to require evidence of bias in fact operate as essentially automatic challenge provisions; others, including several federal statutes, that appear to allow peremptory challenges to judges in fact require some evidence of bias. See, e.g., 28 U.S.C. §144. Is the presumption that judges are neutral stronger than for jurors? Do peremptory challenges to judges undermine public confidence in the judicial system? Should lawyers be required to provide a reason to a judicial review commission even if the effect of a motion to change judges is automatic? See Nancy J. King, *Batson* for the Bench? Regulating the Peremptory Challenge of Judges, 73 Chi.-Kent L. Rev. 509 (1998).

C. JURY DELIBERATIONS AND VERDICTS

Once the jury is seated, the trial begins. In a few jurisdictions, the judge delivers preliminary instructions regarding the task at hand, along with an outline of the procedures for the jury to follow at trial and during deliberation. More often, the jury hears right away the opening statements of the attorneys, followed by the government's case in chief. Assuming that the judge denies the customary defense motion to dismiss the charges at the close of the prosecution's case, the jury then hears the defense evidence, if indeed the defendant chooses to present a defense. After closing statements from the attorneys, the judge instructs the jury on the law relevant to the case, using a combination of standard jury instructions for criminal cases and a few customized instructions that the parties suggest. The case then rests in the hands of the jury. In this section, we consider the rules governing the jury's deliberations at the close of the case.

1. Instructions to Deadlocked Juries

Although most juries reach a unanimous verdict, many start out with divided views among the panel members about the proper outcome. Divisions among jurors may be easier to resolve when juries are presented with a range of offenses, including lesser included charges, that create room for negotiation. But courts are sometimes faced with deadlocked juries. What devices may the court use to encourage the jurors to reach a common decision?

■ NEW YORK CRIMINAL PROCEDURE LAW §310.30

At any time during its deliberation, the jury may request the court for further instruction or information with respect to the law, with respect to the content or substance of any trial evidence, or with respect to any other matter pertinent to the jury's consideration of the case. Upon such a request, the court must direct that the jury be returned to the courtroom and, after notice to both the people and counsel for the defendant, and in the presence of the defendant, must give such requested information or instruction as the court deems proper. With the consent of the parties and upon the request of the jury for further instruction with respect to a statute, the court may also give to the jury copies of the text of any statute which, in its discretion, the court deems proper.

■ DANIEL BAILEY v. STATE

669 N.E.2d 972 (Ind. 1996)

SULLIVAN, J.

We reaffirm that the proper procedure when the jury is apparently deadlocked is for the trial court to call the jury back into open court in the presence of all parties and their counsel and reread all instructions given to them prior to their deliberations, without emphasis on any of them and without further comment. Lewis v. State, 424 N.E.2d 107 (Ind. 1981).

During jury deliberations in defendant Daniel Bailey's trial for murder and [for] carrying a handgun without a license, the jury sent the trial court the following note: "What happens if we cannot come to a unanimous decision this evening?" Interpreting this note as an indication that the jury was deadlocked, the trial court called the jury back into open court and reread to the jury one, but only one, of the final instructions.[3] Defense counsel objected to the procedure, arguing "if one instruction's read to them, . . . they all need to be."

In 1896, the United States Supreme Court reviewed the murder conviction of 14-year-old Alexander Allen for the third time. Allen v. United States, 164 U.S. 492 (1896). Among the assignments of error addressed by the court was a challenge to a jury instruction which has come to be known as the "*Allen* charge." The court described the instruction as follows:

> These instructions were quite lengthy, and were, in substance, that in a large proportion of cases absolute certainty could not be expected; that although the verdict must be the verdict of each individual juror, . . . they should listen, with a disposition to be convinced, to each other's arguments; that, if much the larger number were for conviction, a dissenting juror should consider whether his doubt was a reasonable one which made no impression upon the minds of so many men, equally honest, equally intelligent with himself. If, upon the other hand, the majority was for acquittal, the minority ought to ask themselves whether they might not reasonably doubt the correctness of a judgment which was not concurred in by the majority. [164 U.S. at 501.]

The court found no error in these instructions. This unprepossessing leading authority spawned a host of appellate and scholarly commentary in the three quarters of a century following its pronouncement. One outgrowth of this discussion was the emergence of an approach recommended by the American Bar Association to be used by trial courts in criminal cases when the jury was deadlocked. This standard, adopted by many courts . . . , provided:

> (a) Before the jury retires for deliberation, the court may give an instruction which informs the jury:
>
> (i) that in order to return a verdict, each juror must agree thereto;
>
> (ii) that jurors have a duty to consult with one another and to deliberate with a view to reaching an agreement, if it can be done without violence to individual judgment;
>
> (iii) that each juror must decide the case for himself or herself but only after an impartial consideration of the evidence with the other jurors;
>
> (iv) that in the course of deliberations, a juror should not hesitate to reexamine his or her own views and change an opinion if the juror is convinced it is erroneous; and

3. The instruction reread by the court was as follows:

The Court further instructs you that all verdicts must be unanimous. While it is the duty of each juror to act upon that juror's own individual judgment and determine the issue of guilt or innocence of the defendant of the crime charged and that each juror must look solely to the law and the evidence in the cause in determining the guilt or innocence of the defendant, yet it is likewise the duty of each juror to consult honestly, freely and fairly with the other jurors and endeavor with them, by fair consideration of the law and the evidence in the cause to arrive at a just conclusion as to the guilt or innocence of the defendant. No juror, through carelessness or indifference should yield that juror's own judgment in this cause to the judgment of the other jurors. Neither should any juror allow mere pride or personal opinion to prevent deliberative and reasonable consultation with the other jurors in an honest and good faith effort to arrive at a just verdict in this cause.

(v) that no juror should surrender his or her honest conviction as to the weight or effect of the evidence solely because of the opinion of other jurors, or for the mere purpose of returning a verdict.

(b) If it appears to the court that the jury has been unable to agree, the court may require the jury to continue their deliberations and may give or repeat an instruction as provided in paragraph (a). . . .

(c) The jury may be discharged without having agreed upon a verdict if it appears that there is no reasonable probability of agreement. [American Bar Assn., Project on Minimum Standards for Criminal Justice, Standards Relating to Trial by Jury §5.4, at 145-146 (1969 edition); Standard 15-4.4, at 133 (1980 edition).]

[In Lewis v. State, 424 N.E.2d 107 (Ind. 1981), our court disapproved of giving] any supplemental instructions to deadlocked juries other than rereading all of the original final instructions. [We expressed] concern that a trial judge's necessary discretion "not step over the bounds that limit him in the proper conduct of a trial. He must refrain from imposing himself and his opinions on the jury." We then [reiterated the established principle] that final instructions are not to be orally qualified, modified, or in any manner orally explained to the jury by the trial judge. Ind. Code §35-1-35-1. With this background, we turned to . . . the use of the ABA standard. We said:

> It appears to us . . . that the procedure of paragraph (b) of the above [ABA] Standard in allowing the court to separate this instruction or parts of it from the other instructions and to re-give it to the jury after deliberations re-creates the problem of the "*Allen*" charge situation all over again in a different form. A better solution is . . . for the court to call the jury back into open court in the presence of all of the parties and their counsel, if they desire to be there, and to reread all instructions given to them prior to their deliberations, without emphasis on any of them and without further comment. . . . [424 N.E.2d at 111.]

[The] final instruction dealing with the manner of deliberations . . . is not a housekeeping instruction but an instruction that relates to the very office of the jury. That is, the considerations set forth in this instruction are no more or less important to the jury than the matters set forth in the other final instructions. A jury deadlock could be caused by, e.g., one or more juror's failure to consult "honestly, freely and fairly with the other jurors." But it could also be caused by one or more juror's failure to understand or remember the instruction on reasonable doubt, the instruction on the elements of an offense, or the instruction on the state's burden of proof. The trial court simply does not know whether juror intransigence or a genuine misunderstanding or memory lapse as to the substance of the final instructions has caused the deadlock. By rereading all of the instructions, the jury is taken back to the beginning of its assignment, reminded of all the instructions necessary to decide the case. Not knowing the source of the infection, rereading all the instructions provides a broad spectrum antibiotic for whatever has caused the deadlock. We consider it time well spent.

Despite the many cases and secondary materials addressing the *Allen* charge, our decision in *Lewis* was the first to address the *Allen* charge issue from the perspective that the charge constitutes an embellishment on final instructions and, therefore, can only be read if part of a rereading of all final instructions. We clearly rejected the notion advanced by many jurisdictions . . . that the wording of the ABA standard instruction differs in its impact on juries from the original *Allen* charge.

And as the last of the five members of our court who unanimously decided *Lewis* retires, it is altogether fitting that we reaffirm this important principle of Indiana criminal jurisprudence. We reverse Bailey's convictions and remand to the trial court.

SHEPARD, C.J., concurring.

I join the Court's opinion because it reaffirms our precedent, prohibiting the use of "*Allen* charges" to break jury deadlocks and our rule that if one instruction is to be re-read they should all be re-read. The application of these rules appears awkward in this case because the jury's question to the court seems like a request for information and not a declaration that the jurors were deadlocked. The trial judge interpreted the question as an indication of deadlock, however, and it is possible that she was right. If so, as the Court's opinion indicates, the decision to give an "*Allen* charge" was error.

This appeal also suggests another question which will be ripe for examination when the appropriate case presents itself. Our declaration in Lewis v. State that a judge should re-read instructions to a deadlocked jury was written during an era when it was error to send instructions to the jury room. Now that we regularly give the jury the written instructions, this may be something left to trial court discretion.

Notes

1. *"Dynamite" charges: majority position.* The dynamite charge (or "hammer" charge) originated in Commonwealth v. Tuey, 62 Mass. 1 (1851), and came to national attention in Allen v. United States, 164 U.S. 492 (1896). The instruction produced verdicts, and its use spread rapidly. More recently, many courts have limited or abandoned the *Allen* instruction. About half the states have disapproved dynamite charges, in whole or in part. See People v. Gainer, 566 P.2d 997 (Cal. 1977); Paul Marcus, The *Allen* Instruction in Criminal Cases: Is the Dynamite Charge About to Be Permanently Defused? 43 Mo. L. Rev. 613 (1978). The case law on the subject is extensive. Some courts have limited the instruction through procedural devices, such as preventing judges from giving the instruction too early during the jury's deliberations or from giving it more than once. Along these lines, some courts say that an *Allen* charge is acceptable only if the judge delivered an identical charge to the jury at the start of its deliberations. Other courts focus on the content of the instructions. Appellate courts pay special attention to the balance between statements about the need for agreement and statements about the duty of individual jurors to stand by their own considered opinions. The alternative presented in the ABA standards (as discussed in *Bailey*) influences many courts. See State v. Weidul, 628 A.2d 135 (Me. 1993) (any departure from the ABA alternative will result in summary dismissal). Do you believe that the ABA alternative creates a different reaction among jurors than the traditional *Allen* charge? See also Lowenfield v. Phelps, 484 U.S. 231 (1988) (approving charge that does not instruct minority jurors to reconsider in light of majority views but does tell jurors not to hesitate to "reexamine" their views and to "change" their opinion if they are convinced that they are wrong). According to a study of federal appellate cases between 1964 and 1999, the *Allen* charge tends to hasten process of deliberation once it is given: Jury deliberations averaged about 13 hours before the charge and about 3 hours after the charge. About four percent of cases where a court delivered this charge resulted in mistrials. Appellate courts

overwhelmingly affirm convictions appealed on the basis of such a charge. See Mark Lanier and Cloud Miller, The *Allen* Charge: Expedient Justice or Coercion? 25 Am. J. Crim. Just. 31 (June 2001).

2. *Numerical breakdowns.* When a jury sends out word that it is divided and cannot reach a consensus, two questions spring to mind: How many jurors are "holding out," and which side does the majority favor? Appellate courts usually express concern if a trial judge inquired about the numerical division of the jury, explaining that such inquiries might create undue pressure on the minority jurors to change their votes. However, courts are divided over whether such inquiries, standing alone, constitute legal error. The larger group, including the federal courts, say that a judge's inquiries about the jury's numerical division are per se error. See Brasfield v. United States, 272 U.S. 448 (1926); People v. Wilson, 213 N.W.2d 193 (Mich. 1973). In the other states, this type of inquiry becomes a ground for reversal when combined with other circumstances, such as the judge's further inquiry about whether the majority favors conviction, acquittal, or some other option. On the other hand, if the jury *volunteers* information about its numerical division, the judge typically must inform the parties. Statutes and court rules typically state that the parties must be informed about any statement that the jury makes during its deliberations, and they must have an opportunity to argue to the judge about what she should say to the panel. What sorts of actions by a judge might influence a juror holding a minority view? See Eden v. State, 860 P.2d 169 (Nev. 1993) (no abuse of discretion for trial court to bring lone dissenting juror into chambers, in front of jury forewoman, and ask whether he had seen and heard the evidence and was willing to follow jury instructions). There is some social science evidence that jurors who cling most tenaciously to their views are also those who reach their views most quickly and are most likely to take a more absolutist view of the case. Deanna Kuhn, Michael Weinstock, and Robin Flaton, How Well Do Jurors Reason? Competence Dimensions of Individual Variation in a Juror Reasoning Task, 5 Psychological Science 289 (1994). If this description is generally true, should we give judges more opportunities to convince jurors with minority views to rethink their positions?

3. *The role of lesser included offenses.* Experimental data suggest that juries presented with alternatives for verdicts other than acquittal or the most serious available charge produce fewer acquittals and fewer hung juries. See Neil Vidmar, Effects of Decision Alternatives on the Verdicts and Social Perceptions of Simulated Jurors, 22 J. Personality & Soc. Psych. 211 (1972) (In 54 percent of mock homicide trials, jury acquitted when choice of verdict was guilty of first-degree murder or not guilty; when jury had four options, jurors returned verdicts of first-degree murder in 8 percent of the cases, second-degree murder in 64 percent, manslaughter in 21 percent, and not guilty in 8 percent). Depending on the case, as a strategic matter the prosecution or the defense may favor or oppose the judge instructing the jury about lesser included offenses. The rules governing whether lesser included offenses must be charged are complex and varied among the states; they often turn on judicial assessments of the plausibility of fitting various "stories" to the facts. See Kyron Huigens, The Doctrine of Lesser Included Offenses, 16 U. Puget Sound L. Rev. 185 (1992).

In cases involving lesser included offenses or multiple charges, the judge may encourage agreement among jurors by providing instructions on the order for them to consider lesser included offenses. Two instructions are common. Under an "acquittal first" instruction, the judge tells the jury to reach a unanimous decision to acquit on the most serious charge before moving on to consider conviction for a lesser offense. See State v. Tate, 773 A.2d 308 (Conn. 2001) (if jury that has received "acquittal first" instruction asks for clarification about a lesser included offense and then reports itself deadlocked, trial court should first ask jury if it has reached a partial verdict before declaring mistrial). An alternative is the "unable to agree" or "reasonable efforts" instruction, which permits a jury to consider lesser included offenses if, after reasonable efforts, the jury cannot agree on a verdict on the more serious offense. The acquittal-first instruction was the more traditional of the two, but the reasonable efforts instruction is gaining a strong following among state courts. See State v. Thomas, 533 N.E.2d 286 (Ohio 1988). As defense counsel, which of these instructions would you ordinarily prefer? Under what circumstances might you prefer the other instruction?

4. *Sequestration of juries.* One powerful practical force working in favor of jury agreement is the fact that jurors are forced to remain together in a single room, at least during working hours, until their task is complete. Indeed, for some cases involving an unusual amount of publicity that could taint the jurors, the court will "sequester" the jury and order them to remain together in a hotel during their meals, evenings, and off-days. See Tex. Code Crim. Proc. art 35.23. At one time, this process was much more explicitly designed to produce a verdict. Consider William Blackstone's description of the environment for jury deliberations: "the jury, . . . in order to avoid intemperance and causeless delay, are to be kept without meat, drink, fire, or candle, unless by permission of the judge, till they are all unanimously agreed." Blackstone, 3 Commentaries on the Laws of England 375 (1768).

5. *Alternate jurors.* Another device for producing jury verdicts becomes important when one or more of the sitting jurors cannot proceed with deliberations because of illness or for some other reason. In such a case, the court replaces the departing juror with an alternate juror who heard the evidence at trial and instructs the entire panel to begin its deliberations anew. Statutes and procedure rules authorize this procedure in virtually all jurisdictions, although alternate jurors are typically available only in the most serious or lengthy felony trials. But see Claudio v. State, 585 A.2d 1278 (Del. 1991) (state constitution prohibits use of alternate juror to replace jury member who became sick after one day's deliberations).

6. *Prevalence of hung juries.* In the popular imagination, the "hung jury" is a common occurrence. A study of juries in the 1960s found that hung juries occurred in 5.5 percent of the cases studied. Harry Kalven and Hans Zeisel, The American Jury 57 (1966). During the early 1990s, the Los Angeles County Public Defender collected data over an 18-month period, suggesting that hung juries occurred in approximately 13-15 percent of felony trials. Among the hung juries, the numerical division was 11-1 in 21 percent of the cases (15 percent for guilty and 6 percent for not guilty), while another 21 percent hung 10-2 (16 percent for guilty and 5 percent for not guilty). Clark Kelso, Final Report of the Blue Ribbon Commission on Jury System Improvement, 47 Hastings L.J. 1433 (1996). A more recent study suggests that rates of hung juries in Los Angeles are higher than in other jurisdictions: 13 to 16 percent in Los Angeles, compared to 6.2 percent nationwide. In federal criminal trials, the rate of hung juries remains around 2 to 3 percent. See Paula L. Hannaford, Valerie P. Hans, and G. Thomas Munsterman, How Much Justice Hangs in the Balance? 83 Judicature 59 (1999). Keep in mind that these rates reflect the number of juries that end their deliberations in deadlock; there are no data on the extent to which juries declare themselves deadlocked and ultimately reach a verdict. What outcomes would you expect during any later retrials of cases that initially produced a hung jury?

■ GEORGIA CONSTITUTION ART. I, §I, PARA. XI

(a) The right to trial by jury shall remain inviolate. . . . In criminal cases, the defendant shall have a public and speedy trial by an impartial jury; and the jury shall be the judges of the law and the facts.

(b) A trial jury shall consist of 12 persons; but the General Assembly may prescribe any number, not less than six, to constitute a trial jury in courts of limited jurisdiction and in superior courts in misdemeanor cases. . . .

■ MONTANA CODE §46-16-110

(1) The parties in a felony case have a right to trial by a jury of 12 persons.

(2) The parties may agree in writing at any time before the verdict, with the approval of the court, that the jury shall consist of any number less than that to which they are entitled.

(3) Upon written consent of the parties, a trial by jury may be waived.

Problem 17-3. Non-unanimous Verdicts

> *"A jury too frequently have at least one member, more ready to hang the panel than to hang the traitor."*
>
> *—Abraham Lincoln to Erastus Corning, June 12, 1863*

As in many states, prosecutors and citizens in California have expressed concern that too many trials result in hung juries and that a requirement of unanimity provides radical or irrational jurors with the power to block a just outcome. A 1996 Blue Ribbon Commission on Jury System Improvement in California recommended the following jury reform:

> The Legislature should propose a constitutional amendment which provides that, except for good cause when the interests of justice require a unanimous verdict, trial judges shall accept an 11-1 verdict after the jury has deliberated for a reasonable period of time (not less than six hours) in all felonies, except where the punishment may be death or life imprisonment, and in all misdemeanors where the jury consists of twelve persons. . . .

The commission explained that "eliminating the unanimity requirement is intended primarily to address the problem of an 11-1 or 10-2 hung jury where the hold-out jurors are refusing to deliberate, are engaging in nullification, or are simply [being] unreasonable (e.g., ignoring the evidence)." A slight majority of the commission preferred allowing only 11-1 and not 10-2 verdicts because "where two jurors share the same minority position, it seems less likely that the basis for the minority position is irrationality rather than a legitimate disagreement."

The commission's recommendation was a version of the "modified unanimity" approach — adopted in England and used in civil cases in several states — that gives judges the power to allow non-unanimous verdicts after a period of time (two hours in England). Opting for a time delay before allowing non-unanimous verdicts "forces the jury to begin its deliberations listening to all jurors and counting the votes of all jurors."

As a legislator in California, would you support a bill implementing the commission's recommendation? See Clark Kelso, Final Report of the Blue Ribbon Commission on Jury System Improvement, 47 Hastings L.J. 1433 (1996).

Notes

1. *Jury size: majority position.* Starting in 1970, the Supreme Court permitted experimentation with the size of criminal juries. In Williams v. Florida, 399 U.S. 78 (1970), the Court upheld the use of a six-person jury in a criminal case; however, in Ballew v. Georgia, 435 U.S. 223 (1978), the Court struck down the use of a five-person jury as a violation of the Sixth Amendment. A handful of states took up this invitation, and now allow felonies (other than capital cases) to be tried by juries of either six or eight members, including Arizona (eight-member juries except where sentences are 30 years or more), Utah (eight-member juries), Connecticut (six-member juries), and Florida (six-member juries). Another small group of states, including Indiana and Massachusetts, allow six-member juries for felony trials in limited jurisdiction courts but require full twelve-member juries in general jurisdiction courts. In contrast, for misdemeanors, more than half of the states mandate that juries consist of six members, and another large group of states specify a number between six and twelve members. State Court Organization 1998 at tbl. 42 (June 2000, NCJ 178932). Efforts in a few states to reduce the size of the criminal jury have been rejected on state constitutional grounds. See, e.g., Byrd v. State, 879 S.W.2d 435 (Ark. 1994); Advisory Opinion to the Senate of the State of Rhode Island, 278 A.2d 852 (R.I. 1971). Perhaps reducing the expense and difficulty of selecting and maintaining juries makes it possible to offer juries in a broader range of cases. Will a smaller jury function differently? In a predictable direction?

2. *Does jury size matter?* Social science played a role in the U.S. Supreme Court's decision in Ballew v. Georgia, 435 U.S. 223 (1978), which drew a constitutional line at a jury of six. The *Ballew* Court cited 19 studies on jury size conducted since 1970. An extensive discussion of these studies led the Court to conclude as follows:

> First, recent empirical data suggest that progressively smaller juries are less likely to foster effective group deliberation. . . . Second, the data now raise doubts about the accuracy of the results achieved by smaller and smaller panels. . . . Third, the data suggest that the verdicts of jury deliberation in criminal cases will vary as juries become smaller, and that the variance amounts to an imbalance to the detriment of one side, the defense. . . . Fourth, [smaller juries create] problems not only for jury decisionmaking, but also for the representation of minority groups in the community. . . . We readily admit that we do not pretend to discern a clear line between six members and five. But the assembled data raise substantial doubt about the reliability and appropriate representation of panels smaller than six. [435 U.S. at 232-239].

Does social science offer the best way to answer the question of the proper size of the criminal jury? If so, is study of internal jury dynamics the proper test? Few studies of the role of jury size on decision making in criminal cases have been conducted since the late 1970s. See Michael Saks, Michael J. Saks and Mollie Weighner

Marti, A Meta-Analysis of the Effects of Jury Size, 21 Law & Hum. Behav. 451 (1997) (discussing recent studies, most pertaining to civil juries). For a survey of jury practice in other countries (including New Zealand, Canada, Scotland, Ireland, Spain, Russia, and Japan), see the symposium published at 62 Law & Contemp. Prob. No. 2 (Spring 1999).

3. *Non-unanimous verdicts.* In Apodaca v. Oregon, 406 U.S. 404 (1972), the Supreme Court reversed earlier cases and interpreted the Sixth Amendment right to jury trial to allow convictions based on 11-1 and 10-2 votes. A companion case, Johnson v. Louisiana, 406 U.S. 356 (1972), upheld a conviction based on a 9-3 vote. However, in Burch v. Louisiana, 441 U.S. 130 (1979), the Court concluded that a conviction based on a 5-1 vote violated the right to a jury trial. States have not rushed into this constitutional opening. Only Louisiana and Oregon currently allow juries to convict defendants of felonies on a non-unanimous vote, although this reform is suggested fairly often, as the California proposal in Problem 17-3 illustrates. Some states have adopted non-unanimous verdict rules for misdemeanor trials, and a substantial number allow special exceptions to the unanimity requirement for verdicts, including consent of the parties.

The most famous study of non-unanimous juries is Reid Hastie, Steven D. Penrod & Nancy Pennington, Inside the Jury (1983). The study found several differences between behavior on unanimity-rule and majority-rule juries. Majority-rule juries reach a verdict more quickly; they tend to vote early and conduct discussions in a more adversarial manner; holdouts are more likely to remain at the conclusion of deliberations; members of small groups are less likely to speak; and large factions attract members more quickly. Is there rational explanation for a constitutional doctrine that allows a 9-3 verdict but not a 5-1 verdict? Does democratic theory support any non-unanimous verdict that mimics what a simple majority of society at large would decide in a case? See George Thomas and Barry Pollack, Rethinking Guilt, Juries, and Jeopardy, 91 Mich. L. Rev. 1 (1992) (calculating statistical risk that different jury configurations would mistakenly vote for guilt when majority of society at large would vote for acquittal). If the jury is designed as a protector of individual liberty, would it be appropriate to allow non-unanimous acquittals while requiring unanimity for convictions? Non-U.S. legal systems without a long jury tradition have been more willing to allow non-unanimous verdicts. See EC Legal Systems: An Introductory Guide (Sheridan and Cameron eds., 1995) (discussing non-unanimous verdicts in Great Britain, Greece, Ireland, Italy, and Portugal).

4. *Different rationales for one verdict.* The unanimity requirement calls for each juror to agree to the group outcome, whether it be conviction or acquittal of each possible charge. Jurors may, however, take different routes to reach the same conclusion. For instance, a statute might list more than one method of committing a crime, and jurors may have differing views about which method the defendant used. In Schad v. Arizona, 501 U.S. 624 (1991), a defendant was indicted for first-degree murder, and the prosecutor argued both premeditated and felony-murder theories. It was not clear whether the jurors all agreed on one theory when they returned a guilty verdict. The Court held that there was no due process violation because the state statute treated felony murder and premeditation as alternative *means* of establishing the single criminal element of mens rea. Thus, the key question is whether the statute makes a particular fact an element of the offense or instead an alternative means of establishing a crime element. State courts have also framed the

question in these terms. See State v. Fortune, 909 P.2d 930 (Wash. 1996). However, it has proven difficult to determine which facts are the "means" (over which jurors may disagree) and which are the "elements" (on which jurors must agree). See State v. Boots, 780 P.2d 725 (Or. 1989) (Linde, J.); Richardson v. United States, 526 U.S. 813 (1999) (interpreting the federal Continuing Criminal Enterprise statute to require jury to agree unanimously on the "violations" that make up the "series of continuing violations" that define the enterprise; violations are elements of the offense, not merely the means of committing an element).

5. *Special verdicts: majority position.* Special verdicts require the jury to answer specific questions about its subsidiary findings of fact, and they instruct the jury about the sequence for proceeding from preliminary findings to final conclusions. Proponents of the special verdict argue that it gives the jury valuable information and allows judicial review of improper verdicts. See Larry Heuer & Steven Penrod, Trial Complexity: A Field Investigation of Its Meaning and Its Effects, 18 Law & Hum. Behav. 29, 50 (1994) (survey of 160 actual trials; when special verdict forms were used, jurors reported feeling more informed, better satisfied, and more confident that their special verdict reflected proper understanding of judge's instructions). However, special verdicts are not often used in criminal cases, and some courts have struck down convictions based on special verdicts. According to the seminal case on this question, United States v. Spock, 416 F.2d 165 (1st Cir. 1969), special verdicts may coerce a jury into reaching a guilty verdict: "There is no easier way to reach, and perhaps force, a verdict of guilty than to approach it step by step. A juror, wishing to acquit, may be formally catechized." Could it also be argued that special verdicts might coerce a jury into a verdict of acquittal? Despite this general disinclination to use special verdicts, some state statutes or procedural rules provide for special verdicts in particular types of cases, such as those in which the defendant presents an insanity defense. Does the notion that the jury serves as a way to bring common sense into the process of factfinding suggest a wider reliance on special verdicts?

6. *Inconsistent verdicts.* When there are multiple defendants in a trial or multiple counts against a single defendant, the jury could reach inconsistent conclusions for the different defendants or charges. Yet because of the preference for general verdicts, there is no explanation available for how the jury reached its incongruent outcomes. Faced with this situation, the federal courts have decided that consistency among verdicts is not necessary when a defendant is convicted on one or more counts but acquitted on others. Dunn v. United States, 284 U.S. 390 (1932) (Holmes, J.). The incompatible results, these courts conclude, could be a product of jury lenity, but that does not invalidate the guilty verdict the jury did return. In the federal courts, the presumption that the inconsistent verdict was the product of jury lenity is not rebuttable. Under United States v. Powell, 469 U.S. 57 (1984), defendants cannot present evidence to show that the inconsistent verdict in their particular case resulted from a pro-government error rather than jury lenity. This approach, the Court said, is intended to prevent "speculation" about how the jury reached inconsistent verdicts. State courts have by and large followed the *Dunn* rule for inconsistent verdicts. People v. Caldwell, 681 P.2d 274 (Cal. 1984); Commonwealth v. Campbell, 651 A.2d 1096 (Pa. 1994). A small minority of state courts still hold that inconsistent verdicts require reversal. Many courts, however, recognize an exception for "logically" inconsistent verdicts (as opposed to "factually"

inconsistent verdicts). When a jury has returned verdicts convicting a defendant of two or more crimes, and the existence of an element of one of the crimes negates the existence of a necessary element of the other crime, courts generally say that the verdicts should not be sustained. See United States v. Powell; State v. Hinton, 630 A.2d 593 (Conn. 1993). Why do courts hope to avoid inquiries into the reasons for inconsistent verdicts? If the primary objective is to avoid speculation about the basis for verdicts, would a presumption in favor of dismissing all inconsistent verdicts work just as well as the current majority rule? See Eric L. Muller, The Hobgoblin of Little Minds? Our Foolish Law of Inconsistent Verdicts, 111 Harv. L. Rev. 771 (1998).

7. *Jury reform: juror note-taking.* Traditionally jurors in criminal cases have been barred from taking notes during trial. However, the majority of states (around 35) and the federal courts have begun to allow note-taking subject to judicial approval. See, e.g., Wash. Superior Ct. Crim. R. 6.8; Conn. R. Superior Ct., Crim. §845B; Mich. R. Crim. P. 6.414. Another group of states authorize note-taking without leaving the decision to the trial court in ordinary cases. See Minn. R. Crim. P. 26.03; Md. Crim. R. 4-326; see also ABA Standards for Criminal Justice, Trial by Jury 15-3.5 (3d ed. 1996). About five states still prohibit note-taking. See, e.g., Pa. R. Crim. P. 1113. In states where statutes and procedural rules do not address the question, courts often authorize note-taking. See, e.g., See People v. Hues, 704 N.E.2d 546 (N.Y. 1998) (survey of cases). Research suggests higher juror satisfaction and no change in outcomes when jurors are allowed to take notes. See Larry Heuer and Steven Penrod, Increasing Juror Participation in Trials Through Note Taking and Question Asking, 79 Judicature 256 (1996). Even though the trend is toward letting the trial judge decide the issue, most rules and judicial opinions on the subject call for safeguards, such as the immediate destruction of the notes after the jury completes its deliberations and cautionary instructions to the jury not to rely too heavily on the notes or on other jurors who took notes. See State v. Waddell, 661 N.E.2d 1043 (Ohio 1996). Should note-taking require the consent of the parties? What explains the historical hostility toward note-taking? Do the same attitudes explain the "safeguards" that rules and court decisions impose on the use of notes?

8. *Jury reform: juror questions to witnesses.* Arizona allows jurors to submit written questions to witnesses. Ariz. Crim. P. R. 18.6(e) was amended in 1995 to provide as follows: "Jurors shall be instructed that they are permitted to submit to the court written questions directed to witnesses or to the court; and that opportunity will be given to counsel to object to such questions out of the presence of the jury. [F]or good cause the court may prohibit or limit the submission of questions to witnesses." Commentary to the rules explains what happens if the court refuses to ask a juror's question because it calls for inadmissible evidence: "If a juror's question is rejected, the jury should be told that trial rules do not permit some questions to be asked and that the jurors should not attach any significance to the failure of having their question asked." While it is hard to find other state rules or statutes that allow jurors to submit written questions for witnesses in criminal trials, the great majority of courts allow juror questioning in the sound discretion of the trial judge, even absent a rule or statute addressing the topic. See State v. Culkin, 35 P.3d 233 (Haw. 2001) (approves juror questioning of witnesses through trial judge); Slaughter v. Commonwealth, 744 S.W.2d 407 (Ky. 1987). Fewer than 10 state courts (but a majority of federal courts) have prohibited juror questioning of witnesses. Morrison v. State, 845 S.W.2d 882 (Tex. Crim. App. 1992). These courts have concluded that the power to

question can create in the juror the mindset of an advocate. A nationwide survey of more than 500 trial judges indicated that 77 percent of them never allow jurors to ask witnesses questions. Larry Heuer & Steven D. Penrod, Some Suggestions for the Critical Appraisal of a More Active Jury, 85 Nw. U. L. Rev. 226, 229 (1990). The practice also creates a dilemma for attorneys. If they object to questions posed by the jurors, they risk alienating the jury. If they fail to object, they risk waiving errors that could form the basis of an appeal. Would you like jurors to have this power in a jurisdiction in which you were a prosecutor? A defense attorney?

9. *Non-unanimity in military criminal tribunals.* In the military justice system, a panel of military officers finds the facts to support a criminal conviction and sets the sentence. A three-fourths majority of the panel is necessary to select a sentence more than 10 years. A set of regulations passed soon after the terrorist attacks on September 11, 2001 created specialized courts-martial to try people accused of terrorism. On these panels, a unanimous verdict is required to impose a death penalty, but two-thirds of the panel is enough to find the accused guilty. 66 Fed. Reg. 57833 (Nov. 13, 2001). How might a panel of officers decide criminal matters differently than a panel of citizens on a criminal jury in the civilian system?

2. *Jury Nullification*

During its deliberations, the jury resolves factual disputes based on the evidence the parties present. It then applies the facts to the relevant legal principles that the judge provides in her instructions. But does the jury also have the power to interpret the law in light of its own values and priorities? Can the jury decide that the prosecution has proven a violation of the law but nevertheless choose to acquit because the jury believes that an injustice would otherwise result?

Judicial opinions on this subject widely recognize that the jurors have the "power" to ignore the law or to interpret the law themselves. This power has come to be known as "jury nullification." Nevertheless, judges usually consider jury nullification to be illegitimate. Hence, most courts refuse to instruct a jury that they have the power to "nullify" the law, and most do not allow defense counsel to make such an argument to the jury.

State constitutions and statutes fall into two camps on the issue of the jury's authority to decide questions of law (and thus to decide not to apply the law when an injustice would result). The state constitutions of Georgia (art. I, §1, para. 11, §A), Indiana (art. I, §19), Maryland (art. XXIII), and Oregon (art. I, §16) declare that the jury has authority over both the factual and legal aspects of each case. For example, the Indiana constitution provides: "In all criminal cases whatever, the jury shall have the right to determine the law and the facts." Ind. Const. art. 1, §19. Other state statutes take an opposite view. Cal. Penal Code §1126 ("In a trial for any offense, questions of law are to be decided by the court, and questions of fact by the jury. Although the jury has the power to find a general verdict, which includes questions of law as well as of fact, they are bound, nevertheless, to receive as law what is laid down as such by the court").

Consider the following pamphlet, widely distributed by a private organization that advocates broader use of the jury's power to nullify the criminal law as it applies in individual cases. To the extent that this pamphlet and others like it influence juror behavior, should it be considered a source of law?

■ JURORS' HANDBOOK: A CITIZEN'S GUIDE TO JURY DUTY FULLY-INFORMED JURY ASSOCIATION

Did you know that you qualify for another, much more powerful vote than the one which you cast on election day? This opportunity comes when you are selected for jury duty, a position of honor for over 700 years. . . .

Jury Power in the System of Checks and Balances

In a Constitutional system of justice, such as ours, there is a judicial body with more power than Congress, the President, or even the Supreme Court. Yes, the trial jury protected under our Constitution has more power than all these government officials. This is because it has the final veto power over all "acts of the legislature" that may come to be called "laws."

In fact, the power of jury nullification predates our Constitution. In November of 1734, a printer named John Peter Zenger was arrested for seditious libel against his Majesty's government. At that time, a law of the Colony of New York forbid any publication without prior government approval. Freedom of the press was not enjoyed by the early colonialists! Zenger, however, defied this censorship and published articles strongly critical of New York colonial rule. When brought to trial in August of 1735, Zenger admitted publishing the offending articles, but argued that the truth of the facts stated justified their publication. The judge instructed the jury that truth is not justification for libel. [S]ince the defendant had admitted to the "fact" of publication, only a question of "law" remained. Then, as now, the judge said the "issue of law" was for the court to determine, and he instructed the jury to find the defendant guilty. It took only ten minutes for the jury to disregard the judge's instructions on the law and find Zenger NOT GUILTY.

That is the power of the jury at work; the power to decide the issues of law under which the defendant is charged, as well as the facts. In our system of checks and balances, the jury is our final check, the people's last safeguard against unjust law and tyranny.

A Jury's Rights, Powers, and Duties

But does the jury's power to veto bad laws exist under our Constitution? It certainly does! . . . As recently as 1972, the U.S. Court of Appeals for the District of Columbia said that the jury has an "unreviewable and irreversible power . . . to acquit in disregard of the instructions on the law given by the trial judge" (U.S. v. Dougherty, 473 F.2d 1113 (1972)). Or as this same truth was stated in an earlier decision by the United States Court of Appeals for the District of Maryland: "We recognize, as appellants urge, the undisputed power of the jury to acquit, even if its verdict is contrary to the law as given by the judge, and contrary to the evidence. This is a power that must exist as long as we adhere to the general verdict in criminal cases, for the courts cannot search the minds of the jurors to find the basis upon which they judge. If the jury feels that the law under which the defendant is accused, is unjust, or that exigent circumstances justified the actions of the accused, or for any reason which appeals to their logic or passion, the jury has the power to acquit, and the courts must abide by that decision" (U.S. v. Moylan, 417 F.2d 1002 (1969)).

YOU, as a juror armed with the knowledge of the purpose of a jury trial, and the knowledge of what your Rights, powers, and duties really are, can with your single vote of not guilty nullify or invalidate any law involved in that case. Because a jury's guilty decision must be unanimous, it takes only one vote to effectively nullify a bad "act of the legislature." Your one vote can "hang" a jury; and although it won't be an acquittal, at least the defendant will not be convicted of violating an unjust or unconstitutional law. The government cannot deprive anyone of "Liberty," without your consent! . . .

JURORS MUST KNOW THEIR RIGHTS

You must know your rights! Because, once selected for jury duty, nobody will inform you of your power to judge both law and fact. In fact, the judge's instructions to the jury may be to the contrary. Another quote from U.S. v. Dougherty: "The fact that there is widespread existence of the jury's prerogative, and approval of its existence as a necessary counter to case-hardened judges and arbitrary prosecutors, does not establish as an imperative that the jury must be informed by the judge of that power."

Look at that quote again. The court ruled jurors have the power to decide the law, but they don't have to be told about it. It may sound hypocritical, but the *Dougherty* decision conforms to an 1895 Supreme Court decision that held the same thing. In Sparf v. U.S. (156 U.S. 51), the court ruled that although juries have the right to ignore a judge's instructions on the law, they don't have to be made aware of it by the court.

Is this Supreme Court ruling as unfair as it appears on the surface? It may be, but the logic behind such a decision is plain enough. In our Constitutional Republic (note I didn't say democracy) the people have granted certain limited powers to government, preserving and retaining their God-given inalienable rights. So, if it is indeed the juror's right to decide the law, then the citizens should know what their rights are. They need not be told by the courts. After all, the Constitution makes us the masters of the public servants. Should a servant have to tell a master what his rights are? Of course not, it's our responsibility to know what our rights are! . . .

America, the Constitution and your individual rights are under attack! Will you defend them? READ THE CONSTITUTION, KNOW YOUR RIGHTS! Remember, if you don't know what your Rights are, you haven't got any!

Problem 17-4. Juries and Social Justice

Defense counsel has asked the trial judge to instruct the jury as follows:

> The Court instructs the Jury that under the Constitution of the United States, the Jury has a paramount right to acquit an accused person for whatever reason and to find him not guilty, even though the evidence may support a conviction, and this is an important part of the jury trial system guaranteed by the Constitution.
>
> The Court further instructs the Jury that this principle of jury nullification is just as important to the constitutional process as any other instruction which the Court has given to this Jury, and that in the final analysis, you, the members of the Jury, are the sole judges of whether or not it is right and fair to convict the Accused or whether under the totality of the circumstances, the Accused should be found not guilty. In arriving at your verdict you are not compelled to answer to anyone or to the State, nor

> are you required at any time by the Court or any person or party to give a reason or to be brought to accountability for your decision and vote.

Alternatively, counsel has asked the court for permission to make such an argument to the jury in the closing statement. The prosecutor has objected to the proposed instruction and will object if defense counsel makes such an argument in the closing statement.

This issue has arisen in four cases. In State v. Adams, the defendant is charged with destruction of government property and criminal trespass because she scaled a fence at a military installation and spray-painted antinuclear slogans on military equipment used to maintain nuclear weaponry. In State v. Baker, the defendant is charged with criminal trespass for blocking the doorway to an abortion clinic. He was protesting the practices of the clinic and calling for an end to legal abortions.

In State v. Cunningham, the defendant is charged with robbery in the first degree. The prosecution will present evidence that the defendant took two 12-packs of beer at gunpoint from a convenience store. The minimum sentence for this crime is 10 years. The state has also charged the defendant with being a "persistent felony offender" in the second degree because of his prior felony convictions. If the jury finds him guilty on this charge, the judge will impose a 20-year mandatory minimum sentence.

In State v. Derby, the defendant is an African American man who is charged with distribution of crack cocaine. The government will present evidence that the defendant sold two ounces of crack to an undercover agent. Venue for the trial is set in a location where it is likely that a number of the jurors will be African Americans.

As trial judge in each of these cases, would you grant the motions? What particular circumstances that you do not yet know would influence your decision? Would it matter to you if there were a state constitutional provision stating that the "jury shall have the right to determine the law and the facts"? Compare Davis v. State, 520 So. 2d 493 (Miss. 1988); State v. Wentworth, 395 A.2d 858 (N.H. 1978); Medley v. Commonwealth, 704 S.W.2d 190 (Ky. 1985).

Notes

1. *Authority of jury to nullify: majority position.* There is widespread agreement among state and federal courts that juries have the technical power to "nullify" by issuing general verdicts, thus obscuring whether they have judged only the facts or the law as well. Yet courts in most places refuse to instruct juries about their power to judge the law or to "nullify" the charge, and attorneys are usually not allowed to inform the jury about this power. Typical is the following statements by the Rhode Island Supreme Court:

> While we concede that a jury may render a verdict that violates the law, when this is done, it is a violation of the legal responsibility of the jurors. Certainly, it would be erroneous and improper for a court to lend its approval to such lawless conduct, even if no sanction could be imposed for its exercise. The fact that a person or persons may ignore legal requirements with impunity does not make this failure a right. [State v. Champa, 494 A.2d 102 (R.I. 1985).]

See also Ramos v. State, 934 S.W.2d 358 (Tex. Crim. App. 1996); State v. Ragland, 519 A.2d 1361 (N.J. 1986). Some states acknowledge the power of the jury to assess law and facts by the rather subtle shift from general jury instructions directing the jury that if it finds the facts to be true it "must" find the defendant guilty to language suggesting to the jury that it "should" or "may" find the defendant guilty. A handful of states allow the judge to instruct the jury more directly about its power. Some even allow attorneys to argue nullification directly to the jury if the trial judge allows it. See State v. Bonacorsi, 648 A.2d 469 (N.H. 1994). Limits on jury instructions and arguments about nullification generally apply even in states with constitutional "nullification" provisions. A larger number of states have constitutional provisions recognizing jury nullification powers specifically for libel and sedition cases, no doubt reflecting the tradition sparked by John Peter Zenger. See, e.g., Alabama Const. art. 1, §12; Maine Const. art. 1, §4; New Jersey Const. art. 1, para. 6.

For thorough examinations of the historical origins of jury nullification in the United States, see Clay S. Conrad, Jury Nullification: The Evolution of a Doctrine (1998); Stanton D. Krauss, An Inquiry Into the Right of Criminal Juries to Determine the Law in Colonial America, 89 J. Crim. L. & Criminology 111 (1998). It appears that many of the older cases affirming the power of the jury to "find the law" were intended to limit a judicial practice of directing the jury how to apply the law to particular facts.

2. *The continuing vitality of the nullification debate.* Despite the relatively uniform and restrictive law concerning nullification, the debate over its validity and use continues at a fever pitch. See, e.g., Darryl Brown, Jury Nullification Within the Rule of Law, 81 Minn. L. Rev. 1149 (1997); Andrew Leipold, Rethinking Jury Nullification, 82 Va. L. Rev. 253 (1996). In some cases, scholars have argued that a proper understanding of the power of criminal juries supports jury decision making on questions of law in particular contexts. See, e.g., Colleen Murphy, Integrating the Constitutional Authority of Civil and Criminal Juries, 61 Geo. Wash. L. Rev. 723 (1993); Jack Weinstein, Considering Jury Nullification: When May and Should a Jury Reject the Law to Do Justice, 30 Am. Crim. L. Rev. 239 (1993). Among the more controversial articles is one by Professor Paul Butler, encouraging black jurors to refuse to convict some black defendants in an effort to challenge and change the criminal justice system:

> [F]or pragmatic and political reasons, the black community is better off when some nonviolent lawbreakers remain in the community rather than go to prison. The decision as to what kind of conduct by African-Americans ought to be punished is better made by African-Americans themselves, based on the costs and benefits to their community, than by the traditional criminal justice process, which is controlled by white lawmakers and white law enforcers. Legally, the doctrine of jury nullification gives the power to make this decision to African-American jurors who sit in judgment of African-American defendants. Considering the costs of law enforcement to the black community and the failure of white lawmakers to devise significant nonincarcerative responses to black antisocial conduct, it is the moral responsibility of black jurors to emancipate some guilty black outlaws. . . .
>
> Imagine a country in which more than half of the young male citizens are under the supervision of the criminal justice system, either awaiting trial, in prison, or on probation or parole. Imagine a country in which two-thirds of the men can anticipate being arrested before they reach age thirty. Imagine a country in which there are more young men in prison than in college. Now give the citizens of the country the key to the prison. Should they use it? . . .
>
> In cases involving violent malum in se crimes like murder, rape, and assault, jurors should consider the case strictly on the evidence presented, and, if they have no reasonable doubt that the defendant is guilty, they should convict. For nonviolent malum

> in se crimes such as theft or perjury, nullification is an option that the juror should consider, although there should be no presumption in favor of it. A juror might vote for acquittal, for example, when a poor woman steals from Tiffany's, but not when the same woman steals from her next-door neighbor. Finally, in cases involving nonviolent, malum prohibitum offenses, including "victimless" crimes like narcotics offenses, there should be a presumption in favor of nullification.

Butler, Racially Based Jury Nullification: Black Power in the Criminal Justice System, 105 Yale L.J. 677, 679, 690, 714 (1995). See also Andrew Leipold, The Dangers of Race-Based Jury Nullification: A Response to Professor Butler, 44 UCLA L. Rev. 109 (1996). Jury nullification also becomes a forum for discussing most controversial political and social issues other than race. Robert Schopp, Verdicts of Conscience: Nullification and Necessity as Jury Responses to Crimes of Conscience, 69 S. Cal. L. Rev. 2039 (1996). Would nullification instructions increase or undermine public respect for the justice system? Consider 1 Alexis de Tocqueville, Democracy in America 361 (Francis Bowen trans., 1862) (1835): "He who punishes the criminal is therefore the real master of society. Now, the institution of the jury raises the people itself, or at least a class of citizens, to the bench of judges. The institution of the jury consequently invests the people, or that class of citizens, with the direction of society."

Do the arguments for nullification change when a trial judge refuses to convict based on disagreement with the law as applied to a case? See United States v. Lynch, 952 F. Supp. 167 (S.D.N.Y. 1997) (acquittal of two abortion protesters of criminal contempt charges in bench trial; judge relies in part on "that exercise of the prerogative of leniency which a fact-finder has to refuse to convict a defendant, even if the circumstances would otherwise be sufficient to convict."); Pamela Karlan, Two Concepts of Judicial Independence, 72 S. Cal. L. Rev. 535 (1999) (discussing *Lynch*).

3. *Do nullification instructions and arguments affect jury decisions?* The battles over nullification instructions and arguments — and the efforts of jurors' rights groups — seem to assume that if juries knew they had the power to nullify, they would do so more often. Two studies cast doubt on this assumption. A 1985 study by a psychologist found that juries respond to judicial instructions about nullification only when those instructions are strongly worded; simply informing juries that they have the final authority to decide cases does not change outcomes. Irwin Horowitz, The Effects of Jury Nullification Instructions on Verdicts and Jury Functioning in Criminal Trials, 9 Law & Hum. Behav. 25 (1985). In a second study in 1988, Horowitz found that (1) juries responded to strong instructions about nullification whether those instructions came from the judge or lawyers, (2) strong instructions about the jury's power to "do justice" led both to more acquittals (for sympathetic defendants) and more convictions (for unsympathetic defendants), and (3) cautionary language to the jury from a second actor undermined the inflammatory impact of the instructions. Irwin Horowitz, The Impact of Judicial Instructions, Arguments, and Challenges on Jury Decision Making, 12 Law & Hum. Behav. 439 (1988). See also Keith E. Niedermeier, Irwin A. Horowitz, and Norbert L. Kerr, Informing Jurors of Their Nullification Power: A Route to a Just Verdict or Judicial Chaos? 23 Law & Hum. Behav. 331 (1999); Jeffrey Kerwin and David Shaffer, The Effects of Jury Dogmatism on Reactions to Jury Nullification Instructions, 17 Personality & Soc. Psych. Bull. 140 (1991).

4. *Jury information and jury tampering.* Suppose a nullification enthusiast tries to hand out a jurors' rights tract (like the one distributed by FIJA, reprinted above)

or any other literature at a courthouse to those wearing a juror badge. What can a prosecutor or judge do? The legal lines become quite clear when any person tries to influence an active juror: Such conduct is known as jury tampering, and the right to a free and fair trial overcomes any claim of a right to free speech. Convictions for jury tampering have been upheld against people who distribute FIJA literature or who publicize a FIJA "800" number within a courthouse to jurors with a button indicating their active service. See Turney v. State, 936 P.2d 533 (Alaska 1997). The legal lines are less clear, however, when people distribute literature outside the courthouse to all citizens, or only to those who are not specifically identified as jurors. Professor Nancy King has analyzed these tactics and concludes that they are constitutionally acceptable. King, Silencing Nullification Advocacy Inside the Jury Room and Outside the Courtroom 65 U. Chi. L. Rev. 433 (1998).

5. *Juror misbehavior.* Imagine that a juror lies during voir dire with the goal of exercising the "right" to nullify a conviction (or at least the power of a single juror to hang a jury). Or suppose a juror makes remarks during deliberations suggesting a racial motive in decision making (whether in favor of a guilty or not guilty verdict). What happens in these cases? If jurors violate direct instructions from the judge or lie during voir dire and it comes to light before the jury starts deliberations, the jurors can be removed from the case and alternates put in their place. If their misbehavior comes to light after a verdict has been reached, depending on the nature and severity of the misbehavior, jurors may be prosecuted for jury tampering. Most states and the federal system place sharp limits on the introduction of information from or about jury deliberations in an effort to protect jury secrecy and maintain a focus on issues of guilt and innocence. In addition, a recent survey of judges suggests that serious misconduct is rare (although lesser misconduct, such as failing to be fully honest at voir dire and sleeping during trials, appears to be much more common). See Nancy King, Juror Delinquency in Criminal Trials in America, 1796-1996, 94 Mich. L. Rev. 2673 (1996) ("[O]ur present system enlists reluctant amateurs to perform a demanding and unfamiliar job, in secret, with little accountability. In such a scheme, some degree of misconduct is inevitable").

California now employs a jury instruction that requires jurors to inform the judge whenever a fellow member of the jury refuses to deliberate based on his or her disagreement with the law. People v. Williams, 21 P.3d 1209 (Cal. 2001) (upholding conviction after trial court replaced juror who was reported by fellow juror; replaced juror disagreed with statutory rape law as applied to 18-year-old male defendant and 16-year-old female victim). Do you expect to see this device spread eventually to many other states?

D. THE PUBLIC AS DECISIONMAKER

1. Public Access to Trials

The Sixth Amendment to the U.S. Constitution provides defendants with a right to a "speedy and public trial," as do analogous state constitutional provisions. A public trial might mean that any person could attend, including reporters. Or the right to a public trial might be a personal right of the defendant, giving the defendant a right *not* to have a public trial — to a closed trial — as well.

Courts have recognized both a private and public interest in open trials. The presumption in favor of an open trial is not absolute, and the courts have wrestled with issues such as when the defense or prosecution has a right to a closed proceeding, and when the media has a right of access to proceedings even against the wishes of both parties. Questions regarding media coverage, particularly with cameras and microphones, have taken a higher profile with the creation of specialized television channels devoted to trials, and the increasing capacity through technology to create much wider access to trials. Consider whether the court in the following case properly balances the prosecutor's request to close the trial during the testimony of one key witness and the defendant's request that the trial remain open.

■ STATE v. BARRY GARCIA

561 N.W.2d 599 (N.D. 1997)

MESCHKE, J.

Barry Caesar Garcia appeals a jury verdict and a criminal judgment finding him guilty of murder and aggravated assault, and sentencing him to life imprisonment without parole. We affirm. . . .

During the evening of November 15, 1995, juveniles Jaime Guerrero, Juan Guerrero, Michael Charbonneau, Ray Martinez, Angel Esparza, and Garcia drove around Fargo-Moorhead in a brown, 1975, Minnesota-licensed, Ford sedan owned by Juan Guerrero's mother. The young men took along 10 to 15 red and green shotgun shells and a sawed-off shotgun owned by the Skyline Piru Bloods, a street gang whose members included Jaime Guerrero, Juan Guerrero and Martinez. While driving in a West Fargo residential area near 10 P.M., Garcia asked the driver to stop. Garcia and Charbonneau, who is much taller than Garcia, left the car. Garcia took the shotgun. Their car continued down the street and came to a stop, and Garcia and Charbonneau began walking around the neighborhood.

In the same neighborhood, Pat and Cherryl Tendeland were dropping off their friend, Connie Guler, who had accompanied them to a prayer service in Hillsboro. In the Tendeland car parked in Guler's driveway, while seated and talking, Guler saw a "taller boy . . . maybe six feet or taller" and a "shorter one . . . five feet or less tall" walking down the sidewalk toward them. Guler thought the shorter boy was carrying a gun, but Pat thought it was an umbrella. After the boys stood near Guler's driveway for awhile, they began walking back toward the brown Ford sedan. From their suspicious behavior, Pat decided to back up and follow the boys "to see where they [were] going."

As the Tendeland car slowly approached the Ford sedan, Guler saw the taller boy walking briskly toward the Ford and the shorter boy with the gun lagging behind. The Ford's lights were on, and it started to pull away. Cherryl read off the car's license number. Guler testified about the next thing she remembered:

> I caught out of the sight of my eye something, and I turned, and this shorter boy was coming down off my berm, and he was so close, he could have opened my car door. And the next — our eyes met, and all I remember was these cold, dark eyes. And that's all I know. I don't have a face. And it just — he just raised it. I said, "My God, he's going to shoot," and it went off. I mean, it wasn't a matter of — it was just (indicating), like a click of the finger. It was so quick. . . .

Cherryl was shot in the forehead and shotgun pellets also struck Pat's face, knocking a lens from his glasses. Guler was not struck by the blast. Pat, who had difficulty seeing with blood running down his face and without the lost lens, decided to drive to a nearby police station. [Cherryl Tendeland died from the shotgun wounds.]

Jaime Guerrero, who had remained in the Ford, testified he did not see the gunshot, but he heard it. Guerrero said Charbonneau and Garcia got back in the car about 20 seconds after he heard the shotgun blast. According to Guerrero, Garcia, who was still carrying the shotgun, said "they got her," and "next time, don't look at me." [Based on descriptions of witnesses, the police located the Ford sedan that night.] Police recovered a sawed-off shotgun with a warm barrel from the backseat of the car along with several red and green shotgun shells. Shortly, the police chasing after Garcia captured him in an athletic field at Moorhead State University. When arrested, Garcia possessed one green and three red shotgun shells. . . .

The spent shotgun shell recovered at the scene had been fired from the sawed-off shotgun found in the brown Ford sedan. Neither Pat nor Guler could positively identify Garcia as the person who shot into the Tendeland car. No usable fingerprints were found on the shotgun. Atomic absorption tests on Garcia, Martinez, and Jaime and Juan Guerrero showed significant levels of antimony and barium on all four individuals, thus evidencing each of them could have recently fired a gun or handled a gun that had been recently fired. The pattern on the sole of Garcia's tennis shoes corresponded with shoeprints found at the scene of the shooting.

The Tendeland shooting brought on much publicity, and the trial court allowed expanded media coverage of Garcia's jury trial. See N.D. Admin. R. 21.* At the trial, the State called Jaime Guerrero as a witness. When asked his name, Guerrero replied, "I am not going to say nothing."

Away from the jury, the trial court learned Guerrero had not been granted immunity to testify, warned Guerrero he may be subject to contempt penalties, and also informed him of his Fifth Amendment rights to remain silent and to speak to a lawyer. Guerrero asked to speak with a lawyer, and the trial court appointed the same lawyer who was representing Guerrero in juvenile court to advise him. The court recessed, and Guerrero consulted his lawyer during the lunch hour.

* N.D. Admin. R. 21 provides in pertinent part as follows:

d. "Expanded media coverage" includes broadcasting, televising, electronic recording, or photographing of a judicial proceeding for the purpose of gathering and disseminating information to the public by media personnel. . . .

Section 4. The court may permit expanded media coverage of a judicial proceeding in the courtroom while the judge is present, and in adjacent areas as the court may direct. Expanded media coverage provided for in this rule may be exercised only by media personnel. . . .

b. The judge may deny expanded media coverage of any proceeding or portion of a proceeding in which the judge determines on the record, or by written findings:

1. Expanded media coverage would materially interfere with a party's right to a fair trial;
2. A witness or party has objected and shown good cause why expanded media coverage should not be permitted; . . .
4. Expanded media coverage would include testimony of a juvenile victim or witness in a proceeding in which illegal sexual activity is an element of the evidence. . . .

c. The judge may limit or end expanded media coverage at any time during a proceeding, if the judge determines on the record, or by written findings:

1. The requirements of this rule or additional guidelines imposed by the judge have been violated; or
2. The substantial rights of an individual participant, or rights to a fair trial will be prejudiced by the expanded media coverage if it is allowed to continue.

—Eds.

When the trial court reconvened out of the presence of the jury [t]he State's attorney explained to the court:

> Mr. Guerrero has indicated some willingness to proceed and provide testimony to matters which he has already provided us information. I'm concerned — and it's been relayed to me — that there may be some concern about the media coverage, particularly the television camera, and also the number of viewers and spectators in the audience of the courtroom.
>
> It is — it's my request at this time that, for the testimony of Jaime Guerrero, that the Court terminate expanded media coverage, terminate the use of the television camera, terminate the feed to the television and/or radio just for that testimony, and that the Court also order that anybody other than the family of Barry Garcia or the family of Cherryl Tendeland be excused from the courtroom, to present — to present a more friendly environment, if you will, for the testimony of this child, who is only 15 years of age. I think there are good arguments to be made for the termination of the expanded coverage for a person only 15 years of age. There is some reason to believe that he is concerned about other persons' opinions and feelings and actions if he decides to go ahead and testify. . . .

Garcia's attorney resisted the State's request, arguing there was "no compelling reason to shut things down at this point." . . . The State's attorney explained he had promised to dismiss with prejudice the juvenile court charges against Guerrero if he testified truthfully in Garcia's trial. Guerrero's lawyer told the court Guerrero "is a juvenile, and he is intimidated by the audience and media coverage," and elaborated on Guerrero's reluctance to testify:

> I think he's intimidated by the whole spectacle of the trial, that he will be on television, he will be in the newspaper again. And it would put him at ease not to have to experience this. And he is a juvenile and does want his confidentiality preserved, if possible, but I guess that's . . . not really possible. But those are some of the factors that make him not want to testify. This would put him at ease if he didn't have to kind of run the gauntlet. . . .

Garcia's lawyer again objected to any closure of the trial. The State's attorney explained:

> I would like, just for the record, to note that in support of our request and our position, we are aware of another witness, not Mr. Guerrero, but another witness who has indicated a reluctance to provide testimony, who has been subpoenaed, because of actual repercussions that he's already experienced. So we are basing these requests on some real events, not just speculation. At least that's what I have been told. . . .

The court outlined its "initial thoughts," but recessed and deferred ruling until the media had an opportunity to be heard. After hearing argument from a media representative, the trial court ruled:

> [It] is in the interests of justice to suspend the expanded media coverage order for this witness, and to suspend the rule as regards media coverage. Exercising the inherent powers of the Court to control the courtroom, I am going to order that the courtroom be cleared, that the feeds to the radio and the television be terminated, and that all persons, except for counsel, Mr. Garcia, and Detective Warren, and the immediate family of — was it — of Mr. Garcia, and the immediate family of Mrs. Tendeland. . . .

> The cautionary instruction I intend to give . . . will read as follows: Ladies and gentlemen of the jury, as you are aware, Mr. Guerrero has indicated an unwillingness to testify. He has expressed a concern about all the media coverage, all of the people — and all the people in the courtroom. Taking into consideration the youth of Mr. Guerrero and his concerns, the Court has determined that in order to facilitate his testimony, the courtroom will be cleared of all persons. You are not to draw any conclusions or inferences from the clearance of the courtroom.

The court also allowed a single pool representative, chosen by the media, to remain in the courtroom. The court gave the jury the cautionary instruction, and Guerrero testified in the partially closed courtroom.

Garcia claims his constitutional rights to a public trial were violated when the trial court temporarily terminated expanded media coverage and excluded the general public from the courtroom for Guerrero's testimony.

The Sixth Amendment to the United States Constitution guarantees a criminal defendant "the right to a speedy and public trial. . . ." See also N.D. Const. Art. I, §12. Although the guarantee of a public trial was created for the benefit of criminal defendants, see In re Oliver, 333 U.S. 257 (1948), the right is also shared with the public; the common concern is to assure fairness. Press-Enterprise Co. v. Superior Court of Cal., 478 U.S. 1 (1986). "In addition to ensuring that judge and prosecutor carry out their duties responsibly, a public trial encourages witnesses to come forward and discourages perjury." Waller v. Georgia, 467 U.S. 39 (1984). The Supreme Court explained in Gannett Co., Inc. v. DePasquale, 443 U.S. 368 (1979): "Openness in court proceedings may improve the quality of testimony, induce unknown witnesses to come forward with relevant testimony, cause all trial participants to perform their duties more conscientiously, and generally give the public an opportunity to observe the judicial system." Precedents demonstrate, however, that the right to a public trial is not absolute and must give way in rare instances to other interests essential to the fair administration of justice.

The contours of a criminal defendant's right to a public trial in the context of total closure of an entire pretrial suppression hearing were confronted by the Supreme Court in *Waller*. The *Waller* Court ruled that defendant's public-trial guarantee had been violated, and explained:

> [T]he party seeking to close the hearing must advance an overriding interest that is likely to be prejudiced, the closure must be no broader than necessary to protect that interest, the trial court must consider reasonable alternatives to closing the proceeding, and it must make findings adequate to support the closure. [467 U.S. at 48.]

The *Waller* Court made clear that a trial court's power to exclude the public from a criminal trial should be exercised sparingly and then only for the most unusual of circumstances.

We used the *Waller* standard to measure a trial court's temporary closure of a defendant's criminal trial on charges of gross sexual imposition during the testimony of the child victim, the defendant's adopted son. State v. Klem, 438 N.W.2d 798 (N.D. 1989). Klem's first trial had been entirely open to the public while the child victim testified, and had resulted in a hung jury. At the second trial, when the child witness was first seated to testify, the State's attorney abruptly requested closure of the trial for the child's testimony because the "sensitive nature" of the case "may be very distracting and very embarrassing for him in front of all these people and the people in the Courtroom may inhibit the testimony." After the defendant objected to the proposed closure, the court summarily ruled, "I think I will clear the Courtroom," and did so.

A majority of this Court concluded the trial court, in closing the trial to all but court personnel, parties, attorneys, jurors, and a public media representative during the child's testimony, deprived the accused of his right to a public trial. [The] majority concluded the trial court had failed to satisfactorily comply with the *Waller* requirements: "There was no hearing, no weighing of competing interests, and no findings to support closure." 438 N.W.2d at 801.

Garcia argues the trial court in this case, like the trial court in *Klem,* largely ignored the *Waller* requirements in ordering the partial closure of the courtroom, so that a reversal and a remand for a new trial are necessary. We disagree.

This case differs from *Klem* in several major ways. We pointed out in *Klem* that, ordinarily, a motion to close a trial to the public should be made before trial to avoid unfair surprise and to give the trial court the benefit of research and arguments, but the reasons for closure could not have been reasonably anticipated in this case. The mid-trial motion in *Klem* could have been made before trial, and the reasons for it were given in generalities as the child witness was seated to testify. The witness had in fact testified publicly in the first trial, so there was no apparent reason for either the closure motion or the order.

Here, Guerrero had given a sworn statement in exchange for the State's promise not to attempt to transfer his case from juvenile to adult court. Not until Guerrero was called as a witness for the State, refused to respond to any questions, and consulted with his attorney was the State's attorney or anyone else expecting Guerrero to decline to testify.

This trial court's actions show the careful consideration and weighing of competing interests so sorely lacking in *Klem.* In contrast to the summary ruling in *Klem,* this trial court held an in-chambers hearing, two open court hearings out of the jury's presence, and delayed ruling until the media could also be heard on the request for closure. Although this trial court did not hold a formal evidentiary hearing on the motion, an evidentiary hearing is not necessarily required unless requested.

The *Klem* trial court's exclusion of the general public, except for one media representative, more closely resembled a complete or total closure of the courtroom than what the trial court did here. This court allowed the Tendeland and Garcia family members to remain in the courtroom. This was only a partial closure, one that generally results in the exclusion of certain members of the public while other members of the public are permitted to remain in the courtroom. When a trial court orders a partial, rather than a total, closure of a court proceeding at the request of a party, a "substantial reason," less stringent than the *Waller* "overriding interest" requirement, can justify the closure. We believe this trial court had a substantial reason to partially and temporarily close Garcia's trial during Guerrero's testimony.

This trial court was aware of the widespread publicity generated by this case and the effect of the television camera in the courtroom. Allegations of street-gang activity dramatized this case. The State's attorney told the court about possible "repercussions" experienced by another subpoenaed witness. Guerrero's attorney explained his juvenile client's understandable intimidation from being seen testifying on television and publicized in newspapers that brought about his reluctance to testify. We would have much preferred the trial court to have gotten the explanation for Guerrero's reluctance to testify from Guerrero himself rather than filtered through the State's attorney and Guerrero's lawyer. But extensive interviews with the reluctant witness, while no doubt the better practice, are not constitutionally compelled. . . . Here, Guerrero's intimidation and hesitation to testify were amply demonstrated to the trial court by his opening refusal to even give his name.

A trial court can properly weigh an accused's right to a public trial against the interests of protecting a witness from intimidation to enable the witness to testify with more composure. A trial court may exclude members of the public from a trial if a witness will be inhibited or embarrassed to testify in the presence of an audience from his tender age or the nature of his testimony, from actual threats, or from the possibility of reprisals by others if the witness testifies. In this case, allegations of gang-related activities and possible "repercussions" like those experienced by another potential witness added to the weighing process. . . .

We disagree with Garcia that the trial court's partial closure order went further than necessary. . . . Garcia did not ask the court to allow other relatives or friends to remain in the courtroom during Guerrero's testimony, although he could have. If Garcia wanted others to remain, he should have pointed them out to the trial court and asked they be allowed to stay. The trial court's order for partial closure lasted only during Guerrero's testimony, and then those excluded were readmitted. . . .

A trial court must also consider reasonable alternatives to a partial closure. We recognize that "[c]losure of the courtroom to the public is not the only, nor necessarily the most effective, response to [witness] intimidation." We also recognize, however, that other alternatives sometimes provoke serious confrontation problems. This record is shallow on consideration of reasonable alternatives. The State's attorney, however, identified confrontation problems in possible alternatives in stating: "[W]e're not asking that Mr. Garcia in any way be deprived of any of his rights of confrontation, cross-examination, so forth. We're merely here to try and search for the truth through all the evidence that's available to us. . . ." The trial court considered variations for the partial closure order, at one point telling the attorneys:

> . . . My initial thoughts were — was to clear the courtroom of everyone except the immediate family of the Garcias. And my initial thought was to order the media not to publish in any fashion any of the testimony that's offered, but not necessarily exclude them from the courtroom. . . . Then, you know, as far as the jury is concerned, the only people that would be missing would be all the spectators.

Although this case poses a difficult question, we conclude the court properly considered reasonable alternatives, and found the partial closure to be the only adequate solution for the problem confronting the court. While it would have been helpful if the trial court had made more explicit findings about possible alternatives, we see no constitutional error here. . . .

We stress again that trial courts should not lightly close a criminal trial in any manner, and when dealing with a request for closure, a court must take pains to develop a complete record and make detailed findings about all the circumstances. More explicit findings would have facilitated review in this case. But, considering the circumstances with the findings the trial court did make, we conclude Garcia's constitutional rights to a public trial were not violated by the brief, narrowly tailored, and partial closure ordered for Guerrero's testimony. . . .

Notes

1. *"Public trial": majority view.* The defendant, prosecution, reporters, and the public may all have different interests with respect to whether a trial remains open. The public nature of criminal trials derives both from the express guarantee of the Sixth Amendment and its state analogs and from the First Amendment rights of both the defendant and the press. The presumption of open trials is usually tested when one party wants to close the proceedings and the other does not. A defendant might want to avoid publicity or retribution, exclude people who might provide new evidence, or reduce the risk of a biased jury. The government might want to protect the identity of an informant, undercover police officer, victim, or witness by limiting the number of people who watch the testimony. See, e.g., People v. Jones, 750 N.E.2d 524 (N.Y. 2001) (undercover officer). Courts are often most sympathetic to victim and witness concerns, especially in cases involving children and in cases of sexual assault and abuse. See generally Vivian Berger, Man's Trial, Woman's Tribulation: Rape Cases in the Courtroom, 77 Colum. L. Rev. 1 (1977); Carol Bohmer and Audrey Blumberg, Twice Traumatized: The Rape Victim and the Court, 58 Judicature 390 (1975). In which North Dakota case was the privacy interests of the witness greater — the child sexual victim in *Klem* or the gang member in *Garcia?* In which case did the state have a greater interest in closing the trial?

2. *Media access to the courtroom: majority view.* The press are members of the public and have the same initial rights as any other person to watch trials. In addition to recognizing the right to court access shared by all citizens, the U.S. Supreme Court has enumerated a qualified First Amendment right in the press to attend criminal trials. See Globe Newspaper Co. v. Superior Court for Norfolk County, 457 U.S. 596 (1982); Richmond Newspapers, Inc. v. Virginia, 448 U.S. 555, 572 (1980). But when the defendant or the government makes a strong claim for closure, the Sixth Amendment right to a fair trial and the less specific rights of the government or witnesses conflict with the First Amendment claims of the press. Federal and state law have created a framework governing press access that leaves substantial discretion in the hands of the trial judge, and newspapers and other media regularly sue for access to proceedings or materials. See, e.g., State ex rel. the Missoulian v. Judicial District, 933 P.2d 829 (Mont. 1997).

In addition to general claims for access, reporters often want to bring their cameras and microphones with them. Courts have largely rejected claims that the media have a constitutional right to bring cameras and microphones into the courtroom. However, 47 states currently allow cameras at trials (with various limitations on the placement and use of flash), and 35 states allow trials to be filmed — a dramatic shift since Florida first allowed cameras into its courtrooms in 1977. See Ruth Strickland and Richter Moore, Cameras in State Courts: A Historical Perspective, 78 Judicature (1994). As in North Dakota, state rules often leave the degree of access to the discretion of the trial judge. In contrast, the federal courts have experimented with but largely rejected the use of cameras in the courtroom. Will new technologies such as the Internet or satellite broadcasts that feature many more channels encourage far greater coverage of court proceedings? Will courts become more or less willing to allow video and audio coverage as requests for access expand to everyday proceedings?

3. *What parts of the trial process must be public?* The general requirement of public trials does not mean that all parts of all trials must be open to the public. The trial proceedings may include bench conferences or discussions between judge and

counsel in chambers. Submissions will often be made in writing. Physical evidence may be difficult to view at a distance, or in the form presented in court. Does the defendant have a right to make these proceedings public? Pretrial proceedings often reveal information that, if reported, might influence the judgment of jurors at trial, and courts have been more willing to restrict access at this stage. See, e.g., State v. Archuleta, 857 P.2d 234 (Utah 1993); but see State v. Densmore, 624 A.2d 1138 (Vt. 1993) (allowing media access to psychosexual evaluation submitted by defendant for sentencing). Some information provided at pretrial proceedings, including detention and competency hearings, may be irrelevant to questions of guilt and innocence. Other proceedings, such as voir dire hearings, are closely linked to trial, and for these proceedings the rules governing media at trial apply. See Press-Enterprise Co. v. Superior Court of California, 464 U.S. 501 (1984).

4. *The public as jury.* The demands of the public may change as viewers become increasingly familiar with televised trials. Whether it is the daily fare of Court TV or the exceptional but widely viewed murder trial of O. J. Simpson, an expectation may develop that citizens have a right to see the justice system at work. Has Court TV increased U.S. citizens' respect for the legal system? As media coverage increases, will the pollution of jury pools and the corresponding risk of unfair trials increase?

5. *Televising appeals.* Is there a difference between televising trials and televising appellate arguments? Are trials or appellate proceedings likely to be of greater public interest? It is very difficult for most U.S. citizens to attend arguments in the U.S. Supreme Court, but the Court has fiercely resisted all efforts to film its arguments. Why? Should audio recordings of state and U.S. Supreme Court arguments be made more widely available?

6. *Press shield laws.* Reporters not only cover events in the courtroom, but also interview victims, witnesses and others outside the courtroom. Some states have "press shield" statutes that allow reporters to refuse to reveal their sources of information to criminal investigators. See Miller v. Superior Court, 986 P.2d 170 (Cal. 1999) (interpreting statute to protect reporter's interviews with offender; reporter cannot be jailed for refusing to turn over interview non-broadcast material to court under subpoena from prosecutor). Do these laws promote more active public scrutiny of the criminal justice system?

2. *Community Courts*

Does the criminal justice process require that decisionmakers be judges or juries? A legal realist might point out that the key decisionmakers in modern American criminal justice systems are often prosecutors rather than judges. But both judges and prosecutors are typically lawyers. Must key decisionmakers — those who choose which citizens to bring before a court and who adjudicate and sentence those convicted of offenses — be lawyers? If citizens are to have a voice in criminal justice decisionmaking (beyond the role of complainant, victim or witness), does the long tradition of the American jury satisfy that need? Jurors are chosen for their lack of knowledge. Should they be chosen for their knowledge?

Two substantial movements are changing the forms of criminal adjudication in the United States. Both movements have deep historical roots.

One movement involves the creation of special "drug courts." There are now around 1000 drug courts in the United States in action or in active planning. See

U.S. Department of Justice, Bureau of Justice Assistance, Looking at a Decade of Drug Courts (NCJ 171140) (1998). Drug courts address specific groups of offenders, typically drug offenders whose activities do not include violence. The offenders adjudicated in drug court must plead guilty, and must return to court often as they serve their sentences to update the court on their status. The first modern "drug court" was established in 1989. Drug courts provide a familiar kind of forum (a court) and a familiar decisionmaker (a judge), but with purposes distinct from general criminal courts. Drug courts reflect a rebirth of the goal of rehabilitation as a justification for punishment and social control, and a recognition that a general jurisdiction court handling serious cases of personal violence might have different purposes and priorities than an offense-specific court.

A second and even newer movement appears in the form of "community courts," which in their modern guise have close links to the idea of community policing and the philosophical aim of "restorative justice." The first modern community court opened in New York City in 1993; between 1998 and 2000, around a dozen other community courts were established, with additional courts planned, suggesting that the idea of community courts is spreading, just as the model of drug courts spread a few years ago. See Eric Lee, Community Courts: An Evolving Model (BJS 2000).

Unlike drug courts, community courts typically have a different forum (a conference room) and a different decisionmaker (community members). The goals of community court and the tools to achieve those goals also contrast with traditional criminal courts. Consider the case of four men cited for urinating in public in Manhattan, at different times and in different places. See Center for Court Innovation, "There Are No Victimless Crimes": Community Impact Panels at the Midtown Community Court (BJA 2000). About a month after they were charged, all four were summoned to a meeting with five other people — a "discussion facilitator" and a community panel made up of four people who live or work in the neighborhood: a man and woman in their 60s, a priest, and an out-of-uniform police officer.

The accused citizens are asked to explain what brought them to community court. Two are students from a local university, another is an immigrant cab driver. Each describes the time and place of his infraction. The cab driver explains that "The paper says 'public urination,' [but] it was not in public. It was dark. It was nine o'clock. No people, no vehicles, nothing. [I was] in front of Javits Center, on 38th Street. But there was no single person. Nothing!"

The community members then ask questions, such as "Everyone has to urinate; what do cabbies usually do?" and express their frustrations: "I'm on a community board and I've heard a number of complaints about cabbies who open their door and urinate on the street. It's very offensive, it bothers a lot of people, it's not hygienic. It helps to change the quality of a neighborhood. It's sort of like there's a pact people have in society. You behave in a certain way or you find yourself in a community that's known for breaking the laws."

All participants discuss the reasons for public urination by taxi drivers, students, and others. One of the students says, "I definitely would not want anybody in my doorway using it as a bathroom. But I understand it because I'm on this side. . . . There are a lot of clubs in the area, and a lot of people have the same problem. And it's not a problem that's going to go away by just talking about it; if you have to go and you're drunk, you're going to go."

After two hours of discussion, participants fill out post-meeting questionnaires.

One of the offenders walks around the table to shake hands with each of the community representatives, who have been asked to remain in the room for a short post-meeting debriefing with the facilitator. Outside in the hallway a few moments later, the taxi driver reflects upon what he just experienced as he waits for the elevator. "It's very nice," he says. "We learned to keep the community clean." One of the students, standing nearby, steps forward. "It was nice," he says. "Well, not really 'nice,' but we got to experience the other side. We got to meet with the people, and that was good. We got a sense of the community."

Asked if the experience will influence his decision to urinate in public again, he pauses to think before answering. "I went in there knowing I did something wrong. I pissed in the street. Having to face these people made me feel worse. It gets to you more on a personal level than just having to pay a fine."

Consider what the creation of new kinds of courts says about our current criminal justice process. Should traditional courts be more like community courts? What percentage of the role of traditional criminal courts should be handled in community courts? What percentage of the work of community courts will reflect "net widening"— the assessment of matters that would not have been handled within the criminal justice system? Should participation in community courts be voluntary? Is there any problem with solving the community's problems in the community, with community members as decisionmakers?

■ RESPONDING TO THE COMMUNITY: PRINCIPLES FOR PLANNING AND CREATING A COMMUNITY COURT JOHN FEINBLATT AND GREG BERMAN

NCJ 185986 (Feb. 2001)

For many years an important element has been missing from the criminal justice system. Although courts, police, and prosecutors have become increasingly modernized in recent years, they still often fail to meet the needs of the justice system's primary consumers: the neighborhoods that experience crime and its consequences every day. This problem was first recognized by advocates of community policing, who argued that police officers could address neighborhood crime and disorder more effectively if they established a close relationship with community residents and neighborhood groups. The idea of community justice has since spread to other branches of the justice system including courts, probation departments, prosecutors, and corrections offices. . . .

New York City's Midtown Community Court, which opened in October 1993, differs dramatically from the way that lower courts have operated in the city for many years. Nevertheless, it reflects a return to an old idea. In 1962, New York City closed a network of neighborhood magistrate's courts that handled intake for the city's court system. These courts arraigned defendants and disposed of low-level offenses that did not need to be forwarded to a higher tribunal. . . . While this change increased efficiency to an extent, its cost was remoteness — the new centralized courts were removed from the communities they served. As caseloads increased, felony cases naturally began to claim more and more attention. Fewer resources were devoted to quality-of-life misdemeanors like shoplifting, prostitution, and subway fare cheating, and judges were under tremendous pressure to dispose of such cases quickly. All too often defendants arrested for low-level offenses were released after being sentenced to either "time served" while awaiting their court appearance, a fine that might or might not be paid, or community service that might or might not be performed.

[T]he planners of the Midtown Community Court sought to recreate neighborhood-based intake and arraignment along the lines of the magistrate's courts, but with innovations to meet the needs of the 1990s. It was hoped that such a court could focus on quality-of-life crimes that erode a community's morale. This return to a concern about crimes that affect neighborhood life coincided with the New York City Police Department's new emphasis on community policing, as well as with a growing interest in community-oriented justice on the part of prosecutors, probation offices, and corrections agencies nationwide. . . .

With the help of the local community board — the smallest unit of government in New York City — planners found a location for the court near Times Square on the West Side of Manhattan, an area teeming with quality-of-life crimes. The 1896 building, which was once a magistrate's court, was renovated. . . . The court's location, architecture, and technology are part of a larger strategy to honor the idea of community by making justice restorative. Offenders are sentenced to make restitution to the community through work projects in the neighborhood: caring for trees lining the streets, removing graffiti, cleaning subway stations, and sorting cans and bottles for recycling. At the same time, the court uses its legal leverage to link offenders with drug treatment, health care, education, and other social services.

By the summer of 1996, Midtown had become one of the busiest arraignment courts in the city, arraigning an average of 65 cases per day for an annual total of more than 16,000 cases. Offenders sentenced by the court perform the equivalent of 175,000 dollars' worth of community service work per year. . . . Nearly 75 percent of offenders processed through Midtown complete their community service sentences as mandated, which is the highest rate in the city. . . .

Midtown Community Court's planning team pursued . . . goals they considered to be at the heart of community justice. [The goals included principles for restoring the community:]

- Recognize that communities are victims. Quality-of-life crimes damage communities. If unaddressed, low-level offenses erode communal order, leading to disinvestment and neighborhood decay and creating an atmosphere in which more serious crime can flourish. . . .
- Use punishment to pay back the community. Standard sentences that involve jail, fines, and probation may punish offenders, but they do little to make restitution for the damage caused by crime. A community court requires offenders to compensate neighborhoods through community service.
- Combine punishment with help. By permanently altering the behavior of chronic offenders, social service programs can play an important role in crime control. Encouraging offenders to deal with their problems honors a community's ethical obligation to people who break its laws because they have lost control of their lives.
- Give the community a voice in shaping restorative sanctions. The most effective community courts open a dialog with neighbors, seeking their input in developing appropriate community service projects. A community advisory board can offer residents an institutionalized mechanism for interacting with the judge and court administrators. . . .

[Community courts also embody principles for bridging the gap between communities and courts:]

- Make justice visible. A community court puts offenders to work in places where neighbors can see what they are doing, outfitting them in ways that identify them as offenders performing community service. . . .
- Make justice accessible. A community court welcomes observers and visitors from the community, giving them an opportunity to see justice in action. Calendars and other information about activities in the courtroom are available to the public on computer terminals in the lobby. . . .
- Reach out to victims. A community court can be a safe haven for victims, offering them assistance and a voice in the criminal justice process. Because it is based in the neighborhood where victims live, a community court may be able to provide access to services more quickly and in a less intimidating setting than larger, centralized courts.

[These courts carry out] principles for knitting together a fractured criminal justice system, [and for helping offenders deal with problems that lead to crime:]

- Use the court's authority to link criminal justice agencies. Too often, criminal justice agencies work in isolation, moving cases from street to court to cell and back again without communicating or taking the time to solve problems. . . .
- Explore crossing jurisdictional lines. The problems citizens face often do not conform to the narrow jurisdictional boundaries imposed by modern court systems. A criminal defendant also may be involved in a landlord-tenant dispute or a small claims matter. Handling all of a defendant's cases in one place enhances the court's ability to address the defendant's underlying problems. . . .
- Use the court as a gateway to treatment. The trauma of arrest may prompt a defendant to seek help. A court can use its coercive power to reinforce that impulse.
- Remain involved beyond disposition of the immediate case. A judge in a community court can monitor offenders' experiences in treatment, using the court's authority to reward progress or impose new sanctions for failure.

[S]ome judges, attorneys, and police believe that greater involvement with the community compromises their objectivity. To maintain impartiality, judges traditionally have insulated themselves from the communities and victims affected by the issues they adjudicate, while prosecutors and police have restricted the discretion of frontline attorneys and officers on the beat. . . .

The underlying assumptions and guiding philosophies of law enforcement and social service differ in fundamental ways. Criminal justice professionals operate in a system of escalating sanctions in which defendants are punished more severely each time they fail; criminal courts are not comfortable giving offenders a second chance. Treatment professionals, however, expect relapses and believe that it is critical that clients remain in treatment when a relapse occurs. Addicts may need to hear the same message many times before the message finally sinks in. The community court's approach can work only if criminal justice and social service professionals are willing to adjust their outlooks and work together. . . .

Many quality-of-life problems in a community are not violations of the law and do not come to the attention of the police or the courts. The Midtown Community Court has sought to address these problems in [several] ways. First, the court established a mediation service to resolve neighborhood disputes (for example, the opening of an adult movie house or the operation of a noisy repair shop) before they escalate to legal battles. In addition to helping the community deal with such problems, the service conveys the court's commitment to the community and its quality of life. Second, the court set up a street outreach unit, staffed by police officers and caseworkers from the court, to enroll potential clients in court-based social service programs before they get into trouble with the law. Four mornings a week, outreach teams scour the neighborhood, encouraging likely clients-prostitutes, substance abusers, and homeless people-to come in for help voluntarily. . . .

Police and community groups lose heart in fighting low-level crime when they lack a reliable way to measure progress. To measure its impact on the community, a community court should deploy researchers, compile results, and publicize success. . . . Besides the traditional work of caseload and sentencing outcome analysis, research staff at the Midtown Community Court study problems raised by neighbors. The court's researchers monitor patterns of prostitution and drug dealing as well as street sanitation. To help community groups and police target resources, the researchers have developed neighborhood-specific computer software to map arrests, complaints, and other quality-of-life indicators. When the research confirms success, a community court should be ready to make this success known locally and to other communities that have established community courts. A court can create its own newsletter and Internet Web site and should promote media coverage to ensure feedback on successes to the community.

[T]o be effective a community court must address the needs of the court system's most important constituency: the people who live and work in neighborhoods affected by crime. To address these needs, a community court must ask a new set of questions. What can a court do to solve neighborhood problems? What can courts bring to the table beyond their coercive power and symbolic presence? And what roles can community residents, businesses, and service providers play in improving justice? . . .

Notes

1. *Special courts.* The dramatic emergence in the 1990s of special courts to handle drug offenders, the mentally ill, and now low-level community offenders have their roots in the many police and magistrate courts common throughout the United States until the middle of the twentieth century. Advocates of court unification in the early twentieth century, such as Harvard Law School Dean and jurisprude Roscoe Pound led the elimination of many special courts. Special juvenile courts and family courts remained in place in many jurisdictions through the twentieth century, the remnants of special courts. Other special courts include over 450 tribal forums.

Special courts have reemerged with a vengeance. Indeed some types, like drug courts, are proliferating at such a high rate that it is hard even to count them. From a single drug court in Florida in 1989, there are now around 1000 drug courts operating in at least 48 states — most active, some in the final planning stages.

Now community courts have started their own dramatic upswing. Community courts move farther than drug courts in terms of changing the forum, the decisionmakers, the sentences and the purposes of punishment and social control. By March 2000, community courts were operating in Connecticut, Florida, Georgia, Minnesota, New York, Oregon, Tennessee and Texas; more than dozen others have been proposed, including courts in California, Colorado, Delaware, Hawaii, Indiana, Maryland, and Pennsylvania. See Eric Lee, Bureau of Justice Assistance, Community Courts: An Evolving Model (NCJ 183452) (BJS 2000).

2. *Do special courts work?* Special courts excite their supporters. Whether they work is another question, and one addressed rarely in the burgeoning literature. Indeed, many supporters of special courts do not stop to define the measures of success, pointing instead to the failures of traditional criminal courts, the need to do something different, and to anecdotes of apparent success. Advocates of community courts chose the story about public urination to illuminate the idea and virtue of community courts: Is this a story of success?

Perhaps community courts are still too young for complete assessment. Given the huge number of citizens now passing through drug courts, and the proportion of such offenders who would have been handled through the traditional criminal justice system, there have been strong calls for more formal assessment. In April 2002, the General Accounting Office reported that data was not yet available to make a sound evaluation of drug court effectiveness, and called for a "methodologically sound national impact evaluation." See United States General Accounting Office, Report to Congressional Requesters, Drug Courts: Better DOJ Data Collection and Evaluation Efforts Needed to Measure Impact of Drug Court Programs (GAO-02-434) (April 2002). What should the measures of success for any special court be? Will it vary by the type of court?

3. *The limits of the criminal law.* Community courts, drug courts, family courts and other special courts appear to address problems related to, but beyond, the traditional core of the criminal justice system. Among their common features are less legal process and fewer lawyers, but also less severe sanctions. What are the virtues and dangers and blurring the lines between criminal and civil justice systems? What are, and what should be, the limits of the criminal justice system to respond to the problems of society?

XVIII

Witnesses and Proof

A complete understanding of felony trials requires a knowledge of substantive criminal law, the law of evidence, trial strategy, and procedural rules. Yet it is possible to boil down this wide-ranging material into a few core principles of procedure that define criminal trials. At a general level, these principles are familiar to lawyers and nonlawyers alike.

The first core principle is the presumption of innocence — the idea that a person is not guilty of a crime until the state proves to a fact finder that the person has committed a criminal act with the requisite mental state. The state must prove its case "beyond a reasonable doubt." This is now considered the mirror image of the presumption of innocence.

The second principle — the right to confront witnesses — is our central tool for squeezing truth from the evidence. It is not hard to imagine a system (however unpalatable) that does not presume innocence or that allows conviction on some standard lower than beyond a reasonable doubt, but it is difficult to imagine a system that does not allow a defendant the right to challenge and test witnesses and other evidence.

The defendant can confront any government witness, and the government can confront any defense witness. But can the government call any witness to prove a case? The third principle — the privilege against self-incrimination — recognizes the single great exception to the power of the government to call relevant witnesses. The principle recognizes that a defendant cannot be forced to testify, either by threat of prison or by calling the defendant's silence to the attention of the fact finder. This principle may preclude the government from calling the single person who may know most about the alleged offense.

This chapter explores these core principles. The first section examines the meaning and role of the reasonable doubt standard, since this concept sets up the hurdles that the prosecution must clear during its presentation of witnesses and other evidence. The second section considers the law of confrontation, looking primarily at the defendant's power to test the evidence that the government presents. The third section studies the implementation of the privilege against self-incrimination at trial. The fourth section highlights one of the most important ethical dilemmas in an adversary trial system devoted to finding the truth: What should a defense lawyer do if the lawyer believes the client or a witness is lying? What should a prosecutor do if the prosecutor believes a key witness is lying?

A. BURDEN OF PROOF

Some commentators are skeptical about the practical consequences of using various standards of proof in civil and criminal cases. Perhaps jurors would reach the same verdicts whether they were told to decide cases on preponderance-of-the-evidence, "clear and convincing" proof, or beyond-a-reasonable doubt standards. But the idea (if not the precise language) of the reasonable doubt standard has ancient roots, and the higher burden on the government to obtain a conviction in criminal cases is the cornerstone for principles and practices that appear throughout the criminal trial.

1. *Reasonable Doubt*

How should reasonable doubt be defined? How should juries be instructed to decide when the government has proven its case "beyond" that point? The very phrase "beyond a reasonable doubt" suggests a tension that makes the concept difficult to grasp: Doubt is a negative concept, but to go "beyond" a given amount of evidence is a positive concept. This tension — between a positive and a negative conception of reasonable doubt — is reflected in various definitions and rules that the states have adopted. Is there a single point at which reasonable doubt is passed, or do these positive and negative notions together define a range for juries to apply? Can this tension be resolved?

Some courts simply direct jurors to decide whether the government has proven all elements beyond a reasonable doubt, and allow no further explanation of the reasonable doubt concept. See Romano v. State, 909 P.2d 92 (Okla. Crim. App. 1995). A leading nineteenth-century treatise explains this position: "There are no words plainer than reasonable doubt and none so exact to the idea meant." 1 Joel Prentiss Bishop, New Criminal Procedure, §1094 (1895). Most jurisdictions either direct or allow judges to define reasonable doubt more precisely. Should judges be limited to a standard definition? If so, which one?

■ STEVE WINEGEART v. STATE

665 N.E.2d 893 (Ind. 1996)

DICKSON, J.

How to instruct juries regarding reasonable doubt has long been a subject on which courts, individual judges, and lawyers have taken differing approaches. Today we seek not only to resolve conflicting opinions among different panels of the Court of Appeals but also to foster the improved wording of instructions so that we may achieve greater juror understanding and better application of the rudimentary principle of proof beyond a reasonable doubt.

Following a jury trial, defendant-appellant Steve Winegeart was convicted of the crime of burglary. . . . In his appeal from the conviction, the defendant contends that the trial court erred in instructing the jury regarding reasonable doubt. . . . The defendant asserts that the following instruction, which used the words "actual," "fair," and "moral certainty," permitted the jury to find guilt based upon a degree of proof below that required by the Due Process Clause of the Fourteenth Amendment to the United States Constitution. After stating that the burden is upon the State to prove guilt beyond a reasonable doubt, the challenged instruction explained:

> A reasonable doubt is such doubt as you may have in your mind when having fairly considered all of the evidence, you do not feel satisfied to a moral certainty of the guilt of the defendant. A reasonable doubt is a fair, actual and logical doubt that arises in the mind as an impartial consideration of all the evidence and the circumstances in the case. It is not every doubt, however, it is a reasonable one. You are not warranted in considering as reasonable those doubts that may be merely speculative or products of the imagination, and you may not act upon mere whim, guess or surmise or upon the mere possibility of guilt. A reasonable doubt arises, or exists in the mind, naturally, as a result of the evidence or the lack of evidence. There is nothing in this that is mysterious or fanciful. It does not contemplate absolute or mathematical certainty. Despite every precaution that may be taken to prevent it, there may be in all matters depending upon human testimony for proof, a mere possibility of error.
>
> If, after considering all of the evidence, you have reached such a firm belief in the guilt of the defendant that you would feel safe to act upon that belief, without hesitation, in a matter of the highest concern and importance to you, then you have reached that degree of certainty which excludes reasonable doubt and authorizes conviction. . . .

Winegeart contends that the giving of the reasonable-doubt instruction blatantly violated constitutional principles and deprived his jury trial of fairness. He asserts that in the reasonable-doubt instruction used in his jury trial, the words "actual" and "fair" expand the quantum of doubt needed to constitute "reasonable" doubt, and that the instruction refers to "moral certainty" instead of "evidentiary certainty," thus authorizing the jury to find guilt based on a degree of proof below that required by the Due Process Clause.

The Due Process Clause of the Fourteenth Amendment protects an accused "against conviction except upon proof beyond a reasonable doubt of every fact necessary to constitute the crime with which he is charged." In re Winship, 397 U.S. 358 (1970). Because of the transcending interest a criminal defendant has in his liberty, the risk of an erroneous conviction necessitates that a substantial burden of proof be placed upon the prosecution. The standard of proof beyond a reasonable doubt serves to impress upon the fact-finder "the need to reach a subjective state of near certitude of the guilt of the accused." Jackson v. Virginia, 443 U.S. 307 (1979). While the federal constitution requires that juries be instructed "on the necessity that the defendant's guilt be proven beyond a reasonable doubt," it does not require the use of "any particular form of words." Victor v. Nebraska, 511 U.S. 1 (1994). However, the jury instructions, taken as a whole, must correctly express the concept of reasonable doubt to the jury.

In Cage v. Louisiana, 498 U.S. 39 (1990) (per curiam), a reasonable-doubt instruction was determined to be constitutionally defective. In defining reasonable doubt, the instruction included language that equated reasonable doubt with "a grave uncertainty" and "an actual substantial doubt" and stated, "What is required is not an absolute or mathematical certainty, but a moral certainty." The Court found that the words "substantial" and "grave" suggested a "higher degree of doubt than is required for acquittal under the reasonable-doubt standard," and that these statements, together with the reference to "moral certainty," rather than "evidentiary certainty," permitted a finding of guilt based upon a degree of proof below that required by the Due Process Clause.

These principles were discussed and applied by the United States Supreme Court in the recent companion cases of Victor v. Nebraska and Sandoval v. California, 511 U.S. 1 (1994), which approved reasonable-doubt instructions that included phrases such as "to a moral certainty," and "actual and substantial doubt." In both of the instructions approved in *Victor* and *Sandoval,* the moral certainty language appeared in very similar sentences, which stated that reasonable doubt occurs when, after "consideration of all the evidence," the juror does not have "an abiding conviction, to a moral certainty" of the guilt of the accused. In this context, the Supreme Court explained that "the reference to moral certainty, in conjunction with the abiding conviction language," sufficiently emphasized "the need to reach a subjective state of near certitude of the guilt of the accused." The *Victor* court also distinguished its "moral certainty" instructions from the one in *Cage,* noting that "the problem in *Cage* was that the rest of the instruction provided insufficient context to lend meaning to the phrase." The Court noted, "Instructing the jurors that they must have an abiding conviction of the defendant's guilt does much to alleviate any concerns that the phrase moral certainty might be misunderstood in the abstract." Although clearly stating that the Justices "do not condone" and "do not countenance" the inclusion of the phrase moral certainty in a reasonable-doubt instruction, the Court found that in the context of the entire instruction, which explicitly directed the jurors to base their conclusion on the evidence of the case and not to engage in speculation or conjecture, the inclusion of the moral certainty language did not render the instruction unconstitutional. Similarly, while noting that equating reasonable doubt with substantial doubt is "somewhat problematic," the Court found that the context of the instruction, unlike that in *Cage,* contrasted substantial doubt with fanciful conjecture. It concluded that "taken as a whole, the instructions correctly conveyed the concept of reasonable doubt to the jury."

The challenged words and phrases in the reasonable-doubt instruction given to the *Winegeart* jury contain both significant differences from, and substantial similarities to, the instructions approved in *Victor.* The *Winegeart* instruction's reference to "moral certainty" lacks the "abiding conviction" language noted in *Victor.* On the other hand, the "actual and substantial doubt" wording in the Nebraska instruction in *Victor* is similar to the "fair, actual, and logical doubt" phrase used in Winegeart's trial. Moreover, the *Winegeart* jury was directed to base its decision on all the evidence; to disregard whim, guess, surmise, or mere possibility of guilt; and to consider the "hesitate to act" benchmark—all factors that the *Victor* court found significant. . . .

The proper constitutional inquiry "is not whether the instruction 'could have' been applied in an unconstitutional manner, but whether there is a reasonable likelihood that the jury did so apply it." *Victor.* [W]e conclude that there is not a reasonable likelihood that the jurors who determined the defendant's guilt applied the instruction in a way that violated the Due Process Clause. . . . However, we disapprove of the continued use of this instruction in the future.

The instruction uses 300 words in 11 sentences to explain reasonable doubt. This is not atypical for reasonable-doubt instructions, which often appear to be a conglomeration of phrases providing supplemental or alternative explication of reasonable doubt. Through the years, appellate decisions have held a wide variety of reasonable-doubt instructions to satisfy the minimal constitutional requirements. After a particular phrase has been thus tolerated by appellate courts, trial courts will often — usually in response to requests by counsel — incorporate such "approved" phrases into reasonable-doubt instructions. As a result, most reasonable-doubt instructions commonly in use in our courts today have not been crafted for the purpose of most effectively explaining the concept of reasonable doubt to jurors but rather are used primarily because the language therein is considered adequate to avoid appellate reversal.

As courts utilize such longer, more intricate explanations of reasonable doubt, juries are likely to draw an overall impression which may transcend the literal meaning of the substance of the words. Such lengthy and conceptually challenging instructions often present a drumbeat repetition, declaring that reasonable doubt is not every doubt, not whim, not guess, not surmise, not mere possibility, not fanciful, etc.; and that to qualify as reasonable doubt, such doubt must be fair, actual, logical, natural, etc. It is not surprising that jurors often have difficulty in synthesizing and comprehending reasonable doubt or that they may perceive that the instructing judge is minimizing the degree of doubt that will preclude a finding of guilt.

Although reluctant to find reversible error in instructions purporting to explain reasonable doubt, the United States Supreme Court has acknowledged: "Attempts to explain the term 'reasonable doubt' do not usually result in making it any clearer to the minds of the jury." Miles v. United States, 103 U.S. 304 (1881). The Seventh Circuit has declared:

> "Reasonable doubt" must speak for itself. Jurors know what is "reasonable" and are quite familiar with the meaning of "doubt." Judges' and lawyers' attempts to inject other amorphous catch-phrases into the "reasonable doubt" standard, such as "matter of the highest importance" only muddy the water. . . . It is, therefore, inappropriate for judges to give an instruction defining "reasonable doubt," and it is equally inappropriate for trial counsel to provide their own definition.

United States v. Glass, 846 F.2d 386, 386 (7th Cir. 1988). This view has found support in several other jurisdictions. [The court cited cases from Illinois, Kansas, Missouri, and the U.S. Court of Appeals for the Fourth Circuit.]

Professor Wigmore, noting that "various efforts have been made to define more in detail this elusive and undefinable state of mind," states: "In practice, these detailed amplifications of the doctrine have usually degenerated into a mere tool for counsel . . . to save a cause for a new trial. . . . The effort to [develop these elaborate unserviceable definitions] should be abandoned." 9 John Henry Wigmore, Evidence in Trials at Common Law §2497, 406-409 (James Chadbourn rev. 1981).

Substantial research by linguists, psychologists, and others suggests that many jurors have difficulty understanding jury instructions but much less difficulty understanding those that have been rewritten in light of psycholinguistic principles.

See Peter Tiersma, Reforming the Language of Jury Instructions, 22 Hofstra L. Rev. 37 (1993). Researchers have provided valuable suggestions on how to write more comprehensible jury instructions, including the [elimination] of jargon and modifying clauses and the use of simpler language. Summarizing the suggestions of psycholinguists, Professor Tanford provides ten guidelines for the improvement of instructions.

1. Eliminate nominalizations (making nouns out of verbs) and substitute verb forms; e.g., changing "an offer of evidence" to "items were offered into evidence."
2. Replace the prepositional phrase "as to" with "about"; e.g., changing "you must not speculate as to what the answer might have been" to "you must not speculate about what the answer might have been."
3. Relocate prepositional phrases so they do not interrupt a sentence; e.g., avoiding sentences such as "proximate cause is a cause which, in a natural and continuous sequence, produces the injury."
4. Replace words that are difficult to understand with simple ones; e.g., changing "agent's negligence is imputed to plaintiff" to "agent's negligence transfers to plaintiff."
5. Avoid multiple negatives in a sentence; e.g., "innocent mis-recollection is not uncommon."
6. Use the active rather than passive voice; e.g., changing "no emphasis is intended by me" to "I do not intend to emphasize."
7. Avoid "whiz" deletions (omitting words "which is"); e.g., by changing "statements of counsel" to "statements which are made by counsel."
8. Reduce long lists of words with similar meanings to only one or two; e.g., shortening "knowledge, skill, experience, training, or education" to "training or experience."
9. Organize instructions into meaningful discourse structures that avoid connecting unrelated ideas in ways that make them seem related.
10. Avoid embedding subordinate clauses in sentences; e.g., "you must not speculate to be true any insinuation suggested by a question asked a witness."

J. Alexander Tanford, The Law and Psychology of Jury Instructions, 69 Neb. L. Rev. 71 (1990).

We agree in principle with the . . . jurisdictions that have concluded that the phrase "reasonable doubt" may suffice without further explication and that many attempts to provide effective additional explanation have fallen short. However, we are not convinced that the task is impossible in light of recent and ongoing research, and we thus prefer to endorse for use in Indiana courts a reasonable-doubt instruction that, to the maximum extent possible, reflects the wisdom of the various available resources.

There is an inherent challenge in devising a comprehensible and succinct instruction explaining to lay jurors the concept of reasonable doubt. They must be informed that their determination of guilt depends upon the absence of reasonable doubt. The existence of reasonable doubt precludes a finding of guilt. Viewed in this way, the reasonable-doubt instruction is necessarily an attempt to define a negative concept. When court instructions proceed to define this concept by stating what it is not, the resulting double negative concept diminishes juror comprehension even further. In addition, we perceive that instructions containing repeated statements narrowing the class of doubts eligible for consideration as reasonable doubt may have a cumulative effect of minimizing the value and importance of this bedrock principle of criminal justice.

Although not utilized by the trial court in the present case, one attempt to suggest an improved reasonable-doubt instruction is found in Indiana Pattern Jury Instruction 1.15:

> A reasonable doubt is a fair, actual and logical doubt that arises in your mind after an impartial consideration of all of the evidence and circumstances in the case. It should be a doubt based upon reason and common sense and not a doubt based upon imagination or speculation.
>
> To prove the defendant's guilt of the elements of the crime charged beyond a reasonable doubt, the evidence must be such that it would convince you of the truth of it, to such a degree of certainty that you would feel safe to act upon such conviction, without hesitation, in a matter of the highest concern and importance to you.

1 Indiana Pattern Jury Instructions — Criminal, instruct. 1.15 (2d ed. 1991). This instruction seeks to explain what reasonable doubt is and is not and then proceeds to equate "beyond a reasonable doubt" with the degree of probability a juror would require to act unhesitatingly "in a manner of highest concern and importance to" himself or herself. Such attempts to quantify the degree of probability have received mixed reviews.

The "hesitate to act" analogy is discussed in *Victor.* The *Victor* majority comments that "the hesitate to act standard gives a common-sense benchmark for just how substantial such a doubt must be." [However, a committee of distinguished federal judges, reporting to the Judicial Conference of the United States, has criticized this "hesitate to act" formulation."] The committee explained:

> [T]he analogy it uses seems misplaced. In the decisions people make in the most important of their own affairs, resolution of conflicts about past events does not usually play a major role. Indeed, decisions we make in the most important affairs of our lives — choosing a spouse, a job, a place to live, and the like — generally, involve a very heavy element of uncertainty and risk-taking. They are wholly unlike the decisions jurors ought to make in criminal cases.

Federal Judicial Center, Pattern Criminal Jury Instructions (1987). We find such reasoning persuasive and believe that, while the "hesitate to act" language may bolster an otherwise marginal instruction against constitutional challenge, use of this analogy is neither required nor particularly desirable in explaining the concept of reasonable doubt.

In contrast to the Indiana Pattern Jury Instruction and other common instructions that attempt to define the negative concept of reasonable doubt, a proposal from the Federal Judicial Center focuses upon the positive concept of proof beyond a reasonable doubt. It defines that term, succinctly, as proof "that leaves you firmly convinced," and explains that reasonable doubt is a greater degree of doubt than merely "possible doubt." It explains that a juror's choice between guilty and not guilty should be equated to the distinction between "firmly convinced" of guilt versus "a real possibility" that the defendant is not guilty. The instruction states:

> [T]he government has the burden of proving the defendant guilty beyond a reasonable doubt. Some of you may have served as jurors in civil cases, where you were told that it

is only necessary to prove that a fact is more likely true than not true. In criminal cases, the government's proof must be more powerful than that. It must be beyond a reasonable doubt.

Proof beyond a reasonable doubt is proof that leaves you firmly convinced of the defendant's guilt. There are very few things in this world that we know with absolute certainty, and in criminal cases the law does not require proof that overcomes every possible doubt. If, based on your consideration of the evidence, you are firmly convinced that the defendant is guilty of the crime charged, you [should] find [him/her] guilty. If on the other hand, you think there is a real possibility that [he/she] is not guilty, you [should] give [him/her] the benefit of the doubt and find [him/her] not guilty. [Federal Judicial Center, Pattern Criminal Jury Instructions (1987).]

In the exercise of our inherent and constitutional supervisory responsibilities, see Ind. Const. Art. VII, §4, we seek to assure that juries in criminal cases are equipped with instructions that will allow them to understand and apply correctly the concept of reasonable doubt. Informed by numerous studies and recommendations from academic and judicial authorities, we acknowledge the shortcomings in Indiana Pattern Jury Instruction 1.15, in the instruction at Winegeart's trial, and in the various other reasonable-doubt explanations commonly in use. A substantial improvement in effective communication may be achieved by utilization of the Federal Judicial Center's proposed instruction. We therefore authorize and recommend (but, acknowledging that two of the five members of this Court find the present Indiana Pattern Jury Instruction preferable, do not mandate) that Indiana trial courts henceforth instruct regarding reasonable doubt by giving the above-quoted Federal Judicial Center instruction, preferably with no supplementation or embellishment. We also request that this instruction be added to the next revision of the Indiana Pattern Jury Instructions — Criminal.

While the challenged instruction in the present case is less effective than we would prefer, it is not so deficient as to be constitutionally defective. We therefore reject the defendant's contention of reversible error regarding the trial court's reasonable-doubt instruction. . . .

DEBRULER, J., concurring in result.

I do not share the majority's perception of deep problems within this area, nor the belief that the Federal Judicial Center, Pattern Criminal Jury Instructions are the appropriate remedy. Specifically, I do not believe that "firmly convinced" equates to "beyond a reasonable doubt." Both objectively and subjectively, "firmly convinced" seems more similar to "clear and convincing" than to "beyond a reasonable doubt." I find the Indiana Pattern Jury Instruction more than adequate.

■ JURY INSTRUCTIONS: A PERSISTENT FAILURE TO COMMUNICATE
WALTER STEELE AND ELIZABETH THORNBURG

67 N.C. L. Rev. 77 (1988)

. . . Lawyers and judges have suspected for some time . . . that many jurors do not understand their instructions. These suspicions are confirmed by numerous reported cases in which jury confusion peeks through. Recent social science research has demonstrated empirically that juror comprehension of instructions is appallingly low.

Some of that research further demonstrates that rewriting instructions with clarity as the goal can dramatically improve comprehensibility. Despite these findings, and despite the existence of books and articles explaining how to write instructions more clearly, lawyers and judges continue to produce jury instructions that are incomprehensible to juries. . . .

I. Documented Jury Confusion

. . . Social scientists studying group behavior have conducted tests on juries to determine the uses jurors make of their instructions. Forston [performed empirical studies with jurors in the early 1970s. One such study attempted] to learn what percentage of the instructions individual jurors and deliberating jurors retain and comprehend. . . . His subjects this time were 114 experienced jurors in Polk County, Iowa. [The] jurors were divided into groups. Each group was given detailed background information about its case and read a set of instructions. Each individual juror was given a multiple choice retention-comprehension test. Then the jurors, in groups of six, were given the test as a deliberating group and told that they had to agree unanimously on the answers. The results again showed confusion and misunderstanding. While the deliberating juries scored 10 to 14 percent better than the mean of individual jurors, large numbers of the deliberating juries misunderstood important instructions. "Eighty-six percent of the criminal juries were unable to respond accurately to what constitutes proof of guilt." . . .

Other studies of jury behavior have noted both the influence of instructions and juror misunderstanding of those instructions. In one study, a videotaped reenactment of a murder trial was shown to people called for jury service in three Massachusetts counties. The researchers videotaped and analyzed the jury deliberations. When all the juries were analyzed, the researchers found that an average of 25 percent of the juror discussions referred to the judge's instructions. Analyzing one jury in detail, the researchers [found] that jurors made seven incorrect statements about the meaning of the judge's instructions, only one of which was corrected by other jurors. . . .

Probably the most thorough of the psycholinguistic studies of jury instructions was done by Robert and Veda Charrow in the late 1970s. While the earlier studies revealed that rewriting jury instructions could improve comprehension, they had not tested empirically the linguistic features that impeded comprehension. The Charrows set out to isolate the linguistic features that cause comprehension problems in jury instructions. Their study consisted of two major experiments, each conducted on people called for jury service in Prince Georges County, Maryland.

In the first experiment 35 jurors paraphrased each of 14 pattern jury instructions. In the second experiment the instructions were rewritten to eliminate the words and constructions that seemed to cause confusion in the first experiment. The rewritten instructions then were tested on 48 new jurors. The results showed dramatic improvement in juror comprehension. For example, comprehension of . . . an instruction about the use of evidence improved 52 percent. Overall comprehension improved 35 percent. This improvement occurred even in those instructions which were conceptually quite difficult, casting doubt on many practicing lawyers' argument that it is the conceptual complexity of a jury instruction that creates comprehension problems and that therefore rewriting instructions will not help. . . .

II. Empirical Research: Confusion and Cure

The subjects for our test of juror comprehension of instructions were people called to jury service in Dallas County, Texas, who had not yet served on a jury. Thus, our experimental subjects were actual and potential jurors, demographically identical with the group we wanted to learn about. . . . We selected five pattern jury instructions for testing: (1) proximate cause; (2) new and independent cause; (3) negligence; (4) presumption of innocence; and (5) accomplice testimony. . . .

With two sets of instructions in hand—five pattern instructions and a corresponding set of five rewritten instructions—the next step was to test whether the "simplified" language in the rewritten set enhanced comprehension. To do this we created audio tapes to be played for the jurors. Each tape contained five instructions selected from the five pattern and five rewritten instruction sets. These five were selected in such a way that each tape had both pattern and rewritten instructions; however, to avoid any "learning effect" no tape contained both the pattern and the rewritten version of the same instruction. . . . We used a testing method known as a "paraphrase test": each subject was asked to explain the instructions in her own words. We played each taped instruction for the subject only once. After each instruction was played, we stopped the tape player and started a tape recorder into which the subject stated her understanding of the meaning of the instruction just played. That process was repeated until the subject had heard and paraphrased all five instructions.

In order to calculate the accuracy of each subject's responses, we developed a scoresheet for each instruction that listed the legally significant elements of that instruction. . . . We awarded a score of "1" on the score sheet for each element of the instruction correctly paraphrased by the test subject; " −1" on the score sheet for an incorrect paraphrase of an element; and "0" on the score sheet if the subject failed to mention an element of the instruction indicated on the score sheet. After we scored all responses, as outlined above, the percentages were calculated for each of the three possible responses. . . .

The figures we obtained, expressed in readily comprehensible percentages, confirmed that the jurors understood the rewritten instructions much better than the pattern instructions. Averaging the score sheet results for each set of five instructions revealed that only 12.85 percent of all of the paraphrases of the pattern instructions were correct, compared to 24.59 percent correct paraphrases of the rewritten set of instructions, an impressive 91 percent gain in understanding. [In the table below, the] percentage figures represent the percentage out of the total variables for each instruction. For example, if an instruction had 10 variables on the score sheet, and two of the ten were correctly paraphrased, the percentages would be 0 percent legally incorrect, 80 percent no paraphrase, and 20 percent legally correct. The results for multiple jurors were cumulated to get the results. . . .

Presumption of Innocence

	% of Legally Incorrect Paraphrases	*% of No Paraphrases*	*% of Legally Correct Paraphrases*
Pattern Charge	3.86 percent	78.77 percent	17.37 percent
Rewritten Charge	0.61 percent	76.06 percent	23.3 percent

To the uninitiated, the most telling statistic in our findings may be that the percentage of correct responses is very low in all of the charts. . . . This finding, which is consistent with the findings of other researchers, raises two important concerns. The first relates to the impact of jurors' difficulties in understanding on trial outcome: (1) Will a jury that misunderstands its instructions render the verdict it intends? (2) Will a jury that misunderstands its instructions render the same verdict that it would if it understood the instructions? The second concern relates to the vitality of the jury system regardless of effect on outcome. The use of incomprehensible instructions sends a message to jurors that the law is an undecipherable mystery and that juror understanding of the law is not important.

It seems reasonable to assume that juries render verdicts that are actually incorrect under the law because they do not understand the jury instructions as to that law. This assumption is supported by research and case law. Some of the social science research has demonstrated that the level of juror comprehension affects trial outcome in simulated trials. . . . Elwork and his associates showed identical videotaped trials to juries, half using pattern instructions and half using rewritten instructions. They found a statistically significant difference in the verdicts reached by the two groups. . . .

The integrity of jury verdicts is not the only reason why the clarity of jury instructions should be improved. The right to trial by jury has symbolic as well as actual importance to Americans. For most Americans, jury service is their only contact with the judicial system. Through our traditions and through the physical arrangement of our courtrooms we make clear to jurors that the judge represents the majesty of the law and that the instructions coming from the judge represent objectivity in the heat of battle. Incomprehensible instructions send jurors an undesirable message about the judicial system. . . .

Problem 18-1. A Doubt with a Reason

At 10:40 P.M. on October 29, Trooper Radford stopped Warren Manning on Highway 34 for a defective headlight. After writing Manning a warning ticket, Radford learned from his dispatcher that Manning was driving with a suspended license. Radford placed Manning under arrest and the two left the scene with Manning in the back seat of the patrol car.

Radford's patrol car was spotted early the next morning half-submerged in Reedy Creek Pond, about six and one-half miles from the McInnis residence. He had been shot twice through the head with his own revolver and severely pistol-whipped. The prosecutor charged Manning with murder.

The State's theory of the case was that Manning used his own .25 caliber pistol to threaten Radford. The prosecutor argued that Manning forced the trooper to drive to Reedy Creek Pond, where Manning murdered him and attempted to submerge the patrol car. Radford's revolver was found in a tobacco barn 75 yards behind Manning's home.

Manning testified on his own behalf that after he and Trooper Radford left in the patrol car, the trooper stopped another car traveling in front of them after a bag was thrown from its window. There were four people in the car. Radford approached the vehicle and while he was talking with the driver, Manning ran away from the patrol car unobserved. He walked to a friend's house and was driven back to his car.

After the close of evidence at trial, the judge gave the following charge on reasonable doubt:

> Beyond a reasonable doubt, in telling you that that is the degree of proof by which the State must prove, that phrase means exactly what it states in the English language, and that is a doubt for which you can give a real reason. That excludes a whimsical doubt, fanciful doubt. You could doubt any proposition if you wanted to. A reasonable doubt is a substantial doubt for which honest people, such as you, when searching for the truth can give a real reason. So it's to that degree of proof that the State is required to establish the elements of a charge.

Later in the charge, the judge added this thought about the meaning of reasonable doubt: "I instruct you to seek some reasonable explanation of the circumstances proven other than the guilt of the Defendant and if such a reasonable explanation can be found you should find the Defendant not guilty." As defense counsel, how would you argue that this charge was invalid? Compare State v. Manning, 409 S.E.2d 372 (S.C. 1991).

Notes

1. *Defining reasonable doubt: majority position.* As the Indiana court in *Winegeart* indicated, the federal constitution requires that the government prove all elements of an offense beyond a reasonable doubt, In re Winship, 397 U.S. 358 (1970), but it does not require that courts define reasonable doubt in a particular way. States have adopted a range of positions specifying both what is required and what is forbidden in defining reasonable doubt. Several modern definitions trace their wording back to a famous decision by Chief Justice Lemuel Shaw, in Commonwealth v. Webster, 59 Mass. 295, 320 (1850):

> [W]hat is reasonable doubt? It is a term often used, probably pretty well understood, but not easily defined. It is not mere possible doubt; because every thing related to human affairs, and depending on moral evidence, is open to some possible or imaginary doubt. It is that state of the case, which, after the entire comparison and consideration of all the evidence, leaves the minds of the jurors in that condition that they cannot say they feel an abiding conviction, to a moral certainty, of the truth of the charge.

About 20 states emphasize the negative perspective, defining reasonable doubt as a doubt that would cause a reasonable person to "hesitate to act in their most important affairs." Another group of about 20 states requires the doubt to be "based on reason" or "a valid reason." Roughly 10 states refer to "actual and substantial doubt" or "serious and substantial doubt" or "fair and actual doubt." A handful require that the doubt be articulable, that it be "doubt for which a reason can be given," although some states forbid such formulations because they require jurors to be articulate and place the burden on the defendant to show reasonable doubt. See People v. Antommarchi, 604 N.E.2d 95 (N.Y. 1992). About a dozen states define reasonable doubt in positive terms, focusing on the "moral certainty of guilt" or saying the juror must be "firmly convinced of guilt." (Several states tolerate several different approaches, and thus the preceding categories total more than 50.) See Craig Hemmens, Kathryn Scarborough, and Rolando del Carmen, Grave Doubts About "Reasonable Doubt": Confusion in State and Federal Courts, 25 J. Crim. Just. 231 (1997).

State courts also diverge on the question whether to define reasonable doubt at all. About a dozen states allow the trial judge to avoid the issue by providing no definition to the jury, while two states forbid trial judges from giving definitions. Paulson v. State, 28 S.W.3d 570 (Tex. Crim. App. 2000) (best practice is not to define reasonable doubt for jury). Five states have statutory mandates to define reasonable doubt in all cases; 12 states have reached the same position through case law. A few states require a definition only if the defendant requests it, and another handful require a definition to be given only in complex cases.

One of the dangers of using a negative definition of "reasonable doubt" is that it seems to place a burden on the defendant to show reasonable doubt instead of placing the burden on the government to dispel reasonable doubt (or to offer proof "beyond" reasonable doubt). See Lawrence M. Solan, Refocusing the Burden of Proof in Criminal Cases: Some Doubt About Reasonable Doubt, 78 Tex. L. Rev. 105 (1999) (standard reasonable doubt instructions focus the jury on the defendant's ability to produce alternatives to the government's case, and thereby shift the burden of proof to the defendant). The positive formulation of the instruction — found in the Federal Judiciary Center version of the instruction, which requires a juror to be "firmly convinced that the defendant is guilty of the crime charged"— has gained legal momentum with the decision of the Indiana Supreme Court in *Winegeart* and a 1995 decision by the Arizona Supreme Court mandating the use of this instruction. State v. Portillo, 898 P.2d 970 (Ariz. 1995). The U.S. Supreme Court has refused to mandate a particular definition for all federal courts, and the circuits have adopted a range of positions parallel to those taken among the states. Leading commentators have called for the adoption of a more consistent standard in the federal system. See Jon Newman, Beyond Reasonable Doubt, 68 N.Y.U. L. Rev. 979 (1993).

2. *Do definitions help?* States that forbid trial courts from defining reasonable doubt, or those that leave the decision to the trial judge, echo the long-standing skepticism of observers like Joel Bishop and John Henry Wigmore. Definitions, they say, do not help jurors decide cases. But the difficulty of applying the concept suggests that if states or individual judges want to leave jurors to use their own conceptions of reasonable doubt, they may be saying more about their view of the jury's role than about reasonable doubt. Professor Richard Uviller has observed that "[m]ost people require considerable explanation, example, and parallel articulation to grasp the basic contours of [the concept of reasonable doubt]," and that a reasonable doubt instruction, unadorned by explanation, "is an invitation to clothe it by invention, its flexibility an opportunity to bend it to prefigured purposes." Richard Uviller, Acquitting the Guilty: Two Case Studies on Jury Misgivings and the Misunderstood Standard of Proof, 2 Crim. L.F. 1, 38 (1990). Would the criminal trial be fairer if courts adopted a uniform definition of reasonable doubt? Is such consistency a virtue, or is simply having *some* definition the real virtue? See Peter Tiersma, The Rocky Road to Legal Reform: Improving the Language of Jury Instructions, 66 Brooklyn L. Rev. 1081 (2001) (trial courts unlikely to improve jury instructions; drafters of standardized jury instructions are more likely mechanism for reform).

Problem 18-2. Words and Numbers

Joseph McCullough was charged with possession of a controlled substance (marijuana) and possession of stolen property (a 1974 Chevrolet "Luv" pickup truck). During the voir dire examination of potential jurors, the district judge attempted to illustrate the concept of reasonable doubt with a numerical scale. On a scale of 0 to 10, the judge placed the preliminary hearing standard of probable cause at about 1 and the burden of persuasion in civil trials at just over 5. She then twice described reasonable doubt as about "seven and a half, if you had to put it on a scale." The judge did provide the jurors with the reasonable doubt standard described in Nev. Rev. Stat. §175.211, which provides as follows:

> A reasonable doubt is one based on reason. It is not mere possible doubt, but is such a doubt as would govern or control a person in the more weighty affairs of life. If the minds of the jurors, after the entire comparison and consideration of all the evidence, are in such a condition that they can say they feel an abiding conviction of the truth of the charge, there is not a reasonable doubt. Doubt to be reasonable must be actual and substantial, not mere possibility or speculation.

After introducing the jurors to the reasonable doubt standard provided by the Nevada statute, the judge again noted, "I have tried to give you that on a zero to ten scale." The jury convicted the defendant of both charges. He appeals, claiming that the judge's attempt to quantify reasonable doubt impermissibly lowered the prosecution's burden of proof and confused the jury rather than clarifying the reasonable doubt concept. How would you rule? See McCullough v. State, 657 P.2d 1157 (Nev. 1983).

Problem 18-3. Presumed Innocent or Not Guilty?

Jose Flores was tried and convicted of first-degree murder. The trial court instructed the jury by using a modified version of Oklahoma Uniform Jury Instruction — Criminal No. 903. The instruction read as follows:

> You are instructed that the defendant is presumed to be not guilty of the crime charged against him in the Information unless his guilt is established by evidence beyond a reasonable doubt and that presumption of being not guilty continues with the defendant unless every material allegation of the Information is proven by evidence beyond a reasonable doubt.

This jury instruction reflected the terms of Okla. Stat. tit. 22, §836, which provides that "[a] defendant in a criminal action is presumed to be innocent until the contrary is proved, and in case of a reasonable doubt as to whether his guilt is satisfactorily shown, he is entitled to be acquitted."

Flores now argues that the jury instruction diluted the presumption of innocence and diminished the State's burden of proving him guilty beyond a reasonable doubt. He argues the instruction also failed to advise the jury that the presumption of innocence remains in effect until the jury is convinced of guilt. Was the jury instruction erroneous? Is it more accurate to instruct the jury that a defendant is presumed innocent or presumed not guilty? Compare Flores v. State, 896 P.2d 558 (Okla. Crim. App. 1995); State v. Pierce, 927 P.2d 929 (Kan. 1996).

Notes

1. *Quantifying reasonable doubt.* Most state and federal courts discourage or prohibit trial judges from efforts to quantify the reasonable doubt standard. See State v.

Cruz, 639 A.2d 534 (Conn. 1994). Can the preponderance standard for civil cases be quantified? Don't the preponderance, clear and convincing, and reasonable doubt standards all express degrees of proof? Wouldn't quantitative descriptions help the jury? Did the Nevada judge in Problem 18-2 just choose the wrong numbers? Some judges have used sports analogies rather than numerical descriptions. What if the judge said that the prosecution had to "take the ball way past the 50-yard line, but you don't have to go a hundred yards for a guilty finding"? See State v. DelVecchio, 464 A.2d 813 (Conn. 1983). Studies conducted in the 1970s found that jurors quantified reasonable doubt at around 86 percent certainty of guilt. See Saul Kassin and Lawrence Wrightsman, On the Requirements of Proof: The Timing of Judicial Instruction and Mock Juror Verdicts, 37 J. Personality & Soc. Psych. 282 (1979). A more recent study suggests that jurors take a wide range of positions, associating the concept of "reasonable doubt" with anything from 50 to 100 percent certainty of guilt. See Terry Connolly, Decision Theory, Reasonable Doubt, and the Utility of Erroneous Acquittals, 11 Law & Hum. Behav. 101 (1987).

2. *Statistical proof of reasonable doubt.* What happens if an attorney wants to present statistical "proof" of an element of an offense or a defense? Courts have been generally critical of arguments that statistical evidence shows the likelihood of guilt or the existence of some element of the offense. They often find that such evidence is likely to confuse or mislead the jury. There is an extensive law of evidence related to the use at trial of individual scientific techniques, often limited to specific issues or types of cases. One important illustration is the use of DNA evidence in both criminal and civil cases. See, e.g., State v. Johnson, 922 P.2d 294 (Ariz. 1996) (approving the use of DNA probability evidence in sexual assault cases using restriction fragment length polymorphism (RFLP) protocol and modified ceiling method).

3. *Presumption of innocence and burden of proof.* Is the presumption of innocence anything more than another way to refer to the prosecution's burden of proof? In other words, when a defendant is said to be "presumed innocent," does that statement have legal ramifications beyond requiring the state to prove all elements of the offense beyond a reasonable doubt? Does it remind the jury not to place any evidentiary weight on the mere fact that the defendant has been charged with a crime? Most states declare that a separate instruction on presumption of innocence is not necessary in every case, while about 15 states do require a separate instruction. See, e.g., Ohio Rev. Stat. §2938.08 ("The presumption of innocence places upon the state (or the municipality) the burden of proving him guilty beyond a reasonable doubt. In charging a jury the trial court shall state the meaning of the presumption of innocence and of reasonable doubt in each case"). Does the presumption of innocence tell the jury anything about how long the government bears its burden of proof? Consider this typical description from Horn v. Territory, 56 P. 846, 848 (Okla. 1899):

> A defendant's friends may forsake him, but the presumption of innocence, never. It is present throughout the entire trial; and, when the jury go to their room to deliberate, the "presumption of innocence" goes in with them, protesting against the defendant's guilt. And it is only after the jury has given all the evidence in the case a full, fair, and impartial consideration, and have been able to find beyond a reasonable doubt that the defendant is guilty as charged, that the presumption of innocence leaves him.

In Taylor v. Kentucky, 436 U.S. 478 (1978), the Supreme Court found a federal due process violation when a Kentucky judge refused to instruct the jury on the presumption of innocence. The Court cited Coffin v. United States, 156 U.S. 432

(1895), for the proposition that "[t]he principle that there is a presumption of innocence in favor of the accused is the undoubted law, axiomatic and elementary, and its enforcement lies at the foundation of the administration of our criminal law." A year later, however, the Court held that a presumption-of-innocence instruction was not a constitutional requirement in all cases. Kentucky v. Whorton, 441 U.S. 786 (1979). The instruction was necessary in *Taylor* only because of "skeletal" jury instructions and the prosecutor's repeated suggestions that the defendant's status as a person charged with a crime tended to establish his guilt.

4. *Guilty clothing.* The presumption of innocence can have an impact on the operation of the courtroom. For example, courts generally forbid the state from requiring the defendant to appear in prison garb or surrounded by armed guards. However, the defendant must object to the clothing or other circumstances. Estelle v. Williams, 425 U.S. 501 (1976). Federal and state courts allow the conspicuous use of security guards more readily than they will tolerate shackles or distinctive clothing on the defendant. See Holbrook v. Flynn, 475 U.S. 560 (1986) (upholding four uniformed state troopers sitting in the front spectator row during trial as security measure); Sterling v. State, 830 S.W.2d 114 (Tex. Crim. App. 1992) (seven uniformed deputies in courtroom).

2. *Presumptions*

Judges instruct juries, and lawyers argue to juries, about evidentiary presumptions — asserting either that the jurors should assume a fact to be true or that if one fact is found then another fact or conclusion is more likely to be true. These presumptions can undermine the requirement that crime elements be proven beyond a reasonable doubt. In Sandstrom v. Montana, 442 U.S. 510 (1979), the U.S. Supreme Court rejected an instruction in a deliberate homicide case where intent was an element of the offense. The instruction said, "the law presumes that a person intends the ordinary consequences of his voluntary acts." The defendant had confessed to the killing, making his mental state the key issue. The Court found that, from the standpoint of the reasonable juror, this instruction shifted the burden of proof from the state to the defendant.

In Francis v. Franklin, 471 U.S. 307 (1985), a Georgia prisoner attempting escape killed a man when he fired a gun through a door at the moment the victim slammed it. Again, the sole defense was lack of intent to kill. The trial court, using an instruction with a long pedigree, instructed the jury that "[t]he acts of a person of sound mind and discretion are presumed to be the product of the person's will, but the presumption may be rebutted. A person of sound mind and discretion is presumed to intend the natural and probable consequences of his acts but the presumption may be rebutted. A person will not be presumed to act with criminal intention but the trier of facts . . . may find criminal intention upon a consideration of the words, conduct, demeanor, motive and all of the circumstances connected with the act for which the accused is prosecuted." The jury was also instructed that the defendant was presumed innocent and that the State was required to prove every element of the offense beyond a reasonable doubt. The Supreme Court again rejected the instruction. Even though the trial court had stated that "the presumption may be rebutted," such qualifying language did not prevent a reasonable juror from believing that the defendant bore the burden of showing he did not intend to kill. The *Franklin* Court distinguished valid and invalid instructions involving evidentiary presumptions as follows:

> The court must determine whether the challenged portion of the instruction creates a mandatory presumption, or merely a permissive inference. A mandatory presumption instructs the jury that it must infer the presumed fact if the State proves certain predicate facts. A permissive inference suggests to the jury a possible conclusion to be drawn if the State proves predicate facts, but does not require the jury to draw that conclusion.

471 U.S. at 313. The following case from Washington analyzes jury instructions within this framework of mandatory presumptions and permissive inferences.

■ STATE v. JOHN DEAL

911 P.2d 996 (Wash. 1996)

ALEXANDER, J.

[John Deal was convicted on a charge of first degree burglary. He contends] that the Franklin County Superior Court erred in instructing the jury that it could infer that Deal acted with criminal intent to commit a crime against a person or property, unless he explained with satisfactory evidence why his unlawful entry or remaining in a building was done without criminal intent. Deal asserts that the jury instruction is flawed because it created a mandatory presumption which partially relieved the State of its duty to prove all of the elements of the charged crime and improperly shifted the burden of persuasion from the State to him. [We agree with Deal in part.]

In July 1992, Lori Deal separated from her husband, the Defendant John Deal. . . . In August 1992, [Gerald John Prins] came to Pasco [to help his friend] Jack Carr harvest his potato crop. While there, Prins stayed at Carr's guesthouse. On September 12, 1992, Prins and Lori Deal went out for dinner with some friends. After dinner, Prins and Lori Deal accompanied some members of their party to a club in Kennewick. . . . After Carr noticed that John Deal was also in the club, he suggested to Prins and Lori Deal that they should leave the establishment in order to avoid a "bad situation." Prins and Lori Deal took Carr's suggestion and returned to Carr's guesthouse. Soon thereafter, John Deal appeared at the guesthouse and repeatedly kicked the door in an apparent effort to gain entry. Eventually, Deal picked up a wagon wheel and twice threw it against a window in the door. Deal then reached his arm through the now broken window, opened the door, and walked into the guesthouse where he assaulted Prins for approximately 15 to 20 minutes. He then left.

Deal was subsequently charged in Franklin County Superior Court with first degree burglary. At the ensuing jury trial, he admitted that he kicked the door of the guesthouse several times and that he broke the window in the door in order to gain entry to the residence. Deal also admitted that after entering the house, he remained there and assaulted Prins.

At the close of the trial, the trial court gave the jury the following jury instruction:

> A person who enters or remains unlawfully in a building may be inferred to have acted with intent to commit a crime against a person or property therein unless such entering or remaining shall be explained by evidence satisfactory to the jury to have been made without such criminal intent. This inference is not binding upon you and it is for you to determine what weight, if any, such inference is to be given.

Deal's trial counsel did not except to the giving of this instruction. The jury found Deal guilty of the charge and he was sentenced to serve 23 months in prison. [On appeal,] Deal assails the above jury instruction on several bases.[1] . . .

Deal argues first that the portion of the challenged instruction that precedes the word "unless" violates the due process clause of the Fourteenth Amendment of the United States Constitution, in that it allowed the jury to infer one element of first degree burglary (intent to commit a crime) from an unrelated element (unlawfully remaining in a building), thus, partially relieving the State of its obligation to prove all of the elements of the charged crime.

[B]ecause Deal was charged with first degree burglary, it was incumbent on the State to prove all of the elements of that offense. Those elements are set forth in RCW 9A.52.020(1), as follows:

> A person is guilty of burglary in the first degree if, with intent to commit a crime against a person or property therein, he enters or remains unlawfully in a dwelling and if, in entering or while in the dwelling or in immediate flight therefrom, the actor . . . assaults any person therein.

The State may use evidentiary devices, such as presumptions and inferences, to assist it in meeting its burden of proof. These devices generally fall into one of two categories: mandatory presumptions (the jury is required to find a presumed fact from a proven fact) and permissive inferences (the jury is permitted to find a presumed fact from a proven fact but is not required to do so). Mandatory presumptions potentially create due process problems. Indeed, they run afoul of a defendant's due process rights if they serve to relieve the State of its obligation to prove all of the elements of the crime charged. Sandstrom v. Montana, 442 U.S. 510 (1979). Permissive inferences, on the other hand, do not necessarily relieve the State of its burden of persuasion because the State is still required to persuade the jury that the proposed inference should follow from the proven facts.

We must first determine if the portion of the instruction preceding the word "unless" creates a mandatory presumption or a permissive inference. Significantly, this court recently reviewed a jury instruction that was identical to that portion of the challenged jury instruction. In State v. Brunson, 905 P.2d 346 (Wash. 1995), we held that it was not error for the trial court to give such an instruction because it created a constitutionally valid permissive inference. We also held in *Brunson,* that when permissive inferences are only part of the State's proof supporting an element and not the "sole and sufficient" proof of such element, due process is not offended if the prosecution shows that the inference more likely than not flows from the proven fact.[4] We are not inclined to abandon that holding here.

Deal asserts that even under the lesser standard, the State failed to prove that a necessary element of the charged crime, Deal's intent to commit a crime against a

1. The challenged instruction is identical to a pattern jury instruction. . . . The pattern instruction is based on Rev. Code Wash. §9A.52.040, which reads as follows: "In any prosecution for burglary, any person who enters or remains unlawfully in a building may be inferred to have acted with intent to commit a crime against a person or property therein, unless such entering or remaining shall be explained by evidence satisfactory to the trier of fact to have been made without such criminal intent."

4. The United States Supreme Court has indicated that when an inference is the "sole and sufficient" proof of an element, the prosecution may be required to prove that the inferred fact flows from the proved fact beyond a reasonable doubt. County Court of Ulster County v. Allen, 442 U.S. 140 (1979).

person or property, more likely than not flowed from his unlawful presence at Prins's residence. We disagree, being satisfied that the more likely than not standard was met. We reach that conclusion because the permissive inference contained in the challenged jury instruction was not the sole and sufficient evidence of Deal's intent. As we have observed above, Deal testified at trial that he broke a window in order to enter the premises, and that once inside, repeatedly assaulted Prins. In our judgment, the acts which Deal admitted amply support a conclusion that it was more likely than not that Deal intended to commit a crime against Prins during the time he remained unlawfully on the premises.

Deal's next contention has considerably more merit. He argues that the portion of the challenged instruction that states "unless such entering or remaining shall be explained by evidence satisfactory to the jury to have been made without such criminal intent" created a mandatory presumption which improperly shifted the burden of persuasion to him. . . .

The standard for determining whether a jury instruction creates a mandatory or permissive presumption is whether a reasonable juror might interpret the presumption as mandatory. The constitutionality of mandatory presumptions is examined in light of the jury instructions read as a whole to make sure that the burden of the persuasion on any element of the crime does not shift to the defendant. The burden of persuasion is deemed to be shifted if the trier of fact is required to draw a certain inference upon the failure of the defendant to prove by some quantum of evidence that the inference should not be drawn.

The portion of the instruction we are focusing on in this part of the opinion has the vice identified in *Sandstrom,* in that it essentially requires the Defendant to either introduce evidence sufficient to rebut the inference that he remained on the premises with intent to commit a crime, or concede that element of the crime. In other words, a reasonable juror could have concluded that once Deal's presence on the premises was shown, a finding that he intended to commit a crime was compelled, absent a satisfactory explanation by Deal as to why he was on the premises. This had the effect of relieving the State of its burden of proving beyond a reasonable doubt the element of intent to commit a crime and, therefore, violated Deal's due process rights.

The problem discussed above is not, as the State suggests, mitigated by the last sentence of the jury instruction, which reads: "This inference is not binding upon you and it is for you to determine what weight, if any, such inference is to be given." In our judgment, that additional language does not eliminate the possibility that a reasonable juror could have concluded that a finding of intent to commit a crime was required unless Deal proved otherwise.

We are not unmindful of the fact that we have previously held that the clause following "unless" in the challenged instruction is a production-shifting presumption which, although "rarely necessary and usually ill advised," may be submitted to a jury when the defendant produces evidence on the issue of his or her intent in his or her case in chief. State v. Johnson, 674 P.2d 145 (Wash. 1983). The distinction between production-shifting and persuasion-shifting presumptions is not helpful in this case.[5] The "unless" clause in the instruction here did not require Deal to merely

5. In *Johnson,* we indicated that mandatory presumptions fall into two categories: "persuasion-shifting" presumptions that require a trier of fact to draw an inference unless a defendant by some quantum of evidence proves otherwise and "production-shifting" presumptions that require a trier of fact to draw an inference unless the defendant produces some evidence to the contrary. We cautioned, however,

produce some evidence, but rather it required him to produce "evidence satisfactory to the jury" that he entered the premises without criminal intent. In our judgment, that language could have led a reasonable juror to understand that the burden of persuasion had shifted to Deal. That danger, in our view, did not disappear simply because Deal presented evidence that showed he did not have criminal intent.

Hearkening back to *Johnson*, we observe again that it is unnecessary to include this sort of language in such a jury instruction. Without the language, the instruction permits but does not require jurors to infer criminal intent from unlawful presence. The jury needs no further instruction on that issue because if a defendant is able to credibly explain his unlawful presence on premises, the jurors, as the instruction permits them to do, may simply reject the inferred conclusion of criminal intent.

Because the latter clause in the challenged jury instruction impermissibly shifted the burden of persuasion to Deal, it was error for the trial court to give it. The fact that the instruction is based on a statute, RCW 9A.52.040, does not lessen the violation of the Defendant's due process rights. [The court went on to conclude that the erroneous jury instruction was harmless beyond a reasonable doubt.]

PEKELIS, Justice Pro Tem, concurring.

[T]his court recently reviewed a jury instruction identical to the challenged instruction in this case, except that it did not contain the "unless" clause. In *Brunson*, we held that the inference of intent instruction created a permissive inference. . . . The question before the court in this case is whether the addition to the instruction of the "unless" clause transforms it such that it creates an unconstitutional mandatory inference.

In State v. Johnson, 674 P.2d 145 (Wash. 1983), this court reviewed an instruction substantively identical to the challenged instruction in this case.[2] The *Johnson* court expressed concern that the "unless" clause "might well lead a reasonable juror to interpret the instruction as creating a mandatory production-shifting presumption." The *Johnson* court defined a "production-shifting presumption" as one that requires the trier of fact to draw a certain inference unless the defendant produces some evidence to the contrary. The court then held that, when operative, production-shifting presumptions are impermissible because when the defendant presents no evidence, the jury is required to find the existence of an element of the crime, effectively relieving the State of its burden of persuasion on that element.

The critical difference between *Johnson* and this case is that the defendant did not testify in *Johnson*. The *Johnson* court recognized that "[t]hese constitutional infirmities disappear, however, when the defendant in his own case produces sufficient evidence from which a reasonable juror could find he has met his burden." . . . The issue of whether the jury might feel required to make the inference if

---

that any mandatory presumption could create constitutional concerns in that the State might be relieved of proving every element of the crime charged. We also observed that such a presumption "may also place undue pressure" on a defendant to relinquish his right to remain silent and when those constitutional concerns are operative, production-shifting presumptions are impermissible.

2. The challenged instruction in *Johnson* was as follows: "Any person who enters or remains unlawfully in a building may be inferred to have acted with intent to commit a crime against a person or property therein, unless such entering or remaining shall be explained by evidence satisfactory to you to have been made without criminal intent."

the defendant were to produce no evidence simply does not exist when the defendant has in fact produced such evidence. . . .

Notes

1. *Presumptions: majority position.* The *Deal* case from Washington illustrates the current law regarding burden-shifting presumptions. Both federal and state courts have followed the constitutional structure that the U.S. Supreme Court built in *Sandstrom* and *Franklin.* Federal and state courts differ, however, on the particular kinds of language that create an impermissible mandatory presumption. For instance, courts disagree on whether presumptions such as "a person generally intends the consequences of his acts" can be cured by additional language saying that such presumptions are rebuttable. *Sandstrom* claims apply as well to arguments made by the prosecutor in closing arguments. Should the same standards apply to review of judicial instructions and prosecutorial arguments?

Despite the best efforts of trial courts instructing juries, *Sandstrom* claims continue to arise. Should legislatures bar the use of all evidentiary presumptions? Doesn't all circumstantial evidence require reliance on presumptions? Don't all findings about mens rea require jurors to rely on presumptions even if they are unstated?

2. *Reasonable doubt about what?* Every defendant benefits from the requirement that the state prove all elements of any criminal offense beyond a reasonable doubt. But what are "elements" of offenses, and what are "defenses" that the defendant must prove? Can states define crimes any way they want? The U.S. Supreme Court at times has wrestled with the idea that the federal constitution might place some controls on what the state can designate as an element of a crime or a defense to the charges. Current doctrine, however, reinforces the view that states have substantial discretion in defining crimes. In Patterson v. New York, 432 U.S. 197 (1977), the Supreme Court rejected a due process challenge to a New York law that made the defense of extreme emotional disturbance an affirmative defense that the defendant must prove by a preponderance of the evidence. The Court emphasized that "preventing and dealing with crime is much more the business of the States than it is of the Federal Government." The federal constitution limits the capacity of states to define crimes only to the extent that the state law "offends some principle of justice so rooted in the traditions and conscience of our people as to be ranked as fundamental." The court declined to adopt "as a constitutional imperative, operative countrywide, that a State must disprove beyond a reasonable doubt every fact constituting any and all affirmative defenses related to the culpability of an accused."

Thus, states appear to have substantial discretion within federal constitutional boundaries to define crimes and defenses and to allocate the burden of proving or disproving an element to either the prosecution or the defense. Sometimes the argument is not about whether the state *can* place a particular burden on the state or the defendant, but whether it has in fact done so.

3. *The burden on affirmative defenses: majority view.* States divide on the general issue of whether the prosecution carries the burden of proof on affirmative defenses. Roughly 35 states require the defendant to carry the burden of proof on all affirmative defenses, but they usually require only that the defendant prove the defense by a preponderance of the evidence. See, e.g., Ohio Rev. Code §2901.05 ("[T]he burden of proof for all elements of the offense is upon the prosecution. The burden of

going forward with the evidence of an affirmative defense, and the burden of proof, by a preponderance of the evidence, for an affirmative defense, is upon the accused"). A handful of states require the state to carry the burden of proof on all affirmative defenses, though usually the defendant has the burden of going forward with facts sufficient to raise the defense. It is most common for states to require the prosecution to carry the burden on self-defense, while about half the states place the burden of proving insanity and related defenses on the defendant. See State v. Joyner, 625 A.2d 791 (Conn. 1993) (upholding statute placing burden of insanity defense on defendant).

4. *Elements and facts enhancing punishment.* Are facts that increase punishment—such as a finding that the defendant used a gun during the offense, or the amount of drugs involved—"elements" of the offense that the government must prove beyond a reasonable doubt? In McMillan v. Pennsylvania, 477 U.S. 79 (1986), the Supreme Court held that the reasonable doubt standard applied only to facts that "bear on the defendant's guilt," and upheld a statute enhancing the sentence if the prosecution proved by a preponderance of the evidence that the defendant "visibly possessed a firearm." The majority of states also allow the government to prove sentencing facts, including facts related to the prior criminal history of the defendant, at standards lower than reasonable doubt. See People v. Wims, 895 P.2d 77 (Cal. 1995).

The Supreme Court has spoken again recently on the question of whether particular facts are "elements" of a crime (to be decided by a trial jury using the beyond a reasonable doubt standard) or are instead "sentencing enhancement" (to be decided after trial using a lower standard of proof). The decision in Apprendi v. New Jersey, 530 U.S. 466 (2000), is reprinted in Chapter 19.

5. *Statutory definitions of sufficient evidence.* As we have seen, a legislature is free by and large to define the elements of crimes; it is more limited in its power to declare what inferences about crime elements that a jury must draw from the proven facts. However, the legislature may specify the type of evidence that is *not* sufficient to prove the elements. For instance, some statutes specify the minimum number of witnesses the prosecution must present to support a conviction for a particular crime (e.g., the traditional "two witness rule" for perjury convictions). In Carmell v. Texas, 529 U.S. 513 (2000), the Texas legislature amended its criminal statutes to authorize conviction of certain sexual offenses based on the victim's testimony alone; before that time, the statute required the victim's testimony plus other corroborating evidence to convict the offender. The Court held that when a legislature changes such rules dealing with the sufficiency of evidence, the change may only apply prospectively. Any retroactive application of such a law would amount to an ex post facto law.

Issues about the proper burden of proof and crime definitions draw from a mixture of substantive criminal law, constitutional law, criminal procedure, sentencing law, and evidence, and often from a blend of statutes, case law, and other kinds of legal authority. The mixed nature of questions about defining crimes means that a legislature might accomplish some goal with a rule of evidence that might be invalid as a crime definition. See Montana v. Egelhoff, 518 U.S. 37 (1996) (upholding state statute barring evidence of voluntary intoxication in determining the mental element of an offense); Ronald Allen, Foreward: Montana v. Egelhoff—Reflections on the Limits of Legislative Imagination and Judicial Authority, 87 J. Crim. L. & Criminology 633-691 (1997).

B. CONFRONTATION OF WITNESSES

An adversarial legal system, by its very nature, places great value on the testing of evidence. Cross-examination of witnesses presents the attorneys with their best opportunity to test the reliability of evidence. The cross-examination of a key witness creates high drama for any trial.

State and federal constitutions recognize the importance of this adversarial testing of evidence. Often, however, the constitutional provisions refer to "confrontation" of witnesses rather than to cross-examination. Consider the relevant clause from the Sixth Amendment to the federal constitution: "In all criminal prosecutions, the accused shall enjoy the right . . . to be confronted with the witnesses against him. . . ." In this section, we consider the devices available to test evidence.

1. *The Value of Confrontation*

Ordinarily the prosecution presents witnesses who testify at trial in the presence of the defendant, and the defense counsel cross-examines the witnesses with the defendant present. But does the presence of the defendant add anything? Is there some value in the "confrontation" of witnesses that goes beyond an effective cross-examination? See Richard D. Friedman, Confrontation: The Search for Basic Principles, 86 Geo. L.J. 1011 (1998). The Indiana case reprinted below deals with an unusual trial setting in which the defendant is not physically present during testimony. As you read it, reflect on what makes a cross-examination effective and what additional functions confrontation might serve. The next case, an opinion of the European Court of Human Rights, plays a variation on this theme: efforts by prosecutors in the Netherlands to use witnesses whose names remain unknown to the defendant.

■ MICHAEL BRADY v. STATE

575 N.E.2d 981 (Ind. 1991)

DEBRULER, J.

Following a jury trial, appellant Michael Brady was convicted of child molesting, a Class C felony, and received a sentence of seven years. [Brady contends] that I.C. 35-37-4-8,[1] which authorizes the use of videotaped testimony of child witnesses at

1. At the time of appellant's trial, I.C. 35-37-4-8 read as follows:

(a) This section applies to criminal actions for [child molestation] and for neglect of a dependent, and for attempts of those felonies.

(b) On the motion of the prosecuting attorney, the court may order that:

(1) the testimony of a child be taken in a room other than the courtroom and be transmitted to the courtroom by closed circuit television; and

(2) the questioning of the child by the prosecution and the defense be transmitted to the child by closed circuit television.

(c) On the motion of the prosecuting attorney, the court may order that the testimony of a child be videotaped for use at trial.

(d) The court may not make an order under subsection (b) or (c) unless:

(1) the testimony to be taken is the testimony of a child who:

(A) is less than ten years of age;

(B) is the alleged victim of an offense listed in subsection (a) for which the defendant is being tried or is a witness in a trial for an offense listed in subsection (a);

trial is unconstitutional. Appellant also asserts that the videotaped testimony should not have been admitted into evidence because appellant's right to cross-examine the witness was compromised. . . .

T.B. was born on June 22, 1982. Appellant is her natural father. Appellant and T.B.'s mother, Carla Myers, were married at the time of her birth but were subsequently divorced in November of 1983. . . . Pursuant to a court visitation order in effect in April of 1986, T.B. spent Friday night, April 4, and Saturday night, April 5, with appellant at the home of appellant's mother, Rosemary Brady. Appellant returned T.B. to Carla Myers's home on Sunday, April 6, at 6:00 P.M. On Monday morning, one of T.B.'s teachers discovered T.B. hiding in the bathroom closet and [complaining about genital pain. A physical examination produced evidence of sexual abuse]. During the three months following the discovery of the child's injury, the child made several statements to investigators that it had been appellant who had hurt her. Charges were subsequently filed July 8, 1986.

On January 30, 1987, the State, pursuant to I.C. 35-37-4-8, moved the court to order that T.B.'s testimony be videotaped for use at trial. . . . On February 13, the trial court ruled that it was more likely than not that it would be traumatic for T.B. to testify in court and ordered that the videotape testimony be taken. On March 14, 1987, T.B.'s videotape testimony was taken and was subsequently admitted at trial over appellant's objection and viewed by the jury. The tape had been taken at home in T.B.'s kitchen and bedroom. The judge, prosecutor, defense attorney, investigator, T.B.'s mother, and the operator of the video equipment were present during the videotaping. The videotape session lasted approximately two hours. Appellant was situated in the garage of the house, and he was able to see and hear T.B. via closed circuit television as she was questioned. Appellant was also able to speak with defense counsel by a microphone hook-up. T.B. was not able to see or hear appellant and was not aware of his presence. . . . In sum, the trial court scrupulously followed the statute.

Appellant maintains that this statute is unconstitutional on its face as it infringes upon his right to confront the witnesses against him as guaranteed by the Sixth Amendment of the United States Constitution and Article I, §13 of the Indiana Constitution. . . . The right of confrontation is a fundamental right ensured by the Sixth Amendment, made applicable to the states through the Fourteenth Amendment, wherein it provides that "[i]n all criminal prosecutions, the accused shall enjoy the right . . . to be confronted with the witnesses against him. . . ."

(C) is found by the court to be a child who should be permitted to testify outside the courtroom because . . . evidence has been introduced concerning the effect of the child's testifying in the courtroom, and the court finds that it is more likely than not that the child's testifying in the courtroom would be a traumatic experience for the child. . . .

(f) If the court makes an order under subsection (c), only the following persons may be in the same room as the child during the child's videotaped testimony:

(1) The judge.

(2) The prosecuting attorney.

(3) The defendant's attorney (or the defendant, if the defendant is not represented by an attorney).

(4) Persons necessary to operate the electronic equipment.

(5) The court reporter.

(6) Persons whose presence the court finds will contribute to the child's well-being.

(7) The defendant, who can observe and hear the testimony of the child without the child being able to observe or hear the defendant. However, if the defendant is not represented by an attorney, the defendant may question the child. . . .

The right of confrontation under the Sixth Amendment is honored where "the defense is given a full and fair opportunity to probe and expose [testimonial] infirmities [such as forgetfulness, confusion, or evasion] through cross-examination, thereby calling to the attention of the factfinder the reasons for giving scant weight to the witness' testimony." Delaware v. Fensterer, 474 U.S. 15 (1985) (per curiam). In Maryland v. Craig, 497 U.S. 836 (1990), the Supreme Court went on to state that "we have never insisted on an actual face-to-face encounter at trial in every instance in which testimony is admitted against a defendant." Thus, the defendant's opportunity for cross-examination has been interpreted as being the essential purpose of the federal confrontation right.

The statute in question in this case is similar to the Maryland statute which was reviewed by the United States Supreme Court in *Craig*. The Supreme Court upheld the constitutionality of the Maryland statute as it found that the admission of the child victim's live testimony at the time of trial, transmitted to the courtroom and the trier of fact via one-way closed circuit television, was consonant with the Confrontation Clause. The Supreme Court noted:

> We find it significant . . . that Maryland's procedure preserves all of the other elements of the confrontation right: the child witness must be competent to testify and must testify under oath; the defendant retains full opportunity for contemporaneous cross-examination; and the judge, jury, and defendant are able to view (albeit by videotape monitor) the demeanor (and body) of the witness as he or she testifies. [497 U.S. at 851.]

The Supreme Court went on to state that in some cases the State's interest in protecting a child witness from serious emotional distress and trauma occasioned by testifying in the courtroom and in the presence of the defendant may outweigh a defendant's right to face his or her accusers in court, thus permitting the direct and cross-examination of the child witness to be conducted at a location outside the courtroom, connected to the courtroom by one-way closed circuit television, while the defendant and the trier of fact remain in the courtroom and view the witness on a television screen. In such instances, the Supreme Court concluded that it was not necessary that the child witness be able to view, to hear, or otherwise perceive the presence of the defendant, who is viewing and listening in at the time. . . .

The Indiana statute is, in most respects, like the Maryland statute which the Supreme Court upheld in *Craig*. . . . The single significant dissimilarity in the two statutes appears to be that the Indiana statute, unlike the Maryland statute, authorizes the use of videotaped pre-trial statements as well as the use of closed circuit television during trial. In light of the Supreme Court's analysis in *Craig*, however, we do not believe that the balance struck between the Confrontation Clause and the state interest in protecting the child witness would be different by reason of the differences between these two methods of presenting testimony. We therefore conclude that the Indiana statute, properly construed, satisfies the requirements of the federal confrontation right.

This Court has recently examined the origins and traced the development of the right of criminal defendants to meet the witnesses face to face as this right is guaranteed by Article I, §13 of the Indiana Constitution. State v. Miller, 517 N.E.2d 64 (Ind. 1987). Article I, §13 provides: "In all criminal prosecutions, the accused shall have the right . . . to meet the witnesses face to face. . . ." To a considerable degree, the federal right of confrontation and the state right to a face-to-face meeting are co-extensive. The language employed in the two provisions is different, however, and as we approach the task of construing our state constitution it is appropriate that we start again with the language. The words "face to face" as used in the passage is an adverbial phrase modifying "to meet," and thus describes how a criminal defendant in this state and the State's witnesses are to meet. "Hand in hand" and "back to back" are similar modifiers. The separate definition given it in most dictionaries shows its persistent and common usage. In the first standard English language dictionary, appearing in 1755, it is printed that "face to face" is "without the interposition of other bodies." Johnson's Dictionary. According to the second great standard English language dictionary, published in 1856, "face to face" is defined as the "state of confrontation. The witnesses were presented face to face." An American Dictionary of the English Language, Noah Webster. . . . Of the various meanings which this phrase undoubtedly has in context with the rest of Article I, §13 and in law, its literal meaning is primary, unmistakable, and dominant. A face-to-face meeting occurs when persons are positioned in the presence of one another so as to permit each to see and recognize the other. While the language employed in Article I, §13 of our Indiana Bill of Rights has much the same meaning and history as that employed in the Sixth Amendment, it has a special concreteness and is more detailed. . . .

The right is not absolute. It is secured where the testimony of a witness at a former hearing or trial on the same case is reproduced and admitted, where the defendant either cross-examined such witness or was afforded an opportunity to do so, and the witness cannot be brought to testify at trial again because he has died, become insane, or is permanently or indefinitely absent from the state and is therefore beyond the jurisdiction of the court in which the case is pending. . . . Such an opportunity for cross-examination in a prior civil case, however, will not suffice. . . . In Green v. State, 184 N.E. 183 (Ind. 1933), this Court reversed the defendant's conviction for receiving a deposit, knowing that the bank was insolvent, because the trial court improperly admitted the finding of insolvency from the civil action into the criminal action. . . .

Indiana's confrontation right . . . places a premium upon live testimony of the State's witnesses in the courtroom during trial, as well as upon the ability of the defendant and his counsel to fully and effectively probe and challenge those witnesses during trial before the trier of fact through cross-examination. The defendant's right to meet the witnesses face to face has not been subsumed by the right to cross-examination. . . . While the right to cross-examination may be the primary interest protected by the confrontation right in Article I, §13 of the Indiana Constitution, the defendant's right to meet the witnesses face to face cannot simply be read out of our State's Constitution. . . .

I.C. 35-37-4-8 contains a provision, subsection (f)(7), which specifies that a child who is being videotaped shall not be able to observe or hear the defendant, unless the defendant opts to proceed without counsel. We find that the operation of subsections (c) and (f)(7) of this statute, subsections which the trial judge adhered to in this case, to be violative of Article I, §13 of the Indiana Constitution in that they infringe upon the defendant's right to confront the witnesses against him face to face as they give their trial testimony. When the operation of the subsections is foreclosed in this manner, the statute is nevertheless left in a sensible and administrable form. The trial court retains significant authority under the statute.

The essential purpose of I.C. 35-37-4-8 as a whole is to protect child witnesses and other witnesses who fall within the class of persons labeled "protected persons" from the potentially traumatic experience of having to testify in open court before the person they are accusing. In removing the protected person from the often intimidating and sterile environs of the courtroom to a nearby private room during the trial and interposing a two-way closed circuit television arrangement which would permit the witness to see the accused and the trier of fact and would allow the accused and the trier of fact to see and hear the witness, the witness's testimony would be facilitated and the threat of emotional or mental harm to the witness would be significantly reduced. In such a closed circuit arrangement, there is no person or body interposed between the witness and the accused and a face-to-face meeting as contemplated by the Constitution occurs. In such manner, the main goal of the statute, reducing the trauma caused by in-court testimony before the accused, can still be achieved in large measure without compromising appellant's constitutional right to meet the witnesses face to face.

In light of the foregoing analysis, we hold that the trial court erred in admitting T.B.'s videotaped testimony of March 14, 1987, over appellant's objection that such testimony violated the Confrontation Clause of the Indiana Constitution. Further, we cannot find the admission of this evidence to be harmless as the videotape contained numerous statements incriminating to appellant. Appellant's conviction for child molesting is therefore reversed and the cause is remanded for a new trial. . . .

KRAHULIK, J., dissenting.

Unlike the Sixth Amendment of the United States Constitution, which guarantees the accused in a criminal proceeding the right "to be confronted with the witnesses against him," Article I, §13, of the Indiana Constitution provides that "[i]n all criminal prosecutions, the accused shall have the right . . . to meet the witness face to face." Although little is known about the actual intention of the framers when drafting this language [in 1850], it can naturally be assumed that they were guided by a desire to provide protections similar to those guaranteed by the Sixth Amendment. In accomplishing this task they chose words that conveyed specific meanings. By examining the generally accepted common and legal meanings of the words selected we can ascertain what principles the framers singled out for protection. These are the ideas to which we must be true.

In Noah Webster's American Dictionary of the English Language, published in 1856, "face to face" is defined as the "state of confrontation." Bouvier's Law Dictionary, published in 1883, provides the following definition of confrontation: "The act by which a witness is brought into the presence of the accused, so that the latter may object to him, if he can, and the former may know and identify the accused and maintain the truth in his presence." These definitions suggest that the drafters designed the confrontation provision of Article I, §13 to accomplish three essential objectives: to allow the witness to make an identification of the accused, to afford the defendant the opportunity to challenge or examine the witness, and to create a setting that would impress the witness with the importance of his task and encourage his truthful testimony.

Of these elements, the right of the defendant to examine the witness is most sacred. [In] Miller v. State, 517 N.E.2d 64, 69 (Ind. 1987), a decision upholding the constitutionality of [an earlier version of] I.C. §35-37-4-6, which provided for the admissibility of videotaped statements of sex abuse victims under the age of ten, this court adopted a description of the vital elements of confrontation at trial provided in Mattox v. United States, 156 U.S. 237 (1895), as:

> [A] personal examination and cross-examination of the witness, in which the accused has an opportunity, not only of testing the recollection and shifting the conscience of the witness, but of compelling him to stand face to face with the jury in order that they may look at him, and judge by his demeanor upon the stand and the manner in which he gives his testimony whether he is worthy of belief.

Therefore, confrontation requires the government to provide procedures that give the accused the ability to test the witness' accuracy and credibility before the trier of fact. Any method accomplishing those objectives is sufficient under the Constitution's confrontation provision. . . . The arrangement provided in the statute does not hinder cross-examination, it merely requires that it be done in a less threatening setting than in a full court room.

A second rationale for requiring the witness to make his charges in the defendant's physical presence is that by requiring the accused to look the defendant in the eye he is more likely to be truthful. In molestation cases, however, face to face confrontation may do more to hinder full, honest testimony by the witness than to encourage it. The nature of the relationship between the witness and the accused, the highly embarrassing character of the testimony and the courtroom setting itself combine to create a stressful, traumatic environment likely to make the child a reluctant, unreliable witness. Particularly, in cases where the accused is a family member or trusted friend the child is likely to be intimidated from giving clear, honest testimony out of fear, respect for authority, or even love of the accused.

Opponents of these alternate methods of testimony argue that although it is unfortunate that in-court testimony is difficult for the witness, such "trial by ordeal" is necessary to expose the witness who has been coached or is lying. Although logical, this argument mischaracterizes the nature and purpose of witness examination. Trial testimony, although naturally somewhat stressful, is not intended to be an ordeal for the witness. Rather, it is designed to be an engine for seeking and attaining truth. The revelation of an untruthful witness is properly the result of skillful cross-examination and not of a "stare-down" from the accused. . . .

At least 34 other states have accepted these and other similar arguments and drafted statutes allowing videotaped testimony for child victims of or witnesses to certain types of crimes. Twenty-three have established procedures for testimony over closed-circuit television. Although the statutes vary greatly, each evidences a belief that some measure must be taken to provide additional protection for child witnesses and that these safeguards can be created without endangering the constitutional rights of an accused.

A majority of the statutes challenged in their state court have been upheld. Notably, the constitutions of several of these states contain the same "face to face" language found in our Constitution. See, e.g., Kentucky Constitution section 11. Kentucky's highest court upheld the constitutionality of their statute in Commonwealth v. Willis, 716 S.W.2d 224 (Ky. 1986).

Indiana's requirement of face-to-face meetings is not to be read for its literal language but for the intentions conveyed by that language. The framers' objective in including Article I, Section 13, was to ensure protection of the defendant's right to conduct a cross-examination of the witness that could be viewed by the trier of fact. The choice of the "face-to-face" language stemmed from the inability to predict technology that would meet its objectives without requiring actual physical presence of the witness in the courtroom. The accused does not have a constitutionally protected right to stand eyeball to eyeball with his accuser. The essential issue is whether the procedure in question ensures the rights outlined by the framers. I believe it does.

Notes

1. *Confrontation of child witnesses: majority position.* Under the federal constitution, some witnesses may testify outside the courtroom and outside the presence of the defendant if the defendant is able to monitor the testimony and communicate with the defense attorney conducting the cross-examination. According to Maryland v. Craig, 497 U.S. 836 (1990), the trial court must make a case-specific finding that the witness would suffer from extreme emotional trauma during traditional testimony that would prevent the witness from reasonably communicating. The *Craig* Court distinguished Coy v. Iowa, 487 U.S. 1012 (1988), which struck down a statute protecting child witnesses without an individualized assessment of the potential trauma to the child.

Most high state courts to address this issue (more than 25) follow the federal position and allow prosecuting witnesses to testify outside the courtroom (and outside the defendant's physical presence) so long as the arrangement is "necessary to further an important public policy" and "the reliability of the testimony is otherwise assured." State v. Bray, 535 S.E.2d 636 (S.C. 2000) (lack of case-specific findings invalidated order for televised testimony). The cases often require that the defendant be able to monitor the cross-examination from a remote location or from a hidden or screened location in the room. Another group of high state courts (fewer than 10) have concluded that the defendant must be present (and visible to the witness) during the direct testimony and cross-examination, although some have concluded that it is enough if the defendant's electronic image is present during the testimony. Compare People v. Newbrough, 803 P.2d 155 (Colo. 1990) (approving use of videotaped deposition and questioning by court psychiatrist; defendant and defense counsel monitor questioning by one-way video and relay questions to psychiatrist) and People v. Cintron, 551 N.E.2d 561 (N.Y. 1990) (approving two-way closed-circuit testimony at trial) with People v. Fitzpatrick, 633 N.E.2d 685 (Ill. 1994) (striking down statute that allowed cross-examination on closed-circuit television). The states departing from the federal position, by and large, are those with the specific "face to face" provisions in their state constitutions. Almost 30 state constitutions track the language of the Sixth Amendment to the federal constitution and speak of the right of the accused to be "confronted" with adverse witnesses. About 20 state constitutions mention a defendant's right to meet adverse witnesses "face to face."

Which of the various elements of the classic courtroom confrontation create more reliable testimony? Does it matter that the testimony takes place during trial rather than during an earlier deposition? Does it matter whether the testimony takes place in a courtroom? Note that Indiana required a video image of the defendant to be present during the testimony. Would a cardboard cut-out image of the defendant suffice?

2. *Reliability of out-of-court statements by child witnesses.* As the opinions in *Brady* indicate, a strong majority of states have passed special statutes dealing with the

testimony of child witnesses, including out-of-court statements. The statutes for shielded child testimony typically apply only in sex abuse crimes. In the absence of such a special statute, the rules of evidence (and in particular, rules about untested "hearsay" statements) might prevent the admission of an out-of-court statement. There are, however, exceptions to the hearsay rules that some courts have applied to child witnesses, even when a special child-testimony statute does not apply. In general, these exceptions try to identify out-of-court statements that seem reliable, despite the fact that the person made the statement outside the adversarial courtroom environment. Some courts have concluded that out-of-court statements by children were "excited utterances" or statements made to a professional offering medical diagnosis or treatment (both exceptions to the bar on hearsay).

Social science and psychology researchers have explored at great length the factors associated most strongly with reliable and unreliable child testimony. As one might expect, older children are more reliable witnesses than younger children. Young children depend more heavily than older children on "recognition memory" (responding to specific questions about an event rather than volunteering information in response to a general question). Suggestive questioning is more likely to influence younger children, and small differences in age can mean large differences in reliability. The number of times a child is questioned before trial also affects reliability. See Stephen Ceci and Maggie Bruck, Suggestibility of the Child Witness: A Historical Review and Synthesis, 113 Psych. Bull. 403 (1993). Contrary to expectations, promptness in coming forward with an accusation or consistency in the details of a story are not good indicators of a reliable child witness. If new research indicates that a factor listed in a statute is not a good indicator of reliability, how should the judge interpreting the statute respond?

3. *Defendant's presence during other proceedings.* Both federal and state courts have concluded that defendants have a right, both under confrontation clauses and due process clauses, to be present at "every stage" of the trial. The opinions also declare, however, that some trial or pretrial events do not require the defendant's presence. The defendant must be present only when "his presence has a relation, reasonably substantial, to the fullness of his opportunity to defend against the charge." Snyder v. Massachusetts, 291 U.S. 97 (1934) (Cardozo, J.). In Kentucky v. Stincer, 482 U.S. 730 (1987), the Court held that a defendant must be present for at least some pretrial proceedings; however, there was no error when a trial court held a hearing on the competency of a witness to testify at trial, with the defense counsel present but not the defendant, because the questions asked did not relate to the alleged crime and did not interfere with any opportunity for cross-examination. See People v. Dokes, 595 N.E.2d 836 (N.Y. 1992) (presence required at pretrial conference to decide on prior convictions available for impeaching defendant's testimony).

4. *Waiver of presence.* Does a defendant waive the right to be present during the trial by engaging in disruptive behavior? See Illinois v. Allen, 397 U.S. 337 (1970) (no constitutional error to remove defendant from courtroom after repeated outbursts, if defendant is allowed to return to courtroom after promise of better behavior). By escaping from jail before trial? Crosby v. United States, 506 U.S. 255 (1993) (interpreting Fed. R. Crim. P. 43 to prevent trial in abstentia of defendant who escapes jail before trial begins, but to allow such trials for defendants who escape after trial has begun). By failing to appear on the day set for trial after being released before trial? See People v. Johnston, 513 N.E.2d 528 (Ill. 1987) (failure to appear at trial, after appearing at pretrial hearing, is waiver of right to be present);

Irvin Molotsky, Convicted Killer Arrested Again in France, N.Y. Times, Sept. 23, 1998 at A22 ("Ira Einhorn, an antiestablishment leader who has spent the last 17 years in Europe as a fugitive from justice in the murder of his girlfriend in Philadelphia in 1977, has been arrested again in France and faces possible extradition to the United States. [In 1993, Einhorn] was convicted in absentia of first-degree murder. . . . When Mr. Einhorn was first arrested last year and then freed when a French court refused to allow his extradition, the Pennsylvania law did not have the provision for a new trial upon the defendant's request. So the Pennsylvania Legislature passed a law bringing the state's provision of a retrial on request in line with French law.").

5. *Victims and sequestration of witnesses.* A traditional rule of evidence allows a party to insist that the judge exclude a witness from the courtroom until that witness has testified. This rule of "sequestration of witnesses" makes cross-examination more effective because it prevents the witness from changing her testimony to remain consistent with (or to rebut) the evidence presented up until that time. The judge's power to exclude witnesses existed at common law, and many states now have rules of evidence codifying this discretionary rule. Others, such as Fed. R. Evid. 615, give the parties an absolute right to exclude a witness; the judge has no discretion on the question for most witnesses.

The sequestration rule sometimes conflicts with the notion that the victim of an alleged crime has a special interest in attending a trial. Consider the following typical effort to reconcile these competing principles, contained in Utah R. Evid. 615(1):

> At the request of a party the court shall order witnesses excluded so that they cannot hear the testimony of other witnesses, and it may make the order on its own motion. This rule does not authorize exclusion of . . . a victim in a criminal trial or juvenile delinquency proceeding where the prosecutor agrees with the victim's presence.

Compare Mich. Comp. Laws §780.761(11) ("The victim has the right to be present throughout the entire trial of the defendant, unless the victim is going to be called as a witness. If the victim is going to be called as a witness, the court may, for good cause shown, order the victim to be sequestered until the victim first testifies"). Some states unequivocally grant the victim a right to attend the proceedings, while others grant the trial court discretion to allow the victim to attend. Under these rules and statutes, does the victim now have a right to presence at trial comparable to the defendant's right to be present? Does the presence of the victim in the courtroom influence other witnesses as they testify (creating a sort of "confrontation" right for a crime victim)? Do rules such as these convert the role of the victim from a component of the government's proof into a party in the litigation? See Paul Cassell, Balancing the Scales of Justice: The Case for and the Effects of Utah's Victim's Rights Amendment, 1994 Utah L. Rev. 1373; Robert Mosteller, Victims' Rights and the United States Constitution: An Effort to Recast the Battle in Criminal Litigation, 85 Geo. L.J. 1691 (1997). If you were drafting rules dealing with victim attendance at trial, would you allow all victims to attend the trial from beginning to end? How about victims in assault cases, when the defendants claim that they acted in self-defense or were otherwise provoked by the alleged victim?

The concept of confronting witnesses is a familiar one even in civil law legal systems, which are based on an "inquisitorial" model of factfinding (in which the judge takes responsibility for developing facts) rather than an "adversarial" model (in which the parties present their own facts and take responsibility for testing the factual claims of their adversaries). But the confrontation rights of defendants in civil law systems do not exactly track the confrontation rights of defendants in U.S. courts.

The following case suggests a few of the differences in the rules governing confrontation of witnesses that one might encounter in a civil law system. As you read the case, try to sort out which of the concepts discussed would be familiar to an American court and which would be unthinkable. What does this European decision tell us about criminal justice in the United States?

A word is in order about the court that decided the following case. More than 30 nations have signed a treaty known as the European Convention for the Protection of Human Rights and Fundamental Freedoms. The treaty was signed in 1950, after the revelation of outrageous human rights abuses during World War II and during a time when some European nations felt the need to distinguish their democratic forms of government from Communist legal systems during the Cold War.

Under the European Convention, an individual who is convicted in the criminal courts of a signatory nation can challenge that conviction if it was obtained in violation of the convention. The challenge first goes to the European Commission on Human Rights; either the defendant or the government may appeal the commission's decision to the European Court of Human Rights. The judges of the court are drawn from various signatory nations. They interpret the convention in light of broad principles of international and domestic law. The European Court of Human Rights both reflects and develops a consensus among nations about human rights, including the nature of a fair criminal trial. In the following case, the court considers a challenge to the use of "anonymous witnesses."

■ DÉSIRÉ DOORSON v. NETHERLANDS

22 Eur. Ct. H.R. 330 (1996)

In August 1987 the prosecuting authorities decided to take action against the nuisance caused by drug trafficking in Amsterdam.* The police compiled photographs of persons suspected of being drug dealers, and showed the photos to about 150 drug addicts to collect statements from them. However, most of the witnesses were only prepared to make statements on condition that their identity was not disclosed to the drug dealers they identified. Witnesses who had testified during a similar enforcement effort in 1986 had received threats.

In September 1987 the police received information from a drug addict that Doorson was engaged in drug trafficking. The police then included a 1985 photograph of Doorson in the collection of photographs they showed to other drug addicts. A number of addicts recognized Doorson from his photograph and told police that he had sold drugs. Six of these drug addicts remained anonymous; they were referred to by the police under the code names Y05, Y06, Y13, Y14, Y15 and Y16. The identity of two others was disclosed, namely R and N.

On 12 April 1988 Doorson was arrested on suspicion of having committed drug offenses. During the preliminary judicial investigation, Doorson's lawyer requested an examination of the witnesses referred to in the police report. The investigating

* Material in this opinion preceding paragraph 53 has been edited without indication. — Eds.

judge ordered the police to bring these witnesses before him on 30 May 1988 between 09.30 and 16.00. Doorson's lawyer was notified and invited to attend the questioning of these witnesses before the investigating judge.

On 30 May 1988 Doorson's lawyer arrived at the investigating judge's chambers at 09.30. However, after an hour and a half had elapsed and none of the witnesses had appeared, he concluded that no questioning would take place. The attorney left for another appointment, after the judge promised him that if the witnesses should turn up later that day, they would not be heard but would be required to appear for questioning at a later date so that he would be able to attend. After the lawyer had left, two of the eight witnesses referred to in the police report turned up and were heard by the investigating judge in the absence of the lawyer, witness Y15 at about 11.15 and witness Y16 at about 15.00. Y15 and Y16 did not keep a promise to return for further questioning on 3 June.

In proceedings before the Regional Court, the named witness N appeared, but R did not. Both the prosecution and the defense were given the opportunity to put questions to N. Asked to identify Doorson, N stated that he did not recognize him. On being shown Doorson's photograph, he said that he recognized it as that of a man who had given him heroin when he was ill. However, towards the end of his examination he stated that he was no longer quite sure of recognizing the man in the photograph; it might be that the man who had given him the heroin only resembled that man. He also claimed that when shown the photographs by the police, he had only identified Doorson's photograph as that of a person from whom he had bought drugs because at the time he had felt very ill and had been afraid that the police might not give him back the drugs which they had found in his possession.

After the Regional Court convicted Doorson of drug trafficking and sentenced him to 15 months' imprisonment, he appealed to the Amsterdam Court of Appeal. Doorson's lawyer requested the procurator general of the Court of Appeal to summon the anonymous witnesses and the named witnesses N and R for questioning at that Court's hearing. The procurator general replied that he would summon N and R but not the anonymous witnesses, because he wished to preserve their anonymity.

The Court of Appeal decided to verify the necessity of maintaining the anonymity of the witnesses and referred the case back to the investigating judge for this purpose. The Court of Appeal also requested the investigating judge to examine the witnesses — after deciding whether their anonymity should be preserved or not — and to offer Doorson's lawyer the opportunity both to attend this examination and to put questions to the witnesses.

On 14 February 1990 the investigating judge heard the witnesses Y15 and Y16 in the presence of Doorson's lawyer. The lawyer was given the opportunity to put questions to the witnesses but was not informed of their identity. The identity of both witnesses was known to the investigating judge.

Both witnesses expressed the wish to remain anonymous and not to appear in court. Witness Y16 stated that he had in the past suffered injuries at the hands of another drug dealer after he had cooperated with the police, and he feared similar reprisals from Doorson. Witness Y15 stated that he had in the past been threatened by drug dealers if he were to talk. He also said that Doorson was aggressive. The investigating judge concluded that both witnesses had sufficient reason to wish to maintain their anonymity and not to appear in open court.

At its next hearing on the case, the Court of Appeal heard the witness N in Doorson's presence and his lawyer was given the opportunity to question the witness.

N said that his statement to the police had been untrue and that he did not in fact know Doorson. The named witness R was initially present at these proceedings. Before he was heard, he asked the Court usher who was guarding him for permission to leave for a minute; he then disappeared and could not be found again.

The Court of Appeal decided to refer the case once again back to the investigating judge, requesting her to record her findings as to the reliability of the witnesses Y15 and Y16. On 19 November 1990 the investigating judge drew up a record of her findings regarding the reliability of the statements made to her by Y15 and Y16 on 14 February 1990. She stated in this document that she could not remember the faces of the two witnesses but, having re-read the records of the interrogations, could recall more or less what had happened. She had the impression that both witnesses knew whom they were talking about and had identified Doorson's photograph without hesitation. As far as she remembered, both witnesses had answered all questions readily and without hesitating, although they had made a "somewhat sleepy impression."

On 6 December 1990, the Court of Appeal found Doorson guilty of the deliberate sale of quantities of heroin and cocaine. As regards Doorson's complaint that the majority of the witnesses had not been heard in the presence of Doorson or his lawyer, the Court stated that it had based its conviction on evidence given by the witnesses N, R, Y15 and Y16. Doorson brought this appeal to the European Court of Human Rights.

53. The applicant alleged that the taking of, hearing of and reliance on evidence from certain witnesses during the criminal proceedings against him infringed the rights of the defence, in violation of Article 6(1) and (3)(d) of the Convention, which provide as follows:

> 1. In the determination . . . of any criminal charge against him, everyone is entitled to a fair . . . hearing [by an] impartial tribunal. . . .
>
> 3. Everyone charged with a criminal offence has the following minimum rights: . . . (d) to examine or have examined witnesses against him and to obtain the attendance and examination of witnesses on his behalf under the same conditions as witnesses against him. . . .

54. The applicant claimed in the first place that, in obtaining the statements of the anonymous witnesses Y15 and Y16, the rights of the defence had been infringed to such an extent that the reliance on those statements by the Amsterdam Court of Appeal was incompatible with the standards of a "fair" trial. . . .

Although he conceded that in the course of the appeal proceedings Y15 and Y16 had been questioned by [the Investigating Judge] in the presence of his Counsel and had identified him from a photograph taken several years previously, that was not a proper substitute for a confrontation with him in person. Not knowing the identity of the persons concerned, he could not himself cross-examine them to test their credibility. Nor could the possibility of mistakes be ruled out. It would, in his submission, have been possible to examine the witnesses in his presence, protecting them, if need be, by the use of disguise, voice-distorting equipment or a two-way mirror.

In fact, he questioned the need for maintaining the anonymity of Y15 and Y16 at all. Both had stated before the investigating judge that they feared reprisals but there was nothing to suggest that they were ever subjected to, or for that matter threatened with, violence at the hands of the applicant. Moreover, the basis of the investigating judge's assessment of the need for anonymity was not made clear to the defence. . . .

55. In the second place, the applicant complained about the reliance on the evidence of the named witness R. Although R had been brought to the hearing of the Court of Appeal for questioning, he had — in the applicant's submission — been allowed to abscond under circumstances which engaged the Court of Appeal's responsibility. . . . Since he — the applicant — had not been able to cross-examine R, his statement to the police should not have been admitted as evidence. . . .

67. The Court of Appeal had been entitled to consider the reliability of the statements of Y15 and Y16 sufficiently corroborated by the findings of the investigating judge, as officially recorded on 19 November 1990, and by the statement in open court of the [investigating police officer] that the witnesses in the case had been under no constraint. In any case, the Court of Appeal had noted in its judgment that it had made use of the anonymous statements with "the necessary caution and circumspection." . . .

69. As the Court has held on previous occasions, the Convention does not preclude reliance, at the investigation stage, on sources such as anonymous informants. The subsequent use of their statements by the trial court to found a conviction is however capable of raising issues under the Convention. See Kostovski v. Netherlands, 12 Eur. Ct. H.R. 344 (1990).

[Under the *Kostovski* judgment, the use of statements by anonymous witnesses is acceptable when the statement is taken down by a judge who (a) is aware of the identity of the witness, (b) has expressed, in the official record of the hearing of such a witness, his reasoned opinion as to the reliability of the witness and as to the reasons for the witness's wish to remain anonymous, and (c) has provided the defence with some opportunity to put questions or have questions put to the witness. This rule is subject to exceptions; thus, according to the same judgment, the statement of an anonymous witness may be used in evidence despite the absence of the safeguards mentioned above if (a) the defence has not at any stage of the proceedings asked to be allowed to question the witness concerned, and (b) the conviction is based to a significant extent on other evidence not derived from anonymous sources, and (c) the trial court makes it clear that it has made use of the statement of the anonymous witness with caution and circumspection.]

70. It is true that Article 6 does not explicitly require the interests of witnesses in general, and those of victims called upon to testify in particular, to be taken into consideration. However, their life, liberty or security of person may be at stake, as may interests coming generally within the ambit of Article 8 of the Convention.* Such interests of witnesses and victims are in principle protected by other, substantive provisions of the Convention, which imply that Contracting States should organise their criminal proceedings in such a way that those interests are not unjustifiably imperilled. Against this background, principles of fair trial also require that in appropriate cases the interests of the defence are balanced against those of witnesses or victims called upon to testify.

71. As the Amsterdam Court of Appeal made clear, its decision not to disclose the identity of Y15 and Y16 to the defence was inspired by the need, as assessed by it, to obtain evidence from them while at the same time protecting them against the possibility of reprisals by the applicant. . . .

* Article 8 provides: "Everyone has the right to respect for his private and family life, his home and his correspondence." — Eds.

Although, as the applicant has stated, there has been no suggestion that Y15 and Y16 were ever threatened by the applicant himself, the decision to maintain their anonymity cannot be regarded as unreasonable per se. Regard must be had to the fact, as established by the domestic courts and not contested by the applicant, that drug dealers frequently resorted to threats or actual violence against persons who gave evidence against them. Furthermore, the statements made by the witnesses concerned to the investigating judge show that one of them had apparently on a previous occasion suffered violence at the hands of a drug dealer against whom he had testified, while the other had been threatened. In sum, there was sufficient reason for maintaining the anonymity of Y15 and Y16. . . .

73. In the instant case the anonymous witnesses were questioned at the appeals stage in the presence of Counsel by an investigating judge who was aware of their identity, even if the defence was not. . . . In this respect the present case is to be distinguished from that of *Kostovski.* Counsel was not only present, but he was put in a position to ask the witnesses whatever questions he considered to be in the interests of the defence except in so far as they might lead to the disclosure of their identity, and these questions were all answered. . . .

74. While it would clearly have been preferable for the applicant to have attended the questioning of the witnesses, the Court considers, on balance, that the Amsterdam Court of Appeal was entitled to consider that the interests of the applicant were in this respect outweighed by the need to ensure the safety of the witnesses. More generally, the Convention does not preclude identification — for the purposes of Article 6(3)(d) — of an accused with his Counsel. . . .

76. Finally, it should be recalled that, even when "counterbalancing" procedures are found to compensate sufficiently the handicaps under which the defence labours, a conviction should not be based either solely or to a decisive extent on anonymous statements. That, however, is not the case here: it is sufficiently clear that the national court did not base its finding of guilt solely or to a decisive extent on the evidence of Y15 and Y16.

Furthermore, evidence obtained from witnesses under conditions in which the rights of the defence cannot be secured to the extent normally required by the Convention should be treated with extreme care. The Court is satisfied that this was done in the criminal proceedings leading to the applicant's conviction, as is reflected in the express declaration by the Court of Appeal that it had treated the statements of Y15 and Y16 "with the necessary caution and circumspection." . . .

83. None of the alleged shortcomings considered on their own lead the Court to conclude that the applicant did not receive a fair trial. Moreover, it cannot find, even if the alleged shortcomings are considered together, that the proceedings as a whole were unfair. In arriving at this conclusion the Court has taken into account the fact that the domestic courts were entitled to consider the various items of evidence before them as corroborative of each other. . . . For these reasons, the Court holds, by seven votes to two, that there has been no violation of Article 6(1) taken together with Article 6(3)(d) of the Convention. . . .

RYSSDAL, J., dissenting.

It is not only in drug cases that problems may arise in relation to the safety of witnesses. It is not permissible to resolve such problems by departing from such a fundamental principle as the one that witness evidence challenged by the accused cannot be admitted against him if he has not had an opportunity to examine or have examined, in his presence, the witness in question.

In the instant case the applicant had this opportunity in respect of witness N, who withdrew his earlier statement. The applicant did not have such an opportunity in relation to witness R, who "disappeared," or witnesses Y15 and Y16, who were heard only in the presence of his lawyer. Moreover, Y15 and Y16 were anonymous witnesses whose identity was only known to the investigating judge but not to the applicant and his lawyer, nor to the Regional Court and the Court of Appeal.

Notes

1. *Anonymous witnesses: majority position.* In the United States, a witness is usually required to divulge both his name and address on cross-examination. This is said to allow the defendant to put the witness in a "proper setting" and to test the witness's credibility. See Alford v. United States, 282 U.S. 687 (1931); Smith v. Illinois, 390 U.S. 129 (1968). At the same time, the right to cross-examine prosecution witnesses about their identities or addresses is not considered absolute, and a trial court has discretion to restrict cross-examination on such topics if there is an adequate showing that the safety of the witness is at risk. Alvarado v. Superior Court, 5 P.3d 203 (Cal. 2000) (prosecution may not permanently withhold identities of key witnesses; although disclosure may be delayed until trial, safety concerns of prisoner-witnesses must be addressed by means less drastic than anonymous testimony if testimony is crucial to prosecution's case); State v. Vandebogart, 652 A.2d 671 (N.H. 1994) (witness allowed not to reveal address; she was victim of prior assault by defendant); Randolph N. Jonakait, Secret Testimony and Public Trials in New York, 42 N.Y.L. School L. Rev. 407 (1998). Recall also that the government often may shield the identity of "confidential informants" during the investigation stage.

Courts in a number of nations have upheld convictions based on the testimony of "anonymous witnesses." Legislation in some nations (such as New Zealand) allows undercover police officers to testify without revealing their identities. The general trend has been to allow the use of anonymous witnesses only when accompanied by the sort of safeguards described in the *Doorson* opinion from the European Court of Human Rights. As European nations move toward more of a hybrid between common law and civil law processes (and thus a hybrid between adversarial and inquisitorial development of proof), will they become less likely to rely on devices such as anonymous witnesses?

2. *The value of comparative law.* Do the practices and values of European criminal justice systems have any relevance for American lawyers, legislators, or judges? See Diane Marie Amann, Harmonic Convergence? Constitutional Criminal Procedure in an International Context, 75 Ind. L.J. 809 (2000). Given the perceived differences between adversarial development of proof at trial (dominated by the attorneys) and inquisitorial methods of proof (dominated by the judge), is it fair to conclude that practices relating to confrontation of witnesses are less likely than other practices to interest those who operate within American criminal procedure rules?

2. *Unavailable Prosecution Witnesses*

How can a defendant confront the person who accuses her if the accuser is not present in the courtroom? There are many reasons why a witness or victim may be unavailable in the courtroom. For the most part, the law of evidence dictates when statements made by unavailable witnesses will be admitted at trial. There is, however, a constitutional component to these questions as well. One special class of statements consists of those made at some earlier time by a co-defendant who is in the courtroom but decides not to testify. If statements by one co-defendant directly implicate another defendant, they raise the question of whether the second defendant is able to confront her accuser.

■ KEVIN GRAY v. MARYLAND

523 U.S. 185 (1998)

Breyer, J.

The issue in this case concerns the application of Bruton v. United States, 391 U.S. 123 (1968). *Bruton* involved two defendants accused of participating in the same crime and tried jointly before the same jury. One of the defendants had confessed. His confession named and incriminated the other defendant. The trial judge issued a limiting instruction, telling the jury that it should consider the confession as evidence only against the codefendant who had confessed and not against the defendant named in the confession. *Bruton* held that, despite the limiting instruction, the Constitution forbids the use of such a confession in the joint trial.

The case before us differs from *Bruton* in that the prosecution here redacted the codefendant's confession by substituting for the defendant's name in the confession a blank space or the word "deleted." We must decide whether these substitutions make a significant legal difference. We hold that they do not and that *Bruton*'s protective rule applies.

In 1993, Stacy Williams died after a severe beating. Anthony Bell gave a confession, to the Baltimore City police, in which he said that he (Bell), Kevin Gray, and Jacquin "Tank" Vanlandingham had participated in the beating that resulted in Williams' death. Vanlandingham later died. A Maryland grand jury indicted Bell and Gray for murder. The State of Maryland tried them jointly.

The trial judge, after denying Gray's motion for a separate trial, permitted the State to introduce Bell's confession into evidence at trial. But the judge ordered the confession redacted. Consequently, the police detective who read the confession into evidence said the word "deleted" or "deletion" whenever Gray's name or Vanlandingham's name appeared. Immediately after the police detective read the redacted confession to the jury, the prosecutor asked, "after he gave you that information, you subsequently were able to arrest Mr. Kevin Gray; is that correct?" The officer responded, "That's correct." The State also introduced into evidence a written copy of the confession with those two names omitted, leaving in their place blank white spaces separated by commas. The State produced other witnesses, who said that six persons (including Bell, Gray, and Vanlandingham) participated in the beating. Gray testified and denied his participation. Bell did not testify.

When instructing the jury, the trial judge specified that the confession was evidence only against Bell; the instructions said that the jury should not use the confession as evidence against Gray. The jury convicted both Bell and Gray. Gray appealed. . . .

Bruton, as we have said, involved two defendants — Evans and Bruton — tried jointly for robbery. Evans did not testify, but the Government introduced into evidence Evans' confession, which stated that both he (Evans) and Bruton together had committed the robbery. The trial judge told the jury it could consider the confession as evidence only against Evans, not against Bruton.

This Court held that, despite the limiting instruction, the introduction of Evans' out-of-court confession at Bruton's trial had violated Bruton's right, protected by the Sixth Amendment, to cross-examine witnesses. The Court recognized that in many circumstances a limiting instruction will adequately protect one defendant from the prejudicial effects of the introduction at a joint trial of evidence intended for use only against a different defendant. But it said that

> there are some contexts in which the risk that the jury will not, or cannot, follow instructions is so great, and the consequences of failure so vital to the defendant, that the practical and human limitations of the jury system cannot be ignored. Such a context is presented here, where the powerfully incriminating extrajudicial statements of a codefendant, who stands accused side-by-side with the defendant, are deliberately spread before the jury in a joint trial. Not only are the incriminations devastating to the defendant but their credibility is inevitably suspect. . . . The unreliability of such evidence is intolerably compounded when the alleged accomplice, as here, does not testify and cannot be tested by cross-examination. [391 U.S. at 135-136.]

In Richardson v. Marsh, 481 U.S. 200 (1987), the Court considered a redacted confession. The case involved a joint murder trial of Marsh and Williams. The State had redacted the confession of one defendant, Williams, so as to "omit all reference" to his codefendant, Marsh — indeed, to omit all indication that anyone other than Williams and a third person had participated in the crime. The trial court also instructed the jury not to consider the confession against Marsh. As redacted, the confession indicated that Williams and the third person had discussed the murder in the front seat of a car while they traveled to the victim's house. The redacted confession contained no indication that Marsh — or any other person — was in the car. Later in the trial, however, Marsh testified that she was in the back seat of the car. For that reason, in context, the confession still could have helped convince the jury that Marsh knew about the murder in advance and therefore had participated knowingly in the crime.

The Court held that this redacted confession fell outside *Bruton*'s scope and was admissible (with appropriate limiting instructions) at the joint trial. The Court distinguished Evans' confession in *Bruton* as a confession that was "incriminating on its face," and which had "expressly implicat[ed]" *Bruton*. By contrast, Williams' confession amounted to "evidence requiring linkage" in that it became incriminating in respect to Marsh "only when linked with evidence introduced later at trial." The Court held that "the Confrontation Clause is not violated by the admission of a nontestifying codefendant's confession with a proper limiting instruction when, as here, the confession is redacted to eliminate not only the defendant's name, but any reference to his or her existence." The Court added: "We express no opinion on the admissibility of a confession in which the defendant's name has been replaced with a symbol or neutral pronoun."

Originally, the codefendant's confession in the case before us, like that in *Bruton*, referred to, and directly implicated another defendant. The State, however, redacted that confession by removing the nonconfessing defendant's name. Nonetheless, unlike *Richardson*'s redacted confession, this confession refers directly to the "existence" of the nonconfessing defendant. The State has simply replaced the nonconfessing defendant's name with a kind of symbol, namely the word "deleted" or a blank space set off by commas. The redacted confession, for example, responded to the question "Who was in the group that beat Stacey," with the phrase, "Me, _____, and a few other guys." And when the police witness read the confession in court, he said the word "deleted" or "deletion" where the blank spaces appear. . . .

Bruton, as interpreted by *Richardson,* holds that certain "powerfully incriminating extrajudicial statements of a codefendant"— those naming another defendant — considered as a class, are so prejudicial that limiting instructions cannot work. Unless the prosecutor wishes to hold separate trials or to use separate juries or to abandon use of the confession, he must redact the confession to reduce significantly or to eliminate the special prejudice that the *Bruton* Court found. Redactions that simply replace a name with an obvious blank space or a word such as "deleted" or a symbol or other similarly obvious indications of alteration, however, leave statements that, considered as a class, so closely resemble *Bruton's* unredacted statements that, in our view, the law must require the same result.

For one thing, a jury will often react similarly to an unredacted confession and a confession redacted in this way, for the jury will often realize that the confession refers specifically to the defendant. This is true even when the State does not blatantly link the defendant to the deleted name, as it did in this case by asking whether Gray was arrested on the basis of information in Bell's confession as soon as the officer had finished reading the redacted statement. Consider a simplified but typical example, a confession that reads "I, Bob Smith, along with Sam Jones, robbed the bank." To replace the words "Sam Jones" with an obvious blank will not likely fool anyone. A juror somewhat familiar with criminal law would know immediately that the blank, in the phrase "I, Bob Smith, along with _____, robbed the bank," refers to defendant Jones. A juror who does not know the law and who therefore wonders to whom the blank might refer need only lift his eyes to Jones, sitting at counsel table, to find what will seem the obvious answer, at least if the juror hears the judge's instruction not to consider the confession as evidence against Jones, for that instruction will provide an obvious reason for the blank. A more sophisticated juror, wondering if the blank refers to someone else, might also wonder how, if it did, the prosecutor could argue the confession is reliable, for the prosecutor, after all, has been arguing that Jones, not someone else, helped Smith commit the crime. For another thing, the obvious deletion may well call the jurors' attention specially to the removed name. By encouraging the jury to speculate about the reference, the redaction may overemphasize the importance of the confession's accusation — once the jurors work out the reference. . . .

Finally, *Bruton*'s protected statements and statements redacted to leave a blank or some other similarly obvious alteration, function the same way grammatically. They are directly accusatory. Evans' statement in *Bruton* used a proper name to point explicitly to an accused defendant. And *Bruton* held that the "powerfully incriminating" effect of . . . an out-of-court accusation creates a special, and vital, need for cross-examination — a need that would be immediately obvious had the codefendant pointed directly to the defendant in the courtroom itself. The blank space in an obviously redacted confession also points directly to the defendant, and it accuses the defendant in a manner similar to Evans' use of Bruton's name or to a testifying codefendant's accusatory finger. By way of contrast, the factual statement at issue in *Richardson* — a statement about what others said in the front seat of a car — differs from directly accusatory evidence in this respect, for it does not point directly to a defendant at all.

We concede certain differences between *Bruton* and this case. A confession that uses a blank or the word "delete" (or, for that matter, a first name or a nickname) less obviously refers to the defendant than a confession that uses the defendant's full and proper name. Moreover, in some instances the person to whom the blank refers may not be clear: Although the follow-up question asked by the State in this case eliminated all doubt, the reference might not be transparent in other cases in which a confession, like the present confession, uses two (or more) blanks, even though only one other defendant appears at trial, and in which the trial indicates that there are more participants than the confession has named. . . . We also concede that the jury must use inference to connect the statement in this redacted confession with the defendant. But inference pure and simple cannot make the critical difference, for if it did, then *Richardson* would also place outside *Bruton*'s scope confessions that use shortened first names, nicknames, descriptions as unique as the "red-haired, bearded, one-eyed man-with-a-limp," and perhaps even full names of defendants who are always known by a nickname. This Court has assumed, however, that nicknames and specific descriptions fall inside, not outside, *Bruton*'s protection. . . .

That being so, *Richardson* must depend in significant part upon the kind of, not the simple fact of, inference. *Richardson*'s inferences involved statements that did not refer directly to the defendant himself and which became incriminating "only when linked with evidence introduced later at trial." The inferences at issue here involve statements that, despite redaction, obviously refer directly to someone, often obviously the defendant, and which involve inferences that a jury ordinarily could make immediately, even were the confession the very first item introduced at trial. Moreover, the redacted confession with the blank prominent on its face, in *Richardson*'s words, "facially incriminat[es]" the codefendant. . . .

Nor are the policy reasons that *Richardson* provided in support of its conclusion applicable here. *Richardson* expressed concern lest application of *Bruton*'s rule apply where "redaction" of confessions, particularly "confessions incriminating by connection," would often not be possible, thereby forcing prosecutors too often to abandon use either of the confession or of a joint trial. Additional redaction of a confession that uses a blank space, the word "delete," or a symbol, however, normally is possible. Consider as an example a portion of the confession before us: The witness who read the confession told the jury that the confession (among other things) said, "Question: Who was in the group that beat Stacey? Answer: Me, deleted, deleted, and a few other guys." Why could the witness not, instead, have said: "Question: Who was in the group that beat Stacey? Answer: Me and a few other guys." . . .

The *Richardson* Court also feared that the inclusion, within *Bruton*'s protective rule, of confessions that incriminated "by connection" too often would provoke mistrials, or would unnecessarily lead prosecutors to abandon the confession or joint trial, because neither the prosecutors nor the judge could easily predict, until after the introduction of all the evidence, whether or not *Bruton* had barred use of the confession. To include the use of blanks, the word "delete," symbols, or other indications of redaction, within *Bruton's* protections, however, runs no such risk. Their use is easily identified prior to trial and does not depend, in any special way, upon the other evidence introduced in the case. . . .

For these reasons, we hold that the confession here at issue, which substituted blanks and the word "delete" for the respondent's proper name, falls within the class of statements to which *Bruton*'s protections apply. . . .

Scalia, J., dissenting.

. . . The almost invariable assumption of the law is that jurors follow their instructions. This rule "is a pragmatic one, rooted less in the absolute certitude that the presumption is true than in the belief that it represents a reasonable practical accommodation of the interests of the state and the defendant in the criminal justice process." *Richardson*. . . . In *Bruton,* we recognized a "narrow exception" to this rule. . . .

We declined in *Richardson,* however, to extend *Bruton* to confessions that incriminate only by inference from other evidence. When incrimination is inferential, "it is a less valid generalization that the jury will not likely obey the instruction to disregard the evidence." Today the Court struggles to decide whether a confession redacted to omit the defendant's name is incriminating on its face or by inference. [T]he statement "Me, deleted, deleted, and a few other guys" does not facially incriminate anyone but the speaker. The Court's analogizing of "deleted" to a physical description that clearly identifies the defendant does not survive scrutiny. By "facially incriminating," we have meant incriminating independent of other evidence introduced at trial. Since the defendant's appearance at counsel table is not evidence, the description "red-haired, bearded, one-eyed man-with-a-limp" would be facially incriminating — unless, of course, the defendant had dyed his hair black and shaved his beard before trial, and the prosecution introduced evidence concerning his former appearance. . . . By contrast, the person to whom "deleted" refers in "Me, deleted, deleted, and a few other guys" is not apparent from anything the jury knows independent of the evidence at trial. Though the jury may speculate, the statement expressly implicates no one but the speaker.

Of course the Court is correct that confessions redacted to omit the defendant's name are more likely to incriminate than confessions redacted to omit any reference to his existence. But it is also true — and more relevant here — that confessions redacted to omit the defendant's name are less likely to incriminate than confessions that expressly state it. The latter are "powerfully incriminating" as a class; the former are not so. Here, for instance, there were two names deleted, five or more participants in the crime, and only one other defendant on trial. The jury no doubt may "speculate about the reference" as it speculates when evidence connects a defendant to a confession that does not refer to his existence. The issue, however, is not whether the confession incriminated petitioner, but whether the incrimination is so "powerful" that we must depart from the normal presumption that the jury follows its instructions. I think it is not — and I am certain that drawing the line for departing from the ordinary rule at the facial identification of the defendant makes more sense than drawing it anywhere else.

We explained in *Richardson* that forgoing use of codefendant confessions or joint trials was too high a price to insure that juries never disregard their instructions. The Court minimizes the damage that it does by suggesting that additional redaction of a confession that uses a blank space . . . normally is possible. In the present case, it asks, why could the police officer not have testified that Bell's answer was "Me and a few other guys"? The answer, it seems obvious to me, is because that is not what Bell said. Bell's answer was "Me, Tank, Kevin and a few other guys." Introducing the statement with full disclosure of deletions is one thing; introducing as the complete statement what was in fact only a part is something else. . . . The risk to the integrity of our system (not to mention the increase in its complexity) posed by the approval of such freelance editing seems to me infinitely greater than the risk posed by the entirely honest reproduction that the Court disapproves.

The United States Constitution guarantees, not a perfect system of criminal justice (as to which there can be considerable disagreement), but a minimum standard of fairness. Lest we lose sight of the forest for the trees, it should be borne in mind that federal and state rules of criminal procedure—which can afford to seek perfection because they can be more readily changed—exclude nontestifying-codefendant confessions even where the Sixth Amendment does not. Under the Federal Rules of Criminal Procedure (and Maryland's), a trial court may order separate trials if joinder will prejudice a defendant. . . . Federal and most state trial courts (including Maryland's) also have the discretion to exclude unfairly prejudicial (albeit probative) evidence. Fed. Rule Evid. 403; Md. Rule Evid. 5-403. Here, petitioner moved for a severance on the ground that the admission of Bell's confession would be unfairly prejudicial. The trial court denied the motion, explaining that where a confession names two others, and the evidence is that five or six others participated, redaction of petitioner's name would not leave the jury with the "unavoidable inference" that Bell implicated Gray.

I do not understand the Court to disagree that the redaction itself left unclear to whom the blank referred. That being so, the rule set forth in *Richardson* applies, and the statement could constitutionally be admitted with limiting instruction. . . .

Notes

1. *Out-of-court statements by co-defendants: majority position.* A co-defendant who has confessed and implicated the defendant may be unavailable for testimony or cross-examination at trial because of the co-defendant's privilege against self-incrimination. In Bruton v. United States, 391 U.S. 123 (1968), the Court prevented the use of the co-defendant's statement in a joint jury trial, even if the judge cautions the jury to consider the confession as evidence only against the co-defendant. When the co-defendant takes the stand at trial (and is therefore available for cross-examination), or when the defendant has also confessed and offered enough similar details to make the two confessions "interlocking," the co-defendant's confession may come into evidence. Cruz v. New York, 481 U.S. 186 (1987) (similarities in interlocking confessions provide enough indicia of reliability to satisfy confrontation clause); Nelson v. O'Neil, 402 U.S. 622 (1971) (testimony of co-defendant). Virtually all state courts allow the government to introduce co-defendant confessions under circumstances such as these.

2. *Redacted statements.* The decision in Gray v. Maryland considered the types of redactions to a co-defendant confession that would make the statement admissible against the co-defendant in a joint trial. See also Commonwealth v. Travers, 768 A.2d 845 (Pa. 2001) (*Bruton* not violated by admission of nontestifying co-defendant confession redacted by replacement of the defendant's name with the phrase "the other man"). Before the Supreme Court announced its decision in *Gray,* state courts divided on the question of whether to admit co-defendant confessions when the defendant's name is simply replaced with a neutral pronoun or a word such as "deleted." One group of courts (describing themselves as "facial incrimination" jurisdictions) concluded that replacement of the defendant's name in the confession is enough to prevent the jury from using the evidence improperly. The *Bruton* bar, they said, applies only to co-defendant confessions that facially incriminate the defendant by naming him or making some equivalent identification. Another group of

courts (the "contextual" jurisdictions) looked to the other evidence in the case to determine the probability that the jury would use the other evidence to identify the defendant as the unnamed person mentioned in the co-defendant's confession. See Ex parte Sneed, 783 So. 2d 863 (Ala. 2000) (statement edited to cure *Bruton* problem was irreconcilably inconsistent with theory of defense); People v. Fletcher, 917 P.2d 187 (Cal. 1996). Did the U.S. Supreme Court in *Gray* side with one of these groups of state courts, or did it create a new method of analysis?

Justice Scalia's dissent in *Gray* points out that joinder and severance rules give trial judges discretion to order separate trials for co-defendants if a joint trial would be prejudicial. Would the need to edit a co-defendant's confession convince you, as a trial judge, to adopt a strong presumption in favor of separate trials? Does the operation of the *Bruton* rule call for any changes in joinder and severance rules? See Judith L. Ritter, The X Files: Joint Trials, Redacted Confessions and Thirty Years of Sidestepping *Bruton,* 42 Vill. L. Rev. 855 (1997).

3. *Hearsay exceptions and confrontation.* The *Bruton* issue is one variety of dispute surrounding hearsay statements admitted at trial. Rules of evidence in all jurisdictions exclude out-of-court hearsay statements (that is, statements made out of court by someone other than the witness, offered to prove the truth of the matter addressed in the statement) but then make exceptions to allow into evidence some of the more reliable statements. Because the original declarant of a hearsay statement is not testifying, hearsay evidence raises a constitutional question under the confrontation clause. Supreme Court cases have concluded that the federal confrontation clause allows the government to use hearsay statements of a person who will not testify at trial so long as the evidence falls within a "firmly rooted" exception to the bar on hearsay. When no such exception is available, the confrontation clause prevents use of the evidence unless there are some "particularized guarantees of trustworthiness." See White v. Illinois, 502 U.S. 346 (1992) (spontaneous declarations exception); Idaho v. Wright, 497 U.S. 805 (1990) (no "firmly rooted" exception available; statement presumed inadmissible, presumption overcome by particularized guarantees of trustworthiness); Ohio v. Roberts, 448 U.S. 56 (1980) (business and public records exception). The overwhelming majority of state courts use the same analysis. See People v. Smith, 604 N.E.2d 858 (Ill. 1992); but see State v. Storch, 612 N.E.2d 305 (Ohio 1993) (requiring a showing that a declarant is "unavailable" before allowing use of hearsay evidence that qualifies under traditional exception of spontaneous declarations). Are these cases based on a practical judgment that cross-examination would not provide a useful test of the accuracy of evidence falling under one of the firmly rooted hearsay exceptions?

In Lilly v. Virginia, 527 U.S. 116 (1999), the Supreme Court decided that a defendant's Sixth Amendment right of confrontation prevented the use at trial of the statement made to police by an alleged accomplice, admitting some criminal activity but blaming the defendant for the most serious criminal acts. The accomplice refused to testify at trial and the prosecution sought to introduce the out-of-court statement under an exception to the bar on hearsay evidence, because the statement was against the speaker's penal interest. Four justices (Stevens, Souter, Ginsburg, and Breyer) declared that such statements are not reliable for confrontation clause purposes as falling into a "firmly rooted" exception to the hearsay rule. They reasoned that statements can only qualify as a firmly rooted exception to the hearsay bar when they are "so trustworthy that adversarial testing can be expected to add little to [the statements'] reliability." Justice Scalia joined in the result, concluding that the use of the tape-recorded statements to police at trial without making him available for cross-examination is a "paradigmatic" confrontation clause violation. Other justices concluded that the accomplice's confession does not satisfy a firmly rooted hearsay exception because the statements that were against his penal interest were separate from the statements exculpating him and inculpating Lilly. The case, in their view, did not raise the question whether the confrontation clause permits the admission of a genuinely self-inculpatory statement that also inculpates a co-defendant.

4. *Recorded calls to police as evidence.* In some criminal cases (particularly in domestic violence prosecutions), the government introduces into evidence a recording of the alleged victim's emergency call to the police. This can happen even in cases where the victim does not testify at trial. Consider this description of the evidence in an Ohio prosecution against Jerry Lee for domestic violence:

> In the tape recording, the victim, Lee's wife Kathy, says that her husband stabbed her door, hit her, and tried to throw her out the door. When police officers arrived at the scene, two minutes after receiving a dispatch, the couple's eighteen-year-old son told them, "I think my father is killing my mother." Within five more minutes, Kathy made additional statements to one of the officers, including one that Jerry had tried to stab her. The trial court admitted all these statements. . . . Neither Kathy Lee nor the son testified, and the State made no attempt to account for their absence.

Friedman, Richard D. and Bridget McCormack, Dial-In Testimony, 150 U. Pa. L. Rev. 1171, 1173-74 (2002). Why would the victim and her son not be present at the trial or not be available to testify? What reading of the Sixth Amendment allows this testimony into evidence?

3. Unavailable Topics

Rules of evidence limit the sorts of inquiries a party may pursue at trial. Clearly this has an effect on the defendant's ability to confront and cross-examine prosecution witnesses. Perhaps the most striking of these rules are those that limit the questions the defense may ask about past and current criminal charges against the prosecution's witness. These evidentiary rules are based on the assumption that prior convictions or other wrongdoing could lead the jury to conclude too hastily that the witness is not credible. The following case explores the outer reach of such evidentiary limits on the power to cross-examine.

■ JOHNNY CARROLL v. STATE

916 S.W.2d 494 (Tex. Crim. App. 1996)

BAIRD, J.

Appellant was convicted of murder and sentenced to 30 years confinement. . . . We granted review to determine whether [a State's witness may] be cross-examined concerning pending criminal charges. We will reverse and remand.

The right of confrontation has ancient roots. Over 2,000 years ago the Roman Governor Porcius Festus reported to King Agrippa: "It is not the manner of the

Romans to deliver any man up to die before the accused has met his accusers face to face, and has been given a chance to defend himself against the charges." The right of confrontation was also recognized in English common law. Initially, the right of the accused to confront witnesses was recognized in trials for treason. Arguably, the most notorious treason trial in England was that of the Sir Walter Raleigh, accused of conspiring to overthrow the King of England. Raleigh was charged with treason after a third party, Cobham, confessed under torture, to conspiring with Raleigh. At trial, Raleigh was denied the opportunity to confront Cobham and Cobham's statement was used to convict and ultimately execute Raleigh. . . .

Cross-examination serves three general purposes: cross-examination may serve to identify the witness with his community so that independent testimony may be sought and offered concerning the witness' reputation for veracity in that community; cross-examination allows the jury to assess the credibility of the witness; and, cross-examination allows facts to be brought out tending to discredit the witness by showing that his testimony in chief was untrue or biased. Alford v. United States, 282 U.S. 687 (1931). Cross-examination is by nature exploratory and there is no general requirement that the defendant indicate the purpose of his inquiry. Indeed, the defendant should be granted a wide latitude even though he is unable to state what facts he expects to prove through his cross-examination.

The Constitutional right of confrontation is violated when appropriate cross-examination is limited. The scope of appropriate cross-examination is necessarily broad. A defendant is entitled to pursue all avenues of cross-examination reasonably calculated to expose a motive, bias or interest for the witness to testify. . . . This broad scope necessarily includes cross-examination concerning criminal charges pending against a witness and over which those in need of the witness' testimony might be empowered to exercise control. A witness' pecuniary interest in the outcome of the trial is also an appropriate area of cross-examination.

Nevertheless, there are several areas where cross-examination may be inappropriate and, in those situations the trial judge has the discretion to limit cross-examination. Specifically, a trial judge may limit cross-examination when a subject is exhausted, or when the cross-examination is designed to annoy, harass, or humiliate, or when the cross-examination might endanger the personal safety of the witness. See generally Delaware v. Van Arsdall, 475 U.S. 673 (trial judge may exercise discretion to prevent harassment, prejudice, confusion of the issues, the witness' safety, and repetitive or marginally relevant interrogation.); Tex. R. Crim. Evid. 608, 609, 404 and 405.

In the instant case, the State presented two witnesses who testified they were present at the time of the murder. Charles Fitzgerald testified he and the victim were at a bar when they saw appellant. Appellant showed Fitzgerald a pistol and shortly thereafter got into an argument with the victim. Fitzgerald and the victim moved to a table and appellant followed. Appellant shot the victim with the pistol, and continued shooting as the victim moved toward the back of the bar. Although Fitzgerald testified he only consumed two beers, the officers who interviewed him the night of the murder testified Fitzgerald was intoxicated. Appellant impeached Fitzgerald's testimony with proof of his intoxication at the time of the killing.

Herman Russell testified appellant and the victim argued over a mutual girlfriend. When the victim indicated the girlfriend had moved in with him, appellant pulled a pistol and told the victim he should not talk to the girl. Appellant then put the pistol into his waistband and Russell went to a back room. In less than a minute

Russell heard a gunshot and saw the victim running while holding his arm. Russell testified appellant continued to shoot the victim.[7]

Appellant sought to impeach Russell's testimony with evidence that Russell was currently incarcerated and awaiting trial on an aggravated robbery charge and that he had several prior felony convictions. The State asked the trial judge to prohibit appellant from conducting such cross-examination, contending such evidence was not relevant. Appellant contended Russell's testimony had a potential for bias because Russell's testimony in the instant case might favorably affect the outcome in the aggravated robbery case. Appellant further contended Russell's previous convictions could be used to enhance the felony charge, thus increasing the punishment range and creating a greater likelihood for bias. The trial judge agreed with the State and prohibited the testimony. The Court of Appeals affirmed, holding that Tex. R. Crim. Evid. 608(b) specifically prohibited the use of the pending aggravated robbery charge for impeachment.[9]

There exists a long line of federal and state authority holding a pending criminal charge is an appropriate area of cross-examination. Davis v. Alaska, 415 U.S. 308 (1974); Carmona v. State, 698 S.W.2d 100 (Tex. Crim. App. 1985). Indeed, the instant situation differs little from that confronted by the Supreme Court in Alford v. United States, 282 U.S. 687 (1931), where a prosecution witness testified to Alford's actions and incriminating statements. On cross-examination, Alford sought to elicit testimony that the witness was in federal custody "for the purpose of showing whatever bias or prejudice he may have." However, the trial judge refused to allow such evidence because it was not based upon a final conviction.

The Supreme Court reversed, holding cross-examination is a matter of right. Although the extent of cross-examination is subject to the sound discretion of the trial judge, the trial judge abuses that discretion when he prevents appropriate cross-examination. And inquiry into a witness' potential bias arising from incarceration was appropriate. Indeed, the Supreme Court held Alford should have been allowed to cross-examine the witness to demonstrate the "testimony was biased because given under a promise or expectation of immunity, or under the coercive effect of his detention by officers [who were] conducting the present prosecution." . . .

In Harris v. State, 642 S.W.2d 471 (Tex. Crim. App. 1982), the defendant sought to question the State's witness concerning her pending juvenile charges. The trial judge sustained the State's objections to such cross-examination. On appeal the defendant contended he was entitled to cross-examine the witness concerning any probable bias or interest in her testimony. [W]e reversed stating the defendant "had an unqualified right to ask . . . the only witness linking him with the offense, whether she too had been 'accused' of the offense on trial, and to receive her answer. . . ." The jury was entitled to the "whole picture" in order to evaluate and judge the witness' credibility.

Alford and *Harris* control our resolution of the instant case. Appellant's cross-examination was clearly an attempt to demonstrate that Russell held a possible

7. [Carroll] testified he did not display his weapon. Instead, he and the victim were discussing the mutual girlfriend when the victim used profanity and reached into his pants as if to retrieve a weapon. Appellant shot the victim because the girlfriend had informed him that the victim "had something that would take care of [him]."

9. Tex. R. Crim. Evid. 608(b) provides: "Specific instances of the conduct of a witness, for the purpose of attacking or supporting his credibility, other than conviction of crime as provided in Rule 609, may not be inquired into on cross-examination of the witness nor proved by extrinsic evidence."

motive, bias or interest in testifying for the State. Appellant's inquiry into Russell's incarceration, his pending charge and possible punishment as a habitual criminal, was appropriate to demonstrate Russell's potential motive, bias or interest to testify for the State. A defendant is permitted to elicit any fact from a witness intended to demonstrate that witness' vulnerable relationship with the state.

The State contends appellant's cross-examination was impermissible because no agreement existed between the State and Russell which might affect Russell's motive to testify for the State. However, the existence of such an agreement is not determinative. [It] is possible, even absent an agreement, that Russell believed his testimony in this case would be of later benefit. . . .

Finally, the Court of Appeals' holding that appellant was unable to impeach Russell under Rule 608(b) is erroneous for at least two reasons. First, appellant's cross-examination concerning Russell's incarceration was not an inquiry into a specific instance of conduct. Instead, appellant's cross-examination focused on Russell's possible motive, bias or interest in testifying for the State. To understand this distinction we draw upon . . . Ramirez v. State, 802 S.W.2d 674 (Tex. Crim. App. 1990), which involved the interpretation and application of Rule 608(b). In *Ramirez*, the mother of an eight-year-old victim testified she did not believe appellant sexually assaulted the victim. The State cross-examined the mother regarding her prior use of heroin suggesting that, at the time of the offense, she was under its influence and unaware of what happened to her child. The State offered no evidence to show the mother either previously used heroin, or was under its influence at the time of the incident. Relying on Rule 608(b), we held the State was improperly allowed to question the mother about a specific instance of conduct.

In the instant case the Court of Appeals improperly relied upon Rule 608(b) because appellant . . . did not seek to cross-examine Russell about the underlying facts which gave rise to the aggravated robbery charge. Rather, appellant attempted to inform the jury that Russell had a vulnerable relationship with the State at the time of his testimony. . . . Consequently, the Court of Appeals erred in relying on Rule 608(b) to uphold the trial judge's limitation on appellant's cross-examination of Russell.

Second, although we see no conflict between the right to cross-examine a witness about a pending charge and Rule 608(b), if such a conflict existed, the constitutional right of confrontation would prevail. . . . Accordingly, the judgment of the Court of Appeals is reversed and the case is remanded to that Court. . . .

MEYERS, J., concurring.

In this case the charges pending against the State's witness originated in the same jurisdiction and were brought by the identical authorities as those for which the appellant stands accused. I therefore agree with the decision of our lead opinion to allow the defendant to use these charges for impeachment on cross-examination of this witness. However, in future contexts, should these charges emanate from another jurisdiction or authority, I would hold that release of the information to the jury is subject to a discretionary ruling of the trial court under Rule 403 of the Texas Rules of Criminal Evidence. With these additional comments, I join the opinion of the Court.

MANSFIELD, J., dissenting.

The State presented two witnesses who testified they were in the bar at the time the murder was committed. Charles Fitzgerald testified appellant showed him a pistol and observed him arguing with Robert Brzowski, the victim. Fitzgerald testified further appellant followed him and Mr. Brzowski to another table, shot Mr. Brzowski with the pistol and continued shooting at Mr. Brzowski as he fled toward the back of the bar. Appellant introduced evidence, including the testimony of two police officers who interviewed Fitzgerald after the shooting, that Fitzgerald was intoxicated at the time of the shooting.

The second witness, Herman Russell, the bartender, testified and gave essentially the same version of what occurred as Fitzgerald. Russell testified appellant and Mr. Brzowski argued over a mutual female acquaintance and things went down hill from there, concluding with appellant shooting and killing Mr. Brzowski.

At trial, appellant sought to impeach Russell with evidence of prior felony convictions, i.e., two convictions for cattle theft from 1962 and 1965. Though conceding Texas Rule of Criminal Evidence 609(b)* would ordinarily bar use of the convictions for impeachment as the convictions were too remote (over ten years old), appellant claimed they were relevant as they could be used to enhance punishment if Russell were convicted of his pending charge. Additionally, appellant sought to impeach Russell with evidence of a pending aggravated robbery charge and that he was currently incarcerated awaiting trial on that charge. Appellant alleged Russell was potentially biased because his testimony in the present case might affect the outcome in his pending aggravated robbery case, and he was entitled to show the jury Russell's testimony might be influenced by the charge pending against him.

At the hearing, Russell testified there had been no deals made with the State concerning the pending aggravated robbery charge in relation to his testimony in the present case. He testified he had already given a statement regarding the present case (the killing occurred on April 11, 1992) prior to being arrested on the aggravated robbery charge (the robbery allegedly was committed in 1988). Finally, he testified his testimony in the present case would not be affected by the case pending against him, which was scheduled to be prosecuted in a different court. The trial court denied appellant's motion, and Russell testified without being impeached by evidence of his prior convictions or of the pending aggravated robbery charge. . . .

Texas Criminal Evidence Rule 608(b) does not allow a witness to be impeached, for purposes of attacking his credibility, by proof of specific instances of conduct, other than conviction of crimes as provided by Rule 609, either on cross-examination or by extrinsic evidence. . . . Rule 608(b) is much more restrictive as to impeachment of witnesses by instances of conduct other than convictions than its federal counterpart. . . .

Appellant cites Davis v. Alaska, 415 U.S. 308 (1974), in support of his claim that the Confrontation Clause of the U.S. Constitution requires that he be permitted to show any fact, including a pending charge, which would tend to establish bias or motive of a witness (i.e. Russell) testifying against him. The majority, I respectfully assert, reads *Davis* in a too-broad manner. In *Davis,* counsel for petitioner was denied the opportunity to cross-examine a State's witness as to his status as a probationer, which counsel alleged would tend to show possible motive or bias on the part of the witness. The Supreme Court held "petitioner was thus denied the right of effective

* Rule 609 enables the court to admit into evidence the prior conviction of a witness for impeachment purposes, if the crime was a felony or involved moral turpitude and the court determines that the probative value of admitting this evidence outweighs its prejudicial effect. Evidence of a conviction is not admissible if more than 10 years have elapsed since the date of conviction or release from prison, whichever is later.—EDS.

cross-examination which would be constitutional error of the first magnitude and no amount of showing or want of prejudice would cure it."

The present case differs markedly from the facts of *Davis*. First, the witness in *Davis* was on probation resulting from a recent adjudication of delinquency in a juvenile court and likely could have been impeached with that adjudication under Rule 609(d) had this been a Texas case. Second, unlike in *Davis*, appellant in the present case had available to him, under Rule 612, for impeachment purposes, Russell's statement taken at the time of the killing and before he was arrested on the aggravated robbery charge. Third, in the present case, a hearing was held at which the witness (Russell) testified that he would testify truthfully, he would not be affected by his pending charge as to his testimony and no "deal" had been made with the State concerning his testimony. No such examination of the witness (Green) for bias or motive took place in *Davis*. Fourth, a juvenile adjudication is a final determination by a court and is analogous to a conviction. In the present case the witness had merely been charged with a crime and had not been even tried, much less been convicted. Given these differences, appellant's right to an effective cross-examination was not denied.

There is little doubt—notwithstanding Rule 608(b)—*Davis* mandates that a criminal defendant be permitted to impeach a State witness on cross-examination with evidence of a pending charge against the witness where a deal concerning the witness' testimony with the State existed or was under discussion. Similarly, *Davis* would be implicated where, unlike in the present case, the defendant had no other reasonable means to impeach the witness (e.g. by a prior statement if inconsistent with his testimony) or had not been afforded a hearing by the court at which he could support his claim of bias or motive of the witness which could be shown only by allowing him to cross-examine the witness—before the jury—as to a pending charge. . . . I respectfully dissent.

KELLER, J., dissenting.

. . . Under the majority's analysis the failure to allow cross-examination regarding a pending charge is always error. I agree that, ordinarily, the mere existence of a pending charge gives rise to an inference that the witness may have been influenced. But in some cases, additional facts in the record may show that such an inference is not warranted. . . . When a witness' testimony corresponds with his statement given prior to the point at which the motive for bias arose, and the defendant does not otherwise show that the pending charge may have influenced the witness' testimony at trial, I believe that it is not an abuse of discretion to disallow cross-examination regarding an unrelated pending criminal charge that is alleged to be the motive for bias. Such are the facts in this case. Accordingly, I dissent.

Problem 18-4. Evidence Off Limits

James Egelhoff spent an evening drinking with two friends. Some time after 9 P.M., Egelhoff and his friends left a party in a station wagon. Egelhoff bought beer at 9:20 P.M. At about midnight, the sheriff's department received reports of a possible drunken driver. The deputies who responded to the call discovered the station wagon stuck in a ditch along a U.S. highway. In the front seat were Egelhoff's two friends, each dead from a single gunshot to the head. Egelhoff lay in the rear of the station wagon, yelling obscenities. His blood-alcohol level measured .36, more than one hour later. On the floor of the car, near the brake pedal, lay Egelhoff's .38 caliber handgun, with four loaded rounds and two empty casings. He had gunshot residue on his hands.

At his trial for deliberate homicide, Egelhoff testified that his intoxication made it impossible for him to commit the crime. Although he remembered "sitting on a hill passing a bottle of Black Velvet back and forth" with his friends, he recalled nothing further because of his extreme intoxication. Because he was physically incapable of carrying out the killing and could not remember the events of the evening, Egelhoff concluded that some fourth party had killed his friends.

Deliberate homicide, under state law, occurs when a person "purposely" or "knowingly" causes the death of another human being. Although the trial court allowed Egelhoff to testify about his intoxication, the judge also instructed the jury, consistent with a state statute, that it could not consider Egelhoff's "intoxicated condition in determining the existence of a mental state which is an element of the offense." The jury found Egelhoff guilty as charged.

The defendant argues on appeal that the state statute violated his due process right to present to the jury all relevant evidence to rebut the state's evidence on all elements of the offense charged. Evidence of his intoxication was relevant to deciding whether he had killed the victims "knowingly" or "purposely." The exclusion of this evidence, he says, lessened the government's burden of proof in establishing the mens rea for the crime. How would you rule on the defendant's appeal? Compare Montana v. Egelhoff, 518 U.S. 37 (1996).

Notes

1. *Cross-examination about pending charges: majority position.* As mentioned earlier, rules of evidence control the scope of questions that can be asked during cross-examination. For instance, the rules restrict the cross-examining lawyer to questions related to the subjects covered during direct examination. They also limit questions about prior convictions or pending criminal charges against the witness. However, the constitutional right to confrontation sometimes allows a defendant to go beyond these usual restrictions on cross-examination to ask questions that the prosecuting attorney could not ask. In Delaware v. Van Arsdall, 475 U.S. 673 (1986), the Court held that a defendant's rights secured by the confrontation clause were violated when the trial court prohibited "all inquiry" into the possibility that a witness would be biased after agreeing to testify in exchange for favorable treatment in a different criminal matter. The Court noted that the witness's agreement about the pending charges could show a "prototypical form of bias." The jury "might have received a significantly different impression" of the witness's credibility if defense counsel had been permitted to pursue the proposed line of cross-examination. See also Davis v. Alaska, 415 U.S. 308 (1974) (refusal to allow defendant to cross-examine key prosecution witness to show his probation status for juvenile offense denied defendant his constitutional right to confront witnesses, notwithstanding state policy protecting anonymity of juvenile offenders).

State courts have also concluded that their constitutions allow defendants to pursue lines of cross-examination that the rules of evidence would not allow for other litigants. About 30 states have endorsed the federal position. Like the

Supreme Court in *Van Arsdall,* these courts ask if the proposed questions would explore a "prototypical form of bias." They most often conclude that defense counsel may ask questions about criminal charges pending against the witness. See State v. Mizzell, 563 S.E.2d 315 (S.C. 2002) (trial court violated confrontation rights by forbidding defense counsel to elicit from prosecution witness, charged with same crime as defendant "Tootie" Mizzell, the punishment he could receive if convicted). However, state courts will sometimes uphold a trial court that restricts defense cross-examination on this subject, if the witness asserts that she expects no benefit to flow from testifying. See Marshall v. State, 695 A.2d 184 (Md. 1997). Can an appellate court develop sound rules on this question, or is the issue better left to the discretion of the trial court?

2. *Prior criminal record of prosecution witnesses.* On topics of cross-examination other than pending criminal charges against the witness, trial courts tend to have more discretion to limit cross-examination. This is true, for instance, when defense counsel tries to explore the prior criminal record of prosecution witnesses. Although trial judges often allow at least some cross-examination on this subject, appellate courts uphold most efforts to limit questioning on the topic. Many state courts conclude that the prior convictions of a witness do not demonstrate a "prototypical form" of bias against the defendant, but are simply a generalized attack on the witness's credibility that might confuse the jury. Trial judges can impose reasonable limits on cross-examination to guard against harassment, prejudice, confusion of the issues, or waste of time. See State v. Lanz-Terry, 535 N.W.2d 635 (Minn. 1995). Why do courts treat prior convictions differently from pending criminal charges against a prosecution witness?

3. *Ethics of cross-examination.* Sometimes a judge's evidentiary ruling arrives too late. An attorney's leading question on cross-examination might suggest an answer to the jury, even if the witness never has to answer the question. In response to this problem, rules of legal ethics typically instruct attorneys not to ask a question on cross-examination if there is no reasonable factual basis for the question. See ABA Model Rule of Professional Conduct 3.4(e) (lawyer at trial shall not "allude to any matter that the lawyer does not reasonably believe is relevant or that will not be supported by admissible evidence"). If you were a staff attorney working within the disciplinary body of the state bar, how would you expect to enforce this rule?

4. *Limits on defense evidence.* Our discussion has focused on the defendant's power to "confront" adverse witnesses and test the prosecution's case, mostly through cross-examination of witnesses. Defendants will also answer the prosecution's case by presenting their own evidence. As with cross-examination, a range of legal rules can restrict the evidence a defendant might present. Rules of evidence require generally that any evidence be relevant to an issue in controversy and that its probative value outweigh its prejudicial impact. See Fed. R. Evid. 403 ("Although relevant, evidence may be excluded if its probative value is substantially outweighed by the danger of unfair prejudice, confusion of the issues, or misleading the jury, or by considerations of undue delay, waste of time, or needless presentation of cumulative evidence"). States sometimes enact rules or statutes for a particular subject matter that defendants might try to raise at trial. For instance, most jurisdictions have "rape shield" laws, which limit the power of a defendant in a sexual assault case from inquiring into certain aspects of the sexual history of the victim of the alleged crime.

Statutes and rules of evidence in some jurisdictions also limit the defendant's ability to introduce evidence of voluntary intoxication. In Montana v. Egelhoff, 518

U.S. 37 (1996), the basis for Problem 18-4 above, the Court upheld the constitutionality of a statute that precluded the jury from considering evidence of intoxication when it determined whether the defendant had the mens rea to commit the crime. The Court indicated that 10 states had enacted similar statutes or rules; since the *Egelhoff* decision appeared, the number has grown. The statute in *Egelhoff* appears to place a new type of limit on defense efforts to present evidence. The Montana legislature did not justify its rule by arguing that intoxication evidence is unreliable, cumulative, privileged, or irrelevant. The state instead adopted the rule to deter irresponsible behavior, to incapacitate those who cannot control violent impulses while drunk, and to express society's moral judgment that persons who voluntarily become intoxicated should remain responsible for their actions. After *Egelhoff*, is there any legal or practical limit on the legislature's power to prevent the defendant from presenting evidence that many juries might find convincing? The decision not only addresses the evidence available to the defendant but also reaffirms (and perhaps expands) the state's power to define elements of criminal offenses.

5. *Commentary on evidence.* Although judges constantly evaluate evidence and rule on its admissibility, many states have constitutional or statutory provisions that prohibit the judge from "commenting" on the evidence or the credibility of witnesses. See Wash. Const. art. IV, §16; Ga. Code §17-8-57. There is, however, no federal constitutional bar to judicial commentary on evidence, and some states do not impose such a bar. See Quercia v. United States, 289 U.S. 466 (1933) (no error for judge to comment on evidence so long as the comment does not "excite [in the jury] a prejudice which would preclude a fair and dispassionate consideration of the evidence"; court here committed error by saying that witness displayed mannerisms of a person who is lying).

C. SELF-INCRIMINATION PRIVILEGE AT TRIAL

Once the prosecution has presented its case in chief, the defendant may present evidence as well. The central strategic question for the defendant at this point is whether to testify. While the defendant might present testimony from other witnesses, that evidence is not likely to carry the same weight as a defendant's personal denial of the crime and personal explanation of the prosecution's key evidence. At the same time, a defendant might not feel capable of making a convincing denial at trial, because of nervousness, concern about charges of perjury, or for some other reason.

In the United States, as in most Western legal systems, the law allows the defendant alone to choose whether to testify at trial. The privilege against self-incrimination allows the defendant to refuse to cooperate during certain phases of an investigation, but the privilege provides the clearest protections during a criminal trial. Professor John Langbein has traced the origins of the privilege to the emergence in the eighteenth century of adversary criminal procedure and a prominent role for defense counsel who could speak for the defendant and challenge the government's evidence. See John Langbein, The Historical Origins of the Privilege Against Self-Incrimination at Common Law, 92 Mich. L. Rev. 1047 (1994).

Because of the privilege against self-incrimination, a criminal defendant may refuse to cooperate in some investigative efforts and may refuse to testify at trial. Is there any price for such refusals? As a practical matter, some disadvantages do flow from invoking the privilege. A jury or judge might infer from a defendant's silence that she is guilty or at least that she has no answer to the government's evidence. But can the prosecutor urge the fact finder to draw such inferences? Should the judge do or say anything to prevent the jury from drawing such conclusions? The *Griffin* case reprinted below announced the bright-line constitutional rule that all American courts follow on this question; the following *Murray* opinion from the European Court of Human Rights describes a position encountered in other Western legal systems.

■ EDDIE DEAN GRIFFIN v. CALIFORNIA
380 U.S. 609 (1965)

DOUGLAS, J.

Petitioner was convicted of murder in the first degree after a jury trial in a California court. He did not testify at the trial on the issue of guilt, though he did testify at the separate trial on the issue of penalty. The trial court instructed the jury on the issue of guilt, stating that a defendant has a constitutional right not to testify. But it told the jury:

> As to any evidence or facts against him which the defendant can reasonably be expected to deny or explain because of facts within his knowledge, if he does not testify or if, though he does testify, he fails to deny or explain such evidence, the jury may take that failure into consideration as tending to indicate the truth of such evidence and as indicating that among the inferences that may be reasonably drawn therefrom those unfavorable to the defendant are the more probable.

It added, however, that no such inference could be drawn as to evidence respecting which he had no knowledge. It stated that failure of a defendant to deny or explain the evidence of which he had knowledge does not create a presumption of guilt nor by itself warrant an inference of guilt nor relieve the prosecution of any of its burden of proof.

Petitioner had been seen with the deceased the evening of her death, the evidence placing him with her in the alley where her body was found. The prosecutor made much of the failure of petitioner to testify:

> The defendant certainly knows whether Essie Mae had this beat up appearance at the time he left her apartment and went down the alley with her. . . . He would know that. He would know how she got down the alley. He would know how the blood got on the bottom of the concrete steps. He would know how long he was with her in that box. He would know how her wig got off. He would know whether he beat her or mistreated her. He would know whether he walked away from that place cool as a cucumber when he saw Mr. Villasenor because he was conscious of his own guilt and wanted to get away from that damaged or injured woman. These things he has not seen fit to take the stand and deny or explain. And in the whole world, if anybody would know, this defendant would know. Essie Mae is dead, she can't tell you her side of the story. The defendant won't.

The death penalty was imposed and the California Supreme Court affirmed. The case is here on a writ of certiorari which we granted to consider whether comment on the failure to testify violated the Self-Incrimination Clause of the Fifth Amendment which we made applicable to the States by the Fourteenth in Malloy v. Hogan, 378 U.S. 1 (1964). . . .[3]

If this were a federal trial, reversible error would have been committed. Wilson v. United States, 149 U.S. 60 (1893), so holds. It is said, however, that the *Wilson* decision rested not on the Fifth Amendment, but on an Act of Congress, now 18 U.S.C. §3481.[4] That indeed is the fact. . . . But that is the beginning, not the end, of our inquiry. The question remains whether, statute or not, the comment rule, approved by California, violates the Fifth Amendment.

We think it does. It is in substance a rule of evidence that allows the State the privilege of tendering to the jury for its consideration the failure of the accused to testify. No formal offer of proof is made as in other situations; but the prosecutor's comment and the court's acquiescence are the equivalent of an offer of evidence and its acceptance. The Court in the *Wilson* case stated:

> . . . It is not every one who can safely venture on the witness stand though entirely innocent of the charge against him. Excessive timidity, nervousness when facing others and attempting to explain transactions of a suspicious character, and offences charged against him, will often confuse and embarrass him to such a degree as to increase rather than remove prejudices against him. It is not every one, however honest, who would, therefore, willingly be placed on the witness stand. The statute, in tenderness to the weakness of those who . . . may have been in some degree compromised by their association with others, declares that the failure of the defendant in a criminal action to request to be a witness shall not create any presumption against him.

[C]omment on the refusal to testify is a remnant of the inquisitorial system of criminal justice, which the Fifth Amendment outlaws. It is a penalty imposed by courts for exercising a constitutional privilege. It cuts down on the privilege by making its assertion costly. It is said, however, that the inference of guilt for failure to testify as to facts peculiarly within the accused's knowledge is in any event natural and irresistible, and that comment on the failure does not magnify that inference into a penalty for asserting a constitutional privilege. What the jury may infer, given no help from the court, is one thing. What it may infer when the court solemnizes the silence of the accused into evidence against him is quite another. [We] hold that the Fifth Amendment, in its direct application to the Federal Government, and in its bearing on the States by reason of the Fourteenth Amendment, forbids either comment by the prosecution on the accused's silence or instructions by the court that such silence is evidence of guilt. Reversed.

STEWART, J., dissenting.

. . . Article I, §13, of the California Constitution establishes a defendant's privilege against self-incrimination and further provides: ". . . whether the defendant testifies or not, his failure to explain or to deny by his testimony any evidence or facts

3. [Most states do not allow] comment on the defendant's failure to testify. The legislatures or courts of 44 States have recognized that such comment is, in light of the privilege against self-incrimination, "an unwarrantable line of argument."

4. Section 3481 reads as follows: "In [a federal criminal trial] the person charged shall, at his own request, be a competent witness. His failure to make such request shall not create any presumption against him."

in the case against him may be commented upon by the court and by counsel, and may be considered by the court or the jury." In conformity with this provision, the prosecutor in his argument to the jury emphasized that a person accused of crime in a public forum would ordinarily deny or explain the evidence against him if he truthfully could do so. Also in conformity with this California constitutional provision, the judge instructed the jury [that they could draw a negative inference from the defendant's failure to deny to explain evidence or facts if he had the knowledge to make such an explanation].

We must determine whether the petitioner has been "compelled . . . to be a witness against himself." Compulsion is the focus of the inquiry. Certainly, if any compulsion be detected in the California procedure, it is of a dramatically different and less palpable nature than that involved in the procedures which historically gave rise to the Fifth Amendment guarantee. When a suspect was brought before the Court of High Commission or the Star Chamber, he was commanded to answer whatever was asked of him, and subjected to a far-reaching and deeply probing inquiry in an effort to ferret out some unknown and frequently unsuspected crime. He declined to answer on pain of incarceration, banishment, or mutilation. And if he spoke falsely, he was subject to further punishment. Faced with this formidable array of alternatives, his decision to speak was unquestionably coerced.

Those were the lurid realities which lay behind enactment of the Fifth Amendment, a far cry from the subject matter of the case before us. I think that the Court in this case stretches the concept of compulsion beyond all reasonable bounds, and that whatever compulsion may exist derives from the defendant's choice not to testify, not from any comment by court or counsel. . . .

It is not at all apparent to me, on any realistic view of the trial process, that a defendant will be at more of a disadvantage under the California practice than he would be in a court which permitted no comment at all on his failure to take the witness stand. How can it be said that the inferences drawn by a jury will be more detrimental to a defendant under the limiting and carefully controlling language of the instruction here involved than would result if the jury were left to roam at large with only its untutored instincts to guide it, to draw from the defendant's silence broad inferences of guilt? The instructions in this case expressly cautioned the jury that the defendant's failure to testify "does not create a presumption of guilt or by itself warrant an inference of guilt"; it was further admonished that such failure does not "relieve the prosecution of its burden of proving every essential element of the crime." . . .

I think the California comment rule is not a coercive device which impairs the right against self-incrimination, but rather a means of articulating and bringing into the light of rational discussion a fact inescapably impressed on the jury's consciousness. The California procedure is not only designed to protect the defendant against unwarranted inferences which might be drawn by an uninformed jury; it is also an attempt by the State to recognize and articulate what it believes to be the natural probative force of certain facts. . . .

No constitution can prevent the operation of the human mind. Without limiting instructions, the danger exists that the inferences drawn by the jury may be unfairly broad. Some States have permitted this danger to go unchecked, by forbidding any comment at all upon the defendant's failure to take the witness stand. Other States have dealt with this danger in a variety of ways, as the Court's opinion indicates. Some might differ, as a matter of policy, with the way California has chosen to deal with the problem, or even disapprove of the judge's specific instructions in this case. But, so long as the constitutional command is obeyed, such matters of state policy are not for this Court to decide. I would affirm the judgment.

■ KEVIN SEAN MURRAY v. UNITED KINGDOM

22 Eur. Ct. H.R. 29 (1996)

. . . The applicant was arrested by police officers at 17.40 on 7 January 1990. . . . Pursuant to Article 3 of the Criminal Evidence (Northern Ireland) Order 1988, he was cautioned by the police in the following terms:

> You do not have to say anything unless you wish to do so but I must warn you that if you fail to mention any fact which you rely on in your defence in court, your failure to take this opportunity to mention it may be treated in court as supporting any relevant evidence against you. If you do wish to say anything, what you say may be given in evidence.

In response to the police caution the applicant stated that he had nothing to say. . . .

13. At 21.27 on 7 January a police constable cautioned the applicant pursuant to Article 6 of the Order, inter alia, requesting him to account for his presence at the house where he was arrested. He was warned that if he failed or refused to do so, a court, judge or jury might draw such inference from his failure or refusal as appears proper. He was also served with a written copy of Article 6 of the Order. In reply to this caution the applicant stated: "nothing to say." . . .

15. The applicant was interviewed by police detectives at Castlereagh Police Office on 12 occasions during 8 and 9 January. In total he was interviewed for 21 hours and 39 minutes. At the commencement of these interviews he was either cautioned pursuant to Article 3 of the Order or reminded of the terms of the caution.

16. During the first 10 interviews on 8 and 9 January the applicant made no reply to any questions put to him. He was able to see his solicitor for the first time at 18.33 on 9 January. At 19.10 he was interviewed again and reminded of the Article 3 caution. He replied: "I have been advised by my solicitor not to answer any of your questions." A final interview, during which the applicant said nothing, took place between 21.40 and 23.45 on 9 January. His solicitor was not permitted to be present at any of these interviews.

17. In May 1991 the applicant was tried by a single judge, the Lord Chief Justice of Northern Ireland, sitting without a jury, for the offences of conspiracy to murder, the unlawful imprisonment, with seven other people, of a certain Mr. L and of belonging to a proscribed organisation, the Provisional Irish Republican Army (IRA).

18. According to the Crown, Mr. L had been a member of the IRA who had been providing information about their activities to the Royal Ulster Constabulary. On discovering that Mr. L was an informer, the IRA tricked him into visiting a house in Belfast on 5 January 1990. He was falsely imprisoned in one of the rear bedrooms of the house and interrogated by the IRA until the arrival of the police and the army at the house on 7 January 1990. It was also alleged by the Crown that there was a conspiracy to murder Mr. L as punishment for being a police informer.

19. In the course of the trial, evidence was given that when the police entered the house on 7 January the applicant was seen by a police constable coming down a flight of stairs wearing a raincoat over his clothes and was arrested in the hall of the

house. Mr. L testified that he was forced under threat of being killed to make a taped confession to his captors that he was an informer. He further said that on the evening of 7 January he had heard scurrying and had been told to take off his blindfold. . . . The applicant had told him that the police were at the door and to go downstairs and watch television. While he was talking to him the applicant was pulling tape out of a cassette. On a search of the house by the police . . . a tangled tape was discovered in the upstairs bedroom. The salvaged portions of the tape revealed a confession by Mr. L that he had agreed to work for the police. . . . At no time, either on his arrest or during the trial proceedings, did the applicant give any explanation for his presence in the house.

20. At the close of the prosecution case the trial judge, acting in accordance with Article 4 of the Order, called upon [Murray to give evidence in his own defense]:

> I am also required by law to tell you that if you refuse to come into the witness box to be sworn or if, after having been sworn, you refuse, without good reason, to answer any question, then the court in deciding whether you are guilty or not guilty may take into account against you to the extent that it considers proper your refusal to give evidence or to answer any questions.

21. Acting on the advice of his solicitor and counsel, the applicant chose not to give any evidence. No witnesses were called on his behalf. Counsel . . . submitted, inter alia, that the applicant's presence in the house just before the police arrived was recent and innocent.

22. On 8 May 1991 the applicant was found guilty of the offence of aiding and abetting the unlawful imprisonment of Mr. L and sentenced to eight years' imprisonment. He was acquitted of the remaining charges. . . .

25. In concluding that the applicant was guilty of the offence of aiding and abetting false imprisonment, the trial judge drew adverse inferences against the applicant under both Articles 4 and 6 of the Order. The judge stated that in the particular circumstances of the case he did not propose to draw inferences against the applicant under Article 3 of the Order. . . .

27. Criminal Evidence (Northern Ireland) Order 1988 includes the following provisions:

> Article 3: Circumstances in which inferences may be drawn from accused's failure to mention particular facts when questioned, charged, etc.
>
> (1) Where, in any proceedings against a person for an offence, evidence is given that the accused
>
> (a) at any time before he was charged with the offence, on being questioned by a constable trying to discover whether or by whom the offence had been committed, failed to mention any fact relied on in his defence in those proceedings; or
>
> (b) on being charged with the offence or officially informed that he might be prosecuted for it, failed to mention any such fact, being a fact which in the circumstances existing at the time the accused could reasonably have been expected to mention when so questioned, charged or informed, as the case may be, paragraph (2) applies.
>
> (2) [The] court or jury, in determining whether the accused is guilty of the offence charged, may . . . draw such inferences from the failure as appear proper [and] on the basis of such inferences treat the failure as, or as capable of amounting to, corroboration of any evidence given against the accused in relation to which the failure is material. . . .

Article 4: Accused to be called upon to give evidence at trial . . .

(2) Before any evidence is called for the defence, the court . . . shall tell the accused that he will be called upon by the court to give evidence in his own defence, and . . . shall tell him in ordinary language what the effect of this Article will be if . . . when so called upon, he refuses . . . to answer any question. . . .

(3) If the accused . . . refuses to be sworn, . . . paragraph (4) applies.

(4) The court or jury, in determining whether the accused is guilty of the offence charged, may . . . draw such inferences from the refusal as appear proper [and] treat the refusal as, or as capable of amounting to, corroboration of any evidence given against the accused in relation to which the refusal is material. . . .

Article 6: Inferences from failure or refusal to account for presence at a particular place

(1) Where (a) a person arrested by a constable was found by him at a place or about the time the offence for which he was arrested is alleged to have been committed, and (b) the constable reasonably believes that the presence of the person at that place and at that time may be attributable to his participation in the commission of the offence, and (c) the constable informs the person that he so believes, and requests him to account for that presence, and (d) the person fails or refuses to do so, then if, in any proceedings against the person for the offence, evidence of those matters is given, paragraph (2) applies.

(2) [The] court or jury, in determining whether the accused is guilty of the offence charged, may . . . draw such inferences from the failure or refusal as appear proper [and] treat the failure or refusal as, or as capable of amounting to, corroboration of any evidence given against the accused in relation to which the failure or refusal is material.

(3) Paragraphs (1) and (2) do not apply unless the accused was told in ordinary language by the constable when making the request mentioned in paragraph (1)(c) what the effect of this Article would be if he failed or refused to do so. . . .

40. The applicant alleged that there had been a violation of the right to silence and the right not to incriminate oneself contrary to Article 6(1) and (2) of the Convention. . . . The relevant provisions provide as follows:

1. In the determination of . . . any criminal charge against him, everyone is entitled to a fair and public hearing within a reasonable time by an independent and impartial tribunal. . . .

2. Everyone charged with a criminal offence shall be presumed innocent until proved guilty according to law. . . .

41. In the submission of the applicant, the drawing of incriminating inferences against him under the Criminal Justice (Northern Ireland) Order 1988 violated Article 6(1) and (2) of the Convention. It amounted to an infringement of the right to silence, the right not to incriminate oneself and the principle that the prosecution bear the burden of proving the case without assistance from the accused.

He contended that a first, and most obvious element of the right to silence is the right to remain silent in the face of police questioning and not to have to testify against oneself at trial. In his submission, these have always been essential and fundamental elements of the British criminal justice system. Moreover the Commission in Saunders v. United Kingdom, No. 19187/91, Comm. Rep. 10.5.94 (1994) and the Court in Funke v. France, 1 C.M.L.R. 897 (1993) have accepted that they are an inherent part of the right to a fair hearing under Article 6. In his view these are absolute rights which an accused is entitled to enjoy without restriction.

A second, equally essential element of the right to silence was that the exercise of the right by an accused would not be used as evidence against him in his trial.

However, the trial judge drew very strong inferences, under Articles 4 and 6 of the Order, from his decision to remain silent under police questioning and during the trial. Indeed, it was clear from the trial judge's remarks . . . that the inferences were an integral part of his decision to find him guilty.

Accordingly, he was severely and doubly penalised for choosing to remain silent: once for his silence under police interrogation and once for his failure to testify during the trial. To use against him silence under police questioning and his refusal to testify during trial amounted to subverting the presumption of innocence and the onus of proof resulting from that presumption: it is for the prosecution to prove the accused's guilt without any assistance from the latter being required. . . .

43. The Government . . . emphasised that the Order did not detract from the right to remain silent in the face of police questioning and explicitly confirmed the right not to have to testify at trial. They further noted that the Order in no way changed either the burden or the standard of proof: it remained for the prosecution to prove an accused's guilt beyond reasonable doubt. What the Order did was to confer a discretionary power to draw inferences from the silence of an accused in carefully defined circumstances. [The] Order merely allows the trier of fact to draw such inferences as common sense dictates. The question in each case is whether the evidence adduced by the prosecution is sufficiently strong to call for an answer. . . .

45. Although not specifically mentioned in Article 6 of the Convention, there can be no doubt that the right to remain silent under police questioning and the privilege against self-incrimination are generally recognised international standards which lie at the heart of the notion of a fair procedure under Article 6. By providing the accused with protection against improper compulsion by the authorities these immunities contribute to avoiding miscarriages of justice and to securing the aim of Article 6.

46. The Court does not consider that it is called upon to give an abstract analysis of the scope of these immunities and, in particular, of what constitutes in this context "improper compulsion." What is at stake in the present case is whether these immunities are absolute in the sense that the exercise by an accused of the right to silence cannot under any circumstances be used against him at trial or, alternatively, whether informing him in advance that, under certain conditions, his silence may be used, is always to be regarded as "improper compulsion."

47. On the one hand, it is self-evident that [it] is incompatible with the immunities under consideration to base a conviction solely or mainly on the accused's silence or on a refusal to answer questions or to give evidence himself. On the other hand, the Court deems it equally obvious that these immunities cannot and should not prevent that the accused's silence, in situations which clearly call for an explanation from him, be taken into account in assessing the persuasiveness of the evidence adduced by the prosecution. Wherever the line between these two extremes is to be drawn, it follows from this understanding of "the right to silence" that the question whether the right is absolute must be answered in the negative. . . .

48. As regards the degree of compulsion involved in the present case, it is recalled that the applicant was in fact able to remain silent. Notwithstanding the repeated warnings as to the possibility that inferences might be drawn from his silence, he did not make any statements to the police and did not give evidence during his trial. [H]is insistence in maintaining silence throughout the proceedings did not amount to a criminal offence or contempt of court. . . .

50. Admittedly a system which warns the accused — who is possibly without legal assistance (as in the applicant's case) — that adverse inferences may be drawn from a refusal to provide an explanation to the police . . . involves a certain level of indirect compulsion. However, since the applicant could not be compelled to speak or to testify, as indicated above, this factor on its own cannot be decisive. The Court must rather concentrate its attention on the role played by the inferences in the proceedings against the applicant and especially in his conviction.

51. In this context, it is recalled that these were proceedings without a jury, the trier of fact being an experienced judge. Furthermore, the drawing of inferences under the Order is subject to an important series of safeguards designed to respect the rights of the defence and to limit the extent to which reliance can be placed on inferences.

In the first place, before inferences can be drawn under Article 4 and 6 of the Order appropriate warnings must have been given to the accused as to the legal effects of maintaining silence. Moreover, . . . the prosecutor must first establish a prima facie case against the accused, i.e. a case consisting of direct evidence which, if believed and combined with legitimate inferences based upon it, could lead a properly directed jury to be satisfied beyond reasonable doubt that each of the essential elements of the offence is proved.

The question in each particular case is whether the evidence adduced by the prosecution is sufficiently strong to require an answer. The national court cannot conclude that the accused is guilty merely because he chooses to remain silent. It is only if the evidence against the accused "calls" for an explanation which the accused ought to be in a position to give that a failure to give an explanation "may as a matter of common sense allow the drawing of an inference that there is no explanation and that the accused is guilty." Conversely if the case presented by the prosecution had so little evidential value that it called for no answer, a failure to provide one could not justify an inference of guilt. In sum, it is only common sense inferences which the judge considers proper, in the light of the evidence against the accused, that can be drawn under the Order.

In addition, the trial judge has a discretion whether, on the facts of the particular case, an inference should be drawn. [T]he judge must explain the reasons for the decision to draw inferences and the weight attached to them. The exercise of discretion in this regard is subject to review by the appellate courts.

52. In the present case, the evidence presented against the applicant by the prosecution was considered by the Court of Appeal to constitute a "formidable" case against him. It is recalled that when the police entered the house some appreciable time after they knocked on the door, they found the applicant coming down the flight of stairs in the house where Mr. L had been held captive by the IRA. [Soon after the police arrived, the] applicant was pulling a tape out of a cassette. The tangled tape and cassette recorder were later found on the premises. Evidence by the applicant's co-accused that he had recently arrived at the house was discounted as not being credible. . .

54. In the Court's view, having regard to the weight of the evidence against the applicant, as outlined above, the drawing of inferences from his refusal, at arrest, during police questioning and at trial, to provide an explanation for his presence in the house was a matter of common sense and cannot be regarded as unfair or unreasonable in the circumstances. [T]he courts in a considerable number of countries where evidence is freely assessed may have regard to all relevant circumstances,

including the manner in which the accused has behaved or has conducted his defence, when evaluating the evidence in the case. [W]hat distinguishes the drawing of inferences under the Order is that, in addition to the existence of the specific safeguards mentioned above, it constitutes, as described by the Commission, "a formalised system which aims at allowing common sense implications to play an open role in the assessment of evidence." . . .

55. The applicant submitted that it was unfair to draw inferences under Article 6 of the Order from his silence at a time when he had not had the benefit of legal advice. . . . In this context he emphasised that under the Order once an accused has remained silent a trap is set from which he cannot escape: if an accused chooses to give evidence or to call witnesses, he is, by reason of his prior silence, exposed to the risk of an Article 3 inference sufficient to bring about a conviction; on the other hand, if he maintains his silence inferences may be drawn against him under other provisions of the Order.

56. The Court [will not] speculate on the question whether inferences would have been drawn under the Order had the applicant, at any moment after his first interrogation, chosen to speak to the police or to give evidence at his trial or call witnesses. Nor should it speculate on the question whether it was the possibility of such inferences being drawn that explains why the applicant was advised by his solicitor to remain silent.

Immediately after arrest the applicant was warned in accordance with the provisions of the Order but chose to remain silent. [T]here is no indication that the applicant failed to understand the significance of the warning given to him by the police prior to seeing his solicitor. Under these circumstances the fact that during the first 48 hours of his detention the applicant had been refused access to a lawyer does not detract from the above conclusion that the drawing of inferences was not unfair or unreasonable. . . .

57. [T]he Court does not consider that the criminal proceedings were unfair or that there had been an infringement of the presumption of innocence. . . . For these reasons, the Court [h]olds by 14 votes to 5 that there has been no violation of Article 6(1) and (2) of the Convention arising out of the drawing of adverse inferences on account of the applicant's silence. . . .

WALSH, partly dissenting.

1. In my opinion there have been violations of Article 6(1) and (2) of the Convention. The applicant was by Article 6(2) guaranteed a presumption of innocence in the criminal trial of which he complains. Prior to the introduction of the Criminal Evidence (Northern Ireland) Order 1988 a judge trying a case without a jury could not lawfully draw an inference of guilt from the fact that an accused person did not proclaim his innocence. Equally in a trial with a jury it would have been contrary to law to instruct the jurymen that they could do so. [T]he object and effect of the 1988 Order was to reverse that position. . . .

3. . . . To permit such a procedure is to permit a penalty to be imposed by a criminal court on an accused because he relies upon a procedural right guaranteed by the Convention. I draw attention to the decision of the Supreme Court of the United States in Griffin v. California, 380 U.S. 609 (1965), which dealt with a similar point in relation to the Fifth Amendment of the Constitution by striking down a Californian law which permitted a court to make adverse comment on the accused's decision not to testify. . . .

Problem 18-5. Telling the Jury

Two police officers on patrol learned of an activated security alarm around 2:25 A.M. at Pleasants Hardware Store in the Pinewood Shopping Center. As they approached the plaza, the officers observed a car parked about 100 yards from the shopping center facing away from the hardware store. The store was not lit, and the parking lot was empty. When the officers got out of their car and inspected the premises, they noticed a large hole in the concrete block wall at the rear of the building.

After this initial investigation, the officers drove to the location of the car they had seen earlier to obtain license tag numbers but discovered that it was gone. Within two minutes, they observed the car traveling north on Highway 321 at a high speed with its headlights off. After a brief pursuit, the driver of the car pulled over. The driver, Joseph Reid, told the officers he had stopped in the area of the shopping center because his car had run out of gas. When the officers asked why the car was running at that time, Reid said it had started unexpectedly. The officers found a sledgehammer near the location where Reid stopped his car.

Reid was tried in superior court on the charge of breaking and entering with intent to commit the felony of larceny. During the prosecution's closing argument to the jury, the following exchange took place:

The State: Now defendant hasn't taken the stand in this case —
Defense Counsel: Objection to his remarks about that, Your Honor.
The Court: Overruled.
Defense Counsel: Exception.
The State: The defendant hasn't taken the stand in this case. He has that right. You're not to hold that against him. But we have to look at the other evidence to look at intent in this case.

The prosecutor's remark that the defendant had not testified mirrored the North Carolina Pattern Jury Instructions regarding a criminal defendant's right not to testify. Did the prosecutor commit reversible error by quoting to the jury from the pattern jury instructions? Compare State v. Reid, 434 S.E.2d 193 (N.C. 1993).

Problem 18-6. Pre-arrest Silence

At 2:30 A.M., Patrick Easter's Isuzu Trooper collided with a yellow taxicab. Easter was returning from a wedding reception to his home near the accident site. The cab was carrying six university students. Easter suffered injuries in the accident, and four of the students were seriously injured. A test administered shortly after the accident showed Easter's blood alcohol content was approximately .11. Several days later, Easter was arrested and charged with four counts of vehicular assault.

Easter did not testify at trial. The state and the defense presented evidence supporting different versions of how the accident happened. Officer Fitzgerald's testimony occupied much of the trial, although he did not observe the accident or take a statement from a witness. He testified that he arrived within minutes of the accident and found Easter in the bathroom of a gas station at the intersection, with torn clothes, a cut forehead, and blood on his elbows and knees. He testified that Easter then "totally ignored" him when he asked what happened. He also testified that when he continued to ask questions, Easter looked down, "once again ignoring me, ignoring my questions."

Fitzgerald said that he "felt the defendant was being smart drunk." The officer explained that when he used the term "smart drunk," he meant to say that Easter "was evasive, wouldn't talk to me, wouldn't look at me, wouldn't get close enough for me to get good observations of his breath and eyes, I felt that he was trying to hide or cloak."

Fitzgerald testified he took Easter back to the intersection and told him he would be placed under arrest or he could submit to a voluntary blood-alcohol test at a hospital. Fitzgerald suspected Easter was intoxicated because of Easter's slightly slurred speech, bloodshot eyes, and the odor of alcohol on his breath, although Easter had no coordination problems, walked without difficulty, and produced his license without fumbling or stumbling. After learning that he would be arrested, Easter's attitude changed. He asked for business papers in the truck and for a friend to be telephoned. Easter answered questions about his driver's license and said his home was a mile north of the accident scene.

In closing, the prosecutor argued that the trial testimony was best summed up with the words "smart drunk." He referred several times to testimony that Easter was a "smart drunk" who had ignored Officer Fitzgerald, except when asking about his papers and friend, and concluded, "Easter is a smart drunk." He closed his final argument with these words: "I urge you to find Mr. Easter, the smart drunk in this case, guilty." Did the prosecutor and the prosecution witness improperly comment on the defendant's invocation of his right to silence? See State v. Easter, 922 P.2d 1285 (Wash. 1996).

Notes

1. *Commenting on silence: majority position.* The Supreme Court's broad holding in *Griffin* that a prosecutor may not comment on a defendant's silence at trial has taken an even broader form over time in the state and federal courts. The *Griffin* rule applies not only to a prosecutor's statements literally pointing out that a defendant has not testified. It also prevents the prosecutor from calling the defendant to the witness stand to allow the jury to see the defendant invoke the privilege. The principle also covers veiled references to a defendant's failure to testify. See State v. McLamb, 69 S.E.2d 537 (N.C. 1952) (argument that defendant was "hiding behind his wife's coattail" was equivalent to comment on defendant's failure to testify on his own behalf). Most state courts say that the constitutional rule bars any comments "manifestly intended" to note a defendant's silence, or statements that are reasonably likely to draw a jury's attention to the fact that the defendant did not testify. See Knowles v. United States, 224 F.2d 168 (10th Cir. 1955); People v. Arman, 545 N.E.2d 658 (Ill. 1989). While the prosecutor may usually comment on a defendant's failure to produce *other* witnesses or exculpatory evidence to contradict the government's evidence, even a statement that the government's proof is "uncontradicted" could run afoul of the *Griffin* rule when it is highly unlikely that anyone other than the defendant could rebut the evidence. See Smith v. State, 787 A.2d 152 (Md. 2001) (prosecutor in closing argument improperly commented that the defendant had given "zero" answer to key piece of incriminating evidence; proper test is whether the prosecutor's comment is

"susceptible of the inference" by the jurors that they were to consider silence); but cf. United States v. Robinson, 485 U.S. 25 (1988) (prosecutor may refer to defendant's failure to testify when defense counsel claims in closing argument that government did not allow defendant to explain defendant's side of story). If a prosecutor makes an improper statement and the defense counsel objects, most states require the trial court to give a curative instruction to the jury immediately. Does this vigorous enforcement amount to any real benefit for defendants? Do juries act differently when none of the attorneys mention the defendant's silence, or is that something a jury will consider regardless of what the attorneys say?

2. *Inferences based on silence at trial: other legal systems.* The European Court of Human Rights, as indicated by the *Murray* opinion, reflects a common position in foreign legal systems. Not all systems allow the defendant to remain silent at trial; even among those allowing silence, most empower the judge to draw inferences against the defendant based on this silence. See Criminal Procedure Act of Norway, ch. 9, §93 ("If the person charged refuses to answer, or states that he reserves his answer, the president of the court may inform him that this may be considered to tell against him"); Myron Moskovitz, The O.J. Inquisition: A United States Encounter with Continental Criminal Justice, 28 Vand. J. Transnatl. L. 1121 (1995) (setting the O. J. Simpson murder trial in a typical European civil law courtroom; the presiding judge calls the first witness as follows: "Bailiffs, please bring the Accused forward"). In the United States, the federal and state constitutions as well as some statutes and rules of evidence prevent the fact finder from drawing inferences based on the defendant's silence at trial. See Conn. Gen. Stat. §54-84(b). Is there any value in preventing comments on silence if the fact finder is a judge rather than a jury? Would it be more consistent with truth-seeking if the judge (but not the prosecutor) could tell the jury it may draw inferences from silence?

3. *Incentives to remain silent.* Even if a defendant is convinced that the jury looks unfavorably on a decision not to testify, there are some powerful reasons to remain silent at trial. Once a defendant chooses to take the stand at trial, he may not selectively invoke the privilege to avoid answering the most difficult questions. The defendant is subject to the ordinary scope of cross-examination. For many defendants, this means that the prosecutor can introduce evidence of some prior convictions as a method of impeaching the defendant's credibility as a witness. What remedy is appropriate if a defendant takes the stand but refuses to answer some questions on cross-examination?

4. *Use at trial of pretrial silence.* Although it is clear that a prosecutor cannot make even an indirect reference to the defendant's silence at trial, there is more leeway to comment at trial on some forms of *pretrial* silence by the defendant. The Supreme Court has drawn fine distinctions under the federal constitution. The prosecutor may not use any pretrial silence of the defendant *after* arrest and the delivery of *Miranda* warnings. Doyle v. Ohio, 426 U.S. 610 (1976). However, the government can use a defendant's *pre-arrest* silence as a basis for impeachment during the defendant's testimony at trial. The same is true for postarrest silence when there is no indication that *Miranda* warnings were delivered, or even postarrest silence after a defendant has waived the right to silence after receiving proper warnings. Fletcher v. Weir, 455 U.S. 603 (1982) (postarrest, pre-*Miranda* silence); Jenkins v. Anderson, 447 U.S. 231 (1980) (pre-arrest silence); Anderson v. Charles, 447 U.S. 404 (1980) (selective silence after waiver of right to silence). Is there any real difference in the evidentiary value of these various forms of silence?

State courts are about evenly divided between those that follow this cluster of federal rulings and those that depart from one or more of the components. It is most common to find state courts ruling that postarrest unwarned silence cannot be used as impeachment material at trial. These courts base such rulings both on state constitutional provisions and rules of evidence. See Commonwealth v. DiPietro, 648 A.2d 777 (Pa. 1994); State v. Hoggins, 718 So. 2d 761 (Fla. 1998) (use of pre-*Miranda* silence forbidden as a basis for impeaching the defendant). Note that the prosecutor in Problem 18-6 above used the defendant's pre-arrest silence not for impeachment purposes but during direct examination of a prosecution witness and during closing arguments. Should the use of such evidence depend on the defendant's choice to take the stand at trial?

Chapter 8 discussed 1994 legislation in the United Kingdom that changed the rule regarding silence before trial. A 1984 statute required the police to inform suspects in custody that they have a right to consult an attorney before any interrogation. Under §34 of the Criminal Justice and Public Order Act of 1994, a court may draw inferences from the fact that a person is questioned and fails to mention a fact that an innocent person could reasonably be expected to mention during questioning, so long as the constable warns the accused of this fact at the time of questioning.

5. *Comments on presence at trial.* In Portuondo v. Agard, 529 U.S. 61 (2000), the prosecutor pointed out to the jury that the defendant, who was present in the courtroom, had the opportunity to hear all other witnesses and to tailor his testimony accordingly. Agard claimed that the prosecutor's comments violated his Fifth Amendment right to be present at trial and his Sixth Amendment right to confront his accusers. He drew an analogy to Griffin v. California, suggesting that in his case, just as in *Griffin,* the prosecutor was making the exercise of these constitutional trial rights more costly. Are there meaningful differences between this prosecutor's comment and a comment about a defendant's refusal to testify? The Supreme Court found no constitutional violation.

6. *Compulsory process for defense witnesses.* The defendant who hopes to call witnesses and collect evidence to undermine the prosecution's case receives some significant help from the government. Provisions in the federal constitution and in virtually all state constitutions give the defendant the power of "compulsory process," that is, the power to subpoena witnesses who must inform the court of what they know about the events in question. For instance, the Sixth Amendment to the federal constitution grants to the accused the right "to have compulsory process for obtaining witnesses in his favor." Statutes and rules of procedure also confirm the defendant's power to obtain government support in presenting witnesses.

7. *Threats of perjury charges against defense witnesses.* While it is surely true that the law makes it easier for defendants to obtain favorable testimony, there are also some legal obstacles to finding defense witnesses. To begin with, the defense witnesses might invoke the privilege against self-incrimination. Further, the potential witnesses might fear that if they testify, they will create a risk of perjury charges if the prosecutor believes that the testimony is not truthful. To what extent can government agents, such as judges or prosecutors, use these incentives to make it more difficult for the defendant to obtain witnesses?

The due process clause of the federal constitution controls the statements of prosecutors and judges about possible criminal charges to be filed against defense witnesses. In the leading Supreme Court decision, Webb v. Texas, 409 U.S. 95 (1972), a trial judge warned the defendant's only witness against committing perjury and explained the consequences of a perjury conviction. The Court held that the judge's statements violated due process. See also State v. Finley, 998 P.2d 95 (Kan. 2000) (right to present defense infringed when prosecutor suggests state will charge potential defense witness with felony murder based on her testimony); State v. Goad, 355 S.E.2d 371 (W.Va. 1987).

High state courts have read *Webb* flexibly to mean that the judge or prosecutor can sometimes mention possible criminal charges to a defense witness. Applying federal due process principles rather than state constitutional provisions, the courts often condemn a prosecutor for saying that she "will" bring criminal charges against the defense witness if the witness testifies. See Mills v. State, 733 P.2d 880 (Okla. Crim. App. 1985). However, when a prosecutor tells a defense witness that testimony "could" expose the witness to criminal charges, courts are less likely to find a due process violation. The same distinction applies to a trial judge who informs the witness about possible criminal charges which could result from testifying. See Jones v. State, 655 N.E.2d 49 (Ind. 1995). Should it matter whether the prosecutor speaks directly to the defense witness or instead sends a message by way of the defense attorney or some other third party?

Defendants have much less success when they complain that the government has deported aliens whom the defendant planned to call as defense witnesses. United States v. Valenzuela-Bernal, 458 U.S. 858 (1982) (no due process violation in prosecution for illegal transportation of aliens when government deports all aliens who would have testified for defendant). Can you explain why these claims are more difficult to sustain than those dealing with threats of criminal charges against witnesses?

8. *Defense grants of immunity.* If a prosecution witness invokes her privilege against self-incrimination, the prosecutor has the option of "immunizing" the witness from later prosecution based on the testimony, and the court will compel the witness to testify despite the privilege. (Recall the discussion of this issue in Chapter 10.) However, the defense does not have a comparable power to immunize defense witnesses who invoke the privilege. Defendants sometimes ask the court to order the prosecution to grant immunity to a defense witness, but courts routinely deny the requests. See State v. Roy, 668 A.2d 41 (N.H. 1995). Why have defendants been so unsuccessful in obtaining grants of immunity, even for their most crucial witnesses? When a defendant requests a grant of immunity for a witness and does not receive it, should the judge explain to the jury that the defendant had hoped to call a witness who is now "missing" because of the privilege against self-incrimination?

D. ETHICS AND LIES AT TRIAL

Ethical issues arise at all stages in the prosecution and defense of criminal defendants. Issues before trial include the conduct of interrogations, the grounds for filing charges, and the statements made while negotiating plea bargains. During trial preparation, ethical obligations may require discovery disclosures beyond those required by constitutional doctrine, statutes, or rules of procedure. Throughout the criminal process, ethical dilemmas for defense counsel arise from the tension between the search for truth and the zealous representation of the defendant. For the prosecutor, ethical dilemmas arise from the conflict between the obligation to seek justice on behalf of the public as a whole and the need to consult and defer to the wishes of crime victims.

Some of the most difficult ethical questions in all of legal practice arise when the lawyer believes the client is acting illegally or is lying. Related problems arise when a lawyer believes that a friendly witness is lying. Consider the extent to which the ethical obligations of defense lawyers and prosecutors at trial are — or should be — different.

■ STATE v. TROY JONES

923 P.2d 560 (Mont. 1996)

GRAY, J.

[The State charged Jones with felony assault], alleging that Jones purposely or knowingly caused bodily injury to Kirby Sowers by striking Sowers "about the head and face with a beer bottle. . . ." T.R. Halvorson was appointed to represent Jones and, thereafter, Jones pled not guilty to the charged offense. . . . Two days prior to trial, Halvorson moved to withdraw as Jones' counsel. The State opposed the motion and requested an evidentiary hearing on the grounds for withdrawal. . . . Halvorson based his motion, in part, on Rules 1.16(a)(1) and (b)(1), Montana Rules of Professional Conduct (MRPC). In this regard, Halvorson told the District Court that Jones had stated an intent to testify falsely.

Halvorson also based his motion on Rule 1.16(b)(3), MRPC. The bulk of Halvorson's statements, disclosures and arguments in support of his motion to withdraw were based on his belief that Jones' decision to reject the plea agreement Halvorson had negotiated with the State and proceed to trial was repugnant or imprudent. Halvorson detailed the offense and Jones' role in it, and disclosed Jones' admission that he "punched Sowers with a bottle of beer in [Jones'] right hand." Halvorson indicated that a felony assault had occurred and that Jones admitted having committed it. In addition, Halvorson stated that he did not have a defense to present to a jury on Jones' behalf. He opined that it was repugnant to deny criminal culpability to a jury where on an "open and shut basis . . . there is guilt." Halvorson also indicated that Jones' decision to go to trial rather than accept a plea agreement "when Jones stands virtually no chance of an acquittal" was repugnant to him and constituted good cause for his withdrawal as counsel.

Jones denied that he had communicated an intent to testify falsely to Halvorson and stated that, in fact, he did not intend to testify at his trial. He asserted that Halvorson had "lied about a few things" and that "he disagreed with everything Halvorson said, and that's fine if Halvorson drops out of the case." . . . Based on Jones' statement that he did not intend to testify, the District Court denied Halvorson's motion to withdraw. Several months later, a jury convicted Jones of felony assault and the District Court sentenced him and entered judgment. Jones appeals.

Did the District Court abuse its discretion in denying Halvorson's motion to withdraw as Jones' counsel? . . . Jones' primary contention is that Halvorson had a conflict of interest which resulted in a denial of Jones' constitutional rights to a fair trial and to the effective assistance of counsel. . . .

The Sixth Amendment to the United States Constitution and Article II, §24 of the Montana Constitution guarantee a criminal defendant the right to the assistance of counsel. Mere representation by counsel is not sufficient, however; the assistance must be effective to give true meaning to that right and to the right to a fair trial. Moreover, a criminal defendant's constitutional right to the effective assistance of counsel is comprised of two correlative rights: the right to counsel of reasonable competence and the right to counsel's undivided loyalty. . . . The duty of loyalty is "perhaps the most basic of counsel's duties." Strickland v. Washington, 466 U.S. 668 (1984).

An attorney owes a duty of confidentiality to his or her clients. Rule 1.6, MRPC. The duty of confidentiality is correlative to an attorney's duty of loyalty. Thus, a defense attorney's disclosure of confidential information in violation of Rule 1.6, MRPC, necessarily implicates the attorney's duty of loyalty as well as the defendant's constitutional right to the effective assistance of counsel. Rule 1.16, MRPC, provides in pertinent part:

> (a) [a lawyer] shall withdraw from the representation of a client if: (1) the representation will result in violation of the rules of professional conduct or other law; . . .
>
> (b) [a lawyer] may withdraw from representing a client . . . if: (1) the client persists in a course of action involving the lawyer's services that the lawyer reasonably believes is criminal or fraudulent. . . .

Halvorson contended that his continued representation of Jones would result in a violation of a rule of professional conduct or other law because Jones intended to commit perjury. . . .

Halvorson stated that he had a conversation with Jones in which Jones communicated an intent to testify falsely and, in response, he informed Jones of the consequences of perjury and that he could take no part in presenting perjured testimony to the District Court. He further stated that he gave Jones a weekend over which to further consider Jones' intent to commit perjury and his advice in this regard. The record does not reflect that Halvorson checked back with Jones after the weekend passed, to ascertain whether Jones had reconsidered based on his advice, before filing his motion to withdraw.

Halvorson conceded at the hearing on his motion to withdraw that Jones may have reconsidered and decided not to testify falsely. Thus, the record before us contains only an alleged possible intent to commit perjury. It does not support Halvorson's contention that his continued representation of Jones would result in a violation of the rules of professional conduct or other law. [Furthermore], nothing of record indicates that Jones was "persisting" in his alleged intent to testify falsely after considering Halvorson's advice and warning. The record before us does not support withdrawal based on Rule 1.16, MRPC.

In this regard, Jones and the amici curiae urge our adoption of a variety of standards of knowledge which an attorney should be required to possess prior to moving to withdraw based on a criminal defendant client's intent to commit perjury. Jones contends that a "firm factual basis" must exist. The Criminal Defense Section of the State Bar of Montana asserts that counsel must be "absolutely convinced in his own mind, and in fact beyond a reasonable doubt" that the client will commit perjury before moving to withdraw. The State Bar of Montana Ethics Committee recommends that counsel must "know" that the defendant intends to perjure himself or herself and that a maintained and reiterated statement of intent to do so should be sufficient. We decline to adopt a particular knowledge standard in this case where no findings of fact have been made by the trial court. Moreover, it is unnecessary to do so in this case because it is clear that Halvorson did not meet any standard of knowledge prior to moving to withdraw. . . .

Halvorson also relied on Nix v. Whiteside, 475 U.S. 157 (1986), in support of his motion to withdraw as Jones' counsel because of Jones' alleged intent to commit perjury. In *Nix,* the defendant was charged with murder, but claimed that he had stabbed the victim in self-defense. He told his attorney that the victim was pulling a pistol from underneath the pillow on the bed, but admitted that he had not actually seen a gun. During trial preparation, however, the defendant told his attorney for the first time that he had seen something "metallic" in the victim's hand; his explanation for the change was that "[i]f I don't say I saw a gun, I'm dead." The attorney explained that it was not necessary to prove the victim actually had a gun to succeed on a claim of self-defense, but the defendant continued to insist on testifying falsely. The attorney advised that he would not allow the defendant to testify falsely and that, if the defendant did so, he would be required to advise the court that the defendant was committing perjury and would move to withdraw as counsel.

The defendant testified at trial that he "knew" the victim had a gun, but conceded on cross-examination that he did not actually see a gun in the victim's hand. He was convicted of second-degree murder and subsequently moved for a new trial, claiming that he had been deprived of a fair trial due to his attorney's admonitions. [The trial court denied the motion. In federal habeas corpus proceedings, the] Supreme Court observed that the first part of the Strickland v. Washington, 466 U.S. 668 (1984) [standard for measuring ineffective assistance of counsel] requires a defendant to establish "constitutionally deficient" performance by counsel. Having recognized counsel's duty of loyalty in *Strickland,* the *Nix* Court determined "that duty is limited to legitimate, lawful conduct compatible with the very nature of a trial as a search for truth." While an attorney's duty of confidentiality and loyalty extends to a client's admission of guilt, it does not require the attorney to assist the client in presenting false evidence. Thus, whether the attorney's conduct in *Nix* was seen as a successful attempt to persuade the defendant not to commit perjury, or as a threat to withdraw and disclose the defendant's perjury if and when it occurred, the Supreme Court held that the attorney's representation of the defendant fell "well within accepted standards of professional conduct and the range of reasonable professional conduct acceptable under *Strickland.*"

In reaching its conclusion in *Nix,* the Supreme Court surveyed and set forth various rules of professional conduct and interpretations of such rules. For example, the Supreme Court stated that it is "universally agreed" that an attorney's first duty when confronted with a client's stated intention to testify falsely is to attempt to dissuade the client from the unlawful course of conduct. Moreover, where the client actually gives perjured testimony, an attorney may reveal the perjury to the trial court. In addition, withdrawal may be appropriate where a client states an intent to testify falsely. The Supreme Court was careful to note, however, that it was not intruding into the proper authority of the states to define and apply standards of professional conduct applicable to those admitted to practice in state courts. . . .

Neither the facts nor the holding in *Nix* support Halvorson's motion to withdraw based on Jones' alleged intent to testify falsely in this case. The only pertinent facts in *Nix* were the attorney's advice, in response to the client's stated intent to commit perjury, that he would not allow the client to testify falsely and, if the client did so, he would disclose the perjury to the trial court and move to withdraw; the client did not commit perjury. Here, in response to Jones' alleged intent to testify falsely, Halvorson advised of the potential consequences. To this extent, Halvorson's actions mirrored those of counsel in *Nix.* Halvorson, however, followed his advice by moving to withdraw and making disclosures to the District Court of client confidences. These significant facts were not present in *Nix*. . . .

As a final argument relating to Halvorson's motion to withdraw based on Jones' alleged intent to commit perjury, the State contends that the disclosures Halvorson made to the District Court in this regard were required by Rule 3.3(a)(2), MRPC. Rule 3.3, MRPC, provides, in pertinent part: "A lawyer shall not knowingly: . . . fail to disclose a material fact to a tribunal when disclosure is necessary to avoid assisting a criminal or fraudulent act by the client. . . ." The State asserts that Halvorson knew Jones intended to commit perjury and, as a result, that Rule 3.3(a)(2) imposed an obligation to disclose Jones' intent to testify falsely to the District Court in order to avoid assisting Jones in the criminal or fraudulent act of perjury. However, as discussed above, Halvorson did not know Jones' intent in this regard. Therefore, Rule 3.3 does not support Halvorson's disclosure of Jones' alleged possible intent to commit perjury.

We conclude, on the record before us, that Halvorson's motion to withdraw was improper under Rules 1.16(a)(1) and (b)(1), MRPC, and was not supported by *Nix*. An attorney who abandons his or her duty of loyalty may create a conflict of interest. A defense attorney who essentially joins the prosecution's efforts in obtaining a conviction and acts on a belief that the defendant should be convicted suffers from an obvious conflict of interest. Such an attorney fails to function in any meaningful sense as the Government's adversary. While defense counsel in a criminal case assumes a dual role as a "zealous advocate" and as an "officer of the court," neither role would countenance disclosure to the Court of counsel's private conjectures about the guilt or innocence of his client. It is the role of the judge or jury to determine the facts, not that of the attorney. Where an attorney willfully discloses confidential information communicated by his client, he inhibits mutual trust necessary for effective representation.

Here, the record clearly establishes that Halvorson put his personal interest in not wanting to take Jones' case to trial ahead of Jones' constitutional right to an attorney devoted solely to Jones' interest in exercising his right to a trial by jury. Halvorson informed the District Court that he had negotiated a favorable plea agreement for Jones and indicated that he considered Jones' decision to decline the agreement and exercise his right to trial repugnant. In the course of further explaining Jones' "repugnant" decision, Halvorson reminded the court of the pending felony assault charge, premised on the State's allegation that Jones committed the assault by striking Sowers "with either a beer bottle, or a glass, or some glass object," and disclosed a confidential admission Jones made to him that Jones "punched Sowers with a bottle of beer in Jones' right hand." This disclosure was improper. . . .

Moreover, Halvorson's contention that Jones' "repugnant" decision to exercise his right to a jury trial, rather than accept a plea agreement, constitutes good cause for withdrawal runs directly afoul of Rule 1.2(a), MRPC, which provides in relevant part: "In a criminal case, the lawyer shall abide by the client's decision, after consultation with the lawyer, as to a plea to be entered, whether to waive jury trial and whether the client will testify." The obligations imposed by this Rule are paramount, and unqualified. Thus, while Halvorson may not have agreed with Jones' decision to decline a plea agreement and exercise his right to a jury trial, that decision did not — and cannot — constitute cause for withdrawal.

Halvorson also indicated that, in his opinion, on an "open and shut basis . . . there is guilt and is the plea [sic] that probably should be entered." To illustrate his point, Halvorson detailed for the District Court and the prosecution why he believed Jones was so clearly guilty. He laid out the facts leading up to the alleged assault, which involved Sowers physically removing Jones from a bar and, immediately thereafter, walking into the bar covered with blood. He then stated:

> Now, on probabilities, who else would have done it? [Jones] just had this physical disagreement with [Sowers]. There is no other person that the State has ever suspected, and there's no other person that [Jones] has indicated should be a suspect, and there's no other person that any witness I know of has indicated should be a suspect. So, you know, the range of possible explanations . . . is narrow. It would be like threading a needle to come up with any other explanation. . . . In my mind, under the study of Montana law, there's no doubt but what that [sic] beer bottle is a weapon, and, even if it weren't, there's no doubt in my mind that the degree of injury . . . is serious bodily injury. . . . It's a felony assault, and my client has admitted to me, essentially, that he did it.

Halvorson's narrative detailed for the District Court and the prosecution why he believed Jones was guilty of felony assault and should not go to trial. . . . The record before us establishes that, at the hearing on Halvorson's motion to withdraw, Halvorson totally abandoned his adversarial role on Jones' behalf against the State, essentially joining the prosecution's efforts in obtaining a conviction. In acting on his own belief that Jones should be convicted and in essentially joining the State's efforts in obtaining a conviction, we conclude that Halvorson created "an obvious conflict of interest" and abandoned his duty of loyalty to Jones.

Ordinarily, a criminal defendant's constitutional right to the effective assistance of counsel is violated only when counsel's performance was deficient and the deficient performance prejudiced the defendant's right to a fair trial, and the defendant must establish both elements. The *Strickland* Court noted the availability of "presumed prejudice," however, in situations where counsel is "burdened by an actual conflict of interest. In those circumstances, counsel breaches the duty of loyalty, perhaps the most basic of counsel's duties." . .

The record before us in this case is clear. Halvorson totally abandoned his duties of loyalty and confidentiality to Jones by putting his personal interest in not wanting to take Jones' case to trial ahead of Jones' interest in representation by an attorney devoted solely to his interest in exercising his right to trial. The conflict between Halvorson's sympathies and Jones' rights and interests is unmistakable and egregious and, under such circumstances, Halvorson can be said to have represented Jones only "through a tenuous and unacceptable legal fiction." We conclude that this case constitutes the very rare instance in which a presumption of prejudice is warranted. [W]e refuse to indulge in nice calculations regarding the amount of prejudice attributable to the clear and unequivocal conflict of interest Halvorson created.

We hold that, faced with Halvorson's clear conflict of interest and abandonment of his duty of loyalty to Jones, the District Court abused its discretion in denying Halvorson's motion to withdraw as Jones' counsel. We vacate Jones' conviction and sentence and remand this case to the District Court for a new trial.

■ PEOPLE v. VICTOR REICHMAN

819 P.2d 1035 (Colo. 1991)

PER CURIAM.

This is an attorney discipline case. A hearing panel approved the findings and recommendation of a majority of the hearing board that the respondent receive a public censure for conduct involving dishonesty, fraud, deceit or misrepresentation, and conduct prejudicial to the administration of justice. We accept the recommendation of the hearing panel and publicly censure the respondent and order that he be assessed the costs of these proceedings.

[T]he respondent was the duly appointed or elected District Attorney of the Sixth Judicial District, which includes La Plata County. . . . In the spring of 1987, the respondent and other members of law enforcement in the Sixth Judicial District formed a de facto task force, or "LEADS committee," to conduct undercover operations to investigate and prosecute drug trafficking in the district. A police officer from outside the judicial district was retained to conduct the undercover investigations, and the officer chose the fictitious identity of one "Colton Young," an unemployed biker. The respondent served as the head of the task force.

After several months undercover, "Young" had developed a list of names of suspected drug traffickers in the judicial district. In addition, two individuals had told "Young" that an attorney, Robin Auld, accepted drugs in lieu of fees.[2] Then, in September 1987, "Young" called an emergency meeting of the task force to announce that he believed his undercover identity may have been compromised. The task force decided to rehabilitate "Young's" identity. With the respondent's approval, "Young" was "arrested" for a traffic violation on the main street of Durango outside of the business establishment of a significant target of the task force. Auld was not this target. A search of "Young" was then conducted in such a way that the fruits of the search could be easily suppressed and the charges dismissed. "Young" was instructed to contact Robin Auld and retain him as defense counsel.[3]

As part of the plan, fictitious charges were lodged against "Young" with the respondent's knowledge and approval. The respondent, either personally or through his agents, filed a false criminal complaint against "Young," charging him with the illegal possession of a firearm and of marihuana in the County Court of La Plata County. Other documents filed by or on behalf of the respondent in the "Young" case included a surety bond and an offense report, falsely stating "Young's" name and address, and falsely stating that "Young" had committed certain criminal offenses. In addition, with the respondent's knowledge and approval, "Young" appeared in county court and made false statements to the county judge, who was unaware of the deception.

A majority of the hearing board concluded that the respondent's conduct in filing the false documents and the fictitious criminal complaint, and otherwise creating and maintaining the deception of the county court, violated DR 1-102(A)(4) (conduct involving dishonesty or misrepresentation), and DR 1-102(A)(5) (conduct prejudicial to the administration of justice).

The respondent argues that his conduct was not unethical and he points to a number of cases in which prosecutors engaged in deception during "sting" operations. . . . United States v. Murphy, 768 F.2d 1518 (7th Cir. 1985), discussed the participation of the FBI and federal prosecutors in Operation Greylord. The defendant in Murphy, a former associate judge of the Circuit Court of Cook County, Illinois,

2. On March 19, 1990, this court suspended Robin Auld from the practice of law for six months for his involvement in the occurrences which form the basis for this proceeding.

3. The actual objective of the "arrest" and the filing of the fictitious charges against "Young" was hotly disputed. The special assistant disciplinary counsel sought to establish that the respondent's intention was to coerce Auld into betraying Auld's client or clients. The hearing board did not find that this was the respondent's design by clear and convincing evidence. For the purpose of this opinion, we assume that the respondent's intention was to rehabilitate "Young's" undercover identity.

was convicted of accepting bribes to fix the outcomes of hundreds of criminal cases that came before him. As part of Operation Greylord, FBI agents posed as corrupt lawyers, and other agents testified in made-up criminal cases heard by Judge Murphy. Murphy argued that his convictions were invalid because the Operation Greylord "cases" were frauds on the court, and the undercover agents committed perjury. The court of appeals disagreed, finding that while the agents' acts appeared criminal, the acts were not crimes because they were performed without the requisite criminal intent. Further, *Murphy* held:

> The FBI and prosecutors behaved honorably in establishing and running Operation Greylord. They assure us that they notified the Presiding Judge of the Circuit Court's Criminal Division, the State's Attorney of Cook County, the Attorney General of Illinois, and the Governor of Illinois. Such notice may not be necessary, and certainly a criminal defendant is in no position to complain of the absence of such notice (for he has no personal right to protect the dignity of the Cook County courts), but the notice dispels any argument that the federal Government has offended some principle requiring respect of the internal operations of the state courts. [768 F.2d at 1529.]

Prosecutorial deception may not always constitute prosecutorial misconduct for purposes of determining whether a criminal complaint or indictment must be dismissed. It does not necessarily follow, however, that prosecutorial deception of a type which results in directly misleading a court should be exempted from the proscriptions of the Code of Professional Responsibility simply because the deception is not such as to warrant the dismissal of a criminal case.

In the case of In re Friedman, 392 N.E.2d 1333 (Ill. 1979), the attorney-respondent, Friedman, was a state prosecutor. In two separate investigations involving bribery of two police officers, Friedman instructed the police officers to testify falsely in court hearings. [Defense attorneys had attempted to bribe the officers to testify falsely in favor of their clients, and the prosecutor instructed the officers to do so as part of a bribery investigation directed at the defense attorneys.] Four justices of the Supreme Court of Illinois found that Friedman's conduct violated the Code of Professional Responsibility notwithstanding his motives. Two justices found that Friedman's conduct was unethical but did not merit discipline because he "acted without the guidance of precedent or settled opinion and because there is apparently considerable belief . . . that the respondent acted properly in conducting the investigation. . . ." Two justices concurred in the decision of the court not to impose discipline because they determined that Friedman did not violate the Code of Professional Responsibility. Two justices concluded that Friedman's conduct was unethical and warranted censure.

[The *Friedman* court rejected the argument that the attorney's] conduct was not unethical because he was motivated by . . . his public responsibilities. This argument is the equivalent of the contention that the end justifies the means, and "that pernicious doctrine," Olmstead v. United States, 277 U.S. 438 (1928) (Brandeis, J., dissenting),[5] is unacceptable in the administration of the criminal law.

5. As Justice Brandeis said in dissent in *Olmstead:*

> Crime is contagious. If the Government becomes a lawbreaker, it breeds contempt for law; it invites every man to become a law unto himself; it invites anarchy. To declare that in the administration of the criminal law the end justifies the means — to declare that the Government may commit crimes in order to secure the conviction of a private criminal — would bring terrible retribution. Against that pernicious doctrine this Court should resolutely set its face.

[W]e conclude, as did the hearing panel and the majority of the hearing board, that the respondent's conduct violated DR 1-102(A)(1), and DR 1-102(A)(5). District attorneys in Colorado owe a very high duty to the public because they are governmental officials holding constitutionally created offices. This court has spoken out strongly against misconduct by public officials who are lawyers. The respondent's responsibility to enforce the laws in his judicial district grants him no license to ignore those laws or the Code of Professional Responsibility. While the respondent's motives and the erroneous belief of other public prosecutors that the respondent's conduct was ethical do not excuse these violations of the Code of Professional Responsibility, they are mitigating factors to be taken into account in assessing the appropriate discipline. The respondent has no prior discipline. We find, therefore, that the respondent's misconduct warrants discipline consistent with our duties to protect the public and maintain the integrity of the legal profession.

Accordingly, we accept the recommendation of the hearing panel and publicly censure the respondent Victor Reichman. While the surrounding circumstances may tend to explain and mitigate the misconduct, they do not excuse the deception imposed on the court. We therefore publicly reprimand Reichman and assess him the costs of these proceedings in the amount of $4,851.28. . . .

Notes

1. *Lying clients: majority view.* As the U.S. Supreme Court made clear in Nix v. Whiteside, 475 U.S. 157 (1986), the federal constitutional right to effective counsel does not compel an attorney to remain silent when a client plans to commit perjury during testimony. Nor does the Constitution require the attorney to take any other particular action, such as withdrawing from the case or informing the court of the client's plans. The same can be said for state constitutional rulings: They leave the attorney with several acceptable options. The most pertinent legal requirements in this situation come not from constitutions, but from the rules of legal ethics, often embodied in state statutes. As the Montana court in *Jones* indicates, the first ethical duty of the defense attorney who learns that a client might commit perjury at trial is to convince the client not to commit perjury. What exactly does an attorney tell a client accused of a crime who apparently plans to lie during testimony?

Before taking any further steps, the attorney must have sufficient reason to believe that her client plans to lie during testimony, despite her best efforts to convince him otherwise. State courts sometimes require the attorney to be convinced beyond a reasonable doubt that the client plans to commit perjury. ABA Model Rule of Professional Conduct 3.3(a)(4) phrases it this way: "A lawyer shall not knowingly offer evidence that the lawyer knows to be false." How will an attorney "know" that a client's testimony will be false?

If the attorney faces this problem, several options are open to her under the rules of ethics. One possibility is to withdraw from the case. Ethics rules allow (or even require) the attorney in most pretrial situations to make the motion, although courts often will deny the motion. ABA Model Rule of Professional Conduct 1.16(a)(1) (a lawyer "shall withdraw from the representation of a client if . . . the representation will result in violation of the rules of professional conduct or other law"). What should the attorney say in the motion to withdraw? Suppose the case is set for a bench trial. Does withdrawal prevent any harm from befalling the client or the tribunal? See Norman Lefstein, Client Perjury in Criminal Cases: Still in Search of an Answer, 1 Geo. J. Legal Ethics 521 (1988).

The attorney who does not withdraw must deal with a "trilemma — that is, the lawyer is required to know everything, to keep it in confidence, and to reveal it to the court." Monroe Freedman, Lawyers' Ethics in an Adversary System 28 (1975). The traditional resolution of these conflicting ethical duties was to emphasize the duties to investigate and to hold confidences, and to compromise the duty to reveal matters to the court. However, since the appearance of the ABA's Model Rules of Professional Conduct in 1983 (now adopted in about 40 jurisdictions), the states have moved toward rules requiring counsel to reveal the potential perjury to the court. In the words of Rule 3.3(a)(2), a lawyer "shall not knowingly . . . fail to disclose a material fact to a tribunal when disclosure is necessary to avoid assisting a criminal or fraudulent act by the client." See People v. DePallo, 754 N.E.2d 751 (N.Y. 2001) (no ineffective assistance of counsel when attorney approaches judge in chambers after trial testimony of client and expresses opinion that client committed perjury).

The defense attorney might allow the client to testify but use a "narrative" form of testimony, in which the attorney asks an open-ended question, such as "tell us what happened," and the defendant relates his story without further questions from defense counsel. See People v. Guzman, 755 P.2d 917 (Cal. 1988) (no violation of California constitution or ethics rules). Does this response strike the right balance among the defense lawyer's ethical obligations? Is this an appropriate response to perjury by a defense witness other than the defendant?

2. *Lying prosecution witnesses.* The *Reichman* case from Colorado dealt with perjury by prosecution witnesses in the context of a disciplinary proceeding against a prosecutor. The same issue also comes up when defendants challenge the validity of a conviction based on false testimony by prosecution witnesses. A prosecutor who knowingly allows prosecution witnesses to present false testimony about a material fact violates the federal due process clause. This is true even if the government attorney who knows about the false testimony is not the same as the trial attorney. Once the prosecution witness has delivered the false testimony, the prosecutor must inform the court of the falsehood. See Giglio v. United States, 405 U.S. 150 (1972); Mooney v. Holohan, 294 U.S. 103 (1935); Ex parte Frazier, 562 So. 2d 560 (Ala. 1989) (establishing standard for obtaining new trial when alleging false testimony by prosecution witnesses; prosecution witnesses were "not the prom queen, the Archbishop, or the Mayor of Mobile"); Stephen A. Saltzburg, Perjury and False Testimony: Should the Difference Matter So Much? 68 Fordham L. Rev. 1537 (2000) (*Brady* disclosure obligations have weakened earlier line of cases such as *Mooney,* concerned with presenting false testimony). What inquiries would you expect prosecutors to make about the truthfulness of the testimony from government witnesses? What if the local police department has developed a reputation for "testilying" (providing false testimony to strengthen the prosecution's case)?

Prosecuting attorneys and defense attorneys apparently have different obligations to the court when it comes to false testimony from their witnesses. Is this simply an outgrowth of the burden of proof and the beyond-a-reasonable-doubt standard in criminal cases?

PART FOUR

MEASURING PUNISHMENT AND REASSESSING GUILT

XIX Sentencing

Criminal adjudication points toward sentencing. At sentencing, the system finally announces a "bottom line" outcome for those defendants who have proceeded all the way through the criminal process. Along the way, defense counsel, prosecutors, judges, and police make choices with one eye on the possible sentence. This anticipation of sentencing is perhaps most evident in plea bargaining.

Just as much of criminal procedure looks ahead to sentencing, the sentencing phase offers a chance to look back on the earlier steps in the process. At sentencing, the criminal justice system surveys once again all the major decisions it has reached regarding an offender, from investigation through conviction. It also takes a broader view of the offender's past and future, the victim's past and future, and the community's present attitude toward the crime. After this panoramic survey is complete, the sentencing authority selects a sanction.

One major puzzle for modern sentencing procedures can be summed up in this question: Why go to all the trouble of following intricate procedures for police and prosecutors, before and during trial, if the last step in the system ignores those procedural protections? This question, however, raises another: If the sentencing authority had to be bound by all determinations made prior to conviction, would convicted offenders receive undue protection, as if they were still presumed innocent? How much does sentencing undermine the meaning of conviction?

A. WHO SENTENCES?

In most criminal justice systems, several institutions share the decision about the proper sentence to impose: Legislatures and judges always have a say in the sentence, and juries, parole commissions, or sentencing commissions may participate.

But the precise division of labor in deciding on sentencing policy and sentences in particular cases varies a great deal from place to place. This division of labor in turn shapes the procedures that a court follows as it selects the sanction to impose on a convicted offender.

1. Indeterminate Sentencing

Until recently, sentencing in the United States was an area characterized more by discretion than procedure. In 1950 every state and the federal system had an "indeterminate" sentencing system. Under this type of system, the legislature prescribed broad potential sentencing ranges, and the trial judge sentenced without meaningful legal guidance and typically without offering any detailed explanation for the sentence. An executive branch agency (usually a parole board) ultimately determined the actual sentence each defendant would serve. There were virtually no judicial opinions explaining or reviewing a sentence, and legal counsel ordinarily made oral arguments at sentencing hearings without any written submissions to the court. The unwritten nature of the arguments and the decisions, together with the unavailability of presentence investigation reports, made it difficult to get a handle on sentencing law and practice in an indeterminate system. Perhaps that reveals the most important point about such a system: Sentencing happened without much law.

The following materials offer a glimpse of indeterminate sentencing systems at work. The U.S. Supreme Court decision in Williams v. New York, which came at the high water mark for indeterminate sentencing, captures not only the huge discretion given to trial judges but also some of the principles underlying that discretion. The documents related to the 1989 sentencing of Col. Oliver North were filed after his conviction for obstruction of a congressional investigation into a secret (and illegal) use of funds, derived from a sale of weapons to Iran, to support insurgents in Nicaragua known as "Contras" (hence, the name "Iran-Contra Affair"). The specific charges involved in North's case are less important for our purposes than the style of argument at work. The documents present, in an unusually visible and systematic form, the types of arguments and reasoning that operate in the many cases still sentenced today in indeterminate sentencing systems.

■ SAMUEL WILLIAMS v. NEW YORK

337 U.S. 961 (1949)

BLACK, J.

A jury in a New York state court found appellant guilty of murder in the first degree. The jury recommended life imprisonment, but the trial judge imposed sentence of death. In giving his reasons for imposing the death sentence the judge discussed in open court the evidence upon which the jury had convicted stating that this evidence had been considered in the light of additional information obtained through the court's "Probation Department, and through other sources." [A New York statute authorized the court to consider "any information that will aid the court in determining the proper treatment of such defendant." Williams claimed that the sentence, which was based on information supplied by witnesses, violated due process because the defendant had no chance to confront or cross-examine the witnesses or to rebut the evidence.]

The record shows a carefully conducted trial lasting more than two weeks in which appellant was represented by three appointed lawyers who conducted his defense with fidelity and zeal. The evidence proved a wholly indefensible murder committed by a person engaged in a burglary. . . .

About five weeks after the verdict of guilty with recommendation of life imprisonment, and after a statutory pre-sentence investigation report to the judge, the defendant was brought to court to be sentenced. [T]he judge gave reasons why he felt that the death sentence should be imposed. . . . He stated that the pre-sentence investigation revealed many material facts concerning appellant's background which though relevant to the question of punishment could not properly have been brought to the attention of the jury in its consideration of the question of guilt. He referred to the experience appellant "had had on 30 other burglaries in and about the same vicinity" where the murder had been committed. The appellant had not been convicted of these burglaries although the judge had information that he had confessed to some and had been identified as the perpetrator of some of the others. The judge also referred to certain activities of appellant as shown by the probation report that indicated appellant possessed "a morbid sexuality" and classified him as a "menace to society." The accuracy of the statements made by the judge as to appellant's background and past practices were not challenged by appellant or his counsel, nor was the judge asked to disregard any of them or to afford appellant a chance to refute or discredit any of them by cross-examination or otherwise.

The case presents a serious and difficult question. The question relates to the rules of evidence applicable to the manner in which a judge may obtain information to guide him in the imposition of sentence upon an already convicted defendant. . . . To aid a judge in exercising this discretion intelligently the New York procedural policy encourages him to consider information about the convicted person's past life, health, habits, conduct, and mental and moral propensities. The sentencing judge may consider such information even though obtained outside the courtroom from persons whom a defendant has not been permitted to confront or cross-examine. . . .

Tribunals passing on the guilt of a defendant always have been hedged in by strict evidentiary procedural limitations. But both before and since the American colonies became a nation, courts in this country and in England practiced a policy under which a sentencing judge could exercise a wide discretion in the sources and types of evidence used to assist him in determining the kind and the extent of punishment to be imposed within limits fixed by law. Out-of-court affidavits have been used frequently, and of course in the smaller communities sentencing judges naturally have in mind their knowledge of the personalities and backgrounds of convicted offenders. . . .

In addition to the historical basis for different evidentiary rules governing trial and sentencing procedures there are sound practical reasons for the distinction. In a trial before verdict the issue is whether a defendant is guilty of having engaged in certain criminal conduct of which he has been specifically accused. Rules of evidence have been fashioned for criminal trials which narrowly confine the trial contest to evidence that is strictly relevant to the particular offense charged. These rules rest in part on a necessity to prevent a time consuming and confusing trial of collateral issues. They were also designed to prevent tribunals concerned solely with the issue of guilt of a particular offense from being influenced to convict for that offense by evidence that the defendant had habitually engaged in other misconduct. A sentencing judge, however, is not confined to the narrow issue of guilt. His task within fixed statutory or constitutional limits is to determine the type and extent of punishment after the issue of guilt has been determined. Highly relevant — if not essential — to his selection of an appropriate sentence is the possession of the fullest information possible concerning the defendant's life and characteristics. And modern concepts individualizing punishment have made it all the more necessary that a sentencing judge not be denied an opportunity to obtain pertinent information by a requirement of rigid adherence to restrictive rules of evidence properly applicable to the trial.

Undoubtedly the New York statutes emphasize a prevalent modern philosophy of penology that the punishment should fit the offender and not merely the crime. The belief no longer prevails that every offense in a like legal category calls for an identical punishment without regard to the past life and habits of a particular offender. This whole country has traveled far from the period in which the death sentence was an automatic and commonplace result of convictions — even for offenses today deemed trivial. . . . Indeterminate sentences, the ultimate termination of which are sometimes decided by nonjudicial agencies, have to a large extent taken the place of the old rigidly fixed punishments. . . . Retribution is no longer the dominant objective of the criminal law. Reformation and rehabilitation of offenders have become important goals of criminal jurisprudence. . . .

Under the practice of individualizing punishments, investigation techniques have been given an important role. Probation workers making reports of their investigations have not been trained to prosecute but to aid offenders. Their reports have been given a high value by conscientious judges who want to sentence persons on the best available information rather than on guesswork and inadequate information. To deprive sentencing judges of this kind of information would undermine modern penological procedural policies that have been cautiously adopted throughout the nation after careful consideration and experimentation. We must recognize that most of the information now relied upon by judges to guide them in the intelligent imposition of sentences would be unavailable if information were restricted to that given in open court by witnesses subject to cross-examination. And the modern probation report draws on information concerning every aspect of a defendant's life. The type and extent of this information make totally impractical if not impossible open court testimony with cross-examination. Such a procedure could endlessly delay criminal administration in a retrial of collateral issues.

The considerations we have set out admonish us against treating the due-process clause as a uniform command that courts throughout the Nation abandon their age-old practice of seeking information from out-of-court sources to guide their judgment toward a more enlightened and just sentence. . . . So to treat the due-process clause would hinder if not preclude all courts — state and federal — from making progressive efforts to improve the administration of criminal justice. We hold that appellant was not denied due process of law. Affirmed.

Murphy, J., dissenting.

[Williams] was convicted of murder by a jury, and sentenced to death by the judge. . . . In our criminal courts the jury sits as the representative of the community; its voice is that of the society against which the crime was committed. A judge even though vested with statutory authority to do so, should hesitate indeed to increase the severity of such a community expression.

He should be willing to increase it, moreover, only with the most scrupulous regard for the rights of the defendant. The [evidence here] would have been inadmissible at the trial. Some, such as allegations of prior crimes, was irrelevant. Much was incompetent as hearsay. All was damaging, and none was subject to scrutiny by the defendant.

Due process of law includes at least the idea that a person accused of crime shall be accorded a fair hearing through all the stages of the proceedings against him. I agree with the Court as to the value and humaneness of liberal use of probation reports as developed by modern penologists, but, in a capital case, against the unanimous recommendation of a jury, where the report would concededly not have been admissible at the trial, and was not subject to examination by the defendant, I am forced to conclude that the high commands of due process were not obeyed.

■ UNITED STATES v. OLIVER NORTH

Government's Sentencing Memorandum (June 19, 1989)

The Government respectfully submits this memorandum in connection with the sentencing of Oliver L. North, scheduled for June 23, 1989. [We] focus on those matters we believe are appropriate for the Court to consider in imposing sentence.

The most striking thing about North's posture on the eve of sentencing is his insistence that he has done nothing wrong. Instead, on the day of the verdict, he declared that his "vindication" was not "complete," and promised to "continue the fight" until it is. At the same time, he continues to profit from his notoriety, even while he decries the wastefulness and injustice of his prosecution.

The Government recognizes that sentencing North presents difficult issues. The defendant was a public official who worked tirelessly on programs he and his superiors believed should be pursued. But the crimes of which he was convicted, involving a cover-up even after those programs became known to the public, were crimes designed to protect himself and his associates, not the national security. [North] apparently sees nothing wrong with alteration and destruction of official national security records. His participation in the preparation of a false and misleading chronology [to present during a congressional hearing on the Iran-Contra affair] has not led to any acknowledgment of wrongdoing. Certainly, he sees nothing wrong with lying to Congress, when in the view of himself and his superiors lying is necessary.

His contempt for Congress and the public is accompanied by venality in financial matters. The jury found him guilty of accepting a $13,800 security system from Richard Secord, a man with whom he had been doing business in his official capacity for two years. North does not appear to question the propriety of his other financial relationships with Secord and Hakim, including the use of large amounts of cash without accountability. . . .

In fashioning a just sentence in this case, we urge the Court to consider the seriousness of North's abuse of the public trust, the need for deterrence, North's failure to accept personal responsibility for his actions, his lack of remorse and his perjury on the witness stand. Taking all of these factors into account . . . the Government submits that a term of incarceration is appropriate and necessary.

The conduct of North in this case constituted a serious breach of the public trust. . . . North seems to believe that such activities are business as usual in government or necessary tactics in a "political firestorm." But after a non-political trial and a non-political verdict, the Court, in its sentence, should alert all government officials that such activities are indeed unlawful, and that if officials engaging in such conduct are caught and convicted, the punishment will be severe. Further, the private citizens of this country, who continue to follow this case closely, are entitled to the reassurance only this Court can give that these are serious crimes and that powerful government officials are not accorded special treatment.

Deterrence is particularly important in a case involving not only obstruction, lying and cover-up, but also personal venality. While it is understandable that a person under threat of danger might seek to protect his family, this concern arises frequently for some officials engaged in the areas of intelligence, covert action or, for that matter, law enforcement. They cannot accept private gifts from those doing business with the government. Where, as here, a public official receives a substantial gratuity from an individual with whom he has conducted official business, and proceeds to create fraudulent, back-dated letters to cover it up, the Court must respond.

A sentence in this case that included no period of incarceration would send exactly the wrong message to government officials and to the public. It would be a statement that 15 years after Watergate, government officials can participate in a brazen cover-up, lie to Congress and collect a substantial gratuity and still receive only a slap on the wrist.

[A]cting in his position at the National Security Council, North wielded enormous power in the government. By his own description, he met with presidents and kings. He was the primary official responsible for the coordination of counterterrorism, the release of American hostages and relations with the Contras. . . . Thus, North held a position of substantial public trust that far exceeded his military rank. . . .

North's disregard for this basic precept of a democratic society was graphically demonstrated during his trial testimony. At one point, the Court asked the defendant whether at any time he considered in his own mind not drafting false answers to Congress but, instead, simply saying "no." In a revealing moment, the defendant stated that he never considered the possibility of not doing it. This society cannot tolerate government officials unwilling and unable to exercise independent judgment and responsibility in refusing to perform illegal acts. . . .

Although he calls himself a "scapegoat," he invited this role. He joked about the danger that he would be jailed and bragged that he would be protected because "the old man love[s] my ass." Similarly, his decision to stand trial and gamble on acquittal, a right granted by the Constitution, was also undertaken as a challenge to the capability of our system of justice to respond to crimes with political overtones, given the expressed sympathy and support of this country's then President and Vice President. . . .

North was not content merely to exercise his constitutional right to put the Government to its proof at trial. Instead, he sought to pervert the processes of justice much as he had corrupted the processes of government. With supreme faith in his ability to deceive, North took the stand and perjured himself. For example, his unsupported claim that he had a $15,000 fund in a steel box in his closet echoed the flimsy lies offered by corrupt municipal officials in the days of Tammany Hall.

North's attempt to use the steel box to explain his cash purchase of a car in two installments graphically demonstrated North's penchant for weaving a tale that by its conclusion is preposterous. . . .

North's lack of remorse is particularly troubling in view of the fact that he continues to travel throughout the country, like a politician on the stump, giving speeches and discoursing on his defiance of Congress. Apparently, North has become a wealthy man in the process. The fact that this defendant is cultivating a popular following, which reinforces his lack of remorse, makes it all the more important for the Court to underscore the gravity of North's offenses by imposing a term of incarceration.

Oliver North's sentence will be known to, and closely evaluated by, all who view the perversion of government as a permissible means to the attainment of their goals. The sentence will also be carefully considered by those officials who may now be weighing the advantages of deception, obstruction and personal greed against the risks of punishment. It will also be noted by those serving substantial prison sentences for more personal crimes far less damaging to the nation. Most importantly, the sentence will be closely scrutinized by a citizenry whose confidence in government and the political system has been seriously undermined by the activities of this defendant. . . . Under all these circumstances, we respectfully submit that a term of incarceration is appropriate and necessary.

■ SENTENCING MEMORANDUM ON BEHALF OF OLIVER NORTH

Lt. Col. Oliver L. North is before the court for sentencing upon being found guilty of 3 of the 16 charges brought against him by the IC.* . . .

The IC's memorandum demonstrates that it will stop at nothing in its effort to crush Oliver North. The Supreme Court declared more than 50 years ago that the prosecutor "may strike hard blows, but he is not at liberty to strike foul ones." [Berger v. United States, 295 U.S. 78 (1935).] The IC has ignored the court's command; the blows that it strikes in its memorandum are as foul as any we have seen. It attacks Lt. Col. North for asserting his constitutional right to assert his innocence and stand trial; it ignores his 20 years of loyal and courageous service to this country; it takes him to task for asserting a simple truth — that most of the conduct with which he was charged was authorized by his superiors; and it blasts him for failing to show remorse, when his trial testimony makes clear that he deeply regrets many of his actions.

But the IC does not stop there. Unable to accept the jury's verdict of not guilty on 9 of 12 counts, the IC asks this Court to punish Lt. Col. North for charges on which the jury acquitted him. And not only does the IC ask the Court to disregard the jury's verdict of acquittal; it actually levels new charges, accusing Oliver North of having "supreme faith in his ability to deceive" and claiming without a shred of support that Lt. Col. North committed perjury at trial.

Just as the IC likened Lt. Col. North to Adolf Hitler at trial, it now attacks him for "arrogance"; for "personal venality"; for being "defian[t] of Congress"; and for

* North was prosecuted by a special prosecutor, known at that time in the federal system as an "independent counsel," or IC. — Eds.

possessing a "continuing callous attitude toward the judicial process and our democratic institutions." The IC does not offer evidence to support these charges; it plainly assumes that if it throws enough mud, some will stick. . . .

We submit that Lt. Col. North has already been punished sufficiently for the three offenses of which he was found guilty. He was fired from his job at the NSC. He has lost his career as a Marine Corps officer. He may lose his Marine Corps pension after 20 years of service. He remains under threat of assassination by a dangerous terrorist organization as a direct result of his service to this country. He has been subjected to unrelenting and often hostile press scrutiny for the past two-and-a-half years. Every detail of his life has been probed, first in nationally televised hearings conducted by the joint Iran/Contra committee and then by the IC. He has heard himself likened to Hitler by a prosecutor who appears to lack any sense of fairness and rumors in the press, before Congress, in court, in a nationally televised "docudrama," and now in the IC's memorandum. His children have been tormented. By any standard, the toll that this ordeal has already taken on Lt. Col. North and his family fulfills every legitimate purpose of punishment.

If the Court accepts the IC's view that this punishment is not enough — that Oliver North must be punished further for the three offenses of which he was found guilty — then that punishment should take the form of probation conditioned on community service. As the testimony at trial and letters to the Court demonstrate, Lt. Col. North is a man of extraordinary energy and talents, with remarkable compassion for his fellow man. We urge the Court to permit him to continue using those talents on behalf of the country that he has served with such devotion. A sentence of imprisonment would be cruel and unjust. . . .

In determining the proper sentence for Oliver North, the Court should consider the man as an individual, not — as the IC would have it — merely as a vehicle through which to send a "public message." The Court should weigh carefully Lt. Col. North's service to this country and to society, the devastating impact that imprisonment would have on his family, and the unique confluence of circumstances that gave rise to his conduct. This careful, individualized sentencing is essential to ensure that "the punishment should fit the offender and not merely the crime." Williams v. New York, 337 U.S. 241 (1949).

Oliver North devoted 20 years to the service of this country, from Vietnam to Tehran to Beirut. He has risked his own life and saved the lives of others. We submit that the Court should weigh this service in Lt. Col. North's favor at sentencing.

Upon graduation from the Naval Academy in 1968, Oliver North was commissioned in the United States Marine Corps and served as a platoon commander in Vietnam. His courage protected the lives of many young Marines, including Bill Haskell. In his letter to the Court, Mr. Haskell describes how Oliver North rescued him in the face of hostile fire as he lay wounded:

> . . . Early in the combat I was severely wounded so we needed help quickly. Ollie came to the rescue. In the face of an almost unbelievable barrage of enemy fire, he led a counterattack with his platoon driving the enemy back so that the Marines could medivac their wounded. I think I know Ollie well enough to say that his primary motivation for such heroic action was the desire to save his fellow Marines rather than just to achieve victory over the enemy. Ollie saved my life that day.

Oliver North received the Silver Star Medal for his heroism in saving Bill Haskell and his platoon. He received other medals as well for his service in Vietnam, including two Purple Hearts; a Bronze Star Medal with Combat "V"; and a Navy Commendation Medal with Combat "V." . . .

Following his service in Vietnam, Oliver North became an instructor for other Marines. He devoted himself to ensuring that other young men would be prepared if they were thrust into combat as he had been in Vietnam. . . .

In 1981, Oliver North was assigned to the National Security Council staff. At the NSC, he quickly established himself as a dedicated and hard-working staff officer. . . . Oliver North served initially with distinction on a highly sensitive national security project under the direct supervision of then-Vice President Bush. Lt. Gen. Ben Lewis [says that the project] "put in place, in record time, key mechanisms that were essential to meaningful negotiations with our Allies and the Soviet Union on reducing the size of nuclear forces." . . . As National Intelligence Officer Charles Allen writes, "[I]n a dangerous world, Lt. Col. North has helped make the world safer for every American" through his work on this sensitive project.

By 1984, Oliver North was responsible for two principal areas: counterterrorism and Central America. He worked tirelessly to fulfill these responsibilities. . . .

As a direct result of his critical work to protect Americans from the terrorist threat, Oliver North was targeted for assassination by the Abu Nidal terrorist group — described by Mr. Allen, a counterterrorism expert, as "the most dangerous and capable terrorist group in the Middle East and one of the most dangerous terrorist groups in the world." . . .

A further example demonstrates Lt. Col. North's courageous service to this country. In May 1986, at the President's direction, he and a handful of others undertook a dangerous mission to Tehran in an effort to achieve an opening to Iran and free the American hostages held in Lebanon. This trip entailed great personal danger to Lt. Col. North and his companions; they were the first American officials to travel to Iran since the revolution, and radical Iranians posed a significant threat of death or torture. The danger was particularly great because the trip was absolutely secret. But Lt. Col. North left his family behind — unable even to tell them where he was going — and risked his life for his country and for those held hostage. We ask that the Court give this record of service great weight in choosing the appropriate sentence for Oliver North.

Oliver North . . . has worked to improve society in other ways as well. Since the Congressional hearings of 1987, he has put his unsought and unwanted notoriety to use in service of his fellow citizens, particularly America's youth. Two examples illustrate Lt. Col. North's compassion and concern — and put the lie to the IC's claim that Lt. Col. North displays "contempt for the public."

First, shortly after his Congressional testimony, Lt. Col. North learned that it was the dream of a terminally ill boy to see him before the boy died. Lt. Col. North agreed to meet the boy to give him courage in his final days. The woman who arranged the meeting describes what happened in her letter to the Court:

> [The boy] told me he wanted to meet Lt. Col. North because this was the strongest person that he could ever know. [The boy] said that he needed this man to teach him how to become stronger mentally so that he could deal with his fast-approaching death. . . .
>
> To my amazement and delight, Lt. Col. North brought with him a large Bible with certain scriptures marked throughout the Bible that he said he lives by, that his strength comes from his faith in God. He sat down and read with the child from the Bible and they prayed together that [the boy] would find his answers. Lt. Col. North spent one

> and a half hours alone with [the boy] helping him to find the strength that the child was very much in need of. . . .

Lt. Col. North placed the following inscription on a photograph for the dying boy: "Courageous Hero, Inspiration, Fighter — Semper Fidelis. 18 September '87, Oliver L. North."

Second, Lt. Col. North has spoken out throughout America against drug use and in favor of improved drug prevention and rehabilitation. As but one example, he delivered a speech on behalf of the drug-prevention organization Reach Out America. . . .

Oliver and Betsy North have been married for almost 21 years. They have three daughters and one son. In sentencing Oliver North, the Court should consider both the devastation that this matter has already inflicted on the North family, and the further damage that any term of imprisonment would cause. . . . Two of Oliver North's daughters have been cruelly mocked at school. The family has been portrayed in grossly unfair ways in a nationally televised "docudrama." And the press has forced Oliver North and his family into an inescapable limelight — sometimes cruel, sometimes favorable, but always present.

The Court should also consider the damage that any period of incarceration would cause the North family in the future, particularly the children. . . . It would be wrong to take Oliver North away from his family at this most vulnerable time.

Criminal punishment serves four legitimate purposes: it incapacitates the offender, to prevent him from harming society; it rehabilitates him; it deters him and others from committing further offenses; and it reflects the seriousness of the offenses. The punishment that Oliver North and his family have suffered to date more than adequately fulfills each of these purposes.

1. *Incapacitation.* There is no need to incapacitate Oliver North. Far from representing a threat to society, Lt. Col. North devoted his professional life to ensuring the safety of Americans at home and abroad. . . .

2. *Rehabilitation.* No one can seriously contend that Oliver North needs rehabilitation, and it would be preposterous to suggest that, if rehabilitation *were* necessary, it would occur in prison. . . .

3. *Deterrence.* The punishment that Oliver North has suffered to date fully satisfied any need for deterrence; no additional sentence is necessary.

First, there is no need for a harsh punishment to achieve *specific* deterrence — deterrence of Lt. Col. North from future unlawful acts. In light of his record of service to this country and the excruciating ordeal that he and his family have endured, there is no chance that he will commit offenses in the future.

Second, *general* deterrence — deterrence of those other than Lt. Col. North — provides no basis for harsh punishment. The punishment that Lt. Col. North has suffered to date — including the loss of his position at the NSC, the loss of his career in the Marine Corps, and the minute and public scrutiny of his most private affairs by Congress, the IC, and frequently the media — should amply deter others.

Moreover, a prison sentence for Lt. Col. North would *not* deter high government officials from using their subordinates to carry out actions that are legally or politically risky. It would not escape the notice of such officials if Oliver North were to go to prison while others remain in government in positions of power or return to private-sector sinecures. . . .

4. *The Seriousness of the Offense.* The punishment that Lt. Col. North has suffered to date more than adequately reflects the gravity of the offenses of which he was found guilty. The three offenses — aiding and abetting an obstruction of Congress, destroying, altering, and/or removing official NSC documents, and accepting an unlawful gratuity — are serious. Each is a felony; each has a maximum prison term of between two and five years; and each carries a maximum fine of $250,000. But the seriousness of these offenses is significantly reduced by the unique circumstances of this case.

Lt. Col. North's conduct with respect to the security system is particularly understandable. His life had been threatened and his family placed at risk by one of the world's most dangerous terrorists. He had compelling evidence that Abu Nidal had the ability to carry out the threat in the United States. . . . Oliver North permitted a security system to be installed at his home for the protection of his family. That conduct may have represented poor judgment, but there are powerful mitigating factors, and no one could argue that it was seriously culpable. . . .

■ UNITED STATES v. OLIVER NORTH

Transcript (D.D.C. July 5, 1989)

GESELL, J.

I can assure you, Colonel North, that I'm going to take into full consideration the important fact that before you came to the White House you had served your country with distinction in the highest traditions of the Marine Corps. And the court is not going to overlook that there were major matters of military and quasi-military nature which you performed, again with the highest distinction at great personal risk to yourself after you came to the White House. But I'm sure you realize that this case has little to do with your military behavior, commitment or expertise.

The indictment involves your participation in particular covert events. I do not think that in this area you were a leader at all, but really a low ranking subordinate working to carry out initiatives of a few cynical superiors. You came to be the point man in a very complex power play developed by higher-ups. Whether it was because of the excitement and the challenge or because of conviction, you responded certainly willingly and sometimes even excessively to their requirements. And along the way you came to accept, it seems to me, the mistaken view that Congress couldn't be trusted and that the fate of the country was better left to a small inside group, not elected by the people, who were free to act as they chose while publicly professing to act differently. Thus you became . . . part of a scheme that reflected a total distrust in some constitutional values. . . .

As you stand there now you're not the fall guy for this tragic breach of the public trust. . . . You're here now because of your own conduct when the truth was coming out. Apparently you could not face disclosure and decided to protect yourself and others. You destroyed evidence, altered and removed official documents, created false papers after the events to keep Congress and others from finding out what was happening.

Now, I believe that you knew this was morally wrong. It was against your bringing up. It was against your faith. It was against all of your training. Under the stress of the moment it was easier to choose the role of a martyr but that wasn't a heroic, patriotic act nor was it in the public interest.

You have had great remorse for your family and understandably so. It is often the tragic part of what happens when mistakes are made. I believe you still lack full understanding, however, of how the public service has been tarnished. Nonetheless, what you believe is your own business and jail would only harden your misconceptions. Given the many highly commendable aspects of your life your punishment will not include jail. Indeed, community service may in the end make you more conscious of certain values which at times you and your associates appear to have overlooked in the elite isolation of the White House. . . .

I fashioned a sentence that punishes you. It is my duty to do that. But it leaves the future up to you. This is the sentence of the court. On count six where you are found guilty of aiding and abetting [an] obstruction of Congress, I'm going to impose a sentence of three years and suspend the execution of the sentence, place you on probation for two years, fine you $100,000 and I have to impose a special assessment of $50.

Under count nine, altering, removing and destroying the permanent historical records of the National Security Council I impose a sentence of two years, suspend the execution of sentence, place you on probation for two years, fine you $35,000 and impose a special assessment of $50 and I am required by the statute to impose another mandatory penalty. You are hereby disqualified from holding any office under the United States.

Under count ten, receiving an illegal gratuity, I'll impose a sentence of one year, suspend the execution of that sentence, place you on probation for two years, fine you $15,000 and impose a special assessment again of $50. These sentences and the probation are to run concurrently. The fines are to run consecutively.

Your probation shall consist in addition to the normal requirements of community service in a total amount of 1200, 800 the first year, and 400 the second year and you will remain under the supervision of the District of Columbia probation officer who is familiar with your situation and who has prepared the presentence report. . . .

Notes

1. *Informal procedure at sentencing: majority position.* The New York statute discussed in *Williams,* which allowed the sentencing judge to consider evidence inadmissible under the rules of evidence, typifies sentencing practices in most states. See also Tex. Crim. Proc. Code Ann. §37.07(3). The informal presentation of evidence supposedly supports an effort to obtain the most information possible about the offender and the offense and to make an individualized (perhaps even clinical) decision. Many different actors participate over time in the decision about how best to respond to an individual offender. Thus, the indeterminate sentencing system is one of "multiple discretions." Professor Franklin Zimring describes the system as follows:

> The best single phrase to describe the allocation of sentencing power in state and federal criminal justice is multiple discretion. Putting aside the enormous power of the police to decide whether to arrest, and to select initial charges, there are four separate institutions that have the power to determine criminal sentences — the legislature, the prosecutor, the judge, and the parole board or its equivalent. . . . With all our emphasis on due process in the determination of guilt, our machinery for setting punishment lacks any principle except unguided discretion. Plea bargaining, disparity of treatment

> and uncertainty are all symptoms of a larger malaise — the absence of rules or even guidelines in determining the distribution of punishments. . . .

Zimring, Making the Punishment Fit the Crime: A Consumer's Guide to Sentencing Reform, 12 Occasional Papers of the University of Chicago Law School (1977). More than half of the states use such an indeterminate sentencing system for large groups of cases, although many of these same states might use more narrowly circumscribed sentencing rules for some crimes.

2. *Williams revisited.* Samuel Titto Williams, a black man, was 18 years old at the time he killed 15-year-old Selma Graff, who surprised him during a burglary. He had no record of prior convictions, but he had been accused of burglary at age 11. The judgment in juvenile court was suspended. The probation report — a report prepared by probation officers prior to sentencing, also called a presentence investigation report — informed the judge that Williams was suspected of (but not charged with) committing 30 burglaries during the two months before the murder. A seven-year-old girl who was present during one of those burglaries told the probation department that Williams had molested her sexually. She identified Williams as the perpetrator two weeks after the incident. The probation report also stated that Williams was living with two women, and had brought different men into the apartment for the purpose of having sexual relations with the women. It alleged that he had once gone to a local school to photograph "private parts of young children." Finally, the sentencing judge relied on injuries inflicted on the murder victim's brother during the burglary. The prosecutor had not brought any charges based on the assault. See Kevin Reitz, Sentencing Facts: Travesties of Real-Offense Sentencing, 45 Stan. L. Rev. 523 (1993). Is the problem in *Williams* the new offender information at sentencing or the lack of access to that information?

3. *Capital punishment and informal procedure.* Although the *Williams* Court emphasized that rehabilitative purposes of sentencing required far-reaching information about an offender, the proposed "treatment" for Williams was execution. It brings to mind the statement attributed to the comedian W. C. Fields, who quoted a condemned prisoner on his way to the electric chair, saying, "This will certainly be a lesson to me." *Williams* is still cited with approval in support of informal sentencing procedures generally. However, it has been partially overruled in the context of capital sentencing. In Gardner v. Florida, 430 U.S. 349 (1977), the trial judge sentenced a defendant to death after consulting confidential and unrebutted information in the presentence investigation report. A plurality of the Supreme Court found that due process required, at least in capital cases, that the defendant have access to information that will influence the sentencing judge and have an opportunity to test its reliability.

4. *Discretion in different institutions.* When judges describe the factors they consider in sentencing under an indeterminate system, they often list the types of considerations that the lawyers and the judge discussed in the Oliver North case. One study of sentences in white-collar crime cases in federal court concluded that judges considered three common principles during sentencing: (1) the harm the offense produced; (2) the blameworthiness of the defendant, judged both from the defendant's criminal intent and from other details of the crime and defendant's earlier life; and (3) the consequences of the punishment, both for deterring future wrongdoing and for the well-being of the defendant's family and community. Despite the presence of these common principles for sentencing, judges selected very

different sentences because they did not agree on how to measure each of the principles or the relative weight to place on each. See Stanton Wheeler, Kenneth Mann, and Austin Sarat, Sitting in Judgment: The Sentencing of White-Collar Criminals (1988).

Observers in higher-volume courts, such as state misdemeanor courts, have described a very different reality. During plea bargaining the parties settle quickly on a proper sentence, hinging largely on the charges finally filed and on the parties' interpretation of the facts as reflected in the police reports. These negotiations do not often involve individualized haggling, as in a Middle Eastern bazaar. Rather, they are "more akin to modern supermarkets in which prices for various commodities have been clearly established and labeled." Malcolm Feeley, The Process Is the Punishment: Handling Cases in a Lower Criminal Court 187 (1979). What determines whether a given case will receive the "supermarket" form of sentencing or a more individualized assessment? Is it the presence or absence of a plea agreement?

5. *Sentencing juries.* In some states, juries not only rule on guilt or innocence but also decide the sentence to impose, even in noncapital cases. In about six of these states, the jury's choice is binding; in a few others, the jury only recommends a sentence to the judge. See Fla. Stat. §921.141 (jury recommends sentence); Tex. Crim. Proc. Code Ann. §37.07 (judge can assess punishment if defendant does not request probation or jury sentence; jury must be instructed about parole and other devices for reducing actual amount of prison time offender must serve). The ABA Standards for Criminal Justice, Sentencing 18-1.4 (3d ed. 1994), call for the abolition of jury sentencing. Why do the ABA standards, along with the strong majority of the states, give sentencing responsibilities to the judge and not the jury, the representatives of the community?

Should the sentencing jury be required to vote unanimously for a particular sentence? Should its voting rules be the same as the rules for its vote on guilt and innocence? See Manual for Courts-Martial, Rule 1006(d) (Exec. Order No. 12,473) (members of court martial may propose sentences; panel must consider each proposed sentence from least severe to most severe; unanimous vote needed for death penalty; three-fourths of members must recommend confinement for more than 10 years; two-thirds of members must recommend other sentences). For a proposal to expand the use of jury sentencing, see Adriaan Lanni, Note, Jury Sentencing in Noncapital Cases: An Idea Whose Time Has Come (Again)? 108 Yale L.J. 1775 (1999).

Even in a system that gives no formal sentencing power to juries, the jury might consider likely punishments as it deliberates on the verdict in the case. The jury might acquit if it believes the sanction is too severe.

2. *Legislative Sentencing*

Although indeterminate sentencing has been the norm in this country for most of the twentieth century, new arrangements have emerged over the past generation. Some of those alternative approaches have put the legislature more firmly in control of sentencing. Legislators have decided for themselves the precise sentence that will attach to various types of offenses; other sentencing institutions such as courts are supposed to carry out the choices of the legislature without adding any meaningful choices of their own.

Sentences dominated by legislative choices go back to some of the earliest recorded sources of law. American legislatures during the eighteenth and nineteenth centuries often set specific sentences for designated crimes. Only in the late nineteenth and early twentieth centuries did the state and federal legislatures routinely create more "indeterminate" sentences, authorizing a range of sentences from which a sentencing judge could select a sentence to impose on a particular offender. When legislatures began once again, in the middle of the twentieth century, to designate the specific punishments for certain crimes, they were returning to earlier practices.

■ CODE OF HAMMURABI

(C. H. W. Johns Trans., 1911)

§1: If a man weave a spell and put a ban upon a man, and has not justified himself, he that wove the spell upon him shall be put to death.

§8: If a man has stolen ox or sheep or ass, or pig, or ship, whether from the temple or the palace, he shall pay thirtyfold. If he be a poor man, he shall render tenfold. If the thief has naught to pay, he shall be put to death.

§15: If a man has caused either a palace slave or palace maid, or a slave of a poor man or a poor man's maid, to go out of the gate, he shall be put to death.

§195: If a man has struck his father, his hands one shall cut off.

§196: If a man has caused the loss of a gentleman's eye, his eye one shall cause to be lost.

§197: If he has shattered a gentleman's limb, one shall shatter his limb.

§198: If he has caused a poor man to lose his eye or shattered a poor man's limb, he shall pay one mina of silver.

§209: If a man has struck a gentleman's daughter and caused her to drop what is in her womb, he shall pay ten shekels of silver for what was in her womb.

§210: If that woman has died, one shall put to death his daughter.

§211: If the daughter of a poor man through his blows he has caused to drop that which is in her womb, he shall pay five shekels of silver.

§212: If that woman has died, he shall pay half a mina of silver.

■ U.S. SENTENCING COMMISSION MANDATORY MINIMUM PENALTIES IN THE FEDERAL CRIMINAL JUSTICE SYSTEM

i-ix, 5-8 (1991)

Mandatory minimum sentences are not new to the federal criminal justice system. As early as 1790, mandatory penalties had been established for capital offenses. In addition, at subsequent intervals throughout the 19th Century, Congress enacted provisions that required definite prison terms, typically quite short, for a variety of other crimes. Until recently, however, the enactment of mandatory minimum provisions was generally an occasional phenomenon that was not comprehensively aimed at whole classes of offenses.

A change in practice occurred with the passage of the Narcotic Control Act of 1956, which mandated minimum sentences of considerable length for most drug importation and distribution offenses. . . . In 1970, Congress drew back from the comprehensive application of mandatory minimum provisions to drug crimes enacted 14 years earlier. Finding that increases in sentence length "had not shown the expected overall reduction in drug law violations," Congress passed [legislation] that repealed virtually all mandatory penalties for drug violations.

[Growing criticism of efforts to rehabilitate inmates led lawmakers] to renew support for mandatory minimum penalties. On the state level this trend began in New York in 1973, with California and Massachusetts following soon thereafter. While the trend toward mandatory minimums in the states was gradual, by 1983, 49 of the 50 states had passed such provisions. . . . On the federal level, a comparable but more comprehensive trend was under way. Beginning in 1984, and every two years thereafter, Congress enacted an array of mandatory minimum penalties specifically targeted at drugs and violent crime. . . . There are over 60 criminal statutes that contain mandatory minimum penalties applicable to federal offenses in the federal criminal code today. Only 4 of these 60 statutes, however, frequently result in convictions; the 4 relate to drug and weapons offenses.

Despite the expectation that mandatory minimum sentences would be applied to all cases that meet the statutory criteria of eligibility, the available data suggest that this is not the case. . . . In 35 percent of cases in which available data strongly suggest that the defendant's behavior warrants a sentence under a mandatory minimum statute, defendants plead guilty to offenses carrying non-mandatory minimum or reduced mandatory minimum provisions. [W]hites are more likely than nonwhites to be sentenced below the applicable mandatory minimum; . . . defendants sentenced in some circuits are more likely to be sentenced below the applicable mandatory minimums than defendants sentenced in other circuits.

[Mandatory minimums] are wholly dependent upon defendants being charged and convicted of the specified offense under the mandatory minimum statute. Since the power to determine the charge of conviction rests exclusively with the prosecution for the 85 percent of the cases that do not proceed to trial, mandatory minimums transfer sentencing power from the court to the prosecution.

Notes

1. *Federal constitutional limits on legislative choice of sanctions: majority position.* Courts by and large allow legislatures to choose any punishment for a given crime (with the exception of the death penalty) and turn aside most claims that a punishment is "cruel and unusual" or "disproportionate" to the crime. In Harmelin v. Michigan, 501 U.S. 957 (1991), a statute required a mandatory life sentence for possession of 650 grams or more of cocaine. Justice Scalia and Chief Justice Rehnquist concluded that federal courts should never inquire into the proportionality of noncapital offenses. A group of three additional justices held that federal courts could overturn a disproportionate punishment as "cruel and unusual," but only rarely:

> [T]he primacy of the legislature, the variety of legitimate penological schemes, the nature of our federal system, and the requirement that proportionality review be guided by objective factors [lead us to this conclusion]: the Eighth Amendment does not

require strict proportionality between crime and sentence. Rather, it forbids only extreme sentences that are "grossly disproportionate" to the crime.

501 U.S. at 1001. Courts applying this proportionality test engage in three related inquiries. First, the court makes a threshold comparison of the crime committed and the sentence imposed. If this threshold inquiry leads to an inference of gross disproportionality, the court may compare sentences imposed on other criminals in the same jurisdiction (the "intrajurisdictional" analysis) and compare the sentences imposed for commission of the same crime in other jurisdictions (the "interjurisdictional analysis"). These latter two inquiries can validate the initial judgment that a sentence is grossly disproportionate to a crime.

In *Harmelin,* because of the severe social harms flowing from illegal drugs, the Court decided that there was no gross disparity between the crime and sentence. It therefore did not require any comparison of this statute to other sentencing statutes within the jurisdiction or in other jurisdictions: "intra- and inter-jurisdictional analyses are appropriate only in the rare case in which a threshold comparison of the crime committed and the sentence imposed leads to an inference of gross disproportionality." 501 U.S. at 1005. See also Solem v. Helm, 463 U.S. 277 (1983) (cruel and unusual punishment to impose life imprisonment without possibility of parole on defendant for uttering no account check for $100; defendant had three prior convictions for third-degree burglary, one prior conviction for obtaining money under false pretenses, one prior conviction of grand larceny, and one prior conviction of third-offense driving while intoxicated).

2. *Proportionality in the state courts.* Some state courts have shown a willingness to insist, under various provisions of their state constitutions, that the legislature select a punishment that is proportionate to the crime. See People v. Davis, 687 N.E.2d 24 (Ill. 1997) (statutory penalty for felons convicted of failing to register a firearm violates due process clauses of state and federal constitutions, because penalty is far less severe for more serious offense of unlawful use of weapon by a felon). State courts have also applied the *Harmelin* test under the Eighth Amendment of the federal constitution to bar some disproportionate sentences. State v. Bonner, 577 N.W.2d 575 (S.D. 1998) (15-year sentence for second-degree burglary was disproportionate, cruel and unusual; offender with no prior record was developmentally disabled and accomplices received probation). However, it is most common for state courts to uphold a legislative choice of sanctions in the case at hand, even if they recognize that a proportionality challenge might succeed in theory. State v. Moss-Dwyer, 686 N.E.2d 109 (Ind. 1997) (recognizing possible proportionality challenges under state constitution, but refusing to declare a sentence disproportionate where statute made misinformation on a handgun permit application a greater crime than carrying a handgun without a license).

A few states supplement the review described in *Harmelin* with a different constitutional inquiry, based on the internal consistency of state sentencing laws. In People v. Lewis, 677 N.E.2d 830 (Ill. 1996), the court struck down a statutorily specified sentence for "robbery committed with a category I weapon" because the statute imposed a far more serious penalty for this offense than for the virtually identical crime of "armed violence." The Illinois Supreme Court held that when two statutes punish substantively identical offenses with disproportionate penalties, the prosecutor has overbroad discretion and the statutes violate the "proportionate penalties" clause of the state constitution. What is the likely reaction of a state legislature to a holding such as *Lewis?*

Other state courts turn to non-constitutional methods of reducing sentences in particular cases without declaring a punishment disproportionate for an entire class of cases. See State v. DePiano, 926 P.2d 494 (Ariz. 1996) (despondent mother's unsuccessful attempt to commit suicide and infanticide by asphyxiation was punished by 34-year prison term; court reduced sentence under statute allowing reduction if "the punishment imposed is greater than under the circumstances of the case ought to be inflicted"). Which form of "disproportionality" analysis will place the most significant controls on the choices of the legislature?

3. *The case for legislative determination of sentences.* Although legislatively determined sentences do not often receive a spirited defense in judicial opinions or in the reports of governmental commissions, legislators do from time to time explain why they believe these statutes represent sound policy. As indicated in the report above from the U.S. Sentencing Commission, legislatures in most states have decided from time to time that mandatory minimum statutes are the most appropriate way to set sentences for certain high-priority crimes. Consider the following newspaper op-ed piece written by U.S. Senator Phil Gramm of Texas:

> The fact is that the vast majority of violent crimes in the United States are committed by a relatively small group of predators. University of Pennsylvania criminologist Marvin Wolfgang studied the Philadelphia arrest records of males [and found that 7 percent of all males] committed two-thirds of all violent crime. There is no reason to suppose the same situation doesn't exist in every American city. Combating violent crime is largely a matter of targeting and incarcerating these violent, dangerous, antisocial criminals.
>
> A promising start was made during the 1980s, when Congress enacted mandatory minimum sentences after discovering that defendants with serious criminal records often received very light sentences from judges, which were then further softened by parole boards. By establishing a floor beneath which federal judges could not descend in imposing sentences for certain crimes, such as drug trafficking near schools, and by eliminating the possibility of parole from federal prisons, Congress made sure that hardened criminals would be rendered harmless for substantial periods of time. . . .
>
> Many of the voices urging repeal or modification of mandatory minimum sentences . . . belong to judges who are not pleased that such provisions for the most part do not allow them to impose less stringent sentences on convicted drug traffickers. . . . It should never be forgotten that those who traffic in drugs, whether for the first time — one law enforcement official noted that first-time offender often means nothing more than "first-time caught offender"— or the hundredth time, are never "non-violent criminals." The violence drug-traffickers inflict on society is massive. . . .

Houston Chronicle, Nov. 2, 1993, at A15. Others arguing in favor of mandatory minimum statutes point out that such laws could deter crime by creating a clear and certain punishment that will occur after conviction for the crime. If a legislator supports mandatory minimum penalties on the basis of the *certainty* they might produce in sentencing outcomes, apart from any increase in *severity* they might produce, would she support a statute establishing a fixed sentence that serves as *both* a maximum and a minimum?

4. *Judicial discretion and mandatory penalties.* Many criticisms of mandatory minimum statutes focus on the loss of judicial discretion in sentencing. Consider, for example, the 1970 statement of then-Representative George Bush:

> Federal judges are almost unanimously opposed to mandatory minimums, because they remove a great deal of the court's discretion. In the vast majority of cases which

> reach the sanctioning stage today, the bare minimum sentence is levied — and in some cases, less than the minimum mandatory is given. . . . Probations and outright dismissals often result. Philosophical differences aside, practicality requires a sentence structure which is generally acceptable to the courts, to prosecutors, and to the general public.

116 Cong. Rec. H33314, Sept. 23, 1970. These criticisms and others have led some state and federal judges to believe that mandatory minimum statutes too often force them to impose a fundamentally unjust sentence. A 1993 survey of judicial opinion found that 90 percent of federal judges and 75 percent of state judges believe that mandatory minimum sentences for drug cases were "a bad idea." More than half of the federal judges believed that mandatory minimums were "too harsh" on first-time offenders. A.B.A. J., October 1993, at 78. Are all mandatory minimums subject to the criticisms about uneven enforcement and loss of judicial discretion? Could a legislature address these problems by using only narrow definitions of offenses and offenders eligible for a mandatory sentence?

Can any decisionmaker other than a judge — who decides many individual cases — appreciate the facts about an offender's past that should lead to a lighter sentence? Why do judges sentence below what the legislature might choose as a minimum sentence? Do judges generally share a different political view on crime control? Do they see too many individual cases?

5. *Mandatory mandatories.* Most mandatory minimum statutes instruct the judge to impose a particular sentence for a particular charge, but they do not require the prosecutor to file a given charge when adequate facts are present. Thus, typical mandatory sentencing statutes give prosecutors considerable bargaining power during plea negotiations; they also offer prosecutors opportunities to avoid mandatory minimum sentences when they believe that such sentences would be unjust or a poor use of resources. Legislatures sometimes constrain this prosecutorial power by passing statutes that require the prosecutor to file charges and that prevent plea bargaining. For instance, in 1973 New York passed a "Rockefeller drug law" imposing severe mandatory minimums and restricting plea bargaining. After passage of this law, there were fewer arrests, indictments, and convictions for drug offenses, but those convicted served longer terms. Jacqueline Cohen and Michael Tonry, Sentencing Reforms and the Impacts, in Research on Sentencing: The Search for Reform 348-349 (Alfred Blumstein et al. eds., 1983). This sort of "mandatory mandatory" statute is rare. Why do legislators hesitate to pass statutes that remove the prosecutor's discretion to decline charges or to select a charge not subject to the minimum penalty?

6. *Self-correcting democratic process.* If mandatory minimum sentences truly produce the ill effects described by critics, won't the democratically elected legislature recognize these flaws after a time and abandon the experiment? There are a few examples of this happening. In Connecticut in 2001, the legislature granted judges authority to depart from mandatory minimum sentences for certain drug crimes, such as first-time sales or possession within 1500 feet of a school. A 2001 Indiana law eliminated mandatory 20-year sentences for cocaine dealers (anyone caught with more than 3 grams of cocaine), and Louisiana repealed mandatory sentences for some simple possession and other nonviolent drug offenses. On the other hand, other jurisdictions, such as New York, have debated for years about changing mandatory minimum drug sentences, without ever taking action. See Ronald F. Wright, Are the Drug Wars De-Escalating? Where to Look for Evidence, 14 Fed. Sentencing Reporter 141 (2002). What might prevent the legislature from rethink-

ing self-destructive legislation? Is it a lack of information, a lack of time, or something else?

Problem 19-1. Sentence of Constitutional Proportions

Angela Thompson grew up in a variety of places, living with several different family members and friends. Her uncle, Norman Little, ran a major drug-selling operation in Harlem, and at some point he employed her in his illegal enterprise. Thompson was 17 years old at the time. One summer afternoon, an undercover police officer bought 200 vials of cocaine from her for $2000, on the street outside Little's residence. The officer claimed that it was customary in a sale of this size for him to receive a bonus of 20 additional vials. Thompson, however, gave him only 14 extra vials and promised to "take care" of him personally the next time he made a purchase.

On that same day, officers also made five separate purchases from Little, and one purchase from another of Little's employees, a young woman known as "Shorty." Uniformed officers later arrested Thompson and Little. They decided, however, not to arrest Shorty, because they were afraid that an arrest would reveal the identity of an undercover officer.

Thompson was indicted for the sale of two ounces, 33 grains of cocaine, a class A-I felony that carries a mandatory indeterminate prison sentence. Under the statute, the judge must impose a minimum prison term between 15 and 25 years, and a maximum term of life. If Thompson had not awarded the "bonus" vials to the undercover officer, the government could have charged her only with an A-II sale, whose mandatory minimum sentence is three years.

Little was indicted for five criminal sales of a controlled substance in the first degree. He pleaded guilty to one such sale, in exchange for dismissal of the remaining four counts and a sentence of 15 years to life imprisonment. The prosecutor offered Thompson a plea bargain carrying a sentence of three years to life, but she rejected the offer and went to trial. The jury convicted her of the A-I felony. Thompson had no prior criminal convictions, and no prior arrests. Norman Little had three prior felony and seven prior misdemeanor convictions.

As defense counsel, how would you convince the sentencing judge that a minimum sentence of 15 years for Angela Thompson is cruel and unusual punishment, under either the federal or state constitutions? Compare People v. Thompson, 633 N.E.2d 1074 (N.Y. 1994).

3. Sentencing Commissions

While the legislature always sets the upper and lower boundaries on the permissible punishments for a crime, those boundaries can still leave open many choices about the sentence in particular cases. Rather than leaving the remaining sentencing choices to the discretion of judges and parole authorities, some state legislatures have empowered permanent "sentencing commissions" to create additional rules to guide judges as they select sentences within the statutory range. These guidelines (some embodied in statutes and others in administrative rules) are different from statutory maximum and minimum punishments because they allow judges, under some circumstances, to go above or below the recommended range so long as the final sentence remains within the statutorily authorized range. Sentencing guidelines can be binding or merely advisory for the sentencing judge depending on the judge's statutory authority to "depart" from the guidelines without risking reversal on appeal.

What are the effects of creating a sentencing commission and asking it to formulate sentencing rules more specific than the outer bounds of the statutory maximum and minimum sentence? Will sentencing commissions produce rules that look systematically different from the sentencing rules a legislature would adopt on its own? Will those sentencing guidelines produce a different pattern of sentences in individual cases than judges would impose, if left to their own devices? Whatever other effects a sentencing commission may have, it is certainly true that commissions (and the guidelines they create) give sentencing courts a more refined vocabulary for discussing sentencing choices and make more explicit the types of considerations that matter to a sentencing court. Indeed, without sentencing guidelines and the judicial decisions applying them, it would be difficult to study sentencing at all as a topic in a criminal procedure course.

Sentencing commissions have created sentencing rules in almost half of the states. The materials below introduce the basic structure and functions of such commissions, with particular attention paid to the sentencing commission in Minnesota, one of the earliest and most influential of these bodies.

■ ABA STANDARDS FOR CRIMINAL JUSTICE SENTENCING STANDARD 18-1.3(a)

(3d ed. 1994)

The legislature should create or empower a governmental agency to transform legislative policy choices into more particularized sentencing provisions that guide sentencing courts. The agency should also be charged with responsibility to collect, evaluate and disseminate information regarding sentences imposed and carried out within the jurisdiction.

■ STRUCTURING CRIMINAL SENTENCING DALE PARENT

2-5, 28, 51-53, 57-60 (1988)

For centuries, legislative control over the sentencing process fluctuated between two statutory models of how to formulate punishments for crimes. One model prescribed mandatory penalties, such as capital punishment in nineteenth century England for every theft of fifty shillings or more, or a minimum of two years in prison in twentieth century Michigan for anyone convicted of possessing a gun. The second model prescribed discretionary penalty ranges. [A] person convicted of robbery, for example, could receive probation in the community, or as much as 25 years in prison, or any sanction in between depending on how the facts of the case were assessed in the discretion of the individual judge.

Under the mandatory model, legislatures ousted judges from control over sentencing by stipulating sentences in advance. Every sentencing was required to impose either a stated penalty, or a mandatory minimum sentence, on every offender convicted of the crime, without regard to mitigating circumstances. The judge was permitted no discretion for downward adjustments to reflect either the offender's reduced culpability for the past crime, or his high promise to avoid crime in the future.

The discretionary model exemplified an entirely different approach to the setting of punishment. Under this model, the legislature deferred to the sentencing court's closer opportunity to learn the facts of each crime, to see each offender in person, and to fashion a sentence to fit the particular case. This model left it to the judgment of a single judge to determine how high, or how low, to set the penalty within the authorized sentencing range. The experience or inexperience of the judge, his or her subjective appraisal of the crime's seriousness and the offender's blameworthiness, the decisionmaker's prediction or hunch regarding the offender's likely future conduct — these and similar factors could all influence the discretion to set a severe, moderate, or lenient sentence. . . .

The advantages of each model reflected the disadvantages of the other. By removing all discretion from judges, mandatory sentences sometimes produced punishment that was too severe and disproportionate to the crime. Discretionary sentencing, on the other hand, conferred unguided discretion on judges and inevitably produced unjustifiable discrepancies — unduly lenient sentences for some, undue harshness for others. Whereas mandatory sentences reflected legislative arbitrariness and coerced uniformity, discretionary sentencing power allowed anarchy among judges and produced both arbitrariness and unwarranted disparity.

In at least three major respects, Minnesota's venture altered traditional institutions and concepts in the realm of criminal sentencing:

- It substituted a new system — guided discretion — for the more extreme methods of dividing authority over the punishment process between legislatures and courts.
- It inserted a new governmental entity — the sentencing commission — between the legislature and the judiciary, and authorized the commission to monitor and continuously adjust criminal sentences.
- And it established an unprecedented conceptual connection — known as capacity constraint — between the degree of severity with which guidelines could specify prison sentences and the extent to which state prison resources were available to carry such sentences into effect. . . .

The former system of indeterminate prison sentences set by a judge, subject to the possibility of early release in the discretion of a parole board, was abolished. In its place came a system of determinate sentences, set by the judge under guidance from the sentencing commission, with review by an appellate court. Five key elements were incorporated into this plan:

- First, sentences would be scaled to take account of differences both in the gravity of crimes and the prior records of offenders. Guidance would be specified in the form of sentencing ranges, rather than precise sentences.
- Second, factors relevant to the individualization process would be standardized and weighted in advance. Clear rules would encourage similar outcomes in similar cases. Proportionality among different cases would be facilitated by a carefully constructed hierarchy of offense seriousness.

- Third, a set of departure principles would define the circumstances under which judges could deviate from the guideline sentencing range with good reasons. Judges would thus retain discretion to set the actual sentence, to do justice on a case-by-case basis.
- Fourth, sentencing judges would be required to state reasons for each sentence that differed from the applicable guideline, to assure accountability and reviewability.
- Fifth, all sentences would be subject to review by an appellate court whose written opinions could, over time, evolve finely tuned principles to guide future sentencers. . . .

The [1988 Minnesota] law created a nine-member Sentencing Guidelines Commission, consisting of the chief justice or his designee, two district court judges appointed by the chief justice, the Commission of Corrections, the chairman of the Minnesota Corrections Board, and four gubernatorial appointees — a prosecutor, a public defender, and two citizens. Commission members would serve four-year terms and be eligible for reappointment. The Commission was authorized to hire a director and other staff. . . .

The guidelines . . . were to recommend when state imprisonment was appropriate and to recommend presumptive sentencing durations. The Commission could set ranges of permissible deviation about the fixed sentence of plus or minus 15 percent, which would not constitute departures. The guidelines were to be based on reasonable combinations of offender and offense characteristics. . . . Judges had to give written reasons for sentences that departed from the guidelines recommendation. The state or the defense could appeal any sentence. On appeal, the Supreme Court was to determine if the sentence was illegal, inappropriate, unjustifiably disparate, or not supported by findings of fact. . . .

The Commission sought to assure that guideline punishments would be proportional to the seriousness of offenders' crimes. To achieve that proportionality, it was necessary for the Commission to rank crimes in the order of their seriousness. The seriousness of a crime varies according to the gravity of the offense and the blameworthiness of the offender. Gravity is determined by the harm caused, directly or as a consequence, by the crime. Blameworthiness is determined by the offender's motivation, intent, and behavior in the crime and is enhanced if the offender previously has been convicted of and sentenced for criminal acts. . . .

In devising an offense seriousness ranking, the Commission had to make . . . relatively broad decisions about elements of behavior and intent as they relate to offense seriousness. For example, most would agree that crimes that involve or threaten physical injury generally are more serious than those that involve the loss of property. Case-level judgments involve finer distinctions and are used to distinguish among offenders convicted of similar crimes who have similar prior records.

Although most of us have an intuitive sense of offense seriousness, the concept is highly complex. Most criminal events consist of an offender and a victim linked by an act defined by law as a crime. Thus, judgments about the seriousness of criminal events may involve facts about offenders, victims, and criminal acts.

Some factors can be dismissed because all would agree they are irrelevant to assessing gravity or ascribing blame — for example, that the victim was a Mason or the offender was a Methodist. Some facts are both irrelevant and invidious — such as that the offender and the victim were of the same or different races. But there is a long list of factors that some would consider relevant to assessing harm or ascribing blame.

Most Frequent Offenses in Seriousness Scale

Seriousness Level	*Most Frequent Offenses*
1.	Aggravated forgery, less than $100
	Possession of marijuana (more than 1.5 ounces)
	Unauthorized use of a motor vehicle
2.	Aggravated forgery, $150 to $2,500
	Sale of marijuana . . .
3.	Aggravated forgery, over $2,500
	Arson, third-degree . . .
	Theft crimes, $150 to $2,500
	Sale of cocaine
	Possession of LSD, PCP
4.	Burglary, nondwellings and unoccupied dwellings
	Theft crimes, over $2,500
	Receiving stolen goods, $150 to $2,500
	Criminal sexual conduct, fourth-degree
	Assault, third-degree (injury)
5.	Criminal negligence (resulting in death)
	Criminal sexual conduct, third-degree
	Manslaughter, second-degree . . .
	Witness tampering
	Simple (unarmed) robbery . . .
6.	Assault, second-degree (weapon)
	Burglary (occupied dwelling) . . .
	Criminal sexual conduct, fourth-degree . . .
	Kidnapping (released in a safe place)
	Sale, LSD or PCP
	Sale, heroin and remaining hard narcotics
	Receiving stolen goods, over $2,500
7.	Aggravated (armed) robbery
	Arson, first-degree
	Burglary (victim injured)
	Criminal sexual conduct, second-degree
	Criminal sexual conduct, third-degree
	Kidnapping (not released in a safe place)
	Manslaughter, first-degree
	Manslaughter, second-degree
8.	Assault, first-degree (great bodily harm)
	Kidnapping (great bodily harm)
	Criminal sexual conduct, first-degree
	Manslaughter, first-degree
9.	Murder, third-degree
10.	Murder, second-degree

The victim may be a normal healthy adult or a person who may be especially vulnerable due to age or infirmity. In violent crimes the extent of physical injury may vary from a scratch to death. Some victims may recover fully from physical injuries, while others suffer permanent damage or impairment. In property crimes, the victim's loss could range from a small amount to a fortune. The consequences of property loss may vary greatly with the economic status of the victim. The crime may involve one victim or many. A crime might involve an offender acting alone or in concert with others. The offender might have been immature or mentally impaired and easily induced to participate in a crime. He or she might have been the ringleader who induced others. . . .

The list of factors relevant, or arguably relevant, to assessing offense seriousness is large, and the above variations are a mere sample. Their potential combinations are virtually infinite. Given events as complex and diverse as criminal acts, how was the Commission to go about judging their seriousness?

In the initial unsatisfactory effort [to rank offenses,] each member received a randomly arranged deck of sixty offense cards. Each card listed one offense [and] its statutory maximum sentence. . . . Each member arranged his or her deck in decreasing order of seriousness. [For] the most serious person offenses — homicides — the members' individual ranks clustered together, reflecting a high level of consensus. For less serious person offenses — robberies, sexual assaults, and so forth — consensus declined.

[The] Commission expressed concern about the initial ranking exercise [because it] had overloaded members with information. [The Commission created a subcommittee to divide the task into more manageable components. The subcommittee grouped] crimes into 6 categories — violent, arson, sex, drug, property, and miscellaneous — 5 of which contained 20 or fewer crimes. . . .

The subcommittee instructed the Commission to focus on the usual or typical case in [a] ranking exercise. . . . In phase one individual Commission members ranked crimes within each of the six categories. . . . Phases two, three, and four relied on identification of differences among members, on the articulation of reasons for those differences, and on debate about those reasons. . . . When differences existed it assured that the basis of the differences would be discovered and scrutinized and that the final rankings would reflect a majority opinion.

[T]he Commission divided the overall ranking into ten seriousness levels. . . . [The table on p. 1270 (Table 4.1 in the original text)] shows the most common types of offenses within each of the ten seriousness levels.

■ SENTENCING GUIDELINES AND THEIR EFFECTS
MICHAEL TONRY
17-20 (1987)

The "sentencing commission model" incorporates three main elements — the sentencing commission, presumptive sentencing guidelines, and appellate sentencing review. . . . The *sentencing commission* was indispensable because it possessed the institutional capacity to develop sentencing standards of greater subtlety and specificity than a legislature could. *Presumptive sentencing guidelines* provided a mechanism for expressing sentencing standards in a form that has more legal authority than voluntary guidelines, is less rigid than mandatory sentencing laws, and is much more specific than the maximum and minimum sentences specified by criminal-law statutes. *Appellate sentence review* provided a mechanism for assuring that trial judges either imposed sentences that were consistent with the applicable guidelines or had adequate and acceptable reasons for imposing sentences that were different. The attraction of the sentencing commission model is its merger of the three elements. . . .

When the sentencing commission model was first proposed by Marvin Frankel in 1972, his basic argument was that sentencing was "lawless": no substantive criteria existed to guide either the trial judge's sentence or the appellate judge's review of that sentence. Judge Frankel observed that legislatures are unlikely to be very good at developing detailed sentencing standards. Instead he urged creation of a special-purpose administrative agency that had the institutional capacity, and might develop the institutional competence, to establish substantive sentencing rules.

Minnesota . . . became the first jurisdiction to establish a sentencing commission. . . . The Minnesota commission made a number of bold policy decisions. First, it decided to be "prescriptive" and to establish its own explicit sentencing priorities [rather than] to be "descriptive," to attempt to replicate existing sentencing patterns. Second, the commission decided to de-emphasize imprisonment as a punishment for property offenders and to emphasize imprisonment for violent offenders; this was a major sentencing policy decision, because research on past Minnesota sentencing patterns showed that repeat property offenders tended to go to prison and that first-time violent offenders tended not to. Third, in order to attack sentencing disparities, the commission established narrow sentencing ranges (for example, 30 to 34 months, or 50 to 58 months) and to authorize departures from guideline ranges only when "substantial and compelling" reasons were present. Fourth, the commission elected to adopt "just deserts" as the governing premise of its policies concerning who receives prison sentences. Fifth, the commission chose to interpret an ambiguous statutory injunction that it take correctional resources into "substantial consideration" as a mandate that its guidelines not increase prison populations beyond existing capacity constraints. This meant the commission had to make deliberate trade-offs in imprisonment policies. If the commission decided to increase the lengths of prison terms for one group of offenders, it had also either to decrease prison terms for another group or to shift the in/out line and divert some group of prisoners from prison altogether. Sixth, the commission forbade consideration at sentencing of many personal factors — such as education, employment, marital status, living arrangements — that many judges believed to be legitimate. This decision resulted from a policy that sentencing decisions not be based on factors that might directly or indirectly discriminate against minorities, women, or low-income groups. . . .

Minnesota's guidelines initially proved more successful than even the commission anticipated. Rates of compliance with the guidelines were high. More violent offenders and fewer property offenders went to prison. Disparities in prison sentences diminished. Prison populations remained under control.

Later there was backsliding; as time passed, sentencing patterns came to resemble those that existed before the guidelines were implemented. Few would deny, however, that the Minnesota guideline system has been an impressive effort with important long-term consequences.

Notes

1. *Sentencing commissions and guidelines: majority position.* Almost half the states use sentencing guidelines created by sentencing commissions. The federal system also operates under sentencing guidelines, created in 1987 by the U.S. Sentencing Commission. A state sentencing commission typically drafts the initial set of guidelines

on behalf of the legislature, which then enacts it as an integrated package of sentencing reforms. In other states, the state judiciary adopts a package of guidelines as procedural rules or as informal guidance to judges. Some guidelines are truly "voluntary": There is no practical consequence for a judge who decides to sentence outside the range recommended in the guidelines, so long as the judge remains within the statutory maximum and minimum for the crime. Other guidelines, to some degree or another, are "presumptive." That is, a judge who sentences outside the presumed range for sentences encounters more risk of reversal. Perhaps a reviewing court will reverse the sentence if the sentencing judge did not write an explanation for the unusual sentence; in other states, a sentence could be reversed if the judge's reason does not satisfy some legal standard (in Minnesota, a "substantial and compelling" reason is necessary). Why would a legislature ask a commission to create a set of sentencing guidelines? Does a commission have any advantages over a legislature in setting specific sentencing ranges for particular types of offenses and offenders? Does it have any advantages over a sentencing court with complete discretion to sentence offenders within statutory boundaries?

2. *Amending the rules.* The states that have adopted sentencing guidelines have recognized a need to amend the guidelines over time, and they typically give the leading role in the amendment process to a permanent sentencing commission. However, the extent of the commission's power to amend the guidelines varies. In the largest group of states, the commission only recommends changes to the guidelines, and the legislature (and sometimes the state supreme court) must approve the changes before they become law. Elsewhere, amendments to the guidelines take effect at the end of the commission's administrative rulemaking process or after a waiting period that allows the legislature a chance to pass a statute disapproving of the changes. Do these procedural variations make any difference in the content of sentencing guidelines?

3. *Departures from the rules.* Most guidelines allow the judge to depart from the narrow sentence range designated in the guidelines. The departure could affect either the "disposition" of the sentence (active prison term or nonprison sanctions) or the "duration" of the sentence (the number of months to serve). The departure statutes generally require the judge to explain any departure, and an inadequate explanation can lead to reversal on appeal. Appellate courts in these jurisdictions have developed an extensive case law approving or disapproving of various grounds for departure. However, in theory the sentencing court still retains substantial discretion in deciding whether to depart from the guidelines. See Koon v. United States, 518 U.S. 81 (1996).

In virtually all the guideline systems, the number of departures have remained well below the number of cases sentenced within the guidelines. For instance, in Minnesota "dispositional" departures have occurred in around 10 percent of the total cases sentenced, while "durational" departures have occurred in about 25 percent of the cases involving an active prison term. See Richard Frase, Implementing Commission-Based Sentencing Guidelines: The Lessons of the First Ten Years in Minnesota, 2 Cornell J.L. & Pub. Poly. 279 (1993). By what criteria could a sentencing commission decide how many departures are "too many"?

4. *Appellate courts as the source of sentencing guidelines.* Most sentencing statutes provide only the most general guidance to the sentencing court and do not provide for appellate review of any sentence imposed within the broad statutory limits. Indeed, statutes in about half of the states limit appellate courts to the simple task of

determining whether the sentence of the trial court fell within the statutory minimum and maximum for the charged crimes. A second, large group of states create a more searching appellate review of sentences, in which the appellate court confirms both the legality and the "reasonableness" or "proportionality" of the sentence. Minn. Stat. §244.11. Given that judges see so many individual cases and develop such expertise in sentencing, shouldn't judges develop sentencing rules rather than just apply rules that others create? Statutes establishing sentencing commissions often reserve some commission posts for judges. Are there other ways to involve judges in the creation of general sentencing rules? For two thoughtful proposals to increase the role of federal judges in the creation of federal sentencing rules, see Douglas A. Berman, A Common Law for this Age of Federal Sentencing: The Opportunity and Need for Judicial Lawmaking, 11 Stan. L. & Pol'y Rev. 93 (1999); Joseph W. Luby, Reining in the "Junior Varsity Congress": A Call for Meaningful Judicial Review of the Federal Sentencing Guidelines, 77 Wash. U. L.Q. 1199 (1999).

The law in Great Britain enables the appellate courts themselves to develop more specific guidelines for sentencing, announced in decisions of particular cases. Appellate courts in Great Britain have become one of the main institutions for developing sentencing policy. See R. v. Aramah, 76 Crim. App. Rep. 190 (1982) (conviction for importation of herbal cannabis; court establishes benchmark sentences for importation of various drugs in different amounts); Andrew Ashworth, Three Techniques for Reducing Sentencing Disparity, *in* Principled Sentencing (Andrew von Hirsch and Andrew Ashworth eds., 1992). What sorts of reasons might be a proper or persuasive reason for an appellate court to change its own sentencing guidelines? R. v. Bilinski, 86 Crim. App. Rep. 146 (1987) (amending the *Aramah* guidelines to reflect new increased statutory maximum sentences). See also State v. Wentz, 805 P.2d 962 (Alaska 1991) (limiting use of judicially created "benchmark" sentence for assault).

5. *Research instead of rules.* Are presumptive sentencing rules, created by commissions and approved by legislatures, subject to the same criticisms leveled against legislatively determined sentences? Would sentencing commissions be more valuable if they limited their recommendations to the most commonly encountered "paradigm" cases for sentencing and conducted research into the effects of various types of sanctions? Is lack of knowledge a more pressing concern than lack of uniformity among sentencing judges? See Albert Alschuler, The Failure of Sentencing Guidelines: A Plea for Less Aggregation, 58 U. Chi. L. Rev. 901 (1991).

6. *Parole and parole guidelines.* Wherever judges or juries exercise great discretion in selecting criminal sentences, states have found it necessary to give parole or corrections authorities the power to review those decisions at some later date. This later review imposes a centralized perspective on the decisions of judges or juries from all over the state, and it coordinates the sentences with the amount of correctional resources actually available. In that way, a parole board performs some of the same functions as a sentencing commission. However, parole boards decide on the actual time an offender will serve *after* the judge has already announced a sentence. Some parole boards decide cases according to formal parole guidelines, while others make more ad hoc decisions, depending on prison capacity and other factors. What are the advantages and disadvantages of selecting the release date later in the process through a parole board rather than through a judge applying up-front sentencing rules?

Prison officials also have some influence over the amount of a prison sentence served. In most states, prison officials have the power to reduce the sentence by up to one-third or one-half of the maximum sentence set by the judge or the parole authority. Prison authorities use this discretion to reward good behavior by inmates: The reductions are known as "good time." Jim Jacobs has pointed out the anomaly of placing legal controls on other sentencing decisions, while leaving good time decisions unregulated. Jacobs, Sentencing by Prison Personnel: Good Time, 30 UCLA L. Rev. 217 (1982). Which institutions would be best suited to create legal constraints on good time decisions?

B. REVISITING INVESTIGATIONS AND CHARGES

All sentencing systems must address a few foundational issues. In an indeterminate sentencing system, each sentencing judge addresses these core issues implicitly in individual cases. Sentencing guidelines and other forms of structured sentencing have brought these issues into the open for debate and have given names to practices that have long gone unnoticed or unexamined.

One important facet of the sentencing process is that it involves a reconsideration of earlier decisions, from investigation to adjudication. Sentencing courts never explicitly reverse earlier decisions in the same case, but a sentencing court might allow a close or difficult question decided one way at an earlier stage (for or against the defendant) to influence the sentence. This section evaluates the extent to which courts should reconsider investigative and charging decisions in determining a proper sentence.

1. Revisiting Investigations

Should offenders be punished based on their own choices and behavior or based on choices and behavior by government agents? If some of the defendant's bad acts or statements during investigations are excluded from consideration at a suppression hearing — say because of a *Miranda* violation — should the sentencing judge consider that information after conviction? If some of the government's bad acts during investigations (for example, when government agents propose multiple drug transactions simply to increase the total amount of drugs at issue) do not affect the guilty verdict, should that information nevertheless affect the sentence?

When government agents behave in an outrageous fashion or encourage a person who would not otherwise have committed a crime to do so, the defendant may have a complete defense to the charges, based on entrapment or a due process "outrageous misconduct" claim. See Chapter 10. But entrapment defenses rarely succeed, even when the government agents can control the severity of the defendant's crimes. Entrapment, like other complete defenses, is an all-or-nothing doctrine, allowing no subtlety or gradation in the analysis of government behavior or its effect. Sentencing, defendants claim, is a proper time to make more carefully graded judgments about both the relative culpability of the offender (compared to offenders not subject to government encouragement) and harms more properly attributed to government actions. Claims of "sentencing entrapment" or "sentencing manipulation" often arise in drug cases where the amount of drugs in a transaction can have a major impact on the likely sentence.

■ STATE v. ANTHONY SOTO

562 N.W.2d 299 (Minn. 1997)

TOMLJANOVICH, J.

In February 1993, Soto first met an informant and a police officer who were both working undercover at the time. The informant asked Soto about drugs, but Soto replied that he was not involved in the sale of drugs at that time. After this initial conversation, the informant called Soto approximately three times to discuss a purchase of cocaine. Soto testified that although he was not involved in the sale of drugs at the time, he agreed to try to locate some cocaine for the informant because Soto was in bad financial shape.

Soto subsequently agreed to meet the informant and the undercover police officer in a parking lot on February 8, 1993, at which time the officer informed Soto that he had $1,300 for an ounce of cocaine. Soto left the area for five minutes and returned with a bag containing 27 grams of cocaine, which he exchanged with the officer for the money. At that meeting, the officer asked Soto if he could buy 2 or 3 more ounces of cocaine from him at a later time. Soto responded that it would be no problem.

On February 11, 1993, Soto again met with the informant and the undercover police officer in the same parking lot to sell 2 ounces of cocaine for $2,600. Upon meeting, Soto left the area and went into a nearby restaurant. He returned minutes later with 51 grams of cocaine, which he exchanged for the money. Once again, the officer asked Soto at this meeting if he could buy a larger amount later, and Soto again replied that it was no problem.

On February 18, 1993, Soto agreed to meet the informant and undercover police officer at a bar where they waited for the drugs to arrive. At that time, the officer went into the bar to meet Soto and asked to buy an even larger amount of cocaine from Soto in the near future at a reduced price. Soto replied that he knew someone who was bringing cocaine from Mexico which would sell for $1,000 an ounce. When Soto was informed by a woman that the drugs had arrived, he asked the officer to leave and wait in his car. Soto then went out to the car and gave the officer 27 grams of cocaine in exchange for $1,300.

After the February 18 sale, Soto testified that the informant and the undercover police officer called him at least three times a week to arrange a larger sale of cocaine. On March 11, 1993, the officer met Soto and asked to buy 8 ounces of cocaine. The officer agreed to buy 10 ounces for $1,150 per ounce and they arranged a time to meet later in the day. When the officer arrived at a shopping center to meet with Soto, he was wired with a body microphone and had several officers in the area monitoring him. Soto arrived and gave the officer 279 grams of cocaine in exchange for $11,500. After the exchange was completed, Soto was arrested by the backup officers.

Soto was charged with one count of sale of cocaine in the first degree and the state agreed not to charge him with three additional counts if he would testify against two other accomplices. However, Soto declined the offer and the state amended their complaint by adding the three additional counts for sale of cocaine in the first degree. At trial, Soto asserted the defense of entrapment, but was nevertheless found guilty by the jury of four counts of sale of cocaine in the first degree.

[The sentencing judge] sentenced Soto to the presumptive guidelines sentence for each count, . . . 98 months for Count I, based on a level VIII offense and a criminal history score of 1.5 points. The trial judge then assigned two additional criminal history points for Counts II, III, and IV, resulting in concurrent and presumptive sentences of 122 months, 146 months, and 161 months respectively.

[Soto argues that this court should not use the fact that the government charged multiple counts of drug violations as a reason to enhance the guideline sentence for some of the counts. Such a sentencing rule] would permit police officers and prosecutors to manipulate investigative or charging procedures so as to achieve a specific sentence. For instance, Soto argues that police officers could manipulate the amount of drugs or the number of sales involved, while prosecutors could separate the drug sales into multiple charges in order to ensure that a higher sentence would be imposed. Soto further argues that permitting police officers and prosecutors to have such discretion creates the potential for racially biased decision-making and perpetuates racial disparities in the prosecution of drug crimes. While application of the [traditional charging and sentencing enhancement rules for] undercover drug operations may very well result in such consequences, we have repeatedly recognized that arguments concerning disparities in sentencing are more appropriately addressed to the Sentencing Guidelines Commission. . . .

Soto urges this court to adopt the doctrines of sentencing entrapment and sentencing manipulation to support a downward departure from his presumptive sentence. Soto argues that both doctrines are necessary because . . . the sentencing of multiple sales of controlled substances to undercover police officers allows those officers to manipulate the Sentencing Guidelines by orchestrating the amount of drugs and the number of sales.

Sentencing entrapment occurs when "outrageous official conduct . . . overcomes the will of an individual predisposed only to dealing in small quantities, for the purpose of increasing the amount of drugs . . . and the resulting sentence of the entrapped defendant." United States v. Barth, 990 F.2d 422 (8th Cir. 1993). The Eighth Circuit has recognized that the doctrine of sentencing entrapment may be relied upon to depart from the Federal Sentencing Guidelines. The doctrine of sentencing manipulation is a more recent development. . . . Sentencing manipulation is outrageous government conduct aimed only at increasing a person's sentence. Whereas sentencing entrapment focuses on the predisposition of the defendant, the related concept of sentencing manipulation is concerned with the conduct and motives of government officials.

We are concerned with the disparities which result between similarly situated defendants because of varying law enforcement investigative methods or because of differing charging practices. However, we decline to adopt either doctrine in the absence of egregious police conduct which goes beyond legitimate investigative purposes. Even if we were to adopt either doctrine, the trial record of Soto's case does not support a downward departure based on either doctrine. Under the doctrine of sentencing entrapment, Soto would bear the burden of showing that he was predisposed only to sell smaller amounts of cocaine and that he had neither the intent nor the resources for selling the larger amount he was entrapped into selling. Although the record shows that Soto was asked to sell an increased amount of cocaine in his last sale to the undercover police officer, the record lacks any evidence that Soto was not predisposed to sell the larger amount. Soto argues that the state failed to produce evidence that he had ever been involved in the sale of cocaine prior to the sales at issue. However, it is the defendant who bears the burden of establishing sentencing entrapment, and not the state.

The record in Soto's case similarly lacks support for a finding of sentencing manipulation. Although recognizing the doctrine of sentencing manipulation, the Eighth Circuit has held that it is reasonable for the police to engage in a chain of transactions with a drug dealer in order to establish that person's guilt or to trace the dealer's supplier. Because Soto would bear the burden of establishing the presence of sentencing manipulation, his claim must fail because of the absence of any evidence showing that the drug sales were obtained for the sole purpose of increasing his sentence, rather than to establish his guilt or to trace his supplier. We therefore . . . decline to adopt the doctrines of sentencing entrapment and sentencing manipulation in the absence of egregious police conduct which goes beyond legitimate investigative purposes. Affirmed.

Problem 19-2. Learning a Lesson

Barbara Graham sold a small amount of cocaine to an undercover police officer. The officer selected the location for this sale, an apartment complex that happened to be approximately 650 feet from a private school. The transaction took place on a Friday night at 11:30 P.M. Graham had no prior drug arrests or convictions. A Florida statute requires a mandatory minimum term of three years' imprisonment for any offender who sells illicit drugs within 1,000 feet of a school. If you were the court, would you nevertheless sentence the defendant to less than three years? How would you explain such a decision? Would you reduce the sentence whenever the government provides the defendant with an opportunity to commit an act (such as selling a larger amount of drugs) that will enhance the punishment under sentencing statutes or guidelines? Compare Graham v. State, 608 So. 2d 123 (Fla. Dist. Ct. App. 1992).

Problem 19-3. Reversing the Exclusion

Juan Guzon Valera shot and killed his wife and another man after he discovered them engaging in sexual activity in a car. After inadequate *Miranda* warnings, Valera told a Hawaii County Police Officer about the events leading up to the killings, and where he had illegally obtained the gun. The statement indicated that Valera did not discover his wife's activities by chance, but followed her car to a parking lot expecting to witness her meeting with another man. The statement also showed that he chased the victims on foot a considerable distance away from their car before shooting them. The jury convicted him of manslaughter (but not second-degree murder) and firearms violations. Although the trial judge suppressed these statements during the jury trial, he relied on them during sentencing to enhance the sentence.

The sentencing judge refused to strike from the presentence investigation report several references to Valera's statement to the police. The judge stated: "I think if the jury had heard the evidence which had to be barred because of the way the police questioned Mr. Valera, a different result would have occurred. I think in sentencing, the Court can consider those items which had to be barred. I think in this case, Mr. Valera acted as an executioner. He stalked his victims and shot them one after the other." He sentenced Valera to serve two 10-year consecutive terms of imprisonment for manslaughter, and lesser concurrent terms of imprisonment for the firearms violations.

Valera argues on appeal that the sentencing judge violated his constitutional rights to due process and to counsel, and his privilege against self-incrimination as guaranteed by article I, sections 5, 14, and 10 of the Hawaii Constitution, by relying almost exclusively upon his suppressed statements in determining his sentence. How would you rule? Compare State v. Valera, 848 P.2d 376 (Haw. 1993).

Notes

1. *Sentence entrapment and manipulation: majority position.* Indeterminate sentencing statutes do not tell a judge whether to take corrective action if she believes that government agents have attempted to manipulate a sentence. Likewise, most structured sentencing systems have not addressed the issue of "sentencing entrapment" or "manipulation." A few courts have refused to recognize government behavior as a factor at sentencing. More courts, like the Minnesota Supreme Court in *Soto,* have recognized the possibility of taking account of the behavior of government agents but have not found facts which support a departure in a particular case. A few lower state courts in structured sentencing systems have altered sentences because of investigators' choices. For instance, in State v. Sanchez, 848 P.2d 208 (Wash. Ct. App. 1993), the government arranged a series of three drug transactions between the defendant and one confidential informant, and the trial court departed downward to a sentence greater than the norm for one buy but less than the norm for three independent buys.

> In this case, the difference between the first buy, viewed alone, and all three buys, viewed cumulatively, was trivial or trifling. All three buys were initiated and controlled by the police. All three involved the same buyer, the same seller, and no one else. All three occurred inside a residence within a 9-day span of time. All three involved small amounts of drugs. The second and third buys had no apparent purpose other than to increase Sanchez's presumptive sentence. We conclude, as the sentencing court apparently did, that the second and third buys added little or nothing to the first. Nothing in our holding necessarily applies to drug transactions that are not police-initiated controlled buys, or that involve different sellers or purchasers, or that involve large quantities of drugs, or that have a law enforcement purpose other than to generate an increase in the offender's standard range.

"Reverse buys"—in which the government agent sells to the target of the investigation and can choose the amount and price to offer—highlight claims about sentencing manipulation. The federal sentencing guidelines have a specific instruction for judges facing this situation: "If, in a reverse sting operation . . . , the court finds that the government agent set a price for the controlled substance that was substantially below the market value of the controlled substance, thereby leading to the defendant's purchase of a significantly greater quantity of the controlled substance than his available resources would have allowed him to purchase . . . , a downward departure may be warranted." U.S.S.G. §2D1.1 (Application Note 17). Is this policy an adequate response to potential government manipulation of the sentence?

2. *Developing rules for sentence manipulation.* How might structured sentencing systems take account of manipulative behavior by government agents? Perhaps

government agents could be required to arrest a suspect whenever they have enough proof to make conviction at trial likely. What if government agents wish to continue an undercover operation to obtain information about other suspects? For a year? Two hundred additional transactions? A court might require the government to state its reasons for continuing its investigation after obtaining enough evidence for a conviction. Would a detailed set of rules measuring the contribution of government choices to a defendant's presumptive sentence undermine confidence in the behavior of the government? In the idea of guilt?

3. *Inadequate self-defense and other "partial" substantive criminal law defenses.* Should courts develop refined or modified versions of substantive criminal law defenses other than entrapment, such as self-defense or duress? For instance, a defendant's self-defense argument may not result in an acquittal, but the court may nevertheless rely on the argument to reduce a sentence. Some state sentencing statutes explicitly recognize "partial" or "near-miss" defenses at sentencing: In Tennessee, the court may reduce a sentence if "substantial grounds exist tending to excuse or justify the defendant's criminal conduct, though failing to establish a defense." Tenn. Code §40-35-113(3); see also United States v. Whitetail, 956 F.2d 857 (8th Cir. 1992) (battered woman defense); United States v. Cheape, 889 F.2d 477 (3d Cir. 1989) (duress, defendant participated in robbery at gunpoint). Discussions of criminal law defenses often postpone until sentencing any effort to refine the determination of blameworthiness beyond what is necessary to conclude that a defendant is guilty or not guilty. Does the lack of a more refined set of "partial" defenses undermine the basic principles of liability? The purposes of punishment?

4. *Exclusionary rule at the sentencing hearing: majority position.* Most jurisdictions allow sentencing judges to consider evidence obtained in violation of a defendant's constitutional rights, even when that evidence is suppressed at trial. See Elson v. State, 659 P.2d 1195 (Alaska 1983) (evidence obtained illegally may be used at sentencing unless violation was for purpose of obtaining facts to enhance sentencing); Smith v. State, 517 A.2d 1081 (Md. 1986). The U.S. Supreme Court held in Estelle v. Smith, 451 U.S. 454 (1981), that a sentencing judge in a capital case could not consider a statement obtained in violation of the Fifth Amendment, but it has never addressed whether the exclusionary rule applies generally in sentencing proceedings. Some state statutes and cases allow the introduction of illegally obtained evidence in capital cases, at least within the boundaries of Estelle v. Smith. See, e.g., Utah Code §76-3-207(2) ("Any evidence the court deems to have probative force may be received regardless of its admissibility under the exclusionary rules of evidence"); Stewart v. State, 549 So. 2d 171 (Fla. 1989). Most lower federal courts have decided that the exclusionary rule does not apply at sentencing in noncapital proceedings, concluding that (1) exclusion would not deter police misconduct because the evidence is already excluded at trial, and (2) the sentencing court needs as much information as possible about the offense and offender to select a proper sanction. See, e.g., United States v. Torres, 926 F.2d 321 (3d Cir. 1991). A smaller group applies the exclusionary rule at sentencing. See Pens v. Bail, 902 F.2d 1464 (9th Cir. 1990). If the application of the exclusionary rule to sentencing depends on whether procedural rules at sentencing can truly influence law enforcement officers, do the "sentencing manipulation" cases throw any light on this question? Perhaps the acceptability of illegally obtained evidence should depend on the impact of admitting it in different systems. Where the sentencing judge has only to consult the statutory maximum and minimum sentences, and a list of other factors listed in the statute,

exclusion might have little measurable effect on sentences. Would the importance of an exclusionary rule be different in a more highly structured sentencing system, one that instructed the judge to attach a precise weight to specific facts?

2. *Revisiting Charging Decisions: Relevant Conduct*

It might seem obvious that defendants can be punished only for the crimes of which they have been convicted. Obvious, perhaps, but that is not the law in most jurisdictions. To varying degrees, sentencing laws allow defendants to be punished for the "real offense" and not just for the offense of conviction. When a judge considers a defendant's behavior beyond the facts necessary to prove the offense of conviction, the judge is said to be considering "relevant conduct."

How can defendants be punished for acts that are not the basis for a conviction? Under an unstructured sentencing system, the sentencing court can consider any evidence of the offender's wrongdoing, whether or not the conduct formed the basis of the criminal charges. The statutory floor and ceiling for punishing the crime of conviction leave the sentencing judge with plenty of latitude to set a punishment, even if it is based in part on uncharged conduct. It is difficult and perhaps impossible to define offenses with all of the detail necessary to capture facts that affect the assessment of culpability or harm. Even structured sentencing systems tend to allow a *range* of presumptive sentences, and when choosing a sentence within that range, a judge may account for circumstances that the bare bones elements of the crime cannot capture.

Judges receive information about conduct beyond the offense itself from several sources: during trial, from prosecutors, and in presentence investigation reports. Some of this information, although not strictly necessary to establish the elements of the crime of conviction, nonetheless relates directly to the charged offense. The "relevant conduct" might be an element of an offense other than the crime charged, either more or less serious. For instance, the defendant may have used a gun during the robbery, even though the charge was robbery and not armed robbery. Other facts about the offense, such as the defendant's role in a multiparty offense, may receive no mention in the statutory framework.

The extra information could relate to other uncharged offenses committed during the same time period as the charged crime or as part of the same overarching criminal scheme. A court may also consider all suspected criminal conduct in the past, whether or not it led to a conviction. If a prosecutor ignores some wrongdoing, the judge may nevertheless take it into account. Finally, the court might rely on past noncriminal conduct that is nevertheless blameworthy. The sentencing laws allowing the judge to consider uncharged conduct are sometimes called "real offense" systems (as opposed to "charge offense" systems) because the judge sentences based on the "real" criminal behavior, independent of the prosecutor's charging decisions.

Under indeterminate sentencing, it was possible for a judge to consider all of this information, though some judges would reject some or all of it as irrelevant. Structured sentencing has brought the issue of relevant conduct to a more formal and visible level. Legislatures, sentencing commissions, and judges must now decide explicitly which additional facts a sentencing judge may or may not consider and how much impact the uncharged "relevant conduct" should have.

■ U.S. SENTENCING GUIDELINES §1B1.3(a)

[The seriousness of the offense] shall be determined on the basis of the following:

(1) (A) all acts and omissions committed, aided, abetted, counseled, commanded, induced, procured, or willfully caused by the defendant; and

(B) in the case of a jointly undertaken criminal activity (a criminal plan . . . undertaken by the defendant in concert with others, whether or not charged as a conspiracy), all reasonably foreseeable acts and omissions of others in furtherance of the jointly undertaken criminal activity, that occurred during the commission of the offense of conviction, in preparation for that offense, or in the course of attempting to avoid detection or responsibility for that offense. . . .

(3) all harm that resulted from the acts and omissions specified in [subsection (a)(1)], and all harm that was the object of such acts and omissions. . . .

Illustration of Conduct for Which the Defendant Is Accountable . . .

Defendants F and G, working together, design and execute a scheme to sell fraudulent stocks by telephone. Defendant F fraudulently obtains $20,000. Defendant G fraudulently obtains $35,000. Each is convicted of mail fraud. Defendants F and G each are accountable for the amount he personally obtained under subsection (a)(1)(A). Each defendant is accountable for the amount obtained by his accomplice under subsection (a)(1)(B) because the conduct of each was in furtherance of the jointly undertaken criminal activity and was reasonably foreseeable in connection with that criminal activity.

■ FLORIDA RULE OF CRIMINAL PROCEDURE 3.701(d)(11)

Departures from the recommended or permitted guideline sentence should be avoided unless there are circumstances or factors that reasonably justify aggravating or mitigating the sentence. Any sentence outside the permitted guideline range must be accompanied by a written statement delineating the reasons for the departure. Reasons for deviating from the guidelines shall not include factors relating to prior arrests without conviction or the instant offenses for which convictions have not been obtained.

■ STATE v. DOUGLAS McALPIN

740 P.2d 824 (Wash. 1987)

Callow, J.

Douglas McAlpin received a sentence of 90 months following his plea of guilty to a charge of first degree robbery. [This sentence] exceeded the presumptive sentence range established under the Sentencing Reform Act of 1981 (SRA). The defendant appealed. . . .

Under the SRA the defendant's presumptive sentence range for first degree robbery was 46 to 61 months. This range, which is based on the seriousness of the crime committed and the offender's "criminal history," accounted for: (1) the defendant's two other current convictions for conspiracy and burglary; and (2) two prior juvenile convictions for second degree theft, both crimes being committed while the defendant was between 15 and 18 years of age and both convictions being entered on the same date.

At the defendant's sentencing hearing, it was revealed that his actual record of juvenile crime far exceeded that which was accounted for in determining the standard sentence range. The presentence report confirmed that the defendant had, in fact, amassed a juvenile record of "three files comprising hundreds of pages." The prosecutor supplemented this report with additional information obtained from juvenile court authorities.

The defendant's juvenile record included the following: (1) prior to reaching his 15th birthday he was convicted four times for second degree burglary, and once for taking a motor vehicle without permission (all felonies); (2) between the ages of 15 and 18, he had been found guilty of false reporting and third degree malicious mischief (both misdemeanors); (3) he had been committed to juvenile institutions on four occasions; and (4) he had had "various additional felony arrests which were handled informally."

The presentence report described the defendant as a "textbook sociopath" who had no remorse for his crimes, a long history of drug abuse as a youth, and two episodes in which he had tortured animals. While in the Kitsap County Corrections Center, sharpened toothbrushes were taken away from him. The report aptly characterized the defendant as an "exceedingly dangerous young man." The defendant's counsel did not object to the introduction of the above record at any time prior to the trial court's oral pronouncement of sentence. . . .

In addition to the juvenile record, it was disclosed that the defendant, in entering his guilty plea to the first degree robbery charge, had also signed a plea bargaining agreement. The prosecutor had agreed not to file charges regarding additional crimes to which the defendant had confessed, and for which he had agreed to make restitution.

The prosecutor recommended a sentence of 61 months, the top of the presumptive range. The trial court, however, imposed a 90-month exceptional sentence. The court cited the following reasons for imposing this sentence:

> That the defendant has an extensive criminal history, as set forth in the presentence report. . . . That such criminal history includes at least five felony convictions as a juvenile prior to the defendant's 15th birthday, four commitments to juvenile institutions and various additional felony arrests which were handled informally. That in the course of the police investigations of the instant offenses the defendant also confessed to his involvement in additional burglaries or criminal trespasses with which he was not charged but for which he agreed to make restitution. That such convictions were not computed as prior criminal history and thus the defendant is not being penalized twice for his behavior. . . .

[According to the statute governing appellate review of exceptional sentences,] we must independently determine, as a matter of law, whether the trial court's reasons justify an exceptional sentence. There must be "substantial and compelling" reasons for imposing such a sentence. RCW 9.94A.120(2). . . .

We turn first to the trial court's consideration of the defendant's lengthy record of juvenile felonies. Generally, "criminal history" may not be used to justify an exceptional sentence, because it is one of two factors (the other being the "seriousness level" of the current offense committed) which is used to compute the presumptive sentence range for a particular crime. A factor used in establishing the presumptive range may not be considered a second time as an "aggravating circumstance" to justify departure from the range.

The term "criminal history" as used in the SRA for purposes of the presumptive range calculation includes only certain types of juvenile crimes. Specifically, it is limited to juvenile felonies committed while the defendant was between 15 and 18 years of age. The trial court, recognizing this limitation, did not rely on the defendant's two prior juvenile convictions for second degree theft, both committed while he was between 15 and 18 years of age, as reasons to impose an exceptional sentence. These crimes had already been considered when computing the presumptive sentence range.

On the other hand, the trial court did cite the defendant's five prior pre-age-15 felony convictions as aggravating factors justifying an exceptional sentence. The defendant asserts that this constituted error; he argues that the Legislature, by excluding such crimes from the presumptive range calculation, intended to exclude consideration of them entirely. We disagree.

One of the overriding purposes of the sentencing reform act is to ensure that sentences are proportionate to the seriousness of the crime committed and the defendant's criminal history. This purpose would be frustrated if a court were required to blind itself to a significant portion of a defendant's juvenile criminal record. . . . The trial court here did not err in concluding that a defendant who has amassed an extensive and recent record of pre-age-15 felonies is significantly different from a defendant who has no record at all. . . .

The trial court cited the following two findings as additional aggravating factors:

> [1] That [the defendant's] criminal history includes . . . various additional [juvenile] felony arrests which were handled informally.
>
> [2] That in the course of the police investigations of the instant offenses the defendant also confessed to his involvement in additional burglaries or criminal trespasses with which he was not charged but for which he agreed to make restitution.

We agree with the defendant that the trial court improperly relied on the above findings. The sentencing reform act bars the court from considering unproven or uncharged crimes as a reason for imposing an exceptional sentence. RCW 9.94A.370, at the time of sentencing, provided inter alia: "Real facts that establish elements of a higher crime, a more serious crime, or additional crimes cannot be used to go outside the presumptive sentence range except upon stipulation." In David Boerner, Sentencing in Washington §9.16, at 9-49 to 9-50 (1985), the author states:

> The policy reasons behind this provision are obvious, and sound. To consider charges that have been dismissed pursuant to plea agreements will inevitably deny defendants the benefit of their bargains. If the state desires to have additional crimes considered in sentencing, it can insure their consideration by refusing to dismiss them and proving their existence. . . .

It is not sufficient that the defendant has a record of arrests which were "handled informally." Nor is it sufficient that the defendant confessed to additional uncharged "burglaries or criminal trespasses." Since these arrests and confessions have not resulted in convictions, they may not be considered at all.

We conclude that some of the trial court's reasons for imposing the exceptional sentence could not be considered as aggravating factors. However, the defendant's lengthy record of pre-age-15 felonies, standing alone, is a substantial and compelling reason and justification for imposing the exceptional sentence. The trial court did not err in deciding to impose a sentence outside the standard range. . . .

Notes

1. *Relevant conduct in state sentencing: majority position.* Sentencing judges in indeterminate sentencing systems have always had the power (but not an obligation) to consider any conduct of the defendant, whether charged or uncharged. This conduct might influence the judge's choice of a maximum or minimum sentence from within the broad statutory range. See People v. Lee, 218 N.W.2d 655 (Mich. 1974) (pending charges mentioned in PSI); Anderson v. People, 337 P.2d 10 (Colo. 1959) (conviction for forgery; evidence at sentencing of forgeries submitted to six additional victims); People v. Grabowski, 147 N.E.2d 49 (Ill. 1958) (indictments pending for other crimes in same series of events); see also Williams v. New York, 337 U.S. 961 (1949) (death sentence imposed by judge based on presentence report suggesting defendant had been involved in "30 other burglaries" in area of murder).

States with more structured sentencing systems place more restrictions on the use of the defendant's uncharged conduct. Formally, the structured state systems adopt "charge offense" rather than "real offense" sentencing. The charged offense determines a fairly small range of options available to the judge in the normal case. But "real" and "charge" offense concepts define the ends of a spectrum, and all systems allow varying degrees of real offense conduct to affect the sentencing determination. At a minimum, the uncharged conduct is available to influence the judge's selection of a sentence *within* the narrow range that the guidelines designate for typical cases. Some states go further, and allow judges to use uncharged conduct as a basis for a "departure" from the designated normal range of sentences. Other structured sentencing states (like Florida) prevent the judge from using uncharged conduct to depart from the guideline sentence. Commentary to the Minnesota sentencing guidelines states that "departures from the guidelines should not be permitted for elements of alleged offender behavior not within the definition of the offense of conviction." Minn. Stat. Ann. §244 cmt. II.D.103. The ABA Standards for Criminal Justice, Sentencing 18-3.6 (3d ed. 1994), opt for an offense-of-conviction model.

2. *Relevant conduct in federal sentencing.* In contrast to the states, the federal guidelines create a "modified real offense" system. In a 1995 self-study report, the federal sentencing commission described the tradeoffs at stake in framing a relevant conduct provision:

> If uncharged misconduct is considered, punishment is based on facts proven outside procedural protections constitutionally defined for proving criminal charges,

> introducing an argument of unfairness. . . . The scope of conduct considered at sentencing will also affect, at least to some extent, the complexity of a sentencing system. The scope can be as limited as the conduct defined by the elements of the offense or as broad as any wrongdoing ever committed by the defendant or the defendant's partners in crime. All things being equal, a large scope of considered conduct will require more fact-finding than a more limited scope. . . . Besides fairness and complexity, the scope of conduct considered at sentencing may have serious implications for the balance between prosecutorial and judicial power in sentencing. For example, if the scope of considered conduct is confined to the offense of conviction, many argue that the sentencing system will provide relatively more power to prosecutors to control sentences. . . . Finding the right balance among fairness, complexity, and the role of the prosecutor has been a struggle for sentencing commissions generally. . . .

Discussion Paper, Relevant Conduct and Real Offense Sentencing (1995) (available at *http://www.ussc.gov/simple/relevant.htm*). The federal system uses the offense of conviction as a starting point for guidelines calculations, but then requires many mandatory adjustments and permits a few discretionary adjustments to the "offense level" based on other relevant conduct. The commission explained its support for "real offense" factors on several grounds. First, such a system mirrored prior practices in the indeterminate system. It also gave judges a means to refine and rationalize the chaotic federal criminal code. Finally, the real offense features of the system gave judges a way to check the power of the prosecutor to dictate a sentence based upon the selection of charges. See Julie R. O'Sullivan, In Defense of the U.S. Sentencing Guidelines' Modified Real-Offense System, 91 Nw. U. L. Rev. 1342 (1997).

The use of relevant conduct to enhance sentences in the federal system has come under sharp attack from scholars. See Kate Stith & Jose A. Cabranes, Fear of Judging: Sentencing Guidelines in the Federal Courts 66-77 (1998); Elizabeth Lear, Is Conviction Irrelevant? 40 UCLA L. Rev. 1179 (1993); Kevin Reitz, Sentencing Facts: Travesties of Real-Offense Sentencing, 45 Stan. L. Rev. 523 (1993); David Yellen, Illusion, Illogic and Injustice: Real-Offense Sentencing and the Federal Sentencing Guidelines, 78 Minn. L. Rev. 403 (1993). Critics have attacked the uses of uncharged or dismissed conduct as bad policy, because of the uncertain proof of the uncharged conduct, and the difficulty of achieving uniform practices in deciding how much uncharged conduct is "relevant." They have also raised constitutional questions about whether reliance on such information violates due process (by punishing a person for conduct without proving it beyond a reasonable doubt) or undermines the investigative and charging functions of the grand jury. Does real offense sentencing shift power back toward judges? Are there other ways for courts, legislatures, or commissions to respond to potential prosecutorial abuse?

3. *Varieties of uncharged conduct.* In *McAlpin,* what difference is there, if any, between the aspects of the juvenile record that were proper for the sentencing judge to consider and those aspects of McAlpin's prior conduct that were improper for the court to consider? Some wrongdoing by defendants could form the basis for additional criminal charges, or more serious criminal charges. Other conduct, while blameworthy, does not affect the charging options available to the prosecutor. For example, under the federal criminal code, a mail fraud that nets $10,000 is eligible for the same punishment as a mail fraud that nets $100,000. Should it matter to a sentencing judge (or to a sentencing commission creating sentencing guidelines) whether the conduct in question is an element of some crime for which the defendant

was not charged? Consider this approach to the problem in Kansas Statutes §21-4716(b)(3): "If a factual aspect of a crime is a statutory element of the crime . . . , that aspect of the current crime of conviction may be used as an aggravating or mitigating factor only if [it] is significantly different from the usual criminal conduct captured by the aspect of the crime."

4. *Sentencing for multiple counts.* Defendants are often convicted of multiple offenses arising out of the same transaction or course of conduct. The sentencing judge in an indeterminate system has the discretion to impose separate sentences for the multiple convictions and to decide whether those sentences will be served concurrently (all the terms begin at the same time) or consecutively (a second sentence starts after the first one ends). This gives the judge power to limit the effect of a prosecutor's decision to file multiple charges based on the same conduct. Judges with complete power over the concurrent or consecutive nature of sentences have tended to give what might be termed a "volume discount." Additional convictions will increase the total sentence served, but in decreasing amounts for each additional conviction. Some structured systems limit the judge's ability to adjust a sentence based on multiple convictions. The federal sentencing guidelines have intricate rules for the "grouping" of offenses. See U.S. Sentencing Guidelines ch. 3D. More typical is this provision from the Kansas guidelines, codified in Kan. Stat. §21-4720(b):

> When the sentencing judge imposes multiple sentences consecutively, [t]he sentencing judge must establish a base sentence for the primary crime. The primary crime is the crime with the highest crime severity ranking. . . . The total prison sentence imposed in a case involving multiple convictions arising from multiple counts within an information, complaint or indictment cannot exceed twice the base sentence. . . .

For instance, if a defendant is convicted of aggravated assault and three counts of burglary in one proceeding, the sentence would be limited to twice the guideline sentence for aggravated assault (the more serious charge).

Problem 19-4. Double Counting and Double Jeopardy

In June 1990, Steven Kurt Witte and several coconspirators arranged with Roger Norman, an undercover agent of the Drug Enforcement Administration, to import large amounts of marijuana from Mexico and cocaine from Guatemala. Norman had the task of flying the contraband into the United States, with Witte providing the ground transportation for the drugs once they arrived. The agreement called for delivery of 4,400 pounds of marijuana, plus some cocaine if there was room on the plane. Federal authorities arrested some of the participants in the scheme at an airstrip in Mexico and seized 591 kilograms of cocaine. While still undercover, Norman met Witte the following day to explain that the pilots had been unable to land in Mexico because police had raided the airstrip. Witte was not taken into custody at that time, and the activities of the conspiracy lapsed for several months.

Norman next spoke with Witte five months later, in January 1991, and asked if Witte would be interested in purchasing 1,000 pounds of marijuana. Witte agreed to give Norman $50,000 for the marijuana. When Witte and Norman met in Houston on February 7, Witte delivered half of the cash to Norman and asked that he load the marijuana into a motor home. Undercover agents took the motor home away to load the marijuana; they returned it the next morning loaded with approximately 375 pounds of marijuana, and they arrested Witte when he took possession of the contraband.

In March 1991, a federal grand jury in Texas indicted Witte and Kelly for conspiring and attempting to possess marijuana with intent to distribute it. The indictment was limited on its face to conduct occurring on or about January 25 through February 8, 1991, thus covering only the later marijuana transaction. On February 21, 1992, Witte pleaded guilty to the attempted possession count and agreed to cooperate with the government "by providing truthful and complete information concerning this and all other offenses." In exchange, the Government agreed to dismiss the conspiracy count and to file a motion for a downward departure under the Sentencing Guidelines.

In calculating Witte's base offense level under the federal sentencing guidelines, the presentence report prepared by the U.S. probation office considered the total quantity of drugs involved in all the transactions contemplated by the conspirators, including the planned 1990 shipments of both marijuana and cocaine. The presentence report suggested that Witte was accountable for the 1,000 pounds of marijuana involved in the attempted possession offense to which he pleaded guilty, 4,400 pounds of marijuana that Witte and others had planned to import from Mexico in 1990, and the 591 kilograms of cocaine seized at the Mexican airstrip in August 1990.

At the sentencing hearing, both the defendant and the government urged the court to hold that the 1990 activities concerning importation of cocaine and marijuana were not part of the same course of conduct as the 1991 marijuana offense to which Witte had pleaded guilty, and therefore should not be considered in sentencing for the 1991 offense. The district court concluded, however, that because the 1990 importation offenses were part of the same continuing conspiracy, they were "relevant conduct" under the guidelines and should be taken into account. The court therefore aggregated the quantities of drugs involved in the 1990 and 1991 episodes, resulting in a more severe sentence.

In September 1992, another grand jury in the same district returned a two-count indictment against Witte for conspiring and attempting to import cocaine. The indictment alleged that, between August 1989 and August 1990, Witte tried to import about 591 kilograms of cocaine from Central America. Witte moved to dismiss, arguing that he had already been punished for the cocaine offenses because the cocaine involved in the 1990 transaction had been considered as "relevant conduct" at sentencing for the 1991 marijuana offense. Thus, he said, the court should dismiss the indictment because punishment for these offenses would violate the prohibition against multiple punishments contained in the double jeopardy clause of the Fifth Amendment. Should the court grant the motion? Compare Witte v. United States, 515 U.S. 389 (1995).

Notes

1. *Double jeopardy for enhancing sentences based on prior crimes: majority position.* When criminal conduct gives a sentencing judge the basis for increasing a sentence

against a defendant charged with some separate crime, would a later sentence for the original crime constitute a "multiple punishment" for double jeopardy purposes? In Witte v. United States, 515 U.S. 389, 397 (1995), the Supreme Court rejected a double jeopardy challenge based on the facts described in Problem 19-4:

> Traditionally, sentencing courts have not only taken into consideration a defendant's prior convictions, but have also considered a defendant's past criminal behavior, even if no conviction resulted from that behavior. . . . That history, combined with a recognition of the need for individualized sentencing, [leads us to conclude that] a sentencing judge may appropriately conduct an inquiry broad in scope, largely unlimited either as to the kind of information he may consider, or the source from which it may come. [T]he uncharged criminal conduct was used to enhance petitioner's sentence within the range authorized by statute. . . .
>
> We are not persuaded by petitioner's suggestion that the Sentencing Guidelines somehow change the constitutional analysis. A defendant has not been "punished" any more for double jeopardy purposes when relevant conduct is included in the calculation of his offense level under the Guidelines than when a pre-Guidelines court, in its discretion, took similar uncharged conduct into account. . . . Regardless of whether particular conduct is taken into account by rule or as an act of discretion, the defendant is still being punished only for the offense of conviction.

Can you reconstruct how Witte might have argued that the sentencing guidelines made enhancements based on prior criminal record more like "punishment"? The handful of state high courts that have addressed a double jeopardy challenge on similar facts have reached the same result, holding that there is no constitutional violation in enhancing a sentence based on relevant conduct that is subsequently the basis for a separate indictment, conviction, and punishment. See, e.g., Traylor v. State, 801 S.W.2d 267 (Ark. 1990).

In Monge v. California, 524 U.S. 721 (1998), the Supreme Court decided that the double jeopardy clause does not apply at all to noncapital sentencing proceedings. When Monge was convicted of narcotics crimes, the trial court doubled his sentence based on a previous assault conviction. After a state appeals court overturned the sentence because there was insufficient proof of the details of the assault, Monge argued that a retrial on the sentence enhancement would violate double jeopardy principles. The U.S. Supreme Court disagreed, because double jeopardy protections are inapplicable to sentencing proceedings: The determinations at a sentencing hearing do not place a defendant in jeopardy for an "offense."

2. *Prosecutorial motives and control.* Do rules allowing higher punishment for multiple counts than for a single count give too much power to prosecutors? It is often said that structured sentencing systems shift power from judges to prosecutors. Are there avenues other than "real offense" sentencing to limit these types of prosecutorial control over sentences? In this regard, consider the federal "*Petite* policy" governing successive prosecutions in federal court. See Chapter 14.

When sentencing rules place great weight on the charges and criminal history, the prosecutor has greater influence over the sentence to be imposed. Despite the power of prosecutors to influence sentences in structured sentencing states, research suggests they do not tend to change their charging or plea bargaining practices. Structured systems have not produced dramatically longer sentences or changed rates of guilty pleas. See Dale Parent, Structuring Criminal Sentences

(1988); Terance Miethe, Charging and Plea Bargaining Practices Under Determinate Sentencing: An Investigation of the Hydraulic Displacement of Discretion, 78 J. Crim. L. & Criminology 155 (1987). This is not to say that plea bargains have no effect on the viability or uniformity of sentencing rules. Sometimes the prosecutor and defendant agree to charges and to factual and guideline stipulations that place the sentence outside the range that would ordinarily be prescribed by the guidelines—without asking the judge to depart from the guidelines. See Ilene Nagel and Stephen Schulhofer, A Tale of Three Cities: An Empirical Study of Charging and Bargaining Practice Under the Federal Sentencing Guidelines, 66 S. Cal. L. Rev. 501 (1992).

C. REVISITING PLEAS AND TRIALS

Just as sentencing provides an opportunity to reconsider the significance of events during investigations and charge selection, it also provides an opportunity to reconsider choices made during the resolution of charges. This section reviews the interaction between the sentence, guilty pleas, and decisions made at trial.

1. *Revisiting Proof at Trial*

The prosecution carries the burden of proving all the elements of an offense at trial beyond a reasonable doubt or establishing a factual basis in a guilty plea hearing to show that the government *could have* satisfied this burden. But once the government obtains a conviction, the burden of proving new facts relevant to sentencing becomes easier. Generally, the government need only demonstrate the facts at sentencing by a preponderance of the evidence; there are some sentencing facts for which the *defendant* bears the burden of proof, usually also by a preponderance, such as the facts necessary to justify a downward departure from a presumptive sentence. Hence, it is critical to know which facts must be proven at trial and which can wait until the sentencing hearing.

If the question of which facts are elements of an offense and which are "mere" sentencing facts were left entirely to judgment of the legislature, then the role of courts would be simply to determine legislative intent for each crime. The U.S. Supreme Court and state supreme courts have held that due process requires the government to prove each element of every offense beyond a reasonable doubt. Sullivan v. Louisiana, 508 U.S. 275 (1993); In re Winship, 397 U.S. 358 (1970). See Chapter 18, section A. The courts have also decided that legislatures are not completely free to shift facts from "element" status to "sentencing" status. In McMillan v. Pennsylvania, 477 U.S. 79 (1986), the Court held that the government did not violate due process by proving facts supporting a "sentencing enhancement" for visibly possessing a firearm using the lower preponderance standard of proof. The Court recognized, however, that legislatures could not freely convert offense elements into sentencing facts, and that in some situations sentencing facts would have to be treated as if they were elements and would have to be proved to the jury beyond a reasonable doubt. The following case develops further the idea that some factfinding must happen at trial rather than at sentencing, regardless of the label the legislature uses.

■ CHARLES APPRENDI v. NEW JERSEY

530 U.S. 466 (2000)

STEVENS, J.

A New Jersey statute classifies the possession of a firearm for an unlawful purpose as a "second-degree" offense. Such an offense is punishable by imprisonment for between five years and ten years. A separate statute, described by that State's Supreme Court as a "hate crime" law, provides for an "extended term" of imprisonment if the trial judge finds, by a preponderance of the evidence, that the "defendant in committing the crime acted with a purpose to intimidate an individual or group of individuals because of race, color, gender, handicap, religion, sexual orientation or ethnicity." N.J. Stat. Ann. §2C:44-3(e). The extended term authorized by the hate crime law for second-degree offenses is imprisonment for between 10 and 20 years. The question presented is whether the Due Process Clause of the Fourteenth Amendment requires that a factual determination authorizing an increase in the maximum prison sentence for an offense from 10 to 20 years be made by a jury on the basis of proof beyond a reasonable doubt.

At 2:04 A.M. on December 22, 1994, petitioner Charles C. Apprendi, Jr., fired several .22-caliber bullets into the home of an African-American family that had recently moved into a previously all-white neighborhood in Vineland, New Jersey. Apprendi was promptly arrested and, at 3:05 A.M., admitted that he was the shooter. After further questioning, at 6:04 A.M., he made a statement—which he later retracted—that even though he did not know the occupants of the house personally, "because they are black in color he does not want them in the neighborhood."

A New Jersey grand jury returned a 23-count indictment charging Apprendi with [crimes growing out of] shootings on four different dates, as well as the unlawful possession of various weapons. None of the counts referred to the hate crime statute, and none alleged that Apprendi acted with a racially biased purpose.

The parties entered into a plea agreement, pursuant to which Apprendi pleaded guilty to two counts of second-degree possession of a firearm for an unlawful purpose, and one count of the third-degree offense of unlawful possession of an antipersonnel bomb; the prosecutor dismissed the other 20 counts. Under state law, a second-degree offense carries a penalty range of 5 to 10 years; a third-degree offense carries a penalty range of between 3 and 5 years. As part of the plea agreement, however, the State reserved the right to request the court to impose a higher "enhanced" sentence on [the possession count based on the December 22 shooting] on the ground that that offense was committed with a biased purpose. . . . Because the plea agreement provided that the sentence on the sole third-degree offense would run concurrently with the other sentences, the potential sentences on the two second-degree counts were critical. If the judge found no basis for the biased purpose enhancement, the maximum consecutive sentences on those counts would amount to 20 years in aggregate; if, however, the judge enhanced the sentence on [the December 22 count], the maximum on that count alone would be 20 years and the maximum for the two counts in aggregate would be 30 years, with a 15-year period of parole ineligibility.

After the trial judge accepted the three guilty pleas, the prosecutor filed a formal motion for an extended term. The trial judge thereafter held an evidentiary hearing on the issue of Apprendi's "purpose" for the shooting on December 22. Apprendi adduced evidence from a psychologist and from seven character witnesses who testified that he did not have a reputation for racial bias. He also took the stand himself, explaining that the incident was an unintended consequence of overindulgence in alcohol, denying that he was in any way biased against African-Americans, and denying that his statement to the police had been accurately described. The judge, however, found the police officer's testimony credible, and concluded that the evidence supported a finding that the crime was motivated by racial bias. Having found by a preponderance of the evidence that Apprendi's actions were taken "with a purpose to intimidate" as provided by the statute, the trial judge held that the hate crime enhancement applied [and] sentenced him to a 12-year term of imprisonment on [the December 22 count], and to shorter concurrent sentences on the other two counts. [The New Jersey appellate courts upheld the sentence.]

At stake in this case are constitutional protections of surpassing importance: the proscription of any deprivation of liberty without "due process of law," and the [Sixth Amendment] guarantee that "[i]n all criminal prosecutions, the accused shall enjoy the right to a speedy and public trial, by an impartial jury." Taken together, these rights indisputably entitle a criminal defendant to a jury determination that he is guilty of every element of the crime with which he is charged, beyond a reasonable doubt. . . .

Any possible distinction between an "element" of a felony offense and a "sentencing factor" was unknown to the practice of criminal indictment, trial by jury, and judgment by court as it existed during the years surrounding our Nation's founding. As a general rule, criminal proceedings were submitted to a jury after being initiated by an indictment containing "all the facts and circumstances which constitute the offence, stated with such certainty and precision, that the defendant may be enabled to determine the species of offence they constitute, in order that he may prepare his defence accordingly and that there may be no doubt as to the judgment which should be given, if the defendant be convicted." J. Archbold, Pleading and Evidence in Criminal Cases 44 (15th ed. 1862). . . .

This practice at common law held true when indictments were issued pursuant to statute. Just as the circumstances of the crime and the intent of the defendant at the time of commission were often essential elements to be alleged in the indictment, so too were the circumstances mandating a particular punishment. "Where a statute annexes a higher degree of punishment to a common-law felony, if committed under particular circumstances, an indictment for the offence, in order to bring the defendant within that higher degree of punishment, must expressly charge it to have been committed under those circumstances, and must state the circumstances with certainty and precision. [2 M. Hale, Pleas of the Crown *170]." Archbold, Pleading and Evidence in Criminal Cases, at 51. . . .

We should be clear that nothing in this history suggests that it is impermissible for judges to exercise discretion — taking into consideration various factors relating both to offense and offender — in imposing a judgment within the range prescribed by statute. We have often noted that judges in this country have long exercised discretion of this nature in imposing sentence within statutory limits in the individual case. [O]ur periodic recognition of judges' broad discretion in sentencing — since the nineteenth-century shift in this country from statutes providing fixed-term sentences to those providing judges discretion within a permissible range — has been regularly accompanied by the qualification that that discretion was bound by the range of sentencing options prescribed by the legislature. . . .

As we made clear in In re Winship, 397 U. S. 358 (1970), the "reasonable doubt" requirement has a vital role in our criminal procedure for cogent reasons. Prosecution subjects the criminal defendant both to the possibility that he may lose his liberty upon conviction and the certainty that he would be stigmatized by the conviction. We thus require this, among other, procedural protections in order to "provide concrete substance for the presumption of innocence," and to reduce the risk of imposing such deprivations erroneously. If a defendant faces punishment beyond that provided by statute when an offense is committed under certain circumstances but not others, it is obvious that both the loss of liberty and the stigma attaching to the offense are heightened; it necessarily follows that the defendant should not — at the moment the State is put to proof of those circumstances — be deprived of protections that have, until that point, unquestionably attached.

Since *Winship,* we have made clear beyond peradventure that *Winship*'s due process and associated jury protections extend, to some degree, to determinations that go not to a defendant's guilt or innocence, but simply to the length of his sentence. This was a primary lesson of Mullaney v. Wilbur, 421 U. S. 684 (1975), in which we invalidated a Maine statute that presumed that a defendant who acted with an intent to kill possessed the "malice aforethought" necessary to constitute the State's murder offense (and therefore, was subject to that crime's associated punishment of life imprisonment). The statute placed the burden on the defendant of proving, in rebutting the statutory presumption, that he acted with a lesser degree of culpability, such as in the heat of passion, to win a reduction in the offense from murder to manslaughter (and thus a reduction of the maximum punishment of 20 years).

The State had posited in *Mullaney* that requiring a defendant to prove heat-of-passion intent to overcome a presumption of murderous intent did not implicate *Winship* protections because, upon conviction of either offense, the defendant would lose his liberty and face societal stigma just the same. Rejecting this argument, we acknowledged that criminal law "is concerned not only with guilt or innocence in the abstract, but also with the degree of criminal culpability" assessed. Because the "consequences" of a guilty verdict for murder and for manslaughter differed substantially, we dismissed the possibility that a State could circumvent the protections of *Winship* merely by redefining the elements that constitute different crimes, characterizing them as factors that bear solely on the extent of punishment.

It was in McMillan v. Pennsylvania, 477 U. S. 79 (1986), that this Court, for the first time, coined the term "sentencing factor" to refer to a fact that was not found by a jury but that could affect the sentence imposed by the judge. That case involved a challenge to the State's Mandatory Minimum Sentencing Act. According to its provisions, anyone convicted of certain felonies would be subject to a mandatory minimum penalty of five years imprisonment if the judge found, by a preponderance of the evidence, that the person "visibly possessed a firearm" in the course of committing one of the specified felonies. Articulating for the first time, and then applying, a multifactor set of criteria for determining whether the *Winship* protections applied to bar such a system, we concluded that the Pennsylvania statute did not run afoul of our previous admonitions against relieving the State of its burden of proving guilt, or tailoring the mere form of a criminal statute solely to avoid *Winship*'s strictures.

We did not, however, there budge from the position that (1) constitutional limits exist to States' authority to define away facts necessary to constitute a criminal offense, and (2) that a state scheme that keeps from the jury facts that expose defendants to greater or additional punishment may raise serious constitutional concern. . . . In sum, our reexamination of our cases in this area, and of the history upon which they rely, confirms [that] any fact that increases the penalty for a crime beyond the prescribed statutory maximum [except for the fact of a prior conviction] must be submitted to a jury, and proved beyond a reasonable doubt.

The New Jersey statutory scheme that Apprendi asks us to invalidate allows a jury to convict a defendant of a second-degree offense based on its finding beyond a reasonable doubt that he unlawfully possessed a prohibited weapon; after a subsequent and separate proceeding, it then allows a judge to impose punishment identical to that New Jersey provides for crimes of the first degree, based upon the judge's finding, by a preponderance of the evidence, that the defendant's "purpose" for unlawfully possessing the weapon was to intimidate his victim on the basis of a particular characteristic the victim possessed. In light of the constitutional rule explained above, and all of the cases supporting it, this practice cannot stand.[16]

[New Jersey argues that] the required finding of biased purpose is not an "element" of a distinct hate crime offense, but rather the traditional "sentencing factor" of motive. . . . The text of the statute requires the factfinder to determine whether the defendant possessed, at the time he committed the subject act, a "purpose to intimidate" on account of, inter alia, race. By its very terms, this statute mandates an examination of the defendant's state of mind — a concept known well to the criminal law as the defendant's mens rea.

[Furthermore,] it does not matter whether the required finding is characterized as one of intent or of motive, because labels do not afford an acceptable answer. That point applies as well to the constitutionally novel and elusive distinction between "elements" and "sentencing factors." Despite what appears to us the clear "elemental" nature of the factor here, the relevant inquiry is one not of form, but of effect — does the required finding expose the defendant to a greater punishment

16. The principal dissent would reject the Court's rule as a "meaningless formalism," because it can conceive of hypothetical statutes that would comply with the rule and achieve the same result as the New Jersey statute. While a State could, hypothetically, undertake to revise its entire criminal code in the manner the dissent suggests — extending all statutory maximum sentences to, for example, 50 years and giving judges guided discretion as to a few specially selected factors within that range — this possibility seems remote. Among other reasons, structural democratic constraints exist to discourage legislatures from enacting penal statutes that expose every defendant convicted of, for example, weapons possession, to a maximum sentence exceeding that which is, in the legislature's judgment, generally proportional to the crime. This is as it should be. Our rule ensures that a State is obliged to make its choices concerning the substantive content of its criminal laws with full awareness of the consequence, unable to mask substantive policy choices. . . . Finally, the principal dissent ignores the distinction the Court has often recognized between facts in aggravation of punishment and facts in mitigation. If facts found by a jury support a guilty verdict of murder, the judge is authorized by that jury verdict to sentence the defendant to the maximum sentence provided by the murder statute. If the defendant can escape the statutory maximum by showing, for example, that he is a war veteran, then a judge that finds the fact of veteran status is neither exposing the defendant to a deprivation of liberty greater than that authorized by the verdict according to statute, nor is the Judge imposing upon the defendant a greater stigma than that accompanying the jury verdict alone. Core concerns animating the jury and burden-of-proof requirements are thus absent from such a scheme.

than that authorized by the jury's guilty verdict? [T]he effect of New Jersey's sentencing "enhancement" here is unquestionably to turn a second-degree offense into a first-degree offense, under the State's own criminal code. . . . The New Jersey procedure challenged in this case is an unacceptable departure from the jury tradition that is an indispensable part of our criminal justice system. . . .

SCALIA, J., concurring.

. . . What ultimately demolishes the case for the dissenters is that they are unable to say what the right to trial by jury does guarantee if, as they assert, it does not guarantee — what it has been assumed to guarantee throughout our history — the right to have a jury determine those facts that determine the maximum sentence the law allows. They provide no coherent alternative. . . .

THOMAS, J., concurring.

I join the opinion of the Court in full. I write separately to explain my view that the Constitution requires a broader rule than the Court adopts. . . .

Sentencing enhancements may be new creatures, but the question that they create for courts is not. Courts have long had to consider which facts are elements in order to determine the sufficiency of an accusation (usually an indictment). . . . A long line of essentially uniform authority . . . stretching from the earliest reported cases after the founding until well into the 20th century, establishes that . . . a "crime" includes every fact that is by law a basis for imposing or increasing punishment (in contrast with a fact that mitigates punishment). Thus, if the legislature defines some core crime and then provides for increasing the punishment of that crime upon a finding of some aggravating fact — of whatever sort, including the fact of a prior conviction — the core crime and the aggravating fact together constitute an aggravated crime, just as much as grand larceny is an aggravated form of petit larceny. The aggravating fact is an element of the aggravated crime.

[I]t is fair to say that *McMillan* began a revolution in the law regarding the definition of "crime." Today's decision, far from being a sharp break with the past, marks nothing more than a return to the status quo ante — the status quo that reflected the original meaning of the Fifth and Sixth Amendments. . . .

O'CONNOR, J., dissenting.

. . . Our Court has long recognized that not every fact that bears on a defendant's punishment need be charged in an indictment, submitted to a jury, and proved by the government beyond a reasonable doubt. Rather, we have held that the legislature's definition of the elements of the offense is usually dispositive. [We have] approached each case individually, sifting through the considerations most relevant to determining whether the legislature has acted properly within its broad power to define crimes and their punishments or instead has sought to evade the constitutional requirements associated with the characterization of a fact as an offense element. In one bold stroke the Court today casts aside our traditional cautious approach and instead embraces a universal and seemingly bright-line rule limiting the power of Congress and state legislatures to define criminal offenses. . . .

None of the history contained in the Court's opinion requires the rule it ultimately adopts. [The excerpts from the nineteenth-century Archbold treatise] pertain to circumstances in which a common-law felony had also been made a separate statutory offense carrying a greater penalty. Taken together, the statements from the

Archbold treatise demonstrate nothing more than the unremarkable proposition that a defendant could receive the greater statutory punishment only if the indictment expressly charged and the prosecutor proved the facts that made up the statutory offense, as opposed to simply those facts that made up the common-law offense. . . . Justice Thomas divines the common-law understanding of the Fifth and Sixth Amendment rights by consulting decisions rendered by American courts well after the ratification of the Bill of Rights, ranging primarily from the 1840s to the 1890s. [The] decisions fail to demonstrate any settled understanding with respect to the definition of a crime under the relevant, preexisting common law. . . .

The Court explains Mullaney v. Wilber, 421 U.S. 684 (1975), as having held that the due process proof beyond a reasonable doubt requirement applies to those factual determinations that, under a State's criminal law, make a difference in the degree of punishment the defendant receives. The Court chooses to ignore, however, the decision we issued two years later, Patterson v. New York, 432 U. S. 197 (1977), which clearly rejected the Court's broad reading of *Mullaney.* In *Patterson,* the jury found the defendant guilty of second-degree murder. Under New York law, the fact that a person intentionally killed another while under the influence of extreme emotional disturbance distinguished the reduced offense of first-degree manslaughter from the more serious offense of second-degree murder. Thus, the presence or absence of this one fact was the defining factor separating a greater from a lesser punishment. Under New York law, however, the State did not need to prove the absence of extreme emotional disturbance beyond a reasonable doubt. Rather, state law imposed the burden of proving the presence of extreme emotional disturbance on the defendant, and required that the fact be proved by a preponderance of the evidence. We rejected Patterson's due process challenge to his conviction.

[I]t is possible that the Court's "increase in the maximum penalty" rule rests on a meaningless formalism that accords, at best, marginal protection for the constitutional rights that it seeks to effectuate. [One reading of the Court's holding] requires that a fact be submitted to a jury and proved beyond a reasonable doubt only if that fact, as a formal matter, extends the range of punishment beyond the prescribed statutory maximum. [A]pparently New Jersey could cure its sentencing scheme, and achieve virtually the same results, by drafting its weapons possession statute in the following manner: First, New Jersey could prescribe, in the weapons possession statute itself, a range of 5 to 20 years' imprisonment for one who commits that criminal offense. Second, New Jersey could provide that only those defendants convicted under the statute who are found by a judge, by a preponderance of the evidence, to have acted with a purpose to intimidate an individual on the basis of race may receive a sentence greater than 10 years' imprisonment.

Under another reading of the Court's decision, it may mean only that the Constitution requires that a fact be submitted to a jury and proved beyond a reasonable doubt if it, as a formal matter, increases the range of punishment beyond that which could legally be imposed absent that fact. [Again,] New Jersey could cure its sentencing scheme, and achieve virtually the same results, by drafting its weapons possession statute in the following manner: First, New Jersey could prescribe, in the weapons possession statute itself, a range of 5 to 20 years' imprisonment for one who commits that criminal offense. Second, New Jersey could provide that a defendant convicted under the statute whom a judge finds, by a preponderance of the evidence, not to have acted with a purpose to intimidate an individual on the basis of race may receive a sentence no greater than 10 years' imprisonment. [The] "structural democratic constraints" that might discourage a legislature from enacting either of the above hypothetical statutes would be no more significant than those that would discourage the enactment of New Jersey's present sentence-enhancement statute. . . .

Given the pure formalism of the above readings of the Court's opinion, one suspects that the constitutional principle underlying its decision is more far reaching. The actual principle underlying the Court's decision may be that any fact (other than prior conviction) that has the effect, in real terms, of increasing the maximum punishment beyond an otherwise applicable range must be submitted to a jury and proved beyond a reasonable doubt. . . . The principle thus would apply . . . to all determinate sentencing schemes in which the length of a defendant's sentence within the statutory range turns on specific factual determinations (e.g., the federal Sentencing Guidelines). [T]he apparent effect of the Court's opinion today is to halt the current debate on sentencing reform in its tracks and to invalidate with the stroke of a pen three decades' worth of nationwide reform, all in the name of a principle with a questionable constitutional pedigree. . . .

BREYER, J., dissenting.

[The majority's] rule would seem to promote a procedural ideal — that of juries, not judges, determining the existence of those facts upon which increased punishment turns. But the real world of criminal justice cannot hope to meet any such ideal. It can function only with the help of procedural compromises, particularly in respect to sentencing. . . .

In modern times the law has left it to the sentencing judge to find those facts which (within broad sentencing limits set by the legislature) determine the sentence of a convicted offender. The judge's factfinding role is not inevitable. One could imagine, for example, a pure "charge offense" sentencing system in which the degree of punishment depended only upon the crime charged (e.g., eight mandatory years for robbery, six for arson, three for assault). But such a system would ignore many harms and risks of harm that the offender caused or created, and it would ignore many relevant offender characteristics. [There are] far too many potentially relevant sentencing factors to permit submission of all (or even many) of them to a jury. . . .

At the same time, to require jury consideration of all such factors — say, during trial where the issue is guilt or innocence — could easily place the defendant in the awkward (and conceivably unfair) position of having to deny he committed the crime yet offer proof about how he committed it, e.g., "I did not sell drugs, but I sold no more than 500 grams." And while special postverdict sentencing juries could cure this problem, they have seemed (but for capital cases) not worth their administrative costs. . . .

The majority raises no objection to traditional pre-Guidelines sentencing procedures under which judges, not juries, made the factual findings that would lead to an increase in an individual offender's sentence. How does a legislative determination differ in any significant way? For example, if a judge may on his or her own decide that victim injury or bad motive should increase a bank robber's sentence from 5 years to 10, why does it matter that a legislature instead enacts a statute that increases a bank robber's sentence from 5 years to 10 based on this same judicial finding?

[T]he majority also makes no constitutional objection to a legislative delegation to a commission of the authority to create guidelines that determine how a judge is to exercise sentencing discretion. But if the Constitution permits Guidelines, why does it not permit Congress similarly to guide the exercise of a judge's sentencing discretion? . . .

The source of the problem lies not in a legislature's power to enact sentencing factors, but in the traditional legislative power to select elements defining a crime, the traditional legislative power to set broad sentencing ranges, and the traditional judicial power to choose a sentence within that range on the basis of relevant offender conduct. Conversely, the solution to the problem lies, not in prohibiting legislatures from enacting sentencing factors, but in sentencing rules that determine punishments on the basis of properly defined relevant conduct, with sensitivity to the need for procedural protections where sentencing factors are determined by a judge (for example, use of a reasonable doubt standard), and invocation of the Due Process Clause where the history of the crime at issue, together with the nature of the facts to be proved, reveals unusual and serious procedural unfairness. . . .

Notes

1. *Standard of proof at sentencing: majority position.* In McMillan v. Pennsylvania, 477 U.S. 79 (1986), the Court declared that the federal due process clause allows states to prove some facts affecting the sentence by a preponderance of the evidence. Legislatures, the Court said, ordinarily have the authority to decide which facts are "elements" of a crime, to be proven at trial beyond a reasonable doubt, and which are "sentencing factors," to be proven after conviction by a preponderance of the evidence. Only when an extreme increase in punishment attaches to a sentencing factor (when the "tail" of the sentencing factor "wags the dog" of the substantive offense) will a federal court overturn the legislature's choices. However, in Specht v. Patterson, 386 U.S. 605 (1967), the Court overturned a life sentence imposed under a statute that allowed the trial court to enhance a 10-year maximum sentence for "indecent liberties"; the enhancement was based on a psychiatric examination ordered after conviction, when the defendant was not allowed to cross-examine the psychiatrist about conclusions drawn in the report. How is *McMillan* different from *Specht?*

Nearly all states have adopted by statute the preponderance standard for facts to be proven at sentencing. Most state courts also have held that their state constitutions allow the state to prove certain facts to increase a sentence, using the lower standard of proof at the sentencing hearing. See, e.g., People v. Wims, 895 P.2d 77 (Cal. 1995). Does the issue of allocating facts between the offense and sentencing ever arise in an indeterminate sentencing system? Structured sentencing systems in the states typically provide for a presumptive guideline sentence that is set by reference to the facts underlying a conviction, either proven beyond a reasonable doubt at trial or admitted by the defendant in a guilty plea. Yet these guidelines also allow judges, in varying degrees, to depart from the sentence indicated in the guidelines. The departure might be based on facts proven at the sentencing hearing, and most require the prosecution to show these facts only by a preponderance.

2. *Juries and determinate sentencing laws.* The *Apprendi* decision has created a great deal of upheaval in the state and federal courts. Many defendants have pointed out particular factual findings, especially in drug cases, that increase their sentence in some way or another. Thus, they argue, a jury must make the relevant factual findings. For facts that merely increase a sentence within the designated statutory range, these claims have not succeeded. But what about facts that increase the minimum

sentence that could apply to the crime? In Harris v. United States, 536 U.S. 545 (2002), the Supreme Court reaffirmed *McMillan* and held that a judge rather than a jury could find the facts necessary to increase the minimum sentence. How might you distinguish the increased minimum sentence involved in *Harris* from the increased maximum sentence involved in *Apprendi*?

The *Apprendi* ruling also has implications for capital sentencing, where findings about "aggravating factors" are a precondition to the court imposing the death penalty. See Ring v. Arizona, 536 U.S. 584 (2002) (jury rather than judge must find an aggravating circumstance necessary for imposition of the death penalty).

3. *Rules of evidence at sentencing.* Williams v. New York established that the rules of evidence for criminal trials need not apply in sentencing hearings. This is true both for indeterminate sentencing systems and for most structured sentencing systems. The Federal Rules of Evidence state this explicitly: "The rules (other than with respect to privileges) do not apply in . . . sentencing." Fed. R. Evid. 1101(d)(3). The federal sentencing guidelines also adopt this position: "any information may be considered, so long as it has sufficient indicia of reliability to support its probable accuracy." U.S. Sentencing Guidelines §6A1.3(a). The rules do not apply because of the perceived burden they would place on sentencing judges, converting the sentencing hearing into a second trial. Should Congress or the U.S. Sentencing Commission change positions and apply the rules of evidence to sentencing hearings? Professor Deborah Young favors the rules of evidence over other methods of increasing the reliability of factfinding at sentencing because use of the rules of evidence corrects potential errors whether they benefit the prosecution or the defense. She argues that evenhanded factfinding rules make sense at sentencing precisely because an offender has already been convicted and should no longer be given the benefit of the presumption of innocence. Deborah Young, Fact-Finding at Federal Sentencing: Why the Guidelines Should Meet the Rules, 79 Cornell L. Rev. 299 (1994).

4. *Confrontation of witnesses.* Although the evidentiary rules governing hearsay do not apply to sentencing hearings in federal or state courts, the overlapping protections of the Sixth Amendment's confrontation clause (and the equivalent provisions of the state constitution) still might require that a defendant be allowed to cross-examine witnesses at the sentencing hearing. The small group of courts addressing this question, however, have mostly concluded that the confrontation clause does not apply to the evidence presented during a sentencing hearing. For example, in United States v. Wise, 976 F.2d 393 (8th Cir. 1992), the sentencing court relied on hearsay testimony by a probation officer regarding facts contained in the presentence investigation report. The judge allowed the defendant to cross-examine the probation officer and to introduce witnesses of his own but did not prevent the probation officer from introducing hearsay statements into evidence. The appellate court upheld the sentence and concluded that confrontation of witnesses at sentencing was unnecessary. See also State v. DeSalvo, 903 P.2d 202 (Mont. 1995). Different rules apply to capital sentencing proceedings: The imposition of a death sentence based on information that a defendant does not have the opportunity to deny or explain may run afoul of the confrontation clause. See Gardner v. Florida, 430 U.S. 349 (1977). The Supreme Court has held that the sentencing hearing is part of the "criminal proceedings" and that the right to counsel applies at that stage as well. Mempa v. Rhay, 389 U.S. 128 (1967) (establishing right to counsel at sentencing). If the Sixth Amendment's right to counsel (granted to "the accused") applies at sentencing, why doesn't the Sixth Amendment's right to confront witnesses also apply?

2. *Revisiting Jury Verdicts and Guilty Pleas*

In unstructured sentencing systems the judge may consider at sentencing for one crime some evidence presented during a prosecution for an earlier crime, even if the earlier trial resulted in an acquittal. The idea that a defendant may be punished more severely based on information underlying a prior acquittal may flabbergast nonlawyers, and even some lawyers. But the law explains the use of information underlying acquittals in terms of the different standards of proof at trial and sentencing: Evidence that was insufficient to establish guilt beyond a reasonable doubt might nevertheless be enough to convince the judge to enhance a sentence. In effect, this allows the sentencing judge to ignore the verdict of the jury.

■ UNITED STATES v. VERNON WATTS

519 U.S. 148 (1997)

PER CURIAM

[The] Court of Appeals for the Ninth Circuit held that sentencing courts could not consider conduct of the defendants underlying charges of which they had been acquitted. Every other Court of Appeals has held that a sentencing court may do so, if the Government establishes that conduct by a preponderance of the evidence. [Because the Ninth Circuit's holding conflicts with] the clear implications of 18 U.S.C. §3661, the Sentencing Guidelines, and this Court's decisions, particularly Witte v. United States, 515 U.S. 389 (1995), we grant the petition and reverse in both cases.

[P]olice discovered cocaine base in a kitchen cabinet and two loaded guns and ammunition hidden in a bedroom closet of Watts' house. A jury convicted Watts of possessing cocaine base with intent to distribute, in violation of 21 U.S.C. §841(a)(1), but acquitted him of using a firearm in relation to a drug offense, in violation of 18 U.S.C. §924(c). Despite Watts' acquitted on the firearms count, the District Court found by a preponderance of the evidence that Watts had possessed the guns in connection with the drug offense. In calculating Watts' sentence, the court therefore added two points to his base offense level under [the federal sentencing guidelines]. The Court of Appeals vacated the sentence, holding that a sentencing judge may not, under any standard of proof, rely on facts of which the defendant was acquitted. . . .

We begin our analysis with 18 U.S.C. §3661, which codifies the longstanding principle that sentencing courts have broad discretion to consider various kinds of information. The statute states: "No limitation shall be placed on the information concerning the background, character, and conduct of a person convicted of an offense which a court of the United States may receive and consider for the purpose of imposing an appropriate sentence."

We reiterated this principle in Williams v. New York, 337 U.S. 241 (1949), in which a defendant convicted of murder and sentenced to death challenged the sentencing court's reliance on information that the defendant had been involved in 30 burglaries of which he had not been convicted. We contrasted the different limitations on presentation of evidence at trial and at sentencing: "Highly relevant — if not essential — to [the judge's] selection of an appropriate sentence is the possession of the fullest information possible concerning the defendant's life and characteristics." Neither the broad language of §3661 nor our holding in *Williams* suggests any basis for the courts to invent a blanket prohibition against considering certain types of evidence at sentencing. Indeed, under the pre-Guidelines sentencing regime, it was well established that a sentencing judge may take into account facts introduced at trial relating to other charges, even ones of which the defendant has been acquitted.

The Guidelines did not alter this aspect of the sentencing court's discretion. Very roughly speaking, relevant conduct corresponds to those actions and circumstances that courts typically took into account when sentencing prior to the Guidelines' enactment. Section 1B1.4 of the Guidelines reflects the policy set forth in 18 U.S.C. §3661: "In determining the sentence to impose within the guideline range, or whether a departure from the guidelines is warranted, the court may consider, without limitation, any information concerning the background, character and conduct of the defendant, unless otherwise prohibited by law."

Section 1B1.3, in turn, describes in sweeping language the conduct that a sentencing court may consider in determining the applicable guideline range. The commentary to that section states: "Conduct that is not formally charged or is not an element of the offense of conviction may enter into the determination of the applicable guideline sentencing range." With respect to certain offenses, . . . USSG §1B1.3(a)(2) requires the sentencing court to consider "all acts and omissions . . . that were part of the same course of conduct or common scheme or plan as the offense of conviction." Application Note 3 . . . gives the following example: "Where the defendant engaged in three drug sales of 10, 15, and 20 grams of cocaine, as part of the same course of conduct or common scheme or plan, subsection (a)(2) provides that the total quantity of cocaine involved (45 grams) is to be used to determine the offense level even if the defendant is convicted of a single count charging only one of the sales." Accordingly, the Guidelines conclude that "relying on the entire range of conduct, regardless of the number of counts that are alleged *or on which a conviction is obtained,* appears to be the most reasonable approach to writing workable guidelines for these offenses."

Although the dissent concedes that a district court may properly consider "evidence adduced in a trial that resulted in an acquitted" when choosing a particular sentence within a guideline range, it argues that the court must close its eyes to acquitted conduct at earlier stages of the sentencing process because the "broadly inclusive language of §3661" is incorporated only into §1B1.4 of the Guidelines. This argument ignores §1B1.3 which, as we have noted, directs sentencing courts to consider all other related conduct, whether or not it resulted in a conviction. The dissent also contends that because Congress instructed the Sentencing Commission, in 28 U.S.C. §994(l), to ensure that the Guidelines provide incremental punishment for a defendant who is convicted of multiple offenses, it could not have meant for the Guidelines to increase a sentence based on offenses of which a defendant has been acquitted. The statute is not, however, cast in restrictive or exclusive terms. Far from limiting a sentencing court's power to consider uncharged or acquitted conduct, §994(l) simply ensures that, at a minimum, the Guidelines provide additional penalties when defendants are convicted of multiple offenses. . . . In short, we are convinced that a sentencing court may consider conduct of which a defendant has been acquitted.

As we explained in Witte v. United States, 515 U.S. 389 (1995), . . . sentencing enhancements do not punish a defendant for crimes of which he was not convicted, but rather increase his sentence because of the manner in which he committed the crime of conviction. In *Witte,* we held that a sentencing court could, consistent with the Double Jeopardy Clause, consider uncharged cocaine importation in imposing a sentence on marijuana charges that was within the statutory range, without precluding the defendant's subsequent prosecution for the cocaine offense. We concluded that "consideration of information about the defendant's character and conduct at sentencing does not result in 'punishment' for any offense other than the one of which the defendant was convicted." Rather, the defendant is "punished only for the fact that the *present* offense was carried out in a manner that warrants increased punishment."

The Court of Appeals failed to appreciate the significance of the different standards of proof that govern at trial and sentencing. [A]cquittal on criminal charges does not prove that the defendant is innocent; it merely proves the existence of a reasonable doubt as to his guilt. [I]t is impossible to know exactly why a jury found a defendant not guilty on a certain charge. Thus, contrary to the Court of Appeals' assertion . . . , the jury cannot be said to have "necessarily rejected" any facts when it returns a general verdict of not guilty.

For these reasons, an acquitted in a criminal case does not preclude the Government from relitigating an issue when it is presented in a subsequent action governed by a lower standard of proof. The Guidelines state that it is "appropriate" that facts relevant to sentencing be proved by a preponderance of the evidence, USSG §6A1.3 comment., and we have held that application of the preponderance standard at sentencing generally satisfies due process. McMillan v. Pennsylvania, 477 U.S. 79, 91-92 (1986). . . . We therefore hold that a jury's verdict of acquitted does not prevent the sentencing court from considering conduct underlying the acquitted charge, so long as that conduct has been proved by a preponderance of the evidence.

[In this case], the jury acquitted the defendant of using or carrying a firearm during or in relation to the drug offense. That verdict does not preclude a finding by a preponderance of the evidence that the defendant did, in fact, use or carry such a weapon, much less that he simply *possessed* the weapon in connection with a drug offense.

STEVENS, J., dissenting.

The Sentencing Reform Act of 1984 revolutionized the manner in which district courts sentence persons convicted of federal crimes. . . . Strict mandatory rules have dramatically confined the exercise of judgment based on a totality of the circumstances. . . .

In 1970, during the era of individualized sentencing, Congress enacted the statute now codified as 18 U.S.C. §3661 to make it clear that otherwise inadmissible evidence could be considered by judges in the exercise of their sentencing discretion. The statute, however, did not tell the judge how to weigh the significance of any of that evidence. The judge was free to rely on any information that might shed light on a decision to grant probation, to impose the statutory maximum, or to determine the precise sentence within those extremes. Wisdom and experience enabled the judge to give appropriate weight to uncorroborated hearsay or to evidence of criminal conduct that had not resulted in a conviction. . . . Like a jury in a capital case, the judge could exercise discretion to dispense mercy on the basis of factors too intangible to write into a statute.

Although the Sentencing Reform Act of 1984 has cabined the discretion of sentencing judges, the 1970 statute remains on the books. As was true when it was enacted, §3661 does not speak to questions concerning the relevance or the weight of any item of evidence. That statute is not offended by provisions in the Guidelines that proscribe reliance on evidence of economic hardship, drug or alcohol dependence, or lack of guidance as a youth, in making certain sentencing decisions. Conversely, that statute does not command that any particular weight — or indeed that any weight at all — be given to evidence that a defendant may have committed an offense that the prosecutor failed to prove beyond a reasonable doubt. . . .

A closer examination of the interaction among §3661, the other provisions of the Sentencing Reform Act, and the Guidelines demonstrates that the role played by §3661 is of a narrower scope than the Court's opinion suggests. The Sentencing Reform Act was enacted primarily to address Congress' concern that similar offenders convicted of similar offenses were receiving an unjustifiably wide range of sentences. . . . The [statute requires] that for any sentence of imprisonment in the Guidelines, "the maximum of the range established for such a term shall not exceed the minimum of that range by more than the greater of 25 percent or 6 months," 28 U.S.C. §994(b)(2). The determination of which of these narrow ranges a particular sentence should fall into is made by operation of mandatory rules, but within the particular range, the judge retains broad discretion to set a particular sentence.

By their own terms, the Guidelines incorporate the broadly inclusive language of §3661 only into those portions of the sentencing decision in which the judge retains discretion. [The] Guidelines Manual §1B1.4 provides: "In determining the sentence to impose within the guideline range, or whether a departure from the guidelines is warranted, the court may consider, without limitation, any information concerning the background, character and conduct of the defendant, unless otherwise prohibited by law. *See* 18 U.S.C. §3661."

Thus, as in the pre-Guidelines sentencing regime, it is in the area in which the judge exercises discretion that §3661 authorizes unlimited access to information concerning the background, character, and conduct of the defendant. When the judge is exercising such discretion, I agree that he may consider otherwise inadmissible evidence, including evidence adduced in a trial that resulted in an acquitted. But that practice, enshrined in §3661 and USSG §1B1.4, sheds little, if any, light on the appropriateness of the District Courts' application of USSG §1B1.3, which defines relevant conduct for the purposes of determining the Guidelines range within which a sentence can be imposed. . . .

In 28 U.S.C. §994(l) Congress specifically directed the Commission to ensure that the Guidelines included incremental sentences for multiple offenses. That subsection provides: "The Commission shall insure that the Guidelines promulgated [reflect] the appropriateness of imposing an incremental penalty for each offense in a case in which a defendant is convicted of (A) multiple offenses committed in the same course of conduct . . . and (B) multiple offenses committed at different times. . . ." It is difficult to square this explicit statutory command to impose incremental punishment for each of the "multiple offenses" of which a defendant "is convicted" with the conclusion that Congress intended incremental punishment for each offense of which the defendant has been acquitted. . . .

In my opinion the statute should be construed in the light of the traditional requirement that criminal charges must be sustained by proof beyond a reasonable doubt. That requirement has always applied to charges involving multiple offenses as well a single offense. Whether an allegation of criminal conduct is the sole basis for punishment or merely one of several bases for punishment, we should presume that Congress intended the new sentencing Guidelines that it authorized in 1984 to adhere to longstanding procedural requirements enshrined in our constitutional jurisprudence. The notion that a charge that cannot be sustained by proof beyond a reasonable doubt may give rise to the same punishment as if it had been so proved is repugnant to that jurisprudence. I respectfully dissent.

Notes

1. *Acquitted conduct: majority position.* Although indeterminate sentencing systems typically allow judges to consider prior misconduct when setting a sentence, many states make an exception for acquitted conduct — conduct that formed the basis for a charge resulting in an acquittal at trial. Judges in many states have developed common law rules preventing the use of acquitted conduct at sentencing. See State v. Cobb, 732 A.2d 425 (N.H. 1999); Bishop v. State, 486 S.E.2d 887 (Ga. 1997); Anderson v. State, 448 N.E.2d 1180 (Ind. 1983). On the other hand, some state cases have approved of the use of acquitted conduct. Jones v. State, 156 A.2d 421 (Md. 1959); State v. Woodlief, 90 S.E. 137 (N.C. 1916). Why do so many states limit the use of acquitted conduct, even though they permit sentencing judges to consider prior convictions and prior uncharged conduct more generally?

The Supreme Court in *Watts* confirmed that neither the constitution nor the federal sentencing statutes or guidelines as currently drafted bar a judge from using acquitted conduct. See also Edwards v. United States, 523 U.S. 511 (1998) (sentencing judge can determine defendants were trafficking in both crack and powder, even if jury believed defendants were only trafficking in powder). But the Court did not resolve the policy issue of whether the guidelines *should* limit the use of acquitted conduct. Are sentencing commissions better situated than judges to create limits on the use of acquitted conduct?

2. *Different standards.* Courts allowing the use of acquittal evidence at sentencing have reasoned that juries use a reasonable doubt standard while a sentencing judge uses a preponderance standard. Is this true in practice? Do acquitting juries tend to conclude that a defendant was innocent or that there was a reasonable doubt about guilt? Is it possible to distinguish a jury that found "innocence" from one that found "non-guilty"? See Elizabeth Lear, Is Conviction Irrelevant? 40 UCLA L. Rev. 1179 (1993).

■ UNITED STATES SENTENCING GUIDELINES §3E1.1

(a) If the defendant clearly demonstrates acceptance of responsibility for his offense, decrease the offense level by 2 levels.

(b) If the defendant qualifies for a decrease under subsection (a), the offense [is serious enough to qualify for a level 16 or greater], and the defendant has assisted authorities in the investigation or prosecution of his own misconduct by taking one or more of the following steps:

(1) timely providing complete information to the government concerning his own involvement in the offense; or

(2) timely notifying authorities of his intention to enter a plea of guilty, thereby permitting the government to avoid preparing for trial and permitting the court to allocate its resources efficiently,

decrease the offense level by 1 additional level.

Problem 19-5. Trial Penalty or Reward for Plea?

An experienced police officer watched Milton Coles speak with another person and give that person currency in exchange for a ziplock plastic bag, which the latter retrieved from a hiding place in a nearby tree. A jury found Coles guilty of one count of possessing marijuana. At sentencing, the trial judge made the following statement:

> I never understood why you went to trial in this case, Mr. Coles. Your lawyer did the best he could with no defense at all. I was amazed how successfully he was able to even come up with something plausible. If you had come before the Court and said, "Look, I had a little stuff on me and I needed a little extra money," I would have had some sympathy for you. As it is, though, I don't have any sympathy for you at all. So the Court sentences you to one year.

One year was the maximum available sentence for this offense. Coles has challenged the validity of this sentence, because he claims that the judge penalized him for exercising his constitutional right to stand trial. How would you rule on appeal? Compare Coles v. United States, 682 A.2d 167 (D.C. 1996).

Notes

1. *Sentencing after refusal to plead guilty: majority position.* In a plea agreement a defendant agrees to waive trial, normally in exchange for some perceived advantage at the time of sentencing. In unstructured sentencing systems, judges almost always accept a plea bargain if offered by the parties, but it is not clear what effect the defendant's willingness to plead guilty has on the sentence. Research has shown that defendants pleading guilty tend to receive substantially lower sentences than defendants who go to trial (in some studies the "plea discount" has been one-third or more off post-trial sentences) but that judges tend to sentence based on the original charges filed rather than the charges forming the basis of the guilty plea.

Almost all high state courts say that a sentencing court cannot punish a refusal to plead guilty but can enhance a punishment based on "lack of remorse" or failure to "accept responsibility" for a crime. Jennings v. State, 664 A.2d 903 (Md. 1995). Courts routinely treat an agreement to plead guilty as an appropriate reason for imposing a less severe sentence. State v. Balfour, 637 A.2d 1249 (N.J. 1994) (defendant's agreement to plead guilty can appropriately be weighed in the decision to downgrade an offense to a lower degree at sentencing). In practice, is there a difference between "punishing the exercise of trial rights" and "rewarding acceptance of responsibility"? Do these rules encourage judges to do anything more than choose their words carefully?

2. *Plea bargaining and structured sentencing rules.* Section 3E1.1 of the federal sentencing guidelines, reprinted above, allows the sentencing judge to reduce a

sentence for "acceptance of responsibility," while commentary to that guideline provision insists that courts should not equate acceptance of responsibility with a decision to plead guilty. Rules in various structured sentencing systems give sentencing judges different instructions about the impact of a plea agreement. The possibilities range from rules saying that plea agreements should not change the sentence at all to rules that allow the judge to accept the sentencing recommendations of the parties within certain broad limits. For instance, under the Minnesota sentencing guidelines, judges must impose the sentence indicated in the guideline grid unless there is a valid ground for departure. A plea agreement, standing alone, is not a sufficient reason to depart from the guidelines. In Washington state, statutory guidelines tell the judge to "determine if the agreement is consistent with the interests of justice and with the [statutory] prosecuting standards" and to reject the agreement if it is not. Wash. Rev. Code §9.94A.090(1). The federal sentencing guidelines also advise judges to limit the impact of a guilty plea at sentencing. The court may accept sentencing recommendations offered in a plea agreement "if the court is satisfied either that (1) the recommended sentence is within the applicable guideline range; or (2) the recommended sentence departs from the applicable guideline range for justifiable reasons." U.S. Sentencing Guidelines §6B1.2(b) (reprinted in Chapter 16, section B above).

3. *Sentence enhancements for perjury and obstruction of justice at trial.* Judges who preside at trial also typically impose the sentence on the same defendant after conviction. In United States v. Dunnigan, 507 U.S. 87 (1993), the Court concluded that a sentencing court can enhance a defendant's sentence by a designated amount under the federal guidelines if the court finds that the defendant committed perjury at trial. A defendant's right to testify "does not include a right to commit perjury." To reduce the risk that a court will wrongfully punish a truthful defendant, the court must make "findings to support all the elements of a perjury violation in the specific case." Does the sentencing judge's power to punish perjury without a perjury conviction punish the right to trial?

If perjury at trial can enhance a sentence, this adds to the long list of incentives for defendants not to testify at trial. As we saw in the previous chapter, the Fifth Amendment declares that a factfinder may not draw adverse inferences from this silence at trial. Does the same protection apply to silence at sentencing? In Mitchell v. United States, 526 U.S. 314 (1999), the Supreme Court decided that a guilty plea in federal court does not extinguish the defendant's Fifth Amendment right to remain silent at sentencing. The government in this narcotics case presented testimony from co-defendants at Mitchell's sentencing hearing; the co-defendants claimed that she had sold 1.5 to 2 ounces of cocaine twice a week for 18 months. The sentencing judge found that this testimony established the 5-kilogram threshold for a mandatory 10-year minimum, and noted that Mitchell's failure to testify was a factor in persuading the court to rely on the co-defendants' testimony. The Supreme Court declared that a sentencing judge may not draw adverse inferences from the defendant's silence at the sentencing hearing in selecting a sentence for the defendant.

4. *"Vindictive" sentencing after retrial.* Just as courts insist that a sentence may not be increased to punish a defendant for exercising the right to trial, federal and state courts say that a trial judge may not punish a defendant for exercising the statutory right to appeal. If a defendant successfully appeals a conviction and is convicted again after retrial, a sentence higher than the original sentence imposed is presumed to be a product of "vindictiveness" by the sentencing judge. A sentence motivated by

such vindictiveness violates federal due process. The judge must rebut this presumption by placing on the record his reasons for increasing the sentence after the second conviction. See North Carolina v. Pearce, 395 U.S. 711 (1969). According to *Pearce,* those reasons could be based on "objective information concerning identifiable conduct on the part of the defendant occurring after the time of the original sentence proceeding." Later, the Court said that a court could rebut the presumption of vindictiveness by pointing to any "objective information" that the court did not consider during the first sentencing proceeding. Texas v. McCullough, 475 U.S. 134 (1986).

5. *Probation officers.* Judges who sentence a defendant after a guilty plea have not heard an extensive presentation of the evidence at trial and thus depend heavily on the presentence investigation (PSI) report to inform them about the offender and the offense. Especially in structured sentencing systems in which particular facts have an identifiable impact on the sentence, probation officers (who create the PSI reports) are critical players in the sentencing process. See Charlie Varnon, The Role of the Probation Officer in the Guideline System, 4 Fed. Sentencing Rep. 63 (1991). How might a prosecutor or a defense attorney influence the recommendations of the probation officer? What institutional or individual biases might the probation officer bring to her assessment (and recommendation) of proper sentences?

D. NEW INFORMATION ABOUT THE OFFENDER AND THE VICTIM

We have seen how sentencing courts revisit and refine the choices made prior to conviction. But the sentencing judge does more than this; the judge goes on to consider a broader range of information about the offender's past and future, the broader context of the offense, and the viewpoint of the victim.

1. *Offender Information*

Although the offender's involvement in the crime of conviction is critical to a sentence, judges also consider other aspects of the offender's character and past conduct. In this section, we consider the use at sentencing of the offender's prior criminal record, cooperation with the government in other investigations, and other aspects of an offender's personal history and prospects.

a. Criminal History

At sentencing, the court learns about the defendant's life before the crime of conviction took place. Probation officers collect some of this information; attorneys for either the prosecution or the defense present facts, as well. Often the offender's past will include prior convictions or other encounters with the criminal justice system. Under an unstructured sentencing system, the judge gives the prior criminal record whatever weight she thinks appropriate. Sentencing statutes and guidelines, however, instruct judges in some systems more precisely about the effect that a prior criminal record must have on a sentence.

■ MELVIN TUNSTILL v. STATE
568 N.E.2d 539 (Ind. 1991)

DEBRULER, J.

Appellant was tried to a jury on a charge of murder and was found guilty of voluntary manslaughter, a Class B felony. . . . He received an executed sentence of 20 years [and brought this appeal].

The evidence produced at trial most favorable to the verdict shows that the victim, Jerry Wayne Haggard, died of a single stab wound inflicted by appellant during a scuffle which occurred at a little after 2:00 A.M. on July 19, 1987, in the parking lot of B & B Liquors in Indianapolis. Appellant and Haggard had been acquainted for six or seven years and often socialized and drank together. . . . At approximately 1:45 A.M. on July 19, appellant walked from his house to B & B Liquors to buy some wine before closing time. [S]everal people were congregated in the parking lot, [and] appellant brushed into Haggard. Appellant turned and said to Haggard, "Hey, what's happening?," whereupon Haggard kicked appellant in the groin. Appellant backed away, repeating, "Hey, man, what's going on? What's wrong with you?" and Haggard kicked him again. Haggard kicked appellant a third time, this time in the shins, and appellant pushed Haggard backward. Haggard stumbled, and appellant pulled out a knife and, still backing up but swinging the knife from side to side in front of him, said, "What's wrong with you? You must want to die." [T]he two "clenched," according to one witness, then Haggard staggered back with his hands pressed against his body and fell onto a parked car. He died shortly thereafter. . . .

The trial court enhanced the standard 10-year sentence for a Class B felony by an additional 10 years and imposed a 20-year executed sentence. At the sentencing hearing, the trial court stated that the imposition of an enhanced sentence was warranted by the presence of two aggravating circumstances: 1) appellant was on probation at the time of the instant crime and 2) appellant's criminal history, consisting of three prior arrests. . . .

Appellant first argues that the trial court erred in considering him to have been a probationer at the time the instant offense was committed. Prior to the events at issue here, appellant was convicted of possession of heroin and methadone. He received a suspended sentence, was ordered to pay a $320 fine and court costs, and was placed on a year's probation which was to run from March 7, 1986, to March 7, 1987. In March of 1987, four months before the instant crime, a petition was filed charging that appellant was in violation of his probation because he had not paid the fine and costs. [T]he record indicates that the final hearing on the probation violation was held approximately a week before the sentencing hearing on the instant charge. . . . Appellant's probation period was tolled until the time that a final determination on the violation petition was made, which occurred well after the commission of the charged crime. While not entitled to much weight, appellant's continuing status as a probationer could properly be considered by the trial court as an aggravating circumstance.

Appellant next contends that the trial court committed error by citing three prior arrests as the basis for its finding that his criminal history constituted an aggravating circumstance and in failing to consider evidence of mitigating circumstances apparent on the record. The statement setting out the trial court's rationale for imposing an enhanced sentence read in its entirety as follows:

> The Court does find the following aggravating circumstances: That the defendant was on probation at the time the offense was committed. That the defendant's prior criminal

> history, consisting of an arrest on February 3, 1970, of carrying a concealed weapon, an arrest on May 18, 1971, for assault and battery with intent to kill, an arrest on March 13, 1983 for battery with injury, and other arrests indicating that the defendant's conduct was in fact escalated from carrying a concealed weapon, to in fact, voluntary manslaughter.

At the time of appellant's sentencing hearing, I.C. 35-38-1-7 . . . identified the factors which the court was to take into consideration in imposing sentence. Subsections (b) and (c) set out circumstances which the court was allowed to consider in aggravation and mitigation; subsection (d) stated that "the criteria listed in subsections (b) and (c) do not limit the matters that the court may consider in determining the sentence."

If the sentencing court found that appellant "ha[d] a history of criminal or delinquent activity," the court was authorized to consider that fact as an aggravating circumstance under I.C. 35-38-1-7(b)(2), and it is clear from the court's sentencing statement that it considered appellant's prior arrests to be instances of criminal behavior establishing such a history. In this, the court was in error. A record of arrest, without more, does not establish the historical fact that the defendant committed a criminal offense on a previous occasion such that it may be properly considered as evidence that the defendant has a history of criminal activity. In order to enhance a criminal sentence based, in whole or in part, on the defendant's history of criminal activity, a sentencing court must find instances of specific criminal conduct shown by probative evidence to be attributable to the defendant. A bare record of arrest will not suffice to meet this standard.

An arrest is "the taking of a person into custody, that he may be held to answer for a crime." I.C. 35-33-1-5. An arrest is permissible without a warrant if the arresting officer had, at the time of the arrest, probable cause to believe that the person had committed a felony. An arrest may also be made pursuant to a warrant, which is itself based upon either the return of an indictment or upon probable cause. Probable cause exists when, at the time the warrant is sought or the arrest is made, the arresting officer has knowledge of facts and circumstances which would warrant a man of reasonable caution to believe that the person committed the criminal act in question. The act of placing a person under arrest indicates only a belief, albeit strong, that the arrested person is guilty of a crime, but does not itself constitute a determination of the historical fact of that person's guilt.

The historical fact that a defendant has committed a crime, such that it may then be properly found to constitute the aggravator of a criminal history, may be established upon evidence that the defendant has been convicted of another crime, upon his own admission of guilt of another crime, or upon evidence that the defendant committed another crime which is properly admitted at trial under an exception to the general prohibition against evidence of prior bad acts. Once a defendant's guilt of the other crime is established by conviction, admission, or properly admitted trial evidence, whether or not he was ever placed under arrest is irrelevant. The substance of the aggravator, "history of criminal activity," is the fact that the defendant committed the other crime, not that he was arrested for it.

This is not to say that a record of arrests, particularly a lengthy one, should carry no aggravating weight or that it may not be considered by a sentencing court. A long line of cases from this Court holds that allegations of prior criminal activity need not be reduced to conviction before they may be properly considered as aggravating circumstances by a sentencing court. The court must, however, place this type of information in the proper context when considering it and determining its relative weight. A record of arrests cannot be considered as an aggravator under I.C. 35-38-1-7(b)(2) because it does not reveal to the sentencing court that the defendant has engaged in the kind of behavior which the legislature identified as an aggravator in that subsection. I.C. 35-38-1-7(d), however, gives a sentencing court the flexibility to consider any factor which reflects on the defendant's character, good or bad, in addition to those expressly set out in the rest of the statute when determining the appropriate sentence to impose on that defendant. It is in this category that a record of arrests is properly considered. While a record of arrests does not establish the historical fact of prior criminal behavior, such a record does reveal to the court that subsequent antisocial behavior on the part of the defendant has not been deterred even after having been subject to the police authority of the State and made aware of its oversight of the activities of its citizens. This information is relevant to the court's assessment of the defendant's character and the risk that he will commit another crime and is therefore properly considered by a court in determining sentence.

This Court has also held that criminal charges which are pending at the time of a defendant's sentencing hearing may properly be considered as an aggravating circumstance. Pending charges, like arrests, do not establish the historical fact that the defendant committed the crime alleged, but, like arrests, are relevant and may be considered by a sentencing court as being reflective of the defendant's character and as indicative of the risk that he will commit other crimes in the future.

As noted above, the sentencing statement at issue here makes it clear that the court inferred that appellant actually committed the crimes for which he was arrested, and this inference constitutes error. [A] remand is necessary for the court to conduct a new sentencing hearing and then to issue an order which reflects that the nature of the aggravators and their relative weights were correctly assessed and found to merit an enhanced sentence or to impose a standard sentence. . . .

■ WASHINGTON STATE SENTENCING GUIDELINES

Implementation Manual

The offender score is measured on the horizontal axis of the sentencing guidelines grid. An offender can receive anywhere from 0 to 9 + points on that axis. In general terms, the number of points an offender receives depends on four factors: 1) the number of prior felony criminal convictions; 2) the relationship between any prior offenses(s) and the current offense of conviction; 3) the presence of multiple prior or current convictions; and 4) whether the crime was committed while the offender was on community placement. [A higher number of points translates into a longer prison term or a change from nonprison to prison disposition.] RCW 9.94A.030(12) defines criminal history to include the defendant's prior adult convictions in this state, federal court, and elsewhere, as well as [felonies adjudicated] in juvenile court if [they did not result in a diversion].

"Washout" of Certain Prior Felonies

In certain instances, prior felony convictions are not calculated into the offender score. . . . Prior Class A and sex offense felony convictions are always included in the offender score. Prior Class B felony convictions are not included if 1) the offender has spent ten years in the community; and 2) has not been convicted of any felonies since the most recent of either the last date of release from confinement... or the day the sentence was entered. Prior Class C felonies are not included if the offender has spent five years in the community and has not been convicted of any felonies since the most recent of either the last date of release from confinement... or the day the sentence was entered.

■ CALIFORNIA PENAL CODE §667 ("THREE STRIKES")

(e) (2) (A) If a defendant has two or more prior [serious or violent] felony convictions as defined [elsewhere in the code] that have been pled and proved, the term for the current felony conviction shall be an indeterminate term of life imprisonment with a minimum term of the indeterminate sentence calculated as the greater of:

(i) Three times the term otherwise provided as punishment for each current felony conviction subsequent to the two or more prior felony convictions.

(ii) Imprisonment in the state prison for 25 years. . . .

(f) (1) Notwithstanding any other law, [the sentence enhancement described in subdivision (e)] shall be applied in every case in which a defendant has a prior felony conviction as defined [by this statute]. The prosecuting attorney shall plead and prove each prior felony conviction except as provided in paragraph (2).

(2) The prosecuting attorney may move to dismiss or strike a prior felony conviction allegation in the furtherance of justice . . . or if there is insufficient evidence to prove the prior conviction. If upon the satisfaction of the court that there is insufficient evidence to prove the prior felony conviction, the court may dismiss or strike the allegation.

(g) Prior felony convictions shall not be used in plea bargaining. . . . The prosecution shall plead and prove all known prior felony convictions and shall not enter into any agreement to strike or seek the dismissal of any prior felony conviction allegation except as provided in paragraph (2) of subdivision (f).

Problem 19-6. Striking Out

John Saenz, whose criminal record began in 1959, is 58 years old. He has five felony convictions, including two robberies, assault with a deadly weapon, and auto theft. In a 1985 robbery, Saenz pointed a gun at a San Diego police officer. In 1995 (while still on parole from a prior offense, and while misdemeanor drug charges were still pending against him), Saenz stole $75 worth of clothing, sunglasses, a mustache trimmer, and a birthday card from a discount store in California.

Saenz has admitted stealing the merchandise. His conduct qualifies as petty theft, which is a felony. There is also a provision in the state code for misdemeanor theft. If you were the prosecuting attorney in this case, would you file felony charges against Saenz? If you were the judge, would you grant the defendant's motion to dismiss the felony charge and to accept a proposed guilty plea for misdemeanor theft (which could result in a prison sentence of up to one year)?

Problem 19-7. Personal History and Prospects

Kelley Grady began a love affair with Brenda Croslin while she was living with her husband, Michael, and their two children. Eventually, Brenda left Michael and began renting a home owned by Kelley's mother.

Michael and Brenda had a violent relationship. On more than one occasion Michael choked and beat Brenda in the presence of their children, and threatened to kill her. On March 7, 1993, Michael and Brenda argued on the telephone, and Michael went to Brenda's house, where Kelley and the children were also present. Michael began yelling for Kelley to come out of the house and threatened to kill him. Kelley telephoned the police, and Michael left after the police arrived.

On July 20, 1993, Brenda went to Michael's house after work to pick up their children. When Brenda arrived, Michael began yelling at her, poking her in the chest, slapping her with his hand, and telling her that she was moving back in with him. Brenda told Michael she was not moving back in with him, and Michael became enraged. Michael called Kelley on the telephone and told him Brenda was moving out of the rental house. Kelley heard Brenda crying in the background. Michael began punching, kicking, and choking Brenda.

After his conversation with Michael, Kelley drove his truck to Brenda's house. Finding nobody there, he drove to Michael's house, parked in front, and honked the horn. Kelley had a cellular telephone, a knife, and a semiautomatic handgun in his car. Brenda went onto the porch and told Kelley to leave. But Kelley began yelling "wife beater" and told Michael to come out of the house and pick on someone his own size. Michael took a butcher knife from the kitchen and jumped off the porch into the yard. Kelley saw Michael come out of the house with what he thought was a gun. Kelley reached into his vehicle, retrieved his gun, and began shooting at Michael and running. There were three initial gunshots, a pause, and then another series of shots. Michael fell to the ground face first. Kelley threw the gun down, told Brenda to call 911, and went to his truck.

The police arrested Kelley when they arrived. Michael was pronounced dead immediately after arriving at the hospital, and an autopsy revealed 11 separate bullet wounds. A toxicology report showed a blood alcohol concentration of .164.

Kelley was charged with one count of first-degree premeditated murder in Michael's death. He claimed self-defense, but the jury found him guilty of voluntary manslaughter. At the sentencing hearing, various witnesses testified that Kelley had a reputation as a peaceful, nonaggressive, nonviolent person who sought to avoid conflict. He had no prior criminal history.

Prior to sentencing, the defendant filed a motion for a "downward departure" sentence. Based on the offense of conviction and the defendant's lack of criminal history, the presumptive sentence under the state sentencing guidelines was a term of incarceration of 46-51 months. The defendant requested a nonprison sentence of 36 months, including up to 30 days in jail, up to 180 days in community corrections, a period of probation, and public and monetary restitution. The trial court sentenced the defendant to 30 days in jail, 180 days in residential Community Corrections, 1 year on electronic surveillance, and 1,000 hours of public restitution. The judge also ordered the defendant to make no contact with the Croslin children until later review by the Court, and to pay for a psychological evaluation of the Croslin children.

Under the relevant statute, an appellate court may review a "departure" sentence only to determine whether the findings of fact are "supported by evidence in the record" and whether the reasons justifying the departure are "substantial and compelling." As an appellate judge, would you uphold this sentence? Compare State v. Grady, 900 P.2d 227 (Kan. 1995).

Notes

1. *Prior convictions, prior arrests, and pending charges: majority position.* In all U.S. sentencing systems, the prior convictions of an offender are among the most important determinants of the sentence imposed. In jurisdictions with detailed sentencing rules, prior convictions for more serious offenses typically increase the sentence more than prior convictions for less serious offenses. In some systems (such as the Washington system, illustrated above), prior convictions that occurred long ago have less impact on the current sentence. Prior convictions for the same type of crime as the current offense can increase a sentence more than prior convictions for unrelated wrongdoing. What purposes do these provisions serve? Are they designed to deter the offender, or other offenders, from committing future crimes? Are they designed to select a sentence "proportionate" to the crime committed (that is, to give the offender her "just deserts")? Some sentencing judges are more reluctant to increase a sentence based on a prior arrest or a pending unadjudicated criminal charge. Nevertheless, it is highly unusual for sentencing rules to prevent judges from relying on a prior arrest or a pending charge in setting the current sentence. Under the federal sentencing guidelines, a court may depart from the designated range of sentences if the guidelines' calculation of prior criminal record does not adequately account for "similar adult criminal conduct not resulting in a criminal conviction." U.S. Sentencing Guidelines §4A1.3.

2. *Guidelines versus statutes.* The California code section reprinted above provides an example of a "habitual offender" law popularly known as "three strikes and you're out." Almost all states have habitual felon statutes, which increase sentences by designated amounts for offenders with the necessary prior felony record. The "three strikes" variety is distinctive for the type of prior record necessary and the amount of increase in the sentence; about half the states have statutes of this type.

Both the California statute and the Washington guidelines provisions instruct a sentencing judge on the amount to increase a sentence in light of a prior criminal record. Nonetheless, they function quite differently. Under the Washington guidelines, the amount of increase moves up gradually as the prior record becomes more serious. The judge can depart from the guidelines in exceptional cases. Guidelines also do not allow *prosecutors* to choose whether to use the prior record to increase a sentence; many "habitual offender" laws do allow prosecutors to choose whether to charge a defendant as an "habitual offender." Why would a legislature choose a statute (like California's) rather than guidelines (like the Washington provisions) to control the impact of prior criminal record?

3. *Unreliable prior convictions.* The use of prior convictions to enhance the sentence for the current offense becomes more controversial when there are reasons to question the accuracy of the earlier offense. This is true especially when the earlier conviction occurred without the involvement of defense counsel. The federal constitution bars the use at sentencing of uncounseled prior convictions, but only if the government obtained the prior conviction by violating the defendant's

constitutional right to counsel. See Nichols v. United States, 511 U.S. 738 (1994) (sentencing court may consider defendant's previous uncounseled misdemeanor conviction in sentencing him for subsequent offense); United States v. Tucker, 404 U.S. 443 (1972) (conviction obtained in violation of Sixth Amendment rights cannot enhance later sentence). These questions often arise when the prior conviction took place in the juvenile system or when the earlier case dealt with charges of driving while intoxicated. See State v. LaMunyon, 911 P.2d 151 (Kan. 1996) (juvenile); State v. Brown, 676 A.2d 350 (Vt. 1996) (DUI).

4. *Offender characteristics at sentencing: majority rule.* A criminal defendant is more than the sum of his contacts with the criminal justice system. The sentencing judge in most cases adjusts the sentence in light of the offender's overall character, including the facts known about his family, physical or mental health, and prospects for rehabilitation. In an unstructured sentencing system, it is difficult to say which personal characteristics of an offender tend to influence the sentence. Most structured systems do not consider such personal characteristics at all in setting the presumptive guideline sentence. Nevertheless, most do allow (and even encourage) the sentencing judge to depart from the guidelines on the basis of personal characteristics. Consider the various grounds the defendant in Problem 19-7 might assert as reasons to reduce his sentence. How could a sentencing court in this system best insulate a departure sentence from reversal on appeal?

5. *Family and community.* Sentencing judges also consider the impact of a proposed sentence on the defendant's family and community. The federal sentencing guidelines attempt to limit this practice by declaring that many personal characteristics of the defendant (including the defendant's "family ties and responsibilities") are "not ordinarily relevant" to a sentence. Appellate courts have upheld departure sentences based on such circumstances only when they are present to an "extraordinary" degree. See United States v. Johnson, 964 F.2d 124 (2d Cir. 1992) (upholding downward departure for payroll clerk at VA hospital convicted for defrauding government; defendant was sole support for three children under 7 years of age, institutionalized adult daughter, 17-year-old son, and 6-year-old granddaughter). What are "extraordinary" family circumstances? According to a 1991 survey, 61.6 percent of all federal prisoners and 56.7 percent of all state prisoners had children under age 18. Among female prisoners, the comparable numbers are 61.4 percent and 66.6 percent. In the state systems, 42.9 percent of the prisoners with children under 18 had only one child below that age, 28.9 percent had two, 15.4 percent had three, and 12.8 percent had four or more. Bureau of Justice Statistics, Comparing Federal and State Prison Inmates, NCJ-145864 (1994). See Jack Weinstein, The Effect of Sentencing on Women, Men, the Family, and the Community, 5 Colum. J. Gender & L. 169 (1996).

As a staff attorney for a sentencing commission, how would you draft guidance for sentencing courts in identifying the sorts of family circumstances that should lead to a departure up or down from the ordinary sentence? Would one circumstance be the number of children? The likely home for those children if the parent is incarcerated? Would you follow the ABA approach or would you leave these questions entirely to the discretion of the sentencing courts? See United States v. Monaco, 23 F.3d 793 (3d Cir. 1994) (decreasing sentence because of father's remorse and mental anguish over involving his adult son in a scheme to defraud government during execution of defense contract); United States v. Ledesma, 979 F.2d 816 (11th Cir. 1992) (enhancing sentence because defendant involved her adult daughter in drug trafficking).

b. Cooperation in Other Investigations

Just as a defendant's past conduct can influence the sentence, so can the defendant's future conduct. Perhaps the most important future conduct for sentencing purposes is the defendant's ability and willingness to help the government investigate other suspects. The defendant can tell investigators about past events or can agree to take part in future "sting" operations. In the federal system, "substantial assistance" to the government is by far the most common reason judges give for "departing" downward to give a sentence lower than the range specified in the guidelines. Substantial assistance accounted for more than 70 percent of the downward departures in 1992 (the next most frequent reason appeared in only 7.9 percent of the departures). It is clear that all sentencing systems allow trial judges to reduce a defendant's sentence based on cooperation. What is less clear is exactly who can determine whether the defendant should benefit from an effort to cooperate, and how much the benefit should be.

■ ROBERT MATOS v. STATE

878 P.2d 288 (Nev. 1994)

PER CURIAM.

On February 18, 1993, an informant contacted the Washoe County Consolidated Narcotics Unit ("CNU") and informed officers that appellant Robert Henry Matos was selling methamphetamines out of his Sparks apartment. The informant was concerned that Matos' child was suffering from exposure to this criminal environment. Later, while wearing a police wire, the informant purchased two "eight balls" of crystal methamphetamine from Matos. Matos was arrested and charged with various crimes stemming from this illegal transaction.

In an effort to reduce any forthcoming criminal sentence, Matos offered to assist law enforcement authorities in capturing other individuals involved in trafficking illegal drugs. NRS 453.3405(2) allows the trial judge to "reduce or suspend" an accused's sentence if the accused renders "substantial assistance in the identification, arrest or conviction" of any accomplices, coconspirators or principals. CNU refused to accept Matos' assistance, considering him a danger to law enforcement officers. Undaunted, Matos moved for a sentence reduction under NRS 453.3405(2).

CNU officers testified that on several occasions, Matos threatened to kill various individuals involved with that unit and had a contract put out against a former cooperative. There was also testimony from the informant that Matos had threatened to kill her and her children if she aided in his prosecution. CNU supervisors decided that Matos presented an unreasonable risk to detectives. Therefore, they refused his assistance. The district court denied the sentence reduction, and Matos immediately entered a conditional plea of guilty to one count of trafficking in a controlled substance. He was fined $100,000 and sentenced to ten years in prison. On appeal, Matos claims that the district court erred in its interpretation and application of NRS 453.3405(2). As a related argument, he contends that the denial of the sentence reduction violated his constitutionally protected right to due process of law. . . .

NRS 453.3405(2) allows an accused to file a motion for a sentence reduction in district court when he has provided law enforcement officials with substantial assistance in identifying or apprehending drug traffickers. NRS 453.3405(2) reads as follows:

> The judge, upon an appropriate motion, may reduce or suspend the sentence of any person convicted of violating any [specified narcotics laws] if he finds that the convicted person rendered substantial assistance in the identification, arrest or conviction of any of his accomplices, accessories, coconspirators or principals or of any other person involved in trafficking in a controlled substance. . . . The arresting agency must be given an opportunity to be heard before the motion is granted. Upon good cause shown, the motion may be heard in camera.

In rejecting Matos' request for a reduced sentence under this statute, the district court held that because law enforcement officials had rejected the offer of help, there was no substantial assistance as a matter of law. Matos contends that the district court erred by failing to examine the merits of his motion and inappropriately determining that it lacked jurisdiction to entertain his request because there was no substantial assistance as a matter of law. He argues that there is no requirement in the language of the statute that the government accept the accused's offer of help. By upholding the district court's interpretation, Matos maintains that this court would create dangerous precedent whereby law enforcement officers would have veto power over all possible sentence reductions. Officers could simply refuse to cooperate with an accused and thereby prohibit a willing informant from taking advantage of "rights granted to him under the statute." For support, Matos provides extensive analysis of the legislative history underlying NRS 453.3405(2).

We disagree with these arguments. Matos is unduly confusing a very simple issue. Leaving aside claims regarding veto power, legislative intent, and the accused's rights under the statute, the inescapable question on appeal is whether the district court erred by concluding that Matos did not substantially assist law enforcement officers. No matter how deep Matos tries to bury the question, the answer remains clear. Matos did not render substantial assistance to CNU because, under the facts of this appeal, law enforcement officials legitimately rejected his offer to assist. Matos was a danger to drug agents. Even if the district court erred in its technical interpretation of the statutory language, this is not fatal to its decision. On appeal, this court may imply findings of fact and conclusions of law if the record clearly supports the lower court's ruling. We hold that the record on appeal clearly supports that Matos could not have obtained a sentence reduction under NRS 453.3405(2).

Matos' second claim of error fares no better than his first. He argues that the district court denied his constitutionally protected right of due process by failing to reach the merits of his motion. . . . This aspect of Matos' argument illustrates a fundamental misconception underlying his entire arguing posture on appeal. Matos [claims] that he had a right to a sentence reduction under NRS 453.3405(2). This assertion is incorrect. Granting a sentence reduction under NRS 453.3405(2) is a discretionary function of the district court. Although never addressed in Nevada, federal courts have consistently held that an accused has no protected due process right to a discretionary sentence reduction for offering "substantial assistance" to government officials in apprehending drug criminals. . . .

■ U.S. SENTENCING GUIDELINES §5K1.1

Upon motion of the government stating that the defendant has provided substantial assistance in the investigation or prosecution of another person who has committed an offense, the court may depart from the guidelines.

The appropriate reduction shall be determined by the court for reasons stated that may include, but are not limited to, consideration of the following: (1) the court's evaluation of the significance and usefulness of the defendant's assistance, taking into consideration the government's evaluation of the assistance rendered; (2) the truthfulness, completeness, and reliability of any information or testimony provided by the defendant; (3) the nature and extent of the defendant's assistance; (4) any injury suffered, or any danger or risk of injury to the defendant or his family resulting from his assistance; (5) the timeliness of the defendant's assistance.

Notes

1. *Assisting in other investigations.* In the unstructured sentencing states, cooperation with the government in investigating and trying other criminal cases is generally believed to have some positive effect both on the sentencing court's disposition of the case and on the duration of the sentence imposed. State v. Johnson, 630 N.W.2d 583 (Iowa 2001). Even in highly discretionary sentencing systems, statutes commonly address the sentencing discount a court must give to a defendant who provides assistance to the government. See Brugman v. State, 339 S.E.2d 244 (Ga. 1986) (discussing statute). The more structured sentencing states have followed the same route, instructing the judge that cooperation with the government can serve as a basis for departing from the guideline sentence and imposing some lesser sentence. See Or. Admin. R. 253-08-002(1)(F).

2. *Substantial in whose eyes?* There is some variation in the amount of control the prosecution has over the use of the "substantial assistance" sentencing factor. If the prosecution refuses to accept a defendant's offer of cooperation, then the sentence usually will not be affected, as we saw in the *Matos* case. But what happens if the government accepts the cooperation and later determines that it was not valuable or complete? Section 5K1.1 of the federal guidelines requires a government motion before the court can reduce the sentence based on the defendant's cooperation, while 18 U.S.C. §3553(e) requires the same before a court can reduce a sentence below a statutory mandatory minimum. Should the court have an independent power to reduce a sentence on these grounds, even in the absence of a government motion? State legislatures and courts have been debating this issue for years, although the state debate has not figured at all in the later federal discussions of this question. See La. Rev. Stat. §40:967(G)(2) (allowing reduction or suspension of sentence if district attorney requests reduction for person providing substantial assistance); State v. Sarabia, 875 P.2d 227 (Idaho 1994) (declaring unconstitutional a statute allowing sentence below mandatory minimum only when prosecutor moves for reduction based on substantial assistance).

In Wade v. United States, 504 U.S. 181 (1992), the Supreme Court held that the Constitution does not preserve for federal judges the power to depart for "substantial assistance" without permission of the government. Only when the defendant makes a "substantial threshold showing" of an unconstitutional motive can the court adjust the sentence without a government motion: "Thus, a defendant would be entitled to relief if a prosecutor refused to file a substantial-assistance motion, say, because of the defendant's race or religion." What else might qualify as a constitutionally improper reason for a prosecutor to withhold a motion?

3. *Nonconstitutional controls on assistance discounts.* The real debate over limiting prosecutorial power in this sphere takes place at the non-constitutional level. Legislatures and sentencing commissions must decide whether to make a prosecutor's motion a necessary precondition to this sort of sentence reduction. The concern, of course, is that an unsupervised prosecutor will make the recommendations on arbitrary or inconsistent grounds. In the federal system, prosecutors have attempted to regulate themselves, by creating written policies about which defendants should receive a reduced sentence for substantial assistance. About 80 percent of the federal districts have adopted written guidelines on the subject, and their content is fairly consistent. However, a study sponsored by the U.S. Sentencing Commission (known as the "Maxfield-Kramer Study") found great variety among the 94 federal districts in their granting of substantial assistance motions. Linda Drazga Maxfield and John Kramer, Substantial Assistance: Empirical Yardstick Gauging Equity in Federal Policy and Practice (1998). The study found that demographic characteristics of defendants had some influence on whether they received a motion: defendants who were male, black, Hispanic, noncitizens, and older were all less likely to receive a motion. As a chief prosecutor, how would you react to this news? Could you create guidelines within your office that would promote more consistent decisions about sentence discounts for cooperating defendants? See Frank Bowman, Substantial Assistance: An Old Prosecutor's Meditation on *Singleton, Sealed Case,* and the Maxfield-Kramer Report, 12 Fed. Sent. Reporter 45 (1999); Cynthia Y. K. Lee, From Gatekeeper to Concierge: Reining in the Federal Prosecutor's Expanding Power over Substantial Assistance Departures, 50 Rutgers L. Rev. 199 (1997).

2. *New Information About the Victim and the Community*

What information not related to the offender or the offense may affect the sentence? This section considers two kinds of information beyond the offense and offender: information about the victim, and information about the community.

In a traditional indeterminate sentencing system, victims do not formally address the sentencing court. The trial is seen as a process through which the state prosecutes and punishes individuals for violations of collective norms; individuals are compensated through private law (tort) remedies. Of course, the prosecutor attempts in many cases to bring the victim's concerns or information to the court's attention, and the judge may account for this in imposing a sentence. But until recently, the victim has had little opportunity to speak directly to the sentencing court.

In recent decades, through statutes, state constitutional provisions, and procedural rules, most jurisdictions have created a formal role for victims. Many jurisdictions give victims an opportunity to address the court, both to provide information about the harm caused by the crime and to express an opinion about the proper sentence to impose. But what impact should victims have on individual sentences? Should the personal or family circumstances of the victim matter? Will these factors, if considered, become a cover for invidious factors such as wealth and race?

■ TERRY NICHOLS v. COMMONWEALTH
839 S.W.2d 263 (Ky. 1992)

WINTERSHEIMER, J.

. . . Nichols, while in jail in Ohio, volunteered information regarding a series of unsolved burglaries in Boyd and Greenup Counties, Kentucky. Nichols reached a plea agreement with the prosecution in all cases and the prosecutor recommended a sentence of five years on each of the 11 counts to run concurrently. Nichols appeared in Greenup Circuit Court on January 25, 1989, and pled guilty to 11 counts of burglary in the second degree. . . . He waived formal sentencing and requested to be sentenced immediately. The trial judge indicated that he was inclined to follow the recommendation of the prosecution.

However, before rendering sentence, the judge inquired of the prosecutor if the victims of the burglaries had been consulted in regard to the recommendation, and the prosecutor responded that he did not know. Upon learning that at least one of the victims had not been informed of the proceedings, the trial judge withdrew sentence and set the matter for trial. He advised the prosecution to contact the victims. Three of the 11 victims did not agree with the prosecutor's recommendation. The Greenup County Jailer was one of the victims dissatisfied. These three cases were then sent to a jury only for the purpose of recommending sentence and not for any fact finding of guilt. The jury recommended five year concurrent sentences on the three offenses and indicated that the sentences were to run concurrently with the other eight charges. At final sentencing on May 24, 1989, the trial judge ordered that the three counts run concurrently with each other but further ordered that those terms be served consecutively to the others for a total of ten years in prison. Nichols appealed the ten year sentence, [and] argues that the trial judge should have recused himself because the sentence was motivated by the desire to please the local jailer. . . .

The record indicates that the trial judge directed the prosecution to contact all the victims of the burglaries and not just the jailer. . . . The expression of the concern by the trial judge that the victims of the crimes be informed of the prosecution recommendation does not provide a basis for reversible error based on bias, prejudice or personal knowledge. . . . Clearly the record does indicate that the trial judge was concerned about the views of the victims, including the County Jailer. The trial judge said, "Well, I certainly don't want Mr. Salmons to be mad at the judge. If he, the jailer, thinks he ought to have more . . . I'm not going to give him more. I'm going to give him a fair trial."

K.R.S. 421.500 provides that victims of crimes have a right to make an impact statement for consideration by the court at the time of the defendant's sentencing. The county jailer, who is a victim of crime, has as much right as anyone to make such an impact statement regardless of his official position. The language of the trial judge does not provide a basis for personal bias. The comments of the trial judge were a proper expression of the requirement for notification to all crime victims of their right to express an opinion on a sentencing proceeding. The statement, "I don't want him mad at me," should not be unduly expanded in such a context. [The sentence] is affirmed.

COMBS, J., dissenting.

The Commonwealth recommended a 5-year effective sentence; the trial judge was initially disposed to accept the recommendation; but, to accommodate Jailer

Salmons, the court resolved to impose a harsher penalty; the jury fixed the sentence for the Salmons burglary at 5 years; bound by the verdict as to the term, the court nevertheless sentenced Nichols to 10 years by ordering consecutive service. That is what appears from this proceeding, making it one not distinguished for an appearance of integrity. . . .

The majority would have it that the judge's concern for Mr. Salmons was no more than that due any burglary victim pursuant to KRS 421.500, dealing with victim-impact information as a factor in sentencing. I do not fault a trial court for its concern for a victim, as a victim. Here, however, it is evident that the trial court's solicitude toward Jailer Salmons was due not to the impact of the crime upon the victim, but due to the personal relationship between the victim and the court: "Well, I certainly don't want Mr. Salmons mad at the Judge." While there are a number of salutary reasons for considering genuine victim-impact information, not counted among them, because not relevant to tailoring the penalty to the crime, is the preservation of an individual's personal esteem for the judge.

Moreover, no genuine victim-impact information is to be found in this record. KRS 421.500(3)(c) requires law enforcement personnel to inform the victim as to the "criminal justice process as it involves the participation of the victim"; and subsection (5)(b) requires the prosecutor, "[i]f the victims so desire," to notify a victim of his/her "right to make an impact statement for consideration by the court at the time of sentencing." This right to make an impact statement is more fully discussed in KRS 421.520. . . . Section .520 implies that "the victim has the right to submit a written victim impact statement," which "may contain, but need not be limited to, a description of the nature and extent of any physical, psychological or financial harm suffered by the victim . . . and the victim's recommendation for an appropriate sentence." The statute purports to compel the court to consider the statement prior to making its sentencing decision.

First, deaf to cries of nitpicking, I observe that the present record is devoid of written victim-impact statements. One may also, as I have, search in vain for even an oral statement by any victim. Where does the statute provide for, and why should we (or a trial court) countenance, the prosecutor's hearsay reports of victims' statements?

Second, what the prosecutor did report was that the three victims' objections "boil down to they do not believe in concurrent sentencing for someone who has committed so many offenses." Where in this is any "recommendation for an appropriate sentence"? Where is any information as to impact of a crime upon a victim? I venture that the statute intends that a victim may recommend a "sentence" (that is, a term of years . . .) appropriate for the crime committed against him/her, but not consecutive sentencing for crimes committed against others. This view is neatly supported by the definition of "victim" found in KRS 421.500(1): "'victim' means an individual who suffers direct or threatened physical, financial, or emotional harm as the result of the commission of a crime. . . ." A victim-impact statement is not a committee report. Perhaps the court would have had to consider victim A's (written!) opinion that Nichols should draw 999 years for burglarizing A's home; but the court's consideration of (indeed, deference to) A's opinion that Nichols should be sentenced more harshly (or consecutively) for other crimes, of which A was not a victim, went far beyond the intent of the statute.

Furthermore, it went far beyond the bounds of due process. Concede that the impact upon an individual victim ought to be considered in fixing a sentence for a crime. Concede even that the impact upon each victim is relevant to determining whether multiple sentences should run concurrently or consecutively. But do not concede, I say, that the discretion to assess the effect of accumulated offenses rests elsewhere than in an impartial jury and/or an impartial judge; do not concede that it may be delegated, even in part, to a (justifiably) biased victim. . . .

■ MICHIGAN CONSTITUTION §24

(1) Crime victims, as defined by law, shall have the following rights, as provided by law:

—The right to be treated with fairness and respect for their dignity and privacy throughout the criminal justice process. . . .

—The right to be reasonably protected from the accused throughout the criminal justice process.

—The right to notification of court proceedings.

—The right to attend trial and all other court proceedings the accused has the right to attend.

—The right to confer with the prosecution.

—The right to make a statement to the court at sentencing.

—The right to restitution.

—The right to information about the conviction, sentence, imprisonment, and release of the accused.

(2) The legislature may provide by law for the enforcement of this section.

Problem 19-8. Vulnerable Victim

Billy Creech obtained from a local newspaper a list of recently married men. From that list, he selected a victim to whom he sent a letter threatening to "torture your family members while you watch, or kill one in front of you," unless the victim periodically sent Creech a money order for $100. The letter ended by saying that "Failure to do this will end in bodily harm to your wife!" Creech was convicted for mailing a letter containing a threat to injure the addressee, a federal crime. Can the court consider this newlywed to be a "vulnerable victim"? Compare United States v. Creech, 913 F.2d 780 (10th Cir. 1990).

Notes

1. *Victims' rights at sentencing: majority view.* Over the past 20 years, nearly every state has decided to allow victim involvement at sentencing. See generally National Victim Center, The 1996 Victims' Rights Sourcebook: A Compilation and Comparison of Victims' Rights Laws (1996). It is difficult to capture the depth, range, and impact of this dramatic change in sentencing practice. Almost all states allow victim input through the PSI report. Many allow victims a separate opportunity to make a written or oral statement regarding sentencing, often detailing the kinds of information victims may offer. A few states have retained sharper limits: Several allow judges to choose whether to admit or refuse victim impact information; Texas allows a victim to make a statement only after sentencing, Tex. Code Crim. Proc. art. 42.03.

The Victim and Witness Protection Act of 1982 amended the Federal Rules of Criminal Procedure to require the inclusion of a victim impact statement as a part of the PSI report in federal court. Fed. R. Crim. P. 32 ("The presentence report must contain . . . verified information, stated in a nonargumentative style, containing an assessment of the financial, social, psychological, and medical impact on any individual against whom the offense has been committed"). Federal legislation and constitutional amendments have been proposed that would increase victim participation at sentencing.

The *Nichols* case from Kentucky might at first seem to stress an odd and unlikely event: The jailer was a victim who, being acquainted with the judge, was likely to influence his views at sentencing. But victim impact information is supposed to influence the judge; indeed, many statutes require the judge to take account of victim information. The rich variety of statutes has not produced a substantial case law regarding victim impact statements in the noncapital context. When the impact of such statements is challenged, it often takes the form of the claim in *Nichols*— that the judge was biased, or unduly influenced, by the information. For example, in People v. Vecchio, 819 P.2d 533, 534-535 (Colo. Ct. App. 1991), the court rejected a claim that the trial judge should have recused himself after the prosecutor filed more than 100 victim impact statements.

> The theory behind the collection of these victim impact statements evidently was that all residents of the community were victims of the theft of public property and might properly express their views about the effect of the offenses on them and the community as well as their views of the appropriate sentence which should be imposed upon the defendant. In addition, a considerable number of these statements expressed dissatisfaction with sentences which had previously been imposed by the trial judge's predecessor in office in two unrelated cases involving public figures which, according to the motion and affidavits, had resulted in the removal from office at the retention election of the prior judge. From these facts [the defendant argues that] the "Court is at the mercy of an angry community," and "it must be presumed that this Court is 'interested' in the outcome of this case." . . .
>
> In ruling the allegations here legally insufficient to require disqualification, the trial judge observed, among other things: "Cases which come before this Court are often of such nature as to arouse public passion. . . . If a Court were to find that the grounds in a motion such as this one were sufficient, [j]udges would virtually be unable to serve in communities where they lived." We agree with these statements. Moreover, every sitting judge faces a future retention election and is aware that his conduct in office will have a direct impact upon the outcome thereof. There can be no legal presumption that a judge is intimidated by the outrage of the community in which he serves; retribution at the polls is a risk undertaken by every judicial candidate upon acceptance of appointment in a judicial position. To put it in general parlance, "it goes with the territory."

When 100 people submit impact statements, is that a statement of victims or of the community? Should judges rely on their own sense of the unique nature of harm imposed in particular cases? Does victim impact information differ in kind from other types of new information, such as information about the offender?

2. *Victim impact statements in capital cases.* Courts and legislatures have wrestled with the special problems of integrating victim impact statements with the complex law of capital sentencing. The U.S. Supreme Court limited introduction of victim evidence in capital cases in Booth v. Maryland, 482 U.S. 496 (1987) (victim impact

statement in capital cases leads to arbitrary and capricious decisions because sentencing jury's focus would shift away from the defendant and onto the victim and the victim's family), and South Carolina v. Gathers, 490 U.S. 805 (1989) (rejecting prosecutorial argument about victim impact). The Court reversed itself in Payne v. Tennessee, 501 U.S. 1277 (1991), holding that the jury could hear victim impact information. In *Payne* the Court upheld admission of testimony from a murder victim's mother, describing the impact of the killing on the victim's three-year-old son. The Court held that the victim impact statements "illustrated quite poignantly some of the harm that Payne's killing had caused." State courts and state legislatures have overwhelmingly followed the invitation in *Payne* to allow victim impact evidence in capital cases. See State v. Muhammad, 678 A.2d 164 (N.J. 1996). A few states still ban victim evidence in capital cases or limit the topics that victims can address. See Bivins v. State, 642 N.E.2d 928 (Ind. 1994); Mack v. State, 650 So. 2d 1289 (Miss. 1994).

3. *Implementing victims' rights at sentencing.* As a Michigan legislator, how would you draft legislation to enforce section 24 of the Michigan constitution? Would you provide for victim statements prior to the sentencing hearing, along with any statement at the hearing? If the victim is unwilling to testify, would your statute nevertheless allow the defense or prosecution to subpoena the victim and obtain his evidence under oath? Compare ABA Standards for Criminal Justice, Sentencing §§18-5.9 to 18-5.12.

4. *Vulnerable victims.* Structured sentencing rules often instruct a judge to enhance a sentence if the victim of the crimes was "vulnerable" or otherwise worthy of exceptional protection. The Minnesota Sentencing Guidelines authorize the judge to decrease a sentence if "the victim was an aggressor in the incident," and to increase the sentence if the "victim was particularly vulnerable due to age, infirmity, or reduced physical or mental capacity, which was known or should have been known to the offender" or if the "victim was treated with particular cruelty for which the individual offender should be held responsible." Minn. Sentencing Guidelines II.D.2.a.1, II.D.2.b.1-2. The federal guidelines contain a similar provision for enhancement of the sentence by a designated amount if "the defendant knew or should have known that a victim of the offense was unusually vulnerable due to age, physical or mental condition, or that a victim was otherwise particularly susceptible to criminal conduct." U.S. Sentencing Guidelines §3A1.1. A specified increase is also required when the victim is "a government officer or employee" or a law enforcement officer.

Problem 19-9. Community as Victim

Marvin Jones and Taifi Griffith were members of the "Crips" gang in Seattle. They were on "Black Gangster Disciples" (BGD) turf on Horton Street near John Muir Elementary School talking to some girls, when four members of the BGD gang saw them. Everyone "flashed" their respective gang signs, then one of the BGDs ran away from the group to retrieve a gun. The Crips got into two automobiles and started to drive away. Antwon Johnson, a BGD member who lived across the street from John Muir Elementary School, jumped from some bushes and fired a handgun at the two cars as they passed in front of the school building. The incident occurred while school was in session.

The prosecutor charged Johnson with assault in the first degree. At trial, the prosecution presented testimony from the BGD members, and from several other eyewitnesses. They included William Robbins, a parent picking up his child from school at the time of the shooting, and Roy Dunn, a crossing guard who observed the shooting and collected from the street several spent cartridges following the shooting. The jury found Johnson guilty of assault in the first degree.

At sentencing, Judge Eberharter found that a defendant with Johnson's criminal history, convicted of assault in the first degree, would normally receive a sentence between 85 and 113 months. However, Judge Eberharter found that "substantial and compelling reasons exist which justify a sentence above the Standard range," and he imposed on Johnson an exceptional sentence of 170 months' incarceration. The statutory maximum for the crime is a life term. As the primary reason justifying the exceptional sentence, the Judge pointed to the community impact of the shootings. The judge received several letters from residents of the Mount Baker community near John Muir Elementary School expressing fear and anxiety caused by the shooting. The court's factual findings were as follows: 1) the impact of the Johnson's assaults went far beyond the intended victims; 2) as a result of Johnson's actions, children became frightened to attend school and parents fearful that their children are not safe while at the school; and 3) Johnson invaded the community's zone of safety.

Is the impact of this crime on the community different enough from the typical first degree assault to justify an exceptional sentence? Is the community impact here a "substantial and compelling" reason to justify a sentence higher than the norm for this crime? Compare State v. Johnson, 873 P.2d 514 (Wash. 1994).

Problem 19-10. Local Conditions

An international flight made a scheduled stop at Puerto Rico's airport en route from Colombia to Frankfurt, West Germany. Jorge Armando Aguilar-Pena was aboard. Customs officials conducted an inspection of in-transit passengers and discovered that he was carrying cocaine. After conviction, the probation officer consulted the sentencing guidelines and fixed the sentencing range at 21-27 months. The court accepted the computational conclusions contained in the PSI report, but it departed from the guidelines and sentenced Aguilar to a prison term of 48 months. The court gave the following reasons for its upward departure:

> First, it is a well-known fact that Puerto Rico is being utilized by South American drug traffickers as a convenient stopover point for the distribution of narcotics into the Continental United States and other places in the world via commercial, scheduled airline flights. Second, departure from the guidelines is warranted in order to discourage the utilization of the Puerto Rico International Airport, an airport with lesser law-enforcement capabilities than those in the mainland, as a connecting point for international narcotics trafficking and/or for introduction of narcotics into the Continental United States. Puerto Rico's airport is less secure than airports in cities such as Miami and New York. Third, a sentence within the guidelines in a case of this nature would also be in violation of the Puerto Rico public sentiment, feelings, and mores regarding this type of crime.

Under the federal sentencing guidelines, a sentencing court can depart in a case that presents aggravating or mitigating factors of a kind or to a degree "not adequately considered" by the sentencing commission when formulating guidelines.

The federal guidelines make no provision for "local conditions." The authorizing federal legislation directed the federal sentencing commission to "take into account only to the extent that they do have relevance the community view of the gravity of the offense; . . . the public concern generated by the offense; . . . the current incidence of the offense in the community and in the Nation as a whole." 28 U.S.C. §§994(c)(4), (5), (7). Was this a proper upward departure? Compare United States v. Aguilar-Pena, 887 F.2d 347 (1st Cir. 1989).

Notes

1. *Community views at sentencing: majority position.* Judges do not hand down sentences in a vacuum. Judges may respond implicitly to changing societal conceptions of the seriousness of the offense, or to changes in the prevalence of an offense, or to the particular "message" that a sentence may send to the community. But can judges do so openly? Information about community impact is available much less often than information about the impact on specific victims. One problem with considering community impact is identifying the relevant community. Who should express the community's view? Some courts have allowed victims to offer information about broader community impact. For example, the Pennsylvania Supreme Court in Commonwealth v. Penrod, 578 A.2d 486 (Pa. 1990), allowed victims, family members, and friends to testify at sentencing for drunken-driving defendants "regarding the impact of the offense on the victim, the impact on the community generally, and/or the impact on the family members or friends as members of the community." Should representatives of victims' rights organizations be allowed to speak at every sentencing? Should equal time be given to representatives of those who believe sentences are too severe or that imprisonment harms communities by removing vital members?

2. *Judicial experience and community priorities.* Is it appropriate for judges in the same jurisdiction to weigh community impact differently? Federal judge Reena Raggi argues that federal guidelines should allow local variation among federal districts because particular crimes may create special harms in some localities and because the judges in that area develop special expertise on certain topics:

> I first began to question [the nationally uniform approach of the sentencing guidelines] when I had to impose sentences on a number of defendants who had unlawfully transported firearms into New York from other states. Almost daily my fellow New Yorkers and I would read in the press of the senseless shooting of young children, on the streets, even in their own homes, all victims of random gun fire. Indeed, 16 children were shot in this manner in New York City over approximately 10 weeks [in 1990]; 5 of them died. Almost invariably the guns used in these crimes, as well as most others unlawfully possessed in this area, had come from out of state.
>
> This sort of interstate transportation of guns into the New York area is big business. In the two years between 1990 and 1992, a joint federal-state task force operating in New York arrested 260 people for such trafficking. And yet, when it came time for me to impose sentences in my cases that summer of 1990, I was confronted by a guideline range that rarely exceeded six months' incarceration. . . .
>
> The insight judges have about crimes in their particular districts goes beyond simply recognizing which conduct is more destructive to a community. It also reaches the question of how different levels of conduct contribute to an area's crime problems. For example, despite the fact that no part of the United States is immune from the problem of drugs, few judges have as broad an experience dealing with drug importation and large-scale distribution as my colleagues in the Eastern District of New York. The

> piers and airports of the district make it, for all intents and purposes, the port of New York and, thus, the entry point for a large percentage of the contraband entering this country. Within the district reside the leaders of most of the distribution networks operating in the northeast. . . . District judges should enjoy more discretion — indeed they should be encouraged — to depart from the guidelines to reflect specific local concerns.

Raggi, Local Concerns, Local Insights, 5 Fed. Sentencing Rep. 306 (1993).

3. *Prosecutorial experience and community priorities.* If judges can adjust sentences to take account of local priorities, should prosecutors also be able to make charging decisions on the basis of local needs? Should prosecutorial needs and resources then be allowed to affect sentences? For instance, the U.S. Attorney's Office in San Diego receives far more immigration cases than it can prosecute. Of the 565,581 illegal aliens apprehended in fiscal year 1992, the U.S. Attorney prosecuted 245 felony immigration cases and another 5,000 misdemeanors. Because the San Diego district attorney, as a matter of policy, will not prosecute any cases related to the border, these cases must be prosecuted in federal court or not at all. William Braniff, Local Discretion, Prosecutorial Choices and the Sentencing Guidelines, 5 Fed. Sentencing Rep. 309 (1993). Should the judge enhance a sentence when she knows that an unusually large number of offenders are going unpunished? Should the judge reduce the sentence out of concern for selective and discriminatory treatment or ignore prosecutorial priorities entirely?

E. RACE AND SENTENCING

Race is an unavoidable part of modern American criminal procedure. Difficult questions arise at all stages of the criminal process: What is the role of race in stops and investigations? Can race be an element in the determination of reasonable suspicion or probable cause? When are racial disparities sufficient to justify challenges to charging practices? What role should race play in jury selection? In arguments at trial?

Previous chapters have explored these and other questions about the role that race plays in decisions throughout the criminal process. But perhaps the most common and visible questions about race arise at the end of the process, in the form of claims that black Americans and other minorities are punished more severely than whites. This section considers the charge that racism is an inherent part of the criminal justice process and that its end product is unequal punishment. In some situations, the responsible decisionmakers may be identifiable; in other situations, the source of racial disparities may be hard to specify even when disparity clearly exists.

Discussion of race and punishment must start with some disquieting facts about prison and jail populations. In June 2001, 44.5 percent of the inmates in state and federal prisons and local jails were African American, although African Americans constitute only about 13 percent of the population. The rate of imprisonment for black males aged 25-29 is about 13.4 percent, while the rate for Hispanic males of the same age group is 4.1 percent, and the comparable rate for white males is 1.8 percent. Bureau of Justice Statistics, Prison and Jail Inmates at Midyear 2001, at Table 15 (2002, NCJ 191702). After combining the number of young men on probation or parole with the number in prison or jail, almost a third of young black men are under criminal justice supervision on any given day. African American women remain the fastest growing group in prisons and jails. Drug policies have contributed more than any other crimes to the fast growth in the imprisonment rate for African Americans. As Marc Mauer and Tracy Huling have noted,

> While African American arrest rates for violent crime — 45% of arrests nationally — are disproportionate to their share of the population, this proportion has not changed significantly for twenty years. For drug offenses, though, the African American proportion of arrests increased from 24% in 1980 to 39% in 1993, well above the African American proportion of drug users nationally.

Mauer & Huling, Young Black Americans and the Criminal Justice System (1995).

These materials provoke a recurring question: Does the criminal justice system exacerbate or mediate larger social problems? Can criminal justice systems respond to intentional or unintentional racial bias in society? If so, what is the proper role for courts, police, prosecutors, and legislators in crafting such a response?

1. *Race and the Victims of Crime*

The influence of race on punishment has received the most sustained attention in the context of capital punishment. Many facets of the story of race in American capital punishment emerge in the story of Warren McCleskey and his extraordinary trip through the criminal justice system.

On the morning of May 13, 1978, McCleskey drove to pick up Ben Wright, Bernard Dupree, and David Burney. The four men planned to commit a robbery; they drove from Marietta, Georgia, into Atlanta and decided on the Dixie Furniture Store as a target. McCleskey had a .38 caliber Rossi nickel-plated revolver, which he had stolen in an armed robbery of a grocery store a month earlier. Ben Wright carried a sawed-off shotgun, and the two others had blue steel pistols. McCleskey, who was black, entered the front of the store, and the other three came through the rear by the loading dock. He secured the front of the store by forcing all the customers and employees there to lie on the floor while the other robbers rounded up the employees in the rear and began to bind them with tape. A pistol was taken from George Malcom, an employee, at gunpoint. Before all the employees were tied up, Officer Frank Schlatt, answering a silent alarm, stopped his patrol car in front of the building. Officer Schlatt, who was white, entered the front door and proceeded about 15 feet down the center aisle, where he was shot twice, once in the face and once in the chest. The head wound was fatal. The robbers fled. Sometime later, McCleskey was arrested in Cobb County in connection with another armed robbery. He confessed to the Dixie Furniture Store robbery but denied the shooting. Ballistics showed that Schlatt had been shot by a .38 caliber Rossi revolver. The weapon was never recovered.

McCleskey was convicted in 1978. The jury found two aggravating circumstances that authorized the use of the death penalty: (1) the murder was committed while the offender was committing another capital felony (armed robbery), and (2) the murder was committed against a police officer engaged in the performance of his official duties. The jury sentenced McCleskey to death for murder. Co-defendant Burney was sentenced to life imprisonment, while another co-defendant received a 20-year sentence.

On direct appeal in the Georgia courts, McCleskey first raised the claim that the death penalty violates the due process and equal protection provisions of the federal and state constitutions because prosecutorial discretion permits the government to apply the penalty in a racially discriminatory way. The Georgia Supreme Court rejected this claim as follows: "Appellant's argument is without merit. Gregg v. Georgia, 428 U.S. 153 (1976); Moore v. State, 243 S.E.2d 1 (Ga. 1978)." McCleskey v. State, 263 S.E.2d 146 (Ga. 1980).

Eventually, McCleskey took his claims to federal court: The U.S. district court had the power, under the venerable Habeas Corpus Act of 1867, 28 U.S.C. §2254, to invalidate state convictions obtained in violation of the federal constitution. In federal district court, McCleskey presented the findings of a massive statistical study, dubbed the "Baldus" study (named after its principal author, Professor David Baldus of the University of Iowa). The study analyzed almost 2,500 murder and voluntary manslaughter convictions for crimes committed (or for defendants arrested) between 1973 and 1978 in Georgia. For a random sample of these cases, researchers answered more than 500 questions about each case, such as the defendant's mental and physical condition, the defendant's race and other demographic information, the defendant's prior criminal record, the method of killing, the victim's role in the offense, and so forth. Due to the large number of variables, the researchers could not match many cases that differed in only one respect (for instance, cases that were identical in every respect, except one defendant shot the victim twice while the other defendant shot the victim only once). Thus, they used a statistical technique known as "multivariate regression analysis" to estimate the amount of influence each feature of the case had on the ultimate decision of whether the defendant received the death penalty.

The study concluded that the race of the defendant was not a "statistically significant" factor in the outcome, after "controlling" for all the other factors that could influence the outcome. However, the race of the *victim* remained one of the most important influences on the outcome, even after controlling for other factors.

The district court decided that the study did not establish the intentional discrimination necessary to show a violation of equal protection because the study was flawed. For instance, the court pointed to several errors in the collection of data and noted that "the questionnaire could not capture every nuance of every case." The court also suggested that the study had not successfully isolated the effects of race but instead measured the effects of other permissible factors that were "correlated" with race. McCleskey v. Zant, 580 F. Supp. 338 (N.D. Ga. 1984).

The federal court of appeals took a different approach to the question. It was willing to assume that the study successfully demonstrated "what it purports to prove": Defendants who kill a white victim have a greater chance of receiving the death penalty, and part of that increased risk is based on the race of the victim. Nevertheless, the court of appeals said that this statistical evidence was not enough for McCleskey to prove intentional racial discrimination in his case. When a party relies on statistical patterns of discrimination, the court said, it must show such large racial disparities that the evidence "compels a conclusion that . . . purposeful discrimination . . . can be presumed to permeate the system." The estimated effects of the race of the victim on the death penalty decision were not enough to compel such a conclusion. Indeed, the court said, any statistical study would have difficulty making such a showing about a complex process involving many different decisionmakers. McCleskey v. Kemp, 753 F.2d 877 (11th Cir. 1985). McCleskey then appealed to the U.S. Supreme Court.

■ WARREN McCLESKEY v. RALPH KEMP

481 U.S. 279 (1987)

POWELL, J.

This case presents the question whether a complex statistical study that indicates a risk that racial considerations enter into capital sentencing determinations proves that petitioner McCleskey's capital sentence is unconstitutional under the Eighth or Fourteenth Amendment.

[In support of his habeas claim], McCleskey proffered a statistical study performed by Professors David Baldus, Charles Pulaski, and George Woodworth (the Baldus study) that purports to show a disparity in the imposition of the death sentence in Georgia based on the race of the murder victim and, to a lesser extent, the race of the defendant. The Baldus study is actually two sophisticated statistical studies that examine over 2,000 murder cases that occurred in Georgia during the 1970's. The raw numbers collected by Professor Baldus indicate that defendants charged with killing white persons received the death penalty in 11% of the cases, but defendants charged with killing blacks received the death penalty in only 1% of the cases. . . . Baldus also divided the cases according to the combination of the race of the defendant and the race of the victim. He found that the death penalty was assessed in 22% of the cases involving black defendants and white victims; 8% of the cases involving white defendants and white victims; 1% of the cases involving black defendants and black victims; and 3% of the cases involving white defendants and black victims. . . .

Baldus subjected his data to an extensive analysis, taking account of 230 variables that could have explained the disparities on nonracial grounds. One of his models concludes that, even after taking account of 39 nonracial variables, defendants charged with killing white victims were 4.3 times as likely to receive a death sentence as defendants charged with killing blacks. . . . Thus, the Baldus study indicates that black defendants, such as McCleskey, who kill white victims have the greatest likelihood of receiving the death penalty. . . .

McCleskey's first claim is that the Georgia capital punishment statute violates the Equal Protection Clause of the Fourteenth Amendment.[7] He argues that race has infected the administration of Georgia's statute. . . . McCleskey's claim of discrimination extends to every actor in the Georgia capital sentencing process, from the prosecutor who sought the death penalty and the jury that imposed the sentence, to the State itself that enacted the capital punishment statute and allows it to remain in effect despite its allegedly discriminatory application. [T]his claim must fail.

[To] prevail under the Equal Protection Clause, McCleskey must prove that the decisionmakers in his case acted with discriminatory purpose. He offers no evidence specific to his own case that would support an inference that racial considerations played a part in his sentence. Instead, he . . . argues that the Baldus study compels an inference that his sentence rests on purposeful discrimination. McCleskey's claim that these statistics are sufficient proof of discrimination, without regard to the facts

7. [We] assume the study is valid statistically without reviewing the factual findings of the District Court. Our assumption that the Baldus study is statistically valid does not include the assumption that the study shows that racial considerations actually enter into any sentencing decisions in Georgia. Even a sophisticated multiple-regression analysis such as the Baldus study can only demonstrate a risk that the factor of race entered into some capital sentencing decisions and a necessarily lesser risk that race entered into any particular sentencing decision.

of a particular case, would extend to all capital cases in Georgia, at least where the victim was white and the defendant is black.

The Court has accepted statistics as proof of intent to discriminate in certain limited contexts. First, this Court has accepted statistical disparities as proof of an equal protection violation in the selection of the jury venire in a particular district. Although statistical proof normally must present a "stark" pattern to be accepted as the sole proof of discriminatory intent under the Constitution, because of the nature of the jury-selection task, we have permitted a finding of constitutional violation even when the statistical pattern does not approach such extremes. Second, this Court has accepted statistics in the form of multiple-regression analysis to prove statutory violations under Title VII of the Civil Rights Act of 1964.

But the nature of the capital sentencing decision, and the relationship of the statistics to that decision, are fundamentally different from the corresponding elements in the venire-selection or Title VII cases. Most importantly, each particular decision to impose the death penalty is made by a petit jury selected from a properly constituted venire. Each jury is unique in its composition, and the Constitution requires that its decision rest on consideration of innumerable factors that vary according to the characteristics of the individual defendant and the facts of the particular capital offense. Thus, the application of an inference drawn from the general statistics to a specific decision in a trial and sentencing simply is not comparable to the application of an inference drawn from general statistics to a specific venire-selection or Title VII case. In those cases, the statistics relate to fewer entities, and fewer variables are relevant to the challenged decisions.

Another important difference between the cases in which we have accepted statistics as proof of discriminatory intent and this case is that, in the venire-selection and Title VII contexts, the decisionmaker has an opportunity to explain the statistical disparity. Here, the State has no practical opportunity to rebut the Baldus study. Controlling considerations of public policy dictate that jurors cannot be called to testify to the motives and influences that led to their verdict. Similarly, the policy considerations behind a prosecutor's traditionally wide discretion suggest the impropriety of our requiring prosecutors to defend their decisions to seek death penalties, often years after they were made.[17] Moreover, absent far stronger proof, it is unnecessary to seek such a rebuttal, because a legitimate and unchallenged explanation for the decision is apparent from the record: McCleskey committed an act for which the United States Constitution and Georgia laws permit imposition of the death penalty.

Finally, McCleskey's statistical proffer must be viewed in the context of his challenge. McCleskey challenges decisions at the heart of the State's criminal justice system. One of society's most basic tasks is that of protecting the lives of its citizens and one of the most basic ways in which it achieves the task is through criminal laws against murder. Implementation of these laws necessarily requires discretionary judgments. Because discretion is essential to the criminal justice process, we would demand exceptionally clear proof before we would infer that the discretion has been abused. . . . Accordingly, we hold that the Baldus study is clearly insufficient to support an inference that any of the decisionmakers in McCleskey's case acted with discriminatory purpose.

17. Requiring a prosecutor to rebut a study that analyzes the past conduct of scores of prosecutors is quite different from requiring a prosecutor to rebut a contemporaneous challenge to his own acts. See Batson v. Kentucky, 476 U.S. 79 (1986).

[McCleskey also] contends that the Georgia capital punishment system is arbitrary and capricious in application, and therefore his sentence is excessive [and contrary to the Eighth Amendment], because racial considerations may influence capital sentencing decisions in Georgia. . . . To evaluate McCleskey's challenge, we must examine exactly what the Baldus study may show. Even Professor Baldus does not contend that his statistics prove that race enters into any capital sentencing decisions or that race was a factor in McCleskey's particular case. Statistics at most may show only a likelihood that a particular factor entered into some decisions. There is, of course, some risk of racial prejudice influencing a jury's decision in a criminal case. There are similar risks that other kinds of prejudice will influence other criminal trials. The question is at what point that risk becomes constitutionally unacceptable. McCleskey asks us to accept the likelihood allegedly shown by the Baldus study as the constitutional measure of an unacceptable risk of racial prejudice influencing capital sentencing decisions. This we decline to do.

Because of the risk that the factor of race may enter the criminal justice process, we have engaged in "unceasing efforts" to eradicate racial prejudice from our criminal justice system.[30] [However,] McCleskey's argument that the Constitution condemns the discretion allowed decisionmakers in the Georgia capital sentencing system is antithetical to the fundamental role of discretion in our criminal justice system. Discretion in the criminal justice system offers substantial benefits to the criminal defendant. Not only can a jury decline to impose the death sentence, it can decline to convict or choose to convict of a lesser offense. Whereas decisions against a defendant's interest may be reversed by the trial judge or on appeal, these discretionary exercises of leniency are final and unreviewable. Similarly, the capacity of prosecutorial discretion to provide individualized justice is firmly entrenched in American law. As we have noted, a prosecutor can decline to charge, offer a plea bargain, or decline to seek a death sentence in any particular case. Of course, the power to be lenient also is the power to discriminate, but a capital punishment system that did not allow for discretionary acts of leniency would be totally alien to our notions of criminal justice. . . .

At most, the Baldus study indicates a discrepancy that appears to correlate with race. Apparent disparities in sentencing are an inevitable part of our criminal justice system. [There] can be no perfect procedure for deciding in which cases governmental authority should be used to impose death. Despite these imperfections, our consistent rule has been that constitutional guarantees are met when the mode for determining guilt or punishment itself has been surrounded with safeguards to make it as fair as possible. Where the discretion that is fundamental to our criminal process is involved, we decline to assume that what is unexplained is invidious. In light of the safeguards designed to minimize racial bias in the process, the fundamental value of jury trial in our criminal justice system, and the benefits that discretion provides to criminal defendants, we hold that the Baldus study does not

30. This Court has repeatedly stated that prosecutorial discretion cannot be exercised on the basis of race. Nor can a prosecutor exercise peremptory challenges on the basis of race. More generally, this Court has condemned state efforts to exclude blacks from grand and petit juries. Other protections apply to the trial and jury deliberation process. Widespread bias in the community can make a change of venue constitutionally required. The Constitution prohibits racially biased prosecutorial arguments. If the circumstances of a particular case indicate a significant likelihood that racial bias may influence a jury, the Constitution requires questioning as to such bias. Finally, in a capital sentencing hearing, a defendant convicted of an interracial murder is entitled to such questioning without regard to the circumstances of the particular case.

demonstrate a constitutionally significant risk of racial bias affecting the Georgia capital sentencing process.

Two additional concerns inform our decision in this case. First, McCleskey's claim, taken to its logical conclusion, throws into serious question the principles that underlie our entire criminal justice system. The Eighth Amendment is not limited in application to capital punishment, but applies to all penalties. Thus, if we accepted McCleskey's claim that racial bias has impermissibly tainted the capital sentencing decision, we could soon be faced with similar claims as to other types of penalty. Moreover, the claim that his sentence rests on the irrelevant factor of race easily could be extended to apply to claims based on unexplained discrepancies that correlate to membership in other minority groups, and even to gender. Similarly, since McCleskey's claim relates to the race of his victim, other claims could apply with equally logical force to statistical disparities that correlate with the race or sex of other actors in the criminal justice system, such as defense attorneys or judges. Also, there is no logical reason that such a claim need be limited to racial or sexual bias. If arbitrary and capricious punishment is the touchstone under the Eighth Amendment, such a claim could — at least in theory — be based upon any arbitrary variable, such as the defendant's facial characteristics, or the physical attractiveness of the defendant or the victim, that some statistical study indicates may be influential in jury decisionmaking. As these examples illustrate, there is no limiting principle to the type of challenge brought by McCleskey. . . .

Second, McCleskey's arguments are best presented to the legislative bodies. It is not the responsibility — or indeed even the right — of this Court to determine the appropriate punishment for particular crimes. It is the legislatures, the elected representatives of the people, that are constituted to respond to the will and consequently the moral values of the people. Legislatures also are better qualified to weigh and evaluate the results of statistical studies in terms of their own local conditions and with a flexibility of approach that is not available to the courts. Capital punishment is now the law in more than two-thirds of our States. It is the ultimate duty of courts to determine on a case-by-case basis whether these laws are applied consistently with the Constitution. Despite McCleskey's wide-ranging arguments that basically challenge the validity of capital punishment in our multiracial society, the only question before us is whether in his case the law of Georgia was properly applied. [This] was carefully and correctly done in this case. . . .

Brennan, J., dissenting.

At some point in this case, Warren McCleskey doubtless asked his lawyer whether a jury was likely to sentence him to die. A candid reply to this question would have been disturbing. First, counsel would have to tell McCleskey that few of the details of the crime or of McCleskey's past criminal conduct were more important than the fact that his victim was white. Furthermore, counsel would feel bound to tell McCleskey that defendants charged with killing white victims in Georgia are 4.3 times as likely to be sentenced to death as defendants charged with killing blacks. In addition, frankness would compel the disclosure that it was more likely than not that the race of McCleskey's victim would determine whether he received a death sentence: 6 of every 11 defendants convicted of killing a white person would not have received the death penalty if their victims had been black, while, among defendants with aggravating and mitigating factors comparable to McCleskey's, 20 of every 34 would not have been sentenced to die if their victims had been black.

Finally, the assessment would not be complete without the information that cases involving black defendants and white victims are more likely to result in a death sentence than cases featuring any other racial combination of defendant and victim. The story could be told in a variety of ways, but McCleskey could not fail to grasp its essential narrative line: there was a significant chance that race would play a prominent role in determining if he lived or died. . . .

Evaluation of McCleskey's evidence cannot rest solely on the numbers themselves. We must also ask whether the conclusion suggested by those numbers is consonant with our understanding of history and human experience. Georgia's legacy of a race-conscious criminal justice system, as well as this Court's own recognition of the persistent danger that racial attitudes may affect criminal proceedings, indicates that McCleskey's claim is not a fanciful product of mere statistical artifice.

For many years, Georgia operated openly and formally precisely the type of dual system the evidence shows is still effectively in place. The criminal law expressly differentiated between crimes committed by and against blacks and whites, distinctions whose lineage traced back to the time of slavery. During the colonial period, black slaves who killed whites in Georgia, regardless of whether in self-defense or in defense of another, were automatically executed. A. Higginbotham, In the Matter of Color: Race in the American Legal Process 256 (1978). By the time of the Civil War, a dual system of crime and punishment was well established in Georgia. See Ga. Penal Code (1861). The state criminal code contained separate sections for "Slaves and Free Persons of Color," and for all other persons. . . .

The Court . . . states that its unwillingness to regard petitioner's evidence as sufficient is based in part on the fear that recognition of McCleskey's claim would open the door to widespread challenges to all aspects of criminal sentencing. Taken on its face, such a statement seems to suggest a fear of too much justice. Yet surely the majority would acknowledge that if striking evidence indicated that other minority groups, or women, or even persons with blond hair, were disproportionately sentenced to death, such a state of affairs would be repugnant to deeply rooted conceptions of fairness. The prospect that there may be more widespread abuse than McCleskey documents may be dismaying, but it does not justify complete abdication of our judicial role. . . .

In fairness, the Court's fear that McCleskey's claim is an invitation to descend a slippery slope also rests on the realization that any humanly imposed system of penalties will exhibit some imperfection. Yet to reject McCleskey's powerful evidence on this basis is to ignore both the qualitatively different character of the death penalty and the particular repugnance of racial discrimination, considerations which may properly be taken into account in determining whether various punishments are "cruel and unusual." Furthermore, it fails to take account of the unprecedented refinement and strength of the Baldus study.

In more recent times, we have sought to free ourselves from the burden of [our history of racial discrimination]. Yet it has been scarcely a generation since this Court's first decision striking down racial segregation, and barely two decades since the legislative prohibition of racial discrimination in major domains of national life. These have been honorable steps, but we cannot pretend that in three decades we have completely escaped the grip of a historical legacy spanning centuries. Warren McCleskey's evidence confronts us with the subtle and persistent influence of the past. His message is a disturbing one to a society that has formally repudiated racism, and a frustrating one to a Nation accustomed to regarding its destiny as the product of its own will. Nonetheless, we ignore him at our peril, for we remain imprisoned by the past as long as we deny its influence in the present. . . .

Notes

1. *Compelling evidence of intent.* What sort of statistical study might provide the circumstantial evidence necessary to convince a court that arbitrary racial discrimination plays enough of a role in a sentencing system to invalidate the outcome in one case? Is such a statistical study possible? If racial discrimination does influence some decisionmakers, to some degree, in some cases, how might one demonstrate that fact in a court of law? Both the court of appeals and the Supreme Court concluded that a stronger statistical showing would be necessary before racial influences in sentencing would amount to a constitutional problem. What sort of evidence did the courts have in mind?

2. *Whose race, victim's or defendant's?* Note that the Baldus study found that the race of the *defendant* had no statistically significant effect on the use of capital punishment. In Furman v. Georgia, 408 U.S. 238 (1972), the Supreme Court struck down several capital punishment statutes, declaring that the death penalty (as administered at that time) was "cruel and unusual punishment" and a violation of the Eighth Amendment. Among the many reasons for this decision discussed in the various concurring opinions, several of the justices argued that capital punishment could not stand because it was imposed disproportionately against the poor and racial minorities. Would the Supreme Court have reached a different outcome in *McCleskey* if the Baldus study had pointed to racial discrimination based on the race of the defendant rather than the race of the victim? Can a punishment be racially discriminatory if the government imposes it equally on defendants of all races?

3. *Other venues.* Suppose that on the day after the district court issued its order, the NAACP sends a copy of the Baldus study to a member of the Georgia legislature, and that member distributes copies. As the chair of the senate's committee on criminal justice matters, would you hold hearings? If so, what would be the topic of the hearings — the validity of the study or the most appropriate response to the study? If the Supreme Court had concluded instead that the influence of race in Georgia's capital punishment system rendered McCleskey's sentence unconstitutional, how would you advise Georgia legislators and prosecutors to respond? Would a victory for McCleskey mean abolition of the death penalty in Georgia?

4. *Statistical studies of capital punishment after* McCleskey. The "race of the victim" effect that appeared in the Baldus study in Georgia has also appeared in statistical studies of other states. These claims have gotten very little serious attention from courts; many simply cite *McCleskey* with no further discussion in refusing to consider the studies as relevant evidence of racial discrimination in the use of capital punishment. See People v. Davis, 518 N.E.2d 78 (Ill. 1987). The Supreme Court of New Jersey has indicated that evidence along the lines of that presented in *McCleskey* could be sufficient to establish a prima facie case of a violation of the state constitution. However, the court has also indicated that New Jersey has not yet executed enough people to form the basis for a convincing statistical study. See State v. Bey, 645 A.2d 685 (N.J. 1994) ("The statistics do not support his contention. Our abiding problem with analyzing the effect of race is that the case universe still contains too few cases to prove that the race of a defendant improperly influences death sentencing").

2. *Race and Discretionary Decisions Affecting Punishment*

Racial disparities at sentencing can result from decisions made by actors at early stages of the criminal justice process. A strong bias in investigations or arrests may be passed through and perhaps even validated by studies showing unbiased decision making at a later stage of the process. For example, if whites and blacks who are convicted of a particular offense are punished identically, but members of one race are disproportionately investigated, then the sanction will appear neutral but will in fact be highly disparate, because the investigatory practices do not accurately reflect actual underlying behavior. It is not only police decisions that can generate sharp disparities that are passed through the system: Prosecutors may disproportionately direct cases involving members of one race to state court and identical cases by another race to federal court, where very different punishments attach to analogous state and federal charges. Or prosecutors may offer pleas in a racially disproportionate fashion. Indeed, the impact from an early police or prosecutorial decision can be so strong that the initial decision is in effect also a decision to punish.

This section highlights the difficulty of proving the source of discriminatory effects in large, complicated systems with many participants. Discrimination may be especially hard to unearth when it is the product of repeated, low-level behavior of a large group of individuals, and perhaps the result of unconscious influences on decision making. This section also raises questions about the capacity of the law to change group behavior. A fundamental challenge throughout the law is to design rules and remedies that deter bad conduct. It is hard enough to alter the behavior of individuals; the challenge of developing effective rules is multiplied when disfavored outcomes reflect complex decisions by large groups of people.

■ FREDDIE STEPHENS v. STATE
456 S.E.2d 560 (Ga. 1995)

FLETCHER, J.

Freddie Stephens challenges the constitutionality of OCGA §16-13-30(d), which provides for life imprisonment on the second conviction of the sale or possession with intent to distribute a controlled substance. He contends that the provision as applied is irrational and racially discriminatory in violation of the United States and Georgia Constitutions. . . . The challenged statute states:

> [A]ny person who violates subsection (b) of this Code section . . . shall be guilty of a felony and, upon conviction thereof, shall be punished by imprisonment for not less than five years nor more than 30 years. Upon conviction of a second or subsequent offense, he shall be imprisoned for life.

Subsection (b) makes it unlawful to "manufacture, deliver, distribute, dispense, administer, sell, or possess with intent to distribute any controlled substance." For a defendant to receive a life sentence for a second conviction, the state must notify the defendant prior to trial that it intends to seek the enhanced punishment based on past convictions.

Stephens contends that the statute as applied discriminates on the basis of race. He argues that this court should infer discriminatory intent from statewide and county-wide statistical data on sentences for drug offenders. In Hall County, where

Stephens was convicted, the trial court found that one hundred percent (14 of 14) of the persons serving a life sentence under OCGA §16-13-30(d) are African-American, although African-Americans make up less than ten percent of the county population and approximately fifty to sixty percent of the persons arrested in drug investigations. Relying on evidence provided by the State Board of Pardons and Paroles, the trial court also found that 98.4 percent (369 of 375) of the persons serving life sentences for drug offenses as of May 1, 1994 were African-American, although African-Americans comprise only 27 percent of the state's population. Finally, a 1994 Georgia Department of Corrections study on the persons eligible for a life sentence under subsection (d) shows that less than one percent (1 of 168) of the whites sentenced for two or more convictions for drug sales are serving a life sentence, compared to 16.6 percent (202 of 1219) of the blacks.

In an earlier challenge to death penalty sentencing in Georgia based on statistics showing that persons who murder whites are more likely to be sentenced to death than persons who murder blacks, the United States Supreme Court held that the defendant had the burden of proving the existence of purposeful discrimination and that the purposeful discrimination had a discriminatory effect on him. McCleskey v. Kemp, 481 U.S. 279 (1987). . . .

Stephens concedes that he cannot prove any discriminatory intent by the Georgia General Assembly in enacting the law or by the Hall County district attorney in choosing to seek life imprisonment in this case. His attorney stated at the sentencing hearing: "I cannot prove and I do not feel there is any evidence to show that the district attorney's office is exercising their prosecutorial discretion in a discriminatory manner [and] I don't think I can demonstrate the legislature acted with discriminatory intent in enacting this code section." These concessions preclude this court from finding an equal protection violation under the United States Constitution.

We also conclude that the statistical evidence Stephens presents is insufficient evidence to support his claim of an equal protection violation under the Georgia Constitution. Stephens fails to present the critical evidence by race concerning the number of persons eligible for life sentences under OCGA §16-13-30(d) in Hall County, but against whom the district attorney has failed to seek the aggravated sentence. Because the district attorney in each judicial circuit exercises discretion in determining when to seek a sentence of life imprisonment, a defendant must present some evidence addressing whether the prosecutor handling a particular case engaged in selective prosecution to prove a state equal protection violation. . . .

Stephen's argument about inferring intent from the statistical evidence also ignores that other factors besides race may explain the sentencing disparity. Absent from the statistical analysis is a consideration of relevant factors such as the charges brought, concurrent offenses, prior offenses and sentences, representation by retained or appointed counsel, existence of a guilty plea, circuit where convicted, and the defendant's legal status on probation, in prison, or on parole. Without more adequate information about what is happening both statewide and in Hall County, we defer deciding whether statistical evidence alone can ever be sufficient to prove an allegation of discriminatory intent in sentencing under the Georgia Constitution.

The dissent argues that McCleskey v. Kemp is not the controlling precedent, instead relying on the United States Supreme Court decision on peremptory challenges in jury selections in Batson v. Kentucky, 476 U.S. 79 (1986). We must look to *McCleskey* for a proper analysis of the substantive issue before us, rather than *Batson,* because *McCleskey* dealt with the use of statistical evidence to challenge racial disparity in sentencing, as does this case.

The Supreme Court in *McCleskey* pointed out several problems in requiring a prosecutor to explain the reasons for the statistical disparity in capital sentencing decisions. Many of these same problems exist in requiring district attorneys to justify their decisions in seeking a life sentence for drug offenses based on statewide, and even county-wide, statistics of persons serving life sentences in state prisons for drug offenses.

First, "requiring a prosecutor to rebut a study that analyzes the past conduct of scores of prosecutors is quite different from requiring a prosecutor to rebut a contemporaneous challenge to his own acts. See Batson v. Kentucky, 476 U.S. 79 (1986)." *McCleskey,* 481 U.S. at 296. Second, statewide statistics are not reliable in determining the policy of a particular district attorney. [Even the statistics from Hall County do not accurately reflect the record of the district attorney in this case since she did not assume office until 1993.] Finally, the Court stated that the policy considerations behind a prosecutor's discretion argue against requiring district attorneys to defend their decisions to seek the death penalty. Since district attorneys are elected to represent the state in all criminal cases, it is important that they be able to exercise their discretion in determining who to prosecute, what charges to bring, which sentence to seek, and when to appeal without having to account for each decision in every case. [There] is a rational basis for the sentencing scheme in OCGA §16-13-30(d) and that it does not deprive persons of due process or equal protection under the law.

THOMPSON, J., concurring specially.

[W]e are presented once again with the claim that OCGA §16-13-30(d) is being used in a discriminatory fashion. This time, we are introduced to statewide statistical information which must give us pause: From 1990 to 1994, OCGA §16-13-30(d) was used to put 202 out of 1,107 eligible African-Americans in prison for life. During that same period, the statute was used to put 1 out of 167 eligible whites in prison for life. A life eligible African-American had a 1 in 6 chance of receiving a life sentence. A life eligible white had a 1 in 167 chance of receiving a life sentence. An African-American was 2,700 percent more likely to receive a life sentence than a white. . . . These statistics are no doubt as much a surprise to those who work and practice within the judicial system as to those who do not.

Statistical information can inform, not explain. It can tell what has happened, not why. However, only a true cynic can look at these statistics and not be impressed that something is amiss. That something lies in the fact that OCGA §16-13-30(d) has been converted from a mandatory life sentence statute into a statute which imposes a life sentence only in those cases in which a district attorney, in the exercise of his or her discretion, informs a defendant that the State is seeking enhanced punishment.

McCleskey v. Kemp, 481 U.S. 279 (1987), provides a workable test for determining whether the death penalty statute is being applied discriminatorily. *McCleskey* should continue to be applied in death penalty cases where there is a system of checks and balances to ensure that death sentences are not sought and imposed autocratically. Likewise *McCleskey* should be applied in other cases where the courts have discretion to determine the length of time to be served. However, *McCleskey* probably should not be applied where a district attorney has the power to decide whether a defendant is sentenced to life, or a term of years. . . .

I am persuaded that Batson v. Kentucky, 476 U.S. 79 (1986), could be used to supply a general framework in analyzing cases of this kind. . . . Nevertheless, it is my considered view that the judgment in this case must be affirmed because the defendant has failed to meet his burden even under a *Batson*-type analysis.

In order to establish a prima facie case under *Batson*, a defendant must prove systematic discrimination in his particular jurisdiction. Although the statistics presented by defendant are indicative of a statewide pattern of discrimination in the use of OCGA §16-13-30(d), the Hall County statistics are insufficient to make such a case. They simply show that all the persons in Hall County serving a life sentence under OCGA §16-13-30(d) are African-Americans. They do not show how many African-Americans were eligible to receive a life sentence under the statute; nor do they show how many whites were eligible. Moreover, they offer no information concerning the record of the district attorney in this case. Thus, upon careful review, I must conclude that this defendant, in this case and on this record, failed to prove a pattern of systematic discrimination in his jurisdiction. . . .

Statewide, approximately 15 percent of eligible offenders receive a life sentence under OCGA §16-13-30(d). The statistical evidence presented in this case serves as notice to the General Assembly of Georgia that the mandatory life sentence provision of OCGA §16-13-30(d) has been repealed *de facto*. With such notice, there are at least three courses of action the legislature might now choose to pursue.

One. The General Assembly could choose to leave the mandatory life sentence on the books realizing that it is being used in a small percentage of the eligible cases. Militating against this course of action is the fact that all laws passed by the legislature should be followed. Contempt for and failure to follow any law breeds contempt for and failure to follow other laws.

Two. The General Assembly could reaffirm its commitment to a mandatory life sentence by requiring district attorneys to inform all defendants of prior convictions and thus enforce OCGA §16-13-30(d) with respect to all life eligible offenders. Militating against this course of action is the fact that mandatory life sentences are not favored by the prosecuting bar or by the defense bar. That is evidenced by the fact that from 1990 to 1994 only 203 out of 1,274 life eligible defendants actually received a life sentence under OCGA §16-13-30(d). . . .

Three. The General Assembly could choose to change the mandatory life sentence penalty to one of several sentencing options which the court could impose. For example, the penalty for a second or subsequent sale could be imprisonment for not less than 5 nor more than 30 years, or life. . . . It is my concern that these problems be resolved in whatever way the General Assembly deems best and that, thereafter, the prosecutors and the courts carry out that legislative will.

Benham, P.J., dissenting.

Of those persons from Hall County serving life sentences pursuant to OCGA §16-13-30(d), which mandates a life sentence for the second conviction for sale of or possession with intent to distribute certain narcotics, 100 percent are African-American, although African-Americans comprise only approximately 10 percent of Hall County's population. In our state prison system, African-Americans represent 98.4 percent of the 375 persons serving life sentences for violating OCGA §16-13-30(d). These statistics were part of the finding of the trial court in this case. In the face of such numbing and paralyzing statistics, the majority say there is no need for inquiry. It is with this determination that I take issue.

[In Batson v. Kentucky, 476 U.S. 79 (1986), the Supreme Court] installed a system that shifted the burden to the prosecutor to give race-neutral reasons for the peremptory challenges once the defendant established facts supporting an inference that the prosecutor's use of peremptory challenges was racially motivated. [The] court in *Batson* stated that an inference of discriminatory intent could be drawn from certain conduct or statistical data. Beyond its effect on peremptory challenges, the importance of *Batson* was that it significantly reduced the burden on one claiming discrimination, recognizing that under certain circumstances, the crucial information about an allegedly discriminatory decision could only come from the one who made the decision.

This is the course of reasoning we need to follow in analyzing the issue in this case rather than the more restrictive course taken in McCleskey v. Kemp and applied by the majority. . . . I am not unmindful or unappreciative of the vital and taxing role district attorneys are called upon to undertake in the ongoing battle against the blight of illicit drug trafficking. Throughout this state, they shoulder an enormous burden of responsibility for advancing the fight against drugs, and to do so successfully, they must be invested with considerable discretion in making decisions about ongoing prosecutions. However, it is the very breadth of that discretion, concentrated in a single decision-maker, which makes it necessary that the one exercising the discretion be the one, when confronted with facts supporting an inference of discriminatory application, to bear the burden of establishing that the discretion was exercised without racial influence. This case is more like *Batson* than *McCleskey* because all the discretion in the sentencing scheme involved in this case resides in the district attorney, to the exclusion of the trial court, whereas in death penalty cases such as *McCleskey,* the spread of discretion among the prosecutor, the trial court, and the jurors introduces variables which call for more rigorous statistical analysis. In addition, the complexity of the death penalty procedure, with its many safeguards and the recurring necessity of specific findings at every stage from the grand jury to the sentencing jury, differentiates it from the relative simplicity of the sentencing scheme applicable to this case.

[The] U.S. Supreme Court recognized in *McCleskey* itself that statistical proof which presents a "stark pattern" may be accepted as the sole proof of discriminatory intent. In distinguishing *McCleskey* from such a case, the Supreme Court mentioned in a footnote two cases in which "a statistical pattern of discriminatory impact demonstrated a constitutional violation." One was Gomillion v. Lightfoot, 364 U.S. 339 (1960), where a city's boundaries were altered so as to exclude 395 of 400 black voters without excluding a single white voter, and the other was Yick Wo v. Hopkins, 118 U.S. 356 (1886), in which an ordinance requiring permits for the operation of laundries was applied so as to exclude all of the over 200 Chinese applicants and only one white applicant. The statistics in those cases presented a "stark pattern," but no more stark than the pattern presented in this case. In the present case, based on evidence from law enforcement officers who testified as to arrest rates and other relevant statistics,[2] the trial court found that 100% of the people from that county who were

2. Agent David McIlwraith testified that 50% of the drug investigations involved black males. Investigator Shelly Manny testified that of the 60 drug investigations she conducted in Hall County, only 9 involved blacks and that only 50% of her undercover buys involved black males. Another narcotics investigator testified that since 1989, he had made over 300 cocaine distribution cases in Hall County and only 60% involved black males.

serving life sentences pursuant to OCGA §16-13-30(d) were African-Americans and that statewide, 98.4% of all the persons serving life sentences pursuant to OCGA §16-13-30(d) were African-Americans. . . .

In some instances we must lead the way. [T]his is the time for this Court to draw from our historical strength and our determination that the citizens of this state be treated fairly before the law, and declare that Georgia's constitutional guarantee of equal protection requires that OCGA §16-13-30(d) be applied evenly, in a race-neutral fashion. . . . I would hold, therefore, as a matter purely of state constitutional law, that equal protection of the law in the context of OCGA §16-13-30(d) requires that the prosecution be required, when a defendant has made a prima facie showing sufficient to raise an inference of unequal application of the statute, to "demonstrate that permissible racially neutral selection criteria and procedures have produced the monochromatic result." *Batson*. . . .

Because appellant has made a sufficient showing of discriminatory application of OCGA §16-13-30(d) that the State should be required to give race-neutral reasons for the "monochromatic" application of that statute in Hall County, this court should vacate the life sentences and remand this case to the trial court for a hearing. At such a hearing, should the trial court find that the prosecution could not provide race-neutral reasons for the "monochromatic result" of the application of OCGA §16-13-30(d) in Hall County, sentencing for the offenses involved would still be permissible, but not with the aggravation of punishment authorized by OCGA §16-13-30(d). On the other hand, should the trial court find that the State has provided appropriate race-neutral reasons, the life sentences would be reimposed, whereupon appellant would be entitled to a new appeal. . . .

The statistics offered in this case show an enormous potential for injustice, and those statistics are just like the tip of an iceberg, with the bulk lying below the surface, yet to be realized. And unless we reveal or expose this massive obstacle that lies in the shipping lanes of justice, it will . . . tear a gaping hole in the ship of state, just as a gaping hole was ripped in the Titanic. . . .

Notes

1. *Who discriminates against whom?* What discrimination does Freddie Stephens claim? Who did Warren McCleskey claim had discriminated against him? Other than the fact that both McCleskey and Stephens asserted that race was the basis for discrimination, were these similar claims?

The racial impact of charges under the Georgia statute described above is not the only example of punishment differences that flow from stark racial differences in charging decisions. In a study of charging for crack cocaine offenses in Los Angeles, Richard Berk and Alex Campbell found that black defendants are more likely than white or Latino defendants to be charged in federal court with sale of crack cocaine (which translates into more severe punishments than for comparable charges in state court). While black defendants represented 58 percent of those arrested by the Sheriff's Department for sale of crack cocaine in Los Angeles between 1990 and 1992, they made up 83 percent of the defendants charged with that crime in federal court. White and Latino defendants arrested for this crime were more likely to be prosecuted in state court. Berk & Campbell, Preliminary Data on Race and Crack Charging Practices in Los Angeles, 6 Fed. Sentencing Rep. 36 (1993).

What might be the sources of the racially disparate federal crack prosecutions reported in the Berk and Campbell study?

2. *Competing analogies.* Did the majority in Stephens v. State think that Stephens's claim was the same as McCleskey's? Were you convinced by the competing analogy to discriminatory jury selection in Batson v. Kentucky? Justice Robert Benham, dissenting in *Stephens,* argued that sentencing under the Georgia drug statute was different from capital punishment because it concentrates the decision in the hands of the district attorney. Do you agree? Are there ways a police officer might influence who receives a life sentence under the statute? Do the voters in the county or in the state have some control over this question?

Problem 19-11. The Crack-Powder Differential

In 1986, the United States Congress passed the Anti-Drug Abuse Act to increase the penalties for various drug crimes. The new law imposed heavier penalties on cocaine base (or "crack") than on cocaine powder, a relationship now called the "100 to 1 ratio." An offense involving mixtures weighing 5 grams or more containing cocaine base was subject to the same punishment as an offense involving mixtures weighing 500 grams or more containing cocaine powder. Congress considered crack cocaine to be more dangerous than cocaine powder because of crack's potency, its more highly addictive nature, and its greater accessibility because of its relatively low cost.

Some of the impetus for the federal law came from the news media. Stories associated the use of crack cocaine with social maladies such as gang violence and parental neglect among user groups. Critics of the federal law, however, argued that these social problems did not result from the drug itself, but instead from the disadvantaged social and economic environment in places where the drug often is used.

In practice, the increased penalties for crack meant that African American defendants received heavier penalties than whites for possession and sale of cocaine. Over 90 percent of all people arrested for sale or possession of crack were African American; roughly 80 percent of all people arrested for sale or possession of powder cocaine were white.

By 1989, the Minnesota legislature was debating the same issue. The legislators considered a bill that would make a person guilty of a third degree offense if he or she possessed three or more grams of crack cocaine. Under the same statute, a person who possessed ten or more grams of cocaine powder would be guilty of the same offense; someone who possesses less than 10 grams of cocaine powder would be guilty of a fifth degree offense. The bill became known as the "10 to 3 ratio" law.

The sponsors of the bill argued that this structure facilitated prosecution of "street level" drug dealers. Law enforcement officers who testified at legislative hearings suggested that three grams of crack and ten grams of powder indicated a level at which dealing, not merely using, took place. A person convicted of selling 100 grams of crack may often be characterized as a mid-level dealer (someone who provides the drug to street-level retailers). By comparison, 100 grams of powder usually typifies a low-level retailer; 500 grams is more indicative of a mid-level dealer. However, witnesses from the Department of Public Safety Office of Drug Policy contradicted these estimates for the typical amount of drugs carried by dealers, suggesting that most cocaine powder users are dealers as well.

The customary unit of sales for the two drugs were also different. The normal sales unit of crack was a "rock" weighing .1 gram and selling on the street for $20 or $25. On the other hand, the customary unit of sale for powder was the "8-ball," 1/8 ounce or about 3.5 grams, which sold for about $350. Ten grams of powder cocaine could be easily converted into more than three grams of crack.

Sponsors of the bill also argued that crack is more addictive and dangerous than cocaine powder. Witnesses at the hearings testified that crack cocaine had a more severe effect on the central nervous system and is more addictive than powder cocaine. Other witnesses pointed out, however, that crack and powder cocaine have the same active ingredient, and both produce the same type of pharmacological effects. The differences in effect between the two drugs were based on the fact that cocaine powder is sniffed through the nostrils, while crack cocaine is smoked. If powder cocaine is dissolved and injected, it is just as addictive as crack.

As a member of the Minnesota legislature, would you support the "10 to 3 ratio" bill? What else would you like to know before you vote? Compare State v. Russell, 477 N.W.2d 886 (Minn. 1991).

Notes

1. *Constitutional challenges to punishment differentials: majority position.* Racial disparities in the application of death penalty laws highlight several distinct forms of discrimination. A law could be discriminatory in intent, either at the point of creation or when it is applied. A criminal sanction could also be discriminatory in effect because of uneven (though not intentionally skewed) application of the law. But these are not the only dynamics that create racial differences in criminal punishments. Some laws have racially discriminatory effects, even though the people who create and enforce the law do not intend to burden one racial group more than another and even though they apply the law with complete evenhandedness. These effects occur when the criminal sanctions apply to behavior that people of one race engage in more often than people of other races. Would it ever be unconstitutional for a legislature to criminalize conduct when one racial group is more likely to engage in it?

A number of defendants convicted of trafficking in crack cocaine have argued for a downward departure from the guideline sentence (or an invalidation of the relevant guidelines and statutes) based on an equal protection claim. Federal courts have uniformly rejected this assertion, reasoning that any racial impact of the crack cocaine statutes and guidelines was unintentional. See, e.g., United States v. Reece, 994 F.2d 277 (6th Cir. 1993) (per curiam); United States v. Thomas, 900 F.2d 37 (4th Cir. 1990). While not often addressing such claims, high state courts have usually rejected the constitutional challenges.

2. *Legislative response.* The Minnesota Supreme Court struck down the legislation described in Problem 19-11 on state constitutional grounds in State v. Russell, 477 N.W.2d 886 (Minn. 1991). The legislature responded to the *Russell* decision by increasing the penalties for powder to equal the former penalties for crack. Minn. Stat. §152.021-023. Minnesota's cocaine penalties are now among the toughest in the country, stiffer in some ways than in the federal system.

The federal penalty structure punishes cocaine power and cocaine crack offenders the same for amounts that differ 100 times — the so-called 100-to-1 ratio. Note that this is not a ratio of penalties but of the amounts of drugs that spur similar penalties. In 1994, Congress ordered the U.S. Sentencing Commission, the administrative agency that sets sentencing rules for the federal system, to report on cocaine punishment policies in the federal system. In 1995, the commission issued a report attacking the 100-to-1 ratio, and recommended to Congress a 1-to-1 crack-powder ratio, along with other proposed changes in the federal system that would punish behavior *associated* with crack offenses more severely.

The U.S. Sentencing Commission's recommendation to move to a 1-to-1 quantity ratio came under attack from legislators across the political spectrum. Congress passed legislation to overturn the commission's proposal on October 18, 1995, by a vote of 332 to 83, and President Clinton signed the measure. This was the first time in the history of the commission that Congress voted to override a proposed amendment to the sentencing guidelines. The 100-to-1 quantity ratio remains in effect in the federal system.

As a matter of political reality, how could the U.S. Sentencing Commission recommend the rejection of a policy (the 100-to-1 quantity ratio) that had already received the overwhelming endorsement of the legislative branch when the cocaine penalties were originally enacted? Would Congress have reacted differently to a proposal to reduce, but not eliminate, the differences between crack and powder? Is this equivalent to arguing that a small amount of racial discrimination is acceptable?

3. *Race and crack.* Are you persuaded that racial differentials are the central issue in the crack-cocaine punishment debate? Do different parts of the criminal world just happen to be controlled by groups of a particular race or ethnicity, as an analogy to the use of racketeering laws against the Mafia suggests? Or do you find convincing the argument that racially disproportionate effects (but not intent) justify reworking the system to start with a 1-to-1 quantity ratio?

Michael Tonry surveyed the various causes of the increasing racial divide in criminal punishments in the United States during the 1980s and 1990s. After tracking the steady increase in the proportion of blacks in the nation's prison population during those years, Tonry notes that the increase did not occur because of increased black participation in serious violent crimes: "The proportions of serious violent crimes committed by blacks have been level for more than a decade. Since the mid-1970s, approximately 45 percent of those arrested for murder, rape, robbery, and aggravated assault have been black (the trend is slightly downward)." Instead, most of the changing racial impact of criminal sentences during this time can be traced to drug law enforcement. According to Tonry, politicians pursued the "War on Drugs" with full knowledge of its likely racial impact. Those policies caused

> the ever harsher treatment of blacks by the criminal justice system, and it was foreseeable that they would do so. Just as the tripling of the American prison population between 1980 and 1993 was the result of conscious policy decisions, so also was the greater burden of punishment borne by blacks. Crime control politicians wanted more people in prison and knew that a larger proportion of them would be black.

Michael Tonry, Malign Neglect: Race, Crime and Punishment in America 52 (1995). Is this the sort of "discriminatory intent" that could form the basis for an equal protection challenge? Does this argument create a politically viable basis for revising penalties for violation of the drug laws?

XX Appeals

Errors happen in virtually every felony criminal trial, and in many misdemeanor cases. Appellate courts cannot correct every mistake that occurs at the trial level, but they do try to identify and correct the errors that matter most. Depending on the pertinent double jeopardy rules, an appellate court might respond to a trial error by ordering a new trial or a new sentencing proceeding, by remanding the case for further factual findings by the judge (after a bench trial), or by dismissing the charges.

In this chapter, we explore limits on the power or willingness of appellate courts to correct errors in criminal proceedings. The chapter addresses deceptively simple questions: Who should be able to appeal, and when? How much deference should an appellate court show to findings of fact by the trier of fact? When, if ever, should an appellate court allow a judgment to stand even when it believes that an error occurred? What could be more important than getting the right answer in criminal proceedings?

A. WHO APPEALS?

With rare exceptions (notably in capital cases), appeals are not automatic. Cases can be heard on appeal only when at least one of the parties has the legal authority to request an appeal. This section explores the typical legal limits on the power of parties to file an appeal and the circumstances under which parties are willing to do so.

1. *Right to Appeal*

Most federal and state constitutions do not guarantee criminal defendants any "right to appeal." Instead, statutes and rules of appellate procedure determine who can file an appeal and what issues the parties can raise. What limits do legislatures tend to place on the parties' authority to appeal?

■ ARKANSAS STATUTES §16-91-101

(a) Any person convicted of a misdemeanor or a felony by virtue of a trial in any circuit court of this state has the right of appeal to the Supreme Court of Arkansas. . . .

(c) There shall be no appeal from a plea of guilty or nolo contendere.

■ ARKANSAS RULE OF CRIMINAL PROCEDURE 24.3(b)

With the approval of the court and the consent of the prosecuting attorney, a defendant may enter a conditional plea of guilty or nolo contendere, reserving in writing the right, on appeal from the judgment, to review of an adverse determination of a pretrial motion to suppress evidence. If the defendant prevails on appeal, he shall be allowed to withdraw his plea.

■ CALIFORNIA PENAL CODE §1237.5

No appeal shall be taken by the defendant from a judgment of conviction upon a plea of guilty or nolo contendere, or a revocation of probation following an admission of violation, except where both of the following are met:

(a) The defendant has filed with the trial court a written statement, executed under oath or penalty of perjury showing reasonable constitutional, jurisdictional, or other grounds going to the legality of the proceedings.

(b) The trial court has executed and filed a certificate of probable cause for such appeal with the clerk of the court.

■ CALIFORNIA RULE OF COURT 31(d)

. . . If the appeal from a judgment of conviction entered upon a plea of guilty or nolo contendere is based solely upon grounds (1) occurring after entry of the plea which do not challenge its validity or (2) involving a search or seizure, the validity of which was contested . . ., the provisions of section 1237.5 of the Penal Code requiring a statement by the defendant and a certificate of probable cause by the trial court are inapplicable, but the appeal shall not be operative unless the notice of appeal states that it is based upon such grounds.

Notes

1. *Nonconstitutional basis for right to appeal.* The Supreme Court held long ago in McKane v. Durston, 153 U.S. 684 (1894), that there is no federal constitutional basis for the right to appeal. That holding still accurately describes the law. State

constitutions also do not typically provide for a right to appeal, although there are some exceptions. See Mich. Const. art. I, §20; Wash. Const. art. 1, §22. This is an area dominated by statutes, which address in some detail the types of cases and claims where appeal is available. All states do provide for at least some appellate review of criminal convictions. If one could demonstrate that appellate review is far more common and important today than it was in 1894, might that convince a court to find a new constitutional basis for appeal? How might you demonstrate that appellate review is more common or important today than a century ago?

2. *Appeal after guilty plea: majority position.* Some states (as in Arkansas) allow appeals after guilty pleas only for those issues expressly reserved for appeal in a conditional plea agreement. Others give either the trial court or the appellate court the power to allow the appeal as a completely discretionary matter. Still others (as in California) give the court discretion to allow the appeal only when the defendant meets certain preconditions specified in statute or rule. What variables would be most important in convincing a court to allow an appeal after a plea of guilty? In light of the numbers of appeals and trials occurring each year, how often do you imagine that discretionary appeals after pleas are allowed?

3. *Number of appeals.* The number of defendants who file appeals each year tends to exceed the number of defendants who are convicted at trial. Consider the following statistics for the federal system:

Year	*Criminal Appeals*	*Total Convictions*	*Guilty or Nolo Pleas*	*Conviction After Trial*
1991	9,949	46,768	41,213	5,555
2000	9,162	68,156	64,939	3,217

Bureau of Justice Statistics, Federal Case Processing 2000, with Trends 1982-2000 at tbl. 5, tbl. 7 (2001 NCJ 189737). To the extent that these numbers are typical of other jurisdictions, they suggest that appeal rights may be important to more defendants than trial rights and that a crucial dimension of appeal rights is the availability of appeals after guilty pleas.

4. *Bail pending appeal.* Most felony defendants, in most places, are released at some point prior to their trials or guilty pleas. See Chapter 12. After conviction, however, statutes and court rules make it far less likely that a trial court will release an offender while the appeal is pending. See 18 U.S.C. §§3143(b)(2), 3145(c); Ex parte Anderer, 61 S.W.3d 398 (Tex. 2001) (condition placed on post-conviction bail—prohibition on operating automobile—was aimed at protecting public and "reasonable" under applicable statute). A convicted person who escapes is ineligible to appeal in most systems, although it may be possible to file an appeal upon recapture. See Ortega-Rodriguez v. United States, 507 U.S. 234 (1993) (nonconstitutional federal law creates no absolute bar to escapee's filing of appeal upon recapture); State v. Troupe, 891 S.W.2d 808 (Mo. 1995) ("escape" rule bars appeal, even for those recaptured).

5. *Motions for new trial.* A defendant may convince a trial judge to reconsider a judgment before taking an appeal to another court. A motion for a new trial is, in effect, an "appeal" to the trial court. The motion is made routinely after convictions at trial, and trial judges deny the motion in the overwhelming majority of cases. If you were drafting rules of appellate procedure, would you require such a motion before allowing a party to file an appeal with the appellate court? Would you require it for some issues but not for others?

2. *Appeals by Indigent Defendants*

Although defendants have no federal constitutional right to an appeal, the federal equal protection clause does require states to make its chosen appeals process available to all defendants, even those without the financial resources to pay for an appeal. According to Griffin v. Illinois, 351 U.S. 12 (1956), the state must provide a defendant with a free transcript of a trial record, if such a transcript is necessary to file an appeal. In Douglas v. California, 372 U.S. 353 (1963), the Court extended *Griffin* to require the government to provide indigent appellants with an attorney for an initial "appeal as of right." Even when appellate counsel for an indigent defendant believes the defendant could raise only frivolous issues on appeal, she must advise the appellate court of any colorable issue. Anders v. California, 386 U.S. 738 (1967). Consider the following effort by the state of California to structure the work of appointed defense counsel on appeal.

■ GEORGE SMITH v. LEE ROBBINS

528 U.S. 259 (2000)

THOMAS, J.

Not infrequently, an attorney appointed to represent an indigent defendant on appeal concludes that an appeal would be frivolous and requests that the appellate court allow him to withdraw or that the court dispose of the case without the filing of merits briefs. In Anders v. California, 386 U.S. 738 (1967), we held that, in order to protect indigent defendants' constitutional right to appellate counsel, courts must safeguard against the risk of granting such requests in cases where the appeal is not actually frivolous. We found inadequate California's procedure—which permitted appellate counsel to withdraw upon filing a conclusory letter stating that the appeal had "no merit" and permitted the appellate court to affirm the conviction upon reaching the same conclusion following a review of the record. We went on to set forth an acceptable procedure. California has since adopted a new procedure, which departs in some respects from the one that we delineated in *Anders*. The question is whether that departure is fatal. We hold that it is not. The procedure we sketched in *Anders* is a prophylactic one; the States are free to adopt different procedures, so long as those procedures adequately safeguard a defendant's right to appellate counsel.

Under California's new procedure, established in People v. Wende, 600 P.2d 1071 (Calif. 1979) . . . counsel, upon concluding that an appeal would be frivolous, files a brief with the appellate court that summarizes the procedural and factual history of the case, with citations of the record. He also attests that he has reviewed the record, explained his evaluation of the case to his client, provided the client with a copy of the brief, and informed the client of his right to file a pro se supplemental brief. He further requests that the court independently examine the record for arguable issues. Unlike under the *Anders* procedure, counsel following *Wende* neither explicitly states that his review has led him to conclude that an appeal would be frivolous . . . nor requests leave to withdraw. Instead, he is silent on the merits of the case and expresses his availability to brief any issues on which the court might desire briefing.

The appellate court, upon receiving a "*Wende* brief," must conduct a review of the entire record, regardless of whether the defendant has filed a pro se brief. . . . If the appellate court, after its review of the record pursuant to *Wende*, also finds the appeal to be frivolous, it may affirm. If, however, it finds an arguable (i.e., nonfrivolous) issue, it orders briefing on that issue.

In 1990, a California state-court jury convicted respondent Lee Robbins of second-degree murder (for fatally shooting his former roommate) and of grand theft of an automobile (for stealing a truck that he used to flee the State after committing the murder). Robbins was sentenced to 17 years to life. He elected to represent himself at trial, but on appeal he received appointed counsel. His appointed counsel, concluding that an appeal would be frivolous, filed with the California Court of Appeal a brief that complied with the *Wende* procedure. Robbins also availed himself of his right under *Wende* to file a pro se supplemental brief, filing a brief in which he contended that there was insufficient evidence to support his conviction and that the prosecutor violated Brady v. Maryland, 373 U.S. 83 (1963), by failing to disclose exculpatory evidence. The California Court of Appeal, agreeing with counsel's assessment of the case, affirmed. The court explained that it had "examined the entire record" and [found no support for the two issues that Robbins raised]. After exhausting state postconviction remedies, Robbins filed in [federal district court] for a writ of habeas corpus. . . .

The District Court [concluded] that there were at least two issues that, pursuant to *Anders,* counsel should have raised in his brief (in a *Wende* brief, as noted above, counsel is not required to raise issues): first, whether the prison law library was adequate for Robbins's needs in preparing his defense after he elected to dismiss his appointed counsel and proceed pro se at trial, and, second, whether the trial court erred in refusing to allow him to withdraw his waiver of counsel. . . .

In *Anders,* we reviewed an earlier California procedure for handling appeals by convicted indigents. Pursuant to that procedure, Anders's appointed appellate counsel had filed a letter stating that he had concluded that there was "no merit to the appeal." Anders, in response, sought new counsel; the State Court of Appeal denied the request, and Anders filed a pro se appellate brief. That court then issued an opinion that reviewed the four claims in his pro se brief and affirmed, finding no error (or no prejudicial error). . . .

We held that "California's action does not comport with fair procedure and lacks that equality that is required by the Fourteenth Amendment." We placed the case within a line of precedent beginning with Griffin v. Illinois, 351 U.S. 12 (1956), and continuing with Douglas v. California, 372 U.S. 353 (1963), that imposed constitutional constraints on States when they choose to create appellate review. [A] finding that the appeal had "no merit" was not adequate, because it did not mean that the appeal was so lacking in prospects as to be "frivolous." [We] set out what would be an acceptable procedure for treating frivolous appeals:

> [I]f counsel finds his case to be wholly frivolous, after a conscientious examination of it, he should so advise the court and request permission to withdraw. That request must, however, be accompanied by a brief referring to anything in the record that might arguably support the appeal. A copy of counsel's brief should be furnished the indigent and time allowed him to raise any points that he chooses; the court — not counsel — then proceeds, after a full examination of all the proceedings, to decide whether the case is wholly frivolous. If it so finds it may grant counsel's request to withdraw and dismiss the appeal insofar as federal requirements are concerned, or proceed to a decision on the merits, if state law so requires. On the other hand, if it finds any of the legal points arguable on their merits (and therefore not frivolous) it must, prior to decision, afford the indigent the assistance of counsel to argue the appeal.

We then concluded by explaining how this procedure would be better than the California one that we had found deficient. Among other things, we thought that it would "induce the court to pursue all the more vigorously its own review because of the ready references not only to the record but also to the legal authorities as furnished it by counsel."

The Ninth Circuit ruled that this final section of *Anders,* even though unnecessary to our holding in that case, was obligatory upon the States. We disagree. [This] view runs contrary to our established practice of permitting the States, within the broad bounds of the Constitution, to experiment with solutions to difficult questions of policy.

In McCoy v. Court of Appeals of Wisconsin, Dist. 1, 486 U.S. 429 (1988), we rejected a challenge to Wisconsin's variation on the *Anders* procedure. Wisconsin had departed from *Anders* by requiring *Anders* briefs to discuss why each issue raised lacked merit. The defendant argued that this rule was contrary to *Anders* and forced counsel to violate his ethical obligations to his client. We, however, emphasized that the right to appellate representation does not include a right to present frivolous arguments to the court. [The Wisconsin procedure], by providing for one-sided briefing by counsel against his own client's best claims, probably made a court more likely to rule against the indigent than if the court had simply received an *Anders* brief.

[It] is more in keeping with our status as a court, and particularly with our status as a court in a federal system, to avoid imposing a single solution on the States from the top down. . . . Accordingly, we hold that the *Anders* procedure is merely one method of satisfying the requirements of the Constitution for indigent criminal appeals. States may — and, we are confident, will — craft procedures that, in terms of policy, are superior to, or at least as good as, that in *Anders.* The Constitution erects no barrier to their doing so. . . .

A State's procedure provides [adequate and effective] review so long as it reasonably ensures that an indigent's appeal will be resolved in a way that is related to the merit of that appeal. . . . In determining whether a particular state procedure satisfies this standard, it is important to focus on the underlying goals that the procedure should serve — to ensure that those indigents whose appeals are not frivolous receive the counsel and merits brief required by *Douglas,* and also to enable the State to protect itself so that frivolous appeals are not subsidized and public moneys not needlessly spent. For although, under *Douglas,* indigents generally have a right to counsel on a first appeal as of right, it is equally true that this right does not include the right to bring a frivolous appeal and, concomitantly, does not include the right to counsel for bringing a frivolous appeal. . . . The obvious goal of *Anders* was to prevent this limitation on the right to appellate counsel from swallowing the right itself, and we do not retreat from that goal today.

We think the *Wende* procedure reasonably ensures that an indigent's appeal will be resolved in a way that is related to the merit of that appeal. . . . Although we did not, in *Anders,* explain in detail why the California procedure was inadequate . . . a significant factor was that the old California procedure did not require either counsel or the court to determine that the appeal was frivolous; instead, the procedure required only that they determine that the defendant was unlikely to prevail on appeal. . . . *Wende,* by contrast, requires both counsel and the court to find the appeal to be lacking in arguable issues, which is to say, frivolous.

An additional problem with the old California procedure was that it apparently permitted an appellate court to allow counsel to withdraw and thereafter to decide the appeal without appointing new counsel. . . . Under *Wende,* by contrast, . . . counsel does not move to withdraw and . . . the court orders briefing if it finds arguable issues.

In *Anders,* we also disapproved the old California procedure because we thought that a one paragraph letter from counsel stating only his "bare conclusion" that the appeal had no merit was insufficient. [T]he *Wende* brief provides more than a one-paragraph "bare conclusion." Counsel's summary of the case's procedural and factual history, with citations of the record, both ensures that a trained legal eye has searched the record for arguable issues and assists the reviewing court in its own evaluation of the case.

[The *Anders* procedure] has, from the beginning, faced consistent and severe criticism. One of the most consistent criticisms . . . is that *Anders* is in some tension both with counsel's ethical duty as an officer of the court (which requires him not to present frivolous arguments) and also with his duty to further his client's interests (which might not permit counsel to characterize his client's claims as frivolous). California, through the *Wende* procedure, has made a good-faith effort to mitigate this problem by not requiring the *Wende* brief to raise legal issues and by not requiring counsel to explicitly describe the case as frivolous.

Another criticism of the *Anders* procedure has been that it is incoherent and thus impossible to follow. Those making this criticism point to our language in *Anders* suggesting that an appeal could be both "wholly frivolous" and at the same time contain arguable issues, even though we also said that an issue that was arguable was "therefore not frivolous." In other words, the *Anders* procedure appears to adopt gradations of frivolity and to use two different meanings for the phrase "arguable issue." The *Wende* procedure attempts to resolve this problem as well, by drawing the line at frivolity and by defining arguable issues as those that are not frivolous.[13] . . .

Our purpose is not to resolve any of these arguments. The Constitution does not resolve them, nor does it require us to do so. . . . It is enough to say that the *Wende* procedure . . . affords adequate and effective appellate review for criminal indigents.

[It] may be, as Robbins argues, that his appeal was not frivolous and that he was thus entitled to a merits brief rather than to a *Wende* brief. Indeed, both the District Court and the Ninth Circuit found that there were two arguable issues on direct appeal. The meaning of "arguable issue" as used in the opinions below, however, is far from clear. The courts below most likely used the phrase in the unusual way that we used it in *Anders*—an issue arguably supporting the appeal even though the appeal was wholly frivolous. Such an issue does not warrant a merits brief. But the courts below may have used the term to signify issues that were "arguable" in the more normal sense of being nonfrivolous and thus warranting a merits brief.

[The] proper standard for evaluating Robbins's claim that appellate counsel was ineffective in neglecting to file a merits brief is that enunciated in Strickland v. Washington, 466 U.S. 668 (1984). Respondent must first show that his counsel was objectively unreasonable in failing to find arguable issues to appeal—that is, that counsel unreasonably failed to discover nonfrivolous issues and to file a merits brief raising them. If Robbins succeeds in such a showing, he then has the burden of

13. A further criticism of *Anders* has been that it is unjust. More particularly, critics have claimed that, in setting out the *Anders* procedure, we were oblivious to the problem of scarce resources (with regard to both counsel and courts) and, as a result, crafted a rule that diverts attention from meritorious appeals of indigents and ensures poor representation for all indigents.

demonstrating prejudice. That is, he must show a reasonable probability that, but for his counsel's unreasonable failure to file a merits brief, he would have prevailed on his appeal. . . .

SOUTER, J., dissenting.

In a line of cases beginning with Griffin v. Illinois, this Court examined appellate procedural schemes under the principle that justice may not be conditioned on ability to pay. Even though absolute equality is not required, we held in Douglas v. California that when state criminal defendants are free to retain counsel for a first appeal as of right, the Fourteenth Amendment requires that indigent appellants be placed on a substantially equal footing through the appointment of counsel at the State's expense.

Two services of appellate counsel are on point here. Appellate counsel examines the trial record with an advocate's eye, identifying and weighing potential issues for appeal. This is review not by a dispassionate legal mind but by a committed representative, pledged to his client's interests, primed to attack the conviction on any ground the record may reveal. If counsel's review reveals arguable trial error, he prepares and submits a brief on the merits and argues the appeal.

The right to the first of these services, a partisan scrutiny of the record and assessment of potential issues, goes to the irreducible core of the lawyer's obligation to a litigant in an adversary system. . . . The right is unqualified when a defendant has retained counsel, and I can imagine no reason that it should not be so when counsel has been appointed.

Because the right to the second service, merits briefing, is not similarly unqualified, however, the issue we address today arises. The limitation on the right to a merits brief is that no one has a right to a wholly frivolous appeal, against which the judicial system's first line of defense is its lawyers. Being officers of the court, members of the bar are bound not to clog the courts with frivolous motions or appeals. . . .

The rub is that although counsel may properly refuse to brief a frivolous issue and a court may just as properly deny leave to take a frivolous appeal, there needs to be some reasonable assurance that the lawyer has not relaxed his partisan instinct prior to refusing, in which case the court's review could never compensate for the lawyer's failure of advocacy. A simple statement by counsel that an appeal has no merit, coupled with an appellate court's endorsement of counsel's conclusion, gives no affirmative indication that anyone has sought out the appellant's best arguments or championed his cause to the degree contemplated by the adversary system. [T]here must be some prod to find any reclusive merit in an ostensibly unpromising case and some process to assess the lawyer's efforts after the fact. A judicial process that renders constitutional error invisible is, after all, itself an affront to the Constitution.

In *Anders,* we devised such a mechanism to ensure respect for an appellant's rights. . . . *Anders* thus contemplates two reviews of the record, each of a markedly different character. First comes review by the advocate, the defendant's interested representative. His job is to identify the best issues the partisan eye can spot. Then comes judicial review from a disinterested judge, who asks two questions: whether the lawyer really did function as a committed advocate, and whether he misjudged the legitimate appealability of any issue. In reviewing the advocate's work, the court is responsible for assuring that counsel has gone as far as advocacy will take him with the best issues undiscounted. . . .

Without the assurance that assigned counsel has done his best as a partisan, his substantial equality to a lawyer retained at a defendant's expense cannot be assumed. And without the benefit of the lawyer's statement of strongest claims, the appellate panel cannot act as a reviewing court, but is relegated to an inquisitorial role. It is owing to the importance of assuring that an adversarial, not an inquisitorial, system is at work that I disagree with the Court's statement today that our cases approve of any state procedure that "reasonably ensures that an indigent's appeal will be resolved in a way that is related to the merit of that appeal." . . .

California's *Wende* procedure fails to measure up. Its primary failing is in permitting counsel to refrain as a matter of course from mentioning possibly arguable issues in a no-merit brief; its second deficiency is a correlative of the first, in obliging an appellate court to search the record for arguable issues without benefit of an issue-spotting, no-merit brief to review. . . .

The *Wende* procedure does not assure even the most minimal assistance of counsel in an adversarial role. The Constitution demands such assurances, and I would hold Robbins entitled to an appeal that provides them.

Notes

1. *Counsel for indigent appellants.* The Supreme Court has read the equal protection clause to require equal access to some aspects of the appeals process for both indigent appellants and those who can afford an attorney and various fees. Under Griffin v. Illinois, 351 U.S. 12 (1956), the state must provide an indigent defendant with a free transcript of a trial record, if the rules of appellate procedure require parties to use such a transcript when filing an appeal. In Douglas v. California, 372 U.S. 353 (1963), the Court extended *Griffin* to require the government to provide indigent appellants with an attorney for an initial "appeal as of right." As with the right to appointed counsel at trial, many states use their own constitutions, statutes, or rules of procedure to expand the availability of counsel on appeal beyond what the federal constitution requires.

But not every aspect of the appeals process is available on equal terms to indigent defendants. Under Ross v. Moffitt, 417 U.S. 600 (1974), there is no constitutional requirement to provide counsel for preparation of petitions for discretionary appellate review. As the Supreme Court explained in Smith v. Robbins, when appellate counsel for an indigent defendant believes the defendant could raise only frivolous issues on appeal, states still must have some mechanism for bringing potential issues to the court's attention. See Turner v. State, 818 So. 2d 1186 (Miss. 2001) (counsel who views a defendant's appeal as lacking merit must determine that the defendant is unlikely to prevail on appeal, file a brief referring to anything in record that might arguably support appeal, and advise client of his right to file a pro se supplemental brief). Do the mechanisms described in *Anders* and in the *Wende* case from California give indigent defendants the functional equivalent of retained appellate counsel?

2. *Self-representation on appeal.* In Martinez v. Court of Appeal of California, 528 U.S. 152 (2000), the Supreme Court refused to extend the right of self-representation at trial — established in Faretta v. California, 422 U.S. 806 (1975) — to a direct appeal. The appellate courts may properly appoint counsel for the appellant, even if the appellant objects. One of the Court's reasons to embrace the

right of self-representation at trial was "respect for individual autonomy." Are there any differences between the interests of a defendant at trial and the interests of an appellant when it comes to self-representation?

3. *Interlocutory Appeals*

Appeals usually take place after a final judgment, but on occasion the rules allow for an "interlocutory" appeal of an issue before the proceedings below have reached an end. These interlocutory appeals are especially important to the government. In general, prosecutors have less access to appellate review than defendants. The U.S. Supreme Court noted the state of the common law on prosecutorial appeals in 1892:

> In a few States, decisions denying a writ of error to the State after judgment for the defendant on a verdict of acquittal have proceeded upon the ground that to grant it would be to put him twice in jeopardy, in violation of a constitutional provision. But the courts of many States, including some of great authority, have denied, upon broader grounds, the right of the State to bring a writ of error in any criminal case whatever, even when the discharge of the defendant was upon the decision of an issue of law by the court, as on demurrer to the indictment, motion to quash, special verdict, or motion in arrest of judgment.

United States v. Sanges, 144 U.S. 310, 312-313 (1892). As the Court suggested in *Sanges,* the double jeopardy clauses of the federal and state constitutions have some bearing on when the prosecutor can appeal: They limit the power of the prosecution to request an appeal after jeopardy "attaches," and they bar virtually any prosecutorial appeal after an acquittal. Against this common law presumption against appeals by the state (bolstered by the constitutional limits on double jeopardy), consider the following statute and judicial decision interpreting a rule of appellate procedure.

■ DELAWARE CODE TIT. 10, §§9902, 9903

§9902

(a) The State shall have an absolute right to appeal to an appellate court a final order of a lower court where the order constitutes a dismissal of an indictment or information or any count thereof, or the granting of any motion vacating any verdict or judgment of conviction where the order of the lower court is based upon the invalidity or construction of the statute upon which the indictment or information is founded or the lack of jurisdiction of the lower court over the person or subject matter.

(b) When any order is entered before trial in any court suppressing or excluding substantial and material evidence, the court, upon certification by the Attorney General that the evidence is essential to the prosecution of the case, shall dismiss the complaint, indictment or information or any count thereof to the proof of which the evidence suppressed or excluded is essential. [The] reasons of the dismissal shall be set forth in the order entered upon the record.

(c) The State shall have an absolute right of appeal to an appellate court from an order entered pursuant to subsection (b) of this section and if the appellate court upon review of the order suppressing evidence shall reverse the dismissal, the defendant may be subjected to trial.

§9903

The State may apply to the appellate court to permit an appeal to determine a substantial question of law or procedure, and the appellate court may permit the appeal in its absolute discretion. The appellate court shall have the power to adopt rules governing the allowance of the appeal; but, in no event of such appeals shall the decision or result of the appeal affect the rights of the defendant and he or she shall not be obligated to defend the appeal, but the court may require the Public Defender of this State to defend the appeal and to argue the cause.

■ STATE v. MATTHEW MEDRANO

67 S.W.3d 892 (Tex. Crim. App. 2002)

COCHRAN, J.

The issue in this case is whether article 44.01(a)(5) of the Texas Code of Criminal Procedure[1] permits the State to bring a pretrial appeal of an adverse ruling on a motion to suppress evidence when the trial court does not conclude that the evidence was "illegally obtained." Although this Court, in State v. Roberts, 940 S.W.2d 655 (Tex. Crim. App. 1996), held that the State cannot appeal a pretrial evidentiary ruling unless the defendant claims that the evidence was "illegally obtained," neither the language of the statute nor legislative intent supports this limitation. It is not consistent with the interpretation other state or federal courts have given to the same or similar language in their government-appeal statutes. Moreover, the rule in *Roberts* has proved unworkable in practice. Therefore, we overrule *Roberts* and hold that under article 44.01(a)(5), the State is entitled to appeal any adverse pre-trial ruling which suppresses evidence, a confession, or an admission, regardless of whether the defendant alleges, or the trial court holds, that the evidence was "illegally obtained."

Appellee, Matthew Medrano, was charged with capital murder for the robbery-murder of Benton Smith, a pizza delivery man. The State's only witness to the robbery-murder was Jennifer Erivez, a fourteen-year-old girl, who was standing in the driveway of her home at about 10:00 P.M. waiting for her boyfriend. Jennifer testified that she saw the pizza delivery man drive by and park down the street. Then she saw a maroon car, like a Chrysler LeBaron, drive past slowly and stop under a street light. A man got out of the front passenger side and did something like take the license plate off of the car. Jennifer saw the man's face clearly, but could not

1. Article 44.01(a), in pertinent part, provides:

The State is entitled to appeal an order of a court in a criminal case if the order: . . . (5) grants a motion to suppress evidence, a confession, or an admission, if jeopardy has not attached in the case and if the prosecuting attorney certifies to the trial court that the appeal is not taken for the purpose of delay and that the evidence, confession, or admission is of substantial importance to the case.

recall the car's license plate number. The car then drove further down the street and parked behind the pizza delivery man's truck. The same man got out of the car and walked up to the pizza delivery man. Jennifer heard a gunshot and then saw the man run back to the car. He got in, and the driver sped away.

A few hours later, Jennifer gave police a written description of the person she had seen get out of the car and approach the pizza delivery man. . . . Jennifer also stated that the maroon car contained a total of four people. Because she was unable to recall the car's license plate number, an El Paso police officer, trained in hypnosis, conducted a videotaped hypnotic session the next day. She was still unable to recall the license plate number. About a week later, the police conducted two photo lineups for Jennifer. She did not identify anyone in those lineups, [although Medrano's photo was not in either of those lineups]. After she identified Mr. Medrano as the shooter in a third photo lineup two days later, he was arrested and charged with capital murder.

Defense counsel filed a "Motion to Suppress In Court Identification". . . . After a pretrial suppression hearing, the trial judge orally granted the defense motion. Her written order stated that she granted the motion "for the reasons stated on the record" at the hearing and that she "also f[ound] said identification was obtained in violation of the 4th, 5th, 6th and 14th Amendments of the United States Constitution and Article I, sections 9, 10, 13, and 19 of the Texas Constitution." The State certified that it could not prosecute the case without Jennifer's testimony and filed an appeal. . . .

Article 44.01 was enacted as a vehicle for the State to challenge "questionable legal rulings excluding what may be legally admissible evidence."[5] The purpose of the statute is to permit the pretrial appeal of erroneous legal rulings which eviscerate the State's ability to prove its case. The Texas legislature, in passing Senate Bill 762 in 1987, clearly intended to provide Texas prosecutors with the same vehicle of appeal for pretrial evidentiary rulings as federal prosecutors. . . . There is no question that under 18 U.S.C. §3731, federal prosecutors may appeal a wide variety of pretrial evidentiary rulings — not just those tied to motions to suppress illegally obtained evidence. . . .

All fifty states, as well as the District of Columbia, have provisions permitting the government to appeal adverse rulings of a question of law. Many of those states [at least 18 of them] use the same or very similar language as that contained in art. 44.01(a)(5), and they permit the State to appeal *any* pretrial ruling suppressing evidence if that evidence is likely to be outcome determinative. [At least 13 other] states explicitly grant the prosecution a broad right to appeal any pretrial suppression, evidentiary or other legal ruling which is likely to determine the outcome of the case. A few states explicitly permit the State to appeal only orders excluding "seized evidence," "evidence illegally obtained," or "evidence seized in violation of

5. Bill Analysis, S.B. 762, Acts 1987, 70th Leg., ch. 382, §1. The "Background" Section of the bill analysis begins:

> The Texas Constitution provides that the State has no right to appeal in a criminal case, making Texas the only state that bans all prosecution appeals. This prohibition is viewed as a serious problem in the administration of justice for several reasons: (1) On occasion, defendants are released because of questionable legal rulings excluding what may be legally admissible evidence; (2) Legal issues that have been wrongly decided by trial courts nevertheless stand as precedent, albeit unbinding, for police, prosecutors, and courts; and (3) Trial judges may have a tendency to resolve doubtful legal questions in favor of the defendant because such a ruling cannot harm the judge's reversal rate.

the Constitution." A handful of state courts [four of them] have construed their government-appeal statutes to permit only appeals of constitutionally-based pretrial rulings excluding evidence. State v. Shade, 867 P.2d 393 (Nev. 1994); State v. Counts, 472 N.W.2d 756 (N.D. 1991). At least one state, Ohio, has judicially broadened its government-appeal statute to permit pretrial appeals of nonconstitutional trial rulings excluding evidence, despite language to the contrary. O.R.C. §2945.67; Ohio Crim. R. 12. Although a few states apply their government-appeal statutes narrowly, the vast majority of courts and legislatures across the nation broadly construe their state's-right-to-appeal statutes. They focus upon the same major themes: 1) Does this pretrial ruling effectively prevent the government from presenting its case to a jury? And 2) Is the ruling based upon an erroneous interpretation or application of law?

In *Roberts,* this Court followed that handful of states which have very narrowly construed their state's right-to-appeal statutes. This Court ruled that it lacked jurisdiction to consider a State's appeal from a trial court's ruling that civil deposition testimony was inadmissible. We held that the phrase "motion to suppress evidence," as used in article 44.01(a)(5), was limited to motions which sought to suppress evidence on the basis that such evidence was "illegally obtained." The defendant in *Roberts* contended that a videotaped deposition from a civil case was inadmissible hearsay; he did not claim that the deposition testimony was illegally obtained. Because the defendant's motion was not a "motion to suppress evidence" contemplated under art. 44.01(a)(5), went the logic, the order granting the motion was not appealable. [The *Roberts* Court] relied on the fact that the corresponding federal statute authorizes an appeal by the Government, under 18 U.S.C. §3731, "from a decision or order of a district court suppressing or excluding evidence. . . ." Texas article 44.01(a)(5) authorizes an appeal from a motion to suppress evidence, but it does not explicitly authorize an appeal from a motion to *exclude* evidence. In *Roberts,* this Court reasoned, "[B]y using the term 'suppress' alone, not in conjunction with the broader term 'exclude,' the Legislature meant to limit the State's appeal to those instances where evidence is suppressed in the technical sense, not merely excluded."

The legislative history of article 44.01 shows otherwise. The legislative intent, explicitly stated in the Bill Analysis, was to permit the State to appeal any "questionable legal rulings excluding what may be legally admissible evidence." Period.

[The] Texas Legislature was already familiar with the use of the term "motion to suppress evidence" in the context of pretrial hearings. The Texas Legislature apparently chose the term "motion to suppress evidence" in article 44.01(a)(5) because pretrial "motions to suppress evidence" can be heard under article 28.01. . . . Because the only type of pretrial evidentiary motion mentioned in article 28.01 is a "motion to suppress evidence," it follows that the only type of pretrial evidentiary motion that the State can appeal is the same type that the defendant may file. They are both called a "motion to suppress evidence." Under article 28.01, a motion to suppress evidence is one in which the defendant (or the State) claims that certain evidence should not be admitted at trial for a constitutional, statutory, evidentiary or procedural reason. There is no logical, legal, or linguistic reason that a single phrase concerning the same pretrial evidentiary motion, should bear one meaning for purposes of which pretrial motions a court may consider, but bear a totally different meaning when the State appeals an adverse ruling on that motion. The rule is simple: If the trial court can rule upon a pretrial motion to suppress evidence, the State can appeal it. A motion for the goose is a motion for the gander.

Finally, the rule in *Roberts* is, as this case demonstrates, unworkable. Who decides whether a pretrial motion to suppress evidence is one that seeks to exclude "illegally obtained" evidence? If the defendant labels his motion as one to suppress illegally obtained evidence, is that determinative? If the defendant cites constitutional provisions, is that determinative? If the trial court, in ruling, cites constitutional provisions, is that determinative? Or, as in this case, if the court of appeals determines that, even though both the defendant and trial judge cited constitutional provisions, the motion (and ruling) was not really a motion to suppress illegally obtained evidence? This is a linguistic puzzle that only Humpty Dumpty or a rejection of *Roberts* can resolve. . . .

The trial court's ruling in this case does not involve evidence which would normally be considered "illegally obtained." Still, the ruling excluding Jennifer's identification testimony — which was a legal ruling excluding evidence — is appealable under article 44.01(a)(5) if it could be determined pretrial under article 28.01, §1(6). Relying on the standards concerning the admissibility of post-hypnotic testimony set out in Zani v. State, 758 S.W.2d 233 (Tex. Crim. App. 1988), the trial court orally ruled that Jennifer's identification of Mr. Medrano was inadmissible. After hearing arguments from the prosecutor, the trial court affirmed her oral order with a written ruling that specifically held that the identifications were obtained in violation of the United States and Texas Constitutions. The trial court's written ruling falls squarely within the rulings intended to be appealable under Article 44.01. . . .

WOMACK, J., dissenting.

. . . Today the Court says [our holding in *Roberts*] was wrong because the legislature modeled art. 44.01 after the corresponding federal provision generally, a statute that permits an appeal by the government from suppression or exclusion of evidence. I want to point out four things. First, drafting a statute to apply only to "suppressing" is an odd way of modeling on the federal statute that specifies both "suppressing" and "excluding." Second, our 1996 decision was based on the language of the statute, which is more important than the intentions and interpretations of witnesses who supported the act, which are the primary support for today's decision. "It is the *law* that governs, not the intent of the lawgiver," Antonin Scalia, A Matter of Interpretation 17 (1997), much less the intent of the lawgiver's committee witnesses. But this is only to rehash the 1996 decision of the Court.

In 2002 the more important points are my third and fourth: Today's construction of the ambiguous word increases the scope of the statute, applying it to "excluding" evidence as well as to "suppressing" it. And if that is the correct scope of the statute, the legislature had but to amend the statute by inserting the words "or excluding." Three sessions of the legislature have intervened since our decision, with no action. In this case, that is significant.

If this case were the opposite (if the statute had read "suppressing or excluding evidence," and we had held that it did not apply to the excluding of evidence) legislative inaction might mean little or nothing. What could the legislature do to express more clearly that the statute applied to the excluding of evidence? But when the statute says it applies only to "suppressing" evidence and this Court held that "suppressing" does not mean every "excluding" of evidence, the remedy is quick and easy. If we have misconstrued a statute that is stated clearly, what can the legislature do? Reenact the statute with the additional phrase, "and we really mean it"? When we have misconstrued a criminal-procedure statute that is unambiguous, *stare decisis* has its least force. In such a case we should be more free to overrule our earlier decision. . . .

The Court's other argument that "suppress evidence" means "suppress or exclude evidence" is by reference to Code of Criminal Procedure article 28.01, which provides the procedure for a pretrial hearing like the one that was held in this case. . . . The Court reasons thus: pretrial hearings are to determine motions to suppress evidence; the motion that was filed in this case was decided at a pretrial hearing; therefore it must have been a motion to suppress evidence. . . .

Although pretrial hearings are for motions to suppress evidence (and the other matters that are listed in Article 28.01, section 1), they are not for *only* those matters. There are two reasons. On its face, the statutory list is not exclusive, so the pretrial hearing is not limited to the eleven items on the list. Even if it were exclusive, one item on the list is "(2) Pleadings of the defendant," which include "any other motions or pleadings permitted by law to be filed." Tex. Code Crim. Proc. art. 27.02. It was, therefore, proper for the appellee to file and the court to decide a motion to exclude, not suppress, evidence. So the Court's conclusion that the pretrial motion must be a motion to suppress is invalid.

[There are] strong arguments why the State should be allowed to appeal pretrial rulings excluding evidence. But the statute that was enacted did not allow it, and it still does not. We have no authority to change the statute. I respectfully dissent.

Notes

1. *Appeal of pretrial issues by the government: majority position.* Statutes and procedural rules in most states have now expanded beyond the common law bar on government appeals, granting the government power to appeal certain pretrial rulings. Most of these rules cover a trial judge's decision to dismiss charges before trial or a decision during a suppression hearing to exclude key evidence. The federal statute, 18 U.S.C. §3731, allows the government to appeal the dismissal of an indictment or information as well as a decision "suppressing or excluding evidence . . . not made after the defendant has been put in jeopardy." Under this statute, the government may also appeal a decision to release a person from pretrial detention. Appeals of pretrial rulings do not create double jeopardy problems because double jeopardy does not "attach" in the lower court until the start of a trial.

2. *Appeal after jeopardy attaches.* Once a trial has begun, the government will have more difficulty obtaining appellate review for any errors of the trial judge. If the judge's error leads to an acquittal or a dismissal of the charges, double jeopardy clearly would prevent a second trial for the same offense. But can the government suspend the proceedings at trial once a major error has occurred and obtain appellate review before an acquittal or dismissal? Most criminal procedure rules and statutes block such appeals; there is, however, a small and growing number of states willing to allow the government to bring an appeal after trial has begun but before an acquittal or a dismissal takes place. See, e.g., State v. Malinovsky, 573 N.E.2d 22 (Ohio 1991) (allowing prosecutorial appeal of midtrial evidentiary ruling, based on procedural rule allowing appeal of "motion to suppress evidence").

Double jeopardy clearly bars government appeals after an acquittal. Ball v. United States, 163 U.S. 662 (1896). However, that limit does not matter in the great majority of cases: Acquittals occur in 1 percent of all felony cases filed. Felony Defendants in Large Urban Counties, 1998, NCJ 187232 (November 2001). Dismissals of charges after jeopardy attaches are more common than acquittals, and government appeals after dismissals present more complex legal issues. If a dismissal on a legal question occurs after a conviction, an appellate court can reverse the legal ruling and reinstate the fact finder's verdict without requiring a second trial. For dismissals taking place before a verdict, the government may not appeal if the ruling amounts to a resolution, "correct or not, of some or all of the factual elements of the offense charged." United States v. Scott, 437 U.S. 82, 97 (1978). However, if the preverdict dismissal is based on some legal issue not going to the defendant's guilt or innocence (such as pretrial delay), then a reprosecution after a government appeal is consistent with double jeopardy limits.

When *defendants* appeal after conviction and convince the court to overturn the judgment, the government may ordinarily retry the case without violating double jeopardy. One exception occurs when the fact finder at trial is presented with both a greater and lesser included offense and convicts the defendant only of the lesser offense. In that setting, the "implied acquittal" of the defendant prevents the government from retrying the greater charges if the defendant succeeds on appeal. Green v. United States, 355 U.S. 184 (1957). The government also cannot retry a case after a defendant wins an appeal if the error was the government's failure to present legally sufficient facts to support a conviction.

Do "asymmetric" appeal rights actually hurt defendants? If the prosecutor has only one shot at obtaining a conviction, does that mean the government spends more than it otherwise would on the initial trial? If so, then asymmetric appeal rights might increase the number of false convictions and increase litigation costs for defendants. See Vikramaditya S. Khanna, Double Jeopardy's Asymmetric Appeal Rights: What Purpose Do They Serve? 82 B.U. L. Rev. 241 (2002).

3. *Prosecutorial and appellate court screening of appeals.* Most state statutes leave the chief prosecutor with some control over which issues the government may appeal. The chief prosecutor (or some statewide representative of the government, such as the attorney general) must certify to the appellate court that the trial court's ruling dealt with evidence or some other claim critical to the prosecution of the case and that the appeal is not taken "merely" for purposes of delay. Under what circumstances might the chief prosecutor refuse to certify an issue for appeal? Is this a meaningful limitation on the scope of the government's appeal rights? Should appellate courts themselves sort the important claims from the less important ones? Appellate rules of procedure often give courts the discretion to decline to hear government claims that otherwise qualify for appeal. See State v. Doucette, 544 A.2d 1290, 1293 (Me. 1988).

4. *"Moot" appeals by the prosecution.* A few states, such as Kansas, permit the government to appeal from an acquittal to the state supreme court if the legal issue is of statewide interest and vital to the administration of justice. The appellate decision is only advisory; even if the appellate court sustains the government's position, the trial court acquittal remains final. See Kan. Stat. §3602(b)(1)-(3); State v. Martin, 658 P.2d 1024 (Kan. 1983); State v. Viers, 469 P.2d 53 (Nev. 1970) (striking down a provision similar to Kansas statute on the ground that an advisory appeal presents no case or controversy under the state constitution). In Canada, the appellate court

has discretionary power to hear government claims of legal error leading to an acquittal. See Alan Mewett, An Introduction to the Criminal Process in Canada 209-212 (1988). Will the defense point of view receive adequate representation in such "moot" appeals?

5. *Interlocutory appeals by the defense.* Defendants may also bring interlocutory appeals, although they can do so for fewer issues than the government. Denials of motions for pretrial release and the trial judge's setting of a bail amount are common grounds for defense interlocutory appeals. See Ill. Supreme Ct. R. 604(c). Why do these decisions receive exceptional treatment? What other choices might a defendant most desire to appeal on an interlocutory basis?

B. APPELLATE REVIEW OF FACTUAL FINDINGS

Appellate courts could take a wide range of approaches in selecting which judgments made at trial to review. They could conceivably engage in complete and new ("de novo") review for all issues of fact and law. But this approach would engender huge administrative costs; in effect, the appellate court would retry the entire case. Alternatively, appellate courts might play an extremely limited role in reviewing verdicts, presuming that all judgments of fact and law are correct and reversing only for fundamental failures in process that would undermine confidence in the fairness of the decisionmakers or the ability of the defendant to put on a case (such as a failure to provide counsel, evident bias on the part of the judge, or jury tampering). An even more extreme system might abolish appellate courts altogether, trusting completely in the trial process.

Appellate courts operate under standards that lie somewhere between these conceivable boundaries. Courts distinguish between review of factual findings and legal judgments at trial. The standards of review for factual findings tend to be more deferential because the fact finder at trial (whether a jury or judge) is in a better position to view and weigh evidence. The standard of review on questions of law is different: Appellate courts often assert the same (or greater) competence in assessing legal issues and tend to review questions of law de novo.

Most cases that go to trial (as opposed to those settled through a plea bargain) involve factual disputes. Perhaps the defendant claims she did not do the alleged act at all, or she claims that the facts point to a different crime from the one the prosecution charged (for example, voluntary manslaughter instead of second-degree murder). Whichever side loses at trial will often believe that the factfinder made the wrong decision. Of course, if the defendant is acquitted at trial, then double jeopardy will bar a prosecutorial appeal to reassess her innocence. When should the defendant be able to challenge the factfinder's judgments?

The Supreme Court in Jackson v. Virginia, 443 U.S. 307 (1979), announced the standard that most appellate courts now apply when reviewing the sufficiency of the evidence to support a guilty verdict. James Jackson had been convicted at trial of murdering Mary Cole.

> That the petitioner had shot and killed Mrs. Cole was not in dispute at the trial. The State's evidence established that she had been a member of the staff at the local county jail, that she had befriended him while he was imprisoned there on a disorderly

> conduct charge, and that when he was released she had arranged for him to live in the home of her son and daughter-in-law. Testimony by her relatives indicated that on the day of the killing the petitioner had been drinking and had spent a great deal of time shooting at targets with his revolver. [That evening, Cole drove Jackson] to a local diner. There the two were observed by several police officers, who testified that both the petitioner and the victim had been drinking. The two were observed by a deputy sheriff as they were preparing to leave the diner in her car. The petitioner was then in possession of his revolver, and the sheriff also observed a kitchen knife in the automobile. The sheriff testified that he had offered to keep the revolver until the petitioner sobered up, but that the latter had indicated that this would be unnecessary since he and the victim were about to engage in sexual activity.
>
> Her body was found in a secluded church parking lot a day and a half later, naked from the waist down, her slacks beneath her body. Uncontradicted medical and expert evidence established that she had been shot twice at close range with the petitioner's gun. She appeared not to have been sexually molested. Six cartridge cases identified as having been fired from the petitioner's gun were found near the body.

443 U.S. at 309-310. Following the common law formula, Virginia defined murder as "the unlawful killing of another with malice aforethought." Premeditation distinguished murder in the first degree from murder in the second degree, and the prosecution bore the burden of proof on this element. Jackson admitted shooting Cole but contended that the shooting had been accidental and that the gun had gone off while he was resisting her sexual advances, and that in any case he had been too intoxicated to support a finding of premeditation.

The trial judge found Jackson guilty of first-degree murder. Jackson challenged the conviction in both state and federal court on the grounds that the evidence was constitutionally insufficient. Although the Supreme Court announced in its opinion the standard of review for factual judgments on federal collateral review of state convictions, the constitutional standard in *Jackson* has been applied in state and federal courts for almost all review of factual findings, including on direct appeal. The Court held:

> After *Winship* the critical inquiry on review of the sufficiency of the evidence to support a criminal conviction must be not simply to determine whether the jury was properly instructed, but to determine whether the record evidence could reasonably support a finding of guilt beyond a reasonable doubt. But this inquiry does not require a court to "ask itself whether it believes that the evidence at the trial established guilt beyond a reasonable doubt." Instead, the relevant question is whether, after viewing the evidence in the light most favorable to the prosecution, any rational trier of fact could have found the essential elements of the crime beyond a reasonable doubt. This familiar standard gives full play to the responsibility of the trier of fact fairly to resolve conflicts in the testimony, to weigh the evidence, and to draw reasonable inferences from basic facts to ultimate facts. Once a defendant has been found guilty of the crime charged, the factfinder's role as weigher of the evidence is preserved through a legal conclusion that upon judicial review all of the evidence is to be considered in the light most favorable to the prosecution. The criterion thus impinges upon "jury" discretion only to the extent necessary to guarantee the fundamental protection of due process of law.

443 U.S. at 317-320. Applying this new standard, the Court concluded that "a rational factfinder could readily have found the petitioner guilty beyond a reasonable doubt of first-degree murder under Virginia law."

States modify the *Jackson* standards in two ways. First, as with many other broad standards applied throughout the criminal process, different legal cultures and groups of judges will apply similar standards differently and will reach consistently different outcomes. Thus, the flexibility of the *Jackson* standard allows for more aggressive or more deferential review. Second, some states have supplemented the *Jackson* standard to require from appellate courts an additional task when reviewing the factual support for the guilty verdict. Consider whether Texas has improved on *Jackson* in the following case.

■ ELBERT CLEWIS v. STATE

922 S.W.2d 126 (Tex. Crim. App. 1996)

MALONEY, J.

[In anticipation of a burglary, seven Dallas police officers participated in a covert surveillance operation at Fashionworks, a Dallas business. This location had been burglarized on three previous Monday nights. On Monday, November 11, 1991, at approximately 10:00 P.M., Officers Robert Baird and Mark Sears saw three individuals approach the front of the building. Two of the people pried the front door open with a tire tool and entered the building. The third person, later identified as Elbert Clewis, stood on the porch looking around in all directions, watched the first two suspects open the doors, and then followed them into the building. Baird and Sears saw the three individuals exit the business carrying clothing. Upon seeing the police, they dropped the clothing and fled. The police then apprehended all three suspects. Sears and Baird saw no evidence that Clewis was intoxicated on the night of the offense. Another officer on the scene, Michael Beatty, first saw Clewis that night when he ran around the corner of the Fashionworks building. Beatty noticed that Clewis seemed to be "in a state of shock," and appeared "real nervous and was just real jittery, unsure of what to do" when the police apprehended him. However, Beatty did not believe that Clewis was intoxicated.

After each of the officers testified at trial, defense counsel called Peggy Shivers, mother of one of the suspects. She testified that she had seen Clewis at her house earlier that evening. Mrs. Shivers stated that Clewis was intoxicated at that time: "He was staggering, so I would say on a scale from one to ten, I would give him ten." Clewis argued that his intoxication prevented him from forming the mens rea necessary to establish the elements of burglary. Clewis was convicted of burglary of a building, and the Fifth Court of Appeals affirmed his conviction.]

In his sole ground for review, appellant contends that the court of appeals erred in refusing to review the evidence to determine whether it was factually sufficient to sustain his conviction. Specifically, appellant avers that the evidence was factually insufficient to show that he knowingly and intentionally entered the building. . . .

We hold that the proper standard of review for factual sufficiency of the elements of the offense is [as follows: an appellate court considers] all the evidence without [viewing it] "in the light most favorable to the prosecution" and sets aside the verdict only if it is so contrary to the overwhelming weight of the evidence as to be clearly wrong and unjust.

. . . The Texas Constitution confers appellate jurisdiction upon the courts of appeals, Tex. Const. art. V, §§5 & 6, that includes the power to review questions of fact in criminal cases.[4] [T]he Legislature has consistently recognized the ability of courts with criminal appellate jurisdiction to review the facts of a case and . . . Article 44.25 of the Texas Code of Criminal Procedure[7] has remained nearly identical since 1857 with each subsequent code revision. When their jurisdiction to review fact questions is properly invoked, the courts of appeals cannot ignore constitutional and statutory mandates.

[T]he United States Supreme Court in Jackson v. Virginia, 443 U.S. 307 (1979), set . . . the minimum standard for sustaining a conviction under the Due Process Clause of the Fourteenth Amendment. [Under *Jackson,* an appellate court must ask "whether, after viewing the evidence in the light most favorable to the prosecution, any rational trier of fact could have found the essential elements of the crime beyond a reasonable doubt."] Although Texas courts have adopted the *Jackson* standard as the legal sufficiency standard in direct appeals, we have never held that its application precluded any other type of review. As we explicitly noted in Griffin v. State, 614 S.W.2d 155 (Tex. Crim. App. 1981), "States are free to set higher standards of review than *Jackson.*"

[If] the evidence is insufficient under the *Jackson* standard, it is "legally insufficient." A determination that the evidence is "legally insufficient" means that the case should never have been submitted to the jury. In contrast, the issue of factual sufficiency is a question of fact. A *Jackson* review, "viewing the evidence in the light most favorable to the prosecution," is not a factual sufficiency review; rather, it is an analytical tool used to determine whether there is a fact issue at all.[12] The *Jackson* standard "gives full play to the responsibility of the trier of fact fairly to resolve conflicts in the testimony, to weigh the evidence, and to draw reasonable inferences from basic facts to ultimate facts." *Jackson,* 443 U.S. at 319.

In conducting a factual sufficiency review, an appellate court reviews the factfinder's weighing of the evidence and is authorized to disagree with the factfinder's determination. This review, however, must be appropriately deferential so as to avoid an appellate court's substituting its judgment for that of the jury. . . . If a reviewing court determines that the evidence is insufficient under the *Jackson* standard, it must render a judgment of acquittal. . . . However, when conducting a factual sufficiency review, an appellate court cannot substitute its judgment for that of the factfinder since this would violate the defendant's right to trial by jury. Accordingly, courts of appeals should vacate a conviction based on factually insufficient evidence and remand the cause for a new trial. . . .

Appellant urges us to hold that when the factual sufficiency of an element of the offense is challenged, courts of appeals should apply the *Stone* standard of review,

4. Art. V, §6 of the Texas Constitution provides in relevant part:

> Said Courts of Appeals shall have appellate jurisdiction . . . under such restrictions and regulations as may be prescribed by law. Provided, that the decisions of said courts [courts of appeals] shall be conclusive on all questions of fact brought before them on appeal or error.

The last sentence above is referred to as the "factual conclusivity" clause. [This] clause is a limit on the jurisdiction of the Supreme Court and the Court of Criminal Appeals in discretionary matters.

7. Tex. Code Crim. Proc. Ann. art. 44.25 provides: "The courts of appeals or the Court of Criminal Appeals may reverse the judgment in a criminal action, as well upon the law as upon the facts."

12. [The following example illustrates] the distinction between legal and factual sufficiency: The prosecution's sole witness, a paid informant, testifies that he saw the defendant commit a crime. Twenty nuns testify that the defendant was with them at the time, far from the scene of the crime. Twenty more nuns testify that they saw the informant commit the crime. If the defendant is convicted, he has no remedy under *Jackson* because the informant's testimony, however incredible, is legally sufficient evidence.

articulated by the Third Court of Appeals. Stone v. State, 823 S.W.2d 375 (Tex. Ct. App. 1992). [The] *Stone* court observed that a factual sufficiency review begins with the presumption that the evidence supporting the jury's verdict was legally sufficient, that is, sufficient under the *Jackson* test. In conducting a factual sufficiency review, the court of appeals "views all the evidence without the prism of 'in the light most favorable to the prosecution' . . . and sets aside the verdict only if it is so contrary to the overwhelming weight of the evidence as to be clearly wrong and unjust." . . .

The Code of Criminal Procedure contains two provisions establishing that the jury is the judge of the facts. Tex. Code Crim. Proc. Ann. art. 36.13[17] & 38.04.[18] Notably, Chapter 36, "Trial Before the Jury," and Chapter 38, "Evidence in Criminal Actions," do not reference the appellate process, and no similar provision appears in the Rules of Appellate Procedure. The import of the provisions in the Code is, in part, to distinguish the role of the jury from the role of the judge at trial. [An interpretation of these statutes that precludes] any appellate review of the jury's determination of the facts and the weight to be given the evidence . . . conflicts with appellate courts' jurisdiction and obligation to review criminal convictions "as well upon the law as upon the facts." Tex. Code Crim. Proc. Ann. art. 44.25. The appropriate balance between the jury's role as the judge of the facts and the reviewing court's duty to review criminal convictions is struck by not allowing the appellate court to "find" facts, or substitute its judgment for that of the jury; rather, when it determines that the verdict is against the great weight of the evidence presented at trial so as to be clearly wrong and unjust, it must reverse the verdict and remand for a new trial.

[W]hen the courts of appeals exercise their fact jurisdiction, they [might] substitute their judgment for that of the jury. However, . . . sufficient safeguards can be imposed by this Court to guarantee that the mental processes of the scrivener are reflected in the opinion so that we may ascertain whether the process resulted in a usurpation of the jury function. [In the civil context, the reviewing court in its written opinion must] "detail the evidence relevant to the issue in consideration and clearly state why the jury's finding is factually insufficient . . . as to be manifestly unjust; why it shocks the conscience; or clearly demonstrates bias. . . ." Pool v. Ford Motor Co., 715 S.W.2d 629, 635 (Tex. 1986). [T]hese safeguards help ensure that the factfinder is given the appropriate deference and that the defendant's right to trial by jury remains inviolate.

Neither the federal nor the Texas prohibition against double jeopardy, U.S. Const. amend. V; Tex. Const. art. I, §14, preclude defendants from seeking an acquittal through a new trial. As the United States Supreme Court held, the Double Jeopardy Clause does not prohibit a retrial if the reversal is based on factual insufficiency of the evidence. Tibbs v. Florida, 457 U.S. 31 (1982). However, retrial is prohibited where the reviewing court determines that the evidence is insufficient under *Jackson.* That is, as a practical matter, the State has only one opportunity to present evidence legally sufficient to convict a defendant. [We] hold that the *Stone* standard correctly imports the beyond-a-reasonable-doubt burden of proof and successfully adapts the factual sufficiency standard to the burden of proof at a criminal trial. . . .

17. "Unless otherwise provided in this Code, the jury is the exclusive judge of the facts, but it is bound to receive the law from the court and be governed thereby."

18. "The jury, in all cases, is the exclusive judge of the facts proved, and of the weight to be given to the testimony. . . ."

MEYERS, J., concurring.

. . . Appellant is not contending . . . that there was no evidence to support the verdict (legal insufficiency) or that he was conclusively shown to be not guilty (innocence as a matter of law), either of which argument would present a legal, not a factual, question. [He] is not specifically contending that the evidence supporting conviction was insufficient in itself to prove his guilt. He is only claiming that the contrary evidence was so great that it overwhelmed the evidence of guilt. Under such circumstances, he argues, a guilty verdict is clearly wrong, manifestly unjust, or irrational.

This distinction between the contention that evidence is insufficient to prove a fact and the somewhat different contention that other evidence overwhelmingly disproves that fact is important in the present context because the kind of evidentiary review performed by appellate courts under the rubric established by the United States Supreme Court in Jackson v. Virginia, 443 U.S. 307 (1979), plainly does not contemplate that a reviewing court consider the probative weight of exculpatory evidence when evaluating the sufficiency of inculpatory evidence to sustain a criminal conviction. . . .

Whether it is a good idea for appellate courts to engage in this kind of factual review is a serious question, and one which has sparked intense debate from time to time in the Texas Supreme Court. That debate invariably focuses on the question whether such review effectively denies one or more of the litigants his constitutional right to a jury trial. But, it has been well-established in our civil jurisprudence for many years that the Texas courts of appeals do have the constitutional authority to perform such a review and to reverse judgments upon the facts either because the evidence was factually insufficient to support an affirmative factfinding or because the evidence militating against such factfinding was overwhelmingly greater. It is generally thought that such reversals do not violate the right to a jury trial so long as the appellate court does not render judgment for one of the parties, but rather the cause for another jury determination of the question. Thus, in such circumstances, the appellate court is said not to find facts, as a jury does, but merely to unfind them.

[Our] opinion today only validates a long-standing truth of Texas constitutional law, that the courts of appeals in this state have authority to require a new trial whenever a verdict of guilty is so clearly against the evidence as to be manifestly unjust. The public can be assured that the reversal of criminal convictions on this basis will be most uncommon in practice and that, with few exceptions, there will be no good reason to resent the ones that do occur.

That is why the dissenters' position in this case is so disappointing. Their main complaint seems to be that well-founded convictions will routinely be set aside by appellate judges who are more interested in coddling criminals than in seeing justice done. This attitude toward the courts of appeals is not only unjustified, but it is disrespectful as well. . . . Just because we acknowledge the authority of appellate courts to review jury verdicts on their facts does not mean, therefore, that those courts will perform factual evaluations in an unreasonable, insensitive, or unjust manner. Those who are inclined to be alarmed by our lead opinion should withhold judgment at least until they see how it actually works in practice. . . .

MCCORMICK, P.J., dissenting.

What this case boils down to is whether in criminal cases the appellate courts can substitute their judgment for the jury's on questions of credibility and weight of the evidence. Because the majority does not leave these matters to be resolved at the local level by a jury, I dissent.

A civil "factual sufficiency" standard, which I assume the majority intends to adapt to the criminal side, requires the reviewing court to consider and weigh all the evidence; i.e., the reviewing court considers the evidence without the prism of "in the light most favorable to the verdict." See Pool v. Ford Motor Co., 715 S.W.2d 629 (Tex. 1986). The main difference between the Jackson v. Virginia standard and a "factual sufficiency" standard is the Jackson v. Virginia standard requires the reviewing court to defer to the jury on questions of credibility and weight of the evidence while the "factual sufficiency" standard allows the reviewing court to second-guess the jury on these questions. See Tibbs v. Florida, 457 U.S. 31 (1982) (when a reviewing court reverses the verdict based on the weight of the evidence, the reviewing court sits as a "thirteenth juror" and disagrees with the jury's resolution of conflicting testimony).

The issue here largely involves a question of statutory construction since the grant of appellate jurisdiction is subject to such exceptions and regulations as may be "prescribed by law." See Article V, Sections 5 & 6. The statutory scheme of things on the criminal side shows the Legislature undertook to insure a "factual sufficiency" standard would not be applicable in criminal cases.

The majority relies on Tex. Code Crim. Proc. Ann. Article 44.25, to support its conclusion the courts of appeals have the power to apply a "factual sufficiency" standard. However, the Legislature made significant changes to Article 44.25 in 1981 when the courts of appeals received criminal jurisdiction in noncapital direct appeal cases. The 1981 amendments modified Article 44.25 to its current form: "The courts of appeals or the Court of Criminal Appeals may reverse the judgment in a criminal action, as well upon the law as upon the facts." Prior to this, Article 44.25 and its statutory predecessors provided: "The Court of Criminal Appeals may reverse the judgment in a criminal action, as well upon the law as upon the facts. A cause reversed because the verdict is contrary to the evidence shall be remanded for a new trial." . . .

Therefore, any questions about this Court's and the courts of appeals' power to apply a "factual sufficiency" standard were resolved in 1981 when the Legislature deleted the . . . portions of Article 44.25 which allowed the remedy of a new trial when the verdict was contrary to the weight of the evidence. The legislative changes to Article 44.25 indicate a legislative intent to limit the power of this Court and the courts of appeals to reverse the judgment and remand the case for a new trial when they subjectively believe the verdict is contrary to the weight of the evidence. Any other construction would render the legislative changes to Article 44.25 meaningless. . . .

The majority apparently concludes the 1981 legislative changes to Article 44.25 were [passed simply in an effort to avoid a violation of double jeopardy. Under Burks v. United States, 437 U.S. 1 (1978), and Greene v. Massey, 437 U.S. 19 (1978), an acquittal is necessary when a reviewing court has determined the evidence to be "legally insufficient." However, in Tibbs v. Florida, 457 U.S. 31 (1982), the Supreme Court held that double jeopardy does not bar a retrial when an appellate court reverses a conviction because it was contrary to the weight of the evidence. Thus, the majority argues, the 1981 changes to the statute were a response to a perceived double jeopardy problem that no longer exists.]

More importantly, Article 38.04, Tex. Code Crim. Proc., also shows a legislative intent that a "factual sufficiency" standard is not applicable in criminal cases. Article

38.04, in relevant part, says the jury in all criminal cases "is the exclusive judge of the facts proved and of the weight to be given to the testimony." . . . The majority decides Article 38.04 does not apply to appellate review of sufficiency issues because Article 38.04 is meant "to distinguish the role of the jury from the role of the judge at trial." The majority's interpretation of Article 38.04 is contrary to its "plain language" and exceeds the scope of this Court's power by legislating an "exception" to Article 38.04. Also, it makes no sense to hold the trial judge, who has observed the witnesses testify and their demeanor, has no power to weigh the evidence, while the reviewing court has the power to weigh the evidence on a cold record. . . .

The majority also implicitly explains its holding is necessary to prevent an "unjust" conviction. However, the majority does not explain how this question is relevant to the issue before the Court or how a verdict that meets the Jackson v. Virginia standard can be considered "unjust."[7] Properly applied, the Jackson v. Virginia standard is about as exacting a standard as a "factual sufficiency" standard because both standards require the reviewing court to consider all the evidence. After a reviewing court determines the evidence is sufficient to support the verdict under the Jackson v. Virginia standard, it is practically impossible to say, under a proper application of a "factual sufficiency" standard, the verdict is so contrary to the overwhelming weight of the evidence as to be manifestly unjust. . . .

Law-abiding citizens, who are unconcerned with the legal niceties discussed in these pages, should understand the majority opinion increases the likelihood they will become a victim of violent crime because, according to the majority, this is the only protection a criminal defendant has from an "unjust" conviction. The majority opinion does not cite one instance of an "unjust conviction" under *Jackson,* and, in light of the foregoing discussion, a guilty verdict that meets the Jackson v. Virginia standard can never be considered an "unjust" conviction. The Jackson v. Virginia standard strikes a proper balance between granting defendants a fair evidentiary review of their convictions and protecting society from dangerous criminals. . . .

WHITE, J., dissenting.

Law-abiding Texans, hold on to your hats. We have another "run-away train" and it is again driven by a reckless, careless, and mischievous driver, Judge Maloney. . . . The majority has not provided this Court with a sufficient reason to abandon Jackson v. Virginia's standard for reviewing evidentiary sufficiency as the sole standard for reviewing sufficiency of the evidence and, instead, add the civil standard for reviewing factual sufficiency of the evidence to the review of the appeals in criminal cases.

This holding by the majority represents more than a decision to usurp the role of the jury in our criminal courts; it is no less than a breach of faith by a majority of this Court by which it has abrogated its traditional duty of respecting the abilities of

7. The majority presents a hypothetical in footnote twelve of its opinion to illustrate an "unjust" conviction under the Jackson v. Virginia standard; i.e., the 40 nuns hypothetical. This hypothetical makes two assumptions neither of which [is] very practical. It assumes a prosecutor would choose to prosecute under that fact situation and a jury would actually convict under that fact situation. However, if such a conviction was ever had, the reviewing court in applying Jackson v. Virginia should not have too much trouble concluding that no rational trier of fact could have found beyond a reasonable doubt the essential elements of the offense. Therefore, the 40 nuns hypothetical would not result in an "unjust" conviction under Jackson v. Virginia.

the juries and trial courts of this State to fulfill their responsibility to evaluate and assess the weight and credibility of the evidence presented to them. [There] are mechanisms within place in our criminal justice system which already serve more than adequately to correct manifestly unjust verdicts. [A] defendant can pursue relief from an unjust verdict under the authority of Tex. Code Crim. Proc. art. 11.07. [This provision, dealing with post-conviction challenges to the validity of a conviction,] provides an avenue for relief for a defendant who is asserting a claim of factual innocence. . . . A defendant can also pursue relief through the executive clemency process. . . . Lastly, if a defendant is able to show that the verdict rendered against him at trial is so contrary to the overwhelming weight of the evidence as to be clearly wrong and unjust, then he or she would be eligible to pursue federal habeas relief. . . .

Problem 20-1. Wrong Place, Wrong Time?

An undercover police officer approached an apartment on Sixth Avenue in Saginaw, Michigan, at about 8:30 P.M. on a December evening. He asked a man inside the apartment for a "$10 rock" of crack cocaine and passed two marked $5 bills through an open window. He heard some conversation inside the apartment, then received a small plastic bag containing crack cocaine. Within two hours, the undercover officer returned with a search warrant and several other officers. They found four men inside the apartment: Lemiel Wolfe, Darren Rogers, Alan Wise, and Leonard James.

When the officers entered the apartment, all four of the men in the apartment ran to the back bedroom. The officers found a loaded twelve-gauge shotgun on the floor in the front room. When the police officers entered the back bedroom of the apartment they saw Wise standing over an open vent in the floor, with the grate removed. The officers recovered 27 plastic baggies of crack cocaine from the vent, amounting to less than 50 grams of cocaine. They found no glass pipes or other paraphernalia typically used to smoke cocaine. It appeared to the officers that no one was living in the apartment. The front room contained only a couch, a refrigerator, and a broken television set. The apartment had no running water and the toilet was not in working condition. The bath tub was being used as a toilet.

The officers arrested and searched all four of the men in the apartment. Wolfe was holding $265 in cash, including the two marked $5 bills. In addition, he had a beeper and a key to the back door of the apartment. The search of Rogers revealed a piece of paper with the number of Wolfe's beeper written on it and a shotgun shell of the same type as the shotgun they found in the front room.

The government charged Wolfe and Rogers with possession with intent to deliver less than 50 grams of cocaine, and possession of a firearm during the commission of a felony. Police officers testified at trial to establish the events as described above.

Wolfe testified at trial that he went to Saginaw to visit a friend. He arrived around 6:00 P.M. that evening and went to the Sixth Avenue apartments to visit Sharon Johnson, whose relatives lived in the apartment next to the apartment where the arrest took place. Wolfe visited with her for about five minutes.

Wolfe said that he had invited several friends from Detroit (Rogers, James, and Wise) to visit Johnson. Around 8:00 P.M., he saw his Detroit friends approaching on the street outside the apartments, and he called out to them from the front porch because they were not familiar with the location. Wolfe testified that he left after a few minutes to visit another friend's house. When he returned to Sixth Avenue around 10:00 P.M., Wolfe spoke briefly with the next-door residents, then joined his friends for a party. He went to the local store for food and beer, after collecting money from the others. When Wolfe returned from the store, Leonard James repaid a prior $20 debt with four $5 bills, two of which were the marked bills that James had received earlier that night from the undercover police officer. As the group sat and watched television, Wolfe saw James smoking cocaine, but testified that he saw no other drugs in the apartment. Shortly after his return from the convenience store, the police raided the apartment and arrested Wolfe, along with several others.

Rogers testified as follows:

Q. Wolfe testified that it was about eight o'clock when he saw you. Is he correct?
A. I don't really know what time it was, but when we got there, it was about six when we saw him standing outside. . . .
Q. And how long after Wolfe came back up did he stay upstairs with you?
A. A good little while.
Q. How long is a "good little while"?
A. I'd say an hour, two hours.

Rogers also testified that Leonard James gave Wolfe the marked $5 bills before Wolfe left the Sixth Avenue apartment to visit his other friend.

Wolfe and Rogers were both convicted on both counts; Wolfe appealed. He argues that the government's evidence did not support either of the two charges, because the evidence did not prove that he possessed the cocaine with intent to distribute it, nor did it prove that he possessed a firearm. Under the case law of Michigan, the government can establish possession of cocaine by showing that the defendant physically possessed the cocaine, or that the defendant "had the right to exercise control of the cocaine and knew that it was present." A person's presence, by itself, at a location where drugs are found is insufficient to prove possession. Just as proof of actual possession of narcotics is not necessary to prove possession, actual delivery of narcotics is not required to prove intent to deliver. Intent to deliver has been inferred from the quantity of narcotics in a defendant's possession, from the way in which those narcotics are packaged, and from other circumstances surrounding the arrest.

How would you rule on appeal? Was the evidence sufficient to sustain one or both of the convictions? Were either of the convictions contrary to the weight of the evidence? Would you reach the same outcomes if the police had not found any key on Wolfe when they searched him? Compare People v. Wolfe, 489 N.W.2d 748 (Mich. 1992).

Notes

1. *Sufficiency of the evidence and weight of the evidence.* The federal due process clause, as we have seen, requires a minimum level of evidentiary support for a conviction. Prior to Jackson v. Virginia, 443 U.S. 307 (1979), appellate courts could affirm a conviction so long as there was "some evidence" to support the judgment. In *Jackson,* the Supreme Court decided that a federal court, when reviewing a state court

conviction during postconviction habeas corpus proceedings, must confirm that there was sufficient evidence to support a "reasonable trier of fact" in concluding that the government had proven guilt beyond a reasonable doubt. Does this due process standard for the "sufficiency" of the evidence require the appellate court to consider the inculpatory evidence alone, or to consider it in light of the exculpatory evidence?

Texas is not the only state to create an additional form of appellate review for factual findings. The "weight of the evidence" inquiry was more common years ago than it is today, but some states still grant their appellate courts this authority. Is it necessary, now that the *Jackson* test has replaced the "some evidence" test? Why did the choice among types of appellate factual review generate such strong feelings in the *Clewis* case? Whose right to a jury was at stake?

2. *Evidentiary review and double jeopardy.* The precise type of factual review that an appellate court uses can have double jeopardy consequences. According to Tibbs v. Florida, 457 U.S. 31 (1982), a retrial is possible after an appellate court reverses a conviction because it is contrary to the "weight of the evidence." The prosecution, in such a case, has met the constitutional minimum burden of proof during the first trial, and the defendant's appeal therefore does not bar a second trial. If the prosecution fails to present evidence sufficient to meet the *Jackson* standard in the first trial, it will not receive a second chance. Given this more favorable outcome for the state under the double jeopardy clause, should prosecutors generally favor giving to appellate courts the option of a "weight of the evidence" review?

C. RETROACTIVITY

Appellate courts review questions of law more aggressively than they do questions of fact. Legal questions are typically subject to de novo review. But not every erroneous legal decision by the trial court will lead to a reversal of the judgment. There are several categories of legal errors that will not undermine the judgment below. When lower courts violate rules of law announced in later appellate decisions, appellate courts are sometimes willing to ignore those errors by saying that the new rule of law will not receive "retroactive" application.

The question of which appellate decisions should receive retroactive application seems simple — and until the middle of this century, it was. Common-law systems operated on the assumption that courts "found" the law, and therefore each decision reflected law already in existence. Since the law existed before, during, and after a court's decision, it applied "retroactively" to other active cases, and perhaps (through postconviction review such as habeas corpus) even to defendants who have concluded their direct appeals (sometimes many years ago).

We no longer live in such innocent times. Since the middle of the twentieth century, legal realism has led lawyers and judges to recognize that courts make law, at least interstitially. In light of this honest assessment, some courts have declared that their own rulings will have only prospective application (like statutes) or only limited retroactive effect. When appellate courts say that a decision should receive only prospective application, what conception of judicial powers do they reveal?

The common law, in contrast, recognized legislatures as law "makers" rather than law "finders," and thus statutes were presumed to apply only prospectively. Constitutional doctrine bolstered this assumption: The "ex post facto clause" barred legislation that enhanced the punishment for a prior act. The Supreme Court in Collins v. Youngblood, 497 U.S. 37, 42 (1990), summarized the concept as follows:

> It is settled . . . that any statute [1] which punishes as a crime an act previously committed, which was innocent when done, [2] which makes more burdensome the punishment for a crime, after its commission, or [3] which deprives one charged with [a] crime of any defense available according to law at the time when the act was committed, is prohibited as ex post facto.

Like courts reshaping the concept of judicial power by issuing prospective rulings, legislatures have increasingly enacted laws that apply not only to future but to present and past cases. What limits does the ex post facto principle place on such statutes? Do legislatures think differently about laws if they are limited to prospective application? Do courts think differently about their rulings if decisions are generally applied retroactively?

■ STATE v. CURTIS KNIGHT

678 A.2d 642 (N.J. 1996)

STEIN, J.

After a jury trial, defendant, Curtis Knight, was convicted of first-degree murder, third-degree possession of a weapon for an unlawful purpose, and fourth-degree unlawful possession of a weapon. The Appellate Division reversed defendant's convictions [because] the admission into evidence of defendant's statement to his arresting officer violated defendant's state constitutional right to counsel as construed in State v. Sanchez, 609 A.2d 400 (N.J. 1992). In *Sanchez,* we held that mere recitation of the *Miranda* warnings does not provide an indicted defendant with information sufficient to make a knowing and intelligent waiver of the right to counsel. Recognizing that *Sanchez* was decided after Knight's trial had concluded, the Appellate Division nevertheless determined that the *Sanchez* rule applies retroactively and requires the reversal of Knight's convictions. . . . We affirm.

In March 1990, defendant was tried along with Cesar Glenn for the murder of Glenn Brown, who was also known as Hassan. The State contended that Cesar Glenn held Brown while defendant beat him to death with a pipe. [B]ecause defendant and his girlfriend, Kathy Capella, had moved to California in October of 1988, New Jersey law enforcement authorities had been unable to find defendant prior to or after his indictment. On October 25, 1989, F.B.I. Agent Mark Wilson and local police officers located and apprehended defendant in Palmdale, California. . . . According to Wilson, defendant waived his *Miranda* rights and stated that while he was living in New Jersey he had been robbed by Brown. After the robbery, defendant learned that someone named Rahaem or Knight had beaten up Brown and inflicted serious injuries in the process. Brown's friends apparently believed that defendant was the culprit, and were looking for defendant to exact revenge for the beating. Defendant thus explained to Wilson that he left New Jersey because he feared for his life and that he did not know that the police were looking for him. Although defendant's explanation was not directly inculpatory, at trial the State used defendant's story to connect him to Brown and to argue that defendant killed Brown to get revenge for the robbery. . . . The jury found defendant guilty of all charged offenses: first-degree murder, fourth-degree unlawful possession of a weapon, and third-degree possession of a weapon for an unlawful purpose.

[Knight] contends that his statement to F.B.I. Agent Wilson should not have been admitted into evidence at trial because defendant had not validly waived his right to counsel before speaking with Wilson. The resolution of that issue turns on whether State v. Sanchez, 609 A.2d 400 (N.J. 1992), which we decided after Knight's trial had concluded but before the Appellate Division had ruled on his appeal, applies retroactively to this case. . . .

This Court has four options in any case in which it must determine the retroactive effect of a new rule of criminal procedure. The Court may decide to apply the new rule purely prospectively, applying it only to cases in which the operative facts arise after the new rule has been announced. Alternatively, the Court may apply the new rule in future cases and in the case in which the rule is announced, but not in any other litigation that is pending or has reached final judgment at the time the new rule is set forth. A third option is to give the new rule "pipeline retroactivity," rendering it applicable in all future cases, the case in which the rule is announced, and any cases still on direct appeal. Finally, the Court may give the new rule complete retroactive effect, applying it to all cases, including those in which final judgments have been entered and all other avenues of appeal have been exhausted.

However, before a court chooses from among those four options, it customarily engages in the threshold inquiry of whether the rule at issue is a "new rule of law" for purposes of retroactivity analysis. Our cases have recognized that if a ruling does not involve a "departure from existing law," the retroactivity question never arises and our power to limit the retroactive effect of a decision is not implicated. That approach apparently stems from the concept, prevalent at common law, that the duty of courts was not to pronounce new law but rather to "maintain and expound" extant judicial rulings. See Linkletter v. Walker, 381 U.S. 618, 622 (1965) (quoting 1 William Blackstone, Commentaries 69 (15th ed. 1809)). A court could "discover" what the law had always been, but it could not create new law. The recognition that the retrospective effect of a judicial ruling could be restricted was unknown to the common-law courts and incompatible with the common-law view that an overruled holding was not bad law, it was simply never the law. In time, however, courts came to accept that some decisions represent a break from prior jurisprudence, and that to apply such new rules retroactively could inflict unjustified burdens on the courts and law enforcement personnel.

In State v. Lark, 567 A.2d 197 (N.J. 1989), we discouraged undue emphasis on the old rule/new rule distinction, and noted our reluctance to decide retroactivity questions on the basis of the now-discredited common-law view of law as "perpetual and immutable." [We] cited approvingly the federal Supreme Court's broad definition of "new rule" that provides that a "case announces a new rule when it breaks new ground or imposes a new obligation on the States or the Federal Government [or] if the result was not dictated by precedent existing at the time the defendant's conviction became final." Teague v. Lane, 489 U.S. 288, 301 (1989). Moreover, we held that a decision involving an "accepted legal principle" announces a new rule for retroactivity purposes so long as the decision's application of that general principle is "sufficiently novel and unanticipated."

If a decision indeed sets forth a "new rule," three factors generally are considered to determine whether the rule is to be applied retroactively: "(1) the purpose of the rule and whether it would be furthered by a retroactive application, (2) the degree of reliance placed on the old rule by those who administered it, and (3) the effect a retroactive application would have on the administration of justice." State v. Nash, 317 A.2d 689 (N.J. 1974). Although those three factors have received detailed attention in our retroactivity case law, our cases also indicate that the retroactivity determination often turns more generally on the court's view of what is just and consonant with public policy in the particular situation presented.

The first factor, the purpose of the new rule, is often the pivotal consideration. For example, if the newly announced rule is an exclusionary rule intended solely to discourage police misconduct, then the rule's purpose would not be served by applying the rule to conduct occurring before the rule was announced. For that reason, exclusionary rules are rarely given retroactive effect. On the other hand, if the old rule was altered because it substantially impaired the reliability of the truth-finding process, the interest in obtaining accurate verdicts may suggest that the new rule be given complete retroactive effect.

The second and third factors come to the forefront of the retroactivity analysis when the inquiry into the purpose of the new rule does not, by itself, reveal whether retroactive application of the new rule would be appropriate. The second factor inquires whether law enforcement agents justifiably relied on the old rule in performing their professional responsibilities. The reasoning underlying this inquiry is that state agents should not be penalized for complying in good faith with prevailing constitutional norms when carrying out their duties. In instances where prior judicial decisions gave state officials reason to question the continued validity of the old rule, the significance of the reliance factor correspondingly decreases.

The third factor in the retroactivity analysis, the effect a retroactive application would have on the administration of justice, recognizes that courts must not impose unjustified burdens on our criminal justice system. Thus, we generally have avoided applying new rules retroactively when such an application would undermine the validity of large numbers of convictions. We have noted our concern about overwhelming courts with retrials, and our awareness of the difficulty in re-prosecuting cases in which the offense took place years in the past.

Our three-pronged retroactivity analysis stems from the test set forth by the United States Supreme Court in Linkletter v. Walker, 381 U.S. 618 (1965). Over the years, however, the federal jurisprudence shifted course, and the federal Supreme Court eventually abandoned the *Linkletter* factors in favor of a more mechanical approach. Under current federal law, new rules based on interpretation of the federal Constitution are to be applied to all cases still on direct appeal, see Griffith v. Kentucky, 479 U.S. 314 (1987), but only in rare circumstances to cases in which all avenues of direct review have been exhausted. Teague v. Lane, 489 U.S. 288 (1989). Although we have noted our agreement with some of the principles underlying *Teague,* we have continued to determine the retroactivity of state rules of law under the *Linkletter* test. See State v. Lark. . . .

The threshold retroactivity issue in this case, whether *Sanchez* announced a new rule of law, is a close question. Our analysis begins with Patterson v. Illinois, 487 U.S. 285 (1988), which was decided four years before *Sanchez.* In *Patterson,* the United States Supreme Court held that reading the *Miranda* rights to an indicted defendant enables that defendant to make an informed and valid waiver of the Sixth Amendment right to counsel. The Court rejected the contention that the Sixth

Amendment right to counsel is "more difficult to waive than the Fifth Amendment counterpart." . . .

Four years later, in *Sanchez,* we held that after a defendant has been indicted, administration of *Miranda* warnings during police-initiated interrogation is not adequate to elicit a knowing and voluntary waiver of the right to counsel guaranteed by the State Constitution. We saw *Patterson* as a "change of direction" in the Supreme Court's Sixth Amendment jurisprudence, and found the basis for our decision in "our traditional commitment to the right to counsel." Those observations might imply that the rule set forth in *Sanchez* was not "new," but rather . . . a continuation of traditional adherence to a heightened importance of the right to counsel once the criminal adversarial process has begun. On the other hand, focusing on the period before *Sanchez* was decided, *Patterson* represented the United States Supreme Court's resolution of the question under the federal Constitution, and the *Patterson* Court squarely had rejected the right-to-counsel argument later accepted in *Sanchez*. . . . We therefore conclude that the *Sanchez* rule is "sufficiently novel and unanticipated" to implicate this Court's power to limit the retroactive effect of its decisions. Accordingly, we consider whether retroactive application of the *Sanchez* rule would be appropriate.

To guide us in the inquiry into the purpose of the *Sanchez* rule, we look to the rationale for that rule set forth in *Sanchez* itself:

> The return of an indictment transforms the relationship between the State and the defendant. By obtaining the indictment, the State represents that it has sufficient evidence to establish a prima facie case. Once the indictment is returned, the State is committed to prosecute the defendant. From that moment, if not before, the prosecutor and the defendant are adversaries. . . . Under those circumstances, the perfunctory recitation of the right to counsel and to remain silent may not provide the defendant with sufficient information to make a knowing and intelligent waiver. Such a recitation does not tell the defendant the nature of the charges, the dangers of self-representation, or the steps counsel might take to protect the defendant's interests. [609 A.2d at 408.]

In this case, the inquiry into the purpose of the new rule does not, by itself, reveal whether retroactive application of the rule would be appropriate. Although the *Sanchez* rule is intended, in part, to discourage police interrogation of indicted, unrepresented defendants, it is not solely an exclusionary rule. Similarly, although the rule aims to enhance the reliability of confessions by reducing the inherent coercion of custodial interrogation, it does not replace a rule that substantially impaired the truth-finding function of the criminal trial. Accordingly, we must add to our analysis a consideration of the "reliance" and "administration of justice" factors. Those factors are, to an extent, interrelated in this case.

We fail to discern any appreciable reliance by law enforcement officials on pre-*Sanchez* law. [Only] in exceptional situations would a New Jersey law enforcement officer attempt to interrogate an indicted defendant outside the presence of a defense attorney. We note that in urban counties the first appearance by criminal defendants occurs in Central Judicial Processing (CJP) courts, and in those courts, forms requesting assigned counsel generally are completed by defendants prior to their initial court appearance, and at that court appearance counsel from the public defender's office are generally available to provide representation. . . . Thus, the prevailing practice across much of the State is to provide counsel to defendants immediately after the criminal complaint is filed — even before the grand jury has returned an indictment. . . . Thus, the *Sanchez* rule, which concerns waiver of the right to counsel by indicted yet unrepresented defendants, is implicated only in those unusual cases in which indicted defendants deliberately forgo the right to counsel or absent themselves from their initial court appearance and miss the opportunity to be assigned an attorney. Our assumption is that police do not customarily interrogate indicted and uncounseled defendants.

The third retroactivity factor, the effect retroactive application would have on the administration of justice, militates in favor of limited retroactive application of the *Sanchez* rule. As noted, cases in which the *Sanchez* rule is implicated arise relatively infrequently. Thus, applying *Sanchez* retroactively to cases on direct appeal would neither be chaotic nor overwhelm our courts. However, administration-of-justice considerations counsel against affording *Sanchez* more than "pipeline retroactivity." To accord *Sanchez* complete retroactive effect would impose on the State the burden of reprosecuting some cases in which the offense took place years in the past. Because of failing memories and unavailable witnesses, the problems encountered in prosecuting such cases often are insurmountable.

Based on the three retroactivity factors, we conclude that it would be just and consonant with public policy to apply the *Sanchez* rule in this case. Neither the purpose of the *Sanchez* rule, reliance on pre-*Sanchez* law, nor administration-of-justice considerations justify limiting application of the *Sanchez* rule to cases arising after that decision was announced. Because the pre-*Sanchez* rule did not substantially impair the reliability of the truth-finding process, we will not burden the criminal justice system with the post-conviction-relief applications and retrials that would result from a fully retroactive application of the *Sanchez* decision. *Sanchez* will therefore not apply to those defendants who had exhausted all avenues of direct relief at the time *Sanchez* was decided. . . .

COLEMAN, J., dissenting.

I dissent from the Court's holding that State v. Sanchez should apply retroactively to pipeline cases. The effect of that holding is to require the suppression of an otherwise reliable inculpatory statement by defendant because an F.B.I. Agent in California did not predict that New Jersey would not follow a sixteen-month-old decision of the United States Supreme Court. . . .

As the majority points out, Patterson v. Illinois was consistent with our law and New Jersey did not announce a different rule until nearly four years later when *Sanchez* was decided. Thus, *Sanchez* represented a new rule that could not have been predicted. I fail to see why a rule that served New Jersey well in assuring the reliability of confessions for thirty years under its existing constitution after *Miranda* was decided in 1966 should overnight be found so unreliable as to justify retroactive application of a new rule. The Court rationalizes its conclusion by conjecturing that law enforcement did not rely on *Patterson*. I disagree. It is hard to imagine a rule more deeply etched in the minds of law enforcement agents than the *Miranda* warnings and its progeny, of which *Patterson* is a part. . . . Agent Wilson had every right to rely on the United States Supreme Court's *Patterson* rule when he interrogated defendant only sixteen months after *Patterson* was decided. . . .

Notes

1. *Retroactivity of appellate decisions: majority position.* Historically, appellate courts applied their precedents to all litigants bringing appeals to them, even if the

precedents were announced after the proceedings in the trial court were completed. The Warren Court altered the historical approach to retroactivity in Linkletter v. Walker, 381 U.S. 618 (1965), and Stovall v. Denno, 388 U.S. 293 (1967). *Linkletter* dealt with the retroactivity of Mapp v. Ohio, 367 U.S. 643 (1961), which applied the exclusionary rule in state court proceedings for evidence obtained through unconstitutional searches or seizures. Under the new retroactivity doctrine, the appellate court could refuse to give some appellants the benefit of a new constitutional ruling. The defendant in the original appeal would always receive the benefit of the ruling, but other appellants who were complaining on direct appeal about government conduct taking place before the announcement of the new rule might or might not receive the benefit. The answer would depend on the three factors described in the *Knight* decision from New Jersey.

These changes in retroactivity doctrine appeared at a time when the Supreme Court was expanding the influence of the federal constitution in state criminal proceedings. What part did the retroactivity doctrine play in the "activism" of the Warren Court? Imagine yourself as one of the justices who routinely opposed the Court's expansive reading of the constitution. What would be your views about the new retroactivity doctrine? Did it limit the "damage" of wrongheaded decisions, or did it make them possible? See John C. Jeffries, Jr., The Right-Remedy Gap in Constitutional Law, 109 Yale L.J. 87 (1999).

In Griffith v. Kentucky, 479 U.S. 314 (1987), the Supreme Court abandoned the flexible *Linkletter* approach to retroactivity and announced that it would apply its decisions to all cases on direct appeal, even if the new rule of law did not exist at the time of the defendant's trial. In the wake of the *Griffith* case, some state courts have followed suit and have altered their own "retroactivity" standards (which govern the application of state law rulings). See State v. Waters, 987 P.2d 1142 (Mont. 1999) (follows *Griffith;* new rules of criminal procedure are applicable to cases still subject to direct review regardless of whether those rules represent "clear breaks" with the past). It is still common, however, to find decisions such as the New Jersey opinion in *Knight* that retain some discretion on the retroactivity question. When courts insist on some flexibility in deciding retroactivity, are they proclaiming an "activist" posture toward constitutional criminal procedure? Are they suggesting that their decisions in this field are more legislative than judicial, in the traditional senses of those terms?

2. *Retroactivity and collateral review.* Courts usually treat retroactivity questions differently when they arise during postconviction challenges. Federal courts apply decisions retroactively to cases on direct appeal but not to most defendants who have completed their direct appeals and are bringing a postconviction collateral attack on the judgment. Teague v. Lane, 489 U.S. 288 (1989). If new legal rules were available for postconviction challenges, would new claims flood the court whenever it announced a new procedural rule? Could this problem be solved by allowing retroactive application of a new rule only for prisoners who have *pending* collateral attacks at the time of the decision? Are there reasons other than sheer numbers of claims to treat those on direct appeal differently from those who have filed (or might file) a collateral attack? See Taylor v. State, 10 S.W.3d 673 (Tex. Crim. App. 2000) (rejects federal retroactivity doctrine and adopts a multifactor approach to determine whether new rules of nonconstitutional state law should be retroactively applied in state post-conviction proceedings).

3. *Ex post facto laws and retroactive statutes.* The ex post facto clause of the federal constitution provides that "No state shall . . . pass any . . . ex post facto law." U.S.

Const. art. I, §10, cl. 1. In Calder v. Bull, 3 U.S. (3 Dall.) 386, 390 (1798), the Supreme Court explained that the ex post facto clause prohibited the following kinds of laws:

1) Every law that makes an action done before the passing of the law, and which was innocent when done, criminal, and punishes such action.
2) Every law that aggravates a crime, or makes it greater than it was when committed.
3) Every law that changes the punishment, and inflicts a greater punishment than the law annexed to the crime when committed.
4) Every law that alters the legal rules of evidence, and receives less, or different, testimony, than the law required at the time of the commission of the offense in order to convict the offender.

In Thompson v. Utah, 170 U.S. 343 (1898), the Court held that a Utah law reducing the size of a criminal jury from 12 to 8 deprived a defendant of "a substantial right involved in his liberty" and thus violated the ex post facto clause. The Court overruled *Thompson* in Collins v. Youngblood, 497 U.S. 37 (1990), concluding that the ex post facto clause does not apply to every change of procedure that "alters the situation of a party to his disadvantage." It upheld a statute allowing an appellate court to reform an unauthorized verdict without having to remand for retrial, even for crimes committed before the passage of the statute. Does *Collins* give a legislature flexibility on the retroactivity question comparable to that of the *Linkletter* rule? Most courts limit application of the ex post facto principle to laws that enhance punishment or are found to be "substantive" rather than "procedural." See also Rogers v. Tennessee, 532 U.S. 451 (2001) (state supreme court abolished common law defense in criminal case and applied new rule retroactively to defendant; due process clause rather than the ex post facto clause controls this situation because it involves judicial rather than legislative action).

Problem 20-2. Ex Post Facto

Buford Christmas was indicted in 1992 for the crime of fondling. The date of the crime was listed in the indictment as June 1989. The case went to trial on January 25, 1993, but the jury was unable to reach a verdict, and the judge entered an order of mistrial on January 26, 1993. The case went to trial a second time on March 8, 1993, with the jury returning a verdict of guilty on March 9, 1993. The judge sentenced Christmas to six years in prison.

At the time the crime occurred, the limitations period in the applicable statute, Miss. Code Ann. §99-1-5, was two years for the crime of fondling. On April 21, 1989, the legislature amended the statute, effective July 1, 1989, to extend the limitations period to seven years.

Christmas argues that his prosecution should have been time-barred under the statute of limitations in effect at the time of the crime. He committed the crime in June 1989, but his prosecution did not commence until, at the earliest, January 1992, more than two years later. Christmas contends that his prosecution under the revised seven-year statute of limitations violated the ex post facto clauses in both the federal and state constitutions. How would you rule? See Christmas v. State, 700 So. 2d 262 (Miss. 1997).

D. HARMLESS ERROR

"For every wrong there should be a remedy." This notion entered U.S. legal culture through the words of William Blackstone, conveyed by Chief Justice John Marshall. Marbury v. Madison, 5 U.S. (1 Cranch) 137, 163 (1803) ("it is a settled and invariable principle . . . that every right, when withheld, must have a remedy, and every injury its proper redress") (quoting 3 William Blackstone, Commentaries *109). Indeed, this principle has crystallized in many state constitutions, which include language such as Illinois Constitution article I, section 12: "Every person shall find a certain remedy in the laws for all injuries and wrongs which he receives to his person, privacy, property or reputation. He shall obtain justice by law, freely, completely, and promptly." Surely if this principle applies anywhere, it should apply to the operation of the justice system itself. If a defendant's rights are violated during trial on criminal charges, the error should be correctable on appeal.

Yet criminal trials are complex events, and few long trials occur without some error. If the remedy for every error at trial were a new trial, no major trial would ever end. But in cases where the proof is overwhelming, won't the outcome at the retrial be inevitable? Even for substantial errors, if the outcome is inevitable, why drag witnesses, jurors, and judges through a mere charade? Indeed, can there *ever* be reversible error in obvious cases?

The doctrine of harmless error aims to sort out the tension between a desire to be fair to a wronged defendant and the need to have an efficient system that focuses on errors that may have produced a wrong outcome. If stated too broadly, harmless error rules have the capacity to undermine whatever other procedural rules the system has created.

The U.S. Supreme Court took up this challenge in Fahy v. Connecticut, 375 U.S. 85 (1963), where the defendant was charged with willfully injuring a public building by painting swastikas on a synagogue. The Court found that the erroneous admission of an illegally seized can of paint and paintbrush was not harmless because there was "a reasonable possibility that the evidence complained of might have contributed to the conviction."

In Chapman v. California, 386 U.S. 18 (1967), the Court squarely addressed the issue of whether constitutional errors can be considered harmless. Ruth Chapman and Thomas Teale were convicted in a California state court upon a charge that they robbed, kidnapped, and murdered a bartender. At the trial, the prosecutor commented extensively on the decision by both defendants to remain silent; these comments were in keeping with a provision of the California constitution, which stated that a defendant's "failure to explain or to deny by his testimony any evidence or facts in the case against him may be commented upon by the court and by counsel." The U.S. Supreme Court struck down the California provision in Griffin v. California, 380 U.S. 609 (1965). In concluding that the denial of the federal rights recognized in *Griffin* amounted to harmless error in Chapman's case, the Court wrote:

> In fashioning a harmless-constitutional-error rule, we must recognize that harmless-error rules can work very unfair and mischievous results when, for example, highly important and persuasive evidence, or argument, though legally forbidden, finds its way into a trial in which the question of guilt or innocence is a close one. What harmless-error rules all aim at is a rule that will save the good in harmless-error practices while avoiding the bad, so far as possible.

> [We] do no more than adhere to the meaning of our *Fahy* case when we hold, as we now do, that before a federal constitutional error can be held harmless, the court must be able to declare a belief that it was harmless beyond a reasonable doubt. While appellate courts do not ordinarily have the original task of applying such a test, it is a familiar standard to all courts, and we believe its adoption will provide a more workable standard, although achieving the same result as that aimed at in our *Fahy* case. [386 U.S. at 22-24.]

While allowing harmless error analysis to apply to some constitutional errors, the *Chapman* Court recognized that other constitutional errors are "so basic to a fair trial that their violation can never be treated as harmless error," and cited Gideon v. Wainwright, 372 U.S. 335 (1963) (right to counsel); Payne v. Arkansas, 356 U.S. 560 (1958) (coerced confession); and Tumey v. Ohio, 273 U.S. 510 (1927) (impartial judge).

In Arizona v. Fulminante, 499 U.S. 279 (1991), the Court reconsidered whether a coerced confession was one of the errors "so basic to a fair trial" that harmless error analysis could not apply. *Fulminante* created a new conceptual divide between "trial errors" subject to harmless error analysis and "structural defects" that are not.

> The admission of an involuntary confession — a classic "trial error"— is markedly different from the other two constitutional violations referred to in the *Chapman* footnote as not being subject to harmless-error analysis. One of those violations, involved in Gideon v. Wainwright, was the total deprivation of the right to counsel at trial. The other violation, involved in Tumey v. Ohio, was a judge who was not impartial. These are structural defects in the constitution of the trial mechanism, which defy analysis by "harmless-error" standards. The entire conduct of the trial from beginning to end is obviously affected by the absence of counsel for a criminal defendant, just as it is by the presence on the bench of a judge who is not impartial. Since our decision in *Chapman*, other cases have added to the category of constitutional errors which are not subject to harmless error the following: unlawful exclusion of members of the defendant's race from a grand jury, see Vasquez v. Hillery, 474 U.S. 254 (1986); the right to self-representation at trial, see McKaskle v. Wiggins, 465 U.S. 168 (1984); and the right to public trial, see Waller v. Georgia, 467 U.S. 39 (1993). Each of these constitutional deprivations is a similar structural defect affecting the framework within which the trial proceeds, rather than simply an error in the trial process itself. Without these basic protections, a criminal trial cannot reliably serve its function as a vehicle for determination of guilt or innocence, and no criminal punishment may be regarded as fundamentally fair.
>
> It is evident from a comparison of the constitutional violations which we have held subject to harmless error, and those which we have held not, that involuntary statements or confessions belong in the former category. The admission of an involuntary confession is a "trial error," similar in both degree and kind to the erroneous admission of other types of evidence. . . . When reviewing the erroneous admission of an involuntary confession, the appellate court, as it does with the admission of other forms of improperly admitted evidence, simply reviews the remainder of the evidence against the defendant to determine whether the admission of the confession was harmless beyond a reasonable doubt.

Another example of a "structural error" is the right to a jury verdict of guilt beyond a reasonable doubt, based on a proper instruction to the jury about the meaning of reasonable doubt. See Sullivan v. Louisiana, 508 U.S. 275 (1993). A typical example of a "trial error" that can be ignored if "harmless" is the improper admission of "other crimes" evidence at trial. See State v. Johnson, 664 So. 2d 94 (La. 1995).

States have wrestled with their own harmless error standards, which apply to any errors based in state law. Some apply a unitary rule for constitutional and nonconstitutional errors, while others apply a different standard — usually one that makes it harder to find reversible error — for nonconstitutional errors. Most states have procedural rules that limit reversible error to those errors that affect the outcome or the "substantial rights" of the defendant. The case law on harmless error is often difficult to harmonize even within individual states. Courts still differ on some of the most fundamental questions about this doctrine, such as the burden of proof for establishing the harmlessness of the error.

Harmless error analysis now applies to most kinds of error at trial, but that is only the start of the analysis. In each case courts must also assess whether the error subject to analysis was in fact "harmless." The Supreme Court elaborated on the precise question to ask in the harmless error analysis in Sullivan v. Louisiana, 508 U.S. 275 (1993). The *Sullivan* inquiry "is not whether, in a trial that occurred without the error, a guilty verdict would surely have been rendered, but whether the guilty verdict actually rendered in this trial was surely unattributable to the error."

Few cases in state or federal court spend much time analyzing the legal standard for harmless error, yet the courts apply the doctrine in a huge number of cases. In the end, the rules do not give much guidance. Harmless error analysis is often applied in a single paragraph at the end of opinions, without detailed explanation of the facts. Does harmless error doctrine quietly overwhelm all the meaningful procedural choices made earlier in the case?

■ FEDERAL RULE OF CRIMINAL PROCEDURE 52

(a) Harmless Error. Any error, defect, irregularity, or variance that does not affect substantial rights must be disregarded.

(b) Plain Error. A plain error that affects substantial rights may be considered even though it was not brought to the court's attention.

■ TENNESSEE CRIMINAL PROCEDURE RULE 52

(a) Harmless Error. No judgment of conviction shall be reversed on appeal except for errors which affirmatively appear to have affected the result of the trial on the merits.

(b) Plain Error. An error which has affected the substantial rights of an accused may be noticed at any time, even though not raised in the motion for a new trial or assigned as error on appeal, in the discretion of the appellate court where necessary to do substantial justice.

■ PEOPLE v. WALTER BUDZYN

566 N.W.2d 229 (Mich. 1997)

RILEY, J.

In this appeal, we are asked to review the fairness of the trial for two police officers who were convicted of second-degree murder for killing a suspected drug user while attempting to arrest him while the suspect was holding contraband. We conclude that defendants have demonstrated that their juries were exposed to extrinsic influences that created a real and substantial possibility of prejudice, depriving them of their constitutional rights under the Sixth Amendment. These errors, however, were harmless beyond a reasonable doubt with regard to defendant Larry Nevers. Therefore, we affirm defendant Nevers' conviction. With regard to defendant Walter Budzyn, we conclude that the extrinsic influences were not harmless beyond a reasonable doubt. Accordingly, we vacate defendant Budzyn's conviction and remand for a new trial.

Defendants Budzyn and Nevers were police officers with the Detroit Police Department. They were on duty when the incident occurred that resulted in Malice Green's death. Both were tried at a single criminal proceeding with two different juries.[1]

On November 5, 1992, at approximately 10:15 P.M., defendants were patrolling in the City of Detroit in plain clothes in an unmarked vehicle. They apparently observed a Topaz, driven by Malice Green, with bullet holes in its front passenger door. Defendant Nevers, who only gave testimony before his own jury, testified that he observed the car pull up in front of a house known for its drug activity. Budzyn and Nevers stopped behind the Topaz to investigate. The home, with a storefront attached to it, was occupied by Ralph Fletcher. . . . Robert Hollins and Teresa Pace, witnesses to the event, were present at Fletcher's house and had been smoking cocaine that evening.

Defendant Budzyn, who only testified before his own jury, said that he witnessed Robert Knox running along the building and explained that he chased Knox because, apparently by mistake, he believed that Knox had been in the vehicle with Green. Budzyn caught Knox, brought him around to the front of Fletcher's place, and patted him down for weapons. He also patted down Fletcher, who had been in the car with Green. Manuel Brown, who had been smoking cocaine at Fletcher's place, was walking away from the house, but stopped to watch this activity. Nevers asked Malice Green for his driver's license. Green did not respond to Nevers' request, but walked around to the passenger side of his vehicle and got in. Green was sitting in the passenger seat, with his legs hanging out the open doorway. Budzyn came around to the passenger side, shined his flashlight on him, and asked for his license. Green began to look in the glove compartment, grasped at something that was on the floor, apparently cocaine, and Budzyn asked him to let go of what was in his hand.

At this point, there is substantial disagreement in the testimony given by defendants Budzyn and Nevers and the witnesses to the incident, Brown, Fletcher, Hollins, Knox, and Pace regarding what happened.

The five civilian witnesses testified that after Green refused to open his hand, Budzyn began to hit him repeatedly on the hand with the police flashlight, telling him to open his hand. Budzyn then climbed onto Green, who did not resist but did not comply, straddling him. Brown testified that Budzyn struck Green about ten times on his head with the flashlight. Fletcher, who was only three to five feet away, testified that Budzyn repeatedly hit Green on the hand. Hollins said that he heard Budzyn hit Green six or seven times, and, although he did not see the blows land,

1. There were charges that their crime was racially motivated. Consequently, we note that Budzyn and Nevers are white and Malice Green is black.

that these blows must have landed on Green's head. Knox said that he saw Budzyn hit Green in the hand because Green did not open it when Budzyn asked. Pace testified that from the position on which Budzyn sat on Green, he must have been hitting him on the head.

These five witnesses also said that, while Budzyn was struggling with Green in the Topaz, Nevers struck Green on his knee several times. Brown and Fletcher said that Nevers then went around to the other side of the car, the driver's side, opened the door, and struck Green, who was now lying on the front seat, on the head with his flashlight. Nevers instructed these people to leave the scene.

In contrast to this testimony, Budzyn explained to his jury that while Green was sitting in the passenger side of the vehicle, he suspected that Green was holding narcotics in his fist. He said that he grabbed Green's right arm and that Green kicked him with both his legs. He produced evidence of a small injury to his knee. Budzyn said that he turned and fell backward into the vehicle, dropping his flashlight. Budzyn denied that he ever hit Green at all. Budzyn also said that he only held Green's hands because he suspected that he was holding narcotics. Budzyn called for backup assistance. Budzyn explained that he heard "two hits" after Nevers went around to the driver's door and said that he later was "shocked" to find so much blood on the scene. Budzyn said he retrieved four rocks of cocaine from inside the vehicle.

Like Budzyn, Nevers testified to his jury that he assisted Budzyn when Green resisted Budzyn's efforts to open his hand. Nevers explained that he only hit Green on his knees when Green brought his knees up to stop Nevers from prying open his hand. Nevers then went to the other side of the vehicle because Budzyn told him that Green was attempting to get out of the other side of the car. Nevers then told the people from Fletcher's place to leave. Nevers explained that he hit Green in the head with his flashlight because Green was grabbing for his gun. Nevers said that after he struck him, "[Green] finally let go of my gun and I did not hit him [again]" at that time. Nevers flagged down the EMS medical technicians who had been called to the scene. Green continued to struggle with the officers and Nevers said he saw something "shiny" in Green's right hand and he struck him again, the blow landing on Green's head, because Nevers feared he might be carrying a razor blade or knife. Nevers admitted that, during the course of the incident he hit Green five or six times on the head with his flashlight.

The EMS medical technicians arrived in two vehicles. The first to arrive were Albino Martinez and Mithyim Lewis. The other EMS vehicle soon arrived with two other medical technicians, Lee Hardy and Scott Walsh. Several marked police cars arrived soon after the EMS vehicles. Martinez, Lewis, Hardy, and Walsh all testified that Green was covered with blood and was hanging from the driver's side door when they arrived. There was a pool of blood under his head on the street. These witnesses said that Nevers struck Green in the head with his heavy police flashlight repeatedly even though Green was not offering any significant resistance. Martinez and Walsh said that Nevers told Green to open his hands and hold still, and that, when he did not, Nevers hit him with the flashlight. Martinez and Lewis said that Nevers hit Green four times in the head with the flashlight, while Hardy said he saw Nevers hit Green approximately ten times in the head. Martinez explained that Green was "dazed," and Hardy described him as "stuporous," relating that Green was uttering only a few words like "wait" while Nevers was striking him.

Officer Robert Lessnau, who arrived on the scene in one of the marked police vehicles, pulled Green from the vehicle. The EMS medical technicians testified that

Lessnau hit Green with his fists. Martinez and Walsh said that while Lessnau was striking Green, Nevers also hit Green twice in the ribs. Green finally released the car keys he held in one hand and a piece of white paper, apparently for rolling rock cocaine, he held in the other. The uniformed officers, including Sergeant Freddie Douglas, then cuffed Green's hands behind his back as Green struggled. The EMS medical technicians began rendering care to Green. Green suffered a seizure and, soon after, died.

The people presented Dr. Kalil Jiraki, an assistant Wayne County Medical Examiner, as a medical expert to testify regarding the nature of Green's wounds and the cause of his death. Dr. Jiraki testified that Green died from "[b]lunt force trauma to [his] head" and that he suffered at least fourteen blows to the head. Dr. Jiraki also explained that Green had 0.5 micrograms of cocaine in his body, indicating that he was under the influence of cocaine at the time of his death. He concluded, however, that it had "no bearing on the cause of his death." In response, defendants presented three pathologists, one of whom, Dr. L. G. Dragovic, testified that he identified eleven blunt-force injuries to Green's head.

Budzyn and Nevers were charged with second-degree murder. Beginning with the first reports of Green's death, the case produced a firestorm of media publicity in the Detroit metropolitan area. The incident occurred soon after the California state courts acquitted four white Los Angeles police officers who had been videotaped beating black motorist Rodney King. The acquittal in the King case resulted in a terrible riot in Los Angeles that drew the attention of the national media. The media reports in Detroit of Green's death included a comparison of the two incidents. Before the trial began, the Detroit Police Department fired defendants. The City of Detroit also agreed to a multimillion dollar settlement with Green's estate. In response to some criticisms of the settlement, a city attorney stated that a generous settlement might spare the city the riotous violence that racked Los Angeles after the acquittal of the police officers. These events occurred during the interval between Green's death in November 1992 and the start of defendants' trial in June 1993, seven months later.

Defendants moved to sever the trials, and the trial court refused to separate the proceedings, but did grant defendants separate juries. Nevers asked for a change of venue because of the extensive pretrial publicity, but the trial court denied this motion. The trial court began the voir dire on June 2, 1993. The people began presenting their case on June 18, 1993. During a recess near the end of trial, on August 5 and 6, 1993, the trial court provided the juries with several film videos to watch to entertain themselves, including a copy of *Malcolm X*. The film begins with a video of the Los Angeles police officers beating Rodney King. Defendants moved for a mistrial on this basis, but this motion was denied.[7]

After approximately seven weeks of trial, the juries began deliberating on August 13, 1993. Budzyn and Nevers were convicted of second-degree murder. The jury in Budzyn's trial deliberated for eight days, and, in Nevers' trial, the jury deliberated for nine days. . . .

[The supreme court held that defendants had been denied their right to a fair and impartial jury because they considered extraneous facts not introduced into evidence. It was undisputed that the jurors watched the film *Malcolm X*; it was also

7. The trial judge did not select the movies or approve the selections himself, but he took responsibility for the action taken by the employees of the court. The trial judge disqualified himself on ruling on defendants' motion. The Chief Judge of Recorder's Court referred the motion to a third judge who heard the motion and denied it.

alleged that jurors were made aware of city plans to handle riots after the verdict and that defendants had been involved in a special police anti-drug unit. The film begins with the voice of *Malcolm X*'s character giving a provocative speech charging "the white man with being the greatest murderer on earth" while the viewer is shown footage of Rodney King being beaten by Los Angeles police officers, interspersed with a picture of an American flag. The Rodney King videotape is shown in slow motion, in eight segments, as the American flag begins to burn. The voiceover makes an explicit reference to Detroit, the location of the incident in the instant case, by stating that the black community has been deprived of democracy in the "streets of Detroit." At another point in the film Malcolm X confronts the police, who finally relent and allow him to call an ambulance and take a bleeding man from the police station to the hospital; Malcolm X says "A hundred years ago, they used to put on white sheets and sic bloodhounds on us. Well, nowadays they've traded in the sheets—well, some of them traded in sheets—. . . they have traded in those white sheets for police uniforms. They've traded in the bloodhounds for the police dogs. . . . You've got these Uncle Tom negro leaders today that are telling us we ought to pray for our enemy. We ought to love our enemy. We ought to integrate with an enemy who bombs us, who kills and shoots us, who lynches us, who rapes our women and children. No!"]

[W]e must decide whether any error was harmless beyond a reasonable doubt. There is no dispute that the extrinsic evidence was not duplicative of other properly admitted evidence for either defendant. Hence, we must determine whether the evidence against defendants was overwhelming. We believe that these extraneous influences were harmless for defendant Nevers in light of the overwhelming evidence of his guilt, but that the errors do require reversal for defendant Budzyn because the evidence against him was not overwhelming.

In the Nevers trial, the four EMS witnesses, who had no apparent motive to lie, provided interlocking testimony that Nevers repeatedly bludgeoned Malice Green in the head with his heavy police flashlight while Green was dazed and not offering significant resistance. The medical testimony of the injuries to Green's head also substantiated this testimony. The people have proven that there was unimpeachable, compelling evidence that defendant Nevers harbored, at the very least, an unjustified intent to commit great bodily harm against Green. Thus, . . . the extraneous influences were harmless. . . . In Budzyn's trial, however, we believe that the evidence against defendant Budzyn, particularly considering he was convicted of second-degree murder, was not overwhelming. The evidence against him was fundamentally weaker than the evidence against Nevers for three reasons.

First, of the three civilian witnesses who testified that defendant Budzyn hit Green in the head with his flashlight (Manuel Brown, Robert Hollins, and Teresa Pace), none was able to see the flashlight actually make contact with Green's head. Unlike the EMS witnesses, they did not have a direct view of the blows. Instead, the three witnesses each inferred the fact that the flashlight hit Green in the head from the positions of the two men in the vehicle and from Budzyn's use of the flashlight to strike Green. Brown, who arguably gave the most damaging testimony of any witness, was the farthest witness away, standing fifteen feet from Fletcher, Hollins, Knox, and Pace.

This testimony also contained some inconsistencies. The three key witnesses who testified that Budzyn hit Green on the head with his flashlight gave conflicting testimony on the nature of the blows that Budzyn administered: Pace and Hollins testified that Budzyn lifted the flashlight above his head or shoulders and brought the flashlight down, while Brown insisted that the blows were horizontal, across his body, and that Budzyn did not lift the flashlight above his head. Also, Fletcher, who was only three to five feet away and was the closest of the witnesses to the incident, testified that Budzyn hit Green's clenched fist with the flashlight, but that he did not see Budzyn hit Green anywhere else on his body.

Second, the civilian witnesses admitted that the altercation occurred after Green refused Budzyn's request that he turn over the incriminating evidence he held in his hand. The civilian witnesses all agreed that Green never complied and that he struggled with Budzyn, although they said he never struck him or kicked him. In fact, Fletcher testified that during the entire episode, Budzyn held onto Green's closed fist, attempting to retrieve the contraband. This is a very different setting from the description the EMS medical technicians gave of the situation in which defendant Nevers was striking Green in the head. Because the exchange occurred in the confined context of the car with the car obscuring the witnesses' view, their testimony that Green did not kick Budzyn does not directly rebut his claim that Green did. The medical evidence also does not necessarily contradict Budzyn's claims, because Nevers hit Green with significant force in the head and these blows may have been the cause of Green's extensive head injuries.

Third, in this credibility contest between Budzyn and these witnesses, the civilian witnesses all had either consumed alcohol or cocaine sometime before witnessing the exchange, three of them were friends with Green (Fletcher, Hollins, and Pace), and there was some suggestion from their testimony that they had reason to dislike these officers. This fact is relevant because an inquiry into whether an error was harmless requires a focus on the nature of the error in light of the weight and strength of the other evidence. People v. Mateo, 551 N.W.2d 891 (Mich. 1996). Defendant Budzyn had searched Fletcher and Knox for weapons before defendant Nevers asked to see Malice Green's driver's license. Defendant Budzyn had also broken into Fletcher's home while Fletcher and Hollins among others were there, a week and a half before this incident, searching the house without warrant, and, on another occasion, had arrested two people outside the house. Thus, these witnesses were not in the same objective position as the EMS medical technicians, who, incidentally, did not offer any testimony regarding Budzyn's actions against Green because they had not yet arrived on the scene.

Even if the jury reasonably believed the testimony of the civilian witnesses, they still might not have concluded that Budzyn was guilty of second-degree murder. The question whether Budzyn's unnecessary use of force as described by the civilian witnesses would be second-degree murder or manslaughter is an issue for the jury. We do not believe that the only, possible reasonable conclusion to draw from this evidence is that it established beyond a reasonable doubt that he harbored an intent to kill, an intent to do great bodily harm, or to commit an act in wanton and wilful disregard that the likelihood that the natural tendency of his conduct was to cause death or great bodily harm. In contrast, the testimony from the EMS medical technicians against Nevers made the conclusion inescapable that he was guilty of second-degree murder. We cannot say that the extraneous factors may not have affected the Budzyn jury's verdict. We, therefore, reverse his conviction and remand for a new trial. . . .

Boyle, J., concurring in part and dissenting in part.

I agree with the majority's result and rationale with regard to defendant Nevers, and its result in respect to defendant Budzyn. I write separately to explain my disagreement with certain aspects of the rationale in Budzyn.

First, despite differences of origin, history, class, education, race, ethnicity, sex, economic status, or educational level, it is a fundamental presumption of the judicial system that all Americans are equally capable of fairly discharging their public responsibilities. Batson v. Kentucky, 476 U.S. 79 (1986). Therefore, I disagree with the analysis of the opinions of both Chief Justice Mallett and Justice Riley regarding the showing of the movie, *Malcolm X,* to the extent that each employs assumptions about the predispositions of jurors. The system addresses the mind-set of jurors through voir dire, challenges for cause, and motions for change of venue, all of which require a demonstration of reasons why a prospective juror or a given community may be suspect. The approach is both aspirational and pragmatic. The judiciary has no competence to assess the cultural or psychological mind-set of a given jury and assess its reactions in light of its own assumptions. I also agree with the prosecution that the movie was not an extraneous communication, and find no error in this regard. . . .

However, I agree with the majority that the communication of incorrect information to the jurors during deliberations that defendant Budzyn was a member of STRESS [the special police anti-drug unit] was error requiring reversal. . . . Evaluated in the context of the evidence as a whole, the prejudicial significance is that Budzyn's membership in STRESS indicated a propensity for abuse of young black males. By all accounts, Green had what turned out to be cocaine in his hands and refused to surrender it. Thus, Budzyn's initiation of force against Green was lawful, whichever version of the testimony is believed. The issue in Nevers' trial turned on whether the jury believed Nevers' testimony that the deceased was trying to take his gun, thus justifying the life-threatening response. The issue in Budzyn's trial, by contrast, was whether, and at what point, the lawful use of force became unreasonable.

In substance, the jurors were told that Budzyn was a bad actor with a propensity for violence against young black men. Coupled with other evidence admitted at trial, this information could have persuaded the jurors that Budzyn had a man-endangering state of mind. Thus, it is not only the fact, as the majority observes, that this evidence was relevant to besmirching the defendant's character, but the fact that this information supported the prosecution's theory that defendant was guilty of second-degree murder, that is prejudicial.

Our responsibility is not to decide what we would have done or what we think the jury should have done. It is to hypothesize what the jury would have done had it not been exposed to the extrinsic information. Because there was substantial and real prejudice, I cannot conclude that the error was harmless beyond a reasonable doubt. I join in the opinion for reversal of defendant Budzyn's conviction of second-degree murder. I would affirm the conviction of defendant Nevers.

MALLETT, C.J., concurring in part and dissenting in part.

. . . The issues of greatest concern to both the majority and to myself relate to whether defendants were denied their right to a fair trial as a result of exposure to certain extraneous influences. In particular, I am most concerned with the jurors' exposure to the movie *Malcolm X* and to media accounts of contingency plans of suburban law enforcement in case of a riot. . . . Extensive media coverage continued through the trial, including reports speculating on contingency plans in place in the event of postverdict rioting. Jurors on both Budzyn's and Nevers' panels were exposed to portions of these reports.

[B]eyond showing exposure to an extraneous influence, the defendants . . . must make a showing of prejudice reverberating from the extraneous information. The test for determining whether the threshold level of prejudice is met is whether defendants have established a real and substantial possibility that the extraneous matter could have affected the verdict.

The first factor in this threshold inquiry is the nature and source of the extraneous material. The defendants focus their claim of prejudice resulting from the showing of *Malcolm X* on the opening footage of the movie. In an attempt to make his movie more provocative, producer-director Spike Lee presents opening footage of the beating of motorist Rodney King by Los Angeles police officers against the backdrop of a burning American flag. Along with these images, the viewer hears words from a speech by Malcolm X. Virtually every person in America had been exposed to the footage detailing the brutal beating given Mr. King by members of the Los Angeles Police Department. While it was unfortunate that the jurors were perhaps once again confronted with this footage, is it the defendants' position that the jurors became inflamed and were engulfed by emotion and thus rendered incapable of rendering a fair verdict? The possibility that a few police officers will absolutely violate department rules and procedures is never far from the minds of African-Americans, no matter their station in life. The presence of racism in any community can, and sometimes does, cause American citizens to react emotionally and render less than clear judgment. But there is no reasonable probability that the Rodney King footage affected the jurors in this case.

Racism has not and will not quell the desire of African-Americans to fully exercise all the rights and responsibilities associated with democracy. If this were not true, then the four-hundred-year-old struggle for freedom and economic opportunity would have been abandoned long ago. The defendants have not established that the picture of one black man being beaten by police officers could reasonably have prevented the jurors from rendering a fair verdict.

The words of Malcolm X in the opening sequence are indeed provocative.[12] But when these words are taken in the context of the effect of the overall message of the movie, their effect is greatly lessened. Please be clear, I do not dismiss the power of words. I do dismiss the conclusion that there is a real and substantial possibility that conscientious jurors watching this movie, shown during a recess purely for entertainment purposes, would have allowed it to affect their verdict. . . .

Regarding the nature and source of this extraneous influence, the defendants emphasize that the movie was supplied by the court; this factor alone is not determinative. While this fact does tend to bolster the movie's potential prejudicial effect, the nature of this particular extraneous influence weighs heavily against a finding of prejudice. The movie was chosen by the jurors from three others made available to them purely for purposes of entertainment. The jurors should be credited with enough sophistication to separate entertainment from evidence. . . .

I would further find that, even if the defendants had met their initial burden, a reversal is not required here because it can be said, beyond a reasonable doubt, that the other evidence adduced at trial was so overwhelming that there is no real and substantial possibility that viewing the movie might have contributed to the convictions. I respectfully disagree with the majority's conclusion that the evidence supporting second- degree murder against defendant Budzyn was not overwhelming.

12. For example: "Brothers and Sisters, I am here to tell you that I charge the white man, I charge the white man with being the greatest murderer on earth. . . . I charge him with being the greatest kidnapper on earth. . . . We didn't see any democracy on the streets of Harlem . . . on the streets of Detroit. . . . We've experienced only the American nightmare."

[A]ll five of the eyewitnesses, Fletcher, Pace, Hollins, Brown, and Knox, testified that Budzyn initiated the beating by repeatedly striking Green on the hands. Witnesses Pace and Hollins, who observed the scene from essentially the same vantage point, saw Budzyn swinging his flashlight over his shoulder down toward Green in the direction of Green's head. They both testified that on the basis of the positioning of Budzyn and Green, and the sound of impact, it appeared that Budzyn was repeatedly hitting Green on the head with his flashlight. Further, eyewitness Brown, who observed the scene from a different vantage point, standing on the curb at a slight elevation and to the rear of the car, testified that he actually saw Budzyn strike Green on the head with the flashlight several times. Witness Fletcher's testimony, which did not indicate that Budzyn's blows appeared to land on Green's head, was not necessarily inconsistent with the conclusion of the other witnesses. Fletcher explained that he did not see everything that transpired after observing the blows to Green's hand and after Budzyn positioned himself further into the car on top of Green because Officer Budzyn was positioned in a way that obstructed his view for a period.

I cannot help but conclude that the evidence concerning Budzyn's actions was overwhelming to support the verdict of second-degree murder. This conclusion would not be different even if, as the majority suggests, the injuries actually causing Green's death could have been inflicted solely by Nevers. While Budzyn's actions were perhaps less brutal than Nevers', he initiated the encounter with Green that ultimately resulted in Green's death. His actions went far beyond the level of force necessary in the situation. Rather than calling his partner to assist him in pulling Mr. Green out of the car and handcuffing him, Officer Budzyn exerted excessive force in attempting to get Green to open his clenched fist. Further, Budzyn did not step in to stop Nevers' beating of Green when Nevers continued the beating with actions that were clearly an unjustified and brutal show of force.

The majority attempts to discount the evidence against Budzyn by questioning the credibility of the eyewitnesses. It may or may not be true that because each of these witnesses had been implicated in criminal activity, or because they may have smoked cocaine or consumed alcohol before witnessing the events leading up to Green's death, they were less credible than the EMS witnesses who testified against defendant Nevers. This Court, however, is not in a position to judge the relative credibility of the witnesses against the two officers. The jurors heard the testimony from eyewitnesses Pace, Hollins, Brown, and Fletcher, all of whom were subjected to thorough cross-examination, and evidently found it to be credible. . . .

I recognize that the great majority of police officers conscientiously perform their duties with the utmost regard for the rights of those they seek to protect. However, when police officers cross over the line from keepers of the peace and protectors of lives to aggressors, exerting force far beyond that required in the given situation, the law must treat them no differently than other defendants.

The right to a fair trial by an impartial jury is of paramount importance in securing our liberty. Consequently, this Court has properly taken very seriously the defendants' claims that their juries' exposure to extraneous influences denied them this right. After careful review however, I am left with the distinct and firm impression that the defendants received a fair trial. The potential prejudice from the asserted influences is real. However, it does not rise to a level sufficient to persuade me of a real and substantial possibility that the verdicts were affected. Additionally, given the overwhelming evidence supporting the verdicts, it can be said, beyond a reasonable doubt, that these influences did not contribute to the verdicts.

Notes

1. *Harmless error standards: majority position.* State and federal courts vary widely in the details of their harmless error standards, but most courts apply variations on the standards enunciated by the Supreme Court in *Fahy, Chapman,* and *Sullivan.* Was the U.S. Supreme Court correct when it asserted that the *Chapman* standard assessing whether the errors were harmless "beyond a reasonable doubt" was the same as in *Fahy,* where the test of harmless error was "whether there is a reasonable possibility that the evidence complained of might have contributed to the conviction"? Compare the *Chapman* standard to the newer formulation in *Sullivan,* in which the Court explained that the test "is not whether, in a trial that occurred without the error, a guilty verdict would surely have been rendered, but whether the guilty verdict actually rendered in this trial was surely unattributable to the error." What other standards might courts use? What factors might argue for a standard even more restrictive than "harmless beyond a reasonable doubt"? See State v. Van Kirk, 32 P.3d 735 (Mont. 2001) (applies "cumulative evidence" approach rather than "overwhelming" weight of evidence approach; question is whether fact-finder was presented with admissible evidence that proved same facts as tainted evidence proved).

According to Kotteakos v. United States, 328 U.S. 750 (1946), the "harmless error" standard that applies to non-constitutional errors is slightly different. Non-constitutional error is harmless only when "the error did not influence the jury, or had but very slight effect." Some states create separate standards for reviewing constitutional and non-constitutional errors; most apply a single standard to both types of error, following the unitary direction of rules like the federal and Tennessee procedure rules printed above.

2. *Applying the standard.* One striking feature of harmless error review is how often appellate courts apply the concept, without explanation, to affirm judgments after even substantial errors. Even when harmless error is the central question and there is detailed analysis of the facts, as in *Budzyn,* courts treat the standard of review as so well established that it does not require restating.

But we can learn as much from what courts do as from what they say. A study by Landes and Posner, based on a sample of over 1000 federal appeals, identifies patterns in the outcomes of harmless error cases even if the court opinions do not themselves offer much analysis. Intentional prosecutor and judge errors are more likely than inadvertent errors to be found harmful. Appellate courts are more likely to ignore prosecutor errors than judge errors, possibly because judge errors have a greater influence on jurors. William M. Landes and Richard A. Posner, Harmless Error, 30 J. Leg. Studies, 161 (2001).

3. *Structural and trial error.* As we have seen, courts classify errors under two headings: "trial" errors that are subject to harmless error analysis, and "structural" errors that call for automatic reversal. The admission at trial of unconstitutional confessions — the issue reconsidered in *Fulminante* — is an uncommon issue compared to errors such as faulty jury instructions, since most coerced confessions will be suppressed before trial. Why did most courts, before the U.S. Supreme Court decision in *Fulminante,* place unconstitutional confessions in the automatic reversal category? Only a few courts since *Fulminante* have considered whether state law will allow harmless error analysis for unconstitutional confessions used at trial in state cases, and none so far has rejected the Supreme Court's lead in *Fulminante.* See People v. Cahill, 853 P.2d 1037 (Cal. 1993). Given the willingness of state supreme

courts to adopt their own procedural rules in many areas, why might state courts not wish to reject *Fulminante?* Is *Fulminante* a case that gives state courts more or less power relative to other branches of government? Is it a case that gives state courts more or less power over their own dockets?

One of the most common and difficult harmless error problems arises in assessing the impact of improper jury instructions. The U.S. Supreme Court has wrestled for at least a decade with whether different kinds of instructional error should be subject to harmless error analysis. Is the distinction in *Fulminante* between "trial" and "structural" errors useful in assessing the impact of erroneous jury instructions? Should courts assess whether the outcome (guilt and sentence) would have been the same in the absence of the erroneous instruction, or whether the defendant was clearly guilty of the crime charged? What difference might a proper instruction have made to the jury in determining the proper offense? The proper punishment? In Sullivan v. Louisiana, 508 U.S. 275 (1993), a unanimous Court held that a constitutionally defective reasonable doubt instruction was a "structural error" not subject to harmless error analysis. Most states, however, continue to apply harmless error analysis to most instructional errors. Compare People v. Harris, 886 P.2d 1193 (Cal. 1994) (misinstruction on elements of robbery harmless error) with Commonwealth v. Conefrey, 650 N.E.2d 1268 (Mass. 1995) (harmless error does not apply to failure to give "unanimity" instruction to jury).

Other deviations from the usual procedure for empanelling and instructing a jury are very often deemed to be structural errors in the trial. See State v. LaMere, 2000 Mt. 45 (2000) (summoning jurors by telephone rather than by mail in violation of statute governing juror summonses requires automatic reversal); State v. Cleveland, 959 S.W.2d 948 (Tenn. 1997) (absence of juror during part of closing argument cannot ever be harmless error).

4. *Plain error.* The defendant typically must object to an error at trial; an error not brought to the attention of the trial judge for immediate correction usually cannot form the basis for a later appeal. However, appellate courts make an exception for "plain error," as described in the Rules of Criminal Procedure reprinted above. While the "harmless error" doctrine often involves constitutional arguments, "plain error" is treated as a matter of common law interpretation of the procedural rules. See United States v. Cotton, 525 U.S. 625 (2002) (omission from federal indictment of a fact that enhances the statutory maximum sentence does not amount to plain error); United States v. Vonn, 535 U.S. 55 (2002) (federal defendant who allows Rule 11 error to pass without objections in trial court must satisfy Rule 52(b) plain error rule).

5. *The capacity of harmless error to make procedure irrelevant.* If a harmless error standard allows many cases with clear trial error to be immune from appellate review, then the justice system may lose the shaping function of appellate courts. See Sam Kamin, Harmless Error and the Rights/Remedies Split, 88 Va. L. Rev. 1 (2002). Are not cases that are obvious most likely to be subject to guilty pleas? Are trials — at least difficult or long ones — ever so obvious that the outcome would be the same regardless of how the evidence was presented or the approach taken by the lawyers?

XXI Habeas Corpus

A conviction and appeal are not the end of the line for the criminal defendant. Even after the direct appeal is complete, the offender can still challenge the validity of the conviction in court. These post-conviction review procedures take a variety of names with somewhat different historical roots; the best known form, used in both federal and state constitutions, is the writ of habeas corpus. Some states structure their post-conviction processes around a different historical writ—error coram nobis—which focuses more on new evidence. Others have supplanted the traditional (and quite limited) post-conviction remedies with broader statutes, often simply labeled "post-conviction review" acts. These various post-conviction review procedures are referred to under the general heading of "collateral" review, and they are nominally civil proceedings. If the judge in a collateral proceeding becomes convinced that the government obtained the conviction illegally, she sometimes has the power to grant relief to the "petitioner" and overturn the conviction. In this chapter, we study the conditions under which judges will engage in this collateral review of convictions.

This chapter emphasizes the foundations and future of *judicial* post-conviction review. (There are also executive post-conviction review procedures in most states, including parole and pardon.) The first section of this chapter considers the history and theory behind the common law writ of habeas corpus. The second section considers some of the basic features of collateral review in the states. Two central questions arise here: What distinguishes collateral review procedures from appeals, and to what extent are such procedures necessary at all? The third section considers the particular and highly political debate about federalism that arises when federal courts review and invalidate convictions obtained in state court.

A. HISTORY AND THEORY OF HABEAS CORPUS

Debates today over post-conviction judicial review in the United States focus on what may be a 33-year legal quirk — the expansion of habeas corpus review in federal court of state court convictions. Expanded federal habeas review began around 1963, and has been sharply restricted by judicial decisions and by federal legislation in 1996. But the history of habeas corpus is much older than these recent battles, and is built on concerns about separation of powers and protection of individuals by the judiciary against abuses of power by the executive branch. The future of habeas corpus and other forms of judicial post-conviction review will almost certainly transcend whatever restrictions remain on the special case of federal post-conviction review of state convictions.

The many forms of post-conviction judicial review now available in state courts derive from several historical common law writs; the writ of habeas corpus was the most important of them. In England, even before the time of Magna Carta, courts issued writs of habeas corpus to a government official (usually a jailer or warden) who was detaining a person. The writ, issued after a petitioner established a prima facie case, required the official to appear before the court (along with the prisoner himself — his "corpus") and to present proper justification for detaining the person. The habeas corpus writ became one tool that the English law courts used to release persons held by order of other courts (such as the Chancery and the prerogative courts) and thus to protect the jurisdiction of the law courts. Over time, the habeas corpus writ also became the primary method for challenging royal power to detain a person. Daniel Meador, Habeas Corpus and Magna Carta: Dualism of Power and Liberty 3-9 (1966). In an era of growing distrust of royal power, habeas corpus offered the hope that the rule of law could control executive branch tyranny.

By the early seventeenth century, courts would still refuse to inquire into the validity of a detention in many cases. For instance, in Chamber's Case, 79 Eng. Rep. 746 (K.B. 1629), the petitioner had been detained "by virtue of a decree in the Star Chamber, by reason of certain words he used at the council table, viz. that the merchants of England were screwed up here in England more than in Turkey." He was imprisoned until he agreed to pay a fine of two thousand pounds. When the petitioner asked the royal courts for a writ of habeas corpus to challenge the legality of this confinement, the court refused to grant any relief: "to deliver one who was committed by the decree of one of the Courts of justice, was not the usage of this Court."

However, Parliament strengthened the emerging view of habeas corpus as a writ generally available to challenge illegal detentions in the Habeas Corpus Act of 1679. William Blackstone, in his treatise on English common law, described the terms and significance of this statute:

> [The] glory of the English law consists in clearly defining the times, the causes, and the extent, when, wherefore, and to what degree, the imprisonment of the subject may be lawful. This induces an absolute necessity of expressing upon every commitment the reason for which it is made; that the court upon an *habeas corpus* may examine into its validity; and according to the circumstances of the case may discharge, admit to bail, or remand the prisoner. . . .
>
> [The Habeas Corpus Act of 1679] enacts, 1. That the writ shall be returned and the prisoner brought up within a limited time according to the distance, not exceeding in any case twenty days. . . . 3. That on complaint and request in writing by or on behalf of any person committed and charged with any crime (unless committed for treason or

> felony expressed in the warrant, or for suspicion of the same, or as accessory thereto before the fact, or convicted or charged in execution by legal process) the lord chancellor or any of the twelve judges, in vacation, upon viewing a copy of the warrant or affidavit that a copy is denied, shall . . . award a *habeas corpus* for such prisoner, returnable immediately before himself or any other of the judges; and upon the return made shall discharge the party, if bailable, upon giving security to appear and answer to the accusation in the proper court of judicature. . . . 6. That every person committed for treason or felony shall, if he requires it the first week of the next term or the first day of the next session of *oyer* and *terminer,* be indicted in that term or session, or else admitted to bail; unless the king's witnesses cannot be produced at that time: and if acquitted, or if not indicted and tried in the second term of session, he shall be discharged from his imprisonment for such imputed offence.
>
> [By these] admirable regulations, judicial as well as parliamentary, the remedy is now complete for removing the injury of unjust and illegal confinement. A remedy the more necessary, because the oppression does not always arise from the ill-nature, but sometimes from the mere inattention, of government.

Blackstone, 3 Commentaries on the Laws of England 129-38 (1768).

The American colonists of the eighteenth century were acquainted with the English writ of habeas corpus as it had developed in the seventeenth century. It was often used to challenge custody pending trial, and less often to challenge detention based on a conviction issued by a court without proper jurisdiction, or (later) a conviction obtained through improper procedures. See Dallin Oaks, Habeas Corpus in the States—1776-1865, 32 U. Chi. L. Rev. 243, 258-262 (1965). Despite (or because of) the common use of the writ, most of the earliest state constitutions did not mention habeas corpus or guarantee its availability. One exception was the Massachusetts Constitution of 1780, pt. 2, ch. 6, art. 7, which provided: "The privilege and benefit of the writ of *habeas corpus* shall be enjoyed in this commonwealth, in the most free, easy, cheap, expeditious, and ample manner; and shall not be suspended by the legislature, except upon the most urgent and pressing occasions, and for a limited time, not exceeding twelve months." The federal constitution, in Article I, section 9, clause 2, declared that "The Privilege of the Writ of Habeas Corpus shall not be suspended, unless when in Cases of Rebellion or Invasion, the public Safety may require it." During the ratification debates, some argued that the guarantee of habeas corpus in Article I did not go far enough. In the end, none of the first ten amendments to the federal constitution mentioned habeas corpus. Apparently, the Article I guarantee was thought to be sufficient.

The legislative debate reprinted below deals with an incident early in our nation's history that revealed the purposes and importance of the habeas corpus writ. In 1804, Vice President Aaron Burr, after losing in his bid to win the governorship of New York and killing Alexander Hamilton in a duel, went to Philadelphia where he hatched with others a scheme to create a new empire in the West, including parts of Mexico. By 1807, Burr had purchased 1 million acres in Orleans Territory, had gathered supplies, boats and men, and had sent coded messages to fellow schemers to be ready to attack Mexico.

One of the conspirators, General James Wilkinson (the governor of the Louisiana Territory) revealed the plot. Wilkinson said he had received a coded message from Burr, which indicated that Burr planned to move 500 to 1,000 men in light boats to Natchez by mid-December. In the message, Burr guaranteed the success of the plan with "the lives, the honour, and fortunes of hundreds, the best blood of our country." The people of the region, said Burr, "are prepared to receive us" and he anticipated that "in three weeks all will be settled."

Wilkinson's revelation led President Jefferson to order Burr's arrest. After Burr learned of the proclamation for his arrest from a newspaper story, he surrendered at Natchez, was released on bail, and tried to leave the area. He was captured and taken to Richmond to be arraigned before Chief Justice John Marshall. Burr was later indicted for treason, along with several of his coconspirators. Burr was acquitted on September 1, 1807 when Marshall found a failure of proof of "levying War" against the United States as required by the federal Constitution. See Thomas Abernathy, The Burr Conspiracy (1954). In the midst of this threat to national security, the House of Representatives debated the possibility of suspending the availability of a writ of habeas corpus.

■ SUSPENSION OF THE HABEAS CORPUS U.S. HOUSE OF REPRESENTATIVES

Annals v. 16, 26 Jan. 1807

A message was received from the Senate, by Mr. SAMUEL SMITH, as follows . . .

Gentlemen of the House of Representatives: The Senate have passed a bill suspending for three months the privilege of the writ of habeas corpus, in certain cases, which they think expedient to communicate to you in confidence, and to request your concurrence therein, as speedily as the emergency of the case shall in your judgment require.

Mr. SMITH also delivered in the bill referred to in the said communication, and then withdrew. The bill was read as follows:

A Bill suspending the writ of Habeas Corpus for three months, in certain cases. *Be it enacted, by the Senate and House of Representatives of the United States of America, in Congress assembled,* That in all cases, where any person or persons, charged on oath with treason, misprision of treason, or other high crime or misdemeanor, endangering the peace, safety, or neutrality of the United States, have been or shall be arrested or imprisoned, by virtue of any warrant or authority of the President of the United States, or from the Chief Executive Magistrate of any State or Territorial Government, or from any person acting under the direction or authority of the President of the United States, the privilege of the writ of *habeas corpus* shall be, and the same hereby is suspended, for and during the term of three months from and after the passage of this act, and no longer. . . .

Mr. BURWELL [noted that the] President, in his Message of the 22d, says, "on the whole the fugitives from Ohio and their associates from Cumberland, or other places in that quarter, cannot threaten serious danger to the city of New Orleans." If that be the case, upon what ground shall we suspend the writ of habeas corpus? Can any person imagine the United States are in danger, after this declaration of the President, who unquestionably possesses more correct information than any other person can be supposed to have.

[The] correct and proper mode of proceeding can be had under the existing laws of the United States. These persons may be transferred from the military to the civil authority, and be proceeded against according to law. Those, therefore, who fear the escape of the traitors already apprehended, and would, by this measure, obviate the difficulty, must perceive that consequence would not ensue. [Is] the danger sufficiently great to justify the suspension of this most important right of the citizen, to proclaim the country in peril, and to adopt a measure so pregnant with mischief, by which the innocent and guilty will be involved in one common destruction? [This] was not the first instance of the kind since the formation of the Federal Government; there had been already two insurrections in the United States, both of which had defied the authority of Congress, and menaced the Union with dissolution. Notwithstanding one of them justified the calling out of fifteen thousand men, and the expenditure of one million of dollars, he had not heard of a proposition to suspend the writ of habeas corpus. . . .

What . . . would be the effect of passing such a law? Would it not establish a dangerous precedent? A corrupt and vicious Administration, under the sanction and example of this law, might harass and destroy the best men of the country. It would only be necessary to excite artificial commotions, circulate exaggerated rumors of danger, and then follows the repetition of this law, by which every obnoxious person, however honest, is surrendered to the vindictive resentment of the Government. It will not be a sufficient answer, that this power will not be abused by the President of the United States. He, Mr. Burwell believed, would not abuse it, but it would be impossible to restrain all those who are under him. Besides, he would not consent to advocate a principle, bad, in itself, because it will not, probably, be abused. For these reasons, Mr. Burwell said, he should vote to reject the bill.

Mr. ELLIOT: [Objectionable] as the bill upon the table is in point of principle, it is, if possible, still more objectionable in point of detail. It invests with the power of violating the first principles of civil and political liberty, not only the supreme Executive, and the Executives of individual States and Territories, but all civil and military officers who may derive any authority whatever from the Chief Magistrate. And it extends the operation of the suspension of the privileges of the habeas corpus, not only to persons guilty or suspected of treason, or misprision of treason, but, to those who may be accused of any other crime or misdemeanor, tending to endanger the "peace, safety, or neutrality," of the United States! What a vast and almost illimitable field of power is here opened, in which Executive discretion may wander at large and uncontrolled! A vast and dangerous scene of power, indeed! It gives the power of dispensing with the ordinary operation of the laws to a host of those *little great men,* who are attached to every Government under heaven. . . .

Mr. VARNUM [asked, Will gentlemen] deny that the conspiracy has been formed with deliberation, and has existed for a long time? Is it not evident that it has become very extensive? If, then, this is the case, and the head of the conspiracy has said that he is aided by a foreign Power; if this is true, are we justified in considering the country in a perfect state of safety, until it is brought to a close? I conceive not. I consider the country, in a degree, in a state of insecurity; and if so, the power is vested in the Congress of the United States, under the Constitution, to suspend the writ of habeas corpus. I am also apprehensive that we shall not be able to trace the conspiracy to its source without such a suspension. We have had an instance in which the head of the conspiracy has been brought before a court of justice, and where nothing has been brought against him. It is not my wish to insinuate that any court or public functionary is contemplated by this conspiracy; yet it is possible that this may be the case, and the very existence of the country may depend on tracing it to its source. . . .

Will gentlemen say that any innocent man will have a finger laid upon him, should this law pass? No; there is no probability of it; it is scarcely possible. But, even if it be possible, if the public good requires the suspension of the privilege, every man attached to the Government and to the liberty he enjoys, will be surely willing to submit to this inconvenience for a time, in order to secure the public happiness. The suspension only applies to particular crimes, the liberties of the people will not therefore be touched. . . . I shall, therefore, vote for this bill, under the impression that it will not have the injurious effects that some gentlemen seem to apprehend; and that it will only more effectually consign the guilty into the hands of justice.

. . . The yeas and nays were then taken on the question, "Shall the bill be rejected?"—yeas 113, nays 19.

Twenty-one year old college student Yaser Esam Hamdi was seized by U.S. forces in Afghanistan during the campaign sparked by terrorist attacks on September 11, 2001. Like more than 600 other men seized in that campaign, Hamdi was taken to the U.S. military detention facility set up at Guantanamo Bay, Cuba, colloquially known as Gitmo. Unlike most of the other detainees, Hamdi could claim American citizenship, because he was born on September 26, 1980, in Baton Rouge, Louisiana. His parents were citizens of Saudi Arabia, and Hamdi spent most of his life in Saudi Arabia.

U.S. authorities moved Hamdi from Gitmo to the Naval Brig at the Norfolk Naval Station, and declared him to be an "unlawful enemy combatant." Hamdi's family said that he initially traveled to Pakistan on a religious and humanitarian mission, and when he crossed into Afghanistan to assist refugees, he was swept up by the Taliban and forced to fight.

After his move to Norfolk, Hamdi invoked an ancient Anglo-American tradition: He filed a petition for a writ of habeas corpus, and he sought a lawyer to assist him in challenging his detention. On May 29, Federal district judge Robert Doumar, a 73-year-old Nixon appointee, heard initial arguments. The government argued that in time of war, the Executive Branch should decide who is a threat to national security, without interference by the courts. In response, Judge Doumar asked whether it would be lawful "if the military decided to put him in boiling oil?"

Judge Doumar appointed Federal Defender Frank Durham to represent Hamdi, and found that "Hamdi must be allowed to meet with his attorney because of fundamental justice provided under the Constitution." Frank Durham then invoked the name of Aaron Burr in support of Hamdi's petition for a writ of habeas corpus, claiming that now, like then, the government did not have sufficient proof of treason or any other offense to detain him.

The court ordered the government to grant Hamdi access to his appointed lawyer, and the government appealed to the United States Court of Appeals for the Fourth Circuit. The Fourth Circuit noted the President's "delicate, plenary and exclusive power" in the field of international relations, and the traditional deference that courts give to the President's wartime detention decisions. Because the trial court's order offered "little indication" that the court gave "proper weight to national security concerns," the appellate court reversed the order and remanded for further proceedings. The opinion instructed the trial judge to consider "what effect petitioner's unmonitored access to counsel might have upon the government's ongoing gathering of intelligence" and to give the government "a chance to properly present their arguments." Hamdi v. Rumsfeld, 296 F.3d 278 (4th Cir. 2002).

One week after the Fourth Circuit decision, Judge Doumar held a hearing to ask the government lawyers about the justifications for Hamdi's detention. The government provided a two-page declaration by a government lawyer, Michael H. Mobbs, asserting the basis for Hamdi's detention. On August 16, Judge Doumar filed an order declaring that the Mobbs Declaration was not a sufficient explanation for detaining Hamdi, and requiring the government to produce more information about how it determined that Hamdi was an "enemy combatant." The ruling was based on a close review of the questions that the Mobbs Declaration left unresolved:

> The [Mobbs Declaration] is two pages long and consists of nine numbered paragraphs. . . . The declaration fails to address the nature and authority of Mr. Mobbs to review and make declarations on behalf of the Executive regarding Hamdi's classification. Paragraph 1 of the Mobbs Declaration states that Mr. Mobbs is a Special Advisor to the Undersecretary of Defense for Policy. The declaration does not indicate what authority a "Special Advisor" has regarding classification decisions of enemy combatants. [The declaration also says] nothing to indicate why [Hamdi] is treated differently than all other captured Taliban. There is no reason given for Hamdi to be in solitary confinement, incommunicado for over four months and being held for some eight-to-ten months without charges of any kind. This is clearly an unreasonable length of time to be held in order to bring criminal charges. . . .
>
> In Paragraph 2 of the Mobbs Declaration, Mr. Mobbs claims . . . to have reviewed the relevant records and reports regarding Hamdi's detention and capture. The declaration does not answer under whose authority and by what procedures Mr. Mobbs engaged in such a review. Nor does it explain whether Mr. Mobbs is responsible for supervising the classification decisions of others. These are important considerations for any meaningful judicial review because the Court must be able to determine whether the person(s) making the classification decision did so with the authority of the Executive and pursuant to the statutes, rules, and regulations pertaining to such matters. . . .
>
> Paragraph 6 of the Declaration states Hamdi was originally classified as an enemy combatant by "military forces" based upon his interviews and in light of his association with the Taliban. The document is silent on whose military forces, i.e. U.S. military forces or Northern Alliance forces, [it was] who originally classified Hamdi as an enemy combatant. If it was Northern Alliance forces that originally classified him, then it is unclear how Northern Alliance forces differentiated themselves from Taliban forces during the conflict. Was there some garb of each that made identification easy to participants? . . .
>
> In paragraph 9, the declaration asserts that a "subsequent interview of Hamdi has confirmed the fact that he surrendered and gave his firearm to Northern Alliance forces which supports his classification as an enemy combatant." Again, it appears that Mr. Mobbs is merely paraphrasing a statement supposedly made by Hamdi. Due to the ease with which such statements may be taken out of context, the Court is understandably suspicious of the Respondents' assertions regarding statements that Hamdi is alleged to have made. While it may be premature, and eventually unnecessary, for the Court to bring Hamdi before it to inquire about these statements, the Court finds that it must be provided with complete copies of any statements by Hamdi in order to appropriately conduct a judicial review of his classification. Petitioners' counsel asserted at the hearing that some of these statements were unclassified and provided by the government to counsel for John Phillip Walker Lindh in a companion case in this district.
>
> Without access to the screening criteria and Hamdi's statements, it is impossible to evaluate whether Mr. Mobbs is correct in his assertion that Hamdi's classification as an enemy combatant is justified. The Mobbs Declaration is little more than the government's "say-so" regarding the validity of Hamdi's classification. . . .

Judge Doumar's order was again appealed to the Fourth Circuit, and the appellate opinion is excerpted below. If the United States Supreme Court eventually hears this case or a similar one, how will the Court rule? How should it rule?

■ YASER ESAM HAMDI v. DONALD RUMSFELD

316 F.3d 450 (4th Cir. 2003)

WILKINSON, C.J.

Yaser Esam Hamdi filed a petition under 28 U.S.C. §2241 challenging the lawfulness of his confinement in the Norfolk Naval Brig. . . . The district court certified for appeal the question of whether a declaration by a Special Advisor to the Under Secretary of Defense for Policy setting forth what the government contends were the circumstances of Hamdi's capture was sufficient by itself to justify his detention. Because it is undisputed that Hamdi was captured in a zone of active combat in a foreign theater of conflict, we hold that the submitted declaration is a sufficient basis upon which to conclude that the Commander in Chief has constitutionally detained Hamdi pursuant to the war powers entrusted to him by the United States Constitution. No further factual inquiry is necessary or proper, and we remand the case with directions to dismiss the petition.

[More than 3,000 people were killed on American soil on September 11, 2001.] In the wake of this atrocity, Congress authorized the President "to use all necessary and appropriate force against those nations, organizations, or persons he determines planned, authorized, committed, or aided the terrorist attacks" or "harbored such organizations or persons." The President responded by ordering United States armed forces to Afghanistan to subdue al Qaida and the governing Taliban regime supporting it. During this ongoing military operation, thousands of alleged enemy combatants, including Hamdi, have been captured by American and allied forces.

Although acknowledging that Hamdi was seized in Afghanistan during a time of active military hostilities, the petition alleges that "as an American citizen, . . . Hamdi enjoys the full protections of the Constitution," and that the government's current detention of him in this country without charges, access to a judicial tribunal, or the right to counsel, violates the Fifth and Fourteenth Amendments to the United States Constitution. . . . On June 11, before the government had time to respond to the petition, the district court appointed Public Defender Frank Dunham as counsel for the detainee and ordered the government to allow the Defender unmonitored access to Hamdi. On July 12, we reversed the district court's order granting counsel immediate access to Hamdi. . . .

On July 25, the government filed a [motion to dismiss] the petition for a writ of habeas corpus. Attached to its response was an affidavit from the Special Advisor to the Under Secretary of Defense for Policy, Michael Mobbs, which confirms the material factual allegations in Hamdi's petition — specifically, that Hamdi was seized in Afghanistan by allied military forces during the course of the sanctioned military campaign, designated an "enemy combatant" by our Government, and ultimately transferred to the Norfolk Naval Brig for detention. . . . According to Mobbs, the military determined that Hamdi "traveled to Afghanistan in approximately July or August of 2001" and proceeded to "affiliate with a Taliban military unit and receive weapons training." While serving with the Taliban in the wake of September 11, he was captured when his Taliban unit surrendered to Northern Alliance forces with which it had been engaged in battle. He was in possession of an AK-47 rifle at the time of surrender. . . . According to Mobbs, interviews with Hamdi confirmed the details of his capture and his status as an enemy combatant. . . .

The war powers [described in Articles I and II of the Constitution] invest the President, as Commander in Chief, with the power to wage war which Congress has declared, and to carry into effect all laws passed by Congress for the conduct of war and for the government and regulation of the Armed Forces, and all laws defining and punishing offences against the law of nations, including those which pertain to the conduct of war. These powers include the authority to detain those captured in armed struggle. These powers likewise extend to the executive's decision to deport or detain alien enemies during the duration of hostilities, and to confiscate or destroy enemy property.

Article III contains nothing analogous to the specific powers of war so carefully enumerated in Articles I and II. In accordance with this constitutional text, the Supreme Court has shown great deference to the political branches when called upon to decide cases implicating sensitive matters of foreign policy, national security, or military affairs. The reasons for this deference are not difficult to discern. Through their departments and committees, the executive and legislative branches are organized to supervise the conduct of overseas conflict in a way that the judiciary simply is not. The Constitution's allocation of the warmaking powers reflects not only the expertise and experience lodged within the executive, but also the more fundamental truth that those branches most accountable to the people should be the ones to undertake the ultimate protection and to ask the ultimate sacrifice from them. . . . For the judicial branch to trespass upon the exercise of the warmaking powers would be an infringement of the right to self-determination and self-governance at a time when the care of the common defense is most critical. . . .

Despite the clear allocation of war powers to the political branches, judicial deference to executive decisions made in the name of war is not unlimited. The Bill of Rights which Hamdi invokes in his petition is as much an instrument of mutual respect and tolerance as the Fourteenth Amendment is. It applies to American citizens regardless of race, color, or creed. And as we become a more diverse nation, the Bill of Rights may become even more a lens through which we recognize ourselves. To deprive any American citizen of its protections is not a step that any court would casually take. . . .

Drawing on the Bill of Rights' historic guarantees, the judiciary plays its distinctive role in our constitutional structure when it reviews the detention of American citizens by their own government. . . . Our forebears recognized that the power to detain could easily become destructive "if exerted without check or control" by an unrestrained executive free to "imprison, dispatch, or exile any man that was obnoxious to the government, by an instant declaration that such is their will and pleasure." 4 W. Blackstone, Commentaries on the Laws of England 349-50 (Cooley ed. 1899). The duty of the judicial branch to protect our individual freedoms does not simply cease whenever our military forces are committed by the political branches to armed conflict. The Founders "foresaw that troublous times would arise, when rulers and people would . . . seek by sharp and decisive measures to accomplish ends deemed just and proper; and that the principles of constitutional liberty would be in peril, unless established by irrepealable law." Ex parte Milligan, 71 U.S. (4 Wall.) 2, 120 (1866). While that recognition does not dispose of this case, it does indicate one thing: The detention of United States citizens must be subject to judicial review.

It is significant, moreover, that the form of relief sought by Hamdi is a writ of habeas corpus. In war as in peace, habeas corpus provides one of the firmest bulwarks against unconstitutional detentions. As early as 1789, Congress reaffirmed the courts' common law authority to review detentions of federal prisoners, giving its explicit blessing to the judiciary's power to "grant writs of habeas corpus for the purpose of an inquiry into the cause of commitment" for federal detainees. Act of Sept. 24, 1789, ch. 20, §14, 1 Stat. 81-82. While the scope of habeas review has expanded and contracted over the succeeding centuries, its essential function of assuring that restraint accords with the rule of law, not the whim of authority, remains unchanged. Hamdi's petition falls squarely within the Great Writ's purview, since he is an American citizen challenging his summary detention for reasons of state necessity.

[The] detention of enemy combatants serves at least two vital purposes. First, detention prevents enemy combatants from rejoining the enemy and continuing to fight against America and its allies. In this respect, captivity is neither a punishment nor an act of vengeance, but rather a simple war measure. And the precautionary measure of disarming hostile forces for the duration of a conflict is routinely accomplished through detention rather than the initiation of criminal charges. To require otherwise would impose a singular burden upon our nation's conduct of war. Second, detention in lieu of prosecution may relieve the burden on military commanders of litigating the circumstances of a capture halfway around the globe. This burden would not be inconsiderable and would run the risk of saddling military decision-making with the panoply of encumbrances associated with civil litigation during a period of armed conflict. . . .

Although the district court did not have "any doubts [that Hamdi] had a firearm" or that "he went to Afghanistan to be with the Taliban," the court ordered the government to submit to the court for in camera, ex parte review: (1) "copies of all Hamdi's statements, and the notes taken from any interviews with Hamdi, that relate to his reasons for going to Afghanistan, his activities while in Afghanistan, or his participation in the military forces of the Taliban or any other organization in that country"; (2) "a list of all the interrogators who have questioned Hamdi, including their names and addresses, and the dates of the interviews"; (3) "copies of any statements by members of the Northern Alliance" regarding Hamdi's surrender; (4) "a list that includes the date of Hamdi's capture, and that gives all the dates and locations of his subsequent detention"; (5) "the name and title of the individual within the United States Government who made the determination that Hamdi was an illegal enemy combatant"; (6) "the name and title of the individual within the United States Government who made the decision to move Hamdi from Guantanamo Bay, Cuba to the Norfolk Naval Station"; and (7) "the screening criteria utilized to determine the status of Hamdi." The court's order allows the government to redact "intelligence matters" from its responses, but only to the extent that those intelligence matters are outside the scope of inquiry into Hamdi's legal status. . . .

A review of the court's August 16 order reveals the risk of standing the warmaking powers of Articles I and II on their heads. The district court, for example, ordered the government to produce all Hamdi's statements and notes from interviews. Yet it is precisely such statements, relating to a detainee's activities in Afghanistan, that may contain the most sensitive and the most valuable information for our forces in the field. The risk created by this order is that judicial involvement would proceed, increment by increment, into an area where the political branches have been assigned by law a preeminent role.

[Litigation] cannot be the driving force in effectuating and recording wartime detentions. The military has been charged by Congress and the executive with winning a war, not prevailing in a possible court case. Complicating the matter even further is the fact that Hamdi was originally captured by Northern Alliance forces, with whom American forces were generally allied. The district court's insistence that statements by Northern Alliance members be produced cannot help but place a strain on multilateral efforts during wartime. The court also expressed concern in its order that the Northern Alliance did not "identify the unit to which Hamdi was affiliated," "where or by whom Hamdi received weapons training or the nature and extent thereof," or "who commanded the unit or the type of garb or uniform Hamdi may have worn. . . ." In demanding such detail, the district court would have the United States military instruct not only its own personnel, but also its allies, on precise observations they must make and record during a battlefield capture.

Viewed in their totality, the implications of the district court's August 16 production order could not be more serious. The factual inquiry upon which Hamdi would lead us, if it did not entail disclosure of sensitive intelligence, might require an excavation of facts buried under the rubble of war. The cost of such an inquiry in terms of the efficiency and morale of American forces cannot be disregarded. Some of those with knowledge of Hamdi's detention may have been slain or injured in battle. Others might have to be diverted from active and ongoing military duties of their own. The logistical effort to acquire evidence from far away battle zones might be substantial. And these efforts would profoundly unsettle the constitutional balance. For the foregoing reasons, the court's August 16 production request cannot stand. . . .

To be sure, a capable attorney could challenge the hearsay nature of the Mobbs declaration and probe each and every paragraph for incompleteness or inconsistency, as the district court attempted to do. The court's approach, however, had a signal flaw. We are not here dealing with a defendant who has been indicted on criminal charges in the exercise of the executive's law enforcement powers. We are dealing with the executive's assertion of its power to detain under the war powers of Article II. To transfer the instinctive skepticism, so laudable in the defense of criminal charges, to the review of executive branch decisions premised on military determinations made in the field carriers the inordinate risk of a constitutionally problematic intrusion into the most basic responsibilities of a coordinate branch. . . .

For these reasons, and because Hamdi was indisputably seized in an active combat zone abroad, we will not require the government to fill what the district court regarded as gaps in the Mobbs affidavit. The factual averments in the affidavit, if accurate, are sufficient to confirm that Hamdi's detention conforms with a legitimate exercise of the war powers given the executive by Article II, Section 2 of the Constitution and, as discussed elsewhere, that it is consistent with the Constitution and laws of Congress. Asking the executive to provide more detailed factual assertions would be to wade further into the conduct of war than we consider appropriate and is unnecessary to a meaningful judicial review of this question. . . .

We turn then to the question of whether, because he is an American citizen currently detained on American soil by the military, Hamdi can be heard in an Article III court to rebut the factual assertions that were submitted to support the "enemy combatant" designation. We hold that no evidentiary hearing or factual inquiry on out part is necessary or proper, because it is undisputed that Hamdi was captured in a zone of active combat operations in a foreign country and because any inquiry must be circumscribed to avoid encroachment into the military affairs entrusted to the executive branch. . . .

Article III courts are ill-positioned to police the military's distinction between those in the arena of combat who should be detained and those who should not. Any evaluation of the accuracy of the executive branch's determination that a person is an enemy combatant, for example, would require courts to consider, first, what activities the detainee was engaged in during the period leading up to his seizure and, second, whether those activities rendered him a combatant or not. The first question is factual and, were we called upon to delve into it, would likely entail substantial efforts to acquire evidence from distant battle zones. The second question may require fine judgments about whether a particular activity is linked to the war efforts of a hostile power — judgments the executive branch is most competent to make. . . .

It is important to emphasize that we are not placing our imprimatur upon a new day of executive detentions. We [reject the sweeping proposition] that, with no meaningful judicial review, any American citizen alleged to be an enemy combatant could be detained indefinitely without charges or counsel on the government's say-so. But, Hamdi is not any American citizen alleged to be an enemy combatant by the government; he is an American citizen captured and detained by American allied forces in a foreign theater of war during active hostilities and determined by the United States military to have been indeed allied with enemy forces.

Cases such as Hamdi's raise serious questions which the courts will continue to treat as such. The nation has fought since its founding for liberty without which security rings hollow and for security without which liberty cannot thrive. The judiciary was meant to respect the delicacy of the balance, and we have endeavored to do so.

The events of September 11 have left their indelible mark. It is not wrong even in the dry annals of judicial opinion to mourn those who lost their lives that terrible day. Yet we speak in the end not from sorrow or anger, but from the conviction that separation of powers takes on special significance when the nation itself comes under attack. Hamdi's status as a citizen, as important as that is, cannot displace our constitutional order or the place of the courts within the Framer's scheme. Judicial review does not disappear during wartime, but the review of battlefield captures in overseas conflicts is a highly deferential one. That is why, for reasons stated, the judgment must be reversed and the petition dismissed. It is so ordered.

Notes

1. *Habeas corpus, error coram nobis, and statutory forms of the writs.* In the common law tradition, habeas corpus is the writ allowing a judge to inquire into the lawfulness of detention. The person petitioning for the writ asks a judge with jurisdiction over the detaining official (such as a prison warden) to issue the writ and to require this official to justify the detention. The petitioner could be a criminal defendant awaiting trial, an immigrant in a detention facility, or a convicted person who questions the legal validity of the criminal conviction. The writ of error coram nobis has a different emphasis. It allows the court that entered judgment on a criminal con-

viction to reopen proceedings when presented with new *facts* not available during the earlier proceedings. Every state has statutes or rules to codify and extend the reach of the common law writs, under generic titles such as "post-conviction relief."

2. *Habeas corpus as a post-conviction remedy.* Historians disagree sharply about the types of petitioners who could obtain a writ of habeas corpus. According to one view, the traditional habeas corpus writ in England and the United States was available only to challenge pre-trial detention, or in rare instances for persons convicted of a crime by a court lacking jurisdiction. See Ex parte Watkins, 28 U.S. (3 Pet.) 193 (1830) (convicted person sought habeas relief because federal indictment failed to state an offense; court declined, saying that "the judgment of a court of general criminal jurisdiction justifies his imprisonment, and . . . the writ of habeas corpus ought not to be awarded"); Paul Bator, Finality in Criminal Law and Federal Habeas Corpus for State Prisoners, 76 Harv. L. Rev. 441 (1963) (habeas corpus extended to convictions in courts lacking jurisdiction or to convictions in states which provided no reasonable opportunity to raise claims). Is it relevant that the 1807 debate over suspension of habeas corpus focused on the power of the executive to arrest and detain persons before trial, rather than any unjust detention after conviction?

Other historians contend that habeas corpus was available in the nineteenth century to challenge the validity of criminal convictions obtained through some fundamental injustice, such as a procedural error at trial that violated the due process clause. Gary Peller, In Defense of Federal Habeas Corpus Relitigation, 16 Harv. C.R.-C.L. L. Rev. 579 (1982); see also Ann Woolhandler, Demodeling Habeas, 45 Stan. L. Rev. 575 (1993); James Liebman, Apocalypse Next Time?: The Anachronistic Attack on Habeas Corpus/Direct Review Parity, 92 Colum. L. Rev. 1997 (1992). According to this view, whatever limits may have applied at one time to the common law writ of habeas corpus, courts in the nineteenth century evolved toward using the habeas writ as a method to challenge final convictions on grounds other than jurisdictional defects. Some support for the expansive view comes from Ex parte Lange, 85 U.S. (18 Wall.) 163 (1873). Lange was convicted in federal court of the theft of postal equipment, and he challenged the conviction in habeas corpus on double jeopardy grounds. The Supreme Court declared that a constitutional error in the proceedings, such as a double jeopardy error at sentencing, could deprive a court of jurisdiction. See also Whitten v. Tomlinson, 160 U.S. 231 (1895).

The historical debate over the scope of habeas corpus is important when deciding the type of review that legislators intended when they codified habeas corpus practice in statutes such as the federal Habeas Corpus Act of 1867. In the end, it will prove very difficult to resolve all historical doubts, because the evidence of habeas corpus practice in American and English courts is limited to a handful of arguably atypical appellate decisions.

3. *The federal constitutional guarantee of habeas.* Article I, section 9, clause 2 of the federal Constitution says that habeas corpus "shall not be suspended, unless when in Cases of Rebellion or Invasion the public Safety may require it." The purpose of this constitutional language, like the scope of traditional habeas corpus relief, is not entirely clear today. Perhaps it was designed to prevent the Congress from limiting federal judicial review of federal convictions. See Ex Parte Bollman and Swartout, 8 U.S. (4 Cranch) 75 (1807) (declaring that habeas corpus must be available in federal court for federal prisoners, including those accused of participation in the Burr conspiracy). If so, the Judiciary Act of 1789 avoided any constitutional problems by giving federal judges the power to grant writs of habeas corpus to prisoners in cus-

tody under federal law. On the other hand, perhaps the Article I guarantee was meant to prevent Congress from interfering in *state* court review of those held in federal custody. See William Duker, A Constitutional History of Habeas Corpus 8, 126-80 (1980); but see Tarble's Case, 80 U.S. (13 Wall.) 397 (1871) (rejecting this reading of Article I guarantee).

It is quite clear that the drafters of the federal Constitution did not intend in Article I to guarantee the availability of federal habeas corpus for those convicted in state court. The Judiciary Act of 1789 explicitly barred such federal review, and created no controversy at the time. Nevertheless, it is entirely possible that constitutional change of various sorts (including the process of "incorporation" under the fourteenth amendment) may have converted the Article I guarantee into a constitutional protection for federal habeas review of state convictions. See Jordan Steiker, Incorporating the Suspension Clause: Is There a Constitutional Right to Federal Habeas Corpus for State Prisoners?, 92 Mich. L. Rev. 862, 871-74 (1994).

In Felker v. Turpin, 518 U.S. 651 (1996), the Supreme Court considered the constitutionality of a federal statute placing limits on "successive" federal habeas corpus petitions (petitions after the first one). It held that these statutory limits did not repeal the Supreme Court's authority to entertain original habeas petitions, and were not comprehensive enough to constitute a "suspension" of habeas corpus. Throughout its discussion, the Court assumed that the federal constitution *does* require that state prisoners have some form of habeas corpus writ in federal court: "[W]e assume, for purposes of decision here, that the Suspension Clause of the Constitution refers to the writ as it exists today, rather than as it existed in 1789."

B. THE AVAILABILITY OF POST-CONVICTION REVIEW

Post-conviction review is available to correct some errors in the criminal process even after that process has reached its final conclusion at the close of a direct appeal. Every state currently has a post-conviction review process that has been substantially modernized and restructured in the last 50 years. The major state reforms of post-conviction process took place in the 1960s through the 1980s, though many states have continued to adjust their post-conviction machinery. The post-conviction legal terrain is convoluted, since in a majority of states more than one form of post-conviction remedy applies. For example, in around a dozen states, the writ of habeas corpus is the principal post-conviction remedy, while in almost 40 states the principal form of collateral review is modeled on error coram nobis. The legislature has rewritten the law in the majority of states, but in a few states the modernization of the habeas corpus procedures have come through case law or judicially promulgated court rules. Changes in the past decade or so have tended to make post-conviction review more difficult to obtain. See generally Donald Wilkes, Federal and State Postconviction Remedies and Relief §9-2 (1992) (Appendix A).

Regardless of the form of collateral review allowed in each state, a few central questions define the essential function and scope of such review. For example, post-conviction review is not able to correct every error and every shortcoming of the earlier proceedings. First, there are some *subjects* that are not "cognizable" on post-conviction review: even though the trial court or appellate court may have decided the question wrongly, post-conviction relief is not available for questions dealing with that subject matter and the mistake will go uncorrected for the sake of "finality" in the criminal justice process. Second, there may be some claims that do raise a subject that is cognizable, and yet the claim cannot be heard because the defendant (or the "petitioner" in post-conviction proceedings) failed to follow the proper *procedures* to keep the issue alive, such as objecting to the error at trial, or raising the issue on direct appeal. The following materials consider these two types of limitations on all claims for post-conviction relief. The third part of this chapter considers what has become an especially frequent and compelling claim on collateral review: whether trial or appellate counsel provided adequate assistance.

1. *Cognizable Subject Matter*

There are some subjects that no court will consider in any post-conviction proceeding as a basis for overturning a conviction. States draw different lines to mark the subjects that are off limits for post-conviction review. Sometimes the statutes distinguish between constitutional and non-constitutional claims, with only the former qualifying as a proper subject for post-conviction review. Other statutes reserve collateral review for violations of a criminal defendant's "fundamental" rights. Still others allow challenges based on any "illegal" action. One recurring question deals with claims of actual innocence. When a petitioner claims that there is new evidence to show that she did not commit the crime, will a court ever refuse to hear the claim because of subject matter limits?

■ 42 PENNSYLVANIA CONSOLIDATED STATUTES §9543(a)

To be eligible for relief under this subchapter, the petitioner must plead and prove by a preponderance of the evidence all of the following:

(1) That the petitioner has been convicted of a crime under the laws of this Commonwealth and is at the time relief is granted . . . serving a sentence of imprisonment, probation or parole for the crime . . . .

(2) That the conviction or sentence resulted from one or more of the following:

(i) A violation of the Constitution of this Commonwealth or the Constitution or laws of the United States which, in the circumstances of the particular case, so undermined the truth-determining process that no reliable adjudication of guilt or innocence could have taken place. . . .

(iii) A plea of guilty unlawfully induced where the circumstances make it likely that the inducement caused the petitioner to plead guilty and the petitioner is innocent.

(iv) The improper obstruction by government officials of the petitioner's right of appeal where a meritorious appealable issue existed and was properly preserved in the trial court. . . .

(vi) The unavailability at the time of trial of exculpatory evidence that has subsequently become available and would have changed the outcome of the trial if it had been introduced.

(vii) The imposition of a sentence greater than the lawful maximum.

(viii) A proceeding in a tribunal without jurisdiction.

(3) That the allegation of error has not been previously litigated or waived.

(4) That the failure to litigate the issue prior to or during trial, during unitary review or on direct appeal could not have been the result of any rational, strategic or tactical decision by counsel.

■ OKLAHOMA STATUTES, tit. 22, §1089(c)

The only issues that may be raised in an application for post-conviction relief [by a petitioner sentenced to death] are those that:

1. Were not and could not have been raised in a direct appeal; and
2. Support a conclusion either that the outcome of the trial would have been different but for the errors or that the defendant is factually innocent.

The applicant shall state in the application specific facts explaining as to each claim why it was not or could not have been raised in a direct appeal and how it supports a conclusion that the outcome of the trial would have been different but for the errors or that the defendant is factually innocent. . . .

■ PEOPLE v. KURTIS WASHINGTON

665 N.E.2d 1330 (Ill. 1995)

FREEMAN, J.

The question in this case is whether due process is implicated in a claim of innocence based upon new evidence so as to permit the claim to be raised in a petition under the Post-Conviction Hearing Act (725 ILCS 5/122-1 et seq.). We hold that it is.

In 1982, Kurtis Washington was sentenced to 25 years in prison for murdering Tony Hightie. Hightie had been murdered outside his home in Chicago shortly after 9 P.M. on May 9, 1980. Washington was implicated in the crime by Donna McClure, Hightie's girlfriend, and Ronald Tapes.

McClure and Tapes witnessed the murder. At trial, they said that they had been sitting in a parked car near Hightie's home when they were approached by a man. The man said that he was looking for someone named Will. When McClure and Tapes proved no help, the man approached Hightie just as he left his home. Hightie had been wearing a jacket and hat that belonged to Tapes' brother who was named William. McClure and Tapes said that after a few words with Hightie, the man shot him. The man, McClure and Tapes said, was Washington. Washington's defense was that he had been at a grocery store at the time of Hightie's murder. The store cashier, a person who had accompanied Washington, and Washington's mother all testified to that fact.

The [intermediate] appellate court affirmed the conviction and sentence on direct review. In 1990, Washington filed a post-conviction petition [including a claim that new evidence cast doubt on the accuracy of the verdict. The claim was supported with an affidavit and in camera testimony of Jacqueline Martin]. Martin, who was 16 years old at the time, told how she had been present when Marcus Halsey, then her boyfriend, and Frank Caston had left Halsey's house to revenge an earlier beating of Halsey's brother. She, Halsey, Caston, and Caston's girlfriend drove in a car to an alley in a neighborhood in Chicago. She later learned that it happened to be the neighborhood where Hightie lived. Martin told how, after Halsey and Caston left the car, she had heard two gunshots, and, when the two returned, she had heard Halsey say "it was the wrong guy." . . .

Halsey was questioned by police the next morning. . . . Martin said that after the police questioning, Halsey had threatened to kill her if she told anyone what had happened. Halsey's threats continued, Martin said, and so she eventually stopped going to Halsey's house. Some months later, Halsey's brother confronted her as she was walking near a park and forcibly took her to Halsey. She said that she was kept against her will at Halsey's house for three weeks to a month. She eventually escaped [and] went immediately to her mother's house. That same day she left for Mississippi. She stayed there for six years. Martin told how at the time of the hearing she still feared Halsey. [T]he trial judge granted a new trial on the ground that Martin's testimony was new evidence which, if believed, would have "had some significant impact" upon the jury. The State appealed. . . .

The claim Washington raised is a "free-standing" claim of innocence; the newly discovered evidence is not being used to supplement an assertion of a constitutional violation with respect to his trial [such as a claim that counsel was ineffective in failing to investigate and uncover the new evidence]. The issue is not whether the evidence at trial was insufficient to convict Washington beyond a reasonable doubt. The appellate court rejected that challenge on direct appeal. The issue is whether Washington's claim of newly discovered evidence can be raised in a petition under the Post-Conviction Hearing Act to entitle Washington to a new trial. Post-conviction relief is Washington's remaining hope for a judicial remedy, the time limitations of other avenues offering relief for such a claim having lapsed. See 735 ILCS 5/2-1202(c) (allowing such claims to be made in a motion for a new trial within 30 days); 735 ILCS 5/2-1401(c) (permitting such claims up to two years after a final judgment, the period being excused in certain limited situations, including "fraudulent" concealment of evidence). Executive clemency, of course, would remain available to Washington.

To decide the issue, we must see if either a federal or Illinois constitutional right is implicated in such a free-standing claim of innocence, since Post-Conviction Hearing Act relief is limited to constitutional claims. 725 ILCS 5/122-1. Washington argues that his claim implicates due process protections. The beginning point for addressing that argument is Herrera v. Collins, 506 U.S. 390 (1993), where the Supreme Court rejected the contention as a federal constitutional matter. In light of our own constitution's due process guaranty, we must also assess Washington's argument as a matter of Illinois constitutional jurisprudence.

The issue in *Herrera* was whether a free-standing claim of innocence following a Texas capital conviction could be raised in a habeas corpus petition in view of either the eighth amendment protection against cruel and unusual punishment or the fourteenth amendment due process clause. Ten years after his conviction, Herrera claimed that his brother, who had since died, committed the crimes. The claim was supported by two affidavits. . . .

Looking first to the eighth amendment, the Court admitted an "elemental appeal" in the notion that the Constitution should be construed to prohibit the execution or imprisonment of the innocent. But constitutionally, a newly discovered evidence claim had to "be evaluated in the light of the previous proceedings" in which guilt or innocence was determined. The Court explained that once the usual constitutional safeguards for ensuring against the risk of convicting the innocent in trial proceedings were met, a conviction must mean that the person convicted is no longer "innocent" but is one "who has been convicted by due process of law." Recognizing a free-standing claim of innocence would amount to according "additional process." . . . A claim of innocence itself simply was not, the Court concluded, cognizable under the eighth amendment [or the due process clause].

In the last portion of the opinion, the Court nevertheless addressed "for the sake of argument" the petitioner's claim — rejecting it — as if it were constitutionally cognizable. To do so, the Court proceeded under an assumption that "a truly persuasive demonstration of actual innocence" in a capital case where there was "no state avenue open to process such a claim" would be unconstitutional. . . . On one hand *Herrera* underscores the unkind reality that, though the Constitution offers unparalleled protections against convicting the innocent, it cannot guaranty that result. Then again, the last portion of the opinion suggests that the Constitution must somehow be made to do so, at least in a capital case. . . .

Conflicted or not, at least for noncapital cases, *Herrera* clearly states . . . that a free-standing claim of innocence is not cognizable as a fourteenth amendment due process claim. And so Washington's effort to state a federal constitutional due process claim under the Post-Conviction Hearing Act must fail.

The possibility remains that Washington's claim may be cognizable under the Illinois Constitution's due process protection. . . . Perhaps the closest this court has come to determining that our constitution's due process clause could be a means to recognize a newly discovered evidence claim for post-conviction purposes was in People v. Cornille, 448 N.E.2d 857 (Ill. 1983). There, the court held that a post-conviction claim based upon the discovery that an expert testifying in an arson prosecution lied about his expertise was cognizable under the due process clauses of both the United States and Illinois Constitutions. However, the decision did not turn on a differentiation of the clauses. The State's failure to prevent the perjury by verifying the expert's credentials was sufficient "indicia of State action" which, linked to the "adjudicatory process," made the expert's conduct a due process violation under both. *Cornille* finds its place among a long line of related cases holding that the use of false testimony underlying a conviction is a due process violation.

Those kinds of claims are fundamentally different from ones such as Washington has raised. Washington can claim no state action with regard to the evidence he now relies upon for post-conviction relief. And the "adjudicatory process" by which he was convicted did not otherwise lack due process. Essentially, then, the issue is the time relativeness of due process as a matter of this State's constitutional jurisprudence; that is, should additional process be afforded in Illinois when newly discovered evidence indicates that a convicted person is actually innocent?

We believe so as a matter of both procedural and substantive due process. In terms of procedural due process, we believe that to ignore such a claim would be fundamentally unfair. Imprisonment of the innocent would also be so conscience shocking as to trigger operation of substantive due process. The conflicted analysis in *Herrera* is some proof of that. . . . The Supreme Court rejected substantive due process as means to recognize free-standing innocence claims because of the idea that a person convicted in a constitutionally fair trial must be viewed as guilty. That made it impossible for such a person to claim that he, an innocent person, was unfairly convicted.

We think that the Court overlooked that a "truly persuasive demonstration of innocence" would, in hindsight, undermine the legal construct precluding a substantive due process analysis. The stronger the claim — the more likely it is that a convicted person is actually innocent — the weaker is the legal construct dictating that the person be viewed as guilty. A "truly persuasive demonstration of innocence" would effectively reduce the idea to legal fiction. . . .

We therefore hold as a matter of Illinois constitutional jurisprudence that a claim of newly discovered evidence showing a defendant to be actually innocent of the crime for which he was convicted is cognizable as a matter of due process. That holding aligns Illinois with other jurisdictions likewise recognizing, primarily as a matter of state habeas corpus jurisprudence, a basis to raise such claims under the rubric of due process. [The court cited cases from Texas, Connecticut, and Florida.]

That only means, of course, that there is footing in the Illinois Constitution for asserting free-standing innocence claims based upon newly discovered evidence under the Post-Conviction Hearing Act. Procedurally, such claims should be resolved as any other brought under the Act. Substantively, relief has been held to require that the supporting evidence be new, material, noncumulative and, most importantly, of such conclusive character as would probably change the result on retrial. As for this case, we find neither reason to disagree with the appellate court that those concerns were satisfied nor need to elaborate upon that conclusion. The judgment of the appellate court is affirmed.

McMorrow, J., specially concurring.

. . . The State asks this court to overrule the holding in State v. Molstad, 461 N.E.2d 398 (Ill. 1984), that the defendant's evidence must be "of such conclusive character that it will probably change the result on retrial." The State argues that this court should adopt a more stringent standard by which to gauge a post-conviction petitioner's claim of newly discovered evidence of actual innocence. The State proposes that the defendant should be required to prove that, based upon the newly discovered evidence as well as the other evidence produced at trial, no rational trier of fact could find beyond a reasonable doubt that the defendant was guilty of the crime charged. However, this standard applies to a review of the evidence where the defendant claims that the State's evidence was insufficient to prove him guilty beyond a reasonable doubt. Moreover, where a reviewing court determines that no rational trier of fact could find the defendant guilty beyond a reasonable doubt, the proper remedy is not a new trial but an acquittal on the charges for which there was insufficient evidence to convict the defendant. In light of these considerations, the more stringent standard suggested by the State is not properly applicable to a post-conviction request for a new trial based on newly discovered evidence of actual innocence. . . .

Requests for a new trial based on newly discovered evidence of actual innocence are to be viewed with great caution and are not lightly granted. The trial court's determination is a discretionary one that will be overturned only upon a clear abuse of discretion. There is no basis in the present record to find an abuse of discretion in the trial court's granting of the defendant's request for post-conviction relief because of newly discovered evidence of actual innocence.

The record shows that the defendant could not have discovered Jacqueline Martin or the substance of her testimony while he was standing trial for the Hightie murder. At the time defendant was being prosecuted, Jacqueline had fled to Mississippi and virtually no one knew of her whereabouts. . . .

The record also demonstrates that Jacqueline's testimony was critical to a determination of defendant's guilt. . . . Jacqueline's testimony established that Marcus and

Frank went to Tony Hightie's neighborhood on the night of the shooting, that they had a gun with them, and that they went there in order to retaliate for the beating that Marcus' brother had sustained earlier that day. Jacqueline stated that Marcus and Frank left the car and walked to a nearby location. Jacqueline then heard two gunshots and the boys came running back to the vehicle. Jacqueline heard Marcus tell Frank that they had shot the wrong person. . . .

In light of this evidence, I find no error in the trial court's allowance of the defendant's post-conviction petition. . . . I note that defendant's post-conviction petition included photographs of both the defendant and Frank Caston, an alleged friend of Marcus, and that these photographs show a remarkable facial resemblance between defendant and Frank Caston. For these reasons, I concur in the majority's conclusion that the defendant in the instant cause should receive a new trial.

MILLER, J., dissenting.

. . . Illinois law affords convicted defendants a number of opportunities to raise allegations of newly discovered evidence of innocence; the availability of these forms of relief refutes the majority's conclusion that procedural due process compels a post-conviction remedy for the same claim. First, a defendant may present such evidence in a motion for a new trial, filed within 30 days of the verdict or finding of guilty. If the defendant discovers the evidence too late to satisfy the preceding time limit, relief may be available under section 2-1401 of the Code of Civil Procedure. While at one time it was the rule that claims of newly discovered evidence could not be raised in a petition under [this section], more recent cases have recognized that such claims may be prosecuted under section 2-1401. Notably, the two-year time limit for bringing actions under section 2-1401 corresponds to the two-year limit imposed by Rule 33 of the Federal Rules of Criminal Procedure, which provides the sole means for bringing claims of newly discovered evidence of innocence by convicted defendants in the federal system. . . . Because Illinois law provides convicted defendants with sufficient means by which to raise claims of actual innocence, I do not agree with the majority that considerations of procedural due process mandate an additional remedy under the Post-Conviction Hearing Act.

As an alternative basis for today's holding, the majority concludes that principles of substantive due process also compel recognition of the defendant's claim. This further rationale is equally unpersuasive, however. A defendant seeking to assert a claim of actual innocence in a post-conviction petition has, by definition, been convicted of the charge following a trial or a guilty plea. [T]he majority asserts that the "legal construct" of a convicted defendant's guilt becomes weaker as the showing of actual innocence grows stronger. Although that observation has some theoretical appeal, it slights the role of the trial in our system of criminal justice. At the time a person files a post-conviction petition, he stands before the court, and society, as a convicted defendant, having been found guilty following a trial or guilty plea at which, presumably, all constitutional rights were honored. I do not believe that the legal significance of that event waxes or wanes depending on the strength of a subsequent showing of actual innocence. Given the passage of time, and the fading of memories, there can certainly he no assurance that an adjudication made following a new trial would be any more reliable than the adjudication of the original proceeding, which produced the defendant's conviction. . . .

Finally, I would note that the out-of-state authorities cited by the majority in support of today's decision are fundamentally different from the case at bar. . . .

The cases cited by the majority either involve capital defendants or were maintained under statutes that do not expressly require a constitutional violation as a predicate for relief.

BILANDIC, C.J., dissenting.

. . . What standard for relief should apply to a post-conviction petitioner raising a free-standing claim of actual innocence based on newly discovered evidence? Without any analysis, the majority applies the standard applicable to a defendant's post-trial motion for a new trial: i.e., the newly discovered evidence must be "new, material, noncumulative" and of such conclusive character as would "probably change the result on retrial." The majority then awards the defendant a new trial in which he can present his newly discovered evidence, the testimony of Jacqueline Martin.

This standard is not appropriate for analyzing post-conviction petitioners' claims of actual innocence for many reasons. The standard (1) does not comport with the rationale underlying the majority's recognition of this due process right; (2) wrongly cloaks the already-convicted defendant with a new presumption of innocence; (3) gives no consideration to the need for finality in criminal proceedings; and (4) inappropriately requires a new trial, which may take place decades after the crime and original trial. Also, the standard is not consistent with that applied in other jurisdictions.

The . . . problem with the majority's standard is that it allows the presumption of innocence to survive a constitutionally valid conviction. This happens because the defendant is awarded a new trial in which the State will again bear the burden of proving the defendant's guilt beyond a reasonable doubt. This result is not acceptable. An appropriate standard would recognize that a valid conviction strips the defendant of the presumption of innocence. Accordingly, the defendant should bear the burden of proving his actual innocence.

[T]he majority's standard [also] fails to give due consideration to society's interests in the finality of criminal proceedings. An appropriate standard would take into account the passage of time and would recognize that it becomes substantially more difficult for the State to obtain convictions once memories have faded and evidence has disappeared. . . .

Given the many serious problems with the majority's standard, it is not surprising that other jurisdictions have explicitly rejected it. [The dissenting opinion cited cases from California, Connecticut, and Texas.] This court should not have adopted it either. I urge my fellow justices to rectify this grave error as quickly as possible.

Notes

1. *New facts establishing innocence in post-conviction proceedings: majority position.* Most states have several statutory routes for convicted persons to submit new evidence to demonstrate their innocence. Motions for new trials may be granted on the basis of newly available evidence, although the time limit for such motions is often brief. The ancient writ of error coram nobis focused on the presentation of new evidence, and that practice is now reflected in the post-conviction remedy statutes and case law of most states. See In re Clark, 855 P.2d 729 (Cal. 1993) (habeas corpus available for claims of new evidence, jurisdictional defects, or constitutional claims carrying risk of convicting an innocent person).

The difficult questions arise when the available post-conviction remedy statute limits coverage (as in the Illinois statute at issue in *Washington*) to constitutional questions. Is there a constitutional violation when the state holds a convicted person in custody in the face of convincing evidence of innocence? As we saw, the U.S. Supreme Court declared in Herrera v. Collins, 506 U.S. 390 (1993), that claims of new evidence of innocence do not ordinarily raise due process questions that a federal court must hear on habeas corpus. Only a few state courts have confronted this question, because statutes often provide for methods of considering such evidence regardless of its constitutional status. Those state courts addressing the question have usually agreed with the position of the Illinois court. See Miller v. Commissioner, 700 A.2d 1108 (Conn. 1997).

2. *Constitutional claims on post-conviction.* As we have seen, some state post-conviction remedies are available only to correct state or federal *constitutional* errors in the criminal proceedings: violations of state statutes or procedural rules would not qualify for relief. Federal habeas corpus relief is available for violations of the federal constitution, see Brown v. Allen, 344 U.S. 443 (1953). The federal statute also allows habeas relief for those whose custody violates the "law or treaties" of the United States, see 28 U.S.C. §2241, although it would be rare for a state criminal trial to violate a federal statutory requirement.

Not all constitutional claims are available for post-conviction review in state or federal court. To begin with, the harmless error doctrine applies to post-conviction review. See Milton v. Wainwright, 407 U.S. 371 (1972). Many habeas corpus regimes also block courts from hearing constitutional claims if the constitutional error does not undermine the reliability of the factfinding process. For instance, claims of failure to exclude evidence obtained through an unconstitutional search or seizure are not available in federal court. This was the holding in the famous case of Stone v. Powell, 428 U.S. 465 (1976). The same is true in some state courts. See In re Sterling, 407 P.2d 5 (Cal. 1965).

Note that the Pennsylvania statute reprinted above covers constitutional claims only when the error "so undermined the truth-determining process that no reliable adjudication of guilt or innocence could have taken place." The Oklahoma statute reaches both constitutional and non-constitutional claims, but only when the error supports a conclusion that "the outcome of the trial would have been different but for the errors or that the defendant is factually innocent." Does the public have any legitimate interest in correcting legal errors that occur in criminal proceedings, even when those errors do not undermine the reliability of the guilty verdict?

3. *Jurisdictional and non-constitutional claims on post-conviction.* Some state collateral review statutes adhere to the traditional limit on habeas corpus as a method for correcting only jurisdictional errors. See State ex rel. Dotson v. Roger, 607 N.E.2d 453 (Ohio 1993). Other non-constitutional bases for collateral review appear commonly in the state statutes, such as a challenge to a sentence in excess of the maximum authorized by law. See Florida Rule of Criminal Procedure 3.850.

2. *Procedural Bars*

In addition to subject matter bars, state and federal laws governing post-conviction review place "procedural bars" on the power of the court to hear the merits of a petitioner's claim. State law requires a criminal defendant to take a variety of procedural steps to preserve a claim of error for later review. These steps often include raising an objection at trial or raising a claim on direct appeal—though sometimes having previously raised a claim is itself a reason to bar later review. It is becoming common for statutes of limitations to require petitioners to bring claims promptly—sometimes with periods measured in days rather than months or years. If the defendant fails to take these steps, any later effort to get judicial review of the alleged legal error will be "procedurally barred" because of the petitioner's "procedural default," and the court will refuse to consider the merits of the claim.

Most systems do allow petitioners to raise some claims on collateral review that they did not raise at trial or on direct review, but only if the petitioner provides an adequate reason for that failure. The more extensive the procedural requirements, the more likely a petitioner will fail to preserve some claim and will need to explain the failure to follow those procedures: thus, the bypass standard and its application are critical elements of any system of post-conviction review. As you read the following materials, continue to ask what the role of post-conviction collateral review ought to be. Does a particular view about the role of post-conviction review help to determine the best doctrinal boundaries on procedural defaults? Consider, as well, the relationship of procedural bars to the subject matter bars covered in the previous subsection. Is there a clear distinction between "subject matter" and "procedural" bars?

■ IDAHO CODE §19-4901

(a) Any person who has been convicted of, or sentenced for, a crime and who claims:

(1) That the conviction or the sentence was in violation of the constitution of the United States or the constitution or laws of this state;

(2) That the court was without jurisdiction to impose sentence;

(3) That the sentence exceeds the maximum authorized by law;

(4) That there exists evidence of material facts, not previously presented and heard, that requires vacation of the conviction or sentence in the interest of justice; . . .

(6) [That] the petitioner is innocent of the offense; or

(7) That the conviction or sentence is otherwise subject to collateral attack upon any ground of alleged error heretofore available under any common law, statutory or other writ, motion, petition, proceeding, or remedy:

may institute, without paying a filing fee, a proceeding under this act to secure relief.

(b) This remedy is not a substitute for nor does it affect any remedy incident to the proceedings in the trial court, or of an appeal from the sentence or conviction. Any issue which could have been raised on direct appeal, but was not, is forfeited and may not be considered in post conviction proceedings, unless it appears to the court, on the basis of a substantial factual showing by affidavit, deposition or otherwise, that the asserted basis for relief raises a substantial doubt about the reliability of the finding of guilt and could not, in the exercise of due diligence, have been presented earlier. . . .

■ DENNIS JACKSON v. COMMISSIONER

629 A.2d 413 (Conn. 1993)

BORDEN, J.

The petitioner, Dennis Jackson, appeals from the judgment of the habeas court dismissing his petition for a writ of habeas corpus. The habeas court concluded that the petitioner had failed to demonstrate good cause for his failure to pursue on direct appeal his claim of unconstitutional jury composition that was the basis of his habeas petition. We affirm the judgment of the habeas court.

The record sets forth the facts and lengthy procedural history of this case. At his criminal trial, conducted in May, 1982, the petitioner was represented by Attorney John Buckley. Prior to the trial, Buckley had reached an agreement with assistant state's attorney Patrick Clifford, who Buckley understood would be prosecuting the petitioner's case. Buckley had agreed with Clifford that, in challenging the jury array in the petitioner's case, the petitioner could rely on evidence presented in another case that Buckley and Clifford had tried together and in which a jury array challenge had been brought.

Clifford, however, did not try the petitioner's case, but instead was replaced by assistant state's attorney Robert Devlin. Devlin, unlike Clifford, was unwilling to stipulate to the jury array evidence that had been presented in the case that Buckley and Clifford had tried together. Devlin also argued to the trial court that the petitioner's motion challenging the array was untimely.

In response, the trial court asked Buckley whether he was ready to present evidence necessary to challenge the array. Buckley stated to the court that he would need additional time to subpoena the appropriate witnesses and that he was not prepared to present evidence at that time.[2] Although Buckley informed the trial court that he needed additional time because he had relied on his prior agreement with Clifford, the trial court denied his request for a continuance. The petitioner, therefore, was unable to introduce evidence to support his challenge to the jury array.

The petitioner was subsequently convicted, after a jury trial, of first degree sexual assault, second degree kidnapping and first degree robbery. The petitioner appealed his conviction to this court and we affirmed the judgment of the trial court. In his direct appeal, the defendant did not raise a claim that the trial court had abused its discretion by denying his request for a continuance so that he could produce evidence to challenge the jury array.

In 1987, the petitioner filed a petition for a writ of habeas corpus claiming that the jury array from which his petit jury had been selected had been summoned in violation of his federal and state constitutional rights.[3] The habeas court denied the petition for habeas corpus and the petitioner subsequently appealed. His appeal was consolidated with the appeals of thirty-three other habeas petitioners. [The commissioner of correction] asserted that the proper standard by which to analyze the petitioners' failure to raise their jury array challenges at trial was the cause and

2. The petitioner had previously been granted a two week continuance that began after the jury had been selected but prior to trial.

3. The petitioner, a black male, claimed that members of his race were underrepresented on his jury array in violation of his equal protection rights guaranteed by the fourteenth amendment to the United States constitution and article first, §20, of the Connecticut constitution.

prejudice standard as articulated in Wainwright v. Sykes, 433 U.S. 72 (1977), as opposed to the deliberate bypass rule; see Fay v. Noia, 372 U.S. 391 (1963); upon which the habeas court had relied. We affirmed the judgment of the habeas court. In so doing, we concluded that the appropriate standard by which to analyze procedural defaults at trial was the *Wainwright* standard of cause and prejudice. . . . Johnson v. Commissioner of Correction, 589 A.2d 1214 (Conn. 1991). [We] remanded "the case [to the habeas court] for further proceedings relating to whether there was good cause for [the petitioner's] failure to raise before trial the claim of unconstitutional jury composition that is the basis for his habeas petition." On the remand, the habeas court concluded that there was not adequate cause to excuse the petitioner's failure to pursue the jury array challenge on direct appeal. . . . This appeal followed. . . .

Prior to 1991, we employed the deliberate bypass rule, as articulated in Fay v. Noia, in order to determine the reviewability of constitutional claims in habeas corpus proceedings that had not been properly raised at trial or pursued on direct appeal. In Fay v. Noia (1963), the United States Supreme Court held that federal habeas corpus jurisdiction was not affected by the procedural default, specifically a failure to appeal, of a petitioner during state court proceedings resulting in his conviction. The court recognized, however, a limited discretion in the federal habeas judge to deny relief to an applicant who has deliberately by-passed the orderly procedure of the state courts and in so doing has forfeited his state court remedies. . . . This deliberate bypass standard for waiver required an intentional relinquishment or abandonment of a known right or privilege by the petitioner personally and depended on his considered choice. . . . A choice made by counsel not participated in by the petitioner does not automatically bar relief.

In Wainwright v. Sykes, however, the United States Supreme Court subsequently rejected the sweeping language of *Fay,* which would make federal habeas review generally available to state convicts absent a knowing and deliberate waiver of the federal constitutional contention. The court upheld a state court's refusal to decide the merits of a claimed *Miranda* violation first raised in a posttrial motion and in state habeas corpus proceedings, contrary to a state contemporaneous objection rule. The court adopted as a new standard for federal habeas review . . . that in a collateral attack upon a conviction, the petitioner must make not only a showing of cause for the defendant's failure to challenge the composition of the grand jury before trial, but also a showing of actual prejudice. Thus was born the *Wainwright* cause and prejudice standard for habeas review.

In *Johnson,* the petitioner's original appeal from the judgment of the habeas court, we reconsidered, in light of *Wainwright,* whether the deliberate bypass was the appropriate standard by which to analyze the reviewability of habeas claims that were procedurally defaulted at trial. We decided, after a full review of the relevant considerations, to abandon the deliberate bypass standard of Fay v. Noia, and to adopt the *Wainwright* cause and prejudice standard as the proper standard to determine the reviewability of such claims. In *Johnson,* however, we expressly did not reach the related issue of whether the cause and prejudice standard should replace the deliberate bypass rule for claims procedurally defaulted on appeal.

We now conclude that the *Wainwright* cause and prejudice standard should be employed to determine the reviewability of habeas claims that were not properly pursued on direct appeal. In Johnson v. Commissioner of Correction, we outlined the significant policy reasons for abandoning the deliberate bypass rule and adopting the cause and prejudice standard for claims procedurally defaulted at trial. First, as a general matter, we noted that

> special problems . . . are likely to arise relating to the feasibility of a second trial when a conviction is set aside by a habeas court rather than by an appellate court. These problems are related mainly to the more extended delay of the second trial that frequently results from a reversal of a conviction by a habeas court. There is no statute of limitation or other time limit that would bar a habeas petition. Ordinarily the petition may not be filed until appellate remedies have been exhausted. . . . The greater time lapse that results when a second trial is ordered by a habeas court has a serious impact on the availability of witnesses and other evidence for the second trial. Memories fade with the passage of time, exhibits are lost, and other evidence is less likely to be available. Appellate counsel would have less incentive to raise on appeal all arguable constitutional claims of the defendant if another opportunity to raise such claims were available in the habeas court. . . .
>
> If deliberate bypass were the sole barrier to such review, it could seldom be invoked for a default at trial. It is not common practice and would be unduly cumbersome to establish a record in the trial court showing that the defendant had personally made a knowledgeable waiver of his constitutional procedural rights on each of the myriad occasions that arise during a criminal trial when such rights are involved. Most of these choices during trial, such as whether to move for suppression of evidence or to cross-examine a particular witness, must necessarily be left to counsel, subject to the requirement that his performance satisfy reasonable standards of competency. . . .

The "special problems" regarding procedural defaults at trial that we noted in *Johnson* apply equally to procedural defaults on direct appeal, and militate in favor of our adoption of one standard by which to measure procedural defaults occurring at trial or on direct appeal. As the United States Supreme Court has noted in specifically adopting the cause and prejudice standard to analyze procedural defaults on direct appeal: "A State's procedural rules serve vital purposes at trial, on appeal, and on state collateral attack. [Such rules afford] the opportunity to resolve the issue shortly after trial, while evidence is still available both to assess the defendant's claim and to retry the defendant effectively if he prevails in his appeal. . . . This type of rule promotes not only the accuracy and efficiency of judicial decisions, but also the finality of those decisions, by forcing the defendant to litigate all of his claims together, as quickly after trial as the docket will allow, and while the attention of the appellate court is focused on his case." Murray v. Carrier, 477 U.S. 478 (1986).

We also recognize that the judicial system's legitimate interest in procedural rules is undermined regardless of whether the breach results from counsel's ignorance or inadvertence rather than a deliberate decision, tactical or not, to abstain from raising the claim.[8] Just as with procedural defaults occurring at trial, the costs

8. In adopting the cause and prejudice standard for procedural defaults occurring at trial, we recognized that, particularly in jury array challenges, the deliberate bypass rule would encourage astute counsel to "sandbag" the court by saving their claims until habeas review. Johnson v. Commissioner of Correction, 589 A.2d 1214 (Ct. 1991). This possibility exists because if the time limitations for bringing a challenge at trial were followed, any constitutional defect in the array could be cured, and the trial could be continued. Consequently, "[s]trong tactical considerations would militate in favor of delaying the raising of the claim in hopes of an acquittal, with the thought that if those hopes did not materialize, the claim could be used to upset an otherwise valid conviction at a time when reprosecution might well be difficult."

The same danger of "sandbagging" would exist, albeit to a lesser extent, if we were to continue to apply the deliberate bypass rule to procedural defaults on appeal. The defendant's counsel on appeal might well conclude that the best strategy is to raise a few promising claims on appeal, while reserving others for later habeas review should the direct appeal be unsuccessful.

of violation of our procedural rules are incurred regardless of the kind of attorney error that led to the failure of counsel to pursue a claim on appeal. . . .

One of the underlying rationales for preferring the cause and prejudice standard to the deliberate bypass rule, regarding trial court defaults, is that it is unrealistic and inconsistent with the proper role of trial counsel to require consultation with the client regarding every legal or tactical consideration. The same is true of appellate counsel. It is unrealistic and inconsistent with the proper role of appellate counsel to require consultation with the client, and presumably to secure the client's consent, with respect to the decision of whether to raise or forego particular legal claims on appeal. Indeed, applying the deliberate bypass rule to such decisions of appellate advocacy would create the incentive for counsel to remain silent, rather than to confer with the client because ultimately the client would be better served in a habeas action by remaining ignorant of potential claims on direct appeal. . . .

The petitioner next claims that, even if the cause and prejudice standard is the appropriate standard by which to analyze his failure to pursue his claim on direct appeal, the habeas court improperly concluded that there was insufficient cause for the petitioner's failure to pursue on direct appeal his claim that the composition of the jury array violated his constitutional rights. We are unpersuaded.

[The] denial of a request for a continuance is appealable. Consequently, the petitioner was free to challenge the denial of the continuance on direct appeal if he believed that the denial had been improper under the circumstances of the case. If he then convinced the reviewing court that the denial was reversible error, he would have been entitled, on remand to the trial court, to present the evidence regarding the jury array that he had originally intended to present. Under that scenario, however, if his jury array challenge were successful, a new trial would have ensued shortly after the direct appeal, rather than now, eleven years later.

BERDON, J., dissenting.

At the very least, we should continue to employ the deliberate bypass standard to determine the reviewability of habeas claims that were not properly pursued on direct appeal. The majority's decision closes the door to petitioners who may have meritorious claims to challenge their confinement and who may, in fact, be innocent, but who, through no fault of their own, are precluded from pursuing their claims.

I must confess that the scales weigh heavily, at least for me, in favor of granting a new trial to persons whose claims cast a substantial cloud on the validity of their convictions. The rules established today have equal application for those who are incarcerated for life as well as those who are awaiting the death penalty. The majority, emulating the United States Supreme Court, restricts habeas corpus in the name of finality of decisions. Lest we forget, there is nothing more final than the imposition of the death penalty.

Furthermore, as in the present case, the vast majority of criminal defendants are represented either by public defenders or by special public defenders assigned by the state. These competent and dedicated attorneys carry heavy caseloads, which often play a role in procedural defaults. . . . The state, therefore, must take its share of the blame for the procedural defaults.

[T]he majority notes the problems associated with granting a new trial years after the alleged crime. I too recognize the difficulty of conducting a second trial when memories have faded and evidence is not easily available. In many cases, however, these problems are ameliorated by the rules of evidence permitting admission of a witness' testimony at a prior proceeding under certain circumstances. In addition, a witness' prior inconsistent statement could be introduced into evidence for substantive purposes under certain circumstances.

[T]he majority claims that under the deliberate bypass standard there must be a showing that "the defendant had personally made a knowledgeable waiver of his constitutional procedural rights" and uses this extreme interpretation to reject the deliberate bypass rule. Whether there has been a "deliberate bypass" on appeal should not depend on whether the defendant made a personal, deliberate choice not to pursue a certain claim, but rather, on whether the choice was made by appellate counsel. . . .

Even if the "cause and prejudice" standard is applied, I would get to the merits of the petition in this case. . . . This court has granted the trial court such broad discretion in determining whether to grant or deny a continuance that an appeal on that issue is for all practical purposes frivolous. When the trial court's discretion is so great that it is virtually impossible to obtain reasonable review, the omission of that claim, especially when there is no proof that it was a deliberate omission, should satisfy the "cause" standard.

In addition, the defendant's substantive claim goes to the core of our judicial process. . . . Neither the accused in this case nor the African-American community can possibly believe that the defendant was justly convicted when his jury was not selected from a pool of persons representing a fair cross section of the population. Accordingly, I would find that the "prejudice" has been established. . . .

Notes

1. *Standard for assessing procedural default: majority view.* The trend among the states for assessing a failure to raise a claim prior to a challenge on collateral review has been away from more generous standards such as the "deliberate bypass" standard of Fay v. Noia, 372 U.S. 391 (1963), or simply a general (and sympathetic) "cause" standard. States have moved instead towards the more restrictive requirements of "cause and prejudice" articulated by the U.S. Supreme Court in Wainwright v. Sykes, 433 U.S. 72 (1977), or functional equivalents. Is the Idaho "due diligence" standard more or less exacting than "cause?" Is the Idaho "substantial doubt" standard more or less exacting than the requirement of "prejudice?" Connecticut appears to have been the last state to abandon the "deliberate bypass" standard. However, many states continue to apply a standard different from the "cause and prejudice" standard used in the federal courts and adopted by Connecticut. Utah, for example, requires a showing of "unusual circumstances" to explain any procedural default. See, e.g., Hurst v. Cook, 777 P.2d 1029 (Utah 1989) ("[W]hile habeas corpus is not a substitute for appeal, a conviction may nevertheless be challenged by collateral attack in "unusual circumstances," that is, where an obvious injustice or a substantial and prejudicial denial of a constitutional right has occurred, irrespective of whether an appeal has been taken."). Colorado Rev. Stat. §16-12-206(1)(c) provides:

> A motion for postconviction review may raise only the following issues: (I) Whether there exists evidence of material facts, not previously presented and heard, which by

> the exercise of reasonable diligence could not have been known or learned by the defendant or trial counsel prior to the imposition of the sentence and which require that the conviction or the death sentence be vacated in the interests of justice . . . .

The Connecticut court in *Jackson* applies the same standard to assess failure to raise a claim at trial and on appeal. Should the standard be the same?

Not every procedural default is evaluated under the "cause and prejudice" standard. Some procedural failures in state court are considered unimportant enough to ignore in federal habeas corpus. See Lee v. Kemna, 534 U.S. 362 (2002) (defendant's witnesses did not arrive at courthouse on trial date and defendant moved for continuance but did not file written motion as required by state law; procedural default inadequate to prevent federal habeas review because properly filed motion would not have changed outcome in state court and defendant substantially complied with state rules). In addition, a state might waive its procedural rule requirements. If a state court speaks to the merits of the defendant's claim despite the procedural default, the federal courts are also allowed to address the merits. See Stewart v. Smith, 536 U.S. 856 (2002).

2. *The standard for reassessing facts on habeas.* Often petitioners on collateral review request evidentiary hearings to develop a record supporting their claims. Should courts apply the same standards in deciding whether to hold an evidentiary hearing, and whether to grant relief? In Keeney v. Tamayo-Reyes, 504 U.S. 1 (1992), the Supreme Court directed federal courts to apply the "cause and prejudice" standard in deciding whether to hold evidentiary hearings. *Tamayo-Reyes* overruled Townsend v. Sain, 372 U.S. 293, 313 (1963), one of the linchpin decisions in the expansion of federal collateral review of state convictions. *Townsend* held that a federal court must hold an evidentiary hearing "if the habeas applicant did not receive a full and fair evidentiary hearing in a state court."

Most states, in contrast, apply a lower standard to determine whether a court should hold an evidentiary hearing. Consider the two different standards that Illinois courts use to consider an evidentiary hearing under Ill. Stat. ch. 725 §5/122-2.1:

> (a) Within 90 days after the filing and docketing of each petition the court shall examine such petition and enter an order thereon pursuant to this Section.
>
> (1) If the petitioner is under sentence of death and is without counsel and alleges that he is without means to procure counsel, he shall state whether or not he wishes counsel to be appointed to represent him. If appointment of counsel is so requested, the court shall appoint counsel if satisfied that the petitioner has no means to procure counsel.
>
> (2) If the petitioner is sentenced to imprisonment and the court determines the petition is frivolous or is patently without merit, it shall dismiss the petition in a written order, specifying the findings of fact and conclusions of law it made in reaching its decision. Such order of dismissal is a final judgment and shall be served upon the petitioner by certified mail within 10 days of its entry.
>
> (b) If the petition is not dismissed pursuant to this Section, the court shall order the petition to be docketed for further consideration. . . .

3. *What is sufficient "cause?"* The *Jackson* case raises sharply the question of what is an adequate "cause" for failing to raise a claim. When the U.S. Supreme Court announced the "cause and prejudice" standard in *Sykes,* it chose not to define either term, "leav[ing] open for resolution in future decisions the precise definition of the

cause-and-prejudice standard," emphasizing "only that it is narrower than the [knowing and deliberate waiver] standard" in Fay v. Noia. In Murray v. Carrier, 477 U.S. 478 (1986), the Supreme Court confronted the question whether attorney error in failing to raise a claim that fell short of "ineffective assistance" could nonetheless satisfy the "cause" requirement and thus open the door for habeas review. The Court answered "No," and explained that

> the existence of cause for a procedural default must ordinarily turn on whether the prisoner can show that some objective factor external to the defense impeded counsel's efforts to comply with the State's procedural rule. [A] showing that the factual or legal basis for a claim was not reasonably available to counsel or that "some interference by officials" made compliance impracticable, would constitute cause under this standard. [477 U.S. at 488].

State courts that apply the "cause and prejudice" standard have generally followed federal law in defining these concepts. See Younger v. State, 580 A.2d 552 (Del. 1990); but cf. People v. Reed, 535 N.W.2d 496 (Mich. 1995) (dividing over whether state habeas law should or must follow federal law). Consider the special definition of "cause" used in §99-39-21(4) of the Mississippi Code: "The term 'cause' as used in this section shall be defined and limited to those cases where the legal foundation upon which the claim for relief is based could not have been discovered with reasonable diligence at the time of trial or direct appeal." Under this statute, the burden is on the prisoner to allege any facts necessary to demonstrate that the claims are not procedurally barred.

Remarkable foresight is necessary to assert some claims of "cause" in the federal system. According to Edwards v. Carpenter, 529 U.S. 446 (2000), when a habeas petitioner points to ineffective assistance of counsel as the reason for her failure to raise some challenge within the state system, the ineffective assistance claim itself is also subject to procedural default rules. That is, the petitioner must either follow all state procedural rules when raising the ineffective assistance argument, or show some "cause and prejudice" for failing to raise this "cause" argument in the proper way.

4. *What is "prejudice"?* In United States v. Frady, 456 U.S. 152, 170 (1982), a case involving an erroneous jury instruction on malice murder, the Supreme Court held that a petitioner must show "not merely that the errors at his trial created a possibility of prejudice, but that they worked to his actual and substantial disadvantage, infecting his entire trial with error of constitutional dimensions." State courts applying the "cause and prejudice" default standard have tended to follow federal law. E.g., Turpin v. Todd, 493 S.E.2d 900 (Ga. 1997). However, some legislatures have retained more generous standards. In State v. Bush, 297 S.E.2d 563 (N.C. 1982), the North Carolina Supreme Court applied a statute that employs ordinary harmless error standard for constitutional claims on collateral review, and a standard assessing the "reasonable possibility that . . . a different result would have been reached" for non-constitutional claims.

5. *Procedural bar and statute of limitations.* One of the strongest complaints about habeas corpus and other forms of collateral review is that they undermine finality. Proponents of narrow collateral review standards point to cases — especially capital cases — that have wandered back and forth through state and federal courts for years. One response has been to require that all issues be raised in a single collateral petition, subject to extremely narrow exceptions. A second response has been to

incorporate statutes of limitations where none previously existed. Consider Nev. Stat. §34.726:

> 1. Unless there is good cause shown for delay, a petition that challenges the validity of a judgment or sentence must be filed within 1 year after entry of the judgment of conviction or, if an appeal has been taken from the judgment, within 1 year after the supreme court issues its remittitur. For the purposes of this subsection, good cause for delay exists if the petitioner demonstrates to the satisfaction of the court: (a) That the delay is not the fault of the petitioner; and (b) That dismissal of the petition as untimely will unduly prejudice the petitioner.
>
> 2. The execution of a sentence must not be stayed for the period provided in subsection 1 solely because a petition may be filed within that period. A stay of sentence must not be granted unless: (a) A petition is actually filed; and (b) The petitioner establishes a compelling basis for the stay.

After a long history without any statute of limitations on claims to federal courts in habeas, Congress in 1996 passed the Antiterrorism and Effective Death Penalty Act of 1996. Despite the title, this statute largely focused on adding new limitations to federal review of state convictions. Congress amended 28 U.S.C. §2244(d) to provide:

> (1) A one-year period of limitation shall apply to an application for a writ of habeas corpus by a person in custody pursuant to the judgment of a State court. The limitation period shall run from the latest of (A) the date on which the judgment became final by the conclusion of direct review or the expiration of the time for seeking such review; (B) the date on which the impediment to filing an application created by State action in violation of the Constitution or laws of the United States is removed, if the applicant was prevented from filing by such State action; (C) the date on which the constitutional right asserted was initially recognized by the Supreme Court, if the right has been newly recognized by the Supreme Court and made retroactively applicable to cases on collateral review; or (D) the date on which the factual predicate of the claim or claims presented could have been discovered through the exercise of due diligence.
>
> (2) The time during which a properly filed application for State post-conviction or other collateral review with respect to the pertinent judgment or claim is pending shall not be counted toward any period of limitation under this subsection.

Senator Orrin Hatch (R-Utah) said the law would "stop the frivolous appeals that have been driving people nuts throughout this country and subjecting victims and families of victims to unnecessary pain for year after year after year." See Duncan v. Walker, 533 U.S. 167 (2001) (petitioner filed first federal habeas petition four days before state conviction became final, petition dismissed three months later for failure to exhaust remedies; petitioner filed second federal petition eleven months later; the first petition did not toll the running of limitations period).

Problem 21-1. Successive Petitions

William Andrews was convicted of three counts of first degree murder and two counts of aggravated robbery for the killings of three people in the course of a robbery at the Hi-Fi Shop in Ogden, Utah, and was sentenced to death. The Utah Supreme Court affirmed the conviction in 1977, and the U.S. Supreme Court denied certiorari in 1978. The following month, Andrews filed a petition for post-conviction relief in the district court of Salt Lake County. That court dismissed the petition on the ground that all of the issues raised had been or could have been raised on direct appeal and thus Andrews was barred from any post-conviction review. On appeal, the Utah Supreme Court affirmed this ruling in 1980. Again the U.S. Supreme Court denied certiorari.

Andrews then filed for federal habeas corpus relief in the United States District Court for the District of Utah, Central Division. That court stayed the proceedings and ordered Andrews to return to the state courts to seek possible relief under a decision in another capital case just decided by the Utah Supreme Court. In 1983 the Utah Supreme Court again denied Andrews relief, holding that the decision in the other, newly decided case was not retroactive. Andrews resumed pursuit of his federal habeas corpus petition, but the federal district court denied all requested relief in 1984. The U.S. Court of Appeals for the Tenth Circuit affirmed that decision in 1986, and the U.S. Supreme Court again denied certiorari in 1988.

In October 1987, approximately four months before the United States Supreme Court denied certiorari, Andrews filed a new petition for post-conviction relief in the district court of Salt Lake County. He argued that the court should overturn his death sentence because the trial court committed constitutional error when it did not give the jury a lesser included offense instruction on second degree felony murder. He also alleged that the Utah Supreme Court committed constitutional error when it failed on direct appeal to address sua sponte the trial court's failure to give such an instruction. Andrews pointed out that he was indigent and unable to retain counsel of his choice at trial or on direct appeal, and his court-appointed counsel had failed to effectively research and present these arguments.

The district court denied the petition, because Andrews could or should have raised the issues presented either on appeal or in prior post-conviction petitions. The district judge concluded that the petition was "an abuse of postconviction relief and procedurally defective." Andrews appeals from the denial of his petition, which he filed pursuant to Utah Rule of Civil Procedure 65B(i)(2):

> The complaint shall further state that the legality or constitutionality of his commitment or confinement has not already been adjudged in a prior habeas corpus or other similar proceeding; and if the complainant shall have instituted prior similar proceedings in any court, state or federal, within the state of Utah, he shall so state in his complaint, . . . and shall set forth the reasons for the denial of relief in such other court. In such case, if it is apparent to the court in which the proceeding under this rule is instituted that the legality or constitutionality of his confinement has already been adjudged in such prior proceedings, the court shall forthwith dismiss such complaint, giving written notice thereof by mail to the complainant, and no further proceedings shall be had on such complaint.

Subsection (4) of that rule states that "All claims of the denial of any of complainant's constitutional rights shall be raised in the postconviction proceeding brought under this rule and may not be raised in another subsequent proceeding except for good cause shown therein."

Andrews explains his decision to present this claim in a successive petition for post-conviction relief on these grounds: (1) the case law regarding his right to a lesser included offense instruction at his trial was in an unsettled and evolutionary state during at least part of the period between his conviction and this petition,

(2) there is a strong possibility that he was entitled to a lesser included offense instruction and may have been mistakenly sentenced to death as a result of its absence, and (3) his counsel erred in not making the lesser included offense claim. How would you rule? Compare Andrews v. Schulsen, 773 P.2d 832 (Utah 1989).

Notes

1. *Successive petitions and abuse of the writ: majority view.* Should the procedural hurdles for a second or third petition collaterally attacking a conviction or sentence be the same or higher than for an initial petition? Rules governing review of successive collateral challenges are often referred to under the label "abuse of the writ." The general trend in both federal and state systems has been to severely restrict successive collateral attacks. In the federal system the "cause and prejudice" standard is applied to determine whether a petitioner has abused the writ. See McCleskey v. Zant, 499 U.S. 467 (1991). How much guidance does the "cause" standard provide in the context of successive petitions? States often apply different and more restrictive standards to successive petitions. Under §9-14-51 of the Georgia Code, any grounds for relief not raised by a petitioner in his original or amended petition "are waived unless the Constitution of the United States or of this state otherwise requires or unless [the judge] finds grounds for relief asserted therein which could not reasonably have been raised in the original or amended petition."

In the federal system, the Antiterrorism and Effective Death Penalty Act of 1996 makes it difficult for a federal court to hear claims for a second time. Under the statute, the merits of concluded criminal proceedings should not be revisited in federal court unless the petitioner makes a strong showing of "actual" or "factual" innocence. The Supreme Court has interpreted the federal statute to allow for at least one hearing on the merits in federal court, even if the issue is raised but not resolved in an initial federal petition. See Slack v. McDaniel, 529 U.S. 473 (2000) (federal habeas petition filed after an initial federal petition was dismissed without adjudication on the merits for failure to exhaust state remedies is not a "second or successive" petition; petitioner is not limited in refiled petition to the claims made in the original dismissed petition); Stewart v. Martinez-Villareal, 523 U.S. 637 (1998) (prisoner whose habeas petition was dismissed for failure to exhaust state remedies, and who then did exhaust those remedies and returned to federal court, is not filing a "successive" petition barred by statute; similarly, claim raised in federal court and dismissed as premature can be heard when raised in timely manner in later federal petition).

2. *Successive petitions: Court burden in non-capital and capital cases.* Problem 21-1 is typical for capital cases in terms of the number of successive reviews after conviction, both on direct appeal and collaterally, and in both state and federal systems. However, prisoners in non-capital cases (who are, of course, far more numerous than defendants sentenced to death) are much less likely to file successive petitions.

3. Collateral Review of Ineffective Assistance Claims

How many defendants file collateral attacks on their conviction or sentence? What claims do they typically make? How often do courts grant relief? While reading the following excerpts from a major empirical study of habeas corpus in both state and federal courts, consider whether consistent patterns in collateral review cases throw light on the proper choice of legal doctrines.

■ HABEAS CORPUS IN STATE AND FEDERAL COURTS VICTOR FLANGO

State Justice Institute, 1994

Many of the important points of contention in the current debate about habeas corpus are empirical questions, yet the amount of data brought to bear on these issues is slight. . . . Only a few states report the number of habeas corpus petitions filed or disposed as a separate case category. Data from the California Administrative Office of Courts showed 9,415 petitions were filed in California Superior Court in 1990, while the same year 1,070 habeas petitions were filed in all U.S. District Courts in California. Habeas corpus filings in California have been declining steadily from a high of approximately 15,000 in 1980. In smaller states, the habeas filings in U.S. District Court and state courts of general jurisdiction are roughly equivalent, but small. Examples from 1990 include Connecticut Superior Court 246, U.S. District Court 75; Nebraska District Court 59, U.S. District Court 63; Utah District Court 129, U.S. District Court 24; and Washington Superior Court 114; U.S District Court 195.*

[T]his research was designed to cover all habeas petitions disposed in state and federal court at two separate time periods and so is a snapshot of petitions rather than an historical picture of habeas corpus. [T]he four states chosen for the study were: California, New York, Texas and Alabama. . . .

What types of prisoners file habeas corpus petitions? [O]nly prisoners sentenced to a fairly long term have time to complete the rather lengthy procedures prerequisite to filing a habeas corpus petition. [T]he length of the sentences of habeas petitioners is relatively long, with median times ranging from a minimum sentence of 24 years to a maximum of 30 years in state courts, and 16 to 24 years for petitioners in federal courts.

[Habeas petitioners] are much more likely to have been convicted at trial. Research in 26 urban areas reveals that the jury trial rate for felonies averages 6 percent, yet the majority of habeas petitioners were convicted by a jury trial (62 percent of the state court sample and 66 percent of the federal court sample). [W]hile guilty pleas do not prevent filing of a habeas petition, they may reduce the number of issues over which the petitioner may complain. [I]t is clear that habeas petitions are *not* used by a representative sample of all convicted state prisoners, but rather by the smaller proportion in custody as a result of a jury trial conviction for a serious offense.

Perhaps also as a consequence of the seriousness of the offense, petitioners were likely to have been represented in state court during the original trial. . . . Although the overwhelming number of petitioners were represented by counsel for their initial offense, most were *not* represented by counsel in filing the habeas corpus petitions. . . . Three quarters (75 percent) of the petitioners in state court and 91 percent of the petitioners in federal court represented themselves. . . .

Of the state petitioners, 35 percent were filing their first petition, 15 percent had filed one previous petition, 17 percent had filed two prior petitions, and the

* This paragraph appeared as a footnote.—EDS.

remainder [33 percent] filed three or more prior habeas petitions. Of the federal petitioners, 46 percent were filing their first petition, 18 percent their second, 17 percent their third, while the remainder [19 percent] had previously filed three or more petitions. . . .

Which claims are raised by petitioners? . . . Do petitioners primarily question the practices and procedures of attorneys, the police, the prosecutor, or the courts? . . . Challenges to the competency of the attorney representation were the most common claims in both state and federal court. . . . In one sense, this claim is a precondition for all others because ineffective assistance of counsel is a reason given for not raising related claims previously. . . .

Of the 1,835 petitions in the state sample, 755 (41 percent) raised the claim [of ineffective assistance of counsel] either generally or specifically. . . . Of the 1,626 petitioners in the federal sample, 736 (45 percent) claimed ineffective assistance of counsel. . . . General claims included such allegations as the attorney lacked trial experience, violated the attorney-client privilege, or failed to file a claim or discovery motion, meet with the defendant on a regular basis, or otherwise failed to prepare adequately. . . .

[M]any petitions do not indicate the type of ineffective assistance of counsel received. . . . In both state and federal courts, failure to investigate and failure to object to admissibility or the insufficiency of evidence were not only the claims most likely to be raised, but also the two claims most likely to be raised together. The claim that attorneys misled the defendant was often raised in the context where the attorney failed to explain adequately the plea agreement and its consequences to the

Type of Claims Raised

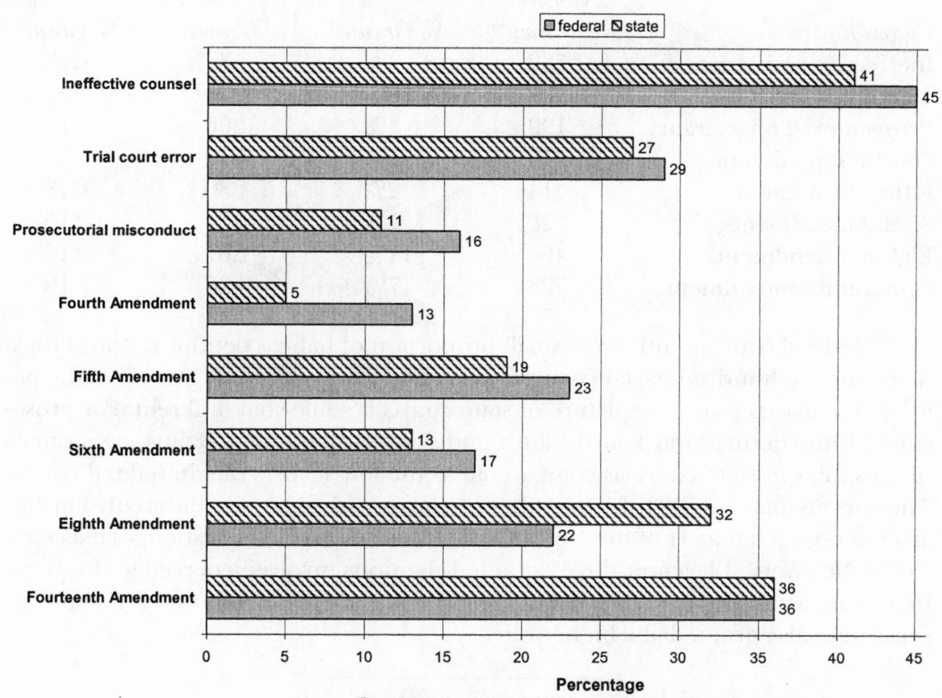

defendant. Forty-three percent (66) of the 152 petitioners in the state sample and 50 percent of the 128 petitioners in the federal sample who claimed a coerced guilty plea, also claimed ineffective assistance of counsel. . . .

Nearly 30 percent of both state and federal court petitioners claimed trial court error. . . . Many of the general claims of trial court error included the claim that the judge failed to explain the charges to the defendant. Detrimental procedural error was the single most frequent trial court error claim specified in state court, whereas failure to suppress improper evidence was the single trial court error most often specified in federal court. . . .

Prosecutorial misconduct was claimed by 11 percent of the state petitioners and 16 percent of the federal petitioners. . . . The specific claim made most frequently by both state and federal prisoners was the failure to disclose. [The second most common specific claim, made by around two percent of state petitioners, was use of perjured testimony, followed by improper comments (one percent), and inflammatory summation (one percent)].

Which claims raised tend to be granted? [B]ecause so few petitions in either the state or federal courts were granted, conclusions drawn from success rates of petitions must be regarded with care. Of the 1,626 federal petitions in the sample, only 17 were granted. Of the petitions filed in state courts, only 1 was granted in California, and only 3 were granted in Alabama. In New York, 48 petitions were granted. [The record-keeping system in Texas made it hard for the researchers to find a comparable number: they noted that in 1992, the Texas Court of Criminal Appeals disposed of 2,244 habeas corpus petitions, sending 116 back to trial courts for additional hearings, setting 152 for hearings before the appellate court, and granting 8 with specific orders.]

	State Courts		*Federal Courts*	
Claims Raised	*Number of Claims*	*% Granted*	*Number of Claims*	*% Granted*
Ineffective assistance	732	8%	584	<1%
Trial court error	528	6%	378	2%
Prosecutorial misconduct	199	3%	206	<1%
Fourth Amendment	79	1%	172	<1%
Fifth Amendment	414	2%	380	<1%
Sixth Amendment	220	1%	224	<1%
Eighth Amendment	463	11%	261	<1%
Fourteenth Amendment	728	7%	426	1%

[F]ederal courts grant a very small proportion of habeas petitions, typically less than one in a hundred in state court and . . . the claims raised do not affect the petitioner's success rate. The picture in state courts is somewhat different. For prosecutorial misconduct and Fourth, Fifth and Sixth Amendment claims, petitioner's success rates in state courts is comparable to the low success rate in federal courts. The success rate for Eighth Amendment claims was markedly different. Further analysis revealed that 41 of the 149 petitions granted involved questions of excessive bail in New York. Eleven of the 41 granted petitions involved coerced guilty pleas. Ineffective assistance of counsel, trial court error and Fourteenth Amendment concerns were also granted at a higher rate. . . .

The Flango study reveals the practical importance of ineffective assistance of counsel claims on collateral challenges made in both state and federal courts. Are there stronger arguments, in general, for using collateral review primarily to assess ineffective assistance claims as opposed to directly addressing the underlying substantive claims (e.g. an issue that an attorney failed to raise, or the impact of facts the attorney failed to develop)? Do the following statutes and case explain the focus on effective assistance issues?

■ 42 PENNSYLVANIA CONSOLIDATED STATUTES §9543

(a) General rule.—To be eligible for relief under this subchapter, the petitioner must plead and prove by a preponderance of the evidence . . .

(2) That the conviction or sentence resulted from one or more of the following: . . .

(ii) Ineffective assistance of counsel which, in the circumstances of the particular case, so undermined the truth-determining process that no reliable adjudication of guilt or innocence could have taken place.

(3) That the allegation of error has not been previously litigated or waived.

(4) That the failure to litigate the issue prior to or during trial, during unitary review or on direct appeal could not have been the result of any rational, strategic or tactical decision by counsel.

■ DONALD DUNCAN v. DARELD KERBY

851 P.2d 466 (N.M. 1993)

FROST, J.

The State of New Mexico appeals from the district court's grant of a writ of habeas corpus to prisoner Donald Duncan. This appeal raises two issues: (1) whether the doctrine of *res judicata* bars a defendant's postconviction claim of ineffective assistance of counsel when the same claim has been denied on the merits in a direct appeal, and (2) whether the trial court erred in granting petitioner's writ of habeas corpus on the grounds of ineffective assistance of counsel. We hold that the doctrine of *res judicata* does not apply in this particular case, and affirm the trial court's grant of habeas corpus relief on the grounds of ineffective assistance of counsel.

Donald Duncan was convicted on six counts of criminal sexual penetration and incest in 1985. On direct appeal with a new attorney, Duncan argued that his conviction should be reversed because he did not receive effective assistance of counsel at trial. The Court of Appeals assessed and rejected the ineffective counsel claim on the merits and affirmed the conviction. Duncan then petitioned the district court for a writ of habeas corpus, requesting post-conviction relief on the grounds of ineffective assistance of counsel. After holding an evidentiary hearing on the issue of counsel's effectiveness, [the judge who] had presided over Duncan's jury trial determined that Duncan had not received effective assistance of counsel at trial, granted the writ of habeas corpus, set aside Duncan's conviction, and ordered a new trial. The judge found that material lapses in the trial attorney's performance leading to a conclusion of incompetent representation included the failure to construct an available and crucial alibi defense, to call key witnesses, and to move to sever offenses.

The State argues that Duncan's ineffective assistance of counsel claim is barred by the doctrine of *res judicata* in this post-conviction action because the same claim was raised and rejected on direct appeal. We have held that New Mexico post-conviction procedures are not a substitute for direct appeal and that our statutes do not require collateral review of issues when the facts submitted were known or available to the petitioner at the time of his trial. When a defendant should have raised an issue on direct appeal, but failed to do so, he or she may be precluded from raising the issue in habeas corpus proceedings. A habeas corpus petitioner will not be precluded, however, from raising issues in habeas corpus proceedings that could have been raised on direct appeal either when fundamental error has occurred, or when an adequate record to address the claim properly was not available on direct appeal. Our habeas corpus cases applying preclusion have not involved instances in which a defendant could not make an evidentiary case for himself on direct appeal because facts supporting his claim were not part of the record. The proper exception to the application of the doctrine of res judicata in such circumstances has been described as follows:

> If an application [for a writ of habeas corpus] is grounded in facts beyond the record previously presented on appeal, and if the additional facts are those which could not, or customarily would not, be developed in a trial on criminal charges, there should be no issue preclusion. . . . When a post-conviction application makes a substantial showing that due process or another fundamental right has been abridged — and the application is supported by facts ill-suited for development in the original trial — it should be addressed on its merits. *Res judicata* does not apply.

State v. Darbin, 708 P.2d 921, 931 (Idaho Ct. App. 1985) (Burnett, J., specially concurring). We adopt this rationale.

[Habeas] corpus proceedings [are] the preferred avenue for adjudicating ineffective assistance of counsel claims. The rationale is that even assuming that a criminal defendant has a new attorney to handle his direct appeal, the record before the trial court may not adequately document the sort of evidence essential to a determination of trial counsel's effectiveness because conviction proceedings focus on the defendant's misconduct rather than that of his attorney. Consequently, an evidentiary hearing on the issue of trial counsel's effectiveness may be necessary. While this may be done through a remand to the trial court during direct appeal when unusual circumstances exist, habeas corpus is specifically designed to address such post-conviction constitutional claims and is the procedure of choice in this situation. It would be inconsistent to recommend habeas corpus for ineffective assistance of counsel claims and then to deny a convicted defendant the ability to use habeas procedure because he was fortunate enough to obtain new counsel on direct appeal and raise the issue at that time. . . .

The State calls our attention to Manlove v. Sullivan, 775 P.2d 237 (N.M. 1989), as part of its argument that Duncan is precluded from relitigating his ineffective assistance of counsel claim in habeas corpus proceedings. *Manlove* observed that when a petitioner brings successive petitions for habeas relief, "collateral estoppel principles may, at the discretion of a subsequent habeas corpus court, prevent relitigation of issues argued and decided on a previous habeas corpus petition." Clearly,

Manlove is procedurally and theoretically distinguishable from this case because it deals with the preclusive effect of issues raised in successive petitions for writs of habeas corpus rather than with the preclusive effect of issues raised initially on direct appeal. The successive-writ petitioner has already enjoyed the opportunity to fully explore his constitutional claims in the postconviction setting, whereas the petitioner who makes his initial claim on direct appeal has not, and consequently, the successive-writ petitioner is in a weaker position to argue that equity confers yet another post-conviction opportunity to make his claim.

Our view of the nature of res judicata in the habeas corpus setting as an equitable, discretionary, and flexible judicial doctrine leads us to conclude that the decision to give preclusive effect to an ineffective assistance of counsel claim rejected on direct appeal but raised again in habeas corpus proceedings is within the sound discretion of the reviewing court. Courts reviewing habeas corpus petitions should decide whether particular claims are *res judicata* based on relevant facts and circumstances, including whether or not a full evidentiary hearing on counsel's effectiveness was previously conducted when that claim is at issue. While redundant claims may be precluded, courts should not impede post-conviction litigation that will provide necessary fuller or fairer procedural opportunities to examine alleged constitutional defects when consideration of an issue on direct appeal is based upon facts which could not, or customarily would not, be developed at trial. . . .

When this Court addresses the propriety of a lower court's grant or denial of a writ of habeas corpus based on ineffective assistance of counsel, findings of fact of the trial court concerning the habeas petition are reviewed to determine if substantial evidence supports the court's findings. Questions of law or questions of mixed fact and law, however, including the assessment of effective assistance of counsel, are reviewed de novo. This approach . . . parallels federal habeas corpus appellate review practice[2] [and] provides logical deference to the trial court fact-finder as first-hand observer. . . .

Duncan's claim of ineffective assistance of counsel was first presented on his direct appeal. Although the grounds alleged in support of Duncan's ineffective assistance of counsel argument were basically the same on direct appeal and in the habeas corpus proceedings, the evidence available in the two proceedings was dramatically different. Duncan's principal contention was that his trial counsel was ineffective because he did not investigate or adequately present Duncan's alibi defense. Reviewing the record to evaluate this argument, the Court of Appeals found on direct appeal that, "the record does not contain any indication whether counsel did or did not investigate this [alibi] defense. It only indicates that counsel chose not to corroborate the defense through witnesses other than defendant."

The evidence available concerning counsel's effectiveness was significantly more extensive at the three-day habeas corpus hearing than at Duncan's direct appeal. Evidence presented at the habeas corpus hearing supporting Duncan's claim included the following: Mr. Arnold Miller, Duncan's trial attorney, did not call five credible and available alibi witnesses; these five witnesses were known to Miller and

2. Federal appellate courts review findings of fact under the clearly erroneous standard of review. Fed. R. Civ. P. 52(a). The New Mexico parallel provision and habeas corpus statute do not adopt the "clearly erroneous" language. See SCRA 1986, 1-052; SCRA 1986, 5-802. Thus, although we review the habeas trial court's findings of fact with deference similar to the federal model, our degree of deference is more accurately termed a review for support by substantial evidence as that standard is applied in New Mexico.

were prepared to testify that Duncan was with them when the crimes allegedly occurred; Miller did not call other witnesses who would have impeached key prosecution witnesses, especially the victims; and several of the defense witnesses who were not called were standing outside the courtroom during Duncan's trial, waiting to be called. The State's evidence at the habeas hearing consisted of Miller's testimony, which attempted to rationalize his alleged failures.

Substantial evidence supports the lower court's conclusion that Duncan did not receive effective assistance of counsel at trial. To succeed on a constitutional claim of ineffective assistance of counsel, the defendant or habeas corpus petitioner must prove that defense counsel did not exercise the skill of a reasonably competent attorney and that such incompetent representation prejudiced his case, rendering the trial court's result unreliable. Strickland v. Washington, 466 U.S. 668 (1984). In considering an ineffectiveness claim, the evaluation should focus on whether an attorney exercised "the skill, judgment and diligence of a reasonably competent defense attorney" in light of the entire proceeding allegedly tainted by incompetent representation. Because substantial evidence supports the district court's findings of fact, we presume these findings to be correct, and undertake de novo review of counsel's effectiveness.

Duncan's trial attorney did not represent him competently. Based on the evidentiary hearing at the trial level of this habeas corpus action, Judge Schnedar found that Miller inexcusably failed to give notice of the alibi defense or call alibi witnesses crucial to Duncan's defense. Miller also did not investigate possible attacks on the credibility of State's witnesses or move to sever counts as related to each victim. Miller's trial preparation was not adequate, and his intentional failure to disclose his mistake of not giving notice of alibi defense compounded his shortcomings, breaching his duty of loyalty to the defendant. We disagree with the State's characterization of these failures as reasonable litigation tactics and find that such a performance falls below an objective level of competent legal representation.

We further agree with the district court that Duncan's incompetent representation prejudiced his case such that but for counsel's error, there is a reasonable probability that the result of the conviction proceedings would have been different. . . . The trial court found that "Miller's conduct undermined the proper function of the adversarial procedure and it cannot be relied upon as having produced a just result." It further found that had Duncan received competent representation, his trial "could have resulted in a prosecution verdict, a defense verdict or a hung jury." . . . Our own review of the trial court's findings enforces our belief that Duncan's defense was prejudiced by his counsel's performance and that his conviction, therefore, cannot stand.

For the foregoing reasons, the decision of the district court granting habeas relief is affirmed.

Notes

1. *Ineffective assistance claims on collateral review: majority position.* The *Duncan* case explains that the capacity for additional factfinding, especially of matters occurring outside of the trial courtroom, makes collateral review especially appropriate for reviewing claims of ineffective assistance of counsel. See People v. Tello, 933 P.2d 1134, 1136 (Cal. 1997) (rules generally prohibiting raising an issue on habeas corpus that

was, or could have been, raised on appeal would not bar an ineffective assistance claim on habeas corpus). Federal courts may grant relief on habeas corpus for an attorney's failure to raise a Fourth Amendment claim at trial or on appeal, even though under the doctrine of Stone v. Powell, 428 U.S. 465 (1976), the federal habeas court could not address the merits of the Fourth Amendment claim itself. See Kimmelman v. Morrison, 477 U.S. 365 (1986).

The Flango study confirms that ineffective assistance of counsel is the most common claim in both state and federal systems. In state systems, claims of ineffective assistance are among the most *successful,* while this does not appear to be true in the federal system. What might be the source of this difference? Is the Pennsylvania statute consistent with or in tension with the generally more sympathetic legal posture towards ineffective assistance claims?

2. *Ineffective assistance by collateral review counsel.* Some states provide appointed counsel for collateral review, at least in cases where courts have determined that a petition raises a substantial claim. For example, Tex. Code. Crim. Pro. 1.051(d)(3) authorizes a trial court to appoint counsel to indigent capital defendants in state habeas corpus proceedings "if the court concludes that the interests of justice require representation." See Tex. Op. Atty. Gen. 1995, No. DM-354. When habeas counsel is appointed by a court, the performance of that counsel can typically be challenged as ineffective in later proceedings. See Crump v. Demosthenes, 934 P.2d 247 (Nev. 1997). However, where there is no statutory or constitutional basis for appointing counsel on habeas corpus review, some courts refuse to consider later ineffective assistance claims regarding representation in prior habeas corpus proceedings. See McKague v. Whitely, 912 P.2d 255 (Nev. 1996). How might you explain this different treatment?

3. *Empirical analysis of collateral review.* The Flango study is one of only a handful of empirical studies of habeas corpus and other forms of collateral review. The years since the Flango study have seen major changes in both federal and state law, and further empirical work is needed. The centrality of ineffective assistance claims to collateral attacks may have become even more pronounced.

The Flango study noted that a majority of habeas petitioners were convicted after trial rather than a plea. Consider the effect and wisdom of Nev. Rev. Stat. §34.810(1): "The court shall dismiss a petition if the court determines that [t]he petitioner's conviction was upon a plea of guilty or guilty but mentally ill and the petition is not based upon an allegation that the plea was involuntarily or unknowingly entered or that the plea was entered without effective assistance of counsel."

The Flango study indicates a very low rate of success for habeas petitioners in both state and federal systems. Why, then, has habeas corpus remained so controversial? First, the tension between finality and continuing claims of denial of justice is a real tension, however a particular court resolves it. This tension is heightened for some classes of cases, especially cases where there is a claim of "true innocence" and in capital cases, where the consequences of finality are obviously more "final" than for other cases. Second, a small handful of habeas corpus petitions are truly silly, but sometimes these cases receive a fair amount of publicity, and therefore help to shape legislative and popular concerns. Under the heading of "ridiculous cases make bad law" are claims by prisoners that the substitution of smooth for chunky peanut butter or nutra loaf for actual meat loaf constitutes "cruel and unusual" punishment. Third, even as collateral review doctrines have tended to restrict access to collateral review in both state and federal courts, the number of cases remains substantial (though the success rate and the grounds for disposition may be changing, along with the time burden on the courts).

4. *Ineffective assistance of counsel in death cases.* Claims of ineffective assistance of counsel take on a special power and poignancy in death penalty cases, where the person responsible for the error and the person suffering the consequences are different. Capital appellate advocate Stephen Bright has noted:

> Poor people accused of capital crimes are often defended by lawyers who lack the skills, resources, and commitment to handle such serious matters. This fact is confirmed in case after case. It is not the facts of the crime, but the quality of legal representation, that distinguishes this case, where the death penalty was imposed, from many similar cases, where it was not. . . .
>
> A poor person facing the death penalty may be assigned an attorney who has little or no experience in the defense of capital or even serious criminal cases, one reluctant or unwilling to defend him, one with little or no empathy or understanding of the accused or his particular plight, one with little or no knowledge of criminal or capital punishment law, or one with no understanding of the need to document and present mitigating circumstances. Although it is widely acknowledged that at least two lawyers, supported by investigative and expert assistance, are required to defend a capital case, some of the jurisdictions with the largest number of death sentences still assign only one lawyer to defend a capital case. . . . Lawyers can make more money doing almost anything else. Even many lawyers who have an interest in criminal defense work simply cannot afford to continue to represent indigents while also repaying their student loans and meeting their familial obligations.

Stephen Bright, Counsel for the Poor: The Death Sentence Not for the Worst Crime but for the Worst Lawyer, 103 Yale L. J. 1835, 1836, 1845-1846, 1850 (1994).

C. FEDERAL HABEAS CORPUS REVIEW OF STATE CONVICTIONS

The modern debate in the United States over habeas corpus has not primarily been a debate about the division of labor between appeals and later collateral reviews of convictions — the topic considered in the prior sections. Instead, the debate has centered on whether and to what extent federal courts (and especially federal district courts) should review final state convictions. This is as much a debate about federalism as about habeas corpus. One reason this topic has generated so much heat in the last few decades may be suggested by the number of habeas corpus petitions filed by state prisoners in federal court (technically petitions under the federal habeas corpus statute, 28 U.S.C. §2254). State prisoners filed 1020 federal petitions in 1961, 8372 petitions in 1971, 7786 petitions in 1981, 10,325 petitions in 1991, and 21,345 petitions in 2000. See Bureau of Justice Statistics, Prisoner Petitions Filed in U.S. District Courts, 2000, with Trends, 1980-2000 (2002) (NCJ 189430).

The absolute number of federal habeas petitions by state prisoners is higher than ever, and reveals that habeas corpus petitions occupy a noticeable portion of the workload for the federal courts. Nevertheless, the absolute number of petitions may overstate the impact of federal review on state criminal justice, because the

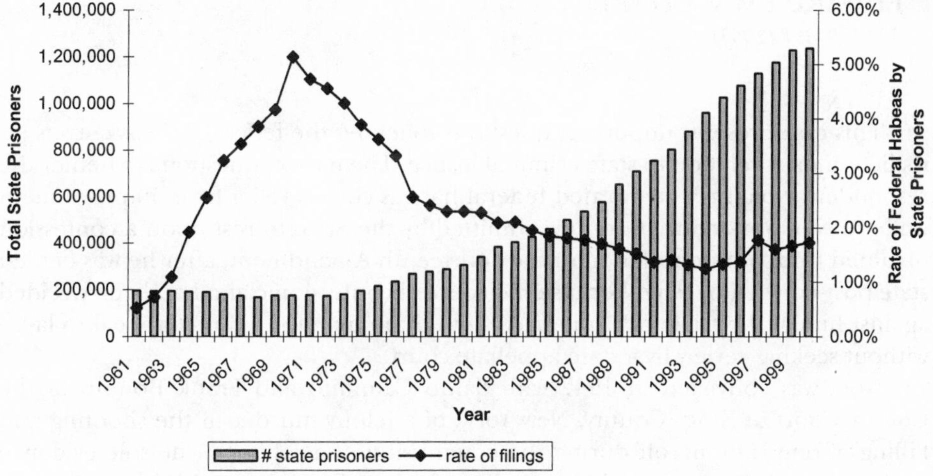

Rate of Federal Habeas Petitioners by State Prisoners

number of state prisoners has increased far more quickly than the number of federal petitions. This data does not describe the rate of federal habeas petitions (i.e., what proportion of state inmates file a federal petition in any given year) or the number of petitions where a federal court actually grants relief. Consider the chart above, illustrating the rate of federal petitions filed by state prisoners between 1961 and 2000.

This chart suggests a dramatic change in federal habeas corpus in the early 1960s. The most important development was the 1963 U.S. Supreme Court decision in Fay v. Noia. The chart also suggests that the rate of federal habeas petitions by state prisoners had returned by 1994 to about what it was in 1963, when *Fay* was decided. This section considers the expansion and contraction of federal review of state convictions through habeas corpus over the past three decades.

1. *Expansion*

Habeas corpus was available in state courts from the earliest days of the nation, but the Judiciary Act of 1789 provided habeas corpus in federal court only for federal prisoners. After the Civil War, the Reconstruction Congress authorized federal courts to review convictions obtained in state courts as part of its general effort to strengthen the national government. However, the Habeas Corpus Act of 1867 did not lead to many challenges of state convictions until the middle of the twentieth century. At about the same time that the U.S. Supreme Court began to expand the influence of the federal constitution in state criminal justice systems (by "incorporating" various parts of the Bill of Rights against the states under the fourteenth amendment), the Court also started to read the habeas corpus statute more broadly. Habeas corpus became the leading procedural mechanism for the federal courts to enforce the new dictates of federal law. As you read the following case, ask whether the Supreme Court had other viable options for enforcing newly announced constitutional requirements.

■ EDWARD FAY v. CHARLES NOIA

372 U.S. 391 (1963)

BRENNAN, J.

This case presents important questions touching the federal habeas corpus jurisdiction in its relation to state criminal justice. The narrow question is whether the respondent Noia may be granted federal habeas corpus relief from imprisonment under a New York conviction now admitted by the State to rest upon a confession obtained from him in violation of the Fourteenth Amendment, after he was denied state post-conviction relief because the coerced confession claim had been decided against him at the trial and Noia had allowed the time for a direct appeal to lapse without seeking review by a state appellate court.

Noia was convicted in 1942 with Santo Caminito and Frank Bonino in the County Court of Kings County, New York, of a felony murder in the shooting and killing of one Hammeroff during the commission of a robbery. The sole evidence against each defendant was his signed confession. Caminito and Bonino, but not Noia, appealed their convictions to the Appellate Division of the New York Supreme Court. These appeals were unsuccessful, but subsequent legal proceedings resulted in the releases of Caminito and Bonino on findings that their confessions had been coerced and their convictions therefore procured in violation of the Fourteenth Amendment. Although it has been stipulated that the coercive nature of Noia's confession was also established, the United States District Court for the Southern District of New York held in Noia's federal habeas corpus proceeding that because of his failure to appeal he must be denied relief. [We hold that federal] courts have power under the federal habeas statute to grant relief despite the applicant's failure to have pursued a state remedy not available to him at the time he applies; the doctrine under which state procedural defaults are held to constitute an adequate and independent state law ground barring direct Supreme Court review is not to be extended to limit the power granted the federal courts under the federal habeas statute. . . . Noia's failure to appeal cannot under the circumstances be deemed an intelligent and understanding waiver of his right to appeal such as to justify the withholding of federal habeas corpus relief. . . .

We do well to bear in mind the extraordinary prestige of the Great Writ, habeas corpus ad subjiciendum, in Anglo-American jurisprudence. [Its] function has been to provide a prompt and efficacious remedy for whatever society deems to be intolerable restraints. its root principle is that in a civilized society, government must always be accountable to the judiciary for a man's imprisonment. . . . There is nothing novel in the fact that today habeas corpus in the federal courts provides a mode for the redress of denials of due process of law. Vindication of due process is precisely its historic office.

[The] nature and purpose of habeas corpus have remained remarkably constant. . . . The principle that judicial as well as executive restraints may be intolerable received dramatic expression in Bushell's Case, 124 Eng. Rep. 1006 (1670). Bushell was one of the jurors in the trial, held before the Court of Oyer and Terminer at the Old Bailey, of William Penn and William Mead on charges of tumultuous assembly and other crimes. When the jury brought in a verdict of not guilty, the court ordered the jurors committed for contempt. Bushell sought habeas corpus, and the Court of Common Pleas, in a memorable opinion by Chief Justice Vaughan, ordered him discharged from custody. The case is by no means isolated, and when habeas corpus practice was codified in the Habeas Corpus Act of 1679, 31 Car. II, c. 2, no distinction was made between executive and judicial detentions.

Nor is it true that at common law habeas corpus was available only to inquire into the jurisdiction, in a narrow sense, of the committing court. Bushell's Case is again in point. Chief Justice Vaughan did not base his decision on the theory that the Court of Oyer and Terminer had no jurisdiction to commit persons for contempt, but on the plain denial of due process, violative of Magna Charta, of a court's imprisoning the jury because it disagreed with the verdict. . . .

Thus, at the time that the Suspension Clause was written into our Federal Constitution and the first Judiciary Act was passed conferring habeas corpus jurisdiction upon the federal judiciary, there was respectable common-law authority for the proposition that habeas was available to remedy any kind of governmental restraint contrary to fundamental law.

[Although the Habeas Corpus Act] of 1867, like its English and American predecessors, nowhere defines habeas corpus, its expansive language and imperative tone, viewed against the background of post-Civil War efforts in Congress to deal severely with the States of the former Confederacy, would seem to make inescapable the conclusion that Congress was enlarging the habeas remedy as previously understood, not only in extending its coverage to state prisoners, but also in making its procedures more efficacious. In 1867, Congress was anticipating resistance to its Reconstruction measures and planning the implementation of the post-war constitutional Amendments. Debated and enacted at the very peak of the Radical Republicans' power, the measure that became the Act of 1867 seems plainly to have been designed to furnish a method additional to and independent of direct Supreme Court review of state court decisions for the vindication of the new constitutional guarantees. Congress seems to have had no thought, thus, that a state prisoner should abide state court determination of his constitutional defense — the necessary predicate of direct review by this Court — before resorting to federal habeas corpus. Rather, a remedy almost in the nature of removal from the state to the federal courts of state prisoners' constitutional contentions seems to have been envisaged. . . .

The breadth of the federal courts' power of independent adjudication on habeas corpus stems from the very nature of the writ. . . . It is of the historical essence of habeas corpus that it lies to test proceedings so fundamentally lawless that imprisonment pursuant to them is not merely erroneous but void. [T]he traditional characterization of the writ of habeas corpus as an original . . . civil remedy for the enforcement of the right to personal liberty, rather than as a stage of the state criminal proceedings or as an appeal therefrom, emphasizes the independence of the federal habeas proceedings from what has gone before. This is not to say that a state criminal judgment resting on a constitutional error is void for all purposes. But conventional notions of finality in criminal litigation cannot be permitted to defeat the manifest federal policy that federal constitutional rights of personal liberty shall not be denied without the fullest opportunity for plenary federal judicial review.

[T]he question of the instant case has obvious importance to the proper accommodation of a great constitutional privilege and the requirements of the federal system. [W]e have consistently held that federal court jurisdiction is conferred by the allegation of an unconstitutional restraint and is not defeated by anything that may occur in the state court proceedings. State procedural rules plainly must yield to this overriding federal policy.

A number of arguments are advanced against this conclusion. One, which concedes the breadth of federal habeas power, is that a state prisoner who forfeits his opportunity to vindicate federal defenses in the state court has been given all the process that is constitutionally due him, and hence is not restrained contrary to the Constitution. . . . But this ignores the important difference between rights and particular remedies. A defendant by committing a procedural default may be debarred from challenging his conviction in the state courts even on federal constitutional grounds. But a forfeiture of remedies does not legitimize the unconstitutional conduct by which his conviction was procured. . . . In what sense is Noia's custody not in violation of federal law simply because New York will not allow him to challenge it? . . .

Although we hold that the jurisdiction of the federal courts on habeas corpus is not affected by procedural defaults incurred by the applicant during the state court proceedings, we recognize a limited discretion in the federal judge to deny relief to an applicant under certain circumstances. [The] federal habeas judge may in his discretion deny relief to an applicant who has deliberately by-passed the orderly procedure of the state courts and in so doing has forfeited his state court remedies. But we wish to make very clear that this grant of discretion is not to be interpreted as a permission to introduce legal fictions into federal habeas corpus. The classic definition of waiver enunciated in Johnson v. Zerbst, 304 U.S. 458 (1938)—"an intentional relinquishment or abandonment of a known right or privilege"—furnishes the controlling standard. If a habeas applicant, after consultation with competent counsel or otherwise, understandingly and knowingly forewent the privilege of seeking to vindicate his federal claims in the state courts, whether for strategic, tactical, or any other reasons that can fairly be described as the deliberate by-passing of state procedures, then it is open to the federal court on habeas to deny him all relief if the state courts refused to entertain his federal claims on the merits—though of course only after the federal court has satisfied itself, by holding a hearing or by some other means, of the facts bearing upon the applicant's default. At all events we wish it clearly understood that the standard here put forth depends on the considered choice of the petitioner. A choice made by counsel not participated in by the petitioner does not automatically bar relief. Nor does a state court's finding of waiver bar independent determination of the question by the federal courts on habeas, for waiver affecting federal rights is a federal question.

The application of the standard we have adumbrated to the facts of the instant case is not difficult. Under no reasonable view can the State's version of Noia's reason for not appealing support an inference of deliberate by-passing of the state court system. For Noia to have appealed in 1942 would have been to run a substantial risk of electrocution. His was the grisly choice whether to sit content with life imprisonment or to travel the uncertain avenue of appeal which, if successful, might well have led to a retrial and death sentence. He declined to play Russian roulette in this fashion. . . . Surely no fair-minded person will contend that those who have been deprived of their liberty without due process of law ought nevertheless to languish in prison. . . . If the States withhold effective remedy, the federal courts have the power and the duty to provide it. Habeas corpus is one of the precious heritages of Anglo-American civilization. We do no more today than confirm its continuing efficacy. . . .

CLARK, J., dissenting.

[There] can be no question but that a rash of new applications from state prisoners will pour into the federal courts, and 98% of them will be frivolous, if history is any guide.[1] This influx will necessarily have an adverse effect upon the disposition of meritorious applications, for, as my Brother Jackson said, they will "be buried in a flood of worthless ones. He who must search a haystack for a needle is likely to end up with the attitude that the needle is not worth the search." Brown v. Allen, 344 U.S. 443 (1953) (concurring opinion). In fact, the courts are already swamped with applications which cannot, because of sheer numbers, be given more than cursory attention.[2] . . .

Essential to the administration of justice is the prompt enforcement of judicial decrees. After today state judgments will be relegated to a judicial limbo, subject to federal collateral attack — as here — a score of years later despite a defendant's willful failure to appeal. . . .

HARLAN, J. dissenting.

This decision, both in its abrupt break with the past and in its consequences for the future, is one of the most disquieting that the Court has rendered in a long time. . . .

The formative stage of the development of habeas corpus jurisdiction may be said to have ended in 1915, the year in which Frank v. Mangum, 237 U.S. 309, was decided. During this period the federal courts, on applications for habeas corpus complaining of detention pursuant to a judgment of conviction and sentence, purported to examine only the jurisdiction of the sentencing tribunal. In the leading case of Ex parte Watkins, 3 Pet. 193 (1830), the Court stated: "An imprisonment under a judgment cannot be unlawful, unless that judgment be an absolute nullity; and it is not a nullity if the court has general jurisdiction of the subject, although it should be erroneous." Many subsequent decisions . . . reaffirmed the limitation of the writ to consideration of the sentencing court's jurisdiction over the person of the defendant and the subject matter of the suit.

The concept of jurisdiction, however, was subjected to considerable strain during this period, and the strain was not lessened by the fact that until the latter part of the last century, federal criminal convictions were not generally reviewable by the Supreme Court. The expansion of the definition of jurisdiction occurred primarily in two classes of cases: (1) those in which the conviction was for violation of an allegedly unconstitutional statute, and (2) those in which the Court viewed the detention as based on some claimed illegality in the sentence imposed, as distinguished from the judgment of conviction. . . .

The next stage of development may be described as beginning in 1915 with Frank v. Mangum, 237 U.S. 309, and ending in 1953 with Brown v. Allen, 344 U.S. 443. In *Frank,* the prisoner had claimed before the state courts that the proceedings in which he had been convicted for murder had been dominated by a mob, and the State Supreme Court, after consideration not only of the record but of extensive affidavits, had concluded that mob domination had not been established. Frank then sought federal habeas, and this Court affirmed the denial of relief. But in doing so the Court recognized that Frank's allegation of mob domination raised a constitutional question which he was entitled to have considered by a competent tribunal uncoerced by popular pressures. Such "corrective process" had been afforded by

1. In the 12-year period from 1946 to 1957 the petitioners were successful in 1.4% of the cases.

2. The increase in number of habeas corpus applications filed in Federal District Courts by state prisoners is illustrated by the following figures: 127 in 1941; 536 in 1945; 560 in 1950; 660 in 1955; 872 in 1960; 906 in 1961; 1,232 in 1962.

the State Supreme Court, however, and since Frank had received "notice, and a hearing, or an opportunity to be heard" on his constitutional claims his detention was not in violation of federal law and habeas corpus would not lie.

It is clear that a new dimension was added to habeas corpus in this case, for in addition to questions previously thought of as "jurisdictional," the federal courts were now to consider whether the applicant had been given an adequate opportunity to raise his constitutional claims before the state courts. And if no such opportunity had been afforded in the state courts, the federal claim would be heard on its merits. . . . But habeas would not lie to reconsider constitutional questions that had been fairly determined. And a fortiori it would not lie to consider a question when the state court's refusal to do so rested on an adequate and independent state ground. . . .

In 1953, this Court rendered its landmark decisions in Brown v. Allen and Daniels v. Allen, 344 U.S. 443, 482-87 (1953). Both cases involved applications for federal habeas corpus by prisoners who were awaiting execution pursuant to state convictions. In both cases, the constitutional contentions made were that the trial court had erred in ruling confessions admissible and in overruling motions to quash the indictment on the basis of alleged discrimination in the selection of jurors.

In *Brown,* these contentions had been presented to the highest court of the State, on direct appeal from the conviction, and had been rejected by that court on the merits, after which this Court had denied certiorari. At this point, the Court held, Brown was entitled to full reconsideration of these constitutional claims, with a hearing if appropriate, in an application to a Federal District Court for habeas corpus. It is manifest that this decision substantially expanded the scope of inquiry on an application for federal habeas corpus. . . .

But what if the validity of the state decision to detain rested not on the determination of a federal claim but rather on an adequate nonfederal ground which would have barred direct review by this Court? That was the question in *Daniels.* The attorney for the petitioners in that case had failed to mail the appeal papers on the last day for filing, and although he delivered them by hand the next day, the State Supreme Court refused to entertain the appeal, ruling that it had not been filed on time. This ruling, this Court held, barred federal habeas corpus consideration of the claims that the state appellate court had refused to consider. [H]abeas corpus would not lie for a prisoner who was detained pursuant to a state judgment which, in the view of the majority in *Daniels,* rested on a reasonable application of the State's own procedural requirements. . . .

The true significance of today's decision can perhaps best be laid bare in terms of a hypothetical case presenting questions of the powers of this Court on direct review, and of a Federal District Court on habeas corpus. Assume that a man is indicted, and held for trial in a state court, by a grand jury from which members of his race have been systematically excluded. Assume further that the State requires any objection to the composition of the grand jury to be raised prior to the verdict, that no such objection is made, and that the defendant seeks to raise the point for the first time on appeal from his conviction. If the state appellate court refuses to consider the claim because it was raised too late, and if certiorari is sought and granted, the initial question before this Court will be whether there was an adequate state ground for the judgment below. If the petitioner was represented by counsel not shown to be incompetent, and if the necessary information to make the objection is not shown to have been unavailable at the time of trial, it is certain that the judgment of conviction will stand, despite the fact the indictment was obtained in violation of the petitioner's constitutional rights. . . .

For this Court to go beyond the adequacy of the state ground and to review and determine the correctness of that ground on its merits would, in our hypothetical case, be to assume full control over a State's procedures for the administration of its own criminal justice. This is and must be beyond our power if the federal system is to exist in substance as well as form. The right of the State to regulate its own procedures governing the conduct of litigants in its courts, and its interest in supervision of those procedures, stand on the same constitutional plane as its right and interest in framing "substantive" laws governing other aspects of the conduct of those within its borders.

The adequate state ground doctrine thus finds its source in basic constitutional principles, and the question before us is whether this is as true in a collateral attack in habeas corpus as on direct review. Assume, then, that after dismissal of the writ of certiorari in our hypothetical case, the prisoner seeks habeas corpus in a Federal District Court, again complaining of the composition of the grand jury that indicted him. Is that federal court constitutionally more free than the Supreme Court on direct review to "ignore" the adequate state ground, proceed to the federal question, and order the prisoner's release?

The answer must be that it is not. . . . In habeas as on direct review, ordering the prisoner's release invalidates the judgment of conviction and renders ineffective the state rule relied upon to sustain that judgment. Try as the majority does to turn habeas corpus into a roving commission of inquiry into every possible invasion of the applicant's civil rights that may ever have occurred, it cannot divorce the writ from a judgment of conviction if that judgment is the basis of the detention. . . . The effect of the approach adopted by the Court is, indeed, to do away with the adequate state ground rule entirely in every state case, involving a federal question, in which detention follows from a judgment.

[The substitute that the Court] has fashioned — that of "conscious waiver" or "deliberate bypassing" of state procedures — is . . . wholly unsatisfactory. [It] amounts to no limitation at all. [The] Court states . . . that "[a] choice made by counsel not participated in by the petitioner does not automatically bar relief." It is true that there are cases in which the adequacy of the state ground necessarily turns on the question whether the defendant himself expressly and intelligently waived a constitutional right. Foremost among these are the cases involving right to counsel, for the Court has made it clear that this right cannot be foregone without deliberate choice by the defendant. See Johnson v. Zerbst, 304 U.S. 458 (1938). But to carry this principle over in full force to cases in which a defendant is represented by counsel not shown to be incompetent is to undermine the entire representational system.

[When] it comes to apply the "waiver" test in this case, the Court . . . seems to be saying . . . that no waiver of a right can be effective if some adverse consequence might reasonably be expected to follow from exercise of that right. Under this approach, of course, there could never be a binding waiver, since only an incompetent would give up a right without any good reason, and an incompetent cannot make an intelligent waiver. . . .

It is the adequacy, or fairness, of the state ground that should be the controlling question in this case. This controlling question the Court does not discuss. . . . Certainly the State has a vital interest in requiring that appeals be taken on the basis of facts known at the time, since the first assertion of a claim many years later might otherwise require release long after it was feasible to hold a new trial. . . .

I recognize that Noia's predicament may well be thought one that strongly calls for correction. But the proper course to that end lies with the New York Governor's powers of executive clemency, not with the federal courts. Since Noia is detained pursuant to a state judgment whose validity rests on an adequate and independent state ground, the judgment below should be reversed.

Notes

1. *Legal revolutions.* How does Justice Brennan cast the majority decision in *Fay* as an extension of tradition rather than a legal revolution? Do the dissents make a compelling case that *Fay* was a revolution? Could both be correct? Arguments about the historical scope of the federal habeas corpus writ must deal with many seemingly inconsistent Supreme Court cases, describing the writ in both broad and narrow terms. Some of the broader pronouncements about the scope of habeas corpus could be explained away (just as Justice Harlan did in his dissent) as aberrations, or as modest extensions of the traditional idea that a habeas court may review the "jurisdiction" of the criminal court or the legality of the sentence. On the other hand, the narrower pronouncements could be explained (as in Justice Brennan's opinion) as the result of the historically narrow scope of Supreme Court criminal appeals jurisdiction, or the narrow scope of the due process concept, rather than the narrow scope of the habeas remedy itself.

Whatever its exact relationship to past developments, the decision in Fay v. Noia marked the beginning of a high-water period of federal habeas corpus review. See Sanders v. United States, 373 U.S. 1 (1963) (expanding availability of successive federal petitions); Townsend v. Sain, 372 U.S. 293 (1963) (expanding availability of factfinding hearing in federal habeas proceedings). At a time when the Court was expanding the reach of the federal constitution, it gave lower federal courts broader authority than ever before to review state convictions. See Robert Cover & Alexander Aleinikoff, Dialectical Federalism: Habeas Corpus and the Court, 86 Yale L.J. 1035 (1977).

The high water of federal habeas corpus started to recede only a decade after the decision in Fay v. Noia. We have already seen that *Fay* itself has been overruled in the federal system. In Wainwright v. Sykes, 433 U.S. 72 (1977), the Court gave renewed importance to the procedural requirements that state courts place on criminal defendants, and replaced the "deliberate bypass" standard with the "cause and prejudice" standard. See also Coleman v. Thompson, 501 U.S. 722 (1991) (rejecting deliberate bypass standard for failure to raise issue on state appeal). Does the relationship between federal and state courts influence the sort of "procedural default" doctrine that should apply on federal habeas corpus, or would the same doctrine be relevant whenever *any* court in collateral proceedings is evaluating earlier criminal proceedings?

2. *Federal factfinding and presumptions.* A federal court ruling on a habeas corpus petition will need to draw some conclusions about facts, that is, historical facts that happened during the investigation and prosecution. What is the impact of the state courts' earlier rulings on questions of fact? For the most part, the federal habeas court must accept the facts as found in the state court proceedings. The federal

statute attaches a "presumption of correctness" to the factual findings of state courts. The party objecting to the state court's factual finding must ordinarily demonstrate to the federal court by "clear and convincing evidence" that the state court's finding was erroneous. The petitioner can avoid this presumption of correctness for state factfinding (and the resulting heavy burden of proof) by showing at the threshold that the state court engaged in a procedurally "unreasonable determination" of the facts "in light of the evidence presented in the State court proceeding." 28 U.S.C. §§2254(d)(2), (e)(1). The federal court reviews "mixed questions" of law and fact (as opposed to pure questions of basic, historical facts) under the same standards as issues of federal law. See Moore v. Dempsey, 261 U.S. 86 (1923) (Holmes, J.). Is the rationale for federal courts deferring to the factual findings of state courts different from the rationale for appellate courts deferring to trial courts on fact questions?

If the state courts have made no finding of facts on a relevant issue, the federal habeas court can conduct its own factfinding hearing only under very limited circumstances. Before 1996, judicial decisions defined the circumstances when a federal court could hold a factfinding hearing. See Townsend v. Sain, 372 U.S. 293 (1963) (creating broad powers for federal courts to hold evidentiary hearings on collateral review); Keeney v. Tamayo-Reyes, 504 U.S. 1 (1992) (applying cause and prejudice standard to determine when to hold evidentiary hearings). Under a 1996 revision to the federal habeas corpus statute, federal courts may conduct a hearing to determine facts that the petitioner "failed to develop" in the state courts only when (1) the petitioner had adequate "cause" for the failure to develop the facts—such as the appearance of a new rule of constitutional law made retroactive to habeas corpus petitions, or the need to determine facts that could not have been developed in state court despite the "due diligence" of the petitioner—*and* (2) the facts in question would establish a constitutional error that resulted in the conviction of an innocent defendant (in other words, "but for" the constitutional error, "no reasonable factfinder" would have found the petitioner guilty). 28 U.S.C. §2254(e)(2).

In Williams v. Taylor, 529 U.S. 420 (2000), the Supreme Court read the statute's "fails to develop" standard to require some showing of "fault" by the petitioner. A failure to develop a claim's factual basis "is not established unless there is lack of diligence, or some greater fault, attributable to the prisoner or his counsel." The necessary "diligence" under the statute requires a petitioner to make "a reasonable attempt, in light of the information available at the time, to investigate and pursue claims in state court." The fact that a particular investigation would have been *successful* is not enough to show that it was a *necessary* part of any reasonable investigation.

3. *Exhaustion of state remedies.* The federal habeas statute requires state prisoners to "exhaust" the remedies available to them in the state court system. The Supreme Court created the exhaustion requirement in Ex parte Royall, 117 U.S. 241 (1886), and Congress codified it in 1948. 28 U.S.C. §§2254(b), (c). To meet this requirement, a petitioner must present a claim of error to the available state courts to hear the claim before including that claim in a federal habeas petition. If a federal petition is "mixed," (that is, if it contains both exhausted and unexhausted claims), the federal court must dismiss the entire petition. Rose v. Lundy, 455 U.S.509 (1982). A federal petition dismissed on exhaustion grounds may be refiled after the petitioner has sought the available remedies from the state courts. See O'Sullivan v. Boerckel, 526 U.S. 838 (1999) (to satisfy the exhaustion requirement, state prisoner must present claims to state supreme court in petition for discretionary review after a ruling

by the intermediate appeals court, if that review is part of the state's "ordinary appellate review procedure"; because the time for requesting leave to appeal to the Illinois Supreme Court was long past, Boerckel's failure to present three of his claims to that court resulted in a procedural default).

Note the interaction between the exhaustion rule described here and the statutes of limitations and limits on "successive petitions" described in Section B of this chapter. As legal counsel for a state prisoner during post-conviction proceedings, would the exhaustion rule influence the specificity of your claims of legal error during state court proceedings?

2. Contraction

Over time, the Supreme Court became more skeptical of the value of federal habeas corpus review of state convictions. In a series of cases interpreting the (still essentially unchanged) federal statute, the Court declared that claims relating to improper searches and seizures would not be "cognizable" in federal habeas corpus, Stone v. Powell, 428 U.S. 465 (1976); and that a federal court would ordinarily not hear the merits of a claim if a petitioner committed "procedural default" by failing to preserve the claim for review in the state system, Wainwright v. Sykes, 433 U.S. 72 (1977). The following case announced what many considered to be the most important limitation on the availability of federal habeas corpus.

■ FRANK DEAN TEAGUE v. MICHAEL LANE

489 U.S. 288 (1989)

O'Connor, J.

In Taylor v. Louisiana, 419 U.S. 522 (1975), this Court held that the Sixth Amendment required that the jury venire be drawn from a fair cross section of the community. . . . The principal question presented in this case is whether the Sixth Amendment's fair cross section requirement should now be extended to the petit jury. Because we adopt Justice Harlan's approach to retroactivity for cases on collateral review, we leave the resolution of that question for another day.

Petitioner, a black man, was convicted by an all-white Illinois jury of three counts of attempted murder, two counts of armed robbery, and one count of aggravated battery. During jury selection for petitioner's trial, the prosecutor used all 10 of his peremptory challenges to exclude blacks. Petitioner's counsel used one of his 10 peremptory challenges to exclude a black woman who was married to a police officer. On appeal, petitioner argued that the prosecutor's use of peremptory challenges denied him the right to be tried by a jury that was representative of the community. The Illinois Appellate Court rejected petitioner's fair cross section claim. The Illinois Supreme Court denied leave to appeal, and we denied certiorari. Petitioner then filed a petition for a writ of habeas corpus in the United States District Court for the Northern District of Illinois. [The District Court declined to grant any relief and the Court of Appeals rejected Teague's fair cross section claim, holding that the fair cross section requirement was limited to the jury venire.]

In the past, the Court has, without discussion, often applied a new constitutional rule of criminal procedure to the defendant in the case announcing the new rule, and has confronted the question of retroactivity later when a different defendant sought the benefit of that rule. [However, we believe that retroactivity] is properly treated as a threshold question, for, once a new rule is applied to the defendant in the case announcing the rule, evenhanded justice requires that it be applied retroactively to all who are similarly situated. Thus, before deciding whether the fair cross section requirement should be extended to the petit jury, we should ask whether such a rule would be applied retroactively to the case at issue. . . .

It is admittedly often difficult to determine when a case announces a new rule, and we do not attempt to define the spectrum of what may or may not constitute a new rule for retroactivity purposes. In general, however, a case announces a new rule when it breaks new ground or imposes a new obligation on the States or the Federal Government. To put it differently, a case announces a new rule if the result was not dictated by precedent existing at the time the defendant's conviction became final. Given the strong language in *Taylor,* application of the fair cross section requirement to the petit jury would be a new rule.

Not all new rules have been uniformly treated for retroactivity purposes. Nearly a quarter of a century ago, in Linkletter v. Walker, 381 U.S. 618 (1965), the Court attempted to set some standards by which to determine the retroactivity of new rules. The question in *Linkletter* was whether Mapp v. Ohio, 367 U.S. 643 (1961), which made the exclusionary rule applicable to the States, should be applied retroactively to cases on collateral review. The Court determined that the retroactivity of *Mapp* should be determined by examining [1] the purpose of the exclusionary rule, [2] the reliance of the States on prior law, and [3] the effect on the administration of justice of a retroactive application of the exclusionary rule. Using that standard, the Court held that *Mapp* would only apply to trials commencing after that case was decided.

The *Linkletter* retroactivity standard has not led to consistent results. Instead, it has been used to limit application of certain new rules to cases on direct review, other new rules only to the defendants in the cases announcing such rules, and still other new rules to cases in which trials have not yet commenced. . . . Dissatisfied with the *Linkletter* standard, Justice Harlan advocated a different approach to retroactivity. He argued that new rules should always be applied retroactively to cases on direct review, but that generally they should not be applied retroactively to criminal cases on collateral review.

In Griffith v. Kentucky, 479 U.S. 314 (1987), [this Court] adopted the first part of the retroactivity approach advocated by Justice Harlan. . . . We gave two reasons for our decision. First, because we can only promulgate new rules in specific cases and cannot possibly decide all cases in which review is sought, "the integrity of judicial review" requires the application of the new rule to "all similar cases pending on direct review." . . . Second, because selective application of new rules violates the principle of treating similarly situated defendants the same, we refused to continue to tolerate the inequity that resulted from not applying new rules retroactively to defendants whose cases had not yet become final. [Thus, under *Griffith,*] a new rule for the conduct of criminal prosecutions is to be applied retroactively to all cases, state or federal, pending on direct review or not yet final, with no exception for cases in which the new rule constitutes a "clear break" with the past. . . .

Justice Harlan believed that new rules generally should not be applied retroactively to cases on collateral review. He argued that retroactivity for cases on collateral review could "be responsibly [determined] only by focusing, in the first instance, on the nature, function, and scope of the adjudicatory process in which such cases arise. The relevant frame of reference, in other words, is not the purpose of the new rule whose benefit the [defendant] seeks, but instead the purposes for which the writ of habeas corpus is made available." Mackey v. United States, 401 U.S. 667, 682 (1971). With regard to the nature of habeas corpus, Justice Harlan wrote:

> Habeas corpus always has been a collateral remedy, providing an avenue for upsetting judgments that have become otherwise final. It is not designed as a substitute for direct review. The interest in leaving concluded litigation in a state of repose, that is, reducing the controversy to a final judgment not subject to further judicial revision, may quite legitimately be found by those responsible for defining the scope of the writ to outweigh in some, many, or most instances the competing interest in readjudicating convictions according to all legal standards in effect when a habeas petition is filed. . . .

Justice Harlan identified only two exceptions to his general rule of nonretroactivity for cases on collateral review. First, a new rule should be applied retroactively if it places "certain kinds of primary, private individual conduct beyond the power of the criminal law-making authority to proscribe." Second, a new rule should be applied retroactively if it requires the observance of "those procedures that . . . are implicit in the concept of ordered liberty." Mackey, 401 U.S. at 693 (quoting Palko v. Connecticut, 302 U.S. 319 (1937) (Cardozo, J.)).

We agree with Justice Harlan's description of the function of habeas corpus. The Court never has defined the scope of the writ simply by reference to a perceived need to assure that an individual accused of crime is afforded a trial free of constitutional error. Rather, we have recognized that interests of comity and finality must also be considered in determining the proper scope of habeas review. Thus, if a defendant fails to comply with state procedural rules and is barred from litigating a particular constitutional claim in state court, the claim can be considered on federal habeas only if the defendant shows cause for the default and actual prejudice resulting therefrom. See Wainwright v. Sykes, 433 U.S. 72 (1977). We have declined to make the application of the procedural default rule dependent on the magnitude of the constitutional claim at issue, or on the State's interest in the enforcement of its procedural rule. . . .

Application of constitutional rules not in existence at the time a conviction became final seriously undermines the principle of finality which is essential to the operation of our criminal justice system. Without finality, the criminal law is deprived of much of its deterrent effect. The fact that life and liberty are at stake in criminal prosecutions "shows only that conventional notions of finality should not have as much place in criminal as in civil litigation, not that they should have none." Friendly, Is Innocence Irrelevant? Collateral Attacks on Criminal Judgments, 38 U. Chi. L. Rev. 142, 150 (1970).

The costs imposed upon the States by retroactive application of new rules of constitutional law on habeas corpus generally far outweigh the benefits of this application. [State] courts are understandably frustrated when they faithfully apply existing constitutional law only to have a federal court discover, during a habeas proceeding, new constitutional commands.

We find these criticisms to be persuasive, and we now adopt Justice Harlan's view of retroactivity for cases on collateral review. Unless they fall within an exception to the general rule, new constitutional rules of criminal procedure will not be applicable to those cases which have become final before the new rules are announced.

Petitioner's conviction became final in 1983. As a result, the rule petitioner urges would not be applicable to this case, which is on collateral review, unless it would fall within an exception. The first exception suggested by Justice Harlan . . . is not relevant here. Application of the fair cross section requirement to the petit jury would not accord constitutional protection to any primary activity whatsoever. The second exception suggested by Justice Harlan — that a new rule should be applied retroactively if it requires the observance of "those procedures that . . . are implicit in the concept of ordered liberty" — we apply with a modification.

[Our] cases have moved in the direction of reaffirming the relevance of the likely accuracy of convictions in determining the available scope of habeas review. See, e.g., Kuhlmann v. Wilson, 477 U.S. 436 (1986) (a successive habeas petition may be entertained only if the defendant makes a "colorable claim of factual innocence"); Murray v. Carrier, 477 U.S. 478 (1986) ("[W]here a constitutional violation has probably resulted in the conviction of one who is actually innocent, a federal habeas court may grant the writ even in the absence of a showing of cause for the procedural default"); Stone v. Powell, 428 U.S. 465 (1976) (removing Fourth Amendment claims from the scope of federal habeas review if the State has provided a full and fair opportunity for litigation creates no danger of denying a "safeguard against compelling an innocent man to suffer an unconstitutional loss of liberty"). [Concerns] about the difficulty in identifying both the existence and the value of accuracy-enhancing procedural rules can be addressed by limiting the scope of the second exception to those new procedures without which the likelihood of an accurate conviction is seriously diminished.

Because we operate from the premise that such procedures would be so central to an accurate determination of innocence or guilt, we believe it unlikely that many such components of basic due process have yet to emerge. We are also of the view that such rules are best illustrated by recalling the classic grounds for the issuance of a writ of habeas corpus — that the proceeding was dominated by mob violence; that the prosecutor knowingly made use of perjured testimony; or that the conviction was based on a confession extorted from the defendant by brutal methods.

An examination of our decision in *Taylor* applying the fair cross section requirement to the jury venire leads inexorably to the conclusion that adoption of the rule petitioner urges would be a far cry from the kind of absolute prerequisite to fundamental fairness that is "implicit in the concept of ordered liberty." [The] fair cross section requirement does not rest on the premise that every criminal trial, or any particular trial, is necessarily unfair because it is not conducted in accordance with what we determined to be the requirements of the Sixth Amendment. Because the absence of a fair cross section on the jury venire does not undermine the fundamental fairness that must underlie a conviction or seriously diminish the likelihood of obtaining an accurate conviction, we conclude that a rule requiring that petit juries be composed of a fair cross section of the community would not be a "bedrock procedural element" that would be retroactively applied under the second exception we have articulated.

Were we to recognize the new rule urged by petitioner in this case, we would have to give petitioner the benefit of that new rule even though it would not be applied retroactively to others similarly situated. . . . But the harm caused by the failure to treat similarly situated defendants alike cannot be exaggerated: such inequitable treatment hardly comports with the ideal of administration of justice with an even hand. . . .

If there were no other way to avoid rendering advisory opinions, we might well agree that the inequitable treatment described above is an insignificant cost for adherence to sound principles of decision-making. But there is a more principled way of dealing with the problem. We can simply refuse to announce a new rule in a given case unless the rule would be applied retroactively to the defendant in the case and to all others similarly situated. We think this approach is a sound one. Not only does it eliminate any problems of rendering advisory opinions, it also avoids the inequity resulting from the uneven application of new rules to similarly situated defendants. We therefore hold that, implicit in the retroactivity approach we adopt today, is the principle that habeas corpus cannot be used as a vehicle to create new constitutional rules of criminal procedure unless those rules would be applied retroactively to all defendants on collateral review through one of the two exceptions we have articulated. Because a decision extending the fair cross section requirement to the petit jury would not be applied retroactively to cases on collateral review under the approach we adopt today, we do not address petitioner's claim.

STEVENS, J., concurring in part and concurring in the judgment.

. . . I am persuaded this petitioner has alleged a violation of the Sixth Amendment. I also believe the Court should decide that question in his favor. I do not agree with Justice O'Connor's assumption that a ruling in petitioner's favor on the merits of the Sixth Amendment issue would require that his conviction be set aside.

When a criminal defendant claims that a procedural error tainted his conviction, an appellate court often decides whether error occurred before deciding whether that error requires reversal or should be classified as harmless. I would follow a parallel approach in cases raising novel questions of constitutional law on collateral review, first determining whether the trial process violated any of the petitioner's constitutional rights and then deciding whether the petitioner is entitled to relief. If error occurred, factors relating to retroactivity — most importantly, the magnitude of unfairness — should be examined before granting the petitioner relief. Proceeding in reverse, a plurality of the Court today declares that a new rule should not apply retroactively without ever deciding whether there is such a rule. . . .

I am persuaded that the Court should adopt Justice Harlan's analysis of retroactivity for habeas corpus cases as well for cases still on direct review. I do not agree, however, with the plurality's dicta proposing a "modification" of Justice Harlan's fundamental fairness exception. [Justice Harlan stated the exception this way]: "[In] some situations it might be that time and growth in social capacity, as well as judicial perceptions of what we can rightly demand of the adjudicatory process, will properly alter our understanding of the bedrock procedural elements that must be found to vitiate the fairness of a particular conviction." [Justice Harlan did not link] the fundamental fairness exception to factual innocence. [A] touchstone of factual innocence would provide little guidance in certain important types of cases, such as those challenging the constitutionality of capital sentencing hearings. Even when assessing errors at the guilt phase of a trial, factual innocence is too capricious a factor by which to determine if a procedural change is sufficiently "bedrock" or "watershed" to justify application of the fundamental fairness exception. In contrast, given our century-old proclamation that the Constitution does not allow exclusion of jurors because of race, Strauder v. West Virginia, 100 U.S. 303 (1880), a rule promoting selection of juries free from racial bias clearly implicates concerns of fundamental fairness. . . .

BRENNAN, J., dissenting.

Today a plurality of this Court, without benefit of briefing and oral argument, adopts a novel threshold test for federal review of state criminal convictions on habeas corpus. It does so without regard for — indeed, without even mentioning — our contrary decisions over the past 35 years delineating the broad scope of habeas relief. . . .

For well over a century, we have read [the Habeas Corpus Act of 1867] to authorize federal courts to grant writs of habeas corpus whenever a person's liberty is unconstitutionally restrained. Nothing has happened since to persuade us to alter that judgment. . . . In particular, our decisions have made plain that the federal courts may collaterally review claims such as Teague's once state remedies have been exhausted. In Brown v. Allen, 344 U.S. 443 (1953), for example, we held that state prisoners alleging discrimination in the selection of members of the grand jury that indicted them and the petit jury that tried them were entitled to reconsideration of those allegations in federal court. . . .

Few decisions on appeal or collateral review are "dictated" by what came before. Most such cases involve a question of law that is at least debatable, permitting a rational judge to resolve the case in more than one way. Virtually no case that prompts a dissent on the relevant legal point, for example, could be said to be "dictated" by prior decisions. By the plurality's test, therefore, a great many cases could only be heard on habeas if the rule urged by the petitioner fell within one of the two exceptions the plurality has sketched. Those exceptions, however, are narrow. . . . The plurality's approach today can thus be expected to contract substantially the Great Writ's sweep.

Its impact is perhaps best illustrated by noting the abundance and variety of habeas cases we have decided in recent years that could never have been adjudicated had the plurality's new rule been in effect. [This observation applies to] numerous right-to-counsel and representation claims we have decided where the wrong alleged by the habeas petitioner was unlikely to have produced an erroneous conviction. See, e. g., Moran v. Burbine, 475 U.S. 412 (1986) (failure of police to inform defendant that attorney retained for him by somebody else sought to reach him does not violate Sixth Amendment); Morris v. Slappy, 461 U.S. 1 (1983) (state court's denial of continuance until public defender initially assigned to represent defendant became available does not violate Sixth Amendment); Ross v. Moffitt, 417 U.S. 600 (1974) (States need not provide indigent defendants with counsel on discretionary appeals).

Likewise, because the Fifth Amendment's privilege against self-incrimination is not an adjunct to the ascertainment of truth, claims that a petitioner's right to remain silent was violated would, if not dictated by earlier decisions, ordinarily fail to qualify under the plurality's second exception. . . . Habeas claims under the Double Jeopardy Clause will also be barred under the plurality's approach . . . , because they bear no relation to the petitioner's guilt or innocence. So, too, will miscellaneous due process and Sixth Amendment claims that relate only tangentially to a defendant's guilt or innocence. See, e.g., Bordenkircher v. Hayes, 434 U.S. 357 (1978) (no due process violation when prosecutor carries out threat to reindict on stiffer charge); Barker v. Wingo, 407 U.S. 514 (1972) (5-year delay does not violate right to speedy trial). . . .

These are massive changes, unsupported by precedent. They also lack a reasonable foundation. By exaggerating the importance of treating like cases alike and granting relief to all identically positioned habeas petitioners or none, the Court acts as if it has no choice but to follow a mechanical notion of fairness without pausing to consider sound principles of decisionmaking. Certainly it is desirable, in the interest of fairness, to accord the same treatment to all habeas petitioners with the same claims. . . . Other things being equal, our concern for fairness and finality ought to . . . lead us to render our decision in a case that comes to us on direct review.

Other things are not always equal, however. Sometimes a claim which, if successful, would create a new rule not appropriate for retroactive application on collateral review is better presented by a habeas case than by one on direct review. In fact, sometimes the claim is only presented on collateral review. In that case, while we could forgo deciding the issue in the hope that it would eventually be presented squarely on direct review, that hope might be misplaced, and even if it were in time fulfilled, the opportunity to check constitutional violations and to further the evolution of our thinking in some area of the law would in the meanwhile have been lost. In addition, by preserving our right and that of the lower federal courts to hear such claims on collateral review, we would not discourage their litigation on federal habeas corpus and thus not deprive ourselves and society of the benefit of decisions by the lower federal courts when we must resolve these issues ourselves. . . .

Notes

1. *New claims on habeas corpus.* Portions of the decision in Teague v. Lane were adopted by a plurality rather than a majority of the court, but later decisions confirmed the basic outlines of that case. See Butler v. McKellar, 494 U.S. 407 (1990). What qualifies as a "new" claim that is now unavailable to state prisoners seeking federal habeas corpus relief? The *Teague* court said that a new claim "breaks new ground or imposes a new obligation" on the government; a rule is new if "the result was not dictated by precedent." This latter formulation suggests that the class of new rules will be very large, for most litigated claims are not "dictated" by precedent. In later cases, the Supreme Court has declared that a decision is new if it rejects any "reasonable, good faith interpretations" of past cases. See O'Dell v. Netherland, 521 U.S. 151 (1997).

2. *Subconstitutional claims.* Federal habeas corpus still extends to all claims alleging violations of previously-established constitutional law. It also reaches some, but not all, non-constitutional claims based on federal law. In Stone v. Powell, 428 U.S. 465 (1976), the Court declared that claims based on the use of evidence obtained through illegal searches and seizures are not available on federal habeas. The exclusionary rule remedy, the Court concluded, is not itself a constitutional requirement and does not contribute to the accuracy of the guilt-innocence determination. On the other hand, in Withrow v. Williams, 507 U.S. 680 (1993), the Court decided that *Miranda* claims are available on federal habeas corpus, despite the fact that the "prophylactic" *Miranda* warnings are not themselves constitutional requirements. Because the *Miranda* rule is a "fundamental" requirement of federal law that protects individual constitutional rights and effectively prevents some violations of those rights, violations of the rule can be presented in a federal habeas claim. See also Reed v. Farley, 512 U.S. 339 (1994) (violations of federal statutes applicable to state criminal proceedings are cognizable on federal habeas corpus if the violation

shows a "fundamental" defect that results in a "miscarriage of justice," or if the violation presents "special circumstances"). Are habeas corpus cases the proper forum for the Supreme Court to signal its retreat from earlier constitutional rulings that it now considers ill-advised or less than "fundamental"? What are the alternatives?

3. *Cognizable issues under the 1996 statute.* The Congress made major changes to the federal habeas corpus statutes in 1996. These changes are probably the most important since the passage of the 1867 Act. A key provision of the new statute, §2254(d), says:

> An application for a writ of habeas corpus on behalf of a person in custody pursuant to the judgment of a State court shall not be granted with respect to any claim that was adjudicated on the merits in State proceedings unless the adjudication of the claim — (1) resulted in a decision that was contrary to, or involved an unreasonable application of, clearly established Federal law as determined by the Supreme Court of the United States; or (2) resulted in a decision that was based on an unreasonable determination of the facts in light of the evidence presented in the State proceeding.

Readers of the revised statute have acknowledged that protracted debate over the statutory language, along with the rich case law at work in the background, makes this an exceptionally difficult statute to interpret. It is clear that the Congress wanted to amend the existing statute to require federal habeas courts to give greater weight to the legal decisions of state courts that have considered a petitioner's claims; it is equally clear that Congress did not intend to give state court decisions binding *res judicata* effect. What would make a state court's application of established federal law "unreasonable"? Does the new statute codify *Teague,* or does it do something more or less than that decision? See Horn v. Banks, 536 U.S. 266 (2002) (*Teague* retroactivity limit is distinct from AEDPA analysis). What has become of *Teague*'s two exceptions?

Other sections of the 1996 statute create filing deadlines for federal petitions: Roughly speaking, federal petitions must be filed within one year of the end of the relevant state proceedings. The statute also limits evidentiary hearings in federal court, limits successive federal petitions, and creates special habeas corpus rules for capital cases in those states that "opt in" to the special rules by appointing counsel for indigent petitioners.

The Supreme Court has begun to answer some of the questions about the meaning of the key statutory language: "a decision that was contrary to, or involved an unreasonable application of, clearly established Federal law." In Williams v. Taylor, 529 U.S. 362 (2000), the Court declared that the 1996 statute placed a "new constraint" on the power of federal courts to hear challenges to state convictions. Under the first clause (the "contrary to" clause), a federal habeas court may grant relief if the state court "arrives at a conclusion opposite to that reached by this Court on a question of law" or "confronts facts that are materially indistinguishable from a relevant Supreme Court precedent and arrives at a result opposite to ours." A routine application of the federal rule to different facts would not qualify for relief under the "contrary to" clause, even if a federal court might have applied the federal rule differently to those facts.

As for the second, "unreasonable application" clause, a federal habeas court should ask whether the state court's application of federal law was "objectively unreasonable." The federal habeas court should not simply ask whether any "reasonable jurist" would apply the federal rule in the same way as the state court did in the case at hand. On the other hand, "unreasonable" is not the same as "incorrect." A federal court might believe that the state court applied federal law incorrectly, and yet decide that the application was reasonable (and therefore unreviewable in habeas corpus).

4. *Harmless error.* As we saw in Chapter 20, when a court declares on direct appeal that some error took place at trial, it will nevertheless uphold the conviction if the error was "harmless beyond a reasonable doubt." Chapman v. California, 386 U.S. 18 (1967). Until recently the same harmless error standard applied to federal habeas corpus proceedings: A cognizable constitutional error would lead the federal court to grant habeas corpus relief (typically ordering a new trial) unless the error was harmless beyond a reasonable doubt. However, in Brecht v. Abrahamson, 507 U.S. 619 (1993), the Court changed the harmless error standard for federal courts to use in habeas corpus proceedings. Now the standard for determining whether habeas relief must be granted is whether the error "had substantial and injurious effect or influence in determining the jury's verdict." Does this change in the harmless error standard further the interest in finality of judgments? Does a federal court respect the comity of state courts by finding that constitutional errors occurred and then leaving the judgment undisturbed unless the error had a "substantial and injurious effect" on the verdict?

5. *Habeas and federal appellate review.* Views about the wisdom of the *Teague* case and the statutory amendments of 1996 depend on what one considers to be the proper function of federal habeas corpus. For those who contend that the basic purpose of habeas corpus is to prevent injustice in individual cases, what would be the best reaction to *Teague* and to the 1996 amendments? Another potential view emphasizes the distinctive abilities of federal courts, and looks to habeas corpus to assure a federal adjudication of every federal claim. This point of view is difficult to square with the reality that state courts often adjudicate federal claims. Professor Barry Friedman has sketched out a third position: Federal habeas corpus is best suited as a proxy for federal direct appellate review. To the extent that a state prisoner could at one time expect the U.S. Supreme Court to exercise direct appellate review in an era when caseload and certiorari practice made that review meaningful, federal habeas corpus could provide state prisoners with an alternative federal appellate court in an era when the U.S. Supreme Court is no longer practically available. See Barry Friedman, Pas de Deux: The Supreme Court and the Habeas Courts, 66 S. Cal. L. Rev. 2467 (1993); Barry Friedman, A Tale of Two Habeas, 73 Minn. L. Rev. 247 (1988). If this is indeed a proper function of federal habeas review, what does it imply about *Teague* and the 1996 amendments?

6. *Appellate courts as gatekeepers.* The Antiterrorism and Effective Death Penalty Act of 1996 gives federal appeals courts the power to block some habeas petitions from reaching the appeals court. The statute says that a party cannot appeal the final order in a post-conviction proceeding to a court of appeals, unless a circuit judge issues a "certificate of appealability," or "COA." The petitioner may obtain such a certificate only by making a substantial showing of the denial of a constitutional right. 28 U.S.C. §2253(c). The federal courts reading this provision broadly to allow appeals in a wide range of claims. See Hohn v. United States, 524 U.S. 236 (1998) (petitioner was complaining about sufficiency of evidence, a constitutional claim covered by COA statute). Petitioners may show a denial of a "constitutional right" even if the district court refused to hear the merits of the claim. According to Slack

v. McDaniel, 529 U.S. 473 (2000), when the district court dismisses a petition on procedural grounds, the "substantial showing necessary to obtain a COA has two components. One component deals with the underlying constitutional claim, while another deals with the district court's procedural holding. A COA should issue if the petitioner shows that "jurists of reason" would find it "debatable" whether 1) the person was denied a constitutional right, and 2) the district court was correct in its procedural ruling.

7. *Judicial attitudes toward habeas corpus.* Do federal and state judges have different attitudes about the importance of federal habeas corpus review of state convictions? In a 1996 survey, federal and state judges were asked if elected state judges have "sufficient independence to make difficult decisions that may favor the rights of convicted offenders." Among federal judges, 74 percent replied "yes," while 81 percent of the state judges replied "yes." When asked if there is a "need for continued existence and availability" of federal habeas review of state convictions, 29 percent of the state judges answered "no," while only 7 percent of the federal judges gave the same answer. Most of the state and federal judges approved of the restrictions on federal habeas review created by Rehnquist Court decisions. See Christopher E. Smith & Darwin L. Burke, Judges' Views on Habeas Corpus: A Comparison of State and Federal Judges, 22 Okla. City U. L. Rev. 1125 (1997). Should legislators consider the views of judges about habeas corpus when debating changes in the statutes governing post-conviction review? If so, for what specific purpose?

Problem 21-2. New Law

The definition of new claims under *Teague* creates a bind for petitioners. They might want to establish that a claim is "new" as a way to explain "cause" for a failure to avoid state procedural default or to obtain a successive federal petition. At the same time, they will need to establish that the claim is not new within the meaning of the retroactivity bar established in *Teague*. Can a claim be considered new for some purposes and not for others? Consider the following facts:

> Henry Griggs and Henry Crawford were accused of murdering James Bush, an enforcer for the then-notorious Phenix City Gang. Griggs and Crawford were tried separately and were defended by lawyers hired by Crawford; both were convicted of murder and sentenced to life imprisonment in 1954. Counsel for Griggs filed a motion for a new trial but evidently did not pursue the appeal. His motion was dismissed for want of prosecution.
>
> In 1990, Griggs petitioned for a writ of habeas corpus, arguing that the trial court erred in not setting aside his conviction because then-Code §38-416, which precluded an accused from testifying under oath on his own behalf, effectively impaired his ability to mount a defense and violated his rights under the Sixth and Fourteenth Amendments. Although the statute did declare an accused incompetent to testify under oath in his own behalf at his trial, §38-415 allowed the accused to make an unsworn statement to the jury, a statement unguided by the accused's counsel and not subject to cross-examination.

If Griggs had filed a federal habeas petition in 1960, before Fay v. Noia, should the court grant relief on a claim that he was denied his Fourteenth Amendment right to due process? (Remember that the Sixth Amendment right to counsel was not incorporated until Gideon v. Wainwright, in 1963, and the Fifth Amendment privilege against self-incrimination was not incorporated until Malloy v. Hogan, in 1964.) How should the court rule if Griggs filed his claim in 1966, after the decision in Fay v. Noia? What result in 1995, post-*Teague*? What result in 1999, after the appearance of new statutory federal standards under the Effective Death Penalty Act of 1996?

In Ferguson v. Georgia, 365 U.S. 570 (1961), the Supreme Court ruled this provision of the Georgia Code unconstitutional, holding: "Georgia, consistently with the Fourteenth Amendment, could not, in the context of §38-416, deny appellant the right to have his counsel question him to elicit his statement." The Georgia statute was unusual at the time. Indeed, Georgia was the only state (and the only jurisdiction in the common-law world) to retain the common-law rule that a criminal defendant is incompetent to testify under oath in his own behalf at his trial. Every other state had abolished the disqualification by the turn of the century. Does this change your analysis in 1960 (pre-*Fay*)? In 1966 (after *Fay*)? In 1995 (after *Teague*)? In 1999 (after the 1996 amendments)? Compare Griggs v. State, 425 S.E.2d 644 (Ga. 1993).

Does this case suggest that Justice Harlan was right to keep a "fundamental fairness" exception to the retroactivity bar, and that *Teague* was wrong to reject that element of Harlan's position? What does this case indicate about the interrelationship between the doctrines of bypass and retroactivity?

Notes

1. *New enough, but not too new.* Before *Teague,* a claim based on "new" law was a strong foundation for a habeas petition. A habeas petitioner who had failed to raise a claim earlier could explain this "procedural default" by saying that the newness of the legal theory was the "cause" of the default. Furthermore, the retroactivity rules on direct appeal and on habeas corpus allowed for a greater "backward" impact from important new decisions. Following *Teague*—which is as much a retroactivity decision as it is a revision of the scope of federal habeas—a claim based on new law has become far more difficult and subtle. The attorney must now demonstrate that the desired outcome would be new enough to meet the "cause and prejudice" standard to avoid a procedural default, but not so new that the claim is barred from federal habeas corpus under *Teague.*

2. *The inevitability of new law claims.* Retroactivity rules respond to a major reality of our legal system: Laws change, and convictions obtained properly under one set of procedural rules would not stand if a newer set of rules were to apply. Persons convicted under the old rules will ask, in any available forum, whether courts (and society at large) can tolerate punishing a person based on procedural rules that are now considered inadequate and unjust. Sometimes these claims will be compelling. A legal culture that aspires to equal treatment of litigants and to the idea of progress (that is, today's understanding of justice is an improvement upon yesterday's understanding of justice) will seek a way to respond to such claims. How would you expect federal habeas corpus to accommodate claims based on new law, even after *Teague* and the 1996 statutory amendments? How would you expect retroactivity rules on appeal and on collateral attack in state courts to change in light of these federal developments? What kind of pressures might restrictive collateral review place on the executive branch in considering requests that it exercise its power to pardon convicted offenders?

Table of Cases

Principal Supreme Court cases are in bold
Other principal cases are in italic

Abbasi v. Secretary of State, 791
Adam, State v., 940
Adams v. New York, 336
Adams, State v., 1067
Addington v. Texas, 782
Adel, State v., 900
Adkins, People v., 707
Advisory Opinion to the Governor (Appointed Counsel), In re, 680
Advisory Opinion to the Senate of the State of Rhode Island, 1143
Agnello v. United States, 338
Agnello, State v., 474
Aguilar v. Texas, 147, 155, 156, 162
Aguilar-Pena, United States v., 1325
Agurs, United States v., 942
Ah Sin v. Wittman, 624, 629
Aime v. Commonwealth, 953
Ajabu v. State, 522
Ake v. Oklahoma, 692
Alabama v. Shelton, 683
Alabama v. White, 55
Alayon, State v., 169
Alcorta v. Texas, 953
Alen, State v., 1133
Alford v. United States, 1205
Allen v. United States, 1139
Allen, People v., 1003
Almeida v. State, 531
Alspach, State v., 701
Alston, State v., 375
Alvarado v. Superior Court, 1205
Alvarez, State v., 899
Amazon Indus. Chem. Corp., United States v., 647
Ammidown, United States v., 1013
Amrein v. State, 1099
Anderer, Ex parte, 1349
Anders v. California, 1348, 1353
Anderson v. Charles, 1233
Anderson v. People, 1285
Anderson v. Peyton, 724
Anderson v. State, 1304
Anderson, State v., 951
Andrei, State v., 260
Andresen v. Maryland, 259, 260
Anonymous, State v., 629
Anthony, People v., 201
Antommarchi, People v., 1180
Anton, State v., 1091
Apelt, State v., 178
Apodaca v. Oregon, 1144
Apprendi v. New Jersey, 1190, **1291,** 1298, 1299
Archuleta, State v., 1161
Arguello, People v., 707
Arizona v. Evans, 358
Arizona v. Fulminante, 558, 1380, 1390, 1391
Arizona v. Hicks, 99

Arizona v. Roberson, 543
Arizona v. Youngblood, 952, 953
Arkansas v. Sullivan, 319
Arman, People v., 1232
Armstrong, United States v., 629, **855,** 861
Arnold v. Kemp, 746
Arroya, People v., 532
Ash, United States v., 611, 696
Ashcraft v. Tennessee, 468
Ashe v. Swenson, 899, 909
Attebury, People v., 513
Atwater v. City of Lago Vista, 312, 318, 319
Ault, State v., 368

Bailey v. State (669 N.E.2d), 1136, 1139
Bailey v. State (972 S.W.2d), 14
Bailey, State ex rel., v. Facemire, 826
Baker, State v., 1099
Baldwin v. New York, 1086
Balfour, State v., 1305
Balicki, Commonwealth v., 100
Ball v. United States, 1360
Ballard, State v., 47
Ballew v. Georgia, 1143
Baltimore City Dept. Soc. Serv. v. Bouknight, 667
Baluyut v. Superior Ct., 625, 629
Banks, People v., 91
Barber, State v., 75
Barella, People v., 1044
Barker v. Wingo, 977, 985
Barnett, State v., 575
Barone v. State, 611
Barron, State v., 636
Bartkus v. Illinois, 878, 889
Barton, State v., 146, 155, 156, 162
Batchelder, United States v., 840
Batson v. Kentucky, 1116, 1130-1135, 1341
Battis, Commonwealth v., 1075
Bauer, State v., 318
Baynes, State v., 813, 819
Beavers v. Haubert, 977
Beavers v. State, 474
Beckett, State v., 358
Beecher v. Alabama, 459
Bell v. Clapp, 174, 176, 177
Bell v. Cone, 726
Bell v. Wolfish, 253
Bellamy, United States v., 75
Benchimol, United States v., 1067
Bender, State v., 815
Benoit, Commonwealth v., 368
Berard, State v., 255
Berger v. New York, 415
Berger, United States v., 829
Bergman, State v., 1067
Berkemer v. McCarty, 505, 506
Berry v. Commonwealth, 901
Bessenecker, State v., 1109
Betts v. Brady, 678, 679, 680
Bey, State v., 1334
Bias, People v., 617, 738
Binegar v. District Ct., 961
Bisaccia, State v., 260
Bishop v. State, 1304
Bittick, State v., 514
Bivens v. Six Unknown Named Agents of Fed. Bureau of Narcotics, 390
Bivins v. State, 1323
Blackledge v. Perry, 862, 1002
Blackmore, State v., 290
Blair v. State, 1099
Blalock, People v., 724
Blanco, Singletary v., 721
Blanton v. City of N. Las Vegas, 1087
Bleyl, State v., 496
Blockburger v. United States, 552, 890, 891, 899, 900-903
Blood, Commonwealth v., 437
Board of Educ. of Ind. School Dist. No. 92 of Pottawatomie County v. Earls, 248, 253
Bobic v. State, 94, 99
Boff, State v., 220
Bollman and Swartout, Ex parte, 1405
Bonacorsi, State v., 1151
Bond v. United States, 96, 99
Bonnell, State v., 236, 239, 240
Bonner, State v., 1263
Boot, In re, 852
Booth v. Maryland, 1322
Boots, State v., 1145
Bordenkircher v. Hayes, 1001
Bouie, State v., 1052
Boulies v. People, 900
Bousman v. District Court, 230
Bowers, State v. (498 N.W.2d), 1087, 1091, 1092
Bowers, State v. (976 S.W.2d), 375
Boyd v. United States, 256, 259-261, 335, 670
Boykin v. Alabama, 1037, 1038, 1045
Bradley v. State, 163
Brady v. Maryland, 942, 950-953, 1244
Brady v. State, 1191
Brady v. United States, 1044, 1051
Bram v. United States, 465, 473, 480
Branch, Ex parte, 1130
Brasfield v. United States, 1140
Brashars v. Commonwealth, 573
Braswell v. United States, 671
Bray, State v., 1197
Brazell, State v., 975
Brecht v. Abrahamson, 1452
Brent v. Commonwealth, 234
Brewer v. Williams, 551
Brewer v. State, 178
Brignoni-Ponce, United States v., 92
Brinegar v. United States, 138, **141**
Brisson, State v., 692
Broce, United States v., 1002

Brochu, State v., 203
Brockman, State v., 455
Brooks, State v., 103
Broom, State v., 619
Brown v. Allen, 1414
Brown v. Bd. of Educ., 615
Brown v. Mississippi, 465, 467-469, 481
Brown v. Ohio, 899
Brown v. People, 177
Brown v. State, 170
Brown v. Texas, 56, 59
Brown, ex rel. State, v. Dietrick, 170, 173
Brown, State v. (588 N.W.2d), 272, 273
Brown, State v. (676 A.2d), 1314
Brown, State v. (783 P.2d), 201
Brown, State v. (940 P.2d), 961
Brugman v. State, 1317
Brunelle, State v., 361
Bruno v. State, 716
Bruton v. United States, 1211, 1212
Buckner v. United States, 179
Budzyn, People v., 1381, 1390
Bumper v. North Carolina, 201
Bunting, Commonwealth v., 992
Burch v. Louisiana, 1144
Burdeau v. McDowell, 240
Burge v. State, 889
Burke, Commonwealth v., 951
Burns v. Reed, 643
Burrows v. Superior Ct., 261
Bush, State v., 1422
Bussey, Commonwealth v., 532
Bustamante, People v., 595
Bustamante-Davila, State v., 201
Butler v. McKellar, 1450
Butts, People v., 638
Byrd v. State, 1143

Caceres, United States v., 810
Cady v. Dombrowski, 9
Cahan, People v., 338, 347, 348, 350, 574
Cahill, People v., 1390
Calandra, United States v., 361
Calder v. Bull, 1378
Caldwell v. Mississippi, 693
Caldwell v. State, 203
Caldwell, People v., 1145
California v. Acevedo, 274, 281, 282, 284
California v. Beheler, 505, 506
California v. Byers, 667
California v. Carney, 284
California v. Ciraolo, 96, 102
California v. Greenwood, 105
California v. Hodari D., 59, 60
California v. Prysock, 514
California v. Trombetta, 952
California Attorneys for Criminal Justice v. Butts, 558
Callahan, People v., 1002
Camara v. Municipal Ct. of San Francisco, 36, 84, **189,** 193
Campbell, Commonwealth v., 1145
Campbell, State v., 411
Canady, State v., 920
Canelo, State v., 188
Canino, People v., 1049
Cantre, People v., 156
Capolongo, State v., 423
Cardwell v. Lewis, 283
Carleton, Commonwealth v., 1134
Carlson v. Landon, 782, 784
Caron, State v., 531
Carper, State v., 267
Carroll v. State, 1213
Carroll v. United States, 141, 282, 283
Carroll, State v., 473
Carty, State v., 202
Casarez v. State, 1134
Caskey, State v., 837
Cason, State v., 1107
Castaneda v. Partida, 1100
Catania, State v., 428
Ceccolini, United States v., 369
Chagnon, State v., 962
Chambers v. Maroney, 283
Chamber's Case, 1394
Champa, State v., 1150
Champion, People v., 119
Chandler v. Miller, 254
Chapman v. California, 1379, 1380, 1390, 1452
Chapman, State v., 534
Cheape, United States v., 1280
Checkley, Commonwealth v., 200
Chenique-Puey, State v., 921
Chimel v. California, 218, 219
Chrisman, State v., 99
Christmas v. State, 1378
Cintron, People v., 1197
Citti v. State, 1069
City of Casper v. Fletcher, 1093
City of Charlottesville v. Schleifer, 23
City of Chicago v. Morales, 16, 21, 24
City of Fargo v. Hector, 899
City of Indianapolis v. Edmond, 84, 89, 90
City of Juneau v. Quinto, 575
City of Los Angeles v. Lyons, 392
City of Los Angeles, United States v., 385
City of Panora v. Simmons, 23
City of St. Paul v. Morris, 14
Clark, In re, 1413
Clark, People v., 532
Clark, State v., 745
Clark, United States v., 1069
Claudio v. State, 1141
Cleary, State v., 534
Cleveland v. State (417 So. 2d), 819
Cleveland v. State (959 S.W.2d), 1391

Clewis v. State, 1363, 1371
Clewley v. State, 1049
Clovis, State v., 922
Cobb, State v., 1304
Cobbs, People v., 1057
Codispoti v. Pennsylvania, 1092
Coffin v. United States, 1183
Cole, State v., 75
Coleman v. Alabama, 700
Coleman v. State (562 A.2d), 75
Coleman v. State (749 So. 2d), 963
Coleman v. State (826 S.W.2d), 184
Coleman v. Thompson, 1442
Coles v. United States, 1305
Coley, State v., 618
Collins v. Youngblood, 1372, 1378
Collins, People v. (27 P.3d), 1057
Collins, People v. (475 N.W.2d), 437
Collins, State v., 454
Collins-Draine v. Knief, 290
Colorado v. Bertine, 265, 266
Colorado v. Connelly, 481, 532, 534
Colorado v. Spring, 523
Colt, State v., 708
Commonwealth v. _______. *See* name of defendant.
Conefrey, Commonwealth v., 1391
Connally v. Georgia, 173
Connecticut v. Barrett, 531
Cook, State v., 273
Coolidge v. New Hampshire, 99
Cooper, People v., 888
Cooper, State v., 73
Corbitt v. New Jersey, 1007
Cordova, State v., 155
Coronado v. State, 247
Cortez, United States v., 70, 73
Costello v. Ocean County Observer, 382
Costello v. United States, 869
Cotton, United States v., 1391
County of Riverside v. McLaughlin, 870
Cowan v. Superior Ct., 1003
Coy v. Iowa, 1197
Craig, State v., 186
Creech, United States v., 1321
Crews, United States v., 369
Cromedy, State v., 613
Cronic, United States v., 725, 726
Crosby v. United States, 1198
Crowder, Commonwealth v., 116, 120
Crowell, State v., 90
Crump v. Demosthenes, 1433
Crump, State v., 543
Cruz v. New York, 1211
Cruz, State v., 1182, 1183
Culbreath, State v., 827, 835
Culkin, State v., 1146
Cunningham, People v., 543
Cuyler v. Sullivan, 71, 713, 726
Dana, Commonwealth v., 335
Danh, State v., 1051
Daugherty, State v., 367
Davidson, State v., 358
Davis v. Alaska, 1219
Davis v. State (520 So. 2d), 1150
Davis v. United States, 530, 531
Davis, People v. (518 N.E.2d), 1334
Davis, People v. (687 N.E.2d), 1263
Davis, State v. (464 S.E.2d), 92
Davis, State v. (504 N.W.2d), 1133
Davis, State v. (804 So. 2d), 638
Deal, State v., 1185
Dean, State v. (543 P.2d), 75
Dean, State v. (645 A.2d), 51, *54,* 75
DeBooy, State v., 90
Defore, People v., 338
DeLancie v. Superior Ct., 255
Delaraba v. Police Dept., 253
Delaware v. Prouse, 90
Delaware v. Van Arsdall, 1219, 1220
DelVecchio, State v., 1183
Densmore, State v., 1161
DePallo, People v., 1244
DePiano, State v., 1264
Derricott v. State, 72
DeSalvo, State v., 1299
DeShields v. State, 559
Diaz, Commonwealth v., 512
Diaz, People v., 119
Dickerson v. Kansas Dept. of Revenue, 1066
Dickerson v. United States, 498, 513, 567
Dionisio, United States v., 662, 672
DiPietro, Commonwealth v., 1234
Ditter, State v., 1057
Dixon, United States v., 891, 898-901
Dixson, State v., 230, 234
Doe, United States v., 668
Doggett v. United States, 985
Dokes, People v., 1198
Domian, State v., 1044
Donnelly, People v., 157
Donovan v. Dewey, 194
Doorson v. Netherlands, 1200
Dorado, People v., 483
Dotson, State ex rel., v. Roger, 1414
Doucette, State v., 1360
Douglas v. California, 701, 1348, 1353
Douglas, Wainwright v., 720
Dow Chemical Co. v. United States, 103, 408
Dowd, State v., 689
Dowling v. United States, 910
Doyle v. Ohio, 1233
Draper, State v., 1044
Drayton, United States v., 48
Drury v. State, 512
Dube, State v., 6
Duckworth v. Eagan, 514
Dudick, State v., 171

Dunaway v. New York, 290
Duncan v. Kerby, 1429, 1432
Duncan v. Louisiana, 1086
Duncan, People v., 869
Dunkerley, In re, 901
Dunn v. State, 169, 523
Dunn v. United States, 1145
Dunn, People v., 408
Dunn, United States v., 229, 230, 234
Dunne, State v., 1093, 1099
Dunnigan, United States v., 1306
Dunnuck v. State, 169
Duren v. Missouri, 1100
Dusina, State v., 1091
Duvernoy, State v., 46
Dye v. State, 506
Dyer, State v., 505

Eason, State v., 357
Easter, State v., 1232
Eastlack, State v., 531
Eden v. State, 1140
Edmonson v. Leesville Concrete, 1134
Edmonson, State v., 864, 869
Edmunds, Commonwealth v., 350, 357, 358
Edwards v. Arizona, 536, 543, 551
Edwards v. Carpenter, 1422
Edwards v. People, 1076
Edwards v. State, 224
Edwards v. United States, 1304
Edwards, United States v., 220
Eisentrager v. Forrestal, 793
Eleneki, State v., 184
Elkins v. United States, 349
Ellis, Commonwealth v., 833-835
Ellis, State v., 202
Elson v. State, 1280
Ely, State v., 655
Engelmann, State v., 1049
England v. State, 636
Entick v. Carrington, 130, 133
Escobedo v. Illinois, 482, 483, 544
Espinoza v. Martin, 1008, 1013, 1014
Espinoza v. State, 235, 619
Estelle v. Smith, 506, 701, 1280
Estelle v. Williams, 1184
Ethington, State v., 1001
Evans v. State, 114
Evans v. Superior Ct., 597

Fahy v. Connecticut, 1379, 1390
Fair v. State, 266
Falkner v. State, 234
Fare v. Michael C., 533,535
Faretta v. California, 702, 703, 707, 1353
Farley, State v., 899
Farmer v. State, 360
Fay v. Noia, 1420, 1422, **1436,** 1442, 1453, 1454
Felix, United States v., 900
Felker v. Turpin, 1406
Fenderson, Commonwealth v., 429
Ferguson v. City of Charleston, 255
Ferguson v. Georgia, 1454
Ferguson, State v., 953
Ferrell v. State, 903, 909
Ferris, State v., 202
Fikes v. Alabama, 468, 482
Filkin, State v., 267
Fini, Commonwealth v., 361
Finley, State v., 1235
Fisher v. State, 1091
Fisher v. United States, 671
Fisher, State v., 1014
Fitzgerald, State v., 52
Fitzpatrick, People v., 1197
Fiumefreddo, People v., 1050
Fleming, State v., 369
Fletcher v. Weir, 1233
Fletcher, People v., 1212
Flippo v. West Virginia, 235
Flores v. State, 1182
Florez, State v., 641
Florida v. Bostick, 48
Florida v. Jimeno, 203
Florida v. J.L., 55, 162
Florida v. Riley, 96, 102
Florida v. Royer, 290
Florida v. Wells, 265
Forbes, State ex rel., v. Canady, 920
Ford, People v., 1044
Fortune, State v., 1145
Foster, State v., 637
Foute, State v., 829
Foy, People v., 1092
FPC v. Tuscarora Indian Nation, 482
Frady, United States v., 1422
Francis v. Franklin, 1184, 1185, 1189
Frank v. Maryland, 190
Franklin, State v., 888
Franks v. Delaware, 179
Franks v. State, 513
Fraternal Order of Police, Miami Lodge 20 v. City of Miami, 254
Frazier, Ex parte, 1244
Frazier v. Cupp, 480
Freeland, State v., 869
Friedman v. Commissioner of Pub. Safety, 694
Frisbie v. Collins, 369
Furman v. Georgia, 1334

Gagnon v. Scarpelli, 701
Gainer, People v., 1139
Garcia, People v., 290
Garcia, State v., 1154, 1160
Gardner v. Florida, 1259, 1299

Garrett v. United States, 900
Gault, In re, 852
George, State v., 202
Georgia v. McCollum, 1134
Gerald, State v., 532
Gerstein v. Pugh, 700, 775
Gesinger, State v., 506
Gibson v. State, 952
Gibson, State v., 1045
Gideon v. Wainwright, 677, 689, 707, 711, 724, 1380, 1454
Giglio v. United States, 953, 1066, 1244
Gilbert v. California, 595, 700
Gillespie, State v., 189
Gindlesperger, Commonwealth v., 403
Giordano, United States v., 424
Glasco v. Commonwealth, 272
Glaspy, Commonwealth v., 1104, 1108
Glass, People v., 869
Glass, State v., 188
Glenn, People v., 61
Globe Newspaper v. Superior Ct. for Norfolk County, 1160
Glosson, State v., 641
Glover, United States v., 724
G.O., In re, 474
Goad, State v., 1235
Go-Bart Importing Co. v. United States, 218
Godinez v. Moran, 1049
Goodwin, United States v., 862
Gordon v. Justice Ct. for Yuba, 1099
Gorton, State v., 573
Goseland, State v., 513
Goss, People v., 909
Grabowski, People v., 1285
Grady v. Corbin, 890, 891, 899, 901
Grady, State v., 1313
Graham v. Connor, 328
Graham v. State, 1278
Graham, People v., 618
Gray v. Maryland, 1206, 1211, 1212
Gray, State v., 975
Green v. United States, 1360
Green, State v., 617, 709, 849, 970
Gregory M., In the Matter of, 241, 246, 247
Grey, State v., 480, 573
Griffin v. California, 1222, 1232, 1234, 1379
Griffin v. Illinois, 1348, 1353
Griffith v. Kentucky, 1377
Griffith, State v., 532
Griggs v. State, 1454
Groom, State v., 394
Grube v. State, 942, 950
Grummon v. Raymond, 175, 176, 177
Guevara, United States v., 999
Guilty Plea Cases, Re, 1049
Guiney v. Police Commr. of Boston, 253
Gustine v. State, 1051
Guzman, People v., 1244
Hackley, State ex rel., v. Kelly, 655
Hagemann, State v., 1049
Hadrick, State v., 617
Hager, State v., 1014
Hale v. Henkel, 671
Haley v. Ohio, 469
Hall, State v., 607
Hamilton v. Alabama, 693
Hambarian v. Superior Court, 835, 836
Hamdi v. Rumsfeld, 1398, *1400*
Hampton, United States v., 631
Hana, People v., 928
Hancich, State v., 820
Hansen, In re, 1099
Hansen, State v., 888
Harding, People v., 899
Harlow v. Fitzgerald, 388
Harman v. Frye, 833
Harmelin v. Michigan, 1262, 1263
Harmon v. Commissioner of Police, 392
Harmon v. State, 205
Harmon, State ex rel., v. Blanding, 819
Harris v. New York, 498, 557
Harris v. Oklahoma, 899
Harris v. United States (331 U.S.), 218
Harris v. United States (536 U.S.), 1299
Harris, Commonwealth v., 455
Harris, People v., 1391
Harrison v. State, 693
Hartgraves v. State, 875
Hatch v. State, 1099
Hathman, State v., 266
Hatten, State v., 235
Hauseman, State v., 266
Havens, United States v., 361
Hawkins v. State, 166, 169
Hawkins, Commonwealth v., 54
Hawkins, People v., 590, 595
Heirtzler, State v., 454
Helfrich, State v., 454
Hempele, State v., 104, 106
Henderson v. Morgan, 1043
Henderson v. People, 101
Henderson, People v., 200
Hensley, United States v., 46
Hernandez v. New York, 1133
Hernandez-Uribe v. United States, 909
Hernley, Commonwealth v., 100
Herrera v. Collins, 1414
Herron, State v., 820
Hessen, State v., 1013, 1014
Hester v. United States, 233
Hickman v. Taylor, 939, 962
Higbee, People v., 168
Higgins, State v., 950
Hightower, State v. (417 S.E.2d), *1111*
Hightower, State v. (680 A.2d), 1108
Hiibel v. District Ct., 121, 127
Hill v. State, 1101, 1107, 1108

Hill, State v., 941
Hinners, State v., 1001
Hinton, State v., 1146
Hitch v. Pima County Superior Ct., 963, 969
Hobbs, People v., 157
Hodge, State v., 1134
Hodson, State v., 228
Hoey, State v., 531
Hofmann, State v., 319
Hogan v. State, 739
Hogg, State v., 888
Hoggins, State v., 1234
Hohn v. United States, 1452
Holbrook v. Flynn, 1184
Holiday, State v., 681, 682
Holloway v. Arkansas, 725
Hope v. Pelzer, 389-391
Horn v. Banks, 1451
Horn v. Territory, 1183
Horton v. California, 99, 178
Hubbell, United States v., 666, 671
Hudson v. Palmer, 254, 255
Hudson v. United States, 1159, 1160
Hues, People v., 1146
Hufnagel, State v., 214, 218
Hughes v. State, 852
Huisman, State v., 266
Hundley, State v., 262
Hurst v. Cook, 1420
Hurtado v. California, 868
Husske v. Commonwealth, 692
Hutchins v. Dist. of Columbia, 23
Hyatt, Commonwealth v., 617

Idaho v. Wright, 1212
Illinois v. Allen, 1198
Illinois v. Gates, 147, 155, 156, 160, 162, 165
Illinois v. Krull, 358
Illinois v. Lafayette, 266
Illinois v. McArthur, 169
Illinois v. Perkins, 513
Illinois v. Rodriguez, 209
Illinois v. Wardlow, 56, 59
Ingram v. Commonwealth, 900
INS v. Cardoza-Fonseca, 92
INS v. Delgado, 239
INS v. Lopez-Mendoza, 361
Isaacson, People v., 641
Isiah B. v. State, 247
Izazaga v. Superior Ct., 961

Jackson v. Commissioner, 1416, 1421
Jackson v. Indiana, 782
Jackson v. Virginia, 1361-1363, 1370, 1371
Jackson, Commonwealth v., 708
Jackson, People v. (217 N.W.2d), 700
Jackson, People v. (452 N.E.2d), 261
Jackson, United States v., 1007
Jacobson v. United States, 631, 636
James v. Illinois, 361
James, State v., 119
Janis, United States v., 348
Janisczak, State v., 10
J.E.B. v. Alabama ex rel. T.B., 1133
Jefferson v. State, 1135
Jenkins v. Anderson, 1233
Jennings v. State, 1305
Jewell v. Maynard, 746
Jiminez, People v., 535
Johns, United States v., 283
Johnson, Ex parte, 1002
Johnson v. Louisiana, 1144
Johnson v. State (922 P.2d), 1044
Johnson v. State (905 P.2d), 206
Johnson v. United States, 3
Johnson v. Zerbst, 197, 691
Johnson, Commonwealth v., 605
Johnson, People v., 992
Johnson, State v. (346 A.2d), 207
Johnson, State v. (606 A.2d), 639, 640
Johnson, State v. (630 N.W.2d), 1317
Johnson, State v. (664 So. 2d), 1380
Johnson, State v. (873 P.2d), 1324
Johnson, State v. (922 P.2d), 1183
Johnson, United States v., 1314
Johnston, People v., 1198
Jones v. State (156 A.2d), 1304
Jones v. State (655 N.E.2d), 1235
Jones v. State (745 A.2d), 60
Jones v. State (798 So. 2d), 14
Jones v. United States, 375
Jones, Commonwealth v., 14
Jones, People v. (375 N.E.2d), 951
Jones, People v. (750 N.E.2d), 1160
Jones, State v. (233 S.E.2d), 1108
Jones, State v. (467 S.E.2d), 992
Jones, State v. (923 P.2d), *1236,* 1243
Joyner, State v., 1190

Kahlbaun, State v., 871, 875
Kahn, United States v., 429
Kansas v. Crane, 790
Kansas v. Hendricks, 790
Karo, United States v., 410, 411
Kastigar v. United States, 655
Katz v. United States, 34, 94, 102, 104, 230, 233, 259, 283, 284, **396,** 403, 404, 408, 412, 414-417, 431, 669
Keeney v. Tamayo-Reyes, 1421, 1443
Keith, State v., 534
Kelekolio, State v., 476, 480
Kelley v. State, 206
Kent v. United States, 843, 851
Kentucky v. Stincer, 1198
Kentucky v. Whorton, 1184

Killackey, Commonwealth v., 189
Killebrew, People v., 1013
Kimmelman v. Morrison, 1433
King, State v., 1069
Kiper, State v., 291, 296
Kirby v. Illinois, 595
Kirby, People v., 1098, 1099
Kirk v. Louisiana, 296
Klopfer v. North Carolina, 985
Knight, State v. (621 P.2d), 408
Knight, State v. (678 A.2d), *1372,* 1377
Knights, United States v., 255
Knotts, United States v., 410, 411
Knowles v. Iowa, 311, 318, 319
Knowles v. United States, 1232
Kock, State v., 282
Kolender v. Lawson, 24, 122
Koon v. United States, 888, 1273
Kotteakos v. United States, 1390
Krueger, People v., 184
Kuhlmann v. Wilson, 545, 551, 552
Kuhn, State v., 80
Kurylczyk, People v., 610, 611
K.W.B., In re, 535
Kyles v. Whitley, 951
Kyllo v. United States, 398, 403, 404

Labron, Commonwealth v., 274
LaCour, State v., 172
Lacy, State v., 975
Ladson, State v., 66
LaFollette v. State, 403
Lagares, State v., 1027, 1030, 1031
La Jeune, United States v., 335
LaMere, State v., 1391
LaMunyon, State v., 1314
Lancaster, People v., 869
Landry v. Attorney General, 450
Lange, Ex parte, 1405
Lanier v. State, 1002
Lanza, United States v., 878
Lanz-Terry, State v., 1220
Larocco, State v., 283
Latimore, Commonwealth v., 1036
Layton, State v., 708
Leach, State v., 206
Ledesma, United States v., 1314
Lee v. Kemna, 1421
Lee v. State, 1066
Lee, People v., 1285
Lee, State v., 630
Lee, United States v., 408
Leftwich, People v., 359
Lego v. Twomey, 532
Lem Woon v. Oregon, 869
Leon, United States v., 357, 358, 360, 361, 391
Lessary, State v., 894
Lettley, State v., 725
Leuthavone, State v., 535
Lewis v. Iowa Dist. Ct. for Des Moines County, 746
Lewis v. United States, 1092
Lewis, Commonwealth v., 72
Lewis, People v., 1263
Leyva, State v., 530
Lilly v. Virginia, 1212
Lindsey, State v., 1091
Lingo v. State, 1122, 1131
Linkletter v. Walker, 1377, 1378
Liteky v. United States, 1114
Lloyd, Commonwealth v., 952
Lo-Ji Sales v. New York, 171, 260
Lombera-Camorlinga, United States v., 524
Long v. United States, 913, 922
Long, Michigan v., 126
Long, State v., 454
Lopez, State v., 611
Losavio v. Mayber, 1109
Lotsch, United States v., 922
Lovasco, United States v., 975
Lovelace v. Commonwealth, 319
Lowenfield v. Phelps, 1139
Lucas v. State, 532
Lucious, State v., 957, 961, 962
Ludecke v. Watkins, 782
Ludwig v. Massachusetts, 1092
Lumzy, People v., 995
Lynch, State v., 737, 746
Lynch, United States v., 1152
Lynumm v. Illinois, 474

Mabry v. Johnson, 1059
MacDonald, United States v., 976
Mack v. State, 1323
Mackintrush v. State, 1131
Maddox v. State, 848, 852
Maestas, State v., 618
Magnusen, State v., 977, 985, 986
Majado, People v., 909
Malinovsky, State v., 1359
Malley v. Briggs, 391
Mallory v. United States, 469
Mandujano, United States v., 506, 648
Manning, State v., 1180
Manson v. Brathwaite, 598, 605, 615
Mapp v. Ohio, 343, 347, 348, 350, 362, 1377
Marbury v. Madison, 1379
Marchetti v. United States, 672
Margali-Olvera v. INS, 1066
Marion, United States v., 975
Maristany, State v., 206, 209
Marron v. United States, 177
Marshall v. Barlow's, Inc., 194
Marshall v. Lonberger, 1043
Marshall v. State, 1220
Martin, Commonwealth v., 404, 407

Martin, State v. (367 S.E.2d), 255
Martin, State v. (495 A.2d), 952
Martin, State v. (658 P.2d), 1360
Martinez v. Ct. of App. of California, 708, 1353
Martinez, People v. (898 P.2d), 180
Martinez, People v. (996 P.2d), 985
Martinez-Fuerte, United States v., 92
Martino, Commonwealth v., 169
Mary Beth G. v. City of Chicago, 224
Maryland v. Buie, 219
Maryland v. Craig, 1197
Maryland v. Garrison, 180
Maryland v. Wilson, 127
Masaniai, State v., 604
Massiah v. United States, 482
Masson v. Netherlands, 790
Mathis v. United States, 514
Matlock, United States v., 204, 205
Matos v. State, 1315, 1317
Mauri v. Smith, 458
Mavredakis, Commonwealth v., 522
Maya, State v., 55
Mayes, State v., 468
Mayo, People v., 991
Mazen v. Seidel, 100
Mazzone, State v., 427
McAlpin, State v., 1282, 1286
McCann v. State, 230
McCarter, State v., 700
McCarthy v. United States, 1045
McCaughey, State v., 209
McCleskey v. Kemp, 1329, 1334, 1340, 1341
McCleskey v. Zant, 1328, 1425
McCloskey v. Honolulu Police Dept., 253
McConkie, State v., 480
McCoy v. State, 254
McCray v. Illinois, 157
McCullough v. State, 1182
McDaniel, People v., 617
McDonald, People v., 614, 618
McDonell, State v., 1033, 1036
McDowell, State v., 202
McFarland v. Texas, 725
McIntosh, People v., 47
McKague v. Whitley, 1433
McKane v. Durston, 1346
McKaskle v. Wiggins, 708
McKay, People v., 319
McKinstry, People v., 349
McLamb, State v., 1232
McLees, State v., 209
McLeod v. State, 474
McMann v. Richardson, 1002
McMillan v. Pennsylvania, 611, 1190, 1290, 1298, 1299
McMorris, State v., 605
McNabb v. United States, 469
McNeil v. Wisconsin, 552
M.E.B., In re, 286, 290
Medeiros, State v., 682
Medford v. State, 289
Medley v. Commonwealth, 1150
Medlock v. 1985 Ford F-150 Pick Up, 1091
Medrano, State v., 1355
Mehner, State v., 177
Melvin, State v., 523
Mempa v. Rhay, 701, 1299
Mendenhall, United States v., 38, 45
Mendes, State v., 483
Mendez, State v., 127
Mendonza v. Commonwealth, 789
Menna v. New York, 1002
Mezzanatto, United States v., 1003
Michigan v. Jackson, 551
Michigan v. Long, 126, 274, 283
Michigan v. Mosley, 536, 543, 544
Michigan v. Thomas, 283
Michigan v. Tucker, 496, 559
Michigan Dept. of Police v. Sitz, 89, 90, 91
Mickens v. Taylor, 725
Midkiff v. Commonwealth, 531
Mierz, State v., 1000
Mikolinski, State v., 90
Miller v. Commissioner, 1414
Miller v. Superior Ct., 1161
Miller, State v. (459 S.E.2d), 910
Miller, State v. (756 P.2d), 1069
Miller, United States v., 260
Mills v. State, 1235
Milton v. Wainwright, 1414
Mincey v. Arizona, 235, 284
Minneapolis v. Buschette, 628
Minnesota v. Carter, 374
Minnesota v. Dickerson, 119
Minnesota v. Murphy, 506
Minnesota v. Olson, 374
Minnick v. Mississippi, 536, 543
Miranda v. Arizona, 197, **483,** 496-499, 506, 513, 514, 522-524, 530-536, 544, 552, 557-560, 563-567, 573-575, 693, 698, 1450
Missoulian, State ex rel. the, v. Judicial Dist., 1160
Missouri v. Hunter, 900
Mitchell v. Superior Ct., 1091
Mitchell v. United States, 1306
Mitchell, State v. (482 N.W.2d), 523
Mitchell, State v. (593 S.W.2d), 596
Mizzell, State v., 1220
Moffett, Commonwealth v., 1108
Mohi, State v., 852
Monaco, United States v., 1314
Monge v. California, 1289
Montana v. Egelhoff, 1190, 1219-1221
Monteiro, State v., 506
Monte Vulture Social Club v. Wallander, 392
Montoya de Hernandez, United States v., 92
Mooney v. Holohan, 942, 1244
Mooney, State v., 236

Moore v. Dempsey, 1443
Moore v. Illinois, 595
Moore v. Michigan, 1044
Morales, State v., 953
Moran v. Burbine, 522, 523
Moran v. State, 103, 105, 106
More, People v., 225, 227, 228
Morris v. Slappy, 709
Morris v. State, 267
Morrison v. State, 1146
Morrow, State v., 408
Moss-Dwyer, State v., 1263
Muetze, State v., 861
Muhammad, State v., 1323
Mu'Min v. Virginia, 1108
Munoz v. State, 638
Munoz, State v., 1069
Murray v. Carrier, 1422
Murray v. Giarratano, 701
Murray v. United Kingdom, 1225
Murray v. United States, 369
Murrell, State v., 272

Nachtigal, United States v., 1087
Napue v. Illinois, 942
National Treasury Employees Union v. Von Raab, 253
Navarroli, People v., 1060
Neahring v. State, 1092
Neely, State v., 273
Neil v. Biggers, 598, 605, 606
Neil, State v., 1116
Nemser, State v., 451, 453, 454
Nelson v. O'Neil, 1211
Nelson, State v., 50, 54
Neuenfeldt v. State, 483
Newbrough, People v., 1197
New Jersey v. T.L.O., 245-247
New York v. Belton, 315, 316
New York v. Burger, 194
New York v. Class, 283
New York v. Quarles, 498, 512, 513
Niblack, State v., 1057
Nichols v. Commonwealth, 1319, 1322
Nichols v. United States, 684, 692, 1314
Nix v. Whiteside, 1243
Nix v. Williams, 362, 368
Nixon v. Singletary, 723, 725
Nixon, State v., 901
Non-testimonial Identification Order, R.H., In re, 228
Norris v. Alabama, 1100
North v. Russell, 1099
North Carolina v. Alford, 1046, 1049, 1050
North Carolina v. Butler, 530, 531
North Carolina v. Pearce, 1307
Novaton v. State, 999

Oates, People v., 411
O'Connor v. Ortega, 240
O'Connor, Commonwealth v., 368
O'Dell v. Netherland, 1450
Ohio v. Johnson, 909
Ohio v. Roberts, 1212
Ohio v. Robinette, 200, 202
Ohio, Reimer v., 658
Oklahoma Press Publishing v. Walling, 662
Oles v. State, 267
Olguin-Rivera, United States v., 273
Olivas, State v., 450
Oliver v. United States, 233
Olivera, State v., 543
Olmstead v. United States, 412, 414, 416, 417
Olwell, State v., 970
O'Meara, State v., 55
One 1985 Ford Thunderbird Auto., Commonwealth v., 102, 361
Opinion of the Justices (DWI Jury Trials), 1091
Oregon v. Bradshaw, 543
Oregon v. Elstad, 557
Oregon v. Hass, 557
Ornelas v. United States, 55, 156
Orozco v. Texas, 505
Ortega-Rodriguez v. United States, 1347
Osakalumi, State v., 955
O'Sullivan v. Boerckel, 1443
Oyler v. Boles, 861

Page v. State, 700
Palmer, State v., 695
Papachristou v. City of Jacksonville, 24
Parent, State v., 186, 188
Patterson v. New York, 1189
Patterson v. State, 1002
Paulson v. State, 1181
Payne v. Arkansas, 468, 1380
Payne v. Tennessee, 1323
Payner, United States v., 375
Payton v. New York, 296
Peart, State v., 732, 745, 747, 748
Peeples, People v., 1108
Peevy, People v., 558
Pelican, State v., 1101
Pennington, State v., 849
Pennsylvania v. Labron, 274
Pennsylvania v. Mimms, 127
Pennsylvania v. Muniz, 513
Pennsylvania v. Ritchie, 952
Pennsylvania Bd. of Probation and Parole v. Scott, 361
Penny-Feeney, United States v., 403
Penrod, Commonwealth v., 1325
Pens v. Bail, 1280
People v. _______. *See* name of defendant.
Perham, State v., 266

Perry, State v., 837
Peters, State v., 840
Peterson, State v., 225
Petite v. United States, 889
Pettingill, People v., 544
Pettitt, State v., 1030
Phelps, State v., 560
Phillips, Commonwealth v., 75
Pierce, State v. (642 A.2d), *268,* 272, 273
Pierce, State v. (927 P.2d), 1182
Pimental v. Dept. of Transportation, 90
Pinder v. State, 1108
Pinder, State v., 234
Piorkowski, State v., 543
Place, United States v., 403, 407
Plaxico v. Michael, 455, 458
Poller, United States v., 214
Portillo, State v., 1181
Portrey, State v., 234
Portuondo v. Agard, 1234
Powell v. Alabama, 676, 678, 679, 711
Powell v. Superior Ct., 888
Powell, State v., 644
Powell, United States v. (34 F.3d), 888
Powell, United States v. (379 U.S.), 663
Powell, United States v. (469 U.S.), 1145, 1146
Powers v. Ohio, 1134
Pratt v. Chicago Hous. Auth., 211
Presha, State v., 474
Press-Enterprise Co. v. Superior Ct. of California, 1161
Pulley, State v., 54
Purkett v. Elem, 1130, 1131

Quarles v. State, 69
Quercia v. United States, 1221

R. v. Aramah, 1274
R. v. Bilinksi, 1274
R. v. Turner, 1013
Rabinowitz, United States v., 218
Ragland, State v., 1150
Rakas v. Illinois, 374
Ramirez, State v., 598, 606
Ramirez, United States v., 183
Ramos v. State, 1150
Randolph, State v., 523
Randy G., In re, 246
Rawlings v. Kentucky, 375
Ray, State v., 9, 273, 283, 770
Reasor v. State, 220
Recorder's Court Bar Assn. v. Wayne Cir. Ct., 743
Reece, United States v., 1342
Reed v. Farley, 1450
Reed, People v., 1422
Reed, State v., 515, 522, 523
Reese v. United States, 770
Reeves, State v., 431, 437
Regina v. Turnbull, 619
Reichman, People v., 1240, 1244
Reid v. Georgia, 72
Reid, State v., 1231
R. Enterprises, Inc., United States v., 659, 662
Resendiz, In re, 1044
Rey v. State, 693
Reynolds v. State, 61, 201
Rezk, State v., 612
Rhode Island v. Innis, 506, 512, 551
Richards v. Wisconsin, 180, 184
Richards, State v., 291
Richardson v. Marsh, 928
Richardson v. State, 441
Richardson v. United States, 1145
Richman, Commonwealth v., 700
Richmond Newspapers v. Virginia, 1160
Ring v. Arizona, 1299
Rivest, State v., 1066
Roberts v. State, 951
Robinson, People v., 60
Robinson, United States v. (414 U.S.), 219
Robinson, United States v. (485 U.S.), 1233
Robinette, State v., 200, 202
Rochin v. California, 227
Rodgers v. State, 724
Roe v. Flores-Ortega, 725
Rogers v. Richmond, 481
Rogers v. Tennessee, 1378
Rogers, People v., 840
Rogers, State v., 60
Rose v. Lundy, 1443
Rose, State v., 95
Ross v. Moffitt, 701, 1353
Ross v. State, 1049
Ross, State v., 1038, 1044
Ross, United States v., 284
Roy, State v., 1235
Royall, Ex parte, 1443
Roye v. United States, 1069
Rubin v. State, 969
Ruiz, United States v., 1040, 1044, 1045
Russell, State v. (343 N.W.2d), 629
Russell, State v. (477 N.W.2d), 1342
Russell, United States v., 631

Sabrina W. v. Willman, 458
Sacramento County v. Lewis, 333
Salaiscooper v. District Ct., 861
Saldana v. State, 445
Salerno, United States v., 780, 788-790
Salvucci, United States v., 375
Samaniego v. City of Kodiak, 328
Sanchez v. State, 1060, 1066

Sanchez, State v. (848 P.2d), 1279
Sanchez, State v. (856 S.W.2d), 90
Sanders v. United States, 1442
Sanders, Commonwealth v., 1108
Sanders, People v., 206
Sandstrom v. Montana, 1184, 1189
Sandy v. District Ct., 1013
Sanges, United States v., 1354
Santiago, State v., 523
Santobello v. New York, 1001, 1059, 1068, 1069
Sapp v. State, 530
Sarabia, State v., 1317
Savva, State v., 281
Scales, State v., 573
Schad v. Arizona, 1144
Schaffer v. United States, 923
Schmerber v. California, 227, 667, 672
Schneckloth v. Bustamonte, 195, 202, 210
Schultz, State v., 261
Schreiber v. Rowe, 729
Scott v. Illinois, 689
Scott v. State, 114
Scott v. United States, 427, 428
Scott, United States v., 1360
Seaberg, People v., 1001
Sealed Case, In re, 440
Sears v. State, 260
Segura v. United States, 169, 369
Semayne's Case, 183
Shapiro v. United States, 667, 672
Sharpe, United States v., 290
Shaw, State v., 1032
Sheridan, State v., 338
Sheriff of Humboldt County v. Marcum, 870
Sheriff, Washoe County v. Bessey, 480
Sherman v. United States, 631, 636
Shumpert v. Department of Highways, 1007
Sibron v. New York, 55
Siebert, People v., 1014
Siegal, State v., 403
Silverman v. United States, 414
Silverthorne Lumber v. United States, 338
Simmons v. United States, 375
Simpson, Ex parte, 876
Singer v. United States, 1098
Singleton, United States v., 1075
Skeleton, State v., 283
Skinner v. Railway Labor Executives' Assn., 253
Slack v. McDaniel, 1425, 1452, 1453
Slamon, State v., 338
Slaughter v. Commonwealth, 1146
Smith v. Hooey, 985
Smith v. Illinois, 1205
Smith v. Maryland, 445
Smith v. Robbins, 1348, 1353
Smith v. State (517 A.2d), 1280
Smith v. State (787 A.2d), 1232
Smith v. State (948 P.2d), 368
Smith, Commonwealth v., 557
Smith, People v., 1212
Smith, State v. (39 S.W.3d), 60
Smith, State v. (488 S.E.2d), 201
Smith, State v. (546 N.W.2d), *499*
Smith, State v. (558 N.W.2d), 725
Smith, State v. (672 P.2d), 1091
Smith, State v. (681 P.2d), 735, 736, 746
Smith, State v. (834 S.W.2d), 553, 557
Smith, State v. (864 P.2d), 902
Smithers, United States v., 618
Sneed, Ex parte, 1212
Snell, United States v., 889
Snyder v. Massachusetts, 1197
Soares, Commonwealth v., 1116
Sokolow, United States v., 72
Solem v. Helm, 1263
Sorrells v. United States, 631, 636
Soto, State v., 1265, 1279
South Carolina v. Gathers, 1323
South Dakota v. Opperman, 265
Spano v. New York, 480, 482
Specht v. Patterson, 1298
Spencer, State v. (519 N.W.2d), *702,* 707, 708
Spencer, State v. (750 P.2d), 697, 700
Spillers v. State, 1108
Spinelli v. United States, 147, 155, 156, 162
Spock, United States v., 1145
Stack v. Boyle, 776, 783
Stagner, Commonwealth v., 1000
Stallworth, Commonwealth v., 220
Stanley, State v., 523, *540,* 543
Stansbury v. California, 505
State ex rel. Brown v. Dietrick, 170
State v. _______. *See* name of defendant.
Staten, State v., 72, 184
Steele v. United States, 177
Stephan v. State, 568, 573, 574
Stephens v. Bonding Assn. of Ky., 770
Stephens v. State, 1335, 1341
Sterling v. State, 1184
Sterling, In re, 1414
Stevens, People v. (597 N.W.2d), 368
Stevens, People v. (610 N.W.2d), 1003
Steven William T., In re, 469
Stewart v. Martinez-Villareal, 1425
Stewart v. Smith, 1421
Stewart v. State, 1280
Stith, People v., 368
Stone v. Bell, 875
Stone v. Powell, 1414, 1433, 1444, 1450
Stoner v. California, 204
Storch, State v., 1212
Stout v. State, 273
Stovall v. Denno, 598, 1377
Stowe, State v., 7
Strain, State v., 470, 474
Strauder v. West Virginia, 1100, 1116

Strecker, State v., 1013
Strickland v. Washington, 710, 723-725, 728, 729, 951
Strickler v. Greene, 951
Strunk v. United States, 986
Stuart v. State, 369
Sudler v. State, 1113
Sugar, State v., 368
Sullivan v. Louisiana, 1290, 1380, 1381, 1390, 1391
Sullivan, State v., 319
Swain v. Alabama, 1116
Swanson v. City of Juneau, 574
Swinehart, Commonwealth v., 650, 655

Tague v. Louisiana, 532
Tarantino, State v., 408
Tarble's Case, 1406
Tate, State v., 1141
Tattered Cover, Inc. v. City of Thornton, 260
Taylor v. Commonwealth, 891, 899
Taylor v. Illinois, 963
Taylor v. Kentucky, 1183
Taylor v. Louisiana, 1100
Taylor v. State, 1377
Taylor, People v. (41 P.3d), 506
Taylor, People v. (541 N.E.2d), 349
Taylor, State v., 1108
Taylor, United States v., 992
Teague v. Lane, 1377, **1444,** 1450-1453
Telfaire, United States v., 615, 618
Tello, People v., 1432
Tennesee v. Garner, 320, 327-329, 334, 390
Terry v. Ohio, 35, 39, 42, 49, 56, 75, **107,** 114-116, 119, 120, 126, 127, 283
Texas v. Cobb, 552
Texas v. McCullough, 1307
Thistlewood v. Trial Magistrate for Ocean City, 24
Thomas, State v. (533 N.E.2d), 1141
Thomas, State v. (540 N.W.2d), 177
Thomas, State v. (798 A.2d), 1108
Thomas, United States v., 1342
Thompson v. Utah, 1378
Thompson, People v. (633 N.E.2d), 1266
Thompson, People v. (820 P.2d), 230
Thompson, State v. (464 A.2d), 428
Thompson, State v. (505 N.W.2d), 228
Thompson, State v. (810 P.2d), 261
Thompson, United States v., 617
Thornley, Commonwealth v., 612
Thrift, State v., 655
Tibbs v. Florida, 1371
Todd v. State, 900
Tollett v. Henderson, 1002
Torres, United States v., 1280
Townsend v. Sain, 1421, 1442, 1443
Travers, Commonwealth v., 1211
Traylor v. State (596 So. 2d), 496
Traylor v. State (801 S.W.2d), 1289
Triplett, Commonwealth v., 557
Trompeter, State v., 972, 975, 976
Troupe, State v., 1347
Trupiano v. United States, 165, 218
Tucker, State v., 1190
Tucker, United States v., 1314
Tuey, Commonwealth v., 1139
Tumey v. Ohio, 171, 1114, 1380
Tunstill v. State, 1308
Turner v. Fouche, 1100
Turner v. State, 1353
Turney v. State, 1153
Turpin v. Todd, 1422
Twigg v. Hercules Corp., 253

United States v. _______. *See* name of defendant.
Unruh, People v., 408
Utterback, State v., 152, 155

Vale v. Louisiana, 220
Valenzuela-Bernal, United States v., 1235
Valera, State v., 1279
Vallejos, State v., 636
Vandebogart, State v., 1205
Van Kirk, State v., 1390
Van Leeuwen, United States v., 73
Vasquez v. State (739 S.W.2d), 296
Vasquez v. State (990 P.2d), 272
Vasquez, State v., 1031
Vasquez-Aerreola, State v., 1014
Vaughn v. Cox, 389, 390
Vecchio, People v., 1322
Vernier v. State, 975
Vernonia Sch. Dist. 47J v. Acton, 85, 253
Viers, State v., 1360
Vilardi, People v., 951
Villalobos, People v., 530
Vineyard, State v., 66, 92
Virdin v. State, 454
Virginia v. Rives, 1108
Vonn v. United States, 1391

Wacker, State v., 408
Waddell, State v., 1146
Wade v. United States (388 U.S.), 667
Wade v. United States (504 U.S.), 1317
Wade, United States v. , 586, 595-598
Wainwright v. Sykes, 1420, 1421, 1442, 1444
Wakefield, State v., 1057
Walker, State v., 851
Walkowiak, State v., 530
Warden v. Hayden, 221, 259

Wardius v. Oregon, 961
Waring v. State, 375
Warner, State v. (762 So. 2d), 1057
Warner, State v. (812 P.2d), 942
Warren, State v., 1014
Washington, People v., 1408, 1414
Washington, United States v., 648
Waters, State v., 1377
Watkins, Ex parte, 1405
Watson, United States v., 201, 297
Watts, United States v., 1300, 1304
Wayte v. United States, 627, 861
Weaver, State v., 203
Webb v. Texas, 1234
Webster, Commonwealth v., 1180
Weeks v. United States, 336, 338, 350
Weidul, State v., 1139
Weis, People v., 369
Welfare of D.A.G., In re, 204
Welsh v. Wisconsin, 168
Wentworth, State v., 1150
Wentz, State v., 1274
West, State v., 266
Westerman v. Cary, 773, 776
Westerman, Commonwealth v., 429
Wheeler, People v., 1116
White v. Illinois, 1212
White, State v., 358
White, United States v., 102, 437
Whitetail, United States v., 1280
Whitfield, People v., 1045
Whitten v. Tomlinson, 1405
Whren v. United States, 66, 83, 87
Wilkes v. Wood, 133
Wilkins, State v., 127
Williams v. Florida, 961, 1143
Williams v. New York, 1248, 1258, 1259, 1285, 1299
Williams v. Taylor (529 U.S. 362), 1451
Williams v. Taylor (529 U.S. 420), 1443
Williams, Commonwealth v., 535
Williams, People v., 1153
Williams, State v., 525, 530
Williams, United States v., 869
Williamson, State v., 951
Willis, People v., 1135
Willis, State v., 617
Wills, State v., 1067
Wilson v. Arkansas, 183, 184
Wilson v. Layne, 185
Wilson v. State (562 S.E.2d), 543
Wilson v. State (874 P.2d), 43, 49-50, 148
Wilson, People v. (213 N.W.2d), 1140
Wilson, People v. (563 N.W.2d), 902
Wims, People v., 1190, 1298
Windsor, State v., 1109
Winegeart v. State, 1170, 1181
Winship, In re, 1180, 1290
Wise, United States v., 1299
Witherspoon v. Illinois, 1114
Withrow v. Larkin, 1114
Withrow v. Williams, 1450
Witte v. United States, 1288, 1289
Wolf v. Colorado, 338, 347, 362
Wolfe, People v., 1370
Wolff, State v., 1044
Wood v. State, 283
Wood, People v., 900
Wood, State v., 370, 374
Woodlief, State v., 1304
Woodruff, State v., 692
Woodward v. State, 146
Woody v. Peairs, 875
Woolverton v. Multi-County Grand Jury, 672
Worthy, State v., 418, 423-425
Wright, People v., 617, 618
Wright, United States v., 889
Wyman v. James, 210, 211
Wyoming v. Houghton, 133, 273, 282

Yarber, Ex parte, 1059
Ybarra v. Illinois, 120
Yick Wo v. Hopkins, 861
Young v. State, 574
Young v. United States ex rel. Vuitton et Fils S.A., 832, 835
Young, State v., 403
Younger v. State, 1422

Zebe v. State, 1066
Ziegler, State v., 240
Zurcher v. Stanford Daily, 664, 665

Index

Abandoned property, 103-106
Abuse of the writ, 1425
Acquittal-first instruction, 1140, 1141
Administrative searches, 189-194
Administrative stops, 84-93
Administrative subpoenas, 663, 664
Administrative warrants, 189-194
Adult curfews, 23, 24
Advisory appeals, 1360, 1361
Aguilar-Spinelli test, 147-155
Alford pleas, 1046-1050
Allen charges, 1136-1141
Allen Report, 744, 745
Alternate jurors, 1141
Anonymous tips
  probable cause, and, 156-161
  reasonable suspicion, and, 55, 161, 162
Anonymous witnesses, 1200-1205
Anticipatory warrants, 186-189
Apparent authority rule, 206-210
Appeals, 1345-1391. *See also* Judicial review
  advisory, 1360, 1361
  bail pending, 1347
  dismissal of charges, after, 1359
  double jeopardy, and, 1359, 1360, 1371
  government, 1354-1361
  guilty pleas, after, 1347
  harmless error, 1379-1391
  indigent appellants, 1348-1354
  interlocutory, 1354-1361
  Jackson standard, 1361-1371
  joinder/severance decisions, 922
  motions for new trials, and, 1347
  number of, 1347
  pretrial rulings, of, 1354-1361
  retroactivity, 1371-1378
  right to appeal, 1346-1347
  right to counsel, 701
Appointed counsel systems, 690, 730-732, 737-742, 745-746
Arrest warrants, 291-297
Arrests, 285-334
  citations, 309-320
  domestic violence, 297-306
  force, 320-334
  Frisbie rule, 369
  police discretion, 297-320
  protective sweeps, 219, 220
  race, and, 306-308
  searches incident to, 214-221
  stop, contrasted, 285-291
  warrants, 291-297
Attorneys. *See* Counsel
At-trial identification, 597
Automatic standing rule, 375
Automobiles, searches of, 267-284

Bail, 759-791
  acquittal rates, and, 771
  appeal, pending, 1347
  bail schedules, 772-776
  bond dealers/bounty hunters, 454, 769, 770
  discretion, 772-778
  domestic assault, 772-779
  excessive bail clause, 776
  failure to appear, and, 768-770
  Federal Bail Reform Act of 1966, 764, 769, 778
  gender bias, 771
  Manhattan Bail Project, 760-765
  nonfinancial release conditions, 766, 768-771
  racial bias, 771, 777
  sentence, and, 760, 764, 765, 771
  station-house, 759, 772, 777
  surety bonds, 767, 769, 770
  victims' rights, 777
Baldus study, 1328-1334
Banking records, 261
Beepers, 409-411
Bentham, Jeremy, 657
Bill of particulars, 941
Binoculars, 50, 408, 409
Bivens actions, 366, 390
Blank lineups, 593, 597
Body cavity searches, 221-228
Bond dealers, 769, 770
Booking questions, 512, 513
Bounty hunters, 769, 770
Brady disclosure requirement, 942-954
Brief searches/stops, 33-127. *See also* Search and seizure
  abandoned property, 103-106
  administrative stops, 84-93
  asking for name/identification, 36, 46, 48, 121-127
  bad neighborhoods, 58, 59
  briefcases, 120
  consensual encounters vs. stops, 38-49
  criminal profiles, 68-84
  detention of luggage, 73
  flyovers, 100-102
  frisks, 106-120
  garbage searches, 103-106
  highway safety, 84-93
  immigration search cases, 92
  orders to exit vehicle, 127
  package profiles, 73
  plain feel doctrine, 116-120
  plain view, 94-103
  police expertise, 54, 68, 72, 73
  pretextual stops, 60-68
  protective *Terry* searches, 106-115
  purses, 120
  pursuit, seizure by, 59, 60
  reasonable person standard, 43-46
  reasonable suspicion, 49-84
  roadblocks, 84-93
  roving stops, 92
  sobriety checkpoints, 84-93
  stops of persons, 36-93
  Terry searches, 106-115
  warrant check, 46
Bugs on government agents, 431-437
Burden of proof
  affirmative defenses, 1189-1190
  entrapment defenses, 637, 638
  presumption of innocence, 1178-1183
  presumptions, 1184-1189
  reasonable doubt standard, 1170-1184
  search warrants, 184, 185
  sentencing, 1290-1299

Canine sniff searches, 404-408
Canons of construction, 120, 425
Capital punishment, 1259, 1299, 1322, 1323, 1327-1334
Case attrition, 798, 825, 826
Cause and prejudice standard, 1420-1425
Cellular phones, 425
Charge bargain, 1000, 1021, 1022
Charge offense sentencing systems, 1281, 1285, 1286
Charging, 797-876. *See also* Double jeopardy, Joinder
  civil law systems, 823, 826
  declination, 802-811
  diversion, 811-820
  domestic violence, 820-826, 835
  factors to consider, 809, 810
  grand jury indictment, 863-876
  information, 863, 868, 869
  juveniles, 842-854
  mandatory charging statutes, 821-823, 826
  mandatory prosecution policies, 820-826
  no-drop policies, 820-826
  overcharging, 841
  police screening, 798-802

preliminary examination, 863-869
private filing of complaints, 835
private prosecution, 827-836
prosecutorial screening, 802-863, 1326
selection among charges, 836-842
selection of system, 842-855
selective prosecution, 855-863
victim input, 835
Checkpoints, 84-93
Child witnesses, 1191-1198
Christopher Commission, 377
Citations, 309-320
Citizen informants, 154, 156
Clearance rates, 566
Cocaine punishment policies, 1341-1343
Code of Hammurabi, 1261
Co-defendant's out-of-court statements, 1205-1213
Cognizable subject matter on habeas, 1407-1414
Collateral attack. *See* Habeas corpus
Collateral consequences of conviction, 1038-1040, 1044
Collateral estoppel, 903-910
Collateral review, 1393
Collective entity doctrine, 671, 672
Collective knowledge doctrine, 290, 291
Communications Assistance for Law Enforcement Act (CALEA), 425
Community caretaker function, 4-10
Community courts, 1161-1167
Community policing, 24-32
Compulsory joinder rules, 911, 919, 920, 923
Compulsory process, 1234, 1235
Computerized government databases, 446-450
Conditional plea, 1000
Confessions, 463-576
corroboration, 474
false physical evidence/false friends, 480
length of interrogation, 468
McNabb-Mallory rule (time rules), 468, 469
Miranda warnings. *See Miranda* warnings
physical abuse, 464-470
physical deprivations, 468
police lies, 475-482
police promises, 470-475
promises/threats, 473-474
videotaping, 567-575
voluntariness, 464-482
vulnerability of suspect, 469, 533-535
Confidential informants
management/control, 638-642
probable cause, and, 146-157
shielding names of, 1205
Confrontation of witnesses. *See also* Witnesses
co-defendants' out-of-court statements, 1205-1213
hearsay statements, 1212, 1213
sentencing, 1299
value of confrontation, 1191-1205
Confrontations, 585. *See also* Showups
Connected pleas, 1050, 1051
Consensual encounters, 38-49
Consensual intercepts, 422, 423
Consensual searches
authority to allow, 204-210
duration of consent, 203
group consent, 210, 211
knowledge and, 201
retroactive consent, 203
scope of consent, 203
third-party consent, 204-210
traffic stops, 200, 202
voluntariness, 194-203, 210
withdrawal of consent, 203
Consistency agreement, 1014
Conspiracies, 903
Container-in-car searches, 267-284
Continuum of force, 329-331
Contract attorney systems, 731, 746-748
Cordless phones, 425
Counsel. *See also* Right to counsel, State-provided counsel
adequacy of, 709-729
ethics of defending criminals, 749-757
grand juries, and, 648
law students as, 709
standby, 708
subpoenas, and, 665, 666
systems for providing, 729-749
Crime control model of criminal procedure, 29, 30, 32
Criminal profiles, 68-84
Critical stage in proceeding, 693-702
Cross-examination, 1191-1221. *See also* Confrontation of witnesses
Curfew laws, 22-24
Curtilage, 106, 230-235
Custody during interrogation, 499-506

Deadlocked juries, 1136-1141
Deadly force, 320-328
Death penalty cases, 1114, 1299, 1322, 1323, 1327-1334
Declination, 802-811
Defense disclosures, 955-963
Deliberate bypass standard, 1420-1425
Delinquency. *See* Juveniles
Demand waiver rule, 985
Desk appearance tickets, 309-320
Detention of luggage, 73
Direct consequences of conviction, 1038-1040, 1044
Discovery, 933-970
  Brady disclosure requirement, 942-954, 1244
  defendant/co-defendant statements, 938
  defense disclosures, 955-963
  depositions, 940, 941
  ethics, 963-970
  guilty pleas, and, 1044, 1045
  materiality of exculpatory evidence, 951
  open file policies, 940
  preservation of evidence, 952-955
  prosecution disclosures, 933-955
  prosecution expert witnesses, 938, 939
  reciprocal, 961, 962
  remedies for violations, 941, 954
  witnesses/potential witnesses, 939, 940
  work product doctrine, 939, 940, 962, 963
Dismissal of jurors for cause, 1109-1114
Disorderly conduct, 13
District attorneys. *See* Prosecutors
Diversion, 811-820
DNA databases, 449, 450
Dog sniff searches, 404-408
Domestic violence
  arrests, 297-306
  bail, 772-778, 789
  charging, 820-826
  protection orders, 920, 921
Double jeopardy
  appeals, and, 1359, 1360, 1371
  collateral estoppel, 903-910
  conspiracies, 903
  dual sovereign doctrine, 878-889
  multiplicity, 901-903
  same offense, 890-903
  sentencing, 1287-1290
Drug courier profiles, 72, 73
Drug courts, 1161, 1162, 1166, 1167
Drug testing, 248-254
Dual juries, 929
Dual sovereign doctrine, 878-889
Due process entrapment, 638-644
Due process model of criminal procedure, 30-32

Electronic Communications Privacy Act of 1986, 445, 446
Electronic records, 445-449
E-mail, 446, 447, 459, 460
Employer-employee relations. *See* Workplaces
Entrapment defenses, 630-644
  burden of proof, 637, 638
  hybrid approach, 636
  objective approach, 636
  outrageous government conduct, 638-644
  physical injury limitation, 637
  sentencing, and, 1275-1280
  subjective approach, 636, 637
  trial strategy, 638
Error coram nobis, 1404
Ethics
  contacting represented persons, 649, 650
  cross-examination, 1220
  defending criminals, of, 749-757
  discovery, and, 963-970
  lying clients and witnesses, 1235-1244
  police experiments, and, 308
European Convention for the Protection of Human Rights and Fundamental Freedoms, 1200
European Court of Human Rights, 1200
Ex post facto principle, 1377, 1378
Excessive bail clause, 776
Exclusionary rule
  causation limits, 362-369
  empirical evidence, 347, 348
  Frisbie rule, 369
  good faith exception, 350-361
  identifications, 585, 586, 597, 598, 605, 606
  impeachment, 361
  independent source rule, 369
  inevitable discovery exception, 362-368
  limitations, 350-375
  Miranda violations, 557-560
  origins, 335-350
  sentencing, and, 1278-1281

standing doctrine, 370-375
wiretaps, 424
Exigent circumstances, 166-170
Expert witnesses
discovery, 938, 939
identifications, 618, 619
Extradition, 889, 890
Eyewitness identifications. *See* Identifications

Failure to appear (FTA), 768-770
Family model of criminal procedure, 32
Fellow officer rule, 145
FinCEN program, 448
Flashlights, 95, 408
Flyovers, 100-102
Four corners rule, 178, 179, 354
Frisbie rule, 369
Frisks, 106-120
Fruit-of-the-poisonous-tree rule, 337, 338, 362, 559, 560
Full searches of people/places. *See also* Search and seizure
balancing methodology, 189-194
consent. *See* Consensual searches
especially intrusive searches, 221-229
lesser invasion/lesser justification, 189-194
medical search techniques, 229
origin of Fourth Amendment, 129-138
probable cause. *See* Probable cause
warrants. *See* Search warrants

Garbage searches, 103-106
Gates totality of the circumstances standard, 147-155
General warrants, 130-138, 193
Good faith exception, 350-361
Government appeals, 1354-1361
Grand jury
document subpoenas, 658-672
immunity, 650-658
indictments, 863-876
makeup/selection, 647
Miranda warnings, 648, 649
origin, 644, 645
reports, 870-876
role of attorneys, 648
secrecy, 645-647
support staff, 870-875
witnesses, 650-658
Guideline (structured) sentencing, 1266-1275, 1281, 1282, 1313
Guilty pleas. *See also* Plea bargains
Alford pleas, 1046-1050
appeals after, 1347
connected pleas, 1050, 1051
discovery, and, 1044, 1045
elements of valid plea, 1037
forfeiture of claims, 1002
harmless error, 1045
incompetent lawyers, and, 1044
involuntary pleas, 1045-1058
nonwaivable claims, 1002, 1003
plea discounts, 1000, 1001
sentencing, and, 1305, 1306
types of pleas, 999, 1000
waiver of appeal, 1001, 1002

Habeas corpus, 1393-1454
abuse of the writ, 1425
Act of 1679, 1394, 1395
Act of 1867, 1405
Act of 1996, 1423, 1425, 1451
availability of, 1406-1434
cause and prejudice standard, 1420-1425
cognizable subject matter, 1407-1414
deliberate bypass standard, 1420-1425
error coram nobis, 1404
evidentiary hearings, 1421
exhaustion of state remedies, 1443, 1444
federal constitutional guarantee, 1405, 1406
federal review of state convictions, 1434-1454
harmless error, 1452
history, 1394-1398
ineffective assistance of counsel, 1425-1433
new claims/law, 1453, 1454
new evidence of innocence, 1408-1414
presumption of correctness, 1442, 1443
procedural bars, 1414-1425
retroactivity, 1444-1450
search and seizure claims, 1414, 1444
statute of limitations, 1422
subject matter bars, 1407-1414
successive petitions, 1424, 1425
suspension, 1393-1406
Habitual offender laws, 1311, 1313, 1314
Harmless error
arrests, 369
doctrine, generally, 1379-1391

Harmless error (*cont.*)
  guilty pleas, 1045
  habeas corpus, 1452
  Miranda warnings, 558
Hearsay statements, 1212, 1213
High-speed chases, 332, 333
Highway safety, 84-93
Houses
  arrests, and, 296
  searches of, 169, 170, 229-236, 404
Hung juries, 1141

Identifications, 577-619
  at-trial, 597
  blank lineups, 597
  corroboration, 619
  cross-racial identification, 584, 612-619
  detention for, 607
  exclusion remedy, 585, 586, 597, 598, 605, 606
  expert testimony, 618, 619
  in-person, 586-609
  jury instructions, 612-618
  memory problems, 577-585
  photographic, 607-612
  police officers as witnesses, 584, 585
  right to counsel, 586-598, 611
  risks of mistaken identification, 577-585
  showups, 585
  suggestive, 598-607
Immigration search cases, 92
Immunity, 650-658, 1235
Impeachment
  exclusionary rule, 361
  Miranda tainted statements, 557, 558
  pre-arrest silence, and, 1233
Impoundment of vehicles, 266
Improperly obtained evidence. *See* Exclusionary rule
In pari materia, 841
Inconsistent verdicts, 1145, 1146
Incorporation of Bill of Rights, 691
Independent and adequate state grounds, 66, 273, 274
Independent counsel, 629, 835, 836
Independent source rule, 369
Indeterminate sentencing system, 1248-1260
Indictments, 863-876
Ineffective counsel claims, 709-729, 1425-1433
Inevitable discovery doctrine, 362-368
Informants. *See also* Confidential informants
  anonymous sources. *See* Anonymous tips
  probable cause, and, 146-157
  undercover agents, 638-642
Information, 863, 868, 869
Informer's privilege, 156, 157
Infrared searches, 403
Initial appearance, 759, 863
Injunctions, 392, 393
In-person identification, 586-609
Interlocking confessions, 1211
Interlocutory appeals, 1354-1361
Interpreting statutes. *See* Statutory interpretation
Interrogation. *See* Confessions
Interstate Agreement on Detainers (IAD), 889, 890
Intrusive body searches, 221-229
Inventory searches, 262-267
Involuntary pleas, 1045-1058

Jeopardy. *See* Double jeopardy
Joinder, 910-929
  compulsory joinder rules, 911, 919, 920, 923
  discretionary joinder of offenses, 911-923
  joint trials of defendants, 923-929
  misjoinder, 923
  permissive joinder rules, 911-923
  severance of offenses, 911-913, 922, 923
Joint trials of defendants, 923-929
Judges
  bench trials, 1086-1100
  commenting on evidence/credibility, 1221
  non-law-trained, 1099
  peremptory challenges to, 1135
  recusal of, 1114
Juries
  alternate jurors, 1141
  availability of jury trial, 1086-1093
  background investigation of jurors, 1109
  deadlocked, 1136-1141
  death-qualified jurors, 1114
  deliberations, 1136-1153
  dismissal for cause, 1109-1114
  excused for hardship, 1113, 1114
  hung, 1141
  inconsistent verdicts, 1145, 1146
  key man selection system, 1100
  lesser included offenses, 1140, 1141

misbehavior, 1153
non-unanimous verdicts, 1144
note-taking, 1146
nullification, 1147-1153
peremptory challenges, 1114-1135
questioning of witnesses, 1146, 1147
race, and, 1101-1109, 1114-1135
selection of jurors, 1100-1135
sentencing, and, 1260, 1298, 1299
sequestration of, 1141
size, 1143, 1144
special verdicts, 1145
tampering with, 1152, 1153
unanimity requirement, 1144
venire, 1100-1135
voir dire, 1101-1109
waiver of jury trial, 1093-1100
Jury instructions
acquittal first instruction, 1140
Allen charge, 1136-1141
dynamite instructions, 1136-1141
hammer charge, 1136-1141
harmless error, and, 1391
identifications, 612-618
reasonable doubt, 1170-1184
unable-to-agree instruction, 1141
Jury nullification, 1147-1153
Jury tampering, 1152, 1153
Juvenile curfews, 22-24
Juveniles
charging, 842-854
interrogation, 469, 472, 473, 499-505, 535
right to counsel, 852, 853

Key man selection system, 1100
Knock and announce rule, 180-184
Knock and talk searches, 201

Lawyers. *See* Counsel
Legislative sentencing, 1260-1266
Legitimately on the premises test for standing, 374
Limited jurisdiction courts, 1099
Lineups, 586-609
Low-level stops/searches. *See* Brief searches/stops
Lying witnesses, 1235-1244

Mandatory charging statutes, 821-823, 826
Mandatory joinder rules, 911, 919, 920, 923
Mandatory minimum penalties, 1260-1266
Mandatory prosecution policies, 820-826
Manhattan Bail Project, 760-765
McNabb-Mallory rule, 468, 469
Medical search techniques, 229
Metal detectors, 93
Minneapolis Domestic Violence Experiment, 299-306
Miranda warnings, 482-576
alternatives to, 566-576
ambiguous waiver/assertion, 525-532
capacity to waive, 533-535
custody, 499-506
effect of invoking rights, 535-544
fifth right, 523
form of warnings, 514-523
grand jury investigations, 648, 649
harmless error, 558
impact, 560-566
impeachment, use of statements for, 557, 558
informing defendant of presence of attorney, 514-523
interrogation, 506-514
invocation/waiver, 524-535
juveniles, 469, 472, 473, 499-505, 535
language barriers, 523, 535
Miranda v. Arizona, 483-495
origins, 482, 483
public safety exception, 512, 513
remedies for violations, 557-560
silence as waiver, 532
statements obtained after violations, 553-557
subsequently acquired evidence, 559-560
translation of warnings, 523, 535
Misjoinder, 923
Motions for new trial, 1347
Multiplicity, 901-903

Nemo tenetur seipsum prodere, 655
Neutral and detached magistrate, 170-174
New judicial federalism, 273, 274
Nighttime searches, 184
No-drop charging policies, 820-826
No-knock entry, 180-184
Nolo contendere, 993, 1000
Nongovernmental infringement of privacy, 450-461
Non-unanimous verdicts, 1144
Nullification by jury, 1147-1153

Official immunity, 383-385, 388-392
Open fields doctrine, 230-235
Open file policies, 940
Open trials, 1160, 1161
Open view. *See* Plain view
Orders to exit vehicle, 127
Outrageous government conduct, 638-644
Overcharging, 841

Package profiles, 73
Pen registers, 440-445
Peremptory challenges, 1114-1135
Permissive joinder rules, 911-923
Petite policy, 883-886, 889, 1289
Petty offenses, no right to jury for, 1091
Photographic identifications, 607-612
Plain feel/touch doctrine, 115-119
Plain hearing, 100
Plain smell, 100
Plain statement rule, 274
Plain view, 93-103, 408
Plea bargains, 993-1084. *See also* Guilty pleas
  bans, 1012, 1013, 1075-1084
  binding nature of agreement, 1000-1003, 1059-1067
  breach of agreement, 1059-1070
  coercive overcharging, 841, 1051
  consistency agreements, 1014
  ethics, 1045
  future of bargaining, 1070-1084
  judicial participation, 1051-1058
  judicial rules, 1007-1014
  knowledge of charges/consequences, 1037-1044
  legislative provisions, 1003-1007
  legitimacy of bargaining, 1070-1075
  package deals, 1050, 1051
  prosecutorial guidelines, 1014-1032
  reasons for, 994-1003
  remedies for breach, 1068-1070
  restrictions on bargaining, 1003-1037
  sentencing, and, 1304-1307
  stipulated sentences, 1013, 1014
  types of bargains, 999, 1000, 1013, 1014
  victim consultation, 1032-1037
Plea discounts, 1000, 1001
Police
  community caretaker function, 4-10
  community policing, 24-32
  discretion in arrest, 297-320
  enforcement of civility, 10-15
  eyewitnesses, as, 584, 585
  review boards, 381, 382
  screening of charges, 798-802
Police courts, 801, 802
Police misconduct
  criminal charges, 393, 394
  equitable relief, 392, 393
  injunctions, 392, 393
  review boards, 381, 382
  tort actions, 383-385, 388-394
Police review boards, 381, 382
Pre-accusation delay, 971-976
Pre-arrest searches, 220, 221
Preliminary examination, 863-869
Presentence investigation (PSI) reports, 1307
Preservation of evidence, 952-955
Presumption of innocence, 1178-1183
Presumptions, 1184-1189
Pretextual arrests, 319
Pretextual stops, 60-68, 319
Pretrial release/detention
  detention, 778-795
  release. *See* Bail
  terrorism, 791-795
Preventive detention, 778-795
Privacy Protection Act of 1980, 665
Private paper searches, 256-261
Private prosecutions, 827-836
Private recording of conversations, 459, 460
Privilege against self-incrimination. *See* Self-incrimination privilege
Probable cause
  alternatives to, 227, 228
  anonymous sources, 157-162
  chart/statutory and case language, 139
  confidential informants, 146-157
  defined, 138-146
  knowledge of officer, 145, 146
  level of certainty, 138, 139, 145
  medical searches, 229
  police expertise, 145, 146
  state statutes/rules of procedure, 162-165
  wiretaps, 428
Probable cause "plus," 227, 228
Procedural bars to habeas review, 1414-1425
Prosecution disclosures, 933-955
Prosecutorial vindictiveness, 862, 863
Prosecutors. *See also* Charging
  contacting represented persons, 649, 650
  grand jury subpoenas, and, 663

immunity, 642
lying witnesses, and, 1240-1244
special, 629, 835, 836
undercover operations, and, 642
Protective sweeps, 219, 220
Protective *Terry* searches, 106-115
Public defender systems, 730-737, 743-748
Public safety exception to *Miranda,* 512, 513
Public trials, 1153-1161
Pursuit, seizure by, 59, 60

Qualified good faith immunity, 391

Race
arrests, and, 306-308
bail, and, 771, 777
capital punishment, 1327-1334
charging, and, 862, 863, 1335-1340
citations, 319, 320
cocaine punishment policies, and, 1341-1343
consensual searches, 77
cross-racial identification, 584, 612-619
discretionary decisions affecting punishment, 1335-1340
force during arrest, and, 328
participation in crimes, and, 307, 308, 1340, 1341, 1343
peremptory challenges, and, 1114-1135
reasonable suspicion, and, 68-84
selective prosecution, and, 855-863
sentencing, and, 1326-1343
stops, 75, 76
victim's race, and, 1327-1334
voir dire, and, 1101-1109
witness descriptions, 75
Rape shield laws, 1220
Real offense sentencing systems, 1281-1287
Reasonable doubt standard, 1170-1184
Reasonable suspicion
beepers, 411
cars, 283
dogs, 404-408
protective sweep, 219, 220
schools, 241-247
stops, 49-84, 161, 162
Reasonable-efforts instruction, 1140, 1141
Reasonableness clause, 91, 136
Reciprocal discovery, 961, 962
Recusal of judges, 1114
Redacted statements of co-defendants, 1211, 1212
Redbook, U.S. Dept. of Justice, 1019-1022
Release from custody. *See* Bail
Relevant conduct, 1281-1287
Reno Bluesheet, 1024-1026
Required records doctrine, 672
Retroactivity, 1371-1378
Reverse buys, 1279
Right to counsel. *See also* Counsel, *Miranda* warnings, State-provided counsel
adequate counsel, 709-729
appeals, 701
constitutional sources, 691
critical stages, 693-702
DWI examinations, 694-700
Fifth Amendment, *Miranda,* 482-576
grand jury, 648
handwriting/blood samples, 700
interrogations after indictment, *Massiah,* 482, 483, 544-552
juveniles, 852, 853
lineups, and, 586-598
photographic identifications, and, 611
psychiatric examinations, 699-701
sentencing, 701
sobriety tests, and, 694-700
statutory provisions, 689, 690
undercover agents, and, 544-552
waiver of right (self-representation), 702-709
when it takes effect, 693-702
Right to silence. *See Miranda* warnings, Self-incrimination privilege
Roadblocks, 84-93
Roving stops, 92
Roving wiretaps, 429

Same conduct test, 890, 891, 894-899
Same elements test, 890, 891, 894-900
Same offense test, 890-903
Same transaction test, 899
Schools
drug testing, 248-254
searches of, 241-247
Scottsboro case, 676, 677
Search and seizure
automobiles, 67, 68, 76-93, 126, 127, 170, 262-284, 332, 333
banking records, 261
drug testing, 248-254
effects (personal property), 262-284
electronic records, 445-449

Search and seizure (*cont.*)
  frisks, 106-120
  full searches. *See* Full searches of people/places
  habeas corpus, 1414, 1440
  houses, 169, 170, 229-236, 404
  independent state decision-making, 66, 273, 274
  intrusive body searches, 221-229
  inventory searches, 262-267
  low-level searches/stops. *See* Brief searches/seizures
  papers, 256-261
  persons, 106-120, 214-229
  pre-arrest searches, 220, 221
  prisons, 254, 255
  private recording of conversations, 459, 460
  remedies for improper. *See* Exclusionary rule, Police misconduct
  schools, 241-254
  searches incident to arrest, 214-221
  technological innovations. *See* Technological innovations and privacy
  workplaces, 236-240
Search incident to arrest, 214-221
Search incident to citation, 311, 312, 318, 319
Search of automobile incident to arrest, 268-274, 283
Search warrants
  administrative warrants, 189-194
  anticipatory warrants, 186-189
  burden of proof, 184, 185
  error in jurisdiction, 180
  execution, 180-185
  exigent circumstances, 166-170
  false statements/errors, 179
  four corners rule, 178, 179, 354
  highly regulated industries, 194
  in writing requirement, 177, 178
  knock-and-announce requirement, 180-184
  listing small items, 178
  neutral and detached magistrate, 170-174
  newspaper offices, 665
  nighttime searches, 184
  no-knock entry, 180-184
  oath/affirmation, 177
  particularity requirement, 174-177
  procedural requirements, 170-180
  subpoenas, contrasted, 664, 665
  telephonic warrants, 177, 178
  third-party searches, 665
Seizure. *See* Search and seizure
Seizure by pursuit, 59, 60
Selective investigations, 621-630
Selective prosecution, 855-863
Self-incrimination privilege. *See also Miranda* warnings
  blood samples/palm prints, 672
  comments on defendant's silence, 1221-1235
  corporations, 671, 672
  document subpoenas, 658-672
  history of, 655, 656
  purpose of privilege, 656, 657
  trial, at, 1221-1235
Self-representation, 702-709
Sense-enhancing devices, 103, 395-412
Sentence bargain, 1000, 1017-1020
Sentencing, 1247-1343
  acceptance of responsibility, 1304-1306
  acquittal evidence, 1300-1304
  bail, and, 771
  capital punishment, 1259, 1299, 1322, 1323, 1327-1334
  commissions, 1266-1275, 1302-1306, 1310, 1311, 1314, 1317, 1318
  community impact, 1323-1326
  cooperation in other investigations, 1315-1318
  crack-cocaine ratio, 1341-1343
  cross-examination of witnesses, 1299
  defendant's family, 1314
  defendant's perjury, 1306
  double jeopardy, 1287-1290
  entrapment/manipulation, 1275-1280
  guidelines, 1018-1026, 1266-1275, 1302-1306, 1310, 1311, 1314, 1317, 1318
  guilty pleas, and, 1304-1307
  habitual offender laws, 1311, 1313, 1314
  illegally obtained evidence, 1278-1281
  indeterminate sentencing systems, 1015, 1248-1260
  informal procedure, 1258, 1259
  juries, 1260, 1298, 1299
  legislative, 1260-1266
  mandatory minimum penalties, 1260-1266
  multiple counts, 1287
  offender information, 1307-1318
  parole boards, and, 1274, 1275
  plea agreements, and, 1014-1027, 1305-1307

presentence investigation reports, 1307
prior convictions/arrests, 1307-1314
probation officers, and, 1307
race, and, 1326-1343
real offense systems, 1017, 1018, 1281-1287
relevant conduct, 1281-1287
retrials, and, 862, 863, 1306, 1307
revisiting charging decisions, 1281-1290
revisiting investigations, 1275-1281
rules of evidence, 1258, 1299
self-defense, and, 1280
standard of proof, 1298
stipulated sentences, 1013, 1014
substantial assistance, 1315, 1318
three strikes and you're out, 1311, 1313
victim information, 1318-1323
vulnerable victims, 1321, 1323
Sentencing commissions, 1266-1275, 1302-1306, 1310, 1311, 1314, 1317, 1318
Sentencing entrapment/manipulation, 1275-1280
September 11 terrorist attacks, 83, 93, 123-125, 469, 791, 1398
Sequestration
juries, of, 1141
witnesses, of, 1199
Serious offenses, jury trial available, 1086-1093
Severance of offenses, 911-913, 922, 923
Showups, 585
Silver platter doctrine, 348, 415, 888, 889
Simple use immunity, 655
Sixth Amendment rights. *See* Confrontation of witnesses, Juries, Right to counsel, Speedy trial
Slow plea, 1000
Sniff searches, 404-408
Sobriety checkpoints, 84-93
Sovereign immunity, 383, 391, 392
Special prosecutors, 629, 835, 836
Special verdicts, 1145
Speedy trial, 970-992
excluded time periods, 992
minimum time requirements, 991, 992
pre-accusation delay, 971-976
prioritizing cases, 992
remedies for violations, 986
statutes, 986-992
statutes of limitations, 971, 972, 976
victim's rights, 986
Speedy trial statutes, 986-992
Standard of proof. *See* Burden of proof
Standby counsel, 708
Standing doctrine, 370-375
State-provided counsel. *See also* Counsel, Right to counsel
appointed counsel systems, 690, 730-732, 737-742, 745, 746
choice of counsel, 708, 709
contract attorney systems, 731, 746-748
indigency, 690
law students as counsel, 709
public defender systems, 730-737, 743-748
replacement of counsel, 708, 709, 1243, 1244
types of charges, 676-672
types of delivery systems, 729-749
State's attorneys. *See* Prosecutors
Station-house bail, 759, 772, 777
Statutes of limitations, 971, 972, 976
Statutory interpretation
canons of construction, 120, 425
constitutions and, 425
in pari materia, 841
legislative history, 92, 93
particular vs. general statutes, 840, 841
purpose of statute, 92, 93, 425
Stipulated sentences, 1013, 1014
Stops, 36-93, 285-291, 506. *See also* Brief searches/stops
Strip searches, 221-229
Structured sentencing, 1266-1275, 1281, 1282, 1313
Subpoenas
administrative, 663, 664
attorneys, of, 665, 666
grand jury, 658-672
search warrants, contrasted, 664, 665
Substantial assistance sentencing factor, 1315, 1318
Successive habeas petitions, 1424, 1425
Suggestive identifications, 598-607
Surety bonds, 767, 769, 770
Suspension of habeas corpus, 1393-1406

Target standing, 375
Technological innovations and privacy, 395-461
beepers, 409-411
binoculars, 50, 408, 409
bugs on government agents, 431-437
computerized government databases, 446-450

Technological innovations and privacy (*cont.*)
dogs, 404-408
electronic records, 445-449
enhancement of senses, 395-412
flashlights, 95, 408
infrared searches, 403
metal detectors, 93
pen registers, 440-445
private recording of conversations, 459, 460
wiretapping. *See* Wiretapping
x-ray machines, 93
Telephonic warrants, 177, 178
Televised trials, 1160, 1161
Terrorism
airports, 93
database searches, 446, 447
detention, 791-795
habeas corpus, 1398, 1404
identification provided to police, 121-127
racial profiling, 83
September 11 attacks, 83, 93, 123-125, 469, 791, 1398
torture during interrogation, 469, 470
wiretaps, 437-440
Terry searches, 106-115
Terwilliger Bluesheet, 1023, 1024
Thermal imaging, 403
Third-degree tactics, 464-468
Third-party consent searches, 204-210
Third-party searches, 665
Thornburgh Bluesheet, 1022, 1023
Three strikes and you're out, 1311, 1313
Tort actions, 383-394, 455-461
Tracking devices, 409-411
Trash, 103-106
Trials
confrontation of witnesses. *See* Confrontation of witnesses
media coverage, 1160, 1161
open (public), 1153-1161
presence of defendant, 1198, 1199
reasonable doubt standard, 1170-1184
self-incrimination privilege, 1221-1235
statistics, 1085
televised, 1160, 1161

Unavailable witnesses, 1205-1213
Unconstitutional conditions, 211
Undercover agents, 544-552, 638-642. *See also* Entrapment defenses
Use/derivative use immunity, 655

Venire, 1100-1135
Victims
bail, and, 777
charging, and, 835
plea bargains, and, 1032-1037
race of victim effect, 1327-1334
right to attend proceedings, 1199
sentencing, and, 1318-1323
speedy trial, and, 986
Vision-enhancing devices, 103, 395-412
Voir dire, 1101-1109
Vulnerable victims, 1321, 1323

Warrant check, 46
Warrant clause, 91, 136
Warrants. *See* Arrest warrants, Search warrants
Weapons frisks, 106-115
Wickersham Commission, 464, 465, 467
Wiretapping, 412-440
application process, 425-430
consensual intercepts, 422, 423
cordless/cellular phones, 425
exclusion remedy, 424
extraterritoriality, 423, 424
frequency, 430
identification of individuals, 428, 429
judicial administration, 425-430
judicial limits, 412-414
length of surveillance, 430
minimization requirement, 425-428
other procedures requirement, 429
probable cause, 428
reports, 428
roving wiretaps, 429
statutory provisions, 414-430
who may apply, 429
Witnesses
anonymous, 1200-1205
availability of defense witnesses, 1234, 1235
child, 1191-1198
confrontation of. *See* Confrontation of witnesses
cross-examination re pending/prior charges, 1213-1221

discovery, 939, 940
expert. *See* Expert witnesses
grand juries, and, 950-958
identifications. *See* Identifications
immunity, 650-658, 1235
lying, 1235-1244
self-incrimination. *See* Self-incrimination privilege
sequestration/exclusion, 1199
unavailable, 1205-1213

Work product doctrine, 939, 940, 962, 963
Workplaces
drug testing, 253, 254
electronic surveillance, 460
searches of, 236-240
Writs of assistance, 132-135

X-ray machines, 93